VideoHound's® DVD Guide (Book 1)
2000. $19.95. ISBN 1-57859-115-5

VideoHound's® DVD Guide (Book 2)
2001. $19.95. ISBN 0-7876-5757-3

VideoHound's Golden Movie Retriever® 2003
2002. $24.95. ISBN 0-7876-5756-5

Also available from Gale

"If you don't have a good story to tell, you're dead."

—John Alonzo, A.S.C.

VideoHound's® DVD GUIDE

BOOK 3

ISSN 1535-3478

VideoHound's® DVD GUIDE

BOOK 3

Mike Mayo

GALE®

THOMSON™

GALE

Detroit • New York • San Diego • San Francisco • Cleveland • New Haven, Conn. • Waterville, Maine • London • Munich

THOMSON
✦
GALE

VideoHound's® DVD Guide, Book 3
Mike Mayo, Editor

Project Editor
Carol A. Schwartz

Product Design
Pamela Galbreath

Manufacturing
Rita Wimberley

Editorial Support Services
Wayne Fong

Most VideoHound books are available at special quantity discounts when purchased in bulk by corporations, organizations, or groups. Customized printings, special imprints, messages, and excerpts can be produced to meet your needs.
For more information, contact:
Special Markets Manager,
The Gale Group, Inc.
27500 Drake Rd.
Farmington Hills, MI 48331-3535

For permission to use material from this product, submit your request via Web at http://www.gale-edito.com/permissions, or you may download our Permissions Request form and submit your request by fax or mail to:

Permissions Department
The Gale Group, Inc.
27500 Drake Rd.
Farmington Hills MI 48331-3535
Permissions Hotline:
248-699-8006 or 800-877-4253, ext. 8006
Fax: 248-699-8074 or 800-762-4058

LIBRARY OF CONGRESS CATALOGING-IN-PUBLICATION DATA

00-043481
ISBN 0-7876-5758-1
ISSN 1535-3478

Printed in the United States of America
10 9 8 7 6 5 4 3 2 1

Contents

When *Rush Hour* came out on DVD, there were only 3 million people out there with DVD players; now there are more than 25 million households with a DVD player. DVD offers something for every kind of film fan—from those who merely want to be entertained to film students who want to uncover the mystery of filmmaking.

by Brett Ratner

In fact, aside from film school, I learned about making movies from listening to directors' commentaries on laserdiscs. Hearing directors speak about how they did something or constructed a scene helped me to understand the process and apply it to my own movies. And with the advent of DVD, the world of filmmaking has been uncovered for a much larger audience.

I am constantly thinking about the DVD when I am shooting a movie. I am always making notes of possible outtakes or a funny moment that might be cool to put on the DVD. I can let a scene go that I would normally never let go from the final cut of the movie because I know that it will end up on the DVD.

DVD is sort of like film school in a box. Every time I make a movie now, I wear a microphone and have a camera follow me around, documenting my experience during the entire movie-making process. I did this with *Rush Hour 2,* and on *Red Dragon,* throughout pre-production, production, and even post. Every meeting I have with the producers, the writers, the cinematographer, and the production designer is documented. There's not enough room to put everything on the DVD, but a vast amount of it will be there. And, I hope, people can experience a part of what I went through in making the movie.

Since I learned so much from laserdiscs and DVD, I'm committed to sharing what I've learned. When you're a kid watching a movie, you can't comprehend how it's done sometimes. Seeing how directors film scenes and interact with the actors, it doesn't seem like brain surgery—something that even I could do. Hearing a director talk about how hard it was to figure out a scene or how something great in the movie happened accidentally makes it all seem possible to do yourself.

I hope you take the chance to enjoy some of the great DVDs outlined in the pages in front of you. I will.

—Brett Ratner

Brett Ratner is the director of Money Talks, Rush Hour, Family Man, Rush Hour 2, *and* Red Dragon. *On DVD,* Rush Hour *was one of the first releases to explore the dimensions of the medium.*

"Film Restoration and DVD"

by Glenn Erickson

Just as home hi-fi sound equipment in the 1950s created high interest in the quality of recorded music, DVD has increased consumer awareness of quality video. There are now entire magazines and websites that review DVD product from a tech-spec point of view. A lot of this is a direct carryover from the audiophile tradition of using high-end calibration instruments to review a sound recording. Many DVD players can display the bit rate of the encoded DVD signal, right as you're watching. VHS was such a low-res format that there wasn't all that much difference between a bad transfer and a good one. Now on DVD, we've seen so much quality video that it's become easy to discriminate between a disc that's been professionally guided through the encoding process, and one that was made on a budget.

As things stand in 2002, all of the big studios are putting out excellent, almost flawless discs of new and recent films. As many of these pictures are at least partially post-produced in the digital realm, you could say that DVD production now begins with the start of filming. The bean-counters are well aware that more than half of their new films will perform far better on disc than they did on theatre screens.

The big word "Restoration" comes into play the moment DVD turns to the issue of older, or library, titles. So many discs come with banners touting a restoration, viewers are getting the impression that all the older movies they see on DVD are undergoing a massive reconstruction process, as was done to *Lawrence of Arabia* about 13 years ago.

The restoration professional Robert A. Harris made headlines with his work on *Lawrence* (as well as *Vertigo, Rear Window,* and others) and performed nothing less than a miracle. David Lean's masterpiece was restored (in the sense of, "returned to a previous state") to its lost Roadshow version. Missing scenes were reinstated, and the original editor from 1962 was brought back to re-cut sequences for which no final print could be found. The entire picture was remixed, with actors like Alec Guinness re-dubbing their roles 30 years after the fact. And all of this had to be done from 70mm elements, mixing and matching a variety of materials that had faded at different rates, to come up with the best possible result. The finished product was dazzling, and 1989 audiences unaccustomed to the clarity of 70mm were thrilled.

But *Lawrence of Arabia* cost millions to restore, as did *Spartacus,* two years later. Mr. Harris himself is quick to point out that the big studios maintain their libraries for revenue, not to preserve film history, nor to rescue deteriorating films that may soon become extinct. Before home video, the films in studio vaults were barely touched, except to provide 16mm elements for degraded television prints. Non-theatrical possibilities for the films have since expanded, from television to VHS to cable and satellite to DVD, and possibly now to the Internet. DVD and other digital delivery formats (cable and HDTV) demand a better source image than VHS did. DVD can now reproduce the finest of theatrical audio systems. Because using a quick telecine transfer for a video master will no longer suffice, studios now have very active "technical service" and "assets management" departments. Although they want to screen theatrical prints of their films on the repertory and museum circuits, the big studios mostly need to make sure the DVD and television sales pipelines are flowing with quality product.

This means that studios no longer routinely dispose of entire vaults of film elements. They also keep practically every piece of film used to make a movie, instead of tossing all but negatives and audio masters. But film holdings aren't exactly being treated as priceless art, either. Market demands and the bottom line are active concepts; film heritage *per se* is not. When a studio hires out services for the kinds of restoration *they* want done, it's likely to be a bulk order to a major lab reading, "Provide new printing elements and video masters for these 100 titles by September 20," or something to that effect. Phrases like, "Research the films to ensure the greatest adherence to the director's vision" don't normally figure in—that kind of pap is generated by the marketing department, to appeal to film fans.

What follows is an overview of the kinds of work done by in-house studio "film managers," and the labs, video technicians, and private restoration companies they hire.

Vault Searches are the first and most frustrating step. Not all studios have a full accounting of their vaulted holdings, and, unfortunately, the average title doesn't usu-

ally merit extensive detective work to locate a better negative, a stereophonic track, or that missing uncut version. But motivated studio personnel have done wonders in this area. Early stereophonic tracks for many Warner's films like *Rebel without a Cause, Land of the Pharaohs,* and *Pete Kelly's Blues* were lost, until an expert got the idea to press the Library of Congress to examine their prints on deposit. The images were faded, but the 4-track magnetic audio stripes were intact. At MGM, a part-time consultant recently found printing elements for several titles thought to be completely lost, or, in studio jargon, "unserviceable." E-mailing dozens of domestic labs, he asked each to look up the titles once again—not by studio, but by the name of the original production company, and received several positive replies, some for elements that hadn't been touched in 40 years.

Choosing the Best Elements is the most critical step. When a DVD blurb reads, "Transferred from the original negative," it simplifies a much more complicated production path. The vault holdings for an old, color film might include several IPs (interpositives) or INs (internegatives) made from the original negative. It's altogether possible that they have faded less than has the ON (original negative), so just making a new IP may not be a fast solution. The best element for overall color may have damaged sections, or splices that fall apart. At this point, the best course of action might be to combine parts of different elements. But if a specific title isn't funded for this extra attention, the best overall element might have to be chosen, and that's that.

Hopeful stories constantly emerge from this jungle of technical problems. Seldom-seen titles have been quietly sitting in the vault for decades, ironically "preserved" by not being pulled out for re-issues or early video work. Sometimes, the lab can print the film fresh out of the can, and it looks terrific. But in the case of most popular movies, there's a history of trouble of various kinds, especially from short term—solution decisions made when they were new. The original negatives of many films from the '30s and '40s no longer exist, because they were unwisely used to make hundreds of release prints, before good intermediate film stocks were developed. The lower-quality dupe negs that do exist may have introduced new flaws. Density fluctuations and poor cropping of compositions, particularly on early talkies, are typical problems.

Usually, an at least passable print can be made, but each title has its own story. Every studio has titles listed as "unserviceable"—no negative, or an incomplete or damaged one. There was a big article last January in *Vanity Fair* magazine, revisiting the idea of finding the lost long version of Orson Welles's *The Magnificent Ambersons,* perhaps by tracking down the print sent to Welles when he was in Brazil. Officially "lost" films have turned up: Tod Browning's silent *The Unknown* was identified and saved a couple of decades ago (so they say) by people re-evaluating a stack of film cans that had been shelved with unidentifiable material. They'd been placed there ages ago, because someone read the word "unknown" on the labels!

Seventy-five years later, nobody expects 40 cans labeled "*Greed*" to magically appear in someone's garage. As unlikely as that might be, even wilder miracles have happened. Criterion's DVD of Carl Theodore Dreyer's *The Passion of Joan of Arc* looks fantastic, and it should. What we saw in film school in the 1970s was impressive, but rather ragged-looking. That's because the film was lost not long after release, and what we saw was an alternate version the director cobbled together as best he could from outtakes. Then, in 1981, a nigh-perfect original print was discovered in, of all places, a Norwegian mental institution. The religious order that ran it had contributed to the production, and was given a copy fresh from the lab, which sat unscreened in a cool, dry corner for 50 years!

The recent re-premiere of another silent movie, Fritz Lang's *Metropolis,* dramatizes the growing potential for the use of digital technology in film restoration. *Metropolis* was severely cut soon after its 1926 release. Further changes made by Paramount for the English-language version radically simplified the story of this science-fiction epic. Using parts of surviving prints and negatives from around the world, a Munich museum pieced together a version that couldn't restore everything, but increased the length of the movie by 50%. Coming as it did from mismatched sources, with some sections looking far worse than others and none free of some kind of damage, their version was about the best that could be done with this title in the photo-chemical realm. But just last year, German technicians finished a *digital* restoration so good, the film looks better than anyone has ever seen it this side of Weimar Berlin. Intense digital matching and cleaning have not only removed scratches, but evened out fluttering contrast, stabilized shaky and warping footage, and restored the detailed gray-on-gray photographic quality that we've previously seen only in stills.

What this *Metropolis* restoration demonstrates is that with enough money, miracles are indeed possible. If expensive computer techniques can finish entire features digitally, they can be of even better use in repairing old films. It's not the same as real film printed from a real negative, but *Metropolis* would never have been restored any other way.

Even better is the knowledge that the sci-fi classic is no longer dependent on a single irreplaceable printing element. A new negative for the restored film can be generated from digital files at any time, so that *Metropolis* need never become lost again. A DVD of this amazing restoration is due within a year.

Digital technology may be a key to the restoration of original Technicolor movies for video formats. Transferring an original Technicolor print to videotape almost always results in a contrasty, inferior result. Truly restoring

Technicolor requires film lab work with three negatives instead of one, and when the old, shrunken "3 strips" are combined now, registration problems between the colors can be serious. For this reason, most DVDs of Technicolor movies are transfers of standard Eastmancolor interpositives made from the "3 strips," that often have uncorrectable registration flaws (seen as color fringing) built in. The expense of going back to the original Technicolor negatives is prohibitive. Warner/Turner's breathtaking DVD of *The Wizard of Oz* was a full-on restoration of this kind, and the results are stunning, but how many films deserve such treatment?

The flexibility of digital tools might be able to simplify the Technicolor compositing process. If digital images can be resized and re-graded for *Metropolis,* it stands to reason that combining the three-color registers for an old Technicolor film might be much simpler in the digital realm than in a film lab.

Naturally, in almost every case, the flexibility of video transfers can make the DVD of a restored film look better than a film print. In a lab, the only latitude is the choice of print stock and the color timing. For video, digital scrubbing and color and density adjustments can often make a bad negative look adequate, and an adequate neg look great. But the overzealous use of some digital tools has become an issue of some controversy.

Digital manipulation is often used during telecine transfers to augment and correct color. The stunning colors in some of the Marilyn Monroe DVDs released last year were achieved by practically re-painting faded negatives. The success of this re-invented color depends on the skill and taste of the colorists.

After telecine, there are digital tools employed at computer workstations that can be used to touch-up a digital master. Criterion has consistently improved the DVD versions of their classic films by manually removing dirt, hair, and scratches frame by frame—making a film like *Children of Paradise* sparkle in comparison to their older, beat-up laserdisc transfer. Disney has been practically repainting its animated classics, removing flaws in the original animation photography. In some cases it's been claimed that colors and textures have been subtly altered, to the displeasure of purists who consider the occasional smudges on the original animation cels to be part of the art, like brushstrokes in a painting.

Other kinds of automatic cleanup and edge-enhancement programs can be grossly misused. The industry finds these tools attractive, because a dull and dirty tape can be quickly made into a "brighter, cleaner" one, for a relatively cheap and predictable price. The programs that isolate and eliminate small anomalies (like dirt and emulsion digs) can also erase detail, and flatten out images. In the wrong hands, a transfer can be so perverted that a film can look as if it were shot on video.

The fact is that all restoration efforts have a revision factor. There's a temptation to "improve" on the original, which is potentially damaging. When George Lucas and Steven Spielberg decide to revise their films, they're extending their controlling egos over film history itself, returning like time travelers to change character motivations and remove unwanted guns from *E.T.* If they want to debase their own work, so be it. The experts who have restored classic Hitchcock or Welles films took on a daunting responsibility *not* to exert their own personalities. An acclaimed film editor recut Orson Welles's *Touch of Evil* from detailed notes, but obviously ran into editing situations that contradicted the deceased director's instructions. At that point, the editor must have been thinking, "What would Welles do now?" His personal judgment has to get involved.

An audio remix is always a matter of personal taste, and there have been objections to new stereophonic tracks that deviate from the originals. *Vertigo*'s sound effects seem distractingly elevated in the new mix. A

1950s battle epic, with its sparse vintage sound effects, can seem too thin when spread out across five or six channels.

The assembly-line approach taken with many library titles can result in unnecessary errors. Audio mixers working on a deadline can scramble tracks, resulting in lost dialogue lines or sound effects that don't jibe with the picture. Studios have plenty of personnel to market their products, but sometimes nobody to ensure quality control. James Bond DVDs are made with scenes missing, and major musicals can have entire reels out of sync, and go uncaught all the way to store shelves. With James Bond, you can bet the problems will be quickly corrected, but if the movie affected happens to be a minor title, it might stay that way for a long time.

The last step in DVD is the actual encoding of the discs. Economics have already resulted in some discs being encoded for DVD at a standard, one-size-fits-all bit rate. This goes against the wisdom that encoding compression needs to be scaled to the demands of individual scenes. With a single bit-rate, a simple shot may look fine, only to be followed by a more complicated one where the details turn into digital mush. This is usually seen only on library titles, and it can be very frustrating.

I've been discussing mostly films owned or controlled by major studios. Restoring independently owned pictures, and those that are in the public domain, brings up new sets of problems. DVD spawned a score of small companies that specialize in licensing and producing discs for films from other sources. Most followed the lead of Criterion, which had been doing the same for laserdisc for years. By and large they've done a great job without the resources of a major studio.

The edge these smaller companies have is their personal commitment to the work—Anchor Bay will lavish attention on an obscure genre title like *The Wicker Man,* while an equivalent movie owned by a major studio might not even merit consideration for

release. Whereas the majors have little incentive to creatively exploit the hundreds (or thousands) of movies they control, tiny companies have successfully created whole new markets for previously obscure filmmakers like Mario Bava and Dario Argento, and reintroduced the early work of directors like Werner Herzog and Paul Verhoeven.

Public domain is a legal sinkhole keeping many, many pictures from decent presentation in any format. Films that fall into this category can simply disappear, because the companies that own the elements that could be used to properly restore them can't protect their investment in the marketplace. Cheap DVDs, sometimes digitized from earlier laserdiscs, are for some titles the only copies available. A rather poor DVD of the originally beautiful *Gorgo* was crudely mastered from a Technicolor print. Turner might have the original MGM-Rank film materials, but if they were to spend the money to turn out a superior product, the fact that the title is in the public domain means anyone could copy their version and re-sell it. It's almost worth allowing studios to reclaim rights to films they long ago let expire, if the result would better ensure that the films would receive proper treatment. It might rescue a forgotten gem like 1951's *Pandora and the Flying Dutchman,* with Ava Gardner and James Mason, that Turner has little incentive to touch.

The jealousy and uncooperative attitudes of some independent collectors can also be an obstacle, as can be seen with the classic film noir *Detour.* Archives around the country hold several original prints, but none are satisfactorily intact. Unfortunately, a collector who has his own damaged print, with the good reels that could restore the film, won't cooperate with any of them.

It needs to be mentioned here that the majority of collectors are highly cooperative and through their "rescued" prints have helped restore many choice items thoughtlessly tossed by the studios. Several parts of the long original cut of the Judy Garland *A Star Is Born* were recovered in this way.

Although DVD is rapidly reaching a wide consumer base, the enthusiastic early adopters of the format continue to watchdog the studios, demanding that features like 16:9 enhancement not be dropped. Although the knowledge base out there is rather high (many DVD aficionados are industry workers), there are still plenty of Internet-based crusaders who make technical demands on the basis of incomplete information. The usual response of studio DVD departments is to be very defensive, and limit contact with outsiders.

After years of ignoring their Hammer films, Warner's remastered the 1959 *The Mummy* beautifully in 16:9. Loud objections on the Web demanded that the film be reissued at 1:66, as it originally screened in the U.K. Like all English films, even the first three James Bond movies, the flat Hammers were composed to be screened in the United States, where standard widescreen projection was 1:85. As few of the big studios transfer their 1:66 films at 16:9 (this requires narrow vertical bars at the sides), the only alternative would be to see *The Mummy* flat, which would defeat DVD's most important benefit, the added resolution of 16:9.

Luckily, Warner Bros. didn't take the uproar as a sign that genre fans weren't worth catering to and have scheduled more Hammer classics for the fall of 2002.

Some parting observations on the subject of restoration for DVD:

Just because a film looks good in your home theatre, it doesn't mean it's been restored. A lab can take a disintegrating film, transfer it to tape, and work miracles on it to produce a presentable DVD. If the deteriorating film is just re-vaulted and left to continue to rot, nothing's been saved. The same studio may return to the vault 15 years from now and find nothing useable to remaster a title for a next-generation format.

Also remember that DVD can't "restore" a grainy, low-budget horror effort to the sheen of a recent film like *Sleepy Hollow*. The new disc of *Last House on the Left* looks better than ever, but it's still a 1972 16mm cheapie shot by a crew used to filming porno movies.

When missing scenes aren't reinstated, or other known-to-exist elements or extras aren't included with a disc, nine times out of ten it's not negligence that gets in the way, but legal restraints. Overworked studio lawyers find "No" to be the safest response to any issue in a gray area, and an exorbitant licensing fee will always foil the best of intentions. A great teaser exists for the film *1941,* a special shoot with an exploding Christmas present, but it couldn't be included on the DVD. Why? A snippet of a Frank Sinatra song can be heard on the soundtrack.

The term "restoration" can be abused too. That severely flawed disc of *Detour* mentioned above proclaims loudly on its cover, "Digitally mastered from original elements." Since the "original element" used was just a beat-up screening print, by the producer's definition, an *unoriginal* element would have to be a copy of a different movie! The best use for reliable online reviewers, and publications like the Video-Hound books, is to get an idea of what the transfer looks like before you buy.

DVD is finally beginning to surpass laserdisc for the breadth and depth availability of those desired library titles. Of course, the class-A special edition treatment, with extensive restoration, isn't enough on just any movie. What really matters is that it's given to the movies *you* want to see. Good luck!

—Glenn Erickson

Glenn Erickson is a film editor and writer with a website called DVD Savant (www.dvdtalk. com/dvdsavant/spec.html), and a member of the Online Film Critics Society. In addition to editing DVD documentaries, he promotes film restorations and consults on film history for studios.

"DVD Regional Codes"
by Mike Long

Have you ever looked at the back of a DVD box and noticed a little picture of a globe with a "1" in it and wondered what that meant? You may have also seen this logo on the box in which your DVD player was packed. This insignia indicates regional coding. Most DVDs carry an embedded code that tells the player which part of the world that the disc is from. Six regional codes coordinate to various geographic areas of the world. They are:

1. U.S., Canada, U.S. Territories

2. Japan, Europe, South Africa, and Middle East (including Egypt)

3. Southeast Asia and East Asia (including Hong Kong)

4. Australia, New Zealand, Pacific Islands, Central America, Mexico, South America, and the Caribbean

5. Eastern Europe, India, Africa, North Korea, and Mongolia

6. China

This regional coding is a fairly new technology and didn't affect the international use of VHS tapes or laserdiscs in the past. The movie studios instituted regional coding to control the availability of films on a global scale. Due to licensing rights and ownership issues, a film that is "owned" by one company in one part of the world, may be "owned" by another company elsewhere. Therefore, the regional coding helps to ensure that the company that owns the film can distribute it appropriately in its part of the world. There is also the matter of timing. For example, many films that have long been available on video in Asia have yet to receive a theatrical release in the U.S. Here, the regional coding cuts down on the likelihood that a viewer in America would see the film before its U.S. theatrical release.

So, that little globe with the "1" represents a region 1 DVD, and this disc is designed to play only on a region 1 DVD player. The vast majority of DVDs sold in the United States are coded for region 1, although some smaller companies do not include a regional code on their discs. These discs are often referred to as all-region DVDs or "region 0" discs (though, technically, there is no region 0). All-region DVDs will play on most region 1 players without any problems. In relation to that, most DVD players available in the U.S. are designed to play region 1 DVDs only. (As if all of this weren't confusing enough, there are some titles available in Canada that, due to licensing issues, are not for sale in the U.S., despite the fact that both are region 1!).

When any new technology like this is introduced, some people will want to defeat it. Because of this, some DVD players are known as "code-free" players. These machines have the ability to play DVDs from any region. Of those players, some may be purchased with that multi-region function easily available, while others must have their hardware modified to achieve it. The powers-that-be have struck back against this technology by creating DVDs with "regional code enhancement." This extra program is designed to detect a "code-free" player and upon doing so, the disc will cease to play.

Regional coding isn't the only thing that differentiates countries. Television broadcast standards also differ. In the United States, as well as other parts of the world, the standard used is called NTSC. In Europe, the PAL (or SECAM) system is used. Put in its simplest terms, the main differences between the two standards deal with the size of the picture and the number of motion-picture frames that are being displayed per second. Also, there are differences in the amount of lines being displayed on the television screen. The NTSC and PAL signals are not compatible, and problems can arise when you attempt to convert from one to the other. (You may have seen a broadcast of a European program and noticed that the image appeared to be "squeezed." This is an example of a PAL to NTSC conversion.) Due to the differences in the broadcast standards, a PAL-encoded DVD won't play on the majority of region 1 DVD players, even if it is "code-free."

DVDs have a worldwide fan-base and the obstacles presented by region coding and conversion issues haven't stopped film fans from realizing that there is a whole world of DVDs outside of the U.S. Due in large part to the Internet, a large community of American "non-region 1" DVD fans has grown up, devotees who seek out popular titles that aren't yet available in the U.S., be they foreign gems or domestic films which have to make their disc debut here.

While such popular television programs as *The Simpsons, Friends,* and *Buffy the Vampire Slayer* have recently been released on DVD in the U.S., these shows have been available overseas for quite some time, and the selection is far greater than the product offered in region 1. Other shows—*Futurama, Xena: Warrior Princess, Will & Grace,* and *Angel*—are already on DVD in other countries, while Americans endure syndicated reruns. Many Hollywood films that are "bare bones" DVD releases in region 1 have received the special edition treatment elsewhere. For example, director John Carpenter has recorded audio commentaries for his films *Starman, Prince of Darkness,* and *They Live,* but these are only available on DVDs in Europe in a region 2 PAL format.

The more technically savvy DVD enthusiasts will often go out of their way to track down an import DVD that has an anamorphic widescreen transfer or DTS audio track, where one doesn't exist in region 1. Finally, there are those foreign films that have yet to be released at all in region 1, such as the Japanese shocker *Ring* (which is being remade by Hollywood) or another hot Japanese title, *Battle Royale,* which plays as a modern updating of *The Lord of the Flies.* Via the Internet and international publications, movie buffs hear about these obscure films and find a way to see them in the U.S. For more information on non–region 1 DVDs, visit International DVD chat forum at www.dvdtalk.com or the forum at www.asiandvdguide.com.

—Mike Long

Mike Long has dedicated most of his life to seeking out obscure movies, cult films, and flicks that no one else has every seen. Because of this passion, he's had to sit through some really bad movies, and at times, sees everyday conversations with subtitles.

DVD has arrived. As of June 2002, about one-third of American households have a DVD player (or players). The Consumer Electronics Association expects about 40% of American homes to have DVD players by the end of 2002, and that number doesn't include the various video game–playing machines (X-Box and Play Station 2) which also play DVDs.

The DVD industry proudly calls itself the most popular form of home entertainment ever released and it's hard to argue with the numbers. How was the revolution accomplished so smoothly?

One obvious reason for the rapid acceptance is that the format is so simple. DVD players are easier to hook up than VCRs or other video recording devices (Tivo, etc.). Plug it into the back of a TV, then slip in a disc and hit play on the menu. Most menus (with the notable exception of the *Memento Special Edition*) are so straightforward that even the seriously technophobic are not intimidated. In the first years, conventional wisdom had it that DVD was for grown-ups while kids' movies were relegated to VHS. Those days are over. If there were any doubts, *Harry Potter and the Sorcerer's Stone* erased them. Younger viewers watch the movie repeatedly, and they have taken to the DVD extras in a mammoth way.

Because DVD is so easy to use, many people don't go beyond the basic "play" option. They don't understand everything that their players will do; don't know about subtitle and captioning options, much less hidden Easter eggs. At the same time, other DVD converts have realized the spectacular difference that Surround sound makes. That accounts for the popularity of five-disc DVD changers. Nobody wants to watch five movies in a row, but when a home theatre system has such superb speakers, it becomes a five-disc CD player.

You don't need an expensive high-end home theatre system to realize that DVD provides a superior picture and stronger sound than VHS, but the medium is really much more than an improvement over videotape. Within the entertainment business in the last year, it has become apparent that DVD is a massive change.

Where VHS was a little version of the movie, DVD is a separate experience with differences that are being manifested in rapidly evolving forms. Note, for example, the two versions of *Kate & Leopold* that are available on disc—the theatrical release and a true director's cut that tells the same story in a different way. Or check out the multiple endings of *Joy Ride*. Younger filmmakers in particular consider DVD to be something more, a forum where they can work through experiments that do not fit within the traditional limitations of a feature film. Even such an established director as David Lynch (more about him later), who has little use for extras, makes sure that his films are transferred to disc with the greatest care possible. Studios understand that viewers expect more from DVD. The studios also know that in the long run (though they say they don't care about the long run) most people are going to see movies at home, not in theatres. Video sales and rentals have been larger than theatrical ticket sales since the mid-1990s and the gap continues to widen as differences in cost lessen.

The famous comparison, which I first saw in Tim Lucas' *Video Watchdog* magazine, is that we've almost reached the point where two tickets to a first-run movie cost about the same as a new DVD release— around $20. Some highly anticipated movies arrive on DVD at huge discounts and catalog titles are routinely put on sale. Recently one of the nationwide retail chains advertised a two-pack of *The Great Escape* and *Run Silent, Run Deep* for $12.99, *Body Heat* for $8.99, *GoodFellas* for $17.99. (By the way, the prices listed with each review in this book are full retail. It's easy to find substantial discounts.)

When two tickets equal one DVD, home entertainment isn't necessarily a second choice to going out to a theatre, particularly in today's market where the theatrical experience has become seriously degraded. In many parts of the United States, mostly outside of the biggest cities, projection is sloppy, prints are banged up, and auditoriums are messy. At the risk of making a crude and unfair generalization, theatre management wants to sell you popcorn and candy. They don't really care about presenting a first-rate visual and auditory experience. DVD producers do.

About midway through the creation of this book, I made the switch to a widescreen HDTV and the results are as significant as I'd hoped they'd be. With an entry-level Surround system and a 36" direct view screen,

most movies look and sound much sharper than they do at the multiplex.

The downside is that the system is unforgiving. Older films that have not been well preserved look terrible. A dinged-up full-frame black-and-white flick can be almost unwatchable, and the problems that have plagued the medium and television in general are still around:

- Pixels or artifacts: sections of the image coalesce into visible squares.

- Flashing patterns: often found in tweed clothes or background mini-blinds. When parallel lines are close together, they may flash stroboscopically or appear to pinwheel.

- Aliasing: diagonal lines break into a shallow stair-step pattern.

- Graininess and artifacts increase in large areas of solid color.

- Digital sound can pop or "clip."

- Surround sound effects, which are meant to place the viewer in the middle of the audio, may be absent or minimal in action scenes.

- As is the case with CDs, surface scratches or blemishes on a disc can cause it to hang up or malfunction in a player.

The point here is that home viewing is becoming better and cheaper very quickly while theatres are attempting to refit themselves with cup holders and stadium seating. Theatres are contemplating a change to digital projection but the motion picture industry understands that digital films bring a host of problems—most notably piracy— and expense. A recent *New York Times* article estimated that it costs around $150,000 to convert a theatre. Digital projection may well be the next step in theatrical presentation, but it is not likely to be available outside of major cities any time soon.

Meanwhile, DVD flourishes, despite some backsliding. One studio, Columbia TriStar, has released a few older titles—*Mountain Men* and *Cowboy* to name two—squeezed into full-frame presentation, rather than re-creating their original widescreen ratio.

But that kind of cavalier treatment of older films is the exception, not the rule. We're actually seeing a second round of "special editions" of titles that were rushed into distribution in the early days of DVD. *Die Hard, Silence of the Lambs, Jerry Maguire,* and even the cult horror favorite *Basketcase* were released when the medium was brand new and have since been polished up and re-released with all the bells and whistles.

The amount and quality of those extras are also subject to considerable discussion these days. Studios are questioning the economics of these sometimes-expensive add-ons. Arnold Schwarzenegger was reportedly paid a substantial sum to record a commentary track. Is that really worth it? Are people going to shell out a couple more dollars per disc—not to mention their irreplaceable time—to listen? On the other hand, take a look at the care that went into the commentary for the new *Jerry Maguire,* which can be accessed either as a standard audio track or, separately, as video commentary with Tom Cruise, Rene Zellweger, Cuba Gooding Jr., and Cameron Crowe sitting around a table with the film they're watching on display at the bottom of the screen.

Steven Spielberg and David Lynch famously decline to do commentary, and any good filmmaker could make the argument that the work should stand on its own. Be that as it may, serious videophiles and casual moviegoers have come to expect commentary tracks on major releases and most writers, directors, producers, and actors seem to consider it something of an honor to be asked to talk about their work. The audience for commentary appears to have grown beyond the hard-core fan base. I've been surprised several times by people who tell me they regularly listen to commentary and can quote what they've learned.

From my point of view, perhaps the most significant development in DVD is the interest it has sparked in older titles. The perfect example is *Joe vs. the Volcano,* a wonderful, quirky, multi-layered comic fantasy which has, since its 1990 release, been dismissed as a so-so entry in the Tom Hanks canon. A second viewing reveals a work of remarkable depth and craftsmanship. The film still has not found the audience or the reputation that it deserves, but, with its release on DVD, interest has been renewed and the word is spreading. As so many of today's biggest releases are nothing more than collections of computer-generated effects—which don't look nearly as believable or realistic as Hollywood executives like to think they do—serious filmgoers are rediscovering the pleasure of a well-told story with serious actors and a sense of reality.

Forget, for the moment, about screen size and sound effects and all of the minutiae that we tend to carp about in the reviews that follow. Which would you rather watch tonight, *Pearl Harbor* or *From Here to Eternity*? Do you want chilly, over-hyped special effects or would you rather spend some more time with Sgt. Warden and Prewitt and Maggio at Schofield Barracks? O.K., I'm letting my biases show. The point is that both films are available in superb special DVD editions. They look as sharp and crisp as the day they came out of the lab. In the long run, viewers will decide how important and enjoyable they are. This book is an unapologetic mixture of the subjective and the objective that tries to describe a growing, changing industry one movie at a time. It's meant to help movie fans make decisions about what they want to buy and rent.

—Mike Mayo

No book like this is the product of a single individual. Without the help of the following people, it would not have been possible.

Alyssa Alison
Danielle Avazian-Reyes
Jane Ayer
Ed Baran
Lana Berman
Chris Bess
Martin Blythe
Tim Brannim
Brian Brown
Jason Campbell
Scott Carlson
Gabriele Caroti
Mike Clarke
Brian Clucas
Josh Davidson
Irene Dean
Suzanne Dobson
Amy Jo Donner
Herb Dorfman
Meg Elliott
Steve Feldstein
Laura Freeman
Danielle Garnier
Cheryl Glenn
Amy Gorton
Jay Grossman
Liz Hagar
Susan Haney
Philip Hansen
Kelly Hargraves

Joe Hatch
Lynne Hillman
Phil Hopkins
Janet Keller
Maral Kaloustian
Jeff Klein
Garrett Lee
Cliff MacMillan
Dianne Malmgren
Andrea Manwaring
Mike Murphy
Jim Newhouse
Steve Newmark
R. O'Donnell
Betty Owen
Ben Pavlovic
Tony Pines
Megan Powers
Sue Procko
Joanna Proctor
Mike Raso
Melisa Richter
Nan Rohr
Leigh Ross
Kimberly Rubin
Greg Saftich
Carl Samrock
Roger Saunden
Spencer Savage
Carl Scarpetti
John Singh
Steve Solomon
John Soo
Mike Steere
Ian Stimler
Bea Suarez
Cheyenne Sweat
Marc Walkow
Steve Wegner
Jay Weisberger
Alex Xagorakis
Joey Zerbo

My most sincere thanks to all.

VideoHound's DVD Guide would not have been possible without the following talented people:

Editors

Mike Mayo (MM) has written three other books for the VideoHound: *Video Premieres, Horror Show,* and *War Movies.* He is host of the nationally syndicated "The Movie Show on Radio" (www.movieshow.com).

Darren Gross (DG) is a Los Angeles–based writer, film preservationist, and researcher. Born and raised in New Jersey (the toll-booth state!), he studied film production, writing, and preservation (thanks to Professor William K. Everson) at New York University. He has contributed reviews and feature articles to *Video Watchdog* and *Worlds of Horror* and is currently composing liner notes for upcoming DVD releases. Mr. Gross also contributed chapters to *The Dark Shadows Movie Book* and the *Dark Shadows Almanac Millennium Edition.* In 1999 after a two year–long, globe-spanning search, he recovered the long lost "director's cut" of *Night of Dark Shadows.* He has worked as a publicist in the home video arena and is currently searching for the lost footage from *House of Dark Shadows* and other films. Darren has just recently discovered some long-lost footage from another cult film, but can't reveal it yet. (What a tease!) For more information on his restoration projects, go to: www.nightofdarkshadows.com

Reviewers

Lisa Andreini (LA) is a freelance writer/screenwriter and award-winning filmmaker living in Los Angeles. In her spare time she both watches and reviews whatever DVDs Mike Mayo sends her from New Jersey or writes book and DVD reviews for Carlye Archibeque's Independent Reviews Site (see below).

Carlye Archibeque (CA) rules the Independent Reviews Site (www.theindependent reviewsite.org) from her castle in Los Angeles, California. Surrounded by feline subjects, she views and reviews film, and reads and writes poetry. Ms. Archibeque favors horror films and romance comedies, especially when they are combined in one film, but her only requirement for a film to be considered good is that it tell any old story in a fresh way. For a film to be considered great, "wow" must be uttered in sincerity (not disbelief) at least once during the viewing. Her film critic career began at the age of four reviewing films for family and friends. A bit of a snob, she never gave a Disney film anything more than a two on the Toddler scale until *Tron* came out. Since then she has contributed movie and music reviews to more widely known Los Angeles magazines such as *No Ho Magazine, LA Village View, Damaged Goods, Next...Magazine, Sic Vice & Verse,* and *Potpourri & Roses.* (She also did time writing for AOL's *Big Brother 2000* web site, but doesn't like to talk about it.) She works at the Academy of Motion Picture Arts and Sciences where she learns something new about film everyday, and lives in said castle with her nerdy husband whom she captured in a cemetery on Halloween.

Aaron Beierle (AB) started a small website (www.currentfilm.com) in 1997 that offered facts on current films. Eventually, the site began offering reviews of theatrical releases and gained a small following. In 1998, DVD reviews began appearing and the site's traffic has grown remarkably since then. He also reviews for www.dvdtalk.com and has a degree in marketing communications.

Mike Brantley (MB) writes about film, television, and other media for the *Mobile Register* newspaper on the Gulf Coast of Alabama. He and his wife Cheryl are avid collectors of cinema in every format, including DVD, laserdisc, 16mm, and even Betamax, when they run across the rare garage sale find. Whenever he gets the chance, Mike rolls his own movies with a vintage Super 8 movie camera. He is webmaster of www.super8filmmaking.com, an Internet gathering place for small-gauge filmmakers.

Justine Elias (JE) is the only film critic to write for both *Film Comment* and *Seventeen* magazine within a single 30-day period. However, she is most notable for pioneering the *Planet of the Apes* Unified Film Theory, which holds that all movies—including those made decades before the 1968 classic—were actually influenced by or conceived as a reaction against it. She writes for the *New York Times, The Village Voice, Premiere,* and *The Guardian.*

Dave Elswick (DE) is a talk show host at Newsradio 920 KARN in Little Rock, Arkansas. He is one of the Top 100 Most Influential Talk Show Hosts in America,

according to *Talkers* magazine, the "bible" of the talk industry. Monthly he sponsors the Dave Elswick Classic Movie at a local theatre. Recent screenings include *Rear Window, Dr. Strangelove,* and *The Deer Hunter.* Dave has been in love with movies since he was a kid. He also does a daily entertainment feature for the Arkansas Radio Network, which is heard throughout the state and in Texas, Mississippi, Oklahoma, and Missouri. He lives in Little Rock with Lynda, his wife of 11 years, and their children.

Glenn Erickson (GE) is a film editor and writer with a website called DVD Savant (www.dvdtalk.com/dvdsavant/spec.html). In addition to editing DVD documentaries, he promotes film restorations and consults on film history for studios.

Brandon Grafius (BG) is a freelance writer, living in northern California with his wife. His experience with film includes writing feature articles and reviews for *DVD Advance* and a short stint as an editor for Valley Media's film database. He earned a master's in poetry from UC Davis, and is currently at work on a novel.

G. Noel Gross (GNG) is a Dallas graphic designer and avowed Drive-In Mutant who specializes in scribbling B-movie reviews. Noel is inspired by Joe Bob Briggs and his gospel of blood, breasts, and beasts. His work can be found on www.dvdtalk.com.

When he is not designing and producing award-winning computer games, **Guido Henkel (GH)** spends most of his time working on www.DVDReview.com, one of the most popular DVD information websites on the Internet. He also writes for a variety of industry and consumer publications.

Mike Long (ML), who has been a film fan since birth, holds a bachelor's degree in film studies from the University of North Carolina and a master's degree in counseling from the University of North Carolina at Charlotte. He has been writing about movies for over a dozen years now, and currently splits his time reviewing DVDs for DVDReview.com and *VideoHound's DVD Guide.* He resides in Fort Mill, South Carolina, with his wife and two daughters.

After a five-year stint irradiating in New Mexico, **Daryl Loomis (DRL)** ventured west to California seeking his fortune in the gold rush. Realizing he was 150 years too late, he got work as a contributor on the *Schwann Opus Classical Music Guide* and *DVD Advance* magazine. When not hunkered down getting his movie fix, he can be found cheering on the bad guys at the local pro wrestling matches.

Erin Lynch (EL). Hidden away somewhere on the West Coast lives the semi-reclusive writer, artist, and self-professed media-junkie known simply as erin. Once a part of the illustrious editorial and freelance magnates of the short-lived publication, *DVD Advance,* he was thrilled to take the next step up to begin working with the staff at what is surely man's best friend: the *VideoHound.* Erin spends most of his time writing stories, spending time with his family, and dreading the upcoming teen-age years of his two children. He also likes to hear from readers via his preferred method of communication: e-mail. Give him a shout at erin@webclique.net.

Jim Olenski (JO) is the owner of Thomas Video (www.thomasvideo.com) in metro Detroit, a fabulous video store that specializes in hard-to-find, cult, foreign, independent, and classic film, on VHS, DVD, and laserdisc. Jim is a frequent contributor to the *VideoHound,* and wrote a weekly column, "Videophile," for *Real Detroit.* Jim's pseudo-elite and sometimes abrasive critical style spawned from the same punk ethic demonstrated in his 26 years as lead guitarist for the Detroit band Cinecyde. Jim is grateful for the opportunity to write for this book, because it gave him the excuse to buy a really expensive home theatre system.

Marc Olmsted (MO) has contributed to *MovieMaker, Tower Video Collector,* and the Independent Reviews Site (www.theindependentreviewssite.org). He also teaches poetry nationally and his book *What Use Am I A Hungry Ghost?* has an introduction by Allen Ginsberg. His M.A. in film can't be revoked for loving *Planet of the Vampires,* ha ha ha ha ha.

Ed Peters (EP) has a bachelor's degree in English from California State University, Northridge. His professional experience includes more than ten years in the electronic public relations industry, specializing in satellite transmission and video production. Ed was there at "the beginning," working with home video companies to promote the first "sell through" titles. The real breakthrough occurred in 1988 when he bought his first laserdisc player. (Despite upgrading several times since, his creditors still have vivid memories of the purchase.) Since March 2000, Ed has been a regular contributor to www.dvdreview.com.

Jack Sanderson (JS) has written entertainment reviews and articles for America Online's Entertainment Asylum, AOL's Kid's Asylum, Hero Magazine, and the Independent Review Site. In live theatre he has made his living as an actor, and he has dallied as a producer, writer, and award-winning director. Jack is currently undergoing aversion therapy for his film addiction by being force-fed bad popcorn.

Although some may argue the point, it's been said that **Brian Thomas (BT)** was conceived (if not born) at the drive-in, most likely during a double feature of *Attack of the Giant Leeches* and *A Bucket of Blood.* Naturally, he was raised as a full-blooded Monster Kid, getting fired up by creatures in movies, comics, and even music—catching scores of strange attractions on Creature Features, Screaming Yellow Theater, Sci-Fi Cinema, and Mystery Science Theater 3000. A fascination with all things weird led him into the study of art, writing, and film. Mr. Thomas became secretly famous drawing and writing hundreds of comic books, including *Teenage Mutant Ninja Turtles, Astro Boy, Speed Racer,* and *Ghostbusters.* Later, he got involved in the fields of new media, website design, computer-based training, video game design, and brain surgery. The video boom only fed the flames of obsession for bizarre cinema. He was a founding member of the Psychotronic Film Society (www.psychotronic.com), in which he still participates as House Critic and Propaganda Minister of the Sinister. As a writer and critic, he has contributed to many print and online film journals, as well as VideoHound's *Cult Flicks & Trash Pics, Sci-Fi Experience,* and his own *VideoHound Dragon: Asian Action & Cult Flicks.* He has also contributed to the mutant TV talk show *Abductions with the Alter Boy* as a writer and actor. Brian Thomas currently resides in his hometown, Chicago, Illinois. In the zoo.

In the dark days before home video, **Ralph Tribbey (RT)** brought *The Rocky Horror Picture Show* to weekly midnight screenings in a chain of small theatres that he owned and operated in southern California. More recently, he has served in various capacities within the entertainment industry. On the publishing side of the business, he has served as managing editor for *American Video Monthly,* editor of *Video $ell Magazine,* and is currently editor and publisher of *The DVD Release Report.* On the manufacturing end of the business he was senior vice president of marketing for West Coast Video Duplicating and is currently a consultant for Technicolor. He also keeps track of DVD releases for *Video Store Magazine.*

Michael J. Tyrkus (MJT) is an independent filmmaker, author, and editor. He has co-written and directed more than a dozen short films. As a writer and editor specializing in biographical and critical reference sources in literature and film, he has contributed to numerous references, including *The International Dictionary of Films and Filmmakers Vol 1: Films, Twentieth-Century Young Adult Writers,* and *The St. James Film Directors Encyclopedia,* edited by Andrew Sarris. He is editor of *Gay & Lesbian Biography* and co-editor of *Outstanding Lives: Profiles of Lesbians and Gay Men.* He has also served as in-house project editor for and contributor to *The St. James Women Filmmakers Encyclope-*

dia. He is co-founder of Lamb-Kiss Productions (www.lamb-kiss.com) and founder of CityScene Productions.

Production Editor

Carol A. Schwartz

Editor without Whom Nothing Would Be Accomplished

Chris Tomassini

The VideoHound Litter

Erin Bealmear, Joann Cerrito, Jim Craddock, Stephen Cusack, Miranda Ferrara, Kris Hart, Melissa Hill, and Margaret Mazurkiewicz

The Big Giant Hound Head

Peter Gareffa

Design Hound

Pamela A.E. Galbreath

Techno Hound

Wayne Fong

Proofreader and Former Hound

Beth Fhaner

Guy Who Spent a Lot of Time on the Phone Checking Facts

Jim Olenski

Production Hounds

Rita Wimberly, Evi Seoud, Mary Beth Trimper, and Dorothy Maki

Hype Hounds

Lauri Taylor and PJ Butland

Special Hound Markets

Inez Torbert

Typesetting

Marco Di Vita of the Graphix Group

This book attempts to review every feature-length film that was released on DVD from roughly June 2001 to May 2002. Following the criteria used for *VideoHound's Golden Movie Retriever* and the first two *DVD Guides,* we don't review works that are shorter than feature length—less than one hour, for practical purposes—but that's sometimes difficult to state precisely. Disney's series of *Baby* discs, for example, state running times of two to two-and-a-half hours each including all extras, but really contain only about a half-hour's worth of programming. We don't review music discs or adult films. We have included cartoon collections and Japanese anime, along with worthy TV shows. The book is meant for people who like to watch movies and want to see them in the best form possible.

Each review begins with a brief plot synopsis and comment on the artistic quality of the film. Following that are remarks—some detailed, some cursory—on the technical details of image and sound. We then give each disc two ratings: one for content and one for presentation, based on the traditional 4-bones to WOOF! scale that judges the quality of storytelling and filmmaking.

♫♫♫♫ Excellent: One of the best of its kind. You want to own this disc.

♫♫♫½ Very good: Prime rental material. Perhaps worth owning.

♫♫♫ Good: Well worth watching.

♫♫ Average: For fans of the genre or star.

♫ Poor: Make sure the scan button is working properly.

woof You have been warned.

The technical rating refers to the quality of image, sound, and extras:

♫♫♫♫ Excellent: Wow! The image approaches or even surpasses theatrical quality. Audio is equally spectacular. Delightful extras are imaginative and abundant.

♫♫♫½ Very good: The image is noticeably sharper and brighter than videotape. The sound is crisp and clear. All the extras you could reasonably expect are present.

♫♫♫ Good: Image and sound are somewhat better than tape but not really special. Extras may or may not be present.

♫♫ Average: Image and sound are not noticeably superior to VHS tape. Extras are minimal.

♫ Poor: Image and sound are substandard, due either to a poor original or transfer. Extras are probably absent.

woof Abysmal.

(Other half-bone ratings indicate the individual reviewer's mixed emotions, second and third thoughts, and free-floating equivocation.)

Each review ends with a listing of the extra features, if any, included on the disc. We also comment on those extras within the review when it's appropriate.

The various sound options available on many DVDs can be confusing and intimidating to those who are not familiar with the medium. This explanation, created by Image Entertainment and included with many discs, illustrates and explains the most popular systems (used with permission):

Dolby Digital Mono

This program features a mono soundtrack encoded to an AC-3 bitstream. When played through Dolby Digital equipment, sound will be heard from the center channel speaker only.

Dolby Digital Stereo

This program features a stereo soundtrack encoded to an AC-3 bitstream. When played through Dolby Digital equipment, sound will be heard from the front left and front right speakers only.

Dolby Digital Surround

This program features a matrixed surround soundtrack encoded to an AC-3 bitstream. When played through Dolby Digital equipment, sound will be heard from all five system speakers. The surround information will be discrete monophonic.

Dolby Digital 4.0

This program features a discrete four channel soundtrack encoded to an AC-3 bitstream. When played through Dolby Digital equipment, sound will be heard from all five system speakers. The surround information will be discrete monophonic.

Dolby Digital 5.0

This program features a discrete five channel soundtrack encoded to an AC-3 bitstream. When played through Dolby Digital equipment, discrete sound will be heard from all five system speakers.

Dolby Digital 5.1

This program features a discrete 5.1 channel soundtrack encoded to an AC-3 bitstream. When played through Dolby Digital equipment, discrete sound will be heard from all five system speakers and a subwoofer.

PCM

This program features an uncompressed digital stereo soundtrack for improved fidelity. When played, discrete stereo sound will be heard from the front right and front left speakers.

DTS

This program features a discrete 5.1 channel soundtrack and must be played through DTS-capable equipment. When played through DTS equipment, sound will be heard from all five system speakers and a subwoofer.

The more advanced stereo Surround systems, which require extra equipment, add a dramatic dimension to newer films, but even without additional speakers and amplifiers, digital sound can be an improvement, particularly when heard through good headphones. (A headphone jack is available on many DVD players.) The soundtracks of some older films still contain static and hiss. Others have been cleaned up admirably.

Format and aspect ratios generally fall into three main categories: Full frame is the general dimensions of your TV screen (usually 1.33:1); if the original film was a different (usually wider) aspect ratio, this picture has probably been cropped or "panned and scanned." Letterboxed video offers a widescreen presentation, with black bands across the top and bottom of the picture, to better approximate the original aspect ratio of the theatrical presentation. The anamorphic format, like letterboxing, preserves the widescreen ratio, but with higher quality. In this book, the specific aspect ratios are provided when available.

While we address the technical questions with each title, we don't obsess over them. This book is for people who like movies. Anyone who discovers (or re-discovers) the wonderful *Atlantic City* and criticizes the image quality is missing the point.

Like videophiles everywhere, reviewers have different tastes, different equipment, different budgets, different living arrangements. It would be wonderful if all of us—and I include readers with reviewers here—could have true home theatre systems with high-definition widescreen monitors, powerful Surround sound systems, and really comfortable chairs. But, alas, that happy day has not yet arrived, and so we do not presume to make definitive judgments. Having played many of the same discs on two different DVD players through the same monitor, I know that no two systems produce precisely the same image and sound.

When you watch a disc at home, your experience may not be the same as our reviewer's. You may see more flaws or fewer. If you enjoy a movie, you're likely to be forgiving. If you don't like it, the errors are going to jump off the screen at you.

In the end, we experience films in our minds. Yes, we use our eyes and ears, but intellect and emotion are much more important.

The various reviewers are identified by their initials at the end of each entry. (Please see their thumbnail biographies beginning on page xxv.) As a group, they are superbly qualified for the job. Each of them has written about film and video for other publications and each brings different priorities to DVD. For example, JO, who belongs to a band, pays more attention to sound than most others. DG is particularly interested in film restoration and is careful to note differences between actual running times and the times claimed by the box copy and/or other reviewers.

The one quality the reviewers share is a love of film.

Most of the entries were written from review copies of DVDs provided by the studios, but not all of them were willing to make their products available. Jim Olenski lent many discs from his store, Thomas Video (www.thomasvideo.com). Other reviewers worked from their personal libraries, and, when necessary, we rented and bought discs wherever we could find them.

Readers should pay little attention to the prices listed here. They are the retail prices suggested by the distributors. DVDs are often put on sale and, after their initial release, catalog titles are routinely marked down.

Finally, I must admit that we weren't able to get to everything. Since the beginning of the DVD business, production and distribution have been troublesome. Even though the industry is only a few years old, it is extremely difficult to find some titles. Several discs have gone out of print after having been released in small numbers. Others have been announced but never delivered. A number of them simply eluded us. We don't know where they are.

With each edition of the *DVD Guide,* we fill in blanks and correct oversights. The book will never be perfect; we try to make it better every time out of the gate.

—MM

Alphabetization

Titles are arranged on a word-by-word basis, including articles and prepositions. Leading articles (A, An, The) are ignored in English-language titles; the equivalent foreign articles are not ignored (because so many people—not you, of course—don't recognize them as articles); thus, *The Abyss* appears in the As, but *L'Enfer* appears in the Ls. Acronyms appear alphabetically as if regular words; for example, *D.O.A.* is alphabetized as "DOA." Common abbreviations in titles file as if they were spelled out, so *Dr. Strangelove* will be alphabetized as "Doctor Strangelove" and *Mr. Nice Guy* as "Mister Nice Guy." Movie titles with numbers, such as *2001: A Space Odyssey,* are alphabetized as if the number were spelled out—so Kubrick's classic would appear in the Ts as if it were "Two Thousand and One: A Space Odyssey." Proper names in titles are alphabetized beginning with the individual's first name; for instance, *Richard Pryor: Live on the Strip* is under "R;" *Stephen King's The Tommyknockers* is under "S."

Country of Origin Codes

The country of origin codes indicate the country or countries in which a film was produced or financed. A listing of films by country may also be found in the **Category Index** under the appropriate term below.

AR	Argentinian	IN	Indian
AU	Australian	IA	Iranian
BE	Belgian	IR	Irish
BR	Brazilian	IS	Israeli
BS	Bosnian	IT	Italian
GB	British	JP	Japanese
CA	Canadian	KO	Korean
CH	Chinese	MX	Mexican
CL	Colombian	NZ	New Zealand
CU	Cuban	NO	Norwegian
CZ	Czech	PL	Polish
DK	Danish	PT	Portuguese
NL	Dutch	RU	Russian
PH	Filipino	SA	South African
FI	Finnish	SP	Spanish
FR	French	SW	Swedish
GE	German	SI	Swiss
GR	Greek	TW	Taiwanese
HK	Hong Kong	VT	Vietnamese
HU	Hungarian	YU	Yugoslavian

Abbreviations

No detailed technical explanations here, just a quick reference list (with a few literal definitions, for the really curious reader) for abbreviations and acronyms used in this book.

AC3	audio coding algorithm (that is, Dolby Digital)
AKA	also known as
B	black and white
B&W	black and white
C	color
CAP:	Closed captions:
Cat.	catalog (number)
CD	compact disc
CD-I	compact disc—interactive
CE	Collector's Edition
CGI	computer-generated image
CS	Collector's Series
DC	Director's Cut
DD	Dolby Digital
DLE	Director's Limited Edition
D.P.	director of photography (cinematographer)
DS	Dolby Surround
DTS	Digital Theater Systems (a surround audio system)
DVD	digital versatile disc
DVD-ROM	digital versatile disc—read only memory
EE	Enhanced Edition
FS	Five Star Edition
f/x	effects
HDTV	high-definition television
LANG:	Language(s):
LD	laserdisc
LE	Limited Edition
ME	Millennium Edition
min.	minute
mm.	millimeter
MPAA	Motion Picture Association of America
NOM:	Nominations:
NSL	no standard list (price)
NYR	not yet reviewed
PCM	pulse code modulation (a sound format)
PE	Platinum Edition
RSDL	reverse spiral dual-layer
SB	Superbit
SE	Special Edition
SF	science fiction
SUB:	Subtitles:
THX	Tomlinson Holman experiment (an audio system certification)
UE	Ultimate Edition
UPC	Universal Product Code (number)
VHS	video helical scan (the predominate videotape format)

Sample Review

Each review contains up to 25 tidbits of information, as enumerated below. Please realize that we faked a bit of info in this review for demonstration purposes.

1. Title; some titles have the designation CE, CS, DC, DLE, EE, FS, LE, ME, PE, SB, SE, or UE (see previous column), as indicated by the distributor

2. Synopsis/review

3. Reviewer's byline; see **Contributors,** p. xxv

4. Alternative title (we faked it here)

5. Critical rating of the movie (♪ to ♪♪♪♪ or woof, ♪♪♪♪ being the ultimate praise)

6. Technical rating of DVD image, sound, and extras (using the same scale); DVDs that were not yet available for review are noted "NYR"

7. Distributor of the DVD

8. Distributor catalog number

9. Distributor UPC

10. Format and aspect ratio (more than one option may be offered)

11. Sound (more than one are possible)

12. Price of DVD

13. Type of DVD case

14. Language(s)

15. Subtitle(s), if any

16. Closed captions, if any

17. Special added features of the DVD

18. Other information about the DVD

19. Year movie was released

20. MPAA rating

21. Length in minutes

22. Black and white (B) or Color (C)

23. Country of origin (if other than the U.S.); see previous page for codes

24. Credits, including cast, voice cast (*V:*), director (*D:*), screenwriter (*W:*), cinematographer (*C:*), and music composer/lyricist (*M:*)

25. Awards and nominations

---

❶ Clerks

❷ Day in the life of a bored convenience store clerk (O'Halloran) and his best friend Randal, who mans the video store next door. Nothing much actually happens—other than a constant parade of crazies, a hockey game on the roof, and even a little necrophilia. Lots of scuzzy fun and non-stop offensive (and hilarious) dialogue. First-time director Smith (Silent Bob in the movie) based this low-budget ($27,575) film on his four years of tormenting customers at the convenience store where he shot on location. The big plus is that the DVD offers all the extras that first appeared on the laserdisc, including the alternate ending and deleted scenes. Unfortunately the video itself looks far worse than the VHS tape. There's so much grain that on most movies it would be unbearable; but because the film's style is so deliberately rough, that's not too aggravating. The contrast and brightness levels are good (about the same as the laserdisc), and the sound is very good, in fact almost too good when the music cuts come in. The bottom line is that, despite the picture, this DVD is worth adding to your collection even if its just for the supplemental material. ❸ —JO ❹ *AKA:* Kevin Smith's Clerks.
❺ *Movie:* ♪♪½ ❻ *DVD:* ♪♪
❼ Miramax ❽ (Cat # 17365, ❾ UPC # 717951002716). ❿ Widescreen (1.85:1) letterboxed. ⓫ Dolby Surround. ⓬ $34.98. ⓭ Keepcase. ⓮ *LANG:* English. ⓯ *SUB:* French, Spanish. ⓰ *CAP:* English. ⓱ *FEATURES:* 18 chapter links · Theatrical trailer · Alternate ending · Deleted scenes · Commentary: director Smith and cast members · Soul Asylum music video. ⓲ Also available as part of a "Kevin Smith" two-pack boxed set.
⓳ 1995 ⓴ (R) ㉑ 89m/ ㉒ B ㉓ US ㉔ Brian O'Halloran, Jef Anderson, Marilyn Ghigliotti, Lisa Spoonhauer, Jason Mewes, Kevin Smith; *D:* Kevin Smith; *W:* Kevin Smith; *C:* David Klein; *A:* David Klein; *M:* Scott Angley. ㉕ Sundance Film Festival '94: Filmmakers Trophy; *NOM:* Independent Spirit Awards '95: Best First Feature, Debut Performance (Anderson), First Screenplay.

Abbott and Costello Meet the Mummy

In their last film for Universal, Abbott & Costello are in Egypt with assorted bad guys, a giant iguana, some so-so effects, and even an interpretative Mummy dance in chapter 15. The slapstick and pratfalls are quickly paced, though this is far from the best for all involved. The black-and-white image is exceptionally sharp. —*MM*
Movie: 🎝🎝 **DVD:** 🎝🎝 ½
Universal Studios (cat #20573, UPC 0251-92057328). Full frame. Dolby Digital Mono. $24.98. Keepcase. *LANG:* English; French; Spanish. *CAP:* English. *FEATURES:* 18 chapters • Trailer • Production notes • Talent files.
1955 90m/B Bud Abbott, Lou Costello, Marie Windsor, Michael Ansara, Dan Seymour, Kurt Katch, Richard Deacon, Mel Welles, Edwin Parker, Richard Karlan, George Khoury; *D:* Charles Lamont; *W:* John Grant; *C:* George Robinson; *M:* Joseph Gershenson, Hans J. Salter.

Aberdeen

Ambitious London attorney Kaisa (Headey) gets a call from her terminally ill mother Helen (Rampling), who lives in Aberdeen, Scotland. Helen wants Kaisa to travel to Oslo and retrieve Tomas (Skarsgard), her alcoholic and estranged father, so Helen and he can have a deathbed reconciliation. Assertive Kaisa tracks the drunk down and makes him come with her on a nightmare trip back. Lead performances are utterly unsentimental. While the video is solid overall, diffusion is present in darker hues. But that is more than likely the intended look of the film and not the fault of the disc. An equally impressive soundtrack features crisp, understandable dialogue and a nice musical score. —*MJT*
Movie: 🎝🎝 **DVD:** 🎝🎝🎝
First Run Features (cat #FRF910095D, UPC 720229910095). Full frame. Dolby Digital 2.0 Surround. $29.95. Keepcase.

LANG: English. *FEATURES:* 12 chapters • Interview with director Hans Petter Moland • Original theatrical trailer • Cast & crew bios • Trailer gallery.
2000 103m/C *NO GB* Stellan Skarsgard, Lena Headey, Ian Hart, Charlotte Rampling; *D:* Hans Petter Moland; *W:* Hans Petter Moland, Kristin Amundsen; *C:* Philip Ogaard; *M:* Zbigniew Preisner.

About Adam

Strange romantic comedy is about an Irish girl (Hudson) who is so sure she's found Mr. Right that she proposes to him in front of a restaurant full of people, and the Mr. Right (Townsend) who literally seduces all her siblings on the way to the alter. In the end, everyone decides that keeping secrets is good, and they live happily ever after. All the players are adorable—especially Kate Hudson, have great Irish accents, and are well dressed. The film is well acted, written, and directed. This will be funny for the open minded and a little weird for most others. The disc looks great with smooth clear color and good sound. The extra featurette offers more fluff and titillation for those not fully satisfied by the film itself. —*CA*
Movie: 🎝🎝 **DVD:** 🎝🎝
Miramax Pictures (cat #23548, UPC 7869-36161656). Widescreen (1.85:1) anamorphic. Dolby Digital 5.1 Surround. $32.99. Keepcase. *LANG:* English; French. *CAP:* English. *FEATURES:* 22 chapters • Behind-the-scenes featurette.
2000 (R) 98m/C *IR GB* Stuart Townsend, Kate Hudson, Frances O'Connor, Charlotte Bradley, Rosaleen Linehan, Brendan F. Dempsey, Alan Maher, Tommy Tiernan, Cathleen Bradley; *D:* Gerard Stembridge; *W:* Gerard Stembridge; *C:* Bruno de Keyzer; *M:* Adrian Johnston.

Abraxas: Guardian of the Universe [BFS]

Please see review for *Great Sci-Fi Thrillers*.
AKA: Abraxas.

Movie: 🎝 ½
1990 (R) 90m/C Jesse Ventura, Sven-Ole Thorsen, Damian Lee, Marjorie Bransfield, Ken Quinn, Marilyn Lightstone, Moses Znaimer, Layne Coleman, Sonja Belliveau, James Belushi; *D:* Damian Lee; *W:* Damian Lee; *C:* Curtis Petersen.

Absolutely Fabulous: Series 1

Absolutely Fabulous began airing in Great Britain in 1992, and was the creation of comedian Jennifer Saunders (of *French and Saunders* TV fame). It stars Saunders as Edina, a fashion-world publicist who attempts to relive her '60s youth with best friend Patsy (Joanna Lumley) by taking massive amounts of drugs and drinking. Meanwhile, they keep running up against Edina's daughter Saffron, who is the exact opposite—politically correct and disapproving of her mother's actions. A fantastic supporting cast of characters adds to the entertainment with particularly hilarious supporting work by Jane Horrocks as Edina's idiotic assistant, Bubble. There are so many great things about the series: hilarious jokes and references to pop culture and society, brilliant writing, perfect comedic timing, and fantastic actors. The two leads wonderfully play up their bad behavior and obviously have fun playing the characters. Season one offers some of the best episodes of the series, including their classic trip to France. If you haven't seen the series before, it's very highly recommended. The disc contains all six episodes of the first season (or "Series," as referred to in the U.K.). All of the episodes look slightly better than they do when broadcast on TV. Sharpness and detail are generally fair; there's a bit of a soft look to many of the episodes, but the image never looks hazy or blurry. Colors are generally strong and well-defined. The most important thing in a show like this one is the dialogue, and every line remains clear and easily understood. The balance between the background laughter, dialogue, and other ambient sounds is fine. All of the discs offer about 15-16 minutes worth of outtakes. The outtakes here aren't quite as funny as the ones included on the second or third seasons, but there are a few very good laughs. One of the outtakes is also a deleted scene. —*AB/DG*

Movie: ♫♫♫ ½ **DVD:** ♫♫♫
BBC/Worldwide Americas (UPC 79405115-3128). Full frame. Dolby Digital Surround. $29.98. Keepcase. *LANG:* English. *CAP:* English. *FEATURES:* 6 chapters per episode • Outtakes • Still gallery • "Making of" featurette.
1994 87m/C *GB* Jennifer Saunders, Joanna Lumley, Julia Sawalha; *W:* Jennifer Saunders.

Absolutely Fabulous: Series 4

Absolutely Fabulous went off the air several years ago, but recently, when writer/star Saunders was producing/writing a new show called *Mirrorball* with the same cast, she decided that things weren't working out, so they produced another season of *Ab Fab* instead. The result is moderately funny, but not up to the same level as the first three seasons of the show. Out of the six episodes, two are better than the rest: "Small Opening," where Saffron puts on one of her plays that tells all about her life with Patsy and her mother, and "Paris," where Patsy tries to revive her modeling career. It's great that all of the old characters returned, but the balance seems off. Julia Sawalha's character has a bit less of a role this time around, and the balance between Saunders and Lumley is off. They're both quite funny, but they're even funnier playing off one another, which they don't do enough of here. Still, the return of *Ab Fab* is welcome, as it's still funnier than much of what's currently on television today. This set presents all six episodes in widescreen. The presentations are a considerable improvement over the full-frame cable TV broadcasts. Sharpness and detail are both excellent. A couple of slight traces of pixelation are visible, but this was hardly noticeable. The colors are nicely rendered. The audio is quite good, and both music and dialogue are well balanced. The most important supplement is the one-off *Mirrorball* special, which was the project that Saunders and much of the rest of the cast were working on. It's funny, but it's clear that Saunders and the rest of the cast have created classic characters in *Ab Fab* that begged to be continued. There are 12 minutes of outtakes and though they're not as funny as some of the ones that were included on the discs for the first three seasons, there are definitely some gems. The commentary is surprisingly subdued; while the two chat throughout all of the episodes, they're rather low-key. Plowman acts as interviewer at times and we learn more about the process of writing and creating these characters and situations. The two also point out some

interesting details and discuss some funny stories from the set. These commentaries are worth a listen, but don't have much repeat value. —*AB/DG*
Movie: ♫♫♫ **DVD:** ♫♫♫ ½
BBC/Worldwide Americas (UPC 79405116-1222). Widescreen (1.85:1) anamorphic. Dolby Digital Surround. $24.98. Keepcase. *LANG:* English. *FEATURES:* Commentary: Jennifer Saunders, series producer Jon Plowman • *Mirror Ball* episode • Outtakes • Who's who guide.
2001 240m/C *GB* Jennifer Saunders, Joanna Lumley, Julia Sawalha, Jane Horrocks; *D:* Bob Spiers; *W:* Jennifer Saunders.

Acceptable Risk

Pharmaceutical scientist Edward Wells (Lowe) discovers a strange fungus in a walled-in part of his basement. He takes it into the lab, finds unusual healing properties in the substance, and immediately begins to test it on himself. At first, he feels superhuman, but monstrous side effects quickly surface. There is some suspense in this TV movie, but the inconsistent story and poor performances are hard to get past. The transfer is simply awful. Colors bleed, artifacts are everywhere, and some of the darker scenes are virtually unwatchable. The stereo sound is much better, but still below average. —*DRL*
Movie: ♫♫ **DVD:** ♫
Artisan Ent. (cat #12675, UPC 70772912-6751). Full frame. Stereo. $19.98. Keepcase. *LANG:* English. *FEATURES:* 14 chapters.
2001 92m/C Chad Lowe, Kelly Rutherford, Sean Patrick Flanery, Patty McCormack, Danielle von Zerneck; *D:* William A. Graham; *W:* Michael J. Murray; *C:* Eyal Grodin.

Accident

As much a Harold Pinter creation as Losey's, this is an intriguing drama among some unusually tight-lipped people, perhaps weighed too heavily in the direction of Meaningful Emptiness, but always engaging and emotionally suspenseful. Romantic entanglements form during summer session at Oxford: dons Stephen (Bogarde) and Charley (Baker), both married, are smitten by the beauty of aloof Austrian exchange student Anna (Sassard). Although young aristocrat William (York) is her supposed beau, relationships thicken at a lunch party that turns into a day-long drunk at Stephen's place. Stephen's wife Rosalind (Merchant) is pregnant, but he's still threatened by his loss of masculinity, trying to secure a BBC deal like the smug Charley, and looking up an old flame (Seyrig) while in London. Stephen's shocked to find Anna sneaking behind William's back to sleep with Charley, as the two young people are practically engaged...but Stephen also discovers he doesn't know the extent of his own desires. DVD is nicely turned out. The 16:9 transfer is strong, showing only the slightest wear and bits of unsteadiness, probably near reel changes. Gerry Fisher's

subtle color values are retained throughout. The color stills I've seen make Jacqueline Sassard's feathery boa a light blue, and on this disc they're plain white, which is probably correct. A lengthy original trailer is included as the only extra. There are no subtitles or closed captioning, which not only makes this a useless disc for the hearing-impaired, but also forces those with American ears to pay close attention to the clipped Brit dialogue. (Title is part of the *Dirk Bogard Collection*.) —*GE*
Movie: ♫♫♫ **DVD:** ♫♫♫ ½
Anchor Bay (cat #DV11666, UPC 013131-166699). Widescreen (1.78:1) anamorphic. Dolby Digital Mono. $39.98. Keepcase. *LANG:* English. *FEATURES:* Trailer • 24 chapters.
1967 100m/C *GB* Dirk Bogarde, Michael York, Stanley Baker, Jacqueline Sassard, Delphine Seyrig, Alexander Knox, Vivien Merchant, Freddie Jones, Harold Pinter; *D:* Joseph Losey; *W:* Harold Pinter; *C:* Gerry Fisher; *M:* John Dankworth. *AWARDS:* Cannes '67: Grand Jury Prize.

The Accused

After a night of drinking and flirting at the local bar, Sarah Tobias (Foster) is brutally raped by three men while a host of onlookers cheer them on. Tobias finds a sympathetic district attorney (McGillis) who thinks their best chance is to accept a plea bargain due to Sarah's questionable behavior that night. Tobias still doesn't feel vindicated and presses charges against the men who encouraged the attack as well. This controversial drama raises many tough questions on the nature of rape and "asking for it," and attempts to answer them all in a brutal flashback scene near the film's conclusion. The anamorphic transfer looks quite good, but dialogue is saddled with a high amount of background hiss on both the 5.1 and Stereo Surround mixes. More extra features should be expected for the release of such a critically acclaimed and commercially successful film. —*BG*
Movie: ♫♫♫ **DVD:** ♫♫ ½
Paramount (cat #01760, UPC 097360176-049). Widescreen anamorphic. Dolby 5.1; Dolby Surround. $24.99. Keepcase. *LANG:* English; French. *SUB:* English. *FEATURES:* 14 chapters • Trailer.
1988 (R) 110m/C Jodie Foster, Kelly McGillis, Bernie Coulson, Leo Rossi, Ann Hearn, Carmen Argenziano, Steve Antin, Tom O'Brien, Peter Van Norden, Woody Brown; *D:* Jonathan Kaplan; *W:* Tom Topor; *C:* Ralf Bode; *M:* Brad Fiedel. *AWARDS:* Oscars '88: Actress (Foster); Golden Globes '89: Actress—Drama (Foster); Natl. Bd. of Review '88: Actress (Foster).

The Acid House

Three Irvine Welsh (*Trainspotting*) short stories combine to create this further portrait of Scottish drug culture. A man who's managed to destroy his life in the span of 24 hours runs into God in a bar; a man finds his lovely bride is cavorting (very

loudly) with a sadistic upstairs neighbor; and an acid trip causes a young man to exchange bodies with a newborn baby. The swearing is continuous, the cuts are sharp, and the hyperactivity is familiar. Colors are rather soft and the picture overall feels a bit hazy. The accents are so thick that subtitles are provided. You'll be glad at first, but they fade in and out at random points and they're burned into the film so it's impossible to turn them off once you've got the hang of the dialect. —*BG*
Movie: 🎵🎵 *DVD:* 🎵🎵 ½
Zeitgeist Films (cat #Z1004, UPC 795975-100434). Widescreen (1.85:1) letterboxed. Dolby Surround. $29.99. Keepcase. *LANG:* English. *SUB:* English. *FEATURES:* 12 chapters ☞ Trailers ☞ Commentary: Irvine Welsh ☞ Glossary ☞ Reprinted interview with Welsh.
1998 118m/C Stephen McCole, Maurice Roeves, Garry Sweeney, Kevin McKidd, Ewen Bremner, Martin Clunes, Jemma Redgrave, Arlene Cockburn, Jenny McCrindle, Michelle Gomez, Tam Dean Burn, Gary McCormack, Jane Stabler; **D:** Paul McGuigan; **W:** Irvine Welsh; **C:** Alasdair Walker.

Across 110th Street
In one of the great blaxploitation movies, both the Mafia and the cops hunt down three hoods who, in a display of extremely bad judgment, knock over a mob-controlled bank while they're disguised as policemen. Lots of bullets create lots of blood. The film was made on location in Harlem and DVD retains the grainy look in both the exteriors and the roughly lit interiors. Mono sound gets the job done. Highly recommended to fans of the genre. —*MM*
Movie: 🎵🎵🎵 *DVD:* 🎵🎵 ½
MGM Home Ent. (cat #1002579, UPC 027-616867803). Widescreen (1.85:1) anamorphic. Dolby Digital Mono. $19.98. Keepcase. *LANG:* English; French; Spanish. *SUB:* French; Spanish. *CAP:* English. *FEATURES:* 16 chapters ☞ Trailer.
1972 (R) 102m/C Anthony Quinn, Yaphet Kotto, Anthony (Tony) Franciosa, Paul Benjamin, Ed Bernard, Antonio Fargas, Tim O'Connor, Lewis Gilbert, Richard Ward; **D:** Barry Shear; **W:** Luther Davis; **C:** Jack Priestley.

Action Arsenal
This five-disc set contains ten really bad, really cheap movies that gain nothing on DVD. Please see individual reviews of *Mind, Body & Soul, Bad Cop 1, Blitz, Kill Cruise, Bad Cop 2, Twisted Justice, Human Prey, Narcotic Justice, Street Vengeance,* and *Revenge Quest.* —*MM*
Movie: 🎵 *DVD:* 🎵🎵
BCI-Eclipse (cat #44076-9, UPC 7873644-07699). Full frame. $19.98. Keepcase (five disc). *LANG:* English.
2001 919m/C

Adrenaline Drive
Meek rental car clerk Suzuki Satoru (Masanobu Ando) is in the local yakuza's office trying to explain a fender bender when there's a gas explosion. He meets meek nurse Sato Shizuko (Hikari Ishida of *Battle Royale*) who comes to help after the explosion. They decide to take a case full of money. The first problem is how to deal with such a load of cash. Their second problem is that the big mean gangster who was harassing Suzuki survived both the explosion and the crash somehow, and he breaks out of the hospital to go after them. And wouldn't you know it, there's nothing like being on the run from a gang of crooks to make a young man and woman fall in love. Yaguchi gives his little adventure just the right understated tone, keeping things light, but not to the point of total caricature, and full of surprises. Ishida is especially good as the little nurse busting loose for the first time in her life. The widescreen image shows off some nice compositions. Though a bit soft, the colors are fresh and vivid. —*BT* **AKA:** Adorenarin Doraibu.
Movie: 🎵🎵🎵 *DVD:* 🎵🎵
Image Ent. (cat #ID0597SLDVD, UPC 014-38105924). Widescreen (1.78:1) anamorphic. $24.99. Keepcase. *LANG:* Japanese. *SUB:* English (non-removable). *FEATURES:* 18 chapters.
1999 111m/C JP Hikari Ishida, Mansanobu Ando, Yataka Matushige, Kazue Tsunogae; **D:** Shinobu Yaguchi; **W:** Shinobu Yaguchi; **C:** Takashi Hamada; **M:** Seiichi Yamamoto.

The Adventures of Buckaroo Banzai Across the Eighth Dimension [SE]
Purposely confusing and sometimes laboring too hard to be off-the-wall flippant, this cult fave nevertheless shapes up as a fun adventure along the lines of a Republic Serial—but with a hip attitude. Surgeon, rock musician, particle physicist, and leader of the Hong Kong Cavaliers, Buckaroo Banzai (Weller) comes back from a trip to the 8th dimension with the ability to see the villainous Red Lectroids who have come from that alternate reality and are living among us. They've taken possession of Doctor Emilio Lizardo (Lithgow), who now goes by the name of Lord John Whorfin. Together with Red Lectroids John Bigboote (Lloyd) and John O'Connor (Schiavelli), they steal the oscillation overthruster invented by Professor Hikita (Ito) to return to the 8th dimension. Unfortunately, the benign Black Lectroids don't want them back, and Black Lectroid John Parker (Lumbly) brings a message from leader John Emdall (Cash) that distills into blackmail: Earth will be destroyed unless Buckaroo and his Cavaliers stop the Red Lectroids in time. Buckaroo enlists stalwarts Reno (Serna) and Rawhide (Brown) and enlists new members New Jersey (Goldblum) and Penny Priddy (Barkin) into the crusade to make the Earth safe from the Red Lectroid scum. DVD presents a fine new transfer of the standard 1984 cut, in 16:9 for the first time on video. There was an early laserdisc that was a collector's treasure even though its squeezed and pan-and-scanned image looked terrible. The transfer is so good, some of the special effects shots are shown to have optical dirt printed in, a flaw that could have been cleaned up digitally, one could suppose. This Special Edition has a number of unusual extras that will either thrill fans or frustrate them, depending on what they expect from their special edition DVDs. The extras address one of the main problems that hurt the show when it was new. At the last minute, extraneous background plotting was removed that would have helped some of the relationships make better sense. Thinking the movie too complicated, they jettisoned a prologue that explained Buckaroo's name and heritage, the genesis of the overthruster, and the relationship between Penny Priddy and Buckaroo's dead wife, who looked just like her. Losing this background info (which was presented in a fairly exciting manner) robbed the film of a lot of needed depth, while alienating literal-minded viewers who wanted all the plot details to add up to an even number. Special edition DVD was not scaled big enough to take in the entire production. Also, although reels of star interviews and behind-the-scenes video were shot, none was retained by anyone except director W.D. Richter, who only had VHS tape copies, often with time-code windows. The extras are consistent with Richter and MacRauch's take on the show, and account for the tongue-in-cheek tone that pretends that Buckaroo is a real historical figure and that the movie is simply an attempt to popularize, for the big screen, a small fraction of his many exploits. This conceit is maintained well by Richter and Earl MacRauch, who pretends to be the real-life Reno on the main commentary track; hopefully it won't be taken as too taxing by fans who'd prefer a straight approach. —*GE* **AKA:** Buckaroo Banzai.
Movie: 🎵🎵🎵 *DVD:* 🎵🎵🎵 ½
MGM Home Ent. (cat #1002040, UPC 027616862785). Widescreen (2.35:1) anamorphic. Dolby Digital 5.1 Surround Stereo. $19.98. Keepcase. *LANG:* English. *SUB:* French; Spanish. *CAP:* English. *FEATURES:* NUON features ☞ Deleted prologue and other scenes ☞ "Making of" featurette ☞ Photo gallery ☞ Commentary ☞ Character profiles.
1984 (PG) 100m/C Peter Weller, Ellen Barkin, Jeff Goldblum, Christopher Lloyd, John Lithgow, Lewis Smith, Rosalind Cash, Robert Ito, Pepe Serna, Vincent Schiavelli, Dan Hedaya, Yakov Smirnoff, Jamie Lee Curtis, Ronald Lacey, Matt Clark, Clancy Brown, Carl Lumbly, Red Morgan; **D:** W.D. Richter; **W:** Earl MacRauch; **C:** Fred W. Koenekamp; **M:** Michael Boddicker.

Adventures of Justine
Compilation of a late-night cable series is a soft-core *Perils of Pauline* with a bit of light bondage. Justine (Boone) is a stu-

dent who accompanies Professor Robson (DiPri) on a series of escapades involving Egyptian tombs, satanists, Nazis, etc. Given the levels of explicitness that have become common in the genre, this is tepid stuff. The cast is thespianically challenged, but attractive and comfortable with nudity. Image is moderately grainy with flatteringly soft focus, but it improves—and the grain is radically lessened—in the sex scenes which occur about every 30 minutes. Sound is fine. The series is a Euro-Irish production. Contents: "In the Heat of Passion," "A Midsummer Night's Sex Comedy," "Object of Desire," "Exotic Liason," "Crazy Love," "A Private Affair," "Seduction of Innocence." —*MM*
Movie: 🎬🎬 ½ **DVD:** 🎬🎬 ½
New Concorde (cat #NH25012 D, UPC 736991050129). Full frame. Stereo. $59.95. Keepcase boxed set. *LANG:* English. *FEATURES:* Trailers ▪ Thumbnail bios ▪ 132 chapters.
2000 638m/C *FR IR* Daneen Boone, Kimberly Rowe, Timothy DiPri, Jennifer Behr, Bo Zena, Alex Veadov; *D:* L.L. Shapira, Kevin Alber, David Cove; *W:* T. C. McKelvey, Noel Harrison, Edward Laraby, Thomas Roberdeau; *C:* Amit Bhattacharya, Nick Hutak, Brad Rushing; *M:* Nigel Holton, Kevin Kiner, Tim Wynn.

The Adventures of Sherlock Holmes, Vol. 3

This disc contains two of the acclaimed Granada television adaptations of Sherlock Holmes stories, "The Blue Carbuncle" and "The Copper Beeches." It shares both the strengths and the weaknesses of the first volume (reviewed in *Book 2*): superb characterizations by Jeremy Brett as Holmes and David Burke as Watson; solid scripts that are faithful to the original; and DVD images that display constant artifacts and pixels. Perhaps that's the best that can be done with the originals, which appear to be in pretty good shape. The "Sherlock Societies" extra is a list of addresses. (Other volumes are also available: Vol. 2, UPC 030306177328, "The Crooked Man" and "The Speckled Band"; Vol. 4, UPC 030306353128, "The Greek Interpreter" and "The Norwood Builder.") —*MM*
Movie: 🎬🎬🎬 ½ **DVD:** 🎬🎬 ½
MPI (cat #3515, UPC 030306351520). Full frame. Dolby Digital Mono. $14.98. Keepcase. *LANG:* English. *SUB:* English. *FEATURES:* 22 chapters ▪ Paget's drawings ▪ Sherlock societies.
1983 100m/C *GB* Jeremy Brett, David Burke.

Adventures of the Kung Fu Rascals

Ultra-low budget juvenile slapstick martial-arts comedy features a few terrific visual effects which lose something on this no-frills DVD. The clarity of the medium makes the film's visual shortcomings all the more glaring. In almost every scene,

heavy grain leads to artifacts. Some objects even appear to "swim" against the background. Anyone who can overlook those massive shortcomings and the silly plot will be rewarded. Chen (writer/director/producer Steve Wang), Lao Zo (Troy Fronin), and Repo (Johnnie Saiko Espiritu) are young warriors (think Larry, Mo, and Curly) who have stolen a treasure map to "the power most big" from the evil Bamboo Man. That leads, at length, to Nio-Titan (Ed Yang), a ponderous stone giant reminiscent of Talos, the bronze man in Ray Harryhausen's *Jason and the Argonauts*. But Wang couldn't afford stop-motion animation effects. Instead, he uses unusual lenses and forced perspective to create the illusion that the guy is 30 feet tall. —*MM* **AKA:** Kung Fu Rascals.
Movie: 🎬🎬 ½ **DVD:** 🎬 ½
York Ent. (cat #YPD-1133, UPC 75072311-3326). Widescreen letterboxed. $14.99. Keepcase. *LANG:* English.
1992 (PG-13) 90m/C Troy Fronin, Johnnie Saiko Espiritu, Steve Wang, Edward Yang; *D:* Steve Wang; *W:* Steve Wang; *C:* Mike Bastings; *M:* Les Claypool.

Advertising Rules!

Extremely sardonic and funny look at the world of advertising. Viktor Vogel (Scheer) bluffs his way into the ad game and gets the responsibility for the new make-or-break account. But when the corporate world collides with his love life, Viktor must make a character-defining decision. This excellent video transfer boasts bright, crisp colors and solid blacks. Some low-end hues do tend to lose clarity, but it is hardly enough to be annoyed by. While dialogue is crisp and discernible on the well-produced soundtrack, some German speech sounds slurred (which is probably due to the actor's thick accents). —*MJT* **AKA:** Viktor Vogel: Commercial Artist.
Movie: 🎬🎬🎬 **DVD:** 🎬🎬🎬
Columbia Tristar (cat #07828, UPC 04339-6078284). Widescreen (1.85:1) anamorphic. Dolby Digital 5.1 Surround; Dolby Digital Stereo. $29.95. Keepcase. *LANG:* German; French. *SUB:* English; French; Spanish; Portuguese; Chinese; Korean; Thai. *FEATURES:* 20 chapters ▪ "Making of" featurette ▪ Deleted scenes ▪ Alternate opening and ending B-roll footage ▪ Theatrical trailers ▪ Filmographies.
2001 (R) 109m/C *GE* Gudrun Landgrebe, Alexander Scheer, Goetz George, Chulpan Khamatova, Maria Schrader, Vadim Glowna; *D:* Lars Kraume; *W:* Lars Kraume, Tom Schlessinger; *C:* Andreas Daub; *M:* Robert Jan Meyer.

Aenigma

A girl is left in a coma from a prank perpetrated by her fellow students at an all girl's college. From her hospital bed, she takes possession of a new student who somehow exacts revenge upon the injured girl's victimizers. Thoroughly inept film from cult director Fulci shows no evidence of any technical, aesthetic, or artistic talent what-

soever. A poor cast of dull, inadequate actors performing terrible lines from an awful script in a totally subpar production. The flat dubbing seems to accurately mirror the lifeless performances and flat characters. The "highlight" is a snail attack scene which is stupid, dull, nauseating, and not in the least bit frightening. This painfully dull and uninteresting "horror" film is an insult to the genre, the audience, and filmmaking in general. It makes you want to abandon watching films altogether. The disc is sharp and free of digital noise. The muted colors appear to be conveyed with accuracy and the mono sound is fairly clean. Volume levels are inconsistent and had to be adjusted several times during playback. —*DG*
Movie: woof **DVD:** 🎬🎬🎬
Image Ent. (cat #ID820GUDVD, UPC 0143-81082029). Widescreen (1.85:1) letterboxed. Mono. $24.99. Keepcase. *LANG:* English. *FEATURES:* Insert card ▪ 12 chapters.
1987 85m/C Jared Martin, Lara Naszinsky; *D:* Lucio Fulci; *W:* Lucio Fulci.

Afraid to Die

Intellectual director Yasuzo Masumura *(The Blind Beast, Giants and Toys)* seems incapable of making an ordinary movie. This would appear to be a response to Yakuza films, and as such it replaces their outlaw-chic celebration of criminal outcasts with a much more downbeat appraisal of the genre. An even greater draw is the fact that the film stars celebrity writer and legendary seppuku suicide Yukio Mishima, playing gangster underboss Takeo Asahina. He hasn't even been released from Tokyo prison, and already his rival underboss Susumu Aikawa (Eiji Funakoshi) is trying to have him murdered. Takeo's wounding of Susumu is what sent him to prison in the first place, and now he finds that an out-of-town asthmatic hitman has been assigned to rub him out. Ditching his old flame Yoshie (Masako Katori), Takeo pursues Ayako (Yoshie Koizumi), a cashier in a movie theatre and the sister of a communist striker. Takeo's adopted brother and uncle Gohei (Takashi Shimura) encourage him to assassinate Susumu without delay, but Takeo openly admits to being a coward—instead, he kidnaps Susumu's child and holds her for ransom. In this film, Yakuza are slime, not citizens. They constantly betray one another. Money is the only thing of value, and beloved relatives are a fatal liability because they are a way to get to men who otherwise have no weaknesses. DVD picture quality is very good in all respects. It tends toward a greenishness that appears to be a part of the production design, but also might be from the filmstock used back in 1960 by Daiei—even the blacks have green in them. But there's still an acceptable range of color, and fleshtones are healthy, so the image has a pleasing originality about it. The punchy jazz score (on the evidence of three films, Masumura seems to go in for this) comes across nicely too. The extras include a trailer full of

spoilers and the usual thorough Fantoma text resources. I was disappointed when I couldn't navigate past the first page of an essay on Mishima, but maybe that glitch was a problem with my specific player. —*GE*
AKA: Karakkaze yaro.
Movie: 🎬🎬🎬 ½ **DVD:** 🎬🎬🎬
Image Ent. (UPC 014381169027). Widescreen (2:35:1) anamorphic. $29.98. Keepcase. *LANG:* Japanese. *SUB:* English. *FEATURES:* Trailer ● Text essays.
1960 96m/C *JP* Yukio Mishima, Ayako Wakao, Keizo Kawasaki, Eiji Funakoshi, Takashi Shimura, Masako Katori, Yoshi Koizumi; *D:* Yasuzo Masumura; *W:* Ryuzo Kikushima, Hideo Ando; *C:* Hiroshi Murai.

After Dark, My Sweet [2]

Artisan corrects the visual flaws of the first full-frame release (reviewed in *Book 1*) of James Foley's neo-noir with this widescreen version. The image is bright and sharp with well-defined colors. Contrast is still high, but that comes from the original. —*MM*
Movie: 🎬🎬🎬 **DVD:** 🎬🎬🎬
Artisan Ent. (cat #12526, UPC 01223612-5266). Widescreen (1.85:1) anamorphic. Dolby Digital Surround. $15.98. Keepcase. *LANG:* English. *CAP:* English. *FEATURES:* 22 chapters.
1990 (R) 114m/C Jason Patric, Rachel Ward, Bruce Dern, George Dickerson, James Cotton, Corey Carrier, Rocky Giordani; *D:* James Foley; *W:* Robert Redlin, James Foley; *C:* Mark Plummer; *M:* Maurice Jarre.

After the Fox

Sellers is a con artist posing as a film director to carry out a bizarre plan to steal gold from Rome. Lackluster comedy (co-written by Neil Simon, not at his best) features occasional backhand slaps at Hollywood with Mature turning in a memorable performance as the past-his-prime actor starring in Sellers's movie. Very light scratches are intermittent. The grain in the desert scenes comes from the original and is not a distraction. Overall, the image is excellent for a film of this age. Sound is acceptable. —*MM* **AKA:** Caccia alla Volpe.
Movie: 🎬🎬 **DVD:** 🎬🎬 ½
MGM Home Ent. (cat #1003133, UPC 027-616872975). Widescreen (2.35:1) anamorphic; full frame. Dolby Digital Mono. $24.98. Keepcase. *LANG:* English; French; Spanish. *SUB:* English; French; Spanish. *CAP:* English. *FEATURES:* 16 chapters ● Trailer.
1966 103m/C *GB IT* Peter Sellers, Victor Mature, Martin Balsam, Britt Ekland; *D:* Vittorio De Sica; *W:* Neil Simon, Cesare Zavattini; *C:* Leonida Barboni; *M:* Burt Bacharach.

After the War

Masterpiece Theatre miniseries follows two young Jewish men—Joe Hirsh (Reynolds) and Michael Jordan (Lukis) (no, not *that* Michael Jordan)—from their meeting at an English private school in 1942 through their careers in the entertainment business. As is so often the case with these imports, the action is talky and supremely well acted. Production values are good. DVD image is roughly of broadcast quality with considerable grain in many scenes, and the occasional dust fleck. A hiss is audible on parts of the soundtrack, too. —*MM*
Movie: 🎬🎬 ½ **DVD:** 🎬🎬
BFS Video (cat #30202-D, UPC 06680530-2022). Full frame. $59.98. Keepcase boxed set. *LANG:* English. *FEATURES:* 28 chapters.
1989 518m/C *GB* Susannah York, Denis Quilley, Adrian Lukis, Robert Reynolds, Caroline Goodall, Serena Gordon, Patrick Malahide, Art Malik; *D:* John Madden, John Glenister, Nicholas Renton; *W:* Frederic Raphael.

Agatha Christie's Miss Marple Set 1

This set includes four films based on the writings of Agatha Christie and the adventures of her most popular character, the prim and proper Miss Jane Marple. The collection includes: *A Caribbean Mystery, The Mirror Cracked from Side to Side, Sleeping Murder,* and *4:50 from Paddington.* In all four films, Miss Marple uses her razor-sharp mind, intuitive understanding of criminal behavior, and trademark knitting needles to solve a variety of murders. The colors are quite good on this video transfer, perfectly representing the diffused colors that are so often used on A&E programs (though this style really doesn't utilize the digital clarity of DVD technology very well). The audio transfer is decent, delivering a solid soundtrack with no noticeable cracks or other problems. —*MJT*
Movie: 🎬🎬 ½ **DVD:** 🎬🎬 ½
A&E (cat #AAE70257, UPC 7339617025-76). Full frame. Dolby Digital Stereo. $39.95. Custom case. *LANG:* English. *FEATURES:* 48 chapters (12 per feature) ● Complete index of all Miss Marple stories.
1987 400m/C *GB*

Agatha Christie's Miss Marple Set 2

This set includes five films based on the adventures of elderly sleuth Miss Jane Marple, created by Agatha Christie. The collection includes: *The Moving Finger, At Bertram's Hotel, Murder at the Vicarage, Nemesis,* and *They Do It with Mirrors.* In all five films, Miss Marple solves case after case using a variety of tactics. The video transfer is decent and perfectly reproduces the diffused colors used on many A&E programs. The audio transfer delivers a solid soundtrack with no noticeable distortion. —*MJT*
Movie: 🎬🎬 ½ **DVD:** 🎬🎬 ½
A&E (cat #AAE70380, UPC 7339617038-01). Full frame. Dolby Digital Stereo. $49.95. Custom case. *LANG:* English. *FEATURES:* 48 chapters (12 per feature) ● Complete index of all Miss Marple stories ● Joan Hickson bio and filmography.
2002 500m/C

Agatha Christie's Poirot: Dumb Witness

Another engaging and period-specific Poirot mystery that is set off when premonitions of a murder prove accurate. Poirot then must solve the crime by communicating with a single, silent witness—the victim's canine companion. While most Poirot adventures are enjoyable from an entertainment standpoint, many discs in the series fail to take advantage of the DVD format. This particular disc features diffused blacks as well as muted colors (a stalwart of the series). However, the transfer is decent enough to be labeled as passable (that is, better than some Poirot adventures on disc, yet not so others). The soundtrack is very solid. Dialogue is reproduced well, as are ambient sounds and the moody musical score. As for the disc's extras, they are trivial but their plentitude make them not a complete waste. —*MJT*
Movie: 🎬🎬🎬 **DVD:** 🎬🎬
Acorn Media (cat #AMP4703, UPC 054-961470396). Full frame. Dolby Digital Stereo. $24.95. Keepcase. *LANG:* English. *FEATURES:* 10 chapters ● Bios of Agatha Christie and David Suchet ● Poirot trivia ● Cast filmographies ● Agatha Christie materials.
2001 103m/C *GB* David Suchet, Hugh Fraser; *D:* Edward Bennett; *W:* Douglas Watkinson; *C:* Simon Kosoff.

Agatha Christie's Poirot: Hercule Poirot's Christmas

When Poirot plans a quiet Christmas in London, it is an inevitability that murder most foul will rear its ugly head. Indeed, when the boiler in his apartment breaks and Poirot takes a diamond baron up on an offer to spend Christmas at his "heated" home and to be on the lookout for a "crime," it's only a matter of time before Poirot winds up with a murder to solve, family politics to unravel, and shocking revelations from the past to sort out. Surprisingly vibrant color definition saves this disc from suffering from the sub-par transfer woes bestowed upon other Poirot adventures. However, blacks do tend to lack crisp definition. Fortunately, this is one of the more "colorful" of the Poirot adventures. A solid soundtrack that reproduces dialogue, ambient sounds, and a musical score quite compliments the above average picture. As for the disc's extras, what they lack in quality they make up for in quantity. —*MJT*
Movie: 🎬🎬 ½ **DVD:** 🎬🎬 ½
Acorn Media (cat #AMP4711, UPC 05496-1471195). Full frame. Dolby Digital Stereo. $24.95. Keepcase. *LANG:* English. *FEATURES:* 10 chapters ● Bios of Agatha Christie and David Suchet ● Poirot trivia ● Cast filmographies ● Agatha Christie materials.
2001 103m/C *GB* David Suchet, Hugh Fraser; *D:* Edward Bennett; *W:* Clive Exton; *C:* Simon Kosoff.

Agatha Christie's Poirot: Peril at End House

Coincidences that lead to murder seem to follow Poirot around like flies. While on holiday in Cornwall, Poirot twists an ankle and encounters the pretty, accident-prone heiress of a local estate and the survivor of several near-fatal mishaps. Of course, Poirot suspects more than mere chance is behind these events when strange connections begin to surface. A rather disappointing video transfer (featuring diffused blacks and muted colors) is redeemed to a certain extent by a solid soundtrack. Dialogue is reproduced well, as are ambient sounds and the moody musical score. The disc's extras, though trivial, are bountiful. —MJT
Movie: 🎬🎬🎬 **DVD:** 🎬🎬
Acorn Media (cat #AMP4436, UPC 054-961443697). Full frame. Dolby Digital Stereo. $24.95. Keepcase. *LANG:* English. *FEATURES:* 10 chapters • Bios of Agatha Christie and David Suchet • Poirot trivia • Cast filmographies • Agatha Christie materials.
1990 103m/C *GB* David Suchet, Hugh Fraser, Pauline Moran; *D:* Renny Rye; *W:* Clive Exton.

Agatha Christie's Poirot: The ABC Murders

It appears as if someone has taken aim at Hercule Poirot (Suchet) when an anonymous letter predicts a murder on a specific date. The police are not convinced, but a murder does occur and the great detective investigates. His only clue is a train schedule, "The ABC Railway Guide." The movie is well paced to capture the growing intensity as the situation gets more desperate. David Suchet is a perfect Poirot, deliberate, tasteful, and superior, but not without his own doubts. Add to that the stylish atmosphere of the British settings during the '30s, and you have a murder mystery of the finest breed. While the opening sequence has a stunning sharp look without the slightest noise, the movie itself exhibits some problems. In dark areas of the picture, a weird comb-pattern artifact is nearly constant. The transfer itself is a bit dark, shrouding almost too many details in blackness, and creating shadows that appear artificially dark and as a result without definition. Highlights are sometimes harsh, giving the presentation a slightly unbalanced look. Dolby stereo has a good frequency response and sounds absolutely natural. High ends are crisp and clear. —GH/MM *AKA:* Poirot: The ABC Murders.
Movie: 🎬🎬🎬 **DVD:** 🎬🎬
Acorn Media (UPC 054961361892). Full frame. Dolby Stereo. $24.98. Keepcase. *LANG:* English. *FEATURES:* Talent files • Reading list • 12 chapters.
1992 103m/C *GB* David Suchet, Hugh Fraser, Philip Jackson; *D:* Andrew Grieve.

The Age of Innocence

Three wealthy New Yorkers (Day-Lewis, Ryder, Pfeiffer) are caught in a tragic love triangle. The cruel irony of this film's title anticipates the elegance and deceit of high society in the 1870s. Scorsese's film is as much a riff on *The Magnificent Ambersons* as a screen version of Edith Wharton's novel. He chooses personal regret over the socio-political comment in Terrence Davies's film of Wharton's *House of Mirth*. As always, astonishingly composed mise-en-scene from Scorsese, with an almost fetishistic noting of table settings' plates and silverware. Breathtaking DVD transfer and sound. —MO
Movie: 🎬🎬🎬 ½ **DVD:** 🎬🎬🎬🎬
Columbia Tristar (cat #52637, UPC 04339-6526372). Widescreen (2.35:1) anamorphic. Dolby Digital 5.1; Dolby Digital 2.0 Surround. $29.95. Keepcase. *LANG:* English; French. *SUB:* English; Spanish; Chinese; Korean; Portuguese; Thai. *CAP:* English; French; Spanish; Chinese; Korean; Portuguese; Thai. *FEATURES:* 28 chapters • Production notes • Theatrical trailer.
1993 (PG) 138m/C Martin Scorsese, Daniel Day-Lewis, Michelle Pfeiffer, Winona Ryder, Richard E. Grant, Alec McCowen, Miriam Margolyes, Mary Beth Hurt, Geraldine Chaplin, Stuart Wilson, Michael Gough, Alexis Smith, Jonathan Pryce, Robert Sean Leonard; *D:* Martin Scorsese; *W:* Martin Scorsese, Jay Cocks; *C:* Michael Ballhaus; *M:* Elmer Bernstein; *Nar:* Joanne Woodward. *AWARDS:* Oscars '93: Costume Des.; British Acad. '93: Support. Actress (Margolyes); Golden Globes '94: Support. Actress (Ryder); Natl. Bd. of Review '93: Director (Scorsese), Support. Actress (Ryder); *NOM:* Oscars '93: Adapt. Screenplay, Art Dir./Set Dec., Support. Actress (Ryder), Orig. Score; British Acad. '94: Support. Actress (Ryder); Directors Guild '93: Director (Scorsese); Golden Globes '94: Actress—Drama (Pfeiffer), Director (Scorsese), Film—Drama.

Agent Red

Naval Special Ops Comm. Matt Hendricks (Lundgren) is aboard a U.S. sub escorting a deadly chemical weapon (which could destroy the world if it got loose, etc., etc.) to a safe storage facility when Russian terrorists take over and threaten to launch the bug at Moscow and New York. With the aid of science babe Dr. Christian (Paul), our hero must save the day. Unapologetically formulaic "B"-movie fare is handled with enough energy to earn at least a qualified recommendation. In part, that's also due to director Lee's commentary track. He talks about the ins and outs of low-budget production and even provides a bit of boosterism for Los Angeles technical professionalism over inexpensive Canadian locations. DVD delivers an exceptionally sharp and clear image for such a modest production. —MM *AKA:* Captured.
Movie: 🎬🎬 **DVD:** 🎬🎬 ½
Columbia Tristar Home Video (UPC 04339-6064829). Widescreen (1.85:1) anamor-phic. Dolby Digital 5.1 Surround. $24.98. Keepcase. *LANG:* English; French. *SUB:* English; Spanish. *FEATURES:* 28 chapters • Trailer • Talent files • Commentary.
2000 (R) 95m/C Dolph Lundgren, Randolph Mantooth, Meilani Paul, Alexander Kuznitsov, Natalie Radford, Steve Eastin, Tony Becker; *D:* Damian Lee; *W:* Damian Lee; *C:* Ken Blakey; *M:* David Wurst, Eric Wurst.

Agnes of God

Stage to screen translation of John Pielmeier's play loses something in the process. Coarse, chain-smoking psychiatrist Dr. Martha Livingston (Fonda) is sent to a convent to investigate whether young nun Agnes (Tilly) is fit to stand trial. It seems that the nun may have given birth to and then strangled her baby, although she denies ever having sexual relations and knows nothing about an infant (or even conception for that matter). Naïve Agnes is frightened by the probing Livingston, while worldly Mother Superior (Bancroft) distrusts the intruder. A melodramatic stew of Catholicism, religious fervor, and science features generally good performances, most notably by Tilly, who won a Golden Globe for her role. Unfortunately, the finale is the epitome of ambiguous and will leave many viewers stumped. The fact that the widescreen image is not anamorphic leads one to believe that this may be an old laserdisc transfer. The picture, while sharp, is very grainy, and generally looks washed-out (although, in all fairness, the entire look of the film is very drab and colorless). The Dolby 2.0 Surround audio track delivers the top-notch dialogue very clearly and there are occasional flourishes of Surround sound effects, mostly musical cues. —ML
Movie: 🎬🎬 ½ **DVD:** 🎬🎬
Columbia Tristar (cat #07759, UPC 04339-6077591). Widescreen (1.85:1) letterboxed. Dolby 2.0 Surround. $24.95. Keepcase. *LANG:* English; French. *SUB:* English; French; Spanish; Portuguese; Chinese; Korean. *CAP:* English. *FEATURES:* Bonus trailers • 28 chapters.
1985 (PG-13) 98m/C Jane Fonda, Anne Bancroft, Meg Tilly, Anne Pitoniak, Winston Rekert, Gratien Gelinas; *D:* Norman Jewison; *W:* John Pielmeier; *C:* Sven Nykvist; *M:* Georges Delerue. *AWARDS:* Golden Globes '86: Support. Actress (Tilly); *NOM:* Oscars '85: Actress (Bancroft), Support. Actress (Tilly), Orig. Score.

A.I.: Artificial Intelligence

In the future, scientists create David (Osment), a robot boy capable of love, and he is given to a family with a comatose child. When the child recovers, the mother leaves David in the woods to fend for himself. David makes friends with sex robot, Gigolo Joe (Law), and the two go on a quest to find the imaginary blue fairy from Pinocchio, in the hopes that she'll be able to turn David into a real boy. Odd dramatization of a Brian Aldiss short story was developed by Stanley Kubrick for over 10 years and was reportedly to be his follow-up to *Eyes Wide Shut*. Oddly enough, it feels neither like a Kubrick nor a Spielberg picture and is occasionally awkward, directionless, and sloppily scripted. Spielberg seems ill at ease with the "sex city" and "flesh fair" sequences and the film is frequently cold, clumsy, and lacking in narrative drive. Knowing that David's quest for the Blue Fairy is totally nonsensical also reduces the urgency of the story. While the striking Gigolo Joe character is totally wasted, David's wry robot Teddy Bear is an absolute delight and nearly steals the show. While not a total success, it does have some thought-provoking moments and an ending that's both beautiful and profoundly depressing. The disc image is grainy and soft with muted colors, but that's an intentional design of the original photography, and theatrical prints looked the same way. With that in mind, the disc reproduces the look perfectly. Images that are supposed to be sharp appear that way and the bright colors (as in "Rouge City") are as vivid as they should be. While much hooharaw has been made about Spielberg's lack of a commentary track, the specially produced featurettes on the disc cover so many aspects of the production, it's really unnecessary. The shorts include interviews with most of the primary cast and highlight some interesting behind-the-scenes footage and special effects demonstrations. Combined, their running time is nearly feature-length. —*DG*

Movie: ♫♫ ½ **DVD:** ♫♫♫
DreamWorks Home Ent. (cat #89567, UPC 667068956726). Widescreen (1.85:1) anamorphic. Dolby Digital 5.1 Surround; Dolby Digital Surround. $29.99. Snapper. *LANG:* English; French. *SUB:* Spanish; French. *CAP:* English. *FEATURES:* Trailers • Storyboards • Still gallery • "Making of" featurettes.
2001 (PG-13) 145m/C Haley Joel Osment, Jude Law, Frances O'Connor, Sam Robards, Brendan Gleeson, William Hurt, Jake Thomas, Clara Bellar, Enrico Colantoni, Adrian Grenier, Emmanuelle Chriqui; *D:* Steven Spielberg; *W:* Steven Spielberg; *C:* Janusz Kaminski; *M:* John Williams; *V:* Robin Williams, Chris Rock, Meryl Streep, Jack Angel; *Nar:* Ben Kingsley. *AWARDS: NOM:* Oscars '01: Visual FX, Score; British Acad. '01: Visual FX; Golden Globes '02: Director (Spielberg), Support. Actor (Law), Score; Broadcast Film Critics '01: Score.

Aimee & Jaguar

Pay little attention to the box art that shows two glamorous women dancing, one mannishly dressed, with a cigarette dangling from her very red lips. The sexual relationship between Lilly (Köhler), sometimes called Aimée and Felice (Schrader), Jaguar, is much more complex. The setting is WWII Germany where Lilly is a proper lady, married to a soldier and mother of four children. Felice is Jewish and a member of the underground. The physical aspects are revealed fairly late in the

story. Most of it is concerned with the two characters—based on real women—and their world. DVD delivers what appears to be an accurate re-creation of a darkish import image. Many interiors are naturally lit and heavily shadowed. In bright exteriors, skin tones look pale. Music effectively employs 5.1, particularly in the concert scene. —*MM*

Movie: ♫♫♫ **DVD:** ♫♫♫
Zeitgeist Films (cat #Z1009, UPC 79597-5100939). Widescreen (1.77:1) anamorphic. Dolby Digital 5.1 Surround. $29.99. Keepcase. *LANG:* German. *SUB:* English. *FEATURES:* 12 chapters • "Making of" featurette • Interviews • Photo gallery of the real Aimée and Jaguar • What happened after *Aimée & Jaguar* • German and American theatrical trailers • Interviews.
1998 125m/C GE Maria Schrader, Juliane Kohler, Johanna Wokalek, Heike Makatsch, Elisabeth Degen, Detlev Buck; *D:* Max Farberbock; *W:* Rona Munro, Max Farberbock; *C:* Tony Imi; *M:* Jan A.P. Kaczmarek.

Air Force One [2 SB]

As is the case with the other "Superbit" releases, improvements are visible, yet rather subtle. If you expect a "Wow!" effect, you won't find it here. Nonetheless, upon close examination and comparison of the images, the "Superbit" release markedly improves on Columbia's previous release (reviewed in *Book 1*) by adding additional detail to the picture, giving it an improved sharpness without the introduction of any artifacts, or ringing from edge-enhancement. In "busy" shots the improvement is most visible, as the picture resolves more definition, bringing out even the subtlest details and shades in the backgrounds. It is clear that this is home video at its very best, as the entire bandwidth of the video stream is allocated to ensure best results throughout. On the audio side, things look the same. The addition of a DTS track gives audiophiles the chance to enjoy the film in their favorite format, while the Dolby Digital track also features an increased data rate for better resolution of the sonic information. Both tracks are phenomenally clear and detailed, creating a very active and aggressive sound field with an incredible dynamic range that allows for faithful reproduction of even the most subtle nuances. The DTS track, especially, manages to impress once again with its full-bodied presentation and a very aggressive bass extension. The layered textures of the score are more transparent, giving the audio track better integration. —*GH* **AKA:** *AFO.*

Movie: ♫♫♫ **DVD:** ♫♫♫ ½
Columbia Tristar (cat #07575, UPC 04339-6075757). Widescreen (2.35:1) anamorphic. Dolby Digital 5.1 Surround Stereo; DTS 5.1. $27.95. Keepcase slipcased. *LANG:* English. *SUB:* English; French; Spanish. *FEATURES:* 28 chapters.
1997 (R) 124m/C Harrison Ford, Gary Oldman, Glenn Close, Dean Stockwell, William H. Macy, Wendy Crewson, Xander Berkeley, Paul Guilfoyle, Liesl Matthews,

Bill Smitrovich, Elya Baskin, David Vadim, Tom Everett, Philip Baker Hall, Spencer Garrett, Donna Bullock, Juergen Prochnow; *D:* Wolfgang Petersen; *W:* Andrew Marlowe; *C:* Michael Ballhaus; *M:* Jerry Goldsmith. *AWARDS: NOM:* Oscars '97: Film Editing, Sound; MTV Movie Awards '98: Villain (Oldman), Fight (Harrison Ford/Gary Oldman).

Air Rage

A rather overdone and overacted action film that amounts to little more than *Die Hard* on a plane. There is an attempt at a "Rock" type vigilante military officer doing all the wrong things for all the right reasons, but it gets lost in a mess of poorly written dialogue and overused clichés. Colors and blacks are extremely well defined and crisp on this above average disc. The soundtrack is similarly impressive and features well-reproduced dialogue, music, and sound effects. A wealth of decent extras round out a well-done disc centered on a below average film. —*MJT*

Movie: ♫♫ **DVD:** ♫♫♫
Paramount (cat #87878, UPC 0973687-87841). Widescreen (1.85:1) anamorphic. Dolby Digital 5.1 Surround; Dolby Digital Surround. $29.99. Keepcase. *LANG:* English. *SUB:* English; Spanish. *FEATURES:* 16 chapters • Commentary: director Ed Raymond, actor Cyril O'Reilly • Director and cast bios • Theatrical trailer • Trailer gallery.
2001 (R) 99m/C Ice-T, Cyril O'Reilly, Steve Hytner, Gil Gerard, Alex Cord, Kim Oja; *D:* Ed Raymond; *W:* Sean O'Bannon; *C:* Mac Ahlberg.

Airheads

Following in the shallow footprints of Bill and Ted and Wayne and Garth, this rock 'n' roll comedy is occasionally as rude and irreverent as its subject matter. At other times—most other times—it's a slow parody that revolves around three sub-genius white boys (Fraser, Buscemi, and Sandler) trying to break into the L.A. music business. Almost all of the humor comes from their plantlike stupidity, and it wears thin about halfway through. The hapless trio decides to raise their profile in the industry by taking over a local radio station with realistic-looking squirt guns. Things get out of hand and a bizarre variation on *Dog Day Afternoon* ensues when the cops, led by Hudson and Farley, surround the station. Overall, director Michael Lehmann comes closer to the satiric tone he hit in *Heathers* than the ridiculous excesses of his mega-flop *Hudson Hawk*, but considering the amount of talent involved, this one should have been much better. DVD image is an accurate re-creation of the unremarkable theatrical release as I remember it. Surround sound is much stronger. The lame 14-minute "special report" extra is an extension of the movie, presenting clips as part of a local TV news special. —*MM*

Movie: ♫♫ **DVD:** ♫♫ ½
MGM Home Ent. (cat #2001945, UPC 024-543019459). Widescreen (1.85:1) ana-

morphic. Dolby Digital 4.0 Surround; Dolby Digital Surround. $19.98. Keepcase. *LANG:* English; French. *SUB:* English; Spanish. *CAP:* English. *FEATURES:* "Special report" featurette ⚫ 16 chapters ⚫ Music videos ⚫ Trailers and TV spots.
1994 (PG-13) 81m/C Brendan Fraser, Steve Buscemi, Adam Sandler, Chris Farley, Michael McKean, Judd Nelson, Joe Mantegna, Michael Richards, Ernie Hudson, Amy Locane, Nina Siemaszko, John Melendez; *D:* Michael Lehmann; *W:* Rich Wilkes; *C:* John Schwartzman; *M:* Carter Burwell.

The Alchemists

A huge pharmaceutical company attempts to cover up the fact that a fertility drug has some serious side effects. Julia Bannerman (Gemmell) and Conner Malloy (Show), a doctor with a secret, try to expose the corporate conspiracy. Film appears to have been made for British TV and so it's well acted with acceptable but less than lavish production values. DVD image and sound are both very nice, a solid cut above broadcast quality. *—MM*
Movie: 🦴🦴½ *DVD:* 🦴🦴½
MTI (cat #50045, UPC 619935404533). Full frame. $24.99. Keepcase. *LANG:* English. *SUB:* Spanish. *FEATURES:* Previews ⚫ Talent files ⚫ 20 chapters.
1999 (PG-13) 150m/C Grant Show, Ruth Gemmell, Edward Hardwicke; *D:* Peter Smith; *C:* Peter Middleton; *M:* Rick Wentworth.

Ali

Mann, a notorious obsessive, couldn't have picked a more ambitious topic. The Herculean task proves too much, yielding a film that lacks focus or insight into its subject. Ali (Smith) is depicted during a contentious decade (1964–74), in which he converted to Islam, befriended civil rights icons, refused the draft, was stripped of his title, married three times, and blurred lines between sport, ethics, and society. Perhaps it's no coincidence that screenwriter Roth, who previously penned *Forrest Gump*, was chosen to chronicle Ali amid such historic happenings. Mann's visual skills are apparent, and Smith gives an inspired performance in and out of the ring. Other note-worthies include Foxx as cornerman "Bundini" Brown, and Voight as verbose sportscaster Cosell. Despite the charisma of its subject (and its lead), film feels distant and subdued. Lands a few clean blows, but certainly not a knockout. For the most part, this is a great-looking DVD with incredibly strong saturated colors, inky grainless blacks, and excellent sharpness. Besides the extreme lack of supplementals, the only thing keeping it from a better technical rating are a few scenes where there are some pesky artifacts, and the mostly sparse use of the Surround tracks. Not that the 5.1 sound is terrible—in fact during the fight sequences (which must bow to Scorsese's *Raging Bull's* brutal bludgeonings for sheer intensity) the Surrounds kick in and you'll want to shout along with the on-screen noisy and rambunctious crowd. As to those limited extras, they include ads, er, trailers for *Spiderman* and *Men in Black 2* which will obviously be included on their respective DVDs. *Ali* is far from director Mann's best film, but it certainly deserves more attention than this. *—JO*
Movie: 🦴🦴½ *DVD:* 🦴🦴🦴
Columbia Tristar (cat #06689, UPC 04339-6066892). Widescreen (2.35:1) anamorphic. Dolby Digital 5.1; Dolby Digital Stereo. $27.95. Keepcase. *LANG:* English; French. *SUB:* English; Spanish; French. *CAP:* English. *FEATURES:* 28 chapters ⚫ Theatrical trailer.
2001 (R) 158m/C Will Smith, Jamie Foxx, Jon Voight, Mario Van Peebles, Ron Silver, Jeffrey Wright, Mykelti Williamson, Jada Pinkett Smith, Michael Michele, Joe Morton, Paul Rodriguez, Nona Gaye, Bruce McGill, Barry (Shabaka) Henley, Giancarlo Esposito, Laurence Mason, LeVar Burton, Albert Hall, David Cubitt, Ted Levine, David Elliott, Michael Bentt, James N. Toney, Charles Shufford, Malick Bowens, Shari Watson, Victoria Dillard, Kim Robillard, Gailard Sartain, Rufus Dorsey, Robert Sale, Damien "Bolo" Wills, Michael Dorn; *D:* Michael Mann; *W:* Michael Mann, Stephen J. Rivele, Christopher Wilkinson, Eric Roth; *C:* Emmanuel Lubezki; *M:* Lisa Gerrard, Pieter Bourke. *AWARDS: NOM:* Oscars '01: Actor (Smith), Support. Actor (Voight); Golden Globes '02: Actor—Drama (Smith), Support. Actor (Voight), Score; Broadcast Film Critics '01: Actor (Smith), Film, Support. Actor (Voight).

The Alice Cooper Story

At age 53, Alice Cooper (AKA Vincent Furnier) seems more vibrant and vigorous than ever, still touring, and still releasing new material (with 2001's *Dragontown* being a very welcome follow-up to 2000's *Brutal Planet*). This limited two-disc edition of 1991's *Alice Cooper—Prime Cuts* features an updated widescreen presentation and 16x9 enhancement plus a highly satisfying bonus disc that includes March 2001 interviews with the Coop as he readies for his new *Dragontown* tour, as well as interviews with former Alice Cooper band members Smith, Dunaway, and Bruce. The anamorphically enhanced rendition of the previously released *Prime Cuts* disc sports the same PCM stereo soundtrack. Though visually enhanced and audibly astute, expect to find the same variation of sound and picture quality as before since much of the concert and television clips are quite rare and, therefore, less than optimal in quality (yet delicious all the same). Disc Two is worth the purchase price alone, as it includes full-length concert excerpts and music videos in wonderful 5.1 sound. The real treat here is the bevy of material from a rehearsal of the *Shake Your Fist and Yell* tour plus interspersed interview clips from the VH1 *Behind the Music* special on Alice Cooper. There's also the terrific title track from the *Brutal Planet—Brutally Live* DVD. Image and sound quality on this one is better than Disc One, yet still varies. Extras on this disc set include a nice little photo gallery, direct song access via a Cooper Jukebox, and the bizarre Coopergame in which the player rolls the dice and attempts to ascend the gameboard made up of snakes and chains (a twisted variation of the kiddie favorite, Chutes and Ladders). *—DP/MM*
Movie: 🦴🦴🦴½ *DVD:* 🦴🦴🦴½
BMG (UPC 06076883159). Widescreen (1.78:1) anamorphic. Dolby Digital 5.1 Surround. $24.98. Keepcase. *LANG:* English. *FEATURES:* Bonus disc ⚫ Photo gallery ⚫ Juke box ⚫ Coopergame.
2001 167m/C Alice Cooper; *D:* D.A. Pennebaker.

Alice in Wonderland

Beyond a minimal backstage bookend device, this is a filmed play, taken from the PBS "Great Performances" series. The relative clarity of DVD makes the limited special effects pretty obvious, but that's not a serious fault. Like other entries in the Broadway Theatre Archives, it's aimed mostly at fans of the cast. Colors are slightly faded. Sound is fine. *—MM*
Movie: 🦴🦴 *DVD:* 🦴🦴½
Image Ent. (cat #ID0871B DDVD, UPC 014-381087123). Full frame. Dolby Digital Mono. $24.98. Keepcase. *LANG:* English. *FEATURES:* 23 chapters ⚫ Trailers ⚫ Filmographies.
1983 87m/C Richard Burton, Kate Burton, Colleen Dewhurst, Donald O'Connor, Nathan Lane, Fritz Weaver, Maureen Stapleton, Eve Arden, Kaye Ballard, James Coco, Andre Gregory; *D:* Kirk Browning; *M:* Richard Addinsell, Jonathan Tunick.

Alien Adventure

While trying to find another planet to colonize and call home, a race of misguided aliens attempts to learn about the planet Earth and whether it would be a suitable environment for their displaced civilization. They decide to land, unknowingly, in a non-operational theme park and use this as their research test bed. During that test, they encounter various high-speed rides and decide that the Earth is not all they thought it would be. Created as a 3-D showcase, the film was originally released on the Imax big screen, and gave a small taste of what new 3-D technology could do. Despite its weak plot and non-developed story line, it reaches the target intended: to provide a powerful display of 3-D CGI animated work. Other features include director's commentary and a very short "making of" featurette. Unfortunately, they also left out a pair of 3-D glasses in the DVD packaging. *—EL*
Movie: 🦴½ *DVD:* 🦴🦴
Ventura Distribution (cat #9264, UPC 017-078926422). Full frame. Dolby Digital 5.1, DTS. $19.99. Keepcase. *LANG:* English. *FEATURES:* Commentary: director ⚫ Photo Gallery (2-D and 3-D) ⚫ "Making of" featurette ⚫ Theatrical trailer.
1999 85m/C *D:* Ben Stassen; *W:* Ben Stassen; *C:* Ben Stassen; *M:* Louis Vyncke.

Alien Exotica: The Secret Files

Agent Preston (Jack Perry) and Agent Forrest (Kira Reed) are in charge of the FBI's "Sex Files" division and are dispatched to Area 69 where a deep-space crew has just returned. While on their coed voyage, they encounter a space-alien fungus that squirts baby powder in the air and makes a frigid scientist strip naked and writhe around on the floor smearing cocoa butter all over herself. The plant then turns itself into a copy of her and runs off to find a man. But—here's the twist—the original can feel all the naughty stuff that's going on, sort of a dirty E.S.P. (Extra Sexual Perception), so she's not all that upset about the predicament. When they get back to Earth, Anne Gallo (Gabriella Hall), the latest alien clone, can't keep her hands and other parts to herself. There are plenty of amusing X-File parallels and the two even run around with flashlights at one point. A seriously ridiculous film that is not soon forgotten. Ms. Reed reprised her role in the somewhat lame sequel *Alien Erotica 2*. Excessively chunky image quality with pronounced digital grain. Presented in its original direct-to-video aspect ratio, but the best viewing option may be premium cable, or gasp, VHS rental. Respectable stereo audio track. Overpriced, poorly produced disc. —GNG/DG **AKA:** The Alien Files.
Movie: ♫♫ ½ *DVD:* ♫ ½
Image Ent. (UPC 619935202535). Full frame. Dolby Digital Surround. $19.98. Keepcase. *LANG:* English. *FEATURES:* Cast bios • Trailers.
1998 C Mark Collver, Kira Reed, Gabriella Hall; *D:* Rolfe Kanefsky.

Alien Visitor

A female extraterrestrial from the Epsilon star system appears in the Australian outback. When she encounters an amiable property surveyor she finds (to her disgust) that she's on Earth. As she waits for her people to locate her, she teleports herself and the surveyor across the world and across time, demonstrating humanity's primitive and self-destructive state as viewed by higher beings. Simple but talky, this ambitious low-budget feature seems a bit silly at first but eventually develops into something intelligent, thought-provoking, and moving. At times it plays like a narrated version of *Koyaanisqatsi* and, like that feature, seems to lack answers to the questions and conundrums it poses. It's a worthwhile film but (admittedly) difficult to market. Miramax's packaging seems designed to be pushing some other kind of film—one much cheesier and probably involving anal probes. The disc features a vivid, sharp, and colorful transfer but is prone to digital noise that interferes with the smooth, 360-degree pans and dissolves that make up the majority of the film. The sound is terrific: clean, full, and involving. —DG **AKA:** Epsilon.
Movie: ♫♫ ½ *DVD:* ♫♫ ½
Miramax Pictures (cat #20767, UPC 7179-5101056). Widescreen (1.85:1) anamor-phic. Dolby Surround 2.0. $29.99. Keepcase. *LANG:* English. *CAP:* English. *FEATURES:* 20 chapters • Insert card with chapter listing.
1995 (PG-13) 92m/C *AU* Syd Brisbane, Alethea McGrath, Chloe Ferguson, Phoebe Ferguson, Ulli Birve; *D:* Rolf de Heer; *W:* Rolf de Heer; *C:* Tony Clark; *M:* Graham Tardiff.

All in the Family: The Complete First Season

Bigoted (but soft-at-heart) Archie (O'Connor) lives with his ditzy wife, Edith (Stapleton), his married daughter, Gloria (Struthers), and her husband, Mike (Reiner). The lower–middle class Archie's uninformed, passed-down values are frequently at odds with Mike and Gloria's much more liberal views. This softer, more compelling remake of the British series *Til Death Us Do Part* uses the central premise and characters but gives the series a moving, emotional quality absent in the original. Edith is much less confrontational than her English counterpart and her innocence is quite lovable. The lead cast is excellent and while topical references are dated, the situations and conflicts are as fresh and relevant today as when the show was originally broadcast. The 13 episodes contained on the disc are all of extremely high caliber but the pilot, "Meet the Bunkers" (which is particularly strong and bold), and the affecting "Gloria's Pregnancy" episodes are both examples of top-notch television. Every episode is filled with hilarious moments. The discs appear to be transferred from sub-sub-syndication masters and are distractingly soft, grainy, and bleary. There are odd, tiny splotches of color distortion, which occasionally appear, but these are camera flaws that would be present on the masters as well. The sound is fine, but occasionally squawks. The chapter links are particularly stingy and the original broadcast dates are, unfortunately, absent. The inclusion of the original opening announcement, "From Television City in Hollywood!" is usually dropped from syndication, and is a very welcome inclusion. This is a worthwhile collection in a series that deserves to continue. Let's hope the studio will return to the original master tapes for improved future season releases. —DG
Movie: ♫♫♫ ½ *DVD:* ♫♫ ½
Columbia Tristar (cat #08207, UPC 04339-6082076). Full frame. Mono. $39.95. Fold out 3-snapcase. *LANG:* English. *SUB:* English; Spanish. *CAP:* English. *FEATURES:* 13 episodes • 1 chapter per episode • Booklet with episode credits.
1971 286m/C Carroll O'Connor, Jean Stapleton, Rob Reiner, Sally Struthers; *D:* John Rich; *M:* Roger Kellaway.

All Night Movies

Four ultra–low budget allegedly erotic comedies are collected on two discs. Please see individual reviews (if you must) of *Bikini Med School*, *Bikini House Calls*, *Illegal Affairs*, and *Brief Affair*. —MM
Movie: ♫ *DVD:* ♫
BCI-Eclipse (cat #44109-9, UPC 7873644-10996). Full frame. $9.98. Keepcase. *LANG:* English.
2000 C

All or Nothing

Here we have yet another urban, hip-hop drama. Mike (Tyrone "June" Gibson) is a young rapper with dreams of making it big. However, he must also devote his time to his girlfriend Gabby (Christine Carlo) and their infant son. Gabby wants Mike to be more realistic about the future, but he can't help but dedicate himself to his craft. After meeting a record promoter, Mike becomes even more determined to be a star. However, Mike's former friend Ice (Adrian R. Mante) and his group Profane are on the hunt for stardom as well, and these two ex-chums begin a rivalry that could become very dangerous. *All or Nothing* certainly presents a gritty and realistic view of the world of hip-hop and the highs and lows of young rappers who want to be like their idols on MTV. But it never really shows us anything new or original. The performances are good and director Adisa Jones gives the movie a nice look and feel, but you may have the feeling that you've seen it all before. Key East Entertainment has put together a fine DVD package, proving that smaller companies can produce fine special editions as well. The film is clear and sharp for the most part, although it is a bit hazy at times. The colors are good and the fleshtones are realistic. The Dolby Digital 5.1 audio track is notably good, producing strong bass response and well-timed Surround sound effects. The disc contains three student films from the director, as well as the director's own cut of *All or Nothing*. Along with this, there are two audio commentary tracks which provide a great deal of insight into the world of low-budget filmmaking. —ML
Movie: ♫♫ *DVD:* ♫♫♫
Key East Ent. (cat #KE-2002, UPC 691597-200227). Widescreen (1.85:1) letterboxed. Dolby Digital 5.1. $19.97. Keepcase. *LANG:* English. *SUB:* Spanish. *FEATURES:* Deleted scenes • Music videos • Photo gallery • Bonus films • Audio commentaries • Featurette • Cast & crew • 20 chapters.
2001 88m/C Christine Carlo, Tyrone Gibson, Adrian R'Mante, Kiko Ellsworth; *D:* Adisa Jones; *W:* Adisa Jones, J. L. Davis.

All over the Guy

Writer/director Don Roos served as executive producer on this film, which re-unites some of the personnel from his hit *The Opposite of Sex*. Unfortunately, the quality of that film isn't reproduced here. Eli (Dan Bucatinsky, who also wrote the film) and Tom (Richard Ruccolo) are two gay men who are set up on a blind date by Brett (Adam Goldberg) and Jackie (Sasha Alexander). They don't really get along, but they

find themselves very attracted to one another. The film then explores the ups and downs of their courtship, as each tries to deal with the baggage from the past which keeps them from succeeding in the present. The problem with *All Over the Guy* is that except for the fact that it deals with a homosexual couple, it's incredibly unoriginal. We've seen this "Oh, they're perfect for each other, why can't they see that?" scenario countless times before. Also, that stereotypical premise doesn't exactly work here, because it's hard for the audience to cheer for this couple to remain together. There doesn't seem to be any real chemistry between them, so whether or not they stay together may become a moot point to some viewers. Some of the performances are good (Goldberg has some good lines), but Ruccolo looks very uncomfortable at times. The DVD provides a satisfactory transfer of the film. The image is sharp, but this reveals some noticeable grain. However, the colors are very realistic and show no signs of oversaturation. The audio offers clear dialogue, but there is little in the way of Surround sound, save for musical cues. The commentary track is great fun and gives insight into the production of the film. Also, the deleted scenes from the film are particularly interesting. —*ML*
Movie: 🎵🎵 ½ **DVD:** 🎵🎵🎵
Studio Home Ent. (cat #VM 7875D, UPC 031398787525). Widescreen (1.85:1) letterbox. Dolby Digital 5.1. $24.99. Keepcase. *LANG:* English. *SUB:* English; Spanish. *CAP:* English. *FEATURES:* Commentary • Deleted scenes • Storyboards • Interviews • Trailer • Short film • 24 chapters.
2001 (R) 95m/C Dan Bucatinsky, Richard Ruccolo, Adam Goldberg, Sasha Alexander, Doris Roberts, Andrea Martin, Tony Abatemarco, Joanna (Joanna DeVarona) Kerns, Nicolas Surovy, Christina Ricci, Lisa Kudrow; *D:* Julie Davis; *W:* Dan Bucatinsky; *C:* Goran Pavicevic.

All Quiet on the Western Front
Big-budget TV remake compares favorably to the 1930 masterpiece. Richard Thomas is fine as Paul Baumer, the German teenager who goes idealistically off to fight in World War I and quickly learns the truth behind the patriotic rhetoric he has heard back home. The real surprise of the production is Ernest Borgnine as the sergeant who takes Paul and his young friends under his wing. It's one of his best performances and he's perfectly suited to the role. There's not much DVD can (or should) do with the full-frame image. It's soft and appropriately grubby. Battle scenes are really remarkable, given their limited scope. Sound is fine, though audiences expecting the sonic assault of *Saving Private Ryan* will find it lacking. In any case, this is one story that should be retold for every generation. —*MM*
Movie: 🎵🎵🎵 ½ **DVD:** 🎵🎵 ½
Artisan Ent. (cat #12448, UPC 01715312-4484). Full frame. Dolby Surround.

$14.99. Keepcase. *LANG:* English. *CAP:* English. *FEATURES:* 21 chapters.
1979 150m/C Richard Thomas, Ernest Borgnine, Donald Pleasence, Patricia Neal; *D:* Delbert Mann; *W:* Paul Monash; *C:* John Coquillon; *M:* Allyn Ferguson.

All That Heaven Allows
Attractive, wealthy middle-aged widow Cary Scott (Wyman) falls for her 15-years-younger gardener, Ron Kirby (Hudson), and becomes the target of small-minded gossips and her disapproving family. Ron's no gigolo or fortune-hunter but societal pressure still gets to Cary and she breaks things off. However, loneliness makes her realize what she's missing and she decides to make things up with Ron and forget her critics. Hopeful Sirk romance still takes some jabs at conformity. This is another gorgeous transfer from Criterion, with the highlight being the incredibly saturated colors that perfectly convey the unique surrealistic look that director Sirk (and the Technicolor process) is noted for. A few minor blemishes show up from the film source itself, but nothing can detract from this stunning presentation. The sound is only mono, but amazingly clear with the dialogue delivered very distinctly. Be sure to watch *Behind the Mirror*, a fine BBC documentary from the late '70s that features great interview footage with Sirk himself. Fassbinder's essay puts Sirk's career into perspective and is very amusing as well. —*JO*
Movie: 🎵🎵🎵 **DVD:** 🎵🎵🎵 ½
Criterion (cat #CC1565D, UPC 71551501-1426). Widescreen (1.77:1) anamorphic. Dolby Digital Mono. $39.95. Keepcase. *LANG:* English. *SUB:* English. *FEATURES:* 21 chapters • Theatrical trailer • Excerpts: *Behind the Mirror: A Profile of Douglas Sirk* • Essay by Rainer Fassbinder • Lobby cards • Production stills.
1955 89m/B Jane Wyman, Rock Hudson, Conrad Nagel, Agnes Moorehead, Virginia Grey, Gloria Talbott, William Reynolds; *D:* Douglas Sirk; *W:* Peggy Fenwick; *C:* Russell Metty; *M:* Frank Skinner, Joseph Gershenson. *AWARDS:* Natl. Film Reg. '95.

All the King's Men
Gritty adaptation of Robert Penn Warren's masterpiece is a bit dated in some respects, but that's mostly due to the familiarity of a story that's been repeated so often in American politics. Almost all of the performances remain forceful and vivid, particularly Broderick Crawford's Oscar-winning portrayal of Willie Stark (loosely based on Huey Long). He's the self-proclaimed "hick" lawyer who rises through the ranks to become governor of an unnamed Southern state. Fellow Oscar-winner Mercedes McCambridge is equally memorable and even less dated as the coolly disillusioned aide. They're absolutely terrific. Some of the supporting cast and third-act plot turns are more melodramatic, but the whole work still holds up. Over-

all, DVD image is very good. Some minor dust flecks show up but director of photography Burnett Guffey's *(From Here to Eternity, Bonnie & Clyde)* superb black and white is rendered flawlessly. Mono sound may disappoint younger viewers. It's true to the era. —*MM*
Movie: 🎵🎵🎵 ½ **DVD:** 🎵🎵🎵
Columbia Tristar (cat #05889, UPC 04339-6058897). Full frame. Dolby Digital Mono. $24.98. Keepcase. *LANG:* English; French; Spanish; Portuguese. *SUB:* English; French; Spanish; Portuguese; Chinese; Korean; Thai. *CAP:* English. *FEATURES:* 28 chapters • Trailers • Filmographies.
1949 109m/B Broderick Crawford, Mercedes McCambridge, John Ireland, Joanne Dru, John Derek, Anne Seymour, Shepperd Strudwick; *D:* Robert Rossen; *W:* Robert Rossen; *C:* Burnett Guffey; *M:* Louis Gruenberg. *AWARDS:* Oscars '49: Actor (Crawford), Picture, Support. Actress (McCambridge); Golden Globes '50: Actor—Drama (Crawford), Director (Rossen), Film—Drama, Support. Actress (McCambridge), Natl. Film Reg. '01; N.Y. Film Critics '49: Actor (Crawford), Film; *NOM:* Oscars '49: Director (Rossen), Film Editing, Screenplay, Support. Actor (Ireland).

All the Right Moves
Tom Cruise stars as a high school football hero Stefan Djordjevic, who is hoping for a college scholarship so that he can vacate the dying Pennsylvania mill town where he grew up. At least that is what he thinks he wants to do. Further mixing up his own mixed feelings are Stefan's pushy, ambitious Coach Nickerson (Nelson), his understanding father "Pop" (Cioffi), and his supportive girlfriend Lisa (Thompson). Despite the somewhat hackneyed story, strong performances push this clichéd melodrama into field-goal range. While Cruise has gone on to make bigger and better films, this one has remained a cult favorite due to the persistent rumor of full-frontal Cruise nudity in the film. (And this urban legend was rekindled in the late '90s, when it was mentioned in *Scream*.) Fox Home Video appears to have ignored the film's title while putting together this DVD. Despite the fact that the disc features a new anamorphic widescreen transfer, the image is lacking in quality. The picture shows visible grain and black spots from the source print. Traces of edge-enhancement are noticeable and the image is hazy at times. The lackluster Dolby Digital 5.1 audio track offers no depth. The dialogue is clear, but the Surround effects are at a very low volume (even during the football game sequences) and there is little bass response. —*ML*
Movie: 🎵🎵 ½ **DVD:** 🎵🎵
20th Century Fox (cat #200807, UPC 024-543008071). Widescreen (1.85:1) anamorphic. Dolby Digital 5.1; Dolby Mono. $19.98. Keepcase. *LANG:* English, French. *SUB:* English; Spanish. *CAP:* English. *FEATURES:* Theatrical trailers • 26 chapters.
1983 (R) 90m/C Tom Cruise, Lea Thompson, Craig T. Nelson, Christopher Penn,

Charles Cioffi, Paul Carafotes, Dick Miller; **D:** Michael Chapman; **W:** Michael Kane; **C:** Jan De Bont; **M:** David (Richard) Campbell.

Almost Famous: Untitled—The Bootleg Cut

Though I was initially unimpressed with the film (see review in *Book 2*), this expanded version corrects virtually all of the faults in the shorter version and brings considerable depth to the story and all of the main characters. The added characterization improves McDormand, Hudson, and Crudup's performances as well. Despite the 35-minute longer running time, this version flows better and is more consistently involving than the shorter edit. The shorter theatrical version is also included, but the HBO "behind-the-scenes" documentary included on the previous disc is not. The picture and sound are as stunning as the previous release but the opening titles (on both versions) are noisy and ugly. The added sequences have been completely finished and look as good as the feature. The commentary is a very personal one, relating the real events behind the film as well as behind-the-scenes anecdotes. The Lester Bangs interview clips are frustratingly short but give one an even greater appreciation of Phil Seymour Hoffman's amazing portrayal of him. The deleted scenes (some included as hidden Easter Eggs—*groan*) are worthwhile but rightfully excluded. One, a grievously indulgent 10-minute sequence where McDormand is forced to listen to the entire "Stairway to Heaven" song could only have been destined for the cutting room floor. Oddly enough, the rights to the song weren't acquired so it plays silent—you'll have to play your own record as accompaniment. Frustratingly, several other deleted sequences (one shown in the trailer) are not on the disc either. The screenplay included is not a complete shooting script, but one cut down to match the feature, so the text for those sequences isn't included either. The album recommendations are inspiring and Crowe's love for the era's music is contagious. —*DG*
Movie: 🦴🦴🦴½ **DVD:** 🦴🦴🦴½
DreamWorks Home Ent. (cat #88751, UPC 667068875126). Widescreen (1.85:1) anamorphic. Dolby Digital 5.1 Surround; Dolby Digital Surround. $34.99. Keepcase. *LANG:* English; French. *SUB:* Spanish; French. *CAP:* English. *FEATURES:* Commentary: Cameron Crowe, Alice Crowe • Interview with Lester Bangs • Behind-the-scenes footage • *Rolling Stone* articles by Crowe • Crowe's top albums of 1973 • Cast and crew filmographies/bios • CD with 6 "Stillwater" songs • Deleted scenes • Outtake • Screenplay • Production notes • Extended Cleveland concert sequence • 30 chapters (bootleg cut) • 24 chapters (theatrical version).
2000 (R) 285m/C Patrick Fugit, Philip Seymour Hoffman, Frances McDormand, Jason Lee, Billy Crudup, Kate Hudson, John Fedevich, Mark Kozelek, Fairuza Balk,

Bijou Phillips, Anna Paquin, Noah Taylor, Jimmy Fallon, Zooey Deschanel, Liz Stauber, Eion Bailey, Mark Pellington, Terry Chen, Peter Frampton, Zack (Zach) Ward, Jann Wenner; **D:** Cameron Crowe; **W:** Cameron Crowe; **C:** John Toll; **M:** Nancy Wilson. *AWARDS:* Oscars '00: Orig. Screenplay; Golden Globes '01: Film—Mus./Comedy, Support. Actress (Hudson); L.A. Film Critics '00: Actor (Douglas), Support. Actress (McDormand); Broadcast Film Critics '00: Orig. Screenplay, Support. Actress (McDormand); *NOM:* Oscars '00: Film Editing, Support. Actress (Hudson, McDormand); Directors Guild '00: Director (Crowe); Screen Actors Guild '00: Support. Actress (Hudson), Support. Actress (McDormand), Cast; Writers Guild '00: Orig. Screenplay.

Alone with a Stranger

Long lost Evil Twin (Moses) learns that he has a rich brother. Evil Twin and girlfriend (Peeples) plan to kidnap Good Twin, sell his company, and scoot with the loot. But what about Good Twin's wife (Niven) and family? Mid-budget genre offering has made-for-TV production values that make few demands on DVD. The image is nice and sharp, but only a scant improvement over VHS tape. —*MM*
Movie: 🦴🦴 **DVD:** 🦴🦴½
New Concorde (cat #NH20784 D, UPC 73-6991478497). Full frame. Stereo. $19.98. Keepcase. *LANG:* English. *FEATURES:* 12 chapters • Talent files • Trailers.
1999 (R) 90m/C William R. Moses, Barbara Niven, Priscilla Barnes, Nia Peeples, Mindy Cohn; **D:** Peter Paul Liapis; **W:** Peter Paul Liapis, Richard Dana Smith; **C:** M. David Mullen; **M:** Alan Howarth.

Along Came a Spider

This second adaptation of James Patterson's feverishly plotted Alex Cross novels actually takes place before *Kiss the Girls*. It's a solidly built but limited thriller that makes the most of star Morgan Freeman's screen presence. His Alex Cross is a detective-psychologist who's called in by an egomaniacal kidnapper who's snatched a senator's daughter from her exclusive private school. As the Secret Service agent who was supposed to protect the girl, Monica Potter continues her uncanny Julia Roberts impersonation. DVD is an essentially flawless reproduction of a big-budget Hollywood mystery. Neither image nor sound will challenge the limits of the medium. —*MM*
Movie: 🦴🦴🦴 **DVD:** 🦴🦴🦴
Paramount (cat #33651, UPC 097363365-143). Widescreen anamorphic. Dolby Digital 5.1 Surround Stereo; Dolby Digital Surround. $29.99. Keepcase. *LANG:* English; French. *SUB:* English. *FEATURES:* 12 chapters • Trailer • "Making of" featurette.
2000 (R) 103m/C Morgan Freeman, Monica Potter, Michael Wincott, Penelope Ann Miller, Michael Moriarty, Dylan Baker, Billy Burke, Jay O. Sanders, Anna Maria Horsford; **D:** Lee Tamahori; **W:** Michael H.

Moss; **C:** Matthew F. Leonetti; **M:** Jerry Goldsmith, Mark Isham.

Along Came Jones

Cowpoke Melody Jones (producer Cooper), who can't handle a gun and pals around with grumpy sidekick Demarest, is the victim of mistaken identity when he is taken for the vicious outlaw Monte Jarrad (Duryea). Both the good guys and the bad guys are after him. The lovely Young is the woman who rides to his defense. Offbeat, charming western parody is based on a novel by Alan le May. The darkness of the early scenes seems to come from the original. There's also a little light snow and some distortion during exterior tracking shots. Coop's patterned shirt tends to flash in some shots, too. Those are comparatively minor flaws in an otherwise fine black-and-white image. —*MM*
Movie: 🦴🦴🦴 **DVD:** 🦴🦴
MGM Home Ent. (cat #1002366, UPC 027-616865779). Full frame. Dolby Digital Mono. $14.95. Keepcase. *LANG:* English. *SUB:* French; Spanish. *CAP:* English. *FEATURES:* 16 chapters • Trailer.
1945 93m/B Gary Cooper, Loretta Young, Dan Duryea, William Demarest; **D:** Stuart Heisler; **W:** Nunnally Johnson; **C:** Milton Krasner; **M:** Arthur Lange.

Along for the Ride

Lulu (Griffith) checks herself out of a San Francisco mental institution and goes to visit her old boyfriend Ben (Swayze), now married to Claire (Miller) in Los Angeles. According to Lulu, she and Ben had a son 16 years before. She put him up for adoption but she has an agreement with the parents that she can visit on the boy's 16th birthday. Would Ben like to go to Wisconsin with her? The main problem here is fundamentally unappealing characters. (They talk in movies.) Pan-'n'-scan DVD image is nice, clear, and sharp; a bit better than VHS tape, but the disc is a bare-bones affair—chapter breaks but no links. —*MM*
Movie: 🦴🦴 **DVD:** 🦴🦴½
Artisan Ent. (cat #12262). Full frame. Dolby Digital Stereo. $14.98. Keepcase. *LANG:* English. *SUB:* English; Spanish. *FEATURES:* 22 chapters • Trailer.
2000 (R) 99m/C Melanie Griffith, Patrick Swayze, Penelope Ann Miller, Joseph Gordon-Levitt, Richard Schiff, Annie Corley, Lee Garlington, Michael J. Pollard, Steven Bauer; **D:** John Kaye; **W:** John Kaye; **C:** Dion Beebe; **M:** Serge Colbert.

Always a Bridesmaid

While most documentaries pick a specific topic and focus on it, *Always a Bridesmaid* presents its main topic and then never revisits it. At the outset, we are lead to believe that filmmaker Nina Davenport has made a film about the pressures that women face concerning marriage and how women over 30 feel like freaks if they aren't married. From here, *Always a Bridesmaid* places the emphasis solely on Davenport and her relationship with boyfriend

Nick. While she does fit into the demographic which the film purports to study, Davenport's story is quite boring and difficult to watch. She interviews family members and ex-boyfriends, all of who look directly into the camera and list off her faults—all of which make Davenport sound like a very troubled person. A documentary on society's views of unmarried women would be very interesting, but *Always a Bridesmaid* doesn't fit that bill. The DVD offers a full-frame transfer of the film, and as the film was shot on 16mm, shows a noticeable amount of grain throughout. This is mixed with wedding videos, which look somewhat better. The image is dark at times, but usually clear. The audio is serviceable, as the dialogue is intelligible, although you probably won't have a clue as to what Nick is talking about when he speaks. —*ML*
Movie: 𝄞 ½ **DVD:** 𝄞𝄞
New Video Group (cat #9486, UPC 76768-5948637). Full frame. Digital 2.0 Surround. $24.95. Keepcase. *LANG:* English. *FEATURES:* Director bio.
2000 98m/C D: Nina Davenport; **W:** Nina Davenport; **C:** Nina Davenport.

Amazing Grace
Some righteous mothers led by Grace Grimes (Mabley) go up against corrupt city politics in a "blaxploitation" comedy that's extremely dated now. The absurdist casting—Butterfly "I don't know nothing about birthin' no babies" McQueen and Stepin Fetchit—remains as jaw-dropping now as it's ever been. On DVD, the soft image ranges between poor and good, though throughout it appears to be a faithful reproduction of the original elements. It's also fairly dim but if it were any brighter some of those mid-'70s clothes would hurt your eyes. —*MM*
Movie: 𝄞𝄞 **DVD:** 𝄞𝄞 ½
MGM Home Ent. (cat #1002880, UPC 027-616870711). Widescreen (1.85:1) letterboxed; full frame. Dolby Digital Mono. $14.98. Keepcase. *LANG:* English. *SUB:* English; French; Spanish. *CAP:* English. *FEATURES:* Trailer • 16 chapters.
1974 99m/C Moms (Jackie) Mabley, Slappy (Melvin) White, Moses Gunn, Rosalind Cash, Dolph Sweet, Butterfly McQueen, Stepin Fetchit; **D:** Stan Lathan; **W:** Matt Robinson; **C:** Edward R. Brown, Sol Negrin.

Amazing Journeys
Documentary shot for IMAX theatres explores the migration habits of seven animal and human cultures. The lush, beautiful photography is absolute eye candy despite the film's own migration to the small screen. Although redone in full frame, the overall feel of this film is still one of enormous size due to breathtaking scenery, wide-open cinematography, and the use of the IMAX camera. Despite its limited scope of material, *Amazing Journeys* is a fun, interesting look into the instinctive migratory qualities of a few of our planet's inhabitants. The DVD also includes a very technical and in-depth fea-

turette on the migration habits of the California gray whale. —*EL*
Movie: 𝄞𝄞𝄞 **DVD:** 𝄞𝄞𝄞
Ventura Distribution (cat #9252, UPC 017-078925227). Full frame. Dolby Digital 5.1 Surround; DTS Surround. $19.99. Keepcase. *LANG:* English; French. *SUB:* English. *FEATURES:* Commentary and intro: director • "Making of" featurette • Theatrical trailers • The Long Journey Home: Migratory Tales of the California Gray Whale • Fun facts trivia.
2002 106m/C

Amazons and Gladiators
This video premiere is a throwback to the sword-and-sandal Italian flicks of the 1960s. General Crassius (Bergin, doing his best not to giggle) is sent to the provinces where he becomes a dictatorial ruler, and disrupts the peaceful existence of Serena (Hiltz), who signs on with the opposition and eventually finds herself in the gladiator's arena. The low-budget production has an autumnal color scheme that gains little on DVD. Night scenes are grainy. Sound is acceptable. —*MM*
Movie: 𝄞 **DVD:** 𝄞𝄞
Studio Home Ent. (cat #ST7921D, UPC 658149792128). Widescreen letterboxed. Stereo. $24.98. Keepcase. *LANG:* English. *FEATURES:* 18 chapters • Trailer.
2001 (R) 89m/C Jennifer Rubin, Patrick Bergin, Nichole Hiltz, Wendi Winburn, Melanie Gutteridge, Richard Norton; **D:** Zachary Weintraub; **W:** Zachary Weintraub; **C:** Thomas Hencz; **M:** Timothy S. Jones.

Ambush
In this Finnish WWII drama, a young officer's platoon is sent to scout behind Russian lines (on bicycles!). While away, word comes that the Russians killed his fiancée, and he throws himself into his work. The beautiful cinematography is compromised by a slightly squeezed transfer that makes everyone look a little taller and thinner. The (non-removable) subtitles are placed flush left, a successful experiment that allows the eye to return to the same spot to read them each time. —*BT*
AKA: Rukajarven Tie.
Movie: 𝄞𝄞𝄞 **DVD:** 𝄞𝄞
Vanguard Intl. Cinema (cat #Vf0245, UPC 658769024531). Widescreen letterboxed. $29.95. Keepcase. *LANG:* Finnish. *SUB:* English. *FEATURES:* 10 chapters • Trailer.
1999 117m/C FI Peter Franzen, Irina Bjorklund, Kari Vaananen, Kari Heiskanen, Taisto Reimalvoto; **D:** Olli Saarela; **W:** Olli Saarela, Antti Tuuri; **C:** Kjell Lagerros; **M:** Tuomas Kantelinen.

American Flyers
Two competitive brothers (Kostner and Grant) train for a grueling three-day bicycle race in Colorado while tangling with personal drama, including the specter that one of them may have inherited dad's tendency for cerebral aneurisms and is sure to drop dead during a bike race soon. Written by

bike movie specialist Steve Tesich (*Breaking Away*) with a lot of the usual clichés, which are gracefully overridden by fine photography and some interesting performances in supporting roles. While the framing of the widescreen version appears to be accurate, the picture itself exhibits problems. The movie has a washed-out quality throughout and appears overly hazy in some shots. The print exhibits some grain, which is even more visible in the blown-up pan and scan version. While the source print is mostly free of major defects, at times the overall quality of the image looks no better than the average VHS copy. During the racing segments, there is a noticeable inconsistency in the image quality. The compression is generally good without introducing artifacts. Surprisingly for its age, the film also contains a good deal of Surround action during the race sequences. The audio is well-balanced, with the dialogue always audible. —*ML/MM*
Movie: 𝄞𝄞 ½ **DVD:** 𝄞𝄞 ½
Warner Home Video (UPC 0853911520-26). Widescreen (2.35:1) anamorphic; full frame. Dolby Surround. $14.98. Snapper. *LANG:* English; French. *SUB:* English; French.
1985 (PG-13) 113m/C Kevin Costner, David Marshall Grant, Rae Dawn Chong, Alexandra Paul, John Amos, Janice Rule, Robert Townsend, Jennifer Grey, Luca Bercovici; **D:** John Badham; **W:** Steve Tesich; **M:** Lee Ritenour, Greg Mathieson.

American Nightmare
Independently made slasher horror is a cut above the norm for the genre. The main reason is a rock-solid performance by Debbie Rochon. She's the avenging killer who's bumping off a group of friends who are listening and calling in to a pirate radio show on Halloween to reveal their deepest fears. There's nothing new about the plotting. Everyone involved understands that, but this is not another "postmodern" *Scream*-themed exercise in hipness. The film hangs on Ms. Rochon's work and she's excellent. The rest of the young cast members don't embarrass themselves, but they're not in her league. DVD image and sound are a slight improvement over VHS tape, but given the film's limited budget, lack of polish, and often harsh lighting conditions—particularly the garish color scheme of the lounge—it's acceptable. —*MM*
Movie: 𝄞𝄞 ½ **DVD:** 𝄞𝄞 ½
Monarch (cat #7588, UPC 7239520758-88). Full frame. $24.98. Keepcase. *LANG:* English. *FEATURES:* 24 chapters • Music video • "Making of" featurette.
2000 (R) 91m/C Debbie Rochon, Brandy Little, Johnny Sneed, Christopher Ryan, Brinke Stevens; **D:** Jon Keeyes; **W:** Jon Keeyes; **C:** Brad Walker; **M:** Peter Gannan, David Rosenblad.

American Ninja
Joe Armstrong (Dudikoff) is a martial arts expert G.I. stationed in the Philippines.

He's a rebel who alienates everyone around him. Then he discovers an arms theft and smuggling operation on his base. Though he's attacked by groups of guys in black jammies at regular intervals, he miraculously manages to prevail and find time to romance the base commander's daughter. Is it the clarity of DVD that makes some of the "schwing" and "bonk" sound effects appear to be just a microsecond off? They've probably always been that way and that carelessness certainly fits with the bad acting and inelegantly choreographed action scenes. Image and sound are a slight improvement over VHS tape. —MM *AKA:* American Warrior.
Movie: 🐾🐾 **DVD:** 🐾🐾
MGM Home Ent. (cat #1002567, UPC 027-616867681). Widescreen (1.85:1) anamorphic. Dolby Digital Mono. $14.98. Keepcase. *LANG:* English. *SUB:* French; Spanish. *CAP:* English. *FEATURES:* 16 chapters.
1985 (R) 96m/C Michael Dudikoff, Guich Koock, Judie Aronson, Steve James; *D:* Sam Firstenberg; *W:* Gideon Amir; *C:* Hanania Baer; *M:* Michael Linn.

American Outlaws

Hollywood tries to wrangle a new generation of western fans, with mixed results. This tale focuses on Jesse James (here played by Irish actor Colin Farrell) and his band of outlaws. After returning home from the Civil War, Jesse and his cohorts find their hometown besieged by an evil railroad baron. These young cowboys decide to take matters into their own hands, thus beginning a war with the railroad and their security expert (played by Timothy Dalton). The film is fast, fun, and never boring, but there's not an original thought in its pretty head, as it delivers every cowboy cliché with predictable timing. Fans of old westerns will probably hate this, but a younger audience may find a new appreciation for men on horseback. The film's muted colors seem to have been a problem for the DVD, and there is considerable grain in any bright portions of the screen (especially in the sky) and some grain in dim earthtones. Other than that the picture is very sharp. Both the DTS and the Dolby Digital 5.1 tracks are excellent delivering gunshots and explosions that are near window-shattering. Imaging and separation are excellent and the Surrounds get a good workout for both ambience and effects. The commentary on the disc is more entertaining than the film itself, with the participants nonchalantly chatting it up, delivering plenty of anecdotes and just enough filmmaking jargon to prove they really know how to make a film (not evidenced by the film itself). Of the four behind-the-scenes featurettes, only "The Making of American Outlaws" feels like a promo. The other three are very interesting, the highlight being "How to Be an Outlaw," where the actors attend a "boot camp" for cowboys and learn the ropes. The supplementals are good enough to make the DVD worth buying. —ML/JO
Movie: 🐾 **DVD:** 🐾🐾🐾

Warner (cat #19031, UPC 0853919031-23). Widescreen (1.85:1) anamorphic. Dolby Digital 5.1; DTS 5.1. $24.98. Snapper. *LANG:* English; French. *SUB:* English; French. *CAP:* English. *FEATURES:* Commentary: director Mayfield, co-writer Rogers, editor Tronick • 4 behind-the-scenes featurettes • Deleted scenes • Storyboards • Production stills • Theatrical trailers • TV spots • Talent files • Film artwork • 28 chapters.
2001 (PG-13) 95m/C Colin Farrell, Gabriel Macht, Scott Caan, Gregory Smith, Will McCormack, Timothy Dalton, Kathy Bates, Nathaniel Arcand, Ali Larter, Ronny Cox, Harris Yulin, Terry O'Quinn, Ty O'Neal, Joe Stevens; *D:* Les Mayfield; *W:* John Rogers, Roderick Taylor; *C:* Russell Boyd; *M:* Trevor Rabin.

American Pie [2 UE]

This "ultimate edition" offers only a few new features which weren't found on the original DVD release, reviewed in *Book 1*. Of the newly added extras, the most impressive one is 10 deleted scenes on the first disc, one featuring an additional appearance by Casey Affleck and another showing a hilarious scene with Stifler's brother. Most of these scenes are brief and were apparently cut to speed up the film. Next, we have a seven-minute audio excerpt from an interview with *American Pie* creators Paul and Chris Weitz, which is accompanied by production stills from the film. The Weitzes discuss the origins of the film and how they came up with the characters. On the musical front, there is a live performance from the band Tonic, who contributed to the film's soundtrack. For you art fans, there is a still gallery featuring nearly 100 movie-poster concepts, most of which bear the film's original title, *Great Falls*. Strangely, the menus are exactly the same as the original release. Image appears to be the same anamorphic widescreen transfer of the unrated version of the film, which appeared on the original DVD. Also, the Dolby Digital 5.1 soundtrack is basically the same. The only new addition here is the inclusion of a DTS 5.1 channel soundtrack, but this is a dialogue-motivated comedy, so the DTS track doesn't differ much from the Dolby track. The second disc in the set contains the full-frame version of the unrated edition (but why would we care about that?) and only a handful of the special features, which are already offered on the first disc. —GH *AKA:* East Great Falls High.
Movie: 🐾🐾 ½ **DVD:** 🐾🐾🐾
Universal Studios (cat #21454, UPC 0251-92145421). Widescreen (1.85:1) anamorphic; full frame. Dolby Digital 5.1 Surround Stereo; DTS Surround. $26.98. Special packaging. *LANG:* English; French. *SUB:* English; Spanish. *FEATURES:* Commentary • Deleted scenes • Outtakes • Featurette • Trailer • Photo montage • Music videos.
1999 (R) 95m/C Jason Biggs, Thomas Ian Nicholas, Chris Owen, Chris Klein, Natasha Lyonne, Tara Reid, Mena Suvari,

Alyson Hannigan, Shannon Elizabeth, Eugene Levy, Seann William Scott, Jennifer Coolidge, Eddie Kaye Thomas, Lawrence Pressman; *D:* Chris Weitz, Paul Weitz; *W:* Adam Herz; *C:* Richard Crudo; *M:* David Lawrence. *AWARDS: NOM:* MTV Movie Awards '00: Film, Breakthrough Perf. (Biggs, Elizabeth), Comedic Perf. (Biggs).

American Pie 2

This sequel to the 1999 boxoffice smash begins one year after the conclusion of the first film. Our four main characters—Jim (Biggs), Kevin (Nicholas), Oz (Klein), and Finch (Thomas)—have returned home to East Great Falls, Michigan, from their freshman year of college. After attending a party ripe with high-school "kids," the four decide to spend their summer at the lake, where they will have a huge party. Unfortunately, to afford the beach house, they must invite everyone's favorite jerk, Stifler (Scott). Once at the lake, the boys find themselves involved in the same sexual hi-jinks viewed in the first film, and each has their own unique problem. Oz misses girlfriend Heather (Suvari), who is studying in Europe. Kevin still pines for ex-girlfriend Vicki (Reid). Finch can't get past the night of passion that he shared with Stifler's Mom (Coolidge). And Jim is anxiously anticipating the arrival of foreign bombshell Nadia (Elizabeth). The film is not without its humorous moments, but it lacks the innocence and heart which made the first a surprise hit. Most of the "big laugh" scenes in the sequel have been presented in the trailers and ad materials, so they aren't that surprising or funny. As in the first film, Eugene Levy steals the show as Jim's dad, and band geek Michelle (Hannigan) really shows her comedic side here. While not a bad film, it must be considered a disappointment. *American Pie 2* is available on DVD in four different incarnations—"R"-rated widescreen and full frame, as well as the unrated widescreen and full frame. (There is also a box set which contains both *American Pie* and the sequel.) As the film is a disappointment, the DVD is as well, despite the fact that it's stuffed with goodies. The widescreen image here is dark and noticeably grainy. This is most likely due to the fact that this single, dual-layer DVD contains seven audio tracks! The Dolby Digital 5.1 and DTS 5.1 tracks both sound fine and there is very little difference between them. (The incidental music sounds better on the DTS track.) Most of the extras on the DVD are typical studio fare, but the outtakes and gag reels shown here are often funnier than the film itself. —ML
Movie: 🐾🐾 ½ **DVD:** 🐾🐾 ½
Universal Studios (cat #21768, UPC 0251-92176821). Widescreen (1.85:1) anamorphic. Dolby Digital 5.1; DTS 5.1. $26.98. Keepcase. *LANG:* English. *SUB:* English; French. *CAP:* English. *FEATURES:* Commentaries • "Making of" featurette • Outtakes and gag reel • Deleted scenes • Audition tapes • Music video • Theatrical trailer • Cast & crew • Production notes • 20 chapters.

2001 (R) 105m/C Jason Biggs, Shannon Elizabeth, Alyson Hannigan, Chris Klein, Natasha Lyonne, Thomas Ian Nicholas, Tara Reid, Chris Owen, Seann William Scott, Mena Suvari, Eddie Kaye Thomas, Eugene Levy, Jennifer Coolidge, Christopher Penn, Eli Marienthal, Casey Affleck, Denise Faye, Molly Cheek; **D:** James B. Rogers; **W:** Adam Herz; **C:** Mark Irwin; **M:** David Lawrence.

American Pimp

The Hughes brothers take a break from conventional features (*Menace 2 Society, From Hell*) to spin out a modest documentary about pimps. They combine interview footage with film clips to let the likes of Rosebudd, C-Note, and Gorgeous Dre tell their own stories. Those already interested in the subject may find it fascinating. Others will see it as all flash and no style. Few-frills DVD presents an accurate re-creation of an image that varies from sharp clarity to intentional roughness. Sound is acceptable throughout. —MM

Movie: 🎘🎘 ½ **DVD:** 🎘🎘 ½
MGM Home Ent. (cat #1001189, UPC 027-616854803). Widescreen anamorphic. Dolby Digital 5.1 Surround Stereo; Dolby Digital Surround. $19.95. Keepcase. *LANG:* English; Spanish. *SUB:* French; Spanish. *CAP:* English. *FEATURES:* 28 chapters.
1999 (R) 87m/C D: Albert Hughes; **W:** Allen Hughes; **C:** Albert Hughes.

An American Rhapsody

To escape their oppressive homeland, a Hungarian couple must enlist the help of a soldier to get them out of Hungary and on their way to America. The family pays the ultimate price as they must leave their youngest daughter, Suzanne (Johansson), behind. After five years, Margit (Kinski) and Peter (Goldwyn) are finally able to bring their adolescent daughter back to the states, but by the time they do, it is too late. Suzanne has come to love the farming family that she was left with and has trouble acclimating to her new American lifestyle and parents. After many years the conflicted, rebellious Suzanne feels the pull of her native homeland and must set out on her own to come to grips with herself, her American paternal family, and the foster parents she left behind many years ago. The film is an engaging look into the struggle of one immigrant family as they learn to adapt to a new country and the loss of their beloved child. Performances are both believable and compelling. The DVD contains a good transfer, the 5.1 Surround track fully utilizes the entire six speakers, and the commentary track by Eva Gardos and Colleen Camp is very insightful. —EL

Movie: 🎘🎘🎘 **DVD:** 🎘🎘🎘
Paramount (cat #33944, UPC 097363394-44). Widescreen anamorphic. Dolby 5.1 Surround, Dolby Surround. $29.99. Keepcase. *LANG:* English. *SUB:* English. *CAP:* English. *FEATURES:* Commentary: writer/director Eva

Gardos, producer Colleen Camp ▪ Theatrical trailer.
2001 (PG-13) 106m/C *US HU* Nastassia Kinski, Scarlett Johansson, Tony Goldwyn, Kelly Endresz-Banlaki, Agnes Banfalvy, Zsuzsi Czinkoczi, Balazs Galko, Zoltan Seress, Mae Whitman, Lisa Jane Persky, Emmy Rossum; **D:** Eva Gardos; **W:** Eva Gardos; **C:** Elemer Ragalyi; **M:** Cliff Eidelman.

American Tragedy

While the events surrounding the OJ Simpson case might not be classified as a true American Tragedy, this dramatization of the trial that riveted a nation truly strikes a chord and raises a fair amount of questions. Quickly stated at the beginning of the DVD is the fact that OJ himself tried to block this film from being made. *American Tragedy* is thorough in its exploration of OJ's side of the case and many of the problems that were unfolding (and almost unraveling) behind the scenes. Ving Rhames and Ron Silver both give strong performances as Johnny Cochran and Ron Shapiro. The DVD sports good sound and picture quality, and also includes a second disc that contains an OJ Simpson documentary and actual trial evidence. —EL

Movie: 🎘🎘🎘 **DVD:** 🎘🎘🎘
Lion's Gate Home Ent. (cat #7683, UPC 031398768326). Widescreen letterboxed. Dolby Stereo. $24.99. Keepcase. *LANG:* English. *SUB:* English; French; Spanish. *CAP:* English. *FEATURES:* OJ Simpson documentary ▪ Trial evidence ▪ 24 chapters.
2000 (PG-13) 170m/C Ving Rhames, Ron Silver, Christopher Plummer, Bruno Kirby, Nicholas Pryor, Robert LuPone, Ruben Santiago-Hudson, Richard Cox, Clyde Kusatsu, Jeff Kober; **D:** Lawrence Schiller; **W:** Norman Mailer; **C:** Bruce Surtees; **M:** Bill Conti.

An American Werewolf in London [CE Universal]

Strange, darkly humorous version of the classic man-into-wolf horror tale became a cult hit, but never clicked with most American critics. Two American college students, David (Naughton) and Jack (Dunne), are backpacking through England when they're viciously attacked by a werewolf one foggy night. Jack is killed, but keeps appearing (in progressively decomposed form) before the seriously wounded David, warning him of impending werewolfdom when the moon is full; Jack advises suicide. Seat-jumping horror and gore, highlighted by intensive metamorphosis sequences orchestrated by Rick Baker, are offset by wry humor, though the shifts in tone don't always work. Universal's new presentation improves upon the old DVD in every department. The film print still has flaws (mainly the occasional speckling), but the transfer itself is far superior, delivering a sharp picture with color that, though not spectacularly vibrant, looks pretty much like it did in the theatre. The biggest complaint about the picture is that

the blacks are often a little grayish and rarely can be called true. The 5.1 soundtracks are fairly crisp and present nicely separated stereo and Surround that is often quite immersing. In the supplemental department (the first release was pretty bare bones), the Rick Baker featurette is short but loaded with info, the Landis interview is funny and insightful, but the commentary track by the two actors is pretty lame and sparse. (They tend to shut up whenever the gorgeous Jenny Agutter is on screen.) All in all though, it's well worth a few bucks to upgrade to this newer edition. —JO/MM

Movie: 🎘🎘🎘 **DVD:** 🎘🎘🎘
Universal Studios (cat #21219, UPC 0251-92121920). Widescreen (1.85:1) anamorphic. Dolby Digital 5.1; DTS 5.1. $26.98. Keepcase. *LANG:* English. *SUB:* French; Spanish. *CAP:* English. *FEATURES:* 20 chapters ▪ Talent files ▪ Production notes ▪ Commentary: David Naughton, Griffin Dunne ▪ John Landis interview ▪ Storyboards ▪ Outtakes ▪ Makeup artist Rick Baker on *Werewolf* ▪ Photo montage.
1981 (R) 97m/C *GB* David Naughton, Griffin Dunne, Jenny Agutter, Frank Oz, Brian Glover, Lila Kaye, David Schofield, John Woodvine, Don McKillop, Paul Kember, Colin Fernandes, Rik Mayall, Paddy Ryan; **D:** John Landis; **W:** John Landis; **C:** Robert Paynter; **M:** Elmer Bernstein. *AWARDS:* Oscars '81: Makeup.

America's Sweethearts

If you're looking for a great romantic comedy starring Julia Roberts, then see *Notting Hill*. But if you're in the mood for a quirky comedy which skewers the Hollywood system, then *America's Sweethearts* is the movie for you. Gwen Harrison and Eddie Thomas (Catherine Zeta-Jones and John Cusack) are America's biggest boxoffice stars, but their highly publicized divorce has tarnished their image. Publicist Lee Phillips (Billy Crystal) is given the task of getting Gwen and Eddie back together for a huge press junket at a secluded Nevada resort. The comedy ensues as Phillips, with his sidekick Danny (Seth Green in a great performance) do everything to get this couple together, while convincing the press that Gwen and Eddie have reconciled. When Eddie runs into Kiki (Julia Roberts), Gwen's sister and personal assistant, he finds himself irresistibly attracted to her, adding more problems to the already hectic situation. The performances in *America's Sweethearts* are fine, but the romantic angles are often hard to swallow. On the other hand, the way in which cutthroat Hollywood politics are portrayed (in the person of vicious studio exec Stanley Tucci) is dead-on and very funny. Unfortunately, many members of the audience will not understand many of the pot-shots taken at the film industry and will thus find the film disappointing. For a big summer release, DVD is surprisingly lacking in extras, but the transfer is impressive. The film is presented in a let-

terboxed format (a full-frame version is also included on the disc) and the transfer is basically flawless. The colors are deep and rich, showing realistic fleshtones. The audio is equally fine, providing clear dialogue and some Surround sound effects. There are some interesting deleted scenes, but otherwise the disc is notable mainly for the great transfer. —ML
Movie: ♫♫ ½ **DVD:** ♫♫♫
Columbia Tristar (cat #06393, UPC 0433-96063938). Widescreen (2.35:1) anamorphic. Dolby Digital 5.1; Dolby Surround. $27.96. Keepcase. *LANG:* English; French. *SUB:* English; French. *CAP:* English. *FEATURES:* Deleted scenes ➤ Theatrical trailers ➤ Filmographies ➤ Production notes. **2001 (PG-13) 103m/C** Julia Roberts, Catherine Zeta-Jones, John Cusack, Billy Crystal, Hank Azaria, Christopher Walken, Seth Green, Stanley Tucci, Larry King; **D:** Joe Roth; **W:** Billy Crystal, Peter Tolan; **C:** Phedon Papamichael; **M:** James Newton Howard.

Amon Saga

To avenge his slain mother, Amon, a young warrior, takes up servitude in the castle of his target, evil lord Valhiss. Amon waits for the perfect opportunity to exact the revenge that he has trained for since childhood. However, once in the service of the army, Amon meets the beautiful Princess Lichia, and his motives begin to change to a desire to protect the princess's endangered life. When Lichia is kidnapped by Valhiss in exchange for a ransom, it is just the reason Amon was waiting for to reveal his true purpose. Unfortunately, *Amon Saga* falls short in several areas. Although the sound and picture on this DVD are decent, the film itself leaves little in the way of unexplored anime territory. The plot rings of about two dozen other anime sword-and-sorcery features and leaves the viewer wondering where he put his 90 minutes. —EL
Movie: ♫ ½ **DVD:** ♫♫
Manga Ent. (cat #40732, UPC 66020040-7322). Full frame. Dolby 5.1 Surround; Stereo. $24.95. Keepcase. *LANG:* English; Japanese. *SUB:* English. *FEATURES:* Rouge's Gallery—character background info ➤ Manga Video previews, DVD catalog, and merchandise info ➤ Palm Pictures DVD previews ➤ Weblinks.
2001 90m/C *JP*

Amores Perros

Alejandro González Iñárritu's brilliant debut tells three interlinked stories, or perhaps, three versions of the same story of broken families and a broken society. The central point is a car accident in Mexico City. Octavio (Bernal) is in one car. He's in love with his sister-in-law Susana (Bauche); their relationship is bound to have unhappy consequences. Valeria (Toldeo), a high fashion model, is in another car. Nearby watching them is El Chivo (Echeverria), an aging grieving revolutionary who's surrounded by his pack of friendly dogs. (Dogs are one of the film's main concerns,

both literally and metaphorically.) That brief description doesn't even hint at the levels of complexity that Iñárritu creates. Krzysztof Kieslowski's *Colors* trilogy is a legitimate comparison. Iñárritu's social criticism is just as sharply pointed and he's working with a more colorful (to be charitable) environment. Few films have made a place look less appealing. DVD re-creates with depressing accuracy the black-green color scheme that Iñárritu favors to make the city's squalid slums seem so rank. He heightens that sense of discomfort by placing his camera too close to his characters in moments of extreme pressure and there are many of those. Only those who have the most serious problems with subtitles should pass this one by. It's nothing less than a masterpiece. —MM *AKA:* Love's a Bitch.
Movie: ♫♫♫♫ **DVD:** ♫♫♫♫
Lion's Gate Home Ent. (cat #ST7864D, UPC 658149786424). Widescreen (1.85:1) anamorphic. Dolby Digital 5.1 Surround; Dolby Surround. $24.98. Keepcase. *LANG:* Spanish; French. *SUB:* English; French; Spanish. *FEATURES:* 24 chapters ➤ Music videos ➤ Commentary (director & writer (Spanish with opt. English subtitles) ➤ 3 featurettes ➤ Music videos ➤ Deleted scenes.
2000 (R) 153m/C *MX* Vanessa Bauche, Emilio Echeverria, Gael Garcia Bernal, Goya Toledo, Alvaro Guerrero, Jorge Salinas, Marco Perez, Rodrigo Murray, Humberto Busto, Gerardo Campbell, Rosa Maria Bianchi, Dunia Saldivar, Adriana Barraza; **D:** Alejandro Gonzalez Inarritu; **W:** Guillermo Arriaga; **C:** Rodrigo Prieto; **M:** Gustavo Santaolalla. *AWARDS:* British Acad. '01: Foreign Film; Natl. Bd. of Review '01: Foreign Film; *NOM:* Oscars '00: Foreign Film; Golden Globes '01: Foreign Film; Ind. Spirit '02: Foreign Film.

The Amphibian Man

At a portside fishing town, a young man named Ichthyander rescues a woman named Gutiere from drowning. Ichthyander is amphibious thanks to the efforts of his benevolent scientist father. Unfortunately, he falls in love with Gutiere and that puts him at odds with a menacing ship captain. Odd but charming fantasy tale is told in contemporary times in realistic locations with a charismatic lead and convincing swimming doubles. The denouement and conventional action of the ending seem a bit at odds with the fantasy, but it's an enjoyable, diverting effort. The disc is transferred from a slightly faded print, but is fairly pristine, features acceptable colors, and is extremely sharp and bright. There's some minimal grain and the last two reels are particularly faded, but this is the best this film has ever looked on video or television. The mono sound is a trifle thin but is clean and noise-free. The various language tracks are performed with much more polish than traditional 1960s U.S. dubbing, which was usually aimed at the kiddie matinee market. The featurettes and behind-the-scenes footage are a real treat for Russian fantasy fans

and the opportunity to see the efforts that went into the production make the disc indispensable. —DG
Movie: ♫♫♫ **DVD:** ♫♫♫
Image Ent. (cat #RUSD0253DVD, UPC 014381025323). Full frame. Dolby Digital 5.1 Surround. $29.99. Keepcase. *LANG:* Russian; English; French; Arabic. *SUB:* Russian; English; French; German; Hebrew; Spanish; Italian; and more. *FEATURES:* Theatrical trailer ➤ Trailers from other releases ➤ Filmographies ➤ Photos ➤ 12 chapters ➤ Insert card with menu guide ➤ 2 featurettes ➤ Behind-the-scenes footage ➤ "Hey, Sailor," isolated song.
1961 93m/C *RU* K. Korieniev, M. Virzinskaya, Mikhail Kozakov, Vladlen Davydov; **D:** Y. Kasancki; **W:** Aleksei Kapler.

The Amy Fisher Story

The real Amy Fisher wishes she looked as good as star Drew Barrymore does in her full-bore bad-girl mode. This made-for-TV sleazefest draws from a variety of sources to dramatize the relationship between the "Long Island Lolita" and Joey Buttafuoco (Denison) and her subsequent attack on his wife. Although the film tries not to take sides, it does include some pretty hot sex scenes (complete with extra footage here) which could explain why this one garnered the highest ratings of the three network productions based on the story. Anchor Bay has done its usual exemplary work with the material, but the full-frame image is still only a modest improvement over broadcast quality. Sound is very good. —MM *AKA:* Beyond Control.
Movie: ♫♫ **DVD:** ♫♫ ½
Anchor Bay (cat #DV12059, UPC 013131-205992). Full frame. Dolby Digital Stereo. $24.98. Keepcase. *LANG:* English. *FEATURES:* 24 chapters.
1993 93m/C Drew Barrymore, Anthony John (Tony) Denison, Harley Jane Kozak, Tom Mason, Laurie Paton, Ken Pogue, Linda Darlow, Garry Davey, Dwight McFee, Gabe Khouth, Philip Granger, Stephen Cooper; **D:** Andy Tennant; **W:** Janet Brownell; **C:** Glen MacPherson; **M:** Michael Hoenig.

Ancient Civilizations

This three-disc set offers a brief overview of ancient Greece, Rome, and Egypt. If you've studied these cultures at all, none of this will be new to you. Video quality is acceptable, though a bit fuzzy, and the audio is serviceable. Each program is also available individually: "Rome and Pompeii," cat. #QD3242, UPC 033937032424; "Athens and Ancient Greece," cat. #QD32-43, UPC 033937032341; "The Land of the Pharoahs," cat. #QD3244, UPC 0339370-32448 (each program is approximately 120 minutes). —BG
Movie: ♫♫ **DVD:** ♫♫
Questar Video (cat #QD3241, UPC 03393-7032417). Full frame. $49.98. Keepcase. *LANG:* English. *FEATURES:* "The Land of the Pharoahs": 10 chapters ➤ "Rome and Pompeii": 12 chapters ➤ "Greece and

Ancient Rome": 12 chapters ● Bonus program on each disc.
2001 360m/C

And God Created Woman

Launching pad for Bardot's career as a sex siren, as she flits across the screen in a succession of scanty outfits and hangs out at the St. Tropez beach in what is euphemistically known as a swimsuit while turning up the heat for the males always in attendance. The plot concerns an 18-year-old nymphomaniac who is given a home by a local family with three handsome young sons. A cutting-edge sex film in its time that was boffo at the boxoffice. Since this is a Criterion DVD, one has to assume that the transfer is as good as it can be, given the source material. While not extremely sharp, the image is still enjoyable. The film is very bright most of the way through, yet there are still a few sequences where a noticeable grain shows up. Because of the lighting, there is not a lot of shadow detail to worry about and not many deep blacks. What's there is pretty good. The biggest complaint about the disc is the sound, which is thin for music and harsh for dialogue and effects. Loud noises are almost painful. This is one DVD where it sounds better just to run the sound through the TV and leave your AV receiver turned off. Luckily, since the dialogue is in French with English subtitles, you can leave the volume set pretty low. —*JO* **AKA:** And Woman...Was Created; Et Dieu Crea la Femme.
Movie: 🐾🐾 ½ **DVD:** 🐾🐾
Criterion (cat #AND110DVD, UPC 037429-147825). Widescreen (2.35:1) anamorphic. Dolby Digital Mono. $29.95. Keepcase. *LANG:* French. *SUB:* English. *FEATURES:* 21 chapters ● U.S. theatrical trailer ● Restoration demonstration.
1957 (PG) 93m/C *FR* Brigitte Bardot, Curt Jurgens, Jean-Louis Trintignant, Christian Marquand; *D:* Roger Vadim; *W:* Roger Vadim, Raoul Levy; *C:* Armand Thirard; *M:* Paul Misraki.

And Now the Screaming Starts [SE]

Handsome, slow-moving period piece begins with voice-over narration suggesting *Rebecca* but the film is really a town-with-a-secret Gothic as young bride Catherine (Beacham) tries to learn what her husband Charles (Ogilvy) is hiding at the Fengriffin estate. Director Roy Ward Baker overplays such non-scary gimmicks as the face at the window but the story does have some suspense, and the disembodied hand machine becomes oddly endearing. The production is well acted throughout, with Peter Cushing bringing his customary grace to the proceedings. On the commentary track, film historian (and assistant editor of this book) Darren Gross and Ian Ogilvy have a comfortable, informative walk down memory lane. They attempt to compare the production to other work being done in the genre by British studios at the time and their talk is often more interesting than the languidly paced action. Exteriors were filmed at the then vacant Oakly Court estate, which served the same function for *The Rocky Horror Picture Show.* —*MM* **AKA:** Bride of Fengriffen; Fengriffen; I Have No Mouth But I Must Scream.
Movie: 🐾🐾 **DVD:** 🐾🐾 ½
Image Ent. (cat #ID6143TVDVD, UPC 014-381614329). Widescreen (1.85:1) letterboxed. Dolby Digital Mono. $24.99. Keepcase. *LANG:* English. *FEATURES:* Trailer ● Commentary ● Still gallery ● 12 chapters.
1973 (R) 91m/C *GB* Peter Cushing, Herbert Lom, Patrick Magee, Ian Ogilvy, Stephanie Beacham, Rosalie Crutchley, Guy Rolfe, Janet Key, Gillian Lind; *D:* Roy Ward Baker; *W:* Roger Marshall; *C:* Denys Coop; *M:* Douglas Gamley.

And Soon the Darkness

Nubile Cathy (Dotrice) and earnest Jane (Franklin) take a bicycling vacation in the French countryside. When Cathy goes missing, Jane frantically tries to find her. Plenty of red herrings here, including the mysterious Paul (Eles) and a creepy gendarme (Nettleton), will keep you wondering how they manage to sustain the stagy action and glacial pacing until the last scenes. Great naturalistic cinematography plays a nice counterpoint to the suspense. Commentary moderated by journalist Jonathan Sothcott covers far more than just this picture since many of the players here also worked on *The Avengers.* Picture looks very good. The sound is unspectacular. —*LA*
Movie: 🐾🐾 ½ **DVD:** 🐾🐾🐾
Anchor Bay (cat #DV11845, UPC 013131-184594). Widescreen (1.77:1) anamorphic. $19.98. Keepcase. *LANG:* English. *FEATURES:* Commentary: director Fuest, co-writer/-producer Clemens ● Theatrical trailer ● Radio spots ● Talent bios ● 24 chapters.
1970 (PG) 94m/C *GB* Pamela Franklin, Michele Dotrice, Sandor Eles, John Nettleton, Claire Kelly, Hanna-Marie Pravda; *D:* Robert Fuest; *W:* Terry Nation, Brian Clemens; *C:* Ian Wilson; *M:* Laurie Johnson.

And Then There Were None [Image]

An all-star cast makes up the 10 colorful guests invited to a secluded estate in England by a mysterious host. What the invitations do not say, however, is the reason they have been chosen to visit—to be murdered, one by one. Cat and mouse masterpiece based on Agatha Christie's book is an entertaining mixture of suspense and black comedy. It's been remade several times as *Ten Little Indians* with varying degrees of success. This remains one of the finest. DVD image is first-rate with a little unavoidable snow the only visual flaw. —*MM*
Movie: 🐾🐾🐾 **DVD:** 🐾🐾 ½
Image Ent. (cat #ID8570CODVD, UPC 01-4381857023). Full frame. Dolby Digital Mono. $24.99. Keepcase. *LANG:* English.

FEATURES: 12 chapters ● British title sequence.
1945 97m/B Louis Hayward, Barry Fitzgerald, Walter Huston, Roland Young, Sir C. Aubrey Smith, Judith Anderson, Mischa Auer, June Duprez; *D:* Rene Clair; *W:* Rene Clair, Dudley Nichols; *C:* Lucien N. Andriot; *M:* Mario Castelnuovo-Tedesco.

Andre

More human-animal interaction from the director of *The Man from Snowy River* and *Zeus & Roxanne,* telling the true story of an orphaned seal that was adopted by the local Marine harbormaster (Keith Carradine) and his family. As they raise their houseguest, the question arises whether the seal, which they've named Andre, should be returned to the wild. It'll remind you of *Free Willy,* with an appealing smaller sea mammal and the equally appealing Tina Majorino, as the youngster who befriends Andre. Look for *Dawson's Creek* heart-throb Joshua Jackson in a small role. (For those who are sticklers for accuracy, Andre is actually portrayed by a sea lion and not a seal.) Based on the book *A Seal Called Andre* by Harry Goodridge and Lew Dietz. Director George Miller should not be confused with the director of *Mad Max,* who shares the same name. While this DVD is shorn of any extra features (even a trailer is absent!), the presentation is fine. The image is sharp and clear, though a bit flat looking at times. There is a slight amount of grain, but the colors look great. The Dolby Digital 5.1 audio mix is quite impressive, as there is a very nice usage of the rear speakers here, most notably during the storm sequence. The dialogue is clear and the track is distortion-free. —*ML*
Movie: 🐾🐾 ½ **DVD:** 🐾🐾🐾
Paramount (cat #09116, UPC 0973609-11640). Widescreen (2.35:1) anamorphic. Dolby Digital 5.1; Dolby Surround; Digital Stereo. $24.99. Keepcase. *LANG:* English; French. *SUB:* English. *CAP:* English. *FEATURES:* 12 chapters.
1994 (PG) 94m/C Keith Carradine, Tina Majorino, Chelsea Field, Keith Szarabajka, Shane Meier, Joshua Jackson; *D:* George Miller; *W:* Dana Baratta; *C:* Thomas Burstyn; *M:* Bruce Rowland.

Angel Eyes

Hard-edged Chicago police officer Sharon Pogue (Lopez) has seen a lot in the line of duty. But when a mysterious civilian saves her life, she is compelled to know more about her savior. As Pogue and her strangely familiar rescuer, Catch (Caviezel), become closer, she finds that there is a dark secret just under the surface—one he is not willing to face. Pogue must come to peace with her own troubled history as she also attempts to help Catch face his. Both Lopez and Caviezel give fine performances despite the film's easily predictable nature. DVD comes with an insightful commentary from director Luis Mandoki. The picture quality is exceptionally crisp with good color and contrast. The sound quality is also impressive, making good use of its Surround capabilities through the chase scenes at the beginning of the film. —EL

Movie: 🎬🎬 ½ **DVD:** 🎬🎬🎬
Warner (cat #21425, UPC 0853921425-21). Widescreen (1.85:1) anamorphic. Dolby 5.1 Surround. $24.98. Snapper. *LANG:* English; French. *SUB:* English; French; Spanish. *CAP:* English. *FEATURES:* Commentary: director Luis Mandoki • Cast and crew bios • 29 chapters.
2001 (R) 104m/C Jennifer Lopez, James Caviezel, Sonia Braga, Terrence DaShon Howard, Jeremy Sisto, Monet Mazur, Victor Argo, Shirley Knight, Jeremy Ratchford, Peter MacNeill, Stephen Kay; *D:* Luis Mandoki; *W:* Gerald Di Pego; *C:* Piotr Sobocinski; *M:* Marco Beltrami.

Angel Sanctuary

Moody, pretty-boy teenager Setsuno discovers he carries the soul of a fallen angel within him. As two violently opposed factions of angels prepare for battle, Setsuno finds himself and his sister in danger and has to use his newly gained supernatural powers to protect them. Similar to *X*, this three-episode condensation of an epic Japanese comic is frequently muddled and ends with confusing supernatural babble that makes little sense. Most distracting of all is the glorification of Setsuno's disturbing incestuous relationship with his sister. Its relation to the plot is tenuous at best and downright unpleasant. The animation is better than average, but the story is a mess. At times the image is a bit grainy and it's streaky in dark scenes. Colors appear accurate and the stereo audio track is excellent. —DG

Movie: 🎬🎬 **DVD:** 🎬🎬🎬 ½
Central Park/U.S. Manga (cat #USMD 2047, UPC 719987204720). Full frame. Stereo Surround. $29.99. Keepcase. *LANG:* Japanese; English. *SUB:* English. *FEATURES:* Making of the English dub • Character sketches, art gallery • Trivia • "Meet the Characters" • 9 chapters • DVD-ROM: art gallery, scripts, production sketches, cast & crew info.
2000 90m/C *JP D:* Seiko Sayama; *W:* Mayori Sekijima.

Angels and Insects

Odd Victorian romantic drama based on A.S. Byatt's novella *Morpho Eugenia* is definitely an acquired taste. The mysteries of nature are nothing compared to the mysteries of human life as naturalist William Adamson (Rylance) discovers when he takes a position at the home of Sir Harold Alabaster (Kemp), amateur insect collector. Adamson falls in love and marries blondly beautiful Eugenia (Kensit), whose outward propriety hides a sensual nature and other secrets. (Do NOT watch the trailer or too many of those secrets will be revealed.) Take note of Paul Brown's costumes, which mimic the exoticness of insects and are positively painful at times. Eugenia's first electric blue and bright red

ball gown is a real dazzler. On DVD, some shimmer is evident in those vibrant fabric patterns and busy stonework. Black clothes display proper detail in close-up. Overall image is no better than average but that's due mostly to the original elements, not the transfer. Sound is weak and muffled but that too appears to come from the original. —MM

Movie: 🎬🎬🎬 **DVD:** 🎬🎬 ½
MGM Home Ent. (cat #1003251, UPC 02-7616874016). Widescreen (1.85:1) letterboxed. Dolby Digital Surround. $19.98. Keepcase. *LANG:* English; Spanish. *SUB:* English; French; Spanish. *CAP:* English. *FEATURES:* 16 chapters • Trailer.
1995 (R) 116m/C *GB* Mark Rylance, Patsy Kensit, Kristin Scott Thomas, Jeremy Kemp, Douglas Henshall, Chris Larkin, Annette Badland, Anna Massey, Saskia Wickham; *D:* Philip Haas; *W:* Belinda Haas, Philip Haas; *C:* Bernard Zitzermann; *M:* Alexander Balanescu. *AWARDS: NOM:* Oscars '96: Costume Des.

Angels Hard As They Come

Opposing biker-gang leaders face off in a ghost town that's been re-populated by hippies. It's a semi-spoof of the genre with an early appearance by Glenn and Busey's film debut. Who'd have thought that producer Demme would go on to make *Silence of the Lambs*? Full-frame image is no better than VHS tape. It's poorly focused with harsh colors. Sound is O.K. Title is available on the *Classic Biker Movies* disc. —MM

Movie: 🎬 ½ **DVD:** 🎬 ½
BFS Video (cat #302910D, UPC 0668053-02916). Full frame. $9.98. Keepcase. *LANG:* English. *FEATURES:* 6 chapters • Talent files.
1971 (R) 86m/C Gary Busey, Scott Glenn, James Iglehart, Gary Littlejohn, Charles Dierkop, Larry Tucker, Gilda Texter, Janet Wood, Brendan Kelly; *D:* Joe Viola; *W:* Jonathan Demme, Joe Viola; *M:* Richard Hieronymous.

Angels in the Outfield

Roger (Gordon-Levitt), a young foster child, is abandoned by his father (Mulroney, looking ridiculous as a biker) as the movie opens. He asks his father when they'll be a family again, and dad replies, "when the Angels win the pennant." In other words, as the Angels are the worst team in baseball...never. Roger prays one night for the Angels to be a winning team again so his family can be reunited. Somewhere, someone or something is listening, and a team of angels is suddenly assisting the players and making spectacular plays. Technically, the film's fine, with sunny cinematography by Matthew Leonetti and fair direction by William Dear. The only lackluster element is a manipulative and sappy score from Randy Edelman. Widescreen image quality is simply passable, as the picture is inconsistent; some scenes are crisp, while oth-

ers are soft and flawed. The 5.1 provides a bit less envelopment than expected. Audio quality is fine, but not too noteworthy, as there's little dynamic range, but passable clarity. —AB

Movie: 🎬🎬 ½ **DVD:** 🎬🎬
Buena Vista Home Ent. (UPC 78693616-9713). Widescreen (1.85:1) anamorphic. Dolby Digital 5.1 Surround. $19.98. Keepcase. *LANG:* English. *SUB:* French; Spanish. *CAP:* English. *FEATURES:* 13 chapters.
1994 (PG) 105m/C Danny Glover, Tony Danza, Christopher Lloyd, Brenda Fricker, Ben Johnson, Joseph Gordon-Levitt, Jay O. Sanders, Dermot Mulroney; *D:* William Dear; *W:* Holly Goldberg Sloan; *C:* Matthew F. Leonetti; *M:* Randy Edelman.

The Angry Red Planet

A Mars-expedition rocket, long thought destroyed, returns to Earth with only two survivors. As one is suffering from an unknown alien infection, the remaining astronaut (Hayden) tries to recall their expedition on Mars in order to find some clue as to the nature of the malady. The scientists' various encounters with hostile forms of life (including the famous "rat-bat-spider" creature who is understandably upset) are told in flashback. This colorful space-exploration thriller is a notch above similar tales from the era thanks to its small cast of likable characters (not an evil commie spy in the bunch!) and the strength of its pacing. There are the usual scientific boners and silly dialogue but the movie is fairly tense and fast-paced. The gruesome death of the comic relief character (Kruschen) only increases the tension, despite the use of Jello for some of the special effects. The Mars sequences are shot using a kind of sepia/orange tinting with dark areas that appear in negative. Mars the orange planet? Hmm. The transfer features strong colors and a nice filmic look, but is marred by sections with poor registration and print damage in later reels. For the most part, this is a sharp though grainy disc, and *does* offer an improvement over VHS. The mono sound is fine. —AB/DG **AKA:** Invasion of Mars; Journey to Planet Four.

Movie: 🎬🎬🎬 **DVD:** 🎬🎬 ½
Paramount (cat #1002638, UPC 0276168-68381). Full frame. Mono. $14.95. Keepcase. *LANG:* English. *SUB:* French; English. *CAP:* English. *FEATURES:* Theatrical trailer • 16 chapters.
1959 83m/C Gerald Mohr, Les Tremayne, Jack Kruschen, Nora Hayden, Paul Hahn, J. Edward McKinley, Tom Daly, Don Lamond; *D:* Ib Melchior; *W:* Ib Melchior, Sidney Pink; *C:* Stanley Cortez; *M:* Paul Dunlap.

Anguish

John Pressman (Lerner) works as an orderly at an ophthalmologist's office. When one of the patients angers him, John's overbearing mother (Rubinstein) hypnotizes him and programs him to kill the offenders. More eyeball-obsessed murders follow. Considering that this is an older Spanish film, the quality of the transfer is quite good. The picture is very clear for the most part, with few signs of artifacting. The only real grain appears to be intentional on the part of the filmmakers. The color balancing on the disc is good, with the red blood standing out against the black backgrounds. The outdoor scenes at the end are quite clear, and show little grain and few defects to the source print. Remastered 5.1 mix gives a very nice balance between dialogue and sound effects, with the latter never drowning out the former. —*GH/MM*

Movie: 🎵🎵 ½ **DVD:** 🎵🎵 ½
Anchor Bay (UPC 013131111392). Widescreen (2.35:1) anamorphic. Dolby Digital 5.1 Surround. $29.98. Keepcase. *LANG:* English. *FEATURES:* Trailer.
1988 (R) 89m/C *SP* Zelda Rubinstein, Michael Lerner, Talia Paul, Clara Pastor; **D:** Bigas Luna; **W:** Bigas Luna; **C:** Josep Civit; **M:** J(ose) M(anuel) Pagan.

Anima

Surreal, fairy-tale tinged story of an aging taxidermist and his wife who are, it would seem, Holocaust survivors. They live in a quiet world of their own making deep in the country, ignoring the past as well as the present world until a Fox Channel–style reporter catches wind of a supposed master of taxidermy who once preserved a jellyfish. He assembles his crew and goes in search of the mystery master and breaks the bubble that the couple has created around themselves. A beautifully shot film—each scene has the feel of a dream—it is also well acted and written. Not a good film for anyone who wants answers spoon-fed to them. The picture looks good and fairly crisp with a little bleeding of the darker colors. A lot of indoor shots and hazy outdoor light give it a faded quality in some scenes, but overall it's a beautiful picture. Also of note, on the review copy there was about 5 seconds of de-pixelation at one point. The sound is slightly above average but not great. —*CA*

Movie: 🎵🎵🎵 **DVD:** 🎵🎵 ½
Vanguard Intl. Cinema (cat #VF0192, UPC 6 58769 01923 0). Full frame. $29.95. Keepcase. *LANG:* English. *FEATURES:* 10 chapters.
1998 88m/C Bray Poor, George Barteni-eff, Jacqueline Bertrand; **D:** Craig Richardson; **W:** Craig Richardson; **C:** Randy Drummond; **M:** Joel Diamond, Adam Hurst.

The Animal

Predictable vehicle for the always annoying Schneider. Wimp Schneider is in a serious car accident and is "rescued" by a mad scientist who replaces his damaged organs with animal parts, which leads to the sort of sophomoric, 10-year-old male bathroom humor we've come to expect from ex-SNLers and their films. Of note, Haskell (from TV's first *Survivor*) makes her acting debut as Schneider's girlfriend. The disc features the kind of care that you wish would go into films of a slightly higher quality. The video transfer is very solid and boasts well-defined colors and very sharp

blacks. A similarly excellent soundtrack exhibits no distortion and reproduces dialogue and music admirably. Of the disc's ample extras, the two commentary tracks stand out as the most enjoyable though they do, from time to time, lack any "real" behind-the-scenes meat. One treat is the substantial amount of bonus footage hidden throughout the disc in the form of deleted scenes, games, etc. —*MJT*

Movie: 🎵🎵 **DVD:** 🎵🎵🎵
Columbia Tristar (cat #06251, UPC 0433-96062511). Widescreen (1.85:1) anamorphic. Dolby Digital 5.1 Surround; Dolby 2.0 Surround. $27.96. Keepcase. *LANG:* English; French. *SUB:* English; French. *FEATURES:* 28 chapters • Commentary: actor Rob Schneider • Commentary: director Luke Greenfield • "Badger Delivery" deleted scenes • Original "making of" featurette • "What's in Marvin?" game • Comedy Central's "Reel Comedy: The Animal" featurette • Theatrical trailers • Filmographies • Production Notes.
2001 (PG-13) 83m/C Rob Schneider, Guy Torry, John C. McGinley, Colleen Haskell, Michael Caton, Louis Lombardi, Ed Asner; **D:** Luke Greenfield; **W:** Rob Schneider, Tom Brady; **C:** Peter Collister; **M:** Teddy Castellucci.

Animals at Play: Cute and Cuddly

This disc is actually a collection of three previously released *Animals at Play* videos. On the DVD, you'll find that each of these selections may be viewed separately, as Parts 1, 2, and 3. It's made up entirely of video footage of animals cavorting at zoos or natural habitat parks. While there is a generous amount of footage given to most of the animals featured, the program has a "cheap" feeling to it, as if someone simply took a camcorder to a zoo, gathered as much footage as possible, and then packaged it for sale. There is very little narration, which gives an occasionally interesting fact about the animals. On the positive side, the range of animals featured here is very wide, going from the familiar (tigers, polar bears) to the exotic (lemurs, meerkats). And, the animals are undeniably cute. Still, this isn't much different from the programs which are featured on Animal Planet around-the-clock. As *Animals at Play* was shot on video, the image is very sharp and clear, showing no defects. The colors are good and the picture is always bright. The Dolby Digital Stereo soundtrack delivers clear narration and unfortunately faithful reproduction of the repetitive music. It should be noted that this music dominates the soundtrack and there are barely any sounds from the animals. —*ML*

Movie: 🎵 ½ **DVD:** 🎵🎵
BFS Video (cat #30280-D, UPC 06680530-2800). Full frame. Dolby Digital Stereo. $19.98. Keepcase. *LANG:* English.
2001 120m/C

Animated Christmas DVD Double Feature

These two animated films are on the general level of old Saturday morning cartoon

fare with fuzzy focus and considerable scratching. Sound is thin. "Santa and the Three Bears" is about a Yellowstone park ranger who saves a mother bear and her cubs. "The Little Christmas Burro" thinks that he's a useless runt until he runs into Joseph and Mary. Both are fine for younger undemanding viewers. —*MM*

Movie: 🎵🎵 **DVD:** 🎵🎵
Marengo Films (cat #0014, UPC 8070130-01426). Full frame. $14.98. Keepcase. *LANG:* English. *FEATURES:* 4 chapters each.
1979 72m/C D: Tony Benedict, Vic Atkinson; **W:** Tony Benedict, Christine Atkinson; **V:** Lorne Greene, Hal Smith, Jean Van Derpyl, Annette Ferrer, Barrie Brooks.

Anne Frank

Solid made-for-TV entry into the pantheon of Anne Frank pathos, legend, or tragedy—take your pick. Romanian-born director Robert Dornhelm does his best work to date by taking a more intimate look at the day-to-day life of the young Anne Frank (played with great precision by Hannah Taylor-Gordon—*Jacob the Liar, Mansfield Park*) during the years she and her family spent in hiding from the German invaders. Anne, as a human being, is fleshed out and painted with more detail than in other biopics covering the same ground (story is based on Melissa Muller's biography and not on the famous diary of the young girl). This has the effect of making her ultimate fate at Auschwitz all the more painful. DVD presentation is sans extras and seems muted, in terms of color, throughout—perhaps intentionally so to create a sense of hopelessness and foreboding. —*RJT*

Movie: 🎵🎵🎵 **DVD:** 🎵🎵 ½
Buena Vista Home Ent. (cat #23528, UPC 786936161434). Full frame. Dolby Digital Surround. $29.99. Keepcase. *LANG:* English. *SUB:* English. *CAP:* English. *FEATURES:* 22 chapters • Cross-promotion trailer for *South Pacific*.
2001 189m/C Ben Kingsley, Brenda Blethyn, Hannah Taylor Gordon, Joachim Krol, Lili Taylor, Tatjana Blacher; **D:** Richard Dornhelm; **W:** Kirk Ellis; **C:** Elemer Ragalyi; **M:** Graeme Revell.

The Anniversary Party

When novelist Joe (Cumming) and actress wife Sally (Leigh) throw themselves a party to celebrate their sixth anniversary, it's only a matter of a few minutes before both hosts and guests resort to the inevitable party-killer—telling the truth. A very funny and well-acted film. An exceptional video transfer boasts bright, vibrant colors and well-defined blacks and other darker hues. The soundtrack is similarly impressive and does justice to the low-noise level of the dialogue throughout the film. The commentary by Leigh and Cumming is the standout of the disc's extras. —*MJT*

Movie: 🎵🎵🎵 **DVD:** 🎵🎵🎵
New Line (cat #N5392, UPC 79404353-9220). Widescreen (1.85:1) anamorphic. Dolby Digital 5.1 Surround; Dolby Digital

Surround. $24.98. Snapper. *LANG:* English. *SUB:* English. *FEATURES:* 22 chapters ● Commentary: actors Jennifer Jason Leigh, Alan Cumming ● Documentary: The Sundance Channel's "Anatomy of a Scene" ● Cast & crew filmographies ● Theatrical trailer ● DVD-ROM: Script-to-screen screenplay; original website.
2001 (R) 117m/C Jennifer Jason Leigh, Alan Cumming, Gwyneth Paltrow, Kevin Kline, Phoebe Cates, John C. Reilly, Jane Adams, John Benjamin Hickey, Parker Posey, Denis O'Hare, Jennifer Beals, Mina (Badiyi) Badie, Michael Panes; *D:* Jennifer Jason Leigh, Alan Cumming; *W:* Jennifer Jason Leigh, Alan Cumming; *C:* John Bailey; *M:* Michael Penn.

Any Which Way You Can

Bare-knuckle boxer Philo Beddoe (Eastwood) and Clyde the orangutang are back in the sequel to *Every Which Way But Loose.* For a plot, Philo gets involved with a big-bucks bout (against Smith) and Clyde wants to procreate. As sequels go, it's O.K. but still feels like a retread. The exceptionally heavy grain comes from the original, as I remember it. I could not pick out any excess artifacts or pixels, even in the dusty outdoor fight scenes. Curiously, the French soundtrack with the original mono sounds more accurate than the beefed-up 5.1, which overdoes everyday sound effects. —*MM*
Movie: 🎵🎵 ½ *DVD:* 🎵🎵 ½
Warner (cat #18586, UPC 0853918586-21). Widescreen (1.85:1) anamorphic. Dolby Digital 5.1 Surround; Mono. $19.98. Snapper. *LANG:* English; French. *SUB:* English; French. *CAP:* English. *FEATURES:* Talent files ● Behind-the-scenes (text) ● Trailer ● 34 chapters.
1980 (PG) 116m/C Clint Eastwood, Sondra Locke, Ruth Gordon, Harry Guardino, William Smith, Geoffrey Lewis, Barry Corbin; *D:* Buddy Van Horn; *W:* Stanford Sherman; *C:* David Worth.

Anzio

The Allied invasion of Italy in 1944 is seen through the eyes of war correspondent Dick Ennis (Mitchum) and Cpl. Rabinoff (Falk). A fine cast waits endlessly to leave the beach in this typically overblown and meandering DeLaurentiis production. (Note how long it takes just to get through the credits!) The big battle scenes are much better. DVD looks exceptionally good for a film from the late '60s. Colors are very bright; signs of wear are minimal. Sound will seem weak to those expecting the full Surround treatment found in contemporary war films. —*MM AKA:* The Battle for Anzio; Lo Sbarco di Anzio.
Movie: 🎵🎵 *DVD:* 🎵🎵🎵
Columbia Tristar (cat #06545, UPC 04339-6065451). Widescreen (2.35:1) anamorphic; full frame. Dolby Digital Mono. $24.98. Keepcase. *LANG:* English; French. *SUB:* English; French; Spanish; Portuguese;

Chinese; Korean; Thai. *CAP:* English. *FEATURES:* 28 chapters ● Trailers.
1968 117m/C Giancarlo Giannini, Robert Mitchum, Peter Falk, Arthur Kennedy, Robert Ryan, Earl Holliman, Mark Damon, Reni Santoni, Patrick Magee; *D:* Edward Dmytryk; *W:* H.A.L. Craig, Frank De Felitta; *C:* Giuseppe Rotunno; *M:* Riz Ortolani.

A*P*E*

A captured giant gorilla (described as "36 feet tall" yet looking as large as Godzilla) escapes from a freighter off the coast of Korea. At the same time an American actress is filming a movie nearby. The ape, per usual, grabs her and rampages through Seoul. So astonishingly bad I was laughing out loud all by myself. Japanese monster movies look like *Star Wars* in comparison. Features maybe not the worst gorilla suit ever, just moth-eaten, with an actor inside prone to some sort of Tai Chi or ballet. His battle with a "giant" dead shark is not to be missed. Too funny to be a total WOOF! The original one-sheet indicates this was released as a 3-D movie, which explains Styrofoam boulders hurtling into your eye over and over. Letter-boxed, but Joanna DeVarona's name doesn't even fit in the screen titles. A mediocre DVD transfer of a mediocre print, which seems to be Image Entertainment's standard. Ditto on sound. —*MO AKA:* Attack of the Giant Horny Gorilla.
Movie: 🎵 *DVD:* 🎵🎵
Image Ent. (cat #ID0309WEDVD, UPC 014-381030921). Widescreen. $24.99. Keepcase. *LANG:* English. *FEATURES:* 13 chapters.
1976 (PG) 87m/C *KN* Rod Arrants, Joanna (Joanna DeVarona) Kerns, Alex Nicol, Francis Lee; *D:* Paul Leder; *W:* Paul Leder, Reuben Leder.

Apocalypse Now [Redux]

New scenes (51 minutes' worth) have been added to the original 1979 cut (reviewed in *Book 1*), and a few scenes shifted. Captain Willard (Sheen) now steals Col. Kilgore's (Duvall) surfboard after the attack on the Viet Cong village. The USO tour, the one with the Playboy Bunnies, is discovered without fuel for their helicopters in a torrential downpour, so Willard plays pimp and trades gasoline for sex for his men. The group comes upon an anachronistic French plantation, intact and surviving in the midst of the war, with bitter Gallic holdouts using a (Kurtz-like) private army and swearing never to leave. Willard listens to at least a reel's worth of mostly unintelligible English and untranslated French sermonizing, and then sensitively beds down an unattached French woman (no Bunnies for him). Later, the deranged Col. Kurtz (Brando) reads randomly to Willard from news magazines, while he's hogtied as a prisoner. This is another case of the deplorable trend to go back and create new marketable items out of established hits, by adding scenes and details that the filmmakers originally did not intend to be included. Francis Coppola has

joined his pals Lucas and Spielberg by pulling his pretty-darn-amazing Vietnam War movie out and retooling it. According to all the hype, this is the "expanded version" that fully expresses the filmmaker's intentions, etc. Hooey. The added "redux" word hangs over the new *Apocalypse* poster like the "now with Bleach" sticker on a box of detergent. The added scenes are very damaging to the film. For curiosity value, plenty of us will want to see this; several nice things from the famous work-in-progress rough cut are here, but all are unnecessary. The original cut, which savagely ejected major scenes left and right, is a model of editorial genius. Coppola and his editors truly fashioned a diamond out of a lot of discordant material, and gave it a consistent through-line. All of the new material either breaks this through-line, or slows what used to be a deliberate picture into a static one. Worse, it re-invents the movie in a way that suggests that something was wrong with it in the first place. DVD looks and sounds pretty much like the first release—excellent. A nice difference between the theatrical release and the DVD is that optional English subtitles are available, so as to better understand the dialogue in the plantation scene. The insert card's scene index (36 chapters) highlights the altered sequences in yellow so as to easily find them. Too bad this wasn't planned as a special DVD from the start; perhaps seamless branching could have been employed to choose between the original version and the 2001 cut. —*GE*
Movie: 🎵🎵 *DVD:* 🎵🎵🎵 ½
Paramount (cat #09629, UPC 097360962-949). Widescreen (2.35:1) anamorphic. Dolby Digital 5.1 Surround Stereo. $29.99. Keepcase. *LANG:* English. *SUB:* English. *CAP:* English. *FEATURES:* 36 chapters ● Trailer.
1979 (R) 202m/C Francis Ford Coppola, Marlon Brando, Martin Sheen, Robert Duvall, Frederic Forrest, Sam Bottoms, Scott Glenn, Albert Hall, Laurence "Larry" Fishburne, Harrison Ford, G.D. Spradlin, Dennis Hopper, Cynthia Wood, Colleen Camp, Linda Carpenter, Tom Mason, James Keane, Damien Leake, Jack Thibeau, R. Lee Ermey, Vittorio Storaro; *D:* Francis Ford Coppola; *W:* Francis Ford Coppola, John Milius, Michael Herr; *C:* Vittorio Storaro; *M:* Carmine Coppola. *AWARDS:* Oscars '79: Cinematog., Sound; AFI '98: Top 100; British Acad. '79: Director (Coppola), Support. Actor (Duvall); Cannes '79: Film; Golden Globes '80: Director (Coppola), Support. Actor (Duvall), Score, Natl. Film Reg. '00; Natl. Soc. Film Critics '79: Support. Actor (Forrest); *NOM:* Oscars '79: Adapt. Screenplay, Art Dir./Set Dec., Director (Coppola), Film Editing, Picture, Support. Actor (Duvall).

The Apocalypse Watch

Will there ever be a time when someone does a Robert Ludlum spy novel right? Here is another low-budget piece of trash that is so boring I had toothpicks holding up my eyelids to get through it. It's all

about a neo-Fascist group trying to start the Fourth Reich. Drew Latham (Patrick Bergin) takes his spy brother's (John Shea) place to infiltrate the group and stop them. He's helped by tasty dish Karin de Vries (Virginia Madsen). Run from this movie. DVD is not as good as VHS and sound is very muddied at times. —DE **AKA:** Robert Ludlum's the Apocalypse Watch.
Movie: 🎬 **DVD:** 🎬½
Artisan Ent. (cat #12434, UPC 07729124-64). Full frame. Dolby 5.1. $19.98. Keepcase. *LANG:* English. *CAP:* English. *FEATURES:* 16 chapters.
1997 176m/C Patrick Bergin, Virginia Madsen, John Shea, Benedick Blythe, Christopher Neame, Malcolm Tierney; **D:** Kevin Connor; **W:** John Goldsmith, Christopher Canaan; **C:** Dennis C. Lewiston; **M:** Ken Thorne.

Arachnid

Once you hit "play" on the *Arachnid* DVD, you'll be forced to view the logos for the 12 production companies and Spanish government agencies who were responsible for the film. With a dozen entities involved, at some point a representative should have said, "Why aren't there any likable characters in this movie?" And that problem is just the tip of the iceberg for this disappointing film. Director Jack Sholder was once on his way to being a favorite amongst genre fans after such low-budget hits as *Alone in the Dark* and *The Hidden*, but his work here is strictly by the books. Chris Potter (of TV's *Silk Stalkings*) stars as Valentine, an ex-Marine, who along with scruffy pilot Mercer (Alex Reid) leads an expedition to a small island in the South Pacific to determine what is killing the locals. After a crashlanding, they find the island to be devoid of humans, but it is teeming with mutated insects, including a giant spider. *Arachnid* plays like a film from the '50s, as the cast is picked off one-by-one by monsters that don't show up until the end. The acting is wooden and the special effects (a mixture of CGI and puppetry) aren't very convincing. Boring and predictable from beginning to end. If you do insist on seeing this film, be sure to view it on DVD, as the quality here is quite good. The picture is very sharp and clear, showing only minor artifacting in some scenes. The colors are bright and true, most notably the green foliage of the island. The Dolby Digital 5.1 audio track is quite good, as it offers accurate stereo separation and nearly constant Surround sound action. The dialogue is clear and there is no distortion on this track. —ML
Movie: woof **DVD:** 🎬🎬🎬
Lion's Gate Home Ent. (cat #VM7974D, UPC 031398797425). Widescreen (1.85:1) anamorphic. Dolby Digital 5.1. $24.99. Keepcase. *LANG:* English. *SUB:* English; Spanish. *CAP:* English. *FEATURES:* Trailer • 24 chapters.
2001 (R) 95m/C Chris Potter, Neus Asensi, Jose Sancho, Alex Reid; **D:** Jack Sholder; **W:** Mark Sevi; **C:** Carlos Gonzalez; **M:** Francesc Gener.

Arbuckle & Keaton, Vol. 1 (1917–19)

As David Pearson explains in his succinct liner notes, Roscoe "Fatty" Arbuckle is remembered today for a scandal—the death of model Virginia Rappe—though he was finally exonerated of any responsibility. No matter; he was blacklisted from the movie business and his early work has been unseen for years. These two discs present some of his best films, two reel comedies that feature a young Buster Keaton as his co-star. Their physical humor contains beautifully timed gags and some of their slapstick is superb. The overt racism of "Out West" is offputting, but it's not unknown in films of that time. Image quality is excellent throughout, perhaps because the films have not been much in demand. A little light snow is visible in some shots. The lively new music by the Alloy Orchestra is up to the group's high standard. These are highly recommended to any student of the silent era. Contents: "The Bell Boy," "The Butcher Boy," "Out West," "Moonshine," and "The Hayseed." —MM
Movie: 🎬🎬🎬 **DVD:** 🎬🎬🎬
Kino on Video (cat #K204, UPC 7383290-20422). Full frame. $29.95. Keepcase. *LANG:* Silent. *SUB:* English intertitles. *FEATURES:* 30 chapters • Liner notes by David Pearson.
2000 125m/B Fatty Arbuckle, Buster Keaton; **D:** Fatty Arbuckle.

Arbuckle & Keaton, Vol. 2 (1918–20)

Image and sound quality are unchanged from *Vol. 1*. Contents: "Back Stage," "Good Night Nurse!," "Coney Island," "The Rough House," and "The Garage." —MM
Movie: 🎬🎬🎬 **DVD:** 🎬🎬🎬
Kino on Video (cat #K205, UPC 7383290-20521). Full frame. $29.95. Keepcase. *LANG:* Silent. *SUB:* English intertitles. *FEATURES:* 15 chapters • Liner notes by David Pearson.
2000 121m/B Fatty Arbuckle, Buster Keaton; **D:** Fatty Arbuckle.

Arctic Blue

Alaskan biologist (Walsh) becomes the local lawman when he's the only one willing to transport a homicidal trapper (Hauer) to a Fairbanks jail. It's one thing after another when their plane crashes; the two leads fight each other and Hauer's vicious pals come after them. DVD image is not much of an improvement over VHS tape. Director Masterton's commentary is a bit technical and stiff. He doesn't sound completely comfortable talking about the film. —MM
Movie: 🎬🎬 **DVD:** 🎬🎬½
Columbia Tristar (cat #06540, UPC 043-39606540). Full frame. Dolby Digital Stereo. $24.98. Keepcase. *LANG:* English; French. *SUB:* English; French. *CAP:* English. *FEATURES:* Commentary: director • 28 chapters • Trailers.

1993 (R) 95m/C Dylan Walsh, Rutger Hauer, Richard Bradford; **D:** Peter Masterson; **W:** Ross LaManna; **C:** Thomas Burstyn; **M:** Peter Melnick.

The Arena

Recently, Roger Corman has been re-making the exploitation pictures he produced in the 1960s and '70s. The results have generally lacked the freshness and verve of the originals. This one is an exception. The Russian production is stylishly filmed and inventively edited. It looks like it cost much more than the Pam Grier version, though the story is just as silly. (*Playboy* Playmates are cast in the leads.) DVD presents a sharp image, with subtle use of color and tinting. The extras are a bit odd. In their commentary/featurettes, stars Dergan and McDougal are like, ohmigod, just, you know, reallyreallyreally happy to talk about how creepy and sort of, like, you know, scary it was to work in Russia. —MM
Movie: 🎬🎬🎬 **DVD:** 🎬🎬🎬
New Concorde (cat #NH20770 D, UPC 736991477094). Full frame. Stereo. $9.98. Keepcase. *LANG:* English. *SUB:* Spanish. *FEATURES:* 24 chapters • Talent files • Commentary: Lisa Dergan, Karen McDougal • Featurettes: Lisa Dergan, Karen McDougal • Trailers.
2001 (R) 92m/C *RU* Lisa Dergan, Karen McDougal, Jennifer Murphy, Georgina Stoll, Solanie Keenan, Victor Verzhbitsky, Anatoly Mambetrov; **D:** Timour Bekmambetov; **W:** John W. Corrington; **C:** Olugbeck Khamraev; **M:** Pavel Karmanov.

Art House

Ray (O'Donahue) and his irritating pal Weston (irritating Hardwick) aspire to be filmmakers, but the road to success is blocked by rocky relationships, money problems, and lack of talent. The comic elements are fitfully funny but the image is so rough that only the most dedicated fans of low-budget ($200,000 according to the director) independent productions will be willing to stick with it. Those hoping to see a lot of Internet babe Weber will be disappointed. DVD probably delivers an accurate reproduction of the original. That is not a recommendation. —MM
Movie: 🎬½ **DVD:** 🎬½
York Ent. (cat #YPD-1085, UPC 75072310-8520). Full frame. $14.99. Keepcase. *LANG:* English. *FEATURES:* Trailers • Director's intro and commentary • Alternate and deleted scenes.
1998 (R) 89m/C Dan O'Donahue, Chris Hardwick, Luigi Amodeo, Rebecca McFarland, Adam Carolla, Cheryl Pollack, Amy Weber; **D:** Leigh Slawner; **W:** Dan O'Donahue, Leigh Slawner; **C:** Billy Beaird; **M:** Christopher Lennertz.

Ashik Kerib

Please see review of *Legend of Suram Fortress*. **AKA:** The Lovelorn Minstrel; The Hoary Legends of the Caucasus.
Movie: 🎬🎬🎬

1988 75m/C *RU* Yiur Mgoyan, Veronkia Metonidze, Levan Natroshvili, Sofiko Chiaureli; *D:* Dodo Abashidze, Sergei Paradjanov; *W:* Giya Badridze; *M:* Djavashir Kuliev.

The Assassin

Young Tong's (Zhang Fengyi) forbidden love for Yiu (Rosamund Kwan) lands him in jail. There he is forced to fight other inmates to the death and as the sole survivor of the massacre is picked as an "assassin," henchman of an evil warlord. He is turned into a killing machine and kills without mercy or second thoughts until he faces Yiu once again. The transfer is a mixed bag that, while serving its purpose, shows a good number of scratches, speckles, and other blemishes and also has a number of registration errors causing the image to waver occasionally. The presentation is also quite grainy and compression artifacts abound, washing out many of the details of the original image. Colors are vibrant but due to the strong compression of the material gradients and falloffs, sometimes look unnatural and show signs of banding. Since this is such a visually sumptuous film, these deficiencies make it a less attractive presentation than it could—or should—have been. Audio is generally clear, although occasionally distortion is evident in some of the louder scenes, as a result of the original elements, not the DVD encoding. —*GH/MM*
Movie: ♫♫♫ *DVD:* ♫♫ ½
Tai Seng (cat #01784, UPC 6016410178-48). Widescreen letterboxed. Dolby Digital Surround. $19.98. Keepcase. *LANG:* Cantonese; Mandarin; English; Vietnamese. *SUB:* English. *FEATURES:* Commentary: Ric Meyers, Bobby Samuels, Frank Djeng.
1993 81m/C *HK* Zhang Fengyi, Rosamund Kwan, Max Mok; *D:* Billy Chung, Sui Hung.

At Bertram's Hotel

Please see review of *Agatha Christie's Miss Marple Set 2.*
Movie: ♫♫ ½ *DVD:* ♫♫ ½
A&E (cat #AAE-70381, UPC 7339617038-18).
1986 100m/C *GB* Joan Hickson, Caroline Blakiston, Helena Michell, George Baker, James Cossins; *D:* Mary McMurray; *W:* Jill Hyem; *C:* John Walker.

At the Earth's Core

Victorian scientist Dr. Perry (Cushing) invents a giant burrowing machine which carries him and his stalwart companion David (McClure) to a prehistoric civilization at the center of the Earth. The men-in-dinosaur-suits are some of the most gloriously goofy you'll ever see. DVD presents an accurate reproduction of the low-budget theatrical release, as I remember it. It makes the antiquated special effects look even more primitive and delightful. —*MM*
Movie: ♫♫ ½ *DVD:* ♫♫ ½
MGM Home Ent. (cat #1002639, UPC 027616868398). Widescreen (1.85:1) anamorphic. Dolby Digital Mono. $14.95. Keepcase. *LANG:* English. *SUB:* French;

Spanish. *CAP:* English. *FEATURES:* 16 chapters ➠ Trailer.
1976 (PG) 90m/C *GB* Doug McClure, Peter Cushing, Caroline Munro, Cy Grant, Godfrey James, Keith Barron; *D:* Kevin Connor; *W:* Milton Subotsky; *C:* Alan Hume; *M:* Michael Vickers.

Atlantic City

Louis Malle's brilliant tale of four characters and a city in transition has never been much to look at in visual terms. The image is cloudy, grainy, grim, and that's exactly as it should be. DVD doesn't change that. The picture is just what I remember from the theatrical release and the film is just as rewarding. Legalized gambling is taking over in Atlantic City and older buildings are being knocked down to make room for casinos. Lou (Lancaster at his mature best), a low-level mobster (very low), ekes out a living by taking care of aging beauty Grace (Reid) and working as a numbers runner. Sally (Sarandon) lives in the apartment next door. She works at a seafood bar and is in training to be a blackjack dealer. Then her faithless husband (Joy) and pregnant sister (McLaren) show up for a visit. He has stolen a shipment of cocaine from a couple of tough guys and wants to make a quick sale. The plot unspools with wonderful unpredictable inevitability to a near perfect ending. Lou and Sally come closer together and the city around them continues to crumble and rebuild. The characters and place have a sense of reality that's been lost in contemporary films, and they make up for any technical deficiencies. Despite the lack of extras, despite the bleached out color, this disc belongs in the library of every serious movie fan. —*MM* *AKA:* Atlantic City U.S.A.
Movie: ♫♫♫ *DVD:* ♫♫ ½
Paramount (cat #01460, UPC 097360146-042). Widescreen (1.85:1) anamorphic. Dolby Digital Mono. $24.98. Keepcase. *LANG:* English. *SUB:* English. *CAP:* English. *FEATURES:* 22 chapters ➠ Trailer.
1981 (R) 104m/C *FR CA* Burt Lancaster, Susan Sarandon, Kate Reid, Michel Piccoli, Hollis McLaren, Robert Joy, Al Waxman; *D:* Louis Malle; *W:* John Guare; *C:* Richard Ciupka; *M:* Michel Legrand. *AWARDS:* British Acad. '81: Actor (Lancaster), Director (Malle); Genie '81: Support. Actress (Reid); L.A. Film Critics '81: Actor (Lancaster), Film, Screenplay; N.Y. Film Critics '81: Actor (Lancaster), Screenplay; Natl. Soc. Film Critics '81: Actor (Lancaster), Director (Malle), Film, Screenplay; *NOM:* Oscars '81: Actor (Lancaster), Actress (Sarandon), Director (Malle), Orig. Screenplay, Picture.

Atlantis: The Lost Empire [CE]

In the summer of 2001 Disney's animated feature was drowned by a tidal wave named "Shrek." It's not a bad film, though the plotting is far too formulaic. Naïve young would-be explorer Milo Thatch (voice of Fox) joins a turn-of-the-(20th)-century expedition to find the lost city. Submarine

captain Rourke (Garner) leads the expedition but the vessel is attacked by a giant robotic squid. (Does any of this sound familiar?) I could not tell a significant difference between the two 5.1 Surround tracks. Both are extremely active. Image is, naturally, superb, and the studio has ladled all the extras onto a second disc that's actually longer than the film itself. Much of the deleted material is presented in storyboard form. The unused "Viking Prologue" is fully animated. The commentary track is serious, providing another detailed look at the entire studio animation process. It's presented in two modes, both standard audio and "visual," where producer Don Hahn and directors Gary Trousdale and Kirk Wise interrupt the film to show what they're talking about, then go back to that point in the action. That option is meant for only the serious student. —*MM*
Movie: ♫♫ ½ *DVD:* ♫♫♫♫
Buena Vista Home Ent. (cat #23835, UPC 786936163872). Widescreen (2.35:1) anamorphic. DTS 5.1; Dolby Digital 5.1 Surround. $39.99. Keepcase. *LANG:* English; French. *CAP:* English. *FEATURES:* 19 chapters ➠ Audio and "visual" commentaries ➠ "DisneyPedia" theories about Atlantis ➠ "Making of" feature (2 hours).
2001 (PG) 95m/C *D:* Gary Trousdale, Kirk Wise; *W:* Tab Murphy; *M:* James Newton Howard; *V:* Michael J. Fox, James Garner, Claudia Christian, Cree Summer, John Mahoney, Leonard Nimoy, David Ogden Stiers, Jim Varney, Phil Morris, Don Novello, Florence Stanley, Corey Burton, Jacqueline Obradors.

The Atomic Cafe [SE]

A popular hit in 1982, as a new wave of anti-nuclear sentiment greeted the Ronald Reagan administration, this "20th Anniversary Edition" brilliantly uses old propaganda films to highlight their own lies. To the tune of songs like "Atomic Cocktail," we see America being taught that its prosperity is threatened and that preparation for massive retaliation is essential. A time capsule of kitschy music and embarrassingly naïve visual mementoes, the compilation of film clips builds to create a vision that sees through the surface of the P.R., to a nation gripped by fear and denial. Using declassified government and military training films, newsreels, civil defense and educational films, and pop songs, the film examines Cold War attitudes toward the nuclear dilemma and the arms race. In the 1950s, our government saw the nuclear threat as simply another public relations problem. The Atomic Energy Commission had been given a free hand, with all the authority and secrecy of a top military project, and public dissent was addressed with a blitz of officially sanctioned information. The fun of the film, of course, is seeing all the out-of-control propaganda methods used to "sell" nuclear complacency as if it were dish soap: misleading semantics ("85% of the fear comes from 15% of the threat"), dramatic animation (heroic USAF bombers wipe out

scores of "hostile enemy cities" in a single strike), and insulting reasoning (the risk of humorous household accidents is equated with the threat of nuclear bombs). The clips are nonsensical and we laugh at them, but it's a nervous laughter that contains the realization that they were made by a self-satisfied Authority convinced of its mandate to mislead the public. Liberals with an agenda to promote will mistakenly label all of the film's original content as government propaganda, which it definitely was not. Once the ball of public sentiment gets rolling in a free society, the flag is soon taken up by all sources of public information and popular entertainment. DVD is a satisfactory presentation that has no extras, even though its controversial subject matter screams out for input from the filmmakers. How do they feel about their film 20 years later? Is raising public consciousness a good thing in the long run? This is an anniversary edition with no commemorative content whatsoever. As the IMDb lists a running time four minutes longer than this edition, I would greatly appreciate any information about possible cuts made to the show. The quality of the print and compression is fine, considering that much of the source material used was rather uneven, showing some scratches (no big deal) but also some unstable footage that jumps in the gate (sometimes distracting). The sound is very clear for audio that probably originated as 16mm optical tracks. —*GE*
Movie: 🎬🎬🎬 ½ ***DVD:*** 🎬🎬🎬 ½
New Video Group (UPC 767685949634). Full frame. $24.98. Keepcase. *LANG:* English.
1982 88m/C D: Kevin Rafferty, Jayne Loader, Pierce Rafferty; **M:** Miklos Rozsa.

Atomic War Bride / This Is Not a Test

We're used to seeing mostly sleez-o exploitation pix in the bizarro Something Weird Video Collection, but this time the Image Entertainment–released branded line brings us a feast of Atomic oddities—two very marginal early '60s Cold War features, and a host of extras that add up to over three and a half hours of radioactive, historical fun. Hacked down by nine minutes, and pan-scanned from its original TotalScope aspect ratio, there's still enough left of the first feature, *Atomic War Bride,* an anti-nuke parable from Marshall Tito's Yugoslavia, to tell that it was no classic. The original title *Rat* translates simply as "war," and the intention was to make an emotional plea for disarmament in the same vein as the previous year's big international success *On the Beach.* John (Antun Vrdoljak) and Maria (Polish actress Ewa Krzyzewska, recent winner of a French film prize for her role in *Ashes and Diamonds*) are preparing for their wedding just as war is announced in their unnamed European country. The ceremony is spoiled by an air raid, and John is shanghaied into the army, where he undergoes silly regimented drills. When his unit is sent into the city to force people into bomb shelters, John is reunited

with his relatives and Maria. Together with others in the shelter, they decide to go to their country's president and plead for peace. In *This Is Not a Test,* deputy sheriff Dan Colter (Seamon Glass) gets word to halt all vehicles in a desert mountain pass, as cities on either side are evacuating under martial law. Colter stops a medley of citizens, who chafe at the inconvenience, bicker, and debate what to do. Word finally comes through that an atomic war has started, and Colter can barely contain the panic. They empty a truck to serve as an impromptu bomb shelter. Among Atom War movies, these two lie fairly near the bottom of the pile, quality-wise. On this themed DVD they're a lot of fun. But even better is the host of Cold War–themed Atomic Short Subjects included as extra content. Getting to them is a hoot, clicking your way through giddy graphics of civil defense signage and mushroom-cloud visuals. The pun-filled text in the graphics and packaging is very funny too. The six short subjects are complete, in reasonable shape, and from the perfect time frame, 1950 and 1951, when the Atomic Energy Commission engaged in a huge PR campaign to convince America to Stop Worrying and...you know. Several were raided for material to create the celebrated *Atomic Café,* and make this disc an excellent companion piece to that show. Image and sound quality on the features and short subjects are up to the studio's standards. They're not perfect but given the age, they're very good. —*GE/MM* **AKA:** Rat.
Movie: 🎬🎬🎬 ***DVD:*** 🎬🎬🎬
Image Ent. (UPC 014381117820). Full frame. Dolby Digital Mono. $24.98. Keepcase. *LANG:* English. *FEATURES:* Atomic Short Subject: You Can Beat the A-Bomb (1950) • Atomic Short Subject: Survival under Atomic Attack (1951) • Atomic Short Subject: Duck and Cover (1951) • Atomic Short Subject: Medical Aspects of Nuclear Radiation (1950) • Atomic Short Subject: One World or None • Atomic Short Subject: Atomic Blonde in Action (OO-la la).
1960 75m/B YU Ljubisa Jovanovic, Eva Krzyzewska, Ita Rina, Antun Vrdoljak; **D:** Veljko Bulajic; **W:** Cesare Zavattini; **C:** Kreso Grcevic; **M:** Vladimir Kraus-Rajteric.

Attack from Mars

Set in the '50s in a movie theatre showing a movie called *Space Patrol* (which refers to an actual TV series of the time). The evil scientist in the movie goes back to the '50s and his crew members have to chase him. Meanwhile at the theatre, an alien has landed and is eliminating staff and patrons. Unredeemably awful, meant to be funny, this crudely cheap film has nothing to recommend it. Dimly referencing the old show, no effort has been made to make *Space Patrol* into an actual product of the '50s. Good DVD transfer of scratchy print with decent sound. —*MO* **AKA:** Midnight Movie Massacre.
Movie: woof ***DVD:*** 🎬🎬🎬
Image Ent. (cat #1D0745CODVD, UPC 01-4381074529). Full frame. $24.99. Keep-

case. *LANG:* English. *FEATURES:* 12 chapters • Alternate title sequence.
1988 86m/C Robert Clarke, Ann (Robin) Robinson; **D:** Mark Stock; **W:** Mark Stock, David Houston.

Attack of the Giant Leeches [Marengo]

Please see review for *A Bucket of Blood / Attack of the Giant Leeches.* **AKA:** The Giant Leeches; She Demons of the Swamp; Demons of the Swamp.
Movie: 🎬
1959 62m/B Kenneth (Ken) Clark, Yvette Vickers, Gene Roth, Bruno VeSota, Michael Emmet, Tyler McVey, Jan Shepard, George Cisar, Dan(iel) White; **D:** Bernard L. Kowalski; **W:** Leo Gordon; **C:** John M. Nickolaus Jr.; **M:** Alexander Laszlo.

Attack of the 60-Foot Centerfold

Angel Grace (North) wants to be Centerfold of the Year so much that she gets a doctor to enhance her endowments even more through a mystery formula. Only there's a little complication and she grows to gargantuan heights. It's intentionally cheesy ultra–low budget exploitation with pretty women and, of course, a spoof on that '58 gem, *Attack of the 50-Foot Woman.* DVD can do nothing to improve the grainy original, particularly in the effects shots. It's equal to tape. —*MM*
Movie: 🎬🎬 ***DVD:*** 🎬🎬
New Concorde (cat #NH20458 D, UPC 736991454897). Full frame. Stereo. $14.98. Keepcase. *LANG:* English. *FEATURES:* 24 chapters • Talent files • Trailers.
1995 (R) 83m/C J.J. North, Tammy Parks, John Lazar, Russ Tamblyn, Tommy Kirk, Stanley Livingston, Michelle (McClellan) Bauer, George Stover, Forrest J Ackerman, Ted Monte, Jim Wynorski, Raelyn Saalman, Tim Abell, Jay Richardson, Nikki Fritz; **D:** Fred Olen Ray; **W:** Steve Armogida; **C:** Gary Graver, Howard Wexler; **M:** Jeff Walton.

Attack—The Battle for New Britain

This compilation is composed of two World War II newsreel documentaries. "Sea Power in the Pacific" (30 minutes) shows the progression of the Japanese takeover of the South Pacific islands and the allied attacks that liberated them. "Attack—The Battle for New Britain" (56 minutes) is narrated by Lloyd Nolan and demonstrates the preparation, training maneuvers, and jungle combat used to break the Japanese hold on the daunting titular island. Both feature plenty of genuine newsreel footage and history amongst the typical newsreel rhetoric of the period. The prints are grainy, bleary, and soft, and the sound is intelligible but poorly reproduced. The opening and end titles on each film are either truncated or nonexistent. —*DG*
Movie: 🎬 ½ ***DVD:*** 🎬
Goodtimes Ent. (cat #05-81234, UPC 018713812346). Full frame. Mono.

$7.49. Keepcase. *LANG:* English. *FEATURES:* 12 chapters.
1944 86m/C

Attraction

Writer/radio personality Matthew (Settle) can't get over Liz (Mol). He parks outside her apartment and shows her how much he still cares by trying to kick down her front door. Then he meets Cory (Mathis), Liz's friend. At about the same time, Liz takes up with Garrett (Scott), Matthew's editor. But when Liz learns about Matthew and Cory, she becomes jealous. This tricky little thriller keeps its focus squarely on the four fully realized, imperfect characters. In his debut, writer/director DeGrazier indulges in some needlessly jitterbug camerawork, but otherwise does more than credible work. DVD delivers an image that ranges between very good and excellent. Surround is employed with intrusive aggressiveness on some music cues. Recommended. —*MM*
Movie: 🐾🐾🐾 *DVD:* 🐾🐾🐾
Studio Home Ent. (cat #7546D, UPC 03-1398754626). Widescreen letterboxed. Dolby Digital 5.1 Surround. $24.98. Keepcase. *LANG:* English. *SUB:* English; French; Spanish. *CAP:* English. *FEATURES:* 24 chapters ▪ Commentary ▪ Music video ▪ Cast, crew, and character interviews.
2000 (R) 95m/C Samantha Mathis, Gretchen Mol, Tom Everett Scott, Matthew Settle; *D:* Russell DeGrazier; *W:* Russell DeGrazier; *C:* Michael Price; *M:* Graeme Revell.

Au Pair Girls

This is a dirty old man movie as only dirty old Englishmen can make them: lots of nudity, a sprinkling of feeble sex jokes that would be rejected by the "Carry On" series, and four leading characters who get into a variety of sexual situations but have no resemblance to human beings living or dead. An Au Pair Girl agency recruits four gorgeous continental women for light household chores in established homes, in exchange for room and board. All come with bright smiles, little clothing, and a completely uninhibited sexuality. Hot number Randi (Gabrielle Drake) spends a wild day in the country with the son of a tycoon that includes a roll in some real hay and a visit to a "poofter" photographer of nudes. Discreet Nan Lee (Me Me Lay) becomes a playmate for a day with a piano prodigy whose mother thinks he needs "inspiration." Christa Geisler (Nanci Wait) gets shown the club scene by her new family's daughter, where she's deflowered by a rock star and learns that free love is no fun. And wild card Anita (Astrid Frank) strips naked as soon as she arrives in her new house, and goes for a gambling jaunt with a cabdriver. For the fadeout, she and all the others eventually end up as the property of a womanizing sheik named El Abab (Ferdy Mayne). DVD is a reasonable-quality disc. Probably originally formatted at 1:66, the full-frame transfer is adequate. Marc Morris's liner notes state that producer Kenneth Shipman was responsible for the previous year's horror film *Burke and Hare,* supposedly a downgrade version of the already saucy 1959 *The Flesh and the Fiends.* —*GE*
Movie: 🐾🐾 *DVD:* 🐾🐾 ½
Image Ent. (cat #ID0915SGDVD, UPC 014381091526). Full frame. Dolby Digital Mono. $14.98. Keepcase. *LANG:* English. *FEATURES:* Stills ▪ Lobby cards ▪ Press book ▪ Marc Morris liner notes ▪ 16 chapters.
1972 86m/C *GB* Gabrielle Drake, Astrid Frank, Nancie Wait, Me Me Lay, Richard O'Sullivan, Johnny Briggs, Ferdinand "Ferdy" Mayne; *D:* Val Guest; *W:* Val Guest, David Adnopoz; *C:* John Wilcox; *M:* Roger Webb.

Audrey Rose

This is one of the films that put Anthony Hopkins on the American map and with good reason. Hopkins plays Elliot Hoover, a sad but gentle man who seems at first to be stalking the Tempeltons (Mason and Beck) and their 11-year-old daughter, Ivy (Swift). Then he finally approaches them with the unbelievable story that Ivy is the reincarnation of his daughter, Audrey Rose, who died in a car accident with her mother 11 years before. Audrey Rose, he sadly tells them, was conscious as the flames engulfed her. They feel sorry for him, but scoff. Then he learns that Ivy is having bad dreams as her birthday approaches and shares his fears that the violent nature of Audrey Rose's death may have led her soul to leap into a new body before it was ready. When Ivy has nightmares, he seems to be the only person who can comfort her. When he steals her from the apartment one night as she hurls through a nightmare, he is arrested and reincarnation goes on trial. The ending is not to be given away, and not to be missed. All the acting in the film is top-notch and this, along with deft direction from Robert Wise and a script from the novelist, is what ultimately makes the story work so well. In addition to Mason's turn as the mother who is willing to be open-minded to save her daughter, Susan Swift is amazing as the sweet Ivy who turns into a six-year-old Audrey Rose, trapped in a burning car with her dead mother, whenever she dreams. The DVD looks like a brand new print with crisp, cleanly separated colors. The only downside is the mono soundtrack, which is minor since this is a character-driven, dialogue film. —*CA*
Movie: 🐾🐾🐾 *DVD:* 🐾🐾🐾 ½
MGM Home Ent. (cat #1002323, UPC 027-616865427). Widescreen (1.85:1) letterboxed. Dolby Digital Mono. $14.98. Keepcase. *LANG:* English; French; Spanish. *SUB:* French; Spanish. *CAP:* English. *FEATURES:* 16 chapters ▪ Theatrical trailer.
1977 (PG) 113m/C Marsha Mason, Anthony Hopkins, John Beck, John Hillerman, Susan Swift, Norman Lloyd; *D:* Robert Wise; *W:* Frank De Felitta; *C:* Victor Kemper.

The Autobiography of Miss Jane Pittman

One hundred and ten–year-old Pittman (Tyson) narrates a tour of American history, starting with her days as a slave and ending with the dawn of the civil rights movement. Managing to be both far-reaching and personal, this is one of the most critically acclaimed made-for-TV movies ever made. Tyson's performance is outstanding, and earned the film one of its nine Emmy Awards. VCI's release, however, leaves quite a bit to be desired. The colors are terribly inconsistent and the sound is often muddy, adding up to an overpriced disc. —*BG*
Movie: 🐾🐾🐾 ½ *DVD:* 🐾 ½
VCI (cat #8307, UPC 089859830723). Full frame. Dolby Mono. $24.99. Keepcase. *LANG:* English. *FEATURES:* 18 chapters ▪ Cicely Tyson at the 1989 National Black Theatre Festival ▪ Cicely Tyson's speech at the 2001 National Theatre Festival ▪ Trailers ▪ Bios.
1974 110m/C Cicely Tyson, Odetta, Joseph Tremice, Richard Dysart, Michael Murphy, Katherine Helmond; *D:* John Korty; *W:* Tracy Keenan Wynn; *C:* James A. Crabe; *M:* Fred Karlin.

Avalanche

Corman's contribution to the '70s disaster cycle finds vacationers at a new winter ski resort at the mercy of a monster avalanche leaving an alleged path of terror and destruction in its wake. A talented cast is buried by weak material, producing a snowbound yawn. The grit and dust you'd expect to see from a film of this age are evident, but there is no excessive artifacting in the snow scenes or the heavy shadows. The grain comes from the original. —*MM*
Movie: 🐾 ½ *DVD:* 🐾🐾
New Concorde (cat #NH20188 D, UPC 736991218895). Full frame. Stereo. $9.98. Keepcase. *LANG:* English. *FEATURES:* 15 chapters ▪ Talent files ▪ Previews.
1978 (PG) 91m/C Rock Hudson, Mia Farrow, Robert Forster, Rick Moses; *D:* Corey Allen; *W:* Corey Allen; *C:* Pierre William Glenn; *M:* William Kraft.

Avalanche Alley

Four extreme snowboarders take an off-limits run known for its frequency of avalanches. While there, an avalanche does hit and they, as well as two others on the hill, are buried in the snow. Now, resort owner and former Olympic skier Rick (Marinaro) and his alcoholic mentor (Mancuso) must race to find survivors before another avalanche hits. Unlike most modern Roger Corman productions, this adventure has a glimmer of the tight, economical filmmaking his pictures used to display. The image shows occasional defects in the bright snow and the stereo sound is adequate. —*DRL*
Movie: 🐾 ½ *DVD:* 🐾🐾
New Concorde (cat #20777, UPC 736991-377790). Full frame. Stereo. $19.98. Keepcase. *LANG:* English. *SUB:* Spanish. *CAP:* English. *FEATURES:* Cast & crew bios ▪ Trailers ▪ 24 chapters.
2001 (PG-13) 86m/C Ed Marinaro, Nick Mancuso, Tobias Mehler, Wolf Larson; *D:* Paul Ziller; *W:* Paul Ziller, Elizabeth Sanchez; *C:* David Pelletier; *M:* George Blondheim.

The Avengers '68

While America was producing hip yet realistic series like *Mod Squad* and *I Spy,* England was pumping out ultra hip, camp spy capers like *The Avengers.* Working for the Ministry, John Steed was the mainstay of the series. Unlike James Bond, Steed solved cases with only his wit, charm, and the other gentlemanly essentials—a deadly umbrella and steel reinforced bowler. Of course there was also his standard-issue babe partner. She was intelligent and witty, but also had curves to match. First there was the slinky Honor Blackman, then the most famous of his partners, the deadly Emma Peel (Diana Rigg), whose costumes were wrapped as tightly as her British manners, and finally, the blonde, mod Tara King (Linda Thorson). This set covers the Tara King section of the series. King did not have quite the chemistry that Peel and Steed did, but these are still fun episodes. Aside from the flirtatious chemistry between the leads, *The Avengers* produced clever story lines and sets from the everyday world. In "Game," a man seeks revenge by placing his enemies in life-size versions of childhood games like Chutes and Ladders. Or "The Super Secret Cypher Caper," where evil window washers try to take over the world, and the Avengers get a few good jabs in on the Bond mystique when an agent from a rival agency ends up dead, despite his many gadgets. This is entertainment for anyone who appreciates their humor as dry as their martinis. The series was shot on film and the transfers are a little faded, and a few scratches show on close inspection, but the bright '60s colors still manage to shine through. The sound is mono and a little muffled which, along with the English accents may have you heading for the up volume button. Set 1 Episodes: Game; The Super Secret Cypher Caper; You'll Catch Your Death; Split; Whoever Shot Poor George Oblique Stroke XR40; False Witness. Set 2 Episodes: All Done With Mirrors; Legacy of Death; Noon Doomsday; Look (Stop Me If You've Heard This One)...But There Were These Two Fellers; Have Guns Will Haggle; The Keep Killing Steed. —CA
Movie: 🎜🎜🎜 **DVD:** 🎜🎜 ½
A&E (cat #AAE 70323, UPC 7339617032-38). Full frame. Dolby Digital Mono. $39.95. Keepcase (2 to a box). *LANG:* English. *FEATURES:* 6 chapters per disc • Production stills.
1968 156m/C *GB* Patrick Macnee, Linda Thorson.

The Avenging Fist

Those that have always wanted to see Yuen Biao and Sammo Hung superheroes need look no further than this film, though they only play supporting roles. In a future megalopolis, only three cops survive the Power Glove project. One goes mad and enslaves another, while the third bides his time waiting for the son of his captive partner to grow up and help him fight the villain. Great CG-eye candy, but fails to make its characters interesting.

The special audio tracks give the sound a big boost, for those with the proper home theatre equipment. —*BT* **AKA:** Kuen San; Quan Shen; Juen Sun; Fight Zone; God of Fist Style; Legend of Tekken; Legend of the Fist Master.
Movie: 🎜🎜 ½ **DVD:** 🎜🎜🎜
Tai Seng (cat #DVD88051, UPC 6016411-20241). Widescreen letterboxed. Dolby Digital 6.1 Surround EX; Dolby Digital DTS ES. $19.95. Keepcase. *LANG:* Cantonese; Mandarin. *SUB:* Chinese; English. *FEATURES:* 12 chapters • Trailer.
2001 96m/C *HK* Lee-hom Wang, Stephen Fung, Kristy Yeung, Gigi Leung, Sammo Hung, Ka-Lok Chin, Yuen Biao, Roy Cheung, Cecilia Yip; *D:* Andrew Lau, Corey Yuen; *C:* Yiu-fai Lai.

The Aviator

Blasé film about Edgar Anscombe (Christopher Reeve), a pilot who carries the baggage of a tragic accident and flies the mail route. He's told to take a teenage passenger, Tillie Hansan (Rosanna Arquette), and crashes in the mountains. Survival story from there with Reeve the hard man who finally melts because of Arquette. We've seen it before and done much better. That said, DVD looks great with very nice sound. —*DE*
Movie: 🎜🎜 ½ **DVD:** 🎜🎜🎜
MGM Home Ent. (cat #1003340, UPC 276-1687489). Full frame; widescreen (1.85:1) anamorphic. Dolby 5.1 Surround. $14.98. Keepcase. *LANG:* English; French; Spanish. *SUB:* English; Spanish; French. *CAP:* English. *FEATURES:* 16 chapters • Theatrical trailer.
1985 (PG) 98m/C Christopher Reeve, Rosanna Arquette, Jack Warden, Tyne Daly, Marcia Strassman, Sam Wanamaker, Scott Wilson; *D:* George Miller; *W:* Marc Norman; *C:* David Connell; *M:* Dominic Frontiere.

The Awful Truth: The Complete Second Season

Roger and Me director Michael Moore triumphs again in his TV series, with 12 episodes that originally aired on Bravo in the U.S. From his election-year political satire (a traveling mosh-pit that attracts only one taker, Republican candidate Allen Keyes) and his born-out-of-outrage drive to put Ficus plants on the ballot against unopposed congressional candidates, Moore manages to skewer both activism and apathy. His social commentary, too, is sometimes sadly on target; watch urban cops turn away, shame faced, as African-Americans march, hands up, pockets turned out, to show they're unarmed. Moore has never been particularly interested in technical sophistication so image does not gain much on DVD. It's roughly equivalent to broadcast or VHS. —*JE*
Movie: 🎜🎜🎜 **DVD:** 🎜🎜 ½
New Video Group (cat #NVG-9494, UPC 76768594933). Full frame. Dolby Digital Stereo. $39.95. Keepcase. *LANG:* English. *FEATURES:* Commentary: director • Direc-

tor bio • Weblinks • Behind-the-scenes footage.
2001 300m/C Michael Moore; *D:* Michael Moore.

Axe

Axe has the distinction of being the best rural shocker shot in Charlotte, North Carolina, in 1974. Other than that, it's not really worth talking about. After a group of thugs kill a man (on an embarrassingly shoddy set), they flee to the country, where they take over a farmhouse. The only residents of this farmhouse are a young girl, Lisa (Leslie Lee), and her invalid grandfather. The criminals force Lisa to cook a chicken dinner (NO!) and then generally terrorize the girl and her grandfather. Eventually, Lisa (who is actively hallucinating throughout this episode) grabs the titular axe and seeks her revenge. The film is slow and boring, and the sub-amateur acting doesn't help. The only positive aspect is the suspense which mounts over the course of the movie. Having seen films like this before, and given the fact that nothing else is happening, the audience knows that Lisa is going to strike back at some time. The image presented on this DVD is full of problems, as defects from the source print are evident. Also, there is visible distortion on the picture and the image jumps at times. The digital mono soundtrack provides mostly clear dialogue, but there is some distorting and hissing as well. This DVD does have plenty of fun goodies attached, as there are bonus trailers, movie poster art, and even an additional feature film. —*ML* **AKA:** Lisa, Lisa; California Axe Massacre.
Movie: 🎜 ½ **DVD:** 🎜🎜 ½
Image Ent. (cat #0796-SWDVD, UPC 0143-81079623). Full frame. Dolby Digital Mono. $24.99. Keepcase. *LANG:* English. *FEATURES:* Theatrical trailer • Bonus trailers • Short films • Radio spots • Promotional art.
1974 (R) 68m/C Leslie Lee, Jack Canon, Frederick Friedel, Frank Jones; *D:* Frederick Friedel; *W:* Frederick Friedel; *C:* Austin McKinney.

Axe 'Em

A group of young people travels to a house in the woods for a relaxing weekend. Unfortunately, this is where, years before, a madman killed his entire family, save his deformed—and equally mad—son who is now ready to follow in Daddy's footsteps. Teens are systematically murdered. This movie is wretched in every way. The only good thing to say is that the film is short. The disc has the absolute worst image and sound quality I've ever seen. Neither rises above awful, but both are, at times, unbearable—not that it matters much. —*DRL*
Movie: woof **DVD:** woof
York Ent. (cat #1182, UPC 7507231188-26). Full frame. Stereo. $14.99. Keepcase. *LANG:* English. *FEATURES:* 15 chapters.
2002 71m/C Joe Clair, Maria Cooper; *D:* Michael Mfume; *W:* Michael Mfume; *C:* Reggie Danials.

Baby Bach

Baby Bach is a perfect example of why adults shouldn't be allowed to critique any medium designed for infants. While the target audience may find themselves enthralled with this DVD, most adults will find it rather uninteresting. The main program on this DVD is a 28-minute segment that offers visuals set to the music of Johan Sebastian Bach. (The 172-minute running time listed on the box is somewhat deceptive.) These visuals include toys, children, and outdoor scenes. These are static images—rather, they are all moving images to hold the little ones attention. The drawback is—that's it. There's no narration or thematic flow here. Once again, this isn't for adults. The only real critique that can be made here is that this DVD is recommended for ages 1 to 36 months. As most 3-year-olds have had a steady diet of *Sesame Street* and *Blue's Clues,* they would probably find this video uninteresting. Along with the main feature, this package offers 34 audio-only tracks of Bach's music. In addition, there is a separate "Language Lab" section which offers "Digital Flash Cards." These cards enable the viewer to learn foreign words by viewing corresponding images. It is exactly the same lesson offered on the *Baby Einstein: Language Lab* DVD, so if you already own that one, this will be of little use. As for the quality of presentation, most of the images presented in the main program were shot on video, which offers a very clear picture that is free from defects. The digital stereo audio does a fine job of reproducing the familiar classical music. —*ML*
Movie: 🎵 ½ **DVD:** 🎵🎵
Buena Vista Home Ent. (cat #25943, UPC 786936179729). Full frame. Digital Stereo. $19.99. Keepcase. *LANG:* English. *FEATURES:* Audio only tracks ‣ Language lab.
2000 28m/C

Baby Boy

John Singleton's third film in a trilogy about black men livin' in the 'Hood. This one is about babies having babies. Even though Jody's (Gibson) old enough to have two baby mamas (each of his girlfriends has his baby), he still lives with his mother (Johnson). He thinks he's trying to protect her from her choice of men, in this case a former tough guy (Rhames). The truth is he doesn't want to grow up. The characters and their situations feel authentic, but the slick look and feel of this picture are pure Hollywood. Lots of extras on the DVD. Technical aspects of image and sound are tops. —*LA*
Movie: 🎵🎵 ½ **DVD:** 🎵🎵🎵 ½
Columbia Tristar (cat #06458, UPC 04339-6064584). Widescreen anamorphic. Dolby Digital 5.1 Surround; Dolby Surround. $27.98. Keepcase. *LANG:* English; French. *SUB:* French; Spanish; Portuguese; Chinese; Korean; Thai. *CAP:* English. *FEATURES:* Commentary: director ‣ Cinemax featurette ‣ Deleted and alternate scenes ‣ Outtakes and bloopers reel ‣ Music videos ‣ Storyboard comparisons

‣ 28 chapters ‣ Trailers ‣ TV spots ‣ Filmographies ‣ Production notes.
2001 (R) 129m/C Tyrese Gibson, Omar Gooding, Taraji P. Henson, Adrienne-Joi (AJ) Johnson, Snoop Dogg, Tamara La Seon Bass, Ving Rhames; **D:** John Singleton; **W:** John Singleton; **C:** Charles Mills; **M:** David Arnold.

Baby Dolittle: Neighborhood Animals

While most of the DVDs in the *Baby Einstein* series deal with abstract concepts, such as colors and sounds, the *Baby Dolittle* discs focus on the very tangible world of animals. "Neighborhood Animals" is designed to give toddlers a primer on the kind of animals that they may see close to home. This 30-minute video has been divided into four sections, each showcasing a different geographical region. "Animals in My House" spotlights dogs, cats, and mice. (Do we really want kids to think that there are mice in the house?) "Animals in My Yard" looks at birds, rabbits, and bugs. "Animals on the Farm" examines cows, horses, and pigs. And finally, "Animals on the River" displays frogs, otters, and ducks. For each animal, the name of the animal is displayed (in lower-case letters for some reason—most toddlers can only read upper-case) and then there are several minutes of video displaying the animal in question doing different things. For dogs and cats, where they come in different shapes and sizes, a variety of animals are shown. Keep in mind that *Baby Dolittle* isn't intended to be a *National Geographic* special. There is no information or facts given about the animals. This video is designed to help children recognize the different animals. The video is hosted by a puppet named Pavlov the Dog (nice), who introduces each animal by following its tracks across the screen. The video is without narration, but does feature soft classical music. Overall, this is one of the best DVDs in the *Baby Einstein* series. The DVD features a full-frame transfer. The show is a mixture of video segments (the puppets) and filmed stock footage (the animals). Both look equally fine, with the filmed footage showing some occasional grain or defect. The colors are very good here. The digital stereo audio track provides clear music with no distortion. The DVD also includes an audio-only track with 12 classical music selections. Also included is a "Digital Flash Card" section where viewers can learn the names of the animals and then learn to identify the animals by their footprints. —*ML*
Movie: 🎵🎵🎵 **DVD:** 🎵🎵 ½
Buena Vista Home Ent. (cat #25947, UPC 786936179767). Full frame. Digital Stereo. $19.95. Keepcase. *LANG:* English. *FEATURES:* Music-only track ‣ Digital flash cards.
2001 30m/C

Baby Dolittle: World Animals

This disc acts as a great companion piece to the "Neighborhood Animals" DVD. Whereas "Neighborhood" focuses on creatures that most children could see in or near their homes, "World Animals" shows animals that live in far-off places. Hosted by a puppet named Jane the Monkey (is that a take-off on Jane from *Tarzan* or Jane Goodall?), this 26-minute program has been divided into three subsections, each focusing on a different part of the world. Each section contains three types of animal. For each animal, the creature is introduced by Jane and then the name of the animal is displayed on-screen. From there, the viewer is treated to video of the creature in their natural habitat. For most of the animals here, these scenes are broken up with shots of toys or objects bearing the likeness of that animal. First, we have "Animals in the Jungle," which features tigers, tropical birds, and monkeys. Next, there is "Animals in the Ocean," which offers sea turtles, dolphins, and fish. Lastly, "Animals on the Savannah" arrive with elephants, giraffe, and lions. This video is a nice way to introduce younger children to exotic animals without bombarding them with a lot of facts that they won't understand. The show is a mixture of video and film elements. Both look fine, with the film elements showing a smattering of grain here and there. The digital stereo audio track does justice to the musical accompaniment. An audio-only track can be found on the DVD which offers 13 classical music tracks. Finally, this DVD offers a learning lab where viewers can master identifying the animals by their appearance and their footprints. —*ML*
Movie: 🎵🎵🎵 **DVD:** 🎵🎵 ½
Buena Vista Home Ent. (cat #25949, UPC 786936179774). Full frame. Digital Stereo. $19.95. Keepcase. *LANG:* English. *FEATURES:* Music-only track ‣ Digital flash cards.
2001 26m/C

Baby Einstein: Language Nursery

The *Baby Einstein: Language Nursery* DVD is aimed at toddlers from ages 1 to 18 months, and it truly believes in the theory of immersion education, as it exposes the viewers to multiple languages. With speakers reading in English, Spanish, French, German, Hebrew, Japanese, and Russian, the program offers common occurrences, such as the alphabet, numbers, and short poems ("Humpty Dumpty") in each language. Each speech is accompanied by video of toys or other common items which would catch the attention of the young audience. The problem here is that the various speeches and languages are presented randomly and in no logical order (without the menu sheet, one would be lost). Also, segments aren't labeled on-screen. For example, it's pretty clear when someone is counting or saying the alphabet in their native tongue, but most won't recognize the poems until they are read in English. This program would have come off far better if each selection had been read in English, and then in the other languages, so that one would know what was happening. Still, this is a minor quibble and this problem won't matter one iota to any 12-month-old watching the DVD. In this reviewer's opinion, a better option is the Language Lab Digital Flash Cards. Here, the viewer is shown a picture of an everyday object or animal and then taught how to say that in one of the eight languages. This provides a concrete experience in language learning. In addition, the DVD offers an audio-only track which features music, nursery rhymes, the alphabet, and counting in the various languages. While it may not matter to young viewers, the DVD offers a fine transfer of this program. Predominantly shot on video, the images here are razor-sharp, showing no distortion or artifacting. Most importantly, the colors are bright and fine, helping to capture those young viewers. The digital stereo sound provides clear speech and the music sounds fantastic. Box copy lists the running time at 162 minutes. That includes all of the extras. The main program itself is only 28 minutes. —ML

Movie: 🎵🎵 *DVD:* 🎵🎵 ½
Buena Vista Home Ent. (cat #25940, UPC 786936179705). Full frame. Digital Stereo. $19.95. Keepcase. *LANG:* English. *FEATURES:* Digital flash cards • Special audio features.
2001 28m/C

Baby Mozart

If you and your child are fans of the minimalist nature of the *Baby Einstein* videos, then you will love *Baby Mozart,* which epitomizes the approach this video series takes. Similar to *Baby Bach, Baby Mozart* offers a 27-minute video of moving images accompanied by the music of Wolfgang Amadeus Mozart. The video combines images of puppets, toys, food, and many other colorful objects. The important thing is that every shot has something that is bright and moving. As is to be expected, the wonderful sounds of Mozart are the real star here, so if the images can capture the child's attention, they will be able to experience the timeless music. The images were captured using high-end video equipment, so they are bright and colorful. There is no grain or distortion to the image, and the colors are very good. The digital stereo audio track delivers a nice reproduction of Mozart's music. This DVD offers an audio-only track containing 29 selections from Mozart. In addition, the disc offers the "Language Lab" portion of the *Baby Einstein: Language Lab* DVD. This offers video flash cards in eight different languages, to enable youngsters to recognize common words in other languages. —ML

Movie: 🎵🎵 *DVD:* 🎵🎵 ½
Buena Vista Home Ent. (cat #25941, UPC 786936179712). Full frame. Digital Stereo. $19.95. Keepcase. *LANG:* English. *FEATURES:* Music-only track • Language lab.
2000 27m/C

Baby Shakespeare

"Thou doth mislead me!" may be a good way to describe The Baby Einstein Company's release of *Baby Shakespeare,* for only one Shakespeare quote appears on the program. The DVD promises "Exploring vocabulary through poems, music, and video," and it does deliver on that front. In the main segment of this disc, which is aimed at viewers age one and up, children are introduced to 12 common words, such as "train," "apple," and "moon." Each introduction is then followed by a quote from a famous poet that includes the word. The authors offered here include the aforementioned Shakespeare, Tennessee Williams, and Robert Frost. Each poem is accompanied by video of the object and other eye-catching items. The program is age-appropriate, and a good way to introduce youngsters to common words and images, but it isn't that different from the contents of the average episode of *Sesame Street.* Also included on the DVD are three audio-only tracks which contain more than 30 selections from Beethoven. In addition, there is an option to view only the poetry sections of the main feature. This program is presented full frame and looks great on this DVD. The vast majority of the imagery here was shot on video and looks crystal clear via the digital transfer. The digital stereo audio track provides a clear presentation of the poetry readings and the orchestral selections sound great. Box copy lists the running time at 101 minutes. That includes all of the extras. The main program itself is only 27 minutes. —ML

Movie: 🎵🎵 *DVD:* 🎵🎵 ½
Buena Vista Home Ent. (cat #25944, UPC 786936179736). Full frame. Digital Stereo. $19.99. Keepcase. *LANG:* English. *FEATURES:* Music-only tracks • 30 chapters.
1999 30m/C

Baby Van Gogh

Most experts agree that newborns have a monochrome view of the world, thus they are fascinated by black-and-white objects. However, once they discover color, things change dramatically. By utilizing the works of Vincent Van Gogh, the *Baby Van Gogh* DVD will help to introduce youngsters into the wonderful world of color. The 24-minute long feature uses six of Van Gogh's most famous works to focus on the colors yellow, green, orange, purple, red, and blue. The program is hosted by a puppet named Vincent Van Goat (adults will notice that his right horn is bandaged) who unveils each of the paintings. Then, the viewer is treated to a series of video images featuring other familiar objects that are also that same color. To help emphasize the theme, the word for the color is spelled out on screen and a narrator reads a poem which deals with that color. This multi-media approach will help toddlers learn to recognize each color by name, while introducing them to the world of fine art. The colorful imagery and the antics of Vincent Van Goat will certainly keep most young children entertained. The

majority of the imagery here is photographed on high-end video and looks quite good. The image is clear and as one would hope, the colors are realistic and true. The digital stereo sound provides clear dialogue and a nice tone for the musical accompaniment. The DVD contains a still gallery where one can study the six Van Gogh paintings and an audio-only section which offers 19 classical music tracks. —ML

Movie: 🎵🎵🎵 *DVD:* 🎵🎵 ½
Buena Vista Home Ent. (cat #25945, UPC 786936179743). Full frame. Digital Stereo. $19.95. Keepcase. *LANG:* English. *FEATURES:* Music-only track • Still gallery.
2000 24m/C

Baby's Day Out

Baby Bink has some unwitting fun with three beleaguered kidnappers-cum-Three Stooges (Mantegna, Pantoliano, Haley) as he leads them on a cartoonish chase through Chicago via the predictable John Hughes. His mother (Boyle) and nanny (Nixon) provide a few fretful moments until the nanny realizes where to find her young charge. The opening credit sequence gives away the entire plot making this a fun ride for very small children only. Particular problem for the filmmakers was that the nine-month-old Worton twins grew past the year mark by the end of the shoot. Blue screens and out-of-sequence shooting were used to overcome the developmental gap. The commentary, which abounds with the myriad ways to distract a baby and detailed explanations of very slick special effects, probably makes it more interesting to adults and techno-geeks than children. Both image and sound are about what you'd expect from a studio release of this age. —LA

Movie: 🎵🎵 ½ *DVD:* 🎵🎵🎵🎵
20th Century Fox (UPC 24543029045). Widescreen (1.85:1) anamorphic; full frame. Dolby Digital 5.1 Surround; Dolby Surround. $19.98. Keepcase. *LANG:* English; French. *SUB:* Spanish. *CAP:* English. *FEATURES:* 20 chapters • Theatrical trailer • Featurette • Commentary: director Patrick Read Johnson.
1994 (PG) 99m/C Adam Worton, Jacob Worton, Joe Mantegna, Lara Flynn Boyle, Joe Pantoliano, Fred Dalton Thompson, John Neville, Brian Haley, Matthew Glave; *D:* Patrick Read Johnson; *W:* John Hughes; *C:* Thomas Ackerman; *M:* Bruce Broughton.

Bachelor Party

He (Hanks) is silly, cute, and poor. She (Kitaen) is intelligent, beautiful, and rich. They're about to get married but her parents hate him and his friends hate her. All is sorted out at the titular bash. It's a light, funny, goodhearted comedy that has aged well. The stars are young, attractive, and sexy. DVD image and sound are a bit above average, but about what you'd expect for a film of this age. Disc is only a minimal improvement over VHS tape in those categories. Extras are studio promotional stuff made for the theatrical release. —*MM*

Movie: ♫♫ ½ **DVD:** ♫♫ ½
20th Century Fox (UPC 024543016441). Widescreen. Dolby Digital 4.0 Surround; Mono. $22.98. Keepcase. *LANG:* English; French. *SUB:* English; Spanish. *FEATURES:* 22 chapters • Trailer • Interviews • Featurettes.
1984 (R) 105m/C Tom Hanks, Tawny Kitaen, Adrian Zmed, George Grizzard, Robert Prescott, William Tepper, Wendie Jo Sperber, Barry Diamond, Michael Dudikoff, Deborah Harmon, John Bloom, Toni Alessandra, Monique Gabrielle, Angela Aames, Rosanne Katon, Bradford Bancroft; *D:* Neal Israel; *W:* Pat Proft; *C:* Hal Trussel; *M:* Robert Folk.

Back to the Secret Garden

This original film continues the story made famous in the novel *The Secret Garden* by Frances Hodgson Burnett and through various film incarnations. The story takes place 30 years after the original tale. Mary (Cherie Lunghi) is now grown up and married to an ambassador. As she is to travel to America, she entrusts the key to the Secret Garden to Martha Sowerby (Joan Plowright), but once Mary leaves, the door to the garden can't be found! In America, Mary visits an orphanage and chooses young Lizzie (Camilla Belle) to journey to England to live at Miseselthwaite Manor. When Lizzie arrives, she discovers the garden and is amazed by its beauty. But the garden appears to be dying. What's causing this? It will be up to Lizzie and Mrs. Sowerby to bring it back to life. The last 30 minutes are quite fun and entertaining, but the first two-thirds of the movie is very boring and convoluted. The film has little of the magic that was present in the popular 1993 *Secret Garden*. Belle and Plowright are very good in their roles, but the film must be viewed as a disappointment. Full-frame image shows some grain in the exterior shots, but otherwise the picture is sharp and the colors are very good. (Unfortunately, the clarity of this transfer makes it quite obvious that the Secret Garden is a set.) With the Surround audio track, we get clear dialogue with no distortion, but very minimal rear-speaker effects. —*ML*

Movie: ♫♫ **DVD:** ♫♫ ½
Artisan Ent. (cat #12588, UPC 01223612-5884). Full frame. Dolby Surround. $19.98. Keepcase. *LANG:* English. *CAP:* English. *FEATURES:* 18 chapters.
2001 100m/C Camilla Belle, Cherie Lunghi, Joan Plowright, David Warner, Leigh Lawson, Florence Hoath; *D:* Michael Tuchner; *W:* Joe Wiesenfeld; *C:* Ian Wilson.

Backyard Dogs

Cole (Hamm) and Lee (Jones) dream of being professional wrestlers. They're working the backyard circuit when they're discovered by aspiring agent Kristy (Turner), who sends them skyrocketing up the ladder of success in that curious subculture.

Given the subject, the ultra-low-budget image is acceptable. On the commentary track, writer/director Robert Boris says that the film was shot on digital video on 18 locations in 18 days. The film makes many of Roger Corman's famous quickie productions look positively polished. But the movie also has the energy and spirit of early Cormans, too. The disc has the requisite extras and, for wrestling fans, is worth a look. Sound is unexceptional. —*MM*

Movie: ♫♫ **DVD:** ♫♫ ½
Artisan Ent. (cat #12250). Full frame. Dolby Digital Surround; Dolby Digital 5.1 Surround. $24.98. Keepcase. *LANG:* English. *SUB:* English; Spanish. *FEATURES:* Talent files • Trailer • Photo gallery • Commentary.
2000 96m/C Scott Hamm, Bree Turner, Walter Emmanuel Jones, Vincent Van Patten; *D:* Robert Boris; *W:* Robert Boris.

The Bad and the Beautiful

In 1952, with the Hollywood system reeling from the first punches that would bring it down, MGM produced this ultra-glossy, hard-hitting "exposé" of what in *Women's Day* might pass for the truth of Hollywood. About as dangerous as an official press release and confirming the greatness of Hollywood traditions that even then had become extinct, this is basically a front office–approved take on *Sunset Boulevard*. Fortunately, it's also a great deal of fun, what with actors chewing the scenery even behind the scenes, writing that assures us that the truth of every character can be grasped in one cliché, and direction that keeps it all exciting—and sometimes even insightful. A famous star, writer, and director are called to the studio by executive Harry Pebbel (Pidgeon) so he can try to convince them to make another movie with exiled producer Jonathan Shields (Douglas). In flashbacks, we learn that Shields and director Fred Amiel (Sullivan) were fast friends learning the business working on B-pictures, until Jonathan filched Fred's script and concept and leapt into A production without him. Georgia Lorrison (Turner), the daughter of an earlier screen great, was a boozing mess until Jonathan turned her into a star, helping her through her problems by feigning a love relationship—until the film was in the can. And writer James Lee Bartlow (Powell) was wooed from a university in the South to the Hollywood bigtime, only to lose his wife Rosemary (Grahame) to the temptations of Tinsel Town. Will they turn their backs on the most hated man in Hollywood, or acknowledge their debt to him? DVD is beautiful, not bad. By the early 1950s, black-and-white studio photography had a silky smoothness that transfers well if the source materials are well prepared. Equally alluring is David Raksin's great score, one of Hollywood's most beautiful. A selection of recovered music cues from the film are included as an extra that soundtrack aficionados will appreciate. I suspect the guiding hand of Turner special projects

whiz George Feltenstein had a hand in this—he's been busy for years making sure that whenever original scoring is found in the vaults, it's brought out for us to enjoy. Also included are trailers for this show and Minnelli's 1962 *Two Weeks in Another Town*, which because of its similarity is often called a sequel, but is not. On the flip side of this two-sided disc is a feature-length documentary on Lana Turner that aired on TCM, *Lana Turner…A Daughter's Memoir*. It's a very entertaining, very slick production that covers Turner's career from a softening, affectionate point of view. The show is very successful at portraying the realities of starting as a naïve girl, who, it is claimed, had no idea she was going to attract so much attention in that tight sweater. Being an MGM starlet was no picnic and most of Turner's allegedly wild private life is not shown. Her relationship with mobster Johnny Stompanato (as celebrated in *L.A. Confidential*) is addressed, which gives us an opportunity to read between the lines. The documentary uses fictional restagings, with stand-ins for Turner and Stompanato, that visually fill out the show but also drag it down to the phony standards of reality televison whenever they appear. They're nicely shot, but a bad idea. —*GE*

Movie: ♫♫♫ **DVD:** ♫♫♫ ½
Warner Home Video (UPC 12569524026). Full frame. $19.98. Snapper. *LANG:* English. *FEATURES:* Trailers • *Lana Turner…A Daughter's Memoir* • Recovered music cues.
1952 118m/B Kirk Douglas, Lana Turner, Dick Powell, Gloria Grahame, Barry Sullivan, Walter Pidgeon, Gilbert Roland, Leo G. Carroll; *D:* Vincente Minnelli; *W:* Charles Schnee; *C:* Robert L. Surtees; *M:* David Raksin. *AWARDS:* Oscars '52: Art Dir./Set Dec., B&W, B&W Cinematog., Costume Des. (B&W), Screenplay, Support. Actress (Grahame); *NOM:* Oscars '52: Actor (Douglas).

Bad Boys [Anchor Bay]

Young thug Mike O'Brien (Penn) is sent to a reformatory for the death of a drug dealer's (Morales) brother. After assorted plot twists, the two antagonists wind up in the same cell block with a lot of issues to settle. The film is not as exploitative as it sounds in synopsis. DVD presents an excellent image, far superior to the earlier release (reviewed in *Book 1*). Mono sound is more than adequate. Director Rosenthal's commentary track shifts between technical talk and chatty gossip. —*MM*

Movie: ♫♫♫ **DVD:** ♫♫♫ ½
Anchor Bay (cat #DV11433, UPC 013131-143393). Widescreen (1.85:1) anamorphic. Dolby Digital Mono. $24.95. Keepcase. *LANG:* English. *CAP:* English. *FEATURES:* 27 chapters • Trailer • Commentary: Rick Rosenthal.
1983 (R) 104m/C Sean Penn, Esai Morales, Reni Santoni, Jim Moody, Eric Gurry, Ally Sheedy, Clancy Brown; *D:* Rick Rosenthal; *W:* Richard Dilello; *C:* Donald E. Thorin; *M:* Bill Conti.

Bad Company

Drew (Brown) and Jake (Bridges) are trying to avoid induction into the Union Army by heading west. The episodic tale is a 19th-century road movie that's never received the credit it's due. This is a terrific film that belongs on the same shelf with *Outlaw Josey Wales*. There may be some surface flaws, but they're lost in the film's inherent grain and softness of image. That comes from the film's age and evocation of the time. Because of it, interiors are realistically dark and reveal few details. Even without extras, the disc is worth your consideration. —*MM*

Movie: 🎬🎬🎬 ½ ***DVD:*** 🎬🎬🎬
Paramount (cat #08476, UPC 097360847-642). Widescreen (1.85:1) anamorphic. Dolby Digital Mono. $24.99. Keepcase. *LANG:* English. *SUB:* English. *CAP:* English. *FEATURES:* 14 chapters.
1972 (PG) 94m/C Jeff Bridges, Barry Brown, Jim Davis, John Savage; ***D:*** Robert Benton; ***W:*** Robert Benton, David Newman; ***C:*** Gordon Willis.

Bad Cop Chronicles: Confessions of a Police Captain

A dedicated Italian police captain (Balsam) tries to wipe out the bureaucratic corruption that infects his city. Balsam gives a fine performance in a turgid, slow-moving tale. DVD image looks like a second-generation VHS dupe with moderate surface damage evident throughout. —*MM*

Movie: 🎬🎬 ***DVD:*** 🎬
BCI-Eclipse (cat #44049-9, UPC 7873644-04995). Full frame. $14.99. Keepcase. *LANG:* English. *FEATURES:* "Spooky Hooky" cartoon • Trivia game • DVD Dictionary • DVD-ROM features • 6 chapters.
1972 (PG) 104m/C *IT* Martin Balsam, Franco Nero, Marilu Tolo; ***D:*** Damiano Damiani; ***W:*** Damiano Damiani, Salvatore Laurani; ***C:*** Claudio Ragona; ***M:*** Riz Ortolani.

Bad Cop Chronicles 2: Corrupt

Bad narcotics cop (Keitel) goes after murderer but mysterious Lydon (AKA Johnny Rotten of the Sex Pistols) gets in the way. Whatever the story has to offer is lost in one of the worst DVDs ever created. Abysmal image looks much worse than the first *Bad Cop Chronicles*. The exceptionally poor sound seems to come from the original. —*MM*

AKA: Order of Death; Cop Killers.
Movie: 🎬 ½ ***DVD:*** 🎬
BCI-Eclipse (cat #44050-9, UPC 7873644-05091). Full frame. $14.99. Keepcase. *LANG:* English. *FEATURES:* "Spooking about Africa" cartoon • Trivia game • DVD Dictionary • DVD-ROM features • 6 chapters.
1984 (PG) 99m/C *IT* Harvey Keitel, John (Johnny Rotten) Lydon, Sylvia Sidney, Nicole Garcia, Leonard Mann; ***D:*** Roberto Faenza; ***W:*** Roberto Faenza, Ennio de Concini, Hugh Fleetwood; ***C:*** Guiseppe Pinori; ***M:*** Ennio Morricone.

The Bad News Bears

Many aspects of *The Bad News Bears* are still as fresh today as they were when the film debuted in 1976. Walter Matthau stars as former minor league baseball player Morris Buttermaker. As his ball-playing days are now long-since behind him, Buttermaker spends his days cleaning swimming pools and drinking beer. He is hired by a local little league to coach a team and soon learns that the team is highly unmotivated and unskilled. Following some embarrassing losses, Buttermaker recruits Amanda (O'Neal), the daughter of an ex-girlfriend, and local bad boy Kelly (Haley) to join the team. As the Bears finally taste success, the once apathetic Buttermaker changes his outlook on the team, but this newfound interest only leads to derision in the ranks. The film is both a classic comedy, and an extremely insightful look at society. The attitudes displayed by the parents and kids are realistic, as the adults become swept up in a game where the children just want to have fun. Along with this biting criticism are some true "laugh out loud" moments, as these vulgar children speak and act the way that kids do in real life. (Actually, the language in this film gets pretty rough at times, so parents, be warned. It would most likely receive a "PG-13" today.) Walter Matthau is brilliant in the lead role. His hang-dog demeanor is perfectly suited to portray the shiftless Buttermaker, but we get to see his true acting skill when Buttermaker begins to actually care about the team. Vic Morrow is also good as the evil coach of a rival team. All of the kids are great, but several of the blonde boys are difficult to tell apart. From the writer of *John Carpenter's The Thing*. Paramount Home Video doesn't quite do the film justice with this DVD release. The image is sharp and clear, but there is some very thick grain at times. Also, some minor artifacting occurs in some scenes. However, the colors are very good, and the fleshtones are realistic. Despite the fact that the DVD packaging proclaims that the DVD offers a Dolby Digital 5.1 Surround soundtrack, the viewer will be hard pressed to find anything coming from the rear speaker, save for an occasional musical cue. Actually, the 5.1 track only sounds slightly better than the digital mono track offered here. Still, both tracks offer clear dialogue and are well-balanced. There are no extra features on this DVD. —*ML*

Movie: 🎬🎬🎬 ½ ***DVD:*** 🎬🎬 ½
Paramount (cat #08863, UPC 097360886-344). Widescreen (1.85:1) anamorphic. Dolby Digital 5.1; Dolby Digital Mono. $24.99. Keepcase. *LANG:* English. *SUB:* English. *CAP:* English. *FEATURES:* 17 chapters • All three *Bears* films are available on DVD, but there is no box set.
1976 (PG) 102m/C Walter Matthau, Tatum O'Neal, Vic Morrow, Joyce Van Patten, Jackie Earle Haley, Chris Barnes, Erin Blunt, Gary Cavagnaro, Alfred Lutter, David Stambaugh, Brandon Cruz, Jaime Escobedo, Scott Firestone, George Gonzales, Brett Marx, David Pollock, Quinn Smith; ***D:***

Michael Ritchie; ***W:*** Bill Lancaster; ***C:*** John A. Alonzo; ***M:*** Jerry Fielding. *AWARDS:* Writers Guild '76: Orig. Screenplay.

The Bad News Bears Go to Japan

This final entry into the *Bad News Bears* series certainly represents the nadir for this rag-tag group of ball-players. When a little-league team backs out of their trip to Japan to play the Japanese champs, the Bears volunteer to go. However, they don't have the funds for the trip, so in steps Hollywood hustler Marvin Lazar (Tony Curtis). Lazar is down on his luck and has decided to sell the TV rights to the international game and make a fortune. What he didn't count on was the outrageous antics. The film is basically 90 minutes of jokes about the Japanese culture. The film focuses too much of its attention on Curtis and not enough on the kids. And while the jokes involving the ball players and their introduction to Eastern ways aren't that funny to begin with, they are far better than the shtick served up by Curtis. This is truly a sad affair, as we witness a film that spells the demise for a once-promising franchise and we view the downfall of a man who was once one of Hollywood's best comedic actors. Today, this film is noteworthy only for an interesting cameo by the one and only Regis Philbin. Interesting, this DVD is actually superior in technical quality than its predecessor. The picture is very sharp and clear, with only some minor artifacting and shimmering present. The colors are good and the only noticeable grain comes during stock footage shots. The Dolby Digital Mono audio track offers clear dialogue and nice reproduction of the musical score. There are no extras. As with the other films in this series, the original "comic-strip" style poster art has been replaced with a photo for the DVD cover. —*ML*

Movie: 🎬 ½ ***DVD:*** 🎬🎬 ½
Paramount (cat #01114, UPC 097360111-446). Widescreen (1.85:1) anamorphic. Dolby Digital Mono. $24.99. Keepcase. *LANG:* English. *SUB:* English. *CAP:* English. *FEATURES:* 12 chapters.
1978 (PG) 92m/C Tony Curtis, Jackie Earle Haley, Tomisaburo Wakayama, George Wyner, Erin Blunt, George Gonzales, Brett Marx, David Pollock, David Stambaugh, Regis Philbin; ***D:*** John Berry; ***W:*** Bill Lancaster; ***C:*** Gene Polito; ***M:*** Paul Chihara.

The Bad News Bears in Breaking Training

Those irrepressible Bad News Bears are back in a very silly movie with a ridiculously long title. Shorn of stars like Walter Matthau and Tatum O'Neal, this sequel brings back most of the original Bears team from the first film and attempts to survive on their talents. The result is a decidedly mixed bag. *Breaking Training* takes place a year after the ending of the original film. In plot-points which are never fully explained, the Bears have won a chance to play a very important game in

the Astrodome (in which the winner will go to Japan, thus setting up the third film in the series) and they have a new coach, who is a tyrant. After dumping this meany, the Bears, under the direction of resident bad-boy Kelly Leak (Jackie Earle Haley), decide to con their parents and travel to Houston on their own. Along the way, they have many crazy adventures. Once in Houston, Kelly has a reconciliation with his estranged father Mike (William Devane), who agrees to coach the team. Of course, the highlight is the game, played under the lights of the Astrodome. *Breaking Training* is simply a rehash of the first film, crossed with a road movie. The story is weak and some of the acting is terrible, but there are some funny moments here. Unfortunately Jimmy Baio (Scott's cousin) creates one of the most annoying on-screen characters ever, as Carmen Ronzonni, which doesn't help the film. *Breaking Training* isn't an altogether awful film, but it is not a worthy successor to the original. Director Michael Pressman would continue his sequel slumming status with *Teenage Mutant Ninja Turtles 2: The Secret of the Ooze* some 14 years later. This DVD image is very sharp and clear, showing only minor grain and slight artifacting at times. The most impressive quality is the colors, which seem to leap off of the screen. The boys on the team have been costumed in contrasting T-shirts, which give the picture a very dynamic quality. The Dolby Digital Mono audio track provides clear dialogue and music reproduction, with no hissing or distortion. There are no extra features on this DVD. —*ML*
Movie: ♫♫ **DVD:** ♫♫ ½
Paramount (cat #08965, UPC 097360896-541). Widescreen anamorphic. Dolby Digital Mono. $24.99. Keepcase. *LANG:* English. *SUB:* English. *CAP:* English. *FEATURES:* 12 chapters.
1977 (PG) 99m/C William Devane, Clifton James, Jackie Earle Haley, Jimmy Baio, Chris Barnes, Erin Blunt, George Gonzales, Jaime Escobedo, Alfred Lutter, Brett Marx, David Pollock, Quinn Smith, David Stambaugh, Dolph Sweet; **D:** Michael Pressman; **W:** Paul Brickman; **C:** Fred W. Koenekamp; **M:** Craig Safan.

Bad Seed

Rising star Luke Wilson is featured in this jarring psychological thriller. The film opens with Emily (Mili Avital) confessing to her husband Preston (Wilson) that she's been having an affair. Enraged, Preston leaves their house, only to return hours later, where he finds that Emily has been murdered. He immediately suspects Jonathan (Norman Reedus), Emily's lover. Preston's thirst for revenge starts him on a bizarre and violent path, which leads him to private detective Dick (Dennis Farina). Preston soon learns that vengeance is a costly enterprise and things aren't always as they seem. Debut from writer/director Jon Bokenkamp certainly offers some exciting thrills and intriguing plot twists. However, the film gets bogged-down in the

middle and the ending is very unsatisfying. Also, some important plot-points are glossed over. Bokenkamp proves that he could bring something new to the genre, but he overextends his reach here. Good performances all around, especially from Wilson. This DVD offers a compelling package, replete with special features. The widescreen transfer looks great, showing minimal grain and good colors. The image is sharp and clear, with only touches of darkness at times. The audio track is puzzling, as it provides clear dialogue and a great presentation of the haunting musical score, but only minimal Surround sound. Save for thunder and musical cues, the rear speakers are silent. Two audio commentaries grace this disc and the one with Bokenkamp and Wilson is especially fun and educational. —*ML* **AKA:** Preston Tylk.
Movie: ♫♫ ½ **DVD:** ♫♫♫
Artisan Ent. (cat #11901, UPC 01223911-9012). Widescreen (1.85:1) anamorphic. Dolby Digital 5.1; Dolby Surround. $24.98. Keepcase. *LANG:* English. *SUB:* English; Spanish. *CAP:* English. *FEATURES:* Audio commentaries • Cast & crew bios • Interviews • Production notes • Trailer • 20 chapters.
2000 (R) 92m/C Luke Wilson, Norman Reedus, Dennis Farina, Mili Avital, Vincent Kartheiser; **D:** Jon Bokenkamp; **W:** Jon Bokenkamp; **C:** Joey Forsyte; **M:** Kurt Kuenne.

Bad Taste [LE]

Before embarking on such high-brow fare as *Heavenly Creatures* and *The Lord of the Rings,* Peter Jackson made the ultimate backyard splatter comedy. Working with his friends, but doing much of the work himself (and also playing several roles in the movie), Jackson created this insane comedy in which an alien fast-food chain ("Crumb's Crunchy Delights") comes to Earth to gather humans to serve in their restaurants. Learning of this threat, the Astro Investigation and Defense Service is called upon to stop the "alien bastards." What results is a film filled with nonstop comic violence, which proves to be one of the goriest films ever made. Just when you think things can't get any wilder, they do. Fans of horror and cult films should not miss out on this one. Since the film was shot on 16mm, past video releases didn't look very good, but that all changes with this DVD. The image has been letterboxed at 1.66:1 and looks great. Yes, there is grain visible in most every shot, but that's to be expected given the low-budget shooting situation. The picture is clear and sharp, and the colors are fine. Both the Dolby Digital 5.1 and DTS-ES 6.1 soundtracks are impressive, but they are obviously remixes and the sounds are a bit exaggerated at times. The Limited Edition DVD includes a 25-minute documentary from 1987, which gives a nice overview of the making of the film. Featuring interviews with Jackson and his parents, the audience learns how Jackson created most of the film from household materials. A less-expensive regular edi-

tion DVD is available, but it does not include the documentary. —*ML*
Movie: ♫♫♫ ½ **DVD:** ♫♫♫ ½
Anchor Bay (cat #DV11657, UPC 013131-165791). Widescreen (1.66:1) anamorphic. Dolby Digital Surround 5.1 EX; 6.1 DTS-ES; Dolby Surround. $39.98. Special packaging. *LANG:* English. *CAP:* English. *FEATURES:* Documentary • Theatrical trailer • Director bio • 25 chapters.
1988 90m/C *NZ* Peter Jackson, Pete O'Herne, Mike Minett, Terry Potter, Craig Smith, Doug Wren, Dean Lawrie, Peter Vere-Jones, Ken Hammon, Michael Gooch; **D:** Peter Jackson; **W:** Tony Hiles, Peter Jackson, Ken Hammon; **C:** Peter Jackson; **M:** Michelle Scullion.

Bagdad Cafe

Jasmin (Saegebrecht), a large German woman, is abandoned by her husband in the middle of the high desert near Las Vegas. She finds her way to the Bagdad Gas and Oil Café and its ill-tempered, irritable owner Brenda (Pounder). The rest of the film is essentially a road movie where the main characters stay in one place and let the colorful supporting cast come to them. Jack Palance all but steals the film as Rudy, the Hollywood artist who becomes obsessed with Jasmin. Not much happens in the quirky story. Conflicts are resolved easily and quickly. Enjoy the offbeat humor and the exceptionally strong sense of place (Newberry Springs, California). The producers of TV's *Northern Exposure* must have taken some inspiration from this one. The low-budget image has always been exceptionally grainy, but I could detect no excessive artifacts. Stereo is serviceable; Surround effects limited. —*MM* **AKA:** Out of Rosenheim.
Movie: ♫♫♫ ½ **DVD:** ♫♫ ½
MGM Home Ent. (cat #1002209, UPC 027-616864406). Widescreen (1.85:1) anamorphic. Dolby Digital Surround Stereo. $19.98. Keepcase. *LANG:* English. *SUB:* French; Spanish. *FEATURES:* 16 chapters • Trailer.
1988 (PG) 91m/C *GE* Marianne Saegebrecht, CCH Pounder, Jack Palance, Christine Kaufmann, Monica Calhoun, Darron Flagg; **D:** Percy Adlon; **W:** Percy Adlon, Eleonore Adlon; **C:** Bernd Heinl; **M:** Bob Telson. *AWARDS:* Cesar '89: Foreign Film; *NOM:* Oscars '88: Song ("Calling You").

Baise Moi

This French exploitation film gives a new meaning to term "bad movie." Two women, Nadine (Karen Bach) and Manu (Raffaela Anderson), meet and go on a crime spree. That's the entire plot of the film. Manu had been raped (which she seemed to take in stride) and had also killed a man. Nadine is a prostitute who killed her nagging roommate. Supposedly, these events freed this duo to travel across France, killing, robbing, drinking, and having sex. The movie is never about anything else but glorifying sex and violence and those who have come away from it having seen

themes involving feminine sexual rage were simply projecting that onto the film. Some have compared the film to *Thelma & Louise*, but that only shows a lack of imagination on their parts. This film was banned in its native France and is referred to in the marketing material as "the most controversial film of the decade." The bottom line is that the gore effects presented in the acts of violence are elementary school level at best, and the only reason that *Baise Moi* has gotten any publicity is due to its realistic portrayal of on-screen sex. As with most "controversial" films, this one is boring and pretentious and should be avoided at all costs. As bad as the movie itself is, the DVD presentation makes things even worse. *Baise Moi* was shot on digital video, but the image here is muddy and grainy. One could assume that the film's look was meant to underscore the gritty realism, but the end result is an extremely ugly transfer. The image is washed-out, dark, and nearly devoid of colors at times. Also, there is shimmering on the image and noticeable lens flare at times. The Dolby 2.0 Surround audio track provides clear dialogue, with only a hint of distortion, but only musical cues from the rear speakers. The most entertaining portions of this DVD are the critical blurbs, with begin with the positive reviews, but then get to the negative ones, some of which are hilarious. —*ML* **AKA:** Rape Me.
Movie: woof **DVD:** ♫
Remstar (cat #REM00131, UPC 6812830-01313). Full frame. Dolby Surround. $29.95. Keepcase. *LANG:* French. *SUB:* English. *FEATURES:* Trailer • Still gallery • Press blurbs • 6 chapters.
2000 77m/C *FR* Raffaela Anderson, Karen Bach; *D:* Virginie Despentes, Coralie Trinh Thi; *W:* Virginie Despentes, Coralie Trinh Thi; *C:* Benoit Chamaillard; *M:* Varou Jan.

Ballad of a Soldier

Private Alyosha (Ivashov) is given a six-day leave to visit his mother as a reward for valor in battle. As he journeys by train to his hometown, moments of human connection are beautifully set against the war-ravaged Russian landscape. An elegant and moving film. The picture has been restored beautifully, with crisp black-and-whites and only occasional grain. The audio has a high level of background hiss, but both the music and dialogue are clear and free of distortion. The only interview with director Chukhraj is embarrassing, as both parties are noticeably frustrated by their language barrier. —*BG* **AKA:** Ballada o Soldate.
Movie: ♫♫♫♫ **DVD:** ♫♫♫
Criterion (cat #148, UPC 037429167922). Full frame. Dolby Mono. $29.95. Keepcase. *LANG:* Russian. *SUB:* English. *FEATURES:* 20 chapters • Audio interviews: Ivashov, Prokhorenko, director Chukhraj.
1960 88m/B *RU* Vladimir Ivashov, Shanna Prokhorenko, Antonina Maximova, Nikolai Kryuchkov; *D:* Grigori Chukhraj; *W:* Grigori Chukhraj, Valentin Yezhov; *C:* Sergei Mukhin; *M:* Mikhail Ziv. *AWARDS:* British

Acad. '61: Film; *NOM:* Oscars '61: Story & Screenplay.

Ballistic Kiss

Donnie Yen (*Iron Monkey*) directs and stars in this film as a highly skilled elite contract killer. An early sequence establishes his abilities, showing the bespectacled hit man taking down a penthouse full of bad guys without even breaking a sweat. Annie Wu is a cop assigned to the many triad execution cases in Hong Kong. Yen falls for Wu from afar. On his next assignment he runs into his old ex-partner Rongguang Yu, who framed him for his secret criminal activities. Before long, the two men are involved in their own private war, with Wu mixed up in the middle of it. Yen makes for a stylish director, mixing up film speeds à la John Woo and painting his screen in monochrome shades for business, wider hues for pleasure. He's a bit too stylish at times, obscuring the action and making frequent back-ups a necessity. —*BT* **AKA:** Sha Sha Ren; Tiao Tiao Miu.
Movie: ♫♫♫ **DVD:** ♫♫ ½
Tai Seng (cat #5243, UPC 48950249056-55). Widescreen letterboxed. $19.95. Keepcase. *LANG:* Cantonese; Mandarin. *SUB:* Chinese; English. *FEATURES:* 8 chapters • Star profile • Trailers.
1998 90m/C *HK* Donnie Yen, Annie (Chen Chun) Wu, Simon Lui, Yu Wing Kwong, Vincent Kok, Karen Tong, Lily Chow, Jimmy Wong; *D:* Donnie Yen; *W:* Bey Logan; *C:* Kai Fei Wong; *M:* Yukie Nishimura.

Balto 2: Wolf Quest

In this sequel to the 1995 original, Balto becomes a father and has to face the task of raising his pups until their adoption. Yet, there's one dog in particular, Aleu (voice of Lacey Chabert) that looks different than the rest—clearly more wolf than the rest. When a near-tragic accident forces Aleu to find out the truth about her wolf heritage, she runs away on a journey to discover her place. Rather than shoving (the very obvious) message at the audience, the film makes its points quietly, across the entire arc of the story. The film also boasts better animation than most non-theatrical family titles usually offer. The vocal talent is particularly good and braced by sincere, involving performances. Even the (refreshingly few) songs are nicely placed. The film will most likely appeal to children age six and above. Some below that might find a few sequences slightly scary. Still, this is a film that both parents and children can enjoy together. The film is presented full-frame which, given the fact that this is a direct-to-video release, is likely the film's original aspect ratio. The animation is crisp throughout, even if it's not particularly detailed. Only a few minor moments of image shimmer appeared and no print problems are present. Colors are bright and vibrant throughout. The Surround soundtrack isn't overtly aggressive, but there were a few action sequences where the channels came to life. Most of

the audio is in the front speakers but the quality is pleasing, as the dialogue is crisp and the score and sound effects are natural and convincing. —*AB/DG*
Movie: ♫♫ ½ **DVD:** ♫♫♫
Universal Studios (cat #21102, UPC 2519-2110221). Full frame. Dolby Digital 5.1 Surround; Dolby Digital Surround. $24.98. Keepcase. *LANG:* English; French; Spanish. *SUB:* English. *CAP:* English. *FEATURES:* 18 chapters • Production notes • Theatrical trailer • "Rescue Aleu" game • "Rescue Heroes" game demo.
2002 (G) 74m/C *D:* Phil Weinstein; *V:* Lacey Chabert, Maurice LaMarche, Jodi Benson, David Carradine, Mark Hamill.

Bandits

One great movie. Brother Joe and Terry (Bruce Willis and Billy Bob Thornton) escape from prison to the music of Led Zepplin. They begin robbing banks in a unique way that gets them the name the "sleeper Bandits." Along the way they hook up with Kate (Cate Blanchett), a bored housewife who falls in love with both the brothers because the two of them make up the perfect man. It's a knock-down laugh fest. The DVD is ultra crisp, loaded with great stuff, and the sound bounced around my living room like a rubber ball. —*DE*
Movie: ♫♫♫ ½ **DVD:** ♫♫♫ ½
MGM Home Ent. (cat #1003235, UPC 027-61687385). Widescreen (2.35:1) anamorphic; full frame. Dolby 5.1 Surround; Dolby Surround. $26.98. Keepcase. *LANG:* English; French; Spanish; Portuguese. *SUB:* English; French; Spanish; Portuguese. *FEATURES:* 32 chapters • Alternate ending • Deleted scenes • "Creating Scene 71" featurette • "Making of" featurette.
2001 (PG-13) 123m/C Bruce Willis, Billy Bob Thornton, Cate Blanchett, Troy Garity, Bobby Slayton, Brian F. O'Byrne, Azura Skye, Stacy Travis, William Converse-Roberts, Richard Riehle, Micole Mercurio, January Jones; *D:* Barry Levinson; *W:* Harley Peyton; *C:* Dante Spinotti; *M:* Christopher Young. *AWARDS:* Natl. Bd. of Review '01: Actor (Thornton); *NOM:* Golden Globes '02: Actor—Mus./Comedy (Thornton), Actress—Mus./Comedy (Blanchett); Screen Actors Guild '01: Support. Actress (Blanchett).

Bar Girls

Based on a play by Lauran Hoffman, this romantic comedy about life and love among the customers at a lesbian bar retains the stiffness of the theatre in presentation, but also has some nice introspective moments for the characters. Even though the lovers and love-ees are all women, the same theme that inhabits heterosexual romantic comedies—fear of intimacy fighting the desire for love—runs through this story. Loretta (Wolfe) is looking for love; Rachel (D'Agostino) walks in the door of the bar and they fall in love, forsaking all others, until the trouble-making JR (Griggs) wanders into the bar and uses the two lovers' weak-

nesses and fears to have her way with them. Long talks ensue and, as the bard says, all's well that ends well. This is a low-budget production with decent production values, including a smooth picture and reasonable sound. —CA
Movie: 🎬🎬 ½ **DVD:** 🎬🎬 ½
MGM Home Ent. (cat #1003252, UPC 027-616874023). Widescreen (1.85:1) anamorphic. Dolby Digital Stereo. $19.90. Keepcase. *LANG:* English. *SUB:* English; French; Spanish. *CAP:* English. *FEATURES:* 16 chapters.
1995 (R) 95m/C Nancy Allison Wolfe, Liza D'Agostino, Justine Slater, Paula Sorge, Camila Griggs, Pam Raines; **D:** Marita Giovanni; **W:** Lauran Hoffman; **C:** Michael Ferris; **M:** Lenny Meyers.

Bar 20 Rides Again

The third entry in the "Hopalong Cassidy" series is one of the best. Hoppy (Boyd) goes undercover, as it were, to infiltrate a gang that's led by the evil Perdue (Worth), who worships Napoleon. For technical comments, please see review of *Hopalong Cassidy.* The title is available on the first volume of *Hopalong Cassidy: The Early Years.* —MM
Movie: 🎬🎬🎬 **DVD:** 🎬🎬 ½
Image Ent. (cat #ID9151UTDVD, UPC 014-381915129). Full frame. Dolby Digital 5.1 Surround Stereo. $24.99. Keepcase. *LANG:* English. *FEATURES:* 12 chapters • Liner notes by Fred Romary.
1935 63m/B William Boyd, James Ellison, George "Gabby" Hayes, Jean Rouveral, Harry Worth, Frank McGlynn, Ethel Wales, Paul Fix, J(ohn) P(aterson) McGowan; **D:** Howard Bretherion; **W:** Doris Schroeder; **C:** Archie Stout.

Barabbas

Imprisoned bandit and ruffian, Barabbas (Quinn) is spared by the Romans, and Christ is crucified in his place. After his Christian girlfriend is stoned for heresy, Barabbas undergoes multiple crises of faith throughout his episodic journey from his tenure in the sulfur mines through to his reign in the gladiatorial arena. An earnest, occasionally poignant biblical drama features a solid performance by Quinn (in a difficult role) and a particularly oily and loathsome characterization by Jack Palace. An actual eclipse was filmed and included in an early sequence, and its effect is quite chilling. The story's lengthy, episodic structure occasionally stalls the picture's momentum and the entirely re-looped dialogue has an unintended distancing effect. Vittorio Gassman is dubbed by at least two different vocal artists: one with a proper English accent and the other with an Italian accent! The gruesome sulfur mine sequence and arena sequences are definite highlights in this often thought-provoking picture. The image is sharp and clean with a minimum of digital artifacts. Unfortunately, the colors are almost non-existent; they've faded so severely, that it raises genuine concern about the preservation and condition of

the master print elements. The multi-channel sound is strong, but naturally doesn't have the presence of later era Surround mixes. The trailer is battered but has stronger color than the feature. —DG
Movie: 🎬🎬🎬 **DVD:** 🎬🎬🎬
Columbia Tristar (cat #07750, UPC 04339-6077508). Widescreen (2.20:1) anamorphic. Dolby Digital 4.0 Surround. $24.95. Keepcase. *LANG:* English. *SUB:* English; French; Spanish; Portuguese. *CAP:* English. *FEATURES:* Theatrical trailer • 28 chapters.
1962 144m/C Anthony Quinn, Silvana Mangano, Arthur Kennedy, Jack Palance, Ernest Borgnine, Katy Jurado, Vittorio Gassman; **D:** Richard Fleischer; **W:** Diego Fabbri, Christopher Fry, Ivo Perilli, Nigel Balchin; **C:** Aldo Tonti; **M:** Mario Nascimbene.

Barbara the Fair with the Silken Hair

To save himself from the diabolical Chudo-Yudo, the Czar offers to reward him with the only thing unknown to him in his kingdom. Ironically, the Czar's wife has just secretly given birth to a son! To save his heir from Chudo-Yudo, the Czar attempts to switch him with the child of a local fisherman. Unfortunately the attempt is bungled. Eighteen years later, Chudo-Yudo comes calling for his prize, hoping to wed his daughter, Barbara, to the heir. It's a lively romp, clearly aimed at children (adult performances are intentionally overdone and silly) but makes memorable use of an incredibly rich (almost Technicolor) color palette and evocative fantastic art direction. The disc is slightly grainy but razor sharp (especially in close-ups) and has a strong filmic look, accurately conveying the bold colors and rich textures. While this would usually rate three bones, the transfer suffers from a terrible visual distortion: the film is presented at 1.85:1 but the film itself appears to be a much wider 'Scope original. The image hasn't been cropped; it's been overly stretched out during mastering. The entire film features a compressed image that no TV settings (not even a 16x9 TV) will reconcile. The sound is fine, but rarely makes use of Surrounds. The "making of" featurette and "excerpts" add up to less than three minutes, but are composed of worthwhile behind-the-camera footage and offer tantalizing glimpses of deleted scenes. —DG
Movie: 🎬🎬 ½ **DVD:** 🎬
Image Ent. (cat #RUSD0249DVD, UPC 014381024920). Widescreen (1.85:1) anamorphic. Dolby Digital 5.1 Surround. $29.99. Keepcase. *LANG:* Russian; English; French. *SUB:* Russian; English; French; German; Hebrew; Spanish; Italian; and more. *FEATURES:* Theatrical trailer • "Making of" featurette • 3 songs from the film • Filmography • Excerpt from a documentary on Alexander Row • Photos • Materials from the Ruscico Museum.
1969 85m/C *RU* Mikhail Pugovkin, Georgy Millyar, Anatoly Kubatsky, Lidya Korolyova; **D:** Alexander Row; **W:** Alexander Row, Mikhail Chuprin; **C:** Dmitry Surensky; **M:** Arkady Filippenko.

Barbarian Queen

Amathea (Clarkson) leads her women warriors on a mission of vengeance against the enemy who captured their men. Energetic home video and cable favorite gains little on DVD because it's such a low-budget, low-light production. —MM
Movie: 🎬 **DVD:** 🎬
New Concorde (cat #NH20256 D, UPC 73-6991425699). Full frame. Stereo. $9.98. Keepcase. *LANG:* English. *SUB:* English. *FEATURES:* 20 chapters • Talent files • Trailers.
1985 (R) 71m/C *IT* Lana Clarkson, Frank Zagarino, Katt Shea, Dawn Dunlap, Susana Traverso; **D:** Hector Olivera; **W:** Howard R. Cohen; **C:** Rudy Donovan; **M:** Christopher Young.

Barbarian Queen 2: The Empress Strikes Back

The buxom battler (Clarkson) is back. This time, she's up against her evil brother. More topless torture, brave band of female rebels, etc. Also the same dimly lit scenes that gain nothing on DVD. Like the first, this one's no better than VHS tape. —MM
Movie: 🎬 ½ **DVD:** 🎬
New Concorde (cat #NH20289 D, UPC 73-6991428997). Full frame. Stereo. $9.98. Keepcase. *LANG:* English. *FEATURES:* 20 chapters • Trailers • Talent files.
1989 (R) 87m/C *IT* Lana Clarkson, Greg Wrangler, Rebecca Wood, Elizabeth Jaegen, Roger Cundy; **D:** Joe Finley; **W:** Howard R. Cohen; **C:** Francisco Bojorquez; **M:** Christopher Young.

Barbarians at the Gate

When the CEO of Nabisco (Garner) decides to buy out the shareholders and take over the company, a comedy about the greed of '80s big business and big bucks is set into motion—based on a true story. An uninspired cable TV movie with decent if tepid DVD transfer and sound to match. —MO
Movie: 🎬🎬 **DVD:** 🎬🎬🎬
HBO (cat #90835, UPC 026359083525). Full frame. Dolby Digital Surround; Dolby Digital Stereo; Dolby Digital Mono. $14.98. Snapper. *LANG:* English; French; Spanish. *SUB:* English; French; Spanish. *CAP:* English; French; Spanish. *FEATURES:* 22 chapters.
1993 (R) 107m/C James Garner, Jonathan Pryce, Peter Riegert, Joanna Cassidy, Fred Dalton Thompson, Leilani Sarelle Ferrer, Matt Clark, Jeffrey DeMunn; **D:** Glenn Jordan; **W:** Larry Gelbart; **C:** Thomas Del Ruth, Nicholas D. Knowland; **M:** Richard Gibbs.

Barbie in the Nutcracker

After a half-century of existence, Barbie finally gets her own movie. Here, she relates (and stars in) the familiar tale of "The Nutcracker." Clara (played by Barbie) is given a nutcracker as a Christmas gift. This enchanted toy leads Clara into a magical world, as she must help the Nutcracker defeat the evil Mouse King. To complete this task, Clara must join the Nutcracker in locating the Sugarplum Princess. Despite the fact that *The Nutcracker* has been performed countless times, there is a fresh quality to this production. While not matching the level of films such as *Toy Story*, the computer animation is quite impressive. (It was done by the same company which produced the popular *ReBoot*.) Clearly, the film is aimed at young girls, but the colorful animation and the well-paced story made it accessible to a wider audience. One can't help but wonder what Barbie's next adventure will be. The movie is offered on this DVD in both full-frame and widescreen formats (note that the full-frame version is the default choice). The image is incredibly sharp and clear, showing no flaws. The picture is very colorful, making it mesmerizing to younger viewers. The Dolby Digital 5.1 audio track is quite impressive for a children's video, offering rich Surround sound and deep bass. The DVD includes a 32-minute documentary filmed at the School of American Ballet, which should certainly appeal to the film's target audience. —ML

Movie: 𝄞𝄞𝄞 **DVD:** 𝄞𝄞𝄞 ½
Artisan Ent. (cat #12061, UPC 012236-120612). Full frame; widescreen (1.85:1) letterboxed. Dolby Digital 5.1; Dolby 2.0 Surround. $19.98. Keepcase. *LANG:* English. *SUB:* English. *CAP:* English. *FEATURES:* Dancing documentary • Interactive game • 22 chapters.
2001 78m/C D: Owen Hurley; **W:** Linda Engelsiepen, Hilary Hinkle, Rob Hudnut; **V:** Kelly Sheridan, Kirby Morrow, Tim Curry, Peter Kelamis.

Barcelona

Metropolitan's Taylor Nichols and Chris Eigeman star as cousins Ted and Fred. Ted is a businessman satisfied with his place in life, living in a terrific apartment in the city of the title in the 1980s. Fred is a Navy officer who generally doesn't get along with his cousin, but the two manage to agree to stay together. It's not long before all manner of arguments, which are at once both intellectual and immature, crop up. Ted even informs Marta (Sorvino) and Ted's friends that Ted happens to be a follower of the Marquis de Sade. The film does not have a sizable plot, instead allowing these characters to talk, flirt, and maybe, intelligently discuss the little things in life. And there are more substantial issues at work. The image quality is O.K., but merely that—a few noticeable flaws keep it from making that next step from "O.K." The picture looks crisp, but detail is wanting. Other problems arise that cause more concern. The print used is not in optimal condition and there are noticeable marks and specks that pop up more frequently than I'd like to see. Mild grain is also apparent, although inconsistent. Some slight pixelation and edge-

enhancement is also seen and occasionally is lightly distracting. Yet colors actually are pleasant, appearing nicely saturated and crisp, with no smearing or other flaws. Flesh tones look natural and accurate, as well. This is a decent transfer; with the vivid cinematography and beautiful locations, I would have hoped for a bit better effort. Dialogue comes through with satisfactory clarity, although it seemed a bit low at times. The commentary from director Whit Stillman and his stars is one of the more entertaining I've heard recently, as the three are very funny and very detailed in their comments about the making of the picture, providing both informative chat about the locations and the shooting schedule and also throwing in a lot of little jokes. —AB/MM

Movie: 𝄞𝄞𝄞 ½ **DVD:** 𝄞𝄞 ½
Warner (cat #C2513, UPC 0539392513-26). Widescreen (1.85:1) anamorphic. Dolby Digital Surround. $19.98. Snapper. *LANG:* English; French; Spanish. *SUB:* English; French; Spanish; Portuguese. *CAP:* English. *FEATURES:* Commentary: Stillman, Nichols, Eigeman • commentary • Deleted scenes with commentary • Alternate ending with commentary • 32 chapters.
1994 (PG-13) 102m/C Taylor Nichols, Christopher Eigeman, Tushka Bergen, Mira Sorvino, Pep Munne, Francis Creighton, Thomas Gibson, Jack Gilpin, Nuria Badia, Hellena Schmied; **D:** Whit Stillman; **W:** Whit Stillman; **C:** John Thomas; **M:** Tom Judson, Mark Suozzo. *AWARDS:* Ind. Spirit '95: Cinematog.

Bare Witness

Erotic thriller is every bit as generic as its title. Hooker Julie (Larranga) has a hidden video camera and gets the wrong guy on tape. After she's killed, her pal (Everhart) looks to be next on the list. A police detective (Daniel, the beefy Baldwin brother, looking even beefier than usual) falls in love with her, etc., etc. The low-budget, poorly lit image gains nothing on DVD. The slow motion sequences are heavy with artifacts. Overall, audio and visuals are equal to VHS. —MM

Movie: 𝄞𝄞 **DVD:** 𝄞𝄞
Columbia Tristar (cat #07117, UPC 043-396071179). Full frame. Dolby Digital Surround. $24.98. Keepcase. *LANG:* English; French. *SUB:* English; French. *CAP:* English. *FEATURES:* 28 chapters • Previews.
2002 (R) 79m/C Angie Everhart, Daniel Baldwin, Catalina Larranaga; **D:** Kelley Cauthen; **W:** Evan Spiliotopoulos, Anthony Laurence Greene; **C:** Kazuo Minami; **M:** Michael Vista.

Basic Instinct [2 SE]

Controversial thriller had tongues wagging months before its theatrical release. Burnt-out detective Douglas falls for beautiful, manipulative murder suspect Stone, perfectly cast as a bisexual ice queen who may or may not have done the deed. Noted for highly erotic sex scenes and an expensive (3 million bucks) script. The main reason to rebuy *Basic Instinct* is that, since this is the direc-

tor's cut (the older DVD is not), it restores a few seconds here and there to a few of the sex scenes, and of course to the opening murder scene with its brutal face stabbing and icepick-through-the-nose intact. (What's missing is the terrific super-steamy Descriptive Video Service audio track included in the first version.) This new anamorphic transfer improves the sharpness a bit, but overall it's still very short of spectacular. At times the image becomes pretty soft for a second generation DVD of a big-buck feature film. Colors are fine but nothing special, and the soundtrack makes very limited use of the Surround channels except when adding ambience to the Jerry Goldsmith soundtrack. The best feature of the new disc is the half-hour documentary "Blonde Poison," which was produced for this DVD and digs into the film's graphic violence, the outrage it caused in the gay community, and the infamous interrogation scene which revealed Stone's true talents. The commentary by feminist Camille Paglia is a great one and far outshines the one by director Verhoeven and cameraman De Bont. Her commentary is pretty much a two-hour love letter to the film with occasionally riotous and silly observations. There's also a "hidden feature" that even the most inept Easter Egg hunter should have no problem finding. The comparison between the theatrical version and TV version is fairly brief, presenting short scenes and then showing their softened TV equivalents. The TV version must be pretty terrible—the revoiced profanity isn't even performed by the actors, but by artists whose voices don't match in the slightest. The worst feature is the insipid case the DVD comes in, which is molded to hold both the DVD and an icepick pen, and is a challenge to open without dropping one or both on the floor, and the tape glue is hard to remove from the case. —JO/DG

Movie: 𝄞𝄞𝄞 **DVD:** 𝄞𝄞 ½
Artisan Ent. (cat #12065, UPC 01223612-0650). Widescreen (1.85:1) anamorphic. Dolby Digital 5.1; Stereo. $26.98. Special packaging. *LANG:* English. *SUB:* English; French; Spanish. *CAP:* English. *FEATURES:* 26 chapters • Theatrical trailer • Talent files • Commentary: feminist critic Camille Paglia • Commentary: Verhoeven, De Bont • Production notes • Storyboard comparisons • Photo gallery • "Making of" documentary, "Blonde Poison" • Dual-layered RSDL.
1992 123m/C Michael Douglas, Sharon Stone, George Dzundza, Jeanne Tripplehorn, Denis Arndt, Leilani Sarelle Ferrer, Bruce A. Young, Chelcie Ross, Dorothy Malone, Wayne Knight, Stephen Tobolowsky; **D:** Paul Verhoeven; **W:** Joe Eszterhas; **C:** Jan De Bont; **M:** Jerry Goldsmith. *AWARDS:* MTV Movie Awards '93: Female Perf. (Stone), Most Desirable Female (Stone); *NOM:* Oscars '92: Film Editing, Orig. Score.

The Basket [SE]

Tells the story of a Pacific Northwest farming community in 1918 struggling to come to terms with the pain and prejudice of wartime America. Compelling performances and exceptional cinematography weaves unlikely threads of forbidden love, racial tensions, and a new game called basketball into an engaging film. The disc boasts a very good video transfer. While colors are eye-popping and extremely well defined, darker hues exhibit some occasional loss of clarity but, are for the most part, well represented. The soundtrack is similarly impressive and features clear and understandable dialogue as well as a very nicely reproduced musical score. Finally, the disc is augmented by quite a few enjoyable extras. —*MJT*

Movie: 🎬🎬 ½ **DVD:** 🎬🎬🎬
MGM Home Ent. (cat #1003127, UPC 027-616872920). Widescreen (1.85:1) anamorphic. Dolby Digital 5.1 Surround; Dolby Digital 2.0 Surround. $26.98. Keepcase. *LANG:* English; Spanish; French; German. *SUB:* English. *FEATURES:* 26 chapters • Deleted scenes with audio commentary • Behind the Basket—Collection of 6 Unique "Making of" Featurettes • Outtakes • Commentary: director Rich Cowan, D.P. Dan Heigh • Photo gallery • Cast & crew bios and filmographies.
1999 (PG) 104m/C Karen Allen, Peter Coyote, Elwon Bakly, Jack Bannon, Robert Karl Burke, Casey Cowan, Eric Dane, Joey Travolta; **D:** Rich Cowan; **W:** Rich Cowan, Frank Swoboda, Tessa Swoboda; **C:** Dan Heigh.

Basket Case [2 SE]

This Special Edition of Frank Henenlotter's cult favorite corrects the main flaw of the original DVD release (reviewed in *Book 1*). The commentary track by filmmaker Henenlotter, producer Ievins, actress Beverly Bonner, and Scooter McRay goes into the production details that true horror fans love. For the most part, they attempt to explain precisely how they managed to make the movie for $35,000. The new transfer is certainly the best the film has ever looked. It's superior to the theatrical print I saw years ago and to older muddy VHS tapes. It appears to be a bit brighter and sharper than the earlier disc, though of course, the image is still very grainy in several scenes. —*MM*

Movie: 🎬🎬🎬 **DVD:** 🎬🎬🎬 ½
Image Ent. (cat #ID07468CDVD, UPC 014-381074628). Full frame. Dolby Digital Mono. $24.99. Keepcase. *LANG:* English. *FEATURES:* 16 chapters • Commentary • Outtakes and bloopers • "In Search of the Hotel Broslin" featurette • Radio spots and interviews • Clips from Beverly Bonner's cable TV show • Trailers • Liner notes by Vince Bonavoglia.
1982 89m/C Kevin Van Hentenryck, Terri Susan Smith, Beverly Bonner, Robert Vogel, Diana Browne, Lloyd Pace, Bill Freeman, Joe Clarke, Ruth Neuman, Richard Pierce, Dorothy Strongin; **D:** Frank Henenlotter; **W:** Frank Henenlotter; **C:** Bruce Torbet; **M:** Gus Russo.

The Bat [Goodtimes]

Mystery writer Cornelia Van Gorden (Moorehead) has rented a remote mansion for the summer. One night, a prowler called The Bat terrorizes Cornelia and her maid. The sleuth-like novelist decides to set a trap to catch him. Based on the Mary Roberts Rinehart and Avery Hopwood play of the early '20s, this already filmed plot had been so completely absorbed into "B"-movies that our late '50s version dodders listlessly in corridors of the Creaky Story line Rest Home. Featuring Vincent Price, who is neither the lead, nor The Bat. A substandard DVD transfer looks like VHS and the sound is no better. —*MO*

Movie: 🎬 **DVD:** 🎬
Goodtimes Ent. (cat #05-81230, UPC 018-713812308). Full frame. Dolby Digital 2.0 Mono. $24.98. Keepcase. *LANG:* English. *FEATURES:* 12 chapters • Theatrical trailer.
1959 80m/B Vincent Price, Agnes Moorehead, Gavin Gordon, John Sutton, Lenita Lane, Darla Hood; **D:** Crane Wilbur; **W:** Crane Wilbur; **C:** Joseph Biroc; **M:** Louis Forbes.

Batman & Mr. Freeze: Subzero

Released in conjunction with the abysmal *Batman & Robin* feature, this one represents a step backwards for the animated *Batman* franchise. While it's still better than most animated features, it fails to live up to its pedigree. Mr. Freeze (voiced by Michael Ansara) is living a quiet life of solitude in the Arctic with his wife Nora, who has been cryogenically frozen. When an uninvited submarine crashes through the ice and ruptures Nora's freezer unit, Mr. Freeze returns to Gotham City to save her. After consulting with the unscrupulous Dr. Belson (voiced by George Dzundza), Freeze learns that Nora can only be saved by an organ transplant and Barbara Gordon (voiced by Mary Kay Bergman), who is the daughter of police commissioner Gordon—and also happens to be Batgirl—is at the top of the unwilling donor list. When Freeze kidnaps Barbara, Batman (voiced by Kevin Conroy) and Robin (voiced by Loren Lester) must rush to save her. As with the *Batman & Robin* film, *Subzero* offers several elaborate set-pieces which ultimately add up to nothing. The story is rather simplistic and it takes far too long for Batman to join the action. The finale is exciting and well done, but it can't save the film. Also, the animation differs somewhat from *Batman: The Animated Series* in that there is more color here and the use of computer-generated image is very noticeable. In short, this will leave the viewer cold. The DVD offers a superior presentation. The picture is very sharp and clear, showing no grain, distortion, or defects from the source material. The image is stable and the colors are quite good. The Dolby Stereo audio track provides clear dialogue and sound effects, along with realistic music reproduction and solid bass. —*ML*

Movie: 🎬🎬 ½ **DVD:** 🎬🎬🎬
Warner (cat #14996, UPC 085391499-26). Full frame. Dolby Stereo. $19.98. Snapper. *LANG:* English; French; Spanish; Portuguese. *SUB:* English; French; Spanish; Portuguese. *CAP:* English. *FEATURES:* Set-top game • "How to Draw Batman" •

Music montage • Cast & crew • Trailers • 21 chapters.
1997 67m/C D: Boyd Kirkland; **W:** Boyd Kirkland, Randy Rogel; **V:** Michael Ansara, George Dzundza, Mary Kay Bergman, Kevin Conroy, Loren Lester.

Batman Beyond: Return of the Joker [2 Uncut]

In December 2000, Warner released a feature-length episode of the *Batman Beyond* TV show entitled "Return of the Joker" (reviewed in *Book 2*). But Bat-fans knew that this was a censored version and demanded that an uncut DVD be released. And now their demands have been fulfilled with a second release, this one offering an additional seven minutes of footage. The world of *Batman Beyond* takes place many years in the future. Bruce Wayne (voiced by Kevin Conroy), the original Batman, is now very old, and teenager Terry McGinnis (voiced by Will Friedle) has donned the Bat-suit. Batman has been trailing a gang called the Jokerz, who have been committing break-ins at technological firms. The real shock comes when it is learned that The Joker (voiced by Mark Hamill) is behind this gang. The problem is that the original Joker is supposed to be dead. This is superior animation in every way, combining the dark look of *Batman: The Animated Series* with a decidedly anime touch. The animation is powerful, sharp, and always professional looking. This is accented by an engrossing story line which is never boring, and doesn't shy away from violence and mature themes (hence the "PG-13" rating). The only real drawback here is that the film doesn't take any time to explain the back-story of this new Batman, so those unfamiliar with the show may be lost at first. Overall, this is a fantastic movie and a fine introduction to the world of *Batman Beyond*. Despite the fact that the DVD box implies that this feature is full frame, it's presented in a letterbox format. The image is incredibly sharp and clear, showing no grain or defects from the source print. The color scheme, which varies from bright and psychedelic to totally dark, looks fine here, with no bleeding or oversaturation. The Dolby Digital 5.1 audio track provides clear dialogue, impressive Surround sound effects, and a nice bass response. This special-edition DVD is loaded with goodies, including a playful audio commentary by the production team and a behind-the-scenes documentary. —*ML*

Movie: 🎬🎬🎬 ½ **DVD:** 🎬🎬🎬🎬
Warner (cat #22355, UPC 085392235-20). Widescreen (1.85:1) letterboxed. Dolby Digital 5.1. $9.98. Snapper. *LANG:* English. *SUB:* English; French. *CAP:* English. *FEATURES:* Commentary • Behind-the-scenes featurette • Animation tests • Deleted scene • Music video • Character bios • Trivia game • Trailers • 18 chapters.
2000 (PG-13) 77m/C D: Curt Geda; **V:** Will Friedle, Mark Hamill, Kevin Conroy, Melissa Joan Hart.

The Batman Superman Movie

The pairing of two of Warner's most popular characters may seem like a simple marketing ploy, but this joint venture is tons of fun and should appeal to fans of both the Dark Knight and the Man of Steel. The Joker (voiced by Mark Hamill) comes to possess an enormous quantity of Kryptonite and makes a deal with Superman's arch-foe Lex Luthor (voiced by Clancy Brown). The Joker will kill Superman (voiced by Tim Daly) for $1 billion. Then, Bruce Wayne AKA Batman (voiced by Kevin Conroy) arrives in Metropolis for a business meeting with Luthor, unaware that he is actually a criminal mastermind. When the Joker makes his move on Superman, Batman intervenes and saves the Last Kryptonian. They then form an uneasy alliance to bring down the Joker and Luthor. To make things even more complicated, Lois Lane (voiced by Dana Delany) decides to shirk her schoolgirl crush on Superman and falls for Bruce Wayne, much to the chagrin of Clark Kent. The film is well-paced and loaded with action. Its greatest accomplishment is the sly way in which it mingles the lives of the two heroes without ever feeling convoluted (and the inclusion of the Lois Lane factor makes things even more fun). The animation style is also a nice combo of the dark *Batman* series and the brighter *Superman* show. The image is sharp and clear, although there is some slight grain at times. Also, the digital transfer has uncovered some minor defects from the source material. The colors are great and there is no visible artifacting. The Dolby Stereo audio track brings the viewer clear dialogue and sound effects and superb music reproduction. —*ML*
Movie: ♪♪♪ ½ **DVD:** ♪♪♪
Warner (cat #16351, UPC 0853916351-23). Full frame. Dolby Stereo. $19.98. Snapper. *LANG:* English; French; Spanish; Portuguese. *SUB:* English; Spanish. *CAP:* English. *FEATURES:* Set-top game • Producer interview • "How to Draw Batman & Superman" • Music montage • Cast & crew listing • Trailers • 18 chapters.
1997 61m/C D: Toshio Masuda; **W:** Stan Berkowitz, Rich Fogel, Steve Gerber; **V:** Mark Hamill, Clancy Brown, Timothy Daly, Kevin Conroy, Dana Delany.

Batman: The Animated Series—The Legend Begins

In 1992, Warner Bros. set the world of animation and "children's programming" on its ear with the introduction of *Batman: The Animated Series.* The show took the noirish look and feel of the Tim Burton *Batman* films to the extreme, while remaining very faithful to the character's comic book origins. This DVD contains the first five episodes. And while this may not represent the best that the series had to offer (it got better as it went along), these shows are still great examples of the style

and storytelling which took place on this landmark television production. The first episode, "On Leather Wings," pits Batman against his natural enemy, the Man-Bat, a giant bat-like creature who has been robbing pharmaceutical companies. The title "Christmas with the Joker" says it all, as Batman and Robin attempt to find the Joker's hideout and rescue his hostages. "Nothing to Fear" introduces us to the Scarecrow, a villain who uses chemicals to induce his victim's darkest fears. (A much scarier-looking Scarecrow would appear on the show in a later episode.) The Joker returns in "The Last Laugh," as he uses a laughing gas to take over Gotham City. And finally, "Pretty Poison" brings in the lovely but deadly Poison Ivy, as she uses her beguiling ways on both Batman and district attorney Harvey Dent, who would eventually become the deadly Two-Face. The most striking thing about the show is the dark animation, which makes any use of bright colors seemingly leap off of the screen. Also, while this is technically a "kids" show, it doesn't shy away from action or darker subject matter, making it something that adults can enjoy as well. While these shows are very good, the DVD does have some minor problems. The shows are presented in their original full-frame format. The image is sharp, but there is some visible grain. Also, some minor defects from the source material can be seen. On the plus side, the dark imagery looks fine, as the true blacks allow for the best possible picture. The Dolby Stereo audio track provides clear dialogue and music reproduction. —*ML*
Movie: ♪♪♪ **DVD:** ♪♪♪
Warner (cat #22319, UPC 085392231928). Full frame. Dolby Stereo. $19.98. Snapper. *LANG:* English; French; Spanish; Portuguese. *SUB:* English; French; Spanish; Portuguese. *CAP:* English. *FEATURES:* Set-top game • "How to Draw Batman" • Producer interview • 5 chapters.
1992 110m/C

Batman: The Movie

In the best comic book manner, the four most powerful villains in the world team up to take down the world's greatest superhero, and take over the world in the course of it. Catwoman (Meriwether), the Penguin (Meredith), the Joker (Romero), and the Riddler (Gorshin) are making plans to rid themselves of Batman (West) and Robin (Ward) so that they would no longer interfere with their villainous deeds. They kidnap Commodore Schmidlapp (Denny) to lure Batman and then begin setting traps for the caped crusader. Meticulously clean and free of defects, specks, or scratches, the transfer makes watching the film a fun experience. There is hardly any grain, producing a very finely defined picture. Colors are powerful and nicely resemble the color schemes of comic books. No distracting signs of edge-enhancement are evident and the compression is flawless without introducing any signs of digital artifacts. Although slightly dated, the audio is also

surprisingly clean and clear. The frequency response is a bit narrow, creating slightly notched dialogues that appear a bit harsh, and the music also suffers notably from the limited spectrum. The commentary track by West and Ward has generally a laid-back and entertaining quality as the two remember the making of this film. They try to keep the track flowing quite well, although occasionally their discussion breaks up. There is not a lot of technical information, but the wealth of anecdotes and information supplied is thoroughly enjoyable. —*GH/MM*
Movie: ♪♪ ½ **DVD:** ♪♪♪
20th Century Fox (UPC 024543019541). Widescreen (1.85:1) anamorphic. Stereo; Mono. $19.98. Keepcase. *LANG:* English; French. *SUB:* English; Spanish. *FEATURES:* 2 featurettes • 2 photo galleries • Trailer • Teasers.
1966 104m/C Burt Ward, Adam West, Burgess Meredith, Cesar Romero, Frank Gorshin, Lee Meriwether, Alan Napier, Neil Hamilton, Stafford Repp, Madge Blake, Reginald Denny, Milton Frome; **D:** Leslie Martinson; **W:** Lorenzo Semple Jr.; **C:** Howard Schwartz; **M:** Nelson Riddle.

Battle of the Planets, Vol. 1

Rhino Home Video provides a treat to all old-school anime fans by bringing the classic *Battle of the Planets* TV show to DVD. This Japanese series aired in the U.S. beginning in 1978 and introduced a generation to Japanimation. The story deals with G-Force, a group of five teenage orphans who have been recruited to fight an army of alien invaders known as Spectra. Each member of G-Force dresses as a different type of bird, and each has their own vehicle. But their main vessel is the *Phoenix,* a massive spaceship, which has the ability to burst into flames to thwart enemies. Volume One of this series includes two episodes from the show, "Attack of the Space Terrapin" and "Rescue of the Astronauts," each of which feature the G-Force team in action. As if this wouldn't be enough to please fans, Rhino has also included the two corresponding episodes from the Japanese version of the show, which is known as *Gatchaman.* These shows feature slightly altered story lines, with more violence and sexual overtones. Also, the DVD includes one episode of *G-Force,* yet another variation of the program, which aired in the '80s. With *Battle of the Planets,* the image is somewhat soft and there are overt defects from the source print. The Dolby Digital 5.1 audio track also shows problems, as the audio is muffled and the voices echo. On *Gatchaman,* the image is much clearer and both the Japanese and English audio tracks are fine. *G-Force* displays the same blur which was evident on *Battle of the Planets.* This DVD is a must-have for any fan of the show. —*ML*
Movie: ♪♪♪♪ **DVD:** ♪♪♪ ½
Rhino (cat #970008, UPC 6034970008-21). Full frame. Dolby Digital 5.1; Dolby

Digital Mono; Dolby Digital Stereo. $19.99. Keepcase. *LANG:* English; Japanese. *SUB:* English. *FEATURES: Gatchaman* episodes ➠ *G-Force* episode.
1978 120m/C *JP*

Battle of the Planets, Vol. 2

Volume Two of the *Battle of the Planets* series actually improves upon the quality shown in Volume One. As with the first DVD, we are treated to two episodes of *Battle of the Planets*—"The Space Mummy" and "The Space Serpent." Along with this are the two episodes from *Gatchaman*, which are entitled "The Giant Mummy That Calls Storms" and "Revenge of the Iron Monster Mechadegon." The *G-Force* episode shown here actually corresponds to the *Rescue of the Astronauts* show from the Volume One DVD. While the *Battle of the Planets* episodes shown here share the same haze and scratches as those from the first disc, the Dolby Digital 5.1 audio is greatly improved, displaying a nice use of Surround sound. The *Gatchaman* episodes both look and sound fine, while *G-Force* shows grain and slight distortion. Despite any technical flaws with these episodes, the sheer depth of this package makes it worth recommending. —*ML*
Movie: 𝅘𝅥𝅮𝅘𝅥𝅮𝅘𝅥𝅮𝅘𝅥𝅮 *DVD:* 𝅘𝅥𝅮𝅘𝅥𝅮𝅘𝅥𝅮 ½
Rhino (cat #970009, UPC 6034970009-21). Full frame. Dolby Digital 5.1; Dolby Digital Mono; Dolby Digital Stereo. $19.99. Keepcase. *LANG:* English; Japanese. *SUB:* English. *FEATURES: Gatchaman* episodes ➠ *G-Force* episode.
1978 120m/C *JP*

Battle of the Planets, Vol. 3

Rhino brings us another fine set from this classic anime series. And while this edition is as impressive on the technical side as the first two editions, it suffers in the quality of the episodes. The first show presented here, "Ghost Ship of Planet Mir," is the disappointing one. The G-Force team is sent to the planet Mir to investigate a series of shipwrecks. (In the corresponding *Gatchaman* episode, the action takes place on Earth!) From there, they simply fight an alien flying saucer and nothing else happens. The second episode, "Big Robot Gold Grab," is much better and features the G-Force versus Spectra action that made the show worth watching in the first place. Here, the team must stop a robot which is stealing gold reserves. As with the previous volumes, the *Gatchaman* episodes, here entitled "The Ghost Fleet from Hell" and "The Grand Mini Robot," are more entertaining due to the fact that the plot is much more linear and often makes more sense. Also included is an episode of the '80s incarnation of the show, *G-Force*, entitled "The Strange White Shadow," which corresponds to "The Space Mummy" episode from Volume Two. With the two *Battle of the Planets* episodes, the image is fuzzy at times, and

a bit soft. The colors are good for the most part, but can be washed-out in certain scenes. The Dolby Digital 5.1 audio track on both shows sounds tinny (as with Volume One) and doesn't offer much bass. The image improves with the *Gatchaman* shows, as it is clearer, but some video artifacting is evident here. Still, this remains a solid package, comparable to the other volumes in the series. —*ML*
Movie: 𝅘𝅥𝅮𝅘𝅥𝅮𝅘𝅥𝅮 ½ *DVD:* 𝅘𝅥𝅮𝅘𝅥𝅮𝅘𝅥𝅮
Rhino (cat #R2 970010, UPC 603497001-026). Full frame. Dolby Digital 5.1; Dolby 2.0 Surround. $19.99. Keepcase. *LANG:* English; Japanese. *SUB:* English. *FEATURES:* Bonus episodes.
1978 125m/C *JP*

The Bear

This film revolves around a young cub adopted by an older bear that helps protect it during its early time in the wilds. Eventually, the two must face their greatest enemy—hunters. The cinematography is nothing short of stunning—many shots are almost too beautiful for words. Although there's not much in the way of plot, it's a well-done movie and successfully tells a good story with little dialogue. The trained bears do an impressive job, and the movie does a fine job bringing us into their world as well. The image quality is amazing; the film is presented with perfect sharpness and magnificent detail throughout. The natural colors of the wilds look flawless. The audio has a magnificent, expansive feel that really puts the viewer right in the great outdoors. The score is also excellent and comes through with clarity on this DVD. Surrounds are put to use often throughout the movie as well to bring the viewer further into the experience of the wilds. The "making of" featurettes are very good and provide plenty of footage of the production crew at work, along with additional interviews. Although they are certainly promotional in nature, they don't feel that way, and go into good detail about the making of the movie. —*AB/DG* *AKA:* L'Ours.
Movie: 𝅘𝅥𝅮𝅘𝅥𝅮𝅘𝅥𝅮 *DVD:* 𝅘𝅥𝅮𝅘𝅥𝅮𝅘𝅥𝅮 ½
Columbia Tristar Home Video (UPC 43396-039940). Widescreen (2.35:1) anamorphic; full frame. Dolby Digital 5.1 Surround; Dolby Digital Surround. $14.95. Keepcase. *LANG:* English; French; Spanish. *SUB:* English; French; Spanish. *CAP:* English. *FEATURES:* 2 featurettes ➠ Trailers ➠ 28 chapters.
1989 (PG) 92m/C *FR* Jack Wallace, Tcheky Karyo, Andre Lacombe; *D:* Jean-Jacques Annaud; *W:* Gerard Brach, Michael Kane; *C:* Philippe Rousselot; *M:* Bill Conti. *AWARDS: NOM:* Oscars '89: Film Editing.

Bear in the Big Blue House: Potty Time with Bear

This DVD represents another compilation of the popular children's show and contains three episodes. "Potty Time with

Bear" is by far the all-time best episode of the program, as it deals frankly with the issue of toilet-training. By using clever songs and Muppet-magic, this show presents potty-training as a fun and natural process that children shouldn't fear. Also, the "Hey, Hey, Hey, Potty!" song is worth the price of admission alone. Up next is "If at First You Don't Succeed," which examines the idea of practice and dedication. Here, Bear explains to Ojo, Pip, and Pop that it's natural to get frustrated when they can't do something at first, but they should keep trying. Note that words such as "failure" aren't used here. The last episode on the DVD, "Call It a Day," is a huge disappointment, as it appears to be made up mainly of clips from other episodes. The idea of exploring the differences between day and night is good, but fans of the show will be bored by this one. However, the "Potty Time with Bear" episode makes this disc a must-have. The image presented here is crystal-clear, showing no defects or distortion. The colorful characters are one of the great things about this show, and those colors look fantastic here. The 2.0 Surround sound offers clear dialogue and the songs sound great. —*ML*
Movie: 𝅘𝅥𝅮𝅘𝅥𝅮𝅘𝅥𝅮 ½ *DVD:* 𝅘𝅥𝅮𝅘𝅥𝅮𝅘𝅥𝅮 ½
Columbia Tristar (cat #07303, UPC 04339-6073036). Full frame. Dolby 2.0 Surround. $24.95. Keepcase. *LANG:* English. *SUB:* English; Spanish. *CAP:* English. *FEATURES:* Sing-alongs ➠ Bonus trailers.
1999 75m/C

The Beast

Long considered taboo due to its erotic subject matter, this 1975 French film from director Walerian Borowczyk arrives in its uncensored form for the first time. Young heiress Lucy Broadhurst (Lisbeth Hummel) arrives at the de l'Esperance chateau, where she is to marry the young Mathurn de l'Esperance (Pierre Benedetti). After retiring to her room, Lucy finds herself dreaming of the 18th-century lady of the chateau, Romilda de l'Esperance (Sirpa Lane), who according to legend, encountered a wild, sexual monster in the forest near the manor. Was this an isolated incident or does the Beast still roam the grounds? The once shocking sex scenes will be considered quite tame by today's audience, and some of them come across as quite silly. Also, *The Beast* is quite uneven, playing as a farcical comedy or a drama, when the brazen Beast isn't on-screen. This DVD offers a widescreen transfer of the film, which looks pretty good given the film's age. While some damage to the source print is evident, the image is clear and the colors are good. The mono soundtrack provides clear dialogue, but there is some audible hissing on the track at times. —*ML* *AKA:* La Bete.
Movie: 𝅘𝅥𝅮 ½ *DVD:* 𝅘𝅥𝅮𝅘𝅥𝅮 ½
Cult Epics (cat #DVD008, UPC 0633900-10080). Widescreen (1.66:1) letterboxed. Dolby Digital Mono. $24.95. Keepcase. *LANG:* English. *FEATURES:* 12 chapters.

1975 94m/C Sirpa Lane, Lisbeth Hummel, Elizabeth Kaza, Pierre Benedetti, Guy Trejan; **D:** Walerian Borowczyk; **W:** Walerian Borowczyk; **C:** Bernard Daillencourt, Marcel Grignon.

The Beast from Haunted Cave

Gold thieves hiding in a wilderness cabin encounter a spiderlike monster. Surprisingly good performances from Richard Sinatra (Frank's nephew) and Sheila Carol. Director Monte Hellman's debut. The film itself is in good condition, although it exhibits quite a few defects. The print used has some scratches and for extended periods of time, lines run along the side of the frame. Slight registration problems create an image that is almost constantly wavering and in certain shots, grain is quite evident. The contrast is well delineated with deep blacks and good highlights and the compression has been done carefully, without introducing artifacts. The audio has been cleaned up to remove defects and excessive hiss and noise, but sadly this is once again a case where the noise removal has done more damage than good. No high ends are left in the track, creating a very harsh presentation that is overly pronounced in the mid-range. As a result, dialogue is sometimes unintelligible and cannot be understood at all. The dynamics of the track also jump quite a bit creating problems where at times dialogue is clearly too shrill and loud, while at others, is hardly audible at all. —MM/GH

Movie: ♫♫ **DVD:** ♫♫
Synapse (cat #B00004REB9). Widescreen (1.85:1) anamorphic; full frame. Dolby Digital Mono. $24.99. Keepcase. *LANG:* English. *FEATURES:* Trailer.
1960 64m/B Michael Forest, Sheila Carol, Frank Wolff, Richard Sinatra, Wally Campo; **D:** Monte Hellman; **W:** Charles B. Griffith; **C:** Andrew M. Costikyan.

Beast Wars: Transformers, Vol. 1

The classic *Transformers* show from the 1980s is updated for the '90s with a sleek new look and style. This computer-animated show debuted in 1996 and comes from the same animators who created *ReBoot*. While the original incarnation of *Transformers* dealt with robots which could turn themselves into vehicles, this show has robots that turn into various animals, hence the title. This DVD contains the first six episodes of the program, in the original order in which they aired. If you can get past the ludicrous explanation as to why the robots must transform into animals, the show is quite engaging and entertaining. The Predacons and Maxamals are constantly fighting and have now arrived on a planet rich with Energon, the element on which they thrive. So, they fight for supreme control of this planet, using their newfound animal skills in the fight. While the animation may not be up

to the level of today's feature-film fare, it is quite good for a TV show from the mid-'90s. The colors are good, and the images never look "cheap." While some members of Generation X may scoff at this representation of *Transformers,* the show is exciting, witty, and never dull. The DVD offers the six episodes in a full-frame format, and they all look fantastic. The image is incredibly sharp and clear, easily rivaling digital broadcast quality. There is no distortion to the image, nor are there any evident problems from the source material. The digital 5.1 audio track is very powerful, as it offers a steady stream of sound from the rear speakers. However, these Surround effects never overpower the dialogue. There are no extras on this disc. —ML

Movie: ♫♫ ½ **DVD:** ♫♫♫
Rhino (cat #R2 976070, UPC 603497607-020). Full frame. Digital 5.1; Digital 2.0. $19.95. Keepcase. *LANG:* English. *FEATURES:* 36 chapters.
1996 140m/C *CA*

The Beast Within

Combination of Southern Gothic and werewolf tale was one of the first to utilize "bladder" type special effects. A young woman (Besch) is attacked in a Mississippi swamp. Seventeen years later, she and her husband (Cox) return to find out what's wrong with their son (Clemens). DVD clarity makes it even easier to spot the massive continuity error in chapter 11. —MM

Movie: ♫♫ ½ **DVD:** ♫♫ ½
MGM Home Ent. (cat #1002336, UPC 027-616865557). Widescreen (2.35:1) anamorphic. Stereo. $14.95. Keepcase. *LANG:* English. *SUB:* French; Spanish. *CAP:* English. *FEATURES:* 16 chapters.
1982 (R) 98m/C Ronny Cox, Bibi Besch, L.Q. (Justus E. McQueen) Jones, Paul Clemens, Don Gordon, Katherine Moffat, John Dennis Johnston, R.G. Armstrong, Logan Ramsey, Ron Soble, Meshach Taylor; **D:** Philippe Mora; **W:** Tom Holland; **C:** Jack L. Richards; **M:** Les Baxter.

Beastmaster

Phantasm auteur Don Coscarelli shifts gears with this sword & sorcery epic. Dar (Marc Singer) is separated from his parents at birth and raised by a farmer. As he ages, Dar realizes that he has the power to communicate with animals, and that he has a mysterious link with the evil cultster Maax. Dar is soon joined by the lovely Kiri (Tanya Roberts) and an adventurer Seth (John Amos), as he faces many challenges in order to confront Maax and fulfill his destiny. *The Beastmaster* is simply a fun film that never slows down to take a breath. The film mixes action, strange creatures, and sex appeal in a way that few '80s films could. Not as serious as some of the other sword & sorcery films of the time, this one is nonetheless great fun to watch and never fails to entertain. Anchor Bay continues their long line of successes with this DVD. The image looks very sharp and shows few defects.

On the entertaining audio commentary, Coscarelli explains that a few shots do look questionable because the director and the financiers couldn't decide how to shoot the picture! The Dolby Digital 5.1 and DTS 5.1 both sound fine, generating nearly constant Surround sound effects. In addition, the booklet included with this DVD contains a nice overview of the film and offers some obscure trivia facts. —ML

Movie: ♫♫♫ **DVD:** ♫♫♫
Anchor Bay (cat #DV12015, UPC 013131-201598). Widescreen (1.85:1) anamorphic. Dolby Digital Surround EX; 6.1 DTS-ES. $19.98. Keepcase. *LANG:* English. *FEATURES:* Commentary • Theatrical trailer • Behind-the-scenes footage • Still gallery • Talent bios • 26 chapters.
1982 (PG) 119m/C Marc Singer, Tanya Roberts, Rip Torn, John Amos, Josh Milrad, Billy Jacoby, Ben Hammer; **D:** Don A. Coscarelli; **W:** Don A. Coscarelli, Paul Pepperman; **C:** John Alcott; **M:** Lee Holdridge.

The Beatles: A Celebration

This cheap, lackluster Beatles documentary features some interesting pictures and other documents that take the viewer through a superficial history of the band. There is none of the band's music and the narration is a bit overdone, but the biggest problem is a slow pace. The video quality varies throughout—although it's never unwatchable, the disc sports a soft and occasionally hazy image. The audio is as variable as the picture. The narration sounds fine, but some of the interviews are thin and harsh. The bonus footage included is simply a little less than two minutes worth of old news footage of the band. —AB/DG

Movie: ♫♫ **DVD:** ♫ ½
Delta/Laserlight (UPC 018111999038). Full frame. Mono. $9.99. Keepcase. *LANG:* English. *SUB:* Spanish; Chinese.
1996 56m/C

Beautiful Beast

Continues Toei's *XX* series of female assassin movies. The mysterious Chinese warrior woman known as Black Orchid arrives in Japan and rubs out mob boss Ishizuka. Fleeing the scene, she hides out with bartender Yoichi Fujinami. Ishizuka's second is hot for revenge. She's come on a personal vendetta against Ishizuka and yakuza boss Ho for murdering her little sister. However, she finds that Ho is not as easy to kill, and Yoichi becomes torn between helping his old pal Yaguchi and the mystery girl that he's falling in love with. Foregoes a lot of empty soft-core sex in favor of providing more action. Director Toshiharu Ikeda is no John Woo, but at least Black Orchid's trunk full of high-powered weaponry provides a little fun. Image and sound are clean. —BT *AKA:* XX: Utukushiki Gakuen; XX Beautiful Beast.

Movie: ♫♫ **DVD:** ♫♫
Central Park/U.S. Manga (cat #APCD2083, UPC 719987208322). Full frame. Dolby

Digital Stereo. $29.99. Keepcase. *LANG:* English; Japanese. *SUB:* English. *FEATURES:* 6 chapters ✱ Character profiles ✱ Trivia quiz ✱ Trailers.
1995 87m/C *JP* Kaori Shimamura, Takanori Kikuchi, Hakuryu, Minako Ogawa; *D:* Toshiharu Ikeda; *W:* Tamiya Takehashi, Hiroshi Takehashi; *C:* Seizo Sengen.

Beautiful Creatures

Fitful comic thriller follows the adventures of Petula (Weisz, unfortunately blonde) and Dorothy (Lynch), two Glasgow lasses with abusive boyfriends. Dorothy escapes a beating from Tony (Glen), only to wind up aiding Petula who's being attacked by Brian (Mannion). Brian dies and the two women decide to make it look like he's been kidnapped and held for ransom. Then a crooked detective (Norton) enters the scene. The overall image is fairly sharp but for a few soft-focus scenes. Colors are solid and accurate as well—although somewhat drab given the setting of Glasgow, Scotland. Black levels are fairly good with only the darkest scenes losing detail. But the transfer does suffer from a few problems as well. Edge-enhancement and compression artifacts are in evidence and the picture is quite grainy, with a surprising number of blemishes for such a recent theatrical release. On the whole, a run-of-the-mill DVD transfer. Audio is presented in both Dolby Digital and DTS 5.1 mixes. As is increasingly the case on these dual format releases, the listener will be hard pressed to find any substantial differences between the two soundtracks. In any case, this isn't really the type of film to take full advantage of a 5.1 mix. The soundstage is firmly anchored to the front speakers with the Surrounds kicking in for the odd musical passage. —*MM/MP*
Movie: 🎬🎬 ½ *DVD:* 🎬🎬 ½
Universal Studios (cat #21262, UPC 0251-92126222). Widescreen (1.85:1) anamorphic. Dolby Digital 5.1 Surround Stereo; DTS 5.1. $26.98. Keepcase. *LANG:* English. *SUB:* French. *CAP:* English. *FEATURES:* 18 chapters ✱ Trailer ✱ Production notes ✱ Talent files.
2000 (R) 88m/C *GB* Rachel Weisz, Susan Lynch, Alex Norton, Iain Glen, Maurice Roeves, Tom Mannion; *D:* Bill Eagles; *W:* Simon Donald; *C:* James Welland; *M:* Murray Gold.

Beautiful Hunter

Shion has been raised since birth to be the perfect assassin and executioner for the Magnificat crime family, a devoutly Catholic gang that do their criminal business in the vestments of priests and nuns. Blind Father Kano fully controls the life of his adopted daughter, until photographer Ito gets photos of her. Sent to collect his evidence, the lethal yet naïve heroine finds herself attracted to Ito, but Father Kano isn't quite so happy about her new boyfriend, and sends Sister Mitsuko and a squad of killers after them. Shion is subjected to a rather elaborate torture ses-

sion in the priory basement, which is outfitted with all manner of bondage gear. Kuno looks—well, beautiful, in and out of a series of foxy outfits, but doesn't display any kind of martial arts to convince us of her master assassin status. The transfer is beautiful, too. What did you expect? —*BT* **AKA:** *XX Beautiful Hunter.*
Movie: 🎬🎬 *DVD:* 🎬🎬
Central Park/U.S. Manga (cat #APCD2154, UPC 719987215429). Full frame. Dolby Digital Stereo. $29.99. Keepcase. *LANG:* English; Japanese. *SUB:* English. *FEATURES:* 11 chapters ✱ Trailers ✱ Character profiles ✱ Trivia quiz.
1994 91m/C *JP* Makiko Kuno, Koji Shimizu; *D:* Masaura Konuma.

Because Why?

Alex has been away from his home town for five years, traveling the world. He returns to find everyone he knew gone, and has to try to find a place to fit in. Image quality is good, while the sound is average for a film of this type. —*BT*
Movie: 🎬🎬 ½ *DVD:* 🎬🎬 ½
Vanguard Intl. Cinema (cat #VF0226, UPC 658769022636). Full frame. $29.95. Keepcase. *LANG:* English. *FEATURES:* 11 chapters.
1993 104m/C *CA* Michael Riley, Martine Rochon, Doru Bandol, Heather Mathieson; *D:* Arto Paragamian; *W:* Arto Paragamian; *C:* Andre Turpin; *M:* Nana Vasconcelos.

The Bedroom

An extra on this disc describes Japanese "pink" films as the rough equivalent of the American exploitation and soft-core films that grew out of the demise of the studio system. In Japan the films are short (little more than an hour long) and filled with as much nudity and sexual content as possible. That certainly describes this entry which has to do with a drug (Halcyon in the film; "hallusion" on the box copy) that renders women unconscious. It's a bit more graphic than late-night cable fare, also more surreal and fetishistic. Sets are minimal; lighting is rough; sound is clear; subtitles are often incoherent. Overall, image is about equal to tape. The spiral of drugs, madness, and death never comes close to *In the Realm of the Senses.* —*MM* **AKA:** *Shisenjiyou No Aria.*
Movie: 🎬🎬 ½ *DVD:* 🎬🎬 ½
Screen Edge Video (cat #EDGE08D, UPC 5060029700089). Widescreen letterboxed. $24.98. Keepcase. *LANG:* Japanese. *SUB:* English. *FEATURES:* 12 chapters ✱ History of "pink" film movement ✱ Director bio and filmography ✱ Stills.
1992 63m/C *JP* Kiyomi Ito, Momori Asano, Kyoko Nakamura, Issei Sagawa; *D:* Hisayasu Sato; *W:* Shiro Yumeno.

Beethoven's 4th

They say that you can't keep a good man down, and this rule apparently applies to huge, unruly dogs as well. Yes, that lovable St. Bernard Beethoven is back for a

fourth installment of this film series. This one finds the awesome canine still living with the Newton family, as seen in *3rd*. As Beethoven is known to wreak havoc around the house (such as ripping the seats off of toilets), the Newtons are at a loss as to how they can control him. Imagine their surprise when Beethoven suddenly becomes very well behaved. Has obedience school actually paid off? No, Beethoven has switched places with an affluent dog named Michelangelo. The mistaken-identity hijinks continue as kidnappers attempt to capture the dog they believe to be Michelangelo. *4th* is a strictly "by the books" direct-to-video family film. It's pretty and everything happens in the right order, but it's also vacuous and predictable. That's a sad statement, considering that director David Mickey Evans wrote the moving *Radio Flyer* and created the fun *The Sandlot*. Younger children will enjoy, but all others need not apply. This unspectacular film looks quite good on DVD, as the image is clear and sharp, showing no defects or distracting grain. A great deal of attention has been paid to the colors, and the palette is very accurate. The Dolby 5.1 Surround track is clear with no distortion, and an appropriate amount of ambient sound from the rear speakers. —*ML*
Movie: 🎬🎬 *DVD:* 🎬🎬🎬
Universal Studios (cat #21266, UPC 0-25192-12662-8). Widescreen (1.85:1) anamorphic. Dolby Digital 5.1. $24.98. Keepcase. *LANG:* English; French; Spanish. *SUB:* English. *CAP:* English. *FEATURES:* Production notes ✱ Bonus trailer ✱ 18 chapters.
2001 94m/C Judge Reinhold, Julia Sweeney, Joe Pichler, Michaela Gallo; *D:* David Mickey Evans.

Behind Enemy Lines

Jingoistic flag-waver is loosely based on the real story of an American military pilot who was shot down during the war in Bosnia. In this version, Owen Wilson is an unlikely but acceptable action hero. He plays Chris Burnett, who sees something he's not supposed to see while on a reconnaissance mission. Evil Serbs shoot down his fighter. While he's trying to get out of the country, his commanding officer, Capt. Reigert (Hackman), must negotiate the treacherous waters of UN diplomacy (embodied in de Almeida), and help his pilot. If you examine the action critically, it adds up to little more than running through the woods, and Wilson does it well. More important to the film's purposes, lots of stuff blows up real good. On their commentary track, director Moore and editor Smith tacitly admit that their post-production work was hurried as the studio wanted to get the film into theatres while patriotic fervor swirling around the events of 9/11/01 was as hot as possible. That's also part of the reason that the ending was clipped short to give the film a happier feel. Their commentary also dwells on the problems that filmmakers face when

they try to cram as much "R"-rated violence as possible into a "PG-13" rating. DVD re-creates the image with a bit more brightness and clarity than was seen in the theatrical release. The cold blue-black color scheme is lighter. Both the Dolby 5.1 and DTS Surround tracks are more effective than the theatrical sound. —MM
Movie: 𝄞𝄞 ½ *DVD:* 𝄞𝄞𝄞 ½
20th Century Fox (UPC 024543038023). Widescreen (2.35:1) anamorphic. Dolby Digital 5.1 Surround; DTS Surround; Dolby Surround. $27.98. Keepcase. *LANG:* English; Spanish. *SUB:* English. *CAP:* English. *FEATURES:* Behind-the-scenes featurette • 7 extended and deleted scenes • 2 commentary tracks.
2001 (PG-13) 106m/C Owen C. Wilson, Gene Hackman, Joaquim de Almeida, David Keith, Gabriel Macht, Charles Malik Whitfield, Olek Krupa, Vladimir Mashkov, Marko Ogonda; *D:* John Moore; *W:* David Veloz, Zak Penn; *C:* Brendan Galvin; *M:* Don Davis.

Behind Locked Doors

Detective Ross Stewart (Carlson) fakes mental illness to have himself committed to a sanitarium where he believes a crooked judge is hiding. It's a fine low-budget noir that mixes period humor with some genuine suspense and strong visuals. The heavily shadowed black-and-white photography is crisp and properly detailed throughout. The sound may strike contemporary viewers as weak but it's accurate. —MM
Movie: 𝄞𝄞 ½ *DVD:* 𝄞𝄞𝄞
Kino on Video (cat #K154, UPC 7383290-15428). Full frame. $29.95. Keepcase. *LANG:* English. *FEATURES:* 12 chapters.
1948 61m/B Lucille Bremer, Richard Carlson, Tor Johnson, Douglas Fowley, Herbert (Hayes) Heyes, Ralf Harolde; *D:* Budd Boetticher; *W:* Eugene Ling, Malvin Wald; *C:* Guy Roe; *M:* Irving Friedman.

Behind Office Doors

Please see *Pre-Code Hollywood: Vol. 3, "Behind Office Doors."*
Movie: 𝄞𝄞
1931 82m/B Mary Astor, Robert Ames, Ricardo Cortez, Charles Sellon; *D:* Melville Brown; *W:* Carey Wilson.

Bela Lugosi Double Feature: The Corpse Vanishes / Invisible Ghost

In the Monogram cheapie *The Corpse Vanishes*, Dr. Lorenz (Lugosi) abducts stricken brides and uses them to create a serum that keeps his wife (Russell) young. It's completely inept but absolutely irresistible. The film itself is ridiculous and irredeemable but it's frequently hilarious and unbelievably loopy. To add to the lunacy, Russell and Lugosi both sleep in twin coffins! If only most comedies were *this* funny.... Both *Corpse* and *Invisible Ghost* (please see review of another edition) are

fairly uniform in print quality. The transfers were taken from scratchy, damaged 16mm prints and are frequently grainy, bleary, and soft. The sound is particularly bad; it's so muffled and crunchy, it sounds like it's emanating from a squawk box. —DG
Movie: woof *DVD:* 𝄞
Marengo Films (cat #MRG-0001, UPC 807013000122). Full frame. Mono. $14.98. Keepcase. *LANG:* English.
2001 128m/C

Bela Lugosi Meets a Brooklyn Gorilla

Mitchell and Petrillo—Dean Martin and Jerry Lewis clones—get lost in the jungle where they meet mad scientist Lugosi. Astonishingly, this ridiculous excuse for a comedy is even worse on the screen than it is in synopsis. DVD is virtually pristine. It looks like it might have been created from elements that were projected once and then locked away for half a century. Given the abysmal nature of the material, that would have been completely just and appropriate. —MM *AKA:* The Boys from Brooklyn; The Monster Meets the Gorilla.
Movie: woof *DVD:* 𝄞𝄞 ½
Image Ent. (cat #ID8696CODVD, UPC 014-381869620). Full frame. Dolby Digital Mono. $24.98. Keepcase. *LANG:* English. *FEATURES:* 16 chapters • Trailer • Interview with Sammy Petrillo.
1952 74m/B Bela Lugosi, Duke Mitchell, Sammy Petrillo, Charlita, Martin Garralaga, Al Kikume, Muriel Landers, Milton Newberger; *D:* William Beaudine; *W:* Tim Ryan; *C:* Charles Van Enger; *M:* Richard Hazard.

Belle de Jour

Based on Joseph Kessel's novel, one of director Buñuel's best movies has all his characteristic nuances: the hypocrisy of our society; eroticism; anti-religion. Deneuve plays Severine, a chic, frigid Parisian newlywed, who decides to become a daytime prostitute, unbeknownst to her husband. Buñuel blends reality with fantasy, and the viewer is never sure which is which in this finely crafted movie. While there are a few noticeable signs of aging courtesy of the source print, the disc provides well-defined blacks and colors. No distortion is present on the French language track. The often silly English dubbed track should be avoided on principle alone. —MJT
Movie: 𝄞𝄞𝄞 ½ *DVD:* 𝄞𝄞𝄞
Buena Vista Home Ent. (cat #24739, UPC 786936169881). Widescreen (1.66:1) letterboxed. Dolby Digital Mono. $32.99. Keepcase. *LANG:* French; English. *SUB:* English. *FEATURES:* 19 chapters • Commentary: Buñuel scholar Julie Jones • Original U.S. theatrical trailer • 1995 rerelease trailer • Miramax trailer gallery.
1967 (R) 100m/C *FR* Catherine Deneuve, Jean Sorel, Genevieve Page, Michel Piccoli, Francesco Rabal, Pierre Clementi, Georges Marchal, Françoise Fabian; *D:* Luis Buñuel; *W:* Luis Buñuel, Jean-Claude Carriere; *C:* Sacha Vierny.

Benji [Ventura]

The Image release of this kid's fav (reviewed in *Book 1*) gets a light nod over this bare-bones edition simply because it comes with a menu. Otherwise, full-frame image and sound are about equal. —MM
Movie: 𝄞𝄞𝄞 *DVD:* 𝄞𝄞
Ventura Distribution (cat #124, UPC 8093-91012407). Full frame. Stereo. $19.95. Keepcase. *LANG:* English.
1974 (G) 87m/C Benji, Peter Breck, Christopher Connelly, Patsy Garrett, Deborah Walley, Cynthia Smith; *D:* Joe Camp; *W:* Joe Camp; *C:* Don Reddy; *M:* Euel Box. *AWARDS:* Golden Globes '75: Song ("I Feel Love"); *NOM:* Oscars '74: Song ("Benji's Theme (I Feel Love)").

Benny Hill Golden Greats

This two-disc set combines material that has been released on tape under the titles *Benny Hill: Golden Chuckles, Golden Guffaws, Golden Laughs, Golden Smiles, Golden Sniggers, Golden Yucks,* and *Benny Hill: The World's Favorite Clown.* I thought I had seen most of the British comedian's skits on various late-night broadcasts but much of this material was new to me. For fans, the material is terrific—inspired slapstick, sight gags, and sexual humor. Benny Hill deserves to be ranked up there with Sid Caesar and Milton Berle as an innovator who understood TV comedy and created some routines that will always inspire laughter. Feminists who object to Hill's understanding of the advantages that women have over men have never appreciated him, and these discs probably won't change their minds. That's their loss. DVD is a nice package. The image is clear but on the light side and lacking depth, basically all you should expect from '80s TV. A few inconsequential glitches appear in a couple of the production numbers. The "favorite scenes" option arranges material from the shows by theme. The thumbnail biography combines text and narration. —MM
Movie: 𝄞𝄞𝄞 *DVD:* 𝄞𝄞𝄞
HBO (cat #99245, UPC 026359924521). Full frame. Mono. $39.98. Boxed set. *LANG:* English. *FEATURES:* 106 chapters in programs • "Benny Hill: The World's Favorite Clown" documentary • Favorite scenes • Thumbnail bio • Photo gallery.
1989 398m/C *GB* Benny Hill; *W:* Benny Hill.

Best Men

An uneven mixture of dark comedy and family drama marks this engaging tale of a groom (Wilson) trying to get to the church on time on the day that he is released from prison in the small town where he grew up. Thwarting him are his four buddies, first Billy (Flanery, most notable for his role as Young Indiana Jones) asks to be dropped off at the bank for some cash. Things get more complicated when he turns out to be a bank robber known as Hamlet and it just goes downhill from there. One by one, the men go looking for Billy, until presto, instant small-town siege. Oh yeah, and

Billy's dad (Ward) is the sheriff. The FBI shows up, the bride shows up, and most of all Brad Dourif shows up. (His character is self-described as "What people commonly refer to as a disgruntled Vietnam vet.") Along for the ride are Wilson's Marine buddy (Cain), who has been recently discharged from the Marines, and the friend/lawyer whose ineptitude put Wilson in jail in the first place. This is not a perfect film but has some memorable moments. The disc looks really good with rich colors and clear sound. —CA **AKA:** Independence.

Movie: 🎬🎬 ½ **DVD:** 🎬🎬🎬 ½
MGM Home Ent. (cat #1003341, UPC 027-616874900). Widescreen (2.35:1) anamorphic; full frame. Dolby Digital Surround 5.1. $14.95. Keepcase. *LANG:* English. *SUB:* English; French; Spanish. *CAP:* English. *FEATURES:* 16 chapters.
1998 (R) 89m/C Sean Patrick Flanery, Dean Cain, Luke Wilson, Andy Dick, Mitchell Whitfield, Drew Barrymore, Fred Ward, Raymond J. Barry, Brad Dourif, Art Edler Brown, Tracy Fraim; **D:** Tamra Davis; **W:** Art Edler Brown, Tracy Fraim; **C:** James Glennon; **M:** Mark Mothersbaugh.

The Best of Resfest: Resfest Shorts 1

An assortment of 16 animated and live-action films from Res Fest, an innovative traveling international festival of film, video, and design. From the satirical propaganda of "Pasta for War" (directed by Zack Schlappi) to the stop-motion action of "Max" (by "AWOL"), these are the voices of the future. Full frame image is generally very good. The main benefit of DVD is access to individual films. —JE
Movie: 🎬🎬 ½ **DVD:** 🎬🎬🎬
Palm Pictures (cat #3041, UPC 66020-0304126). Full frame. $19.95. Keepcase. *LANG:* English. *FEATURES:* Commentary: director.
2002 C

The Best of the Blues Brothers

Oh how I wish John Belushi were still with us. His early death robbed us not only of his comic genius, but the Blues Brothers. This look back by Rhino is a must-have for anyone who loved *Saturday Night Live*, John Belushi, and Dan Aykroyd. It needs to be remembered that these two talented comics and musicians produced the album *A Briefcase Full of Blues*, which went double platinum and gave us a great movie and a fantastic soundtrack. Drop this disc in and sit back and let the remembrances of great talent wash over you. DVD image quality is quite good, even the early tape from *Saturday Night Live*. The sound is very good capturing the tin side of TV and the fullness of in concert sound. —DE
Movie: 🎬🎬🎬 ½ **DVD:** 🎬🎬🎬
Rhino (cat #972779, UPC 603497277926). Full frame. Dolby 5.1 Surround. $14.98. Keepcase. *LANG:* English. *FEATURES:* 15 chapters • Blues Brothers Trivia • Selective discography.

1993 60m/C John Belushi, Dan Aykroyd, Tom Davis; **W:** Dan Aykroyd, Tom Davis.

The Best of Tromadance

Independent short films are assembled under the umbrella of Troma Studio's unique alternative decay. Though I'm not a huge fan of their Z-movie efforts to replace Roger Corman as this century turns (with films such as *Toxic Avenger* and *Tromeo and Juliet*), I have to admit that they have managed to assemble a truly high quality and hilarious group of shorts, the best being "Please Kill Mr. Kinski," a nine-minute account of how the director of *Crawlspace* (David Schmoeller) was nearly driven to do just that—with previously unseen footage of actor Klaus Kinski at his most impossible. Among others, "The Psychotic Odyssey of Richard Chase," "Zit-lover," and "H.R. Pukenshette" also go where angels fear to tread. Excellent DVD transfer and sound. —MO
Movie: 🎬🎬🎬 **DVD:** 🎬🎬🎬 ½
Troma Team Video (cat #9039, UPC 7903-57903931). Full frame. $14.95. Keepcase. *LANG:* English. *FEATURES:* 11 film chapters • Lloyd Kaufman (Tromadance assembler) featurette • Filomographies • Troma Team theatrical trailers.
2002 180m/C D: Lloyd Kaufman.

Best Seller

Dennis Meechum (Dennehy) is a cop turned author and Cleve (Woods) is an assassin who wants a book written about his career and corruption in politics. Against his better judgment, Meechum agrees to write the book, but Cleve uses the research to find the men he wants to kill. When the bad guys figure out what's going on, they kidnap Meechum's daughter. That's right, they're bad. And sneaky too. Woods works a little too hard here to make his character mean and creepy and Dennehy is just walking through, taking home a check. If it were a movie of the week it would be impressive, but as it is, about the only missing cliché is a stressed out weepy wife for Meechum. But she died long before the story begins. The sound and picture qualities are a little below par, but so is the whole movie, so it kind of fits. —JAS
Movie: 🎬🎬 **DVD:** 🎬🎬 ½
MGM Home Ent. (cat #1003505, UPC 027-616876553). Full frame; widescreen anamorphic. Dolby Digital. $14.95. Keepcase. *LANG:* English; French; Spanish. *SUB:* English; French; Spanish. *FEATURES:* 16 chapters • Original theatrical trailer.
1987 (R) 112m/C James Woods, Brian Dennehy, Victoria Tennant, Paul Shenar, Seymour Cassel, Allison Balson, George Coe, Anne Pitoniak; **D:** John Flynn; **W:** Larry Cohen; **C:** Fred Murphy; **M:** Jay Ferguson.

Better Dayz

Another tale of life in the 'Hood, where the good people try to stay away from drugs and gangs. Faye (Cargle) is working

towards a college scholarship, but might be held back by her no-good brother and her new mobster boyfriend. The picture is grainy and lacks focus, but is still much better than the sound. —BG
Movie: 🎬 **DVD:** 🎬
York Ent. (cat #YPD-1189, UPC 7507231-18925). Full frame. Dolby Stereo. $14.99. Keepcase. *LANG:* English. *SUB:* Spanish. *FEATURES:* 30 chapters • Trailers.
2002 101m/C Erik Williams, Shantel Cargle, Rich Odell; **D:** Norman C. Linton; **W:** Norman C. Linton; **C:** Brenden Flint.

Beverly Hills Bordello

Late-night cable series may gain a hint of clarity on DVD, but only a hint. This collection of four episodes looks fine. A fair amount of grain leads to artifacts in the few establishing shots. Both the people and the sets are attractive and brightly lit. The stories are excuses for fairly energetic writhings that are handled with soft-focus romanticism. Disc is a barebones presentation with no menu. Contents: "The Bachelor Party," "Things Your Wife Won't Do," "Janet and the Professor," "Research." A second volume (cat. #YPD-1049) has identical production values; contents: "Taboo," "Adultery Cyber Style," "Wish List," "The Witness."
Movie: 🎬🎬 **DVD:** 🎬🎬 ½
York Ent. (cat #YPD-1050, UPC 75072310-5024). Full frame. Dolby Digital 5.1 Surround. $14.98. Keepcase. *LANG:* English.
2001 90m/C Gabriella Hall, Monique Parent, Debra Summers, Shauna O'Brien, Alexis Blair, Chris Kapanke; **D:** Jon Burroughs; **C:** Conrad Dobler; **M:** Herman Beeftink.

Beverly Hills Cop [CE]

One of Eddie Murphy's best makes a delightful debut on DVD. He plays Axel Foley, a Detroit police detective who goes to Beverly Hills in a battered Chevy Nova to investigate the murder of a high school friend. The culture clash between the politically sensitive, white-wine sipping local cops (Reinhold and Ashton) and the Rust Belt refugee generates some grand comic moments. The first scene between Axel and Serge (Pinchot) is still one of the funniest moments ever put on screen. Director Martin Brest revisits the film on his commentary track and often sounds as astonished and delighted by his work as any fan taking another look after a long absence. In fact, Brest often goes silent and appreciates the comedy. Image is fine but anyone expecting the high polish of contemporary star vehicles will be disappointed. Sound is fine. —MM
Movie: 🎬🎬🎬 ½ **DVD:** 🎬🎬🎬 ½
Paramount (cat #01134, UPC 097360113-440). Widescreen anamorphic. Dolby Digital 5.1 Surround Stereo; Dolby Digital Surround; Stereo. $24.99. Keepcase. *LANG:* English; French. *SUB:* English. *CAP:* English. *FEATURES:* 11 chapters • Commentary: director • Cast and crew interview • Casting featurette • Music featurette • Location map • Photo gallery • Trailer.

1984 (R) 105m/C Eddie Murphy, Judge Reinhold, John Ashton, Lisa Eilbacher, Ronny Cox, Steven Berkoff, James Russo, Jonathan Banks, Stephen Elliott, Bronson Pinchot, Paul Reiser, Damon Wayans, Rick Overton; **D:** Martin Brest; **W:** Danilo Bach, Dan Petrie Jr.; **C:** Bruce Surtees; **M:** Harold Faltermeyer. *AWARDS: NOM:* Oscars '84: Orig. Screenplay.

Beverly Hills Cop 2

Highly successful sequel spins essentially the same plot, only this time, Axel Foley (Murphy) is dealing with a band of international thieves and arms smugglers. DVD image is fine, as good as any big-budget studio production from 1987. The 5.1 remix is way better than the theatrical release. The deleted scene was wisely cut. —*MM*
Movie: ♪♪ ½ **DVD:** ♪♪♪ ½
Paramount (cat #01860, UPC 0973601-86048). Widescreen anamorphic. Dolby Digital 5.1 Surround; Dolby Surround; Stereo. $24.99. Keepcase. *LANG:* English; French. *SUB:* English. *CAP:* English. *FEATURES:* 13 chapters ● Interviews ● "Making of" featurette ● Deleted scene ● Music featurette ● Trailer.
1987 (R) 103m/C Eddie Murphy, Judge Reinhold, Juergen Prochnow, Ronny Cox, John Ashton, Brigitte Nielsen, Allen (Goorwitz) Garfield, Paul Reiser, Dean Stockwell, Chris Rock, Gil Hill, Robert Ridgely, Gilbert Gottfried, Todd Susman, Robert Pastorelli, Tommy (Tiny) Lister, Paul Guilfoyle, Hugh Hefner; **D:** Tony Scott; **W:** Larry Ferguson, Warren Skaaren; **C:** Jeffrey L. Kimball; **M:** Harold Faltermeyer. *AWARDS: Golden Raspberries '87: Worst Song ("I Want Your Sex"); NOM:* Oscars '87: Song ("Shakedown").

Beverly Hills Cop 3

Alex Foley (Murphy) finds yet another case that takes him back to his pals on the Beverly Hills P.D. This time, he uncovers a criminal network fronting WonderWorld, an amusement park with a squeaky-clean image. Fast-paced action, lots of gunplay, and the star wisecracking his way through the slow spots. DVD delivers everything that you'd expect from a hit movie with a roman numeral on the end of the title. Image and sound are flawless. So? —*MM*
Movie: ♪ ½ **DVD:** ♪♪ ½
Paramount (cat #32219, UPC 09736322-1944). Widescreen anamorphic. Dolby Digital 5.1 Surround; Dolby Digital Surround; Stereo. $24.98. Keepcase. *LANG:* English; French. *SUB:* English. *CAP:* English. *FEATURES:* 14 chapters ● Trailer ● Interviews.
1994 (R) 105m/C Eddie Murphy, Judge Reinhold, Hector Elizondo, Timothy Carhart, Stephen McHattie, Theresa Randle, John Saxon, Alan Young, Bronson Pinchot, Al Green, Gil Hill; **D:** John Landis; **W:** Steven E. de Souza; **C:** Mac Ahlberg; **M:** Nile Rodgers.

Beverly Hood

Offensive and stereotype-riddled take on the Beverly Hillbillies mythos. Although some might find this kind of humor enjoyable, the lack of technical prowess displayed by the filmmakers makes it a near complete waste of time. A poor video transfer features muted colors and darker colors that display little or no definition. The soundtrack fares better but it's still rather awful (dialogue is coarse and occasionally completely unintelligible). The musical score is the only aspect that doesn't seem to suffer. —*MJT*
Movie: ♪ ½ **DVD:** ♪
York Ent. (cat #YPD1147, UPC 75072311-4729). Full frame. Dolby Digital 5.1 Surround. $14.99. Keepcase. *LANG:* English. *SUB:* Spanish. *FEATURES:* 24 chapters ● Star filmographies ● Trailer gallery.
1999 (R) 90m/C Arif S. Kinchen, Buddy Lewis, Kym E. Whitley, Leila Arcieri, Lavell Crawford; **D:** Tyler Maddox-Simms; **W:** Tyler Maddox-Simms, Melissa Balin, Yolanda Sherman, Troy Stroud; **C:** Christopher Poncin.

Beyond Barbed Wire

Heartfelt documentary tells the story of the Japanese-Americans (who mostly detested that hyphenated status) who fought in the 442 Division. These were young men who were sent to "assembly centers" and "pioneer communities" (as our government called the concentration camps where Americans of Japanese descent were sent in 1942) and then volunteered to fight. The filmmakers use the same techniques seen in the HBO series *Band of Brothers*, combining contemporary (late 1990s) interviews with the surviving veterans and archival footage of their combat action. The quality of the older film varies; the new stuff looks fine. The disc also contains a pristine version of the fictional film *Go for Broke* (reviewed in *Book 2*) and three short films about the internment produced by the War Dept. This is a terrific disc for any fan or student of war movies. —*MM*
Movie: ♪♪♪ ½ **DVD:** ♪♪♪ ½
VCI (cat #8272, UPC 089859827228). Full frame; widescreen (1.66:1) letterboxed. Dolby Digital Mono. $24.99. Keepcase. *LANG:* English. *FEATURES:* 13 chapters, *Beyond Barbed Wire* ● 12 chapters, *Go for Broke* ● Short films: "Japanese Relocation," "Challenge to Democracy" ● Previews ● Filmmakers' bios.
1997 88m/C D: Steve Rosen; **W:** Steve Rosen; **C:** Steve Rosen; **Nar:** Noriyuki "Pat" Morita.

Beyond Suspicion

Video premiere is a solid thriller that actually contains some great elements and dark, gritty moments of real mystery. Jeff Goldblum is good as insurance salesman John Nolan, who assumes another identity, but this is yet another film that is ultimately destroyed by Anne Heche's inability to play believable characters. The characters in this story are clearly too complex for her to grasp, which is actually a compliment to the film and its script—albeit hardly to the actress. The definition and sharpness of the transfer is extremely good and it is also mostly free of edge-enhancement, creating a very solid look. The presentation is also free of blemishes, giving the image a very clean and stable look throughout. Colors are beautifully rendered and powerful without ever being oversaturated. The blacks in the transfer are very deep, giving outstanding depth to the image itself, while the compression, too, is without any artifacts or problems. The 5.1 track is nicely produced. Surrounds are used frequently and effectively, but are never obtrusive. —*GH*
AKA: Auggie Rose.
Movie: ♪♪ ½ **DVD:** ♪♪♪
20th Century Fox (cat #2001986). Widescreen (1.85:1) letterboxed. Dolby Digital 5.1 Surround Stereo; Dolby Digital Surround. $34.98. Keepcase. *LANG:* English; French. *SUB:* English; Spanish. *CAP:* English. *FEATURES:* Alternate ending ● 3-minute featurette ● Commentary: director Matthew Tabak, Jeff Goldblum ● Commentary: Matthew Tabak, producer Daniel Stone.
2000 108m/C Jeff Goldblum, Anne Heche, Timothy Olyphant, Nancy Travis, Richard T. Jones, Kim Coates, Joe Santos; **D:** Matthew Tabak; **W:** Matthew Tabak; **C:** Adam Kimmel; **M:** Don Harper, Mark Mancina.

Beyond the Law

Ex-undercover cop Danny Saxon (Sheen) is recruited by the FBI to infiltrate a biker gang involved in drugs and gun smuggling. But he finds himself being drawn into the unconventional lifestyle and a friendship with the leader, Blood (Madsen). Clumsy and derivative video premiere gains nothing on DVD. No-frills disc is identical to VHS tape. —*MM* **AKA:** Fixing the Shadow.
Movie: ♪ ½ **DVD:** ♪♪
Artisan Ent. (cat #11798, UPC 01223611-7988). Full frame. Dolby Digital Surround. $14.98. Keepcase. *LANG:* English. *CAP:* English. *FEATURES:* 26 chapters ● Talent files ● Production notes.
1992 (R) 101m/C Charlie Sheen, Michael Madsen, Linda Fiorentino, Courtney B. Vance, Leon Rippy, Rip Torn; **D:** Larry Ferguson; **W:** Larry Ferguson; **C:** Robert Stevens; **M:** Cory Lerios, John D'Andrea.

Beyond Tomorrow

Please see review for *A Classic Christmas.*
Movie: ♪♪
1940 84m/B Richard Carlson, Sir C. Aubrey Smith, Jean Parker, Charles Winninger, Harry Carey Sr., Maria Ouspenskaya, Rod La Rocque; **D:** Edward Sutherland; **W:** Adele Comandini; **C:** Lester White.

The Bible

The book of Genesis is depicted in episodic, poetic vignettes illustrating the stories of Adam and Eve, Cain and Abel, Sarah and Abraham, The Tower of Babel, Noah's Ark, and others. The common wisdom with *The Bible* is to say that John Huston makes a great Noah but the rest of the show is a saggy mess that isn't saved by great performances from the likes of George C. Scott and Ava Gardner. John Huston is a great filmmaker but it is true that some of his latter-day efforts have an air of indifference about them, as if they had been conceived as a way to shore up the director's gambling debts. The look is still big-budget glossy, and many scenes, like the Tower of Babel, use very elaborate production values, but the impact on the screen just isn't there. DVD is a great improvement on earlier home video incarnations. The widescreen laserdisc of more than 15 years ago was a washed-out, colorless failure. Visually, this is still not a dazzling experience, but I have to guess that the original roadshow might have looked very similar. —GE

Movie: 🎬🎬 ½ *DVD:* 🎬🎬 ½
20th Century Fox (UPC 24543020790). Widescreen (2.35:1) anamorphic. Dolby Digital 5.1 Surround Stereo. $19.98. Snapper. *LANG:* English. *FEATURES:* Trailer.
1966 174m/C Michael Parks, Ulla Bergryd, Richard Harris, Stephen Boyd, George C. Scott, Ava Gardner, Peter O'Toole, Franco Nero, John Huston; *D:* John Huston; *W:* Christopher Fry, Vittorio Bonicelli; *C:* Giuseppe Rotunno; *M:* Toshiro Mayuzumi; *Nar:* John Huston. *AWARDS:* NOM: Oscars '66: Orig. Score.

Big Bad Mama 2

So what if the title character (Dickinson) was dead at the end of the first movie? Picky, picky, picky! On his commentary track, director Wynorski breezes right past that little detail and focuses largely on his better memories of the production. He doesn't make too much of this little low-budget effort, and he even deflects most criticism of the DVD image by noting when he was losing sunlight. That's why two consecutive shots in the same scene look markedly different. Overall, image is fine, and the disc is unusually well-produced for a Corman production, with smoothly transitioning menus. —MM

Movie: 🎬🎬 *DVD:* 🎬🎬 ½
New Concorde (cat #NH20285 D, UPC 736991428591). Full frame. $14.98. Keepcase. *LANG:* English. *FEATURES:* 18 chapters • Commentary: Jim Wynorski • Interview with Roger Corman • Trailers.
1987 (R) 85m/C Angie Dickinson, Robert Culp, Danielle Brisebois, Julie McCullough, Bruce Glover, Jeff Yagher, Jacque Lynn Colton, Ebbe Roe Smith, Charles Cyphers; *D:* Jim Wynorski; *W:* Jim Wynorski, R.J. Robertson; *C:* Robert New; *M:* Chuck Cirino.

The Big Bird Cage

Jack Hill's spoofy sequel to *The Big Doll House* is still one of the best Philippine babes-behind-bars exploitation flicks. Check out the early '70s fashions—bell-bottoms, hip huggers, and hot pants. The humor is broad and ribald with Rocco, the gay guard suffering a fate worse than death—actually a couple of fates worse

than death. Bizarre moments are sprinkled throughout, none stranger than the scene where one skinny inmate slathers her body with chicken fat, and runs naked through a coconut-filled river. On his 30-years-after-the-fact commentary track, Hill remembers the film with fondness and has good stories to tell. There's not much in visual terms for DVD to work with but this is still the best-looking version of the film I've seen in theatres or home video. —MM
AKA: Women's Penitentiary 2.
Movie: 🎬🎬🎬 *DVD:* 🎬🎬🎬
New Concorde (cat #NH20119 D, UPC 736991411999). Full frame. $14.98. Keepcase. *LANG:* English. *FEATURES:* Commentary: Jack Hill • 24 chapters • Trailers • Talent files.
1972 (R) 93m/C Pam Grier, Sid Haig, Anitra Ford, Candice Roman, Teda Bracci, Carol Speed, Karen McKevic, Vic Diaz; *D:* Jack Hill; *W:* Jack Hill; *C:* F. Sacdalan; *M:* William Allen Castleman, William Loose.

The Big Broadcast of 1938

In one half of his dual role, Fields is the owner of an ocean liner which he enters in a transatlantic race. The ship can convert the electricity from radio broadcasts into power for its airplane-like propellers. No, it doesn't make any sense, as it's just an excuse for various radio stars to show off their routines in the ship's entertainment room. Hope, in his first feature, sings his Oscar-winning signature tune "Thanks for the Memories" and he really does it well. According to one of the featurettes on another disc in this Bob Hope Collection, he got the role after Jack Benny turned it down. DVD image is superb. There are virtually no signs of wear. The black-and-white photography is crisp and very well detailed. Mono sound is equally clear. If only all films this old looked this good. Disc also contains *College Swing*. (Please see review.) Curiously, you cannot switch from one to the other without removing the disc from the player. —MM
Movie: 🎬🎬 *DVD:* 🎬🎬🎬
Universal Studios (cat #21462, UPC 025-192146220). Full frame. Dolby Digital Mono. $24.98. Keepcase. *LANG:* English. *SUB:* French; Spanish. *CAP:* English. *FEATURES:* 18 chapters • Production notes • Talent files.
1938 94m/B W.C. Fields, Martha Raye, Dorothy Lamour, Shirley Ross, Russell Hicks, Bob Hope, Ben Blue, Leif Erickson; *D:* Mitchell Leisen; *W:* Walter DeLeon, Francis Martin; *C:* Harry Fischbeck; *M:* Boris Morros, Ralph Rainger, Leo Robin. *AWARDS:* Oscars '38: Song ("Thanks for the Memories").

Big Empty

Neo-noir is a solid addition to the field. Lloyd Matthews (writer McManus) is a private eye who's burned out on divorce work when he's hired by a suspicious wife (Goldwasser) to find the truth about her too-good-to-be-true husband (Bryan). Compar-

isons to Coppola's *The Conversation* are not out of place. DVD can't do much for the image. This one has an indie-prod look with pale color and understated lighting, but it's handled with real style by director Perez. He and McManus combine deadpan humor with a real understanding of their material. I could have done without McManus's *Pulp Fiction* hairdo, but that's a quibble. This one's a sleeper. Find it. —MM
Movie: 🎬🎬🎬 *DVD:* 🎬🎬🎬
Vanguard Intl. Cinema (cat #VF0186, UPC 658769018639). Full frame. $29.95. Keepcase. *LANG:* English. *FEATURES:* 11 chapters • Trailer • Commentary: McManus, Perez • Behind-the-scenes rough footage.
1998 93m/C James McManus, Pablo Bryant, Ellen Goldwasser, H.M. Wynant; *D:* Jack Perez; *W:* James McManus; *C:* Shawn Maurer; *M:* Jean-Michael Michenaud.

Big Fella

Please see review of *Song of Freedom*.
Movie: 🎬🎬 ½
1937 73m/B GB Paul Robeson, Elisabeth Welch, Eldon Grant; *D:* J. Elder Wills; *W:* Ingram D'Abbes, Fenn Sherie; *C:* Cyril Bristow; *M:* Eric Ansell.

The Big Heat

When police detective Bannion's (Ford) wife (Brando, sister of Marlon) is killed in an explosion meant for him, he pursues the gangsters behind it and uncovers a police scandal. His appetite is whetted after the discovery and he involves mobster Vince Stone's (Marvin) brassy moll Debby (Grahame). Seminal film noir hasn't lost a step. DVD exhibits very mild flaws—light flecks and snow—that are unimportant. One of the best. —MM
Movie: 🎬🎬🎬 ½ *DVD:* 🎬🎬🎬
Columbia Tristar (cat #06532, UPC 04339-6065321). Full frame. Dolby Digital Mono. $24.98. Keepcase. *LANG:* English; French. *SUB:* English; French; Spanish; Portuguese; Chinese; Korean; Thai. *CAP:* English. *FEATURES:* 28 chapters • Vintage advertising and trailers.
1953 90m/B Glenn Ford, Lee Marvin, Gloria Grahame, Jocelyn Brando, Alexander Scourby, Carolyn Jones; *D:* Fritz Lang; *W:* Sydney Boehm; *C:* Charles B(ryant) Lang Jr.

The Big Hit [2 SB]

The "Superbit" edition of this featherweight action thriller (first reviewed in *Book 1*) loses the French language and two commentary tracks. It's got more subtitles and even more intense sound effects. If there were any visual flaws, I could not see them. The first DVD release is superior to the version I saw in the theatre. This disc is noticeably better, though it is one of the first I've viewed on a widescreen monitor, and so perhaps I'm easily impressed. —MM
Movie: 🎬🎬 ½ *DVD:* 🎬🎬🎬 ½
Columbia Tristar (cat #08835, UPC 0433-96088351). Widescreen (1.85:1) anamorphic. Dolby Digital 5.1 Surround; DTS Sur-

round. $27.95. Boxed keepcase. *LANG:* English. *SUB:* English; French; Spanish; Portuguese; Chinese; Korean; Thai. *FEATURES:* 28 chapters.
1998 (R) 91m/C Mark Wahlberg, Lou Diamond Phillips, Bokeem Woodbine, Antonio Sabato Jr., Christina Applegate, Avery Brooks, China Chow, Lainie Kazan, Elliott Gould, Lela Rochon, Sab Shimono; *D:* Kirk Wong; *W:* Ben Ramsey; *C:* Danny Nowak; *M:* Graeme Revell.

Biker Zombies

What happens when a John Hughes film clashes with a George Romero movie? A huge mess, that's what. *Biker Zombies* (AKA *Biker Zombies from Detroit*) attempts to meld a teenage drama with a "NC-17"-caliber zombie film with disastrous results. The film opens with an unidentified presence (Satan?) wandering the streets of Detroit, possessing "evil" people. (This presence is illustrated via Steadi-cam and an incredibly distorted voiceover.) As an example of where *Biker Zombies* is headed, this scene lasts about 10 minutes and is incredibly boring. The scene then shifts to Grosse Pointe, Michigan, where teen Ken (Tyrus Woodson) has just moved to town. He finds the other kids to be stuck-up until he meets Courtney (Jillian Buckshaw) and strikes up a relationship. We eventually learn that the "evil" folks from the beginning have become a zombie biker gang (although we're never told why they've become a zombie biker gang). Why not zombie flight attendants?) and the two story lines intersect near the end of the movie. But by that time, any interest in this snoozefest has long since vanished. The teen angle is unoriginal and contrived, while the zombie aspect is silly and confusing. (This is the sort of film where a character is shown reading *Fangoria* magazine, in hopes that the movie will look hip...or get free publicity.) Also, please note that the 76-minute running time is very misleading, as the film is full of padding and the slowly crawling end credits last about 5 minutes. The film was shot on digital video and for the most part, the image looks fine. It shows little evidence of video distortion or artifacting, although there are some incidences of these problems. The colors are good and the daytime scenes are very clear. The audio is another story altogether. The DVD is listed as having a Digital 5.1 Stereo Surround Sound mix. The problem is that what would normally be the center channel track comes out of all five speakers. So, yes, the viewer is surrounded by sound, but it is quite disorienting. —*ML*
AKA: Biker Zombies from Detroit.
Movie: woof *DVD:* ♪ ½
Spectrum Films (cat #DA3835, UPC 7335-65338355). Widescreen (1.85:1) letterboxed. Digital 5.1 Stereo Surround. $24.99. Keepcase. *LANG:* English. *FEATURES:* Trailer ⬤ Still gallery.
2001 76m/C Tyrus Woodson, Jillian Buckshaw; *D:* Todd Brunswick; *W:* John Kerfoot.

Bikini Med School / Bikini House Calls

Combine a couple of cheap sets, a stripper who keeps her clothes on mostly, bad jokes, and a few tame sex scenes and you've got two of the worst movies ever made with the word "bikini" in the title. So much of the same or similar footage is also used in both that the two movies are essentially identical and neither gains anything on DVD. Titles are part of the "All Night Movies" collection. —*MM*
Movie: ♪ *DVD:* ♪
BCI-Eclipse (cat #44109-9, UPC 7873644-10996). Full frame. $9.98. Keepcase. *LANG:* English. *FEATURES:* 10 chapters, *Med School* ⬤ 11 chapters, *House Calls.*
1998 87m/C Kim (Kimberly Dawn) Dawson, Tamara Landry, Thomas Draper, Sean Abbananto; *D:* Michael Paul Girard; *W:* Michael Paul Girard; *C:* Denis Maloney; *M:* Miriam Cutler.

Bill & Ted's Bogus Journey

Big-budget sequel to B & T's first movie has better special effects and about the same number of laughs. Slain by look-alike robot duplicates from the future, our subgenius heroes pass through heaven and hell before tricking the Grim Reaper into bringing them back for a second duel with their most heinous terminators. Most excellent closing montage. DVD does a fine job with the film's funky neon-pastel future, grubbier present, and the afterlife. Grain in the night scenes comes from the original. Sound is very good. —*MM*
Movie: ♪♪ ½ *DVD:* ♪♪ ½
MGM Home Ent. (cat #1002727, UPC 027-616869258). Widescreen (1.85:1) anamorphic. Dolby Mono. $14.98. Keepcase. *LANG:* English; French; Spanish; Portuguese. *SUB:* English; French; Spanish; Portuguese. *CAP:* English. *FEATURES:* Featurette ⬤ 2 trailers ⬤ 16 chapters.
1991 (PG) 98m/C Keanu Reeves, Alex Winter, William Sadler, Joss Ackland, Pam Grier, George Carlin, Amy Stock-Poynton, Hal Landon Jr., Annette Azcuy, Sarah Trigger, Chelcie Ross, Taj Mahal, Roy Brocksmith, William Shatner; *D:* Peter Hewitt; *W:* Chris Matheson, Edward Solomon; *C:* Oliver Wood; *M:* David Newman.

Bill & Ted's Excellent Adventure

The years have been kind to this sweet-natured comedy about a couple of loveable doofuses (or should that be doofi?) who must save the world by passing history. Bill (Winter) and Ted (Reeves) are guided on this quest by Rufus (Carlin) who transports them in his telephone booth/time machine to visit the old west, ancient Greece, and the Middle Ages. Many have worked with similar "dumb" comic material in the years since but seldom with such breezy pleasing results. DVD delivers a most excellent image; not that the limited

special effects really need it. The 5.1 sounds way better than it did in theatres. Party on! —*MM*
Movie: ♪♪♪ *DVD:* ♪♪ ½
MGM Home Ent. (cat #1002728, UPC 027-616869265). Widescreen (2.35:1) anamorphic. Dolby Digital 5.1 Surround Stereo. $14.98. Keepcase. *LANG:* English. *SUB:* English; French; Spanish. *CAP:* English. *FEATURES:* Trailer ⬤ 16 chapters.
1989 (PG) 105m/C Keanu Reeves, Alex Winter, George Carlin, Bernie Casey, Dan Shor, Robert V. Barron, Amy Stock-Poynton, Ted Steedman, Terry Camillieri, Rod Loomis, Al Leong, Tony Camilieri; *D:* Stephen Herek; *W:* Chris Matheson, Edward Solomon; *C:* Tim Suhrstedt; *M:* David Newman.

Billy Bragg & Wilco: Man in the Sand

This documentary is not always terribly interesting and not always completely informative about its subject, but the film's peaceful, relaxed nature and the heart and spirit of the performers still make it more than worthwhile viewing. It focuses on the work of singer/songwriter Woody Guthrie. Thirty years after Woody's passing, daughter Nora Guthrie brought in British songwriter Billy Bragg to record and sing some of the thousands of Woody's songs that have recently been discovered, leading to the album *Mermaid Avenue.* Stretches of the early part of the film take too long trying to develop a look at the music of Guthrie through the opinions of others, but doesn't give the viewer enough direct information about his work. The narration of daughter Nora Guthrie presents us with more interesting and engaging information about what his music means to people. The passion of the musicians shines through, but a better film may have had it shining even brighter. The film is obviously a fairly low-budget affair with some well-preserved stock footage. The result varies somewhat throughout the presentation—occasionally some of the shots look soft, but mostly, the film looks crisp and clear. The audio track is a notch above the picture quality. The musical score and performances are certainly the most important element, and they come through quite well, sounding clear and easily understood. —*AB/DG AKA:* The Making of Mermaid Avenue.
Movie: ♪♪ ½ *DVD:* ♪♪♪
Rykodisc USA (UPC 660200303327). Widescreen (1.77:1) anamorphic. Dolby Digital Surround. $24.95. Keepcase. *LANG:* English. *FEATURES:* Direct song access ⬤ Artist discographies.
2001 89m/C

Billy Liar

Billy Fisher (Courtenay) is a youthful clerk with a big problem. Absorbed by a fantasy where he imagines himself the president of a country called Ambrosia, the immature Billy is so dissatisfied with his life in a dismal Yorkshire town that he fabricates all kinds of unsupportable and embarrassing lies. Only when the gorgeous, adventurous Liz (Christie) comes back to town, willing to run away to London with him to start a real life together, does the vocally ambitious Billy's character even begin to come into focus. The photography is remarkable, and the wide anamorphic screen is essential to "get" all of the fantasy moments that pop in and out. Schlesinger does a lot of literal "architectural" framing on the crumbling streets with walls coming down and new structures being built in their place, and only in the widescreen can you even begin to become comfortable with the show. Add to that 16:9 enhancement, and the disc is a stunner. An excerpt from a British BBC show, *Hollywood U.K.: British Cinema in the Sixties,* shows not only Schlesinger and his collaborators Waterhouse and Hall, but snippets of new interviews with Courtenay and (a still-arresting) Christie, and provides even more great background on the picture. Avoid the well-cut trailer until you see the film because it's something of a spoiler. Courtenay and Christie join Schlesinger for an audio commentary track, which is fairly absorbing. —GE

Movie: 𝄢𝄢𝄢 ½ **DVD:** 𝄢𝄢𝄢𝄢
Criterion (cat #121, UPC 037429159224). Widescreen (2.35:1) anamorphic. Dolby Digital Mono. $39.95. Keepcase. *LANG:* English. *SUB:* English. *FEATURES:* Commentary: Courtenay, Christie, Schlesinger • Excerpts from *Northern Lights* • Trailer • 16 chapters • Liner notes by A.O. Scott • Liner notes by Bruce Goldstein.
1963 94m/B *GB* Tom Courtenay, Julie Christie, Finlay Currie; **D:** John Schlesinger; **W:** Willis Hall, Keith Waterhouse; **C:** Denys Coop; **M:** Richard Rodney Bennett.

Bingo Long Traveling All-Stars & Motor Kings

In 1939, ace pitcher Bingo Long (Williams) and catcher Leon Carter (Jones) organize a traveling team of black baseball players to compete with the Negro League. Eventually, they prove so popular that the league arranges a challenge game to settle the matter. The film has aged beautifully. Its reputation as a pioneering "black" film has never been questioned. What may surprise even its fans is what a terrific baseball picture it is. Part of director Badham's commentary track is essentially an introduction to the game. He sounds comfortable and seems to enjoy a trip back to one of his better early efforts. He also says that Billy Dee Williams's character is based on Satchel Paige and Jones's Carter is a thinly disguised Josh Gibson. DVD image is very good, actually excellent considering the film's age. It re-creates a slightly soft, pastel image that's perfect for a period piece. Surface damage is almost non-existent. Mono sound is fine. Admittedly, I'm not an objective reviewer here; this is one of my favorites. —MM
Movie: 𝄢𝄢𝄢 ½ **DVD:** 𝄢𝄢𝄢 ½
Universal Studios (cat #21773, UPC 0251-92177323). Widescreen (1.85:1) anamor-

phic. Dolby Digital Mono. $19.98. Keepcase. *LANG:* English. *SUB:* Spanish; French. *CAP:* English. *FEATURES:* 18 chapters • Commentary • Production notes • Talent files • Trailer • DVD-ROM features.
1976 (PG) 111m/C Billy Dee Williams, James Earl Jones, Richard Pryor, Stan Shaw; **D:** John Badham; **W:** Matthew Robbins, Hal Barwood; **C:** Bill Butler; **M:** William Goldstein.

Bio-Dome

While trying to find a restroom, extremely stupid buddies Shore and Baldwin get sealed inside a scientifically created "pure environment." Immediately, they trash the place, much to the aggravation of the team of scientists. Insane plotting and stupid dialogue permeate the film, not to mention Shore's lame gimmick and Baldwin's lame attempt at Shore's gimmick. Its only redemption is the soundtrack, highlighted by a performance from Tenacious D (featuring Jack Black), which shows off the good Surround mix. The transfer is pristine. Regardless of the audio and video quality, however, please stay away. —DRL
Movie: woof **DVD:** 𝄢𝄢 ½
MGM Home Ent. (cat #100342, UPC 0276-16874917). Widescreen (1.85:1) anamorphic. Dolby 5.1 Surround; Dolby Stereo Surround. $14.95. Keepcase. *LANG:* English; French; Spanish. *SUB:* English; French; Spanish. *CAP:* English. *FEATURES:* Theatrical trailer • 16 chapters.
1996 (PG-13) 94m/C Pauly Shore, Stephen Baldwin, William Atherton, Henry Gibson, Joey Lauren Adams, Teresa Hill, Kylie Minogue, Kevin West, Denise Dowse, Dara Tomanovich; **D:** Jason Bloom; **W:** Kip Koenig, Scott Marcano; **C:** Phedon Papamichael; **M:** Andrew Gross. *AWARDS:* Golden Raspberries '96: Worst Actor (Shore).

Biozombie

Playing as a mixture of *Mallrats* and *Dawn of the Dead,* this Hong Kong import is aimed squarely at a Generation-X audience. The film introduces us to Woody (Jordan Chan) and Bee (Sam Lee), two slackers who work at a video store. While on an errand to pick up their boss's car, they hit a strange pedestrian and take him back to the mall. This stranger turns out to be a zombie, and he soon infects several others. With the mall locked up for the night, Woody and Bee must take it upon themselves to protect the few humans remaining...while doing the least amount of work possible. The film turns into a true rollercoaster ride, as we start with the comedic opening, then move into the action-horror, and finally, a very nihilistic ending. The image is sharp and clear, but the transfer has exposed some defects in the low-budget film. Scratches and white blemishes from the source print are noticeable at times, and there is some overt grain during the brightly lit scenes. The colors are true and realistic for the most part, but things do appear slightly blanched in some

scenes. However, taking the film's origins into consideration, this is probably the best that the film has ever looked. Stereo offers clear, audible dialogue and sound effects, in both the original Cantonese dialogue track, or with an English dubbed version (which, for once, isn't all that bad). The English subtitles are in white with a black backing and easy to read. There are some typos, but they appear to be fairly accurate. —ML
Movie: 𝄢𝄢 ½ **DVD:** 𝄢𝄢 ½
Media Blasters (UPC 631595010688). Full frame. Dolby Digital Stereo. $24.98. Keepcase. *LANG:* Cantonese; English. *SUB:* English. *FEATURES:* Still gallery • Trailers.
1998 94m/C *HK* Jordan Chan, Sam Lee; **D:** Wilson (Wai-Shun) Yip.

Bite the Bullet

In the first decade of the 20th century, a newspaper promotes a 700-mile endurance horse race that attracts adventurers, gamblers, cowboys, and wannabes from across the globe. News magnate Jack Parker (Coleman) enters a picked rider on his champion steed, and a real knight, Sir Norfolk (Bannen) arrives with his English riding gear and a hearty attitude. Punk Carbo (Vincent) arrogantly thinks he has what it takes to win, and aging cowpoke "Mister" (Johnson) signs on because he desperately wants to be somebody before he dies. Miss Jones (Bergen) is an ex-prostitute who may have an ulterior motive for giving the race a go. A Mexican vaquero (Arteaga) needs the money for his family. Gambler Luke Matthews (Coburn) has foolishly bet his bankroll on winning; he and horse-loving, thoughtful Sam Clayton (Hackman) are ex–Rough Riders with differing philosophies of life. When the grueling race begins, it's a test of both beast and character. This still may be not the "real" West, but even in its glorification, the film abandons the usual western movie vendettas and shootouts in favor of details and events that are far more credible than fast guns or moral mythmaking. We do get a little gunplay in the last act, but the main delight of the show is watching men and horses go through the physical beating of a race that we feel, the kind of thing that can't be faked in CGI. Ace cameraman Harry Stradling Jr. uses long lenses but few zooms and stays away from the filters that mar some contemporary period pictures. DVD is a no-extras beauty. As with many a superior film ghetto-ized in home video by the unimpressive stats from an unimportant theatrical run, this picture deserves the great transfer it's been given. One reason it failed at the boxoffice was its ill-conceived ad campaign: the illustration on the insert sheet shows the faux-Remington picture of galloping horses with our stars' foolish faces pasted in. Audiences in 1975 rejected what looked like a very corny picture. Columbia does great work with their transfers, but still needs better proofreaders; multiple Oscar winner and Hollywood writer/director legend Richard Brooks is clumsily misidentified as Robert Brooks on the package text.

Movie: 🐾🐾🐾 ½ **DVD:** 🐾🐾🐾
Columbia Tristar (cat #07761, UPC 04339-6077614). Widescreen (2.35:1) anamorphic; full frame. Dolby Digital Mono. $19.98. Keepcase. *LANG:* English. *SUB:* English; French; Spanish; Portuguese; Chinese; Korean; Thai. *CAP:* English.
1975 (PG) 131m/C Gene Hackman, James Coburn, Candice Bergen, Dabney Coleman, Jan-Michael Vincent, Ben Johnson, Ian Bannen, Paul Stewart, Sally Kirkland, Mario Arteaga; *D:* Richard Brooks; *W:* Richard Brooks; *C:* Harry Stradling Jr.; *M:* Alex North. *AWARDS: NOM:* Oscars '75: Sound, Orig. Score.

Black and Blue

Determined to rid his neighborhood of the influences of gang violence, RoRo (Burce) organizes law-abiding citizens to reclaim their turf. A valiant effort done on video with an extremely clean and bright DVD transfer. Director Hollins shows his competence in film language as much as his screenplay suffers. Matters aren't helped by his cast. Still, it seems likely you'll see Hollins's name on tomorrow's television dramas. Decent sound, too. —*MO*
Movie: 🐾🐾 ½ **DVD:** 🐾🐾🐾
York Ent. (cat #YPD1100, UPC 75072311-0028). Full frame. 5.1 Stereo Surround Sound. $14.99. Keepcase. *LANG:* English. *FEATURES:* 24 chapters ⬤ Theatrical trailer.
2001 105m/C Cedric Pendleton, Angela Ardis, Cedric Moore, Steve Burce; *D:* William A. Hollins; *W:* William A. Hollins; *C:* Leroy Patton; *M:* Ricky Keller, Oliver Wells.

The Black Cat / The Fat Black Pussycat

These two '60s rarities are astonishing. In *The Black Cat,* young drunken Southern husband Lou (Frost) is more interested in his various pets than in his blonde wife. His many problems find a focus in Pluto, the feline of the title. The updated story sticks fairly close to Poe—much closer than Roger Corman did in his more successful contemporaneous adaptations—even though the film features a rocking bar-band version of "Candy." *Fat Black Pussycat* posits a psycho killer who's running amuck among the beatniks of Greenwich Village. The camp humor value is incalculable. Look for Geoffrey Lewis and Hector Elizondo making their cinematic debuts in small roles. Both black-and-white films look remarkably good. *Fat Black* is the sharper of the two, with higher production values. The odd bits of dust show up and there are a few registration blips, but nothing serious. Considering the age of these two, image quality is excellent. Mono sound delivers easily understandable dialogue. —*MM*
Movie: 🐾🐾🐾 **DVD:** 🐾🐾🐾
Image Ent. (cat #ID0797SWDVD, UPC 014-381079722). Widescreen (1.85:1) letterboxed; full frame. Dolby Digital Mono. $19.98. Keepcase. *LANG:* English. *FEATURES:* 15 chapters ⬤ 7 deleted scenes from *Fat Black Pussycat* ⬤ Trailers for cat-

themed films ⬤ Cat-girl short film ⬤ Gallery of exploitation art ⬤ Radio spots.
1965 73m/B Robert Frost, Robyn Baker, Sadie French, Anne MacAdams; *D:* Harold Hoffman; *W:* Harold Hoffman; *C:* Walter Schenk; *M:* Scotty McKay.

The Black Cobra

After photographing a psychopath in the process of killing someone, a beautiful woman seeks the help of a tough police sergeant (Williamson) to protect her. DVD is simply awful. It contains some of the heaviest artifacts you'll ever see. Weak sound wavers its wan on the *Dealin' Dirty* collection. —*MM* **AKA:** *Cobra Nero.*
Movie: woof **DVD:** woof
BCI-Eclipse (cat #44295-9, UPC 7873644-29592). Full frame. $9.98. Keepcase. *LANG:* English. *FEATURES:* 12 chapters.
1987 (R) 90m/C *IT* Fred Williamson, Karl Landgren, Eva Grimaldi; *D:* Stelvio Massi.

Black Godfather

JJ (Perry) works his way to the top of a drug-selling mob. It's a fairly standard gangster story made on a low budget. The image is very grainy, making DVD no better than tape, beyond the curious extras. —*MM*
Movie: 🐾 ½ **DVD:** 🐾🐾
BCI-Eclipse (cat #44115-9, UPC 787364-411597). Full frame. $9.98. Keepcase. *LANG:* English. *FEATURES:* 6 chapters ⬤ "Spooking about Africa" cartoon ⬤ Trivia game ⬤ DVD dictionary ⬤ DVD-ROM features.
1974 (R) 90m/C Rod Perry, Damu King, Don Chastain, Jimmy Witherspoon, Diane Summerfield; *D:* John Evans; *W:* John Evans; *C:* Jack Steely.

Black Hawk Down

Based on actual events, this intense, violent action film follows a group of U.S. soldiers on a disastrous mission. During a well-planned seek-and-capture mission in Somalia, one of the powerful Black Hawk support helicopters is shot down. As things proceed to go horribly awry, the group of lost and confused soldiers tries to make its way back to base while fighting off vengeful mobs of highly armed native militia. It's a gripping, frequently terrifying illumination of little-known recent history. It frequently plays like a modern update of *Zulu Dawn* as the scattered soldiers are besieged by thousands of furious, machine gun-toting Africans. Moment-to-moment reality is the focus here, and the well-chosen settings and air of human confusion only amplify the believability of the enacted events. The film shows what good work that slickmeister producer Jerry Bruckheimer *(Pearl Harbor, Armageddon)* is capable of if given a good script and fine director. The epilogue features some awkward cliché spouting, but it's a minor quibble. The film has a very stylized, occasionally grainy look and the disc captures the variant tones and photographic techniques perfectly. Faces are sharp and well defined,

and the colors are strong. The Surround mix is of demo quality; sound effects, dialogue, and the terrific score are carefully balanced to sweep viewers into the story and make them feel as if they're in the middle of it. The featurette is just under a half hour and utilizes some excellent behind-the-scenes footage of both the film's production and the Ranger training the cast underwent. Excellent and worthwhile. —*DG*
Movie: 🐾🐾🐾 ½ **DVD:** 🐾🐾🐾 ½
Columbia Tristar (cat #06766, UPC 0433-96067660). Widescreen (2.40:1) anamorphic. Dolby Digital 5.1 Surround. $27.96. Keepcase. *LANG:* English; French. *SUB:* English; French; Chinese; Thai. *CAP:* English. *FEATURES:* Insert booklet ⬤ Filmographies ⬤ Trailers ⬤ "On the Set" featurette ⬤ 28 chapters ⬤ Production notes.
2001 (R) 143m/C Josh Hartnett, Eric Bana, Ewan McGregor, Tom Sizemore, William Fichtner, Sam Shepard, Gabriel Casseus, Kim Coates, Hugh Dancy, Ron Eldard, Ioan Gruffudd, Tom Guiry, Charlie Hofheimer, Danny Hoch, Jason Isaacs, Zeljko Ivanek, Glenn Morshower, Jeremy Piven, Brendan Sexton III, Johnny Strong, Richard Tyson, Brian Van Holt, Steven Ford, Gregory Sporleder, Carmine D. Giovinazzo, Chris Beetem, George Harris, Ewen Bremner, Boyd Kestner, Nikolaj Coster-Waldau, Ian Virgo, Thomas (Tom) Hardy, Tac Fitzgerald, Matthew Marsden, Orlando Bloom, Kent Linville, Enrique Murciano, Michael Roof, Treva Etienne, Ty Burrell; *D:* Ridley Scott; *W:* Ken Nolan; *C:* Slawomir Idziak; *M:* Hans Zimmer. *AWARDS:* Oscars '01: Film Editing, Sound; *NOM:* Oscars '01: Cinematog., Director (Scott); British Acad. '01: Cinematog., Film Editing, Sound; Directors Guild '01: Director (Scott); Writers Guild '01: Adapt. Screenplay.

Black Knight

Subtlety and the element of surprise are two things that all of the great comic actors know how to use to their advantage. Obviously, Martin Lawrence was absent on that day of Comic School, as evidenced here, where he begins the film at full-speed and never comes back down. The plot is an urban updating of *A Connecticut Yankee in King Arthur's Court.* Jamal (Lawrence) is an apathetic employee at an amusement center (which is shaped like a castle). He attempts to retrieve a strange-looking amulet while cleaning the moat and falls into the water. When he resurfaces, he finds himself in 16th-century England, although he thinks that he is at a new entertainment complex called "Castle World." *Black Knight* is one of the worst films to come along in quite some time, as it offers poorly drawn characters, giant plotholes, and most importantly, no laughs. Director Gil Junger has a long sit-com history and was responsible for *10 Things I Hate About You,* one of the smartest comedies of the '90s, but he certainly stumbles here. Viewers would be much better off checking out one of the classic versions of *A Connecticut Yankee...* or Sam Raimi's brilliant *Army of Darkness.*

While *Black Knight* is a stinker of a movie, the DVD is technically superior. The image is very sharp and clear, showing only some minor artifacting and edge-enhancement at times. There is virtually no grain to be had here, and the colors are excellent. The Dolby Digital 5.1 audio track is equally impressive, as it immerses the viewer into the film. The dialogue is crystal clear, and the frequent Surround sound effects (such as crowd noises or horse hooves) add to the experience. The audio commentary with director Junger is entertaining and informative. (Be sure to look for him in one very funny outtake.) The remainder of the extra features are "by the book" behind-the-scenes featurettes. —*ML*

Movie: 🎬 **DVD:** 🎬🎬🎬 ½
20th Century Fox (cat #2003988, UPC 024543039884). Widescreen (2.35:1) anamorphic. Dolby Digital 5.1; Dolby Surround. $26.98. Keepcase. *LANG:* English; Spanish; French. *SUB:* English. *CAP:* English. *FEATURES:* Commentary • Actor's comments • Deleted scenes • Outtakes • Choreography featurette • Storyboards • Behind-the-scenes • Theatrical trailers.
2001 (PG-13) 95m/C Martin Lawrence, Tom Wilkinson, Vincent Regan, Marsha Thomason, Kevin Conway, Darryl (Chill) Mitchell, Jeannette Weegar, Michael Burgess, Isabell Monk, Helen Carey; **D:** Gil Junger; **W:** Darryl Quarles, Peter Gaulke, Gerry Swallow; **C:** Ueli Steiger; **M:** Randy Edelman.

Black Like Me

Independent feature based on Howard Griffin's account of his "passing for black" in the American South of the early 1960s will strike younger viewers as bizarre. Griffin had his skin chemically darkened and traveled through the Deep South to experience life as a black man and then recounted those events in a series of articles and a book. On film, star James Whitmore's makeup may appear comical. It looks like, well, blackface, and in these sensitive times, that's a line that some refuse to cross. But the film is an adaptation of a true story and to dismiss it out of hand is wrong. It describes a time and place that are (mostly) gone now. All of the disc's flaws come from the original material (as I hazily remember it from a college screening decades ago). The opening theme is shrill; otherwise the sound delivers dialogue without a problem. The black-and-white image is often muddy. The natural-light location night scenes are difficult to make out, as they have always been. If the film is more instructive as history than enjoyable as entertainment, it is still well worth watching again—for just that reason. —*MM*

Movie: 🎬🎬🎬 **DVD:** 🎬🎬 ½
VCI (cat #8309, UPC 08959830921). Full frame. Dolby Digital Mono. $14.99. Keepcase. *LANG:* English. *FEATURES:* 18 chapters • Trailer.
1964 107m/B James Whitmore, Roscoe Lee Browne, Will Geer, Walter Mason, John Marriott, Clifton James, Dan Priest; **D:** Carl Lerner; **W:** Carl Lerner, Gerda Lerner; **C:** Victor Lukens, Henry Mueller; **M:** Meyer Kupferman.

The Black Raven

It was a dark and stormy night outside the old dark house that is the Black Raven Inn. The usual suspects are taking refuge from the storm when they learn that there's $50,000 in stolen money hidden there. Public domain title is no better than VHS tape with bad scratches, serious registration instability, and poor sound. The image is exceptionally dark—as such films from that era tend to be—and DVD does nothing to brighten the murk. Title is available as part of the *Crime Stoppers* triple feature. —*MM*

Movie: 🎬🎬 **DVD:** 🎬
Triton Multimedia (cat #TDVD9166, UPC 017078916621). Full frame. Dolby Digital Mono. $19.98. Keepcase. *LANG:* English. *FEATURES:* 12 chapters • Popeye cartoon • Radio program.
1943 64m/B George Zucco, Wanda McKay, Glenn Strange, I. Stanford Jolley; **D:** Sam Newfield; **W:** Fred Myton; **C:** Robert C. Cline.

Black Robe [MGM]

In 1634, young Jesuit priest, Father Laforgue (Bluteau), journeys across the North American wilderness to bring the church to Canada's Huron Indians. Widescreen image here may be a bit better than the earlier Trimark disc (reviewed in *Book 2*), but that release also offers a full-frame option. —*MM*

Movie: 🎬🎬🎬 ½ **DVD:** 🎬🎬🎬
MGM Home Ent. (cat #1002204, UPC 027-616864352). Widescreen (1.85:1) anamorphic. Dolby Digital Surround. $14.98. Keepcase. *LANG:* English. *SUB:* French; Spanish. *CAP:* English. *FEATURES:* 16 chapters • Trailer.
1991 (R) 101m/C *AU CA* Lothaire Bluteau, Aden Young, Sandrine Holt, August Schellenberg, Tantoo Cardinal, Billy Two Rivers, Lawrence Bayne, Harrison Liu, Marthe Tungeon; **D:** Bruce Beresford; **W:** Brian Moore; **C:** Peter James; **M:** Georges Delerue. *AWARDS:* Australian Film Inst. '92: Cinematog.; Genie '91: Director (Beresford), Film.

Black Spring Break 2

Cheerful comedy rises above the level of the genre. If Greg (Rod Z.) doesn't lose his virginity soon, he won't be accepted into Beta Phi Beta fraternity. His pal Southboy (producer Fordham) has the answer. They'll go to Black Spring Break in Daytona, where they'll hire a hooker and videotape the encounter. Problem solved. Of course, it doesn't work. The film was made on such a tiny budget that the image is exceptionally grainy and there was apparently no money to re-loop dialogue that's occasionally harsh and muffled by wind. And at one point an inexplicable green artifact blooms right in the middle of the screen. But those flaws are relatively unimportant at this level. The film has a good heart; the performances lack polish but the cast is attractive. That's director Zirilli as the agent. —*MM*

Movie: 🎬🎬 ½ **DVD:** 🎬🎬 ½
Steeplechase Ent. (cat #2001-9, UPC 808-837200194). Full frame. $19.98. Keepcase. *LANG:* English. *FEATURES:* Deleted scenes • "Making of" footage • Bloopers • Casting clips • Songs • 8 chapters.
2001 83m/C Keisha Lewis, Divine Brown, Rod Z., G. Thang, Daniel Zirilli; **D:** Daniel Zirilli; **W:** Keisha Lewis; **C:** Nikolas Mann; **M:** Daniel Zirilli.

Blackheart

A pair of con artists have their scam down—the seductive Annette (Alonso) picks up wealthy men, then Ray (Grieco) steps in, roughs them up, and takes their cash. Things get messy when they discover a young woman (Loewi) who has yet to learn of an enormous inheritance, and Ray steps into the role of seducer. Although the film runs out of steam in the last 20 minutes, Grieco and Loewi are likeable in the lead roles. The picture quality is excellent, even in the numerous exterior night scenes. The audio is not quite as good, but this is probably due more to mumbling actors than the DVD itself. —*BG*

Movie: 🎬🎬 **DVD:** 🎬🎬🎬
Image Ent. (cat #OVED1131DVD, UPC 014-381113129). Full frame. Dolby Stereo. $19.99. Keepcase. *LANG:* English. *SUB:* Spanish. *FEATURES:* 15 chapters • Optional music-only soundtrack.
1998 (R) 95m/C Maria Conchita Alonso, Richard Grieco, Fiona Loewi, Christopher Plummer; **D:** Dominic Shiach; **W:** Brock Simpson, Brad Simpson; **C:** Ousama Rawi.

The Blackout

Movie star Matty (Modine) indulges in multiple addictions on a trip home to Miami. He proposes to pregnant girlfriend Annie (Dalle) but when he learns that she's had an abortion, Matty goes on a binge and suffers a blackout. In New York 18 months later, Matty has kicked his addictions and found Susan (Schiffer) but nightmares compel him back to Miami and the possibility that he committed murder. It's all sleazy, symbolic, and as feverishly unfocused as most of director Ferrara's films tend to be. DVD appears to be an accurate reproduction of a so-so image. Colors are either a little off or, more likely, deliberately ugly, particularly the skin tones. Sound is fine. —*MM*

Movie: 🎬 **DVD:** 🎬🎬 ½
Columbia Tristar (cat #06447, UPC 04339-6064478). Full frame; widescreen (1.85:1) anamorphic. Dolby Digital Surround. $24.98. Keepcase. *LANG:* English. *SUB:* English; Spanish. *CAP:* English. *FEATURES:* 28 chapters • Filmographies • Trailers.
1997 (R) 100m/C Matthew Modine, Beatrice Dalle, Claudia Schiffer, Dennis Hopper, Sarah Lassez; **D:** Abel Ferrara; **W:** Abel Ferrara, Chris Zois, Marla Hanson; **C:** Ken Kelsch; **M:** Joe Delia.

Blacktop

While on vacation, Sylvia (Davis) walks away from an argument with David (Munro), her comedian boyfriend. Intent on returning home, she accepts a ride in an 18-wheeler called Goliath with seemingly harmless trucker Jack (Aday, who's hard to swallow in the role) and her scenic countryside tour quickly becomes a road trip of terror. Sylvia has three tools in this cat-and-mouse game, however: time, her own strength, and David, who is hot on their tail. This HBO production is full of car chases and bad dialogue, some of which is pretty amusing. The picture and sound are average, no better than its original broadcast. —DL
Movie: 🎬 ½ **DVD:** 🎬🎬
HBO (cat #91900, UPC 026359190025). Full frame. Dolby Surround; Stereo. $24.98. Snapper. *LANG:* English; Spanish. *SUB:* English; French; Spanish. *CAP:* English. *FEATURES:* Cast and crew bios ▪ 17 chapters.
2001 (R) 100m/C *CA* Meat Loaf Aday, Kristen Davis, Lochlyn Munro, Victoria Pratt; *D:* T.J. Scott; *W:* Kevin Lund; *C:* Attila Szalay; *M:* Ennio di Berardo.

The Blair Thumb

The Blair Witch Project spoofed as a 28-minute short with the characters played by human thumbs in little costumes and matted-in human eyes and mouths (the trademarked "Thumbation"). "In October of some year, three student filmmakers went into the woods to shoot a documentary about 'The Blair Thumb'...." So funny I forgot to die. An amusing premise carried off with a major lack of humor, but already a burgeoning franchise as evidenced by "Thumb Wars" and the apparent promise of future thumb-headed parodies from the bountiful writer who gave us *Patch Adams*. The eyes and mouths move with the same gut-turning obscenity I remember feeling when watching "Clutch Cargo" cartoons. Only a brain soaked in too much bong water will find this a thumb-slapper. Excellent DVD transfer and sound wasted utterly. —MO
Movie: 🎬🎬 **DVD:** 🎬🎬🎬 ½
Image Ent. (cat #ID0362BODVD, UPC 014-381036220). Full frame. Dolby Digital 5.1 Surround; Surround. $9.99. Keepcase. *LANG:* English. *FEATURES:* 9 chapters ▪ Commentary: Steve Oedekerk ▪ Outtakes ▪ Storyboards ▪ Coming attraction trailers.
2001 28m/C *D:* Steve Oedekerk; *W:* Steve Oedekerk; *V:* Megan Cavanagh, Steve Oedekerk, Paul Greenberg, Jim Jackman.

Blankman

Self-appointed Chicago superhero Daryl Walker (Wayans) tries to make up in creativity what he lacks in superpowers. (All he has is a bulletproof union suit, rubber gloves, an old towel for a cape, and a mask made out of a sock.) A subplot involving a crooked politician is half-baked but it does serve to introduce glamorous TV reporter Kimberly Jonz (Givens). The scenes between them are the best in the film. One is a night ride on the El, followed by a visit to Blankman's junk-filled "fortress of solitude," a wonderful creation by production designer James Spencer. The softish image is only slightly better than VHS tape. The screen size and language options are the only real improvements. —MM
Movie: 🎬🎬 **DVD:** 🎬🎬 ½
Columbia Tristar Home Video (UPC 04339-6065499). Widescreen (1.85:1) letterboxed; full frame. Dolby Digital 5.1 Surround Stereo; Dolby Digital Surround. $24.95. Keepcase. *LANG:* English; French. *SUB:* English; French; Spanish; Portuguese; Chinese; Korean; Thai. *FEATURES:* Trailer ▪ 28 chapters.
1994 (PG-13) 96m/C Damon Wayans, Robin Givens, David Alan Grier, Jason Alexander, Jon Polito, Nick(y) Corello; *D:* Mike Binder; *W:* J.F. Lawton, Damon Wayans; *C:* Newton Thomas (Tom) Sigel; *M:* Miles Goodman.

Blast-Off Girls / Just for the Hell of It

Blast-Off Girls is the story of a boy band's sputtering blast-off toward stardom—a tale that's every bit as relevant today as it was then. Boojie Baker (Conway) is a dapper dandy who struts around twirling a cane, with a dingy blonde on his other arm, a babe who performs certain favors to assure business dealings go Boojie's way. Though he's actually more of a pimp, he fancies himself as a hot-shot talent promoter, and with the aid of his lady friends, he successfully cons a homely garage band into a less-than-financially lucrative contract. But Boojie's steady stream of party girls keeps the boys of the Big Blast pacified for only so long before they start yammering for an actual paycheck. Trouble intensifies when the group heads into the studio and realizes they're woefully unprepared to make it as real musicians, no matter how much pot they smoke. Sexual innuendo is pervasive, but the flick is ultimately chaste and lean on charm. KFC's "Colonel Sanders" appears in a cameo. Juvenile delinquent pictures really had their heyday in the '50s, but that didn't dissuade director Lewis from putting his spin on the genre in *Just for the Hell of It* and his kids are MEAN. To them, it isn't a good party if there's a recognizable stick of furniture in the room after it's over. Keith Moon and Johnny Cash have left hotel suites in better shape than these punks. Only they don't LOOK like delinquents; in fact, they look more like members of the Young Republicans. Still, they wander the city engaging in random acts of willful and wanton destruction. They pick fights with little leaguers. One of them burns a poor lady's newspaper WHILE SHE'S READING IT! These cackling teenagers even steal a blind man's cane, for heaven's sake! Such reckless behavior can only go on for so long without someone getting hurt—and tragically, they do. The second feature on this disc, *Just for the Hell of It* (see separate entry for credits), looks acceptable, with a vividly colored transfer that's a bit soft. *Blast-off* is presented at 1.66 and fares worse, with a faded, exceedingly grainy and damaged print source. Audio on both is sharp and muddy, more of a reflection of the incompetent original recording than an aspect of the transfer. The extras are, as usual, terrific. —GNG/DG
Movie: 🎬 **DVD:** 🎬🎬
Image Ent. (cat #ID9740SWDVD, UPC 014-381974027). Full frame; widescreen (1.66:1) letterboxed. Mono. $24.99. Keepcase. *LANG:* English. *FEATURES:* Theatrical trailers ▪ Trailers for other H.G. Lewis films ▪ H.G. Lewis short, "Hot Night at the Go-Go Lounge" ▪ Drive-in intermission shorts ▪ Facts of life drive-in pitch book ▪ Gallery of drive-in exploitation art ▪ Radio spots.
1967 83m/C Ray Sager, Dan Conway, Harland "Colonel" Sanders; *D:* Herschell Gordon Lewis; *W:* Herschell Gordon Lewis.

The Blind Beast

This unique horror is a big surprise in every respect, a serious work of art about sex pushed way beyond human barriers. An easy film to dismiss or reject out of hand, the work is honest and legitimate, on a subject that usually surfaces only as exploitative trash. Blind sculptor Michio (Eiji Funakoshi), helped by his doting Mother (Noriko Sengoku), creates a huge studio-prison packed with gigantic sculptures of female torsos and outsized anatomical features. He kidnaps Aki (Mako Midori), a model whose body he admires, and forces her to submit to his plan to sculpt a masterpiece from her, by feel alone. Aki tries deception and seduction in attempts to escape, but her efforts take an unexpected turn. She reacts positively to his repeated rapes and buys into the psychological side of his transgressive art, in which touch and tactile sensation are all. Herself going blind in the dimly lit studio, Aki eagerly joins Michio in a descent into a sado-masochistic obsession that spirals out of control toward pain, mutilation, and death. With a minimal cast, and mostly confined to one elaborate, bizarre set, director Masumura manages to communicate ideas about extreme erotic obsession without being revolting. I have to admit experiencing shivers of dread, expecting something abominable to occur at any moment. *The Blind Beast* is conceptually extreme, graphically restrained, and very interesting. That's not to recommend this erotic ordeal for any but adults who know what they're getting into...yet I can affirm that this is not quasi-porn chic, or the faux-artsy, pandering kind of junk which seems to cross all national boundaries nowadays. Masumura's aim is direct and his method unfussy. The visuals are strikingly sensual, but not overaestheticized. This DVD is beautifully produced, the best Fantoma disc I've yet seen. The DaieiScope image is in excellent shape and has very good color. The soundtrack is strong, and there are good removable subtitles. —GE *AKA:* Moju.

Movie: ♪♪♪ DVD: ♪♪♪ ½
Image Ent. (UPC 014381132427). Widescreen (2.35:1) anamorphic. $29.95. Keepcase. *LANG:* Japanese. *SUB:* English. *FEATURES:* Biographical notes ▪ Still gallery ▪ Trailer.
1969 86m/C *JP* Eiji Funakoshi, Mako Midori, Noriko Sengoku; *D:* Yasuzo Masumura; *W:* Yoshio Shirasaka; *C:* Setsuo Kobayashi.

Blind Date

A blind date between workaholic Walter (Willis) and gorgeous Nadia (Basinger) starts off well but then her alcohol intolerance throws the relationship off track. Then there's her psychotic ex-boyfriend David (Larroquette) to be dealt with. This is one of the worst-looking DVDs ever released by a major studio. Image is soft with heavy grain that leads to swimming artifacts even in conventionally illuminated interiors. (Did the original look this poor in theatres? I don't remember.) On a conventional monitor, the full-frame version is slightly superior to the widescreen, but neither is really an improvement over VHS tape. —*MM*
Movie: ♪♪ DVD: ♪
Columbia Tristar (cat #07746, UPC 0433-96077461). Widescreen (2.35:1) anamorphic; full frame. Dolby Digital Surround. $24.98. Keepcase. *LANG:* English; French. *SUB:* English; French; Spanish; Portuguese; Chinese; Korean; Thai. *CAP:* English. *FEATURES:* 28 chapters ▪ Trailer.
1987 (PG-13) 95m/C Kim Basinger, Bruce Willis, John Larroquette, William Daniels, George Coe, Mark Blum, Phil Hartman, Stephanie Faracy, Alice Hirson, Graham Stark; *D:* Blake Edwards; *W:* Dale Launer; *C:* Harry Stradling Jr.; *M:* Henry Mancini.

Blitz

A German car designer's (Prochnow) pet project, a vehicle that runs without gas, is halted by the influence of an Arab conglomerate. DVD delivers an unbelievably poor image. Daylight scenes are washed-out; night scenes are virtually opaque. Title is available as part of the *Action Arsenal* collection. —*MM* *AKA:* Killing Cars.
Movie: ♪ DVD: ♪
BCI-Eclipse (cat #44076-9, UPC 7873644-07699). Full frame. $19.98. Keepcase. *LANG:* English. *FEATURES:* 8 chapters.
1985 (R) 104m/C Juergen Prochnow, Senta Berger, William Conrad, Agnes Soral; *D:* Michael Verhoeven; *W:* Michael Verhoeven; *C:* Jacques Steyn; *M:* Michael Landau.

Blood and Sand

In the film that made him a star, Rudolph Valentino plays Gallardo, the young matador who finds success in the bullring and the bedroom. The expected signs of wear and registration woes are much in evidence, but the image is remarkably sharp and presented with careful attention to corrected tinting and with a new score by Mont Alto Motion Picture Orchestra. It's still easy to see why Valentino became so popular. A nice assortment of extras accompany the film. Don't miss Orson Welles's introduction and outro for a TV broadcast of the film, or "Valentino Speaks," excerpts of admittedly "dubious authenticity" from a *Photoplay* magazine article. —*MM*
Movie: ♪♪ DVD: ♪♪♪
Kino on Video (cat #K214, UPC 7383290-21429). Full frame. $29.95. Keepcase. *LANG:* Silent. *SUB:* English intertitles. *FEATURES:* 16 chapters ▪ Intro by Orson Welles ▪ Trailer ▪ Funeral footage ▪ "Valentino Speaks" ▪ Essay about the Ibanez novel ▪ Score credits.
1922 87m/B Rudolph Valentino, Nita Naldi, Lila Lee, Walter Long; *D:* Fred Niblo; *W:* June Mathis; *C:* Alvin Wyckoff.

Blood Cult

Bizarre mutilation murders take place on a small Midwestern college campus. On their commentary track, the filmmakers boast that this gruesome little slasher was the very first feature produced to be a video premiere. That might be true. They also admit that it cost a whopping $25,000 to make and that's certainly easy to believe. The grainy shot-on-video image is no better than VHS tape. Extras are relatively extensive. —*MM*
Movie: ♪ DVD: ♪♪♪
VCI (cat #8260, UPC 089859826023). Full frame. Dolby Digital Stereo. $24.99. Keepcase. *LANG:* English. *FEATURES:* 16 chapters ▪ Commentary: Christopher Lewis, Linda Lewis, Rod Slane ▪ Talent files ▪ Photo gallery ▪ Interviews ▪ Trailer ▪ Promotional video.
1985 (R) 89m/C Chuck Ellis, Julie Andelman, Jim Vance, Joe Hardt; *D:* Christopher Lewis; *M:* Rod Slane.

Blood from the Mummy's Tomb

The immortal spirit of Tera, Egyptian queen of evil, haunts Margaret (Leon), the daughter of an archaeologist who discovered her tomb. As a long-prophesied conjunction of stars begins to occur, Margaret finds herself enthralled by Tera's power and finds herself becoming possessed by Tera's spirit. This adaptation of Bram Stoker's *The Jewel of Seven Stars* begins well, with a wonderfully mysterious and moody first half, but it loses steam in the somewhat muddled (and tedious) second half. Cou.louris (without the old age makeup) looks exactly like his Thatcher character in *Citizen Kane*, 30 years earlier, but sadly is given not much to do other than roll his eyes and scream. Leon is a likable heroine but that wig and false eyelashes have got to go! Remade in post-*Omen* fashion as *The Awakening*. Unavailable in the U.S. for years, the film presented on DVD is in fine shape. The transfer is generally grainy and a tad soft, but colors are rich and vibrant and close-ups tend to be razor sharp. The first 10 minutes have a light scratch running down the center of the frame. Audio is strong for mono. The brief (10-minute) featurette showcases screenwriter Wicking and star Leon, who share behind-the-scenes stories highlighting what is considered to be a "jinxed" production. We learn that director Holt died suddenly during filming and original star Peter Cushing had to be replaced after several days so that he could tend to his dying wife. The stories are tragic but they are completely undercut and cheapened by the insertion of quick cutaways to characters reacting in horror from the film itself. Shameful, immature, and cruel. The bonus Hammer trailer disc presents 20 theatrical previews from other films from the studio released by Anchor Bay with highlights being *Shatter* and *A Challenge for Robin Hood*, which are unavailable on DVD. Almost all of the trailers are presented in fine, if not pristine shape. This disc is identical to one given out as a freebie back in 1999. —*DG*
Movie: ♪♪ ½ DVD: ♪♪♪
Anchor Bay (cat #DV11440, UPC 013131-144093). Widescreen (1.85:1) anamorphic. Mono. $24.98. Keepcase. *LANG:* English. *FEATURES:* Bonus disc: "Hammer Trailer Collection" ▪ Featurette ▪ Trailer ▪ TV spot ▪ Radio spots with poster gallery ▪ Still gallery.
1971 94m/C *GB* Andrew Keir, Valerie Leon, James Villiers, Hugh Burden, George Coulouris, Mark Edwards; *D:* Seth Holt; *W:* Christopher Wicking; *C:* Arthur Grant; *M:* Tristram Cary.

Blood of the Dragon

A dying Ming patriot gives a beggar boy a list of rebels to deliver to the rebel leader. Heroic outlaw the White Dragon (Jimmy Wang Yu) defends the boy from the formidable Red Wolf General Tai (Yee Yuen) and his legion. The epic final bloody battle is worth the wait. Distributor Michael Thevis saw fit to provide fresh main credit animation (which gives a lot more space to those involved with the dubbing than the original cast and crew), and a new rock soundtrack for its 1978 U.S. debut. The print is in decent shape for its age and origin, with reasonably good sound. Available as a triple feature on one disc under the title *Great Martial Arts Movies*. Cover art features Sonny Chiba, though none of his movies are included. —*BT* *AKA:* The Desperate Chase; The Dangerous Chase.
Movie: ♪♪ ½ DVD: ♪ ½
BFS Video (cat #30236D, UPC 066805-302367). Full frame. $9.98. Keepcase. *LANG:* English. *FEATURES:* 5 chapters ▪ Glossary of martial arts weapons.
1971 (R) 96m/C *HK* Wang Yu, Lung Fei, Chiao Chiao, Yau Tin, Tin Miu, Yuen Yee; *D:* Pao Shu Kao; *W:* Pao Shu Kao, Hong Ngai; *C:* Fang Chi Kuo.

Blood on the Sun [Image]

This release corrects the main flaw in the earlier version (reviewed in *Book 2*), by cleaning up the soundtrack a bit. Light

audio crackle is intermittent. This disc looks terrific, with a superb black-and-white image created, according to the box copy, from the original nitrate camera negative. —*MM*
Movie: 𝄞𝄞𝄞 **DVD:** 𝄞𝄞𝄞 ½
Image Ent. (cat #HRS9444, UPC 0143819-44426). Full frame. Dolby Digital Mono. $19.98. Snapper. *LANG:* English. *FEATURES:* 9 chapters.
1945 98m/B James Cagney, Sylvia Sidney, Robert Armstrong, Wallace Ford; **D:** Frank Lloyd; **W:** Lester Cole, Nathaniel Curtis, Frank Melford; **C:** Theodor Sparkuhl; **M:** Miklos Rozsa.

Blood Simple

Bartender Ray (Getz) is helping his boss's disaffected wife Abby (McDormand) flee across Texas when they decide to stop at a motel instead and begin a torrid affair. Unbeknownst to them, her husband Marty (Hedaya) has hired detective Loren Visser (Walsh) to shadow them—and then in a jealous fever hires the same detective to kill them both. From then on it's noirish twist upon twist upon double-cross, as a murder-for-hire becomes a study in desperate characters. DVD is a distinct improvement on the grainy theatrical prints seen back in 1984. For the 2000 theatrical reissue, the Coens were able to reinstate some editorial differences that their original distributor had made them remove, for clarity's sake. But they've gone a bit further than that with the addition of a *Forever Young* preface, a talking-head introduction that confused everyone in the theatre. In this strange 60 seconds of film, a gentleman identifies himself as Mortimer Young and lets us know how happy he is that this masterpiece has been restored for mankind: "digitally swabbed" and with the "boring parts taken out and replaced with other material." It's plenty weird, an in-joke or a rib that we aren't quite in on. Even more weird, but less welcome, is the "commentary" by Kenneth Loring (a real person?) that plays like a low-key version of a Monty Python sketch. He ever-so-politely explains every ridiculous detail of the show, and you aren't very far in before realizing that his whole commentary track is a gag. It also seems intentionally/unintentionally contemptuous of its audience, if only in a vague sense. On the other hand, it's no more insulting than most television sports commentaries. Perhaps because of the theatrical re-issue, the print used for the transfer appears to have been pretty much flawless. The transfer is sharp enough to show the film grain that shows up in the darker scenes. Even then, the image remains steady and the blacks very inky. Colors are generally saturated without any bleed and during the nighttime scenes are extremely vibrant. Thankfully, the DVD doesn't have one of those hopped-up fake 5.1 soundtracks and opts to go with the more natural sounding original soundtrack, which is pretty much just dialogue from the center channel and a left or right effect here and there. You'll have to listen hard to hear anything from the rear. Don't let that turn you off because anything more might have ruined the effect of the film. —*GE/JO*
Movie: 𝄞𝄞𝄞 ½ **DVD:** 𝄞𝄞𝄞
Universal Studios (cat #21425, UPC 0251-92142529). Widescreen (1.85:1) anamorphic. Dolby Surround. $24.98. Keepcase. *LANG:* English. *SUB:* Spanish; French. *CAP:* English. *FEATURES:* Commentary: "Kenneth Loring of Forever Young Films" • Theatrical trailer • Production notes • 18 chapters • Talent files.
1985 (R) 96m/C John Getz, M. Emmet Walsh, Dan Hedaya, Frances McDormand, Samm-Art Williams, Van Brooks, Lauren Bivens, Holly Hunter; **D:** Joel Coen; **W:** Joel Coen, Ethan Coen; **C:** Barry Sonnenfeld; **M:** Carter Burwell. *AWARDS:* Ind. Spirit '86: Actor (Walsh), Director (Coen); Sundance '85: Grand Jury Prize.

Blood Surf

This low-budget no-brainer tells of a small group who go to Australia to tape a new sensation in exploitative reality-TV: "Blood Surfing." Essentially, it's surfing in shark-infested waters. Oddly enough, the group finds themselves under attack from a giant crocodile and from a band of mercenaries who seemed to have popped over from another film. Regehr is a hoot (in obvious Ahab/Quint form) and seems to be enjoying himself. The movie itself is unintentionally funny and not frightening in the least—it's exactly what you'd expect. It also features some hilarious deaths and rubbery special effects; again, exactly what you'd expect from the premise. The cover art is pretty nifty, though. The disc is bright and clear with strong colors but some digital shimmer is occasionally visible around edges of moving objects. Sound is strong for a low-budget effort. The bonus behind-the-scenes outtakes are fun. —*DG* **AKA:** Crocodile.
Movie: 𝄞 ½ **DVD:** 𝄞𝄞 ½
Lion's Gate Home Ent. (cat #VM7666D, UPC 031398766629). Widescreen (1.85:1) anamorphic. Dolby Digital 5.1. $24.99. Keepcase. *LANG:* English. *SUB:* English; French; Spanish. *CAP:* English. *FEATURES:* 24 chapters • Alternate angle storyboard option for action scenes • Bonus footage.
2000 (R) 88m/C Matt Borlenghi, Duncan Regehr, Kate Fischer, Taryn Reif, Joel West, Dax Miller; **D:** James D.R. Hickox; **W:** Sam Bernard, Robert L. Levy; **C:** Christopher Pearson; **M:** Jim Manzie.

Blood: The Last Vampire

In contemporary Japan, Saya is the last original vampire. She's employed by an American intelligence agency to hunt down a new type of shape-shifting monster and goes undercover as a high school student on the Yokota Air Force Base in Japan. The story is told with an effective mix of conventional hand-drawn animation and computer-generated work. That fits the combination of fantasy with an ultra-realistic setting and very expressive lighting. Filmmakers play against current trends in anime with a very dark image, pale desaturated colors and character-drawing that avoids most stereotypes. DVD image is flawless. On a good widescreen monitor, the film looks as sharp as a theatrical presentation (which, remarkably, the film enjoyed in America) and sound is equally good. Highly recommended to horror fans. —*MM*
Movie: 𝄞𝄞𝄞 **DVD:** 𝄞𝄞𝄞
Manga Ent. (cat #4078-2, UPC 66020-0407827). Widescreen (1.85:1) anamorphic. Dolby Digital 5.1 Surround Stereo; Dolby Digital Surround. $24.95. Keepcase. *LANG:* English and Japanese. *SUB:* English. *FEATURES:* "Making of" featurette • Trailer • Photo gallery • Weblinks.
2000 40m/C JP **D:** Hiroyuki Kitakubo.

Blood Thirst

Deservedly obscure Philippine horror concerns a woman who maintains eternal youth by indulging in ritual killings and strange experiments. The black-and-white image has been well maintained. Overall, the film looks better than the first feature on this double feature, *Bloodsuckers.* (Please see review.) It is of interest to only the most dedicated fan. —*MM*
Movie: 𝄞 **DVD:** 𝄞𝄞 ½
Image Ent. (cat #ID0585SWDVD, UPC 014-381058529). Full frame. Dolby Digital Mono. $24.99. Snapper. *LANG:* English. *FEATURES:* 12 chapters • Trailer • Trailers for 12 more horror films • Featurette: "The Horny Vampire" • Archival short subject: "Midsummer Nightmare" • Drive-in intermission shorts and announcements • Gallery of drive-in exploitation art.
1965 B PH Robert Winston, Yvonne Nielson, Vic Diaz; **D:** Newton Arnold.

Bloodfight

A martial arts tournament movie, and not a particularly good one, obviously hoping to cash in on the success of Jean-Claude Van Damme's hit *Bloodsport.* Bolo Yeung even plays the same character. Yasuaki Kurata stars as a champion who enters the big tournament to avenge the death of his student (Simon Yam). The film's lack of English dubbing is actually a detriment, as the Asian cast members all struggle to speak their dialogue in English, with varying levels of comprehensibility. The image transfer is fine, though cropped. But the sound is a real problem, reducing an obvious stereo track to mono, doing further damage to the dialogue. Available as a triple feature on one disc under the title *Great Martial Arts Movies.* Cover art features Sonny Chiba, though none of his movies are included. —*BT*
Movie: 𝄞 ½ **DVD:** 𝄞
BFS Video (cat #30236D, UPC 06680530-2367). Full frame. $9.98. Keepcase. *LANG:* English. *FEATURES:* 5 chapters • Glossary of martial arts weapons.
1989 96m/C HK JP Bolo Yeung, Yasuka Kurata, Simon Yam, Ken-ming Lum, Christina Lawson; **D:** Shuji Goto; **W:** Sawaguchi Yoshiaki; **C:** Murano Nobuaki; **M:** Oguchi Yuji.

Bloodfist 5: Human Target

When undercover FBI agent Jim Roth (Wilson) attempts to unravel an international arms deal, he's found out and left for dead. He comes to with amnesia and finds himself caught between the arms dealers and the FBI who think he's turned double agent. The DVD image is nice and clear, though dark areas tend to lose detail. Night exteriors are expectedly grainy. Stereo is O.K. —MM

Movie: ♪♪ ½ **DVD:** ♪♪ ½
New Concorde (cat #NH20478 D, UPC 736991447899). Full frame. Stereo. $14.98. Keepcase. *LANG:* English. *FEATURES:* 24 chapters • Trailer • Talent files.
1993 (R) 84m/C Don "The Dragon" Wilson, Denice Duff, Yuji Okumoto, Don Stark, Danny Lopez, Steve James, Michael Yama; *D:* Jeff Yonis; *W:* Jeff Yonis; *C:* Michael G. Wojciechowski; *M:* David Wurst, Eric Wurst.

Bloodfist 6: Ground Zero

Nick Corrigan (Wilson) must battle terrorists who have taken over a nuclear missile silo and threaten New York. This low-budget effort doesn't look as good as the best entries in the series. Lackluster fight direction and choreography. DVD cannot improve VHS tape.

Movie: ♪♪ **DVD:** ♪♪
New Concorde (cat #NH20491 D, UPC 7366991449190). Full frame. Stereo. $14.99. Keepcase. *LANG:* English. *FEATURES:* 24 chapters • Trailers • Talent files.
1994 (R) 86m/C Don "The Dragon" Wilson, Cat Sasson, Steve Garvey; *D:* Rick Jacobson; *W:* Brendan Broderick, Rob Kerchner; *C:* Michael Gallagher; *M:* John Graham.

Bloodfist 7: Manhunt

Martial arts expert Jim Trudell (Wilson) is accused by corrupt cops of murder and is forced to prove his innocence while on the run. Mediocre genre piece is no more inspired than its synopsis. Neither is the DVD. It's no better than VHS tape. —MM
Movie: ♪♪ **DVD:** ♪♪
New Concorde (cat #NH20501 D, UPC 73699145196). Full frame. Stereo. $14.99. Keepcase. *LANG:* English. *FEATURES:* 24 chapters • Trailers • Talent files.
1995 (R) 95m/C Don "The Dragon" Wilson, Jonathan Penner, Jillian McWhirter, Stephen Davies, Cyril O'Reilly, Eb Lottimer, Steven Williams; *D:* Jonathan Winfrey; *W:* Brendan Broderick, Rob Kerchner; *C:* Michael Gallagher; *M:* Elliot Anders, Mike Elliot.

Bloodfist 8: Hard Way Out

Rick Cowan (Wilson) is a CIA agent turned teacher who's drawn back into the game after a team of assassins comes after him. DVD image here is a distinct improvement over more recent entries in the long-lived series. Perhaps the filmmakers were inspired by the Irish locations. Sound is acceptable. —MM *AKA:* Hard Way Out.
Movie: ♪♪ ½ **DVD:** ♪♪ ½
New Concorde (cat #NH20502 D, UPC 736991450295). Full frame. Stereo. $14.99. Keepcase. *LANG:* English. *FEATURES:* 24 chapters • Trailers • Talent files.
1996 (R) 78m/C Don "The Dragon" Wilson, John Patrick White, Warren Burton, Richard Farrell; *D:* Barry Samson; *W:* Alex Simon; *C:* John Aronson; *M:* John Faulkner.

The Bloodsuckers

Oxford Don Richard Fountain (Mower) heads off to Greece where he is seduced by Chrises (Hassall) in a really funny drug orgy scene, complete with grand '60s music. His pals, led by Patrick Macnee, attempt to bring him back. Overall, the acting is fine; the ending is unfortunate. The film curiously intermixes elements of drug use, sexual obsession, and vampirism. DVD is a good re-creation of a flawed original. Black splicing tape is an intermittent distraction. Surface flaws are light and numerous. The extras include the usual Something Weird drive-in double feature shorts, filler material, trailers for nine other horror features, and goofy short subjects. The second feature is the black-and-white *Blood Thirst.* (Please see review.) For those who wish to re-create the full drive-in experience, the two films can be played straight through with intermission materials. —MM *AKA:* Incense for the Damned; Doctors Wear Scarlet; The Freedom Seekers.
Movie: ♪♪ ½ **DVD:** ♪♪
Image Ent. (cat #ID0585SWDVD, UPC 014381058529). Full frame. Dolby Digital Mono. $24.99. Snapper. *LANG:* English. *FEATURES:* 12 chapters • Trailer • Trailers for 12 more horror films • Featurette: "The Horny Vampire" • Archival short subject: "Midsummer Nightmare" • Drive-in intermission shorts and announcements • Gallery of drive-in exploitation art.
1970 90m/C *GB* Patrick Macnee, Peter Cushing, Patrick Mower, Edward Woodward, Alex Davion, Imogen Hassall, Madeline Hinde, Johnny Sekka; *D:* Robert Hartford-Davis; *W:* Julian More; *C:* Desmond Dickinson.

Bloody Proof

A serial killer is stalking well-to-do women in Mexico. Detective Ibarra (Bauer) is assigned to the case. Rookie tabloid reporter Estela (Arizmendi) finds an important clue. The resolution of the stereotypical premise runs true to form, but the characters are treated seriously and the film is stylishly made with a few moments of abrupt, shocking violence. DVD image is not a major improvement over VHS tape, but the film rates a recommendation to fans. —MM
Movie: ♪♪♪ **DVD:** ♪♪
Vanguard Intl. Cinema (cat #VF9182, UPC 658769918236). Full frame. Dolby Digital Stereo. $29.95. Keepcase. *LANG:* English. *FEATURES:* 10 chapters.
1999 99m/C Steven Bauer, Yareli Arizmendi, Olivia Hussey; *D:* Gabriel Beristain; *W:* M. Francesconi, Tim Hoy; *C:* Andres Leon Becker; *M:* Eduardo Gamboa.

Blow

In adapting Bruce Porter's book about the true story of 1970's cocaine impresario George Jung, director Ted Demme, screenwriters David McKenna and Nick Cassavetes, and an impressive roster of actors including Johnny Depp, Penelope Cruz, Paul Reubens, and Ray Liotta, have wrought a multi-million dollar narrative about a man with the morals of a gnat. Though pictorially stunning and featuring stellar performances from Depp as the likable drug-dealing Jung, and Liotta as his tortured father, the filmmakers seem ambivalent to draw any judgments about the man who became the largest Colombian cocaine importer in this country. With visual references to *Goodfellas, Traffic,* and *Boogie Nights,* perhaps the filmmakers thought that throwing in bits of other good movies will rub off on theirs. No such luck. Whatever qualms I may have about the film, the DVD certainly impresses. The late Demme contributed heavily to the supplements, not only conducting a feature-length commentary (with the real-life Jung), but offering his observations on deleted scenes as well as moderating interviews with Jung that can be accessed while viewing the film. The 2.35 anamorphic transfer is picture-perfect: colorful, sharp, and blemish-free. Both the 5.1 discrete and matrix Surround tracks offer a very busy sound field, with constant rear channel activity and full-blooded low-frequency punch. There's even a documentary about the Colombia drug trade and the tragic impact on the country's history. While I cannot fault the disc from its thoroughness, I find the entire enterprise itself rather tough to swallow as appropriate for popular, mass entertainment. While watching it, I kept thinking about a line from Shakespeare, something about a tale "full of sound and fury, signifying nothing." —EP
Movie: ♪ ½ **DVD:** ♪♪♪ ½
New Line (cat #N5284, UPC 7940435284-22). Widescreen (2.35:1) anamorphic. Dolby Digital 5.1; Dolby Digital Stereo Surround. $24.98. Keepcase. *LANG:* English. *SUB:* English. *FEATURES:* 25 chapters • Commentary: Director Ted Demme, George Jung • Deleted scenes with director commentary • Ted Demme's production diary • Nikka Costa music video • Theatrical teaser and trailer • George Jung interviews by director Ted Demme • Trivia subtitle track • "Lost Paradise: Cocaine's Impact on Colombia" documentary • DVD-ROM features: script-to-screen access • Link to original website.
2001 (R) 124m/C Johnny Depp, Penelope Cruz, Jordi Molla, Franka Potente, Rachel Griffiths, Ray Liotta, Ethan Suplee, Paul (Pee-wee Herman) Reubens, Max Perlich, Clifford Curtis, Miguel (Michael) Sandoval,

Kevin Gage, Jesse James, Dan Ferro, Emma Roberts, Bob(cat) Goldthwait, James King; **D:** Ted (Edward) Demme; **W:** David McKenna, Nick Cassavetes; **C:** Ellen Kuras; **M:** Graeme Revell.

Blow Dry

Comedic situations and family healing make for an uncomfortable mix when the National British Hairdressing Championships come to a sleepy English town. An odd assortment of Brits and Yanks populate this familiar tale and even the dependable Rickman can't save the film. Writer Simon Beaufoy tries to re-create the success of *The Full Monty* but doesn't hit the mark. Director Breathnach also fared better with his previous effort, *I Went Down.* DVD delivers a very good image with crisp bright interiors and softer exteriors, familiar to fans of British imports, due to the gray light. —MM
Movie: ♫♫ **DVD:** ♫♫♫
Miramax Pictures (cat #21647, UPC 7869-36144697). Widescreen (1.85:1) anamorphic. Dolby Digital 5.1 Surround Stereo. $32.99. Keepcase. *LANG:* English. *CAP:* English. *FEATURES:* 20 chapters ▪ Trailers.
2000 (R) 91m/C *GB* Alan Rickman, Natasha Richardson, Rachel Griffiths, Rachael Leigh Cook, Josh Hartnett, Bill Nighy, Warren Clarke, Rosemary Harris, Hugh Bonneville, Peter McDonald, Heidi Klum, Michael McElhatton; **D:** Paddy Breathnach; **W:** Simon Beaufoy; **C:** Cian de Buitlear; **M:** Patrick Doyle.

Blow Out

Sound-effects expert Jack Terri (Travolta) inadvertently tapes an auto crash that kills a presidential candidate and finds himself being stalked by a spooky assassin (Lithgow). This homage to Antonioni's *Blow Up* is marred by self-conscious, show-off stylistic devices that have become DePalma's signature. (Note the spinning camera in chapter 9.) DVD presents an O.K. image which, if memory serves, is an accurate re-creation of the original. Sound is adequate. —MM
Movie: ♫♫ ½ **DVD:** ♫♫ ½
MGM Home Ent. (cat #1000982, UPC 027-616852885). Widescreen (2.35:1) anamorphic; full frame. Dolby Digital Surround. $19.98. Keepcase. *LANG:* English; Spanish. *SUB:* French; Spanish. *CAP:* English. *FEATURES:* 16 chapters ▪ Trailer.
1981 (R) 108m/C John Travolta, Nancy Allen, John Lithgow, Dennis Franz; **D:** Brian DePalma; **W:** Brian DePalma; **C:** Vilmos Zsigmond; **M:** Pino Donaggio.

The Blue and the Gray

Jonathan (Hammond) leaves his home in Virginia to pursue his dream of making a living as an artist in Gettysburg. When the Civil War breaks out, he finds himself staring across the Mason-Dixon line at his family. Like most miniseries, it's overly long (3 discs and 6 1/2 hours!), melodra-

matic, and with some suspect dialogue, but for those looking for a sweeping epic it will certainly fit the bill. Gregory Peck is stately as always in his portrayal of Abraham Lincoln. Picture quality is quite grainy even in daylight scenes, and gets worse in large patches of darkness. This DVD is the full 381-minute version. —BG
Movie: ♫♫ **DVD:** ♫♫
Columbia Tristar (cat #06544, UPC 043-396065444). Full frame. Dolby Mono. $27.95. Keepcase. *LANG:* English; French. *SUB:* English; French; Spanish; Portuguese; Chinese; Korean; Thai. *CAP:* English. *FEATURES:* 84 chapters.
1982 381m/C Gregory Peck, Lloyd Bridges, Colleen Dewhurst, Stacy Keach, John Hammond, Sterling Hayden, Warren Oates; **D:** Andrew V. McLaglen; **M:** Bruce Broughton.

The Blue Angel

One of the greats receives the treatment it deserves on this two-disc set. Stuffy, pompous Prof. Immanuel Rath (Jannings) goes to a nightclub where he hopes to catch some of his students who have been passing around pictures of the lovely Lola Lola (Dietrich). The teacher falls hard and eventually loses everything he has cared for. Dietrich's smoldering sexuality made her a star. It also makes Rath's obsession easy to identify with. The film was shot in English and German versions and both are included here. The "scene comparison" extra shows how subtle the differences in editing are. Both look and sound very good, with the edge going to the English version (which was probably made from elements that had seen less wear). Both look much better than any other presentations I've seen on tape or conventional projection. A light crackle is more audible on the German disc. Optional English subtitles are white on black background; easy to read unobtrusive. —MM **AKA:** Der Blaue Engel.
Movie: ♫♫♫♫ **DVD:** ♫♫♫♫
Kino on Video (cat #K226, UPC 738329-022624). Full frame. $24.98. Keepcase. *LANG:* English; German. *SUB:* English. *FEATURES:* Commentary: film historian Werner Sudendorf ▪ Scene comparison ▪ Dietrich screen test ▪ Trailers ▪ Dietrich interview ▪ Dietrich performance ▪ Photo gallery ▪ Illustrated production notes ▪ Talent files ▪ DVD credits ▪ 21 chapters.
1930 90m/B *GE* Marlene Dietrich, Emil Jannings, Kurt Gerron, Rosa Valetti, Hans Albers; **D:** Josef von Sternberg; **W:** Robert Liebmann, Carl Zuckmayer, Karl Vollmoller; **C:** Gunther Rittau; **M:** Frederick "Friedrich" Hollander.

Blue Moon

An older couple (Gazzara and Moreno) tries to rekindle love one night in the Catskills. Hard to fault the stellar performances of these giants in this tepid if honest effort obviously destined for cable. Excellent DVD transfer and sound. —MO

Movie: ♫♫ ½ **DVD:** ♫♫ ½
Winstar Home Ent. (cat #FLV5316, UPC 7220917531625). Full frame. $24.98. Keepcase. *LANG:* English. *FEATURES:* 16 chapters ▪ Theatrical trailer ▪ Filmographies.
2000 (PG-13) 90m/C Ben Gazzara, Rita Moreno, Alanna Ubach, Brian Vincent, Heather Matarazzo, Vincent Pastore, Burt Young, Victor Argo, Lillo Brancato; **D:** John A. Gallagher; **W:** John A. Gallagher, Steve Carducci; **C:** Craig DiBona; **M:** Stephen Endelman.

Blue Submarine No. 6—Episode 1: Blues

This is the opening volume of a limited series based on the titular Japanese comic. At an undisclosed time in the future, the seas have risen dramatically and coastal cities are partially submerged. Ex-sub commander Tetsu (now a somewhat amoral scavenger) is sought out by young pilot Miyumi in an attempt to persuade him to take command of Blue Submarine No. 6. Humanity is engaged in constant battle with a race of technologically advanced humanoid sea creatures and it is hoped that No. 6 will be able to turn the tide of battle. This exciting, kinetic, somewhat experimental combination of traditional cell animation and computer animation is entertaining but somewhat awkward. The shift between the two different types of animation is a distraction and pulls the viewer out of the story. Though the backstory is only mentioned minimally, it's intriguing enough to entice one to watch the follow-up episodes. The picture quality is top-notch and vivid, and the rapidly cut action scenes suffer no digital artifacts or noise. The terrific Surround track packs quite a wallop, and is loudly mixed and tremendously involving. The subtitled version is the preferred viewing option. (It should be noted that the discs are quite pricey for the minimal contents they contain. A single disc containing a truncated version of the entire series is available but omits a considerable amount of story material.) —DG
Movie: ♫♫ ½ **DVD:** ♫♫♫ ½
Pioneer Ent. (cat #0940, UPC 669198094-095). Full frame. Dolby Digital 5.1. $19.98. Keepcase. *LANG:* Japanese; English. *SUB:* English. *FEATURES:* Booklet with chapter listing ▪ 8 chapters ▪ 4 anime trailers.
1998 29m/C *JP* **D:** Mahiro Maeda; **W:** Hiroshi Yamaguchi.

Blue Submarine No. 6—Episode 2: Pilots

As a group of submariners prepare to engage their amphibious enemies in a final battle, it becomes clear that the true enemy is evil scientist Zorndyke. Zorndyke has created the race of humanoid sea creatures and is planning on causing massive global destruction to weaken humanity's hold over the Earth. When a fleet of organic battleships attacks Blue 6's home base, broody pilot Tetsu goes off on his own to prevent its destruction. While the two types of animation still serve as a distraction, the story in this episode continues to evolve and improve. There are some interesting creatures and colorful, impressive designs for the enemy craft. The animation uses a groundbreaking cinematic style, where different areas of the frame show variant areas of focus unlike traditional cell animation where all planes of distance are sharply delineated. Also impressive are several scenes with a very quiet, visual, observant and filmic pace. The disc features a stunning picture and a very impressive Surround track. —DG

Movie: 🦴🦴½ **DVD:** 🦴🦴🦴½
Bandai Ent. (cat #0941, UPC 669198094-194). Full frame. Dolby Digital 5.1 Surround. $19.98. Keepcase. *LANG:* Japanese; English. *SUB:* English. *FEATURES:* Booklet with chapter listing ➤ 8 chapters.
1998 30m/C *JP D:* Mahiro Maeda; *W:* Hiroshi Yamaguchi.

Blue Submarine No. 6—Episode 3: Hearts

The story finally clicks in this exciting, opulent episode. Reluctant pilot Tetsu is rescued by the mermaid girl he saved in "Episode 1." As a bond forms between the two, one of Zorndyke's creatures—an intelligent whale that has rebelled—rescues them and takes them to meet up with Blue 6, which has escaped the base's destruction. Computer animation is used sparingly and poetically in this episode and the plot threads start to merge in gripping fashion. The excellent disc is equivalent in quality to previous volumes. —DG

Movie: 🦴🦴🦴 **DVD:** 🦴🦴🦴½
Bandai Ent. (cat #0942, UPC 669198094-293). Full frame. Dolby Digital 5.1 Surround. $19.98. Keepcase. *LANG:* Japanese; English. *SUB:* English. *FEATURES:* Booklet with chapter listing ➤ 8 chapters.
1998 30m/C *JP D:* Mahiro Maeda; *W:* Hiroshi Yamaguchi.

Blue Submarine No. 6—Episode 4: Minasoko

Tetsu and Kino set off to Antarctica to confront evil scientist Zorndyke while Blue 6 and the rest of the submarine fleet prepare a nuclear missile strike on Zorndyke's base. Low-key somewhat disappointing conclusion goes the intellectual route but still leaves too many questions unanswered. The Zorndyke character is so low-key and depressive that he almost completely vanishes from the screen. The mood and tone of the entire show are quite evocative and the last shot is absolutely perfect. The "Creator's Eyes" video is fairly substantial, if a bit dull and experimental. Some aliasing and edge shimmer is visible in this "making of" program. The episode itself looks and sounds as terrific as previous episodes in the set. While it is extremely pricey to purchase the

series as individual discs, the one-disc "movie" compilation that is available is cut down and censored. The four-disc version is the preferred format. —DG

Movie: 🦴🦴🦴 **DVD:** 🦴🦴🦴½
Bandai Ent. (cat #0943, UPC 669198094-392). Full frame. Dolby Digital 5.1 Surround. $19.98. Keepcase. *LANG:* Japanese; English. *SUB:* English. *FEATURES:* Booklet with chapter listing ➤ 10 chapters ➤ "Creator's Eyes" video.
1998 41m/C *JP D:* Mahiro Maeda; *W:* Hiroshi Yamaguchi.

Blue Thunder

Police helicopter pilot Frank Murphy (Scheider) is chosen to test a high-tech chopper that can see through walls, record a whisper, and level city blocks. Seems the antiterrorist toy is needed for security during the 1984 Olympics, but other nefarious forces are at work. Plotting and script are both clichéd but lively, and the cast is solid from top to bottom. On DVD, blacks are on the soft side but grain is at a minimum in the night scenes, and the aerial work looks as good as I remember it from the theatrical release. Sound is adequate. —MM

Movie: 🦴🦴½ **DVD:** 🦴🦴
Columbia Tristar (cat #1389). Widescreen anamorphic; full frame. Dolby Digital Surround. $19.95. Keepcase. *LANG:* English; French. *SUB:* English; French. *FEATURES:* 28 chapters ➤ Trailer.
1983 (R) 110m/C Roy Scheider, Daniel Stern, Malcolm McDowell, Candy Clark, Warren Oates; *D:* John Badham; *W:* Dan O'Bannon, Don Jakoby; *C:* John A. Alonzo. *AWARDS: NOM:* Oscars '83: Film Editing.

Bluebeard

Artist and puppeteer Albert Garron (Carradine) strangles his lovers when he becomes aware of their human imperfections. As he falls in love with a pretty young dressmaker (Jean Parker), an undercover policewoman (the dressmaker's sister) puts herself in danger to catch him. A labor of love for Ulmer, this stylish and atmospheric B-film wrings every last penny out of the minuscule budget and tells its story in evocative, foggy, 18th-century Paris settings. The performances are strong for a quickie such as this, but some awkward plotting and a technically fumbled ending take this one down a notch. Previously available only in hideous-looking video versions, this edition is the best yet available. Made primarily from a 35mm French archival print this version isn't perfect, but the best this film will probably ever find. The print is fairly clean but has a few splices; it is also a bit dark and the sound is on the squawky side. The supplements, including rare behind-the-scenes color footage of the puppet featured in the film, are interesting. For fans of the film, this version is a must-have. —DG

Movie: 🦴🦴½ **DVD:** 🦴🦴
All Day Ent. (cat #99010002, UPC 64968-6988129). Full frame. Dolby Digital Mono. $24.98. Keepcase. *LANG:* English. *FEA-*

TURES: Still and artwork gallery ➤ "Bluebeard Revealed" featurette with color footage ➤ Insert booklet with notes ➤ 11 chapters.
1944 73m/B John Carradine, Jean Parker, Nils Asther; *D:* Edgar G. Ulmer; *W:* Pierre Gendron; *C:* Jock Feindel.

Boa

Relentlessly nonsensical sci-fi horror imagines that a maximum-security prison is being built in Antarctica. Construction awakens a giant sleeping computer-generated boa constrictor. Princeton professor (Cain) and wife (Lackey) are brought in by the warden (Wasson) to set things right. Minimal sets are kept deliberately dark to hide their impoverished look, and Surround effects are heightened in a futile effort to distract viewers from the silly visuals. Overall, the film attempts to do far too much with far too little money and talent. On any medium, this one's good for *MST3K* laughs and little else. —MM

Movie: 🦴½ **DVD:** 🦴½
Columbia Tristar (cat #09316, UPC 043-396093164). Full frame. Dolby Digital 5.1 Surround; Dolby Surround. $24.98. Keepcase. *LANG:* English. *SUB:* English; Spanish. *CAP:* English. *FEATURES:* 20 chapters ➤ Talent files ➤ Trailers.
2002 (R) 95m/C Dean Cain, Mark Sheppard, Grand Bush, Craig Wasson, Elizabeth Lackey; *D:* Phillip J. Roth; *W:* Phillip J. Roth, Terry Neish; *C:* Todd Barron; *M:* Rich McHugh.

Bob le Flambeur

Paris. Bob Montagné (Duchesne) is a professional gambler who's managed to stay clear of criminal activity for 20 years, after serving time for a bank job in the '30s. He plays paternalistic mentor for Paolo (Cauchy) and looks after Anne (Corey), a promiscuous young thing whom the unscrupulous Marc (Buhr) wants to put out on the streets. Even though he's a good friend of inspector Ledru (Decomble), bad gambling luck tempts him to put together a caper with the aim of knocking off a large casino in Deauville. It's a gamble few have won, and Bob seems to be doing it for almost existential reasons. Even though its modest budget shows every so often, the film is an engrossing crime tale set amid the French equivalent of the lowlifes who animated John Huston's *The Asphalt Jungle.* Criterion's DVD looks stunning, as if we were seeing a 1955 answer print in Paris. A few cuts rock at the splice point, and that is literally it. The soundtrack is also very clean for an independent film, suggesting that the dialogue was post recorded; what little music there is sounds good as well. The film has lots of odd cues that don't add up to much and haven't dated well, along with some clunky optical transitions. They're details that add to the curio interest, such as the director billing himself as simply "Melville." The two extras start with a great interview with actor Daniel Cauchy, now an elderly producer. He very quickly gives us a good idea of the unusual way *Bob* was filmed—two years of work whenever Melville could round up more production cash. The radio interview with Melville is from 1960 and spends a lot of time comparing his work to the New Wave directors who were then the rage. —*GE* **AKA:** *Bob the Gambler.*

Movie: 🎵🎵🎵 ½ **DVD:** 🎵🎵🎵🎵
Criterion (cat #150, UPC 037429165928). Full frame. Dolby Digital Mono. $29.98. Keepcase. *LANG:* French. *SUB:* English. *FEATURES:* 27 chapters ▪ Liner notes by Luc Sante ▪ 1970 text interview from "Melville on Melville" by Rui Nogueira ▪ Video interview with Daniel Cauchy ▪ Trailer ▪ Radio interview with Melville.
1955 97m/B *FR* Roger Duchesne, Isabel Corey, Daniel Cauchy, Howard Vernon, Gerard Buhr, Guy Decomble; **D:** Jean-Pierre Melville; **W:** Jean-Pierre Melville, Auguste Le Breton; **C:** Henri Decae; **M:** Jean Boyer, Eddie Barclay.

The Body

Would-be religious thriller with wooden acting, laughable dialogue, and clunky plot. In modern-day Jerusalem, Israeli archeologist Sharon Golban (Williams) checks out a tomb discovered beneath a shop and finds the skeleton of a crucified man. Could it be the remains of Jesus? When word reaches the Vatican, Cardinal Pesci (Wood) dispatches Father Matt Gutierrez (Banderas) to deal with the provocative situation. This is a very average DVD. The image varies from sharp to soft and there are some real problems with shots featuring a lot of detail. On occasion the picture shimmers and injects a pattern on the screen. Colors are undersaturated yet still bleed—reds are a real problem. Blacks are also inconsistent, ranging from almost there to gray and grainy. The 5.1 soundtrack does fine for the music score, but is otherwise nothing special, if anything at times inducing an artificial sound to the dialogue. Rent it if you just gotta see it, but you won't be missing much if you don't. —*JO*
Movie: 🎵 **DVD:** 🎵 ½
Columbia Tristar (cat #06595, UPC 04339-6065956). Widescreen (2.35:1) anamorphic; full frame. Dolby Digital 5.1; Dolby Surround. $24.95. Keepcase. *LANG:* English. *SUB:* English; French. *CAP:* English. *FEATURES:* 28 chapters ▪ Theatrical trailer ▪ Talent files.
2001 (PG-13) 108m/C Antonio Banderas, Olivia Williams, John Wood, John Shrapnel, Derek Jacobi, Jason Flemyng, Makram Khoury, Vernon Dobtcheff, Ian McNeice; **D:** Jonas McCord; **W:** Jonas McCord; **C:** Vilmos Zsigmond; **M:** Serge Colbert.

Body Count

Daniel (Theroux) takes his fiancée Suzanne (Milano) home to meet his wealthy family. The couple is out of the immediate line of fire when thieves (led by Ice-T) break in to steal the art collection. An elaborate game of hide and seek ensues and before it's all over the place is littered with dead and almost-dead bodies. The full-frame image is very sharp, making it a bit better than VHS tape. —*MM* **AKA:** *Below Utopia.*
Movie: 🎵🎵 **DVD:** 🎵🎵 ½
Artisan Ent. (cat #10201, UPC 01223610-2014). Full frame. Dolby Digital Stereo. $14.98. Keepcase. *LANG:* English. *CAP:* English. *FEATURES:* 16 chapters.
1997 (R) 88m/C Ice-T, Alyssa Milano, Justin Theroux, Tommy (Tiny) Lister, Jeannette O'Connor, Nicholas Walker, Eric Saiet, Marta Kristen, Ron Harper, Robert Pine, Richard Danielson; **D:** Kurt Voss; **W:** David Diamond; **C:** Denis Maloney; **M:** Joseph Williams.

The Bodyguard [BFS]

Sonny Chiba, pretty much playing himself, vows to smash a whole drug ring. He offers himself as bodyguard to anyone who will step forward to testify against them. A young woman takes his offer, but what Chiba actually wants is someone to act as bait for the bad guys. The script is a bit of a mess, so you'd expect a Chiba picture to pay off with more action. Unfortunately, outside of a few scenes, he does more dodging around than direct fighting. The U.S. version is padding with scenes shot in New York City. Available as part of a triple feature on one disc entitled *Classic Sonny Chiba Movies.* The image is vibrant, if a bit soft, and cropped on the sides. —*BT*
Movie: 🎵 ½ **DVD:** 🎵 ½
BFS Video (cat #30235D, UPC 06680530-2350). Full frame. $9.98. Keepcase. *LANG:* English. *FEATURES:* 4 chapters ▪ Bio ▪ Filmography ▪ Trivia.
1976 (R) 89m/C *JP* Sue Shiomi, Sonny Chiba, Aaron Banks, Bill Louie, Judy Lee; **D:** Maurice Sarli.

Boesman & Lena

The adaptation of the apartheid-era play by Athol Fugard follows the travails of downtrodden couple Boesman (Glover) and Lena (Bassett). Their shanty-town home in Cape Town has been bulldozed by the government, so they take to the dusty road with their meager belongings, constantly bickering about their plight. The couple constructs a makeshift adobe for the night, which attracts the attention of an old man (Jonah), who is even lower on the economic ladder. Lena allows the man to stay, much to Boesman's displeasure. The performances in this film are outstanding, but the story gets to be grating after a while. This DVD offers both a letterboxed and full-frame transfer of the film. The image here is very good, showing little grain and only the slightest edge-enhancement. Also of note are the rich colors on this transfer. The audio track is especially good, offering a rich bass and impressive Surround sound effects. Interviews with the cast and crew offer insight into the making of the film. A bit of trivia: director John Berry, known for making such serious films as this one, directed 1978's *The Bad News Bears Go to Japan!* —*ML*

Movie: 🎵🎵 ½ **DVD:** 🎵🎵🎵 ½
Kino on Video (cat #K209 DVD, UPC 7383-29020927). Widescreen (2.35:1) letterboxed; full frame. Dolby 2.0 Surround. $29.95. Keepcase. *LANG:* English. *FEATURES:* Cast & crew interviews ▪ Theatrical trailer ▪ Cast & crew bios ▪ 12 chapters.
2000 86m/C *FR* Danny Glover, Angela Bassett, Willie Jonah; **D:** John Berry; **W:** John Berry; **C:** Alain Choquart; **M:** Wally Badarou.

Bones

Bones offers the odd combination of Italian Gothic horror with an urban, hip-hop attitude. The result is a film that feels very unoriginal, and yet, is like nothing that you've seen before. The story concerns a haunted house in the heart of a rundown city. (The house itself resembles a skull.) When four young entrepreneurs, Patrick (Khalil Kain), Bill (Merwin Mondesir), Tia (Katharine Isabelle), and Maurice (Sean Amsing), decide to buy the house and transform it into a nightclub, they inadvertently awaken the ghost that resides inside. It seems that gentleman gangster Jimmy Bones (Snoop Dogg) was murdered in the house by a group of rivals, and his soul is still hungry for revenge. Following his grisly resurrection, Jimmy decimates the club and takes to the streets, seeking his vengeance. Director Ernest Dickerson *(Tales from the Crypt: Demon Knight)* has given *Bones* a fantastic look and keeps things moving at a nice pace, but he never slows down long enough to explain exactly what is going on. Parts of the film are extremely confusing and seemingly major plot points (such as a demonic dog which roams the house) are never explained. Also, we are never given a clear idea of exactly what Jimmy's motivation is. At first, he appears to be like *The Crow,* simply looking to avenge his death, but then, the movie takes an odd turn and only gets more confusing. These plot problems aside, *Bones* is by no means the worst horror film of the year, and it does manage to scare up a creepy atmosphere and some goopy special effects. The *Bones* DVD is anything but bare-bones, as New Line offers us a jam-packed special edition. The image here borders on perfect, as there is basically no grain, distortion, or artifacting. The colors are very deep and true, and the rich blacks make the oft-used reds and blues look even better. The DTS ES 6.1 audio track is incredibly textured and detailed, offering a booming bass and a plethora of Surround effects. The Dolby Digital 5.1 track offered here isn't quite as rich as the DTS audio, but it is impressive as well. The DVD contains a wealth of special features, including a featurette which explores the European horror films which influenced *Bones.* The audio commentary with director Dickerson, Snoop Dogg, and co-writer Adam Simon is very good, although Snoop doesn't speak very often and his voice is so soft that he's often difficult to hear. Dickerson is technically oriented and is perhaps most interesting during the deleted scenes where he talks about the various pressures (most involving time) that caused scenes to be cut or shortened. —*ML/MM*

Movie: 🦴🦴 ***DVD:*** 🦴🦴🦴🦴

New Line (cat #5407, UPC 7940435407-21). Widescreen (2.35:1) anamorphic. DTS ES 6.1; Dolby Digital EX 5.1; Stereo Surround. $24.95. Keepcase. *LANG:* English. *SUB:* English. *FEATURES:* Commentary • Featurettes • Deleted scenes • Music videos • Theatrical trailer • Bios • Production notes • 19 chapters.

2001 (R) 94m/C Snoop Dogg, Pam Grier, Michael T. Weiss, Clifton Powell, Ricky Harris, Bianca Lawson, Khalil Kain, Katharine Isabelle, Merwin Mondesir, Sean Amsing; ***D:*** Ernest R. Dickerson; ***W:*** Adam Simon; ***C:*** Flavio Labiano; ***M:*** Elia Cmiral.

Bongwater

This is a wacky film that would have been so much better with a coherent story line and characters you care about. Of course it is a film about chronic pot smokers in their 20s, so that might be a lot to ask for if it wasn't based on a book that did have a real beginning, middle, and an end. Bitter literature-major blues aside, it is still fun to watch, if not for the film as a whole, then for Alicia Witt's costumes and the cool set decoration, both of which give the film a cartoon feel, and the snortingly funny characters. David (Wilson) is the local pot dealer. His friends include a gay couple (Dick and Sisto), a Humboldt supplier (Black), a crazy rich girl (Murphy), and a semi-slutty girl (Locane). He meets slutty-girl's friend (Witt) and falls in love. It's not a love that shows much on the screen, but we go with it. When she bails to follow a guitar player to New York, the ensuing fight causes him to go to the nearest strip bar to drink, and her to knock over a candle on the way out that ends up burning down his house. Witt and Wilson spend the rest of the time talking to their friends about how they don't care about each other (her in N.Y. and he in Seattle) and sleeping with other people. It's all worth it for the '80s party that Dick and Sisto throw towards the end. The color on the disc is fabulous. Reds, greens, and the occasional blacks all get their due and the sound is very good. —*CA*

Movie: 🦴🦴 ***DVD:*** 🦴🦴🦴 ½

Image Ent. (cat #OVED 323 DVD, UPC 014-38103231). Full frame. Dolby Digital 5.1; Dolby Digital Surround. $19.99. Keepcase. *LANG:* English. *FEATURES:* 12 chapters.

1998 (R) 98m/C Luke Wilson, Alicia Witt, Amy Locane, Brittany Murphy, Jack Black, Andy Dick, Jeremy Sisto, Jamie Kennedy, Scott Caan, Patricia Wettig; ***D:*** Richard Sears; ***W:*** Nora Macoby, Eric Weiss; ***C:*** Richard Crudo; ***M:*** Mark Mothersbaugh, Josh Mancell.

Boogeymen

Compilation DVD focuses on 17 villains from the world of horror films, presenting them neatly arranged, with an introduction, three trivia facts, and two film clips each. The villains featured range from well-known baddies such as Michael Myers, Jason Voorhees, and Freddy Krueger, and lesser-known villains such as Camilla from *The Guardian* and the Djinn from *Wishmaster.* The quality of the video varies, but it's never bad. Some clips are grainier than others, but it's clear that an attempt was made to clean up many of the scenes. Aspect ratios also vary, but NO clips are shown in 2.35:1, and the clip from *Halloween* is even shown full-frame! The audio is a Dolby Digital 5.1, which, once again varies from clip to clip. For some there is a nice use of Surround sound, while the rear speakers stay silent for others. —*GH/ML*

Movie: 🦴🦴 ***DVD:*** 🦴🦴

Universal Studios (cat #21371, UPC 0251-92127129). Full frame. Dolby Digital 5.1 Surround Stereo. $1998.00. Keepcase. *LANG:* English. *SUB:* French; Spanish. *CAP:* English. *FEATURES:* Commentary: Robert Englund • Character thumbnail bios • Stills • Trailers • DVD-ROM features.

2001 58m/C

Borderline

MacMurray and Trevor play undercover agents trying to infiltrate a Mexican drug ring. With their real identities hidden, they fall for each other. The leads work well together but director Seiter seems unsure whether the material is comic or dramatic. Title is available on the *Great Cop Movies* triple feature and it's the sharpest of the three, with only light static on the soundtrack. Image is a shade sharper than VHS tape. —*MM*

Movie: 🦴🦴 ***DVD:*** 🦴🦴

BFS Video (cat #30174-D, UPC 066805-301742). Full frame. $9.98. Keepcase. *LANG:* English. *FEATURES:* 4 chapters.

1950 88m/B Fred MacMurray, Claire Trevor, Raymond Burr, Roy Roberts, Jose Torvay, Morris Ankrum, Charles Lane, Don Diamond, Nacho Galindo, Pepe Hern, Richard Irving; ***D:*** William A. Seiter; ***C:*** Lucien N. Andriot; ***M:*** Hans J. Salter.

Boris Karloff DVD Double Feature

In the first entry in the series, the cunning detective Mr. Wong (Karloff) traps a killer who feigns guilt to throw suspicion away from himself. In the second, Mr. Wong aids the police in solving the murder of a detective. Both films contain a fair amount of light scratching. *Mr. Wong* generally has a good image for a film of its age. Though two years younger, *Fatal Hour* looks much grainier. That appears to come from the original, not the DVD transfer. (See separate entries for credits.) —*MM*

Movie: 🦴🦴 ***DVD:*** 🦴🦴

Marengo Films (cat #0011, UPC 807013-001129). Full frame. $14.98. Keepcase. *LANG:* English. *FEATURES:* 4 chapters each.

2000 138m/C

Born Romantic

Three men chase three women around contemporary London in hopes of making a genuine emotional connection, albeit in a lightweight fashion. Frankie (Ferguson) woos ice cold Eleanor (Williams); Fergus searches for his former fiancée; Jocelyn (Horrocks) tries to dodge a petty criminal. A philosophizing taxi driver holds them all together. Charming, but not a classic. DVD looks and sounds great. —*LA*

Movie: 🦴🦴 ½ ***DVD:*** 🦴🦴🦴

MGM Home Ent. (UPC 027616874795). Widescreen anamorphic. Dolby Digital Stereo. $26.98. Keepcase. *LANG:* English.

2000 (R) 97m/C *GB* Craig Ferguson, Adrian Lester, Catherine McCormack, Jimi Mistry, David Morrissey, Olivia Williams, Jane Horrocks, Hermione Norris, Ian Hart, Kenneth Cranham, John Thompson, Paddy Considine; ***D:*** David Kane; ***W:*** David Kane; ***C:*** Robert Alazraki; ***M:*** Simon Boswell.

Borough of Kings

Jimmy O'Conner (Stanek) is trying to get away from a life of crime in Brooklyn but the ties are hard to cut. Similar stories have been told dozens of times before. This little independent production has a strong spirit and commitment to the characters on its side. Those outweigh its predictability. On their commentary track, director Lewin and producer/writer/actor Newall round up the usual indie-prod stories, and their affection for the work is evident throughout. The deleted scenes are very rough looking, and Lewin must be thanking her lucky stars that she was talked out of the romantic love scene that's filled with floating feathers. The shot-on-location, grainy image gains nothing on DVD. Extras are the main drawing point. —*MM*

Movie: 🦴🦴🦴 ***DVD:*** 🦴🦴 ½

Studio Home Ent. (cat #AV1586D, UPC 806469158623). Full frame. Dolby Digital 5.1 Surround Stereo. $19.98. Keepcase. *LANG:* English. *SUB:* English; French; Spanish. *CAP:* English. *FEATURES:* 24 chapters • Commentary • Deleted scenes • Interviews • Trailers.

1998 (R) 95m/C Philip Bosco, Jim Stanek, Kerry Butler, Joseph Lyle Taylor, Erik Jensen, Patrick Newall, Olympia Dukakis; ***D:*** Elyse Lewin; ***W:*** Patrick Newall; ***C:*** Nils Kenaston; ***M:*** Alan Elliott.

Boss of Bosses

Chazz Palminteri stars in made-for-cable gangster flick as Paul Castellano, who is shot repeatedly in the opening scene. Flashback to his youth in 1933. Production values are a solid cut above average and so are the image and sound. The film looks as sharp as a big-budget theatrical release. Alas, that clarity makes both the strenuous overacting by the supporting cast and their cartoon-ish Italian accents even more egregious. —*MM*

Movie: 🦴🦴 ***DVD:*** 🦴🦴 ½

Warner (cat #T6603, UPC 0539396603-26). Widescreen (1.85:1) letterboxed. Dolby Surround. $19.98. Snapper. *LANG:* English; French. *SUB:* English; French; Spanish. *FEATURES:* 27 chapters.

1999 94m/C Chazz Palminteri, Daniel Benzali, Jay O. Sanders, Clancy Brown, Al Ruscio, Steven Bauer, Angela Alvarado, Sonny Marinelli; **D:** Dwight Little; **W:** Jere P. Cunningham; **C:** Brian Reynolds; **M:** John Altman.

Boundaries

Standard video premiere erotic thriller revolves around Reggie (Shower, miscredited as "Showers" on the box copy) who thinks that her hubby is having an affair so she sets out for a fling herself. It's fairly tepid stuff that gains nothing on this bare-bones DVD. No menu; image and sound are identical to VHS tape. —*MM* **AKA:** Erotic Boundaries.
Movie: 🎵🎵 **DVD:** 🎵🎵
York Ent. (cat #YPD-1161, UPC 75072311-6129). Full frame. $14.98. Keepcase. *LANG:* English.
1997 (R) 90m/C Kathy Shower, Tim Agee, Lisa Comshaw, Carolyn Smith; **D:** Mike Sedan; **W:** Helen Haxton; **C:** Chris Moreman.

Bowery at Midnight

Lugosi plays a dual role as a psychologist who runs a soup kitchen and a criminal mastermind who recycles criminals into zombies that commit crimes for his benefit. Even a double shot of Bela can't raise this fast-moving silliness from the realm of pulp entertainment. DVD does a fine job with imperfect source material that suffers from registration woes, murky photography, light snow, and the tinny, distorted sound typical of the era. —*MM*
Movie: 🎵½ **DVD:** 🎵🎵½
Troma Team Video (cat #AED-2054, UPC 785604205425). Full frame. Dolby Digital Mono. $24.99. Keepcase. *LANG:* English. *FEATURES:* 7 chapters • Credits • Film background (text).
1942 60m/B Bela Lugosi, Tom Neal, Dave O'Brien, Wanda McKay; **D:** Wallace Fox; **W:** Gerald Schnitzer; **C:** Mack Stengler; **M:** Edward Kay.

Boxcar Bertha

Scorsese's vivid portrayal of the South during the 1930s' Depression is *Bonnie and Clyde* with an unapologetic political bias. Barbara Hershey is a free-wheeling, free-thinking woman who winds up in cahoots with anti-establishment train robber David Carradine. Based on the book *Sister of the Road* by Boxcar Bertha Thomson, the film contains few hints of the talent Martin Scorsese would show later. DVD looks good but it's no better than the source material. Overall, it's certainly superior to the picture I first saw at the drive-in all those years ago and to full-frame video-tapes. —*MM*
Movie: 🎵🎵½ **DVD:** 🎵🎵½
MGM Home Ent. (cat #1003247, UPC 027-616873972). Widescreen (1.85:1) anamorphic. Dolby Digital Mono. $19.98. Keepcase. *LANG:* English; French. *SUB:* English; French; Spanish. *CAP:* English. *FEATURES:* 16 chapters • Trailer.
1972 (R) 90m/C Barbara Hershey, David Carradine, John Carradine, Barry Primus, Bernie Casey, Victor Argo, Martin Scorsese, John Stephens; **D:** Martin Scorsese;

W: John W. Corrington, Joyce H. Corrington; **C:** John Stephens; **M:** Gib Guilbeau, Thad Maxwell.

The Boy in the Plastic Bubble [2]

Please see review of *Killer B Double Feature*.
Movie: 🎵🎵½
1976 100m/C John Travolta, Robert Reed, Glynnis O'Connor, Diana Hyland, Ralph Bellamy, Anne Ramsey, Vernee Watson-Johnson, P.J. Soles, John Friedrich; **D:** Randal Kleiser; **W:** Douglas Day Stewart; **C:** Arch R. Dalzell; **M:** Paul Williams, Mark Snow.

Boycott

A solid, well scripted, beautifully acted slice of a pivotal event in the fight for civil rights. Starting from Rosa Park's refusal to move to the back of the bus simply because she is black, the story chronicles the upheaval that follows her act. Delving into the positive and negative reactions of both the black and the white communities gives the work an evenhanded feel absent in films like *The Long Walk Home*. Rising to the top of the pro side in the black community is the little known Reverend Martin Luther King (a restrained Wright). Sappy as it sounds, this is the kind of film that makes you believe in heroes and the ability of humanity to rise above its limitations. Of note, it's directed by Clark Johnson, who played Meldnk on the underrated series *Homicide: Life on the Streets*. The film was shot for television and has a nice color mix with good definition and good sound. —*CA*
Movie: 🎵🎵🎵 **DVD:** 🎵🎵🎵½
HBO (cat #91779, UPC 026359177927). Full frame. Dolby Digital Surround; Stereo. $24.90. Snapper. *LANG:* English; Spanish. *SUB:* English; French; Spanish. *CAP:* English. *FEATURES:* 17 chapters • Cast & director bios.
2002 112m/C Jeffrey Wright, Terrence DaShon Howard, CCH Pounder, Carmen Ejogo, Reg E. Cathey, Brent Jennings, Shawn Michael Howard, Erik Todd Dellums, Iris Little-Thomas, Whitman Mayo, E. Roger Mitchell, Mike Hodge, Clark Johnson; **D:** Clark Johnson; **W:** Timothy J. Sexton, Herman Daniel Farrell III; **C:** David Hennings; **M:** Stephen James Taylor.

Brain Drain

Young Argentine street kids are thieves who specialize in car radios. Their dreams of a better life are at odds with their surroundings. Things go wrong when they make false accusations against a cop and he comes after them. Full-frame image is no better than VHS tape or broadcast. Bright yellow colloquial subtitles are burned in and easy to read. —*MM*
Movie: 🎵🎵 **DVD:** 🎵🎵
Vanguard Intl. Cinema (cat #VF9206, UPC 658769920635). Full frame. $29.98. Keepcase. *LANG:* Spanish. *SUB:* English. *FEATURES:* 11 chapters.

1998 92m/C Nicolas Cabre, Luis Quiroz, Enrique Liporace; **D:** Fernando Musa; **W:** Fernando Musa, Branko Andjic; **C:** Carlos Torlaschi; **M:** Luis Maria Serra.

The Brain that Wouldn't Die

Please see review for *Mystery Science Theater 3000: "The Brain that Wouldn't Die."*
AKA: The Head that Wouldn't Die.
Movie: 🎵🎵½
1963 92m/B Herb Evers, Virginia Leith, Adele Lamont, Leslie Daniel, Bruce Brighton, Paula Maurice; **D:** Joseph Green; **W:** Joseph Green; **C:** Stephen Hajinal; **M:** Tony Restaino.

Bram Stoker's Dracula [SB]

While the previous DVD release (reviewed in *Book 1* as *Dracula*) had excellent picture and sound quality, this one pushes it a notch higher. Some dark scenes are still grainy but that's how they appeared in theatres. Fleshtones, faces, and close-ups look stunning. The opening studio logo is surprisingly filthy and marked, and of course, being "Superbit," there are no extras. —*DG* **AKA:** Dracula.
Movie: 🎵🎵🎵 **DVD:** 🎵🎵🎵½
Columbia Tristar (cat #07909, UPC 0433-96079090). Widescreen (1.85:1) anamorphic. DTS; Dolby Digital Surround. $27.95. Keepcase. *LANG:* English. *SUB:* English; French; Spanish; Portuguese; Chinese; Korean; Thai. *CAP:* English. *FEATURES:* 28 chapters • "Superbit" info booklet.
1992 (R) 128m/C Gary Oldman, Winona Ryder, Anthony Hopkins, Keanu Reeves, Richard E. Grant, Cary Elwes, Billy Campbell, Sadie Frost, Tom Waits; **D:** Francis Ford Coppola; **W:** Jim V. Hart; **C:** Michael Ballhaus; **AWARDS:** Oscars '92: Costume Des., Makeup, Sound FX Editing; **NOM:** Oscars '92: Art Dir./Set Dec.

Brannigan

John Wayne makes a not-completely comfortable transition to the *Dirty Harry*–style crime movie. He plays a rough-and-tumble Chicago cop who travels to London to arrest a racketeer who has fled the States rather than face a grand jury indictment. DVD image is on the bright, pale side with very little surface damage. Some flashing background patterns are the only real distraction. —*MM*
Movie: 🎵🎵½ **DVD:** 🎵🎵½
MGM Home Ent. (cat #1002568, UPC 027-616867698). Widescreen (2.35:1) anamorphic. Dolby Digital Mono. $14.95. Keepcase. *LANG:* English; French; Spanish. *SUB:* French; Spanish. *CAP:* English. *FEATURES:* Trailer • 16 chapters.
1975 (PG) 111m/C John Wayne, John Vernon, Mel Ferrer, Daniel Pilon, James Booth, Ralph Meeker, Lesley-Anne Down, Richard Attenborough; **D:** Douglas Hickox; **W:** Michael Butler, William W. Norton Sr.; **C:** Gerry Fisher; **M:** Dominic Frontiere.

Bravo

Low-budget action film attempts to take a standard Chuck Norris–style plot and jazz it up with *El Mariachi* locales and attitude. Carlos Bravo (Callardo) is a secret service agent whose loyalty to President Montana (Ganem) knows no bounds. Even after Bravo's been sacked, he comes back to rescue his peerless leader from kidnappers. The young filmmakers had neither the budget nor the experience to stage exciting fight scenes. These are fairly slow and pedestrian. On the other hand, the cast is attractive and fresh and the plotting is fervid. Full-frame DVD image is generally very good but is still not a huge improvement over VHS tape. The filmmakers' commentary has a strong "can you believe we're doing this?" quality. —*MM*
Movie: 🎬🎬 **DVD:** 🎬🎬 ½
Xenon Ent. (cat #XE XX4092DVD, UPC 000-799409220). Full frame. $24.98. Keepcase. *LANG:* English; Spanish. *FEATURES:* 12 chapters • Behind-the-scenes featurette • Talent files • Trailers • Commentary: producer, director.
1998 85m/C Carlos Gallardo, Richard Livingston, Gustvo Ganem; *D:* Lorena David; *W:* Eric P. Sherman.

Bravo Two Zero

During the Persian Gulf War, a British Special Forces team infiltrates Iraq on a mission to cut the communication line from Baghdad to mobile SCUD launchers. A good portion of the film involves their torture at the hands of Iraqi soldiers after they are captured. The film tries to convince us we are witnessing courage against the odds, but it might be just sadistic. The picture has a grainy look to it, and background detail is minimal. The soundtrack is a good 2-channel mix, and features lots of loud things. The disc is pretty bare bones, considering its high price tag. —*BG*
Movie: 🎬🎬 **DVD:** 🎬🎬 ½
Buena Vista Home Ent. (cat #23954, UPC 786936164763). Widescreen (1.85:1) anamorphic. Dolby Surround. $32.95. Keepcase. *LANG:* English. *CAP:* English. *FEATURES:* 20 chapters • Trailer.
1999 115m/C Sean Bean, Steve Nicolson, Rick Warden; *D:* Tom Clegg.

Bread and Chocolate

Brilliant satire on the very real problems of immigrant Italian workers living in Switzerland. Italian-to-the-core Nino (Manfredi) attempts to build a better life for his family back in Italy by trying his hand at a number of menial jobs in a spotless Swiss city. To the uptight Swiss, he might as well be an animal. He fails so miserably that he finally doesn't know whether he's coming or going. The sound is typically mediocre for an Italian film of this era. Unfortunately, the grainy transfer was made from a beat-up release print of the film. —*LA* **AKA:** Pane e Cioccolata.
Movie: 🎬🎬🎬 ½ **DVD:** 🎬 ½

Hen's Tooth Video (cat #4050, UPC 75973-1405027). Widescreen (1.85:1) letterboxed. $24.98. Keepcase. *LANG:* Italian. *SUB:* English. *FEATURES:* Original theatrical trailer • 12 chapters.
1973 110m/C *IT* Nino Manfredi, Anna Karina, Johnny Dorelli, Paolo Turco; *D:* Franco Brusati; *W:* Nino Manfredi, Franco Brusati, Iaia Fiastri; *C:* Luciano Tovoli; *M:* Daniele Patrucchi. *AWARDS:* N.Y. Film Critics '78: Foreign Film.

Bread and Roses

This eye-opening and political charged film should be a wake-up call to many Americans. Maya (Pilar Padilla) illegally crosses the border from Mexico into the United States to live with her sister Rosa (Elpidia Carrillo). After taking a disastrous job as a cocktail waitress, Maya goes to work with Rosa as a housekeeper in a high-rise office building. But she soon learns that the "American Dream" can be difficult to obtain. Her boss, who was nice enough to give her the job, attempts to extort money from her and the work is very demanding. She then meets Sam (Adrien Brody), an idealistic young man who is attempting to unionize the immigrant workers so that they can get the salaries and benefits which they deserve. What Sam, Maya, and their compatriots find is that they have a great battle ahead of them. This important and moving film realistically portrays the plight of the exploited workers and attempts to convey the hardships they endure. It's a bit talky and preachy at times, but it's also engaging, right up to the surprising ending. While shorn of any extra features (a look at real-life workers would have been nice), this is still an adequate DVD. The film is presented in a letterboxed format and the transfer is quite good. The image is sharp and clear, showing a minimal amount of grain and some sporadic defects from the source print. The Dolby Digital 5.1 audio track is clean and free from distortion, although the sound coming from the rear speakers is typically limited to musical cues. —*ML*
Movie: 🎬🎬🎬 **DVD:** 🎬🎬🎬
Studio Home Ent. (cat #7886D, UPC 658-149788626). Widescreen (1.85:1) letterboxed. Dolby Digital 5.1. $24.95. Keepcase. *LANG:* English. *SUB:* English; Spanish. *CAP:* English. *FEATURES:* Trailer • 24 chapters.
2000 (R) 106m/C *GB* Adrien Brody, Elpidia Carrillo, Pilar Padilla, George Lopez, Jack McGee, Alonso Chavez; *D:* Ken Loach; *W:* Paul Laverty; *C:* Barry Ackroyd; *M:* George Fenton.

Bread and Tulips

The incredibly charming adventures of an unappreciated housewife. On a coach tour vacation with her cranky husband and two self-absorbed teenage sons, Rosalba (Maglietta) is left behind at a rest stop. Instead of waiting for the bus to return for her, she hitchhikes toward home, intending to spend a little time alone, but on a whim she gets a job in Venice. When her hus-

band sends a wannabe private eye to find her, unintended but liberating results ensue. DVD picture and sound quality show that Italy has caught up with the rest of the world. —*LA* **AKA:** Pane e Tulipani.
Movie: 🎬🎬🎬 ½ **DVD:** 🎬🎬🎬
Columbia Tristar (cat #08697, UPC 43396-086975). Widescreen (1.85:1) letterboxed. Dolby Digital 5.1 Surround. $29.98. Keepcase. *LANG:* Italian. *SUB:* English. *FEATURES:* Bonus trailers • 28 chapters.
2001 (PG-13) 105m/C *IT SI* Licia Maglietta, Bruno Ganz, Marina Massironi, Guiseppe Battiston, Antonio Catania, Felice Andreasi, Vitalba Andrea; *D:* Silvio Soldini; *W:* Silvio Soldini, Doriana Leondeff; *C:* Luca Bigazzi; *M:* Giovanni Venosta.

Break of Dawn

Clumsily made-for-TV re-creation of the true story of 1930s Mexican radio personality Pedro Gonzalez (Chavez). After Gonzalez persuades a station to give him an early morning slot, his Spanish broadcasts thrust him into the center of the struggle for immigrant rights in Los Angeles. When Gonzalez won't play ball with the evil Anglo District Attorney (Schroeder), he is set up on a phony rape charge and sentenced to 50 years in San Quentin. A grave disservice is done to this very interesting story by a rudimentary script, flat performances, and the unnecessary inclusion of scratchy archival footage of old Los Angeles. The particularly murky image transfer from what appears to be a videotape of a release print of the film contributes to the general cheesiness of the enterprise. —*LA*
Movie: 🎬🎬 ½ **DVD:** 🎬
Vanguard Intl. Cinema (cat #VF0214, UPC 658769021431). Full frame. $29.98. Keepcase. *LANG:* Spanish and English. *SUB:* English. *FEATURES:* 11 chapters.
1988 105m/C Oscar Chavez, Maria Rojo, Tony Plana, Peter Henry Schroeder; *D:* Isaac Artenstein; *W:* Isaac Artenstein; *C:* Stephen Lighthill.

Breakdown

Director Mostow debuted with this stunningly tense and effective thriller. The film is essentially a waking nightmare as a couple (Russell and Quinlan) find themselves stranded in the wide-open desert country. After Quinlan takes a ride from a helpful truck driver (Walsh), Russell can't find her at their designated rendezvous point. He catches up to Walsh, who says he doesn't know where she is. With no help whatsoever, he has to find out what has become of her. The film is a solid piece of work, constantly upping the tension. Russell delivers one of his most powerful and intense performances, making for a successful and engaging character, while Walsh plays the villain perfectly with a subtle, yet incredibly menacing portrayal. The screenplay is solid and intense and the film races along at a rapid clip. DVD image is clear and sharp with nicely saturated colors. Flesh tones are natural, if sometimes a little red. There are quite a few instances of distracting shimmer; the print used shows occasional signs of wear and is occasionally grainy. The soundtrack is very good, but not particularly stunning. Surround use is occasionally aggressive, but could be stronger. The dialogue sounds clear and natural. —AB/DG

Movie: 🎬🎬🎬 **DVD:** 🎬🎬 ½
Paramount (cat #0334547, UPC 973633-45473). Widescreen (2.35:1) letterboxed. Dolby Surround 5.1; Dolby Stereo. $24.99. Keepcase. *LANG:* English; French. *SUB:* Spanish. *CAP:* English. *FEATURES:* Trailer • 31 chapters.
1996 (R) 93m/C Kurt Russell, Kathleen Quinlan, J.T. Walsh, M.C. Gainey, Jack Noseworthy, Rex Linn, Ritch Brinkley, Kim Robillard; **D:** Jonathan Mostow; **W:** Jonathan Mostow; **C:** Doug Milsome; **M:** Basil Poledouris.

Breaking Away

Spirited, imaginative, lighthearted coming-of-age drama revolves around Dave (Christopher), who's just graduated from high school in Bloomington, Indiana, and is trying on the identity of an Italian bicycle racer. His three friends (Quaid, Haley, and Stern) understand because they're at a similar loose end, as "townies" or "cutters" as they're called in this university 'burg. Dave's mom (Barrie) puts up with him but his dad (Dooley at his best) thinks that it's time for his son to grow up and be miserable, just as he did at that age. There's not a false note in Steve Tesich's Oscar-winning script, and producer/director Yates handles it with rare understanding. Image is acceptable for a film of this age; it's not going to dazzle anyone but the disc does offer both wide and full versions. Of the audio options, the mono sounds crisper than the Surround to my ears. —MM

Movie: 🎬🎬🎬 ½ **DVD:** 🎬🎬🎬
20th Century Fox (cat #2002908, UPC 024543029083). Widescreen (1.85:1) anamorphic; full frame. Dolby Digital Surround; Mono. $19.98. Keepcase. *LANG:* English; French. *SUB:* English; Spanish. *CAP:* English. *FEATURES:* 16 chapters • Trailer and TV spots.
1979 (PG) 100m/C Dennis Christopher, Dennis Quaid, Daniel Stern, Jackie Earle Haley, Barbara Barrie, Paul Dooley, Amy Wright; **D:** Peter Yates; **W:** Steve Tesich; **C:** Matthew F. Leonetti; **M:** Patrick Williams. *AWARDS:* Oscars '79: Orig. Screenplay; Golden Globes '80: Film—Mus./Comedy; Natl. Bd. of Review '79: Support. Actor (Dooley); N.Y. Film Critics '79: Screenplay; Natl. Soc. Film Critics '79: Film, Screenplay; Writers Guild '79: Orig. Screenplay; *NOM:* Oscars '79: Director (Yates), Picture, Support. Actress (Barrie), Orig. Song Score and/or Adapt.

Breaking In

Odd buddy heist film with Burt Reynolds as Ernie, a successful lifetime safecracker who stumbles upon Mike (Siemaszko) one night on a job. He decides to take the kid on as an apprentice and an awkward relationship forms between the natural loner

and the born loser. The script was written by John Sayles, whose work is amazing when he directs his own material, but is a little uneven when it's picked up by others; in this case Bill Forsyth, who directed the amazing *Gregory's Girl* but went on to drown in the horrible *Being Human*. In the end it's the surrogate family relationship created by the male leads that makes the film worth watching...that and a scene with a Doberman, well, two Dobermans. This disc looks good with some fading between colors and the sound is average. —CA

Movie: 🎬🎬 **DVD:** 🎬🎬🎬
MGM Home Ent. (cat #1003343, UPC 027-616874924). Widescreen (1.66:1) letterboxed. Dolby Digital Stereo Surround; Mono. $14.95. Keepcase. *LANG:* English; French; Spanish. *SUB:* English; French; Spanish. *CAP:* English. *FEATURES:* 16 chapters.
1989 (R) 95m/C Burt Reynolds, Casey Siemaszko, Sheila Kelley, Lorraine Toussaint, Albert Salmi, Harry Carey Jr., Maury Chaykin, Stephen Tobolowsky, David Frishberg; **D:** Bill Forsyth; **W:** John Sayles; **C:** Michael Coulter; **M:** Michael Gibbs.

Breakout

Jon Wagner (Duvall) is framed by his grandfather (Huston) for a murder he didn't commit. He's held captive in a Mexican prison with seemingly no hope of release. Ann (Ireland), Jon's wife, schemes for his escape. At every turn, however, someone is a step ahead of her. Frustrated and overwhelmed, she hires adventurer and expert pilot Nick Colton (Bronson) to get him out at any cost. With three cohorts and a helicopter, Colton gets set to fight for Jon's freedom. A convoluted script and wooden performances make this a barely average actioner. The good-looking DVD transfer shows off Ballard's fine photography. The mono sound is clear, if a little light. —DRL

Movie: 🎬🎬 **DVD:** 🎬🎬 ½
Columbia Tristar (cat #4862, UPC 043-396048621). Widescreen (2.35:1) anamorphic. Dolby Digital Mono. $19.95. Keepcase. *LANG:* English. *SUB:* Chinese; English; French; Korean; Portuguese; Thai. *CAP:* English. *FEATURES:* 28 chapters.
1975 (PG) 96m/C Charles Bronson, Jill Ireland, Robert Duvall, John Huston, Sheree North, Randy Quaid; **D:** Tom Gries; **W:** Howard B. Kreitsek, Marc Norman, Elliott Baker; **C:** Lucien Ballard; **M:** Jerry Goldsmith.

Breast Men

Loosely based on the true story of the two doctors (Schwimmer and Cooper) who developed silicone breast implants, the title refers to the movie's target audience as much as to the movie itself. The film follows both partners across three decades, but doesn't incorporate enough period details to make the journey truly engaging. The picture quality is crisp and clear, which aids in distinguishing between the various flesh tones that are on display. Sound is also good, although extra features are scarce. —BG

Movie: 🎬🎬 **DVD:** 🎬🎬🎬
HBO (cat #91470, UPC 026359147029). Full frame. Dolby Surround. $14.98. Keepcase. *LANG:* English. *SUB:* English; Spanish; French. *CAP:* English; Spanish; French. *FEATURES:* 10 chapters • Cast and crew bios and filmographies.
1997 (R) 95m/C John Stockwell, Terry O'Quinn, Kathleen Wilhoite, Lisa Marie, David Schwimmer, Chris Cooper, Louise Fletcher, Emily (Proctor) Procter, Matt Frewer; **D:** Lawrence O'Neil; **W:** John Stockwell; **C:** Robert Stevens; **M:** Dennis McCarthy.

Breathless

One of the pinnacle films of the French New Wave movement. The story follows Michel (Belmondo), a handsome car thief who is on the run after shooting a cop, and Patricia (Seberg), a beautiful American student living in Paris writing for the *Herald*. The story is just a frame for conversations about the differences between men and women, and the French and Americans, as the couple does the dance of love. She doesn't want to be held down; he believes love is the cornerstone of existence. Only when she makes her final, fatal act of independence does the core difference between the two become painfully apparent. Today the film is sensual and thought provoking, but when it was made it was startling for the conventions it broke. Godard directed the film from a two-page treatment written by Truffaut. He filmed the scenes without sound and gave the actors most of their dialogue from the sidelines and then looped in the sound during the editing process. The cinematography was also against the grain of normal filmmaking. Rather than focus on the characters and their movements, he chose to widen the narrative to include the landscapes and activities going on around the actors. He rigged his cinematographer Coutard up in everything from wheelchairs to mail carts so that the shoot was stealthy and captured natural life. Godard was a fan of the American Beat movement and tried to encompass their love of spontaneity into his filmmaking. The result is amazing and engaging to watch. Originally shot on 16mm, the film has been digitally re-mastered and looks really good with a few residual scratches here and there, and the sound is average. The critical commentary is really interesting for anyone who wants a crash course on the French New Wave and its importance to modern filmmaking. —CA *AKA:* A Bout de Souffle.

Movie: 🎬🎬🎬 ½ **DVD:** 🎬🎬🎬
Winstar Home Ent. (cat #FLV5266, UPC 72-0917526621). Full frame. $24.90. Keepcase. *LANG:* French. *SUB:* English. *FEATURES:* 16 chapters • Commentary: film critic David Sterritt • Weblinks.
1959 90m/B *FR* Jean-Paul Belmondo, Jean Seberg, Daniel Boulanger, Jean-Pierre Melville, Liliane Robin; **D:** Jean-Luc Godard; **W:** Jean-Luc Godard; **C:** Raoul Coutard; **M:** Martial Solal. *AWARDS:* Berlin Intl. Film Fest. '60: Director (Godard).

The Breed

Set in a noir-ish anytime, this horror film tells the story of an FBI agent Grant (a very stiff Woodbine), who starts out searching for a serial killer and ends up teamed with Aaron Grey (Paul), who turns out to be a vampire. It seems that the vampires who walk among us are ready to come out of the closet and join society, but a political dissident in the vampire ranks is trying to start a war, or is he? Could there be crosses and double-crosses afoot? Grant, a black man, is less than thrilled at being teamed with a vampire, which results in not-too-subtle moral banter about racism and the Nazis to explain the vamps' fear of the humans and condemn the human sense of self preservation. There is a little bit of *Dark City* and Philip Marlowe in the art direction and mood of the film and it has moments of promise, but the poor acting and choppy editing and direction make everyone look uncomfortable amid the atmospheric scenery. This is a rental at best, slightly above-average sound and good picture quality. —CA

Movie: ♫♫ **DVD:** ♫♫♫
Columbia Tristar (cat #06783, UPC 043-396067837). Widescreen letterboxed; full frame. Dolby Digital 5.1 Surround; Dolby Surround Stereo. $24.95. Keepcase. *LANG:* English; French. *SUB:* English; French; Spanish; Portuguese; Chinese; Korean; Thai. *CAP:* English. *FEATURES:* 28 chapters ▪ Commentary: director, Adrian Paul ▪ Filmographies.
2001 (R) 91m/C Adrian Paul, Bai Ling, Bokeem Woodbine, Zen Gesner, Jake Eberle; *D:* Michael Oblowitz; *W:* Christos N. Gage, Ruth Fletcher.

Breeders

Vintage exploitation has a ridiculous foam rubber monster attacking and impregnating women in New York. It's all an excuse to show as much female nudity as possible. DVD presents a remarkably clear and unblemished image. Mono sound is acceptable. —MM

Movie: ♫ ½ **DVD:** ♫♫
MGM Home Ent. (cat #1002324, UPC 027616865434). Widescreen (1.85:1) anamorphic. Dolby Digital Mono. $14.95. Keepcase. *LANG:* English. *SUB:* French; Spanish. *CAP:* English. *FEATURES:* 16 chapters ▪ Trailer.
1986 (R) 77m/C Teresa Farley, Frances Raines, Amy Brentano, Lance Lewman, Natalie O'Connell; *D:* Tim Kincaid; *W:* Tim Kincaid; *C:* Arthur Marks.

Brewster's Millions [Universal]

Montgomery Brewster (Pryor) is an ex–big league pitcher who is down on his luck in both his career and life. All of that changes when Brewster's deceased uncle leaves him a massive fortune. But before he can claim his inheritance, though, he must overcome one condition of the will: Montgomery has to spend $30 million in a period of 30 days and have nothing to show for

it or he forfeits the larger sum of money. Always up to a challenge, Brewster wholeheartedly accepts the conditions of the will and sets about the task of disposing of the cash. The transfer is both crisp and clear, and there were no noticeable artifacts throughout the course of the film. Surround sounds good and makes good use of both speakers on the Dolby stereo track. —EL

Movie: ♫♫♫ **DVD:** ♫♫ ½
Universal Studios (cat #21954, UPC 0251-92195426). Widescreen (1.85:1) anamorphic. Dolby Digital Surround. $19.66. Keepcase. *LANG:* English; French; Spanish. *SUB:* Spanish; French. *CAP:* English. *FEATURES:* Production notes ▪ Cast and filmmaker bios ▪ Theatrical trailer ▪ 18 chapters.
1985 (PG) 101m/C Richard Pryor, John Candy, Lonette McKee, Stephen Collins, Jerry Orbach, Pat Hingle, Tovah Feldshuh, Hume Cronyn, Rick Moranis; *D:* Walter Hill; *W:* Timothy Harris, Herschel Weingrod; *C:* Ric Waite; *M:* Ry Cooder.

The Bride

On a dark and stormy night, Dr. Frankenstein (Sting) and his pal (Crisp) are working in a glorious Rube Goldberg–inspired lab. Their goal is to create a mate for the doctor's original creation Viktor (Brown) who appears none too happy about the entire situation. He's right. When it turns out that Eva (Beals), the would-be bride, is a hottie, Dr. Frank tells Vik to take a hike and keeps her for himself. The rest of the film follows two plotlines. In one, the monster has a series of picaresque adventures with a dwarf (Rappaport, who easily steals the film); the other follows the jealousies that emerge as Eva matures. On his commentary track, director Roddam refreshingly admits the film's flaws and his own mistakes. To my taste, at least, the film improves on a second viewing. It looks terrific on DVD, which provides a very nice reproduction of an often dark image. —MM

Movie: ♫♫ **DVD:** ♫♫♫
Columbia Tristar (cat #05924, UPC 0433-96059245). Widescreen (1.85:1) anamorphic. Dolby Digital Surround. $19.98. Keepcase. *LANG:* English; French; Spanish; Portuguese. *SUB:* English; French; Spanish; Portuguese; Chinese; Korean; Thai. *CAP:* English. *FEATURES:* 28 chapters ▪ Trailers ▪ Filmographies ▪ Commentary.
1985 (PG-13) 118m/C *GB* Sting, Jennifer Beals, Anthony (Corlan) Higgins, David Rappaport, Geraldine Page, Clancy Brown, Phil Daniels, Veruschka, Quentin Crisp, Cary Elwes; *D:* Franc Roddam; *W:* Lloyd Fonvielle; *C:* Stephen Burum; *M:* Maurice Jarre.

Bride of the Wind

The story of Alma Mahler, reputed to be a genuine muse for the likes of her first husband, composer Gustave Mahler, rebound lover, artist Oskar Kokoschka; second husband, architect Walter Gropius; and finally, her last husband, novelist Franz Werfel. Beautifully shot and perfectly acted, this is

a period piece for the bodice-ripping crowd. Married to Mahler at a young age, Alma stands by his side until his death, even when he denies her the freedom to create on her own, and then she launches into a series of affairs and marriages to decidedly talented men, all the while continuing to ignore her own talent as a composer until her last husband pushes her to continue her work. The movie never manages to explain exactly how she inspires the artists she dallies with, but it is still the story of an extraordinary time and extraordinary people. The picture on the disc is beautiful, making the heavily filtered cinematography as smooth as silk with very little bleeding, and the sound is very good highlighting the beautiful soundtrack of turn of the century music. —CA

Movie: ♫♫ **DVD:** ♫♫♫ ½
Paramount (cat #33946, UPC 097363394-648). Widescreen anamorphic. Dolby Digital 5.1 Surround. $29.95. Keepcase. *LANG:* English. *SUB:* English. *CAP:* English. *FEATURES:* 13 chapters.
2001 (R) 99m/C Sarah Wynter, Jonathan Pryce, Vincent Perez, Simon Verhoeven, August Schmolzer, Gregor Seberg, Dagmar Schwarz, Wolfgang Hubsch, Johannes Silberschneider; *D:* Bruce Beresford; *W:* Marilyn Levy; *C:* Peter James; *M:* Stephen Endelman.

Bridget Jones's Diary

So you've got this petite (but slightly pudged up) sunny-faced Texan playing a "singleton" Brit who drinks and smokes and consumes too many calories and has man trouble and is the beloved heroine of Helen Fielding's international best-selling novel. No wonder the English got a bit upset—but, as it turns out, not for a good reason since Zellweger is ab fab as Bridget. Zellweger understands Bridget and the humor of her situation as she tries to take control of her chaotic life. She begins with her caddish, clever boss Daniel Cleaver (Grant) and ignores the handsome but apparently stuffy Mark Darcy (Firth). From start to finish, the movie is delightful, and so is the disc. Of course, the DVD delivers a fine reproduction of a big-budget Hollywood romantic comedy. The extras are well chosen. Director Maguire is unashamedly tickled to be doing a commentary of her hit debut. The seven deleted scenes are good enough (and short enough) that they could have been re-incorporated into the film, particularly the final one, without making the film too long. The menus are cool but a bit on the slow side. Even some of Bridget's fans may not know that Fielding first told her story in a series of newspaper columns, which are included as text. —MM

Movie: ♫♫♫ **DVD:** ♫♫♫
Miramax Pictures (cat #23598, UPC 786-936161977). Widescreen (2.35:1) anamorphic. Dolby Digital 5.1 Surround. $29.99. Keepcase. *LANG:* English; French. *CAP:* English. *FEATURES:* 17 chapters ▪ Commentary: Sharon Maguire ▪ Behind-the-scenes featurette ▪ 2 music videos

• 7 deleted scenes • Original newspaper columns.
2001 (R) 115m/C Renee Zellweger, Hugh Grant, Colin Firth, Gemma Jones, Jim Broadbent, Embeth Davidtz, Shirley Henderson, James Callis, Sally Phillips; **D:** Sharon Maguire; **W:** Richard Curtis, Andrew Davies, Helen Fielding; **C:** Stuart Dryburgh; **M:** Patrick Doyle.

Brief Affair

Please see review of *Illegal Affairs*.
1996 C D: Louis Lewis.

Bright Eyes

Shirley Temple stars as an adorable orphan caught between foster parents. The original black-and-white version gets a fine DVD transfer, though the sound is spotty at times. The two-bone rating is for the B&W transfer. Ignore the garish, flickering colorized version; it is blecherous and deserves a derisive WOOF! —*JE*
Movie: 🦴🦴 **DVD:** 🦴🦴
20th Century Fox (cat #2002969, UPC 0245029694). Full frame. Stereo; Mono. $19.98. Keepcase. *LANG:* English. *SUB:* English; Spanish.
1934 (PG) 84m/B Shirley Temple, James Dunn, Lois Wilson, Jane Withers, Judith Allen, Jane Darwell, Charles Sellon; **D:** David Butler; **W:** David Butler, Edwin Burke, William Conselman; **C:** Arthur C. Miller.

Bring It On

Toros' head cheerleader Torrance Shipman (Dunst) inherits a scandal when she learns that the routines her school has been tearing up national competitions with were stolen from an East Compton soul squad called the Clovers. This is the story of the Toros' struggle toward redemption, and ultimately to a team-to-team competition with their wronged rivals. It's anything but easy. One teammate tumbles from atop a human pyramid. They ALL fall victim to the inhumanity of "spirit fingers" when Torrance decides to hire a choreographer to create a new, ORIGINAL routine. The 17-year-old starlet also makes time to fall in love with the brother of her punk-gymnast-turned-spirit-queen best friend (Dushku). At long last, the Clovers and Toros meet in the sort of Jock Jams extravaganza that ESPN airs over and over, and by way of this national cheerleading competition comes greater racial understanding. A high-five to screenwriter Jessica Bendinger for such politically incorrect lines as: "Cheerleaders are dancers gone retarded." So infectiously upbeat and funny that the lack of carnality typical of the cheerleader genre almost goes unnoticed. The disc features a first-rate rendition of the film. The anamorphic transfer is faultless. Both the 5.1 and DTS tracks are excellent and they especially thump during the musical bass riffs, while the dialogue is also crisp. The audio commentary by director Reed is fun. There's nothing overly surprising, except when he jokingly tattles on Ms. Dushku for showing up hung over to the car wash

shoot. He also introduces three extended scenes and 10 deleted scenes (about 14 minutes). There's also a three-minute car wash video. The film can also be viewed with Universal's version of "Pop Up Video" in which factoids appear on screen throughout. Recommended. —*GNG/DG*
Movie: 🦴🦴 **DVD:** 🦴🦴🦴½
Universal Studios (cat #020960, UPC 025-192096020). Widescreen (1.85:1) anamorphic. DTS; Dolby Digital 5.1 Surround. $26.98. Keepcase. *LANG:* English; French. *CAP:* English. *FEATURES:* "Making of *Bring It On*" • Deleted scenes • Extended scenes • Commentary: Reed • Home movies of car wash scene • Wardrobe, makeup tests • "As If" video • Trailers • DVD-ROM features • "Did you know that?" animated anecdotes.
2000 (PG-13) 98m/C Kirsten Dunst, Eliza Dushku, Jesse Bradford, Gabrielle Union, Clare Kramer, Nicole Bilderback, Tsianina Joelson, Rini Bell, Ian Roberts, Richard Hillman, Lindsay Sloane, Cody McMains; **D:** Peyton Reed; **W:** Jessica Bendinger; **C:** Shawn Maurer; **M:** Christophe Beck.

Britannia Hospital

Britannia Hospital undergoes a fateful, fitful day of escalating madness and tension, into which devious reporter Mick Travis (McDowell) penetrates with his spy television camera. Her Royal Highness is scheduled to visit to celebrate the building's 500th year of service, and hospital director Vincent Potter (Rossiter) is desperately trying to keep this on track while fending off union work actions by the cooking staff, orderlies, and painters. Added to the rage of the strikers is a demonstration by black activists demanding the surrender to trial of President Ngami, an African despot claimed to be a murdering cannibal, who's a patient in the hospital's swank VIP ward. A new adjunct to the hospital is a modernistic and supersecret research facility run by the utterly insane Professor Millar (Crowden), a latter-day Frankenstein who has a plan to assemble an entire human from spare parts. He also claims to have created a living creature that will be the evolutionary successor to troubled modern man. DVD is a very proper presentation with an easily understood dialogue track, which helps us Yanks follow the starched U.K. accents. There are no subtitles or closed captions, not a plus. An interview with McDowell is a welcome extra; he talks about director Anderson and writer Sherwin and theorizes that this flag-bashing feature died at the U.K. boxoffice because it premiered right in the middle of the Falklands, make that Malvinas, war. This DVD supposedly has five minutes reinstated that were trimmed in the U.S.; I don't remember seeing the full frontal nudity of McDowell on the stitch 'n' paste operating table, but other than that can't speculate on what might have been cut. —*GE*
Movie: 🦴🦴🦴 **DVD:** 🦴🦴🦴
Anchor Bay (cat #DV11413, UPC 013131-141399). Widescreen (1.78:1) anamorphic. $19.98. Keepcase. *LANG:* English.

FEATURES: Malcolm McDowell interview • Trailers • Talent files • 29 chapters.
1982 (R) 111m/C *GB* Malcolm McDowell, Leonard Rossiter, Graham Crowden, Joan Plowright, Mark Hamill, Alan Bates, Dave Atkins, Marsha A. Hunt; **D:** Lindsay Anderson; **W:** David Sherwin; **C:** Mike Flash; **M:** Alan Price.

Broadway Danny Rose

Standup comics at a deli listen to Sandy Baron's tale of show business's most loveable and least successful "personal manager," Danny Rose (Allen). He's a dedicated plodder, cultivating ungrateful talents who invariably dump him the moment he gets them somewhere. This leaves Danny with a steady corral of incompetent hypnotists, hopeless balloon acts, women who play tunes on glassware, and an adorable guy whose bird act keeps being eaten by cats. Danny's big hope for the big time is Lou Canova (Forte), an over-the-hill lounge singer whose charm is outweighed by his vanity and infidelity. Yet Danny supports Lou's big break, even going so far as to play the "beard" for his girl on the side, Tina Vitale (Farrow), a tough cookie who rankles at Danny's ethics and lack of ruthlessness. DVD is plainwrap as only a Woody Allen disc can be—his unique deal with Orion (which carried through to MGM) is complete control over the content of video presentations, and besides the theatrical trailer, there are no extras whatsoever. Perhaps emulating his hero European masters, Allen doesn't always like his own work but he wants it to speak for itself. Flawless 16:9 transfer is able to give the fairly short movie a high compression rate, and the result is sparkling, even on a big screen. —*GE*
Movie: 🦴🦴🦴 **DVD:** 🦴🦴🦴
MGM Home Ent. (cat #1001744, UPC 027-616860446). Widescreen (1.78:1) anamorphic. Dolby Digital Mono. $19.98. Keepcase. *LANG:* English; French. *SUB:* English; French; Spanish. *CAP:* English. *FEATURES:* Booklet • Trailer • 16 chapters. Also available as part of the *Woody Allen Collection* (cat. #1001750, $99.96).
1984 (PG) 85m/B Woody Allen, Mia Farrow, Nick Apollo Forte, Sandy Baron, Milton Berle, Howard Cosell; **D:** Woody Allen; **W:** Woody Allen; **C:** Gordon Willis. *AWARDS:* British Acad. '84: Orig. Screenplay; Writers Guild '84: Orig. Screenplay; *NOM:* Oscars '84: Director (Allen), Orig. Screenplay.

Broken Blossoms [Kino]

This edition of one of D.W. Griffith's best earns a slight recommendation over the Image release (reviewed in *Book 1*) because the new score by Joseph Turrin is superior, and the disc contains more extras. Image appears to be about the same. DVD presents an excellent re-creation of damaged original elements. Signs of wear vary from light to heavy. Some of the scratchiness is very rough. —*MM*
Movie: 🦴🦴🦴 **DVD:** 🦴🦴🦴

Kino on Video (cat #K196, UPC 7383290-19624). Full frame. $24.98. Keepcase. *LANG:* Silent (English intertitles). *FEATURES:* 12 chapters • Filmed intro by Lillian Gish • Complete text of original story • Recording of 1919 song "Broken Blossoms" • Notes on score • D.W. Griffith on leading ladies, excerpts from "Photoplay" magazine.
1919 89m/B Lillian Gish, Richard Barthelmess, Donald Crisp; *D:* D.W. Griffith; *W:* D.W. Griffith; *C:* Billy (G.W.) Bitzer; *M:* Louis F. Gottschalk. *AWARDS:* Natl. Film Reg. '96.

Brooklyn Babylon

The story of Solomon and Sheba is retold (roughly) in contemporary New York when black musician Sol (Trotter) and the strictly religious Sara (Goberman) fall in love. Writer/director Marc Levin's intentions are high-minded and he succeeds, at least in part, in creating believable sympathetic characters. That said, those not already involved with hip-hop will find the music irritating. Some aliasing is noticeable in the opening pan, but otherwise, the image is fine. Interiors are diamond sharp. Sound is excellent. Given the seriousness of the filmmakers, a commentary track might have been illuminating. —MM
Movie: 🎬🎬½ *DVD:* 🎬🎬🎬
Artisan Ent. (cat #11783, UPC 0122361-17834). Widescreen (1.85:1) letterboxed. Dolby Digital Surround. $19.98. Keepcase. *LANG:* English. *SUB:* Spanish. *CAP:* English. *FEATURES:* 27 chapters • Talent files.
2000 (R) 90m/C Bonz Malone, David Vadim, Tariq Trotter, Karen Goberman, Rahzel; *D:* Marc Levin; *W:* Marc Levin; *C:* Mark Benjamin.

Brother

Takeshi "Beat" Kitano's films are something of an acquired taste. He mixes abrupt graphic (and usually brief) violence with prolonged scenes of introspection. And when it comes to expressing emotion, he seldom does more than twitch or take off his sunglasses. But the man is cool, and to those (like me) who accept his measured pace, his work has a hypnotic quality. In his first film set in America, he plays an exiled Japanese yakuza who partners up with a street hustler (Epps) and takes on the local drug gangs. Yes, that's the stuff of hundreds of video premiere action flicks. He transcends the clichés. DVD image ranges between good and very good with only the slightest distortion in bright exterior panning shots. The 5.1 Surround is very good to excellent making very good use of ambient sounds. Subtitles are helpful with both the Japanese dialogue and the often softly delivered English. —MM
Movie: 🎬🎬🎬 *DVD:* 🎬🎬🎬
Columbia Tristar (cat #06388, UPC 04339-6063884). Widescreen (1.85:1) anamorphic. Dolby Digital 5.1; Dolby Digital Surround. $24.95. Keepcase. *LANG:* English and Japanese. *SUB:* English; French; Spanish. *CAP:* English. *FEATURES:* 28 chapters • Trailers.

2001 (R) 118m/C *JP* Takeshi "Beat" Kitano, Omar Epps, Kuroudo Maki, Masaya Kato, Susumu Terajima; *D:* Takeshi "Beat" Kitano; *W:* Takeshi "Beat" Kitano; *C:* Katsumi Yanagishima; *M:* Joe Hisaishi.

Brother of Darkness

Another HK crime horror story, though this one is about the lurid details of a single murder, rather than the depravity of a serial killer. Wong Kuen To (Hugo Ng, later a director) has been arrested for the bloody murder of his brother Wah (Ho Ka-Kui). Court testimony flashbacks explain why he did it. It's not much of a mystery, just a terrific excuse to show a lot of sadism, sex, and violence. The evil brother proves worthy of painful death within the first reel. Growing up, To trains in the martial arts to defend himself. Finally, when Wah tries to rape his girlfriend and with his mother driven nearly into insanity, To goes over the edge. Wah is such a thoroughly nasty villain that it's almost comical, and Ho Ka-Kui hams it up terrifically. As an amusing twist, frequent screen psycho Anthony Wong is cast as the prosecutor. It's all completely sordid. The image and sound quality are average, though it looks good considering how dark the picture is most of the time. —BT *AKA:* Ti Tian Xing Dao Zhi Sha Xiong.
Movie: 🎬🎬½ *DVD:* 🎬🎬
Tai Seng (cat #5397, UPC 4895024). Widescreen letterboxed. $14.95. Keepcase. *LANG:* Cantonese; Mandarin. *SUB:* Chinese; English. *FEATURES:* 8 chapters.
1994 84m/C *HK* Lily Chung, Hugo Ng, William Ho, Lai Yee, Anthony Wong; *D:* Billy Tang; *W:* Billy Tang; *C:* Tony Miu; *M:* Wong Bong.

The Brotherhood

This study of two mafia brothers struggling for respect features good performances, if not the most interesting story. Frank (Douglas), a middle-aged Mafioso, brings his much younger brother Vince (Cord) into "The Family." Vince has new-fangled ideas which are exciting to the syndicate, but don't sit well with Frank. Tired of Frank's resistance, the syndicate orders Vince to prove himself by making a hit on his own flesh and blood. The transfer, rich in color, looks good, with only occasional dirt from the source material. The mono sound is clear, emphasizing Lalo Schifrin's fine score. —DRL
Movie: 🎬🎬½ *DVD:* 🎬🎬🎬
Paramount (cat #6815, UPC 097360681-543). Widescreen (1.85:1) anamorphic. Mono. $24.99. Keepcase. *LANG:* English; French. *SUB:* English. *CAP:* English. *FEATURES:* 16 chapters.
1968 96m/C Kirk Douglas, Alex Cord, Irene Papas, Luther Adler, Susan Strasberg, Murray Hamilton; *D:* Martin Ritt; *W:* Lewis John Carlino; *C:* Boris Kaufman; *M:* Lalo Schifrin.

Brothers in Arms

This 3-episode TV documentary relates the history of the 101st Airborne Division—the first U.S. regiment of paratroopers. "Date

with Destiny" (40 min.) details the formation of the division leading up to the landings at Normandy, "Fire and Ice" (43 min.) follows the troops in Europe, and "In Their Father's Footsteps" (40 min.) tells of the conversion of the 101st into the Air Mobile during the war in Vietnam. A fairly well-done documentary knitted together with personal recollections that are funny, interesting, and frequently moving. The footage shown matches the stories but at times seems a bit arbitrary. The third episode is the strongest, featuring the most vivid and affecting stories. The black & white stock footage is generally grainy, in poor condition, and suffers from severe digititis. The interview segments feature accurate colors and are much better. The audio is fine, though a few of the participants' stories are a bit hard to discern. The bonus documentary matches the stock footage in quality and sounds muffled. —DG
Movie: 🎬🎬½ *DVD:* 🎬🎬½
BFS Video (cat #30219-D, UPC 06680530-2190). Full frame. Mono. $19.98. Keepcase. *LANG:* English. *FEATURES:* Historical time line from WW II to Vietnam • "The True Glory" bonus documentary (31 min.) • Photo gallery.
2001 120m/C

The Brothers Quay Collection

This film highlights 10 shorts from the celebrated animators, the Brothers Quay. Spanning the period from 1984–1993, this compilation gives one a nice overview of the work of the Brothers. The films range in length from 1 minute to 21 minutes, and all feature the Quay's trademark use of unique sets, disturbing puppets, and bizarre camera movements. While fans of this style of animation will simply love this collection, newcomers or the curious may quickly become bored, as there isn't much to differentiate each short. Add to this the fact that the Quays leave a lot open to interpretation, and we're left with something that won't appeal to a mass audience. (Although MTV fans will recognize at least one of the shorts as an old MTV promo and also the influence that this work has had on bands such as Tool.) The DVD renders this collection very watchable, although it does enhance some defects in the older films. The images are sharp and clear, showing no distortion. The audio (which is mainly music) sounds fine. The DVD includes a bonus film, "Nocturna Arrificialia," from 1979, which was the Brothers Quay's first short. Purists should note the interview included on this disc is the same as the one found on the *Institute Benjamenta* DVD. —ML
Movie: 🎬🎬 *DVD:* 🎬🎬
Kino on Video (cat #K170 DVD, UPC 738329017026). Various (full frame and letterboxed). Digital Stereo. $29.98. Keepcase. *LANG:* English. *FEATURES:* Bonus short film • Bonus theatrical trailer • Filmmaker interview • 11 chapters.
2000 102m/C *D:* Stephen Quay, Timothy Quay.

Bruce Lee: A Warrior's Journey

An excellent documentary on Bruce Lee, focusing on the events leading up to—and philosophy behind—his unfinished film *The Game of Death*. Recently unearthed footage from the film has been assembled according to Lee's own notes into a 41-minute featurette. For the most part, it's all action footage, and damn good, and contains three of the best fight scenes of Bruce Lee's career. It's as close as we're likely to get to Lee's true vision of *The Game of Death*, and should be considered required viewing. The sleeve lists an audio commentary track and a music video among the special features, but they do not appear on the disc. (The screener may have been missing some extras because it's an advance review copy.) Other than that, the transfer is flawless. —*BT*
Movie: 🎵🎵🎵🎵 **DVD:** 🎵🎵🎵
Warner (cat #37275, UPC 08539372-7529). Full frame; widescreen letterboxed. Dolby Digital 5.1 Surround. $19.98. Keep-case. *LANG:* English. *SUB:* English; French; Spanish; Portuguese. *CAP:* English. *FEATURES:* 26 chapters ☞ Trailer.
2001 100m/C HK KN US Bruce Lee, Kareem Abdul-Jabbar, Grandmaster Han Jae Ji, Dan Inosanto, Taky Kimura, Linda Lee Caldwell, James Tien, James Franciscus; *D:* John Little, Bruce Lee; *W:* John Little, Bruce Lee; *C:* Hoo-gon Lee; *M:* Wayne Hawkins.

Bruce Lee and Kung Fu Mania

Another low-rent (made for SLP or EP VHS) compilation of Bruce Lee, Kung-Fu, and '70s Hong Kong action and swordplay trailers, this one makes an attempt to structure itself as a documentary. The first half hour focuses on Bruce Lee and is made up of clips (a "Making of *Enter The Dragon*" is a fairly lengthy highlight but is given a much better presentation on Warner's *Enter the Dragon* disc) and trailers in order of production, with on-screen titles telling the basics of Lee's life story. Liberal use is made of the song "Kung Fu Fighting." The rest of the program is excused (er, introduced) as "Here are some other films *influenced* by Bruce Lee...." The trailers are fun but their claims of relevance can be a bit tenuous at times. Relating the terrific Japanese comic-book adaptation and swordplay film *Lightning Swords of Death (Lone Wolf and Cub: Baby Cart to Hell)* to Bruce Lee is stretching it a bit. Any chance to see the trailer from *The Flying Guillotine* is always appreciated, and thankfully, most of the clips are from fairly obscure films. The prints are faded, battered, and scratched for the most part but the contemporary lab work and exhibition of these films was never too polished to begin with. There's a fair amount of digital noise around the edges of objects and the flat, thin sound has a slight bit of hiss to it. (As several of the trailers are squeezed anamorphic 35mm, they can be unsqueezed on a 16x9 TV and look a bit less distorted that way.) —*DG*

Bruce Lee Fights Back from the Grave

A kung fu instructor travels to Los Angeles to visit a friend, but arrives just in time for the man's funeral. He vows to track down the five mysterious men responsible for the murder. Le's acting and martial arts are standard—during slow-motion replays, you can see that he actually misses with kicks by a good 12 inches. The main attraction should be Le's duels with the five different styled killers, but they're all sloppy and fake looking, with stuntmen waiting around to get hit. The producers even think of a way to pad out the running time with footage from a Hollywood Boulevard parade. Shot by an Italian crew disguised with Chinese credits. The print has some splices and scratches, the transfer (on a triple feature *Classic Kung Fu Fighting Movies* DVD) is smeary, and the full-frame image is still cropped off on all four sides, and squeezed during the title sequence. —*BT*
Movie: 🎵½ **DVD:** 🎵🎵
BFS Video (cat #30230D, UPC 06680530-2305). Full frame. $14.98. Keepcase. *LANG:* English. *FEATURES:* 4 chapters ☞ Bio ☞ Selected filmography ☞ Trivia.
1976 (R) 84m/C Bruce Le, Deborah Chaplin, Anthony Bronson; *D:* Umberto Lenzi.

Bruce Lee the Invincible

When a Chinese martial arts pupil goes bad, his master sends him to Malaysia to reform. When another student is sent to check on his progress, he finds that the misguided student has become even worse. The martial arts master and his loyal pupils head to Malaysia to straighten out the baddie. Dull, clichéd, cheap-looking martial arts picture is exploitatively packaged as if it was a Bruce Lee film. Lee appears nowhere in the film, which was made several years after his death. The dubbing is hilariously bad, the fight scenes are unimaginatively choreographed, and it features one of the worst gorilla costumes ever used in a film. If the music seems better than usual, that's because it was lifted from *The Outlaw Josey Wales, Star Wars,* and other much better films. The disc is just as bad as the movie. The film was shot at a much wider aspect ratio and the cropping on the disc causes fight scenes to occasionally occur partially offscreen. It was transferred from a pale, battered theatrical print with abundant splices and twitchy frames. Some sections of the film are presented out of focus and there are dramatic color shifts around the beginning of each reel. Perhaps the print was stored next to a sunny window.... The sound is thin and full of crackle. —*DG* **AKA:** Nan Yang Tang Ren

Jie; Game of the Dragon; The Invincible; Bruce Li the Invincible.
Movie: woof **DVD:** woof
Goodtimes Ent. (cat #05-81190, UPC 018-713811905). Full frame. Mono. $7.49. Keepcase. *LANG:* English. *FEATURES:* 12 chapters ☞ Insert card with chapter listings.
1977 83m/C Bruce Li, Ho Chung Dao, Chen Sing.

Bruiser

The first film from horror icon George A. Romero in more than seven years offers a great central premise, but little else. Henry Creedlow (Flemyng) is a nice guy who gets used by everyone around him. His cheating wife, his overbearing boss, and his dishonest stock broker all push Henry around, but he never stands up for himself. That is, until the day that he wakes up to find that his face has been replaced by a blank white mask. Being "faceless" allows Henry to assert himself and get revenge. *Bruiser* is boring and filled with many unlikable characters, the worst of which is Henry. If we had liked him more, it would have been entertaining to witness his vengeance, but sadly, that's not the case. The last act is simply absurd and one can't help but wonder what has happened to the once great Romero. On the plus side, the DVD offers a lush anamorphic transfer, which offers a sharp and clear picture. This clean image helps to highlight the stunning production design which inhabits this low-budget film. The audio is O.K., but there is little sound from the rear speakers. Romero completists will enjoy the audio commentary included on the disc, although it does get a bit too "chatty" at times. —*ML*
Movie: 🎵½ **DVD:** 🎵🎵🎵
Studio Home Ent. (cat #7772D, UPC 031-398777229). Widescreen (1.85:1) anamorphic. Dolby 2.0 Surround. $24.99. Keepcase. *LANG:* English. *SUB:* English; Spanish. *CAP:* English. *FEATURES:* Commentary ☞ Music video.
2000 99m/C Jason Flemyng, Peter Stormare, Leslie Hope, Nina Garbiras, Tom Atkins, Jeff Monahan; *D:* George A. Romero; *W:* George A. Romero; *C:* Adam Swica; *M:* Donald Rubinstein.

Bubble Boy

While *Bubble Boy* found its way onto some critics "Worst of 2001" lists, it would be much more appropriate to call it "The Most Flawed Film of the Year." For the movie offers an ingenious and promising premise and then deflates right before the viewer's eyes. Jimmy (Jake Gyllenhaal) is a young man who was born without any "immunities" and is forced to live life in a large plastic bubble, lest he die. His religious fanatic mother (Swoosie Kurtz) shelters Jimmy from the outside world and fills his head with lies and propaganda. Things begin to change when he meets Chloe (Marley Shelton), his beautiful and friendly neighbor. A friendship blooms between the two teenagers, but the relationship can't go any further, due to Jimmy's disease. Because of

this, Chloe decides to marry a cad named Mark (Dave Sheridan) and travels to Niagara Falls for the wedding. Realizing that he will be losing the love of his live, Jimmy constructs a bubble-suit, and leaves his house for the first time to pursue his lost love. This is where the film totally falls apart. The filmmakers could have had a great time showing Jimmy being perplexed by everyday events and objects, because of his isolated existence. Instead, they elected to have him confront a religious cult, circus freaks, a biker gang, and mud wrestlers. The result is a film that is uneven, convoluted, and rarely funny. *Bubble Boy* came under fire upon its initial release due to the unsympathetic portrayal of a person who suffers from an immune system disorder. But the real protests should have been against the film itself. While *Bubble Boy* is certainly a disappointment, the DVD gets a good grade. The image is very sharp and clear, showing minimal grain and zero distortion. The film has a wide color palette, which plays well on this transfer. There are no obvious defects from artifacting or edge-enhancement. The Dolby Digital 5.1 audio track is nice as well, offering impressive Surround sound effects and a deep bass response. The commentary from the director and star Gyllenhaal is fun, but the best extra feature is the documentary on the creation of the bubble suit, which is simply fascinating. —*ML*
Movie: 🦴🦴 ½ **DVD:** 🦴🦴🦴
Buena Vista Home Ent. (cat #24020, UPC 786936165401). Widescreen (2.35:1) anamorphic. Dolby Digital 5.1. $32.98. Keepcase. *LANG:* English. *SUB:* English; French; Spanish. *CAP:* English. *FEATURES:* Commentary • Director's Diary • Special effects featurette • Production design gallery • Storyboards • Sing-along • 14 chapters.
2001 (PG-13) 84m/C Jake Gyllenhaal, Swoosie Kurtz, Marley Shelton, Danny Trejo, John Carroll Lynch, Stephen Spinella, Verne Troyer, Dave Sheridan, Brian George, Patrick Cranshaw, Fabio; **D:** Blair Hayes; **W:** Ken Daurio, Cinco Paul; **C:** Jerzy Zielinski; **M:** John Ottman.

A Bucket of Blood / Attack of the Giant Leeches [Marengo]

Both of these public domain titles are reviewed in *Book 2*. Here, the print used for *A Bucket of Blood* is clean and fairly splice-free. The one used for *Attack of the Giant Leeches* is more worn and has light scratches and a fair amount of splices. Both show very little digital grain or noise, making these a notch above the usual bargain bin disc. Contrasts are stronger on *Bucket* but both are fairly soft and black levels are chalky. The sound is thin and a bit squawky. (The critical rating is an average of 3 bones for *Bucket* and 2 bones for *Leeches*.) —*DG*
Movie: 🦴🦴 ½ **DVD:** 🦴🦴
Marengo Films (cat #MRG-0024, UPC 807-013002492). Full frame. Mono. $14.98. Keepcase. *LANG:* English. *FEATURES:* 4 chapters per film.

1959 66m/B Dick Miller, Barboura Morris, Antony Carbone, Julian Burton, Ed Nelson, Bert Convy, Judy Bamber, John Brinkley, Myrtle Domerel, John Herman Shaner, Bruno VeSota; **D:** Roger Corman; **W:** Charles B. Griffith; **C:** John Marquette; **M:** Fred Katz.

Bucktown

Dean Johnson (Williamson) reopens his murdered brother's bar and finds that he's got to fight against rednecks and racist cops. Things don't get much easier after he brings in some of his pals to clean up the town. Mono sound can do little to improve the often-unintelligible dialogue. Overall, the DVD image looks about as good as it could be expected to look, given the film's slap-dash production values. Most of the bright reds glow and there are a lot of them. Pam Grier has seldom been sexier. —*MM*
Movie: 🦴🦴 **DVD:** 🦴🦴
MGM Home Ent. (cat #1002580, UPC 027-616867810). Widescreen (1.85:1) anamorphic. Dolby Digital Mono. $19.98. Keepcase. *LANG:* English. *SUB:* French; Spanish. *CAP:* English. *FEATURES:* 16 chapters • Trailer.
1975 (R) 95m/C Fred Williamson, Pam Grier, Bernie Hamilton, Thalmus Rasulala, Art Lund; **D:** Arthur Marks; **W:** Bob Ellison; **C:** Robert Birchall; **M:** Johnny Pate.

Buddha Assassinator

It's not easy trying to figure out who the bad guys are in this kung fu comedy. Both political factions are equally ruthless, and even the monks are a pretty rude bunch. The designated young hero acts like such a jerk for most of the film that it's tough to root for him. An introduction explains how the modest Buddha Fist Style came into conflict with the greedy Lo Han Style. Then, everyone is in a flurry of activity because Prince Tsoi is visiting the district. Abbot Fung Yung scolds dirty Abbot Sun Lu (Chen Yueh-Sheng) to clean up for the visiting royalty, and his rascal adopted nephew Shao Hai (Mang Hoi) is told to keep out of the way. Luckily, he disobeys, and saves the Prince from an assassination. He's rewarded with a job as the Prince's personal guard. However, the real plan is for the brash Shao Hai to act as bait for the assassins. Shao Hai gets the Prince to teach him his crazy Lo Han style of kung fu. Afterward, Sun Lu teaches him his own Buddhist Fist style. Eventually, Prince Tsoi faces off against Shao. Can his Five Element Buddha Palm win out over Tsoi's Lo Han Sleeping Kick? Fight scenes are nicely acrobatic, but bear no similarity to any kind of actual fighting. The print is in horrible shape—scratched, speckled, squeezed, and cropped. —*BT*
AKA: Fo Zhang Huang Di; Shogun Massacre.
Movie: 🦴 ½ **DVD:** 🦴 ½
Xenon Ent. (cat #XEXA6087DVD, UPC 000-799608722). Full frame. Dolby Digital 2.0. $14.98. Keepcase. *LANG:* English. *FEATURES:* 6 chapters • Clips from other Xenon martial arts titles.

1979 85m/C *HK* Hwang Jang Lee, Mang Hai, Lung Fei, Chien Yueh Sheng; **D:** Kar Wu Tung; **W:** Yi Kuang, Tu Liang-Ti; **C:** Woo Kuo-Hsiao; **M:** Chen Hsun-Chi.

Buffy the Vampire Slayer

Today, we think of *Buffy, The Vampire Slayer* as the popular television series. But there was a time when *Buffy* was known as a mediocre horror spoof. Kristy Swanson stars as the title character, a cheerleader who is destined to be a vampire slayer. After a series of murders in her California town, Buffy meets the mysterious Merrick (Donald Sutherland), who trains her to defend herself against a powerful vampire named Lothos (Rutger Hauer). The central premise is quite engaging, but the film is very uneven and is never able to balance the horror and comedy. Small roles from Paul Reubens and Luke Perry are the real highlights of the film. Neither funny nor scary, it's amazing that writer Joss Whedon was able to go on and create the TV series from this. Fortunately, the DVD fares somewhat better. The letterboxed image looks fine, showing only minor grain and occasional defects from the source print. The bright colors are rich and true. The Dolby 4.0 audio track sounds good, but there is noticeable hissing during chapter 12. —*ML*
Movie: 🦴🦴 **DVD:** 🦴🦴 ½
20th Century Fox (cat #2001650, UPC 02-4543016502). Widescreen (1.85:1) anamorphic. Dolby 4.0 Surround; Dolby 2.0 Surround. $19.98. Keepcase. *LANG:* English. *SUB:* English; Spanish. *CAP:* English. *FEATURES:* Featurette • Theatrical trailer • TV spots • 30 chapters.
1992 (PG-13) 98m/C Kristy Swanson, Donald Sutherland, Luke Perry, Paul (Pee-wee Herman) Reubens, Rutger Hauer, Michele Abrams, Randall Batinkoff, Hilary Swank, Paris Vaughan, David Arquette, Candy Clark, Natasha Gregson Wagner; **D:** Fran Rubel Kuzui; **W:** Joss Whedon; **C:** James Hayman; **M:** Carter Burwell.

Buffy the Vampire Slayer: Season 1

Buffy Summers (Gellar) is a girl destined to fight vampires and throw around campy dialogue like it was Shakespeare. She's aided by the "Scooby Gang" (so called before her casting as Daphne, by the way), a collection of her fellow high school friends. There's Willow (Hannigan), a budding witch, and Zander (Brendon), who has a long-term crush on Buffy. He is also the funniest Greek chorus of one since Lou Costello. To a lesser extent, Cordelia (Carpenter), the school princess, joins in the adventures and makes a great elitist naysayer. They in turn are watched over by Giles (Head), the most English of librarians who works for a secret society of Watchers, who find and train the Slayers. On the bad guy's team is the Master, an ages old, ugly vampire trapped in a cavern over the Hellmouth waiting for "the harvest" to set him free. This season boasts the rise and

fall of Darla and the introduction of Spike, a very sexy British punk vampire and his psychic/psycho girlfriend Drucillia. As the show goes on the Scooby Gang enlarges and the concept of a single Slayer existing in the world becomes the biggest Elephant in the room since the coupling of the McGregor boys in the television version of *Highlander*. The good and the evil lines also get fuzzy. The story lines themselves are amazing, doing what all good fantasy and sci-fi were made to do—take real-life trauma and build a metaphor that makes the horror bearable. The scary tones that high school competition can take on are covered in "Witch" when competitors for the cheerleading squad start spontaneously combusting. Child abuse and overdemanding sports coaches are brought to light in "Nightmares," when a comatose child makes his nightmares a reality for the inhabitants of Sunnydale by allowing the nightmare Freddy Kruger–style shadow of his coach to terrorize the teens. All the acting is top-notch and the players work together like the Olympic hockey team of olden days. If you're a supporter of *Buffy*, there's no need to go on, and if you're not a watcher, you should give the set a rental audition before buying it. The picture and sound quality are good for a series produced for television. If you're a fan of Buffy, the only thing that could ruin this set is the rest of the world getting it before you could...oh wait, that happened. And while after all that waiting it's good to be able to sit your friends down and make them watch the complete first season of the show that made Sarah Michelle Gellar able to forget her failing film career, it would have been nice if the set weren't so extras-light. There are some mini-interviews with Joss Wheden and one with Boreanaz, who plays Angel, Buffy's soon-to-be boyfriend, but seriously, the series isn't called "Angel, Buffy's the Vampire Slayer's Boyfriend." Next time, a SMG interview would be nice. (Season 2 is also available on DVD.) —CA
Movie: ♫♫♫ ½ **DVD:** ♫♫♫
20th Century Fox (cat #2000828, UPC 024543008286). Full frame. Dolby Digital Surround. $39.90. Box case, 3 discs. *LANG:* English; French. *FEATURES:* 12 episodes, with chapters. ▪ Interview with Joss Whedon and David Boreanaz ▪ Additional interviews with Whedon on select episodes ▪ TV trailers ▪ Whedon commentary on "Welcome to the Hellmouth," "The Harvest."
1997 600m/C Sarah Michelle Gellar, Anthony Head, Alyson Hannigan, Nicholas Brandon, Kristine Sutherland, Charisma Carpenter; **D:** Charles Martin Smith, John Kretchmer; **W:** Joss Whedon.

Bull Durham [MGM SE]
This "Special Edition" improves on the previous Image release (reviewed in *Book 1*) with more extras and a full-frame screen size option. A second commentary track features Kevin Costner and Tim Robbins who do their best to come across as just a

couple of good ol' boys remembering what a fine time they had making a movie that was instrumental in putting both of them on the map. (They *do* laugh a lot.) Shelton's commentary is more serious. DVD image is fine, though on the soft side, reflecting the film's tone and modest budget. Those who have the Image disc may not need to replace it, but for everyone else, this is one of the best sports movies ever made and it belongs in your library. —*MM*
Movie: ♫♫♫ ½ **DVD:** ♫♫♫ ½
MGM Home Ent. (cat #100331, UPC 0276-16874801). Widescreen (1.85:1) anamorphic; full frame. Dolby Digital 5.1 Surround; Dolby Digital Surround; Mono. $24.98. Keepcase slipcase. *LANG:* English; French; Spanish; Portuguese. *SUB:* English; French; Spanish; Portuguese. *CAP:* English. *FEATURES:* 28 chapters ▪ "Making of" documentaries ▪ Commentary: Ron Shelton ▪ Commentary: Kevin Costner, Tim Robbins ▪ Trailers ▪ Photo gallery ▪ Liner notes.
1988 (R) 107m/C Kevin Costner, Susan Sarandon, Tim Robbins, Trey Wilson, Robert Wuhl, Jenny Robertson; **D:** Ron Shelton; **W:** Ron Shelton; **C:** Bobby Byrne; **M:** Michael Convertino. *AWARDS:* L.A. Film Critics '88: Screenplay; N.Y. Film Critics '88: Screenplay; Natl. Soc. Film Critics '88: Screenplay; Writers Guild '88: Orig. Screenplay; *NOM:* Oscars '88: Orig. Screenplay.

A Bullet for the General
Just another Communist agitprop ultra-violent semi-closeted gay spaghetti western made by Italians, set in Mexico and filmed in Spain. Chuncho (Volonte) is the revolutionary leader who's stealing arms. American dandy Bill Tate (Castel) signs on to help but his motives are questionable. This is a big-budget production that looks very good on DVD. Blacks are deep; the minimal grain comes from the original. Audio is fine for the familiar dubbed voices. Don't look at the trailers if you want to enjoy the film; they reveal far too much. —*MM* **AKA:** Quien Sabe?.
Movie: ♫♫♫ **DVD:** ♫♫♫
Anchor Bay (cat #DV11544, UPC 013131-154498). Widescreen (2.35:1) anamorphic. Dolby Digital Mono. $24.98. Keepcase. *LANG:* English. *FEATURES:* 2 trailers ▪ 23 chapters ▪ Liner notes by Steven Paul Davies.
1968 95m/C *IT* Martine Beswick, Lou Castel, Gian Marie Volonte, Klaus Kinski; **D:** Damiano Damiani; **W:** Salvatore Laurani, Franco Solinas; **C:** Antonio Secchi; **M:** Luis Bacalov.

Bully
Larry Clark, the director who brought us the highly disturbing *Kids*, returns with another bleak look at teenage life with *Bully*. However, this film is much more focused and watchable, but no less eerie. Brad Renfro stars as Marty, a slacker who enjoys surfing and hanging out with his best friend Bobby (Nick Stahl). The problem is that Bobby constantly abuses Marty, both physically and verbally. When Marty's new girlfriend Lisa

(Rachel Miner) witnesses this behavior, she convinces Marty that he should stand up for himself. After Bobby rapes several girls, Marty and Lisa hatch a plan to kill Bobby and end his reign of terror. *Bully* is a harsh and challenging film, which is filled with unlikable characters. Much of the first hour drags, as Clark explicitly depicts the sexual behaviors and substance abuse carried out by these teenagers. But the second half of the film, in which the murder plot transpires, is riveting. The unique factor here is that not one of the participants in the murder scheme seems to have any moral objection to the act. While *Bully* is far too general in its portrayal of all teens as pot-smoking losers, the film is based on a true story, and should be an eye-opening one to many viewers. The DVD offers the film in a widescreen format and delivers a nice transfer. The image is clear and sharp, displaying an image that is free from any distortion or artifacting and only shows a slight bit of grain. The colors are good and the image is always stable. The audio track delivers clean dialogue and a nice bass response from the hip-hop soundtrack. An interview with the director, which is included on the disc, helps to explain some of his motivations. —*ML*
Movie: ♫♫♫ **DVD:** ♫♫♫
Studio Home Ent. (cat #VM7898D, UPC 031398789321). Widescreen (1.85:1) anamorphic. Dolby Digital 5.1. $24.99. Keepcase. *LANG:* English. *SUB:* English; Spanish. *CAP:* English. *FEATURES:* Cast & crew interviews ▪ Theatrical trailer ▪ Music-only track ▪ 24 chapters.
2001 113m/C Brad Renfro, Nick Stahl, Bijou Phillips, Rachel Miner, Michael Pitt, Kelli Garner, Daniel Franzese, Leo Fitzpatrick; **D:** Larry Clark; **W:** Zachary Long, Roger Pullis; **C:** Steve Gainer.

Bummer
Please see review of *Johnny Firecloud*.
Movie: ♫♫ **DVD:** ♫♫
Something Weird Video (cat #ID0804SW-DVD, UPC 014381080421). Widescreen (1.85:1) letterboxed. $24.99. Keepcase. *LANG:* English.
1973 (R) 90m/C Kipp Whitman, Dennis Burkley, Carol Speed, Connie Strickland; **D:** William Allen Castleman; **W:** Alvin L. Fast.

Burn the Floor
This isn't actually a movie; it's a presentation of a touring group that puts on a wonderfully high-energy dance performance. There are a number of different styles of dance that are used to tell the story, including ballroom dancing. The result is a funkier, more stylish *Lord of the Dance*, with a number of young dancers who are remarkably talented. Even if you're not a big fan of dance, you should be able to appreciate the talent involved and practice needed to reach this level. The costumes are magnificent, and a large portion of the budget is devoted to them. The lighting and general production values are top-notch, and it's highly entertaining—the audience in the background during this performance cer-

tainly sounds as if they were enjoying it, as well. The image is slightly on the soft side, but is very clean looking and crisp throughout. Lighting plays a major role in the performance as well, and colors look pure—without any problems. There are occasional moments of shimmer but overall, this is very strong for a non-anamorphic transfer. The audio is presented with the choice of 5.1 or DTS sound. While the two are not tremendously different, there are some noticeable improvements in the DTS version. The DTS version sounds more dynamic, and has a livelier presence. While both soundtracks offer an enjoyable listening experience, the DTS version provides a more enveloping, rich presentation. A 30-minute documentary details the incredible effort that this group of dancers had to go through to bring together a live show. It takes the viewer right behind-the-scenes of every element of the production, and the details are both informative and entertaining. Highly recommended. —*AB/DG*
Movie: 🎵🎵🎵 **DVD:** 🎵🎵🎵
Universal Studios Home Video (UPC 251-92071324). Widescreen (1.77:1) letterboxed. DTS; Dolby Surround 5.1. $24.99. Keepcase. *LANG:* English. *SUB:* French. *CAP:* English. *FEATURES:* Production notes ▪ Featurette ▪ Trailer ▪ Cast & crew bios. **2000 97m/C**

Burnzy's Last Call

Sal (McCaffrey) tends bar at Eppy's, a Manhattan joint where Burnzy (Gray), a retired newspaperman, is a regular. The film is an ensemble piece that focuses on the various colorful characters who drift in and out of the place. The independent production has never had particularly lush production values. DVD appears to have been made from a videotape which displays various glitches that might come from a dirty head on the playback machine. The minimal extras are all the disc has to offer. —*MM*
Movie: 🎵🎵½ **DVD:** 🎵🎵
Vanguard Intl. Cinema (cat #VF9196, UPC 658769919639). Widescreen (1.66:1) letterboxed. $29.98. Keepcase. *LANG:* English. *FEATURES:* 12 chapters ▪ Director's intro ▪ Trailer.
1995 88m/C Sam Gray, David Johansen, James McCaffrey, Christopher Noth, Sherry Stringfield, Roger Robinson, Tony Todd; **D:** Michael de Avila; **W:** George Gilmore; **C:** Scott St. John.

Bury Me High

No, it's not another Cheech & Chong movie, but an epic adventure film based on the traditional Chinese practice of feng shui, or geomancy. In China, Wisely is a hero on par with Indiana Jones, and the character has appeared in several films. In the tiny nation of Carrinan, megalomaniac millionaire Nguen uses geomancy to select the perfect burial site, guaranteeing that his descendants will conquer the world. His associate Wei objects, and takes steps to warn the world with the help of his friend Wong. Two dozen years later, daughter Anna Wong

(Moon Lee) is busting hackers as a computer security expert. Wisely Wei (Chin Ka-Lok) has not only become a computer expert, but has mastered mathematics and martial arts like his father. But x-rays reveal an inoperable brain tumor, and the once rich Wong family is on the brink of bankruptcy. Anna hires Wisely to go to Carrinan with her to move their fathers' graves to reverse their bad luck. Wisely's feng shui expert friend Chen Chang-Ching (Tsui Siu-Ming) gives up his job teaching at UCLA to help him out. The night of their arrival in Carrinan, brutal General Nguen (Yuen Wah) stages a coup and assassinates the president. The heroes discover his plan to build a city over the five peaks of the Conqueror's Locale, changing the topography in his favor so he can conquer the world. This grand adventure has a lot going for it, including good action scenes and marvelous locations, and the premise of using topography to influence events is also engaging. However, the story meanders quite a bit. Star Chin has the moves, but not the charisma to make an engaging hero, and he's only indirectly involved in too much of the action. Tsui's character gets more centrally involved in the action, and he's the sidekick—perhaps a benefit of also being the director. The transfer is above average for a Universe title, showing off the breathtaking camera artistry of Peter Pau *(Crouching Tiger Hidden Dragon).* —*BT* **AKA:** Wei Si Li Zhi ba Wang Xie Ji; The Legend of Wisely.
Movie: 🎵🎵½ **DVD:** 🎵🎵
Tai Seng (cat #5100, UPC 4895024906-416). Widescreen letterboxed. $19.95. Keepcase. *LANG:* Cantonese; Mandarin. *SUB:* Chinese; English; Bahasa. *FEATURES:* 8 chapters ▪ Trailers.
1990 97m/C HK Moon Lee, Ka-Lok Chin, Sibelle Hu, Yuen Wah, Tsui Siu Ming, Paul Chu; **D:** Corey Yuen; **W:** Corey Yuen; **C:** Peter Pau; **M:** Chris Babida.

Business Is Business

Early Verhoeven film is a loosely plotted series of sketches involving Amsterdam prostitutes. On DVD, it looks much better than a lot of American features from 1971, particularly the low-budget sex comedies. Some faint vertical scratches are the only noticeable flaw. Verhoeven's commentary is to the point. —*MM* **AKA:** Diary of a Hooker; Any Special Way.
Movie: 🎵🎵½ **DVD:** 🎵🎵🎵
Anchor Bay (cat #DV11255, UPC 0131-31125597). Widescreen (1.66:1) anamorphic. Dolby Digital Mono. $24.99. Keepcase. *LANG:* Dutch. *SUB:* English. *FEATURES:* 23 chapters ▪ Verhoeven thumbnail bio ▪ Stills gallery ▪ Trailer.
1971 89m/C NL Ronnie Bierman, Sylvia De Leur, Piet Romer, Jules Hamel, Bernard Droog, Henk Molenberg, Albert Mol; **D:** Paul Verhoeven; **W:** Gerard Soeteman; **C:** Jan De Bont; **M:** Mulius Steffaro.

The Butcher's Wife

A blonde Demi Moore stars in this bizarre and boring film. Greenwich Village butcher Leo (George Dzundza) returns from a fishing

vacation with a new wife, Marina (Moore). She felt compelled to marry Leo because she thought it was her destiny. Marina has an immediate impact on the neighborhood and begins to influence the love lives of everyone she meets, most notably psychiatrist Jeff Daniels. Is Marina simply a charming woman, or does she have some sort of special powers that influence others? That interesting premise goes nowhere, as the viewer finds it difficult to really care about the fates of the characters. Also, Moore's accent jumps around like a hyperactive child, which makes it challenging to take the film seriously. On the plus side, the DVD offers a sharp and crisp transfer, showing little grain or distortion. The audio is satisfactory, but there is little in the way of Surround sound or subwoofer effects. —*ML*
Movie: 🎵 ½ **DVD:** 🎵🎵🎵
Paramount (cat #32312, UPC 0973632-31240). Widescreen (1.85:1) anamorphic. Dolby Digital 5.1; Dolby 2.0 Surround. $29.99. Keepcase. *LANG:* English; French. *SUB:* English. *FEATURES:* Theatrical trailer.
1991 (PG-13) 104m/C Demi Moore, Jeff Daniels, George Dzundza, Frances McDormand, Margaret Colin, Mary Steenburgen, Max Perlich, Miriam Margolyes, Christopher Durang, Diane Salinger; **D:** Terry Hughes; **W:** Ezra Litwack, Marjorie Schwartz; **C:** Frank Tidy; **M:** Michael Gore.

Butterflies Are Free

Goldie Hawn stars as aspiring actress Jill Tanner, who moves into an apartment next door to a cute, wise, blind guy, Don Baker. Played by Edward Albert, Baker has a deal with his mom: if he can survive in his own apartment for two months, he doesn't have to live with her anymore. Eileen Heckart plays the overprotective mom to perfection: a performance for which she received a Best Supporting Actress Oscar. The romance between Hawn and Albert is charming. The comedy is funny. Hawn is very likable, despite being ditzy. Albert is stifled by playing blind, working hard to make others comfortable with his handicap and being super cool about it himself. Mom tries to throw a wet blanket over her son's new love interest, taking Jill to lunch and swearing her to secrecy as she reveals the difficulties of dating a blind person. Jill gets tangled up with a director who wants more from her than is appropriate. Will love triumph? Oh, yeah. The transfer to DVD provides a crisp image, and the sound is good. Nothing to shout about, but a nice innocuous movie with some good laughs. —*JAS*
Movie: 🎵🎵½ **DVD:** 🎵🎵🎵
Columbia Tristar (cat #07754, UPC 04339-6077546). Widescreen; full frame. Mono. $19.95. Keepcase. *LANG:* English. *SUB:* English; Spanish; French; Portuguese; Chinese; Korean; Thai. *CAP:* English. *FEATURES:* 28 chapters.
1972 (PG) 109m/C Goldie Hawn, Edward Albert, Eileen Heckart, Michael Glaser; **D:** Milton Katselas; **W:** Mary St. Feint; **C:** Charles B(ryant) Lang Jr.; **M:** Robert Alcivar. *AWARDS:* Oscars '72: Support. Actress (Heckart); *NOM:* Oscars '72: Cinematog., Sound.

Cabeza de Vaca

In 1528, a Spanish expedition shipwrecks off the Florida coast. Sole survivor Cabeza de Vaca (Diego) is captured by the Iguase Indian tribe and made a slave to their shaman. He's later freed but leaves with respect for their culture. When Spanish soldiers find him and want his help in subduing the natives, he is outraged by their cruelty. This one's a genuine sleeper that deserves a wide audience. It's a beautifully made film from first-time director Echevarria. DVD is able to handle the potentially troublesome wilderness landscapes without excess artifacts. It is however, only a small improvement over a good VHS tape. —MM

Movie: 🎬🎬🎬 **DVD:** 🎬🎬🎬
New Concorde (cat #NH20456 D, UPC 73-6991445697). Full frame. Stereo. $9.98. Keepcase. *LANG:* Spanish and Indian. *SUB:* English. *FEATURES:* 24 chapters • Talent files • Trailers.
1990 (R) 111m/C *MX SP* Juan Diego, Daniel Gimenez Cacho, Roberto Sosa, Carlos Castanon, Gerardo Villarreal, Roberto Cobo, Jose Flores, Ramon Barragan; **D:** Nicolas Echevarria; **W:** Guillermo Sheridan, Nicolas Echevarria; **C:** Guillermo Navarro; **M:** Mario Lavista.

Cabin by the Lake / Return to Cabin by the Lake

This DVD offers both the original film and its sequel on one disc. In the first film, Judd Nelson stars as Stanley Caldwell, a screenwriter who takes his work a little too seriously when he does research on a story about a serial killer who kidnaps and drowns his female victims. Stanley creates his own garden of victims in the lake by his house, until one young woman escapes and a trap is laid for the killer. The film doesn't offer anything truly original, but Nelson is very good as the subdued psychopath, and the underwater garden of victims is certainly a disturbing sight. Also, some of the kidnap scenes are quite intense for a TV movie. In the sequel, Stanley returns when his screenplay is actually put into production. He sneaks onto the movie set and begins to take control of "his" movie. As the filming continues, Stanley returns to his psychopathic ways. This sequel is much looser than the first and many of the scenes are played tongue in cheek. Nelson is good once again, but the movie needs to be more serious to succeed. Both images here are very sharp and clear, showing only the slightest amount of grain and rivaling digital broadcast quality. The picture shows no distortion and the colors are very good. For a TV production, the Dolby 2.0 Surround audio tracks are surprisingly good, offering very clear dialogue and nicely placed Surround effects. There are no extras whatsoever on this DVD. —ML

Movie: 🎬🎬 **DVD:** 🎬🎬 ½
USA Home Ent. (cat #96306 0313-2, UPC 696306031321). Full frame. Dolby 2.0 Surround. $19.95. Keepcase. *LANG:* English. *CAP:* English. *FEATURES:* Production notes • 10 chapters (each).
2000 91m/C Judd Nelson, Hedy Burress, Michael Weatherly, Bernie Coulson, Susan Gibney; **D:** Po Chich Leong; **W:** C. David Stephens; **C:** Philip Linzey; **M:** Frankie Blue, Daniel Licht.

Cabiria

Episodic spectacle tells the travails (and travels) of young child Cabiria, who is assumed dead after parts of her house collapse during the eruption of Mount Etna in the 3rd century B.C. When her nanny is sold for slavery, Cabiria is nearly sacrificed to the god Moloch during a pagan ceremony but is rescued by a noble Roman soldier and his amiable strongman sidekick, Maciste. From there, the three become embroiled in many misadventures. Entertaining, groundbreaking Italian epic was a reported inspiration to D.W. Griffith but occasionally displays the formative era of its style of storytelling. The titles are excessively "purple prosey" but they were written by a well-known novelist and were meant to add respectability to the production. The volcano eruption, the burning of the Roman fleet, and the temple Moloch scenes are strong highlights, but lovable Maciste steals the show. In fact, several silent films were made featuring the character and his popularity carried on into the "Peplum" genre of the '60s. Considering the age of the film, the disc is fine. Images are occasionally soft and contrasts a bit bright, but digital noise is kept to a minimum and detail is scarcely lacking. The sound is excellent and captures the piano soundtrack well. A full orchestra would have been even better. —DG

Movie: 🎬🎬🎬 **DVD:** 🎬🎬🎬
Kino on Video (cat #K187DVD, UPC 73832-9018726). Full frame. Stereo. $29.95. Keepcase. *LANG:* Silent. *SUB:* English intertitles. *FEATURES:* 14 chapters • Insert card with notes.
1914 123m/B *IT* Lidia Quaranta, Bartolomeo Pagano, Umberto Mozzato; **D:** Giovanni Pastrone; **W:** Giovanni Pastrone, Gabriele D'Annunzio; **C:** Segundo de Chomon.

Cactus Flower

"Sock It to Me Girl" Goldie Hawn gives her Oscar-winning performance in this American film of a French farce far removed from its original material. Walter Matthau plays Dr. Julian Winston, a dentist who lies to his mistress, Toni Simmons (Hawn). The lie Winston tells Toni is that he is married. He thinks this will help him maintain a happy single life and keep things spicy between Toni and him. When Simmons attempts suicide, Dr. Winston proposes marriage. Not wanting to be a home wrecker, she insists on meeting Mrs. Winston to make sure things are done correctly. Winston convinces his nurse (Bergman) to pretend to be his wife. The older woman does too good a job and complications occur when Hawn misinterprets Bergman's blasé nature as concealed love for her "estranged husband." This flick is not as stilted as other film relics from the '60s. The dialogue waxes between witty and flat but the actors are great. The picture quality on both widescreen and full-frame versions is crisp and the sound is clear. —JAS

Movie: 🎬🎬 ½ **DVD:** 🎬🎬
Columbia Tristar (cat #07757, UPC 04339-6077577). Full frame; widescreen (1.85:1) letterboxed. Mono. $19.95. Keepcase. *LANG:* English. *SUB:* English; French. *CAP:* English. *FEATURES:* 28 chapters.
1969 (PG) 103m/C Walter Matthau, Goldie Hawn, Ingrid Bergman, Jack Weston, Rick Lenz; **D:** Gene Saks; **W:** I.A.L. Diamond; **C:** Charles B(ryant) Lang Jr.; **M:** Quincy Jones. *AWARDS:* Oscars '69: Support. Actress (Hawn); Golden Globes '70: Support. Actress (Hawn).

Cadfael—The Raven in the Foregate

After the murder of a local priest for not baptizing the illegitimate son of a woman, Brother Cadfael (Jacobi), the medieval sleuth, must discover which of the local inhabitants of Shrewsbury was out for revenge. Cadfael must hurry if he is to locate the killer before he can strike again. The picture quality of this DVD release is good although some of the colors do look a little oversaturated. The stereo track makes good use of both speakers and contains no noticeable flaws, however both sound and picture do not seem to be noticeably improved over the VHS version. —EL

Movie: 🎬🎬 **DVD:** 🎬🎬
Acorn Media (cat #476, UPC 0549614762-99). Full frame. Dolby Stereo. $19.95. Keepcase. *LANG:* English. *CAP:* English. *FEATURES:* Commentary: Derek Jacobi • Bio and booklist of Ellis Peters • Production scrapbook • Filmographies • 8 chapters.
1994 75m/C Derek Jacobi; **D:** Ken Grieve.

Cadillac Man

Robin Williams stars as Joey O'Brien, a slimy car salesman with his hands in a few too many cookie jars, so to speak. When a cuckolded husband (Robbins) goes around the bend and takes the dealership hostage, O'Brien is forced to make the sales pitch of his life. Even Williams fans will have a hard time with this one, unless you find adultery and hostage situations inherently funny. The dubbed versions are much more amusing. The focus is a bit soft, causing for some shots to look extremely hazy. The soundtrack handles the large doses of yelling quite well. —BG

Movie: 🎬 ½ **DVD:** 🎬🎬 ½
MGM Home Ent. (cat #1003344, UPC 027-616874931). Widescreen (1.85:1) anamorphic; full frame. Dolby Surround; Mono. $14.95. Keepcase. *LANG:* English; French; Spanish. *SUB:* English; French; Spanish. *CAP:* English. *FEATURES:* 16 chapters • Trailer.

1990 (R) 95m/C Robin Williams, Tim Robbins, Pamela Reed, Fran Drescher, Zack Norman, Annabella Sciorra, Lori Petty, Paul Guilfoyle, Tristen Skylar; **D:** Roger Donaldson; **W:** Ken Friedman; **C:** David Gribble; **M:** J. Peter Robinson.

Caged Heat

Low-budget babes-behind-bars film touted as the best sexploitation film of its day. Demme's directorial debut—now a cult favorite—is a genre-altering installment in producer Roger Corman's formulaic Cinderella cycle. Familiar plot: innocent woman lands behind bars, where she loses some of her innocence, gets a certain updating. These babes may wear hot pants and gratuitously bare their midriffs, but they're not brainless bimbos—they're strong individuals who work together to liberate themselves. Horror diva Barbara Steele returned to the big screen to portray the wheelchair-bound, cabaret-dreaming prison warden, a part written specifically for her. DVD probably presents as good an image as we're likely to see. This is still modestly produced drive-in fare. —JE **AKA:** Renegade Girls; Caged Females. **Movie:** ♫♫ **DVD:** ♫♫ ½
New Concorde (cat #NH20134, UPC 7369-91413498). Widescreen. Dolby Digital Mono. $14.98. Keepcase. LANG: English. FEATURES: Leonard Maltin interview with Roger Corman ● Original theatrical trailers. **1974 (R) 83m/C** Juanita Brown, Erica Gavin, Roberta Collins, Barbara Steele, Ella Reid, Cheryl "Rainbeaux" Smith, John Aprea, Amy Barrett, Gary Goetzman; **D:** Jonathan Demme; **W:** Jonathan Demme; **C:** Tak Fujimoto; **M:** John Cale.

Caillou: Family Collection, Vol. 1

This is the first DVD collection of the popular animated children's program which is broadcast on PBS. The show centers around Caillou (pronounced ki-yu), a 4-year-old boy who is constantly on the go. Caillou lives with his parents, his sister Rosie, and their cat, Gilbert. A typical young boy, he likes to play, uses his imagination, and sometimes gets fussy if things don't go his way. Unlike many children's shows, Caillou doesn't dabble in the fantastic. The show presents the realistic (if not mundane) adventures of a child. According to the "Parent's Corner" information on the DVD, the show was designed to mirror the actual experiences of children, so that they could relate to the program. Thus, children find the show fascinating. Also, the program makes fine use of primary colors, so younger children, who don't necessarily understand the stories, will find the show interesting to watch. This DVD contains two episodes. "Caillou's Fabulous Fall" deals with the autumn holiday season, and includes segments which focus on pumpkins, Thanksgiving, and Christmas. The second, "Dr. Caillou," deals with medical matters. In the first segment, Caillou visits the dentist; in the second, Caillou's Daddy gets

sick and Caillou helps to care for him; and in a third part, Caillou loses his voice. The animated segments are broken up by "live action" portions in which puppets (who are based on Gilbert and Caillou's toys) act out skits that relate to the themes of the episode. While Caillou may not be very appealing to adults, it is one of the few children's shows that doesn't talk down to kids or treat them as if they are only consumers. The DVD offers the two episodes in a full-frame mode and the presentation is equal to digital broadcast quality. The image is very sharp and clear, making the bright colors look great. The digital stereo sound provides clear dialogue free of distortion. The extras on this disc are quite a disappointment, as the interactive games are far too brief, the sing-along is only one song (and that's the opening theme!), and the character bios are taken directly from the show. —ML **Movie:** ♫♫♫ **DVD:** ♫♫ ½
Sony Wonder (cat #CVD 4771, UPC 07464-0477195). Full frame. Digital Stereo. $24.95. Keepcase. LANG: English; French. FEATURES: Interactive games ● Sing-along ● Character bios ● Parent's corner. **2001 80m/C** CA

Calamity Jane

In one of her best Warner musicals, Day stars as the rip-snortin', gun-totin' Calamity Jane of western lore, in an on-again, off-again romance with Wild Bill Hickok. Great songs including "A Woman's Touch," "Whip Crack Away," and the Oscar-winning "My Secret Love." It's always good to see any classic film released on DVD and Calamity Jane will certainly be welcome to the collection of any fan of the great "old-fashioned" musicals. At first look, there is some distraction due to a few film scratches and some white speckling, but within a few minutes you're used to it and you can sit back and enjoy this fine presentation. The colors are particularly vibrant (Wesson's drag performance is a standout) and the blacks, contrast, and brightness levels give the film more zing than remembered from any previous viewing (televised or home video). Warner's inclusion of two newsreels from 1953 are welcome supplementals and should produce a few chuckles. —JO **Movie:** ♫♫♫ **DVD:** ♫♫♫
Warner (cat #22292, UPC 08539229222). Full frame. Dolby Digital Mono. $19.98. Snapper. LANG: English; French. SUB: English; Spanish; French; Portuguese; Japanese. CAP: English. FEATURES: 34 chapters ● Theatrical trailer ● "Western Style" Premiere Newsreel ● Photoplay Magazine's Film Award Newsreel. **1953 101m/C** Doris Day, Howard Keel, Allyn Ann McLerie, Dick Wesson; **D:** David Butler; **W:** James O'Hanlon; **C:** Wilfrid M. Cline; **M:** Sammy Fain, Paul Francis Webster. AWARDS: Oscars '53: Song ("Secret Love"); NOM: Oscars '53: Sound, Scoring/Musical.

Calendar

A photographer (played by writer/director Egoyan) reminisces about an assignment that sent him to Armenia to work on a calendar of the country's ancient churches. His wife comes along as a translator, but begins to fall for their Armenian guide. While extremely intricate and tightly constructed, this elegant film still manages to work on an emotional level as well. The picture quality is inconsistent, at times being detailed and rich but falling prey to heavy grain and shimmering at others. The audio quality is excellent, which is very important for the film's complicated layering of sound. Students of Egoyan's films will be interested in his commentary track and the 50-minute documentary. —BG **Movie:** ♫♫♫ ½ **DVD:** ♫♫♫
Zeitgeist Films (cat #Z1002, UPC 79757-5100234). Full frame. $29.99. Keepcase. LANG: English and Armenian. FEATURES: 12 chapters ● Commentary: Atom Egoyan ● Bio/filmography ● Stills gallery ● Interview ● Documentary. **1993 73m/C** CA Atom Egoyan, Arsinee Khanjian, Ashot Adamian; **D:** Atom Egoyan; **W:** Atom Egoyan; **C:** Norayr Kasper.

California Suite

The posh Beverly Hills Hotel is the setting for four unrelated Neil Simon skits, ranging from a battling husband (Matthau) and wife (May) to a sparring divorced couple (Alda and Fonda) to feuding friends (Cosby and Pryor). Smith is notable as a neurotic English actress in town for the Oscar awards while Caine is effectively low-keyed as her bisexual husband. Simonized dialogue (the place is "like paradise with a lobotomy") is crisp and funny and so DVD's visual quality is relatively unimportant. Disc presents a nice pastel color scheme that's completely appropriate to the setting and mood. Monaural sound makes the dialogue completely understandable. —MM **Movie:** ♫♫♫ **DVD:** ♫♫ ½
Columbia Tristar (cat #07727, UPC 0433-96077270). Widescreen (1.85:1) anamorphic; full frame. Dolby Digital Mono. $24.98. Keepcase. LANG: English; French. SUB: English; French; Spanish; Portuguese; Chinese; Korean; Thai. CAP: English. FEATURES: 28 chapters. **1978 (PG) 103m/C** Alan Alda, Michael Caine, Bill Cosby, Jane Fonda, Walter Matthau, Richard Pryor, Maggie Smith, Elaine May; **D:** Herbert Ross; **W:** Neil Simon; **C:** David M. Walsh; **M:** Claude Bolling. AWARDS: Oscars '78: Support. Actress (Smith); Golden Globes '79: Actress—Mus./Comedy (Smith); NOM: Oscars '78: Adapt. Screenplay, Art Dir./Set Dec.

Call Me Claus

This is a surprisingly good made-for-TV holiday movie, due mostly to the talent involved, both in front of and behind the camera. In 1965, young Lucy Cullins visits Santa Claus (Nigel Hawthorne) and makes

a very specific Christmas wish (which we won't divulge here). When that wish is not fulfilled, Lucy turns her back on Christmas. Now an adult, Lucy (Whoopi Goldberg) is a producer at the "Shop-A-Lot" home shopping channel. When the time arrives for the big holiday rush, Nick (Hawthorne, again) is hired to be the on-air Santa Claus. What no one realizes is that Nick is the real Santa. A pesky elf (Taylor Negron) arrives to remind Nick that his 200-year contract is about to expire, and he needs to choose a successor to be the next Santa. Nick decides that Lucy would make the perfect Santa and he sets out to melt her heart and transform her into Father Christmas. The film is predictable and manipulative at times, but it is also very entertaining. Hawthorne is brilliant as Nick/Santa, and Whoopi (who was also executive producer on the film) is her usual playful self. Garth Brooks provides original songs for the movie. Fun fare for the whole family imparts an important reminder of what the holidays are all about. The image offered on this DVD is nearly pristine and certainly rivals digital broadcast quality. It's very sharp and clear, showing zero distortion and basically no grain. The colors, most notably the reds and greens, are very good here. The Dolby Surround Sound offers clear dialogue and a good bass response, but very little in the way of rear speaker effects. —ML
Movie: 🎵🎵🎵 **DVD:** 🎵🎵 ½
Columbia Tristar (cat #06832, UPC 04339-6068322). Full frame. Dolby Surround. $19.95. Keepcase. *LANG:* English. *SUB:* English; French; Spanish; Portugese; Chinese; Korean; Thai. *CAP:* English. *FEATURES:* Bonus trailers ⚬ Filmographies ⚬ 28 chapters ⚬ Music featurette.
2001 90m/C Whoopi Goldberg, Nigel Hawthorne, Taylor Negron; *D:* Peter Werner; *M:* Garth Brooks.

Calle 54

Arguably one of the more enjoyable films ever made about music, this one is a thoroughly engrossing behind-the-scenes glimpse into the lives of some of the greatest Latin jazz artists of the 20th century. A wonderful video transfer is highlighted by superb color reproduction (particularly during the concert sequences). The soundtrack is even more astounding as it encompasses the viewer and manages to actually do the music justice. A superb documentary on the history of Latin jazz rounds out this excellent collection. —MJT
Movie: 🎵🎵🎵 **DVD:** 🎵🎵🎵
Miramax Pictures (cat #22597, UPC 7869-36153675). Widescreen (1.85:1) anamorphic. Dolby Digital 5.1 Surround; Dolby Digital Stereo. $32.99. Keepcase. *LANG:* Spanish; French. *SUB:* English. *CAP:* English. *FEATURES:* 13 chapters ⚬ Commentary: producer/Latin jazz historian Nat Chediak ⚬ Documentary on the history of Latin jazz ⚬ Musician bios and discographies ⚬ Theatrical trailer ⚬ Trailer gallery.
2001 (G) 105m/C *D:* Fernando Trueba; *W:* Fernando Trueba; *C:* Jose Luis Lopez-Linares.

Candyman 2: Farewell to the Flesh

Good, solid "B"-movie sequel to the original *Candyman*. The film boasts direction by Bill Condon, who later went on to write and direct *Gods and Monsters,* and story credit to Clive "hit or miss" Barker (he hits here.) The story takes place in New Orleans as the first days of Mardi Gras get into full swing. The Candyman legend is alive and well with everyone but the police, who believe they have a, you guessed it, serial killer on their hands. We meet Annie, whose father died at the hands of the Candyman (once again played with dignity by Tony Todd), but Annie doesn't believe it, even when her brother Ethan tells her he saw the one-armed man in question. Ethan also says that their father found a way to kill the Candyman, but it's hard for Annie to believe him when he's in jail for a Candyman-style murder. One thing leads to another and Annie finds herself on the lam and learning about the darker side, so to speak, of her family history. The only annoying part of the film is the voice-over by a New Orleans DJ. We can only hope that a director's cut, à la *Blade Runner,* is in the works. All the technical elements of the film are top-notch and the acting is good with fine little roles for character actors Veronica Cartwright and Bill Nunn. The disc looks very good, slightly above VHS quality and sounds good. —CA
Movie: 🎵🎵 ½ **DVD:** 🎵🎵🎵
MGM Home Ent. (cat #1002325, UPC 027-616865441). Widescreen (1.85:1) anamorphic. Stereo Surround. $14.95. Keepcase. *LANG:* English; French. *SUB:* French; Spanish. *CAP:* English. *FEATURES:* 16 chapters ⚬ Theatrical trailer ⚬ Commentary: director.
1994 (R) 99m/C Tony Todd, Kelly Rowan, Veronica Cartwright, Timothy Carhart, William O'Leary, Bill Nunn, Fay Hauser; *D:* Bill Condon; *W:* Rand Ravich, Mark Kruger; *C:* Tobias Schliessler; *M:* Philip Glass.

Cane Toads: An Unnatural History

Entertaining, informative, and frequently fall-down funny, this documentary relates the history of the Cane Toad. Originally brought to Australia to eliminate the beetles that were eating the valuable sugar cane crops, the toads were not only unsuccessful, but have since grown to enormous numbers, way beyond any sort of control. Director Lewis constructs his film with sincere and hilarious interviews with toad lovers (who seem right out of a Monty Python sketch), toad haters, zoologists, and toad substance abusers (?!). The comedic highlights have to be the "menacing toad," and "toad's world view" sequences that are absolutely wonderful and uproarious. Jaunty, clever, and fascinating, this is the kind of film you want to show to your friends. Double-feature it with *Frogs* for maximum effect. Originated on 16mm, the disc is free of digital arti-

facts, but the film itself is extremely grainy and soft. The disc is recorded at an extremely high bit rate, so it's probably the best it could look. The sound is clear but undistinguished. The short film is worthwhile and looks much, much clearer. A must-have for lovers of the strange and unusual. —DG
Movie: 🎵🎵🎵 ½ **DVD:** 🎵🎵 ½
First Run Features (cat #FRF909723D, UPC 720229909723). Full frame. Dolby Digital Mono. $24.95. Keepcase. *LANG:* English. *FEATURES:* 12 chapters ⚬ Bonus 15-min. short film, "Signing Off."
1987 47m/C *D:* Mark Lewis; *W:* Mark Lewis.

Cannibal Apocalypse

Over the years, *Cannibal Apocalypse* has played under many different titles, but that doesn't change the fact that it's an odd movie. The film offers a serious sub-text comparing war to a contagious disease, but then loses sight of this lofty goal as it devolves into an incredibly violent horror film. Genre-vet John Saxon stars as Captain Norman Hopper, a Vietnam veteran who is still plagued by nightmares of the war, in which he rescued POWs Charlie (John Morghen) and Tommy (Tony King), only to find that they had become cannibals. During the rescue, Tommy bites Hopper. The conceit of *Cannibal Apocalypse* is that a single bite can transmit a disease which causes the carrier to become a cannibal. Following the war, Hopper makes a comfortable living with his lovely wife in suburban Atlanta. One day, he receives a phone call from Charlie, who is out on leave from a psychiatric hospital. This call brings back disturbing impulses in Hopper and leads Charlie on a rampage. Once he is captured by the police, Charlie is returned to the hospital, where Tommy is a patient as well. Together, they flee from captivity and begin a cannibalistic onslaught of the city. Will Hopper join them, or can he resist the urge to devour another human? *Cannibal Apocalypse* is not a very good movie, in that it's full of mistakes, and it's slow and boring at times. However, the film doesn't shy away from controversial issues as it contains a smorgasbord of gory special effects. But the most disturbing aspect is Saxon's unnatural attraction to his teenage neighbor. *Cannibal Apocalypse* is one sick puppy, but it should please fans of Italian cannibal films. This DVD should please fans as well, as the film has been beautifully transferred here. The anamorphic image looks great. The colors are fantastic and the image is very clear. There is some minor artifacting and some flaws from the source print, but otherwise it looks fine. The Dolby Digital Mono audio track provides clear dialogue and no hissing or distortion. The extra features here are a mixed bunch, with the video location tour of Atlanta being the lowpoint. This DVD does offer a nice text essay which outlines the differences in the many cuts of the film. —ML *AKA:* Cannibals in the

Streets; Savage Apocalypse; The Slaughterers; Cannibals in the City; Virus; Invasion of the Flesh Hunters.
Movie: 🎵🎵 **DVD:** 🎵🎵🎵
Image Ent. (cat #ID0640SRDVD, UPC 014-381064025). Widescreen (1.85:1) anamorphic. Dolby Digital Mono. $24.99. Keepcase. *LANG:* English. *FEATURES:* Cast & crew interviews • Location featurette • Trailers • Filmographies • Still gallery • Alternate opening credits • Liner notes • 12 chapters.
1980 96m/C *IT* John Saxon, Elizabeth Turner, John Morghen, Tony King; **D:** Anthony (Antonio Margheriti) Dawson; **W:** Anthony (Antonio Margheriti) Dawson, Dardano Sacchetti, Jimmy Gould; **C:** Fernando Arribas; **M:** Alexander Blonksteiner.

Cannibal! The Musical

It's a musical comedy based (loosely) on the true story of Alferd Packer, the only American ever to be convicted for cannibalism. Reporter Toddy Walters gets the real story from Packer (*South Park* creator Trey Parker) himself as he sits in jail, awaiting his date with the hangman. Asked to lead Utah miners into the gold country of his native Colorado, Packer agrees. One night, his beloved horse Liane disappears, and a heartbroken Packer tends to lead the group around in circles looking for her, rather than toward their intended destination. Swept off course while crossing rivers, led astray by Packer's lovesick woodcraft, captured by Japanese Indians, troubled by trappers, menaced by a Cyclops—there seems to be no end to the party's tribulation. When one of the party is killed, they turn to cannibalism, bad wigs, and false beards. Packer is the only one to make it out of the wilderness alive, and he's immediately accused of foul play. But since this is based on Packer's own version of the tale, first we get to see some rather extreme carnage for which he claims no responsibility, and some catchy song and dance numbers. The commentary track reveals that Parker made the film to get back at a girlfriend that dumped him, and that a lot of DVD commentaries might be improved with a couple bottles of whiskey, as the cast puts alcohol to good use while watching the film. Includes on-set footage of the film being made, two (!) introductions from Troma's Lloyd Kaufman, some documentary bits, the original promotional trailer for both *Alferd Packer* (the film's original title) and *Cannibal!*, a look at Trey Parker's beach house, a tour of Troma studios, a Troma quiz, and much more! —*BT*
Movie: 🎵🎵🎵 **DVD:** 🎵🎵🎵
Troma Team Video (cat #9986, UPC 7903-57998630). Full frame. $29.98. Keepcase. *LANG:* English. *FEATURES:* Trailers • Behind-the-scenes footage • Documentary features • Trivia game • Commentary.
1996 (R) 105m/C Ian Hardin, Jason McHugh, Matt Stone, Trey Parker, Juan Schwartz; **D:** Trey Parker; **W:** Trey Parker.

Can't Stop the Music

'80s kitsch classic! Jack (Guttenberg), a songwriter/DJ in New York, wants to make it big. His retired supermodel roommate Samantha (Perrine) gets him a deal with her ex-boyfriend. Very loosely based on the story of how the real Village People were assembled during the disco era. Production numbers provide maximum entertainment value. It's a miracle Steve Guttenberg didn't blow a gasket. He didn't need a microphone; they could probably hear him in New Jersey. The "Village People Story" extra is an earnest, almost reverent documentary about the real group. DVD looks and sounds fabulous. Don't watch it alone. —*LA*
Movie: woof **DVD:** 🎵🎵🎵
Anchor Bay (cat #DV11561, UPC 0131311-56195). Widescreen (2.35:1) anamorphic. Dolby Digital Surround; 6.1 DTS-EX. $19.98. Keepcase. *LANG:* English. *CAP:* English. *FEATURES:* Theatrical trailer • Still gallery • Photo essay: The Village People Story • 24 chapters.
1980 (PG) 120m/C Valerie Perrine, Bruce Jenner, Steve Guttenberg, Paul Sand, Leigh Taylor-Young, Village People; **D:** Nancy Walker; **W:** Bronte Woodard, Allan Carr; **C:** Bill Butler; **M:** Jacques Morali. *AWARDS:* Golden Raspberries '80: Worst Picture, Worst Screenplay.

Cape Fear

Former prosecutor turned small-town lawyer Peck and his family are plagued by the sadistic attentions of criminal Mitchum, who just finished a six-year sabbatical at the state pen courtesy of prosecutor Peck. Taut and creepy; Mitchum's a consummate psychopath. Based on (and far superior to) John MacDonald's *The Executioners*. Don't pass this one up in favor of the Scorsese remake. Superb blacks and excellent graytones make this anamorphic transfer of a classic film noir one of the best-looking black-and-white DVDs available. Both detail and sharpness are amazing and the resulting depth of picture gives *Cape Fear* the treatment it deserves. The mono sound delivers composer Bernard Herrmann's score quite impressively (although it can't compete with the adapted score's 5.1 presentation on the Scorsese remake) and the dialogue is always crisp. The only time the audio sounds harsh is when the music reaches into the higher frequencies. Though the DVD is slim on extras, "The Making of *Cape Fear*" is well worth it, with Peck and director Thompson doling out interesting anecdotes (many involving co-star Mitchum) and even technical details from the film they made 40 years ago. Both reminisce about the production, co-stars, censor battles, and Scorsese's remake with surprising candor and affection. —*JO/EP*
Movie: 🎵🎵🎵 ½ **DVD:** 🎵🎵🎵 ½
Universal Studios (cat #20634, UPC 0251-92063428). Widescreen (1.85:1) anamorphic. Dolby Digital Mono. $24.98. Keepcase. *LANG:* English. *SUB:* French; Spanish. *CAP:* English. *FEATURES:* 18 chapters • "The Making of *Cape Fear*" featurette •

Trailer • Production notes and photos • Talent files • DVD-ROM features.
1961 106m/B Gregory Peck, Robert Mitchum, Polly Bergen, Martin Balsam, Telly Savalas, Jack Kruschen, Lori Martin; **D:** J. Lee Thompson; **C:** Sam Leavitt; **M:** Bernard Herrmann.

Cape Fear

Scorsese lets out all the stops in his overachieving remake of the 1961 film. Paroled convict Max Cady (De Niro) haunts lawyer Sam Bowden (Nolte) and his family (Lange and Lewis). The difference here is that Bowden has a degree of guilt himself. The cast does tremendous work and the director may never have been more flamboyant. (Note the cameos by Mitchum, Peck, and Balsam, stars of the first version. Elmer Bernstein adapted the original score by Bernard Herrmann.) Just as Scorsese's remake cranked up the intensity from the original, Universal's 2-DVD set cranks up the presentation as well. The first disc contains the film itself and both the image and the audio are top-notch and hard to beat. This may be Universal's best-looking DVD to date. The colors amaze with both their finely detailed hues and their complete saturation. Every scene is as sharp as the last with no artifacting or other signs of digital compression. Both 5.1 soundtracks make full use of their capabilities with full-bodied dynamic music, crisp dialogue, and energetic Surround effects, particularly during the houseboat sequence. When the action's at a lull, the rears revert to very spacious ambience. Disc two contains all the supplementals and there are plenty of them, starting with "The Making of Cape Fear," by producer Laurent Bouzereau, who also did the "making of" for the '61 film. Other highlights include the how-to of matte paintings and a photo montage on De Niro's physical transformation into the evil Max Cady. This set delivers all the way and is worth adding to any library. —*JO*
Movie: 🎵🎵🎵 **DVD:** 🎵🎵🎵🎵
Universal Studios (cat #20567, UPC 0251-92056727). Widescreen (2.35:1) anamorphic. Dolby Digital 5.1 Surround; DTS 5.1; Dolby Surround. $24.98. Keepcase. *LANG:* English; French; Spanish. *CAP:* English. *FEATURES:* 18 chapters • Theatrical trailer • Talent files • Production notes • Deleted scenes • Photo montages • Matte paintings • "Making of" documentary • "On the Set of the Houseboat."
1991 (R) 128m/C Robert Mitchum, Gregory Peck, Martin Balsam, Robert De Niro, Nick Nolte, Jessica Lange, Juliette Lewis, Joe Don Baker, Illeana Douglas, Fred Dalton Thompson; **D:** Martin Scorsese; **W:** Wesley Strick; **C:** Freddie Francis; **M:** Bernard Herrmann, Elmer Bernstein. *AWARDS:* NOM: Oscars '91: Actor (De Niro), Support. Actress (Lewis).

Capitaine Conan

On the Bulgarian border in 1918, during the last clashes of WWI, Conan (Torreton) is a fearless, impulsive warrior, reserving his respect only for his men. Although

armistice is finally declared, the troops stationed in the Balkans are not demobilized and become increasingly fractious. This causes a rift between Conan and his educated friend Norbert (Lebihan), who's been appointed a military legal representative. They are warily reunited in defense of a soldier (Val) charged with desertion, while still dealing with the ravages of the long conflict. With the DVD, we get a letterboxed transfer which is clear, but not very sharp. The picture is dark at times, and often appears hazy. Also, defects from the source print are visible in this transfer. The sound is adequate, but the wartime explosions would have been much better had they offered some resonance from the rear speakers. A 54-minute documentary about director Bertrand Tavernier and the making of *Capitaine Conan* is included on the DVD, and gives an exhaustive overview of the filmmaker and his cinematic style. —*ML* **AKA:** Captain Conan.
Movie: 🎵🎵🎵 **DVD:** 🎵🎵 ½
Kino on Video (cat #K188 DVD, UPC 7383-29018825). Widescreen (1.85:1) letterboxed. Digital Stereo. $29.95. Keepcase. *LANG:* French. *SUB:* English. *FEATURES:* "Making of" documentary ● 22 chapters.
1996 129m/C FR Philippe Torreton, Samuel Le Bihan, Bernard Le Coq, François Berleand, Claude Rich, Catherine Rich, Pierre Val; **D:** Bertrand Tavernier; **W:** Bertrand Tavernier, Jean Cosmos; **C:** Alain Choquart; **M:** Oswald D'Andrea. *AWARDS:* Cesar '97: Actor (Torreton), Director (Tavernier), Film.

Captain Corelli's Mandolin

On the Greek island of Cephallonia during WWII, a romance springs up between a free-spirited Italian captain (Cage) and a lovely local girl, Pelagia (Cruz). Things get complicated when the Italians are forced to surrender to the Germans. Based on the novel by Louis de Bernieres. The entire international cast is forced to speak clumsily accented English that doesn't flatter any of them, especially Cage. Features great music, and beautiful natural light cinematography. DVD looks and sounds great; the extras not terribly interesting. —*LA*
Movie: 🎵🎵 **DVD:** 🎵🎵🎵
Universal Studios (cat #21378, UPC 0251-92137 822). Widescreen (2.35:1) anamorphic. Dolby Digital 5.1 Surround; DTS 5.1 Surround. $26.98. Keepcase. *LANG:* English; French. *CAP:* English. *FEATURES:* Commentary: John Madden ● Russell Watson: "Ricordo Ancor" (Pelagia's Song) music video ● Theatrical trailer ● Production notes ● 18 chapters ● Cast & filmmaker bios ● DVD-ROM features.
2001 (R) 127m/C GB US Nicolas Cage, Penelope Cruz, Christian Bale, John Hurt, David Morrissey, Irene Papas, Patrick Malahide; **D:** John Madden; **W:** Shawn Slovo; **C:** John Toll; **M:** Stephen Warbeck.

Captain Kidd [Marengo]

Please see review for *Pirates!: Long John Silver / Captain Kidd.*

Movie: 🎵 ½
1945 83m/B Charles Laughton, John Carradine, Randolph Scott, Reginald Owen, Gilbert Roland, Barbara Britton, John Qualen, Sheldon Leonard; **D:** Rowland V. Lee; **W:** Norman Reilly Raine; **C:** Archie Stout. *AWARDS: NOM:* Oscars '45: Orig. Dramatic Score.

Careful

In the mountain community of Tolzbad the residents live under the constant threat of avalanche. In the midst of this strange environment, two families are plagued by incest, tragedy, and sibling rivalry. This is another unique, completely artificial, stylized work from director Maddin. Bizarre and visually impressive, the film is realized in the style of silent expressionist classics and was filmed entirely on soundstages in a process similar to Two-Strip Technicolor. It's frequently hilarious and features many wonderful set-pieces. A film as unusual as this one begs for a commentary and the excellent, revealing one included here is a must. Maddin and Toles both reveal very strange inspirations for their dialogue and offbeat ideas. Maddin is clearly a very unsettling, disturbed person who sees the world in ways as odd as his films. The documentary functions mostly as a portrait of the filmmaker during the making of *Twilight of the Ice Nymphs* and features some excellent behind-the-scenes footage and interviews. Maddin has a tendency to make disturbing, revealing admissions but rarely elaborates on them. One wonders what a team of Viennese shrinks would make of this man's life and points of view! The film is intentionally soft, grainy, and bathed in odd colors. The disc displays the challenging imagery with accuracy and without digital noise. Soundtrack is designed to sound like a crackly, old record and the dialogue is mostly post-synched. The dialogue is clear and the soundtrack is conveyed without additional noise or hiss. —*DG*
Movie: 🎵🎵🎵 **DVD:** 🎵🎵🎵 ½
Kino on Video (cat #K184DVD, UPC 7383-29018429). Full frame. Mono. $29.95. Keepcase. *LANG:* English. *FEATURES:* Commentary: Maddin, Toles ● 60 min. documentary, "Guy Maddin: Waiting for Twilight" ● 16 chapters—"Careful" ● 12 chapters—"Waiting for Twilight" ● Insert card with chapter listings.
1992 100m/C Kyle McCulloch, Gosia Dobrowolska, Jackie Burroughs, Sarah Neville, Brent Neale, Paul Cox, Victor Cowie, Michael O'Sullivan, Vince Rimmer, Katya Gardner; **D:** Guy Maddin; **W:** Guy Maddin, George Toles; **C:** Guy Maddin; **M:** John McCulloch.

Careful, He Might Hear You

Abandoned by his father, six-year-old P.S. becomes a pawn between his dead mother's two sisters, working-class Lila (Nevin) and the wealthy Vanessa (Hughes). Things

are further unsettled by the reappearance of prodigal dad (Hargreaves). Set in Depression-era Australia, Schultz's vision is touching and keenly observed, and manages a sort of child's-eye sense of proportion. DVD image ranges between good and very good, but when viewed on a standard-sized TV screen, an odd distracting double letterbox—with gray bars at the top and bottom and black inner bars closer to the image—is visible. —*MM*
Movie: 🎵🎵🎵 **DVD:** 🎵🎵 ½
Image Ent. (cat #ID0772DADVD, UPC 014-381077223). Widescreen (2.35:1) anamorphic. Dolby Digital Stereo. $24.98. Keepcase. *LANG:* English. *FEATURES:* 18 chapters.
1984 (PG) 113m/C AU Nicholas Gledhill, Wendy Hughes, Robyn Nevin, John Hargreaves; **D:** Carl Schultz; **W:** Michael Jenkins; **C:** John Seale; **M:** Ray Cook. *AWARDS:* Australian Film Inst. '83: Actress (Hughes), Film.

A Caribbean Mystery / The Mirror Cracked from Side to Side

Please see review of *Agatha Christie's Miss Marple Set 1.*
Movie: 🎵🎵 ½ **DVD:** 🎵🎵 ½
A&E (cat #AAE-70258, UPC 7339617025-83). Full frame. Dolby Digital Stereo. Keepcase. *LANG:* English.
1989 100m/C Joan Hickson, Donald Pleasence, T.P. McKenna, Michael Feast, Sheila Ruskin, Adrian Lukis, Frank Middlemass; **D:** Christopher Petit; **W:** T.R. Bowen; **C:** John Walker.

Carl Theodore Dreyer Box Set

This four-disc set contains three of director Dreyer's best films, *Gertrud, Day of Wrath, Ordet* (please see individual reviews), and a documentary, *Carl Theodore Dreyer—My Métier* (94 mins.). This plain-spoken and visually distinguished show covers the director's unique life and films with a nice balance of clips and interviews. The cameramen and actors all behave as if working with Dreyer was the high point of their lives. Dreyer only made 13 features, and went through long periods of inactivity, but he never seems to have become frustrated and bitter, or to have turned into an unfulfilled genius with a career made up of partially filmed and abandoned "masterpieces." The idea of a film director as an uncompromising artist is quickly becoming extinct in a film world dominated by commercialism, and Dreyer's story is as inspirational and as spiritual as the movies he made. Image and sound quality are up to Criterion's high standards. —*GE*
Movie: 🎵🎵🎵🎵 **DVD:** 🎵🎵🎵🎵
Criterion (cat #DRE090, UPC 037429158-425). Widescreen anamorphic; full frame. $79.95. Keepcase. *LANG:* Danish. *SUB:* English.
2000 432m/C

Carmen Jones

Bizet's tale of fickle femme fatale Carmen heads south with an all black cast and new lyrics by Hammerstein II. Soldier Belafonte falls big time for factory working belle Dandridge during WWII, and runs off with her after he kills his commanding officer and goes A.W.O.L. Tired of prettyboy Belafonte, Dandridge's eye wanders upon pugilist Joe Adams, and fatal passion ensues. Though the stars were superb singers, they didn't have operatic voices; real divas, like Marilyn Horne, did the dubbing. New widescreen transfer looks gorgeous. Surround remix is excellent. —JE
Movie: 🎵🎵🎵 **DVD:** 🎵🎵🎵 ½
20th Century Fox (cat #2001882, UPC 02-45018827). Widescreen anamorphic. Dolby Digital 4.0 Surround; Dolby Surround. $19.98. Keepcase. LANG: English. SUB: English; Spanish. FEATURES: Theatrical trailer • Original one-sheet.
1954 105m/C Dorothy Dandridge, Harry Belafonte, Pearl Bailey, Roy Glenn, Diahann Carroll, Brock Peters; **D:** Otto Preminger; **W:** Harry Kleiner; **C:** Sam Leavitt; **M:** Oscar Hammerstein, Georges Bizet. AWARDS: Golden Globes '55: Film—Mus./Comedy, Natl. Film Reg. '92; NOM: Oscars '54: Actress (Dandridge), Scoring/Musical.

Carnegie Hall

Widowed Irish-American Nora (Hunt) gets a job at Carnegie Hall and raises her son Tony to be a pianist. But the adult Tony (Prince) develops an interest in jazz. Ma hates it; they have a rift; Tony goes on the road with a band. He marries Ruth (O'Driscoll) and becomes famous. Years later, Ruth decides to reunite mother and son. The famous Carnegie Hall plays a big part in her scheme. The schmaltzy story showcases some of the big musical stars of the day. DVD image is virtually damage free. It appears to have been made from well-preserved original elements. Sound is typical of the era, and so is on the thin side. Should it have been beefed up or remixed? Probably not. —MM
Movie: 🎵🎵 ½ **DVD:** 🎵🎵 ½
Kino on Video (cat #K199, UPC 73832901-9921). Full frame. $24.98. Keepcase. LANG: English. FEATURES: 20 chapters • Production stills • Music notes • "Piano Scene" from Ulmer's Detour • Trailer.
1947 134m/B Marsha Hunt, William Prince, Martha O'Driscoll, Frank McHugh; **D:** Edgar G. Ulmer; **W:** Karl Kamb; **C:** William J. Miller.

Carnival of Blood / Curse of the Headless Horseman [SE]

If you're looking for a couple of stinkers, then this double-feature is perfect for you. These low-budget horror quickies mimic the style of the "Godfather of Gore" Herschell Gordon Lewis. But while Lewis's films were bad in a fun way, these two sickos are just bad. Carnival of Blood focuses on a series of murders that have taken place at the Coney Island amusement park. An aspiring district attorney takes his girlfriend there to investigate. What we get is three semi-gory murders, a great deal of amusement park footage, and some incredibly bad acting. The trailer should have gone something like this: "See! The microphone enter the shot at the 19:50 point! See! A guy's butt for 15 seconds because he won't move out of the way of the camera! See! Rocky actor Burt Young (here using the name John Harris) as Gimpy the Hunchback!" (I wish I was making that up.) This film is silly, boring, and pointless. Two years later, the same director made Curse of the Headless Horseman, which follows roughly the same formula. A young hippie, who's also a doctor in residence, inherits his uncle's "ranch," which is really a Wild West amusement park. He and his hippie friends decide to check it out. For most of the film, we simply watch the characters as they examine each of the attractions. Fifty minutes into the film, the titular headless horseman shows up and throws blood on some people. Amazingly, it's even worse than Carnival of Blood. These two movies cannot be recommended to general audiences, but fans of "so bad it's good" fare should love them. Both images are littered with defects from the source prints (which were clearly well-used theatrical prints), such as green lines, scratches, missing frames, and white specs. Surprisingly, the colors are fine on both. Both offer Dolby Digital Mono soundtracks, which provide adequate dialogue, but both have hissing. The best parts of this DVD are the bonus trailers for other bad drive-in movies. The trailers of Asylum of Satan and The Hunchback of the Morgue are both funny and intriguing. If only this DVD had contained those films.... —ML **AKA:** Death Rides a Carousel.
Movie: woof **DVD:** 🎵
Image Ent. (cat #ID1180SWDVD, UPC 014-381118025). Full frame. Dolby Digital Mono. $24.99. Keepcase. LANG: English. FEATURES: Bonus trailers • Still gallery • Bonus short films.
1971 (PG) 80m/C Earle Edgerton, Judith Resnick, Martin Barlosky, John Harris, Burt Young, Kaly Mills, Gloria Spivak; **D:** Leonard Kirtman; **W:** Leonard Kirtman; **C:** David Howe.

Carnival of Souls [DC]

Cult-followed zero-budget zombie opera has young Hilligoss and girlfriends taking a wrong turn off a bridge into a river. Mysteriously unscathed, Hilligoss rents a room and takes a job as a church organist, but she keeps running into dancing dead people, led by director Harvey. High on atmosphere, low on acting talent. Spooky, very spooky. This genuine cult classic gets the treatment it deserves. This great 2-DVD set from Criterion includes both the original 78-minute release and a new 84-minute cut. The new director's cut looks great and the print used for the transfer is near perfect. What's most amazing is that the original cut looks just as good. Sure, an occasional blemish shows up, as one would expect with a low-budget flick of this vintage, but both transfers have very good blacks and excellent graytones. Even the low-fi soundtrack sounds good, with the eerie Gene Moore organ score never sounding better. Expect a full compliment of supplementals including 45 minutes of outtakes backed by the aforementioned organ score in its entirety. —JO
Movie: 🎵🎵🎵 **DVD:** 🎵🎵🎵
Criterion (cat #CC1553D, UPC 71551501-0221). Full frame. Dolby Digital Mono. $39.95. Keepcase. LANG: English. SUB: English. FEATURES: 15 chapters • Theatrical trailer • Extended 84-minute director's cut • Original 78-minute theatrical version • "The Movie That Wouldn't Die: The Story of Carnival of Souls" • "The Carnival Tour": video update on the film's locations • Illustrated history of the Saltair resort • 45 minutes of outtakes accompanied by Gene Moore's organ score • 60 minutes of excerpts from films made by Centron Corp. • Commentary: director Herk Harvey, screenwriter John Clifford • Essay on the history of Centron Corp. • Printed interviews illustrated with photos and memorabilia • Dual-layered RSDL.
1962 72m/B Candace Hilligoss, Sidney Berger, Frances Feist, Stan Levitt, Art Ellison, Bill de Jarnette, Steve Boozer, Pamela Ballard, Harold (Herk) Harvey; **D:** Harold (Herk) Harvey; **W:** John Clifford; **C:** Maurice Prather; **M:** Gene Moore.

Carnival of Souls / Dementia 13

A drag-racing car crashes through a bridge railing and disappears into the river below. Although a rescue crew is unable to retrieve the car, a single shocked survivor staggers out of the river. The survivor, Mary (Hilligoss), a church organist, quickly packs up her things and moves into a boarding house in another town. As Mary tries to adjust to her new surroundings she is haunted by a ghoulish apparition (Harvey) that seems to be following her. This atmospheric low-budget production is (sadly) the only feature film produced by director Harvey's Kansas industrial film and commercial production company. The film is hampered by the amateur performances but the actors' flat and mannered behavior somehow helps contribute to the strange mood of the film. Director Harvey makes terrific use of wide-open, near abandoned locations, particularly the abandoned amusement park Saltair. This real, but completely surreal location is a fantasist's dream (an enormous abandoned, ornate boardwalk and amusement park in the middle of the desert), and fits this story like a glove. Though the basic idea and final twist are extremely similar to similar Twilight Zone episodes, the rich black-and-white photography and unusual organ score help set it apart. Carnival of Souls comes from a fairly clean 16mm

print and features a better range of contrasts and gray tones than *Dementia 13* does, but is nowhere near the clarity of the stupendous Criterion edition. The sound is a bit rough and it's hard to discern the dialogue at times. Both discs have minimal shimmer around the edges of moving people and objects. This print runs a few minutes shorter than other releases. While the print used for *Dementia 13* (first reviewed in *Book 2*) is in better condition and less scratchy than the one used on the Roan/Troma DVD, the contrasts are too strong. Images are either solid black or bright white; there are almost no gray shadings. The sound is muffled though fairly coherent. —*DG*
Movie: ♫♫♫ **DVD:** ♫♫
Marengo Films (cat #MRG-0017, UPC 807-013001792). Full frame. Mono. $14.98. Keepcase. *LANG:* English. *FEATURES:* 6 chapters per film.
1962 72m/B Candace Hilligoss, Sidney Berger, Frances Feist, Stan Levitt, Art Ellison, Bill de Jarnette, Steve Boozer, Pamela Ballard, Harold (Herk) Harvey; **D:** Harold (Herk) Harvey; **W:** John Clifford; **C:** Maurice Prather; **M:** Gene Moore.

Carnivore

Combining "Resident Evil" (the video game, not the film) and a variation on *Scooby-Doo* probably seemed like a good idea at the time, but the resulting film is nothing but gristle. It opens in a dilapidated house, which is actually a secret government lab. We learn through an incredibly muffled voice-over, that the goal of the operation was to create an organic weapon, which has come to be known as "The Carnivore" or "Carni." (Are we supposed to be afraid of a monster that has a nickname?) As Dr. Westmont is attempting to subdue the creature, it attacks him and escapes...although it can't leave the house. As government agents race to the scene to contain the situation, a group of local teenagers decide to have a private party there. From this point on, the characters wander through the house and are killed off one-by-one by "Carni." Despite the fact that this one's only 81 minutes long, it seems to drag on forever. There are long stretches where nothing happens and the monster attacks are brief and far between. "Carni" appears to be a person wearing a spandex leotard with a monkey mask. The acting is awful and the technical problems (see below) are the final nail in the coffin. This DVD offers the film in a letterboxed format. Despite the information in the film's credits stating that it was shot on film, the movie has the appearance of a video production. The image is somewhat dark and grainy, and there is a fair amount of video distortion. The worst problem is the audio. The dialogue is so muffled that it's usually impossible to understand what the actors are saying. The film's opening narration is even worse. To confound matters, the sound effects have been recorded much louder than the dialogue, making the overall volume incredibly unbalanced. There is also a low-frequency hum present on the soundtrack. *Carnivore* is a bloody mess of a movie and the poor DVD presentation does not help matters. —*ML*
Movie: woof **DVD:** ♫
MTI (cat #1091, UPC 039414510911). Widescreen (1.85:1) letterboxed. Dolby Surround. $24.95. Keepcase. *LANG:* English. *SUB:* Spanish. *FEATURES:* Commentary • Featurette • Trailer • 8 chapters.
2001 81m/C Jill Adcock, Steven W. Cromie, John C. Jacob, Lori Johnson, Jeff Swan; **D:** Kenneth Mader, F. Joseph Kurtz; **W:** Kenneth Mader, F. Joseph Kurtz; **M:** Doug Lofstrom.

Carrie

Overprotected and brutalized by her religious fanatic mother (Laurie) and mocked by the popular kids at her high school, Carrie White (Spacek) possesses incredible psychic powers. She's invited to the prom and, when she finds that she's the butt of a cruel joke (by Allen and Travolta), she cuts loose. The milestone horror movie has become a perennial favorite and it looks just fine on DVD. Image is a sterling re-creation of a well-preserved original. Extras are acceptable with two documentaries. "Carrie the Musical" featurette is a six-minute reminiscence by Betty Buckley and Lawrence D. Cohen. "Stephen King and the Evolution of Carrie" is text. —*MM*
Movie: ♫♫♫ **DVD:** ♫♫♫
MGM Home Ent. (cat #1002332, UPC 027-616865519). Widescreen (1.85:1) anamorphic. Dolby Digital 5.1 Surround Stereo; Mono. $19.98. Keepcase. *LANG:* English; French; Spanish. *SUB:* French; Spanish. *CAP:* English. *FEATURES:* 32 chapters • "Acting Carrie" documentary • "Visualizing Carrie" documentary • "Carrie the Musical" featurette • "Stephen King and the Evolution of Carrie" • Photo gallery • Trailer.
1976 (R) 98m/C Sissy Spacek, Piper Laurie, John Travolta, William Katt, Amy Irving, Nancy Allen, Edie McClurg, Betty Buckley, P.J. Soles, Sydney Lassick, Stefan Gierasch; **D:** Brian DePalma; **W:** Lawrence D. Cohen; **C:** Mario Tosi; **M:** Pino Donaggio. *AWARDS:* Natl. Soc. Film Critics '76: Actress (Spacek); *NOM:* Oscars '76: Actress (Spacek), Support. Actress (Laurie).

Carrington

England's artistic Bloomsbury group is examined through the eccentric relationship of artist Dora Carrington (Thompson) and her love for homosexual Lytton Strachey (Pryce), celebrated author of *Eminent Victorians*. There's many a menage as the duo live together with Carrington's husband (Waddington), on whom Strachey has a crush, and both their various amours (though Carrington's heart is reserved for Lytton). Film is distractingly divided into titled segments (from 1915 to 1932) and, while Pryce gives a bravura performance, Thompson is merely enigmatic. Based on Michael Holyrod's biography *Lytton Strachey*. Hampton's directorial debut. The disc's decent video transfer is hampered occasionally by blandness found in the bright hues. Overall, however, the disc reproduces colors and blacks quite well and looks decent throughout. The soundtrack is a bit superior to the video transfer as it features clear and discernible dialogue and no disagreeable distortion. The behind-the-scenes featurette found on the disc amounts to little more than an elongated trailer, which makes it a bit of a disappointment. —*MJT*
Movie: ♫♫ ½ **DVD:** ♫♫ ½
MGM Home Ent. (cat #1002749, UPC 027-616869470). Widescreen (1.85:1) anamorphic. Dolby Digital Surround. $19.98. Keepcase. *LANG:* English; French; Spanish. *FEATURES:* 16 chapters • Behind-the-scenes featurette • Theatrical trailer • Trailer gallery.
1995 (R) 120m/C *FR GB* Emma Thompson, Jonathan Pryce, Steven Waddington, Samuel West, Rufus Sewell, Penelope Wilton, Jeremy Northam, Peter Blythe, Janet McTeer, Alex Kingston, Sebastian Harcombe, Richard Clifford; **D:** Christopher Hampton; **W:** Christopher Hampton; **C:** Denis Lenoir; **M:** Michael Nyman. *AWARDS:* Cannes '95: Special Jury Prize, Actor (Pryce); Natl. Bd. of Review '95: Actress (Thompson); *NOM:* British Acad. '95: Actor (Pryce), Film.

Cast a Giant Shadow

Based on Israel's post-WWII fight for independence, with Douglas starring as an American military hero who serves as a consultant and strategist for the Jewish army. In Israel, he learns that the Arabs are all power-hungry and consumed with greed, while the Jews just want to dance around a fire and sing folk songs in their homeland. The film proceeds to waste an amazing cast. The picture quality is astonishing, considering the age of the film. The same cannot be said of the audio; the actors often sound as if they were trapped in a shoebox while their dialogue was being recorded. —*BG*
Movie: ♫ ½ **DVD:** ♫♫ ½
MGM Home Ent. (cat #1003134, UPC 027-616872982). Widescreen (2.35:1) anamorphic. Dolby Mono. $14.95. Keepcase. *LANG:* English; French; Spanish. *SUB:* English; French; Spanish. *FEATURES:* 16 chapters • Trailer.
1966 138m/C Kirk Douglas, Senta Berger, Angie Dickinson, John Wayne, James Donald, Chaim Topol, Frank Sinatra, Yul Brynner; **D:** Melville Shavelson; **W:** Melville Shavelson; **C:** Aldo Tonti; **M:** Elmer Bernstein.

The Castle of Cagliostro

Master thief Lupin III, AKA The Wolf, and his right-hand gunman Jigen, are on the trail of a counterfeiter. Their search leads them to the secluded European country of Cagliostro. Lupin unwittingly attracts the attention of the nation's mysterious monarch when he tries to help a damsel in distress. From the creators of *Princess Mononoke,* this much earlier effort has a beautiful stylization reminiscent of a Tin-Tin comic strip. Still, a considerable technical leap has been made to *Mononoke,* so only anime completists will really be pleased with these relatively primitive roots. Wonderful DVD transfer with good sound. —*MO*

Movie: 🎬🎬 **DVD:** 🎬🎬🎬🎬
Manga Ent. (cat #MANG4051-2 WR02, UPC 660200405120). Widescreen letterboxed. Dolby Digital Stereo. $29.95. Keepcase. *LANG:* Japanese; English. *SUB:* English. *FEATURES:* 11 chapters ● Theatrical trailer.
1980 100m/C *JP D:* Hayao Miyazaki.

Castles of War

Informative yet overly dramatic documentary focuses on the history of castles. It discusses architecture, history, legends, etc., and is a very thorough and complete examination of the topic. However, many of the reenactments can grow tiresome. Most bright colors are represented well by the video transfer as are blacks and other darker colors. But the overall presentation lacks crisp definition, which often results in a bland, washed-out look. The soundtrack reproduces the narration well, with no distortion or other noticeable flaws. The bonus feature included on the disc, "Castles of Fear," is as enjoyable as the main feature. —*MJT*

Movie: 🎬🎬 ½ **DVD:** 🎬🎬 ½
BFS Video (cat #30225-D, UPC 06680530-2251). Full frame. Dolby Digital Stereo. $19.98. Keepcase. *LANG:* English. *FEATURES:* 8 chapters ● Bonus program: "Castles of Fear" ● Siege weapons glossary.
2000 90m/C D: Andre Jansen, Oscar de Waard, Mark Verkerk.

Casualties of War

A Vietnam war morality play about army private Fox in the bush who refuses to let his fellow soldiers and commanding sergeant (Penn) skirt responsibility for the rape and murder of a native woman. Fox achieves his dramatic breakthrough. Based on the true story by Daniel Lang. An excellent video transfer is highlighted by vibrant colors and accented by solid blacks (though some "jungle" scenes may exhibit a loss of clarity and appear a bit dark, this can be excused as an aesthetic choice). The superb soundtrack features crisp, clear dialogue and wonderfully explosive music and sound effects. Of the disc's extras the "making of" documentary and the interview with Fox standout as well produced, informative, and extremely entertaining. —*MJT*

Movie: 🎬🎬🎬 **DVD:** 🎬🎬🎬
Columbia Tristar (cat #06292, UPC 0433-96062924). Widescreen (2.35:1) anamorphic. Dolby Digital 5.1 Surround; Dolby Surround. $19.95. Keepcase. *LANG:* English; French; Spanish; Portuguese. *SUB:* English; French; Spanish; Portuguese; Chinese; Korean; Thai. *FEATURES:* 28 chapters ● "Eriksson's War: A Conversation with

Michael J. Fox" featurette ● "The Making of *Casualties of War*" featurette ● Theatrical trailers ● Deleted scenes ● Production notes.
1989 (R) 120m/C Sean Penn, Michael J. Fox, Don Harvey, Thuy Thu Le, John Leguizamo, Sam Robards, John C. Reilly, Erik King, Dale Dye; *D:* Brian DePalma; *W:* David Rabe; *C:* Stephen Burum; *M:* Ennio Morricone.

The Cat o' Nine Tails

A blind puzzle maker (Malden) and a reporter (Franciscus) investigate a series of murders. Though the action is not nearly as graphically violent as it would become later in his career, the film marks Argento's debut as a suspense director to be reckoned with. This one has suffered from poor distribution, both theatrically and on home video. Though I'm not one of Argento's biggest fans, I have to admit that the DVD is simply spectacular, giving the director's famous camerawork the treatment it deserves. Image is superb and the extras are well chosen. Sound is very good. —*MM*

Movie: 🎬🎬 ½ **DVD:** 🎬🎬🎬 ½
Anchor Bay (cat #DV11333, UPC 0131311-33394). Widescreen (2.35:1) anamorphic. Dolby Digital Surround Stereo. $24.99. Keepcase. *LANG:* English; French; Italian. *FEATURES:* Interviews ● Trailers ● TV and radio spots ● Poster and still gallery ● 27 chapters ● Talent files.
1971 (PG) 112m/C *GE FR IT* Karl Malden, James Franciscus, Catherine Spaak, Cinzia de Carolis, Carlo Alighiero; *D:* Dario Argento; *W:* Dario Argento; *C:* Erico Menczer; *M:* Ennio Morricone.

Catherine Cookson's The Girl

The illegitimate child of an affair, Hannah is sent to live with her wealthy father after her mother dies from illness. But her new stepmother refuses to accept her, and uses all of her power to make Hannah's life miserable for years to come. It's even more melodramatic than it sounds, and any sensible person would turn it off about 15 minutes in, when our seven-year-old heroine is given a brutal whipping. Picture and sound are about average for a made-for-TV production. —*BG* **AKA:** The Girl.

Movie: 🎬 ½ **DVD:** 🎬🎬 ½
BFS Video (cat #30139-D, UPC 06680530-1391). Full frame. Dolby. $29.98. Keepcase. *LANG:* English. *FEATURES:* 15 chapters.
1996 148m/C *GB* Siobhan Flynn, Malcolm Stoddard, Jonathan Cake, Jill Baker, Mark Benton; *D:* David Wheatley; *W:* Gordon Hann.

Catherine the Great

Teenaged German princess Sophia (Zeta-Jones) marries into Russian royalty in 1744 when she weds Peter (Jaenicke), nephew of the Empress Elizabeth (Moreau), and has a name change when she's crowned Catherine II. The marriage is a

disaster and with the help of her lover Gregory Orlov (McGann), Catherine eventually gets rid of Peter and is crowned Empress and Czarina of all the Russias as she struggles to drag her medieval empire into the modern world. Typically lavish and simplistic historical retelling. Originally released as a two-part miniseries. The average video transfer's problems begin with brighter scenes that are washed-out to the point of being downright blurry. Some darker-lit scenes have virtually no clarity, which results in even worse bleeding of colors. Still, many scenes in between these two extremes feature adequately sharp and clear image reproduction (though not of a redeeming sort). The soundtrack fares a bit better and manages to reproduce dialogue crisply as well as a distortion-free musical track. —*MJT*

Movie: 🎬🎬 ½ **DVD:** 🎬🎬
A&E (cat #AAE-70154, UPC 7339617015-48). Full frame. Dolby Digital Stereo. $19.95. Keepcase. *LANG:* English. *FEATURES:* 9 chapters ● Cast filmographies.
1995 100m/C *GE* Catherine Zeta-Jones, Paul McGann, Ian Richardson, Jeanne Moreau, Mark McGann, Hannes Jaenicke, Mel Ferrer, Omar Sharif, John Rhys-Davies, Brian Blessed; *D:* Marvin J. Chomsky; *W:* John Goldsmith; *C:* Elemer Ragalyi; *M:* Laurence Rosenthal.

Cats [UE Universal]

Capitalizing on the success of the *Cats: Commemorative Edition* DVD release, Universal unleashes a second helping of *Cats* with some new extras. The first half of this two-disc set features a filmed performance of *Cats* the musical. Director David Mallet has shot the performance in an unobtrusive manner, giving one the illusion of being in the front row. Elaine Page leads the competent cast here as Grizabella, and as always, *Cats* is a stirring and engrossing show. The second disc offers a sneak-peek behind the curtain with interviews, a "making of" featurette, and a demonstration of the famous *Cats* makeup. The audio and video of the performance film are stellar, giving us a very clear picture, which displays a realistic rainbow of colors. The Dolby Digital 5.0 sound brings the all-important music to life, furthering the illusion of attending a live performance. —*ML*

Movie: 🎬🎬🎬 **DVD:** 🎬🎬🎬 ½
Universal Studios (cat #21472, UPC 02-5192147227). Widescreen (1.78:1) letterboxed. Dolby Digital 5.0 Surround. $26.98. Special packaging. *LANG:* English. *FEATURES:* Cast and crew interviews ● Makeup demonstration ● "Making of" featurette ● 21 chapters.
1998 121m/C Elaine Page, Ken Page, John Mills; *D:* David Mallet, Trevor Nunn; *C:* Nicholas D. Knowland; *M:* Andrew Lloyd Webber.

Cave Girl

After falling through a time warp while on a field trip, geeky Rex (Roebuck) finds himself in prehistoric times where he falls for cute cavebabe Iba (Thompson). This is lightweight low-budget exploitation. DVD makes the often exceptionally grainy image look about as good as it can, though that's certainly not saying much. —MM **AKA:** Cavegirl.

Movie: 🎬🎬 **DVD:** 🎬🎬 ½
Rhino (cat #R2 975737, UPC 603497573-721). Widescreen anamorphic. $9.95. Snapper. *LANG:* English. *FEATURES:* Trailer • 12 chapters.
1985 (R) 85m/C Daniel Roebuck, Cindy Ann Thompson, Saba Moor, Jeff Chayette; **D:** David Oliver; **W:** David Oliver; **C:** David Oliver; **M:** Jon St. James.

Caveman

Ringo Starr stars as Atouk, the caveman with designs on the hottest cave-girl (Bach) in the tribe. Shelly Long plays the less voluptuous but more righteous girl with an eye on Atouk. Dennis Quaid is Atouk's hunky friend. Character actors Jack Gilford and Avery Schrieber round out the cast for blind jokes and overacting, respectively. The dialogue is grunted. The jokes are lousy and the story flimsy. The only funny part is that the subtitles are the same whether you watch them in Spanish, French, or English. And so is the dubbing. Cavemen were apparently fluent in several tongues. It makes one wonder who got paid for that job at MGM. The picture quality looks like film stock from the '80s, mostly hindered by the stop-action dinosaurs and the milky backgrounds used to make it appear as though they and the cavemen existed together. The film was directed and written, if there was any writing, by Carl Gottlieb, who co-wrote *Jaws* after a brief career in TV. If you have to watch a bad prehistoric caveman comedy, there are two *Flintstones* films to chose from. Move along, there's nothing to see here. —JAS

Movie: woof **DVD:** 🎬🎬🎬
MGM Home Ent. (cat #1003507, UPC 027-616876577). Full frame, widescreen (1.85:1) anamorphic. Dolby Digital. $14.95. Keepcase. *LANG:* English; French; Spanish. *SUB:* English; French; Spanish. *CAP:* English. *FEATURES:* Original theatrical trailer.
1981 (PG) 92m/C Ringo Starr, Barbara Bach, John Matuszak, Dennis Quaid, Jack Gilford, Shelley Long, Cork Hubbert, Avery Schrieber; **D:** Carl Gottlieb; **W:** Carl Gottlieb, Rudy DeLuca; **C:** Alan Hume; **M:** Lalo Schifrin.

The Caveman's Valentine

Romulus Ledbetter (Jackson), once a promising Julliard-trained pianist, is now a homeless cave dweller in Central Park. He's convinced that his mortal enemy lives atop the Chrysler Building and is attacking him with X- and Z-rays. When a friend is found dead hanging from a tree outside his cave, Romulus believes in his heart that he knows who the villain is. His daughter (Ellis), a cop, is doubtful, as is everyone who was disappointed by Romulus's descent into mental illness. The plot of the film is so old it has hair (as Rex Reed would say). There is never any doubt that despite his mental limitations, Romulus will find the killer, but Jackson's even-handed portrayal of Romulus as a man who has a firm grip on the insanity that creates great art, but a tenuous grip on reality, is well worth watching. Anthony Michael Hall has a great bit part as the yuppie who lends Romulus a suit in exchange for hearing him play. There are shades of David Helfgott in Romulus, but in this case, the genius of his own piano playing is terrifying to him because of the visions it brings. In the course of trying to solve the murder of his friend, he must twice conquer his fear of playing. He has a muse to help him, which can only be described as the ghost of his wife past. The real wife is alive and well, but her younger, wiser image follows him around, strangely giving him his strongest link to reality. Jackson's acting coupled with Kasi Lemmon's (*Eve's Bayou*) bold direction in attempting to use light, color, and sound to show us what Romulus sees when he is caught up in his illness makes the film worth a look-see. The color on the disc is great with firm blacks and deep browns and reds that texture the New York City grime and architecture. The sound is crisp and clear and uses the multi-channel systems well. —CA

Movie: 🎬🎬 ½ **DVD:** 🎬🎬🎬
Universal Studios (cat #21376, UPC 025-192137624). Widescreen (1.85:1) letterboxed. Dolby Digital 5.1 Surround, DTS 5.1 Surround. $26.90. Keepcase. *LANG:* English; French. *SUB:* English; French. *CAP:* English. *FEATURES:* 18 chapters • Commentary: director, editor • Deleted scenes • Theatrical trailer.
2001 (R) 105m/C Samuel L. Jackson, Aunjanue Ellis, Colm Feore, Ann Magnuson, Rodney Eastman, Tamara Tunie, Anthony Michael Hall, Jay Rodan; **D:** Kasi Lemmons; **W:** George Dawes Green; **C:** Amelia Vincent; **M:** Terence Blanchard.

C.C. & Company

C.C. Ryder (Namath) is an uneasy rider who challenges Moon (Smith) for leadership of the Heads motorcycle gang. He also rescues fashion babe Ann (Ann-Margret) from a fate worse than death at the hands of a couple of his fellow gang members. Namath's acting skills are of a piece with the rest of this ridiculous goof of a movie. It stinks in almost every respect. If the love scene with Ann-Margret were more professionally lit, the picture wouldn't stink as bad, but it would still stink. DVD stinks, too. It appears to have been made from a VHS tape with washed-out colors and fuzzy focus throughout. Title is also available on *Classic Biker Movies* disc. Image is the same on both releases. —MM **AKA:** Chrome Hearts.

Movie: 🎬 **DVD:** 🎬
Platinum Disc (cat #00329, UPC 0960-09003296). Full frame. Dolby Digital Mono. $9.98. Modified jewelcase. *LANG:* English. *FEATURES:* 12 chapters • Ann-Margret thumbnail bio and filmography.
1970 (R) 91m/C Joe Namath, Ann-Margret, William Smith, Jennifer Billingsley, Teda Bracci, Greg Mullavey, Sid Haig, Bruce Glover; **D:** Seymour Robbie; **W:** Roger Smith; **C:** Charles F. Wheeler; **M:** Lenny Stack.

The Celluloid Closet

Fascinating, eye-opening documentary charts the history of gay cinematic portrayals from silent films up into the early 1990s. The clips are well-chosen and the interview subjects are lucid and insightful. It's an entertaining overview but occasionally lacks the richness and depth of author Russo's work. In retrospect, the championing of the limp, timid *Philadelphia* as some kind of pinnacle of gay film respectability is quite awkward. It'd certainly be interesting to see a sequel brought up to contemporary times. The film transfer is bright and sharp if a bit grainy and shimmery. The sound is fine. The group audio commentary lacks focus and seems ill-prepared, but the recorded lecture (erroneously listed as a commentary on the package) by Russo is an absolute must. The outtake interviews (which feature some actors not included in the film) are terrific and are just as compelling (if not more) than the feature. —DG

Movie: 🎬🎬🎬 **DVD:** 🎬🎬🎬
Columbia Tristar (cat #82107, UPC 04339-6821071). Full frame. Dolby Digital Surround. $29.95. Keepcase. *LANG:* English. *SUB:* English. *CAP:* English. *FEATURES:* Commentary: Epstein, Friedman, Tomlin, Rosenman, Glassman • 28 chapters • Insert booklet with notes from Charlton Heston and Gore Vidal • Commentary: author Vito Russo • Trailers • Outtake interviews • Talent files • Direct weblink to GLAAD website.
1995 (R) 102m/C D: Robert Epstein, Jeffrey Friedman; **W:** Armistead Maupin; **C:** Nancy Schreiber; **M:** Carter Burwell; **Nar:** Lily Tomlin.

Cement

L.A. undercover detectives Holt (Penn) and Nin (Wright) are deeply troubled in many ways, but the immediate focus of their woes is a mobster's brother (De Sando) who fooled around with Holt's girl (Fenn) and is now about to be encased in the titular cement overcoat. The moderate grain in the opening scenes appears to be deliberate. Overall, DVD presents a flawless, accurate reproduction of a mid-budget original. —MM

Movie: 🎬🎬 **DVD:** 🎬🎬 ½
Studio Home Ent. (cat #7891D, UPC 658-149789128). Widescreen (1.85:1) letterboxed. Dolby Digital Stereo. $24.99. Keepcase. *LANG:* English. *SUB:* English; Spanish. *CAP:* English. *FEATURES:* Trailer • 24 chapters.
1999 (R) 100m/C Christopher Penn, Jeffrey Wright, Sherilyn Fenn, Anthony De Sando, Henry Czerny; **D:** Adrian Pasdar; **W:** Justin Monjo; **C:** Geary McLeod; **M:** Doug Caldwell.

The Center of the World

Several recent French films have presented explicit sexual matters while remaining staunchly anti-erotic. Writer Paul Auster and director Wayne Wang assay similar territory here with results that will not please all viewers. Imagine the flip side of *Pretty Woman*. Richard (Sarsgaard) is a wealthy dot.com geek who offers stripper Florence (Parker) a major wad of dough to spend a few days with him in Las Vegas. She lays down strict rules about what she will and won't do for him—and promptly breaks them. They're both immature and vulnerable and inclined to play humiliating mind games with each other. The sex show turns out to be little to get overwrought about, though both leads give as credible performances as the narrowness of their characters allow. The film was shot on digital video, so DVD presents what appears to be a totally accurate recreation of an image that often shifts into pale colors with brighter highlights. Some shots are desaturated almost to sepia. Sound is fine. *—MM*
Movie: 🦴🦴🦴 **DVD:** 🦴🦴🦴 ½
Artisan Ent. (cat #11963, UPC 0122361-19630). Widescreen anamorphic. Dolby Digital 5.1 Surround; Dolby Digital Surround. $24.98. Keepcase. *LANG:* English. *CAP:* English. *FEATURES:* 28 chapters ⁍ Trailer and teaser ⁍ "Making of the Website" featurette ⁍ Commentary: Wayne Wang, consultant Patrick Lindenmaier ⁍ 2 alternate endings ⁍ DVD-ROM features ⁍ Talent files ⁍ Production notes.
2001 86m/C Peter Sarsgaard, Molly Parker, Carla Gugino, Balthazar Getty; *D:* Wayne Wang; *W:* Wayne Wang, Paul Auster, Siri Hustvedt; *C:* Mauro Fiore.

Chac: The Rain God

Drought threatens a Mayan village. In desperation, the Cacique (Mendez Ton) and the villagers pay a reluctant visit to the ancient Diviner (Balam) on the mountaintop hoping he'll awaken Chac to save their crops. Beautifully photographed allegorical representation of the myths and customs of the Mayan people effectively uses nonprofessional actors. An excellent, but underdeveloped subplot pertains to a mute village boy (Santis) who begins to learn the ancient ways of the Diviner. The story leads up to a rain ceremony inspired by Klein's research, but essentially choreographed by him. Klein's commentary is full of fascinating historical and anecdotal information. Unfortunately, it was apparently written instead of being told off-the-cuff so it tends to be a bit stiff and, in places, doctrinaire. This DVD looks and sounds fantastic. *—LA*
Movie: 🦴🦴🦴 **DVD:** 🦴🦴🦴 ½
Image Ent. (cat #ID9525MLSDVD, UPC 01-4381952520). Widescreen (1.85:1) letterboxed. Dolby Digital Mono. $29.98. Keepcase. *LANG:* Tzeltal and Mayan dialects. *SUB:* English. *FEATURES:* Photo gallery ⁍ Theatrical trailer ⁍ Commentary: director Ronaldo Klein ⁍ 18 chapters.
1974 94m/C *MX* Pablo Canche Balam, Alonzo Mendez Ton, Sebastian Santis; *D:* Ronaldo Klein; *W:* Ronaldo Klein; *C:* Alex Phillips Jr., William Kaplan Jr.

Champ against Champ [BFS]

Dragon Lee returns to his village to fight against the evil Master Kai. Injured fighting Kai's men, he has his leg amputated and replaced with a freshly made steel leg. The music is provided by anachronistic cues from '70s action pictures. Good for a Saturday afternoon of camp, this one gets an extra bone for sheer goofiness. The print is in decent shape for its age and origin, with reasonably good sound. Available as a triple feature on one disc under the title *Great Martial Arts Movies*. Cover art features Sonny Chiba, though none of his movies are included. *—BT* *AKA:* Wu Tang Champ vs. Champ.
Movie: 🦴🦴 **DVD:** 🦴 ½
BFS Video (cat #30236D, UPC 0668053-02367). Full frame. $9.98. Keepcase. *LANG:* English. *FEATURES:* 5 chapters ⁍ Glossary of martial arts weapons.
1983 88m/C *HK* Dragon Lee, Charles Han, Mark Wong, Doris Tsui, Antonio Sieou, Danny Hung, Stan Yuen, David Yuen; *D:* Godfrey Ho; *W:* Richard Sam; *C:* Joey Mah; *M:* Ricky Chan.

Champ vs. Champ [Xenon]

Godfrey Ho, the master of bad kung fu movies, presents another flick where there's more chopping in the editing than in the choreography. Li Wan (Dragon Lee) finds his homecoming cold. The evil Master Kai fears there's a plot against him, and wants to eliminate all possible opponents, even though he's protected by his magic handmaidens. He rightfully suspects Master Ti is leading the resistance, and is after a list Ti holds of his secret enemies. Li Wan is injured fighting Kai's men, and his leg has to be amputated. Inspired by the great one-legged hero Ti Kong, and with a freshly made steel leg, Li Wan learns the famed 18 Kicking Styles that can grant him victory. The snowy mountain locations provide a fresh backdrop for the action, but Lee's movements are relatively lacking in grace even before his leg gets cut off, and many of the battles rely on gimmicks like steel legs, fighting rings, fire breathing, and magic bolts. The music is provided by anachronistic cues from '70s action pictures. Good for a Saturday afternoon of camp, this one gets an extra bone for sheer goofiness. A horrible print—scratched, speckled, squeezed, and cropped. Except for the leads, the credits on the package are wrong. *—BT* *AKA:* Wu Tang Champ vs. Champ.
Movie: 🦴🦴 **DVD:** 🦴🦴
Xenon Ent. (cat #XEXA6291DVD, UPC 000-799629123). Full frame. Dolby Digital 2.0. $14.98. Keepcase. *LANG:* English. *FEA-TURES:* 6 chapters ⁍ Clips from other Xenon martial arts titles.
1983 88m/C *HK* Dragon Lee, Charles Han, Mark Wong, Doris Tsui, Antonio Sieou, Danny Hung, Stan Yuen, David Yuen; *D:* Godfrey Ho; *W:* Richard Sam; *C:* Joey Mah; *M:* Ricky Chan.

The Charcoal People

Film document of the beautiful, horrible lives of migrant charcoal workers in the eucalyptus rain forests of Brazil. Clear transfer from what is almost entirely hand-held camera. The picture is cropped off slightly on the sides. The "interview" touted on the menu with Brazilian soccer star Renaldo is actually a 10-second endorsement clip, useless to anyone who has already picked up the DVD. *—BT* *AKA:* Os Carvoeiros; The Charcoal People of Brazil.
Movie: 🦴🦴 **DVD:** 🦴🦴 ½
Vanguard Intl. Cinema (cat #VF0234, UPC 658769023435). Full frame. $24.95. Keepcase. *LANG:* Portuguese. *SUB:* English. *FEATURES:* 8 chapters ⁍ Photo gallery ⁍ Trailer ⁍ Interview.
2001 65m/C *BR US D:* Nigel Noble; *W:* Jose Padilha; *C:* Flavio Zangrandi.

The Charge of the Light Brigade

Revisionist retelling of the notorious English defeat by the Russians at Balaclava is a political indictment of the British military and class structure. Though the battle scenes in the last reels are impressive, the filmmakers take liberties with historical fact and are just as interested in generational conflicts as in international matters. With the exception of Vanessa Redgrave (who is untypically simpering), the ensemble cast is excellent, particularly Howard's phlegmatic Cardigan. The evocation of time and place is unusually strong. DVD delivers the best version of the film I've seen on home video, worlds superior to the full-frame VHS tape. By contemporary standards, the image is softly focused and often grainy. (It sharpens in chapter 9 when the scene shifts to Turkey.) Sound is slightly clipped but that seems to come from the original recording. Skin tones seem very reddish, but again I hesitate to fault the transfer. Dark, grubby interiors look fine. A historian's commentary could have been a valuable addition, but given the film's modest American success and reputation, that would have been too much to ask for. *—MM*
Movie: 🦴🦴🦴 **DVD:** 🦴🦴🦴
MGM Home Ent. (cat #1003427, UPC 027-616875761). Widescreen (2.35:1) anamorphic. Dolby Digital Mono. $14.98. Keepcase. *LANG:* English; French. *SUB:* English; French; Spanish. *CAP:* English. *FEATURES:* 16 chapters ⁍ Trailer.
1968 (PG-13) 130m/C *GB* Trevor Howard, John Gielgud, David Hemmings, Vanessa Redgrave, Harry Andrews, Jill Bennett, Peter Bowles, Mark Burns, Alan Dobie, T.P. McKenna, Corin Redgrave, Norman Rossington, Rachel Kempson, Donald Wolfit,

Howard Marion-Crawford, Mark Dignam, Ben Aris, Peter Woodthorpe, Roger Mutton, Joely Richardson; **D:** Tony Richardson; **W:** Charles Wood; **C:** David Watkin; **M:** John Addison.

Chasing Sleep

A fascinating thriller that ought to find its audience on DVD. Jeff Daniels stars as college professor Ed Saxon, who wakes up one morning to find that his wife hasn't come home. He informs the police, who send a detective (Gil Bellows) to investigate. The disappearance renders Ed unable to sleep. The anxiety and the insomnia take a toll on him and he begins to hallucinate. As the story unfolds, Ed learns more about his wife than he ever knew, and his grip on reality begins to slip. *Chasing Sleep* is a fascinating thriller, which should remind some viewers of the work of David Lynch. There seems to be something happening here just beneath the surface, which neither Ed nor the viewer can identify, but it's certainly eerie. The film is well constructed, having a dream-like air, and the unique production design (Ed's house is full of holes and leaky pipes) adds to the film's strange look. It also contains one scene in the bathroom which may cause the viewer to lose sleep. The image on this DVD is acceptable, but there are some ringing artifact issues and the image is a bit hazy at times. The brown color-scheme to the film makes the accuracy of the palette hard to judge. The Dolby Digital 5.1 soundtrack is very effective, as a great deal of care has gone into the sound design of this film. Many scenes are accompanied by ambient sounds from the rear and a low rumbling from the subwoofer, which only enhance the uneasy feel of the movie. —*ML*
Movie: 🎵🎵🎵 ½ **DVD:** 🎵🎵 ½
Studio Home Ent. (cat #7779D, UPC 031-398777922). Widescreen (1.85:1) letterboxed. Dolby Digital 5.1. $24.99. Keepcase. *LANG:* English; French. *SUB:* English; French; Spanish. *CAP:* English. *FEATURES:* Trailer.
2000 (R) 104m/C Jeff Daniels, Emily Bergl, Gil Bellows, Zach Grenier, Julian McMahon, Ben Shenkman, Molly Price; **D:** Michael Walker; **W:** Michael Walker; **C:** Jim Denault.

Chato's Land

Half-breed Apache Chato (Bronson) is tracked by a posse eager to resolve a racist sheriff's killing. Former Confederate Quincey Whitmore (Palance) leads the hunt. The conventionally plotted western is bolstered by an above-average cast. DVD image exhibits some signs of fading and wear, but it looks fine for a film of its age. Mono sound is acceptable. —*MM*
Movie: 🎵🎵 ½ **DVD:** 🎵🎵 ½
MGM Home Ent. (cat #1002367, UPC 027-616865786). Widescreen (1.85:1) letterboxed. Dolby Digital Mono. $19.98. Keepcase. *LANG:* English. *SUB:* French; Spanish. *CAP:* English. *FEATURES:* 16 chapters • Trailer.

1971 (PG) 100m/C Charles Bronson, Jack Palance, Richard Basehart, James Whitmore, Simon Oakland, Richard Jordan, Ralph Waite, Victor French, Lee Patterson; **D:** Michael Winner; **W:** Gerald Wilson; **C:** Robert Paynter; **M:** Jerry Fielding.

The Cheap Detective

Neil Simon's parody of *The Maltese Falcon* gloriously exploits the resourceful Falk in a Bogart-like role (clearly reminiscent of his Bogie impression in Simon's *Murder by Death*). After Falk's character is accused of killing his own partner, he must rush to prove his innocence. This leads him on many comic capers, involving many strange characters. A vast supporting cast—notably Brennan, DeLuise, and Kahn—is equally game for fun in this consistently amusing venture, which also spoofs *Casablanca*. Fans of '40s film noir will find this hysterical, while some younger viewers may not get many of the jokes or references. The DVD offers the film in both a letterboxed and full-frame format. The image is clear, but there is some slight artifacting. The color scheme is nice and the deep blacks add to the noir feel. The Dolby Digital Mono soundtrack provides clear dialogue, but little else. An interview with author Neil Simon is included on this disc, and it sheds some light onto the creative process behind the film. —*ML*
Movie: 🎵🎵🎵 **DVD:** 🎵🎵 ½
Columbia Tristar (cat #90399, UPC 04339-6903999). Widescreen (2.35:1) anamorphic; full frame. Dolby Digital Mono. $19.95. Keepcase. *LANG:* English; Spanish. *SUB:* English; Spanish; Portuguese; Chinese; Korean; Thai. *CAP:* English. *FEATURES:* Featurette • Talent files • 28 chapters.
1978 (PG) 92m/C Peter Falk, Ann-Margret, Eileen Brennan, Sid Caesar, Stockard Channing, James Coco, Dom DeLuise, Louise Fletcher, John Houseman, Madeline Kahn, Fernando Lamas, Marsha Mason, Phil Silvers, Vic Tayback, Abe Vigoda, Paul Williams, Nicol Williamson; **D:** Robert Moore; **W:** Neil Simon; **C:** John A. Alonzo.

Cheap Trick: Music for Hangover

This disc attempts to combine the experience of a live concert with the extra properties of DVD. It's a small less-than-completely-successful step. The disc contains 14 songs performed by Cheap Trick at a 1998 concert at the Metro in Chicago. Of course, the songs can be accessed individually. The disc also contains a rudimentary commentary by the band members. That's presented MST3K-style with silhouettes at the bottom of the screen. The band members do not introduce themselves and really don't have much of anything worthwhile to say. With their occasional burps, they sound like Spinal Tap without the humor or self-awareness. Image quality is exceptionally

rough throughout. Some shots approach mediocrity; most of the footage might have come from a surveillance camera. Sound and image on the interview extra is even worse. —*MM*
Movie: 🎵🎵 **DVD:** 🎵 ½
Rhino (cat #R2 976071, UPC 603497607-129). Full frame. Dolby Digital 5.1 Surround; Dolby Stereo. $19.98. Keepcase. *LANG:* English. *FEATURES:* 14 chapters • Commentary • Interview • Liner notes by Billy Corgan • Discography • Promotional material.
1998 65m/C

The Cheat [Kino]

Please see review for *Manslaughter / The Cheat.*
Movie: 🎵🎵🎵
1915 55m/B Jack Dean, James Neill, Dana Ong, Hazel Childers, Fannie Ward, Sessue Hayakawa; **D:** Cecil B. DeMille; **W:** Alvin Wyckoff, Hector Turnbull. *AWARDS:* Natl. Film Reg. '93.

The Cheaters

A gang of con men tries to skim off the scam of the infamous King of Ghosts Lun Yan (Simon Lui), who is working his way to the top of a media company, but they bite off more than they can chew. Those hoping for a twisty puzzle thriller on the order of *Sneakers* should look elsewhere, as the intent here is to place noir drama in some new modern context. Director Billy Chung seems to build his film toward some sort of climax, but instead lets it drift away. Jordan Chan is becoming one of the more interesting Hong Kong stars of the past few years. Image and sound are both excellent. —*BT*
Movie: 🎵🎵 **DVD:** 🎵🎵🎵
Tai Seng (cat #5581, UPC 601643968841). Widescreen letterboxed. Dolby Digital 5.1 Surround. $19.95. Keepcase. *LANG:* Cantonese; Mandarin. *SUB:* Chinese; English. *FEATURES:* 8 chapters • Star profiles • Trailers.
2000 80m/C *HK* Jordan Chan, Simon Lui, Ken Wong, Thomas Lam, Alex Fong; **D:** Billy Chung; **W:** Edmand Pang, Paul Chung; **C:** Daniel Chan; **M:** Kin Law.

Cheech and Chong's Nice Dreams

Director Tommy Chong is at the helm a second time as he and his lowrider compadre, Cheech, are in business selling hefty amounts of herb from their "Nice Dreams" truck under the guise of ice cream novelties (the "Big Stick" treat). They amass quite a fortune in cash, guitars, and a beachside manor that can only be considered a thumbing of the nose at the conservative capitalists of the then-presiding Regan Administration. Though presumably inspired by Paramount's wonderful *Up in Smoke* DVD, Columbia sadly misses the mark here with a noticeably inferior transfer that's upstaged by a distracting level of graininess and noticeably dirty source print. It's not an unwatchable presentation by any means—the color is actually quite rich as is most of the shadow detail—but knowing the product Columbia TriStar is capable of turning out, this appears to be an uninspired attempt at best. The monaural sound field has a reasonable span, kicking off with some nice wailing guitar riffs at the film's opening. The musical numbers, varied and vibrant, provide an energetic audio presence without ever challenging the clarity of the dialogue, which is always easily understandable. —DP

Movie: ♪♪ ½ **DVD:** ♪♪

Columbia Tristar (cat #05855, UPC 04339-6058552). Widescreen (1.85:1) anamorphic; full frame. Dolby Digital Mono. $24.98. Keepcase. *LANG:* English; French; Spanish; Portuguese. *SUB:* English; French; Spanish; Portuguese; Korean; Chinese; Thai. *FEATURES:* Trailers.

1981 (R) 97m/C Richard "Cheech" Marin, Thomas Chong, Evelyn Guerrero, Stacy Keach, Paul (Pee-wee Herman) Reubens; ***D:*** Timothy Leary, Thomas Chong; ***W:*** Richard "Cheech" Marin, Thomas Chong; ***C:*** Charles Correll; ***M:*** Harry Betts.

Cheech and Chong's The Corsican Brothers

Possibly the worst of the duo's spotty cinematic efforts finds them in a variety of roles, from bad rock musicians in the present to participants in the French Revolution. There's not a single genuine laugh in the 90-minute running time. The cheaply made production looks pretty poor on DVD. (It looked pretty poor in theatres, too.) Faces appear too red, and the brighter reds of costumes and set design are almost radioactive. The whole film has a grotesque color scheme that's meant to be humorous, I think. —MM

Movie: woof **DVD:** ♪♪

MGM Home Ent. (cat #1003508, UPC 027-616876584). Widescreen (1.85:1) anamorphic; full frame. Dolby Digital Surround; Mono. $14.98. Keepcase. *LANG:* English; French. *SUB:* English; French; Spanish. *CAP:* English. *FEATURES:* Trailer • Teaser • 16 chapters.

1984 (PG) 91m/C Richard "Cheech" Marin, Thomas Chong, Roy Dotrice, Rae Dawn Chong, Shelby Fiddis, Rikki Marin, Edie McClurg; ***D:*** Thomas Chong; ***W:*** Richard "Cheech" Marin, Thomas Chong; ***C:*** Harvey Harrison.

Chicks, Man

Pals Jack (Priest) and Rod (Roberts) have multifaceted problems with women. They fall for the wrong ones and can't connect with the right ones. The film looks and feels a bit like the cult favorite *The Tao of Steve,* with interesting characters, but it lacks the snappy humor and the budget was obviously much smaller. Widescreen image is not much of an improvement over VHS tape. —MM

Movie: ♪♪ **DVD:** ♪♪

York Ent. (cat #YPD-1116, UPC 75072311-1629). Widescreen letterboxed. $14.99. Keepcase. *LANG:* English. *FEATURES:* Trailers • Deleted scenes • Director's commentary and intro • Behind-the-scenes featurette • Rehearsal footage.

1999 93m/C Aaron Priest, Robia LaMorte, Krista Gano, Nick Wechsler, Scott Roberts, Renee Humphrey; ***D:*** Jeremy Wagener; ***W:*** Jeremy Wagener; ***C:*** Michael J. Bruggemeyer; ***M:*** David Stout.

The Child

Combining elements of *The Bad Seed, The Omen,* and *Night of the Living Dead, The Child* is a low-budget horror-quickie that attempts to cash in on the fright-film craze of the early '70s. What we get is a poorly dubbed film that makes little sense, but does offer some interesting shocks. In the film, a young woman returns to her hometown to be the nanny for a disturbed girl named Rosalie (Rosalie Cole). Little Rosalie has a bad habit of killing neighbors and talking to zombies in the local graveyard, all the way harping on her mother's mysterious death. This is one of those movies where everyone acts very eccentric, but said behavior doesn't add anything to the plot. The finale offers some excitement, but overall the film is more of a curiosity than a "must-see." The DVD offers a full-frame transfer of the film, which looks as if it were found in a decaying drive-in. There are scratches and defects galore, but that will only add to the charm for fans of the obscure and bizarre. The mono sound only enhances the atrocious dubbing. On the plus side, this disc is crammed with trailers and movie posters from drive-in shockers, making for nostalgic fun. As if that weren't enough, another movie, *I Eat Your Skin,* is included on the disc. —ML **AKA:** Kill and Go Hide.

Movie: ♪ ½ **DVD:** ♪♪

Image Ent. (cat #ID0798SWDVD, UPC 014-381079821). Full frame. Dolby Digital Mono. $24.99. Keepcase. *LANG:* English. *FEATURES:* Theatrical trailer • Bonus trailers • Short films • Bonus feature: *I Eat Your Skin* (1964) • Still gallery • Radio spots • 12 chapters.

1976 (R) 95m/C Laurel Barnett, Rosalie Cole, Frank Janson, Richard Hanners, Ruth Ballan; ***D:*** Robert Voskanian; ***W:*** Ralph Lucas; ***C:*** Mori Alavi; ***M:*** Rob Wallace.

Child Star: The Shirley Temple Story

Made-for-TV film gives an overview of Shirley Temple's early career, starting from birth. George and Gertrude Temple (Colin Friels and Connie Britton) enroll young Shirley (Ashley Rose Orr) in dance class, where she is immediately "discovered" and placed into low-budget musicals. A talent scout from Fox studios sees one of these films and Shirley instantly becomes a contract player with the studio. From there, she goes on to become "America's Sweetheart," making five films a year, and earning a great deal of money for her fami-

ly. But the career is a strain on the young star and at times, her parents feel that she is simply a pawn for the money men. This is a very poorly paced film and does a terrible job of telling what could be a very compelling story. It glosses over the first few years of Shirley's life, so the viewer never knows exactly why her parents wanted her to get into show business or what exactly happened with those early films. These details clearly weren't deleted due to running time, because the middle of the film is padded with several montages. The film attempts to make some statements about the treatment of youngsters by the studios, and the trappings of early success, but the bulk of the film seems content to merely pick and choose the highlights of Temple's young life and spend a few moments exploring them. DVD presents the film in its original full-frame aspect ratio. The picture here is nearly pristine, as it is very sharp and clear, and shows no defects. The colors are rich and true, and the fleshtones are very realistic. Surround provides clear dialogue and nice reproduction of the music, with occasional Surround sound effects (mostly musical cues and crowd noise). Surprisingly, the audio commentary with executive producer Melissa Joan Hart is quite good, as she fills in many of the gaps missing from the story. —ML

Movie: ♪ ½ **DVD:** ♪♪♪

Buena Vista Home Ent. (cat #23614, UPC 786936162110). Full frame. Dolby 2.0 Surround. $29.99. Keepcase. *LANG:* English. *SUB:* French; Spanish. *CAP:* English. *FEATURES:* Commentary • Featurette • 14 chapters.

2001 88m/C Ashley Rose Orr, Connie Britton, Steven Vidler, Colin Friels, Emily Anne Hart, Hinton Battle; ***D:*** Nadia Tass; ***W:*** Joe Wiesenfeld; ***C:*** David Parker; ***M:*** Bill Elliot.

Children of Paradise

Once again, Criterion has made "one of those movies you're supposed to see but you avoided half your life" into an experience better than what can be gotten in an art theatre. As sweeping as *Gone with the Wind* and as literate as a great novel, *Children of Paradise* is the intellectual's epic, a vast saga that for many represents the screen's most sophisticated depiction of the mystery of romance. In an impressive reconstruction of a lost age, four men seek the same elusive woman, whose love means something completely different to each of them. For the beautiful "free soul" Garance (Arletty), love is something simple, to be given to those who please her. The mime Baptiste Debureau (Jean-Louis Barrault) is consumed with an ideal he sees within Garance, and is tortured because she can't love him back in the same way. Actor Frédérick LeMaitre (Pierre Brasseur) amuses Garance, and doesn't complicate matters as does Baptiste, but he can't hold her either. The megalomanic criminal Lacenaire (Marcel Herrand) boasts contemptuously to Garance that he

loves no one, and that their pairing would represent two superior intellects above the filthy mob. The nobleman Edouard de Montray (Louis Salou) offers his property and protection, but sets himself up to be despised. Garance eventually has need of his help when she's falsely implicated in Lacenaire's skullduggery. Finally, to the side of this four-way tug of war is Nathalie (Maria Casares), who adores Baptiste as deeply as he loves Garance, a cruel trick of fate that spells guilt and pain for all. This all plays out in an incredibly dense and alive Parisienne Boulevard of actors, beggars, and criminals. The backstage atmosphere is intoxicating, a whirlwind of tempers and egos in a setting that constantly threatens to become a fantasy itself. The entertainments are the dreams of the citizenry brought to life. DVD does the film a great service. The picture quality is so good that the slight imperfections are easily overlooked—I thought the laserdisc was just fine until I saw this. There are still a few short passages where original elements haven't survived and the quality drops momentarily. As demonstrated in the digital restoration extra, thousands of instances of frame damage, hair, dirt, and various other kinds of crud have been removed, resulting in the show being the cleanest it's looked since it was new. Those looking for expert analysis are provided with the very incisive commentary from the laser version; between that and the essay and interview in the printed booklet, a good overview of the production story comes together. The notes do a good job of placing the production in the context of the Nazi occupation of Paris. —GE **AKA:** Les Enfants du Paradis.
Movie: 🐾🐾🐾🐾 **DVD:** 🐾🐾🐾🐾
Criterion (UPC 37429151723). Full frame. $39.98. Keepcase. *LANG:* French. *SUB:* English. *FEATURES:* Commentary: film scholars Brian Stonehill & Charles Affron • Booklet: interview by Brian Stonehill, essay by Peter Cowie • Notes • Intro by Terry Gilliam • Restoration demonstration • Jacques Prévert's film treatment • Production designs • Stills gallery • Filmographies • U.S. theatrical trailer.
1944 188m/B *FR* Jean-Louis Barrault, Arletty, Pierre Brasseur, Maria Casares, Albert Remy, Leon Larive, Marcel Herrand, Pierre Renoir, Gaston Modot, Jane (Jeanne) Marken, Louis Salou; **D:** Marcel Carne; **W:** Jacques Prevert; **C:** Roger Hubert; **M:** Maurice Thiriet, Joseph Kosma. *AWARDS: NOM:* Oscars '46: Orig. Screenplay.

Children of the Corn 4: The Gathering

The corn cult is back for more horror in the heartland in another franchise that won't die. The town's children are being taken over by a mysterious presence, causing them to dispatch of grown-ups in various creative ways, often involving rusty farm tools. It's time to put this series out to pasture. Heroine Naomi Watts later went on to critical acclaim in David Lynch's

Mulholland Drive. The picture looks fine and the soundtrack offers enough punch to help deliver the attempted shocks, but it's hard to justify the disc's price tag. —BG **AKA:** Deadly Harvest.
Movie: 🐾 **DVD:** 🐾🐾 ½
Buena Vista Home Ent. (cat #23354, UPC 786936160291). Widescreen (1.85:1) anamorphic. Dolby Surround. $32.99. Keepcase. *LANG:* English; French. *SUB:* Spanish. *CAP:* English. *FEATURES:* 13 chapters.
1996 (R) 85m/C Naomi Watts, Brent Jennings, Jamie Renee Smith, William Windom, Karen Black; **D:** Greg Spence; **W:** Stephen Berger, Greg Spence; **C:** Richard Clabaugh; **M:** David Williams.

Children of the Corn 5: Fields of Terror

The children's cult has returned for another bloodbath. This time they've mellowed out and settled into a commune, but they're still up to their murderous ways. Poor Stephen King is still getting "Based on the short story by" credits. The picture quality is pretty good, although it suffers during nighttime scenes, when heavy grain becomes visible. Surround effects are kept to a minimum. —BG
Movie: 🐾 ½ **DVD:** 🐾🐾 ½
Buena Vista Home Ent. (cat #23355, UPC 786936160307). Widescreen (1.85:1) anamorphic. Dolby Surround. $32.99. Keepcase. *LANG:* English. *CAP:* English. *FEATURES:* 14 chapters • Trailers.
1998 (R) 85m/C Alexis Arquette, Greg Vaughan, Stacy Galina, Eva Mendez, Adam Wylie, Dave Buzzotta, David Carradine, Fred Williamson; **D:** Ethan Wiley; **W:** Ethan Wiley; **C:** David Lewis; **M:** Paul Rabjohns.

Children of the Corn: Revelation

The basic plotline of this tedious sequel is that Jamie (Mink), our dim-witted heroine, can't contact her grandmother in Nebraska so she goes there only to find that the apartment building her grandmother lives in is condemned and Granny is nowhere to be found. (They obviously condemn buildings differently in Nebraska than anywhere else because there are people living in it. Of course they are necessary because you can't have a mounting body count without bodies, but still....) The story attempts to explain the origin of the corn god and the children who loved him but succeeds only in being fodder for the next *Scary Movie/Scream*–type knock off. At one point, after ignoring a big sign that says "Go home, Jamie," Jamie sees a glowing green light emanating from a door that not only has a "do not enter" sign posted, but a chain and padlock hanging from it. She takes the open padlock as a sign that she should enter the room, and even though it looks good for her untimely death, she manages to live through seven or eight more bad choices. If you didn't already know from the opening scene that her grandmother had been converted into one of the evil children loitering around the

apartment, then I would say that Grandma had left her apartment without telling Jamie just to get away from such an obviously genetically inferior offspring. It's sad to mention, but Michael Ironside has a brief part as a priest of unknown origin who tries to warn Jamie about something, something vague that she never understands. Bad script, mediocre acting, and general stupidity make this a beer-drinking, group watching rental at best. The disc sound and color are slightly above video quality. —CA
Movie: 🐾 ½ **DVD:** 🐾🐾
Buena Vista Home Ent. (cat #23359, UPC 7 86936 16034 5). Widescreen (1.85:1) anamorphic. Dolby Digital 5.1 Surround. $32.99. Keepcase. *LANG:* English. *CAP:* English. *FEATURES:* 13 chapters.
2001 81m/C Claudette Mink, Michael Ironside, Troy Yorke; **D:** Guy Magar.

Children of the Living Dead

Standard *...of the Living Dead* fare has only producer John Russo as a connection to the original. It is one of the worst of these seemingly endless low-budget horrors. The voice dubbing sounds exceptionally unnatural; lighting is amateurish with the odd flash when someone behind the camera mishandles a mirror; acting is poor. Story is the same old same old. DVD magnifies all of these flaws and so the whole thing is essentially unwatchable. —MM
Movie: woof **DVD:** 🐾🐾
Artisan Ent. (cat #12272). Widescreen letterboxed. Dolby Digital 5.1 Surround; Dolby Surround. $14.98. Keepcase. *LANG:* English. *SUB:* English; Spanish. *FEATURES:* 16 chapters • Trailer • Photo gallery.
2000 (R) 90m/C Tom Savini, A. Barrett Worland, Jamie McCoy; **D:** Tor Ramsey; **W:** Karen Wolf.

Chill Factor

In this variant on *Speed*, if the temperature of a top secret weapon goes above 50 degrees, it will blow up, and probably take a good chunk of a state with it. When the scientist behind the making of the weapon needs help, he turns to Arlo (Gooding Jr.) and Tim (Ulrich). Tim forces Arlo at gunpoint to help him transport the weapon across the desert. Most of the film involves them arguing with each other while being chased. In between, stuff blows up real good. The actors are energetic, but the script doesn't give them any help. Gooding Jr. simply screams at Ulrich and swears every few minutes, which becomes tiring. The picture's attempts at humor fall completely flat and despite a few tense moments, it just never manages to work. DVD image is very strong with a sharp picture and rich, strong colors. Flesh tones are natural, and black level is solid as well. There are few instances of pixelation. The soundtrack makes effective use of the Surrounds. Even subtle sounds, such as the sound of the jungle in the early scenes, are involving. The text for the cast/crew bios scrolls slowly upward rather than just being basic text. The score also plays in the background. Under the bios for director Hugh Johnson, Skeet Ulrich, Peter Firth, and actress Hudson Leick, you'll find interviews with each that run about a minute or two in length. —AB/DG

Movie: 🎵 ½ **DVD:** 🎵🎵🎵
Warner Home Video (UPC 85391804628). Widescreen (2.35:1) anamorphic. Dolby Surround 5.1. $14.98. Snapper. *LANG:* English. *CAP:* English. *FEATURES:* Trailers • 26 chapters • Cast & crew bios • Production notes • DVD-ROM: Game & weblinks • Visual effects documentary.
1999 (R) 102m/C Skeet Ulrich, Cuba Gooding Jr., Peter Firth, David Paymer, Daniel Hugh-Kelly, Kevin J. O'Connor, Judson Mills, Hudson Leick, Jim Grimshaw; **D:** Hugh Johnson; **W:** Drew Gitlin, Mike Cheda; **C:** David Gribble; **M:** Hans Zimmer, John Powell.

China Moon

Beautiful Rachel (Stowe) is married to rich-but-abusive Rupert (Dance). Kyle (Harris) is the lonely Florida homicide detective who's besotted by Rachel and conveniently helps her dispose of murdered hubby's body. Their problems increase when his rookie partner (Del Toro) turns out to be smarter than anyone thinks. Good performances can't ratchet up the suspense. Another *Body Heat* it is not. Some bad shimmer and distortion are apparent in fast panning shots, along with grain in others. Overall, acceptable image and sound are not a large improvement over VHS tape, but disc does offer two screen ratios. —MM

Movie: 🎵🎵 ½ **DVD:** 🎵🎵 ½
MGM Home Ent. (cat #1002750, UPC 027-616869487). Widescreen (2.35:1) anamorphic; full frame. Dolby Digital Surround. $19.98. Keepcase. *LANG:* English; French; Spanish. *SUB:* English; French; Spanish. *CAP:* English. *FEATURES:* Trailers • 16 chapters.
1991 (R) 99m/C Ed Harris, Madeleine Stowe, Benicio Del Toro, Charles Dance; **D:** John Bailey; **W:** Roy Carlson; **C:** Willy Kurant; **M:** George Fenton.

Choke

This direct-to-video film offers a story with an intriguing twist. The film opens with Gena (Chelsy Reynolds, who looks exactly like Alicia Silverstone) running over a pedestrian. She immediately contacts her father Henry (Dennis Hopper), who agrees to help her cover up the hit-and-run. Unfortunately, sleazy businessman Ron (Roy Tate) overhears Henry's conversation and decides to use this information to blackmail Henry. This leads Henry to seek retaliation against Ron. Not knowing where to turn next, Henry receives assistance from a most unexpected source—Will (Michael Madsen), an edgy serial killer. Their bizarre arrangement leads to twists and turns, which may put Gena in even more danger. The unique story is undermined by the strange pacing of the film. There are several scenes of padding, but there are

also many shots of Dennis Hopper simply looking at the camera. Also, Michael Madsen appears to be in a totally different film at times. Still, *Choke* is better than most of its low-rent brethren. The image shown on this DVD is presented full frame and is very clear and sharp, showing no defects or distortion. The quality of this transfer is superior for a film of this caliber. The colors are true and the picture is never overly bright. The audio track offers clear dialogue, but little in the Surround sound department. —ML

Movie: 🎵🎵 ½ **DVD:** 🎵🎵 ½
MTI (cat #8115, UPC 039041581157). Full frame. Digital Surround. $24.95. Keepcase. *LANG:* English. *SUB:* Spanish. *FEATURES:* Trailers • Cast bios • 20 chapters.
2001 (R) 95m/C Dennis Hopper, Michael Madsen, L.P. Brown III, Chelsy Reynolds, Roy Tate; **D:** John Sjogren.

Choose Me

A fun romance about losers finding love in the big city. Dr. Nancy Love (Bujold), a radio show love-talk guru, has never been in love, but of course this doesn't keep her from being good at her job. Eve (Warren) owns a bar and makes regular calls to Dr. Love about her unhappy relationship with the married Zack (Patrick Bauchau from *The Pretender*). Unknown to Eve, her lover's wife Pearl sits at the bar every night and chats with her. Billy Ace (Larroquette), a slick motorcycle-riding hormone in tight black pants, bartends at Eve's place and pines for her nightly. Mickey (Carradine) has just been released from a mental hospital and never kisses a girl he wouldn't marry. Mickey kisses a lot of girls and makes a lot of proposals in this story. When Dr. Love, using a fake name to keep her privacy, becomes Eve's roommate, things get even more complicated. This is a film that takes its time to develop the situations and characters giving them as much plausibility as possible for bedroom farce. All the players are great and the script is more than competent. The picture is clean, with a little fuzzing around the edges of things and the sound is a bit muffled and run together, none of which is distracting. —CA

Movie: 🎵🎵 ½ **DVD:** 🎵🎵 ½
MGM Home Ent. (cat #1002627, UPC 027-616868275). Widescreen (1.85:1) anamorphic. Dolby Digital Stereo. $19.90. Keepcase. *LANG:* English. *SUB:* English; French; Spanish. *CAP:* English. *FEATURES:* Theatrical trailer.
1984 (R) 106m/C Keith Carradine, Genevieve Bujold, Lesley Ann Warren, Rae Dawn Chong, John Larroquette, John Considine, Patrick Bauchau; **D:** Alan Rudolph; **W:** Alan Rudolph; **C:** Jan Kiesser; **M:** Phil Woods.

Chopper

Biopic of famous Aussie criminal Mark "Chopper" Read is highlighted by Bana's extraordinary performance in the title role. Dominik's directorial debut follows Read's career from prison—where he murders

one inmate, forces another to cut off his ears, and generally makes hardened criminals fear for their lives—to his old haunts where he seeks revenge for past wrongs. Full of gore, violence, and wild humor, it's not for everyone, but it does make its points about society's preoccupation with the "celebrity criminal." Read didn't participate directly in the production, but it was based on one of his best sellers and he provides a boastful commentary track. (Director Dominik's commentary is more low-keyed and technical.) DVD image appears to be an accurate translation of the original, but Dominik uses the odd "acid" color process so popular these days, that gives the film an ugly look. Surround tracks are strong. Subtitles would help with some of the more difficult accents. —MM

Movie: 🎵🎵🎵 **DVD:** 🎵🎵🎵
Image Ent. (cat #ID2020VDVD, UPC 0143-81120226). Widescreen (1.78:1) anamorphic. Dolby Digital 5.1 Surround; Dolby Digital Stereo; DTS 5.1. $24.98. Keepcase. *LANG:* English. *FEATURES:* Trailer • 2 commentary tracks • Deleted scenes • "Weekend with Chopper" featurette • 28 chapters.
2001 94m/C *AU* Eric Bana, Vince Colosimo, Simon Lyndon, David Field, Daniel Wyllie, Bill Young, Gary Waddell, Kate Beahan, Kenny Graham; **D:** Andrew Dominik; **W:** Andrew Dominik; **C:** Geoffrey Hall; **M:** Mick Harvey. *AWARDS:* Australian Film Inst. '00: Actor (Bana), Director (Dominik), Support. Actor (Lyndon); *NOM:* Australian Film Inst. '00: Adapt. Screenplay, Cinematog., Film, Film Editing, Sound, Score.

The Choppers

No, it's not a movie about false teeth. Teen punk Hall operates a car theft ring made of fellow punksters. Rock 'n' roll tunes by the Hallmeister include the much-overlooked "Monkey in My Hatband." Disc was made from seriously damaged original elements. So much footage is missing from the opening shot that it's virtually unintelligible. Considering how fuzzily focused the murky black-and-white photography is, that might be a blessing. The film is also available on a Something Weird double feature with *Wild Guitar* from Image (please see review). —MM

Movie: 🎵 ½ **DVD:** 🎵 ½
BCI-Eclipse (cat #44112-9, UPC 7873644-11290). Full frame. $9.98. Keepcase. *LANG:* English. *FEATURES:* 6 chapters • "Have You Got Any Castles" cartoon • DVD dictionary • Trivia game • DVD-ROM features.
1961 66m/B Arch Hall Jr., Marianne Gaba, Robert Paget, Tom Brown, Rex Holman, Bruno VeSota; **D:** Leigh Jason; **W:** Arch (Archie) Hall Sr.; **C:** Clark Ramsey; **M:** Al Pellegrini.

Christianity: The First Two Thousand Years

This mammoth miniseries, stretching over six hours, covers the history of Christianity from the birth of Christ to the present. If you're interested in the subject matter, a better introduction can hardly be imagined—it's exhaustive, insightful, and impressively objective, for the most part. The ending is disappointing, as the program focuses too much on Catholicism and ignores other denominations. The first half is narrated expertly by Ossie Davis and Ruby Dee. The picture often looks fuzzy, both colors and outlines, but the sound quality is very good. —BG

Movie: 🐾🐾🐾 **DVD:** 🐾🐾½
A&E (cat #AAE-71000, UPC 7339617100-07). Full frame. Dolby Stereo. $39.95. Keepcase. *LANG:* English. *CAP:* English. *FEATURES:* 48 chapters • Historical time line. **2000 365m/C Nar:** Ossie Davis, Ruby Dee.

Christina's House

Christina's House is a poor excuse for a slasher film—a genre which isn't exactly known for quality to begin with. Christina (Allison Lange) lives with her father (John Savage) and her brother Bobby (Lorne Stewart) in a large, old house. After hearing some strange noises coming from the attic, she begins to think that there is someone in the house besides her family. After several young girls disappear in the vicinity of Christina's house (which is apparently in the median strip of a highway!), Christina must determine who is terrorizing her family. The film borrows heavily from classics such as *Black Christmas*, but never finds its own voice. What remains is scene after scene of John Savage yelling and bursting into rooms for no apparent reason. The last scene is intriguing, but it is far too late to save this film. Savage and Brad Rowe (who was very promising in *Body Shots*) should have known better. The image on the DVD shows a noticeable amount of black grain throughout the film, and there are also occasional blemishes from the source print. The colors are fine and there is little artifacting. The Dolby Digital 5.1 soundtrack is effective, offering clear dialogue and some Surround sound effects. The DVD contains both the widescreen and full-frame versions of the film. —ML

Movie: 🐾 **DVD:** 🐾🐾
MGM Home Ent. (cat #1002653, UPC 027-616868510). Widescreen (1.85:1) anamorphic; full frame. Dolby Digital 5.1. $26.98. Keepcase. *LANG:* English. *SUB:* English; French; Spanish. *FEATURES:* 16 chapters. **1999 97m/C CA** Brendan Fehr, Brad Rowe, John Savage, Allison Lange, Lorne Stewart; **D:** Gavin Wilding.

Christmas Evil

Traumatized as a child by seeing his mother and Santa 'neath the Christmas tree, knife-wielding Harry (Maggart) dresses up as the jolly old elf to strike terror into the hearts of children. Of all the holiday-themed horrors that have flourished as video premieres, this may be the cheapest looking and the relative clarity of this DVD

makes that all the more apparent. Snow and other surface damage are in evidence, too, along with the occasional digital hiccup that results in massive, albeit brief artifacts. Looking at the extras, even a fan must ask: Do we really need a director's commentary track? —MM *AKA:* Terror in Toyland; You Better Watch Out.

Movie: 🐾½ **DVD:** 🐾🐾½
Troma Team Video (cat #9021, UPC 790-357902132). Full frame. $24.99. Keepcase. *LANG:* English. *FEATURES:* 10 chapters • Lewis Jackson and Brandon Maggart interviews and commentary • Storyboard to film • Preview audience response cards. **1980 (R) 92m/C** Brandon Maggart, Jeffrey DeMunn, Dianne Hull, Scott McKay, Peter Friedman, Joe Jamrog, Rutanya Alda, Raymond J. Barry, Andy Fenwick, Sam Gray, Patricia Richardson; **D:** Lewis Jackson; **W:** Lewis Jackson; **C:** Ricardo Aronovich.

Christmas Past

These nine silent films are primarily of historic value. As entertainment they're dated and they're so old that even their nostalgia value is limited. "A Trap for Santa" is a D.W. Griffith melodrama. "A Winter Straw Ride" appears to be a home movie of a school outing. The new score by Al Kryszak employs a small orchestra and handbell choir and sounds very nice. There's a lot of light surface damage and graininess, but overall the films look very good for works that are more than a century old. Contents: "A Holiday Pageant at Home" (1901), "A Winter Straw Ride" (1906), "A Trap for Santa" (1909), "A Christmas Accident" (1912), "The Adventure of the Wrong Santa Claus" (1914), "Santa Claus vs. Cupid" (1915), "Santa Claus" (1925), "A Christmas Carol" (1910), "The Night Before Christmas" (1905). —MM

Movie: 🐾🐾½ **DVD:** 🐾🐾½
Kino on Video (cat #K232). Full frame. $24.99. Keepcase. *LANG:* Silent (English intertitles). *FEATURES:* 9 chapters. **2000 121m/B**

Christoph Von Dohnanyi: In Rehearsal— Philharmonia Orchestra

Christoph Von Dohnanyi performs Haydn's "Symphony No. 88 in G" with the Philharmonia in this entertaining look and the backstage preparations and execution of a classical music concert. Among the highlights: Dohnanyi discusses his approach to rehearsals and communicating with the orchestra. This above-average video transfer displays a nice color palette as well as admirably defined blacks. It's not spectacular, but it's impressive enough. The soundtrack is excellent, featuring a superbly reproduced musical score that really sounds full despite not being a 5.1 mix. —MJT

Movie: 🐾🐾½ **DVD:** 🐾🐾🐾

Image Ent. (cat #ID9323RADVD, UPC 014-381932324). Full frame. Dolby Digital Stereo. $19.99. Keepcase. *LANG:* English. *FEATURES:* 9 chapters. **1998 58m/C**

Christy— A Change of Seasons

Developed for the PAX television network, this is a miniseries adaptation of the acclaimed novels by author Catherine Marshall. In *A Change of Seasons*, the first half of a two-part miniseries, typhoid fever sweeps through Tennessee's Cutter Gap. When it takes a young mother's life, Christy (Lee Smith) is left questioning her faith. This DVD sports a good transfer with a quality picture with no noticeable defects. The addition of a Surround track might have been nice, but the stereo track is utilized perfectly with full sound out of both speakers. Unfortunately, both parts of this miniseries are a rather weak adaptation of story line and plot. —EL

Movie: 🐾🐾 **DVD:** 🐾🐾½
Lion's Gate Home Ent. (cat #7711, UPC 031398771128). Widescreen letterboxed. Stereo. $19.99. Keepcase. *LANG:* English. *SUB:* English; French; Spanish. *CAP:* English. *FEATURES:* Trailer. **2001 (PG) 87m/C** Lauren Lee Smith, Diane Ladd, Stewart Finlay-McLennan, James Waterson, Ingrid Torrance; **D:** George Kaczender; **W:** Catherine Marshall; **C:** Laszlo George; **M:** Ron Ramin.

Christy— A New Beginning

In the second half of the two-part miniseries, Christy (Lee Smith) prepares to settle down and marry, but when an unexpected suitor comes calling, she must decide between the two men who both seek her heart. Image and sound quality are identical to *A Change of Seasons*. —EL

Movie: 🐾🐾 **DVD:** 🐾🐾½
Lion's Gate Home Ent. (cat #7714, UPC 031398771425). Widescreen letterboxed. Stereo. $19.99. Keepcase. *LANG:* English. *SUB:* English; French; Spanish. *CAP:* English. *FEATURES:* Trailer • 24 chapters. **2001 (PG) 89m/C** Lauren Lee Smith, Diane Ladd, Stewart Finlay-McLennan, James Waterson; **D:** Don McBearty; **W:** Catherine Marshall; **C:** Laszlo George; **M:** Ron Ramin.

Christy— Return to Cutter Gap

In another TV movie from a Catherine Marshall novel, Christy remembers her time as a missionary teacher in Cutter Gap, Tennessee. Young Christy (Smith) is an outsider who, because of her urban attitude and message of progress, becomes the object of the rural townspeople's suspicion and anger. When a rash of thievery causes a panic, everyone must work together to save the town and learn something about each other in the process. A simplistic story and unconvincing perfor-

mances make this hard to endure. The image and sound are equal to its original PAX network broadcast. —DRL
Movie: 🦴 **DVD:** 🦴🦴 ½
Lion's Gate Home Ent. (cat #7729, UPC 031398772927). Widescreen (1.85:1) letterboxed. Stereo. $19.99. Keepcase. *LANG:* English. *SUB:* English; French; Spanish. *FEATURES:* Trailer ● 24 chapters.
2001 (PG) 89m/C Lauren Lee Smith, Stewart Finlay-McLennan, James Waterson, Diane Ladd; *D:* Chuck Bowman; *W:* Tom Blomquist; *C:* Laszlo George; *M:* Ron Ramin.

Chunhyang
Korean costume drama is a lavishly produced romance. In the 18th century, Mongryong, the son of the governor, falls in love with Chunhyang, the daughter of a courtesan. Their relationship involves secrecy and various jealousies. It's a slowly paced story and, even though the setting and time are remote from most western viewers, surprisingly involving. DVD image has the proper clarity for a period piece, with exceptionally bright vibrant colors and no serious flaws. But why isn't the introductory singer subtitled? —MM
Movie: 🦴🦴🦴 **DVD:** 🦴🦴🦴
New Yorker Video (cat #82601, UPC 7171-19826147). Widescreen letterboxed. $29.98. Keepcase. *LANG:* Korean. *SUB:* English. *FEATURES:* 20 chapters ● Trailer.
2000 120m/C *KN* Hyo Jung Lee, Seung Woo Cho, Jung Hun Lee, Sung Nyu Kim; *D:* Kwon Taek Im; *W:* Myoung Kon Kim; *C:* Il Sung Jung; *M:* Jung Gil Kim.

The Church
In 1988, Italian horror legend Dario Argento and exciting newcomer Michele Soavi teamed up to make *Demons 3*. The resulting film was eventually titled *The Church* and showed none of the spunk that the first two *Demons* films had displayed. The movie opens during the Crusades, as a group of Christian knights slaughter an entire village of suspected satanists. To purify the ground, a cathedral is built on the sight of the massacre. Jump ahead to present day, where the huge Gothic church is undergoing renovations. The new church librarian Evan (Tomas Arana) decides to investigate the church basement and accidentally unleashes the evil spirits of the dead. This causes a chain reaction in which the church is completely sealed-off from the outside world. After that...not much happens. Director Soavi fills the film with bizarre images, but the story never moves forward and there is neither terror nor suspense. A creative subplot concerning the church's architect gets left behind in favor of Soavi's beautiful, yet hollow shots. The possessions don't begin until well over an hour into the movie and many will find *The Church* to be excruciatingly slow. The film shows true promise, but is never able to deliver. Despite the flawed pedigree, Anchor Bay has done a fine job with this transfer. The prologue is slightly

soft and washed-out (this may have been intentional), but the rest of the film looks fine. The image is sharp and mostly clear, although there is some overt grain at times. The colors are good, although not terribly striking. There is no interference from edge-enhancement or artifacting here. The Dolby Digital Surround EX audio track is very good, although not as impressive as the audio on Anchor Bay's *Suspiria*. The dialogue is clear, and the Surround effects are well-balanced and plentiful. —ML **AKA:** La Chiesa.
Movie: 🦴🦴 **DVD:** 🦴🦴🦴
Anchor Bay (cat #DV11748, UPC 0131-31174892). Widescreen (1.85:1) anamorphic. Dolby Digital Surround EX. $19.98. Keepcase. *LANG:* English. *FEATURES:* Theatrical trailer ● Director bio ● 25 chapters.
1998 102m/C *IT* Tomas Arana, Hugh Quarshie, Feodor Chaliapin Jr., Barbara Cupisti, Antonella Vitale, Asia Argento; *D:* Michele (Michael) Soavi; *W:* Dario Argento, Michele (Michael) Soavi, Franco Ferrini; *C:* Renato Tafuri; *M:* Keith Emerson.

Cinderella
The 1965 television adaptation by the famed duo of Richard Rodgers and Oscar Hammerstein remains true to the story line of the oft-told tale; the music and songs make this version a unique experience. Lesley Ann Warren stars as Cinderella, the girl who must live by the fireplace and work for her wicked stepmother and stepsisters. When the Prince (Stuart Damon, Dr. Allen Quartermaine of *General Hospital* and *Port Charles*) holds a ball, the stepmother and her daughters can't wait to attend and meet the young bachelor. Cinderella has no hopes of joining in on the fun, until her Fairy Godmother (Celeste Holm) arrives to transform the young girl into a beauty the Prince will never forget. While some of the acting is a bit wooden and the cheap set design is laughable at times, the songs never fail to impress. Fans of Rodgers & Hammerstein will adore this and it is appropriate for viewers of all ages. This TV special is presented full frame and suffers from the technological limitations of 1965. The special was captured on videotape, and offers all of the flaws that come with it. The image is sharp and clear, but there is a great deal of video noise and lens flare here. The colors are good, but they do appear slightly washed-out at times. The Dolby Surround audio track does a fine job of re-creating the music from the show, but the only Surround effects are musical cues. The DVD contains a retrospective featurette, which outlines the origins of the special and gives background on the featured players. —ML
Movie: 🦴🦴 ½ **DVD:** 🦴🦴
Columbia Tristar (cat #07320, UPC 0433-96073203). Full frame. Dolby 2.0 Surround. $24.95. Keepcase. *LANG:* English. *SUB:* English; Spanish. *CAP:* English. *FEATURES:* Featurette ● Sing-along ● Filmographies ● Bonus trailers ● 28 chapters.
1964 83m/C Lesley Ann Warren, Ginger Rogers, Walter Pidgeon, Stuart Damon,

Celeste Holm; *D:* Charles S. Dubin; *W:* Joseph Schrank; *M:* Richard Rodgers, Oscar Hammerstein.

Cinderella 2: Dreams Come True
Anyone who's seen the animated classic *Cinderella* (or read the fairy tale for that matter) knows that the story is wrapped up very nicely at the end when the handsome Prince discovers that Cinderella is his true love. It would seem that any attempt at a continuation of that story would be a stretch. Well, the creative minds at Disney appear to have been stumped by this task as well, as the belated animated sequel *Cinderella 2: Dreams Come True* is an anthology, proving that creating a feature-length story was a daunting task. The wrap-around story deals with the familiar mice from the first film, notably Jaques (voiced by Rob Paulsen) and Gus (voiced by Corey Burton), who, with the help of the Fairy Godmother (voiced by Russi Taylor), decide to create a scrapbook for Cinderella. (Apparently, the Fairy Godmother just hangs around the castle, talking to mice.) In the first story, Cinderella (voiced by Jennifer Hale) has just returned from her honeymoon with the Prince (voiced by Christopher Daniel Barnes), when she is placed in charge of planning a banquet by Prudence (Holland Taylor), who oversees the castle. Cinderella isn't happy or comfortable with the traditional way the banquet is done, so she decides to take matters into her own hands. The second tale deals with the mice, and here we find Jaques being pursued by Pom Pom, the castle's resident cat. With some help from the Fairy Godmother, he turns the tables on the confused feline. In the final tale, Anastasia (voiced by Tress MacNeille), one of Cinderella's stepsisters, falls in love with the local baker, and Cinderella helps her prepare for a date. While any of the animated Disney films which feature strong female characters could be said to have a feminine slant, *Cinderella 2* seems to be particularly aimed at the little girls in the audience. The stories are basic, simple, and easy-to-follow, so some viewers may be a bit bored by them, especially the second and third episodes, as they drag quite a bit. The animation is acceptable, but not up to the caliber of Disney's theatrical features. This is an unnecessary sequel and a mediocre movie. DVD picture is extremely sharp and clear, showing no distortion, artifacting, or defects from the source material. The colors are beautiful and vibrant, seemingly leaping off of the screen at times. Both Dolby and DTS tracks provide clear dialogue, nice musical reproduction, and some Surround sound effects, but neither is outstanding. The LFE response is weak and the stereo separation is adequate. —ML
Movie: 🦴🦴 **DVD:** 🦴🦴🦴
Buena Vista Home Ent. (cat #22033, UPC 786936148435). Widescreen (1.66:1) anamorphic. Dolby Digital 5.1; DTS 5.1.

$29.99. Keepcase. *LANG:* English; French; Spanish. *SUB:* English. *CAP:* English. *FEATURES:* Featurette • Set-top games • Music video • 14 chapters. **2002 (G) 73m/C D:** John Kafka; **V:** Jennifer Hale, Rob Paulsen, Corey Burton, Russi Taylor, Holland Taylor, Tress MacNeille, Christopher Daniel Barnes.

The Circle

Engaging almost documentary-like story of a day in the life of several Middle Eastern women whose paths cross as they take different routes but ultimately come face to face with a similar fate. Three of the women are recently released from prison and on the streets of Iran where they find little to sustain them. One of the women believes that she will find acceptance and joy by returning to her husband and son, who did not visit her once during the five years of her confinement. A fourth woman released from prison returns home only to be driven out by her brothers who try to beat her for her transgressions. As for their crimes, we are never told. The fourth woman is pregnant, a gift from the last night of her lover's life. He too, it seems, was imprisoned and executed for the unknown crime. She wants to have an abortion, but without the consent of the father or each of the couple's fathers, she cannot. Another woman abandons her daughter on the street hoping that a kind stranger can give her a better life. What becomes painfully clear as the filmmaker artfully allows the film to unfold is that the most likely crime each woman is guilty of is simply wanting to live her own life in a culture that considers women to be invisible citizens at best, and nuisances at worst. The filmmaker makes what can best be described as brave cinematic choices, using pictures to make you feel the story rather than beating you over the head with dialogue or in-your-face violence. A perfect example occurs when two of the women converse behind the ticket window of a theatre. Each time a customer, always a man, steps up, the entire screen is taken up by the man's back as he blocks out the smaller figures of the women sitting behind the bars of the window. The backs of the men take up the screen for at least 10 or 15 seconds, which is a long time in a film, but ultimately the effect is just that—effective. The print looks marvelous with rich blacks and skin tones and the sound is good. —*CA* **AKA:** Dayereh.
Movie: 🎬🎬🎬 **DVD:** 🎬🎬🎬 ½
Winstar Home Ent. (cat #FLV5307, UPC 720917530727). Widescreen anamorphic. $24.90. Keepcase. *LANG:* Farsi. *SUB:* English. *FEATURES:* 12 chapters • Director interview • Trailers.
2000 91m/C *IA* Mariam Palvin Almani, Nargess Mamizadeh, Fereshteh Sadr Orfani, Fatemeh Naghavi, Monir Arab, Elham Saboktakin, Mojhan Faramarzi; **D:** Jafar Panahi; **W:** Kambozia Partovi; **C:** Bahram Badakhshami. *AWARDS:* Venice Film Fest. '00: Film.

Circuitry Man

In a post-Apocalyptic future America, tough gal Lori (Wheeler-Nicholson) tries to deliver a briefcase full of computer chips to the underground Big Apple. Along the way, she runs into Plughead (Wells), a humanoid with electrical outlets that allow him to "plug in" to other people's fantasies and pain. It's fairly standard fare that's handled with a lively sense of humor and good characters. Deborah Holland's score is terrific, and for once, the filmmakers elected to include a composer on the commentary track. She, Wells, and the Lovy brothers seem to enjoy looking back at their sleeper hit. Image is very good, but not quite as bright or sharp as the sequel, *Plughead Rewired* (please see review), which is included on the flip side of the disc. —*MM*
Movie: 🎬🎬 ½ **DVD:** 🎬🎬🎬 ½
Columbia Tristar (cat #04865, UPC 043-396048652). Widescreen (1.85:1) anamorphic. Dolby Digital Surround; Dolby Stereo. $24.98. Keepcase. *LANG:* English. *SUB:* English; Spanish. *CAP:* English. *FEATURES:* 28 chapters • Trailers • Commentary: Steven & Robert Lovy, Wells, Holland.
1990 (R) 85m/C Jim Metzler, Dana Wheeler-Nicholson, Lu Leonard, Vernon Wells, Barbara Alyn Woods, Dennis Christopher; **D:** Steven Lovy; **W:** Robert Lovy, Steven Lovy; **C:** Jamie Thompson; **M:** Deborah Holland.

Circus of Horrors

After botching an illegal experimental plastic surgery technique on socialite Evelyn Morley Finsbury (Wilde), Dr. Rossiter (Diffring) crashes his car and requires some repair work on his own face from his ever-loyal assistants Angela (Hylton) and Martin (Griffth). Hiding under the name of "Dr. Bernard Schüler" in France, Rossiter inveigles himself into the good graces of Vanet (Pleasence), the owner of a small circus, by repairing the face of Vanet's daughter Nicole (Challoner). Rossiter stands by as a performing bear kills the drunken Vanet. He then appropriates the circus, and populates it with ex-prostitutes and criminals, all of whom are females whose faces he's fixed with his brilliant reconstructive techniques. It all moves at an extremely fast pace with an unbroken succession of shock scenes made believable by just enough of a plot to motivate the mayhem. The odd structure relates plastic surgery horror to the war, where it is said Dr. Rossiter got lots of practice mending soldiers. Beyond that, it's Grand Guignol all the way, with Rossiter a conscienceless fiend. Great color lensing by Douglas Slocombe effortlessly mixes the backstage action with the staged acts and real ones. Only some audience reaction shots where the focus is bad shows anything less than perfect camerawork. DVD is brightly colored, sharply detailed in 16:9 and comes with a very clear soundtrack. Some erroneous filmographies list the original film as anamorphic, but it is really flat 1:85. An earlier Image laserdisc was both squeezed and pan-and-scanned,

which added to the impression of this being a wider film. —*GE*
Movie: 🎬🎬🎬 ½ **DVD:** 🎬🎬🎬 ½
Anchor Bay (UPC 013131414390). Widescreen (1.78:1) anamorphic. Dolby Digital Mono. $24.98. Keepcase. *LANG:* English. *FEATURES:* Trailer • TV spots • Stills and ad materials • Anton Diffring bio • 27 chapters.
1960 92m/C *GB* Donald Pleasence, Anton Diffring, Erika Remberg, Yvonne Monlaur, Jane Hylton, Kenneth Griffith, Colette Wilde, Charla Challoner; **D:** Sidney Hayers; **W:** George L. Baxt; **C:** Douglas Slocombe; **M:** Muir Mathieson.

Cirque du Soleil— A Baroque Odyssey

For die-hard Cirque du Soleil fans who want to know more about this highly original performance group, this disc is a must-see. All others may find this documentary a bit boring. Made in 1994, *A Baroque Odyssey* gives an overview of Cirque du Soleil up to that point (when they had been in existence for 10 years). This program contains home movies of the troupe's early street performances, long before they were captivating audiences worldwide. There are interviews with the troupe's founder Guy Laliberte, and Gilles Ste-Croix, the artistic director. Highlights from the group's most famous performances, "Cirque Reinvente," "Nouvelle Experience," "Mystere," and "Saltimbanco" are featured here. The piece shows how the troupe progressed from a small band of performers to a traveling group. As the program on this DVD offers a mixed bag of media, the quality here fluctuates. The interviews were shot on film in the desert, and while they are sharp and clear, there is a noticeable amount of grain here. The modern-day performances were captured on video and look quite good, offering nice colors and only a slight amount of distortion. The early shows were filmed on a home movie camera (possibly 8mm) and they present the grain, haze, and defects which are inherent with this visual medium. The stereo sound on this DVD is consistent throughout, offering clear dialogue and nice musical reproduction. —*ML*
Movie: 🎬🎬 ½ **DVD:** 🎬🎬🎬
Columbia Tristar (cat #07075, UPC 0433-96070752). Full frame. Dolby Digital Stereo. $24.95. Keepcase. *LANG:* English. *FEATURES:* Bonus trailers • 24 chapters.
1994 56m/C

Cirque du Soleil— La Magie Continue

Today, audiences the world over know Cirque du Soleil, either from catching the group on tour, or by visiting their now-famous act in Las Vegas. But nearly 20 years after their inception, there are fans who want to know what the early days were like for this group. Enter *La Magie Continue*, a DVD which chronicles the sophomore tour of Cirque du Soleil. The performance contains a wide variety of traditional selections, including tumbling, trapeze, acrobatics, and the Cirque du Soleil clowns. This troupe's inventiveness can be seen in these early shows, through their takes on soccer and the old gym-class favorite, the parachute. At under an hour, this program is somewhat brief, but it does manage to capture the magic of Cirque du Soleil. The performance offered on this DVD was shot on video and displays some of the limitations in that medium which existed in 1986. The image is sharp and clear, but there is a noticeable amount of video distortion and some artifacting. Still, the colors are very good and the presentation is far from unacceptable. The Dolby Digital Stereo sound offers a nice reproduction of the music which accompanies the performances and there is no distortion or hissing. —ML

Movie: ♫♫♫ **DVD:** ♫♫ ½
Columbia Tristar (cat #07071, UPC 0433-96070714). Full frame. Dolby Digital Stereo. $24.95. Keepcase. *LANG:* English. *FEATURES:* Bonus trailers • 8 chapters.
1986 50m/C

Cirque du Soleil— Nouvelle Experience

Cirque du Soleil has become one of the most beloved attractions in the world, and their series of DVD releases is a fantastic way to relive the magic in your home. The *Nouvelle Experience* DVD represents the group's 1990–91 tour and features the usual array of dazzling performances. This show is hosted by a ringmaster who bears a striking resemblance to the Heat Miser from the holiday special *Year without a Santa Claus*. This figure with large red hair introduces the various acts. The show starts with an exhibition of one of the traits which has made Cirque du Soleil famous—contortionist. These talented females bend their bodies into incredible and painful-looking shapes in a segment which lasts several minutes. The remainder of the program features a nice mixture of such familiar elements as trapeze, tightrope walking, juggling, and acrobatics. Aside from the great contortionists, the other highlight of the show is a segment in which a clown pulls a volunteer from the audience to aid in the performance. That poor woman! As with any Cirque du Soleil video, *Nouvelle Experience* is a nice representation of the group in action, but is no substitute for seeing them live. The performance presented here was captured on videotape. The source material shows some anomalies which are exaggerated on this digital transfer. The image is somewhat hazy at times, and the lights create some video distortion. Still, the image is sharp and the colors are quite good. The Dolby stereo audio track provides a very nice reproduction of the music used in the production and the scant dialogue is clear. —ML

Movie: ♫♫ ½ **DVD:** ♫♫
Columbia Tristar (cat #07074, UPC 04339-6070745). Full frame. Dolby Digital Stereo. $24.95. Keepcase. *LANG:* English. *FEATURES:* Bonus trailers • 12 chapters.
1991 85m/C

Cirque du Soleil Presents Circue Reinvente

Emmy Award–winning performance by the famed troupe in all of their colorful splendor, performing all of their best-loved feats. From acrobatics to tightrope walking and clowns to contortionists, there is something here for everyone and *Cirque Reinvente* puts the viewer at ringside for this hour-long performance. Shot on video, the program looks very good on DVD. There is some occasional flaring from the lights (which appears as a white "blooming" on the screen), but otherwise the image is very clear and rivals broadcast quality. Most notable here are the splendid colors of the performers' costumes. The stereo sound gives a faithful reproduction of the lively music that accompanies this show. —ML

Movie: ♫♫♫♫ **DVD:** ♫♫♫ ½
Columbia Tristar (cat #07073, UPC 0433-96010738). Full frame. Dolby Digital Stereo. $24.95. Keepcase. *LANG:* English. *FEATURES:* 8 chapters.
1989 56m/C

Cirque du Soleil— Saltimbanco

The eclectic circus/theatre troupe returns for another exciting performance with *Saltimbanco*. As per usual, the show is full of amazing acrobatic feats, but the ever-evolving Cirque du Soleil adds some interesting new exhibitions to the mix to spice things up. The first thing that one notices here are the elaborate costumes. While this troupe has always been known for their elaborate dress, the costumes here are extremely colorful and eye-catching. Also, in many of the performances, the group members wear very unusual masks (which resemble something from *Pink Floyd: The Wall*), heightening the surrealistic nature of the show. The most interesting new attraction here is a master ball-bouncer. He performs an unusual variation on juggling, where he bounces the balls on the floor, instead of tossing them into the air. The speed at which he can do this is simply amazing. While some of the segments here are a bit dark in tone, there is a very humorous section where a mime taunts a member of the audience. For you purists, *Saltimbanco* contains the usual tightrope walkers, contortionists, and acrobats who made the troupe famous. While this can't reproduce the magic of a live performance, this is a nice representation of Cirque du Soleil's work. The performance was shot on video and there is some occasional video distortion and blurring here. However, the colors are fantastic, and the image is very clear. The Dolby Digital Stereo sound offers a nice reproduction of the haunting music which accompanies the show. —ML

Movie: ♫♫♫ **DVD:** ♫♫ ½
Columbia Tristar (cat #07070, UPC 0433-96070707). Full frame. Dolby Digital

Stereo. $24.95. Keepcase. *LANG:* English. *FEATURES:* Bonus trailers • 12 chapters.
1994 78m/C

Citizen Cohn

James Woods does a fine job of playing Roy Cohn, the closeted gay Jewish lawyer who became notorious for ensuring the death penalty for the Rosenbergs, the famous Jewish couple accused of spying. He was Joe McCarthy's lead attorney during the Communist witch hunts of the 1950s, beating out Robert Kennedy for the job. The story is framed by Cohn's revisiting his past on his way to death. In the end he is surrounded by the people he has wronged. They needle him with his lack of honor and his hollow achievements. The cast is excellent; the story is intriguing but low on facts. You could almost argue that Hollywood is still holding a grudge for the famous blacklist of writers from that time, but it hardly comes up in the film. More likely it was the fuel that got this made for HBO. A lifetime of anger, denial, and tyranny does not easily fit into 112 minutes, but the highlights from Cohn's life of bitterness and power lust prove entertaining enough. The picture quality is just slightly less than crisp, which is surprising for a HBO product. —JAS

Movie: ♫♫♫ **DVD:** ♫♫♫
HBO (cat #90826, UPC 026359082627). Widescreen anamorphic. Dolby Surround; Mono. $19.95. Snapper. *LANG:* English; Spanish; French. *SUB:* English; Spanish; French. *FEATURES:* Cast & crew bios • 23 chapters.
1992 (R) 112m/C James Woods, Joe Don Baker, Joseph Bologna, Ed Flanders, Frederic Forrest, Lee Grant, Pat Hingle; *D:* Frank Pierson; *W:* David Franzoni; *C:* Paul Elliott.

Citizen Kane

Welles's masterpiece is an American tragedy of newspaper tycoon Charles Foster Kane. To a degree, the character is based on William Randolph Hearst and now the two are often confused in the public imagination. That's somehow appropriate for this ambitious work that's lost none of its fierce originality. The film's technical brilliance—fragmented narrative structure, stunning deep-focus photography from Gregg Toland, vivid soundtrack, fabulous ensemble acting—has never been given a better showcase on home video. Both image and sound have been carefully restored, but the film retains its dark, heavily shadowed look. Of the many extras, the most valuable may be critic Roger Ebert's commentary. He has studied the film in the most minute detail through shot-by-shot classes that he teaches at film festivals and his observations have real merit. "The Battle over Citizen Kane" is a PBS American Masters episode that's included on a second disc. —MM

Movie: ♫♫♫♫ **DVD:** ♫♫♫♫
Warner (cat #T6565, UPC 05393965-6527). Full frame. Dolby Digital Mono.

$24.95. 2-disc slipcase. *LANG:* English. *SUB:* English; French; Spanish; Portuguese. *CAP:* English. *FEATURES:* 31 chapters (film) ● 11 chapters (documentary) ● Commentary: Roger Ebert ● Commentary: Peter Bogdanovich ● 1941 premiere newsreel ● Gallery of storyboards, photos, promotional material ● "The Battle over Citizen Kane" documentary.
1941 119m/B Orson Welles, Joseph Cotten, Everett Sloane, Dorothy Comingore, Ruth Warrick, George Coulouris, Ray Collins, William Alland, Paul Stewart, Erskine Sanford, Agnes Moorehead, Alan Ladd, Gus Schilling, Philip Van Zandt, Harry Shannon, Sonny Bupp, Arthur O'Connell; *D:* Orson Welles; *W:* Orson Welles, Herman J. Mankiewicz; *C:* Gregg Toland; *M:* Bernard Herrmann. *AWARDS:* Oscars '41: Orig. Screenplay; AFI '98: Top 100, Natl. Film Reg. '89; N.Y. Film Critics '41: Film; *NOM:* Oscars '41: Actor (Welles), B&W Cinematog., Director (Welles), Film Editing, Picture, Sound, Orig. Dramatic Score.

Citizen Welles

Judging by the handsome packaging of this DVD set, and reading the claims on the cover, one would think this an attractive bargain. It isn't. Both *The Stranger* and *The Trial* are already available separately on DVD (reviewed in *Book 1*) in very good-looking editions taken from excellent elements. This set makes the deceptive claim that the films are fully restored. As explained in the restoration documentary, each transfer was optimized for contrast and cleaned up digitally to some extent. But the source materials were obviously 16mm public domain–quality prints. Both features are dupey, with bad contrast and poor definition. The digital work improves their looks, but much better copies of both titles can be seen free of charge on the Turner Classic Movies. The set is almost a parody of a Criterion-style presentation. A quote on the back from critic Jeffrey Lyons reads, "This restoration is in perfect condition. Orson Welles would have loved seeing it." I'm not particularly enamored of Lyons as a reviewer, but the nerve of this flimflam takes the cake, as Lyons is a contributor to the disc itself, in commentaries on the features, and in narration on the extras. Those commentaries are simply terrible. For anyone with even a cursory knowledge of Welles, he's a bore, and his explanations about the director are so confused that beginners won't have a clue to what he's talking about. Just when you thought things couldn't be worse, the documentary about the "restoration" of the pictures does little more than assure the viewer that all the bad visuals you are looking at actually look great. —GE
Movie: 🐶🐶🐶½ **DVD:** 🐶
FOCUSfilm (UPC 683070935528). Full frame; widescreen (1.66:1) letterboxed. $29.98. Keepcase. *LANG:* English. *FEATURES:* "The Hearts of Age" short subject ● Restoration documentaries ● Photo galleries.
2001 213m/C

City Hunter: Secret Service

World renowned detective Ryo "Joe" Saeba, better known as City Hunter, is hired as a bodyguard for a foreign politician. Though incorrigible horndog Saeba insists he only guards women, he changes his tune when he learns threats have been made against the man's daughter. The animation here is flat and dull, perhaps in response to the plot, which favors melodrama over action and comedy. The disc version includes, without explanation, an extra three-minute sequence, which may be part of another City Hunter adventure, or a deleted scene from this one. —BT *AKA:* City Hunter: Secret Police.
Movie: 🐶½ **DVD:** 🐶🐶🐶
A.D.V. Films (cat #DCH005, UPC 702727-013126). Full frame. $29.98. Keepcase. *LANG:* Japanese; English. *SUB:* English; English song. *FEATURES:* 8 chapters ● TV spots ● Trailers ● Extra scene.
1996 (R) 90m/C *JP D:* Kenji Kodama; *W:* Kenji Kodama, Akinori Endo; *C:* Youichi Hasegawa; *M:* Tatsumi Yano.

City of Glass

In London, on New Year's Eve 1997, a car crash kills Raphael (Lai) and Vivian (Qi). Back in Hong Kong, their respective families are mystified, and when his son and her daughter go to England to claim the bodies, they learn another side of their parents' lives. Much of the story is told as flashbacks to their college days in the turbulent 1970s. Performances are generally fine, but the soft focus and sappy music are slapped on with a trowel. DVD image is about what you'd expect from a well-produced import. It lacks the sharpness of a big-budget Hollywood production, but that is in part intentional. Reds and whites tend to glow. The 5.1 is active for this kind of story. —MM *AKA:* Boli Zhi Cheng.
Movie: 🐶🐶🐶 **DVD:** 🐶🐶🐶
Tai Seng (cat #5234, UPC 60164345841). Widescreen (1.85:1) letterboxed. Dolby Digital 5.1 Surround. $24.98. Keepcase. *LANG:* English; Cantonese; Mandarin. *SUB:* English; Trad. & Simpl. Chinese. *FEATURES:* Trailer ● 9 chapters ● Talent files.
1998 111m/C *HK* Leon Lai, Shu Qi, Nicola Cheung, Daniel Ng; *D:* Mabel Cheung; *W:* Alex Law; *C:* Jingle Ma.

The City of the Dead

Previously released on disc under the title *Horror Hotel* (reviewed in *Book 2*), this version is far superior. Both image and sound are excellent and it contains two commentary tracks, one by star Christopher (at his imperious best) and one by director Moxey. There's also an interview with star Venetia Stevenson. The only flaws are achingly slow menus. —MM *AKA:* Horror Hotel.
Movie: 🐶🐶🐶 **DVD:** 🐶🐶🐶½
VCI (cat #8274, UPC 089859827426). Widescreen (1.66:1) anamorphic. Dolby Digital Mono. $19.98. Keepcase. *LANG:* English. *FEATURES:* 18 chapters ● Commentary: Christopher Lee ● Commentary:

John Moxey ● Interviews with Lee, Moxey, and Venetia Stevenson ● Trailer ● Talent files ● Photo gallery.
1960 76m/B *GB* Christopher Lee, Patricia Jessel, Betta St. John, Dennis Lotis, Venetia Stevenson, Valentine Dyall; *D:* John Llewellyn Moxey; *W:* George L. Baxt; *C:* Desmond Dickinson.

City on Fire [Dimension]

One of the most important early Hong Kong action films arrives on DVD in a thoroughly "westernized" edition. The voice dubbing has a generic sound and the audio appears to have been redone. Both detract somewhat from fine performances in the leads. Ko Chow (Chow Yun-Fat) is an undercover cop who has more troubles with his ambitious, venal fellow cops than with the gang he's attempting to infiltrate. By the end, he's closer to criminal Lee Fu (Danny Lee) than to his bosses. The rest of the plot covers territory familiar to fans. Image is superior to the Tai Seng release (reviewed in *Book 1*); the lack of an option for the original sound is an unforgivable oversight. —MM
Movie: 🐶🐶🐶 **DVD:** 🐶🐶
Buena Vista Home Ent. (cat #23142, UPC 786936158496). Widescreen (1.85:1) anamorphic. Dolby Digital 5.1 Surround Stereo. $29.99. Keepcase. *LANG:* English. *CAP:* English. *FEATURES:* 16 chapters ● Trailer.
1987 98m/C *HK* Chow Yun-Fat, Sun Yueh, Danny Lee, Carrie Ng, Roy Cheung; *D:* Ringo Lam; *W:* Tommy Sham; *C:* Andrew Lau; *M:* Teddy Robin Kwan.

Clambake

In the long and ignominious string of big-budget Hollywood musicals that Elvis made, this may be the very worst and, appropriately, this DVD may be the ugliest of his entire oeuvre. In a relentlessly toxic vehicle, Elvis plays a rich man's son who wants success on his own terms so he trades places with a water-skiing teacher (Hutchins). Some print damage is evident but the intense graininess and lack of detail appear to come mostly from the original. (The famous Elvisian pompadour is a solid black mass in most shots.) The film simply lacks polish at every level and the image reflects it. —MM
Movie: 🐶 **DVD:** 🐶½
MGM Home Ent. (cat #1002569, UPC 027-616867704). Widescreen (2.35:1) letterboxed. Dolby Digital Mono. $24.98. Keepcase. *LANG:* English; Spanish. *SUB:* French; Spanish. *CAP:* English. *FEATURES:* 16 chapters ● Trailer.
1967 98m/C Elvis Presley, Shelley Fabares, Bill Bixby, James Gregory, Gary Merrill, Will Hutchins, Harold (Hal) Peary, Suzie Kaye, Angelique Pettyjohn; *D:* Arthur Nadel; *W:* Arthur Browne Jr.; *C:* William Margulies; *M:* Jeff Alexander.

Classic Biker Movies

Please see reviews of *Evel Knievel, C.C. & Company,* and *Angels Hard As They Come.* BFS Video (cat #302910D, UPC 0668053-02916). $9.98. Keepcase.
2002 263m/C

A Classic Christmas: Scrooge / Beyond Tomorrow

In *Scrooge,* this edition of the popular Christmas tale follows the usual plot points and features a fairly nasty Scrooge but the abbreviated ghost visits (Marley is invisible!) and fantasy sequences are unsatisfying. The Bob Cratchit and Tiny Tim subplot is weakened by maudlin, uninteresting performances. The original release version ran longer but as it's rarely screened, it's difficult to make a definitive evaluation of the film. In *Beyond Tomorrow,* on Christmas eve, three older businessmen befriend a young man (Carlson) and woman and help them become a couple. Shortly afterward, the three are killed in a plane crash, but they come back as ghosts to help the troubled couple. Clumsily designed holiday movie oddly starts off with Christmas instead of building up to it. The cast is likable (though Carlson's horse-obsessed Texan seems a bit odd) but the romantic couple is underdeveloped and the film is marred by a seriously wrongheaded denouement. Both films have been transferred from grainy, soft, and battered 16mm prints. The image is dark overall and blacks tend to be thick and muddy, but there isn't much in the way of digital noise. Sound is intelligible if a bit thin and warbled. —DG
Movie: ♪♪ *DVD:* ♪♪
Marengo Films (cat #MRG-0013, UPC 807013001327). Full frame. Mono. $14.98. Keepcase. *LANG:* English. *FEATURES:* 6 chapters per film.
2000 145m/C

Classic Dick Tracy Movies

The three Dick Tracy movies on this disc look pretty good for public domain titles. Black and white is clear enough with only the expected signs of wear. Please see individual reviews of *Dick Tracy Meets Gruesome, Dick Tracy vs. Cueball,* and *Dick Tracy's Dilemma.* —MM
Movie: ♪♪ *DVD:* ♪♪
BFS Video (cat #30172-D, UPC 0668053-01728). Full frame. $9.98. Keepcase. *LANG:* English. *FEATURES:* 12 chapters ● Boris Karloff bio and filmography ● Chester Gould bio ● Trivia.
2001 188m/C

Classic Family DVD Double Feature: "The Little Princess" & "Heidi"

The first half of this double-bill is the Shirley Temple version of *The Little Princess.* Minor print damage and fading are evident, but no more than you'd expect for a film of this age. Overall, it looks very good, but is not as sharp as the SlingShot edition (reviewed in *Book 2*). The second feature is the 1967 *Heidi* with Maximillian Schell. It's not quite as sharp with considerable grain (coming from the original, I think) and faded colors that are no better than tape. —MM
Movie: ♪♪♪ *DVD:* ♪♪ ½
Marengo Films (cat #MRG-0022, UPC 807-013002294). Full frame. $14.98. Keepcase. *LANG:* English. *FEATURES:* 6 links each feature.
2000 199m/C

Classic Heist Movies

Please see reviews of *The Great St. Louis Bank Robbery, High Risk,* and *The Squeeze.* BFS Video (cat #30295-D, UPC 06680530-2954). $9.98. Keepcase.
2002 277m/C

Classic Seventies Movies

Please see reviews of *Born to Win* (in *Book 2), Katherine,* and *The Harrad Experiment.* BFS Video (cat #30290-D, UPC 06680530-2909). $9.98. Keepcase.
2002 271m/C

Classic Sonny Chiba Movies

Please see individual reviews of *The Bodyguard, Shogun's Ninja,* and *Sister Streetfighter.* BFS Video (cat #30235D, UPC 06680530-2350). Widescreen letterboxed. $9.98. Keepcase. *LANG:* English.
2001 282m/C

Cleo from 5 to 7

A simple story makes for a moving and effective movie in this French film that traces a pair of hours in a beautiful French singer's life as she waits to find out if she has cancer. As she walks the streets of the city, she begins to learn more about herself and the world around her and she comes to terms with what her future just might be. The main performance by Marchand is strong, and the cinematography does a wonderful job of capturing the world of Paris, from the streets to the people. This is an engaging piece of cinema that's well written and beautifully photographed. The color opening sequence that opens the film looks a little bit spotty, with marks and other damage, as well as colors that seemed faded. The rest of the film is in black and white. If not sharp, images are at least crisp and never wanting in clarity. Detail is also pleasing. There are some sequences where marks or scratches on the print do appear, but they are never terribly distracting. The mono French soundtrack is enjoyable, but has a slight background hiss. The music sounds light and crisp, and is enjoyable. —AB/DG
AKA: Cleo de 5 a 7.
Movie: ♪♪♪ *DVD:* ♪♪♪
Criterion (UPC 37429149027). Widescreen (1.66:1) letterboxed. Mono. $29.98. Keepcase. *LANG:* French. *SUB:* English. *FEATURES:* 18 chapters ● Restored color opening sequence.
1961 90m/B *FR* Corinne Marchand, Antoine Bourseiller, Dorothee Blanck, Michel Legrand, Jean-Claude Brialy, Jean-Luc Godard, Anna Karina, Eddie Constantine, Sami Frey; *D:* Agnes Varda; *W:* Agnes Varda; *C:* Jean Rabier; *M:* Michel Legrand.

Clint Eastwood: Out of the Shadows

This entry in public television's "American Masters" series is an uncritical look at one of America's most important filmmakers. The focus is not on Eastwood's personal life but on his professional career. In that regard, Eastwood was one of the first actors to form a production company, Malpaso, and take control of his own career. All of the usual suspects are rounded up to say the right things and the clips are well chosen. Image quality is generally good to very good, somewhat better than broadcast quality. Recommended. —MM
Movie: ♪♪♪ *DVD:* ♪♪♪
Warner (cat #21514, UPC 0853921514-24). Full frame and widescreen. Dolby Digital Surround. $19.98. Snapper. *LANG:* English. *SUB:* English; French; Spanish; Portuguese; Japanese; Chinese; Korean; Thai. *CAP:* English. *FEATURES:* 23 chapters.
2000 87m/C *D:* Bruce Ricker; *W:* Dave Kehr; *C:* Bruce Ricker; *M:* Lennie Niehaus; *Nar:* Morgan Freeman.

The Clockmaker

Contemplative drama about a clockmaker (Noiret) whose life is shattered when his son (Rougerie) is arrested and charged as a political assassin. Cast is excellent, as always, and Tavernier handles the material with his usual sure grasp. DVD image is very good, even excellent considering the age of the film. Yellow subtitles are burned in and easily legible. —MM **AKA:** L'Horloger de Saint-Paul.
Movie: ♪♪♪ ½ *DVD:* ♪♪♪
Kino on Video (cat #K234, UPC 738329-023423). Widescreen (1.66:1) letterboxed. $29.98. Keepcase. *LANG:* French. *SUB:* English. *FEATURES:* 14 chapters.
1973 105m/C *FR* Philippe Noiret, Jean Rochefort, Jacques Denis, William Sabatier, Christine Pascal; *D:* Bertrand Tavernier; *W:* Bertrand Tavernier, Jean Aurenche, Pierre Bost; *C:* Sylvain Rougerie; *M:* Philippe Sarde.

Clockwise

John Cleese plays Brian Stimpson, the overly English headmaster of a British high school who is overly attached to time. He runs his—and everyone's—life by the clock. One day on the way to his train, which will

take him to give a very important speech, he goes right instead of left and a cross-country flight to make it to the speech on time becomes one long chance to watch Cleese prove why he's the undisputed successor to Peter Sellers. Weird monks, helpful people who aren't, and the need to steal clothing are all foils for this master of physical comedy. Another Anchor Bay transfer that looks great; the sound is mono though, and it can only go so far. —CA
Movie: 🎬🎬 ½ **DVD:** 🎬🎬🎬 ½
Anchor Bay (cat #DV11571, UPC 01313-1157192). Widescreen (1.66:1) anamorphic. Dolby Digital Mono. $19.90. Keepcase. *LANG:* English. *FEATURES:* 23 chapters ● John Cleese interview & bio ● Theatrical trailer.
1986 (PG) 96m/C *GB* John Cleese, Penelope Wilton, Alison Steadman, Stephen Moore, Sharon Maiden; **D:** Christopher Morahan; **W:** Michael Frayn; **C:** John Coquillon; **M:** George Fenton.

Close-Up

Hossain Sabzian, an uneducated laborer who escapes his everyday life through cinema, is convicted of fraud when he poses as a famous director. He portrays himself as Mohsen Makhmalbaf, a well-respected Iranian filmmaker, and attempts to deceive an innocent family into believing he will be using them in his next feature. When his deception is discovered, he must strive to make amends not only with the family he betrayed, but with the court system as well. *Close-Up* provides a poignant view of the effect cinema can have on the human psyche when it is used as a tool of escapism. Although the film itself is entertaining, there were many noticeable visual artifacts in the picture quality throughout the movie. Probably the most upsetting is the loss of dialogue sound during one of the most crucial parts at the end of the film. —EL
Movie: 🎬🎬 ½ **DVD:** 🎬
Facets Multimedia, Inc. (cat #3106, UPC 736899031060). Widescreen letterboxed. $29.95. Keepcase. *LANG:* Iranian. *SUB:* English. *FEATURES:* Interview with Abbas Kiarostami ● Abbas Kiarostami filmography ● Mohsen Makhmalbaf filmography ● 16 chapters.
1990 100m/C *IA* Hossain Sabzian, Mohsen Makhmalbaf, Abolfazi Ahankhah, Mehrdad Ahankhah; **D:** Abbas Kiarostami; **C:** Ali Reza Zaiindast.

Closely Watched Trains

Railroad trainee Milos Hrma (Neckar) follows in the family footsteps but has grievous problems finding his sexual identity. Smitten by every girl he sees and flabbergasted by the wanton excesses of his dispatcher colleague Hubicka (Somr), Milos tries to find his footing but is terminally shy, especially with the ready and willing conductress Masa (Bendova). His efforts to counteract his personal sexual problems lead to more embarrassing, and seri-

ous, misadventures. DVD is a handsome flat transfer of this Czech feature, with a nice liner essay from Richard Schickel to help place it in historical context (all news to this viewer) and a cheesy American "art movie" trailer which tries to make it seem like a bawdy sex romp. That makes sense when you realize that the American distributor was Sigma III, an outfit also responsible for unleashing *The Horrible Dr. Hichcock* on U.S. audiences. Technical quality and presentation are up to Criterion's usual high standards. —GE **AKA:** Ostre Sledovane Vlaky.
Movie: 🎬🎬🎬 ½ **DVD:** 🎬🎬🎬 ½
Criterion (cat #131, UPC 037429161524). Full frame. $29.95. Keepcase. *LANG:* Czech. *SUB:* English. *FEATURES:* 20 chapters ● Liner essay by Richard Schickel ● Trailer.
1966 89m/B *CZ* Vaclav Neckar, Jitka Bendova, Vladimir Valenta, Josef Somr; **D:** Jiri Menzel; **W:** Jiri Menzel; **C:** Jaromir Sofr; **M:** Jiri Sust. *AWARDS:* Oscars '67: Foreign Film.

The Closet

François (Auteuil) is about to be fired. He's not bad at his job, he's just a dullard with no friends and no life. His ex-wife ignores his calls and his son just ignores him. As he ponders leaping off his balcony he meets the new neighbor, a kind older man, who hits on a plan to save his job. In order to make himself more interesting and politically correct, he should start a rumor he's gay. They doctor some questionable photos placing François in the forefront and send them to his work. People begin falling over themselves to get close to François, who is no longer a boring nobody but a discreet employee by day and a wild man by night, or so everyone thinks. Auteuil's quiet underplaying of François is a joy to behold as he is constantly amazed by his fellow man, especially co-worker Felix (Depardieu), a macho brute, who becomes obsessed with the fact that François doesn't find him attractive. This film is full of the kind of humor that inspires spontaneous laughter and has the bonus of a feel-good ending. The disc looks and sounds very good. The subtitles are easy to read, though the translation is not as good as it could be with obvious phrases that have been made awkward due to a misunderstanding of colloquial English. —CA **AKA:** Le Placard.
Movie: 🎬🎬🎬 **DVD:** 🎬🎬🎬 ½
Miramax Pictures (cat #23826, UPC 786936163803). Widescreen anamorphic. Dolby Digital. $32.99. Keepcase. *LANG:* French. *SUB:* English. *CAP:* English. *FEATURES:* 16 chapters ● Theatrical trailer.
2000 (R) 86m/C *FR* Daniel Auteuil, Gerard Depardieu, Thierry Lhermitte, Michel Aumont, Michele Laroque, Jean Rochefort, Alexandra Vandernoot; **D:** Francis Veber; **W:** Francis Veber; **C:** Luciano Tovoli; **M:** Vladimir Cosma.

Cobra Verde

Even by Herzog/Kinski standards, their final collaboration was a wild trip. (On his

commentary track, Herzog notes the moment when Kinski physically attacked him.) Kinski is Cobra Verde, a 19th-century Brazilian bandit who finds work as a slave overseer on a sugar plantation. When he impregnates all three of the owner's daughters, he's sent on an impossible mission to re-open the slave trade with a mad African king. Discovering that he's been betrayed, CV trains an army of women to overthrow the ruler and take control of the business himself. Kinski is at his most messianic throughout and the sharp DVD image captures every maniacal nuance of his performance. Grain is minimal even in the desert exteriors. Even though the English dubbing is pretty good, I'd recommend the 5.1 German-dialogue option just to make the most of Popol Vuh's terrific score. —MM **AKA:** Slave Coast.
Movie: 🎬🎬🎬 **DVD:** 🎬🎬🎬 ½
Anchor Bay (cat #DV11098, UPC 013131-109894). Widescreen (1.77:1) anamorphic. Dolby Digital 5.1 Surround; Dolby Digital Surround. $24.98. Keepcase. *LANG:* German; English. *SUB:* English. *FEATURES:* Text Herzog interview (on reverse side of sleeve) ● Trailers ● Commentary: Herzog ● 28 chapters ● Talent files.
1988 110m/C *GE* Klaus Kinski, Peter Berling, Jose Lewgoy, Salvatore Basile; **D:** Werner Herzog; **W:** Werner Herzog; **C:** Viktor Ruzicka; **M:** Popul Vuh.

The Coca-Cola Kid

This strange comedy finds Coca-Cola's top marketing man (Roberts) sent to the outback to develop some new strategies. After learning of a region controlled by a local soft drink tycoon where no Coca-Cola is sold, he becomes determined to force his product into the market. The film's not quite clever enough to be taken as satire, so it comes off as the world's longest product placement. We do get to see quite a bit of the beautiful Greta Scacchi as the secretary/love interest. The sound mix seems a bit off—you'll strain to hear the dialogue, then be blown away by cheesy '80s music. Both the widescreen and full-frame versions look quite good and handle the plentiful reds, although the pan and scan version is a bit grainier. —BG
Movie: 🎬🎬 **DVD:** 🎬🎬 ½
MGM Home Ent. (cat #1003345, UPC 027616874948). Widescreen (1.85:1) anamorphic; full frame. Dolby Surround. $14.95. Keepcase. *LANG:* English; French; Spanish. *CAP:* English. *FEATURES:* 16 chapters ● Trailer.
1984 (R) 94m/C *AU* Eric Roberts, Greta Scacchi, Bill Kerr, Chris Haywood, Kris McQuade, Max Gilles; **D:** Dusan Makavejev; **W:** Frank Moorhouse; **C:** Dean Semler; **M:** William Motzig.

Cocaine Fiends

Please see review of *The Madness Trilogy*.
AKA: The Pace That Kills.
Movie: 🎬🎬
1936 74m/B Lois January, Noel Madison, Willy Castello, Dean Benton, Lois Lindsay,

Sheila (Manors) Mannors; **D:** William A. O'Connor.

Cold War

This hit-man thriller is mostly a routine affair, looking like a much older picture than it is, and distinguished only by the novelty of the South Korean locations and actors. Yam does little to define his character—his lone personality trait is the way he stubs out cigarettes. It makes little sense that Yung, now head of a huge criminal organization, would be hunting down a hired assassin on his own, but that's what he does. At least the ending shows a little spirit, but not much. The print looks worn and dark. —*BT*
Movie: ♫ ½ **DVD:** ♫♫
Tai Seng (cat #84814, UPC 6016438481-43). Widescreen letterboxed. $14.95. Keepcase. *LANG:* Cantonese; Mandarin; Vietnamese; Cambodian. *SUB:* English. *FEATURES:* 8 chapters • Trailers.
2000 91m/C *HK KN* Simon Yam, Kar-yan Leung, Christy Chung, Vincent Wan, Yak-choi Lee, On-tung Yeung, Kinko; **D:** Kar-yan Leung; **W:** Kar-yan Leung; **C:** Ross Clarkson.

College Swing

Lightweight, dated musical has Gracie Allen inheriting a small-town college which she turns into a hangout for her vaudeville pals. The top cast goes through some lively musical numbers and routines. Anyone who has ever wondered why Betty Grable was called the Sweater Girl will figure it out here. DVD image borders on the miraculous. The crisp black-and-white photography is reproduced with no serious signs of wear. Mono sound is distortion free. Disc also contains *Big Broadcast of 1938.* (Please see review.) You cannot switch from one film to the other without removing the disc from the player. —*MM* **AKA:** Swing, Teacher, Swing.
Movie: ♫♫ **DVD:** ♫♫♫
Universal Studios (cat #21462, UPC 025-192146220). Full frame. Dolby Digital Mono. $24.98. Keepcase. *LANG:* English. *SUB:* French; Spanish. *CAP:* English. *FEATURES:* 18 chapters • Production notes • Talent files • Trailer.
1938 86m/B George Burns, Gracie Allen, Martha Raye, Bob Hope, Edward Everett Horton, Ben Blue, Betty Grable, Jackie Coogan, John Payne; **D:** Raoul Walsh; **W:** Walter DeLeon, Francis Martin; **C:** Victor Milner; **M:** Boris Morros, Hoagy Carmichael, Burton Lane, Frank Loesser.

Colonel Redl

An absorbing and intricately rendered psychological study of an ambitious officer's rise and fall in pre–World War I Austria. Brandauer (best known to American audiences for his Oscar-nominated performance in *Out of Africa*) is excellent as the vain, insecure homosexual ultimately undone by his own ambition and his superior officer's smug loathing. Mueller-Stahl and Landgrebe are particularly distin-

guished among the supporting players. This film is the second in the Szabo/Brandauer trilogy, coming after *Mephisto* and before *Hanussen*. Nominated for an Academy Award (Best Foreign Language Film) and a Golden Globe (Best Foreign Film). The DVD offers an adequate full-frame transfer of the film. The image is clear and sharp for the most part, but there is some mild grain and the image shimmers at times. Also, the picture is slightly dark. The digital mono audio track offers clear dialogue with no ambient hissing. The English subtitles are yellow and very easy to read. —*ML*
Movie: ♫♫♫♫ **DVD:** ♫♫♫
Anchor Bay (cat #DV11414, UPC 01313-1141498). Full frame. Dolby Digital Mono. $29.98. Keepcase. *LANG:* German. *SUB:* English. *FEATURES:* Theatrical trailer • Featurette • Talent bios • 28 chapters.
1984 (R) 142m/C *GE HU* Klaus Maria Brandauer, Armin Mueller-Stahl, Gudrun Landgrebe, Jan Niklas, Hans-Christian Blech, Laszlo Mensaros, Andras Balint; **D:** Laszlo Szabo; **W:** Laszlo Szabo, Peter Dobai; **C:** Lajos Koltai; **M:** Zdenko Tamassy. *AWARDS:* British Acad. '85: Foreign Film; Cannes '85: Special Jury Prize; *NOM:* Oscars '85: Foreign Film.

The Color of Pomegranates

Paradjanov's depiction of the life of Armenian poet Arutium Sayadin, known as Sayat Nova, who rises from carpet weaver to court minstrel to archbishop, is told without conventional narrative tools. There's a Fellini-esque quality to the editing of the often-surrealistic images. Eloquent symbols are derived from Armenian paintings, poetry, and history. The disc also includes a 1994 documentary about the filmmaker, *Paradjanov: A Requiem,* and an early short feature, "Hagop Hovnatanian." Image appears slightly faded, but I have not seen a theatrical release, so it may be accurate. Sound is fine and the yellow subtitles are easy to read. The documentary is in Russian and English and presents Paradjanov as a sort of Russian Hemingway. —*MM*
AKA: Sayat Nova; Tsvet Granata.
Movie: ♫♫♫ **DVD:** ♫♫♫
Kino on Video (cat #K201, UPC 73832902-0125). Full frame. $29.95. Keepcase. *LANG:* Russian. *SUB:* English. *FEATURES:* 12 links (feature) • 10 links (documentary) • Documentary: *Paradjanov: A Requiem* • Short feature: "Hagop Hovnatanian."
1969 80m/C *RU* Sofiko Chiaureli, M. Aleksanian, V. Galstian; **D:** Sergei Paradjanov; **W:** Sergei Paradjanov; **C:** A. Samvelyan.

Colors

Vivid, realistic cop drama pairs sympathetic veteran Bob Hodges (Duvall) with trigger-tempered Danny McGavin (Penn) on the gang-infested streets of East Los Angeles. Fine play from the leads and Don Cheadle, but the film is still controversial

in its unsettling depiction of streetlife. Colorful, free-wheeling direction from Hopper. Director of photography Haskell Wexler gives the film a deliberately unpolished look, but the grain does not lead to any extra artifacts. Recommended on any medium. —*MM*
Movie: ♫♫♫ **DVD:** ♫♫ ½
MGM Home Ent. (cat #1002570, UPC 027616867711). Widescreen (1.85:1) anamorphic. Dolby Digital Surround. $14.95. Keepcase. *LANG:* English; French; Spanish. *SUB:* French; Spanish. *CAP:* English. *FEATURES:* Trailer • 16 chapters.
1988 (R) 120m/C Glenn Plummer, Sy Richardson, Damon Wayans, Fred Asparagus, Sherman Augustus, R.D. Call, Seymour Cassel, Nick(y) Corello, Virgil Frye, Courtney Gains, Clark Johnson, Leon, Tina Lifford, Micole Mercurio, Jack Nance, Tony Todd, Gerardo Mejia, Sean Penn, Robert Duvall, Maria Conchita Alonso, Trinidad Silva, Randi Brooks, Grand Bush, Don Cheadle, Rudy Ramos; **D:** Dennis Hopper; **W:** Michael Schiffer; **C:** Haskell Wexler; **M:** Herbie Hancock.

Come and See

Byelorussia, 1943. When teenage Floriya finds a rifle, he joins with the homefront army who are protecting the rural villages from the Germans. He narrowly escapes the grisly fate of most of the troops and makes a shattering return home. Forced to hide out in another village, he is witness to devastating atrocities by the Germans who lay siege to the town. This haunting, devastating film re-creates the horrors that were committed in over 600 towns in Byelorussia by the retreating Nazis. The tangible reality of the sets, locations, and battles help this film achieve the terrifying believability of a documentary. The surreal forest attack is presented in chilling, dreamlike fashion, and is a superb orchestration of image, music, and sound. The film frequently uses the device of having characters act directly into the camera, as if it's adopted the point of view of the person they're speaking to. Having our primary characters shamelessly emote into the camera (as if to convince us of their sincerity) is artificial and distracting. A film as powerful as this doesn't need such gimmickry. The title is a biblical quote concerning the beckoning four horsemen of the apocalypse. The disc features a heavily grainy image, with rich, somewhat muted hues. It appears to be an aspect of the original photography. There's a bit of edge shimmer and the layer change on disc two is very awkward. Although the film is presented full frame, the framing never appears compromised—it was probably shot at academy aperture for artistic reasons. The 5.1 sound is excellent and involving, but sounds more like a strong stereo track. The introduction by director Klimov is informative and interesting, but it runs for almost 20 minutes and is best viewed after the film. The additional interviews are brief, but worthwhile. The archival doc-

umentary footage runs about 5 minutes and the explicit nature of its images drives home the real-life horror of these atrocities. —*DG AKA:* Idi i Smotri; Go and See. *Movie:* 🎬🎬🎬 ½ *DVD:* 🎬🎬🎬
Kino on Video (cat #K219DVD, UPC 738-329021924). Full frame. Dolby 5.1 Surround. $29.95. Keepcase. *LANG:* Russia; English; French. *SUB:* English; Russian; French; Spanish; Dutch; Japanese; and others. *FEATURES:* Intro by director Klimov • 2 photo galleries • Interviews with the cast & crew • Cast & crew filmographies • "Partisans in Belarus" materials • "Nazis' Brutalities" materials • 22 chapters • Insert booklet with notes.
1985 137m/C *RU* Alexei Kravchenko, Olga Mironova, Lubomiras Lauciavicus, Vladas Bagdonas, Viktor Lorents, Juris Lumiste, Kazimir Rabetsky, Yevgeni Tilicheyev; *D:* Elem Klimov; *W:* Elem Klimov, Alex Adamovich; *C:* Alexei Rodionov; *M:* Oleg Yanchenko.

Comedy in Da Hood
Terrible collection of black-oriented humorous bits and routines wants to be funny but only proves that poorly written comedy is never funny. Features Tony Roberts, Kool Bubba Ice, Gerald Kelly, and Jay. DVD is VHS quality, sound is thin, and the added laugh track is just plain irritating. —*DE*
Movie: 🎬 *DVD:* 🎬 ½
Warner (cat #A56134-2, UPC 085365613-423). Full frame. Stereo. $19.98. Keepcase. *LANG:* English. *FEATURES:* 21 chapters.
2001 101m/C

Comes a Horseman
Robards is a cattle baron attempting to gobble up all the oil-rich land of his neighbors. His ex-lover Fonda stands up to him, with the help of World War II veteran Caan and old-timer Farnsworth, in a slow-moving but intriguing western. DVD looks fine, but there's little to be done with the softish image and often-underlit interiors. Some edge-enhancement is obvious in exteriors. Mono sound is fine for the thundering hoofbeats. —*MM*
Movie: 🎬🎬 ½ *DVD:* 🎬🎬 ½
MGM Home Ent. (cat #1002368, UPC 027616865793). Widescreen (2.35:1) anamorphic. Dolby Digital Mono. $19.98. Keepcase. *LANG:* English; French; Spanish. *SUB:* French; Spanish. *CAP:* English. *FEATURES:* 16 chapters • Trailer.
1978 (PG) 119m/C James Caan, Jane Fonda, Jason Robards Jr., George Grizzard, Richard Farnsworth, Jim Davis, Mark Harmon; *D:* Alan J. Pakula; *W:* Dennis Lynton Clark; *C:* Gordon Willis; *M:* Michael Small. *AWARDS:* Natl. Bd. of Review '78: Support. Actor (Farnsworth); Natl. Soc. Film Critics '78: Support. Actor (Farnsworth); *NOM:* Oscars '78: Support. Actor (Farnsworth).

Comic King
Two friends work themselves up the corporate ladder in the competitive field of Japanese comic books, finally becoming successful enough to launch their own

company. All the while, they're fighting for the attention of their executive assistant. To help them out of their romantic quandary, two of their creations (both played by Tse) spring to life to offer advice. Manga readers will appreciate the numerous industry jokes, but others may be bored. The picture is a bit fuzzy around the edges, but the Cantonese soundtrack is good. Stay away from the dubbed Mandarin track, and beware of the special features, which are in unsubtitled Cantonese. —*BG*
Movie: 🎬 *DVD:* 🎬🎬 ½
Tai Seng (cat #WSDVD1196, UPC 601643-938646). Full frame. Dolby 5.1. $19.95. Keepcase. *LANG:* Cantonese; Mandarin. *SUB:* English; Chinese. *FEATURES:* 6 chapters • Behind-the-scenes featurette.
2000 100m/C *HK* Chi Lan Cheung, Chan Eason, Nicholas Tse, Ruby Lin, Julian Cheung; *D:* Sing Pui O; *W:* Chris Lou.

Coming Apart
Free love was never really very free as shrink Joe Glazer (Torn) finds when he secretly films his sexual escapades with a variety of women, leading to his own emotional breakdown. Comparisons to *I Am Curious, Yellow* and *sex, lies, and videotape* are not out of place. This one's avant-garde, daring, over-the-top and, perhaps, very funny. Or is the story about the duck in chapter 2 meant to be taken seriously? Whatever, DVD presents an accurate reproduction of an intentionally distressed image with coarse sound. —*MM*
Movie: 🎬🎬 *DVD:* 🎬🎬🎬
Kino on Video (cat #K155, UPC 73832901-5527). Widescreen (1.66:1) letterboxed. $29.95. Keepcase. *LANG:* English. *FEATURES:* 18 chapters • "City below the Line" autobiographical featurette • "How to Fall into Oblivion and Take Your Movie with You" • "Cominga Part 2: Adventures in Re-releasing" featurette.
1969 111m/B Rip Torn, Sally Kirkland, Viveca Lindfors; *D:* Milton Moses Ginsberg; *W:* Milton Moses Ginsberg; *C:* Jack Yager.

Coming Home
Though this Oscar-winning film is an accurate portrayal of some attitudes toward the Vietnam war and the 1960s, it also carries such heavy political baggage that anyone who doesn't share its left-wing values will be hard pressed to appreciate it. At the beginning of the Tet Offensive, Marine Captain Bob Hyde (Dern) goes to Vietnam. His wife Sally (Fonda) begins to do volunteer work at a V.A. hospital. That's where she finds Luke Martin (Voight), a veteran who's paralyzed from the waist down. A few years before, he was the star quarterback and she was a cheerleader at the same high school. From the beginning, there's a sexual element to their relationship. The film is at its best when it focuses on the veterans. In that regard, it deserves to be ranked with *The Best Years of Our Lives* and *Born on the Fourth of July*. But the resolution of the romantic triangle at the center of the film is so pat that it's

almost insulting. That said, the emotions are honest, if one-sided. On their commentary track, Voight, Dern, and director of photography Haskell Wexler present an excellent defense of the film. They discuss the genesis of the project and, not surprisingly, remember it as one of the high points of their careers. They also provide much of the content for the two featurettes, "Coming Back Home" and "Hal Ashby: A Man Out of Time," both well worth watching for fans of the film. On DVD, as it was in theatrical release, the image is a bit soft and grainy, befitting the documentary look that the filmmakers were trying to achieve. It's never going to look any better than it does here, and it shouldn't. —*MM*
Movie: 🎬🎬 *DVD:* 🎬🎬🎬 ½
MGM Home Ent. (cat #1003333, UPC 027616874825). Widescreen (1.85:1) anamorphic. Dolby Digital Mono. $19.98. Keepcase. *LANG:* English; French; Spanish. *SUB:* English; French; Spanish. *CAP:* English. *FEATURES:* 16 chapters • Commentary: Jon Voight, Bruce Dern, Haskell Wexler • "Coming Back Home" featurette • "Hal Ashby: A Man Out of Time" featurette • Trailer.
1978 (R) 130m/C Jane Fonda, Jon Voight, Bruce Dern, Penelope Milford, Robert Carradine, Robert Ginty, Mary Gregory, Kathleen Miller, Beeson Carroll, Willie Tyler, Charles Cyphers, Olivia Cole, Tresa Hughes, Bruce French, Richard Lawson, Rita Taggart, Pat Corley; *D:* Hal Ashby; *W:* Robert C. Jones; *C:* Haskell Wexler. *AWARDS:* Oscars '78: Actor (Voight), Actress (Fonda), Orig. Screenplay; Cannes '78: Actor (Voight); Golden Globes '79: Actor—Drama (Voight), Actress—Drama (Fonda); L.A. Film Critics '78: Actor (Voight), Actress (Fonda), Film; N.Y. Film Critics '78: Actor (Voight); Writers Guild '78: Orig. Screenplay; *NOM:* Oscars '78: Director (Ashby), Film Editing, Picture, Support. Actor (Dern), Support. Actress (Milford).

Coming Out
Quiet Philipp is a gay teacher maintaining a passionless straight relationship. After meeting a young uncloseted teenager, he struggles to confront his desires. This landmark East German gay film tells an oft-told story but ends it in a more downbeat fashion than most. Philipp is a bit cold and not as interesting as the teenager he mistreats. The film's depiction of gay life is gaudy, unreal, and exotic but the story is rather dreary. The disc is sharp, but colors are drab and the film is overly grainy and prone to digital shimmer. The sound is excellent. —*DG*
Movie: 🎬🎬 *DVD:* 🎬🎬 ½
First Run Features (cat #FRF903924D, UPC 679126903924). Widescreen (1.85:1) letterboxed. Stereo. $29.95. Keepcase. *LANG:* German. *SUB:* English. *FEATURES:* 6 chapters • Theatrical trailer • Trailers from East German films • Guide to Queer Berlin • Director bio/filmography.
1989 113m/C *GE* Matthias Freihof, Dagmar Manzel, Dirk Kummer; *D:* Heiner Carow; *W:* Wolfram Witt; *C:* Martin Schlesinger; *M:* Stefan Carow.

Committed

Graham plays Joline, who does booking at a New York nightclub and is almost weirdly obsessed with keeping her marriage to Carl (Wilson) working. She even has her wedding ring tattooed on her finger. When Carl believes that things aren't quite working out for the best, she goes out West to get him back. Strangely, she chooses to give him his space and simply follows him as he lives in El Paso. She makes friends with the locals, which include Neil (Visnjic), who instantly likes Joline; Carmen (Velasquez), who becomes Joline's friend; and others. Joline is an odd and not always likable character, but because she is played with such warmth, we choose to follow her along on her weird journey. An amusing film but not a laugh-out-loud comedy. Sharpness and detail are both excellent, but there's a moment or two which suffer from pixelation. Colors are solid, bold, and nicely saturated. Although the score doesn't make much of an impression, it comes through clearly and sounds fine throughout the picture. Surround use is limited, as expected. Dialogue is clear and natural. —AB/DG

Movie: 🎵🎵 **DVD:** 🎵🎵🎵
Buena Vista Home Ent. (cat #18281, UPC 717951004710). Widescreen (1.85:1) anamorphic. Dolby 5.1 Surround. $24.99. Keepcase. *LANG:* English; French. *FEATURES:* Trailer • 30 chapters.
1999 (R) 98m/C Heather Graham, Luke Wilson, Casey Affleck, Goran Visnjic, Patricia Velasquez, Alfonso Arau; *D:* Lisa Krueger; *W:* Lisa Krueger; *C:* Tom Krueger. *AWARDS:* Sundance '00: Cinematog.

Companeros

The Mexican revolution. Shoeshine boy Vasco (Tomas Milian) kills a federale officer and is made a lieutenant by General Mongo (Francisco Bódalo), one of many warring revolutionary warlords. Vasco and Swedish gun salesman Yodlof Pederson (Franco Nero) become unlikely companions when Mongo sends them to Yuma, to liberate authentic revolutionary Xantos (Fernando Rey), a pre-Gandhi preacher of nonviolence imprisoned by American oil interests in the hope of extorting oil leases from him. Some critics credit Sergio Corbucci with "politicizing" the subgenre. The locale has been shifted from a vague "West" to revolutionary Mexico, where violent upheaval reigned from before the turn of the century, well into the 1920s. The conflict is a simple one between virtuous Communists and oppressive generals and capitalists. Corbucci's mood is less cynical, and more inclined toward comedy. The comedy direction is broader than broad, and obvious to the point of playing to juveniles. There is plenty of action in the film, guaranteeing a shootout or stunt every few minutes. None of it is very serious, but things never stay calm for long. The acting is broad and basic. Disc is very, very good looking. The colors are bright, and the wide image is clean and clear. I watched it with

the Italian track, which seemed preferable to the English dub. —GE
Movie: 🎵🎵 ½ **DVD:** 🎵🎵🎵 ½
Anchor Bay (UPC 013131154399). Widescreen (2.35:1) anamorphic. Mono. $24.98. Keepcase. *LANG:* Italian; English. *FEATURES:* "Making of" documentary.
1970 (R) 118m/C *IT SP GE* Franco Nero, Tomas Milian, Jack Palance, Fernando Rey, Iris Berben, Francisco Bodalo; *D:* Sergio Corbucci; *W:* Sergio Corbucci, Massimo De Rita, Arduino (Dino) Maiuri, Fritz Ebert; *C:* Alejandro Ulloa; *M:* Ennio Morricone.

Company Man

Inventive satire about the Bay of Pigs invasion is never quite as funny as it's trying to be. Co-writer and -director McGrath stars as Allan Quimp, a grammar teacher who unwittingly becomes a CIA agent and causes the famous Cold War debacle. His wife (Weaver, misused and made up to look hideous) is really behind it all. The big-name cast seems to be having fun—too much fun, really—but the absurdity is unfocused. Look for Woody Allen as a CIA chief. DVD delivers the sharp image you'd expect from a major (albeit underperforming) studio release. Otherwise sound is O.K. and the disc is unexceptional. —MM
Movie: 🎵🎵 **DVD:** 🎵🎵 ½
Paramount (cat #33797, UPC 097363379-744). Widescreen anamorphic. Dolby Digital Surround Stereo. $29.99. Keepcase. *LANG:* English. *SUB:* English. *FEATURES:* 14 chapters • Trailer.
2001 (PG-13) 81m/C Douglas McGrath, Sigourney Weaver, John Turturro, Anthony LaPaglia, Ryan Phillippe, Denis Leary, Alan Cumming, Woody Allen, Paul Guilfoyle; *D:* Douglas McGrath, Peter Askin; *W:* Douglas McGrath, Peter Askin; *C:* Russell Boyd; *M:* David Lawrence.

Confessions of a Police Captain

Please see review of *Bad Cop Chronicles: Confessions of a Police Captain.*
1972 m/C

Confessions of a Psycho Cat / Hot Blooded Woman

Virginia (Lord) has just had a nervous breakdown so she does not accompany her brother on an African safari. Instead, she chooses three men (including boxer Jake LaMotta!) to hunt down in Manhattan. Yes, this is a bizarrely deranged variation on *The Most Deadly Game.* The second feature is an equally unhinged exploitation flick from 1965, *Hot Blooded Woman.* Both present relatively well-preserved black-and-white images. Some scratches are visible, and the sound on *Hot Blooded* is distorted; *Confessions* displays less damage, but it's pointless to criticize that aspect of the disc. This rare '60s exploitation is recommended to fans of the era and the genre. Nobody else will last five minutes with this low-budget fare. —MM

Movie: 🎵🎵 ½ **DVD:** 🎵🎵🎵
Something Weird Video (cat #ID07995SW-DVD, UPC 014381079920). Full frame. Dolby Digital Mono. $24.99. Keepcase. *LANG:* English. *FEATURES:* 16 chapters • 10 sexploitation trailers • Archival short film "Preface to Life" • Gallery of exploitation art • Radio spots.
1968 69m/B Eileen Lord, Ed Brandt, Frank Grace, Dick Lord, Jake LaMotta; *D:* Herb Stanley; *W:* Bill Boyd; *C:* Paul Guffee.

Confessions of Robert Crumb

The self-portrait of R. Crumb that emerges here is a very levelheaded assessment of a truly unusual artist. It was originally a documentary from the BBC, made seven years before the Terry Zwigoff examination *Crumb,* which more or less picks up where this good set-up leaves off. And it's a great piece of work. Using examples of his artwork, home movies, personal photos, and some rare footage, the underground comic artist tries to explain his middle-class background, the circumstances that turned him into a cult legend, and his rocky life dealing with the accompanying notoriety. Staged and unstaged video footage shows him living with his wife and child, in general pleased with how his life turned out...and amused by the surviving remnants of his previous paranoid self. The film gets off to a rocky start with Crumb and Aline, his long-time wife, addressing the camera directly. For a moment we think we're going to get a poor imitation of David Byrne in *True Stories,* feeding us a line of gab. But it very quickly becomes clear that Crumb is sincere. His on-camera monologues are self-aware, perceptive, and funny. He has no particular axe to grind, nor any inclination to paint a rosy picture of himself. DVD is a simple package: an attractive cover (there's a folding poster of same inside) the disc with the show, a cute animated menu, and chapter stops. That's it; there's no further documentation on the artist or on how the show came to be. It's very satisfying just the same. —GE
Movie: 🎵🎵🎵 ½ **DVD:** 🎵🎵🎵 ½
Home Vision Cinema (cat #CON 100, UPC 037429164129). Full frame. $19.98. Keepcase. *LANG:* English. *FEATURES:* 8 chapters.
1987 55m/C Robert Crumb, Aline Kominsky Crumb; *D:* Mary Dickinson; *W:* Robert Crumb; *C:* Colin Chase, Patti Musicaro.

The Conqueror of Atlantis

See review for *Goliath and the Dragon.*
1965 C *IT* Kirk Morris; *D:* Alfonso Brescia; *W:* Alfonso Brescia.

Conspiracy

On January 20, 1942, key members of the Nazi party and the German government met at a house in the Berlin suburb of Wannsee. The two-hour meeting was

called by Chief of Security Reinhard Heydrich (Branagh). The purpose was to discuss the logistics of the Holocaust. Critical decisions about the extermination of European and Russian Jews had already been made. At Wannsee, the details were settled. One participant took fairly detailed notes. Those are the basis for this film, and for a 1984 German production (not yet available on DVD) that's actually superior in many important ways. It is more low-keyed and quietly more damning, if that's possible. This adaptation by HBO boasts much more polished production values, but many of the characters border on caricature. The leads, including Stanley Tucci as Heydrich's aide Adolf Eichmann, are fine. Image is superior to cablecast. Not much use is made of Surround capabilities (not much is needed). With a serious film like this, some sort of historical commentary or background could have been extremely useful. The extras are all promotional material. —*MM*
Movie: 🎬🎬🎬 ***DVD:*** 🎬🎬🎬
HBO (cat #91783, UPC 026359178320). Widescreen (1.85:1) anamorphic. Dolby Digital Surround; Stereo. $19.98. Snapper. *LANG:* English; French; Spanish. *SUB:* English; French; Spanish. *CAP:* English. *FEATURES:* 18 chapters • Talent files • 2 featurettes.
2001 (R) 96m/C Stanley Tucci, Kenneth Branagh, Colin Firth, Barnaby Kay, Ben Daniels, David Threlfall, Jonathan Coy, Brendan Coyle, Ian McNeice, Owen Teale, Nicholas Woodeson, Ewan Stewart, Kevin McNally, Brian Pettifer; *D:* Frank Pierson; *W:* Loring Mandel; *C:* Stephen Goldblatt.

Conspirators of Pleasure

From noted Czech animator Jan Svankmajer comes a live-action film which displays style over substance. With virtually no dialogue, six characters go through the motions of preparing their bizarre sexual rituals. Full of dark and disturbing imagery, the movie wants to make statements about society, but will be far too shocking and weird for most viewers. *Conspirators of Pleasure* epitomizes "art-house" strangeness and will only be gratifying to the most patient of audiences. The film is presented full-frame and is quite sharp and clear. There is the occasional defect from the source print, and the image is slightly dark at times, but otherwise it's fine. The digital stereo is adequate, as it includes mostly music and sound effects. Also included on the DVD is a 14-minute short by Svankmajer called "Food." This brief film also has little dialogue, but is far more watchable, and the disturbing images here are much more universal. —*ML* *AKA:* Spiklenci Slasti.
Movie: 🎬 ***DVD:*** 🎬🎬
Kino on Video (cat #K146 DVD, UPC 738-32901462). Full frame. Digital Stereo. $29.95. Keepcase. *LANG:* English. *FEATURES:* Bonus film.
1993 83m/C *CZ SI GB* Petr Meissel, Gabriela Wilhelmova, Barbora Hrzanova,

Anna Wetlinska, Jiri Labus, Pavel Novy; *D:* Jan Svankmajer; *W:* Jan Svankmajer; *C:* Miloslav Spala.

The Contaminated Man

An infectious disease expert (Hurt) loses his family to an unknown disease. Now some years later at an "infectious disease laboratory" in a vaguely defined Russia, disgruntled security guard Muller (Weller) has been infected with a deadly pathogen, where one drop of his blood will now kill a person in a matter of seconds. Soon word gets out. The disease expert is called in to investigate and teams up with an American reporter, as Muller is determined to get home to see his wife and son, even if it means infecting the entire Russian population. TV movie dull beyond belief. Poor William Hurt in a long blond wig. Peter Weller getting to do an eccentric Olivier-like turn as the Russian-accented, bald Muller—the only fun in the whole film. Barely routine image transfer and sound. —*MO*
Movie: 🎬 ***DVD:*** 🎬🎬🎬
Studio Home Ent. (cat #7833D, UPC 6581-4978332). Widescreen anamorphic. $24.99. Keepcase. *LANG:* English. *CAP:* English. *FEATURES:* 24 chapters • Trailer.
2001 (R) 98m/C William Hurt, Natascha (Natasha) McElhone, Peter Weller, Katja Woywood, Michael Brandon; *D:* Anthony Hickox; *W:* John Penney; *C:* Bruce Douglas Johnson; *M:* Michael Hoenig.

Contraband

Ship captain (Veidt) held in a contraband inspection port, tracks ship-jumping British spy (Hobson) to fogbound London where they become embroiled in a battle of wits with Nazi spies. A delightful, entertaining comedy-thriller filled with wonderful performances and lively vignettes. Hay Petrie is a delight in two different roles and it's nice to see the usually menacing Veidt in the good-guy role. His talent for dry wit is quite wonderful; too bad it wasn't exploited in other comedies. A smash hit of its time, and well deserved. The U.S. version (entitled *Blackout*) was shortened by several minutes. This disc presents the uncut full-length British version. The image is a tad soft and grainy with milky contrasts. The sound is intelligible but has audible hiss and crackle. Not perfect, but it does the job. —*DG* *AKA:* Blackout.
Movie: 🎬🎬🎬 ***DVD:*** 🎬🎬½
Kino on Video (cat #K211DVD, UPC 738-329021122). Full frame. Mono. $29.95. Keepcase. *LANG:* English. *FEATURES:* 14 chapters • Insert card.
1940 88m/B *GB* Conrad Veidt, Valerie Hobson, Esmond Knight, Hay Petrie, Raymond Lovell, Harold Warrender, Charles Victor; *D:* Michael Powell; *W:* Michael Powell; *C:* Frederick A. (Freddie) Young.

The Convent

Touted by many horror websites as the "next big thing," this fun film fails to deliver on that promise, but is mildly entertain-

ing nonetheless. In 1960, a young woman enters a church, shoots several nuns and a priest, and then torches the place. Jump ahead to the present, as a group of college kids enter the now-condemned convent to perform a fraternity prank. Elsewhere in the dilapidated convent, amateur satanists perform a ritual, releasing the evil spirits held captive in the sanctuary. From this point on, *The Convent* becomes a monster mash, as each character is either possessed, killed, or both. The only hope for the trapped youngsters is the now-grown girl who started all of this in 1960. The film is creatively shot by director Mike Mendez, and the demon makeup is unusual, but the action owes too much to *Night of the Demons 2, The Church,* and the "Goth Talk" skit from *Saturday Night Live.* With a running time of only about 76 minutes, the film is short and sweet, but horror aficionados will feel as if they've seen it all before. The DVD offers a letterboxed transfer of the film, which is clear, but shows some noticeable grain in the daytime shots. The Dolby Digital 5.1 audio track actually offers too much in the way of rear sound, making the dialogue difficult to hear at times. The production commentary track is great fun, demonstrating the camaraderie which emerged during the making of the film. (Box claims that a French 2.0 track is on the DVD, but there is not one.) —*ML*
Movie: 🎬🎬½ ***DVD:*** 🎬🎬🎬½
Studio Home Ent. (cat #VM 7863D, UPC 031398786320). Widescreen letterboxed. Dolby Digital 5.1. $24.99. Keepcase. *LANG:* English. *SUB:* English; Spanish. *CAP:* English. *FEATURES:* Audio commentaries • Deleted scene • Featurette • Trailer • 24 chapters.
2001 (R) 79m/C Adrienne Barbeau, Coolio, Bill Moseley, Joanna Canton, Megahn Perry; *D:* Mike Mendez.

Cool and Crazy

After a slow start, this film becomes an endearing portrait of a half-dozen Norwegian men living in what looks like the coldest place on Earth. With the narrative interrupted by frequent choral performances out in the freezing snow in all kinds of weather, we can't help but love the spirit of these guys. Their sentimentality and sense of humor are infectious. A number of mostly elderly gentlemen in the tiny seacoast town of Berlevag, Norway, consider choir practice the highlight of their week. We hear and see them talk about themselves and their quiet lives. Eventually, they take an extended bus ride to Murmansk, across the border in Russia, to perform. It is what it is and it's not going to appeal to those who can't wait to get back to the latest studio blockbuster. Frankly, it helps to have a few years on you to appreciate the great bunch of men you meet here. It's not that we're given any deep insights into human nature; the picture just lets these guys talk, whether it's making fun of each other over the potato pot, or reminiscing about their checkered pasts. We get a good idea of what life might be like way North of the Arctic Circle, where the only real livelihood is the town's one remaining fish cannery. DVD is a very pleasant show. I can't be sure, but it looks as if it were shot in PAL digital video and converted to NTSC. Sometimes the image is film-like, but the conversion gives it a video look as well. The subtitles are easy to read, with the exception that whoever produced them allowed some far-right letters to be cropped off once in awhile. It's no big flaw. The subs cannot be removed. A little more clumsy are the cuts made to the picture. Sixteen minutes were lopped out for export, and in several places there are edits with flash-frames revealing a field or two of excised material. As I can't see the film becoming more exciting if it were longer (it's on the slow side as it is), I just hope that no transcendent footage was jettisoned. Watching this, you can't tell if the director would be infuriated, or just glad that his show was picked up for U.S. distribution. —GE **AKA:** Heftig og begeistret.

Movie: ♪♪♪ **DVD:** ♪♪
First Run Features (UPC 720229910064). Widescreen (1.66:1) letterboxed. $29.98. Keepcase. *LANG:* Norwegian. *SUB:* English. *FEATURES:* Trailers ● Photos ● Text bios ● Choir roster.
2001 **89m/C** *NO* **D:** Knut Erik Jensen; **C:** Aslaug Holm, Svein Krovel.

Cops

Two-disc collection includes *Bad Cop 1, Bad Cop 2, Narcotic Justice,* and *Street Vengeance.* Please see individual reviews. —MM

Movie: ♪ **DVD:** ♪
BCI-Eclipse (cat #44268-9, UPC 7873644-26898). Full frame. $9.98. Keepcase. *LANG:* English.
2001 **360m/C**

Cops and Robbersons

Bored, dim-witted dad Norman Robberson (Chevy Chase), a TV cop-show junkie, wishes his life had a little more danger and excitement. How lucky for him when hard-nosed cop Jake Stone (Jack Palance) sets up a command post in his house to stake out the mobster living next door (Robert Davi). Predictable plot isn't funny and drags Chase's bumbling idiot persona on for too long (even a scene with an angry cat attacking Chase isn't funny). Diane Wiest and Davi are two bright spots, but their talents are wasted, while Palance does little more than reincarnate his *City Slickers* character. Poor effort from otherwise notable director Michael Ritchie, who had scored twice before with Chase with *Fletch* and *Fletch Lives.* This film receives the standard bare-bones treatment from Columbia TriStar. Both full-frame and widescreen images are clear, but somewhat dark. There is a modest amount of grain visible, but there are some defects from the source print, mostly white spots. The Dolby Surround audio track offers

clear dialogue, and occasional Surround sound effects, such as musical cues and gunfire. Despite "PG" rating, there is some brief nudity. —ML
Movie: ♪♪ **DVD:** ♪♪ ½
Columbia Tristar (cat #05892, UPC 0433-96058927). Widescreen (1.85:1) anamorphic; full frame. Dolby Surround. $19.95. Keepcase. *LANG:* English; French; Spanish; Portuguese. *SUB:* English; French; Spanish; Portuguese; Chinese; Korean; Thai. *CAP:* English. *FEATURES:* Filmographies ● Theatrical trailer ● Bonus trailers ● 28 chapters.
1994 (PG) **93m/C** Chevy Chase, Jack Palance, Dianne Wiest, Robert Davi, Jason James Richter, Fay Masterson, Miko Hughes, Richard Romanus, David Barry Gray; **D:** Michael Ritchie; **W:** Bernie Somers; **C:** Gerry Fisher; **M:** William Ross.

Cops on a Mission

Patrolman Daniel Wu is sent undercover within the Hung Hing triad organization, headed by Eric Tsang. As he's promoted within the organization, he starts an affair with his boss's wife, kills his undercover partner to avoid detection, and leads ruthless raids against rival gangs. Is he still working to bust the triad, or has he become one? Director Marco Mak does a fine job in this crime drama presenting the gradual blurring of the lines between hero and villain. Wu is good in the lead, but Eric Tsang easily walks off with the movie as the noble mob boss. A crisp and lovely image transfer highlights this DVD release from Tai Seng, which bears more than their usual amount of extra features. However, there's a glitch on the disc that sometimes makes a bit of trouble playing the main feature. —BT
Movie: ♪♪♪ **DVD:** ♪♪♪ ½
Tai Seng (cat #03324, UPC 601641033-244). Widescreen letterboxed. Dolby Digital 5.1. $19.95. Keepcase. *LANG:* Cantonese; Mandarin; Vietnamese. *SUB:* English. *FEATURES:* 12 chapters ● Commentary ● Filmographies ● Image gallery ● Trailers.
2001 **102m/C** *HK* Daniel Wu, Eric Tsang, Kwan Suki, David Lee, Frankie Ng; **D:** Marco Mak; **C:** Tony Miu; **M:** Lincoln Lo.

Cor, Blimey!

From the 1950s through the '70s, the British film industry produced a smashingly successful series of sex romp comedies called the *Carry On* films. The lead players in most of them were Sid James and Barbara Windsor, who had an on-again off-again relationship despite Windsor's marriage to famous gangster Ronnie Kray. This made-for-TV film tells their story with amusing re-creations of the period, lively behind-the-scenes trickery, and a painfully poignant ending. Spiro is note-perfect as Windsor, and the rest of the cast is terrific. Windsor appears herself in the heart-tugging epilogue. Important people like Jim Dale and Gerald Thomas and Peter Rogers (creators of the *Carry On* films) are conspicuously absent and the Krays never appear. A worthwhile portrait of bawdy

times past, told in a very personal way. The disc is bright, colorful, and sharp. The image is slightly grainy but digital noise is scarce. The sound (mostly dialogue) is excellent. —DG
Movie: ♪♪♪ **DVD:** ♪♪♪
BFS Video (cat #30124-D, UPC 0668053-01247). Widescreen letterboxed. Dolby Stereo. $19.98. Keepcase. *LANG:* English. *FEATURES:* 12 chapters.
2000 **96m/C** *GB* Geoffrey Hutchings, Samantha Spiro, Adam Godley, Barbara Windsor; **D:** Terry Johnson; **W:** Terry Johnson; **C:** Paul Wheeler; **M:** Barrington Pheloung.

Corky Romano

Halfwit black sheep of the family Corky Romano (Kattan) has been recruited by his two older brothers (Berg, Penn), mysterious henchman Leo Corrigan (Ward), and "Pops" (Falk), Corky's Mafia head father, for a special job. Tired of being spied upon by the FBI, the Romano clan decides to even the playing field by putting their own informant on the inside of the Bureau. Corky's main task is to retrieve the FBI file being used to try his father, but as easy and straightforward as the job appears from the outside, for Corky it is almost impossible. The comedy adds another notch in the belt of SNL players venturing onto the silver screen, and while this film has a couple of shining moments of decent laughs, overall the film lacks anything that would make it something worth investing a lot of time or money in. The DVD features a clean transfer with good color quality and no noticeable distortions or ghosting. Surround is underutilized and does not have a lot to offer from the rear speakers, however the overall sound quality is decent. Extras include extended scenes, which do not add much to the bone rating. —EL
Movie: ♪♪ **DVD:** ♪♪ ½
Buena Vista Home Ent. (cat #24024, UPC 786936165449). Widescreen (1.85:1) anamorphic. Dolby 5.1 Surround Sound. $29.99. Keeper. *LANG:* English. *SUB:* French; Spanish. *CAP:* English. *FEATURES:* "Corky Romano: All Access" featurette ● Extended scenes ● 16 chapters.
2001 (PG-13) **85m/C** Chris Kattan, Vinessa Shaw, Peter Falk, Peter Berg, Christopher Penn, Fred Ward, Richard Roundtree, Matthew Glave, Dave Sheridan, Roger Fan; **D:** Rob Pritts; **W:** David Garrett, Jason Ward; **C:** Steven Bernstein; **M:** Randy Edelman.

Cornbread, Earl & Me

Superficial melodrama is notable mostly for the presence of a very young Laurence Fishburne III. The story revolves around the murder of a high school basketball star by cops who take him for a rapist, and the repercussions of that act. Sound is no better than it's ever been. The soft, grainy image is really no better than a widescreen VHS tape. —MM
Movie: ♪♪ **DVD:** ♪♪

MGM Home Ent. (cat #1002581, UPC 027616867827). Widescreen (1.85:1) anamorphic. Dolby Digital Mono. $14.98. Keepcase. *LANG:* English. *SUB:* French; Spanish. *CAP:* English. *FEATURES:* 16 chapters ☛ Trailer.
1975 (R) 95m/C Moses Gunn, Rosalind Cash, Bernie Casey, Tierre Turner, Madge Sinclair, Keith Wilkes, Antonio Fargas, Laurence "Larry" Fishburne; *D:* Joseph Manduke; *W:* Leonard Lamensdorf; *C:* Jules Brenner; *M:* Donald Byrd.

The Corpse Vanishes

Please see review for *Bela Lugosi DVD Double Feature: The Corpse Vanishes / Invisible Ghost.*
Movie: 🎜🎜½
1942 64m/B Bela Lugosi, Luana Walters, Tristram Coffin, Elizabeth Russell, Vince Barnett, Joan Barclay, Angelo Rossitto; *D:* Wallace Fox.

Corrupt

Please see review of *Bad Cop Chronicles 2: Corrupt.*
1984 m/C

The Cotton Club

In 1928, jazzman Dixie Dwyer (Gere) makes the mistake of falling in love with Vera Cicero (Lane), gangster Dutch Schultz's (Remar) moll. At the same time, tap dancer Sandman Williams (Hines) falls in love with Lea Rose Oliver (McKee), who can pass for white. If director Coppola and writer Puzo don't re-create the success of *The Godfather,* they do put together an entertaining and beautifully filmed story. The print used for this DVD is generally clean and free of defects or mars, but slight registration errors are evident in some portions of the film, causing the image to waver slightly. No edge-enhancement is evident, which gives the transfer a rather natural look. Coppola has used a noticeably muted color palette for this film that makes strong use of shadows and highlights. The DVD restores this flair perfectly, creating bold blacks and well-delineated shadows that also carry enough image information to create a highly detailed picture. Flesh tones are natural and no compression artifacts are visible. John Barry's jazz score is perfectly represented here with a wide sound field that creates an intimate atmosphere of a bustling and busy club. Surround usage is good throughout. The audio is free of distortion or sibilance and has a very good frequency response. —*MM/GH*
Movie: 🎜🎜🎜 **DVD:** 🎜🎜🎜
MGM Home Ent. (cat #1002205, UPC 027616864369). Widescreen (1.85:1) anamorphic. Dolby Digital 5.1 Surround Stereo; Dolby Digital Mono. $24.99. Keepcase. *LANG:* English; French. *SUB:* French; Spanish. *CAP:* English. *FEATURES:* 16 chapters.
1984 (R) 121m/C Diane Lane, Richard Gere, Gregory Hines, Lonette McKee, Bob Hoskins, Fred Gwynne, James Remar,

Nicolas Cage, Lisa Jane Persky, Allen (Goorwitz) Garfield, Gwen Verdon, Joe Dallesandro, Jennifer Grey, Tom Waits, Diane Venora; *D:* Francis Ford Coppola; *W:* William Kennedy, Mario Puzo, Francis Ford Coppola; *C:* Stephen Goldblatt; *M:* John Barry. *AWARDS: NOM:* Oscars '84: Art Dir./Set Dec., Film Editing.

Count Yorga, Vampire

A European vampire (Quarry) relocates to trendy L.A., sets up shop as a spiritualist and sets about gathering a harem. The film is a veritable postcard of the late 1960s. The script and the acting are more polished than the production values, but the location work is typical of the time. Quarry is properly seductive and regal, though his wardrobe looks like it came from Liberace's garage sale. There's little DVD can do with the image. It's as dark and grainy as it was at the drive-in so long ago. But this version of the film adds 3 minutes to the previous running time of 90 minutes and the "PG" rating has been upgraded to "PG-13." —*MM AKA:* The Loves of Count Yorga, Vampire.
Movie: 🎜🎜½ **DVD:** 🎜🎜
MGM Home Ent. (cat #1002337, UPC 027616865564). Widescreen (1.85:1) anamorphic. Dolby Digital Mono. $19.98. Keepcase. *LANG:* English; French. *SUB:* French; Spanish. *CAP:* English. *FEATURES:* 16 chapters ☛ Trailer.
1970 (PG-13) 93m/C Robert Quarry, Roger Perry, Michael Murphy, Michael Macready, Donna Anders, Judith Lang, Marsha Jordan, Julie Conners, Paul Hansen; *D:* Bob Kelljan; *W:* Bob Kelljan; *C:* Arch Archambault; *M:* Bill Marx.

Courage Under Fire

Suffering crippling doubts about his own conduct in the Gulf War, Col. Nat Serling (Washington) receives an assignment to validate a medal of honor that could be awarded to a Karen Walden (Ryan), a woman who gave her life to save her crew. As Serling interviews the remaining crew members (Damon, Phillips) he is told conflicting stories about Walden and her leadership capabilities. It's up to Serling to put all the puzzle pieces together. We are shown the events as told by each person (à la *Rashomon*), and the flashbacks change to reflect the characters' points of view, revealing just a little bit more than the previous tale. Washington's performance is detailed, complex, and emotional. Although she's mostly cast in comedies, Ryan really does well in this dramatic role. This is an intelligent, moving, powerful picture and one of the better dramas in recent years. Deakins's excellent cinematography provides a bit of a washed-out, bleak look to the battle scenes and a more natural one during the current sequences. Sharpness and detail are both excellent; the DVD provides crisp, clear, bright images that are natural looking and free of all but a few very minor flaws. There are a few instances prone to pixelation, but these are too brief to be distract-

ing. The colors look accurate throughout. Flesh tones also are natural. Surrounds play a heavy factor in the battle scenes; these scenes are so enveloping and will have you ducking in your living room. Bass during the more intense sequences is powerful and deep. The impressive audio is superior to that on the theatrical screening I viewed. Although the differences between them are slight, the DTS track is slightly more dynamic. On the commentary track, director Zwick discusses the actors in the film and how they went about building characters and giving their performances. He provides an interesting analysis for many of the performances of the film. Although he seems to lose steam a quarter of the way through the film, Zwick provides some very interesting comments. It would have been better if he had been paired up with another person involved in the production to provide a fuller, more involved analysis. The featurette is mainly promotional, offering interviews and some behind-the-scenes footage. —*AB/DG*
Movie: 🎜🎜🎜 ½ **DVD:** 🎜🎜🎜 ½
20th Century Fox (UPC 24543010821). Widescreen anamorphic. Dolby Surround 5.1. $19.98. Keepcase. *LANG:* English; French. *SUB:* English; Spanish. *CAP:* English. *FEATURES:* Commentary ☛ "Making of" featurette.
1996 (R) 120m/C Denzel Washington, Meg Ryan, Matt Damon, Lou Diamond Phillips, Michael Moriarty, Scott Glenn, Bronson Pinchot, Seth Gilliam, Sean Astin, Regina Taylor, Tim Guinee, Ken Jenkins, Kathleen Widdoes, Zeljko Ivanek, Tim Ransom, Ned Vaughn; *D:* Edward Zwick; *W:* Patrick Sheane Duncan; *C:* Roger Deakins; *M:* James Horner.

Cousins

An American remake of *Cousin, Cousine,* in which two distant cousins-by-marriage meet at a wedding and, due to their respective spouses' infidelities, fall into each other's arms. A gentle love story with a humorous and biting look at the foibles of extended families. Nicely defined colors highlight an above average video transfer, though some darker hues do display a slight loss of clarity. The soundtrack is superior to the video transfer. Dialogue is crisp and clear and music is reproduced well. Where the disc falters is in the underutilization of ambient sound effects, which makes the 5.1 mix simply good. —*MJT*
Movie: 🎜🎜🎜 ½ **DVD:** 🎜🎜 ½
Paramount (cat #32181, UPC 0973632-18142). Widescreen (1.85:1) anamorphic. Dolby Digital 5.1 Surround; Dolby Digital Surround; Dolby Digital Stereo. $24.99. Keepcase. *LANG:* English; French. *SUB:* English. *FEATURES:* 16 chapters.
1989 (PG-13) 110m/C Isabella Rossellini, Sean Young, Ted Danson, William L. Petersen, Norma Aleandro, Lloyd Bridges, Keith Coogan; *D:* Joel Schumacher; *W:* Stephen Metcalfe; *C:* Ralf Bode; *M:* Angelo Badalamenti.

Cowboy

Western roundup based on the memoirs of tenderfoot-turned-cowpoke Frank Harris. Harris (Lemmon) is a Chicago hotel clerk who meets cattle boss Tom Reece (Ford), who's in the city on business. Losing his money in a poker game, Reece reluctantly accepts a loan from Harris in exchange for a piece of his cattle business. So Harris and Reece hit the dusty trail on a cattle drive that takes them into Mexico where Harris falls in love with Maria (Kashfi), the daughter of a wealthy rancher, and gradually turns from city slicker into hardened trail boss. Good cast, no fuss. Right out of the gate, this oater's DVD presentation is a big disappointment—it's full frame and for the most part lacking any sharpness. Add to that the excessive grain that comes into play during almost any daylight scene, and it's quite a workout on the eyes to get through this one. The good news is that the colors are actually pretty good with great fleshtones and not much bleed. Most likely, there wasn't much Columbia could have done about the mono sound, but when combined with the poor picture quality, the total lack of dynamics and fidelity are more aggravating than they need be. Other than *Cowboy's* trailer and a couple other "bonus" trailers, there are no supplementals. Even at half its $19.95 prices, this disc would be no bargain. —JO
Movie: 🎬🎬🎬 **DVD:** 🎬
Columbia Tristar (cat #07874, UPC 0433-96078741). Full frame. Dolby Digital Mono. $19.95. Keepcase. *LANG:* English. *SUB:* English; Spanish; French; Portuguese. *CAP:* English. *FEATURES:* 28 chapters • Theatrical trailer.
1958 92m/C Jack Lemmon, Glenn Ford, Anna Kashfi, Brian Donlevy, Dick York, Victor Manuel Mendoza, Richard Jaeckel, King Donovan; **D:** Delmer Daves; **W:** Edmund H. North; **C:** Charles Lawton Jr.; **M:** George Duning. *AWARDS: NOM:* Oscars '58: Film Editing.

The Cranes Are Flying

When her lover goes off to fight during WWII, a girl is seduced by his cousin. Touching love story is free of politics. Like many Criterion discs, the video transfer is excellent. Blacks are extremely sharp, and lighter hues are as equally crisp and impressive. The soundtrack is just as flawless. One small shortcoming of the disc, however, is the curious lack of extras. It would have been nice to hear a film scholar or the like discuss the film's place in history on a commentary track. —MJT
AKA: Letyat Zhuravit.
Movie: 🎬🎬🎬 ½ **DVD:** 🎬🎬🎬 ½
Criterion (cat #CRA040, UPC 0374291680-28). Full frame. Dolby Digital Mono. $29.95. Keepcase. *LANG:* Russian. *SUB:* English. *FEATURES:* 21 chapters.
1957 91m/B RU Tatyana Samoilova, Alexei Batalov, Vasily Merkuryev, A. Shvorin; **D:** Mikhail Kalatozov; **W:** Viktor Rozov; **C:** Sergei Urusevsky; **M:** Moisej Vajnberg. *AWARDS:* Cannes '58: Film.

Crash & Byrnes

Video premiere is a run-of-the-mill action picture. Young hotshot DEA agent Roman Byrnes (Ellis) is teamed with ex-CIA agent "Crash" Riley (writer Larson) to save the world from a virus attack by terrorist Lissette Martineau (Pacula). Lots of stuff blows up, and many bullets are fired. Beyond some aliasing and flashing within parallel lines, full-frame DVD image ranges between very good and excellent. Sound is fine. —MM
Movie: 🎬🎬 **DVD:** 🎬🎬
Pioneer Ent. (cat #PEAD-11547D, UPC 013-023154797). Full frame. Dolby Digital Surround. $19.98. Keepcase. *LANG:* English. *FEATURES:* 16 chapters.
1999 92m/C CA Wolf Larson, Greg Ellis, Joanna Pacula, Steven Williams, Sandra Lindquist, Terry Chen, Melanie Angel; **D:** Jon Hess; **W:** Wolf Larson; **C:** Anthony C. Metchie; **M:** Ken Williams.

The Crater Lake Monster

This "monster-mash" film from the late '70s tries to re-capture some of the innocent fun of the creature films of the 1950s, but fails miserably. After a meteor falls into Crater Lake, a dinosaur emerges from the water and begins to eat tourists and locals. The monster was created by stop-motion effects master Dave Allen, but this clearly isn't his best work. The beast is quite fake looking and the atrocious optical effects which put man and beast in the same shot don't help. None of the "actors" in the film appear to be professionals and the "plot" is simply one scene after another of characters finding reasons to be standing by the lake, so that they may be eaten by the monster. Shockingly, a subplot concerning a criminal on the run is thrown in, but it doesn't add to the film. Those who love "so bad it's good" movies will have a field day and one can't help but wonder how this one never wound up on *Mystery Science Theater 3000*. The film is presented in a full-frame format on this DVD and gets a better transfer than it deserves. The image is sharp and clear, although this does reveal some flaws in the source print. The colors are quite good, especially the occasional splashes of blood. The Dolby Stereo soundtrack offers clear dialogue, but there are some audible clicks and pops on the track. —ML
Movie: woof **DVD:** 🎬🎬
Rhino (cat #976063-2, UPC 6034976063-20). Full frame. Digital Mono. $9.95. Keepcase. *LANG:* English. *FEATURES:* Trailer • 12 chapters.
1977 (PG) 85m/C Richard Cardella, Glenn Roberts, Mark Siegel, Bob Hyman, Kacey Cobb; **D:** William R. Stromberg; **W:** Richard Cardella; **C:** Paul Gentry.

The Crawling Eye

Paranormal scientific investigator Alan Brooks (Tucker) comes to the Trollenberg in the Alps to investigate strange killings of climbers up on the mountain's cloudy slopes. The facts parallel an earlier experience in South America where extraterrestrials were theorized to be involved. Also drawn to the mountain is the sister team of Sarah (Jayne) and Anne (Munro) Pilgrim. Anne's clairvoyance is receiving psychic mindstorms from the Trollenberg mountain, and she's thrown into a state of near-hysteria by visions of climbers being menaced by horrible things coming out of the darkness. DVD is a great treat, as it presents the first watchable version of the movie since its short theatrical run in 1958. I'd seen it on television throughout the '60s in splicey, murky prints that always started with the Trollenberg valley out of focus, and with a big tear in the first shot. Come the '80s, it disappears from TV, to be replaced by awful-looking video and laser versions, with the same poor picture, the same flaws. Cannon Films in 1988 had a video transfer in its library (oh boy!), but popping it into the tape deck revealed that they'd obviously just duped an even worse copy to pirate in some territory or another. The "Widescreen European Edition" herein is actually the original *The Trollenberg Terror*, complete with the U.K. Certificate X card, "Eros Films" logo, and a couple of instances of restored frames, showing a bit more when decapitated bodies are pulled out from under bunks, and the like. These moments had had big sloppy splices in the American cut. The sound is also greatly improved from the muffled and warbly 16mm prints that were all I had seen before. Finally, the widescreen enhancement reveals an image as sharp as a tack, fully demonstrating that the film was carefully photographed, with superior atmospherics in many scenes. Besides the beautiful close-ups of Janet Munro's anguished eyes, we do see the mechanics behind most of the effects, and the various dodges used to make a location Alpine story solely on English sound stages. The miniatures don't look any smaller, but there are wires on view where none are wanted—the sort of thing that I readily forgive, but don't necessarily expect you to. —GE **AKA:** The Trollenberg Terror.
Movie: 🎬🎬🎬 **DVD:** 🎬🎬🎬
Image Ent. (cat #ID8701CODVD, UPC 014381870121). Widescreen (1.66:1) anamorphic. Dolby Digital Mono. $19.98. Keepcase. *LANG:* English. *FEATURES:* 16 chapters • Liner notes by David Del Valle • Trailer.
1958 87m/B GB Forrest Tucker, Laurence Payne, Janet Munro, Jennifer Jayne, Warren Mitchell; **D:** Quentin Lawrence; **W:** Jimmy Sangster; **M:** Stanley Black.

The Crawling Hand

Mild-mannered student Paul (Peter Breck) turns into a raccoon-eyed homicidal zombie after he and his Swedish girlfriend Marte (Sirry Steffen) find the hand of an astronaut on the beach. With Gilligan's "Skipper" Alan Hale as the Sheriff and the Rivingtons' "The Bird Is the Word" on the soundtrack, the comic side is complete. But toward the end, Breck manages to make his character sympathetic. DVD image and sound are not much of an improvement over VHS tape. Light static is audible throughout and one shirt pattern goes into black-and-white psychedelic flashing. *—MM*

Movie: 🎵🎵🎵 **DVD:** 🎵🎵 ½
Rhino (cat #R2 971484, UPC 603497148-424). Full frame. $14.98. Snapper. *LANG:* English. *FEATURES:* 12 chapters.
1963 98m/B Kent Taylor, Peter Breck, Rod Lauren, Sirry Steffen, Alan Hale Jr., Richard Arlen, Allison Hayes, Arline Judge; *D:* Herbert L. Strock; *W:* Herbert L. Strock; *C:* Willard Van der Veer.

crazy/beautiful

Nicely realistic tale of teen love, angst, and dreams uses a little role reversal. Nicole (Dunst) is a white girl from a privileged family. Her father is a congressman, but her mother's suicide has given her a short life of misery and mental illness resulting in wild and self-destructive behavior. Enter Carlos (Hernandez) and it's true love at first sight. Carlos is from a tight-knit Mexican family that is placing all their hopes on his talent and intelligence. He rides the bus two hours each way to attend the school that Nicole spends all her time trying to ditch. He's an A student, on the football team, and madly in love with Nicole. As she tries to spiral down, he desperately tries to pull her up. The film is unflinching in its portrayal of modern youth and faulty parenting, but it also allows the characters to be empathetic and hopeful. Without falling prey to clichéd writing or performances, the story manages to give the power of true love a good name, whether it is between man and woman or parent and child. Dunst and newcomer Hernandez are perfectly cast as the lovers from opposite sides of the tracks who blindly find their way through the wreckage of Nicole's life to some middle ground. Beautifully lit and directed, the disc looks great and the sound is very good. *—CA*

Movie: 🎵🎵🎵 **DVD:** 🎵🎵🎵 ½
Buena Vista Home Ent. (cat #23951, UPC 786936164725). Widescreen (1.85:1) anamorphic. Dolby Digital 5.1; DTS 5.1. $29.99. Keepcase. *LANG:* English. *SUB:* French; Spanish. *CAP:* English. *FEATURES:* 14 chapters • "Making of" featurette • Deleted scenes • Commentary: Dunst, Stockwell.
2001 (PG-13) 99m/C Kirsten Dunst, Jay Hernandez, Taryn Manning, Rolando Molina, Bruce Davison, Lucinda Jenney, Soledad St. Hilaire; *D:* John Stockwell; *W:* Phil Hay, Matt Manfredi; *C:* Shane Hurlbut; *M:* Paul Haslinger.

Crazy Horse and Custer: "The Untold Story"

Long before Little Big Horn, two legendary enemies find themselves trapped together in deadly Blackfoot territory. George Armstrong Custer and Crazy Horse are forced

to form a volatile alliance in the struggle against the murderous tribe. History takes a back seat to Hollywood fantasies. Disc appears to have been made from substandard elements. Colors are faded; dark areas are harsh. Title is also available as part of "The Wild West" set. *—MM*

Movie: 🎵 **DVD:** 🎵 ½
BCI-Eclipse (cat #44056-9, UPC 7378644-05695). Full frame. $9.98. Keepcase. *LANG:* English. *FEATURES:* 6 chapters • "Have You Got Any Castles" cartoon • Movie trivia game • DVD dictionary • DVD-ROM features.
1990 (R) 120m/C Slim Pickens, Wayne Maunder, Mary Ann Mobley, Michael Dante.

Creature Comforts

This disc compiles animators Nick Park and Peter Lord's (of *Wallace and Gromit* fame) early shorts. The Oscar-winning "Creature Comforts" is the most popular, focusing on a group of zoo animals who comment on the living conditions, providing some very funny remarks. "Wat's Pig" is the story of two brothers—one raised by royalty, the other by a pig. "Not without My Handbag" is the tale of a woman who won't go to hell without her favorite handbag. Those not used to the duo's more comedic efforts might be a bit surprised by these shorts. Some of them, such as "Handbag," might be a bit scary for younger kids. "Adam" rounds out the set. The four shorts aren't always humorous, but it's still amazing to see the early work from Park and Lord. Although these certainly aren't nearly as complex as *Chicken Run* in terms of the claymation, they are very impressive. The four shorts are presented differently, and are varied in terms of quality. "Creature Comforts" generally looks very good, although it's a bit soft at times, with a couple of marks on the print used. "Wat's Pig" fares about as well, with rich colors and good sharpness, although a bit of grain is visible. The last two are full-frame presentations and generally look fine. The four shorts are either presented in stereo or mono ("Creature Comforts"). Aside from sounding a little bit harsh at times, the audio is clear and acceptable. *—AB/DG*

Movie: 🎵🎵🎵 **DVD:** 🎵🎵 ½
Image Ent. (UPC 014381010626). Widescreen (1.66:1) letterboxed; (1.85:1) anamorphic. Stereo. $9.99. Snapper. *LANG:* English. *FEATURES:* 4 chapters.
1990 33m/C *D:* Nick Park.

Creature from the Black Lagoon

An anthropological expedition in the Amazon stumbles upon the Gill-Man, a prehistoric humanoid fish monster who takes a fancy to fetching Adams, a coed majoring in "science," but the humans will have none of it. Originally filmed in 3-D, this was one of the first movies to sport top-of-the-line underwater photography and remains one of the most enjoyable monster movies ever made. This isn't the best of Universal's Classic Monster Collection, but it'll

do. Though there are more print flaws than in the older titles in the series, the transfer itself is near excellent with good blacks and graytones with only the underwater sequences proving to be a bit sub-par and occasionally not so sharp. Overall, an easy-to-watch DVD. The sound has the expected tinny quality, but is certainly crisp enough. Film historian Tom Weaver provides his usual in-depth commentary. *—JO*

Movie: 🎵🎵🎵 **DVD:** 🎵🎵🎵
Universal Studios (cat #20760, UPC 025192076022). Full frame. Dolby Digital Mono. $24.98. Keepcase. *LANG:* English. *SUB:* French. *CAP:* English. *FEATURES:* 18 chapters • Theatrical trailers • Talent files • Production notes • Production photos • Commentary: film historian Tom Weaver • "Back to the Black Lagoon."
1954 79m/B Richard Carlson, Julie Adams, Richard Denning, Antonio Moreno, Whit Bissell, Nestor Paiva, Ricou Browning, Ben Chapman, Bernie Gozier; *D:* Jack Arnold; *W:* Arthur Ross, Harry Essex; *C:* William E. Snyder, Charles S. Welbourne; *M:* Hans J. Salter, Henry Mancini.

Creatures from the Abyss

Horror fans looking for something a bit different should check out this Italian feature. After being stranded on a raft, five young people board an abandoned yacht. The boat is an oceanographic research vessel where very strange fish were being studied. The five youngsters decide to make the yacht their party-place, but things get nasty once they realize that killer fish are running wild on board the ship. As if that weren't bad enough, exposure to these aquatic nasties causes humans to mutate into monsters! On the surface (?!), this looks like the average Italian thriller, with bad acting, atrocious dubbing, and lackluster pacing. But the odd plot concerning mutant plankton ("Plankton" being the film's original title) and the fact that *Creatures from the Abyss* consistently crosses the line with its disturbing special effects make it stand out. The timid will find the last act revolting, but those looking for a throwback to the gore-soaked '80s will love it. An adequate anamorphic widescreen transfer is offered on this DVD, providing a sharp picture that unfortunately shows some defects from the source print. Considering the lack of video quality which these films usually produce, the disc looks fine. The mono soundtrack offers clear dialogue, but little else. *—ML* **AKA:** Plankton.

Movie: 🎵🎵 ½ **DVD:** 🎵🎵🎵
Media Blasters (cat #SSDVD-0106, UPC 631595010695). Widescreen (1.85:1) anamorphic. Dolby Digital Mono. $24.95. Keepcase. *LANG:* English. *FEATURES:* Still gallery • Director interview • Bonus trailers • 11 chapters.
1994 86m/C *IT*

Creepin'

The 'Hood has its very own slasher, as Shameeka searches out victims who

haven't paid child support. This painfully long movie is nothing more than marginally related sketch pieces, and another parody of slasher movies that makes both *Scary Movies* look really funny. The production values of this film are so low that even on DVD it looks and sounds like a home movie. —*BG*

Movie: woof **DVD:** ♪
York Ent. (cat #YPD-1109, UPC 75027311-0929). Full frame. Dolby 5.1. $14.99. Keepcase. *LANG:* English. *SUB:* Spanish. *FEATURES:* 24 chapters • Trailers.
2001 122m/C Tim Greene, Denny Live, Michael Shaun, Bobby Holiday; ***D:*** Tim Greene; ***W:*** Tim Greene; ***C:*** Tim Greene.

Cremains

Anthology film centers on a mortician (Chester Delacruz), who is being investigated for cremating two bodies at once. As he is questioned by an unseen panel of inquisitors, who ask if he's ever dealt with the supernatural in his profession, he relates three stories. In the first tale, a young woman (Wanda Plimmer) makes the mistake of driving through a small town famous for its ritual sacrifices. In the next story, a serial killer (Chris Williams) captures a hitchhiker and then the mind-games begin. The third story features a woman (Kimberly Lynn Cole) who seeks out the help of a horror author (R.W. Smith), as she's convinced that a female vampire is after her. The final segment comes back to the story of the mortician and deals with the macabre results of his double-cremation. The film is a great example of how one must take the good with the bad when dealing with low-budget efforts. The good here are the stories themselves. While they aren't incredibly original, they all have that "urban legend" feel to them which makes them easily accessible. The bad lies in the fact that at 107 minutes, it is way too long, and all of the segments feel padded. Also, there are multiple problems with the audio, and the dialogue is often out of sync with the actor's mouths. This independent production isn't perfect, but it's actually better than some studio horror films released lately. —*ML*

Movie: ♪♪½ **DVD:** ♪♪½
BCI-Eclipse (cat #9505, UPC 6123859505-99). Widescreen (1.78:1) letterboxed. Dolby Digital Surround. $19.95. Keepcase. *LANG:* English. *FEATURES:* Deleted scenes • Outtakes • Trailers.
2000 107m/C Chester Delacruz, Wanda Plimmer, Chris(topher) Williams, Kimberly Lynn Cole, R.W. Smith; ***D:*** Steve Sessions; ***W:*** Steve Sessions.

Cries and Whispers

The greatest American success by the acclaimed Swedish filmmaker Bergman is the story of three sisters—one of whom is dying a protracted, horrible death of tuberculosis. The setting is rural Sweden, more than 100 years ago, and a series of flashbacks and dream sequences are among

the storytelling methods utilized by the director. As Agnes (Andersson) slowly succumbs to her disease, she is cared for by her two sisters and a servant. One sister is sexually repressed, while the other is promiscuous, but each is too wrapped up in her own life to be of much help to their diminishing sibling. Only the devoted maid Anna (Sylway) seems capable of ministering to Agnes's spiritual and physical pain. The imagery is beautiful, earning cinematographer Sven Nykvist a deserved Oscar for his effort. Although many studios choose not to provide anamorphic enhancement to 1.66:1 ratio films, this DVD does feature such enhancement—a boon to the widescreen crowd. The image, while occasionally exhibiting slight imperfections of the source, is quite good, and the monaural Swedish soundtrack is just fine. English subtitles are optional. There is an English-dubbed soundtrack as well, although dubbing is pooh-poohed by the purists. An in-depth, 52-minute interview with Bergman and his collaborator Erland Josephson focuses not just on this film, but on the director's storied career. It was originally broadcast on Swedish Television. —*MB* **AKA:** Viskingar Och Rop.

Movie: ♪♪♪ **DVD:** ♪♪♪
Criterion (cat #CRI070, UPC 037429-156322). Widescreen (1.66:1) anamorphic. Dolby Digital 1.0. $29.95. Keepcase. *LANG:* Swedish; English. *CAP:* English. *FEATURES:* 18 chapters • Interview with Bergman and collaborator Erland Josephson • Optional English-dubbed soundtrack.
1972 (R) 91m/C *SW* Harriet Andersson, Ingrid Thulin, Liv Ullmann, Kary Sylway, Erland Josephson, Henning Moritzen; ***D:*** Ingmar Bergman; ***W:*** Ingmar Bergman; ***C:*** Sven Nykvist. *AWARDS:* Oscars '73: Cinematog.; Natl. Bd. of Review '73: Director (Bergman); N.Y. Film Critics '72: Actress (Ullmann), Director (Bergman), Film, Screenplay; Natl. Soc. Film Critics '72: Cinematog., Screenplay; *NOM:* Oscars '73: Costume Des., Director (Bergman), Picture, Story & Screenplay.

Crime Stoppers, Vol. 2

Please see individual reviews of *Fog Island, The Black Raven,* and *Dick Tracy vs. Cueball.*

Movie: ♪♪ **DVD:** ♪ ½
Triton Multimedia (cat #TDVD9166, UPC 017078916621). Full frame. Dolby Digital Mono. $19.98. Keepcase. *LANG:* English. *FEATURES:* Popeye cartoon • Radio program.
2001 199m/C

Crimes of Passion [2]

Director Ken Russell is fearless. I do not believe that this movie could be made today. Joanna Crane (Kathleen Turner) is a sportswear designer by day and a $50/a trick hooker by night. John Laughlin is married to a frigid woman (Annie Potts) and finds sexual release with Turner. Anthony Perkins plays a priest who makes Norman Bates look like a choirboy. This one isn't

for the kids. It's uncensored and depicts sex acts that many will find repulsive. The only thing that keeps this movie from being completely stellar is a soundtrack by Rick Wakeman ("Yes") that just plain sucks. DVD is loaded with cool stuff, not found on Anchor Bay's earlier release. The commentary with Russell and writer/producer Barry Sandler is eye-opening, going so far as to explain why certain works of art were on the wall of Turner's crib. Deleted scenes weren't remastered, which was a bummer, and they really don't add anything. Movie is super crisp and sound is good. —*DE*

Movie: ♪♪♪ ½ **DVD:** ♪♪♪
Anchor Bay (cat #DV11393, UPC 131311-3939). Widescreen (1.85:1) anamorphic. Dolby Digital 5.1 Mono. $15.98. Keepcase. *LANG:* English. *FEATURES:* 29 chapters • Commentary: Ken Russell, writer/producer Barry Sandler • Deleted scenes with commentary by Sandler • Theatrical trailer.
1984 101m/C Kathleen Turner, Anthony Perkins, Annie Potts, John Laughlin, Bruce Davison, Norman Burton; ***D:*** Ken Russell; ***W:*** Barry Sandler; ***C:*** Dick Bush; ***M:*** Rick Wakeman. *AWARDS:* L.A. Film Critics '84: Actress (Turner).

The Crimson Rivers

Two crime threads become one in this intricate French thriller. Commisairre Niemans (Reno) is investigating a series of gruesome murders in which each victim represents a clue to the next. Miles away, Kerkerian (Cassel) is assigned to the desecration of a young girl's grave. When his investigation leads to Niemans's next victim, the two combine forces to uncover a bizarre plot of kidnapping and genetic experimentation. An intelligent script (from Grange's own novel) and fabulous editing build the suspense very well. A clear transfer, excellent Surround sound, and informative extras compliment the movie. The one problem with the DVD is the commentary track, which is in French and, without knowledge of the language, is useless. —*DRL* **AKA:** Les Rivieres Pourpres.

Movie: ♪♪♪ **DVD:** ♪♪♪
Columbia Tristar (cat #6593, UPC 04339-6065932). Widescreen (2.35:1) anamorphic. Dolby 5.1 Surround; Dolby Digital Stereo. $24.95. Keepcase. *LANG:* French; English. *SUB:* English; French. *CAP:* English. *FEATURES:* Commentary: director & cast • "The Investigation" documentary • 3 production featurettes • Filmographies • Production notes • Trailer • 28 chapters.
2001 (R) 105m/C *FR* Jean Reno, Vincent Cassel, Nadia Fares, Dominique Sanda, Laurent Avare, Jean-Pierre Cassel, Didier Flamand; ***D:*** Mathieu Kassovitz; ***W:*** Mathieu Kassovitz, Jean-Christophe Grange; ***C:*** Thierry Arbogast; ***M:*** Bruno Coulais.

Crocodile Dundee

New York newspaper reporter Sue Charlton (Kozlowski) is assigned to the Outback to interview living legend Mick Dundee

(Hogan). When she finally locates the man, she's so taken that she brings him back to the Big Apple with her. The naïve Aussie wanders about, amazed at the wonders of the city and unwittingly charms everyone he comes into contact with, from high-society transvestites to street hookers. The sleeper hit of '86 has aged nicely. DVD image is fine, though a bit soft, as it has always been. The Surround remix is fine. —*MM*

Movie: ♫♫♫ ***DVD:*** ♫♫ ½
Paramount (cat #32029, UPC 097363202-943). Widescreen anamorphic. Dolby Digital Surround; Mono. $24.98. Keepcase. *LANG:* English; French. *SUB:* English. *CAP:* English. *FEATURES:* Trailer • 16 chapters.
1986 (PG-13) 98m/C *AU* Paul Hogan, Linda Kozlowski, John Meillon, David Gulpilil, Mark Blum; **D:** Peter Faiman; **W:** Paul Hogan, John Cornell; **C:** Russell Boyd; **M:** Peter Best. *AWARDS:* Golden Globes '87: Actor—Mus./Comedy (Hogan); *NOM:* Oscars '86: Orig. Screenplay.

Crocodile Dundee 2

Having conquered New York City, Mick Dundee (Hogan), the loveable rube, returns to his native Australia looking for adventure. Crooks are involved in a sequel that's notably lacking in the original's charm. Image is slightly softer than the other two films in the series. Sound is a bit better. —*MM*

Movie: ♫♫ ***DVD:*** ♫♫
Paramount (cat #32147, UPC 097363214-748). Widescreen anamorphic. Dolby Digital 5.1 Surround; Dolby Digital Surround; Stereo. $24.98. Keepcase. *LANG:* English; French. *SUB:* English. *CAP:* English. *FEATURES:* 20 chapters • Trailer • Behind-the-scenes featurette.
1988 (PG) 110m/C Stephen (Steve) Root, Jace Alexander, Luis Guzman, Colin Quinn, Paul Hogan, Linda Kozlowski, Kenneth Welsh, John Meillon, Ernie Dingo, Juan Fernandez, Charles S. Dutton; **D:** John Cornell; **W:** Paul Hogan; **C:** Russell Boyd; **M:** Peter Best.

Crocodile Dundee in Los Angeles

Mick (Hogan) is back in America. The happy couple returns so that Sue (Kozlowski) can investigate a movie studio that may be involved in a smuggling ring and, even worse, keeps cranking out dumb sequels. Meanwhile, Mick introduces their son (Cockburn) to life in the big city while working as an extra on the suspicious studio lot. The series' downward spiral continues, though the DVD image and sound are the strongest of the three. That is NOT a recommendation. —*MM*

Movie: ♫ ½ ***DVD:*** ♫♫ ½
Paramount (cat #33932, UPC 097363393-245). Widescreen anamorphic. Dolby Digital 5.1 Surround; Dolby Digital Surround. $24.98. Keepcase. *LANG:* English. *SUB:* English. *CAP:* English. *FEATURES:* 14 chapters • Trailers • "Making of" featurette.

2001 (PG) 95m/C Paul Hogan, Linda Kozlowski, Jere Burns, Jonathan Banks, Paul Rodriguez, Mike Tyson, Alec Wilson, Serge Cockburn; **D:** Simon Wincer; **W:** Matthew Berry, Eric Abrams; **C:** David Burr; **M:** Basil Poledouris.

Cross Creek

To become more confident in her writing, and to break away from the confines of modern civilized life, frustrated writer Marjorie Kinnan Rawlings (Steenburgen) trades in her neo-cosmopolitan lifestyle for a subdued, less-bohemian existence in the remote forests and swamps of Cross Creek. From her new home in Florida she discovers her inner voice and style as she weaves tales of the colorful inhabitants and rich landscapes of this small swampy town. While produced more than 10 years ago, *Cross Creek* maintains a rather modern feel. The picture quality is stunning. It really shows off the colorful, rich, exotic swamp locations, giving the viewer a sense of almost being there. The inclusion of a 5.1 Surround track would have been nice as there are plenty of outdoor nature and weather scenes that could have been enhanced by 360-degree sound; however, the stereo track is well done and makes full use of both speakers. Also included is an interesting 17-minute interview with Mary Steenburgen about the making of the film and what it was like working with an all-star cast. While overtly sentimental in parts, this is an enjoyable story of a writer overcoming personal obstacles and rising to a new artistic level. —*EL*

Movie: ♫♫ ½ ***DVD:*** ♫♫♫
Anchor Bay (cat #11444, UPC 01313114-4499). Widescreen (1.85:1) anamorphic. Dolby Digital Stereo; Mono. $19.98. Keepcase. *LANG:* English. *CAP:* English. *FEATURES:* Theatrical trailer • "Cross Creek: A Look Back with Mary Steenburgen" featurette • 26 chapters.
1983 (PG) 120m/C Mary Steenburgen, Rip Torn, Peter Coyote, Dana Hill, Alfre Woodard, Malcolm McDowell; **D:** Martin Ritt; **W:** Dalene Young; **C:** John A. Alonzo; **M:** Leonard Rosenman. *AWARDS: NOM:* Oscars '83: Costume Des., Support. Actor (Torn), Support. Actress (Woodard), Orig. Score.

Crossfire Trail

Rafe Covington (Selleck) promises a dying man to take care of his family; to protect them from harm and most importantly from unscrupulous land-grabbers and their henchmen. Soon he finds himself in the middle of a private war! The transfer is free of speckles or blemishes, rendering a very stable and clear image. The level of detail found in the picture is very good and colors are rich and vibrant throughout, without ever being oversaturated. The transfer is free of edge-enhancement, and therefore always pleasing and never appears unnaturally sharpened. Blacks are very deep and solid, and shadows are perfectly balanced. With a natural-sounding frequency response, the audio has a very pleasing quality, bringing the film to

life without ever coming across as artificial. —*GH*

Movie: ♫♫♫ ***DVD:*** ♫♫♫
Warner Home Video (UPC 53939662221). Widescreen (1.78:1) anamorphic. Dolby Digital Stereo. $24.98. Snapper. *LANG:* English; French. *SUB:* English; French. *FEATURES:* Talent files.
2001 100m/C Tom Selleck, Virginia Madsen, Mark Harmon, Wilford Brimley, David O'Hara, Christian Kane, Barry Corbin, Brad Johnson, William Sanderson, Joanna Miles, Ken Pogue, Rex Linn; **D:** Simon Wincer; **W:** Charles Robert Carner; **C:** David Eggby; **M:** Eric Colvin.

Crouching Tiger, Hidden Dragon [2 SB]

Like the first DVD release (reviewed in *Book 2*), this disc looks noticeably sharper than the version I saw in the theatre. Sound is equally flawless. Columbia TriStar makes sure that these "Superbit" editions present the best image and audio possible by paring away the extras and using all available space on the disc for the film itself. Both the dusty deserts and the bamboo forest, which could induce pixelation, look fine. —*MM*

Movie: ♫♫♫ ***DVD:*** ♫♫♫♫
Columbia Tristar (cat #07577, UPC 0433-96075771). Widescreen (2.35:1) anamorphic. Dolby Digital 5.1 Surround Stereo; DTS Surround Stereo. $27.95. Slipcase keepcase. *LANG:* Mandarin. *SUB:* English; French; Spanish; Portuguese; Chinese; Korean; Thai. *FEATURES:* 28 chapters.
2000 120m/C Chow Yun-Fat, Michelle Yeoh, Zhang Ziyi, Chang Chen, Cheng Pei-Pei, Sihung Lung; **D:** Ang Lee; **W:** James Schamus, Wang Hui Ling, Tsai Kuo Jung; **C:** Peter Pau; **M:** Tan Dun. *AWARDS:* Oscars '00: Art Dir./Set Dec., Cinematog., Foreign Film, Orig. Score; Australian Film Inst. '01: Foreign Film; British Acad. '00: Director (Lee), Foreign Film, Score; Directors Guild '00: Director (Lee); Golden Globes '01: Director (Lee), Foreign Film; Ind. Spirit '01: Director (Lee), Film, Support. Actress (Ziyi); L.A. Film Critics '00: Cinematog., Film, Score; Natl. Bd. of Review '00: Foreign Film; N.Y. Film Critics '00: Cinematog.; Broadcast Film Critics '00: Foreign Film; *NOM:* Oscars '00: Adapt. Screenplay, Costume Des., Director (Lee), Film, Film Editing, Song ("A Love Before Time"); Writers Guild '00: Adapt. Screenplay.

Cruel and Unusual

Adam Turrell (Berenger) is another of those darned serial killers. He goes to a small fishing village and insinuates his way into the lives of Mike O'Connor (Runyan) and his sister Kate (Hayward), who have yet to fully recover from the death of their father. The story is economically and competently constructed from overly familiar elements. The cool blue-black production design and soft Canadian light make an effortless transition to DVD. Sound is acceptable. —*MM* **AKA:** Watchtower.

Movie: 🎵🎵 **DVD:** 🎵🎵
Columbia Tristar (cat #07371, UPC 04339-6073715). Widescreen (1.85:1) anamorphic. Dolby Digital 5.1 Surround; Dolby Surround. $24.98. Keepcase. *LANG:* English. *SUB:* English; Spanish. *FEATURES:* 20 chapters ▪ Filmographies ▪ Trailer ▪ Still gallery.
2001 (R) 100m/C Tom Berenger, Rachel Hayward, Tygh Runyan, Mitchell Kosterman; **D:** George Mihalka; **W:** Robert Geoffrion, Rod Browning, Dan Witt; **C:** Peter Benison; **M:** Michel Cusson.

Cruel Intentions [2]

Star power aside, this is a better, more watchable film than the original. A prequel to the Sarah Michelle Gellar/Reese Witherspoon vehicle, it begins when stepsister Kathryn and Sebastian first meet. Sebastian (Dunne) comes to live with his father and his rich wife (Mimi Rogers), who does a fabulous flip on the stepmother joke. She is the original parent here and as evil as anything Cinderella could imagine. This film is far more realistic teen fodder than the original. The teenagers are awkward, and everything doesn't always go as planned. Director Kumble has tried to explain how the Kathryn and Sebastian of the first film came to be so cynical and vengeful, and he does a pretty good job. There are no loving parents in this Peyton Place, only big sharks grooming their little sharks. Kathryn and Sebastian circle each other like caged cats, but when Kathryn moves in for the kill, Sebastian backs off in favor of changing his bad ways for the love of the school virgin, Danielle (Thompson). One thing leads to another, and in the end there is a nasty curve on the road to true love, but not one you would expect (amazingly enough). Make no mistake, this is still a B-grade psycho teen film with plenty of teen girls in and out of uniform, but it does have more heart than most. As with the first, there is a lot of sex and not all of it is straight, so it might not be a good film for everyone. The color suffers from a little fuzziness and bleeding but nothing serious. Mostly the film looks overlit, or maybe it's all those blonde girls reflecting the light. The sound is good. —CA *AKA:* Manchester Prep.
Movie: 🎵🎵 **DVD:** 🎵🎵🎵
Columbia Tristar (cat #05841, UPC 0433-96058415). Widescreen (1.85:1) anamorphic; full frame. Dolby Digital 5.1 Surround, Dolby Digital Surround. $24.95. Keepcase. *LANG:* English. *SUB:* English; Spanish. *CAP:* English. *FEATURES:* 28 chapters ▪ Theatrical trailer ▪ Cast and crew bios.
1999 (R) 87m/C Amy Adams, Mimi Rogers, Robin Dunne, Sarah Thompson, Keri Lynn Pratt, David McIlwraith; **D:** Roger Kumble; **W:** Roger Kumble; **C:** James R. Bagdonas.

Cry Blood, Apache

An old man (Joel McCrae) remembers when, as a young man (Jody McCrae) he and his sadistic friends massacred a group of Apaches and were hunted by the husband of one of their victims. It's violent but not as sadistic as some. DVD presents an acceptable reproduction of a faded, snowy low-budget image. Title is available as part of "The Wild West" five-disc set. —MM
Movie: 🎵🎵 **DVD:** 🎵🎵
BCI-Eclipse (cat #44213-9, UPC 7873644-21398). Full frame. $19.98. Keepcase. *LANG:* English. *FEATURES:* "Spooking about Africa" cartoon ▪ 8 chapters ▪ Trivia game ▪ DVD dictionary ▪ DVD-ROM features.
1970 (R) 90m/C Joel McCrae, Jody McCrae, Robert Tessier, Marie Gahva, Don Henley; **D:** Jack Starrett; **W:** Sean McGregor; **C:** Bruce Scott; **M:** Elliot Kaplan.

The Cry of the Owl

Chilly thriller by Claude Chabrol weaves a tale of romance, jealousy, and murder in the most ordinary circumstances imaginable. Taken, like *Purple Noon*, from a Patricia Highsmith novel, it proves once again that mentally troubled characters make for interesting noirish movies. Robert (Christophe Malavoy) is an artist separated from his wife Veronique (Virginie Thévenet) and working in Vichy. She won't let him forget his history of nervous breakdowns, and likes to torment him as best she can. Robert's been peeping into the window of Juliette (Mathilda May), watching her innocuously interact with her fiancé Patrick (Jacques Penot). He seeks not a sexual thrill, but simply the calm of imagining a peaceful life with a stable person. One day he stops being a passive observer, introduces himself, and finds her completely receptive. Claude Chabrol is the least experimental and the least flashy of the New Wave directors, and his controlled, subdued style is a perfect match for the quiet menace of Patricia Highsmith's story. DVD is technically a decent effort. The image is not top standard, but it looks as if the element provided may have been a pre-existing transfer, probably from when the film was prepared for home video in the late 1980s. A company that specializes in films that it describes as "fallen through the cracks," All Day would seem to have rescued this title from oblivion. A nicely recorded commentary track from Chabrol author Ric Menello (and given life by an unbilled David Kalat) explains that after a successful theatrical run, the film disappeared because its rights were confused with a string of other Chabrol pictures. An ensuing court case tied up the title beyond what was considered a reasonable window for a video release. The color is a bit murky and dark scenes that must have been unreadable on the screen are a bit blotchy, but the grim lighting always looks appropriate to the on-screen mood. The soundtrack is basic but clear. All Day is once again to be commended for casting about for lost and abandoned titles and coming up with a winner. —GE *AKA:* Le Cri du Hibou.
Movie: 🎵🎵🎵 **DVD:** 🎵🎵 ½

All Day Ent. (UPC 014381150223). Widescreen (1.66:1) letterboxed. $24.98. Keepcase. *LANG:* French. *SUB:* English. *FEATURES:* Commentary: critic/author Ric Menello, producer David Kalat.
1987 102m/C *FR IT* Christophe MaLavoy, Mathilda May, Virginie Thevenet, Jacques Penot, Jean-Pierre Kalfon, Patrice Kerbrat; **D:** Claude Chabrol; **W:** Claude Chabrol, Odile Barski; **C:** Jean Rabier; **M:** Matthieu Chabrol.

Cuando Habla El Corazon

Childhood friends Miguel and Cruz must pass their test of manhood: given one bullet each, they are to return home with an animal. When Miguel misses his shot, Cruz gives up his only bullet rather than watch his friend suffer disgrace, at the cost of failing the test himself. This decision causes their lives to take very different paths. Unfortunately, there's lots of singing. The film's age is evident in both picture and sound, making it hard to distinguish from tape. The running time is 85 minutes, not the 130 claimed on the packaging. —BG *AKA:* When the Heart Speaks.
Movie: 🎵 ½ **DVD:** 🎵🎵
VCI (cat #KPF 522, UPC 089859052224). Full frame. Dolby Mono. $19.99. Keepcase. *LANG:* Spanish. *SUB:* English. *FEATURES:* 12 chapters ▪ Trailers ▪ Poster gallery ▪ Bios.
1942 85m/B *MX* Pedro Infante, Victor Manuel Mendoza, Maria Luisa Zea; **D:** Jose Segura.

Cuba

This forgotten Sean Connery vehicle finds the Scot travelling to Cuba on the brink of the 1959 revolution as an anti-terrorist advisor to Batista. He runs into an old flame (Adams) and tumbles deeper into the political turmoil than he had planned. The film spends most of its time on the image of Cuba as a corrupt playground for the elite where violence can erupt at any moment. Colors are a bit soft but the picture still looks nice overall. Sound quality is inconsistent, with some dialogue being buried beneath an entourage of microphone hiss. Somehow, this slipped through MGM's cracks and wound up non-anamorphic. —BG
Movie: 🎵🎵 **DVD:** 🎵🎵 ½
MGM Home Ent. (cat #1003334, UPC 027616874832). Widescreen (1.85:1) letterboxed. Dolby Mono. $19.98. Keepcase. *LANG:* English; French; Spanish. *SUB:* English; French; Spanish. *CAP:* English. *FEATURES:* 16 chapters ▪ Trailer.
1979 (R) 121m/C Sean Connery, Brooke Adams, Jack Weston, Hector Elizondo, Denholm Elliott, Chris Sarandon, Lonette McKee; **D:** Richard Lester; **W:** Charles Wood; **C:** David Watkin; **M:** Patrick Williams.

Cuban Story

This curious propaganda film espousing the merits of Fidel Castro's revolution and the ousting of Batista was filmed prior to the decay of U.S. relations with Cuba. A rather insincere (and seemingly soused) Errol Flynn appears during brief wraparound segments in an astonishingly unfocused, distracted performance. The lion's share of the footage is excellent silent documentary material backed with Flynn's ass-kissing narration, library music, and stock sound effects of (what seems to be) a dinner party in progress. One silent scene apparently features Flynn drunkenly accusing a casino dealer of cheating! Despite the pro-Castro nature of the material, the film ends with a series of speedy trials and executions (one of which is graphically depicted) that strongly implicate a troublesome new state of affairs. This film and the cheapie *Cuban Rebel Girls* were to be Flynn's last efforts. Unreleased (except in Russia), this fascinating piece of film history has only recently surfaced in the U.S. thanks to the efforts of David Kalat and Kyra Pahlen. It would be absolutely *perfect* double-billed with Woody Allen's *Bananas*. The quality of the film transfer is acceptable, given the poor condition of the original materials and the cheapness of the production. The majority of it is sharp and clear with strong contrasts, but some stock footage sections are overbright with poorer tone balance. There are print speckles and marks throughout the presentation but no digital artifacts. The sound is muffled and squawky (it sounds as if taken from a decaying optical track) and there's a distracting background buzz that appears about 20 minutes in. This is probably the best this film will ever look and sound; the technical defects should not deter the curious. The introduction by the director's daughter is brief but interesting. —*DG* **AKA:** The Truth about Fidel Castro Revolution. **Movie:** 🎭🎭 **DVD:** 🎭🎭🎭 Image Ent. (cat #ADED1712DVD, UPC 014-381171228). Full frame. Mono. $24.99. Keepcase. *LANG:* English. *FEATURES:* 10 chapters ➨ Insert booklet with notes ➨ Intro by Kyra Pahlen. **1959 50m/B** Errol Flynn; **D:** Victor Pahlen.

Curse of the Headless Horseman

Please see review for *Carnival of Blood / Curse of the Headless Horseman*.
1972 80m/C Don Carrara, Claudia Dean, B.G. Fisher, Margo Dean, Lee Byers, Joe Cody; **D:** John Kirkland.

The Curse of the Jade Scorpion

Ace insurance investigator CW Briggs (Allen) finds his old methods clashing with new efficiency expert Betty Ann Fitzgerald (Hunt) in this 1940s Tracy/Hepburn wannabe. At an office party held at the Rainbow Room, Briggs and Fitzgerald are subjects of the unscrupulous hypnotist Voltan (Stiers), who sends each of them off to steal the jewelry of prominent New Yorkers and deliver it to his lair. He also makes them believe they're madly in love with each other, setting them up for an

"opposites attract" kind of romance. It's a snappy, funny idea that falls flat because the script needed one more pass and there's no chemistry whatsoever between Allen and Hunt. The funny-again Woody Allen needs a sharp collaborator to help him with his new sloppier writing habits. It's difficult to tell if they were trying for an old-timey look or if the transfer was bad, but the picture has an overall orange glow that overwhelms both the actors and the sets. The titles bleed across the entire frame. —*LA*
Movie: 🎭🎭 ½ **DVD:** 🎭🎭 DreamWorks Home Ent. (cat #89268, UPC 667068926828). Widescreen (1.85:1) anamorphic. Dolby Mono. $34.98. Keepcase. *LANG:* English; Spanish; French. *SUB:* English. *CAP:* English. *FEATURES:* 24 chapters ➨ Cast and filmmaker bios ➨ Production notes ➨ Theatrical trailer.
2001 (PG-13) 103m/C Woody Allen, Helen Hunt, Dan Aykroyd, Elizabeth Berkley, Charlize Theron, Wallace Shawn, David Ogden Stiers, John Schuck, Brian Markinson, Michael Mulheren, Peter Linari, Prof. Irwin Corey, Peter Gerety; **D:** Woody Allen; **W:** Woody Allen; **C:** Zhao Fei.

Curse of the Vampires

Philippine vampire movie is atrocious in every sense. DVD looks like it was created from a third-generation VHS dupe. Sound appears to have been deliberately distressed in the drive-in "wraparounds." Give the producers credit for attempting to use the film's many deficiencies to their advantage, but this is still a rotten movie. —*MM*
Movie: 🎭 ½ **DVD:** 🎭 ½ Retromedia Entertainment Inc. (cat #010, UPC 802993101197). Keepcase. *LANG:* English. *FEATURES:* Intermission spots ➨ Photo gallery ➨ Trailers ➨ Bloopers ➨ 8 chapters.
1970 85m/C *PH* Eddie Garcia, Amalia Fuentes, Romeo Vasquez, Mary Walter; **D:** Gerardo (Gerry) De Leon; **W:** Pierre L. Salas, Ben Fello; **C:** Mike Accion; **M:** Tito Arevalo.

Cut and Run

In this disappointing jungle action picture, a small camera crew (Blount and Mann) travels to the Columbian jungle to track down the son of their boss (Aames). Unfortunately, Aames has gotten himself involved with a group of drug smugglers who are being stalked and eliminated by natives in thrall to the Colonel (Lynch). Deodato repeats several ideas (exploitative camera crews, ultraviolence, etc.) from his earlier (and better) *Cannibal Holocaust,* but illogical contrivances, uninteresting characters, and limp action sequences make for a fairly undistinguished work. The on-location photography gives the film greater production values but the extremely fake-looking gore effects seem even more bogus in this realistic setting. This disc restores several gory death sequences that were cut or refilmed

for the previous U.S. release. These gruesome additions add tension to what must have been a fairly tame and bloodless picture. Because a few of these scenes were never dubbed into English, they are presented on the disc in Italian with English subtitles. The disc features a very clear and colorful transfer, though one particularly gory shot looks terrible—almost as if it was artificially zoomed in during telecine. Framing seems tight on the bottom and there's a bit of grain to the image but it's probably the best this has ever looked on video. The mono sound (featuring a very funky Simonetti score) is limited (and aside from some difficult to understand Lynch dialogue) is clean and intelligible. The featurette is interesting and showcases welcome comparisons between a few of the violent scenes and their refilmed "soft" versions. It's a very informative short and packs a lot of information in its 17-minute running time. Deodato is refreshingly candid and Lynch makes for a surprisingly warm and funny interview subject. —*DG* **AKA:** Inferno in Diretta; Amazon: Savage Adventure; Straight to Hell.
Movie: 🎭🎭 **DVD:** 🎭🎭🎭 Anchor Bay (cat #DV11683, UPC 013131-168396). Widescreen (1.85:1) anamorphic. Mono. $19.98. Keepcase. *LANG:* English; Italian. *FEATURES:* Director's intro ➨ "Uncut and Run" featurette ➨ Trailer ➨ Director bio ➨ 25 chapters.
1985 (R) 91m/C *IT* Lisa Blount, Leonard Mann, Willie Aames, Richard Lynch, Michael Berryman, Karen Black, Eriq La Salle; **D:** Ruggero Deodato; **W:** Cesare Frugoni; **C:** Alberto Spagnoli; **M:** Claudio Simonetti.

Cutter's Way

Disenchanted yacht bum Richard Bone (Bridges) hangs out a lot with Vietnam double-amputee survivor Alex Cutter (Heard), an alienated malcontent with an extremely volatile personality that is somehow attractive to his alcoholic wife Mo (Eichhorn). One late night, Richard thinks he sees local oil millionaire J.J. Cord in an alley where the bludgeoned body of a teenaged girl is found the next day. Richard would like to forget it all, but Alex seizes upon the possibility that the arrogant Cord might truly be brought to account for the crime. The film is poignant, powerful, funny, and tragic. The vivid characters perfectly embody the fringe dwellers in the lush California lifestyle: educated bums, resentful, self-loathing intellectuals. Every scene in this gem is a keeper, with dialogue and situations that surpass anything in Stone, Lynch, or Tarantino's entire output, put together. All three leads have an incredible commitment to their roles, with Heard taking top honors by convincingly portraying a one-legged, one-armed, one-eyed cripple mostly by simply acting. DVD is a simple affair with a great transfer that brings out the richness in Jordan Cronenweth's often dark and moody photography. The neon El

Encanto sign in one of the very first shots is finally completely legible. Jack Nitzsche's haunting, quirky score and the brassy mariachis used to represent J.J. Cord's Santa Barbara empire come across alive and kicking on the soundtrack. —GE
AKA: Cutter and Bone.
Movie: 🎬🎬🎬 ½ **DVD:** 🎬🎬🎬
MGM Home Ent. (cat #1002206, UPC 027616864376). Widescreen (1.78:1) anamorphic. Dolby Digital Mono. $14.98. Keepcase. *LANG:* English; French; Spanish. *SUB:* French; Spanish. *CAP:* English. *FEATURES:* 16 chapters • Trailer.
1981 (R) 105m/C Jeff Bridges, John Heard, Lisa Eichhorn, Ann Dusenberry, Stephen Elliott, Nina Van Pallandt, George Dickerson; *D:* Ivan Passer; *W:* Jeffrey Alladin Fiskin; *C:* Jordan Cronenweth; *M:* Jack Nitzsche.

Cybercity
In 2017, mercenary Dakota's (Howell) family is murdered by a virtual prophet (Piper) who's trying to take over the world. Dakota seeks revenge with the help of assassin Lilith (von Palleske). It's standard-issue post-apocalypse hokum that gains absolutely nothing on DVD, beyond the meager extras. —MM
Movie: 🎬 ½ **DVD:** 🎬🎬
New Concorde (cat #NH20712 D, UPC 73-6991471290). Full frame. Stereo. $19.98. Keepcase. *LANG:* English. *FEATURES:* 24 chapters • Talent files • Trailers.
1999 86m/C C. Thomas Howell, Roddy Piper, Heidi von Palleske, David Carradine; *D:* Peter Hayman; *W:* Nehu Ghiran; *C:* Graeme Mears; *M:* Donald Quan.

Cypress Edge
The murder of Louisiana Senator Woodrow McCammon's (Steiger) daughter brings her estranged family back together. The motive is clear—the $18 million estate—and the benefactors are the usual suspects. DVD image gains nothing on VHS tape. The presence of genre stalwarts Dourif and Napier in the supporting cast is the main draw. —MM
Movie: 🎬🎬 **DVD:** 🎬🎬
MTI (cat #8114, UPC 039414581140). Full frame. $24.98. Keepcase. *LANG:* English. *SUB:* Spanish. *FEATURES:* 20 chapters • Trailers.
1999 (R) 90m/C Rod Steiger, Damian Chapa, Brad Dourif, Ashley Laurence, Charles Napier; *D:* Serge Rodnunsky; *W:* Serge Rodnunsky; *M:* Carl Dante.

Cyrano de Bergerac
Please see review of *Dueling DVD*.
Movie: 🎬🎬🎬 **DVD:** 🎬🎬
Marengo Films *FEATURES:* 12 chapters.
1950 113m/B Jose Ferrer, Mala Powers, William Prince, Elena Verdugo, Morris Carnovsky; *D:* Michael Gordon; *W:* Carl Foreman; *C:* Franz Planer; *M:* Dimitri Tiomkin. *AWARDS:* Oscars '50: Actor (Ferrer); Golden Globes '51: Actor—Drama (Ferrer).

Daisies
Banned during the communist invasion of Czechoslovakia, this film was considered to be a shining example of the short-lived "Czech New Wave" movement. Through its use of enigmatic imagery and experimental cinematography, it weaves a surreal tale of two prankish women, both named Marie, who ensnare and control the people around them according to their inane sense of humor. It is not difficult to see why a film portraying women in the '60s with so much freedom would have stirred up quite a bit of trouble in communist Russia. The film and sound quality are both decent despite its lack of a remastered digital soundtrack and many dust artifacts on the negatives. —EL *AKA:* Sedmikrasky.
Movie: 🎬🎬 **DVD:** 🎬🎬 ½
Facets Multimedia, Inc. (cat #92, UPC 736-899009236). Full frame. $29.95. Keepcase. *LANG:* Russian. *SUB:* English. *FEATURES:* Vera Chytilova filmography and bio sketch • Documents related to the banning of *Daisies* • 14 chapters.
1996 74m/C CZ Jitka Cerhova, Ivana Karbanova, Julius Albert; *D:* Vera Chytilova; *W:* Ester Krumbachova, Vera Chytilova; *C:* Jaroslav Kucera; *M:* Jiri Sust, Jiri Slitr.

Dance 'til Dawn
Prom night serves as an excuse to trot out high school stereotypes where unlikely couples—most popular boy dates nerdy girl, nerdy boy rescues most popular girl, etc.—end up together with predictable, mildly amusing results. The only aspect of the 1980s that hasn't dated badly is the absence of gross-out humor in a teen comedy. All the familiar faces here don't particularly add to the entertainment value except for Edie McClurg and Kelsey Grammar who, as overly concerned parents, seem to be in a much funnier movie than the rest of the cast. Made-for-TV movie has the quality of broadcast television. —LA
Movie: 🎬 **DVD:** 🎬🎬 ½
Hen's Tooth Video (cat #4080, UPC 75973-1408028). Full frame. Dolby Digital. $24.98. Keepcase. *LANG:* English. *FEATURES:* 12 chapters.
1988 96m/C Christina Applegate, Alan Thicke, Tempestt Bledsoe, Tracey Gold, Edie McClurg, Alyssa Milano, Brian Bloom, Matthew Perry, Chris Young, Kelsey Grammer, Cliff DeYoung; *D:* Paul Schneider; *W:* Andrew Guerdat, Steven Kreinberg; *C:* Stevan Larner.

Dancing at the Blue Iguana
Going behind the scenes of the Blue Iguana, we learn that strippers are people too, although, judging by this film, very shallow and uninteresting ones. The plot follows five of the club's dancers over the course of a week in an almost random fashion, with significant plot developments introduced and then dropped without a second mention. The result is the worst kind of soft-core movie—one with pretensions of being an art-house film. A good deal of bleeding is present in many of the colors, especially whites, and the dialogue is often drowned out by music or other commotion. The DVD contains a documentary on Daryl Hannah's "research" and two different commentary tracks, but why? —BG
Movie: 🎬 **DVD:** 🎬🎬 ½
Studio Home Ent. (cat #VM7870D, UPC 031398787020). Widescreen letterboxed. Dolby 5.1. $19.98. Keepcase. *LANG:* English. *SUB:* English; Spanish. *CAP:* English. *FEATURES:* 24 chapters • Production commentary • Director commentary • Deleted and alternate scenes • Trailer.
2000 (R) 123m/C Charlotte Ayanna, Kristin Bauer, W. Earl Brown, Daryl Hannah, Chris Hogan, Sheila Kelley, Elias Koteas, Vladimir Mashkov, Sandra Oh, Rodney Rowland, Jennifer Tilly; *D:* Michael Radford; *W:* Michael Radford, David Linter; *C:* Ericson Core; *M:* Tal Bergman, Renato Neto.

Dancing in September
If you're interested enough to look up this DVD, you may as well go ahead and watch it. Isaiah Washington and Nicole Ari Parker give fine performances as a producer and a sitcom writer who fall in love while developing a new half-hour comedy called *Just Us*. The story follows the rise and fall of producer George Washington and writer Tommy Crawford's relationship, the sitcom they create, and the star they make: Vicellous Reon Shannon plays James, a mentally unbalanced teen with a daughter and an ungrateful girlfriend. James has fame thrust upon him; because of his natural behavior in the sitcom role and his ability to memorize lines after one read, he suddenly finds himself rising from candy hustler on the street to pop icon. The girlfriend and her mother tolerate James as long as he supplies them and the baby with money, and when the show starts to go down the tubes and he stops taking his medication, James's story heads for a tragic conclusion. The characters are more often righteous than right, leading to trite scenes about entitlement and misguided values. The acting is good, and overall it's a decent "B"-movie of cultural relativism, if there is such a thing. The transfer from film to DVD is nothing to get excited about. It retains the film feel to no ill affect or boon. On the back of the DVD box you'll see the unaccredited quote "Has the sharp savvy tone of an insider's account" in bold red letters. The movie does offer a glimpse into the sitcom world, but through frosted glass. The industry does need to be confronted with its racial bias, but ultimately, it comes down to which audience is watching and how they are going to spend their money. Yes, we all agree it would be nice to have the actual make up of society reflected on television, but that is not what TV's about. The old adage has not changed: TV is all about selling the soap. —JAS

Movie: ♫♫ ½ **DVD:** ♫♫♫
HBO (cat #91778, UPC 026359177828). Full frame. Dolby Surround. $19.98. Snapper. *LANG:* English; Spanish. *SUB:* Spanish; French; English. *CAP:* English. *FEATURES:* Cast and crew bios ▪ Chapter selections ▪ 18 chapters.
2000 (R) 106m/C Nicole Ari Parker, Isaiah Washington IV, Vicellous Reon Shannon, Malinda Williams, Jay Underwood, Michael Cavanaugh, Chi McBride, James Avery, LeVar Burton, Peter Onorati, Kadeem Hardison, Jenifer Lewis, Anna Maria Horsford; *D:* Reggie Rock Bythewood; *W:* Reggie Rock Bythewood; *C:* Bill Dill.

Danger beneath the Sea

What appears to be a made-for-TV adventure trots out every known submarine movie cliché. The massively jawed Casper Van Dien is Capt. Sheffield, who's been given command of the *Lansing,* much to the dismay of many of the boat's officers. A nuclear incident occurs while the sub is in the China Sea, and he must deal with uncertainties about a possible war and a mutinous crew. The pace moves along nicely and production values are on the high side. DVD delivers an excellent image. The 5.1 mix is fine, but this one won't make fans forget the incredible aural experience of *Das Boot* (reviewed in Book 1). —*MM*
Movie: ♫♫ **DVD:** ♫♫ ½
York Ent. (cat #YPD-1181, UPC 75072311-8123). Full frame. Dolby Digital 5.1 Surround Stereo. $14.99. Keepcase. *LANG:* English. *SUB:* Spanish. *FEATURES:* 30 chapters ▪ Trailers ▪ Filmographies.
2002 93m/C Casper Van Dien, Gerald McRaney; *D:* Jon Cassar; *W:* Lucien K. Truscott IV; *C:* Derick Underschultz; *M:* Norman Orenstein.

Dangerous Summer

American architect Howard Anderson (Skerritt) is building a luxury resort in the Australian mountains when he becomes the victim of an elaborate arson/murder scheme. DVD can do nothing for a production that looks like an aged made-for-TV movie. Registration jitters, near constant static, heavy grain, and artifacts are all evident. —*MM* **AKA:** The Burning Man.
Movie: ♫♫ **DVD:** ♫
BFS Video (cat #30293-D, UPC 06680530-2930). Full frame. $9.98. Keepcase. *LANG:* English. *FEATURES:* 6 chapters ▪ Talent files.
1982 100m/C *AU* Tom Skerritt, James Mason, Ian Gilmour, Wendy Hughes; *D:* Quentin Masters; *W:* David Ambrose; *C:* Peter Hannan.

Daniel Boone: Trail Blazer

Low-budget rendition of the famous frontiersman's heroics (filmed in Mexico) is fairly well acted. It's not surprising that

such an old film is in pretty rough shape with lots of snow and bad splices particularly evident. DVD is equal to tape. Title is available as part of "The Wild West" boxed set. —*MM*
Movie: ♫♫ ½ **DVD:** ♫♫
Brentwood (cat #44213-9, UPC 78736442-1398). Full frame. $19.95. Keepcase. *LANG:* English. *FEATURES:* 8 chapters ▪ "Good Boos Night" cartoon ▪ DVD dictionary ▪ DVD-ROM features ▪ Trivia game.
1956 75m/B Bruce (Herman Brix) Bennett, Lon Chaney Jr., Faron Young, Damian O'Flynn, Fred Kohler Jr., Claudio Brook, Kem Dibbs; *D:* Ismael Rodriguez, Albert C. Gannaway; *W:* Tom Hubbard, John Patrick; *C:* Jack Draper; *M:* Raul Lavista.

Daria, The Movie: Is It Fall Yet?

The first feature based on the popular MTV animated series has some fine characters and attitude to burn, but far too much of its humor is standard sit-com insult material. (Think *Ghost World* without the complexity.) It's summer vacation and Daria (voice of Grandstaff), the smart teenager who wears her alienation as a badge of honor, finds herself working as a counselor at the touchy-feely "OK to Cry Corral" summer camp while her sister Quinn (Hoopes) hires a tutor to boost her test scores. Their friends are likewise engaged in activities they'd rather not be doing. The animation is exceptionally simple with large patches of color, a generally autumnal palette, and limited character movement. It's nothing DVD can't handle easily. —*MM*
Movie: ♫♫♫ **DVD:** ♫♫♫
Paramount (cat #87189, UPC 097368718-944). Full frame. Dolby Digital Surround. $24.98. Keepcase. *LANG:* English. *CAP:* English. *FEATURES:* 2 extra episodes ▪ Music video.
2001 75m/C *D:* Karen Disher, Guy Moore; *W:* Glenn Eichler, Peggy Nicoll; *V:* Tracy Grandstaff, Wendy Hoopes, Sarah Drew, Bart Fasbender.

Dario Argento: An Eye for Horror

This documentary focuses on the film and the life of Italian horror director Dario Argento. Through clips from his various films and interviews with both fans and collaborators, it examines the history of Argento's films, while giving an autobiographical view of his life. It is this probing into Argento's personal life which makes *An Eye for Horror* different from the other documentaries which have focused on the filmmaker. This means that this essay will appeal to longtime Argento-philes and newcomers interested in his work. Also, horror film fans will enjoy the interviews with icons John Carpenter, George Romero, and Tom Savini. This DVD certainly does justice to the piece, as the interviews and behind-the-scenes footage are letterboxed at 1.78:1, and even more

impressive, all of the clips are presented in their original aspect ratio. Not surprisingly, the image quality varies throughout, but the picture is clear and sharp for the most part. The audio track is serviceable, as the interviewees are all clear and distinguishable, but should not be compared to the recent DVD releases of Argento films. —*ML*
Movie: ♫♫♫ ½ **DVD:** ♫♫♫
Image Ent. (cat #ID0846NB DVD, UPC 014-381084627). Full frame. Dolby Digital Stereo. $19.98. Keepcase. *LANG:* English. *FEATURES:* 16 chapters.
2000 57m/C

Dark Asylum

Dr. Maggie Belham (supermodel Porizkova) is called to examine a captured serial killer (Drake), who is being held in an asylum while the FBI are on their way to claim him. Of course he escapes, and Dr. Belham finds herself trapped in the institution with him. The thin plot is stretched too far but there's a high level of tension, mostly due to Drake's screen presence. The level of grain is made more noticeable by the numerous scenes that take place in darkness. Dialogue is sometimes lost beneath the music and sound effects, but is adequate overall. —*BG*
Movie: ♫♫ **DVD:** ♫♫ ½
Studio Home Ent. (cat #ST7896D, UPC 658149789623). Widescreen letterboxed. Dolby Stereo. $24.99. Keepcase. *LANG:* English. *SUB:* English; Spanish. *CAP:* English. *FEATURES:* 24 chapters ▪ Trailers.
2001 (R) 96m/C Paulina Porizkova, Larry Drake, Judd Nelson, Juergen Prochnow; *D:* Gregory Gieras; *W:* Gregory Gieras; *C:* Viorel Sergovici Jr.

Dark Blue World

Ambitious film follows the relationship between two Czech pilots, Franta Slama (Vetchy) and his young friend Karel Vojtisek (Hadek), from the 1930s through their years in England flying for the R.A.F. against the Germans, and finally their return home after the war when they're imprisoned by the Communists. Director Sverak moves fluidly back and forth in time. The key subplot involves the two men and Susan (Fitzgerald), an English woman whose husband is in the Navy. DVD image is so sharp and richly detailed that the computer-generated special effects during the aerial sequences are much too clear. (That's a flaw that the film shares with the similar but much less successful *Pearl Harbor.*) The planes are far too bright and shiny to be real, and some of the action sequences are ridiculously far-fetched. That said, some of the flying scenes are well choreographed and the use of Surround effects puts you right in the middle of things. Also, do not watch the "Aerial Symphony" before the film itself. It contains all the best flying bits and spoils them in narrative terms. Two documentaries cover the film's production

and visual effects. —*MM* **AKA:** Trmavomodry Svet.
Movie: 🎬🎬🎬 **DVD:** 🎬🎬🎬
Columbia Tristar (cat #08275, UPC 043396082755). Widescreen (2.35:1) anamorphic. Dolby Digital 5.1 Surround. $29.98. Keepcase. *LANG:* Czech and English. *SUB:* English. *CAP:* English. *FEATURES:* 28 chapters ▪ Commentary: director, producer ▪ Documentaries ▪ "Aerial Symphony" ▪ Photo montage ▪ Weblink ▪ Trailers.
2001 (R) 115m/C *CZ GB* Ondrej Vetchy, Tara Fitzgerald, Krystof Hadek, Oldrich Kaiser, Charles Dance, Linda Rybova, Hans-Jorg Assmann, Anna Massey; *D:* Jan Sverak; *W:* Zdenek Sverak; *C:* Vladimir Smutny; *M:* Ondrej Soukup.

Dark Shadows: DVD Collection 1

Dark Shadows, (1966–1971) was originally designed as the soap opera equivalent of the Gothic romance paperbacks that were popular at the time. As the half-hour series progressed, lackluster ratings inspired the producers (Dan Curtis and Robert Costello) to add supernatural elements to the show. They struck gold when they introduced a character named Barnabas Collins, a reluctant vampire whose popularity turned the show into a smash hit. This DVD collection contains 40 episodes (essentially eight weeks of broadcast episodes) and begins (wisely) with Episode 210, where Barnabas was introduced. Conniving punk Willie Loomis breaks into the Collins crypt in an attempt to steal long-lost jewels, and unwittingly unleashes Barnabas from his imprisonment in a chained coffin. Pretending to be a long-forgotten cousin from the British branch of the family, Barnabas is able to convince the family to give him the dilapidated Old House on the property. As he and Willie (who is now Barnabas's slave) restore the house, Barnabas becomes obsessed with waitress Maggie, who bears a startling resemblance to his long-lost love. The series, taped without edits, sometimes has the feeling of a live performance; actors occasionally fumble for their lines, and (unbelievably) cameras and boom microphones appear in shots now and again. Somehow it adds to the charm. The series creates a wonderfully moody, twilight world that is frequently evocative and oft poetic. The black-and-white camerawork and stage-bound, fog-laden sets create an atmosphere akin to that in Universal's horror classics. Barnabas is quite an original creation and stage actor Frid brings him to vivid, sinister, and palpably threatening life. The episodes are several notches above their previous videotape releases. The images are razor sharp and feature much better contrasts. There's a layer of near-microscopic grain and instances of damage (due to the condition of the original masters) and occasional digital edge noise. The transitions between episodes are sometimes abrupt and the opening slates

(which were on the VHS tapes) are not included. The mono audio is clean but limited and often reveals the crude sound recording present on the masters. The "Introduction" featurette is a brief 15-minutes overview of the first 209 episodes and it does an admirable job of conveying the essential backstory. It should be viewed prior to the episodes. The interviews are very brief (5 minutes) and subject to digital noise at edit points. The chapter stops are rather stingy. The booklet features a short breakdown of the episodes and includes the original air-dates. Highly recommended. —*DG*
Movie: 🎬🎬🎬 **DVD:** 🎬🎬🎬
MPI (cat #DVD7403, UPC 0303067403-93). Full frame. Mono. $59.98. Boxed snap-case. *LANG:* English. *FEATURES:* 1 chapter per episode ▪ Interview clip with Jonathan Frid ▪ Interview clip with Kathryn Leigh Scott ▪ Interview clip with John Karlen ▪ Insert booklet with disc episode guide ▪ "Dark Shadows Introduction" featurette.
1967 440m/B Jonathan Frid, Joan Bennett, John Karlen, Kathryn Leigh Scott, Louis Edmonds, Dennis Patrick, Mitchell Ryan; *D:* Lela Swift, John Sedwick; *W:* Malcolm Marmorstein, Ron Sproat; *M:* Robert Cobert.

The Darling Buds of May

This miniseries (more accurately a series of films) was a huge hit in England in the early 1990s. In no small measure, that's because it's the debut of a lovely young Catherine Zeta-Jones, playing Mariette Larkin, who, when we first meet her, has just learned that she's pregnant. Not that it bothers her perpetually joyful dad, "Pop" Larkin (Jason), or her understanding mother (Ferris). They live with Mariette's several sibs on an idyllic Yorkshire farm. It's a place of sun-splashed fields and woods. When a young tax inspector (Franks) shows up, he's out of his league. DVD can do little to improve the soft, overlit image. Heavy artifacts show up in every pan or fast movement. The occasional pause or jump in the picture may come from missing frames in the original. Overall, picture and sound are of broadcast quality. Five 200-minute discs are in the set (they are also available individually for $19.98). Contents: "The Darling Buds of May," "When the Green Woods Laugh" (cat. #30191-D, UPC 066805301919); "A Breath of French Air," "Oh! To Be in England" (cat. #30192-D, UPC 066805301926); "Stranger at the Gates," "A Season of Heavenly Gifts" (cat. #30193-D, UPC 066805301933); "The Happiest Days of Your Life," "Cast Not Your Pearls Before Swine" (cat. #30194-D, UPC 066805301940); "Climb the Greasy Pole," "Christmas Is Coming," "Le Grand Weekend" (cat. #30195-D, UPC 066805301957). —*MM*
Movie: 🎬🎬🎬 **DVD:** 🎬🎬 ½
BFS Video (cat #30190, UPC 066805301-902). Full frame. Stereo. $89.98. Boxed set keepcase. *LANG:* English. *FEATURES:* 4

chapters per show ▪ Photo gallery ▪ Catherine Zeta-Jones interview ▪ Selected filmographies ▪ Thumbnail bios.
1991 1015m/C *GB* David Jason, Pam Ferris, Philip Franks, Catherine Zeta-Jones; *D:* Rodney Bennett, David Giles, Robert Tronson, Steve Goldie; *W:* Paul Wheeler, Barrie Guard, Bob Larbey, Robert Banks Stewart, Richard Harris; *M:* Pip Burley.

Date with an Angel

When aspiring musician Jim (Knight) fishes a beautiful angel (Beart) out of the swimming pool, he is simply trying to rescue her. But the beauty of the heavenly creature overwhelms him and he finds himself questioning his wedding to the stuck-up Patty (Cates), the daughter of a cosmetics mogul (Dukes). (In a nice touch, the cosmetic company is called Ethereal Beauty.) Sickeningly cute and way too sentimental, the film will be enjoyed only by those looking for the sappiest of romances, although Beart's beauty is other-worldly. Writer/director Tom McLoughlin had previously made *Friday the 13th Part 4: Jason Lives,* so this was a slight change of pace for him. Despite this film's bad reputation, Anchor Bay has cleaned it up quite well for its DVD debut with a widescreen transfer. (This is one of those films which is simply unwatchable in its full-frame state, as the image gets far too soft.) The image here is sharp (although it is still a bit hazy in certain shots) and the colors are good. An occasional defect from the source print is visible. Surround audio track offers clear dialogue with no distortion. —*ML*
Movie: 🎬 ½ **DVD:** 🎬🎬 ½
Anchor Bay (cat #DV12115, UPC 01313-1211597). Widescreen (2.35:1) anamorphic. Dolby Surround. $14.98. Keepcase. *LANG:* English. *FEATURES:* Theatrical trailer ▪ 25 chapters.
1987 (PG) 105m/C Charles Lane, Emmanuelle Beart, Michael E. Knight, Phoebe Cates, David Dukes, Bibi Besch, Albert Macklin, David Hunt, Michael Goodwin; *D:* Tom McLoughlin; *W:* Tom McLoughlin; *C:* Alex Thomson; *M:* Randy Kerber.

Daughter of Darkness

This true crime shocker is more a bizarre black comedy during its first half, quite unlike its totally grim follow-up *Brother of Darkness* (which was shot with much of the same cast). Even during the second half there are moments of unusual humor. A young woman reports her family has been wiped out. The oafish police captain follows all clues back to the witness, and she goes into her confessional flashback. That's when things get really sleazy and unpleasant. The print has a few scratches and splices, but otherwise the transfer is fine. The footage of more explicit scenes are of slightly lower quality. —*BT*
Movie: 🎬🎬 **DVD:** 🎬🎬

Tai Seng (cat #5396, UPC 48950249092-95). Widescreen letterboxed. $14.95. Keepcase. *LANG:* Cantonese; Mandarin. *SUB:* Chinese; English. *CAP:* Chinese. *FEATURES:* 8 chapters.
1993 93m/C *HK* Anthony Wong, Lily Chung, Hugo Ng, William Ho; *D:* Ivan Lai; *W:* Ivan Lai, Ging On Suen; *C:* Kwok Keung Lee; *M:* Wong Bong.

The Daughter of Dr. Jekyll

On her 18th birthday, Janet (Talbott) and her fiancé (Agar) find out she is the daughter of the infamous Dr. Jekyll. As a series of grisly murders suddenly occur, Janet finds herself troubled by horrible dreams that seem to suggest that she has inherited her father's dementia! Fast-paced, enjoyable little B-film by cult director Ulmer. The performers do a thoroughly professional job, but the script (which has Jekyll not only turning into Mr. Hyde, but a werewolf!) is a bit of a clumsy muddle. Previously available in bleary cropped video editions, this disc, made from the original masters, is a revelation to behold. The opening scenes are prone to a bit of digital noise caused by the on-screen fog, but the rest of the film is crystal clear with excellent contrasts. There are a few minor moments of print damage, but as they occur during intermittent shots within the same scene, they are most likely due to a technical camera problem during filming and would be evident on all prints. The sound is clear and appealing and the isolated music track is a fun bonus. The interviews are interesting but very static. Recommended! —DG
Movie: 🎬🎬 **DVD:** 🎬🎬🎬
All Day Ent. (cat #ADED9648, UPC 014-381964820). Widescreen (1.85:1) letterboxed. Dolby Digital Mono. $24.99. Keepcase. *LANG:* English. *FEATURES:* Isolated music and effects track • Theatrical trailer • Rare stills and artwork • Interviews with John Agar and Arianne Ulmer Cipes • Insert booklet with notes • 18 chapters.
1957 71m/B John Agar, Arthur Shields, John Dierkes, Gloria Talbott; *D:* Edgar G. Ulmer; *W:* Jack Pollexfen; *C:* John F. Warren; *M:* Melvyn Lenard.

Daughters of the Dust

Five women of a Gullah family living on the Sea Islands off the Georgia coast in 1902 contemplate moving to the mainland in this emotional tale of change. The Gullah are descendants of West African slaves and their isolation has kept their superstitions and native dialect (a mixture of West African, Creole, and English) intact. Family bonds and memories are celebrated with a quiet narrative and beautiful cinematography in Dash's feature-film directorial debut. Fans of this film will definitely want to check out this comprehensive DVD release. The beautiful transfer is letterboxed at 1.85:1 and shows few defects. The image is sharp and the colors are

quite good. The 45-minute documentary gives an in-depth look into the making of the film and offers interviews with the cast and crew. Also of interest is the never-before-seen footage from a preliminary version of the film. —ML
Movie: 🎬🎬🎬 ½ **DVD:** 🎬🎬🎬🎬
Kino on Video (cat #K1333 DVD, UPC 738-329013328). Widescreen (1.85:1) letterboxed. Dolby Digital Surround. $34.95. Keepcase. *LANG:* English. *FEATURES:* Commentary • Behind-the-scenes documentary • Deleted scenes • Isolated musical score • Bonus featurette • Historian interview • Theatrical trailer • 14 chapters.
1991 113m/C Cora Lee Day, Barbara O, Alva Rogers, Kaycee Moore, Cheryl Lynn Bruce, Adisa Anderson, Eartha D. Robinson, Bahni Turpin, Tommy Redmond Hicks, Malik Farrakhan, Cornell (Kofi) Royal, Vertamae Crosvenor, Umar Abdurrahman, Sherry Jackson, Rev. Ervin Green; *D:* Julie Dash; *W:* Julie Dash; *C:* A. Jafa Fielder; *M:* John Barnes. *AWARDS:* Sundance '91: Cinematog.

David Blaine: Fearless

This disc hooks together the best from Blaine's three TV specials: *Street Magic* (1996), *Magic Man* (1998), and *Frozen in Time* (2000). Hailed as the successor to Houdini (but what young magician isn't?), Blaine mixes magic and spirituality into entertainment for the average person. Both *Street Magic,* shot in the U.S., and *Magic Man,* shot in South America, show Blaine doing tricks for random citizens. The fan of sleight of hand will be amazed, and the critic of magic will be able to wonder how much of the magic was manipulated by clever film editing...except for the part where Blaine puts a diamond in his mouth and has it come out his eye lid, ick. The third show, *Frozen in Time,* is more of a spiritual journey than magic. Staying awake for three days with constant public watching while avoiding touching the ice, which could give him frostbite, is more than magic, it's insanity. Overall enjoyable and interesting if you like magic shows or want to see what Blaine is all about. Lots of video footage leads to uneven picture and sound quality, but it is never BWC ("Blair Witch Quality"). —CA
Movie: 🎬🎬 ½ **DVD:** 🎬🎬 ½
Buena Vista Home Ent. (cat #24395, UPC 0788832468). Full frame. Dolby Digital Surround. $19.99. Keepcase. *LANG:* English. *SUB:* French; Spanish. *CAP:* English. *FEATURES:* 11 chapters • "Unseen Blaine" material • Behind-the-scenes footage • Newspaper articles.
2002 110m/C

Day of Wrath

In the 1600s, elderly pastor Absalon Pedersson (Roose) presides over the trial of a harmless woman, Herlofs Marte (Svierker) denounced as a witch. But she knows that

Absalon once spared another accused witch, the mother of the young girl he married, Anne (Movin). Herlofs threatens to denounce Anne at the point of death at the stake, unless Absalon spares her. Back home, robbed of her youth by marriage to an old man, Anne blooms into happiness and rebellion by the return of Absalon's son Martin (Lerdorff) from school. As Absalon remains aloof to all but his spiritual duties, his household is coming apart, and his mother Meret (Neiiendam), who hates Anne enough to have already convinced herself that her daughter-in-law is an evil spirit, suspects that the abomination of adultery is also afoot. It's amazing how well preserved (restored) this movie is, considering its age and the fact that it was filmed during the Nazi occupation of Denmark. This disc must be from prime elements; it makes older prints seem dank and fuzzy. The movie has beautifully designed settings, now full of details not visible before. The title is available as part of the *Carl Theodor Dreyer Box Set* (see separate entry). —GE **AKA:** *Vredens Dag.*
Movie: 🎬🎬🎬🎬 **DVD:** 🎬🎬🎬🎬
Criterion Coll. Full frame. Keepcase. *LANG:* Danish. *SUB:* English. *FEATURES:* Stills gallery • Cast interviews.
1943 110m/B *DK* Thorkild Roose, Sigrid Neiiendam, Lisbeth Movin, Preben Lerdorff, Anna Svierker; *D:* Carl Theodor Dreyer; *W:* Carl Theodor Dreyer; *C:* Karl Andersson; *M:* Poul Schierbeck.

Daydream Believers: The Monkees Story

Made-for-TV biopic of the original "boy band" is a curious overachiever on DVD. This modest little movie comes with a wealth of extras, including commentary by some of the people whose lives are being depicted. For those who don't remember, the Monkees were created by TV executives who wanted to re-create the screen success of the Beatles' Richard Lester films in a half-hour TV show. First they needed a band, so they hired four telegenic young guys (Geddis, Lohr, Stanchev, Fisher) and, amazingly, they became a hit. Modestly budgeted film actually does a fairly good job of recounting the major events of the time and the cast's impersonation of the individuals is O.K. DVD image is slightly sharper than broadcast quality with the expected aliasing as the main flaw. Sound is fine. —MM
Movie: 🎬🎬 ½ **DVD:** 🎬🎬🎬
New Concorde (cat #NH20787D, UPC 736-991378797). Full frame. $19.98. Keepcase. *LANG:* English. *CAP:* English. *FEATURES:* 18 chapters • Commentary: director Neill Fearnley • Commentary: Micky Dolenz • Commentary: Davy Jones • Commentary: Peter Tork • Trailers • Interviews • Filmographies.
2000 (PG-13) 91m/C George Stanchev, L.B. Fisher, Jeff Geddis, Aaron Lohr, Colin Ferguson, Wallace (Wally) Langham; *D:* Neill Fearnley; *W:* Ron McGee; *C:* David Makin; *M:* Fred Mollin.

De Sade

Bizarre look at a portion of the Marquis de Sade's life. The brutal nature of de Sade's (Dullea) fetishes and actions are re-created with an intoxicating, psychedelic feel that is certainly circa the 1960s. The film itself is a bit confusing (it bounces between flashbacks, reality, insane dementia, reality, etc.), but is viewable for its acting and set design. The disc features exceptional reproduction of colors and blacks. The bright, vibrant colors used throughout the film really stand out and are quite well defined. Unfortunately, the soundtrack is a disappointment to the video presentation. The sound often comes across as muddied, which makes dialogue somewhat hard to understand. —*MJT*
Movie: ♫♫ ½ **DVD:** ♫♫♫
MGM Home Ent. (cat #1002965, UPC 027616871527). Widescreen (1.85:1) anamorphic. Dolby Digital Mono. $19.98. Keepcase. *LANG:* English; French. *SUB:* English; French; Spanish. *FEATURES:* 16 chapters ▪ Theatrical trailer ▪ Episode of the *Richard Matheson, Storyteller* series.
1969 104m/C Senta Berger, Keir Dullea, John Huston, Anna Massey, Lilli Palmer, Sonja Ziemann; **D:** Cy Endfield; **W:** Richard Matheson; **C:** Richard Angst.

Dead and Rotting

This home-grown horror film proves to be above average, despite its low-budget drawbacks. It distances itself from other direct-to-video horror films by keeping the story serious and never devolving into a simple series of references to other scary movies. The story focuses on three construction workers: Hollis (Stephen O'Mahoney), J.B. (Tom Hoover), and Eric (Trent Haaga), who love to play pranks on people. After trespassing on the property of a local witch (Barbara Katz-Norrod), the three have a run-in with her son, Pox (Christopher Suciu). The witch retaliates by poisoning the trio. They in turn seek revenge by hiring two local stoners, Asher (Jeff Dylan Graham) and Shugi (Jamie Star), to vandalize the witch's house, but they accidentally murder her son. This infuriates the witch, so she transforms herself into a young, sexy woman (Debbie Rochon) and proceeds to seduce each of the three men. Shot on high-end video, the film certainly stays true to its low-budget roots, as the acting is pretty bad for the most part and most of the locations appear to simply be the homes of the crew members. Also, director David P. Barton doesn't do very much to add any distinctive style to the film. Still, it's the twisted story that will make this one appealing to hard-core horror fans. The film presents some very brutal ideas (although little in the way of gore) and sees them through to the end. Once the main story has been established, things are fairly predictable, but the movie has a unique way of presenting some old ideas. It's a good example of the kind of gung-ho filmmaking that is still taking place in America's heartland. As with most Tempe DVDs, this one comes packed with goodies. The image is sharp, but it can't hide the flaws inherent with video productions. There is a noticeable blurring of the image at times, and in most scenes, any light source shows signs of bleeding and oversaturation. Also, there is some video distortion. However, the colors are good. The Dolby Digital 5.1 audio track is an impressive mix, as there is constant Surround sound action throughout the movie. The DVD provides several nice extras, such as an audio commentary by director Barton and several behind-the-scenes featurettes. But be warned—avoid the bonus feature "Filthy McNasty" at all costs. This video quickie appears to have been shot over a long-weekend at a very boring party. —*ML*
Movie: ♫♫ ½ **DVD:** ♫♫♫
Full Moon Pictures (cat #TD-1105, UPC 922928110599). Widescreen (1.85:1) anamorphic. Dolby Digital 5.1. $19.99. Keepcase. *LANG:* English. *FEATURES:* Commentary ▪ "Making of" featurette ▪ Director interview ▪ Makeup effects featurette ▪ Isolated musical score ▪ Still galleries ▪ Bonus shorts ▪ Bonus feature ▪ Bonus trailers ▪ 30 chapters. There is no chapter/scene selection menu on this DVD.
2002 72m/C Stephen O'Mahoney, Tom Hoover, Trent Haaga, Barbara Katz-Norrod, Christopher Suciu, Jeff Dylan Graham, Jamie Star, Debbie Rochon; **D:** David P. Barton.

Dead Creatures

A close-knit group of British twentysomething women travels around the dingy areas outside of London satiating their need for human flesh with saran-wrapped body parts they carry in their luggage. The girls are all suffering from a kind of zombie-disease that is inflicted by a bite and eventually results in the victim's literal decomposition. The dreary tone of the film echoes that of lower-class British TV dramas: heavy grainy images, squalid locations with minimal lighting and makeup. Parkinson directs this low-key horror drama without the usual female nudity prevalent in today's micro-budgeted horror films, but the lack of a thriller element or traditional genre structure works against it. Without anywhere to go with the story, this one peters out around the halfway mark. The gore effects, though used minimally, are repugnant and truly nauseating. The picture is soft and grainy with drab, dull hues. The color scheme would seem to be designed intentionally, but what a waste that this was shot on 35mm. The behind-the-scenes featurette is fairly lengthy video footage that shows some glimpses behind the scenes, including the gore effects. The audio commentary is excellent, and provides tremendous insight into this guerilla production, though it can be a bit difficult to tell the different commentators apart at times. —*DG*
Movie: ♫ **DVD:** ♫♫ ½
MTI (cat #50047, UPC 619935404731). Widescreen (1.85:1) letterboxed. Stereo.

$24.95. Keepcase. *LANG:* English. *SUB:* Spanish. *FEATURES:* Behind-the-scenes featurette ▪ Commentary: Parkinson, dubbing mixer Davies, Shepherd ▪ 20 chapters ▪ Additional previews ▪ *Fangoria* article on the film.
2001 89m/C Beverly Wilson, Antonia Beamish, Brendan Gregory; **D:** Andrew Parkinson; **W:** Andrew Parkinson; **C:** Jack Shepherd; **M:** Andrew Parkinson.

The Dead Hate the Living

Young filmmakers sneak into an abandoned medical research facility to make a low-budget horror feature about a scientist who raises the dead to be his zombie slaves. Little do they know that the facility was abandoned after a scientist's experiments to revive the dead through alchemical means went horribly wrong. When they discover the scientist's body, they decide to go ahead and use what they've found to add to the film's production value. They accidentally manage to open a rift into the dimension of the dead. The script is a patchwork of influences, and horror fans can play a little game of "spot the reference" while they watch. There are some really spectacular (and gruesome) zombie monsters—the f/x makeup throughout the film is terrific. Sound quality is O.K., but the image transfer is excellent. There's a music video, trailers, and a very good documentary feature. Writer/director Parker gets involved beyond the commentary track he shares with the lead actors, which gives the disc a surprisingly chummy feel. In the cast section, he writes a short essay about his feelings about each actor and what it was like working with them. —*BT*
Movie: ♫♫ ½ **DVD:** ♫♫♫
Full Moon Pictures (cat #FUMDV8045, UPC 763843804562). Full frame. $24.99. Keepcase. *LANG:* English. *FEATURES:* 30 chapters ▪ Trailer ▪ Documentary featurette ▪ Image gallery ▪ Commentary ▪ Music video ▪ Filmographies.
1999 90m/C Eric Clawson, Jamie Donahue, Brett Beardslee, Wendy Speake; **D:** Dave Parker; **W:** Dave Parker; **C:** Tom Calloway; **M:** Jared DePasquale.

Dead in the Water

Dead in the Water comes across as a combination of *Dead Calm* and *Diabolique*, and while it offers a good cast, it brings nothing new to the genre. Three Americans, Gloria (Dominique Swain), her boyfriend Danny (Scott Bairstow) and their friend Jeff (Henry Thomas) are vacationing in Brazil. There, they meet Marcos (Sebastian DeVincente), who is immediately taken with Gloria. When the trio decides to take a boat-ride along the coast, Gloria invites Marcos along. Things are fine until Danny notices Marcos intentions towards Gloria and a heated dispute begins. Danny's plan to give Marcos his comeuppance backfires, and the three young friends sudden-

ly find themselves in a great deal of trouble. As they try to decide on the best course of action to cover their tracks, the friendship begins to disintegrate and no one can be trusted. Very weak (and unoriginal plot) is given some help by the competent acting (especially the reliable Thomas) and the beautiful scenery. As the film is relatively brief, one could do a lot worse. DVD image is very sharp and clear, showing only a minute amount of grain. The colors are good, and the brilliance of the image showcases the location photography. With the Dolby Digital 5.1 audio track, we get clear dialogue, but there is not a great deal of Surround sound presence. The audio from the rear speakers consists mainly of musical cues and certain sound effects. For a direct-to-video feature, this DVD offers many sound extras, including an audio commentary and an original short film from director Gustavo Lipsztein. —ML
Movie: 🎬🎬 **DVD:** 🎬🎬 ½
Lion's Gate Home Ent. (cat #ST7931D, UPC 658149793125). Widescreen (1.78:1) anamorphic. Dolby Digital 5.1 Surround. $24.99. Keepcase. *LANG:* English. *SUB:* English; Spanish. *CAP:* English. *FEATURES:* Commentary • Alternate ending • Behind-the-scenes footage • Short film • Trailer • 24 chapters.
2001 (R) 89m/C Dominique Swain, Henry Thomas, Scott Bairstow, Renata Fronzi, Sebastian DeVincente; **D:** Gustavo Lipsztein.

Dead or Alive

It's almost impossible to make an effective action movie without a substantial budget, and auteur Lowry Brooks Jr. proves it. He's the producer/writer/director/star of this effort. Parris Bally is a bounty hunter who alone can defeat an international terrorist. The acting is amateurish; the lighting is dim; the action sequences are slow; the image is exceptionally grainy with heavy artifacts; much of the dialogue is unintelligible. —MM
Movie: woof **DVD:** woof
York Ent. (cat #YPD-1180, UPC 75072311-8024). Full frame. Dolby Digital 5.1 Surround Stereo. $14.95. Keepcase. *LANG:* English. *SUB:* Spanish. *FEATURES:* Trailers • 24 chapters.
2002 84m/C Lowry Brooks Jr., Simeon Ndi, Gregory Dorsey, Veronica Pitts, Linda Floyd, Brian Horsey; **D:** Lowry Brooks Jr.; **W:** Lowry Brooks Jr.; **C:** Dominic Desantis; **M:** Gabriel Holden.

Dead Pet

Kevin Coetteleer follows in the footsteps of Adam Sandler as a likeable, slightly geeky nice guy. He plays Jake Thompson who comes home from college to find that his repulsive parents have forgotten to pick him up at the airport and they've spent the rest of his education fund on an operation for their beloved poodle. From there, the comedy is nicely deadpan and inventive. Low-budget image lacks any pol-

ish but DVD delivers an acceptable picture. Sound is unremarkable. —MM
Movie: 🎬🎬 ½ **DVD:** 🎬🎬 ½
York Ent. (cat #YPD-1117, UPC 75072311-1728). Widescreen letterboxed. $14.99. Keepcase. *LANG:* English. *FEATURES:* Trailers • Director's intro.
2001 93m/C Kevin Cotteleer, Gina Doctor, Brian Sostek; **D:** Kevin Cotteleer; **W:** Kevin Cotteleer; **C:** Dan Ming.

The Dead Pool

The death of substance-abusing rock star Johnny Squares (Carrey) while filming a music video with obnoxious English director Peter Swan (Neeson) introduces detective Harry Callahan (Eastwood) to the morbid game called The Dead Pool. A group of bettors guess which celebrities might die next—Squares was on the list, and now Harry's name is too. With help from his partner Al Quan (Kim) and feisty reporter Samantha Walker (Clarkson), Harry faces a number of bizarre assassination attempts, not knowing if his assailants are hoods avenging a mob boss he's put in prison, or the Dead Pool Killer in person. DVD is a solid addition to the line, with a new, clean 2001 transfer, picture, and sound. Colors are good, even in the numerous dark scenes, and the audio has been remixed to 5.1. —GE
Movie: 🎬🎬 ½ **DVD:** 🎬🎬🎬
Warner Home Video (UPC 0853918590-24). Widescreen (1.85:1) anamorphic. Dolby Digital 5.1 Surround Stereo. $19.98. Snapper. *LANG:* English. *SUB:* English; French; Spanish; Portuguese; Japanese; Chinese; Thai; Korean. *FEATURES:* Trailer.
1988 (R) 92m/C Clint Eastwood, Liam Neeson, Patricia Clarkson, Evan C. Kim, David Hunt, Michael Currie, Michael Goodwin, Jim Carrey; **D:** Buddy Van Horn; **M:** Lalo Schifrin.

Dead Sexy

The Indefatigable Shannon Tweed (also executive producer) is police detective Kate McBain, who's investigating a series of murders of young women. Someone plies them with champagne, then kills them. Her prime suspect is wealthy "Blue" Dresden (Enos). But as the carefully darkened faces in key scenes indicate, McBain's colleague Rackles (Jones), who's equally beefy and brunette, could be the culprit. Kate falls for Blue because he's rich and studly, thereby raising the question so often asked in direct-to-video erotic thrillers: Is he Mr. Right or a serial killer? Production values and image are a bit sharper than most of these cable-ready flicks. Sound is unremarkable. —MM
Movie: 🎬🎬 ½ **DVD:** 🎬🎬
Columbia Tristar (cat #06995, UPC 043396069954). Full frame. Dolby Digital Stereo. $29.98. Keepcase. *LANG:* English; French. *SUB:* English; Spanish; Portuguese; French; Chinese; Korean; Thai. *CAP:* English. *FEATURES:* 28 chapters • Trailers.
2001 (R) 89m/C Shannon Tweed, John Enos, Kenneth White, Sam Jones, Eric

Keith; **D:** Robert Angelo; **W:** Anthony Laurence Greene, Elroy Canton; **C:** Kazuo Minami; **M:** Nicholas Rivera.

Dead Silence

Renata (Edwards) is a small-town girl who's always the butt of vicious jokes. She's pushed to the breaking point and decides enough is enough. Dull "dark comedy" minus laughs, a straight-to-video David Lynch wannabe, particularly obvious from the original title, *Wilbur Falls.* Barely average image transfer and sound. —MO
AKA: Wilbur Falls.
Movie: 🎬🎬 **DVD:** 🎬🎬🎬
MTI (cat #50048, UPC 619935404830). Full frame. $22.49. Keepcase. *LANG:* English. *SUB:* Spanish. *FEATURES:* 20 chapters • Theatrical trailer • Cast bios • Trivia.
1998 95m/C Danny Aiello, Sally Kirkland, Suzanne Cryer, Shanee Edwards; **D:** Juliane Glantz; **W:** Juliane Glantz; **C:** Kurt Brabbee; **M:** Jim Halfpenny.

Dead Simple

Motel-owner and wannabe singer (Stern) gets hooked up with a floozie (Kohl) and her boyfriend (Caan). Before long, his wife (Richardson) is dead and other bodies are piling up faster than he can plant them. It's a supposed goof on *Blood Simple* (though the shooting title was "Viva Las Nowhere" according to director Bloom). The deft Coen brothers touch is absent. For a mid-budget Canadian production, the image is fine but not spectacular in any way. Same for sound. The commentary track is sporadic with long stretches of silence. —MM **AKA:** Viva Las Nowhere.
Movie: 🎬🎬 **DVD:** 🎬🎬 ½
Artisan Ent. (cat #11979, UPC 01223611-9791). Widescreen. Dolby Digital 5.1 Surround; Dolby Digital Surround. $14.98. Keepcase. *LANG:* English. *SUB:* English; Spanish. *FEATURES:* 24 chapters • Commentary • Filmographies • Trailer • Behind-the-scenes featurette • Photo gallery.
2001 (R) 98m/C Daniel Stern, James Caan, Patricia Richardson, Sherry Stringfield, Lacey Kohl, Tim Abell; **D:** Jason Bloom; **W:** Richard Uhlig, Steve Seitz; **C:** James Glennon; **M:** Andrew Gross.

Dealin' Dirty

These four "urban" thrillers are cheaply made and show all of the flaws of low-budget works. They're amateurish in every respect and most of them show signs of age and damage. Both *Dealin' Dirty* and *Rockin' with a Bullet* appear to have been titled *Sugar Hill* and *Sugar Hill, Pt. 2* at one time. They have to do with drugs and the music business. Also included are *Black Cobra* and *Black Godfather.* (Please see reviews.) —MM
Movie: woof **DVD:** woof
BCI-Eclipse (cat #44295-9, UPC 7873644-29592). Full frame. $9.98. Keepcase. *LANG:* English. *FEATURES:* 10 chapters • Commentary: J. Vincent Parris • Interview

with Leonard Turner • Interview with Divina Harris • Music videos.
19?? 70m/C Leonard Turner; **D:** J. Vincent Parris; **W:** J. Vincent Parris.

Dean Koontz's Black River

The Stepford Wives meets *The Truman Show* as Jay Mohr finds himself stranded in the perfect town, with unknown forces conspiring to keep him there. Dean Koontz's story is unintentionally funny, and poor special effects ruin the rest of the suspense. The picture quality is a small step up from VHS, with faded colors and a lack of detail. The background hiss often threatens to stage a rebellion, placing the sound quality a notch below DVD standards. —*BG*
Movie: ♫ **DVD:** ♫ ½
MTI (cat #8121, UPC 039414581218). Full frame. $24.98. Keepcase. *LANG:* English. *SUB:* Spanish. *FEATURES:* 20 chapters • Trailers • Cast bios.
2001 (PG) 87m/C Jay Mohr, Lisa Edelstein, Ann Cusack, Ron Canada, Stephen Tobolowsky; **D:** Jeff Bleckner; **W:** Daniel Taplitz; **C:** John Bartley.

Death Before Dishonor

Sergeant Joseph "Gunny" Burns (Dryer) has recently been transferred to a Middle Eastern country, where he must deal with nasty Arab terrorists who shoot women and children, smash up vegetable carts, and even burn the American flag to let us know how bad they are. But when they kidnap his commanding officer, Gunny decides he's had enough diplomacy. The "Don't Tread on Me" patriotism that follows makes Chuck Norris films look like liberal propaganda. Picture quality is inconsistent, with some fairly major flaws every now and then, but is very good in most places. The audio track has lots of explosions. —*BG*
Movie: ♫ ½ **DVD:** ♫♫ ½
Anchor Bay (cat #DV11407, UPC 013131140798). Widescreen (1.85:1) anamorphic. Dolby Ultra-Stereo 2.0. $24.98. Keepcase. *LANG:* English. *CAP:* English. *FEATURES:* 28 chapters • Trailer.
1987 (R) 95m/C Fred (John F.) Dryer, Brian Keith, Joanna Pacula, Paul Winfield; **D:** Terry J. Leonard; **W:** John Gatliff; **C:** Don Burgess; **M:** Brian May.

The Death Curse of Tartu / Sting of Death

An ancient Seminole witch doctor (Doug Hobart) lies entombed deep in the Everglades having left express notice that he NOT be disturbed. Sure enough, folks rudely come snooping around his damp cave, noising up the place with their wild dance music, so ever-cranky Tartu (who prefers tribal rhythms) takes to bumping them off in fiendish ways as random critters. In the second half of this double bill, *Sting of Death*, again deep in the Everglades, scientists tinker in ways they shouldn't with ordinary jellyfish and pretty soon a loathsome half-man half-jellyfish creature is draggin' beach bunnies into the surf. Typically, word spreads slowly about these attacks, as Karen (Valerie Hawkins) and her college cutie friends arrive at her family's secluded estate for spring break with no inkling of their impending doom. Both are presented in full frame, but astonishingly, given the state of *Sting*'s original negative (the only existing print was covered with mold!), its color is a heckuvalot more vibrant than *Tartu*! Both exhibit a fair amount of scratches and blemishes typical to these sorts of pictures. The same is true for the mono tracks with *Tartu* having consistent background static and *Sting* fairing much better. —*GNG/MM*
Movie: ♫♫ ½ **DVD:** ♫♫♫
Something Weird Video (UPC 0143810-80025). Full frame. $24.98. Keepcase. *LANG:* English. *FEATURES:* Commentaries • Exploitation shorts • Trailers.
1966 84m/C Fred Pinero, Doug Hobart, Babette Sherrill, Mayra Christine, Bill Marcos, Sherman Hayes, Gary Holtz, Frank Weed; **D:** William Grefe; **W:** William Grefe; **C:** Julio Chavez; **M:** Al Greene, Al Jacobs.

Deathstalker

This low-budget sword-and-sorcery non-epic has become a perennial favorite on cable and home video because it has a brief but intense love scene involving co-star Lana Clarkson, and an exceptional amount of incidental nudity among the supporting cast. Beyond that, it's standard stuff about a bare-chested warrior (Hill), evil wizard, kidnapped princess (Benton), etc. It's spawned three sequels to date. Since so much of the action is set in dark crowded interiors, DVD offers an image that's only a marginal improvement over VHS tape. —*MM* **AKA:** El Cazador de la Muerte.
Movie: ♫♫ **DVD:** ♫♫ ½
New Concorde (cat #NH20247 D, UPC 73-6991424791). Full frame. Stereo. $9.98. Keepcase. *LANG:* English. *FEATURES:* 20 chapters • Trailers • Talent files.
1983 (R) 80m/C Richard (Rick) Hill, Barbi Benton, Richard Brooker, Victor Bo, Lana Clarkson; **D:** John Watson; **W:** Howard R. Cohen; **C:** Leonardo Solis; **M:** Oscar Cardozo Ocampo.

Deathstalker 2: Duel of the Titans

On DVD, this sequel is superior to the original because it contains a wonderfully breezy commentary track by exploitation auteur Wynorski, abetted by stars Terlesky and Naples. They have a lot of fun remembering the spoofy material. Otherwise, DVD does about as much with the cheapjack image as any medium could. —*MM*
Movie: ♫♫ **DVD:** ♫♫♫
New Concorde (cat #NH20279 D, UPC 73699142990). Full frame. Stereo. $9.98. Keepcase. *LANG:* English. *FEATURES:* 20 chapters • Trailers • Talent files • Commentary: Wynorski, Terlesky, Naples.
1987 (R) 85m/C John Terlesky, Monique Gabrielle, John Lazar, Toni Naples, Maria Socas, Queen Kong; **D:** Jim Wynorski; **W:** Jim Wynorski; **C:** Leonardo Solis; **M:** Chuck Cirino.

Deceived

Trapped in a scientific outpost, a motley crew of opportunists (including tech-geek Nelson and military officer Gossett Jr.) listens to a message from space. The signal immediately begins to change them, and it becomes apparent that it is not coming from space after all, but from somewhere far more sinister. There is a solution, however, and it has something to do with believing in God. This faith-based thriller from the *Left Behind* team has some tension, but the overt propaganda and phoned-in performances make it hard to handle. However, the DVD is as enjoyable as it could be with quality picture and sound, and many informative and funny extras. —*DRL*
Movie: ♫ ½ **DVD:** ♫♫♫
Cloud Ten Pictures (UPC 745638006030). Full frame. Dolby 5.1 Surround; Stereo. $19.95. Keepcase. *LANG:* English; Spanish. *CAP:* English. *FEATURES:* Deleted scenes • Bloopers and outtakes • 5 featurettes • Trailers for other Cloud Ten films • Bios • 30 chapters.
2001 99m/C Judd Nelson, Louis Gossett Jr., Stewart Bick, Michelle Nolden, Deborah Odell; **D:** Andre Van Heerden; **W:** Paul LaLonde, John Patus; **C:** George Tirl, Jiri Tirl; **M:** Gary Koftinoff.

Deceiver

Warning: Don't watch this film unless you're willing to watch it a couple of times to catch all the nuances in the script and performances. A really good psychological thriller with a layered, complex script. James Wayland (Tim Roth) is a murder suspect undergoing a lie detector test. Detectives Braxton (Chris Penn) and Kennesaw (Michael Rooker) are trying to tie Roth to the murder of a call girl (Renee Zellweger) but find Roth's intelligence too much for them. If you're looking for action, look elsewhere. If you're looking for a smart script and good acting, this one is right up your alley. DVD has clean picture and good sound although whispered dialogue is sometimes hard to hear. That's what optional subtitles are for. —*DE* **AKA:** Liar.
Movie: ♫♫♫ **DVD:** ♫♫♫
MGM Home Ent. (cat #1003346, UPC 027-61687495). Widescreen (2.35:1) anamorphic; full frame. Dolby Stereo Surround. $14.98. Keepcase. *LANG:* English; Spanish. *SUB:* English; Spanish. *FEATURES:* 16 chapters • Original theatrical trailer.
1997 (R) 102m/C Renee Zellweger, Tim Roth, Christopher Penn, Michael Rooker, Ellen Burstyn, Rosanna Arquette; **D:** Jonas Pate, Josh Pate; **W:** Jonas Pate, Josh Pate; **C:** Bill Butler; **M:** Harry Gregson-Williams.

December 7th / The Fleet That Came to Stay

It should be noted that this disc contains the shorter cut of *December 7th* (36 minutes) which is the one that won the Academy Award. As such, though still racist, this version is nowhere near as hysterical and shows less knee-jerk anti-Asian paranoia than is on display in the extremely longer version (reviewed in *Book 2*). Director Budd Boetticher's *Fleet that Came to Stay* is a short portrayal of the war in the Pacific, focusing on the taking of Okinawa. Constructed almost entirely of documentary footage of the actual events, it has much more punch and gives one a strong sense of what it was like to be present during the battles. *December 7th*, with its bogus reenactments, can't come close. My only qualm: the footage leads one to believe in the U.S. fleet's total success while the disastrously high body count given in the newspaper headline at the end tells another, more chilling tale. Both discs are equal to VHS but the prints used are extremely ratty, with a constant stream of scratches and cinch marks. The sound on both is fairly poor with *Fleet* audio sounding fairly muffled and squawky. Contrasts are better on *December 7th* while *Fleet* is dark and murky. —DG

Movie: 🎵🎵 **DVD:** 🎵
Goodtimes Ent. (cat #05-81186, UPC 018-713811868). Full frame. Mono. $7.49. Keepcase. *LANG:* English. *FEATURES:* 9 chapters ∘ Insert card with chapter listings.
1943 60m/B D: John Ford; **C:** Gregg Toland; **M:** Alfred Newman.

The Deep End

Margaret Hall (Swinton) is a typical mother who is forced to perform remarkable acts when her college-bound son Beau (Tucker) becomes involved with a corrupt older man who demands money to keep the boy's sexual orientation secret from his absent father. To reveal almost anything else about the plot would be unfair. It unfolds through complex characters and their relationship to an astonishingly vivid environment. Lake Tahoe is more than a backdrop for the action; it's part of the story. Graduate students could write papers on the directors' use of water images. Their commentary track is one of the more thoughtful and soft-spoken. Who'd have thought that this story came from a novel first condensed for the *Ladies Home Journal* and that it's a remake of Max Ophuls's *Reckless Moment* with one significant change in character? DVD does justice to director of photography Giles Nuttgens's remarkable work. This is one of the nicest images you'll see, capturing the blue/green/auburn color scheme with more detail than the theatrical release. Strongest recommendations. Fans of the directors' cult favorite *Suture* will not be disappointed. —MM
Movie: 🎵🎵🎵 **DVD:** 🎵🎵🎵 ½

20th Century Fox (UPC 024543031666). Widescreen (2.35:1) anamorphic. Dolby Digital 5.1 Surround; Dolby Digital Surround. $29.98. Keepcase. *LANG:* English; French. *SUB:* English; Spanish. *CAP:* English. *FEATURES:* 25 chapters ∘ Commentary: Scott McGehee, David Siegel ∘ Sundance Channel "anatomy of a scene" featurette ∘ "Making of" featurette ∘ Photo gallery ∘ Trailer and TV spot.
2001 (R) 99m/C Tilda Swinton, Goran Visnjic, Jonathan Tucker, Raymond J. Barry, Joshua Lucas, Peter Donat, Tamara Hope, Jordan Dorrance; **D:** Scott McGehee, David Siegel; **W:** Scott McGehee, David Siegel; **C:** Giles Nuttgens; **M:** Peter Nashel. *AWARDS:* Sundance '01: Cinematog. (Nuttgens); *NOM:* Golden Globes '02: Actress—Drama (Swinton); Ind. Spirit '02: Actress (Swinton), Cinematog.

Deep in the Woods

A group of young actors is invited to an isolated country manor to perform "Little Red Riding Hood" for a strange, mute child's birthday. As night falls, the dark house and the woods nearby become the stalking grounds of a wolf-like killer, who may be supernatural in origin. A French response to the *Scream* films, *Deep in the Woods*'s strongest element is a tangible, unnerving mood of fear and lurking danger. The photography is exquisitely framed and lit; the interiors of the house are reduced to pools of light and chasms of darkness that seem alive with unseen terrors. The cast is attractive and likable, but the character relationships are a bit confusing on first viewing. Director Delplanque admirably sustains the high level of tension from first frame to last, but the conventional ending is a bit of a letdown. The disc features a satisfyingly accurate transfer with perfect blacks and rich colors. There's some slight grain on the odd shot or two, but these seem to be part of the source print. Shot in a format similar to Super35, the full-frame title sequence reveals more on the bottom than in the widescreen edition. The preferred format is the widescreen edition, as it features stronger compositions. A few beautifully composed shots (particularly the exquisite dressing room tracking shot) are ruined by the full-frame cropping. The Surround track is excellent, fully enveloping the viewer and featuring sound effects channeled for maximum fright. The French dialogue is preferred, naturally. The commentary by Yuzna is surprisingly strong; he frequently quotes the non-English speaking director and gives background information and behind-the-scenes stories provided by Delplanque. A well-done "fan" commentary. As nice as the disc is, the film works even better in the theatre. —DG **AKA:** *Promenons Nous dans les Bois.*
Movie: 🎵🎵🎵 **DVD:** 🎵🎵🎵 ½
Artisan Ent. (cat #12182, UPC 01223612-1824). Widescreen (2.35:1) anamorphic; full frame. Dolby Surround 5.1. $24.98. Keepcase. *LANG:* French; English. *SUB:* English. *CAP:* English. *FEATURES:* 20 chapters ∘ Commentary: horror expert Brian Yuzna ∘ Cast & filmmaker bios and filmographies ∘ Trailer ∘ Photo gallery ∘ Insert card with chapter listings.
2000 (R) 88m/C *FR* Clotilde Courau, Clement Sibony, Vincent Lecoeur, Alexia Stresi, Maud Buquet; **D:** Lionel Delplanque; **W:** Annabelle Perrichon; **C:** Denis Rouden; **M:** Jerome Coullet.

Deep Trouble

It's strictly amateur hour in this hip-hop urban drama. New York drug kingpin Perry (Count Stovall) decides that the world of organized crime simply isn't enough, and decides to overtake the business of Star (Janel C. Scarborough). Star is an entertainment manager, who represents up-and-coming actress Diana (Alyah Horsford), as well as several stand-up comics. Star and Diana decide that they aren't going to be pushed around by this bully, so they take a stand and the "trouble" begins. The film is filled with bad acting and amateurish special effects (several characters get shot in the head, which is represented by a simple trickle of blood). Writer/director Juney Smith, shouldn't quit his day job as an actor. The film is very poorly paced, having more scenes of pointless dialogue than action. The DVD doesn't fare much better. The image is presented full frame, and despite being sharp, shows considerable grain. The audio is a mess, with the dialogue either being muffled and unintelligible or loudly distorted and unintelligible. Either way, it's difficult to understand what anyone is saying in the film...which may not be such a bad thing. —ML
Movie: 🎵 ½ **DVD:** 🎵🎵
MTI (cat #7016, UPC 039414570168). Full frame. Digital Stereo. $24.95. Keepcase. *LANG:* English. *FEATURES:* Trailers ∘ Director bio.
2001 102m/C Count Stovall, Janel C. Scarborough, Alyah Horsford; **D:** Juney Smith; **W:** Juney Smith.

Deep Water

Ambitious and busy little video premiere finds room for all of your favorite sea-going thriller clichés. We've got the terrorists who want to hold the ocean liner hostage; we've got the explosion that causes a tidal wave that capsizes the aforementioned liner so that we then have the upside-down ship; not to mention the sharks, and the aircraft carrier (under the command of Coburn), and the lone Marine (Mandylor) on board the upside-down ship who can stand up to the bad guys, and romance the newsbabe (Hughes). With all that going on, punctuated by some not-very-special-but-still-kind-of-neat computer effects, one has to wonder why the studio elected to release a pan-and-scan full-frame version. The image is fine for what it is, but that's not much. Surround effects are excellent, too. —MM
Movie: 🎵🎵 ½ **DVD:** 🎵🎵 ½
20th Century Fox (cat #2002799, UPC 024543027997). Full frame. Dolby Digital

5.1 Surround; Dolby Surround. $14.98. Keepcase. *LANG:* English. *SUB:* English; Spanish. *CAP:* English. *FEATURES:* Trailer ▪ 12 chapters ▪ Talent files.
1999 (R) 101m/C James Coburn, Costas Mandylor, Finola Hughes, Alex Hyde-White, Larry Poindexter, Chick Vennera; *D:* John Putch; *W:* J. Everitt Morley, Darby Black; *C:* James Mathers; *M:* Alexander Baker.

Deeply
Off the coast of Nova Scotia, a secluded fishing island is haunted by a curse. Once every 50 years, the fish disappear until a sacrifice is made. Kirsten Dunst stars as a young woman caught within this strange cycle. The film begins with undertones of *The Stepford Wives* and *The Wicker Man*, hinting at the dark secret of an idyllic village, but tips its hand too early and decides it would rather be a romance. A good deal of grain is present and the colors are too dull to truly capture the grandeur of the film's setting. The stereo soundtrack is adequate, but also fails to take full advantage of the film's setting. —*BG*
Movie: ♫♫ *DVD:* ♫♫ ½
Studio Home Ent. (cat #ST7906D, UPC 65-8149790629). Full frame. Dolby Stereo. $24.98. Keepcase. *LANG:* English. *SUB:* English; Spanish. *CAP:* English. *FEATURES:* 24 chapters ▪ Trailers.
1999 102m/C *CA* Alberta Watson, Lynn Redgrave, Kirsten Dunst, Julia Brendler, Brent Carver; *D:* Sheri Elwood; *W:* Sheri Elwood; *M:* Micki Meuser.

The Defiant Ones
Stanley Kramer's powerful examination about the shackles of racial prejudice revolves around two escaped prisoners, one black and one white, in the rural South. Bound by a chain and their societal resentments towards one another, convicts Joker Jackson (Curtis) and Noah Cullen (Poitier) face constant peril as the law and bloodhounds close in. A prime example of a Stanley Kramer "message" movie, this one may not have the same groundbreaking sheen as when it was first released in 1958, but it still dazzles with that timeless technique of good storytelling. The chemistry between Curtis and Poitier is still intact, despite the heavy handed dialogue-as-sermon in some scenes. In fact, the strength of the acting keeps the whole affair from devolving into a political polemic. Not only do the leads hold their own, but the supporting roles shine equally bright, including Theodore Bikel as the pursuing sheriff and Lon Chaney as the rational voice of a bloodthirsty lynch mob. The 1.66 non-anamorphic transfer looks gorgeous with sharp gray tones and dead-on contrast levels. The source print shows nary a blemish or speckle and, despite some edge-enhancement, details come through strong and distinct. The Dolby Digital mono soundtrack exhibits no hiss or distortion, just crisp and clean dialogue. Compare the worn theatrical trailer with the sparkling feature presentation and one can appreciate the care MGM put into this edition. As far as movie-only DVDs go, this one ranks as reference quality. —*EP*
Movie: ♫♫♫ *DVD:* ♫♫♫ ½
MGM Home Ent. (cat #1002738, UPC 027616869364). Widescreen (1.66:1) letterboxed. Dolby Digital Mono. $14.98. Keepcase. *LANG:* English; French; Spanish. *SUB:* French; Spanish. *FEATURES:* 16 chapters ▪ Theatrical trailer.
1958 97m/B Tony Curtis, Sidney Poitier, Theodore Bikel, Lon Chaney Jr., Charles McGraw, Cara Williams; *D:* Stanley Kramer; *W:* Nedrick Young, Harold Jacob Smith; *C:* Sam Leavitt; *M:* Steve Dorff. *AWARDS:* Oscars '58: B&W Cinematog., Story & Screenplay; British Acad. '58: Actor (Poitier); Golden Globes '59: Film—Drama; N.Y. Film Critics '58: Director (Kramer), Film, Screenplay; *NOM:* Oscars '58: Actor (Curtis), Actor (Poitier), Director (Kramer), Film Editing, Picture, Support. Actor (Bikel), Support. Actress (Williams).

Dementia 13 [Marengo]
Please see review for *Carnival of Souls / Dementia 13.*
1963 m/C

Dementia 13 [Roan]
This popular public domain title (first reviewed in *Book 2*) has never looked very good on video, but this version (identical to the Roan laserdisc) looks better than most. The transfer was made from an extremely grainy print with scratches and an occasionally unstable image. While contrasts are still too bright, there's more visible detail in the lighter areas than on other tapes and discs. Sound is fairly thin, but coherent and not too crackly. The commentary is interesting and informative but Campbell is a slow and repetitive commentator. The trailer and the text from the D-13 mental fitness test (designed to tell whether an audience member was mentally stable enough to see the film) are appreciated bonuses not included on other releases. —*DG* *AKA:* The Haunted and the Hunted.
Movie: ♫♫♫ *DVD:* ♫♫ ½
Troma Team Video (cat #ROAN AED-2056, UPC 785604205623). Widescreen (1.66:1) letterboxed. Mono. $19.95. Keepcase. *LANG:* English. *FEATURES:* Commentary: Campbell ▪ Theatrical trailer ▪ Original D-13 test ▪ 12 chapters.
1963 75m/B William Campbell, Luana Anders, Bart Patton, Patrick Magee, Barbara Dowling, Ethne Dunn, Mary Mitchell, Karl Schanzer; *D:* Francis Ford Coppola; *W:* Francis Ford Coppola; *C:* Charles Hannawalt; *M:* Ronald Stein.

Demon Lust
The Sopranos meets *Dracula* in this ultra low-budget New Jersey independent production. Nick (Teller) and Tony (Vincent) owe $5,000 to a mobster who has sent a thug (Savini) to collect. After some allegedly comic bits, the two guys find themselves hooked up with Amanda (Stevens), a beautiful babe who's really a monster. DVD really can't do anything but provide room for the extras. Shot-on-video image is so underlit throughout that grain is exceptional. Most of the lead roles are well acted. —*MM*
Movie: ♫♫ *DVD:* ♫♫ ½
El Independent Cinema (cat #vo-9501, UPC 612385950193). Full frame. $19.99. Keepcase. *LANG:* English. *FEATURES:* "Demon Affairs" short film ▪ Outtakes ▪ Brinke Stevens interview.
2001 140m/C Edward Lee Vincent, Zander Teller, Brinke Stevens, Tom Savini; *D:* David A. Goldberg; *W:* Coven Balfour; *C:* Joseph Robert Jobe; *M:* Coven Balfour.

Demonia
Italian horror director Lucio Fulci certainly had his ups and downs during his long career, and *Demonia* is definitely a "down." Archaeologists digging in Sicily uncover a sealed convent where five nuns were crucified in the 15th century. This discovery unleashes an ancient evil and bizarre murders begin to take place. Unfortunately, that's about it as far as the plot goes. Even by Fulci's standards, *Demonia* is slow and pondering, with many scenes taking place twice, once in reality and then again in a dream (nightmare?). Fulci's trademark gore is scant and the special effects are laughable. Even die-hard Fulci fans will be disappointed. This DVD release doesn't fare much better. The image is nicely framed at 1.66:1, but the transfer seems to have come from two source prints. Most of the scenes are incredibly soft and hazy, looking very washed-out, while others are very sharp, clear, and colorful. And one shot appears to have been done through a screen door! Fulci completists should like the brief interview with the late director that is included on the disc. —*ML*
Movie: woof *DVD:* ♫♫ ½
Media Blasters (cat #SSDVD-0102, UPC 631595010299). Widescreen (1.66:1) letterboxed. Dolby Digital Mono. $24.95. Keepcase. *LANG:* English. *FEATURES:* Director bio ▪ Director filmography ▪ Actor interview ▪ Behind-the-scenes footage ▪ 12 chapters.
1990 90m/C *IT* Brett Halsey, Meg Register, Carla Cassola, Al Cliver, Lucio Fulci; *D:* Lucio Fulci; *W:* Lucio Fulci, Piero Regnoli; *C:* Luis Ciccarese.

The Demon's Baby
Five demons, summoned in the Ching Dynasty, can enter the physical plane by possessing babies. If all five demons incarnate, they will terrorize the world. These demons are imprisoned in vases, which are guarded by a gold Buddha statue. General Hsu (Elvis Tsui) discovers the jars among the treasures in a cave, and he has them brought to his house. But when the sneaky butler steals the golden

Buddha, replacing it with a copy, the jars are left unprotected and the demons escape. That night, the demon-occupied general runs around the house impregnating all four of his wives. A possessed chef seduces a maid for the fifth pregnancy. Before long, the possessed women have bulging bellies that break open into fanged, ravenous mouths—and the tentacled demon fetuses are demanding a blood feast, scarfing down livestock, priests, and servants. A kooky priest (Anthony Wong) is sent for, and a furious supernatural battle commences! Despite the large amount of gore on display here, *The Demon's Baby* never quite crosses the line into bad taste. Helping keep things light is Wong, who gives his character an amusing devil-may-care attitude, even while in combat with Hellspawn. The transfer is generally O.K., but the poorly translated actors' profiles are a hoot. —*BT*

Movie: 🎵🎵 ½ **DVD:** 🎵🎵

Tai Seng (cat #5221, UPC 48950249014-59). Widescreen letterboxed. Dolby Digital 5.1 Surround. $18.95. Keepcase. *LANG:* Cantonese; Mandarin. *SUB:* Chinese; English. *CAP:* English. *FEATURES:* 8 chapters • Star files • Trailers.

1998 85m/C *HK* Emotion Cheung, Anthony Wong, Annie (Chen Chun) Wu, Elvis Tsui; *D:* Kant Leung; *W:* Kant Leung; *C:* Chung Yun Chan; *M:* Lincoln Lo.

Desert Trail

Please see review for *John Wayne: Western Classics.*

Movie: 🎵 ½

1935 57m/B John Wayne, Paul Fix, Mary Kornman; *D:* Robert North Bradbury; *W:* Lindsley Parsons; *C:* Archie Stout.

Designing Woman

Slick MGM romantic farce somehow earned the Oscar for Best Original Screenplay in 1957. It no longer seems very funny, but it's certainly fun watching the classy, natural Lauren Bacall. Gregory Peck can be called a good sport in his role, and that's about it. Vincente Minnelli keeps things percolating, but the show has limitations—mainly its script, which is efficient but not much else. But there's the always-fun Dolores Gray, who I'll watch any day. Sports writer Mike Hagen (Peck) meets and weds Marilla (Bacall) so fast that he doesn't find out that she's a prominent dress designer until they're back in New York. His card-playing cronies don't get along with her hoity-toity fashion and Broadway associates. The plot gets a double burner when a gangster (Platt) sics thug Johnny O (Connors) onto Mike for exposing the fight rackets. This becomes confused with Marilla's suspicions that Mike is still carrying on with showgirl Lori Shannon (Gray). Add to this punchy boxer Maxie Stultz (Shaughnessy) who sleeps with his eyes open and decks anyone who looks at Mike cross-eyed, and there's

enough trouble for everyone. DVD begins well, using clever original artwork on the cover...instead of the usual collage of star faces. The transfer is only the tiniest bit faded, which is great considering the leached look of earlier videos and prints I've seen. Like most Minnelli pictures in 'Scope, the pan-and-scan versions of this were particularly bad, and this 16:9 image at least represents his framing properly. The sound is in mono, even though there is a Perspecta Stereo notice in the main titles...a track configuration that's probably lost now, and wasn't true stereo anyway. The featured extra is a mock interview with costume designer Helen Rose, essentially a set of answers with blank spaces in between for the questions to be filled in later. It's rather confusing—this woman who's supposed to be Helen Rose is first shown sitting down and addressing someone offscreen—named Helen. —*GE*

Movie: 🎵🎵🎵 **DVD:** 🎵🎵🎵🎵

Warner Home Video (UPC 12569545328). Widescreen (2:35:1) anamorphic. Mono. $19.98. Snapper. *LANG:* English. *FEATURES:* Trailer • "Interview" with Helen Rose.

1957 118m/C Gregory Peck, Lauren Bacall, Dolores Gray, Sam Levene, Tom Helmore, Mickey Shaughnessy, Jesse White, Chuck Connors, Edward Platt, Alvy Moore, Jack Cole; *D:* Vincente Minnelli; *W:* George Wells; *C:* John Alton; *M:* Andre Previn. *AWARDS:* Oscars '57: Story & Screenplay.

Desperado [2 SB]

This "Superbit" edition clears up the only significant flaw in the first DVD release (reviewed in *Book 1*)—relatively weak sound. Here, the terrific Los Lobos soundtrack, which is more fun than the movie in some ways, gets all that it's due. Image is equally sharp. This disc is sharper than the theatrical release I saw. If only the film were as energetic as Rodriguez's first telling of the story in the micro-budget *El Mariachi*. —*MM* **AKA:** El Mariachi 2.

Movie: 🎵🎵🎵 **DVD:** 🎵🎵🎵🎵

Columbia Tristar (cat #07576, UPC 0433-96075764). Widescreen (1.85:1) anamorphic. Dolby Digital 5.1 Surround Stereo; DTS Surround. $27.95. Slipcase keepcase. *LANG:* English. *SUB:* English; French; Spanish; Portuguese; Chinese; Korean; Thai. *FEATURES:* 28 chapters.

1995 (R) 103m/C Antonio Banderas, Salma Hayek, Joaquim de Almeida, Steve Buscemi, Richard "Cheech" Marin, Carlos Gomez, Quentin Tarantino, Carlos Gallardo; *D:* Robert Rodriguez; *W:* Robert Rodriguez; *C:* Guillermo Navarro; *M:* Los Lobos. *AWARDS: NOM:* MTV Movie Awards '96: Most Desirable Male (Banderas), Kiss (Antonio Banderas/Salma Hayek).

Desperate Hours

Sometimes you just shouldn't remake a classic. Humphrey Bogart would be spinning in his grave if he saw this mish mash. Escaped convict Michael Bosworth (Mickey Rourke) holes up in the Cornell house.

There's Papa Cornell (Anthony Hopkins, in a role he probably wishes he'd never taken), Momma Cornell (Mimi Rogers), and their two kids. Kelly Lynch (ohhh, baby) stars as Rourke's lawyer accomplice. This movie is just way over the top, and the ending is utter stupidity. DVD boasts good picture, O.K. sound. —*DE*

Movie: 🎵🎵 ½ **DVD:** 🎵🎵🎵

MGM Home Ent. (cat #1003348, UPC 027-61687497). Widescreen (1.85:1) anamorphic. Stereo Surround. $19.98. Keepcase. *LANG:* English; French; Spanish. *SUB:* English; French; Spanish. *FEATURES:* Trailer • 16 chapters.

1990 (R) 105m/C Mickey Rourke, Anthony Hopkins, Mimi Rogers, Kelly Lynch, Lindsay Crouse, Elias Koteas, David Morse, Shawnee Smith, Danny Gerard, Matt McGrath; *D:* Michael Cimino; *W:* Mark Rosenthal, Larry Konner, Joseph Hayes; *C:* Doug Milsome; *M:* David Mansfield.

Desperate Living (John Waters Collection Vol. 2)

Recently released from an asylum, Peggy Gravel (Stole) finds herself on the run after her enormous maid (Hill) suffocates Mr. Gravel. They flee to Mortville, a town comprised of degenerates and ruled with an iron fist by the ridiculous Queen Carlotta (Massey). One of Waters's sleaziest efforts, with 400-pound lesbians, a nudist camp, rat eating, glory holes, and a botched sex-change. Even without Divine, the best of Waters's early output. All right, it's not so bad that New Line forces you to buy *Polyester* if you want to own *Desperate Living* on DVD. The worst thing about the whole John Waters Collection discs are the crappy cardboard cases that they come in. *Desperate Living* looks as good as you'd want it to on DVD, with all the rough edges preserved—scratchy sound (not to mention a healthy dose of wow-and-flutter here and there) and film grain included. In this case, saying that the DVD is an improvement over the VHS version actually means that the film looks a little worse, since the lower resolution tape couldn't convey the raw grit delivered here on the DVD. In addition to the better/bad picture delivered by the DVD, you also get another one of those amazing John Waters commentaries that are always as entertaining as the films themselves. He's accompanied on this one by actress Liz Renay, who seems like a wacky real-life version of a Waters's screen character. —*BG/JO*

Movie: 🎵🎵 **DVD:** 🎵🎵🎵

New Line (cat #N5231, UPC 7940435231-20). Full frame. Dolby Mono. $30.99. Custom cardboard. *LANG:* English. *CAP:* English. *FEATURES:* 18 chapters • Trailer • Commentary.

1977 90m/C Mink Stole, Jean Hill, Edith Massey, Liz Renay, Mary Vivian Pearce, Cookie Mueller, Susan Lowe, Ed Peranio, Pat Moran, George Stover, Turkey Joe, Channing Wilroy; *D:* John Waters; *W:* John Waters; *C:* Thomas Loizeaux.

Destination Nightmare

For those of you still playing "Six Degrees of Kevin Bacon," here is where you can connect George Hamilton to Boris Karloff. *Destination Nightmare* is an anthology of four stories from the short-lived TV show *The Veil*. Karloff introduces the stories and plays a small role in each. In "The Return of Madam Vernoy," George Hamilton plays a supporting role and was sporting the perfect tan, even at the ripe age of 19. In that story, a reincarnated woman has full recall of her past life and insists on going to see her old husband before she can commit to marry another. In "The Birthday," a 16-year-old girl wakes up with the memories of another girl. In the next tale, a young pilot discovers the murderous sins of his father. And there is the old stand-by of the ghostly hitchhiking girl, who died on prom night oh-so-many years ago and still "wanders these roads each year." More amazing than the high quality of the image transfer is how the whole disc is oddly entertaining. Karloff is a charmer and each of his acting appearances is amusing. It's very unusual to see the host of an anthology series actually appear in the stories as someone else. —JAS

Movie: ♫♫ ½ **DVD:** ♫♫♫ ½
Rhino (cat #R2972756, UPC 603497275-625). Full frame. $9.95. Snapper. *LANG:* English. *FEATURES:* 4 chapters.
1954 100m/C Boris Karloff, Tod Andrews, Whit Bissell, George Hamilton, Myron Healey; **D:** Paul Landres.

The Devil Bat

Lugosi stars as a scientist who has marked for death the men who cheated him. After giving them bat-attracting cologne, he releases his pet—a gigantic bat—which seeks out the victims and tears out their throats. Probably the most fun of all of Lugosi's low-budget cheapies, this one's a fast-paced, roughly hewn, and silly time-waster. The transfer may have been cribbed from store-bought laserdisc. Image is grainy, smeary, soft, and prone to digital shimmer and pixelation. The sound is frequently scratchy and prone to distortion. Title is available on the *Great Bloodsucking Movies* disc. —DG **AKA:** Killer Bats.

Movie: ♫♫ **DVD:** ♫♫
BFS Video (cat #30237-D, UPC 06680530-2374). Full frame. Mono. $9.98. Keepcase. *LANG:* English. *FEATURES:* 6 chapters • Cast bios/filmographies.
1941 67m/B Bela Lugosi, Dave O'Brien, Suzanne Kaaren, Yolande Donlan; **D:** Jean Yarbrough; **W:** John Thomas Neville; **C:** Arthur Martinelli.

Devil Girl from Mars

In a small Scottish inn known as the Bonnie Charlie, a slice-of-life group of characters see a huge and noisy spaceship land in the meadow. They're held prisoner by Nyah, a one-woman army sent to conquer the Earth in the name of her home planet Mars. She looks spectacular in her black leather miniskirt with matching boots, cape, and cowl, and she's after male prisoners to help repopulate Mars. Stuffy Brits resist. Image has packaged the DVD attractively but woefully bereft of any bonuses or extras. The picture looks fine, but the Dolby mix makes all but the most strident sound effects difficult to pick up. They would have done better to keep the mono soundtrack. —BT

Movie: ♫♫ ½ **DVD:** ♫♫
Image Ent. (cat #ID8589CODVD, UPC 014-381858921). Full frame. $24.99. Snapper. *LANG:* English. *FEATURES:* 12 chapters.
1954 76m/B *GB* Hugh McDermott, Hazel Court, Patricia Laffan, Peter Reynolds, Adrienne Corri, Joseph Tomelty, Sophie Stewart, John Laurie, Anthony Richmond; **D:** David MacDonald; **W:** John C. Mather, James Eastwood; **C:** Jack Cox; **M:** Edwin Astley.

Devil Hunter Yohko: The Complete Collection, Vol. 1

Sixteen-year-old Yohko Mano is finding stranger things happening to her than the urges of her post-pubescent sexuality. Her grandmother reveals the truth: Yohko has inherited the mantle of Devil Hunter from a line of 107 previous warriors. Produced before *Buffy the Vampire Slayer*, this anime—which recounts the adventures of a teenage girl assigned to protect the world from demon invaders—was the first title imported by ADV Films, and this DVD collection marks their 10th anniversary. The "special edition" version of part 1, which contains the original cut never released anywhere before, is in English only without subtitles. The Japanese version with optional English subtitles is only accessible via the special features menu, which also has rarity on anime **DVD:** an audio commentary on which ADV Films folks reminisce about the anniversary of this, a reissue of their debut title. —BT

Movie: ♫♫ **DVD:** ♫♫ ½
A.D.V. Films (cat #DY001, UPC 70272703-0925). Full frame. $29.98. Keepcase. *LANG:* Japanese; English. *SUB:* English. *FEATURES:* 15 chapters • Commentary • Art gallery • Trailers.
1993 43m/C *JP* **D:** Tetsuro Aoki, Katsuhisa Yamada; **W:** Yoshihiro Tomita, Hisaya Takabayashi; **C:** Kinichi Ishikawa, Hiroshi Isakawa; **M:** Hiroya Watanabe, Toshiyuki Omori.

Devil Man

Manga Video presents two "Devil Man" anime adaptations in one package, running about 55 minutes each. In "The Birth," the parents of our hero release a monster from an ice cave in Antarctica. Teen Akira's pal Ryu reveals how his father went insane and killed himself, but the secret behind the madness is a demon skull mask found in an Aztec cave. It (the mask, not the cave) allows one to see into the ancient demonic world. Unfortunately, the boys' knowledge of this world makes them a target for demons still roaming the Earth. The only way to protect themselves is to attempt to merge with demons. The ultimate danger is that their human spirit will become completely dominated by that of the demon. Ryu fails in his attempt, but Akira succeeds in his transformation, able to become a demon-shredding Devil Man when the need arises. In "The Demon Bird," the Devil Man fights soul-snatching demon Jinmen, Gelmar the water demon, and Shirnu the bird demon. A splatterpunk series that broke through sex and gore barriers in a Hellish fantasy setting. The few extras on the DVD are mostly of a purely promotional nature. There's a video trailer for "Devil Man," plus a music video made up of Manga title clips, a weblink to the Manga Video website, and some catalogue information. —BT

Movie: ♫♫♫ **DVD:** ♫♫ ½
Manga Ent. (cat #MANGA40502WR01, UPC 660200405021). Full frame. Dolby Digital 5.1 Surround. $29.95. Keepcase. *LANG:* English. *FEATURES:* 12 chapters • Trailers • Bios • Filmographies • Image gallery.
1987 120m/C *JP* **D:** Tsutomu Iida; **W:** Tsutomu Iida, Nagai Go; **M:** Kenji Kawai; **V:** Alan Marriott, Adam Matalon.

The Devil's Brigade

Dirty Dozen–style film with Holden as the leader of a special commando brigade consisting of the usual misfits and oddballs. The team is trained to take on the Nazis in Scandinavia but has their assignment cancelled. Instead, they take them on in the Italian Alps, making for some perilous adventures. Non-acting notables include former football great Hornung and former boxing champ Gene Fullmer. The video transfer is passable. There are some distracting pixelation problems present in both light and dark colors. These flaws manifest themselves in peripheral images (e.g. power lines, cinder blocks, license plates, etc.). Though it is a minor quibble, the problem occurs often enough, that it tends to ruin a few scenes. The soundtrack is solid, but is ultimately nothing special. —MJT

Movie: ♫♫ **DVD:** ♫♫ ½
MGM Home Ent. (cat #1003428, UPC 027616875778). Widescreen (2.35:1) letterboxed. Dolby Digital Mono. $14.95. Keepcase. *LANG:* English; Spanish. *SUB:* English; Spanish; French. *FEATURES:* 16 chapters • Original theatrical trailer.
1968 130m/C William Holden, Cliff Robertson, Vince Edwards, Andrew Prine, Claude Akins, Michael Rennie, Dana Andrews, Gretchen Wyler, Carroll O'Connor, Richard Jaeckel, Jack Watson, Paul Hornung, Jeremy Slate, Don Megowan, Patric Knowles, James Craig, Richard Dawson, Tom Stern, Luke Askew, Harry Carey Jr., Tom Troupe, Norman Alden, David Pritchard, Gene Fullmer; **D:** Andrew V. McLaglen; **W:** William Roberts; **C:** William Clothier; **M:** Alex North.

The Devil's Prey

Full of bare breasts and clichés so bold they hurt the eyes, *Devil's Prey* is so bad it's boring. Misogyny is high and IQs are low as a group of teens goes to a rave out in the middle of nowhere. Between the alcohol and the ecstasy the girls in the group are targeted for sacrifice. As they drive away from the party, they run into a blood-soaked girl on a deserted stretch of highway. In the tradition of *Children of the Corn,* there is nowhere to run or hide as the teens are chased by a scripted group of devil worshipers led by the town priest (Bergin, obviously still being punished for *Sleeping with the Enemy*). The picture is very pretty, the blood and bare skin looks great, and the sound is better than average. —CA
Movie: woof *DVD:* ♫♫♫
Studio Home Ent. (cat #ST7859D, UPC 6 58149 78592 2). Full frame. Stereo. $24.99. Keepcase. *LANG:* English. *SUB:* English; Spanish; French. *CAP:* English. *FEATURES:* 24 chapters.
2001 (R) 91m/C Patrick Bergin, Ashley Jones, Charlie O'Connell, Bryan Kirkwood, Tim Thomerson; *D:* Bradford May.

The Diamond of Jeru

A rare adaptation of one of Louis L'Amour's non-western stories finds jungle guide Billy Zane leading an American couple into the wilds of Borneo. He then has to rescue them from hostile natives when they try to steal their sacred gem. O.K. action and adventure, mixed with mediocre drama. Picture and sound are both solid. —BT
Movie: ♫♫ *DVD:* ♫♫
USA Home Ent. (cat #9630603182, UPC 696306031826). Full frame. Dolby Digital 5.1 Surround. $19.95. Keepcase. *LANG:* English. *CAP:* English. *FEATURES:* 8 chapters. • Interviews.
2001 89m/C Billy Zane, Keith Carradine, Paris Jefferson, Jackson Raine, Khoa Do; *D:* Ian Barry, Dick Lowry; *W:* Beau L'Amour; *C:* Stephen Windon; *M:* Christopher Tyng.

Diary of a Lost Girl

Second Louise Brooks/G.W. Pabst collaboration was made after the star left Hollywood to pursue more challenging roles under Pabst's guidance. This one follows a frail but mesmerizing German girl through a series of problems that begin with rape and pregnancy, and lead to prostitution. This version was created from a restoration using various elements found in Europe. The new running time is 116 minutes (as opposed to the 99-minute running time of earlier tapes). Some damage is still apparent—scratches, sprocket wear, snow—but overall, the image ranges between fair and good. The short film, "Windy Riley Goes Hollywood," looks much worse. —MM *AKA:* Das tagebuch einer verlorenen.
Movie: ♫♫♫ ½ *DVD:* ♫♫♫
Kino on Video (cat #K225, UPC 73832902-2525). Full frame. $24.98. Keepcase. *LANG:* Silent. *SUB:* English intertitles. *FEATURES:* 16 chapters • 1930 short film, "Windy Riley Goes Hollywood."
1929 116m/B GE Louise Brooks, Fritz Rasp, Josef Rovensky, Sybille Schmitz; *D:* G.W. Pabst; *W:* Rudolf Leonhard; *C:* Sepp Allgeier, Fritz Arno Wagner; *M:* Timothy Brock.

Diary of a Sex Addict

Curious film is part "erotic thriller," part serious character study. Sammy Horn (Des Barres) is a successful chef and family man who risks his professional and personal happiness with a series of sexual encounters, which he recounts to his psychiatrist Dr. Bordeaux (Kinski). It's depressing stuff with moments of very strange humor which may be intentional. Performances are generally good and DVD appears to be a completely faithful re-creation of an original image that was shot on high-definition video. That gives the film an underfed look and a sense of depravity that's almost necessary for the story to be successful. Sound is fine, but again has a certain "unenhanced" quality that fits the mood. —MM
Movie: ♫♫ ½ *DVD:* ♫♫ ½
Columbia Tristar (cat #07067, UPC 04339-6070677). Full frame; widescreen (1.78:1) anamorphic. Dolby Digital 5.1 Surround Stereo; Dolby Digital Surround. $29.98. Keepcase. *LANG:* English; French. *SUB:* English; Spanish; French; Portuguese; Chinese; Korean; Thai. *CAP:* English. *FEATURES:* 28 chapters • Trailers.
2001 93m/C Michael Des Barres, Rosanna Arquette, Nastassia Kinski, Alexandra Paul, Ed Begley Jr.; *D:* Joseph Brutsman; *W:* Joseph Brutsman, Tony Peck; *C:* Nathan Hope; *M:* Doug Smith.

Dick Tracy [Marengo]

In this 15-episode serial, Chester Gould's legendary comic strip character (Byrd) pits himself against the ruthless "Spider" crime ring. Led by a mysterious club-footed mastermind, the gang kidnaps Tracy's brother and turns him into an evil cohort thanks to brain surgery. As Tracy tries to locate his missing brother, he fights the crime-ring's attempts at murder and mass destruction. A fun, cheap serial told at breakneck speed and featuring a likeable Byrd as the titular hero in his first screen incarnation. The gripping, unpolished thrill-ride that is let down by some clumsy editing. The action sequences are exciting but typical for a low-budget serial and are supported by the usual assembly of library music and stock shots. The disc is transferred from grainy, soft, cropped, and overbright prints. Facial and other details are present, but whites are lacking in detail. The noise reduction program used during the transfer apparently interpreted some fast movement (such as waving arms, etc.), as dirt and accidentally eliminated those bits of information from the frame. This causes some odd distortions at times. The sound is tinny and flat, but coherent. Fairly entertaining barnstormer deserves a more pristine presentation. —DG
Movie: ♫♫ ½ *DVD:* ♫ ½
Marengo Films (cat #MRG-0023, UPC 807013002393). Full frame. Mono. $14.98. Keepcase. *LANG:* English. *FEATURES:* 15 episodes.
1937 290m/B Ralph Byrd, Smiley Burnette, Irving Pichel, Jennifer Jones; *D:* John English, Alan James, Ray Taylor.

Dick Tracy [VCI]

Serial based on the popular comic strip character sets him against "The Spider." DVD boasts an image that might be a slight improvement over VHS tape, but given the age of the work, there's little to be done. The extras on this two-disc set are nice, particularly the commentary track in the early episodes by Max Allan Collins, who wrote the strip for several years, and a 1945 radio show, *Dick Tracy in B-Flat* with Bing Crosby as the detective, Bob Hope, Frank Sinatra, Judy Garland, and Dinah Shore. —MM
Movie: ♫♫ *DVD:* ♫♫♫
VCI (cat #8273, UPC 089859827327). Full frame. Dolby Digital Mono. $24.99. Keepcase. *LANG:* English. *FEATURES:* 15 chapters • Commentary: Max Allan Collins • Photo gallery with commentary • *Dick Tracy in B-Flat* radio show.
1937 290m/B Ralph Byrd, Smiley Burnette, Irving Pichel, Jennifer Jones; *D:* John English, Alan James, Ray Taylor.

Dick Tracy

Warren Beatty leads an all-star cast on a wild romp through the Prohibition Era. The yellow-coated gumshoe finds himself up against a slew of mobsters and one dangerous dame (Madonna) as he tries to make the city safe again. Beatty's direction is sometimes flat and Madonna isn't quite up to the role of femme fatale, but the pace is brisk and the art direction wonderful. The transfer does an excellent job of bringing out the plentiful reds, though other colors appear a tad muted. Both soundtracks add punch to the explosions and Sondheim tunes, but the dialogue is sometimes lost. There isn't even a trailer to be found. —BG
Movie: ♫♫♫ *DVD:* ♫♫ ½
Buena Vista Home Ent. (cat #18372, UPC 717951005298). Widescreen (1.85:1) anamorphic. Dolby 5.1; DTS 5.1. $19.99. Keepcase. *LANG:* English; French. *CAP:* English. *FEATURES:* 12 chapters.
1990 (PG) 105m/C Warren Beatty, Madonna, Charlie Korsmo, Glenne Headly, Al Pacino, Dustin Hoffman, James Caan, Mandy Patinkin, Paul Sorvino, Charles Durning, Dick Van Dyke, R.G. Armstrong, Catherine O'Hara, Estelle Parsons, Seymour Cassel, Michael J. Pollard, William Forsythe, Kathy Bates, James Tolkan; *D:* Warren Beatty; *W:* Jim Cash, Jack Epps Jr.;

C: Vittorio Storaro; **M:** Danny Elfman, Stephen Sondheim. *AWARDS:* Oscars '90: Art Dir./Set Dec., Makeup, Song ("Sooner or Later"); *NOM:* Oscars '90: Cinematog., Costume Des., Sound, Support. Actor (Pacino).

Dick Tracy, Detective

Please see review of *Dick Tracy DVD Double Feature.*
Movie: 🎵🎵
1945 62m/B Morgan Conway, Anne Jeffreys, Mike Mazurki, Jane Greer, Lyle Latell; **D:** William Berke; **W:** Eric Taylor; **C:** Frank Redman; **M:** Roy Webb.

Dick Tracy DVD Double Feature

In the first feature film, Splitface (Mazurki) is on the loose, a schoolteacher is murdered, the Mayor is threatened, and a nutty professor uses a crystal ball to give Tracy the clues. The second film on this disc is much more fun. Please see review of *Dick Tracy Meets Gruesome.* Light registration jitters and mild surface damage are visible on both. Otherwise, they're the equal of a good VHS tape and look as good as you could expect for low-budget series entries of a certain age. —*MM*
Movie: 🎵🎵 ½ **DVD:** 🎵🎵
Marengo Films (cat #0006, UPC 8070130-00627). Full frame. $14.95. Keepcase. *LANG:* English. *FEATURES:* 4 chapters each.
1945 126m/C

Dick Tracy Meets Gruesome

Gruesome (Karloff) uses "suspended animation gas" to stage bank robberies and such. The public domain title is available on both *Dick Tracy DVD Double Feature* and *Classic Dick Tracy Movies* discs (see separate entries). Image is about the same on either. —*MM* **AKA:** Dick Tracy's Amazing Adventure; Dick Tracy Meets Karloff.
Movie: 🎵🎵
1947 66m/B Boris Karloff, Ralph Byrd, Lyle Latell, Anne Gwynne, Edward Ashley, June Clayworth, Tony Barrett, Skelton Knaggs; **D:** John Rawlins; **W:** Eric Taylor, Robertson White; **C:** Frank Redman; **M:** Paul Sawtell.

Dick Tracy vs. Cueball

The famous detective from the comics page has his work cut out for him when the evil gangster Cueball shows up. Public domain title is equal to VHS tape. It's available on the *Classic Dick Tracy Movies* triple feature (see separate entry). —*MM*
Movie: 🎵🎵
FEATURES: 4 chapters.
1946 62m/B Morgan Conway, Anne Jeffreys, Lyle Latell, Rita (Paula) Corday, Ian Keith, Dick Wessel, Skelton Knaggs; **D:** Gordon Douglas; **W:** Robert E. Kent, Dane

Lussier; **C:** George E. Diskant; **M:** C. Bakaleinikoff, Phil Ohman.

Dick Tracy's Dilemma

Stop me if you've heard this one before; the Claw has a steel hook for a hand. In this incarnation, he's up against Dick Tracy. Public domain title is available on the *Classic Dick Tracy Movies* triple feature (see separate entry). DVD is identical to tape. —*MM* **AKA:** Mark of the Claw.
Movie: 🎵🎵
FEATURES: 4 chapters.
1947 60m/B Ralph Byrd, Lyle Latell, Kay Christopher, Jack Lambert, Ian Keith, Jimmy Conlin; **D:** John Rawlins; **W:** Robert Stephen Brode; **C:** Frank Redman; **M:** Paul Sawtell.

Die Hard [FS 2]

This "Five Star" edition improves on the first release (reviewed in *Book 1*) with more sound options, three commentary tracks (two aural, one subtitled), and a second disc filled with extras. The two extended scenes don't really add much. One involving the power shutdown can be incorporated into a "branched" version of the entire film. Like so much of the deleted material you find on discs, it was wisely edited; the film is stronger without it. The commentaries are very nicely done. McTiernan and production designer Jackson DeGovia are particularly instructive. It should go without saying that image and sound are exemplary. This release is also available as part of the *Die Hard: Ultimate Edition* boxed set ($79.98; UPC 024543012610), in which the two sequels also get the royal treatment. —*MM*
Movie: 🎵🎵🎵 **DVD:** 🎵🎵🎵 ½
20th Century Fox (cat #2001252, UPC 024543012528). Widescreen (2.35:1) anamorphic. DTS 5.1 Surround; Dolby 5.1 Surround; Dolby Surround. $29.98. 2-disc keepcase. *LANG:* English; French. *SUB:* English; Spanish. *CAP:* English. *FEATURES:* 40 chapters ▪ Liner notes ▪ 3 commentary tracks ▪ Script ▪ Deleted scenes ▪ "Making of" featurette ▪ Gag reel ▪ Interactive magazine articles ▪ Still gallery ▪ Trailers and TV spots ▪ DVD-ROM features.
1988 (R) 114m/C Bruce Willis, Bonnie Bedelia, Alan Rickman, Alexander Godunov, Paul Gleason, William Atherton, Reginald Vel Johnson, Hart Bochner, James Shigeta, Mary Ellen Trainor, De'voreaux White, Robert Davi, Ric(k) Ducommun; **D:** John McTiernan; **W:** Jeb Stuart, Steven E. de Souza; **C:** Jan De Bont; **M:** Michael Kamen. *AWARDS: NOM:* Oscars '88: Film Editing, Sound.

Dillinger and Capone

As this micro-budget wonder has it, John Dillinger (Sheen) was not killed in front of the Biograph Theater in Chicago. That was his brother (Estevez), and Public Enemy Number One retired to a farm in Bakersfield, California, and got married. Years

later, Al Capone (Abraham), more than half mad from syphilis, is released from prison and forces Dillinger back into the business for the proverbial one last job. It's an energetic story, told in a dark red-brown color scheme. DVD image is very soft and grainy, no better than VHS tape. Sound is much much worse. Dialogue has a clipped, swallowed quality that makes it difficult to understand in many scenes. —*MM*
Movie: 🎵🎵🎵 **DVD:** 🎵 ½
New Concorde (cat #NH20429 D, UPC 736991442993). Full frame. $14.98. Keepcase. *LANG:* English. *FEATURES:* Trailers ▪ Talent files ▪ 18 chapters.
1995 (R) 95m/C Martin Sheen, F. Murray Abraham, Catherine Hicks, Stephen Davies, Don Stroud, Clint Howard, Joe Estevez; **D:** Jon Purdy; **W:** Michael B. Druxman; **C:** John Aronson; **M:** David Wurst, Eric Wurst.

The Dimension Travelers

The screenwriter of the celebrated animes *Perfect Blue* and *Cowboy Bebop* tries his hand at a live-action feature, with mixed results. Based on a novel by Taku Mayumura, the film offers an intriguing idea, but becomes overly convoluted as it goes on. Teenaged schoolgirl Midori (Chiharu Niiyama) is popular with her schoolmates, but often feels disconnected from her peers. She then meets Mayumi (Yasue Sato), who claims to be from a parallel dimension. Mayumi tries to convince Midori that anyone can pass between dimensions and that she does it all the time. Midori doesn't believe Mayumi's claims at first, but she then begins to experience episodes where she finds herself in strange places, where she is treated as if she were a different person. Can Midori and Mayumi really travel between worlds, or are they both suffering from delusions? This interesting idea is never really allowed to develop, as the story gets bogged down in detailing the activities of the alternate dimensions. The viewer isn't given enough clues as to whether or not what we're seeing is real and the ending is convoluted. On the plus side, the characters are genuinely drawn and all of the young actors are fine. The image is alternately hazy and grainy at times, showing some artifacting and distortion. Also, there are some visible defects from the source print. The colors are good for the most part, although some shots are slightly washed-out. The Dolby Digital stereo audio track provides clear dialogue and adequate stereo separation. The English subtitles are clear and easy to read. —*ML*
Movie: 🎵🎵 **DVD:** 🎵🎵
Central Park/U.S. Manga (cat #APCD 2170, UPC 719987217027). Widescreen (1.85:1) letterboxed. Dolby Digital Stereo. $29.99. Keepcase. *LANG:* English; Japanese. *SUB:* English. *FEATURES:* Character profiles ▪ Actress profile ▪ Trivia ▪ Trailer ▪ Bonus trailers ▪ 10 chapters.
1998 95m/C *JP* Chiharu Niyama, Yasue Sato; **D:** Kazuya Konaku.

Dimples

Shirley Temple stars in this lightweight film made during the Great Depression. Set in the 1850s, it stars Temple as Sylvia Dolores Appleby, who is better known as Dimples. She performs with a group of street musicians who work under the tutelage of Dimples's grandfather, Professor Eustace Appleby (Frank Morgan). Unbeknownst to Dimples, Professor Appleby is a crook who uses the musicians as a way to distract potential targets. While performing at the home of the wealthy Caroline Drew (Helen Westley), Appleby steals several furs, but returns them when Dimples is held by Mrs. Drew for questioning. Mrs. Drew is immediately taken by Dimples, and offers to let the young girl come live with her, so that she may have a proper upbringing. Meanwhile, Mrs. Drew's nephew, Allen (Robert Kent) is opening a theatrical company, much to the chagrin of his aunt, and wants to hire Dimples to be in his production of *Uncle Tom's Cabin*. Professor Appleby agrees to let Dimples live with Mrs. Drew and work with Allen, as he sees it as a money-making scheme. Will Professor Appleby redeem himself so that Dimples can become a star of the stage? This is one of those old-fashioned films which has a story, but no plot. Dimples meets the Drews, performs in a show, etc., but nothing ever really happens. Still, the pace is brisk, and there are some nice musical numbers. Be warned, this film has some controversial elements, as it features the now-famous actor Stepin Fetchit doing his shtick and some very racist moments during the performances of *Uncle Tom's Cabin*. This DVD gives the viewer the choice of either watching the original black-and-white version of *Dimples*, or a new colorized version. This transfer looks fine given the film's age, but there are some obvious defects from the source print and visible grain in many scenes. Also, the image flickers in certain shots. The digital stereo sound doesn't sound all that different from the digital mono track, but both provide clear dialogue and a nice reproduction of the music. —ML
Movie: 🎬🎬 **DVD:** 🎬🎬
20th Century Fox (cat #2002970, UPC 024543029700). Full frame. Digital Stereo; Digital Mono. $19.98. Keepcase. *LANG:* English. *SUB:* English; Spanish. *CAP:* English. *FEATURES:* 24 chapters.
1936 (PG) 78m/B Shirley Temple, John Carradine, Frank Morgan, Helen Westley, Berton Churchill, Robert Kent, Delma Byron; **D:** William A. Seiter; **W:** Nat Perrin, Arthur Sheekman; **C:** Bert Glennon; **M:** Louis Silvers.

Diner

At the end of 1959, six friends (Stern, Bacon, Guttenberg, Rourke, Daly, Reiser) hang around "their" Baltimore diner and try to figure out what's happening. Loosely plotted film is a sharply observed character study with some terrific laughs and a young cast on the verge of fame. The print

is basically very clean, with excellent compression, though there are occasional scratches. Some of the night shots lose a bit of detail in the shadows, but the problem seems to be in the source print rather than the transfer. Colors are crisp with no bleeding; there is a scene in front of a church with a stained glass window in the background that is a great reference point for the chroma noise; the colors on the glass were sharp and detailed. Mono is just fine for an excellent, evocative soundtrack full of '50s rock and roll and R&B, and a stereo remix would have been nice, but in the end is not necessary. We get the sound as the characters in the movie so often did, without reengineering...like listening to an old car radio, though much clearer. In a new documentary, "Diner: on the Flip Side," most of the major stars (Mickey Rourke is conspicuously absent) and Barry Levinson reminisce about their experiences during the production. Fun and offering some good insights, it's much like the movie; similar to sitting with friends and hearing various perspectives about a shared experience. The "All-New Introduction" by the director is simply cuts from the documentary placed before the film and is not skippable, though I found that I could fast-forward past it. —PT/MM
Movie: 🎬🎬🎬 ½ **DVD:** 🎬🎬🎬
Warner Home Video (UPC 0125695077-22). Widescreen (1.66:1) anamorphic. Dolby Digital Mono. $14.98. Snapper. *LANG:* English; French. *SUB:* English; French. *FEATURES:* Trailers • Documentary • Intro.
1982 (R) 110m/C Steve Guttenberg, Daniel Stern, Mickey Rourke, Kevin Bacon, Ellen Barkin, Timothy Daly, Paul Reiser, Michael Tucker, Jessica James, Kathryn Dowling, Colette Blonigan; **D:** Barry Levinson; **W:** Barry Levinson; **C:** Peter Sova; **M:** Bruce Brody, Ivan Kral. *AWARDS:* Natl. Soc. Film Critics '82: Support. Actor (Rourke); *NOM:* Oscars '82: Orig. Screenplay.

Dinner with Friends

Gabe and Karen (Quaid and MacDowell) host a dinner for their closest friends, Beth and Tom (Kinnear and Collette), but only Tom shows up to tell them that he and Beth are getting a divorce because he has met someone new. The result is a dissection of both relationships by Gabe and Karen as they try to decide what makes a relationship work or fail, and what it means to them. That's the stuff of soap operas, but a really good soap opera directed by Norman Jewison (*Moonstruck*, the original *Thomas Crown Affair*). Flashbacks tell the story from the day that Gabe and Karen introduced Tom to Beth. You begin to choose sides, but once Tom shows up to tell his side, it becomes apparent that there are no sides and Gabe and Karen will find no easy answers. Based on a play by David Margulies. Shot for HBO, the disc is above standard TV quality, and the sound is very good for a dialogue-driven film. —CA
Movie: 🎬🎬 ½ **DVD:** 🎬🎬🎬

HBO (cat #91893, UPC 026359189326). Full frame. Dolby Digital Surround; Stereo. $24.90. Snapper. Great. *LANG:* English; Spanish. *SUB:* English; French; Spanish. *CAP:* English. *FEATURES:* 14 chapters • Cast & crew bios.
2001 95m/C Dennis Quaid, Andie MacDowell, Greg Kinnear, Toni Collette; **D:** Norman Jewison; **W:** Donald Margulies.

Directed by Andrei Tarkovsky

Please see review of *The Sacrifice*.
1988 101m/C SW Andrei Tarkovsky; **D:** Michael Leszcylowski; **W:** Michael Leszcylowski; **Nar:** Brian Cox, Erland Josephson.

The Directors: Roger Corman

Fast, cheap, and in control might well serve as the motto for Hollywood's wily independent king, producer/writer/director (and talent-spotter) extraordinaire Roger Corman, who has hundreds of films on his credit list. Though he's not known for his artistic touch, Corman is witty, well-spoken, and a truly savvy businessman. Though this documentary tactfully omits mention of his later, uglier output—sexually violent video garbage—much of Corman's output is lively, fun, or least notable for who was in it or behind the camera. A must for aspiring filmmakers. Image is a slight improvement on broadcast quality. The only extra is a filmography and it's just a simple list of movies—if you want to see which movies the interviewees (Ron Howard, Martin Scorsese, James Cameron) worked on, you have to refer to the documentary itself. —JE
Movie: 🎬🎬🎬 **DVD:** 🎬🎬🎬
Winstar Home Ent. (cat #WHE73155, UPC 720917315522). Full frame. Dolby Digital Stereo. $9.98. Keepcase. *LANG:* English. *FEATURES:* Filmography.
2001 60m/C

Dirty Harry [2]

Detective Harry Callahan (Eastwood) is a dedicated cop and working-class hero disgusted by the sexual degeneracy that The Summer of Love has brought to his city. He bristles with undisguised contempt at spineless city officials who are soft on crime and criminals, and who object to his cowboy methods of dealing with criminals: shoot first, and threaten later. Callahan meets his match with The Scorpio Killer (Robinson), who commits horrible crimes while taunting Harry personally. The film demonizes the liberal authorities, who are seen as cowardly bureaucrats more interested in punishing Harry than neutralizing a killer. The mayor and police chief roles are filled by actors John Vernon and John Larch, who normally play slimy villains. Shot in zoom-happy, grainy, ugly Panavision, this is efficient and cruel propaganda, and still has a hell of a macho kick. It's an irresponsible film that claims a higher morality while making sadism and social vigilantism into a

feel-good spectacle. Warner Bros. brought out the first DVD (reviewed in *Book 1*) a few years back, in the same "Clint Eastwood Collection" packaging, so you have to look carefully to see if you have the new disc or the old one. The new disc says "all new 2000 digital transfer" in the box on the back. The transfer is better, much better than the old one, which came out soon after the launch of DVD. Both were anamorphic 16:9, but this one is obviously from a much better element, for the colors are better and the picture sharper, cleaner, and far less grainy. Now the grainy, dark night scenes look appropriately grainy—not just a sludge of black. (If you have the old disc, don't dump it if you want a Spanish language track or a pan 'n' scan version of the movie, as the new disc has neither.) —*GE*
Movie: 🎬🎬🎬 ½ **DVD:** 🎬🎬🎬 ½
Warner (cat #21516, UPC 0853921516-22). Widescreen (2.35:1) anamorphic. Dolby Digital 5.1 Surround; Mono. $19.98. Snapper. *LANG:* English; French. *SUB:* English; French; Spanish. *CAP:* English. *FEATURES:* Documentary: "Dirty Harry: The Original" ❧ Trailer ❧ "Making of" featurette ❧ Interview excerpts.
1971 (R) 103m/C Clint Eastwood, Harry Guardino, John Larch, Andrew (Andy) Robinson, Reni Santoni, John Vernon, Albert "Poppy" Popwell; *D:* Donald Siegel; *W:* Dean Riesner, Harry Julian Fink, Rita M. Fink; *C:* Bruce Surtees; *M:* Lalo Schifrin.

Dirty Kopz

McCord (writer/director Combs) is a corrupt cop who's trying to steal $8 million from a drug kingpin. This ultra–low budget effort is more talk-fest (with some very funny lines) than action picture. The grain is very heavy with all the expected artifacts. Lighting is almost non-existent. Score thumps right along. —*MM*
Movie: 🎬 ½ **DVD:** 🎬 ½
York Ent. (cat #YPD-1156, UPC 75072311-5627). Full frame. $14.99. Keepcase. *LANG:* English. *SUB:* Spanish. *FEATURES:* 24 chapters.
2001 C Ryan Combs, Jules Dupree, Mark Denegal, Kevin Parker, Cesar Gomez; *D:* Ryan Combs; *W:* Ryan Combs; *C:* Corwin Bibb.

Dirty Rotten Scoundrels [MGM]

When the French Riviera becomes too small for two con artists, a winner-takes-all battle sets the stage for 1988's *Dirty Rotten Scoundrels*, a charming, utterly ruthless comedy that seemed almost anachronistic upon its first release. That might be because the film was a remake of 1963's *Bedtime Story*, which featured urbane con man David Niven and boorish swindler Marlon Brando vying for the affections and fortunes of wealthy ingenue Shirley Jones. In *Scoundrels*, Michael Caine's sophisticated Lawrence Jamieson and Steve Martin's uncouth Freddy Benson set their sights on Glenne Headley's

slightly bumbling American soap heiress Janet Colgate. Director Frank Oz nimbly juggles the actors, their frequently hilarious escapades and the European scenery while never letting the audience forget they are rooting for a couple of scam artists. The script, crediting three writers including *Ruthless People*'s Dale Launer (with lots of input from Steve Martin, according to Oz in his very scene-specific commentary track), ingeniously piles on the sight gags and somehow manages to make the more unsavory undertones of the story not only palatable but downright tasty. The 1.85:1 anamorphic transfer dazzles with rich colors and sharp, detailed images. The remastered 5.1 Surround is no slouch either. Oz goes into great detail in the commentary, determined to discuss virtually every scene and cut. What makes the disc a keeper (along with the earlier Image release, reviewed in *Book 1*) is the inclusion of the teaser trailer, where Martin gently pushes an old woman off a dock as he and Caine calmly stroll by. Listen to the Oz commentary here, too; he points out a Caine sight gag as well. —*EP*
Movie: 🎬🎬🎬 **DVD:** 🎬🎬🎬
MGM Home Ent. (cat #1002729, UPC 027616869272). Widescreen (1.85:1) anamorphic. Dolby Digital 5.1 Surround; Dolby Surround. $19.98. Keepcase. *LANG:* English; French; Spanish. *SUB:* English; French; Spanish; Portuguese. *FEATURES:* 16 chapters ❧ Commentary: director Frank Oz ❧ Behind-the-scenes featurette ❧ Teaser trailer with optional commentary by director Oz ❧ Theatrical trailer.
1988 (PG) 112m/C Steve Martin, Michael Caine, Glenne Headly, Anton Rodgers, Barbara Harris, Dana Ivey; *D:* Frank Oz; *W:* Stanley Shapiro, Paul Henning, Dale Launer; *C:* Michael Ballhaus; *M:* Miles Goodman.

The Disappearance of Flight 412

Please see review of *Great Sci-Fi Thrillers*.
1974 74m/C Glenn Ford, Bradford Dillman, David Soul, Guy Stockwell; *D:* Jud Taylor; *W:* Neal R. Burger, George Simpson.

The Dish

Chock full of more smiles than laughs, *The Dish* is about an Australian team of radio scientists who use their local radio dish to receive and share the transmissions from the Apollo 11 moon landing. It's based on a true story; the historic landing and first steps could not have been broadcast without them. The tiny farming town of Parkes, Australia, gets a taste of fame as they share in the anticipation and excitement surrounding the moon landing. Sam Neil plays the head scientist and recent widower, Cliff Buxton. Patrick Warburton plays the American representative from NASA who has come to make sure things run correctly. The conflicts are less important to this story than the charm. The mayor and his family are getting caught up in the excitement of being important while not really

understanding much about the Apollo mission itself. It's a crisp, clear transfer from film for this DVD and if you've finished watching *Waking Ned Devine* and you're yearning for another small-town charmer with warm accents, here it is. —*JAS*
Movie: 🎬🎬🎬 **DVD:** 🎬🎬🎬
Warner (cat #21249, UPC 0853921249-23). Widescreen letterboxed. Dolby Digital Surround 5.1. $19.98. Snapper. *LANG:* English. *SUB:* English; French; Spanish. *FEATURES:* Theatrical trailers ❧ 27 chapters.
2000 (PG-13) 104m/C *AU* Sam Neill, Patrick Warburton, Tom Long, Kevin Harrington, Bille Brown, John McMartin, Tayler Kane, Eliza Szonert, Carl Snell; *D:* Rob Sitch; *W:* Rob Sitch, Santo Cilauro, Tom Gleisner, Jane Kennedy; *C:* Graeme Wood; *M:* Edmund Choi.

Disney's American Legends

A collection of classic stories of great American heroes. Included on this disc are the tales of: John Henry, Johnny Appleseed, Paul Bunyan, and Casey Jones. Each story is introduced by James Earl Jones. The disc includes a sublime video transfer featuring bright colors that virtually pop off the screen as well as vividly reproduced blacks that are crisp and solid throughout. The soundtrack is similarly impressive. However, the sound does get a bit muffled during the "Johnny Appleseed" segment, but it's quickly resolved. While the introductions by James Earl Jones are a nice touch, they seem quickly put together and almost an afterthought. It might also have been nice to have included some filmmaker insights, or perhaps the musings of an expert on American folklore discussing the importance of these figures in history rather than the minimal extras found on the disc. —*MJT*
Movie: 🎬🎬🎬 **DVD:** 🎬🎬🎬
Buena Vista Home Ent. (cat #24239, UPC 786936167245). Full frame. Dolby Digital Surround. $29.99. Keepcase. *LANG:* English. *FEATURES:* 10 chapters ❧ Celebrity host intros by James Earl Jones ❧ American Legends: A Learning Adventure, 2 interactive games ❧ Walt Disney's TV intro to "Johnny Appleseed" ❧ Trailer gallery ❧ DVD-ROM weblinks.
2002 58m/C *Nar:* James Earl Jones.

Diva [Anchor Bay]

The Anchor Bay edition corrects the flaws of the earlier release (reviewed in *Book 1*) with a fine 5.1 audio remix and an anamorphic image transfer. Some grain crops up in the darker scenes but that has always been there. Highly recommended. —*MM*
Movie: 🎬🎬🎬 ½ **DVD:** 🎬🎬🎬 ½
Anchor Bay (cat #DV11399, UPC 01313-1139990). Widescreen (1.66:1) anamorphic. Dolby Digital 5.1 Surround Stereo. $24.98. Keepcase. *LANG:* English; French. *SUB:* English. *FEATURES:* 27 chapters ❧ Interview with director Jean-Jacques Beineix ❧ Thumbnail Beineix bio ❧ Trailer.

1982 (R) 123m/C *FR* Frederic Andrei, Roland Bertin, Richard Bohringer, Gerard Darmon, Jacques Fabbri, Wilhelmenia Wiggins Fernandez, Dominique Pinon; **D:** Jean-Jacques Beineix; **W:** Jean-Jacques Beineix; **C:** Philippe Rousselot; **M:** Vladimir Cosma. *AWARDS:* Cesar '82: Cinematog., Sound, Score; Natl. Soc. Film Critics '82: Cinematog.

Divided We Fall

This Czechoslovakian film was nominated for an Academy Award (Best Foreign Language Film, 2000) and swept the Czech equivalent to the Oscars. It takes place during World War II and is set in a quiet Czech village. That peacefulness is shattered when Nazis take over the town. Despite this madness, Josef (Boleslav Polivka) and his wife Marie (Anna Siskova) attempt to maintain their usually calm lives. Things change, however, when this couple agrees to hide David (Csongor Kassai), a young Jewish man, in their apartment. The tension mounts as an old friend, Horst (Jaroslav Dusek), who is working with the Nazis, begins to frequent the apartment. While the story here may sound similar to *The Diary of Anne Frank*, *Divided We Fall* shows the other side of the coin. Here, the story focuses on the parties responsible for hiding a Jewish person, and not the fugitives themselves. There is a great deal of suspense in the film, but also a fair share of heart as well, as we come to know Josef and Marie. Director Jan Hrebejk uses an interesting technique, shooting the scenes involving the Nazis in a highly stylized way, as if those images were taken from a nightmare. The DVD is equally impressive in its presentation. The 1.78:1 anamorphic image is quite sharp. Subtle grain is visible in some shots, but for the most part, the image is clear and the colors are good. The Dolby Digital 5.1 audio track is very good, offering dynamic Surround sound from the outset. The sound field here is very wide, giving clear dialogue, but robust rear speaker effects as well. —*ML* **AKA:** Musime si Pomahat. **Movie:** ♫♫♫ **DVD:** ♫♫♫
Columbia Tristar (cat #07169, UPC 04339-6071698). Widescreen (1.78:1) anamorphic. Dolby Digital 5.1; Dolby 2.0 Surround. $29.95. Keepcase. *LANG:* Czech. *SUB:* English. *CAP:* English. *FEATURES:* Theatrical trailer ▪ Filmography ▪ 28 chapters.
2000 (PG-13) 123m/C *CZ* Boleslav Polivka, Anna Siskova, Csongor Kassai, Jaroslav Dusek, Jiri Pecha, Simona Stasova, Marin Huba, Vladimir Marek, Jiri Kodet, Richard Tesarik; **D:** Jan Hrebejk; **W:** Petr Jarchovsky; **C:** Jan Malir; **M:** Ales Brezina. *AWARDS:* NOM: Oscars '00: Foreign Film.

Dixie Dynamite

When a Georgia moonshiner is killed, his two lissome daughters, suspecting foul play, make like a pair of Nancy Brew detectives. The music is performed by Duane Eddy and Dorsey Burnette. Image quality is notably poor, with distorted colors, really peachy skin tones, and oddly bluish cast to the whole print. Interactive menu is very hard to read—contrast doesn't light up very well. When you hit "extras" it goes straight to the theatrical trailer, and then into a trailer for another movie called *Any Gun Can Play*. There is no intermediate menu step. —*JE* **Movie:** ♫ **DVD:** ♫ ½
VCI (cat #8280, UPC 089859828027). Full frame. Dolby Digital Mono. $9.99. Keepcase. *LANG:* English. *FEATURES:* Original theatrical trailer.
1976 (PG) 88m/C Warren Oates, Christopher George, Jane Anne Johnstone, Kathy McHaley, R.G. Armstrong, Wes Bishop; **D:** Lee Frost; **W:** Lee Frost, Wes Bishop.

D.O.A.: The End

Documentary from 1990 on the reunion of punk band D.O.A. at the DNA Lounge, a San Francisco night club. I was around in the late '70s when D.O.A. was playing at S.F.'s Mabuhay Gardens (AKA The Fab Mab), a club that hosted countless punk and new wave bands at a time when everyone had a band—even me (The Job). D.O.A. was a hard-core act from Canada that was neither the best or the worst of its kind. Dirk Dirksen emcees this comeback in 1990. He's a host everyone in the Bay Area knew from those original legendary days and he hasn't aged a jot from his middle-aged hedgehog curmudgeon self. This alone brings back memories, but D.O.A. is just not particularly worth the trip, at least not until the Dead Kennedys' lead vocalist and poet, Jello Biafra (who came in third when he ran for San Francisco mayor in the '80s—one vote was mine) takes the stage for the last few numbers. This shows how D.O.A. clearly needed a better front man, just as its covers (Subhumans, Iggy) are often better than its original material. Very average video source does not help the DVD transfer or sound. —*MO* **Movie:** ♫♫ ½ **DVD:** ♫♫ ½
Rhino (cat #R2 972781, UPC 6034972-78121). Full frame. $19.99. Keepcase. *LANG:* English. *FEATURES:* 22 chapters ▪ Interview with lead singer Joe Keithly ▪ Band photos, original concert posters and reviews ▪ D.O.A. coloring book ▪ D.O.A. music videos.
1999 90m/C

Dr. Dolittle 2

Those of you who were annoyed by the first *Dr. Dolittle* film with Eddie Murphy may want to give this sequel a try. This film is much quieter, and while it will never be confused with a Merchant-Ivory film, does a much better job of focusing on characters and plot. Here, Dr. Dolittle (Murphy) is called upon to help save a forest from destruction by loggers. The humorous aspect is that it's a mafioso beaver (Richard C. Sarafian) and his raccoon henchman (Michael Rapaport) who summon Dolittle to this task. The doctor decides that he can save the forest if he can successfully mate two rare Grizzly bears (Steve Zahn and Lisa Kudrow), but that won't be an easy task, as the male bear has never been in the wild. To make matters worse, Charisse (Raven-Symone), Dolittle's oldest daughter, is having trouble handling her father's fame. This is a surprisingly funny and sweet film, and except for the expected toilet humor, it's fun for the whole family. The animals here are cute and charming for the most part, and a chameleon named Pepito steals the show. DVD offers a pristine transfer of the film, which gives us a razor-sharp picture which shows virtually no flaws. In addition, the 5.1 audio mix is crystal clear, offering dialogue with no distortion, nice Surround sound effects, and substantial subwoofer response. The generous extras will enable both young and old alike to learn how all of the special effects involving the animal actors were done. —*ML* **Movie:** ♫♫♫ ½ **DVD:** ♫♫♫♫
20th Century Fox (cat #2002667, UPC 024543026679). Widescreen (2.35:1) anamorphic. Dolby Digital 5.1; Dolby Surround. $26.98. Keepcase. *LANG:* English; French. *SUB:* English; Spanish. *CAP:* English. *FEATURES:* Commentary ▪ "Making of" featurette ▪ Storyboards ▪ Music video ▪ Theatrical trailers ▪ TV spots ▪ "Tank the Bear" featurette ▪ Grizzly Bear Guide ▪ 24 chapters.
2001 (PG) 87m/C Eddie Murphy, Jeffrey Jones, Kevin Pollak, Raven-Symone, Kyla Pratt, Kristen Wilson, Zane R. (Lil' Zane) Copeland Jr.; **D:** Steve Carr; **W:** Larry Levin; **C:** Daryn Okada; **M:** David Newman; **V:** Norm MacDonald, Lisa Kudrow, Steve Zahn, Mike Epps, Michael Rapaport, Jacob Vargas, Isaac Hayes, Andy Dick, Joey Lauren Adams, Richard Sarafian.

Dr. Jekyll and Mr. Hyde [Kino]

This edition of the Barrymore *Dr. Jekyll* is shorter (73 minutes) than the Image edition (reviewed in *Book 1*). It also has different extras. Otherwise, light to moderate print damage is in evidence throughout. The new score is nice. —*MM* **Movie:** ♫♫ **DVD:** ♫♫ ½
Kino on Video (cat #K217, UPC 738329-021726). Full frame. $24.98. Keepcase. *LANG:* Silent. *SUB:* English intertitles. *FEATURES:* 12 chapters ▪ 1909 audio recording of "The Transformation Scene" ▪ 1925 parody "Dr. Pyckle and Mr. Pride" with Stan Laurel ▪ Excerpt from another 1920 version starring Sheldon Lewis ▪ Essay about the story's origins and variations ▪ About the Mont Alto score.
1920 73m/B John Barrymore, Martha Mansfield, Brandon Hurst, Charles Lane, J. Malcolm Dunn, Nita Naldi, Louis Wolheim; **D:** John S. Robertson; **W:** Clara Beranger; **C:** Karl Struss, Roy F. Overbaugh.

Dr. Jekyll & Mr. Hyde

Successful Dr. Henry Jekyll (Baldwin) is caught in the middle of a violent gang war

while on his honeymoon and is altered physically and infused with a driving intensity and anger after his wife's murder in this awful, plodding mess of a movie that has nothing to do with its namesake. The whole thing gets worse when Jekyll discovers that he is fated to become the legendary crime fighter the White Tiger. (Executive producer Francis Ford Coppola should be ashamed that his name is associated with this project.) The video transfer does little to salvage the disc with a blurry color spectrum. The soundtrack fares a bit better with the sound effects being the apparent beneficiary of the sound mixer's time. —*MJT*
Movie: 🎜🎜 ½ ***DVD:*** 🎜🎜
MTI (cat #50051, UPC 619935405134). Full frame. Dolby Digital Stereo. $24.95. Keepcase. *LANG:* English. *SUB:* Spanish. *FEATURES:* 20 chapters • Cast bios • Theatrical trailer • Trailer gallery.
2000 (R) 90m/C *CA AU* Adam Baldwin, Steve Bastoni, Chang Tseng, Jason Chong, Richard Chong, Kira Clavel, Karen Cliche; ***D:*** Colin Budds; ***W:*** Peter M. Lenkov; ***C:*** Mark Wareham; ***M:*** Garry McDonald.

Dr. Jekyll and Sister Hyde

Tongue-in-cheek variation on the split-personality theme also tosses in a Jack-the-Ripper angle. The good doctor (Bates) of the title transforms himself into a sultry knife-wielding babe (Beswick) who kills prostitutes. DVD does the best job possible with a low-budget image. The film was made on a few sets and lacks the usual opulence that Hammer lavished upon its best productions. Fans of the studio's work should make a point of listening to the group commentary track by star Martine Beswick, director Roy Ward Baker, writer/co-producer Brian Clemens, and film historian Marcus Hearn. —*MM*
Movie: 🎜🎜 ½ ***DVD:*** 🎜🎜🎜
Anchor Bay (cat #DV11446, UPC 01313-1144697). Widescreen (1.85:1) anamorphic. Dolby Digital Mono. $24.98. Keepcase. *LANG:* English; French. *FEATURES:* 25 chapters • Talent files • Still and poster gallery • Commentary.
1971 (R) 94m/C *GB* Ralph Bates, Martine Beswick, Gerald Sim; ***D:*** Roy Ward Baker; ***W:*** Brian Clemens; ***C:*** Norman Warwick; ***M:*** Philip Martell, David Whitaker.

Dr. Lamb

This feature, based on the crimes of serial killer Lam Guo-wen, helped set off a whole wave of True Crime films in Hong Kong. Police trace snuff photographs to taxi driver Simon Yam, who eventually breaks down and confesses. Once the confessions start, all pretense of suspense disappears, and there's no disguising that *Dr. Lamb*'s main purpose is to provide shocks and horror for its leering audience. As such, it's an excellent piece of work. The Cantonese tracks have repeated odd

beeps to cover profanity (Cantonese only, not the frequent English uttered by Eric Kai), as if a few foul words should be hidden in the midst of murder, madness, and perversity. A vertical digital line passes across the screen at around the 72-minute mark. By the way, the keepcase is actually a bit smaller than usual—wish it would become standard, saving us all some space! —*BT*
Movie: 🎜🎜 ½ ***DVD:*** 🎜🎜
Winsom Ent. (cat #WDV3080D, UPC 4895-067302305). Widescreen letterboxed. Dolby Digital 5.1. $14.95. Keepcase. *LANG:* Cantonese; Mandarin. *SUB:* Chinese; English. *FEATURES:* 9 chapters.
1992 89m/C *HK* Simon Yam, Danny Lee, Kent Cheng, Parkman Wong, Siu-ming Lau; ***D:*** Danny Lee; ***W:*** Kam Fai Law; ***C:*** Tony Miu; ***M:*** Jonathan Wong.

Dr. Mabuse, The Gambler

Dr. Mabuse (Klein-Rogge) is a mastermind criminal who moves through society wearing any one of a score of clever disguises. His only aides are a handful of loyal agents, who carry out his brilliant instructions to commit audacious crimes without knowing their exact purpose. He engineers a daring train robbery that helps him to commit stock fraud on a giant scale. He suborns people by winning against them at cards. In the posh gambling houses of Berlin, he manipulates a number of characters, such as the foolish playboy Edgar Hull (Paul Richter) and an exotic dancer, Cara Carozza (Aud Egede Nissen). He uses his influence to control the weak Count Told (Alfred Abel) and eventually kidnaps and imprisons the Countess Told (Gertrude Welcker). Only Chief Gaming Inspector von Wenk (Bernhard Goetzke) has enough information to even detect the possibility of a single intelligence behind the crimes and destabilizing schemes; he gets close to the disguised Mabuse, but is foiled by Mabuse's incredible skills of mind control. He can hypnotize many people to obey his will, and has the power to "cloud men's minds" when necessary. As an embodiment of his time, Mabuse is a brilliant construction, especially after commentator David Kalat explains that author Jacques's intention was the conservative championing of the lost system of noblesse against the more democratic Weimar Republic, whose freedoms and lack of class distinction, he thought, brought chaos. It's a very slow web that the film weaves, and by the end it's as if you've been watching a thriller that really means something. Image's double disc has a very good visual look, far better than extant versions available of *Metropolis* made four years later. The playback speed is smooth and large sections of the film appear to be in great shape, difficult to imagine for a 1922 release. Robert Israel has assembled a gigantic scene-specific score that uses the instruments and rhythms of the day; much of the music is reminiscent of the feel of Weill's *Three Penny Opera*. Restorer

David Shepard and author Kalat provide that annotation in the form of a commentary that stretches throughout the almost four-hour length of the film. Mr. Kalat's commentary is extremely well delivered. Only once on part 2 does his editor let him down, allowing a couple of false starts of one paragraph through before the correct take continues the show. It's frankly a relief to know that Kalat couldn't come up with such a fluid discourse off the top of his head! This old film that has to be judged as "special viewing." It's a rarified kind of art cinema, a pulp legend from the distant past, and a special treat for people who love movies. —*GE* **AKA:** Doktor Mabuse der Spieler; Dr. Mabuse, Parts 1 & 2.
Movie: 🎜🎜🎜 ½ ***DVD:*** 🎜🎜🎜 ½
Image Ent. (UPC 14381941227). Full frame. $29.99. Keepcase. *LANG:* Silent. *SUB:* English intertitles.
1922 242m/B *GE* Rudolf Klein-Rogge, Aud Egede Nissen, Alfred Abel, Gertrude Welcker, Lil Dagover, Paul Richter, Bernhard Goetzke; ***D:*** Fritz Lang; ***W:*** Fritz Lang, Thea von Harbou; ***C:*** Carl Hoffmann.

Doctor of Doom

A killer known in the press as "The Mad Doctor" abducts women for brain transplant experiments. Wrestler Gloria Venus (Lorena Velázquez) and her roommate Golden Rubi, the "American Cyclone" (Elizabeth Campbell), get involved in the hunt for the killer. The Mad Doctor sends his "greatest triumph" Gomar (Gerardo M. Zapeda)—a man given a gorilla's brain—out to capture the fighting femmes. Saturday matinee action fare from Mexico. Packaged with horrible graphics and no extras. This edition is from an American International 16mm TV print that has some fingerprints, speckles, and flat sound, but the transfer is reasonably good—probably better than most people would think the film deserves. But fans of cheesy Mexican horror movies will consider themselves lucky to have it. —*BT* **AKA:** Wrestling Women vs. the Aztec Ape.
Movie: 🎜🎜 ½ ***DVD:*** 🎜 ½
Beverly Wilshire Filmworks (cat #BWFD881-19, UPC 026617881191). Full frame. $14.99. Keepcase. *LANG:* English.
1962 111m/C *MX* Elizabeth Campbell, Lorena Lalazquez, Armando Silvestre, Roberto Canedo, Chucho Salinas, Sonia Infante; ***D:*** Rene Cardona Sr.; ***W:*** Alfredo Salazar; ***C:*** Enrique Wallace; ***M:*** Antonio Diaz Conde.

Dr. Orloff's Monster

The evil Dr. Fisherman (Dr. Orloff's apprentice, you see) has been experimenting in electromagnetics, and may have developed a way to animate and control the dead. And for some reason, this means sending his new robot off to murder prostitutes and strippers. There's some Gothic family intrigue thrown in as well. The picture has quite a few scratches from the source, but the transfer still looks good given the film's budget and age. The sound is still tinny and the music often sounds warped, but this too is probably due to the source materials. —BG

Movie: 🎵 ½ **DVD:** 🎵🎵 ½
Image Ent. (cat #ID9104BIDVD, UPC 0143-81910421). Widescreen (1.66:1) anamorphic. Dolby Mono. $24.95. Keepcase. *LANG:* French; English. *SUB:* English. *FEATURES:* 12 chapters ▪ Alternate and deleted footage ▪ Trailers.
1964 88m/B *SP* Jose Rubio, Agnes Spaak; *D:* Jess (Jesus) Franco; *C:* Alfonso Nieva.

Dr. Seuss' How the Grinch Stole Christmas

This adaptation of Dr. Seuss's famous children's book may take liberties that the Chuck Jones's cartoon did not, but it's faithful to the original spirit and Jim Carrey's interpretation of the title character as a Nixonian blusterer is truly inspired. So is the intricate production design by Michael Corenblith recalling an even more demented Munchkinland. DVD retains the soft focus and pastel colors of the theatrical release—both fitting for a story that takes place within a snowflake. (It's impossible to be more precise about the full-frame version made available for review. Doubtless, the widescreen version—cat. #20677—is more visually impressive.) Surround effects are not overdone. The dual-layer disc is jammed with all the extras that you'd expect from a studio-produced hit. Curiously (or not), this story decries the commercialism of the holiday, but many of the extras are amazingly heavy on product placement. —MM *AKA:* How the Grinch Stole Christmas; The Grinch.
Movie: 🎵🎵🎵 **DVD:** 🎵🎵🎵 ½
Universal Studios (cat #21275). Full frame. Dolby Digital 5.1 Surround Stereo; DTS Surround. $26.98. Keepcase. *LANG:* English; French. *CAP:* English. *FEATURES:* 20 chapters ▪ Deleted scenes montage ▪ "Spotlight on Location" featurette ▪ Who School featurette ▪ Makeup design featurette ▪ Seussian set decoration featurette ▪ Visual effects featurette ▪ Music video ▪ Descriptive Video Service soundtrack ▪ "Wholiday" recipes ▪ Trailer ▪ "By the Numbers" statistics ▪ Production notes ▪ Talent files ▪ DVD-ROM features ▪ Max's playhouse games.
2000 (PG) 102m/C Jim Carrey, Jeffrey Tambor, Christine Baranski, Taylor Momsen, Molly Shannon, Josh Ryan Evans, Clint Howard, Bill Irwin; *D:* Ron Howard; *W:* Jeffrey Price, Peter S. Seaman; *C:* Don Peterman; *M:* James Horner; *Nar:* Anthony Hopkins. *AWARDS: NOM:* Oscars '00: Art Dir./Set Dec., Costume Des., Makeup; Golden Raspberries '00: Worst Remake/Sequel, Worst Screenplay.

Doctor Zhivago

Loving husband, doctor, and poet, Yuri Zhivago (Sharif) has his life turned inside out by the Russian revolution and (while separated from his family) falls in love with sensitive nurse, Lara (Christie). This extraordinarily beautiful filming of the Boris Pasternak novel substitutes the author's richly evocative descriptions with sumptuous visuals. While the plot has been (necessarily) clarified and simplified for the film, the essential set pieces and overarching story line are the same. Lean captures exquisite imagery in the snowy Russian landscapes in the same way he conveyed beauty with the desert surroundings in *Lawrence of Arabia*. A great romantic epic filled with memorable sequences, an incredible cast, and evocative sets. Highly recommended. The stunning picture quality of this disc blows all previous video and laserdisc editions out of the water. The imagery is always razor sharp, and clean, and colors are rich and smooth with a dense, nearly three-dimensional, filmic look. The newly rebalanced Surround sound is terrific. The disc is packed with fascinating contemporary featurettes and interviews and the newly produced documentary is exemplary. Running over an hour, it covers the making of the film as well as the history of the original novel. Most illuminating are interview clips with the real-life basis for Lara and home movie footage of her and author Boris Pasternak. The audio commentary appears only sporadically and overlaps much material that is covered elsewhere, but there are some worthwhile stories to be heard. It's a beautiful, exemplary release of a terrific film. —DG
Movie: 🎵🎵🎵 ½ **DVD:** 🎵🎵🎵🎵
Warner (cat #65571, UPC 0125695571-23). Widescreen (2.35:1) anamorphic. Dolby Surround 5.1. $29.98. Keepcase (slipsleeve box). *LANG:* English; French. *SUB:* English; French; Spanish. *CAP:* English. *FEATURES:* 61 chapters ▪ Commentary: Sharif, Steiger, Sandra Lean ▪ Intro by Omar Sharif ▪ "Doctor Zhivago: The Making of a Russian Epic" documentary ▪ 10 vintage documentaries ▪ Music-only audio track ▪ Vintage audio interviews ▪ 1965 New York Premiere coverage ▪ Cast/director career highlights ▪ Theatrical trailer.
1965 (PG-13) 197m/C Omar Sharif, Julie Christie, Geraldine Chaplin, Rod Steiger, Alec Guinness, Klaus Kinski, Ralph Richardson, Rita Tushingham, Siobhan McKenna, Tom Courtenay, Bernard Kay, Gerard Tichy, Noel Willman, Geoffrey Keen, Adrienne Corri, Jack MacGowran, Mark Eden, Erik Chitty, Peter Madden, Jose Maria Caffarell, Jeffrey Rockland, Wolf Frees, Lucy Westmore; *D:* David Lean; *W:* Robert Bolt; *C:* Frederick A. (Freddie) Young; *M:* Maurice Jarre. *AWARDS:* Oscars '65: Adapt. Screenplay, Art Dir./Set Dec., Color, Color Cinematog., Costume Des. (C), Orig. Score; AFI '98: Top 100; Golden Globes '66: Actor—Drama (Sharif), Director (Lean), Film—Drama, Screenplay, Score; Natl. Bd. of Review '65: Actress (Christie); *NOM:* Oscars '65: Director (Lean), Film Editing, Picture, Sound, Support. Actor (Courtenay).

Dodsworth [MGM]

The lives of a self-made American tycoon and his wife are drastically changed when they take a tour of Europe. The success of their marriage seems questionable as they reevaluate their lives. Huston excels, as does the rest of the cast in this film, based upon the Sinclair Lewis novel. The video transfer, which is merely adequate, lacks crisp, well-defined blacks (a necessity with a black-and-white film). It appears the disc is the victim of a sub-par source print. Similarly, the soundtrack features decently reproduced dialogue, but becomes muddied far too often. The musical score is also far too intrusive in some scenes to be deemed enjoyable. —MJT
Movie: 🎵🎵🎵 ½ **DVD:** 🎵🎵
MGM Home Ent. (cat #1002739, UPC 027616869371). Full frame. Dolby Digital Stereo; Dolby Digital Mono. $19.98. Keepcase. *LANG:* English; French. *SUB:* English; French; Spanish. *FEATURES:* 18 chapters.
1936 101m/B Walter Huston, David Niven, Paul Lukas, John Payne, Mary Astor, Ruth Chatterton, Maria Ouspenskaya, Charles Halton; *D:* William Wyler; *W:* Sidney Howard; *C:* Rudolph Mate; *M:* Alfred Newman. *AWARDS:* Natl. Film Reg. '90; N.Y. Film Critics '36: Actor (Huston); *NOM:* Oscars '36: Actor (Huston), Director (Wyler), Picture, Screenplay, Sound, Support. Actress (Ouspenskaya).

Dogma [2 SE]

Film transfer is identical to the previous disc, reviewed in *Book 2*. The full-frame presentation that was included on the original edition that is not included here. The difference is in the extras. The cast and crew commentary is an incredibly funny affair, with some great jokes and smart humor about production obstacles, as well as stories from the set. Affleck dominates quite a bit of the proceedings, joking about what's going on in the scene as well as pointing out areas where Smith is lacking as a director. Smith also has some great stories, such as the difficulties working with Fiorentino. The commentary track can be viewed with the "Follow the Buddy Christ" feature, where an icon pops up for about five seconds every so often throughout the picture, which allows you to view the group of commentators. This track, though funny, is slightly more serious than the other tracks. Occasional references to Miramax/Disney are bleeped out at the studio's insistence. The second commentary was made because the first track didn't give much information about the making of the picture. In this one, the group talks in depth about the making of the picture and features more technical information. There are still some jokes on this commentary, but it's more about the behind-the-scenes on the roles of the crew in certain scenes and how scenes were filmed and where. About 100 minutes worth of deleted scenes are included. Separated and with introductions from Pereira, Smith (as well as Smith's new child), and others, the scenes fall into a couple of categories—some are just nice to have on the disc, but certainly wouldn't have worked as they don't push the plot or really go anywhere. Some of the other scenes are very funny and could have worked, but the picture was already a little lengthy. The famous "Fat Albert" sequence has made it onto the disc, for those who have been following its history. Also included are about 13 minutes worth of various goofs, alternate takes, and funny bits. Some bits, especially a couple of Affleck gags, are incredibly funny. —AB/DG

Movie: 🦴🦴 ½ **DVD:** 🦴🦴🦴🦴
Columbia Tristar Home Video (UPC 433-96056145). Widescreen (2.35:1) anamorphic. Dolby Surround 5.1. $29.98. 2-disc slip sleeve. LANG: English. CAP: English. FEATURES: Cast & crew outtakes ▪ Commentary: Smith, Affleck, Lee ▪ Commentary: producer Scott Mosier, Vincent Pereira ▪ Commentary: Smith, Mosier, View Askew historian Vincent Pereira ▪ Complete set of storyboards from 3 major scenes ▪ 100 minutes of deleted scenes with View Askew crew intros ▪ Jay and Silent Bob's Secret Stash Spot ▪ Bonus! Follow the Buddy Christ for More Hijinks ▪ Talent files.
1999 (R) 125m/C Ben Affleck, Matt Damon, Linda Fiorentino, Chris Rock, Salma Hayek, Jason Lee, George Carlin, Alan Rickman, Jason Mewes, Janeane Garofalo, Kevin Smith, Alanis Morissette, Bud Cort, Jeff Anderson, Guinevere Turner; **D:** Kevin Smith; **W:** Kevin Smith; **C:** Robert Yeoman; **M:** Howard Shore. AWARDS: NOM: Ind. Spirit '00: Screenplay; Golden Raspberries '99: Worst Support. Actress (Hayek).

The Dogs of War

Severely underrated action film follows a group of mercenaries led by Jamie Shannon (Walken) as they prepare for the overthrow of a small African country. Performances are first rate, as is the adaptation of Frederick Forsythe's carefully detailed novel. DVD is the best the film has ever looked on home video. Very faint snowy flecks are visible in some scenes. DVD is a far better-looking show than the previous dull VHS and laser versions. Legendary cameraman Jack Cardiff, who made a career out of shooting in difficult locations, goes against his Technicolor style and tries to make the image look as natural as possible, with subdued colors in the jungle. He excels with his night photography, where the entire African township is realistically illuminated without our questioning where all the light is coming from. MGM's Technical Services division, which conscientiously strives to maintain the longest and most original version of its movies, apparently did the right thing and located the original version. So why isn't there at least a mention of the fact that the show has been lengthened by 15 minutes? The film probably doesn't register as a major title on the sales charts, so perhaps touting the longer

cut wouldn't have been that big a deal, especially when there are no new scenes of marketable bloodshed or mayhem. What we do get are interesting details, 15 minutes' worth spread throughout nine scenes in the first 2/3 of the film. And the rescue of JoBeth Williams's role, which was reduced to almost nothing in the first U.S. cut. —MM/GE

Movie: 🦴🦴🦴 ½ **DVD:** 🦴🦴 ½
MGM Home Ent. (cat #1001826, UPC 027616860965). Widescreen (1.85:1) anamorphic. Dolby Digital Surround. $14.95. Keepcase. LANG: English. SUB: French; Spanish. CAP: English. FEATURES: Trailer ▪ 16 chapters.
1981 (R) 102m/C GB Christopher Walken, Tom Berenger, Colin Blakely, Paul Freeman, Hugh Millais, Victoria Tennant, JoBeth Williams; **D:** John Irvin; **W:** Gary De Vore; **C:** Jack Cardiff; **M:** Geoffrey Burgon.

Dogs: The Rise and Fall of an All-Girl Bookie Joint

On the surface, this is a story about some twentysomething women who are bad at relationships and can't pay the rent. To solve one of their problems they turn their apartment into a bookie joint. However, underneath there is the story of the girl who has just lost her mother and needs money to pay for her funeral. The thread that weaves it all together is the drive to survive and rise above what life has given you, or sometimes what you give yourself. This is an indie, low-budget film and the acting and lighting reflect its limitations, but overall it is a good story with competent acting. Well worth a rental, and probably worth buying for those of you who like a good female-centric underdog story. The picture is about video quality with no obvious artifacts and the sound is good, though muffled in some places. —CA

Movie: 🦴🦴 **DVD:** 🦴🦴
Vanguard Intl. Cinema (cat #VF00194, UPC 658769019438). Full frame. $29.95. Keepcase. LANG: English. FEATURES: 10 chapters ▪ Theatrical trailer.
1996 88m/C Pam Columbus, Pam Gray, Eve Annenberg, Toby Huss, Leo Marks, Amedo D'Adamo; **D:** Eve Annenberg; **W:** Eve Annenberg; **C:** Wolfgang Held.

The Doll Squad

An ex-CIA agent, apparently escaped from a James Bond movie, threatens to take over the world through various dastardly schemes. For some reason, only a top-secret force of women in spandex can stop his evil plans. The lousy special effects and awful fight scenes make this a perfect film for late nights with sarcastic friends. Just don't watch it alone. Picture and audio are a slight improvement over tape, but don't expect too much. —BG
AKA: Hustler Squad.
Movie: 🦴 **DVD:** 🦴🦴 ½
Image Ent. (cat #ID0833TGDVD, UPC 014381083323). Widescreen (1.78:1)

anamorphic. Dolby Mono. $24.99. Keepcase. LANG: English. FEATURES: 16 chapters ▪ Commentary: Ted V. Mikels ▪ Interview: Tura Satana ▪ Trailers ▪ Mikels filmography.
1973 (PG) 93m/C Michael Ansara, Francine York, Anthony Eisley, John N. Carter, Rafael Campos, William Bagdad, Lisa Todd, Lillian Garrett, Herb Robbins, Tura Satana; **D:** Ted V. Mikels; **W:** Ted V. Mikels, Jack Pichesin, Pam Eddy; **C:** Anthony Salinas; **M:** Nicholas Carras.

Domestic Disturbance

Why is it that John Travolta, who has done great films, seems to pick stupid scripts with such frequency? In this cliché-ridden film he is a divorced dad with a great relationship with his son. His ex decides to marry a guy (Vince Vaughn) who is perfect in outward appearance but hides a dark past. His violent tendencies boil over and Travolta must save his son and ex-wife. For only the die-hard Travolta fan who loves anything he does. DVD colors are not clean, and dialogue is sometimes almost inaudible but with this script, that might be a blessing in disguise. —DE
Movie: 🦴 ½ **DVD:** 🦴🦴
Paramount (cat #33772, UPC 09736337-722). Widescreen anamorphic. Dolby Digital 5.1 Surround; Dolby Surround. $29.98. Keepcase. LANG: English; French. SUB: English. CAP: English. FEATURES: 15 chapters ▪ Commentary: director ▪ Deleted scenes with director's commentary ▪ Storyboards ▪ Theatrical trailer.
2001 (PG-13) 89m/C John Travolta, Vince Vaughn, Teri Polo, Matt O'Leary, Ruben Santiago-Hudson, Susan Floyd, Steve Buscemi, Angelica Torn; **D:** Harold Becker; **W:** Lewis Colick; **C:** Michael Seresin; **M:** Mark Mancina.

Dominick & Eugene

This severely overlooked sleeper is a bittersweet joy. Dominick (Liotta) and Eugene (Hulce) are fraternal twins, but due to a childhood accident Eugene is mentally slow. In a strange turn of events, Eugene works as a garbage man to support Dominick as he trains to be a doctor. The script was co-written by Alvin Sargent (Ordinary People, Paper Moon) and he is in top form here using the illusively simple dialogue and actions between the brothers to build a relationship that is full of the joys and pitfalls of interdependence. Who is really taking care of whom here? When Dominick finds out that he has been accepted to a school far away to finish up his medical degree, he doesn't tell Eugene. His inner conflict over wanting to be on his own and not wanting to leave his brother leads to a tension between the two that grows to an almost unbearable level when Dominick also starts sharing his time with a beautiful fellow student (Curtis). But this isn't a story about con-

flict, it's a story about conflict resolution and how love and loyalty can overcome not only fear of abandonment but abandonment itself. The final act of the film may be a little forced depending on your mood, but the revelations made there are well worth a little suspension of disbelief, and unless the audience is comprised of rocks, there won't be a dry eye in the house. The acting by Liotta and Hulce is top-notch and if it hadn't been released the same year as *Rain Man* there surely would have been more buzz about the film. The disc has decent color and sound, not as crisp and clear as they might have been on either front, but fine for a story- and character-driven film. —CA
Movie: 🎵🎵🎵 ½ **DVD:** 🎵🎵 ½
MGM Home Ent. (cat #1002628, UPC 027616868282). Widescreen (1.85:1) anamorphic. Dolby Digital Stereo; Dolby Digital Stereo Surround; Mono. $19.90. Keepcase. *LANG:* English; French; Spanish. *SUB:* English; French; Spanish. *CAP:* English. *FEATURES:* 16 chapters • Theatrical trailer.
1988 (PG-13) 96m/C Ray Liotta, Tom Hulce, Jamie Lee Curtis, Todd Graff, Bill Cobbs, David Strathairn; *D:* Robert M. Young; *W:* Alvin Sargent, Corey Blechman; *C:* Curtis Clark; *M:* Trevor Jones.

Don Giovanni

Joseph Losey is so faithful to Mozart's plot that this nearly three-hour adaptation is meant for devoted opera lovers. Neophytes will find their patience tested by the lengthy introduction and the dark Venetian locations. The story follows the famous lover (Raimondi) from a glass blowing factory to the flames of hell. DVD image is a faithful re-creation of an original that's more than 20 years old. It's grainy with some harsh colors. Details are lost in voluminous dark clothes. Sound is excellent. —MM
Movie: 🎵🎵 ½ **DVD:** 🎵🎵 ½
Columbia Tristar (cat #07212, UPC 043396072121). Widescreen (1.85:1) letterboxed. Dolby Digital Surround. $29.98. Keepcase. *LANG:* Italian. *SUB:* English; French; Spanish; Chinese; Korean; Thai. *CAP:* English. *FEATURES:* 28 chapters • Trailers.
1979 176m/C Ruggero Raimondi, John Macurdy, Edda Moser, Kiri Te Kanawa, Kenneth Riegel; *D:* Joseph Losey; *C:* Pierre Saint-Blancat.

Don Juan (Or If Don Juan Were a Woman)

In her final film, Bardot once again plays every man's fantasy and nightmare, this time as a reincarnation of Don Juan whose sole desire is to seduce and destroy men. It's good risqué, retro fun, but it's hard to tell if the film is a celebration of sexuality, Bardot's final stab at the (male) audience that exploited her throughout her career, or just another movie where the woman who takes control of her own sexuality is pun-

ished. Home Vision's transfer is excellent, with appropriately soft and dreamy colors, and the stereo soundtrack is quite good as well. The tray card includes an excellent essay by Nathan Rabin. —BG *AKA:* Don Juan 73; Ms. Don Juan; Si Don Juan Etait une Femme.
Movie: 🎵🎵 ½ **DVD:** 🎵🎵🎵
Home Vision Cinema (cat #DON230, UPC 037429161128). Widescreen (1.66:1) anamorphic. Dolby Stereo. $29.98. Keepcase. *LANG:* French. *SUB:* English. *FEATURES:* 15 chapters • Trailers for other Bardot films • Bardot filmography.
1973 94m/C FR Brigitte Bardot, Jane Birkin, Matthieu Carriere, Robert Hossein, Maurice Ronet, Michele Sand; *D:* Roger Vadim; *W:* Jean Cau; *C:* Henri Decae.

Don Q, Son of Zorro

Please see review for *Mark of Zorro / Don Q, Son of Zorro.*
Movie: 🎵🎵
1925 111m/B Douglas Fairbanks Sr., Mary Astor, Donald Crisp; *D:* Donald Crisp; *W:* Jack Cunningham; *C:* Henry Sharp.

Dona Herlinda & Her Son

Rodolfo has a relationship with young music student, Ramon. When Rodolfo's widowed mother invites Ramon to live with them, he accepts. As the days stretch on, Rodolfo and Ramon become pawns in the subtle, but disturbing machinations of Dona Herlinda, who has her own plans for Rodolfo and a way to fit Ramon into them. What seems a superficially gentle and simple movie hides a thoroughly depressing, aggravating story of manipulation. Herlinda is portrayed with such kind simplicity that it becomes hard to target her as the villain of the story, which she certainly is. Rodolfo agrees to enter into a heterosexual marriage of convenience which leaves Ramon demoted to a combination babysitter and plaything. The filmmaker seems unaware of this aspect in the finished motion picture and some critics have embraced the film as a warm ode of parental acceptance, which seems unfathomable, given the way the two lovers are quietly wrenched apart. This Mexican production was filmed entirely on location and betrays its extremely low-budget with an overly naturalistic look and cheap "home-movie" quality photography. A terrible quality disc by any standard, the image is pale, grainy, and ugly, with excessive amounts of smearing, print marks and muddy blacks. The images tend to look "blocky" with very detectable pixels and a slight twitch is evident at the start of nearly every cut. The disc reviewed also had several moments of programming glitches where the picture jumps. Sound is muddy and poor with the occasional audible digital click. —DG *AKA:* Dona Herlinda y Su Hijo.
Movie: 🎵🎵 **DVD:** woof
Vanguard Intl. Cinema (cat #VF0252, UPC 658769025231). Full frame. Mono.

$29.95. Keepcase. *LANG:* Spanish. *SUB:* English. *FEATURES:* 12 chapters.
1986 90m/C MX Guadalupe Del Toro, Arturo Meza, Marco Antonio Trevino, Leticia Lupersio; *D:* Jaime Humberto Hermosillo; *W:* Jaime Humberto Hermosillo; *C:* Miguel Ehrenberg.

Donnie Darko

Image a *Twilight Zone* version of *American Beauty.* That's more or less what Richard Kelly is up to with this festival favorite, and he's more or less successful. (Hints of David Lynch, *Magnolia,* and even *Harvey* are evident, too.) Donnie Darko (Gyllenhaal) is a bright high school student who's troubled by dreams or fantasies concerning a nightmarish rabbit figure called Frank who tells him that the world is going to end in less than a month. As Donnie counts down the days, Frank orders him to do odd, destructive things. To reveal any more of the plot would spoil much of the film. Its unpredictability is much of the fun. The inventive casting (welcome back, Katherine Ross) helps, too. On the other hand, the supposedly shocking revelations of the seething underside of suburbia are familiar, far too familiar, and Gyllenhaal's mopey interpretation of the protagonist is a bit offputting. DVD looks as sharp and crisp as you'd expect from a new big-budget studio release. The 5.1 mix is exceptionally active and strong. Perhaps because of that and the tendency of the leads to mumble, much of the dialogue is very difficult to decipher. I found myself backing up to re-hear significant bits of information and finally turned on the English subtitles for the second half. —MM
Movie: 🎵🎵🎵 **DVD:** 🎵🎵🎵 ½
20th Century Fox (cat #2003640, UPC 024543036401). Widescreen (2.35:1) anamorphic. Dolby Digital 5.1 Surround Stereo; Dolby Surround. $24.98. Keepcase. *LANG:* English; French. *SUB:* English; Spanish. *CAP:* English. *FEATURES:* 2 director and cast commentaries • Extended & deleted scenes with commentary • "Cunning Visions" infomercials • Music video • "Philosophy of Time Travel" book • Talent files • Stills gallery • Trailer and TV spots • 28 chapters.
2001 (R) 113m/C Jake Gyllenhaal, Jena Malone, Drew Barrymore, Mary McDonnell, James Duval, Maggie Gyllenhaal, Holmes Osborne, Katharine Ross, Patrick Swayze, Noah Wyle, Arthur Taxier, Stuart Stone; *D:* Richard Kelly; *W:* Richard Kelly; *C:* Steven Poster; *M:* Michael Andrews. *AWARDS: NOM:* Ind. Spirit '02: Actor (Gyllenhaal), First Feature.

Don't Bother to Knock

An older New York hotel. Flyer Jed Towers (Richard Widmark) arrives to find out why his singer girlfriend Lyn Lesley (Anne Bancroft) is calling off their romance. Incensed when she criticizes him as too cold, Jed retires to his room, but strikes up a flirtation with a blonde he sees in a window across the way. Nell Forbes (Monroe) is actually a babysitter who's seriously unbalanced—wearing the jewelry and clothing of the woman whose child she is minding. Nell has been released from the asylum too soon, and is dangerous. DVD apparently includes an entire replacement reel transferred from print, and the digital correction makes any mismatch with the rest of the film imperceptible. Title is part of the *Marilyn Monroe: The Diamond Collection, Vol. 2.* —GE

Movie: 🎵🎵 ½ **DVD:** 🎵🎵🎵
20th Century Fox (cat #2003504, UPC 024543035046). Full frame. Stereo; Mono. $19.98. Keepcase. *LANG:* English. *SUB:* English; Spanish. *CAP:* English. *FEATURES:* Restoration comparison • Still gallery • Trailer.
1952 76m/B Richard Widmark, Marilyn Monroe, Anne Bancroft, Elisha Cook Jr., Jim Backus, Lurene Tuttle, Jeanne Cagney, Donna Corcoran; *D:* Roy Ward Baker; *W:* Daniel Taradash; *C:* Lucien Ballard; *M:* Lionel Newman.

Don't Say a Word

Douglas stars as Nathan Conrad, a successful Manhattan psychologist who has a young daughter and a wife (Janssen) who has recently injured her leg in an accident. Conrad is called in one night to analyze a seriously disturbed young girl named Elisabeth (Murphy). The next morning, Conrad discovers that a group lead by Patrick (Bean) has abducted his daughter. They don't want money—they want information that's in Elisabeth's memory. Unfortunately, director Fleder and writer Kelly don't seem to have worked out all the details. Only the Douglas character seems to be even somewhat developed. Most of the other roles are one-dimensional and rather thankless (which director Fleder occasionally seems to admit on the commentary), and are enlivened slightly by what the actors bring to the screen. Several plot threads are dull, insufficiently developed, or altogether unnecessary. Towards the end, the film attempts to build up intensity, but the intercutting has the opposite effect, further draining the tension that has been built up. The picture quality is about as good as one might expect from a big studio new release. Sharpness and detail are strong but there is some noticeable edge-enhancement. The Surround track is quite rich across-the-board, with deep bass at times. Fleder's commentary provides a solid amount of details about the day-to-day production of the film, and work with the actors, as well as some technical information about specific sequences. One gets the feeling he's disappointed in the end result, though. There's a second commentary track featuring several of the actors' reflections on two specific scenes. The results are variable but interesting. The majority of the extras detail the production process and would be of particular inter-est to film students, but having a section entitled "Cinema Master Class" for such a clinker must be facetious. —AB/DG

Movie: 🎵🎵 **DVD:** 🎵🎵🎵 ½
20th Century Fox (UPC 24543034056). Widescreen (2.35:1) anamorphic. DTS; Dolby Digital 5.1 Surround. $27.98. Keepcase. *LANG:* English. *CAP:* English. *FEATURES:* Commentary: director Gary Fleder • Scene-specific commentary: Douglas, Platt, Bean, Murphy, Jansen • Trailers • Deleted scenes • Chapters • "Making of" featurette • "Set tour" featurette • "Film scoring" featurette • Dailies screening • Brittany Murphy screen test • Storyboard-to-scene comparisons.
2001 (R) 112m/C Michael Douglas, Sean Bean, Brittany Murphy, Skye McCole Bartusiak, Famke Janssen, Guy Torry, Jennifer Esposito, Shawn Doyle, Victor Argo, Oliver Platt, Conrad Goode, Paul Schulze, Lance Reddick; *D:* Gary Fleder; *W:* Patrick Smith Kelly, Anthony Peckham; *C:* Amir M. Mokri; *M:* Mark Isham.

Doomsdayer

This film has it all—bad acting, clichéd plot, Brigitte Nielsen, and characters you could never care about no matter how much Prozac the director gave you. There's an elite force, a romantic triangle, and something about a bomb that could destroy the world. Of course, if the world were really this dull and meaningless it would probably be a good idea, but luckily this is just a film and you can avoid it. Disc does, however, have pretty good picture quality and sound. —CA

Movie: woof **DVD:** 🎵🎵 ½
MTI (cat #50050, UPC 619935405035). Full frame. $24.95. Keepcase. *LANG:* English. *SUB:* Spanish. *FEATURES:* Extra trailers.
1999 93m/C Joe Lara, Udo Kier, Brigitte Nielsen, Sandra Gomez; *D:* Michael J. Sarna.

Doomwatch

During a routine sampling survey, a member of the titular ecological team discovers some strange findings on an isolated island. The hostile, secretive community is undergoing the disfiguring effects of industrial water pollution, which their local priest has interpreted as divine retribution for years of inbreeding. To help them, the scientist must go against the villagers. This fairly taut drama is mistakenly sold as a horror film. Based on a British TV series, the film occasionally feels episodic, but is well paced and features fairly strong performances. The lead scientist (Bannen) could certainly benefit from a friendlier bedside manner, though! The full-frame disc never seems cropped, so it is most likely an unmatted transfer. It features a very sharp image and a clean soundtrack, but it features a slightly grainy print source and occasionally is a bit smeary during movement in night scenes. (The disc runs 89 minutes, not 88 as listed on package. The original was 92 min-utes. There are no cuts; the discrepancy is due to its origin as a PAL master.) —DG

Movie: 🎵🎵 ½ **DVD:** 🎵🎵 ½
Image Ent. (cat #ID9891EUDVD, UPC 014381989120). Full frame. Dolby Digital Mono. $24.99. Keepcase. *LANG:* English. *FEATURES:* 12 chapters.
1972 89m/C *GB* Ian Bannen, Judy Geeson, John Paul, Simon Oates, George Sanders; *D:* Peter Sasdy; *W:* Clive Exton; *C:* Ken Talbot.

Dot & the Kangaroo

Based on the book by Ethel Pedley, *Dot & the Kangaroo* tells the story of a young girl who gets lost in the bush, and must rely on the help of many clever animals to get back home. Dot (voiced by Barbara Frawley) wanders away from home. Alone and scared, she meets a red kangaroo (voiced by Joan Bruce), who agrees to help her. We learn that the kangaroo recently lost her own joey, so she feels very protective of Dot. They explore the bush together, seeking assistance from other animals, such as a kookaburra and a duck-billed platypus. The film teaches about animals and also touches on the history of the Australian Outback. It also features many rousing songs, including "Riding in the Pouch of a Red Kangaroo" (which will surely get stuck in your head). The animation is a combination of animated drawings placed over live-action backgrounds (years before Disney's *Dinosaur*). Unfortunately, the quality of the animation varies greatly throughout the film. Also, there are some very dull moments which only pad the running time. Still, *Dot & the Kangaroo* is inoffensive fun and children will most likely enjoy it. Followed by at least seven sequels, which explore the further adventures of Dot. This animated film shows its age on this DVD. While the picture is clear for the most part, the image is somewhat dark and the colors seem faded. Also, there are scratches and blemishes evident from the source print. The Dolby Digital Mono soundtrack provides clear dialogue, but there is an audible hiss on the track. —ML

Movie: 🎵🎵 ½ **DVD:** 🎵🎵
Hen's Tooth Video (cat #4078, UPC 759731407823). Full frame. Dolby Digital Stereo. $24.95. Keepcase. *LANG:* English. *FEATURES:* Theatrical trailer • 12 chapters.
1977 75m/C *AU D:* Yoram Gross; *V:* Barbara Frawley, Joan Bruce.

Double Bang

Dull, boring, overdrawn crime caper is a chore to watch unless you are related to the Baldwin family and then you watch it out of respect to your relatives. Billy Benson (William Baldwin) is a dead cop whose partner gets whacked. Billy goes after bad guy Solly Fish (Jon Seda) and has to protect a witness (Elizabeth Mitchell in a throw-away role) along the way. In the real world Solly wouldn't last 20 minutes with his Mafia Uncle. Bad movie but the disc itself is good. Great sound and crisp colors. —DE

Movie: 🎵 **DVD:** 🎵½
Artisan Ent. (cat #12519, UPC 01223-6125198). Full frame; widescreen (1.85:1) anamorphic. 2.0 and 5.1 Dolby Digital Surround. $24.98. Keepcase. *LANG:* English. *SUB:* English; Spanish. *FEATURES:* 20 chapters ⚫ Director and cast filmographies (these are very thin) ⚫ Trailer ⚫ Interactive motion menus.
2001 (R) 104m/C William Baldwin, Adam Baldwin, Jon Seda, Elizabeth Mitchell; **D:** Heywood Gould; **W:** Heywood Gould; **C:** David Rush Morrison.

Double Deception

Bodyguard Luke Campbell (Mandylor) is hired to protect Lisa Ozaki (Kikukawa), the daughter of a wealthy businessman. Mr. Ozaki (Nakata) suspects a kidnapping plot and sets a double in Lisa's place. When the abduction occurs and Ozaki refuses to pay the ransom, Luke takes it upon himself to rescue her. He kidnaps the real Lisa and uses her as bait, which leads to schemes and double-crosses that defy logic. Cheap suspense and a strange appearance by Udo Kier are all that's going for this dull, poorly acted thriller. The sound is always clear, but the image suffers badly from artifacts. —DRL

Movie: 🎵½ **DVD:** 🎵½
MTI (cat #1092, UPC 039414510928). Full frame. Dolby Digital Stereo. $24.95. Keepcase. *LANG:* English. *SUB:* Spanish. *FEATURES:* Filmographies ⚫ 8 chapters.
2001 (R) 87m/C Louis Mandylor, James Russo, Rei Kikukawa, Kouji Nakata, Jim Stathis, Udo Kier, Joe Estevez; **D:** Shundo Ohkawa; **W:** Shundo Ohkawa, Chris Chan Lee; **C:** Blain Brown; **M:** Jeremy C. Grody.

Double Down

Although Jason Priestley gets top billing in this film, the story actually focuses on a group of four friends. David (Priestley), Mike (Kane Picoy), Cory (Peter Dobson), and Brett (Orien Richman) are four young hustlers who love to gamble and hang out at Zigs, the restaurant owned by David's father. This quartet dreams of opening their own eatery and plans to use their gambling earnings to finance the establishment. The movie is narrated by Mike and the film mainly explores his sad existence, in which he vacillates between out-of-control gambling and his pipe dreams of being a restaurateur. The problem with *Double Down* is that nothing really happens. The movie is made up mostly of scenes in which the four buddies talk and harass one another. There is no real drama here. Given the fact that we've seen films like this before (and the clues given by the text from the DVD box), the audience expects one of the characters (i.e. Mike) to get into very serious trouble because of the gambling, but this never materializes. The film offers some nice performances, most notably from Dobson, and some funny lines, but not much else.

Even more surprising than the lack of action in the movie is how nice this film looks on DVD. The transfer is sharp and very clear, showing very little grain and no distortion. The colors are great, especially those in the final scene. The digital stereo audio track provides clear dialogue, with no discernible hissing. —ML **AKA:** Zigs.

Movie: 🎵🎵 **DVD:** 🎵🎵½
Avalanche Ent. (cat #1568D, UPC 8064-69156827). Widescreen (1.85:1) letterboxed. Digital Stereo. $19.99. Keepcase. *LANG:* English. *SUB:* English; French; Spanish. *CAP:* English. *FEATURES:* Trailer ⚫ Bonus trailers.
2001 (R) 93m/C Peter Dobson, Jason Priestley, Orien Richman, Kane Picoy, Richard Portnow, Luca Palanca, Alicia Coppola, Alexandra Powers, David Proval; **D:** Mars Callahan; **W:** Mars Callahan; **C:** Christopher Pearson.

Down from the Mountain

This documentary revolves around a concert that took place on May 24, 2000, at Nashville's Ryman Auditorium, by the musicians—Ralph Stanley, Alison Krauss, John Hartford, Emmylou Harris, the Fairfield Four and Gillian Welsh, among others—who performed on the surprise hit soundtrack to the Coen brothers's *Oh, Brother, Where Art Thou?* Directors Nick Doob, Chris Hegedus and D.A. Pennebaker follow the participants (and the city) as they get ready and then as they perform. Like the soundtrack, this presentation of the music is so accessible that it's recommended even to those who don't think of themselves as fans of bluegrass or "roots" music. The image, which appears to have been shot on 16mm, is absolutely nothing special. Picture goes in and out of focus and some of the lighting is abominable. But that rough, intentionally unpolished quality is fine for the subject. Sound is everything that the music needs. Recommended. —MM

Movie: 🎵🎵🎵½ **DVD:** 🎵🎵🎵
Artisan Ent. (cat #12324). Widescreen (1.85:1) anamorphic. Dolby Digital 5.1 Surround; Dolby Digital Surround. $19.98. Keepcase. *LANG:* English. *FEATURES:* Synopsis ⚫ 12 chapters ⚫ Talent files ⚫ Credits ⚫ Song list ⚫ Trailer.
2000 (G) 98m/C D: Chris Hegedus, D.A. Pennebaker, Nick Doob.

Down to Earth

In a remake of Warren Beatty's *Heaven Can Wait* (itself a remake of 1941's *Here Comes Mr. Jordan*), Chris Rock stars as struggling stand-up comic Lance Barton. When he rides his bicycle into the path of an oncoming truck, angel Mr. Keyes (Levy) plucks Lance from the scene of the accident before the truck can hit him, and takes him to heaven. Once there, Lance pleads his case to Mr. King (Palminteri), who agrees to send Lance back to Earth, but in another body. The image transfer is crystal clear, showing little grain and no

noise or distortion. The colors, most notably the background lighting at the Apollo Theatre, are very impressive, showing a very nice spectrum of hues. The framing appears to be accurate, as there is no warping of the frame. The 5.1 sound gives the viewer an exceptional Surround display for a comedy, as the applause at the Apollo flow from every speaker (creating the "You Are There!" feel). The rap music that dominates the soundtrack will have your subwoofer working overtime. Of course, these goodies never drown out the dialogue and the track is free from any distortion. —ML

Movie: 🎵🎵½ **DVD:** 🎵🎵🎵½
Paramount (cat #33778, UPC 097363377-849). Widescreen (1.85:1) anamorphic. Dolby Digital 5.1 Surround Stereo; Dolby Digital Surround Stereo. $29.99. Keepcase. *LANG:* English; French. *SUB:* English. *CAP:* English. *FEATURES:* 14 chapters ⚫ "Making of" featurette ⚫ Trailer.
2001 (PG-13) 87m/C Chris Rock, Regina King, Chazz Palminteri, Eugene Levy, Frankie Faison, Mark Addy, Greg Germann, Jennifer Coolidge, Mario Joyner; **D:** Chris Weitz, Paul Weitz; **W:** Chris Rock, Lance Crouther, Ali LeRoi, Louis CK; **C:** Richard Crudo; **M:** Jamshield Sharifi.

Down to the Sea in Ships

Please see review for *Parisian Love / Down to the Sea in Ships.* **AKA:** The Last Adventurers.

Movie: 🎵🎵½
1922 83m/B Marguerite Courtot, Raymond (Ray) McKee, Clara Bow; **D:** Elmer Clifton; **W:** John L.E. Pell; **C:** Alexander Penrod.

Dracula: The Dark Prince

This attempt to tell the true story behind the Dracula myth, while historically suspect, is a surprisingly interesting and gory period piece. In 15th-century Romania, it is Prince Vlad the Impaler's (Martin) destiny to deliver his people from the oppression of Turkish rule, by any means necessary. This was foretold by the church, but is Vlad a messiah or the antichrist? That depends on which side you ask. The fighting scenes are shot in a dizzying way and some of the casting choices are insane (Daltrey as the King of Hungary?), but Martin is good and the movie is pretty entertaining. The full-frame presentation is crisp, with a clean transfer, and the Surround mix is used well for atmosphere. —DRL **AKA:** Dark Prince: The True Story of Dracula.

Movie: 🎵🎵½ **DVD:** 🎵🎵🎵
Artisan Ent. (cat #12701, UPC 01223612-7017). Full frame. Dolby 5.1 Surround; Dolby Stereo. $24.98. Keepcase. *LANG:* English. *SUB:* Spanish. *CAP:* English. *FEATURES:* Director and cast filmographies ⚫ Photo gallery ⚫ Trailers ⚫ 20 chapters.
2001 (R) 89m/C Rudolf Martin, Jane March, Peter Weller, Roger Daltrey, Michael

Sutton, Christopher Brand; **D:** Joe Chappelle; **W:** Thomas Baum; **C:** Dermott Downs; **M:** Frankie Blue.

Dracula 2000

Dracula (Butler) goes to present-day New Orleans. So does Van Helsing (Plummer). The filmmakers attempt to add some new twists to the familiar (but stylish) material with mixed results. There's little to recommend it beyond the audience of horror fans. The image is sharp and very clear, giving us a transfer that is essentially pristine. There is no distortion or noise, and the picture is stable throughout. The colors are very lush and rich, and as is to be expected, the reds, which dominate the film, look great. While the 5.1 track offers sufficient audio quality throughout the movie, it really comes to life at the 1:08:00 point, a scene which can well be used by many as a Surround sound demo! The extensive extras are listed below. —MM/ML *AKA:* Wes Craven Presents: Dracula 2000.

Movie: 🎬🎬 **DVD:** 🎬🎬🎬 ½
Buena Vista Home Ent. (cat #21678, UPC 786936145038). Widescreen (2.35:1) anamorphic. Dolby Digital 5.1 Surround Stereo. $24.99. Keepcase. *LANG:* English; French. *SUB:* English; Spanish. *CAP:* English. *FEATURES:* Commentary: Patrick Lussier, Joel Soisson ● Deleted scenes and extended scenes with commentary ● Behind-the-scenes featurette ● Auditions ● Storyboards ● Trailer.
2000 (R) 98m/C Jonny Lee Miller, Justine Waddell, Gerard Butler, Colleen (Ann) (Vitamin C) Fitzpatrick, Jennifer Esposito, Danny Masterson, Jeri Ryan, Lochlyn Munro, Sean Patrick Thomas, Omar Epps, Christopher Plummer; **D:** Patrick Lussier; **W:** Joel Soisson; **C:** Peter Pay; **M:** Marco Beltrami.

Dracula's Daughter

Count Dracula's daughter, Countess Marya Zaleska, heads to London supposedly to find the cure to a mysterious illness. Instead she finds she has a taste for human blood, especially female blood. She also finds a man, falls in love, and tries to keep him by casting a spell on him. A good script and cast keep this sequel to Bela Lugosi's *Dracula* entertaining. The print used for the DVD transfer is in a lot worse shape than those used for the bigger Universal Monster Collection DVDs (the prime Karloffs and Lugosis, for instance) but, the occasional scratch and speckling almost add something to the charm. The only real aggravation is the one or two times that the film flutters up and down a bit, most likely due to sprocket damage. The image, though, is very sharp and the graytones full of detail. The mono sound is scratchy but distinct. Maybe to make the film source appear better than it is, Universal has included the theatrical trailer that looks like it's been through several wars and sitting in a

swamp for years. Available only as part of a double feature with *Son of Dracula* (see separate entry). —JO
Movie: 🎬🎬🎬 **DVD:** 🎬🎬🎬
Universal Studios (cat #21398, UPC 025192139826). Full frame. Dolby Digital Mono. $29.98. Keepcase. *LANG:* English; Spanish. *SUB:* Spanish; French. *CAP:* English. *FEATURES:* Theatrical trailer ● Talent files ● Production notes ● Dual-layered RSDL.
1936 71m/B Gloria Holden, Otto Kruger, Marguerite Churchill, Irving Pichel, Edward Van Sloan, Nan Grey, Hedda Hopper; **D:** Lambert Hillyer; **W:** Garrett Fort; **C:** George Robinson.

Dragon Inn

Rebels protect two children during a power struggle in the Ming dynasty. Power-hungry eunuch Tsao Siu Yan (Donnie Yen), leader of the East Chamber, is intent on destroying all who oppose him. He sets up a trap to bring out the rebel leader Chow Wai-on (Tony Leung), but instead, a small group of rebels is prey. Lead by Yau Mo-yan (Brigitte Lin Ching Hsia), the group escapes into the desert before Tsao Siu Yan's Black Arrow soldiers can track them. They go to "Dragon Inn," a remote tavern in the desert, where they meet with Chow Wai-on, but Tsao and his men seek shelter in the same tavern. The rebels try to stay alive, while Tsao's men slowly close the net. But Jade (Maggie Cheung), the rogue owner of the inn, and a master thief herself, is not obligated to either group. With its good humor and the beautiful photography, the film almost feels like the Hong Kong version of *The Old Dark House,* making the most of a limited location. When the action explodes with full force during its final third act, there are no holds barred and the viewers are treated to some absolutely spectacular stunts. The movie's original length is 88 minutes, but Tai Seng has been able to obtain a 103-minute cut for DVD release. The transfer is mostly free of defects or blemishes, although in certain scenes, dust is quite evident. The colors are vibrant and natural. The black level is good, creating solid blacks, while shadows still maintain good definition at all times. Since the disc defaults to the Cantonese track with the English subtitles turned on, let's quickly forget that there is such a thing as an English audio track. The Chinese tracks, though presented only in mono, are of very good quality however, with a good dynamic range. On his commentary track, Ric Meyers from *Inside Kung Fu* magazine fills in background on the actors and the stature many of them have in Hong Kong cinema. He also discusses thematic elements and technical aspects. —GH/MM
Movie: 🎬🎬🎬 **DVD:** 🎬🎬🎬
Tai Seng (UPC 601643877648). Widescreen (1.85:1) letterboxed. Dolby Digital Mono. $29.98. Keepcase. *LANG:* Cantonese; Mandarin; English. *SUB:* English.

FEATURES: Commentary ● Trailers ● Filmographies.
1992 103m/C HK Tony Leung Ka-Fai, Brigitte (Lin Chinag-hsia) Lin, Maggie Cheung, Donnie Yen; **D:** Raymond Lee.

Dragon Tales

"I wish, I wish with all my heart, to fly with dragons, in a land apart." With this rhyme, thus begins an animated children's series originating from PBS. It follows the adventures of Emmy and her brother Max, as they use a magical dragon's scale to visit Dragon Land. Once there, they play with the strong, but shy Ord, the young, but smart Cassie, and the two-headed dragon siblings, Wheezie and Zak, who have a flair for music. In each episode, the group has a task or a goal which is intended to teach a valuable lesson. The problem with *Dragon Tales* is that the educational value of the show can get lost in the shuffle at times. In some episodes, the lesson is quite clear, making it a valuable tool for parents. But in others, the show seems to be focused more on pure entertainment, so the message goes unnoticed. And while each dragon is given a distinct personality, they are also caricatures, the most insulting being Ord—yes, it's unique that the largest dragon is also afraid of everything, but it's not very original that the big, strong guy isn't very smart. On top of all of this, the animation varies in quality. At times, the drawings are very distinct, while others look rushed and blurry. The show can be entertaining and is on target at times, but the bottom line is that there are better children's programs out there. Interesting trivia—Wesley Eure, one of the show's developers, starred as Will Marshall on the cult TV series *Land of the Lost.* This DVD series offer five episodes per disc, with each show running between 11–15 minutes. These are pristine reproductions of the programs, as they show bright colors, with no grain or artifacting. The image is very clear, and there is no on-screen distortion. Surround audio tracks provide clear dialogue and nice reproduction of the music. Each DVD also contains four sing-alongs, taken from the musical numbers used to break up the episodes on the TV show. —ML
Movie: 🎬🎬 **DVD:** 🎬🎬 ½
Columbia Tristar (cat #08601, UPC 043396086012). Full frame. Dolby 2.0 Surround. $19.95. Keepcase. *LANG:* English; Spanish. *SUB:* English. *CAP:* English. *FEATURES:* Sing-alongs ● Bonus trailers.
1999 69m/C V: Andrea Libman, Danny McKinnon, Ty Olsson, Chantal Strand, Kathleen Barr, Jason Michas.

Dragon's Claws

Originally planned to star Jackie Chan, this one contains all the marks of a classic kung fu flick, plus some interesting twists. There's a young hero who needs to learn a thing or two, the sinister villainy (and powerful legs) of the great Hwang Jang Lee, a respected kung fu style that must be learned and surpassed, a dirty old mendicant who is really a grandmaster in disguise, creative training sequences, colorful villains, and kick-ass martial arts action. The plot and settings keep you interested in the story without becoming too complicated. Image and sound are surprisingly crisp. Much superior to more expensive releases of the same title, which are from cropped, edited, and English-dubbed prints. —*BT* **AKA:** Dragon's Claw; Dragon Claw.

Movie: *♪♪♪* **DVD:** *♪♪* ½
Tai Seng (cat #DVD470, UPC 489039110-4700). Widescreen letterboxed. $14.95. Keepcase. *LANG:* Cantonese; Mandarin. *SUB:* Chinese; English. *FEATURES:* 9 chapters.
1979 91m/C *HK* Jang-Lee Hwang, Jimmy Liu, Kar Wing Lau, Dragon Lee; **D:** Joseph Kuo; **W:** Ping Han Chiang; **C:** Kuan Wah Ma; **M:** Tsun Chi Chen.

Dragstrip Girl

Toothless remake-in-title-only comes from the Showtime cable network's *Rebel Highway* series. Johnny (Dacascos) is a working class Mexican-American kid who's trying to better himself by working with a car theft ring. He falls for rich girl Laura (Wagner), but their dragstrip to romance is rocky. Production is second-rate in every respect. The filmmakers don't really understand what makes the original teen exploitation pictures so much fun and try to clean things up. A few fleeting moments of Traci Lords doing a credible Marilyn Monroe imitation beneath a fluffy platinum blonde wig is all the film has to offer. Image is unusually grainy and prone to artifacts even in bright interiors. —*MM*
Movie: *♪* **DVD:** *♪* ½
Buena Vista Home Ent. (cat #24569, UPC 786936168402). Full frame. Dolby Digital Surround Stereo. $34.98. Keepcase. *LANG:* English. *CAP:* English. *FEATURES:* 15 chapters.
1994 82m/C Mark Dacascos, Natasha Gregson Wagner, Raymond Cruz, Traci Lords; **D:** Mary Lambert; **W:** Jerome Gary; **C:** Sandi Sissel.

Drawing Flies

Kevin Smith served as executive producer of this low-budget independent production and he appears in a cameo as Silent Bob. The story concerns five young Canadian slackers (Mewes, Lee, Humphrey, Lee, Brooks) who are booted off of welfare and decamp for the woods where they hope to find Bigfoot. They also talk a lot. That's right, it's "The Blair Clerks Project." It's difficult to say much about the image quality because the black-and-white photography is so rough. It appears to be an accurate reproduction of the original. The commentary track with the cast members is a veritable auditory food fight as everyone concerned whoops it up. Filmmakers Ingram

and Gissing are more restrained, but annoyingly knock their cigarette lighters (or something) against an ashtray near the microphone. —*MM*
Movie: *♪♪* **DVD:** *♪♪* ½
Indie DVD (cat #00079, UPC 802695000-798). Full frame. Dolby Digital Surround. $19.98. Keepcase. *LANG:* English. *FEATURES:* 19 chapters • 2 commentary tracks • Director's cut • Bloopers, outtakes, deleted scenes • Intro by Kevin Smith and Scott Mosier.
2002 76m/B *CA* Jason Lee, Jason Mewes, Renee Humphrey, Carmen Lee, Martin Brooks, Kevin Smith; **D:** Matthew Gissing, Malcolm Ingram; **W:** Matthew Gissing, Malcolm Ingram; **C:** Brian Pearson.

Dreaming Fists with Slender Hands

Two boys, raised together by a kung fu master, are hired to defend a town from gangsters. Beaten and separated, they're each trained in different fighting styles for the return match. Shot in the backyards of Taiwan, it features lame kung fu and lamer comedy. The image is cropped severely and the dubbed soundtrack is scratchy. —*BT* **AKA:** Kung Fu Kids.
Movie: *♪* **DVD:** *♪♪*
Tai Seng (cat #84114, UPC 6016438411-44). Full frame. $14.95. Keepcase. *LANG:* English. *FEATURES:* 8 chapters.
1980 90m/C *TW* Lung Fei, Chin Hu, Lap Cho Lau, Leung Tai; **D:** Karl Liao; **W:** Yao Chung; **C:** How-chung Chen; **M:** Mao-shan Huang.

The Dress Code

Bruno (Linz), his mother Angela (Halprin), and friend Shawniqua (Davael) are all outsiders. Driven by a recurrent angel dream, Bruno's decision to wear a dress may not have anything to do with his sexual identity. He competes in a series of Catholic school spelling bees that culminate in a national contest and an opportunity for the winner to have an audience with the Pope. A comedy by definition, Shirley MacLaine's turn as a director is competent if pedestrian. The script is distantly charming. Some good performances from peripheral characters played by Gary Sinise, Kathy Bates, Jennifer Tilly, and MacLaine herself, but *Dress Code* lacks any real bite or energy. This film apparently surfaced somewhere before going straight to video. Decent DVD transfer and sound. —*MO* **AKA:** Bruno.
Movie: *♪♪* **DVD:** *♪♪♪* ½
MGM Home Ent. (cat #1001824, UPC 027616890401). Full frame. Dolby Digital Stereo. $24.98. Keepcase. *LANG:* English. *CAP:* English. *FEATURES:* 24 chapters.
1999 (PG-13) 108m/C Alex D. Linz, Gary Sinise, Jennifer Tilly, Kathy Bates, Joey Lauren Adams, Shirley MacLaine, Brett Butler, Gwen Verdon, Stacey Halprin, Kiami Davael;

D: Shirley MacLaine; **W:** David Ciminello; **C:** Jan Kiesser; **M:** Chris Boardman.

Dressed to Kill [SE]

The 11-minute museum sequence at the center of Brian DePalma's erotic thriller remains a bravura piece of filmmaking. The rest of the film hasn't aged quite so well. The plot lapses and asinine ending are the most blatant shortcomings, but this disc is still a nice package. It contains both the "R"-rated theatrical release and an unrated version. A short featurette compares scenes from both along with the third broadcast television version. It demonstrates that—in the mind of the MPAA ratings board, at least—the difference between a potential "X" rating and prime-time TV lies in nuance. Beyond a few seconds of body-double nudity and slashing violence, the three versions are identical. On DVD the film looks good but not great; it never has. The extensive extras make the difference for this one. —*MM*
Movie: *♪♪* ½ **DVD:** *♪♪♪* ½
MGM Home Ent. (cat #1002333, UPC 027-6167865526). Widescreen (2.35:1) anamorphic. Dolby Digital 5.1 Surround; Mono. $24.98. Keepcase. *LANG:* English; French. *SUB:* French; Spanish. *CAP:* English. *FEATURES:* 16 chapters • 2 photo galleries • "R"-rated and unrated versions • 3 featurettes • "Making of" documentary • Keith Gordon appreciation featurette • Advertising gallery.
1980 (R) 105m/C Angie Dickinson, Michael Caine, Nancy Allen, Keith Gordon, Dennis Franz, David Margulies, Brandon Maggart; **D:** Brian DePalma; **W:** Brian DePalma; **C:** Ralf Bode; **M:** Pino Donaggio.

Drive By

Ceasar (Acosta), the young brother of the leader of the neighborhood gang, hates the drugs and murder on the streets, but the pull of gang life is strong. He is tipped off about a set-up of his brother, and must choose between his future and his family. Expertly filmed and acted it is not, but the artistry of this movie is secondary to its message. The film's emotion and sincerity come through in the credible script (from obvious life experience). The non-professional actors and location shooting add to the realism. The image and sound are both adequate, but the film's budget is especially evident here. —*DRL*
Movie: *♪♪♪* **DVD:** *♪♪♪*
Artisan Ent. (cat #12437, UPC 01223612-4375). Widescreen (1.78:1) anamorphic. Dolby 5.1 Surround; Dolby Stereo Surround. $24.98. Keepcase. *LANG:* English. *SUB:* English; Spanish. *CAP:* English. *FEATURES:* Commentary: director & producer • Deleted scenes • Isolated music track • Music video • Screen tests • Photo gallery • Trailer • 20 chapters.
2001 (R) 98m/C Mario Acosta, Felipe Camacho, Alberto Viruena, Raul Salinas, Vincente Zuniga C; **D:** Juan J. Frausto; **W:**

Vincente Zuniga C, Juan J. Frausto; **C:** Gennadi Balitski; **M:** Christopher Morford.

Drive-in Discs, Vol. 2

This is the second volume of a proposed 15-disc collection of delightful drive-in dreck (*Vol. 1* is reviewed in *Book 2*), containing a double feature: 1959's *The Wasp Woman* and *The Giant Gila Monster*. The DVD re-creates the full drive-in experience for those who choose it, complete with window-boxed cartoons, national anthem, countdown clock, and more. The widescreen prints themselves are surprisingly clean, with *The Wasp Woman* showing more stable gray tones and black levels than the sporadically inky *Gila Monster*. Both prints are remarkably free of source defects considering they've likely been stored in a brown paper sack all these years. The audio, presented in Dolby Digital mono, is suitable for standard viewing. However, to get the most of the drive-in experience, choose the "Distorto" option at the ticket booth—it's the latest in low-fidelity sound that perfectly re-creates that tinny quality of those battered cast aluminum window speakers of your favorite outdoor cinema. Distorto delivers the program soundtrack solely from your left-front speaker (clever) while ambient sounds of cars pulling in, footsteps in the gravel, and crickets chirping are delivered from the remaining channels. —*DP*
Movie: 🎵🎵 ½ **DVD:** 🎵🎵🎵
Elite Entertainment, Inc. (cat #EE3749, UPC 790594374921). Widescreen (1.85:1) anamorphic. Dolby Digital Mono; "Distorto" sound. $29.95. Keepcase. *LANG:* English. *FEATURES:* Trailer ▪ Cartoons ▪ Snack bar promos ▪ Countdown clock, national anthem, etc. ▪ 16 chapters.
2001 147m/C

Driven

A state-of-the-art disc in service to utter drivel. *Driven* ostensibly stars Sylvester Stallone (also responsible for the turgid screenplay) as Joe Tanto, a defrocked racing legend pulled back onto the track to mentor brilliant but undisciplined hotshot driver Jimmy Bly (Kip Pardue). Director Renny Harlin keeps the narrative going fast, leaving little time to dwell on the more clichéd aspects of Stallone's screenplay, which is pretty much everything between the main titles and end credits. The DVD itself is as perfect as the format allows. The 2.35 anamorphic transfer presents smooth, detailed images with vibrant colors and excellent detail definition. The Dolby Digital 5.1 audio never lets up, whether the constant, circling whir of race cars or the incessant pulsing music track. Director Harlin and Stallone chime in with two audio commentaries, Harlin giving scene-by-scene analysis and Stallone explicating the deleted scenes. While the documen-

tary about the special effects makes one marvel at what can be accomplished with digital technology, it only underscores the idea that this movie was manufactured rather than filmed. Besides, the puns are too good to resist. "Rocky Road?" "Rambo: First Gear?" —*EP*
Movie: 🎵🎵 **DVD:** 🎵🎵🎵 ½
Warner (cat #21013, UPC 0853921013-20). Widescreen (2.35:1) anamorphic. Dolby Digital 5.1. $24.98. Snapper. *LANG:* English; French. *SUB:* English; French; Spanish. *FEATURES:* 34 chapters ▪ Commentary: director Renny Harlin ▪ Additional scenes with audio commentary by Sylvester Stallone ▪ Behind-the-scenes documentaries ▪ Theatrical trailer.
2001 (PG-13) 117m/C Sylvester Stallone, Burt Reynolds, Kip Pardue, Til Schweiger, Gina Gershon, Robert Sean Leonard, Stacy Edwards, Estella Warren, Christian de la Fuente; **D:** Renny Harlin; **W:** Sylvester Stallone, Renny Harlin; **C:** Mauro Fiore; **M:** BT (Brian Transeau).

Druids

This "historical epic" is neither historical nor epic. Lambert plays Vercingetorix, a Gallic king who tries to drive the invading Romans from his land. He gathers his native brothers and rallies them for the fight of their lives. Von Sydow plays the leader of the Druids and Lambert's spiritual advisor, but only occasionally bothers to show up to spout some esoteric drivel about the price of destiny. There is some dust on the image during outdoor scenes, but the transfer is otherwise fine. The 5.1 Surround mix is pretty good, and the rear channels are heavily employed during the battle scenes, but that can't help this movie. —*DRL* **AKA:** Vercingetorix.
Movie: 🎵 ½ **DVD:** 🎵🎵 ½
Columbia Tristar (cat #6445, UPC 04339-6064454). Widescreen (2.35:1) anamorphic; full frame. Dolby 5.1 Surround; Dolby Surround. $27.96. Keepcase. *LANG:* English. *SUB:* Chinese; English; Korean; Thai. *CAP:* English. *FEATURES:* Trailers ▪ 28 chapters.
2001 (R) 115m/C Christopher Lambert, Klaus Maria Brandauer, Max von Sydow, Ines Sastre, Stefan Ivanov, Barnard Pierre Donnadieu; **D:** Jacques Dorfman; **W:** Jacques Dorfman, Rospo Pallenberg, Norman Spinrad; **M:** Pierre Charvet.

Drunken Master

Wong Fei-hung (Jackie Chan) is the most brash, stubborn, and spoiled young man studying at Po Chi Lam martial arts academy and clinic. Completely overconfident in his fighting abilities, he would rather cut up in class than do his exercises. Wong ends up being punished by training with crazy Uncle So, but runs afoul of contract killer Thunderleg Yen. The alcoholic So (perhaps a descendant of the famous Beggar So) teaches him his secret Drunken Fist style. The freshly inebriated young hero then takes on all com-

ers, especially Yen. Chan performs what look like grueling training exercises, but the meat of the movie is its classic fight scenes. For those of us who have only had the opportunity to see this film in scratched, squeezed, and cropped television prints on blurry "public domain" label transfers, this widescreen DVD edition is a refreshing revelation. The clear, less crowded frames are easier on the eyes, and make following the action more enjoyable. It also shows how many shots actually *are* out of focus. The original English dub is a much more faithful (and profane) translation, and much easier to hear. Ric Meyers is an acknowledged expert in martial arts cinema, and Jeff Yang, co-author of Jackie Chan's autobiography, team up for the best commentary for a Chan film to date. —*BT* **AKA:** Drunken Monkey in a Tiger's Eye; Chui Kuen; Zui Quan; The Story of Drunken Master; Drunk Monkey; Challenge; Eagle Claw Snake Fist Cat's Paw Part 2.
Movie: 🎵🎵🎵 ½ **DVD:** 🎵🎵🎵 ½
Columbia Tristar (cat #08390, UPC 0433-96083905). Widescreen (2.35:1) anamorphic. $24.95. Keepcase. *LANG:* English; Cantonese. *SUB:* English; French; Spanish; Portuguese; Korean; Thai. *CAP:* English. *FEATURES:* 28 chapters ▪ Commentary ▪ Trailers.
1978 (PG-13) 111m/C *CH* Jackie Chan, Simon Yuen, Jang-Lee Hwang, Kau Lam; **D:** Woo-ping Yuen; **W:** See Yuen Ng; **C:** Hai Chang; **M:** Fu-Liang Chou.

Dude, Where's My Car?

Slow-witted roommates Jesse and Chester wake one morning to a bizarre, seemingly unexplainable situation. To make matters worse, they appear to have trashed their girlfriends' home the night before and, of course, their car is missing, dude. Too hung over to remember how this all came to be, the two boys set out to piece things together and, in the process, involve themselves with angry transsexuals, ostriches, and extraterrestrials. Follows the grand tradition of stoned and/or goofball duos like Cheech and Chong, Bill and Ted, and Wayne and Garth, but just can't reach their level. If you like this film at all, the DVD is worth acquiring just for hilarious commentary by the director and Kutcher and Scott. It's one of the funniest ever, right up there with those by the Pythons or Bruce Campbell. The transfer is a good one, too; super sharp, with near stunning colors. Blacks are near perfect except in a couple of scenes. The soundtrack really throws in some good Surround effects and is full bodied and powerful throughout. Getting back to the supplementals, the "making of" featurette is a goodie, too, particularly when Kutcher is manning the "Dude-Cam." The extended scenes are worth a watch as well, with some of them funnier than what ended up in the film. —*JO*
Movie: 🎵🎵 ½ **DVD:** 🎵🎵🎵 ½

20th Century Fox (cat #2001793, UPC 024543017936). Widescreen (1.85:1) anamorphic. Dolby Digital 5.1; Dolby Surround. $26.98. Keepcase. *LANG:* English. *SUB:* English; Spanish. *CAP:* English. *FEATURES:* 22 chapters • Theatrical trailer • TV spots • Commentary: Danny Leiner, Ashton Kutcher, Seann William Scott • "Making of" featurette • 7 extended scenes • Music video, "Stupid Ass" by Grand Theft Auto.
2000 (PG-13) 83m/C Ashton Kutcher, Seann William Scott, Jennifer Garner, Marla Sokoloff, Kristy Swanson; *D:* Danny Leiner; *W:* Philip Stark; *C:* Robert Stevens; *M:* David Kitay.

The Duel

In imperial China, men are celebrated for their martial arts and sword fighting skills as they are typically hired for various jobs to protect royalty, the wealthy, or the poor. But two men stand out among all sword-fighters of the country: Snow (Ekin Cheng), the "God of Sword," and Yeh (Andy Lau), the "Sword Saint." To determine the world's finest swordmaster, Yeh challenges Snow for a life-and-death duel atop the apex of the Forbidden City, but as the date of the duel draws nearer, strange things happen in the Imperial city. Valuable items are stolen, people are killed, and above all the spoiled Princess Phoenix is determined to have things her way. The transfer shows a few nicks but is generally clean and free of distracting defects. The presentation is stable and only slight grain is evident in the movie. The colors are powerfully rendered, bringing out the best of the movie's atmospheric cinematography with its cold blue tones and the contrasting hot colors. Skin tones are natural. The black level is solid and deep. The DVD contains a 5.1 channel Cantonese Dolby Digital track as well as Dolby Surround tracks in Mandarin and English. The 5.1 mix is especially energetic and creates a wide sound field. Often used to enhance the moody ambience, the Surround channels are also engaged for effects purposes, making the disc a dynamic and immersive experience. —GH/MM
Movie: ♪♪♪ **DVD:** ♪♪♪
Tai Seng (UPC 601643928142). Widescreen (2.35:1) letterboxed. Dolby Digital 5.1 Surround. $29.98. Keepcase. *LANG:* Cantonese; Mandarin; English. *SUB:* English. *FEATURES:* Isolated music and effects track • Commentary: Ric Meyers • "Making of" featurette • Photo gallery • Trailers.
2000 106m/C *HK* Andrew Lau, Ekin Cheng, Nick Cheung, Patrick Tam; *D:* Andrew Lau.

Dueling DVD: Cyrano de Bergerac / The Son of Monte Cristo

Cyrano de Bergerac, the first feature on this disc, is the adventures of a witty, brilliant swordsman who happens to have a giant proboscis; a literate, well-acted version of the oft-filmed tale. Ferrer delivers a rich, absorbing performance, in a story both dramatic and thrilling. Occasionally the film feels a bit stagy but it's a minor quibble in a sumptuous independent production. In *The Son of Monte Cristo*, Louis Hayward stars as the titular character who (in Zorro-like fashion) works with rebels to turn the people against evil Count Gurko (Sanders). A classic but by-the-numbers golden age Hollywood swashbuckler with good production values and a solid cast. Sanders essays the villain with typical glee and Bennett makes a strong and intelligent love interest. The odd soup of clashing accents is occasionally distracting. Both films are transferred from fairly clean and intact 16mm prints with minimal digital noise. *Cyrano* has richer blacks and *Cristo* tends to be a tad grainy and soft but both films display good contrast. The audio for both is intelligible but a bit muffled and squawky. —DG
Movie: ♪♪♪ **DVD:** ♪♪
Marengo Films (cat #MRG-0020, UPC 807013002096). Full frame. Mono. $14.98. Keepcase. *LANG:* English. *FEATURES:* 12 chapters.
2001 212m/C

Dumbo

Disney's animated feature about a baby elephant remains one of the studio's best efforts. Dumbo is ridiculed for his large ears until he discovers that he can fly and becomes a star. If the animation lacks the depth and complexity of *Snow White* or *Fantasia,* the emotions of the story are honest and moving. The hallucinatory dream sequence is still frightening. Disc comes with all the extras that the studio lavishes on its proven crowd-pleasers. Image is excellent with grain that comes from the original. The 5.1 remix is not overly aggressive or intrusive. This one belongs in every library. —MM
Movie: ♪♪♪♪ **DVD:** ♪♪♪♪
Buena Vista Home Ent. (cat #21615, UPC 786936144390). Full frame. Dolby Digital 5.1 Surround Stereo. $29.99. Keepcase. *LANG:* English; French; Spanish. *CAP:* English. *FEATURES:* Commentary: film historian John Canemaker • 17 chapters • "Celebrating Dumbo" featurette • Art gallery • "Reluctant Dragon" sound design featurette • TV introduction by Walt Disney • DVD storybook • Publicity materials • Previews • Michael Crawford music video • Animated shorts: "Elmer Elephant" and "The Flying Mouse" • 2 sing-along songs • DVD-ROM weblinks.
1941 63m/C *D:* Ben Sharpsteen; *W:* Joe Grant, Dick Huemer; *M:* Frank Churchill, Oliver Wallace; *V:* Sterling Holloway, Edward Brophy, Verna Felton, Herman Bing, Cliff Edwards. *AWARDS:* Oscars '41: Scoring/Musical; *NOM:* Oscars '41: Song ("Baby Mine").

Dune [2 SE]

This three-disc "special edition" corrects the flaws noted in the review of the first DVD release in *Book 2.* The widescreen transfer is flawless and serves to make the computer-generated effects more obvious. (The blue eyes are never remotely believable.) The Surround options deliver very good sound, notable in the big action scenes and crowd scenes with offscreen voices. It appears that all of the extras from the earlier release are here, along with about 15 minutes that was cut from various TV versions. It's an exceptionally nice package. If only someone would put as much effort into a full restoration of the David Lynch version. —MM *AKA:* Frank Herbert's Dune.
Movie: ♪♪♪ **DVD:** ♪♪♪ ½
Artisan Ent. (cat #12529, UPC 01223-6125297). Widescreen (1.77:1) anamorphic. DTS Surround; Dolby Digital 5.1; Dolby Surround. $26.98. Special packaging. *LANG:* English. *CAP:* English. *FEATURES:* Commentary • 5 featurettes • John Harrison interview • Vittorio Storaro essay • Photo gallery • Talent files • 84 chapters.
2000 270m/C Alec Newman, William Hurt, Saskia Reeves, Ian McNeice, P. H. Moriarty, Julie Cox, Matt Keeslar, Giancarlo Giannini, Barbara Kodetova, Robert Russell, Miljen Kreka Kljakovic; *D:* John Harrison; *W:* John Harrison; *C:* Vittorio Storaro, Harry B. Miller III; *M:* Graeme Revell.

The Dunwich Horror

Young warlock Wilbur Whatley (Stockwell) steals a copy of the "Necronomicon" from the library of Miskatonic University and sets about to restore his family to their rightful place as rulers of the known universe. He also needs the co-operation of a blonde co-ed (Dee). Stockwell is wonderfully hammy throughout; the trippy dream sequence is among the most irritating of the era and those who have always wanted to see the original Gidget (and her body double) stretched out on a satanic altar will find what they're looking for. This is far and away the sharpest-looking version of the film I've seen. Some grain appears in the special effects shots, but that comes from the original. This is a very good image. Mono sound is fine. —MM
Movie: ♪♪♪ **DVD:** ♪♪♪
MGM Home Ent. (cat #1002338, UPC 027616865571). Widescreen (1.85:1) anamorphic. Dolby Digital Mono. $19.98. Keepcase. *LANG:* English; French. *SUB:* French; Spanish. *CAP:* English. *FEATURES:* 16 chapters • Trailer.
1970 90m/C Sandra Dee, Dean Stockwell, Lloyd Bochner, Ed Begley Sr., Sam Jaffe, Joanna Moore, Talia Shire, Barboura Morris, Beach Dickerson, Michael Fox, Donna Baccala; *D:* Daniel Haller; *W:* Curtis Hanson, Henry Rosenbaum, Ronald Silkosky; *C:* Richard C. Glouner; *M:* Les Baxter.

Eagle Fist

A militiaman trains in the temple with an old man, who teaches him Eagle Fist– and Toad Fist–style kung fu. He also learns the secret weapon of hitting pressure points to lock the nerves. Then he sets out on a mission to retrieve the manual for unlocking nerves, stolen by the mysterious Red Dart. A traditional kung fu movie with a multiple twist ending, and bits of gentle comedy. The nerve-locking techniques central to the plot are the same ones conspiracy theorists still claim killed Bruce Lee. The soundtrack uses the theme from *True Grit*. The full-frame transfer, from a decent print for its age, is reasonably vivid. Released as a *Brooklyn Zoo Double Feature* with *Lady Iron Monkey*. The packaging prominently features the World Trade Center towers and the package notes that "A portion of proceeds to benefit NYC relief charities." —*BT* **AKA:** Eagle's Claw.

Movie: ♪♪ ½ **DVD:** ♪♪
Xenon Ent. (UPC 694795305626). Full frame. Dolby Digital 2.0. $9.99. Keepcase. *LANG:* English. *FEATURES:* 6 chapters • Trailers.
1977 93m/C *HK* Kwan Chun Chi, Chang Yi, Don Wong, Philip Ko; *D:* Tso Nam Lee; *W:* San Yee Cheung.

Eagle vs. Silver Fox

More Godfrey Ho hokum, sloppily constructed with flashbacks within flashbacks that easily confuses the viewer, should any be trying to pay attention. Sly villain Silver Fox works for the Northern lords trying to destroy the Southern rebels and restore the Manchurians to Chinese ruler. Li So goes with his father to carry a message, but they're ambushed by the Silver Fox gang, stabbed, and thrown in the river. But the villains fail to find the message, and Li survives. He beats up some toughs in a restaurant, and is joined by girl pickpocket Yuen Ling. Li and Ling go out and get in more fights with the gang, working their way up to the Silver Fox himself. The story is so poorly constructed that it's hard to tell what's going on at any given moment. Characters jump forward and back in time, one character seems to be telling a story that's another character's flashback, and so on. There are some weird sequences in slow motion that have a disturbing dreamlike quality. The dance-like choreography is too seldom and too little, failing to make up for all the other nonsense. The picture is squeezed at an angle in some shots, and so badly cropped that often no one appears on screen during a conversation. —*BT*

Movie: ♪ **DVD:** ♪ ½
Xenon Ent. (cat #XEXA6286DVD, UPC 000-799628621). Full frame. $14.98. Keepcase. *LANG:* English. *FEATURES:* 6 chapters • Clips from other Xenon kung fu titles.
1983 85m/C *KN* Hwang Jang Lee, Mario Chan, Pui-Shan Wing, Richard Kong, Simpson Yuen; *D:* Godfrey Ho; *W:* Kun Lung; *C:* Jimmy Wang Yu; *M:* Ricky Chan.

Earth

The third in a triptych of films (after *Zvenigora* and *Arsenal*), *Earth* is a visual masterpiece from a giant of early Soviet cinema. Dovzhenko's love for the Ukranian land and people is evident in every haunting and poetic image. The story, about a young man who ushers in the industrial age by bringing a tractor to his town, is mostly Soviet propaganda, and comes secondary to the style and emotion put into the production. The picture has suffered little degradation and has a fine orchestral score. Also included is a reconstruction of Eisenstein's *Bezhin Meadow*, tragically destroyed during WWII. It was painstakingly remade with stills, intertitles, and selections from Prokofiev to tell the story of a young boy, new Russia, and the struggle with his evil father, old Russia. The downside to this otherwise great release is the preface to the reconstruction. It begins with both Russian and English intertitles, after which is an English-dubbed narration, but the dubbing soon stops and there are no subtitles. It is as confusing as it sounds. —*DL* **AKA:** Zemlya; Soul.

Movie: ♪♪♪♪ **DVD:** ♪♪♪
Image Ent. (cat #1411, UPC 014311411-22). Full frame. Mono. $24.99. Keepcase. *LANG:* Silent/Russian and English. *SUB:* English. *FEATURES:* Reconstruction of Eisenstein's *Bezhin Meadow* • 16 chapters.
1930 101m/B *RU* Semyon Svashenko, Mikola Nademsy, Stephan Shkurat, Yelena Maximova, Yulia Solntseva; *D:* Alexander Dovzhenko; *W:* Alexander Dovzhenko; *C:* Daniil Demutsky.

Earth vs. the Spider

Lab security guard Quentin (Gummersall) is an introverted comic book lover until his elderly partner is killed during a shootout. Taking advantage of the destroyed lab, Quentin rashly injects himself with an experimental spider serum. As his relationship with the girl down the hall (Heinle) improves, Quentin begins to display the physical strengths of a spider (à la Spiderman) and commences a gruesome physical transformation (à la *The Fly*) as well. This is one in a series of five made-for-cable-TV movies, all based on the original AIP drive-in classics. The story bears little resemblance to the original version, making the title rather inaccurate. Though clearly a low-budget effort, the production is glossier than most TV movies, has a consistent sense of humor and provides some diverting matinee-style thrills. The beginning is fairly strong but as Quentin becomes less sympathetic, the story shifts focus to Aykroyd's noirish and less interesting detective character. A scene-stealing dog and funny comic shop owner are highlights, and Russell is obviously having a ball. Though fitted for television, the disc is presented in both widescreen and full-frame versions. The widescreen edition is preferred as it adds slightly to the periphery of the framing. Colors are strong and the image is sharp and pleas-

ing. Except for a few digitally noisy newspaper close-ups, the disc is free of artifacts. The sound is particularly effective: cleanly recorded with strong Surround presence, particularly with the music score. Unfortunately, the dialogue is occasionally mixed too low. The "featurette" is really just a teaser and is less than two minutes long. The photo gallery is bountiful but the images are presented at too low a resolution and look particularly "blocky." —*DG*

Movie: ♪♪ **DVD:** ♪♪♪ ½
Columbia Tristar (cat #07363, UPC 04339-6073630). Widescreen (1.78:1) anamorphic; full frame. Dolby Digital 5.1 Surround. $24.95. Keepcase. *LANG:* English; French. *SUB:* English; French; Spanish; Portuguese; Korean; Thai; Chinese. *CAP:* English. *FEATURES:* "Making of" featurette • Photo gallery • DVD-ROM weblink • Trailers • Filmographies.
2001 (R) 90m/C Devon Gummersall, Dan Aykroyd, Amelia Heinle, Christopher Cousins, John Cho, Theresa Russell, Mario Roccuzzo; *D:* Scott Ziehl; *W:* Cary Solomon, Chuck Konzelman, Max Enscoe, Annie de Young; *C:* Thomas Callaway; *M:* Charles Bernstein.

East Side Story

Between 1934 and 1973, the Soviet Union and Eastern bloc countries produced more than 40 musicals. Under strict socialist control, the films were a constant source of irritation to the censors and governing board. Working within communist strictures, the filmmakers had to produce stories that toed the party line, focusing the songs and dance numbers on the joys of working in the fields and the factories and producing for the common good. Though technically and aesthetically limited, the films were a fascinating mirror of their Western counterparts and were much appreciated by the oppressed workers. Although most of the films surveyed are fairly awkward, the ground-breaking *My Wife Wants to Sing* and the self-reflexive *Midnight Revue* both seem very enticing. Especially thrilling are a short series of teenage musicals starring the Eastern equivalent of Frankie Avalon and Annette Funicello. This is an important document for film historians and world cinema buffs. It's only marred by flat narration and the end of the musical era isn't elaborated on in enough detail. The non-anamorphic disc appears to be taken from an older transfer—it's fairly grainy and has instances of digital noise, especially prevalent in some of the black-and-white films. The films themselves seem in desperate need of restoration—colors are faded, prints frequently display damage, and the sound on most is a bit harsh. The sound and picture of the modern interviews and segments is much more colorful (though bleedy) and sounds better. —*DG*

Movie: ♪♪♪ **DVD:** ♪♪
Kino on Video (cat #K161DVD, UPC 7383-29016128). Full frame. Mono. $29.95. Keepcase. *LANG:* Several, mostly Russian.

SUB: English. FEATURES: 14 chapters ☞ List of the featured films ☞ Insert card with chapter listings.
1997 79m/C GE D: Dana Ranga; W: Andrew Horn, Dana Ranga.

Eat Drink Man Woman

On Taiwan, master chef Tao Chu (the wonderful Sihung Lung) has his hands full with his three daughters. His wife died several years before, and the three young women are about to strike out on their own. Jia-Chien (Chien-Lien Wu) is an aggressive young executive who's ready to announce that she has bought a condo. Jia-Jen, a devout Christian, is a high school teacher, and appears content to stay in the family home. The youngest, Jia-Ning (Yu-Wen Wang), has just begun an improbable romance. Their next-door neighbor Jin Rong (Sylvia Chang) and her young daughter are almost members of the family; at least until Jin's overbearing mother (Ah-Leh Gua) arrives for an open-ended visit. Mom's all-purpose advice is "Don't marry the bastard" but she has her eye on Master Chu. Initially, it may be difficult to keep the characters straight but that passes quickly and the film is as easy to follow—and as interesting—as a good soap opera and it ends with a letter-perfect twist. Don't miss the wonderful Scorsese shot when Master Chu first goes to his restaurant kitchen. And the key sequences of food preparation are astonishing. (The first chapter alone is almost worth the price of the disc.) Image quality is fine throughout and sound is superior to the theatrical presentation. One quibble: Why aren't the opening credits translated? —MM
Movie: 🐾🐾🐾🐾 **DVD:** 🐾🐾🐾
MGM Home Ent. (cat #1002584, UPC 02-7616867858). Widescreen (1.85:1) anamorphic. Dolby Digital Surround. $19.98. Keepcase. LANG: Mandarin Chinese. SUB: English. CAP: English. FEATURES: 16 chapters ☞ "A Feast for the Eyes: Ang Lee in Taipei" featurette ☞ Trailer.
1994 (R) 123m/C TW Sihung Lung, Kuei-Mei Yang, Yu-Wen Wang, Chien-Lien Wu, Sylvia Chang, Winston Chao, Ah-Leh Gua, Lester Chen; D: Ang Lee; W: Ang Lee, James Schamus, Hui-Ling Wang; C: Jong Lin; M: Mader. AWARDS: Natl. Bd. of Review '94: Foreign Film; NOM: Oscars '94: Foreign Film; Golden Globes '95: Foreign Film; Ind. Spirit '95: Actor (Lung), Actress (Wu), Cinematog., Director (Lee), Film, Screenplay.

Eat My Dust

Gangster Bill and his thugs gun down Hung and his wife, leaving their son Hank in an orphanage. Years later, Bill is doing very well in the triads, and is working on a big counterfeiting deal. Meanwhile, street chestnut vendors Rob (Mark Ng) and Hank (Michael Tsang) rescue Wendy (Cynthia Lam) from her triad pursuers. They think she's a hooker, but Wendy Ho is actually a cop trying to bust Bill, and hopes she can

trace the murder back to him. When Hank coincidentally meets up with a dying friend of his father, and learns how his parents died, he decides to get revenge. Eat My Dust can't decide which direction to go, and doesn't accomplish any of them all that well. The comic segments are a waste of time, but the fighting (what there is of it) is a highlight, and there are some nice explosion f/x. The climax features a lot of unbelievable gunplay. One curious detail: chestnut vendors who have access to bazookas, explosives, and machine guns. For some reason, Tai Seng didn't give this movie their usual widescreen and multiple language release, going with this bargain priced full-frame dubbed mono package, which has a jittery image and flaring highlights. Actual running time is 89 minutes, not the 94 printed on the back cover. The print doesn't have any proper credits, just a credit slide at the end—which may be made up of phony names. —BT
Movie: 🐾🐾 **DVD:** 🐾
Tai Seng (cat #44464, UPC 6016434446-42). Full frame. $9.95. Keepcase. LANG: English. FEATURES: 10 chapters ☞ Trailers.
1993 89m/C HK Michael Tsang, Mark Ng, Cynthia Lam, Paul Tai, Philip Cheng, Johnny Chu; D: Philip So; W: Man Cheng; M: Bob Yuen.

Echo of Murder

Based on the true story of Spin reporters (played here by Belushi and Hines) who revisited the Atlanta Child Murders, four years after the case was officially closed. From 1979–81, almost 30 children, all of them young African-American boys, were killed in this horrifying spree, but the investigation was over when one man was convicted of two of the murders. Was that really the end, or is there more to the story? There's some very good information about an important part of our history, although the sensationalism is sometimes over the top. The film has a good deal of grain, as is often the case with cable premieres, but they really blew the chance to provide useful historical information with the extras—the "historical texts" are just a summary of the movie's events, and the weblink is to Showtime's site. —BG AKA: Who Killed Atlanta's Children?.
Movie: 🐾🐾 ½ **DVD:** 🐾🐾 ½
Showtime Networks, Inc. (cat #SHO1041, UPC 758445104127). Full frame. Dolby Digital. $24.95. Keepcase. LANG: English; Spanish. FEATURES: 12 chapters ☞ Interviews with Belushi and Hines ☞ Cast bios ☞ Historical info.
2000 105m/C James Belushi, Gregory Hines; D: Charles Robert Carner; W: Charles Robert Carner; C: Michael Goi; M: James Verboort.

Echo Park

Unsung ensemble comedy about three roommates—a body builder, a single-mother waitress, and an itinerant songwriter—living in Los Angeles's Echo Park charts

their struggles as they aim for careers in showbiz. The video transfer is decent enough. Although it features nice definition for brighter colors, darker hues tend to bleed and lose definition. Overall, the picture is not as crisp as it could have been (but, it is important to note, the widescreen version is far better off than the full-frame version included on the disc). The soundtrack fares better than the video. Yet, while there is no noticeable distortion and music was reproduced well, some parts were a bit muffled and hard to discern. —MJT
Movie: 🐾🐾 ½ **DVD:** 🐾🐾
MGM Home Ent. (cat #1002751, UPC 027616869494). Widescreen (1.85:1) anamorphic; full frame. Dolby Digital Mono. $19.98. Keepcase. LANG: English; French. SUB: English; French; Spanish. FEATURES: 16 chapters ☞ Theatrical trailer ☞ Trailer gallery.
1986 (R) 93m/C AU Tom Hulce, Susan Dey, Michael Bowen, Richard "Cheech" Marin, Christopher Walker, Shirley Jo Finney, Cassandra Peterson, Yana Nirvana, Timothy Carey; D: Robert Dornhelm; W: Michael Ventura; C: Karl Kofler; M: David Rickets.

Ecstasy

Young Eva (Hedy Kiesler, later known as Hedy Lamarr) marries Emile (Zvonomir Rogoz), only to discover he's a closed-off man concerned only about having absolute order in his life. Despondent, she returns to her father's horse farm, "to find peace." Divorce proceedings are begun. While swimming, her horse runs off with her dress on its back, causing her to meet Adam (Aribert Mog), a construction foreman, under revealing conditions. They begin a torrid affair. All seems well until Emile and Adam meet up independently. Despite its racy reputation, this is a very artistic and emotionally valid exploration of the sensual life of a troubled young woman. There's almost no dialogue, and the story is told in the "pure visual" style of Dreyer's Vampyr: slow scenes, beautiful photography, a lingering attention to details of decor, and the subtle expressions on the actor's faces. The plot is reduced to the bare minimum. All the time and attention is spent on contrasts of light and dark, and symbolically charged imagery. Some of the symbolism is rather thin, but accepted as expressionist shorthand, it serves the same purpose as whole paragraphs of text. DVD comes from the Austrian Film Archive and is clearly the German version of the movie, entitled "Ekstasy" in the dreamy opening visual that almost reminds of the beginning of Blue Velvet. The image is not terrific, but not bad either. The movie is quite intact, but it's also several dupey generations away from prime material—the grain is severe, and the framing way too tight. Several scenes crop Lamarr down almost to the eyes, and it's obvious that some optical dupe in the past cropped way in on all four sides. That said, it's also very watch-

able and few details are lost. Perhaps the Czechs or the French have miraculously kept some superior version somewhere, but this version is not at all bad. —*GE*
AKA: Extase; Ekstase; Symphony of Love.
Movie: 🎵🎵🎵 **DVD:** 🎵🎵 ½
Image Ent. (cat #ID1444CLDVD, UPC 014-381144420). Full frame. Dolby Digital Mono. $24.98. Keepcase. *LANG:* German. *SUB:* English.
1933 90m/B *CZ* Hedy Lamarr, Jaromir Rogoz, Aribert Mog; **D:** Gustav Machaty; **W:** Gustav Machaty.

Eddie and the Cruisers

Offbeat rock variation on *Citizen Kane* caused barely a ripple in its theatrical release but went on to become one of home video's original sleeper hits. The title refers to an early '60s rock group clearly patterned on Bruce Springsteen and the E Street Band. Eddie (Pare) may have been killed in a car wreck on the eve of stardom. Years later, reporter Maggie Foley (Barkin) resurrects the story with the idea that he might be alive. Though the pace is sluggish and the story line thin, the film boasts good performances and an enjoyable (if derivative) soundtrack. DVD image ranges between fair and good; sound between good and very good. —*MM*
Movie: 🎵🎵 ½ **DVD:** 🎵🎵 ½
MGM Home Ent. (cat #1002358, UPC 027-616865694). Widescreen (1.85:1) anamorphic. Dolby Digital Surround Stereo. $14.95. Keepcase. *LANG:* English. *SUB:* French; Spanish. *CAP:* English. *FEATURES:* 16 chapters • Trailer.
1983 (PG) 90m/C Tom Berenger, Michael Pare, Ellen Barkin, Joe Pantoliano, Matthew Laurance, Helen Schneider, David Wilson, Michael "Tunes" Antunes, Joe Cates, John Stockwell, Barry Sand, Howard Johnson, Robin Karfo, Rufus Harley, Bruce Brown, Louis D'Esposito, Michael Toland, Bob Garrett, Joanne Collins; **D:** Martin Davidson; **W:** Martin Davidson, Arlene Davidson; **C:** Fred Murphy; **M:** John Cafferty.

The Education of Little Tree

Adapted from a children's book by Forrest Carter, this film presents a child's-eye view of a large-scale epic on par with such modern classics as *The Secret Garden.* In 1935, poor, orphaned, and part–Native American Little Tree (Joseph Ashton) is sent to live with his grandfather (James Cromwell) and Native American grandmother (Tantoo Cardinal) in the Smokey Mountains of Tennessee. There, he learns "The Way" of his Cherokee ancestors and how to make moonshine from his Scottish/Irish grandfather. A nosy, Bible-thumping aunt tips off authorities and soon Little Tree is shipped off to an evil state institution to cure him of his inappropriate Indian ways. There, the old-fashioned discipline (which helped to garner the film's "PG" rating) runs fierce and abusive. Cardinal and

Cromwell carve out memorable performances alongside first-rate newcomer Ashton. Also first-rate is the transfer on this DVD. The image is very sharp and clear, showing only touches of darkness at times. There is basically no grain to be found here, and only a slight amount of artifacting. The colors are fine, and the crisp image helps to bring the beautiful locations to life. The Dolby Digital 5.1 channel audio track sounds very good, as it offers clear dialogue, without a hint of distortion. The audio from the rear channels is used sparingly here, and due to the thematic nature of the film, is limited mostly to musical cues and select sound effects. —*ML*
Movie: 🎵🎵🎵 **DVD:** 🎵🎵 ½
Paramount (cat #33614, UPC 097363361-442). Widescreen (1.85:1) anamorphic. Dolby Digital 5.1; Dolby 2.0 Surround. $24.99. Keepcase. *LANG:* English; French. *SUB:* English. *CAP:* English. *FEATURES:* 26 chapters.
1997 (PG) 112m/C James Cromwell, Tantoo Cardinal, Joseph Ashton, Graham Greene; **D:** Richard Friedenberg; **W:** Richard Friedenberg; **C:** Anastas Michos; **M:** Mark Isham.

The Educational Archives Volume 1: Sex & Drugs

Skip Elsheimer, co-founder and curator of the A/V Geeks Educational Film Archive, has put together a wonderful collection of short educational films for this DVD series. These are the 16mm films that school-aged children were subjected to from the '50s to the '80s. With the advent of videotape, these gems were all but lost. Now, however, you can re-live those memories in the comfort of your own home. *The Educational Archives Volume 1* focuses on films which deal with sex and drugs. On the sex side, the topics range from simple human growth, to the dangers of syphilis. With the drug films, most of the major illegal substances are featured, and these shorts simply attempt to scare the viewer into just saying "no." These old movies are very dated, inaccurate, embarrassing, and most importantly, entertaining. Viewers should be warned: the subject matter on this DVD is at times very frank and should be considered the equivalent of an "R" rating. Anyone who remembers watching these old films in school will recall the frequent technical problems, and they are lovingly reproduced here. The films are all grainy and very scratchy. With most of them, there are bumps, skips, and missing frames. The mono soundtrack is frequently accompanied by a hissing sound. The only thing missing is the rumble of the old 16mm projector. —*ML*
Movie: 🎵🎵 ½ **DVD:** 🎵🎵
Fantoma Films (cat #FAN1260DVD, UPC 014381126020). Full frame. Dolby Digital Mono. $24.99. Keepcase. *LANG:* English. *FEATURES:* Bonus filmstrip.
2001 120m/C

The Educational Archives Volume 2: Social Engineering 101

Volume 2 of *The Educational Archives* series is much more lighthearted and fun than Volume 1. This series of short educational films from yesteryear deals with hygiene, manners, and social skills. The psychology at work in these shorts is dated and often ludicrous. For example, in "Shy Guy," a young Dick York is urged by his father to conform in order to fit in. But here, "conforming" basically means picking one person and becoming their clone. Another highlight is "Lunchroom Manners," in which a kid puts WAY too much thought into getting his lunch and not getting it on him. The most bizarre entry is "The Outsider," in which the oddly named Susan Jane is convinced that there's something wrong with her and that everyone hates her. What is presented as a simple social phobia more closely resembles a persecutor complex. The 10 short films presented here are all very entertaining and funny. True, some of the basic lessons taught here still hold true today, but the presentation is just wacky. As with Volume One, the films vary in quality, but most are quite worn, showing scratches and lines. The black-and-white films are grainy and most have at least one jump. The mono sound provides clear dialogue and distorted music, which adds to the nostalgia. This DVD is a lot of fun and would make a great party film. —*ML*
Movie: 🎵🎵🎵 ½ **DVD:** 🎵🎵 ½
Fantoma Films (cat #FAN1261DVD, UPC 014381126129). Full frame. Dolby Digital Mono. $24.99. Keepcase. *LANG:* English. *FEATURES:* Bonus filmstrip.
2001 120m/C

Eegah!

Please see review for *Mystery Science Theater 3000: "Eegah!"*
Movie: woof
1962 93m/C Marilyn Manning, Richard Kiel, Arch Hall Jr., William Waters, Carolyn Brandt, William Lloyd, Ray Dennis Steckler; **D:** Arch (Archie) Hall Sr.; **W:** Bob Wehling; **C:** Vilis Lapenieks; **M:** Arch Hall Jr.

The Eel

After serving an eight-year sentence for killing his wife during a jealous fit, Yamashita (Koji Yakusho, best known to Western filmgoers from *Shall We Dance*) tries to make a fresh start by opening a barbershop in a small town near Tokyo. Outside of his parole officer, Yamashita's only friend is his pet eel, which he found and cared for in prison. When he saves Keiko (Misa Shimizu) from suicide, an intimate relationship tenuously blossoms, but not before secrets from both their pasts threaten to undue the small amount of happiness they have rebuilt for themselves. A delicate, earthy character study about passion and redemption, Shohei

Imamura's film unfolds like a beautiful flower, telling its story gently and without ornamentation. In *Eel*, as in *Dance*, Yakusho plays another protagonist struggling to make peace with the confines of societal expectation. His Yamashita is fractured, not so much from his contradictions, but in his stoic refusal to pardon himself from his psychological prison...much like his watery (and silent) friend. The 1.78 transfer exhibits slightly high contrast levels, but otherwise colors are solid and details come through, even in nighttime scenes. Audio may be mono, but sounds clean and surprisingly detailed. No extras, other than a theatrical trailer and some biographical notes. For purists, the English subtitles may be turned off. Winner of the Palme D'Or at Cannes, Imamura's compelling examination of healing through acceptance resoundingly delivers. Don't let this *Eel* slip through your fingers. —EP
AKA: Unagi.
Movie: 🐾🐾🐾 **DVD:** 🐾🐾 ½
New Yorker Video (cat #DVD67901, UPC 717119679149). Widescreen. Dolby Digital Mono. $29.95. Keepcase. *LANG:* Japanese. *SUB:* English. *FEATURES:* 29 chapters ▪ Theatrical trailer ▪ Cast/director filmographies.
1996 117m/C *JP* Koji Yakusho, Misa Shimizu, Mitsuko Baisho, Shou Aikawa, Fujio Tsuneta, Akira (Tsukamoto) Emoto, Etsuko Ichihara, Tomoroh Taguchi, Ken Kobayashi, Sabu Kawara; **D:** Shohei Imamura; **W:** Shohei Imamura, Motofumi Tomikawa, Daisuke Tengan; **C:** Shigeru Komatsubara; **M:** Shinichiro Ikebe. *AWARDS:* Cannes '97: Film; *NOM:* Ind. Spirit '99: Foreign Film.

8 1/2

Celebrated filmmaker Guido Anselmi (Mastroianni) is surrounded, attended, patronized, seduced, and in general overwhelmed by endless armies of assistants, producers, writers, agents, and prospective actresses, all of whom want to know about his new picture and what's in it for them. On good terms with his wife Luisa (Aimee), Guido clearly is at odds about everything to do with both his movie and his life; and he keeps ruminating over childhood scenes and various fantasies involving his family and the women he's known. Outside Rome, a gigantic set representing a futuristic rocketship launching pad is being erected for him to film, but Guido doesn't have the slightest idea of what to do with it, a fact that might drive him crazy, if he had the time. *8 1/2* is essentially Fellini's self-portrait, a circus-like fantasy that expresses the unique weirdness of being a celebrated genius that the whole world seems to want a part of. Fellini doesn't seem to be complaining about his state of affairs, but rather, honestly acknowledging that this is just how it is for, "sigh," such a wonderboy as himself. An egocentric person tries to pretend that everyone he knows is a bit player in a movie where he is the star. Fellini's fame makes everyone he comes in contact with

act like bit players, depending on him to behave as the star, so naturally there's a strong tendency to become egocentric! (Take the Fellini test: Do you imagine everyone you know dancing to your tune in long lines, as if Life were a big party convened to celebrate You? I wish.) The film is interesting because Guido (like Fellini) is fighting the riptide towards egomania as strongly as he can. He's helped by the honesty of his plain-speaking wife, his candidly critical writer, and his own conscience in the form of truths speaking in his fantasies. When Guido just gives up and turns the visit to his rocketship set into a big-top parade, the film does come together as an abstract of Fellini's professional, spiritual, and mental condition—it is a big cinematic self-portrait. In the lavish Criterion two-disc set, you simply can't get a better introduction to Fellini or his masterpiece. The 16:9 image has been digitally scrubbed, and looks luminous and free of anything remotely resembling a ding or dirt. The mono sound is fresh and clear, and the subtitles have been reworked from the theatrical originals. The feature transfer on disc one includes a commentary by Gideon Bachmann, a film critic, and Antonio Monda, a NYU film professor. Terry Gilliam introduces the picture in an interview-like essay that is polished and entertaining. It contains so many key clips from the film that it shouldn't be seen before the movie and would be better titled, "Spoiler Introduction." The 1963 trailer rounds out disc one, which sits in the case alongside a 22-page booklet with writings by Fellini, critic Tulio Kezich, and film teacher and writer Alexander Sesonske. Disc two has two lengthy documentaries: "Nino Rota: Between Cinema and Concert," and "Fellini: A Director's Notebook," directed by Fellini himself. Interviews are taken with Sandra Milo, Lina Wertmuller, and Vittorio Storaro. There are also two galleries of rare photos and production stills. In the end, *8 1/2* is enjoyable for the same reason all pictures are—the people are interesting and glamorous, and Italian films of this era seem to be populated by the most beautiful women ever to walk the Earth. There's also a constantly changing musical feeling to the picture, that goes well with Gianni Di Venanzo's sleek camerawork—the picture has a surface you can enjoy without understanding a bit of what's happening, which, admittedly, is how I've related to it for a long, long time. —GE **AKA:** Otto E Mezzo; *Federico Fellini's 8 1/2.*
Movie: 🐾🐾🐾🐾 **DVD:** 🐾🐾🐾🐾
Criterion (cat #140, UPC 037429135624). Widescreen (1.85:1) anamorphic. Dolby Digital Mono. $39.95. Keepcase. *LANG:* Italian. *SUB:* English. *FEATURES:* Booklet ▪ Commentary: Gideon Bachmann, Antonio Monda ▪ Intro by Terry Gilliam ▪ Trailer ▪ 28 chapters ▪ Documentaries ▪ Interviews.
1963 135m/B *IT* Marcello Mastroianni, Claudia Cardinale, Anouk Aimee, Sandra Milo, Barbara Steele, Rossella Falk, Eddra Gale, Mark Herron, Madeleine LeBeau,

Caterina Boratto; **D:** Federico Fellini; **W:** Tullio Pinelli, Ennio Flaiano, Brunello Rondi, Federico Fellini; **C:** Gianni Di Venanzo; **M:** Nino Rota. *AWARDS:* Oscars '63: Costume Des. (B&W), Foreign Film; N.Y. Film Critics '63: Foreign Film; *NOM:* Oscars '63: Art Dir./Set Dec., B&W, Director (Fellini), Story & Screenplay.

800 Leagues down the Amazon

An overqualified cast and crew is left with little to do in an adaptation of this lesser Jules Verne work. In the 19th century, Garral (Bostwick) and his daughter Minha (Zuniga) take a voyage down the Amazon in a massive ark-like vessel. They encounter mildly entertaining complications. Full-frame DVD offers only a minor improvement over VHS tape. —MM
Movie: 🐾 ½ **DVD:** 🐾🐾 ½
New Concorde (cat #NH20434 D, UPC 73-6991343498). Full frame. Stereo. $19.98. Keepcase. *LANG:* English. *FEATURES:* 24 chapters ▪ Talent files ▪ Trailers.
1993 (PG-13) 100m/C Daphne Zuniga, Barry Bostwick, Adam Baldwin, Tom Verica, E.E. Bell; **D:** Luis Llosa; **W:** Laura Schiff, Jackson Barr; **C:** Pili Flores-Guerra; **M:** Jorge Tafur.

18 Again!

An accident on his 81st birthday causes Jack Watson (Burns) to switch bodies with his grandson, college student David (Schlatter). Once he recovers from the shock, Jack uses his charm, his experience, and his grandson's youthful body to make David's college life a little better. Pauly Shore co-stars—enough said. There's a little nudity and enough sexual innuendo that it's hard to imagine how this film got away with a "PG." The picture is soft but relatively grain-free, while the soundtrack is marred by consistent microphone cracks and hisses. —BG
Movie: 🐾 **DVD:** 🐾🐾 ½
Anchor Bay (cat #DV11447, UPC 0131311-44796). Widescreen (1.85:1) anamorphic. Dolby Mono. $14.98. Keepcase. *LANG:* English. *CAP:* English. *FEATURES:* 24 chapters ▪ Trailer.
1988 (PG) 100m/C George Burns, Charlie Schlatter, Anita Morris, Jennifer Runyon, Tony Roberts, Red Buttons, Miriam Flynn, George DiCenzo, Pauly Shore, Anthony Starke; **D:** Paul Flaherty; **W:** Jonathan Prince, Josh Goldstein; **C:** Stephen M. Katz; **M:** Billy Goldenberg.

84 Charing Cross Road

In the early 1950s, New Yorker Helen Hanff (Bancroft) begins a correspondence with reserved English bookseller Frank Doel (Hopkins). Helen's tastes in books and Frank's reserved demeanor create a swirl of intellectual charm and humor on the screen that make for a fine film. The screenplay is by Hugh Whitemore, adapted from the play written by the real Helen

Hanff, who really corresponded with a real Frank Doel. Helen's gifts to Frank and his co-workers in the story show the devastating power of blind kindness. These characters exude a level of charm and civility almost lost in modern society. Hanff's typewriter and Frank's handwritten notes border on historic; a tale such as this would be impossible today thanks to the Internet, e-mail, and Amazon.com. The film transfer to DVD is sharp and clean, but lacks a widescreen presentation. The sound quality is no frills, but acceptable. This DVD edition offers no special features, but then what more could there be than a reading list? The screenplay under the direction of David Jones manages to open up the stage version beyond the reading of letters to show the everyday lives of those involved. The one flaw—Helen's moments of talking directly to the camera. —JAS

Movie: 𝄞𝄞𝄞 **DVD:** 𝄞𝄞 ½
Columbia Tristar (cat #07762, UPC 0433-96077621). Full frame. Mono. $24.95. Keepcase. *LANG:* English. *SUB:* English; French; Spanish; Portuguese; Chinese; Korean; Thai. *CAP:* English. *FEATURES:* Bonus trailers.
1986 (PG) 100m/C Anne Bancroft, Anthony Hopkins, Judi Dench, Jean De Baer, Maurice Denham, Eleanor David, Mercedes Ruehl, Daniel Gerroll, Hugh Whitemore; *D:* David Hugh Jones; *W:* Hugh Whitemore; *C:* Brian West; *M:* George Fenton. *AWARDS:* British Acad. '87: Actress (Bancroft).

Electra

Engaging and powerful adaptation of the story of Electra by gifted director Cacoyannis. This classic story of love, betrayal, lust, and vengeance is boldly directed, brilliantly acted (Papas is superb as Electra), and masterfully photographed. The excellent video transfer is evident in the clarity of the image. Blacks have very nice definition, as do lighter hues. The soundtrack boasts excellent dialogue reproduction as well as an exceptional musical score. —MJT *AKA:* Elektra.

Movie: 𝄞𝄞𝄞 **DVD:** 𝄞𝄞𝄞
MGM Home Ent. (cat #1002585, UPC 027-616867865). Widescreen (1.66:1) letterboxed. Dolby Digital Mono. $19.98. Keepcase. *LANG:* Greek; English; French. *SUB:* English; French; Spanish. *FEATURES:* 16 chapters ⚬ Theatrical trailer.
1962 113m/C Irene Papas, Aleka Katselli, Yarmis Fertis; *D:* Michael Cacoyannis; *W:* Michael Cacoyannis; *C:* Walter Lassally.

The Elephant Man

Dr. Frederick Treves (Hopkins), a surgeon at London Hospital where progressive work is being done with anaesthetics, takes an interest in a sideshow freak exhibited by a scurrilous mountebank named Bytes (Jones). John Merrick (Hurt) is a disgustingly deformed young man who must wear a hood in public, and cannot walk straight, or even lie down without

risking asphyxiation. Treves "rents" Merrick for some study and conferences, but loses track of him when the abusive Bytes takes him to France. Merrick eventually escapes his owner, and makes his way back to London where Treves finds him residence in the hospital, winning approval from the institution's Governor (Gielgud) and head nurse (Hiller). Cleaned up, and treated with respect, John shows himself to be a sensitive gentleman, even a bit vain, and publicity surrounding his case attracts the attention of the charitable well-to-do. Visited by royalty and celebrities like actress Mrs. Kendal (Bancroft), John also falls victim to a thuggish night porter (Elphick), who secretly exhibits him at night in his own rooms atop the hospital. In the midst of all this, Treves has to ask himself if he's really helping John, or just using his notoriety to advance his own career, as sort of a gentleman version of Bytes. In the very first scene, Treves states his hate of the age of machines, revealing himself as a closet romantic, looking for truth and beauty in places as unlikely as a dirty circus sideshow. He's a horror hero, like director Lynch, convinced there's some greater grace to be discovered examining the loathsome but God-created crawling things to be found under mossy stones. Paramount's DVD is immediately to be seized, just to feast one's eyes on Francis's B&W photography in its original Panavision format. Unseen except for revival screenings and a Japanese subtitled video release, cable and television screenings have all been of a revolting pan 'n' scan version further insulted with an overzealous squeeze. The image looks just great, and the 5.1 mix of Lynch's weird personal soundtrack is excitingly rendered. There are no chapter selections, as with *The Straight Story*; this is the only evidence that David Lynch had an involvement in the disc. —GE

Movie: 𝄞𝄞𝄞𝄞 **DVD:** 𝄞𝄞𝄞𝄞
Paramount (cat #01347, UPC 097360134-742). Widescreen (2.35:1) anamorphic. Dolby Digital 5.1 Surround; Dolby Digital Surround; Mono. $29.99. Keepcase. *LANG:* English; French; Spanish. *SUB:* English. *FEATURES:* Short interviews ⚬ Make-up documentary ⚬ Still gallery ⚬ Trailer.
1980 (PG) 125m/B Michael Elphick, Anthony Hopkins, John Hurt, Anne Bancroft, John Gielgud, Wendy Hiller, Freddie Jones, Kenny Baker; *D:* David Lynch; *W:* Eric Bergren, Christopher DeVore, David Lynch; *C:* Freddie Francis; *M:* John Morris, Samuel Barber. *AWARDS:* British Acad. '80: Actor (Hurt), Film; Cesar '82: Foreign Film; *NOM:* Oscars '80: Actor (Hurt), Adapt. Screenplay, Art Dir./Set Dec., Costume Des., Director (Lynch), Film Editing, Picture, Orig. Score.

Elizabeth

I'd recommend this A&E biography (from Britain's Channel 4 TV) to younger viewers who are taken with the Cate Blanchett feature *Elizabeth*. Historian David Starkey sets out the facts of her incredible life

without the more egregious dramatic embellishments. It's one of the greatest stories in our cultural history. This presentation combines Starkey's assured narration and comments by other historians with period re-creations. DVD image is a solid cut above cablecast quality. Stereo sound is the same. Fine, accessible popular history. —MM

Movie: 𝄞𝄞𝄞 **DVD:** 𝄞𝄞𝄞
A&E (cat #AAE-70489, UPC 7339617048-91). Full frame. Dolby Digital Stereo. $39.98. Keepcase boxed set. *LANG:* English. *CAP:* English. *FEATURES:* 24 chapters ⚬ Chronology of English monarch.
2002 200m/C Imogen Slaughter, Miles Richardson, Abigail Harrison; *D:* Mark Fielder; *W:* David Starkey; *C:* Chris Openshaw; *M:* Andy Price.

Elvis: '68 Comeback Special

The one-hour special—Elvis's first—was broadcast on December 3, 1968, at a time when the British invasion had past its peak and psychedelia was on the rise. Conventional wisdom has it that this TV appearance revitalized Elvis's career. That's not really true. He was always popular with one generation of fans while younger people would never take him seriously because his films were (and largely still are) a joke. The posturing, the sneer, and the leather outfits are all on display here. The songs are not the King's best. The title is in public domain. This DVD can boast an image that's about as good as anyone can expect of a 1968 commercial broadcast. (This version runs 73 minutes.) Both the 5.1 remix and the original mono are clear, but they shouldn't be compared to contemporary sonic compositions. —MM

Movie: 𝄞𝄞 **DVD:** 𝄞𝄞 ½
Lightyear Entertainment (UPC 085365408-821). Full frame. Dolby Digital 5.1 Surround; Mono. $24.98. Keepcase. *LANG:* English. *FEATURES:* 30 chapters ⚬ Web connections ⚬ Photo gallery.
1968 73m/C Elvis Presley; *D:* Steve Binder.

Elysia

Please see review for *Sex and Buttered Popcorn, Vol. 3.*
1934 m/B

Emmet Otter's Jug-Band Christmas

This holiday classic is a welcome addition to DVD and has only improved with age. Turning away from the usual "slapstick" Muppet style, the film finds Jim Henson and company presenting a tale which is more serious and somber, while maintaining all of the Muppet charm. Also, marionettes are used here. Emmet Otter and his mother are a poor family who take odd jobs to make ends meet. With Christmas approaching, both trying to find ways to scrape together some money to buy a

Christmas present for the other. As fate would have it, a talent show is being held in town with a cash prize. Emmet puts together the titular jug-band, while his mother opts to sing a solo. This touching film offers a poignant story, while teaching a great lesson about the importance of love, family, and the Christmas spirit. And the cameo by Kermit the Frog doesn't hurt either. This one should be adored by young and old alike. As *Emmet Otter* was shot on video, the DVD offers a pristine picture which rivals digital broadcast quality. The colors are true and there is no distortion on the image. The Dolby Digital 5.1 audio mix sounds fine (despite a noticeable lack of bass response) and truly brings the rousing music to life. —ML

Movie: 🎬🎬🎬🎬 ½ **DVD:** 🎬🎬🎬 ½
Columbia Tristar (cat #07816, UPC 043-396078161). Full frame. Dolby Digital 5.1; Dolby 2.0 Surround. $19.95. Keepcase. *LANG:* English; French; Spanish. *SUB:* English; French; Spanish. *CAP:* English. *FEATURES:* Bonus trailers • 28 chapters.
1977 50m/C D: Jim Henson; **W:** Jerry Juhl; **M:** Paul Williams; **V:** Jerry Nelson, Frank Oz, Marilyn Sokol, Richard Hunt.

Empire of the Ants

Enormous ants mutated by nuclear waste stalk a real estate dealer (Collins) and prospective buyers of undeveloped oceanfront property. The script is a long way from the H.G. Wells source material. Softish DVD image is typical of a mid-'70s monster picture. It is all that the movie needs, particularly in the quaint special effects scenes. Sound is equally dated and weak. —MM

Movie: 🎬 ½ **DVD:** 🎬🎬
MGM Home Ent. (cat #1002633, UPC 027-616868336). Full frame. Dolby Digital Mono. $14.95. Keepcase. *LANG:* English. *SUB:* French; Spanish. *CAP:* English. *FEATURES:* 16 chapters • Trailer.
1977 (PG) 90m/C Joan Collins, Robert Lansing, John David Carson, Albert Salmi, Jacqueline Scott, Robert Pine; **D:** Bert I. Gordon; **W:** Bert I. Gordon; **C:** Reginald Morris.

Empire of the Sun

Spielberg's second attempt at epic drama (the first was *The Color Purple*) is this beautifully photographed and produced tale of Shanghai during the Japanese occupation. British child Jim finds himself separated from his parents and interned at a POW camp where his humanity and worldview are tested constantly. Based on Ballard's semi-autobiographical novel, the film evinces the director's strong visual eye but has many script and pacing problems. While Bale delivers a strong performance, the role seems to be written for a child much younger. The character's childish, naïve, goofy, annoying (and sometimes downright stupid) behavior doesn't seem sincere from a kid whose eyes betray so much intelligence. After a strong, fairly serious first half, the film

takes a bad turn into POW camp whimsy, gratingly emphasized by Williams's occasionally overdone music. The use of chorus during parts of the film *is* beautiful; it's a shame that the Chinese lyrics are not translated or presented phonetically in the DVD's optional subtitles. The disc features a stunning transfer of a frequently smoky, cloudy movie. Except for one twitchy, digitized shot, the film looks superb. The remixed 5.1 soundtrack is terrific, as expected for a big studio release such as this. "The China Odyssey" is a 1987 featurette that was originally shown on TV. Narrated by Martin Sheen, it's a substantial examination of the historical events behind the story and is filled with terrific behind-the-scenes footage. —DG

Movie: 🎬🎬🎬 **DVD:** 🎬🎬🎬 ½
Warner (cat #11753, UPC 0853911753-22). Widescreen (1.85:1) anamorphic. Dolby Surround 5.1; Dolby Stereo. $24.98. Snapper. *LANG:* English; French. *SUB:* English; French; Spanish; Portuguese; Japanese; Thai; Korean. *CAP:* English. *FEATURES:* Behind-the-scenes documentary "The China Odyssey" • Theatrical trailer • 45 chapters, feature • 14 chapters, documentary.
1987 (PG) 153m/C Christian Bale, John Malkovich, Miranda Richardson, Nigel Havers, Joe Pantoliano, Leslie Phillips, Rupert Frazer, Ben Stiller, Robert Stephens, Burt Kwouk, Masato Ibu, Emily Richard, David Neidorf, Ralph Seymour, Emma Piper, Peter Gale, Zhai Nai She, Guts Ishimatsu, J.G. Ballard; **D:** Steven Spielberg; **W:** Tom Stoppard, Menno Meyjes; **C:** Allen Daviau; **M:** John Williams. *AWARDS:* Natl. Bd. of Review '87: Director (Spielberg); *NOM:* Oscars '87: Art Dir./Set Dec., Cinematog., Costume Des., Film Editing, Sound, Orig. Score.

The Enemy

At first glance, *The Enemy* may appear to be a stylish, by-the-numbers espionage thriller, but a second glance will reveal that the film is worth watching. Luke Perry stars as Dr. Mike Ashton, a geneticist who lives with his elderly father, Dr. George Ashton (Horst Buchholz), a retired chemist. When Mike's young assistant is murdered, the police in the guise of Robert Ogilvie (Roger Moore), John Creger (Tom Conti), and Penny Johnson (Olivia D'Abo), arrive to investigate. It appears that Ogilvie and Creger are more interested in the older Dr. Ashton, but won't tell Mike why. When Mike's dad suddenly disappears, Mike and Penny team up to find him. As Mike follows his father's trail, he learns that his entire life has been a lie and that he may have to come close to death to learn the truth about his father's past. At times, *The Enemy* plays like any other spy thriller, but the solid performances and quick pace keep the film from becoming mere video-store fodder. The story is quite predictable at times, and the stunts are clichéd, but the mysterious circumstances concerning Mike's dad are maintained until the finale, making the film a solid watch. Despite the fact that

the DVD case lists the film as being full frame, it is in fact letterboxed at 1.85:1. The image is very sharp and clear, showing only minor grain during the daytime scenes and some slight shimmering when horizontal lines are on-screen. The colors are good and the image is never dark. The Dolby Stereo audio track offers clear dialogue, well-balanced sound effects, and no distortion. The only extra on the disc is a trailer for the film. —ML

Movie: 🎬🎬 ½ **DVD:** 🎬🎬 ½
Avalanche Ent. (cat #AV1580D, UPC 806-469158029). Widescreen (1.85:1) letterboxed. Dolby Stereo. $19.99. Keepcase. *LANG:* English. *SUB:* English; Spanish. *CAP:* English. *FEATURES:* Trailer • 24 chapters.
2001 (R) 98m/C Luke Perry, Olivia D'Abo, Roger Moore, Horst Buchholz, Tom Conti, Hendrick Haese; **D:** Tom Kinninmont, Charlie Watson; **W:** John Penney; **C:** Mike Garfath; **M:** Gast Waltzing.

Enemy at the Gates

Jean-Jacques Annaud uses the Battle of Stalingrad to tell a story of the individual heroics and bravery of two snipers, the Russian Vassili Zaitsev (Law) and the German Konig (Harris). Also involved are a propaganda officer (Fiennes), who wants to turn Zaitsev into an inspirational hero, and Tania (Weisz), a soldier who loves Zaitsev. The horrors of the battle are as well realized as any since *Saving Private Ryan*, and the characters emerge as fully believable human beings. In short, this is the epic war movie that the elephantine *Pearl Harbor* so desperately tried to be. Though virtually the entire story is set in bomb-blasted city rubble, DVD re-creates the image with no significant flaws. The 5.1 Surround isn't as intense as the opening scenes of *Ryan*, but it does its job nicely. My only complaint is the relative obviousness of the CGI effects in the shots involving aircraft, but that has nothing to do with the disc. Filmmakers and studio executives these days simply refuse to admit computer-generated special effects call attention to themselves. —MM

Movie: 🎬🎬🎬 ½ **DVD:** 🎬🎬🎬 ½
Paramount (cat #33862, UPC 097363386-247). Widescreen anamorphic. Dolby Digital 5.1 Surround Stereo; Dolby Digital Surround. $29.99. Keepcase. *LANG:* English; French. *SUB:* English. *CAP:* English. *FEATURES:* 20 chapters • 9 deleted scenes • 2 "making of" featurettes • Trailer.
2000 (R) 131m/C *GE GB IR* Jude Law, Ed Harris, Joseph Fiennes, Rachel Weisz, Bob Hoskins, Gabriel Marshall-Thomson, Eva Mattes, Ron Perlman, Matthias Habich; **D:** Jean-Jacques Annaud; **W:** Jean-Jacques Annaud, Alain Godard; **C:** Robert Fraisse; **M:** James Horner.

Enemy Mine

As Earthlings attempt to colonize space in the near future, they run into competition from the Dracs. Davidge (Quaid) and Drac (Gossett Jr. under amphibian makeup) are fighter jocks who find themselves stranded on a barren planet. They learn they must cooperate to survive, and then there's Drac's unorthodox method of pro-creation to deal with. DVD delivers the image with occasionally unforgiving clarity. Davidge's crashlanding is only a short step above the *Flash Gordon* serial. And while the production design used to create the planet's surface is impressive, it's production design and that, too, looks a little old-fashioned. That dated quality is further heightened by the strident music. Those criticisms not withstanding, the film has become a favorite on home video and it looks very good here. Sound is up to the task but not spectacular. —*MM*

Movie: 🦴🦴 **DVD:** 🦴🦴 ½

20th Century Fox (UPC 024543012993). Widescreen (2.35:1) anamorphic. Dolby Digital 4.0 Surround; Dolby Surround. $24.98. Keepcase. *LANG:* English; French. *SUB:* English; Spanish. *FEATURES:* 20 chapters • Behind-the-scenes featurette • Trailer.

1985 (PG-13) 108m/C Dennis Quaid, Louis Gossett Jr., Brion James, Richard Marcus, Lance Kerwin, Carolyn McCormick; **D:** Wolfgang Petersen; **W:** Edward Khmara; **C:** Tony Imi; **M:** Maurice Jarre.

The Enforcer

Third in Eastwood's Dirty Harry series may be the most ham-fisted. The various liberal-conservative conflicts are reduced to silly sloganeering on both sides and the bad guys (SLA-inspired domestic terrorists) are caricatures. Tyne Daley makes an early appearance as Harry's new partner. DVD image is very sharp with bright unfaded colors. A few instances of little digital burps and blips pop up occasionally, but you've got to search them out. Harry's potentially difficult herringbone sport coat does not flash. Surround is effective. If only the movie itself were better. Several of the extras are nothing more than a few short paragraphs of text. —*MM*

Movie: 🦴🦴 **DVD:** 🦴🦴 ½

Warner (cat #18593, UPC 0853918593-21). Widescreen (2.35:1) anamorphic. Dolby Digital Surround. $19.98. Snapper. *LANG:* English; French. *SUB:* English; French; Spanish; Portuguese; Japanese; Chinese; Thai; Korean. *FEATURES:* 30 chapters • Talent files • Trailer • "Making of" featurette • "Behind the scenes" (text) • "On location" (text) • "Memorable lines" (text).

1976 (R) 96m/C Clint Eastwood, Tyne Daly, Harry Guardino, Bradford Dillman, John Mitchum, Albert "Poppy" Popwell; **D:** James Fargo; **W:** Stirling Silliphant, Stuart Hagmann; **C:** Charles W. Short; **M:** Jerry Fielding.

The Erotic Mirror

The gimmick that fueled the *Mirror, Mirror* series is resurrected for another bit of El soft-core. Amy (Wallace) buys an antique mirror that's haunted by a ghost (Caine) who seduces her, etc., etc. Lots of ecstat-

ic rubbing and moaning and lots of tattoos and piercings. (One woman has absolutely grotesque implants.) This production was shot on video and looks a bit better than some of the studio's other recent releases. The focus is hazy throughout with over-exposed exteriors. DVD does nothing to improve the grainy image. —*MM*

Movie: 🦴 **DVD:** 🦴🦴

El Independent Cinema (cat #sc-1024, UPC 612385102493). Full frame. $19.98. Keepcase. *LANG:* English. *FEATURES:* 20 chapters (no menu) • Trailers • 3 behind-the-scenes featurettes.

2001 160m/C Laurie Wallace, Misty Mundae, Darian Caine, Esmeralda DeLarocca; **D:** Pete Jacelone; **W:** Clancy Fitzsimmons; **C:** Giorgyorgy Benaskovich; **M:** Francis Anthony McGlynn, Dennis Peterson.

The Erotic Rites of Countess Dracula

In 1966, Scarlet Brooks's rock star breakthrough is cut short when she's bitten by Count Dracula. Thirty-five years later and yearning for death, she's sick of being a vampire. Renfield (now her own trusted assistant) has a supernatural lesbian solution to restore her as a mortal, but not without complications. Donald F. Glut, *Famous Monsters of Filmland* contributor and prominent member of the Count Dracula Society, writes and directs this dreadfully weird indulgence into Russ Meyer and Jess Franco territory. Unfortunately, it clunks along with the listless pacing of a high school play. Completely soft-core (even the lesbo-vampire Eurotrash fans will probably be disappointed) and shot on video by what appears to be a professional porno crew, it is lit very well on a super-clean DVD transfer with excellent sound for the mediocre pseudo-Goth score. Though advertised on the box, there is no Chapter Index on my copy. The "trailer vault," besides more video soft-core trailers, also includes a special Retro section with grind-house pre-porn film trailers of the late '60s and early '70s, such as *Inga*. It's pop cultural archive of greater interest than the main feature. —*MO* **AKA:** Scarlet Countess.

Movie: woof **DVD:** 🦴🦴🦴 ½

El Independent Cinema (cat #SC 1018-DVD, UPC 612385101892). Full frame. $19.98. Keepcase. *LANG:* English. *FEATURES:* 13 (get it?) chapters • Commentary: director Donald F. Glut • Outtakes and outtakes interview • Trailer and Seduction Cinema "trailer vault."

2001 90m/C Brick Randall, Del Howison, Meredith Rinehart, Nicole Liberty, Julia Anna Thurman; **D:** Don Glut; **W:** Don Glut; **C:** Steven R. Rocha.

Erotic Survivor 2

As in the previous film, contestants compete to survive in the wilderness to win a $20 prize, but this time they're all women tramping through the veldt in "Africa." There are some silly picnic games, lots of nudity, and an informative trivia quiz. Their

easiest challenge seems to be finding something to eat in the bush. Sound and picture are of camcorder quality. —*BT*

Movie: 🦴 **DVD:** 🦴🦴

El Independent Cinema (cat #sc1021dvd, UPC 612385102196). Full frame. $19.98. Keepcase. *LANG:* English. *FEATURES:* Trailers • Behind-the-scenes featurette.

2001 86m/C Katie Jordan, Allanah Rhoades, Vanessa Del Sol, Tiffany Sonders, Syndy Devil; **D:** John Bacchus; **W:** John Bacchus; **C:** Giorgyorgy Benaskovich, Hector Rosario Sanchez.

Escape from Alaska

Some fair snow footage and avalanche effects are the only things worth mentioning in this otherwise pedestrian adventure. Evil oil company executives are hiding things. It's up to Neal (Griffith) and Lea (Feeney) to set things right. Some of the avalanche effects look pretty neat. Those shots are much clearer and sharper than the conventional nature footage, and despite the brightness, pixels and artifacts are at a minimum. Otherwise, the full-frame image is a bit better than VHS tape. —*MM* **AKA:** Avalanche.

Movie: 🦴🦴 **DVD:** 🦴🦴

First Look Pictures (cat #FLP-94803). Full frame. $24.98. Keepcase. *LANG:* English. *FEATURES:* Trailer • 10 chapters.

2002 (PG-13) 96m/C Thomas Ian Griffith, Caroleen Feeney, R. Lee Ermey, John Ashton, C. Thomas Howell; **D:** Steve Kroschel; **W:** Steve Kroschel; **C:** Richard Pepin; **M:** Alex Wilkinson.

Escape to Grizzly Mountain

Dan Haggerty stars in this film, which according to the disclaimer at the outset, is "not related to *Grizzly Adams*." The story deals with a young boy, Jimmy (Miko Hughes), who lives with his sister and has few friends. One day, Jimmy visits the circus and meets an adorable bear cub, which he named "Dudley." Jimmy is disgusted by the way in which the circus performers treat the bear, so he kidnaps Dudley with hopes to set him free. While exploring a cave in Grizzly Mountain State Park with the cub, Jimmy is suddenly transported back in time to the year 1841! There, he meets a kindly mountain man named Jeremiah (Haggerty). Jimmy and Jeremiah travel back to the present, where Jimmy introduces the ancient time-traveler to the wonders of modern life. They also act to outsmart Aunt Molly (Cynthia Palmer), the owner of the circus, so that Dudley may remain free. This bizarre and confusing film is saved only by the bear cub Dudley, who is incredibly cute. Other than that, we have tired old actors such as Haggerty and Jan Michael Vincent wandering through this lackluster production. The animal-rights angle is handled appropriately, but most viewers, especially adolescents, will be turned off by the inanity of the movie. The full-frame picture is sharp, but there is a fine amount of grain in most of the shots. The colors are good, and the fleshtones are realistic. A small amount of artifacting can be seen in several scenes. The Dolby Stereo Surround audio offers clear dialogue and some Surround sound effects, mostly musical cues. —ML

Movie: ♫♫ **DVD:** ♫♫

MGM Home Ent. (cat #1003250, UPC 027-616874009). Full frame. Dolby Digital Stereo Surround. $14.95. Keepcase. *LANG:* English. *SUB:* English; Spanish. *CAP:* English. *FEATURES:* 16 chapters.

1999 95m/C Dan Haggerty, Miko Hughes, Jan-Michael Vincent, Cynthia Palmer; **D:** Anthony Dalesandro; **W:** Boon Collins.

Eva

Writer Tyvian Jones (Baker) falls in love with hooker Eva (Moreau) and leaves his fiancée Francesca (Lisi) for her, thereby beginning a descent into obsession. DVD contains two versions of the film, the theatrically released *Eva*, and the "director's cut" *Eve*, 16 minutes longer with burned-in Swedish subtitles. Unfortunately, that second version is also in much poorer shape. Compared to the theatrical release, it's harsh, sometimes muddy, high-contrast black and white. The first has a pale cast but is much sharper and easier to make out. Sound is acceptable on both. —MM

AKA: Eva the Devil's Woman.

Movie: ♫♫ ½ **DVD:** ♫♫♫

Kino on Video (cat #K169, UPC 73832901-6920). Widescreen (1.85:1) letterboxed. $24.98. Keepcase. *LANG:* English. *SUB:* Swedish. *FEATURES:* 15 chapters.

1962 103m/B *FR IT* Jeanne Moreau, Stanley Baker, Virna Lisi, James Villiers, Giorgio Albertazzi, Riccardo Garrone; **D:** Joseph Losey; **W:** Hugo Butler, Evan Jones; **C:** Gianni Di Venanzo; **M:** Michel Legrand.

Evel Knievel

George Hamilton seems to be having a whale of a good time playing the famous dare-devil, but you'll be hard pressed to appreciate his performance on this rotten transfer. DVD was made from exceptionally poor elements—a worn VHS tape, perhaps? Wavering sound is filled with static. Surface damage includes the normal dust and lots of film splices. Title is available on the *Classic Biker Movies* disc. —MM

Movie: ♫♫ **DVD:** ♫

BFS Video (cat #302910D, UPC 0668053-02916). Full fram. $9.98. Keepcase. *LANG:* English. *FEATURES:* 6 chapters • Talent files.

1972 (PG) 90m/C George Hamilton, Bert Freed, Rod Cameron, Sue Lyon; **D:** Marvin J. Chomsky; **W:** John Milius; **C:** David M. Walsh; **M:** Patrick Williams.

An Everlasting Piece

In a unique and entertaining comedy, noted American filmmaker Barry Levinson turns his sites on Ireland, setting his story against the war-torn world of Belfast in the 1980s. Colm (Barry McEvoy) is a shiftless young man who gets a job as a barber in the local mental institution. There, he discovers fellow barber George (Brian F. O'Byrne). When the only toupee salesman in the area (played by comic Billy Connolly) is admitted to the institution, Colm and George convince the man to give them the names of his customers. From there, they set out to corner the toupee market, and be the sole supplier of hairpieces in the Belfast area. But along the way, they meet with irate customers, competition, and even the IRA. This is a hilarious comedy, featuring the British irreverence seen in such films as *Saving Grace* and *The Full Monty*. Levinson shows great confidence with the foreign dialects and the thick Irish accents (the subtitles come in handy here), but the film does get too serious at times, focusing on the religious fighting, as opposed to using it as a backdrop. This DVD offers a crisp transfer of the film, delivering a clear image, with only a subtle amount of grain at times. The colors are nice, as Levinson juxtaposes the drab roadhouses with other brighter colors. The audio tracks provide consistent Surround sound effects and a nice bass response, which helps to accent the '80s tunes used on the soundtrack. —ML

Movie: ♫♫♫ **DVD:** ♫♫♫ ½

DreamWorks Home Ent. (cat #87820, UPC 667068782028). Widescreen (1.85:1) anamorphic. DTS 5.1 Surround; Dolby Digital 5.1; Dolby 2.0 Surround. $26.99. Keepcase. *LANG:* English. *SUB:* English. *CAP:* English. *FEATURES:* Production notes • Cast & crew • Theatrical trailer • 20 chapters.

2000 (R) 103m/C Barry McEvoy, Brian F. O'Byrne, Anna Friel, Billy Connolly, Pauline McLynn, Laurence Kinlan, Ruth McCabe; **D:** Barry Levinson; **W:** Barry McEvoy; **C:** Seamus Deasy; **M:** Hans Zimmer.

Every Which Way But Loose

This change-of-pace blue-collar comedy was a surprise hit for Eastwood. He's beer-drinking trucker Philo Beddoe who moonlights as a bare-knuckle boxer. He and his orangutan Clyde travel to Colorado in search of would-be country singer Lynne (Locke) with whom Philo is smitten. It's loose, sloppy, and enjoyable. DVD image is a bit sharper than the sequel *Any Which Way You Can*, but that's a moot point with these grainy films. Disc is an accurate re-creation of the theatrical release. —MM

Movie: ♫♫♫ **DVD:** ♫♫ ½

Warner (cat #18594, UPC 0853918594-20). Widescreen (1.85:1) anamorphic. Dolby Digital 5.1 Surround; Mono. $19.98. Snapper. *LANG:* English; French. *SUB:* English; French. *CAP:* English. *FEATURES:* Talent files • Trailer • Behind-the-scenes (text) • 30 chapters.

1978 (R) 119m/C Clint Eastwood, Sondra Locke, Geoffrey Lewis, Beverly D'Angelo, Ruth Gordon; **D:** James Fargo; **W:** Jeremy Joe Kronsberg; **C:** Rexford Metz; **M:** Steve Dorff.

Everybody's Famous!

A delightful film full of humor and hope with an undercurrent of satire and true wit. Jean believes in the talent of his overweight bitter teenage daughter, who spends her time at local talent shows impersonating Madonna. He's desperate to make her a star. How far will Jean go to make sure Marva will become a singing sensation? How far will anyone go to be famous? At one point Jean's wife exclaims at the point of hysteria, "Why can't anyone be happy being normal anymore?" If this story is any example, the reason is it's so much more fun when everybody's famous. The wonderful ending more than makes up for the fact that some of the twists and turns are so old they keep their teeth in a jar by the bed. Colorful and full of fun music, the disc looks and sounds very good. —CA *AKA:* Iedereen Beroemd!.

Movie: ♫♫♫ ½ **DVD:** ♫♫♫ ½

Miramax Pictures (cat #23830, UPC 786-936163858). Widescreen (1.85:1) anamorphic. Dolby Digital 5.1 Surround. $32.99. Keepcase. *LANG:* Dutch. *SUB:* English. *CAP:* English. *FEATURES:* 17 chapters • Theatrical trailer.

2000 (R) 99m/C *BE* Josse De Pauw, Eva Van der Gucht, Werner De Smedt, Thekla Reuten, Victor Low, Gert Portael; **D:** Dominique Deruddere; **W:** Dominique Deruddere; **C:** Willy Stassen; **M:** Raymond van het Groenewoud. *AWARDS: NOM:* Oscars '00: Foreign Film.

Evil Dead [LE]

Shot on grainy 16mm, the film (previously reviewed in *Book 1*) has suffered a fair number of awful video incarnations, but Anchor Bay has resurrected it in what has to be a definitive version: 16:9 remastered from the original negative, and brimming with the kinds of goodies fans want. For icing on a grisly cake, the packaging mimics the film's "Book of the Dead" central prop, complete with a rubbery "human skin" binding. Horror addicts already know all about the film and its sequels and their many versions, etc. The troubled history of the second sequel, *Army of Darkness,* has filled more than one article in *Video Watchdog* magazine. A very comprehensive account of the filming of this show can be found in Bill Warren's recent book, *The Evil Dead Companion.* Anchor Bay should get the P.T. Barnum award for their fun and attention-getting marketing of this limited edition. It comes wrapped in a cello box like a packet of expensive stationery: inside is an ugly brown mass of rubber. (For a moment I thought someone had sent me a monster mask.) Inside is a creepy reproduction of the book from the film itself, with the movie disc enveloped near the back, as if just along for the ride. The disc is handsomely mounted and packed with extras. Dolby Digital and THX logos herald the show, which comes up looking grainy but solid, and in more colors than just the green I'd seen on VHS 15 years ago. Anchor Bay always has solidly produced extras, and with full cooperation from the principals involved (Bruce Campbell was a producer as well as the star), the documentaries here are authoritative. The above-mentioned Bill Warren, a solid choice for a literary perspective, can be seen in one of them. As seen in both the stills and an 18-minute selection of raw outtakes that are included, the kids making the movie seem to be having one heck of a fun time, even when drenched in sickening makeup or putrid gore. The film's prop and makeup designer, Tom Sullivan, opened his bag of tricks for this limited edition—the eye-catching packaging was his work. —GE

Movie: ♫♫♫ **DVD:** ♫♫♫♫
Anchor Bay (cat #DV11904). Widescreen (1.85:1) anamorphic. DTS Surround; Dolby Digital 5.1 Surround. $49.98. Special packaging. *LANG:* English; French. *CAP:* English. FEATURES: 2 commentary tracks ♦ Behind-the-scenes footage and outtakes ♦ 2 featurettes and documentaries ♦ Trailers & TV spots ♦ Poster & still gallery ♦ Talent files.
1983 (NC-17) 85m/C Bruce Campbell, Ellen Sandweiss, Betsy Baker, Hal Delrich, Sarah York, Theodore (Ted) Raimi, Sam Raimi, Scott Spiegel; *D:* Sam Raimi; *W:* Sam Raimi; *C:* Tim Philo; *M:* Joseph LoDuca.

The Evil That Men Do

Charles Bronson once again dons the mantle of justice for another brain-dead revenge flick. This time out, his target is a torture expert known as the Doctor (Maher), who makes a living by sharing his knowledge with Central American dictators. This movie makes you appreciate the simple things in life, such as owning genitals that haven't been crushed, electrocuted, or otherwise abused. Picture quality is inconsistent, with some colors appearing faded, but both widescreen and full-frame versions are offered. The mono track sounds like a warped record, having an especially difficult time handling the music. —BG

Movie: ♫ **DVD:** ♫♫ ½
Columbia Tristar (cat #06691, UPC 043-396066915). Widescreen (1.85:1) anamorphic; full frame. Dolby Mono. $19.95. Keepcase. *LANG:* English. *SUB:* English; French; Spanish; Portuguese. *CAP:* English. FEATURES: 28 chapters ♦ Trailers.
1984 (R) 90m/C Charles Bronson, Theresa Saldana, Joseph Maher, Jose Ferrer, Rene Enriquez, John Glover, Raymond St. Jacques, Antoinette Bower, Enrique Lucero, Jorge Luke; *D:* J. Lee Thompson; *W:* John Crowther; *C:* Xavier Cruz; *M:* Ken Thorne.

Evolution

Ghostbusters director Ivan Reitman returns with another sci-fi/comedy. And while it may not be as good as that ghostbusting classic, it is certainly entertaining. A meteorite crashes to Earth and local community college scientist Ira Kane (David Duchovny) and Harry Block (Orlando

Jones) investigate. They discover that the seemingly innocent space-rock is carrying alien organisms which begin to grow at an alarming rate, threatening the local area. The government arrives to intervene in the guise of evil General Woodman (Ted Levine) and clumsy CDC official Allison Reed (Julianne Moore). Of course, the attempts to contain the growing alien threat fails, forcing the comedic duo of Kane and Block, along with bumbling fireman-wannabe Wayne Grey (Seann William Scott) to stop the extraterrestrial baddies. While there is some scientific mumbo-jumbo in *Evolution* (the script was originally a horror film!), the movie simply wants to be a fun thrill-ride and it delivers. Duchovny (whose role is like a goofier version of his famous character from *The X-Files*) is very funny in the lead, with Jones and Scott both attempting to steal the show with their shenanigans. The special-effects suffer at times (Reitman admits that they were rushed), but the aliens are convincing for the most part. The DVD from Dreamworks is good, but doesn't live up to their usual standards. Due to all of the information crammed onto this single, one-sided disc, the image is a bit soft at times. The colors are good and the image is clear, but is not always sharp. The audio tracks, both the Dolby Digital 5.1 and the DTS 5.1, are very good, giving rich Surround and throbbing bass. The most exciting extra on the DVD is the audio commentary with Reitman, Duchovny, Jones, and Scott. This track is very funny, as the quartet reminisce about the production and poke fun at one another. —ML

Movie: ♫♫♫ **DVD:** ♫♫♫
DreamWorks Home Ent. (cat #88923, UPC 667068892321). Widescreen (1.85:1) anamorphic. Dolby Digital 5.1; DTS 5.1; Dolby 2.0 Surround. $26.99. Keepcase. *LANG:* English. *SUB:* English; French. *CAP:* English. FEATURES: Commentary ♦ "Making of" featurette ♦ Deleted scenes ♦ Storyboards ♦ Visual effects featurette ♦ Photo gallery ♦ Talent files ♦ Production notes ♦ 22 chapters.
2001 (PG-13) 101m/C David Duchovny, Julianne Moore, Orlando Jones, Seann William Scott, Ted Levine, Ethan Suplee, Michael Ray Bower, Katharine Towne, Dan Aykroyd, Richard Moll, Gregory Itzin, Ty Burrell; *D:* Ivan Reitman; *W:* David Diamond, David Weissman, Don Jakoby; *C:* Michael Chapman; *M:* John Powell.

Exit Wounds

Unpredictable, unorthodox Detroit police detective Orin Boyd (Seagal, of course) gets sent to the baddest part of town after successfully, but unconventionally, breaking up a plot to kill the Vice President. There, along with his rambunctious new partner (Washington), he uncovers corrupt cops and a drug-running scheme involving the notorious crime lord Walker (DMX). Lots of martial arts sequences and loads of gunfire from, presumably, really bad shots. Romance also blossoms between Mr. Loose Canon and a precinct comman-

der played by Hennessey. Typical Seagal flick, sure to be enjoyed by fans. Others should be wary. The film presents no major challenges for the DVD. Colors are nowhere near saturated (as in the theatre) so there is never a risk of bleed and the picture remains sharp. Blacks and grays get an A, and considering the lack of variance to enhance detail, the color is very good. The 5.1 sound is full bodied and powerful, but seems artificial at times, sort of like Spock in *Star Trek The Motion Picture*. The supplementals are mostly a waste with the nine-minute "On the Set with Anthony Anderson" making you want to find him and punch him hard, very hard. —JO

Movie: ♫♫ **DVD:** ♫♫♫
Warner (cat #21069, UPC 0853921069-29). Widescreen (2.35:1) anamorphic. Dolby Digital 5.1. $24.98. Snapper. *LANG:* English; French. *SUB:* English; Spanish; French. *CAP:* English. FEATURES: 32 chapters ♦ Theatrical trailer ♦ "Making of" documentary ♦ "On the set with Anthony Anderson" ♦ DMX music video "No Sunshine."
2001 (R) 98m/C Steven Seagal, DMX, Isaiah Washington IV, Anthony Anderson, Michael Jai White, Bill Duke, Jill(ian) Hennessey, Tom Arnold, Bruce McGill, David Vadim, Eva Mendez; *D:* Andrzej Bartkowiak; *W:* Ed Horowitz, Richard D'Ovidio; *C:* Glen MacPherson; *M:* Jeff Rona, Damon Blackman.

The Exorcist [2]: The Version You've Never Seen

This new release is essentially a longer rough-cut, which author William Peter Blatty has always favored over director William Friedkin's more elliptical vision. It offers plenty of additional scenes that help draw a much more clearly defined picture of the characters and events in the film. But the inclusion of these additional scenes, which consist of a lot of dialogue, results in a significantly slower pace. In many instances where the original cut was pounding along, the story is now larded with more exposition and dialogue. In other places the editing has changed, creating a faster pace on purpose, where the slow creepiness of the original was the key to success. The largest difference is certainly the ending of the film, long a sore point between Blatty and Friedkin. While the original cut featured an ending that was considered bleak—unintentionally so I may add, as many viewers weren't able to correctly interpret Friedkin's final frames—the new cut is much more clearly defined. The transfer on this DVD comes from a great looking film print that looks noticeably better than the print used for the 25th Anniversary Edition (reviewed in *Book 1*). Although the film still shows quite a bit of grain—a direct result of the film stock—it is nonetheless visibly subdued. The new transfer also offers a better level of detail, which is mostly also a direct effect of the reduced graininess of the print.

While the previous release suffered from some edge-enhancement, these problems are practically gone in the new presentation. At the same time contrast is slightly improved, creating a much nicer definition without the inclusion of distracting ringing artifacts. The framing of both versions is absolutely identical and in terms of color reproduction, both films look equally strong. The newly remixed Dolby Digital 5.1 EX adds an additional center channel to the Surrounds, is even more impressive. While this improvement does not necessarily stem from the additional channel information, the entire track feels more dynamic and explosive. —GH/MM
Movie: 🎵🎵🎵 **DVD:** 🎵🎵🎵
Warner Home Video (UPC 0853918632-29). Widescreen (1.85:1) anamorphic. Dolby Digital 5.1 EX. $24.98. Snapper. *LANG:* English. *SUB:* English; French; Spanish; Portuguese. *FEATURES:* Production notes • Trailers • TV and radio spots.
1973 (R) 132m/C Ellen Burstyn, Linda Blair, Jason Miller, Max von Sydow, Jack MacGowran, Lee J. Cobb, Kitty Winn, Barton Heyman, Peter Masterson; **D:** William Friedkin; **W:** William Peter Blatty; **C:** Owen Roizman, Billy Williams; **M:** Jack Nitzsche; **V:** Mercedes McCambridge. *AWARDS:* Oscars '73: Adapt. Screenplay, Sound; Golden Globes '74: Director (Friedkin), Film—Drama, Screenplay, Support. Actress (Blair); *NOM:* Oscars '73: Actress (Burstyn), Art Dir./Set Dec., Cinematog., Director (Friedkin), Film Editing, Picture, Support. Actor (Miller), Support. Actress (Blair).

Exorcist 3: Legion

George C. Scott turns in an excellent performance as police Lt. Kinderman, in William Peter Blatty's underrated horror sequel. Wisely, it discards whatever happened in *Exorcist 2:The Heretic,* and builds a new tale using scraps of story elements from the original. The mysterious patient in Room X holds the key to a rash of serial killings in Washington, but the man's identity could be either of two men both thought long dead. The DVD delivers solid visuals, and also has a very good audio track, providing clarity to Blatty's subtle multilayered soundtrack. —BT
Movie: 🎵🎵🎵 **DVD:** 🎵🎵🎵
Warner (cat #17488, UPC 0853917488-23). Widescreen letterboxed. Dolby Digital 5.1 Surround. $19.99. Snapper. *LANG:* English; French. *CAP:* English. *FEATURES:* 31 chapters • Trailer.
1990 (R) 105m/C George C. Scott, Ed Flanders, Jason Miller, Nicol Williamson, Scott Wilson, Brad Dourif, Nancy Fish, George DiCenzo, Viveca Lindfors, Patrick Ewing, Fabio; **D:** William Peter Blatty; **W:** William Peter Blatty; **C:** Gerry Fisher; **M:** Barry de Vorzon.

Expresso Bongo

Low rent wheeler-dealer Johnny (Harvey) discovers talented teenaged schlub Herbert (Richard) singing at a club and suc-

cessfully launches his career. By way of his "no surrender" personality, Johnny is able to get Herbert much-needed television exposure and a gig performing with an older singer, Dixie Collins (Donlan), who's on the downward spiral. A fast-paced (occasionally stylish) film adaptation of the Wolf Mankowitz play. Director Guest exquisitely uses the widescreen framing like an "Old Master" and the film frequently plays like a British version of *Jailhouse Rock.* This revealing look behind the curtains of the music industry is as relevant today as it was on original release. Harvey (whose Lithuanian accent occasionally sneaks out) manages to make his character quite sympathetic and he appears to he having great fun with the role. C'mon, how dastardly can a man be when he wears a Don Knotts hat? While there are a few brief song sequences, it's not a musical by any means. The liner notes compare it to *The Sweet Smell of Success* but this is a much lighter, kinder film. The disc utilizes a transfer with rich contrasts but the original print displays occasional damage and the odd wobbly frame. Digital shimmer appears infrequently around diagonal lines. While the framing is very wide, it's just a hair shy of its full aspect ratio. It's a minor quibble, though; this must look downright awful in pan 'n' scan! The sound is fine and the inclusion of the production and cast notes from the original pressbook is an inspired touch. —DG
Movie: 🎵🎵🎵 **DVD:** 🎵🎵🎵
Kino on Video (cat #K229DVD, UPC 7383-29022921). Widescreen (2.35:1) anamorphic. Mono. $24.95. Keepcase. *LANG:* English. *FEATURES:* 12 chapters • Insert card • Excerpts from the original pressbook.
1959 111m/B *GB* Laurence Harvey, Sylvia Syms, Yolande Donlan, Cliff Richard; **D:** Val Guest; **W:** Wolf Mankowitz; **C:** John Wilcox.

The Extreme Adventures of Super Dave

Super Dave Osborne was a hilariously inept stuntman comic who appeared on the TV series *Bizarre* about a decade ago. All his stunts would end in disaster: things would fall on him; he would fall off of things; he'd get dragged down the road, etc. This film comes about 10 years too late. The "plot" involves Dave failing at his latest attempt to pull off a big stunt, and deciding to go into retirement. Hedaya stars as Dave's evil promoter and Carides stars as a cute mother Dave befriends. Of course Super Dave has to return to stunts in the end to save the day, but by this point you'll probably be beyond caring. If you thought some skits from *Saturday Night Live* were stretched thin to make movies, this film makes those seem relatively rich and inventive. None of it is terribly funny, and the ever-dry Super Dave isn't exactly one of the best actors. The disc is passable with images remaining adequately sharp throughout. Colors are

pleasant and look vibrant throughout. The occasional mark on the print is noticeable, but not distracting. The sound is fairly limited but the sparse use of the Surrounds (used every time Dave gets crushed by a large object) comes through clearly. The dialogue seems very poorly dubbed. —AB/DG
Movie: 🎵🎵 **DVD:** 🎵🎵🎵
MGM Home Ent. (UPC 27616837028). Widescreen (1.85:1) anamorphic. Dolby Digital Surround. $14.95. Keepcase. *LANG:* English. *CAP:* English. *FEATURES:* Trailer • Booklet • 32 chapters.
1998 (PG) 91m/C Bob Einstein, Gia Carides, Carl Michael Lindner, Steve Van Wormer, Dan Hedaya; **D:** Peter Macdonald; **W:** Lorne Cameron, Don Lake; **C:** Bernd Heinl; **M:** Andrew Gross.

Extreme Heist

Two bumbling crooks (Bosch and Narvy) screw up a sting operation when they steal a book of bank codes worth millions. With the gang they stole from and the FBI both trying to recover the book, the thieves are in for a wild ride. This plot is just an excuse for the comic martial arts and extreme stunts that make this a fun, fast-paced action movie. Bosch has skill and charisma in the fight scenes, if not in the dramatic ones. The stereo sound is clear, but the sub-par image has a lot of dirt from the original and edges are often fuzzy. —DRL
Movie: 🎵🎵 ½ **DVD:** 🎵🎵
MTI (cat #1093, UPC 039414510935). Full frame. Dolby Digital Stereo. $24.95. Keepcase. *LANG:* English. *SUB:* Spanish. *FEATURES:* Filmographies • Trailer • 8 chapters.
1999 (PG-13) 95m/C John Yong Bosch, Jason Narvy, Motoko Nagino, Michael Hexum; **D:** Koichi Sakamoto, Makoto Yokoyama; **W:** Carlton Holder; **C:** David Wald; **M:** Mike Verta.

Extreme Honor

Video premiere action/heist picture is mostly standard-issue stuff. Navy SEAL John Kennedy Brascoe (Anderson) becomes involved in a plot to breach the security of a millionaire's (Ironside) mansion to win a million bucks for his son's cancer treatment. The idea of having a serious illness involving a child in a cheap flick like this is distasteful, and what does the nutty title mean? DVD offers nothing but the optional Spanish subtitles over VHS tape. Pale image is identical. —MM
Movie: 🎵🎵 **DVD:** 🎵🎵
MTI (cat #8117, UPC 039414581171). Full frame. $24.98. Keepcase. *LANG:* English. *SUB:* Spanish. *FEATURES:* 20 chapters • Trailers • Cast bios.
2001 (R) 95m/C Dan Anderson, Michael Ironside, Michael Madsen, Olivier Gruner, Grand Bush, Martin Kove, Antonio Fargas, Edward Albert, Charles Napier, Odile Corso; **D:** Steven Rush; **W:** Steven Rush; **C:** Ken Blakey; **M:** David Powell, Geoff Levin.

Extreme Limits

Dr. Hunter (John Beck) and his lovely daughter Nadia (Julie St. Claire) are on an expedition in Siberia to uncover the long-lost Tesla Ray. Devised by famed scientist Nikola Tesla, the test of this mental weapon caused the great Tunguska explosion of 1908 and led Tesla to hide the weapon in a cave (actually the Bat Cave of 1960s television fame, if you must know). Recovering the little shoeshine box that holds the death ray, the Hunters hop on board a charter flight full of lovely soap opera stars and head back to the States. Terrorists hitch a ride at the last minute; the plane crashes—you know the drill. For a viewer, the only redeeming feature is found in trying to name all of the films that contributed stock footage. Flight and mountain sequences were pulled directly from *Cliffhanger*, the train footage and some helicopter gunplay come from *Narrow Margin*, and the final scene liberally borrows from *The Long Kiss Goodnight*. Original footage shot for the film is static, bland, and uninteresting, so when you see something that looks intriguing, start guessing as to what movie it's from. Technical quality is decent with a fairly sharp image and good color saturation and black levels. Although some of the stock footage is of noticeably lesser quality, this is a solid transfer of a very low-budget production. The soundtrack is clear enough but the sound effects have a very tacked-on feel and the use of the Surround is overly obvious and distracting. —*MP*
Movie: *♪ ½* ***DVD:*** *♪♪*
20th Century Fox (cat #2002371). Widescreen (1.78:1) anamorphic. Dolby Digital 5.1 Surround Stereo; Dolby Digital Surround. $34.98. Keepcase. *LANG:* English. *SUB:* English. *FEATURES:* Commentary: Jim Wynorski, Julie St. Claire, Andrea Rossoto ● Photo gallery ● Trailer.
2001 (R) 105m/C Treat Williams, Hannes Jaenicke, John Beck, Susan Blakely, Gary Hudson, Julie St. Clair; *D:* Jim Wynorski; *C:* Andrea V. Rossotto.

Extremities

An adaptation of William Mastrosimone's play about a woman and her would-be attacker. When Joe (Russo) comes to Marjorie's (Fawcett) house to rape and kill her, she turns the tables on him, finding herself in the unintended position of victimizing him. It's violent and strangely ambiguous. Fawcett famously breaks out of her *Charlie's Angels* mold. Russo is suitably creepy in snakeskin cowboy boots. The underutilized Alfre Woodard serves as the voice of reason. The full-frame version looks grainy, but the widescreen version looks very good. The sound is fine. —*LA*
Movie: *♪♪ ½* ***DVD:*** *♪♪♪*
MGM Home Ent. (cat #1003349, UPC 276-16874986). Widescreen (1.85:1) anamorphic; full frame. $14.98. Keepcase. *LANG:* English. *SUB:* French; Spanish. *CAP:* English. *FEATURES:* Original theatrical trailer ● 16 chapters.

1986 (R) 83m/C Farrah Fawcett, Diana Scarwid, James Russo, Alfre Woodard; *D:* Robert M. Young; *W:* William Mastrosimone; *C:* Curtis Clark; *M:* J.A.C. Redford.

An Eye for an Eye

San Francisco cop Sean Kane (Norris) is pitted against drug kingpin Morgan Canfield (Lee). It's a standard-issue martial arts exercise. The harsh colors and high grain gain little on DVD. This one's virtually identical to VHS tape. —*MM*
Movie: *♪♪* ***DVD:*** *♪♪*
MGM Home Ent. (cat #1002633, UPC 027-616868336). Full frame. Dolby Digital Mono. $14.95. Keepcase. *LANG:* English. *SUB:* French; Spanish. *CAP:* English. *FEATURES:* 16 chapters ● Trailer.
1981 (R) 106m/C Chuck Norris, Christopher Lee, Richard Roundtree, Matt Clark, Mako, Maggie Cooper; *D:* Steve Carver; *W:* James Bruner; *C:* Roger Shearman; *M:* William Goldstein.

An Eye for an Eye

Karen McCann (Field) listens on the phone as her 17-year-old daughter is raped and murdered, then watches as the killer is released on a technicality. When he strikes again, Karen decides to take the law into her own hands, Charles Bronson style. It's even more shallow and manipulative than it sounds, preying shamelessly on middle-class fears and mistrust of the legal system. The biggest mystery is how so many big names got caught up in this clunker. Picture quality is average, with heavy grain in dark scenes but several steps above tape. There's not much difference between the original Dolby Surround track and the 5.1 remix. —*BG*
Movie: *♪* ***DVD:*** *♪♪ ½*
Paramount (cat #33091, UPC 097363309-123). Widescreen anamorphic. Dolby 5.1; Dolby Surround. $24.99. Keepcase. *LANG:* English; French. *SUB:* English. *CAP:* English. *FEATURES:* 10 chapters.
1995 (R) 102m/C Sally Field, Ed Harris, Kiefer Sutherland, Beverly D'Angelo, Joe Mantegna, Keith David; *D:* John Schlesinger; *W:* Amanda Silver, Rick Jaffa; *C:* Amir M. Mokri; *M:* James Newton Howard.

Eye Witness

Witnessing an assassination, a boy claims the killers are hunting him. He and his older sister escape numerous attacks and are aided by their grandfather and a resourceful young bystander even under the shadow of martial law. Director Hough, who also did Hammer's *Twins of Evil* and some *Avengers* TV, at times shows flashes of Sam Fuller's graphic sensibility. Anchor Bay's revival of this film shows a curious if pure nostalgia for a movie neither camp nor innovative enough to transcend its "B"-movie conventions. Excellent DVD transfer and the best sound one could hope for given the source. —*MO* *AKA:* Sudden Terror.

Movie: *♪♪ ½* ***DVD:*** *♪♪♪ ½*
Anchor Bay (cat #DV12049, UPC 0131312-04995). Widescreen anamorphic. Dolby Digital Mono. $19.98. Keepcase. *LANG:* English. *FEATURES:* 23 chapters ● Commentary: director John Hough, (uncredited) writer Bryan Forbes ● Theatrical trailer ● John Hough bio.
1970 (PG) 95m/C *GB* Mark Lester, Lionel Jeffries, Susan George, Tony Bonner; *D:* John Hough; *W:* Bryan Forbes; *C:* David Holmes.

Faces of Death 2

The second installment in the disgusting series, which purports to show actual footage of death and dismemberment. The truth is even more irresponsible—obviously staged scenarios are intermixed with documentary footage of animal slaughter and the Vietnam War. While the free mixture of fictionalized and "actual" death is awful enough, more appalling is the film's attempt to rationalize itself as sociology. This DVD also includes a bonus program, "The Worst of Faces of Death," comprised of highlights from the series. In both picture and sound, the presentation is indistinguishable from video. —*BG*
Movie: *woof* ***DVD:*** *♪ ½*
Gorgon Video (cat #DVD2201, UPC 7421-07220126). Full frame. $19.98. Keepcase. *LANG:* English. *SUB:* English; Spanish. *FEATURES:* 21 chapters ● Trailers ● "The Worst of Faces of Death."
1981 85m/C *D:* Conan LeClaire; *W:* Alan Black; *Nar:* Frances B. Gross.

Faces of Death 3: Scenes from the Underground

The appalling series continues, with more "gory, real-life footage of death." Although most of the scenes are obvious fakes, the inclusion of some actual animal slaughter and footage from the Vietnam War makes this truly reprehensible. Think carefully before you watch this series, even as a guilty pleasure. The picture is soft and grainy while the audio is flat and muffled, making for an overall product that is barely distinguishable from tape. —*BG*
Movie: *woof* ***DVD:*** *♪ ½*
Gorgon Video (cat #DVD2202, UPC 74210-7220225). Full frame. $19.98. Keepcase. *LANG:* English. *SUB:* English; Spanish. *FEATURES:* 20 chapters ● Trailers.
1981 84m/C Frances B. Gross; *D:* Conan LeClaire; *W:* Alan Black.

Facing the Enemy

Otherwise acceptable domestic thriller begins with the death of a child in a particularly strong scene, and that's really too heavy for this kind of escapism. The death seriously damages the marriage of cop McCleary (Ashby) and Olivia (Paul). They're separated when he begins a murder investigation. A complex plot sets McCleary against a nasty conman (producer Caulfield). Acting is above average. Image is only so-so. Most interiors are fine. Heavy artifacts and aliasing appear in exterior pans. Sound delivers understandable dialogue. —MM

Movie: 🎬🎬 ½ **DVD:** 🎬🎬

New Concorde (cat #NH20788 D, UPC 736991478893). Full frame. $19.98. Keepcase. *LANG:* English. *SUB:* Spanish. *FEATURES:* Trailers ▪ Filmographies ▪ 18 chapters.

2000 (R) 98m/C Linden Ashby, Maxwell Caulfield, Alexandra Paul, Cynthia Preston, Max Gail, Bruce Weitz, Melanie Wilson; **D:** Rob Malenfant; **W:** Martin Kitrosser; **C:** Steve Adcock; **M:** Richard Bowers.

Falling in Love

Two New Yorkers unexpectedly fall in love when their relationship develops into more than just friendship. Now each must face their own feelings, confront their spouses, and come to grips with their mutual desires to be together. The film attempts to recapture the on-screen passion between Robert De Niro and Meryl Streep that was so prevalent in the 1978 classic *The Deer Hunter*. Although this film is decently produced and well acted, it lacks much of the plot cohesiveness and strength of dialogue that would be expected from a film with actors of this caliber. DVD picture looks good and the sound quality is decent, but due to a few scenes with dust artifacts and the exclusion of a Surround track this DVD release makes its VHS cousin a close second. —EL

Movie: 🎬🎬 **DVD:** 🎬🎬

Paramount (cat #01628, UPC 097360162-844). Widescreen anamorphic. Dolby Digital Mono. $24.99. Keepcase. *LANG:* English; French. *CAP:* English. *FEATURES:* 14 chapters.

1984 (PG-13) 106m/C Robert De Niro, Meryl Streep, Harvey Keitel, Dianne Wiest, George Martin, Jane Kaczmarek, David Clennon; **D:** Ulu Grosbard; **W:** Michael Cristofer; **C:** Peter Suschitzky; **M:** Dave Grusin.

Fallout

It is horribly ironic that filmmaker Robert Palumbo chose to film the introduction to his independent feature on top of one of the World Trade Center towers. His film concerns the interplay among four high-rise office workers who flee a disaster of uncertain origin and find themselves trapped in a basement fallout shelter. His story really has nothing to do with the 9/11/01 atrocities. It's a well-made character study that attempts to work within the limitations of a modest budget. It's mostly successful, too, and certainly doesn't need any extra baggage. Parallels to reality are difficult to ignore, however. Palumbo and some of his cast members have some interesting things to say on their commentary track. Full-frame DVD image is no significant improvement over VHS tape. Heavy grain and artifacts are visible throughout. —MM

Movie: 🎬🎬 ½ **DVD:** 🎬🎬🎬

York Ent. (cat #YPD-1087, UPC 75072310-8728). Full frame. $14.98. Keepcase. *LANG:* English. *FEATURES:* Trailers ▪ Director's intro ▪ Commentary.

2001 88m/C Claire Beckman, Mark Deakins, Keith Randolph Smith, David Wasson; **D:** Robert Palumbo; **W:** Robert Palumbo, Mark Gallini; **C:** Wolfgang Held; **M:** Frank Ferrucci.

Family Man

Nicolas Cage stars in this odd mixture of *A Christmas Carol* and *It's a Wonderful Life*. On Christmas Eve, Wall Street power-broker Jack Campbell is suddenly transported to the life that he could have had with college sweetheart Kate (Tea Leoni). This captain of industry now finds himself living in the New Jersey suburbs, changing diapers, and working as a tire salesman. This forces Jack to look at his priorities and contemplate the choices he has made in his life. This is an entertaining film, with some touching moments, but it is ultimately flawed. The film preaches the importance of love and the evils of greed, but it never seems to accurately portray the wants and desires of middle America. Also, the story is meant to be character-driven, yet we never really get to know Jack and Kate, nor does the movie explain why life-changes would suddenly totally skew someone's priorities. DVD is loaded with goodies, most notably the gorgeous anamorphic widescreen transfer, which offers a crystal clear picture. (Notice the lack of distortion in the all-white snow shots.) The disc offers both a Dolby Digital 5.1 and a DTS 5.1 soundtrack, and both are outstanding, adding to the mood of the film. The two audio commentaries deliver a wealth of information about the movie, but it would have been nice to have heard from Nicolas Cage on these tracks. The highlight of the bonus features is an outtake with an overactive toddler. —ML

Movie: 🎬🎬 **DVD:** 🎬🎬🎬 ½

Universal Studios (cat #20941, UPC 025-192094125). Widescreen (2.35:1) anamorphic. Dolby Digital 5.1; DTS. $26.98. Keepcase. *LANG:* English; French. *SUB:* English. *CAP:* English. *FEATURES:* "Spotlight on Location" featurette ▪ "Making of" featurette ▪ Audio commentaries ▪ Music score commentary ▪ Deleted scenes ▪ Outtakes ▪ Music video ▪ Set-top game ▪ Production notes ▪ Cast & filmmakers ▪ DVD-ROM features.

2000 (PG-13) 125m/C Nicolas Cage, Tea Leoni, Don Cheadle, Amber Valletta; **D:** Brett Ratner; **W:** David Diamond, David Weissman; **C:** Dante Spinotti; **M:** Danny Elfman.

Family Viewing / Next of Kin

Two early features from Canadian auteur Atom Egoyan, both exploring technology, ideas of truth, and family relationships. In his first feature, *Next of Kin,* an unhappy young man sees a chance to do good

when he learns of an Armenian family who still misses the son they gave up for adoption many years ago. *Family Viewing* follows a young man who schemes to release his near-comatose grandmother from her nursing home, against his father's wishes. Also included are three of Egoyan's earlier short films, which take different approaches to the same issues. The picture and sound are quite good for such low-budget films, and Egoyan's audio commentaries are among the most insightful this reviewer has heard. —BG

Movie: 🎬🎬🎬 **DVD:** 🎬🎬🎬

Zeitgeist Films (cat #Z1003, UPC 797575-100333). Full frame. $34.99. Keepcase. *LANG:* English. *SUB:* English. *FEATURES:* 24 chapters ▪ 3 Egoyan short films ▪ Commentary: director ▪ Photo gallery ▪ Rehearsal footage ▪ Bio/filmography.

1987 92m/C CA David Hemblen, Adian Tierney, Gabrielle Rose, Arsinee Khanjian; **D:** Atom Egoyan; **W:** Atom Egoyan; **C:** Robert MacDonald, Peter Mettler; **M:** Mychael Danna. *AWARDS:* Toronto-City '87: Canadian Feature Film.

Fantastic Dinosaurs of the Movies

Harmless, undistinguished made-for-video junk compilation of clips, trailers, and featurettes from dinosaur, stop-motion animation, and fantasy films. Naturally, snippets from Ray Harryhausen's considerable body of work are in the majority here. The clips come fast and furious and the program isn't dull, but the print quality varies. All the trailers are transferred from well-worn (and some cases, disastrously damaged) theatrical exhibition prints that appear somewhat soft. The color clips are terribly faded, with most of the variant hues either non-existent or else entirely pink, typical of older faded Eastmancolor print stock. Digital noise is minimal but present. The sound features consistent volume levels and a minimum of crackle, but is still fairly nasal and flat. —DG

Movie: 🎬 ½ **DVD:** 🎬

Goodtimes Ent. (cat #05-81220, UPC 018-713812209). Full frame. Mono. $7.49. Keepcase. *LANG:* English. *FEATURES:* 12 chapters ▪ Insert card with chapter listings.

1990 74m/C

Farscape, Vol. 1

Sci-Fi channel space opera is about Crichton (Browder), an astronaut from Earth who's zipped through a wormhole and finds himself with a mixed-race (very mixed) crew on a ship that's alive in a galaxy far far away. Yes, it's standard stuff for the genre, but it's done up with superb production values that include good writing and acting, and inventive, funny creatures from the Jim Henson shop. DVDs are a substantial improvement over broadcast, cablecast, or tape, with the show's use of Surround tracks in key scenes. (Many feature films don't sound this good on disc.) The shows are carefully transferred with bright colors (also important in

context) and deep blacks. Volumes 2 and 3 are reviewed in *Book 2*. (Go figure.) The demanding technical standards are constant throughout the series. To date, 10 discs have been released. Contents: (1) Premiere; I, E.T. (UPC 702727009624); (4) PK Tech Girl; That Old Black Magic (702727009921); (5) DNA Mad Scientist; They've Got a Secret (702727010026); (6) Till the Blood Runs Clear; Rhapsody in Blue (702727101125); (7) The Flax; Jeremiah Crichton (702727100224); (8) Durka Returns; A Human Reaction (702727010323); (9) Through the Looking Glass; A Bug's Life (702727010422); (10) Nerve; The Hidden Memory (702727010521). —MM
Movie: 🎵🎵🎵 **DVD:** 🎵🎵🎵 ½
A.D.V. Films (cat #DFS001, UPC 702727-009624). Full frame. Dolby Digital 5.1 Surround; Dolby Digital Surround. $24.98. Keepcase. *LANG:* English. *FEATURES:* 4 chapters per episode • Previously unbroadcast footage • Actor profiles • Previews • Conceptual drawings.
2000 118m/C Ben Browder, Claudia Black, Anthony Simcoe, Virginia Hey; *D:* Rowan Woods; *V:* Jonathan Hardy, Lani Tapu.

Farscape, Vol. 6
While "Till the Blood Runs Clear" is a rather formulaic and straightforward episode from the sci-fi series, borrowing from *Star Wars* on occasion, "Rhapsody in Blue" is a cleverly written, mind-boggling episode. It is episodes of this caliber that give the series its excellent reputation and fans of the series definitely want to look out for this one. The transfer of these episodes is once again superb. Even upon closest scrutiny, the image quality is absolutely fantastic and reveals an incredible level of detail. Presented in the series's full-frame aspect ratio, the transfer is free of any blemishes and has an incredibly rich color reproduction that saturates the screen with otherworldly tinges at one time, and beautifully golden desert tones at others. Blacks are very deep, rendering a very dimensional image with great shadow delineation. The full-blown 5.1 channel makes aggressive use of the Surround channels. The quality by far exceeds any broadcast presentation of the films, as the wide frequency response creates bombastic explosions and crystal-clear high ends. —GH
Movie: 🎵🎵🎵 **DVD:** 🎵🎵🎵 ½
A.D.V. Films (UPC 702727010125). Full frame. Dolby Digital 5.1 Surround Stereo; Dolby Digital Surround Stereo. $24.98. Keepcase. *LANG:* English. *FEATURES:* Previously unbroadcast footage • Video profile of spaceship Mora • Conceptual drawings • Trailers.
2001 100m/C

Fashionably L.A.
Kassidy (Olson), Simone (Arnold), Tatia (Lano), Arielle (Laningham), and Jessalyn (Gibson) endure the insanity and depreda-

tions of the L.A. fashion scene. On her commentary track, filmmaker Olson says that the film is partly autobiographical and that's obvious in some scenes. The extensive (for a low-budget film) extras are the main difference between this disc and tape. The image switches between very grainy black and white and "gritty, authentic, nasty color," according to Olson. Sound is acceptable. The commentary track adds a lot. —MM
Movie: 🎵🎵🎵 **DVD:** 🎵🎵🎵
York Ent. (cat #YPD-1088, UPC 75072310-8827). Full frame. $14.95. Keepcase. *LANG:* English. *FEATURES:* Commentary: Olson, Arnold, Patricia Hampton, Esse Carter • Bikini garage sale fund raiser featurette • Trailers • 10 chapters.
1999 95m/C Tamara Olson, Darienne Arnold, Holly Laningham, Miranda Gibson, Jenya Lano; *D:* Tamara Olson; *W:* Tamara Olson; *M:* Mark Killian.

The Fast and the Furious
On the lam after being falsely accused of murder, co-director Ireland takes Malone and her Jaguar hostage and makes a run for the border by entering the Pebble Beach race. So-so transfer seems to have been made from inferior original elements. Title is available as part of the *Great Racing Movies* triple feature (see separate entry). —MM
Movie: 🎵🎵 **DVD:** 🎵🎵
Full frame. *LANG:* English. *FEATURES:* 4 chapters.
1954 73m/B John Ireland, Dorothy Malone, Bruce Carlisle, Iris Adrian, Jean Howell; *D:* Edwards Sampson, John Ireland; *W:* Jerome Odlum, Jean Howell; *C:* Floyd Crosby; *M:* Alexander Gerens.

The Fast and the Furious
This boxoffice hit doesn't pack the same punch on the small screen. Paul Walker stars as Brian, an undercover police officer attempting to infiltrate the world of illegal street racing. A gang has been using fast yet small cars to rob 18-wheelers, and Brian must uncover the mastermind behind these thefts. He befriends Dominic (Vin Diesel), the local street-racing champ, to gain info, but unexpectedly falls for Dominic's sister, Mia (Jordana Brewster). While the film does contain some spectacular stunts during the racing scenes and the truck robberies, the remainder is an unfocused mess. The film tries to intertwine several plots, but never takes any time to focus on any of them, nor do we ever learn much about the world of illegal racing. For Vin Diesel or Paul Walker enthusiasts only. The transfer on this DVD isn't nearly as disappointing, as it offers a nearly pristine transfer of the film, showing only the slightest defects. The audio tracks (both Dolby Digital 5.1 and DTS 5.1) sound fantastic, adding to the illusion of actually being in the driver's seat. The extras on the disc vary in quality, with the

highlight being the magazine article which inspired the film. —ML
Movie: 🎵 **DVD:** 🎵🎵🎵 ½
Universal Studios (cat #21270, UPC 0251-9212702-1). Widescreen (2.35:1) anamorphic. Dolby Digital 5.1; DTS 5.1. $26.99. Keepcase. *LANG:* English; French. *SUB:* English. *CAP:* English. *FEATURES:* Commentary • "Making of" featurette • Magazine article • Deleted scenes • Visual effects featurettes • Editing demo • Storyboards • Music videos • Theatrical trailer • Production notes • Cast & crew filmographies.
2001 (PG-13) 101m/C Vin Diesel, Paul Walker, Jordana Brewster, Michelle Rodriguez, Rick Yune, Ted Levine, Ja Rule, Thom Barry, Chad Lindberg, Johnny Strong, Matt Schulze, Vyto Ruginis; *D:* Rob Cohen; *W:* Gary Scott Thompson, Erik Bergquist, David Ayer; *C:* Ericson Core; *M:* BT (Brian Transeau).

Fast Sofa
Rick (Busey), a restless urban cowboy, takes his hedonistic lifestyle on the road after his apartment is robbed. Interesting direction and quirky story can't fix the error of casting Busey (son of Gary) in the lead. He's more appropriate for character roles than a dashing hooligan carrying the picture. Better-than-average DVD transfer and sound. —MO
Movie: 🎵🎵 **DVD:** 🎵🎵🎵
Studio Home Ent. (cat #ST7946D, UPC 658149974627). Widescreen letterboxed. Dolby Stereo. $24.99. Keepcase. *LANG:* English. *SUB:* Spanish. *CAP:* English; Spanish. *FEATURES:* 24 chapters • Theatrical trailer.
2001 (R) 95m/C Jake Busey, Jennifer Tilly, Eric Roberts, Adam Goldberg, Crispin Glover, Natasha Lyonne, Bijou Phillips; *D:* Salome Breziner; *W:* Salome Breziner, Peter Chase, Bruce Craven; *C:* Dean Lent; *M:* William V. Malpede.

The Fat Black Pussycat
Please see review of *The Black Cat / The Fat Black Pussycat*.
1963 89m/B Frank Jamus, Janet Damon, Patricia McNair, Hugh Romney, Geoffrey Lewis, Hector Elizondo; *D:* Harold Lea; *W:* Harold Lea; *C:* Beat Carroll.

Fata Morgana
Please see review of *Lessons of Darkness*.
1992 m/C *D:* Werner Herzog; *W:* Werner Herzog; *M:* Leonard Cohen.

Fatal Attraction [SCE]
The movie that defines the genre of "be careful who you have a fling with, because she just might be a real nutcase." Glenn Close is excellent as Alex, the obsessive one-night stand of Dan (Douglas). Anne Archer is his busy wife, who is just too much the wife to be the hot seductress. Hot sex, Glenn Close naked when she was

in her prime, animals in the stew pot—this is one wild ride. If only the studio had taken the time to make sure the technical elements of this DVD were up to the movie itself. The colors are muddy, the sound is just plain jarring at times, and the DVD looks old. What a waste when you get all these cool extra features—including the famous original ending—that really add so much to the enjoyment of the movie. —DE

Movie: 🎞🎞🎞 ½ **DVD:** 🎞🎞

Paramount (cat #01762, UPC 097360176-247). Widescreen anamorphic. Dolby 5.1; Dolby Surround; Dolby Stereo. $24.98. Keepcase. *LANG:* English; French. *SUB:* English. *FEATURES:* Forever Fatal: new cast & crew interviews • Social Attraction: the cultural phenomenon of Fatal Attraction • Visual Attraction: behind-the-scenes production featurette • Rehearsal footage • Alternate ending with commentary from director Adrian Lyne • Commentary: director • Theatrical trailer.

1987 (R) 120m/C Michael Douglas, Glenn Close, Anne Archer, Stuart Pankin, Ellen Hamilton-Latzen, Ellen Foley, Fred Gwynne, Meg Mundy, J.J. Johnston; *D:* Adrian Lyne; *W:* James Dearden; *C:* Howard Atherton; *M:* Maurice Jarre. *AWARDS: NOM:* Oscars '87: Actress (Close), Adapt. Screenplay, Director (Lyne), Film Editing, Picture, Support. Actress (Archer).

Fatal Blade

Top yakuza assassin Kiyoshi Nakajo is sent to L.A. to take revenge on a Mafioso for some thefts, and ends up crossing paths with British-born LAPD detective Gary Daniels. The two end up working toward the same goal, and develop respect for each other. A pretty good direct-to-video action film. Kentaro Shimizu makes a standout villain, cackling evilly at his every misdeed. Cinematographer Michael Goi does a great job making this look like a more expensive production. Transfer quality is better than average. —BT *AKA:* Gedo.

Movie: 🎞🎞 ½ **DVD:** 🎞🎞 ½

MTI (cat #9702, UPC 03941459702). Full frame. $24.95. Keepcase. *LANG:* English. *FEATURES:* 8 chapters • Trailer • Filmographies.

2000 (R) 99m/C *JP* Gary Daniels, Kioshi Nakajo, Eric Lutes, Victor Rivers, Kentaro Shimizu, Seiko Matsuda, Barry Sattels, Cuba Gooding Sr., Jack McGee; *D:* Talun Hsu; *W:* Talun Hsu, Simon Tse, Bill Zide, Nao Sakai; *C:* Michael Goi; *M:* Robert Douglas.

Fatal Error

Robin Cook isn't losing any sleep over this conventional made-for-TV medical thriller. Something is turning Seattle citizens into pillars of salt (sort of). Have no fear, beautiful doctors Samantha Carter (Turner) and Nick Baldwin (Sabato) are on the case. The solution is pretty silly but the cast is attractive and the production values are relatively high. DVD image is only slightly sharper than broadcast quality. So is sound. —MM

Movie: 🎞🎞 **DVD:** 🎞🎞 ½

Artisan Ent. (cat #12460, UPC 70772-9124603). Full frame. Dolby Digital Surround. $24.98. Keepcase. *LANG:* English. *CAP:* English. *FEATURES:* 6 chapters.

1999 91m/C Antonio Sabato Jr., Janine Turner, Robert Wagner, Malcolm Stewart; *D:* Armand Mastroianni; *W:* Rockne S. O'Bannon; *C:* David Geddes; *M:* Ron Ramin.

The Fatal Hour

Please see review of *Boris Karloff DVD Double Feature.*

Movie: 🎞 ½

1940 68m/B Boris Karloff, Marjorie Reynolds, Grant Withers, Charles Trowbridge, John Hamilton, Frank Puglia, Jason Robards Sr.; *D:* William Nigh; *W:* W. Scott Darling, George Waggner; *C:* Harry Neumann.

Father Frost

An old "babushka" recites the familiar "once upon a time" fairy tale invitation. In a small village, the kindhearted Nastenka lives a miserable life, ever-suffering under the cruel heel of her stepmother and stepsister, while her father caters to his demanding wife's whims and endures her incessant insults. In another village far away, Ivanushka begins his journey to manhood by leaving home. However, Ivanushka's pride must be tamed if he is to be the worthwhile man his elderly mother wishes him to be. Among the trials he must face are an attack by bloodthirsty forest bandits, the transforming spells of Grandfather Mushroom (!), and the evil witch Baba Yaga, who lives in a house perched atop giant chicken legs. Yet the forest also houses kindly Father Frost, who paints the landscape with snow and offers guidance to those who seek wisdom. Needless to say, Nastenka and Ivanushka meet and fall in love. Whether they have a happy ending depends on how they conquer the fantastic obstacles before them. The most impressive aspect of this film and the other Russian "fairy tale" imports is the conviction of the actors and the direction. For example, Ivanushka must face an army of living trees come to life under Baba Yaga's spell. Men in rubber suits? You betcha. Look fake after the first cut? Yup. But for that initial moment, the magic is absolutely there. The same applies with Ivanushka's transformation into a bear-man. Definitely low-tech, but his desire to do a good deed to break the spell speaks to the child—and responsible adult—in everyone. The full-frame transfer bursts with saturated, storybook colors. Detail delineation is superb, with deep blacks and excellent contrast. I may remember seeing the movie from holiday morning reruns on television, but the movie never looked this crisp and clean. The source material shows a few blemishes (as well as editor marks for the opening and closing narrator scenes) but not to distraction. Digital or compression artifacts? Nyet. The audio and subtitles come in three flavors: Russian, English, and French. The 5.1 audio contain quite a bit of dynamic range and envelopment, mainly exhibited in N. Budashkin's whimsical balalaika-heavy compositions. The English audio is the original dubbed soundtrack from the American release. The Russian soundtrack shows subtle differences in the dialogue (obviously with the English subtitles engaged). Purists will hate me, but I prefer the dubbed version and suggest this audio option to first-time viewers. —GH/MM *AKA:* Morozko; Jack Frost.

Movie: 🎞🎞🎞 **DVD:** 🎞🎞🎞

Image Ent. (UPC 014381024821). Full frame. Dolby Digital 5.1 Surround. $24.99. Keepcase. *LANG:* Russian; French; English. *SUB:* English; French; Russian. *FEATURES:* Theatrical trailers • Photo gallery • Archival materials • Video interview with Natalya Sedakh • Folk songs.

1966 84m/C *RU* Aleksandr Kyvylya, Natalya Sedykh, Eduard Izotov, Inna Churikova, Georgy Millyar, Anatoly Kubatsky; *D:* Alexander Row; *W:* Alexander Row; *C:* Dmitry Surensky.

Faust

Mephistopheles (Jannings under a host of disguises) wagers an angelic emissary that he can corrupt Faust's spirit, with the damnation of all humanity as the prize. The aging sage Faust (Ekman) indeed sells his soul in exchange for easing the misery of the townspeople struck with the Plague. Once seduced by the promise of renewed youth, however, Faust trades his altruistic intentions for soulless gratification. When he falls in love with the innocent Gretchen (Horn), Faust may yet have one final chance at saving his soul (and humanity's) from the encroaching inferno. Kino Video recently released a new DVD boasting digital mastering from "35mm archival materials." Unfortunately, the source elements exhibit quite a bit of damage and decay. The full-frame transfer varies in quality. Sometimes the image is crisp and clear with excellent contrast, while in other moments (mostly contained in the second half) the fuzzy, murky picture drowns all details. Deep black levels and good gray tones help flesh out the cleaner sections. Timothy Brock's expansive symphonic score (specially composed for the film and performed by the Olympia Chamber Orchestra) echoes Wagnerian motifs and Bernard Herrmann orchestrations as well as serving up tender and comical passages. The Dolby Digital stereo projects amply, sometimes sounding a little too "big" against the aging visuals. —EP *AKA:* Faust-Eine deutsche Volkssage.

Movie: 🎞🎞🎞 ½ **DVD:** 🎞🎞 ½

Kino on Video (UPC 738329020729). Full frame. Dolby Digital Stereo. $29.95. Keepcase. *LANG:* Silent. *FEATURES:* Photo gallery.

1926 117m/B *GE* Emil Jannings, Warner Fuetterer, Gosta Ekman, Camilla Horn; *D:* F.W. Murnau; *W:* Hans Kyser; *C:* Carl Hoffmann; *M:* Timothy Brock, Werner R. Heymann.

Faust: Love of the Damned

Following in the footsteps of *The Crow* and *Spawn,* another tortured comic book hero is resurrected to seek revenge with cape, super powers, attitude, etc. Mark Frost is fine in the title role. Providing able assistance are genre stalwarts Jeffrey Combs and Andrew Divoff. DVD handles the many dark scenes quite well. The Barcelona locations look enough like America. Given the genre and the budget, DVD image is very good. The story is not nearly as violent or sexually explicit as the source material. On his commentary track, director Yuzna takes an explanatory approach. —*MM*

Movie: 🎬🎬 ½ **DVD:** 🎬🎬🎬 ½
Lion's Gate Home Ent. (cat #7702, UPC 031398770220). Widescreen. Dolby Digital 5.1 Surround Stereo. $24.99. Keepcase. *LANG:* English. *SUB:* English; French; Spanish. *CAP:* English. *FEATURES:* 24 chapters • Commentary: director • Production commentary • Trailer.
2000 (R) 96m/C Mark Frost, Andrew Divoff, Jeffrey Combs, Isabel Brook; *D:* Brian Yuzna; *W:* David Quinn; *C:* Jacques Haitkin; *M:* Xavier Capellas.

The Favor

In a change of pace, men take a backseat to the women in this diverting romantic comedy. Kathy (Kozak) seeks to relieve the boredom of her marriage through best friend Emily's (McGovern) tryst with Kathy's old beau Tom (Wahl). Or so she thinks until Em spills all the juicy details. Good comic performances, an attractive cast, and witty dialogue help overcome the plot's sheer silliness. DVD presents an acceptably bright image and clear sound for the material. On a conventional TV monitor, the full-frame option looks slightly sharper, though this is not a film that's going to test the limits of anyone's video system. —*MM*

Movie: 🎬🎬 ½ **DVD:** 🎬🎬🎬
MGM Home Ent. (cat #1002962, UPC 027616871497). Widescreen (1.85:1) anamorphic; full frame. Dolby Digital Surround. $14.98. Keepcase. *LANG:* English; French; Spanish. *SUB:* English; French; Spanish. *CAP:* English. *FEATURES:* 16 chapters • 4 trailers.
1992 (R) 97m/C Harley Jane Kozak, Elizabeth McGovern, Bill Pullman, Brad Pitt, Ken Wahl, Larry Miller, Holland Taylor; *D:* Donald Petrie; *W:* Josann McGibbon, Sara Parriott; *C:* Tim Suhrstedt; *M:* Thomas Newman.

The Fear Chamber

Near the end of his career, Boris Karloff made this and three other Mexican "horror films" in L.A. Fortunately, he was written out of the story before he could be completely embarrassed by the silliness of the rest of it involving a mutant rock monster and topless go-go dancing. (Trust me, it's not fun.) The credits on this disc are in Spanish. Overall image quality is poor. Disc looks like it was made from a duplicated tape. The wraparound material is deliberately distressed. —*MM* *AKA:* Torture Zone; Chamber of Fear; La Camara del Terror; Torture Chamber.

Movie: woof **DVD:** 🎬 ½
Retromedia Entertainment Inc. (cat #008, UPC 802993789197). Widescreen letterboxed. $12.99. Keepcase. *LANG:* English. *FEATURES:* 8 chapters • Intermission spots • Trailers • Bloopers.
1968 88m/C *MX* Boris Karloff, Yerye Beirut, Julissa, Carlos East, Sandra Chavez, Eva Muller, Pamela Rosas, Santanon, Isela Vega; *D:* Juan Ibanez, Jack Hill; *W:* Jack Hill, Luis Enrique Vergara; *C:* Austin McKinney, Raul Dominguez.

Fearless Dragon

A pedicab driver (Philip Ko) and a travelling student (Leung Ka-Yan) are accused of stealing a treasure meant to help refugees. They try to capture each other to claim the reward, while staying one step ahead of the law. After getting in various scrapes together, the pair team up to catch the real thief. The team of Leung and Ko are good at both fighting and knockabout comedy, but both performers were capable of better things. Leung was a regular fixture in Sammo Hung's films of the period, and all three leads ended up directing later in their careers. The overall attitude is tiresomely juvenile, though there's damn fine fighting in the finale. Though apparently set in old China, references are made to modern superheroes and the movie *Midnight Express.* The tape version was hosted by Rudy Ray Moore as part of the *Shaolin Dolemite Collection,* but the DVD is much more straightforward. Despite the "full frame" notice on the back cover, the picture is nicely letterboxed and looks reasonably good for a film of its age. —*BT* *AKA:* Fearless Dragons.

Movie: 🎬🎬 **DVD:** 🎬 ½
Xenon Ent. (cat #XEXA6089DVD, UPC 000799608920). Widescreen letterboxed. $14.98. Keepcase. *LANG:* English. *FEATURES:* 6 chapters.
1979 83m/C *HK* Philip Ko, Kar-Yan Leung, Lung-Wai Wang; *D:* Lee Chiu; *C:* Wan Shing Law; *M:* Tai Kong Ng.

Female Trouble

Divine leads a troublesome existence in this $25,000 picture. She turns to a life of crime and decadence, seeking to live out her philosophy: "Crime is beauty." Look closely at the Divine rape scene where she plays both rapist and victim. Climax of her deviant ways comes with her unusual night club act, for which the law shows no mercy. Trashy, campy; for die-hard Waters fans. It's hard to tell, but overall this transfer seems to be the worst one in the New Line John Waters Collection series. The picture seems slightly grungier than even the old original VHS release, and there are even some artifacts, something that is not a problem with any of the other discs. The original mono soundtrack is included, as is a new Dolby Surround remix. As with the *Pink Flamingos* soundtrack, there's not a whole lot of difference; in fact, I prefer the mono. Add another Waters commentary where he's having as much fun talking as we are listening and how can you go wrong? Available only as part of a double feature with *Pink Flamingos* (see separate entry). —*JO*

Movie: 🎬🎬 ½ **DVD:** 🎬🎬 ½
New Line (cat #N5232, UPC 7940435232-29). Widescreen (1.85:1) letterboxed. Dolby Digital Mono. $30.99. Custom. *LANG:* English. *SUB:* English. *FEATURES:* 24 chapters • Theatrical trailer • Commentary: John Waters.
1974 (R) 95m/C Divine, David Lochary, Mary Vivian Pearce, Mink Stole, Edith Massey, Cookie Mueller, Susan Walsh, Michael Potter, Ed Peranio, Paul Swift, George Figgs, Susan Lowe, Channing Wilroy, Pat Moran, Elizabeth Coffey, George Stover; *D:* John Waters; *W:* John Waters; *C:* John Waters.

Ferngully

When the evil Hexxus (voice of Curry) threatens to destroy the magical Ferngully, its woodland inhabitants band together to put a stop to his deadly plans. Led by Crysta (Mathis), an impetuous young fairy, and Zak (Ward), a human caught in the middle of their perilous crusade, a small band of unlikely heroes stands up against the most dangerous threat to ever face their magical wooded home: deforestation. A shout to the deforestation conflicts that plagued the planet during the mid-'90s, this animated feature sports an A-list of voice talent including Robin Williams, Christian Slater, and Cheech Marin teaming up to create forestry awareness. This film lacks much in the way of a solid and cohesive plotline, and does little to educate its intended younger audience beyond what they may already know of the dangers facing this planet's rainforests. This picture quality on this DVD release is crisp and clear. There are no noticeable defects in the film quality, and no noticeable degradation in the image. The included 5.1 Surround track sounds good and makes adequate use of all six speakers. The Surround effects are nicely done in some of the scenes with the tractors and heavy equipment, and Silvestri's musical score still sounds clean and new. —*EL*

Movie: 🎬🎬 ½ **DVD:** 🎬🎬🎬
20th Century Fox (cat #2003297, UPC 0245420032977). Widescreen (1.85:1) anamorphic; full frame. English Dolby 5.1 Surround; Dolby Surround. $19.98. Keepcase. *LANG:* English; French. *SUB:* English; French; Spanish. *CAP:* English. *FEATURES:* Theatrical trailer • 24 chapters.

1992 (G) 80m/C D: Bill Kroyer; **W:** Jim Cox; **M:** Alan Silvestri; **V:** Samantha Mathis, Christian Slater, Robin Williams, Tim Curry, Jonathan Ward, Grace Zabriskie, Richard "Cheech" Marin, Thomas Chong, Tone Loc, Jim Cox.

Fever

Artist Nick Parker (Thomas) struggles to make ends meet by teaching a night class at the local community college and living in a run-down apartment. When his landlord is murdered, Parker is visited by fits of sleepwalking and begins to question his sanity. The film is atmospheric and tense, but can't quite sustain its momentum all the way through. The disc looks good, with a gritty feel that helps create suspense, but the advertised 5.1 sound is actually a two-channel mix. —BG
Movie: 🎵🎵 ½ **DVD:** 🎵🎵🎵
Studio Home Ent. (cat #7655D, UPC 6581-49765528). Widescreen anamorphic. Dolby 2.0. $24.99. Keepcase. *LANG:* English. *SUB:* English; French; Spanish. *FEATURES:* 30 chapters ➡ Commentary: director ➡ Cast & crew interviews ➡ Behind-the-scenes ➡ Trailers.
1999 (R) 90m/C Henry Thomas, David O'Hara, Bill Duke, Teri Hatcher, Sandor Tecsi, Irma St. Paul, Marisol Padilla Sanchez; **D:** Alex Winter; **W:** Alex Winter; **C:** Joe DeSalvo; **M:** Joe Delia.

Fiddler on the Roof [2 SE]

Based on the long-running Broadway musical. The poignant story of Tevye, a poor Jewish milkman at the turn of the century in a small Ukrainian village, and his five dowry-less daughters, his lame horse, his wife, and his companionable relationship with God. Topol, an Israeli who played the role in London, is charming, if not quite as wonderful as Zero Mostel, the Broadway star. (The film might have had a longer cinematic shelf life if Mostel had reprised his role with Richard Lester directing him, as Lester did in *A Funny Thing Happened on the Way to the Forum*.) Finely detailed set decoration and choreography, and strong performances from the entire cast create a sense of intimacy in spite of near-epic proportions of the production. This is the second release of *Fiddler* on DVD and the improvement is immediately noticeable. The anamorphic is far sharper than the letterboxed edition, and the 5.1 soundtrack is much more full bodied and ambient. There's not too much on the low end, but that's most likely because of the film's vintage. Colors are vivid and contrasts are good. The only problem seems to be in darker shots (and dimmer parts of the screen overall) where some detail is lost. Overall though, the upgrade is worth it. The new disc also includes more supplementals than the previous edition, including a hit and miss commentary by Jewison and Topol. —JO/MO
Movie: 🎵🎵🎵 ½ **DVD:** 🎵🎵🎵🎵

MGM Home Ent. (cat #1002566, UPC 027616867674). Widescreen (2.35:1) anamorphic. Dolby Digital 5.1. $19.98. Keepcase. *LANG:* English. *SUB:* English; Spanish; French. *CAP:* English. *FEATURES:* 36 chapters ➡ Commentary: Norman Jewison, Topol ➡ New DVD intro by Norman Jewison ➡ *Norman Jewison, Filmmaker* documentary ➡ "Any Day Now," sung by Paul Michael Glaser (Perchik) deleted from film ➡ "Tevye's Dream" in full color with Norman Jewison commentary ➡ Stories of Sholom Aleichem read by Norman Jewison ➡ Historical background with Norman Jewison commentary ➡ Storyboard-to-film comparison ➡ 1979 re-release theatrical trailer.
1971 (G) 184m/C Chaim Topol, Norma Crane, Leonard Frey, Molly Picon, Paul Mann, Rosalind Harris, Michele Marsh, Neva Small, Paul Michael Glaser, Ray Lovelock; **D:** Norman Jewison; **W:** Joseph Stein; **C:** Oswald Morris; **M:** John Williams. *AWARDS:* Oscars '71: Cinematog., Sound, Orig. Song Score and/or Adapt.; Golden Globes '72: Actor—Mus./Comedy (Topol), Film—Mus./Comedy; *NOM:* Oscars '71: Actor (Topol), Art Dir./Set Dec., Director (Jewison), Picture, Support. Actor (Frey).

Fidel

Biopic of the life and revolutionary struggles of Fidel Castro (Martin). It's clear that writer Stephen Tolkin and director David Attwood admire Castro's efforts to fashion Marxist theory into real life, but this is fundamentally a political tract, more honest than Maoist "people's art" but with too much of an agenda to go over without viewers' wariness and some genuine tedium. Very clean DVD transfer and good sound. —MO
Movie: 🎵🎵 ½ **DVD:** 🎵🎵🎵
Artisan Ent. (cat #11519, UPC 70772911-5199). Full frame. Dolby Digital Surround. $19.98. Keepcase. *LANG:* English. *CAP:* English. *FEATURES:* 36 chapters ➡ Production notes and cast bios ➡ John F. Kennedy's speech on the Cuban Missile Crisis.
2002 140m/C Victor Huggo Martin, Gael Garcia Bernal, Patricia Velasquez, Maurice Compte, Tony Plana, Guillermo Diaz, Margarita d'Francisco, Enrique Arce; **D:** David Attwood; **W:** Stephen Tolkin; **C:** Checco Varese; **M:** John Altman.

The Field [Artisan]

This should in no way be mistaken as part of the "quaint village comedy" genre movies, such as *Waking Ned Devine* or *Chocolat*. This is real drama. Richard Harris plays "Bull" McCabe, a cattle farmer who rents the field he has used to tend his herd for decades. McCabe's son Tadgh (Bean) terrorizes the widow that owns the field, prompting her to return to her own people in England and put the field up for auction. The small Irish town where the story is set is divided between those residents who agree with McCabe, that the land should be his, and those who think he's a mean bastard and should shut up about it. Tom Berenger plays an American

investor, returning to his Irish roots with the intention of lifting up this little town's economy with limestone mining. He intends to buy the field, and pave it over for his factory. As in the great tragedies of old, two well-intended characters, possessed of specific goals, collide with explosive results. The character of McCabe is part King Lear, part Brecht's Mother Courage, sacrificing everything in a desperate attempt for what he believes is right, while entirely unaware that he is his own worst enemy. Richard Harris is perfect in this role, cutting to the bone of McCabe with an actor's scalpel in a scene at the local priest's home, where he explains what the land means to him while finding himself surrounded by betrayal. It's a rare piece of acting and well worth the viewing. The DVD transfer is clean, the sound is good, but you may have to strain a little to hear through the thick Irish accents. —JAS
Movie: 🎵🎵🎵🎵 **DVD:** 🎵🎵🎵 ½
Artisan Ent. (cat #12494, UPC 01223612-4948). Widescreen anamorphic. Mono. $24.98. Keepcase. *LANG:* English. *FEATURES:* 19 chapters ➡ Cast & crew information.
1990 (PG-13) 113m/C *GB* Richard Harris, Tom Berenger, John Hurt, Sean Bean, Brenda Fricker, Frances Tomelty, John Cowley, Sean McGinley, Jenny Conroy; **D:** Jim Sheridan; **W:** Jim Sheridan; **C:** Jack Conroy; **M:** Elmer Bernstein. *AWARDS: NOM:* Oscars '90: Actor (Harris).

15 Minutes

New York cop (and unapologetic publicity hound) De Niro teams up with arson investigator Burns to track down a couple of European immigrant murderers who are videotaping their violent crimes for celebrity purposes. The few valid points that filmmaker Herzfeld has to make about society's fascination with the dark side are undermined by a conclusion that's equally predictable and ridiculous. The surprise is Grammer who's very good as a sleazy talk-show host. DVD delivers an absolutely accurate reproduction of the big-screen image and sound field. The main attractions here are New Line's extensive "Infinifilm" extras (listed below) which take a deeper look at the film's serious side. —MM
Movie: 🎵🎵 ½ **DVD:** 🎵🎵🎵 ½
New Line (cat #N5166, UPC 7940435166-27). Widescreen anamorphic. Dolby Digital 5.1 Surround Stereo; Dolby Digital Surround. $26.98. Keepcase. *LANG:* English. *CAP:* English. *FEATURES:* 21 chapters ➡ "Making of" featurette ➡ "Does Crime Pay?" featurette ➡ Trivia subtitle track ➡ Commentary: John Herzfeld ➡ Deleted scenes with commentary ➡ Video footage from actor's perspective ➡ Music video ➡ Trailer ➡ DVD-ROM features.
2001 (R) 120m/C Robert De Niro, Edward Burns, Kelsey Grammer, Avery Brooks, Melina Kanakaredes, Vera Farmiga, Karel Roden, Oleg Taktarov, John DiResta, James Handy, Darius McCrary, Charlize Theron, Kim Cattrall, David Alan

Grier; **D:** John Herzfeld; **W:** John Herzfeld; **C:** Jean-Yves Escoffier; **M:** Anthony Marinelli, J. Peter Robinson.

The Fifth Element [2 SB]

"Superbit" edition improves upon the earlier release (reviewed in *Book 1*) by making the riotously colorful image even brighter and sharper. The DTS sound is as aggressive as the picture. The movie itself is still a mixed bag, but it has never looked better, even compared to the theatrical version which I saw at the MPAA's delightful screening room. —*MM*
Movie: 🎬🎬 ½ **DVD:** 🎬🎬🎬🎬
Columbia Tristar (cat #07574, UPC 0433-96075740). Widescreen (2.35:1) anamorphic. Dolby Digital 5.1 Surround Stereo; DTS 5.1. $27.95. Slipcased keepcase. *LANG:* English. *SUB:* English; French; Spanish; Portuguese; Chinese; Thai. *FEATURES:* 28 chapters.
1997 (PG-13) 125m/C Bruce Willis, Gary Oldman, Ian Holm, Milla Jovovich, Luke Perry, Lee Evans, Chris Tucker, Brion James, Tommy (Tiny) Lister, John Neville, John Bluthal, Maiwenn Le Besco, Mathieu Kassovitz; **D:** Luc Besson; **W:** Luc Besson; **C:** Thierry Arbogast; **M:** Eric Serra. *AWARDS:* British Acad. '97: Visual FX; Cesar '98: Art Dir./Set Dec., Cinematog., Director (Besson); *NOM:* Oscars '97: Sound FX Editing; MTV Movie Awards '98: Fight (Milla Jovovich/aliens); Golden Raspberries '97: Worst Support. Actress (Jovovich), Worst New Star (Tucker).

Fifth of July

Theatre is a medium best experienced live, so it was a wise move on the part of the makers of this television production of Langford Wilson's award-winning play *Fifth of July* to construct it more as a movie than as a stage play. While the production does utilize what is essentially one set, the action is given enough freedom to escape the confines of the typical stage and take on a more three-dimensional feel. The play is set in Lebanon, Missouri, and takes place on the fourth and fifth of July, 1977. Richard Thomas stars as Kenneth Talley, a physically impaired Vietnam veteran who has come to Lebanon to take on a job as a teacher. He lives with his lover, Jed (Jeff Daniels), who is supportive of Kenneth, but despises his alcoholism and mood swings. While there is already tension in the household, things get even more heated when Kenneth's boyhood friend John Landis (Jonathan Hogan) and his wife Gwen (Swoosie Kurtz) come to visit. Kenneth is sitting on a great deal of rage and secrets, and they will all spill out before the holiday is over. The story is quite gripping from the outset and the characters are wonderfully realized. Co-director Marshall W. Mason helmed the original stage play, and does a fine job here. Kurtz won a Tony for her part in the original production. Look for *Sex and the City*'s Cynthia Nixon in a small role. This production was shot on video and is presented full frame on this DVD. Due to the limitations in video technology in 1982, there are some problems revealed by this digital transfer. The image is cloudy and there is a great deal of video artifacting and streaking. The image is blurry at times and the colors are quite dull. On a positive note, the Dolby Digital Mono audio track provides crisp dialogue, with no overt hissing, which allows Wilson's poignant dialogue to come through clearly. —*ML* **AKA:** Lanford Wilson's Fifth of July.
Movie: 🎬🎬🎬 **DVD:** 🎬🎬
Image Ent. (cat #ID875B DDVD, UPC 0143-8108759). Full frame. Dolby Digital Mono. $24.99. Keepcase. *LANG:* English. *FEATURES:* Filmographies ● Bonus trailers ● 16 chapters.
1982 116m/C Richard Thomas, Jeff Daniels, Swoosie Kurtz, Cynthia Nixon, Jonathan Hogan; **D:** Marshall Mason; **W:** Lanford Wilson.

Fighting Ace

An orphan sets out to avenge the murder of his parents, but must first learn enough kung fu to beat up the villain. He finds several capable masters, and schemes to keep them from knowing he has more than one teacher. Chopsocky mayhem ensues. I'm sure the picture and audio quality is better than some VHS tapes. —*BG*
Movie: 🎬 ½ **DVD:** 🎬 ½
Xenon Ent. (cat #XE XA 6287DVD, UPC 000799628720). Full frame. $14.98. Keepcase. *LANG:* English (dubbed). *FEATURES:* 6 chapters ● "Best Chops & Kicks:" scenes from Wu-Tang Collection DVDs.
1979 77m/C Liu Chang Liang, Lung Chun Erl.

Fighting Rats of Tobruk

Australian film about the Egyptian campaign in World War II attempts to take a slightly documentary approach to the subject. It's notable mostly for providing an early role for Peter Finch. DVD is not much of an improvement over VHS tape, though the title appears never to have been available on home video. Night scenes are extremely muddy, but that appears to come from the original. Normal signs of wear are obvious throughout, as is a light static hiss. —*MM*
Movie: 🎬🎬 **DVD:** 🎬🎬
Winstar Home Ent. (cat #FLV5300, UPC 720917530024). Full frame. $14.98. Keepcase. *LANG:* English. *FEATURES:* DVD production credits ● Filmographies ● Trailers ● 16 chapters.
1944 71m/C *AU* Grant Taylor, Peter Finch, Chips Rafferty, Pauline Garrick; **D:** Charles Chauvel; **C:** George Heath.

Final

Actor Campbell Scott makes his solo directorial debut (after co-directing the critical hit *Big Night* and a TV version of *Hamlet*) with this Kafkaesque psychological thriller. Denis Leary stars as Bill, a man who wakes up in a hospital with no real recollection of how he got there. He is convinced that he is in the future, having been cryogenically frozen, and that the hospital is actually a government facility, where he will soon be executed. Dr. Ann Robinson (Hope Davis) is the psychiatrist assigned to Bill's case, and she does her best to comfort and convince him that as soon as he is stable and can remember what brought him to the hospital, he will be released. Bill is very resistant, and even violent, at first, but as his memories begin to return, he realizes that his situation is much more serious than he first thought. Most of *Final* could have easily been staged as a play, as the majority of the action takes place in Bill's room. But Scott has chosen to intercut the conversations between Ann and Bill with flashbacks to Bill's past, which help to tell his story. The film is masterfully edited and the cutting between past and present is seamless. However, the movie is too long for its own good and it takes 70 minutes for anything to really happen. At that point, the film takes a sudden, jarring shift which definitely increases the drama, but also brings many plot inconsistencies to light as well. Leary is excellent in this dramatic role, and Davis's cold performance is good as well. Scott shows great promise, but the finished product is disappointing. The movie was shot on digital video, but has a polished, professional look that resembles film in most shots. Minor artifacting and video distortion are to be seen here, but for the most part, the image is stable and the colors are good. The Dolby Stereo provides clear dialogue and fine reproduction of the grating score. Do not watch the trailer first, as it gives away many of the film's secrets. —*ML*
Movie: 🎬🎬 ½ **DVD:** 🎬🎬 ½
Lion's Gate Home Ent. (cat #8064D, UPC 031398806424). Widescreen (1.85:1) anamorphic. Dolby Stereo. $24.99. Keepcase. *LANG:* English. *CAP:* English. *FEATURES:* Trailer ● 24 chapters.
2001 (R) 111m/C Denis Leary, Hope Davis, J.C. MacKenzie, Jim Gaffigan; **D:** Campbell Scott; **W:** Bruce McIntosh; **C:** Dan Gillham; **M:** Guy Davis.

Final Fantasy: The Spirits Within

This animated film has the distinction of being the first feature-length computer-animated work to use photo-realistic artificial actors. It also has the distinction of being a movie that killed the film production company which created it, due to its lack of performance at the boxoffice. Despite that, the film is a fun and fascinating sci-fi romp. *Final Fantasy* takes place in the future, where alien invaders have made Earth a desolate wasteland. Dr. Aki Ross (voiced by Ming Na) is a scientist hard at work on finding a way to stop the aliens. With the help of a group of soldiers led by ex-flame Captain Gray Edwards (voiced by Alec Baldwin), Aki travels the globe looking

for elements with which to destroy the invaders. However, the evil military leader General Hein (voiced by James Woods) disagrees with Aki's methods and wants to take an offensive approach. The animation in *Final Fantasy* is simply fascinating, as the characters truly resemble actual humans at times. The problem with the film is the needlessly convoluted plot, which some will find very hard to follow. Science-fiction enthusiasts will love the film, but a general audience may only appreciate the pretty pictures. With the *Final Fantasy* DVD, we get a stupendous 2-disc set that boasts a flawless transfer of the film (which was taken directly from a digital source). The picture is sharp and clear, bereft of any flaws. The colors are splendid and the picture shows a true depth. The Dolby Digital 5.1 audio track also performs well, offering clean dialogue, crisp music, nice Surround sound effects, and a very rich bass. Many times while watching a movie, the viewer may wonder "How did they do that?" Well, the *Final Fantasy* DVD will certainly answer that question, as it contains hours of documentaries and behind-the-scenes footage, which explain how the digital magic was created. —*ML*
Movie: 🎞🎞🎞 **DVD:** 🎞🎞🎞🎞
Columbia Tristar (cat #06249, UPC 04339-6062498). Widescreen (1.85:1) anamorphic. Dolby Digital 5.1; Dolby Surround. $29.95. Keepcase. *LANG:* English; French. *SUB:* English; French. *CAP:* English. *FEATURES:* Audio commentaries • Isolated score with commentary • Storyboards • Theatrical trailers • Production notes • "Making of" documentary • Deleted scenes • Editing workshop • Character files • 28 chapters.
2001 (PG-13) 104m/C D: Hironobu Sakaguchi; **W:** Al Reinert, Jeff Vintar; **M:** Elliot Goldenthal; **V:** Ming Na, Alec Baldwin, Steve Buscemi, Peri Gilpin, Ving Rhames, Donald Sutherland, James Woods, Keith David, Jean Simmons.

The Final Programme

Groovy '70s style sci-fi based on the popular (popular among the LSD crowd anyway) novel by Michael Moorcock. The art director must have borrowed every colored floodlight in London, just as the costume designer gobbled up all the white polyester, to give the film its "unique" futuristic look. What the film lacks in plot logic, it more than makes up for with plain old charisma. This, no doubt, comes from the leads Jon Finch *(The Horror of Franken-stein, Frenzy)*, who plays swinging Pulitzer prize–winning physicist and all-around swinging guy Jerry Cornelius, and his match, the bisexual, possibly cannibalistic computer expert, Miss Brunner (Jenny Runacre); who is trying to put together the final program for immortality. There are also nice bit parts from Patrick Magee and Sterling Hayden. The film borrows heavily in tone and pace from fun British shows like *The Avengers* and *The Prisoner*. Memo-

rable dialogue includes "Throw out your needle and come out with your veins clean." This is not a good show for anyone who wants to know what just happened once the credits roll. The print has some dust specks and there is the occasional bad looping on the soundtrack, but overall it's still a passable transfer for a cultish '70s acid flick. —*CA* **AKA:** The Last Days of Man on Earth.
Movie: 🎞🎞½ **DVD:** 🎞🎞
Anchor Bay (cat #DV11642, UPC 0131311-64299). Widescreen (1.77:1) anamorphic. Dolby Digital Mono. $24.90. Keepcase. *LANG:* English. *FEATURES:* 24 chapters • Commentary: Fuest, Runacre, moderated by journalist Jonathan Sothcott • U.S. theatrical trailer.
1973 85m/C *GB* Hugh Griffith, Harry Andrews, Jon Finch, Jenny Runacre, Sterling Hayden, Patrick Magee, Sarah Douglas; **D:** Robert Fuest; **W:** Robert Fuest; **C:** Norman Warwick; **M:** Gerry Mulligan, Paul Beaver, Bernard Krause.

Find a Place to Die

It's difficult to judge the content of this little-known spaghetti western because the image and sound are so degraded on this disc. Story concerns Lisa (Petit), whose brother is killed guarding their gold mine. She enlists the help of gunfighter Joe (Hunter) as dozens of other baddies try to get the gold and her. Soundtrack is filled with constant low-level static. There are some registration jitters. Colors are harsh with heavy grain leading to some of the thickest and most artistic pixels I've ever seen. At times, the whole screen seems to swim. —*MM* **AKA:** Joe! Cercati un Posto Per Morire.
Movie: 🎞🎞 **DVD:** 🎞½
VCI (cat #8313, UPC 089859831324). Widescreen letterboxed. Dolby Digital Mono. $9.99. Keepcase. *LANG:* English. *FEATURES:* 12 chapters • Trailers: *Cattle Queen of Montana, Tennessee's Partner*.
1968 89m/C *IT* Jeffrey Hunter, Pascale Petit, Pierro Lulli, Daniela Giordano; **D:** Anthony (Giuliano Carnimeo) Ascot; **W:** Ralph Grave, Al Hine; **C:** Riccardo (Pallton) Pallottini; **M:** Gianni Ferrio.

Finding Buck McHenry

Yet another movie that shows the magic power of baseball. Young Jason Ross (Michael Schiffman) knows everything that there is to know about baseball...or so he thinks. After being cut from his little league team, Jason falls under the tutelage of school custodian Mack Henry (Ossie Davis), who tells Jason all about the great players from the Negro Leagues. Having never heard of these players, Jason does some research and learns of a forgotten player named Buck McHenry. Could Mr. Henry be this famous player? Jason convinces Mr. Henry to coach an expansion team of all of the kids who have been cut from the neighborhood teams, where Mr. Henry's knowledge

about the game of baseball only deepens the mystery. This is a gentle and fun film, which relays an important message about tolerance, acceptance, and honesty. The DVD brings us the film in a full-frame format, offering a clear image, free from major defects. The audio is crisp, providing audible dialogue with no distortion. It would have been nice if the DVD could have contained some information about the real players from the Negro Leagues. —*ML*
Movie: 🎞🎞½ **DVD:** 🎞🎞
Showtime Networks, Inc. (cat #SHO3024, UPC 758445302424). Full frame. Digital Stereo. $19.98. Keepcase. *LANG:* English. *FEATURES:* 18 chapters.
2000 88m/C Ossie Davis, Ruby Dee, Ernie Banks, Michael Schiffman, Duane McLaughlin, Karl Pruner, Megan Bower, Catherine Blythe; **D:** Charles Burnett; **W:** Alfred Slote; **C:** John L. Demps Jr.; **M:** Stephen James Taylor.

Fiona

Abandoned as a baby, Fiona (Thomson) was raised in an abusive home and is now a crack-smoking hooker on the streets of New York. After she kills three cops, she takes refuge in a crackhouse where she hooks up with another burnt-out case who turns out to be her long-lost mom. Film is a blend of harshly lit fiction and footage of real prostitutes and drug addicts. DVD delivers a properly rough, grainy image that's loaded with artifacts. Sound is equally poor. —*MM*
Movie: 🎞½ **DVD:** 🎞½
Vanguard Intl. Cinema (cat #VF9176, UPC 658769917635). Full frame. $29.95. Keepcase. *LANG:* English. *FEATURES:* 12 chapters.
1998 85m/C Anna Thomson, Mike Hodge, Anna Grace, Felicia Maguire; **D:** Amos Kollek; **W:** Amos Kollek; **C:** Ed Talavera; **M:** Alison Gordy.

Fire Alarm

Western star Johnny Mack Brown tries another genre as firefighter Charlie who spends some time romancing career girl Patricia (Francis) after he rescues her kitten. (Really!) Ancient feature is riddled with every flaw imaginable: flecks, blobs, and an intermittent vertical scratch down the left side. Bad static, too. Title is available on the *Great Fire Movies* disc. —*MM*
Movie: 🎞 **DVD:** 🎞½
BFS Video (cat #30293-D, UPC 06680530-2930). Full frame. $9.98. Keepcase. *LANG:* English. *FEATURES:* 6 chapters.
1932 67m/B Johnny Mack Brown, Noel Francis; **D:** Karl Brown; **W:** Karl Brown, I.E. Chadwick.

Firehouse

Tempers and racial prejudices ignite in a lily-white firehouse when a black rookie (Roundtree) replaces a veteran. This made-for-TV emergency drama ran briefly as a series (with a different cast) in 1974.

It's difficult to tell where the deliberately rough-edged cinéma-vérité production values end and the grain begins. In any case, this one has a nice feel for location. It looks better than most of the features in BFS Video's *Great* and *Classic* series. Title is available on the *Great Fire Movies* disc. —*MM*

Movie: 🎬🎬 ½ **DVD:** 🎬🎬
BFS Video (cat #30293-D, UPC 06680530-2930). Full frame. $9.98. Keepcase. *LANG:* English. *FEATURES:* 6 chapters • Talent files.
1972 73m/C Richard Roundtree, Vince Edwards, Andrew Duggan, Richard Jaeckel, Sheila Frazier, Val Avery, Paul LeMat, Michael Lerner; *D:* Alex March; *M:* Tom Scott.

The Firemen's Ball

A movie tailor-made for Western critics, who could praise its artfulness and at the same time trumpet its anti-Communist theme, this one was an instant hit in the U.S., becoming forever associated with the artistic stand made against Soviet oppression in Czechoslovakia. Along with the allegorical animated films of Jiri Trinka and a host of others, an entire liberal wing of Czechoslovensky Film was proud to be a thorn in the side of the Commies. All were promptly put out of business when the Russian tanks rolled into Prague. In their small-town meeting hall, a maladroit committee of volunteer firefighters holds a ball to celebrate the retirement of one of their own, but thanks to poor planning and lack of leadership, the evening quickly devolves into a catastrophe. Nobody can prevent the lottery prizes from being stolen out from under the very noses of those guarding them. A beauty contest turns into an embarrassing farce, and the brigade can't even respond properly to a real fire next door. Even without the production notes on this Criterion DVD, the wit of the film quickly makes it obvious that the stuffy, quarreling, infantile leadership of the volunteer fire brigade represents the ruling politbureau of Communist Czechoslovakia. Everything about the ball is out of control, owing to a total lack of ethics. DVD has a great color transfer, supervised by cameraman Miroslav Ondrícek *(If..., Amadeus)* himself. One of the interesting interviews with director Forman spends a few minutes watching Ondrícek supervise the colorist in the transfer room. —*GE*
AKA: Hori, ma panenko.
Movie: 🎬🎬🎬 ½ **DVD:** 🎬🎬🎬 ½
Criterion (cat #145, UPC 037429165522). Full frame. Dolby Digital Mono. $29.95. Keepcase. *LANG:* Czechoslovakian. *SUB:* English. *FEATURES:* Forman interview • Transfer featurette • 18 chapters • Liner notes by J. Hoberman.
1968 73m/C CZ Vaclav Stockel, Josef Svet; *D:* Milos Forman; *W:* Ivan Passer, Jaroslav Papousek, Vaclav Sasek, Milos Forman; *C:* Miroslav Ondricek; *M:* Karel Mares. *AWARDS:* NOM: Oscars '68: Foreign Film.

Fires Within

Curiously flat romance wastes an attractive cast. After eight years as a political prisoner in Cuba, Nestor (Smits) is released and goes to Miami to be reunited with his wife Isabel (Scacchi) and daughter. Once there, he finds that Isabel has fallen in love with another man (D'Onofrio). Nestor must then choose between attempting to save his family or engaging in more political activism. Performances are restrained but secondary plotlines fizzle. Both wide and full images are fine with no noteworthy flaws. —*MM*
Movie: 🎬 **DVD:** 🎬🎬🎬
MGM Home Ent. (cat #1002752, UPC 027616869500). Widescreen (1.85:1) anamorphic; full frame. Dolby Digital Surround; Mono. $14.95. Keepcase. *LANG:* English; French; Spanish. *SUB:* English; French; Spanish. *CAP:* English. *FEATURES:* 16 chapters • 4 trailers.
1991 (R) 90m/C Jimmy Smits, Greta Scacchi, Vincent D'Onofrio; *D:* Gillian Armstrong; *W:* Cynthia Cidre; *C:* David Gribble; *M:* Maurice Jarre.

Firestarter 2: Rekindled

Sci-Fi Network miniseries sequel to the Stephen King/Drew Barrymore 1984 film finds Charlene "Charlie" McGee (Marguerite Moreau) in heat. Literally. Since last we saw her, she's all grown up, smokin' hot, and shaking her groove thang at a nightclub. Her dance floor grinding resumes outside on the hood of an exceedingly lucky stranger's car, but just before wanton diddling is to commence, she pulls away from Mr. Right Now and slinks down a deserted alley. Passion has stirred her Curse!!! A fiery aura forms around her and soon a wall of flame follows as Ms. Moreau struts toward the camera looking ever-so scrumptious. If only her love life weren't the least of her problems. Enter Malcolm McDowell, who completely steals the flick as über–mad scientist John Rainbird who's obsessed with "his Charlie" and a gaggle of new young mutant marvels he's cooked up. Each of these nose-miners has his own "gift." One can impose his will on others. Another reads minds. There's even a kid whose screams create devastating shockwaves. Comic book sorta fun. Anyway, there's all sorts of plot flying around with nearly three hours to kill. Mostly it boils down to Charlie getting into scraps with the killer kiddos where she growls something like, "You Know What I Can Do!!!" That's when you know it's time to get out the marshmallows. Ogle Ms. Moreau. Savor Malcolm. But ignore Charlie's weenie boy toy (Danny Nucci) and the insufferable post-mondo meltdown epilogue. On DVD, the widescreen image transfer suffers from pronounced grain in darker scenes. Surround audio is mildly explosive. —*NGN*
Movie: 🎬🎬 ½ **DVD:** 🎬🎬 ½

MGM Home Ent. (UPC 696306031727). Widescreen (1.85:1) anamorphic. Dolby Digital 5.1 Surround; Dolby Surround. $19.98. Keepcase. *LANG:* English. *CAP:* English. *FEATURES:* Abbreviated filmographies • Trailers • 20 chapters.
2002 168m/C Marguerite Moreau, Malcolm McDowell, Danny Nucci, Dennis Hopper, Skye McCole Bartusiak, John Dennis Johnston, Darnell Williams, Deborah Van Valkenburgh; *D:* Robert Iscove; *W:* Philip Eisner; *C:* David Boyd.

Firetrap

Crack thief Max Hooper (Cain) is trying to go straight but he takes on the proverbial "one last job" to steal a new computer chip from a highrise. When it's set afire, the burglar must become a hero. Video premiere is built on even more clichés, which are handled with dispatch. Full-frame image and sound are no real improvement on the VHS tape. The transparency of the cut-rate pyrotechnics and other CGI effects will be about the same on either medium. —*MM*
Movie: 🎬🎬 **DVD:** 🎬🎬 ½
Studio Home Ent. (cat #ST7926D, UPC 658149792623). Full frame. Dolby Digital Stereo. $24.98. Keepcase. *LANG:* English. *SUB:* English; Spanish. *CAP:* English. *FEATURES:* 24 chapters • Trailer.
2001 (R) 99m/C Dean Cain, Richard Tyson, Lori Petty, Mel Harris, James Storm, Vanessa Angel, John O'Hurley, Elena Sahagun, Steven Williams; *D:* Harris Done; *W:* Richard Preston Jr., Diane Fine; *C:* Mark W. Gray; *M:* Sean Murray.

First Degree

The smallest company barbecue in history finds six high-strung tech employees getting on each other's nerves. No one seems to care that the company's president was kidnapped and murdered a few months ago except his wife (Black), who's determined to make life difficult for the remaining employees, who may or may not have been involved in her husband's death. The haphazard timeframe of this suspense-comedy makes Tarantino's films seem linear. Picture and sound are adequate, but this reviewer's DVD didn't include any extra features, such as a menu or chapter links. —*BG*
Movie: 🎬 ½ **DVD:** 🎬🎬
York Ent. (cat #YPD-1172, UPC 75072311-7225). Full frame. Dolby 5.1. $14.99. Keepcase. *LANG:* English.
2001 83m/C Karen Black, Jack Scalia, Kimberley Kates, Erika Eleniak, James Wilder, C. Thomas Howell; *D:* Stephen Eckelberry; *W:* Karen Black, Richmond Riedel; *C:* Susan Emerson.

First Love and Other Pains / One of Them

This program consists of two gay-themed films, both slightly less than feature length. In *First Love*, a Hong Kong college student falls in love with an older British

professor. In *One of Them,* two New Zealand youths struggle with their sexual identity and its place in their society. Both stories are predictable, and don't have much new to offer. Picture and sound quality aren't much improved over tape. —*BG*
Movie: 🎵 ½ **DVD:** 🎵🎵 ½
First Run Features (cat #FRF 909815D, UPC 720229909815). Widescreen letterboxed. $29.95. Keepcase. *LANG:* Cantonese and English. *SUB:* English. *FEATURES:* 21 chapters • Stills gallery • Trailer.
1999 97m/C Edward Strode, Alex Wong, Ciaran Pennington, Cameron J. Watt; *D:* Simon Chung, Stewart Main; *W:* Simon Chung, Peter Wells; *C:* Ping Hung Wong, Stewart Main.

First Men in the Moon
An International team of astronauts lands on the moon and discovers an aged British flag and a note. They track the note to elderly Arnold Bedford (Judd) where he recounts an amazing tale: in 1899, oddball experimenter Cavor (Jeffries) succeeds in launching a ship with himself, ne'er do-well Bedford, and his fiancée, Kate (Hyer). Arriving on the moon, they encounter a strange race of insect-like men. This, the only Ray Harryhausen film shot in a 'Scope, widescreen format, successfully utilizes the panoramic compositions to create a complete, involving world. The story and characters are particularly strong and the film has a wonderful sense of adventure. It bares strong similarities to the many Jules Verne adaptations of the period and has a similarly merry (and oft silly) sense of humor. The music by Laurie Johnson is a worthy successor to Bernard Herrmann's Harryhausen scores. The transfer is richly colored and razor sharp. Grain is minimal and digital edging is kept to a minimum. The multi-channel sound conveys the involving theatrical experience perfectly. The impressive, bold music score sounds terrific. The small photo gallery and menu images are typical of most Columbia releases; that is, presented at a painfully low resolution with images that are hideous and noisy. The sleeve art is particularly lousy. ("This Is Dynamation" featurette and "The Ray Harryhausen Chronicles" documentary are covered in *Book 2* in the review for *Sinbad and the Eye of the Tiger.*) —*DG*
Movie: 🎵🎵🎵 **DVD:** 🎵🎵🎵 ½
Columbia Tristar (cat #05845, UPC 04339-6058453). Widescreen (2.35:1) anamorphic. Dolby Digital 4.0 Surround. $24.95. Keepcase. *LANG:* English. *SUB:* English; French; Spanish; Portuguese; Chinese; Korean; Thai. *CAP:* English. *FEATURES:* 28 chapters • Photo gallery • "This Is Dynamation" featurette • "The Harryhausen Chronicles" featurette • Trailers.
1964 103m/C *GB* Martha Hyer, Edward Judd, Lionel Jeffries, Erik Chitty, Peter Finch; *D:* Nathan (Hertz) Juran; *W:* Nigel Kneale, Jan Read; *C:* Wilkie Cooper; *M:* Laurie Johnson.

The First Power
A detective (Phillips) and a psychic (Griffith) join forces to track down a serial killer (Kober) who, after being executed, uses his satanic powers to kill again. DVD delivers this unmitigated junk with a pale color scheme and often hazy light. —*MM*
Movie: 🎵 ½ **DVD:** 🎵🎵 ½
MGM Home Ent. (cat #1002326, UPC 027616865458). Widescreen (1.85:1) anamorphic. Dolby Digital Surround Stereo. $14.98. Keepcase. *LANG:* English. *SUB:* French; Spanish. *CAP:* English. *FEATURES:* 16 chapters • Trailer.
1989 90m/C Lou Diamond Phillips, Tracy Griffith, Jeff Kober, Mykelti Williamson, Elizabeth Arlen; *D:* Robert Resnikoff; *W:* Robert Resnikoff; *C:* Theo van de Sande; *M:* Stewart Copeland.

First Time Felon
Engrossing made-for-cable feature based on the true story of Greg Yance (Omar Epps), a young Chicago drug dealer who commutes his conviction by participating in a prison boot camp program. Daniel Therriault's gritty script keeps the more inspirational story elements from becoming *"An Officer and a Gentleman* meets *Boyz N the Hood."* Charles S. Dutton's no-nonsense direction elicits knockout performances from Epps and Delroy Lindo as a brutally sage drill sergeant. The 1.85 anamorphic transfer looks exceptionally clean and crisp, with solid colors and superb detail delineation. A few scenes suffer from overly zealous edge-enhancement. Surround sound is full-bodied and aggressive. —*EP*
Movie: 🎵🎵🎵 **DVD:** 🎵🎵🎵
HBO (cat #91465, UPC 026359146527). Widescreen (1.85:1) anamorphic. Dolby Digital Stereo Surround. $14.98. Snapper. *LANG:* English; French; Spanish. *SUB:* English; French; Spanish. *FEATURES:* 14 chapters • Cast/crew bios.
1997 (R) 106m/C Omar Epps, William Forsythe, Rachel Ticotin, Delroy Lindo; *D:* Charles S. Dutton; *W:* Daniel Therriault.

First Turn On [DC]
Summer camp sex comedy follows the adventures of several young campers who decide to die happy when a rock fall traps them in a cave. It's very silly stuff, featuring an early appearance by Vincent D'Onofrio. Don't miss Kaufman's memories of what a joy *Penthouse* Pet Sheila Kennedy was to work with. For comments on image quality and extras, please see review of *Squeeze Play.* —*MM*
Movie: 🎵🎵 ½ **DVD:** 🎵🎵🎵
Troma Team Video (cat #9013, UPC 790-357901333). Full frame. $19.98. Keepcase. *LANG:* English. *FEATURES:* 9 chapters • Troma materials • Featurette • Commentary: director.
1983 (R) 88m/C Georgia Harrell, Michael Sanville, Googy Gress, Jenny Johnson, Heide Basset, Vincent D'Onofrio, Sheila Kennedy; *D:* Michael Herz, Lloyd Kaufman;

W: Michael Herz, Lloyd Kaufman, Stuart Strutin, Georgia Harrell; *C:* Lloyd Kaufman.

Fishing with Gandhi
Roy and Gil (the Reichmuth twins) are rednecks who make the guys in *Dumb and Dumber* look like Rhodes Scholars. They pick up Dan (Klein) and meditate, with alleged humor, on the ways of the world for another hour or so. The budget is as minimal as the laughs. Image quality is equal to tape. —*MM*
Movie: 🎵🎵 **DVD:** 🎵🎵 ½
York Ent. (cat #YPD-1089, UPC 75072310-8926). Full frame. $14.99. Keepcase. *LANG:* English. *FEATURES:* Trailers • Director's intro and commentary • Animated short film • Outtakes.
1998 73m/C John Reichmuth, James Reichmuth, Dan Klein, Gabe Weisert, William Birdthistle, Christina Milano, Dan Hunt; *D:* Gabe Weisert; *W:* John Reichmuth, James Reichmuth, Gabe Weisert, William Birdthistle; *C:* Matthew Uhry; *M:* Paul Stasi.

Fist of Fear, Touch of Death
Among the many features robbing the grave of Bruce Lee throughout is this hilarious oddity, part phony documentary and part action comedy. Announcer Adolf Caesar interviews celebrities at a martial arts show at Madison Square Garden, recaps Lee's biography, and shows scenes from old Hong Kong features, redubbed to represent events from early in Lee's life. Tedious at times, but this concoction is so completely ludicrous that it can't help but be somewhat entertaining. Image and sound quality are a bit sharper on this release of this common title (on a triple feature *Classic Kung Fu Fighting Movies* DVD), but the letterbox matte is tighter, cutting off the top of heads. —*BT* *AKA:* Fist of Fear; The Dragon and the Cobra.
Movie: 🎵 ½ **DVD:** 🎵🎵
BFS Video (cat #30230D, UPC 06680530-2305). Widescreen letterboxed. $14.99. Keepcase. *LANG:* English. *FEATURES:* 4 chapters • Bio • Selected filmography • Trivia.
1980 (R) 81m/C Fred Williamson, Ron Van Cliff, Adolph Caesar, Aaron Banks, Bill Louie; *D:* Matthew Mallinson; *W:* Ron Harvey; *C:* John Hazard; *M:* Keith Mansrod.

Fist of Fury
This feature was compiled from a 30-hour TV series based on the Bruce Lee classic *The Chinese Connection.* Donnie Yen stars and provides some incredible action choreography, especially for a TV show. All efforts are somewhat compromised by the cheap-looking video image. There are some glitches in the programming, easily overcome with a tap to the fast-forward button. Two audio commentary tracks (with Yen and actor Robin Shou, plus others) and a 22-minute documentary cover the project's production. —*BT*

Movie: 🎵🎵 ½ **DVD:** 🎵🎵🎵 ½
Tai Seng (cat #06974, UPC 6016410697-48). Full frame. Dolby Digital 5.1. $19.95. Keepcase. *LANG:* Cantonese; English. *SUB:* English. *FEATURES:* 16 chapters • 2 audio commentaries • Documentary featurette • Trailers • Filmographies.
1995 120m/C Donnie Yen, Joey Meng, Eddy Ko, Chi Wing Lau, Jang-Lee Hwang; *D:* Benny Chan, Yun-chuen Leung, Gummiu Wong, Wai-man Cheng, Ming-hoi Wu, Mau-sing Tang, Shiu-kee Lung; *M:* Bon Yin Wong.

The Fist Power
This exercise in action and suspense, produced by Wong Jing, is kind of like the kung fu version of *Kramer vs. Kramer* and *Dog Day Afternoon*. Ex-British Marine Charles (Anthony Wong), stepdad to son Tung (Tony in English dub), will fight for custody against the boy's mother Sara (Li Fei) and her new husband George Chiu. Officer Brian Cheuk (Vincent Zhou) is a top security expert. A police inspector proves to be no help whatsoever to Charles, telling him that ex-British officers have no rights since the reunification. Increasingly frustrated, Charles assembles a squad of his buddies to take a school class hostage, a class that includes the son of the police inspector—and Brian's nephew. He demands his son be handed over to him before he can be sent to America. Brian vows to get Tony for Charles, but he has to fight both the cops and George's triad thugs to the airport and back. Director Aman Chang does a good job keeping the action going at a brisk pace, though his fight scenes tend toward fast cuts that obscure movement too much. The DVD provides plenty of language options along with a crisp letterboxed transfer. As is the usual case, the English dubbed dialogue is less polite than the subtitle translation. Highlights are way too hot throughout, though this may be the fault of the original print. *—BT* *AKA:* Sang sei Kuen Chuk; Sheng Si Quan Su.
Movie: 🎵🎵🎵 **DVD:** 🎵🎵 ½
Tai Seng (cat #00304, UPC 6016410030-49). Widescreen letterboxed. Dolby Digital 5.1. $19.95. Keepcase. *LANG:* Cantonese; English; Mandarin; Vietnamese. *SUB:* English. *FEATURES:* 8 chapters • Trailers • Filmographies.
1999 89m/C *HK* Anthony Wong, Vincent Zhou, Sam Lee, Gigi Lai, Pei Pei Cheng, Kar Wing Lau, Fei Li, Suet Lam; *D:* Aman Chang; *M:* Tommy Wai.

Fistful of Lead
Bounty hunter Sartana (Hilton) is a Man With No Name wannabe. Some of the movie might have been filmed on sets left over from *For a Few Dollars More*. Plot and execution are generic spaghetti western. DVD looks like a dupe of an old VHS tape. Pan 'n' scan treatment cramps the widescreen framing. Title is available as part of "The Wild West" boxed set. *—MM*
Movie: 🎵🎵 **DVD:** 🎵🎵

Brentwood (cat #44213-9, UPC 78736442-1398). Full frame. $19.95. Keepcase. *LANG:* English. *FEATURES:* 8 chapters • "Have You Got Any Castles" cartoon • DVD dictionary • DVD-ROM features • Trivia game.
1970 92m/C *IT* George Hilton, Charles Southwood, Pierro Lulli, Erika Blanc; *D:* Giuliano Carnimeo; *W:* Tito Carpi; *C:* Stelvio Massi; *M:* Francesco De Masi.

Fists of Bruce Lee
A triad boss hires electronic expert Bruce Li to install a security system. Rival mobsters try to force Li to spy on his boss, so they can kidnap his daughter for leverage. Lo Lieh appears as a noble rival mobster with a prosthetic hand he can whip out on a chain. The cinematography is rarely in focus. Frames are removed from some fight footage to speed up blows. The soundtrack borrows from *Live & Let Die* and other '70s pop tunes. Some of the dubbing actors don't speak English much better than the original Chinese actors. Image and sound quality are a bit sharper on this release of this common title (on a triple feature *Classic Kung Fu Fighting Movies* DVD), but the full-frame image crops off real estate on all four sides of the frame. The image is squeezed and windowboxed for the credit sequence. *—BT*
Movie: 🎵 **DVD:** 🎵🎵
BFS Video (cat #30230D, UPC 06680530-2305). Full frame. $14.99. Keepcase. *LANG:* English. *FEATURES:* 4 chapters • Bio • Selected filmography • Trivia.
1978 (R) 94m/C *HK* Bruce Li, Lo Lieh, Tong Lung, Wai Lau Chan, Paul Wei; *D:* Bruce Li; *C:* Wan Hsiung Lai.

Five Card Stud
Formulaic Hollywood western is tired and dated. Five members of a lynching party are being killed one by one. Gambler Van Morgan (Martin) tried to stop the lynching and now tries to stop the killer. Also involved is pistol-packing preacher Jonathan Rudd (Mitchum) and the lovely Lily Langford (Stevens). Surface damage is evident throughout. Heavy grain gives a harsh quality to the bright, unfaded colors. Blacks lose all detail in most shots. *—MM*
Movie: 🎵🎵 **DVD:** 🎵🎵 ½
Paramount (cat #06737, UPC 097360673-746). Widescreen (1.85:1) anamorphic. Dolby Digital Mono. $24.99. Keepcase. *LANG:* English; French. *SUB:* English. *CAP:* English. *FEATURES:* 12 chapters.
1968 (PG) 103m/C Robert Mitchum, Dean Martin, Inger Stevens, Roddy McDowall, Yaphet Kotto, John Anderson, Katherine Justice; *D:* Henry Hathaway; *W:* Marguerite Roberts; *C:* Daniel F. Fapp; *M:* Maurice Jarre.

The Five Heartbeats
Well-acted and -directed story of an all-black singing group that makes it big in the '60s chronicles the ups and downs in

their musical and personal lives. Townsend again shows the cruelty and racism that exist in both the black and white worlds but mostly in the music industry in general. Finally, though, through all the sweaty singing, illicit sex, and infighting, the film never really heats up. There are bold moments that work really well—a roadside rousting by Southern cops is an especially fine standout—but overall the story's scenes seem stilted and contrived. Much more enjoyable and groundbreaking is Townsend's *Hollywood Shuffle*. The disc has bold bright colors and deep blacks and the sound is really good. *—CA*
Movie: 🎵🎵 ½ **DVD:** 🎵🎵🎵 ½
20th Century Fox (cat #2001876, UPC 02454301876). Widescreen (1.85:1) anamorphic. Dolby Digital 4.0 Surround. $19.90. Keepcase. *LANG:* English. *SUB:* English; Spanish. *CAP:* English. *FEATURES:* Chapter links • Robert Townsend profile • Trailer.
1991 (R) 122m/C Robert Townsend, Tressa Thomas, Michael Wright, Harry J. Lennix, Diahann Carroll, Leon, Hawthorne James, Chuck Patterson, Roy Fegan, Tico Wells, John Canada Terrell, Harold Nicholas, Paul Benjamin, Norma Donaldson, Eugene Glazer; *D:* Robert Townsend; *W:* Robert Townsend, Keenen Ivory Wayans; *C:* Bill Dill; *M:* Stanley Clarke.

Five on the Black Hand Side
Barber Brooks (Jackson) tries to rule his family with dictatorial powers until his wife (Taylor), who has submitted graciously to his will, decides to rebel. This family-oriented comedy is a distinct departure from the normal "blaxploitation" of the early '70s. Today, it's more interesting as nostalgia for the clothes and the hairstyles, but it's still enjoyable enough. DVD image is very grainy and that appears to come from the original. The studio has done its usual competent work with a catalog title. The only extra is a trailer and it is not to be missed. *—MM*
Movie: 🎵🎵 ½ **DVD:** 🎵🎵 ½
MGM Home Ent. (cat #1002582, UPC 027616867834). Widescreen (1.85:1) letterboxed. Dolby Digital Mono. $14.98. Keepcase. *LANG:* English. *SUB:* French; Spanish. *CAP:* English. *FEATURES:* 16 chapters • Trailer.
1973 (PG) 96m/C Clarice Taylor, Leonard Jackson, Virginia Capers, Glynn Turman, D'Urville Martin; *D:* Oscar Williams; *W:* Charlie Russell; *C:* Gene Polito; *M:* H.B. Barnum.

Flambards
In the early 1900s, teenaged orphan Christine is sent to live with her tyrannical uncle Russell and his two sons on their crumbling English estate, Flambards. Bitter rivalries and jealousies abound between arrogant tradition-bound Mark and younger William, who's obsessed with the new-fangled airplanes. The situation

intensifies as both young men fall in love with Christine and World War I begins. DVD image is very grainy, leading to heavy pixels in some scenes. Dark clothes lack detail. Sound is thin. All of the flaws are typical of British TV productions of the era. —MM

Movie: 🎞🎞 ½ **DVD:** 🎞 ½
BFS Video (cat #95027-D, UPC 06680591-027). Full frame. $59.98. Keepcase. *LANG:* English. *FEATURES:* 52 chapters.
1978 676m/C *GB* Christine McKenna, Stephen Grives, Alan Parnaby, Edward Judd, Sebastian Abineri, Peter Settelen, Carol Leader, Frank Mills; **D:** Lawrence Gordon Clark, Peter Duffell.

Flash Gordon: Spaceship to the Unknown

This is the feature-length abridgement of the original serial in which the evil Ming (Middleton) is about to crash his planet Mongo into Earth, only to be thwarted by Flash Gordon (Crabbe), Dr. Zarkov (Shannon), and Dale Arden (Rogers), not to mention his own hubba-hubba daughter (Lawson) who falls for Flash even before his shirt is torn. The delightful effects, including the famous rocketship and dueling iguanas, look very good here. DVD image is remarkably clean throughout. Sound is dated. —MM

Movie: 🎞🎞 ½ **DVD:** 🎞🎞 ½
Image Ent. (cat #ID0289HEDVD, UPC 014-381028928). Full frame. Dolby Digital Mono. $19.98. Keepcase. *LANG:* English. *FEATURES:* 16 chapters.
1936 98m/B Buster Crabbe, Jean Rogers, Charles Middleton, Priscilla Lawson, Frank Shannon; **D:** Frederick Stephani.

Flash Gordon: The Deadly Ray from Mars

Edited from the original serial, Flash (Crabbe) must, once again, squelch the evil plans of Emperor Ming. This time, Ming is on Mars and is threatening to destroy the Earth with his new death ray. The usual cheesy fun is loused up by "comic relief" from an annoying reporter who is trying to get the big intergalactic scoop. The image, considering its age, looks great, though it's not as clear as others in the series. The mono sound is above average. —DRL **AKA:** The Deadly Rays from Mars; Flash Gordon's Trip to Mars.

Movie: 🎞 🎞 ½ **DVD:** 🎞🎞 ½
Image Ent. (cat #286, UPC 0143810286-21). Full frame. Mono. $19.99. Keepcase. *LANG:* English. *FEATURES:* 16 chapters.
1939 97m/B Buster Crabbe, Jean Rogers, Charles Middleton; **D:** Robert F. "Bob" Hill, Ford Beebe.

Flash Gordon: The Peril from Planet Mongo

The nefarious Emperor Ming threatens to destroy the peaceful kingdom of Arboria

with heat projectiles. Flash, Dale Arden, and Dr. Zarkov must step in to rescue the poor people, but Ming soon reveals even more diabolical plans that put the entire universe in jeopardy. Can the heroic trio save the day? This image and sound are very good considering the film's age. There is almost no degradation of the original and the transfer is free from defect. The mono sound is crisp, with only slight traces of noise. This re-edit from the original serial is hokey, but good-natured, sci-fi fun. —DRL

Movie: 🎞🎞 **DVD:** 🎞🎞🎞
Image Ent. (cat #287, UPC 0143810287-20). Full frame. Mono. $19.99. Keepcase. *LANG:* English. *FEATURES:* 12 chapters.
1940 82m/B Buster Crabbe, Carol Hughes, Charles Middleton, Frank Shannon; **D:** Ford Beebe, Ray Taylor; **W:** George Plympton, Basil Dickey; **C:** Jerome Ash, William Sickner.

Flash Gordon: The Purple Death from Outer Space

That darn Ming (Middleton) is trying to conquer the Earth again, this time by spreading "electrified dust" from his spaceship and causing a plague of the "purple death." It's up to Flash (Crabbe) and company to fly back to Mongo and save the day. All of your favorite cheesy effects are trotted out in this condensation of the famous serial. Sound is a bit shrill and thin but the image looks as good as it ever has. —MM

Movie: 🎞🎞 **DVD:** 🎞🎞 ½
Image Ent. (cat #ID0288HEDVD, UPC 014-381028829). Full frame. Dolby Digital Mono. $19.98. Keepcase. *LANG:* English. *FEATURES:* 16 chapters.
1940 88m/B Buster Crabbe, Carol Hughes, Charles Middleton, Frank Shannon; **D:** Ford Beebe, Ray Taylor.

The Fleet that Came to Stay

Please see review for *December 7th / The Fleet that Came to Stay.*
1946 C

Flesh and Bone

Moody, atmospheric suspense film is hard to categorize. Viewers will be reminded at various times of *Blood Simple,* Terrence Malick's *Badlands, The Grifters,* and even *The Last Picture Show.* It begins with a frightening introductory scene in the early 1960s. Flash forward to the present where Arliss Sweeney (Quaid) makes the rounds of small Texas towns restocking his vending machines and collecting quarters. He's a quiet, careful man who minds his own business but doesn't miss much, either. He catches a sexy, penny-ante crook (Paltrow in a memorable debut) in the act but since she hasn't harmed him, he does nothing. Through an odd coincidence—the film is filled with them—Arliss

meets Kay Davies (Ryan), who's making a halfhearted escape attempt from a bad marriage. The fourth member of this curious quartet is Arliss's father (Caan), a spooky and cheerful personification of evil. Though the plot appears to wander far afield at times, it never strays far from its central themes. The problem is that it moves so slowly. It takes writer/director Kloves more than two hours to tell an essentially simple tale of familial guilt and individual responsibility. If the film had been 15–20 minutes shorter, as it could have been, it would have been much stronger. The less scenic side of rural Texas—all dust, rust, and barbed wire—is almost as important as the human characters. The actors are understated and believable throughout. Dennis Quaid is particularly good. He's much more restrained and introspective than he normally is and that's exactly what the part calls for. DVD handles the slightly soft image with no problems. Both dark, cramped interiors and overly bright sunlit exteriors are fine. Surround effects are spare but effective. A commentary track really is called for. —MM

Movie: 🎞🎞🎞 **DVD:** 🎞🎞🎞
Paramount (cat #32899, UPC 097363289-944). Widescreen anamorphic. Dolby Digital 5.1 Surround; Dolby Digital Surround. $24.98. Keepcase. *LANG:* English. *SUB:* English. *CAP:* English. *FEATURES:* 12 chapters.
1993 (R) 127m/C Dennis Quaid, Meg Ryan, James Caan, Gwyneth Paltrow, Scott Wilson, Christopher Rydell; **D:** Steven Kloves; **W:** Steven Kloves; **M:** Thomas Newman.

The Flesh and the Fiends

The best of the many films telling the story of Burke (Rose) and Hare (Pleasence), two lower-class Edinburgh ne'er-do-wells who discover a novel way to make an extra buck: by selling recently expired townsfolk to nearby Doctor Knox (Cushing) for use as a teaching tool to his students. Unfortunately, the two "resurrectionists" are a bit impatient and turn to murder to keep the doctor (and their pockets) freshly supplied. Featuring terrific, multi-layered performances by Cushing and Pleasence, this version is gripping, atmospheric, and strongly dramatic. The only weak element is an underdeveloped love story that at least serves a plot function. Previously available in awful, censored, and pan-and-scan versions, this disc is a revelation to behold. The wide Dyaliscope framing is perfectly preserved and absolutely essential to an appreciation of the film. While objects on the edges of the frame seem a little thin and distorted, this is due to the original limitations of the lenses, and is not a problem with the transfer. The contrasts are perfect; rich blacks, strong grays and contrasts, and a clean, grain-free image. The sound is strong for a mono track. Also included is a "Continental" version (designed for distribution on the European

continent), which features nudity and somewhat stronger violence. Though this alternate version is a worthwhile inclusion and a historical curiosity, the nudity is distracting and the transfer is made from a fairly battered, overly contrasty print source. The standard version is a better film and is definitely the preferred viewing option. The extras are nice additions, especially for the horror completist. —DG *AKA:* Mania; Fiendish Ghouls; Psycho Killers.
Movie: 🎬🎬🎬 *DVD:* 🎬🎬🎬
Image Ent. (cat #ID9811IIDVD, UPC 014-38198112). Widescreen (2.35:1) anamorphic. Dolby Digital Mono. $24.99. Keepcase. *LANG:* English. *FEATURES:* Theatrical trailer • Alternate title sequence from *Mania,* the U.S. version • Filmographies • Photo and poster gallery • 26 chapters • Insert booklet with notes.
1960 87m/B *GB* Peter Cushing, June Laverick, Donald Pleasence, George Rose, Dermot Walsh, Renee Houston, Billie Whitelaw, John Cairney, Michael Balfour; *D:* John Gilling; *W:* John Gilling, Leon Griffiths; *C:* Monty Berman; *M:* Stanley Black.

Fleshburn

Calvin Duggai (Landham), an Indian Vietnam veteran, escapes from a mental institution and seeks vengeance on the five psychiatrists who had him committed. The grainy, low-budget image is identical to tape, and probably identical to the theatrical release. —MM
Movie: 🎬🎬 *DVD:* 🎬🎬
Rhino (cat #R2 876010, UPC 603497601-028). Full frame. $19.98. Snapper. *LANG:* English. *FEATURES:* 15 chapters.
1984 (R) 91m/C Steve Kanaly, Karen Carlson, Sonny Landham, Macon McCalman; *D:* George Gage; *W:* George Gage, Beth Gage, Brian Garfield; *M:* Arthur Kempel.

Flight to Mars

The best words *Daily Variety*'s review of November 7, 1951, could find for this early space movie were "singularly unexciting," and for once their lack of enthusiasm is shared by the rest of us. The first Mars rocket (called Rocket M.A.R.S.) is launched successfully, but crashlands on the red planet after being damaged in a meteor shower. An advanced civilization greets the astronauts and welcomes them to their underground utopia, offering to help make repairs for a return flight. The flight leader, Dr. Jim Barker (Franz), falls in love with Martian scientific assistant Alita (Chapman), much to the consternation of Earth scientist Carol Stafford (Huston). She had set her slide rule for him, but there's romantic compensation in the form of Steve Abbott (Mitchell), an amorous newswriter along for the ride. Things get dicey when Alita reports that all the cooperation is a ruse—as soon as the rocket is ship-shape, the Martians will seize it to begin an invasion of Earth. DVD doesn't give the show the presentation it needs. We may be looking at the only surviving

print of the movie, and it is interesting to observe the original two-color Cinecolor process hues. But the print is damaged in distracting ways. Respliced film breaks occur every couple of minutes, not interfering with the continuity—until a key scene late in the show. Then, a storm of splices frustratingly interrupts important dialogue lines. It would have been better if this section were replaced with a substitute source, even a B&W one. Almost as annoying are a small series of bubble-dots just below center screen that pop up constantly during the movie. From my experience, they look like the result of the film scorched by a projector with a too-hot lamp. The trailer has the same flaw. Besides those rather glaring flaws, the picture is handsomely transferred. The opening shots have the same Cinecolor feel as *Invaders from Mars,* with a similar title design. The subdued hues of Cinecolor have the look of a faded paint-by-numbers watercolor, and it is interesting to see how the art directors tried to accommodate the limited palette. —GE
Movie: 🎬🎬 *DVD:* 🎬🎬 ½
Image Ent. (UPC 014381967821). Full frame. $24.98. Keepcase. *LANG:* English. *FEATURES:* Liner notes by Tom Weaver • Trailer • Interview with Cameron Mitchell.
1952 72m/C Cameron Mitchell, Marguerite Chapman, Arthur Franz, Virginia Huston; *D:* Lesley Selander; *W:* Arthur Strawn; *C:* Harry Neumann; *M:* Marlin Skiles.

Flooding

This independent festival pleaser by writer/producer/director Portugal is a clever homage to Alfred Hitchcock on a budget. Joyce Calloway (Gibson) has become agoraphobic after the unsolved murder of her husband and has spent the past six months since his death in her house. She is working with a new doctor (who comes to the house, of course) to get over her fear of the outside world, and she better hurry, because her parents are selling the house in an effort to get her to go outside. She orders food via the Web and has a close next-door neighbor who helps her pick her one-night stands from the personals. They also come to the house, of course. After a fling, a man—who has the name of the one-night stand, but is not the man she slept with—comes to her back door, falls inside, and dies after uttering a name she doesn't recognize. A detective with an eye patch shows up. He is mean; his partner is nice. The tension mounts as it becomes clear that her subconscious mind is holding out on her and that someone wants her dead or at least out of the way. The why of the story is the weak link in the film; it is the journey to the answer that is absorbing. This is not a perfect film, but it is worth watching for fans of suspense. The director's commentary is fairly interesting as Portugal takes you through the technical nightmare and joy of making a film on a budget. The deleted scenes leave you

wishing for a director's cut as a few of the plot holes and characters are filled in with the cut footage rather nicely. The disc looks washed-out and the sound has the quality of a student film despite the 5.1 Surround, but overall it gives the feeling of watching a Bava or Argento film late at night when no digital TV was in sight. —CA
Movie: 🎬🎬 ½ *DVD:* 🎬🎬
York Ent. (cat #YPD 1090, UPC 75072310-9022). Widescreen letterboxed. 5.1 Surround. $14.99. Keepcase. *LANG:* English. *FEATURES:* 13 chapters • Theatrical trailer • Commentary: director • Deleted scenes.
1997 86m/C Brenna Gibson, Lauren Bailey, Kary Cawley; *D:* Todd Portugal; *W:* Todd Portugal.

Flowers of Shanghai

Elegant but tedious period drama set in the brothels of late 19th-century Shanghai. Director Hou Hsai-Hsien guides an almost static camera through the sexual intrigue of the graceful "flower girls" who held court among—and emotional sway over—their wealthy clientele. Scenarist Chu Tien-Wen (adapting from the novel *Biographies of Flowers of Shanghai*) juggles multiple plotlines in soap opera fashion but with no urgency. Conflicts range from flower girl Jade (Fang Hsuan) refusing other clients because she believes Zhu (Simon Chang) will marry her, to the fears of the veteran Crimson (Michiko Hada) that she is slowly becoming a wilting blossom in the eyes of her dwindling patrons. Re-creating such a stifling environment risks losing dramatic impact. Unfortunately, Hsien captures the stylized rituals of the milieu all too accurately; the turgid pacing of *Flowers* makes Merchant-Ivory look like Sam Peckinpah. Cinematographer Mark Lee Ping-Bin bathed every frame in a golden color wash. While the effect may have looked great when projected, on video the gimmick is just left of annoying. The 1.85 non-anamorphic transfer does what it can with the film's monochromatic color spectrum. Details are sharp enough, but the image exhibits some edge-enhancement and fleshtones are non-existent. —EP *AKA:* Haishang Hua.
Movie: 🎬🎬 *DVD:* 🎬🎬
Winstar Home Ent. (cat #FLV5289, UPC 720917528922). Widescreen (1.85:1) letterboxed. Dolby Digital Stereo. $24.98. Keepcase. *LANG:* Mandarin. *SUB:* English. *FEATURES:* 16 chapters • Theatrical trailer • Cast/director filmographies.
1998 125m/C *JP TW* Tony Leung Chiu-Wai, Michiko Hada, Hsiao-hui Wei, Jack Kao, Michelle Reis, Annie Shizuka Inoh, Fang Hsuan, Simon Chang; *D:* Hsiao-Hsien Hou; *W:* Tien-wen Chu; *C:* Mark Lee Ping-Bin; *M:* Yoshihiro Yanno.

Fly Away Home [2 SE]

Young Amy (Anna Paquin) withdraws when she loses her mother in a car crash and is forced to live with her estranged father, Thomas (Jeff Daniels), a scruffy

sculptor/inventor, in rural Ontario. Still dealing with her mother's death, Amy suddenly becomes a mother herself to a tiny gaggle of goslings, when she happens upon a nest of uprooted eggs. Director Carroll Ballard, who did such an amazing job with *The Black Stallion*, shows that he hasn't lost his knack for making great films about animals. Based on the true story of inventor Bill Lishman, who took domesticated geese on a winter migration from Toronto, Canada, to North Carolina, leading the formation in his motor-powered glider. This "Special Edition" DVD offers a fine transfer and much more. The image is very sharp and clear, although there is a slight bit of grain on the image. The colors are fine, but the picture is dark in some shots. The Dolby Digital 5.1 audio track is very impressive, as it provides clear dialogue, nice reproduction of the music, and well-placed Surround sound effects. The audio coming from the rear perfectly compliments the on-screen action. The audio commentary with the director and cinematographer (who have a long-standing relationship) is very informative and relaxed. Also, the DVD includes several segments which focus on the making of the film and the real-life story behind the movie. —*ML* **AKA:** *Father Goose; Flying Wild.*
Movie: 🎲🎲🎲 **DVD:** 🎲🎲🎲 ½
Columbia Tristar (cat #06046, UPC 043396060463). Widescreen (1.85:1) anamorphic. Dolby Digital 5.1; Dolby Surround. $24.95. Keepcase. *LANG:* English; French; Spanish; Portuguese. *SUB:* English; French; Spanish; Portuguese; Chinese; Korean; Thai. *CAP:* English. *FEATURES:* Commentary ▪ Isolated music score with commentary ▪ Featurettes ▪ Documentary ▪ Theatrical trailer ▪ Filmographies ▪ Bonus trailers.
1996 (PG) 107m/C Jeff Daniels, Anna Paquin, Dana Delany, Terry Kinney, Jeremy Ratchford; **D:** Carroll Ballard; **W:** Robert Rodat, Vince McKewin; **C:** Caleb Deschanel; **M:** Mark Isham. *AWARDS: NOM:* Oscars '96: Cinematog.

Focus

Playwright and novelist Arthur Miller made his mark with *The Crucible,* which used the Salem Witch Trials to mirror the anti-communist McCarthy-ism of the 1950s. With *Focus,* he spins a Kafka-esque tale of mistaken identity which becomes a cautionary story of anti-Semitism. William H. Macy stars as Lawrence Newman, an upright citizen of Brooklyn, New York, who seems to have everything going for him. He has a good job, he's well-liked by his neighbors, and he's just married the lovely Gertrude (Laura Dern). But things change when Lawrence gets a new pair of glasses. Suddenly, everyone mistakes this Christian man for someone who is Jewish. Lawrence doesn't think much of these odd occurrences at first, but then he realizes that familiar people are treating him differently, that he's being spied upon, and that his life might be in danger. To protect

Gertrude and himself, Lawrence realizes that he must stand up against this bigotry. *Focus* is a very intense and emotional film, which spins an intriguing story. As usual, Macy is perfect, and the supporting cast, which includes David Paymer and Meatloaf (here acting under the name Michael Lee Aday) is excellent. The only real drawback to the film is the odd nature of the central premise. Some audience members may not buy the "Clark Kent"–like transformation which Lawrence undergoes once he dons his new glasses. To us, he's the same person, but suddenly the other characters see him as a threat. This plot-device points out the illogical aspects of racism, but it may be too much of a *Twilight Zone* spin for some people. DVD image is very sharp and clear, free from any major overt defects. There is minor grain in some shots and a couple of the nighttime scenes are a bit too dark. The Dolby Digital 5.1 audio track is quite impressive (even during the opening credit sequence!). The dialogue is clear and audible at all times, and the Surround sound effects are good. A featurette includes interviews with the cast and crew, but most importantly, with Miller, as he gives his thoughts on *Focus.* Strangely, the trailer for *Focus* is present in this featurette, but it's been split in two—with the opening showing at the start of the featurette and the remainder of the trailer coming at the end. —*ML*
Movie: 🎲🎲🎲 **DVD:** 🎲🎲🎲
Paramount (cat #34034, UPC 097363403-649). Widescreen (1.78:1) anamorphic. Dolby Digital 5.1; Dolby Surround. $29.98. Keepcase. *LANG:* English. *SUB:* English. *CAP:* English. *FEATURES:* Featurette ▪ 15 chapters.
2001 (PG-13) 106m/C William H. Macy, Laura Dern, David Paymer, Meat Loaf Aday, Michael Copeman, Kenneth Welsh, Kay Hewtrey, Joseph Ziegler, Arlene Meadows; **D:** Neil Slavin; **W:** Kendrew Lascelles; **C:** Juan Ruiz-Anchia; **M:** Mark Adler.

Fog Island

Framed for a crime and then sprung from the clink, an inventor (Zucco) invites those who done him wrong to his island estate. They drop like flies until the identity of the true villain is revealed. Formula public domain picture gains little on DVD. There's heavy grain and artifacting in the titular foggy scenes. Film breaks are evident throughout. Sound might come from a transistor radio in another room. Title is available as part of the *Crime Stoppers* triple feature. —*MM*
Movie: 🎲🎲 **DVD:** 🎲
Triton Multimedia (cat #TDVD9166, UPC 017078916621). Full frame. Dolby Digital Mono. $19.98. Keepcase. *LANG:* English. *FEATURES:* 12 chapters ▪ Popeye cartoon ▪ Radio program.
1945 72m/B George Zucco, Lionel Atwill, Terry Morse, Jerome Cowan, Veda Ann Borg; **D:** Terry Morse; **W:** Pierre Gendron; **C:** Ira Morgan.

Follow the Stars Home

In San Francisco, Dianne (Williams) is seriously injured in a car accident. Flashback to her meeting with charming fisherman Mark (Close). They marry and she becomes pregnant but when they learn that their daughter will be born with severe disabilities, Mark can't cope and bolts. Flash forward to Dianne making a life for herself and her daughter—aided by her mother (Brown) and Mark's steadfast pediatrician brother David (Scott), who obviously loves her. Since this is a Hallmark made-for-TV tearjerker, production values are first-rate. Full-frame image ranges between good and very good with only a little inconsequential flashing within complex patterns. Sound is O.K. —*MM*
Movie: 🎲🎲 ½ **DVD:** 🎲🎲 ½
Artisan Ent. (cat #12011). Full frame. $19.98. Keepcase. *LANG:* English. *FEATURES:* 20 chapters ▪ Production notes ▪ Talent files.
2001 97m/C Kimberly Williams, Campbell Scott, Eric Close, Blair Brown, Alexa Vega, Roxanne Hart; **D:** Dick Lowry; **W:** Sally Robinson.

Following

It's easy to spot some of the same elements that made *Memento* so much fun in Christopher Nolan's low-budget debut. As it begins, down-on-his-luck Bill (Theobold) has taken to following strangers he sees on London streets. He claims to be a writer gathering material. One of his subjects, Cobb (Haw), turns out to be a thief—or is he? Nolan fractures time, moving back and forth in his story. At least, that's the way the film was released theatrically. You have the option on DVD of watching it chronologically. That's one of the more interesting extras. There's also a commentary track—something curiously lacking on the first DVD release of *Memento.* It's difficult to say much about the image quality. Disc provides a clear transfer of a picture that was shot in 16mm black and white. Stereo is more than adequate for the film's limited aural range. The limited production values will never recommend this one to a large mainstream audience, but it's a terrific find for more adventurous suspense fans. —*MM*
Movie: 🎲🎲🎲 **DVD:** 🎲🎲🎲 ½
Columbia Tristar (cat #07603, UPC 04339-6076037). Full frame. Dolby Digital Stereo. $24.98. Keepcase. *LANG:* English. *SUB:* English; Spanish. *CAP:* English. *FEATURES:* Commentary: Christopher Nolan ▪ Angle with director's shooting script ▪ Chronological structure option ▪ 14 chapters.
1999 (R) 71m/B Jeremy Theobald, Alex Haw, Lucy Russell, John Nolan; **D:** Christopher Nolan; **W:** Christopher Nolan; **C:** Christopher Nolan; **M:** David Julyan.

A Fool There Was

Adapted from Rudyard Kipling's poem, this film tells the story of a man (Jose) led to ruin by a cruel "Vampire" woman (Bara). The term was quickly shortened to "Vamp" and the rest is history. Bara controls the screen as well as the men in this star-making performance. Everyone mercilessly overacts, although a dark, surprising, conclusion helps the overall feel. All the blemishes in the picture are from the source material, and the transfer is as good as can be expected. The modern piano score adds nothing; it merely reflects the on-screen action. —*DRL*

Movie: ♫♫ ½ **DVD:** ♫♫ ½
Kino on Video (cat #241, UPC 738329024-123). Full frame. Mono. $29.95. Keepcase. *LANG:* Silent. *SUB:* English intertitles. *FEATURES:* 10 chapters • Complete text of Rudyard Kipling's "The Vampire" • Excerpt from Terry Ramsaye's "A Million and One Nights" • Photo gallery • Original 1915 review.
1914 70m/B Mabel Frenyear, Victor Benoit, Theda Bara, Edward Jose, Runa Hodges, Clifford Bruce; *D:* Frank Powell; *W:* Roy L. McCardell; *C:* George Schneiderman.

For Sale

After France Robert (Kiberlain) leaves her intended (Stevenin) standing at the altar, he hires his friend Luigi (Castellitto), a detective, to find out why. As Luigi learns more and more about the woman's past, he finds that her sexual life is an adventure. Essentially, this is another of the anti-erotic romances that have been coming out of France in recent years. It's also an intriguing psychological puzzle. DVD image is slightly subdued compared to a similar American studio production. It appears to be an accurate reproduction of the original. Optional subtitles are easy to read. —*MM*

Movie: ♫♫♫ **DVD:** ♫♫♫
Image Ent. (cat #ID9604SIDVD, UPC 014-381960426). Widescreen (2.35:1) anamorphic. Dolby Digital Stereo. $24.98. Keepcase. *LANG:* French. *SUB:* English. *FEATURES:* 12 chapters.
1998 116m/C *FR* Sandrine Kiberlain, Sergio Castellitto, Jean-François Stevenin; *D:* Laetitia Masson; *W:* Laetitia Masson; *C:* Antoine Hebale; *M:* Siegfried.

Forbidden Sins

Video premiere is slightly better than the generic title would suggest. Defense attorney Maureen Doherty (Shannon Tweed) is hired to defend multi-millionaire David Mulholland (Timbrook), who's accused of murdering a stripper during kinky sex. Once again an erotic thriller asks the question: Is he Mr. Right or is he a serial killer? Complicating matters further, Maureen's ex- is the detective assigned to the case. The script actually manages a bit of originality and humor within the limits of the genre. There's not much to be said for the DVD, however. Full-frame image and sound are not really much better than VHS tape. Disc is a double feature with *Human Desires*. —*MM*

Movie: ♫♫ **DVD:** ♫♫
Columbia Tristar (cat #05287, UPC 04339-6052871). Full frame. Dolby Digital Stereo. $19.98. Keepcase. *LANG:* English. *SUB:* English; French; Spanish; Portuguese. *FEATURES:* 28 chapters.
1999 (R) 87m/C Shannon Tweed, Corbin Timbrook; *D:* Robert Angelo; *W:* Daryl Haney, Hel Styverson; *C:* Michael Goi; *M:* Herman Beeftink.

Force 10 from Navarone

The most curious thing about this completely mediocre adventure is the difference in running times. The widescreen version is eight minutes longer than the full frame that's on the flip side of the disc. The introductions, taken from *The Guns of Navarone,* are slightly different and different studio logos appear before the films start (MGM and Columbia for the widescreen; Orion and American International on the full frame). Unfortunately, Barbara Bach's fleeting bathtub scene is all too brief in both. Other sources claim that differences within the body of the film are incidental. Director Guy Hamilton, known best for his work on James Bond films, doesn't come close to re-creating the original. This one's a fairly silly story with Shaw and Fox taking over the Peck and Niven roles, with most of the heroics handled by Ford. Image is barely acceptable. Heavy grain in large areas of solid color—a bright blue sky, a field—leads to artifacts. Aliasing is a problem for any diagonal line, particularly in the widescreen. —*MM*

Movie: ♫♫ **DVD:** ♫♫ ½
MGM Home Ent. (cat #908418, UPC 027-616841827). Widescreen (2.35:1) letterboxed; full frame. Dolby Digital Mono. $14.98. Keepcase. *LANG:* English. *SUB:* French; Spanish. *CAP:* English. *FEATURES:* Trailer • 32 chapters • Booklet.
1978 (PG) 118m/C Robert Shaw, Harrison Ford, Barbara Bach, Edward Fox, Carl Weathers, Richard Kiel, Franco Nero; *D:* Guy Hamilton; *W:* Robin Chapman; *C:* Christopher Challis; *M:* Ronald Goodwin.

Forgive and Forget

David (Shepherd), an extremely repressed gay construction worker, is attracted to longtime friend Theo (Simm). Making a terrible mistake in judgment, David comes out to his friends and family on a TV chat show, with disastrous repercussions. A surprisingly depressing, low-key drama that seems at odds with its sitcom premise. Unfortunately, David is too enigmatic and unreadable (and somewhat unlikable) a character for his predicament to be affecting. His coming out also seems highly contrived but the irresolute ending is effective. The image is sharp with vivid colors and accurate fleshtones, but is slightly grainy and occasionally displays light amounts of digital ghosting and edging. The sound is terrific: crisply recorded and richly balanced. The audio

commentary is informative, but ponderous and dull. —*DG*

Movie: ♫♫ **DVD:** ♫♫ ½
TLA Video (cat #TLAD004, UPC 80783900-0078). Widescreen (1.78:1) anamorphic. Dolby Digital Surround. $29.99. Keepcase. *LANG:* English. *FEATURES:* TV spots • Cast & crew bios • Commentary: Walsh, Burt • 24 chapters • Other TLA trailers.
1999 96m/C *GB* Steve John Shepherd, John Simm, Laura Fraser, Maurice Roeves, Ger Ryan, Meera Syal; *D:* Aisling Walsh; *W:* Mark Burt; *C:* Kevin Rowley; *M:* Hal Lindes.

Forgotten

Ben Turner (McGann) runs a hotel in rural England. Rachael Monroe (Burton) thinks that he's a killer. In the end, the more important questions involve reasons and motivations, not actual crimes. This is a nicely complicated British TV import, exceptionally well acted and handsomely produced. Image is very good, much better than similar American productions. Sound is fine. —*MM*

Movie: ♫♫♫ **DVD:** ♫♫ ½
BFS Video (cat #30137-D, UPC 06680530-1377). Full frame. $19.98. Keepcase. *LANG:* English. *FEATURES:* 12 chapters.
1999 153m/C *GB* Geraldine Alexander, Paul McGann, Caleb Ranson, Christopher Villiers, Ian Hogg, Adrian Rawlins, Gwyneth Strong; *D:* Ben Bolt; *W:* Spencer Eastman.

Forrest Gump [SCE]

The Oscar-winning crowd-pleaser arrives on DVD with all of the extras that viewers have come to expect in a special edition. In this case, those also include some candid admissions on the commentary track. Tom Hanks plays the "stupid is as stupid does" goodhearted hero of an unlikely epic that attempts to make sense of the 1960s and '70s. Forrest grows up in Alabama where he becomes a football star, falls in love with the free-spirited Jenny (Penn), then goes to Vietnam where he meets Lt. Dan (Sinese) and Bubba Bufford-Blue (Williamson). He returns a hero and, in one way or another, stumbles into every major moment of popular culture in the next years. DVD makes the computer-generated special effects more obvious than I remember them from the theatrical release. They're most noticeable in the 1968 Washington demonstration scene. That's also where producer Wendy Finerman admits that the infamous cop-out moment—when Forrest is to deliver his thoughts on the Vietnam war, only to have them muted by interfering cops—occurred because the filmmakers could not think of anything for him to say. (She also thinks that the Washington Monument is called the "Washington Memorial.") Some grain crops up there, too, and the scenes where Hanks and other characters are inserted into TV broadcasts look as intentionally bad as they always have. Those criticisms not withstanding, Hanks's performance remains courageous and winning, and the soundtrack is a fine collection of oldies.

The documentary and featurettes are on a second disc. —MM
Movie: 🎬🎬 ½ **DVD:** 🎬🎬🎬 ½
Paramount Home Video (UPC 097361564-449). Widescreen (2.35:1) anamorphic. Dolby Digital 5.1 Surround; Surround. $29.99. Keepcase. *LANG:* English; French. *SUB:* English. *CAP:* English. *FEATURES:* 19 chapters • Commentary: Zemeckis, Starkey, production designer Rick Carter • Commentary: Wendy Finerman • "Through the Eyes of Forrest Gump" documentary • 4 featurettes • 2 deleted scenes • Photo gallery • Talent files • Screen tests • 2 theatrical trailers. **1994 (PG-13) 142m/C** Sonny Shroyer, Mary Ellen Trainor, Tom Hanks, Robin Wright Penn, Sally Field, Gary Sinise, Mykelti Williamson; *D:* Robert Zemeckis; *W:* Eric Roth; *C:* Don Burgess; *M:* Alan Silvestri. *AWARDS:* Oscars '94: Actor (Hanks), Adapt. Screenplay, Director (Zemeckis), Film Editing, Picture, Visual FX; AFI '98: Top 100; Directors Guild '94: Director (Zemeckis); Golden Globes '95: Actor—Drama (Hanks), Director (Zemeckis), Film—Drama; Natl. Bd. of Review '94: Actor (Hanks), Film, Support. Actor (Sinise); Screen Actors Guild '94: Actor (Hanks); Writers Guild '94: Adapt. Screenplay; Blockbuster '95: Movie, T., Drama Actor, T. (Hanks); Blockbuster '96: Drama Actor, V. (Hanks); *NOM:* Oscars '94: Art Dir./Set Dec., Cinematog., Make-up, Sound, Support. Actor (Sinise), Orig. Score; Golden Globes '95: Screenplay, Support. Actor (Sinise), Support. Actress (Wright Penn), Score; MTV Movie Awards '95: Film, Male Perf. (Hanks), Breakthrough Perf. (Williamson); Screen Actors Guild '94: Support. Actor (Sinise), Support. Actress (Field, Wright Penn).

The Forsaken

Since the invention of film, there have been hundreds of vampire movies and apparently with *The Forsaken,* we've reached the saturation point. This bloodsucker epic combines elements of *Near Dark, The Lost Boys,* and *The Hitcher,* and rarely has anything original to say. Sean (Kerr Smith) is driving cross-country, when he picks up a hitchhiker named Nick (Brandon Fehr). Nick is actually a vampire-hunter, aiming to stop a band of the undead who have been terrorizing the local desert area. From this point on, everything that takes place in the film is very predictable and *The Forsaken* becomes very tedious. The film mixes car-chases and shootouts, but the action is never engaging. A new origin for vampirism is given, but this unique touch is nowhere near enough to save this anemic film. One would be much better off watching one of the films that influenced *The Forsaken.* Having said that, the DVD features a nearly flawless transfer of the film, which shows no grain during the daytime scenes and accurately balances the darkness in the nighttime shots. There are no conspicuous defects on this transfer. The audio is excellent as well, with the 5.1 track providing a nice dynamic range.

There is always realistic Surround sound and the bass response is nice as well. If you must watch this DVD, be sure to watch the featurette about the true stars of the film—the cars. —ML
Movie: 🎬 ½ **DVD:** 🎬🎬🎬
Columbia Tristar (cat #06453, UPC 04339-6064539). Widescreen (1.85:1) anamorphic. Dolby Digital 5.1. $24.95. Keepcase. *LANG:* English; French. *SUB:* English; French; Chinese; Korean; Thai. *CAP:* English. *FEATURES:* Commentary • Featurettes • Theatrical trailer • Deleted scenes • Cast & crew. **2001 (R) 90m/C** Kerr Smith, Izabella Miko, Johnathon Schaech, Brendan Fehr, Simon Rex, Carrie Snodgress, Phina Oruche; *D:* J.S. Cardone; *W:* J.S. Cardone; *C:* Steven Bernstein; *M:* Johnny Lee Schell, Tim Jones.

Fortune Quest: Journey to Terrason

Anime does little to distinguish itself from other entries into the fantasy genre, save for the fact that the story line resembles a game of "Dungeons & Dragons" at times. At the outset, we are introduced to our five main characters: Pastel, a young poet and topographer; Clay, a fighter; Trapp, a thief; Rumy, an elf-kid; and Shiro, a baby white dragon. This quintet is a "gang" that likes to go on adventures. Having recently returned from an excursion, the group is recuperating at Trapp's mansion. When Trapp's father, who is a world-renowned thief, comes home with a strange jewel, a new adventure unfolds. Trapp mysteriously disappears and the team must confront a group of white dragons to save their friend. *Fortune Quest* offers an engaging story and interesting characters, but at times fall prey to its own silliness. Fantasy fans will certainly enjoy the action here, however, those who prefer more mature anime may find themselves annoyed by Rumy and Shiro. The title is appropriate for the "Pokemon" and "Digimon" crowd, as it features only cartoonish violence. As far as style goes, *Fortune Quest* looks like any number of Japanimation offerings, as it features the stereotypical wide-eyed characters and multi-plain animation. The DVD yields a good transfer of the program, and is presented in a full-frame manner. The image is sharp and clear, although it is a bit soft at times. The color scheme is excellent, highlighting the bold yellows and reds used here. Both the original Japanese dialogue and a newly created dubbed English track are offered here. The audio is crisp and clear, giving us intelligible dialogue and good sound effects. However, the sound from the rear speakers is so low as to be almost non-existent. The subtitles are yellow and very easy to read. —ML
Movie: 🎬🎬 ½ **DVD:** 🎬🎬 ½
Media Blasters (cat #EFDVD-8906, UPC 631595890679). Full frame. Dolby Surround. $29.95. Keepcase. *LANG:* English; Japanese. *SUB:* English. *FEATURES:* Bonus trailers • 25 chapters. **1997 125m/C** *D:* Rubin Arvizu, Eiichi Sato.

42 Up

Important, irreverent entry in the "Up" documentary series. In 1964, a TV documentary was made focusing on 14 seven-year-old English children from various classes and backgrounds. Every seven years since then, another documentary has been produced in which the growing children discuss and reflect on their career and life goals, hopes, triumphs, and failures. This sixth film finds all the interviewees now 42 and in various states of personal happiness, fulfillment, or disillusionment. An amazing, moving, distressing, and eye-opening examination of life and what it is to be human. Clips from the other "Up" series are featured in the profiles, so prior viewing of the earlier installments is not a requirement. When finished, copies of the entire series should be launched into space for other civilizations to find. I can think of no greater record of human growth and values. The colors on the disc are rich and vivid for the most part. The various clips from previous installments showcase grainier and less-pristine film elements. The grainy black-and-white footage is occasionally prone to digital noise, but the whole package is highly satisfying. Apted fills the commentary with behind-the-scenes information but the track is a little bit dry and is better sampled in sections. —DG
Movie: 🎬🎬🎬🎬 **DVD:** 🎬🎬🎬 ½
First Run Features (cat #FRF909754D, UPC 720229909754). Full frame. Dolby Digital Mono. $29.95. Keepcase. *LANG:* English. *FEATURES:* Commentary: Apted • Director bio and filmography • 12 chapters. **2000 139m/C** *GB D:* Michael Apted.

Fosse

Filmed performance of the stage play of the same name. The play celebrates the work of one of Broadway's greatest talents—Bob Fosse. Features such memorable songs as: "Life Is Just a Bowl of Cherries," "Steam Heat," "Dancin' Man," and "Big Spender." Unfortunately, like most filmed Broadway performances, it fails to capture the spirit and exuberance of the "live" performance. Which makes the disc more enjoyable as a soundtrack rather than a film. That being said, the disc is exceptional in its presentation. The video transfer is very good and boasts extremely well-defined colors and blacks. The re-mixed soundtrack is the real standout. Music is spread out over the different channels very well which results in a lush yet sharp sound. —MJT
Movie: 🎬🎬 ½ **DVD:** 🎬🎬🎬
Image Ent. (cat #ID1527WNDVD, UPC 014381152722). Widescreen (1.78:1) anamorphic. Dolby Digital 5.1 Surround; Dolby Digital Stereo; DTS 5.1 Surround. $24.99. Keepcase. *LANG:* English. *FEATURES:* 33 chapters. **2001 127m/C** Ben Vereen, Ann Reinking; *D:* Matthew Diamond.

Four Dogs Playing Poker

Down in Rio, four friends (Getty, Edwards, London, and Williams) steal a valuable Degas statue with the help of Felix (Curry). But it disappears en route to Los Angeles and the buyer, Mr. Ellington (Whitaker), is none too happy. He demands a cool million. The four buds decide to take out life insurance policies and then to have one kill another to raise the money. The plot echoes *Usual Suspects* and *Shallow Grave* but lacks the fresh nastiness of those two originals. The widescreen image is acceptable, not exceptional. It's clear enough but soft and lacking fine detail. Overall, it appears to be an accurate re-creation of a mid-budget original. Sound is all the film demands. —*MM*
Movie: ♪♪ ½ **DVD:** ♪♪ ½
Warner (cat #37410, UPC 0853937410-20). Widescreen (1.85:1) letterboxed. Dolby Digital Surround. $19.98. Snapper. *LANG:* English. *SUB:* English; French; Spanish. *FEATURES:* 25 chapters • Trailer • Talent files.
2000 (R) 98m/C Olivia Williams, Balthazar Getty, Stacy Edwards, Daniel London, Tim Curry, Forest Whitaker, George Lazenby, John Taylor; **D:** Paul Rachman; **W:** Thomas Durham, William Quist; **C:** Claudio Rocha; **M:** Brian Tyler, Scott Hackwith.

4:50 from Paddington

Please see review for *Sleeping Murder / 4:50 from Paddington.*
1987 100m/C Joan Hickson, David Horovitch, David Waller, Maurice Denham, Joanna David; **D:** Frank Conniff; **W:** T.R. Bowen; **C:** John Walker.

Four for Texas

Ponderous, poorly made western appears to be serious at times—with Bronson as a cold-eyed villain—spoofy at others—note the cameos by the Three Stooges and Arthur Godfrey. Joe Jarrett (Martin) and Zach Thomas (Sinatra) are dueling conmen in Galveston. Anita Ekberg and Ursula Andress provide plenty of pulchritude as their leading ladies. DVD presents a nice image with very bright colors—reds on the riverboat scenes are really red—with only the usual amount of grain in the dusty exteriors. I spotted no artifacts even in the panning stagecoach chase scenes. Clipped dialogue sounds like it comes from the original dubbing. —*MM*
Movie: ♪ **DVD:** ♪♪ ½
Warner (cat #21495, UPC 0853921495-20). Widescreen (1.85:1) letterboxed. $19.98. Snapper. *LANG:* English; French. *SUB:* English; French; Spanish; Portuguese; Japanese; Chinese; Korean; Thai. *FEATURES:* 30 chapters • Behind-the-scenes featurette • Talent files • Trailer.
1963 124m/C Frank Sinatra, Dean Martin, Anita Ekberg, Ursula Andress, Charles Bronson, Victor Buono, Jack Elam, Arthur Godfrey, Moe Howard, Larry Fine, Joe DeRi-

ta; **D:** Robert Aldrich; **W:** Robert Aldrich, Teddi Sherman; **C:** Ernest Laszlo; **M:** Nelson Riddle.

Four of the Apocalypse

Bizarre spaghetti western is an adaptation of Brett Harte's *The Outcasts of Poker Flats* that's played out over a '70s hippie rock score. Gambler Stubby (Testi), pregnant prostitute Bunny (Frederick), drunk Clem (Pollard), and possibly mad Buck (Baird), who sees dead people, are thrown out of town. Out in the desert, they run across the vicious Chaco (Milian) and the plotting gets very inventive. Different scenes will also remind you of *McCabe & Mrs. Miller* and *High Plains Drifter.* Production values are roughly on a par with those contemporaneous releases. DVD image is a bit pale and overexposed but that seems to come from the original elements. Almost no signs of wear are visible. Sound is fine. Some scenes that were cut from the American release have been restored with the original Italian dialogue and subtitles. —*MM* **AKA:** I Quattro dell'apocalisse; Four Horsemen of the Apocalypse.
Movie: ♪♪♪ **DVD:** ♪♪♪
Anchor Bay (cat #DV11955, UPC 0131311-95590). Widescreen (1.85:1) anamorphic. Dolby Digital Mono. $24.98. Keepcase. *LANG:* English; Italian. *SUB:* English. *FEATURES:* 25 chapters • Trailer • New "making of" featurette • Talent files.
1975 87m/C IT Fabio Testi, Tomas Milian, Lynne Frederick, Michael J. Pollard, Harry Baird; **D:** Lucio Fulci; **W:** Ennio de Concini.

Frances [Anchor Bay]

Heartbreaking story of 1930s starlet Frances Farmer (Lange), who was so far ahead of her time that she spent most of her career in and out of mental hospitals. It's a story about what happened to an eccentric woman who spoke her mind in the '30s, a time before Madonna and Rosanne, when anti-social behavior could get your adult rights revoked and turned over to your husband or mother. In this case, Frances is raised by a domineering mother (played to rationalized perfection by Kim Stanley), who repeatedly commits her to asylums, hoping Frances will come to her senses and return to her life as a "star." The primitive "mental health" scenes are painfully realistic, far beyond the simple glimpses films like *The Snake Pit* gave. The story seamlessly goes from Frances's teen years to her broken down adulthood with sad grace, and Lange flows with it effortlessly. She perfectly captures the helpless hysteria brought on by involuntary commitment to a system, both medical and studio, which has no idea how to treat her except with shock therapy and lobotomy. Both Lange and Stanley were nominated for Academy Awards. The extra featurette is a good companion to the movie in that it explains enough about the times that Frances lived in to make

the surreal aspects of the film a little more believable. The disc is beautiful with mostly solid blacks and colors that highlight the fabulous cinematography, and the sound is very good. —*CA*
Movie: ♪♪♪ ½ **DVD:** ♪♪♪ ½
Anchor Bay (cat #DV11559, UPC 0131311-55590). Widescreen (1.85:1) anamorphic. Dolby Digital Surround. Mono. $19.90. Keepcase. *LANG:* English; French. *CAP:* English. *FEATURES:* 30 chapters • "Remembering Frances" featurette • Trailer.
1982 134m/C Jessica Lange, Kim Stanley, Sam Shepard, Jeffrey DeMunn, Gerald S. O'Loughlin, Chris Pennock, John Randolph, Lane Smith; **D:** Graeme Clifford; **W:** Christopher DeVore, Nicholas Kazan, Eric Bergren; **C:** Laszlo Kovacs; **M:** John Barry. *AWARDS: NOM:* Oscars '82: Actress (Lange), Support. Actress (Stanley).

Frank Lloyd Wright— A Film by Ken Burns and Lynn Novick

PBS and famed director Ken Burns team up to bring viewers an intimate look into the life and works of this country's most famous architect, Frank Lloyd Wright. This powerful documentary chronicles Wright's personal and professional vision as he paved a prolific and staggering career that influenced generations of architects and spoke to the world. This documentary provides a plethora of archival interview footage in addition to gorgeous cinematography of the buildings he created. Stereo soundtrack is more than adequate for this type of documentary. Overall the video quality is superb. Some artifacts occur during the black-and-white interview and archival video footage, but that's to be expected. The picture quality of the housing footage is lush with gorgeous color that seems to jump off the screen. —*EL*
Movie: ♪♪♪ ½ **DVD:** ♪♪♪
Warner (cat #3675, UPC 794054367522). Full frame. Stereo. $29.98. Keepcase. *LANG:* English. *CAP:* English. *FEATURES:* "Ken Burns: Making History" behind-the-scenes featurette • Ken Burns interview • Ken Burns and Lynn Novick interview with Charlie Rose • Weblinks • 16 chapters.
1998 153m/C D: Ken Burns, Lynn Novick; **W:** Geoffrey C. Ward; **Nar:** Edward Herrmann.

Frankenstein Meets the Wolfman

Guilty and weary, Lawrence Talbot (Chaney Jr.) comes to "Visaria" under the assumed name Taylor, in hopes of locating Dr. Frankenstein's notebooks. Larry wants to learn the long-dead Doctor's secrets of life and death with the aim of ending his own life: he somehow reasons that his supernatural existence as the lycanthropian "Wolf Man" can only be terminated through Frankenstein's alchemistic science. In short order he finds Visaria a backward hamlet of burghers and peasants terrified of the castle above them on the hill. He finds no diaries but does uncover the frozen, intact Frankenstein Monster (Lugosi), who needs merely to be pulled from the ice to pop back to life. The film looks fine on DVD, with the same intermittent speckling here and there but mostly sharp looking. Frequent series cameraman George Robinson's lighting is the best thing in the movie. Many of the setups look great and there's nothing lazy about the look of the film. It's available as a double feature with *House of Frankenstein* (see separate entry). —GE

Movie: 🐾🐾 ½ **DVD:** 🐾🐾🐾
Universal Studios (cat #21401, UPC 0251-92140129). Full frame. Dolby Digital Mono. $29.98. Keepcase. *LANG:* English. *SUB:* Spanish; French. *CAP:* English. *FEATURES:* Trailer • Production notes.
1942 73m/C Lon Chaney Jr., Bela Lugosi, Patric Knowles, Lionel Atwill, Maria Ouspenskaya, Ilona Massey, Dwight Frye; *D:* Roy William Neill; *W:* Curt Siodmak; *C:* George Robinson.

Frankie and Johnny

Ex-con gets a job as a short-order cook and falls for a world-weary waitress. She doesn't believe in romance, but finally gives in to his pleas for a chance and finds out he may not be such a bad guy after all. Nothing can make Pfeiffer dowdy enough for this role, but she and Pacino are charming together. In a change-of-pace role, Nelligan has fun as a fellow waitress who loves men. Based on the play *Frankie and Johnny in the Clair de Lune* by McNally who also wrote the screenplay. The disc showcases an impressive video transfer that features well-defined colors and blacks (though some darker scenes exhibit a drop in clarity). The disc features solid dialogue as well as ambient sounds and a musical score that are remarkably well reproduced. —MJT

Movie: 🐾🐾🐾 **DVD:** 🐾🐾 ½
Paramount (cat #32222, UPC 097363222-248). Widescreen (1.85:1) anamorphic. Dolby Digital 5.1 Surround; Dolby Digital Surround. $24.99. Keepcase. *LANG:* English. *SUB:* English. *FEATURES:* 17 chapters • Theatrical trailer.
1991 (R) 117m/C Al Pacino, Michelle Pfeiffer, Hector Elizondo, Nathan Lane, Kate Nelligan, Jane Morris, Greg Lewis, Al Fann, K. Callan, Phil Leeds, Tracy Reiner, Dey Young; *D:* Garry Marshall; *W:* Terrance McNally; *C:* Dante Spinotti; *M:* Marvin Hamlisch. *AWARDS:* British Acad. '91: Support. Actress (Nelligan); Natl. Bd. of Review '91: Support. Actress (Nelligan).

Fraternity Vacation

Two frat boys (Robbins and Dye) go on spring break with geeky pledge Wendell (Geoffreys), since his family owns a Palm Springs condo. Things get out of control when they make a bet with a rival fraternity over which one of them can score with their beautiful neighbor (Wilson). A typical '80s college movie that Tim Robbins has

long since dropped from his résumé. The picture is clear and relatively free of grain, though the colors seem exceptionally soft. The soundtrack frequently bumps its head on a low ceiling. —BG

Movie: 🐾 ½ **DVD:** 🐾🐾 ½
Anchor Bay (cat #DV11452, UPC 0131-31145298). Widescreen (1.85:1) anamorphic. Dolby Mono. $14.98. Keepcase. *LANG:* English. *CAP:* English. *FEATURES:* 25 chapters • Trailers • Liner notes interview with star Leigh McCloskey.
1985 (R) 95m/C Stephen Geoffreys, Sheree J. Wilson, Cameron Dye, Leigh McCloskey, Tim Robbins, Matt McCoy, Amanda Bearse, John Vernon, Nita Talbot, Barbara Crampton, Kathleen Kinmont, Max Wright, Julie Payne, Franklin Ajaye, Charles Rocket, Britt Ekland; *D:* James Frawley; *W:* Lindsay Harrison; *C:* Paul Ryan; *M:* Brad Fiedel.

Freddy Got Fingered

Legitimate contender for Worst-Movie honors stars first-time director Green as Gord, a dedicated slacker who refuses to get a job and move out of his father's (Torn) house. Green's trademarked bad taste jokes include horses, elephants, and kinky sex from a wheelchair-bound girlfriend. Are you laughing yet? If not, how about Gord's falsely accusing his overbearing father of abusing his younger son, thereby explaining the title? The film is appallingly bad in every respect; the DVD is fine in image, sound, and extras. It looks terrific. Green's commentary track is inane, though his ineptitude may have been meant to be humorous. Other commentaries are limited to a few scenes. A very short "PG"-rated version is also included. —MM

Movie: woof **DVD:** 🐾🐾🐾
20th Century Fox (UPC 024543024590). Widescreen (2.35:1) anamorphic. Dolby Digital 5.1 Surround; Dolby Surround. $19.98. Keepcase. *LANG:* English; French. *SUB:* English; Spanish. *FEATURES:* 28 chapters • Commentary: Tom Green • Scene-specific commentary: Wilson, Coughlan, Torn • "PG" version.
2001 (R) 88m/C Tom Green, Rip Torn, Harland Williams, Eddie Kaye Thomas, Julie Hagerty, Anthony Michael Hall, Marisa Coughlan; *D:* Tom Green; *W:* Tom Green, Derek Harvie; *C:* Mark Irwin; *M:* Mike Simpson. *AWARDS:* Golden Raspberries '01: Worst Picture, Worst Actor (Green), Worst Director (Green), Worst Screenplay.

Free to Be... You and Me

In 1972, *That Girl!* star Marlo Thomas noticed that most programming for children was either gender or racially biased. So, she decided to create a work which would be free from such stereotypes and encourage children to be themselves. The result was the Peabody and Emmy Award–winning TV special, *Free to Be...You and Me*. Thomas was able to recruit many celebrity guests, such as Michael Jack-

son, Alan Alda, Mel Brooks, Kris Kristofferson, Harry Belafonte, and many more to assist with the project. The result is a celebration of human beings expressed through music, skits, and animation. The program offers 15 different sections, which explore such topics as gender stereotypes, parental roles, emotions, and manners. Many of the topics are still relevant, but some come across as very dated. The segment in which Thomas and Belafonte sing about the jobs that mommies and daddies have feels quite awkward, but shows how far working mothers have come. And while some of the skits are quite hokey (the Michael Jackson segment is fascinating, given how he's changed over the years), overall, it's a positive piece. So, this DVD can be a nostalgia piece for those who grew up with this special and the series of guidance films that it spawned (I can still remember watching them in school), but it could potentially be a good learning tool for parents and families. The image varies greatly in quality throughout the show. The opening credits and the last segment were both clearly shot on film and haven't held up very well, as they are riddled with scratches and blemishes. The bulk of the live-action skits were captured on video and they look fine, offering clear images and no distortion. The same goes for the animated segments, which look fine as well. The Dolby Digital Mono sound offers clear dialogue, but there is a low-frequency hum audible throughout. —ML

Movie: 🐾🐾 **DVD:** 🐾🐾 ½
Hen's Tooth Video (cat #4079, UPC 759-731407922). Full frame. Dolby Digital Mono. $19.95. Keepcase. *LANG:* English. *FEATURES:* 16 chapters.
1974 45m/C Marlo Thomas, Alan Alda, Harry Belafonte, Mel Brooks, Diana Ross, Roosevelt "Rosie" Grier, Michael Jackson, Kris Kristofferson.

Freez'er

JM (Walker III) catches his wife Andrea (Walrond) in bed with another man. In a moment of passion, he smacks her with a baseball bat. What to do next? Hide the body, of course, and that leads to an efficient little horror. Writer/director Avenet-Bradley squeezes every penny out of a modest budget and wisely limits himself to a few characters and settings. He also got surprisingly good performances from his cast. Minimal score is effective. This is what independently produced genre pictures ought to be but so seldom are. DVD can do little to improve the grainy image, but then, that's what this kind of movie is supposed to look like. His commentary track is fine. Recommended to fans. —MM

Movie: 🐾🐾🐾 **DVD:** 🐾🐾 ½
Steeplechase Ent. (cat #2005-9, UPC 808-837200590). Full frame. $19.98. Keepcase. *LANG:* English. *FEATURES:* 9 chapters • 2 deleted scenes • Commentary: director • Behind-the-scenes featurette • Photo gallery • Trailer • Internet links.

2000 83m/C Barnes Walker III, Carrie Walrond, John L. Altom; **D:** Brian Avenet-Bradley; **W:** Brian Avenet-Bradley; **C:** Brian Avenet-Bradley; **M:** Mark Lee Fletcher.

The French Connection [SE]

Popeye Doyle (Hackman) and his partner Buddy Russo (Scheider) are a couple of hard-nosed NYC narcotics detectives who stumble onto what turns out to be one of the biggest narcotics rings of all time, involving French mastermind Alain Charnier (Rey). Cat-and-mouse thriller will keep you on the edge of your seat; contains one of the most exciting chase scenes ever filmed. Hackman's portrayal of Doyle is exact and the teamwork with Scheider special. Based on a true story from the book by Robin Moore. Followed in 1975 by *French Connection 2*. Friedkin's film is harsh and dirty looking, so don't blame it on the DVD. In fact, on this excellent DVD, *The French Connection* looks pretty much exactly as it did when it hit the big screen decades ago. There is grain present but it is again an accurate representation of the grain of the film stock that director Friedkin employed. Imagewise, the disc appears to be perfect. The 5.1 remix created for the DVD is a good one, giving more depth and power to the score, and having none of that artificial and fake sound that comes through on a lot of remixes. This is a two-DVD set: the first includes the feature itself and two commentary tracks. The Friedkin track is the most interesting with the director supplying plenty of info on both the pre-production and the shoot itself. Disc two is nothing but supplementals including two recent hour-long documentaries, with the BBC piece by far the best of the two. The deleted scenes are O.K., but it's Friedkin's introductions to them that make them of interest. (Also available in *The French Connection 1 & 2* box set, cat. #20028, $39.98.) —JO
Movie: 🎜🎜🎜 ½ **DVD:** 🎜🎜🎜🎜
20th Century Fox (cat #2002065, UPC 24543020653). Widescreen (1.78:1) anamorphic. Dolby Digital 5.1 Surround Stereo; Dolby Digital Surround; Mono. $26.98. Keepcase. *LANG:* English; French. *SUB:* Spanish. *CAP:* English. *FEATURES:* Commentary: Friedkin, Hackman, Scheider • Theatrical trailer • "Making *The French Connection*: The Untold Stories" • Deleted scenes documentary hosted by Friedkin • Photo gallery • 32 chapters • *Poughkeepsie Shuffle* BBC documentary • *French Connection 2* theatrical trailer • Dual-layered RDSL. Also available in *The French Connection 1 & 2* box set (cat. #20028), $39.98.
1971 (R) 102m/C Gene Hackman, Roy Scheider, Fernando Rey, Tony LoBianco, Eddie Egan, Sonny Grosso, Marcel Bozzuffi; **D:** William Friedkin; **W:** Ernest Tidyman; **C:** Owen Roizman; **M:** Don Ellis. *AWARDS:* Oscars '71: Actor (Hackman), Adapt. Screenplay, Director (Friedkin), Film Editing, Picture; AFI '98: Top 100; British

Acad. '72: Actor (Hackman); Directors Guild '71: Director (Friedkin); Golden Globes '72: Actor—Drama (Hackman), Director (Friedkin), Film—Drama; Natl. Bd. of Review '71: Actor (Hackman); N.Y. Film Critics '71: Actor (Hackman); Writers Guild '71: Adapt. Screenplay; *NOM:* Oscars '71: Cinematog., Sound, Support. Actor (Scheider).

French Connection 2

New York policeman "Popeye" Doyle goes to Marseilles to crack a heroin ring headed by his arch nemesis, Frog One, whom he failed to stop in the United States. Dour, super-gritty sequel to the 1971 blockbuster, and featuring one of Hackman's most uncompromising performances. Fox has given this sequel as good a transfer as the original. The film itself is sharper, less grainy, and more colorful, so in many ways this DVD looks better than the first. Colors are saturated and strong. Blacks are always dead-on and the shadow detail high, even in the numerous night and indoor scenes. The stereo sound is not as powerful as the 5.1 remix that was done for the first film but is always more than adequate. Like *The French Connection*, the sequel features two commentary tracks, the first by director Frankenheimer, who does as good a job as Friedkin had on the first. It's clear that Frankenheimer still considers the making of *The French Connection 2* and working with Hackman one of the best experiences of his entire career. The second track pales in comparison but is still pretty good. Well worth spending the extra $13.00 (above the cost of the original by itself) to get this conclusion to the Frog One saga. (Only available as part of *The French Connection 1 & 2* box set, cat. #20028, $39.98.) —JO
Movie: 🎜🎜🎜 ½ **DVD:** 🎜🎜🎜 ½
20th Century Fox Widescreen (1.85:1) anamorphic. Dolby Digital Stereo; Dolby Digital Mono. Keepcase. *LANG:* English (Stereo, Mono); French (Mono). *SUB:* English; Spanish. *CAP:* English. *FEATURES:* 32 chapters • Theatrical trailer • Photo gallery • Storyboard gallery • Commentary: Frankenheimer, Hackman, Rosen.
1975 (R) 118m/C Gene Hackman, Fernando Rey, Bernard Fresson; **D:** John Frankenheimer; **W:** Robert Dillon; **C:** Claude Renoir; **M:** Don Ellis.

The French Lieutenant's Woman

A film is being made of a 19th-century English romance, where Charles (Irons), a biologist who's engaged to be married, falls in love with outcast Sarah (Streep) in a short but passionate affair. Anna and Mike, who play the characters of Sarah and Charles, have a relationship that runs parallel to that of their characters. Script by Harold Pinter adds the element of film-within-a-film as an externalized metaphor for novelist John Fowles's own omniscient, self-reflexive commentary from the pre-

sent of 1967. Freddie Francis, who directed some Hammer films, lends his Gothic eye as cinematographer. Director Karel Reisz has made some good films, such as *Morgan* and *Who'll Stop the Rain?*, but Pinter's script, per usual, is so detached that it seems at odds with Reisz's more passionate energies. However intriguing the idea of contrasting a time of suffocating morals with a time of no morals (with heartbreak the inevitable result in both), I prefer other film-within-film musings such as the Dionysian if erratic Dennis Hopper's *Last Movie*. Another first-rate transfer from MGM/UA does complete justice to the DVD image and, though not Dolby Digital 5.1, dialogue and score are crisp and clean. —MO
Movie: 🎜🎜🎜 **DVD:** 🎜🎜🎜🎜
MGM Home Ent. (cat #1002458, UPC 027616866653). Widescreen (1.85:1) anamorphic. Dolby Digital 2.0 Mono. $19.98. Keepcase. *LANG:* English; French; Spanish. *SUB:* French; Spanish. *CAP:* English; French; Spanish. *FEATURES:* 16 chapters • Theatrical trailer.
1981 (R) 124m/C Meryl Streep, Jeremy Irons, Leo McKern, Lynsey Baxter; **D:** Karel Reisz; **W:** Harold Pinter; **C:** Freddie Francis; **M:** Carl Davis. *AWARDS:* British Acad. '81: Actress (Streep); Golden Globes '82: Actress—Drama (Streep); L.A. Film Critics '81: Actress (Streep); *NOM:* Oscars '81: Actress (Streep), Adapt. Screenplay, Art Dir./Set Dec., Costume Des., Film Editing.

Fresh

In this urban drama, an intelligent 12-year-old boy named Fresh (Nelson) runs heroin in the morning and sells crack after school in a tough Brooklyn neighborhood. This enterprising young man draws life-lessons from chess-hustler father Sam (Jackson) and heroin-dealing mentor Esteban (Esposito), so he looks for a way out of the dead-end business. First time writer/director Boaz Yakin plays it straight, foregoing the usual Hollywood-style rap and automatic weapons approach to convey the message that circumstances can kill innocence just as effectively as a bullet. Startling, but subdued, the atmosphere allows the plot and characters to become more complicated than first expected. Excellent performance by newcomer Nelson and, as usual, Jackson is electric. Yakin would go on to make a hit family film for Disney with *Remember the Titans*. This DVD release is part of Miramax's "Collector's Series." Despite the relatively low-budget nature of this film, this transfer is outstanding. The image is very sharp and clear, showing practically no grain and only minor defects from the source print. There is little artifacting and the colors are superb. On the audio side, the Dolby Surround track provides a robust soundtrack, which gives clear dialogue, nice Surround effects, and realistic bass response during a shootout scene. In his informative commentary, writer/director Yakin discusses the mak-

ing of the film and his inspirations for the story. —*ML*
Movie: 🎵🎵 ½ **DVD:** 🎵🎵🎵
Miramax Pictures (cat #25013, UPC 7869-36172058). Widescreen (1.85:1) anamorphic. Dolby Digital Surround Sound. $32.99. Keepcase. *LANG:* English; French. *SUB:* English. *CAP:* English. *FEATURES:* Commentary • Featurette • Storyboards • Gag reel • Cast audition tapes • 20 chapters.
1994 (R) 114m/C *FR* Samuel L. Jackson, Giancarlo Esposito, Sean Nelson, N'Bushe Wright, Ron Brice, Jean LaMarre, Luis Lantigua, Yul Vazquez, Cheryl Freeman; *D:* Boaz Yakin; *W:* Boaz Yakin; *C:* Adam Holender. *AWARDS:* Ind. Spirit '95: Debut Perf. (Nelson); Sundance '94: Special Jury Prize, Filmmakers Trophy; *NOM:* Ind. Spirit '95: Support. Actor (Esposito).

Friction
Poor Natalie (Wagner) works as a secretary and is having trouble making ends meet. While a mechanic is telling her about the bill for her car repairs, she runs into an old pal who seems to be rolling in dough. What's the secret? She's a lap dancer. Natalie considers a career change, or at least a little moonlighting. Tepid material looks pretty bad on disc. Excessive grain makes the image worse than most VHS tapes of comparable low-budget stuff. No-frills disc lacks even a menu. —*MM* *AKA:* Lap Dancer.
Movie: 🎵 ½ **DVD:** 🎵 ½
York Ent. (cat #YPD-1160, UPC 75072311-6020). Full frame. $14.98. Keepcase. *LANG:* English. *FEATURES:* 15 chapters.
1995 80m/C Elizabeth Wagner, Steve Kesmodel, Jennifer Wolf; *D:* Arthur Egeli; *W:* Michael Paul Girard, D. Avelo; *C:* Felipe Alba.

Friday the 13th, Part 5: A New Beginning
Jason rises from the dead to slice up the residents of a secluded halfway house. The sequels and the sameness never stop, but this one does boast more polished production values than many entries in the series and those are the highlight of the DVD. Image and monaural sound are excellent. —*MM*
Movie: woof **DVD:** 🎵🎵🎵
Paramount (cat #01823, UPC 097360182-347). Widescreen anamorphic. Dolby Digital Mono. $24.98. Keepcase. *LANG:* English; French. *SUB:* English. *CAP:* English. *FEATURES:* Trailer • 14 chapters.
1985 (R) 92m/C John Shepherd, Melanie Kinnaman, Shavar Ross, Richard Young, Juliette Cummins, Corey Feldman, Carol Lacatell, Vernon Washington; *D:* Danny Steinmann; *W:* Danny Steinmann, David M. Cohen, Martin Kitrosser; *C:* Stephen Posey.

Friday the 13th, Part 6: Jason Lives
In a beginning borrowed from *Ghost of Frankenstein*, Jason is revived and the same old slice-'n'-dice follows. Tired

sequel was followed by even more that became even worse. DVD presents one of the sharpest images in the series. Film looks and sounds very good, not that those matter. —*MM*
Movie: woof **DVD:** 🎵🎵 ½
Paramount (cat #31982, UPC 097363198-246). Widescreen anamorphic. Dolby Digital Surround. $24.98. Keepcase. *LANG:* English. *SUB:* English. *CAP:* English. *FEATURES:* Teaser trailer • 16 chapters.
1986 (R) 87m/C Thom Mathews, Jennifer Cooke, David Kagen, Kerry Noonan, Renee Jones, Tom Fridley, C.J. Graham, Darcy Demoss; *D:* Tom McLoughlin; *W:* Tom McLoughlin; *C:* Jon Kranhouse; *M:* Harry Manfredini.

Friends: The Complete First Season
This four-disc set features the first 23 episodes of the definitive Generation X sitcom, about six Manhattan residents who only occasionally do anything besides sit in a coffee bar. The first season follows Ross (Schwimmer) as he deals with his ex-wife's new lesbian partner; Rachel (Aniston) as she learns to live in the real world; and the exploits of ugly naked guy. If the *Best of Friends* collections weren't enough for you, this should do the trick. The picture is nice overall, although color inconsistency shows up occasionally. The soundtrack has been remastered in Dolby 5.0, but little use is made of the rear speakers. —*BG*
Movie: 🎵🎵🎵 **DVD:** 🎵🎵🎵
Warner (cat #17804, UPC 0853917804-27). Full frame. Dolby 5.0. $69.98. Custom cardboard. *LANG:* English. *SUB:* English; French; Spanish; Korean. *CAP:* English. *FEATURES:* 23 chapters • Pilot episode commentary: producers • Central Perk interactive map • Trivia quiz • Trailer • Cast career highlights.
1995 587m/C Jennifer Aniston, Courteney Cox Arquette, Lisa Kudrow, Matt LeBlanc, Matthew Perry, David Schwimmer; *D:* James Burrows, Peter Bonerz; *W:* David Crane, Marta Kaurmann.

Fright
Before *Halloween* and *When a Stranger Calls,* this British import gave us a babysitter in jeopardy. Amanda (George) is sitting for Mrs. Lloyd (Blackman), who's more than a little nervous before leaving for her night on the town. Could it have anything to do with an escaped mental patient (Bannen)? Don't watch the incredibly lurid, spoiler-filled trailer on the disc if you want any suspense. In her tight little minidress, Susan George is a fetching heroine and the whole thing is carried off pretty well with fairly restrained exploitation elements. DVD was up to Anchor Bay's high standards. It was created from excellent original elements. The ornate, busy interior of the house looks fine; colors are bright. Light static is audible on the soundtrack, but dialogue is understand-

able throughout. Overall, the image is remarkable for a film of this age. —*MM*
AKA: Night Legs.
Movie: 🎵🎵 ½ **DVD:** 🎵🎵🎵
Anchor Bay (cat #DV12050, UPC 0131312-05091). Widescreen (1.66:1) anamorphic. Dolby Digital Mono. $19.98. Keepcase. *LANG:* English. *FEATURES:* 22 chapters • Trailer • Peter Collinson thumbnail bio.
1971 87m/C *GB* Susan George, Honor Blackman, Ian Bannen, John Gregson, George Cole, Dennis Waterman, Tara Collinson, Maurice Kaufmann, Michael Brennan, Roger Lloyd Pack; *D:* Peter Collinson; *W:* Tudor Gates; *C:* Ian Wilson; *M:* Harry Robinson.

Fritz the Cat
Ralph Bakshi's animated tale for adults about a cat's adventures as he gets into group sex, college radicalism, and other hazards of life in the 1960s. Loosely based on the underground comics character by Robert Crumb. Originally X-rated. The video transfer features reasonably well-defined colors (some loss of definition is apparent) and blacks are not as crisp or clear as they should be (which might have been caused by the state of the transfer print). The adequate soundtrack features occasionally muffled dialogue and a reasonably well-done musical score. —*MJT*
Movie: 🎵🎵🎵 **DVD:** 🎵🎵
MGM Home Ent. (cat #1002730, UPC 027616869289). Widescreen (1.85:1) anamorphic. Dolby Digital Mono. $19.98. Keepcase. *LANG:* English; French. *SUB:* English; French; Spanish. *FEATURES:* 16 chapters • Theatrical trailer.
1972 77m/C *D:* Ralph Bakshi; *W:* Ralph Bakshi; *C:* Ted C. Bemiller, Gene Borghi; *M:* Ed Bogas, Ray Shanklin; *V:* Skip Hinnant, Rosetta Le Noire, John McCurry.

From Hell [DLE]
Despite the liberties that they take with the suspects they finger (not to mention the casting of a glamorous Hollywood star as an allegedly hard-bitten prostitute), the Hughes Brothers have created a Jack the Ripper film that sticks close to the known historical facts of the famous case. Making good use of Prague locations and a superb Whitechapel set, they re-create Victorian London with remarkable effectiveness. Their storytelling techniques, though, are completely 21st century. Johnny Depp is believable enough as the opium-smoking Inspector Abberline. Heather Graham is gorgeous as activist hooker and potential victim Mary Kelly. Unfortunately, the plot finally boils itself down to yet another psychic detective on the trail of a serial killer, a story that's been told far too many times lately. DVD re-creation of an often dark and difficult image is near perfect. I could spot no flaws even in the foggy night scenes. In this special edition, the first disc contains the feature, with commentary track and more than 20 deleted scenes. The second has more short features and trailers, many

emphasizing details of the production design, the factual basis of the film, and the various sources of the story, including the complex graphic novel by Alan Moore and Eddie Campbell. A standard DVD release, without the extras, is scheduled for later in 2002. —MM

Movie: 🐾🐾🐾 **DVD:** 🐾🐾🐾🐾
20th Century Fox (cat #2003560). Widescreen (2.35:1) anamorphic. Dolby Digital 5.1 Surround; DTS 5.1 Surround; Dolby Surround. $29.98. Keepcase. *LANG:* English; French; Spanish. *SUB:* English. *CAP:* English. *FEATURES:* 32 chapters • Commentary • Deleted scenes • 6 featurettes • Trailers.

2001 (R) 121m/C Johnny Depp, Heather Graham, Ian Holm, Robbie Coltrane, Ian Richardson, Jason Flemyng, Katrin Cartlidge, Terence Harvey, Susan Lynch, Leslie Sharp, Annabelle Apsion; *D:* Albert Hughes, Allen Hughes; *W:* Terry Hayes, Rafael Yglesias; *C:* Peter Deming; *M:* Trevor Jones.

From Here to Eternity

In late 1941, Pvt. Robert E. Lee Prewitt (Clift) joins Sgt. Milt Warden's (Lancaster) outfit at Schofield Barracks. Capt. Holmes (Ober) wants the new man to box on the regimental team but Prewitt refuses; he'd rather bugle. The boxers, all NCOs, then give him "the treatment"—endless rounds of punishment for invented infractions. With the help of his friend Maggio (Sinatra), Prewitt perseveres. At the same time, Warden puts some moves on Holmes's unhappy wife Karen (Kerr) and Prewitt meets Lorene (Reed), a professional "conversationalist" at the Congress Club. The great WWII romance arrives on DVD looking about as good as it ever has. Though the film has been digitally "washed," a few dust flecks are still there, but only the picky will complain about them. Movies from the '50s aren't supposed to be visually flawless. This one has character. The extras are nice enough but really cannot really add much to a film that's just about perfectly realized. Mono sound is crisp and clear for some of the sharpest dialogue you'll ever hear. This one belongs in every library. —MM

Movie: 🐾🐾🐾🐾 **DVD:** 🐾🐾🐾 ½
Columbia TriStar (cat #05319, UPC 043396053199). Full frame. Dolby Digital Mono. $24.98. Keepcase. *LANG:* English; French; Spanish; Portuguese. *SUB:* English; French; Spanish; Portuguese; Chinese; Korean; Thai. *CAP:* English. *FEATURES:* 28 chapters • Commentary: Tim Zinnemann, Alvin Sargent • "Making of" featurette • Trailers • Filmographies • Production notes • Excerpt from "Fred Zinnemann: As I See It."

1953 118m/B Burt Lancaster, Montgomery Clift, Frank Sinatra, Deborah Kerr, Donna Reed, Ernest Borgnine, Jack Warden, Philip Ober, Mickey Shaughnessy, George Reeves, Claude Akins, Harry Bellaver, John Dennis, Tim Ryan, John Bryant, John Cason, Doug(las) Henderson, Robert Karnes, Robert J. Wilke, Carleton Young, Merle Travis, Arthur Keegan, Barbara Morrison, Tyler McVey; *D:* Fred Zinne-

mann; *W:* Daniel Taradash; *C:* Burnett Guffey; *M:* George Duning. *AWARDS:* Oscars '53: B&W Cinematog., Director (Zinnemann), Film Editing, Picture, Screenplay, Sound, Support. Actor (Sinatra), Support. Actress (Reed); AFI '98: Top 100; Director's Guild '53: Director (Zinnemann); Golden Globes '54: Support. Actor (Sinatra); N.Y. Film Critics '53: Actor (Lancaster), Director (Zinnemann), Film.

Full Eclipse

A clean-looking, well-acted take on werewolf lore. Max (Van Peebles) is despondent and confused after the suicide of his partner. Adam Garou (no foreshadowing there), who runs a special unit of the LAPD, wants to help Max in his time of need by making him part of his crack team where he will be able to make a difference in the community. The only catch is the unit shoots up a mysterious golden liquid that gives them superhuman powers and some of the worst prosthetic claws ever seen growing out of their knuckles. At first Max is hesitant, but when Casey (Kensit) seduces then shoots Max, he has little choice but to take the potion and live. Garou (Payne) leads the group on nightly hunts and there is slaughter and it is good. Max researches Garou and finds out that he's lived a really long time, especially for a drug addict. But is he a drug addict? Where does this mysterious liquid come from? The final revelation is no revelation at all, and the same can be said for the entire story. The film and the people all look good; the actors act well, everything is lit right, but in the end there is no passion and you really don't care who lives or dies. Well, actually you root for Garou, cause he seems to know how to have fun and act in a real monster movie. The disc is fabulous, the scenes are mostly at night with the actors in black clothing and the lead actor is black, but there's not trouble seeing the action due to clever use of neon light and night vision goggles. The sound is above average. —CA

Movie: 🐾🐾 **DVD:** 🐾🐾🐾 ½
HBO (cat #91130, UPC 026359113024). Full frame. Dolby Surround; Dolby Digital Stereo; Stereo. $14.98. Snapper. *LANG:* English; Spanish. *SUB:* English; French; Spanish. *CAP:* English. *FEATURES:* 15 chapters • Cast and crew bios.

1993 (R) 97m/C Mario Van Peebles, Patsy Kensit, Bruce Payne, Anthony John (Tony) Denison; *D:* Anthony Hickox; *W:* Richard Christian Matheson; *C:* Sandi Sissel.

Full Metal Jacket [2 SE]

Kubrick's Vietnam film is re-released on DVD in a newly remastered edition. (The first disc is reviewed in *Book 1*.) The movie is presented full-frame, just as the director intended, but the image presented in this new transfer is definitely an improvement. The picture is sharp and clear, showing little grain and no overt noise. Also better is the newly mastered Dolby Digital 5.1 soundtrack. While this track is a little light on the

Surround sound, it does offer clear dialogue and no distortion. The rear channels are used mostly for musical cues and major sound effects, but the battle scenes do sound very nice. The sound field isn't very wide, but once again, this is better than the previous 2-channel soundtrack. —ML

Movie: 🐾🐾🐾 **DVD:** 🐾🐾🐾 ½
Warner (cat #21154, UPC 0853921154-26). Full frame. Dolby Digital 5.1 Surround Stereo. $24.98. Snapper. *LANG:* English; French. *SUB:* English; French; Portuguese; Spanish. *FEATURES:* Trailer.

1987 (R) 116m/C Matthew Modine, R. Lee Ermey, Vincent D'Onofrio, Adam Baldwin, Dorian Harewood, Arliss Howard, Kevyn Major Howard, Ed O'Ross, John Terry, Jon Stafford, Marcus D'Amico, Kieron Jecchinis, Bruce Boa, Kirk Taylor, Tim Colceri, Ian Tyler, Gary Landon Mills, Sal Lopez, Ngoc Le, Peter Edmund, Tan Hung Francione, Leanne Hong, Costas Dino Chimona; *D:* Stanley Kubrick; *W:* Stanley Kubrick, Michael Herr, Gustav Hasford; *C:* Doug Milsome; *M:* Abigail Mead. *AWARDS:* NOM: Oscars '87: Adapt. Screenplay.

Full Moon in Blue Water

Widower Floyd (the always fine Hackman) is in imminent danger of losing his café. He owes back taxes and the local real estate slimeball wants to trick him out of his property. Luckily for him, school bus driver Louise (Garr) not only wants to save his business, she wants to save him, too. Fine comic performances, especially by Garr and Meredith, and charming atmosphere. Visual quality is above average on both screen formats. Sound is crisp and clear. —LA

Movie: 🐾🐾 ½ **DVD:** 🐾🐾🐾
MGM Home Ent. (cat #1003350, UPC 027616874993). Widescreen (1.85:1) anamorphic; full frame. $14.98. Keepcase. *LANG:* English. *SUB:* French; Spanish. *CAP:* English. *FEATURES:* Original theatrical trailer • 16 chapters.

1988 (R) 96m/C Gene Hackman, Teri Garr, Burgess Meredith, Elias Koteas, Kevin Cooney, David Doty; *D:* Peter Masterson; *W:* Bill Bozzone; *C:* Fred Murphy; *M:* Phil Marshall.

Funeral in Berlin

Second of the Caine/Harry Palmer espionage films (following up *Ipcress File*), in which the deadpan anti-hero British secret serviceman arranges the questionable defection of a Russian colonel (Homolka). Good look at the spy biz and post-war Berlin. Based on the novel by Len Deighton. *Billion Dollar Brain* continues the series. Paramount has done a fine job on the transfer, but the truth is, the rating should be knocked down a bit due to the outrageous $29.95 suggested retail price on a movie from 1966. And the only supplemental included is the theatrical trailer. This isn't the first time Paramount has done this, and it most likely won't be the last. But back to the transfer: fairly good source material with very little damage; sharp, detailed

image; excellent color, contrast, and brightness; no artifacts. Overall, the picture is much more polished than *Ipcress,* but again, it's not nearly as memorable. The mono sound delivers crisp distinct dialogue but the music is pretty thin, even considering the age of the film. —*JO/MM*
Movie: 🎼🎼🎼 **DVD:** 🎼🎼
Paramount (cat #06609, UPC 097360660-944). Widescreen (1.85:1) anamorphic. Dolby Digital Mono. $29.98. Keepcase. *LANG:* English; French. *SUB:* English. *CAP:* English. *FEATURES:* Trailer (full frame) ◦ 12 chapters.
1966 (R) 102m/C Michael Caine, Eva Renzi, Oscar Homolka, Paul (Christian) Hubschmid, Guy Doleman, Hugh Burden; *D:* Guy Hamilton; *W:* Evan Jones; *C:* Otto Heller; *M:* Konrad Elfers.

Funny, Dirty Little War

A microcosm of Argentinean politics is played out in the small town of Colonia Vela between the Peronistas and the Communists in a black comedy with a brutal message about dictatorships and the consequences of power. You don't have to know anything about Argentine politics to get the satire. Based on the novel by Osvaldo Soriano. This transfer from an old, scratched release print looks and sounds mediocre. —*LA* *AKA:* No Hambra mas Penas ni Olvido; Funny Little Dirty War.
Movie: 🎼🎼 ½ **DVD:** 🎼🎼
Vanguard Intl. Cinema (cat #VF0250, UPC 658769025033). Full frame. $29.95. Keepcase. *LANG:* Spanish. *SUB:* English. *FEATURES:* 9 chapters.
1983 80m/C *AR* Federico Luppi, Julio de Grazia, Miguel Angel Sola; *D:* Hector Olivera; *W:* Hector Olivera, Roberto Cassa; *C:* Leonardo Solis; *M:* Oscar Cardozo Ocampo.

Funny Girl

Film follows the early career of comedienne Fanny Brice (Streisand), her rise to stardom with the Ziegfeld Follies, and her stormy romance with gambler Nick Arnstein (Sharif) in a beautifully produced and funny look at backstage music hall life in the early 1900s. Wyler and Stradling outdo themselves on the fantastic widescreen compositions. Great songs, such as "People" and "Don't Rain on My Parade." Perfectly cast. The image and sound quality couldn't be better. The bonus features are remarkably well produced, but for the Streisand fan only. —*LA*
Movie: 🎼🎼🎼 **DVD:** 🎼🎼🎼🎼
Columbia Tristar (cat #03089, UPC 04339-6030893). Widescreen (2.35:1) anamorphic. Dolby Digital 5.0; Dolby Surround. $24.98. Keepcase. *LANG:* English; French. *SUB:* French; Spanish; Portuguese; Chinese; Korean; Thai. *CAP:* English. *FEATURES:* Bonus featurettes: "Barbra in Movieland," "This Is Streisand" ◦ Song highlights ◦ Filmographies ◦ Bonus trailers ◦ Production notes ◦ 28 chapters.
1968 (G) 151m/C Barbra Streisand, Omar Sharif, Walter Pidgeon, Kay Medford, Anne

Francis; *D:* William Wyler; *W:* Isobel Lennart; *C:* Harry Stradling Sr.; *M:* Jule Styne, Walter Scharf. *AWARDS:* Oscars '68: Actress (Streisand); Golden Globes '69: Actress—Mus./Comedy (Streisand); *NOM:* Oscars '68: Cinematog., Film Editing, Picture, Song ("Funny Girl"), Sound, Support. Actress (Medford), Scoring/Musical.

Funny Lady

Generally considered the inferior sequel to 1968's *Funny Girl,* wherein Barbara Streisand cemented her name as a movie star, *Funny Lady* is a reasonable follow-up with a few laughs and even a nice song or two. It's held back by a script that never seems more than a rehash of musical biography clichés, and by Ms. Streisand herself, who may sing about needing People, but doesn't convince us that she's anywhere near that human. Divorced by a humbled Nicky Arnstein (Sharif), Fanny Brice (Streisand) embarks on the second stage of her career with the pushy, obnoxious yet charming Billy Rose (Caan). If you worship the ground this woman walks on, then you've already seen this one 20 times and it's Perfect. If, like me, you think her personality is just too powerful to let anything as insignificant as a story, drama, or other actors interrupt her star aura, then the film will have you shaking your head. The problem can be seen in every frame where Streisand is on screen. Whatever the original intent of a particular scene was, it's been creatively killed by the Prime Directive: All Streisand, All the Time. She's the center of the cosmos; nothing is allowed to hold attention for more than a few milliseconds. It's no myth that stars with too much power use the post-production process to whittle away at anything and anybody who crowds their spotlight, and *Funny Lady* has all the earmarks of this kind of futzing in the cutting room. DVD has a scratch here and there but otherwise looks terrific, with vibrant colors and very clear audio. It's the last credited film by the great James Wong Howe. I hope it was his age and not this assignment that prompted the camera stylist to retire. The only extra is a menu choice that allows one to go directly to the songs in the show. Fans of Barbara Streisand will love this disc. —*GE*
Movie: 🎼🎼 **DVD:** 🎼🎼🎼
Columbia Tristar (cat #06676, UPC 043396066762). Widescreen (2:35:1) anamorphic; full frame. Dolby Digital Mono. $24.98. Keepcase. *LANG:* English; French. *SUB:* English; French; Spanish; Portuguese; Chinese; Korean; Thai. *FEATURES:* Filmographies of Herbert Ross, Barbra Streisand, James Caan ◦ Trailers.
1975 (PG) 137m/C Barbra Streisand, Omar Sharif, James Caan, Roddy McDowall, Ben Vereen, Carole Wells, Larry Gates, Heidi O'Rourke; *D:* Herbert Ross; *W:* Jay Presson Allen, Arnold Schulman; *C:* James Wong Howe. *AWARDS: NOM:* Oscars '75: Cinematog., Costume Des., Song ("How Lucky Can You Get"), Sound, Orig. Song Score and/or Adapt.

A Funny Thing Happened on the Way to the Forum

A historical farce as told by a Borscht Belt comic, set in ancient Rome, with baggy pants replaced by baggy togas. It's a door-slamming romantic (and Romanic) comedy of errors based on the hit Broadway show. Zero Mostel, star of the Broadway version, is the laziest, most conniving slave in Rome. When his master goes out of town, he's instructed to keep an eye on the master's son, but the son has fallen for the girl next door, and next door happens to be the ill-reputed house of Phil Silvers, a dealer in beautiful female slaves. The foxy slave makes a deal to get the boy his dream girl in exchange for his freedom. Complications pile on top of each other, and Mostel stays a hairbreadth ahead of getting busted every minute. Fortunately, the material is strong enough to win out over its interpretation. The DVD extras here are next to non-existent. However, the transfer is excellent. —*BT*
Movie: 🎼🎼 ½ **DVD:** 🎼🎼
MGM Home Ent. (cat #908091, UPC 027616809124). Widescreen anamorphic. $24.98. Keepcase. *LANG:* English; Spanish. *SUB:* French; Spanish. *CAP:* English. *FEATURES:* 28 chapters ◦ Trailer ◦ Booklet insert.
1966 100m/C Zero Mostel, Phil Silvers, Jack Gilford, Buster Keaton, Michael Hordern, Michael Crawford, Annette Andre; *D:* Richard Lester; *W:* Melvin Frank, Michael Pertwee; *C:* Nicolas Roeg; *M:* Ken Thorne. *AWARDS:* Oscars '66: Adapt. Score.

The Fury

The head of a government institute for psychic research finds that his own son is snatched by supposed terrorists who wish to use his lethal powers. The father tries to use another young woman with psychic power to locate him, with gory results. The visceral highlight is the sprinkler of blood near the end of the film. A real chiller. It's about time that one of my favorite DePalma films got the proper treatment, although the DVD is not without its flaws, some of them due to film print damage. The colors are vastly improved over any of the earlier video releases and they are generally strong with little or no bleed. The image stays fairly sharp except during some of the darker scenes, where there is some grain. The film was available letterboxed on laserdisc previously, and though all of the director's films are among those that truly benefit from being seen in their original aspect ratio, the LD was fairly lackluster. Fox's DVD also features a new 4.0 mix that adds a lot of power to the excellent John Williams score (my favorite of his) but is pretty much just a stereo mix with the dialogue sent to the center. Not perfect, but sure worth the upgrade. —*JO*
Movie: 🎼🎼🎼 **DVD:** 🎼🎼🎼
20th Century Fox (cat #2001387, UPC 24543013877). Widescreen (1.85:1) anamorphic. Dolby Digital 4.0; Dolby Sur-

round; Dolby Digital Mono. $19.98. Keepcase. *LANG:* English (DD4.0; DS); French (Mono). *SUB:* English; Spanish. *CAP:* English. *FEATURES:* Theatrical trailers ▪ Stills gallery ▪ 20 chapters.

1978 (R) 117m/C Kirk Douglas, John Cassavetes, Carrie Snodgress, Andrew Stevens, Amy Irving, Charles Durning, Carol Rossen, Rutanya Alda, William Finley, Jane Lambert, Joyce Easton, Daryl Hannah, Dennis Franz, James Belushi; *D:* Brian DePalma; *W:* John Farris; *C:* Richard H. Kline; *M:* John Williams.

Fury in the Shaolin Temple

Two kung fu masters secretly trade sons, agreeing to teach them their two kung fu styles. The Eagle Fist Clan kills the fathers, and the two sons are manipulated into fighting each other. A standard story of separated boys and kung fu styles, guided only by Gordon Ho's listless direction. The monks of Shaolin, though supposedly the defenders of China, are portrayed to be just as sinister as the enemy clan. The highlight is surely the appearance of the fabled robot-like 18 Bronzemen of Shaolin. The sound is of the usual poor quality of a dubbed 1970s kung fu flick. The image is squeezed and cropped. Volume 7 of the *Wu Tang Clan Hidden Chambers Collection,* a series which makes up for the often poor quality of the prints presented with quite extensive extras. These include short bios of cast and crew members, contemporary interviews, clips from cast members' other films, image galleries, trailers, nice 3-D animated menus, interview footage of the Shaolin Temple Abbots, and more. —*BT*

Movie: 🎬🎬 *DVD:* 🎬🎬 ½
Xenon Ent. (cat #7, UPC 694795302120). Full frame. $14.95. Keepcase. *LANG:* English. *FEATURES:* Cast bios ▪ Trailers ▪ Interviews ▪ Wu Tang Clan music video ▪ Wu Tang Clan interview.

1982 83m/C *HK KN* Gordon Liu, Philip Ko, Philip Cheung, Kei Chu Gam; *D:* Godfrey Ho; *W:* Stephen So; *C:* Kwok Wah Mah; *M:* Ricky Chan.

Gadget Trips— Mindscapes

Combining the talents of three music and multi-media wizards, *Gadget Trips / Mindscapes* brings the experience of free-form music and cutting-edge animation into the living room. This DVD was designed to be a visual and aural journey into sight and sound, while portraying the surreal story line of *Gadget,* a popular mystery/puzzle-based video game from the mid-'90s. The DVD release features an almost flawless transfer with no visible artifacts. The main complaint, which garnered the disc a lower bone rating, is due to the video quality in some of the CGI animation. The scenes that were taken straight from the video game unfortunately show their age. Quite a few of the scenes are grainy with some aliasing during the pans. This is possibly

due to the use of the original CD-ROM based animations, which have a lot of detail sacrificed for file size, and do not transfer well to a larger format screen. The sound on this disc is extremely crisp and the music really captivates and draws in the listener. There were no noticeable anomalies in the soundtrack, and it sounded especially good at louder volumes. —*EL*

Movie: 🎬🎬🎬 *DVD:* 🎬🎬🎬
Image Ent. (cat #9370, UPC 0143810937-28). Full frame. Dolby Digital Surround. $24.99. Keepcase. *LANG:* English. *FEATURES:* 23 chapters.

1995 79m/C *D:* Haruhiko Shono; *M:* Koji Ueno, Shin'ichi Tanaka.

Galaxina

On the galactic Space Police ship *Infinity* in the year 3009, Captain Avery Schreiber and crew are all horny for the ship's only other crew member—the robot Galaxina (Dorothy Stratton). The ship is attacked by the Vader-like villain Ordric and crashlands on the outlaw planet Altair 1. With the entire crew suffering from whiplash, Galaxina must go to an old western town to complete their mission. Early spoof of *Star Wars* has a few decent laughs in it, but only has the distinction of making a lot of lame jokes on screen first. It manages to make the most of its cheap f/x, classical music, and borrowed sound effects, but that's about all. The DVD universe is not very impressive. The smeary full-frame picture looks squeezed, with hunks sliced off both sides, and the editing seems a bit choppy. The "hilarious" Easter Egg noted on the package is easy to find—and turns out to be a short collection of unfunny, computer-animated "screen tests" for the title role. Also, the cast biography section is difficult to read, and the feature lacks subtitle or language options. However, the menu design is fittingly cheesy, in keeping with the nature of the film. —*BT*

Movie: 🎬🎬 *DVD:* 🎬🎬
Rhino (cat #R26627, UPC 0812276627-21). Full frame. Dolby Digital 5.1. $19.95. Keepcase. *LANG:* English. *FEATURES:* 16 chapters ▪ Trailer ▪ Bios ▪ Image gallery.

1980 (R) 95m/C Dorothy Stratten, Avery Schreiber, Stephen Macht, James D. Hinton, Ronald J. Knight, Lionel Smith, Tad Horino, Herb Kaplowitz, Nancy McCauley; *D:* William Sachs; *W:* William Sachs; *C:* Dean Cundey.

A Galaxy Far Far Away

This documentary introduces a screaming horde of *Star Wars* fans, and chronicles the 42 days they spent waiting in line for the premiere of *The Phantom Menace.* You also get to meet a Jedi/Rapper and a Boba Fett impersonator, and to hear discussions on the Force as religion. None of the fans are terribly articulate, and the film doesn't seem to have a clear idea of what it wants to do. The low budget is apparent on this DVD release, which features grainy picture and dialogue that is

often lost in the background noise. Once again, Vanguard has inflated the running time on their packaging by almost 15 minutes. —*BG*

Movie: 🎬 ½ *DVD:* 🎬🎬
Vanguard Intl. Cinema (cat #VFO270, UPC 658769027136). Full frame. $19.95. Keepcase. *LANG:* English. *FEATURES:* 12 chapters ▪ Deleted scenes ▪ Commentary: director, editor, producer.

2000 65m/C *D:* Tariq Jalil; *W:* Tariq Jalil, Terry Tocantins; *C:* Jeremy Ides.

The Gambler

Axel (Caan), college professor by day and world's worst gambler by night, loses $44,000 in one evening. With the mafia after him, Axel tries increasingly pathetic schemes to raise the money. This mildly interesting, occasionally tedious character study is helped by good performances (most notably from Brookes, who gives an emotional performance as Axel's mother). Dirt and scratches from the source material mar an otherwise good transfer. The mono sound is clear, but unspectacular. —*DRL*

Movie: 🎬🎬 *DVD:* 🎬🎬 ½
Paramount (cat #8678, UPC 0973608678-48). Widescreen (1.85:1) anamorphic. Mono. $24.99. Keepcase. *LANG:* English; French. *SUB:* English. *CAP:* English. *FEATURES:* 13 chapters.

1974 (R) 111m/C James Caan, Lauren Hutton, Paul Sorvino, Burt Young, James Woods, Jacqueline Brookes, M. Emmet Walsh; *D:* Karel Reisz; *W:* James Toback; *C:* Victor Kemper; *M:* Jerry Fielding.

Gandhi

The biography of Mahatma Gandhi from the prejudice he encounters as a young attorney in South Africa, to his role as spiritual leader to the people of India and his use of passive resistance against the country's British rulers, and his eventual assassination. Kingsley is a marvel in his Academy Award–winning role and the picture is a generally riveting epic worthy of its eight Oscars. There's not much to say about the DVD transfer of the film other than...it's gorgeous. The 5.1 soundtrack is also a good one, with the Ravi Shankar pieces the highlight of the score. The music sounds so good that it makes up for the near non-existent use of the Surround tracks. The worthwhile supplementals include a recent interview with Ben Kingsley and the newsreel footage of the real Gandhi that includes some of the most important moments of his life and serve to show how accurate Kingsley's performance was. —*JO*

Movie: 🎬🎬🎬 ½ *DVD:* 🎬🎬🎬 ½
Columbia Tristar (cat #03297, UPC 04339-6032972). Widescreen (2.35:1) anamorphic. Dolby Digital Stereo. $24.05. Keepcase. *LANG:* English; Spanish; French. *SUB:* English; Spanish; French; Chinese; Korean; Thai; Portuguese. *CAP:* English. *FEATURES:* 28 chapters ▪ Theatrical trailer ▪ Talent files ▪ Production notes ▪ Original Gand-

hi newsreel footage ☞ Ben Kingsley talks about Gandhi ☞ "Making of" photo montage ☞ The words of Mahatma Gandhi.
1982 (PG) 188m/C *GB* Ben Kingsley, Candice Bergen, Edward Fox, John Gielgud, John Mills, Saeed Jaffrey, Trevor Howard, Ian Charleson, Roshan Seth, Athol Fugard, Martin Sheen, Daniel Day-Lewis, Rohini Hattangady; *D:* Richard Attenborough; *W:* John Briley; *C:* Billy Williams; *M:* George Fenton. *AWARDS:* Oscars '82: Actor (Kingsley), Art Dir./Set Dec., Cinematog., Costume Des., Director (Attenborough), Film Editing, Orig. Screenplay, Picture, Sound; British Acad. '82: Actor (Kingsley), Director (Attenborough), Film, Support. Actress (Hattangady); Directors Guild '82: Director (Attenborough); Golden Globes '83: Actor—Drama (Kingsley), Director (Attenborough), Foreign Film, Screenplay; L.A. Film Critics '82: Actor (Kingsley); Natl. Bd. of Review '82: Actor (Kingsley); N.Y. Film Critics '82: Actor (Kingsley), Film; *NOM:* Oscars '82: Makeup, Orig. Score.

Gang of Four

Four theatre students, sharing a house together, find that a former roommate left some secrets behind when a police detective starts snooping around. Slow paced and very talky, with minimal payoff and endless scenes of the characters rehearsing their lines. The dialogue is clear, which is about all you can ask from the sound for a film with this much conversation. The picture is fine, but non-anamorphic. —*BG*
Movie: 🎬🎬½ *DVD:* 🎬🎬½
Image Ent. (cat #ID071951DVD, UPC 014-381071924). Widescreen (1.85:1) letterboxed. Dolby Mono. $24.99. Keepcase. *LANG:* French. *SUB:* English. *FEATURES:* 16 chapters.
1988 155m/C *FR SW* Bulle Ogier, Benoit Regent, Laurence Cote, Fejria Deliba, Ines de Medeiros; *D:* Jacques Rivette; *W:* Jacques Rivette, Pascal Bonitzer, Christian Laurent; *C:* Caroline Champetier.

Gang Related

Rodriguez (Shakur) and Divinci (Belushi) are corrupt homicide cops who set up drug deals with impounded dope, then kill the customers. Their plans unravel when they whack an undercover DEA agent posing as a dealer. This film, Shakur's last, is a genuine sleeper that shows the potential he had as an actor. Both leads are fine. The production values are actually a bit too clean and neat for the subject and its allegedly gritty treatment. Image is essentially flawless. Surround effects are fairly restrained. —*MM*
Movie: 🎬🎬🎬 *DVD:* 🎬🎬🎬
MGM Home Ent. (cat #1002635, UPC 027616868350). Widescreen (2.35:1) anamorphic. Dolby Digital 5.1 Surround Stereo; Dolby Digital Surround. $14.95. Keepcase. *LANG:* English; French; Spanish. *SUB:* English; French; Spanish. *CAP:* English. *FEATURES:* Trailer ☞ "Making of" featurette ☞ 16 chapters.

1996 (R) 109m/C James Belushi, Tupac Shakur, Dennis Quaid, Lela Rochon, James Earl Jones, David Paymer, Wendy Crewson, Gary Cole, Terrence "T.C." Carson, Brad Greenquist, James Handy, Victor Love, Robert LaSardo, Gregory Scott Cummins; *D:* Jim Kouf; *W:* Jim Kouf; *C:* Brian Reynolds; *M:* Mickey Hart.

Ganja and Hess

Upper-class museum curator Hess (Jones) has his married friend George (Gunn) over for the weekend. The depressive George stabs Hess several times with an ancient bone dagger before committing suicide. Hess finds he has been infected with a form of vampirism and brings Ganja (Clark) into his world when she comes searching for George. Crude, low-budget but ground-breaking and absolutely essential art film is part genre film, part African spiritual examination. This difficult-to-classify work was reedited in a clumsy attempt to turn it into a *Blacula*–type genre picture and re-titled *Blood Couple* (amongst others). This disc presents director Gunn's original uncut edit. It's a film with some scenes of incredible potency and imagery. Its richness rewards repeated viewings and should not be dismissed on cursory examinations. The exotic music soaks the film in an exotic atmosphere. Transferred from one of the last remaining 35mm blow-up prints (the original Super 16mm material was disassembled into the re-edited version), the film is extremely grainy and soft with muted colors and the occasional tightly framed shot. This film looked fairly poor in the theatre and this disc is the best this film will probably ever look on home video. It shouldn't affect one's appreciation of the film. The mono sound is fine. The commentary is funny, appreciative, and affectionate. Producer Schultz and cinematographer Hinton have the strongest memories but all make comments worth hearing. The essay (taken from an issue of *Video Watchdog* magazine) is worthwhile and puts the film, its re-editing, and director Gunn's careers in perspective. —*DG* *AKA:* Blood Couple; Black Vampire; Double Possession; Black Out: The Moment of Terror; Black Evil.
Movie: 🎬🎬🎬 *DVD:* 🎬🎬🎬
All Day Ent. (cat #98040001, UPC 649-686984121). Widescreen (1.85:1) anamorphic. Mono. $27.99. Keepcase. *LANG:* English. *FEATURES:* Still and artwork gallery ☞ Text essay by Tim Lucas and David Walker ☞ Commentary: Schultz, Clark, Hinton, Sam Waymon ☞ 22 chapters.
1973 (R) 110m/C Duane Jones, Marlene Clark, Bill Gunn, Sam Waymon, Leonard Jackson, Candece Tarpley, Mabel King; *D:* Bill Gunn; *W:* Bill Gunn; *C:* James E. Hinton; *M:* Sam Waymon.

Gappa the Trifibian Monster

Gappa represents a more obscure example of the rubber-suit monster trend in Japanese films which was made famous

by Godzilla and his numerous foes. However, unlike those famous monsters from Toho Studios, *Gappa* is neither much fun nor very exciting. An expedition is sent to the South Seas to discover rare and exotic animals to be placed on Playmate Island, an amusement park which is the brainchild of the editor of Playmate Magazine. The adventurers discover what they believe to be a dinosaur egg and when it hatches, a baby dinosaur is born. They capture the creature and return with it to Tokyo. Of course, the creature isn't a baby dinosaur, but a little Gappa monster, and soon Mom and Dad Gappa are rampaging through Tokyo searching for their child. The plot is taken directly from the British film *Gorgo* and the building-crushing action quickly becomes tiresome. The film has been letterboxed at 2.35:1 for this DVD release. The print shows some defects and the image is quite dark at times. Otherwise, the image is clear and displays only a slight amount of grain. The subtitles fall below the letterboxed frame and are easy to read. —*ML* *AKA:* Daikyoju Gappa; Monster from a Prehistoric Planet.
Movie: 🎬½ *DVD:* 🎬🎬½
Media Blasters (cat #TSDVD-0180, UPC 631595018028). Widescreen (2.35:1) letterboxed. Dolby Digital Mono. $19.95. Keepcase. *LANG:* English; Japanese. *SUB:* English. *FEATURES:* Production notes.
1967 (PG) 90m/C *JP* Tamio Kawaji, Yoko Yamamoto, Tatsuya Fuji, Koji Wada, Yuji Okada; *D:* Haruyasu Noguchi; *W:* Ryuzo Nakanishi; *C:* Muneo Ueda.

Garden of Eden

Chick flick finds three women searching for answers to the Big Questions on the border between America and Mexico in Tijuana. The independent production was clearly made on a strict budget and so there's little that DVD can do for the unpolished image. Colors are harsh. Sound is acceptable. Subtitles for the Spanish dialogue are small but readable. —*MM* *AKA:* El Jardin del Eden.
Movie: 🎬🎬½ *DVD:* 🎬🎬
Vanguard Intl. Cinema (cat #VF9210, UPC 658769921038). Full frame. $29.98. Keepcase. *LANG:* English and Spanish. *SUB:* English. *FEATURES:* 12 chapters.
1994 104m/C Renee Coleman, Bruno Bichir, Gabriela Roel, Rosario Sagrav; *D:* Maria Novaro; *W:* Maria Novaro, Betriz Novaro; *C:* Eric Alan Edwards.

The Garden of the Finzi–Continis

Acclaimed film by De Sica about an aristocratic Jewish family living in Italy under increasing Fascist oppression on the eve of WWII. The garden wall symbolizes the distance between the Finzi-Continis and the Nazi reality about to engulf them. Flawless acting and well-defined direction. Based on the novel by Giorgio Bassani, who collaborated on the script but later repudiated the film. Music by De Sica's son, Manuel. In the hit-and-miss world of

Columbia DVDs, this one is right in the middle. The film print shows substantial damage and the transfer seems soft and grainy at times. Like the colors, which are fairly weak, this may be due to the source material. The disc does handle blacks very well, and they are usually dark and inky. The stereo soundtrack seems to lack any separation and sounds more like mono. It also clips and distorts on almost any louder music or dialogue. In addition, all we get for supplementals are the trailer and talent files. One would have hoped for a much better DVD of this exceptionally fine foreign film. —JO **AKA:** Il Giardino Del Finzi-Contini.

Movie: ♫♫♫♫ **DVD:** ♫♫
Columbia Tristar (cat #06201, UPC 04339-6062016). Widescreen (1.85:1) anamorphic. Dolby Digital Stereo. $29.95. Keepcase. *LANG:* Italian. *SUB:* English. *CAP:* Italian. *FEATURES:* 28 chapters • Theatrical trailer • Talent files.
1971 (R) 94m/C *IT* Dominique Sanda, Helmut Berger, Lino Capolicchio, Fabio Testi, Romolo Valli; **D:** Vittorio De Sica; **W:** Cesare Zavattini; **C:** Ennio Guarnieri; **M:** Bill Conti, Manuel De Sica. *AWARDS:* Oscars '71: Foreign Film; Berlin Intl. Film Fest. '71: Golden Berlin Bear; *NOM:* Oscars '71: Adapt. Screenplay.

The Gatchaman Collection

DVD contains three separate episodes, each running about 45 minutes, together making up an entire story arc. "The Dragon King" introduces the viewer to all of the main players. First, we have the villainous aliens, the Galactor, led by the evil Solaris. The Galactor have been on Earth for 3 million years, and have now decided to take the planet for their own. They have allied themselves with the Republic of Hontworl, and have unleashed a giant war machine shaped like a dragon. Fortunately, Dr. Nanbu, head of the International Science Organization, has created the Science Ninja Team. These five teenagers, who have taken on the likeness of different birds for their uniforms, are specially trained to fight the Galactors. In Volume 2, "The Red Specter," the Science Ninja Team visit a mysterious Galactor island, where they are assisted by the rogue Red Specter team. In Volume 3, the Galactor launch their final assault to destroy humanity. Disc is slightly different from the American version of the original series. While the five team members essentially look the same, their names are obviously different. There is more violence and sexuality than Americans were used to. (Also, there's some profanity in the subtitled version.) The image is sharp and clear, showing only a fine sheen of grain, with some minor defects from the source print evident. The colors look good, but like many anime aren't very bold. The exception here is that the blacks are very deep and rich. Both English and Japanese tracks offer clear and audible dialogue with no discernible hiss or distortion.

There isn't a great deal of Surround action, but the audio from the rear speakers does add some depth to the presentation. The English subtitles are yellow and quite easy to read. —ML
Movie: ♫♫ ½ **DVD:** ♫♫♫
Urban Vision Entertainment (UPC 638652-107008). Full frame. Dolby Digital Surround Stereo. $29.98. Keepcase. *LANG:* English; Japanese. *SUB:* English. *FEATURES:* Music video at end of episode 3 • Trailers.
1994 135m/C *JP* **D:** Hiroyuki Fukushima, Akihiko Nishiyama; **M:** Maurice White, Bill Myers.

Gator King

Villainous Santos (Fargas) imports Chinese crocodiles to serve them up as dinner at his restaurant and for other nefarious purposes. Spunky journalist Maureen (Foley) and her ex-beau Ranger Ronny (Richardson) decide to investigate. It's a standard-issue micro-budget action flick with nothing really to recommend it, even to fans of the genre. Image and sound are identical to VHS tape. —MM
Movie: ♫ ½ **DVD:** ♫ ½
Rhino (cat #R2 976007, UPC 603497600-724). Full frame. $19.98. Snapper. *LANG:* English. *FEATURES:* 15 chapters.
1970 (R) 86m/C Antonio Fargas, Jay Richardson, Shannon K. Foley, Michael Berryman, Joe Estevez; **D:** Grant Austin Waldman; **W:** John L. Denk; **C:** Richard Lacy; **M:** Joe Pegram.

Gattaca [2 SB]

Ethan Hawke stars as Vincent, a young man whose genes have conspired to keep him away from his dream of becoming an astronaut in a future world where genetics mean everything. Unwilling to accept his fate, he develops an elaborate scheme to adopt the identity of the genetically superior Jerome (Law), who became paralyzed in a car accident. But when one of Vincent's supervisors is murdered, the added attention threatens to blow his scheme wide-open. This is slower and more contemplative than many films in the genre, and even with a disappointing ending is still a cut above average. Columbia's "Superbit" DVD looks and sounds amazing, but viewers without a high-end system may be unable to tell the difference between this version and the previous (and cheaper) edition reviewed in *Book 1.* —BG
Movie: ♫♫♫ **DVD:** ♫♫♫ ½
Columbia Tristar (cat #07963, UPC 043396079632). Widescreen (2.35: 1) anamorphic. Dolby 5.1; DTS. $27.96. Keepcase. *LANG:* English. *SUB:* English; French; Spanish; Portuguese; Chinese; Korean; Thai. *CAP:* English. *FEATURES:* 28 chapters.
1997 (PG-13) 112m/C Ethan Hawke, Uma Thurman, Jude Law, Gore Vidal, Alan Arkin, Loren Dean, Jayne Brook, Elias Koteas, Tony Shalhoub, Ernest Borgnine; **D:** Andrew Niccol; **W:** Andrew Niccol; **C:** Slawomir Idziak; **M:** Michael Nyman.

AWARDS: NOM: Oscars '97: Art Dir./Set Dec.; Golden Globes '98: Score.

General Idi Amin Dada: A Self Portrait

This one-of-a-kind documentary was made with the full cooperation of the titular dictator, whose reign of terror began in Uganda in 1971. Director Schroeder seldom preaches or manipulates, but gives Amin enough space to reveal himself in all his egomaniacal and delusional glory. The result is a fascinating portrait of a human face behind unthinkable acts of evil. For a documentary from the 1970s, the picture is remarkably sharp and clear, with extremely vibrant colors for the most part. The sound is slightly less consistent, at times coming across as muffled or distorted. For this DVD, the cuts General Amin extorted (using 150 French captives as leverage) from Schroeder have been restored. —BG
Movie: ♫♫♫ ½ **DVD:** ♫♫♫
Criterion (cat #153, UPC 037429166529). Full frame. Dolby Mono. $29.95. Keepcase. *LANG:* English. *SUB:* English. *FEATURES:* 17 chapters • Video interview: Barbet Schroeder • Time line of Ugandan History • Documentation of Idi Amin's requested cuts.
1974 90m/C D: Barbet Schroeder; **W:** Barbet Schroeder; **C:** Nestor Almendros.

George Washington

As Armond White recognizes in his liner notes, the influences of Haskell Wexler's *Medium Cool,* and even more importantly, Terrence Malick's *Days of Heaven,* are easy to spot in David Gordon Green's remarkable debut. In simplest terms, it's a coming-of-age story about a group of black children in rural North Carolina. Nasia (Candace Evanofski) and Buddy (Curtis Cotton III) believe that their friend George Richardson (Damien Jewan Lee) is destined for greatness. It's easy to accept; he has a stillness and maturity well beyond his years. (These non-professional young actors are astonishing.) Plot is secondary to Green's meditative, lyrical style, which is lovingly captured on a DVD that ranks with Criterion's best. The carefully photographed image and sound are flawless. Extras include Green's short films, Clu Gulager's 1969 short "A Day with the Boys," interviews with the cast, a deleted scene, and a Charlie Rose interview. The film made something of a splash on the festival circuit, but has enjoyed only limited commercial distribution. To anyone who's interested in serious independent filmmaking, it's required viewing. —MM
Movie: ♫♫♫ ½ **DVD:** ♫♫♫ ½
Criterion (cat #152, UPC 037429166123). Widescreen (2.35:1) anamorphic. Dolby Digital Surround. $39.95. Keepcase. *LANG:* English. *SUB:* English. *FEATURES:* 16 chapters • Short films • Cast interviews • Deleted scene • Charlie Rose interview • Commentary: Green, Tim Orr, Paul Schneider • Trailer.

2000 90m/C Candace Evanofski, Donald Holden, Damien Jewan Lee, Curtis Cotton III; **D:** David Gordon Green; **W:** David Gordon Green; **C:** Tim Orr; **M:** Michael Linnen, David Wingo.

German Silent Masterpieces

These public domain silent titles are acceptable, at this price. The Image edition of *The Last Laugh* (please see review) is much better in one other respect. This version of *Nosferatu,* Murnau's adaptation of *Dracula,* has new credits and music (by Peter Shirmann). Registration woes and a crackle on the soundtrack are the most glaring flaws. *Der Golem* is the story of a huge clay figure that's given life by a rabbi in hopes of saving the Jews in the ghetto of medieval Prague. Image is very dark, as it has been in every version I've ever seen. This version has no musical accompaniment. *—MM*
Movie: ♫♫♫ ½ **DVD:** ♫♫
Triton Multimedia (cat #TDVD9127, UPC 017078912722). Full frame. Dolby Digital Mono. $12.98. Keepcase. *LANG:* Silent (English intertitles). *FEATURES:* 15 chapters, *Nosferatu* ▪ 8 chapters, *Last Laugh* ▪ 10 chapters, *Der Golem.*
2000 m/C

Gertrud

Gertrud Kanning (Rode) surprises her husband Gustav (Rothe) with a blunt statement: she doesn't want to be the wife of a government minister, and she's going to leave him for another man because there is no love in her marriage and she'll no longer compromise. Expecting to find joy in the arms of classical pianist Erland Jannsson (Owe) she learns from old flame and celebrated poet Gabriel Lidman (Rode) that the pianist considers her a cheap conquest. Gabriel, her first love of long ago, mawkishly tries to entice her to run away with him instead, and her husband Gustav makes a clumsy effort to get her back. Gertrud must choose among the three men in her life, all who have betrayed her love in different ways. This is an extremely stylized and slow film, appearing at first to be almost a parody of the Bergman-type of story where the characters are morbidly obsessed with their own inner beings. Everyone moves slowly, the settings and camera viewpoints are rigidly restrained, and the characters never seem to make eye contact with each other, delivering their lines to the opposite wall instead of their fellow actors, barely blinking. Hailing from 1964, this widescreen black-and-white film is represented in a flawless anamorphic transfer, with crystal clear sound. The title is available as part of the *Carl Theodor Dreyer Box Set* (see separate entry). *—GE*
Movie: ♫♫♫♫ **DVD:** ♫♫♫♫
Criterion Widescreen (1.78:1) anamorphic. Keepcase. *LANG:* Danish. *SUB:* English. *FEATURES:* Archival footage ▪ Stills gallery ▪ Cast interviews.

1964 116m/B *DK* Nina Pens Rode, Bendt Rothe, Ebbe Rode, Baard Owe; **D:** Carl Theodor Dreyer; **W:** Carl Theodor Dreyer; **C:** Arne Abrahamsen, Henning Bendtsen; **M:** Jorgen Jersild.

Gesualdo: Death for Five Voices

Produced for German television, and apparently shot on digital video, this is a quirky and uneven documentary about a very obscure composer, who led a horrid life worthy of Vincent Price and Edgar Allan Poe. A short history is offered of the Italian prince Don Carlo Gesualdo (1560–1613), a renowned composer of very strange and very progressive madrigals, usually sung by five voices without accompaniment. Gesualdo's eerie, melancholy music is a mirror of a bizarre and morbid life—after murdering his first wife Maria Davalos and her lover, he spent the rest of his days composing, tormenting others, and festering in despair and remorse. We hear testimonies about Gesualdo by musical experts, one of the Prince's descendants, and even a woman who claims to be the incarnation of his murdered love. This is apparently an English re-edit of a German original, for the titles all come up in English, with a few misspelled. Werner Herzog, a great raconteur on his Anchor Bay DVDs, revoices the many Italians on screen. This is hard to follow sometimes, prompting the wish that the picture had simply been subtitled. The madrigal performances are outstanding. The musical performances are good, and the input from the experts on Gesualdo's violent and cruel life is well presented, if a bit dry. One excellent passage has all five singers sing their parts separately, and then together. When the harmony (is that weird sound a harmony?) combines, the sum of the voices is far, far more than its parts. But when dealing with Gesualdo's life, there's a problem navigating through some of Herzog's embellishments. Various guides in Venosa and Naples show us the actual locations of Gesualdo's crimes. But Herzog throws in a busty woman who the camera pursues through the ruined castle, until she claims to be the reincarnation of Gesualdo's lost wife. O.K. Unfortunately, Herzog never explains whether she's a real kook or (we suspect) an actress helping in a restaging. DVD is a featureless but good-looking show with a 16:9 image. I'm guessing that it was shot in PAL digital video, perhaps with some sort of added film-look that coarsens the image. Some scenes look much more like video than others. There's nothing extra at all with the disc, nothing from Herzog or about the shooting that might neutralize concerns about the show. *—GE* **AKA:** Death for Five Voices.
Movie: ♫♫♫ **DVD:** ♫♫ ½
Image Ent. (UPC 014381933024). Widescreen (1.78:1) anamorphic. $29.98. Keepcase. *LANG:* Italian & English.
1995 60m/C *GE* **D:** Werner Herzog; **W:** Lucki Stepetic; **C:** Peter Zeitlinger.

Get Down on It

Two of the dumbest characters you'll ever meet, Kinky (Tempest) and Ta-Ta (Jones) need someone to take care of their kids, so they place a bet on who will find a husband first. Their only criteria are that he has a three-bedroom house and he can't be on welfare. It's even more idiotic (and less funny) than its plot summary, and the DVD looks and sounds like it was taped from a public access channel. *—BG*
Movie: woof **DVD:** woof
York Ent. (cat #YPD-1099, UPC 75072310-9923). Full frame. $14.99. Keepcase. *LANG:* English. *FEATURES:* 24 chapters ▪ Trailers.
2001 104m/C Tempest, Keisha Jones, Kimberely Scott Stein, Mac Bootsie; **D:** Simuel Rankins; **W:** Simuel Rankins; **C:** Dexter Parks.

Get Out Your Handkerchiefs

An absolutely stunning, funny, intelligent, and clever film. Depardieu is afraid he is losing his wife so he picks out an attractive man at the restaurant where they are eating and makes a gift of her. He just wants to make her smile, he tells the befuddled man. One thing leads to another and soon they are both taking care of her as she goes from one strange fainting fit to another. Slowly they come to relate to each other better than they ever could to the woman of their affections. They decide she needs to get pregnant to be happy and set about making it happen. Finally on vacation she finds what she really needs to be happy, a 13-year-old genius who boldly proclaims to her after being caught peeking up her nightgown, "I'm 13, I'm not made of stone." There's also a running gag with sweaters that is subtle but hysterical. Perfectly timed and acted with a script that is both mildly slapstick and sensitive, this is a crowd pleaser. The print is pristine and the sound is good. It also won the Academy Award for best foreign film the year it was released, proving that the Academy can sometimes be very open minded (it was the '70s...). *—CA* **AKA:** Preparez Vous Mouchoirs.
Movie: ♫♫♫♫ **DVD:** ♫♫♫ ½
All Day Ent. (cat #Dv11590, UPC 0131311-59097). Widescreen (1.66:1) anamorphic. Dolby Digital Mono. $19.90. Keepcase. *LANG:* English; French. *SUB:* English. *FEATURES:* 25 chapters ▪ Theatrical trailer.
1978 (R) 109m/C *FR* Gerard Depardieu, Patrick Dewaere, Carole Laure; **D:** Bertrand Blier; **W:** Bertrand Blier; **C:** Jean Penzer; **M:** Georges Delerue. *AWARDS:* Oscars '78: Foreign Film; Cesar '79: Score; Natl. Soc. Film Critics '78: Film.

Get Over It!

Teenaged Berke (Foster) has just been dumped by his childhood sweetheart Allison (Sagemiller), and becomes determined to win her back when she falls for heartthrob and boy-band member, Striker

(West). Ignoring the advice of friends Felix (Hanks) and Dennis (Sisqo), Berke tries out for the school play, so that he can be close to Allison. When Berke's dramatic and singing talents prove to be questionable, Felix's sister Kelly (Dunst) volunteers to help. Will Berke win Allison back, or will a love blossom between him and Kelly? The movie does have some funny moments, but any film that relies on reaction shots from Tom Hanks's son for laughs is in trouble. You'd be better off sticking to the similar but superior *10 Things I Hate About You*. Image is very sharp and clear, although there is a minute amount of grain during the early chapters. The bright colors that dominate the film look very good, and the fleshtones are realistic. No discernible problem from artifacting; no distortion. There is constant use of Surround effects and the sound field is quite good. The constant music sounds nice, and there is noteworthy bass response. —*ML*
Movie: 🦴🦴 **DVD:** 🦴🦴🦴
Miramax Pictures (cat #23295, UPC 786936159974). Widescreen (2.35:1) anamorphic. Dolby Digital 5.1 Surround Stereo. $29.99. Keepcase. *LANG:* English; French. *SUB:* English. *CAP:* English. *FEATURES:* Commentary: director Tommy O'Haver, writer R. Lee Fleming Jr. ● Deleted and extended scenes with commentary ● Martin Short outtakes ● Music video ● Behind-the-scenes featurette.
2001 (PG-13) 90m/C Kirsten Dunst, Ben Foster, Colin Hanks, Melissa Sagemiller, Sisqo, Shane West, Martin Short, Swoosie Kurtz, Ed Begley Jr., Zoe Saldana, Coolio, Mila Kunis; *D:* Tommy O'Haver; *W:* R. Lee Fleming Jr.; *C:* Maryse Alberti; *M:* Steve Bartek.

The Ghost Breakers

Funny, snappy horror-comedy produced after the success of Hope's *The Cat and the Canary*. Mary Carter (Goddard) inherits a haunted castle in Cuba and is targeted by nefarious forces. Larry Lawrence (Hope) plays a tell-all radio host who joins Mary on her cruise to Cuba. Hope and Goddard are a fun team and the fast-paced film is filled with witty repartee and atmosphere. The inclusion of a genuine supernatural zombie (Noble Johnson) adds a nice creepy tension. Hope's valet, Alex (Willie Best), is a shufflin' black character typical of the era. He's fairly funny, but may offend some. The disc utilizes a terrific transfer from near-pristine elements. The black-and-white imagery is slightly grainy, but consistently sharp and rich in contrasts. The sound is strong for a mono track. The short featurettes are a nice collection of bonus material on Hope, and "Hollywood Victory Caravan" includes some funny (historically interesting) routines and guest spots by Alan Ladd, Barbara Stanwyck, and Bing Crosby. —*DG*
Movie: 🦴🦴🦴 ½ **DVD:** 🦴🦴🦴 ½
Universal Studios (cat #21213, UPC 0251-92121326). Full frame. Mono. $19.98. Keepcase. *LANG:* English. *SUB:* Spanish;

French. *CAP:* English. *FEATURES:* 18 chapters ● Trailer ● Photo gallery ● "Entertaining the Troops" ● "Command Performance 1944" ● "Hollywood Victory Caravan" ● Production notes ● Cast and filmmaker bios ● DVD-ROM Features.
1940 83m/B Bob Hope, Paulette Goddard, Richard Carlson, Paul Lukas, Willie Best, Pedro de Cordoba, Noble Johnson, Anthony Quinn; *D:* George Marshall; *W:* Walter DeLeon; *C:* Charles B(ryant) Lang Jr.

The Ghost of Frankenstein

Having somehow survived Wolf Frankenstein's bullets in *Son of*, Ygor (Lugosi) frees the Monster (Chaney Jr.) from the hardened sulphur pit when the villagers foolishly attempt to dynamite the ruins of castle Frankenstein. Ygor then spirits the Monster across Bavaria to the mental clinic of the other Frankenstein son, Ludwig (Hardwicke), who is using his father's secrets to cure insanity. Once again, the less well-traveled title looks splendid, far better than the television prints we used to see. These films weren't terribly expensive, but the production values are not compromised, especially the careful and moody photography, and the occasional spiffy special effect. Universal has gone rather skimpy with the extras, however, with just the Realart trailer and a few sketchy production facts text pages. Title is part of a double feature with *Son of Frankenstein* (please see review). Since some of these programmers are fairly short, they fit nicely onto a single disc, without any compromise of quality. This DVD appears to have been made from a newer remaster, not the VHS version, and is stunning. —*GE*
Movie: 🦴🦴 **DVD:** 🦴🦴🦴
Universal Studios (cat #21404, UPC 025192140426). Full frame. Dolby Digital Mono. $24.99. Keepcase. *LANG:* English; French; Spanish. *SUB:* French; Spanish. *CAP:* English. *FEATURES:* Trailer ● Production notes.
1942 68m/B Cedric Hardwicke, Lon Chaney Jr., Lionel Atwill, Ralph Bellamy, Bela Lugosi, Evelyn Ankers, Dwight Frye; *D:* Erle C. Kenton; *W:* W. Scott Darling; *C:* Milton Krasner; *M:* Charles Previn.

Ghost World

Terry Zwigoff's adaptation of Daniel Clowes's cult favorite comic book captures the spirit and complex characters of the original. The result is a rare comedy that's equally perceptive, funny, and touching. Enid (Birch) and Rebecca (Johansson) graduate from high school and face an uncertain summer. Enid still has to take a make-up art class, but they really want to get an apartment together. They're defiant misfits who desperately want to be unique individuals while, with equal desperation, seeking acceptance from the peers they disdain. In short, they're mercurial adolescents filled with promise, humor, and doubt. Their curiosity (and a streak of

meanness) leads them to Seymour (Buscemi), an adult who's not far removed from their own particular quirkiness. The film's real success is its commitment to these characters and its refusal to turn them into stereotypes or to make cheap jokes. And though it seems loosely plotted, it builds to a strong, satisfying conclusion. DVD image is an accurate re-creation of an image that's built on a slightly uncomfortable color scheme and production design. From the opening theme (which will worm its way into your brain) to Seymour's apartment to the final shot, the film has a disquieting quality. Sound is more than adequate to the story. My only criticism is the relative lack of extras which are limited to the usual "making of" featurette and a few deleted scenes. A commentary track might have been illuminating. —*MM*
Movie: 🦴🦴🦴🦴 **DVD:** 🦴🦴🦴
MGM Home Ent. (cat #1002564, UPC 027616867650). Widescreen (1.85:1) anamorphic. Dolby Digital 5.1 Surround Stereo. $24.98. Keepcase. *LANG:* English. *SUB:* English; French; Spanish. *CAP:* English. *FEATURES:* 16 chapters ● 4 deleted and alternate scenes ● Music video ● "Jaan Pehechaan Ho" music video ● Trailer.
2001 (R) 111m/C Thora Birch, Scarlett Johansson, Steve Buscemi, Brad Renfro, Illeana Douglas, Bob Balaban, Teri Garr, Stacy Travis, Dave Sheridan, Brian George; *D:* Terry Zwigoff; *W:* Daniel Clowes, Terry Zwigoff; *C:* Alfonso Beato; *M:* David Kitay. *AWARDS:* Ind. Spirit '02: Support. Actor (Buscemi); N.Y. Film Critics '01: Support. Actor (Buscemi); Natl. Soc. Film Critics '01: Support. Actor (Buscemi); *NOM:* Oscars '01: Adapt. Screenplay; Golden Globes '02: Actress—Mus./Comedy (Birch), Support. Actor (Buscemi); Ind. Spirit '02: First Feature; Writers Guild '01: Adapt. Screenplay.

Ghosts of Mississippi

Seen simply as a Hollywood courtroom melodrama, this fact-based story about the assassination of Medgar Evers and the long-delayed trial of Byron De La Beckwith (Woods) is moderately entertaining. Star Alec Baldwin's engaging performance as an idealistic Assistant D.A. helps to offset a leisurely pace, too many clichés, and a lack of suspense. Though her role is central to the story, Whoopi Goldberg has nothing to do but stand around looking brave and sad, and to deliver a key piece of evidence when it's needed. Working under thick layers of prosthetic makeup, James Woods is a repellant but somehow fussy villain. He was nominated for an Oscar for his work. The widescreen transfer is highly detailed, finely restoring every bit of information from the original film print. Defects in the print are limited to a few dust marks. Colors are well delineated in this transfer and always natural. Blacks are deep and solid, but never wash out the shadows. However quite a bit of edge-enhancement has been applied to this transfer to give it a "sharper" appearance.

The enhancement is a tad exaggerated at times, creating almost noticeable halos around high contrast areas of the image. Frequency response is wide and unexaggerated, creating a natural sound field. —GH/MM *AKA:* Ghosts from the Past.
Movie: 🎬🎬 *DVD:* 🎬🎬🎬
Warner Home Video (UPC 0539392507-25). Widescreen (1.85:1) anamorphic; full frame. Dolby Digital 5.1 Surround. $19.98. Snapper. *LANG:* English; French. *SUB:* English; French. *FEATURES:* Trailer.
1996 (PG-13) 123m/C Alec Baldwin, Whoopi Goldberg, James Woods, Craig T. Nelson, Wayne Rogers, William H. Macy, Michael O'Keefe, Yolanda King, Susanna Thompson, Lucas Black, James Pickens Jr., Virginia Madsen, Bill Cobbs; *D:* Rob Reiner; *W:* Lewis Colick; *C:* John Seale; *M:* Marc Shaiman. *AWARDS: NOM:* Oscars '96: Makeup, Support. Actor (Woods); Golden Globes '97: Support. Actor (Woods).

The Giant Gila Monster
Please see review for *Drive-in Discs, Vol. 2.*
Movie: 🎬 ½
1959 74m/B Don Sullivan, Lisa Simone, Shug Fisher, Jerry Cortwright, Beverly Thurman, Don Flourney, Pat Simmons; *D:* Ray Kellogg; *W:* Jay Simms; *C:* Wilfrid M. Cline; *M:* Jack Marshall.

Giants and Toys
Director Yasuzo Masumura and writer Ishio Shirasaka present a knife-edged picture of the 1950s Japanese consumer landscape devoured by American values and business practices. World Candy Company is engaged in a media advertising war for the Japanese candy market, against Giant and Apollo, their main competitors. World's publicity men feel constant pressure to make dramatic sales increases, which prompts desperate efforts to find out what's going on at the other companies. Nishi (Hiroshi Kawaguchi) is the eager assistant to Goda (Hideo Takamatsu), whose job is on the line to produce sales results. Together they decide to place World's hopes on a "space" themed campaign, and they find a spunky and photogenic model in Kyoko Shima (Hitomi Nozoe), a gamin with terrible teeth, but the desirable (?) ability to touch her nose with her long tongue. The pressure gets higher as Giant's caveman spokesman and World's space girl travel in dueling loudspeaker buses. Magazines and television shows are saturated with captivating images of Kyoko. All seems well, especially when Apollo Candy suffers a catastrophic fire, but Kyoko's celebrity is going to her head, and Nishi's attempts to sort out his love life with his World duties come to ruin. The ending slides toward some crazy climax of death and failure, but the filmmakers surprise us with a much more memorable image of debasement at the fade-out. All of this is played out at the frantic pace of something like Billy Wilder's *One, Two, Three,* and is both convincing and entertaining. The story is easy to follow (for being so complicated) and the characters are very accessible—they could have walked out of *The Apartment* or *Patterns.* The screen is constantly bombarded with mass-produced images celebrated for their Pop-Art qualities—years before Pop Art hit American culture. Even the titles look 10 years ahead of their time, with a snapshot of Kyoko Sushi multiplying into rows of Warhol-like repeated images. DVD is very good-looking, with muted colors in the "business" scenes and blaring hues whenever toys, neon, or the glitzy TV shows take over. The music varies from Latin Mambo rhythms to a savage Gorath-like march that enforces the relentless, breakneck pace of the advertising machine. A Japanese trailer stresses the fact that the movie is a serious adult offering; excellent liner notes and biographical information help clue Western viewers into the picture. The clarity of the removable subtitles is also a big help, considering the pace of this audiovisual juggernaut. —GE *AKA:* Kyojin to Gangu.
Movie: 🎬🎬🎬 ½ *DVD:* 🎬🎬🎬 ½
Image Ent. (UPC 014381145625). Widescreen (2.35:1) anamorphic. $29.98. Keepcase. *LANG:* Japanese. *SUB:* English. *FEATURES:* Trailer ▪ Chuck Stephens's printed text essay ▪ Photos ▪ Yasuzo Masumura bio and filmography.
1958 95m/C *JP* Hiroshi Kawaguchi, Hitomi Nozoe, Yunosuke Ito, Kinzo Shin; *D:* Yasuzo Masumura; *W:* Ishio Shirasaka; *C:* Hiroshi Murai; *M:* Tetsuo Tsukahara.

The Gift
Effectively spooky Southern Gothic revolves around the widow Annie (Blanchett), a psychic who winds up helping the police find the killer of a rich girl (Holmes). Among those involved are battered wife Swank, abusive hubby Reeves, Holmes's fiancé Kinnear, and not-quite-right mechanic Ribisi. Cast and production values are first-rate all the way through and anyone who can accept the premise will be entertained. Image is very crisp and you'll probably notice this the most in Annie's own house. Take a moment to look at all the little details of the rooms, from the chipped paint early in the movie to the red cover-up applied by the kids later in the film. The sharpness is quite nice and the black level is right on the money. The 5.1 is very suitable for this type of film. Dialogue is dominant throughout and sounds good and absolutely distortion-free. Your other four speakers will get some play in the numerous scenes where Annie's gift presents itself. —GH/MM
Movie: 🎬🎬🎬 *DVD:* 🎬🎬🎬
Paramount Home Video (UPC 097363289-548). Widescreen (1.85:1) anamorphic. Dolby Digital 5.1 Surround. $29.98. Keepcase. *LANG:* English; French. *SUB:* English; French. *FEATURES:* "Making of" featurette ▪ Music video ▪ Trailer.
2000 (R) 112m/C Cate Blanchett, Katie Holmes, Hilary Swank, Keanu Reeves, Greg Kinnear, Giovanni Ribisi, Michael Jeter, Gary Cole, Kim Dickens, Rosemary Harris, J.K. Simmons, Chelcie Ross, John Beasley; *D:* Sam Raimi; *W:* Billy Bob Thornton, Tom Epperson; *C:* Jamie Anderson; *M:* Christopher Young. *AWARDS: NOM:* Ind. Spirit '01: Support. Actor (Ribisi).

Ginger Snaps
Hailed by many as "the next big thing," this Canadian werewolf film does offer some unique aspects, but is ultimately disappointing. Brigitte (Emily Perkins) and Ginger (Katharine Isabelle) Fitzgerald are very strange sisters who embrace death and despise conformity. Their bizarre relationship changes when Ginger is attacked by a werewolf. She then becomes a sexual predator who is after every boy in school. Disgusted by this, Brigitte searches for a way to cure her sister. The film takes a uniquely feminine approach to the werewolf myth, and also treats the condition as a disease (similar to the approach of fellow Canadian David Cronenberg in *The Fly*). Yet, *Ginger Snaps* moves at a snail's pace, and it's not until the last 15 minutes that anything actually happens. Also, Brigitte and Ginger are both so difficult to like that it makes the film hard to access. Artisan has simply thrown *Ginger Snaps* onto DVD, delivering a full-frame version with no extras and showing little respect for the film. Those who are truly interested should look to the North, as the Canadian version is letterboxed and loaded with special features. —ML
Movie: 🎬🎬 ½ *DVD:* 🎬
Artisan Ent. (cat #12211, UPC 01223612-2111). Full frame. Dolby 2.0 Surround. $19.98. Keepcase. *LANG:* English.
2000 (R) 107m/C *CA* John Bourgeois, Peter Keleghan, Emily Perkins, Katharine Isabelle, Kris Lemche, Mimi Rogers, Jesse Moss, Danielle Hampton; *D:* John Fawcett; *W:* Karen Walton; *C:* Thom Best; *M:* Michael Shields.

Girl in Gold Boots
A naïve small-town waitress decides to make good on her dream of becoming a dancer and hitches a ride to Los Angeles. She lands a job at a seedy club, and finds that the fast life isn't all she'd hoped for. A lousy script, incompetent editing and continuity, and some of the worst dancing you'll ever see combine to make this prime MST3K fodder. There's only so much DVD can do to help a film like this—even with digital remastering, the picture is marred with plenty of scratches and more serious flaws, and the dialogue ranges between adequate and abysmal. —BG
Movie: woof *DVD:* 🎬🎬 ½
Image Ent. (cat #ID0834TGDVD, UPC 014381083422). Widescreen (1.78:1) anamorphic. Dolby Mono. $24.99. Keepcase. *FEATURES:* 18 chapters ▪ Commentary: Ted V. Mikels ▪ Trailers ▪ Lobby card gallery ▪ Mikels filmography.
1969 91m/C Jody Daniels, Leslie McRae, Tom Pace, Mark Herron; *D:* Ted V. Mikels;

W: Art Names; **C:** Robert Maxwell; **M:** Nicholas Carras.

A Girl Thing

A series of four female-oriented vignettes center on the clients of a New York psychiatrist (Channing.) In the first, an uptight, commitment-phobic lawyer (Macpherson) finds herself attracted to and begins to date another woman (Capshaw). Some soft porn and heartache ensues. The next story is about three sisters (DeMornay, Janney, Headly), two of whom would rather poke their eyes out than spend time together. Their mother has died and left a most unusual demand in her will. Top-notch acting and well planned plotting make this the best of the four stories. The last two revolve around a woman scorned who takes revenge on her cheating husband, and a gun-toting malcontent who takes the psychiatrist's office and patients hostage. While the series is well produced and the themes are important, ultimately the series lacks heart. Everything is too clean and polished to give the feel of any real threat and you never worry about any of the characters. Shot for television, the picture is very good and so is the sound. —CA
Movie: 🎞🎞 ½ **DVD:** 🎞🎞🎞
Showtime Networks, Inc. (cat #SHO 1048, UPC 75844510482). Widescreen. Dolby Digital 5.1. $24.90. Keepcase. *LANG:* English; Spanish. *FEATURES:* 4 chapters ▪ Interviews with actresses & director ▪ Filmographies.
2001 237m/C Stockard Channing, Elle Macpherson, Kate Capshaw, Glenne Headly, Rebecca DeMornay, Allison Janney, Lynn Whitfield, Linda Hamilton, Camryn Manheim, Scott Bakula, Bruce Greenwood, Brent Spiner, Mia Farrow; **D:** Lee Rose.

A Girl, 3 Guys and a Gun

Three friends (Clark, Florence, Holland), tired of their lives as air-conditioning repair men, decide to hit the open road in the hopes of starting new lives in the big city. The only thing that stands in the way of them and their dreams is the needed funding to make it happen. To remedy this problem, the boys come to the logical conclusion that they should rob the local bingo game. This one was produced by the Roger Corman startup New Concorde, and like many of the films he has produced and directed in his varied career, it's exceptionally one-dimensional. While the film allows viewers to think that they are in for a coming-of-age road adventure, the fact is that the main characters never get more than 20 miles from their hometown. The audience is expected to believe by the end of the movie that these disgruntled gentlemen have come to grips with their mundane existence and feel settled. Plagued by a shallow plot and even shallower acting, this film leaves you wondering where you left your hour and a half. DVD picture quality is good with crisp edges and nice color throughout the fea-

ture. There are no noticeable defects in the transfer save a couple of outdoor scenes when the actor's skin color seems a bit over saturated. The sound quality in certain scenes seems to be a little muddled when the actors are speaking, a case where the art of overdubbing prior to the DVD's release probably should have been employed. —EL
Movie: woof **DVD:** 🎞🎞
New Concorde (cat #20782, UPC 736991-478299). Widescreen letterboxed. Stereo. $19.98. Keepcase. *LANG:* English. *FEATURES:* Commentary: director Brent Florence ▪ Actors' commentary ▪ Bloopers and outtakes ▪ Theatrical trailer ▪ Cast and crew bios ▪ Preview attractions ▪ 24 chapters.
2001 (R) 88m/C Robin Clark, Josh Holland, Tracy Zahoryin, Christian Leffler, Brent Florence, Michael Trucco, Tava Smiley; **D:** Brent Florence; **W:** Brent Florence; **C:** Matt Davis.

Girl with Green Eyes

Kate Brady (Tushingham) is a young Catholic farm girl who comes to Dublin for work and falls in love with much older divorced writer Eugene Gaillard (Finch). She moves in with him despite her moral misgivings but both discover their differences are too great to sustain their relationship. O'Brien adapted the screenplay from her novel *The Lonely Girl.* The video transfer features a very well reproduced black-and-white image. The film's shadows are crisp and clear and darker scenes do not lose definition. The soundtrack is decent, but not as impressive as the video. There is no noticeable distortion, but the thick Irish accents make some dialogue hard to understand (thankfully, the disc comes enhanced with subtitles). —MJT
Movie: 🎞🎞 ½ **DVD:** 🎞🎞 ½
MGM Home Ent. (cat #1003135, UPC 027-616872999). Widescreen (1.66:1) letterboxed. Dolby Digital Mono. $14.95. Keepcase. *LANG:* English. *SUB:* English; French; Spanish. *FEATURES:* 16 chapters ▪ Theatrical trailer.
1964 91m/B *GB* Peter Finch, Rita Tushingham, Lynn Redgrave, Marie Kean, Julian Glover, T.P. McKenna, Yolande Finch, Arthur O'Sullivan; **D:** Desmond Davis; **W:** Edna O'Brien; **C:** Manny Wynn; **M:** John Addison.

The Glass House

When their parents are killed in a car accident, Ruby (Sobieski) and Rhett (Morgan) are sent to live with the Glasses, a middle-aged, childless couple living in the hills of Malibu. But something is hiding below the surface, and Ruby begins to wonder if the Glasses' intentions are the purest. This below-average thriller is never threatening enough and doesn't make enough sense to be truly effective. Skarsgard is excellent as the menacing father, but he's swimming upstream. The film looks and sounds excellent, with a dark palate that does justice to the inspired art directing. Extra features are plentiful, but uninteresting. And

what's a major studio doing still putting out DVDs that aren't anamorphic? —BG
Movie: 🎞 ½ **DVD:** 🎞🎞🎞
Columbia Tristar (cat #06252, UPC 04339-6062528). Widescreen (2.35:1) letterboxed; full frame. Dolby 5.1, Dolby Surround. $27.96. Keepcase. *LANG:* English; French. *SUB:* English; French. *FEATURES:* 28 chapters ▪ Commentary ▪ Trailers ▪ Interviews ▪ Deleted scene ▪ Filmographies ▪ Production notes.
2001 (PG-13) 111m/C Leelee Sobieski, Stellan Skarsgard, Diane Lane, Trevor Morgan, Bruce Dern, Kathy Baker, Christopher Noth, Rita Wilson, Michael O'Keefe, Vyto Ruginis; **D:** Daniel Sackheim; **W:** Wesley Strick; **C:** Alar Kivilo; **M:** Christopher Young.

The Glass Shield

Fact-based story recounts the education of young J.J. (Boatman), who arrives fresh from the police academy as the only black officer in a division of a Southern California Sheriff's department where he encounters several varieties of racism, both overt and hidden, from both his superiors (Anderson, Walsh, Ironside) and fellow officers. Then there are the pressures to maintain loyalty to the department, no matter what. When a young black man named Teddy (Ice Cube) is arrested for no reason and then framed for another crime, J.J. has to decide which side he's on. His only ally is Deborah (Petty), a fellow rookie who's also a woman and a Jew. At times, writer/director Charles Burnett makes things look too slick and polished, when the story would have been more effective with a layer of *Hill St. Blues* grittiness, and the bad guys are too one-dimensional. For the most part, though, Burnett is successful in making J.J.'s hard decisions seem real and important, and they're what the film is really about. Also, Burnett tells the story without using any profanity, and he keeps the violent content to a minimum. As far as the language is concerned, that may be unrealistic for these characters, but it somehow strengthens the performances. DVD image is a solid cut above full-frame VHS tape, though it is not the most sharply focused you'll ever see. Surround sound is well used, too. No extras, but on any medium, this one's a sleeper worth finding. —MM
Movie: 🎞🎞🎞 **DVD:** 🎞🎞 ½
Miramax Pictures (cat #16580, UPC 7179-51001702). Widescreen (1.85:1) anamorphic. Dolby Digital Surround. $29.98. Keepcase. *LANG:* English. *CAP:* English. *FEATURES:* 21 chapters.
1995 (PG-13) 109m/C Michael Boatman, Lori Petty, Michael Ironside, M. Emmet Walsh, Ice Cube, Richard Anderson, Elliott Gould; **D:** Charles Burnett; **W:** Charles Burnett; **C:** Elliot Davis; **M:** Stephen James Taylor.

A Glimpse of Hell

Overachieving made-for-TV movie examines the 1989 explosion in a gun turret on the USS *Iowa* and the Navy's attempts to shift blame for the incident onto an alleged "suicidal homosexual" crew member. Lt. JG Dan Meyer (Leonard) is the young officer who tries to see that the truth comes out. Captain Fred Moosally (Caan) is the commanding officer who finally has to decide whether to follow the official story or his conscience. The film is actually more nuanced than it sounds in synopsis, and the acting is mostly understated, though the villains are a bit broad. It also makes for a very nice DVD. Both sound and image are far superior to broadcast standards. Lighting is dramatic. Blacks are solid but details are clear in dark uniforms. Surround is limited. Some sort of commentary or other extra explaining the reality behind this version might have been valuable. —MM

Movie: 🎬🎬 ½ **DVD:** 🎬🎬 ½
20th Century Fox (UPC 024543034766). Widescreen (1.78:1) anamorphic. Dolby Digital 5.1 Surround Stereo; Dolby Surround. $34.98. Keepcase. *LANG:* English. *SUB:* English; Spanish. *FEATURES:* 20 chapters.
2001 (PG-13) 85m/C Robert Sean Leonard, James Caan, Daniel Roebuck, Jamie Harrold, Cherie Devanney; **D:** Mikael Salomon; **W:** Charles C. Thompson II, David Freed.

Glitter

Mariah Carey's disastrous debut makes *Showgirls* look like *Driving Miss Daisy.* The synthetic diva plays Billie Frank, a young singer completely without guile or ambition whose natural talent carries her inevitably and swiftly to the top of the music world. To appreciate how truly and thoroughly bad the film is, just listen to director Vondie Curtis-Hall's commentary track. It is so halting, unfocused, and embarrassing that there might well have been someone holding a gun to his head and forcing him to think up something...*anything* to say. He seems profoundly depressed by the entire enterprise and who could blame him? Of course, DVD image and sound are all that you'd expect of a big-budget studio release, even one as insubstantial as this. —MM

Movie: 🎬 **DVD:** 🎬🎬
Columbia Tristar (cat #08194, UPC 04339-6081949). Widescreen (2.40:1) anamorphic; full frame. Dolby Digital 5.1 Surround; Dolby Digital Surround. $27.98. Keepcase. *LANG:* English; French. *SUB:* English; French. *CAP:* English. *FEATURES:* 28 chapters • 2 music videos • Commentary: director • Trailers.
2001 (PG-13) 104m/C Mariah Carey, Max Beesley, Tia Texada, Da Brat, Valarie Pettiford, Ann Magnuson, Terrence DaShon Howard, Dorian Harewood, Grant Nickalls, Eric Benet, Padma Lakshmi, Isabel Gomes; **D:** Vondie Curtis-Hall; **W:** Kate Lanier; **C:** Geoffrey Simpson; **M:** Terence Blanchard.

Go Fish

A sweet story about a close-knit group of friends who share apartments, their lives, and their loves. And, oh yeah, they are all lesbians. The film was shot in black and white for cost considerations and for the most part it was probably the hand of fate pitching in. The B&W format gives the film a documentary feel that keeps the love scenes from becoming prurient and makes the filmmakers occasional intersplicing between the real life action and fantasy elements of sight, sound, and inner dialogue feel avant garde rather than gratuitous. In a particularly funny bit, one of the more loose women is accosted in her mind by a jury of her peers after she has slept with a man just for the fun of it and because he is a friend. She is forced to defend herself as a lesbian to the jury in her mind and is left uneasy for days around her friends. The film does its best to discuss the issues that lesbians face, from finding love to choosing clothes. Its frame is the casual meanderings and musings by the group about two of its members who are fumbling through the first days of dating. Max (Turner, also the co-writer) is pretty, outgoing, and single. Ely (Brodie) is older and more reclusive. Their friends think they are perfect for each other. The rest of the film is a casual portrait of the group and their daily lives as Max and Ely grow closer together. The acting in the film seems mostly non-professional, but the direction, editing, and cinematography are all amazing. The B&W stock makes the film grainy and the sound is decent. It definitely has a student film quality to it, but overall it is good fare for lovers of independent films about counter-culture. —CA

Movie: 🎬🎬🎬 ½ **DVD:** 🎬🎬
MGM Home Ent. (cat #1002210, UPC 027-616864413). Full frame. Dolby Digital Mono. $19.98. Keepcase. *LANG:* English; Spanish. *SUB:* French; Spanish. *CAP:* English. *FEATURES:* 16 chapters • Theatrical trailer.
1994 (R) 87m/B Guinevere Turner, V.S. Brodie, T. Wendy McMillan, Anastasia Sharp, Migdalia Melendez; **D:** Rose Troche; **W:** Guinevere Turner, Rose Troche; **C:** Ann T. Rossetti; **M:** Brendan Dolan, Jennifer Sharpe. *AWARDS: NOM:* Ind. Spirit '95: Support. Actress (Brodie).

Go for Broke! [VCI]

In 1943, wet-behind-the-ears Lt. Michael Grayson (Johnson) is less than thrilled to learn that his first command after Officer Candidate School is to be the 442nd Regimental Infantry. It's composed of Japanese-Americans. At first, he sees them as "stinkin' Jap" stereotypes, but, of course, he comes to understand them as the unit distinguishes itself in the European Theatre. Robert Pirosh handles the material well, though this one isn't nearly as ambitious (or as successful) as *Battleground,* which he wrote. The title is in public domain and the film is available on other discs. (See reviews of *Legendary World War II Films, Book 2,* and *Beyond Barbed Wire.*) This version looks very good. Very faint surface damage is visible on the black-and-white image, but it's negligible. Mono sound is true to the era and delivers understandable dialogue. —MM

Movie: 🎬🎬🎬 **DVD:** 🎬🎬🎬
VCI (cat #8279, UPC 089859827921). Full frame. Dolby Digital Mono. $14.99. Keepcase. *LANG:* English. *FEATURES:* Trailer • 12 chapters.
1951 92m/B Van Johnson, Gianna Maria Canale, Warner Anderson, Lane Nakano, George Miki; **D:** Robert Pirosh; **W:** Robert Pirosh; **C:** Paul Vogel; **M:** Alberto Colombo. *AWARDS: NOM:* Oscars '51: Story & Screenplay.

Godmonster of Indian Flats

How can you not like a flick whose titular character is an eight-foot mutant sheep created from ancient gasses released from a mine in a historical wild (and in this case wooly) west town? Eddie (Richard Marion) is a dim-witted shepherd who wanders into Reno, hits it big at the slots, and wins a lot of attention from shady new friends who relieve him of his loot and send him home to sob himself to sleep among his flock. He then has a wacky nightmare that could very well have been a bad LSD trip and is found in a stable by a local college professor (E. Kerrigan Prescott). Beside Eddie is a wet knot of mutant wool that the professor decides warrants further study. After interminable subplots involving a corrupt nearby town, the sheep monster finally lumbers out of the lab on a rampage. Generous supplements only sweeten this goof fest that's too insane to resist. Don't try and demonstrate your home theatre with this one unless you enjoy being laughed at. The full-frame transfer shows its age. Image and mono sound are consistently nothing special but certainly more than adequate. Something Weird Video opens their schlock vaults to reveal a bonus picture called *Passion in the Sun* (1964, 70 minutes) about a sideshow freak in pursuit of the stripper of his dreams. There's a musical number from Hobbs' Roseland affectionately dubbed "You Cannot Fart Around with Love." But what really makes this disc a keeper is a sick little 15-minute short called "The Geek" about this group of long-hairs who wander into the woods in search of Bigfoot (or his brother Kyle), who has a good time with a blonde as her hippie friends look on. Also included are two fascinating public health reels on fly and rat control (30 minutes). —JO/GNG/DG

Movie: 🎬 **DVD:** 🎬🎬 ½
Image Ent. (cat #ID0801SWDVD, UPC 014-381080124). Full frame. Mono. $24.99. Snapper. *LANG:* English. *FEATURES:* 12 chapters • 70-minute horror nudie, *Passion in the Sun* • Short subject, "Rural Rat Control" • Short subject, "Community Fly Control Operations" • Short subject, "You Cannot Fart Around with Love" • Short subject, "The Geek" • Horror drive-in exploitation art • Horrorama radio spot rarities.
1973 89m/C Stuart Lancaster, E. Kerrigan Prescott, Richard Marion; **D:** Fredric Hobbs; **W:** Fredric Hobbs; **M:** Henry Price.

God's Little Acre

Hard as it may be to believe, the cast of this Southern soap opera went on to populate *Gilligan's Island*, *Hawaii Five-0*, *Combat*, and *Bonanza*. Crazed family patriarch Ty Ty (Ryan) believes that there's gold buried on his property and so he and his sons (Lord and Morrow) dig vast holes. Meanwhile, Buddy Hackett is running for sheriff and tough guy Ray is sniffing around sexy daughter-in-law Louise, and then there's albino Landon out in the barn. DVD contains two versions of the film, the 111-minute theatrical release and the 118-minute "uncensored" version. Neither will raise many eyebrows today. Image is much crisper and sharper in the "uncensored" version. Some minor aliasing is visible in both but the image holds true in panning shots. —*MM*

Movie: 𝄞𝄞𝄞 **DVD:** 𝄞𝄞𝄞 ½

Image Ent. (cat #ID6162TVDVD, UPC 014-381616224). Widescreen (1.85:1) letterboxed. Dolby Digital Mono. $24.98. Keepcase. *LANG:* English. *FEATURES:* 16 chapters each ⚬ 2 trailers.

1958 110m/B Robert Ryan, Tina Louise, Michael Landon, Buddy Hackett, Vic Morrow, Jack Lord, Aldo Ray, Fay Spain; **D:** Anthony Mann; **W:** Philip Yordan; **C:** Hans J. Haller; **M:** Elmer Bernstein.

Godzilla, King of the Monsters [Goodtimes]

Several versions of the debut of the long-lived Japanese monster are available on DVD. (Please see *Book 1*.) Most are better than this lackluster effort that looks like it was transferred from VHS tape. —*MM* **AKA:** *Gojira*.

Movie: 𝄞𝄞𝄞 **DVD:** 𝄞𝄞

Goodtimes Ent. (cat #05-81221, UPC 018-713812216). Full frame. Dolby Digital Mono. $7.49. Keepcase. *LANG:* English. *FEATURES:* 12 chapters.

1956 80m/B *JP* Raymond Burr, Takashi Shimura, Akira Takarada, Akihiko Hirata, Momoko Kochi, Sachio Sakai, Fuyuki Murakami, Ren Yamamoto; **D:** Inoshiro Honda, Terry Morse; **W:** Inoshiro Honda, Takeo Murata; **C:** Masao Tamai, Guy Roe; **M:** Akira Ifukube.

Godzilla vs. Destroyah

Please see review of *Godzilla vs. Space Godzilla / Godzilla vs. Destroyah*. **AKA:** Godzilla vs. Destroia; Godzilla vs. Destroyer; Godzilla vs. Desutoroia.

1995 103m/C *JP* Megumi Odaka, Momoko Kochi, Kenpachiro Satsuma, Takehiro Murata; **D:** Takao Okawara; **W:** Kazuki Omori; **M:** Akira Ifukube.

Godzilla vs. Space Godzilla / Godzilla vs. Destroyah

In the 1994 *Godzilla vs. Space Godzilla*, we are witnesses to a truly otherworldly encounter. While Japan's secret military bureau messes with Godzilla's brain in an attempt to gain control over the behemoth, a mutant Space Godzilla has set its eyes on Earth. It travels through space and lands on Earth to destroy Godzilla and to make the planet its own. In an explosive showdown, Godzilla and Space Godzilla square off against each other, leaving most of their surroundings in waste. One year later, Toho had reassembled all the set pieces from the previous movie and started a new attack. In *Godzilla vs. Destroyah* a new Godzilla emerges. Powered by radioactivity, the monster's body is threatening to overheat and cause a China Syndrome nuclear meltdown. While scientists try to find ways to safely destroy Godzilla a new threat appears in the shape of Destroyah. This ferocious creature and its descendants have set their eyes on mankind and Godzilla Junior. To save the planet, the scientists try to freeze the explosive monster while attempting to find a way to stop Destroyah on its path of destruction. The only solution, it seems, is to have the monsters battle things out among themselves. Taken from rather clean film prints, the material shows little to no damage and a high level of detail. Colors are strong but not oversaturated, making both the *Mothra* (please see review) and *Godzilla* double features spectacularly flashy movies. Shadow delineation is also perfect, with deep shadows that always maintain a high level of definition. The discs contain dubbed audio tracks in English language only and sadly the original Japanese language tracks are not part of the release. Presented in stereo, the audio tracks are well produced however, and although the dubs are oftentimes out of sync and a little weary, the overall experience of the movies is great. —*GH*

Movie: 𝄞𝄞 ½ **DVD:** 𝄞𝄞𝄞

Columbia Tristar Home Video (UPC 04339-6046900). Widescreen (1.85:1) anamorphic. Dolby Stereo. $27.98. Keepcase. *LANG:* English. *SUB:* English; French; Spanish. *CAP:* English. *FEATURES:* 28 chapters each.

1994 175m/C *JP* Megumi Odaka, Akira (Tsukamoto) Emoto, Jun Hashizume; **D:** Kensho Yamashita.

Goin' South

Sub-genius outlaw Henry Moon (Nicholson) is saved from the gallows by Julia Tate (Steenburgen), who agrees to marry him, but really wants him to work on her secret gold mine. Then they try to get to the loot before his old gang catches wind of it. It's tongue-in-cheek, rough-hewn comedy that gains no polish on this barebones DVD. Nor should it. The image is as grainy as it's ever been, and the movie itself is still a delight. Particularly recommended to fans of the cast who may have missed this one. —*MM*

Movie: 𝄞𝄞𝄞 **DVD:** 𝄞𝄞 ½

Paramount (cat #01133, UPC 097360113-341). Widescreen (1.85:1) anamorphic. Dolby Digital Mono. $24.99. Keepcase. *LANG:* English. *SUB:* English. *CAP:* English. *FEATURES:* 12 chapters.

1978 (PG) 109m/C Jack Nicholson, Mary Steenburgen, John Belushi, Christopher Lloyd, Veronica Cartwright, Richard Bradford, Danny DeVito, Luana Anders, Ed Begley Jr., Anne Ramsey; **D:** Jack Nicholson; **W:** Charles Shyer; **C:** Nestor Almendros; **M:** Perry Botkin.

Going Places

Though the box copy and art would lead you to think that this is a lighthearted Gallic sex romp, it's much darker and not really much fun. Jean-Claude (Depardieu) and Pierrot (Dewaere) are a couple of petty thieves who don't mind a bit of kidnapping and forcible sex now and again. No matter, though, because the extraordinarily attractive women don't really mind. DVD presents an image that's good but on the soft side. It's about average for an import of this age. French dialogue track is more expressive than the English. Optional subtitles are white. —*MM* **AKA:** *Les Valseuses*; *Making It*.

Movie: 𝄞𝄞 **DVD:** 𝄞𝄞 ½

Anchor Bay (cat #DV11588, UPC 013131-158892). Widescreen (1.66:1) anamorphic. Dolby Digital Mono. $24.98. Keepcase. *LANG:* French; English. *SUB:* English. *FEATURES:* Trailers ⚬ 30 chapters.

1974 (R) 122m/C *FR* Gerard Depardieu, Patrick Dewaere, Miou-Miou, Isabelle Huppert, Jeanne Moreau, Brigitte Fossey; **D:** Bertrand Blier; **W:** Bertrand Blier; **C:** Bruno Nuytten; **M:** Stephane Grappelli.

The Golden Bowl

Beautiful but bloodless Merchant/Ivory adaptation of Henry James's complex 1904 novel set in turn-of-the-century London. Wealthy American aesthete Adam Verver (Nolte) dotes on his only daughter, Maggie (Beckinsale), and even buys her a husband—an impoverished Italian aristocrat, Prince Amerigo (a miscast Northam), whom she loves. But unknown to both Ververs, the prince and Maggie's best friend, the equally poor Charlotte (Thurman), had a long-ago affair that gets rekindled, even though Charlotte has become the wife of Adam. A studied menage à quatre where just what anyone knows (or suspects) is never made clear. The wonderful cast and excellent cinematography make this another feather in the Merchant/Ivory cap. The lush look of the film is only enhanced by the DVD presentation. The widescreen transfer looks good, offering a clear and sharp image, with only the slightest evidence of artifacting. The colors are very nice, showing realistic fleshtones and warm hues all around. The 5.1 audio track is perfect, bringing clear dialogue, lovely music reproduction, and very impressive Surround sound. —*ML*

Movie: 𝄞𝄞𝄞 **DVD:** 𝄞𝄞𝄞

Lion's Gate Home Ent. (cat #VM7834D, UPC 031398783428). Widescreen (2.35:1) letterboxed. Dolby Digital 5.1. $24.99. Keepcase. *LANG:* English. *SUB:* English; Spanish.

CAP: English. *FEATURES:* Trailer ▪ 30 chapters.
2000 (R) 130m/C *GB* Nick Nolte, Uma Thurman, Kate Beckinsale, Jeremy Northam, Anjelica Huston, James Fox, Madeleine Potter, Peter Eyre; *D:* James Ivory; *W:* Ruth Prawer Jhabvala; *C:* Tony Pierce-Roberts; *M:* Richard Robbins.

Goldwyn: The Man and His Movies

Based on Scott Berg's excellent biography, this look at the career of Sam Goldwyn is a capsule history of Hollywood. Goldwyn, famous for his malapropisms, was one of the great showmen. His fortunes rose and fell so often and so far that his life was more eventful than many of his movies. The film makes good use of clips, but the real value comes from Berg's source material. Image quality varies, as expected, but it's still an improvement over broadcast quality. This one earns highest recommendations to anyone who's interested in the film industry. —*MM*
Movie: ♫♫♫ *DVD:* ♫♫ ½
Columbia Tristar (cat #07801, UPC 04339-6078017). Full frame. Dolby Digital Stereo. $24.98. Keepcase. *LANG:* English. *SUB:* English. *CAP:* English. *FEATURES:* 28 chapters ▪ Goldwyn filmography ▪ Trailers.
2001 118m/C *D:* Peter Jones, Robert Israel, Mark Catalena; *W:* Peter Jones, Scott Berg; *Nar:* Dustin Hoffman.

The Golem

Please see review for *German Silent Masterpieces*. *AKA:* Der Golem, wie er in die Welt kam.
Movie: ♫♫♫ ½
1920 80m/B *GE* Paul Wegener, Albert Steinruck, Ernst Deutsch, Lyda Salmonava, Otto Gebuehr, Max Kronert, Loni Nest, Greta Schroder, Hans Sturm; *D:* Carl Boese, Paul Wegener; *W:* Henrik Galeen, Paul Wegener; *C:* Karl Freund; *M:* Hans Landberger.

Golf Balls!

This is the kind of exploitation fluff that became popular during the first days of home video. It's a silly comedy about the guys and girls at the low-rent Pennytree golf club who are put upon by the snotty rich folk over at the Bentwood Country Club. The plot makes *Caddyshack 2* look like *King Lear*. The film appears to have been shot on video and just about every visual flaw imaginable shows up. The most important are incredibly heavy artifacts and pixelation in the darker scenes. —*MM*
Movie: ♫ ½ *DVD:* ♫ ½
Key East Ent. (cat #KE2001, UPC 691597-200128). Full frame. Dolby Digital Surround. $24.98. Keepcase. *LANG:* English. *SUB:* English; Spanish. *FEATURES:* 30 chapters.
1999 (R) 87m/C George Longenhagen, Todd Allen Durkin, Dan Barkley, Naia Kelly, Amy Lynn Baxter; *D:* Steve Procko; *W:* Bob Small, Steve Procko; *C:* Steve Fraasa.

Goliath and the Dragon

Formulaic but enjoyable sword-and-sandals genre film is filled with English-named Italian actors, bare-chested heroes, beautiful busty women, evil opponents, and plenty of mythological creatures. Although the film is generally clean and mostly free of defects, it is quickly noticeable that this DVD seems to be produced from a mediocre quality laserdisc transfer. Edge-enhancement is prevalent throughout the film and a number of video artifacts, ranging from shimmering to weird interlaced effects, plague the presentation. Although colors are generally well reproduced, a number of scenes have noticeable blue tinge, unbalancing the image, giving the film a very unnatural look that was certainly not desired. The transfer is also very dark and not much shadow detail is left in the majority of the film. Disc also includes a second feature, the full-length 1965 *The Conqueror of Atlantis* in a full-frame transfer—most likely a TV version, as the opening credits are actually in widescreen. However, the presentation is pretty bad. The film is riddled with scratches and blemishes of all sorts. Registration problems and emulsion degradation add to the problems and worst of all, the entire film has a giant "SWV" ("Something Weird Video") logo on the right side of the screen, about 2/3rds down. —*GH* *AKA:* La Vendetta di Ercole.
Movie: ♫♫♫ *DVD:* ♫♫ ½
Image Ent. (cat #ID0802SWDVD, UPC 014-381080223). Widescreen (2.35:1) letterboxed. Dolby Digital Mono. $24.98. Keepcase. *LANG:* English. *FEATURES:* Trailers ▪ 3 "sword and sandal" short subjects ▪ Full-length feature, *The Conqueror of Atlantis* ▪ Gallery of "sword and sandal" exploitation art.
1961 90m/C *IT FR* Bruce Cabot, Mark Forest, Broderick Crawford, Gaby Andre, Leonora Ruffo; *D:* Vittorio Cottafavi; *W:* Marco Piccolo, Archibald Zounds Jr.; *C:* Mario Montuori; *M:* Les Baxter.

Gonin

Five Japanese businessmen who have been devastated by the economy find their lives further complicated by Yakuza gangsters. They retaliate, successfully. But their troubles are just starting because the bad guys hire an assassin ("Beat" Takashi, at his deadpan best) to get them. Yes, it's a lot more of the old ultra-violence, which loses some of its effectiveness when experienced behind burned-in white subtitles. Those are unreadable in bright scenes, and sometimes unintentionally funny in their mistranslation. Image ranges between some sharp, well-detailed interiors to action scenes which may have been shot on high definition video. Pixelation and artifacts appear to be intentional in those moments. A bit of surface damage is evident, too. —*MM*
Movie: ♫♫ ½ *DVD:* ♫♫ ½

Tai Seng (UPC 677880102591). Widescreen letterboxed. Dolby Surround. $19.98. Keepcase. *LANG:* Japanese. *SUB:* English. *FEATURES:* 12 chapters ▪ Trailer ▪ Synopsis (text).
1995 109m/C *JP* Koichi Sato, Masahiro Motoki, Naoto Takenaka, Takeshi "Beat" Kitano; *D:* Takashi Ishii; *W:* Takashi Ishii; *C:* Yasushi Sasakibara; *M:* Goro Yasukawa.

Good Advice

Stock broker Ryan Turner (Sheen) gets in trouble with the powers-that-be and finds himself unemployed and reduced to living with his shallow girlfriend Cindy (Richards). Then she dumps him and takes off with a rich guy. To keep body and soul together, Ryan takes over the advice column she has been writing. Since Cindy works at home (when she works), her editor Page (Harmon) won't know the difference, right? But can Ryan think like a woman? O.K., Charlie Sheen is no Dustin Hoffman and this ain't *Tootsie*, but it is an acceptable little low-budget comedy. Director Steve Rash admits as much on his "everyone was wonderful" commentary track. For a film that was made on a TV schedule, this one looks pretty good on disc. Image is on the soft side but is presented without any visual flaws. Sound is fine for the low- to mid-budget production. —*MM*
Movie: ♫♫ ½ *DVD:* ♫♫ ½
Artisan Ent. (cat #12237, UPC 0122361-22371). Widescreen (1.85:1) anamorphic. Dolby Digital 5.1 Surround; Dolby Surround. $19.98. Keepcase. *LANG:* English. *SUB:* Spanish. *CAP:* English. *FEATURES:* Talent files ▪ Production notes ▪ Trailers ▪ Commentary: Steve Rash ▪ 21 chapters.
2001 (R) 93m/C Charlie Sheen, Denise Richards, Angie Harmon, Jon Lovitz, Rosanna Arquette, Estelle Harris, Barry Newman; *D:* Steve Rash; *W:* Robert Horn, Daniel Margosis; *C:* Daryn Okada; *M:* Teddy Castellucci.

Good Guys Wear Black

Mild-manner professor John T. Booker (Norris) keeps his former life as a leader of a Vietnam commando unit under wraps until he discovers that he's number one on a CIA hit list. Action scenes set on ski slopes and auto race tracks follow. DVD delivers a fair to good image. It's about equal to VHS tape and all that should be expected of a film this old. Sound is weak. —*MM*
Movie: ♫♫ *DVD:* ♫♫
HBO (cat #90611, UPC 026359061127). Widescreen letterboxed. $24.98. Snapper. *LANG:* English. *SUB:* English; French; Spanish. *CAP:* English. *FEATURES:* 16 chapters.
1978 (PG) 96m/C Chuck Norris, Anne Archer, James Franciscus; *D:* Ted Post; *W:* Mark Medoff; *M:* Craig Safan.

Good Men, Good Women

This story within a story within a story, possibly within another story, is strictly for the art-house film crowd. Based on a book by Bi-Yu Chiang, a heroine of the Taiwanese revolution, it tells the story of an actress who is acting in a film about Chiang. During the filming someone is faxing pages of her own diary to her home. The diary tells the story of her wild days with the love of her life. The film was shot with the world's most stationary crowd and never bothers to explain even as much as the DVD box does. You will either consider this a work of genius or a sleep aid. The landscape cinematography is beautiful; the print is beautiful, too, and clean with clear color and sound. —*CA* **AKA:** Haonan haonu.

Movie: ♫♫ ½ **DVD:** ♫♫♫
Winstar Home Ent. (cat #FLV5294, UPC 720917529424). Widescreen (1.85:1) letterboxed. Stereo. $24.90. Keepcase. *LANG:* Taiwanese with some Chinese. *SUB:* English. *FEATURES:* 16 chapters ● Weblinks.
1995 108m/C *JP TW* Lim Giong, Jack Kao, Vickey We, Jieh-Wen King, Ben Hsier; *D:* Hsiao-Hsien Hou; *W:* Tien-wen Chu; *C:* Hwai-en Chen.

The Good Wife

Set in 1939 Australia, this story of obsession and unconditional love is flawlessly acted and beautifully filmed. Marge (Ward) is married to a good, loving man, Sonny (Brown), but she feels the call of the illusive "something" she's missing. Her longing takes the form of an obsession with the new bartender (Neill), a womanizing, vain man who roams from town to town looking for his own illusive something. It only fuels her desire when he refuses to have anything to do with her. Sonny gives Marge enough rope to hang herself, to the delight of the town gossips, and hopes against hope that she will come to realize what's important. Sets, costumes, and landscapes all combine to create an atmospheric morality play that is at times predictable. Filled with beautiful people, passion both fulfilled and denied, and a decent ending, this disc is a fine girls' night or date film. The picture quality is good with a little fuzzing around the edges of objects and the sound is also good. —*CA* **AKA:** The Umbrella Woman.

Movie: ♫♫ ½ **DVD:** ♫♫ ½
MGM Home Ent. (cat #1002745, UPC 027616869432). Widescreen (1.85:1) anamorphic; full frame. Dolby Digital Stereo. $14.95. Keepcase. *LANG:* English. *SUB:* English; French; Spanish. *CAP:* English. *FEATURES:* 16 chapters ● Theatrical trailer.
1986 (R) 97m/C *AU* Rachel Ward, Bryan Brown, Sam Neill, Steven Vidler, Bruce Barry, Jennifer Claire; *D:* Ken Cameron; *W:* Peter Kenna; *C:* James Bartle; *M:* Cameron Allan.

Goodbye, Mr. Cool

Released from prison after six years, Lung (Ekin Cheng) decides to retire from the world of gangs and take a job at his friend's restaurant. But both the gangs he ruled and the ones he fought with have different ideas. Soon, Lung discovers there is more than his life at stake—while in prison, his girlfriend Helen (Karen Mok) had a son, and Lung will be forced to fight for his newfound family. More reflective and sentimental than one might expect, but there's still a healthy dose of martial arts action. The picture is quite good, but the dialogue is heavy on background hiss. This disc is double-sided, single-layered, with half of the film on each side. The only way to access the chapters is from the main menu, as the DVD itself is not broken into tracks. —*BG*

Movie: ♫♫ ½ **DVD:** ♫♫ ½
Tai Seng (cat #DVD-472, UPC 489039110-4724). Widescreen letterbox. Dolby 5.1; Dolby Surround; DTS Surround. $24.95. Keepcase. *LANG:* Cantonese; Mandarin. *SUB:* English; Simplified Chinese; Traditional Chinese. *FEATURES:* 10 chapters.
2001 101m/C *HK* Ekin Cheng, Karen Mok; *D:* Jingle Ma.

Goodbye South, Goodbye

Two small time crooks—beleaguered Kao (Kao) and hotheaded Flatty (Taiwanese pop star Giong)—piss off some very influential people. Their problems don't kick in until halfway through the movie, but so little actually happens it's difficult to tell if their actions indeed trigger the pathetic consequences. This movie seems to consist of the parts that usually get cut out or are not written at all. There's lots of driving from place to place, smoking, and one-sided telephone conversations made somewhat interesting by the use of extremely long takes and desaturated natural light cinematography. Unfortunately, there's no story to serve. At one point, Kao goes through a car wash inside his car and he's not even on the phone or smoking a cigarette. It's almost worth sitting through the entire movie just to hear a Taiwanese gentleman do a karaoke bit about the virtues of being a man. Transfer from release print flattens available light photography. Sound is fine. —*LA* **AKA:** Nanguo Zaijian, Nanguo.

Movie: ♫♫ **DVD:** ♫♫ ½
Winstar Home Ent. (cat #FLV5285, UPC 720917528526). Widescreen (1.85:1) letterboxed. Stereo. $24.98. Keepcase. *LANG:* Taiwanese. *SUB:* English. *FEATURES:* 16 chapters ● Awards and filmographies ● *Flowers of Shanghai* trailer ● Weblinks.
1996 116m/C *JP TW* Jack Kao, Lim Giong, Kuei-ying Hsu, Annie Shizuka Inoh; *D:* Hsiao-Hsien Hou; *W:* Tien-wen Chu; *C:* Mark Lee Ping-Bin, Hwai-en Chen; *M:* Lim Giong.

The Goonies

Wacky, obnoxious teen adventure pic about a group of kids searching through subterranean catacombs for buried treasure in the hopes that it might save their town from developers. Hot on their trail is the evil Fratelli family, whose deformed son Sloth (Matuszak) is kept chained to a wall. The story is pure Little Rascals, and Spielberg's touch is extremely evident. It features topnotch camerawork and grand, impressive sets, but the kids are so annoying and tiresome you wish a boulder would fall on them. The depiction of the obese "Chunk" is insulting and borders on being offensive. Most of the jokes are dumb and childish but Ramsey and Matuszak provide some strong laughs. Twelve-year-olds will probably love the film (I did when I was that age) but adults will probably find it a trying experience. The disc is gorgeous, sharp, and colorful if a tad grainy in the dimly lit scenes. The remix isn't as strong as a modern track (naturally) but it is well done and exciting. The commentary is more anecdotal than informative, and Astin makes a sudden departure just before the one-hour mark. The audio track features occasional video cutaways of the recording session that are fun, though one wishes they had shown the recording session a bit more. The complete two-part Lauper video that is included is an appreciated extra and is a few notches in quality below the feature. The deleted scenes are presented at 1.85 and are worthwhile, but more would be nice. The famous deleted "Octopus" scene is included and it's pretty lame. —*DG*

Movie: ♫♫ **DVD:** ♫♫♫ ½
Warner (cat #11474, UPC 0853911474-28). Widescreen (2.35:1) anamorphic. Dolby Surround 5.1. $24.98. Snapper. *LANG:* English; French; Spanish. *SUB:* English; French; Spanish; Portugese. *CAP:* English. *FEATURES:* "The Making of Goonies" featurette ● Trailer ● Cyndi Lauper music video ● Commentary: Donner, Feldman, Quan, et al ● 3 deleted scenes ● 37 chapters.
1985 (PG) 114m/C Sean Astin, Josh Brolin, Jeff B. Cohen, Corey Feldman, Martha Plimpton, John Matuszak, Robert Davi, Anne Ramsey, Mary Ellen Trainor, Jonathan Ke Quan, Kerri Green, Joe Pantoliano; *D:* Richard Donner; *W:* Chris Columbus, Steven Spielberg; *C:* Nick McLean; *M:* Dave Grusin.

Goose Boxer

Gray-haired master picks fights with kung fu students, looking for the man who killed his brother using Crane Style. A new teacher at one school is abducted by White Crested Crane to teach him better kung fu, leading to a confrontation between students and master. Much of the running time is full of insufferable "comedy" music. If you can stand that, and the mostly lame gags, there's some fine Crane Style kung fu on display here. The widescreen transfer, from a decent print for its age, is reasonably vivid, but skips a few times near the start as if there's a crease in the tape master. Released as a *Brooklyn Zoo Double Feature* with *Tiger Over Wall*. The packaging prominently features the World Trade Center towers and the package notes that "A portion of proceeds to benefit NYC relief charities." —BT

Movie: 🎬🎬 **DVD:** 🎬 ½

Xenon Ent. (UPC 694795305527). Widescreen letterboxed. Dolby Digital 2.0. $9.99. Keepcase. *LANG:* English. *FEATURES:* 6 chapters • Trailers.

1978 79m/C *HK* Charles Heung, Philip Ko, Bolo Yeung, Hoi Sang Lee; *D:* See Fu Tai; *W:* Hoi Ching Cheung; *C:* Law Wan Shing, Fook Leung Chow.

Gormenghast

Adapted by Malcolm McKay from the novels by British author Mervyn Peake, this miniseries follows a literary tradition dating back to Thomas More's *Utopia* and Plato's *Republic,* creating a completely fictitious world to expose the foibles and follies of the human condition. At times modern, Medieval, and futuristic, the monarchy of Gormenghast prides itself on maintaining its rituals and traditions to preserve society. The rich stay rich, the poor remain poor, and everyone knows their place. Yet like most utopian and dystopian literature, our story begins with the birth of change...usually in the form of a child, in this case Titus, the 77th Earl of Groan and future lord of Gormenghast. The perpetually brooding 76th Earl, Lord Groan (Richardson), sees fatherhood as another bothersome activity, keeping him from his library and his love for ornithology, particularly owls. Daughter Lady Fuchsia (McIntosh) first greets her newborn brother with jealousy, but eventually overcomes her envy when she realizes that Titus may be the first opportunity to develop a "normal" familial relationship. Steerpike (Rhys Meyers) is an abused kitchen helper, terrorized by the corpulent royal cook Swelter (Griffiths). Flay (Lee), royal manservant to the Earl, witnesses the porcine chef's brutality and intercedes. Steerpike pledges his devotion and obedience to Flay and very soon starts his path up the courtly ladder, gaining confidences and increasing his visibility amongst the privileged class. Proper deference and humility endears him to the hierarchy, all the better to conceal his pathological thirst for power and rebellion of Gormenghast's caste system. Soon, Steerpike counsels Lord Groan's scheming twin sisters, Cora and Clarice (Baxter and Wanamaker), on how to wrest power away from the Earl and back into their hands. With a ruthlessness and bearing that would shame Machiavelli, Steerpike manipulates virtually all who cross his path, instantly sizing how their standing may or may not aid his rise to the throne. And that's just in the first hour! Luckily, each episode ends with a review of the cast list, like getting an hourly reminder; they come in handy. The full-frame transfer exhibits strong color fidelity and excellent detail delineation. Even though the costumes and art direction favor reds and purples, hues are strong but not brilliant, likely an intentional effect. Despite the numerous process shots and occasional photographic diffu-

sion, the image reads sharp and clean. Stereo packs more punch than one would expect for a made-for-TV production. Each episode starts with a madrigal-like chant. With the Pro-Logic mode engaged, my home theatre literally sounded like a cathedral. Richard Rodney Bennett's music score reflects the timelessness of the setting, drawing upon Elizabethan and contemporary music styles. Dialogue is clear and intelligible. Surround channel activity occurs frequently, with whistling wind, forest sound effects, and music fill. While not exactly subwoofer busting, there is some low-end energy in the soundtrack, primarily used in magnifying voice timbre and the heavier musical passages. —GH

Movie: 🎬🎬🎬 **DVD:** 🎬🎬🎬

Warner Home Video (UPC 7940511545-21). Full frame. Dolby Digital Surround. $34.98. Keepcase. *LANG:* English. *CAP:* English. *FEATURES:* "Making of" documentary • Trailers • Enhanced "making of" documentary.

2000 232m/C *CA GB US* Jonathan Rhys Meyers, Ian Richardson, Neve McIntosh, Christopher Lee, Richard Griffiths, June Brown; *D:* Andy Wilson; *W:* Malcolm McKay.

The Grapes of Death

French horror auteur Jean Rollin takes a stab at the zombie genre, and the result falls somewhere between *Night of the Living Dead* and the Italian "gut-muncher" films which would follow. As with most films in this genre, the plot is wafer-thin. A young woman named Elizabeth (Marie-Georges Pascal) must vacate the train in which she is traveling after she is attacked by a strange man. Once off the train, Elizabeth finds herself lost in the French wine-country. Upon seeking help in a nearby village, she soon learns that most of the locals have become crazed, homicidal zombies. She attempts to get assistance from the villagers who are still "normal," but then realizes that she must face this evil alone. Elizabeth's only hope is to find her way to a nearby vineyard, where her fiancé is waiting for her. However, the pesticide used for the grape harvest may be behind the odd behavior of the town's inhabitants, and Elizabeth could be walking into a trap. While most European horror films are more leisurely paced than their American cousins, *Grapes* is just plain slow. The film contains far too many scenes of Elizabeth walking through fields. Yes, the scenery is beautiful, but we didn't come here for a travelogue. Rollin is famous for his erotic-vampire films, and he is certainly out of his mode here. This one has the distinction of being the first French "gore film," but the special effects here are cheesy and unconvincing. To his credit, Rollin does create a dream-like atmosphere that is effective at times, but for the most part, the movie is simply boring. Synapse Films has done a fine job of restoring the film for this DVD. The image is sharp and clear, although the film does show its age by

revealing scratches and white marks. The colors are good and there is only a small amount of grain on the image. The mono soundtrack is adequate, as it provides clear dialogue with no hissing. The yellow subtitles are clear and very easy to read. A 33-minute featurette is included on the DVD, which includes an in-depth interview with Rollin in which he discusses his career. —ML **AKA:** Les Raisins de la Mort.

Movie: 🎬 ½ **DVD:** 🎬🎬 ½

Synapse (cat #SFD0016, UPC 65493030-1692). Widescreen (1.66:1) anamorphic. Dolby Digital Mono. $24.98. Keepcase. *LANG:* French. *SUB:* English. *FEATURES:* Theatrical trailers • Director interview • Director filmography • Director bio • Still gallery • 18 chapters.

1978 90m/C *FR* Marie-Georges Pascal, Jean-Pierre Bouyxou, Christian Meunier, Brigitte Lahaie, Serge Marquand, Felix Marten; *D:* Jean Rollin; *W:* Jean Rollin.

Grass

This documentary uses animation, newsreel footage, and clips from government propaganda films to give a legal history of marijuana. The old films are often hilarious, and do a good job of illustrating how the government has tried to link this drug with whatever social fear was popular at the time, be it heroin, immigrants, or even Red China. The picture quality is inconsistent due to the variety of source materials, but Paul Mavrides' imaginative animation comes through beautifully, and the soundtrack is uniformly excellent. —BG

Movie: 🎬🎬🎬 **DVD:** 🎬🎬🎬 ½

Home Vision Cinema (cat #GRA 170, UPC 037429167625). Widescreen (1.85:1) anamorphic. Dolby 5.1. $29.95. Keepcase. *LANG:* English. *FEATURES:* 13 chapters • Interview with Ron Mann • Deleted scene • High Times Magazine gallery • Trailer • Quick reference guide to state-by-state marijuana laws.

2000 80m/C *CA* Ron Mann; *D:* Ron Mann; *W:* Soloman Vesta; *M:* Guido Luciani; *Nar:* Woody Harrelson.

The Grass Is Greener

Talented cast delivers something of a dull dud. An American millionaire (Mitchum) takes over part of an impoverished British Earl's (Grant) mansion and falls in love with the lady of the house (Kerr). The Earl enlists the aid of an old girlfriend (Simmons) in a feeble attempt to make her jealous. Guess how it ends. Aliasing is a major problem in most panning shots and it's obvious in others. Otherwise DVD image is nice and bright. —MM

Movie: 🎬🎬 **DVD:** 🎬🎬

Artisan Ent. (cat #10246, UPC 01715312-0462). Widescreen letterboxed. Dolby Digital Mono. $19.98. Keepcase. *LANG:* English. *CAP:* English. *FEATURES:* 18 chapters.

1961 105m/C Cary Grant, Deborah Kerr, Jean Simmons, Robert Mitchum; *D:* Stanley Donen; *W:* Hugh Williams; *C:* Christopher Challis; *M:* Noel Coward.

Grateful Dawg

This documentary features home video, studio, and concert footage of Jerry Garcia and Dave Grisman as they experiment with bluegrass and other traditional forms of American music. We can thank Grisman for insisting the film consist of complete performances, since the music is far more interesting than the interviews. The film doesn't offer much insight into this interesting collaboration, but it does provide plenty of solid acoustic music. Picture and sound are both wildly inconsistent due to the wide range of source materials. The packaging says the program is pan and scan, but the disc appears to be letterboxed at a 1.66:1 ratio. A major studio ought to know better. —BG

Movie: 🎵🎵 ½ **DVD:** 🎵🎵 ½
Columbia Tristar (cat #07168, UPC 0433-96071681). Widescreen letterboxed. Dolby 5.1. $24.95. Keepcase. *LANG:* English. *SUB:* English; French; Spanish. *CAP:* English. *FEATURES:* 20 chapters • Commentary: Gillian and David Grisman • Bonus performances • Discographies • Outtakes • Music video • Production notes.
2001 81m/C Jerry Garcia, David Grisman; **D:** Gillian Grisman.

Graveyard Shift

There have been many bad movies based on the novels of Stephen King, but this is the worst of the lot. And that's saying quite a bit! Based on a relatively benign short story from King's *Night Shift* collection, this 90-minute film stretches a simple idea too far and becomes a chaotic mess in the process. The Bachman Textile Mill (Richard Bachman is a pseudonym of King's) has recently been re-opened, and several deaths have occurred on the night shift. Drifter John Hall (Andrews) comes to the town of Gates Falls, Maine, looking for work and takes a job at the mill. The work is awful and the foreman Warwick (Macht) is a royal jerk, but meeting Jane (Wolf) makes things a bit better for John. When Warwick assembles a crew to clean out the mill's basement over the Fourth of July weekend, John volunteers, as he needs the money. Little does the clean-up crew know that the monstrous terror that has been killing the mill workers is waiting in the catacombs beneath the mill. The film is slow, corny, predictable, and utterly boring. When the monster finally appears at the end, it's a big let-down. Any sane viewer will certainly stop the movie during the scene where a group of rats are shown floating on debris while "Surfing USA" plays on the soundtrack. If one insists on watching this film, then DVD is the way to go. The image is very sharp and clear, showing virtually no grain and little artifacting. The colors are very good, and the dark photography is handled well. Dolby 5.1 offers clear dialogue, very good stereo separation and well-placed Surround effects. There are no extras. —ML **AKA:** Stephen King's Graveyard Shift.
Movie: woof **DVD:** 🎵🎵 ½

Paramount (cat #32512, UPC 097363251-248). Widescreen anamorphic. Dolby Digital 5.1; Dolby Surround; Stereo. $24.99. Keepcase. *LANG:* English; French. *SUB:* English. *CAP:* English. *FEATURES:* 11 chapters.
1990 (R) 89m/C David Andrews, Kelly Wolf, Stephen Macht, Brad Dourif; **D:** Ralph S. Singleton; **W:** Stephen King, John Esposito; **C:** Peter Stein; **M:** Brian Banks.

Great Adventures

Two-disc set includes *Rescue from Gilligan's Island, Over the Hill Gang, Seven Lucky Ninja Kids,* and *White Fang to the Rescue*. Please see individual reviews. —MM
Movie: 🎵 **DVD:** 🎵
BCI-Eclipse (cat #44274-9, UPC 7873644-27499). Full frame. $9.98. Keepcase. *LANG:* English.
2000 m/C

Great Balls of Fire

Jerry Lee Lewis (Quaid) starts down the path to fame and makes the misstep of marrying his second cousin Myra (Ryder). His cousin Jimmy Swaggart (Baldwin) tries to lead him down the path of the righteousness, to use his God-given talent for the Lord. Jerry Lee is too much of an egomaniac to believe in God. When Jerry embarks on a British concert tour, the British press skewers him for "robbing the cradle" after they discover that Myra is not just his cousin, but is only 13 years old. The story of his music makes a nice subplot to his fame and marriage. The song "Great Balls of Fire" was partly inspired by Myra's fear of the hydrogen bomb. The film also illustrates Lewis's other inspirations, black rhythm and blues, and a strong desire to dethrone Elvis. The quality of the film transfer to DVD is O.K. and the digital sound shows off the vocal excursions of the Killer himself as Dennis Quaid lip-synchs. More worth a look than you'd expect. —JAS
Movie: 🎵🎵🎵 **DVD:** 🎵🎵🎵
MGM Home Ent. (cat #1003509, UPC 027616876591). Widescreen (1.85:1) anamorphic. Dolby Digital Surround; Dolby Stereo. $14.95. Keepcase. *LANG:* English; French. *SUB:* English; French; Spanish. *FEATURES:* 16 chapters • Original trailer.
1989 (PG-13) 108m/C Dennis Quaid, Winona Ryder, Alec Baldwin, Trey Wilson, John Doe, Lisa Blount, Steve Allen, Stephen Tobolowsky, Lisa Jane Persky, Michael St. Gerard, Peter Cook; **D:** Jim McBride; **W:** Jack Baran, Jim McBride; **C:** Alfonso Beato; **M:** Jack Baran, Jim McBride.

Great Bloodsucking Movies

Please see reviews of *The Satanic Rites of Dracula* (in *Book 1*), *The Devil Bat,* and *The Last Man on Earth*.
BFS Video (cat #30237-D, UPC 06680530-2374). $9.98. Keepcase. *FEATURES:* 6 chapters per film • Cast bios/filmographies.
2001 251m/C

Great Cop Movies

Please see individual reviews of *A Real American Hero, He Walked by Night* and *Borderline*. —MM
Movie: 🎵🎵 **DVD:** 🎵🎵
BFS Video (cat #30174-D, UPC 06680530-1742). Full frame. $9.98. Keepcase. *LANG:* English. *FEATURES:* Thumbnail bios and filmographies • Trivia • 12 chapters.
1978 260m/C

Great Detective Movies

Please see reviews of *They Call It Murder, Murder Once Removed,* and *A Tattered Web*.
BFS Video (cat #30292-D, UPC 066805302923). $9.98. Keepcase.
2002 248m/C

Great Fighting Machines of WWII

This boxed set contains the discs *Great Fighting Machines of WWII: Allied & Axis Bombers, ...Fighters,* and *...Tanks*. Please see individual reviews. —MM
Movie: 🎵🎵 ½ **DVD:** 🎵🎵 ½
Questar Video (cat #QD3252, UPC 033-937032523). Full frame. $44.99. Keepcase.
2001 360m/C

Great Fighting Machines of WWII: Allied & Axis Bombers

Like the other discs in this series, this one is aimed solidly at the military history buff. The visuals are a combination of fairly familiar combat footage and what appear to be training or promotional films. The subjects are American, German, Russian, British, and Japanese bombers. The Brit narration is heavy on statistics and other numbers. The moderately scratchy image (both black and white and color) ranges between good and very good. The copy of William Wyler's "Memphis Belle" that's included as an extra is no better or worse than other versions of the public domain title that are available on other labels. —MM
Movie: 🎵🎵 ½ **DVD:** 🎵🎵 ½
Questar Video (cat #QD3255, UPC 0339-37032554). Full frame. $19.99. Keepcase. *LANG:* English. *FEATURES:* 12 chapters • "Memphis Belle" • "Bombers in the News" featurette • "B-25s: Target Tokyo" featurette.
2001 120m/C D: Jonathan Moore; **W:** Chris Chant; **Nar:** Robert Booth.

Great Fighting Machines of WWII: Allied & Axis Fighters

This is probably the most interesting disc in the series simply because fighter planes are more photogenic and fast moving than bombers or tanks. They're essentially the rock stars of WWII weaponry. The usual suspects are rounded up here—Spitfire, Mustang, Lightning, Zero, etc.—though the most interesting footage is of the German jet fighters that were developed at the end of the war. Again, the black-and-white footage is scratchy. The best extra is a War Department short film, "Japanese Zero," about aircraft identification that stars Ronald Reagan.

Movie: 🎞🎞 ½ **DVD:** 🎞🎞 ½
Questar Video (cat #QD3253, UPC 03393-7032530). Full frame. $19.99. Keepcase. *LANG:* English. *FEATURES:* 12 chapters ▪ "Japanese Zero" ▪ "Fighters in the News" featurette ▪ "Flying the P-47 Thunderbolt" featurette.
2001 120m/C D: Jonathan Moore; **W:** Chris Chant; **Nar:** Robert Booth.

Great Fighting Machines of WWII: Allied & Axis Tanks

The lack of a really strong soundtrack makes this the weakest of the three films in the series. For tanks to be really impressive and frightening on screen, the image must be accompanied by loud, rumbling, threatening sound effects and those are lacking. Instead, the producers do their usual good dry job of spinning out facts and figures to go along with stock footage that is of interest to military history fans only. All others are warned. —*MM*
Movie: 🎞🎞 ½ **DVD:** 🎞🎞 ½
Questar Video (cat #QD3254, UPC 03393-7032547). Full frame. $19.99. Keepcase. *LANG:* English. *FEATURES:* 12 chapters ▪ "Killing a Russian Tank" German training film ▪ "Tanks in the News" featurette ▪ "The Pershing Tank" featurette ▪ "Mass-Producing Armor" featurette.
2001 120m/C D: Jonathan Moore; **W:** Bruce Quarrie; **Nar:** Robert Booth.

Great Fire Movies

Please see reviews of *Firehouse, A Dangerous Summer,* and *Fire Alarm.*
BFS Video (cat #30293-D, UPC 06680530-2930). $9.98. Keepcase.
2002 231m/C

The Great Gatsby

World War I vet Jay Gatsby (Stephens) falls in love with the aloof Daisy Buchanan (Sorvino). Spurned because he is poor, Gatsby transforms himself into an enigmatic playboy amongst the rootless Long Island rich. In the meantime, Daisy marries the wealthy but emotionally abusive Tom Buchanan (Donovan). Gatsby plots to get Daisy back, but as witnessed by the story's narrator Nick Carraway (Rudd), the difference between having and wanting sometimes exacts a price of mythic proportions. Mira Sorvino makes for an ethereal but all too distant Daisy, Paul Rudd embues Carraway with a "Call me Ishmael" innocence that's waiting to be shattered, and Donovan shades Tom Buchanan with enough humanity so that one can almost understand his treatment

of people as puppets. The major flaw is Toby Stephens's Gatsby; in his hands, Gatsby is far from "Great." The man who supposedly incites mystery, romance, and drama instead plops around his mansion like he's forgotten he owns it. All the socialites speak his name like a god, but when on-camera, Gatsby is as exciting as a mashed potato sandwich. The full-frame transfer is proficient enough with accurate and consistent colors, natural fleshtones, and sharp details. I detect slight pixelation in some shots, but overall the presentation is free from digital artifacts. Colors are well reproduced, creating a natural palette. Blacks are deep and solid, while shadows always maintain good definition. The contrast of the transfer is generally good, although at times the image appears overly harsh. Dolby Surround works just as capably. Dialogue is clearly reproduced in the track and well integrated in the overall mix. Intermittent rear speaker action helps to punctuate Carl Davis's evocative period score. —*EP*
Movie: 🎞🎞 ½ **DVD:** 🎞🎞🎞
A&E Home Video (UPC 733961701272). Full frame. Dolby Surround Stereo. $19.98. Keepcase. *LANG:* English. *FEATURES:* 12 chapters ▪ Filmographies ▪ A&E Biography of F. Scott Fitzgerald.
2001 100m/C Toby Stephens, Mira Sorvino, Martin Donovan, Paul Rudd, Francie Swift, Matt Malloy; **D:** Robert Markowitz; **W:** John McLaughlin; **C:** Guy Dufaux; **M:** Carl Davis.

Great John Wayne Movies

Triple feature includes *Lawless Frontier* and *Sagebrush Trail* (both reviewed in *Book 2*) and *Helltown,* another low-budget western based on a Zane Grey novel. Image is dark; focus is poor; static is heavy in all three. —*MM*
Movie: 🎞🎞 **DVD:** 🎞 ½
BFS Video (cat #83955-D, UPC 06680583-9559). Full frame. $9.98. Keepcase. *LANG:* English. *FEATURES:* John Wayne thumbnail bio and filmography ▪ Trivia ▪ 12 chapters.
2000 158m/C

Great Mafia Movies 2

You get what you pay for. These three made-for-TV movies look about as bad as any you'll ever see on disc. *Mob Story* (reviewed in *Book 1*) is the best of the bunch and it's poor. Yvette Mimieux, at her most wooden, plays the title character in *Hit Lady. Incident on a Dark Street* is the most complex of the three. It concerns Justice Department efforts to bust big-time racketeers and features a cast familiar to television viewers. All three appear to have been made from heavily damaged original elements. They display considerable wear and look no better than second generation VHS dupes. —*MM*
Movie: 🎞 **DVD:** 🎞
BFS Video (cat #30228-D, UPC 06680530-2282). Full frame. $9.98. Keepcase. *LANG:*

English. *FEATURES:* 12 chapters ▪ Thumbnail bios and filmographies.
2002 270m/C

Great Martial Arts Movies

Please see individual reviews of *Blood of the Dragon, Champ Against Champ,* and *Bloodfight.*
BFS Video (cat #30236D, UPC 06680530-2367). Full frame. $9.98. Keepcase. *LANG:* English.
2002 284m/C

The Great Muppet Caper

Kermit, Fozzie, and Gonzo play investigative journalists traveling to London to crack the case of Lady Holiday's stolen diamond necklace. The transfer is mostly free of blemishes and defects, but sadly, it is fairly soft and the level of grain evident throughout the films borders on the distracting; the grain is heavy and permeates every frame, no matter what the lighting conditions of these scenes are. Colors are vibrant and lively, although the entire film has a bit of a dull, grayish sheen to it that visibly dates the movie. Once again, with a fully cleaned-up transfer, the film could have boasted colors richer than anything we have seen. The compression is good without introducing noticeable compression artifacts. All of the language tracks are adequate but exhibit signs of sibilance and distortion. However, the disc also boasts a newly remixed 5.1 channel Dolby Digital mix, which corrects most of the deficiencies found in these other audio tracks—although the disc does not default to this clearly improved audio track. —*GH*
Movie: 🎞🎞 ½ **DVD:** 🎞🎞 ½
Columbia Tristar Home Video (UPC 4339-6056183). Widescreen (1.85:1) letterboxed; full frame. Dolby Digital 5.1 Surround Stereo; Dolby Digital Surround Stereo. $24.95. Keepcase. *LANG:* English; French; Spanish. *SUB:* English; French; Spanish. *FEATURES:* Trailers ▪ "Muppetisms" introductions to characters.
1981 (G) 95m/C Charles Grodin, Diana Rigg, John Cleese, Robert Morley, Peter Ustinov, Peter Falk, Jack Warden; **D:** Jim Henson; **W:** Jack Rose; **C:** Oswald Morris; **V:** Frank Oz. *AWARDS: NOM:* Oscars '81: Song ("The First Time It Happens").

Great Racing Movies

Triple feature includes *The Big Wheel* (reviewed in *Book 2*), *The Fast and the Furious* (1954), and *Hot Rod Girl* (1956). Please see individual reviews. —*MM*
Movie: 🎞🎞 **DVD:** 🎞 ½
BFS Video (cat #30175-D, UPC 06680530-1759). Full frame. $9.98. Keepcase. *LANG:* English. *FEATURES:* Thumbnail bios and filmographies ▪ "Many Wives of Mickey Rooney" text ▪ Trivia ▪ 12 chapters.
2000 235m/C

The Great St. Louis Bank Robbery

Three career criminals recruit young George Fowler (McQueen) to be the wheelman in a bank job. The fact-based story follows two plotlines. One is an almost documentary re-creation of the robbery and, as such, it's a fascinating snapshot of American city life in the late 1950s. When the focus shifts to the histories of the characters, the film is on less solid footing. The more restrictive times forced the filmmakers to be circumspect about sexual motivations and there are enough Oedipal conflicts and repressed urges at work to fill a textbook. The violence, on the other hand, is remarkably realistic for the time. On balance, the film earns a solid recommendation to McQueen fans, particularly those who think they've seen all of his work. DVD presentation is acceptable for a film of this age and budget. It's not the sharpest black-and-white photography you've ever seen but it looks pretty good. Sound is a little harsh with some static, but again, standard for the late '50s. The image is presented with black borders on all four sides, retaining the original ratio. Title is available on *Classic Heist Movies* and from the Roan Archives (cat. #AED-2018, $19.98). —*MM*
Movie: ♪♪♪ *DVD:* ♪♪ ½
BFS Video (cat #30295-D, UPC 06680530-2954). Widescreen (1.66:1) letterboxed. $9.98. Keepcase. *LANG:* English. *FEATURES:* 6 chapters ● Talent files.
1959 86m/B Graham Denton, David Clarke, James Dukas, Steve McQueen, Molly McCarthy; *D:* Charles Guggenheim; *W:* Richard T. Heffron; *C:* Victor Duncan; *M:* Bernardo Segall.

Great Scary Movies

The transfers utilized for this budget disc often look profoundly digitized. *The Terror* (reviewed in *Book 1*) features a soft image with poor, yellow-tinted colors and occasional print damage. *House on Haunted Hill* (also in *Book 1*) seems cribbed from another company's transfer. The print is clean and contrasts are excellent, but the image is plagued by digital noise and shimmer. *Night of the Living Dead* (reviewed in *Book 2*) has the same overbright, ugly contrasts that plagued public domain video transfer for years. The Elite disc is still the best option for that film. Sound on all discs tends to be hissy and poor. *The Terror* and *Night of the Living Dead* sound particularly warbled and murky. —*DG*
Movie: ♪♪ *DVD:* ♪ ½
BFS Video (cat #30232-D, UPC 06680530-2329). Full frame. Mono. $9.98. Keepcase. *LANG:* English. *FEATURES:* 6 chapters per episode ● Cast bios/filmographies.
2001 250m/C

Great Sci–Fi Thrillers

Collection of three SF films was made from original elements that are no better

than VHS tape. *Disappearance of Flight 412* is an early made-for-TV UFO drama that posits a military cover-up of the whole business. It has not been available on home video and this version appears to be a shortened (74 minutes) version of the 120-minute original. *Slipstream* is the most interesting of the bunch. It's a big-budget production about a post-apocalyptic future where cop Mark Hammill chases dim-witted bounty hunter Bill Paxton who's made off with prisoner Bob Peck. Some fine aerial photography and exotic Turkish landscapes lose a lot with this weak image and sound. The third feature, *Abraxas*, is reviewed in *Book 1*. —*MM*
Movie: ♪♪ *DVD:* ♪♪
BFS Video (cat #30229-D, UPC 06680530-2299). Full frame. $9.98. Keepcase. *LANG:* English. *FEATURES:* 12 chapters ● Thumbnail bios and filmographies.
2002 263m/C

Great Spy Movies

Triple feature includes *Hangmen* (reviewed in *Book 1*), *The Inside Man* (reviewed in *Book 2*), and *The Sell Out*. Please see individual reviews. —*MM*
Movie: ♪♪ *DVD:* ♪♪
BFS Video (cat #30176-D, UPC 06680530-1766). Full frame. $9.98. Keepcase. *LANG:* English. *FEATURES:* Thumbnail bios and filmographies ● Trivia ● 12 chapters.
2000 280m/C

The Great Texas Dynamite Chase

One of the genuinely great drive-in films arrives on DVD looking about as good as it has to. At the beginning, a fair amount of dust and snow are in evidence, but that clears up quickly and the rest of the full-frame image looks very good. The plot is archetypal exploitation material that follows Candy (Jennings) and Ellie-Jo (Jones) as they rob banks from one end of Texas to the other, with dynamite as their chosen weapon. —*MM* *AKA: Dynamite Women.*
Movie: ♪♪♪ *DVD:* ♪♪ ½
New Concorde (cat #NH20158 D, UPC 736991415898). Full frame. $19.98. Keepcase. *LANG:* English. *FEATURES:* 24 chapters ● Talent files ● Trailers.
1976 (R) 90m/C Claudia Jennings, Jocelyn Jones, Johnny Crawford, Chris Pennock, Tara Strohmeier, Miles Watkins, Bart Braverman; *D:* Michael Pressman; *C:* Jamie Anderson; *M:* Craig Safan.

Great WWII Movies

Please see reviews of *A Walk in the Sun* (in *Book 2*), *We Dive at Dawn*, and *The North Star*.
BFS Video (cat #30294-D, UPC 06680530-2947). $9.98. Keepcase.
2002 307m/C

The Greatest

Muhammad Ali stars as himself in this biopic, tracing the fighter's rise to fame,

his conversion to Islam, his refusal to serve in the Vietnam War, and his return to the top of the boxing world. Large gaps are left in the story, and "The Greatest Love of All" is played one too many times. Ali is terribly earnest; this movie makes him look like an all-around swell guy, which is probably far less interesting than reality. The picture quality is fairly good, but the dialogue suffers from a poor mix and is often lost beneath music or background noise. —*BG*
Movie: ♪ ½ *DVD:* ♪♪ ½
Columbia Tristar (cat #06205, UPC 04339-6062054). Widescreen (1.85:1) anamorphic; full frame. Dolby Mono. $19.95. Keepcase. *LANG:* English; French. *SUB:* English; French; Spanish; Portuguese; Chinese; Korean; Thai. *CAP:* English. *FEATURES:* 28 chapters ● Trailers.
1977 (PG) 100m/C Muhammad Ali, Robert Duvall, Ernest Borgnine, James Earl Jones, John Marley, Roger E. Mosley, Dina Merrill, Paul Winfield; *D:* Tom Gries; *W:* Ring Lardner Jr.; *C:* Harry Stradling Jr.; *M:* Michael Masser.

Green

Four drugged up friends—Eric (Patterson), Ralph (Gallagher), Dave (director Hirsch), and Joanna (Millican)—cruise around suburban Phoenix, Arizona, and wonder why their lives are so unsatisfying. Hirsch makes the most of an obviously limited budget by tossing in every imaginable low-cost trick: mixing black and white and color, stop-motion animation, fast motion live action, etc. The young cast is engaging enough to keep the navel-gazing material from becoming too self-conscious. DVD is sharp throughout. Hirsch is properly modest on his commentary track. Fans of *Go* and *The Tao of Steve* should take a look. —*MM*
Movie: ♪♪♪ *DVD:* ♪♪♪
York Ent. (cat #YPD-1092, UPC 75072310-920). Full frame. $19.99. Keepcase. *LANG:* English. *FEATURES:* Short film "Karl's in a coma" ● Trailers ● Commentary.
2001 88m/C Hyrum Patterson, Matt Gallagher, Karl T. Hirsch, Dana Millican; *D:* Karl T. Hirsch; *W:* Karl T. Hirsch; *C:* Dave Long; *M:* Ben Scribner.

Greenfingers

British import suffers from a certain over-familiarity. We've seen this before in *Waking Ned Divine*, *The Full Monty*, *Saving Grace*, and many other quirky-character comedies. Hardened inmate Colin Briggs (Owen) is reluctant to accept a transfer to the Edgefield minimum security prison, but he is seduced by the joys of gardening, particularly after he meets celebrity author/gardener Georgina Woodhouse (Mirren) and her daughter (Little). A strong cast carries it off, particularly the two leads, with good support from Kelly. DVD image ranges between very good and excellent, sound from good to very good. —*MM*
Movie: ♪♪♪ *DVD:* ♪♪ ½

Columbia Tristar (cat #07065, UPC 0433-96070653). Widescreen (1.85:1) anamorphic; full frame. Dolby Digital 5.1 Surround; Dolby Digital Surround. $24.98. Keepcase. *LANG:* English. *SUB:* English; Spanish. *CAP:* English. *FEATURES:* 28 chapters • Trailers.
2000 (R) 90m/C *GB US* Clive Owen, Helen Mirren, David Kelly, Warren Clarke, Danny Dyer, Paterson Joseph, Natasha Little, Adam Fogerty; *D:* Joel Hershman; *W:* Joel Hershman; *C:* John Daly; *M:* Guy Dagul.

Gregory's Girl

Gregory (Sinclair) is an average adolescent boy about to embark on the greatest adventure of his life: girls. Of course he has to get up the courage to actually ask the girl of his dreams, Dorothy (Hepburn), out on a date. Dorothy happens to be the beautiful girl who is the rage of the soccer team and may take Gregory's position as goalie away, but he doesn't really care because he fully admits that she is the better player. What he doesn't know is that when it comes to love and dating, girls are way ahead of that particular game. This is a fabulous realistic tale of the awkward stage between childhood and adulthood that takes its time with story development. There is never any rush to force the teens together or have them go beyond awkward exchanges of kisses, and the dialogue is humorous and witty without seeming out of place for the age of the characters. Written and directed by Bill Forsyth, who was thought to be Scotland's gift to filmmaking before the better forgotten *Being Human,* this is both enjoyable family fare and an intelligent piece of filmmaking—a genuine must-see. As for the quality of the disc itself, it's clear that the elements it was struck from were less than perfect. The picture is clean, but the colors are dull and bleed a bit. The sound is clear but presented in a mono format. —*CA*
Movie: 🐾🐾🐾 ½ **DVD:** 🐾🐾
MGM Home Ent. (cat #1002629, UPC 027616868299). Widescreen (1.85:1) anamorphic. Dolby Digital Mono. $19.90. Keepcase. *LANG:* English/Scottish. *SUB:* English; French; Spanish. *CAP:* English. *FEATURES:* 16 chapters.
1980 91m/C *GB* Gordon John Sinclair, Dee Hepburn, Jake D'Arcy, Chic Murray, Alex Norton, John Bett, Clare Grogan; *D:* Bill Forsyth; *W:* Bill Forsyth; *C:* Michael Coulter. *AWARDS:* British Acad. '81: Screenplay.

Grey Gardens

Famous non-fiction cult film charts the day-to-day existence of Big Edie and Little Edie Beale, an elderly mother-and-daughter pair (aunt and cousin to Jacqueline Kennedy) who live in a dilapidated, filth-ridden East Hampton mansion. The bold contrast between the beautiful, expensive properties in the neighborhood and the festering dump the Beales have allowed their manor to become is startling. The

film is a veritable catalog of bizarre behavior. The Beales live in a miserable codependent purgatory in which they argue endlessly (and have been for 23 years!) about their failed lives and the perceived blame they lay on each other. The two are such wackos that it never really becomes depressing, just funnier, especially with repeated viewings. Big Edie almost never moves from her bed while Little Edie dances, sings, and wears the most horrid outfits. It's full of very strange and quotable dialogue and the whole thing must have influenced the family in *Pink Flamingoes.* The commentary is terrific; excellent, funny, and informative, though Maysles's input is minimal and it's a bit hard to tell who's speaking at times. Stay tuned after the color bars for a recent phone conversation between Little Edie and Albert Maysles. The disc is a gorgeous, accurate rendition of the grainy original and features strong, vivid colors and a very sharp crisp image. The sound is clear, if occasionally sharp and limited due to the raw source recordings. The contemporary trailers have very bizarre hyperbole from mainstream papers and the additional interviews and filmographies are all worthwhile. The essay is short but sensitively written. Very effective if watched just before Spring Cleaning. —*DG*
Movie: 🐾🐾🐾 **DVD:** 🐾🐾🐾 ½
Criterion (cat #GRE300, UPC 03742915-9125). Full frame. Dolby Digital Mono. $39.95. Keepcase. *LANG:* English. *SUB:* English. *FEATURES:* 25 chapters • Booklet with notes • Commentary: Albert Maysles, Hovde, Meyer, Froemke • Excerpt from an audio interview with Little Edie Beale • Interviews with Todd Oldham and John Bartlett on the fashions • Trailers • Behind-the-scenes photographs • Filmographies.
1975 95m/C *D:* Albert Maysles, David Maysles, Ellen Hovde, Muffie Meyer, Susan Froemke; *C:* Albert Maysles, David Maysles.

Groundhog Day [2 SE]

This Special Edition complements the fine image transfer of the first release (reviewed in *Book 1*) with a nice commentary track by director Harold Ramis. As expected from the creator of such a massive commercial and critical hit, he's understated and modest, mostly focusing on details of the creation and praise for his collaborators. —*MM*
Movie: 🐾🐾🐾 **DVD:** 🐾🐾🐾 ½
Columbia Tristar (cat #05816, UPC 043396058163). Widescreen (1.85:1) anamorphic. Dolby Digital 5.1 Surround; DTS Surround. $24.98. Keepcase. *LANG:* English; French; Spanish; Portuguese. *SUB:* English; French; Spanish; Portuguese; Chinese; Korean; Thai. *CAP:* English. *FEATURES:* 28 chapters • Commentary: director • "Weight of Time" documentary • Trailers • Filmographies • Production notes.
1993 (PG) 103m/C Bill Murray, Andie MacDowell, Chris Elliott, Stephen

Tobolowsky, Brian Doyle-Murray, Marita Geraghty, Angela Paton; *D:* Harold Ramis; *W:* Harold Ramis, Daniel F. Rubin; *C:* John Bailey; *M:* George Fenton. *AWARDS:* British Acad. '93: Orig. Screenplay.

Guadalcanal Diary

Captains Cross (Roberts) and Davis (Conte) lead the first detachments of Marines onto the Japanese stronghold of Guadalcanal, braving snipers and bombing raids and holding territory for our invading regular Army. Based on the popular Tregaskis book, this saga of the Marines was filmed practically before the fighting had finished on Guadalcanal. It's one of the key combat films of the war, and survives better as a document of the times than as an entertainment. Calculated to indoctrinate civilian audiences to the realities of combat, it's also encumbered with scenes to reassure the folks back home that their boys are in good hands in the military. The spectacle of the Marines driving an enemy regiment into the sea, and massacring them in the surf, is the kind of scene best appreciated by an audience that feels threatened. Fox's DVD is a spotless transfer that looks better than the studio print that I saw at UCLA 30 years ago. It's so clear that the occasional bit of real combat footage really sticks out. —*GE*
Movie: 🐾🐾 ½ **DVD:** 🐾🐾 ½
20th Century Fox (cat #2002532). Full frame. Stereo; Mono. $19.98. Keepcase. *LANG:* English. *SUB:* English; Spanish. *CAP:* English. *FEATURES:* Trailer.
1943 93m/B Preston Foster, Lloyd Nolan, William Bendix, Richard Conte, Anthony Quinn, Richard Jaeckel, Roy Roberts, Minor Watson, Miles Mander, Ralph Byrd, Lionel Stander, Reed Hadley, John Archer, Eddie Acuff, Selmer Jackson, Paul Fung; *D:* Lewis Seiler; *W:* Lamar Trotti, Jerome Cady; *C:* Charles Clarke; *M:* David Buttolph.

The Guardian

An archaeological expedition unleashes the ancient Telal, a demon who jumps from body to body, *Fallen*-style. A boy has been chosen to defeat him, but only exarmy agent Kross (Van Peebles) can protect this young messiah long enough to fulfill his destiny. In the meantime, lots of people mutter pseudo-prophetic gibberish and lots of guns are fired. A highpoint is Ice-T receiving repeated roundhouse kicks to the head. The picture quality is quite good, although the soundtrack doesn't pack as much punch as might be desired. —*BG*
Movie: 🐾 ½ **DVD:** 🐾🐾 ½
Studio Home Ent. (cat #7816D, UPC 658149781627). Widescreen anamorphic. Dolby Stereo. $24.99. Keepcase. *LANG:* English. *SUB:* English; Spanish; French. *FEATURES:* 24 chapters • Trailers.
2000 (R) 89m/C Mario Van Peebles, James Remar, Ice-T, Daniel Hugh-Kelly, Stacy Oversier; *D:* John Terlesky; *W:* John

Terlesky, Jeff Yagher, Gary J. Tunnicliffe; **C:** Maximo Munzi.

Gumby, Vol. 1

Rhino Home Video has set out to introduce Gumby to a new generation and to delight the long-time fans of the stretchy, green character. This DVD contains 21 classic Gumby adventures from the 1950s and '60s. In these timeless stories, we are introduced to Gumby and his pals Pokey, Prickle, and Poo. Also along for the ride are Gumby's parents. The shows average five to seven minutes in length and vary in narrative structure. Some feature Gumby going on fantastic journeys, such as when he visits the moon, or when he travels to a land composed of musical instruments. Others focus on Gumby and Pokey's adventures around the house (usually to the chagrin of Mom and Dad), the best episodes being the ones where Gumby allows a group of robots to do his chores and they get out of control. At times, these shows come across as just plain weird, and almost trippy. But no matter how strange the show gets, Gumby is always polite, courteous, and forthright, making the show appropriate for all ages. (And Gumby seems to subsist on crackers and milk.) Gumby fans (such as Nigel Tufnel of Spinal Tap) should find this set very satisfying. The DVD case states "This video contains technical anomalies inherent in historic footage." In other words, there are some cosmetic flaws to be found in this transfer. The shows are presented full frame. There are scratches and blemishes from the source prints and at times, the colors are slightly subdued. Still, considering the age of these programs, the image quality isn't all that bad—especially since there are no major scratches or missing frames. The digital mono audio track provides clear dialogue, music, and sound effects, but there is some isolated hissing and popping. (This DVD is also available as part of the *Gumby Box Set*, which offers several bonus features.) —*ML*
Movie: 🎬🎬 ½ **DVD:** 🎬🎬
Rhino (cat #R2 976078, UPC 603497607-822). Full frame. Digital Mono. $19.95. Keepcase. *LANG:* English. *FEATURES:* 21 chapters.
2002 121m/C

The Gunfighters

Lackluster pilot of a proposed Canadian series pits three individualistic relatives against a powerful empire-builder (Kennedy). DVD offers a cleaner image than other titles in "The Wild West" set, but it's still no better than broadcast TV. —*MM*
Movie: 🎬 ½ **DVD:** 🎬🎬 ½
Brentwood (cat #44213-9, UPC 78736442-1398). Full frame. $19.95. Keepcase. *LANG:* English. *FEATURES:* "Cobweb Hotel" cartoon ● 8 chapters ● Trivia game ● DVD dictionary ● DVD-ROM features.
1987 100m/C *CA* Art Hindle, Reiner Schoene, Anthony Addabbo, George

Kennedy, Michael Kane, Lori Hallier; **D:** Clay Borris.

Gunman in the Streets

Billed as a "lost film noir," this minor crime film predates so many trends, it might be called the first Euro Noir. "La Traqué" was the title of a simultaneously made French version. The real attraction here is a very young Simone Signoret, whose beauty and talent carry the picture, even when it comes up wanting in other departments. Tough bank robber Eddy Roback (Clark) is sprung from a police van on his way to trial by the rest of his gang, who are all quickly captured by wily police inspector Dufresne (Gravet). In desperation, Eddy turns to his old flame Denise Vernon (Signoret), who manages to make Dufresne think she has no interest in the gangster, when in actuality she's totally committed to him. Her present date is American newspaperman Frank Clinton (Duke), from whom she borrows money for Eddy to escape to Belgium. But to prove his love to Denise, Frank invites himself along on the getaway, forming a tense romantic triangle that could get them all shot! The French cast is colorful but speaks their English lines awkwardly. Some of it is natural enough but the majority of the dialogue must have been dubbed phonetically, or by voice-over specialists who were non-natives. So for all the authentic French sets, this always seems like a poverty-row American production transplanted to Paris. All Day Entertainment has done a fine job on yet another rare film, obtaining good original elements (an heir of the producer is listed as the copyright holder on the box) and producing a top-quality disc. The transfer quality is on a par with major studio work. All Day's menu design is also an improvement, with handsome graphics and easy-to-use navigation. There's a good photo gallery, and the censored snippets are included. —*GE* **AKA:** Time Running Out; La Traque; Gangster at Bay.
Movie: 🎬🎬 ½ **DVD:** 🎬🎬🎬
All Day Ent. (UPC 014381137422). Full frame. $24.98. Keepcase. *LANG:* English. *FEATURES:* Deleted scenes ● Photo gallery ● Booklet.
1950 88m/B *FR* Dane Clark, Simone Signoret, Fernand Gravet, Robert Duke; **D:** Frank Tuttle; **W:** Jacques Companeez, Victor Pahlen; **C:** Claude Renoir, Eugene Schufftan; **M:** Joe Hajos.

Haiku Tunnel

Josh Kornbluth slogs his way through the day as a temp worker who surreptitiously writes a novel as he pretends to work. When his new employer asks him to "go perm" his life takes a turn for the unmanageable. Jacob and Josh Kornbluth strung together three monologues about Josh's now-former life as a temp worker. They actually admit in their commentary that the theme of their movie, developed at the

Sundance Institute, is Josh's inability to mail 17 letters, which hardly merits 90 minutes of your undivided attention. It shouldn't come as too much of a surprise that the result is uncinematic and decidedly unfunny. Sony went to some pains to make sure the DVD package was top-notch, but the information here could be of interest to their immediate circle of friends or to other Kornbluths only. —*LA*
Movie: 🎬 **DVD:** 🎬🎬🎬
Columbia Tristar (cat #07473, UPC 43396074736). Widescreen anamorphic. Dolby Digital 5.1 Surround; Dolby Surround. $29.98. Keepcase. *LANG:* English. *SUB:* French. *FEATURES:* Commentary: Jacob and Josh Kornbluth ● Deleted scenes ● Theatrical trailers ● Filmographies ● Outtakes ● 28 chapters.
2000 (R) 88m/C Josh Kornbluth, Warren Keith, Helen Shumaker, June Lomena, Amy Resnick; **D:** Josh Kornbluth, Jacob Kornbluth; **W:** Josh Kornbluth, Jacob Kornbluth, John Bellucci; **C:** Don Matthew Smith.

Hairdo U

Gay hairdresser Tiny (Stevenson) narrates this knockabout little comedy. After an unfortunate incident, macho construction workers David (producer Smith) and Wayne (Connors) are sentenced to community service at Tiny's Beauty Academy. There, David falls in love with Tiny's roommate Aqua (Askew). But she'll have nothing to do with such a lout and so he turns to Tiny for sensitivity training. Acting is all over the map with every funny, natural performance matched by another that's amateurish. The bawdy comedy is based on racial and sexual stereotypes which are handled with a bracing lack of tact. There's little DVD can do to improve the ultra-low-budget, shot-on-location in St. Louis image. It's as rough and grainy as any you've ever seen. —*MM*
Movie: 🎬🎬 ½ **DVD:** 🎬
York Ent. (cat #YPD-1200, UPC 75072312-0027). Full frame. Dolby Digital 5.1. $14.99. Keepcase. *LANG:* English. *SUB:* Spanish. *FEATURES:* 30 chapters ● Trailers.
2002 92m/C Jason Smith, Eric Connors, Que Stevenson, Monica Askew, Jeff Jefferson; **D:** Dee Ross McKissic; **W:** Dee Ross McKissic; **C:** Christopher Benson; **M:** Mykk C.

Hairspray (John Waters Collection Vol. 1)

Waters's first truly mainstream film, if that's even possible, and his funniest. In 1962, big hairdos rule, the *Corny Collins Show* is the hippest thing in Baltimore, and segregation's still hanging around. Teenager Tracy Turnblad (Lake) is caught in the middle of all these forces, dancing her way to the top of the *Collins Show* before she stops to look around at its "Whites Only" policy. Deals with racism and stereotypes, as well as typical "teen" problems (hairdo's and don'ts). Filled with refreshingly tasteful, subtle social satire (although not without typical Waters touches that will please die-hard fans). Lake is lovable and appealing as Divine's daughter; Divine, in his last film, is likeable as an iron-toting mom. This newer Waters film looks great on DVD and, as far as the New Line "John Waters Collection" goes, is only surpassed by *Pecker. Hairspray* is a vividly colorful film and the DVD delivers them fully saturated without a hint of bleed. The picture's pretty sharp as well being marred only occasionally by what appears to be some added grain. Not much use is made of the Surround tracks, but the 5.1 soundtrack gives plenty of force to all the music and might have you dancing in your seat. Another great commentary by Waters, this time accompanied by Ricki Lake. Available only as a double feature with *Pecker* (see separate entry). —JO/BG

Movie: 🐾🐾🐾 **DVD:** 🐾🐾🐾
New Line (cat #N5230, UPC 79404). Widescreen (1.85:1) letterboxed. Dolby Digital 5.1; Dolby Surround. $29.95. Custom. *LANG:* English. *CAP:* English. *FEATURES:* 19 chapters • Commentary: John Waters, Ricki Lake.
1988 (PG) 94m/C Ricki Lake, Divine, Jerry Stiller, Colleen (Ann) (Vitamin C) Fitzpatrick, Sonny Bono, Deborah Harry, Ruth Brown, Leslie Ann Powers, Michael St. Gerard, Shawn Thompson, Clayton Prince, Pia Zadora, Ric Ocasek, Mink Stole, Mary Vivian Pearce, Alan J. Wendl, Susan Lowe, George Stover, Toussaint McCall, John Waters; *D:* John Waters; *W:* John Waters; *C:* David Insley; *M:* Kenny Vance.

Hallelujah, I'm a Bum

Perfectly delightful comedy/musical done in recitative (basically talking on-pitch) style and featuring a charming central performance by Jolson. The mayor of New York (Morgan) is a friend of well-known bum Bumper (Jolson), who is called "The Mayor of Central Park" by his fellow transients. When Morgan's girlfriend attempts suicide, Bumper rescues her and falls in love with her. Dropping his life of leisure, Bumper and pal Acorn (Edgar Connor) get jobs at a bank to support the amnesiac girl. The charm of this fairly saucy (pre-code) depression-era comedy is still tangible and the songs are short, playful, and funny. And can you think of a better movie title?! The film has been re-released many times under different titles, and so MGM has probably done all it could with a grainy, somewhat contrasty and damaged print master. The image is still acceptable except for some instances of aliasing and digital noise—most likely caused by the noise reduction technology mistaking some of the grain for dirt. The audio is sharp and tinny, typical of unpreserved audio elements for the era and subtitles are frequently necessary to make out some of the dialogue and lyrics. The miserable condition of the trailer makes one appreciate the image of the film itself. Still highly recommended, despite the caveats. —DG **AKA:** Hallelujah, I'm a Tramp; The Heart of New York; Happy Go Lucky; Lazy Bones.

Movie: 🐾🐾🐾 **DVD:** 🐾🐾
MGM Home Ent. (cat #1003136, UPC 027-616873002). Full frame. Mono. $14.95. Keepcase. *LANG:* English. *SUB:* English; French; Spanish. *CAP:* English. *FEATURES:* Trailer.
1933 83m/B Al Jolson, Madge Evans, Frank Morgan, Chester Conklin, Edgar Connor; *D:* Lewis Milestone; *W:* Ben Hecht, S.N. Behrman; *M:* Richard Rodgers, Lorenz Hart.

Halloween [EE]

This version of Carpenter's low-budget masterpiece contains the extra footage that was shot for its network television presentation. The new scenes were needed to fill a two-hour time slot (not including commercials). They really add nothing to an admirably tight horror film. Chapter links identify the new material for the curious. Image and sound are fine. The disc has been available as part of the Special Edition set. —MM

Movie: 🐾🐾 ½ **DVD:** 🐾🐾 ½
Anchor Bay (cat #DV11959, UPC 0131311-95996). Widescreen (2.35:1) anamorphic. Dolby Digital Mono. $24.98. Keepcase. *LANG:* English. *FEATURES:* 30 chapters.
1978 (R) 90m/C Jamie Lee Curtis, Donald Pleasence, Nancy Loomis, P.J. Soles, Charles Cyphers, Kyle Richards, Brian Andrews, John Michael Graham, Nancy Stephens, Arthur Malet, Mickey Yablans, Brent Le Page, Adam Hollander, Robert Phalen, Sandy Johnson, David Kyle, Nick Castle; *D:* John Carpenter; *W:* John Carpenter, Debra Hill; *C:* Dean Cundey; *M:* John Carpenter.

Halloween 2: The Nightmare Isn't Over! [Universal]

Universal takes a giant step sideways with this DVD release, which isn't terribly different from a product already on the market. In this much-maligned sequel, escaped murderer Michael Myers continue to stalk babysitter Laurie Strode (Jamie Lee Curtis) after she is transported to the local hospital following the horrific events which transpired in the original *Halloween.* Once at the hospital, Myers hacks his way through the sparse staff in order to reach Laurie. Meanwhile, Myers's psychiatrist, Dr. Sam Loomis (Donald Pleasence), is hot on the butcher's trail and is Laurie's only hope. Granted, this film makes little sense (why is the hospital so big and so dark?) and is often just an exercise in violence, but director Rick Rosenthal is able to retain some of John Carpenter's style from the first film and *Halloween 2* is still much better than many of the films from the slasher cycle. This DVD presents the film in an anamorphic widescreen, but that is the only difference between this release and the previous DVD from GoodTimes Home Video. The image is sharp and clear, and isn't as dark as the GoodTimes version.

Also, the colors really stand out here, especially reds. The audio is fine, as there are some subtle Surround effects, but it's almost identical to the previous release. Also, the production notes shown here closely match those on the previous incarnation. So, buyer beware, as this Universal release costs over three times more than the very similar GoodTimes DVD. —ML

Movie: 🐾🐾🐾 **DVD:** 🐾🐾
Universal Studios (cat #21427, UPC 0251-92142727). Widescreen (2.35:1) anamorphic. Dolby 2.0 Stereo. $24.98. Keepcase. *LANG:* English. *SUB:* English; Spanish; French. *CAP:* English. *FEATURES:* Theatrical trailer • Production notes • Cast & crew bios • 18 chapters.
1981 (R) 92m/C Jamie Lee Curtis, Donald Pleasence, Jeffrey Kramer, Charles Cyphers, Lance Guest; *D:* Rick Rosenthal; *W:* John Carpenter, Debra Hill; *C:* Dean Cundey; *M:* John Carpenter.

Halloween 4: The Return of Michael Myers [MGM LE]

Ten years after his rampage in *Halloween* & *Halloween 2,* masked killer Michael Myers escapes during a stormy patient transfer. Returning to Haddonfield, Illinois, Michael sets his murderous eyes on his last remaining relative—his cute little niece! Better than average entry in the series with some fairly likable characters, strong camerawork, effective suspense, and a few good scares. Pleasence is entertaining as the obsessed Dr. Loomis, but it's a shame his role is so underwritten. A fine moody opening sequence and a shocking, effective ending make this worthwhile for fans. The picture transfer is sleek, with a slightly grainy print source that seems to match my memories of seeing the film theatrically. The newly created 5.1 Surround track is nice but only a slight step up from the stereo track. The featurette is interesting but rather insubstantial. Too bad a few deleted scenes (photos of which were included in the original press kit) aren't included. The slight amount of extras doesn't seem to really warrant a limited edition tin. —DG

Movie: 🐾🐾 ½ **DVD:** 🐾🐾🐾
MGM Home Ent. (cat #DV11890, UPC 013131189094). Widescreen (1.85:1) anamorphic. Dolby Surround 5.1; Stereo. $39.98. Tin and jewelcase. *LANG:* English. *CAP:* English. *FEATURES:* Booklet with notes • Theatrical trailer • 26 chapters • "Halloween: Final Cut" featurette.
1988 (R) 89m/C Donald Pleasence, Ellie Cornell, Danielle Harris, Michael Pataki, George P. Wilbur, Beau Starr, Kathleen Kinmont, Sasha Jenson, Gene Ross; *D:* Dwight Little; *W:* Alan B. McElroy; *C:* Peter Collister; *M:* Alan Howarth, John Carpenter.

The Halls of Montezuma

High-strung Lieutenant Carl Anderson (Widmark) has to pop painkillers given him by soulful medic "Doc" Jones (Malden) to keep on going. His Marines, trapped on a post-Guadalcanal, post-Tarawa island, are pinned down by Japanese rockets and must go on a hazardous patrol to learn their location. His colorful squad consists of Sgt. Randolph Johnson (Gardiner), an interpreter, the cheerful Pvt. Coffman (Wagner), sometimes jittery Corporal Conroy (Hylton), psychotic Pvt. "Pretty Boy" Riley (Homeier), journalist Dickerson (Webb), busted Pvt. Slattery (Freed), tough guy Sgt. Zelenko (Brand), green recruit Private Whitney (Milner), and nice-guy Pidgeon Lane (Palance). Released in 1950, this Marine combat film doubtlessly was produced before the outbreak of the Korean conflict, and doesn't have the confused attitudes of the few war dramas made concurrent with that war. It attempts to be as true as possible to the fighting experience, and does a fairly good job of it, even if the gloss of Technicolor candy-colors everything in sight. DVD simply looks great. It's obviously not mastered from original Technicolor elements but whatever they did use is in very good shape, with strong colors. The trailer included looks like a Marine Corps recruiting film. —GE

Movie: 🎭🎭 **DVD:** 🎭🎭🎭
20th Century Fox (cat #2002544, UPC 024543025443). Full frame. Stereo; Mono. $19.98. Keepcase. *LANG:* English; French. *SUB:* English; Spanish. *CAP:* English. *FEATURES:* Trailer.
1950 113m/C Richard Widmark, Jack Palance, Reginald Gardiner, Robert Wagner, Karl Malden, Richard Boone, Richard Hylton, Skip Homeier, Jack Webb, Neville Brand, Martin Milner, Bert Freed; **D:** Lewis Milestone; **W:** Michael Blankfort; **C:** Winton C. Hoch, Harry Jackson; **M:** Sol Kaplan.

Hamlet

In 1964, the "electronovision" process may have been pretty hot stuff. In an extra, Richard Burton attempts to talk about its superiority to conventional film or video cameras in recording a theatrical production of his *Hamlet* at the Lunt-Fontanne Theater. Apparently it was less intrusive than conventional film or video cameras, and the lenses do provide some close-ups. Even so, this black-and-white image is pretty poor. Some scenes look like they were filmed through the wrong end of a telescope. There's really nothing DVD can do to improve the dark, cavernous image. The production is of genuine historical interest to students of the theatre, but it has little to offer in the way of entertainment. Monaural sound is clear but limited. —MM

Movie: 🎭🎭 ½ **DVD:** 🎭🎭
Image Ent. (UPC 014381588026). Full frame. $29.98. Keepcase. *LANG:* English. *SUB:* English. *FEATURES:* 26 chapters • Filmographies and awards • Richard Burton discusses "electronovision."
1964 190m/B Richard Burton, John Gielgud; **D:** Bill Colleran.

Hamlet

Filmed version of a Joseph Papp stage production is part of the Broadway Theatre

Archive series. Kline's interpretation of the Danish prince is generally low-keyed and intelligent. Though camera movement and sets are minimal, the acting style has been toned down so the production doesn't feel so much like a filmed play. Even so, it never moves out from under the proscenium and so this version is recommended mostly to actors and serious students of Shakespeare, not general audiences. DVD image is no better than VHS tape but the accessibility of the disc makes it more valuable. Sound is suitable. —MM

Movie: 🎭🎭🎭 **DVD:** 🎭🎭 ½
Image Ent. (cat #ID0876B DDVD, UPC 014381087628). Full frame. Dolby Digital Stereo. $24.98. Keepcase. *LANG:* English. *FEATURES:* 19 chapters • Filmographies.
1990 173m/C Kevin Kline, Dana Ivey, Diane Venora, Brian Murray; **D:** Kevin Kline, Kirk Browning; **M:** Bob James.

Hammer House of Horror

This 13-episode anthology series, produced by the classic Hammer Films studio, features strong casts and interesting, macabre scripts all set in modern times. Apart from a few clinkers ("Visitor from the Grave," and "Charlie Boy" are quite poor), the lion's share is effectively creepy. Most episodes are extremely downbeat with gloomy endings. "The Silent Scream" featuring Peter Cushing as a deranged pet shop owner has a particularly nasty denouement. The locally filmed settings turn up in multiple episodes and many sets are clearly redressed from other episodes. The episodes are presented uncut, restoring scenes of gore and nudity ("Witching Time" and "Rude Awakening" are particularly sexual) absent from previous video releases and from U.S. TV broadcasts. A worthwhile collection of late era Hammer. The discs utilize stunning new transfers that are quite a revelation; previous editions have looked murky, colorless, and indistinct. The image is frequently razor sharp and brightly colored. Fleshtones are perfect, blacks are rich, and all the episodes have a strong, filmic look. There are occasional instances of ghosting (a result of the PAL to NTSC conversion of the masters) but it's a minor quibble. The mono sound is clean and strong. —DG

Movie: 🎭🎭🎭 **DVD:** 🎭🎭🎭 ½
A&E (cat #AAE-70310, UPC 7339617031-08). Full frame. Mono. $69.95. Keepcase (4 discs). *LANG:* English. *FEATURES:* Hammer filmography • Photo gallery • Essay on Hammer films • 5 chapters per episode.
1980 676m/C

Hammers over the Anvil

This turn-of-the-century Australian coming-of-age story is most noteworthy for its early Russell Crowe performance; the film even starts with an odd scene of him riding horses in the buff. The story is about a

crippled boy, Alan (Outhred), who is obsessed with horseback riding. His mentor, horse-tamer East (Crowe) has a disastrous affair with a married British woman (Rampling) that eventually provides Alan with a chance to prove himself. While the production is earnest, it's somewhat unfocused and missing the spark of life. Some of the character relationships are unclear and Outhred's performance is limited which inspires some unintentionally funny moments. The disc features a poor transfer from a projection print, complete with reel change marks. Although cropped, the compositions don't appear compromised. The colors are disastrous; the entire image is brownish and blacks have a green cast to them. It's both unflattering to the actors (whose faces suffer) and poorly represents the cinematography. The stereo soundtrack utilizes both channels in a surprisingly effective, involving mix. —DG

Movie: 🎭🎭 **DVD:** 🎭 ½
Fox/Lorber (cat #FLV5258, UPC 7209175-2582). Full frame. Stereo. $24.98. Keepcase. *LANG:* English. *FEATURES:* Filmographies • Weblinks • 16 chapters.
1991 98m/C *AU* Charlotte Rampling, Russell Crowe, Alexander Outhred, John Rafter Lee, Kirsty McGregor, Jake Frost; **D:** Ann Turner; **W:** Ann Turner, Peter Hepworth; **C:** James Bartle.

The Handmaid's Tale

Adaptation of Margaret Atwood's novel wears its politics on its sleeve. Even the box copy proudly notes "The women in the film were given a week off from shooting to march in Washington against the revising of abortion laws." Strongly held convictions do not necessarily make for good entertainment. In the near-future society of Gilead, a sterile society forces fertile women (including Richardson) into bearing children for the elite. Once again, DVD delivers an excellent reproduction of a first-rate image that ranges between very good and excellent. Sound is fine. —MM

Movie: 🎭🎭 **DVD:** 🎭🎭🎭
MGM Home Ent. (cat #1002731, UPC 027616869296). Widescreen (1.85:1) anamorphic. Dolby Digital Surround. $19.98. Keepcase. *LANG:* English. *SUB:* English; French; Spanish. *CAP:* English. *FEATURES:* 16 chapters • Trailer.
1990 (R) 109m/C Natasha Richardson, Robert Duvall, Faye Dunaway, Aidan Quinn, Elizabeth McGovern, Victoria Tennant, Blanche Baker, Traci Lind; **D:** Volker Schlondorff; **W:** Harold Pinter; **C:** Igor Luther; **M:** Ryuichi Sakamoto.

Hannah and Her Sisters

Hannah (Farrow) is divorced from Mickey Saxe (Allen) and is raising her two children while managing the emotional lives of her parents (O'Sullivan & Nolan) and her sisters Lee (Hershey) and Holly (Wiest). But Hannah's husband Elliot (Caine) is straying in the direction of Lee, who's having problems with her dour artist boyfriend

Frederick (von Sydow). And Holly is despondent at not achieving success either in show business or with men; her latest find, David (Waterston), is being poached by rival April (Fisher). To top it all off, Mickey's doctors have him thinking he has a brain tumor, which causes him to go on a multi-faith search for a God to believe in before it's all over! DVD is extras-light (trailer only) but presents the feature in an unblemished and clear 16:9 transfer that makes you feel like you're walking the New York streets with Woody's actors. He's quoted in the nicely chosen (for once!) liner notes on the disc insert, that the secret to making New York look luscious and vibrant on film is to shoot only on overcast days, which accounts for the darkness and frequent raininess of scenes. But with the life that's injected into the story, none of this ever looks gloomy. —GE

Movie: ♫♫♫ ½ **DVD:** ♫♫♫ ½
MGM Home Ent. (cat #1001745, UPC 027616860453). Widescreen (1.78:1) anamorphic. Dolby Digital Mono. $19.98. Keepcase. *LANG:* English; French. *SUB:* English; French. *CAP:* English. *FEATURES:* Trailer • Booklet • 16 chapters. Also available as part of the *Woody Allen Collection* (cat. #1001750, $99.96).

1986 (PG) 103m/C Mia Farrow, Barbara Hershey, Dianne Wiest, Michael Caine, Woody Allen, Maureen O'Sullivan, Lloyd Nolan, Sam Waterston, Carrie Fisher, Max von Sydow, Julie Kavner, Daniel Stern, Tony Roberts, John Turturro; **D:** Woody Allen; **W:** Woody Allen; **C:** Carlo Di Palma. *AWARDS:* Oscars '86: Orig. Screenplay, Support. Actor (Caine), Support. Actress (Wiest); British Acad. '86: Director (Allen), Orig. Screenplay; Golden Globes '87: Film—Mus./Comedy; L.A. Film Critics '86: Film, Screenplay, Support. Actress (Wiest); Natl. Bd. of Review '86: Director (Allen), Support. Actress (Wiest); N.Y. Film Critics '86: Director (Allen), Film, Support. Actress (Wiest); Natl. Soc. Film Critics '86: Support. Actress (Wiest); Writers Guild '86: Orig. Screenplay; *NOM:* Oscars '86: Art Dir./Set Dec., Director (Allen), Film Editing, Picture.

Hanover Street

In this World War II romance, an American bomber pilot (Ford) begins a relationship with married nurse, Margaret (Down). Complications ensue when he has to team up with Margaret's unknowing husband (Plummer) during an espionage assignment behind enemy lines. Slushy contrived drama in the style of popular supermarket romance paperbacks is most successful during the adventures in the latter half. The John Barry score is laid on quite thick. The film itself is pleasantly functional but never superlative and occasionally awkward. Particularly fascinating are the action scenes that frequently prefigure similar ones in Ford's later Indiana Jones vehicles. Romance novel fans will probably rate this a bit higher (heck, my mom loved it) and will get much enjoyment from seeing Ford at his most handsome.

The image is sharp and appears accurately colored, occasionally revealing variable lighting in the outdoor sequences. There's a thin layer of visible grain and occasional digital edging is evident. The sound is strong, giving the majority of presence to the loud, lush score. The sound effects seem a bit undermixed and Ford's frequent mumblings are occasionally incoherent. On the commentary, director Hyams reveals that he hasn't viewed the film since just prior to release. His memories of the production are fairly vivid and involving but he tends to drop out occasionally to watch the film. —DG

Movie: ♫♫ ½ **DVD:** ♫♫♫
Columbia Tristar (cat #05831, UPC 0433-96058316). Widescreen (2.35:1) anamorphic. Dolby Digital 4.0 Surround; Dolby Digital Surround. $19.95. Keepcase. *LANG:* English; French; Spanish. *SUB:* English; French; Spanish; Portuguese; Chinese; Korean; Thai. *CAP:* English. *FEATURES:* 28 chapters • Trailers • Commentary: director Peter Hyams.

1979 (PG) 109m/C Harrison Ford, Lesley-Anne Down, Christopher Plummer, Alec McCowen; **D:** Peter Hyams; **W:** Peter Hyams; **C:** David Watkin; **M:** John Barry.

Happenstance

Is it fate, destiny, or chance that brings people together? Clerk Irene (Tautou) chats with a woman on the subway who tells her that she will meet her true love that day. He turns out to be Younes (Faudel) but of course the made-for-each-other duo's actually getting together is a maze of complications. Amusing romantic comedy. Crisp, bright colors and well-defined blacks help the video transfer rise above average. While many darker scenes that appear extremely grainy keep it from being anything other than just this. Lack of distortion allows for nice, crisp dialogue. —MJT **AKA:** The Beating of the Butterfly's Wings; Le Battement d'Ailes du Papillon.

Movie: ♫♫ ½ **DVD:** ♫♫♫
New Yorker Video (cat #DV84902, UPC 717119849245). Widescreen (1.85:1) anamorphic. Dolby Digital Surround. $29.95. Keepcase. *LANG:* French. *SUB:* English. *FEATURES:* 20 chapters • Original theatrical trailer • New Yorker films trailer gallery.

2000 (R) 97m/C FR Audrey Tautou, Faudel, Eric Savin, Eric Feldman, Nathalie Besancon, Lysaine Meis, Lily Boulogne, Françoise Bertin, Frederique Bouraly, Irene Ismailoff; **D:** Laurent Firode; **W:** Laurent Firode; **C:** Jean-Rene Duveau; **M:** Peter Chase.

Happy Campers

One would expect the directorial debut from Daniel Waters, the writer of *Heathers*, to be a bit strange, but the offbeat nature of this film will take most viewers by surprise. The action takes place at Camp Bleeding Dove. As the story opens, we are introduced to the camp's seven counselors: Wichita (Brad Renfro), a rebellious

anarchist; Wendy (Dominique Swain), a bubbly overachiever; Pixel (James King), a waifish free-spirit; Talia (Emily Bergl), who's followed Wichita to the camp; Adam (Jordan Bridges), a chauvinist jock; Donald (Justin Long), an obsessive geek; and Jasper (Kerram Malicki-Sanchez), an openly gay dreamer. The seven personalities immediately clash and a boys-against-girls standoff begins. When camp director Oberon (Peter Stormare) is suddenly incapacitated, the young counselors are left in charge, and the activities fall into disarray, as the entire camp becomes focused on the budding relationship between Wichita and Wendy. While the campers are left to their own devices, the counselors find themselves experimenting with sex and love. To say that this is an unfocused film would be a gross understatement. There is no true plot here, as the story meanders from one counselor to the next. As the attraction between Wichita and Wendy becomes the focus of the camp, it is the glue that holds the film together. Much of the story is told through diary-like voice-overs from the seven counselors and the movie does resemble randomly chosen journal entries. The characters are likable and interesting and there are some truly funny lines here, but most will be thrown off by the film's odd tone. The image is very sharp and clear, showing only slight grain during the daytime scenes. The colors are very good and the image is stable. With the Dolby Digital 5.1 audio track, we get clear dialogue, and well-timed Surround sound effects. There are no extras on this DVD. —ML

Movie: ♫♫ **DVD:** ♫♫ ½
New Line (cat #5520, UPC 7940435520-21). Widescreen (1.85:1) anamorphic; full frame. Dolby Digital 5.1; Stereo Surround. $24.98. Snapper. *LANG:* English. *SUB:* English. *CAP:* English.

2001 (R) 94m/C Brad Renfro, Dominique Swain, Emily Bergl, James King, Jordan Bridges, Peter Stormare, Justin Long, Keram Malicki-Sanchez; **D:** Daniel Waters; **W:** Daniel Waters; **C:** Elliot Davis; **M:** Rolfe Kent.

Happy End

The story of a love triangle that takes an unexpected twist, this film caused a lot of controversy upon its release in Korea. Sound and image are faithfully transferred from a film that purposely goes for a rough, handheld camera look. Subtitles are crisp and easy to read. —BT

Movie: ♫♫♫ **DVD:** ♫♫
Tai Seng (cat #00904, UPC 6016410090-41). Widescreen letterboxed. $24.95. Keepcase. *LANG:* Cantonese; Mandarin. *SUB:* English. *FEATURES:* 8 chapters.

1999 99m/C KN Mink-sik Choi, Do-yeon Chun, Jin-mo Joo; **D:** Ji-woo Chung; **W:** Ji-woo Chung; **C:** Woo-Hyoung Kim.

Hard As Nails

Overachieving video premiere is a genre piece that leaves no cliché unturned, but it also has moments of real style. Gangster Alex (Scotti) and stripper Kat (Yates) are caught between Russian and Japanese gangs in Los Angeles. A cop (Craig) and a hooker (Farentino) are involved, too. Double-crosses abound. Some of the stunt work is wonderfully acrobatic. Director Katkin makes the most of a pocket-change budget. Night scenes, apparently shot on video, are exceptionally grainy, though, in this case, that fits the story. DVD image is no real improvement over VHS tape. —*MM*

Movie: ♫♫ ½ **DVD:** ♫♫ ½
New Concorde (cat #NH20772 D, UPC 736991477292). Full frame. Stereo. $19.98. Keepcase. *LANG:* English. *SUB:* Spanish. *FEATURES:* 12 chapters • Trailers • Thumbnail bios.
2001 (R) 88m/C Allen Scotti, Kim Yates, Andrew Craig, Matt Westmore, Lorissa McComas, Stella Farentino; *D:* Brian Katkin; *W:* Brian Katkin; *C:* Marco Cappetta; *M:* Chris Farrell.

Hard Cash

Unlucky thief Thomas (Slater) gets his hands on millions in marked money. The problem is the FBI-agent-gone-bad Cornell (Kilmer) wants it, too. Suspense elements take a backseat to comedy. The presence of Verne Troyer (*Austin Powers's* Mini-me) pretty much guarantees that. Unfortunately the bizarre comic elements are neither bizarre nor comic enough. Technically, the DVD delivers the goods. Image looks just fine with no surface damage. For a caper flick, the Surround is reasonably active. Overall, an acceptable video premiere. —*MM* **AKA:** Run for the Money.

Movie: ♫♫ **DVD:** ♫♫♫
Artisan Ent. (cat #12779, UPC 01223612-7796). Widescreen (1.85:1) anamorphic; full frame. Dolby Digital 5.1; Dolby Surround. $19.98. Keepcase. *LANG:* English. *SUB:* Spanish. *CAP:* English. *FEATURES:* 24 chapters • Trailer.
2001 (R) 98m/C Christian Slater, Bokeem Woodbine, Val Kilmer, Daryl Hannah, Verne Troyer, Balthazar Getty, Vincent Laresca, Peter Woodward, William Forsythe, Sara Downing; *D:* Pedrag (Peter) Antonijevic; *W:* Willie Dreyfus; *C:* Phil Parmet; *M:* Steve Edwards.

Hard Lessons

In a fact-based story, Washington stars as George McKenna, the newly appointed principal of George Washington High in Los Angeles. The school is located in South Central, a gang- and drug-infested war zone where the students are armed for their own protection. The situation appears hopeless but McKenna refuses to give up. The video transfer is often too dark (a trait repeated in many TV movies hastily put out on DVD). A lack of the crispness that usually accompanies even the worst discs makes this transfer too dull to surpass average DVD standards. However, it is an improvement over a

straight VHS copy. Similarly, the soundtrack is solid yet hindered by an occasional "murky" sound that again makes the disc hover just around average. —*MJT*
AKA: The George McKenna Story.

Movie: ♫♫ ½ **DVD:** ♫♫ ½
Artisan Ent. (cat #12758, UPC 01223612-7581). Full frame. Dolby Digital Surround. $14.98. Keepcase. *LANG:* English. *FEATURES:* 13 chapters.
1986 95m/C Denzel Washington, Lynn Whitfield, Akosua Busia, Richard Masur; *D:* Eric Laneuville; *W:* Charles Eric Johnson; *C:* Isidore Mankofsky; *M:* Herbie Hancock.

Hard Luck

Lucky O'Donnell (Harris) breaks out of the mental institution to spend a final few days with best friend Eric (Faber), who's dying of cancer. Along the way they pick up Lucky's reluctant childhood sweetheart, Sheryl (Humphrey), and take a road trip down memory lane. While the plot is fairly predictable, a few very good performances make this a somber and enjoyable film. The picture shows a good deal of grain, but the soundtrack handles dialogue quite well. The packaging makes several false claims, advertising non-existent outtakes and inflating the film's running time by almost 15 minutes. —*BG*

Movie: ♫♫ ½ **DVD:** ♫♫♫
Vanguard Intl. Cinema (cat #VFO256, UPC 658769025637). Full frame. $29.95. Keepcase. *LANG:* English. *FEATURES:* 12 chapters • Commentary: director Jack Rubio, actor/writer Kirk Harris • Trailers.
2001 85m/C Kirk Harris, Renee Humphrey, Matthew Faber, Ron Gilbert, Gareth Williams, Karen Black, Joannne Baron, Darrell Bryan, Tony Longo, Luca Bercovici, Jon Jacobs; *D:* Jack Rubio; *W:* Kirk Harris.

The Hard Road

Two-disc collection includes *Born to Win* (reviewed in *Book 2*), *One for the Road, The Last Train,* and *Murder in the Orient.* Please see individual reviews. —*MM*

Movie: ♫ **DVD:** ♫
BCI-Eclipse (cat #44302-9, UPC 7873644-30291). Full frame. $9.98. Keepcase. *LANG:* English.
2000 m/C

Hard Ticket to Hawaii

Donna (Spier) and Taryn (Carlton) are undercover agents who, between hot tub sessions, stumble across a diamond smuggling/drug dealing operation in Hawaii. To many of his fans, this is Andy Sidaris's finest film. It certainly highlights all of the elements that have made his movies perennial guilty-pleasure favorites: lots of Playboy Playmates, jut-jawed heroes so dense they couldn't pour lemonade out of a boot with instructions on the heel, really neat toys, gorgeous scenery. DVD also provides the extras that the cognoscenti want to see. On the commentary track he and Arlene (his wife and producer) talk about the details of low-budget

filmmaking. He seems a bit uncomfortable with a bit of violence early on and says that it's the most graphic moment in any of his work. At other times, he feigns distraction at the abundant amounts of nudity on display. DVD image is about as clear as anyone could expect. The film was made for video and so it's not the most opulent. Some parts of the featurette are a short step above home video quality and that's fine. —*MM*

Movie: ♫♫♫ **DVD:** ♫♫♫
Ventura Distribution (cat #1132-7, UPC 634991113229). Full frame. $19.98. Keepcase. *LANG:* English. *FEATURES:* 12 chapters • Behind-the-scenes featurette • Trailers • Andy Sidaris thumbnail bio • Liner notes • Commentary: Andy and Arlene Sidaris • Still gallery.
1987 (R) 96m/C Ron Moss, Dona Speir, Hope Marie Carlton, Cynthia Brimhall, Harold Diamond, Rodrigo Obregon, Rustam Branaman, Kwan Hi Lim; *D:* Andy Sidaris; *W:* Andy Sidaris; *C:* Howard Wexler; *M:* Gary Stockdale.

Hardball

Schizophrenic baseball film can't decide whether it wants to be another *Bad News Bears* kid-oriented story or a foul-mouthed morality tale of redemption. Reeves stars as a compulsive gambler who agrees to coach a group of inner-city kids to relieve his gambling debts. Predictably, the movie becomes a lesson in "showing up" with Reeves learning the lesson right along with the kids. Unfortunately, what could have been a pleasant family film is overcome by swearing (mostly by the kids) and an act of violence that just makes the film all that more confusing and painful. The video transfer is well done. Colors and blacks are nicely defined and no loss of definition is evident. The soundtrack is similarly impressive particularly the musical score. A few moderately decent extras are included. —*MJT*

Movie: ♫♫ **DVD:** ♫♫♫
Paramount (cat #33079, UPC 097363307-921). Widescreen (1.85:1) anamorphic. Dolby Digital 5.1 Surround; Dolby Digital Surround. $29.99. Keepcase. *LANG:* English; French. *SUB:* English. *FEATURES:* 16 chapters • Commentary: director Brian Robbins, writer John Gatins • "Making of" featurette • 3 deleted scenes • Interstitials • Music video by Lil Bow Wow, Lil' Wayne, Lil' Zane & Sammie.
2001 (PG-13) 106m/C Keanu Reeves, Diane Lane, John Hawkes, Bryan C. Hearne, Julian Griffith, A. Delon Ellis Jr., DeWayne Warren, Michael Jordan, D.B. Sweeney, Mike McGlone, Graham Beckel, Mark Margolis; *D:* Brian Robbins; *W:* John Gatins; *C:* Tom Richmond; *M:* Mark Isham.

Harlan County War

Based-on-truth story recounts the saga of a Kentucky coal-mining town in the early 1970s. After two miners are killed in a cave-in, the mine foreman forces everyone back to work the next day. As fate would

have it, a new union organizer (Stellan Skarsgard) comes to town. Ruby (Holly Hunter), furious that her husband (Ted Levine) had to return to the mine after witnessing such a tragedy, begins to talk with the union rep to learn what she can do to help. Soon, the miners go on strike. As "scabs" are brought in to replace the miners, Ruby encourages the other women of Harlan to join the men on the picket line and stand up to the company. What results is a long struggle that turns violent at times. This is a moving film, with great performances by Skarsgard and Hunter. And for once, the DVD contains notes that detail how the events on which the film is based occurred in real life. Disc displays a sharp, sometimes grainy picture, which accurately captures the dark mood of the film. The audio is clean and clear, and there is an impressive use of Surround sound at times. We also get interviews with Hunter, Skarsgard, and director Tony Bill, which shed more light on the importance of this project. —ML
Movie: ♫♫♫ ½ **DVD:** ♫♫♫
Showtime Networks, Inc. (cat #SHO1040, UPC 758445104028). Full frame. Dolby Surround. $24.98. Keepcase. *LANG:* English; Spanish. *FEATURES:* Cast & crew interviews ▪ Actor bios ▪ Background information on film ▪ Weblinks ▪ 12 chapters.
2000 104m/C Holly Hunter, Stellan Skarsgard, Ted Levine, Wayne Robson; **D:** Tony Bill; **W:** Peter Silverman; **C:** Flavio Labiano; **M:** Van Dyke Parks.

Harlem Nights
Star Murphy's directorial debut is a slow, poorly plotted but exceptionally attractive showcase for a talented ensemble cast. He and Richard Pryor star as the owners of a profitable Harlem nightclub-casino in 1938. Things are going so well that a gangster (Lerner) and his pal, a crooked cop (Aiello), try to take over. The rest is a simplified version of *The Sting*. Herbie Hancock's jazzy score is terrific; so is the glossy production design. DVD delivers first-rate eye candy. The 5.1 is used for some nice ambient effects. If the story were as strong as everything else, this would be a knock-out. —MM
Movie: ♫♫ **DVD:** ♫♫♫
Paramount (cat #32316, UPC 097363231-646). Widescreen anamorphic. Dolby Digital 5.1 Surround; Dolby Digital Surround; Stereo. $24.98. Keepcase. *LANG:* English; French. *SUB:* English. *CAP:* English. *FEATURES:* 18 chapters ▪ Trailer.
1989 (R) 118m/C Eddie Murphy, Richard Pryor, Redd Foxx, Danny Aiello, Jasmine Guy, Michael Lerner, Arsenio Hall, Della Reese, Eugene Glazer; **D:** Eddie Murphy; **W:** Eddie Murphy; **M:** Herbie Hancock. *AWARDS:* Golden Raspberries '89: Worst Screenplay; *NOM:* Oscars '89: Costume Des.

Harlock Saga
Villainous Alberich steals a lump of enchanted gold from the planet Rhine and has it forged into a magic ring. He intends to destroy the universe with it, so space pirate Captain Harlock and his band intervene in an attempt to stop him. A needlessly muddled science-fiction rendition of Richard Wagner's "Ring of the Nibelung" opera cycle. This ambitious idea has great potential but unfortunately, it's executed in an awkward, sometimes static fashion and only the barest of story elements is actually used. None of the characters are given much depth and the story often descends into babble. The excellent music uses a few of Wagner's themes but is mainly built on new compositions. A disappointment. The disc features strong colors and a sharp image but is marred by edge noise and digital grain during camera pans. Compositions seem a bit tightly framed at times. The sound is strong but low-end sounds tend to warble and distort. The Japanese language track is far superior to the English dub. —DG
Movie: ♫♫ **DVD:** ♫♫ ½
Central Park/U.S. Manga (cat #USMD20-32, UPC 719987203228). Full frame. Dolby Digital Surround. $29.99. Keepcase. *LANG:* Japanese; English. *SUB:* English. *FEATURES:* All 6 episodes ▪ 12 chapters ▪ Reversible sleeve with chapter listing ▪ "Making of the English dub" featurette ▪ Text interviews ▪ Textless credits ▪ "The World of Harlock" character bios ▪ DVD-ROM: art, character sketches, cast, scripts, reviews, interviews.
1999 137m/C *JP* **D:** Yoshio Takeuchi; **W:** Leiji Matsumoto; **M:** Kaoru Wada.

Harold Robbins' Body Parts
First, the title is not to be taken literally. This movie is not about the organs and appendages of the late trash novelist. Instead, it's an unsurprising formula revenge flick. Ty Kinnick (Grieco) is double-crossed by his best friend (Stewart) and wife (Massey) during a drug deal. Five years later, he's back and finds that the intrigues are still being played out. Both production values and acting are a bit above average for a Corman picture. DVD delivers a good to very good full-frame image. Sound is fine. —MM *AKA:* Body Parts.
Movie: ♫♫ **DVD:** ♫♫ ½
New Concorde (cat #NH20745 D, UPC 736991474598). Full frame. Stereo. $19.98. Keepcase. *LANG:* English. *SUB:* Spanish. *FEATURES:* 24 chapters ▪ Trailers ▪ Talent files.
2001 86m/C Richard Grieco, Will Foster Stewart, Athena Massey; **D:** Craig Corman; **W:** Craig Corman.

The Harp in the South
Australian miniseries follows the Darcys, a working class Irish/Australian family in the late 1940s. Engaging characters highlight this tale of solid, god-fearing immigrants as they wrestle with poverty and prejudice in the crowded streets of Surry Hills, a suburb of Sydney. Mumma Darcy's (Phelan) wit and humor hold her husband and two growing daughters together. Even though the film was made for TV, there are fine period details and excellent performances. The picture is grainy and contrasty—not up to broadcast quality—but the sound is fine. —LA
Movie: ♫♫♫ ½ **DVD:** ♫♫
BFS Video (cat #30262-D, UPC 66805302-626). Full frame. Dolby Digital. $19.98. Keepcase. *LANG:* English. *FEATURES:* 18 chapters.
1986 282m/C *AU* Anne Phelan, Martyn Sanderson, Anna Hruby; **D:** George Whaley; **W:** George Whaley, Ruth Park; **C:** Paul Murphy.

Harrad Experiment
Please see review of *Killer B Double Feature*.
Movie: ♫ ½
1973 (R) 98m/C James Whitmore, Tippi Hedren, Don Johnson, Bruno Kirby, Laurie Walters, Victoria Thompson, Elliot Street, Sharon Taggart, Robert Middleton, Billy (Billie) Sands, Melanie Griffith; **D:** Ted Post; **W:** Ted Cassedy, Michael Werner; **C:** Richard H. Kline; **M:** Artie Butler.

Harry Potter and the Sorcerer's Stone
Enchanting, well-produced, and faithful adaptation of the novel tells the tale of young Harry Potter (Radcliffe), who is rescued from his abusive adoptive parents by giant Hagrid (Coltrane) and taken on a journey to Hogwarts, a school of magic. Making friends with fellow students, Ron (Grint) and Hermione (Watson), Harry attempts to discover the secret of the sorcerer's stone. Author Rowling's world is re-created in believable, big-budget fashion and the cast is uniformly excellent. The story is quite entertaining and involving, and the young leads carry the film with skill. The majority of the special effects are excellent but the "Quidditch" match is a confusing, unbelievable mess. The climax is visually interesting but fairly humdrum. The British prints are entitled *Harry Potter and the Philosopher's Stone* (as that was the original book title) and all dialogue and visual references to the titular object were shot in two variants (*Sorcerer's* and *Philosopher's*). The U.K. and Canadian video releases contain the *Philosopher* version; this U.S. disc contains the *Sorcerer* edition. The disc is gorgeous with a sharp, defined image; perfect colors; and a smooth filmic texture. There's a slight bit of grain in night scenes, but it's a quibble. The film, shot in Super35, is available in widescreen and full frame. The widescreen edition adds to the left and right sides of the frame and accurately reflects the theatrical prints. The full-frame edition reveals more on the top and bottom of the frame, but shaves off the peripheral imagery. Each is watchable, but the widescreen edition features stronger compositions. The Surround sound is top-notch and fully utilizes all the channels in

its involving mix. The supplements are fun and will mostly appeal to children. The deleted scenes are fully finished and worthwhile. Finding them is a bit of a challenge. —DG **AKA:** Harry Potter and the Philosopher's Stone.

Movie: 🎬🎬🎬 **DVD:** 🎬🎬🎬 ½
Warner (cat #22467, UPC 0853922467-24). Widescreen (2.35:1) anamorphic. Dolby Digital 5.1 Surround. $26.99. 2-disc foldout snapcase. *LANG:* English; Spanish. *SUB:* English; Spanish. *CAP:* English. *FEATURES:* 7 deleted scenes • 35 chapters • Interactive tour of Hogwarts • Design gallery • Interview featurette • Interactive games. DVD-ROM: Hat sorting, games, weblink.
2001 (PG) 152m/C Daniel Radcliffe, Rupert Grint, Emma Watson, Robbie Coltrane, Richard Harris, Maggie Smith, Zoe Wanamaker, Alan Rickman, Ian Hart, John Hurt, Tom Felton, Harry Melling, Richard Griffiths, Fiona Shaw, John Cleese, Warwick Davis, Julie Walters, Sean Biggerstaff, David Bradley, Matthew Lewis; *D:* Chris Columbus; *W:* Steven Kloves; *C:* John Seale; *M:* John Williams. *AWARDS: NOM:* Oscars '01: Art Dir./Set Dec., Costume Des., Score; British Acad. '01: Costume Des., Film, Sound, Support. Actor (Coltrane), Visual FX; Broadcast Film Critics '01: Score.

Harvesters
Small-time crooks cross paths with a family of organ thieves in this ultra low-budget splatterfest. Gore effects (as well as cars and helicopters) are rendered through extraordinarily bad computer graphics, adding camp value to an otherwise predictable tale. Heavy grain is present throughout this straight-to-video production, and the halo effect is so pronounced that characters often seem to be glowing. —BG
Movie: 🎬 **DVD:** 🎬🎬
Key East Ent. (cat #KE 2005, UPC 691597-200524). Full frame. Dolby Stereo. $24.95. Keepcase. *LANG:* English. *FEATURES:* 28 chapters • Trailers • "Making of" featurette.
2002 90m/C Donna Sherman, George Stover, Patty Cipoletti, Steven King; *D:* Joe Ripple; *W:* Donald M. Dohler; *C:* Joe Ripple.

The Harvey Girls
Fans of musicals will enjoy this film and fans of Judy Garland will love it. Garland plays a hopeful mail-order bride traveling west to meet her intended only to discover that he is a dried-up old cowboy. The letters that seduced her to California were written by the dashing owner of the saloon that stands defiantly across from a new restaurant run by the Harvey Girls of the title, beautiful women traveling westward as a "symbol of the promise of what is to come," also known as waitresses in the first chain restaurant in the West. She breaks it off with the agreement of her fiancé and becomes a Harvey girl. Competition develops between the Harvey girls and the bar girls, led by a vivaciously evil

Angela Lansbury, and a Wild West version of the Jets and Sharks with petticoats. It's a musical, though, so where normally gang fights, gunfire, and arson might mean something, here it just means they all live happily ever after. Directed by George Sidney, the same guy who did *Bye Bye Birdie* and *Viva Las Vegas*, the movie is just plain fun. It's also beautiful to look at with a great Technicolor transfer. The costume designer took complete advantage of that color scheme, from Lansbury's Macy's parade dresses to the cowboy extras with their fuchsia, green, and red neck scarves. Sound is good and the lyrics by Johnny Mercer, are all sing-along quality. —CA
Movie: 🎬🎬 ½ **DVD:** 🎬🎬🎬
Warner (cat #65348, UPC 0 12569 534-82). Full frame. Dolby Digital Mono. $19.90. Snapper. *LANG:* English. *SUB:* English. *FEATURES:* 26 chapters • Inside & CD art work by Al Hirschfeld • 3 deleted musical numbers • Commentary: director.
1946 102m/C Judy Garland, Ray Bolger, John Hodiak, Preston Foster, Angela Lansbury, Virginia O'Brien, Marjorie Main, Chill Wills, Kenny L. Baker, Selena Royle, Cyd Charisse; *D:* George Sidney; *C:* George J. Folsey; *M:* Harry Warren, Johnny Mercer. *AWARDS:* Oscars '46: Song ("On the Atchison, Topeka and Santa Fe"); *NOM:* Oscars '46: Scoring/Musical.

Hatari!
Some spectacular African scenery and a dandy Mancini score have aged more gracefully than the sluggish pace of this lumbering adventure. John Wayne is the blustering boss of a gang of hunters who capture wildlife for zoos. It's hard to watch these days without feeling for the rhinos and giraffes. Remember, though, that the film was relatively enlightened for its time. It's still far from the best for director Hawks, veteran writer Brackett, or the cast. Though DVD image is not spectacular, it is good, perhaps even very good considering how difficult the bright, dusty exteriors can be, particularly in the long tracking shots that Hawks favors for the action scenes. Mono sound is true to the original. —MM
Movie: 🎬🎬 ½ **DVD:** 🎬🎬 ½
Paramount (cat #06629, UPC 097360662-948). Widescreen (1.85:1) anamorphic. Dolby Digital Mono. $29.99. Keepcase. *LANG:* English; French. *SUB:* English. *FEATURES:* Trailer • 17 chapters.
1962 158m/C John Wayne, Elsa Martinelli, Red Buttons, Hardy Kruger, Gerard Blain, Bruce Cabot; *D:* Howard Hawks; *W:* Leigh Brackett; *C:* Russell Harlan; *M:* Henry Mancini. *AWARDS: NOM:* Oscars '62: Color Cinematog.

Haunted
In 1925, David Ash (Quinn), who teaches a university course debunking the supernatural, is drawn to a supposedly haunted mansion where artist Robert Mariell (Andrews) lives with his sister Christina (Beckinsale), brother Simon (Lowe), and

their elderly nanny (Massey). Many inexplicable manifestations occur and they all seem to be connected to the three sibs. Production is solidly handled at all levels—writing, acting, direction—with some good twists at the end. Highly recommended. Unfortunately, the full-frame image is no real improvement over VHS tape. —MM
Movie: 🎬🎬🎬 **DVD:** 🎬🎬
Artisan Ent. (cat #11484, UPC 70772911-484). Full frame. Dolby Digital Stereo. $19.98. Keepcase. *LANG:* English. *CAP:* English. *FEATURES:* 19 chapters.
1995 (R) 108m/C *GB* Aidan Quinn, Kate Beckinsale, Anthony Andrews, Alex Lowe, Anna Massey, Geraldine Somerville, Victoria Shalet, John Gielgud; *D:* Lewis Gilbert; *W:* Lewis Gilbert, Bob Kellett, Tim Prager; *C:* Tony Pierce-Roberts; *M:* Debbie Wiseman.

Haunted Castle
An aspiring musician is summoned to his mother's castle to receive information on her dying wishes. Once he's there, things begin to go wrong as the castle takes on a mysterious life of its own. Johnny meets Mr. D (Shearer), a mysterious figure inhabiting his mother's estate. Mr. D presents a once in a lifetime deal, and Johnny must choose between the enticing offer of fame and fortune in exchange for his soul, or giving up his life's dreams and vying for the freedom of his mother's life. Created as a 3-D showcase, *Haunted Castle* was originally released on the Imax big screen, and gave a small taste of what new 3-D technology could do. The entire feature is done in 3-D and is shot from a first person perspective, which greatly enhances the 3-D experience. The picture quality is good and the sound gives an adequate sense of things moving all around as you walk through this mysterious castle. The plot is a little weak, and like other films in this series does not provide much except an enticing look at what can be done with CGI animation and 3-D technology. —EL
Movie: 🎬🎬 **DVD:** 🎬🎬 ½
Ventura Distribution (cat #9263, UPC 017-078926323). Full frame. Dolby Digital 5.1; DTS. $19.99. Keepcase. *LANG:* English. *FEATURES:* Commentary: director • "Making of" featurette • Theatrical teaser & trailer • Arid biography • Photo gallery (2-D & 3-D).
2001 38m/C *D:* Ben Stassen; *W:* Ben Stassen, Kurt Frey; *V:* Jasper Steverlinck, Kyoko Baertsoen, Harry Shearer.

Haunted Honeymoon
Arthritic horror-comedy about a couple of radio stars (Wilder and Radner) in a haunted house on a dark and stormy night. Sad times for the Mel Brooks alumni and Gilda Radner in her final screen appearance. Dark exteriors are very grainy. Interiors look much better. In fact, the DVD image is much sharper than it needs to be. Sound is fine with Surround effects that are not as intrusive as they might have been. —MM

Movie: ♫ **DVD:** ♫♫ ½
MGM Home Ent. (cat #1002328, UPC 027616865472). Widescreen (1.85:1) anamorphic. Dolby Digital 5.1 Surround; Mono. $14.98. Keepcase. *LANG:* English; Spanish. *SUB:* French; Spanish. *CAP:* English. *FEATURES:* 16 chapters • Trailer.
1986 (PG) 82m/C Gene Wilder, Gilda Radner, Dom DeLuise, Jonathan Pryce, Paul Smith, Peter Vaughan, Bryan Pringle, Roger Ashton-Griffiths, Jim Carter, Eve Ferret; *D:* Gene Wilder; *W:* Terence Marsh, Gene Wilder; *C:* Fred Schuler.

The Haunted World of Edward D. Wood Jr.

There's a good documentary here, but it suffers from the fact that it's an inside job. One of the producers was an old associate of Wood, which gives the show very good access to all the classic characters who became part of Ed Wood lore. And Wade Williams is also involved, so we're spared the dodges of low-budget Hollywood documentaries, such as using trailers to illustrate movies that can't be licensed. But the film loses focus and perspective on its subject, who is presented as if he were a great filmmaker, instead of what he was—a guy who wanted to make films so badly he couldn't be stopped. The interviewees, who are mostly still Hollywood wannabes as they slip into retirement and beyond, are allowed to prattle on far too long and too repetitively. The show has some good qualities, but comes off as a big valentine from the "Ed Wood gang," mailed to themselves. The life and wild times of maverick underachieving director are covered through most of the key people in his life—his wives, his close-knit group of actors, the wonderful Maila Nurmi who resents him even as she proudly talks of their history together. Woods's transvestism is covered in detail (and tastefully) and many of the small distortions (and a few big ones) of the Tim Burton feature are corrected. DVD is nicely tricked out. The well-produced film looks fine and plays well. The menu takes you to a host of extras introduced by the Vampira impersonator. The personal stills and home videos of most of the cast are on display, with publicity video coverage of the actors and producer coming together for screening parties. Philip Chamberlain and Forrest Ackerman (here's Bela's ring!) are there for the *The Haunted World* premiere at the Nuart theatre in West L.A. Coverage of the shoots for the new material get pretty tedious, but there are a lot of classic stills included as well. The producer has the rights to Wood's semi-amateur western "Crossroads of Laredo" so it makes an appearance, with a new track, new video titles, and rather annoying narration. Director's commentary is mostly about the production of the documentary. —*GE*
Movie: ♫♫ ½ **DVD:** ♫♫ ½
Image Ent. (cat #ID1551CODVD, UPC 014381155129). Full frame. Dolby Digital Mono. $24.98. Keepcase. *LANG:* English. *FEATURES:* "Crossroads of Laredo," Wood's 23-minute first film • Commentary • Unedited A&E interview • SciFi Channel coverage of the world premiere • "Behind the Camera," collection of outtakes from the interview shoots • Ed Wood reunion and Hollywood Premiere video footage • Galleries of Ed Wood rarities and photos.
1995 112m/C D: Brett Thompson.

Hav Plenty

Moving in the circles of young black professionals, Lee Plenty (Cherot) is an unemployed would-be writer who doesn't seem to care very much about getting a job. The beautiful, materialistic, and ambitious Havilland (Maxwell), a friend from college, invites Lee to a New Year's Eve party when she (Hav) finds that her fiancé Michael (Harper) is playing around on her. The sedate holiday weekend turns into a frenzy of surprises, as Lee is chased by Hav's hairdo-happy friend Caroline (Jones) and newlywed sister Leigh (Lee). This film is a screwball romantic comedy which comes off as a hybrid of Spike Lee and Woody Allen, with writer/director/editor Cherot's own personal touches thrown in. The performances are excellent, especially Cherot himself, who only starred when the actor hired to play his part bowed out as filming started. On this DVD, the film's low-budget roots show through. The image is sharp, but noticeably grainy, and there are some visible defects from the source print. Otherwise, the colors are good and there is only a minimal amount of artifacting. The Dolby Digital 5.1 audio track provides clear dialogue, but little else. There aren't many Surround sound effects and the LFE response is 0. —*ML*
Movie: ♫♫♫ **DVD:** ♫♫ ½
Miramax Pictures (cat #18531, UPC 7179-51005489). Widescreen (1.85:1) anamorphic. Dolby Digital 5.1 Surround. $29.99. Keepcase. *LANG:* English. *SUB:* English. *CAP:* English. *FEATURES:* 15 chapters.
1997 (R) 87m/C Christopher Scott Cherot, Chenoa Maxwell, Hill Harper, Tammi Katherine Jones, Robbine Lee, Betty Vaughn, Reginald James, Kenneth "Babyface" Edmonds; *D:* Christopher Scott Cherot; *W:* Christopher Scott Cherot; *C:* Kerwin Devonish; *M:* Wendy Melvoin, Lisa Coleman.

Haxan: Witchcraft through the Ages

Everywhere you read about this film, the stress is put upon how shocking it is purported to be, sort of a pornographic/satanic combination of taboo subjects. What it really is, is an excellent silent documentary that incorporates some very sophisticated styles in a very modern way. Some of the content might disturb a fundamentalist viewer, but all in all, one should expect a sharp documentary with some very imaginative and evocative "re-creations" of demonic activity. Witches, devils, and possession have been a part of humanity since before recorded history, and haven't changed much in content or principle from the Middle Ages to the present (make that 1922 Sweden). Starting out with a slide-show technique (graphics and other visual examples intercut with explanatory text), the film soon brings its weird subject to life through very convincing re-creations. Some of these re-creations naturalistically show historical events, such as a witch hunt and the roles played by citizens and church officials. Christensen himself plays Satan as a pot-bellied, hairy horror who constantly leers and waggles his tongue obscenely. Besides tormenting and raping novitiate witches, the kinds of "authentic" witch activity pictured are flights through the sky on brooms, boiling a meal of toads and unbaptized infants (pretty disturbing), and rituals where the witches must kiss Satan on his filthy-looking rump, or worse. Sickness is blamed on witches who throw pots of their own urine onto people's doors, and devils are shown parading as grotesque giant pigs and cats. The most horrific vision of all is an image of a woman giving birth to a succession of crawling, verminous insectoid demons that would give Dario Argento or David Cronenberg the willies. Criterion has given an exemplary presentation to yet another classic film that needs a lot of explanation to relate to modern viewers. The extra material complements and validates Christensen's already authoritative grasp of his subject matter. This is no jazz-age Chariots of the Gods–style trash feature, but an academically precise document. Besides a commentary, the disc has two versions of the film encoded together: the 104-minute original feature, beautifully restored, and the 76-minute 1968 reissue version, which substitutes an odd William Burroughs narration for Christensen's intertitles and adds a strange jazz score. —*GE* **AKA:** Haxan; Witchcraft through the Ages.
Movie: ♫♫♫ ½ **DVD:** ♫♫♫ ½
Criterion (UPC 37429161722). Full frame. $29.98. Keepcase. *LANG:* English. *FEATURES:* Music from the original Danish premiere • Commentary: scholar Caspar Tybjerg • Director's intro to 1941 re-issue • Glossary of Christensen's historical sources • Stills gallery.
1922 74m/B SW Maren Pedersen, Clara Pontoppidan, Oscar Stribolt, Benjamin Christiansen, Tora Teje, Elith Pio, Karen Winther, Emmy Schonfeld, John Andersen, Astrid Holm, Gerda Madsen; *D:* Benjamin Christiansen; *W:* Benjamin Christiansen; *C:* Johan Ankerstjerne; *Nar:* William S. Burroughs.

He Said, She Said

This film plays like the romantic comedy version of *Rashomon*, which couples should definitely enjoy. After an on-air fight, the lives of TV personalities Dan (Kevin Bacon) and Lorie (Elizabeth Perkins) are revealed from their unique perspectives. The story re-traces how their relationship formed and we get to see how their recollections of specific incidents differ. *He Said, She Said* makes some funny and poignant comments about the distinct ways that men and women view the world and the story offers some surprises once it shifts to Lorie's point of view. Still, this "men and women are different" vibe is nothing new, and the film seems to have difficulty balancing the drama and comedy. (The hallucination scenes are funny, but seem oddly out of place.) The DVD offers an anamorphic widescreen transfer which is clear, but often appears dark. There is some visible grain at times, but no artifacting or distortion. The Dolby Digital 5.1 soundtrack gives us clear dialogue, but little Surround sound effects and no real bass response. The audio commentary featuring the directors, writer, and cinematographer is very entertaining and gives insight into the views behind the film. —*ML*

Movie: 🐾🐾🐾 **DVD:** 🐾🐾 ½
Paramount (cat #32343, UPC 097363234-340). Widescreen (2.35:1) anamorphic. Dolby Digital 5.1; Dolby 2.0 Surround. $24.99. Keepcase. *LANG:* English; French. *SUB:* English. *FEATURES:* Commentary • Theatrical trailer.
1991 (R) 115m/C Elizabeth Perkins, Kevin Bacon, Sharon Stone, Nathan Lane, Anthony LaPaglia, Stanley Anderson, Charlaine Woodard, Danton Stone, Phil Leeds, Rita Karin; *D:* Marisa Silver, Ken Kwapis; *W:* Brian Hohlfield; *C:* Stephen Burum; *M:* Miles Goodman.

He Walked by Night [BFS]

Los Angeles homicide investigators track down cop killer Ray Morgan (Basehart) in this excellent fact-based drama that was the inspiration for Jack Webb's *Dragnet*. The final confrontation in underground tunnels rivals *The Third Man*. Title is available on the *Great Cop Movies* disc. DVD image shows some signs of wear. Black-and-white photography ranges between fair and good. Only a minor improvement over VHS tape, but the price is right. —*MM*
Movie: 🐾🐾🐾 ½ **DVD:** 🐾🐾
Full frame. *LANG:* English. *FEATURES:* 4 chapters.
1948 80m/B Richard Basehart, Scott Brady, Roy Roberts, Jack Webb, Whit Bissell; *D:* Alfred Werker, Anthony Mann; *W:* John C. Higgins; *C:* John Alton; *M:* Leonid Raab.

Head

Infamously plotless feature is essentially a long-form version of the Monkees (Tork, Dolenz, Jones, Nesmith) television show. The film attempts to deflect criticism by admitting up front that it (and its stars) are shallow and pointless, but that doesn't really wash. It's interesting as a historical artifact of the late '60s and for the curious collection of guest stars who are quickly found by way of a "cameo" feature on the menu which takes you right to each appearance. Songs can be reached the same way. Given the loosey-goosey nature of the production, it seems pointless to criticize image and sound but both are really quite good with bright trippy colors

and only occasional surface damage. Production values are no better than made-for-TV. —*MM*
Movie: 🐾🐾 ½ **DVD:** 🐾🐾 ½
Rhino (cat #R2 4460). Full frame. Dolby Mono. $19.98. Keepcase. *LANG:* English. *FEATURES:* 20 chapters • TV spots and trailers • Jump to cameo • Jump to song.
1968 (G) 86m/C Peter Tork, Mickey Dolenz, Davy Jones, Michael Nesmith, Frank Zappa, Annette Funicello, Teri Garr, Timothy Carey, Logan Ramsey, Victor Mature, Jack Nicholson, Bob Rafelson, Dennis Hopper; *D:* Bob Rafelson; *W:* Jack Nicholson, Bob Rafelson; *C:* Michael Hugo; *M:* Ken Thorne.

Head over Heels

Freddie Prinze Jr. and Monica Potter star in a surprisingly funny and effective film, which rises above the typical "chick flick" fare. Potter plays an artist who moves in with four supermodels. She then meets Prinze, whom she considers to be the perfect guy...until she witnesses him committing murder! Despite the predictable *Rear Window* subplot, the film is just quirky enough to set it apart from the pack, and the supermodel roommates are particularly funny. Along with the typical romantic fare, there are scenes of "gross-out" humor and some moments of action, which would make *Head over Heels* a good choice for a date movie. Stellar presentation is free of blemishes and creates an intensely clear image without noise, grain, or other distractions. Colors are absolutely natural looking and faithfully rendered in all circumstances the film has to offer. Blacks are deep, giving the image a refreshing dimensionality, and the incredibly high level of detail that is found through the picture is also perfectly maintained in the image's shadows. The compression is flawless and no compression artifacts are visible. Both language tracks are beautifully mastered and make good use of Surround, creating an engaging presentation that is active, yet never obtrusive. —*ML/GH*
Movie: 🐾🐾 **DVD:** 🐾🐾🐾
Universal Studios (cat #20937, UPC 0251-92093722). Widescreen (2.35:1) anamorphic. Dolby Digital 5.1 Surround Stereo; Dolby Digital Surround; DTS Surround. $26.94. Keepcase. *LANG:* English; French. *SUB:* English. *CAP:* English. *FEATURES:* "Making of" featurette • Talent files • Production notes • Trailer • DVD-ROM features • 18 chapters.
2001 (PG-13) 86m/C Monica Potter, Freddie Prinze Jr., Shalom Harlow, Ivana Milicevic, China Chow, Jay Brazeau, Stanley DeSantis, Tomiko Fraser, Sarah O'Hare; *D:* Mark Waters; *W:* Ron Burch, David Kidd; *C:* Mark Plummer; *M:* Randy Edelman, Steve Porcaro.

The Hearse

The Hearse was released in 1980 and attempted to mix two horror genres which

were very popular at the time—haunted houses and stalkers. The result is a film that has some scary moments, but is ultimately a convoluted mess. School teacher Jane Hardy (Trish Van Devere) decides to leave her troubled life in San Francisco behind and retreat to the country. She moves into her late aunt's house, but soon learns that the suspicious locals regard the house as being cursed. A strange black hearse appears in Jane's front yard, and at times, attempts to run her off the road while driving. Jane finds comfort in the arms of Tom (David Gautreaux), a handsome, but mysterious man, who appears to have many secrets. When Jane finds her aunt's diary, she begins to learn why the townspeople fear her house, and realizes that her aunt had been involved with the forces of darkness. This is a very slow-paced film that, in the first half, appears to be building to an exciting climax. Unfortunately, the second half of the film proves to be redundant and boring, and the exact same shot of Jane running to her car is shown three times! (Ironically, director George Bowers went on to edit such well-known films as *From Hell, A League of Their Own,* and *How Stella Got Her Groove Back.*) The film does contain some creepy images, and at least one classic "jump" scare, but the repetitive scenes of the hearse pursuing Jane grow very tiresome. The twist ending is nice and pre-dates many recent shockers, but the actual finale is a low-budget letdown. DVD looks pretty good. The image is clear and shows few defects from the source print. The colors are good, and there is little distortion to the image. While the picture is quite soft at times, this transfer is surprisingly sufficient, given the age and relative obscurity of the title. The Dolby stereo soundtrack provides clear dialogue. This DVD contains the theatrical trailer for the film, which turns out to be as repetitive as the movie—"I'm possessed...I'm possessed." —*ML*
Movie: 🐾 ½ **DVD:** 🐾🐾
Rhino (cat #976064-2, UPC 6034976064-29). Widescreen (1.85:1) letterboxed. Digital Mono. $9.95. Keepcase. *LANG:* English. *FEATURES:* Trailer • 12 chapters.
1980 (PG) 100m/C Trish Van Devere, Joseph Cotten, Donald Hotton, David Gautreaux; *D:* George Bowers; *W:* William Bleich; *C:* Mori Kawa.

The Heart of Dixie

Three co-eds (Sheedy, Madsen, Cates) at a southern university in the 1950s see their lives and values changed by the influence of the civil rights movement. Filmmakers manage to drain all drama and significance from one of the most important chapters in American history. DVD does nothing to improve the softish image. Curiously, the two dubbed monaural soundtracks are much brighter and livelier than the English Surround. And if you don't understand French or Spanish, you don't have to listen to the inane dialogue. —*MM*
Movie: 🐾 ½ **DVD:** 🐾🐾

MGM Home Ent. (cat #1002571, UPC 027616867728). Widescreen (1.85:1) anamorphic. Dolby Digital Surround; Mono. $14.98. Keepcase. *LANG:* English; French; Spanish. *SUB:* French; Spanish. *CAP:* English. *FEATURES:* 16 chapters • Trailer. **1989 (PG) 96m/C** Virginia Madsen, Ally Sheedy, Phoebe Cates, Treat Williams, Kyle Secor, Francesca Roberts, Barbara Babcock, Don Michael Paul, Kurtwood Smith, Richard Bradford; *D:* Martin Davidson; *W:* Tom McCown; *C:* Robert Elswit; *M:* Kenny Vance.

Heart of Glass

One of Herzog's stranger attempts at filmmaking. Famous for improvisation of both script and direction that drives his cast to jump ship, Herzog is responsible for films like *Aguirre, The Wrath of God* and the remake of *Nosferatu* (which had a stable script, by the way.) A small German town that lives on the profits of the famous Ruby glass it makes is thrown into hysteria when the keeper of the glass formula dies suddenly without letting anyone in on the secret. There's a foppish rich boy who relies on the town crier to guide him and who says things like, "The chaos of the stars makes my head ache." What seems like three hours into the film, the crier begins a half hour of strange prophecies including a bishop appointing a goat as pope. Then we're introduced to characters we've never seen before who "Set out pathetic and senseless in a boat that was way too small," and end the story. If you don't like art films, do not go near this. If you like to live in ignorance of what just transpired on the screen, this is your baby. The disc looks splendid and the film was given a German film award for cinematography. Even on the small screen of a TV you can appreciate the spectacular shots. The sound is decent. —CA *AKA:* Herz aus Glas.
Movie: ♫ ½ *DVD:* ♫♫♫ ½
All Day Ent. (cat #DV11566, UPC 013131-156690). Widescreen (1.66:1) anamorphic. Dolby Digital Mono. $29.90. Keepcase. *LANG:* German. *SUB:* English. *FEATURES:* 23 chapters • Commentary: director • Theatrical trailer • Production notes.
1974 93m/C GE Josef Bierbichler, Stefan Guttler, Clemens Scheitz, Volker Prechtel, Sonia Skiba; *D:* Werner Herzog; *W:* Werner Herzog, Herbert Achternbusch; *C:* Jorge Schmidt-Reitwein; *M:* Popul Vuh.

Heartbreakers

This is a good fun, funny, romantic comedy about a mother-daughter team who set up rich men to take a fall, and spill a lot of money on their way down, tripping over the duo's good looks. Maxine (Weaver) and Paige (Hewitt) are adorable as the cons who put the fun in dysfunction. Max marries the men and passes out on the wedding night, and then Paige swoops in and creates a divorce case for infidelity faster than you can say "sweet young thing." None of the men know the two women are related. Liotta is Dean, a man who just lost a fortune to Weaver, but still loves her even when he stumbles on the girls and their latest con and realizes he's been scammed (maybe even more). Lee is the soft-spoken, genuinely nice rich guy who makes it hard for Paige to keep her mind on business. He's also the man she wants to swindle to prove to Maxine that she can work on her own. Will these two women continue to fleece the rich to get more body-hugging clothing or is there a double wedding in their future? While there may be no real mystery here, between the beautiful scenery, both human and environmental, the great acting, and the marvelous script, it is fun to watch the obvious unfold. The DVD transfer is very inconsistent, with varying sharpness and a lot of film damage for a newer film. In fact, at times it appears that the film print was actually dirty and that a good cleaning would have resulted in a much better transfer. Where the disc excels is in its excellent handling of the colors, which are rich and fully saturated. Blacks are also very deep and inky with very little grain in the dimmer scenes. The 5.1 sound shows nothing special but is very consistent and features well-mixed ambience and a clear dialogue track. There are plenty of supplementals, but the "making of" documentary is kind of boring, as is Mirkin's commentary—mainly because of all the empty spaces. —CA/JO
Movie: ♫♫♫ *DVD:* ♫♫ ½
MGM Home Ent. (cat #1002357, UPC 027616865687). Widescreen (2.35:1) anamorphic. Dolby Digital 5.1 Surround. $26.98. Keepcase. *LANG:* English; French; Spanish. *SUB:* English; French; Spanish. *CAP:* English. *FEATURES:* 26 chapters • Making of *Heartbreakers* and "Laffs & Gaffes" featurettes • 22 deleted scenes with optional director's commentary • Commentary: Mirkin, Weaver, Hewitt • Theatrical trailer.
2001 (PG-13) 123m/C Sigourney Weaver, Jennifer Love Hewitt, Gene Hackman, Ray Liotta, Jason Lee, Anne Bancroft, Jeffrey Jones, Nora Dunn, Julio Mechoso, Ricky Jay; *D:* David Mirkin; *W:* Paul Guay, Robert Dunn, Steve Mazur; *C:* Dean Semler; *M:* John Debney.

Hearts in Atlantis

Eleven-year-old Bobby Garfield (Yelchin) is a child of a widowed mother (Davis) who struggles to make ends meet. One day, mysterious stranger Ted Brautigan (Hopkins) comes to live in the apartment above them. Soon enough, he becomes a father figure of sorts for Bobby, teaching him about the world around them and providing sound advice about life. Ted's also got a secret, and is on the run from some very ominous people. Hopkins gives (another) brilliant, subtle, understated performance that makes some of the film's more clichéd dialogue emotional and moving, and he works well with Yelchin. Technically, the film is also quite solid, with an enjoyable and not-too-sappy score, fine period detail (the film takes place in the early '60s), and beautiful cinematography. Somewhat episodic tale is based on only one ("Low Men in Yellow Coats") of the five interconnected stories that make up Stephen King's book and shoehorns in an explanation of the title that's neither present in nor relevant to the original story. Fans of the book will also find that while the core of this story is unchanged, Ted's secret (and the nature of his pursuers) is jettisoned in favor of conventional explanations. Overall, this is a slight film, but it's also bittersweet, well acted, and enjoyable. DVD captures the remarkably attractive cinematography beautifully. Sharpness and detail are excellent, as small details are clearly visible, even in some of the low-light sequences. A minimal layer of grain is visible during some of the darker sequences. The audio track is involving, but fairly subtle in its Surround uses. "Remembering *Hearts in Atlantis*" is a 30-minute interview/featurette with director Scott Hicks interviewing star Anthony Hopkins, who shares stories about working with his co-stars on the film, as well as his career. The commentary by Hicks is enjoyable but it does get a bit praise-heavy at times. He provides great insight about specific scenes; he breaks down a sequence into its elements and discusses how these pieces of the puzzle came together. It's a satisfying track that does a nice job covering all aspects of the production. —AB/DG
Movie: ♫♫ ½ *DVD:* ♫♫♫ ½
Warner (cat #22081, UPC 0853922081-28). Widescreen (2.35:1) anamorphic. Dolby Digital 5.1 Surround. $24.98. Snapper. *LANG:* English; French. *SUB:* English; French. *FEATURES:* Trailer • Cast/filmmaker profiles • Commentary: director Scott Hicks • Chapters • "Remembering Hearts in Atlantis": Hicks interviews Anthony Hopkins.
2001 (PG-13) 101m/C Anthony Hopkins, Anton Yelchin, Hope Davis, Mika Boorem, David Morse, Alan Tudyk, Tom Bower, Celia Weston, Adam LeFevre, Timothy Reifsnyder, Deirdre O'Connell, Will Rothhaar; *D:* Scott Hicks; *W:* William Goldman; *C:* Piotr Sobocinski; *M:* Mychael Danna.

Heathers [2 THX]

This edition improves on the first release (reviewed in *Book 1*) with beefed up 5.1 Surround stereo and a lively commentary track. Another unusual extra is the original ending, presented as pages from the screenplay. —MM
Movie: ♫♫♫ ½ *DVD:* ♫♫♫ ½
Anchor Bay (cat #DV11405, UPC 01313-1140590). Widescreen (1.85:1) anamorphic. Dolby Digital 5.1 Surround Stereo. $24.99. Keepcase. *LANG:* English. *CAP:* English. *FEATURES:* 29 chapters • "Swatch Dogs and Diet Coke Heads" featurette • Commentary: director Lehmann, producer Di Novi, writer Waters • Trailer • Screenplay excerpt.
1989 (R) 102m/C Winona Ryder, Christian Slater, Kim Walker, Shannen Doherty,

Lisanne Falk, Penelope Milford, Glenn Shadix, Lance Fenton, Patrick Laborteaux, Jeremy Applegate, Renee Estevez; *D:* Michael Lehmann; *W:* Daniel Waters; *C:* Francis Kenny; *M:* David Newman. *AWARDS:* Ind. Spirit '90: First Feature.

Hedwig and the Angry Inch

The "angry inch" of the title refers both to glam rocker Hedwig's (Mitchell) back-up band and to his/her botched sex change operation. Though the film is based on a popular stage play, it's definitely an acquired taste. For my money, the energy of *Rocky Horror* is lacking; the music is clichéd; the lyrics are pretentious; the script is thoughtlessly profane; and filmmakers would have us believe that sexual confusion has a larger meaning. DVD delivers the film's deliberate tackiness intact. Sound is excellent. Extras are numerous. —*MM*
Movie: 🎵🎵 *DVD:* 🎵🎵🎵 ½
New Line (cat #N5401, UPC 7940435401-27). Widescreen (1.85:1) anamorphic. Dolby Digital 5.1 Surround; DTS 5.1; Dolby Digital Stereo. $24.98. Snapper. *LANG:* English. *SUB:* English. *CAP:* English. *FEATURES:* Commentary • Deleted scenes • Select a song option • Trailer • Talent files • "Making of" featurette • DVD-ROM extras • 26 chapters.
2000 (R) 95m/C John Cameron Mitchell, Michael Pitt, Andrea Martin, Miriam Shor, Alberta Watson, Maurice Dean Wint, Rob Campbell, Stephen Trask, Theodore Liscinski, Michael Aranov; *D:* John Cameron Mitchell; *W:* John Cameron Mitchell; *C:* Frank DeMarco; *M:* Stephen Trask. *AWARDS: NOM:* Golden Globes '02: Actor—Mus./Comedy (Mitchell).

Heidi

The famous novel by Johanna Spyri is probably best known through this cinematic adaptation starring Shirley Temple. In the timeless story, Heidi is the poor little girl no one seems to want. The film opens with Heidi's aunt leaving her to live with her gruff grandfather, Adolph Kramer (Jean Hersholt). Kramer is known to the townspeople as a hermit and a "heathen," but he and Heidi soon strike up a deep relationship. Unfortunately, the scheming aunt returns, and sells Heidi to Sesemann (Sidney Blackmer) to be a companion to his invalid daughter, Klara (Marcia Mae Jones). Once in this household, Heidi tries to avoid the evil governess Fraulein Rottenmeier (Mary Nash) and finds a friend in the butler Andrews (Arthur Treacher). While Heidi is able to survive with the Sesemanns, she never stops thinking of a way to return to her beloved grandfather. The story offers many emotional highs and lows, which may be too strong for smaller children, but the rest of the family should enjoy it. Temple is especially good here, as she displays true acting ability, as opposed to getting by on her sheer cuteness. This DVD offers both the original

black-and-white version of *Heidi*, as well as a colorized version. The image here is surprisingly clear for a film of this advanced age. There are some noticeable defects in the source print, and at times, it is clear that frames are missing, but otherwise, this transfer is quite good. There is some minor grain in some shots and occasional flickering of the image, but this won't interfere with the viewing. The digital stereo track offers clear dialogue with little hissing, and the original mono track is free from defects as well. The original theatrical trailer is offered here, but the years haven't been as kind to it, as it is riddled with defects. —*ML*
Movie: 🎵🎵🎵 *DVD:* 🎵🎵
20th Century Fox (cat #2002971, UPC 02-4543029717). Full frame. Digital Stereo; Digital Mono. $19.98. Keepcase. *LANG:* English. *SUB:* English; Spanish. *CAP:* English. *FEATURES:* Theatrical trailer • 22 chapters.
1937 88m/B Shirley Temple, Jean Hersholt, Helen Westley, Arthur Treacher, Sidney Blackmer, Marcia Mae Jones, Mary Nash; *D:* Allan Dwan; *W:* Walter Ferris; *C:* Arthur C. Miller; *M:* Julien Josephson.

Heidi

Please see review for *Classic Family DVD Double Feature.*
Movie: 🎵🎵
1967 100m/C Maximilian Schell, Jennifer Edwards, Michael Redgrave, Jean Simmons; *D:* Delbert Mann; *W:* Earl Hamner; *M:* John Williams.

Heist

David Mamet has put together a satisfying, somewhat soulless caper flick. The script is tight; the plotting assured; the cast couldn't be better. Joe Moore (Hackman) is a professional thief who needs one more score to retire. Actually, he could retire on his most recent job, but Bergman (DeVito), the moneyman behind it, won't pay up unless Joe agrees to do "the Swiss thing," whatever that is. Mamet never reveals any more information than the viewer absolutely must know to follow what's happening. Joe's guys Bobby (Lindo) and Pinky (Jay) agree to go along. So does Joe's wife Fran (Pidgeon). Bergman sends his greasy nephew Jimmy Silk (Rockwell) along to keep tabs on Joe. Let the double-crosses begin. DVD image is a flawless re-creation of the theatrical release. It's actually a bit sharper, but then, at my local multiplex we're lucky to get the reels on the projector in the proper order. Sound is equally good. A commentary track with Mamet, Pidgeon (Mrs. Mamet), and Hackman might have been cool. —*MM*
Movie: 🎵🎵🎵 *DVD:* 🎵🎵🎵
Warner (cat #21321, UPC 85392132126). Widescreen (1.85:1) anamorphic. Dolby Digital Surround. $24.98. Snapper. *LANG:* English; French. *SUB:* English; Spanish. *FEATURES:* 28 chapters • Talent files • Trailer.

2001 (R) 107m/C Gene Hackman, Danny DeVito, Delroy Lindo, Sam Rockwell, Rebecca Pidgeon, Ricky Jay, Patti LuPone, Jim Frangione; *D:* David Mamet; *W:* David Mamet; *C:* Robert Elswit; *M:* Theodore Shapiro.

Hell Asylum

Indie horror company Tempe Video has released some impressive DVDs lately, but that winning streak ends abruptly here. This bargain-basement cheapie looks as if it were shot over a weekend by someone who lost a bet. The story (?!) is a bizarre mixture of the TV show *Fear Factor* and *House on Haunted Hill,* with a bit of *The Haunting* (1999) thrown in for good measure. A sleazy producer (Tim Muskatell) recruits five beauties (Debra Mayer, Tanya Dempsey, Sunny Lombardo, Stacey Scowley, and Olympia Fernandez) to spend the night in a haunted mental hospital. The person who survives the night will win $1 million. While this is all supposed to be an elaborate gag for the cameras, the building really is haunted...by a guy in a cloak. Wooden acting, predictable plot, and zero-budget special effects ruin any potential fun that the film may have offered. It's not even worth watching to make fun of it. *Hell Asylum* was shot on video. DVD image is sharp, but some video artifacting is evident. Also, the colors are a bit flat. The Dolby Digital 5.1 audio track sounds fine and is the highlight of this otherwise disappointing film. While *Hell Asylum* is a bummer, the extras on the disc, most notably the bloopers and the commentary, are actually entertaining. This DVD receives a rating of one bone for the inclusion of the short film "Mulva: Zombie Ass Kicker." Mulva is a teenage girl (?) who appears to be mentally challenged, is addicted to chocolate syrup, and is afraid of Halloween. On the night that she (?) decides to face her fear of trick or treating, the undead invade her neighborhood. This grade-Z video is actually funny and is unlike anything you've ever seen before. If only Mulva could have infiltrated the *Hell Asylum.* —*ML*
Movie: 🎵 *DVD:* 🎵🎵 ½
Full Moon Pictures (cat #TD-1104, UPC 822928110490). Widescreen (1.85:1) anamorphic. Dolby Digital 5.1. $19.95. Keepcase. *LANG:* English. *FEATURES:* Commentary • Director's production diary • Cast & crew interviews • Bloopers & outtakes reel • Still gallery • Trailer • Bonus trailer • Bonus film.
2001 72m/C Tanya Dempsey, Stacey Scowley, Debra Mayer, Olympia Fernandez, Sunny Lombardo; *D:* Danny Draven.

Hell Comes to Frogtown

In a post-nuclear holocaust land run by giant frogs, a renegade who is one of the few non-sterile men left on Earth must rescue some fertile women and impregnate them. Sci-fi spoof is extremely low-budget, poorly scripted and acted, but fun

nonetheless. Stars "Rowdy" Roddy Piper of wrestling fame, who actually wears a bomb as a codpiece. Another fine transfer of a below B-grade movie from Anchor Bay. The image is sharp with vivid colors and makes the film look far better than you'd ever expect. Blacks are deep and inky, never graying or graining. The stereo soundtrack sounds more like mono but is fairly strong with super-clear dialogue. The most disappointing aspect of the disc is the commentary which, though loaded with plenty of info, is not nearly as much fun as a commentary about a giant frog movie should be. —JO/MO
Movie: ♪♪ **DVD:** ♪♪♪
Anchor Bay (cat #DV11390, UPC 0131311-39099). Widescreen (1.85:1) anamorphic. Dolby Digital 2.0 Stereo. $24.98. Keepcase. *LANG:* English. *CAP:* English. *FEATURES:* 22 chapters • Commentary: director Donald G. Jackson, writer Randall Frakes • Theatrical trailer.
1988 (R) 88m/C Roddy Piper, Sandahl Bergman, Rory Calhoun, Donald G. Jackson, Cec Verrell; *D:* Robert J. Kizer, Donald G. Jackson; *W:* Randall Frakes; *C:* Donald G. Jackson.

Hell of the Living Dead

Following the success in Italy of *Dawn of the Dead* and *Zombie*, director Bruno Mattei attempted to make a film which combined elements of the two hits. Unfortunately, he also added several reels of stock footage to the mix, making *Hell of the Living Dead* (AKA *Night of the Zombies*) a laughably bad film. When a chemical leak turns the native population in New Guinea into shuffling zombies, a SWAT team is dispensed to help...or are they on vacation?...anyway, once they arrive in the tropical paradise, the blue-suited SWAT guys meet a reporter, Lia (Margit Evelyn Newton) and her cameraman, Max (Selan Karay), and they all make their way to the chemical plant to attempt to solve the problem. *Hell of the Living Dead* is about 30 minutes too long and much of that running time is made up of the aforementioned stock footage, showing wild animals and native rituals. The film's few zombie attack scenes are fun, but the special effects are laughable. Worst of all are the bloopers, such as when a SWAT member's knife slowly works its way out of his boot during a shot. Italian zombie film completists should certainly seek this one out, as they may find it charming. All others should simply watch a documentary on New Guinea. Anchor Bay has attempted to polish some quality into this DVD release. The image quality varies from shot to shot, as the real movie and the stock footage look totally different. The movie looks fine, although there is some grain and some noticeable defects from the source print. Also, the image is washed-out and the colors (save for those blue jumpsuits) are very dull. The mono soundtrack is serviceable, as it offers clear dialogue and no hissing. The DVD contains an interview with director Mattei, wherein he admits that *Hell of the Living Dead* isn't a good movie. Amen, brother. —ML *AKA:* Apocalipsis Canibal; Night of the Zombies; Zombie Creeping Flesh.
Movie: ♪ **DVD:** ♪♪ ½
Anchor Bay (cat #DV11750, UPC 0131311-75097). Widescreen (1.85:1) anamorphic. Dolby Digital Mono. $19.98. Keepcase. *LANG:* English. *FEATURES:* Director interview • Theatrical trailer • Still gallery • 24 chapters.
1983 103m/C *IT SP* Margit Evelyn Newton, Frank Garfield, Selan Karay; *D:* Bruno Mattei; *W:* J.M. Cunilles, Claudio Fragasso; *C:* John Cabrera.

Hell up in Harlem

Sequel to *Black Godfather* finds Tommy Gibbs (Williamson) surviving the attack at the end of the first film and going on to take on crooked cops and the mob—in short, the usual suspects. On his commentary track, director Larry Cohen is enthusiastic about this seminal "blaxploitation" picture, and he should be. DVD delivers a very nice re-creation of an unpolished "B"-movie image. Mono sound is true to the period. Right on! —MM
Movie: ♪♪♪ **DVD:** ♪♪♪
MGM Home Ent. (cat #1002583, UPC 027616867841). Widescreen (1.85:1) anamorphic. Dolby Digital Mono. $14.98. Keepcase. *LANG:* English; French. *SUB:* French; Spanish. *CAP:* English. *FEATURES:* Trailers • 16 chapters • Commentary.
1973 (R) 98m/C Fred Williamson, Julius W. Harris, Margaret Avery, Gerald Gordon, Gloria Hendry; *D:* Larry Cohen; *W:* Larry Cohen; *C:* Fenton Hamilton; *M:* Fonce Mizell, Freddie Perren.

Hellbound: Hellraiser 2 [2 THX]

Anchor Bay corrects the errors in the first release (reviewed in *Book 1*) with an anamorphic widescreen transfer and a 5.1 Surround remix. They've also added a commentary track. The film looks and sounds great, but it's still a so-so sequel. —MM *AKA:* Hellraiser 2.
Movie: ♪♪ **DVD:** ♪♪♪
Anchor Bay (cat #DV11233, UPC 01313-1123395). Widescreen (1.85:1) anamorphic. Dolby Digital 5.1 Surround Stereo. $29.98. Keepcase. *LANG:* English. *CAP:* English. *FEATURES:* 30 chapters • Commentary: Ashley Laurence, Tony Randel, Peter Atkins • "Lost in the Labyrinth" featurette • Trailer • Still gallery.
1988 (R) 96m/C *GB* Ashley Laurence, Clare Higgins, Kenneth Cranham, Imogen Boorman, William Hope, Oliver Smith, Sean Chapman, Doug Bradley; *D:* Tony Randel; *W:* Peter Atkins; *C:* Robin Vidgeon; *M:* Christopher Young.

Helltown

Please see review of *Great John Wayne Movies*. *AKA:* Born to the West.
Movie: ♪ ½
1938 60m/B John Wayne, Marsha Hunt, Johnny Mack Brown, Monte Blue, Syd Saylor, John D. Patterson; *D:* Charles T. Barton; *W:* Stuart Anthony, Robert Yost; *C:* Devereaux Jennings.

Helmut Newton: Frames from the Edge

Maben's documentary about German photographer Helmut Newton only skims the surface really, but some would say the same of Newton's vampy pictures. For his part, Newton insists he's not a voyeur. He's completely unapologetic about liking to photograph beautiful naked women in high heels. The most enlightening interview is with British actress Charlotte Rampling. Documentary looks like it was shot on 16mm and badly transferred. Picture is soft focus and the sound is muddy. —LA
Movie: ♪♪ **DVD:** ♪ ½
Image Ent. (cat #ID9270RADVD, UPC 014-381927023). Full frame. Dolby Digital Mono. $24.98. Keepcase. *LANG:* English. *SUB:* English. *FEATURES:* 14 chapters.
1988 100m/C *D:* Adrian Maben; *Nar:* Adrian Maben.

Helter Skelter Murders

Independently made version of the Manson family killings is one of the most amateurish depictions of real events ever committed to film. Sequences were filmed at the Spahn ranch. Manson's own recordings of his songs "Mechanical Man" and "Garbage Dump" are included though they're barely audible through the constant and loud static hiss and the frequent pops. Heavy artifacts and bad aliasing are common. Almost none of the dialogue is synched with mouth movement. Overall, the muddy black and white is no better than an old VHS tape. —MM
Movie: woof **DVD:** ♪ ½
Image Ent. (cat #ID0591CODVD, UPC 014-381059120). Full frame. Dolby Digital Mono. $24.98. Keepcase. *LANG:* English. *FEATURES:* 14 chapters.
1971 (R) 83m/B Brian Klinknett, Debbie Duff, Phyllis Estes; *D:* Frank Howard; *W:* J.J. Wilkie, Duke Howze; *C:* Frank Howard.

Hermes— Winds of Love

Atmospheric anime adaptation retools the Minotaur and the Labyrinth myth to encompass a battle royal between good Prince Hermes and evil King Minos for control of Greece. First half suffers from meandering exposition but makes up for it in the second half with turbo-charged battle scenes and a killer climax in the bowels of Hades. Fans of anime may be disappointed in the restrained graphic imagery but the mythological setting makes for a nice change of pace from the *Blade Runner*-esque environs made famous by *Akira*. The transfer looks sharp with brilliant colors, but frequently buckles under excessive edge-enhancement. The discrete 5.1 track surpasses the matrixed Surround audio with numerous directional sound

effects. As an extra, the disc includes a deleted scene, listed on the cover as "outtake." Could anime bloopers during the end credits be far behind? —*EP*
Movie: 🐾🐾 ½ **DVD:** 🐾🐾 ½
Image Ent. (cat #ID1015SIDVD, UPC 0114-381101522). Widescreen (1.85:1) letterboxed. Dolby Digital 5.1; Dolby Digital Stereo Surround. $24.98. Keepcase. *LANG:* Japanese. *SUB:* English. *FEATURES:* 20 chapters • Theatrical trailers • Isolated music & effects track • Deleted scene.
1997 114m/C *JP D:* Tesuo Imazawa; *M:* Yuichi Mizusawa; *V:* Taketo Koyasu, Miki Ito, Koji Nabara, Katsuosuke Hori.

Hero and the Terror
Danny O'Brien (Norris) was labeled "Hero" by the local press when he captured serial killer Simon Moon (Jack O'Halloran) AKA "the Terror." Danny caught Moon by accident and as a result is as uncomfortable about being called "Hero" as Chuck Norris should be about being called an actor. Norris is a performer, posturing with line readings and posing for oddly lit camera shots. This film underutilizes his fighting skills, and overemphasizes bad writing and clichéd line deliveries. Simon Moon escapes, providing Danny with a chance to be a real hero by catching him again, this time with a fight. Danny leaves his girlfriend's bedside in the maternity ward where she has just delivered their baby girl. Why? He has to. It's what a hero does. Heroes also ignore their bosses when told to wait for back-up. They know where killers hide and they won't share that information, lest in bring those who want to help into danger. Of course in the end, Danny is a real hero, not just because he kills Simon Moon, but also because he marries the girl. The weak script relies on the music to tell us when to be nervous, sad, pensive, or happy and the transfer to DVD reveals a cheap print and mediocre sound. —*JAS*
Movie: 🐾 ½ **DVD:** 🐾🐾🐾
MGM Home Ent. (cat #1003510, UPC 027-616876607). Widescreen (1.85:1) anamorphic. Dolby Digital Surround. $14.95. Keepcase. *LANG:* English. *SUB:* English; Spanish; French. *CAP:* English. *FEATURES:* 16 chapters • Original trailer.
1988 (R) 96m/C Chuck Norris, Brynn Thayer, Steve James, Jack O'Halloran, Ron O'Neal, Billy Drago; *D:* William Tannen; *W:* Michael Blodgett; *C:* Eric Van Haren Noman; *M:* David Michael Frank.

Heroes of Iwo Jima
A&E channel documentary looks at the controversies that have surrounded Joe Rosenthal's famous photograph of the Marines raising the flag on Mt. Suribachi. Actually, there are two pictures and that's part of the story. Gene Hackman narrates. The producers combine color and black-and-white archival footage—almost all of it in excellent shape—with contemporary interviews. Image and sound are excel-

lent, both a cut above conventional broadcast quality. —*MM*
Movie: 🐾🐾🐾 **DVD:** 🐾🐾🐾
A&E (cat #AAE70336, UPC 7339617033-68). Full frame. Dolby Digital Stereo. $19.98. Keepcase. *LANG:* English. *FEATURES:* Time line of the battle • 12 chapters.
2001 100m/C *D:* Arnold Shapiro; *W:* Arnold Shapiro, Lauren Lexton; *M:* John Thomas, Marie Maxwell; *Nar:* Gene Hackman.

Hidden Agenda
Before Frances McDormand won an Oscar for *Fargo*, she appeared in this intriguing political thriller as Ingrid Jessner. Ingrid and her fiancé Paul Sullivan (Dourif) are in Belfast, Northern Ireland, investigating allegations of cruel and unusual punishment by the local police force. After they go public and report their findings in a news conference, Paul is murdered. The authorities tell Ingrid that Paul was helping the Irish Republican Army and close the case. With the aid of a skeptical British policeman Kerrigan (Cox), Ingrid begins to investigate the murder on her own and discovers a web of lies and deceit. The film gets too talky and bogged down in politics for its own good, but still manages to be suspenseful. Director Ken Loach has made a career of tackling controversial political topics and he doesn't shy away from the violence and corruption of Northern Ireland here. McDormand is excellent as the frightened and frustrated Ingrid, and Cox is very good in his role as well. DVD image is mostly sharp, but also blurry and hazy at times. There is some grain, as well as some defects from the source print, in the form of white dots. With the Surround audio, we get clear dialogue with no distortion, but there is a mild hissing on the track. —*ML*
Movie: 🐾🐾 ½ **DVD:** 🐾🐾
MGM Home Ent. (cat #1003335, UPC 027-616874849). Widescreen (1.85:1) anamorphic; full frame. Dolby Digital Surround. $19.98. Keepcase. *LANG:* English. *SUB:* English; French; Spanish. *CAP:* English. *FEATURES:* Theatrical trailer • 16 chapters.
1990 (R) 108m/C Frances McDormand, Brian Cox, Brad Dourif, Mai Zetterling, John Benfield, Des McAleer, Jim Norton, Maurice Roeves; *D:* Ken Loach; *W:* Jim Allen; *C:* Clive Tickner; *M:* Stewart Copeland. AWARDS: Cannes '90: Special Jury Prize.

The Hidden Fortress
Sniveling failures at soldiery, peasants Tahei (Minoru Chiaki) and Matakishi (Kamatari Fujiwara) try to stumble back home, constantly blaming one another for their ill fortune. Captured by the victorious Yamana clan, and forced with hundreds of other slave laborers to search a pit for missing pieces of gold, they escape when the mine is attacked, only later to find some of the missing gold hidden in sticks in a mountain spring. That's when they meet the formidable General Rokurota Makabe

(Toshiro Mifune), a resourceful warrior who's in a tight spot. Stuck behind Yamana lines, Makabe has to find a way to smuggle both the gold, and the Princess Yukuhime (Misa Uehara) back into their own kingdom of Hayakawa. Much to their chagrin, the lowly Tahei and Matakishi find themselves aiding in a bold adventure. Criterion again makes DVD better than going to the movies. Their disc restores the film to its full 139 minutes, and presents it in full Tohoscope widescreen, anamorphically enhanced. Better yet, the original Perspecta-Sound multitrack audio configuration has been restored to the disc. This '50s phenomenon spread a mono track to three speakers in a fairly sophisticated faux-stereo using selected frequencies. (Or so I've been explained.) The subtitles are newly translated and reportedly an improvement over the originals, which didn't keep the various names and warring provinces straight. This time, the principals say things like, "This sucks!" and "Whatever," contemporary jargon that will surely be an embarrassment later when it dates. Also included is a trailer, and a video testimonial from George Lucas. Obviously Criterion could not resist, but even with Mr. Lucas's later involvement with Kurosawa, his insights are not all that dazzling. —*GE* *AKA:* Kakushi Toride No San Akunin; Three Rascals in the Hidden Fortress; Three Bad Men in the Hidden Fortress.
Movie: 🐾🐾🐾🐾 **DVD:** 🐾🐾🐾🐾
Criterion (UPC 37429135129). Widescreen (2.35:1) anamorphic. $29.98. Keepcase. *LANG:* Japanese. *SUB:* English. *FEATURES:* George Lucas appraisal • Trailer.
1958 139m/B *JP* Toshiro Mifune, Misa Uehara, Kamatari (Keita) Fujiwara, Susumu Fujita, Eiko Miyoshi, Takashi Shimura, Kichijiro Ueda, Koji Mitsui, Minoru Chiaki, Toshiko Higuchi, Shiten Ohashi; *D:* Akira Kurosawa; *W:* Akira Kurosawa, Shinobu Hashimoto, Ryuzo Kikushima, Hideo Oguni; *C:* Kazuo Yamazaki; *M:* Masaru Sato. AWARDS: Berlin Intl. Film Fest. '59: Director (Kurosawa).

Hidden Hollywood: Treasures from the 20th Century Fox Vaults
Compilation (in the style of the *That's Entertainment!* features) examines the history of 20th Century Fox by showcasing never-before-seen musical numbers and comedy routines cut from the studio's films. An absolutely fascinating glimpse at some charming, oddball, and interesting sequences, all of which are presented in their entirety. Tap-dancing star Bill "Bojangles" Robinson's two cut routines from *Café Metropole* are interesting, if not very impressive, and most of the Betty Grable and Alice Faye clips are charming. A bizarre Bert Lahr song must be seen to be believed. The highlight of the program is a long, funny sequence cut from *We're Not Married* featuring Walter Brennan. Joan Collins makes a fine, appropriate host (a test sequence of hers finishes off the pro-

gram) and the program is handsomely shot and well produced. Film preservationists Bob Gitt and Anthony Slide are also featured in interesting interview segments where they offer insights into the nature of the clips and film restoration in general. This AMC television special is given an excellent presentation on disc. The video originated wraparound segments are razor sharp and colorful and nearly all of the film clips are in pristine condition. There's some occasional shimmer in the video segments, but it's a minor quibble. Sound is excellent. Highly recommended. —DG

Movie: ♪♪♪ ½ **DVD:** ♪♪♪♪ ½
Image Ent. (cat #ID0962FSDVD, UPC 014-381096224). Full frame. Dolby Digital Surround. $24.99. Keepcase. *LANG:* English. *FEATURES:* 16 chapters.
1999 91m/C Joan Collins, Betty Grable, Shirley Temple, Al Jolson, Bert Lahr, Don Ameche, Alice Faye; **D:** Shelley Lyons; **W:** Brian Anthony, Kevin Burns, Michael Matessino.

Hidden Hollywood 2: More Treasures from the 20th Century Fox Vaults

This return trip to 20th Century Fox showcases a plethora of curiosities from the cutting-room floor. Host Joan Collins lends only her voice this time and there's a stronger focus on nitrate film decay and restoration. Most of the musical segments were cut for obvious reasons, but from a film historian's perspective, they're absolutely fascinating. Deleted musical numbers featuring lunky Victor Mature certainly fall into the "what were they thinking?" category. Most interesting are the brief "flash-frame" sequences shown before and after a take has begun. These priceless, candid moments reveal the actors out of character as they wind themselves up for a take, or reacting afterwards to a fumbled line or misstep. A long, complete W.C. Fields sequence that was cut from *Tales of Manhattan* is a comedic highlight. Maddeningly, while an existing tantalizing alternate cut of *My Darling Clementine* is discussed, no clips are shown. The quality of the film and video segments is terrific, with the exception of the W.C. Fields sequence which (presumably because of print damage) is pristine but tends to jitter. Sound is cleanly recorded and noise-free. —DG

Movie: ♪♪♪♪ **DVD:** ♪♪♪
Image Ent. (cat #ID0963FSDVD, UPC 014-381096323). Full frame. Dolby Digital Surround. $24.99. Keepcase. *LANG:* English. *FEATURES:* 17 chapters.
1999 91m/C Joan Collins, Betty Grable, W.C. Fields, Carmen Miranda, Ginger Rogers, Alice Faye; **D:** Shelley Lyons; **W:** Brian Anthony, Kevin Burns, Michael Matessino.

Hiding Out

A young stockbroker testifies against the Mafia and must find a place to hide to avoid being killed. He winds up at his cousin's high school in Delaware, but can he really go through all those teenage troubles again? Despite some funny moments, this film can never overcome the fact that it's a strange hybrid between teen-comedy and an "R"-rated action film. Cryer is very good in the lead role, and Keith Coogan has some great moments as his confused and frustrated cousin. While most viewers remember the "Maxwell House" angle, the rest of the film is ultimately forgettable. This DVD provides a clear transfer, which is sharp, but slightly dark at times. Also, there are some noticeable problems caused by edge-enhancement. The 2.0 Surround audio track provides clear dialogue, and there is some occasional action from the rear speakers. —ML

Movie: ♪♪ **DVD:** ♪♪ ½
Anchor Bay (cat #DV11402, UPC 0131311-40293). Widescreen (1.85:1) anamorphic. Dolby Surround. $9.98. Keepcase. *LANG:* English. *CAP:* English. *FEATURES:* Theatrical trailer.
1987 (PG-13) 99m/C Jon Cryer, Keith Coogan, Gretchen Cryer, Annabeth Gish, Tim Quill; **D:** Bob Giraldi; **W:** Jeff Rothberg, Joe Menosky; **C:** Daniel Pearl; **M:** Anne Dudley.

High Heels and Low Lifes

London nurse Shannon (Driver) and actress Frances (McCormack) innocently stumble across evidence of a $10 million bank heist and not-so-innocently decide to blackmail the thieves for a cut of the loot. So begins a comic caper movie, not unlike *Beautiful Creatures* (please see review), but lighter in tone. Director Mel Smith is also responsible for *The Tall Guy*. Like that cult fave, it will have to find an audience on home video since it has received scant theatrical distribution. Widescreen image is as sharp and colorful as a major Hollywood production. Sound is equally strong. This one's a lightweight sleeper that's worth seeking out. —MM

Movie: ♪♪♪ **DVD:** ♪♪♪
Buena Vista Home Ent. (cat #24405, UPC 786936080230). Widescreen (1.85:1) anamorphic. Dolby Digital 5.1 Surround. $29.98. Keepcase. *LANG:* English. *SUB:* French; Spanish. *CAP:* English. *FEATURES:* "Making of" featurette ▪ Commentary: Smith, Fuller ▪ Montage set to music.
2001 (R) 85m/C *US GB* Minnie Driver, Mary McCormack, Kevin McNally, Mark Williams, Danny Dyer, Michael Gambon, Kevin Eldon, Len Collin, Darren Boyd, Julian Wadham; **D:** Mel Smith; **W:** Kim Fuller; **C:** Steven Chivers; **M:** Charlie Mole.

High Noon

Generally faithful but unnecessary TV remake of the famous 1952 western is an exceptionally handsome production. Stoic marshal Will Kane (Skerritt) has just married Quaker Amy (Thompson) and is about to hand in his badge when he learns that bad guy Frank Miller (Madsen) will be coming to town on the noon train with revenge on his mind. DVD offers a superb reproduction of a very good widescreen image. The commentary track by the director of photography and a producer sticks to the point and is only slightly defensive about the whole remake business. Sound is completely adequate to the task at hand. —MM

Movie: ♪♪ ½ **DVD:** ♪♪♪
Artisan Ent. (cat #11860, UPC 01223611-8602). Widescreen (1.85:1) anamorphic. Dolby Digital 5.1 Surround; Dolby Digital Surround. $24.98. Keepcase. *LANG:* English; Spanish. *SUB:* English; Spanish. *CAP:* English. *FEATURES:* 24 chapters ▪ Trailers ▪ Interviews ▪ Behind-the-scenes feature ▪ Commentary: David A. Rosemont, Robert McLachlan.
2000 (PG-13) 93m/C Tom Skerritt, Susanna Thompson, Reed Edward Diamond, Maria Conchita Alonso, Michael Madsen, Dennis Weaver, August Schellenberg; **D:** Rod Hardy; **W:** Carl Foreman, T.S. Cook; **C:** Robert McLachlan; **M:** Allyn Ferguson.

High Risk

Goofy crime flick posits four Americans (Brolin, Little, Davison, Vennera) who tell wives and girlfriends they're going fishing for the weekend when actually they're going to fly down to Colombia and knock over a drug deal. Coburn is the expatriate kingpin they've targeted. DVD image is nothing less than atrocious. It might have been copied from a well-worn VHS tape and is no better than broadcast. Title is available on the *Classic Heist Films* disc. —MM

Movie: ♪♪ **DVD:** ♪ ½
BFS Video (cat #30295-D, UPC 06680530-2954). Full frame. $9.98. Keepcase. *LANG:* English. *FEATURES:* 6 chapters ▪ Talent files.
1981 (R) 94m/C James Brolin, Anthony Quinn, Lindsay Wagner, James Coburn, Ernest Borgnine, Bruce Davison, Cleavon Little, Chick Vennera; **D:** Stewart Raffill; **W:** Stewart Raffill; **C:** Alex Phillips Jr.; **M:** Mark Snow.

High Spirits

Peter Plunkett (O'Toole) is about to lose the family castle to an American investor. He recruits his staff to play ghosts in an effort to attract travelers seeking the best "haunts" in Ireland. The staff does such a lousy job of being ghouls that the real ghosts come forward in disgust. Mary Plunkett (Hannah) and her murderous fiancé, Martin Brogan (Neeson), continue the fight they started over 200 years ago on their wedding eve when he killed her. Jack (Guttenberg) and Sharon (D'Angelo) from America are also a bickering couple, but they're alive. Jack falls for Mary, Martin is attracted to Sharon, and hilarity ensues. Brother Tony (Gallagher) and Miranda (Tilley) are thrown into the mix for a little more forbidden love. Brother Tony is close to taking his vows of celibacy and Miranda sees him as a delectable challenge. Writer/director Neil Jordan *(The Crying Game)* puts together an entertaining diversion that has just slightly sharper teeth than the Disney live-action comedies of the '70s. The sound is nothing to shout about and the picture quality is not a lot better than VHS. —*JAS*

Movie: 🦴🦴 **DVD:** 🦴🦴🦴
MGM Home Ent. (cat #1003511, UPC 027616876614). Full frame; widescreen (1.85:1) anamorphic. Dolby Surround. $14.95. Keepcase. *LANG:* English. *SUB:* English; Spanish; French. *CAP:* English. *FEATURES:* 16 chapters • Original trailer.
1988 (PG-13) 99m/C Daryl Hannah, Peter O'Toole, Steve Guttenberg, Beverly D'Angelo, Liam Neeson, Martin Ferrero, Peter Gallagher, Jennifer Tilly; **D:** Neil Jordan; **W:** Neil Jordan; **C:** Alex Thompson; **M:** George Fenton.

Higher Learning

Malik (Epps), attending a multi-racial college on an athletic scholarship, encounters racism, motivational inertia, and love. It's an entertaining, frequently funny, and insightful drama for the majority of the running time. Unfortunately, the movie goes awry with a wrong-headed, cartoonish white supremacist subplot involving Remy (Rapaport). Singleton sets up several involving dramatic ideas but instead of developing or resolving the conflicts, he clumsily resorts to a campus shootout to end his film. A bi-sexual subplot is a bit muddled, as well. It's certainly watchable, but could have been much better. The disc features a bright, sharp image transfer that seems a bit grainy, with some digital edging and noise. The Surround track is terrific, giving greatest depth to the music track. Dialogue is always clear and sound effects are frequently directional. Singleton's commentary is reflective and biographical, but also provides interesting anecdotes and production info. —*DG*

Movie: 🦴🦴🦴 **DVD:** 🦴🦴🦴
Columbia Tristar (cat #06768, UPC 043-396067684). Widescreen (1.85:1) anamorphic. Dolby Digital 5.1 Surround; Dolby Digital Surround. $19.95. Keepcase. *LANG:* English; French; Spanish; Portuguese. *SUB:* English; French; Spanish; Portuguese; Chinese; Korean; Thai. *CAP:* English. *FEATURES:* 28 chapters • Commentary: director John Singleton • Trailers • Filmographies.
1994 (R) 127m/C Omar Epps, Kristy Swanson, Michael Rapaport, Laurence "Larry" Fishburne, Jennifer Connelly, Ice Cube, Tyra Banks, Jason Wiles, Cole Hauser, Regina King; **D:** John Singleton; **W:** John Singleton; **C:** Peter Collister.

Highlander [Anchor Bay]

A race of immortals must fight each other until only one is left, for reasons the mere humans watching this film are not privy to. The paper-thin plot follows Connor (Lambert) from his kilt-wearing days as a Scottish warrior to present-day New York as he prepares for the final battle. While receiving little notice at the boxoffice, the film has gradually turned into a cult classic, spawning three sequels to date and a TV series. While much of it is still enjoyable, a few cheap shots spoil some of the fun. Anchor Bay's edition is a deluxe box set, with a bonus disc containing three songs from Queen's soundtrack. The transfer is sometimes astonishing and sometimes heavy on the grain, with occasional inconsistent colors. The soundtrack handles the music and special effects better than the dialogue, which never settles into a consistent volume. —*BG*

Movie: 🦴🦴 ½ **DVD:** 🦴🦴🦴
All Day Ent. (cat #DV11723, UPC 013131-172393). Widescreen (1.85:1) anamorphic. Dolby Surround EX; DTS 6.1. $39.98. Keepcase, metal sleeve. *LANG:* English; French. *CAP:* English. *FEATURES:* 28 chapters • Commentary: Russell Mulcahy, producers Davis, Panzer • Talent bios • Poster and still gallery • Queen music videos.
1986 (R) 110m/C Christopher Lambert, Sean Connery, Clancy Brown, Roxanne Hart, Beatie Edney, Alan North, Sheila Gish, Jon Polito; **D:** Russell Mulcahy; **W:** Gregory Widen, Peter Bellwood, Larry Ferguson; **C:** Gerry Fisher; **M:** Michael Kamen.

Highway

Gen-X slacker Jack (Leto) is caught with a mobster's woman and decides to skip town before his feet end up broken. He takes his buddy, Pilot (Gyllenhaal), on the road to Seattle and falls in love with the proverbial "hooker with the heart of gold" (Blair) on the way. The film tries to capture the spirit of the mid-'90s grunge era but doesn't nail enough of the details to be convincing. The anamorphic picture is quite good, boasting sharp colors and good detail. The soundtrack seems a bit bass-heavy, making it less vibrant than it should be. —*BG*

Movie: 🦴 ½ **DVD:** 🦴🦴🦴
New Line (cat #N5477, UPC 7940435477-20). Widescreen (2.35:1) anamorphic; full frame. Dolby Digital 5.1; Stereo Surround Sound. $24.98. Snapper. *LANG:* English. *SUB:* English. *CAP:* English. *FEATURES:* 20 chapters.
2001 (R) 97m/C Jared Leto, Selma Blair, Jake Gyllenhaal, Kimberley Kates, Jeremy Piven, John C. McGinley; **D:** James Cox; **W:** Scott Rosenberg; **C:** Mauro Fiore.

Himalaya

The age-old struggle of generations deciding between tradition and progress plays itself out once more against the spectacular scenery of the Tibetan mountains. Although the story is nothing new, the film gives a detailed look into a traditional lifestyle that is fast dying out, using non-professional actors, location shooting, and not an ounce of special effects. A bit of the film's grandeur is lost on the small screen, but it is still breathtaking. The sharp colors and distinct backgrounds work to convey the harsh environment that is so important. The subtitles are burned into the picture, rather than being placed outside in the large black bars offered by the aspect ratio. —*BG* **AKA:** Himalaya—L'Enfance d'un Chef; Himalaya—The Youth of a Chief; Caravan.

Movie: 🦴🦴🦴 ½ **DVD:** 🦴🦴🦴
Kino on Video (cat #K235, UPC 73832902-3522). Widescreen (2.35:1) anamorphic. Dolby 5.1. $29.95. Keepcase. *LANG:* Tibetan. *SUB:* English. *FEATURES:* 16 chapters • Commentary • "Making of" documentary • Electronic press kit • Trailer.
1999 104m/C *FR SI GB* Thinlen Lhondup, Karma Wangiel, Lhakpa Tsamchoe; **D:** Eric Valli; **W:** Eric Valli, Olivier Dazat; **C:** Eric Guichard, Jean-Paul Meurisse; **M:** Bruno Coulais. *AWARDS: NOM:* Oscars '99: Foreign Film.

The Hippie Revolt

Please see review for *Mondo Mod / The Hippie Revolt.*
1967 75m/C D: Edgar Beatty; **C:** Laszlo Kovacs, Vilmos Zsigmond.

His Majesty, the Scarecrow of Oz

An early cinematic attempt to bring L. Frank Baum's imaginative Oz series to the screen, this film has the benefit of being written and directed by Baum himself. A rough adaptation of *The Scarecrow of Oz*, the film tells of evil King Krewl and his attempt to thwart the love of Princess Gloria and gardener Pon. Dorothy, the Scarecrow (who looks like another creepy cinematic clown), the Tin Man, the Cowardly Lion and others all try to help save Gloria and defeat witch Mombi and Krewl. As the grammar of film storytelling was still being developed during this era, the film evinces the pacing difficulties and clumsiness typical of the time. Actors approach the camera and enact scenes in front of it in fairly static shots, characters frustratingly chatter reams of dialogue which is never communicated in the intertitles, and the focus is on a series of short visual vignettes, rather than a tight, coherent story. Much of it feels like a home movie filming of a costume garden party in a loony bin. There are enough enjoyable instances of early cinematic trickery to make this entertaining. The witches taking off on broomsticks, Mombi turned into a can of "preserved sandwiches," the Scarecrow's adventure under the sea, the Scarecrow decapitating Mombi, and other scenes all have an undeniable primitive charm. The disc features a print that's surprisingly clean for its vintage. There are a few splices and sections of damage, but overall it's pleasing, if a bit tightly framed on top. The image is a bit pasty and features very low contrasts, but all the details are readable and there's very little digital noise. The disc features a passable score, but the intertitles are read aloud which is unnecessary. Sound is adequate.

The disc uses cover artwork from the same company's awful release of *Wizard of Oz.* (Please see review.) —DG
Movie: 🎬🎬 **DVD:** 🎬🎬
Brentwood (cat #44070-9, UPC 78736440-7095). Full frame. Mono. $4.99. Keepcase. *LANG:* English. *FEATURES:* "Little Rascals: Came the Brawn" short • Trivia game • DVD dictionary • 6 chapters.
1914 59m/B Violet MacMillan, Frank Moore, Pierre Couderc, Raymond Russell; *D:* L. Frank Baum; *W:* L. Frank Baum; *C:* James A. Crosby.

Hit Lady

Please see review for *Great Mafia Movies 2.*
Movie: 🎬🎬
1974 74m/C Yvette Mimieux, Dack Rambo, Clu Gulager, Keenan Wynn; *D:* Tracy Keenan Wynn; *W:* Yvette Mimieux; *M:* George Aliceson Tipton.

Hitch Hike to Hell / Kidnapped Coed

Unfortunately, neither of these two refugees from the drive-in delivers the tawdry pleasures promised in the titles. In *Hitch Hike to Hell,* psycho mama's boy Howard (Gribbin) drives around in a laundry delivery van and picks up young women to kill. He's still got issues with his sister who ran away from home. *Kidnapped Coed* might have served as the model for the strange "medieval" section of *Pulp Fiction.* Eddie Mattlock (Canon on the screen, Cannon on the box) kidnaps heiress Sandra Morley (Rivers). He makes the first ransom demand from a telephone booth that's inexplicably in the middle of a field. The two spend the rest of the film engaged in incredibly bizarre complications. The features are not up to the standards of Something Weird's best vintage exploitation. On disc, signs of wear are minimal and colors are bright, but the films were made on such low budgets that those same colors are harsh, and sound is muffled. —MM
Movie: 🎬 **DVD:** 🎬🎬 ½
Image Ent. (cat #ID1176SWDVD, UPC 014-381117622). Full frame. Dolby Digital Mono. $24.98. Keepcase. *LANG:* English. *FEATURES:* 3 psycho-on-the-loose short subjects • Trailers • Gallery of exploitation art • Harry Novak featurette • 23 chapters.
1997 (R) 88m/C Robert Gribbin, John Harmon, Randy Echols, Dorothy Bennett, Russell Johnson; *D:* Irvin Berwick; *W:* John Buckley; *C:* William de Diego.

Hitched

Marriage is like a ball and chain. Eve (Lee) marries salesman Ted (Hall). She finds out what a heel he truly is when he gets into an automobile accident with another woman. To "protect" their marriage, she chains him to a pillar in their soundproof basement and reports him missing to deflect attention from her action. Cary Grant (Carter), the detective on the case, becomes smitten with her. Hall overdoes it. Lee acts like David Lynch is still directing her. Carter exhibits the right combination of earnestness and charm. Looks and sounds like broadcast television. —LA
Movie: 🎬🎬 ½ **DVD:** 🎬🎬 ½
USA Home Ent. (cat #96306 0342-2, UPC 696396 034223). Full frame. Dolby Digital Surround. $19.95. Keepcase. *LANG:* English. *CAP:* English. *FEATURES:* 10 chapters.
2001 89m/C Sheryl Lee, Anthony Michael Hall, Alex Carter; *D:* Wesley Strick; *W:* Wesley Strick; *C:* Jonathan Freeman; *M:* Randy Miller.

The Hitcher

Halsey (Howell) is driving cross-country on his way to San Diego, when he tries to break up the monotony of the open road by picking up a hitchhiker (Hauer). Something his mother (and mine) warned him against ever doing. Turns out mom knew best, because the passenger starts babbling about the previous pickup he just dismembered. Halsey manages to dispose of his unwanted passenger, but the hitcher takes a real shine to the boy and commences high-speed stalking. It's pretty satisfying thriller fare with several twists and turns and lots of shocking deaths. Hauer is almost too convincing and there are some genuinely suspenseful moments. During the first 20 minutes of the movie, the image appears as if it's being projected through a screen door and is a terrible mess during night scenes. It clears up, more or less, later on and some of the widescreen vistas are extremely sumptuous. —GNG/DG
Movie: 🎬🎬 ½ **DVD:** 🎬🎬
HBO (cat #93756, UPC 026359375620). Widescreen (2.35:1) letterboxed. Dolby Digital 5.1 Surround; Dolby Digital Surround. $14.98. Keepcase. *LANG:* English. *SUB:* English; Spanish; French. *FEATURES:* 13 chapters • Cast & crew bios.
1986 (R) 98m/C Rutger Hauer, C. Thomas Howell, Jennifer Jason Leigh, Jeffrey DeMunn, John M. Jackson, Billy Green Bush; *D:* Robert Harmon; *W:* Eric Red; *C:* John Seale; *M:* Mark Isham.

The Hobbit

Animated adaptation of Tolkien's book as perceived by Arthur Rankin and Jules Bass. While the film captures the story in essence, the visual presentation is extremely rough with crude animation and a washed-out art style that does not adequately reflect the beauty and richness of Tolkien's work. It tells the story of the hobbit Bilbo Baggins as he is recruited for a treasure hunt. Although adventure is against the very nature of Hobbits, he accepts the challenge and goes out for the adventure of his lifetime, facing dark foes, perilous creatures, and even a dragon! DVD transfer is marred with stains and dirt and exhibits excessive grain throughout. The result is an image that always appears muddy and dirty, and never stable. The compression also adds to this feeling as it introduces noticeable pixelation and other digital artifacts. Audio also shows signs of age and neglect. The frequency response is very limited, resulting in a harsh-sounding presentation that is occasionally exhibiting some hiss and slight distortion. —GH
Movie: 🎬🎬 ½ **DVD:** 🎬🎬
Warner Home Video (UPC 12569056626). Full frame. Dolby Digital Mono. $19.98. Snapper. *LANG:* English. *SUB:* English; French; Spanish. *FEATURES:* Tolkien highlights.
1978 76m/C *D:* Arthur Rankin Jr., Jules Bass; *M:* Maury Laws; *V:* Orson Bean, John Huston, Otto Preminger, Richard Boone.

A Hole in the Head

One of the underappreciated final efforts in Capra's directing career, this lighthearted comedy stars Sinatra as a shiftless but charming lout who tries to raise money to save his hotel from foreclosure. Avoiding financial ruin is but one of his two aims; the other is learning to be responsible for his young son. Robinson plays Sinatra's older brother, and he attempts to get custody of the boy because his slacker sibling is on the verge of bankruptcy and eviction. Sinatra, still riding high on his Oscar success for *From Here to Eternity* six years earlier, gives a solid performance. Notable for the introduction of the song "High Hopes," sung by Sinatra and his on-screen son. The monaural sound is full, adequately conveying the brassy, jazzy soundtrack, and all dialogue is distinct. The very wide image would have benefited from anamorphic enhancement, but no dice. The source elements suffer from nicks here and there, but the color is vibrant—particularly on the kid's carrot-red top and the 1950s costumes and decor. The No. 1 complaint about the video transfer is the excessive edge-enhancement, causing visual ringing and halos around actors and scenery. The only extra is the theatrical trailer. —MB
Movie: 🎬🎬🎬 **DVD:** 🎬🎬
MGM Home Ent. (cat #1002378, UPC 027-616865892). Widescreen (2.35:1) letterboxed. Dolby Digital 1.0. $14.95. Keepcase. *LANG:* English; French; Spanish. *SUB:* Spanish; French. *CAP:* English. *FEATURES:* 16 chapters • Original theatrical trailer.
1959 120m/C Frank Sinatra, Edward G. Robinson, Thelma Ritter, Carolyn Jones, Eleanor Parker, Eddie Hodges, Keenan Wynn, Joi Lansing; *D:* Frank Capra; *W:* Arnold Schulman; *C:* William H. Daniels. *AWARDS:* Oscars '59: Song ("High Hopes").

Holiday in the Sun

When the DVD box promises "Filmed at The Bahamas," you know you're in for a treat. "At" The Bahamas? Shouldn't that be "in" The Bahamas? Is The Bahamas a specific address now? That grammatical mystery aside, this Olsen Twins opus is

nothing but a thinly disguised advertisement for the Atlantis Resort at—that is, in—The Bahamas. The girls star as Madison and Alex Stewart, two fun-loving junior high students who are looking forward to the class trip to Hawaii for winter break. But their father surprises them with a trip to The Bahamas in his private jet. (Man, life is rough.) The girls are disappointed that they won't get to be with their friends, but they decide to make the most of visiting the tropical paradise. Once there, they ride horses, meet boys, and foil a smuggling ring. While Mary-Kate and Ashley fans will probably love this, anyone over the age of 12 will most likely find it annoying and insulting. Why would you want to watch someone else have a dream vacation? This DVD is certainly no dream come true. As it was made for TV, the film is presented in a full-frame format. The image is noticeably grainy and there are obvious defects from the source material. The colors are good and there are no distracting artifacting problems. Surround provides clear dialogue, but there are Surround effects only during the musical numbers. (Speaking of the audio, Weezer should be truly ashamed for lending their song "Island in the Sun" to this movie!) —*ML*
Movie: woof **DVD:** 🎵🎵
Warner (cat #37441, UPC 08539367441-20). Full frame. Dolby Surround Stereo. $24.98. Snapper. *LANG:* English. *SUB:* Spanish; French. *CAP:* English. *FEATURES:* Behind-the-scenes • Fashion Close-up • Music video • Bonus trailers • Cast & crew • 15 chapters.
2001 (G) 88m/C Mary-Kate Olsen, Ashley (Fuller) Olsen, Ben Easter, Ashley Hughes, Markus Flanigan, Jamie Rose, Jeff Altman, Wendy Schaal; **D:** Steve Purcell; **W:** Brent Goldberg, David T. Wagner; **C:** David Lewis; **M:** Mark Isham, Steve Porcaro.

The Hollow Man [2 SB]

This "Superbit" release corrects the minor problems of the "Special Edition" (reviewed in *Book 2*). The feature is on one disc; all the extras are on a second. DTS Surround is much more effective than theatrical sound. Even the image is sharper. The film seems to pop right out of a good widescreen monitor with brilliant colors and crisp focus to highlight the dandy (though unrealistic) effects. If there are any flaws, I could not see them. Use this one to show off your system. —*MM*
Movie: 🎵🎵½ **DVD:** 🎵🎵🎵🎵
Columbia Tristar (cat #08997, UPC 04339-6089976). Widescreen (1.85:1) anamorphic. DTS 5.1 Surround; Dolby Digital 5.1 Surround. $29.98. Special packaging. *LANG:* English. *SUB:* English; French; Spanish; Portuguese; Chinese; Korean; Thai. *FEATURES:* 28 chapters (film) • "Making of" featurette • 3 deleted scenes • 15 behind-the-scenes featurettes • Picture-in-picture comparisons • Trailers • Filmographies.
2000 (R) 114m/C Kevin Bacon, Elisabeth Shue, Josh Brolin, William Devane, Kim

Dickens, Greg Grunberg, Mary Jo Randle, Joey Slotnick; **D:** Paul Verhoeven; **W:** Andrew Marlowe; **C:** Jost Vacano; **M:** Jerry Goldsmith. *AWARDS: NOM:* Oscars '00: Visual FX.

Hollywood at Your Feet: The Story of the Chinese Theater Footprints

The story of Sid Grauman's famous Chinese Theater forecourt is loaded with great archival photographs, fun newsreels, and contemporary videotaped ceremonies of hand and foot prints being made from 1927 to the present. The chapter headings are cleverly divided into each star's segment so you can flip directly to the story that interests you. Hosted by Raquel Welch for American Movie Classics, this TV documentary contains a wealth of highlights, but it left me wanting more details, more color. The narration—and Ms. Welch's delivery of it—are a little too flat and unceremonious. DVD looks and sounds just like broadcast television. —*LA*
Movie: 🎵🎵🎵 **DVD:** 🎵🎵🎵
Image Ent. (cat #ID964FSDVD, UPC 0143-81096422). Full frame. Dolby Digital Stereo. $24.98. Keepcase. *LANG:* English. *FEATURES:* 41 chapters.
2000 53m/C D: Michele Farinola; **W:** Ed Singer.

Hollywood Chainsaw Hookers

Private detective Jack Chandler (Jay Richardson) has been hired to find young runaway Samantha (Linnea Quigley). When he inquires at the police station for leads on the case, Chandler learns that a series of murders have been taking place in Los Angeles in which unsuspecting men are dismembered with a chainsaw. Despite the fact that this is supposed to be a campy "B"-movie/cult film, it isn't particularly funny nor exciting. There is little on-screen violence and the acting is horrible. The DVD image is clear and fairly sharp, although there is some softness at the edges. The defects from the source print are constantly evident, as there are scratches and white & black dots on most of the scenes. The colors are O.K., but appear washed-out in several scenes. The audio on the DVD is a digital mono soundtrack, which offers inconsistent volume (which may have more to do with poor mike placement during production than with this transfer) and some hissing. —*ML*
Movie: 🎵🎵 **DVD:** 🎵🎵½
Navarre (UPC 802993123496). Widescreen (1.66:1) letterboxed. Dolby Digital Mono. $24.95. Keepcase. *LANG:* English. *FEATURES:* "Making of" featurette • Fred Olen Ray's "Night Owl Theater."
1988 (R) 90m/C Linnea Quigley, Gunnar Hansen, Jay Richardson, Michelle (McClellan) Bauer, Dawn Wildsmith, Dennis Mooney, Jerry Fox; **D:** Fred Olen Ray; **W:**

Fred Olen Ray, T.L. Lankford; **C:** Scott Ressler; **M:** Michael Perilstein.

Hollywood Rhythm, Vol. 1: Best of Jazz and Blues (1929—41)

Almost all of these short films were produced by the Paramount studio (in Astoria, Queens) to fill the running times of their programs. (Three were not produced by Paramount.) They can be seen now as precursors to music videos. Some are simple staged performances. Others create light narratives to surround the playing. Print damage is evident in almost all of them—light scratches, the occasional blip and registration slip (particularly irritating in one Cab Calloway number), even a few missing frames here and there. There's also some static on the soundtrack and anyone expecting full-bodied sound will be disappointed. Still, this is great stuff for fans of the bands and the singers, including a young Billie Holiday and George Dewey Washington. Contents: "A Rhapsody in Black and Blue" (1932; Louis Armstrong), "A Bundle of Blues" (1933; Duke Ellington, Ivie Anderson), "Cab Calloway's Hi-De-Ho" (1933), "Ain't Misbehaving" (1941; Fats Waller), "Symphony in Black" (1935; Duke Ellington, Billie Holiday), "Jitterbug Party" (1934; Cab Calloway), "St. Louis Blues" (1929; Bessie Smith), "Hoagy Carmichael" (1939; with Jack Teagarden), "Ol' King Cotton" (1930; George Dewey Washington), "Black and Tan Fantasy" (1929; Duke Ellington, Fredi Washington, Arthur Whetsol), "Those Blues" (1932; Vincent Lopez). —*MM*
Movie: 🎵🎵🎵 **DVD:** 🎵🎵
Kino on Video (cat #K197, UPC 73832901-9723). Full frame. $24.98. Keepcase. *LANG:* English. *FEATURES:* 12 chapters • "Jazz à la Cuba" with Don Aspiazu and his orchestra • Liner notes by Richard Barrios.
2000 123m/B

Hollywood Rhythm, Vol. 2: Best of Big Bands Swing (1929—39)

Technical quality of this disc is roughly equal to *Vol. 1*. The funniest entry is "Singapore Sue," where a very young Cary Grant sounds like he's doing an impression of himself. Contents: "Blue of the Night" (1933; Bing Crosby), "Musical Doctor" (1932; Rudy Vallee, Mae Questel), "Singapore Sue" (1931; Anna Chang, Cary Grant), "Office Blues" (1930; Ginger Rogers), "Artie Shaw's Class in Swing" (1931), "Her Future" (1930; Ethel Merman), "A Lesson in Love" (1931; Helen Kane), "Favorite Melodies" (1929; Ruth Etting), "Meet the Boyfriend" (1930; Lillian Roth), "Dream House" (1932; Bing Crosby), bonus performances by Bob Wills and His Texas Playboys, Ginger Rogers & Jack Oakie, Tallulah Bankhead, Kate Smith, Jeanette McDonald, Maurice Chevalier, and the Boswell Sisters. —*MM*

Movie: 🎬🎬🎬 **DVD:** 🎬🎬
Kino on Video (cat #K198, UPC 73832901-9822). Full frame. $24.98. Keepcase. *LANG:* English. *FEATURES:* 11 chapters • Bonus performances • Liner notes by Richard Barrios.
2000 118m/B

Hollywood Screen Tests: Take 1

Robert Culp narrates this interesting look at the screen test, which broke in new stars and rekindled the careers of veterans. Highlights include Ann-Margret singing a fantastically seductive number that got her into *State Fair*, Marlon Brando's test for *Viva Zapata*, and a collection of tests to find the perfect combination for *The Sound of Music*. Most entertaining however, are the tests that paired Adam West and Burt Ward for the *Batman* television series, as well as an alternate duo that couldn't quite cut it. While image and sound quality vary by segment, they are much better than could be expected. —*DRL*
Movie: 🎬🎬🎬 **DVD:** 🎬🎬🎬
Image Ent. (cat #968, UPC 0143810968-28). Various. Dolby Stereo. $24.99. Keepcase. *LANG:* English. *FEATURES:* 24 chapters.
2000 90m/C Julie Andrews, Ann-Margret, Marlon Brando, Sean Connery, Dustin Hoffman, Christopher Plummer, Raquel Welch, Burt Ward, Adam West; *M:* Chris Many, Andy Williams, Tom Jenkins; *Nar:* Robert Culp.

Hollywood Screen Tests: Take 2

This second volume of screen test rarities from the studio vaults is not quite as entertaining as the first. The highlights—including a display of amazing skill and charisma from Bruce Lee, Barbra Streisand's test that landed her *Hello, Dolly*, and a Judy Garland wardrobe test for *Valley of the Dolls*—are on par with anything on the first disc, but the rest is a little dull. Less care was taken on the image and sound, as the picture is grainier, with more artifacts in the transfer, and the sound is very low. Still, it contains rare, interesting footage and is well worth a look. —*DRL*
Movie: 🎬🎬 ½ **DVD:** 🎬🎬 ½
Image Ent. (cat #969, UPC 0143810969-27). Various. Dolby Stereo. $24.99. Keepcase. *LANG:* English. *FEATURES:* 36 chapters.
2000 91m/C James Coburn, Judy Garland, Elliott Gould, Rock Hudson, Martin Landau, Bruce Lee, Leslie Nielsen, Barbra Streisand, Tuesday Weld; *M:* Chris Many, Tom Jenkins; *Nar:* Robert Culp.

Hollywood Shuffle

Young black actor Bobby Taylor (a very charismatic Townsend) struggles to break into the big time, but finds himself conflicted with the role he's just been assigned: a stereotypical jive-talking gangster in a film written, produced, and directed by white people. A handsome but amateur production (funded on Townsend's credit cards and featuring a cast of friends, relatives, and other stand-up comics), the film spends the lion's share of its running time on hit-or-miss fantasy sequences (Townsend as Rambo, a Bogart-esque detective, Stepin Fetchit, etc.) which sometimes stall the dramatic flow of the main story. Though sincerely intentioned, this amusing "message" picture intends to break black stereotypes, but resorts to using clichéd, archly portrayed "evil white men" and overdone gay characters. Sadly, though the film did lead to much movie and television success for Townsend and the Wayans brothers, they've broken none of the ground one would have expected. Instead they've been producing the same type of stereotypical characterizations as parodied in this film. It is amusing, though, and worth a look, if only for the "Attack of the Street Pimps" segment. Though unfortunately not 16x9 enhanced, the disc is a clean, bright, and colorful transfer that gives the low-budget film a nice degree of gloss. The sound is clear and pleasing with not much Surround presence. The trailer features exclusive footage and is worth a look. —*DG*
Movie: 🎬🎬 **DVD:** 🎬🎬🎬
MGM Home Ent. (cat #1002211, UPC 027616864420). Widescreen (1.85:1) letterboxed. Dolby Digital Mono. $19.98. Keepcase. *LANG:* English; Spanish. *SUB:* Spanish; French. *CAP:* English. *FEATURES:* Theatrical trailer • 16 chapters • Insert card with chapter listing.
1987 (R) 81m/C Robert Townsend, Anne-Marie Johnson, Starletta DuPois, Helen Martin, Keenen Ivory Wayans, Damon Wayans, Craigus R. Johnson, Eugene Glazer; *D:* Robert Townsend; *W:* Robert Townsend, Keenen Ivory Wayans; *C:* Peter Deming; *M:* Patrice Rushen, Udi Harpaz.

Home for the Holidays

Claudia Larson (Hunter) is heading home for yet another chaotic and exasperating family Thanksgiving. But a new visitor (McDermott) offers romance. The proceedings are pepped up by Robert Downey Jr.'s turn as Claudia's brother, Jodie Foster's direction, and W.D. Richter's script. But they're still not sufficiently penetrating to deliver a first-rate film. Interesting to see *The Practice*'s McDermott in an early role. Good DVD transfer and sound. —*MO*
Movie: 🎬🎬🎬 **DVD:** 🎬🎬🎬 ½
MGM Home Ent. (cat #1002359, UPC 027-616865700). Widescreen (1.85:1) anamorphic. Dolby Digital 5.1; Dolby Digital Stereo; Dolby Digital Mono. $19.98. Keepcase. *LANG:* English; French; Spanish. *SUB:* French; Spanish. *CAP:* English; French; Spanish. *FEATURES:* 16 chapters • Commentary: director Jodie Foster • Theatrical trailer.
1995 (PG-13) 103m/C Holly Hunter, Anne Bancroft, Charles Durning, Robert Downey Jr., Dylan McDermott, Cynthia Stevenson, Geraldine Chaplin, Steve Guttenberg, Claire Danes, David Strathairn, Austin Pendleton; *D:* Jodie Foster; *W:* W.D. Richter; *C:* Lajos Koltai; *M:* Mark Isham.

Homicidal

William Castle's *Psycho* imitation is an alternative gem that makes a belated debut on home video. He takes all the key elements of Hitchcock's original and reshuffles them. We've got the big old house with the steep staircase, the creepy invalid older woman, a troubled young man, the blonde who's up to something, the cheap hotel, the vaguely threatening cops, the unexpectedly graphic knife violence, the young couple who investigates. And, of course, there's the central gimmick which is cheesily transparent. Most viewers will tumble to it early on and that's part of the fun, too. It will not be even hinted at here. With enthusiastic overacting from all the leads, the whole thing becomes a minor camp masterpiece. DVD delivers a beautifully photographed black-and-white image that ranges between very good and excellent. Mono sound is fine for the action. —*MM*
Movie: 🎬🎬🎬 **DVD:** 🎬🎬🎬
Columbia Tristar (cat #06930, UPC 04339-6069305). Full frame. $24.98. Keepcase. *LANG:* English. *SUB:* English; French. *CAP:* English. *FEATURES:* 28 chapters • Trailers • Featurette.
1961 87m/B Glenn Corbett, Patricia Breslin, Alan Bunce, James Westerfield; *D:* William Castle; *W:* Robb White; *C:* Burnett Guffey; *M:* Hugo Friedhofer.

Honky Tonk Freeway

An odd assortment of travelers become involved in the mayor's (Devane) attempts to get an interstate ramp that will funnel suckers into his little town of Ticlaw, Florida. The general level of comedy is established by one character's proposed children's book, *Ricky, the Carnivorous Pony*. Are you laughing yet? Grain is heavy in some bright tropical exteriors but the overall image is acceptable for a work of this age. Monaural sound is all that's required. —*MM*
Movie: 🎬 **DVD:** 🎬🎬 ½
Anchor Bay (cat #DV11455, UPC 0131311-45595). Widescreen (1.85:1) anamorphic. Dolby Digital Mono. $24.98. Keepcase. *LANG:* English. *CAP:* English. *FEATURES:* 26 chapters • Trailers.
1981 (PG) 107m/C Teri Garr, Howard Hesseman, Beau Bridges, Hume Cronyn, William Devane, Beverly D'Angelo, Geraldine Page; *D:* John Schlesinger; *W:* Edward Clinton; *C:* John Bailey; *M:* Elmer Bernstein, Steve Dorff.

Hook

Though he said he was never going to do it, Peter Pan has grown up. He has become uptight Peter Banning (Williams), who places work before family, forgetting

all about Neverland and the evil Captain Hook (Hoffman), until Hook kidnaps the Banning kids. With the help of Tinkerbell (Roberts), her magic pixie dust, and many happy thoughts, Peter sets out to rescue his kids and recapture his lost youth. Sets and special effects are dazzling, but the big-budget fantasy lacks a certain charm, at least for adults. Kids generally love it, and the truth is that it's better the second time around, particularly on this handsome disc. The level of detail found in this transfer is breathtaking, as every bit of information from the film print is preserved without any loss or artifacting. Color delineation is also perfect, creating an image that features powerful colors and restores even the most subtle hues from the film's colorful production design. Both audio tracks are very well done but the 5.1 mix's expansive sound field creates an atmosphere that gives the presentation much more dimension. Surrounds are used frequently and effectively, sometimes for effects purposes, sometimes to create a richer ambient atmosphere. The frequency response of the track is very natural with deep low ends and brilliant high ends. But there is a slight distortion in some dialogue. This does not appear to be digital distortion but sounds more like a slightly overdriven signal during the actual recording of the lines. —MM/GH

Movie: ♫♫ ½ **DVD:** ♫♫♫ ½
Columbia Tristar Home Video (UPC 04339-6039308). Widescreen (2.35:1) anamorphic. Dolby Digital 5.1 Surround; Dolby Surround. $19.98. Keepcase. *LANG:* English. *SUB:* English. *FEATURES:* 28 chapters • Trailer • Talent files.
1991 (PG) 142m/C Dustin Hoffman, Robin Williams, Julia Roberts, Bob Hoskins, Maggie Smith, Charlie Korsmo, Caroline Goodall, Amber Scott, Phil Collins, Arthur Malet, Dante Basco, Gwyneth Paltrow, Glenn Close, David Crosby; **D:** Steven Spielberg; **W:** Nick Castle; **C:** Dean Cundey; **M:** John Williams. *AWARDS: NOM:* Oscars '91: Art Dir./Set Dec., Costume Des., Makeup, Song ("When You're Alone"), Visual FX.

Hopalong Cassidy

In this first of the popular series, Hoppy (Boyd) and his friends intervene in a brewing range war. Rustlers are helped by a two-timing foreman who's playing both sides against each other. After a career in silent films, Boyd was having trouble finding work. He was initially approached to play the villain. He declined but agreed to be the good guy if the character were cleaned up. He was, and the series went on for more than 60 installments. "Gabby" Hayes's stock character was killed off in this episode but was brought back for the rest. For a low-budget movie more than half a century old, this one looks astonishingly good. The Lone Pine, California, locations are still impressive and so is William Boyd. The 5.1 soundtrack option delivers more detail, but it also contains a considerable increase in

static. Fred Romary's extensive liner notes provide an excellent introduction to the series, explaining its beginnings and development over the years. The title is available with *Bar 20 Rides Again* on the first volume of *Hopalong Cassidy: The Early Years.* —MM **AKA:** Hopalong Cassidy Enters.

Movie: ♫♫ ½ **DVD:** ♫♫ ½
Image Ent. (cat #ID9151UTDVD, UPC 014-381915129). Full frame. Dolby Digital 5.1 Surround Stereo. $24.99. Keepcase. *LANG:* English. *FEATURES:* 10 chapters • Liner notes by Fred Romary.
1935 60m/B William Boyd, James Ellison, Paula Stone, Robert Warwick, Charles Middleton, Frank McGlynn, Kenneth Thomson, George "Gabby" Hayes, James Mason, Franklyn Farnum, Doris Schroeder; **D:** Howard Bretherton; **C:** Archie Stout.

Hopalong Cassidy Returns

In the seventh entry in the "Hopalong Cassidy" series, Hoppy (Boyd) faces a lady outlaw, Lilli Marsh (Brent), who, of course, falls hard for our stalwart hero. If this is not one of the best in the series, it maintains the high production standards, and it contains the debut of series regular Morris Ankrum as a villain. The disc itself is equally impressive. For technical comments, please see review of *Hopalong Cassidy.* Title is available on a double feature with *Three on the Trail* on *Hopalong Cassidy: The Early Years.* —MM

Movie: ♫♫ ½ **DVD:** ♫♫ ½
Image Ent. (cat #ID9152UTDVD, UPC 014-38191528). Full frame. Dolby Digital 5.1 Surround Stereo; Dolby Digital Mono. $24.99. Keepcase. *LANG:* English. *FEATURES:* 12 chapters • Liner notes by Fred Romary.
1936 74m/B William Boyd, George "Gabby" Hayes, Evelyn Brent, Morris Ankrum, William Janney; **D:** Nate Watt; **W:** Doris Schroeder; **C:** Archie Stout.

Horatio Hornblower

Adventure bounds on the high seas in these adaptations of C.S. Forester's popular novels set in the late 18th century. Hornblower (Gruffudd) is a young recruit who rises through the ranks of the King's Navy as the British battle the French. "The Duel" provides an introduction to Hornblower and his mentor, Captain Pellew (Lindsay). "The Fire Ships" has Hornblower preparing for his lieutenant's exam. "The Duchess and the Devil" finds our man escorting the Duchess of Wharfedale (Lunghi) to England with important naval dispatches. In "The Wrong War," the Brits prepare a coup against the French Republican government. Compared to other British TV imports, this one looks very good, but don't expect the sharpness of American theatrical releases. Dark clothes reveal nice details which tend to be lost in dim below-decks interiors. Some pixels are visible in bright seascapes, too. The

"England's Royal Warships" extra is very nice. —MM

Movie: ♫♫♫ **DVD:** ♫♫♫
A&E (cat #AAE-70062, UPC 733961700-626). Full frame. $59.95. Keepcase boxed set. *LANG:* English. *SUB:* English. *FEATURES:* 74 chapters • C.S. Forester thumbnail bio • "Making of" featurette • Nautical terms and definitions.
1999 400m/C *GB* Ioan Gruffudd, Robert Lindsay, Denis Lawson, Cherie Lunghi, Anthony Sher, Samuel West, Andrew Tiernan, Ronald Pickup; **D:** Andrew Grieve; **W:** Russell Lewis, Mike Cullen, Patrick Harbinson; **C:** Alec Curtis, Neve Cunningham.

Horatio Hornblower: The Adventure Continues

Young British naval officer Hornblower's (Gruffudd) career continues with two linked stories, "Mutiny" and "Retribution." Horatio recounts to Capt. Pellew (Lindsay) the reasons for his imprisonment on mutiny charges after confining his insane captain Sawyer (Warner) to his quarters to prevent his sending the crew into a suicidal battle. Then Hornblower must lead a force to recapture an enemy fort. Image is just as good as the first series; the only drawback here is the lack of subtitles. The "3-D cannon" extra is pretty cool but simple. —MM

Movie: ♫♫♫ **DVD:** ♫♫ ½
A&E (cat #AAE-70199, UPC 7339617019-99). Full frame. Dolby Digital Stereo. $39.98. Keepcase boxed set. *LANG:* English. *FEATURES:* 40 chapters • 3-D cannon • Classes of ships (text) • C.S. Forester thumbnail bio.
2001 200m/C *GB* Ioan Gruffudd, Robert Lindsay, David Warner, Jamie Bamber, Paul McGann, Nicholas Jones, Philip Glenister, David Rintoul; **D:** Andrew Grieve; **C:** Chris O'Dell; **M:** John Keane.

The Horror of Hammer

Exhaustive compilation of trailers from British studio Hammer Films, whose popular and classy series of colorful horror films (during the late '50s through the '70s) stretched the limits of screen violence and catapulted actors Christopher Lee and Peter Cushing to international stardom. Though nobly intentioned, the trailers on this collection look thoroughly miserable, all deriving from scratched, battered, and faded collector's prints. The terrible condition of the trailers conveys none of the beauty and elegance of the film's original photography and set design and so this is a poor representation of that studio's work. The disc is also prone to excessive digital noise, aliasing, artifacting, and other authoring problems. On the plus side, the audio commentary (though poorly miked and occasionally more opinionated than scholarly) does cover a lot of ground and features some interesting second- and third-hand anecdotes. Also of

interest are the two rarely seen featurettes (showcasing behind-the-scenes footage of *Dracula A.D. 1972* and *When Dinosaurs Ruled the Earth*) and a few trailers for rarely screened Hammer films such as *Night Creatures*, *Stranglers of Bombay*, and the William Castle remake of *The Old Dark House*. The sound is just as scratched and muddy as the visual presentation of the trailers. —*DG*
Movie: ♪ **DVD:** woof
All Day Ent. (cat #ADED0904DVD, UPC 01-4381090420). Full frame. Dolby Digital Mono. $24.99. Keepcase. *LANG:* English. *FEATURES:* 53 trailers from Hammer films ● 4 alternate trailers ● "Beauties and Beasties" featurette ● "Prince of Terror" featurettes ● Commentary: Ted Newsom, Gary H. Smith, Stuart Galbraith.
2001 115m/C

Horror 101

"Witnesses are never a good thing; if you take anything away from this class, I hope it's that." So begins Miss James's (Bo Derek) Horror 101 class. Aside from some cool art direction and that single snippet of dialogue, this is a fairly rote horror film. It manages to sustain some tension for the audience about the true identity of the killer for a while, that is if the audience is composed entirely of four-year-old children who have never seen a horror film. The class is made up of standard college-issue cut outs: the loose girl, the prissy girl, the jock, etc., who are led down the blood-covered primrose path toward their untimely demise. Surprisingly, Derek plays bad better than she ever played good, and the rest of the cast runs from competent to "nephew of the director." A definite rental with a good picture and average muffled "B"-movie sound. —*CA*
Movie: ♪ **DVD:** ♪♪♪
Taurus (cat #KE 203, UPC 6915972003-26). Full frame. Dolby. $19.95. Keepcase. *LANG:* English. *FEATURES:* 20 chapters ● Behind-the-scenes featurette.
2000 120m/C Justin Urich, Bo Derek; **D:** James Glenn Dudelson.

The Horse's Mouth

Star Alec Guinness wrote the script for this glorious comedy about half-mad (or is he just extremely creative?) painter Gulley Jimson. In pursuit of his Muse, Gulley will do anything. That's why he's being released from jail as we meet him. The result is one of the best of those uniquely British character-based comedies—smart, funny, perceptive, and surprising. There may well be some flaws on this disc, but the truth is that I love this movie so much I'll forgive it almost anything. It looks simply splendid with bright rich colors and no grain that's not present on the original. Criterion has done its usual good work. The short film that's included—D.A. Pennebaker's "Daybreak Express" actually ran with the feature when it was released in New York. English subtitles are recommended for Guinness's gravelly interpreta-

tion and some of the other accents. —*MM*
AKA: The Oracle.
Movie: ♪♪♪ ½ **DVD:** ♪♪♪ ½
Criterion (cat #154, UPC 037429168721). Widescreen (1.66:1) anamorphic. Dolby Digital Mono. $29.95. Keepcase. *LANG:* English. *SUB:* English. *FEATURES:* Liner notes by Bruce Eder ● Liner notes by Ian Christie ● Liner notes by Ronald Neame ● 15 chapters ● Interview with Ronald Neame ● Short film, "Daybreak Express" with intro by D.A. Pennebaker ● Trailer.
1958 93m/C *GB* Alec Guinness, Kay Walsh, Robert Coote, Renee Houston, Michael Gough; **C:** Arthur Ibbetson; **M:** Kenneth V. Jones. *AWARDS:* Natl. Bd. of Review '58: Support. Actress (Walsh); *NOM:* Oscars '58: Adapt. Screenplay.

Hostage High

Synopsis makes this fact-based thriller sound like exploitation, but it's a fairly serious effort. Disgruntled former student Jason Copeland (Schroder) attempts to take over his school. Police negotiator Skip Fine (Winkler) tries to defuse the situation. DVD delivers an excellent full-frame image of a production that has a shot-on-location indie look. The best thing about the disc is a perceptive commentary track by producer Steve Natt and Winkler. Recommended. —*MM* **AKA:** Detention: The Siege at Johnson High.
Movie: ♪♪♪ **DVD:** ♪♪♪
Artisan Ent. (cat #12004, UPC 122361-20049). Full frame. Dolby Digital 5.1 Surround; Dolby Digital Surround. $24.98. Keepcase. *LANG:* English; Spanish. *SUB:* English. *CAP:* English. *FEATURES:* 20 chapters ● Talent files ● Trailer ● Photo gallery ● Commentary: Steve Natt and Henry Winkler.
1997 (R) 93m/C Rick Schroder, Henry Winkler, Freddie Prinze Jr., Ren Woods, Katie Wright, Alexis Cruz, Patrick Malone; **D:** Michael W. Watkins; **W:** Larry Golin; **C:** Bill Roe; **M:** Brian Adler.

Hot Blooded Woman

Please see review for *Confessions of a Psycho Cat / Hot Blooded Woman*.
1965 68m/B D: Dale Berry.

Hot Pursuit

Prep-school bookworm Dan Bartlett (Cusack) is all set to spend a week in the Caribbean with his willing girlfriend Lori (Gazelle) and her disapproving parents (Markham and Fabares). But Dan fails a test and thinks that he can't go. A none-too-persuasive plot twist has him trailing the family by a few hours, trying to make his way to his love while Ben Stiller (in his debut) is putting some moves on her. As teen comedies go, this one is relatively inoffensive and ephemeral. Even Cusack's undeniable charm can't make it really interesting. DVD looks about as good as a mid-budget, mid-'80s studio release could be expected to look. It's not a huge

improvement over VHS tape and there's no need for it to be. —*MM*
Movie: ♪♪ ½ **DVD:** ♪♪ ½
Paramount (cat #32082, UPC 09736320-8242). Widescreen anamorphic. Dolby Digital Surround. $24.99. Keepcase. *LANG:* English. *SUB:* English. *CAP:* English. *FEATURES:* 14 chapters.
1987 (PG-13) 93m/C Monte Markham, Shelley Fabares, Ben Stiller, John Cusack, Robert Loggia, Jerry Stiller, Wendy Gazelle; **D:** Steven Lisberger; **W:** Steven V. Carabatsos; **C:** Frank Tidy; **M:** Joseph Conlan.

Hot Rod Girl

A concerned police officer (Connors) organizes supervised drag racing after street racing gets out of hand. Typically low-budget Corman production is so rough that it gains nothing on DVD. Image looks like a dupe of a poor tape. Title is available on the *Great Racing Movies* disc (see separate entry). —*MM* **AKA:** Hot Car Girl.
Movie: ♪ **DVD:** ♪ ½
Full frame. *LANG:* English. *FEATURES:* 4 chapters.
1956 75m/B Lori Nelson, Chuck Connors, John W. Smith; **D:** Leslie Martinson; **W:** John McGreevey; **C:** Sam Leavitt.

Hot Summer

A hard film to classify and critique, this one's a winner for sheer voyeur value. The sight of Eastern Block teens singing and dancing in their bathing suits is worth the price of admission. Shot in East Germany while the wall was still up and released while a rebellion was going on in the streets of Prague, this is a musical that follows 11 boys and girls (17-year-olds) on a summer vacation to the Baltic Sea. Along the way they develop antagonistic crushes on each other, which result in a lot of pranks accompanied by song and dance routines. This is cheese so well processed that it reaches Velveeta status, but fun for anyone who likes the old '60s Beach Party movies. Of course, Frankie never got in trouble for stealing the "collective's" boat to take Annette out on a date. The picture on the disc is good but a little faded and the sound is average. —*CA* **AKA:** Heisser Sommer.
Movie: ♪♪ **DVD:** ♪♪ ½
First Run Features (UPC 67912691126). Full frame. $29.95. Keepcase. *LANG:* German. *SUB:* English. *FEATURES:* 12 chapters ● Music video ● Filmographies ● Best of German Cinema featurette.
1968 91m/C *GE* Frank Schobel, Chris Doerk, Madeleine Lierck, Hanns-Michael Schmidt, Regine Albrecht; **D:** Joachim Hasler.

The Hotel New Hampshire

Tony Richardson's disjointed, sluggish adaptation of John Irving's novel charts the tribulations of the oddball Berry clan. How weird are they? "Father" (Bridges) perpetually dreams of running any hotel named "New Hampshire," adult sister

Fran (Foster) and brother John (Lowe) sexually tease each other, younger sister Lilly (Dundas) is convinced she has stopped growing, and youngest son Egg (a very young Green, from the *Austin Powers* films) keeps plopping Sorrow, their dead dog's stuffed carcass, all over the house. While colors, like blue pom-poms and bright red-shingled roofs, transmit vibrantly and without bleed, the contrast levels vary widely. Hot background light sources practically burn out foreground shadow detail while nighttime or low-lit interior scenes drown the image in an inky darkness. Mastered from a clean source print, the video shows minimal but detectable edge-enhancement. At least there are no digital or compression artifacts. Surround audio might just as well have been in mono. —*EP*
Movie: 🎵🎵 **DVD:** 🎵🎵 ½
MGM Home Ent. (cat #1002207, UPC 02-7616864383). Widescreen (1.85:1) letterboxed. Dolby Digital Surround Stereo; Dolby Digital Mono. $24.98. Keepcase. *LANG:* English; French. *SUB:* English; Spanish. *CAP:* English. *FEATURES:* Trailer • 16 chapters.
1984 (R) 110m/C Jodie Foster, Rob Lowe, Beau Bridges, Nastassia Kinski, Wallace Shawn, Wilford Brimley, Amanda Plummer, Anita Morris, Matthew Modine, Lisa Banes, Seth Green, Jennifer (Jennie) Dundas Lowe; **D:** Tony Richardson; **W:** Tony Richardson; **C:** David Watkin; **M:** Jacques Offenbach.

The Hound of the Baskervilles

If this adaptation of the famous Sherlock Holmes tale lacks the atmosphere (and pedigree) of the 1939 version, it earns a solid recommendation for the casting of the three leads. Christopher Lee is fine as Sir Henry, who fears returning to the estate he has inherited because someone's trying to kill him (with a tarantula!). Andre Morell's Dr. Watson is the embodiment of Conan-Doyle's original character, and so is Peter Cushing's Holmes. He is much more aloof and prickly than Rathbone. If all of the details don't follow the book, that's to be expected. The production values are up to the Hammer studio's standards. (Fans of the horror films will recognize the sets and costumes.) An excellent widescreen image preserves the sharp Hammer look, too. Some of the shots involving heavy mist and ground fog lose a bit of definition, but that looks to come from the original. The busy interior of 221-B Baker Street is flawless. Recommended. —*MM*
Movie: 🎵🎵🎵 **DVD:** 🎵🎵🎵
MGM Home Ent. (cat #1003429, UPC 027-616875785). Widescreen (1.66:1) letterboxed. Dolby Digital Mono. $14.98. Keepcase. *LANG:* English; French; Spanish. *SUB:* English; French; Spanish. *CAP:* English. *FEATURES:* Christopher Lee featurette • Readings from the book by Christopher Lee • Trailer • 16 chapters.
1959 86m/C *GB* Peter Cushing, Christopher Lee, Andre Morell; **D:** Terence Fisher; **W:** Peter Bryan; **C:** Jack Asher; **M:** James Bernard.

House

Horror novelist Roger Cobb (Katt) moves into his dead aunt's supposedly haunted house only to find that the monsters don't necessarily stay in the closets. His worst nightmares come to life as he writes about his Vietnam experiences and is forced to relive the tragic events, but these aren't the only visions that start springing to life. It sounds depressing, but is actually a funny, intelligent "horror" flick. Followed by several lesser sequels. The long out-of-print VHS edition of *House* looked pretty average and sounded pretty bad. This Anchor Bay DVD looks great and sounds good. The anamorphic transfer is incredibly sharp with saturated colors and subtle hues. The commentary is pleasant to listen to, as it's obvious the four sincerely like each other and the film they made together. The rest of the supplementals don't count for much since the 12-minute "making of" featurette is just a big ad and one of the two trailers is the worst looking trailer in recent memory. The photo gallery is definitely worth a look. (Formerly available as part of *House / House 2* limited edition set, same catalog number.) —*JO*
Movie: 🎵🎵🎵 **DVD:** 🎵🎵🎵
Anchor Bay (cat #DV11424, UPC 0131311-42495). Widescreen (1.85:1) anamorphic. Dolby Digital Mono. $29.98. Keepcase. *LANG:* English. *CAP:* English. *FEATURES:* 26 chapters • 2 theatrical trailers • Photo gallery • Commentary: Miner, Cunningham, Wiley, Katt • "Making of" featurette.
1986 (R) 93m/C William Katt, George Wendt, Richard Moll, Kay Lenz, Michael Ensign, Mary Stavin, Susan French; **D:** Steve Miner; **W:** Ethan Wiley; **C:** Mac Ahlberg; **M:** Harry Manfredini.

House 2: The Second Story

The flaccid and seemingly unrelated sequel to the haunted-house horror flick concerns two innocent guys who move into the family mansion and discover Aztec ghosts. Has none of the personality or humor which helped the first movie along. The transfer and sound are as good as the DVD for the first film, but that doesn't really make the movie much more enjoyable. The commentary by Wiley and Cunningham is full of dead space and lacking the personality that made the *House* commentary so good. (Only available as part of the out-of-print 2-disc *House / House 2* limited edition set.) —*JO*
Movie: 🎵 **DVD:** 🎵🎵 ½
Anchor Bay Widescreen (1.85:1) anamorphic. Dolby Digital Mono. Keepcase. *LANG:* English. *CAP:* English. *FEATURES:* 25 chapters • Theatrical trailer • Commentary: Ethan Wiley, Sean Cunningham.
1987 (PG-13) 88m/C John Ratzenberger, Arye Gross, Royal Dano, Bill Maher, Jonathan Stark, Lar Park Lincoln, Amy Yasbeck, Devin Devasquez; **D:** Ethan Wiley; **W:** Ethan Wiley; **C:** Mac Ahlberg.

House Arrest

Kyle Howard and Amy Sakasitz star as Grover and Amy Beindorf, two children who have just realized that their parents, Ned (Pollock) and Janet (Curtis) are about to divorce. Aware of a better time when the grown-ups showed more affection towards one another, the two children manage to lock their parents in the basement to force them to sort out their differences. DVD looks like it was transferred from someone's VHS copy. Pan 'n' scan picture has three stages—soft, softer, and softest, the last of which has the image practically looking blurry. Edge-enhancement is present and although not consistently visible, is irritating. Pixelation, some annoying shimmering, and print flaws all team up to give an already soft picture a rough, digital appearance. Colors look rather smeary throughout, as well. Though the film was presented in Dolby Digital 5.1 in theatres, disc is only stereo, with weakly delivered music and dialogue that can sound rough. —*AB/MM*
Movie: 🎵 ½ **DVD:** 🎵 ½
HBO Home Video (UPC 26359129629). Full frame. Dolby Stereo. $19.98. Snapper. *LANG:* English. *FEATURES:* Trailer • Talent files.
1996 (PG) 107m/C Jamie Lee Curtis, Kevin Pollak, Christopher McDonald, Jennifer Tilly, Caroline Aaron, Wallace Shawn, Sheila McCarthy, Ray Walston, Kyle Howard, Amy Sakasitz, Jennifer Love Hewitt; **D:** Harry Winer; **W:** Michael Hitchcock; **C:** Ueli Steiger; **M:** Bruce Broughton.

House of Frankenstein

Dr. Gustav Niemann (Karloff) breaks from Neustadt Prison with the deadly assistance of hunchbacked inmate Daniel (Naish). A couple of murders later, they have disguised themselves as carnival mountebanks. Their display of the skeleton of Dracula turns out to be the real McCoy, materializing into the Count (Carradine) when the stake is removed. After the Count fails to return to his coffin before dawn and becomes a skeleton once more, Niemann moves on to Frankenstein's castle, where they find the Doctor's records, the Monster (Strange), and the "Wolf Man" Larry Talbot (Chaney Jr.). On DVD the film looks even better than its co-feature, *Frankenstein Meets the Wolfman* (transferred later, it got higher-tech attention), but gets short shrift in the extras department. The production notes this time around are a single uninformative paragraph, and the cast bios consist of one tidbit each, such as J. Carroll Naish getting hired as a movie actor by donating blood to the head of Fox films. The trailer amusingly ticks off the five monsters packed into this monochrome monster rally, counting Karloff's Mad Scientist (number 4!) and J. Carroll Naish's The Hunchback (number 5!). Of interest is the fact that once you choose between the two titles on the disc, you can't switch to the other without first turning off your DVD player. (Someone please correct me here if I'm wrong.) Since the menu designs for the two shows are dissimilar, maybe the idea to double-bill these lower-tier monster movies was made after individual mastering was done. —GE

Movie: 🎵🎵 **DVD:** 🎵🎵🎵
Universal Studios (cat #21401, UPC 025192140129). Full frame. Dolby Digital Mono. $29.98. Keepcase. *LANG:* English. *SUB:* French; Spanish. *CAP:* English. *FEATURES:* Trailer • Production notes.
1944 71m/B Boris Karloff, J. Carrol Naish, Lon Chaney Jr., John Carradine, Elena Verdugo, Anne Gwynne, Lionel Atwill, Peter Coe, George Zucco, Glenn Strange, Sig Rumann; *D:* Erle C. Kenton; *W:* Edward T. Lowe; *C:* George Robinson.

The House of the Spirits

An ambitious, yet ultimately disappointing film adaptation of the Isabel Allende book of the same title. The story covers three generations of a rich South American family, but mostly focuses on the blindly ambitious middle patriarch Esteban (Irons) as he destroys almost everyone and everything he loves trying to fill his insatiable thirst for more of everything. The cast is a tabloid who's who: Jeremy Irons, Meryl Streep, Winona Ryder, etc., and while they all hold their own with their roles, each one, with the exception of—amazingly enough—Antonio Banderas, are horribly miscast. Also, the magical realism that is usually present in Allende's stories falls deaf under the cold Swedish direction of Bille August, and ultimately we're left with a soap opera that touts an amazing cast and great cinematography. It might still be worth watching for anyone who likes their tragedy pretty, like a traffic accident in Beverly Hills or the neighbors arguing in the driveway of Rodeo Drive. The film looks great and the sound is good. —CA

Movie: 🎵🎵 ½ **DVD:** 🎵🎵🎵
Artisan Ent. (cat #11797, UPC 01223611-7971). Widescreen (1.85:1) anamorphic. Dolby Digital Surround. $14.90. Keepcase. *LANG:* English. *CAP:* English. *FEATURES:* Cast & crew bios • Production notes.
1993 (R) 109m/C Meryl Streep, Jeremy Irons, Glenn Close, Winona Ryder, Antonio Banderas, Armin Mueller-Stahl, Vanessa Redgrave, Sarita Choudhury, Maria Conchita Alonso, Vincent Gallo, Miriam Colon, Jan Niklas, Teri Polo, Jane Gray; *D:* Bille August; *W:* Bille August; *C:* Jorgen Persson; *M:* Hans Zimmer.

House on Bare Mountain

If Frank Henenlotter's liner notes are to be believed, this "nudie-cutie" is most famous for being the subject of a raid by a Boston police chief who was up for re-election. It's a silly movie with star Bob Cresse doing a bad imitation of Jonathan Winters's little old lady character, and lots of young women taking off some of their clothes.

DVD presents a clear reproduction of a fairly soft-focused image. Sound is completely adequate to the task at hand. Title is available as the second feature on the *Monster Nudie Double Feature* with *Kiss Me Quick!* (Please see review.) —MM

Movie: 🎵 **DVD:** 🎵🎵
Image Ent. (cat #ID9738SWDVD, UPC 014-381973822). Full frame. Dolby Digital Mono. $24.99. Snapper. *LANG:* English. *FEATURES:* 12 chapters • Theatrical trailers • 4 archival exploitation short subjects • Gallery of exploitation art.
1962 62m/C Robert W. Cresse, Laura Eden, Angela Webster, Hugh Cannon, Warren Ames; *D:* Lee Frost.

House Party 4: Down to the Last Minute

When Uncle Charles (David Roberson) goes on vacation, teenager Jon Jon (Marques Houston) volunteers to housesit, much to the chagrin of his sister, Monique (Alexis Fields). Of course, despite the warnings from his uncle, Jon Jon has no intention of spending the weekend alone. He immediately calls his best friends, Mark (Jerome Jones) and T (Kelton Kessee), and they plan a huge party, going as far as to put out invitations on the Internet. As is to be expected, things get out of hand, and Jon Jon faces his worst nightmare when Monique learns of the party and threatens to expose the shindig to their parents. *House Party 4* is predictable from beginning to end and has none of the charm found in the first two films of this series. R&B group IMX (formerly Immature) star in the film, and their fans are probably the only ones who will enjoy this movie, but I doubt they'll forgive the way that Houston is constantly mugging for the camera. Ironically, this is an impressive DVD. The film can be viewed in either a full-frame or widescreen mode. The preferable widescreen image looks very good, showing strong colors and no grain. The picture is clear and sharp with no distortion. The Dolby Digital 5.1 sound mix is very good as well, bringing us clear dialogue and occasional Surround sound effects. Surprisingly, the bass on the ambient music isn't very powerful. —ML

Movie: woof **DVD:** 🎵🎵
New Line (cat #N5295, UPC 7940435295-28). Widescreen (1.85:1) anamorphic; full frame. Dolby Digital 5.1; Dolby 2.0 Surround. $24.98. Snapper. *LANG:* English. *SUB:* English. *CAP:* English. *FEATURES:* Featurette • Music video • Bonus trailers • 15 chapters.
2000 (R) 79m/C Marques Houston, David Roberson, Jerome Jones, Alexis Fields, Kelton Kessee.

How High

Rappers Method Man and Redman star as Silas and Jamal, two stoners from New Jersey who have different blends of marijuana for different illnesses and other problems. One of their friends lights himself on fire after falling asleep with a joint,

and they use his ashes to plant their latest strain of pot. When they smoke their old friend, his ghost appears and, smart as he is, tells the two all the answers they need to get perfect scores on their SATs. Offered a scholarship to any school they want, they pick Harvard. There's nothing in the way of plot and even less in the way of lessons—it's all about weed jokes, women, and dialogue that strings together more curse words than one can count. Spalding Gray (yes, *that* Spalding Gray) is amusing as an African-American history professor. The picture looks consistently sharp and well defined, with no instances of even slight softness that I noticed. Shadow detail is also strong. The presentation's only noticeable flaws are a couple of tiny instances of pixelation and edge-enhancement, neither of which cause much in the way of distraction. The print used was crystal clear throughout, with no specks, marks, grain, or other flaws. While 5.1 is certainly not aggressive, a few scenes have some decent sound effects placed in the Surrounds. The film's rap soundtrack could have benefited from a bit more reinforcement from the rear speakers, but the music does sound bassy and rich coming from the fronts. Dialogue sounded clear and crisp throughout, as well. Both stars sound a bit high on their commentary track. —AB/MM

Movie: 🎵🎵 **DVD:** 🎵🎵🎵
Universal Studios Home Video (UPC 025-192195129). Widescreen (1.85:1) anamorphic. Dolby Digital 5.1 Surround; DTS 5.1. $26.98. Keepcase. *LANG:* English. *FEATURES:* Commentary • Deleted scenes (22 min.) • Outtakes • Trailers • Production notes • Talent files • Music videos • "Making of" featurette.
2001 (R) 93m/C Method Man, Redman, Obba Babatunde, Chuck Davis, Anna Maria Horsford, Fred Willard, Lark Voorhies, Essence Atkins, Jeffrey Jones, Mike Epps, Hector Elizondo, Chris Elwood, Spalding Gray, Tracey Walter; *D:* Jesse Dylan; *W:* Dustin Lee Abraham; *C:* Francis Kenny; *M:* Rockwilder.

How to Get Ahead in Advertising

Ostensibly a companion piece to the 1987 cult classic *Withnail and I*, this 1988 satire reunites writer/director Bruce Robinson and star Richard E. Grant. Grant plays Dennis Bagley, a hyper advertising man who begins to unravel when trying to conceptualize a pitch for an innocuous pimple cream. Bagley gets so obsessed, he starts spouting off: first about the evils of advertising and then, literally, when a boil appears on his shoulder. However, this carbuncle has a mind and an id of its own. Cynical and energetic, *How to Get Ahead* sports a satiric bent so ferocious it makes *Withnail* seem downright submissive by comparison. If *Withnail* charted the turbulent seas of iconoclastic behavior, then *Advertising* attacks the compliance of middle-class consumerism with two formidable weapons: Robinson's acerbic, hilari-

ous dialogue and Grant's virtuoso performance. From the first scene, where Bagley addresses new recruits about the dos and don'ts of advertising, the satiric echoes to the opening speech of *Patton* ring loud and clear. For proof of Grant's conviction to the role, look no further than when the feral Bagley, complete with foaming ketchup mouth, gorges his face on hospital food (chapter 13). The 1.85 non-anamorphic transfer looks sharp and clean, with bright colors and solid image detail. The crisp Surround soundtrack allows for clear dialogue and even manages some envelopment when the classical music kicks in (Robinson's ironic use of Holst and Saint-Saens excerpts border on the inspired). Alas, there are no extras other than the wacky theatrical trailer. Even a simple current interview with Robinson and/or Grant would have been fascinating. —*EP*
Movie: 🎬🎬🎬 ***DVD:*** 🎬🎬🎬
Criterion (cat #CC1574D, UPC 71551501-2324). Widescreen (1.85:1) letterboxed. Dolby Digital Surround. $29.98. Keepcase. *LANG:* English. *SUB:* English. *FEATURES:* 20 chapters • Theatrical trailer.
1989 (R) 95m/C *GB* Richard E. Grant, Rachel Ward, Susan Wooldridge, Mick Ford, Richard Wilson, John Shrapnel, Jacqueline Tong; ***D:*** Bruce Robinson; ***W:*** Bruce Robinson; ***C:*** Peter Hannan; ***M:*** David Dundas, Rick Wentworth.

How to Kill Your Neighbor's Dog

Struggling playwright Peter McGowen (Branagh) is stuck with writer's block, made worse by the neighbor's barking dog, a stalker, and his wife's aggressive maternal instincts. In an effort to boost the dialogue of his new play he befriends a neighbor, a young girl with cerebral palsy. The results are predictable, and the turn into drama is a bit sudden, but Branagh plays an excellent curmudgeon and the script is full of catchy one-liners. Picture quality is fairly grainy and the dialogue is often muddled, making for a merely average disc. —*BG*
Movie: 🎬🎬 ½ ***DVD:*** 🎬🎬 ½
Artisan Ent. (cat #12608, UPC 012-236126089). Full frame. $24.98. Keepcase. *LANG:* English. *SUB:* Spanish. *CAP:* English. *FEATURES:* 28 chapters • Trailer.
2001 (R) 108m/C Kenneth Branagh, Robin Wright Penn, Jared Harris, Suzi Hofrichter, Johnathon Schaech, Peter Riegert, Lynn Redgrave; ***D:*** Michael Kalesniko; ***W:*** Michael Kalesniko; ***C:*** Hubert Taczanowski; ***M:*** David Robbins.

How to Succeed in Business without Really Trying

Classic musical comedy about a window-washer who charms his way to the top of a major company. Robert Morse repeats his Tony-winning Broadway role. Loosely based on a non-fiction book of the same title by Shepherd Mead, which Morse purchases on his first day of work. Excellent transfer of stage to film, with choreography by Moreda expanding Bob Fosse's original plan. The film is dynamite from start to finish, but this DVD is very sub-par for MGM. Maybe an anamorphic transfer (instead of letterboxed) would have helped, but the image is soft and there are scenes where unacceptable amounts of artifacts appear. On the plus side, the colors are very good and bleed is almost non-existent, which is rare when the image is this soft. The only supplemental, the original theatrical trailer, looks even worse. Almost all MGM's lower priced DVD releases are far superior to this one. —*JO*
Movie: 🎬🎬🎬 ½ ***DVD:*** 🎬 ½
MGM Home Ent. (cat #908095, UPC 027-616809520). Widescreen (2.35:1) letterboxed. Dolby Digital Mono. $24.98. Keepcase. *LANG:* English; Spanish. *SUB:* Spanish; French. *CAP:* English. *FEATURES:* 28 chapters • Theatrical trailer.
1967 121m/C Robert Morse, Michele Lee, Rudy Vallee, Anthony Teague, George Fenneman, Maureen Arthur; ***D:*** David Swift; ***W:*** David Swift, Abe Burrows; ***C:*** Burnett Guffey; ***M:*** Frank Loesser.

The Howling

John Sayles and Joe Dante create one of the finest modern horror movies. It's filled with jokes and celebrity appearances. The mixture of comedy with real scares is rare. A TV newswoman (Stone) must face real horror in the form of a serial rapist-killer (Picardo) and a town that's filled with werewolves. (By the way, this film has nothing to do with the title-only sequels that have followed.) DVD presents a fine re-creation of an image that's often very dark. Mono sound does the job. A special edition with a commentary track by the writer and director is definitely called for. —*MM*
Movie: 🎬🎬🎬 ***DVD:*** 🎬🎬 ½
MGM Home Ent. (cat #1002329, UPC 027-616865489). Widescreen (1.85:1) anamorphic. Dolby Digital Mono. $19.95. Keepcase. *LANG:* English. *SUB:* French; Spanish. *CAP:* English. *FEATURES:* 16 chapters • Trailer.
1981 (R) 91m/C Dee Wallace Stone, Patrick Macnee, Dennis Dugan, Christopher Stone, Belinda Balaski, Kevin McCarthy, John Carradine, Slim Pickens, Elisabeth Brooks, Robert Picardo, Dick Miller, Kenneth Tobey, Meshach Taylor, John Sayles, Roger Corman, Forrest J Ackerman; ***D:*** Joe Dante; ***W:*** John Sayles, Terence H. Winkless; ***C:*** John Hora; ***M:*** Pino Donaggio.

Howling 3: The Marsupials

Werewolves (who raise their young in pouches like marsupials) live in the Australian outback. Escaping to the city, wolf woman Jerboa (Biolos) falls in love with Donny (Biolos) and runs off to the wilderness with the help of a benevolent scientist (Otto) to escape pursuit by government medics. This jaw-dropping mess seems to switch gears every 10 minutes and features some of the worst werewolf effects in the history of the genre. On the commentary track, Mora insists it was all supposed to be funny, but just because nobody takes a bad script seriously doesn't make the film a comedy. The few laughs there are seem awkward. On the plus side is some very pretty location photography; Otto is likable and Biolos and Annesley are attractive leads. (Except when Annesley's pouch is showing! Yecch!) The disc seems to be framed correctly and features a bright, colorful, and near-stunning transfer of the film. The remixed soundtrack is light on multi-channel effects but does have strong presence. The audio commentary (though dubious) is consistently interesting and worth listening to. Heck, watch it with the film! It's more enjoyable that way. —*DG* **AKA:** The Marsupials: Howling 3.
Movie: 🎬 ***DVD:*** 🎬🎬🎬 ½
Elite Entertainment, Inc. (cat #EE6672, UPC 790594667221). Widescreen (1.85:1) anamorphic. Dolby Surround 5.1. $29.95. Keepcase. *LANG:* English. *FEATURES:* Commentary: Mora • Still gallery • Trailer and TV spot • 12 chapters • Insert card.
1987 (PG-13) 94m/C *AU* Barry Otto, Imogen Annesley, Dasha Blahova, Max Fairchild, Ralph Cotterill, Leigh Biolos, Frank Thring Jr., Michael Pate; ***D:*** Philippe Mora; ***W:*** Philippe Mora; ***C:*** Louis Irving; ***M:*** Allan Zavod.

Human Desires

A search for a new model to represent a line of lingerie provides a bevy of beauties for disheveled P.I. Dean Thomas (Noble) to investigate when one of them turns up dead. The death is ruled a suicide but fellow model Zoe (Billings) thinks it was murder, and Thomas is ready to go to the mats, if necessary, to find out. The action is generally well lit and photographed, so it looks fine, but the full-frame image and sound are not noticeably superior to VHS tape. Disc is a double feature with *Forbidden Sins*. —*MM*
Movie: 🎬🎬 ***DVD:*** 🎬🎬
Columbia Tristar (cat #05287, UPC 04339-6052871). Full frame. Dolby Digital Stereo. $19.98. Keepcase. *LANG:* English. *SUB:* English; French; Spanish; Portuguese. *CAP:* English. *FEATURES:* 28 chapters.
1997 (R) 95m/C Shannon Tweed, Christian Noble, Dawn Ann Billings, Duke Stroud; ***D:*** Ellen Earnshaw; ***W:*** Todd Smith; ***C:*** Carl Oakwood; ***M:*** Ed Korvin.

Human Prey

A psychologist goes nuts and kills people at random. No-budget action flick was shot on video and is amateurish in every respect—acting, direction, writing, lighting. DVD can do nothing to improve it. Title is available as part of the "Action Arsenal" collection. —*MM*
Movie: 🎬 ***DVD:*** 🎬

BCI-Eclipse (cat #44076-9, UPC 7873644-07699). Full frame. $19.98. Keepcase. *LANG:* English. *FEATURES:* 7 chapters. **1995 85m/C** Cliff Drew, Mickey Levy, Gloria Lusiak; *D:* James Tucker; *W:* James Tucker.

The Hunchback of Notre Dame

The only real attraction here is Gina Lollobrigida at the height of the mid-'50s cheese-cake phase of her career, and there's a lot to be said for that. Otherwise, this one's a product of its time—slow, showy, long, and overacted. In terms of plot, the film is fairly faithful to Victor Hugo's novel. Gina Lollobrigida is a spirited Esmeralda, the sultry gypsy who catches the eye of bell-ringer Quasimodo (Quinn) and his boss at the cathedral, Claude Frollo (Cuny). Director Jean Delannoy has problems keeping the two conflicting sides of the film in sync. At the beginning, for example, when the characters and conflicts are being laid out, the action stops cold for several minutes while La Lollo does a sexy dance in a very red, very tight dress. Alas, the rest of the film can't match that moment, though the plot often pauses to admire the leading lady. Quinn is trapped under heavy, stiff prosthetic makeup and Cuney is a mopey villain. In the end, this live-action version runs a distant fourth behind Lon Chaney's 1923 silent film, the brilliant 1939 William Dieterle-Charles Laughton picture, and the underrated 1982 made-for-TV movie with Anthony Hopkins, Leslie Anne Down, and Derek Jacobi (the last as yet unavailable on disc). DVD appears to be an accurate reproduction of a bright, slightly harsh image with strong supersaturated colors. Gina's dress is astonishing. Shingle patterns flash strongly, particularly in panning shots. Surround delivers understandable dialogue. —MM **AKA:** Notre Dame de Paris.
Movie: 🎵🎵 *DVD:* 🎵🎵
Miramax Pictures (cat #24738, UPC 786-936169874). Widescreen (2.35:1) letterboxed. Dolby Digital Surround. $34.98. Keepcase. *LANG:* English. *CAP:* English. *FEATURES:* 19 chapters.
1957 (PG) 104m/C *FR* Anthony Quinn, Gina Lollobrigida, Alain Cuny, Jean Danet, Robert Hirsch, Jean Tissier; *D:* Jean Delannoy; *W:* Jacques Prevert, Jean Aurenche; *C:* Michel Kelber; *M:* Georges Auric.

The Hunchback of Notre Dame

Disney's animated version of the famous novel is a true enigma. It works perfectly fine as a movie, but it doesn't work at all as a Disney family film. While recent Disney entries such as *The Emperor's New Groove* and *Hercules* have been hip and sassy, *Hunchback* throws in far too many mature themes for the film to be accepted as children's fare. Gary Trousdale and Kirk Wise, the directors of the classic *Beauty and the Beast*, head to France again for this film. Here we meet Quasimodo (voice of Hulce), the hunchbacked bell-ringer of

Notre Dame cathedral, who has been raised by the evil Frollo (Jay). After spending 20 years exiled in the church, Quasimodo decides to venture out into the world, against his master's wishes, and attend a festival. There, he meets the enchanting gypsy dancer Esmeralda (Moore). When the crowd turns on Quasimodo, Esmeralda rushes to his aid. Disgusted by this display, Frollo orders her to be arrested by soldier Phoebus (Kline). Quasimodo offers sanctuary to Esmeralda, who is taken by Phoebus's bravery and chivalry. Together, this trio decides that Frollo has oppressed the people of Paris long enough, and fights back. The film tells a wonderful story, which teaches a fine lesson about inner strength and beauty, and the animation is breathtaking at times. (The use of stained glass in Notre Dame is awesome.) But any film which has a sexually repressed puritan as the villain and a scantily clad gypsy dancer as the love interest isn't exactly aimed at the pre-school set, so parents should certainly take note. The songs here, by *Beauty* composer Alan Menken with lyrics by Stephen Schwartz, are good for the most part, and do help to advance the story. Despite digital remastering for DVD, the film does show some grain and assorted defects from the source print. Otherwise, the image is sharp and clear. The colors here are excellent, as the hues aid in telling the story. The DVD contains both a DTS 5.1 and Dolby Digital 5.1 audio track, both of which sound fine. The DTS track is a bit louder and offers more dynamic range, but otherwise, both are identical. The dialogue is clear, the songs sound great, and the stereo separation is superb. There is a lack of bass response at times. (One would think that the bells of Notre Dame would create more of a rumble). This DVD contains a spirited audio commentary with Trousdale and Kirk and producer Don Hahn, where they discuss the making of the film. —ML
Movie: 🎵🎵🎵 *DVD:* 🎵🎵🎵
Buena Vista Home Ent. (cat #23315, UPC 786936160079). Widescreen (1.85:1) anamorphic. Dolby Digital 5.1; DTS 5.1. $29.99. Keepcase. *LANG:* English; French; Spanish. *SUB:* English. *CAP:* English. *FEATURES:* Featurette ● Commentary: Trousdale, Kirk, producer Don Hahn ● Sing-a-long ● Set-top game ● 30 chapters.
1996 (G) 91m/C *D:* Kirk Wise, Gary Trousdale; *W:* Irene Mecchi, Tab Murphy, Jonathan Roberts, Bob Tzudiker, Noni White; *M:* Stephen Schwartz, Alan Menken; *V:* Tom Hulce, Demi Moore, Kevin Kline, Tony Jay, Charles Kimbrough, Jason Alexander, Mary Wickes, David Ogden Stiers. *AWARDS: NOM:* Oscars '96: Orig. Score; Golden Globes '97: Score.

The Hunchback of Notre Dame 2

Over the years, Disney's direct-to-video animated sequels have ranged from good (*Pocahontas 2*) to awful (*Return of Jafar*). This one falls somewhere in-between. The

story picks up a few years after the conclusion of the first film. Quasimodo (voiced by Hulce) still lives in the belfry of Notre Dame and still talks to the gargoyles, but has been accepted by the citizens of Paris. Phoebus (Kline) has married Esmeralda (Moore) and they now have a young son, Zephyr (Osment). When the circus comes to town, everyone is excited about going, especially Quasimodo and Zephyr. However, the evil Sarousch (McKean) has more in mind than putting on an exciting show. His circus is merely a cover for a band of thieves, and he plans to steal a jewel-encrusted bell from Notre Dame. He enlists Madeline (Hewitt) to gain the trust of Quasimodo, and thus, access to the bell-tower. When Madeline approaches the Hunchback, he is shy at first, but soon begins to fall in love with Madeline. Can she return this love, or does she intend to steal Quasimodo's heart, as well as the priceless bell? Sequel brings back all of the familiar characters (and the actors who portrayed them as well), but the story is too predictable and the animation is horrible. From the outset, it is very clear what's going to happen to Quasimodo and which direction the story is going to take. Also, the movie hits the viewer over the head with its message—the bell in question looks ordinary from the outside, but the inside is beautiful, just like Quasimodo. Get it? The animation ranges from mediocre to awful, as there isn't much detail in the drawings. (It definitely pales in comparison to the first film.) Some of the drawings resemble Saturday-morning cartoon work, while others have an anime look to them. One positive thing about this film is that it doesn't contain the mature themes that plagued the first film, thus making it much more appropriate for family viewing. The image is very sharp, crisp, and clear, showing no defects or distortion. The colors are excellent and the picture has real depth. Both Dolby and DTS tracks offer clear dialogue and music, but lack the dynamic range and bass response that one would expect from a fairly new film. —ML
Movie: 🎵🎵 *DVD:* 🎵🎵 ½
Buena Vista Home Ent. (cat #21317, UPC 786936141450). Widescreen (1.66:1) anamorphic. Dolby Digital 5.1; DTS 5.1. $29.99. Keepcase. *LANG:* English; French; Spanish. *SUB:* English. *CAP:* English. *FEATURES:* Featurettes ● Set-top games ● 24 chapters.
2001 (G) 68m/C *D:* Bradley Raymond; *V:* Tom Hulce, Demi Moore, Kevin Kline, Jennifer Love Hewitt, Haley Joel Osment, Michael McKean, Jason Alexander, Jane Withers.

The Hunger: Smoke, Mirrors, and Paranoia

This cable TV series bears little resemblance to the 1983 vampire film. The only connection is David Bowie, who introduces each half-hour episode. The films themselves are imaginative, in a way, but also undernourished and lacking in sex appeal,

which, apparently, is the selling point. Given the arty, distressed, shot-on-video look to which the filmmakers aspire, there's little improvement to be gained on DVD. Bottom line: The image is ugly and the stories aren't very interesting. Contents: "Bottle of Smoke," "Approaching Desdemona," "The Seductress," and "Skin Deep." Other available collections of the series include: *Bump in the Night* (UPC 750723105529); *Soul Snatcher* (UPC 750723105420); *Soul for Sale* (UPC 750723103129); *Vampires* (UPC 750723-103020); and *Wicked Dreams* (UPC 75-0723103228). —*MM*
Movie: 𝆕𝆕 **DVD:** 𝆕𝆕
York Ent. (UPC 750723105321). Full frame. Dolby Digital 5.1 Surround. $14.98. Keepcase. *LANG:* English. *FEATURES:* 24 chapters • Trailers • Filmographies.
2000 120m/C David Bowie, Cathy Moriarty.

The Hunter

Steve McQueen's last movie is an enjoyable if somewhat subdued and thoughtful combination of action and character study, based on a real character, Ralph "Papa" Thorson. He's a contemporary bounty hunter and so the role eerily echoes McQueen's early success on the TV series *Wanted: Dead or Alive*. The plotting is episodic with heavy emphasis on the supporting characters, particularly Kathryn Harrold as Thorson's very pregnant girlfriend, and LeVar Burton as a young guy who begins as the object of one of Thorson's hunts but becomes an employee. DVD is an accurate re-creation of the theatrical image, with the muted colors and relatively soft focus typical of the period. Mono sound is just fine. —*MM*
Movie: 𝆕𝆕𝆕 **DVD:** 𝆕𝆕 ½
Paramount (cat #01192, UPC 097360119-244). Widescreen anamorphic. Dolby Digital Mono. $29.98. Keepcase. *LANG:* English. *SUB:* English. *CAP:* English. *FEATURES:* 14 chapters • Trailer.
1980 (PG) 97m/C Steve McQueen, Eli Wallach, Kathryn Harrold, LeVar Burton; **D:** Buzz Kulik; **W:** Peter Hyams; **C:** Fred W. Koenekamp; **M:** Charles Bernstein.

Hurlyburly

Casting agents Eddie (Penn) and Mickey (Spacey) share a Hollywood apartment with out-of-work actor Phil (Palminteri). Eddie uses cocaine almost constantly; Phil has just been dumped by his wife; and Mickey, although more low-key, is ready to explode. They're all desperate to be huge "Hollywood" successes. The plot pretty much consists of the men venting their spleens and treating women like crap, particularly Bonnie (Ryan), a slutty exotic dancer traded among the boys. Snappy dialogue-happy script might have worked on the stage, but here, with the camera in close, the mean spirit becomes tiring very quickly. Paquin shows confidence in her first adult role, as a drifter girl-toy. The soundtrack is crisp and clear, which is essential since dialogue runs this

movie and needs to be understood. On disc, the video transfer is also exceptional, although fine detail in darker colors is occasionally lost. Of particular note is the extensiveness of the audio commentaries. After listening to them all, you will get the feeling that you've watched a completely different movie each time. —*MJT*
Movie: 𝆕𝆕 **DVD:** 𝆕𝆕𝆕
New Line (cat #N4746, UPC 7940434746-20). Widescreen (1.85:1) anamorphic. Dolby Digital 5.1 Surround; Dolby Digital Surround. $24.98. Snapper. *LANG:* English. *SUB:* English. *FEATURES:* 29 chapters • Commentary: Anthony Drazan, David Rabe • Commentary: Penn, Baerwald, social commentator Janet Brown • Cast & crew filmographies and bios • Theatrical trailer.
1998 (R) 122m/C Sean Penn, Kevin Spacey, Chazz Palminteri, Meg Ryan, Robin Wright Penn, Anna Paquin, Garry Shandling; **D:** Tony Drazan; **W:** David Rabe; **C:** Gu Changwei; **M:** David Baerwald. *AWARDS: NOM:* Ind. Spirit '99: Actor (Penn).

Husbands and Wives

When Jack (Pollack) and Sally (Davis) announce that they are getting divorced, it throws their friends' own marriage into chaos. As Judy (Farrow) and Gabe (Allen) examine their own relationship, they find it lacking and begin looking for love with other partners. Bold and often screamingly funny examination of marriage feels painfully autobiographical at times (scenes between Allen and Farrow seem extremely revelatory and private) and is utterly convincing. Pollack's relationship with fruitcake Sam (Lysette Anthony, whose "valley girl" accent is a bit dodgy) is uproarious and Davis's anger feels almost tangibly real. The subtle character role reversals that happen during the film are a delight to behold. The image is sharp, warmly colored, and very grainy, though the grain is an intentional part of the documentary-style of the camerawork. The sound is clean and strong; it's another terrific Woody Allen mono sound mix. As usual, it's comparable to most stereo tracks. —*DG*
Movie: 𝆕𝆕𝆕 **DVD:** 𝆕𝆕𝆕
Columbia Tristar (cat #51557, UPC 043-396515574). Widescreen (1.85:1) anamorphic. Mono. $24.95. Keepcase. *LANG:* English. *SUB:* English; French; Spanish; Portuguese. *CAP:* English. *FEATURES:* 28 chapters • Trailers.
1992 (R) 107m/C Woody Allen, Mia Farrow, Judy Davis, Sydney Pollack, Liam Neeson, Juliette Lewis, Lysette Anthony, Blythe Danner; **D:** Woody Allen; **W:** Woody Allen; **C:** Carlo Di Palma. *AWARDS:* British Acad. '92: Orig. Screenplay; L.A. Film Critics '92: Support. Actress (Davis); Natl. Bd. of Review '92: Support. Actress (Davis); Natl. Soc. Film Critics '92: Support. Actress (Davis); *NOM:* Oscars '92: Orig. Screenplay, Support. Actress (Davis).

I Am Sam

Cliché-ridden drama is a four-hankie wallow for some; an embarrassment to oth-

ers. Sean Penn is the title character, a slightly retarded man who must battle the legal system for custody of his darling little daughter (Fanning). Will he win over a harried, cynical lawyer (Pfeiffer, looking even more gorgeous than normal)? Yet another stellar transfer from the folks at New Line. The image is nice and sharp with no glaring edge-enhancement or film grain. Colors are deep and natural and black levels are spot-on. It should be mentioned that the color blue is used as an artistic device throughout the film and much of the movie is seen with a blue tint or blue backgrounds. As is to be expected for such a new film, there are no nicks or blemishes of any sort on the print. The film looks great from beginning to end. As for audio, this isn't a real whiz-bang picture designed to make full use of your sound system and much of the dialogue-oriented action is firmly anchored to the center speaker. But John Powell's almost whimsical musical score as well as the half dozen or so covers of Beatles songs performed by artists such as Eddie Vedder and Aimee Mann really make full use of the 5.1 mixes. The score swells up to engulf the listener and the great dynamic range allows for a very lifelike audio experience. —*MM/MP*
Movie: 𝆕𝆕 ½ **DVD:** 𝆕𝆕𝆕 ½
New Line Home Video (UPC 7940435537-21). Widescreen (1.85:1) anamorphic. DTS 5.1 Surround; Dolby 5.1 Surround; Dolby Surround. $24.98. Snapper. *LANG:* English. *SUB:* English. *FEATURES:* Commentary • Documentary • Deleted scenes • Production notes • Theatrical press kit • Trailer.
2001 (PG-13) 93m/C Sean Penn, Michelle Pfeiffer, Dakota Fanning, Dianne Wiest, Loretta Devine, Richard Schiff, Laura Dern, Brad Allan Silverman, Stanley DeSantis, Doug Hutchison, Joseph Rosenberg, Mary Steenburgen; **D:** Jessie Nelson; **W:** Jessie Nelson, Kristine Johnson; **C:** Elliot Davis; **M:** John Powell. *AWARDS: NOM:* Oscars '01: Actor (Penn); Screen Actors Guild '01: Actor (Penn), Support. Actress (Fanning); Broadcast Film Critics '01: Actor (Penn).

I Bury the Living

Newly arrived cemetery manager Robert Kraft (Boone) sticks pins in a map of the graveyard and people mysteriously die. Does he have some unexplained power or is it merely coincidence? Suspense/horror film makes the most of a modest budget. Boone is particularly good in the lead. DVD presents an ultra-sharp undamaged black-and-white image. Mono sound is strong, too, making this one a nicely understated sparkler. Producer/director Band is father of Charles Band, founder of Full Moon Entertainment. —*MM*
Movie: 𝆕𝆕𝆕 **DVD:** 𝆕𝆕𝆕
MGM Home Ent. (cat #1002642, UPC 027-616868428). Full frame. Dolby Digital Mono. $14.95. Keepcase. *LANG:* English. *SUB:* French; Spanish. *CAP:* English. *FEATURES:* Trailer • 16 chapters.

1958 76m/B Richard Boone, Theodore Bikel, Peggy Maurer, Herbert Anderson, Howard Smith, Robert Osterloh, Russ Bender, Matt Moore, Ken Drake, Glenn Vernon, Lynn Bernay, Cyril Delevanti; **D:** Albert Band; **W:** Louis Garfinkle; **C:** Frederick Gately; **M:** Gerald Fried.

I Never Promised You a Rose Garden

Deborah (Quinlan), a disturbed 16-year-old girl, spirals down into madness while hospital psychiatrist Dr. Fried (Andersson) attempts to bring her back. Compelling exploration of the clinical treatment of schizophrenia is based on the Joan Greenberg best-seller. DVD presents a very grainy image that is, for the most part, an accurate reproduction of a mid-budget '70s image. Sound is poor and the print displays some snow and nicks. The feature-length commentary by Kathleen Quinlan advertised on the box copy is not there. —MM

Movie: 🐾🐾🐾 **DVD:** 🐾🐾 ½
New Concorde (cat #N20174 D, UPC 736-991417496). Full frame. $19.98. Keepcase. *LANG:* English. *FEATURES:* 24 chapters • Interview with Kathleen Quinlan • Trailers • Thumbnail bios.
1977 (R) 90m/C Kathleen Quinlan, Bibi Andersson, Sylvia Sidney, Diane Varsi, Dennis Quaid, Jeff Conaway; **D:** Anthony Page; **W:** Gavin Lambert, Lewis John Carlino; **C:** Bruce Logan; **M:** Paul Chihara. *AWARDS: NOM:* Oscars '77: Adapt. Screenplay.

I Spit on Your Corpse, I Piss on Your Grave

Kidnapped Sandy (Haack) turns the table on her captor, then continues to torture the other captives. Just what we need—a revival of the '70s rape-revenge movies. This film is depraved from start to finish, and some sort of prize should be given to anyone who can sit through the final 10 minutes. The extremely low budget makes for a fairly poor DVD that looks and sounds like a bad VHS tape. An amusing extra chronicles the director's encounters with police after a nosy neighbor finds a slew of prosthetic body parts in the dumpster. —BG

Movie: woof **DVD:** 🐾
Sub Rosa Studios (cat #SREDVD1000). Full frame. $29.99. Keepcase. *LANG:* English. *FEATURES:* 10 chapters • Commentary: writer/director Stanze, star Haack • Trailers • "Making of" featurette • "The Dumpster Incident."
2002 70m/C Emily Haack, Scot Spookytooth, Shaun Snow, John Specht, Jeff Atwater; **D:** Eric Stanze; **W:** Eric Stanze.

I Vampiri

This is the first time that Mario Bava's film has been presented in its original form in this country. (The story of a Paris newspaperman's journey into an underground network of mad scientists and vampires was

released with "extra" scenes under the title *Devil's Commandment*.) The movie makes frequent use of stock footage and although the quality is not quite as good in many of those shots, as soon as Bava's own material comes into play, the image is remarkably sharp, clean, and bold. Contrast is very good with very deep blacks and good shadow fall-offs. Highlights are usually rendered very well without bleeding, although occasionally some overexposure is evident in selected shots. Although the frequency response is limited on the Dolby mono and some sibilance is evident, the track is in good shape without notable defects or problems. As usual, Bava biographer Tim Lucas's liner notes are a great read and full of valuable information. —MM/GH **AKA:** The Devil's Commandment; Lust of the Vampires.

Movie: 🐾🐾🐾 **DVD:** 🐾🐾🐾
Image Ent. (cat #ID8481FDVD, UPC 014-381848120). Widescreen (2.35:1) anamorphic. Dolby Digital Mono. $24.99. Keepcase. *LANG:* Italian. *SUB:* English. *FEATURES:* Liner notes by Tim Lucas • Photo and poster gallery • Trailers • 12 chapters.
1956 78m/B *FR* Gianna Maria Canale, Dario Michaelis, Carlo D'Angelo, Wandisa Guida, Paul Muller, Renato Tontini; **D:** Riccardo (Robert Hampton) Freda, Mario Bava; **C:** Mario Bava.

I Want to Live!

Bad girl Graham (Hayward) tries to settle down and raise a family, but is drawn back into some shady dealings to make ends meet. When her partners in crime finger her for a murder she had nothing to do with, Graham finds herself in an uphill battle for her life. While the film made quite a splash on its release, catching six Oscar nominations with Hayward winning for Best Actress, it hasn't aged particularly well. The last half-hour is tense and moving but much of the rest is melodramatic and overly sentimental. The picture contains the expected amount of grain for a film from the 1950s, but the non-anamorphic widescreen is a mystery. John Mandel's jazz score comes across nicely, though the dialogue meets with frequent distortion. —BG

Movie: 🐾🐾 **DVD:** 🐾🐾 ½
MGM Home Ent. (cat #1003430, UPC 027-616875792). Widescreen (1.66:1) letterboxed. Dolby Mono. $14.95. Keepcase. *LANG:* English. *SUB:* English; French; Spanish. *CAP:* English. *FEATURES:* 16 chapters • Trailer.
1958 120m/B Susan Hayward, Simon Oakland, Theodore Bikel, Virginia Vincent, Wesley Lau; **D:** Robert Wise; **W:** Nelson Gidding, Don Mankiewicz; **C:** Lionel Lindon; **M:** Johnny Mandel. *AWARDS:* Oscars '58: Actress (Hayward); Golden Globes '59: Actress—Drama (Hayward); N.Y. Film Critics '58: Actress (Hayward); *NOM:* Oscars '58: Adapt. Screenplay, B&W Cinematog., Director (Wise), Film Editing, Sound.

Ice Grill

Strictly amateur production is a lame action/heist flick. The so-called Ice Grill bandits steal jewels and decide to double-cross another gangster. Visual and aural flaws are numerous and constant: serious aliasing, grain leading to heavy artifacts in dim shots (and lighting is poor to non-existent throughout), harsh sound that renders some dialogue unintelligible. —MM

Movie: 🐾 **DVD:** woof
York Ent. (cat #YPD1182, UPC 75072311-8222). Full frame. $14.99. Keepcase. *LANG:* English.
2002 98m/C Travis Johnson, Jay Parris, Johnny Kitt, Crystal Hyman, Hope Harris, Jane Blaze; **D:** John Stu; **W:** John Stu; **C:** Weiner Milien.

The Ice Rink

This fabulously funny French farce is focused on filmmaking. A small film crew has come to an ice rink to make a film that mixes hockey and romance. What seems like a relatively simple shoot turns into a disaster. No one on the crew can ice-skate. The hockey team doesn't speak French. And the American film star (Bruce Campbell) tapped for the lead in the film seems bored. And these dilemmas are just the tip of the "ice" berg. The comedy is a mixture of very subtle humor (the director and his megaphone) and comedy of the "pratfall" variety (someone falls on the ice in every scene). The film moves along at a nice pace, and one is almost sad to see it end so quickly. Fans of foreign comedies will certainly enjoy it, and cult-film followers will delight in seeing horror-icon Campbell in a different role. The DVD offers a transfer which is sharp, but riddled with problems. There are scratches and blemishes from the source print evident throughout the film. Also, the transfer is very bright, making the colors look washed-out. The digital stereo provides clear dialogue, but the white subtitles are difficult to read at times. —ML **AKA:** La Patinoire.

Movie: 🐾🐾🐾 ½ **DVD:** 🐾🐾
Kino on Video (cat #K212 DVD, UPC 738-329021221). Widescreen (1.85:1) letterboxed. Digital Stereo. $29.98. Keepcase. *LANG:* French. *SUB:* English. *FEATURES:* Theatrical trailer • 14 chapters.
199980m/C *FR* Tom Novembre, Marie-France Pisier, Bruce Campbell, Dolores Chaplin, Mireille Perrier, Jean-Pierre Cassel; **D:** Jean-Philippe Toussaint; **W:** Jean-Philippe Toussaint; **C:** Jean-François Robin.

The Ice Storm

Muted, but occasionally funny tale about two suburban Connecticut families and their crises of fidelity and sexual exploration during the 1970s. Though the production and performances are top-notch (with Weaver a standout as a chilling ice queen), the film never really gels. The ending achieves poignancy, but the young characters in the film are so strange and quirky, they're almost creepy. Despite its

'70s era story line, the film (refreshingly) doesn't poke fun at the styles and clothing of the era; it's merely background for the tale. In retrospect, it seems like a rough draft for *American Beauty,* which features strong similarities to this film and also focuses on infidelity and suburban angst. The disc is sharp and pleasing with a minimum of grain. The sound is excellent, with the Surround track particularly effective once the titular ice storm begins. The featurette is extremely short and insubstantial. —*DG*

Movie: 🎬🎬½ **DVD:** 🎬🎬🎬½
20th Century Fox (cat #2001224, UPC 024543012245). Widescreen (1.85:1) anamorphic. Dolby Surround 5.0; Dolby Surround. $24.98. Keepcase. *LANG:* English; French. *SUB:* English; Spanish. *CAP:* English. *FEATURES:* Featurette • Theatrical trailer • 24 chapters.
1997 (R) 113m/C Kevin Kline, Sigourney Weaver, Joan Allen, Christina Ricci, Tobey Maguire, Elijah Wood, Katie Holmes, Henry Czerny, Adam Hann-Byrd, David Krumholtz, Jamey Sheridan, Maia Danzinger, Kate Burton, John Benjamin Hickey, Allison Janney, Byron Jennings; *D:* Ang Lee; *W:* James Schamus; *C:* Frederick Elmes; *M:* Mychael Danna. *AWARDS:* British Acad. '97: Support. Actress (Weaver); *NOM:* Australian Film Inst. '98: Foreign Film; British Acad. '97: Adapt. Screenplay; Golden Globes '98: Support. Actress (Weaver); Writers Guild '97: Adapt. Screenplay.

The Iceman Cometh

As part of the "Broadway Theatre Archive" series, this double-disc set doesn't have much to offer in terms of image. It shouldn't. This is a 1960 TV production of O'Neill's famous play. Its value is mostly historic, particularly for serious students of drama (not that the credits aren't impressive). This represents, I think, the only recorded version of Jason Robards's Hickey. Considering the age of the production and the conditions under which it was made, DVD image is very good. —*MM*

Movie: 🎬🎬🎬 **DVD:** 🎬🎬½
Image Ent. (cat #ID0877B DDVD, UPC 014381087727). Full frame. Dolby Digital Mono. $24.98. Keepcase. *LANG:* English. *FEATURES:* Intro by Brooks Atkinson • Liner notes • 24 chapters • Jason Robards filmography.
1960 210m/B Jason Robards Jr., Myron McCormick, Tom Pedi, James Broderick, Robert Redford, Ronald Radd; *D:* Sidney Lumet.

Idiot Box

Lazy and brainless, Kev (Mendelsohn) and Mick (Sims) spend most of their time watching violent cop shows and old videos while drinking themselves to oblivion. It's from the "idiot box" that the dim duo gets the idea that they've learned enough to rob banks, but it just so happens that a pair of crooks wearing clown masks are already on a bank crime spree. Naturally both sets of robbers eventually target the same bank and the cops just happen to be waiting. For a true exercise in delusion, be sure to watch the "Behind the Scenes" portion of the DVD. The filmmakers are more than happy to tell you how this "film" is a window in to Australian suburban life and what a great job they did making it. They refer to their work as darkly comic, but true dark comedy has either something so say that rings true or is bitterly sarcastic. This film is barely amusing, proving that it's hard to be cool when you have nothing to say. The transfer to DVD is passable, and overall captures the poor quality of the film. —*JAS*

Movie: 🎬½ **DVD:** 🎬🎬🎬
Winstar Home Ent. (cat #FLV5283, UPC 720917528328). Full frame. Dolby Digital. $24.98. Keepcase. *LANG:* English. *FEATURES:* Weblinks • Behind-the-scenes featurette • Trailer.
1997 83m/C *AU* Ben Mendelsohn, Jeremy Sims, John Polson, Robyn Loau, Graeme Blundell, Deborah Kennedy, Stephen Rae, Andrew S. Gilbert, Amanda Muggleton, Paul Gleeson, Susie Porter; *D:* David Caesar; *W:* David Caesar; *C:* Joseph Pickering; *M:* Tim Rogers, Nick Launay. *AWARDS: NOM:* Australian Film Inst. '97: Actor (Sims), Art Dir./Set Dec., Director (Caesar), Film Editing, Sound, Score.

Il Grido

When his girlfriend of seven years leaves him, Aldo (Cochran) takes their daughter to find a new life in the Italian countryside. His wanderings lead him into the lives of several women, but he finds himself unable to shake his hometown and his lost love. Fans of Antonioni's work will be interested, but others may find themselves bored by the film's slow pace and lack of plot. The picture and audio are not a notable improvement over VHS, and the burned-in subtitles leave entire conversations untranslated. —*BG* *AKA:* The Cry; The Outcry.

Movie: 🎬🎬½ **DVD:** 🎬🎬
Kino on Video (cat #K176, UPC 7383290-1762). Full frame. $29.95. Keepcase. *LANG:* Italian. *SUB:* English. *FEATURES:* 15 chapters.
1957 116m/B *IT* Steve Cochran, Alida Valli, Dorian Gray, Betsy Blair, Gabriella Pallotta; *D:* Michelangelo Antonioni; *W:* Michelangelo Antonioni, Ennio de Concini; *C:* Gianni Di Venanzo; *M:* Giovanni Fusco.

Illegal Affairs

The sleazy firm of Grimes and Peterson specializes in divorce cases and that provides the framework for a series of soft-core sex scenes all performed by actors who are familiar with the genre. Cast and crew are identical in *Brief Affair.* Both are video premieres with exceptionally poor images that gain nothing on DVD. They are part of the *All Night Movies* collection. —*MM*

Movie: 🎬 **DVD:** 🎬
BCI-Eclipse (cat #44109-6, UPC 7873644-10996). Full frame. $9.98. Keepcase. *LANG:* English. *FEATURES:* 11 chapters, *Illegal* • 10 chapters, *Brief.*
1996 87m/C Jay Richardson, Monique Parent, Christian Noble; *D:* Michael Paul Girard; *W:* Michael Paul Girard; *C:* Denis Maloney; *M:* Miriam Cutler.

Illicit Confessions

Poor Erica (Pickett). Because she works as a lap dancer (with a little hooking on the side), the judge won't grant her custody of her daughter. Actually, there's an attempt at some seriousness in this otherwise pedestrian stripper flick, but not enough to recommend it. DVD looks worse than most VHS tapes with poor production values and very heavy grain leading to heavy artifacts. No menu. —*MM* *AKA:* Confessions of a Lap Dancer.

Movie: 🎬½ **DVD:** 🎬½
York Ent. (cat #YPD-1162, UPC 7507231-16228). Full frame. $14.98. Keepcase. *LANG:* English.
1977 (R) 90m/C Blake Pickett, Amy Lindsey, Doug Jeffrey, Julia Kruise; *D:* Mike Sedan; *W:* Helen Haxton; *C:* Chris Moreman.

Immortal Beloved

On his deathbed, Beethoven (Oldman) writes a testament that declares his "Immortal Beloved" as the only heir. The enigmatic letter is found shortly after his death and questions arise as to who this anonymous heir is. Anton Schindler (Krabbé), his long-time friend, takes it upon himself to find the mysterious lover to have the testament executed. He meets with the women Beethoven loved and leads the viewer into the past of Beethoven's life and work. Oldman is darkly intense, and a scene in which the aged composer remembers his terrifying childhood amid the strains of "Ode to Joy" is simply stunning. DVD image is absolutely clean and of pristine quality without the slightest film artifacts. The picture is incredibly detailed with well-defined edges, but never appears overenhanced. Shadows are deep and solid, but always maintain plenty of detail, even in the darkest scenes. The color reproduction is breathtaking and entirely faithful. All shades and hues are perfectly reproduced and fleshtones are absolutely natural. The 5.1 mix is so engulfing that it will bathe your entire home theatre or living room in music. The mix is so wide and makes fantastic use of the Surrounds that you oftentimes feel as if you were sitting right there in the room with the orchestra. —*MM/GH*

Movie: 🎬🎬½ **DVD:** 🎬🎬🎬½
Columbia Tristar Home Video (UPC 043-396747692). Widescreen anamorphic. Dolby Digital 5.1 Surround. $19.98. Keepcase. *LANG:* English; Spanish. *SUB:* English; Spanish. *FEATURES:* Commentary • 2 documentaries • Theatrical trailer.
1994 (R) 121m/C Gary Oldman, Jeroen Krabbe, Isabella Rossellini, Johanna Ter Steege, Marco Hofschneider, Miriam Margolyes, Barry Humphries, Valeria Golino,

Christopher Fulford; **D:** Bernard Rose; **W:** Bernard Rose; **C:** Peter Suschitzsky.

Impromptu

This one is an intelligent, sharp, funny romantic comedy set in 1830s Europe among the era's artistic greats—here depicted as scalawags, parasites, and early beatniks. The main characters are mannish author George Sand (Davis), who falls hard for Frederick Chopin (Grant) and arranges to spend some time with him. The middle section is a grand bedroom farce, but from beginning to end, this is a sleeper meant for adults. Image is generally very good but not spectacular, an accurate re-creation of the theatrical release as I recall it. Sound is similarly fine but unimpressive. —*MM*
Movie: ♫♫♫ ½ **DVD:** ♫♫♫
MGM Home Ent. (cat #1002967, UPC 027616871541). Widescreen (1.66:1) letterboxed. Dolby Digital Surround; Mono. $19.98. Keepcase. *LANG:* English; French. *SUB:* English; French; Spanish. *CAP:* English. *FEATURES:* 16 chapters • Trailer.
1990 (PG-13) 108m/C Judy Davis, Hugh Grant, Mandy Patinkin, Bernadette Peters, Julian Sands, Ralph Brown, Georges Corraface, Anton Rodgers, Emma Thompson, Anna Massey, John Savident, Elizabeth Spriggs; **D:** James Lapine; **W:** Sarah Kernochan; **C:** Bruno de Keyzer. *AWARDS:* Ind. Spirit '92: Actress (Davis).

In a Class of His Own

High-school janitor Rich Donato (Lou Diamond Phillips) is an ex-teen bad boy who has formed a close relationship with both the teachers and the students at the school where he works. However, to keep his job, he must pass the GED exam, which isn't an easy task. When his wife appeals for help, Rich finds himself becoming a school project. Teacher Linda Ching (Joan Chen) and a group of students band together to aid Rich in his time of need. Based on a true story, *In a Class of His Own* is standard made-for-TV fare, but the story is uplifting, and both Phillips and Chen give outstanding performances. Originally presented on Showtime, the film is offered in a full-frame format on this DVD. The image is quite sharp and clear, showing only a fine grain at times. The colors are good, although the image is somewhat dark in some scenes. The Dolby 2.0 Surround audio track provides surprisingly deep bass from the hip-hop ambient music. The dialogue is typically clear, but the sound is muffled at times. Unfortunately, there is very little in the way of Surround sound. —*ML*
Movie: ♫♫ ½ **DVD:** ♫♫
Showtime Networks, Inc. (cat #SHO3031, UPC 758445303124). Full frame. Dolby Surround. $19.98. Keepcase. *LANG:* English; Spanish. *CAP:* English. *FEATURES:* 12 chapters.
1999 94m/C Lou Diamond Phillips, Cara Buono, Joan Chen, Nathaniel DeVeaux; **D:**

Robert Munic; **W:** Robert Munic; **C:** Ron Stannett; **M:** Sharon Farber.

In His Life: The John Lennon Story

Made-for-TV biopic covers some of the same ground as *Backbeat* but not nearly as well. The subject is the early years of John Lennon (McQuillan). Performances are acceptable and since the film was shot in Liverpool, it has a nice look that may or may not be authentic. DVD is a slight improvement over broadcast quality, but the film has little to recommend it. —*MM*
Movie: ♫♫ **DVD:** ♫♫
Studio Home Ent. (cat #ST 7848D, UPC 658149784826). Full frame. Stereo. $24.98. Keepcase. *LANG:* English. *SUB:* English; French; Spanish. *CAP:* English. *FEATURES:* 24 chapters • Trailers.
2000 87m/C Phillip McQuillan, Daniel McGowan, Mark Rice-Oxley, Lee Williams, Jamie Glover, Scot Williams, Blair Brown, Kristian Ealey, Christine Kavanagh, Gillian Kearney, Palina Jonsdottir; **D:** David Carson; **W:** Michael O'Hara; **C:** Lawrence Jones; **M:** Dennis McCarthy.

In Love and War

British officer Eric Newby (Blue) is captured during WWII and put into an Italian POW camp. The prisoners escape once the Fascist government falls, but German Panzer Units are hot on their trail. Eric finds Wanda (Bobulova), and they quickly fall in love. She will risk anything to save him but, as the Germans close in, Eric is the one who must take the ultimate risk. This Hallmark Hall of Fame production is sanitized, but an emotional script (from the novel by Newby, fictionalized from his own experiences) and strong performances make it an above-average TV movie. Image and sound are identical to its original broadcast. —*DRL*
Movie: ♫♫ **DVD:** ♫♫ ½
Artisan Ent. (cat #12492, UPC 707729-124924). Full frame. Dolby 2.0 Surround. $19.98. Keepcase. *LANG:* English. *FEATURES:* Production notes • Filmographies • 20 chapters.
2001 98m/C Callum Blue, Barbara Bobulova, Peter Bowles, Nick Reding, John Warnaby, Toby Jones, Robert Weatherby, Nicholas Gallagher; **D:** John Kent Harrison; **W:** John Mortimer; **C:** Giovanni Fiore Coltellacci; **M:** Nicola Piovani.

In the Country Where Nothing Happens

This oddball comedy of errors follows crooked businessman Enrique (Lujan), who's been using his company to launder money to his assumed identity. When he is kidnapped, his wife could care less, his kidnappers can't figure out who he is, and his company tries to use the event as a smokescreen for their financial scandal. Although inconsistent, there are some good laughs and plenty of insight into Mexican society. The sound is adequate

but the picture is marred by a good deal of grain and excessive digital artifacts. The special features are in Spanish with no subtitles. —*BG* **AKA:** En el Pais de No Pasa Nada.
Movie: ♫♫ ½ **DVD:** ♫♫
Vanguard Intl. Cinema (cat #VF9128, UPC 658769912838). Widescreen letterboxed. $29.95. Keepcase. *LANG:* Spanish. *SUB:* English. *FEATURES:* 12 chapters • Trailer • "Making of" featurette.
1999 92m/C MX Fernando Lujan, Julieta Egurrola, Maria (Isasi-Isasmendi) Isasi, Alvaro Guerrero, Zaide Silvia Gutierrez; **D:** Maricarmen de Lara; **W:** Maricarmen de Lara, Laura Sosa; **C:** Arturo de la Rosa.

In the Footsteps of the Holy Family

A&E special (three programs on two discs) combines dramatizations, discussions with scholars, and contemporary footage shot in the Middle East to tell various stories concerning the birth of Jesus. Several opinions are presented but the producers know their audience so they stick close to biblical ideas, seasoned with a dash of "unexplained mysteries" hyperventilation. DVD image is generally a bit superior to cablecast, but some aliasing does crop up. Sound is fine. —*MM*
Movie: ♫♫ **DVD:** ♫♫ ½
A&E (cat #AAE-70337, UPC 7339617033-75). Full frame. Dolby Digital Stereo. $29.98. Keepcase. *LANG:* English. *FEATURES:* 18 chapters.
2001 150m/C Nar: Roger Moore.

In the Mood for Love [SE]

A woman and a man live next door to each other in 1962 Hong Kong, each with their respective spouses. When they start to suspect that their spouses may be seeing each other, they begin to fall in love. Due to the tight quarters in Hong Kong, both physically and morally, they conduct their affair mostly with a subtle knowing look and very little else. The incredible skill of Kar-Wai as a director and Cheung and Leung as the couple make what could be an exercise in tedium a monument to smoldering passion. Of the more interesting extras are the deleted scenes, some of which are of scenes that are already in the film but shot in different locations by Kar-Wai. It is enthralling to listen to the director talk about his work and how he made the cinematic decisions that go into making the film. As this is a Criterion disc, it is loaded with extras and a fabulous companion booklet. The print transfer is beautiful and the sound is very good. —*CA*
Movie: ♫♫♫ ½ **DVD:** ♫♫♫ ½
Criterion (cat #147, UPC 715515012928). Widescreen (1.66:1) anamorphic. Dolby Digital 5.0. $39.95. Keepcase. *LANG:* Cantonese; Shanghai. *SUB:* English. *FEATURES:* 28 chapters • Deleted scenes • Commentary: director • 48-page booklet • Short film, interviews, press conferences.

2000 (PG) 98m/C *HK* Tony Leung Chiu-Wai, Maggie Cheung, Rebecca Pan, Lai Chen, Siu Ping-Lam; *D:* Wong Kar-Wai; *W:* Wong Kar-Wai; *C:* Christopher Doyle, Mark Lee Ping-Bin; *M:* Michael Galasso, Umebayashi Shigeru. *AWARDS:* Cannes '00: Actor (Leung Chiu-Wai); N.Y. Film Critics '01: Cinematog., Foreign Film; *NOM:* Ind. Spirit '01: Foreign Film; Natl. Soc. Film Critics '01: Cinematog., Foreign Film; Broadcast Film Critics '01: Foreign Film.

In the Time of the Butterflies

Based on the true story of the Mirabal sisters (Hayek, Maestro, Cavazos) who resisted the reign of fear, violence, and repression at the hands of General Leonidas Trujillo (Olmos) and died for it. Made-for-TV movie has unfortunate little plot gaps that lessen the emotional impact of an otherwise very interesting story. Fine performance; production values are high. Very good Mexico locations stand in for the Dominican Republic in the 1940s. Image quality and sound are excellent. *—LA*
Movie: 🎬🎬🎬 **DVD:** 🎬🎬🎬
MGM Home Ent. (cat #1002802, UPC 27616869999). Full frame. Dolby Digital 5.1 Surround. $26.98. Keepcase. *LANG:* English. *SUB:* English; French; Spanish. *CAP:* English. *FEATURES:* 16 chapters • Theatrical trailer.
2001 (PG-13) 97m/C Salma Hayek, Lumi Cavazos, Mia Maestro, Edward James Olmos, Marc Anthony, Pilar Padilla, Demian Bichir, Fernando Becerril; *D:* Mariano Barroso; *W:* Judy Klass, David Klass; *C:* Xavier Perez Grobet; *M:* Van Dyke Parks.

Inbred Rednecks

A lighthearted hillbilly comedy, shot in and around North Carolina. Billy Bob and his buddies, seeking fame and fortune via the cock-fighting circuit, have bred a gigantic mutant cock dubbed "Big Ass Rooster." Of course, the cock fighting story is only the central theme running through a rambling collection of sub-plots, satires, and old jokes illustrated. Along the way, there's UFOs, state fair vomit rides, bar fights, scalping, an escaped lab monkey with the e coli virus, and a million dollar nut sack. The DVD features a commentary track that actually delays the start of the feature by several minutes. There's also a half-hour section of odds & ends, with outtakes, bloopers, and interviews with the cast and crew. Most of this footage has the sound running out of synch. Toward the end, the image erupts in some major digital glitches while the soundtrack drops out entirely. *—BT*
Movie: 🎬🎬 ½ **DVD:** 🎬 ½
Sub Rosa Studios (cat #SRDVD0000, UPC 674945102138). Full frame. $19.95. Keepcase. *LANG:* English. *FEATURES:* 24 chapters • Commentary • Documentary featurettes.
1997 135m/C Joshua P. Warren, Brent Ponder, Steve Lewis; *D:* Joshua P. Warren; *W:* Joshua P. Warren; *M:* Joshua P. Warren.

Incident on a Dark Street

Please see review for *Great Mafia Movies 2*.
1972 (PG-13) 96m/C James Olson, David Canary, Robert Pine, Richard S. Castellano, William Shatner, Murray Hamilton, Gilbert Roland; *D:* Buzz Kulik; *W:* E. Jack Neuman.

Indecent Proposal

Remember all the controversy that surrounded this movie when it came out? Would you let your wife sleep with a total stranger for a million dollars? It helped fuel early talk radio for weeks. Demi Moore and Woody Harrelson are Diana and David Murphy, a young married couple who have overstepped their financial bounds. Enter billionaire John Gage (Robert Redford), who offers financial freedom. A lame and thin look at trust, love, and marriage. Directed by Adrian Lyne, the film loses its steam quickly. DVD is O.K., but beyond the extras, nothing that you couldn't get with tape. *—DE*
Movie: 🎬🎬 ½ **DVD:** 🎬🎬
Paramount (cat #32453, UPC 09736-324534). Widescreen anamorphic. 5.1 Dolby Surround; Stereo. $24.98. Keepcase. *LANG:* English; French. *SUB:* English. *CAP:* English. *FEATURES:* 16 chapters • Commentary: Adrian Lyne.
1993 (R) 119m/C Robert Redford, Demi Moore, Woody Harrelson, Seymour Cassel, Oliver Platt, Billy Bob Thornton, Rip Taylor, Billy Connolly, Joel Brooks, Sheena Easton, Herbie Hancock; *D:* Adrian Lyne; *W:* Amy Holden Jones; *C:* Howard Atherton; *M:* John Barry. *AWARDS:* MTV Movie Awards '94: Kiss (Demi Moore/Woody Harrelson); Golden Raspberries '93: Worst Picture, Worst Support. Actor (Harrelson), Worst Screenplay; *NOM:* MTV Movie Awards '94: Female Perf. (Moore), Most Desirable Female (Moore).

The Indian in the Cupboard

It's rare for a film to live up to its pedigree, but this one succeeds. With the director of *What about Bob?* (Frank Oz), the writer of *E.T.* (Melissa Mathison), and the producers of *Raiders of the Lost Ark* (Kathleen Kennedy and Frank Marshall) working behind the camera, one expects magic, and this film delivers. Omri (Hal Scardino) is a somewhat lonely boy who receives an antique cupboard for his birthday. When he places a toy Indian in the cupboard, it comes to life as Little Bear (Litefoot). Amazed at this event, Omri shares the occurrence with his friend Patrick (Rishi Bhat), who decides to put a toy cowboy, Boo-hoo Boone (David Keith) in the cupboard and the magic works again. Omri is able to see the world through Little Bear's small eyes, and they make several enchanting discoveries together. The film delivers a satisfying message about friendship, tolerance, and magic, without becoming overly sappy. Scardino is very

good in the lead role, and there is a nice use of special effects here, to create the illusion of a miniature Indian and a full-size boy. This DVD presentation is nearly as satisfying as the film. The image is very clear and sharp, showing very natural colors and fleshtones. There is little grain and the only real problem here is that the image is slightly dark in some scenes. The Dolby 2.0 Surround audio track provides clear dialogue and some impressive Surround effects. Also, there is noticeable quality in the stereo separation and the score sounds wonderful. The audio commentary from director Oz is engaging and informative...and a bit odd, as he is the voice of Miss Piggy. *—ML*
Movie: 🎬🎬🎬 **DVD:** 🎬🎬🎬
Columbia Tristar (cat #11642, UPC 04339-6116429). Widescreen (1.78:1); full frame. Dolby Surround. $24.95. Keepcase. *LANG:* English; Spanish; French. *SUB:* English; Spanish; French. *CAP:* English. *FEATURES:* Commentary • Photo gallery • Talent files • Production notes • Trailers.
1995 (PG) 97m/C Hal Scardino, Litefoot, Lindsay Crouse, Richard Jenkins, Rishi Bhat, David Keith; *D:* Frank Oz; *W:* Melissa Mathison; *C:* Russell Carpenter; *M:* Miles Goodman.

The Indian Tomb

Sequel to *The Tiger of Eschnapur* finds Harald Berger (Hubschmid) and Seetha (Paget) managing to elude Chandra's soldiers until Seetha's faith in her gods results in her capture and her apparent death. Berger's partner Dr. Rhode (Holm) and Berger's sister Irene (Bethmann) discover they're in the hands of a madman when Chandra lies about Berger's whereabouts. Along the way is another knockout dance (with Ms. Paget in an even more revealing costume), encounters with a horde of lepers locked away in the catacombs, and a full-scale palace revolt. Please see review of *Tiger* for technical comments. *—GE* *AKA:* Das Indische Grabmal.
Movie: 🎬🎬🎬 **DVD:** 🎬🎬🎬
Fantoma Films (UPC 14381123920). Full frame. Snapper. *LANG:* German and English. *SUB:* English. *FEATURES:* Stills collection.
1959 102m/C *GE* Debra Paget, Paul (Christian) Hubschmid, Sabine Bethmann; *D:* Fritz Lang; *W:* Werner Jorg Luddecke; *C:* Richard Angst; *M:* Michel Michelet.

Indiscreet

This romantic comedy directed by Stanley Donen and starring Cary Grant and Ingrid Bergman may seem a little out of date in the 21st century. If you can take yourself back to a time when having an affair wasn't just another type of romantic relationship, it can still be entertaining. Bergman is a famous actress who feels that all the good men are taken, and Grant is the charming man that would be perfect for her if he weren't married. She resists becoming his mistress, and just when she is about to give in she discovers the ugly truth. He's not married at all; he's a playboy who lies to keep his freedom. She indignantly states, "How dare he make love to me and not be a married man," and plots her revenge just as he is considering marriage for the first time in his life. The mixed signals lead to romance and a really silly dance scene. This is pure frothy fun. It was a little disappointing to see that they had used a print to strike the DVD, but who knows what elements they had at their disposal? There are obvious scratch and dust marks on the film and the sound is poor. —CA

Movie: 🎬🎬🎬 ***DVD:*** 🎬 ½
Artisan Ent. (cat #12047, UPC 017153-120479). Widescreen letterboxed. Dolby Digital Stereo. $19.90. Keepcase. *LANG:* English. *SUB:* English. *CAP:* English. *FEATURES:* 10 chapters.
1958 100m/C Cary Grant, Ingrid Bergman, Phyllis Calvert; ***D:*** Stanley Donen; ***W:*** Norman Krasna; ***C:*** Frederick A. (Freddie) Young; ***M:*** Richard Rodney Bennett.

Indochine

Eliane Devries (Catherine Deneuve) is the owner of a rubber plantation in the French colony of Indochina (now called Vietnam). Repressed and with many personal problems, she lives a prosperous life while exploiting the local people for her own wealth. Unlike many of her French colleagues, however, she seeks the closeness to the local people to an extent. She even adopts an Indochinese daughter when her parents die, and follows many of the local customs and habits—including the smoking of opium. Her harsh exterior serves as a disguise for inner torment, torrid love affairs, and lack of acceptance within the French upper-class society. Although signs of film grain are evident in a handful of scenes, the transfer exhibits a very high level of detail. The color reproduction is phenomenal, bringing out the best of the beautiful and often majestic photography. Fleshtones are absolutely natural and the colorful costumes and production designs practically leap off the screen. French/Vietnamese Surround audio track is well produced and integrated with good spatial integration. —GH

Movie: 🎬🎬🎬 ***DVD:*** 🎬🎬🎬
Columbia Tristar Home Video (UPC 0433-96272392). Widescreen (1.85:1) anamorphic. Dolby Surround. $27.98. Keepcase. *LANG:* French. *SUB:* English; French; Spanish. *FEATURES:* Trailers.
1992 (PG-13) 155m/C *FR* Catherine Deneuve, Linh Dan Pham, Vincent Perez, Jean Yanne, Dominique Blanc, Henri Marteau, Carlo Brandt, Gerard Lartigau; ***D:*** Regis Wargnier; ***W:*** Erik Orsenna, Louis Gardel, Catherine Cohen, Regis Wargnier; ***C:*** François Catonne; ***M:*** Patrick Doyle. *AWARDS:* Oscars '92: Foreign Film; Cesar '93: Actress (Deneuve), Art Dir./Set Dec., Cinematog., Sound, Support. Actress (Blanc); Golden Globes '93: Foreign Film; Natl. Bd. of Review '92: Foreign Film; *NOM:* Oscars '92: Actress (Deneuve); British Acad. '93: Foreign Film.

Inga

Back in 1968, *Inga* was one hot number. Now it's much more notorious for its depiction of mid-'60s clothes, haircuts, and (cue scary music) dancing. The story concerns virginal young Inga (Liljedahl), who goes to live with her worldly aunt Greta and becomes the object of lust for every man she meets. By current standards, the sexual content is tepid, but the dialogue is uproarious. The black-and-white photography looks pretty good on DVD, though it's not as detailed as contemporaneous American studio productions. The Swedish version is much grainier than the American. Light hiss and static are audible throughout. —MM

Movie: 🎬🎬 ***DVD:*** 🎬🎬 ½
El Independent Cinema (cat #sc-2204-dvd, UPC 612385220494). Full frame. $19.98. Keepcase. *LANG:* English; Swedish. *SUB:* English. *FEATURES:* Trailers • Commentary • Audio interview with Marie Liljedahl • Swedish version.
1967 86m/B *SW* Marie Liljedahl, Monica Strommerstedt; ***D:*** Joe Sarno; ***W:*** Joe Sarno; ***C:*** Bruce G. Sparks.

Inherit the Wind

Powerful courtroom drama, based on the Broadway play, is a fictionalized version of the infamous Scopes "Monkey Trial" of 1925. Tracy is defense attorney Clarence Darrow for the small-town school teacher (York) on trial for teaching Darwin's Theory of Evolution. March is prosecutor William Jennings Bryan seeking to restore religion to the public schools. Strong performances make the dramatic confrontations more important than the politics involved. DVD image is very nice. Some grain is evident in a few scenes but nothing excessive for Ernest Laszlo's excellent black-and-white photography. —MM

Movie: 🎬🎬🎬 ½ ***DVD:*** 🎬🎬🎬
MGM Home Ent. (cat #1002740, UPC 027616869388). Widescreen (1.66:1) letterboxed. Dolby Digital Mono. $14.98. Keepcase. *LANG:* English; French; Spanish. *SUB:* French; Spanish. *CAP:* English. *FEATURES:* 16 chapters • Trailer.
1960 128m/B Spencer Tracy, Fredric March, Florence Eldridge, Gene Kelly, Dick York, Donna Anderson, Harry (Henry) Morgan, Elliott Reid, Philip Coolidge, Claude Akins, Noah Beery Jr., Norman Fell; ***D:*** Stanley Kramer; ***W:*** Nedrick Young, Harold Jacob Smith; ***C:*** Ernest Laszlo; ***M:*** Ernest Gold. *AWARDS:* Berlin Intl. Film Fest. '60: Actor (March); *NOM:* Oscars '60: Actor (Tracy), Adapt. Screenplay, B&W Cinematog., Film Editing.

Institue Benjamenta or This Dream People Call Human Life

The Brothers Quay, whose animation has fascinated the world for years, now try their hands at a live-action film. Mark Rylance (*Angels and Insects*) stars as Jakob Von Gunten, who enters the Institute Benjamenta, where he will be trained as a domestic servant. What he finds instead is a surreal world run by Herr Benjamenta (Gottfried John) and his sister Lisa (Alice Krige, *Ghost Story*). This story takes a back-seat to the Quay's unique and disturbing visuals. The black & white photography and bizarre mise en scene are clearly tributes to the German expressionist films of the 1930s. Fans of the Quays' animation may be disappointed by the film, but followers of filmmakers like David Lynch will eat this up. The DVD features a brief interview with the reclusive brothers. The monochrome image on the DVD is very clear and free from obtrusive grain, and the digital stereo brings the odd score and sound effects to life. —ML

Movie: 🎬🎬 ½ ***DVD:*** 🎬🎬🎬
Kino on Video (cat #K171 DVD, UPC 738-329017125). Widescreen (1.66:1) letterboxed. Stereo. $29.95. Keepcase. *LANG:* English. *FEATURES:* Theatrical trailer • Filmmaker interview • On-set featurette • 14 chapters.
1995 105m/B *GB* Mark Rylance, Alice Krige, Gottfried John; ***D:*** Stephen Quay, Timothy Quay; ***W:*** Stephen Quay, Timothy Quay, Allan Passes; ***C:*** Nicholas D. Knowland; ***M:*** Lech Jankowski.

Intersection

Successful architect Vincent (Gere) is torn between his aloof wife/partner, Sally (Stone), and a sexy journalist mistress, Olivia (Davidovitch). Whom to choose? Since he's a completely self-involved boor, you won't care either way. Another retooling of a French film (*Les Choses de la Vie*) as a Hollywood star vehicle that doesn't work. Lousy dialogue doesn't help. The film does boast some nice location shots of Vancouver, B.C. The disc reproduces colors well, though a slight loss of clarity is noticeable in darker hues. The soundtrack is a bit more impressive with crisp, clear dialogue and a nicely produced musical score. —MJT

Movie: 🎬 ½ ***DVD:*** 🎬🎬 ½
Paramount (cat #32242, UPC 097363224-242). Widescreen (1.85:1) anamorphic. Dolby Digital 5.1 Surround; Dolby Surround. $24.99. Keepcase. *LANG:* English. *SUB:* English. *FEATURES:* 10 chapters.
1993 (R) 98m/C Richard Gere, Sharon Stone, Lolita (David) Davidovich, Martin Landau, David Selby, Jenny Morrison; ***D:*** Mark Rydell; ***W:*** Marshall Brickman, David Rayfiel; ***C:*** Vilmos Zsigmond; ***M:*** James Newton Howard. *AWARDS:* Golden Raspberries '94: Worst Actress (Stone).

Intimacy

Dark and haunting drama explores the lives and desires of people who are flawed, lonely, and in pain, seeking emotional comfort and not finding it in brief physical encounters. Jay (Rylance) and Claire (Fox) meet every Wednesday for a wordless sexual encounter. There is no love evident in their actions. It's a search for contact—for someone to see and feel and find comfort with. As Jay says at one point when asked if he's seeing anyone else besides Claire, "this woman, she's all I've got." After it's over, they go their separate ways until Jay decides he wants to know more and follows her. He finds out what she does and even meets her not-so-dim husband (the great Spall). The documentary-like cinematography is striking and makes the film feel even more raw and realistic. Its bleakness is crisp and cool, but not so grim as to be depressing. The film has become somewhat notorious for its graphic and raw portrayal of sex, but with its sad tone and low-key surroundings, there's nothing particularly erotic about these scenes. This is a low-budget drama, often filmed with handheld cameras and what looks to be available light. DVD presentation is an enjoyable one, though, and offers the film in a way that I'd guess is about as good as it can look. Sharpness and detail are solid throughout; there are some dark or dimly lit scenes, but they still show a satisfactory amount of detail. The 5.1 stays very front-focused, but pleasing. Surrounds occasionally come in with very subtle ambient sounds, but most of the audio comes from the front. Dialogue and a mild score are clear, but there are also a good deal of environmental sounds, whether the characters are in a crowded pub or out on the streets. —AB

Movie: 𝄞𝄞𝄞 **DVD:** 𝄞𝄞𝄞
TVA International (cat #09339, UPC 043-39609339). Widescreen (2.35:1) letterboxed. Dolby Digital 5.1 Surround. $21.90. Keepcase. *LANG:* English; French. *SUB:* English. *FEATURES:* Trailer.
2000 119m/C *GB FR* Mark Rylance, Kerry Fox, Timothy Spall, Alastair Galbraith, Marianne Faithfull, Susannah Harker, Philippe Calvario, Rebecca Palmer, Fraser Ayres; *D:* Patrice Chereau; *W:* Patrice Chereau, Anne-Louise Trividic; *C:* Eric Gautier; *M:* Eric Neveux.

Into the Arms of Strangers: Stories from the Kindertransport

An emotionally wrenching roller coaster of historical import that reminds you how, sometime, there is a thin line between hope and hopelessness. Covering the lives of several children, now adults, who were saved when Great Britain agreed to take refugee children from the countries being invaded by Hitler. Known as the Kindertransport, the program saved the lives of 10,000 children who would surely have perished under the Nazi regime. Of the six million people—mostly Jewish—who were killed during the Holocaust, one and a half million were children. Through interviews and historical footage, we learn of the invasion of the children's homelands, their parents' decision to sign them up for the Kindertransport, and the aftermath that is their lives. Most of the children lost their parents, but some were reunited. One boy who spent 11 years with an English family only to be reunited with his parents, who then seemed like strangers, reflects as an adult how lucky he was to have two families who loved him and to have survived the Holocaust. "What more could you ask for?" he says, choking back tears; what more indeed? It is difficult emotionally to watch the surviving children, now older than the parents who sent them to England, still trying to come to terms with the parental abandonment that saved their lives. As with *Shindler's List,* there is hope in the photos of the large families reminding us that the Kinder survived for reasons far larger than themselves. This is not an easy film to watch, but it seems important to watch such heartfelt testimony to man's ability to do good painfully juxtaposed beside his ability to do evil, if it's only to lend an ear to the survivors. And the film stands high in the forest of Holocaust documentaries. It is well made, well presented, and takes time with its subject. The extras are also painful but hopeful, especially the interview with Lord Richard Attenborough whose family actually adopted two of the Kindertransport children. The film is comprised of a mix of old footage, and video and film interviews, so the picture quality is mixed, and the sound is very good. —CA

Movie: 𝄞𝄞𝄞 ½ **DVD:** 𝄞𝄞 ½
Warner (cat #18872, UPC 0853918872-25). Full frame. Dolby Digital 5.1 Surround. $24.90. Snapper. *LANG:* English; French. *SUB:* English; French; Spanish. *CAP:* English. *FEATURES:* 28 chapters • Filmmaker commentary • Interviews with Lord Attenborough and others • Survivor profiles; weblinks, photo gallery, theatrical trailer.
2000 117m/C *D:* Mark Jonathan Harris; *W:* Mark Jonathan Harris; *C:* Don Lenzer; *Nar:* Judi Dench.

Into the Woods

A delightful cluster of fractured fairy tales, this Broadway musical has great music, comedy, and heart. It manages to strike at the universal concerns behind them: our desires, our problems, and our fears in the real world. And in a daring midpoint twist, it becomes a parable that ranges way beyond the realm of children's stories. To remove the curse of a Witch (Peters) that prevents them from having children, the Baker (Zien) and his wife (Gleason) go into the woods to find several magical items. There they meet Red Riding Hood (Ferland), who's just escaped the clutches of the Wolf (Westenberg) and enlist the aid of a number of other characters from other stories (Jack and the Beanstalk, Cinderella, Rapunzel). The search becomes entangled with a half-dozen familiar story lines, yet all is wonderful by the time intermission rolls around...after which the show does a complete reversal on our expectations, pitting the characters not against fairy tale lightness, but instead the sometimes insoluble problems of the real world. Lapine and Sondheim are known for their radical story structures, but *Into the Woods* is very audience-friendly. The various intrigues seem to have sorted themselves out at the mid-point, but then the playwrights push their characters into a life beyond "happily ever after," where princesses find out their perfect mates aren't so perfect, and even the most powerful characters have painful lessons to learn. DVD is from a videotaped television show (shown first on PBS, I think) that is excellently directed and covered. It doesn't try to escape artificial stage trappings, like Jack's plastic Cow, but the settings and costumes are more than enough to inspire the suspension of disbelief—a literal film version with "real" settings and splashy special effects would just dissipate the impact of this great show. —GE

Movie: 𝄞𝄞𝄞 ½ **DVD:** 𝄞𝄞𝄞 ½
Image Ent. (UPC 014381596724). Full frame. $34.98. Keepcase. *LANG:* English.
1990 153m/C Bernadette Peters, Joanna Gleason, Chip Zien, Tom Aldredge, Kim Crosby, Ben Wright, Barbara Byrne, Chuck Wagner, Robert Westenberg, Danielle Ferland; *D:* James Lapine; *W:* James Lapine; *M:* Stephen Sondheim.

Into Thin Air: Death on Everest

Based on the book by Jon Krakauer (played in the telepic by McDonald) about the tragic May 1996 climbing expedition to Mount Everest that resulted in the deaths of eight climbers. The beauty of the mountain cinematography is done justice with extremely well-defined blacks and colors. Unfortunately, this clarity is showcased only in daylight scenes. Night scenes, particularly those during snowstorms, lack definition and are extremely blurry. Dialogue is reproduced well on a slightly above-average soundtrack that lacks the intensity that a survival-of-the-fittest movie like this requires. —MJT

Movie: 𝄞𝄞 **DVD:** 𝄞𝄞 ½
Columbia Tristar (cat #06462, UPC 043-396064621). Full frame. Dolby Digital Surround; Dolby Digital Stereo. $19.95. Keepcase. *LANG:* English; French; Spanish; Portuguese. *SUB:* English; French; Spanish; Portuguese; Chinese; Korean; Thai. *FEATURES:* 28 chapters • Theatrical trailer gallery • Talent files.
1997 90m/C Peter Horton, Christopher McDonald, Nathaniel Parker, Richard Jenkins; *D:* Robert Markowitz; *W:* Robert J. Avrech.

Introducing Dorothy Dandridge

Beautiful, sexy singer/actress Dorothy Dandridge (Berry) was the first black woman to be nominated for a Best Actress Academy Award for her title role in 1955's *Carmen Jones.* Ten years later, at age 42, she was dead from an overdose of anti-depressants after suffering a lifetime of sadness—an abusive childhood, two failed marriages, a brain-damaged child, tumultuous affairs, limited career choices, and bad financial decisions. Berry, who was also one of the executive

producers on the film, appears in practically every scene and gives 100% in each one. The film covers more than 20 years of Dandridge's life and Berry shows every conceivable emotion during that time. (Berry is also the first black woman to win a Best Actress Academy Award for 2001's *Monster's Ball*.) Spiner's portrayal of Earl Mills, whose book was the inspiration for the film, shows us a man who was very good in show business, but also truly cared for Dorothy on a very human level. The picture itself is clear for the most part, but a bit dark and the colors are somewhat drab. A small amount of grain is noticeable. This may be due to the fact that the nearly two-hour film was squeezed onto a single-layer disc. The audio is well-balanced, with both the dialogue scenes and the musical numbers sounding equally good. There isn't much of a presence of any spectacular Surround effects, but the sound of the musical numbers is well-mixed and takes good advantage of the multiple-speaker format. The audio sounds natural without exaggerated high ends. —*MM/GH*
Movie: 🎬🎬🎬 *DVD:* 🎬🎬🎬
HBO Home Video (UPC 026359156922). Full frame. Dolby Digital Surround Stereo; Mono. $14.98. Snapper. *LANG:* English; Spanish. *SUB:* English; French; Spanish. *FEATURES:* Talent files.
1999 (R) 115m/C Halle Berry, Brent Spiner, Obba Babatunde, Loretta Devine, Cynda Williams, Latanya Richardson, Tamara Taylor, Klaus Maria Brandauer, D.B. Sweeney, William Atherton; *D:* Martha Coolidge; *W:* Scott Abbott, Shonda Rhimes; *C:* Robbie Greenberg; *M:* Elmer Bernstein.

Introduction to Antiques

This Australian production delivers nothing more than the title promises. It's a brief introduction to an unbelievably complex subject. Writer Anna Clark chooses a few examples to demonstrate the differences that separate real antiques from replicas and fakes. The disc contains three programs, "The Introduction," "English Style," and "French Style." All were shot on video and so the image is not a significant improvement over VHS tape. The programs are not divided into chapters. Sound is fine for the narration and the middle-of-the-road classical score. Overall, it's not as much fun as a good episode of public TV's *Antiques Roadshow*. —*MM*
Movie: 🎬½ *DVD:* 🎬½
BFS Video (cat #30265-D, UPC 06680530-2657). Full frame. Dolby Digital Stereo. $19.98. Keepcase. *LANG:* English. *FEATURES:* 4 chapters • Price information on selected items • "History of Sotheby's" • Sotheby's addresses.
1995 150m/C Anna Clark; *W:* Anna Clark.

Invaders from Mars [MGM]

MGM edition is a slight improvement over the earlier non-anamorphic Anchor Bay

release (reviewed in *Book 1*). This remake has never had a particularly sharp image. DVD makes the deliberately fake-looking optical effects all the more so. Some shimmering artifacts are visible in the establishing shots of the house. —*MM*
Movie: 🎬🎬 *DVD:* 🎬🎬
MGM Home Ent. (cat #1002339, UPC 027616865588). Widescreen (2.35:1) anamorphic. Dolby Digital Surround Stereo. $19.98. Keepcase. *LANG:* English. *SUB:* French; Spanish. *CAP:* English. *FEATURES:* 16 chapters • Trailer • "Making of" featurette • Sci-fi promo featurette.
1986 (PG) 102m/C Hunter Carson, Karen Black, Louise Fletcher, Laraine Newman, Timothy Bottoms, Bud Cort, Dale Dye; *D:* Tobe Hooper; *W:* Dan O'Bannon, Don Jakoby; *C:* Daniel Pearl; *M:* Sylvester Levay, David Storrs, Christopher Young.

Invasion of the Animal People

Jerry Warren re-edited Virgil Vogel's *Terror in the Midnight Sun* (please see review), added needless footage of John Carradine as a narrator, and completely muddled an already silly Swedish sci-fi film. DVD reveals how much poorer this version looks with a fuzzy black-and-white image. Frank Henenlotter's liner notes attempt to explain the film's various incarnations and the differences between versions. —*MM*
AKA: Terror in the Midnight Sun; Space Invasion of Lapland; Horror in the Midnight Sun; Space Invasion from Lapland.
Movie: woof *DVD:* 🎬🎬
Image Ent. (cat #ID9751SWDVD, UPC 014-381975123). Full frame. Dolby Digital Mono. $24.99. Snapper. *LANG:* English. *FEATURES:* 15 chapters • Swedish exploitation trailers • 2 Swedish short subjects • "Girl in the Glacier" episode of TV show *13 Demon Street* • Gallery of exploitation art.
1962 73m/B SW Robert Burton, Barbara Wilson, John Carradine; *D:* Jerry Warren, Virgil W. Vogel; *W:* Arthur C. Pierce; *C:* Hilding Bladh; *M:* Harry Arnold, Allan Johansson.

Invasion of the Blood Farmers

In a small New York town, members of an ancient Druidic cult murder young women, taking their blood in the hope of finding the precise, rare blood type to keep their queen alive. A fearlessly awful, out-and-out drive-in movie that entertains in classic splatter style. Loads of unintentional laughs. You'll want this one on your shelves just for the great title alone. And the DVD is plenty good enough for this sort of low-budget offering. First off, the film is presented letterboxed while the only previous version was full frame on a hard-to-find out-of-print VHS tape that made an appearance early in the history of home video. And the image is much sharper than anyone could expect with decent blacks and healthy color. Extras include an episode of *Fred Olen Ray's*

Night Owl Theater with the cult film director and his wife hamming it up. —*JO*
Movie: 🎬🎬 *DVD:* 🎬🎬½
Ventura Distribution (cat #RMED006, UPC 802993678996). Widescreen (1.85:1) letterboxed. Dolby Digital Stereo. $19.95. Keepcase. *LANG:* English. *SUB:* English. *FEATURES:* Chapter links • Theatrical trailer • Photo gallery • *Fred Olen Ray's Night Owl Theater.*
1972 (PG) 86m/C Norman Kelley, Tanna Hunter, Bruce Detrick, Jack Neubeck, Cythia Fleming, Paul Craig Jennings; *D:* Ed Adlum; *W:* Ed Adlum, Ed Kelleher.

Invasion U.S.A.

Key picture for the '50s is a bizarre call to arms against the Communist threat, not some insidious subversion from within, but an all-out military onslaught. The orgy of military stock footage used to depict the Soviet juggernaut is ridiculous but effective, thanks to excellent editing and graphic, if crude, special effects. The strange framing story, with a Criswell-like "forecaster" cryptically informing a group of bar patrons that their futures will grow out of their present and past behaviors, is rather well-handled, even if the dialogue and characterizations hit the heights of camp hilarity. With an exciting roster of "explosive supplementary material," this is a strongly recommended DVD, both for jaw-dropping sociology, and group viewing fun. In a Manhattan bar, newscaster Vince Potter (Mohr); the beautiful Carla Sanford (Castle); George Sylvester (Bice), the owner of a tractor factory; Arizona rancher Ed Mulfory (Blythe); and blustering congressman Arthur Harroway (Crosby) are entranced by the confident attitude of a mysterious Mr. Ohman (O'Herlihy), who asks them to think about their country. While they're talking, war breaks out in the form of a full-scale Russian military invasion, using Atomic bombs to knock out airstrips in the Northwest. The Navy is said to have resisted well in the Pacific, but Alaska and Washington State are overrun. Sylvester and Mulfory fly to the coast on one of the last flights out, but meet horrible fates at the hands of ruthless invaders, who take out Boulder dam in a nuclear strike. New York City is nuked as well, with skyscrapers collapsing as enemy troops blast their way in; the newscaster tries to shield his new girlfriend Carla, but to no avail. All wish they had been a trifle more committed to their country's defense. The transfer looks very good, with almost no print damage. The 1.37:1 aspect ratio has a lot of dead space at the top and bottom. 1952 is technically too early for films to be composed wider, even 1.66:1, so this must be the exception. Synapse has thoughtfully windowboxed the picture slightly, which helps keep all the action on-screen—even expensive monitors routinely crop off picture extremes on all sides of the image. The best extra is a 30-minute version of the originally hour-long public information short subject "Red Nightmare" (AKA "Freedom and You," AKA "The Commies Are Coming, the Commies Are Coming"). It was made in 1962 by Warner's for the Defense Department; the title of the specific agency on-screen reads like double-speak dis-information. Jack Kelly, Jack Webb, and Andrew Duggan star, and Robert Conrad and Peter Breck show up in bits. It's directed by the famous *Wolf Man* auteur, George Waggner, here unaccountably billed as WaGGner, and liberally uses themes from paranoid science-fiction movies. —GE

Movie: 🎬🎬🎬 **DVD:** 🎬🎬🎬
Synapse (cat #SFD0018, UPC 65493030-1890). Full frame. Dolby Digital Mono. $24.98. Keepcase. *LANG:* English. *FEATURES:* Interviews with Dan O'Herlihy, William Schallert, Noel Neill • Liner notes by Bill Geerhart • 2 Defense Department audio recordings • Theatrical trailer.
1952 73m/B Gerald Mohr, Peggy Castle, Dan O'Herlihy, Robert Bice, Tom Kennedy, Phyllis Coates, Erik Blythe, Wade Crosby, William Schallert, Noel Neill; **D:** Alfred E. Green; **W:** Robert Smith; **C:** John L. "Jack" Russell; **M:** Albert Glasser.

Invasion U.S.A.

Mercenary Matt Hunter (Norris) defends all of America—including its shopping malls and suburbs—against Russian terrorists who land in Florida and look for condos. Image ranges between good and very good in this low-budget exercise in mindless jingoism. —MM

Movie: 🎬 **DVD:** 🎬🎬½
MGM Home Ent. (cat #1002636, UPC 027616868367). Widescreen (1.85:1) anamorphic. Dolby Digital Surround Stereo; Mono. $14.95. Keepcase. *LANG:* English; French. *SUB:* French; Spanish. *CAP:* English. *FEATURES:* 16 chapters • Trailer.
1985 (R) 108m/C Chuck Norris, Richard Lynch, Melissa Prophet, Alex Colon, Billy Drago; **D:** Joseph Zito; **W:** James Bruner; **C:** Joao Fernandes; **M:** Jay Chattaway.

The Invincible Killer

Wang Chun (Wai-man) leaves his gang to settle down with a family, but boss Lo frames Wang Chun for a murder and kidnaps his family. Only Wang Chun's powers of kung fu can save him now. The story and dialogue are as bad as most of the genre's low-budget entries, but extra time is spent on the plot (unfortunately), which only makes it more incomprehensible and unbelievable. By the time the action has started, it's already an hour into the movie. Complete with disco-era mutton chops and a soft-core scene. Presented in full-frame, but it seems to have been cropped from a widescreen image. —BG

Movie: 🎬 **DVD:** 🎬½
Tai Seng (cat #77744, UPC 6016437774-43). Full frame. $9.98. Keepcase. *LANG:* English (dubbed). *FEATURES:* 9 chapters • Trailer for other Martial Arts Theatre titles.
1981 89m/C Weiman Chan.

Invincible Obsessed Fighter

In this one, Elton Chong is obsessed mainly with dressing up in silly outfits. Chuck (Elton Chong) arrives home too late and finds his father dead, killed by Eagle Tse. The youth uses a variety of disguises to hide from Eagle, but it doesn't really matter what disguise he picks, since he always picks fights with Eagle's men anyway. Having run out of disguises, Chuck just puts on a funny hat and goes out where the bad guys can find him, whereupon he faces and beats each in turn. The fight choreography isn't that interesting, leaving it to a parade of gimmicks—and Chong's insane schtick—to maintain interest. Haphazardly edited, the DVD confuses matters further by cropping the film severely. —BT

Movie: 🎬½ **DVD:** 🎬½
Xenon Ent. (cat #XAXE6288DVD, UPC 000-799628829). Full frame. $14.98. Keepcase. *LANG:* English. *FEATURES:* 6 chapters.
1982 84m/C *HK* Elton Chong, Michael Wong, Shirley Mak; **D:** John King; **W:** Stephen To; **C:** James Fan; **M:** Roman Sang.

The Invisible Ghost

Mr. Kessler (Lugosi) sits down to dinner and orders his servant Evans (Muse) to serve an empty setting where he addresses his wife. The rest of the situation involves mysterious murders and is much much wackier, so wacky that any synopsis would spoil the fun. This one's similar to the Universal features that were being cranked out at the same time, but without the crystalline production values. Vertical scratches and dust flecks are visible throughout. The thin sound and light static are typical of the period. Flaws and all, this is as good an image as you're likely to find. Also, it's worth noting that the film is respectful of its sole black character, and that was almost unknown in mainstream Hollywood films of the '40s. —MM

Movie: 🎬🎬 **DVD:** 🎬🎬½
Troma Team Video (cat #AED-2040, UPC 785604204023). Full frame. Dolby Digital Mono. $19.98. Keepcase. *LANG:* English. *FEATURES:* 17 chapters • Cast and credits • Film background • Trailer.
1941 70m/B Bela Lugosi, Polly Ann Young, John McGuire, Clarence Muse, Betty Compson; **D:** Joseph H. Lewis; **W:** Helen Martin, Al Martin; **C:** Marcel Le Picard.

The Irishman

Based on Elizabeth O'Connor's award-winning novel, this film paints a portrait of life in Australia in the 1920s, a time when industrialization and motorization were beginning to filter into the once untamed land. Here, we meet the Doolan family, a clan of Irish descent who are trying to make ends meet. Paddy (Michael Craig) refuses to abandon his horse-drawn carts in favor of a motor-driven truck. Paddy's son Michael (Simon Burke) respects his father's wishes, but young Will (Lou Brown) is determined to embrace technology. Will leaves the family, with Paddy and Michael trying to keep the business running. Can Paddy make it using the old ways, or will he have to give in to progress? Good old-fashioned drama focuses on the struggles of one family and how familial love doesn't always mix well with business. Craig is wonderful in the lead role and young Lou Brown is very good as the fiery Will. This film marks the second appearance by familiar Aussie actor Bryan Brown *(F/X).* Despite the quality of this film, the DVD suffers from many problems. The film is presented in a full-frame format. The image is grainy and quite blurry at times (as if it were taken from a PAL source). There are multiple defects from the source print such as scratches and black dots. The image also suffers from noticeable artifacting and drab colors. The Dolby Digital mono audio track offers clear dialogue, with some distortion. There is also a faint hiss on the track. —ML

Movie: 🎬🎬½ **DVD:** 🎬½
BFS Video (cat #30263-D, UPC 06680530-2633). Full frame. Dolby Digital Mono. $19.98. Keepcase. *LANG:* English. *FEATURES:* Bios • Production notes • Trivia • 12 chapters.
1978 108m/C *AU* Lou Brown, Michael Craig, Simon Burke, Robyn Nevin, Bryan Brown; **D:** Donald Crombie; **W:** Donald Crombie; **C:** Peter James; **M:** Charles Marawood.

Irma La Douce

A young gendarme pulls a one-man raid on a back-street Parisian joint and falls in love with one of the hookers he arrests. Lemmon is great as the well-meaning incompetent boob, and MacLaine gives her all as the hapless demimondaine. Pace plods, however. The film is based on a successful Broadway musical, though the songs were jettisoned. DVD presents a very nice image. This one looks as good as a big-budget 1960s studio production could look. Mono sound is rich and full. —MM

Movie: 🎬🎬½ **DVD:** 🎬🎬½
MGM Home Ent. (cat #1002379, UPC 027-616865908). Widescreen (2.35:1) anamorphic. Dolby Digital Mono. $14.99. Keepcase. *LANG:* English; French; Spanish. *SUB:* French; Spanish. *CAP:* English. *FEATURES:* 16 chapters.
1963 144m/C Jack Lemmon, Shirley MacLaine, Herschel Bernardi; **D:** Billy Wilder; **W:** Billy Wilder, I.A.L. Diamond; **M:** Andre Previn. *AWARDS:* Oscars '63: Adapt. Score; Golden Globes '64: Actress—Mus./Comedy (MacLaine); *NOM:* Oscars '63: Actress (MacLaine), Color Cinematog.

The Iron Mask

In a final "Ho—LA!" to the silent screen, Fairbanks takes on Dumas's heroic D'Artagnan in a story that combines *The Three Musketeers* and *The Man in the Iron Mask.* D'Artagnan joins his three heroic buddies to stop a plot to kidnap the prince. Dwan's fine direction and Fairbanks's stunts make for almost as exciting a picture as *Mask of Zorro* a decade earlier. The disc features a good orchestral score by Carl Davis and the print, restored by the Museum of Modern Art, looks almost pristine. Outtakes and an excerpt from the film's 1952 re-release (with narration from Fairbanks Jr.) make this a fantastic disc for armchair swashbucklers. —*DRL*

Movie: ♫♫♫ **DVD:** ♫♫♫ ½
Kino on Video (cat #248, UPC 738329024-826). Full frame. Mono. $29.95. Keepcase. *LANG:* Silent. *FEATURES:* Outtakes ☞ Excerpt from the 1952 re-release (narrated by Fairbanks Jr.) ☞ Photo gallery ☞ Essays ☞ 12 chapters.
1929 103m/B Douglas Fairbanks Sr., Nigel de Brulier, Marguerite de la Motte, Ullrich Haupt, William "Billy" Bakewell; **D:** Allan Dwan; **W:** Douglas Fairbanks Sr.; **C:** Henry Sharp.

Iron Monkey [Miramax]

The whole city quakes as the thief named Iron Monkey strikes, robbing the rich to give to the poor. Shaolin monks brought in by the governor are ineffective. Mild mannered Dr. Yang at the Pa Cho Tong clinic, along with his nurse Miss Orchid Ho (Jean Wang), are in reality the ones behind the black mask. The Legate officer is due to inspect the region, so the governor cracks down harder on Fox to catch the outlaw. Doctor Wong Kei-ying is passing through town with his precocious son Wong Fei-hung, and a demonstration of Wong's kung fu prowess is enough to make him a suspect. With Fei-hung held as security, Wong is given a week to prove his innocence by catching Iron Monkey. The main attraction: Yuen Woo-ping's stunningly choreographed superhero action sequences. This American re-release cleans up the image and sound, replacing the original score with one by James L. Venable on both language tracks (which you cannot toggle between). Interview segments with Donnie Yen and Quentin Tarantino make you wish they'd sat together for a full commentary. —*BT*
AKA: Siunin Wong Fei-hung Tsi Titmalau; Shao Nian Huang Fei Hong Zhi Tie Ma Liu; Iron Monkey: The Young Wong Fei-hung.
Movie: ♫♫♫ ½ **DVD:** ♫♫♫ ½
Miramax Pictures (cat #25132, UPC 7869-36173123). Widescreen (1.85:1) anamorphic. Dolby Digital 5.1 Surround. $29.95. Keepcase. *LANG:* Chinese; English. *SUB:* English. *CAP:* English. *FEATURES:* 18 chapters ☞ Interviews ☞ Score medley.
1993 (PG-13) 87m/C *HK* Rongguang Yu, Donnie Yen, Yam Sai-kun, Tsing-ying Wong; **D:** Woo-ping Yuen; **W:** Tseng Pik-Yin, Tsui Hark, Tai-Muk Lau, Cheung Tan, Pik-yin Tang; **C:** Arthur Wong; **M:** James L. Venable.

The Island of Dr. Moreau

Remake of *Island of Lost Souls* lacks the intensity of the original, but Burt Lancast-

er turns in another solid performance as the scientist who has isolated himself on a Pacific island to continue his chromosome research—he can transform animals into near-humans and humans into animals. Some of the critters are a bit too obviously created with rubber masks. DVD image is slightly pale and not particularly sharp throughout. It is, however, an accurate reproduction of the low- to mid-budget original. —*MM*
Movie: ♫♫ **DVD:** ♫♫ ½
MGM Home Ent. (cat #1002334, UPC 027-616865533). Widescreen (1.85:1) anamorphic. Dolby Digital Mono. $19.98. Keepcase. *LANG:* English; French; Spanish. *SUB:* French; Spanish. *CAP:* English. *FEATURES:* 16 chapters ☞ Trailer.
1977 (PG) 99m/C Burt Lancaster, Michael York, Nigel Davenport, Barbara Carrera, Richard Basehart, Nick Cravat; **D:** Don Taylor; **W:** John Herman Shaner, Al Ramrus; **C:** Gerry Fisher.

It

Clara Bow, already a star, made herself an icon with this romantic comedy. Defined as the power of magnetism, confidence, sex appeal, and all the intangibles, Bow became the epitome of the "It" girl for the jazz era. A department store girl, she sets her sights on the owner, but a friend's illegitimate child throws a wrench in Bow's plans. Although a bit simple-minded, it's still very amusing. Also included is an interesting documentary on Bow's life, narrated by Courtney Love. The DVD's beginning is a bit rocky, with a storm of cracks and specks, but it settles down into a rather remarkable transfer. —*BG*
Movie: ♫♫♫ **DVD:** ♫♫♫
Kino on Video (cat #K195, UPC 7383-29019525). Full frame. $29.95. Keepcase. *LANG:* Silent. *FEATURES:* 18 chapters ☞ Documentary.
1927 71m/B Clara Bow, Antonio Moreno, Jacqueline Gadsdon, William Austin, Gary Cooper, Julia Swayne Gordon; **D:** Clarence Badger, Josef von Sternberg; **W:** Hope Loring, Louis D. Lighton; **C:** Kinley Martin. *AWARDS:* Natl. Film Reg. '01.

It Came from Outer Space

John (Carlson) and Ellen (Rush) watch a great fireball going down near a mine and believe it's an alien starship. Townspeople disappear and return, behaving in a strange way. The sheriff and his men are ready to exterminate the aliens, but John hopes to reach a peaceful solution. Originally released in 3-D and based on Ray Bradbury's "The Meteor," this is one of the most interesting of '50s sci fi and directed by one of its best, Jack Arnold, whose muscular exposition always propels everything along with earnestness and economy. You can even catch some Bradbury atmosphere and dialogue through the "B"-movie conventions. Film historian Tom Weaver's commentary is also a great plea-

sure. A pristine DVD transfer with excellent sound. —*MO*
Movie: ♫♫♫ **DVD:** ♫♫♫♫
Universal Studios (cat #20435, UPC 025-192043529). Full frame. Dolby Digital Surround. $19.98. Keepcase. *LANG:* English. *SUB:* French; Spanish. *CAP:* English; French; Spanish. *FEATURES:* 18 chapters ☞ "The Universe According to Universal," original documentary ☞ Commentary: film historian Tom Weaver ☞ Photography and poster gallery ☞ Theatrical trailer ☞ Production notes ☞ Cast and filmmakers.
1953 81m/B Richard Carlson, Barbara Rush, Charles Drake, Russell Johnson, Kathleen Hughes; **D:** Jack Arnold; **W:** Harry Essex, Ray Bradbury; **C:** Clifford Stine; **M:** Henry Mancini, Herman Stein, Irving Gertz.

It! The Terror from Beyond Space

The sole survivor of the first Martian expedition is believed to have murdered his colleagues. He's arrested and brought back to Earth via space ship. En route, a vicious alien (a guy in a fairly generic rubber suit) begins killing the crew members. Curiously enjoyable low-budget SF would provide Ridley Scott with the basic plot for *Alien*. Artifacts are heavy in the dark opening shot, and infrequent light scratches appear later. Overall though, the DVD image is fine for 1950s black and white, and it's all the film needs. —*MM* **AKA:** It! The Vampire from Beyond Space.
Movie: ♫♫ ½ **DVD:** ♫♫ ½
MGM Home Ent. (cat #1002340, UPC 027-616865595). Full frame. Dolby Digital Mono. $19.98. Keepcase. *LANG:* English. *SUB:* French; Spanish. *CAP:* English. *FEATURES:* 16 chapters ☞ Trailer.
1958 68m/B Marshall Thompson, Shawn Smith, Kim Spalding, Ann Doran, Dabbs Greer, Paul Langton, Ray Corrigan; **D:** Edward L. Cahn; **W:** Jerome Bixby; **C:** Kenneth Peach Sr.; **M:** Paul Sawtell, Bert Shefter.

The Item

Bizarre little festival fave was shot on video and, to be blunt about it, the DVD image is simply butt-ugly. It's grainy, unfocused, poorly lighted, and the sound has a hollow booming quality. A game young cast valiantly attempts to overcome the pervasive cheapness of the production and a patchwork script. The story has to do with a group of unpleasant people (allegedly tough criminal types) who have agreed to guard a heavy strongbox for a few hours. Turns out that it contains a supernatural critter which shows them their worst fears. Lots of gory violence and special effects borrowed from better films (most obviously *Jacob's Ladder*) fill out the running time. Disc comes with a full complement of extras, including an allegedly humorous "Gun Safety" bit of business. —*MM*
Movie: ♫♫ **DVD:** ♫♫
Artisan Ent. (cat #12011). Widescreen letterboxed. Dolby Digital 5.1 Surround; Dolby

Digital Surround. $14.98. Keepcase. *LANG:* English. *SUB:* English; Spanish. *FEATURES:* 16 chapters • Commentary • 3 behind-the-scenes featurettes • 2 deleted scenes • "Gun Safety" short • Trailer.
2001 100m/C Dawn Marie Velasquez, Dave Pressler, Dan Clark; ***D:*** Dan Clark; ***W:*** Dan Clark; ***C:*** Michael Mayhew; ***M:*** Howard Drossin.

It's a Mad, Mad, Mad, Mad World

If you had to pick just one word to describe director Stanley Kramer's 1963 epic caper comedy, it would be "timeless." The inspired casting of the great comedians of the day as the film's central characters, hell-bent on finding a fortune in stolen cash, continues to pay dividends again and again as the years pass. Indeed, the greats of those days—Milton Berle, Sid Caesar, and Jonathan Winters—have in time become legends, and the film remains both knock-out funny and something of a time capsule honoring them. MGM makes excellent use of the rarely used DVD-14 configuration, placing the entire feature film on the DVD-9 side of this double-sided disc, and the bonus features on the reverse DVD-5 side. The only real negative here is the lack of a commentary track. —*RT*
Movie: 🎵🎵🎵 ½ *DVD:* 🎵🎵🎵
MGM Home Ent. (cat #1002380, UPC 027-616865915). Widescreen (2.55:1) anamorphic. Dolby Digital 5.1 Surround. $19.98. Keepcase. *LANG:* English; French. *SUB:* English; French; Spanish. *CAP:* English; French; Spanish. *FEATURES:* 32 chapters • 2 theatrical trailers • "Something a Little Less Serious" documentary • "Extented" scenes.
1963 155m/C Spencer Tracy, Sid Caesar, Milton Berle, Ethel Merman, Jonathan Winters, Jimmy Durante, Buddy Hackett, Mickey Rooney, Phil Silvers, Dick Shawn, Edie Adams, Dorothy Provine, Buster Keaton, Terry-Thomas, Moe Howard, Larry Fine, Joe DeRita, Jim Backus, William Demarest, Peter Falk, Leo Gorcey, Edward Everett Horton, Joe E. Brown, Carl Reiner, ZaSu Pitts, Eddie Anderson, Jack Benny, Jerry Lewis, Norman Fell, Stan Freberg, Don Knotts; ***D:*** Stanley Kramer; ***W:*** William Rose, Tania Rose; ***C:*** Ernest Laszlo; ***M:*** Ernest Gold. *AWARDS:* Oscars '63: Sound FX Editing; *NOM:* Oscars '63: Color Cinematog., Film Editing, Song ("It's a Mad, Mad, Mad, Mad World"), Sound, Orig. Score.

Ivanhoe

Sir Walter Scott's legendary epic is done justice in this detailed and action-packed miniseries from BBC. After returning from the Crusades in Palestine, Sir William of Ivanhoe (Waddington) must battle the deceitful Prince John (Brown) and the insane Grand Master of the Templar Order (Lee) to win his love and reseat King Richard (Edwards) upon his rightful English throne. The beautiful landscapes and constant swordplay keep the action flowing, but uneven performances limit its overall effectiveness. The transfer looks the same as its original broadcast, though there are some artifacts in the darker scenes. The stereo sound is nothing special. On two DVDs. —*DRL*
Movie: 🎵🎵🎵 *DVD:* 🎵🎵 ½
A&E (cat #70422, UPC 733961704228). Full frame. Dolby Digital Stereo. $39.95. Keepcase (2 DVD boxed set). *LANG:* English. *FEATURES:* Sir Walter Scott bio • 36 chapters.
1997 292m/C *GB* Steven Waddington, Susan Lynch, Ciaran Hinds, Victoria Smurfit, Ralph Brown, Rory Edwards, Ronald Pickup, David Horovitch, Trevor Cooper, Valentine Pelka, Nick Brimble, Jimmy Chisholm, Christopher Lee, Aden (John) Gillett, James Cosmo, Sian Phillips, Ciaran Madden; ***D:*** Stuart Orme; ***W:*** Deborah Cook; ***C:*** Clive Tickner; ***M:*** Colin Towns.

Jabberwocky

Pythonesque chaos prevails in the medieval cartoon kingdom of King Bruno the Questionable, who rules with cruelty, stupidity, lust and dust. Jabberwocky is the big dragon mowing everything down in its path until hero Palin decides to take it on. Uneven, but really funny at times. The otherworldly hue of most of director Gilliam's films is reproduced admirably here. The base, non-flamboyant colors are nicely done while blacks are similarly well-defined. The overall look of the film does lend itself to softer blacks and a more muted color scheme, however. The able soundtrack provides understandable dialogue (though you might need to turn the volume up in a few sections) as well as an equally impressive musical score. As with other Gilliam discs, the commentary track proves both insightful and entertaining. But what else would you expect from an American Python? —*MJT*
Movie: 🎵🎵 ½ *DVD:* 🎵🎵🎵
Columbia Tristar (cat #92249, UPC 043-396922495). Widescreen (1.85:1) letterboxed; full frame. Dolby Digital 5.1 Surround; Dolby Surround. $24.95. Keepcase. *LANG:* English; French. *SUB:* English; French; Spanish. *FEATURES:* 28 chapters • Commentary: director Terry Gilliam, actor Michael Palin • International photo gallery • Sketch-to-screen comparisons • Theatrical trailer.
1977 (PG) 104m/C *GB* Michael Palin, Eric Idle, Max Wall, Deborah Fallender, Terry Jones, John Le Mesurier, Annette Badland, Warren Mitchell, Harry H. Corbett, David Prowse, Neil Innes; ***D:*** Terry Gilliam; ***W:*** Charles Alverson, Terry Gilliam; ***C:*** Terry Bedford; ***M:*** De Wolfe.

Jack and Sarah

Widowed London lawyer Jack (Grant) hires American waitress Amy (Mathis) to help raise his infant daughter Sarah. Complications arise because Amy has no child-rearing skills and Jack's parents and in-laws disapprove of the whole situation. Performances are uniformly excellent from both the scene-stealing toddlers and Ian McKellen. But the plot is thin with some uncomfortable moments. According to some sources, the film exists in an "R"-rated version. This disc is "PG" and a disappointment all the way around. Flashing in tight patterns is excessive. So is aliasing. Both may come from edge-enhancement. Whatever the reason, disc is no better than tape. —*MM*
Movie: 🎵🎵 ½ *DVD:* 🎵🎵
MGM Home Ent. (cat #1002753, UPC 027-616869517). Full frame. Dolby Digital Surround. $19.98. Keepcase. *LANG:* English; French. *SUB:* English; French; Spanish. *CAP:* English. *FEATURES:* 16 chapters • 4 trailers.
1995 (PG) 110m/C *GB* Richard E. Grant, Samantha Mathis, Ian McKellen, Judi Dench, Cherie Lunghi, Eileen Atkins, Imogen Stubbs; ***D:*** Tim Sullivan; ***W:*** Tim Sullivan; ***C:*** Jean-Yves Escoffier; ***M:*** Simon Boswell.

Jack and the Beanstalk: The Real Story

This TV miniseries is a co-production of Jim Henson's company and Hallmark Entertainment, and does a wonderful job of updating and twisting the classic "Jack and the Beanstalk" fairy tale. This contemporary version stars Matthew Modine as Jonathan William Von Hapsburg Robinson, known to his friends as Jack. He runs a powerful global empire and is hard at work on building a new casino. But the construction unearths a finding that unveils a dark secret which hangs over the Robinson family. Jack is a direct descendant of the Jack who climbed that famed beanstalk, killed the giant, and made off with the goose and harp. In a very detailed flashback, we are told the original story again, but with a new twist. As it turns out, the giant was actually a peaceful soul and the original Jack was a thief. Now, present-day Jack is being put on trial by the giants and his only hope is to return the goose and harp, with the aid of Ondine (Mia Sara), a mysterious woman who has chosen to help Jack. This updated fairy tale is very imaginative and entertaining. The way the story builds upon the original tale is ingenious and the pacing never drags. Also, the special effects are quite impressive for a made-for-TV film. Modine leads a great cast, which includes such familiar faces as Vanessa Redgrave, Jon Voight, and Darryl Hannah. Parents, be warned: While this one is taken from the classic tale, the new version contains some rather dark sequences, so it may not be suitable for the younger viewers. Although the DVD box claims that the film is presented full frame, in actuality, it is letterboxed at 1.78:1. The image is fantastic, rivaling digital broadcast quality. There are no distracting imperfections to be found here, as the image is very sharp and clear, showing great colors and virtually no grain. The Dolby Digital 5.1 audio track is impressive as well, providing nearly con-

stant Surround effects and booming bass response. A nice featurette gives an overview of how the special effects were created. —*ML* **AKA:** Jim Henson's Jack and the Beanstalk.
Movie: 🎵🎵🎵 **DVD:** 🎵🎵🎵
Artisan Ent. (cat #11867, UPC 70772911-8671). Widescreen (1.78:1) letterboxed. Dolby Digital 5.1; Dolby Surround. $19.98. Keepcase. *LANG:* English. *CAP:* English. *FEATURES:* Special effects featurette • Production notes • Behind-the-scenes featurette • 11 chapters.
2001 184m/C Matthew Modine, Vanessa Redgrave, Mia Sara, Jon Voight, Daryl Hannah, Richard Attenborough; **D:** Brian Henson; **W:** Jim V. Hart, Brian Henson.

Jack the Giant Killer

A young farmer (Mathews) and a princess (Meredith) battle an evil wizard (Thatcher), dragons, giants, sea monsters, and other mystical creatures. Cast and effects attempt to re-create the magic of *Seventh Voyage of Sinbad* but the effects lack the magic that Ray Harryhausen created. Somewhat faded image is not a striking improvement over a good VHS tape. It has the slightly thin quality associated with duplication from an imperfect original. There appears to be little surface damage, however. —*MM*
Movie: 🎵🎵 ½ **DVD:** 🎵🎵
Goodtimes Ent. (cat #05-81211, UPC 018-713812117). Full frame. Dolby Digital Mono. $24.98. Keepcase. *LANG:* English. *FEATURES:* 12 chapters.
1962 (G) 95m/C Kerwin Mathews, Judi Meredith, Torin Thatcher, Walter Burke, Roger Mobley, Barry Kelley, Don Beddoe, Anna Lee, Robert Gist; **D:** Nathan (Hertz) Juran; **W:** Nathan (Hertz) Juran, Orville H. Hampton; **C:** David S. Horsley; **M:** Paul Sawtell, Bert Shefter.

Jack the Ripper: 4 Tales of the Supernatural

Boris Karloff hosts and acts in four half-hour stories from an old series called *The Veil*, no doubt some network's answer to *The Twilight Zone*. You couldn't ask for a better transfer—the image quality is terrific. In a supernatural twist on *Rear Window*, a man sees a woman across the alley murdered in her apartment a few days before the murder actually occurs. When he reports the crime to the police, he becomes the number one suspect. In the second story a man returns from the grave in response to his son's horrid behavior. In the third story, illness aboard an old sailing vessel prompts the captain to commit an act that forever places a ghost at the Mariner's Club. In the final story a man suffers horrible dreams where he watches the details of Jack the Ripper's crimes as they are happening in real time. Karloff takes a role in each story and introduces with quaint aplomb. If you have a taste for decent "B"-movie classics, eat up this television take on the genre. —*JAS*

Movie: 🎵🎵🎵 **DVD:** 🎵🎵🎵 ½
Rhino (cat #R2972758, UPC 603497275-823). Full frame. $9.95. Snapper. *LANG:* English. *FEATURES:* 4 chapters.
1958 70m/B Boris Karloff, Niall MacGinnis, Kay Stewart, Morris Ankrum, Harry Bartell, Clifford Evans, Robert E. (Bob) Griffin, Thomas B(rowne). Henry; **D:** David MacDonald; **W:** Jimmy Sangster.

The Jackals

Six bandits threaten a miner (Price) and his granddaughter (Ivarson) to get their gold. The setting is 19th-century South Africa and so the film looks like a western with lions and elephants. Faded image and sound make for a DVD that's no improvement over VHS tape. Title is also available as part of "The Wild West" collection. —*MM*
Movie: 🎵🎵 **DVD:** 🎵 ½
BCI-Eclipse (cat #44073-9, UPC 7873644-07392). Full frame. $9.98. Keepcase. *LANG:* English. *FEATURES:* 6 chapters • "Cobweb Hotel" cartoon • DVD dictionary • Trivia game • DVD-ROM features.
1967 105m/C Vincent Price, Diana Ivarson, Robert Gunner, Bob Courtney, Patrick Mynhardt; **D:** Robert D. Webb.

Jackie's Back

Faux bio-pic was produced for the Lifetime cable network. It tells the story of second-rate soul singer and blaxploitation star Jackie Washington (producer Lewis), who's trying to mount a comeback. Tim Curry plays the filmmaker who's following her around. Some of the jokes are funny but the film lacks the rare tone of, say, *This Is Spinal Tap*. The list of guest stars is pretty impressive. DVD can do nothing to improve the low-budget and often intentionally rough-looking image. Only the extras differentiate this disc from cablecast or VHS tape. —*MM*
Movie: 🎵🎵 ½ **DVD:** 🎵🎵
Xenon Ent. (cat #XE XX 4202DVD). Full frame. $19.98. Keepcase. *LANG:* English. *FEATURES:* Commentary: Robert Townsend • Trailers • 12 chapters.
1999 (R) 91m/C Jenifer Lewis, Tim Curry, Tangie Ambrose, Whoopi Goldberg, David Hyde Pierce, Tom Arnold, Julie Hagerty, JoBeth Williams, Dolly Parton, Grace Slick, Liza Minnelli; **D:** Robert Townsend; **W:** Mark Brown, Dee La Duke; **C:** Charles Mills; **M:** Marc Shaiman.

Jackpot

Sunny Holiday (Gries) is on the road with his manager (Morris), travelling the country to compete in karaoke shows. They hope it will lead Holiday to stardom and his own record contract, but in the meantime it subjects the audience to lots of bad singing, which might sound better after several drinks. It's all curiously detached, and doesn't amount to much. The colors seem faded and washed-out, but that might have been the filmmakers' intentions, and the sound comes off as

muffled in both the 5.1 and 2-channel mix. The disc contains both wide- and full-frame versions of the film. —*BG*
Movie: 🎵🎵 ½ **DVD:** 🎵🎵 ½
Columbia Tristar (cat #06903, UPC 0433-96069039). Widescreen (2.35:1) anamorphic; full frame. Dolby 5.1; Dolby Surround. $29.95. Keepcase. *LANG:* English. *SUB:* English. *CAP:* English. *FEATURES:* 28 chapters • Filmmakers' commentary track • Filmographies • Trailers for other Sony Pictures Classics films.
2001 (R) 100m/C Jonathan (Jon Francis) Gries, Garrett Morris, Daryl Hannah, Peggy Lipton, Adam Baldwin, Mac Davis, Crystal Bernard, Anthony Edwards; **D:** Michael Polish; **W:** Michael Polish, Mark Polish; **C:** M. David Mullen; **M:** Stuart Matthewman; **V:** Patrick Bauchau.

Jackson Pollock: Love and Death on Long Island

This BBC-produced documentary is a companion piece or introduction to Ed Harris's feature *Pollock*. It's a fairly standard once-over of the famous artist's short, eventful life, quoting friends and associates and using footage of the subject. The new footage looks fine. Overall, the image is acceptable though it has been deliberately "distressed" in many scenes in an attempt to re-create or suggest Pollock's drippy style. Disc is only a marginal improvement over VHS tape or broadcast, for that matter, but the film tells an interesting story that's worth watching on any medium. —*MM*
Movie: 🎵🎵 ½ **DVD:** 🎵🎵 ½
Home Vision Cinema (cat #POL 050, UPC 037429164020). Full frame. $19.98. Keepcase. *LANG:* English. *FEATURES:* 8 chapters.
1999 46m/C Ed Harris, Lee Krasner; **D:** Teresa Griffiths; **Nar:** Neil Pearson.

Jacob the Liar

In a Polish ghetto during WWII, Jacob overhears a radio report at the police station and quickly perpetuates the fiction that he possesses the forbidden radio. The entire ghetto and even the Germans become unwitting participants in Jacob's well-meaning, but ultimately destructive fantasy. Their whole world collapses when they get rounded up and sent to a concentration camp. A sentimental American remake came out in 1999. Beyer documentary is pretty well produced. DEFA trailer is just clips from their many films. DVD has a low contrast picture that looks dull and lifeless. Sound is fine. (Review disc had problems. It played fine until the last three chapters when it began to freeze and pixelate. I tried cleaning it with a special wiper three times and playing it again. I also tried on a friend's machine and it was still glitchy and wouldn't play correctly in the same spots, but it didn't do the same things. That was a little weird, but there's definitely something wrong with the disc.) —*LA* **AKA:** Jakob der Lugner.

Movie: ♫♫ ½ **DVD:** ♫♫ ½
Hen's Tooth Video (cat #69083, UPC 679-126908325). Full frame. MPEG 2 Stereo. $29.98. Keepcase. *LANG:* German. *SUB:* English; French; Spanish; Hebrew. *FEATURES:* "Traces of Time," documentary about director Frank Beyer • Introductory trailer for DEFA Films • Bios of Becker and Beyer • 11 chapters.
1974 (PG-13) 101m/C *GE* Armin Mueller-Stahl, Vlastimil Brodsky, Erwin Geschonneck, Henry Hubchen, Blanche Kommerell, Manuela Simon; *D:* Frank Beyer; *W:* Jurek Becker; *C:* Gunter Marczinkowski. *AWARDS: NOM:* Oscars '76: Foreign Film.

Jade Claw

Kwan Master Kwan is killed by Yen, who uses his famed Double Phoenix Eye Fist, leaving Kwan's son Wen an orphan. Years later, youngster Kwan Wen enters a school to learn kung fu. Chang the cook is the guy who defeated Yen and handicapped his two aides. Beaten by the villains who killed his father, Wen receives instruction from Chang in his top secret Shadow Eagle Fist and Claw techniques, though most of Wen's training comes in the form of altered cooking chores. All this comedy in the kitchen is reminiscent of Jackie Chan's *Half A Loaf of Kung Fu,* this film's obvious inspiration. Though no match for Chan's hit in the martial arts department, *Jade Claw* at least achieves a bit of character and some decent gags, unlike its fellow imitators. The widescreen image (despite what it says on Xenon's generic packaging) is slightly squeezed and a bit soft, but in keeping with the condition of Hong Kong films of the period. —*BT* **AKA:** Kei Chiu; Ji Zhao; Crystal Fist.
Movie: ♫ ½ **DVD:** ♫♫
Xenon Ent. (cat #XAXE6092DVD, UPC 00079960922). Widescreen letterboxed. $14.98. Keepcase. *LANG:* English. *FEATURES:* 6 chapters.
1979 84m/C *HK* Billy Chong, Simon Yuen, Brandy Yuen, Jim James, Chiu Sing Hau; *D:* Hwa Yi Hung; *W:* Chan Wai Li; *C:* Man-Wan Wong; *M:* Shung Chi Chen.

Jailbreakers

Featherweight made-for-cable flick is an exercise in shallow style. High school cheerleader Angel (Doherty, who's at least 15 years too old for the role) falls for bad-boy Tony (Sabato, ditto the age thing). They steal stuff. Her folks (Edwards and Barbeau) are appalled. None of it is meant to be taken seriously, but that's no excuse, and what is Friedkin doing here? Extras-free DVD provides slight if any improvement over broadcast quality. —*MM*
Movie: ♫♫ **DVD:** ♫♫
Buena Vista Home Ent. (cat #21686, UPC 786936145113). Full frame. Dolby Digital Surround. $29.99. Keepcase. *LANG:* English. *CAP:* English. *FEATURES:* 13 chapters.
1994 (R) 76m/C Shannen Doherty, Antonio Sabato Jr., Adrienne Barbeau, Adrien Brody, Vince Edwards, George Gerdes; *D:*

William Friedkin; *W:* Debra Hill, Gigi Vorgan; *C:* Cary Fisher; *M:* Hummie Mann.

Jane Austen: Her Life, Her Works, Her Society

Three programs examine the life, times, and writings of Jane Austen, with excerpts from her novels and letters as well as location footage, complete with a stuffy British narrator and Baroque chamber music. The bone ratings are irrelevant; if you're interested in Austen or Victorian England you'll like this. If not, you'll fall asleep. Sound and picture are both what should be expected from a TV production. (Packaging lists runtime of 156 mins. for the three episodes; my calculations come out to 174 mins.) —*BG*
Movie: ♫♫ **DVD:** ♫♫ ½
BFS Video (cat #81791-D, UPC 07733179-10). Full frame. $29.98. Keepcase. *LANG:* English. *FEATURES:* 20 chapters.
1998 60m/C

The January Man

This had the makings of a classic, great story, great actors, but then the script was changed and the greatness became crap. Nick Stanley (Kevin Kline) is an ex-cop called back to duty because he has a knack for getting the bad guy. He's hated by his brother (Harvey Keitel), desired by the Mayor's (Rod Steiger) daughter (Mary Elizabeth Mastrantonio), despised by his superior (Danny Aiello), and helped by his painter friend (Alan Rickman). Oh yeah, let's not forget his ex-wife (Susan Sarandon) in a throw-away role. Now with that cast, you'd think this movie would be great. But it gets lost, not knowing where it's going. Is it a thriller, a comedy, both? Who knows? Worth watching just to see Kline do his thing. DVD is of good quality. Picture is true and sound is crisp. —*DE*
Movie: ♫♫ ½ **DVD:** ♫♫♫
MGM Home Ent. (cat #1003351, UPC 276-1687500). Widescreen (1.85:1) anamorphic; full frame. Dolby 5.1 Surround. $14.98. Keepcase. *LANG:* English; French; Spanish. *SUB:* English; French; Spanish. *CAP:* English. *FEATURES:* 16 chapters • Original theatrical trailer.
1989 (R) 97m/C Kevin Kline, Susan Sarandon, Mary Elizabeth Mastrantonio, Harvey Keitel, Rod Steiger, Alan Rickman, Danny Aiello; *D:* Pat O'Connor; *W:* Pat O'Connor, John Patrick Shanley; *C:* Jerzy Zielinski; *M:* Marvin Hamlisch.

Jaws 2

When last we found Chief Martin Brody (Scheider), he was dog-paddling his way back to Amity. Nearly five years later, divers are exploring the wreck of the *Orca* when surprise, surprise, ANOTHER toothy beast stops by for dinner. But the poor fella is horribly burned when, after swallowing down an Olympic skier, he attempts to have the speed boat and its remaining occupant for dessert and the whole thing

BLOWS UP in his snout. Ouch! Naturally, pre-chewed lunchables start washing up and Brody starts seeing great big sharks everywhere. This being a movie, no one believes him and—presto—we have suspense. Steven Spielberg's original was a transcendent piece of cinema, and while its twin pales cerebrally, it delivers what audiences wanted without insulting them in the process. The widescreen transfer is generally pretty good, but there are a fair amount of artifacts present throughout. The mono track is crisp and serves the score reasonably well. Included is a 45-minute documentary about why making mechanical shark movies is really, really hard. It's clip-heavy but features fairly candid interviews with the producers, director, and screenwriter. The separate interview with Keith Gordon is interesting. As a member of the teen cast, he hints about on-set romances over the protracted shoot, but stops short of any juicy details. In another interview, composer John Williams swears to us that he really did write new music for the film. In an amusing segment, director Jeannot Szwarc explains how the flick's title had to be changed in France to avoid an unfortunate play on words. About four minutes of mostly forgettable deleted scenes, but the underwater shot of the shark attacking the chopper pilot is fun to see. There's also an extensive collection of production photos, storyboards, shark facts, cast bios, and theatrical trailers. —*GNG/DG*
Movie: ♫♫ **DVD:** ♫♫♫
Universal Studios (cat #20928, UPC 0251-92092824). Widescreen (2.35:1) anamorphic. Mono. $26.98. Keepcase. *LANG:* English; French. *SUB:* Spanish. *CAP:* English. *FEATURES:* "Making of *Jaws 2*" • "Jaws 2: A Portrait" by Keith Gordon • "The Music of *Jaws 2*" • The French joke • Deleted scenes • Photo gallery • Storyboards • Shark facts • Trailer • Production notes • Cast & crew bios.
1978 (PG) 116m/C Roy Scheider, Lorraine Gary, Murray Hamilton, Joseph Mascolo, Jeffrey Kramer, Collin Wilcox-Paxton, Keith Gordon; *D:* Jeannot Szwarc; *W:* Carl Gottlieb, Howard Sackler; *C:* Michael C. Butler; *M:* John Williams.

Jay and Silent Bob Strike Back

Slackers Jay (Mewes) and Silent Bob (director Smith) are mortified to learn that Miramax Pictures is going to make a movie of Bluntman and Chronic, comic book characters based on them, and that people on the Internet are saying nasty things about them. They elect to go from New Jersey to Hollywood and put a stop to the production. O.K., there are about three times too many gay jokes in this road movie, but the humor is not mean-spirited; much of the action is inventive and Smith's silent mugging is terrific. Many characters and cast members from Smith's earlier movies show up again. Of course, image and sound quality are first-rate. The package is a two-RSDL disc set with film and commentary on one; the rest of the features on the other. Those tend to be long on quantity, short on quality. No less than 42 extended and deleted scenes are included, each with an extended introduction by the filmmakers, where they shamelessly promote their various products. —*MM*

Movie: 🐾🐾🐾 **DVD:** 🐾🐾🐾 ½
Buena Vista Home Ent. (cat #24665, UPC 786936169195). Widescreen (2.35:1) anamorphic. Dolby Digital 5.1 Surround. $29.98. Keepcase. *LANG:* English; French. *SUB:* Spanish. *CAP:* English. *FEATURES:* Commentary: filmmakers • 18 chapters • Gag reel • TV spots • Music videos • Behind-the-scenes featurette • Comedy Central featurette • Guide to Morris Day and the Time • DVD-ROM features • Talent files • Internet trailers.
2001 (R) 95m/C Kevin Smith, Jason Mewes, Jason Lee, Ben Affleck, Shannon Elizabeth, Eliza Dushku, Ali Larter, Jennifer Schwalbach, Chris Rock, Will Ferrell, Brian O'Halloran, Seann William Scott, George Carlin, Carrie Fisher, Judd Nelson, Jon Stewart, Mark Hamill, Diedrich Bader, Wes Craven, Gus Van Sant, Matt Damon, Shannen Doherty, Jason Biggs, James Van Der Beek, Joey Lauren Adams, Alanis Morissette, Renee Humphrey; *D:* Kevin Smith; *W:* Kevin Smith; *C:* Jamie Anderson; *M:* James L. Venable.

J.D.'s Revenge

Attorney in training Ike (Turman) is possessed by the spirit of a gangster who was murdered on Bourbon Street in the early 1940s. That adds an element of horror to a lively, nicely done piece of "blaxploitation." DVD image quality ranges between fair and very good, depending on the lighting conditions. Mono sound is fine. —*MM*

Movie: 🐾🐾 ½ **DVD:** 🐾🐾 ½
MGM Home Ent. (cat #1002855, UPC 027-616870452). Widescreen (1.85:1) anamorphic; full frame. Dolby Digital Mono. $14.98. Keepcase. *LANG:* English; French. *SUB:* French; Spanish. *CAP:* English. *FEATURES:* 16 chapters • Trailer.
1976 (R) 95m/C Louis Gossett Jr., Glynn Turman, Joan Pringle, David McKnight, James L. Watkins; *D:* Arthur Marks; *W:* Jaison Starkes; *C:* Harry J. May; *M:* Prince.

Jealousy

In Spain, Carmen (Sanchez-Gijon) and Antonio (Cacho) are about to be married. But he discovers a photograph of her and a man named Jose. Doubts grow to plague him. The simple story is played out with conviction by all concerned. DVD delivers a clear, sharp, bright image—surprisingly good for an import. Sound is fine too, and the burned in English subtitles are easy to read. —*MM* *AKA:* Celos.

Movie: 🐾🐾🐾 **DVD:** 🐾🐾 ½
Vanguard Intl. Cinema (cat #VF0174, UPC 658769017434). Widescreen (1.66:1) letterboxed. Dolby Digital Stereo. $29.95.

Keepcase. *LANG:* Spanish. *SUB:* English. *FEATURES:* 12 chapters.
1999 105m/C *SP* Daniel Gimenez Cacho, Aitana Sanchez-Gijon, Maria Botto, Luis Tosar; *D:* Vicente Aranda; *W:* Vicente Aranda, Alvaro del Amo; *C:* Jose Luis Alcaine; *M:* Jose Nieto.

Jeepers Creepers

Fantastically fun and scary horrorfest harkens back to the visceral fright films of the '70s. College-student siblings Darry (Justin Long) and Trish (Gina Phillips) are taking the back roads home when they witness a mysterious figure apparently dumping bodies down a drain pipe. When they choose to investigate, they find themselves being pursued by a being of relentless evil. Unlike other recent horror fare, *Jeepers Creepers* doesn't try to be a horror-comedy and the film never fails to shock. Writer/director Victor Salva has set up a fairly familiar premise, which he then proceeds to tear down as the story gets weirder by the moment. Salva has also given the film a very nice look, as the dark photography and the use of action in the background are reminiscent of John Carpenter. Some may be turned off by the bizarre plot twists and dark nature of the film, but horror fans should eat this up. DVD offers a nice transfer of the film, but the daytime scenes are noticeably grainy, especially when compared to the same shots from the trailer (also included on the disc). The Dolby Digital 5.1 audio track is very impressive, as the score by Bennet Salvay and the constant use of rear speaker action helps to intensify the horror. Behind-the-scenes featurettes included on the disc give a dearth of information on the film, and Salva's audio commentary is especially good. —*ML*

Movie: 🐾🐾🐾🐾 **DVD:** 🐾🐾🐾 ½
MGM Home Ent. (cat #1002776, UPC 027-616869753). Widescreen (1.85:1) anamorphic; full frame. Dolby Digital 5.1; Dolby Surround. $26.98. Keepcase. *LANG:* English; French; Spanish. *SUB:* English; French; Spanish. *CAP:* English. *FEATURES:* Commentary • Deleted scenes • "Making of" featurette • Still gallery • Theatrical trailer • Cast & crew • 24 chapters.
2001 (R) 89m/C Gina Phillips, Justin Long, Jonathan Breck, Patricia Belcher, Brandon Smith, Eileen Brennan; *D:* Victor Salva; *W:* Victor Salva; *C:* Don E. Fauntleroy; *M:* Bennett Salvay.

Jeeves & Wooster: The Complete Second Season

The continuing adventures of the bumbling gentleman, Wooster (Laurie), and his butler, Jeeves (Fry), who always manages to get him out of trouble. A series of misadventures, which are compounded by Wooster's incompetence, befall these good chaps in each episode. The series is amiable if not often hilarious, and the two-disc set is probably most suited for palates that have already been acclimated

to British comedy. The picture is adequate, with the soft hues that identify a BBC production, and the clean dialogue helps in deciphering those confounded accents. —*BG*

Movie: 🐾🐾 ½ **DVD:** 🐾🐾 ½
A&E (cat #AAE-70212, UPC 7339617021-25). Full frame. Dolby Stereo. $39.95. Keepcase. *LANG:* English. *FEATURES:* 6 chapters per episode.
1996 300m/C *GB* Hugh Laurie, Stephen Fry; *D:* Simon Langton; *W:* P.G. Wodehouse.

Jekyll & Hyde: The Musical

Baywatch producer/star Hasselhoff stars in a filmed version of the Broadway stage production and does a credible job with the crowd-pleasing material. His voice is good enough to handle the songs, and the demands of the sometimes silly role are within his grasp. DVD image is slightly better than broadcast quality and the 5.1 track is much better. 2.0 Surround isn't bad either though subtitles or captions would have been welcome for some of the lyrics. —*MM*

Movie: 🐾🐾 ½ **DVD:** 🐾🐾 ½
Goodtimes Ent. (cat #05-81303, UPC 018713813039). Widescreen letterboxed. Dolby Digital 5.1 Surround Stereo; Dolby Digital Surround. $24.98. Keepcase. *LANG:* English. *FEATURES:* 12 chapters • Prelude with David Hasselhoff • Talent files.
2001 134m/C David Hasselhoff, George Merritt, Coleen Sexton, Andrea Rivette.

Jerry Maguire [2 SE]

The first release of this hit (reviewed in *Book 1*) earned high marks for the quality of both widescreen image and sound. But that was about it; no extras. This "Special Edition" has everything that serious videophiles have come to expect, along with curious "video commentary track" on disc two that takes full advantage of the cast. At the top of the screen, Tom Cruise, Rene Zellweger, Cuba Gooding Jr., and Cameron Crowe (dressed down in jeans, shorts, and shades) sit around a table and comment on the film, which is displayed in the bottom third of the screen. Those who prefer the standard audio commentary can hear the same thing by watching the conventional film on disc one. On both, they're chummy and lighthearted, revisiting the film that seriously boosted their careers. Of the other extras, perhaps the most impressive are Jay Mohr's astonishing one-take "are you in or are you out" telephone scene and Kelly Preston's "Chicago style" moment. They're part of the deleted scenes where Crowe is joined on his commentary by editor Joe Hutchins. As for the image, it's better than the theatrical release, as I remember it. —*MM*

Movie: 🐾🐾🐾 ½ **DVD:** 🐾🐾🐾🐾
Columbia Tristar (cat #02066, UPC 0433-96020665). Widescreen (1.85:1) anamorphic. Dolby Digital 5.1 Surround; Dolby Surround. $27.98. Special packaging. *LANG:* English; French; Spanish; Portuguese. *SUB:*

English; French; Spanish; Portuguese; Chinese; Korean; Thai. *CAP:* English. *FEATURES:* 28 chapters ▪ Audio & video commentary: Crowe, Cruise, Gooding, Zellweger ▪ Deleted scenes with commentary ▪ "Secret Garden" music video by Bruce Springsteen ▪ "Making of" featurette ▪ Trailers ▪ Mission statement (text) ▪ Talent files ▪ Photo gallery ▪ Rehearsal footage ▪ "My First Commercial" with Rod Tidwell ▪ Sports agent featurette.
1996 (R) 135m/C Tom Cruise, Cuba Gooding Jr., Renee Zellweger, Kelly Preston, Bonnie Hunt, Jerry O'Connell, Jay Mohr, Regina King, Glenn Frey, Jonathan Lipnicki, Todd Louiso, Mark Pellington, Eric Stoltz; *D:* Cameron Crowe; *W:* Cameron Crowe; *C:* Janusz Kaminski; *M:* Nancy Wilson. *AWARDS:* Oscars '96: Support. Actor (Gooding); Golden Globes '97: Actor—Mus./Comedy (Cruise); MTV Movie Awards '97: Male Perf. (Cruise); Natl. Bd. of Review '96: Actor (Cruise); Screen Actors Guild '96: Support. Actor (Gooding); Broadcast Film Critics '96: Breakthrough Perf. (Zellweger), Support. Actor (Gooding); *NOM:* Oscars '96: Actor (Cruise), Film Editing, Orig. Screenplay, Picture; Directors Guild '96: Director (Crowe); Golden Globes '97: Actor—Mus./Comedy (Cruise), Film—Mus./Comedy, Support. Actor (Gooding); MTV Movie Awards '97: Film, Breakthrough Perf. (Zellweger); Screen Actors Guild '96: Actor (Cruise), Support. Actress (Zellweger); Writers Guild '96: Orig. Screenplay.

Jiang Hu— "The Triad Zone"

Fans of HBO's *The Sopranos* should definitely see this. Jim Yam (Tony Leung Ka-Fai), boss of the Hung Bo gang, narrates the tale. Yam is a stylish fellow—even his bullet-proof vest is Versace. Word comes that someone will try to kill Jimmy in the next 24 hours. Proof of the validity of this rumor comes almost immediately when a sniper strikes. Trying to determine the identity of the assassin, and who hired him, causes Yam to re-examine every facet of his life and everyone he's close to. Beautifully photographed and creatively directed, *Jiang Hu* mixes *King of New York* brashness with *Goodfellas* wit and a huge romantic streak. Anthony Wong stops the show as a benevolent god who appears to save Yam's life. Transfer image is sharp and vivid. —*BT*
Movie: 🎬🎬🎬 ½ *DVD:* 🎬🎬🎬
Tai Seng (cat #DVD357, UPC 489039110-3574). Widescreen letterboxed. Dolby Digital 5.1. $19.98. Keepcase. *LANG:* Cantonese; Mandarin. *SUB:* Chinese; English. *FEATURES:* 9 chapters.
2000 107m/C HK Tony Leung Ka-Fai, Sandra Ng, Anthony Wong, Roy Cheung; *D:* Dante Lam; *W:* Hing Kai Chan, Amy Chin; *C:* Man Po Cheung; *M:* Tommy Wai.

Jill the Ripper

Functioning alcoholic and ex-cop Matt Wilson (Dolph Lundgren) launches his own investigation after his brother is murdered. This takes him into a world of political corruption and kinky sex, circa 1977 in Boston. An S&M thriller along the lines of *8mm*. It's hard to believe that a major player like Columbia would release such a bad looking DVD, even for this low-budget offering. The disc is so bad that I started watching the movie, got sick of the disc but wanted to finish the film, and switched to VHS. The image goes beyond soft—it can actually be called fuzzy. It's like looking through a layer of gauze that softens the picture and steals the color. Once in a while the picture becomes sharper for a moment or two but then goes back to its unwatchable condition. While not as horrible as the picture, the soundtrack is pretty unspectacular with very few Surround effects (it's 5.1), poor imaging, and a too-lean bass track. Director Hickox's commentary manages to be boring even though it pretty much nonstop complaining about the making of the film and a little more venom could have made it all worthwhile. —*JO*
Movie: 🎬🎬 *DVD:* 🎬
Columbia Tristar (cat #05004, UPC 0433-96050044). Widescreen (1.85:1) anamorphic. Dolby Digital 5.1; Dolby Surround; Dolby Digital Stereo. $29.95. Keepcase. *LANG:* English (DD5.1; DS); Spanish (Stereo); French (Stereo). *SUB:* English; Spanish. *CAP:* English. *FEATURES:* 28 chapters ▪ Trailer ▪ Talent files ▪ Commentary: directory Anthony Hickox.
2000 (R) 94m/C Dolph Lundgren, Danielle Brett; *D:* Anthony Hickox; *W:* Kevin Bernhardt, Gareth Wardell; *C:* David Pelletier; *M:* Steve Gurevitch, Thomas Barquee.

Jimmy Zip

Troubled pyromaniac teen Jimmy (Fletcher) runs away from his abusive home and winds up on the streets of the city where he's taken in by the silky Rick (Mulkey) who turns him into a drug courier. Circumstances bring Jimmy into contact with Horace (Gossett) who tries to turn him around. Give this Canadian production credit for energy and inventiveness, if nothing else. DVD image is good for a modestly budgeted little work, with only some minor flashing within clothing patterns. Sound is acceptable. —*MM*
Movie: 🎬🎬 ½ *DVD:* 🎬🎬 ½
Vanguard Intl. Cinema (cat #VF0180, UPC 658769018035). Widescreen letterboxed. $29.95. Keepcase. *LANG:* English. *FEATURES:* Trailer ▪ Director intro ▪ Music track ▪ 12 chapters.
2000 (R) 112m/C CA Brendan Fletcher, Chris Mulkey, Robert Gossett, Adrienne Frantz, James Russo, Kim (Kimberly Dawn) Dawson; *D:* Robert McGinley; *W:* Robert McGinley; *C:* Christopher Tufty; *M:* Geoff Levin.

Jo Jo Dancer, Your Life Is Calling

Pryor's directorial debut is a pseudonymous autobiographical portrait of his rise to stardom, descent into drugs, and well-publicized self immolation. Despite the personal and revealing nature of the material, the film just glosses the surface. The haphazard, episodic construction is unfocused and plodding at times and never adequately explains Pryor's relationships, the root causes of his addictions, or his self-destructive personality. A better script and less-involved director might have pulled some real gold from the material, but the final result here is cold and unsatisfying. Shot in Super35, each framing has its benefits. The full-frame rendition has more foot room and (despite some cropping at the edges) seems stronger compositionally. The picture is clean and free of noise, but the photography is generally grainy and bland. Sound is fine. —*DG*
Movie: 🎬🎬 *DVD:* 🎬🎬🎬
Columbia Tristar (cat #06673, UPC 04339-6066731). Widescreen (2.35:1) anamorphic; full frame. Mono. $19.95. Keepcase. *LANG:* English. *SUB:* English; French. *CAP:* English. *FEATURES:* 28 chapters.
1986 (R) 97m/C Richard Pryor, Debbie Allen, Art Evans, Fay Hauser, Barbara Williams, Paula Kelly, Wings Hauser, Carmen McRae, Diahnne Abbott, Scoey Mitchell, Billy Eckstine, Virginia Capers, Dennis Farina; *D:* Richard Pryor; *W:* Richard Pryor, Rocco Urbisci; *C:* John A. Alonzo; *M:* Herbie Hancock.

Joe

An odd friendship grows between a businessman and a blue-collar worker as they search together for the executive's runaway daughter. Thrust into the midst of the counter-culture, they react with an orgy of violence. Rich, vibrant colors are showcased by a video transfer that also admirably defines blacks. It should be noted, however, that while most scenes retain clarity, some darker-lit ones do seem a bit diffused. In short, the film looks like an early '70s movie. The soundtrack provides decent dialogue reproduction, though it does sound tinny in some spots. But it is clear and understandable throughout. The musical score is also nicely represented. —*MJT*
Movie: 🎬🎬 ½ *DVD:* 🎬🎬 ½
MGM Home Ent. (cat #1003336, UPC 027616874856). Widescreen (1.85:1) letterboxed; full frame. Dolby Digital Mono. $19.98. Keepcase. *LANG:* English. *SUB:* English; French; Spanish. *FEATURES:* 16 chapters ▪ Theatrical trailer.
1970 (R) 107m/C Peter Boyle, Susan Sarandon, Dennis Patrick; *D:* John G. Avildsen; *W:* Norman Wexler; *C:* John G. Avildsen, Henri Decae; *M:* Bobby Scott. *AWARDS:* *NOM:* Oscars '70: Story & Screenplay.

Joe Dirt

Joe Dirt (Spade) is the janitor at a radio station when the DJ (Miller) wants to use him as the butt of his show. But soon it becomes evident that the joke is really on him and that the seemingly dim-witted geek has a story to tell that amazes the DJ as well as audiences around the country. DVD creates a sparkling image that is absolutely clean and stable. No grain is visible in the film and it's mostly free of edge-enhancement and its accompanying ringing artifacts; the transfer looks phenomenal. Colors are very rich and vibrant without being oversaturated, and flesh-tones are naturally rendered at all times. Definition is very high, bringing out even the most subtle information in the film print while the solid black levels render deep blacks and well delineated shadows. The compression is also very good without notable compression artifacts. The 5.1 mix is very active throughout, creating a lively sound field that makes good use of the Surround channels and has a wide spatial integration in the front field. —GH

Movie: 🎞🎞🎞 **DVD:** 🎞🎞🎞 ½
Columbia Tristar (cat #06161, UPC 0433-96061613). Widescreen (1.85:1) anamorphic; full frame. Dolby Digital 5.1 Surround Stereo; Dolby Digital Surround Stereo. $24.98. Keepcase. *LANG:* English; French. *SUB:* English; French. *FEATURES:* Commentary: director Dennie Gordon • Commentary: David Spade • Deleted scenes and outtakes • Trailers.
2001 (PG-13) 91m/C David Spade, Dennis Miller, Adam Beach, Christopher Walken, Jaime Pressly, Caroline Aaron, Fred Ward, Bob Zany, Liz Torres, Joe Don Baker, Blake Clark, Tyler Mane, Steve Schirripa, Bob (Kid Rock) Ritchie, Erik Per Sullivan, Megan Taylor Harvey, Fred Wolf; *D:* Dennie Gordon; *W:* David Spade, Fred Wolf; *C:* John R. Leonetti; *M:* Waddy Wachtel.

Joe versus the Volcano

Here's a wonderful comedy that needs to be re-evaluated by as many people as can muster the imagination to give it another try. Joe Banks (Hanks) works in a demoralizing drudge job for a medical-supply firm, under the petty tyranny of boss Frank Waturi (Hedaya). After losing his nerve on his previous job as a fireman, he's become a chronically congested and miserable hypochondriac. A visit to mysterious Dr. Ellison (Stack) confirms Joe's worst nightmares—he's dying from a terminal disease. Awareness of his imminent death brings Joe back to life, so to speak, and he quits his job and goes out on a date with DeDe (Ryan), a fear-constipated co-worker. In the morning, Samuel Harvey Graynamore (Bridges), an eccentric millionaire industrialist, shows up at Joe's door with a wild offer: he needs an essential resource, from the Waponis, a weird tribe on an island in the South Pacific. They won't cooperate unless Graynamore provides them with a sacrifice to appease their Volcano God. That's where Joe comes in—he's given a sheaf of credit cards and told to go on a spree on his way to certain doom...he's going to die anyway, so why not a short, lavish, glorious life instead of a slow painful demise? From its cheapo font main titles, the film is visually deceiv-

ing. Director Shanley sets up brilliantly composed scene shots that express just the right mood, and moves on. The details are great, too. There's a wonderful on-the-town sequence in New York that ranks among the best. There's sharply observed criticism in all of this, softened by the fairy-tale approach. People remark that the volcano action at the end is silly and unrealistic, when the picture never tried to be realistic for a moment...some fantasies you reject and some you embrace. DVD has been a long time a' coming, down its own crooked road. The reputation of this film being what it is, I'm grateful to see it come out at all. The colors are much sharper on the DVD, with the sickly greens of the fluorescents that "suck out your soul" at American Panascope, pulsing like electricity. The restaurant's scarlet hues are stable, and the amusing illustration-like views of the volcano at the end are a lot sharper, because of DVD's ability to handle reds better. This movie cries for extras, or anything to help place it in context. A chance to learn more about John Patrick Shanley would be welcome, but the "cast and crew" production notes link only to more info on Hanks and Ryan. The "behind-the-scenes documentary" turns out to be a woebegone featurette from 1990, where the actors pay lip service to the "existential" nature of the film, and then basically give up. Shanley smiles and answers the final question, "Who Wins, Joe or the Volcano?," with a meaningless laugh that indicates total editorial desperation. A music video for the Eric Burdon version of "16 Tons," which opens the film, is fairly unimpressive, and the big-faces cover art stinks. —GE

Movie: 🎞🎞🎞 ½ **DVD:** 🎞🎞🎞 ½
Warner Home Video (UPC 85391606024). Widescreen (2.35:1) anamorphic. Dolby Digital 5.1 Surround; Dolby Surround. $19.98. Snapper. *LANG:* English; French; Japanese. *SUB:* English; French; Japanese; Spanish; Portuguese. *CAP:* English. *FEATURES:* Featurette • Music video.
1990 (PG) 106m/C Tom Hanks, Meg Ryan, Lloyd Bridges, Robert Stack, Amanda Plummer, Abe Vigoda, Dan Hedaya, Barry McGovern, Ossie Davis; *D:* John Patrick Shanley; *W:* John Patrick Shanley; *C:* Stephen Goldblatt; *M:* Georges Delerue.

John Carpenter's Ghosts of Mars

Despite the fact that he is now well into his 50s, horror veteran Carpenter sets out to prove that he can still rock 'n' roll with this sci-fi shockfest. The story is set in the future, where Mars has been colonized, and in an interesting twist is ruled by women. Police officer Melanie (Natasha Henstridge) is found alone and unconscious on a ghost-train. She then recounts her tale of the tragedy which befell the mining town of Shining Canyon. She had been dispatched there with her squad (which includes Pam Grier) to retrieve "Desolation" Williams (Ice Cube), a wanted murderer. What they find is a ghost-town overrun

by zombie-like savages, bent on killing every human in sight. A stand-off ensues as the few survivors hole-up in the town's police station. Playing as a greatest hits package, *Ghosts of Mars* is reminiscent of Carpenter's earlier films, *The Thing, Assault on Precinct 13,* and *Escape from New York.* The film is very well-paced and Carpenter keeps the action coming from all sides. However, don't dwell too much on the plot or continuity, for this will sour a potentially fun experience. The image offered on this DVD is stunning, as it shows a flawless image, which shows no grain, distortion, or artifacting. The colors (dominated by Martian red) are good. The Dolby Digital 5.1 audio track rocks, as it offers sweeping Surround sound effects and great bass. The handful of featurettes on the disc are shockingly useless, but the commentary with Carpenter and Henstridge is a lot of fun. —ML *AKA:* Ghosts of Mars.

Movie: 🎞🎞🎞 **DVD:** 🎞🎞🎞 ½
Columbia Tristar (cat #06250, UPC 0433-96062504). Widescreen (2.40:1) anamorphic; full frame. Dolby Digital 5.1. $27.96. Keepcase. *LANG:* English. *SUB:* English; French. *CAP:* English. *FEATURES:* Commentary • Actor video diary • Special effects featurette • Score featurette • Cast & crew filmographies • 28 chapters.
2001 (R) 98m/C Natasha Henstridge, Ice Cube, Clea DuVall, Pam Grier, Jason Statham, Joanna Cassidy, Wanda De Jesus, Liam Waite; *D:* John Carpenter; *W:* John Carpenter, Larry Sulkis; *C:* Gary B. Kibbe; *M:* John Carpenter.

John Wayne: Western Classics (1932–35)

Duke fans delight, because here he is in six early roles. The worst, *Two Fisted Law,* is a Columbia matinee. The others are five of sixteen "Lone Star Westerns," five-reel pictures produced by Monogram from 1933–35. They are extremely cheap and the acting is bad but, with a stock company that includes Wayne, Hayes, and Canutt, there is definite interest for fans of vintage westerns. The images for all six films are above average, but the five "Lone Stars" have the same score (badly synthesized western music) and the sixth has none. Contents: *Desert Trail* (1935), *Paradise Canyon* (1935), *The Trail Beyond* (1934), *Two-Fisted Law* (1932), *Riders of Destiny* (1933), and *West of the Divide* (1933). —DRL

Movie: 🎞 ½ **DVD:** 🎞🎞
Columbia Tristar (cat #5823, UPC 043396-058231). Full frame. Mono. $26.95. Keepcase (2-case box). *LANG:* English. *SUB:* English; French; Spanish. *CAP:* English. *FEATURES:* 48 chapters.
2001 318m/B

Johnny Firecloud / Bummer

The real treat on this disc is the commentary track by Dave Friedman, Frank Henenlotter, and Mike Vraney, that accompanies *Johnny Firecloud.* They discuss the film about half the time; the rest is cheerful nostalgia that's much more interesting than the events on-screen. The story is a *Billy Jack* retread about a Native American Vietnam vet (Mohica, who's Puerto Rican, according to the producer) who exacts violent revenge on the rednecks (led by Meeker) who lynch his grandpa. Sacheen Littlefeather, whose claim to fame is her *Godfather* Oscar acceptance speech for Marlon Brando, appears briefly as a rape victim. The second half of the double feature, *Bummer* is a low-budget tale of a second-rate rock band who abuse groupies. Where *Firecloud* is bright and sharp, *Bummer* is very dark and poorly lit. It's difficult to make out any of the action in many scenes. Both appear to have been made from virtually pristine original elements. —*MM*

Movie: 🎵🎵 ½ **DVD:** 🎵🎵🎵
Image Ent. (cat #ID0804SWDVD, UPC 014-381080421). Widescreen (2.35:1) letterboxed. Dolby Digital Mono. $24.99. Keepcase. *LANG:* English. *FEATURES:* 16 chapters each • Commentary • 6 trailers • Gallery of exploitation art • 2 short subjects.
1975 94m/C Victor Mohica, Ralph Meeker, Frank De Kova, Sacheen Little Feather, David Canary, Christina Hart; *D:* William Allen Castleman; *W:* Wilton Denmark; *M:* William Loose.

Johnny Mnemonic [2 SB]

With his storage capacity greatly exceeded, wet-wired mnemonic courier, Johnny (Reeves), has uploaded information into his brain that could change the world. The only problem is that he only has so much time before the overloaded data within his mind begins to kill him. With the help of a cyber-enhanced body guard (Meyer) and one-third of the needed download code, Johnny races against the clock, and the corporation that is seeking the same information, to extract the data from his mind. This version of *Johnny Mnemonic* (the first is reviewed in *Book 1*) is coded with the "Superbit" technology, which greatly enhances the sound and picture quality. The difference is absolutely astounding. The sound effects on the 5.1 track are loud, engrossing, and make over-the-top use of all six speakers throughout the film. The picture is equally impressive, with rich, dynamic color and extra crisp, clean images. There is no noticeable haloing or strange fast panning issues, which makes for clean, smooth action sequences. Even though this release lacks any special features, the dynamic sound and ultra-impressive picture quality makes this DVD worth the purchase price alone. —*EL*

Movie: 🎵🎵 ½ **DVD:** 🎵🎵🎵🎵
Columbia Tristar (cat #07573, UPC 0433-96075733). Widescreen (.85:1) anamorphic. DTS; Dolby Digital 5.1 Surround. $27.96. Boxed keepcase. *LANG:* English.

SUB: English; Spanish; Chinese; Korean; Thai. *CAP:* English. *FEATURES:* 28 chapters.
1995 (R) 98m/C Keanu Reeves, Dina Meyer, Ice-T, Takeshi "Beat" Kitano, Dolph Lundgren, Henry Rollins, Udo Kier, Barbara Sukowa, Denis Akiyama; *D:* Robert Longo; *W:* William Gibson; *C:* François Protat; *M:* Brad Fiedel.

Joseph Campbell Mythos

This three-disc set is a direct, quality recording of a series of Joseph Campbell lectures from 1986 and '87. We should consider ourselves lucky that someone had the presence of mind to undertake them while he was still in a state of good health. Using simple slides projected on a blackboard, Campbell takes us methodically through his concept of the human experience as "one great story." Instead of being prompted by an interviewer, the content is presented as if we were his undergraduates. Susan Sarandon's introductions and "bumpers" interpolated between major lecture topics are mainly a commercial marketing hook, that don't quite mesh. They're rather dry, and you get the idea that the packagers are trying to make the show sexy. The video recording of the late '80s still holds up. Whoever organized the shooting of the lectures did a nice job of catching Campbell's rhythm on the fly, with few technical problems. It's much closer to studio stage-lighting than the ragged quality we're used to seeing on universities' own AV tapes of lectures...not polished, but never distracting from the content. (The programs are also available on individual discs.) —*GE*

Movie: 🎵🎵🎵 ½ **DVD:** 🎵🎵🎵
Winstar Home Ent. (UPC 790658999008). Full frame. $99.98. 3-disc keepcase. *LANG:* English. *FEATURES:* Bibliography • Bio.
1997 600m/C Joseph Campbell, Susan Sarandon.

Joseph Campbell: The Power of Myth

Bill Moyers's contribution to Public Television has been nothing short of remarkable. A son of Texas ministers whose compassionate, humanistic point of view is politically unclassifiable, he's the perfect conduit to the wisdom of Joseph Campbell. The shows are models of organization and presentation, each a direct interview where Moyers brings out Joseph's ideas, richly illustrated with museum-quality images of ancient cosmologies and art. Very good college lecturers give us the illusion that they're pulling back the curtains of our dulled minds to expose real Truths—and Campbell does that every few minutes. Part of Campbell's credibility is that he's not selling anything—he's not a crackpot, and he hasn't any belief system or ideology he wants to inculcate. Contents: 1. *The Hero's Adventure*—links the mythical heroic figure to our own life adventures. 2. *The Message of the Myth*—Creation myths that served in ancient

times are no longer providing what modern man needs. 3. *The First Storytellers*—The place of ritual and the tribal Shaman is discussed in terms of sacrifice, rites of passage, and accepting Death as rebirth. 4. *Sacrifice and Bliss*—Finding our place in our personal world requires creating a new concept of the mythic role of sacrifice. 5. *Love and the Goddess*—The idea of romance is a fairly new one, but not the various erotic objectifications of women. 6. *Masks of Eternity*—Campbell tackles the big issues—God, eternity, religion, as addressed by several religions. (The six programs are also available as individual discs.) DVD image quality is excellent; sound is good. Both are less important than content. A final extra is an interview with George Lucas, who holds the status of Campbell's "most famous acolyte," because of his acknowledgment of the master's first book, *The Hero with a Thousand Faces*, as a core influence on the *Star Wars* cultural empire. This is perhaps the best side effect of *Star Wars*, and it in no way interferes with the messages, but the added interview is mildly irritating just the same. Lucas credits his pastiche of themes as being inspired by the mythical teachings of the master. As popular as *Star Wars* is, the idea that it is a new "classic" myth should be resisted in any form. Yes, its outline conforms to some of Campbell's concepts, but the very idea that this basically shallow screenplay is a new myth that's re-invigorating our species is a good example of the debasing power of commercialism. —*GE*

Movie: 🎵🎵🎵🎵 **DVD:** 🎵🎵🎵 ½
Winstar Home Ent. (UPC 715098764627). Full frame. $59.98. 2-disc keepcase. *LANG:* English. *FEATURES:* George Lucas interview • Text bios and bibliographies • Art gallery • Trailer.
1988 360m/C Joseph Campbell, Bill Moyers.

Josie and the Pussycats

Think *Spice World,* not *Wayne's World,* and you're in the right pew for this dumber-than-dumb comedy about a rock band's rocky road to fame. Rachael Leigh Cook (*AntiTrust, Texas Rangers*), Tara Reid (*American Pie*), and Rosario Dawson (*He Got Game*) are recruited by evil rock promoter Wyatt Frame (played by Alan Cumming, *Circle of Friends*) to deliver an encoded message on their hit CD. Will they turn their fans into mindless zombies, or will anyone notice, or care? Slick, but pointless girl-band comedy fails to be either a digging satire or an all-that-funny comedy. DVD presentation far exceeds the content of the film itself. Director commentary, deleted scenes, music videos, and more back this less-than-worthy effort. —*RT*

Movie: 🎵🎵 **DVD:** 🎵🎵🎵
Universal Studios (cat #21377, UPC 0251-92137723). Widescreen (1.85:1). AC3 - 5.1 Dolby Digital. $26.98. Keepcase. *LANG:* English; French. *SUB:* English. *CAP:* English. *FEATURES:* 18 chapters • Theatri-

cal trailer ▪ Backstage Pass featurette (24 min.) ▪ 3 deleted scenes ▪ Music video—"Three Small Words" by Josie and the Pussycats ▪ Music video—"Backdoor Lover" by DuJour.
2001 (PG-13) 99m/C Rachael Leigh Cook, Tara Reid, Rosario Dawson, Parker Posey, Alan Cumming, Gabriel Mann, Paulo Costanzo, Tom Butler, Missi Pyle, Carson Daly, Seth Green, Breckin Meyer, Donald Adeosun Faison; *D:* Deborah Kaplan, Harry Elfont; *W:* Deborah Kaplan, Harry Elfont; *C:* Matthew Libatique; *M:* John (Gianni) Frizzell.

The Journey of Natty Gann

Meredith Salenger is Natty Gann, a young woman living in Depression-era Chicago. When times get tough and her father (Wise) must move out West to work, Natty is left behind in the care of a woman who runs the apartments where she lives. Saddened after being left on her own, Natty hops onto a train to look for her father, eventually befriending a wolf and a drifter (Cusack). Meanwhile, her father has found out about Natty's disappearance and, seriously worried, sets out to look for her. A film that was originally presented in 2.35:1 widescreen is presented only in a severely cropped pan and scan with a terrible transfer. Aside from some brighter outdoor sequences, the picture either looks soft or excessively soft, lacking in detail. The darkest scenes especially suffer, appearing murky and undefined. Grain ranges from mild to heavy, while there are a fair amount of marks and specks on the print. Registration problems are evident in the opening credits. Sound is actually quite good for an older release. Some sound effects, such as the powerful engine of the train that Natty sneaks away in, have respectable power and clarity. Dialogue remains clear, as does James Horner's enjoyable score. —*AB*
Movie: ♪♪♪ ½ **DVD:** ♪
Buena Vista Home Ent. (UPC 786936178-159). Full frame. Dolby Surround. $14.98. Keepcase. *LANG:* English. *CAP:* English.
1985 (PG) 101m/C Meredith Salenger, John Cusack, Ray Wise, Scatman Crothers, Lainie Kazan, Verna Bloom; *D:* Jeremy Paul Kagan; *W:* Jeanne Rosenberg; *C:* Dick Bush; *M:* James Horner. *AWARDS: NOM:* Oscars '85: Costume Des.

Joy Ride

Road/suspense/horror thriller does just about everything right. College student Lewis (Walker) is driving home for break. He's going to pick up his pal Venna (Sobieski), with whom he'd like to be more involved, but first he's got to bail out his ne'er-do-well brother Fuller (Zahn). Fuller talks him into playing a teasing game with a trucker named Rusty Nail (voice of Levine) on the CB radio. That leads to an increasingly violent cross-country game of cat-and-mouse that's filled with intriguing complications. On his commentary track,

writer/director Dahl admits that some of those got a bit difficult to handle. That's why the disc includes three extra endings. (The one the producers finally decided to use was filmed nine months after photography had finished.) DVD image is as sharp as you'd expect from a contemporary release. The extra footage, which can be incorporated into the body of the film or viewed separately, has not been polished and is barely watchable. Those who have not seen the film should watch it straight through without any of the various commentary tracks or the scene-switching option. (An option allows you to toggle a mudflap logo. When it appears, you can switch to an alternative version of the scene. I could not access Dahl's commentary on one of them.) 5.1 Surround is much more impressive than the theatrical release. —*MM*
Movie: ♪♪♪ **DVD:** ♪♪♪
20th Century Fox (cat #2003625, UPC 024543036258). Widescreen (2.35:1) anamorphic. Dolby Digital 5.1 Surround; Dolby Surround. $24.98. Keepcase. *LANG:* English; French. *SUB:* English; Spanish. *CAP:* English. *FEATURES:* Alternate endings ▪ Commentary: John Dahl ▪ Commentary: Steve Zahn, Leelee Sobieski ▪ Commentary: writers Clay Tarver, J.J. Abrams ▪ Voice auditions for Rusty Nail ▪ "Making of" featurette.
2001 (R) 96m/C Paul Walker, Steve Zahn, Leelee Sobieski, Jessica Bowman, Stuart Stone, Basil Wallace, Brian Leckner; *D:* John Dahl; *W:* J.J. Abrams, Clay Tarver; *C:* Jeffrey Jur; *M:* Marco Beltrami; *V:* Ted Levine.

Judgment

This film is part of the "Left Behind" series of biblical thrillers. Roma Downey (AKA Leigh Lewis) returns as Helen Hannah. It seems the Anti-Christ, ahem, Franco Macalousso (Nick Mancuso) wants to put the poor girl on trial for her crimes against humanity. Namely by refusing to take "the mark" and join the rest of One Nation Earth in world bliss—eternal damnation be, well, damned. Thus, a courtroom drama is born. Because it's really hard to work explosions into the courtroom, the director tacked on a subplot about Helen's hand-wringing comrades watching the trial on the tube, while Mr. T threatens to go down to the courthouse and lay down a righteous hiney whuppin—*A-Team* style. While few actors command the screen like the incomparable Mr. T, Bernsen comes very close with a truly inspired and moving performance that elevates the entire movie. There's an honesty that comes through, as though he's wrestling with the same root questions his character must face. Somewhere amid the Revelation lore are intriguing, even thought-provoking, moments of honest debate about the whys of religious faith. The disc features a full-frame transfer with nary a blemish. The 5.1 track is the wind beneath Gary Koftinoff's soaring score. The music is such a strong pres-

ence that it becomes almost another character—one that demands to be noticed; it's crucial to the film's impact. Also included is an overzealous behind-the-scenes featurette that explores new heights in horn-tooting. The half-hour pep rally touts Cloud Ten Pictures' latest via cast interviews and more. —*GNG/DG* **AKA:** Apocalypse 4: Judgment.
Movie: ♪♪ **DVD:** ♪♪
Cloud Ten Pictures (UPC 745638003633). Full frame. Dolby Digital 5.1 Surround. $29.95. Keepcase. *LANG:* English; Spanish. *FEATURES:* Behind-the-scenes footage ▪ Interviews ▪ Deleted scenes ▪ The making of *Judgment* ▪ Creating the film score ▪ Trailers.
2001 105m/C Jessica Steen, Corbin Bernsen, Mr. T, Leigh Lewis, Nick Mancuso; *D:* Andre Van Heerden; *M:* Gary Koftinoff.

Juliet of the Spirits [Criterion]

Like all Criterion discs, this one looks just fine. Image and sound are everything that anyone could ask of a 1965 release, and the short television interview is delightful. That said, there's not much difference between this disc and the Image edition, reviewed in *Book 1*. Both are excellent. —*MM* **AKA:** Giulietta Degli Spiriti.
Movie: ♪♪♪♪ **DVD:** ♪♪♪ ½
Criterion (cat #149, UPC 037429165829). Widescreen (1.85:1) anamorphic. Dolby Digital Mono. $29.98. Keepcase. *LANG:* Italian. *SUB:* English. *FEATURES:* 26 chapters ▪ 1966 interview with Ian Daniels ▪ Liner notes by John Baxter.
1965 142m/C *IT* Giulietta Masina, Valentina Cortese, Sylva Koscina, Mario Pisu, Sandra Milo, Caterina Boratto, Valeska Gert; *D:* Federico Fellini; *W:* Federico Fellini, Tullio Pinelli, Ennio Flaiano, Brunello Rondi; *C:* Gianni Di Venanzo; *M:* Nino Rota. *AWARDS:* N.Y. Film Critics '65: Foreign Film; *NOM:* Oscars '66: Art Dir./Set Dec., Color, Costume Des. (C).

The Jungle Book

An Indian storyteller relates the tale of a young boy who is raised by wolves after his father is attacked by a tiger. Twelve years later the boy stumbles across a human city where his mother lives and complications ensue. Charming British production in the style of the same team's *The Thief of Baghdad* features colorful, glistening photography and ambitious special effects. An entertaining adventure that still holds up. Kipling's tale was also adapted (with liberal changes) into the later Disney feature. Both are worth seeing. This budget disc is presented in a very clean print with a muted but acceptable representation of the Technicolor original. The mono sound is fine. Virtually free of digital noise, this is more than acceptable for the price. —*DG* **AKA:** Rudyard Kipling's Jungle Book.
Movie: ♪♪♪ **DVD:** ♪♪ ½
Goodtimes Ent. (cat #05-81213, UPC 018-713812131). Full frame. Mono. $7.49.

Keepcase. *LANG:* English. *FEATURES:* 12 chapters.
1942 109m/C Sabu, Joseph Calleia, Rosemary DeCamp, Ralph Byrd, John Qualen; *D:* Zoltan Korda; *W:* Laurence Stallings; *C:* Lee Garmes; *M:* Miklos Rozsa. *AWARDS: NOM:* Oscars '42: Color Cinematog., Orig. Dramatic Score.

Jungle Girl
This Republic adventure serial is wonderfully dated. Don't miss the scene where our hero (Neal) sneaks up on a village while hiding behind a handful of branches. Apparently, he is attempting to disguise himself as a moving bush, but the moment is worthy of Monty Python. He and our heroine (Gifford) valiantly dash from crisis to crisis for more than four hours. Beyond a bit of static on the soundtrack, the DVD presents a very nice black-and-white image. For fans of the era. —*MM*
Movie: 🎵🎵 *DVD:* 🎵🎵 ½
VCI (cat #8265, UPC 089859826528). Full frame. Dolby Digital Mono. $24.99. Keepcase. *LANG:* English. *FEATURES:* 15 chapters ▪ Photo gallery ▪ Talent files.
1941 267m/B Frances Gifford, Tom Neal, Trevor Bardette, Gerald Mohr, Eddie Acuff, Frank Lackteen; *D:* John English; *W:* William Witney.

Jurassic Park 3 [CE]
Remarkable and economical sequel delivers all the cool dinosaur effects that fans expect. Dr. Alan Grant (Neill), who evaded the lame *JP2* is inveigled into a return trip to the island by a millionaire (Macy) and his wife (Leoni) to hunt for their adolescent son. The film works because it moves so swiftly and sticks to the point: dinosaurs. Hungry dinosaurs, flying dinosaurs, hatching dinosaurs, cooperative dinosaurs you get the idea. And it clocks in at a sleek 93 minutes. It could go without saying that the DVD image is flawless. DTS and 5.1 Surround are far superior to that offered in many neighborhood multiplexes. The film is also available in a full-frame version (UPC 025192-146923). —*MM*
Movie: 🎵🎵🎵 *DVD:* 🎵🎵🎵 ½
Universal Studios (cat #21101, UPC 025-192110122). Widescreen (1.85:1) anamorphic. Dolby Digital 5.1 Surround; DTS. $26.98. Keepcase. *LANG:* English; French. *SUB:* Spanish. *CAP:* English. *FEATURES:* "Making of" featurette ▪ Commentary: special effects team ▪ Tour of Stan Winston studio ▪ 20 chapters ▪ Visit ILM ▪ Dinosaur turntables computer effects demonstration ▪ Storyboard-to-film comparison ▪ Trailers ▪ DVD-ROM features ▪ New dinosaurs featurette.
2001 (PG-13) 90m/C Sam Neill, William H. Macy, Tea Leoni, Alessandro Nivola, Michael Jeter, Trevor Morgan, John Diehl, Bruce A. Young, Taylor Nichols, Mark Harelik, Julio Mechoso, Laura Dern; *D:* Joe Johnston; *W:* Peter Buchman, Alexander Payne, Jim Taylor; *C:* Shelly Johnson; *M:* Don Davis.

Just for the Hell of It
Please see review for *Blast-Off Girls / Just for the Hell of It. AKA:* Destruction, Inc.
Movie: woof
1968 85m/C Rodney Bedell, Ray Sager, Nancy Lee Noble, Agi Gyenes, Steve White; *D:* Herschell Gordon Lewis; *W:* Allison Louise Downe; *C:* Roy Collodi; *M:* Larry Wellington.

Just One Night
Standard night-in-the-life film follows a man (Hutton) on a layover (pun intended) in San Francisco the night before his wedding. A hooker accidentally comes to his door; he loses a shoe; he meets an unhappy bombshell of a married woman on his hunt for a new shoe and the expected occurs. There are some nice moments and Seymour Cassel is great, but ultimately wasted, as the trash bin tycoon who the hooker ultimately services. This is a nice time passer if you haven't got anything else to do and it's on cable. A good-looking disc with above average picture and sound. —*CA*
Movie: 🎵 ½ *DVD:* 🎵🎵🎵
Image Ent. (cat #OVED0302DV2, UPC 014-381030228). Full frame. Dolby Digital 5.1 Surround; Surround Stereo. $19.99. Keepcase. *LANG:* English. *FEATURES:* 12 chapters.
2000 (PG-13) 90m/C Timothy Hutton, Maria Grazia Cucinotta, Udo Kier, Michael O'Keefe, Robert Easton, Don Novello, Seymour Cassel, Natalie Shaw; *D:* Alan Jacobs; *W:* Alan Jacobs; *C:* John Campbell; *M:* Anthony Marinelli.

Just Visiting
This is an American remake of the French film *Les Visiteurs,* directed and written by the same director and writer. Usually American remakes of European films are either tedious or embarrassing for all concerned. In this case, the French version had just as much bawdy toilet and slapstick humor as any American film, so it translates nicely. Not that this is a bad thing, as all the actors have great comedic timing and delivery with both the verbal and physical antics. Reno plays a 12th-century knight, Count Thibault, who, on the day of his wedding, is bewitched into killing his bride. As he waits to be put to death, his trusty but dense companion André (Clavier, the co-writer) brings a wizard who will send Thibault and André back in time to stop the evil deed. But the wizard is English, a running joke for the French it seems, and the predictable occurs when Thibault and André end up in current day New York in a museum where Thibault's descendent (Applegate) works. Food is flung, baths are taken poorly, and cars are battled with swords, but eventually all's well that ends well. This is a fun film if you're looking to avoid any deep thought beyond wondering what a knight wears under his armor. Reno, Clavier, and Applegate are all onboard with the material and their acting abilities no doubt con-

tribute to this film being a rental suggestion rather than a woof. The extra featurette on the excellent special effects is rather lacking in depth but still worth a look. The disc looks great with bright full-bodied colors and great sound. —*CA*
Movie: 🎵🎵 ½ *DVD:* 🎵🎵🎵 ½
Hollywood Pictures (cat #23620, UPC 786936162141). Widescreen (2.35:1) anamorphic. Dolby Digital 5.1 Surround. $32.99. Keepcase. *LANG:* English. *CAP:* English. *FEATURES:* Theatrical trailer ▪ "The Magic behind the Magic" featurettes.
2001 (PG-13) 88m/C Jean Reno, Christian Clavier, Christina Applegate, Tara Reid, Matt Ross, Bridgette Wilson, John Aylward, George Plimpton, Malcolm McDowell, Sarah Badel, Bill Bailey, Kendra Torgan, Richard Bremner, Robert Glenister; *D:* Jean-Marie Poire; *W:* Christian Clavier, Jean-Marie Poire, John Hughes; *C:* Ueli Steiger; *M:* John Powell.

Justice League
Following the success and critical praise for *Batman: The Animated Series* and *Batman Beyond,* Warner Bros. brings us yet another great animated show with a strong comic book pedigree. This DVD contains the first three episodes of *Justice League,* which—for all intents and purposes—constitutes a pilot film. As part of a political endeavor, Superman is enlisted to help the world dispose of its nuclear stockpiles. Meanwhile, Batman is investigating strange happenings at a deep-space communications lab. These two story lines converge when a huge meteor crashes in Metropolis, releasing a horde of giant alien invaders. Superman and Batman attempt to battle these extraterrestrial foes, but to no avail. But they are soon joined in their fight by Green Lantern, Hawkgirl, The Flash, Wonder Woman, and a newcomer to Earth, Martian Manhunter. Together, these seven super-heroes combine their might to thwart this overwhelming foe. *Justice League* represents another high watermark in animation for Warner and their compatriots at Cartoon Network. The show is fast-paced, exciting, dramatic, and more involving than most live-action shows. While the story line presented here suffers from a severe lack of originality (it's basically a re-hashing of *Independence Day* and *The War of the Worlds*), it gives the audience a chance to focus on the characters and their dynamics, which is basically the purpose of these episodes. We get to see how the Justice League was formed and learn each character's unique traits. Granted, some liberties are taken in relation to the comic books (Wonder Woman can fly? And the usually invulnerable Superman is constantly wounded here?!?), but long-time fans should love the look and feel of this show. A word of caution for parents—the action gets pretty violent at times here, and the alien invaders are goopy. This DVD brings the viewer a pristine presentation of the show, which rivals (at times beats) digital broadcast resolution. The

image is incredibly sharp and clear, showing no distortion or defects from the source material. Also, the colors are very rich and brilliant. The only flaw is that during some sweeping shots, there is some artifacting. The audio track provides clear dialogue with no interference and a nice amount of Surround effects, making the on-screen battles really come to life. —ML
Movie: 🎵🎵🎵 **DVD:** 🎵🎵🎵
Warner (cat #22236, UPC 0853922236-26). Full frame. Dolby Surround Stereo. $19.98. Snapper. *LANG:* English. *CAP:* English. *FEATURES:* Character bios • Cast & crew list • Bonus trailers • 12 chapters. **2002 60m/C**

K-PAX

When a strange man (Spacey) appears in Grand Central Station, he is taken to the city's mental hospital. He insists that his name is Prot and that he comes from the planet K-PAX. His doctor (Bridges) finds information that corroborates Prot's story and tries to piece together his origins. A frustrating and mostly successful drama with terrific performances and an interesting (though familiar) premise. Unfortunately the ending of the film is badly bungled; this kind of story needs a strong, definitive conclusion. Instead the filmmakers try to have their cake and eat it too with a cryptic, possibly uplifting, possibly depressing ending that's completely unsatisfying. The weak ending only helps magnify some creaky aspects of the script (such as modern mental hospital procedure) and awakens familiarity of the film's revelations with previous Jeff Bridges films. A true shame, as it could have been something wonderful. Fault cannot be found with the disc, however, which features a stunning, perfect image that's both sharp and noise-free. Colors are fairly muted which is by design. The Surround track is also magnificent and enveloping. The "alternate" ending isn't much different and the deleted scenes don't contribute much. The photo gallery is brief but the images are rich and evocative. The commentary is informative, but the movie soundtrack intrudes constantly and it's pretty dull. —DG
Movie: 🎵🎵½ **DVD:** 🎵🎵🎵🎵
Universal Studios (cat #21553, UPC 0251-92155321). Widescreen (2.35:1) anamorphic. DTS; Dolby Digital 5.1 Surround. $26.98. Keepcase. *LANG:* English; French. *SUB:* Spanish. *CAP:* English. *FEATURES:* Booklet with notes • 18 chapters • Alternate ending • "Making of" featurette • Commentary: director Iain Softley • Deleted scenes • Storyboard comparison • Jeff Bridges's photo gallery • Trailer • DVD-ROM website link and other features.
2001 (PG-13) 120m/C Kevin Spacey, Jeff Bridges, Mary McCormack, Alfre Woodard, David Patrick Kelly, Saul Williams, Peter Gerety, Celia Weston, Ajay Naidu, John Toles-Bey, Kimberly Scott, Mary Mara, Aaron Paul, William Lucking; **D:** Iain Softley; **W:** Charles Leavitt; **C:** John Mathieson; **M:** Ed Shearmur.

Kadosh

Meir (Hattab) and his wife Rivka (Abecassis) are ultra-Orthodox Jews living in the Mea Shearim quarter of Jerusalem. They have been married for 10 years and are still childless, so Meir is pressed by his rabbi father to divorce his wife (though they love each other) and remarry. Rivka learns the fertility problem is with her husband but can do nothing because of religious tenets, so she leaves her home. Meanwhile, Rivka's younger sister, Malka (Barda) contemplates abandoning her unhappy arranged marriage to be with the man she loves. With this DVD, we get a letterboxed transfer that is slightly dark and shows some minor grain. Otherwise, the image is clear and the colors are natural. However, the white subtitles are nearly impossible to read at times. The audio is average, rendering the dialogue clear and audible. The disc includes a 24-minute behind-the-scenes look at the film, which offers footage of the filmmakers attending the Cannes Film Festival. —ML
Movie: 🎵🎵 **DVD:** 🎵🎵½
Kino on Video (cat #K193 DVD, UPC 7383-29019327). Widescreen (1.85:1) letterboxed. Digital 2.0 Surround. $29.95. Keepcase. *LANG:* Hebrew. *SUB:* English. *FEATURES:* Theatrical trailer • "Making of" featurette • 12 chapters.
1999 110m/C *IS* Yael Abecassis, Yoram Hattab, Meital Barda, Sami Hori, Uri Klauzner, Yussef Abu-Warda; **D:** Amos Gitai; **W:** Amos Gitai, Eliette Abecassis; **C:** Renato Berta; **M:** Louis Sclavis.

Kansas

Wild rebel Doyle Kennedy (Dillon) involves loner nice-guy Wade Corey (McCarthy) in a bank heist. They go on the lam but Corey tries to straighten himself out. Curious little film isn't completely successful but the stars make it more than watchable. DVD presents an excellent widescreen image that captures the flat dramatic landscapes with no serious flaws. Use of Surround is subdued. —MM
Movie: 🎵🎵 **DVD:** 🎵🎵½
MGM Home Ent. (cat #1002572, UPC 027-616867735). Widescreen (2.35:1) anamorphic. Dolby Digital Surround. $14.95. Keepcase. *LANG:* English. *SUB:* French; Spanish. *CAP:* English. *FEATURES:* 16 chapters • Trailer.
1988 (R) 111m/C Matt Dillon, Andrew McCarthy, Leslie Hope, Kyra Sedgwick; **D:** David Stevens; **W:** Spencer Eastman; **C:** David Eggby; **M:** Pino Donaggio.

The Karate Kid: Part 2

This sequel to the 1984 hit attempts to re-capture some of the magic and success of the first film, with mixed results. The story picks up six months later. Mr. Miyagi (Noriyuki "Pat" Morita) is summoned to his home in Okinawa, Japan. His father is ill. As things haven't been going very well for Daniel (Ralph Macchio) at home, he decides to accompany Miyagi. Once they arrive in Japan, romance blossoms all around, as Miyagi rekindles a romance with his childhood sweetheart (Nobu McCarthy) and Daniel falls in love with Kumiko (Tamlyn Tomita). But as Miyagi discovers his long-lost love, he also discovers that an old grudge with Sato (Danny Kamekona) is still standing. From this point on, the film parallels the first one, as both Miyagi and Daniel must prove themselves as both worthy fighters and worthy men. (Although, the inclusion of a typhoon does help to break up the repetition.) As with *The Karate Kid,* this sequel is far from original, but veteran director John G. Avildsen is able to pull at the heartstrings and keep the action moving at a nice pace. Once again, Morita steals the show as the lovable and wise Miyagi. DVD is a fairly straightforward release. This image in both the widescreen and full-frame transfers are sharp and clear, with only minor grain and some slight artifacting at times. The colors are good and the image shows no distortion. The Dolby 2.0 Surround track is very impressive, as it offers clear dialogue and some dynamic Surround effects in chapter 23. —ML
Movie: 🎵🎵½ **DVD:** 🎵🎵½
Columbia Tristar (cat #05991, UPC 043396059917). Widescreen (1.85:1) anamorphic; full frame. Dolby Surround. $19.95. Keepcase. *LANG:* English; Spanish; French; Portuguese. *SUB:* English; Spanish; French; Portuguese; Chinese; Korean; Thai. *CAP:* English. *FEATURES:* Featurette • Theatrical trailer • Bonus trailers • Filmographies.
1986 (PG) 95m/C Ralph Macchio, Noriyuki "Pat" Morita, Danny Kamekona, Martin Kove, Tamlyn Tomita, Nobu McCarthy, Yuji Okumoto, William Zabka; **D:** John G. Avildsen; **W:** Robert Mark Kamen; **C:** James A. Crabe; **M:** Bill Conti. *AWARDS:* NOM: Oscars '86: Song ("Glory of Love").

The Karate Kid: Part 3

In the *Karate Kid* films, the Daniel (Ralph Macchio) character has a "Never Say Die!" attitude. Unfortunately, so do the filmmakers behind these movies, as they trot out this tired re-tread. This film picks up where the events of *The Karate Kid: Part 2* ended. Daniel and Mr. Miyagi (Noriyuki "Pat" Morita) have returned from their adventures in Japan, and are ready to resume their normal lives. But Daniel learns that his mother is on the move again, and Miyagi is out of a job. Also, Daniel decides to forego the annual karate tournament. This leads to a story line of revenge, as Kreese (Martin Kove), the evil karate instructor from the first film, teams up with millionaire Terry Silver (Thomas Ian Griffith) to seek vengeance. Using student Mike (Sean Kanan), they are able to bully Daniel into entering the tournament, much to the dismay of Miyagi. Daniel finds himself lost on a sea of turmoil and he must regain his competitive spirit to prove himself and win back the trust of Miyagi. Basically, if you've seen the first two films, then you've seen this one as well, as there are no surprises here. Macchio seems far too old for the role and Morita looks bored. The only bright spot here is Robyn Lively as Daniel's new love interest. We get a fairly basic DVD release. The image is grainy, but sharp and the colors are quite good. The Dolby Surround audio track is quite dynamic, as it offers some superb Surround sound during the fight sequences, pulling the viewer into the cheering crowds. —ML

Movie: 🎵🎵 **DVD:** 🎵🎵 ½
Columbia Tristar (cat #05992, UPC 0433-96059924). Widescreen (1.85:1) anamorphic; full frame. Dolby Surround. $19.98. Keepcase. *LANG:* English; Spanish; French; Portuguese. *SUB:* English; Spanish; French; Portuguese; Chinese; Korean; Thai. *CAP:* English. *FEATURES:* Theatrical trailer • Bonus trailers • Filmographies.
1989 (PG) 105m/C Ralph Macchio, Noriyuki "Pat" Morita, John G. Avildsen, Thomas Ian Griffith, Martin Kove, Sean Kanan, Robin (Robyn) Lively; *D:* John G. Avildsen; *W:* Robert Mark Kamen; *C:* Steve Yaconelli; *M:* Bill Conti.

Kate & Leopold

This pleasant little romantic comedy ought to be a preview of the future of DVD. According to director James Mangold on his commentary track, he had serious differences with the studio on the form that the theatrical release should have. He did not want to add more graphic elements. He had one conception of the way the story should be told; executives (and test audiences) had others. DVD contains both the theatrical release and a true "director's cut." There's no clicking on an icon to reincorporate scenes; the disc simply has two versions of the film, both with commentary. Your choice. The story is your basic time-travel romance with Kate McCoy (a haggard-looking Ryan, whose hair might have been attacked by rabid chipmunks), a slightly burnt-out New York pollster (who works with test audiences) meeting Leopold (Jackman), third Duke of Albany. How does he get from an "amber glowing wonderful" late 19th century to the present day? It has to do with Stuart (Schreiber, providing superb support again), Kate's ex-beau. The film looks and sounds as good as any contemporary big-budget star vehicle, but the real value of the disc lies in that second version of the film. The deleted scenes can be viewed separately, but the medium has always promised that it would not be merely a "little" version of the theatrical experience, and would offer more. This disc shows that special treatment need not be reserved only for blockbusters. —MM

Movie: 🎵🎵🎵 **DVD:** 🎵🎵🎵 ½
Buena Vista Home Ent. (cat #25747, UPC 786936178258). Widescreen (1.85:1) anamorphic. Dolby Digital 5.1 Surround. $29.99. Keepcase. *LANG:* English; French (director's cut only). *SUB:* Spanish. *CAP:* English. *FEATURES:* Director's cut • Commentary: director • "On the Set" featurette • Deleted scenes with commentary • Music video • Costumes featurette.

2001 (PG-13) 121m/C Meg Ryan, Hugh Jackman, Liev Schreiber, Breckin Meyer, Natasha Lyonne, Bradley Whitford, Paxton Whitehead, Spalding Gray, Philip Bosco, David Aaron Baker; *D:* James Mangold; *W:* James Mangold, Steven Rogers; *C:* Stuart Dryburgh; *M:* Rolfe Kent. *AWARDS:* Golden Globes '02: Song ("Until"); *NOM:* Oscars '01: Song ("Until"); Golden Globes '02: Actor—Mus./Comedy (Jackman); Broadcast Film Critics '01: Song ("Until").

Katherine

Made-for-TV flick is a rough fictionalization of the events surrounding Patty Hearst. Katherine Alman (Spacek) is the heiress who becomes a violent revolutionary. A first-rate cast cannot do much with the thin material. DVD image is terrible. It looks like a worn VHS tape. Soundtrack is filled with static. Title is available on the *Classic Seventies Movies* disc. The "Seventies Time Travel" text extra is actually kind of neat. —MM *AKA:* The Radical.

Movie: 🎵 **DVD:** 🎵
BFS Video (cat #30290-D, UPC 06680-5302909). Full frame. $9.98. Keepcase. *LANG:* English. *FEATURES:* 6 chapters • Talent files • "Seventies Time Travel."
1975 98m/C Sissy Spacek, Art Carney, Jane Wyatt, Henry Winkler, Julie Kavner, Hector Elias, Jenny Sullivan; *D:* Jeremy Paul Kagan.

Katie Tippel

In 19th-century Amsterdam, a young woman (Van De Ven in a moving performance) works her way out of poverty and into a world of wealth and education. It's a Dickensian tale of prostitution told with lush production values. DVD presents an excellent image with the proper amount of detail visible in dark interiors and costumes. Grain appears to come from the original. Optional white subtitles are easy to read. As always, Verhoeven's commentary track is nicely done. —MM *AKA:* Katie's Passion; Cathy Tippel; Hot Sweat; Keetje Tippel.

Movie: 🎵🎵🎵 **DVD:** 🎵🎵🎵 ½
Anchor Bay (cat #DV11254, UPC 0131311-25498). Widescreen (1.66:1) anamorphic. Dolby Digital Mono. $24.99. Keepcase. *LANG:* Dutch. *SUB:* English. *FEATURES:* 25 chapters • Trailers • Talent files • Commentary.
1975 (R) 104m/C NL Monique Van De Ven, Rutger Hauer, Eddie Brugman, Hannah De Leeuwe, Andrea Domburg; *D:* Paul Verhoeven; *W:* Gerard Soeteman; *C:* Jan De Bont; *M:* Roger van Otterloo.

Ken Burns: Jazz

With 1140 minutes—that's 19 hours—at his disposal, documentarian Ken Burns has indeed given himself ample time to explore the origins and history of jazz music, starting in the 1890s in New Orleans. From there he moves on in 10 episodes, each on a separate disc, to tell the entire story. For fans of the music, this documentary is a treasure trove of information, memories, and rare glimpses at some of Jazz's best and most influential performers. Burns uses a combination of interviews, photographs, recordings, and commentary. Many of the episodes are further accompanied by full performances and live recordings of memorable pieces and artists—Louis Armstrong's "I Cover the Waterfront," Duke Ellington's "C-Jam Blues," and Mile Davis doing "New Rhumba," to cite just three. Presented as a respectable box set, the package makes a great impression from the get-go. The episodes are presented in extremely clean full-frame transfers. The image quality is quite remarkable, considering that this documentary makes heavy use of rare photographs, recordings, and film footage. The transfer features great black levels, making sure the documentary looks rock-solid at all times, never giving way to faded shots that may really date the material. Without the hiss, noise, or frequency limitations that you would initially expect from such old recordings, all tunes and tracks are beautifully balanced and sound natural. The narration is well integrated with the rest of the audio, creating a coherent feel throughout the 19 hours of presentation. Perhaps the most interesting extras are the "Music Information Cards": for every piece of music there's a card with information about composer, performers, recording dates, and the like. The cards also allow you to jump directly to the section within the documentary where the piece is played. —GH

Movie: 🎵🎵🎵 ½ **DVD:** 🎵🎵🎵 ½
Warner Home Video (UPC 7940548262-27). Full frame. $119.98. Special packaging. *LANG:* English. *FEATURES:* Music information cards • "Making of" documentary • Special performances.
2000 1140m/C *D:* Ken Burns; *W:* Geoffrey C. Ward; *C:* Ken Burns, Buddy Squires.

Ken Burns' Mark Twain

Mark Twain was the wiseguy who was wise beyond his age. Filled with quotes, excerpts, and interpretations of Twain's work, as well as insightful explanation about his personality and worldviews, this three-hour documentary goes into considerable detail. Burns manages to show us just how remarkable the man really was. Featuring good detail and delineation, the DVD presentation is beautiful and without any flaws. The audio is presented in a good stereo track, which fully serves the purpose for this documentary. It consists almost entirely of narration with very little music interspersed for atmosphere. —GH/MM *AKA:* Mark Twain.

Movie: 🎵🎵🎵 **DVD:** 🎵🎵🎵
Warner Home Video (UPC 7940548608-25). Full frame. Dolby Digital Stereo. $29.98. Keepcase. *LANG:* English. *FEATURES:* "Making of" featurette • Interview outtakes • Conversation with Ken Burns.
2001 220m/C *D:* Ken Burns; *C:* Ken Burns; *Nar:* Keith David, Kevin Conway.

Kennedy

This miniseries originally debuted in 1983 on the 20th Anniversary of the death of John Kennedy and follows his life from election night to his assassination in Dallas 1000 days later. The five-hour series is absorbing and fairly accurate historically. The producers skirt over both Kennedy's and Hoover's private lives and extracurricular activities, which is a great relief when all is said and done. Private conversations are obviously fiction and Jackie seems to be presented as a bit of an airhead who thinks the best thing about her husband's Presidency is all the free clothes. However, the depiction of violence during the civil rights clashes is brutally and realistically depicted. The best part of the disc is the extras section; here you find the real Kennedy. Footage of his inaugural address and his trip to Berlin are especially interesting, but the featurette on the Cuban missile crisis is riveting. The film was made for TV and the picture reflects this with a general dullness of color and less than perfect sound. —CA

Movie: 🎕🎕🎕 **DVD:** 🎕🎕 ½
Carlton Intl. Media (cat #82036, UPC 679398203623). Full frame. $49.95. Keepcase. *LANG:* English. *FEATURES:* 36 chapters ▪ Kennedy Inaugural Address ▪ "One Week in October" documentary short ▪ "One Day in Berlin" documentary short ▪ "The Last Two Days" documentary short.
1983 278m/C Martin Sheen, Blair Brown, Vincent Gardenia, Geraldine Fitzgerald, E.G. Marshall, John Shea; **D:** Richard Hartley.

Keoma

Tight little spaghetti western, with a simple story of loner Keoma (Nero) searching for freedom from oppression. While it visually and stylistically borrows more than an ample amount of Sam Peckinpah, there is some terrific camerawork and composition on display here that feels quite original. Fans of gunplay will be delighted as scores of bad guys fall (dramatically so) victim to the bullet, yet actual bloodshed is minimal. Those who are unfamiliar with spaghetti westerns are given a great sample with *Keoma,* and it will likely create an immediate interest in the genre. Detail is sharp and strong in the numerous extreme close-ups, and colors are vivid and bold when they appear in this dirt-filled environment. The print is in pretty good shape, though some of the night scenes are faded and grainy. Audio is satisfactory. Extras include a very informative and enjoyable commentary with director Castellari (his English isn't too bad) and journalist Waylon Wahl (his is fine), a 10-minute interview with Nero. —SH

Movie: 🎕🎕🎕 **DVD:** 🎕🎕🎕
Anchor Bay (UPC 13131158199). Widescreen (2.35:1) anamorphic. Dolby Digital Surround. $24.95. Keepcase. *LANG:* English. *FEATURES:* Commentary ▪ Franco Nero interview ▪ Trailer ▪ Talent files.
1976 101m/C *IT* Franco Nero, Woody Strode, William Berger, Donald O'Brien; **D:** Enzo G. Castellari; **W:** Enzo G. Castellari,

George Eastman, Mino Roli; **C:** Aiace Parolini; **M:** Guido de Angelis, Maurizio de Angelis.

Key Largo

A group of people are held prisoner at a Florida hotel by the elements and by a gang of ruthless thugs led by the sadistic Johnny Rocco (Robinson). As the storm swirls around the captives and their captors, inner tempests rage within the hostages as well, which include soul-shocked ex-G.I. Frank McCloud (Bogart), war widow Nora Temple (Bacall), and her disabled father-in-law (Barrymore). Rocco's alcoholic moll (Trevor, in an Oscar-winning performance) and his sweaty goons (among them, character actors par excellence Thomas Gomez and Dan Seymour) round out the gritty cast of characters. In the eye of the storm, both literally and figuratively, is Robinson's played-to-the-hilt performance as gangster leader Rocco. At first glance, the contrast seems wrong. Daytime scenes look so bright, the blacks appear practically washed-out, but the effect is intentional. Huston, in collusion with legendary cinematographer Karl Freund, conducts a symphony of shadows...as only that mysterious mix of black & white creates. The beaming daylight scenes lull the viewer into a false sense of security. At first, nothing appears out of the ordinary in the seemingly normal hotel environs. As night falls and the storm approaches, our antagonists make their real presence and dark purpose known. The audio exhibits some wear and signs of distortion, on par for a monophonic track its age. Occasionally, when the music swells, the center channel sounds a little congested. Yet the picture is so good, you will be hard pressed to find fault with the audio. The French soundtrack has just enough crackles and hiss to suggest the dubbing is from the period. —EP

Movie: 🎕🎕🎕 ½ **DVD:** 🎕🎕🎕
Warner Home Video (UPC 12569501027). Full frame. Dolby Mono. $19.98. Snapper. *LANG:* English; French. *SUB:* English; French. *FEATURES:* Talent files ▪ Production notes ▪ Trailer.
1948 101m/B Humphrey Bogart, Lauren Bacall, Claire Trevor, Edward G. Robinson, Lionel Barrymore, Thomas Gomez, Dan Seymour; **D:** John Huston; **W:** Richard Brooks, John Huston; **C:** Karl Freund; **M:** Max Steiner. *AWARDS:* Oscars '48: Support. Actress (Trevor).

Khartoum

When the situation demands it, a great actor can really turn on the ham and that's precisely what Laurence Olivier does with this eye-rolling performance. His "Islamic extremist," the Mahdi seems to have been based on Leo McKern's cult leader in *Help!* filmed a year before. The bizarre accents are almost identical but Olivier is forced to go an extra step with some of the most outrageous makeup and costuming he ever wore. The combination of

blackface with bright red lipstick and a turban must be seen to be appreciated. (Think Joan Crawford channeling Peter Sellers.) Co-star Charlton Heston has merely an uncomfortable-sounding British accent to work with. He plays Gen. Charles George Gordon, who's sent to the city of Khartoum in 1883 by an ineffective British government to prevent it from being taken over by the Muslim hordes. It's a lumbering, leisurely paced epic that begins with a musical overture before the feature starts. That's followed by a long narrative introduction to set the scene. When they finally do arrive, the large-scale action set-pieces seem a bit clumsy and slow by today's standards. DVD appears to have been made from very well-preserved original elements. Since the theatrical release was in Cinerama, it may be slightly cropped even at 2.35:1 but nothing significant was lost. The odd white fleck shows up here and there but the colors remain bright and vivid, and you have to look hard to spot any artifacts in the desert landscapes. Surround remix is pretty good. Dialogue is easy to understand. —MM

Movie: 🎕🎕 ½ **DVD:** 🎕🎕 ½
MGM Home Ent. (cat #1003431, UPC 027-616875808). Widescreen (2.35:1) anamorphic. Dolby Digital Surround. $14.98. Keepcase. *LANG:* English; Spanish. *SUB:* English; French; Spanish. *CAP:* English. *FEATURES:* 20 chapters ▪ Trailer.
1966 134m/C Charlton Heston, Laurence Olivier, Ralph Richardson, Richard Johnson, Alexander Knox, Hugh Williams, Nigel Green, Michael Hordern, Johnny Sekka; **D:** Basil Dearden; **W:** Robert Ardrey; **C:** Edward Scaife; **M:** Frank Cordell. *AWARDS:* NOM: Oscars '66: Story & Screenplay.

The Kid

The packaging declares that this one is *Rocky* meets *The Karate Kid,* and for once, the studio's description is accurate. Jimmy Albright (Jeff Saumier) is a good kid from a normal middle-class family, who often studies with his friends. But what his parents don't know is that instead of going to his friend's house, Jimmy treks across town to a gym where he secretly trains with Harry (Rod Steiger). Jimmy dreams of being a boxer, but he knows that his parents would never allow it. Jimmy's training is going well, and he is showing great promise, until pompous bully Trey (Daniel Brochu) enters the picture. Intimidated by Jimmy's natural talent, Trey threatens to expose Jimmy's secret life and ruin his chances of becoming a junior champion. This is by no means a bad movie, but it is incredibly benign, and one can't help but feel that we've seen it all before. The performances are good and the fight scenes are well shot, but on the whole, the movie pales in comparison to the classic with which it has been compared. The image is very sharp and clear, showing very little grain and no artifacting. The colors are good and the image is stable. The Dolby Surround audio track offers some nice

Surround effects during the fight scenes, and the dialogue is always clear and audible. —ML
Movie: 🎵🎵 **DVD:** 🎵🎵 ½
Miramax Pictures (cat #26562, UPC 786-93618542). Widescreen (1.85:1) anamorphic. Dolby Digital Surround. $29.99. Keepcase. *LANG:* English. *CAP:* English. *FEATURES:* Bonus trailers • 16 chapters.
1997 (PG) 89m/C *CA* Jeff Saumier, Rod Steiger, Ray Aranha, Mark Camacho, Jane Wheeler, Tod Fennell, Daniel Brochu, Jason Tremblay; *D:* John Hamilton; *W:* Seymour Blicker; *M:* Normand Corbeil.

The Kid Brother

Thirteen-year-old Kenny just wants to be a normal boy, but he was born without legs. A French TV crew comes to film his family life, causing them to examine the ways in which they've all been manipulated. It's a bit darker than one might think, but not terribly interesting. The sound quality is adequate, but the picture is pretty bad, with heavy grain and an overall lack of detail. —BG
Movie: 🎵 ½ **DVD:** 🎵🎵
Vanguard Intl. Cinema (cat #VFO269, UPC 658769026931). Full frame. Dolby Stereo. $29.95. Keepcase. *LANG:* English. *FEATURES:* 11 chapters.
1987 95m/C Caitlin Clarke, Henry Easterday, Lane Curtis, Zach Grenier, Jesse Easterday Jr.; *D:* Claude Gagnon; *W:* Claude Gagnon; *C:* Yudeo Hato.

Kidnapped Coed

Please see review of *Hitch Hike to Hell / Kidnapped Coed*.
1977 (R) 76m/C Jack Canon, Leslie Ann Rivers, Gladys Lavitan, Larry Lambeth; *D:* Frederick Friedel; *W:* Frederick Friedel; *C:* Austin McKinney; *M:* George Newman Shaw, John Willhelm.

Kill by Inches

Curious, creepy horror/thriller has strong overtones of David Lynch. The story concerns Thomas (Salinger), a tailor who is obsessed with proper measurement, and his relationship with his sister (Cyr). DVD delivers a very good image, though this independent production is not as bright as studio releases. Sound is fine. —MM
Movie: 🎵🎵 ½ **DVD:** 🎵🎵 ½
Winstar Home Ent. (cat #FLV5291, UPC 720917529127). Widescreen (1.66:1) letterboxed. $24.98. Keepcase. *LANG:* English. *FEATURES:* 16 chapters • Trailer • Filmographies • Production credits • Weblinks.
1999 85m/C *FR* Emmanuel Salinger, Myriam Cyr, Marcus Powell, Peter McRobbie; *D:* Diane Doniol-Valcroze, Arthur Flam; *W:* Diane Doniol-Valcroze, Arthur Flam; *C:* Richard Rutkowski; *M:* Geir Jenssen.

Kill Cruise

The depressed alcoholic, drug-abusing skipper (Prochnow) of the yacht Bella Donna gives up sailing until he meets two beautiful young women (Hurley and Kensit) who want to sail to Bermuda for a taste of the good life. Three-character study actually develops some tension. DVD image is no improvement over VHS tape. Title is available as part of the "Action Arsenal" collection. —MM
Movie: 🎵🎵 **DVD:** 🎵🎵
BCI-Eclipse (cat #44076-9, UPC 7873644-07699). Full frame. $19.98. Keepcase. *LANG:* English. *FEATURES:* 12 chapters • Patsy Kensit thumbnail bio.
1990 (R) 99m/C Juergen Prochnow, Patsy Kensit, Elizabeth Hurley; *D:* Peter Keglevic; *W:* Peter Keglevic; *C:* Edward Klosinski; *M:* Brynmor Jones.

Kill Me Later

A dark comedy about a depressed bank teller (Blair) who is contemplating suicide when her bank is robbed. She agrees to help the thief (Beesley) escape if he makes a promise to kill her later. In these post-Prozac times it's hard to have patience with our bank teller's angst qualifying as anything but a bad date to avoid and, while ambitious and almost succeeding, this story requires first-rate exposition to pull quirky out of sophomoric. Clean DVD transfer and sound. —MO
Movie: 🎵🎵 **DVD:** 🎵🎵 ½
Studio Home Ent. (cat #ST7911D, UPC 658149791121). Widescreen letterboxed. Dolby Stereo. $24.99. Keepcase. *LANG:* English. *SUB:* English; Spanish. *FEATURES:* 25 chapters • Commentary: director Dana Lustig, writer Annette Goliti Gutierrez • Cast interviews • Theatrical trailer.
2001 (R) 89m/C Selma Blair, Max Beesley, Lochlyn Munro, O'Neal Compton, Brendan Fehr, D.W. Moffett; *D:* Dana Lustig; *W:* Annette Goliti Gutierrez; *C:* David Ferrara; *M:* Tal Bergman, Renato Nero.

Killer

Yet another portrait of triad society, this one focusing more on the sadness and drama, with little violence. Tung (Jordan Chan) and his three buddies became a legend by killing a triad member in their Hong Kong neighborhood, after which they joined and ascended rapidly within a rival triad. However, Tung has grown weary of the gangster life. Po (Simon Lui), on the other hand, loves the triad life, and fits in perfectly. Internal and external forces alike conspire to unravel all their lives. This gangster melodrama gets by on Billy Chung's stylish direction, and the personality of stars Chan and Lui. The DVD transfer does a good job of keeping the mostly dark scenes readable, and has good sound. Interviews with the cast at the premiere are in Chinese only. —BT *AKA:* Diy Sau; Dao Shou.
Movie: 🎵🎵 ½ **DVD:** 🎵🎵 ½
Tai Seng (cat #5391, UPC 48950249088-54). Widescreen letterboxed. Dolby Digital 5.1 Surround. $19.98. Keepcase. *LANG:* Cantonese; Mandarin. *SUB:* Chinese; English; Bahasa; Korean. *CAP:* English. *FEATURES:* 8 chapters • Star profiles • Trailers • Interviews.
2000 88m/C *HK* Jordan Chan, Simon Lui, Ken Wong, Mark Cheng; *D:* Billy Chung; *W:* Simon Lui, Billy Chung, Edmand Pang; *C:* Chi Ken Kwan.

Killer B Double Feature: Boy in the Plastic Bubble & The Harrad Experiment

In the first half of this double-bill, Travolta plays a young man who's forced by immunity deficiencies to live in a carefully controlled environment, separated from virtually all direct human contact. The title has earned something of a reputation (mainly for its scarcity, I think), but it's pretty much standard disease-of-the-week fare recommended to Travolta completists only. In the second, a callow Don Johnson matriculates at a college that's experimenting with sexual freedom. There's much more talk than tease'n'sleaze, alas. Both films have a fuzzy, faded look that's actually a little worse than most VHS tapes. —MM
Movie: 🎵 ½ **DVD:** 🎵 ½
Marengo Films (cat #MRG-0018, UPC 807-013001891). Full frame. $19.99. Keepcase. *LANG:* English. *FEATURES:* 6 chapters each feature.
2000 184m/C

Killer Barbys

The titular punk band is on the road to their next gig when their car breaks down. Fortunately, they are close to a hospitable castle. Unfortunately, it is owned by the ancient Countess Von Fledermaus, who needs fresh blood to keep her young. Typical Franco silliness, with more clichés, continuity errors, and gaps in logic than you can count. The low rating for the DVD is due to a major technical flaw—although plenty of special features are available, they forgot to include a cursor or any other way of indicating which menu option has been selected. Unless you're using a DVD-ROM player, you'll find yourself counting beeps to guess where you are. —BG
Movie: woof **DVD:** 🎵
Media Blasters (cat #SSDVD-0108, UPC 631595010893). Full frame. $24.95. Keepcase. *LANG:* English; Spanish. *SUB:* English. *FEATURES:* 10 chapters • Trailers • Music videos • Behind-the-scenes • Production notes.
1996 87m/C *SP* Santiago Segura, Maria Angela Giordano, Aldo Sambrel, Silcia Superstar; *D:* Jess (Jesus) Franco; *W:* Jess (Jesus) Franco, Paxti Irigoyen; *C:* Piluca Banquero.

Killer Instinct

Teen horror is aimed at the *Scream* crowd and manages to generate some nice suspense and scares. A group of kids decide to spend the night in an abandoned insane asylum where—surprise, sur-

prise—they are bumped off in inventive ways. This is a modestly budgeted production that really gains little in visual terms on DVD. Image is only acceptable with some grain in darker scenes that appears intentional. But the whole thing is carried off with some style, wit, and originality. Fans have seen much worse. —MM
Movie: 🐾🐾🐾 **DVD:** 🐾🐾
Lion's Gate Home Ent. (cat #VM7695D, UPC 031398769521). Widescreen anamorphic. Dolby Digital Stereo. $24.98. Keepcase. *LANG:* English. *SUB:* English; French; Spanish. *CAP:* English. *FEATURES:* 24 chapters • Previews.
2000 (R) 87m/C Corbin Bernsen, Paige Moss, Jeannie Meyers, Brigitte Brooks, Dee Wallace Stone; **D:** Ken Barbet; **W:** Christopher Stone, Bruce Cameron; **C:** Richard Ashbury; **M:** Timothy S. Jones.

Killer Klowns from Outer Space
A spaceship crashes on Earth and from it emerge three clowns who kill people and turn them into cotton candy. Mike and Debbie see them and try to convince the inhabitants of the small town that this is an alien attack, but of course no one pays heed to their words. The transfer is generally clean and without overt defects other than occasional speckles, and the print shows a good level of detail throughout. Color reproduction is very strong and faithful, but never appears oversaturated. Overall, the Surround audio fulfills the needs of the movie and certainly exceeds expectations. The commentary track by the Chiodo Brothers, who wrote, directed, and produced the film, is a great addition, as it oozes enthusiasm for the movie. Without interruption, the trio talks about the production, the shooting, the cast, the problems, the low budget, and more as they revisit the film with the viewer. —GH
Movie: 🐾🐾 ½ **DVD:** 🐾🐾🐾 ½
MGM Home Ent. (cat #1002350, UPC 027-616865618). Widescreen (1.85:1) anamorphic. Dolby Digital Surround Stereo. $24.98. Keepcase. *LANG:* English. *SUB:* English; French; Spanish. *CAP:* English. *FEATURES:* Commentary • 5 featurettes • Deleted scenes and bloopers • Storyboard • Trailer.
1988 (PG-13) 90m/C Grant Cramer, Suzanne Snyder, John Allen Nelson, Royal Dano, John Vernon, Peter Licassi, Michael Siegel, Charles Chiodo; **D:** Stephen Chiodo; **W:** Stephen Chiodo, Charles Chiodo; **C:** Alfred Taylor; **M:** John Massari.

King Lear
TV adaptation of the Joseph Papp Shakespeare Festival performance is for fans of the cast. Everyone else is likely to be disappointed by the poverty-row production values of interpretation of the Bard's great tragedy. Sound is poor (the most glaring failure); the image is dimly lit; colors are faded. Most of the flaws appear to come from substandard original elements. —MM
Movie: 🐾🐾 ½ **DVD:** 🐾🐾

Image Ent. (cat #ID0883B DDVD, UPC 014381088328). Full frame. Dolby Digital Mono. $24.98. Keepcase. *LANG:* English. *FEATURES:* 28 chapters • Filmographies.
1974 176m/C James Earl Jones, Raul Julia, Paul Sorvino, Rene Auberjonois, Rosalind Cash, Ellen Holly, Douglas Watson, Tom Aldredge; **D:** Edwin Sherin; **M:** Charles Gross.

King of the Pecos
John Clayborn (Wayne), a young lawyer who can also handle a shootin' iron, exacts revenge on his parents' killer in the courtroom. This is an ambitious early outing for the star, with good character development, an interesting plot, taut pacing, and beautiful photography that's captured on a sparkling DVD. Some aliasing crops up during fast pans, but otherwise, the image is splendid. The disc looks about 1,000% better than the public domain titles of the same vintage. Recommended. —MM
Movie: 🐾🐾 ½ **DVD:** 🐾🐾 ½
Artisan Ent. (cat #12042, UPC 01715312-0424). Full frame. Dolby Digital Mono. $14.98. Keepcase. *LANG:* English. *FEATURES:* 16 chapters.
1936 54m/B John Wayne, Muriel Evans, Cy Kendall, Jack Clifford, John Beck, Yakima Canutt; **D:** Joseph Kane; **W:** Dorrell McGowan, Stuart E. McGowan, Bernard McConville; **C:** Jack Marta.

King Solomon's Mines
The search for King Solomon's Mines leads a safari through the treacherous terrain of the desert, fending off sandstorms, Zulus, and a volcanic eruption. Adapted from the novel by H. Rider Haggard and remade twice. The disc boasts a very decent video transfer. Black-and-white definition is above average and features a crispness that is usually missing from older films when first transferred to DVD. Consequently, the shortcomings of this transfer probably have more to do with the lack of a decent source print than the disc's actual production. The soundtrack fares similarly well and is clear and is only distorted in a few isolated pockets. However, the disc would indeed benefit from a decent audio remix. —MJT
Movie: 🐾🐾🐾 **DVD:** 🐾🐾
MGM Home Ent. (cat #1002381, UPC 027616865922). Full frame. Dolby Digital Mono. $19.98. Keepcase. *LANG:* English. *SUB:* French; Spanish. *FEATURES:* 16 chapters.
1937 80m/B Cedric Hardwicke, Paul Robeson, Roland Young, John Loder, Anna Lee; **D:** Robert Stevenson; **W:** Michael Hogan, Roland Pertwee; **C:** Cyril Knowles, Glen MacWilliams; **M:** Mischa Spoliansky.

Kingdom Come
The death of a black family's patriarch (director McHenry) brings far-flung archetypical relatives to the funeral. There's the wise, saintly widow (Goldberg); the stoic,

hardworking son (L.L. Cool J., in a solid breakout performance) and his eager-to-please wife (Fox); the ne'er-do-well son (Anderson) and his shrewish wife (Pinkett Smith); the Bible-thumper (Devine); and the gold-digger (Braxton, in her debut). Throw in an overly officious and unfortunately flatulent preacher (Cedric), let simmer, and bring to a boil. Does the mix of comedy and drama work? Not always, but often enough to earn a recommendation. DVD delivers an accurate re-creation of an often warm, fairly soft image. McHenry's commentary is low-keyed, serious, and tends toward the day-to-day business of filmmaking. —MM
Movie: 🐾🐾🐾 **DVD:** 🐾🐾🐾
20th Century Fox (UPC 024543023968). Widescreen letterboxed. Dolby Digital 5.1 Surround; Dolby Surround. $19.98. Keepcase. *LANG:* English. *SUB:* English; Spanish. *CAP:* English. *FEATURES:* 28 chapters • "Making of" featurette • Music video • Commentary: Doug McHenry • Trailer • TV spots.
2001 (PG) 89m/C L.L. Cool J., Jada Pinkett Smith, Vivica A. Fox, Loretta Devine, Anthony Anderson, Cedric the Entertainer, Darius McCrary, Whoopi Goldberg, Toni Braxton, Masasa, Clifton Davis, Richard Gant, Doug McHenry; **D:** Doug McHenry; **W:** Jessie Jones, David Bottrell; **C:** Francis Kenny; **M:** Tyler Bates.

Kings Go Forth
Hormones and war rage in a love triangle set against the backdrop of WWII France. Sgt. Loggins (Sinatra) loves Monique (Wood) who loves Cpl. Harris (Curtis). When Sgt. Loggins asks for her hand in marriage, she refuses because she is mixed—half black, half white. He says it doesn't matter, but she still demurs because she's in love with Cpl. Harris, who says that it doesn't matter either because he has no intention of marrying her. Meanwhile, there's a war going on. Film is not particularly satisfying on either the war, the racial, or romantic fronts. The black-and-white image ranges between very good and excellent on DVD. Monaural sound is no better than fair. —MM
Movie: 🐾🐾 ½ **DVD:** 🐾🐾 ½
MGM Home Ent. (cat #1003137, UPC 027-616873019). Full frame. Dolby Digital Mono. $14.98. Keepcase. *LANG:* English; French. *SUB:* English; French; Spanish. *CAP:* English. *FEATURES:* 16 chapters • Trailer.
1958 109m/B Frank Sinatra, Tony Curtis, Natalie Wood, Leora Dana; **D:** Delmer Daves; **W:** Merle Miller; **C:** Daniel F. Fapp; **M:** Elmer Bernstein.

The King's Guard
This is, strange to say, a porn film without any porn. It's all there—the contrived scenes, the remote, yet undecorated locations, the poor dialogue and unmemorable soundtrack that seems to be leading up to casual sex, but then all there is, is more poor dialogue. The film is shot entirely outside with everyone running around in Renaissance garb. Perhaps one of the

actors said to the other, "my aunt has two acres of woodland, let's make a bodice ripper." But then the aunt said no to the ripping part which just left the bodices...anyway the film is poor at best, with funny, surreal moments, and a guy with a really strong Scottish accent who, when he addresses the princess as "your highness," sounds like he's saying, "you're heinous." Aside from the sophomoric humor you can derive from the suffering of the players, there is little to be said to recommend the film. Oh, the plot, you ask: a princess is being escorted by the handsome king's guard when the group is set upon by a group of cutthroats led by the ex-leader of the king's guard (Eric "my sister won an Academy Award and all I got was this lousy "B"-movie career" Roberts) who wants the princess for himself. The color and clarity are decent—it was all shot outside in heavy daylight—but the sound is fairly bad and you need to turn the TV up high to make out the dialogue. —CA
Movie: ♪ ½ **DVD:** ♪♪ ½
Studio Home Ent. (cat #1571D, UPC 806-469157121). Full frame. Stereo. $19.99. Keepcase. *LANG:* English. *SUB:* English; French; Spanish. *CAP:* English. *FEATURES:* 24 chapters ▪ Trailer.
2001 (PG-13) 94m/C Ashley Jones, Eric Roberts, Ron Perlman, Trevor St. John, Lesley-Anne Down; **D:** Jonathan Tydor; **W:** Jonathan Tydor.

Kiss Me Quick!

As Frank Henenlotter explains in his liner notes, this movie was one of the first "nudie-cuties" inspired by Russ Meyers's *Immoral Mr. Teas*. It's a virtually plotless excuse to display topless women. Made a few months after *The Munsters* and *The Addams Family* appeared on TV, it also features a guy made up to look like the Frankenstein monster who tries to make the semi-naked ladies dance. The commentary track with Something Weird's Mike Vraney and producer Harry Novak is mostly about the early days of the exploitation business, not the film itself. DVD image is an accurate reproduction of a well-preserved low-budget original. Extras are abundant but not as extensive as some of the studio's other "drive-in double features." Disc also contains *House on Bare Mountain* (please see review). —MM
Movie: ♪ ½ **DVD:** ♪♪ ½
Image Ent. (cat #ID9738SWDVD, UPC 014381973822). Full frame. Dolby Digital Mono. $24.99. Snapper. *LANG:* English. *FEATURES:* 16 chapters ▪ Theatrical trailers ▪ Commentary: Mike Vraney, Harry Novak ▪ Four archival exploitation short subjects ▪ Gallery of exploitation art.
1964 66m/C Frank Coe, Max Gardens, Althea Currier, Jackie DeWitt, Claudia Banks; **D:** Peter Berry; **C:** Laszlo Kovacs.

Kiss of the Dragon

Jet Li stars in what is essentially a Luc Besson French action thriller. Chinese Intelligence officer Liu Jian, a kung fu master and acupuncture expert, is sent to Paris to work with Inspector Tchéky Karyo. Karyo is really planning to kill a drug lord and any witnesses, including convenient fall guy Li. Karyo's favorite little reluctant junkie hooker Bridget Fonda witnesses the murders, putting her in danger as well. Corey Yuen's fight choreography is the highlight, with Li's attack on Paris Police HQ a kung fu classic. With Li and director Chris Nahon edited together with Fonda, the audio commentary track needs subtitles. The film transfer is top-notch —BT
Movie: ♪♪♪ **DVD:** ♪♪♪ ½
20th Century Fox (cat #2003046, UPC 024543030461). Widescreen letterboxed. Dolby 5.1 Surround; Dolby 2.0 Surround. $26.98. Keepcase. *LANG:* English; Spanish. *SUB:* English. *CAP:* English. *FEATURES:* 24 chapters ▪ Trailers ▪ Documentary featurettes ▪ Storyboard comparison.
2001 (R) 98m/C *FR US* Jet Li, Bridget Fonda, Tcheky Karyo, Burt Kwouk; **D:** Chris Nahon; **W:** Luc Besson, Robert Mark Kamen; **C:** Thierry Arbogast; **M:** Craig Armstrong.

Kiss Tomorrow Goodbye

After a night of hard-partying Dustin (Lea) wakes up on the beach next to a dead woman. Homeless Minnow (McCallany) says that Dustin killed her, and offers to get rid of the body for certain considerations. Before long, Dustin finds his life being taken over. Jason Priestley's directorial debut is an acceptable video premiere thriller. DVD presents a very nice full-frame image with a thumpy score. —MM
Movie: ♪♪ **DVD:** ♪♪ ½
MTI (cat #8120, UPC 039414581201). Full frame. $24.95. Keepcase. *LANG:* English. *SUB:* Spanish. *FEATURES:* 20 chapters ▪ Trailers ▪ Talent files.
2000 (R) 90m/C Nicholas Lea, Holt McCallany, Kari Wuhrer, Jason Priestley, Philip Casnoff, Jennifer Blanc; **D:** Jason Priestley; **W:** Ozzie Cheek; **C:** Bruce Logan; **M:** Harold Kloser.

The Kiss You Gave Me

Angela (Aviles) is a successful TV reporter in Puerto Rico. Her husband Armando (Alvarez) takes their son to live in the United States without her consent. She hooks up with an old flame Pedro Juan (Navarro), who was an activist during their college days, to search for her son. It gets more and more preposterous as the plot thickens. Lame, simplistic treatment of a very dramatic story combined with quick fade-outs and cheesy lighting give away its TV origins. Transfer from videotape looks O.K. Sound is fine. —LA *AKA:* El Beso Que Me Diste.
Movie: ♪♪ **DVD:** ♪♪ ½
Vanguard Intl. Cinema (cat #VF0208, UPC 658769020830). Widescreen (1.85:1) letterboxed. $29.98. Keepcase. *LANG:* Spanish. *SUB:* English. *FEATURES:* 11 chapters.
2000 90m/C Maricarmen Aviles, Jimmy Navarro, Rene Monclova, Carola Garcia, Ernesto Concepcion, Humberto Gonzales; **D:** Sonia Fritz; **W:** Sonia Fritz; **C:** Augustin Cubano; **M:** Miguel Cubano.

Kizuna

This offbeat Japanese animated tale tells of the relationship between Ranmaru and Enjoji. Ranmaru is a legendary fencing champion until he is hit by a car that is trying to run down Enjoji, who is a mobster's son. After Enjoji nurses Ranmaru back to health, they become a couple. When Kai, another mobster's son, rescues Ranmaru from the clutches of a lecherous professor, he becomes enmeshed with the two, eventually revealing his own crush on Ranmaru. Undistinguished melodrama/comedy which seems to occur in a predominantly gay world and the constant slobbering the characters do over Ranmaru becomes a bit silly at times. There's certainly a novelty in seeing an anime obsessed with male eros (instead of the usual hypersexualized females) but the Ranmaru character is underdeveloped and the story is insubstantial. The disc is a slight step above the VHS. There's a bit of shimmer around edges at times, the subtitles are not removable and there are no chapter stops. Unfortunately, the subtitles occur about a beat or two before the characters speak their lines of dialogue. Sound is average. —DG
Movie: ♪♪ **DVD:** ♪♪
Ariztical Ent. (cat #CQC502, UPC 6310-08050232). Full frame. Stereo. $29.95. Keepcase. *LANG:* Japanese. *SUB:* English.
1994 55m/C *JP* **D:** Rin Hiroo; **W:** Miyoo Morita, Kazuma Kodaka; **M:** Fujio Takano.

Klute

Small-town policeman Klute (Sutherland) comes to New York in search of a missing friend and becomes involved with prostitute/would-be actress Bree (Fonda) in an intelligent, gripping crime drama. DVD transfer is mostly clean with few minor blemishes. Since the color scheme is equally important to this film as its aspect ratio, it is great to see that it also has been perfectly reproduced on this release. The film is made up of many very dark shots and contrast of the presentation is well preserved with deep solid blacks that don't break up. Image detail is a bit lacking in the shadow areas with slight dot crawl, but for the most part, the image is without flaws, creating a very pleasant presentation. The compression is free of artifacts, further making for a stable and detailed presentation. The original mono soundtrack has been left untouched. As a result it clearly shows the limitations of the technology at the time, but also maintains its very vintage quality. The track is a bit muddy at times and the narrow frequency response gives it a harsh quality, but somehow it perfectly befits the movie itself. —GH/MM
Movie: ♪♪♪ ½ **DVD:** ♪♪♪
Warner Home Video (UPC 0125691027-29). Widescreen (2.35:1) anamorphic.

Dolby Digital Mono. $19.98. Snapper. *LANG:* English; French. *SUB:* English; French; Spanish; Portuguese; Japanese; Korean; Thai; Chinese. *CAP:* English. *FEATURES:* 1971 featurette ● Trailer ● Filmographies.

1971 (R) 114m/C Jane Fonda, Donald Sutherland, Charles Cioffi, Roy Scheider, Rita Gam, Jean Stapleton; *D:* Alan J. Pakula; *W:* Andy Lewis, Dave Lewis; *C:* Gordon Willis; *M:* Michael Small. *AWARDS:* Oscars '71: Actress (Fonda); Golden Globes '72: Actress—Drama (Fonda); N.Y. Film Critics '71: Actress (Fonda); Natl. Soc. Film Critics '71: Actress (Fonda); *NOM:* Oscars '71: Story & Screenplay.

Knight Chills

For those who enjoy role-playing games, such as Dungeons & Dragons, getting lost in an adventure can be quite thrilling. However, watching others play a role-playing games isn't very exciting or interesting. But that's what we're treated to during the first 20 minutes of *Knight Chills*, a low-budget movie which offers a compelling premise, but simply collapses under its own weight. John (Michael Wayne Walton) is a young man who is obsessed with role-playing games and meets every Saturday night to play with a group led by local teacher, Jack Nixon (Tim Jeffrey). John is constantly teased by the other players (although we're never told why) and this abuse leads to a psychotic break, where he begins to take the games far too seriously. After John dies in a mysterious car accident, the players who taunted him find themselves being stalked by a black knight on a steed. As with many low-budget fright flicks, this one features far too many dialogue scenes and not enough action. The acting is amateurish, but director Katherine Hicks has tried to give the movie a nice look. Viewers will be better off checking out the similarly themed Tom Hanks vehicle *Mazes and Monsters*. *Knight Chills* was shot on video and the process suffers in this DVD transfer. The picture is sharp, but there is a great deal of video distortion, artifacting, and pixelation. (Candlelight looks especially bad here.) On the positive side, the colors are bright and realistic. The Dolby Digital 5.1 audio track is also bad, as the same audio portion comes from all five speakers. So technically it is Surround sound, but not in the traditionally accepted sense. For a low-budget film, the DVD includes some nice behind-the-scenes extras. —*ML*

Movie: ♪ *DVD:* ♪♪
Spectrum Films (cat #VF3833, UPC 73356-5338331). Widescreen (1.85:1) letterboxed. Digital 5.1 Stereo Surround. $24.99. Keepcase. *LANG:* English. *FEATURES:* Trailer ● Still gallery ● Behind-the-scenes featurette ● FX featurette.
2001 (PG-13) 82m/C Tim Jeffrey, Michael Wayne Walton; *D:* Katherine Hicks.

A Knight's Tale

A peasant (Ledger) poses as a knight to compete in prestigious jousting tourna-ments. Struggling to keep his identity a secret, he falls in love with lady Jocelyn (Sossamon) and finds a rival in evil (boo, hiss!) Count Adhemar (Sewell). Columbia was rightfully slammed for posting supposed raves from a non-existent critic in newspaper advertisements. They needn't have bothered; this is a terrific, funny, and highly satisfying picture. Sewell is loaded with charisma and his compadres (Tudyk, Addy, and Bettany) almost steal the film with their hilarious characterizations. The story strikes a strong balance between action, drama, and comedy. The use of modern rock songs in the film is absolutely inspired; this is a gleefully (intentionally) anachronistic period film and it works like gangbusters. Why it wasn't a smash is a mystery. Stick through the end credits for a post-credit gag sequence. The picture quality is strong; colors are accurate, though subdued and the image is sharp. There's a bit of digital grain throughout, especially prevalent in wide shots. The Surround sound has strong presence and a lot of punch to it. You'll certainly feel the impact of those lances with the appropriate Surround sound system. The disc is jammed to the gills with worthwhile extras. There's some overlap between the 11 very brief featurettes and the HBO special but a plethora of exciting behind-the-scenes footage is utilized. The commentary is informative and frequently riotous; Helgeland and Bettany are old friends and take great pleasure in ribbing each other, the film, and its participants. About a half hour in they crack open the beers and it becomes even funnier. The deleted scenes are given extensive introductions and commentary by Helgeland and the editor. All are worth watching but would certainly have been distractions from the main story. Highly recommended. —*DG*

Movie: ♪♪♪ ½ *DVD:* ♪♪♪ ½
Columbia Tristar (cat #06143, UPC 0433-96061439). Widescreen (2.35:1) anamorphic. Dolby Digital 5.1 Surround; Dolby Digital Surround. $27.96. Keepcase. *LANG:* English; French. *SUB:* English; French. *FEATURES:* Commentary: director Helgeland, Paul Bettany ● Insert booklet with notes ● 28 chapters ● Deleted scenes with filmmaker intros ● 11 behind-the-scenes featurettes ● HBO "making of" special ● Music video ● Website link ● Trailers ● Filmographies ● Production notes ● DVD-ROM features including screensaver.
2001 (PG-13) 132m/C Heath Ledger, Mark Addy, Rufus Sewell, Shannyn Sossamon, Paul Bettany, Laura Fraser, Christopher Cazenove, Alan Tudyk, James Purefoy; *D:* Brian Helgeland; *W:* Brian Helgeland; *C:* Richard Greatrex; *M:* Carter Burwell.

The Knights Templar

Documentary on the history and mythology of the Knights Templar. While the subject matter is interesting and engaging, the documentary frequently becomes tedious with over-long interviews and overused reenactments. Not recommend-ed for the ardent Templar scholar or the casual observer, but somewhere in-between. The disc displays a sharp picture via a good video transfer. Colors and blacks are crisp and well defined. The soundtrack is similarly well done and features crisp, understandable dialogue and narration. The musical score is also reproduced nicely, although a slight volume increase is evident between a few chapters. —*MJT*

Movie: ♪♪ *DVD:* ♪♪ ½
BFS Video (cat #30244-D, UPC 06680-5302442). Full frame. Dolby Digital Stereo. $19.98. Keepcase. *LANG:* English. *FEATURES:* 11 chapters ● "The Mythology of the Knights Templar" interactive text.
2000 120m/C *D:* James Wignall; *W:* James Wignall.

Knives of the Avenger

This rarely seen Bava film is actually a Viking permutation of *Shane*. Rurik (Mitchell) is the stranger who arrives at the cottage where Queen Karin (Pichelli) is in hiding until her missing husband returns. She has a young son and both are in need of the protection that Rurik and his lethal throwing knives can provide. In his liner notes, Tim Lucas details the production's financial troubles. Though the film certainly doesn't rank among Bava's best, it's not bad and the performances are effective despite the dubbing, even of Mitchell. DVD image is exceptional. Only minor signs of wear are visible. The film looks much better than many Hollywood productions of its era. Curiously, the trailer is in battered black and white. —*MM* *AKA:* Viking Massacre; I Coltelli Del Vendicatore.

Movie: ♪♪♪ *DVD:* ♪♪♪
Image Ent. (cat #ID9713AODVD, UPC 014-381971323). Widescreen (2.35:1) anamorphic. Dolby Digital Mono. $24.98. Keepcase. *LANG:* English; Italian. *FEATURES:* Liner notes by Tim Lucas ● Mario Bava bio and filmography ● Cameron Mitchell filmography ● Trailer ● Photo and poster gallery ● 12 chapters.
1965 85m/C *IT* Cameron Mitchell, Elissa Pichelli, Luciano Pollentin, Fausto Tozzi, Giacomo "Jack" Rossi-Stuart; *D:* Mario Bava; *W:* Mario Bava, Alberto Liberati, Giorgio Simonelli; *M:* Marcello Giombini.

The Korean War in Color

This documentary is essentially an introduction to the Korean War. That's all anyone could expect of a 90-minute feature about an exceptionally complex subject. It's been created from various sources, American and Korean, with the unifying feature being color, as opposed to black-and-white photography. But this is very rough color, often shot under harsh conditions. The dated look is accentuated by occasionally heavy surface damage. It's virtually all grim stuff, often washed-out and pale. At times, the heavy grain leads to the expected artifacts and pixels. Despite the title, many of the extras are in black and white, most notably the Marilyn Monroe visit (silent with musical accompaniment) and the 1952 television interview with Sen. Joseph McCarthy. The Korean footage of the execution of spies and guerrillas before the war is shocking. The 3-bone technical rating is due to the amount of extra material, not the quality of the picture or sound. —MM

Movie: 🦴🦴 ½ **DVD:** 🦴🦴🦴
Goldhil Home Media (cat #GH1571, UPC 743457157124). Full frame. Dolby Digital 5.1 Surround; Dolby Surround. $29.95. Keepcase. *LANG:* English. *FEATURES:* Slide show • 15 chapters • Execution of spies and guerrillas • Gun camera compilation • Interview with Sen. Joseph McCarthy • Featurette on Korean War Veterans' Memorial • Newsreel bios • Korean War time line.
2002 90m/C W: Chris Cassell.

Kramer vs. Kramer

Workaholic ad man Ted Kramer (Hoffman) is shocked when his unhappy wife Joanna (Streep) simply leaves one night, giving little reason beyond the fact that "she can't live with him anymore." Faced with the problem of taking care of their five-year-old son Billy (Henry) on his own, Ted must neglect his coveted new position at work, and soon is in danger of losing his job altogether. Columbia TriStar's DVD transfer starts with a very grainy torch lady logo that thankfully gives way to a pristine 16:9 transfer of the film. Nestor Almendros's muted and soft colors are rendered beautifully; this is a film with a very clean look, and few opticals. Every shot is a model of carefully graded light and shade. The camera does few "tricks," and supports the drama between the characters with an almost-invisible non-presence. A lengthy documentary features a detailed and frank account of the shooting of the film, with excellent interviews of the producers and key actors. Dustin Hoffman gives a very open and generous interview and is obviously very proud of the film. Meryl Streep is just as charming as you'd think she'd be. —GE

Movie: 🦴🦴🦴🦴 **DVD:** 🦴🦴🦴 ½
Columbia Tristar (cat #04858, UPC 0433-96048584). Widescreen (1.85:1) anamorphic. Dolby Digital 5.1 Surround. $24.95. Keepcase. *LANG:* English. *FEATURES:* Trailers • "Making of" documentary.
1979 (PG) 105m/C Dustin Hoffman, Meryl Streep, Jane Alexander, Justin Henry, Howard Duff, JoBeth Williams; **D:** Robert Benton; **W:** Robert Benton; **C:** Nestor Almendros. *AWARDS:* Oscars '79: Actor (Hoffman), Adapt. Screenplay, Director (Benton), Picture, Support. Actress (Streep); Directors Guild '79: Director (Benton); Golden Globes '80: Actor—Drama (Hoffman), Film—Drama, Screenplay, Support. Actress (Streep); L.A. Film Critics '79: Actor (Hoffman), Director (Benton), Film, Screenplay, Support. Actress (Streep); Natl. Bd. of Review '79: Support. Actress (Streep); N.Y. Film Critics '79: Actor (Hoffman), Film, Support. Actress

(Streep); Natl. Soc. Film Critics '79: Actor (Hoffman), Director (Benton), Support. Actress (Streep); Writers Guild '79: Adapt. Screenplay; *NOM:* Oscars '79: Cinematog., Film Editing, Support. Actor (Henry), Support. Actress (Alexander).

La Cage aux Folles

This is the well-oiled French farce that inspired *The Birdcage*. The film is adapted from Jean Poiret's stage play of the same name. The script is from the old school of "the well-made play" where the first two acts are entertaining exposition for a hilarious third act. Michel Serrault's outrageous performance as Albin keeps the flick funny from start to finish. The comedy holds up despite the historical snapshot of a time when homosexuality was just barely becoming acceptable, only a few years before the AIDS crisis began. In the story, Renato's son Laurent announces his engagement to Andrea, the daughter of the leader of the Morality Political Party. Unable to tell her parents the truth about Laurent's father (owner of a cabaret of female impersonators), Andrea says Renato is a diplomat in the arts. Her parents are anxious to meet the prospective in-laws and drive to St. Tropez for dinner with them. The problem is, they live above the nightclub, the décor of their apartment borders on brothel, and Albin refuses to make himself scarce. Hiding the erotic art and getting the flighty maid to wear his shoes are just the beginning of what turns out to be a spontaneously combustible evening. The print used for the DVD is not the best, but it's outweighed by the quality of the comedy. If you can handle the subtitles, you'll find it's funnier than watching the dubbed version, and well worth the effort. —JAS **AKA:** Birds of a Feather.

Movie: 🦴🦴🦴 ½ **DVD:** 🦴🦴
MGM Home Ent. (cat #1002216, UPC 027-616844475). Widescreen (1.66:1) letterboxed. Dolby Digital Mono. $19.98. Keepcase. *LANG:* English; French. *SUB:* English; French; Spanish. *FEATURES:* Original theatrical trailer.
1978 (R) 91m/C *FR* Ugo Tognazzi, Michel Serrault, Michel Galabru, Claire Maurier, Remy Laurent, Benny Luke, Carmen Scarpitta, Luisa Maneri; **D:** Edouard Molinaro; **W:** Edouard Molinaro, Francis Veber, Jean Poiret, Marcello Danon; **C:** Armando Nannuzzi; **M:** Ennio Morricone. *AWARDS:* Cesar '79: Actor (Serrault); Golden Globes '80: Foreign Film; *NOM:* Oscars '79: Adapt. Screenplay, Costume Des., Director (Molinaro).

La Cage aux Folles 2

What a drop in quality from the original this piece of tripe turns out to be. If it weren't for the fact that the lead characters are gay, this could be a bad sequel to *That Darn Cat*. In an effort to prove he can still turn heads while in drag, Albin (Serrault) plants himself at a café and waits for attention. What he gets is a spy on the

run dragging him to a hotel room—Albin mistakes the gent's intentions—where the spy dies. The guy chasing him dies, and our two heroes suddenly find themselves entangled with the Secret Service, who now want to use Albin as bait. Most farce is an amalgam of contrivances for the purpose of humorously plucking the strings of tension, but this one fails to establish an even remotely believable situation, resulting in weak jests and poorly played chords. Renato (Tognazzi) had forbidden Albin to dress as a woman, and now the Secret Service wants Albin in drag for their mission. When Albin and Renato escape both sides of the spy game for Italy, Albin must keep wearing dresses and pass for a real woman when he meets Renato's mother. The problem is, Albin loves being in drag. It's not very funny to dress up a duck as a duck. Who cares? To escape Italy, Albin has to maintain his charade as a woman but dressed as a man. The print used in the making of this DVD version contains all the charm of a film print from the '80s. It can be a bit cloudy at points with the occasional scratch. The music gets monotonous, the story is lame, and the actors make valiant efforts to make it all fly, but the comedy never really lasts beyond an occasional chuckle. It is, however, funnier in French. Stick to the subtitles and avoid the dubbed version. What a pity they tried for a trilogy. —JAS

Movie: 🦴 **DVD:** 🦴🦴
MGM Home Ent. (cat #1002217, UPC 027-616864482). Widescreen (1.66:1) letterboxed. Dolby Digital Mono. $19.98. Keepcase. *LANG:* French; English; Spanish. *SUB:* English; French; Spanish. *FEATURES:* Original theatrical trailer • 22 chapters.
1981 (R) 101m/C *FR* Ugo Tognazzi, Michel Serrault, Marcel Bozzuffi, Michel Galabru, Benny Luke; **D:** Edouard Molinaro; **W:** Francis Veber; **C:** Armando Nannuzzi; **M:** Ennio Morricone.

La Promesse

Young Igor (Renier) and his father Roger (Gourmet) are out to make a buck, but not by the most scrupulous of measures. They have horned out a living by bringing immigrants over the borders into France and providing them with illegal paperwork and substandard housing. Despite the less than ideal lifestyle that Igor has grown up in, he still cares for his father very much. Those feelings begin to change when the young boy witnesses his father cover up an accident involving one of the boarders, which results in the loss of a life. Now, Igor must betray a father's trust as he struggles to honor a promise made to care for the surviving family of the deceased man. This is an engaging and powerful story of a boy who must reconcile his devotion to his father with his own ethical standing. This movie is truly a triumph of independent film. The DVD release sports a very nice transfer with crisp edges, good coloring, and no noticeable dusty artifacts on the film. The Dolby Digital soundtrack on the film makes good

use of the speakers. It provides a clear and clean dialogue track with no noticeable hissing, popping, or other audible anomalies. The original trailer is included, but unfortunately there is no commentary track. —EL **AKA:** The Promise.
Movie: ♪♪♪ ½ **DVD:** ♪♪♪
New Yorker Video (cat #62402, UPC 7171-19624248). Widescreen anamorphic. Dolby Digital Surround. $29.95. Keepcase. *LANG:* French. *SUB:* English; Italian. *FEATURES:* European trailer ⁕ Cast and crew filmographies ⁕ Photo gallery ⁕ 16 chapters.
1996 93m/C *FR BE* Jeremie Renier, Olivier Gourmet, Assita Ouedraogo, Rasmane Ouedraogo; *D:* Jean-Pierre Dardenne, Luc Dardenne; *W:* Jean-Pierre Dardenne, Luc Dardenne; *C:* Alain Marcoen; *M:* Jean-Marie Billy. *AWARDS:* L.A. Film Critics '97: Foreign Film; Natl. Soc. Film Critics '97: Foreign Film.

La Sentinelle

Deliberately paced Hitchcockian suspense film begins with morose Mathias (Salinger) travelling by train from Germany to France to attend medical school. The sinister Bleicher (Richard), who seems to be a customs official, grills Mathias in a very strange scene but lets him go. Later, the younger man discovers a shrunken head in his luggage. The film is never as fully engaging as a thriller needs to be, but it does have its moments. Unfortunately, DVD is little improvement over tape. Artifacts are exceptionally heavy in exterior panning shots and most interiors are very dim. The unflattering lighting seems to come from the original. The subtitles are burned in. —MM **AKA:** The Sentinel.
Movie: ♪♪♪ **DVD:** ♪♪
Winstar Home Ent. (cat #5116). Widescreen (1.66:1) letterboxed. $29.98. Keepcase. *LANG:* French. *SUB:* English. *FEATURES:* Production notes ⁕ Cast and crew thumbnail bios ⁕ 8 chapters.
1992 139m/C *FR* Emmanuel Salinger, Jean-Louis Richard, Thibault de Montalembert, Valerie Dreville, Marianne (Cuau) Denicourt, Bruno Todeschini, Jean-Luc Boutte; *D:* Arnaud Desplechin; *W:* Arnaud Desplechin; *C:* Caroline Champetier; *M:* Marc Oliver Sommer.

The Lady and the Highwayman

TV adaptation of Barbara Cartland novel finds a rogue (Grant) falling for the lady (Anthony) he is protecting. Naturally, there's a happy ending but only the most dedicated viewer will reach it. This DVD is one of the very worst ever made. Image looks like a third generation dupe created on cheap dirty equipment. Absolutely unwatchable. —MM
Movie: ♪♪ ½ **DVD:** woof
BCI-Eclipse (cat #44077-9, UPC 7873644-07798). Full frame. Dolby Digital Stereo. $14.99. Keepcase. *LANG:* English. *FEATURES:* "Came the Brawn" Little Rascals short ⁕ DVD Dictionary ⁕ Trivia game ⁕ DVD-ROM features ⁕ 6 chapters.

1989 100m/C *GB* Hugh Grant, Emma Samms, Oliver Reed, Michael York, Robert Morley, John Mills, Lysette Anthony; *D:* John Hough; *W:* Terence Feely; *M:* Laurie Johnson.

Lady Blue

Distasteful animated horror/erotica is more of the same old schoolgirls, monsters, and magic. Nothing about the animation or the characters is notable. Image and sound are equal to VHS tape. Language options are the only improvement. —MM
Movie: ♪ ½ **DVD:** ♪♪
Central Park/U.S. Manga (UPC 71998718-3520). Full frame. $29.98. Keepcase. *LANG:* Japanese; English. *SUB:* English. *FEATURES:* 9 chapters ⁕ About Toshio Maeda ⁕ Meet the cast excerpts ⁕ Trailers ⁕ Art gallery.
1996 60m/C *D:* Toshio Maeda.

The Lady Eve

Perhaps the best Sturges comedy of them all. Stanwyck is the playfully conniving junior member of a father-and-daughter card shark team who demonstrates her playful wickedness when she drops an apple core on the head of Fonda, the wealthy-but-naïve snake enthusiast and beer tycoon who is their latest prey. But Stanwyck is knocked off her game when she falls hard for Fonda, whom she affectionately calls "Hopsy." They enjoy a shipboard romance, but their fun is over when Fonda discovers who she really is and dumps her. Later, Stanwyck exacts her revenge on him by pretending to be the Lady Eve, a rich British visitor who winds up winning Fonda's affection all over again. Then they bust up again, only he still doesn't realize it's the same dame. It'll all work out in the end, but getting there is the fun. The situations are frankly ridiculous, but writer/director Sturges manages to keep the flick believable and funny every preposterous step of the way. He is helped mightily in this endeavor by the sincere performances of his leads, who are backed convincingly by screwball comedy veterans Pallette, Demarest, and Blore, among others. Based on the story "The Faithful Heart" by Monckton Hoffe. Later remade as *The Birds and the Bees*. The DVD gets the predictably first-rate Criterion treatment, with a beautiful B&W transfer and a quite serviceable monaural soundtrack. Contrast is quite good, with deep blacks in the relatively blemish-free image. Extras are generous, as is the case also with Criterion's disc of *Sullivan's Travels*, also by Sturges. —MB
Movie: ♪♪♪♪ **DVD:** ♪♪♪ ½
Criterion (cat #CC1567D, UPC 7155150-11624). Full frame. Dolby Digital Mono. $39.95. Keepcase. *LANG:* English. *SUB:* English. *FEATURES:* 26 chapters ⁕ Commentary: film scholar Marian Keane ⁕ Video intro by writer/director Peter Bogdanovich ⁕ 1942 radio adaptation performed by Stanwyck and Milland ⁕ Edith Head costume designs ⁕ Scrapbook of

original publicity materials and production stills ⁕ Original theatrical trailer.
1941 93m/B Barbara Stanwyck, Henry Fonda, Charles Coburn, Eugene Pallette, William Demarest, Eric Blore, Melville Cooper; *D:* Preston Sturges; *W:* Preston Sturges; *C:* Victor Milner. *AWARDS:* Natl. Film Reg. '94; *NOM:* Oscars '41: Story.

Lady for a Day

Frank Capra Jr. provides an introduction and a nostalgic commentary track for the DVD of one of his father's early hits. It's an adaptation of a Damon Runyon story about an apple peddler (Robson) who is transformed into a grand dame by gambler Dave the Dude (William) to fool her visiting daughter. It's very light material, handled with the Capra touch that would strike gold the next year—1934—with *It Happened One Night*. A minimum amount of flecks and dust are visible, but the image is in excellent shape for a film of this age. Sound is typical of the era. Capra remade the film as *Pocketful of Miracles* in 1961. —MM
Movie: ♪♪♪ **DVD:** ♪♪♪
Image Ent. (cat #ID0853FCDVD, UPC 014-381085327). Full frame. Dolby Digital Mono. $24.98. Keepcase. *LANG:* English. *FEATURES:* 19 chapters ⁕ Intro and commentary by Frank Capra Jr.
1933 96m/B May Robson, Warren William, Guy Kibbee, Glenda Farrell, Ned Sparks, Jean Parker, Walter Connolly; *D:* Frank Capra; *W:* Robert Riskin; *C:* Joseph Walker. *AWARDS: NOM:* Oscars '33: Actress (Robson), Adapt. Screenplay, Director (Capra), Picture.

Lady Frankenstein

Frankenstein's (Cotton) beautiful daughter (Neri) graduates from med school and comes back home. When she sees what dear old dad's been up to, she gets some ideas of her own. Cotton brings some brief class to this drive-in exploitation before making an early exit. With the familiar dubbing, the film sounds a bit like a gladiator movie. DVD can do little to improve this exceptionally grainy, poorly focused image. The funky chapter titles show that the disc's producers understand the nature of the material perfectly. The Rosalba Neri interview was shot on video with poor lighting and sound. —MM **AKA:** La Figlia di Frankenstein; The Daughter of Frankenstein; Madame Frankenstein.
Movie: ♪ ½ **DVD:** ♪♪
DVD Drive-In (cat #F1M1S390106). Widescreen anamorphic. $29.95. Keepcase. *LANG:* English. *FEATURES:* 27 chapters ⁕ Photo and stills gallery ⁕ Trailer and TV spot ⁕ Cast and crew thumbnail bios ⁕ Interview with director Mel Welles.
1972 (R) 84m/C *IT* Joseph Cotten, Rosalba (Sara Bay) Neri, Mickey Hargitay, Paul Muller, Herbert (Fuchs) Fux, Renate Kasche, Ada Pometti, Lorenzo Terzon, Paul Whiteman; *D:* Mel Welles; *W:* Edward Di Lorenzo; *C:* Riccardo (Pallton) Pallottini.

Lady in Blue

L.A. police detective Carla (Reed) has bodice-ripping fantasies and goes undercover as a hooker in this very low-budget, tepid soft-core frippery. Production values are so low that it's difficult to tell where the graininess of the original image ends and the digital artifacts begin. Whatever the case, the pixelation is so heavy that it appears to be painted on in some shots. This one really looks worse than tape. No-frills disc lacks even a menu. —MM
Movie: ♪ **DVD:** woof
York Ent. (cat #YPD-1163, UPC 75072311-6327). Full frame. $14.98. Keepcase. *LANG:* English. *FEATURES:* 15 chapters.
1996 (R) 90m/C Kira Reed, Larry Gund, Jyl Dillon, John St. John, Kimberly Blair, Steve Long; **D:** Michael Paul Girard; **W:** Michael Paul Girard; **C:** Denis Maloney; **M:** Michael Paul Girard.

Lady in Red

John Sayles wrote this early script for a Corman production that's almost a companion piece to Martin Scorsese's *Boxcar Bertha*. Trying to make her way in the tough times of the 1930s, Polly Franklin (Martin) finds herself in all sorts of trouble, and finally winds up at Anna's (Fletcher) bordello. Then she meets John Dillinger (Conrad). Christopher Lloyd has a nice supporting role as a mobster and James Horner *(Titanic)* wrote the score. The whole thing is fast-paced with oodles of violence, sex, and humor. There's not much DVD can do with the low-budget image. Very heavy artifacts bloom from the original heavy grain. Even daylight exteriors tend to look dim. Only the extras differentiate this one from VHS tape, but it's still a lot of fun. —MM **AKA:** Guns, Sin and Bathtub Gin.
Movie: ♪♪♪ **DVD:** ♪♪
New Concorde (cat #NH20199 D, UPC 736991419995). Full frame. $14.98. Keepcase. *LANG:* English. *FEATURES:* 24 chapters • Filmographies • Trailers.
1979 90m/C Pamela Sue Martin, Louise Fletcher, Robert Conrad, Christopher Lloyd, Dick Miller, Laurie Heineman, Robert Hogan, Glenn Withrow, Rod Gist, Mary Woronov; **D:** Lewis Teague; **W:** John Sayles; **C:** Daniel Lacambre; **M:** James Horner.

Lady Iron Monkey

A girl is raised by apes and ends up in the court of the Ching Dynasty. Her simian upbringing makes her a natural at Monkey Style kung fu. When the Emperor betrays the 8 Heroes, killing half of them in an explosion, she joins them in open rebellion. A fanciful and offbeat kung fu movie from director Chen Chi-hwa, who made the early Jackie Chan vehicles *Half a Loaf of Kung Fu* and *Snake & Crane Arts of Shaolin*. The full-frame transfer, from a decent print for its age, is reasonably vivid, but slightly squeezed horizontally. Released as a *Brooklyn Zoo Double Feature* with *Eagle Fist*. The packaging promi-

nently features the World Trade Center towers and the package notes that "A portion of proceeds to benefit NYC relief charities." —BT **AKA:** Ape Girl; Fighting Justice.
Movie: ♪♪ ½ **DVD:** ♪♪
Xenon Ent. (UPC 694795305626). Full frame. Dolby Digital 2.0. $9.99. Keepcase. *LANG:* English. *FEATURES:* 6 chapters • Trailers.
1983 85m/C *TW* Fung Kam, Ringo Chan, Lo Lieh; **D:** Chi-Hwa Chen; **W:** Juen Hau; **C:** Chung Yun Chan; **M:** Sat San Wang.

Lagaan: Once upon a Time in India

A beautiful epic story of life and death in India, somewhat on the scope of Sergio Leone's best films. The film's cinematography is a highlight of this disc and is really showcased by the exceptional video transfer. Colors are bright and sharp, and blacks are well-defined. While some print flaws are evident, they are minimal. The similarly well-done soundtrack boasts crisp, clear dialogue and an impressive musical score. —MJT
Movie: ♪♪♪ **DVD:** ♪♪♪
Columbia Tristar (cat #07961, UPC 0433-96079618). Widescreen (2.35:1) anamorphic. Dolby Digital 5.1 Surround; Dolby Digital Surround. $27.96. Keepcase. *LANG:* English; Hindi. *SUB:* English; Spanish; French; Portuguese; Chinese; Korean; Thai. *FEATURES:* 52 chapters • "Scene Unseen" • Filmographies • Production notes.
2001 225m/C *IN* Aamir Khan, Gracy Singh, Rachel Shelley, Paul Blackthorne, Suhasini Mulay, Kulbasan Kharbanda, Raghubir Yadav; **D:** Ashutosh Gowariker; **W:** Ashutosh Gowariker; **C:** Anil Mehta; **M:** A.R. Rahman.

Lantana

The densely tangled Australian plant that provides the title is a reflection of the lives of the characters in this complex psychological mystery. Police detective Leon Zat (LaPaglia, at his considerable best) is investigating a missing-person case while attempting to deal with his own infidelity and guilt. Do NOT watch the trailer before the feature because it contains some spoilers. The film works through careful revelation of characters who are notably lacking in the glamour that a Hollywood production typically applies to this kind of story. Instead, they're much more real and the film is all the more compelling for that. DVD image and sound are everything you'd expect from a contemporary studio release—flawless. The film is serious enough to rate a commentary track. —MM
Movie: ♪♪♪ ½ **DVD:** ♪♪♪
Lion's Gate Home Ent. (cat #VM8020D, UPC 031398802020). Widescreen (2.35:1) anamorphic. Dolby Digital 5.1 Surround. $24.98. Keepcase. *LANG:* English. *SUB:* English; Spanish. *CAP:* English. *FEATURES:* Trailers • "Nature of Lantana" featurette • 24 chapters.

2001 (R) 120m/C *AU* Anthony LaPaglia, Kerry Armstrong, Geoffrey Rush, Barbara Hershey, Rachael Blake, Vince Colosimo, Peter Phelps, Daniela Farinacci, Leah Purcell, Glenn Robbins; **D:** Ray Lawrence; **W:** Andrew Bovell; **C:** Mandy Walker; **M:** Paul Kelly. *AWARDS:* Australian Film Inst. '01: Actor (LaPaglia), Actress (Armstrong), Adapt. Screenplay, Director (Lawrence), Film, Support. Actor (Colosimo), Support. Actress (Blake).

L.A.P.D.: To Protect and Serve

Fact-based story focuses on a group of bad cops led by Lt. Alexander (Madsen). Officer Steele (Singer) has to decide what to do after he catches them in the act. It's a fair police drama that gains little on this no-frills DVD. Image and sound are equal to VHS tape. —MM
Movie: ♪♪ **DVD:** ♪♪
MTI (cat #9701, UPC 039414597011). Full frame. Dolby Digital Surround. $24.95. Keepcase. *LANG:* English. *FEATURES:* 12 chapters.
2001 98m/C Dennis Hopper, Michael Madsen, Charles Durning, Marc Singer; **D:** Ed Anders; **W:** Rob Neighbors; **C:** Michael Balery.

Lara Croft: Tomb Raider

Adaptation of the popular game has all the depth of characterization found in the original, along with star Angelina Jolie's really weird-looking lips. The obligatory (but essentially unnecessary) plot has to do with a gizmo that can alter space and time. The Illuminati, long-time favorite villains of assorted conspiracy-theorists, are the bad guys. The British accents affected by Jolie and her father Jon Voight are rotten. DVD presents the flawless image you expect from a big-budget studio release. Surround effects are well integrated and impressive in the overly frantic action scenes. Intricate menus are neat. Click on the squiggle at the bottom of Special Features to go to an interview with Jolie and Voight. —MM **AKA:** Tomb Raider.
Movie: ♪♪ **DVD:** ♪♪♪
Paramount (cat #33675, UPC 097363367-543). Widescreen anamorphic. Dolby Digital 5.1 Surround Stereo; Dolby Digital Surround. $29.99. Keepcase. *LANG:* English; French. *SUB:* English. *CAP:* English. *FEATURES:* 12 chapters • "Making of" featurette • Commentary: Simon Weist • "Crafting Lara Croft" featurette • Visual effects featurette • Game featurette • 4 deleted scenes • DVD-ROM features • Alternate title sequence • U2 Music video.
2001 (PG-13) 96m/C Angelina Jolie, Iain Glen, Daniel Craig, Leslie Phillips, Jon Voight, Noah Taylor, Richard Johnson, Julian Rhind-Tutt, Chris (Christopher) Barrie; **D:** Simon West; **W:** Patrick Massett, John Zinman; **C:** Peter Menzies Jr.; **M:** Graeme Revell.

Larceny

Two Canadian TV miniseries, *Love and Larceny* and *Grand Larceny*, are combined in the story of 19th-century conwoman Betsy Bigley (Dale). Comparisons to *Moll Flanders* are appropriate but only to a point. This one's not quite as raunchy and rambunctious as it could have been. Still, production values are fine. Grain and irritating pixels are fairly heavy in the first disc. Image is better in the second, but still won't knock anyone's eyes out. Acting is excellent throughout. —*MM* **AKA:** Love and Larceny; Grand Larceny.
Movie: 🎬🎬 ½ **DVD:** 🎬🎬
BFS Video (cat #30196-D, UPC 06680530-1964). Full frame. $39.98. Keepcase boxed set. *LANG:* English. *FEATURES:* 24 chapters ● Cast thumbnail bios ● Production stills.
1991 243m/C CA Jennifer Dale, Victor Garber, Douglas Rain, Kenneth Welsh, Robert Joy, Brent Carver, Sheila McCarthy; **D:** Robert Iscove, Stephen Surjik; **W:** Douglas Bowie.

The Larry Sanders Show: The Complete First Season

Ever wonder what the late-night host and guest are chatting about as they go to commercial? This HBO series, starring Garry Shandling as the wildly insecure comic Larry Sanders, broke new ground in TV comedy, acknowledging that Letterman, Leno, and Carson-savvy viewers were plenty educated in the late night ratings wars, and were ready to go backstage. As Sanders, Shandling parlayed his neurotic stage persona into a lovable comic character who can't help sabotaging his romances (with first season girlfriend Linda Doucette), and his working life (with sidekick Jeffrey Tambor). Image quality is not a huge improvement over broadcast or VHS. —*JE*
Movie: 🎬🎬🎬 ½ **DVD:** 🎬🎬
Columbia Tristar (cat #04759, UPC 043-396047594). Full frame. Dolby Digital Surround. $50.95. Keepcase. *LANG:* English. *SUB:* English; Spanish. *FEATURES:* Shandling interview with critic Tom Shales.
1992 322m/C Garry Shandling, Jeffrey Tambor.

Las Vegas Lady

Three shrewd casino hostesses (Stevens, Moody, Scruggs) plot a multi-million dollar heist. The machinations of the caper are distinctly non-captivating. In the second half, however, Ms. Stevens is constantly in danger of falling out of her low-cut dress. She succeeds in maintaining her modesty. Image and sound are indistinguishable from VHS tape. —*MM*
Movie: 🎬 ½ **DVD:** 🎬 ½
Rhino (cat #R2 976011, UPC 603497601-127). Full frame. $19.98. Snapper. *LANG:* English. *FEATURES:* 15 chapters.
1976 (PG) 90m/C Stella Stevens, Stuart Whitman, George de Cecenzo, Andrew

Stevens, Lynne Moody, Linda Scruggs; **D:** Noel Nosseck; **W:** Walter Dallenbach; **C:** Stephen M. Katz; **M:** Alan Silvestri.

Lassie

This feature film updates the classic *Lassie* story to a modern setting, but never tampers with the tried-and-true formula of the old TV show and movies. To try and change their luck, the Turner family moves away from the city and into the Virginia countryside. There, troubled youngster Matthew Turner (Tom Guiry) meets a stray collie, Lassie. Parents Laura (Helen Slater) and Steve (Jon Tenney) are pleased to see that befriending the dog has helped to bring Matthew out of his shell. Things go sour when a local rancher begins to make trouble for the Turners. It's up to Lassie to save the day, as he (she?) proves that this dog will go to any lengths to protect Matthew. This is wholesome family fun that will entertain youngsters and remind older viewers of the *Lassie* stories on which they were raised. The mountain scenery is beautiful and veteran director Daniel Petrie keeps things moving along at a nice pace. Look for *Dawson's Creek* star Michelle Williams, making her film debut. As with most Paramount discs, the *Lassie* DVD looks and sounds fantastic. The transfer is free from any serious defects; the image is very sharp and clear, and there is only a minute amount of grain. The colors are fantastic, and the clarity of the image gives great depth and texture to the landscape shots. The Dolby Digital 5.1 audio track provides clear dialogue and really comes to life during the exciting finale, when the Surround sound action adds a great deal of depth to the scene. —*ML*
Movie: 🎬🎬 ½ **DVD:** 🎬🎬 ½
Paramount (cat #33034, UPC 0973633-03442). Widescreen (1.85:1) anamorphic. Dolby Digital 5.1; Dolby Surround. $24.99. Keepcase. *LANG:* English. *SUB:* English. *CAP:* English. *FEATURES:* 11 chapters.
1994 (PG) 92m/C Helen Slater, Jon Tenney, Tom Guiry, Brittany Boyd, Richard Farnsworth, Frederic Forrest, Michelle Williams; **D:** Daniel Petrie; **W:** Matthew Jacobs, Gary Ross, Elizabeth Anderson; **C:** Kenneth Macmillan; **M:** Basil Poledouris.

The Last Castle

When decorated military hero Gen. Eugene Irwin (Redford) is convicted of a military crime and sent to prison for 10 years, the last thing he expects is to face another war, but that is exactly what he gets. After witnessing the brutal force employed by the ruthless prison warden (Gandolfini), Irwin decides he must earn the prisoners' confidence, and help them to rise above their mistreatment and make a change for the better. This soggy action-packed romp is designed to glorify nationalism and the determination of the human spirit. It's hindered by a soft, unbelievable story line. The jewel of this release, however, is the quality of picture and sound.

The image is exceptionally clear with vibrant color and no noticeable artifacts. The action sequences are smooth and clear with no aliasing on fast pans. The 5.1 Surround track is scorching. It makes complete use of all five speakers while being crisp and clear and it delivers great sound quality at high-volume levels. —*EL*
Movie: 🎬🎬 ½ **DVD:** 🎬🎬🎬 ½
DreamWorks Home Ent. (cat #89870, UPC 67068987027). Widescreen (2.40:1) anamorphic. Dolby 5.1 Surround; DTS 5.1 Surround; Dolby Surround. $26.99. Keepcase. *LANG:* English; French; Spanish. *SUB:* French; Spanish. *CAP:* English. *FEATURES:* Deleted scenes with commentary ● HBO Special: *Inside the Castle Walls* ● Commentary: director ● Theatrical trailer ● Production notes ● Cast and filmmaker bios.
2001 (R) 133m/C Robert Redford, James Gandolfini, Mark Ruffalo, Delroy Lindo, Steve (Stephen) Burton, Paul Calderon, Samuel Ball, Clifton (Gonzalez) Collins Jr., Frank Military, George W. Scott, Brian Goodman, Michael Irby, Maurice Bullard, Jeremy Childs; **D:** Rod Lurie; **W:** Graham Yost, David Scarpa; **C:** Shelly Johnson; **M:** Jerry Goldsmith.

The Last Days of Pompeii

This silent Italian costume drama is really more theatrical than cinematic. As the brief liner notes explain, it was made before the advent of many modern techniques. A title card describes what's about to happen; then the scene is played out before a motionless camera in one wide shot. Given the age and stodginess of the material, it's recommended now only to serious students of the silent era. DVD is made from a print that looks pretty good early on, but deteriorates toward the end as minimal signs of wear become very rough. Some stretches are almost blank. —*MM*
Movie: 🎬 ½ **DVD:** 🎬🎬 ½
Kino on Video (cat #K186, UPC 73832901-8627). Full frame. $29.95. Keepcase. *LANG:* Silent. *SUB:* English intertitles. *FEATURES:* 12 chapters ● New piano score by Beatrice Jona Affron.
1913 88m/B IT Fernanda Negri Pouget, Eugenia Tettoni Fior; **D:** Mario Caserini; **W:** Mario Caserini; **M:** Martha Koeneman.

The Last Dragon

Harlem homeboy Leroy Green (Taimak), AKA Bruce Leroy or "the walking fortune cookie," is a kung-fu student looking to attain the highest level of enlightenment. He is sidetracked by Sho'nuff (Carry III), a loony who considers himself to be the Shogun of Harlem, leading to lots of kung-fu fighting and bad '80s music. It's hard to tell how much of this is intentionally campy and how much is simply misguided, but the film is certainly good for some laughs. As is often the case with movies from this period, the picture is a bit hazy and low on detail. The two-channel soundtrack handles the punches and funky

dance grooves nicely. —*BG* **AKA:** Berry Gordy's The Last Dragon.
Movie: 🎵🎵 ½ **DVD:** 🎵🎵 ½
Columbia Tristar (cat #05985, UPC 04339-6059856). Widescreen (1.85:1) anamorphic. Dolby Surround. $19.95. Keepcase. *LANG:* English; French; Portuguese. *SUB:* English; French; Portuguese; Chinese; Korean; Thai; Spanish. *CAP:* English. *FEATURES:* 28 chapters • Trailers • Filmographies • Production notes.
1985 (PG-13) 108m/C Taimak, Vanity, Christopher Murney, Julius J. Carry III, Faith Prince; **D:** Michael A. Schultz; **W:** Louis Venosta; **C:** James A. Contner; **M:** Misha Segal.

Last Hurrah for Chivalry

Kao's wedding is vehemently disrupted by his arch-enemy Pai, who kills Kao's entire family. Kao seeks vengeance, but knowing that Pai is too much for him to handle, Kao decides to hire the best swordsman in the country. Eventually he meets Chang, a young man with a reputation as a superb blademaster. Kao helps the impoverished young man and builds a friendship with him, so that he can use him for his plans and then sends Chang off to finish Pai. But it appears as if Kao has more on his mind than simply revenge. Although the story itself is developing very slowly and drags at many points, the countless sword fighting sequences are mesmerizing and absolutely amazing. Especially the climactic fights—each of them running for well over five minutes of man-to-man dueling—are masterfully executed. As with most Hong Kong imports, there are some blemishes in the transfer, but for the most part I was pleasantly surprised by the clean transfer offered on this release. Although inconsistent, the color reproduction is well done, bringing us strong colors that are free of noise or bleeding. Skin tones are naturally rendered. Blacks are deep throughout with good shadow definition. Some pixelation is evident but I never found it distracting. The DVD contains three separate language tracks. The first one is what seems to be the original Cantonese track. Presented in 5.1 Dolby Digital, this track has a very pleasing quality with a good frequency response and good dynamics. However, the Surrounds are mostly dead, and only the stereo field is used quite effectively. The second track is a Dolby Digital 5.1 Mandarin track, which to my surprise also features different music than the Cantonese track. This language track is also quite good, although a bit harsh-sounding in quality and with less transparence. Last up is the English track, but you might as well forget it's there, because the quality is quite poor. The dub is poorly synched up with the video and, even worse, it's distorted from beginning to end. That's not really a big drawback since most fans will want to watch the film in the Cantonese version anyway. —*GH/MM* **AKA:** Hao xia.

Movie: 🎵🎵 ½ **DVD:** 🎵🎵🎵
Tai Seng (UPC 601643045344). Widescreen (2.35:1) letterboxed. Dolby Digital 5.1 Surround. $29.98. Keepcase. *LANG:* Cantonese; Mandarin; English. *SUB:* Chinese; English. *FEATURES:* Trailer • Filmographies.
1978 108m/C *HK* Damian Lau, Wei Pei, San Lee Hoi; **D:** John Woo; **W:** John Woo; **C:** Ching Yu, Yao Chu Chang.

The Last Laugh

In this classic silent film, a hotel doorman (Jannings), who takes an inordinate amount of pride in the job and his uniform, is crassly demoted to a men's room attendant. His family and his neighbors, who had previously shown much affection and respect for him, mock his plight, which brings him to the edge of despair. *The Last Laugh* is almost unbearably sad until the wonderful (studio imposed) upbeat finale. This highly influential film is told kinetically with an active, frequently moving camera and surreal sections that convey the interior paranoia and despair of the doorman. The "hangover" sequence is a must-see; it's delightfully evocative and loopy. The transfer features an overbright print with low contrasts. Though frequently scratched and prone to all manner of damage, the content of the images is always readable. The edges of objects tend to show some digital shimmer. The effective orchestral score by Timothy Brock sounds terrific. Although the story is told virtually without intertitles, there is a small section about 3/4 into the film that requires them. It is told in English on this disc, but the original hand-written German intertitle sequence is included as a bonus. The photo gallery is excellent and the insert card is a reproduction of a promotional card from the original U.S. release. It features an amusingly overwrought synopsis. —*DG* **AKA:** Der Letzte Mann.
Movie: 🎵🎵🎵 **DVD:** 🎵🎵🎵
Kino on Video (cat #K206DVD, UPC 73832-9020620). Full frame. Dolby Stereo. $29.95. Keepcase. *LANG:* Silent. *FEATURES:* 12 chapters • Insert card • Photo gallery • German intertitle sequence.
1924 88m/B *GE* Emil Jannings, Maly Delshaft, Max Hiller; **D:** F.W. Murnau; **W:** Carl Mayer; **C:** Karl Freund; **M:** Giuseppe Becce.

The Last Man on Earth

In this adaptation of Richard Matheson's novel *I Am Legend*, Price stars as the titular character. After a plague kills most of the world, immune scientist Morgan hunts down the vampiric population by day and fends off his home by night. This U.S./Italian co-production is an interesting attempt but becomes clunky about halfway through. Despite some location filming, the production values occasionally seem cheap. The image is grainy, smeary, soft, and prone to digital shimmer and pixelation. Audio is O.K. Title is available on the

Great Bloodsucking Movies disc. —*DG* **AKA:** L'Ultimo Uomo Della Terra.
Movie: 🎵🎵 **DVD:** 🎵🎵
BFS Video (cat #30237-D, UPC 066805-302374). Widescreen (2.35:1) letterboxed. Mono. $9.98. Keepcase. *LANG:* English. *FEATURES:* 6 chapters • Cast bios/filmographies.
1964 86m/B *IT* Vincent Price, Franca Bettoya, Giacomo "Jack" Rossi-Stuart, Emma Danieli; **D:** Ubaldo Ragona, Sidney Salkow; **W:** Richard Matheson, William P. Leicester, Furio M. Menotti; **C:** Franco Delli Colli; **M:** Paul Sawtell, Bert Shefter.

The Last of the Blue Devils

This documentary focuses on the reunion of some of the most famous jazzmen from Kansas City. Forty years after they got their start, such jazz and blues greats as Count Basie, Big Joe Turner, and Jay McShann return to the hall where they first begin to play. The film features performances by the aforementioned legends, being accompanied by other greats such as Eddie Durham, Eric Dixon, and Charles McPherson. Along with the reunion footage, there are archival clips showing these in earlier performances, as well as interviews. This one's a must for jazz enthusiasts and those who enjoy tracing the history of American music. Unfortunately, the DVD is a disappointment. The image is cloudy and very grainy at times, showing the film's age. Also, the colors are washed-out and the picture is often quite soft. The audio is clear, reproducing the music and dialogue well, but as the music is the true star of the movie, a Surround sound remastering would have been much more appropriate. On the plus side, the disc does offer four performances which were left out of the original cut of the film. —*ML*
Movie: 🎵🎵 ½ **DVD:** 🎵🎵
Kino on Video (cat #K168 DVD, UPC 7383-29016821). Widescreen (1.66:1) letterboxed. Digital Hi-Fi. $29.98. Keepcase. *LANG:* English. *FEATURES:* Commentary • Outtakes • 24 chapters.
1980 90m/C D: Bruce Ricker.

The Last of the Dogmen

Clichéd modern western with an intriguing premise and good actors. Montana bounty hunter Lewis Gates (Berenger) is recruited to nab three escaped cons but finds them dead and a Cheyenne arrow nearby. Gates does some investigating (in a library no less!) and discovers that maybe some descendants of the 1864 Sand Creek massacre are living in the woods. He gets anthropologist Lillian Sloan (Hershey) involved, discovers a tribe of modern-day dog soldiers, and finds a very angry sheriff (Smith) on their trail. The DVD is only a slight improvement over the VHS version due to an intermittently soft image with numerous occurrences of artifacts. (This problem gets better the further you get into the disc.) Colors don't bleed but are a little weak. Overall the picture could use a boost in contrast. The 5.1 soundtrack is good enough with good low end during music and occasional effect. The alternate soundtrack is director Murphy's preferred version, which leaves out the Wilfred Brimley narration. —JO

Movie: ♫♫ ½ **DVD:** ♫♫ ½
HBO (cat #91202, UPC 026359120220). Widescreen (1.85:1) letterboxed. Dolby Digital 5.1; Dolby Digital Stereo. $19.98. Snapper. *LANG:* English; French. *SUB:* English; Spanish; French. *FEATURES:* 34 chapters • Theatrical trailer • TV spots • Talent files • Alternate soundtrack • Commentary: director Tab Murphy • Costume sketch gallery • "Making of" featurettes.
1995 (PG) 117m/C Tom Berenger, Barbara Hershey, Kurtwood Smith, Steve Reevis, Andrew Miller, Gregory Scott Cummins; **D:** Tab Murphy; **W:** Tab Murphy; **C:** Karl Walter Lindenlaub; **M:** David Arnold; **Nar:** Wilford Brimley.

The Last Place on Earth
Epic tale of bitter hardship and ambition depicts the 1911 race between the British Antarctic Expedition led by Capt. Robert Falcon (Shaw) and his Norwegian rival Roald Amundsen (Ousdal) to reach the South Pole. DVD exhibits the heavy grain you should expect to find in older TV productions, but it's not really excessive in the many snowscapes. Image is about equal to VHS tape. —MM

Movie: ♫♫♫ **DVD:** ♫♫
BFS Video (cat #98581-D, UPC 06680591-5819). Full frame. $39.98. Keepcase boxed set. *LANG:* English. *FEATURES:* 28 chapters.
1994 385m/C *CA* Martin Shaw, Sverre Anker Ousdal, Max von Sydow, Susan Wooldridge; **D:** Ferdinand Fairfax; **W:** Trevor Griffiths; **C:** John Coquillon; **M:** Trevor Jones.

The Last Siege
Despite a severe lack of originality, this cross between *Passenger 57* and *Under Siege 2* still manages to be moderately entertaining. Jeff Fahey stars as ATF agent Eddie Lyman. After being suspended from duty, he decides to accompany his wife on a train trip, where she is working with Senator Douglas Wilson (Hudson). Terrorist David Anderson (Huff), whom Lyman had been tracking before his suspension, is on board the train and is armed with a nuclear weapon. It is now up to Lyman to defuse the bomb and save the passengers. The film is not full of surprises or ingenious plot twists, but director Worth Keeter keeps things moving along at a nice pace. Fahey does a good job as Lyman, and Hudson (who seems to be the hardest working man in direct-to-video movies) is intriguing as the friendly and regal senator. The video premiere is certainly a knock-off of many more familiar theatrical releases, but it's a fun ride. The

full-frame image is sharp, however there is some slight grain and noticeable artifacting in some shots. The colors are good and there is no overt distortion to the image. Audio offers clear dialogue and some very nice Surround effects. The mix takes advantage of the train sound effects and distributes them nicely throughout the speakers. —ML **AKA:** Hijack.

Movie: ♫♫ **DVD:** ♫♫
Artisan Ent. (cat #12626, UPC 70772912-6263). Full frame. Dolby Surround. $19.98. Keepcase. *LANG:* English. *CAP:* English. *FEATURES:* 22 chapters.
1999 94m/C Jeff Fahey, Ernie Hudson, Brent Huff, Patrick Kilpatrick; **D:** Worth Keeter; **W:** Steve Latshaw.

The Last Tattoo
In WWII New Zealand, Captain Starwood (Goldwyn) is investigating the murder of an American soldier when he crosses paths with a local nurse (Fox) trying to track the spread of a particularly nasty strain of gonorrhea. As their investigations converge, they begin to suspect a conspiracy that leads to the top of the American military base. The medical aspects of the case are perhaps the most interesting, as the mystery itself requires several plot twists that stretch credibility. Anchor Bay's transfer looks good and only stumbles a tad in exterior night scenes, in which a good deal of grain is present. The Dolby Mono track is serviceable. —BG

Movie: ♫♫ ½ **DVD:** ♫♫♫
Anchor Bay (cat #DV11618, UPC 0131311-61892). Widescreen (1.66:1) anamorphic. Dolby Mono. $24.98. Keepcase. *LANG:* English. *FEATURES:* 33 chapters • Trailer.
1994 111m/C *NZ* Kerry Fox, Tony Goldwyn, Robert Loggia, Rod Steiger; **D:** John Reid; **W:** Keith Aberdein; **C:** John Blick; **M:** John Charles.

The Last Train
Romance is almost hopeless at the beginning of World War II in France. During the 1940 invasion of Paris, a man (Trintignant) and woman (Schneider) turn to each other for comfort when separated from their families while trying to escape the city. French, very French. Serious early registrations are a hint of what's to come. Image is grainy and harsh; no better than a well-worn tape. —MM

Movie: ♫♫ **DVD:** ♫ ½
BCI-Eclipse (cat #44078-9, UPC 7873644-07897). Full frame. $9.98. Keepcase. *LANG:* English. *FEATURES:* 6 chapters • "Cobweb Hotel" cartoon • Trivia game • DVD dictionary • DVD-ROM features.
1974 101m/C *FR* Romy Schneider, Jean-Louis Trintignant, Maurice Biraud; **D:** Pierre Granier-Deferre; **W:** Pierre Granier-Deferre; **C:** Walter Wottitz; **M:** Philippe Sarde.

The Last Waltz [SE]
When The Band decided to call it quits in 1976, Martin Scorsese was enlisted by Robbie Robertson to find a way to com-

memorate it on film. It started out to be the usual 16mm catch-as-catch-can show, but as enthusiasm and backing grew, it evolved into a full-on 35mm multicamera recording, with state-of-the-art audio work and professional lighting and design. For their farewell concert at Bill Graham's Winterland in San Francisco on Thanksgiving, 1976, The Band are seen performing a slate of their best songs, joined by a score of top names who do their own material and join in a final song together. Several songs are performed under studio conditions as a change of pace. Scorsese wanted to thoroughly cover the performances with multiple 35mm cameras, working with stage lighting and camera moves coordinated and choreographed to the lyric lines of the songs being sung. And he wanted to do this all for a live show without interfering with the performer-audience connection; cameras on cranes hovering over the stage and blocking views would make the audience mere accessories to a filming session. Although he sometimes acts as if the final show were a bit overproduced, Scorsese's use of Hollywood professionals to dress up the movie was a very good move. Frankly, most earlier concert films tend to become repetitious and boring, unless one is a fanatic music fan. The carefully planned lighting changes and nicely designed stage sets give the show an edge. For once, a concert film isn't a poor substitute for really being there. DVD presents the footage in a masterfully transferred presentation, with a number of great extras. The documentary does an excellent job of explaining the genesis of the show as told in retrospect by Scorsese and Robertson, who are both still proud as Punch over it. The diagrams of the lighting and the script—basically a camera and lighting cue sheet coordinated to each bar of music for each song—are fascinating to look at. There are two audio commentaries with Scorsese and the musicians that are going to be must-hears for fans who are more music-oriented. There's also a comprehensive essay by Robbie Robertson in the insert. A special bonus is a long jam with the assembled Band and guests that served as the encore after the show. It's not transferred as well as the rest of the film, and the visual quits before the track does, because one camera's magazine ran out. All of these are going to be treasured items. I have the old 1989 flat laserdisc, and there's just no comparison. —GE

Movie: ♫♫♫ ½ **DVD:** ♫♫♫ ½
MGM Home Ent. (cat #1003426, UPC 027-616875754). Widescreen (1.85:1) anamorphic. Dolby Digital 5.1 Surround. $24.98. Keepcase. *LANG:* English. *FEATURES:* Audio commentaries • New documentary • Outtake performance.
1978 (PG) 117m/C D: Martin Scorsese; **C:** Michael Chapman.

The Last Warrior
An earthquake turns California into Mojave Island. Capt. Nick Preston (Lundgren) is

trapped in a desert military junkyard. He must lead a group of survivors against prison inmates and the usual post-apocalyptic folderol. Some aliasing is visible within tight lines. Otherwise image is fine, perhaps a bit better than VHS tape. —*MM*
Movie: 🎬🎬 ***DVD:*** 🎬🎬 ½
Artisan Ent. (cat #11970, UPC 01223611-9708). Full frame. Dolby Digital Surround. $24.99. Keepcase. *LANG:* English. *CAP:* English. *FEATURES:* 34 chapters ▪ Trailer ▪ Talent files.
1999 (PG-13) 95m/C Dolph Lundgren, Rebecca Cross, Julino Mer, Sherrie Alexander, Joe Michael Burke; ***D:*** Sheldon Lettich; ***W:*** Stephen J. Brackely, Pamela K. Long; ***C:*** David Garfinkel; ***M:*** David Michael Frank.

The Last Wave

Director Peter Weir's follow-up to the enigmatic *Picnic at Hanging Rock* is the equally haunting tale of a lawyer (Chamberlain) defending a group of aborigines against charges of murder. He begins to have vivid dreams of an impending cataclysm, which he believes might be tied to the spiritual beliefs of his clients. The film is hypnotic, and crawls under the skin with a subtle sense of terror. The transfer is excellent—colors are vivid, details are amazing, and the only noted flaws occurred in scenes with large patches of darkness. The original stereo audio track is included, along with a 5.1 remix; both are excellent, with heavy use of the subwoofer helping to create the sense of impending doom. —*BG*
Movie: 🎬🎬🎬 ½ ***DVD:*** 🎬🎬🎬 ½
Criterion (cat #142, UPC 037429161920). Widescreen (1.77:1) anamorphic. Dolby Stereo; Dolby 5.1. $29.95. Keepcase. *LANG:* English. *CAP:* English. *FEATURES:* 23 chapters ▪ Trailer ▪ Interview with director Peter Weir.
1977 (PG) 109m/C *AU* Richard Chamberlain, Olivia Hamnett, David Gulpilil, Frederick Parslow, Vivean Gray, Nadjiwarra Amagula, Roy Bara, Walter Amagula, Cedric Lalara, Morris Lalara, Peter Carroll; ***D:*** Peter Weir; ***W:*** Peter Weir, Tony Morphett, Petru Popescu; ***C:*** Russell Boyd.

Late Night Sessions

Movies about the rave scene tend to follow similar "hey, kids, let's put on a show" plotlines and this extremely low-budget Vancouver production is no exception. It is made with some inventive techniques and genuine concern for its characters, and those make up for a lot of shortcomings. DVD image is a slight improvement over VHS tape; so is sound. As usual, York has provided an abundance of extras for a modest video premiere. —*MM*
Movie: 🎬🎬 ½ ***DVD:*** 🎬🎬 ½
York Ent. (cat #YPD-1093, UPC 75072310-9329). Widescreen (1.66:1) letterboxed. $14.99. Keepcase. *LANG:* English. *FEATURES:* 10 chapters ▪ Director's intro and commentary ▪ Trailers.
1999 90m/C *CA* Caterpillar MacLaggan, Zak Santiago Alam, Michael Nyuis; ***D:*** Joshua B. Hamlin.

Lawman

Tough western follows U.S. Marshal Jered Maddox (Lancaster) to the town of Sabbath where Vincent Bronson (Cobb) runs things. Maddox means to bring in Bronson and six of his cowboys for the accidental death of a man in another town. Bronson wants to make a deal; Maddox says no. The film is brooding and relentless with fine performances, particularly by Ryan as the local lawman who understands how the power works. Grain is noticeable in bright exteriors, but the overall DVD quality is very good for a film of this age. Mono sound is fine. Particularly recommended to fans of late-'60s westerns. —*MM*
Movie: 🎬🎬🎬 ***DVD:*** 🎬🎬 ½
MGM Home Ent. (cat #1002369, UPC 027-616865809). Widescreen (1.85:1) anamorphic. Dolby Digital Mono. $19.95. Keepcase. *LANG:* English; French; Spanish. *SUB:* French; Spanish. *CAP:* English. *FEATURES:* 16 chapters ▪ Trailer.
1971 (PG) 95m/C Burt Lancaster, Robert Ryan, Lee J. Cobb, Sheree North, Joseph Wiseman, Robert Duvall, Albert Salmi, J.D. Cannon, John McGiver, Richard Jordan, John Beck, Ralph Waite, John Hillerman, Richard Bull; ***D:*** Michael Winner; ***W:*** Gerald Wilson; ***C:*** Robert Paynter; ***M:*** Jerry Fielding.

Le Dernier Combat

Director Luc Besson's first feature tells the tale of a bleak post–nuclear war world where survival is a day-to-day struggle. One man builds an airplane so that he can fly about in search of a mate. Shot in black and white with no dialogue, it's a kind of silent *Road Warrior*, with an extremely clean DVD transfer of its silver-and-licorice black-and-white. Besson (*Le Femme Nikita, Leon/The Professional, The Fifth Element*) has been faulted for favoring form over content, meaning at his worst he's an ad executive's dream, with meaningless close-ups of cigarette tips and light through liquor glasses, but I have for the most part enjoyed his comic book style which has already been thoroughly absorbed into American film and TV with barely a nod to his originality. *Le Dernier Combat (The Last Battle)* is more a curiosity than an out-and-out good film. However, it is also more than just for the Besson completist. If anything, it shows how a good-looking feature film can be made with virtually nothing. Excellent sound for some superb Foley work. —*MO* **AKA:** The Last Battle.
Movie: 🎬🎬🎬 ***DVD:*** 🎬🎬🎬 ½
Columbia Tristar (cat #06509, UPC 043-39606509). Widescreen anamorphic. Dolby Digital. $29.95. Keepcase. *LANG:* Sound effects only. *CAP:* Sound effects. *FEATURES:* 28 chapters ▪ Theatrical trailer.
1984 (R) 93m/B *FR* Pierre Jolivet, Fritz Wepper, Jean Reno, Jean Bouise, Christiane Kruger; ***D:*** Luc Besson; ***W:*** Luc Besson; ***C:*** Carlo Varini; ***M:*** Eric Serra.

Le Magnifique

Whimsical spy spoof stars Belmondo as a novelist who's also his fictional hero, secret agent Bob St. Clare, who must save the world, etc., etc. For fans of the period, the young and impossibly lovely Jacqueline Bissett is Bob's contact Tatiana, and that's all the recommendation they need. Some of the humor is a bit dated and, for my money, it's not quite as much fun as the similar (but still unavailable on home video) *Modesty Blaise,* but it (and *Austin Powers*) are cut from the same cloth. DVD image is pretty astonishing. It's excellent, with bright unfaded colors and no flaws worth mentioning. Bright yellow subtitles are not removable. —*MM* **AKA:** The Magnificent One.
Movie: 🎬🎬🎬 ***DVD:*** 🎬🎬🎬
Image Ent. (cat #ID0664SRDVD, UPC 014-381066425). Widescreen (1.66:1) anamorphic. Dolby Digital Mono. $24.99. Keepcase. *LANG:* French. *SUB:* English. *FEATURES:* 12 chapters.
1976 84m/C *FR* Jean-Paul Belmondo, Jacqueline Bisset, Hans Meyer, Vittorio Caprioli; ***D:*** Philippe de Broca; ***W:*** Francis Veber, Philippe de Broca; ***C:*** Rene Mathelin; ***M:*** Claude Bolling.

Le Petit Soldat

The passage of time has softened the controversy that swirled about Godard's second film (after *Breathless*) in the initial release. It's the story of photographer Bruno Forestier (Subor), who joins the French nationalist movement against Algeria. While he tries to decide whether to follow orders to kill one of the opposition, he falls in love with a model (the lovely Karina, in her debut), unaware of her political beliefs. Godard's once-revolutionary on-the-fly filmmaking techniques seem completely contemporary and natural now. One extra is a text explanation of the restoration process that the film has undergone. It leads a viewer to expect the worst but the DVD is astonishingly sharp for a film shot on 16mm more than 40 years ago. Both image and sound are first-rate. Curiously, optional English subtitles cannot be triggered if you choose to listen to critic David Sterritt's abbreviated commentary track. That's a quibble. For serious students of film, this one makes a long-overdue debut on home video. —*MM*
Movie: 🎬🎬🎬 ***DVD:*** 🎬🎬🎬 ½
Winstar Home Ent. (cat #FLV5267, UPC 720917526720). Full frame. $24.98. Keepcase. *LANG:* French. *SUB:* English. *FEATURES:* Restoration text ▪ DVD production credits ▪ Abbreviated commentary by David Sterritt ▪ 16 chapters ▪ Filmographies.
1960 88m/B *FR* Michel Subor, Anna Karina, Henri-Jacques Huet, Paul Beauvais, Georges De Beauregard, Jean-Luc Godard, Laszlo Szabo; ***D:*** Jean-Luc Godard; ***W:*** Jean-Luc Godard; ***C:*** Raoul Coutard; ***M:*** Maurice Leroux.

Le Professionnel

French assassin Joss Beaumont (Belmondo) returns from the African republic of Malagasy, where he's been imprisoned for two years because his own superiors

turned him in to the Malagassic authorities when they decided to abort his mission. Instantly his old department is mobilized to eliminate him, but Beaumont is faster and smarter than all of them put together. Fast, clever, and beholden to nothing done before, the film is a slick package, a spy thriller that relies on brains instead of guns. Jean-Paul Belmondo has the years on him finally to reflect a level of experience and weariness befitting a believable noir-ish hero, yet he's in superb shape. There's a constant flow of fistfights and combat encounters in the picture, none of which are hyped with cutting or music. Belmondo makes them all credible. DVD is very plain-wrap. This is no liability because the show is nicely self-contained, and you don't walk away needing outside explanations or context. The enhanced picture looks pristine, and the mysterious score by Ennio Morricone, which sounds at first like it belongs in a sensitive love story instead of a spy chase, sounds great. This is a surprise picture for people who like intelligent thrillers. —GE *AKA:* The Professional.
Movie: 🎬🎬🎬 ½ *DVD:* 🎬🎬🎬
Image Ent. (cat #ID0666SRDVD, UPC 014-381066623). Widescreen (1.78:1) anamorphic. $24.99. Keepcase. *LANG:* French. *SUB:* English.
1981 109m/C FR Jean-Paul Belmondo, Jean Desailly, Robert Hossein, Michel Beaune, Cyrielle Claire, Jean-Louis Richard, Sidiki Bakaba; *D:* Georges Lautner; *W:* Georges Lautner, Michel Audiard; *C:* Henri Decae; *M:* Ennio Morricone.

Le Trou

Four long-term convicts in a Paris prison cell are planning to escape by tunneling to freedom. Then a fifth inmate joins them. Is he going to betray them or is there already a Judas among the men? Based on a true story, the film has no musical score to detract attention from the growing tension. Criterion has done its usual splendid job with a virtually flawless transfer of a richly detailed black-and-white image. The extras are all text—liner notes by Chris Fujiwara and excerpts from the original U.S. pressbook. Don't read them until you've watched the film. —MM *AKA:* The Hole; The Night Watch; Il Buco.
Movie: 🎬🎬🎬🎬 *DVD:* 🎬🎬🎬 ½
Criterion (cat #129, UPC 037429156223). Widescreen (1.66:1) anamorphic. Mono. $29.95. Keepcase. *LANG:* French. *SUB:* English. *FEATURES:* 19 chapters • Liner notes by Chris Fujiwara • Excerpts from the 1964 U.S. pressbook.
1959 123m/B FR Phillippe LeRoy, Marc Michel, Catherine Spaak, Andre Bervil, Michel Constantin, Jean-Paul Coquelin, Jean Keraudy, Raymond Meunier, Eddy Rasimi, Dominique Zardi; *D:* Jacques Becker; *W:* Jacques Becker, Jose Giovanni, Jean Aurel; *C:* Ghislan Cloquet.

The Learning Curve

When Paul and Georgia (Giovinazzo and Mazur), lovers and partners in crime, try to swindle corrupt businessman Marshal (Ventresca), he brings them into his fold to commit some petty crimes. But as Marshal gives them more dangerous responsibilities, their passion fades. This is a labor of love for writer/director Schwab, but the plot centers on the crimes instead of the characters and it moves much too slowly. The Surround channels are heavy with music and gunfire and the transfer is good, though the edges tend to blur. A director's commentary would have been a welcome addition to this release. —DRL
Movie: 🎬🎬 *DVD:* 🎬🎬 ½
MGM Home Ent. (cat #1003129, UPC 027-616872944). Widescreen (1.85:1) anamorphic; full frame. Dolby 5.1 Surround. $26.98. Keepcase. *LANG:* English. *SUB:* English; French; Spanish. *CAP:* English. *FEATURES:* 16 chapters.
2001 (R) 97m/C Carmine D. Giovinazzo, Monet Mazur, Vincent Ventresca, Steven Bauer, Majandra Delfino, Richard Erdman, Jack Laufer; *D:* Eric Schwab; *W:* Eric Schwab; *C:* Michael Hofstein; *M:* Zoran Boris.

Left Luggage

After a deceptively slow beginning, veteran actor-turned-director Jeroen Krabbé manages to draw together a minor fable, anchored by solid performances throughout. In Antwerp in 1972, student Laura Fraser *(Virtual Sexuality, Vanilla Sky),* who's in need of a job, reluctantly becomes a nanny to a family of Hasidic Jews. After some rough beginnings—especially with Krabbé as the overbearing father—she comes to care for the family, mentor their youngest son, and rediscovers her own roots. Lackluster DVD presentation for this minor theatrical release—strictly for viewers drawn to the subject. —RT
Movie: 🎬🎬 ½ *DVD:* 🎬🎬
Wellspring Media, Inc. (cat #FLV5282, UPC 720917528229). Full frame. Dolby Digital Surround. $24.98. Keepcase. *LANG:* English. *FEATURES:* 11 chapters • Theatrical trailer • Filmographies.
1998 100m/C Laura Fraser, Isabella Rossellini, Jeroen Krabbe, Maximilian Schell, Marianne Saegebrecht, Chaim Topol; *D:* Jeroen Krabbe; *W:* Edwin de Vries; *C:* Walther Vanden Ende; *M:* Henry Vrienten.

Legally Blonde

Southern California babe Elle (Witherspoon) thinks that her beau is about to propose. But he dumps her and says that he'll need someone more "serious" because he's off to Harvard Law School. She decides that she'll apply there, too, and she's accepted. Yes, it's *Clueless* meets *The Paper Chase* with the emphasis on light, sweet-natured comedy. It all works because Reese Witherspoon has such an intelligent appreciation of the material and handles it perfectly. MGM has done a superb job on this disc. Both the full-frame and widescreen presentations are on one side; most extras on the flip, and they are well chosen. It could go without saying that image and sound are flawless, though Surround effects are needed only sparingly. The "trivia track" option is a series of pop-up captions that comment (with questionable authenticity) on the action. Example: "In the U.S. 58% of women paint their nails...and so do 6% of straight rural men." The two commentary tracks take different approaches. The one with director Luketic and Witherspoon is lighter in tone; the second more technical. A real treat all the way through. —MM
Movie: 🎬🎬🎬 ½ *DVD:* 🎬🎬🎬 ½
DreamWorks Home Ent. (cat #1002626, UPC 027616868268). Widescreen (2.35:1) anamorphic; full frame. Dolby Digital 5.1 Surround; Dolby Digital Surround. $26.98. Keepcase. *LANG:* English; French; Spanish. *SUB:* English; French; Spanish. *CAP:* English. *FEATURES:* 32 chapters • 8 deleted scenes • Trivia track • 2 featurettes • 2 commentary tracks • Music video • Theatrical trailer.
2001 (PG-13) 95m/C Reese Witherspoon, Matthew Davis, Selma Blair, Luke Wilson, Ali Larter, Holland Taylor, Victor Garber, Jessica Cauffiel, Jennifer Coolidge, Osgood Perkins II, Alanna Ubach, Raquel Welch, Linda Cardellini, Meredith Scott Lynn; *D:* Robert Luketic; *W:* Karen McCullah Lutz, Kirsten Smith; *C:* Anthony B. Richmond; *M:* Rolfe Kent.

Legend [UE]

A naïve forest dweller, Jack (Cruise), allows his girlfriend, Princess Lily (Sara), to view the sacred unicorns. Unfortunately, three foul demonic creatures take advantage of the situation, poisoning one of the unicorns and abducting the other. Lily is also captured and brought before the lord of evil, Darkness (Curry) to witness the slaying of the last unicorn, which will plunge the world into eternal night. Jack and his friends attempt to rescue Lily and save the Unicorn. Simple mythic fable is told on a gigantic scale and filled with impressive visuals. The story is fairly basic, but the film is an opulent, richly designed work. Curry is excellent as the demonic Darkness and the role makes perfect use of his wonderful voice. Director Scott, unsure of his original cut, had the film trimmed by over 20 minutes and had the incredible orchestral Jerry Goldsmith score replaced with one by synthesizer artists, Tangerine Dream. The director's cut disc presents Scott's never-before-released original version, complete with the Goldsmith music. It's a richer, much more coherent work, clearly delineating the characters and dramatic situations. The Goldsmith score is evocative and thrilling; it's one of his absolute best. The U.S. version is choppy and plays almost like an extended music video. (Where the "director's cut" gets 3.5 bones, the U.S. version earns only two.) The Tangerine Dream score, while fine on its own, is limp and ill suited to the film. The use of a Bryan Ferry pop song to end the film is quite nauseating. The director's cut ending is much more satisfying. For the first time on video, the film is presented in its original widescreen dimensions. The framing is exquisitely composed and absolutely essential. The transfer is sharp and richly colored. Dark scenes display some grain but digital noise is kept to a minimum. The Surround track is sweeping and involving. Goldsmith's score is given tremendous presence and the soundscape is detailed and impressive. The U.S. cut looks fine, but it features a less crisp transfer and the sound is nowhere near as rich as in the director's cut. Scott's commentary is filled with interesting stories and reflections, but there's no information about the longer opening, the various versions, the cut "Faerie Dance" sequence, or the process of restoration. The documentary is just shy of an hour and interviews most of the key participants (except for Cruise, who must have been too busy hawking copies of *Dianetics*). The rest of the extras are further icing on an already wonderfully rich cake. The alternate opening is of poor quality, but it's from a video source. Since it was considered lost, we're lucky it even exists in this form. It was rightly dropped for the film, as it's rather lengthy and meandering. The non-relooped dialogue is near impossible to make out and sound effects are absent. The reconstruction of lost "The Faerie Dance" sequence is interesting, but was probably correctly left out; it's simply too clumsy and annoying. The storyboards highlight an interesting scene that was never shot. A beautiful, essential special edition of an underrated film—it deserves much better packaging. Highly recommended. —DG

Movie: ♪♪♪ ½ **DVD:** ♪♪♪ ½
Universal Studios (cat #21775, UPC 0251-92177521). Widescreen (2.35:1) anamorphic. DTS; Dolby Digital 5.1 Surround; Dolby Digital Surround. $24.98. Keepcase. *LANG:* English. *SUB:* Spanish; French. *CAP:* English. *FEATURES:* 114-minute director's cut • 90-minute original release cut • Commentary: Ridley Scott • 18 chapters • Isolated Tangerine Dream music score • Insert booklet • 3 photo galleries • Storyboards for 3 sequences • Trailers & TV spots • Production notes • Cast & filmmaker bios • "Creating a Myth: The Making of *Legend*" • Re-creation of "Faerie Dance" with audio track, storyboards, photos • Alternate opening sequence: "Four Goblins" • Brian Ferry music video, "Is your love strong enough?" • DVD-ROM: Script-to-scene comparison.
1986 (PG) 114m/C *GB* Tom Cruise, Mia Sara, Tim Curry, David Bennett, Billy Barty, Alice Playten; *D:* Ridley Scott; *M:* Jerry Goldsmith. *AWARDS: NOM:* Oscars '86: Makeup.

The Legend [2]

Kung fu cinema's most famous mama's boy hero returns for more adventures. Fong Sai-yuk (Jet Li) comes home to serve the rebel Red Lotus Society. Sent to retrieve a red box from some traveling samurai, Fong runs into trouble when he has to protect the Mandarin's daughter and rescue his mom from traitors. Uneven and awkwardly paced, *Legend 2* nevertheless contains all the comic complications and elaborate acrobatic fight sequences that fans of the first film should expect. Josephine Siao once again steals the show with her charm and comic timing. Image and sound quality are excellent, though it would have been nice to have more language and subtitle options. —BT
AKA: Fong Sai-yuk 2.
Movie: ♪♪♪ **DVD:** ♪♪♪
Buena Vista Home Ent. (cat #21653, UPC 786936144741). Widescreen letterboxed. Dolby Digital 5.1 Surround. $29.99. Keepcase. *LANG:* English. *SUB:* English. *CAP:* English. *FEATURES:* 18 chapters • Trailers.
1993 (R) 95m/C *HK* Corey Yuen, Jet Li, Josephine Siao, Adam Cheng, Michelle Reis; *D:* Corey Yuen; *W:* On Kay; *C:* Pin Bang Lee; *M:* Lowell Lo.

The Legend of a Professional

Anthony Wong stars as a working class hitman. He can't find a girl to settle down with; his mom nags; and he's still haunted by thoughts of the one honest man among hundreds he killed years ago. To find a wife, he pretends to be casting for a movie. Josie Ho is one of those answering his ad, and he hires her to pose as his girlfriend for his mother's benefit when she visits from Vietnam. Learning his true business, Josie cuts herself in as a partner, though neither of them can see their deadliest enemy coming. Not as much action as you'd like to see in your hitman movies, but the tough sell romance works. Image transfer is a bit smeary, though the cinematography has a hazy look. —BT
Movie: ♪♪♪ **DVD:** ♪♪
Tai Seng (cat #5631, UPC 6016439689-40). Widescreen letterboxed. Dolby Digital 5.1 Surround. $19.95. Keepcase. *LANG:* Cantonese; Mandarin. *SUB:* Chinese; English. *CAP:* Chinese. *FEATURES:* 8 chapters • Star profiles • Trailers.
2000 92m/C *HK* Anthony Wong, Thomas Lam, Josie Ho, Helena Law, Kon Lan Law, Karel Wong, Ka Chun Ho, Gabriel Harrison; *D:* Billy Chan; *W:* Billy Chan; *C:* Tak Yip Pun.

The Legend of Hell House

Although very similar in plot to *The Haunting* (both versions), *The Legend of Hell House* brings some originality to the haunted house genre. Dr. Barrett (Revill), a physicist, is recruited by a tycoon to search for evidence of life after death. His assignment is to enter Hell House, which is known as "the Mount Everest of haunted houses," and discover proof of ghostly activity. Barrett takes along his wife (Hunicutt), and two mediums (Franklin and McDowall). Things start off innocently enough, but soon these guests find themselves in an all-out war with the ghosts. While the film is deliberately paced and there's not a great deal of action until the finale, *The Legend of Hell House* doesn't pull any punches and we get to see just how nasty these spirits can get. A suspenseful, scary screamfest. Matheson wrote the screenplay from his novel. The DVD transfer blows away the previous video editions, even the laserdisc. Still, it's definitely not a show piece, with varying degrees of sharpness being the main flaw. Colors are excellent and even the saturated reds do not bleed. The 4.0 soundtrack opens things up a bit more than the older versions but the fidelity is limited, which is a shame since the soundtrack by Delia Derbyshire and Brian Hodgson is eerie and atmospheric. With such a reasonable price, you can't gripe too much about the lack of supplementals, but putting trailers for other totally unrelated movies seems to be much too aggravating (just makes one wish there were some real extras) to be a very good selling tool. —ML/JO
Movie: ♪♪♪ **DVD:** ♪♪ ½
20th Century Fox (cat #2001384, UPC 024543013846). Widescreen (1.85:1) letterboxed. Dolby 4.0 Surround; Dolby Mono. $19.98. Keepcase. *LANG:* English; French. *SUB:* English; Spanish. *CAP:* English. *FEATURES:* Theatrical trailer • 30 chapters.
1973 (PG) 94m/C Roddy McDowall, Pamela Franklin, Clive Revill, Gayle Hunnicutt, Peter Bowles, Roland Culver, Michael Gough; *D:* John Hough; *W:* Richard Matheson; *C:* Alan Hume; *M:* Brian Hodgson, Delia Derbyshire.

The Legend of 1900

Told in a fanciful style that constantly threatens to edge over into fantasy, this film features a great performance from Tim Roth, and some of the most interesting musical sequences in a modern movie. Image's disc does justice to this beautifully produced 1998 gem, which won a Golden Globe for best music score. A stoker on the luxury liner *Virgina*, Danny Boodman (Nunn) finds a baby in the year 1900, and gives it that for a name: 1900. As he grows up on the liner, a stateless person with no identity on any shore, 1900 (now Roth) discovers a marvelous musical talent and becomes the ship's star pianist. He lives a strangely charmed existence, soundly defeating a challenge by jazz great Jelly Roll Morton (Williams III) for the title of world's greatest man behind a piano. 1900's best friend, trumpet soloist Max (Vince), tries to get him to leave the ship, at least once, but 1900 never does, even though the vision of a beautiful Girl (Thierry) tempts him. And all along, he develops his own unique philosophy for dealing with the world. If this were all there was to the film, it would be interesting, but Tornatore has turned the movie into a musical feast more compelling than most musicals. 1900 plays arrangements of vintage jazz and ragtime, and his own personal music. The movie is transformed by his playing, and Tornatore's direction brings the magic of his performances to life in highly stylized, emotional scenes that make us as excited about 1900 as are his passenger audiences. DVD is a beauty, with a great Technovision widescreen image. It's originally a Fine Line arthouse release, which raises interesting questions of how it got into Image Entertainment's lineup, but nobody here is complaining. The IMDb lists an original Italian running time almost 40 minutes longer...this version is so entirely satisfying I'm tempted to wonder how more scenes could improve it. —GE **AKA:** The Legend of the Pianist on the Ocean; La Leggenda del Pianista Sull'Oceano.

Movie: ♪♪♪ ½ **DVD:** ♪♪♪ ½
Image Ent. (cat #ID1442LIDVD, UPC 0143-81144222). Widescreen (2.35:1) anamorphic. DTS 5.1; Dolby 5.1. $24.99. Keepcase. *LANG:* English. *FEATURES:* Trailer • Filmographies • Music video • Isolated music and effects track.
1998 (R) 116m/C Tim Roth, Pruitt Taylor Vince, Clarence Williams III, Bill Nunn, Melanie Thierry; **D:** Giuseppe Tornatore; **W:** Giuseppe Tornatore; **C:** Lajos Koltai; **M:** Ennio Morricone. *AWARDS:* Golden Globes '00: Score.

The Legend of Rita

Import is set in a turbulent Germany of the 1970s and follows the life of a young anarchist. After her bank-robbing anti-government group is disbanded, Rita (Bibiana Beglau) flees to communist East Germany to begin a new life. There, she is forced to take on a new identity and drifts from job to job, lover to lover. As Rita moves through life, changing her name and her situation, she begins to fully understand the differences between East and West Germany, and she becomes increasingly alienated. Beautifully shot and well acted, *Rita* paints a haunting picture of a period of history which many would choose to forget. An educational film for Americans who aren't familiar with what was happening in Germany during this time. The DVD brings a transfer with a clear picture, but the colors are somewhat muted at times. The dialogue is clear, but there is very little use of any true Surround sound. The subtitles are easy to read. —ML **AKA:** Die Stille Nach Dem Schuss; The Silence After the Shot.

Movie: ♪♪♪ **DVD:** ♪♪♪
Kino on Video (cat #K218 DVD, UPC 738-329021825). Widescreen (1.85:1) letterboxed. Dolby Digital Surround. $29.95. Keepcase. *LANG:* German. *SUB:* English. *FEATURES:* Commentary • Theatrical trailer • 14 chapters.
1999 101m/C GE Bibiana Beglau, Martin Wuttke, Nadja Uhl, Harald Schrott, Alexander Beyer, Jenny Schily; **D:** Volker Schlöndorff; **W:** Volker Schlöndorff, Wolfgang Kohlhaase; **C:** Andreas Hofer.

The Legend of Suram Fortress / Ashik Kerib

The first film on this double-bill is based on a Georgian folktale about a medieval fortress that collapses as soon as it is built. The village soothsayer tells a young man he must sacrifice himself, by bricking himself up alive within the fortress walls, if the building is ever to stand. *Ashik Kerib* is the story of a wandering minstrel who is rejected by a rich merchant as his daughter's suitor. He then journeys for 1,000 days trying to earn enough money to marry his beloved. Along the way, he's imprisoned by an evil sultan and rides a flying horse among other adventures. The exotic makeup and non-linear natures of both films are going to put off those in search of conventional narrative storytelling. With both films, DVD appears to present an accurate re-creation of unpolished originals, though *Ashik* suffers from registration problems. At times, the burned-in subtitles are written over the original credits, making them difficult to read. —MM **AKA:** Legenda Suramskoi Kreposti.

Movie: ♪♪ **DVD:** ♪♪ ½
Kino on Video (cat #K203, UPC 73832902-0323). Full frame. $29.99. Keepcase. *LANG:* Russian. *SUB:* English. *FEATURES:* 15 chapters each.
1985 89m/C RU Levan Outchanechvili, Zourab Kipchidze; **D:** Sergei Paradjanov; **W:** Vaja Gigashvili; **C:** Yuri Klimenko.

Legend of the Chupacabra

Yet another "found footage" horror film, in which a group of intrepid youngsters treks into the wilderness armed with video cameras, in search of a mythical "goat sucking" beastie—an old-fashioned monster movie dressed up in the current (or current in 1997) wave of documentary-style fiction. If you want to see a Chupacabra autopsy, this is the movie for you. It's a monster rampage! The full-frame presentation gives a pretty good approximation of an actual amateur documentary, intercut with studio interview footage of talking head "experts." Sometimes it seems like they're almost taking it seriously. At other times, it seems like they're just trying not to laugh. The DVD features a poorly recorded commentary with director Castro and unidentified cast and crew members. As a commentary track, it's a bit lacking, but as a party it works just fine. A couple of deleted scenes are on the disc, including an "alternate ending" which is even sillier and not as scary as the one they ended up with. —BT

Movie: ♪♪ ½ **DVD:** ♪♪
Troma Team Video (cat #9018, UPC 790-35790183). Full frame. $19.98. Keepcase. *LANG:* English. *FEATURES:* 9 chapters • Trailers • Commentary • Deleted scenes • Documentary featurettes • Unused footage.
1997 71m/C Katsy Joiner, Stan McKinney, J. T. Trevino, Chris Doughton; **D:** Joe Castro; **W:** Mark Stephens; **C:** Christian Remde.

The Legend of the Lone Ranger

TV feature film compilation of the original episodes from *The Lone Ranger* TV series. Ambushed, along with his brother and several other rangers, our titular hero (Moore) survives thanks to Tonto (Silverheels) and decides to fight injustice with his trademark mask, white hat, and horse. Sincere but unintentionally hilarious adaptation of the legendary radio character features guffaw-inducing, innuendo-filled dialogue, wooden performances, and creaky stock library music. Moore's Ranger seems like a dazed, stiff dope and the Silverheels's Tonto seems nearly as daft. The picture source is clean with nice contrasts but there's an abundance of digital noise. The mono sound is adequate. The TV episode included features strong color but is slightly soft and suffers from the same digital noise. —DG **AKA:** The Lone Ranger; Enter the Lone Ranger.

Movie: ♪♪ **DVD:** ♪ ½
Marengo Films (cat #MRG-0002, UPC 807-013000221). Full frame. Mono. $14.98. Keepcase. *LANG:* English. *FEATURES:* 10 chapters • 1966 color episode from TV series, 23 mins.
1959 65m/B Clayton Moore, Jay Silverheels, Glenn Strange; **D:** George B. Seitz; **W:** George B. Seitz; **C:** Mack Stengler.

Legend of the Red Dragon

Li plays Hung Hei-Kwun. He and his grown-up son (the fantastic Tse Miu) are hired to guard a rich man who comes in contact with a mother/daughter team of con artists. Together, they must save five children who have pieces of a map leading to hidden treasure tattooed on their backs. In other words, there's enough plot to be interested, but the constant—and occasionally spectacular—fight scenes are the main draw. Li is engaging as usual, and the kids are skilled martial artists. It's entertaining and fairly well acted, and the action comes at a brisk pace. Given Hong Kong's terrible archival history, this 1994 picture actually looks decent. Sharpness and detail are lacking and the transfer is fairly soft throughout. Specks, marks, and other print flaws are noticeable. Colors are occasionally bold, but slightly smeary at times and subdued at others. Overall, this is a decent presentation. Unfortunately, the original language track is *not* included. The English dub tracks make minimal use of Surrounds and the majority of the action utilizes the front speakers. —AB

Movie: ♪♪♪ **DVD:** ♪♪
Columbia Tristar (cat #06597, UPC 04339-6065970). Widescreen (1.85:1) letterboxed. Dolby Digital 5.1 Surround; Dolby Digital Stereo. $24.98. Keepcase. *LANG:* English. *FEATURES:* Chapter links • Bonus trailers • Cast & director filmographies • Trailer • Photo gallery.
1994 94m/C HK Jet Li, Tse Miu, Damian Lau, Chingmy Yau, Deannie Yip, Lung-Wai Wang, Jing Wong; **D:** Jing Wong, Corey Yuen; **W:** Jing Wong; **C:** Tom Lau.

Legendary Sherlock Holmes Movies

The features on this triple bill—*Dressed to Kill, The Woman in Green,* and *Terror by Night*—are public domain titles that are

reviewed in *Book 2*. These are poor image and sound transfers. —*MM*
Movie: 🐶🐶 ½ **DVD:** 🐶 ½
BFS Video (cat #30173-D, UPC 06680530-1735). Full frame. $9.98. Keepcase. *LANG:* English. *FEATURES:* Thumbnail bios and filmographies ▪ Trivia ▪ 12 chapters.
2000 200m/C

The Legendary Strike

Ching Dynasty Prince Carter Wong hires a Japanese warrior to take the Buddha's Relic to its new owners in Japan. A Shaolin monk objects to the sale of the holy Buddhist object to foreigners, and kills the samurai to get it, swallowing the prize before he's killed in turn. Another Shaolin, another samurai, a Ching official and his troops, Korean agents, and Ming patriots all come running after the corpse, trying to keep it out of the others' hands. There's entirely too much talk and intrigue going on, but eventually all the players' alliances and identities are revealed, and everyone chooses partners for the kung fu dance. Unfortunately, the action doesn't justify the intricate build up. The full-frame image chops off the sides, and the mono soundtrack is a bit tinny. The disc comes with an informative commentary track by Martial Arts Theater's resident expert Ric Meyers. —*BT* **AKA:** Long Ji Yat Chiu; Lang Zi Yi Zhao; A Fist Too Fast; Iron Maiden.
Movie: 🐶 ½ **DVD:** 🐶🐶 ½
Tai Seng (cat #84064, UPC 6016438406-42). Full frame. $14.95. Keepcase. *LANG:* English. *FEATURES:* 8 chapters ▪ Commentary.
1978 89m/C *HK* Carter Wong, Angela (Mao Ying) Mao, Casanova Wong, Sing Chan, Kam Kong; **D:** Fung Wong; **W:** Lung Ku; **M:** Frankie Chan.

Lena's Dreams

A day in the life of gifted Latina actress in New York. After years of slogging from audition to audition, Lena (Forte), at the end of her rope and ready to quit, finally gets the call she's been hoping for: a part in a big Broadway show. Excellent performance by Forte stands out in otherwise overwrought drama. Unfortunately, the contrasty transfer from a digital video original obscures details especially in actors' faces. Beware of handheld movement if you're prone to motion sickness. Sound is fine and adds to the intimate atmosphere. —*LA*
Movie: 🐶🐶 **DVD:** 🐶🐶
MTI (cat #7018, UPC 03941470182). Full frame. $24.98. Keepcase. *LANG:* English. *SUB:* Spanish. *FEATURES:* 20 chapters ▪ Cast bios ▪ Trailers.
1997 97m/C Marlene Forte, Gary Perez, Susan Perez, Jeremiah Birkett; **D:** Gordon Eriksen, Heather Johnston; **W:** Gordon Eriksen, Heather Johnston; **C:** Armando Basulto; **M:** Don Braden.

Lena's Holiday

Cabdriver (Lemmon) comes to the aid of East German tourist Lena (Waterman) when, during a switcheroo at the airport,

she comes into the possession of a box of diamond-filled condoms. She hides the box in the mansion of eccentric photographer Corey Flynn (Mancuso) and tries to hide from bad guy (Sarrazin) as he tracks her all over Los Angeles. The forced wackiness rapidly wears thin. Image and sound quality are mediocre. —*LA*
Movie: 🐶 ½ **DVD:** 🐶🐶
Rhino (cat #R2 976065, UPC 603497606-528). Widescreen anamorphic. $9.98. Snapper. *LANG:* English. *FEATURES:* 12 chapters.
1990 (R) 97m/C Felicity Waterman, Chris Lemmon, Noriyuki "Pat" Morita, Susan Anton, Michael Sarrazin, Nick Mancuso, Bill Dana, Liz Torres; **D:** Michael Keusch; **W:** Michael Keusch, Deborah Tilton; **C:** Louis DiCesare.

Lenny

Smoky nightclubs, drug abuse, and raunchy language abound in the Hoffman/Fosse collaboration on the life of controversial comedian Lenny Bruce, whose provocative routines and self-destructive tendencies eventually led to an untimely end. Perrine is wonderful as his stripper wife. Her opening routine, artfully edited between audience and dancer, is the finest strip show ever put on film. The whole film has a feeling of authenticity that has largely been lost in American movies. DVD captures Bruce Surtees's evocative black-and-white cinematography with no flaws worth noting. Mono sound is fine, and the yellow subtitles are easy to read for those who have trouble catching every word. Caustic, sharp, unsentimental, it's one of Fosse's best. —*MM*
Movie: 🐶🐶🐶 ½ **DVD:** 🐶🐶🐶 ½
MGM Home Ent. (cat #1003337, UPC 027-616874863). Widescreen (1.85:1) anamorphic; full frame. Dolby Digital Mono. $19.98. Keepcase. *LANG:* English; French. *SUB:* English; French; Spanish. *CAP:* English. *FEATURES:* 16 chapters ▪ Trailer.
1974 (R) 111m/B Dustin Hoffman, Valerie Perrine, Jan Miner, Stanley Beck; **D:** Bob Fosse; **W:** Julian Barry; **C:** Bruce Surtees; **M:** Ralph Burns. *AWARDS:* Cannes '75: Actress (Perrine); Natl. Bd. of Review '74: Support. Actress (Perrine); N.Y. Film Critics '74: Support. Actress (Perrine); *NOM:* Oscars '74: Actor (Hoffman), Actress (Perrine), Adapt. Screenplay, Cinematog., Director (Fosse), Picture.

Les Bonnes Femmes

A character study of a small group of Parisian shopgirls contrasts their wild explorative nightlife and their humdrum jobs. At the periphery of their adventures lurks a young, romantic motorcyclist who seems particularly fascinated by Jacqueline (Clotilde Joano). It's an interesting, occasionally funny drama with a somewhat formless structure and a frightening, unsettling ending. Though foreshadowed earlier, the events of the conclusion are still shocking and are depicted in a matter-of-fact style, which only amplifies the horror. Kino's disc is a non-anamorphic trans-

fer of a theatrical print with burned-in subtitles. The subtitles are fairly accurate but occasionally simplify or modify the dialogue. Contrasts are fairly strong, but the image is a tad soft and light scratches are prevalent. The sound conveys the limitations of an old optical soundtrack and occasionally squawks. —*DG* **AKA:** The Good Girls; The Girls.
Movie: 🐶🐶🐶 **DVD:** 🐶🐶 ½
Kino on Video (cat #K165DVD, UPC 738-329016524). Widescreen (1.66:1) letterboxed. Mono. $29.95. Keepcase. *LANG:* French. *SUB:* English. *FEATURES:* 14 chapters ▪ Insert card.
1960 105m/B *FR* Bernadette LaFont, Stephane Audran, Clothilde Joano, Lucile Saint-Simon; **D:** Claude Chabrol; **W:** Paul Geoauff; **C:** Henri Decae; **M:** Pierre Jansen, Paul Misraki.

Les Carabiniers

Godard's grim anti-war tract details the pathetic adventures of two young bums (Mase and Juross) who are lured into enlisting with promises of rape, looting, torture, and battle without justification. The film was controversial in its day and remains typically elliptical and non-linear. DVD presents a first-rate re-creation of an image that has always been meant to be unpleasant. As David Sterritt explains in his abbreviated commentary, Godard worked hard to give the footage he shot a distressed, fuzzy quality that would match the newsreel footage he incorporates. Any comment on picture quality is beside the point. —*MM* **AKA:** The Soldiers.
Movie: 🐶🐶🐶 **DVD:** 🐶🐶🐶
Winstar Home Ent. (cat #FLV5268, UPC 720917526829). Full frame. Mono. $24.99. Keepcase. *LANG:* French. *SUB:* English. *FEATURES:* 16 chapters ▪ Commentary: David Sterritt ▪ Filmographies ▪ DVD production credits ▪ Weblinks.
1963 80m/B *GB IT FR* Albert Juross, Marino (Martin) Mase, Catherine Ribeiro, Genevieva Galea, Anna Karina; **D:** Jean-Luc Godard; **W:** Jean-Luc Godard; **C:** Raoul Coutard; **M:** Philippe Arthuys.

Less Than Zero

Life has certainly imitated art with this adaptation of Bret Easton Ellis's novel of drugged-out Beverly Hills rich kids. Over the years, Robert Downey Jr.'s portrayal of a young man's spiraling descent into addiction has gained an added level of verisimilitude. The scant story follows him and two friends, Clay (McCarthy) and Blair (Gertz), who have taken different paths since their recent graduation from high school. True, it's difficult to work up much sympathy for the rich and pampered but their story is not without fascination. For a late '80s film, DVD image is really very good. It's a little on the soft side, even in the black-and-white sequences, but it's a true reproduction of the original, as I remember it. Surround isn't overly impressive but it delivers the dialogue without problem. —*MM*

Movie: ♪♪♪ **DVD:** ♪♪♪
MGM Home Ent. (cat #2002517, UPC 024-543025177). Widescreen (1.85:1) anamorphic. Dolby Digital 4.0 Surround; Dolby Surround; Mono. $19.98. Keepcase. *LANG:* English; French. *SUB:* English; Spanish. *CAP:* English. *FEATURES:* Trailers ▪ TV spots ▪ 28 chapters.
1987 (R) 98m/C Andrew McCarthy, Jami Gertz, Robert Downey Jr., James Spader; *D:* Marek Kanievska; *W:* Harley Peyton; *C:* Edward Lachman; *M:* Thomas Newman.

Lessons of Darkness

With documentaries such as *Little Dieter Needs to Fly,* director Werner Herzog has proven himself to be a master of the form. But when is a documentary not a documentary? This occurs when Herzog takes footage which he shot on location, and then adds a fictional story line to match the images. This DVD set offers two such films. First, there is *Lessons of Darkness,* which is made up of footage shot in Kuwait in 1991, following Operation Desert Storm. Herzog photographed the oil-field fires and burned-out machinery, and then added narration concerning a doomed alien race and the war which has taken place on their planet. A second disc contains the 76-minute film from 1971 *Fata Morgana,* which literally means "mirage." With this film, Herzog traveled to Africa and photographed many mirages and other optical tricks played by the desert sun. Again, a narration track was added, creating a story of aliens visiting another planet. Clearly, neither is aimed at the average filmgoer. Both contain fantastic imagery, but the peculiar narration may turn some viewers away. *Fata Morgana* includes an audio commentary with Herzog (and actor Crispin Glover!), whose stories about the making of the film are far more interesting than the bizarre narration. *Lessons of Darkness* is presented in a letterboxed format and looks quite good. The image is clear, but there is some minor artifacting and a small amount of grain. The grain is much more prevalent in *Fata Morgana,* which is presented full frame. The colors here are especially good, as the bleak desert contrasts with the bright blue sky. Both DVDs offer mono audio tracks which provide clear dialogue and music, but little else. —*ML*
Movie: ♪♪ **DVD:** ♪♪♪
Anchor Bay (cat #DV11542, UPC 01313-1154290). Widescreen (1.77:1) anamorphic. Dolby Digital Mono. $29.98. Keepcase. *LANG:* English. *SUB:* English. *FEATURES:* Bonus film, *Fata Morgana* ▪ Production notes ▪ Director bio.
1992 54m/C *GE FR GB D:* Werner Herzog; *W:* Werner Herzog; *C:* Paul Berriff; *Nar:* Werner Herzog.

Let Freedom Ring: Images of the American Spirit

A collection of clips, newsreels, and other vignettes that depict some of the most memorable acts of patriotism in American history, beginning with World War II and ending with the events of September 11, 2001. Also included are sections on Pearl Harbor, the Iwo Jima flag raising, VE and VJ Days, JFK's inauguration, the moon landing, the Challenger explosion, and President George W. Bush's address to the nation following September 11. A valuable collection in terms of preserving the events that have helped shape our national identity, yet a disturbing use of the media to rally the masses to the cause of patriotism. Considering the variety of source materials used in this disc's creation, the video quality is surprisingly good. Or it's at least as good as can be expected. For the most part, colors are represented well and blacks are well-defined. —*MJT*
Movie: ♪♪ ½ **DVD:** ♪♪ ½
MPI (cat #DVD3540, UPC 0303063540-26). Full frame. Dolby Digital Stereo. $19.98. Keepcase. *LANG:* English. *SUB:* English. *FEATURES:* 22 chapters ▪ The 9-20-01 declaration of George W. Bush in its entirety.
2001 150m/C

Let It Ride

Dreyfuss is a small-time gambler who finally hits it big at the track. Some funny moments but a generally lame script cripples the talented cast. Garr is fine as the wife who slips further into alcoholism with each race. For a studio production of this age, DVD image ranges between very good and good. Same for sound. —*MM*
Movie: ♪♪ **DVD:** ♪♪
Paramount Home Video (UPC 097363220-046). Widescreen letterboxed. Dolby Digital 5.1 Surround; Dolby Digital Surround. $29.98. Keepcase. *LANG:* English; French. *SUB:* English. *FEATURES:* 18 chapters ▪ Behind-the-scenes featurette.
1989 (PG-13) 91m/C Richard Dreyfuss, Teri Garr, David Johansen, Jennifer Tilly, Allen (Goorwitz) Garfield, Ed Walsh, Michelle Phillips, Mary Woronov, Robbie Coltrane, Richard Edson, Cynthia Nixon; *D:* Joe Pytka; *W:* Nancy Dowd; *C:* Curtis J. Wehr; *M:* Giorgio Moroder.

Let's Make Love

Billionaire playboy Jean-Marc Clement (Montand) visits a theatre to quash plans to parody him on stage, and falls in love with performer Amanda Dell (Monroe). But the theatre people think Clement is an actor looking to play the part of Clement, and he has to keep up the deception to stay close to Amanda. From then on, Clement strives to become stage-worthy, hiring help from pros Milton Berle, Bing Crosby, and Gene Kelly. He seems to be getting through to Amanda, but what happens when she finds out who he is? This is a pretty dreadful movie, and shows what might have become of Marilyn had she lived. Audiences rejected her in this generic-Marilyn role, and for all we know, her star might have faded as other iconic attractions took over in the '60s. DVD looks stunning. Title is part of the *Marilyn Monroe: The Diamond Collection, Vol. 2.* —*GE*
Movie: ♪ ½ **DVD:** ♪♪♪
20th Century Fox (UPC 024543035084). Widescreen (2.35:1) anamorphic. Dolby Digital 4.0 Surround; Mono. $19.98. Keepcase. *LANG:* English; French. *SUB:* English; Spanish. *CAP:* English. *FEATURES:* Restoration comparison ▪ Still gallery ▪ Trailer.
1960 118m/C Yves Montand, Marilyn Monroe, Tony Randall, Frankie Vaughan, Bing Crosby, Gene Kelly, Milton Berle; *D:* George Cukor; *W:* Norman Krasna; *C:* Daniel F. Fapp; *M:* Lionel Newman. *AWARDS: NOM:* Oscars '60: Scoring/Musical.

Letters from a Killer

Race Darnell (Patrick Swayze) has been sent to Death Row for a murder he did not commit. Only weeks before his final execution date, his attorney finds evidence that could prove his innocence and quickly seeks a retrial. With the new evidence, the jury immediately comes to a new decision and acquits Race of all charges. Overnight he comes from Death Row to be a free man! But during his time in prison Race was writing recorded love letters to four different women to burn his time. He made each one of them believe he loved her and did not mention the others until the day when the letters get mixed up and are sent to the wrong "girlfriends." As a result, Race receives an enraged hate letter from a woman who threatens to kill him for the betrayal, but he is unable to recognize the voice. Immediately after being released from prison he tries to find out which one of the four has decided to kill him. The soft transfer lacks the definition you would expect for a high-resolution 16x9 presentation, but nonetheless creates a detailed picture. The color reproduction is very good, creating natural fleshtones, with vivid and strong colors. The 5.1 mix is well integrated and uses the discrete Surrounds quite effectively. Creating a busy atmosphere throughout and some great effects, the soundtrack has a good and unexaggerated bass extension. —*GH*
Movie: ♪♪ ½ **DVD:** ♪♪♪
Studio Home Ent. (UPC 658149739529). Widescreen (1.78:1) anamorphic. Dolby Digital 5.1 Surround. $14.98. Keepcase. *LANG:* English; French. *SUB:* Spanish. *FEATURES:* Commentary ▪ Behind-the-scenes montage ▪ Interviews ▪ Photo gallery ▪ Trivia game ▪ Trailers.
1998 (R) 103m/C Patrick Swayze, Gia Carides, Kim Myers, Olivia Birkelund, Tina Lifford, Elizabeth Ruscio, Roger E. Mosley, Bruce McGill, Mark Rolston; *D:* David Carson; *W:* Nicholas Hicks-Beach; *C:* John A. Alonzo; *M:* Dennis McCarthy.

Lewis and Clark: Journey of the Corps of Discovery

Ken Burns combines some spectacular nature photography with his familiar mix of paintings, maps, period photographs, and interviews to tell the story of the Lewis and Clark expedition. The ambitious documentary tries to delve beneath the usual schoolbook recitation of the facts to find the men and women who made the trip. Writers Stephen Ambrose and William Least-Heat Moon are quoted often. Full-frame image and sound may be a slight improvement over broadcast or VHS tape, but not much. The main value of the double-sided disc is in the extensive extras. —MM

Movie: 🎜🎜🎜 **DVD:** 🎜🎜 ½
Warner (cat #B3499D, UPC 7940543499-24). Full frame. Stereo. $29.98. Keepcase. *LANG:* English. *FEATURES:* 15 chapters ● Interview with Ken Burns, Stephen Ambrose, Dayton Duncan ● Conversation with Ken Burns ● "Making of" featurette ● "Ken Burns Making History" featurette. **1997** 240m/C **D:** Ken Burns; **W:** Dayton Duncan; **C:** Ken Burns, Buddy Squires, Allen Moore; **M:** Bobby Horton; **V:** Hal Holbrook, Adam Arkin, Murphy Guyer, Sam Waterston, Matthew Broderick, Kevin Conway, Gene Jones.

Lexx Series 2, Vol. 1

German/Canadian TV sci-fi series borrows from *Star Trek, Lost in Space, Dune, Alien,* and others but manages to be fresh and original. The title refers to a living dragonfly-shaped spaceship the size of Manhattan. Aboard are the usual suspects: space babe (Eva Habermann and then Xenia Seeberg), emotionless guy with really bad hair (Michael McManus), comic coward (Brian Downey), and disembodied guy (Jeffrey Hirschfield) trapped in a machine. Some of the content (particularly the medical stuff) is extremely graphic. (The box copy claims these are "uncut" episodes containing material never broadcast.) Each disc contains four shows and extras. Image in conventional scenes is excellent and production values for television are top-drawer. Some shimmering and aliasing are evident in special effects shots. Computer-generated effects are plentiful and well done but, well, still computer effects. Contents: "Mandrid," "Terminal," "Lyekka," "Luvliner." Three other volumes are also available (UPCs 054961449590, 054961473892, 054961475490) of equal image and audio quality. —MM

Movie: 🎜🎜🎜 **DVD:** 🎜🎜🎜
Acorn Media (cat 054981447992). Full frame. Dolby Digital Stereo. $29.98. Keepcase. *LANG:* English; French. *FEATURES:* "Making of" featurette ● Cast and character bios ● "Rated Lexx" featurette ● Trivia questions ● Cast interviews. **1998** 192m/C **GE CA** Eva Habermann, Michael McManus, Brian Downey, Xenia Seeberg, Jeff Hirschfield.

Liam

Stuttering little Liam (Burrows) and his family live in 1930s Liverpool among unemployment and incipient Fascism. His sister Teresa (Burns) lies about being Catholic to get a job as a maid in a Jewish home where some of her obligations cause her to question her faith. An undercurrent of Catholic hellfire grimly links Liam with his doomed sister. This film plays like a very personal memoir without achieving any universal appeal. The children's performances are very good. DVD looks and sounds good, but the cinematography is oddly colorful for the somber tone of the film. —LA

Movie: 🎜🎜 ½ **DVD:** 🎜🎜🎜
Lion's Gate Home Ent. (cat #ST7941D, UPC 658149794122). Widescreen letterboxed. Dolby Stereo. $24.98. Keepcase. *LANG:* English. *SUB:* English; Spanish. *CAP:* English. *FEATURES:* Theatrical trailer ● 24 chapters ● Interactive menus. **2000 (R)** 90m/C **GE GB** Ian Hart, Claire Hackett, David Hart, Anthony Borrows, Megan Burns, Anne Reid, Russell Dixon, Julia Deakin, Andrew Schofield, Bernadette Shortt, David Corey; **D:** Stephen Frears; **W:** Jimmy McGovern; **C:** Andrew Dunn; **M:** John Murphy.

The Libertine

After her husband's funeral, Mimi (Spaak) receives a key to an apartment that proves to be a secret pad he'd kept for illicit lovemaking. Investigating, she finds the place decked out as a sex palace, complete with movie projectors that show earlier orgies. Incensed that her husband sought his happiness elsewhere, Mimi embarks on a one-woman crusade of free sex and licentious seduction, with her hubby's business partner, doctors, strangers, even one of his female ex-lovers. But along the way she meets Dr. De Marchi (Trintignant), who patiently shows her that sexual adventure is where you find it, and that a good marriage can have it too. Shot in English, the movie has plenty of restrained nudity but no graphic sex. DVD is an interesting package that makes a case for the film being sophisticated adult fare. That reads well but is supported only tenuously by the picture itself. Liner notes author Nathaniel Thompson (whose Mondo Digital site is the most intelligent and worthwhile of sites devoted to fringe pictures like this) does an excellent job of explaining how serious adult filmmaker and importer Radley Metzger ran his Audubon Films. The transfer is adequate but nothing exceptional. One commendable aspect is the effort taken to reconstruct the full-length film; the quality drops a few notches every once in awhile, where reconstituted foreign material excised from the American release pops back in. —GE
AKA: La Matriarca.
Movie: 🎜🎜 ½ **DVD:** 🎜🎜 ½
First Run Features (UPC 72022299100-26). Widescreen (1.85:1) letterboxed. $24.98. Keepcase. *LANG:* English. *FEATURES:* Text essay ● Trailers ● Artwork. **1969** 90m/C **IT** Catherine Spaak, Jean-Louis Trintignant, Luigi Pistilli, Luigi Proietti, Renzo Montagnani; **D:** Pasquale Festa Campanile; **C:** Alfio Contini; **M:** Armando Trovajoli.

L.I.E.

Howie (Dano) is a lonely boy. His mother died on the Long Island Expressway (the L.I.E. of the title) and his father has little time for him after a hard day at work scamming construction clients and an evening in the arms of his new girlfriend. "The Long Island Express way has lanes going east, lanes going west, and lanes going straight to hell," he narrates at the beginning of the film as he walks the overpass railing. His best friend is Gary, a shady boy with a sexuality beyond his years. Howie has a schoolboy crush on him, which Gary uses to manipulate him into criminal acts. When Gary up and leaves town, he leaves Howie at the mercy of Marine Big John (Cox), a lover of young boys. When Howie's dad goes to the big house, he becomes emotionally dependent on Big John, who is in turn drawn to Howie's innocence. This is a deeply complicated and disturbing film about human desire—in this case, that of an aging Marine for young boys, and in some cases their desire for him. The most disturbing thing about the film is its ability to take characters that are so often stereotyped (a pedophile, a boy hustler) and make them realistic and incredibly three dimensional so that their relationships are a complex web, not a simple prey-and-predator scenario. Cox is nothing short of brilliant, walking the thin line between paternal and creepy, and Paul Franklin Dano won an award for Best Debut Performance from the IFP/West Independent Spirit Awards for his portrayal of the vulnerable young Howie. The script and direction by Michael Cuesta are right on target. The commentary by Cuesta and Cox isn't the normal extra fluff and goes a long way toward explaining the choice to make such a controversial film. They are well worth listening to. There are interesting film stock tricks and the cinematography is amazing. The transfer looks like it was overexposed leading to some oversaturation of color on the DVD, but it's nothing distracting. The sound is better than VHS quality. —CA

Movie: 🎜🎜🎜 **DVD:** 🎜🎜🎜
New Yorker Video (cat #DVD 85002, UPC 717119850241). Widescreen anamorphic. $29.95. Keepcase. *LANG:* English. *FEATURES:* 12 chapters ● Commentary: director ● Commentary: Brian Cox ● Deleted scenes. **2001 (NC-17)** 97m/C Brian Cox, Paul Franklin Dano, Billy Kay, Bruce Altman, James Costa, Tony Donnelly, Walter Masterson, Marcia DeBonis, Adam LeFevre; **D:** Michael Cuesta; **W:** Michael Cuesta, Stephen M. Ryder, Gerald Cuesta; **C:** Romeo Tirone; **M:** Pierre Foldes. *AWARDS:* Ind. Spirit '02: Debut Perf. (Dano); *NOM:* Ind. Spirit '02: Actor (Cox), Director (Cuesta), Film, Support. Actor (Kay).

Liebestraum

Underwritten, overdirected story attempts to be a combination of *Barton Fink* and *Body Heat.* Architecture professor Nick

(Anderson) moves to a small town to be near his dying mother (Novak). He meets old friend Paul (Pullman) and becomes infatuated with Paul's unhappy wife Jane (Gidley). The film has been available in "R"- and unrated editions. Here the scene that makes a difference is included as an extra. DVD does a good job—good enough, anyway—with an image that's often dark and deliberately murky. Style is much more important than substance here. —MM

Movie: 🎵🎵 ½ **DVD:** 🎵🎵🎵
MGM Home Ent. (cat #1002212, UPC 027-616864437). Widescreen (1.85:1) anamorphic. Dolby Digital Surround. $14.95. Keepcase. *LANG:* English; French. *SUB:* French; Spanish. *CAP:* English. *FEATURES:* 16 chapters • Trailer.
1991 (R) 109m/C Kevin Anderson, Bill Pullman, Pamela Gidley, Kim Novak; *D:* Mike Figgis; *W:* Mike Figgis; *C:* Juan Ruiz-Anchia; *M:* Mike Figgis.

Lies

Jang Sun Woo's film has been rightly compared to *Last Tango in Paris* and *In the Realm of the Senses*. It's about the mutual sexual obsession that grows between established sculptor J (Lee Sang Hyun) and teenager J (Kim Tae Yeon). Their physical affair quickly progresses from kinkiness to serious sado-masochism involving whipping. The subject is handled with a frankness that's rare in mainstream American films. It will make many viewers (including this one) uncomfortable, in part because the performances are so natural that they seem real. DVD appears to be completely accurate visually. Some grain crops up in darker scenes, but well-lit shots are completely clear. Sound is natural. Optional yellow subtitles are clear. The "director's statement" extra is text. —MM
AKA: Gojitmal.

Movie: 🎵🎵 ½ **DVD:** 🎵🎵🎵
Winstar Home Ent. (cat #FLV5315, UPC 720917531526). Widescreen anamorphic. $24.98. Keepcase. *LANG:* Korean. *SUB:* English. *FEATURES:* Director's statement • Trailer • 16 chapters.
1999 115m/C *KN* Sang Hyun Lee, Tae Yeon Kim; *D:* Sun Woo Jang; *W:* Sun Woo Jang; *C:* Woo-Hyoung Kim; *M:* Palan Dal.

The Life and Times of Hank Greenberg

Documentarian Aviva Kempner looks at the considerable impact that Detroit Tigers slugger Hank Greenberg had on America's Jewish community. The film is put together in fairly standard fashion, combining archival footage of Greenberg in action with reminiscences of friends and family, and some film taken of Greenberg shortly before his death. It's an unashamedly loving portrait. Even to such notables as Walter Matthau and Alan Dershowitz, Greenberg was a hero, one of the few Jews who rose to any prominence in professional baseball. Given the nature of the material, DVD is scant improvement

over VHS tape. The older film is supposed to look old and the contemporary interviews are mostly talking heads. Sound is fine. —MM

Movie: 🎵🎵 **DVD:** 🎵🎵 ½
20th Century Fox (UPC 024543025788). Full frame. Dolby Digital Stereo. $29.98. Keepcase. *LANG:* English. *SUB:* English; Yiddish; Spanish. *FEATURES:* 20 chapters • Commentary: Aviva Kempner • Trailer • Hank Greenberg statistics • Aviva Kempner thumbnail bio • Extended interviews.
1999 (PG) 95m/C *D:* Aviva Kempner; *W:* Aviva Kempner.

Life As a House

Things are not going very well for George Monroe (Kline). He lives alone in a dilapidated shack. He's fallen out of touch with his ex-wife Robin (Scott Thomas) and his troubled son Sam (Christensen). He's just been "let go" from his architectural firm. But worst of all, he has just learned that he is dying. So George decides to live life to the fullest by tearing down his old shack and building his dream house. Soon, everyone begins to see that George's dream is a reality and his family and neighbors rally around him to see the house completed. But as George is succeeding at building his new house, his real goal is to re-build his family. The film is a unique entry into the "terminally ill" genre, as it doesn't really focus on dying. Instead the film is about living, and how we must make the most of the time that we are given. Also, it's not until the very end that the movie becomes sappy and overly emotional. But *Life As a House* does have its share of problems. There are far too many characters in the film and too many subplots. Often, we find ourselves wishing the film would get back to Sam and George. Also, things get wrapped up a bit too nicely in the end. Still, the film is a nice drama for adults with an honest view of life, death, and family. For this "Platinum Series" DVD the image is sharp, but not without its problems. There are some shots which are visibly blurry and one shot becomes unusually dark. Also, the amount of grain fluctuates throughout. Despite this, the colors are fine. The DTS 5.1 audio track provides a great dynamic range, with clear dialogue and fantastic stereo separation. Also, there are some nice Surround effects to be had here. The Dolby Digital 5.1 track is impressive as well, but not quite as crisp as the DTS track. As a well-built special edition DVD, this disc is loaded with extras, most notably an informative audio commentary, and two interesting documentaries, the better of which is "From the Ground Up," a 10-minute look at the production design. —ML/LA

Movie: 🎵🎵 ½ **DVD:** 🎵🎵🎵
New Line (cat #5471, UPC 7940435471-26). Widescreen (2.35:1) anamorphic. Dolby Digital 5.1; DTS 5.1; Dolby Surround. $24.98. Snapper. *LANG:* English. *SUB:* English. *CAP:* English. *FEATURES:* Documen-

tary, "Character Building: Inside Life As a House" • Documentary, "From the Ground Up" • Deleted scenes with optional commentary • Commentary: Winkler, producer Rob Cowan, writer Mark Andrus • Theatrical trailer • Theatrical press kit • 22 chapters • DVD-ROM features.
2001 (R) 124m/C Kevin Kline, Hayden Christensen, Kristin Scott Thomas, Jena Malone, Mary Steenburgen, Jamey Sheridan, Scott Bakula, Sam Robards, Mike Weinberg, Scotty Leavenworth, Ian Somerhalder, Sandra Nelson; *D:* Irwin Winkler; *W:* Mark Andrus; *C:* Vilmos Zsigmond; *M:* Mark Isham. *AWARDS:* Natl. Bd. of Review '01: Breakthrough Perf. (Christensen); *NOM:* Golden Globes '02: Support. Actor (Christensen); Screen Actors Guild '01: Actor (Kline), Support. Actor (Christensen).

Life Is to Whistle

A charming love letter to Cuba. Mariana, a passionate ballerina, Elpidio, a sensitive musician, and Julia, a middle-aged social worker who faints at the mention of the word "sex," seem to symbolize the exuberance of Cuban life. The younger two were orphaned as young children; the social worker gave up her baby at the same orphanage. Their meeting in Havana's Plaza de la Revolution represents a king of healing. The image quality suffers from desaturated color cinematography, which also detracts from a vibrant story. Sound quality is fine. —LA **AKA:** La Vida Es Silbar.

Movie: 🎵🎵🎵 **DVD:** 🎵🎵 ½
New Yorker Video (cat #75601, UPC 71-7119756147). Widescreen letterboxed. $29.98. Keepcase. *LANG:* Spanish. *SUB:* English. *FEATURES:* 16 chapters • Original theatrical trailer.
1998 106m/C *SP CU* Luis Alberto Garcia, Isabel Santos, Coralia Veloz, Claudia Rojas; *D:* Fernando Perez; *W:* Fernando Perez, Eduardo Del Llano, Humberto Jimenez; *C:* Raul Perez Ureta; *M:* Bola de Nieve, Benny More.

Life on a String

Set in the distant past, this is a lyrical story of a young boy searching for a cure for his blindness. His possible cure involves a myth which requires him to devote his life to music and the breaking of 1,000 strings on a banjo. Adapted from a story by Shi Tiesheng. The disc's video transfer reproduces colors nicely, though a loss of clarity on borders is occasionally noticeable. While no distortion is noticeable on the decent soundtrack, the musical track was far too loud during some scenes and did suffer as a result. —MJT

Movie: 🎵🎵 **DVD:** 🎵🎵
Kino on Video (cat #K233, UPC 738329-023324). Widescreen (1.85:1) letterboxed. Dolby Digital Stereo. $29.95. Keepcase. *LANG:* Mandarin. *SUB:* English. *FEATURES:* 13 chapters.
1990 110m/C *CH* Xu Qing; *D:* Chen Kaige; *W:* Chen Kaige; *C:* Gu Changwei; *M:* Xiao-Song Qu.

Life with Judy Garland— Me and My Shadows

Based on daughter Lorna Luft's book, this film explores the life of the wildly popular and much-loved Judy Garland (Davis). From her young childhood in which she was signed to a contract at MGM at 14, to her later years when addiction to barbiturates and alcohol had consumed her life, this Emmy award–winning made-for-television biopic is riveting. Judy Davis is compelling in her portrayal of Garland, and a life that was overrun with insecurity and frailty. The full-frame picture is stunningly clear and crisp with no defects in the transfer. The real jewel on this release, however, is the 5.1 Surround track. It completely utilizes all six speakers to produce walls of sound (and emotion) during the beautiful performance scenes with Garland singing. This film is a captivating dose of reality into a woman most people only know as the girl with the ruby slippers. —EL
Movie: ♫♫♫ ½ **DVD:** ♫♫♫ ½
Miramax Pictures (cat #24792, UPC 786-936170399). Full frame. Dolby Digital 5.1 Surround. $22.99. Keepcase. *LANG:* English; French. *CAP:* English. *FEATURES:* Commentary: daughter Lorna Luft • Behind-the-scenes featurette • "I Play the Palace" deleted scene • 32 chapters.
2001 (PG) 107m/C Judy Davis, Victor Garber, Hugh Laurie; **D:** Robert Ackerman.

Life without Dick

Colleen (Parker) inadvertently kills her boyfriend Dick (Knoxville) before inept Irish hitman Daniel (Connick) gets the chance to rub him out at the behest of his underworld boss (Ferguson). Colleen is easily persuaded to do Daniel's hits for him so he can retire and resume his singing career. Connick wouldn't look more uncomfortable if a gun were pointed at his head. It's flat unfunny exploitation of the incomprehensible popularity of Parker. The one bright spot is a cameo of Garr as an emotional fortune teller. Both the widescreen and full-frame versions look sharp and bright. Sound is excellent. —LA
Movie: ♫ ½ **DVD:** ♫♫♫
Columbia Tristar (cat #06671, UPC 0433-96066717). Widescreen (1.85:1) anamorphic; full frame. English 5.1 Dolby Digital. $24.98. Keepcase. *LANG:* English; Spanish; Portuguese. *SUB:* English; French; Spanish; Portuguese; Chinese; Korean; Thai. *CAP:* English. *FEATURES:* Bonus trailers • Interactive menus • 28 chapters.
2001 (PG-13) 96m/C Sarah Jessica Parker, Harry Connick Jr., Teri Garr, Johnny Knoxville, Craig Ferguson, Geoffrey Blake, Brigid Conley Walsh, Ever Carradine, Erik Palladino, Claudia Schiffer; **D:** Bix Skahill; **W:** Bix Skahill; **C:** James Glennon; **M:** David Lawrence.

Light at the Edge of the World

Based on the Jules Vern novel, this film recounts the story of Will Denton (Dou-glas), a lighthouse guard with a mysterious past. When the island is taken over by Captain Kongre (Brynner) and his band of pirates to be used as a hideout and merciless trap for unsuspecting ships, Denton must make a life altering decision of whether to help the unsuspecting ships and their crews or to safely wait it out until the militia arrives to roust the high seas riffraff. This film is an enjoyable yet rather surreal vision of one man's struggle against forces beyond his control. Kirk Douglas and Yul Brynner are in fine form and ably backed by a talented supporting cast. There were some noticeable dust artifacts that made it onto this film, but they are few and far between. The color has held up fairly well in this more than three-decade old release and the transfer contains a crisp and clear picture. The Dolby Mono track is decent but gives itself away during certain scenes. This release certainly could have benefitted from a re-mastered stereo soundtrack, but overall it does not detract horribly. —EL
Movie: ♫♫♫ **DVD:** ♫♫♫
Image Ent. (cat #680, UPC 0143810680-23). Widescreen (2.35:1) anamorphic. Dolby Digital Mono. $22.49. Keepcase. *LANG:* English. *FEATURES:* 20 chapters.
1971 (PG) 126m/C Kirk Douglas, Yul Brynner, Samantha Eggar; **D:** Kevin Billington; **W:** Tom Rowe; **C:** Henri Decae; **M:** Piero Piccioni.

Light Keeps Me Company

Considering that Carl-Gustaf Nykvist was making a documentary about his father, this look at the famous cinematographer is remarkably candid. It touches on the more painful parts of his life—divorce, a child's suicide, the onset of aphasia in 1998 that ended his professional career—as well as the expected compliments and honors. More importantly, the film is made very much in the Bergman/Nykvist style. It's quiet, calm, and illuminated with fine winter light. Sven Nykvist himself comes across with the same kind of cool reserve. The son of missionaries who were absent from his life for years at a time, he realizes how much his life has mirrored theirs. Many of the directors and actors he has worked with are interviewed here. They say all of the right things and their affection seems completely genuine. The most important part of Nykvist's career was his work with Ingmar Bergman and that is given its full due. DVD image is very good with only some minor distortion in exterior panning shots. Sound is particularly strong. Recommended to anyone who wants to know about the real wear of filmmaking. —MM
Movie: ♫♫♫ ½ **DVD:** ♫♫♫
First Run Features (UPC 720229909891). Widescreen (1.66:1) letterboxed. $24.98. Keepcase. *LANG:* English; Swedish. *SUB:* English. *FEATURES:* 12 chapters • Trailers • Sven Nykvist filmography • Director's foreword (text).

2000 78m/C *DK SW* **D:** Carl-Gustaf Ny-kvist; **Nar:** Erland Josephson, Melinda Kinnaman, Rikard Wolff.

Lilies

Strange revenge fantasy is set in a northern Quebec men's prison in 1952. A bishop (Sabourin) goes to hear the confession of a dying convict and is taken hostage in the chapel by the prison's homosexual population. There, he is forced to watch a play that re-creates a 40-year-old incident in his own life. As the prison walls fade away, the actor/prisoners turn into students Simon (Cadieux) and Vallier (Gilmore), who take the lovers' roles in the pageant about the martyrdom of St. Sebastien too seriously for comfort. The female roles are played by men. The language choices and the minimal extras are really all that differentiate DVD from VHS. The menu is exceptionally slow to respond. —MM **AKA:** Les Feluettes.
Movie: ♫♫ **DVD:** ♫♫ ½
Wolfe Video (cat #5195). Full frame. Dolby Digital Stereo. $24.95. Keepcase. *LANG:* English; French. *FEATURES:* 9 chapters • Trailers.
1996 (R) 95m/C *CA* Marcel Sabourin, Jason Cadieux, Danny Gilmore, Brent Carver, Matthew Ferguson, Alexander Chapman, Aubert Pallascio; **D:** John Greyson; **W:** Michel Marc Bouchard; **C:** Daniel Jobin; **M:** Mychael Danna. *AWARDS:* Genie '96: Art Dir./Set Dec., Costume Des., Film, Sound; *NOM:* Genie '96: Actor (Cadieux), Actor (Ferguson, Gilmore), Adapt. Screenplay, Cinematog., Director (Greyson), Film Editing, Support. Actor (Chapman), Score.

Link

Primatologist Dr. Phillip (Stamp) and his nubile assistant Jane (Shue) find that their experiment has gone awry and their hairy charges are running amok. It's as ridiculous as it sounds. DVD image often looks grainy and the colors are fairly muted. Still, it is generally a clean print and there is little edge-enhancement or noise. Audio, presented in Dolby 2.0, is basically satisfactory. —MM/SH
Movie: woof **DVD:** ♫♫ ½
Anchor Bay (UPC 13131142396). Widescreen (2.35:1) anamorphic. Dolby Digital Stereo. $24.99. Keepcase. *LANG:* English. *FEATURES:* Trailer.
1986 (R) 103m/C *GB* Elisabeth Shue, Terence Stamp, Steven Piner, Richard Garnett; **D:** Richard Franklin; **W:** Everett DeRoche; **C:** Mike Molloy; **M:** Jerry Goldsmith.

Lionheart

When 17-year-old Jesse Martin set out to be the youngest person to circumnavigate the globe unaided, many people thought he was crazy. Who had ever heard of a young person, with virtually no sailing experience, undertaking such a dangerous adventure? But after sailing into an Australian harbor after 329 days at sea, there would be few that would ever ask that question again. This documentary is comprised of footage taken on his boat during the course of his trip and news file footage. It's a captivating and appealing adventure. DVD picture is crisp, and the Dolby Digital stereo track is very clear. —EL

Movie: 🎵🎵🎵 **DVD:** 🎵🎵🎵
Image Ent. (cat #1021, UPC 014381102-123). Widescreen letterboxed. Dolby Digital Stereo. $24.99. Keepcase. *LANG:* English. *FEATURES:* Lionheart featurette ▪ Jesse Martin bio ▪ 15 chapters.
2000 70m/C **D:** Paul Currie; **C:** Jessie Martin; **M:** Christine Woodruff.

Lip Service

Allison (Temchen) and Kat (Gertz) were fast friends in college. Years later, they're reunited. By then, Allison is a conservative designer. Kat is boozed-up free spirit who moves in with Allison and takes over her life. Though the trailer makes the film look like a lesbian-awakening story, that's really a minor subplot which is dispensed with quickly. Neither the characters nor their conflicts are particularly engaging. The grainy, indie prod, full-frame DVD image is no improvement over VHS tape. Sound is better. —MM **AKA:** Kat and Allison.

Movie: 🎵🎵 **DVD:** 🎵🎵 ½
MTI (cat #8112, UPC 039414581126). Full frame. $24.98. Keepcase. *LANG:* English. *SUB:* Spanish. *FEATURES:* 20 chapters ▪ Talent files ▪ Trailers.
2000 (R) 95m/C Jami Gertz, Sybil Temchen, Jonathan Silverman, Christian Camargo, Adewale Akinnuoye-Agbaje, Jenna Byrne; **D:** Shawn Schepps; **W:** Shawn Schepps; **C:** Feliks Parnell.

Listen to Britain and other Films by Humphrey Jennings

Documentarians point to American Flaherty and Englishmen John Grierson and Humphrey Jennings as three of the most influential pioneers. This DVD collects a series of Humphrey Jennings's most famous works, all of which center on England during or just after WWII. Jennings's most famous film, "London Can Take It!" (1940; 9 min.) almost offhandedly shows the utter destruction raining on London (including the tossed bus on the DVD cover illustration). The shots are more newsreel-oriented than later Jennings films, but they're very carefully arranged. By openly, proudly showing the bomb hits instead of trying to minimize them, the film concentrates on honoring the character of the Londoners, going so far as to make little jokes about the wrecked stores, etc. The message to Londoners and enemies alike is that the bombing isn't going to put the nation out of business, far from it. It was wildly popular in the U.K. and very influential in America, where it had an enormous impact on public opinion to support the besieged Brits. In "Words for Battle" (1941; 8 min.) a medley of visuals accompanies Laurence

Olivier as he quotes great Englishmen like Milton, Blake, and Browning, as well as Winston Churchill and Abraham Lincoln. Jennings reportedly assembled this brief and verbally poetic film from found footage instead of shooting new scenes. The quiet reserve in Olivier's voice is hypnotizing, as he reads some of the most famous and stirring words written in the English language. "Listen to Britain" (1942; 18 min.) is a montage of wartime activity, focusing on naturalistic montages of trains, people dancing and working, and preparing defenses for the country—but concentrating on an audio montage of noises, voices, and music. It's a more extended tone poem that has no formal narration or set plot. Instead, we're given an aural portrait of a nation working, fighting back day to day. "Fires Were Started" (1943; 70 min.) is a day in the life of a fire crew that must fight to keep the docks functioning during the Nazi air raids. Organization, teamwork, and sacrifice are required as the firemen fight through the night, with bombs falling around them. Jennings's second most famous film, this feature-length documentary is the most dated, simply because it goes on so long and is so literal. In "A Diary for Timothy" (1945; 39 min.), a baby arrives exactly five years after the start of the war, and the film reviews events to catch him up on the violent and uncertain world into which he's been born. The sacrifices of his parents, and their hopes for the future are what young Timothy has for a legacy. The most all-round satisfying of the films, this imaginative chronicle welcomes the brand-new Tim into a struggle-in-progress, telling him times are tough but he's part of a good crew. Jennings mixes some of his most beautiful and carefully shot images with famous author E.M. Forster's compelling narration. Made for a celebration of Britain, "Family Portrait" (1951; 26 min.) examines the English character and its new place in the post-war world. Sort of a letdown after the at-sword's-point eloquence of the wartime films, this show does its best to talk about the better aspects of the British political system ("where politicians dine with the opposition") and the desire to make the classed society more equitable. DVD is a well-assembled group of great films in only passable condition. None are broken, but all are well scratched from wear, and are too grainy and contrasty to be from archive-quality materials. David Shepard is the producer, so it might be surmised that these prints are all there are to be had, except that since they come from the Blackhawk Collection, we can also assume that these are not from original English sources. In general, the audio is serviceable, but almost always has some distortion. "Fires Were Started" suffers the most, as it has the most dialogue, often delivered off the cuff by non-actors. Much of it is just unintelligible, which may have contributed to its lack of impact on this reviewer. And the disc had no closed captions or subtitles that would have

helped one through (or, God forbid, make the disc accessible to deaf viewers). Yet, the beauty here comes through largely unimpaired. The films should be required viewing for film students. Better yet, today's television "journalists" with their trash "news" should be forced to watch these elegant and responsible works of art. The extra of Myra Hess playing Beethoven on the piano is a full short-subject extension of a segment in "Listen to Britain." —GE

Movie: 🎵🎵🎵 ½ **DVD:** 🎵🎵 ½
Image Ent. (cat #ID1488DSDVD, UPC 014-381148824). Full frame. Dolby Digital Mono. $24.99. Keepcase. *LANG:* English. *FEATURES:* Myra Hess playing Beethoven on the piano.
1940 182m/C *GB* **D:** Humphrey Jennings.

Little City

Bland, lifeless "romantic comedy" about a group of tempestuous heterosexual and lesbian couples living and loving in San Francisco. Handsomely photographed production takes full advantage of the beautiful location scenery, but is missing any trace of chemistry between the attractive cast members. Sciorra is fine, but Going and Williams are unconvincing as lesbians. Jon Bon Jovi barely registers on-screen. It's hard to blame the cast, though, as there seems to be no spark of life during any of the proceedings. The denouement is clichéd, manipulative, and lame. The disc features a sharp, colorful transfer with only minimal grain. The sound is clean and clear, but lacks Surround presence—appropriate for this dialogue heavy picture. —DG

Movie: 🎵 ½ **DVD:** 🎵🎵🎵 ½
Miramax Pictures (cat #21631, UPC 786-93614454). Widescreen (1.85:1) anamorphic. Dolby Surround 2.0. $29.99. Keepcase. *LANG:* English. *SUB:* English. *CAP:* English. *FEATURES:* Behind-the-scenes featurette ▪ 24 chapters ▪ Insert card with chapter listing ▪ Trailers for other Miramax titles.
1997 (R) 90m/C Jon Bon Jovi, Penelope Ann Miller, Annabella Sciorra, Josh Charles, Joanna Going, JoBeth Williams; **D:** Roberto Benabib; **W:** Roberto Benabib; **C:** Randall Love.

Little Dieter Needs to Fly

Acclaimed documentary filmmaker Werner Herzog here turns his cameras on a man with a truly unique story. Dieter Dengler grew up in Bavaria, and witnessed much of the carnage caused by World War II. Seeing the battles from a first-hand perspective, Dieter was determined to become a pilot. He went to the U.S., joined the Navy, and fulfilled his dream of becoming a combat-fighter pilot. He was sent to Vietnam, where his plane was shot down over Laos, and he became a prisoner of war. He eventually escaped and was rescued. Herzog interviews Dengler in his home in San Francisco, but also takes him

back to his boyhood home and then to Laos, so that Dengler can relate his story. *Little Dieter Needs to Fly* is a compelling, engrossing, and moving story, which is not always uplifting, but is hard to turn away from. The typically flamboyant Herzog pulls back here, letting Dieter's story play out on its own. The film has been lauded with awards, and Herzog is now working on a feature-film version of Dieter's story. The DVD offers the film in a letterboxed format and gives the viewer a fine transfer. The image is sharp and clear, showing minimal grain and very true colors. The mono audio track provides clear dialogue, but lacks any real presence during the war footage. The detailed production notes which accompany this DVD give a great deal of insight into the making of the film and Dieter's story. —*ML*
Movie: 🎬🎬🎬 ½ **DVD:** 🎬🎬 ½
Anchor Bay (cat #DV11541, UPC 013131-154191). Widescreen (1.85:1) anamorphic. Dolby Digital Mono. $29.98. Keepcase. *LANG:* English. *FEATURES:* Production notes • Director bio • 16 chapters.
1997 74m/C *GE GB* **D:** Werner Herzog; **W:** Werner Herzog; **C:** Peter Zeitlinger.

The Little Foxes [MGM]

Nineteen hundred. The avaricious Hubbard family has pretty much sewn up the economic opportunities in their southern hometown, but the prospect of a deal with a Chicago investor to build a cotton gin has brothers Ben (Dingle) and Oscar (Reid) hot for more riches. The problem is their sister Regina (Davis), whose sickly husband Horace (Marshall) is too ethical to allow his savings to be used on the deal. The heartless Regina wants the money so badly, she doesn't care whether her husband lives or dies. Oscar pushes his dimwit bank teller son Leo (Duryea) to simply steal Horace's money from his safe deposit box. The only comfort to Horace is his virtuous daughter Alexandra (Wright). She doesn't understand how venal her relatives are, but by just observing her mother Regina, gets a chance to learn quickly. MGM's DVD would seem to be a reasonable repressing of HBO video's earlier disc (reviewed in *Book 1*), and looks and sounds fine. The Toland photography is very well represented, with his deep-focus mastershots looking especially good on a large monitor. Alternate French and Spanish language tracks are included, but they're of a very poor quality. —*GE*
Movie: 🎬🎬🎬 ½ **DVD:** 🎬🎬🎬
MGM Home Ent. (cat #1002382, UPC 027616865939). Full frame; widescreen (1.85:1) anamorphic. Stereo; Mono. $14.95. Keepcase. *LANG:* English; French. *SUB:* English; French; Spanish. *CAP:* English. *FEATURES:* Trailer.
1941 116m/B Bette Davis, Herbert Marshall, Dan Duryea, Teresa Wright, Charles Dingle, Richard Carlson, Carl Benton Reid; **D:** William Wyler; **W:** Lillian Hellman; **C:** Gregg Toland; **M:** Meredith Willson. *AWARDS:* NOM: Oscars '41: Actress

(Davis), Director (Wyler), Film Editing, Picture, Screenplay, Support. Actress (Collinge, Wright),Orig. Dramatic Score.

Little Man Tate

Seven-year-old genius Fred (Hann-Byrd) is the prize in a tug-of-war between his mother (Foster) who wants him to lead a normal life and a psychologist (Weist) who loves him for his intellect. The acclaimed directorial debut for Foster contains overtones of her own life as a child actor. She quickly admits as much on a very relaxed, nostalgic commentary track. DVD image and sound are fine but unspectacular. That's fine; the performances are the heart of the film. —*MM*
Movie: 🎬🎬🎬 **DVD:** 🎬🎬🎬
MGM Home Ent. (cat #1002361, UPC 027-616865724). Widescreen (1.85:1) anamorphic. Dolby Digital 5.1 Surround Stereo; Dolby Digital Surround. $19.98. Keepcase. *LANG:* English; French; Spanish. *SUB:* French; Spanish. *CAP:* English. *FEATURES:* 16 chapters • Commentary: Jodie Foster • Trailer.
1991 (PG) 99m/C Jodie Foster, Dianne Wiest, Harry Connick Jr., Adam Hann-Byrd, George Plimpton, Debi Mazar, Celia Weston, David Hyde Pierce, Danitra Vance, Josh Mostel, P.J. Ochlan; **D:** Jodie Foster; **W:** Scott Frank; **C:** Mike Southon; **M:** Mark Isham.

The Little Princess [Marengo]

Please see review for *Classic Family DVD Double Feature.*
Movie: 🎬🎬🎬 ½
1939 (G) 91m/B Shirley Temple, Richard Greene, Anita Louise, Ian Hunter, Cesar Romero, Arthur Treacher, Sybil Jason, Miles Mander, Marcia Mae Jones, E.E. Clive; **D:** Walter Lang; **W:** Ethel Hill, Walter Ferris; **C:** Arthur C. Miller; **M:** Walter Bullock.

Little Shots of Happiness

Frances (Dickenson), a bored office drone, decides to leave her husband and begins to live out of her office secretly. Each night she goes to a nightclub or a bar in Boston, picking up different men. A very pleasant surprise in the endless DVDs that make up these pages. Winner of the John Cassavetes Award at the Cine Arts U.S. International Film Festival, this one harkens back very much to the work of that great director, with a crude video DVD transfer replacing the grainy & shaky 16mm black-and-white of Cassavetes's early days (and equally to the enrichment of its presentation). An indie gem that once more suggests the possibility of film liberated from commerce, as Cocteau once hoped. With a well-mixed alternative rock score. —*MO*
Movie: 🎬🎬🎬 **DVD:** 🎬🎬
Vanguard Intl. Cinema (cat #VF0128, UPC 658769021837). Full frame. $29.95. Keepcase. *LANG:* English. *FEATURES:* 12 chapters • Commentary: director Todd

Verow • Theatrical trailer • Deleted scenes • "Making of" featurette.
1997 (R) 85m/C Bonnie Dickenson, Todd Verow, Linda Ekoian, Rita Gavelis, P.J. Marino, Castalia Jason, Leanne Whitney, Bill Dwyer, Eric Sapp, Maureen Picard, Eric Romley; **D:** Todd Verow; **W:** Jim Dwyer, Todd Verow; **C:** Todd Verow.

Little Women

Louisa May Alcott's Civil War story of the four March sisters—Jo, Beth, Amy, and Meg, who share their loves, their joys, and their sorrows—has been adapted for the screen numerous times. The 1994 version starring Winona Ryder is solid. A 1949 version with June Allyson has merit, whereas the 1978 TV adaptation is more forgettable. But this 1933 vintage edition—the one with Hepburn, directed by Cukor—is the one to choose before the others. Everything about this classic film is wonderful, from the lavish period costumes to the excellent script, and particularly the captivating performances by the cast. Another fine black-and-white transfer from Warner Bros., the disc comes close to the picture standards set by WB's DVD issues of *Now, Voyager* and *Citizen Kane* in terms of stunning B&W eye candy. Occasional white specks and very occasional visual noise in the darkest scenes are all that mar the presentation. Don't fret too much over these minor criticisms, however, because few vintage classics look better on home video. Needless to say, this DVD eclipses previous VHS and LD issues of *Little Women*, which were more seriously hindered by scratches and wear that have been digitally concealed for the DVD. This presentation is not just black and white; it's all the grays in between—and you get to see every monochromatic hue. The monaural soundtrack is all that can be expected from an almost 70-year-old film; that is, the dialogue is distinct and clear, and the snap, crackle, and pop usually associated with early sound films is minimal. Max Steiner's score sounds great given the limited fidelity of the source material. —*MB*
Movie: 🎬🎬🎬🎬 **DVD:** 🎬🎬🎬 ½
Warner (cat #65159, UPC 0125695159-25). Full frame. Dolby Digital Mono. $19.98. Snapper. *LANG:* English. *SUB:* English; Spanish; French; Portuguese; Chinese; Korean. *CAP:* English. *FEATURES:* 33 chapters • Scoring session music cues • Notes on the Hepburn/Cukor collaboration and awards • Theatrical trailer.
1933 107m/B Katharine Hepburn, Joan Bennett, Paul Lukas, Edna May Oliver, Frances Dee, Spring Byington, Jean Parker, Douglass Montgomery; **D:** George Cukor; **W:** Victor Heerman, Sarah Y. Mason; **C:** Henry W. Gerrard; **M:** Max Steiner. *AWARDS:* Oscars '33: Adapt. Screenplay; Venice Film Fest. '34: Actress (Hepburn); *NOM:* Oscars '33: Director (Cukor), Picture.

Live Nude Girls Unite!

Julia Query was a dancer at San Francisco's Lusty Lady peep show who "never dreamed that her first attempt at labor activism would be as a stripper." Quirks of the trade began to irk her, and when she realized her "co-workers" felt the same—it was time for action. Together they set out to unionize and secure a contract to fight back against bizarre industry rules. However, the Lusty Lady's ownership cringed at the possibility of bending to the will of militant showgirls, so more than six months of brutal negotiating against high-priced union-bustin' attorneys ensued. From that conflict (and another more personal story) spawns genuine emotion. Query somehow couches her first-hand account of the sex industry with an aura of "normalcy" that adeptly avoids muffling the beat of her political diatribe. Outrageously absurd and, at moments, oddly moving. Full-frame image quality is consistent with other documentaries shot on consumer video with natural lighting. Voice-overs are strong, but some girl-on-the-street interviews can get a little iffy. The deleted scenes are funny and the image gallery is tiny. —GNG/DG

Movie: 🎾🎾½ **DVD:** 🎾½

First Run Features (UPC 720229909747). Full frame. $29.95. Keepcase. LANG: English. FEATURES: Deleted scenes ● Image gallery ● Trailer.

2000 75m/C D: Vicky Funari, Julia Query; **C:** Vicky Funari.

Living It Up

Despondent bus driver Martin (Gomez) stands on an overpass and is about to jump when the Spanish equivalent of Clarence talks him down with the promise of one week to spend 100 million pesetas, then die. Martin rents a villa, throws a lavish party, and meets Lola (Hayek), a gorgeous but inept member of the catering staff. It's love at first sight for Martin. Lola has something else in mind. The charming Gomez makes up for all sins of sappiness. The DVD looks and sounds great. The featurette contains a tiny bit of honesty along with the usual lovefest. —LA AKA: La Gran Vida.

Movie: 🎾🎾🎾 **DVD:** 🎾🎾🎾

Columbia Tristar (cat #06446, UPC 0433-96064461). Widescreen (2.35:1) anamorphic. 5.1 Dolby Digital (Spanish); Dolby Surround. $29.98. Keepcase. LANG: Spanish; English; French. SUB: English; French; Portuguese; Chinese; Korean; Thai. CAP: English. FEATURES: "Making of" featurette ● Hayek filmography ● Bonus trailers ● Animated menus ● 28 chapters.

2000 (R) 114m/C SP Salma Hayek, Carmelo Gomez, Tito Valverde; **D:** Antonio Caudri; **W:** Carlos Asorey Brey, Fernando Leon de Aranda; **C:** Nesto Calvo; **M:** Manuel Villalta.

The Locusts

Backwater beefcake Clay Hewitt (Vaughn) swaggers into sleepy little Seely, Kansas, where everyone has a lit cigarette and a secret, and nobody is safe from hopeless clichés and corny dialogue. Clay's sweaty sleeveless T-shirts and choirboy face (both attempting to channel Brando's Stanley

Kowalski) soon have the women swarming and swooning, but he's only interested in helping the emotionally damaged Flyboy (Davies) get out from under his emasculating and abusive mother Delilah (Capshaw), who's also Clay's boss and overly ardent admirer. Judd is barely used (lucky her) as Clay's spunky squeeze. First time director Kelley is as blatant with his visuals—note the big spider in the first shots—as the character names and metaphors. (Delilah has workers castrating bulls a lot.) DVD delivers a solid re-creation of a good but unspectacular image that's appropriately soft for a 1950s period piece. Sound is fine. —MM

Movie: 🎾½ **DVD:** 🎾🎾½

MGM Home Ent. (cat #1002968, UPC 027-616871558). Widescreen (2.35:1) anamorphic. Dolby Digital Surround. $19.95. Keepcase. LANG: English. SUB: English; French; Spanish. CAP: English. FEATURES: 16 chapters ● Trailer.

1997 (R) 123m/C Kate Capshaw, Jeremy Davies, Vince Vaughn, Ashley Judd, Paul Rudd, Daniel Meyer, Jessica Capshaw; **D:** John Patrick Kelley; **W:** John Patrick Kelley; **C:** Phedon Papamichael; **M:** Carter Burwell.

Lone Ranger

Clayton Moore gallops onto the big screen to halt an impending war between the settlers and Native Americans. To succeed, he'll have to handle bigshot rancher Kilgore (Bettger), who's got his eyes on the Natives' land. All the good-natured excitement and moral instruction from the TV series have made their way into this film, along with a condescending and paternalistic attitude towards the Native Americans. The picture is clean and free of grain but often appears tinted in various shades of blue, gray, and red, sometimes even within the same frame. The sound quality is slightly better, although with a good deal of background hiss. VCI has tried to make this a deluxe edition, including a bonus disc of interviews and bios. —BG

Movie: 🎾🎾½ **DVD:** 🎾🎾

VCI (cat #8252, UPC 089859825224). Widescreen letterboxed; full frame. $24.99. Keepcase. LANG: English. FEATURES: 18 chapters ● Cast bios ● Trailers ● Photo gallery ● Interview: Dawn Moore ● Interview: Michael Ansara.

1956 87m/C Clayton Moore, Jay Silverheels, Lyle Bettger, Bonita Granville; **D:** Stuart Heisler; **W:** Herb Meadow; **C:** Edwin DuPar; **M:** David Buttolph.

Lone Ranger and the Lost City of Gold

Clayton Moore rides again as the masked avenger, this time crossing paths with a band of hooded outlaws who have been terrorizing Native Americans and settlers alike in a small frontier town. Each of the victims owned a piece of a golden medallion that could reveal the location of the titular city. Less engaging than its predecessor, but still an enjoyable western romp. As in VCI's release of the previous

film, colors are extremely inconsistent and often show a sharp tint, and the sound is merely average. The second disc contains Moore and Silverheels's induction into the Cowboy Hall of Fame. —BG

Movie: 🎾🎾 **DVD:** 🎾🎾

VCI (cat #8254, UPC 089859825422). Widescreen letterboxed; full frame. $29.99. Keepcase. LANG: English. FEATURES: 18 chapters ● Photo gallery ● Cowboy Hall of Fame Induction Ceremony ● Trailers.

1958 80m/C Clayton Moore, Jay Silverheels, Douglas Kennedy, Noreen Nash, Ralph Moody; **D:** Lesley Selander; **W:** Eric Freiwald, Robert Schaefer; **C:** Kenneth Peach Sr.; **M:** Les Baxter.

The Lone Ranger: Volume 1

The masked crusader (Moore) and Tonto (Silverheels) save the day in Episodes 183–187 of the original television series. They travel the West making the land a save place to live. More interesting than the main program are the special features: the first two episodes of the series, first aired in 1949. These give the origins of the Lone Ranger, which are often taken for granted. The image for both the color and B&W episodes is close to the original broadcast and, though there is some dirt from the source material, the image is vibrant and well defined. The mono sound is very clear and free of noise. —DRL

Movie: 🎾🎾 **DVD:** 🎾🎾½

Rhino (cat #976623, UPC 6034976623-26). Full frame. Mono. $19.95. Keepcase. LANG: English. FEATURES: Episodes 1 and 2 of the series ● 24 chapters.

1956 134m/C Clayton Moore, Jay Silverheels, Slim Pickens, William Challee, Ron Hagerthy; **D:** Earl Bellamy, George B. Seitz, Oscar Rudolph; **W:** George B. Seitz, Doane R. Hoag, Wells Root, Tom Seller; **C:** William F. Whitley, Mack Stengler.

Lone Wolf McQuade

Martial arts action abounds as unorthodox Ranger Norris goes up against gun-running mercenaries led by Carradine. Good to very good DVD image handles the wide desert landscapes without any serious problems. It's actually better than the cartoonish story requires. —MM

Movie: 🎾🎾 **DVD:** 🎾🎾½

MGM Home Ent. (cat #1002573, UPC 027-616867742). Widescreen (1.85:1) anamorphic. Dolby Digital Mono. $14.95. Keepcase. LANG: English; French; Spanish. SUB: French; Spanish. CAP: English. FEATURES: 16 chapters ● Trailer.

1983 107m/C Chuck Norris, Leon Isaac Kennedy, David Carradine, L.Q. (Justus E. McQueen) Jones, Barbara Carrera; **D:** Steve Carver; **W:** H. Kaye Dyal; **C:** Roger Shearman; **M:** Francesco De Masi.

Lonely Hearts

Odd, quirky film about two shy hopeless people finding each other. Peter (Kaye) is

an aging man who has lived with his mother all of his life. Now that she has died he begins a search for a mate. As a 50-year-old mama's boy, he has a daunting task, so he goes to a dating agency. Patricia (Hughes) is younger than Peter and has been controlled by her parents all of her life. The agency sets them up and their dates include bingo and neighborhood theatre, where they each are cast for an upcoming production. Through their awkward fumblings and missteps they come to a better understanding of themselves and a hope of knowing each other. This is a slow-paced film with a real feel for the discomfort of dating and reaching out for something you're not sure you know what to do with. Good for lovers of foreign and independent films but not a good date film. Picture quality is slightly above VHS quality and the sound is average. —CA
Movie: 🎵🎵 **DVD:** 🎵🎵 ½
MGM Home Ent. (cat #1002754, UPC 027-616869524). Widescreen (1.85:1) anamorphic; full frame. Dolby Digital Mono. $19.90. Keepcase. *LANG:* English. *SUB:* English; French; Spanish. *CAP:* English. *FEATURES:* 16 chapters.
1982 (R) 95m/C *AU* Wendy Hughes, Norman Kaye, Jon Finlayson, Julia Blake, Jonathan Hardy; *D:* Paul Cox; *W:* Paul Cox, John Clarke; *C:* Yuri Sokol; *M:* Norman Kaye. *AWARDS:* Australian Film Inst. '82: Film.

Lonely Wives
Please see review for *Pre-Code Hollywood: Vol. 4, Lonely Wives.*
1931 m/C

The Long Gray Line
John Ford's long love affair with the military reaches its full flower with this fact-based tale. Marty Maher (Power) is an Irish immigrant who rises through the ranks to become an instructor at West Point. He knows virtually nothing about what goes on at the academy when he arrives, fresh from the Auld Sod. He takes to the place and the life there. Ford regulars O'Hara, Bond, and Carey turn in their usual competent work. The film was made with the cooperation of the Army and Ford uses the wide screen to create impressive post-card vistas of West Point. Much is lost with the full-frame version. Both were created from exceptionally well-preserved or restored original elements. Sound is equally impressive. —MM
Movie: 🎵🎵🎵 **DVD:** 🎵🎵🎵
Columbia Tristar (cat #06546, UPC 0433-96065468). Widescreen (2.55:1) anamorphic; full frame. Dolby Digital 3.0 Surround. $24.98. Keepcase. *LANG:* English. *SUB:* English; French; Spanish; Portuguese; Chinese; Korean; Thai. *FEATURES:* Trailer • 28 chapters.
1955 138m/C Tyrone Power, Maureen O'Hara, Robert Francis, Donald Crisp, Ward Bond, Betsy Palmer, Phil Carey; *D:* John Ford; *W:* Edward Hope; *C:* Charles Lawton Jr.

Long John Silver
Please see review for *Pirates!: Long John Silver / Captain Kidd.* **AKA:** Long John Silver Returns to Treasure Island.
Movie: 🎵 ½
1954 103m/C *AU* Robert Newton, Connie Gilchrist, Kit Taylor, Grant Taylor, Rod Taylor; *D:* Byron Haskin; *W:* Martin Rackin; *C:* Carl Guthrie; *M:* David Buttolph.

The Long Night
WWII vet Joe Adams (Fonda) is having a hard time adjusting to civilian life. In fact, he has just killed con man/magician Maximilian (Price) and barricaded himself inside his apartment. Flashbacks serve to show how Joe got into this predicament. What this remake of *Le Jour se lève* lacks in narrative drive it makes up for with superb set design that recalls *Night of the Hunter.* DVD presents a well-maintained image of crystalline black-and-white photography. Light strobing in some check patterns is easy to ignore. Sound is less than perfect, but this rarely seen noir is a treat for fans. —MM
Movie: 🎵🎵🎵 **DVD:** 🎵🎵🎵 ½
Kino on Video (cat #K156, UPC 73832901-5626). Full frame. $29.95. Keepcase. *LANG:* English. *FEATURES:* 16 chapters • Production design essay • Photo gallery.
1947 101m/B Henry Fonda, Vincent Price, Barbara Bel Geddes, Ann Dvorak, Howard Freeman, Moroni Olsen, Elisha Cook Jr.; *D:* Anatole Litvak; *W:* John Wexley; *C:* Sol Polito; *M:* Dimitri Tiomkin.

The Long Run
The Comrades Marathon is the most grueling running race in the world—54 miles through the Africa terrain. Berry (Armin Mueller-Stahl) has been a coach for runners entering this race for years. But now that he is three years away from retirement, the company which sponsors his team decides to replace him with a new, younger coach. As running and coaching are all Berry knows, he's suddenly stuck with nothing to do. Until the day that he sees Christine (Nthati Moshesh) jogging down the road. *The Long Run* is a beautifully shot film, with director Jean Stewart making great use of the African landscapes. Mueller-Stahl (who received an Oscar nomination for his work in *Shine*) and newcomer Moshesh are both very good in their roles and the tale of the physical and mental challenges involved in the race is quite interesting. The problem is that it is a sports film, and like every sports film before it, there are some clichéd traps into which it falls. DVD image is very sharp and clear, although there is some visible grain in the daylight shots. The colors are good and the fleshtones are realistic. The Dolby Surround audio track is surprisingly good, providing clear dialogue and very active Surround effects (especially during the finale). However, note that there is a slight hiss. A trailer and filmographies are the only extras. —ML

Movie: 🎵🎵 ½ **DVD:** 🎵🎵 ½
Universal Studios (cat #21488, UPC 0251-92148828). Widescreen (1.85:1) anamorphic. Dolby Surround. $29.98. Keepcase. *LANG:* English; French. *SUB:* English. *CAP:* English. *FEATURES:* Theatrical trailer • Filmographies • 18 chapters.
2000 113m/C *SA* Armin Mueller-Stahl, Nthati Moshesh, Paterson Joseph, Desmond Dube, Septula Sebogodi; *D:* Jean Stewart; *W:* Johann Potgieter; *C:* Cinders Forshaw.

Look Back in Anger
Brilliant film version of John Osborne's famous play that ushered in the "angry young man" dramas of late 1950s British cinema. Jimmy Porter (Burton) seethes with resentment about everything. Unable to cope with the ever-present squalor around him, he rails incessantly with his ever-suffering wife Alison (Mary Ure) and his sweet but hapless friend Cliff (Gary Raymond) bearing helpless witness. While a modern sensibility might deem Porter's self-pitying rants too narcissistic, the power of Burton's performance ranks alongside Marlon Brando's Stanley Kowalski as one of the great depictions of caged masculinity. The mildly letterboxed (1.66 non-anamorphic) transfer looks quite good with sharp image quality and excellent detail delineation. Gray tones and contrast are nicely balanced, the only distraction being intermittent speckles in the source print. The Dolby Digital mono soundtrack plays cleanly without distortion. —EP
Movie: 🎵🎵🎵 ½ **DVD:** 🎵🎵🎵
MGM Home Ent. (cat #1002741, UPC 027-616869395). Widescreen (1.66:1) letterboxed. Dolby Digital Mono. $14.95. Keepcase. *LANG:* English. *SUB:* French; Spanish. *FEATURES:* 16 chapters • Theatrical trailer.
1958 99m/B *GB* Richard Burton, Claire Bloom, Mary Ure, Edith Evans, Gary Raymond, Glen Byam Shaw, George Devine, Donald Pleasence, Phyllis Neilson-Terry; *D:* Tony Richardson; *W:* John Osborne, Nigel Kneale; *C:* Oswald Morris; *M:* John Addison.

Look Who's Talking Now
Continuing to wring revenue from a tired premise, the family dogs throw in their two cents in the second sequel to *Look Who's Talking.* For anyone who thinks Diane Keaton's hair makes her look a little like a hound dog, here's a chance to visualize her as a similarly long-eared poodle with an attitude. Danny DeVito is also cast in character as the voice of a rough street-smart mutt, who happens to get thrown into the same household as the bosses' pure-bred poodle. Sparks, Alpo, and butt-jokes fly as the dogs mark their territory, emulating the relationship between James (Travolta) and Mollie (Alley). Meanwhile, dimwit wife Mollie is worried that James is having an affair and is determined to get back at him. The voice of Bruce Willis is

sorely missed here. Surprisingly, there is little grain to be had here and the full-frame image is sharp and clear. There is no distortion to the image and the colors are fine. With the Dolby Surround audio track, the viewer is treated to clear dialogue, and occasional Surround effects, limited mostly to musical cues. Stereo separation is noticeably good. —ML

Movie: ♫ ½ **DVD:** ♫♫
Columbia Tristar (cat #07732, UPC 04339-6077324). Full frame. Dolby Surround. $24.95. Keepcase. *LANG:* English. *SUB:* English; French; Spanish; Portuguese; Chinese; Korean. *CAP:* English. *FEATURES:* Trailers • 28 chapters.
1993 (PG-13) 95m/C John Travolta, Kirstie Alley, Olympia Dukakis, George Segal, Lysette Anthony; **D:** Tom Ropelewski; **W:** Leslie Dixon, Tom Ropelewski; **C:** Oliver Stapleton; **M:** William Ross; **V:** Diane Keaton, Danny DeVito.

Looking for an Echo

Warm, friendly, reclaiming-your-mojo tale is from the guy who did *Eddie and the Cruisers*, a film about a hot young '50s-style rock-and-roll guy who disappears and makes a comeback. This film is about an older '50s-style guy who used to be the hot young rock-and-roll lead singer for a doo-woop band who makes a comeback. The script, directing, and acting are all well above competent but not everyone will be able to find enough empathy for the characters to care whether they make a comeback or not. However, the cinematography by Charles Minsky is awe-inspiring and well worth watching. The DVD transfer and sound are decent. —CA

Movie: ♫♫ **DVD:** ♫♫♫
USA Home Ent. (cat #96306 0368 2, UPC 696306036821). Full frame. Dolby Stereo. $26.90. Keepcase. *LANG:* English. *SUB:* English. *CAP:* English. *FEATURES:* 19 chapters • Cast & crew booklet.
1999 (R) 97m/C Armand Assante, Diane Venora, Joe Grifasi, Tom Mason, Anthony John (Tony) Denison, Edoardo Ballerini, David Margulies, Christy Romano; **D:** Martin Davidson; **W:** Martin Davidson, Jeffrey Goldenberg, Robert Held; **C:** Charles Minsky.

The Lord of Hangzhou

After his travels abroad, wealthy Master Mi is reluctant to settle down to running his estate. The poor scholar he hires to keep his accounts conspires with local rascals to steal his fortune. Ruined, Mi heads for the capital to get help from his friend Chin. After a long arduous journey with many hardships, Mi is shocked to learn that Chin is actually the Emperor! Action fans may be disappointed that it fails to live up to promise of opening battle, but those that stick with it should find that *The Lord of Hangzhou* holds up on its own terms as a captivating drama. Image is sharp and colorful. —BT *AKA:* Hong Chow Wong Yow; Hang Zhou Wang Ye.
Movie: ♫♫♫ **DVD:** ♫♫ ½

Tai Seng (cat #5223, UPC 48950249026-85). Widescreen letterboxed. $19.95. Keepcase. *LANG:* Cantonese; Mandarin. *SUB:* Chinese; English. *FEATURES:* 8 chapters • Trailers • Star profiles.
1998 96m/C *HK* Kwan Ho Tse, Waise Lee, Kwok-Bong Chan; **D:** Andy (Wing Keung Chien) Chin; **W:** Ma Chi Tsuen; **C:** Peter Ngo.

Lord of the Flies

Proper English schoolboys stranded on a desert island during a nuclear war are transformed into savages. A study in greed, power, and the innate animalistic/survivalistic instincts of human nature. Based on William Golding's novel, which he described as a "journey to the darkness of the human heart." The film print used is in far better condition than what was used for the earlier VHS release and, when combined with the Criterion transfer, the result is a very good looking black-and-white DVD. In fact if you've only seen the film on TV or on the old VHS version, you'll be simply amazed at the quality. The mono sound is still edgy, but there is far less hiss than before. The commentary is among the best there is of the analytical variety (don't expect to yuck it up on this one) and the wealth of information delivered by the four participants should satisfy even the most fanatical film student looking for an in-depth film perspective. Another excellent Criterion DVD that is a must for any serious collector. —JO

Movie: ♫♫♫ ½ **DVD:** ♫♫♫
Criterion (cat #LOR020, UPC 0374291367-20). Full frame. Dolby Digital Mono. $39.95. Keepcase. *LANG:* English. *SUB:* English. *FEATURES:* 31 chapters • Theatrical trailer with commentary • Commentary: Peter Brook, Lewis Allen, Tom Hollyman, Gerald Feil • Deleted scene with a reading by author William Golding • Excerpts from the novel read by author William Golding • Production scrapbook • Home movies • Outtakes • Gerald Feil's documentary "The Empty Space."
1963 91m/B *GB* James Aubrey, Tom Chapin, Hugh Edwards, Roger Elwin, Tom Gamen; **D:** Peter Brook; **W:** Peter Brook; **C:** Tom Hollyman; **M:** Raymond Leppard.

Lord of the Flies

Inferior second filming of William Golding's famous novel of schoolboys marooned on a jungle island is notable for the lush photography. That's captured in a fine DVD image that handles both intricate jungle backgrounds and dark campfire scenes with the proper level of detail. Use of Surround effects is limited. —MM

Movie: ♫♫ **DVD:** ♫♫ ½
MGM Home Ent. (cat #1002637, UPC 027-616868374). Widescreen (1.85:1) anamorphic. Dolby Digital Surround Stereo. $14.95. Keepcase. *LANG:* English. *SUB:* French; Spanish. *CAP:* English. *FEATURES:* 16 chapters.

1990 (R) 90m/C Balthazar Getty, Danuel Pipoly, Chris Furrh, Badgett Dale, Edward Taft, Andrew Taft; **D:** Harry Hook; **W:** Sara Schiff; **C:** Martin Fuhrer; **M:** Philippe Sarde.

The Lord of the Rings

Animated interpretation tackles the first two books of Tolkien's trilogy. Hobbits, wizards, elves, dwarves, and other inhabitants of Middle Earth are brought to life by Ralph Bakshi's animation, which combines conventional drawing with "roto-scope" techniques which draw over film of "real" people. It's less than completely successful and there's nothing that DVD can do about that. Disc appears to have been made from very good original elements. In fact, the film looks as good as I've ever seen it, and it sounds better. —MM

Movie: ♫♫ **DVD:** ♫♫ ½
Warner (cat #37408, UPC 0853937408-25). Widescreen anamorphic. Dolby Digital Surround; Mono. $19.98. Snapper. *LANG:* English; French. *SUB:* English; French; Spanish; Portuguese; Mandarin; Thai; Korean; Japanese. *CAP:* English. *FEATURES:* 38 chapters • Talent files • Trailer • Trivia.
1978 (PG) 128m/C D: Ralph Bakshi; **W:** J.C. (Chris) Conkling, Peter S. Beagle; **V:** Christopher Guard, John Hurt.

Lorna Doone

Lavish translation of R.D. Blackmore's classic tale of star-crossed love proffers the typical made-for-cable deference to the source but little in the way of adventurous filmmaking. Set in 17th-century England, the swashbuckling romance concerns the impossible love between common farmer John Ridd (Richard Coyle) and Lorna Doone (Amelia Warner) a member of the renegade Doone clan. Once respected but now outlaws, the Doones pillage the shire as they please. Bitter familial rivalries may be no match for true love, but John must also contend with the violent Carver Doone (Aidan Gillen), who murdered John's father and intends to have Lorna as his bride. After decades of Hollywood bowdlerization of classic literature, one can certainly appreciate treating the source with respect and dignity. However, just because a novel-to-film adaptation is literal does not make it thematically faithful. Adrian Hodges's script reverently brims with Age of Enlightenment cadences and epic romance amid the verdant English countryside, but Mike Barker's generic direction takes no chances with visualizing the 130-year-old text. Frequent pixelation, mostly in the numerous cloudy landscape shots, and excessive film grain mar the otherwise sharp, colorful full-frame transfer. The stereo soundtrack adequately serves John Lunn's "o'er the heather" music score and chimes in with occasional ambience effects. —EP

Movie: ♫♫♫ **DVD:** ♫♫
A&E (cat #AAE-70224, UPC 7339617022-48). Full frame. Dolby Digital Stereo. $24.98. Keepcase. *LANG:* English. *FEATURES:* 14 chapters.

2001 150m/C *GB* Richard Coyle, Amelia Warner, Aidan Gillen, Martin Clunes, Michael Kitchen, Martin Jarvis, Barbara Flynn, Peter Vaughan, Anton Lesser, Jack Shepherd; **D:** Mike Barker; **W:** Adrian Hodges; **C:** Chris Seager; **M:** John Lunn.

Loser

Very low-budget ($38,000) street drama concerns young small-time drug dealer James Dean Ray (Harris) and his self-destructive slide toward oblivion. Festival-circuit hit. DVD can do nothing to improve the primitive look and sound of the film. Extras are more important. —*MM*
Movie: 🎬🎬 **DVD:** 🎬🎬 ½
York Ent. (cat #YPD-1144, UPC 75072311-4422). Full frame. $14.99. Keepcase. *LANG:* English. *FEATURES:* Director's intro and commentary • Trailers.
1997 (R) 90m/C Kirk Harris, Jonathon Chaus, Peta Wilson, Norman Salect, Jack Rubio; **D:** Kirk Harris; **W:** Kirk Harris; **C:** Kent Wakeford.

Lost and Delirious

Unevenly told tale of young girls who fall in love at boarding school as told through the eyes of their naïve new roommate. When Mouse (Mischa Barton) discovers that Pauline (a very dynamic Piper Perabo in her pre–*Coyote Ugly* days) and Troy (Jessica Pare, the poor man's Liv Tyler) are lovers, she turns a blind eye, living more in awe than in judgment of the two seniors. When their secret is discovered, Troy, who is from an upright moneyed family, denies their relationship, blames Pauline for stalking her, and immediately starts bonding with a guy from the school across the forest. Pauline, who is adopted and a bit of a rebel, begins quoting Shakespeare and practicing fencing in the hopes of dueling for the hand of her true love. Melodramatic at times, the film still manages a feel for real teen angst, and cinematically it is a work of art. One scene in particular is shot entirely in silhouette in the forest just outside the school. Pauline is working with a hawk that she has rehabilitated from a broken wing as Mouse looks on and they discuss the true nature of love. The lighting and dialogue create an ethereal matte painting that stays with you. Based on Susan Swan's *The Women of Bath*, it's well worth a look for anyone who likes romantic drama and beautiful cinematography. The picture is clean with good, solid blacks, even in the night scenes, and the sound is a little above average. —*CA*
Movie: 🎬🎬 ½ **DVD:** 🎬🎬🎬
Studio Home Ent. (cat #ST7901D, UPC 658149790124). Widescreen anamorphic. Dolby Digital Surround 5.1. $24.98. Keepcase. *LANG:* English. *SUB:* English; Spanish. *FEATURES:* 24 chapters • Trailer.
2001 100m/C *CA* Mischa Barton, Piper Perabo, Jessica Pare, Jackie Burroughs, Graham Greene, Mimi Kuzyk, Luke Kirby; **D:** Lea Pool; **W:** Judith Thompson; **C:** Pierre Gill; **M:** Yves Chamberland. *AWARDS:*

Genie '01: Cinematog; *NOM:* Genie '01: Screenplay, Support. Actress (Kuzyk).

The Lost Battalion

It was called the war to end all wars, and quite simply it was one of the most violent periods in human history. *The Lost Battalion* recounts the true story of the United States' 77th division, 308th battalion and their struggle to take German occupied land. This A&E production takes made-for-television movies to a new level. With great effects cinematography much in the vein of *Saving Private Ryan*, it is an intense, gripping view into the dysfunctional war machine, and what it takes for a soldier to be a part of it. Rick Schroeder continues to impress with his strong dramatic acting ability, which is further complemented by a talented supporting cast. The picture and sound quality are decent, but this is an occasion where the inclusion of a 5.1 Surround track would have only made this a stronger release. Accompanying the film is a great History Channel documentary, which gives an intimate view into the First World War and some of the individuals who played a part in it. —*EL*
Movie: 🎬🎬🎬 **DVD:** 🎬🎬🎬 ½
A&E (cat #70399, UPC 733961703993). Full frame. Dolby Digital. $19.95. Keepcase. *LANG:* English. *FEATURES:* History Channel's *Dear Home: Letters from World War I* • Rick Schroder bio and filmography.
2001 100m/C Rick Schroder, Phil McKee, Jamie Harris, Jay Rodan; **D:** Russell Mulcahy; **W:** James (Jim) Carabatsos; **C:** Jonathan Freeman; **M:** Rick Marvin.

The Lost Continent

A rocket fired from White Sands Missile Base is lost and an expedition to locate it leads to an uncharted island of dinosaurs. This print is restored to the original theatrical version with green-tinted "lost world" sequences. A childhood favorite best left to memory, where even the death of Sgt. Willie (Melton) by goring Triceratops is far creakier than the trauma it inspired. Perhaps the crudest stop-motion animation of dinosaurs in film history, but preferable to men in suits or puppets. Good DVD transfer and sound, better than Image's usual. —*MO*
Movie: 🎬🎬 ½ **DVD:** 🎬🎬🎬
Image Ent. (cat #109215CDVD, UPC 0143-81921526). Full frame. $24.99. Keepcase. *LANG:* English. *FEATURES:* 12 chapters.
1951 82m/B Cesar Romero, Hillary Brooke, Chick Chandler, John Hoyt, Acquanetta, Sid Melton, Whit Bissell, Hugh Beaumont; **D:** Sam Newfield; **W:** Richard H. Landau; **C:** Jack Greenhalgh; **M:** Paul Dunlap.

Lost in Yonkers

I consider this Pulitzer Prize winner to be one of the best Neil Simon plays. A strong cast is led by Richard Dreyfuss in probably his best role and Mercedes Ruehl, excellent as usual. This film deals with family

dynamics many of us have experienced in our own lives. DVD looks great and sound is clean and clear. —*DE* **AKA:** Neil Simon's Lost in Yonkers.
Movie: 🎬🎬🎬 **DVD:** 🎬🎬🎬
Columbia Tristar (cat #08204, UPC 0433-96082045). Widescreen anamorphic. Dolby Surround. $24.98. Keepcase. *LANG:* English. *SUB:* English; French. *CAP:* English. *FEATURES:* 28 chapters • Theatrical trailers.
1993 (PG) 114m/C Mercedes Ruehl, Irene Worth, Richard Dreyfuss, Brad Stoll, Mike Damus, David Strathairn, Robert Miranda, Jack Laufer, Susan Merson; **D:** Martha Coolidge; **W:** Neil Simon; **M:** Elmer Bernstein.

Love and Basketball

Childhood friends and high school sweethearts Monica (Lathan) and Quincy (Epps) pursue their dreams of pro basketball careers and sort out their feelings for each other over a 12-year period. First-time director Prince-Bythewood avoids the clichés of most sports movies by removing the Big Game climax and replacing it with thoughtful character study and an understanding of the sacrifices that athletes make to excel in their chosen profession. DVD image quality is outstanding. Colors are deep and rich, giving this transfer a very lifelike feel. Black level is also solid and even the darkest scenes show fine detail. The transfer exhibits absolutely no edge-enhancement, compression problems, artifacts, or grain of any kind. Audio is clear and dialogue is never muddled or overwhelmed. That said, there really isn't much in the way of range or atmospheric effects to really give this mix a workout. —*MM/GH*
Movie: 🎬🎬🎬 **DVD:** 🎬🎬🎬
New Line Home Video (UPC 7940435064-20). Widescreen (1.85:1) anamorphic. Dolby Digital 5.1 Surround; Dolby Surround. $19.98. Snapper. *LANG:* English. *SUB:* English. *FEATURES:* Commentary • Isolated score • Documentary • Deleted scenes • Bloopers • Audition reels • Animated storyboards • Music video • Trailers • Talent files.
2000 (R) 124m/C Omar Epps, Sanaa Lathan, Alfre Woodard, Dennis Haysbert, Debbi (Deborah) Morgan, Harry J. Lennix, Kyla Pratt, Glenndon Chatman; **D:** Gina Prince-Bythewood; **W:** Gina Prince-Bythewood; **C:** Reynaldo Villalobos; **M:** Terence Blanchard. *AWARDS: NOM:* Ind. Spirit '01: Actress (Lathan), First Feature.

Love Beat the Hell outta Me

Using the frame of four friends getting together for a night of dominos, this film attempts to show how men deal with the emotional trauma brought on by their relationships with women. Unfortunately, it fails miserably, or maybe it doesn't. If most men deal with their emotional trauma by sitting around for hours calling women dirty names and hiding their affairs with their friends' girlfriends, then maybe it succeeds. If you put aside the bad dialogue and poor direction, there is always the mediocre acting to dwell on. After that there's the horrible transfer. As the film cuts from one domino player to the other, the lighting and color saturation change. The sound is average. —CA

Movie: ♫ ½ **DVD:** ♫
Warner (cat #A54094 2, UPC 085365409-422). Full frame. Dolby Digital Stereo. $19.90. Snapper. LANG: English. FEATURES: 10 chapters ⚬ Bonus music videos.
2000 (R) 89m/C Glenn Plummer, Terrence DaShon Howard; **D:** Kennedy Goldsby; **W:** Kennedy Goldsby.

Love Can Seriously Damage Your Health

In 1965 when Diana and Santi first met, he was the bellman tasked with guarding the Beatles' suite at their hotel in Spain and she was the beautiful Beatles fan who got one over on him. Thirty years later and many break ups and make ups, he is the personal assistant of the King of Spain and she is a woman bent on reclaiming their relationship. It's an amusing though not exceptional romantic comedy. Penelope Cruz is adorable as Spain's answer to Meg Ryan and should look into doing a few more romantic comedies. The print transfer is clean though not vibrant and the sound is good. —CA **AKA:** Amor Perjudica Seriamente la Salud.

Movie: ♫♫ ½ **DVD:** ♫♫ ½
Vanguard Intl. Cinema (cat #VF9149, UPC 658769914931). Full frame. $29.95. Keepcase. LANG: Spanish. SUB: English. FEATURES: 14 chapters.
1996 118m/C SP Ana Belen, Penelope Cruz, Gabino Diego, Janjo Puigcorbe, Carles Sans, Lola Herrera; **D:** Manuel Gomez Pereira; **W:** Manuel Gomez Pereira; **C:** Juan Amoros.

Love Come Down

Two brothers (Larenz Tate and Martin Cummins) fight through the killing of their father, the imprisonment of their mother, and the younger brother's drug addictions. If this weren't a movie it would make a great country song. Not much here to watch; basically a waste of good film stock for a below average made-for-cable movie. Theme of the film is "sometimes falling in love means falling apart," which is what this script does all too often. Disc passes muster with O.K. sound and true colors. —DE

Movie: ♫ **DVD:** ♫♫
Studio Home Ent. (cat #VM7937D, UPC 31398793724). Full frame. Dolby 5.1. $24.98. Keepcase. LANG: English. SUB: Spanish. CAP: English. FEATURES: Trailer ⚬ 28 chapters.
2000 (R) 102m/C CA Larenz Tate, Martin Cummins, Sarah Polley, Deborah Cox, Travis Davis, Jake Le Doux, Rainbow Sun Francks, Barbara Williams, Peter Williams, Clark Johnson, Kenneth Welsh, Jennifer Dale, Naomi Gaskin; **D:** Clement Virgo; **W:** Clement Virgo; **C:** Dylan Mcleod; **M:** Aaron Davis, John Lang. AWARDS: Genie '01:

Sound, Support. Actor (Cummins); NOM: Genie '01: Film, Screenplay, Support. Actress (Williams), Score.

Love Film

A train ride from Hungary to France gives Jansci (Balint) time to reminisce on Kata (Halasz), his childhood love, whom he is going to visit. In turn, other memories from his youth during the Soviet occupation of Hungary come flooding back. This quiet, emotional story feels inspired by Proust in the way that small thoughts trigger waves of memory. The film is artfully shot, though the washed-out, dirty print and sub-par transfer don't do it justice. The mono sound is occasionally difficult to hear, but the subtitles, burned on the image, are easy to read. —DRL **AKA:** Szerelmesfilm; A Film about Love.

Movie: ♫♫♫ **DVD:** ♫ ½
Kino on Video (cat #224, UPC 73832902-2426). Widescreen (1.66:1) letterboxed. Mono. $29.95. Keepcase. LANG: Hungarian. SUB: English. FEATURES: 15 chapters.
1970 123m/C HU Andras Balint, Judit Halasz, Edit Kelemen, Andras Szamosfalvi; **D:** Istvan Szabo; **W:** Istvan Szabo; **C:** Josef Lorinc.

Love Goggles

In the tradition of Two Can Play at That Game and Booty Call comes this exploration of the love lives of young, urban African Americans. Ollie (Steven Peacock Jacoby) and Topcat (Trevor David) are best friends. Topcat owns a nightclub and is a smooth ladies' man. Ollie considers himself to be a player, but has decided that it's time to settle down and find "Mrs. Right." When Ollie meets Mona (Ruby Campbell), all seems well. Ollie appears to have found the woman of his dreams, but Topcat thinks otherwise and begins to offer Ollie tons of advice. Should Ollie follow his heart, or listen to his heartless friend? The film has some funny moments, but the movie never really finds its voice. The characters are all stereotypical and at times the movie plays like a re-run of Martin. The film has been edited in a very strange manner, with scenes that begin and end seemingly at random, which doesn't help the cause. This one is a worthy imitator of the more popular films listed above, but view it only if you've exhausted all other possibilities. DVD image is somewhat sharp, but is also blurry and hazy at times. There is quite a bit of artifacting, as well as noticeable grain. The digital stereo audio offers clear dialogue, but the sound is distorted at times. On a more positive note, the director's commentary is playful and well worth a listen. —ML

Movie: ♫ ½ **DVD:** ♫♫
Delta/Laserlight (cat #7015, UPC 039414-570151). Widescreen (1.77:1) letterboxed. Digital Stereo. $24.95. Keepcase. LANG: English. SUB: Spanish. FEATURES: Commentary: director ⚬ Trailers ⚬ 20 chapters.
1999 106m/C Trevor David, Ruby Campbell, Steven Peacock Jacoby, Q-Tip; **D:** Anthony Travis.

Love Is a Many Splendored Thing

A married American war correspondent (Holden) and a beautiful Eurasian doctor (Jones) fall in love in post–World War II Hong Kong. They struggle with racism and unhappiness until he's sent to Korea to observe the Army's activities there. Some surface damage is intermittent and light pixelation crops up in the brightest exteriors. Otherwise, the image is very good. Colors are unfaded and if the lushly romantic theme song had been remixed into Surround, it might be more than viewers could bear. —MM

Movie: ♫♫ ½ **DVD:** ♫♫♫
20th Century Fox (UPC 024543000327). Widescreen (2.35:1) anamorphic. Dolby Digital Stereo. $24.98. Keepcase. LANG: English; French. SUB: English; Spanish. CAP: English. FEATURES: 18 chapters ⚬ Trailers ⚬ Photo gallery.
1955 102m/C William Holden, Jennifer Jones, Torin Thatcher, Isobel Elsom, Jorja Curtright, Virginia Gregg, Richard Loo; **D:** Henry King; **W:** John Patrick; **C:** Leon Shamroy; **M:** Alfred Newman. AWARDS: Oscars '55: Costume Des. (C), Song ("Love Is a Many-Splendored Thing"), Orig. Dramatic Score; NOM: Oscars '55: Actress (Jones), Art Dir./Set Dec., Color, Color Cinematog., Picture, Sound.

The Love of Jeanne Ney

Wildly convoluted silent film begins in Russia where Jeanne's (Jehanne) Bolshevik lover (Henning) kills her father for betraying the cause, and then shifts to Paris where the pair face even more daunting obstacles. DVD makes the film look remarkably fresh with only moderate signs of wear and registration problems. The new score by Timothy Brock is engaging and effective. —MM

Movie: ♫♫ ½ **DVD:** ♫♫ ½
Kino on Video (cat #K208, UPC 73832902-0828). Full frame. Stereo. $29.95. Keepcase. LANG: Silent. SUB: English intertitles. FEATURES: 16 chapters.
1927 113m/B GE Edith Jehanne, Brigitte Helm, Uno Henning, Eugen Jenson, Fritz Rasp; **D:** G.W. Pabst; **W:** Ilya Ehrenburg, Ladislaus Vayda.

Love on a Diet

A romantic comedy about a woman who wants to lose the weight she's gained in time to reunite with her concert pianist boyfriend, and the fat salesman who helps her beyond the call of duty for reasons even he can't explain. Most productions that involve beautiful actors cutting up in fat makeup are either maudlin pity parties or mean-spirited farces, but this one works surprisingly well by treating the leads as characters first. The humor and drama come from their personalities rather than from their weight problems. Instead of the usual dual language menus that come on

Chinese discs, this one has separate menus in Chinese and English. —*BT*
Movie: 🎦🎦🎦 ½ ***DVD:*** 🎦🎦 ½
China Star (cat #HF501545D, UPC 48950-80001391). Widescreen letterboxed. Dolby Digital 5.1. $24.95. Keepcase. *LANG:* Cantonese; Mandarin. *SUB:* Chinese; English. *FEATURES:* 16 chapters ▪ Documentary featurette ▪ Trailers.
2001 95m/C *HK* Sammi Cheng, Andrew Lau, Rikiya Kurokawa, Suet Lam; ***D:*** Johnny To, Kai-Fai Wai; ***W:*** Kai-Fai Wai, Hoi Nai; ***C:*** Siu Keung Cheng; ***M:*** Cacine Wong.

Love Potion #9

An early role finds Sandra Bullock doing a Jerry Lewis *Nutty Professor* riff. She's Diane, a nerdy biochemist who, along with equally nerdy co-worker Paul (Donovan), takes a sip of "love potion no. 8" which he got from Madame Ruth (Bancroft). It's lightweight material with several missteps along the way, and a pretty good ending. Recommended mostly to fans of the star. DVD delivers a near-perfect image. Sound is acceptable with limited Surround effects. Not many are really needed. —*MM*
Movie: 🎦🎦 ***DVD:*** 🎦🎦🎦
20th Century Fox (UPC 024543018704). Widescreen anamorphic. Dolby Digital 4.0 Surround; Dolby Surround. $19.98. Keepcase. *LANG:* English. *SUB:* English; Spanish. *FEATURES:* 24 chapters ▪ Featurette ▪ Trailers ▪ TV spot.
1992 (PG-13) 96m/C Tate Donovan, Sandra Bullock, Mary Mara, Dale Midkiff, Hillary Bailey Smith, Dylan Baker, Anne Bancroft; ***D:*** Dale Launer; ***W:*** Dale Launer; ***C:*** William Wages; ***M:*** Jed Leiber.

Love Songs

Three actors direct interrelated stories by Charles Fuller. In "A Love Song for Champ," a boxer (Townsend) has financial problems. "A Love Song for Jean and Ellis" is about an unlikely romance between a sophisticated lady (Whitfield) and a fruit vendor (Braugher), and "A Love Song for Dad" is about a bartender (Gossett Jr.) who tries to help his son. Made-for-cable production is an overachiever on DVD. Image is bright, colorful, and sharply focused. Sound is fine. —*MM*
Movie: 🎦🎦🎦 ***DVD:*** 🎦🎦🎦
Showtime Networks, Inc. (cat #SHO1039, UPC 758445103922). Full frame. Stereo. $24.98. Keepcase. *LANG:* English; Spanish. *CAP:* English. *FEATURES:* 12 chapters ▪ Filmographies ▪ 4 interviews.
1999 101m/C Robert Townsend, Andre Braugher, Louis Gossett Jr., Rachael Crawford, Carl Gordon, Lynn Whitfield, Brent Jennings, Dule Hill, Sandra Caldwell; ***D:*** Robert Townsend, Andre Braugher, Louis Gossett Jr.; ***W:*** Charles Fuller; ***C:*** James R. Bagdonas; ***M:*** Pete Anthony, Ronnie Laws.

The Lover

In 1929 Vietnam, a poor French teenaged girl (March) meets a wealthy Chinese young man (Leung) on a ferry. He's imme-diately taken by her beauty. Detached, determined, and unromantic, she allows herself to be seduced for the experience and the money he offers. It's based on Marguerite Duras's autobiographical novel, but she repudiated the film when it was released in France. Director Annaud takes a remote but unashamedly erotic approach to the situation and creates some of the most beautiful and intense sexual scenes ever put on film. DVD recreates them with the right degree of softness for an exotic period piece. Sound is equally evocative. This is the "unrated" version, 10 minutes longer than the theatrical release. —*MM* **AKA:** *L'Amant.*
Movie: 🎦🎦🎦 ***DVD:*** 🎦🎦🎦
MGM Home Ent. (cat #1002733, UPC 027-616869319). Widescreen (1.85:1) anamorphic. Dolby Digital Surround. $19.98. Keepcase. *LANG:* English; French. *SUB:* English; French; Spanish. *CAP:* English. *FEATURES:* 16 chapters ▪ Trailer.
1992 113m/C *FR* Jane March, Tony Leung Ka-Fai, Frederique Meininger, Arnaud Giovanietti, Melvil Poupaud, Lisa Faulkner, Xiem Mang; ***D:*** Jean-Jacques Annaud; ***W:*** Gerard Brach, Jean-Jacques Annaud; ***C:*** Robert Fraisse; ***M:*** Gabriel Yared; ***Nar:*** Jeanne Moreau. *AWARDS:* Cesar '93: Score; *NOM:* Oscars '92: Cinematog.

Lover's Prayer

Unconvincing and frequently silly period romantic tragedy in the Merchant-Ivory vein. A rich boy (Stahl) falls in love with the girl next door (Dunst). Unfortunately, she is the daughter of a nearly ruined woman of little class (Walters) and other people are interested in her as well. It's a clunky combination of two different stories (by Chekhov and Turgenev) filmed in pastoral surroundings with a talented but miscast troupe of actors. All the cast play the Russian drama with British accents, but Stahl's is fairly dodgy and he mumbles most of his lines to hide it. The dialogue is stiffly poetic and hilariously overwritten, and the narration is obvious and unnecessary. The cartoonish suitors are particularly disastrous and the last reels of gloom and doom seem contrived. The preprint material used in the transfer has the occasional mark or blemish, but overall the image quality is colorful and sharp, capturing the lush photography and scenery with accuracy. The sound is excellent but not as fully mixed as most Surround tracks. Disc contains an isolated music track that is not mentioned anywhere on the package but can be accessed by using the remote control on your DVD player. —*DG* **AKA:** *All Forgotten.*
Movie: 🎦🎦 ***DVD:*** 🎦🎦🎦
Image Ent. (cat #OVED0367DVD, UPC 014-38103672). Widescreen (1.78:1) anamorphic. Dolby Digital 4.0 Surround. $19.99. Snapper. *LANG:* English. *FEATURES:* 18 chapters ▪ Theatrical trailer ▪ Isolated music and effects track.
1999 (PG-13) 106m/C Nick Stahl, Kirsten Dunst, Julie Walters, Geraldine

James, Nathaniel Parker, James Fox; ***D:*** Reverge Anselmo; ***W:*** Reverge Anselmo; ***C:*** David Watkin; ***M:*** Joel McNeely.

Loves of a Blonde

Factory committee members air their worries to Army officials. Relocating soldiers to their town will create havoc among the local girls, who outnumber the local boys 16 to 1 and have to work in a dull shoe factory. At a dance, the girls are disappointed to find out that most of the soldiers are dumpy-looking older men. Andula (Hana Brejchová) and her two girlfriends have a bad time fending off the crude advances of three men in uniform, but Andula's heart is captured by the pianist with the band, Milda (Vladimir Pucholt). She allows herself to be seduced by this junior league ladies' man, and becomes petulant when he doesn't contact her again. Irked by the "stay virginal" party line of her dorm committee, Andula hitches a ride to Prague, right to Milda's front door, only to find him out working (read: chasing other girls). Milda's parents allow her in, but Milda's mother (Milada Jezková) is not at all pleased by her presence! Once again Mr. Forman proves that observing human behavior is one of the best uses for a movie camera. Criterion's disc is a charmer, with a few scratches here and there and extras that help fill in the holes for the uninitiated, 35 years after the fact. In an excellent interview, Forman tells us how he blended the efforts of amateurs and pro actors, and about his reaction to the film's Oscar nomination. His anecdotes paint a larger picture of filmmaking in Prague at the time. The boy who plays Milda was a professional who surprised everyone by taking off for London, where he spent 10 years working menial jobs to put himself through medical school. The deleted scene is an oddity because it was included in the export prints shown in the U.S., but not in the official negative stored in Prague and used to make this disc. It's a totally new scene where Milda tries to talk his way into the bed of yet another girl he's picked up, and it's just as funny and tense as the rest of the film. —*GE* **AKA:** *A Blonde in Love;* Lasky Jedne Plavovlasky.
Movie: 🎦🎦🎦 ½ ***DVD:*** 🎦🎦🎦 ½
Criterion (cat #144, UPC 037429165423). Full frame. Dolby Digital Mono. $29.98. Keepcase. *LANG:* Czechoslovakian. *SUB:* English. *FEATURES:* Director interview ▪ Deleted scene ▪ 14 chapters.
1965 88m/B *CZ* Hana Brejchova, Josef Sebanek, Vladimir Pucholt, Milada Jezkova; ***D:*** Milos Forman; ***W:*** Milos Forman, Vaclav Sasek, Ivan Passer, Jaroslav Papousek; ***C:*** Miroslav Ondricek; ***M:*** Evsen Illin. *AWARDS:* *NOM:* Oscars '66: Foreign Film.

Luck of the Draw

Video premiere is a low-budget *Get Shorty* that's moderately entertaining for its familiar cast, if for nothing else. Ex-con Jack Sweeney (Marshall) has just been turned

down for a job at a bank when he wanders into a shoot-out. It involves bad guys and cops. The object is a pair of plates that can make perfect $100 bills. When the gunsmoke clears, Jack has the goods. The rest involves quickly paced double- and triple-crosses and some various comic bits. Action scenes are so-so. Such genre stalwarts as Eric Roberts, William Forsythe, Ice-T, Michael Madsen, and Frank Gorshin (the Riddler in TV's *Batman*) show up before it's over. Full-frame DVD image is sharp with bright colors within relatively subdued production values. Sound delivers clear dialogue and gunshots. —*MM*
Movie: 🎞 ½ **DVD:** 🎞 ½
Artisan Ent. (cat #12146). Full frame. Dolby Digital Stereo. $24.98. Keepcase. *LANG:* English. *FEATURES:* 21 chapters ▪ Talent files ▪ Trailer.
2000 (R) 108m/C James Marshall, Michael Madsen, Ice-T, Frank Gorshin, Eric Roberts, Dennis Hopper, Wendy Benson, William Forsythe, Sasha Mitchell, Richard Ruccolo; **D:** Luca Bercovici; **W:** Namon Ami, Rick Bloggs, Kandice King; **C:** Keith L. Smith; **M:** Steve Edwards.

Luckytown

Average story with great cast and production values. Lidda (Dunst) goes to Las Vegas looking for her card shark father (Caan) who's gotten himself into trouble with the local hard-nosed strip club owner. The film is competent but derivative to the point of boredom and the acting talents of Caan and Dunst are wasted on the film. The disc looks good, above average, and the sound is also good. —*CA*
Movie: 🎞 ½ **DVD:** 🎞🎞🎞
Studio Home Ent. (cat #7838D, UPC 6581-49783829). Widescreen letterboxed. Dolby Stereo. $24.99. Keepcase. *LANG:* English. *SUB:* English; French; Spanish. *FEATURES:* 24 chapters ▪ Trailer.
2000 (R) 101m/C Kirsten Dunst, Vincent Kartheiser, James Caan, Robert Miano, Luis Guzman, Jennifer Gareis, Theresa Russell; **D:** Paul Nicholas; **W:** Brendon Beseth; **C:** Denis Maloney; **M:** Greg Edmonson.

Luminarias

Based on Fernandez's play and directed by her husband, Valenzuela, this film plays like a Latina version of *Waiting to Exhale*. Andrea (Fernandez) and her friends spend most of their time grousing about their love lives at a restaurant called Luminarias. The story is told with love and pride, but it plays like a soap opera with no subtext or subtlety at all. The DVD looks pretty good, but the sound effects come across so crisply that they're intrusive. Extras are not very illuminating. —*LA*
Movie: 🎞🎞 ½ **DVD:** 🎞🎞 ½
MTI (cat #8122, UPC 039414581225). Widescreen letterboxed. $24.98. Keepcase. *LANG:* English. *SUB:* Spanish. *FEATURES:* Commentary: Valenzuela, producer Sal Lopez, Fernandez ▪ Behind-the-scenes ▪ 20 chapters ▪ Cast bios ▪ Trailers ▪ Interactive menus.

1999 (R) 101m/C Evelina Fernandez, Marta DuBois, Dyana Ortelli, Angela Moya, Scott Bakula, Robert Beltran, Sal Lopez, Andrew C. Lim, Geoffrey Rivas, Richard "Cheech" Marin; **D:** Jose Luis Valenzuela; **W:** Evelina Fernandez; **C:** Alex Phillips Jr.; **M:** Eric Allaman.

Luminous Motion

Bright 10-year-old Phillip (Lloyd) lives a gypsy existence traveling with his alcoholic mother (Unger) and a series of men she seduces, robs, and leaves. They spend some time with Pedro (Kinney), a carpenter, and Phillip has a curious relationship with his father (Sheridan). Nothing's quite what it first appears to be in this adaptation of Scott Bradford's novel *The History of Luminous Motion*. The film alternates between a grainy, gritty look and more conventional visuals. Both are rendered accurately on DVD though the image is never meant to be excellent. It is right for the story. —*MM*
Movie: 🎞🎞 ½ **DVD:** 🎞🎞 ½
Winstar Home Ent. (cat #FLV5295, UPC 720917529523). Widescreen (1.85:1) letterboxed. Dolby Digital 5.1 Surround; Stereo. $24.98. Keepcase. *LANG:* English. *FEATURES:* 16 chapters ▪ Trailer ▪ Filmographies ▪ DVD production credits.
2000 94m/C Eric Lloyd, Deborah Kara Unger, Jamey Sheridan, Terry Kinney, Paz de la Huerta, James Berland; **D:** Bette Gordon; **W:** Scott Bradfield, Robert Roth; **C:** Teodoro Maniaci; **M:** Lesley Barber.

Lured

A down-on-her-luck American dance-hall girl (Ball) is enlisted by Scotland Yard to help track down the murderer of several young women. Using herself as bait, the crafty femme encounters several oddball suspects (including Karloff) and is also wooed by a distinguished Lothario (Sanders). A terrific, well-utilized cast of character actors elevates this fairly formulaic romantic thriller. Ball manages to be believable, likeable, smart, and funny as the lead and it's an absolute treat to see perennial madman George Zucco playing one of the good guys for a change. Karloff only has a brief scene, but it's a delicious highlight. This independent production (from Hunt Stromberg) is just as slick and glossy as other big studio productions of the time (it particularly evokes the look of a Warners or RKO production) and is just as entertaining. The final third feels a bit padded but Sirk's direction is always assured and effective. The image is presented with rich contrasts, and a wide range of gray tonalities, and is predominantly sharp and textured. The print source used has minor damage, reel change marks, and speckles, but it's rarely distracting and digital shimmering is kept to a minimum. The sound is always clear and intelligible. —*DG*
Movie: 🎞🎞🎞 **DVD:** 🎞🎞🎞
Kino on Video (cat #K164DVD, UPC 73832-9016425). Full frame. Mono. $29.95.

Keepcase. *LANG:* English. *FEATURES:* 16 chapters ▪ Insert card.
1947 103m/B Lucille Ball, George Sanders, Charles Coburn, Cedric Hardwicke, Boris Karloff, Alan Mowbray, George Zucco, Joseph Calleia, Tanis Chandler, Alan Napier, Robert Coote; **D:** Douglas Sirk; **W:** Leo Rosten; **C:** William H. Daniels; **M:** Michel Michelet.

Lush

Lionel (Campbell Scott) is an alcoholic golfer who returns home to face his demons. It's just too bad it was in this film. A rambling mish-mash where we're supposed to wait around till all the parts come together. Your wait is in vain as the film never jells. The acting of Laura Linney (Rachel) and the look at the seamy side of New Orleans society helps this film avoid a woof. Maybe if viewed through a drunken stupor this film would make some sense. Isn't it amazing how DVDs that lack story and acting can deliver decent technical merit? This disc boasts good colors and sound, but it can't save the anemic scripting and acting in the film. —*DE*
Movie: 🎞 ½ **DVD:** 🎞🎞
Studio Home Ent. (cat #ST79360, UPC 658149793620). Full frame. Stereo. $24.99. Keepcase. *LANG:* English. *SUB:* Spanish. *FEATURES:* 28 chapters ▪ Trailer ▪ Interactive menus.
2001 (R) 94m/C Campbell Scott, Laura Linney, Jared Harris, Laurel Holloman; **D:** Mark Gibson; **W:** Mark Gibson; **C:** Caroline Champetier; **M:** Barrett Martin.

Lust for a Vampire

This, the second film in Hammer's "Karnstein trilogy" (following *The Vampire Lovers* and preceding *Twins of Evil*), finds beautiful Carmilla (Stensgaard) resurrected by her parents. Initially preying upon the buxom girls at a nearby girl's finishing school, Carmilla reluctantly falls in love with an author (Johnson) who has been hired as a teacher. This odd mixture of poetic, camp, erotic, and pulp horror is awkwardly scripted (several ideas and possible plot threads are introduced and abandoned) and features a clumsily motivated finale. The performances are strong and Stensgaard is a likable lead. The shameless casting of Raven (made-up and dubbed by Valentine Dyall to sound like Christopher Lee) seems like a lame attempt to fool audiences into thinking this is one of the Lee Dracula pictures. The gratuitous nudity of the early sections is quite silly but the love scene between Stensgaard and Johnson is surprisingly suggestive and erotic. The framing seems a tad tight, but compositions rarely seem to suffer. Except for a few dirty, grainy shots during the title sequences, this is a handsome transfer with a rich palette. One brief shot is prone to digital noise, but the rest of the program is free from digital artifacts. The mono sound is excellent. Sangster's memories of the film are fairly limited but Leigh and Hearn fill in the

gaps. Their dialogue frequently dwells outside the film itself, but is always interesting. The talent bios are well written and the art and poster galleries are nicely done. —AB/DG **AKA:** To Love a Vampire.
Movie: 🎵🎵 ½ **DVD:** 🎵🎵🎵
Anchor Bay (cat #DV11460, UPC 0131311-46097). Widescreen (1.78:1) anamorphic. Mono. $19.98. Keepcase. *LANG:* English. *FEATURES:* Commentary: Sangster, Leigh, Hammer historian Marcus Hearn • Theatrical trailer • Radio spots • Poster and still gallery • Talent bios • Yutte Stensgaard still gallery easter egg • 21 chapters • Insert card.
1971 (R) 95m/C *GB* Ralph Bates, Barbara Jefford, Suzanna Leigh, Michael Johnson, Yutte Stensgaard, Pippa Steele, Helen Christie, David Healy, Mike Raven; **D:** Jimmy Sangster; **W:** Tudor Gates; **C:** David Muir.

The Luzhin Defence
John Turturro plays Alexander Luzhin, a chess master so eccentric he borders on savant. His chaotic childhood has left him with no social skills, but his genius has left him with little need to socialize until he meets a beautiful woman (Watson), who just may be his soul mate, at the Italian resort where a major chess tournament is being played. He proposes and life seems grand until the dark figure of the mentor who abandoned him shows up and starts undermining his game and his sanity. Watson and Turturro are hot, hot, hot together as the star-crossed couple. The scenic locations and beautiful camerawork, given its full due with a superb transfer, are coupled with the pitch perfect acting to make this one a good choice for lovers of serious films that don't coddle. Based on a novel by Vladimir Nabokov. —CA
Movie: 🎵🎵🎵 ½ **DVD:** 🎵🎵🎵 ½
Columbia Tristar (cat #06389, UPC 04339-6063891). Widescreen anamorphic. Dolby Digital 5.1, Dolby Digital Surround. $29.95. Keepcase. *LANG:* English. *SUB:* English; French; Spanish. *CAP:* English. *FEATURES:* 28 chapters • Commentary: director • "Making of" featurette • Theatrical trailers.
2000 (PG-13) 106m/C *FR GB* John Turturro, Emily Watson, Geraldine James, Stuart Wilson, Christopher Thompson, Peter Blythe, Orla Brady, Fabio Sartor; **D:** Marleen Gorris; **W:** Peter Berry; **C:** Bernard Lutic; **M:** Alexandre Desplat.

MacArthur
Disappointing biopic is bookended by General MacArthur's (Peck) appearance at West Point in 1961 in which he offered his famous "Duty, Honor, Country" speech. Walking among the Corps of Cadets, the aging general recalls a life filled with both triumphs and tragedies. From Bataan to Inchon, the military feats are shown in all their glory. But so too does the film give equal time to the flaws of character that ultimately led President Truman to dismiss the general in 1951. The image is by no means spectacular but it is decent

enough. The overall look is somewhat soft and both colors and black levels are muted. It's also a bit on the dark side and features a fair amount of film grain. But the film elements appear to have been in good shape as there are only minor nicks and blemishes to mar the transfer. This looks like a film that was shot in the 1970s and no amount of work is going to change that. —MP
Movie: 🎵🎵 **DVD:** 🎵🎵 ½
Universal Studios Home Video (UPC 2519-2054426). Widescreen (1.85:1) anamorphic. Dolby Digital Mono. $24.98. Keepcase. *LANG:* English. *SUB:* English; French; Spanish. *FEATURES:* Trailer • Production notes • Talent files.
1977 (PG) 130m/C Gregory Peck, Ivan Bonar, Ward (Edward) Costello, Nicolas Coster, Dan O'Herlihy; **D:** Joseph Sargent; **W:** Hal Barwood, Matthew Robbins; **C:** Mario Tosi; **M:** Jerry Goldsmith.

Macbeth
This adaptation is one of Polanski's very best. Seen previously only in Shakespeare film festivals, and fatally pan-scanned on cable TV, the DVD will be the first time most consumers will be able to appreciate it in its full glory. After helping to put down a rebellion, Macbeth (Finch) is rewarded with the post of Thane by good king Duncan (Selby). But he bitterly thirsts for even faster advancement, as a cackle of witches has forecast his eventual rise to the crown. Macbeth and his scheming wife (Annis) plot first the murder of Duncan, and then the demise of heirs that stand to secede to the throne before him. But as they start down the path of killing, the ambitious couple is beset with strange visions and hallucinations. The print looks somewhat darkish, as it did in theatres. It isn't in perfect shape. The opening sequence is rather dirty, with a scratch running through half the titles—a scary beginning that thankfully doesn't continue through the rest of the show. The mono sound is solid, with voices particularly well-recorded. Of enormous use are the English subtitles, which make the Shakespearean speeches exponentially more accessible. —GE
Movie: 🎵🎵🎵 ½ **DVD:** 🎵🎵🎵
Columbia Tristar Home Video (UPC 04339-6077805). Widescreen (2.35:1) anamorphic. Dolby Mono. $29.98. Keepcase. *LANG:* English. *SUB:* English. *FEATURES:* Trailers • 28 chapters.
1971 (R) 139m/C Jon Finch, Nicholas Selby, Martin Shaw, Francesca Annis, Terence Baylor, John Stride, Stephan Chase, Noelle Rimmington, Maisie Farquhar, Elsie Taylor; **D:** Roman Polanski; **W:** Roman Polanski, Kenneth Tynan; **C:** Gilbert Taylor.

MacKenna's Gold
Grim desperados trek through Apache territory to uncover legendary cache of gold in this somewhat inflated epic. Subdued stars Peck and Sharif vie for attention here with such overactors as Cobb, Meredith,

and Wallach. Meanwhile, Newmar (Catwoman of TV's *Batman*) swims nude. A must for all earthquake buffs. The western scenery looks nothing short of spectacular on this DVD. The image is sharp, colors are vibrant, and there is incredible detail even in the harsher shadows of the outer scenes. It's too bad that Columbia couldn't come up with a better film print to work from because there is almost always some sort of film damage on the screen. Mostly it's in the form of flecks and speckling and it doesn't detract too much from the overall image. The new 5.0 mix is a good one, adding natural sounding Surround tracks that greatly enhance any of the action sequences. —JO
Movie: 🎵🎵 ½ **DVD:** 🎵🎵🎵
Columbia Tristar (cat #03709, UPC 04339-6037090). Widescreen (2.35:1) anamorphic; full frame. Dolby Digital 5.0; Dolby Digital Stereo. $14.95. Keepcase. *LANG:* English. *SUB:* English; Spanish; Chinese; Korean; Thai; Portuguese. *CAP:* English. *FEATURES:* 28 chapters • Talent files • Production notes • Theatrical poster.
1969 (PG) 128m/C Gregory Peck, Omar Sharif, Telly Savalas, Julie Newmar, Edward G. Robinson, Keenan Wynn, Ted Cassidy, Eduardo Ciannelli, Eli Wallach, Raymond Massey, Lee J. Cobb, Burgess Meredith, Anthony Quayle, John David Garfield; **D:** J. Lee Thompson; **W:** Carl Foreman; **C:** Joe MacDonald; **M:** Quincy Jones.

Macross: Box Set
In the late 20th century an abandoned spaceship of unknown origin crash-lands on Earth. Ten years later, as the ship is preparing for a test launch, an armada of alien spacecraft appears, attempting to retrieve the vessel. After a disastrous "space fold" operation whisks the ship to the far side of the universe, the crew (and its civilian inhabitants) must constantly fight their gigantic alien adversaries to return home. Filled with interesting characters, gripping plot developments, and original ideas, *Macross* is a memorable, trendsetting space-opera. This 36-episode Japanese animated series was recut, redubbed, rescored, and rewritten to become the backbone of the U.S. series *Robotech*. This edition presents the series in its original, unaltered version. The additional plot elements, character moments, and scenes of violence and human despair give the series a more satisfyingly adult tone than the U.S. version. Elements of the original backstory (which were given a severe overhaul) are much clearer and more intriguing here than the technobabble it was turned into. While the U.S. series is an enjoyable alternate version, the original is a more compelling work. The transfers utilized for the disc are far cleaner and more colorful than the *Robotech* discs. Layers of grain and haze present on those transfers are completely absent from these, which reveals more intricate details in the animation and richer colors. Unfortunately, the episodes are prone to instances of digital shimmer and

edge noise, which are especially noticeable on diagonal lines and during horizontal pans. The mono sound is limited, but clean and satisfying. The box set itself is beautifully designed and the liner notes are incredibly informative and well done. The nine discs will reportedly be released separately in the future. —DG

Movie: 🎵🎵🎵 **DVD:** 🎵🎵🎵 ½
AnimEigo Inc. (cat #AV001-250, UPC 7371-87003752). Full frame. Mono. $360.00. Keepcase. *LANG:* Japanese. *SUB:* English. *FEATURES:* 4 episodes per disc • 4 chapters per episode • Textless title sequence • Insert hologram card • Detailed liner notes and song lyrics • Noburo Ishiguro audio interview track with subtitles (Easter egg) • Unrestored demo clip (Easter egg) • Line-art sideshow (Easter egg).
1985 900m/C JP Noboru Ishiguro.

Mad Max [MGM SE]

This "Special Edition" corrects the faults of the first Image release (reviewed in *Book 1*). The transfer is very good. The aspect ratio is not as wide as on an earlier letterboxed laserdisc, perhaps 2.10 to 1 by my guess. The disc is two-sided, with a choice of 16:9 and flat transfers on one side and the majority of the extras on the other. Those are slick and informative, but overly packed with film footage that's a spoiler if you've not seen the film, and redundant if you have. The Mel Gibson career piece is very fluffy, concentrating on his beginnings in Australia and then by necessity glossing over most of Mel's entire superstar career, because none of his big successes are MGM properties. You get plenty of people just falling over themselves to say how beautiful a young man he was. Original crewmembers Jon Dowding, David Eggby, Chris Murray, and Tim Ridge provide a nice commentary track that betrays their excitement filming this thing when they were young and very, very reckless. A second "Road Rants" track is a subtitle track that pops up with a wealth of detailed information, naming the actors and specifying all the cars. It's like having a know-it-all telling you to watch for continuity errors and the like, and is a lot more appealing than it sounds. TV spots and a trailer are included, and although the trailer is menu'ed as Australian, it starts out with an MPAA notice! The big thrill of this DVD, and the extra we've all been waiting for, is hearing the Australian dialogue track. In their original dialects, with their voices matching their mouths, the cop characters come off as a lot more interesting and human, more "natural" actually than the comicbook characters of *The Road Warrior*. That optional subtitle fact track is useful here too, as it explains some thicker instances of Oz jargon in the dialogue, including profanity that doesn't sound profane at all to us Yanks. The now-intolerable American track is included as well, along with French and Spanish dubs that are nice; overall, there's a high ratio of useful extras on this disc and not just fluff. —GE

Movie: 🎵🎵🎵 ½ **DVD:** 🎵🎵🎵 ½
MGM Home Ent. (cat #1002726). Widescreen anamorphic; full frame. Dolby Digital 5.1. $19.98. Keepcase. *LANG:* English; Australian. *SUB:* English. *CAP:* English. *FEATURES:* 2 documentaries.
1980 (R) 93m/C AU Mel Gibson, Joanne Samuel, Hugh Keays-Byrne, Steve Bisley, Tim Burns, Roger Ward, Vincent (Vince Gill) Gil; *D:* George Miller; *W:* George Miller; *C:* David Eggby; *M:* Brian May.

Mad Youth

Please see review of *Sex and Buttered Popcorn, Vol. 2.*
Movie: 🐕
1940 61m/B Mary Ainslee, Betty Atkinson, Willy Castello, Betty Compson, Tommy Wonder; *D:* Melville Shyer; *W:* Willis Kent.

Madame Butterfly

Opera for people who don't like opera works beautifully on DVD. The widescreen image contains no flaws and the sound—even through headphones—is equally lush and clear. Performances are fine, but I'm hardly one to comment on that aspect. To my taste, it's more successful than the similar *Moulin Rouge*. (I'm able to accept this "singing" of dialogue, where Luhrman's anachronistic songs simply do not work.) The French production is set in 1904 Nagasaki (actually Tunisia, with some archival footage of old Japan), where the rotten American Lt. Pinkerton (Troxell) seduces and abandons young Butterfly (Ying Huang). By placing the action in a realistic setting and having the cast underplay the more flamboyant aspects of the piece, director Mitterand makes the opera work as a film. Clear yellow subtitles are not distracting and so those who (like me) are unfamiliar with the details of the story will have no trouble following it. —MM

Movie: 🎵🎵🎵 **DVD:** 🎵🎵🎵 ½
Columbia Tristar (cat #05670, UPC 0433-96056701). Widescreen (1.85:1) anamorphic. Dolby Digital Surround. $29.98. Keepcase. *LANG:* Italian. *SUB:* English; Spanish; Portuguese; Chinese; Thai. *CAP:* English. *FEATURES:* "Making of" featurette • 16 chapters.
1995 129m/C FR Ying Huang, Richard Troxell, Ning Liang, Richard Cowan; *D:* Frederic Mitterrand; *W:* Frederic Mitterrand; *C:* Philippe Welt.

Made [SE]

Jon Favreau and Vince Vaughn try to recapture the spirit and sense of fun that made *Swingers* such a hit. They don't. Bobby (Favreau) and his friend Ricky (Vaughn) are low-level would-be mob guys in Los Angeles. When their boss Max (Falk) sends them to New York on a sketchily defined job, Ricky thinks it's their ticket to the big time. But then, Ricky's wrong about everything and that's the film's main problem. Writer Favreau attempts to make Ricky funny by exaggerating all of his most irritating qualities. Instead of being funny, though, he's just supremely irritating, beyond-belief irritating—so irritating that it's all but impossible to keep your finger from the scan-forward button. On the plus side, the plot is intriguingly spun out and the supporting cast—including many familiar faces from *The Sopranos* and a surprisingly assured turn from Sean Combs—is excellent. DVD image and sound are flawless, and the disc is packed with extras. —MM

Movie: 🎵 ½ **DVD:** 🎵🎵🎵 ½
Artisan Ent. (UPC 012236122456). Widescreen anamorphic. Dolby Digital 5.1 Surround; Dolby Digital Surround. $24.98. Keepcase. *LANG:* English. *SUB:* Spanish. *CAP:* English. *FEATURES:* 16 chapters • Trailers • Deleted and alternate scenes • Commentary • Scene editing workshop • Talent files • Production notes • Music cues.
2001 (R) 94m/C Jon Favreau, Vince Vaughn, Famke Janssen, Faizon Love, David O'Hara, Vincent Pastore, Peter Falk, Sean (Puffy, Puff Daddy, P. Diddy) Combs; *D:* Jon Favreau; *W:* Jon Favreau; *C:* Christopher Doyle; *M:* John O'Brien, Lyle Workman.

Madeline at the North Pole

This DVD presents three episodes from the *Madeline* animated television show, which is, of course, based on the popular children's tales by Ludwig Bemelmans. All of the episodes here deal with winter and Christmas. In the first show, Madeline and her friends visit the North Pole, where Madeline dazzles everyone (including Santa Claus) with her culinary skills. The second episode finds Santa too portly to slide down chimneys, so Madeline must assist him. "Madeline and the Ice Skates" is a "bonus" episode, in which Madeline receives a pair of skates for her birthday, and can't wait to try them out. Fans of Madeline, and most younger children for that matter, should love these short and sweet segments. Madeline's enthusiasm is infectious and each show teaches a subtle lesson. The shows here look great, as they are very colorful and show no defects or distortion. The digital stereo audio track is acceptable, as it provides clear dialogue and crackle-free music. —ML

Movie: 🎵🎵🎵 **DVD:** 🎵🎵🎵
Studio Home Ent. (cat #VM7815D, UPC 03-1398781523). Full frame. Digital Stereo. $14.99. Keepcase. *LANG:* English; Spanish. *SUB:* English. *FEATURES:* Bonus episode • Bonus trailers • Trivia game.
2000 70m/C

Mademoiselle

A secret sociopath, known in her small French village only as Mademoiselle (Moreau), wreaks havoc on the villagers by starting fires and poisoning livestock. Inflamed by an obsession with hunky Italian migrant worker Manou (Manni), Mademoiselle manages to place the blame for her creepy crimes squarely on him. The xenophobic villagers are happy to blame a man they already don't trust. Based on a story by Jean Genet; British director Tony Richardson beautifully captures the oddball essence of Jeanne Moreau as the virgin/whore. The black-and-white cinematography by David Watkin is so stunning it's worth watching even if you don't like Jean Genet's story. (Some sources list Marguerite Duras as the screenwriter, crediting only the story to Genet. The movie titles mention only Genet.) The transfer is beautiful. —LA

Movie: 🎵🎵🎵 ½ **DVD:** 🎵🎵🎵 ½
MGM Home Ent. (cat #1003248, UPC 027-616873989). Widescreen (2.35:1) anamorphic. Mono. $19.98. Keepcase. *LANG:* French. *SUB:* English; French; Spanish. *CAP:* French. *FEATURES:* Original theatrical trailer ● 16 chapters.
1966 105m/B *FR GB* Jeanne Moreau, Ettore Manni, Umberto Orsini, Keith Skinner, Jane Berretta, Mony Rey; **D:** Tony Richardson; **W:** Jean Genet; **C:** David Watkin.

The Madness Trilogy: Reefer Madness, Cocaine Fiends, Sex Madness

In *Cocaine Fiends,* Jane gets slipped some "headache powder" that makes her want to run off to the big city with a complete stranger. She's forced to sing and dance at the Dead Rat Café by the man she loves—who's also her supplier. Her brother comes a-lookin' for her and winds up on nose candy himself. Jane discovers her brother in a flop house and resolves to set things right once and for all. In *Sex Madness,* Millicent is the beauty queen who chases her stage dreams in the big city and ends up with a nasty case of syphilis. Now she can't go home to her high-school sweetheart. Until cured, doctors say she can never get married, but what they're really saying is she can't have sex. After going to a quack doctor she believes she's cured but after she's married and has a child, the scourge of "social disease" wreaks terrible vengeance. Not exactly Ibsen's *Ghosts,* but it's an entertaining period exploitation quickie. Pretty racy stuff for its day: Men and women dancing and pairing off to "go upstairs." Secretaries admire each other's figures. And there's even a disturbing allusion to a sexual predator of children. Given the age and cult popularity of the films, they're bound to be in poor condition. *Reefer Madness* (reviewed in *Book 2*) is in the best shape, while *Cocaine Fiends* is in the worst, with several points where the image and sound skip missing frames. However, there is little or no evidence of digital grain or shimmering too often associated with black-and-white budget DVDs. *Reefer Madness* also has the best audio quality. A real source of frustration, though, is that each movie is on a single continuous track without chapter stops. —GNG/DG
Movie: 🎵🎵 ½ **DVD:** 🎵🎵

Whirlwind Media (UPC 688321201223). Full frame. Mono. $24.95. Keepcase. *LANG:* English.
2000 187m/C

The Magic Show

Filmed Broadway stage production gains little on DVD. Within the framework of a minimal plot, chipmunk-cheeked magician Doug Henning performs several of his tricks. The early '80s outfits are almost as astonishing. Image and sound are about equal to tape. Lighting is dim. —MM
Movie: 🎵🎵 **DVD:** 🎵🎵
Image Ent. (cat #ID0697CODVD, UPC 014-381069723). Full frame. Dolby Digital 5.1 Surround Stereo; Mono. $24.98. Keepcase. *LANG:* English. *FEATURES:* 18 chapters.
1981 105m/C Doug Henning, Didi Conn, Anita Morris, Sandee Currie; **D:** Norman Campbell; **W:** Jerry Ross; **C:** Harry Lake; **M:** Stephen Schwartz.

The Magnificent Ambersons

Orson Welles's original version of *The Magnificent Ambersons* (1942) is one of the most highly sought after "lost grails" in cinema history. The film was butchered by the studio, which cut out an enormous chunk and had sections indifferently reshot by other Welles's associates. That compromised version is still considered one of film history's masterworks while the legendary original cut has never been found. This remake was produced with the intention of shooting Welles's original screenplay in an attempt to re-create the richness and rhythms of that long-lost masterpiece. Unfortunately, the producers chose a director with no affinity for the material (Arau has stated publicly that he does not like the original) and whose endless "improvements," revisions, additions, and reworkings both undermine the stated intent of the project and cripple the delicate story structure. *Amberson*-philes hoping to see faithful restagings of famous lost scenes will be quite disappointed—all have been reworked, rewritten, or omitted. Worst of all, the richly written narration is nowhere to be found. In simple terms, the film tells of a rich Indianapolis family who lose their fortune through bad investments, untimely deaths, and the selfishness of young upstart George. Arau fights the material from first frame to last, frequently turning quiet dramatic passages into telenovella-esque histrionics, adding unnecessary Tango dance numbers, overplaying the Oedipal element of the story, and including point-of-view shots of George in the womb. The cast struggles as best it can under extremely poor direction. Greenwood, Cromwell, and Hootkins manage to steal a few genuine moments from the ashes but period colloquialisms stick like fish bones in Mol and Rhys-Meyers's throats. Preview audiences in 1942 complained that Tim Holt's "George" was too unsympathetic—one wonders what they would have made of this film's inter-

pretation of him. Meyers's preening, arrogant, contemptuous, and loathsome "George" is overacted with such intense, eye-rolling hatred, it burns away any ounce of sympathy. He spends the film looking like a bug-eyed goldfish and behaving like an ass. Instead, one is left cheering at his comeuppance instead of empathizing. Tilly reaches new depths in overblown hysteria—her characterization is painfully redesigned and seems unbelievable, awkward, and near psychotic. She plays spinsterish Aunt Fanny like a blowsy, manipulative prostitute. The film is much like Van Sant's unnecessary remake of *Psycho* in that it only serves to remind audiences of the quality of the previous work. (Note: It should be said that a remake doesn't need to slavishly follow every verse of the original script, but a work such as this, which claims to be a faithful re-creation of the original, sets itself up for brickbats by evoking Welles name to authenticate this dreck.) Booth Tarkington's story *is* still there (and most of the actual lines of dialogue) and the dissipation of the family's wealth is much more understandable here. The production is handsomely mounted and nicely photographed. This disc is sharp, colorful, and pleasing. There's a bit of shimmer in eyes visible only in medium-wide shots, but close-ups look razor sharp. The sound is crisp and clear, though the dialogue is a bit under-mixed. The descriptive hyperbole on the back of the package is a total boondoggle, making bogus claims that this travesty is a faithful "restoration" of Welles's version. For contrast, it points out that in 1942, the studio had changed Welles's ending—something *this* one does as well. The "making of" featurette is the same insubstantial 1/2 hour commercial/puff piece that aired on A&E during the week of broadcast. —DG
Movie: 🎵🎵 **DVD:** 🎵🎵🎵
A&E (cat #AAE-70340, UPC 7339617034-05). Full frame. Dolby Digital Surround. $24.95. Keepcase. *LANG:* English. *FEATURES:* "Making of" featurette ● Talent bios ● 18 chapters.
2002 139m/C Madeleine Stowe, Bruce Greenwood, Jonathan Rhys Meyers, Jennifer Tilly, William Hootkins, James Cromwell; **D:** Alfonso Arau.

Magnificent Butcher

Lam Sai-Wing (Sammo Hung) is an almost childlike, innocent student of the martial arts school of Master Wong Fei Hung, but the young man constantly runs into problems with the rival kung fu school of the Five Dragons. Helping the weak, and good in his heart, Wing is entirely unsuspecting as Da-Hoi (Yuen Biao), son of the Master of the Five Dragons, plots against him. First Da-Hoi rapes Wing's sister-in-law, then kills her brother and finally creates a set up, blaming Wing for the death of his own sister. Hot for vengeance, Wing perfects his martial arts skills to face off against Da-Hoi. Staggering kung fu sequences, choreographed by Sammo

Hung and Woo-ping Yuen, are among the best ever put on film. The image shows some signs of wear in the form of speckles and scratches and the occasional registration problem that causes the image to jitter slightly. Colors are bold and beautiful, and the film has a very natural quality throughout without the faded discoloration found in so many imports. The 5.1 audio has a very narrow frequency response without notable bass and I was unable to spot any Surround usage. As such, this is actually more of a mono audio track with some subtle stereo effects. —GH

Movie: 🎚🎚 ½ **DVD:** 🎚🎚 ½
Tai Seng (UPC 601643564944). Widescreen (2.35:1) letterboxed. Dolby Digital 5.1. $29.98. Keepcase. *LANG:* Cantonese; Mandarin; English. *SUB:* English; Japanese; Chinese. *FEATURES:* Trailers • Talent files.
1987 108m/C *HK* Sammo Hung, Yuen Biao; *D:* Woo-ping Yuen; *W:* Jing Wong.

Magnum Force

Harry Callahan's (Eastwood) second outing is a real let-down after the seminal *Dirty Harry* but it's enjoyable enough as a cop-action movie. This time out, Harry finds himself against a group of young vigilante cops (Matheson, Soul, Niven, and Uhrich). DVD comes from a careful transfer of original elements that have been well preserved. Colors are bright and the source material exhibits no damage. Sound is fine for the film's age. —MM

Movie: 🎚🎚 ½ **DVD:** 🎚🎚 ½
Warner Home Video (UPC 0853918599-25). Widescreen anamorphic. Dolby Digital 5.1. $19.98. Snapper. *LANG:* English; French. *SUB:* English; French; Spanish; Portuguese; Japanese; Chinese; Thai; Korean. *FEATURES:* 36 chapters • Talent files • "Making of" featurette • Behind the scenes—text • Memorable lines—text.
1973 (R) 124m/C Clint Eastwood, Hal Holbrook, Mitchell Ryan, David Soul, Robert Urich, Tim Matheson, Kip Niven, Albert "Poppy" Popwell; *D:* Ted Post; *W:* Michael Cimino, John Milius; *C:* Frank Stanley; *M:* Lalo Schifrin.

Major League 2

This sequel plays out a continuation of the first story. Many of the same characters return; most importantly, Charlie Sheen as Ricky "Wild Thing" Vaughn. The team has been having trouble for the majority of the season. The predictable track the film takes leads the audience through the season, and asks "Will the team bounce back or not?" Is there really any doubt of the outcome? *ML2* retains the similar comedic strengths of the first film as well as many of the same cast members. It's certainly not art, but it does provide for a few laughs. The best part has to be Randy Quaid as a loud-mouthed fan shouting from the stands. Besides Quaid, most of the cast does a mediocre job. Not a total loss, but it could have used some more originality. Images are sharp, detailed, and nicely rendered throughout. Colors are fine

as well, looking solid and nicely saturated, with no problems. Black level is good and flesh tones are accurate and natural. There are a few minor print flaws and a few moments that suffer from pixelation. Not a home run, but at least a strong double. The newly created 5.1 soundtrack offers limited Surround effects use, as well as a strong presentation of the score, however cheesy it may be. Dialogue is clear for the majority of the time, but occasionally, it seemed a little thin. —AB/DG

Movie: 🎚🎚 ½ **DVD:** 🎚🎚 ½
Warner Home Video (UPC 85391688228). Widescreen letterboxed. Dolby Surround 5.1. $14.98. Snapper. *LANG:* English; French. *SUB:* English; French; Spanish. *CAP:* English. *FEATURES:* 31 chapters • Trailers • Bios.
1994 (PG) 105m/C Charlie Sheen, Tom Berenger, Corbin Bernsen, James Gammon, Dennis Haysbert, Omar Epps, David Keith, Bob Uecker, Alison Doody, Michelle Burke, Margaret Whitton, Eric Bruskotter, Takaaki Ishibashi, Randy Quaid; *D:* David S. Ward; *W:* R.J. Stewart; *C:* Victor Hammer; *M:* Michel Colombier.

Major League 3: Back to the Minors

Scott Bakula (why'd they have to go and cancel *Quantum Leap?*) stars as Gus Cantrell, pitcher for the Twins. He's a player with considerable skills, but he's having a hard time, so the owner offers him a job as manager of a AAA farm team. Of course, the team turns out to be a new bunch of weirdos that Bakula has to pull together to win the day when they find out they're playing the big-league team in a promotional game. Predictable and silly, the film offers a good performance from Bakula, who holds together what's otherwise a fairly low-key, low-budget effort. And what *Major League* film would be complete without the commentary from Bob Uecker's character? Going to the trough a third time stretches this series a bit thin, but there are a few scattered laughs. Images are sharp and colors are strong but there are trace amounts of pixelation, print marks, and a little bit of shimmering. The DVD contains a fairly unremarkable audio track but during the baseball games it really opens up. The music has a fairly appealing presence, sounding clear and clean. —AB/DG

Movie: 🎚🎚 ½ **DVD:** 🎚🎚
Warner Home Video (UPC 85391593423). Widescreen (1.85:1) letterboxed. Dolby Surround 5.1. $14.98. Snapper. *LANG:* English; French. *SUB:* English; French; Spanish. *CAP:* English. *FEATURES:* 24 chapters.
1998 (PG-13) 90m/C Scott Bakula, Corbin Bernsen, Dennis Haysbert, Takaaki Ishibashi, Jensen Daggett, Eric Bruskotter, Walton Goggins, Ted McGinley, Kenneth Johnson, Peter M. MacKenzie, Bob Uecker, Steve Yeager, Larry Brandenburg, Judson Mills, Lobo Sebastian, Thom Barry, Tim DiFilippo, Tom DiFilippo, Ted DiFilippo; *D:* John Warren; *W:* John Warren; *C:* Tim Suhrstedt; *M:* Robert Folk.

Making the Grade

Jersey tough kid (Nelson) owes the mob (Clay), and so he attends prep school in place of a rich kid (Olsen) who can't be bothered. It's better than similar '80s teen flicks, but not by much, and then there's the Diceman's overbearing hambone act. DVD image is completely adequate to the material. —MM **AKA:** *Preppies.*

Movie: 🎚🎚 **DVD:** 🎚🎚 ½
MGM Home Ent. (cat #1002574, UPC 027-616867759). Widescreen (1.85:1) anamorphic. Dolby Digital Surround. $14.98. Keepcase. *LANG:* English. *SUB:* French; Spanish. *CAP:* English. *FEATURES:* 16 chapters • Trailer.
1984 (PG) 105m/C Judd Nelson, Joanna Lee, Dana Olsen, Ronald Lacey, Scott McGinnis, Gordon Jump, Carey Scott, Andrew (Dice Clay) Silverstein; *D:* Dorian Walker; *W:* Gene Quintano; *C:* Jacques Haitkin; *M:* Basil Poledouris.

Mama Flora's Family

Based on the novel by Alex Haley (*Roots*), which was finished by co-author David Stevens after Haley's 1992 death. It's about Haley's mother, Mama Flora (Cicely Tyson), who endures one tragedy after another while raising her family. First, as a teenaged servant, Flora gets pregnant and is forced to give up the child. Then, when she does marry, her husband is killed and their property burned. Meanwhile, her other children and grandchildren struggle with discrimination and grow up angry and resentful. The film holds together because of the force of Tyson's portrayal. The film is presented full frame on this DVD. The picture is clear, although there is some occasional shimmering of the image. Good, true colors are to be had here, although there is some slight grain in some shots. The audio track offers a striking deep bass and subtle Surround effects. The score is nicely represented on this track. The DVD would have benefited from some further background information on Haley and the origins of the story. —ML

Movie: 🎚🎚 ½ **DVD:** 🎚🎚 ½
Artisan Ent. (cat #12337, UPC 70772912-3378). Full frame. Dolby Surround. $19.98. Keepcase. *LANG:* English. *CAP:* English. *FEATURES:* 20 chapters.
1998 175m/C Cicely Tyson, Mario Van Peebles, Blair Underwood, Queen Latifah, Hill Harper, Shemar Moore, Della Reese; *D:* Peter Werner; *W:* David Stevens, Carol Schreder; *C:* Neil Roach.

Man Next Door

Serial killer thriller is notable mostly for the return to the screen of Virginia Mayo. The story is fairly standard stuff, though the Louisiana locations are used well. DVD image is no improvement over VHS tape. Extras are notable. —MM

Movie: 🎚🎚 **DVD:** 🎚🎚 ½
York Ent. (cat #YPD-1174, UPC 75072311-7423). Full frame. $14.99. Keepcase. *LANG:* English. *FEATURES:* Director's intro

and commentary ● Auditions ● Music video ● Trailers.
1997 (R) 104m/C Virginia Mayo, Karen Carlson, John Furlong; **D:** Rod C. Spence.

The Man Who Cried

Suzie (Ricci), a young Jewish girl, emigrates from war-torn Russia and is taken in by an English family. As she grows older she is haunted by the memories of her estranged father who went to America in search of a better life for himself and his family. Her one dream is to find her remaining paternal link and once again become a family. But before she can undertake the journey, she must come to grips with her Jewish heritage, her gypsy lover, Cesar (Depp), and the pressing onslaught of the fear-inspiring Nazi regime. Although the performances by the all-star cast are enjoyable, the plot is one-dimensional and seems rushed and underdeveloped towards the end. DVD sports a crisp transfer, and aside from a few noticeable points where the soundtrack is out of sync with the actors, the overall sound of the film is well done. —EL
Movie: 🎬🎬 ½ **DVD:** 🎬🎬 ½
Universal Studios (cat #21475). Widescreen (1.85:1) anamorphic. Dolby Digital 5.1; DTS; Surround. $29.98. Keepcase. *LANG:* English; French. *CAP:* English. *FEATURES:* Theatrical trailer ● Production notes ● Cast and filmmakers ● DVD-ROM features ● Recommendations.
2000 (R) 97m/C *GB FR* Christina Ricci, Johnny Depp, Cate Blanchett, John Turturro, Harry Dean Stanton, Oleg Yankovsky; **D:** Sally Potter; **W:** Sally Potter; **C:** Sacha Vierny; **M:** Osvaldo Golijoy. *AWARDS:* Natl. Bd. of Review '01: Support. Actress (Blanchett).

The Man Who Haunted Himself

While driving one evening, Harold Pelham (Moore) has a car accident. When he awakes, people claim they have seen him in places that he has never been. Does Pelham have a doppelganger—or is he going insane? With a story line far more fitting for the *Alfred Hitchcock* TV hour it comes from, it's hard to remain interested in much besides the hallucinogenic visuals that accompany the finale. Director *(Dead of Night)* Basil Dearden's last film; Bryan Forbe's uncredited script does its best to flesh out a simple idea. Excellent DVD transfer and reasonable sound given its origin. —MO
Movie: 🎬🎬 ½ **DVD:** 🎬🎬🎬 ½
Anchor Bay (cat #DV12051, UPC 0131312-05190). Widescreen anamorphic. Dolby Digital Mono. $19.98. Keepcase. *LANG:* English; French. *FEATURES:* 23 chapters ● Commentary: director Roger Moore, (uncredited) writer Bryan Forbes ● Theatrical trailers ● Roger Moore bio.
1970 94m/C *GB* Roger Moore, Hildegard(e) Neil, Olga Georges-Picot; **D:** Basil Dearden; **W:** Bryan Forbes; **C:** Tony Spratling; **M:** Michael Lewis.

The Man Who Loved Women

This remake proves—though no proof is needed—that Blake Edwards is no François Truffaut. The original (reviewed in *Book 2*) is a sleek French romance and character study. In this iteration, the humor is broader, the sexual content is a bit more graphic, and it all seems heavier. David Fowler (Reynolds) is a successful sculptor and womanizer. He seduces them and they flock to him. It's all so trying that he goes to a shrink (Andrews) and talks and talks and talks. You know where they're headed. Both wide- and full-frame images are very grainy, but then, that's the way director of photography Haskell Wexler's films tend to look. The disc is an accurate reproduction of the theatrical release as I remember it. Mono sound delivers understandable dialogue and does nothing for Henry Mancini's score. —MM
Movie: 🎬🎬 **DVD:** 🎬🎬 ½
Columbia Tristar (cat #06675, UPC 04339-6066755). Widescreen anamorphic; full frame. Mono. $24.98. Keepcase. *LANG:* English; French. *SUB:* English; French. *CAP:* English. *FEATURES:* 28 chapters.
1983 (R) 110m/C Burt Reynolds, Julie Andrews, Kim Basinger, Marilu Henner, Cynthia Sikes, Jennifer Edwards; **D:** Blake Edwards; **W:** Blake Edwards; **C:** Haskell Wexler; **M:** Henry Mancini.

The Man Who Wasn't There

Ed Crane (Thornton, in a masterfully underplayed performance) is a small-town barber who goes unnoticed by many. He suspects that his wife Doris (McDormand) is cheating on him with Dave (Gandolfini), who owns the store where she works. When Ed wants to invest in the new "dry cleaning" process that a stranger tells him about, he decides to try blackmail. What follows is a series of stately paced twists and complications. Sharpness and detail are excellent throughout, as Roger Deakins's brilliant black-and-white cinematography remains crisp and well-defined, even into the shadows. Slight grain was present theatrically and remains slightly visible at times here, as well. The print used is beautiful, as no specks, marks, or scratches are present. One or two little traces of edge-enhancement and pixelation don't present major concerns. The 5.1 soundtrack seems to fold into mono for a good deal of the film, only lightly opening up now and then, mainly for Carter Burwell's beautiful score. Still, this works for the movie—the subdued soundtrack is appropriate for the material and tone. Dialogue and Thornton's narration remain clear and natural. This is the first commentary from Joel and Ethan Coen, who are joined by actor Billy Bob Thornton, who has also never participated in a commentary track. This effort is not particularly structured. Instead it seems like the three are simply stating whatever occurs to them while they're watching. It's a nice mix of jokes and some tidbits about the production. —AB/MM
Movie: 🎬🎬🎬 ½ **DVD:** 🎬🎬🎬 ½
USA Home Ent. (cat #963960319-2, UPC 696306031925). Widescreen (1.85:1) anamorphic. Dolby Digital 5.1 Surround. $26.98. Keepcase. *LANG:* English; French. *SUB:* French; Spanish. *CAP:* English. *FEATURES:* Commentary ● Interview with Roger Deakins ● 5 deleted scenes ● Trailer ● TV spots ● "Making of" featurette ● Photo gallery ● Filmographies.
2001 (R) 116m/B Billy Bob Thornton, Frances McDormand, Michael Badalucco, James Gandolfini, Katherine Borowitz, Jon Polito, Scarlett Johansson, Richard Jenkins, Tony Shalhoub; **D:** Joel Coen; **W:** Joel Coen, Ethan Coen; **C:** Roger Deakins; **M:** Carter Burwell. *AWARDS:* L.A. Film Critics '01: Cinematog; *NOM:* Oscars '01: Cinematog.; Golden Globes '02: Actor—Drama (Thornton), Film—Drama, Screenplay; Writers Guild '01: Orig. Screenplay; Broadcast Film Critics '01: Film, Screenplay.

The Man with the Golden Gun

James Bond (Moore, in his second outing in the role) receives a cryptic message—a golden bullet that carries his number, 007. To the secret agent, this message is a clear warning, however, telling him that Scaramanga (Lee) has set his sights on him as a target. Scaramanga is a highly paid assassin, known for his distinctive golden gun and many rumors surround the enigmatic man. No one has ever seen Scaramanga—and lived. Unfortunately, the source print used for this transfer exhibits blemishes and speckles that have not been cleaned up for the DVD release. As a result, dust and scratches are present almost throughout the presentation. The image features some great colors, while maintaining a natural balance. Blacks are deep without losing detail. While the music presentation is rich, dialogue comes across a bit thin, due to the material's age. —GH
Movie: 🎬🎬 ½ **DVD:** 🎬🎬🎬 ½
MGM Home Ent. (UPC 027616273437). Widescreen (1.78:1) anamorphic. Dolby Stereo. $9.94. Keepcase. *LANG:* English. *SUB:* French; Spanish. *FEATURES:* Commentary ● 2 documentaries ● Photo gallery ● Trailers and TV spots ● Booklet.
1974 (PG) 134m/C *GB* Roger Moore, Christopher Lee, Britt Ekland, Maud Adams, Herve Villechaize, Clifton James, Soon-Teck Oh, Richard Loo, Marc Lawrence, Bernard Lee, Lois Maxwell, Desmond Llewelyn; **D:** Guy Hamilton; **W:** Tom Mankiewicz; **C:** Ted Moore; **M:** John Barry.

The Mangler 2

The haunted laundry machine in the abominable first film has become a computer virus in this inexplicable sequel-in-number-only. The setting is a private school where Jo (Swain) unleashes the bug into the security system thereby turning everyday appliances into killing machines, etc., etc. Not even the presence of the redoubtable Lance Henriksen is enough to elevate this formulaic dreck. Curiously, it gets the full treatment on DVD, complete with commentary track where writer/director Michael Hamilton-Wright admits that it took him all of eight days to write the script. There's nothing special about either the sound or the softish image that lacks detail in dark areas. That's to be expected of such a low-budget, quickly made (48 camera set-ups per day) Canadian effort. —*MM*

Movie: 🎬🎬 **DVD:** 🎬🎬 ½
Artisan Ent. (cat #12490, UPC 01223612-8359). Widescreen anamorphic. Dolby Digital 5.1 Surround; Dolby Surround. $24.98. Keepcase. *LANG:* English. *SUB:* English; Spanish. *FEATURES:* 20 chapters • Commentary • Behind-the-scenes featurette • 2 music videos • Outtakes • Talent files.
2001 (R) 96m/C *CA* Lance Henriksen, Chelse Swain, Phillipe Bergerone; **D:** Michael Hamilton-Wright; **W:** Michael Hamilton-Wright.

The Manhattan Project

The threat of nuclear devastation hits a small town as Paul (Collet), a young science whiz, creates the first personal-sized nuclear bomb from stolen materials at a local military testing lab. As Paul heads to the national science fair to show his newest invention, the lab discovers the missing plutonium and the military starts a nationwide search to find the boy and his life-threatening device. It is up to Dr. Mathewson (Lithgow), the scientist/boyfriend of Paul's mother, to find the young boy and convince him to give up his project before the military takes more drastic steps. Playing on the early '80s fear of nuclear holocaust, the film is a well-done, complex thriller. While it lacks much of the larger-than-life plotting and special effects produced by today's standards, this film still provides an engaging viewing experience. This DVD release sports both widescreen and full-frame versions. The color and picture look good with no noticeable distortions or artifacts on the transfer. The Dolby digital Surround track sounds good; there are no noticeable distortions in the quality and it makes good use of the front three speakers. The back two speakers seemed to be underutilized. —*EL* **AKA:** Manhattan Project: The Deadly Game.

Movie: 🎬🎬🎬 **DVD:** 🎬🎬🎬
MGM Home Ent. (cat #1003512, UPC 027-616876621). Widescreen (1.85:1) anamorphic; full frame. Dolby Digital Surround. $14.95. Keepcase. *LANG:* English; French; Spanish. *CAP:* English. *FEATURES:* Theatrical trailer • 16 chapters.
1986 (PG-13) 112m/C John Lithgow, Christopher Collet, Cynthia Nixon, Jill Eikenberry, John Mahoney, Sully Boyer, Richard Council, Robert Schenkkan, Paul Austin; **D:** Marshall Brickman; **W:** Marshall Brickman, Thomas Baum; **C:** Billy Williams.

Manhunter [LE]

Will Graham (Petersen) was the FBI's top guy in their Behavioral Science Unit until he retired after a harrowing pursuit of a serial killer. Now, he's called back to duty to find a psychotic family killer by colleague Jack (Farina). Will's technique: to match the thought processes of serial killers and thus anticipate their moves. Intense thriller, based on the Thomas Harris novel *Red Dragon.* Harris also wrote *The Silence of the Lambs,* whose most notorious character, Hannibal "The Cannibal" Lecter, appears in this movie as well (spelled Lektor and played by Cox). Graham visits the prisoner to get fresh insights into his new case and Lektor plays his usual nasty mind games. Director Mann applies the slick techniques he introduced in the popular TV series *Miami Vice,* creating a quiet, moody intensity broken by sudden onslaughts of violence. This Anchor Bay limited edition two-DVD set features both the original theatrical release version and the "restored" director's cut of the film. While the first looks near spectacular, with strong saturated colors and a very sharp image, the director's cut (which many would prefer with its extra three minutes of character development) looks amazingly bad with a picture so soft that you'd think they had nobody on the set to focus the camera. The other problem with this cut is that, for some reason, it has a muffled-sounding Dolby Surround soundtrack, while the theatrical version has a new 5.1 mix that is much stronger. The two have very similar sounding Surround tracks but the 5.1 blows the other away when it comes to fidelity and presence. If you're someone who enjoys collecting numbered limited edition sets, then buy this one, otherwise just stick to the single-disc theatrical release edition, which is only half the cost. —*JO* **AKA:** Red Dragon.

Movie: 🎬🎬🎬 **DVD:** 🎬🎬🎬
Anchor Bay (cat #DV11692, UPC 013131-169294). Widescreen (2.35:1) anamorphic. Dolby Digital 5.1; Dolby Surround. $39.98. Keepcase. *LANG:* English. *CAP:* English. *FEATURES:* 30 chapters • Theatrical trailer • Talent files • "Making of" featurette • "The Manhunter Look," with cinematographer Dante Spinotti • 24-page collector's booklet.
1986 (R) 100m/C William L. Petersen, Kim Greist, Joan Allen, Brian Cox, Dennis Farina, Stephen Lang, Tom Noonan, Benjamin Hendrickson, David Seaman; **D:** Michael Mann; **W:** Michael Mann; **C:** Dante Spinotti; **M:** Michel Rubini.

Maniac [LE]

This slasher film is a cult classic and completely deserves high placement in the genre. Joe Spinell plays a sadistic maniac terrorizing New York with his nightly outings. Who can blame him, though, with the annoying voice of his mother in his head singing in "I told you so" verse every time he comes back to the apartment with a new scalp, "I warned you not to go out tonight." What difference does it make that he's really talking to himself in his mother's own voice? Spinell's portrayal of the killer is amazing. Unlike most films that show serial killers as either omnificent or moronic, Maniac shows the ups and downs of the daily life of a killer. Spinell portrays him with the same grace that Shakespearian actors give to Hamlet. When he returns home after trying one more time to have a good relationship with a hooker only to end up strangling, slicing, and scalping her, his weary movements as he replaces the mannequin that wears the scalp from his last experience with the new one have a surreal working man quality to them. The script, direction, and acting are all good here, and the slow quiet pacing of the film brings to mind an extreme *Henry: Portrait of a Serial Killer,* only with a lot more gore. Tom Savini's visual effects are amazing, especially given the time frame. He saves the best for himself, playing a sleazy guy seducing a girl in a car. In one of the most effective sequences of the film, his head is blown completely off, and we get the view from behind his head with a view of the killer standing on the hood of Savini's car, and it looks pretty real (having never actually seen someone's head blown off, that is). The set decoration of Spinell's mannequin-heavy apartment is also a wonder to behold. Neither over the top or shy about its subject, the room reflects the mixture of madness and hopefulness that are at war in the killer. For lovers of the splatter genre, this is a keeper. Anchor Bay has put this disc out so, of course, it looks and sounds great. No scratches or sound problems, but it was a low-budget '80s film so the production quality is mid-range at best. The extras are fun, especially the Anchor Bay–produced "The Joe Spinell Story," which chronicles his amazing life as a fringe player in Hollywood to his untimely death. There is also a CD of the soundtrack in the shape of Spinell's head that is pretty cool and it's all wrapped up in a collectable tin. —*CA*

Movie: 🎬🎬🎬 **DVD:** 🎬🎬 ½
Anchor Bay (cat #DV11850, UPC 01313-1185096). Widescreen (1.85:1) anamorphic. Dolby Digital Surround Ex; DTS-ES; Dolby Digital Surround 2.0. $39.90. Keepcase. *LANG:* English; French; Italian. *SUB:* Spanish. *CAP:* English. *FEATURES:* 23 chapters • "The Joe Spinell Story," documentary • Radio interviews with filmmakers • Commentary: Lustig, Savini, Marinelli, Walter • Gallery of Outrage • Stills • Talent bios • Theatrical trailer.
1980 91m/C Joe Spinell, Caroline Munro, Gail Lawrence, Kelly Piper, Tom Savini, Rita Montone, Hyla Marrow, William Lustig, Sharon Mitchell; **D:** William Lustig; **W:** C.A. Rosenberg, Joe Spinell; **C:** Robert Lindsay; **M:** Jay Chattaway.

Manji

Practically unclassifiable in terms of Western movies, from its bare outline Yasuzo Masumura's *Manji* resembles the exploitative sex movies of Radley Metzger. Its subject matter moves from lesbian love, to

adultery, to multiple sexual relationships tangled in webs of deceit, blackmail, and maybe even murder. Austere in scope and pared down to the raw emotions shared by its four mad lovers, the film is a contemplative mass of interesting ideas about human behavior. Housewife Sonoko Kakiuchi (Kyoko Kishida) falls madly in love with fellow art student Mitsuko Tokumitsu (Ayako Wakao), the daughter of a wealthy industrialist. Mitsuko plays coy, but allows a secret relationship to begin. It becomes so intense that Sonoko is soon flaunting it before her uncomprehending husband Kotaro (Eiji Funakoshi). But the supposedly faithful Mitsuko has a male lover, Eijiro Watanuki (Yusuke Kawazu) she manipulates as cleverly as she does Sonoko; Eijiro wheedles Sonoko into a secret blood contract, to hold Mitsuko for both of them forever. This 1964 film transcends the entire sex revolution in Western movies with an erotic picture outside and beyond anything I've seen. It's not pornographic at all, and has very limited nudity. It doesn't play or behave like an exploitative picture, and makes many standard "meaningful" European films look like cheap pandering in comparison. Precious little time is wasted with anything but the developing psychosexual tangle between its characters. The lesbian theme is confronted directly, without comment or context that would prejudge it. DVD the best-looking yet of Fantoma's Masumura collection. The image is practically flawless, and the delicate color brings out the sensual aspects of clothing, printed stationery, settings, and skin. The trailer is loaded with spoilers, and shots not seen in the film proper, including some lesbian kissing in a wooded exterior that seems lamely conventional when compared to the originality of what was kept in the show. I can't think of a better choice for the cover of the box than the bare-shoulders double portrait of the actresses. "Manji" is the name of the written character that we call a backwards swastika. It has no relationship to Nazism, but the resemblance makes the cover look very sinister. Word of mouth will be needed to get this extremely adult, extremely thought-provoking film the audience it deserves. There are obviously many Japanese cinema fans who've known about Yasuzo Masumura for decades, but as cult discoveries go, he deserves to be the next Mario Bava. —GE *AKA:* All Mixed Up.
Movie: ♫♫♫ ½ *DVD:* ♫♫♫ ½
Image Ent. (UPC 014381169126). Widescreen (2:35:1) anamorphic. $29.98. Keepcase. *LANG:* Japanese. *SUB:* English. *FEATURES:* Trailer • Masumura text bio and filmography • Photo gallery.
1964 91m/C *JP* Ayako Wakao, Kyoko Kishida, Yusuke Kawazu, Eiji Funakoshi; *D:* Yasuzo Masumura; *W:* Kaneto Shindo; *C:* Setsuo Kobayashi; *M:* Tadashi Yamauchi.

Mannequin

Sleeper hit revolves around Jonathan (McCarthy), an innocent young department store window dresser, and the spirit of an ancient Egyptian princess (Cattrall) who comes to life in one of his mannequins. It's every bit as frivolous as it sounds and more fun than it ought to be. The grainy DVD image is not much of an improvement over VHS tape. (It is, however, accurate.) Sound is unusually weak. —MM
Movie: ♫♫♫ *DVD:* ♫♫
MGM Home Ent. (cat #1002746, UPC 027-616869449). Widescreen (1.85:1) anamorphic; full frame. Dolby Digital Surround Stereo. $14.98. Keepcase. *LANG:* English; French. *SUB:* English; French; Spanish. *CAP:* English. *FEATURES:* 16 chapters • Trailers.
1987 (PG) 90m/C Andrew McCarthy, Kim Cattrall, Estelle Getty, James Spader, Meshach Taylor, Carole (Raphaelle) Davis, G.W. Bailey; *D:* Michael Gottlieb; *W:* Ed Rugoff; *C:* Tim Suhrstedt; *M:* Sylvester Levay. *AWARDS: NOM:* Oscars '87: Song ("Nothing's Gonna Stop Us Now").

Manos, the Hands of Fate

Please see review of *Mystery Science Theater 3000: "Manos: Hands of Fate."*
Movie: woof
1966 74m/C Tom Nayman, Diane Mahree, Hal P. Warren, John Reynolds; *D:* Hal P. Warren; *W:* Hal P. Warren.

Manslaughter / The Cheat

Brimming with silent sexuality, this double feature shows two sides of DeMille. *Manslaughter* is about a mislead debutante (Joy) whose wild ways cause the death of a police officer. Her lover is also the District Attorney (Meighan) who must prosecute her. Here, in his typical fashion, DeMille uses spectacle (this time, it's Roman orgies) to titillate. On the other hand, *The Cheat* utilizes sadomasochism and exoticism to rouse the senses. Here, a socialite (Ward), after her ivory trader friend settles a large debt for her, is literally branded with the trader's mark. Her shame causes both her own, and her husband's, downfall. The prints for both films show some signs of degradation, though *The Cheat*, for its age, looks outstanding. (The Image edition is reviewed in *Book 2.*) Both boast new, better than average, orchestral scores. —DRL
Movie: ♫♫ ½ *DVD:* ♫♫♫
Kino on Video (cat #244, UPC 738329024-420). Full frame. Mono. $29.95. Keepcase. *LANG:* Silent. *SUB:* English intertitles. *FEATURES:* 18 chapters.
1922 159m/B Leatrice Joy, Thomas Meighan, Lois Wilson; *D:* Cecil B. DeMille; *W:* Jeanie Macpherson; *C:* Alvin Wyckoff.

Manufacturing Consent: Noam Chomsky and the Media

Slick and informative documentary looks at the background and career of American linguist, educator, and political activist Noam Chomsky, including his seminal linguist work "Synactic Structures." It also examines his outspoken criticism of the American power elite and the media. This admirable video transfer showcases well-reproduced colors and blacks. However, due to the varying sources used throughout, this quality does vary considerably. But overall, the disc is a solid presentation. The soundtrack is also quite good and features clear, understandable dialogue, which is important for this film since it's comprised of Chomsky talking for about two hours. Of the extras on the disc, the debate with Buckley stands out as an entertainment highlight. —MJT
Movie: ♫♫♫ *DVD:* ♫♫♫
Zeitgeist Films (cat #ZV1013, UPC 795-975101325). Full frame. Dolby Digital 2.0 Surround. $29.99. Keepcase. *LANG:* English. *FEATURES:* 24 chapters • Noam Chomsky reflects on the film • Excerpts from 1969 "Firing Line" debate with William F. Buckley Jr. • 1971 discussion with Michel Foucault • Filmmaker bios and production notes.
1993 167m/C *D:* Mark Achbar, Peter Wintonick.

The Many Adventures of Winnie the Pooh

This is a collection of animated shorts based on the stories and characters of A.A. Milne's world of Winnie the Pooh. Animation is quite clean and has not degenerated like later straight-to-video efforts from Disney. However, there is an absence of backgrounds, cheating by repeatedly showing book illustrations that come to life. A tepid if not shameful entry in the Disney canon. Clean DVD transfer and excellent sound. —MO
Movie: ♫♫ ½ *DVD:* ♫♫♫ ½
Buena Vista Home Ent. (cat #24452, UPC 786936126433). Full frame. Dolby Digital 5.1. $29.99. Keepcase. *LANG:* English; French; Spanish. *SUB:* English. *CAP:* English. *FEATURES:* 21 chapters • Behind-the-scenes "Making of" footage • "A Day for Eeyore" short • "Winnie the Pooh Theme Song" performed by Carly Simon • Sing-along song, "The Wonderful Thing About Tiggers" • Sneak peek at two new Pooh films • Child-friendly game, "The 100 Acre Wood Challenge" • Winnie the Pooh scrapbook • Art gallery • "Pooh's Shadow" DVD storybook • "Pooh's Pop-Up Fun Facts."
1977 (G) 83m/C

Mararia

Love tragedy is set on the volcanic island of Lanzarote during the Spanish Civil War. Dr. Fermin (Gomez) arrives and immediately is smitten by Mararia (Toledo). Then English surveyor Bertrand (Glen) shows up and is equally smitten. So is she, this time. Even though the handsome film doesn't have the production values of an American studio work, it is carefully lit and photographed and is graced with a fine score. Unfortunately, the DVD is riddled with every visual flaw imaginable—distracting aliasing and horrible artifacts in almost all of the impressive exteriors. Burned in subtitles are bright. —*MM*

Movie: *🦴🦴🦴* **DVD:** *🦴*
Vanguard Intl. Cinema (cat #TF1010). Widescreen letterboxed. $29.98. Keepcase. *LANG:* Spanish. *SUB:* English. *FEATURES:* Trailer ⬤ 12 chapters.
1998 109m/C *SP* Goya Toledo, Carmelo Gomez, Iain Glen, Mirta Ibarra; **D:** Antonio J. Betancor; **W:** Antonio J. Betancor, Carlos Alvarez; **C:** Juan Ruiz-Anchia; **M:** Pedro Guerra.

Margaret Cho: I'm the One That I Want

Margaret Cho is a comedic genius. This does not mean that she is universally funny or that her humor is pleasing to everyone, but it does mean that she can glean the humor out of the most delicate situations and can follow the acorn of a thought through to its big oak of a laugh in no time at all. This disc covers her live show at the Warfield in San Francisco where she plays to, if applause is any indication, a predominantly gay audience. Be ready for a frank, funny whirlwind ride on the gender express. Starting her routine with a review of her last show for PETA, she segues from Karl Lagerfield as murderer, to fag hags being the backbone of the gay community, to her own phobia of straight men and to her experience aboard a lesbian cruise. It's all smooth and funny and fun. Good show for anyone who likes irreverent humor. The picture on the disc is good, but it is a live show and the lighting is not always the best, but the sound is very good, crisp and clear. —*CA*

Movie: *🦴🦴🦴* **DVD:** *🦴🦴* ½
Winstar Home Ent. (cat #WHE73146, UPC 720917314624). Full frame. $19.90. Keepcase. *LANG:* English. *FEATURES:* 28 chapters ⬤ Commentary ⬤ Filmography ⬤ Behind-the-scenes featurette.
2000 96m/C Margaret Cho; **D:** Lionel Coleman; **W:** Margaret Cho.

Maria's Lovers

Maria (Kinski) is married to Ivan (Savage), an impotent WWII vet, and succumbs to the charms of a rakish lady-killer (Spano). Ivan falls for an older woman. After even more complications, she turns to a wandering musician (Carradine). Russian director Konchalovsky's first American film is offbeat and uneven but gorgeously lit and photographed. DVD delivers a virtually flawless image; even the gauzy romantic scenes look good with no excess grain or artifacts. —*MM*

Movie: *🦴🦴* ½ **DVD:** *🦴🦴🦴*
MGM Home Ent. (cat #1002755, UPC 027-616869531). Widescreen (1.85:1) anamorphic; full frame. Dolby Digital Stereo; Mono. $19.98. Keepcase. *LANG:* English; French. *SUB:* English; French; Spanish. *CAP:* English. *FEATURES:* 16 chapters ⬤ Trailers.
1984 (R) 103m/C Nastassia Kinski, John Savage, Robert Mitchum, Keith Carradine,

Anita Morris, Bud Cort, Karen Young, Tracy Nelson, John Goodman, Vincent Spano; **D:** Andrei Konchalovsky; **W:** Gerard Brach, Marjorie David, Andrei Konchalovsky; **C:** Juan Ruiz-Anchia; **M:** Gary S. Remal.

Marilyn Monroe: The Diamond Collection, Vol. 2

The second boxed set of Marilyn Monroe's 20th Century Fox features wraps up the rest of her starring roles for the studio, as well as one very good comedy where she's just in for support. Although none of these contain her iconic or best performances, each is a fascinating piece of MM history—roles charting sometimes-awkward attempts to graduate to full dramatic stardom, with varying degrees of success. And they also show how Fox attempted to package and re-package MM as a star by shifting her from genre to genre, and trying her out with a number of directors. Please see individual reviews of *Don't Bother to Knock, Let's Make Love, Monkey Business, Niagara,* and *River of No Return.*

Movie: *🦴🦴🦴* **DVD:** *🦴🦴🦴*
20th Century Fox (UPC 024543035428). Various. $79.98. Keepcase boxed set. *LANG:* English.
2002 476m/C

The Mark

Convicted child molester Jim Fuller (Whitman) cannot escape his past upon release from prison. Whitman turns in a brilliant performance and is given his own commentary track to reminisce about his work. Director Green takes a similar but more technical approach. DVD image is near perfect, capturing excellent black-and-white photography. Monaural sound is fine, too. Over the years this film has developed a strong reputation for its handling of a difficult subject and it deserves the special attention it receives here. —*MM*

Movie: *🦴🦴🦴* ½ **DVD:** *🦴🦴🦴* ½
VCI (cat #8271, UPC 089859827129). Widescreen (2.35:1) anamorphic. Dolby Digital Mono. $24.99. Keepcase. *LANG:* English. *FEATURES:* Commentary: Guy Green ⬤ Commentary: Stuart Whitman ⬤ 2000 ASC Awards presentation to Green ⬤ Trailer ⬤ Photo gallery ⬤ Talent files ⬤ 18 chapters.
1961 127m/B *GB* Stuart Whitman, Maria Schell, Rod Steiger, Brenda de Banzie, Maurice Denham, Donald Wolfit, Paul Rogers, Donald Houston, Amanda Black, Russell Napier, Marie Devereux; **D:** Guy Green; **W:** Sidney Buchman, Raymond Stross; **C:** Dudley Lovell; **M:** Richard Rodney Bennett. *AWARDS: NOM:* Oscars '61: Actor (Whitman).

Mark of Zorro [2] / Don Q, Son of Zorro

Fairbanks's athletic ability shines in two original swashbucklers. In *Mark,* he portrays both the hero and his bumbling alter

ego, Don Diego de Vega, in the quest to free California and win the heart of Marguerite de la Motte. Fairbanks's stunts are amazing in this, one of the most exciting silent adventures. Its sequel is less exciting, but features a better story and some great whip tricks. Don Cesar, Zorro's son, must beat a murder rap and court Mary Astor. An aged Zorro (Fairbanks in a dual role) makes a cameo appearance. Neither piano score is very thrilling, but both prints are well preserved and look good. With unique extras (including Fairbanks's "fight" with Jack Dempsey), this disc is a treat for silent adventure fans. (The Image edition of *Mark* is reviewed in *Book 1.*) —*DRL*

Movie: *🦴🦴🦴* **DVD:** *🦴🦴🦴* ½
Kino on Video (cat #249, UPC 738329-024925). Full frame. Mono. $29.95. Keepcase. *LANG:* Silent. *FEATURES:* Intro by Orson Welles ⬤ Excerpts from Fairbanks's home movies ⬤ "Fairbanks v. Jack Dempsey" excerpt from a Pathe newsreel ⬤ Excerpt from Fairbanks's book *Making Life Worth While* ⬤ 24 chapters.
1920 80m/B Douglas Fairbanks Sr., Marguerite de la Motte, Noah Beery Sr., Mary Astor, Noah Beery Jr., Milton Berle, Charles Stevens; **D:** Fred Niblo; **W:** Douglas Fairbanks Sr.; **C:** William McGann, Harris (Harry) Thorpe.

Marnie

Marnie (Hedren), a pathological thief and compulsive liar, takes jobs using fake references and false names. When she has the trust of her co-workers, she empties the company safe before disappearing into thin air—until she applies for a job at Rutland's, unaware that Mark Rutland (Connery) is a friend of a businessman she robbed in an earlier heist. Mark is making a move on Marnie and soon the two are entangled in an affair and possibly even marriage. A commercial flop during its theatrical release, the film has since been recognized as one of Hitchcock's better works, the completion of his career-long quest to possess the icy blonde heroine. Highly detailed, the transfer restores a very faithful representation of the movie. However, the film's age is evident in the graininess of the picture, although it never becomes distracting. The image is generally sharp and restores every bit of detail from the film print. Colors are vividly reproduced with absolutely natural fleshtones and the original silky color scheme. The cleaned-up mono soundtrack is free of distortion and background noise. Nonetheless, the film's age is noticeable in the limited frequency response. Without bass extension, the track always appears a bit harsh with an overemphasis in the midrange. —*MM/GH*

Movie: *🦴🦴🦴* ½ **DVD:** *🦴🦴🦴*
Universal Studios Home Video (UPC 0251-92058721). Widescreen (1.85:1) anamorphic. Dolby Digital Mono. $29.98. Keepcase. *LANG:* English; French. *SUB:* English. *FEATURES:* Documentary ⬤ Photo gallery ⬤ Theatrical trailer ⬤ Production notes ⬤ Bios.

1964 130m/C Tippi Hedren, Sean Connery, Diane Baker, Bruce Dern, Louise Latham, Martin Gabel, Henry Beckman, Mariette Hartley, Alan Napier; **D:** Alfred Hitchcock; **W:** Jay Presson Allen; **C:** Robert Burks; **M:** Bernard Herrmann.

Marquis de Sade

Innocent Justine (Gunn) searches for her sister Juliette in 17th-century Paris and is drawn into the sexually deviant world of the Marquis de Sade (Mancuso). It's impossible to take this exploitation in the proper spirit once you notice that Mancuso's hair, costume, and mustache make him a dead ringer for Captain Hook in Disney's animated *Peter Pan.* Full-frame DVD image is really no improvement over VHS tape. —*MM* **AKA:** Dark Prince: Intimate Tales of Marquis de Sade.
Movie: ♫ ½ **DVD:** ♫♫
New Concorde (cat #NH20656 D, UPC 73-6991465695). Full frame. Stereo. $14.98. Keepcase. *LANG:* English. *FEATURES:* 24 chapters ▪ Trailers ▪ Talent files.
1996 (R) 88m/C Nick Mancuso, Janet Gunn, John Rhys-Davies; **D:** Gwyneth Gibby; **W:** Craig J. Nevius; **C:** Eugeny Guslinsky.

Mars Needs Women

When the Martian singles scene starts to drag, the Red Planet boys cross the solar system in search of fertile Earth babes to repopulate the planet. Seems ex-Batgirl Craig, the go-go dancing lady scientist, is at the top of their dance cards. There's some print damage evident, but that, like the slightly out-of-sync dialogue and grainy color, is altogether appropriate for this alternative gem. Meant to be watched with a group of like-minded friends. —*MM*
Movie: ♫ **DVD:** ♫♫
MGM Home Ent. (cat #1002351, UPC 027-616868525). Full frame. Dolby Digital Mono. $14.95. Keepcase. *LANG:* English; Spanish. *SUB:* French; Spanish. *CAP:* English. *FEATURES:* 16 chapters.
1966 80m/C Tommy Kirk, Yvonne Craig, Warren Hammack, Tony Houston, Larry Tanner, Cal Duggan; **D:** Larry Buchanan; **W:** Larry Buchanan; **C:** Robert C. Jessup.

Mars: The Red Planet

The first thing you'll notice with this disc is that it offers an interactive mode as well as an entertainment mode. The interactive mode is perfect if you know what you're looking for and you actually want to dig directly into some of the materials on the disc, whereas the entertainment mode allows you to sit back, and simply enjoy the ride. And it's a good ride; this DVD contains EVERYTHING you could possibly want to know about Mars. The opening minutes are some of the most visually powerful images on the disc. From a rocket-mounted camera we get to witness the craft's ascent into the sky, and within little more than two minutes we see the Earth shriveling to a blue orb. The speed of this spacecraft is mesmerizing and seeing the Earth grow smaller and

smaller with every second is an experience you have to see. From there, the disc takes us through photographs and computer-generated imagery that show details of Mars, and maps of the planet's surface. All of it incredibly well presented and great looking. The quality of the images and the ability to go back and forth, zoom in and out of them is quite stunning. The interactive version of the disc includes listings of every Mars mission ever attempted or flown. Information like Launch Sites, Launch Vehicles and Dates, Mission Objectives and Results, every bit of detail is nicely catalogued and presented on this disc. The disc even contains 3-D images of the Mars surface and when viewed with the 3-D glasses that come with the package, you get indeed a good depth of field out of those pictures. On top of the program is a newly recorded version Gustav Holst's "The Planets" by Ryan Shore. In total, the disc offers four audio tracks during the Planetary View section of the disc, as well a six different camera angles. Considering how much information and images DVD International managed to stuff onto this single-layer disc, it is surprising the video and audio quality did not suffer. Images are crisp and clear, footage is also without problems or notable compression artifacting, and the audio track is always clear. —*GH*
Movie: ♫♫♫ **DVD:** ♫♫♫ ½
A-PIX Entertainment Inc. (UPC 647715072-122). Full frame. $24.98. Keepcase. *LANG:* English. *FEATURES:* Multi-angle video ▪ 3-D video and still Images ▪ Isolated Score ▪ 200 Easter eggs.
1999 90m/C

Martian Successor Nadesico: Endgame

The sixth and final installment in ADV Films's line of DVD releases of the *Martian Successor Nadesico* series is once again a showcase for the quality DVD can achieve with animation films, when treated properly. An alien triggers the final showdown with the Jovians, destroying the slim chance of peace that existed. To bring back peace, the crew of Nadesico decides to return to Mars to put an end to the war. DVD contains five episodes. The image is sharp and clean without notable defects or blemishes. Only the slightest sheen of grain is visible in some shots and without edge-enhancement, the picture is rendered very faithfully, maintaining the bold strokes of the cell animation, as well as the subtle nuances in the image. Both language tracks are in stereo and well produced with a natural sounding frequency response. —*GH*
Movie: ♫♫ ½ **DVD:** ♫♫♫
A.D.V. Films (UPC 702727009426). Full frame. Dolby Digital Stereo. $24.98. Keepcase. *LANG:* Japanese; English.
1996 (PG-13) 125m/C *JP* **D:** Tatsuo Sato.

Mary Pickford: A Life on Film

Whoopi Goldberg narrates a fairly comprehensive biography of one of the great

female pioneers of moviemaking. By age 17, Pickford had become the first actress to rise to international superstar status in the exciting, burgeoning world of the movies. Pickford deservedly was America's Sweetheart. In addition to recent and old interviews and vintage photographs and newsreel footage, this title boasts clip after wonderful clip of Pickford's silver screen performances. Documentary credits her for being one of the first thespians to understand how to correctly act for the camera, not the stage. She was also a cunning businesswoman, and by the time she was 30 she was the first and only woman to ever own a major movie studio. She belongs on a short list that also includes names like Griffith, DeMille, Chaplin, and Keaton—creative giants who contributed mightily to the early development of the cinema. The DVD's sound and picture are more than adequate, although—ironically—many of the vintage clips from Pickford's movies are cleaner than newer interview footage apparently captured on visually noisy videotape, not high-resolution film. —*MB*
Movie: ♫♫♫ **DVD:** ♫♫♫
Image Ent. (cat #ID9794MLSDVD, UPC 014381979428). Full frame. Dolby Digital Stereo. $29.95. Keepcase. *LANG:* English. *FEATURES:* 13 chapters.
1999 96m/C *Nar:* Whoopi Goldberg.

M*A*S*H [FS]

Because the long-running TV series was so popular, many viewers have forgotten what a blistering anti-war comedy Robert Altman's original film is. For this "Five Star Collection" special edition, it's been restored to its original grubbiness, and a second disc full of extras have been created. Though the setting is a Mobile Army Surgical Hospital in Korea, the real subject is Vietnam. The doctors (Sutherland, Gould, and Skerritt) are anti-establishment rebels; that establishment is represented by the pious Frank Burns, who's such a formidable figure as portrayed by Robert Duvall that he makes an early exit. A restoration demonstration recounts the studio's efforts to re-create the film. (The original negative has been lost for years.) That work was not as difficult as it might have been because Altman was trying to create an image that was "dirty, not crisp and clear." He wanted a muddy, dirty, olive-drab look and he got it. He also used filters to diffuse the focus. On disc, the film looks as good as it ever has, and the subtitles are a real help in understanding the sometimes muffled dialogue. At times, though, the subtitle simply reads "all talking at once" when the overlapping speech is intentionally impossible to understand. On his commentary track, Altman often pauses to appreciate his work. What he does have to say is worth listening to. The extras on the second disc are something more than the usual "weren't-we-all-wonderful?" self-congratulation that you usually find with older hits. Though the box copy claims that this is the "restored uncut original version!," the running time is 116 minutes, the same as the widely available VHS tape. —*MM*

Movie: 🎬🎬🎬🎬 **DVD:** 🎬🎬🎬🎬
20th Century Fox (cat #20022709, UPC 024543027096). Widescreen (2.35:1) anamorphic. Dolby Stereo; Mono. $26.98. Keepcase. *LANG:* English; French. *SUB:* English. *CAP:* English. *FEATURES:* 40 chapters (feature) • Commentary: Robert Altman • Backstory featurette • Trailer • Still gallery • Menu soundbites • Restoration featurette (text and film) • "M*A*S*H Comedy under Fire" featurette • "M*A*S*H Reunion" featurette • "Enlisted" featurette.
1970 (R) 116m/C Franz Gottlieb, Donald Sutherland, Elliott Gould, Tom Skerritt, Sally Kellerman, JoAnn Pflug, Robert Duvall, Rene Auberjonois, Roger Bowen, Gary Burghoff, Fred Williamson, John Schuck, Bud Cort, G(eorge) Wood, David Arkin, Michael Murphy, Indus Arthur, Ken Prymus, Bobby Troup, Kim Atwood, Timothy Brown; *D:* Robert Altman; *W:* Ring Lardner Jr.; *C:* Harold E. Stine; *M:* Johnny Mandel; *V:* Sal Viscuso. *AWARDS:* Oscars '70: Adapt. Screenplay; AFI '98: Top 100; Cannes '70: Film; Golden Globes '71: Film—Mus./Comedy, Natl. Film Reg. '96; Natl. Soc. Film Critics '70: Film; Writers Guild '70: Adapt. Screenplay; *NOM:* Oscars '70: Director (Altman), Film Editing, Picture, Support. Actress (Kellerman).

The Mask of Zorro [2SE]

This two-disc Special Edition corrects the negligible flaws in the first release (reviewed in *Book 1*). One disc contains the widescreen version; the second is full frame. Both have the director's comfortable commentary and a full slate of extras is divided between the two. This is a good choice to show off a fancy new monitor and sound system. —*MM* **AKA:** Zorro.

Movie: 🎬🎬🎬 **DVD:** 🎬🎬🎬🎬
Columbia Tristar (cat #04061, UPC 043396040618). Widescreen (2.35:1) anamorphic; full frame. Dolby Digital 5.1 Surround Stereo; DTS 5.1. $27.98. Keepcase. *LANG:* English; French; Spanish. *SUB:* English; French; Spanish. *CAP:* English. *FEATURES:* Commentary: director • "Unmasking Zorro" featurette • Deleted scenes • Costume designs • Advertising materials • 2 music videos • Trailers • Talent files • Production notes.
1998 (PG-13) 136m/C Antonio Banderas, Anthony Hopkins, Catherine Zeta-Jones, Stuart Wilson, Matt Letscher, Maury Chaykin, Tony Amendola, Pedro Armendariz Jr., L.Q. (Justus E. McQueen) Jones; *D:* Martin Campbell; *W:* Ted Elliott, Terry Rossio, John Eskow; *C:* Phil Meheux; *M:* James Horner. *AWARDS:* *NOM:* Oscars '98: Sound, Sound FX Editing; British Acad. '98: Costume Des.; Golden Globes '98: Actor—Mus./Comedy (Banderas), Film—Mus./Comedy; MTV Movie Awards '99: Breakthrough Perf. (Zeta-Jones), Fight.

Masquerade: Eternal Life

After the death of his mother, teenaged Gen goes to visit his grandmother. He meets a woman he's already seen in a dream and is accosted by a pushy American blonde who's hot for his bod. Eroticism is less important than some very stylish visuals and occasional slapstick humor. Given the excesses of adult anime, this one's fairly sedate. Image has the bright translucence familiar to fans of the form. English dialogue is corny. —*MM*

Movie: 🎬🎬 **DVD:** 🎬🎬
Central Park/U.S. Manga (cat #A18D-2078, UPC 719987207820). Full frame. $29.99. Keepcase. *LANG:* English; Japanese. *SUB:* English. *FEATURES:* Meet the characters • Art and sketch gallery • Storyboards • 16 chapters • DVD-ROM features • Previews.
2000 120m/C

Master of Death

If you're the kind of person who enjoyed watching Kung-Fu Theater on TV as a child, then this DVD is for you. Especially if you would watch the movies on a television which had poor reception, as this disc will effectively re-create that experience. The film itself tells the story of a young man named Chow (Chi Kwan Chun) who leaves his Shaolin monk master in order to search for the villains who killed his parents. To complete his quest, Chow must fight a seemingly never-ending stream of opponents in order to seek out his vengeance. The movie is definitely your standard "chop-socky" affair, with exaggerated sound effects and battle cries. The film has been dubbed into English, and the dubbing is atrocious, with the characters spouting inane lines which rarely come close to matching the movements of their lips. The movie was clearly shot in a (very) widescreen format, but it presented full frame on this DVD. The result is a picture that looks squeezed and very ugly. The image is constantly filled with defects from the source print, consisting primarily of scratches and white spots. The image looks faded and the colors are washed-out. The digital mono audio track does a fine job of delivering the hackneyed dialogue, but there is a faint hiss on the track. Actually, if you must watch this film, skip the primary audio track and listen to the audio commentary from Hong Kong film expert Ric Meyers and martial artist Bobby Samuels, as it is very entertaining and informative. The pair know a lot about this movie and give a great overview of Hong Kong films. —*ML*

Movie: 🎬 **DVD:** woof
Tai Seng (cat #86614, UPC 6016438661-47). Full frame. Digital Mono. $14.95. Keepcase. *LANG:* English. *FEATURES:* Commentary • 8 chapters.
1975 90m/C *HK* Lo Lieh, Kwan Chun Chi.

The Master of the Rings

Somebody desperate for cash must have come up with this boring documentary that purports to be a biography of cult writer J.R.R. Tolkien. About a half hour is devoted to Tolkien's life and the balance of the film concentrates on fans, role players, a fantasy artist (Roger Garland) whose work has been associated with Tolkien, and musician Bob Catley, who writes songs based on Tolkien's work. The whole thing is rather dull (Catley's music is embarrassingly bad) and this is a disc for die-hard fans only. Actually, I can't believe that there isn't a less boring way to gather this information, so it's probably a disc for nobody. The image on the DVD is pretty good except for dark scenes and backgrounds where enormous amounts of grain appear. Colors are vibrant enough and there are quite a few scenes that are lushly pleasing to the eye. The stereo audio is good enough for the interviews and even the background music—you'll probably want to turn it off when that Catley guy starts a-croakin' (although if you're masochistic enough to watch this disc, you should probably punish your eardrums a bit for full effect). —*JO*

Movie: 🎬 **DVD:** 🎬 ½
Lion's Gate Home Ent. (cat #VM7881D, UPC 031398788126). Full frame. Dolby Digital Stereo. $14.99. Keepcase. *LANG:* English. *SUB:* English. *CAP:* English. *FEATURES:* 15 chapters.
2001 61m/C

Masters of the Universe

Planet Eternia's mightiest hero, He-Man (Lundgren), must once again face off against his mortal enemy Skeletor (Langella) as they battle for supremacy and the power of Castle Greyskull. This over-the-top, Flash-esque adaptation of the popular Saturday morning cartoon series represents many of the problems experienced in '80s cinematic fare. Laden with bad dialogue, unbelievable effects, and an uninteresting plot, *Masters* does nothing to entice the viewer. DVD picture quality is good, as should be expected from a major studio release, and the Dolby Surround track makes very adequate use of all six speakers in the high action battle sequences. An unbelievably serious commentary track is provided by director Gary Goddard, who talks about many of the obstacles he faced in filming his first big feature. —*EL*

Movie: woof **DVD:** 🎬🎬 ½
Warner (cat #37073, UPC 0853937073-23). Widescreen anamorphic. Dolby 5.1 Surround. $19.98. Snapper. *LANG:* English; French. *SUB:* English; French; Spanish. *CAP:* English. *FEATURES:* Commentary: director Gary Goddard • Character profiles • Theatrical trailer • 30 chapters.
1987 (PG) 109m/C Dolph Lundgren, Frank Langella, Billy Barty, Courteney Cox

Arquette, Meg Foster; **D:** Gary Goddard; **W:** David Odell; **C:** Hanania Baer; **M:** Bill Conti.

The Matrix Revisited

Featurette turned to feature at 163 minutes in length, this is essentially the bonus disc that got away, with never-before-seen footage and actor interviews, the nuts and bolts from storyboard to computer graphics of *The Matrix*. The box hints that we're going to see some of the sequel, currently called *The Matrix Reloaded*, but the truth is almost as disappointing as when I first learned Jet Li wasn't going to be in the new one. A few quick scenes from *Reloaded* minus the effects are mostly actors on wires or standing in front of a green screen, however fetching Carrie-Ann Moss may be in her new PVC duster. First glance into animators working on an upcoming "Matrix Anime" project proves to be just a series of sketches. Even the original blocking tapes of Yuen Wo Ping's fight choreography grow tedious. Too evasive in packaging to be respectful to its hard-core followers, this disc wants to be a tantalizing commercial for fanning any dying embers in the franchise. Decent DVD transfer of average video material, with super sound tweaking the techno score. —*MO*
Movie: 🐾🐾 **DVD:** 🐾🐾🐾🐾
Warner (cat #19007, UPC 0853919007-26). Full frame. Dolby Digital 5.1. $19.98. Snapper. *LANG:* English. *SUB:* English; Spanish; French. *CAP:* English; Spanish; French. *FEATURES:* 33 chapters • "What Is to Come?" featurette • "What Is Animatrix?" featurette • "Dance of the Master" featurette (Yuen Wo Ping's blocking tapes).
2001 163m/C D: Josh Oreck.

Matter of Trust

Another one of those pesky serial killers is on the loose, with a penchant for large-breasted prostitutes. Alcoholic cop D'Angelo (Howell) might be the city's only hope. It's a hackneyed and amateurish production, lacking enough sex even to serve as decent soft-core. The picture quality is extremely grainy with washed-out colors, and the audio is merely average. —*BG*
Movie: 🐾 **DVD:** 🐾🐾
USA Home Ent. (cat #0615, UPC 9630600-982). Full frame. Dolby 2.0. $19.95. Keepcase. *LANG:* English. *CAP:* English. *FEATURES:* 12 chapters.
1998 (R) 90m/C C. Thomas Howell, Joan Severance, Nick Mancuso, Robert Miano, Jennifer Leigh Warren, Randee Heller; **D:** Joey Travolta; **W:** John Penney; **C:** Dan Heigh; **M:** Jeff Lass.

Matthew Blackheart: Monster Smasher

Thawed out after over 50 years of icy imprisonment, the titular smasher (Bogue, doing his best Bruce Campbell), created during WWII from the body parts of dead war heroes, returns to New York with a '40s attitude and one mission: to defeat his arch-nemesis Mortas (Heyerdahl), who has created a monster race and is bent on ruling the world. While strictly "B"-movie fare, the funny script and bizarre concept make it worth watching. The below-average image transfer and noisy stereo mix reveal the disc to be as low-budget as the movie. —*DRL*
Movie: 🐾🐾 **DVD:** 🐾 ½
MTI (cat #50052, UPC 619935405233). Full frame. Stereo. $24.95. Keepcase. *LANG:* English. *SUB:* Spanish. *FEATURES:* Cast bios • Trailers • 20 chapters.
1999 (R) 93m/C Robert Bogue, Chris Heyerdahl, Jay Baruchel, Karen Elkin; **D:** Erik Canuel; **W:** Robert Engels; **C:** John Dyer; **M:** Michael Corriveau.

Mau Mau Sex Sex

David Friedman and Dan Sonney independently produced dozens of exploitation pictures that broke new ground in depicting screen sex and violence. Frequently at odds with censors, the two helped create or develop the gore film, the nudie-cutie film, the nudist camp picture, the roughie, and other essays in cinematic sleaze over a 60-year period. This affectionate documentary is a portrait of the two pioneers as they are today: Friedman, ever the pitchman, runs a fairground in Alabama, while Sonney is retired and lives in California. As the two are followed around their daily routines, we are introduced to their friends, wives, and families and given an overview of their works in the exploitation film industry. It's hard to imagine the two unctuous elderly fellows as the guiding force behind such controversial smut, but they occasionally drop saucy and hilarious bon-mots that help the viewer reconcile the two parts of their lives. Director Frank Henenlotter provides frequently hilarious commentary, historical information, and analysis of the duo's films. While the historical information never really develops beyond an overview (it has been mined elsewhere), the film is intended as a portrait of the two men, *not* as a history of the genre. The lounge-music soundtrack is terrific and helps keep things bouncy and fun. Shot on video, the disc seems to accurately convey the colors and exposure of the original videography and is only marred by some video noise that tends to appear around eyes during some interview segments. The clips are in fine shape for the most part, though some are quite faded and scratched. The Friedman and Sonney commentary is frequently repetitive to the on-screen information but it's enjoyable and features interesting production anecdotes. A highlight: As the end credits play, it becomes clear that Sonney has no idea what an audio commentary is and is skeptical about how such a thing could be profitable! The track by Muller (author of *Grindhouse*) and Bonnitt is the best of the two; filled with behind-the-scenes anecdotes, it gives a complete picture of the thought and work that went into the production and complements the historical information offered in the film itself. Created, market-ed, exhibited, and sold in the spirit and style of Friedman and Sonney's pictures, *Mau Mau Sex Sex* is irresistible. Though available in some stores, the best outlet is www.maumausexsex.com, where it can be ordered directly from the filmmakers themselves. —*DG*
Movie: 🐾🐾🐾 **DVD:** 🐾🐾🐾
Seventh Planet Productions (UPC 000007-770036). Full frame. $24.95. Keepcase. *LANG:* English. *FEATURES:* 32 chapters • Commentary: Bonnitt, Muller • Commentary: David Friedman, Dan Sonney • Filmographies & bios • Soundtrack samples • Theatrical trailer • Gallery of exploitation trailers • Gallery of promotional art.
2000 80m/C David Friedman, Dan Sonney, Frank Henenlotter; **D:** Ted Bonnitt; **W:** Ted Bonnitt, Eddie Muller.

Max Fleischer's Superman

Most of these cartoons (and the extras) are available on other discs. This collection looks and sounds pretty good, actually very good for the age of the short films. Contents: "The Mad Scientist," "The Mechanical Monsters," "Electronic Earthquake," "Billiar Dollar Limited," "Arctic Giant," "Bulleteers," "Magnetic Telescope," "Volcano," "Terror on the Midway," "Play Safe." —*MM*
Movie: 🐾🐾 ½ **DVD:** 🐾🐾 ½
Winstar Home Ent. (cat #WHE73010, UPC 720917301020). Full frame. Dolby Digital Prologic; Dolby Digital Stereo. $24.98. Keepcase. *LANG:* English. *FEATURES:* 15 chapters • Restoration demonstration • Trailers.
1998 100m/C D: Max Fleischer.

Maybe Baby

This British dramedy tackles the sensitive subject of infertility, but never lives up to its potential, instead coming across as a made-for-TV movie. Sam (Hugh Laurie) and Lucy (Joely Richardson) are a loving couple who have been unable to conceive a child, despite numerous attempts. Lucy encourages Sam to capture his emotions in a diary, but instead he turns their problems into a screenplay for his job at the BBC. After the script is enthusiastically accepted by his superiors, Sam must keep the production a secret from Lucy, who would be disgusted by having her life splashed upon the screen. While *Maybe Baby* has the makings of a madcap English comedy, it never goes that route, choosing to attempt a balance between humor and drama. The result is a film which isn't very funny and is actually quite depressing at times. Cameos by Rowan Atkinson, Joanna Lumley, and Emma Thompson do spice things up a bit, as does the performance by Tom Hollander as the insane Scottish director who is chosen to film Sam's script. Directed by popular British writer/comedian Ben Elton, based on his novel *Inconceivable*. DVD looks quite good. There is some minor artifacting at times, but otherwise the image is sharp

and clear, with little grain. The colors are quite nice and director Elton has allowed natural hues to populate his film. The Dolby 2.0 Surround audio track is serviceable, as it offers clear dialogue and occasional Surround effects. The trailer included on the DVD portrays the film as a wild comedy. It's unfortunate that the DVD doesn't include production notes, as it would have been interesting to learn if art is imitating life in this film, with the frustrated husband turned screenwriter. —*ML*
Movie: ♫♫ **DVD:** ♫♫ ½
USA Home Ent. (cat #963060245-2, UPC 696306024521). Widescreen (1.85:1) letterboxed. Dolby Surround. $19.95. Keepcase. *LANG:* English. *FEATURES:* Theatrical trailer • 12 chapters.
1999 (R) 93m/C *GB FR* Hugh Laurie, Joely Richardson, Adrian Lester, James Purefoy, Tom Hollander, Joanna Lumley, Rowan Atkinson, Dawn French, Emma Thompson, Rachael Stirling; *D:* Ben Elton; *W:* Ben Elton; *C:* Roger Lanser; *M:* Colin Towns.

Maze

A very solid romantic comedy starring Rob Morrow who also helped write the screenplay and directed. Talented but handicapped artist Lyle Maze (Morrow) wants to work in nudes. His best friend's girlfriend Callie (Laura Linney) volunteers to pose. A relationship develops and watching it grow and mature is truly very enjoyable. The disc is fine. Sound is good and colors are fine, but I sure wish we had a director's commentary from Morrow who put together this smart piece of film. —*DE*
Movie: ♫♫♫ **DVD:** ♫♫
Studio Home Ent. (cat #VM7932D, UPC 03139879322). Full frame. Dolby Digital 5.1. $24.98. Keepcase. *LANG:* English. *SUB:* Spanish. *CAP:* English. *FEATURES:* Trailer • 24 chapters • Interactive menus.
2001 (R) 98m/C Rob Morrow, Laura Linney, Craig Sheffer, Gia Carides, Rose Gregorio, Robert Hogan; *D:* Rob Morrow; *W:* Rob Morrow, Bradley White; *C:* Wolfgang Held; *M:* Bobby Previte.

McKenzie Break

Irish intelligence officer John Connor (Keith) is sent to Scotland to POW Camp McKenzie during WWII. Captured U-boat commander Schluetter (Griem) is suspected of planning a mass break-out and Connor is supposed to stop the action. The battle of wills between the hard-headed Irishman and the wily German makes for an interesting escape tale where viewers' sympathies and expectations are neatly turned around. DVD image is an acceptable transfer of a soft original that's mostly composed of deliberately drab, desaturated colors. Sound gets the job done. Don't miss the trailer. Even in its banged up, faded condition, it's completely bizarre with dialogue that often has nothing to do with the movement of the mouths of the characters on screen. —*MM*
Movie: ♫♫♫ **DVD:** ♫♫ ½

MGM Home Ent. (UPC 027616799326). Widescreen letterboxed. Dolby Digital Stereo. $14.98. Keepcase. *LANG:* English; French. *SUB:* English; French. *FEATURES:* 32 chapters • Trailer.
1970 106m/C Brian Keith, Helmut Griem, Ian Hendry, Jack Watson, Horst Janson, Patrick O'Connell; *D:* Lamont Johnson; *W:* William W. Norton Sr.; *C:* Michael Reed; *M:* Riz Ortolani.

Me & Isaac Newton

A compelling, intriguing portrait of seven cutting-edge scientists whose work covers the gamut of human experience. From language to cancer research to the origins of the universe, the scientists interviewed and profiled offer an eye-opening contradiction to the introverted, white lab coated cliché of years past. All are passionately dedicated to their work, were driven to it by personal reasons, and are extremely compassionate in their attempts to better humanity and combat disease. Deceptively simple, and delicately structured, it's essentially a talking-head piece, but what the participants are saying is well worth listening to. The use of the scientists' home movies and personal photographs complements the interviews and delivers an even stronger insight into these people's lives. Perhaps because of director Apted's previous work on the *Up* films (*42 Up,* etc.), the ending feels a bit inconclusive. One wants to revisit these people in a few years to see what has happened to them since this documentary was filmed. The images are sharp, clear, and colorful. The interview sections (with the exception of the one with Gertrude Elion) look excellent but the location footage suffers from digital shimmer and noise, especially evident in horizontal panning movements. The sound is less limited than most documentaries and is crisp, clear, and excellent. —*DG*
Movie: ♫♫♫ **DVD:** ♫♫♫
Home Vision Cinema (cat #ISA 020, UPC 037429166925). Widescreen (1.77:1) letterboxed. Dolby Digital Surround. $29.95. Keepcase. *LANG:* English. *FEATURES:* 21 chapters • Insert booklet with notes.
1999 107m/C *D:* Michael Apted; *C:* Maryse Alberti; *M:* Patrick Seymour.

Me, Myself, and Irene

Carrey plays Charlie, a Rhode Island state trooper who has an evil second personality. Irene (Zellweger) is in trouble with the law, due to the fact that she's involved with some sort of plot having to do with a country club and environmental problems. It doesn't really make much sense, nor is it really that interesting. It drags down the pace of the movie. I'm sure there could have been a simpler way to have Irene join Charlie/Hank for a road trip. The two go on the run and begin to fall in love. Carrey steals every set he's in and gets to showcase his brand of physical comedy. The Farrelly humor only works about half the time. Some jokes are dragged on too long,

while others barely register or fall flat. Some are too gross for their own good. But for every joke that flops there's still quite a few that do work. It's a moderately funny movie for those who don't mind very raunchy humor. The image is well-defined and crisp with accurate colors. Some scenes suffer from slight edge-enhancement flaws and pixelation. The sound is fine, but not remarkable. The commentary track is pretty good—the brothers talk a great deal about crafting some of the humor of the movie as well as working with the various actors. It's their best commentary by far, and definitely worth a listen. The deleted scenes can be added back to the film via seamless branching and they can also be viewed in a separate section. —*AB/DG*
Movie: ♫♫ **DVD:** ♫♫♫
20th Century Fox (UPC 24543006251). Widescreen (1.85:1) anamorphic. Dolby Digital 5.1 Surround; Dolby Digital Surround. $22.98. Keepcase. *LANG:* English; French. *SUB:* English; Spanish. *CAP:* English. *FEATURES:* The Farrelly brothers • Deleted scenes with optional commentary • Trailer • "Making of" featurettes • "Breakout" music video.
2000 (R) 117m/C Jim Carrey, Renee Zellweger, Robert Forster, Chris Cooper, Richard Jenkins, Traylor Howard, Daniel Greene, Zen Gesner, Tony Cox, Anthony Anderson, Lenny Clarke, Shannon Whirry, Rob Moran, Mongo Brownlee, Jerod Mixon, Michael Bowman, Mike Cerrone, Anna Kournikova, Cam Neely, Brendan Shanahan; *D:* Bobby Farrelly, Peter Farrelly; *W:* Bobby Farrelly, Peter Farrelly, Mike Cerrone; *C:* Mark Irwin; *M:* Peter Yorn, Lee Scott; *V:* Rex Allen.

Me You Them

Inspired by a true story about a woman with three husbands. When earthy beauty Darlene (Brazilian talk show hostess Casé) returns to her village in the Brazilian countryside, Osias (Duarte) immediately proposes marriage. Soon Osias's cousin Zezinho (Garcia) moves in, then young handsome Ciro (Vasconcelos) catches her attention. The movie keeps getting better as the ménage coalesces. Full frame version looks great, but it's the widescreen compositions that show off the spectacular locations shot in a palette of deep golds and blues best. Music by the great Gilberto Gil. This movie is so well done it doesn't need a director's commentary. The sound is good. —*LA* *AKA:* Eu Tu Eles.
Movie: ♫♫♫ ½ **DVD:** ♫♫♫ ½
Columbia Tristar (cat #06387, UPC 0433-96063877). Widescreen (2.35:1) anamorphic; full frame. Dolby Digital Portuguese 5.1; Dolby Surround. $29.98. Keepcase. *LANG:* Portuguese; French. *SUB:* English; French; Spanish; Chinese; Korean; Thai. *CAP:* English. *FEATURES:* Commentary: director • Theatrical trailers • 28 chapters • Interactive menus.
2000 (PG-13) 107m/C *BR PT* Regina Case, Lima Duarte, Stenio Garcia, Luiz Carlos Vasconcelos, Nilda Spencer; *D:*

Andrucha Waddington; **W:** Elena Soarez; **C:** Breno Silveira; **M:** Gilberto Gil.

Medium Cool [SE]

John Cassellis (Forster) is fired from a television news program for taking an interest in the subject matter of his work, and for protesting that his newsfilm is being forward to the FBI by his superiors. Leaving his nurse girlfriend Ruth (Hill), he becomes involved with Eileen (Bloom) and her young son, Harold (Blankenship). who are new to the Chicago slums from Appalachia. John attaches himself to a documentary crew covering the convention, just as Eileen takes to the streets to search for the runaway Harold...right in the middle of the very dangerous antiwar demonstrations. Through its terrific commentary track, this new disc can address the specific mysteries and concerns that the film has always raised: How much of the show was documentary? Were those actors or real people? And the most pressing question: how did they get the yellow-clad actress Verna Bloom in the middle of all those real events? The commentary, by filmmaker (and revered cameraman) Haskell Wexler, editor Paul Golding, and actress Marianna Hill, reveals that the movie was not made by magic, only by very intelligent people with brilliant ideas. The revelations about the shooting of the picture are pretty impressive, especially the idea that as early as January 1968, before the assassinations, even, Wexler and company were writing scenes to take place amid the anticipated riots in Chicago. Like the "summer of love" the year before in which we heard everyone was going to go to San Francisco, in 1968 the word on the street was that it was "all going to come down" in Chicago at the convention. The anti-war movement was still a grass-roots protest thing and not yet the media circus it later became, with hippies and yippies and Nixon's counterattack and fatuous pop music pretending it was issuing calls to revolution. Chicago indeed became ground zero for this major event. Haskell's camera was only able to enter black neighborhoods in Chicago through the intervention of Studs Terkel, and with the cooperation of the black citizens themselves. And while clearly liberal (defined here as open-minded, concerned with truth and not the status quo), the filmmakers admit their desire to present a point of view they felt was going unexpressed. They present, for instance, the National Guard as relatively benign (except as a harbinger of more use of military against the public) compared to Daley, who gave his cops direct orders to teach the long-haired flag-burners a lesson. Haskell Wexler's skills as a dramatist rarely surface in discussions of the film. His direction of actors is so good that you think the little hillbilly kid isn't acting at all. Verna Bloom comes off as authentic West Virginia and not the professional actress she is. There's some technical full-frontal nudity in a scene between Forster and Marianna Hill that was shocking beyond belief back then, yet seems benign now. Ms. Hill reacts with modest restraint on the commentary track, but nobody comments why they felt the movie needed that kind of controversial content. The impression is that the movie earned its "X" more for its dangerous political attitudes, and profanity. When the picture gets intellectual in the camera-looking-at-the-camera ending, it strives for artsy significance, and succeeds better than most. DVD looks as if the negative elements have been sitting in a time warp waiting to be transferred for this DVD. The 16x9 enhancement helps prove that it was shot 35mm; it doesn't look grainy or hastily improvised. The sound is clear, and, yes, those are Frank Zappa songs in the middle of the show, making fun of phony hippies. The menu design is clear and functional. The feature has a new "R" rating up front, but the old "X" rating card remains at the end, a nice touch. —GE
Movie: 🎬🎬🎬🎬 **DVD:** 🎬🎬🎬🎬
Paramount (cat #06907, UPC 097360690-743). Widescreen anamorphic. Dolby Digital Mono. $29.99. Keepcase. *LANG:* English. *SUB:* English. *FEATURES:* 19 chapters ● Commentary: Wexler, Golding, Hill ● Trailer. **1969 111m/C** Robert Forster, Verna Bloom, Peter Bonerz, Marianna Hill, Peter Boyle, Harold Blankenship, Charles Geary, Sid McCoy, Christine Bergstrom, William Sickingen; **D:** Haskell Wexler; **W:** Haskell Wexler; **C:** Haskell Wexler; **M:** Michael Bloomfield.

Meet the Feebles

Now that director Peter Jackson has garnered international fame and fortune for his work on *The Lord of the Rings,* audiences will begin to see more of the twisted films that he has been making in his native New Zealand. And *Meet the Feebles* is arguably the sickest of his films (although that's a tough call). The film poses this simple premise: What goes on backstage at an all-puppet revue (a la the Muppets)? The answer is, everything that you can think of! The Feebles are a semi-talented group of performers who are gearing up for their first national TV broadcast, which will be going out live. As the animals rehearse, star Heidi Hippo begins to suspect that boyfriend and Feebles manager Bletch (a walrus) is cheating on her and wants to replace her with Samanta, a Siamese cat. Also, the emcee appears to have a venereal disease, and an elephant performer is being slapped with a paternity suit. Into this menagerie comes Robert, a shy porcupine, who has just joined the chorus. He immediately falls in love with Lucille, a poodle. In the meantime, as show time approaches, tempers flare, and it becomes clear that not all of the Feebles will survive the night. Will Robert be able to save Lucille? It should be made very clear that despite the fact that *Meet the Feebles* deals with the lives of puppets, it is not for children...or most adults for that matter. The film is very frank in its depiction of sex, drug use, and profanity among the creatures made of felt. In lesser hands, this would have been a one-joke film, but Jackson and his crew are able to make it both shocking and fun. And while the activities of the puppets will leave most viewers flabbergasted on their initial viewing, a second pass will reveal the sly humor and good nature which are at work. Unfortunately, seemingly little work went into this DVD release. The film is presented full frame and is marred by many problems. First, this transfer came from a print which has clearly seen a great deal of use, as it is fraught with scratches, lines, and blemishes. The image is very dark and the colors are washed-out. The video quality is actually worse than VHS at times. The audio track is a Dolby Digital 5.1 mix, which has been recorded at a very high volume. This results in an overpowering rear channel effect, which makes one feel as if they were sitting with their backs towards the TV. There is also a low-frequency hum on this track. The DVD contains the theatrical trailer for the film, but it is in bad shape as well. So, it looks as if Jackson's fans will have to continue to wait for the definitive version of *Meet the Feebles.* (This DVD has no chapter menu and there are no chapter stops during the film. It's a Region 1 release that has previously been available in Canada.) —ML
Movie: 🎬🎬 ½ **DVD:** woof
Spectrum Films (cat #DA3129, UPC 7335-65031294). Full frame. Dolby Digital 5.1. $14.98. Keepcase. *LANG:* English. *FEATURES:* Theatrical trailer ● Bonus trailers. **1989 94m/C** *NZ* **D:** Peter Jackson; **W:** Peter Jackson, Danny Mulheron, Frances Walsh, Stephen Sinclair; **C:** Murray Milne; **M:** Peter Dasent; **V:** Peter Vere-Jones, Mark Hadlow, Stuart Devine, Donna Atkinson, Mark Wright, Brian Sergent.

Megiddo: The Omega Code 2

Michael York reprises his role as Stone Alexander: Antichrist. This "sequel" is the original story retold with emphasis on the action instead of the dogma. This time, the savior is David (Biehn), U.S. President and Stone's brother. The plot is much more broad and unfocused than the original, but decent character performances and a slightly more subtle agenda make this version easier to watch. Occasional artifacts and grids are present on the transfer, but it is mostly clean. The Surround sound gets heavy use during the battle scenes and the dialogue is clear. Really, though, this film has little appeal beyond its established audience. —DRL
Movie: 🎬 ½ **DVD:** 🎬🎬 ½
Goodtimes Ent. (cat #81304, UPC 0787-13813046). Widescreen (1.85:1) anamorphic. Dolby Digital 5.1; Dolby Surround. $24.95. Keepcase. *LANG:* English. *CAP:* English. *FEATURES:* 22 chapters ● Special effects featurette ● 2 interviews ● Trailer. **2001 (PG-13) 106m/C** Michael York, Michael Biehn, Diane Venora, R. Lee

Ermey, Udo Kier, Franco Nero; **D:** Brian Trenchard-Smith; **W:** John Fasano, Stephan Blinn; **C:** Bert Dunk; **M:** Peter Bernstein.

Mein Krieg

Curious German documentary is similar to the HBO miniseries *Band of Brothers*. Filmmakers Harriet Eder and Thomas Kufus interview six men who, as teenagers, served in the German Wehrmacht and carried movie cameras with them as they trained and again later as they invaded Russia. Contemporary interviews are combined with footage they shot 50 years before. Though the older film has been very well preserved, it is grainy. These are, after all, home movies, and that's the point. Subtitles are burned in. —*MM* **AKA:** My Private War.
Movie: ♫♫ ½ **DVD:** ♫♫ ½
Kino on Video (cat #K192, UPC 73832901-9228). Full frame. $29.95. Keepcase. *LANG:* German. *SUB:* English. *FEATURES:* 14 chapters.
1990 90m/C GE **D:** Harriet Eder, Thomas Kufus.

Memento [1]

Twisty and engaging noir thriller follows a man searching for his wife's killer in Los Angeles. Only problem is, Leonard Shelby (Pearce) lost his short-term memory after the attack and forgets all current events every 15 minutes, or so. Problem solved as Lenny tattoos the most vital info all over his body and leaves less permanent "clues" for himself on Post-Its and Polaroids of the suspects. He meets Natalie (Moss) and Teddy (Pantoliano), who may want to help him, but—like his own memory—cannot be trusted. Ingeniously constructed story is told backwards (sort of) from Pearce's shooting of the presumed killer to his puzzle-like reconstruction of events, and leaves the audience as perplexed as the impaired hero. Clever use of flashbacks and black-and-white segments help define events in time, and make it clear that the film really is about the act of memory. DVD is probably a better medium for the film than conventional theatre projection. It's certainly fine for a second viewing (definitely warranted). Image and sound are excellent, of course, and the extras are fine, but where's the commentary track? That's the most glaring missed opportunity of this otherwise excellent package. —*MM*
Movie: ♫♫♫ ½ **DVD:** ♫♫♫
Columbia Tristar (cat #06598, UPC 04339-6065987). Widescreen (2.35:1) anamorphic. Dolby Digital 5.1 Surround; Dolby Digital Surround. $24.98. Keepcase. *LANG:* English. *SUB:* English; Spanish. *CAP:* English. *FEATURES:* IFC interview with Christopher Nolan and Elvis Mitchell • Trailer and TV spot • Talent files • Tattoo gallery • "Memento Mori" short story by Jonathan Nolan (text) • "OTNEMEM" notes.
2000 (R) 116m/C Guy Pearce, Carrie-Anne Moss, Joe Pantoliano, Mark Boone Jr., Stephen Tobolowsky, Callum Keith Ren-

nie, Harriet Harris, Jorja Fox; **D:** Christopher Nolan; **W:** Christopher Nolan; **C:** Wally Pfister; **M:** David Julyan. *AWARDS:* L.A. Film Critics '01: Screenplay; Broadcast Film Critics '01: Screenplay; *NOM:* Directors Guild '01: Director (Nolan); Golden Globes '02: Screenplay; Broadcast Film Critics '01: Film.

Memento [2 SE]

The packaging of this special edition appears to be designed to re-create the frustrations felt by the film's protagonist Leonard. First, how do you get the discs out of the damn box? (I finally pried open the back and pushed them out.) Once a disc is in the player, the menus present more problems. Like the inserts, they're designed to mimic a mental patient's case file. To play the movie, highlight the word "watch," which is near the middle of the group of 50 words on the screen. The second disc with the extras is more difficult to navigate and I eventually gave up after having found the script. Apparently, you have to take a test and get the right answers to access certain features. Life is short. As for image and sound, both are aces. In a side-by-side comparison with the first release (see review above), it's difficult to spot any significant differences. The main extra is Christopher Nolan's commentary track. He's soft-spoken, scene-specific, and tightly focused on matters at hand. (Those who, like me, cannot find the commentary option on the menu can start the film and use the audio selection on the remote to go to the fourth language track.) For the casual viewer, the standard release is just fine. More serious fans will want to own this one even if they can't figure out how to get to everything. Now, how do I get all this stuff back into the box? —*MM*
Movie: ♫♫♫ ½ **DVD:** ♫♫♫
Columbia Tristar (cat #07646, UPC 0433-96076464). Widescreen (2.35:1) anamorphic. DTS 5.1 Surround; Dolby 5.1 Surround; Dolby Surround. $27.98. Special packaging. *LANG:* English. *SUB:* English; Spanish. *CAP:* English. *FEATURES:* 16 chapters • Commentary: Christopher Nolan • "Anatomy of a Scene" featurette • Shooting script • Original short story • Production stills and sketches • Promotional material.
2000 (R) 116m/C Guy Pearce, Carrie-Anne Moss, Joe Pantoliano, Mark Boone Jr., Stephen Tobolowsky, Callum Keith Rennie, Harriet Harris, Jorja Fox; **D:** Christopher Nolan; **W:** Christopher Nolan; **C:** Wally Pfister; **M:** David Julyan. *AWARDS:* Ind. Spirit '01: Director (Nolan), Screenplay; Ind. Spirit '02: Film, Support. Actress (Moss); L.A. Film Critics '01: Screenplay; Broadcast Film Critics '01: Screenplay; *NOM:* Oscars '01: Film Editing, Orig. Screenplay; Directors Guild '01: Director (Nolan); Golden Globes '02: Screenplay; Ind. Spirit '02: Cinematog.; Broadcast Film Critics '01: Film.

Memoirs of a Survivor

Painfully artistic and full of trite literary, political, and social references, this adaptation of Doris Lessing's book is better left to first-year film students. It's full of promising touches: a newspaper stand that reads "Talks Continue," in the first scene, moves to "No News Is Good News," by the last scene. And the score is nice, but it seems to rise and fall for no good reason, making it the score of impending nothing. "D" (Christie) is living in a seemingly post-apocalyptic society. We're never told how it got that way or what anyone thinks about it. Everyone seems to go around in a daze including D until the arrival of Emily (Mellinger) and her dog, who are mysteriously dropped off to live with D one day. D takes this in stride. Emily meets up with a cute guy who organizes the local child gangs into productive gardeners. One thing leads to another and the three of them walk through a wall at the end. The picture on the disc is fairly clean and the colors are good. Mono sound is decent. —*CA*
Movie: ♫ **DVD:** ♫♫ ½
All Day Ent. (cat #DV11644, UPC 013131-16447). Widescreen (1.85:1) anamorphic. Dolby Digital Mono. $24.90. Keepcase. *LANG:* English. *FEATURES:* 27 chapters • Trailer.
1981 (R) 115m/C Julie Christie, Christopher Guard, Leonie Mellinger, Nigel Hawthorne; **D:** David Gladwell; **W:** Kerry Crabbe, David Gladwell; **C:** Walter Lassally; **M:** Mike Thron.

Men Are from Mars, Women Are from Venus

This ABC News special, narrated by Barbara Walters at her smarmiest, aims at the lowest common denominator among middle-aged American couples. Six couples have been carefully chosen to illustrate John Gray's dishonest "interplanetary" conceit: men and women don't speak the same language. Gray's theorizing never goes beyond sloganeering and cheap jokes. Ultimately his advice boils down to this: lie to your wife about how you understand her feelings and you'll have her eating out your hands in no time. He seems to be preying upon the culture of the victim where everyone blames someone else for his or her unhappiness. He never coaches them to take responsibility for their own actions. One of the husbands "got it"; he learned how to placate his wife by saying the right things. How he really feels is his dirty little secret. The DVD looks just like a TV broadcast. —*LA*
Movie: ♫ **DVD:** ♫♫
MPI (cat #DVD3529). Full frame. $19.98. Keepcase. *LANG:* English. *CAP:* English. *FEATURES:* 17 chapters.
1997 60m/C

Men at Work

Carl (Sheen) and James (director Estevez) are underachieving garbage men whose boss has assigned his large brother-in-law Louis (David) to observe their work. The first day Louis goes out with them they find the body of a dead politician among the trash cans. Don't you just hate when that happens? This is one of the ugliest images ever to appear from a major studio on DVD. Did the film look this bad in theatres? I don't remember, but this version is so exceptionally grainy that it's painful to watch. It's also poorly focused with pale colors. —*MM*

Movie: 🎬🎬 ½ **DVD:** 🎬 ½
MGM Home Ent. (cat #1003513, UPC 027-616876638). Widescreen (1.85:1) anamorphic; full frame. Dolby Digital Surround. $14.98. Keepcase. *LANG:* English. *SUB:* English; French; Spanish. *CAP:* English. *FEATURES:* 16 chapters ▪ Trailer.
1990 (PG-13) 98m/C Charlie Sheen, Emilio Estevez, Leslie Hope, Keith David; **D:** Emilio Estevez; **W:** Emilio Estevez; **C:** Tim Suhrstedt; **M:** Stewart Copeland.

Mephisto

This 1982 winner of the Academy Award for best foreign film is stunning and disturbing and...disturbing. Brandauer plays Hendrik Hofgen, a struggling actor trying to make it big in 1930s Germany. He believes himself to be morally bound to his art but as the Nazis come to power and he realizes his desire to perform in the motherland can only be met by performing propaganda plays, he is shown to be morally bound only to fame. His greatest role is Mephisto, but he is slowly revealed to be more like the easily bought Faustus, thinking that he is going to beat the devil. Brandauer's portrayal of Hendrik is flawless. His ability to show Hendrik as a morally blank slate who believes himself to be above the everyday politics of the world without appearing to be acting is incredible. Dark and penetrating, this is an important film. The print transfer is beautiful. The rich reds and blacks of the costumes and uniforms are beautiful and the sound is very good for mono. —*CA*

Movie: 🎬🎬🎬 ½ **DVD:** 🎬🎬🎬 ½
Anchor Bay (cat #DV11240, UPC 013131-124095). Widescreen (1.77:1) anamorphic. Dolby Digital Mono. $29.90. Keepcase. *LANG:* German. *SUB:* English. *FEATURES:* 26 chapters ▪ Conversations with Szabo and Brandauer.
1981 144m/C *HU* Klaus Maria Brandauer, Krystyna Janda, Ildiko Bansagi, Karin Boyd, Rolf Hoppe, Christine Harbort, Gyorgy Cserhalmi, Christiane Graskoff, Peter Andorai, Ildiko Kishonti; **D:** Istvan Szabo; **W:** Istvan Szabo, Peter Dobai; **C:** Lajos Koltai; **M:** Zdenko Tamassy. *AWARDS:* Oscars '81: Foreign Film.

Mermaid

Family-oriented tale is based on the true story of a woman who, after the death of her husband, returns with her young daughter, Desi, to the small town where she grew up. The woman (Mathis) is determined to keep the harsh truth about death

from her daughter and in some small way, herself, while her mother (Burstyn) pushes for honesty and the sharing of grief. As Desi's birthday approaches, her mother consents to let the daughter write a letter to her daddy in heaven as a way of saying good-bye. Desi attaches the letter to a Mermaid balloon, which floats all the way to—believe it or not—a town called Mermaid, where it is found by one of the nicest families ever made. The rest would be an urban legend if not for good record-keeping. Strictly after-school special material, this is a sweet but not overly candy-coated material that will be uplifting for those who like hopeful stories, but could leave the cynic with a bit of a tummy ache. Especially enjoyable is the footage during the closing titles with the real families involved watching the shooting of the story they lived. The color and sound on the disc are TV quality. It was shot for Showtime, and is presented in the original full-frame format. —*CA*

Movie: 🎬🎬 ½ **DVD:** 🎬🎬 ½
Showtime Networks, Inc. (cat #SHO3025, UPC 758445302523). Full frame. Stereo. $19.90. Keepcase. *LANG:* English. *CAP:* English. *FEATURES:* 18 chapters.
2000 94m/C Samantha Mathis, Ellen Burstyn, David Kaye, Jodelle Ferland, Blu Mankuma, Tom Heaton; **D:** Peter Masterson; **W:** Todd Robinson; **C:** Jon Joffin; **M:** Peter Melnick.

Metropolis

An elaborate and expensive anime from the top names in the field, this one is based upon a comic book from the late '40s, when it must have seemed very ahead of its time. A reworking of ideas in Fritz Lang's classic *Metropolis*, the comic either predated the central visions of films like *Blade Runner*, or this 2001 adaptation chose to copy them too. What one is left with are reels of beautiful animation, in service of a story where a lot happens but no great drama emerges. Wonder city Metropolis is celebrating its new super-tower called the Ziggurat. It's the brainchild of Duke Red (voice: Jamieson Price), a megalomaniac who has no political ambitions for himself, but has secretly hired outlaw scientist Dr. Laughton (voice: Junpei Takeguchi) to make a super-robot duplicate of his dead daughter Tima (voice: Yuka Imoto). Metropolis is served by thousands of robot slaves but Tima is a hybrid programmed to rule in a special throne atop the tower. Before she can be announced, hitman Rock (voice: Kouki Okada) blows up the lab. Rock, the adopted son of Duke Red, is also an anti-robot zealot. Meanwhile, young Kenichi (voice: Kei Kobayashi) and his detective Uncle arrive from Japan to arrest Dr. Laughton, just in time to rescue the glowing, magical Tima and go on the run. Double-disc set is a very lavish special edition that comes in one of those multifold card packages that you want to be very careful with (don't get it wet). The feature is by itself on its own disc, and is mastered at a fat bit rate. It

looks consistently great, even in those scenes when brown characters hide in dark brown backgrounds. A second smaller-format DVD disc houses the extras, which cover the history and production of the concept very nicely. There's an abundance of art galleries, animation evolution comparisons, interviews, and a full documentary for Japanese television. Some of the compositions on the feature transfer looked tight top to bottom; in the documentary, the letterboxed clips from the film were composed at a less-wide 1:66, leading me to wonder if the perceived over-matting will upset anime experts. It was only noticeable on a few wide shots where small figures walked at the bottom of the frame. —*GE*

Movie: 🎬🎬 ½ **DVD:** 🎬🎬🎬 ½
Columbia Tristar (cat #07796, UPC 04339-6077966). Widescreen (1.78:1) anamorphic; full frame. DTS 5.1; Dolby Digital 5.1; Dolby Surround. $27.98. Special packaging. *LANG:* English; Japanese; French. *SUB:* English; French; Spanish. *CAP:* English. *FEATURES:* Trailers ▪ Documentary, "The Making of Metropolis" ▪ Filmmaker interviews ▪ Multi-angle animation comparisons ▪ History of the comic book ▪ Thumbnail bios ▪ Conceptual art gallery.
2001 109m/C *JP* **D:** Rin Taro; **W:** Katsuhiro Otomo; **M:** Toshiyuki Honda; **V:** Yuka Imoto, Kei Kobayashi, Kouki Okada, Jamieson Price, Toshio Furukawa, Junpei Takeguchi.

The Mexican

South-of-the-border snorer has Jerry (Pitt), an inept go-fer for mobster Margolese (Hackman), on a mission to retrieve a priceless antique pistol called The Mexican. Girlfriend Samantha (Roberts) wants Jerry to go straight and, when he refuses, she heads to Las Vegas, only to be kidnapped by gay hitman Leroy (Gandolfini), who steals the rest of the uneven film). It's difficult to say much about the look of the DVD. It appears to be an accurate reproduction of the original, which relies on an acid-etched, dirty-dusty, yellow-brown color scheme. Superior audio makes the monotonous faux heroic Mexican score even more irritating than it might have been otherwise. The commentary track is really more detailed and serious-minded than the film warrants. —*MM*

Movie: 🎬🎬 **DVD:** 🎬🎬🎬
DreamWorks Home Ent. (cat #87822, UPC 667068782226). Widescreen (2.35:1) anamorphic. Dolby Digital 5.1 Surround Stereo; DTS Surround; Dolby Digital Surround. $26.99. Keepcase. *LANG:* English. *SUB:* English. *CAP:* English. *FEATURES:* 8 deleted scenes with optional commentary ▪ Commentary: Vrebinski, Wyman, editor Craig Wood ▪ "Making of" featurette ▪ Production notes ▪ Talent files ▪ 28 chapters.
2001 (R) 123m/C Brad Pitt, Julia Roberts, James Gandolfini, Bob Balaban, Gene Hackman, J.K. Simmons, David Krumholtz, Michael Ceveris; **D:** Gore Verbinski; **W:** J.H. Wyman; **C:** Darius Wolski; **M:** Alan Silvestri.

Mexico City

Decent thriller concerns Mitch (Stacy Edwards) searching for her missing brother (Johnny Zander). She becomes embroiled in political intrigue and has to deal with corrupt police and politicians who only care when it's in their best interests. DVD has a quality picture and sound is very good. —DE

Movie: 🎬🎬🎬 **DVD:** 🎬🎬🎬
Buena Vista Home Ent. (cat #2482803, UPC 8693617068). Widescreen (1.85:1) anamorphic. Dolby Digital Surround. $29.98. Keepcase. *LANG:* English; Spanish. *CAP:* English. *FEATURES:* 17 chapters • Commentary: director Richard Sheppard • Spanish language track.
2001 (R) 88m/C Stacy Edwards, Jorge Robles, Johnny Zander, Robert Patrick; *D:* Richard Shepard; *W:* Richard Shepard, Jonathan Stern.

Mickey Blue Eyes

Michael Felgate (Grant) is a polished and successful Manhattan art auctioneer who is steadily climbing the ladder of corporate success. After dating Gina (Tripplehorn), an enchanting teacher, for three months, he proposes and plans to meet her family. But there's a secret she has kept from him for these three months. She is the daughter of a Mafia kingpin (Caan), a gangster who extracts money for the mob. Unafraid of the implications it could have to date and marry a mobster's daughter and warned by Gina about the tactics of her family, Michael goes ahead and meets the family, starting with her father Frank, making it all the way to "Uncle" Vito Graziosi (Young). Immediately the mobsters try to include Michael in their intimate ring of business, but Michael refuses, firmly intent to stay clean. The widescreen transfer is highly detailed. Although the full-frame presentation crops the image, it is an open matte transfer, revealing more picture information at the top and bottom of the screen. Both have vibrant colors with well-saturated hues and without any signs of chroma noise. Blacks are very well defined and solid while the highlights are always balanced and natural. The same is true for flesh-tones, which are rendered accurately, even under difficult lighting conditions. The soundtrack has a natural quality. Although there is some bass extension and Surround usage, the audio is front loaded, as expected, and makes use of the discrete Surround channels sparingly, only in a handful of scenes. Kelly Makin's commentary is informative, although a bit dry and slow at times. —GH

Movie: 🎬🎬🎬 **DVD:** 🎬🎬🎬 ½
Warner Home Video (UPC 0539392565-29). Widescreen (1.85:1) anamorphic; full frame. Dolby Digital 5.1 Surround. $14.98. Snapper. *LANG:* English. *SUB:* English. *FEATURES:* Commentary • Trailer.
1999 (PG-13) 103m/C Hugh Grant, Jeanne Tripplehorn, James Caan, Burt Young, Gerry Becker, James Fox, Joe (Johnny) Viterelli, Maddie Corman, Tony Darrow,

Paul Lazar, Vincent Pastore, Frank Pellegrino, Scott Thompson, John Ventimiglia; *D:* Kelly Makin; *W:* Robert Kuhn, Adam Scheinman; *C:* Donald E. Thorin; *M:* Wolfgang Hammerschmid.

Mickey Mouse in Living Color

This irresistible collection presents the first 26 color cartoons starring Mickey Mouse in chronological order. Spanning the years 1935–1938, the perky, amusing 6–9 minute shorts feature vivid and rich use of bright primary colors for the characters and more muted hues for the beautifully painted backgrounds. Secondary Disney characters like Donald Duck, Goofy, Pluto, et al, also figure into most of the cartoons. While the legendary "The Band Concert" is fine, "Thru the Mirror," "Mickey's Garden," and "Brave Little Tailor" are even better. While all the cartoons are worthwhile, they are more genial and amusing than laugh-out-loud funny. A bit of a contrast from the more violent, hilarious Warner Bros. cartoons, but the animation is wonderful. This set ("limited" to 150,000 copies) presents the cartoons in the full richness of their Technicolor hues in print masters that are nearly spotless. The sharpness and clarity of them is eye-opening, but moments featuring fast movement are prone to distracting digital distortion. The mono sound is terrific—the only limitations are those found on the original source recordings. The bonus featurettes are brief but interesting. Also included are several rough draft pencil tests of the cartoons. They're worthwhile, especially for animation scholars. Unfortunately the pencil tests had several glitches on the discs we previewed. —DG

Movie: 🎬🎬🎬 ½ **DVD:** 🎬🎬🎬
Buena Vista Home Ent. (cat #21541, UPC 786936158243). Full frame. Mono. $32.99. Keepcase, tin. *LANG:* English. *CAP:* English. *FEATURES:* 26 original cartoons • Intro by Leonard Maltin • Original concept art • Theatrical poster art • Interview featurette • Pencil and audio tests.
2001 217m/C

Mickey's Magical Christmas

This DVD may be the ultimate example of a "mixed" bag. The "House of Mouse" is a nightclub overseen by Mickey Mouse and where dozens of notable animated Disney characters can be spotted. When a Christmas party at the "House of Mouse" runs longer than expected when a snowstorm traps the patrons in the club, everyone is O.K. with this, save for Donald Duck, who has no Christmas spirit. Mickey attempts to rectify this by showing several Christmas-themed films. Some of these are new, such as Huey, Dewey, and Louie building a snowman, or old, as in a classic short in which Mickey chops down Chip 'n' Dale's tree to use as a decoration. There is also a new version of *The Nutcracker* featuring Donald, Mickey, and Minnie.

These shorts and the wrap-around story are fair at best, but the saving grace of this collection is the inclusion of *Mickey's Christmas Carol*, a re-telling of the Dickens's classic, with Scrooge McDuck playing Ebenezer. This segment is the only part which overcomes the special's TV roots, but it makes the DVD worth checking out. The image on this disc is fine, with some of the older segments showing some small flaws from their source prints. The colors are bright, with no bleeding or oversaturation. Both the Dolby 5.1 and DTS 5.1 audio tracks provide clear dialogue and distortion-free music. The disc includes a bonus episode of *House of Mouse* (which shows how weak the show is) and some sing-alongs. —ML

Movie: 🎬🎬🎬 **DVD:** 🎬🎬🎬
Buena Vista Home Ent. (cat #22950, UPC 786936157000). Full frame. Dolby Digital 5.1; DTS 5.1. $29.99. Keepcase. *LANG:* English. *SUB:* English. *CAP:* English. *FEATURES:* Bonus episode • Sing-alongs • Sound effects demo • 12 chapters.
2001 62m/C

A Midnight Clear

Keith Gordon's low-budget high-quality war film is a brilliant sleeper. It's set in December 1944 in the Ardennes Forest, in either France, Luxembourg, or Belgium. Nobody in the six-man recon patrol is really sure where they are. Will Knott (Hawke) is the nominal leader of the group, though Avakian (Dillon) really knows more about soldiering. Mother (Sinise) is half mad; Stan (Gross) is a tough Jew who's ready to fight; Miller (Berg) wants the war to be over; Father (Whaley) refuses to admit that their unit is even part of the army. They arrive at an abandoned house in the middle of the snow-covered woods and find that the Germans are there, too, but these Germans are not the enemy they're used to fighting. Though the film certainly has a contemporary sensibility, it is not revisionist history. On their commentary track, Gordon and Hawke try to make that clear. They also address the politics of filmmaking with more candor than most filmmakers. Every decision costs money; producers make demands; some battles are won while others are not really fought. Those ideas are most clearly illustrated in the deleted scenes section. Perhaps the film is better without most of those moments, but the long scene with Sgt. Hart, even in its rough state, is impressive. DVD presentation of the full-frame image is very good. (This is the original aspect ratio; not pan-and-scan.) Sound is fine. —MM

Movie: 🎬🎬🎬 ½ **DVD:** 🎬🎬🎬 ½
Columbia Tristar (cat #09230, UPC 043-396092303). Full frame. Dolby Surround. $24.98. Keepcase. *LANG:* English. *SUB:* English; French. *CAP:* English. *FEATURES:* Commentary: Gordon, Hawke • Deleted scenes • 28 chapters.
1992 (PG) 107m/C Peter Berg, Kevin Dillon, Arye Gross, Ethan Hawke, Gary Sinise, Frank Whaley, John C. McGinley, Larry Joshua, Curt Lowens, David Jensen,

Rachel Griffin, Tim Shoemaker; **D:** Keith Gordon; **W:** Keith Gordon; **C:** Tom Richmond; **M:** Mark Isham.

Midnight Madness

Five teams of college stereotypes search the city of Los Angeles for clues as part of a wacky scavenger hunt designed by a fellow student. Features the big-screen debut of Michael J. Fox as the little brother of David "I'm a Pepper" Naughton (look closely to see the former Pepper pitchman drinking a bottle of the stuff; it's the only near-witty moment). Also casts Stephen "Flounder" Dorf, making this flick somewhat of an *It's a Mad, Mad, Mad, Mad Animal House,* but to say that is an insult to both of those films. Even the presence of arch-geek Eddie Deezen can't save the outing. Though this is the best this film has ever looked, Anchor Bay's DVD is, at best, only average. The film print itself looks like it should have been cleaned before the transfer—maybe it was, but it still looks pretty nasty at times. Sharpness comes and goes and the colors are generally pretty weak. On the other hand, blacks, brightness, and contrast are all better than expected. The soundtrack claims to be Dolby Surround, but even under torture I couldn't say that it sounded like anything more than stereo. —JO
Movie: 🎬 **DVD:** 🎬🎬
Anchor Bay (cat #DV11404, UPC 0131311-40491). Full frame. Dolby Surround. $14.98. Keepcase. *LANG:* English. *FEATURES:* 20 chapters.
1980 (PG) 110m/C David Naughton, Stephen Furst, Debra Clinger, Eddie Deezen, Michael J. Fox, Maggie Roswell; **D:** David Wechter; **W:** David Wechter; **C:** Frank Phillips; **M:** Julius Wechter.

A Midsummer Night's Sex Comedy

A warm, sumptuous gem of a comedy set during the early 1900s at a beautiful, romantic country house. Andrew (Allen), a wisecracking inventor, is having sexual problems with his wife (Steenburgen) when he invites intellectual snob Dr. Leopold (Ferrer) and his fiancée, Ariel (Farrow), for a weekend getaway. Also in attendance is lothario, Doctor Jordan (Roberts) and the nurse (Hagerty) he's having a fling with. A comedy of manners (and errors) ensues with Andrew and Jordan chasing after Ariel with Leopold chasing after the two with a bow and arrow! This beautifully photographed film features a terrific cast, knockout jokes, and a touching and magical denouement. Designed as a tribute to similar comedies by Renoir and Bergman, it's much better, in my humble opinion. Look quick for the crewmember (in modern jeans and T-shirt!) glimpsed during the morning pastoral sequence. The picture transfer is slightly grainy, but bright and colorful with perfect fleshtones. The sound (with omnipresent crickets and beautiful Mendelssohn music) shows just

how good mono tracks are capable of sounding. —DG
Movie: 🎬🎬🎬 ½ **DVD:** 🎬🎬🎬🎬
MGM Home Ent. (cat #1001746, UPC 027-616860460). Widescreen (1.85:1) anamorphic. Mono. $19.98. Keepcase. *LANG:* English. *SUB:* English; French; Spanish. *CAP:* English. *FEATURES:* Booklet with notes • Theatrical trailer • 16 chapters.
1982 (PG) 88m/C Woody Allen, Mia Farrow, Mary Steenburgen, Tony Roberts, Julie Hagerty, Jose Ferrer; **D:** Woody Allen; **W:** Woody Allen; **C:** Gordon Willis.

Midway [Universal CE]

U.S. intelligence deciphers encoded Japanese transmissions that hint at an upcoming invasion at Midway Island. This all-star re-creation of the important WWII battle is an accurate but uneven work. Blessed with a terrific cast (another strong Heston performance) and a gripping first half, the film goes somewhat limp in its battle sequences. While it's interesting to see the epic chess match being played by the two opposing leaders, the overuse of stock footage and static character scenes in the battle re-creations drain the film of its dramatic energy. While the use of the actual Midway battle footage works well with the filmmakers' proposed intentions, the cannibalization of UNCREDITED scenes from *Away All Boats, Tora! Tora! Tora!,* and another Japanese-made films seems crass and cheap. The use of dubbing on Japanese actor Toshiro Mifune gives his scenes an unintentional '70s dubbed-*Godzilla* film feel. The disc is a gorgeous transfer of the somewhat blandly (khaki, khaki, khaki!) colored film. The clarity of the image reveals the stock footage even more clearly and the wide framing is essential. The sound is mono, but you'll want to crank up the bass to re-create that "Sensurround" feel. The featurettes are all excellent, substantial and filled with interesting anecdotes and reminiscences. The only disappointment in this disc is the inclusion of only 10 minutes of the scenes shot for the TV broadcast. About a half-hour of additional footage depicting the battle of the Coral Sea (featuring Mitchell Ryan and others) is not included on the disc, though it's discussed and a brief clip is shown on the documentary. One of the featurettes is contemporary to the film and features Charlton Heston (replete with stylish cravat!) discussing the real-life events behind the story. —DG
Movie: 🎬🎬 ½ **DVD:** 🎬🎬🎬
Universal Studios (cat #21220, UPC 0251-92122026). Widescreen (2.35:1) anamorphic. Mono 1.1. $24.98. Keepcase. *LANG:* English; Spanish; French. *CAP:* English. *FEATURES:* 18 chapters • Booklet with notes • Original featurette • "Making of" documentary • Featurette on John Williams • Featurette on Sensurround Sound • Photos and portraits montage with music • Additional scenes shot for television • Theatrical trailer • Production notes • Cast & filmmaker bios.

1976 (PG) 132m/C Charlton Heston, Henry Fonda, James Coburn, Glenn Ford, Hal Holbrook, Robert Mitchum, Cliff Robertson, Robert Wagner, Kevin Dobson, Christopher George, Toshiro Mifune, Tom Selleck; **D:** Jack Smight; **W:** Donald S. Sanford; **C:** Harry Stradling Jr.; **M:** John Williams.

Millennium Dragon

The plot to this one is a muddle that only starts to unwind midway through. Yuen Biao (called "Yuen Bill" here) gets star billing, but only has a supporting role. Chu Lai-Yee is the real star, playing South Korean government agent Kim, sent to Russia to investigate a smuggling ring. The likely head of the ring is rich antiquities fan Cho Dai-foo (Charlie Cho), but Cho's real scheme is to get his hands on the powerful Millennia Luminant Pearl. Terrorist Hon Foh-lui (Chin Siu-Ho) has it, and wants to trade Cho for a classified computer chip in his possession. Kim successfully infiltrates Hon's organization, and finds that Chinese spies Yuen and Ben Ng are working undercover on the case as well. Once everyone gets his or her cover blown, it ends up in a big running gun battle with everyone after the pearl. Considering the cast, there's precious little kung fu fighting to speak of. One would think that the Moscow and Mongolian locations would at least add some visual interest, but except for a few shots, the whole thing might as well have been shot in suburban New Mexico. The print quality is O.K., but the transfer isn't. Colors and textures are stable only when there's no movement, which is almost never. The highlights are much too hot. White subtitles disappear completely over frequent light backgrounds. —BT
AKA: Red Square Thieves; Hung Cheung do Ying; Hong Qiang dao Ying.
Movie: 🎬 ½ **DVD:** 🎬
Tai Seng (cat #80694, UPC 6016438069-45). Widescreen letterboxed. Dolby Digital 5.1. $14.95. Keepcase. *LANG:* Cantonese; Mandarin. *SUB:* Chinese & English (nonremoveable). *FEATURES:* 6 chapters.
1993 93m/C HK Yuen Biao, Chu Lai-Yee, Chin Siu Ho, Lily Chung, Charlie Cho, Ben Ng; **D:** Philip Ko; **W:** Li Ngai Chi.

Mimic 2

The giant mutant cockroaches from *Mimic* are back in an economical but effectively told little sf/horror film. Story is tight; effects are excellent; pace is quick. DVD transfer is perfectly clean without even the slightest defect, rendering a very clean and clear picture that is also mostly free of grain. Some edge-enhancement is visible in the transfer, creating unnaturally hard edges in some instances but for the most part, the artifacts remain undetectable in the elaborate shots. The image reveals a high level of detail and looks much more like a full-budget film production than a direct-to-video sequel. The presentation offers powerful colors that help the mood of the film immensely and blacks that are as deep as one could wish. With a wide frequency response, the audio manages to produce earth-shattering booms and ominous ostinati with its powerful bass extension, yet at the same time keeps the high ends clear and free of distortion. —MM/GH

Movie: 🎬🎬🎬 **DVD:** 🎬🎬🎬
Buena Vista Home Ent. (cat #21646, UPC 786936144680). Widescreen (1.85:1) anamorphic. Dolby Digital 5.1 Surround Stereo. $29.99. Keepcase. *LANG:* English. *SUB:* English. *CAP:* English. *FEATURES:* 6 deleted scenes • "Making of" featurette • Video diary • 11 chapters.
2001 (R) 82m/C Alix Koromzay, Bruno Campos, Will Estes, Edward Albert, Jon Polito, Gaven Eugene Lucas; *D:* Jean De Segonzac; *W:* Joel Soisson; *C:* Nathan Hope.

The Mind Benders

This serious movie about sensory deprivation experiments is often listed as a science-fiction story, but it doesn't play like one. It's an espionage tale, a psychothriller, and a love story. It also would seem to connect up a half-dozen different threads in the history of fantastic films...although technically, there's nothing fantastic about it. Professor Sharpey (Goldblatt) has apparently sold secrets to the Russians, and kills himself. MI5 Major Hall (Clements) investigates Sharpey's experiments in Isolation studies, and concludes that the once-loyal Professor has indeed turned traitor. But Sharpey's partner Dr. Henry Longman (Bogarde) is determined to prove that the Isolation experiments were responsible, and reluctantly offers to undergo a long immersion in the sense-depriving water tank, even though he's barely recovered from the psychic effects of a previous experiment. Longman's wife Oonagh (Mary Ure), knowing the danger, dreads the thought of Henry returning to the tank. DVD looks and sounds great. Georges Auric's stirring score comes across strong in the tense main titles, and the B&W photography of Oxford in 1963 (and dumb meaningless details, like Longman's antique car) is very good. There are some atmospheric angles and double exposures in the isolation tank, but in general, the movie doesn't go in for dramatic staging or visual fireworks. Neither subtitles nor closed captioning are on the disc, so it's good that the dialogue is recorded so clearly, a problem with the earlier *Day the Earth Caught Fire*, where closed captioning saved the day. A very strange trailer tries to present *The Mind Benders* as a shocking adult exposé. It's hosted by a man in a room full of posters for the film, who soberly states that he can't show us any scenes, but they crop up anyway. The science and politics of the show probably threw the original marketers, who wisely decided to stress the sex angle. The complexity seems to have thrown Anchor Bay's copywriters as well, as they posit *The Mind Benders* as an inspiration for *The Manchurian Candidate*. How can an English film released in 1963 be the inspiration for an American film released in 1962? (The film is also available as part of "The Dirk Bogarde Collection" boxed set.) —GE

Movie: 🎬🎬🎬 **DVD:** 🎬🎬🎬½
Anchor Bay (cat #DV11579, UPC 0131311-57994). Widescreen (1.78:1) anamorphic. Dolby Digital Mono. $19.98. Keepcase. *LANG:* English. *FEATURES:* Trailer • Dirk Bogarde bio.
1963 99m/C Dirk Bogarde, Mary Ure, John Clements, Michael Bryant, Wendy Craig, Harold Goldblatt, Geoffrey Keen; *D:* Basil Dearden; *W:* James Kennaway; *C:* Denys Coop; *M:* Georges Auric.

Mind, Body & Soul

When a woman (Allen) witnesses a human sacrifice performed by her boyfriend's satanic cult, she goes to the police (Hauser). The cops, however, believe that she's part of the cult so she is forced to rely on a public defender to protect her from not-exactly-Mr.-Right and his pals. This extremely cheaply made video premiere gains nothing on DVD. Sound is hollow, image is grainy, and there's a weird hangup between two chapters. Title is available on the *Action Arsenal* collection. —MM

Movie: 🎬🎬 **DVD:** 🎬½
BCI-Eclipse (cat #44076-9, UPC 7873644-07699). Full frame. $19.98. Keepcase. *LANG:* English. *FEATURES:* 11 chapters.
1992 (R) 93m/C Wings Hauser, Ginger Lynn Allen, Jay Richardson, Ken Hill, Jesse Kaye, Tami Bakke; *D:* Rick Sloane; *W:* Rick Sloane; *C:* Robert Hayes; *M:* Alan Der Marderosian.

Mind Meld: Secrets behind the Voyage of a Lifetime

In this long interview piece, *Star Trek* stars William Shatner (Captain Kirk) and Leonard Nimoy (Mr. Spock) meet in Nimoy's beautiful backyard to discuss the making of the original TV series, the fans, clashes with management, the phenomenon, and their personal struggles. This absolutely terrific "talking heads" documentary is consistently fascinating, honest, and informative. The two have been friends for over 35 years and their ability to put their guard down in front of themselves (and the camera) is a brave and revealing thing to behold. At times, this intensely personal discussion can seem like we're sitting in on a private psychotherapy session but some of their comments and stories will stay with you for days. Rumors of Shatner producing his own "gaseous anomaly" during the interview are indeed true. In fact he audibly does it multiple times! Trek fans will get the most out of this program, but actors and students of human behavior will find something to enjoy as well. The documentary is beautifully shot and warmly lit. The image increases in grain in the wide shots but the rest of the program looks terrific, with vivid fleshtones and strong colors. The sound recording and reproduction are excellent. The featurette is just a commercial and there is no time encoding on the disc. —DG

Movie: 🎬🎬🎬 **DVD:** 🎬🎬🎬½
Creative Light Video (cat #CL12067, UPC 692187112067). Widescreen (1.85:1) anamorphic. Dolby Digital Stereo. $24.95. Keepcase. *LANG:* English. *SUB:* English. *FEATURES:* "Making of" featurette • Shatner & Nimoy bios • 8 chapters.
2001 75m/C William Shatner, Leonard Nimoy; *D:* Peter Jaysen; *C:* Adam Biggs.

The Miracle of the Cards

The healing power of faith is the focus of this sappy and vacant drama from the studio that brought you *Left Behind*. The true story of Craig Shergold (Sangster), a terminally ill boy who breaks the Guinness record for receiving get-well cards, from sickness to doubt and redemption, is told to reporter Kirk Cameron through flashbacks from the family. The picture looks no better than a video and the Surround channels are only used for the light classical soundtrack. Fans of *Left Behind* are the only people who will have their lives affirmed by this tale. —DL

Movie: 🎬 **DVD:** 🎬🎬
Cloud Ten Pictures (cat #776, UPC 745-68007136). Full frame. Surround. $19.95. Keepcase. *LANG:* English. *FEATURES:* Cast and crew bios • Production notes • Audio interviews • Trailers • 8 chapters.
2000 89m/C Catherine Oxenberg, Thomas Sangster, Kirk Cameron, Peter Wigfield, Richard Thomas; *D:* Mark Griffiths; *W:* Lee Wilson; *C:* Henry Lebo; *M:* Ken Harrison.

The Mirror

Wonderful child's view of life in Russia during WWII is told through haunting images. Black-and-white flashbacks of important events in the country's history are interspersed with scenes of day-to-day family life. DVD presents an excellent re-creation of both the black-and-white and color footage. Burned-in yellow subtitles are easy to read. —MM **AKA:** Zerkalo; A White White Boy.

Movie: 🎬🎬🎬 **DVD:** 🎬🎬🎬
Kino on Video (cat #K150, UPC 73832901-5022). Full frame. $29.95. Keepcase. *LANG:* Russian. *SUB:* English. *FEATURES:* 14 chapters.
1975 106m/C RU Margarita Terekhova, Philip Yankovsky, Ignat Daniltsev, Oleg (Yankovsky) Jankowsky; *D:* Andrei Tarkovsky; *W:* Andrei Tarkovsky; *C:* Georgy Rerberg; *M:* Eduard Artemyev.

The Mirror Cracked from Side to Side

Please see review for *A Caribbean Mystery / The Mirror Cracked from Side to Side*.
1992 100m/C Joan Hickson, Claire Bloom, Barry Newman, Glynis Barber, John Castle, Judy Cornwell, Margaret Courtenay,

David Horovitch, Norman Rodway; **D:** Norman Stone; **W:** T.R. Bowen; **C:** John Walker.

Mishima: A Life in Four Chapters

One of Japan's most important modernist writers, Yukio Mishima led a failed and largely symbolic coup against the capitalist government, then committed ritual suicide. This biopic examines his life and final day, weaving in re-creations from three of his novels. The rigidly formal structure keeps the audience at a distance, though much of it is still fascinating. The colors aren't sharp enough to do justice to Eiko's imaginative set designs. Dialogue is clear, though the rear speakers aren't used much. —BG
Movie: 🎬🎬🎬 **DVD:** 🎬🎬🎬
Warner (cat #11530, UPC 0853911530-23). Widescreen anamorphic. Dolby Surround; Dolby Mono. $19.98. Snapper. *LANG:* English; Japanese; French. *SUB:* English; Japanese; French. *CAP:* English. *FEATURES:* 34 chapters • Behind-the-scenes featurette • Commentary: Paul Schrader • Deleted scene • Trailer • Production notes.
1985 (R) 121m/C Ken Ogata, Kenji Sawada, Yasosuke Bando; **D:** Paul Schrader; **W:** Leonard Schrader, Paul Schrader; **C:** John Bailey; **M:** Philip Glass; **Nar:** Roy Scheider.

Mission Kashmir

A boy's parents are killed by accident by the Indian Paramilitary. The head of the unit takes him into his home. When the boy finds out his adopted father killed his parents he becomes a terrorist bent on destroying his adopted father. This is a good movie that could have been an absolute classic if the musical numbers had been left out. Some of the lines are chilling in light of 9/11. DVD is beautiful, the colors are vivid, the sound outstanding. —DE
Movie: 🎬🎬🎬 **DVD:** 🎬🎬🎬½
Columbia Tristar (cat #08736, UPC 043-396087361). Widescreen anamorphic. 5.1 Dolby Digital. $24.98. Keepcase. *LANG:* Hindi and English. *SUB:* English; French; Spanish; Portuguese; Chinese; Korean; Thai. *CAP:* English. *FEATURES:* 28 chapters • Theatrical trailers.
2000 (R) 157m/C IN Hrithik Roshan, Sanjay Dutt, Jackie Shroff, Preity Zinta, Sonali Kulkarni; **D:** Vidhu Vinod Chopra; **W:** Vidhu Vinod Chopra, Vikram Chandra; **C:** Vinod Pradhan.

Mission Manila

Ex-CIA agent Web (Wilcox) goes to Manila to find his brother who's in trouble with drugs and mobsters. The standard-issue plot is enlivened by some very good performances (particularly from Robin Eiseman and Sam Hennings), a knock-about sensibility, and surprising humor. Don't miss the scene where the heroine is tied to the railroad track. DVD image is generally good to very good with only one striped shirt that flashes badly. —MM

Movie: 🎬🎬½ **DVD:** 🎬🎬½
Image Ent. (cat #0VED9030DVD, UPC 014381903027). Full frame. Dolby Digital Stereo. $24.98. Keepcase. *LANG:* English. *FEATURES:* 12 chapters.
1987 (R) 98m/C Larry Wilcox, Tetchie Agbayani, Sam Hennings, Al Mancini, James Wainwright, Robin Eisenman; **D:** Peter M. MacKenzie; **W:** Peter M. MacKenzie; **C:** Les Parrott; **M:** Nicholas Pike.

Mission to Death

Second-rate rip-off of *Dirty Dozen* follows 10 G.I.s on a commando mission to take a German radar station at the end of WWII. Plot is essentially a series of scenes where our "heroes" sneak up and stab guys in the back. DVD is equal to tape in every way. —MM
Movie: 🎬 **DVD:** 🎬🎬
Winstar Home Ent. (cat #FLV5302, UPC 72-0917530222). Full frame. $24.98. Keepcase. *LANG:* English. *FEATURES:* Trailers • 16 chapters.
1966 71m/C Jim Brewer, James E. McLarty, Jim Westerbrook, Robert Stolper, Dudley Hafner, Jerry Lasater; **D:** Kenneth W. Richardson; **C:** Ronald Perryman; **M:** Emil Cadkin, William Loose.

Mrs. Winterbourne

Unmarried, homeless, and pregnant, Connie Doyle (Lake) is whisked into the lap of luxury when she's assumed to be the widowed Patricia Winterbourne after a train wreck. The grieving in-laws (who had never met the bride) take her in and accept her and her baby as part of the household. Since things are finally going her way, Connie elects not to disabuse them while she falls for faux-brother-in-law Bill (Fraser). MacLaine is fine as the spirited matriarch. Not surprisingly, the comic story has a darker side. It's based on Cornell Woolrich's noirish novel *I Married a Dead Man* and it's a remake of the equally grim 1950 film *No Man of Her Own*. Both wide- and full-frame images are generally very good. No flaws; the picture is simply not as sharp or as bright as some big-budget studio comedies. Sound is O.K. on a no-frills disc. —MM
Movie: 🎬🎬🎬 **DVD:** 🎬🎬🎬
Columbia Tristar (cat #07742, UPC 0433-96077423). Widescreen (1.85:1) anamorphic; full frame. Dolby Digital 5.1 Surround; Dolby Stereo. $24.98. Keepcase. *LANG:* English; French. *SUB:* English; French; Spanish; Portuguese; Chinese; Korean; Thai. *CAP:* English. *FEATURES:* 28 chapters.
1996 (PG-13) 106m/C Ricki Lake, Brendan Fraser, Shirley MacLaine, Miguel (Michael) Sandoval, Loren Dean, Susan Haskell, Paula Prentiss; **D:** Richard Benjamin; **W:** Phoef Sutton, Lisa-Marie Rodano; **C:** Alex Nepomniaschy; **M:** Patrick Doyle.

Mr. Bill Goes to Hollywood / Mr. Bill Does Vegas

This is a collection of 25 short *Mr. Bill* films. Since these nasty little comedies

are meant to be consumed in small doses, the DVD really provides more than most viewers will be interested in watching. Image and sound remain true to their home video roots and so DVD adds nothing but accessibility to the individual films. All but one are full frame. Given its epic stature, "The Biliad and the Odyssey," is presented widescreen. —MM
Movie: 🎬🎬 **DVD:** 🎬🎬
Lion's Gate Home Ent. (cat #VM 7901D, UPC 031398790129). Full frame; widescreen letterboxed. Stereo. $24.98. Keepcase. *LANG:* English. *FEATURES:* 25 chapters.
2001 94m/C Wayne Newton, Jenna Elfman, Tom Smothers, Dick Smothers, Don Novello; **D:** Walter Williams.

Mr. Deeds Goes to Town

Small-town idealist Longfellow Deeds (Cooper, at his best) inherits $20 million and promptly sets about to giving it away to the needy. That lands him in a courtroom for a hearing to judge his sanity. He also manages to find time to fall in love with beautiful tough cookie Babe Bennett (Arthur), a reporter who's determined to fathom the good guy's motivation. One of Capra's best and they don't get much better than that. DVD was created from a print with some registration problems, resulting in a slight occasional jitter, and many of the film's splices seem to be damaged as well, causing visible jumps when cuts occur. Although some of those signs of age and damage are still evident in the source print, the film looks great with a perfect balance of contrast that creates a pleasing picture. The blacks are deep and solid and the film's highlights are pronounced but never overemphasized. The monaural audio has been nicely restored. —MM/GH
Movie: 🎬🎬🎬½ **DVD:** 🎬🎬🎬
Columbia Tristar Home Video (UPC 04-3396894396). Full frame. Dolby Digital Mono. $24.98. Keepcase. *LANG:* English; Spanish. *SUB:* English; French; Spanish; Portuguese; Chinese; Korean; Thai. *FEATURES:* Commentary • Featurette • Vintage advertising • Production notes.
1936 118m/B Gary Cooper, Jean Arthur, Raymond Walburn, Walter Catlett, Lionel Stander, George Bancroft, H.B. Warner, Ruth Donnelly, Douglass Dumbrille, Margaret Seddon, Margaret McWade; **D:** Frank Capra; **W:** Robert Riskin; **C:** Joseph Walker. *AWARDS:* Oscars '36: Director (Capra); N.Y. Film Critics '36: Film; *NOM:* Oscars '36: Actor (Cooper), Picture, Screenplay, Sound.

Mr. Rice's Secret

Ailing youngster Owen Walters (Switzer) inherits a medieval code ring from Mr. Rice (Bowie). It leads him on a magical quest. The filmmakers deserve credit for attempting to combine a serious story with the fantastic elements, and they get credible performances from the cast. But the well-intentioned story tends toward the preachy and the production values leave much to be desired. DVD image is good to very good but not really superior to VHS tape. —*MM*

Movie: 🎵🎵 **DVD:** 🎵🎵 ½
MTI (cat #8119, UPC 039414581195). Widescreen (1.85:1) letterboxed. $24.95. Keepcase. *LANG:* English. *SUB:* Spanish. *FEATURES:* 20 chapters ● Talent files.
2000 (PG) 113m/C *CA* David Bowie, Garwin Sanford, Bill Switzer, Teryl Rothery; **D:** Nicholas (Nick) Kendall; **W:** J.H. Wyman; **C:** Gregory Middleton; **M:** Simon Kendall, Al Rodger.

Mr. Sardonicus

In the 19th century, a doctor is summoned to Baron Sardonicus's castle to cure him of his facial affliction. Since Sardonicus witnessed a horrible shock, his mouth has been frozen in a hideous grin (similar looking to Conrad Veidt in *The Man Who Laughs*). At the film's original theatrical showings, audience members were given a "Thumbs Up/Thumbs Down" card. The viewers would then vote on the ultimate fate of Sardonicus by voting. Sardonicus was always doomed, though, as a happy ending was never filmed. The lack of subplots, suspense, and surprise makes this a fairly flat and unremarkable picture. Sardonicus is often masked and inexpressive, leaving his assistant Krull (Homolka) to chew the scenery. Homolka has fun with the role, but the rest of the characters are pretty dull. Surprisingly limp for a William Castle picture. The disc uses a near-pristine print source with terrific contrasts and rich blacks. The image is sharp but occasionally suffers from instances of digital noise. Some shots occasionally look sped-up, leading one to believe there were problems transferring from a PAL master. Sound is excellent. The featurette focuses solely on interviews with genre historians and collectors, but is lively and funny. Too bad they didn't think to include a punishment poll card as an insert. —*DG*
AKA: Sardonicus.

Movie: 🎵🎵 **DVD:** 🎵🎵🎵
Columbia Tristar (cat #06931, UPC 0433-96069312). Widescreen (1.85:1) anamorphic. Mono. $24.95. Keepcase. *LANG:* English. *SUB:* English; French. *CAP:* English. *FEATURES:* Trailers ● "Taking the Punishment Poll" featurette ● 28 chapters.
1961 89m/B Guy Rolfe, Ronald Lewis, Oscar Homolka, Audrey Dalton, Vladimir Sokoloff; **D:** William Castle; **W:** Ray Russell; **C:** Burnett Guffey; **M:** Von Dexter.

Mr. Saturday Night [MGM]

Despite a successful career, Billy Crystal always strikes me as having been born a has-been. In this film he plays Buddy Young Jr., a Catskills comedian past his prime. The story flits through Buddy's life, from his days as a boy entertaining the family with his brother Stan (Paymer) to his life on the "retirement home comedy

circuit." Oy. The story has great potential and there are some lovely melancholy moments, but ultimately, Buddy is a schmuck and it's Stan you feel for. If it were based on a real person it might at least contain the interest of juicy biography gossip, but Crystal himself scripted this. Who else but a male writer would script a wife so understanding and tolerant of her husband's need to screw around? Sound and picture are standard DVD quality. The bonus materials will show you how much Crystal loves this movie, as he chatters about his inspiration and his boyhood summers in the Catskills. Buddy Young Jr. is the screen manifestation of Crystal's muse and career inspiration. A pity his muse is too self-centered and selfish to pony up some real comedy. —*JAS*

Movie: 🎵 ½ **DVD:** 🎵🎵🎵
MGM Home Ent. (cat #1003514, UPC 027-616876645). Widescreen (1.85:1) anamorphic. Dolby Digital Surround. $14.95. Keepcase. *LANG:* English. *SUB:* French; Spanish. *FEATURES:* 16 chapters ● Deleted scenes ● 3 "making of" featurettes ● Gag reel.
1992 (R) 118m/C Billy Crystal, David Paymer, Julie Warner, Helen Hunt, Mary Mara, Jerry Orbach, Ron Silver, Sage Allen, Jackie Gayle, Carl Ballantine, Slappy (Melvin) White, Conrad Janis, Jerry Lewis; **D:** Billy Crystal; **W:** Babaloo Mandel, Lowell Ganz, Billy Crystal; **C:** Don Peterman; **M:** Marc Shaiman. *AWARDS: NOM:* Oscars '92: Support. Actor (Paymer).

Mr. Show: The Complete First & Second Seasons

Bob Odenkirk and David Cross star in this inconsistent, subversive, and often brilliant sketch comedy series that blasts everything from politics to consumer culture to popular television, with hilarious results. Definitely not for all tastes, since it frequently ignores the conventions of decency. Highlights include the Mom and Pop porno store, and Mr. Show's secession from the union, where they declare themselves a sovereign nation. The picture and sound aren't vastly improved over the show's run on late-night HBO, but the extras are plentiful and enjoyable. All 10 episodes are complete with audio commentary. —*BG*

Movie: 🎵🎵🎵 **DVD:** 🎵🎵🎵
HBO (cat #99212, UPC 026359921223). Full frame. Dolby Surround. $34.98. Custom cardboard. *LANG:* English. *CAP:* English. *FEATURES:* Commentary: cast and crew ● "Fuzz" the Musical ● "Before It Was a TV Show" ● The Best of Mr. Show ● Original TV spots ● Bios.
2002 288m/C Bob Odenkirk, David Cross; **D:** Bob Odenkirk, David Cross; **W:** Bob Odenkirk, David Cross.

Mr. Vincent

Johnny Vincent (Hughes) is a would-be singer-songwriter who becomes easily

obsessed by women. Lisa (LoCicero) appears to be the most recent. Vincent's love is transformed into something more dangerous. Director Celestino tells the story with black-and-white, cinema verité techniques. Unfortunately, the disc is marred by some inexplicable pixels that crop up intermittently. Stripes in clothing patterns tend to flash, too. The director's commentary mentioned on the box copy is a short filmed introduction. —*MM*

Movie: 🎵🎵 ½ **DVD:** 🎵🎵 ½
Vanguard Intl. Cinema (cat #VF0196). Widescreen (1.66:1) letterboxed. $29.95. Keepcase. *LANG:* English. *FEATURES:* 13 chapters ● Trailer.
1997 90m/B Frank John Hughes, Lisa LoCicero, Mimi Scott, Robert Bruzio; **D:** Robert Celestino; **W:** Robert Celestino, John Mollica; **C:** Dick Fisher; **M:** Chris Hagian.

Mr. Wong, Detective

Please see review for *Boris Karloff DVD Double Feature*.
Movie: 🎵🎵
1938 69m/B Boris Karloff, Grant Withers; **D:** William Nigh; **W:** Houston Branch; **C:** Harry Neumann.

Mists of Avalon

Variation of the Arthurian legends is told from the perspective of the women who shape the events with their own spiritual powers. The result is a tale that is no less thrilling and exciting than the real story about Arthur, Excalibur, and the knights of the roundtable. Featuring a stellar cast and a $20 million budget, the film is rich and colorful, filled with little details and a lush production design. But ultimately it is the high-caliber performances from the likes of Anjelica Huston and Julianna Margolies that put this production on the map. Presented in a finely defined anamorphic widescreen presentation in the film's original 1.85:1 aspect ratio—as opposed to the open matte transfer seen on TV—the image now displays the real composition of the frames, showing off the beautifully framed pictures that Edel and his crew captured. Colors are vibrant and natural, creating the fantastic but realistic look the filmmakers strived for. Flesh tones are neutral and colors are strong without oversaturation. Blacks are deep, giving the image very good visual depth without breaking up. The compression has also been done carefully and doesn't show any signs of pixelation or other artifacting. With active Surrounds, a wide sound stage, and an impressively wide dynamic range, the audio track finally lives up to the epic scale of the movie and creates an immersive sonic experience. —*GH/MM*

Movie: 🎵🎵🎵 **DVD:** 🎵🎵🎵 ½
Warner Home Video (UPC 0539396636-24). Widescreen (1.85:1) anamorphic. Dolby Digital 5.1 Surround. $19.98. Snapper. *LANG:* English; French. *SUB:* English; French; Spanish; Portuguese. *FEATURES:*

Costume designs • Additional scenes • Photo gallery • Storyboards.

2001 180m/C Julianna Margulies, Anjelica Huston, Samantha Mathis, Edward Atterton, Joan Allen, Michael Vartan, Hans Matheson, Caroline Goodall, Michael Byrne, Clive Russell, Mark Lewis Jones; *D:* Uli Edel; *W:* Gavin Scott; *C:* Vilmos Zsigmond; *M:* Lee Holdridge.

Mitchell

Please see review for *Mystery Science Theater 3000 "Mitchell."*
Movie: ♫

1975 (R) 90m/C Joe Don Baker, Linda Evans, Martin Balsam, John Saxon, Merlin Olsen, Harold J. Stone; *D:* Andrew V. McLaglen; *W:* Ian Kennedy Martin; *C:* Harry Stradling Jr.; *M:* Jerry Styner.

Mo' Money

If you like the Wayans Brothers then expect to laugh your butt off at this uneven comedy. Damon is an ex-con trying to make it in the outside world. His girlfriend is helping him along. Things get out of hand; thin comedy ensues. Film does have a few good laughs but they're too few and far between. Thank goodness these guys got better. DVD is in good form. Sound is crisp. —*DE*
Movie: ♫♫ *DVD:* ♫♫ ½
Columbia Tristar (cat #07880, UPC 04339-6078802). Widescreen; full frame. Dolby Surround. $24.98. Keepcase. *LANG:* English. *SUB:* English; French. *CAP:* English. *FEATURES:* 28 chapters.
1992 (R) 97m/C Damon Wayans, Marlon Wayans, Stacey Dash, Joe Santos, John Diehl, Harry J. Lennix, Mark Beltzman, Quincy Wong, Larry Brandenburg, Almayvonne; *D:* Peter Macdonald; *W:* Damon Wayans; *C:* Don Burgess; *M:* Jay Gruska.

Mob Story [BFS]

Please see review for *Great Mafia Movies 2.*
Movie: ♫ ½
1990 (R) 98m/C John Vernon, Margot Kidder, Al Waxman, Kate Vernon; *D:* Gabriel Markiw, Jancarlo Markiw.

Mobile Suit Gundam: The Battle Begins! Vol. 1

This is the Japanese-animated giant robot series that started it all. While the initial run of the series was a flop, hit reruns, a Gundam cult following, and immense tie-in toy success led to a plethora of spin-offs, rip-offs, and further developments in the Gundam story line. Far in the future, mankind has spread to floating space-colonies contained within gigantic rotating space stations (designs which were clearly the "inspiration" for the station in *Babylon 5*). When the republic of Zeon wages a war of independence against Earth, heavy casualties are inflicted on both sides. Armed with gigantic "Mobile Suits" (giant robot-sized battle armor manned by a sin-

gle pilot) the republic is unstoppable, until one of the colonies develops a powerful suit of their own—"Gundam." In these episodes, teenager Amuro finds his colony attacked and becomes the pilot of the Gundam, facing off in battles with the enemies. He finds himself pitted repeatedly with the charismatic leader of Zeon, Char, who pilots a fast mobile suit called "The Red Comet." Exciting and original, the series exists in a well-thought-out world full of rich story possibilities. The teenaged robot pilot has become a staple (or cliché) of the genre, but seems fresh and well-motivated here. Most refreshing is the adult tone of the story. Despite the primary marketing focus of giant robot battles, the focus is on the characters, and the various battles always have a death-toll. While it takes a few episodes to establish the world of the story, it's the feeling of entering a self-contained world (which is revealed in pieces) that makes the series so compelling. This disc contains episodes 1–5 of the 43-episode series. The disc series should run to 10 volumes. The disc features a pristine print source with stunning, bright colors. Detail is so good that it reveals occasional scuff marks and flaws in the original animation. Aside from a digitized look to the diagonal edges of objects, this is a superb rendition. Although the episodes in this series are only presented in a dubbed English-language version, the quality of the voicework is excellent and fits the animation perfectly. The sound is surprisingly full, bold, and exciting for a mono track. Except for the end credit song (which reveals a flawed source recording), the entire program sounds excellent. —*DG* **AKA:** *Kido Senshi Gundam; First Gundam.*
Movie: ♫♫♫ *DVD:* ♫♫♫ ½
Bandai Ent. (cat #1770, UPC 669198177-095). Full frame. Mono. $24.98. Keepcase. *LANG:* English. *FEATURES:* Episodes 1–5 • Mobile Suite Encyclopedia • Insert card • Sticker. Also available: Vol. 2, cat.#1771; Vol. 3, #1772; Vol. 4, #1773; Vol. 5, #1774.
1979 125m/C *JP D:* Yoshiyuki Tomino; *M:* Takeo Watanabe, Yuji Matsuyama.

Mobile Suit Gundam Wing: Operation 1

Far in the future, mankind is living both on Earth and in enormous floating space colonies that orbit the Earth. As tensions between the two domains increases, the colonies launch five powerful battle suits to Earth, disguised as falling meteors. The five disparate 15-year-old pilots, including the psychotic suicidal lead Heero, begin to launch a series of destructive attacks on Earth military installations. This spinoff of the *Mobile Suit Gundam* series is interesting and ambitious, but difficult as entertainment. The protagonists are essentially terrorists and their rampant destruction and murder of unknowing military personnel and pilots only serves to reduce audience sympathy. The first few episodes start off a bit slow, focusing primarily on the unsympa-

thetic Heero's many irrational outbursts and suicide attempts before building a stronger sense of story and character in episode 5. Although the series seems to attempt a kind of moral ambiguity for both warring factions, the morally reprehensible actions of both sides are very troubling. The episodes are colorful and the character designs are strong, but the animation is fairly undistinguished. The disc features colors that are vivid and distortion-free, though there's a surplus of digital edge noise on moving objects. The multi-channel sound is excellent. —*DG*
Movie: ♫♫ ½ *DVD:* ♫♫♫
Bandai Ent. (cat #1670, UPC 669198167-096). Full frame. Dolby Digital Surround. $24.98. Keepcase. *LANG:* Japanese. *SUB:* English. *FEATURES:* Insert booklet with episode listings • 5 chapters per episode. Also available: "Operation 2," cat.#1671, "3," #1672; "4," #1673; "5," #1674.
1995 125m/C *JP*

Molly

Elizabeth Shue plays Molly, a 28-year-old woman who is mentally handicapped. The way Shue plays the role combined with the situations she's put into make the character seem too cartoonish. The film involves Molly's brother (the fantastic Eckhart, who is wasted in this role), who finds himself taking care of her, and deciding to go through with hospital tests that could improve her mental ability. Lines fall flat one right after another and the general level of dialogue makes the lowest of TV movies look like Shakespeare—everything is so overly dramatic that the film becomes unbearable. Eckhart and the rest of the supporting cast are fine, but don't make much of an impression. Scenes are incredibly manipulative, the music is overdone, and the plotting is simply bizarre. This is a particularly awful movie—it's been edited down to 87 minutes and even that feels like absolute torture. Disc looks decent overall; the picture has a rather flat look to it, with images that are adequately sharp and show good detail. Colors are natural and occasionally bright and never suffer from bleeding. There are a few marks and scratches on the print material used for the transfer. Sound is fine, if unremarkable. —*AB/DG*
Movie: ♫ *DVD:* ♫♫♫
MGM Home Ent. (UPC 027616744821). Widescreen (1.85:1) anamorphic. Dolby Digital Surround. $14.95. Keepcase. *LANG:* English. *CAP:* English. *FEATURES:* Theatrical trailer • 24 chapters.
1999 (PG-13) 87m/C Elisabeth Shue, Aaron Eckhart, Jill(ian) Hennessey, Thomas Jane, D.W. Moffett, Elizabeth Mitchell, Robert Harper, Elaine Hendrix, Michael Paul Chan, Lucy Alexis Liu; *D:* John Duigan; *W:* Dick Christie; *C:* Gabriel Beristain; *M:* Trevor Jones.

Mommie Dearest

A biographic film (spanning over two decades) about actress Joan Crawford based on the book by her revenge-seeking adopted daughter, Christina. Intense drama is paced and written more like a thriller. It features an incredible performance by Dunaway and a fantastic supporting cast headed by Forrest and Scarwid. Crawford is depicted as a true obsessive-compulsive psycho, unable and unwilling to give her children any more than token affection. Under the mistaken impression that she'll spoil them, she ends up terrorizing them into obeying her, treating them more like dogs. It's gripping and entertaining, but some characters and events are only given cursory development. The "wire-hangers" scene where Crawford goes berserk in her daughter's room for no discernible reason has become a classic. The film's highly quotable dialogue, histrionics, and psychotic depiction of Crawford have made it a camp favorite in some circles, but it's a much more frightening and well-crafted film than that honor would suggest. The disc features a beautiful transfer with a rich "filmic" look and perfect colors and flesh tones. The subject matter doesn't necessitate much demand on a Surround system but the sound is crisp, warm, and satisfying. The trailer is interesting and the photos are fairly slim. —DG

Movie: 🎬🎬🎬 **DVD:** 🎬🎬🎬 ½
Paramount (cat #01263, UPC 097360126-341). Widescreen (1.85:1) anamorphic. Dolby Digital 5.1. $29.99. Keepcase. *LANG:* English; French. *SUB:* English. *CAP:* English. *FEATURES:* Theatrical trailer • Photo gallery • 15 chapters • Insert card with chapter listings.
1981 (PG) 129m/C Faye Dunaway, Diana Scarwid, Steve Forrest, Mara Hobel, Rutanya Alda, Harry Goz, Howard da Silva; **D:** Frank Perry; **W:** Frank Perry, Robert Getchell, Frank Yablans; **C:** Paul Lohmann; **M:** Henry Mancini. *AWARDS:* Golden Raspberries '81: Worst Picture, Worst Actress (Dunaway), Worst Support. Actor (Forrest), Worst Support. Actress (Scarwid), Worst Screenplay.

Mom's Outta Sight

Substandard kiddie SF comedy exudes cheapness. Special effects and props are bargain-basement material. The story has something to do with a matter transmission machine that turns a sexy woman into a mincing man and makes another (Williamson) invisible. The only redeeming feature is an all-too-brief cameo by Brinke Stevens. The dim DVD image is indistinguishable from VHS tape. —MM

Movie: 🎬 **DVD:** 🎬
20th Century Fox (cat #2002162, UPC 024543021629). Full frame. Dolby Digital Surround Stereo. $19.98. Keepcase. *LANG:* English. *SUB:* English. *FEATURES:* Trailer • Talent files • 16 chapters.
2001 (PG) 89m/C Hannes Jaenicke, Melissa Williamson, Steve Scionti, Ariauna Albright, Brinke Stevens; **D:** Peter Stewart; **W:** Sean O'Bannon; **C:** Theo Angell; **M:** Jay Bolton.

Mondo Balordo

Please see review of *Mondo Drive-In Double Feature*.
Movie: 🎬
1964 86m/C Franz Drago; **D:** Robert Montero; **W:** Albert T. Viola; **Nar:** Boris Karloff.

Mondo Drive-In Double Feature

This nutzo double feature begins with *Primitive Love*, part–"mondo" compilation, part–Jayne Mansfield sex comedy involving a dance in a grass skirt and a modest striptease. Neither is very entertaining, but Jayne does have to deal with a comedian who must somehow be genetically linked to Jim Carrey. The second half, *Mondo Balordo*, is a more conventional "mondo" that juxtaposes shots of a beauty contest in Las Vegas with Japanese female wrestling/bondage stuff and wild animals feeding on each other and being slaughtered. Though both are a bit faded, image quality is generally very good, with surprisingly little print damage. Sound is fine. —MM

Movie: 🎬 **DVD:** 🎬🎬🎬
Image Ent. (cat #ID0809SWDVD, UPC 014-381080926). Full frame. Dolby Digital Mono. $24.98. Keepcase. *LANG:* English. *FEATURES:* 32 chapters • "Let's Go to the Drive-In" wraparound material • 11 trailers • 5 short films • Gallery of exploitation art with announcements.
1964 C

Mondo Mod / The Hippie Revolt

Younger viewers in the early years of the 21st century will watch these films with astonishment and (possibly) convulsive laughter. True, they exaggerate certain aspects of the reality of the late 1960s, but the attitudes, clothes, and hairstyles on display here are real. Lamentable, but real. The films are less true documentaries than compilations of found footage. Most of it seems to have been found in Los Angeles and San Francisco. Using real footage and staged scenes, they show people shopping, riding motorcycles and surfboards, dancing (oh, how we danced), taking drugs, protesting this and that, attending love-ins, etc. *Mondo Mod* claims to star "The Youth of the World." For all their flaws and limitations, the films do a pretty good job of showing just how obnoxious everybody could be in those years. On *Hippie* the image is generally grainy with some harsh colors (photography is from young Laszlo Kovacs and Vilmos Zsigmond); *Mondo* generally looks better. Mono sound is O.K. The technical bone rating is based on the quantity of the extras, not quality. Peace. —MM

Movie: 🎬🎬🎬 **DVD:** 🎬🎬🎬
Image Ent. (cat #ID10375SWDVD, UPC 014381103724). Full frame. Dolby Digital Mono. $24.98. Keepcase. *LANG:* English. *FEATURES:* 12 chapters per film • Commentary: Johnny Legend, Eric Caidin • 7

trailers • Alternate footage • 3 short features • Gallery of drive-in exploitation art.
1967 72m/C D: Peter Perry; **C:** Laszlo Kovacs, Vilmos Zsigmond; **Nar:** Harve Humble.

Money Buys Happiness

Money (Weatherford) and Georgia (Murphy) are on the verge of divorce when a friend commits suicide and leaves them an upright piano. Their problems crystallize as they attempt to transport the instrument 50 blocks across town. That's a curious premise for a comedy but this one manages to generate some genuine wit. The film has that familiar, slightly underfed indie-prod look, and there's little that DVD can do to improve it. Sound is fine for the sharp dialogue. The director's introduction mentioned on the box copy is nowhere to be found. —MM

Movie: 🎬🎬 ½ **DVD:** 🎬🎬
Vanguard Intl. Cinema (cat #VF9172, UPC 658769917239). Widescreen letterboxed. $29.95. Keepcase. *LANG:* English. *FEATURES:* 12 chapters • Trailer.
1999 104m/C Megan Murphy, Jeff Weatherford, Michael Chick, Cynthia Whalen, Caveh Zahedi; **D:** Gregg Lachow; **W:** Gregg Lachow; **C:** Jamie Hook; **M:** Jim Ragland.

Money Talks

Slightly above-average action/buddy comedy stars Tucker and in a nonexistent performance, Charlie Sheen. The film mainly revolves around Tucker, who plays Franklin Hatchett, a small-time ticket scalper/con-artist who is sent off to prison after being busted early on in the film. On the way to the jail, he gets tangled up in a getaway put together by Villard. The police, though, think he was behind the whole affair and are out to get him—unfortunately, so is Villard and his entire team. Not knowing what to do, Franklin calls James Russell (Sheen) and offers the reporter an exclusive interview in exchange for a place to hide out. Tucker steals each and every scene. He carries the movie wonderfully and it's fun to watch him work with the lines, which are standard action movie fare. There are a few good action sequences, but everything takes a background role to Tucker, and in this case, that's O.K. The picture is sharp and smooth, and detail is consistently good. Colors are strong as well, although not always terribly vibrant; just accurate and natural. Flesh tones are fine, and black level remains solid. A full-frame version is on the flip side. The Surround soundtrack is good, but its use is not predominant. Effects are most strong in the action sequences and for the funky Lalo Schifrin score. —AB/DG

Movie: 🎬🎬🎬 **DVD:** 🎬🎬🎬
New Line Home Video (UPC 7940434634-26). Widescreen (2.35:1) anamorphic; full frame. Dolby Digital 5.1 Surround. $19.98. Snapper. *LANG:* English; French. *SUB:* English; French; Spanish. *CAP:* English. *FEA-*

TURES: Trailer ● Production notes ● 24 chapters.
1997 (R) 92m/C Chris Tucker, Charlie Sheen, Heather Locklear, Paul Sorvino, Veronica Cartwright, Elise Neal, Paul Gleason, Larry Hankin, Daniel Roebuck, David Warner, Michael Wright, Gerard Ismael; **D:** Brett Ratner; **W:** Joel Cohen, Alec Sokolow; **C:** Russell Carpenter, Robert Primes; **M:** Lalo Schifrin. AWARDS: NOM: Golden Raspberries '97: Worst New Star (Tucker).

Monkey Business

Absent-minded scientist Barnaby Fulton (Grant) and his wife Edwina (Rogers) are settling into middle age, when his experiments with vitality result in a rejuvenation formula. Unfortunately, Barnaby doesn't know he's succeeded, because a lab chimpanzee has done the final mixing of ingredients by accident, and dumped the dose in the lab water cooler. After he takes a drink, Barnaby's eyesight improves, along with his attitude: like a teenager, he takes an immediate interest in fast cars, silly pranks, and the office secretary, Lois (Monroe). DVD has no trouble with the full-frame black-and-white image. Title is part of the Marilyn Monroe: The Diamond Collection, Vol. 2. —GE/MM
Movie: ♫♫♫ **DVD:** ♫♫♫
20th Century Fox (UPC 024543035121). Full frame. Dolby Digital Stereo; Mono. $19.98. Keepcase. LANG: English; French. SUB: English; Spanish. CAP: English. FEATURES: Restoration comparison ● Still gallery ● Trailer.
1952 97m/B Cary Grant, Ginger Rogers, Charles Coburn, Marilyn Monroe, Hugh Marlowe, Larry Keating, George Winslow; **D:** Howard Hawks; **W:** Ben Hecht, Charles Lederer, I.A.L. Diamond; **C:** Milton Krasner; **M:** Leigh Harline.

Monkeybone

Weird comedy about comatose cartoonist Stu Miley (Fraser), who must escape from his own comic fantasy world in order to return to consciousness after an accident. Monkeybone, a chimp embodiment of a teenager's libido from Stu's Show Me the Monkey animated pilot, is the focus of the rest of the film as he escapes from the underworld and "steals" Stu's body to romance his awaiting girlfriend (Fonda). Kattan is funny as the organ donor and Turturro, who puts his considerable talent to voicing a monkey, is successful, although some may tire of the one-note libidinous simian humor. Based on the graphic novel Dark Town by Kaja Blackley. I'll admit this is one of my guilty pleasures but I really got a kick out of the film. This is a good-looking and loaded DVD. The scenes in the underworld are stunningly colorful and the saturated colors never bleed a speck. The image stays sharp with the exception of a couple of obvious bluescreen scenes where some grain is apparent. Most of the time, though, the disc will blow you away. The DTS soundtrack is spectacular and the Dolby Digital 5.1 is not far behind. When you've finished the movie, there are some extended scenes, several of which add significantly to the story, and an interesting "animation study" of seven scenes in which the before and after CGI composites are compared. The commentary is a bit slow; director Selick seems a little put out or bored. —JO
Movie: ♫♫♫ **DVD:** ♫♫♫ ½
20th Century Fox (cat #2001935, UPC 024543019350). Widescreen (1.85:1) anamorphic. Dolby Digital 5.1; DTS 5.1; Dolby Surround. $26.98. Keepcase. LANG: English (DD5.1; DTS5.1; DS); French (DS). SUB: English; Spanish. CAP: English. FEATURES: 22 chapters ● Theatrical trailer ● TV spots ● Commentary: director Henry Selick ● 11 extended scenes with optional commentary ● Alternate ending ● 7 animation studies with optional commentary ● Photo gallery ● Dual-layered RSDL.
2001 (PG-13) 92m/C Brendan Fraser, Bridget Fonda, Whoopi Goldberg, Chris Kattan, Dave Foley, Giancarlo Esposito, Rose McGowan, Megan Mullally, Lisa Zane; **D:** Henry Selick; **W:** Sam Hamm; **C:** Andrew Dunn; **M:** Anne Dudley; **V:** John Turturro.

Monster from the Ocean Floor

This is not really a monster movie. It's a film about a vacuous blonde and her fantasies about a one-eyed amoeba, and the man she loves, a scientist with an underwater pod who doesn't believe her story about the amoeba. There is a semi-interesting (for 1954) Jules Vernesque side plot about using the sea for farmland. The action starts after an inane "World of Disney"–style voice-over informs us that the beach scenes were filmed on the beach in Mexico and the underwater scenes were filmed underwater in Mexico. Then we are treated to our heroine Julie (Kimball) speaking with a little Mexican boy. He tells her the story of the sea monster and swears that his father was eaten by it. "He went out and never came back," he tells her. "Was he drinking?" she replies. She becomes obsessed with finding the one-eyed monster and even plies Pablo, "the reprobate," as it says in the titles, with tequila. Pablo, by the way, is played by the director, Ordung (I know, you're thinking, or dung what?). There is some talk by Pablo and his mother of feeding "the fair one" to the monster because legend has it that the attacks will stop if they do, and hey, they can't afford to lose anymore cows. I became excited at the prospect, but Pablo loses his nerve to too much tequila and the sight of Julie's unbridled cleavage. Julie finds the monster, which looks like a giant Chinese lantern with arms, and a big magic marker pupil drawn on its head. As harp music swells and it seems the slow-moving lantern of a monster may finally get his blonde, Julie is rescued by the man she loves as he drives his underwater pod where the sun doesn't shine (underwater that is). Overall, this is a great way to waste 64 minutes and a bottle of tequila. (Invite friends.) The sound is mono and the picture is TV broadcast quality. —CA AKA: It Stalked the Ocean Floor; Monster Maker.
Movie: ♫♫ **DVD:** ♫♫
Rhino (cat #R2972467, UPC 603497246-724). Full frame. $9.95. Snapper. LANG: English. FEATURES: 12 chapters.
1954 66m/C Anne Kimball, Stuart Wade, Jonathan Haze, Wyott Ordung, David Garcia, Dick Pinner; **D:** Wyott Ordung; **W:** William Danch; **C:** Floyd Crosby; **M:** Andre Brummer.

The Monster That Challenged the World

Huge eggs are discovered in the Salton Sea. They eventually hatch into huge, carnivorous pop-eyed caterpillars. The creatures are really too silly to move this one into the first rank of 1950s big critter SF movies, but the action is still enjoyable. DVD appears to have been made from very well-preserved original elements. The underwater scenes are as murky as they've ever been, but the rest is fine black and white. —MM
Movie: ♫♫ ½ **DVD:** ♫♫ ½
MGM Home Ent. (cat #1002352, UPC 027-616865632). Full frame. Dolby Digital Mono. $19.98. Keepcase. LANG: English. SUB: French; Spanish. CAP: English. FEATURES: 16 chapters.
1957 83m/B Tim Holt, Audrey Dalton, Hans Conried, Harlen Ward, Max (Casey Adams) Showalter, Mimi Gibson, Gordon Jones; **D:** Arnold Laven; **W:** Pat Fielder; **C:** Lester White; **M:** Heinz Roemheld.

Monsters Crash the Pajama Party Spook Show Spectacular

Spook Shows were traveling live-acts featuring magicians, monsters, and funhouse antics. Usually presented late at night, after the main feature was over or as a counterpart to a feature film, the acts were interactive, with monsters grabbing girls out of the audience, etc. This collection of oddball shorts and strange vignettes were utilized in Spook Shows around the country. Monsters Crash the Pajama Party features a mad scientist (and his gorilla) preying on a group of teenagers who elect to spend the night in a haunted house. It's more of a curio than anything else. There's no acting or story on display and it sorely needs the interactive environment of its original venue. A second feature, Tormented, is a fairly standard cheapie from schlockmeister Bert I. Gordon. A doctor drowns his girlfriend and is haunted by guilt, and her specter. More silly than scary, it's filled with some unintentional laughs and a moment or two of suspense. The rest of the clips are fun and valuable as historical documents, but have no real artistic value. Overall, it's an entertaining package that conveys a nos-

talgic sense of an extinct form of entertainment. As expected, the quality of the materials used varies wildly. The opening of *Monsters Crash* is very battered and scratchy, but afterwards is fairly clean (if occasionally soft) with seemingly accurate colors. *Tormented* is somewhat grainy with contrasts that are a bit harsh. It's obviously a well-used print, but it's probably the best the film has looked on video. The audio is usually intelligible, if a bit crackly and squawky at times. The commentaries do a nice job of detailing the world of the traveling Spook Show and the booklet is terrific. The menus are designed to challenge. There are several graphics featuring skeletons, graveyards, etc., and clicking on one of the objects takes you to a short or feature. Nothing is labeled, and it's a chore for those who only want a fully functional menu. For those who like exploring Easter eggs, it's a fun feature, done in the spirit of the collection. —DG
Movie: 🦴🦴 **DVD:** 🦴🦴
Image Ent. (cat #ID08055SWDVD, UPC 01-4381080520). Full frame. Mono. $19.99. Keepcase. *LANG:* English. *FEATURES:* "Hypnoscope!" intro • Commentary: Philip Morris • Commentary: Harry Wise • Illustrated essay: "How to Put on Your Own Spook Show!" • Insert booklet "Secrets of the Spook show" • "The Asylum of the Insane" 3-D short • 2 pairs of 3-D glasses • 48 minutes of Spook Show previews • Horror Home Productions shorts • "Don't Be Afraid" short short • "Spook House Ride" • "Drive-In Werewolf" • "Chased by Monsters" • Stills and exploitation art with radio spot rarities.
1965 31m/C Peter J. D'Noto, Vic McGee, James Reason, Pauline Hilcurt, Charles Egan, Joseph Ormond; **D:** David L. Hewitt; **W:** David L. Hewitt, Jay Lister; **C:** David L. Hewitt, Austin McKay.

Monty Python Live

This box-set should be a must-have for Python fans. The two-disc set contains four different programs. First, there is the 1982 concert film, *Monty Python Live at the Hollywood Bowl,* which offers the troupe doing some of the best-known skits in a live forum. Next, we have "Monty Python's Flying Circus: Live at Aspen" (AKA "U.S. Comedy Arts Festival Tribute to Monty Python") from 1998. This is more of a tribute/retrospective, with host Robert Klein taking the group through their more memorable moments. This is followed by "Parrot Sketch Not Included: 20 Years of Python," which is simply a collection of clips from the *Monty Python's Flying Circus* TV show. Other than the clips, the highlight of this segment is the cynical quips from host Steve Martin. Finally, we have "Fliegender Zirkus," which is an episode of *Flying Circus* which was prepared for German television with English subtitles that aren't exactly right and has never before been available in America. As this DVD set features many different source materials, the quality varies. *Hollywood Bowl* shows noticeable grain, while

"Live at Aspen" is broadcast quality. Also, the various clips from *Flying Circus* show different degrees of quality. Overall, the material presented here looks fine and true Python fans won't let any minor defects get in their way. —ML/CA
Movie: 🦴🦴🦴 **DVD:** 🦴🦴🦴
A&E (cat #AAE-70353, UPC 7339617035-35). Full frame. Dolby Digital Stereo. $39.95. Box-set: Keepcase. *LANG:* English. *FEATURES:* Cast filmographies • Glossary • Bonus footage • 2 chapters per disc • Post-Python troupe highlights • Pythonisms • Confusing Musings • Bleeding Critics.
1972 270m/C *GB*

Monty Python's Flying Circus Set 1

The winning combination of dry British humor and some of the most clever skits ever thought up made Monty Python one of the most consistently funny and amazing comedy teams ever to hop the pond. It also helps that the material was presented by a troupe with near-perfect timing with both physical comedy and line delivery. Their biggest talent is making fun of British manners and presentation. Skits like "How to Recognize Different Types of Trees from Quite a Long Way Away," or "Undressing in Public," are hilarious for their dedication to mimicking PBS—PBS on a bender that is. They also love to parody the British documentary as shown by the humorously slow burning, "The Funniest Joke in the World," about a joke created as a tool against the Germans during World War II. The group is, however, true to the memory of Shakespeare with most of the women's roles played by the six men that made up Python, resulting in some of the ugliest, funniest hags ever to take the stage. Also of note is the amazing animation segues created by Terry Gilliam, before computers mind you, that are shows in themselves. The box states that the DVD format allows you to enjoy the original scratches, pops, and hisses with crystal clarity and much of that is true. The series was shot on film and very little restoration, short of cleaning, has been done for the film. It still looks fairly good with clear color and good sound. (Sets #2–7 are also available on DVD.) —CA
Movie: 🦴🦴🦴 ½ **DVD:** 🦴🦴 ½
A&E (cat #AAE-70041, UPC 7339617004-11). Full frame. $39.95. Keepcase (2 to a box). *LANG:* English. *FEATURES:* 6 chapters per disc • Pythonisms Glossary • Gilli-animations art gallery.
1969 204m/C *GB*

Mood Swingers

A group of British friends living in an inherited mansion invite some American friends over for a Dionysian weekend. But a terrorist group known as "the Conceptualists" seems to be moving closer. Another British drug film that's far too hip for its own good; its attempts to be clever and meaningful come off as merely preten-

tious. The picture quality is very good in places, but suffers from inconsistent colors. The dialogue is delivered clearly, but the music lacks energy. —BG
Movie: 🦴 **DVD:** 🦴🦴 ½
Image Ent. (cat #OVED1132DVD, UPC 014381113228). Widescreen (2.35:1) anamorphic. Dolby Stereo. $19.99. Keepcase. *LANG:* English. *FEATURES:* 16 chapters • Music and sound effects track.
2000 (R) 101m/C Paul Bettany, Hayley Carr, Katy Carmichael, Charlie Condou, Alexandra Gilbreath, William Marsh; **D:** William Marsh; **W:** Martin Amis, William Marsh; **C:** Daniel Cohen.

A Moon for the Misbegotten

In Eugene O'Neil's classic play, an Irish-American tenant farmer (Flanders) convinces his daughter to spend a night with their landlord, in hopes of convincing him to sell them the farmland. Through the course of the evening, facades are pulled back and some surprising truths emerge. Dewhurst and Robards are excellent in the lead roles, building the drama towards a well-earned emotional payoff. The picture is a bit soft and low on detail, but the mono soundtrack serves its purpose quite well. —BG
Movie: 🦴🦴🦴 ½ **DVD:** 🦴🦴🦴
Image Ent. (cat #ID1476B DDVD, UPC 014381147629). Full frame. Dolby Mono. $24.99. Keepcase. *LANG:* English. *FEATURES:* 17 chapters • Trailers • Cast bios.
1975 135m/C Jason Robards Jr., Colleen Dewhurst, Ed Flanders; **D:** Jose Quintero, Gordon Rigsby; **W:** Eugene O'Neill.

Moon of the Wolf

Sheriff Whitaker (Janssen) investigates the death of a young woman seemingly mauled by wild dogs in the bayou. While her brother Lawrence (Lewis) insists it was the man who was secretly seeing his sister, his Cajun father insists it was the "loup garou." Undistinguished, unpolished TV film features a likeable Janssen (in desperate need of an authoritative haircut), an abundance of red herrings, superfluous scripting, and needlessly developed characters. The audience is about 20 minutes ahead of the characters in this one and the majority of the running time is spent waiting for them all to catch up. Though structured like a thriller, director Petrie deprives us of a thrilling (though obvious) revelation scene and instead unveils the identity of the wolfman matter-of-factly. Though manipulative, the last reel manages to conjure up some tension and thrills. The DVD is a notch below VHS, featuring a battered, soft print source and digital shimmer around the edges of objects. Sound is passable. The quality of the short is no better. The "DVD Dictionary" has erroneous information. —DG
Movie: 🦴🦴 **DVD:** 🦴
Brentwood (cat #44081-9, UPC 78736440-8191). Full frame. Mono. $4.99. Keep-

case. LANG: English. FEATURES: "Casper: A-Haunting We Will Go" short ● Trivia game ● DVD dictionary ● 6 chapters.
1972 74m/C David Janssen, Barbara Rush, Bradford Dillman, John Beradino, Geoffrey Lewis, Royal Dano; **D:** Daniel Petrie; **W:** Alvin Sapinsley; **C:** Richard C. Glouner; **M:** Bernardo Segall.

Moon over Tao

In 16th-century Japan, a Samurai (Hiroshi Abe) and a sorcerer (Toshiyuki Nagashima) are dispatched to discover the origins of a strange sword which can cut through solid stone. Once on their quest, they learn that the sword was forged from a meteorite, which also housed a strange orb. This orb contains the power to destroy the world. Meanwhile, three mysterious alien females are dispatched to Earth to retrieve the orb. Unfortunately, it has fallen into the hands of an evil tyrant (Takaaki Enoki) who wants to use its powers to rule the planet. Moon over Tao successfully mixes sword & sorcery action with a science-fiction slant. Director Keita Amemiya is best known for making films featuring futuristic creatures, but he tones that down here, evoking an interesting narrative and impressive fight scenes. American viewers familiar with similar films will find the pacing here a bit different, but the film is engrossing all the same. This DVD offers a beautiful widescreen transfer. The image is rich and true, showing only slight artifacting at times. The colors are impressive, and the image is always bright and consistent. The 2.0 Surround audio mix delivers clear dialogue and some well-placed rear speaker action. The lack of any real extras (even a trailer) is the only thing which hurts this DVD release. —ML
Movie: 🎵🎵🎵 **DVD:** 🎵🎵🎵
Media Blasters (cat #TSDVD-0114, UPC 631595011487). Widescreen (1.85:1) letterboxed. Dolby Surround. $29.95. Keepcase. LANG: English; Japanese. SUB: English. FEATURES: Bonus trailers ● 14 chapters.
1997 96m/C JP Toshiyuki Nagashima, Hiroshi Abe, Takaai Enoki; **D:** Keito Amamiya.

Morgan: A Suitable Case for Treatment

Offbeat comedy finds deranged artist/communist Morgan Delt (Warner) coping with his divorce from the lovely Leoni (Redgrave) by donning an ape suit. Some of the frantic humor has aged poorly, but the strong performances are still fresh. The black-and-white photography is good but somehow not as sharp as it is in Billy Liar, a similar British comedy made four years before. DVD appears to be an accurate re-creation of the original. —MM AKA: Morgan!; A Suitable Case for Treatment.
Movie: 🎵🎵🎵 **DVD:** 🎵🎵🎵
Anchor Bay (cat #DV11461, UPC 0131311-46196). Widescreen (1.66:1) anamorphic. Dolby Digital Mono. $24.98. Keepcase.

LANG: English. FEATURES: Trailer ● Talent files ● 27 chapters.
1966 93m/B GB Vanessa Redgrave, David Warner, Robert Stephens, Irene Handl, Bernard Bresslaw, Arthur Mullard, Newton Blick, Nan Munro, Graham Crowden, John Rae, Peter Collingwood, Edward Fox; **D:** Karel Reisz; **W:** David Mercer; **C:** Larry Pizer; **M:** John Dankworth. AWARDS: British Acad. '66: Screenplay; Cannes '66: Actress (Redgrave); NOM: Oscars '66: Actress (Redgrave), Costume Des. (B&W).

Morons from Outer Space

Slow-witted aliens from elsewhere in the universe crash into Earth, and become internationally famous, despite their intellectual limitations. The sight gags begin with a space ship that has fuzzy dice hanging over the fur-covered steering wheel and continue virtually nonstop until the closing credits. Most of the humor is right on target with some very good effects. Softish focus and pastel colors lead to a DVD image that displays moderate grain but no serious flaws. —MM
Movie: 🎵🎵🎵 **DVD:** 🎵🎵 ½
MGM Home Ent. (cat #1002644, UPC 027616868442). Widescreen (1.85:1) anamorphic. Dolby Digital 5.1 Surround Stereo; Mono. $14.95. Keepcase. LANG: English; French. SUB: French; Spanish. CAP: English. FEATURES: 16 chapters ● Trailer.
1985 (PG) 87m/C GB Griff Rhys Jones, Mel Smith, James B. Sikking, Dinsdale Landen, Jimmy Nail, Joanne Pearce, Paul Brown; **D:** Mike Hodges; **W:** Griff Rhys Jones, Mel Smith; **C:** Phil Meheux; **M:** Peter Brewis.

Moscow on the Hudson

In this good-natured 1984 comedy about what it means to willingly embrace the American Dream, Robin Williams plays Vladimir Ivanoff, a circus musician who takes advantage of his troupe's visit to New York City by defecting in Bloomingdale's. With only his saxophone and the bittersweet memories of the family he left behind, Vladimir jumps into the melting pot of Manhattan feet first, only to find that freedom isn't just a word but a state of mind. Williams is particularly endearing as the naïve jazzman, a Russian Alice lost in a Wonderland that grows curiouser and curiouser with each encounter. Good supporting cast helps, with Maria Conchita Alonso as Vladimir's Italian girlfriend and Cleavant Derricks as the security guard who gives Vlad his first taste of American hospitality. The disc offers full-frame and widescreen viewing options. Both transfers deliver a superb, colorful picture, if slightly grainy at times. Whether listening to the discrete Surround remix or standard Dolby Surround track, the main audio attraction is that every word of Paul Mazursky's winning script can be heard clearly. —EP

Movie: 🎵🎵🎵 **DVD:** 🎵🎵🎵
Columbia Tristar (cat #06536, UPC 04339-6065369). Widescreen (1.85:1) anamorphic; full frame. Dolby Digital 4.0; Dolby Digital Surround. $19.98. Keepcase. LANG: French. SUB: English; French; Spanish; Portuguese; Chinese; Korean; Thai. FEATURES: 28 chapters ● Commentary: director Paul Mazursky ● Theatrical trailers.
1984 (R) 115m/C Robin Williams, Maria Conchita Alonso, Cleavant Derricks, Alejandro Rey, Elya Baskin; **D:** Paul Mazursky; **W:** Paul Mazursky, Leon Capetanos; **C:** Donald McAlpine; **M:** David McHugh.

The Mothman Prophecies

With his first feature film Arlington Road, director Mark Pellington was able to combine his aggressive cinematic style with a jolting story to create a truly entertaining film. With his sophomore effort, his style is still intact, but the script never truly gels. Richard Gere stars as Washington Post reporter John Klein, who is on top of the world until he suddenly loses his wife (Messing). Two years later, while traveling to Richmond, Virginia, to interview the governor, Klein finds himself in Point Pleasant, West Virginia, with no recollection of how he got there. He learns from local police officer Connie Mills (Linney) that the local residents have been hearing and seeing strange things lately—things that look similar to drawings that Klein found in his wife's journal. These sightings of a "moth-like" creature, and the strange connection to his late wife, pique Klein's curiosity, so he decides to investigate further. Soon, Klein himself experiences odd happenings and suspects that these strange phenomenon may be an omen for an impending disaster. But what, when, and where? The film introduces an intriguing premise and certainly has a handful of creepy scenes (the "psychic phone call" being the best), but the film is far too long and never seems to really decide what it wants to be. Once the finale begins, the viewer will be impressed by how many aspects of the story are tied together, but this comes far too late, as the second act becomes redundant. Gere and Linney are very good in their roles, as is Will Patton in a supporting role as a paranoid local. Pellington's constantly moving camera and the film's great sound design add to the tension here, but the bottom line is that the picture comes off as a second-rate episode of The X-Files. This DVD does a fantastic job of presenting the film in both widescreen and full frame. The image is very sharp and clear, showing off the unusual visual style. The colors are rich and true, and the picture is relatively free from grain, although the director obviously pushes the grain at times. The Dolby Digital 5.1 audio track is very good. The atmosphere relies heavily on the use of Surround effects and a low, rumbling bass. However, the center channel has been mixed a bit low, so the dialogue is hard to hear at times. Surprisingly, the

DVD is nearly devoid of extras, containing only a trailer and a music video. —ML
Movie: 🎵🎵 ½ **DVD:** 🎵🎵🎵
Columbia Tristar (cat #07808, UPC 0433-96078086). Widescreen (2.35:1) anamorphic; full frame. Dolby Digital 5.1. $27.96. Keepcase. *LANG:* English; French. *SUB:* English; French; Spanish. *CAP:* English. *FEATURES:* Theatrical trailer • Music video • 28 chapters.
2002 (PG-13) 119m/C Richard Gere, Laura Linney, Will Patton, Debra Messing, Lucinda Jenney, Alan Bates, David Eigenberg, Nesbitt Blaisdell; *D:* Mark Pellington; *W:* Richard Hatem; *C:* Fred Murphy; *M:* Tomandandy.

Motorama
The tale of the most bizarre road trip ever taken by a 10-year-old. Gus (Michael) runs, or more to the point, drives away from his constantly bickering, battering parents in a stolen red hot rod, and all the cash from his piggy bank, in a quest to win $5 million by collecting all of the letters in the word "Motorama." He picks up letters on cards at each participating gas station with a minimum purchase of $5 worth of gas. It sounds easy, but this was written by Joseph Minion, the guy who wrote *After Hours,* and you know how that turned out (and if you don't, get thee to a video rental house right away). What starts out as a search for riches and the girl in his 10-year-old dreams leaves him with an eye patch and a full-sleeve tattoo that says "TORA." Ambiguous to the end, unexplainable to your friends, and populated by every wacky star of the '80s from Martha Quinn to Meat Loaf, *Motorama* is quite the trip. The picture looks pretty good, but there is some bleed in the reds, of which there are quiet a few, and the sound is decent but not fabulous with some muffling which requires a trip to the volume button. —CA
Movie: 🎵🎵 ½ **DVD:** 🎵🎵 ½
Columbia Tristar (cat #06531, UPC 04339-6065314). Full frame. Dolby Digital. $19.95. Keepcase. *LANG:* English. *SUB:* English; French; Spanish; Portuguese; Chinese; Korean; Thai. *CAP:* English. *FEATURES:* 28 chapters • Trailer.
1991 (R) 89m/C Jordan Christopher Michael, Martha Quinn, Flea, Michael J. Pollard, Meat Loaf Aday, Drew Barrymore, Garrett Morris, Robin Duke, Sandy Baron, Mary Woronov, Susan Tyrrell, John Laughlin, John Diehl, Robert Picardo, Jack Nance, Vince Edwards, Dick Miller, Allyce Beasley, Shelley Berman; *D:* Barry Shils; *W:* Joe Minion; *C:* Joseph Yacoe; *M:* Andy Summers.

Moulin Rouge [SE]
Director Baz Luhrmann's tale of turn-of-the-(19th) century Paris is so furiously paced with such aggressive musical numbers that it feels like an MTV pep rally. The story concerns the romance between courtesan Satine (Kidman) and innocent writer Christian (McGregor), but the spectacle is Luhrmann's real point. The movie's key

gimmick of incorporating late 20th-century rock music into the period setting simply doesn't work for many viewers (this one included). That said, the production is high-energy, high-calorie eye candy with supersaturated colors and near constant movement. DVD captures all of that flamboyance, and may actually provide a better medium for the film than the theatre. To my tastes, this one is much more enjoyable in measured doses. The extensive extras are on the second disc. —MM
Movie: 🎵🎵 ½ **DVD:** 🎵🎵🎵 ½
20th Century Fox (UPC 024543008705). Widescreen (1.85:1) anamorphic. Dolby Digital 5.1 Surround Stereo; DTS 5.1 Surround. $29.98. Special packaging. *LANG:* English; Spanish. *SUB:* English. *FEATURES:* 36 chapters • Commentaries • "Making of" featurettes • Script development featurettes • Multi-angle scene options • Deleted and extended scenes • Many Easter eggs • Music videos • Trailers • Still gallery.
2001 (PG-13) 126m/C *AU US* Nicole Kidman, Ewan McGregor, John Leguizamo, Jim Broadbent, Garry McDonald, Kylie Minogue, Richard Roxburgh, David Wenham, Natalie Mendoza; *D:* Baz Luhrmann; *W:* Baz Luhrmann, Craig Pearce; *C:* Donald McAlpine; *M:* Craig Armstrong. *AWARDS:* Australian Film Inst. '01: Cinematog., Costume Des., Film Editing, Sound; Golden Globes '02: Actor—Mus./Comedy, Actress—Mus./Comedy (Kidman), Score; L.A. Film Critics '01: Support. Actor (Broadbent); Natl. Bd. of Review '01: Film, Support. Actor (Broadbent); *NOM:* Directors Guild '01: Director (Luhrmann); Golden Globes '02: Actor—Mus./Comedy (McGregor), Director (Luhrmann), Song ("Come What May"); Broadcast Film Critics '01: Actress (Kidman), Director (Luhrmann), Film.

The Mountain Men
DVD takes a baby step backward with this release. There's not much to the story of Bill Tyler (Heston) and Henry Frapp (Keith), two frontier fur trappers whose ruggedness is pure Hollywood. But why would the studio release a big outdoor adventure like this only in a full-frame ratio? That effectively eliminates any worth the DVD might have had. Otherwise, image is acceptable. —MM
Movie: 🎵 ½ **DVD:** 🎵 ½
Columbia Tristar (cat #08999, UPC 04339-6089990). Full frame. Dolby Digital Stereo. $24.95. Keepcase. *LANG:* English; French. *SUB:* English; French; Spanish; Portuguese; Chinese; Korean; Thai. *CAP:* English. *FEATURES:* 28 chapters.
1980 (R) 102m/C Charlton Heston, Brian Keith, John Glover, Seymour Cassel, Victor Jory; *D:* Richard Lang; *W:* Fraser Heston; *C:* Michael Hugo; *M:* Michel Legrand.

Mountain of the Cannibal God
Susan Stevenson (Andress) persuades Dr. Edward Foster (Keach) to accompany her

into the jungle to find her missing anthropologist husband. They find a tribe of cannibals who indulge in all sorts of nasty practices that run the gamut from bestiality (in an indescribably grotesque and funny moment) to coating a naked Ursula with mud. Despite the content, this is one of the most polished of the cannibal/mondo exploitation that was briefly popular in the late '70s. DVD image ranges from good to very good. —MM
AKA: Il Montagna di Dio Cannibale; Slave of the Cannibal God.
Movie: woof **DVD:** 🎵🎵🎵
Anchor Bay (cat #DV11858, UPC 0131311-85898). Widescreen (2.35:1) anamorphic. Dolby Digital Mono. $24.98. Keepcase. *LANG:* English. *FEATURES:* 27 chapters • Trailer • "Legacy of the Cannibal God" featurette • Poster and still gallery.
1979 103m/C *IT* Stacy Keach, Ursula Andress, Claudio Cassinelli, Franco Fantasia; *D:* Sergio Martino; *M:* Guido de Angelis, Maurizio de Angelis.

The Movies Begin (1894–1913)
This superb collection is essentially Film 101 in a box. It illustrates the first days of moving images from Eadweard Muybridge's 1880s consecutive photographs that approximate motion to the narratives of D.W. Griffith. Nobody should be surprised that these works begin with naked women, explore violence and special effects, and end with powerful images of a speeding train chasing a heroine in distress. (That film, *The Girl and Her Trust,* also uses a gimmick with a bullet that could be reused today.) Winsor McCay's animation, slapstick, and social realism are included, too. Most of the images are simple black and white; some are brightly tinted. Thomas Edison, George Méliès, Louis Lumière, and Edwin S. Porter are also represented. Most of the films are very short. Some contain brief explanatory commentary by Barry Salt. More substantial text notes by Charles Musser are a separate option. DVDs were created from materials of the British Film Institute and the overall level of quality is excellent. Of course, given the age of the 133 works, many display considerable damage in places. That should not deter anyone with an interest in early cinema. Select contents: *Homage to Eadweard Muybridge, The Kiss, The Great Train Robbery, The Golden Beetle, A Trip to the Moon, The Impossible Voyage, The Black Imp, The Mysterious Retort, Aladin Or the Wonderful Lamp, Ali Baba and the Forty Thieves, Revolution Russia, History of a Crime, Dewar's—It's Scotch, The Dream of a Rarebit Fiend, How It Feels To Be Run Over, Winsor McCay and His Animated Pictures, The Girl and Her Trust.* —MM
Movie: 🎵🎵🎵🎵 **DVD:** 🎵🎵🎵 ½
Kino on Video (cat #K236A-E, UPC 73832-9123621). Full frame. $99.95. Keepcase boxed set. *LANG:* English narration.
2002 379m/C

The Moving Finger

Please see review of *Agatha Christie's Miss Marple Set 2.*

Movie: ♫♫ ½ **DVD:** ♫♫ ½

A&E (cat #AAE-70381, UPC 7339617038-18).

1985 100m/C *GB* Joan Hickson, Michael Culver, Richard Pearson, Andrew Bicknell, Sandra Payne; **D:** Roy Boulting; **W:** Julia Jones; **C:** Ian Hilton.

Muhammad Ali— Through the Eyes of the World

To complement the Will Smith blockbuster *Ali,* Universal has released the 104-minute documentary. This intimate portrait of the legendary boxer turned Islamic civil rights leader is a poignant vision of the influence that Ali had over the world, not only for his skill as an athlete but for his magnetic, captivating goodwill. The documentary is filled to capacity with interview footage from well-known celebrities such as Billy Crystal, Rod Steiger, and Maya Angelou, in addition to fallen competitors who tried to stand up to the greatest fighter to ever step into the ring. The picture on this DVD is perfect, and the 5.1 soundtrack is very clean. —EL

Movie: ♫♫♫ **DVD:** ♫♫♫ ½

Universal Studios (cat #21658, UPC 0251-92165825). Widescreen (1.78:1) anamorphic. Dolby Digital 5.1 Surround. $19.98. Keepcase. *LANG:* English; French; Spanish. *SUB:* French; Spanish. *CAP:* English. *FEATURES:* Interviews on how Muhammad Ali affected people • Unseen interviews • Photo gallery • Music video by Faithless • Fight chronology • Ali featurette • Theatrical trailer • Ali Center promotional video.

2002 104m/C

Mulholland Drive

Canadian hopeful Betty Elms (Watts) arrives in Hollywood and moves into her aunt's apartment while she's away. But an amnesia-stricken woman known only as Rita (Harring) has already sneaked in. Instead of calling the police, Betty tries to help Rita recover her memory and discover her identity. On the first of many parallel stories, film director Adam (Theroux) is being forced to use an actress he doesn't want, by shadowy forces who freeze his accounts and make him a veritable fugitive in just a few hours. Rita and Betty grow closer as they collect clues that eventually lead them to the bungalow apartment of someone named Diane Selwyn. Corpses, a weird homeless man, lesbian sex, a phantom nighttime stage show, a mysterious "whatzit" box, and incredibly shrunken relatives are only the surface symptoms of a puzzle that recasts the women in strangely related roles. If the puzzle aspect of the film is a good one, it's because the original piece was clearly developing hints that would have been addressed as the miniseries went on. The characters dress up like one another—Rita and Betty seem interchangeable at one point, an idea interestingly timed with their sexual collision. The theme is nicely echoed through the semi-interchangeable actresses Adam is trying to cast for his lip-synching pop-song scene. Lynch does a great job of handling the way one plane appears to intersect with another. Some events definitely happen in a specific timeline, and others, like the dead-of-night performance of a Roy Orbison song in Spanish, are isolated dream experiences that seemingly happen out of time, outside the story we are watching. What works best are the same elements we're always attracted to—interesting and sensual characters, and perplexing plot turns that make us want to see more and find out what's going to happen next. DVD is a careful transfer that makes the many dark-on-dark scenes look as attractively murky as they did in the theatre. Jack Fisk's wholly believable settings often look better on DVD, as many theatres chose to project the show narrower than 1:85, cropping off many compositions too tightly. Lynch probably did some vertical repositioning in his transfer, while selectively darkening parts of Laura Harring's nude scene to frustrate DVD weenies with nothing better to do than to surf for celebrity private parts. The lack of chapters is a bother, but understandable. —GE

Movie: ♫♫♫ **DVD:** ♫♫♫ ½

Universal Studios (cat #21780, UPC 0251-92178023). Widescreen (1.85:1) anamorphic. Dolby Digital 5.1 Surround; DTS 5.1. $24.98. Keepcase. *LANG:* English. *SUB:* Spanish; French. *CAP:* English. *FEATURES:* David Lynch's "10 Clues to Unlocking This Thriller" (text).

2001 (R) 146m/C Naomi Watts, Laura Harring, Justin Theroux, Ann Miller, Dan Hedaya, Lafayette Montgomery, Michael J. Anderson, Scott Coffey, Chad Everett, Melissa George, James Karen, Katharine Towne, Billy Ray Cyrus, Angelo Badalamenti, Mark Pellegrino, Lee Grant, Kathrine (Kate) Forster, Missy (Melissa) Crider, Brent Briscoe, Marcus Graham, Vincent Castellanos, Michael Des Barres, Robert Forster; **D:** David Lynch; **W:** David Lynch; **C:** Peter Deming; **M:** Angelo Badalamenti. *AWARDS:* Cesar '01: Foreign Film; Ind. Spirit '02: Cinematog.; L.A. Film Critics '01: Director (Lynch); Natl. Bd. of Review '01: Breakthrough Perf. (Watts); N.Y. Film Critics '01: Film; Natl. Soc. Film Critics '01: Actress (Watts), Film; *NOM:* Oscars '01: Director (Lynch); British Acad. '01: Score; Golden Globes '02: Director (Lynch), Film—Drama, Screenplay, Score; Broadcast Film Critics '01: Film.

Mummies Alive!

This action-packed cartoon series finds four Egyptian mummies brought back to life in modern-day San Francisco to continue their battle against the evil Scarab. The action quotient is high enough to keep children entertained. The colors are bright and vivid, but edges are not always distinct and some bleeding occurs. The dialogue is sometimes drowned out by sound effects. —BG

Movie: ♫♫ **DVD:** ♫♫ ½

Lion's Gate Home Ent. (cat #VM 7722D, UPC 031398772224). Full frame. $19.99. Keepcase. *LANG:* English; Spanish. *SUB:* English. *FEATURES:* 5 chapters • Trivia game • Interview with executive producer Ivan Reitman • Trailer.

1997 103m/C D: Seth Kearsley; **V:** Graeme Kingston, Scott McNeil, Pauline Newstone.

The Mummy

The theme of a living mummy was revitalized by the creative team at Hammer, and this film remains—with the Karloff original from 1932—the best Mummy movie ever made. Archeologist John Banning (Peter Cushing) is so intent on staying with his father's expedition to unearth the Egyptian tomb of Ananka that he refuses to have his broken leg properly set. He's therefore unable to assist when his father Stephen (Felix Aylmer) is unaccountably driven mad just as his dream of discovery comes true. Years later back in England, the now-crippled John again fails his asylum-restrained father when he discounts the old man's claims that a living mummy is loose in the world, much to John's later regret. Mehemet Bey, an Egyptian adept of the god Karnak, has both the holy scroll of life, and the mummy Kharis (Christopher Lee) as well, and plans to use him to murder the English infidels. DVD is beautifully detailed and lushly colored, making the previous flat and pale laserdiscs and VHS versions totally disposable. Some shots look a bit soft—but only parts of the frame, indicating that there may be a bit of softness in some of the elements, but none of this is the least bit distracting. The image has been cleaned of scratches and other blemishes. It simply looks great. —GE

Movie: ♫♫♫ ½ **DVD:** ♫♫♫

Warner Home Video (UPC 85392203420). Widescreen (1.78:1) anamorphic. Dolby Digital 5.1 Surround. $19.98. Snapper. *LANG:* English; French. *SUB:* English; French. *FEATURES:* 25 chapters • Trailer • Talent files.

1959 88m/C *GB* Peter Cushing, Christopher Lee, Felix Aylmer, Yvonne Furneaux, Eddie Byrne, Raymond Huntley, George Pastell, Michael Ripper, John Stuart; **D:** Terence Fisher; **W:** Jimmy Sangster; **C:** Jack Asher.

Mummy Raider

Give the guys at EI Independent credit for killing two birds with one knockoff. Alleged parody of *The Mummy* and *Lara Croft: Tomb Raider* looks like it was taped in a garage. The plot has to do with some shootouts and, very briefly, a guy wrapped in burlap. Then it's fast-forward to (or through) the soft-core lesbian scenes. Only the extras differentiate disc from tape. —MM

Movie: woof **DVD:** ♫♫ ½

El Independent Cinema (cat #sc-1020-dvd, UPC 612385102097). Full frame. $24.98. Keepcase. *LANG:* English. *FEATURES:* Trailers • Behind-the-scenes featurette • 2 music videos • Outtakes • "My First Female Lover" featurette.
2001 80m/C Misty Mundae, Darian Caine, Esmeralda DeLarocca, Jayne Ester; *D:* Brian Paulin; *W:* Bruce G. Hallenbeck.

The Mummy Returns

Bombastic sequel to the not-quite-as-bombastic 1999 hit is set a decade later and finds married Rick (Fraser) and Evelyn (Weisz) having adventures with their eight-year-old son Alex (Boath). The reincarnated Anck-Su-Namun (Velasquez) manages to bring crispy Imhotep (Vosloo) back again. He wants to rule the world; so does his archenemy the Scorpion King (Dwayne "The Rock" Johnson). It's virtually impossible to keep all the characters straight but that's not really necessary. This is less a movie than a theme-park ride, demanding no emotional involvement from the audience. Tellingly, the commentary track begins with director Sommers and editor Ducsay talking about the film's $200 million domestic boxoffice. Many of the other extras are little more than promotional opportunities for other Universal Studios enterprises. Of course, the film looks and sounds so good that the many computer-generated effects are robbed of any power they might have had. (The film is also available in a widescreen version.) Surround sound channels are an integral part of the loud, emotion-free action. —*MM*
Movie: ♫♫ *DVD:* ♫♫♫ ½
Universal Studios (cat #21379, UPC 0251-92137921). Full frame. Dolby Digital 5.1 Surround Stereo. $26.98. Keepcase. *LANG:* English; French. *CAP:* English. *FEATURES:* 20 chapters • Outtakes • Special effects featurette • Trailers • Production notes • Talent files • DVD-ROM features • Music video • Game.
2001 (PG-13) 129m/C Brendan Fraser, Rachel Weisz, Oded Fehr, John Hannah, Patricia Velasquez, Dwayne "The Rock" Johnson, Arnold Vosloo, Freddie Boath, Adewale Akinnuoye-Agbaje, Shaun Parkes, Alun Armstrong; *D:* Stephen Sommers; *W:* Stephen Sommers; *C:* Adrian Biddle; *M:* Alan Silvestri.

The Mummy's Curse

Sequel to *The Mummy's Ghost* and Chaney's last outing as Kharis. Construction by a government order causes Kharis and Ananka (Christine) to be dug up in a Louisiana bayou (how they got there from a New England swamp is anyone's guess) and taken to Cajun country for study by archaeologists. The usual havoc ensues. Includes lots of stock footage from earlier mummy movies. Based on a story by Leon Abrams and Dwight V. Babcock. The print for *The Mummy's Curse* seems to have been in better condition than the other *Mummy's* in this series and there are far fewer blemishes to interfere with the

enjoyment of the film. For some reason, though, the graytones and blacks don't seem as good as and, as a result, the cinematography seems to lack some of the depth present on the other features. Hey, and what a coincidence, like all the others, this one's got 18 chapters too! Universal's not the only company to do this—a couple of years ago a DVD manufacturer called up to ask if there a few spots that might warrant a chapter link on a certain well-known film. Seems they were short of the number required by the studio issuing the film. Kind of a backwards mindset. Only available as part of a double feature with *The Mummy's Ghost* (see separate review). —*JO*
Movie: ♫♫ *DVD:* ♫♫ ½
Universal Studios (cat #21405, UPC 0251-92140525). Full frame. Dolby Digital Mono. $29.98. Keepcase. *LANG:* English; Spanish. *SUB:* French. *CAP:* English. *FEATURES:* 18 chapters • Trailer • Production notes • Talent files.
1944 61m/B Lon Chaney Jr., Peter Coe, Virginia Christine, Kay Harding, Dennis Moore, Martin Kosleck, Kurt Katch; *D:* Leslie Goodwins; *W:* Bernard Schubert; *C:* Virgil Miller.

The Mummy's Ghost

The fourth in the Universal series and the sequel to *The Mummy's Tomb* has Kharis (Chaney Jr.) searching for the reincarnation of his ancient love, Princess Ananka, who just happens to be New England college coed Amina (Ames). The high priest (Zucco) sends fellow priest Yousef Bey (Carradine) along to assist but he makes the mistake of declaring his own love for Amina and the mummy gets very, very mad. Oh, and both Kharis and Amina sink into a swamp, thus setting up the next (and last) film in the series. Once again the DVD gets the same review as with most others in this series: good transfer, so-so source material. Worth owning since it looks better than the VHS tape as well as better than it looked on the Saturday Afternoon Movie. Available as a double feature with *The Mummy's Curse* (see separate review). —*JO*
Movie: ♫♫ *DVD:* ♫♫♫
Universal Studios (cat #21405, UPC 0251-92140525). Full frame. Dolby Digital Mono. $29.98. Keepcase. *LANG:* English; Spanish. *SUB:* French. *CAP:* English. *FEATURES:* 18 chapters • Trailer • Production notes • Talent files.
1944 61m/B Lon Chaney Jr., John Carradine, Ramsay Ames, Robert Lowery, Barton MacLane, George Zucco; *D:* Reginald LeBorg; *W:* Griffin Jay, Henry Sucher, Brenda Weisberg; *C:* William Sickner; *M:* Hans J. Salter.

The Mummy's Hand

Although this is the followup to 1932's *The Mummy*, it actually has little to do with the original film. Archaeologists Steve Banning (Foran) and Babe Jensen (Ford) are searching for the tomb of ancient

Egyptian Princess Ananka. Crazy high priest Andoheb (Zucco) sends mummy Kharis (Tyler), who is the tomb's guardian, to kill anyone who defiles her rest. So Kharis shuffles off but finds Marta (Moran) instead. And being a guy, albeit a long-dead guy, he wants to make the beauty his bride. Low-budget but the mix of scares and comedy makes this worth watching. The film prints used for most of these secondary (although still well-lensed and entertaining) titles in the Universal Classic Monster series haven't been preserved very well. There is considerable film damage, including scratches and speckling. Still, the DVD image is sharp and full of depth thanks to the combination of good blacks, contrast, and graytones. The sound is crisp, and the dialogue is easy to distinguish, but a lot of hiss comes along with it. No supplementals other than the production notes and talent files. It seems like Universal is treating these like bargain discs and may not want to shell out the bucks for a film historian's commentary. Available as a double feature with *The Mummy's Tomb* (see separate review). —*JO*
Movie: ♫♫ ½ *DVD:* ♫♫♫
Universal Studios (cat #21407, UPC 0251-92140723). Full frame. Dolby Digital Mono. $29.98. Keepcase. *LANG:* English; Spanish. *SUB:* French. *CAP:* English. *FEATURES:* 18 chapters • Trailer • Production notes • Talent files.
1940 70m/B Dick Foran, Wallace Ford, Peggy Moran, Cecil Kellaway, George Zucco, Tom Tyler, Eduardo Ciannelli, Charles Trowbridge; *D:* Christy Cabanne; *W:* Griffin Jay, Maxwell Shane; *C:* Elwood "Woody" Bredell; *M:* Hans J. Salter.

The Mummy's Tomb

Chaney Jr. is in wraps for the first time in this sequel to *The Mummy's Hand*. Kharis is transported to America by a crazed Egyptian high priest to kill off surviving members of the expedition, weakened by a lame script and too much stock footage. Pretty much the same review as for it partner (*The Mummy's Hand*) on this Universal double-feature DVD. Excellent transfer of a print showing much wear and tear and sounding like it's being screened in front of an army of hissing snakes. Still, this is the best way to see the film and certainly worth the price, especially when you're getting two classic monster flicks. The technical bone rating is based on the assumption that this is most likely the best Universal could have done with these prints. Only available as part of a double feature with *The Mummy's Hand* (see separate review). —*JO*
Movie: ♫♫ *DVD:* ♫♫♫
Universal Studios (cat #21407, UPC 0251-92140723). Full frame. Dolby Digital Mono. $29.98. Keepcase. *LANG:* English; Spanish. *SUB:* French. *CAP:* English. *FEATURES:* 18 chapters • Trailer • Production notes • Talent files.
1942 71m/B Lon Chaney Jr., Dick Foran, John Hubbard, Elyse Knox, George Zucco,

Wallace Ford, Turhan Bey; **D:** Harold Young; **W:** Griffin Jay, Henry Sucher; **C:** George Robinson.

Muppet Family Christmas

A Muppet Family Christmas is a great holiday offering and a must for fans of the Muppets. The Muppets converge on the farm of Fozzie Bear's mother to celebrate Christmas. Kermit, Gonzo, and all the gang make merry, as they wait for Miss Piggy to arrive. As is to be expected, the songs are great and the slapstick comedy will appeal to all ages. This special is notable because it's one of the rare occurrences where the characters from *The Muppet Show* mingle with the familiar creatures from *Sesame Street*. (A pre-hype Elmo can be viewed in several scenes.) The show is also a bit dated, as most young viewers will not recognize the Fraggles, from the '80s HBO series. The DVD gives us a super-sharp image, which is equivalent to digital-broadcast quality. The 2.0 Surround audio track isn't spectacular, but it does provide clean dialogue and the songs sound fine. Muppet purists will need to take note—for reasons unexplained, the scene in which Fozzie first meets the Talking Snowman has been removed from this version. —*ML*
Movie: 🎵🎵🎵 ½ **DVD:** 🎵🎵🎵
Columbia Tristar (cat #07814, UPC 04339-6078147). Full frame. Dolby Digital Stereo. $19.95. Keepcase. *LANG:* English. *SUB:* English; French; Spanish. *CAP:* English. *FEATURES:* Bonus trailers • 20 chapters. **1995 47m/C**

The Muppet Movie

The Muppets make the jump to the silver screen in this highly successful, sweet, and funny musical feature. This witty and self-reflexive film is a road movie telling (loosely) how the Muppets first met. Kermit the Frog encounters Fozzie the Bear, Miss Piggy, etc., and they all join him on his journey to Hollywood to seek stardom. The songs are a mixed bag of cute, memorable numbers and flat, middling songs that tend to stall the narrative. The Muppets' charm is considerable and makes up for any awkward moments or distractions. Filled with cameos by contemporary comedians and an absolutely inspired, brilliantly relevant use of Orson Welles. The film was shortened by two minutes after release. That footage has *not* been reinstated in this edition. The first 10 minutes of the film are terribly grainy and prone to an atrocious amount of digital video noise and smearing. The full-frame edition is preferable as the digital noise is less noticeable. After the problematic opening sequences, the image quality improves drastically, with a sharp (if grainy) image and bold, vibrant colors. The audio doesn't make much use of Surrounds but is fairly clean. The "Muppet test footage" is a test reel shot by director James Frawley with Kermit and Fozzie

interacting on location in British surroundings. It's loose, improvised, and absolutely hilarious. Fozzie and Kermit make observations that are somewhat more adult than usual. A terrific extra. —*DG*
Movie: 🎵🎵🎵 **DVD:** 🎵🎵
Columbia Tristar (cat #05393, UPC 04339-6053939). Widescreen (1.85:1) anamorphic; full frame. Dolby Digital 5.1 Surround; Dolby Digital Surround. $19.95. Keepcase. *LANG:* English; Spanish; French. *SUB:* English; Spanish; French. *CAP:* English. *FEATURES:* 28 chapters • Muppet test footage • Muppetism commercials • Trailers • 28 chapters.
1979 (G) 94m/C *GB* **Cameos:** Edgar Bergen, Milton Berle, Mel Brooks, Madeline Kahn, Steve Martin, Carol Kane, Paul Williams, Charles Durning, Bob Hope, James Coburn, Dom DeLuise, Elliott Gould, Cloris Leachman, Telly Savalas, Orson Welles; **D:** James Frawley; **W:** Jack Burns, Jerry Juhl; **C:** Isidore Mankofsky; **M:** Paul Williams; **V:** Jim Henson, Frank Oz, Jerry Nelson, Richard Hunt, Dave Goetz. *AWARDS: NOM:* Oscars '79: Song ("The Rainbow Connection"), Orig. Song Score and/or Adapt.

The Muppets Take Manhattan

In this, the third Muppet film, the group of disparate pals journey to Manhattan to try to sell their college musical show to Broadway. Sweet, charming songs and a warm, moving script elevate this a notch above previous entries. Filled with hilarious and dramatic incidents and featuring the requisite cameos and gags, it manages to be satisfying for both adults and children. This was Frank Oz's welcome directorial debut. The preferred viewing option for this film is the widescreen edition. Although both versions offer satisfying compositions, the full frame is a tad dark. The widescreen is sharp, bright, and colorful but moderately grainy. The sound is clean but dated and limited. The interview with Henson is individually indexed per question. Navigating the questions is tedious and labored; it even locked-up our player twice. Henson isn't a very dynamic subject, but it's a valid inclusion. The three "Muppetism" commercials are brief but hilarious. —*DG*
Movie: 🎵🎵🎵 ½ **DVD:** 🎵🎵🎵
Columbia Tristar (cat #05616, UPC 04339-6056169). Widescreen (1.85:1) anamorphic; full frame. Mono. $19.95. Keepcase. *LANG:* English; Spanish; French; Portuguese. *SUB:* English; Spanish; French; Portuguese; Chinese; Korean; Thai. *CAP:* English. *FEATURES:* 28 chapters • Trailers • Muppetism commercials • Interview with Jim Henson.
1984 (G) 94m/C **Cameos:** Dabney Coleman, James Coco, Art Carney, Joan Rivers, Gregory Hines, Linda Lavin, Liza Minnelli, Brooke Shields, John Landis; **D:** Frank Oz; **W:** Frank Oz; **C:** Robert Paynter; **M:** Ralph Burns; **V:** Frank Oz, Tom Patchett, Jim Henson. *AWARDS: NOM:* Oscars '84: Orig. Song Score and/or Adapt.

Murder at the Vicarage

Please see review of *Agatha Christie's Miss Marple Set 2.*
Movie: 🎵🎵 ½ **DVD:** 🎵🎵 ½
A&E (cat #AAE-70382, UPC 7339617038-25).
1986 100m/C *GB* Cheryl Campbell, Robert Lang, Polly Adams, Joan Hickson, Paul Eddington; **D:** Julian Amyes; **W:** T.R. Bowen; **C:** John Walker.

Murder by Death

A group of famous sleuths are invited to the isolated mansion of one Lionel Twain (Capote) where they are challenged to solve a murder that has yet to be committed. Neil Simon's satire of classic mystery detectives features an inspired cast playing characters based on Sam Spade, Charlie Chan, Miss Marple, Hercule Poirot, and Nick and Nora Charles. While the entire cast is perfection, Falk's "Sam Diamond" is a pitch perfect and hilarious characterization that deserves special mention. In fact, all of the cast's characterizations are so strong, one could easily visualize them in further films as these characters. Simon's script is a Chinese puzzle box of mysteries within mysteries, inside jokes, and verbal puns. It's a virtual funhouse of a movie, with well-timed visual gags (that almost seem designed to be performed live on the stage), and juicy, hilarious lines for all. Simon's affection for the mystery genre is infectious and makes this frequently uproarious film a virtual love letter to the detectives it ribs. Best of all, Simon knows how to pace a script, giving the plentiful gags room to breath, while building up suspense. A follow-up (but not a sequel) featuring many of the same cast was produced called *The Cheap Detective.* The disc features a stunning, sharp transfer from a near-pristine print. Fleshtones and colors are perfect though some digital grain appears fleetingly in a few scenes. The mono audio is clean and free of noise. Atmospheric effects and the music score are given the strongest amount of sonic presence. The full-frame edition sacrifices no peripheral information, but reveals more foot and headroom instead. It's a viable alternative for widescreen-phobics, but the compositions on the widescreen version are stronger. The interview with Simon is interesting but only touches the surface of the project. —*DG*
Movie: 🎵🎵🎵 ½ **DVD:** 🎵🎵🎵 ½
Columbia Tristar (cat #07934, UPC 04339-6079342). Widescreen (1.85:1) anamorphic; full frame. Mono. $24.95. Keepcase. *LANG:* English; Spanish. *SUB:* English; Spanish; Portuguese; Chinese; Korean; Thai. *CAP:* English. *FEATURES:* Interview with Neil Simon • Trailers • Talent files • 28 chapters • Insert booklet with notes.
1976 (PG) 95m/C Peter Falk, Alec Guinness, David Niven, Maggie Smith, Peter Sellers, Eileen Brennan, Elsa Lanchester, Nancy Walker, Estelle Winwood, Truman Capote, James Coco; **D:** Robert Moore; **W:** Neil Simon; **C:** David M. Walsh; **M:** Dave Grusin.

Murder in Coweta County

This made-for-CBS breakthrough was directed by Gary Nelson and based on true events first popularized in Margaret Anne Barnes's book. The story itself is compelling enough, but what broadens the flick's appeal is beholding Mayberry's finest Andy Griffith seethe pure evil as a 1940s Southern land baron, while legendary country-music outlaw Johnny Cash sets aside his Man in Black persona as a Man in Blue determined to see justice prevail. John Wallace (Griffith) is a mean son of a gun. He's beloved by the people of Meriwether County only for fear of what'd happen to them if they didn't. But when he takes his criminal business into Coweta County, where Sherrif Lamar Potts (Cash) runs the show, things change. Presented in full frame as originally broadcast, the image quality exhibits improvement over previous VHS releases, although digital grain is evident in isolated scenes. This is seemingly acknowledged by a box cover note: "There may be some slight visual variances due to the state of the original master." Utilitarian Dolby Digital 2.0 track. Cash and Griffith deliver powerful performances that belie the low-budget nature of this bargain-bin jewel. Highly recommended. —NGN
Movie: 🐾🐾🐾 **DVD:** 🐾🐾 ½
Studio Home Ent. (cat #UAV40290DVD, UPC 084296402908). Full frame. Dolby Stereo. $14.98. Keepcase. *LANG:* English. *FEATURES:* Talent files.
1983 100m/C Johnny Cash, Andy Griffith, Earl Hindman, June Carter Cash, Cindi Knight, Ed Van Nuys; **D:** Gary Nelson; **W:** Dennis Nemec; **C:** Larry Pizer; **M:** Brad Fiedel.

Murder in the Orient

Low-budget Philippine martial arts flick scrapes the bottom of the barrel. Paul Marcelli (Marchini) is an American secret agent searching for $10 million in gold buried by Japanese at the end of the war. The supporting cast is remarkably chubby. The image is faded and scratched. A loud hiss and intermittent crackling make the soundtrack even worse. —MM
Movie: 🐾 **DVD:** 🐾
BCI-Eclipse (cat #44082-9, UPC 7873644-08290). Full frame. $9.98. Keepcase. *LANG:* English. *FEATURES:* 6 chapters • "There's Good Boos To-Night" cartoon • Trivia game • DVD dictionary • DVD-ROM features.
1973 (R) 90m/C *PH* Ron Marchini, Leo Fong, Leila Hermosa, Eva Reyes; **D:** Manuel G. Songo; **W:** Manuel G. Songo.

Murder Once Removed

The good doctor (Forsythe) has a bedside manner that's too friendly for some of his upscale female patients. This is movie-of-the-week stuff. DVD does nothing to improve the cheap-looking image. It's full of artifacts and the soundtrack is full of

static. Title is available on the *Great Detective Movies* disc. —MM
Movie: 🐾 **DVD:** 🐾
BFS Video (cat #30292-D, UPC 06680530-2923). Full frame. $9.98. Keepcase. *LANG:* English. *FEATURES:* 6 chapters • Talent files.
1971 74m/C John Forsythe, Richard Kiley, Barbara Bain, Joseph Campanella; **D:** Charles S. Dubin; **M:** Robert Jackson Drasnin.

The Musketeer

Follow the epic adventures of D'Artagnan (Chambers), Porthos (Spiers) and Athos (Gregor Kremp) as they battle to protect the sovereignty of the Queen of England (Deneuve) from the evil, power-hungry Cardinal Richelieu (Rea) and his murderous henchman, Febre (Roth). Unfortunately, this adaptation of the timeless classic falls flat. Sagging dialogue, corny one-liners, and some non-believable performances by Suvari and Chambers paralyze the story. While the inclusion of martial arts–style theatrics and Tim Roth's hideously evil Febre make for some fun viewing, it is not enough to bring the film back into good graces. The Dolby Surround track makes good use of all six speakers, and the picture looks fantastic. —EL
Movie: 🐾🐾 **DVD:** 🐾🐾🐾 ½
Universal Studios (cat #21765, UPC 0251-92176524). Widescreen (2.35:1) anamorphic. Dolby 5.1 Surround; DTS Surround. $26.98. Keepcase. *LANG:* English; French. *CAP:* English. *FEATURES:* "Casting Justin Chambers" featurette • Behind-the-scenes on the stunts • Theatrical trailer • Production notes • Cast and crew bios and film highlights • 18 chapters.
2001 (PG-13) 105m/C Justin Chambers, Mena Suvari, Tim Roth, Catherine Deneuve, Stephen Rea, Daniel Mesguich, David Schofield, Nick Moran, Jeremy Clyde, Michael Byrne, Steve Spiers, Jan Gregor Kremp, Jean-Pierre Castaldi; **D:** Peter Hyams; **W:** Gene Quintano; **C:** Peter Hyams; **M:** David Arnold.

My Best Friend's Wedding [2 SE]

This "special edition" lacks the full-frame version available on the first release (reviewed in *Book 1*). It adds an anamorphic widescreen transfer, more language and subtitle options, and a few more extra features. The new image is essentially flawless—everything anyone could expect of a glittering big-budget star vehicle. The "I Say a Little Prayer" restaurant scene is one of the funniest moments in any romantic comedy. This one belongs in every library. —MM
Movie: 🐾🐾🐾 **DVD:** 🐾🐾🐾 ½
Columbia Tristar (cat #05817, UPC 0433-96058170). Widescreen (2.35:1) anamorphic. Dolby Digital 5.1; Dolby Surround. $24.98. Keepcase. *LANG:* English; French; Spanish; Portuguese. *SUB:* English; Spanish; Portuguese; Chinese; Korean; Thai. *CAP:* English. *FEATURES:* 28 chapters

• 3 featurettes • "Say a Little Prayer" sing-along • Wedding album • Trailers • Filmographies • Production notes • DVD-ROM features.
1997 (PG-13) 105m/C Julia Roberts, Dermot Mulroney, Cameron Diaz, Rupert Everett, Philip Bosco, M. Emmet Walsh, Rachel Griffiths, Susan Sullivan, Paul Giamatti; **D:** P.J. Hogan; **W:** Ronald Bass; **C:** Laszlo Kovacs; **M:** James Newton Howard. *AWARDS: NOM:* Oscars '97: Orig. Mus./Comedy Score; British Acad. '97: Support. Actor (Everett); Golden Globes '98: Actress—Mus./Comedy (Roberts), Film—Mus./Comedy, Support. Actor (Everett); MTV Movie Awards '98: Female Perf. (Roberts), Breakthrough Perf. (Everett), Comedic Perf. (Everett).

My Bodyguard

To escape the constant poundings by the local school bully, Moody (Dillon), Clifford Peach (Makepeace) enlists the help of school outcast Ricky Linderman (Baldwin) as his personal bodyguard. As Clifford begins to make peace with his new school surroundings he becomes closer to his new guardian and protector; as their business deal develops into friendship, though, Clifford finds out that the mysterious stories circulating about his new friend's past may not be so far-fetched. This charming and enjoyable coming-of-age film is a shining example of a simple and well-developed plotline that engages while entertaining the viewer. This DVD release features a very clear and crisp transfer. There were no noticeable anomalies or defects, and very few dust artifacts clouding the picture. The DVD offers both a 1.85:1 widescreen presentation, as well as a pan-and-scan version for viewers who detest the black bars across the top and bottom of their screen. The sound quality is equally strong with no noticeable defects. The Surround track makes good use of the front three speakers, but leaves the back two underutilized. —EL
Movie: 🐾🐾🐾 **DVD:** 🐾🐾🐾
20th Century Fox (UPC 02454302916). Widescreen (1.85:1) anamorphic; full frame. Dolby Surround; Mono. $19.98. Keepcase. *LANG:* English; French. *SUB:* English; Spanish. *CAP:* English. *FEATURES:* Theatrical trailer and TV spots • 18 chapters.
1980 (PG) 96m/C Chris Makepeace, Adam Baldwin, Martin Mull, Ruth Gordon, Matt Dillon, John Houseman, Joan Cusack, Craig Richard Nelson, Tim Kazurinsky, George Wendt, Jennifer Beals; **D:** Tony Bill; **W:** Alan Ormsby; **C:** Michael D. Margulies; **M:** Dave Grusin.

My Favorite Blonde

Beautiful British spy Carroll convinces Hope to aid her in carrying out a secret mission. It's lots of fun as Hope, his trained penguin, and Carroll embark on a cross-country chase to elude the Nazis. Hope's behavior is hilarious and the pace is zippy. Image is simply superb. The black-and-white photography has been well

preserved or restored. Heavy fog scenes are as soft as they have always been but conventional interiors are crystalline and details in dark clothing are sharp. Mono sound is clear. RSDL disc also includes *Star Spangled Rhythm*.
Movie: 🦴🦴🦴 **DVD:** 🦴🦴🦴
Universal Studios (cat #21363, UPC 025-192136320). Full frame. Dolby Digital Mono. $24.98. Keepcase. *LANG:* English. *SUB:* French; Spanish. *CAP:* English. *FEATURES:* 18 chapters • Trailer • Production notes • Talent files.
1942 78m/B Bob Hope, Madeleine Carroll, Gale Sondergaard, George Zucco, Lionel Royce, Walter Kingsford, Victor Varconi, Bing Crosby; **D:** Sidney Lanfield; **W:** Frank Butler, Don Hartman; **C:** William Mellor; **M:** David Buttolph.

My First Mister

Coming-of-age story revolves around 17-year-old narrator Jennifer Wilson (Sobieski), who's enamored of piercings, black lipstick, her own alienation. On a whim, she applies for a job at a conservative clothing store managed by Randall Harris (Brooks) in a suburban mall. Against all his instincts, he says yes. Though they could not be more different in attitude and age, they are two lonely people. Each sees something that he or she needs in the other, and eventually, the two form an unconventional friendship. Yes, the story is very similar to *Ghost World* released the same year, but it lacks the spark that drives that underground hit, and the ending takes an abrupt and not completely satisfying turn. In many ways, this is a "Hollywood" version of the same story and it's not nearly as sharp. Performances are excellent, though, and they carry the story over many of the rough spots. Actress-turned-director Christine Lahti won an Academy Award for a short film. This is her first feature and on the commentary track she recounts her education as a filmmaker. DVD has no trouble with the character-driven drama's subdued color scheme and production design. Image and sound are all they ought to be for a new studio release. Recommended. —*MM*
Movie: 🦴🦴🦴 **DVD:** 🦴🦴🦴
Paramount (cat #33891, UPC 09736-3389149). Widescreen anamorphic. Dolby Digital 5.1 Surround; Dolby Surround. $29.99. Keepcase. *LANG:* English. *SUB:* English. *CAP:* English. *FEATURES:* 18 chapters • Commentary: director.
2001 (R) 109m/C Albert Brooks, Leelee Sobieski, Desmond Harrington, Carol Kane, Michael McKean, Mary Kay Place, John Goodman, Lisa Jane Persky; **D:** Christine Lahti; **W:** Jill Franklyn; **C:** Jeffrey Jur; **M:** Steve Porcaro.

My Little Margie: Collection 2 (1952–55)

This '50s sitcom features Farrell and Storm as Vern and Margie Albright, a middle-aged father and his twentysomething daughter. Their comic circumstances are often the result of a ridiculous misunderstanding, but everything gets tied together with a nice moral. This two-disc set contains 12 episodes, although they don't seem to be in any particular order or even from the same season. The picture is grainy and not particularly sharp, and the sound runs into some distortion. —*BG*
Movie: 🦴 ½ **DVD:** 🦴 ½
VCI (cat #8267, UPC 089859826726). Full frame. $29.99. Keepcase. *LANG:* English. *FEATURES:* 12 chapters • Bios.
2002 345m/B Gale Storm, Charles Farrell, Hillary Brooke.

My Man Godfrey [Criterion]

The Criterion edition of this magnificent comedy is worlds better than the earlier public domain discs (reviewed in *Book 1*). Though the image isn't as sharp as contemporary black and white, it looks very good for 1936. Bob Gilpen's commentary is professorial. The other extras are well chosen. This title isn't as well known as some others of its time, and so for many fans of star William Powell in particular and of screwball comedy in general, it's a rare treat. Find it. —*MM*
Movie: 🦴🦴🦴🦴 **DVD:** 🦴🦴🦴 ½
Criterion (cat #114, UPC 715515011921). Full frame. Dolby Digital Mono. $39.98. Keepcase. *LANG:* English. *SUB:* English. *FEATURES:* 21 chapters • Commentary: Bob Gilpen • Lux Radio Theater program • Archival newsreel footage • Outtakes • Trailer • Stills.
1936 95m/B William Powell, Carole Lombard, Gail Patrick, Alice Brady, Mischa Auer, Eugene Pallette, Alan Mowbray, Franklin Pangborn, Jane Wyman; **D:** Gregory La Cava; **W:** Gregory La Cava, Morrie Ryskind; **C:** Ted Tetzlaff; **M:** Charles Previn. *AWARDS:* Natl. Film Reg. '99; *NOM:* Oscars '36: Actor (Powell), Actress (Lombard), Director (La Cava), Screenplay, Support. Actor (Auer), Support. Actress (Brady).

Mysterious Mr. Wong

If he can just collect the 12 coins of Confucius, Mr. Wong (Lugosi), like his soulmate Fu Manchu, will be able to rule the world. Lucky for him, they're all in New York's Chinatown. All of the problems you'd expect to encounter in a low-budget film more than half a century old are here—heavy static on the soundtrack, registration jitters, obvious print damage. The result is an image that's only a scant improvement over VHS. —*MM*
Movie: 🦴 ½ **DVD:** 🦴🦴
Troma Team Video (cat #AED-2042, UPC 785604204220). Full frame. Dolby Digital Mono. $24.99. Keepcase. *LANG:* English. *FEATURES:* 11 chapters • Credits • Film background (text).
1935 56m/B Bela Lugosi, Arline Judge, Wallace Ford, Fred Warren, Lotus Long; **D:** William Nigh; **W:** Nina Howatt; **C:** Harry Neumann.

Mystery Science Theater 3000: "Eegah!"

This cult show revolves around a human (Joel Hodgson) who is forced in an experiment by Dr. Forrester (Trace Beaulieu) to sit in a satellite with two robots he created and watch bad horror and sci-fi flicks. While the movies are running, we see the three in shadow, and listen to their comments about just how bad the movie is. *EEGAH!* is another absolutely awful movie, which opens up the forum nicely, with the gang providing some screamingly funny observations. Rhino has put together a really fine DVD as well, even though MST3K never really offered great audio/video quality. Although a scene or two actually looks halfway decent, the majority of the movie looks extremely soft, and is plagued with numerous flaws such as scratches, lines, marks, and a generally worn and dated appearance. Colors are generally a little pale, and the picture has a bland appearance. The TV series skits themselves fare much better. Just like the movie's image quality, the sound quality is pretty funky at times as well. Although we can always hear the comments of the gang about the movie, the movie itself sounds very thin and occasionally harsh. The option to view the film uncut without commentary is appreciated. (Critical rating is an average of 3 bones for the show, but a WOOF! for the movie.) —*AB/DG*
Movie: 🦴 ½ **DVD:** 🦴🦴
Rhino Home Video (UPC 81227660222). Full frame. Stereo. $19.98. Keepcase. *LANG:* English. *FEATURES:* 18 chapters • Film without commentary.
1993 90m/C

Mystery Science Theater 3000: "Manos, the Hands of Fate"

The *Mystery Science Theater 3000* gang is back, with what has to be one of the funniest episodes of the show. Joel, Tom Servo, and Crow are forced to watch *Manos: Hands of Fate*. This is a truly bizarre horror film in which a family gets lost in the desert and finds themselves at a "hotel," which is apparently the doorway to hell. Or something like that. *Manos* doesn't make any sense, and the guys have a great time making fun of it. The jokes about the caretaker, Torgo, are enough to make this DVD worth buying. The best line is "Every frame of this movie looks like someone's last known photograph." Before *Manos*, we are treated to an old Chevrolet training film entitled "Hired, Part Two." As an added bonus, the DVD includes "Poopie!," a 30-minute outtake reel of many jokes and blunders from the taping of the show. Most of these concern Tom Servo's head falling off, but the gag never gets old. The DVD presents *MST3K: Manos* in its original full-frame aspect ratio. The image on the "skits" is

sharp and clear, and, as is to be expected, the image on *Manos* looks terrible, but this only adds to the fun. The audio is fine, making all of the jokes clear and audible. —ML
Movie: 🎬🎬🎬🎬 **DVD:** 🎬🎬 ½
Rhino (cat #R2 2274). Full frame. Dolby 2.0 Surround. $19.95. Snapper. *LANG:* English. *FEATURES:* Outtakes reel ➠ 20 chapters.
1993 97m/C

Mystery Science Theater 3000: "Mitchell"

As with any television series, *Mystery Science Theater 3000* had its high points and low points. Despite the fact that *Mitchell* is an important episode in the *MST3K* continuum, it represents a low point. The film *Mitchell* is an average cop thriller starring Joe Don Baker and John Saxon. The film isn't good, but it isn't unusually bad either, so the jokes from Joel, Tom Servo, and Crow come across as very run-of-the-mill. The wisecracks about Joe Don Baker's physique grow tiresome quickly, and there just isn't enough material in the movie for the guys to work with. On an historical note, this episode does portray the departure of Joel Robinson (played by Joel Hodgson) from the "Satellite of Love," and the introduction of Mike Nelson as the resident human aboard the satellite. With this DVD, we get a full-frame presentation of the program, which offers a very clear picture when Joel and the robots are taking their breaks, and a noticeably grainy picture during the viewing of *Mitchell*. The sound is adequate, providing clear dialogue, with no distortion. —ML
Movie: 🎬🎬 **DVD:** 🎬🎬 ½
Rhino (cat #R2 2265). Full frame. Dolby 2.0 Surround. $19.95. Snapper. *LANG:* English. *FEATURES:* Trailer ➠ 20 chapters.
1993 97m/C

Mystery Science Theater 3000: "Red Zone Cuba"

A trio of convicts assaulting a Cuban stronghold get captured, then escape. Back in the American Southwest, they go on a robbing and killing spree. However awful this is, it's a shame that this DVD can't click out of Mystery Theater mode so we also can watch the film as it was released. Unlike MST3K's cult following, if I want to hear jokes, I'll ask my friends over. Worse, what is already a bad print looks far worse framed within its standard "back row" silhouette proscenium. Very ordinary DVD transfer of the MST3K video shenanigans with equally mediocre sound. —MO
Movie: 🎬🎬 **DVD:** 🎬🎬 ½
Rhino (cat #R2 2334, UPC 6034972334-27). Full frame. $19.95. Keepcase. *LANG:* English. *FEATURES:* 20 chapters.
1994 97m/C

Mystery Science Theater 3000: "The Brain that Wouldn't Die"

This is one of the first shows with second host Mike Nelson. The episode does provide the occasional big laugh, but it doesn't take its place among the series' best. The film doesn't quite provide the opportunity for the usual commentary. Still, for fans of the series, the chance to own these shows on DVD is fantastic, and even some of the weaker episodes like this one still have their moments. The film looks worn, with a rough look that includes a number of scratches and marks on the print used. It also utilizes a cut version of the film. The skit scenes on the ship also have a few minor instances of shimmering. Just like the image quality, the sound quality is pretty funky at times as well. Although we can always hear the comments of the gang about the movie, the movie itself sounds very thin and occasionally harsh. (For a review of the film, please see *Book 2*) —AB/DG
Movie: 🎬🎬 ½ **DVD:** 🎬🎬
Rhino Home Video (UPC 81227660321). Full frame. Stereo. $19.98. Keepcase. *LANG:* English. *FEATURES:* Film presented without commentary ➠ 18 chapters.
1993 90m/C

Nadia: Secret of Blue Water, Vol. 1: The Adventure Begins

Young inventor Jean rescues the mysterious young Nadia and her pet lion cub, King, during the Paris World's Fair of 1889. Doggedly pursued by a trio of bumbling oddballs, the three end up inside Captain Nemo's legendary submarine, the *Nautilus,* where things get even stranger. The delightful period farce is loosely based on *20,000 Leagues under the Sea* and filled with the wit and adventure of Jules Verne's other works. (Disney's later *Atlantis* feature bears uncomfortable similarities with some of the story elements and the character designs of this production.) A light, absolutely charming animated series (39 episodes total) with energy and humor to spare. Look quick for a fun in-joke for fans of *Those Magnificent Men in Their Flying Machines.* While the packaging recommends this for people 12 and up, the subject matter is fit for all ages (adults included). The series will stretch to a projected 10 volumes on DVD. The disc features bright, vivid, perfect colors and a terrific soundtrack. The only distraction is some digital noise during panning movements and some edge shimmer. Highly recommended. This disc contains episodes 1–4. Also available: "Vol. 2: The Dark Kingdom" (cat. #DNS/002, UPC 702727016721), "Vol. 3: Aboard the Nautilus" (cat. #DNS/003, UPC 702727012426), "Vol. 4: Battleground" (cat. #DNS/004, UPC 702727016820), "Vol. 5: Nadia's Island" (cat. #DNS/005, UPC 702727012624),

"Vol. 6: The Deep Blue Sea" (cat. #DNS/006, UPC 702727016929), "Vol. 7: Nemo's Fortress" (cat. #DNS/007, UPC 702727012525). —DG **AKA:** The Secret of Blue Water.
Movie: 🎬🎬🎬 ½ **DVD:** 🎬🎬🎬
A.D.V. Films (cat #DNS/001, UPC 702727-012327). Full frame. Dolby Digital Surround. $29.98. Keepcase. *LANG:* Japanese; English. *SUB:* English. *FEATURES:* Anime previews ➠ Textless opening and closing ➠ 4 chapters per episode.
1989 100m/C *JP D:* Hideaki Anno; *M:* Shiroh Sagisu.

Narcotic Justice

A Los Angeles detective goes rogue after his girlfriend is killed. Shot-on-video action flick is strictly amateur hour. DVD is equal to VHS. Title is available as part of the *Action Arsenal* collection. —MM
Movie: 🎬 **DVD:** 🎬
BCI-Eclipse (cat #44076-9, UPC 7873644-07699). Full frame. $19.98. Keepcase. *LANG:* English. *FEATURES:* 7 chapters.
19?? 75m/C Karl Niemiec, Stuart Wilson, Blumen Young, Wendi Westbrook; *D:* Randy Misho; *W:* Karl Niemiec.

National Lampoon's European Vacation

For anyone not familiar with the Griswalds, they are the American family you don't want traveling to Europe because they can in no way improve international relations. They win a trip that allows them access to destroy all the European high points, humiliating themselves along the way. There are some truly funny moments, such as the reoccurrence of Eric Idle as the English traveler who is repeatedly injured by patriarch Clark Griswald (Chase) as they travel parallel itineraries across Europe. Overall, nowhere near as funny as the original *Vacation,* but still funnier than *Dr. Dolittle 2* (but then so are a lot of movies). Pretty picture, good sound. —CA **AKA:** European Vacation.
Movie: 🎬🎬 ½ **DVD:** 🎬🎬🎬
Warner (cat #11521, UPC 0853911521-25). Widescreen. Dolby Digital Mono. $19.90. Snapper. *LANG:* English. *SUB:* English; French; Spanish; Portuguese. *CAP:* English. *FEATURES:* 27 chapters ➠ Original credits *Holiday Road* ➠ Theatrical trailer.
1985 (PG-13) 94m/C Chevy Chase, Beverly D'Angelo, Dana Hill, Jason Lively, Victor Lanoux, John Astin, William Zabka; *D:* Amy Heckerling; *W:* John Hughes, Robert Klane, Eric Idle; *M:* Charles Fox.

Naughty Stewardesses

This famously successful bit of early '70s exploitation is a cinematic time capsule. The looks and attitudes of that era are in full flower in this story of three adventurous, independent young women (Hoffman, Joi, Jordan) who run across kidnappers, pornographers, and a dead-eye sugardaddy (Livingstone). The whole film is a snapshot of a distant era, and now, even the title is politically incorrect. (*Naughty Flight Attendants* just doesn't have the same ring, does it?) On his commentary track, producer/writer Sherman takes his time explaining how the film came to be made, and he seems to have a pretty good memory for details of the production. (He's even embarrassed by one scene.) Though some surface damage and fading are noticeable in a few shots, for the most part the film is in good shape. DVD image ranges between good and excellent for a work of this age and budget. —*MM*

Movie: 🎬🎬🎬 **DVD:** 🎬🎬🎬
El Independent Cinema (cat #sc-2205, UPC 612385220593). Full frame. $19.99. Keepcase. *LANG:* English. *FEATURES:* 24 chapters ▪ Trailers ▪ Outtakes and one deleted scene ▪ Commentary: Sam Sherman ▪ TV spot ▪ Weblink.
1974 (R) 96m/C Connie Hoffman, Donna Desmond, Sydney Jordan, Marilyn Joi, Robert Livingstone, Richard Smedley; **D:** Al Adamson; **W:** Sam M. Sherman.

Nekromantik

Robert (Daktari Lorenz) is a skinny, ineffectual employee of Joe's Streetcleaning Agency. It's a gruesome job, scraping up what's left of folks after car accidents, but Robbie loves his work. In fact, he takes it home with him. There in his dingy apartment are shelves lined with mason jars filled with human remains. He shares this flat with his gorgeous girlfriend Betty (Monika M.) who coos with delight upon each addition to their macabre menagerie. Their blood lust reaches critical mass when Rob totes home a rotting body he's fished out of the drink. The young lovers paw and caress the slimy unfortunate until they work themselves into a fevered depravity that climaxes in them having sex with the corpse. It's vile. Disgusting. Disturbing. And intentionally so. Revulsion is its sole purpose. And as a testament to Jorg's success, his film has been censored or banned in most every country it ever managed to play. It also features genuine footage of animal cruelty. Proceed with caution and an empty stomach. The commentary is in English with the director and co-author Franz Rodenkirchen, in which they joke about Jorg's cameo in the film and the movie's cheap, crude effects. Also included is an early short film by Buttgereit called "Horror Heaven." —*GNG/DG*
Movie: 🎬 **DVD:** 🎬🎬½
Image Ent. (UPC 690816600190). Full frame. Mono. $34.98. Keepcase. *LANG:* German. *SUB:* English. *FEATURES:* Production stills ▪ Commentary: Buttgereit, Franz Rodenkirchen ▪ Liner notes ▪ Trailer ▪ Short, "Horror Heaven." ▪ 2 featurettes.
1987 74m/C GE Monika M., Daktari Lorenz, Harald Lundt, Henri Boeck, Clemens Schwenter, Holger Suhr, Jorg Buttgereit; **D:** Jorg Buttgereit; **W:** Franz Rodenkirchen, Jorg Buttgereit; **C:** Uwe Bohrer; **M:** Herman Kopp.

Nelly et Monsieur Arnaud

Wafer-thin tale about a would-be romance between 25-year-old secretary Nelly (the always luminescent Emmanuelle Beart) and 60-ish retired magistrate Pierre Arnaud (Michel Serrault) she works for. What initially seems headed for a May–December affair turns out to be the Gallic version of *The Odd Couple:* Nelly exudes calm and grace while Arnaud bellows his memoirs and frustrations about life and his failed marriage. Complications arise when Nelly starts seeing Arnaud's book editor (Jean-Hugues Anglade). While charming and chatty, the narrative conflicts are slight at best and at times I felt that this was a story told many times before and with nothing new to say this go around. Presented in 1.66 aspect ratio with anamorphic enhancement, the image undergoes "reverse letterboxing," with thin black bars on the sides instead of the top and bottom. Transfer is sharp and stable with colors muted but solid. Mono sound is fine. In French with optional English subtitles. —*EP* **AKA:** *Nelly and Mr. Arnaud.*
Movie: 🎬🎬½ **DVD:** 🎬🎬½
New Yorker Video (cat #DVD61401, UPC 7171196614140). Widescreen (1.66:1) anamorphic. Dolby Digital Mono. $29.95. Keepcase. *LANG:* French. *SUB:* English. *FEATURES:* 16 chapters ▪ Theatrical trailer ▪ Cast/director filmographies ▪ Photo gallery.
1995 105m/C IT GE FR Emmanuelle Beart, Michel Serrault, Jean-Hugues Anglade, Françoise Brion, Claire Nadeau, Michael (Michel) Lonsdale, Charles Berling, Michele Laroque; **D:** Claude Sautet; **W:** Jacques Fieschi, Claude Sautet; **C:** Jean-François Robin; **M:** Philippe Sarde. *AWARDS:* Cesar '96: Actor (Serrault), Director (Sautet); *NOM:* British Acad. '96: Foreign Film; Cesar '96: Actress (Beart), Film, Film Editing, Sound, Support. Actor (Anglade, Lonsdale), Support. Actress (Nadeau), Writing, Score.

Nemesis

Please see review of *Agatha Christie's Miss Marple Set 2.*
Movie: 🎬🎬½ **DVD:** 🎬🎬½
A&E (cat #AAE-70382, UPC 7339617038-25).
1986 100m/C GB Joan Hickson, Margaret Tyzack, Ann Cropper, Valerie Lush; **D:** David Tucker; **W:** T.R. Bowen; **C:** John Walker.

The Nest

An island community is overcome by nasty mutant cockroaches created by that old stand-by, a scientific experiment gone wrong. The formula horror pushes all the right buttons delivering some good scares along with intentional humor. Great fun for fans. The image is so rough and grainy that DVD can do nothing to improve it. —*MM*
Movie: 🎬🎬½ **DVD:** 🎬🎬
New Concorde (cat #NH20294 D, UPC 73-6991429499). Full frame. $14.98. Keep-

case. *LANG:* English. *FEATURES:* 24 chapters ▪ Trailers ▪ Talent files.
1988 (R) 89m/C Robert Lansing, Lisa Langlois, Franc Luz, Terri Treas, Stephen Davies, Diana Bellamy, Nancy Morgan; **D:** Terence H. Winkless; **W:** Robert King; **C:** Ricardo Jacques Gale; **M:** Rick Conrad.

The Net [2 SE]

This "Special Edition" of Irwin Winkler's Hitchcockian thriller eliminates the few flaws on the first release (reviewed in *Book 1*), though it does eliminate the full-frame screen-size option. I could see no visual flaws in the image transfer. If anything, it looks a bit sharper than the theatrical presentation. DVD also includes two filmmakers' commentaries, one from the writers and one from the director and producer. My only quibble is the inventive menus, which can be a bit difficult to decipher at first. They are, however, appropriate to the tricky nature of the plot. —*MM*
Movie: 🎬🎬🎬 **DVD:** 🎬🎬🎬½
Columbia Tristar (cat #07731, UPC 043396-077317). Widescreen (1.85:1) anamorphic. Dolby Digital 5.1 Surround; Dolby Stereo. $24.98. Keepcase. *LANG:* English; French; Spanish; Portuguese. *SUB:* English; French; Spanish; Portuguese; Chinese; Korean; Thai. *CAP:* English. *FEATURES:* 28 chapters ▪ Liner notes ▪ Commentary: John Brancato, Michael Ferris ▪ Commentary: Irwin Winkler, Rob Cowan ▪ HBO featurette ▪ Trailers ▪ Talent files.
1995 (PG-13) 114m/C Sandra Bullock, Jeremy Northam, Dennis Miller, Diane Baker, Ken Howard, Wendy Gazelle, Ray McKinnon; **D:** Irwin Winkler; **W:** John Brancato, Michael Ferris; **C:** Jack N. Green; **M:** Mark Isham.

Never Say Never Again

James Bond matches wits with a charming but sinister tycoon who is holding the world nuclear hostage as part of a diabolical plot by SPECTRE. Connery's return to the world of Bond after 12 years is smooth in this remake of *Thunderball* hampered by an atrocious musical score. Carrera is stunning as Fatima Blush. Although Connery is back, purists will have qualms considering this to be part of the "official" Bond series, since longtime Bond producer, Albert "Cubby" Broccoli, had nothing to do with this endeavor. The DVD transfer looks worse than those for the much older Connery Bonds that are better films as well. The image has a lot of blurring and it starts right off the bat before the film really gets rolling. There is also much more film print damage than there should be on a film of this vintage. At a couple of spots, the film actually shakes. Colors are only O.K., and there is more bleed than there should be as well. The Dolby Surround is fine (at least more enjoyable than the image) but offers nothing too spectacular and practically no Surround at all. —*JO*
Movie: 🎬🎬½ **DVD:** 🎬🎬

MGM Home Ent. (cat #1001098, UPC 027-616853981). Widescreen (2.35:1) anamorphic. Dolby Surround. $14.95. Keepcase. *LANG:* English; Spanish. *SUB:* Spanish; French. *CAP:* English. *FEATURES:* 32 chapters ▪ Theatrical trailer.
1983 (PG) 134m/C Sean Connery, Klaus Maria Brandauer, Max von Sydow, Barbara Carrera, Kim Basinger, Edward Fox, Bernie Casey, Pamela Salem, Rowan Atkinson, Valerie Leon, Prunella Gee, Saskia Cohen Tanugi; *D:* Irvin Kershner; *W:* Lorenzo Semple Jr.; *C:* Douglas Slocombe; *M:* Michel Legrand.

Never 2 Big

A young record company executive wants to prove that someone at the company murdered his singer sister to prevent her from leaving and signing with another label. Of course, he's been framed for the crime and has to stay out of jail to prove his own innocence before the entire capable cast is suffocated by the accumulated clichés. Full-frame image might be slightly sharper than VHS tape. —MM
Movie: ♫♫ *DVD:* ♫♫
Artisan Ent. (cat #12035, UPC 01223612-0353). Full frame. Dolby Digital Stereo. $14.98. Keepcase. *LANG:* English. *CAP:* English. *FEATURES:* 17 chapters ▪ Talent files.
1998 (R) 100m/C Ernie Hudson, Nia Long, Tony Todd, Donnie Wahlberg, Terrence DaShon Howard, Donald Adeosun Faison, Tommy (Tiny) Lister, Salli Richardson, Shemar Moore; *D:* Peter Gathings Bunche; *W:* Peter Gathings Bunche; *C:* Nancy Schreiber; *M:* Joseph Williams.

The NeverEnding Story

A lonely young boy (Oliver) helps a warrior (Hathaway) save the fantasy world in his book from destruction by the Nothing. Wonderful, intelligent family movie is about imagination with swell effects and a sweet but not overly sentimental script. The anamorphic transfer exhibits a sharp, detailed picture. The laserdisc looks smudgy by comparison. (Another one bites the dust!) Colors are bold and slightly saturated, completely understandable for a fairy-tale setting. The source print looks very clean but graininess pops up in some process shots. Deep black levels and the increased resolution bring out the finer details with minimal aliasing. Despite pixelation occurring a couple of times (noticeable in the cloud effects), there are no digital artifacts. Surround audio could have used some tinkering. The front soundstage sounds spacious, but feels less energetic than the laserdisc's PCM track. The mono Surround channel houses some ambience effects and music, but not with much impact. Low-end energy is also lacking. The Rock Biter's entrance in chapter 6 could have used much more rumble. —EP
Movie: ♫♫♫ *DVD:* ♫♫♫
Warner Home Video (UPC 85391327721). Widescreen (2.35:1) anamorphic; full frame. Dolby Digital Stereo. $19.98. Keep-

case. *LANG:* English; French. *SUB:* English; French; Spanish. *FEATURES:* Trailer ▪ Production notes.
1984 (PG) 94m/C Barret Oliver, Noah Hathaway, Gerald McRaney, Moses Gunn, Tami Stronach, Patricia Hayes, Sydney Bromley, Thomas Hill; *D:* Wolfgang Petersen; *W:* Wolfgang Petersen; *C:* Jost Vacano; *M:* Klaus Doldinger, Giorgio Moroder.

NeverEnding Story 2: The Next Chapter

Bastian (Brandis of the *Seaquest* series) finds himself generally in the same place this time around. He's still not getting along with the other children in school and he's at odds with his father. Again, he seeks out the old man's bookstore and, soon, hears the pleas of the Childlike Empress asking the young lad to return to Fantasia and save the day with his imagination once more. Image transfer for this sequel is generally superb, with fine sharpness and detail, even though a few scenes do appear to be shot in an intentionally "soft" focus. Slight pixelation is occasionally apparent, as are a few tiny instances of edge-enhancement; yet the picture seems almost completely free of wear. Soundtrack is generally pleasant, although a newly done 5.1 presentation would have been appreciated. Some of the sound effects are rather primitive, while others are clean and crisp. —AB/MM
Movie: ♫♫ *DVD:* ♫♫♫
Warner Home Video (UPC 0853913278-20). Widescreen (2.35:1) anamorphic. Dolby Digital Surround Stereo. $19.99. Snapper. *LANG:* English. *FEATURES:* Trailer ▪ "Bastian's Challenge" game.
1991 (PG) 90m/C Jonathan Brandis, Kenny Morrison, Clarissa Burt, John Wesley Shipp, Martin Umbach; *D:* George Miller; *W:* Karin Howard; *C:* David Connell; *M:* Robert Folk.

The New Daughters of Joshua Cabe

Sequel to the made-for-TV movie finds Sheriff Cabe (McIntire) unjustly accused and jailed. His adopted daughters must save the day. DVD is an accurate reproduction of a scratched, faded cut-rate original. Title is also available as part of *The Wild West* boxed set (cat.# 44213-9). —MM
Movie: ♫♫ *DVD:* ♫♫
Brentwood (cat #44083-9, UPC 78736440-8399). Full frame. $9.98. Keepcase. *LANG:* English. *FEATURES:* "Spooky Hooky" cartoon ▪ 6 chapters ▪ DVD dictionary ▪ DVD-ROM features ▪ Trivia game.
1976 80m/C John McIntire, Jack Elam, Geoffrey Lewis, John Dehner; *D:* Bruce Bilson; *W:* Margaret Armen, Paul Savage.

The New Gladiators

In the distant future, reality television has upped the ante. The newest show pits death row criminals against each other (on motorcycles!) in a fight to the death.

Even though it was made in the '80s, the set design and special effects make the film look like a forgotten episode of *Lost in Space*. Picture and audio are both video quality, and Troma doesn't seem to want to tell us if the film was originally full frame or if this is a pan-and-scan version. The extras are of marginal quality and questionable relevance. —BG
Movie: woof *DVD:* ♫½
Troma Team Video (cat #9033, UPC 7903-57903337). Full frame. $19.95. Keepcase. *LANG:* English. *FEATURES:* 9 chapters ▪ Commentary ▪ Interview with Dario Argento ▪ Interview with Antonella Fulci ▪ Trailers.
1983 90m/C IT Jared Martin, Fred Williamson, Eleanor Gold, Howard (Red) Ross, Claudio Cassinelli; *D:* Lucio Fulci; *W:* Elisa Briganti, Dardano Sacchetti; *C:* Guiseppe Pinori; *M:* Riz Ortolani.

New Port South

Disaffected high school student Maddox (Shields) takes a cue from a now-institutionalized former student and attempts to disrupt the power structure at his suburban Chicago school. His fellow students help him for awhile, but they don't share his troubled convictions. The teachers struggle to maintain a balanced approach to keeping control of their territory. Only marred by occasional flashes of excess, John Hughes's son James has crafted a very thoughtful and provocative story about student/teacher relations. Beautifully photographed by Ruiz-Anchia and stylishly directed by title designer Cooper. Soundtrack adds to the atmosphere as opposed to simply trying to sell records. This movie is for intelligent teenagers. Image and sound quality is tiptop in keeping with the excellent production values on this picture. —LA
Movie: ♫♫♫ ½ *DVD:* ♫♫♫ ½
Buena Vista Home Ent. (cat #21677, UPC 786936145021). Widescreen (1.85:1) anamorphic. Dolby Digital 5.1 Surround; DTS 5.1 Surround. $29.98. Keepcase. *LANG:* English. *CAP:* English. *FEATURES:* 18 chapters.
2000 (PG-13) 97m/C Todd Field, Will Estes, Melissa George, Gabriel Mann, Blake Shields; *D:* Kyle Cooper; *W:* James Hughes; *C:* Juan Ruiz-Anchia.

New York in the Fifties

Modest little documentary is little more than a collection of talking heads, but the talk is fascinating and crisply edited. It's based on Dan Wakefield's book. He and several other people who were involved in the New York literary/artistic scene of the 1950s reminisce about those halcyon days. Subjects include Robert Redford, Joan Didion, John Gregory Dunne, Nat Hentoff, Nan and Gay Talese, and Calvin Trillin. (William F. Buckley also appears but he seems properly mortified to be in this group.) Film clips of Jack Kerouac, Steve Allen, and Stormin' Norman Mailer enliven the relatively static action. It was essentially a man's world then, ruled by the returning World War II veterans. The main subjects of discussion are sex and literature; the participants divide their comments between the expected nostalgic musings and clear-eyed analysis of the changes that rolled through those years, ending on November 22, 1963. DVD quality is very good. Archival footage hasn't been cleaned up too much, and that's fine. —*MM*

Movie: 𝄞𝄞𝄞 **DVD:** 𝄞𝄞𝄞

First Run Features (UPC 720229909839). Full frame. $29.95. Keepcase. *LANG:* English. *FEATURES:* 12 chapters ● Trailer ● Director's interview.

2001 72m/C Robert Redford, Joan Didion, John Gregory Dunne, Nat Hentoff, Nan Talese, Gay Talese, Calvin Trillin, William F. Buckley; *D:* Betsy Blankenbaker; *C:* Bobby Shepard; *M:* Steve Allee.

Newsies

An unfortunate attempt at an old-fashioned musical with a lot of cute kids and cardboard characters and settings. (The film plays like *Annie* with boys instead of girls.) The plot, such as it is, concerns the 1899 New York City newsboys strike against penny-pinching publisher Joseph Pulitzer. Christian Bale (who would later go on to be the *American Psycho*!) plays the newsboys' leader and at least shows some charisma in a strictly cartoon setting. The songs are mediocre, but the dancing is lively. However, none of it moves the story along. This was the directorial debut of choreographer Kenny Ortega (*Dirty Dancing, Shag, Xanadu*). Add a bone to the critical rating for viewers under 12. Despite the somewhat dubious reputation of *Newsies,* Disney has given the DVD the Special Edition treatment. The 2.35:1 anamorphic image looks very good: sharp and clear, showing no grain or artifacting. The image does get soft at times, but these instances are rare. The color scheme, made up mostly of dark, drab colors, looks fine here. The Dolby Digital 5.1 audio track is splendid, giving fresh life to the musical score. The dialogue is clear and there is a nice use of Surround sound, but there is a noticeable lack of bass response. This DVD is loaded with extra features, the best of which is a featurette which focuses on the true story behind the film. The audio commentary is also informative and entertaining. —*ML*

Movie: 𝄞 ½ **DVD:** 𝄞𝄞𝄞 ½

Buena Vista Home Ent. (cat #23688, UPC 786936162783). Widescreen (2.35:1) anamorphic. Dolby Digital 5.1. $29.99. Keepcase. *LANG:* English; Spanish. *SUB:* English; Spanish; French. *CAP:* English. *FEATURES:* Commentary ● Featurettes ● Storyboards ● Theatrical trailers ● Sing-a-long ● 22 chapters.

1992 (PG) 121m/C Christian Bale, Bill Pullman, Robert Duvall, Ann-Margret, Michael Lerner, Kevin Tighe, Charles Cioffi, Luke Edwards, Max Casella, David Moscow; *D:* Kenny Ortega; *W:* Bob Tzudik-

er; *C:* Noni White; *M:* Alan Menken, Jack Feldman. *AWARDS:* Golden Raspberries '92: Worst Song ("High Times, Hard Times").

Next of Kin

Please see review of *Family Viewing.*

Movie: 𝄞𝄞𝄞 ½ **DVD:** 𝄞𝄞𝄞

Zeitgeist Films (cat #Z1003, UPC 797575-100333). Full frame. $34.99. Keepcase. *LANG:* English. *SUB:* English; French. *FEATURES:* 18 chapters ● Commentary: director ● Bio/filmography ● Rehearsal footage ● Photo gallery.

1984 72m/C *CA* Patrick Tierney; *D:* Atom Egoyan; *W:* Atom Egoyan.

Next Time

Offbeat romance tells the story of the relationship between Matt (Campbell), a young white guy, and Evelyn (Allen), a 39-year-old black woman, who meet at a laundrette. The film was made on the tiniest of budgets and the bare-bones DVD cannot improve the exceptionally grainy and harsh image. It's equal to VHS tape. —*MM*

Movie: 𝄞𝄞 ½ **DVD:** 𝄞𝄞

Vanguard Intl. Cinema (cat #VF0184). Full frame. $29.95. Keepcase. *LANG:* English. *FEATURES:* Trailer ● 12 chapters.

1999 97m/C Jonelle Allen, Christian Campbell, Ishtar Robert Harper, Iona Morris; *D:* L. Alan Fraser; *W:* L. Alan Fraser; *C:* William Hooke; *M:* James S. Mulhollan Jr.

Niagara

Honeymooners Polly and Ray Cutler (Peters and Adams) are enjoying a belated Niagara Falls honeymoon until they become involved in the noirish misery of the couple in the bungalow next door: George Loomis (Cotten) is insanely jealous of his floozie wife Rose (Monroe), a knockout mantrap with a boyfriend on the side. Polly is drawn to the melancholy George, which is a bad idea as the whole situation is about to turn homicidal. DVD delivers a film that looks better than I've ever seen it before. Title is part of the *Marilyn Monroe: The Diamond Collection, Vol. 2.* —*GE*

Movie: 𝄞𝄞𝄞 **DVD:** 𝄞𝄞𝄞

20th Century Fox (UPC 024543035169). Full frame. Stereo. Mono. $19.98. Keepcase. *LANG:* English; French. *SUB:* English; Spanish. *CAP:* English. *FEATURES:* Restoration comparison ● Trailer ● Still gallery.

1952 89m/B Joseph Cotten, Jean Peters, Marilyn Monroe, Max (Casey Adams) Showalter, Don Wilson; *D:* Henry Hathaway; *W:* Charles Brackett, Walter Reisch; *C:* Joe MacDonald; *M:* Sol Kaplan.

Nico and Dani

During summer vacation, two teenaged friends experiment with each other sexually. As the holiday progresses, their differing sexual identities begin to emerge and they make tentative steps towards manhood. A sweet and affecting coming-of-

age tale told with a refreshingly naturalistic approach. Director Gay avoids knee-jerk melodrama and clichéd plot twists in a very quiet, likable film. Though based on a play, the film never feels static and the production makes picturesque use of its Spanish seaside locations. The young leads turn in remarkable performances that successfully convey both the awkwardness and excitement of adolescence. While not perfect, the disc is perfectly acceptable. Colors appear accurate, the image is sharp and the print source is clean. The image tends to be a bit grainy and panning movements (such as the opening sequence which is shot from a moving train) tend to look overtly noisy. The sound recording and Surround mix are terrific, drawing the audience into the atmosphere of the film. The worthwhile featurette showcases behind-the-filming footage and interviews with the principal participants. —*DG* **AKA:** *Krampack.*

Movie: 𝄞𝄞𝄞 **DVD:** 𝄞𝄞𝄞

New Yorker Video (cat #DVD82801, UPC 717119828141). Widescreen (1.85:1) anamorphic. Dolby Digital Surround. $29.95. Keepcase. *LANG:* Spanish. *SUB:* English; Spanish. *FEATURES:* 6 chapters ● "Making of" featurette ● Interviews with director and cast ● 2 music videos ● Theatrical trailer ● Insert foldout with chapter listings.

2000 90m/C *SP* Fernando Ramallo, Jordi Vilches, Marieta Orozco, Esther Nubiola, Chisco Amado, Ana Gracia; *D:* Cesc Gay; *W:* Cesc Gay, Tomas Aragay; *C:* Andreu Rebes; *M:* Riqui Sabates, Joan Diaz, Jordi Prats.

Night Divides the Day

A serial killer is stalking the students at Hollow Pointe University. The exceptionally low-budget film is more of a serious independent effort than exploitation. Production values are strictly on the *Blair Witch* level, so DVD does little more than provide extras. —*MM*

Movie: 𝄞𝄞 **DVD:** 𝄞𝄞

El Independent Cinema (cat #vo-9503, UPC 612385950391). Full frame. $19.95. Keepcase. *LANG:* English. *FEATURES:* Outtakes ● Trailers ● "911" short film ● "The Initiation" short film.

2001 125m/C Tiffany Richards, John Stump, David Strowell, Jeff Burton, Michael McCallum, Lynn Wolfbrandt; *D:* Jeff Burton; *W:* Alex Hencken, Joe Cottonmouth, Jeff Burton; *M:* Jeff Burton.

The Night Heaven Fell

Ursula (Brigitte Bardot) returns from the convent to the Spanish town where her Aunt Florentine (Alida Valli) lives unhappily with Count Ribera (Pepe Nieto), a macho brute and womanizer. A local malcontent, Lambert (Stephen Boyd) has returned from political exile to find his sister dead by suicide over the Count; and a deadly feud is reignited. Complicating matters is Aunt Florentine's unwillingness to admit

her love for Lambert, and virgin Ursula's instantaneous attraction to him. It's serious, overheated melodrama in a commercial package that reveals Roger Vadim to be basically the sex merchant everyone accuses him of being. DVD is beautiful-looking and sounding, plain and simple. Again, the extras are slim but the presentation attractive, with the film's original artwork on the insert. Liner notes are split between Michael Frost's informative essay, and more muck from Chris Gore about his adolescent masturbatory fantasies. The cover art has a provocative still of an arm about to yank a Spanish mantilla from the naked body of our beloved BB. She's pouting, probably trying to figure out just what kind of career she's gotten herself into. —GE **AKA:** Les Bijoutiers du Clair de Lune.
Movie: 🎬🎬 ½ ***DVD:*** 🎬🎬🎬
Home Vision Cinema (cat #NIG 100, UPC 037429161029). Widescreen (2.35:1) anamorphic. $29.95. Keepcase. *LANG:* French. *SUB:* English. *FEATURES:* 19 chapters ▪ Michael Frost essay ▪ Liner notes by Chris Gore.
1957 95m/C *FR IT* Brigitte Bardot, Stephen Boyd, Alida Valli, Pepe Nieto; ***D:*** Roger Vadim; ***W:*** Roger Vadim, Peter Viertel, Jacques Remy; ***C:*** Armand Thirard; ***M:*** Georges Auric.

Night of the Ghouls

This is the second to last in Ed Wood's celebrated series of inept horror movies that began with *Bride of the Monster* and *Plan 9 from Outer Space,* and if it doesn't quite sink to the wonderful depths of those alternative gems, it contains enough silliness for fans. The nutball plot concerns a cop (Moore) in evening dress who investigates a fake psychic (Duncan) in a turban. DVD image is as good as it could possibly be. To give Ed his due, he could produce clearly focused black-and-white photography in some interiors. At other times, of course, the image is far too dark and murky to make anything out, and the writing and acting exist in their own Woodsian universe. —MM **AKA:** Revenge of the Dead.
Movie: 🎬 ***DVD:*** 🎬🎬
Image Ent. (cat #ID8697CODVD, UPC 014-381869729). Full frame. Dolby Digital Mono. $24.99. Keepcase. *LANG:* English. *FEATURES:* 12 chapters ▪ Trailers.
1959 69m/B Paul Marco, Tor Johnson, Duke Moore, Kenne Duncan, John Carpenter, Criswell, Bud Osborne, Anthony Cardoza, Vampira, Valda Hansen, Tom Mason; ***D:*** Edward D. Wood Jr.; ***W:*** Edward D. Wood Jr.; ***C:*** William C. Thompson.

Night of the Living Dead [Elite ME]

(For film review see *Book 2.*) The primary difference in this second Elite DVD release is the inclusion of all the extras that were part of the label's groundbreaking laserdisc release. This edition looks nearly identical to the previous release;

that is to say, perfect. A 5.1 Surround mix is also exclusive to this version and it's a bit clearer and bolder than the mono track. It offers little Surround presence, though. The additional interviews, memorabilia, and script-viewing options make this the best edition of the film on the market. —DG **AKA:** Night of the Flesh Eaters; Night of the Anubis.
Movie: 🎬🎬🎬 ½ ***DVD:*** 🎬🎬🎬🎬
Elite Entertainment, Inc. (cat #EE1117, UPC 790594111724). Full frame. Dolby Digital 5.1 Surround; Mono. $24.95. Keepcase. *LANG:* English. *FEATURES:* Liner notes by Stephen King ▪ Liner notes by George Romero ▪ 12 chapters ▪ 2 audio commentaries ▪ THX Optimizer ▪ Script ▪ Scrapbooks/memorabilia gallery ▪ "Night of the Living Bread" short ▪ Audio interview with Duane Jones ▪ Judith Ridley interview ▪ Scenes from "There's Always Vanilla" ▪ Stills and poster gallery from "There's Always Vanilla" ▪ Trailer and TV spot ▪ Outtakes from "The Derelict" ▪ Notes on Image Ten/The Latent Image ▪ 8 Image Ten commercials.
1968 90m/B Judith O'Dea, Duane Jones, Karl Hardman, Marilyn Eastman, Keith Wayne, Judith Ridley, Russell Streiner, Bill "Chilly Billy" Cardille, John A. Russo, Kyra Schon, Bill (William Heinzman) Hinzman, John Simpson, Vincent Survinski, George A. Romero; ***D:*** George A. Romero; ***W:*** John A. Russo, George A. Romero; ***C:*** George A. Romero. *AWARDS:* Natl. Film Reg. '99.

Night on the Galactic Railroad

Lonely student Giovanni, alone and caring for his sick mother, is out watching the stars one night when a gigantic train appears out of nowhere. Boarding it, he finds his sole friend Campanella, and embarks on an interstellar journey that might also be transporting the dead to the afterlife. This slow and somewhat ponderous animated feature is based on a novel written by Kenji Mayazawa, but recasts the characters as cats. There are some haunting moments (an episode involving victims of the "R.M.S. Titanic" is particularly effective) and a sad ending, but it somehow misses the mark. The music (which should be much stronger and virtually omnipresent) is more quirky than appropriate. The disc features strong colors but some very fine digital smear is occasionally noticeable on the image. The presentation seems to be a 1.66 version of a 1.85 original. It's still a better choice than VHS, and boasts a crisp (though fairly quiet) sound mix. The DVD-ROM features are an appreciated bonus. Will most likely improve on repeated viewings where the problems with the pacing should be less obvious. The original language is the preferred option. —DG **AKA:** Night on the Milky Way Railroad; Ginga Tetsudo No Yoru.
Movie: 🎬🎬 ½ ***DVD:*** 🎬🎬 ½
Central Park/U.S. Manga (cat #CPMD20-71, UPC 719987207127). Widescreen (1.66:1) letterboxed. Dolby Stereo. $29.99. Keepcase. *LANG:* Japanese; English. *SUB:*

English. *FEATURES:* 21 chapters ▪ Trailer ▪ Art gallery ▪ Production history ▪ DVD-ROM: Cast & production info ▪ DVD-ROM: Script ▪ DVD-ROM: Art Gallery & History.
1985 108m/C *JP* ***D:*** Gisaburo Sugii; ***W:*** Minoru Betsuyaku; ***M:*** Haruomi Hosono.

Night Orchid

Filmmaker Mark Atkins heads for Stephen King territory with the story of a young psychic (Paris) who arrives in a rural hamlet and has visions of murders. For a low-budget video premiere, this one looks very good. It's made with a degree of style and originality, and the extras are well-chosen. Fans have seen much worse. —MM
Movie: 🎬🎬🎬 ***DVD:*** 🎬🎬🎬
York Ent. (cat #YPD-1145, UPC 75072311-4521). Widescreen letterboxed. $14.99. Keepcase. *LANG:* English. *FEATURES:* Trailers ▪ Deleted scenes and outtakes ▪ Director's intro and outtakes.
1997 (R) 93m/C Dale Paris, Alyssa Simon, Mary Ellen O'Brien; ***D:*** Mark Atkins; ***C:*** Paul Atkins; ***M:*** C.C. Adcock.

Night to Dismember

Director Doris Wishman has the reputation that equals Ed Wood Jr.'s as an auteur of alternative classics. This piece of junk cements her place in the cinematic hall of shame. On her commentary track, she admits that the original negative was lost/ruined in the lab and she had to salvage this footage. It apparently has something to do with a psychotic killer but characters wander in and out for no reason, as does Wishman's camera. It's simply incoherent crap filled with lots of fake blood. Lighting is so poor that any comment on DVD image quality is pointless. —MM
Movie: woof ***DVD:*** 🎬 ½
Elite Entertainment, Inc. (cat #EE3674, UPC 790594367428). Widescreen (1.85:1) anamorphic. $24.95. Keepcase. *LANG:* English. *FEATURES:* Trailer ▪ 8 chapters ▪ Commentary: Doris Wishman, D.P. C. Davis Smith.
1983 69m/C Samantha Fox, Diane Cummings, Saul Meth; ***D:*** Doris Wishman; ***W:*** Doris Wishman; ***C:*** C. Davis Smith.

Nightbreed

A teenager flees a chaotic past to slowly become a member of a bizarre race of demons that live in a huge, abandoned Canadian graveyard; a place where every sin is forgiven. Based on Barker's novel *Cabal,* and appropriately gross, nonsensical, and strange. Good special effects enhance the overall creepiness. Horror director David Cronenberg's performance is a definite plus. A lot of the atmosphere was lost in the previous video editions of *Nightbreed,* but it's all back on this fine transfer to DVD by Warner. The DVD is able to convey the subtle difference in hues and that may be all it took to make the difference. The image is also very sharp with excellent contrast and brightness levels. Another big difference is in the soundtrack, with the 5.1 delivering plenty of information to the Surround channels. The improved sound also allows the eerie Danny Elfman score to mingle well with the crisp dialogue and aforementioned Surround effects. Unfortunately, there are basically no supplementals—a commentary by Barker would have been especially appreciated. —JO

Movie: 🎬🎬🎬 **DVD:** 🎬🎬🎬 ½
Warner (cat #18537, UPC 0853918537-25). Widescreen (1.85:1) anamorphic. Dolby Digital 5.1; Dolby Digital Stereo. $19.98. Snapper. *LANG:* English. *SUB:* English; Spanish; French. *CAP:* English. *FEATURES:* 30 chapters ● Theatrical trailer ● Talent files.
1990 (R) 102m/C *CA* Craig Sheffer, Anne Bobby, David Cronenberg, Charles Haid; *D:* Clive Barker; *W:* Clive Barker; *C:* Robin Vidgeon; *M:* Danny Elfman.

Nightmaster

A handful of karate students practice their homework with much higher stakes away from the classroom. For them, deadly Ninja games are the only way to study. Early Kidman outing lensed in Australia is a bit befuddling to watch thanks to useless flashbacks and plot elements thrown in seemingly for no other reason than to gain a little running time. If you just want to see a young Nicole Kidman, maybe you can suffer through this DVD. But is the headache caused by your eyes trying to focus on the soft, grainy picture really worth it? It doesn't matter if the scene is brightly lit, dark, full of detail, or just a simple close-up, the image is consistently atrocious. Reds bleed horribly. Amazingly enough, the blacks are pretty good with very little grain. The sound fares much better and, though just stereo, there is nice imaging and separation, particularly during music numbers, which although not terrible in an '80s power pop way, seem there only to help the film achieve feature length. —JO

Movie: 🎬 **DVD:** 🎬
Lion's Gate Home Ent. (cat #VM7945D, UPC 031398794523). Full frame. Dolby Digital Stereo. $14.99. Keepcase. *LANG:* English. *SUB:* English; Spanish. *CAP:* English. *FEATURES:* 24 chapters.
1987 (R) 91m/C *AU* Nicole Kidman, Tom Jennings, Vince Martin, Joanne Samuel; *D:* Mark Joffe; *W:* Michael McGennan.

Nine Lives of Fritz the Cat

Fritz gets fed up with his '70s lifestyle, so he sets out on a new series of "wild" adventures. Without the involvement of originator R. Crumb or the first film's director, Ralph Bakshi (already a fall from Zap Comics), this pale sequel is almost criminal. MGM lists this as an entry in its "Avant Garde" category, a sad commentary in itself. The usual top-notch MGM DVD transfer and sound, however. —MO

Movie: 🎬🎬 **DVD:** 🎬🎬🎬 ½

MGM Home Ent. (cat #1002735, UPC 027-616869333). Widescreen anamorphic. Dolby Digital 2.0 Mono. $19.98. Keepcase. *LANG:* English. *SUB:* English; Spanish; French. *CAP:* English; Spanish; French. *FEATURES:* 16 chapters ● Theatrical trailer.
1974 77m/C *D:* Robert Taylor; *W:* Robert Taylor, Eric Monte; *V:* Skip Hinnant.

1969

Absolutely nothing about rotten little movie rings true. The title leads you to believe that it has something significant to say about a very difficult, complicated time. It does try to do that, but writer/novice director Ernest Thompson gets it all wrong. Ralph and Scott (Downey Jr. and Sutherland), longtime neighbors and best friends, are sophomores at a small Maryland college. Scott's parents (Dern and Hartley) don't agree with his long hair and weird ideas. Ralph's mother (Cassidy) drinks too much and talks too loud. Ralph's younger sister (Ryder) thinks Scott is "beautiful." Scott's brother (Wynne) goes to fight in Vietnam. Near the beginning, the moms and the sister come to visit the guys at college. After a contrived accident, they all get caught up in the occupation of a building by students. The cops come bursting in and club everyone in sight. But they stop when Scott gets mad. He yells, "Stupid cops," the police back off, and they all walk away. Riiiight. From there, it gets even worse. Thompson tries to impose his own saccharine Norman Rockwell, *On Golden Pond* sensibility on that confrontational year and it just doesn't work. The actors may have sensed the basic falseness of the material because they're stiff and numb throughout. The story wanders aimlessly in the middle, with a lot of second-rate oldies on the soundtrack, and then arrives at a conclusion that defies description. In clear defiance of the material, the DVD image is nothing less than excellent. Adding insult to absurdity, the film is presented in both full-frame and anamorphic widescreen versions. Inexplicable. —MM

Movie: woof **DVD:** 🎬🎬🎬
MGM Home Ent. (cat #1003339, UPC 027-616874887). Widescreen (1.85:1) anamorphic; full frame. Dolby Digital Surround. $14.98. Keepcase. *LANG:* English. *SUB:* English; French; Spanish. *CAP:* English. *FEATURES:* 16 chapters ● Trailer.
1989 (R) 96m/C Kiefer Sutherland, Robert Downey Jr., Winona Ryder, Bruce Dern, Joanna Cassidy, Mariette Hartley, Christopher Wynne; *D:* Ernest Thompson; *W:* Ernest Thompson; *C:* Jules Brenner; *M:* Michael Small.

1999

A New Year's Eve party provides a group of New Yorkers with the opportunity to kvetch, flirt, and generally get silly. Some of it—notably the scenes with Buck Henry and Stephen Wright—is very funny. Other parts are less successful. Throughout, the image ranges between poor and very poor. DVD

appears to provide a good reproduction of an atrociously lighted original. —MM
Movie: 🎬🎬 **DVD:** 🎬🎬
York Ent. (cat #YPD-1084, UPC 75072310-8421). Widescreen letterboxed. $14.99. Keepcase. *LANG:* English. *FEATURES:* Trailers ● Director's intro and commentary ● Audition tape.
1998 (R) 93m/C Dan Futterman, Jennifer Garner, Matt McGrath, Amanda Peet, Steven Wright, Sandrine Holt, Buck Henry, Margaret Devine, Daniel Lapaine, David Gelb, Nick Davis; *D:* Nick Davis; *W:* Nick Davis; *C:* Howard Krupa; *M:* Sue Jacobs, Lynne Geller.

Ninja in the Deadly Trap

Ming Dynasty General Ti Lung succeeds in repelling marauding Japanese troops, but a band of ninja fighters led by Yasuaki Kurata still resists. The general sends his son to seek out the old Master of the 3 Arts, who knows the ways of the ninja, to help them learn how to catch the assassins. The Master offers the help of his three students: Philip Kwok is expert at acrobatics; Lu Feng is a weapons and combat master; and Chiang Sheng is an adept hand-to-hand fighter. Meanwhile, the assassins work their way into the general's household. The three students secretly take jobs on the staff as well, and wait for the assassins to make their move. Director Philip Kwok takes far too long to gather his three ninja-teers, wasting time with meaningless intrigues, but things really start hopping in the third act. The ninja techniques and weaponry are reasonably historically accurate, though some cinematic license is taken The full-frame image transfer is soft, but surprisingly colorful for its age, but the cropping from widescreen does serious damage to the composition of almost every shot. The audio commentary by HK film expert Ric Meyers and martial artist Bobby Samuels provides a rambling but informative commentary track. —BT **AKA:** Heroes Defeat Japs; Hero Defeating Japs; Ninja Kung Fu; Ninjutsu; Ruthless Tactics.
Movie: 🎬🎬🎬 **DVD:** 🎬🎬 ½
Tai Seng (cat #84094, UPC 6016438409-49). Full frame. $14.95. Keepcase. *LANG:* English. *FEATURES:* 8 chapters ● Video trailers ● Commentary.
1983 92m/C *TW* Philip Kwok, Ti Lung, Sheng Chiang, Feng Lu, Kurata Yasuaki, Chuen Yung Chung; *D:* Philip Kwok; *W:* Saishing Sum; *C:* Kam-chun Yu.

Ninja in the U.S.A.

Evil drug kingpin Tyger McFerson (George Nicholas Albergo) is acquitted of murder charges because all witnesses against him have been killed by his ninja army. Cops Rodney Kuen and Jerry Wong (Alexander Lou) give McFerson the benefit of the doubt because he saved their lives in Vietnam. But when Jerry's reporter wife is kidnapped by Tyger's ninjas to suppress evidence against him, Jerry suits up with all his ninja gear and storms McFerson's compound. Despite the video release title, there's no reason to believe any of this takes place anywhere in the United States. The dubbing is absolutely horrendous. The picture is severely cropped from widescreen. Enjoy! —BT

Movie: ♫ ½ **DVD:** ♫
Tai Seng (cat #86594, UPC 6016438659-42). Full frame. $14.95. Keepcase. *LANG:* English. *FEATURES:* 8 chapters • Martial Arts Theater ad • Video trailers.
1988 93m/C *TW* Alexander Lou, George Nicholas Albergo, Eugene Thomas, Alex Yip; *D:* Dennis Wu; *W:* Ed Jones; *C:* Owen Casey; *M:* Sherman Chow.

Ninja vs. Shaolin Guards

Four monks are entrusted to take the Golden Sutra of Da Mor to Tibet, as New Republic assassins pursue. There's also a ruthless bounty hunter on their trail. Robert Tai's fight choreography is excellent, and there's some awesome action scenes here, especially those set in the snowy mountain forests. As usual, the fanciful ninja hijinks are highly entertaining. The cropped image, from a slightly speckled print, seriously impairs viewing. —BT
AKA: Guards of Shaolin.
Movie: ♫♫ ½ **DVD:** ♫ ½
Tai Seng (cat #91594, UPC 6016439159-44). Full frame. $14.95. Keepcase. *LANG:* English. *FEATURES:* 8 chapters.
1984 86m/C *TW* Alexander Lou, Robert Tai, Alan Chui, Fun Kim, Lung Wong; *D:* William Chung Kei; *W:* George Ma; *C:* Miyaki Yukio.

No Man's Land

Brilliant Oscar-winning satire on the futility of war with the added distinction of being highly entertaining. Bosnian soldier Ciki (Djuric) finds himself in a trench between the Bosnian line and the Serbian line. The Serbs have planted a mine under one of his comrades that will explode when the body is moved, but his comrade isn't dead. When a Serbian soldier becomes trapped along with them, they have to pool their resources to survive. Sound and image qualities are excellent. —LA
Movie: ♫♫♫♫ **DVD:** ♫♫♫♫
MGM Home Ent. (cat #1003329, UPC 027-626874788). Widescreen (2.35:1) anamorphic; full frame. 5.1 Surround. $26.98. Keepcase. *LANG:* Serbo-Croatian. *SUB:* English; French; Spanish. *CAP:* English. *FEATURES:* Original theatrical trailer • 16 chapters.
2001 (R) 98m/C *BS FR IT BE GB* Branko Djuric, Rene Bitoraje, Filip Sovagovic, Georges Siatidis, Serge-Henri Valcke, Simon Callow, Katrin Cartlidge; *D:* Danis Tanovic; *W:* Danis Tanovic; *C:* Walther Vanden Ende; *M:* Danis Tanovic. *AWARDS:* Oscars '01: Foreign Film; Cannes '01: Screenplay; L.A. Film Critics '01: Foreign Film; *NOM:* Broadcast Film Critics '01: Foreign Film.

Nomads

Famous anthropologist Jean Pommier (Brosnan, sporting a lumberjack beard and a goofy French accent) moves to the U.S. to settle down. But his new home seems to attract a strange group of vagabonds, who may be tied to the house's past. If you can get by the '80s hard rock score there are some genuine chills in this understated horror film. MGM's DVD is from their bargain basement-priced series, so not much should be expected. Given that, the film looks fine, and handles the music and dialogue well. MGM has settled into the groove of releasing double-sided discs with both full frame and anamorphic versions; let's hope this practice continues. —BG
Movie: ♫♫ ½ **DVD:** ♫♫ ½
MGM Home Ent. (cat #1003352, UPC 027-616875013). Widescreen (1.85:1) anamorphic; full frame. Dolby Mono. $14.95. Keepcase. *LANG:* English. *SUB:* English; French; Spanish. *CAP:* English. *FEATURES:* 16 chapters • Trailer.
1986 (R) 91m/C Pierce Brosnan, Lesley-Anne Down, Adam Ant, Anna Maria Monticelli, Mary Woronov, Hector Mercado; *D:* John McTiernan; *W:* John McTiernan; *C:* Stephen Ramsey; *M:* Bill Conti.

The North Star

Given the reputation of the talent behind the screen—script by Lillian Hellman, direction by Lewis Milestone, music by Aaron Copland, cinematography by James Wong Howe—this is an unusually ham-fisted bit of propaganda. It was made at a time when Russians were our valiant Soviet allies (not Godless Communists they had been and would become after the war) but that's no excuse. The story concerns the efforts of a collective village to resist the German army. DVD image appears to be a relatively accurate re-creation of an exceptionally grainy and/or well-worn original. Sound is shrill at times with near constant static. Title is part of the *Great WWII Movies* disc. —MM **AKA:** Armored Attack.
Movie: ♫ ½ **DVD:** ♫♫
BFS Video (cat #30294-D, UPC 06680530-2947). Full frame. $9.98. Keepcase. *LANG:* English. *FEATURES:* 6 chapters • Talent files.
1943 108m/B Dana Andrews, Walter Huston, Anne Baxter, Farley Granger, Walter Brennan, Erich von Stroheim, Jack Perrin, Dean Jagger; *D:* Lewis Milestone; *W:* Lillian Hellman; *C:* James Wong Howe; *M:* Aaron Copland. *AWARDS:* NOM: Oscars '43: B&W Cinematog., Orig. Screenplay, Sound, Orig. Dramatic Score.

Nosferatu [Triton]

Please see review for *German Silent Masterpieces*. **AKA:** Nosferatu, Eine Symphonie des Grauens; Nosferatu, A Symphony of Terror; Nosferatu, A Symphony of Horror; Nosferatu, the Vampire; Terror of Dracula; Die Zwolfte Stunde.
Movie: ♫♫♫♫

1922 63m/B *GE* Max Schreck, Alexander Granach, Gustav von Wagenheim, Greta Schroder, John Gottowt, Ruth Landshoff, G.H. Schnell; *D:* F.W. Murnau; *W:* Henrik Galeen; *C:* Fritz Arno Wagner, Gunther Krampf.

Nostradamus: His Life and Prophecies / Prophecy and Prediction

These sensationalist programs should give conspiracy hounds something to sink their teeth into. "Nostradamus" details the life and examines the prophecies of the famous seer, discussing what has come true and what is yet to be. "Prophecy and Prediction" uses the foresight of both ancient and modern prophets to tell of the coming Armageddon. Both programs focus on what will happen just before and at the dawn of the millennium, making what is being said more outdated, and more humorous, every day. Both the DVD's image and sound are average, no better than a video. —DRL
Movie: ♫ ½ **DVD:** ♫♫
BFS Video (cat #30285, UPC 066805302-855). Full frame. Mono. $19.95. Keepcase. *LANG:* English. *FEATURES:* 12 chapters.
1994 142m/C *D:* Kevin Jordan, Klaus Kamphausen.

Not Another Teen Movie

Mostly on-target (and proudly tasteless) parody hits all of the conventions of Hollywood movies aimed at young audiences. But it is also remarkable for the amount of raunchy sexual humor that the MPAA allowed within the limits of an "R" rating. (Nothing in the 18 deleted scenes comes close to the nasty stuff that was left in the opening scenes!) Janey Briggs (Leigh) is the smart teenaged beauty who hides behind glasses, books, severe hair-do, and paint-spattered clothes. She's secretly in love with the handsome quarterback (Evans), who asks the ugly duckling to the prom on a bet. We've also got the Cruel girl (Kirshner), the cheerleader (Pressley), etc. Cinematic targets include *16 Candles, American Beauty,* and dozens of others. Molly Ringwald's cameo at the end is inspired. DVD image looks fine for a movie that was never meant to be polished in any regard, and the package contains an abundance of extras. As is so often the case, the deleted scenes were wisely cut. —MM
Movie: ♫♫♫ **DVD:** ♫♫♫
Columbia Tristar (cat #07602, UPC 0433-96076020). Widescreen (1.85:1) anamorphic. Dolby Digital 5.1 Surround. $27.96. Keepcase. *LANG:* English; French. *SUB:* English; French. *CAP:* English. *FEATURES:* 28 chapters • 2 commentary tracks • 18 deleted scenes • Unrated Marilyn Manson music video • Teen movie quiz • Talent files • Trailers • Auditions montage • Joel Gallen's short film "Car

Ride" ▪ 3 behind-the-scenes featurette ▪ Teen movie factoids track.

2001 (R) 90m/C Chyler Leigh, Chris Evans, Eric Jungmann, Eric Christian Olsen, Cody McMains, Sam Huntington, Ron Lester, Samm Levine, Deon Richmond, Jaime Pressly, Mia Kirshner, Riley Smith, Lacey Chabert, Cerina Vincent, Beverly Polcyn, Joanna Garcia, Randy Quaid, Ed Lauter, Mr. T, Paul Gleason, Molly Ringwald; **D:** Joel Gallen; **W:** Michael G. Bender, Adam Jay Epstein, Andrew Jacobson, Phil Beauman, Buddy Johnson; **C:** Reynaldo Villalobos; **M:** Theodore Shapiro.

Not Love Just Frenzy

Max (Novo), Yeye (Rubio), and Monica (Cuervo) swap bodily fluids and bitch slaps in this weirdly dated, nihilistic, ultimately very shallow look at sex-obsessed Madrid youth. Their kooky friends love them anyway. The lesbian madam is not a reincarnation of Bergman alum Bibi Andersson; she's just another blonde Spanish bombshell. Look for useless cameos by such famous contemporary Spanish stars as Javier Bardem and Penelope Cruz. Transfer from release print actually looks pretty good. The reel changes are pretty clean and the image doesn't pick up too much contrast. Sound is unspectacular. —LA **AKA:** Mas Que Amor Frenesi.

Movie: 🎬🎬 ½ **DVD:** 🎬🎬 ½
Image Ent. (cat #ID0757JDDVD, UPC 0143-81075724). Widescreen (1.85:1) anamorphic. Dolby Digital Stereo. $24.98. Keepcase. *LANG:* Spanish. *SUB:* English. *FEATURES:* 14 chapters.
1996 104m/C *SP* Nancho Novo, Cayetana Guillen Cuervo, Ingrid Rubio, Beatriz Santiago, Javier Bardem, Penelope Cruz; **D:** Alfonso Albacete, Miguel Bardem, David Menkes; **W:** Alfonso Albacete, Miguel Bardem, David Menkes; **C:** Nesto Calvo; **M:** Juan Antonio Bardem.

Not without My Daughter

Based-on-truth story of Betty Mahoody (Field) who goes to Iran with her Iranian husband (Molina). He decides that they and their daughter will stay. Then she learns that she has no rights in the Islamic country. The transfer is generally good looking, although not spectacularly so. The print shows signs of dirt and speckles, and the image has a fairly soft quality. Nonetheless it is a well-defined presentation with good detail and strong colors throughout. Whether it's the earthen tones of Iran's (actually Israel's) landscape and cities, or the colorful clothing, the image is always stable and faithfully restores the look of the original movie. No serious edge-enhancement has been applied to the transfer, giving it a balanced look. However, compression artifacts in the form of pixelation are evident throughout the movie and can become noticeable especially during some of the grainier shots. —GH
Movie: 🎬🎬 ½ **DVD:** 🎬🎬 ½

MGM Home Ent. (cat #1002576, UPC 027-616867773). Widescreen (1.85:1) anamorphic. Dolby Digital Stereo; Mono. $14.95. Keepcase. *LANG:* English; French; Spanish. *SUB:* French; Spanish. *CAP:* English. *FEATURES:* "Making of" featurette ▪ Trailer.
1990 (PG-13) 116m/C Sally Field, Alfred Molina, Sheila Rosenthal, Roshan Seth, Sarah Badel, Mony Rey, Georges Corraface; **D:** Brian Gilbert; **W:** David W. Rintels; **C:** Peter Hannan; **M:** Jerry Goldsmith.

Nothing in Common

Jackie Gleason's final film is one of the first to show just how good Tom Hanks can be. It's also an early example of director Garry Marshall's ability to craft crowd-pleasing, character-based entertainment. Hanks is David Basner, swiftly rising young Chicago advertising executive. Gleason is his father Max, an irascible, self-centered old coot who calls at midnight to announce that David's mother (Saint) has left him. It's then up to David to take care of dear old dad and to learn how similar and different the two are. The expected heavy grain shows up in exteriors. Interiors aren't that great, either, but DVD is accurate as I remember the theatrical release. The main selling point of the disc is the choice of screen ratios. —MM
Movie: 🎬🎬🎬 ½ **DVD:** 🎬🎬🎬
Columbia Tristar (cat #07748, UPC 04339-6077485). Widescreen (1.85:1) anamorphic; full frame. Dolby Digital Mono. $19.98. Keepcase. *LANG:* English; French. *SUB:* English; French; Spanish; Portuguese; Chinese; Korean; Thai. *CAP:* English. *FEATURES:* Trailer ▪ 28 chapters.
1986 (PG) 119m/C Tom Hanks, Jackie Gleason, Eva Marie Saint, Bess Armstrong, Hector Elizondo, Barry Corbin, Sela Ward, John Kapelos, Jane Morris, Dan Castellaneta, Tracy Reiner; **D:** Garry Marshall; **W:** Rick Podell; **C:** John A. Alonzo; **M:** Patrick Leonard.

Novocaine

Frank Sangster (Martin) is a dentist who works alongside his hygienist and fiancée, Jean (Dern). But when visited by sexy junkie Susan (Bonham Carter), Frank's tidy, prosperous life becomes a darkly comic hell of drugs and murder. Neither the retro chic of *Man Who Wasn't There* nor the realist noir of *The Deep End*, fence-straddling *Novocaine*, despite its clever graphics, never manages to shake off the anesthetic and become involving. Above average DVD transfer and excellent sound, though. —MO
Movie: 🎬🎬 ½ **DVD:** 🎬🎬🎬 ½
Artisan Ent. (cat #12350, UPC 01223612-350). Widescreen anamorphic. Dolby Digital 5.1. $24.98. Keepcase. *LANG:* English. *SUB:* Spanish. *CAP:* English; Spanish. *FEATURES:* 15 chapters ▪ Commentary: director David Atkins ▪ Theatrical trailer ▪ "Getting the Shot—The Making of *Novocaine*" featurette ▪ Special documentary

"Bitten"—An Exploration into Forensic Dentistry ▪ Deleted scenes ▪ Isolated score.
2001 (R) 95m/C Steve Martin, Helena Bonham Carter, Laura Dern, Elias Koteas, Scott Caan, Keith David, Lynne Thigpen, Kevin Bacon; **D:** David Atkins; **W:** David Atkins; **C:** Vilko Filac; **M:** Steve Bartek.

Now, Voyager

Davis plays Charlotte Vale, a lonely ugly duckling who is repressed by a domineering mother (Cooper). But she begins to shine after temporarily escaping the stifling maternal influence when she goes to a sanatorium for therapy. That's when the spinster undergoes a marvelously played transformation into a vibrant young woman with a new love for life and a growing sense of confidence. Out of her shell, she takes a sea cruise and has a shipboard romantic affair with a suave European. Turns out he is married and their relationship is doomed, but she nonetheless finds inspiration to utter the famous dialogue, "Oh, Jerry, we have the stars. Let's not ask for the moon." In the end, she's a more-than-even match for dear old mum. Definitely melodramatic, but an involving story nonetheless. Based on a novel by Olive Higgins Prouty—actually the third book in Prouty's four-volume saga about the Vales family of Boston. On DVD, it doesn't seem possible for any black-and-white film to look better than *Now, Voyager* does. Blacks are deep and there are plenty of glorious shades of gray between those blacks and whites. It looks as though it could have been filmed yesterday, with hardly a blemish or even a digital compression artifact present to spoil that illusion. The original 1.37:1 compositions are preserved by the full-frame presentation, because that's how they made movies back then. The limitations of the soundtrack's fidelity reveal its age, but the dialogue nevertheless is easily understood, and Max Steiner's fine score is never shrill nor distorted. Extras are thin, but film score buffs will appreciate the musical cues from the original scoring session. There is a theatrical trailer and a biography of Davis, but these extras will leave fans of the movie wanting more. —MB
Movie: 🎬🎬🎬 ½ **DVD:** 🎬🎬🎬 ½
Warner (cat #65301, UPC 0125695031-20). Full frame. Dolby Digital Mono. $19.98. Snapper. *LANG:* English. *SUB:* English; Spanish; French; Portuguese. *CAP:* English. *FEATURES:* 38 chapters ▪ Scoring session music cues ▪ Theatrical trailer ▪ Cast career highlights.
1942 117m/B Bette Davis, Gladys Cooper, Claude Rains, Paul Henreid, Bonita Granville; **D:** Irving Rapper; **W:** Casey Robinson; **C:** Sol Polito; **M:** Max Steiner. *AWARDS:* Oscars '42: Orig. Dramatic Score; *NOM:* Oscars '42: Actress (Davis), Support. Actress (Cooper).

Nowhere in Sight

Rehash of *Wait until Dark* has little to add to that masterpiece of suspense/horror. This

time, Carly Bauer (Slater) is the blind woman who's tormented in her apartment by a couple of nasty thugs. The cast does credible work with familiar material. Barebones (not even a menu) DVD is identical to VHS tape in all important respects. —*MM*
Movie: 🎬🎬 ½ **DVD:** 🎬🎬
Studio Home Ent. (cat #VM#7842D, UPC 031398784227). Full frame. Stereo. $14.99. Keepcase. *LANG:* English.
2001 94m/C Helen Slater, Mark Camacho, Richard Jutras, Max Perlus, Andrew McCarthy; *D:* Douglas Jackson; *W:* James (Momel) Lemmo; *C:* Bruno Philip; *M:* Helen Slater, David Findlay.

The Nude Set
Wealthy and spoiled rotten, Sophie Durville (Agnes Laurent) heads to Paris, hot on the trail of love—in this case a study med student who has left her in mid-heat. Once there, Sophie takes a liking to the popular Bohemian strip clubs and decides to give things a whirl herself. Wild (for the time) charming sex comedy originally titled *Mademoiselle Striptease* features lots of sexy girls and even a few cool cabaret performances. This was the first feature released by Radley Metzger's Audubon Films. The DVD delivers a solid black-and-white picture with good contrast and brightness levels. There are a few scratches and some speckling on the film itself (and the picture is a little soft), but it sort of puts things in the right vintage perspective. As expected, the audio offers little to get excited about, but is more than adequate in delivering undistorted sound and dialogue, even if the overall soundtrack is less than dynamic. Extras include trailers from several vintage Audubon films. —*JO* **AKA:** Mademoiselle Strip-tease.
Movie: 🎬🎬🎬 **DVD:** 🎬🎬 ½
First Run Features (cat #FRF9100400, UPC 720229910040). Full frame. Dolby Digital Stereo. $29.95. Keepcase. *LANG:* English. *FEATURES:* 12 chapters ▪ Theatrical trailer ▪ Photo gallery ▪ Vintage trailer gallery.
1961 86m/C *FR* Agnes Laurent, Dora Doll, Vera Valmont, Philippe Nicaud, Simone Paris; *D:* Pierre Foucaud; *W:* Alice Colaris.

Nureyev
Enjoyable documentary on the life of legendary dancer Rudolf Nureyev. The film traces Nureyev's life using a variety of insightful interviews and entertaining performances. A good video transfer boasts well-represented colors and blacks. Some of the archival video footage is a little less impressive, but it's not overly noticeable. Dialogue is crisp and understandable and there is no distortion on the very solid soundtrack. —*MJT*
Movie: 🎬🎬 ½ **DVD:** 🎬🎬 ½
Image Ent. (cat #ID9317RADVD, UPC 014-381931723). Full frame. Dolby Digital Mono. $24.99. Keepcase. *LANG:* English. *FEATURES:* 23 chapters.
1991 90m/C Rudolf Nureyev; *D:* Patricia Foy.

O
The theatrical release of *O* was delayed due to its "controversial" subject matter, but now the film is available on DVD, so you can judge it for yourself. The film is a modern-day re-telling of Shakespeare's classic *Othello*. Odin James (Mekhi Phifer), better known as O to his friends, is the star basketball player at a southern prep school. The team's coach, Duke Goulding (Martin Sheen), treats Odin as if he were his own son. This makes Hugo Goulding (Josh Hartnett), Duke's actual son, jealous. Hugo is on the basketball team as well, and is tired of having the spotlight and his father's affection showered on Odin, so he devises a plan to get his revenge. Hugo begins to convince Odin that his girlfriend Desi (Julia Stiles) is secretly seeing fellow player Mike (Andrew Keegan). Hugo accents these lies by staging scenes in which Odin will witness Desi with Mike. As Odin's jealously begins to grow, his concentration on the basketball court dwindles, sending his entire life spiraling out of control. Not content with having Odin fail in his greatest talent, Hugo devises a plan which will throw everyone's lives into turmoil and grant him the attention he feels he deserves. *O* is a powerful film and does a great job of updating the Bard's work. The high-school violence and inter-racial relationship which got the film so much negative attention are handled very well, and certainly aren't the focus of the movie. Director Tim Blake Nelson (best known for his role as Delmar in *O Brother, Where Art Thou?*) has given the film a dream-like look and never allows the story to drag. The two male leads, Phifer and Hartnett, are very good, while Stiles appears to be sleepwalking through the film. *O* is a challenging film and an excellent morality tale. It may not have the timeless quality of *Othello*, but it does work well for today's audience. Lions Gate has given *O* the Deluxe Edition treatment with this two-disc set. Disc One offers *O* in either an anamorphic widescreen or full frame. The image here is clear and very sharp, showing only some very fine grain in the daylight scenes. There is no distortion to the image, nor are there any defects from the source print. The colors are good and the fleshtones are natural. The Dolby Digital 5.1 audio track offers good Surround effects and a throbbing bass with the film's hip-hop soundtrack. Director Nelson's commentary is engaging and informative. The second disc offers several special features including a bonus film—the 1922 silent version of *Othello* which, unfortunately, is very difficult to watch. —*ML*
Movie: 🎬🎬🎬 **DVD:** 🎬🎬🎬
Studio Home Ent. (cat #VM 7911D, UPC 031398791128). Widescreen (1.85:1) anamorphic; full frame. Dolby Digital 5.1. $24.99. Keepcase. *LANG:* English. *SUB:* English; Spanish. *CAP:* English. *FEATURES:* Commentary ▪ Interviews ▪ Deleted scenes ▪ Trailer ▪ Scene analysis ▪ Bonus film ▪ 24 chapters. 2-disc set.
2001 (R) 94m/C Mekhi Phifer, Josh Hartnett, Julia Stiles, Elden (Ratliff) Henson, Andrew Keegan, Rain Phoenix, John Heard, A.J. (Anthony) Johnson, Martin Sheen; *D:* Tim Blake Nelson; *W:* Brad Kaaya; *C:* Russell Fine; *M:* Jeff Danna.

The Object of My Affection
Nina (Aniston) is a Brooklyn social worker who breaks up with her overbearing boyfriend Vince (Pankow). At about the same time, gay schoolteacher George (Rudd) breaks up with his boyfriend Joley (Daly). Nina invites him to rent her spare room. When she discovers that she's pregnant, she asks him to help her raise the baby. They try to create something like a conventional relationship, but the sexual/social cards are stacked against them. Playwright Wendy Wasserstein does a very nice job adapting Stephen McCauley's novel. This kind of studio-produced character-driven drama is easy for DVD. Both image and sound are first rate. —*MM*
Movie: 🎬🎬 ½ **DVD:** 🎬🎬🎬
20th Century Fox (UPC 024543027522). Widescreen (1.85:1) anamorphic. Dolby Digital Surround; Dolby Stereo. $19.98. Keepcase. *LANG:* English; French. *SUB:* English; Spanish. *CAP:* English. *FEATURES:* 20 chapters ▪ Trailer ▪ "Making of" featurette.
1998 (R) 112m/C Jennifer Aniston, Paul Rudd, John Pankow, Timothy Daly, Alan Alda, Nigel Hawthorne, Allison Janney, Amo Gulinello, Steve Zahn, Daniel Cosgrove; *D:* Nicholas Hytner; *W:* Wendy Wasserstein; *C:* Oliver Stapleton; *M:* George Fenton.

Obsession
In Italy, a rich, lonely businessman (Robertson) meets a mysterious young girl (Bujold), the mirror image of his late wife who was killed by kidnappers. Intriguing suspense film is not quite up to some comparisons with Hitchcock thrillers, and in fact, it drags a little as DePalma builds the suspense and heaps on the atmosphere. Don't get your hopes up; this isn't going to be one of those DVDs that improves the presentation of a film so much that you can ignore all its weaknesses. The truth is, the DVD may be the worst version available; even the VHS edition looks a little sharper. Things seem to run together, and it not just because of color bleed, which is also quite noticeable. There is a ghosting to bright images that often shows up on an old black-and-white film where age may excuse it, but here it's incredibly aggravating. On the plus side, the 5.1 sound is pretty good, although lacking in Surround except for a little ambience and a couple of effects. The "Obsession Revisited" documentary is fairly trite and, since its image is sharper than that of the movie itself, only serves to confirm the poor transfer of the film. —*JO*
Movie: 🎬🎬 ½ **DVD:** 🎬
Columbia Tristar (cat #04181, UPC 04339-6041813). Widescreen (2.35:1) anamorphic. Dolby Digital 5.1; Dolby Surround;

Dolby Digital Mono. $24.95. Keepcase. *LANG:* English; French. *SUB:* English; French; Spanish. *CAP:* English. *FEATURES:* Documentary • Trailers • Filmographies • 28 chapters.
1976 (PG) 98m/C Cliff Robertson, Genevieve Bujold, John Lithgow; *D:* Brian DePalma; *W:* Paul Schrader; *C:* Vilmos Zsigmond; *M:* Bernard Herrmann. *AWARDS: NOM:* Oscars '76: Orig. Score.

Ocean's 11

Crooked moneyman Sypros Acebos (Tamiroff, as comedy relief) thinks he's organizing a fantastic plan to rob five Las Vegas casinos simultaneously, but the real force behind the caper is gambler Danny Ocean (Sinatra). He assembles 10 of his ex-paratroop buddies in the desert Mecca, and they prepare themselves to tap each casino's cash bin by knocking out the power at the stroke of the New Year and using night-vision specs to navigate amid the confusion. Pal Sam Harmon (Martin) is a popular crooner who takes a singing engagement in a casino bar; others like-wise take inside jobs to get near the tills. Wealthy Jimmy Foster (Lawford) attracts the suspicions of his stepfather Duke San-tos (Romero), a gangster who doesn't fig-ure out what's going on in time. Garbage-man Josh Howard (Davis Jr.) also has a key role in the robbery, which goes alarm-ingly well. But with Las Vegas sealed off, the boys take desperate measures to sneak the loot out of the city, a gambit that has some drawbacks. The movie is lavish and slick, accurately imparting the feel of Vegas at the time with its still fairly stylish hotels and casinos. Large but not gargantuan as they are now, they seem like movie sets and were probably simple to re-create on sound stages. There's nothing cheap about the production, much of which was filmed in the real hotels (a coup of cooperation only the Rat Pack could achieve) and the big New Years' party scenes make the 2001 remake look chintzy in comparison. DVD is a great improvement on the 1990 laserdisc in both color and image quality, although it must be said that the picture never looked anything less than good on television. Fans of the Rat Pack with large monitors will enjoy the relaxed Panavision composi-tions and the frequent guest cameos from the likes of George Raft, Red Skelton (whose schtick seems to be a concession to the image requirements of the Vegas chamber of commerce), and Shirley MacLaine. There's a feature-length com-mentary from Frank Sinatra Jr., and Angie Dickinson. A nice clip from the *Tonight Show* has Frank Sr. hosting with Angie as a guest, reminiscing about the experience. Besides the usual trailers, there's a very welcome extra that comes in the form of a map of the Vegas hotels: clicking on each in turn brings up an interesting mini docu-mentary on the hotel and an aspect of the Vegas lifestyle of the time, with ex show-girls, croupiers, and other non-celebrities providing testimonials. —GE

Movie: 𝄪𝄪 ½ *DVD:* 𝄪𝄪𝄪 ½
Warner Home Video (UPC 85392149421). Widescreen (2:35:1) anamorphic. Dolby Digital Mono. $19.98. Snapper. *LANG:* Eng-lish. *SUB:* English; French; Spanish. *FEA-TURES:* Commentary • *Tonight Show* clip • Trailers • Las Vegas featurette • 38 chapters.
1960 148m/C Frank Sinatra, Dean Mar-tin, Sammy Davis Jr., Angie Dickinson, Peter Lawford, Richard Conte, Cesar Romero, Joey Bishop, Akim Tamiroff, Henry Silva, Buddy Lester, Norman Fell, Red Skel-ton, Shirley MacLaine, George Raft; *D:* Lewis Milestone; *W:* Harry Brown, Charles Lederer; *C:* William H. Daniels; *M:* Nelson Riddle.

Ocean's Eleven

Funny, smart, and refreshingly insignifi-cant, Steven Soderbergh's remake is a fine big-time entertainment. Newly released from prison, ambitious thief Danny Ocean (Clooney) rounds up a team of experts to pull an amazing heist in Las Vegas: to knock off an impregnable vault used by three casinos. Reuben Tishkoff (Gould) bankrolls the caper to get back at casino owner Terry Benedict (Garcia). Ocean's number one man is Dusty Ryan (Pitt), a jack of all crooked trades who spends his honest time teaching Holly-wood actors how to look professional while playing poker. Together they enlist Linus (Damon), a Chicago pickpocket; Saul Bloom (Reiner), an aging conman with a bad heart; the Malloy brothers (Affleck and Caan), a pair of electronic experts who bicker like magpies; Frank Catton (Mac), a blackjack dealer who knows the ropes; Yen (Qin), a circus dare-devil; and Basher Tarr (Cheadle), a demoli-tions expert. The heist has just kicked into high gear when Dusty discovers that Danny has an ulterior motive for the rob-bery: Terry Benedict's present paramour is Danny's ex, Tess (Roberts). Dusty thinks Danny is in far over his head, and he con-siders calling off the whole shebang. It's a fantasy from the word Go. But instead of being insulting, this is exactly the kind of plausible silliness we love in caper films. DVD does a good job jumping between visual extremes without missing a beat, from the grainy contrast of the parole meeting, to lush casino interiors. The jazzy bass rhythm score sounds particularly lush. Audio is Dolby Digital and Dolby Sur-round, but no DTS. The extras are numer-ous. I sampled the laid-back commentary with Matt Damon, Andy Garcia, and Brad Pitt, but listened to all of Steven Soder-bergh and Ted Griffin's track. They strike a nice balance between clever wisecracking and very interesting, confessional insights. The trailers are nice—this show had a great ad campaign—but the HBO and EPK derived "documentaries" are the kind of promo junk you can find on *ET* any night of the week. —GE

Movie: 𝄪𝄪𝄪 ½ *DVD:* 𝄪𝄪𝄪 ½
Warner Home Video (UPC 0853922634-24). Widescreen (2.35:1) anamorphic.

Dolby Digital 5.1 Surround. $26.98. Snap-per. *LANG:* English. *FEATURES:* 2 commen-tary tracks • Promotional documentaries • Trailers • Filmographies • DVD-ROM features.
2001 (PG-13) 116m/C George Clooney, Brad Pitt, Andy Garcia, Matt Damon, Julia Roberts, Don Cheadle, Casey Affleck, Scott Caan, Elliott Gould, Bernie Mac, Carl Reiner, Edward Jemison, Shaobo Qin, Henry Silva, Angie Dickinson, Holly Marie Combs, Joshua Jackson, Topher Grace, Steve Lawrence, Eydie Gorme, Wayne New-ton; *D:* Steven Soderbergh; *W:* Ted Griffin; *C:* Steven Soderbergh; *M:* David Holmes. *AWARDS: NOM:* Broadcast Film Critics '01: Cast.

The Odyssey

Lavish TV miniseries based on Homer's 2,700-year-old epic poem, relating the adventures of King Odysseus of Ithaca. On the day his son is born to faithful wife Penelope (Scacchi), Odysseus (Assante) is commanded by the goddess Athena (Rossellini) to leave his home and travel to battle the Trojans. Little does he realize that this is the beginning of a 20-year sojourn, where additional trials include sea monsters, the Cyclops, the Kingdom of the Dead, enchantress Circe (Peters) and getting shipwrecked on the isle of Calypso (Williams), who wants to keep the hunk around. But even Odysseus realizes there's no place like home. Well-paced and exciting, this is one of the better examples of the recent big-budget made-for-TV movies. The DVD offers the film full frame (naturally) and brings a glorious transfer. The image is crystal-clear, show-ing only minute grain at times. The colors are fine, as the picture rivals digital broad-cast quality. The audio is fine as well, delivering clear dialogue and well-placed Surround sound effects. —ML

Movie: 𝄪𝄪𝄪 *DVD:* 𝄪𝄪𝄪 ½
Artisan Ent. (cat #12039, UPC 70772912-0391). Full frame. Dolby 2.0 Surround. $14.98. Keepcase. *LANG:* English. *FEA-TURES:* "Making of" featurette • 30 chap-ters.
1997 (PG-13) 203m/C Armand Assante, Greta Scacchi, Geraldine Chaplin, Eric Roberts, Bernadette Peters, Irene Papas, Vanessa L(ynne) Williams, Christopher Lee, Isabella Rossellini, Jeroen Krabbe, Nicholas Clay, Ron Cook, Michael J. Pol-lard, Paloma Baeza, Alan Cox, Heathcote Williams; *D:* Andrei Konchalovsky; *W:* Andrei Konchalovsky, Chris Solimine; *C:* Sergei Koslov; *M:* Eduard Artemyev.

Of Mice and Men

Director Gary Sinise and writer Horton Foote are scrupulously faithful to John Steinbeck's famous novel in this terribly underrated film. Sinise also plays George, protector of Lennie (Malkovich), as they try to find work on California farms during the Depression. Sherilyn Fenn is very good as the neglected wife of the ranch owner's son Curley (Siemaszko). DVD image and

sound are superior to the theatrical release. This one really deserves the full slate of extras, including a commentary track. Maybe some day. —MM
Movie: 🎬🎬🎬 ½ **DVD:** 🎬🎬 ½
MGM Home Ent. (cat #1000680, UPC 027-616850119). Widescreen (1.85:1) anamorphic. Dolby Digital Surround; Mono. $19.98. Keepcase. *LANG:* English; French; Spanish. *SUB:* English; French; Spanish. *CAP:* English. *FEATURES:* 16 chapters • Trailer.
1992 (PG-13) 110m/C John Malkovich, Sherilyn Fenn, Casey Siemaszko, Joe Morton, Ray Walston, Gary Sinise, John Terry, Richard Riehle; **D:** Gary Sinise; **W:** Horton Foote; **C:** Kenneth Macmillan; **M:** Mark Isham.

The Ogre

Misfit Abel (Malkovich) desperately believes in his own personal power to change the world around him. He winds up captured by the Germans in 1939 and is held in a POW camp until chance lands him in the service of a group of high-ranking Nazis, including Hermann Goring (Spengler). Goring sends Abel out to recruit young boys into becoming military conscripts and he gains the nickname of the Ogre, the mythic devourer of children. DVD presents a very good image, often on the dark side and lacking Hollywood polish. Sound is good, too. —MM *AKA:* Der Unhold.
Movie: 🎬🎬 **DVD:** 🎬🎬🎬
Kino on Video (cat #K148, UPC 73832901-4827). Widescreen (1.66:1) letterboxed. $29.95. Keepcase. *LANG:* German. *SUB:* English. *FEATURES:* 13 chapters • Trailer.
1996 117m/C *GE FR GB* John Malkovich, Volker Spengler, Armin Mueller-Stahl, Gottfried John; **D:** Volker Schlondorff; **W:** Volker Schlondorff, Jean-Claude Carriere; **C:** Bruno de Keyzer; **M:** Michael Nyman.

Oh My Goddess! Vol. 1

Young college student Keiichi, trying to order take-out food, accidentally calls a Celestial Help Line and conjures up dainty goddess Belldandy. Offered one wish, the shy, diminutive Keiichi wishes for Belldandy to stay with him as his girlfriend. As Belldandy and Keiichi begin to fall for each other, the agreeable goddess's two sisters show up to cause goofy havoc. Essentially a Japanese take on *I Dream of Jeannie*, *Oh My Goddess* is light, bright, cheery fare told with a surplus of humor and charm. While some critics have remarked about Belldandy's characterization as an endlessly submissive woman, it should be stated that both she and Keiichi are complete innocents and not intended as gender role models. (And, "Hello?! This is a FANTASY!") The chief asset is the irresistible and cute characters and story lines. The disc is brilliantly colorful and sharp, but fast movements tend to suffer from digital noise. Vertical tilt movements look particularly bad, but the clarity and crisp sound make the DVD still preferable to the VHS. The program offered without

dialogue is a fun feature—dub your own episode with friends!—but the audio commentary is fairly insubstantial. It's essentially chit chat and laughs in the dubbing studio with the actors with very little production information of background offered. A second volume is also available. —DG
Movie: 🎬🎬🎬 **DVD:** 🎬🎬 ½
AnimEigo Inc. (cat #AV201-063, UPC 737-187003486). Full frame. Dolby Stereo. $21.49. Keepcase. *LANG:* Japanese; English. *SUB:* English. *FEATURES:* 6 chapters per episode • Insert notes • Textless credit sequences • Commentary: dubbing director and artists • Music and effects track for each episode • Slide show with cels and drawings.
1993 87m/C *JP* **D:** Hiroaki Gohda; **W:** Naoko Hasegawa; **M:** Takeshi Yasuda.

Old Yeller

Disney Studios' first and best boy-and-his-dog film, set in Texas in 1869. Fifteen-year-old Travis Coates (Kirk) is left in charge of the family farm while dad Jim (Parker) is away on a cattle drive. When his younger brother Arliss (Corcoran) brings home a stray dog, Travis is displeased but lets him stay. Yeller saves Travis's life, but contracts rabies in the process. Keep tissue handy, especially for the kids. Strong acting, effective scenery—all good stuff. Like all the Vault Disney releases, this one really excels in the extras department. The commentary is particularly enjoyable as the participants trade off anecdotes rather than just talking about what is currently happening on the screen. On disc 2, in addition to all the production archives, is a wonderfully produced documentary with new interviews, a warm and interesting conversation with Tommy Kirk where he recounts numerous films he made for Disney; an interesting "Lost Treasures" featurette focusing on the ranch where *Old Yeller* was filmed; and tons more. The movie itself fares a little worse than the supplementals. The colors vary in intensity and accuracy, and the picture is soft throughout. Since the DVD boasts THX certification, it could be that there was no better preprint material available, but one would expect better for this classic. The 5.1 remix is a definite improvement with considerable fidelity, dynamics, and separation during music sequences, although the dialogue remains mono and flat. The Pluto cartoon that precedes the movie is apropos and benefits from better image quality than the film. —JO
Movie: 🎬🎬🎬 ½ **DVD:** 🎬🎬 ½
Buena Vista Home Ent. (cat #21554, UPC 786936143843). Widescreen (1.75:1) anamorphic. Dolby Digital 5.1. $29.99. Keepcase. *LANG:* English. *SUB:* Spanish. *CAP:* English. *FEATURES:* 14 chapters • Theatrical trailer • Commentary: Kirk, Parker, Bob Weatherwax, Kevin Corcoran • Original theatrical animated short "Bone Trouble" • Featurette: "Old Yeller: Remembering a Classic" • Featurette: "Dogs!" • Conversations with Tommy Kirk • Featurette Lost Treasures—"Ranch of

the Golden Oak" • Production archives • 1957 Disney studio album.
1957 (G) 84m/C Dorothy McGuire, Fess Parker, Tommy Kirk, Kevin Corcoran, Jeff York, Beverly Washburn, Chuck Connors; **D:** Robert Stevenson; **W:** Fred Gipson, William Tunberg; **C:** Charles P. Boyle; **M:** Oliver Wallace.

Olive Juice

Insipid featherweight romantic comedy boasts appearances by members of the Backstreet Boys. Keeler (Berlau) falls for Michelle (Littrell) but she's about to marry. DVD image and sound equal VHS tape and that's all the film requires. —MM
Movie: 🎬🎬 **DVD:** 🎬
Studio Home Ent. (cat #ST7871D, UPC 658149787124). Full frame. Dolby Digital Stereo. $24.99. Keepcase. *LANG:* English. *SUB:* English; Spanish. *CAP:* English. *FEATURES:* 24 chapters.
2001 (PG-13) 90m/C Leighanne Littrell, James Berlau, Michael Hartson, Jay Love, Ginger King; **D:** Ken Hastings; **W:** Ken Hastings; **C:** Alex D. Darvounis; **M:** Jason Libs, Michael Tscanz.

Oliver & Company

Highly simplified animated version of Dickens's *Oliver Twist* finds a kitten (voice of Lawrence) abandoned in New York where he falls under the spell of Dodger (Joel), a charismatic mongrel. Bette Midler, as the snooty poodle Georgette, has the best moment in a real Ethel Merman–style show stopper, "Perfect Isn't Easy," when she sings, "I'm pretty and classy; we're not talking Lassie." Admittedly, the animation is not the studio's best, and the rough-and-tumble of the Big Apple at street level isn't exactly the setting most people think of for a Disney movie. But the film still earns a solid recommendation, and it comes with the usual full plate of extras. The simple drawing style presents no problems for DVD. Image and sound are both excellent. —MM
Movie: 🎬🎬🎬 **DVD:** 🎬🎬🎬
Buena Vista Home Ent. (cat #25047, UPC 786936172423). Widescreen (1.66:1) anamorphic. Dolby Digital 5.1 Surround. $29.98. Keepcase. *LANG:* English; French; Spanish. *CAP:* English. *FEATURES:* "Disney's Animated Animals" featurette • 2 Pluto cartoons • Scrapbook art gallery • 2 sing-alongs • Publicity materials • "Making of" featurette • 24 chapters.
1988 (G) 72m/C D: George Scribner; **W:** Jim Cox, James Mangold; **V:** Joey Lawrence, Billy Joel, Richard "Cheech" Marin, Bette Midler, Dom DeLuise, Roscoe Lee Browne, Richard Mulligan, Sheryl Lee Ralph, Robert Loggia, Taurean Blacque, Carl Weintraub, Natalie Gregory, William Glover.

Oliver Stone Collection

This collection is made up of *Any Given Sunday, JFK, Natural Born Killers, Born on the 4th of July, The Doors,* and *Wall Street*

(all reviewed in *Book 1* and *Book 2*), and the documentary "Oliver Stone's America." That film seems to be Stone's summary of his previous audio commentaries, where he talks about the inspirations and experiences that he has had during his years directing. The disc also seems to be designed as a wrap-up of the "Oliver Stone Collection," and is available only as part of the set. Stone's commentaries are actually a bit more interesting than the areas covered in this documentary. The interviewer, Charles Kiselyak, doesn't ask particularly probing questions and often simply lets Stone go down the path of whatever is on his mind. Stone can be an engaging speaker, but this program doesn't go into enough depth about any one topic to be very engaging. The film is presented in full-frame, with the exception of some of the clips from Stone's movies, which are in different aspect ratios. Sharpness and detail are generally good; the clips from the movies look crisp and clear, although some noticeably don't look quite as pristine as their actual DVD releases. Although the interview segments are a little dark now and then, the picture is fairly free of problems. The documentary is presented entirely in stereo sound, and for the interviews, the dialogue between the two is generally clear and easily understood. The inclusion of Stone's short film is an appreciated extra. —*AB/DG*
Movie: 🎬🎬 **DVD:** 🎬🎬 ½
Warner Home Video (UPC 85392571222). Full frame. Dolby Digital Surround. $166.88. Snapper boxed set. *LANG:* English. *FEATURES:* "Last Year in Vietnam" student film.
2000 951m/C

On Her Majesty's Secret Service
Early entry in the 007 series delivers strong characters and a romantic story as well as action. What it doesn't provide is a great Bond. George Lazenby gives the role a try, and it just doesn't seem to suit him. He has none of the snappy delivery that the other Bonds have, and doesn't pull off the humor like Connery, or even Brosnan does. In this entry Bond falls in love with a Countess (Rigg) after saving her life, and also goes after his arch enemy, Blofeld (Savalas), who plans to use biological warfare in his attempt to take over the world. Director Hunt keeps things moving at a rapid clip, and although Lazenby occasionally seems awkward, the film moves on with or without him. Even considering the few tiny problems, this is definitely an enjoyable entry in the series. The general quality of the picture is pleasing, with images that are solid, acceptable colors, and sharp images. The print source used featured several scratches and marks. This edition contains the original mono soundtrack. It's limited (naturally) compared to more recent films but it's clean and has punch. The commentary is narrated and hosted by a member of the Ian Fleming Foundation. Director Hunt does much of the talking, and he's very funny at

times, sharing his comments with humor and energy. A rather huge crowd of cast and crew populate this commentary track, from the cinematographer to the actors to the director and other members of the crew. Edited together, their comments reveal a great amount of detail about this film. There are plenty of amusing stories in addition to the technical information. A 43-minute documentary examines the history of the story, from the difficulty of choosing a new Bond for the series to the problems with shooting on locations, all the way through to the film's release. Lazenby shares his thoughts on his role in the series in interviews, and gives quite a few interesting opinions on what it was like to step into a role as popular as 007. —*AB/DG*
Movie: 🎬🎬🎬 **DVD:** 🎬🎬🎬
MGM Home Ent. (cat #908126, UPC 0276-16812629). Widescreen (2.35:1) anamorphic. Mono. $29.98. Keepcase. *LANG:* English; Spanish. *SUB:* French; Spanish. *CAP:* English. *FEATURES:* Booklet with notes ● Commentary: Hunt, cast and crew ● "Inside *On Her Majesty's Secret Service*" documentary ● "Inside Q's Laboratory" documentary ● "Above It All" featurette ● Still gallery ● Trailer ● TV spots ● Radio spots ● 32 chapters.
1969 (PG) 144m/C *GB* George Lazenby, Diana Rigg, Telly Savalas, Gabriele Ferzetti, Ilse Steppat, Bernard Lee, Lois Maxwell, Desmond Llewelyn, Catherine Schell, Julie Ege, Joanna Lumley, Mona Chong, Anouska (Anoushka) Hempel, Jenny Hanley; *D:* Peter Hunt; *W:* Richard Maibaum; *M:* John Barry.

On Our Merry Way
Episodic comedy stars Meredith as Oliver Pease, a would-be newspaper reporter (actually he works in the classifieds) who asks the question, "How has a child changed your life?" Among those queried are a couple of jazz musicians (Fonda and Stewart), Hollywood bit players (Lamour and Moore), and con men (Demerest and MacMurray). Knock-out Goddard, who was married to Meredith at the time, plays his wife in the film. DVD presents a terrific black-and-white image that's virtually flawless. —*MM* **AKA:** *A Miracle Can Happen.*
Movie: 🎬🎬 ½ **DVD:** 🎬🎬🎬
Kino on Video (cat #K166, UPC 73832901-6623). Full frame. $29.95. Keepcase. *LANG:* English. *FEATURES:* 16 chapters ● Alternate opening.
1948 107m/B Burgess Meredith, Paulette Goddard, Dorothy Lamour, Victor Moore, James Stewart, Henry Fonda, Fred MacMurray, William Demarest, Hugh Herbert, Eilene Janssen, Dorothy Ford, David Whorf; *D:* King Vidor, Leslie Fenton; *W:* Laurence Stallings, Lou Breslow; *C:* John Seitz, Ernest Laszlo, Gordon Avil, Joseph Biroc, Edward Cronjager; *M:* Heinz Roemheld.

On the Beach
Survivors attempt to live normal lives in post-apocalyptic Australia while waiting for

the inevitable arrival of lethal radiation that's floating through the air toward them. Astaire is very strong in his first dramatic role, Peck is his usual solid self as an American sub commander, and all the performances are believable. But the whole thing has a very heavy-handed Cold War feel (particularly the ominous music). That's almost inevitable with "message movies" of the era. Insignificant dust and surface damage show up from time to time. Black-and-white photography ranges between good and very good; not the most detailed you'll ever see. —*MM*
Movie: 🎬🎬🎬 **DVD:** 🎬🎬🎬
MGM Home Ent. (cat #908372, UPC 0276-16837226). Widescreen (1.85:1) letterboxed. Dolby Digital Mono. $14.98. Keepcase. *LANG:* English; French. *SUB:* French; Spanish. *CAP:* English. *FEATURES:* 32 chapters ● Booklet.
1959 135m/B Gregory Peck, Anthony Perkins, Donna Anderson, Ava Gardner, Fred Astaire; *D:* Stanley Kramer; *W:* John Paxton; *C:* Daniel F. Fapp; *M:* Ernest Gold. *AWARDS:* Golden Globes '60: Score; *NOM:* Oscars '59: Film Editing, Orig. Dramatic Score.

On the Borderline
On their way to California with their new baby, Luke (Mabius) and Nicole (Shelton) find themselves short of funds in a border town. She takes work as a waitress while he becomes involved with transporting Mexican aliens. Curious little road thriller actually works pretty well. The leads and a solid supporting cast handle the material well. Some scenes are curiously tinted to disguise the less-than-lavish production values. Otherwise, DVD image is fine, if unspectacular. —*MM*
Movie: 🎬🎬 ½ **DVD:** 🎬🎬 ½
Studio Home Ent. (cat #AV1583D, UPC 806469158326). Widescreen letterboxed. Stereo. $19.99. Keepcase. *LANG:* English. *SUB:* English; Spanish. *CAP:* English. *FEATURES:* 24 chapters ● Trailer.
2001 (R) 93m/C Eric Mabius, Marley Shelton, Elizabeth Pena, R. Lee Ermey; *D:* Michael Oblowitz; *W:* Kevin R. Frech; *C:* Michael Barrow; *M:* Michael Wandmacher.

On the Edge
Heartfelt, engaging look at a group of hopeless teens hospitalized for their interest in committing suicide and the paths each of their lives take under the care of an insightful doctor (Rea). It beats the pants off the star-bloated, self-important *Girl, Interrupted* in character development without resurrecting any songs from the '60s. The story follows Jonathan (Murphy), who comes under the care of Rea after he decides to drive a convertible car off a cliff. For extra measure he leaves his seatbelt undone, which is his undoing as he is thrown free from the car and ends up institutionalized. While there he meets Toby (American actor Jonathan Jackson, sporting a fabulous Irish accent) and Rachael (Vessey), and learns to develop a sense of humor and a ray of hope.

Great script deals with the subject of teen depression in a realistic manner and is supported by great performances. Clean smooth picture with sold colors and very good sound. —CA

Movie: 🎞🎞🎞 ½ **DVD:** 🎞🎞🎞 ½
Universal Studios (cat #21771, UPC 0251-92177125). Widescreen (1.85:1) anamorphic. Dolby Digital 5.1. DTS 5.1. $26.90. Keepcase. *LANG:* English; French; Spanish. *SUB:* English; French; Spanish. *CAP:* English. *FEATURES:* 18 chapters • Theatrical trailer.
2000 (R) 86m/C *IR* Cillian Murphy, Tricia Vessey, Jonathan Jackson, Stephen Rea; **D:** John Carney; **W:** Daniel James, John Carney; **C:** Eric Alan Edwards.

On the Line

Clearly an excuse for 'Nsync's Lance Bass and Joey Fatone to set a few teenaged hearts aflutter, this romantic comedy hits a bull's eye. Kevin Gibbons (Bass), playing an ad guy, "chokes" whenever he meets a cute girl. He meets a cute girl, Abby (Chriqui), on the L train, they bond over the Cubs and go their separate ways. Kicking himself for letting her get away, Gibbons plasters Chicago with posters begging her to call him. Director Bross cleverly allows Bass maximum screen time without jeopardizing the availability of his star by keeping Chriqui at bay until the last reel. Director's commentary is a lovefest recommended for hard-core 'Nsync fans only. Slickly made on a short shooting schedule, the film looks and sounds really good on DVD. —LA

Movie: 🎞🎞 **DVD:** 🎞🎞🎞 ½
Miramax Pictures (cat #25503, UPC 7869-36176308). Widescreen (1.85:1) anamorphic. Dolby Digital 5.1 Surround. $29.98. Keepcase. *LANG:* English; French. *FEATURES:* Commentary: Eric Bross, Emmanuelle Chriqui • Behind-the-scenes featurette • Storyboard comparison • Outtakes, deleted and alternate scenes with commentary • Music video • Director's home video • Talent files • Interviews • Trailer • 15 chapters.
2001 (PG) 90m/C Lance Bass, Joey Fatone, Emmanuelle Chriqui, GQ, Al Green, Tamala Jones, Dave Foley, Dan Montgomery Jr., Jerry Stiller; **D:** Eric Bross; **W:** Paul Stanton, Eric Aronson; **C:** Michael Bernard; **M:** Stewart Copeland.

On the Waterfront

Federal investigations of corruption on the New York docks put pressure on Union boss Johnny Friendly (Cobb), a coarse thug who silences squealer Joey Doyle by having him thrown from a roof to his death. Young Terry Malloy (Brando), a not-too-bright ex-boxer and kid brother of Friendly's lawyer Charley (Steiger) is appalled by the murder, and drawn to the victim's sister Edie (Saint). Both she and activist priest Father Barry (Malden) are desperate to find more "squealers" who could help the feds rid the docks of racketeers, and Terry is soon in what seems a no-win predicament, having to choose between loyalties to family and friends, to his new girlfriend, and to what is right. DVD is a

kind of miss for Columbia TriStar, one studio that rarely even stumbles. The film looks fine, but the chosen aspect ratio is 1.37:1 flat. I've seen the picture at festivals, at the very formal Academy, at UCLA, and it's always projected at 1.85:1 widescreen. The titles are composed in horizontal blocks of text. In 16mm flat prints, microphones frequently intruded into the upper frame, especially in the scene of the interrupted meeting in the church. Those shots must have been slightly blown up here. The movie looks much better when matted to widescreen with tighter compositions. The extras are rather a mixed bag. The commentary track by Richard Shickel and author Jeff Young is informative but still comes off as analysis instead of testimony. These oral documents have tremendous historical value (even more so when they're done by principals), but sometimes they're much easier to read in print than to sit through for hours at a time. The featurette is the most frustrating extra. The famous taxicab scene between Rod Steiger and Brando is analyzed by the filmmakers and critics in an endless repetition of the same information. That fellow who interviews movie greats on the Bravo channel says the same thing at least three times, and the overkill is numbing. Much better is a rambling interview with Kazan himself (looking very spry and with a very sharp mind) about the wild relationships between the main creatives on the picture. Wildcat producer Sam Spiegel was apparently the kind of guy his writers and directors wanted to kill half the time! —GE

Movie: 🎞🎞🎞 ½ **DVD:** 🎞🎞 ½
Columbia Tristar Home Video (UPC 43396-784093). Full frame. Dolby Digital 5.1 Surround Stereo. $19.98. Keepcase. *LANG:* English. *FEATURES:* Commentary: Richard Shickel, Jeff Young • "Making of" featurette • Interview with Elia Kazan.
1954 108m/B Marlon Brando, Rod Steiger, Eva Marie Saint, Lee J. Cobb, Karl Malden, Pat Henning, Leif Erickson, Tony Galento, John Hamilton, Nehemiah Persoff; **D:** Elia Kazan; **W:** Budd Schulberg; **C:** Boris Kaufman; **M:** Leonard Bernstein. *AWARDS:* Oscars '54: Actor (Brando), Art Dir./Set Dec., B&W, B&W Cinematog., Director (Kazan), Film Editing, Picture, Story & Screenplay, Support. Actress (Saint); AFI '98: Top 100; British Acad. '54: Actor (Brando); Directors Guild '54: Director (Kazan); Golden Globes '55: Actor—Drama (Brando), Director (Kazan), Film—Drama, Natl. Film Reg. '89; N.Y. Film Critics '54: Actor (Brando), Director (Kazan), Film; *NOM:* Oscars '54: Support. Actor (Cobb), Support. Actor (Malden, Steiger), Orig. Dramatic Score.

One Fine Day

Clichés have a soft marshmallow center. This movie is light, fluffy, sugary, with very little substance, but enjoyable if you're in the mood. A nod to the classic screwball comedies of the '40s and '50s. Harried single mom/architect Pfeiffer and political

columnist/weekend dad Clooney get tangled up together with their bratty kids when they all arrive late to a school field trip. Naturally they hate each other, but they are forced to work together to solve their day-care dilemma. They accidentally switch cell phones, and then have to rely on each other for the rest of the day. You can see the jokes and mishaps coming two blocks away. Pfeiffer always looks good and Clooney is adorable as the single dad with heart. The screenplay by Ellen Simon is a paint by numbers knock-knock joke with as much substance as junk mail to which the actors have a hard time anything anything. Without Clooney and Pfeiffer, this flick would be a Lifetime movie of the week flop. The DVD sound quality is good. The image quality is better than video, but there's no reason to get excited about it. —JAS

Movie: 🎞🎞 **DVD:** 🎞🎞🎞 ½
20th Century Fox (cat #2000006, UPC 024543000068). Widescreen (1.85:1) anamorphic. Dolby Surround. $19.98. Keepcase. *LANG:* Spanish. *SUB:* English; Spanish. *FEATURES:* 25 chapters.
1996 (PG) 108m/C Michelle Pfeiffer, George Clooney, Alex D. Linz, Mae Whitman, Charles Durning, Jon Robin Baitz, Ellen Greene, Joe Grifasi, Pete Hamill, Anna Maria Horsford, Sheila Kelley, Barry Kivel, Robert Klein, George Martin, Michael Massee, Amanda Peet, Bitty Schram, Holland Taylor, Rachel York; **D:** Michael Hoffman; **W:** Terrel Seltzer, Ellen Simon; **C:** Oliver Stapleton; **M:** James Newton Howard. *AWARDS: NOM:* Oscars '96: Song ("For the First Time"); Golden Globes '97: Song ("For the First Time").

One for the Road

Michael Madsen's screen debut is unwatchable on this atrocious DVD. He plays alcoholic Cecil Moe who's trying to straighten himself out. The image might be a second generation EP VHS dupe—pale and unfocused. —MM **AKA:** Against All Hope.

Movie: 🎞 **DVD:** woof
BCI-Eclipse (cat #44085-9, UPC 7873644-08597). Full frame. $19.98. Keepcase. *LANG:* English. *FEATURES:* "Spooky Hooky" cartoon • 6 chapters • DVD dictionary • DVD-ROM features • Trivia game.
1982 90m/C Michael Madsen, Maureen McCarthy, Rex Flores, Tim Joosten, Herb Harms, Ron Schultz; **D:** Edward T. McDougal.

100 Girls

Here's an odd little video premiere which mixes campus-comedy with sexual politics. During a party in an all-girls dormitory (dubbed "The Virgin Vault"), a blackout occurs, trapping Matthew (Jonathan Tucker) in an elevator with a mystery girl. They connect both mentally and physically, but when the lights come on, she's gone. Now, Matthew must scour the dorm, attempting to find his unknown soulmate. As males are not commonly allowed inside, he must find new and creative ways to get inside

and learn about each resident. During his search, Matthew learns a great deal about women and begins to appreciate the differences and similarities between the genders. *100 Girls* is certainly entertaining and engaging, and one can't help but watch until the end to see who the "mystery girl" is. But the film is wildly uneven, combining crude humor with deadly serious gender rhetoric. Also, the ending is a bit anti-climatic. Still, there are some very funny moments, and viewers could certainly do worse. This DVD brings us the film in a letterbox format which accompanies a nice-looking transfer. The image is sharp and clear, showing only slight grain and no defects. There are some artifacting effects at times, but not too many. The audio is clean, giving the audience clear dialogue and no distortion. Packaging claims Dolby Digital 5.1, but the disc is Dolby 2.0 Surround. —*ML*
Movie: 🎧🎧 ½ **DVD:** 🎧🎧
Studio Home Ent. (cat #VM#7739D, UPC 03139877392). Widescreen (1.85:1) letterboxed. Dolby 2.0 Surround. $24.98. Keepcase. *LANG:* English. *SUB:* English; French; Spanish. *FEATURES:* Theatrical trailer • Bonus trailers • 24 chapters.
2000 (R) 95m/C Jonathan Tucker, James DeBello, Emmanuelle Chriqui, Larisa Oleynik, Jaime Pressly, Katherine Heigl; **D:** Michael Davis; **W:** Michael Davis; **C:** James Lawrence Spencer; **M:** Kevin Bassinson.

One Night at McCool's
Randy (Dillon), a laid-back bartender, finds himself hip deep in love and murder when gold-digging femme fatale Jewel (Tyler) seduces him and convinces him not only to kill her former partner in crime, but to let her move in with him. Carl (Reiser), Randy's cousin, cannot get Jewel out of his mind after seeing her, and when she turns to him to steal Randy's house, Carl stops at nothing to help her. Detective Dehling (Goodman) also cannot live without Jewel after seeing her at McCool's, and when an opportunity presents itself to get Randy out of the picture by framing him for a crime, Dehling takes matters into his own hands. The film recounts the story of three inept men, one controlling woman, and the bizarre love quadrangle that destroys them all. The plot and attempted comedy in this film lack quite a bit in the way of entertaining fare, and while Michael Douglas does a good job as ruthless hitman Mr. Burmeister, the overall film leaves the viewer lacking. Picture and sound are good; extras are extensive. —*EL*
Movie: 🎧🎧 **DVD:** 🎧🎧🎧
USA Home Ent. (cat #28, UPC 696306002-826). Widescreen (1.77:1) anamorphic. Dolby Digital 5.1. $19.95. Keepcase. *LANG:* English. *SUB:* English; French; Spanish. *CAP:* English. *FEATURES:* Behind-the-scenes: director's "making of" *McCool's* • Theatrical trailers and TV spots • Deleted scenes • Wardrobe, hair, and makeup tests • First cast read through • "Where Did We Shoot That?" (maps of locations)

• Shot-by-shot: storyboards to finished film • 16 chapters.
2001 (R) 93m/C Liv Tyler, Matt Dillon, Paul Reiser, John Goodman, Michael Douglas, Reba McEntire, Richard Jenkins, Andrew (Dice Clay) Silverstein, Leo Rossi, Eric Schaeffer; **D:** Harald Zwart; **W:** Stan Seidel; **C:** Karl Walter Lindenlaub; **M:** Marc Shaiman.

Open Your Eyes
Far superior to Cameron Crowe's remake *Vanilla Sky*, Alejandro Amenabar's original is a must-see for fans of psychological thrillers. As with his U.S. hit *The Others*, Amenabar lets the story unfold slowly and then wows the viewer with a surprise ending. Eduardo Noriega stars as the handsome and vain Cesar, a rich playboy who can have any woman that he wants. When he meets Sofia (Penelope Cruz, who played the same role in *Vanilla Sky*), he is immediately smitten, despite the fact that she is with Pelayo (Fele Martinez), Cesar's best friend. After spending a quiet evening with Sofia, Cesar is involved in an auto accident and is left disfigured. Following this, he begins to lose his grip on reality and is accused of murder. As with his previous film *Thesis*, here Amenabar makes many statements about the act of seeing and believing what one sees. *Open Your Eyes* is a great thriller and even those who are usually cautious of foreign films will enjoy it. Sadly, *Open Your Eyes* only gets a lukewarm reception on DVD. The anamorphic widescreen transfer is very nice, as it is sharp and shows only minute grain and a gentle softness at times. The bass from the 2.0 Surround track is impressive, but there is little action from the rear speakers. Some scenes would have been even more effective with a true Surround track. Also, the lack of any substantial extras is disappointing, as it would be nice to know more about some of the shots and effects in the film. —*ML* *AKA:* Abre Los Ojos.
Movie: 🎧🎧🎧🎧 **DVD:** 🎧🎧🎧
Artisan Ent. (cat #12159, UPC 0122-36121596). Widescreen (1.85:1) anamorphic. Dolby 2.0 Surround. $14.98. Keepcase. *LANG:* Spanish. *SUB:* English. *FEATURES:* Production notes • Cast & crew bios • 19 chapters.
1997 (R) 117m/C SP Eduardo Noriega, Penelope Cruz, Najwa Nimri, Chete Lera, Fele Martinez, Gerard Barray; **D:** Alejandro Amenabar; **W:** Alejandro Amenabar, Mateo Gil; **C:** Hans Burman; **M:** Alejandro Amenabar, Mariano Marin.

Opera
Many consider this to be Dario Argento's last great film, but newcomers to the Argento oeuvre will simply find it bloody and confusing. The story is centered on an opera troupe performing *MacBeth*. After the star is injured, young understudy Betty (Cristina Marsillach) takes over the lead and is an immediate smash. Unfortunately, a black cloud spreads over the production as several members of the cast and

crew turn up dead. The killer attacks the victims when they are with Betty, and forces her to watch the brutal slayings. Argento dazzles the viewer with many elaborate camera tricks, the most notable being a swirling, bird's-eye view of the opera house, but the story leaves much to be desired. The killings happen at random, and the ending is a mess. There are no clear suspects until chapter 17, and by then most viewers will be bored. Still, the "peephole" killing remains one of Argento's most creative death scenes, making this a must-have for fans of the director. The new anamorphic transfer on this DVD is incredibly sharp, showing only minor defects. The audio tracks on this DVD are impressive as well, mixing clear dialogue, sharp sound effects, and the operatic score. There are some sudden shifts in volume, but this happens rarely. A 36-minute documentary on the making of the film is included here and remains one of the best featurettes ever on a DVD. Those involved with the film give honest and often shocking details about the film's production, separating this from the usual corporate featurette. The Limited Edition DVD contains a CD with the film's soundtrack. —*ML* *AKA:* Terror at the Opera.
Movie: 🎧🎧 ½ **DVD:** 🎧🎧🎧 ½
Anchor Bay (cat #DV11854, UPC 0131311-85492). Widescreen (2.35:1) anamorphic. Dolby Digital Surround EX; 6.1 DTS-ES. $34.98. Keepcase. *LANG:* English. *CAP:* English. *FEATURES:* Theatrical trailers • Music video • Director bio • Soundtrack CD.
1988 (R) 107m/C IT Christina Marsillach, Ian Charleson, Urbano Barberini, William McNamara, Antonella Vitale, Barbara Cupisti, Coralina Cataldi Tassoni, Daria Nicolodi; **D:** Dario Argento; **W:** Dario Argento, Franco Ferrini; **C:** Ronnie Taylor; **M:** Claudio Simonetti.

Operation Petticoat
Submarine captain Sherman (Grant) teams with wheeler-dealer Holden (Curtis) to make the *Sea Tiger* seaworthy. They're joined by a group of nurses, and the gags—often rampantly sexist—begin. Great teamwork from the stars keeps things rolling merrily along. Unfortunately, this is a substandard release. No extra care appears to have been taken in making the disc. The grainy image suffers from some bad aliasing along bright lines, but the worst aspect is the sound—it has a curiously flat quality throughout and at times, it even drops out completely for short moments. A restored "Special Edition" is in order. —*MM*
Movie: 🎧🎧🎧 ½ **DVD:** 🎧🎧
Artisan Ent. (cat #12045, UPC 01715312-0455). Widescreen (1.66:1) letterboxed. Dolby Digital Mono. $24.99. Keepcase. *LANG:* English. *CAP:* English. *FEATURES:* 18 chapters.
1959 120m/C Cary Grant, Tony Curtis, Joan O'Brien, Dina Merrill, Gene Evans, Arthur O'Connell, Virginia Gregg; **D:** Blake Edwards; **W:** Stanley Shapiro, Maurice

Richlin; **C:** Russell Harlan; **M:** David Rose. *AWARDS: NOM:* Oscars '59: Story & Screenplay.

The Opponent

Patty Sullivan (Eleniak) takes up boxing to build her self esteem and escape an abusive relationship and just about every other cinematic psychobabble cliché you've ever seen in a movie of the week. To the film's credit, it does a good job of establishing a beaten-up lived-in world—it was shot in Port Chester, New York—with modest production values that gain nothing on DVD. Acting is fine. Disc is marred by a couple of curious little digital pauses where the image freezes momentarily and almost imperceptibly. —*MM*

Movie: 🐾🐾 ½ **DVD:** 🐾🐾 ½
Lion's Gate Home Ent. (cat #7820D, UPC 031339782025). Widescreen letterboxed. Dolby Digital Stereo. $24.98. Keepcase. *LANG:* English. *SUB:* English; Spanish. *CAP:* English. *FEATURES:* 24 chapters ● Trailer.
2001 (R) 90m/C Erika Eleniak, Aunjanue Ellis, James Colby, John Doman; **D:** Eugene Jarecki; **W:** Eugene Jarecki; **C:** Joe Di Gennaro.

The Order

Stupid but entertaining flick finds Van Damme kicking butt in the Holy Land; first, as a crusading knight who sickens of the slaughter, and then a millennium later as he pursues a lost scripture (and his kidnapped father) in modern-day Jerusalem. Seems Dad and the scroll have fallen into the hands of a ruthless and fanatical cult intent upon instigating all-out Holy War. If it sounds deep…it ain't. Most of the time it's just one can of whupass after another, with the result being exactly what you expect from Jean-Claude. So, if you're looking for religious philosophy or a solution to the Middle East crisis, look somewhere else. Columbia has given this Van Damme actioner a pretty good DVD. Visually, the only problem seems to be a varying color accuracy that is most noticeable when fleshtones become a little reddish. Other than that, the colors are bold, the blacks and contrasts are excellent, and the picture is very sharp—even on the full-frame side of the two-sided disc. The 5.1 sound is better than most with some good booming (but not boomy) bass, crisp high ends, and excellent use of the Surround channels. There aren't any extras other than trailers for *The Order* and a few other Columbia Tristar films, but really, who would bother to watch 'em? —*JO*

Movie: 🐾🐾 **DVD:** 🐾🐾 ½
Columbia Tristar (cat #08426, UPC 04339-6084261). Widescreen (1.85:1) anamorphic; full frame. Dolby Digital 5.1. $24.95. Keepcase. *LANG:* English. *SUB:* English; French. *CAP:* English. *FEATURES:* 28 chapters ● Theatrical trailer.
2001 (R) 89m/C Jean-Claude Van Damme, Ben Cross, Charlton Heston, Brian Thompson, Sofia Milos; **D:** Sheldon Lettich; **W:** Jean-Claude Van Damme, Les Weldon.

Ordet

A crisis of faith and love is coming to head at the Borgen farm. Patriarch Morten (Malberg) is adamant that his son Anders (Cay Kristiansen) should not marry the tailor's daughter, as her family is of a different faith. Morten feels that the Christian ways are falling by the wayside, as his eldest son Mikkel (Emil Hass Christiansen) is a non-believer. Mikkel's dedicated and loving wife Inger (Birgitte Federspiel) gently accepts her husband's lack of faith, as she awaits her third child. Morten is determined to defend the church of his forefathers, but his third son Johannes is a mental case, who believes himself to be Jesus Christ and is beginning to become a serious embarrassment. And then one night, events transpire that change all of their lives. Like the other films in the *Carl Theodor Dreyer Box Set, Gertrud* and *Day of Wrath* (please see reviews), the DVD presents flawless image and sound. —*GE*
AKA: The Word.

Movie: 🐾🐾🐾🐾 **DVD:** 🐾🐾🐾🐾
Criterion Full frame. Keepcase. *LANG:* Danish. *SUB:* English. *FEATURES:* Birgitte Federspiel interview.
1955 126m/B *DK* Henrik Malberg, Birgitte Federspiel, Cay Kristiansen, Emil Hass Christiansen; **D:** Carl Theodor Dreyer; **W:** Carl Theodor Dreyer, Kaj Munk; **C:** Henning Bendtsen. *AWARDS:* Golden Globes '56: Foreign Film; Venice Film Fest. '55: Film.

Ordinary People

Robert Redford's directorial debut is a stunning drama that hit 1980 America with the downer news that not only was there such a thing as dysfunctional families (a newish term at the time), but that understanding and awareness of real interpersonal problems didn't provide the instant cures we were used to seeing in movies. The Jarrett family has had two crises and is heading for a third. The favorite son has been lost in a boating accident, and the resulting misery has incited the second son, Conrad (Hutton), to attempt suicide. Now he's recovered, but struggles to keep up a stoic emotional front, while his caring father (Sutherland) and his rather cold mother (Moore) try to help him shake off the problem by minimizing it. Conrad finally accepts the help of psychiatrist Dr. Berger (Hirsch) and confides in a potential girlfriend, Jeannine (McGovern), in an attempt to make the pain go away and to "stop worrying other people." But the problem goes much deeper than that, to the emotional roots of the whole Jarrett family. Paramount's DVD is the studio's usual quality package. The film has been given a superior transfer with clear sound; on a large monitor it looks very handsome, far better than the rental VHS I saw when it was new, at the very beginning of home video. A brilliantly constructed trailer is included as well. —*GE*

Movie: 🐾🐾🐾 ½ **DVD:** 🐾🐾🐾 ½
Paramount (cat #08964, UPC 097360896-442). Widescreen (1.78:1) anamorphic.

Dolby Digital Mono. $29.99. Keepcase. *LANG:* English; French. *SUB:* English. *FEATURES:* 10 chapters ● Trailer.
1980 (R) 124m/C Mary Tyler Moore, Donald Sutherland, Timothy Hutton, Judd Hirsch, M. Emmet Walsh, Elizabeth McGovern, Adam Baldwin, Dinah Manoff, James B. Sikking, Frederic Lehne; **D:** Robert Redford; **W:** Alvin Sargent; **C:** John Bailey; **M:** Marvin Hamlisch. *AWARDS:* Oscars '80: Adapt. Screenplay, Director (Redford), Picture, Support. Actor (Hutton); Directors Guild '80: Director (Redford); Golden Globes '81: Actress—Drama (Moore), Director (Redford), Film—Drama, Support. Actor (Hutton); L.A. Film Critics '80: Support. Actor (Hutton); Natl. Bd. of Review '80: Director (Redford); N.Y. Film Critics '80: Film; Writers Guild '80: Adapt. Screenplay; *NOM:* Oscars '80: Actress (Moore), Support. Actor (Hirsch).

Organ

Two cops try to bust organ thieves, but a warehouse battle results in one being captured and the other mentally damaged. A mad scientist performs strange biological and "psychotronic" experiments on the captive policeman, while his victim's twin brother, also a cop, searches for his sibling. Though the plot is hard to follow, *Organ* emerges as one of the better entries in the new wave of Japanese horror films. Nearly every frame has something unpleasant going on—there's so much gory violence that it's surprising when some occurs *off*screen! Amid the horror, there's also beauty—some shots are so lovely that they become disturbing themselves. Even the soundtrack sounds infected—a wonderful mix of pulsing electronic music and hellish moans and growls, perfectly punctuating the visual nightmare. Shot on 16mm, the full-frame transfer looks surprisingly good. There's a 22-minute preview of the sequel, narrated by a Fujiwara. The menu is difficult to navigate. —*BT*

Movie: 🐾🐾 ½ **DVD:** 🐾🐾 ½
Synapse (cat #SFD0006, UPC 65493030-0695). Full frame. $29.99. Keepcase. *LANG:* Japanese. *SUB:* English. *FEATURES:* 20 chapters ● Trailers ● Sequel footage.
1996 105m/C *JP* Kei Fujiwara, Nasa Kenjin, Hirota Reona, Okubo Ryu; **D:** Kei Fujiwara; **W:** Kei Fujiwara; **C:** Kei Fujiwara.

Original Sin

Eighteen-eighties Cuban coffee-plantation owner Luis (Banderas) sends to America for a mail-order bride, seeking only someone loyal and of child-bearing years. To discourage gold diggers, he describes himself as a clerk. When his bride-to-be Julia (Jolie) shows up, Luis discovers that she's much more attractive than her picture. She claims that she wanted to be desired for something other than her beauty. With a start like that, what could go wrong? Well, betrayal, murder, and theft, for starters. An American private detective arrives on the scene, hired by Julia's family to report on her well-being. This fuels doubts in Luis, but a little too late. Soon he's cleaned out, shamed, and on the trail of his former "wife." Banderas and Jolie torch the scenes as the couple in lust, but the ham-handed dialogue and direction derail this period potboiler. The above-average video transfer features bright and vivid colors. Blacks are also well defined though there is some slight diffusion in darker hues. The soundtrack is similarly impressive and boasts clear dialogue, impressive sound effects, and a lush musical score. The extras included on the disc are decent, but there's nothing spectacular here. —*MJT*

Movie: 🎵🎵 ½ **DVD:** 🎵🎵 ½
MGM Home Ent. (cat #1003049, UPC 027-616872302). Widescreen (2.35:1) anamorphic. Dolby Digital 5.1 Surround. $26.98. Keepcase. *LANG:* English; Spanish; French; Portuguese. *SUB:* English; Spanish; French; Portuguese. *FEATURES:* 16 chapters • Commentary: director Michael Cristofer • "You Can't Walk Away from Love," music video by Gloria Estefan • Animated photo gallery • Original theatrical trailer.
2001 188m/C Antonio Banderas, Angelina Jolie, Thomas Jane, Jack Thompson, Gregory Itzin, Joan Pringle, Allison Mackie, Cordelia Richards, Pedro Armendariz Jr.; *D:* Michael Cristofer; *W:* Michael Cristofer; *C:* Rodrigo Prieto; *M:* Terence Blanchard.

Orloff and the Invisible Man

Extremely silly "horror" movie tells the story of the long night Dr. Carondet (Valladares) spends at the castle of Orloff (genre staple Vernon) and his daughter Cecile (Carva). Yes, there's an invisible man around, too. The box copy accurately compares his encounter with a scullery maid to Bela Lugosi's wrestling with the stuffed octopus in *Bride of the Monster*. DVD quality varies with the source material. Some stretches exhibit quite a lot of surface damage; others are completely clear. Sound is adequate. —*MM AKA:* Orloff Against the Invisible Man; The Invisible Dead; Dr. Orloff's Invisible Monster.
Movie: 🎵 **DVD:** 🎵🎵 ½
Image Ent. (cat #ID91088IDVD, UPC 0143-81910827). Widescreen (1.66:1) anamorphic. Dolby Digital Mono. $24.99. Snapper. *LANG:* English; French; German. *FEATURES:* 10 chapters • Trailer (in French) • Alternate "clothed" scenes.
1970 76m/C IT FR Howard Vernon, Brigitte Carva, Fernando (Fernand) Sancho, Isabel Del Rio, Paco Valladares; *D:* Pierre Chevalier; *W:* France Villon; *M:* Camile Sauvage.

Orphans

A dark, dark, dark, dark Scottish comedy. Did I say dark? Written and directed by Peter Mullan *(Session 9)*, *Orphans* tells the disturbing tale of four siblings and their attempt to cope with their mother's death the night before her funeral. This is highly reminiscent of Dunne's *After Hours,* only darker and with a funeral...and lots of blood. While the quad is at a pub at the beginning of the very long night, Thomas (Lewis), the oldest son, gets up and sings Karaoke for his mother, which is funny, until he starts to sob. Then some patrons start to laugh and Michael (Henshall), the next brother in line, gets in a fight and gets knifed. Of course he doesn't tell Thomas or his sister, the wheelchair-bound Sheila (Stevenson). Instead he tells the youngest brother, John (McCole), who decides that he should find a gun and shoot the knife-wielding Karaoke heckler. Michael wants to wait for medical care until he clocks in to work in the morning so he can make a claim against his employer. (His scene at work the next day is not to be missed.) So off they go into the night; Michael bleeding and passing time in bars; Thomas in denial locking himself in the church with their dead mum; Sheila losing all patience and deciding to get herself home in her wheelchair by herself but being waylaid to a stranger's birthday party; and John looking for a gun. There is so much to see in this film. The dialogue is witty—and subtitled for the Scottish impaired—and the acting is great and there are moments of what can only be described as visual irony. There is also a lot of harsh language that is evident even if you don't get the Scots. The disc looks great, with rich blacks in the night scenes, which is most of the film, and the sound is very good, with exception made for the accents which makes the dialogue sound muffled. —*CA*
Movie: 🎵🎵🎵 **DVD:** 🎵🎵🎵
Image Ent. (cat #2DO598SLDVD, UPC 014-381059823). Widescreen (1.85:1) letterboxed. Dolby Digital 5.1 Surround; Dolby Digital 4.0 Matrix Surround. $24.98. Keepcase. *LANG:* English. *SUB:* English. *FEATURES:* 16 chapters.
1997 102m/C GB Douglas Henshall, Gary Lewis, Stephen McCole, Rosemarie Stevenson, Alex Norton, Frank Gallagher, Malcolm Shields; *D:* Peter Mullan; *W:* Peter Mullan; *C:* Grant Scott Cameron; *M:* Craig Armstrong.

Osmosis Jones

Osmosis Jones is a great family film that should actually appeal to most of the family. Bill Murray is hilarious as Frank, a man who eats a tainted egg. Once he ingests the egg, the action moves inside his body, which is an animated world filled with great characters. The title character, Osmosis Jones (voiced by Chris Rock), is a white-blood cell who is after the germs that rode in on the egg. What Jones doesn't know is that the virus Thrax (voiced by Laurence Fishburne) has entered Frank and wants to kill Frank. Jones is joined by a cold-pill named Drix (voiced by David Hyde Pierce) to combat the evil Thrax. The film is full of clever in-jokes and film references. Frank's body is littered with funny signs and markers, and the whole thing plays like a buddy-cop movie. The animation is fun and colorful and the scenes with Murray are worth checking out on their own. With the *Osmosis Jones* DVD, we get a picture-perfect transfer that renders the animated scenes extremely striking. The live-action scenes look great as well, being free from overt grain or distortion. The audio track is impressive as well, offering nearly constant Surround sound effects. The extras on the DVD are somewhat lacking (the commentary is especially bad), making the brilliant transfer the highlight of this package. —*ML*
Movie: 🎵🎵🎵🎵 **DVD:** 🎵🎵🎵
Warner (cat #21323). Widescreen (2.35:1) anamorphic. Dolby Digital 5.1. $24.98. Snapper. *LANG:* English; French; Spanish. *SUB:* English; French. *CAP:* English. *FEATURES:* Commentary • Interactive game • Documentaries • Deleted scenes • Theatrical trailer • 12 chapters.
2001 (PG-13) 95m/C Bill Murray, Molly Shannon, Chris Elliott, Elena Franklin; *D:* Bobby Farrelly, Peter Farrelly, Piet Kroon, Tom Sito; *W:* Marc Hyman; *C:* Mark Irwin; *M:* Randy Edelman; *V:* Chris Rock, Laurence "Larry" Fishburne, David Hyde Pierce, Brandy Norwood, William Shatner, Ron Howard.

Othello

Silent version of Shakespeare's tragedy features Jannings as the Moor. The film has a strong reputation but this disc was made from damaged original elements, and displays all the problems you'd expect to find in a work of this age—registration bounce, lots of scratches and snow and larger white blobs. It is of historic value only. Four silent Shakespearian short films are included too: "Duel Scene from Macbeth" (1905), "Taming of the Shrew" (1908), "Romeo Turns Bandit" (1910), and "Desdemona" (1911). —*MM*
Movie: 🎵🎵 ½ **DVD:** 🎵🎵
Kino on Video (cat #K181, UPC 73832901-8122). Full frame. $29.95. Keepcase. *LANG:* Silent. *SUB:* English intertitles. *FEATURES:* 16 chapters • Liner notes by Douglas Brode.
1922 81m/B GE Emil Jannings, Lya de Putti, Werner Krauss; *D:* Dimitri Buchowetzki.

The Others

Ultra low-budget comedy features more heart than most. On the eve of their graduation, five friends (Aspen, Brady, Elfman, Rhys, and Livingston) have to deal with the bullying jocks and the principal (Linden), and try to pull a prank. The film certainly lacks polish, but it's well acted (by a cast that's a bit too old) and it's told with some real humor and appreciation for the characters. DVD is a slight improvement visually over VHS tape with considerable extras. —*MM*
Movie: 🎵🎵🎵 **DVD:** 🎵🎵🎵
York Ent. (cat #YPD-1143, UPC 75072311-4323). Widescreen letterboxed. $14.99. Keepcase. *LANG:* English. *FEATURES:* Direc-

tor's intro and commentary • "Making of" featurette • Deleted scenes • Trailers. **1997 (R) 85m/C** Phillip Rhys, Jennifer Aspen, John Livingston, Derrex Brady, Hal Linden, Bodhi (Pine) Elfman; **D:** Travis Fine; **W:** Travis Fine.

The Others [CE]

Defiantly old-fashioned ghost story is one of the most effective in recent years. The setting is a brooding estate on the Jersey Channel Islands, 1945. That's where Grace (Kidman) lives with her children Anne (Mann) and Nicholas (Bentley), waiting for her husband who's been declared missing and presumed dead. She needs new servants because the previous bunch disappeared. Three creepy applicants (Flanagan, Sykes, and Cassidy) show up at the front door. The main problem within the strange house is that the children are so extremely photosensitive that doors must be kept locked and heavy curtains drawn over the windows. The plot unfolds at a measured pace with some neatly arranged scares. Those come from really strong performances, and brilliant use of sound. This is perhaps the best narrative incorporation of 5.1 Surround effects I've ever experienced. The exceptionally dark image is flawless, though I should confess that I became so involved in the film that I wasn't as critical as I might have been. Even so, I looked for pixels and artifacts in the heavy fog scenes and found none. The surprise ending is honestly arrived at, but this one is engrossing from the first frame. The film is on one disc of this set; extras are on the other. —*MM*
Movie: ♫♫♫ ½ **DVD:** ♫♫♫ ½
Buena Vista Home Ent. (cat #24168, UPC 786936166552). Widescreen (1.85:1) anamorphic. Dolby Digital 5.1 Surround. $29.99. 2-disc keepcase. *LANG:* English; French. *SUB:* English; Spanish. *CAP:* English. *FEATURES:* 19 chapters • 3 documentaries • Still gallery • Trailer • visual effects featurette.
2001 (PG-13) 101m/C Nicole Kidman, Fionnula Flanagan, Alakina Mann, James Bentley, Christopher Eccleston, Elaine Cassidy, Eric Sykes, Renee Asherson; **D:** Alejandro Amenabar; **W:** Alejandro Amenabar; **C:** Javier Aguirresarobe; **M:** Alejandro Amenabar. *AWARDS: NOM:* British Acad. '01: Actress (Kidman), Orig. Screenplay; Golden Globes '02: Actress—Drama (Kidman).

Our Lady of the Assassins

Gay writer Fernando (Jaramillo) returns to his hometown of Medellin, Colombia (misspelled on the box copy), and immediately begins a relationship with Alexis (Ballesteros), a teenaged street kid, whose understanding of the violent nature of the city is deeper than the older man's. Of course, that violence eventually affects their lives intimately. Reportedly to minimize his time in the dangerous city, director Schroeder shot the film on digital

video. That gives the DVD image a flat quality in many scenes and it's heightened by some unrealistic lighting. Sound is fine but the English subtitles are burned in. Jorge Arriagada's score is terrific. Curiously, nothing about the box copy or art refers to the sexual elements of the story. They suggest that it's a political thriller or action picture, when that is not the case. —*MM AKA:* La Virgen de los Sicarios.
Movie: ♫♫♫ **DVD:** ♫♫♫
Paramount (cat #33979, UPC 097363397-940). Widescreen anamorphic. Dolby Digital 5.1 Surround; Dolby Surround. $29.98. Keepcase. *LANG:* Spanish. *SUB:* English. *FEATURES:* 16 chapters.
2001 (R) 98m/C CL FR German Jaramillo, Anderson Ballesteros, Juan David Restrepo, Manuel Busquets; **D:** Barbet Schroeder; **W:** Fernando Vallejo; **C:** Rodrigo Lalinde; **M:** Jorge Arrigagda.

Out Cold

Typical teen T&A fest sprinkled with bodily function jokes, body part jokes, and nice snowboard stunts. Using *Casablanca* loosely as a story model (yes, the one with Bogart) it tells the sordid tale of Rick Rambis, who was dumped by the girl he loved and lives in a constant state of depression over why she left him while working at a ski resort. One day she walks into the town bar and he learns that she was, yes, already engaged to someone else. There's a subplot about her evil corporate father (Majors) trying to turn the ski resort into a...ski resort. Nice stunt reel in the extras and everybody does their part to act as immature as possible. Fun waste of time. Very good picture with nice color and a clean transfer and the sound is above average. —*CA*
Movie: ♫♫ ½ **DVD:** ♫♫♫ ½
Buena Vista Home Ent. (cat #24025, UPC 786936165456). Widescreen (1.85:1) anamorphic. Dolby Digital Surround. $29.95. Keepcase. *LANG:* English. *SUB:* French; Spanish. *CAP:* English. *FEATURES:* 18 chapters • Commentary: director • "Making of" featurette • King of the Mountain action footage.
2001 (PG-13) 90m/C Jason London, Willie Garson, Lee Majors, A.J. Cook, Derek Hamilton, Zach Galifianakis, Flex Anderson, Caroline Dhavernas, Victoria Silvstedt; **D:** Brendan Malloy, Emmett Malloy; **W:** Jon Zack; **C:** Richard Crudo; **M:** Michael Andrews.

Out of Africa

This multi award–winning drama stars Meryl Streep as Baroness Karen Blixen, who comes to Africa with her husband, but finds love with another man (Redford). Highlighted by absolutely stunning cinematography and great performances from both Redford and Streep. Images are, for the most part, consistently sharp. The colors of Africa look beautiful and are very pleasing with no problems. Black level is average, and flesh tones remain fine throughout. There are a couple of scenes that look slightly grainy, and there are a

few small marks on the print source. The audio does sound a bit thin, lacks bass, and isn't as dramatic as current Surround tracks. Much of the film is dialogue, but there are scenes (such as the flight over Africa and the lion attack) where the audio opens up nicely. The commentary is excellent. Pollack is a fascinating speaker; he keeps his comments organized and his thoughts go into further depth about the tale on-screen. He also discusses the origin of the project and talks about the difficulties with telling a story like this on the big screen. The "Song of Africa" documentary is an impressively done 50-minute retrospective look at the making of the film. Interviews with everyone from Pollack and Streep to composer John Barry are included. In between interview segments are examinations of the history of the story and Africa itself. —*AB/DG*
Movie: ♫♫♫ ½ **DVD:** ♫♫♫ ½
Universal Studios Home Video (UPC 251-92025020). Widescreen (1.85:1) anamorphic. Dolby Digital 5.1 Surround. $29.98. Keepcase. *LANG:* English; French. *CAP:* English. *FEATURES:* Commentary: Pollack • Trailer • "Song of Africa" documentary • Production notes • Cast bios.
1985 (PG) 161m/C Meryl Streep, Robert Redford, Klaus Maria Brandauer, Michael Kitchen, Malick Bowens, Michael Gough, Suzanna Hamilton, Rachel Kempson, Graham Crowden, Shane Rimmer, Donal McCann, Iman, Joseph Thiaka, Stephen Kinyanjui; **D:** Sydney Pollack; **W:** Kurt Luedtke; **C:** David Watkin; **M:** John Barry. *AWARDS:* Oscars '85: Adapt. Screenplay, Art Dir./Set Dec., Cinematog., Director (Pollack), Picture, Sound, Orig. Score; British Acad. '86: Adapt. Screenplay; Golden Globes '86: Film—Drama, Support. Actor (Brandauer), Score; L.A. Film Critics '85: Actress (Streep), Cinematog.; Natl. Bd. of Review '85: Support. Actor (Brandauer); N.Y. Film Critics '85: Cinematog., Support. Actor (Brandauer); *NOM:* Oscars '85: Actress (Streep), Costume Des., Film Editing, Support. Actor (Brandauer).

Out of Sync

Gypsy DJ Jason St. Julian (L.L. Cool J.) gets in trouble with his bookies and L.A. detectives, one of whom forces him into an undercover job with a drug-dealing club owner (Zada). Then Jason falls for the bad guy's girlfriend (Dillard). When he made the film, L.L. Cool J.'s acting chops had yet to be developed, but he's still the best thing on screen. Some minor artifacts crop up in the many dark smoky nightclub scenes. Disc is essentially equal to VHS tape. —*MM*
Movie: ♫♫ **DVD:** ♫♫
Artisan Ent. (cat #12040, UPC 01223612-0407). Full frame. Dolby Digital Stereo. $14.98. Keepcase. *LANG:* English. *CAP:* English. *FEATURES:* 18 chapters • Talent files • Production notes.
1995 (R) 105m/C L.L. Cool J., Victoria Dillard, Howard Hesseman, Ramy Zada, Don Yesso, Yaphet Kotto; **D:** Debbie Allen;

W: Robert E. Dorn; **C:** Isidore Mankofsky; **M:** Steve Tyrell.

Out of Time

Modern-day Rip van Winkle tale is directed and written by the man who wrote the play *On Golden Pond*. Jack Epson (McDaniel) has time for everything but his wife (Harris) and daughter. When the pioneer ghosts of the small woodland town where he lives decide they need him to monkey wrench the expansion plans of the town bad boy, they put him to sleep for 20 years so he can be fresh for the fight. There is nothing new or exciting here for seasoned filmgoers, but it is a competent film with no violence or sex to spoil the scenery. The acting is good overall, worthy of early Disney B-family films. It's also nice to see a story where the lead couple is bi-racial and it's never mentioned as a plot-point, just accepted as part of the framework. Filmed for the Showtime cable channel, the disc has TV quality sound and picture and is shown in its original 1.33 format. —*CA*
Movie: 🦴🦴 ½ **DVD:** 🦴🦴 ½
Showtime Networks, Inc. (cat #SH03026, UPC 758445302622). Full frame. Stereo. $19.90. Keepcase. *LANG:* English. *CAP:* English. *FEATURES:* 18 chapters.
2000 94m/C James McDaniel, Mel Harris, August Schellenberg, Ken Pogue; **D:** Ernest Thompson; **W:** Ernest Thompson, Rob Gilmer; **C:** Stephen McNutt; **M:** Terry Frewer.

The Outlaw Josey Wales [2]

The "Clint Eastwood Collection" incarnation of his seminal western/war movie appears to be identical to the first edition (reviewed in *Book 1*). That disc, however, contained both widescreen and full-frame versions. This one's widescreen only. It also features a new (1999) "making of" featurette, "Hell Hath No Fury," and a brief introduction by Eastwood. —*MM*
Movie: 🦴🦴🦴 ½ **DVD:** 🦴🦴🦴
Warner (cat #21517, UPC 0853921517-21). Widescreen (1.85:1) anamorphic. Dolby Digital 5.1 Surround Stereo; Dolby Digital Mono. $19.98. Snapper. *LANG:* English; French. *SUB:* English; French; Spanish. *CAP:* English. *FEATURES:* 35 chapters • 2 "making of" featurettes • Adapting the novel (text) • Casting (text) • Shooting (text) • Trailer • Talent files • Intro by Eastwood.
1976 (PG) 135m/C Clint Eastwood, Chief Dan George, Sondra Locke, Matt Clark, John Vernon, Bill McKinney, Sam Bottoms, Will Sampson, Woodrow Parfrey, Royal Dano, John Quade, John Russell, John Mitchum, Kyle Eastwood; **D:** Clint Eastwood; **W:** Philip Kaufman; **C:** Bruce Surtees; **M:** Jerry Fielding. *AWARDS:* Natl. Film Reg. '96; *NOM:* Oscars '76: Orig. Score.

Outpost in Morocco

A womanizing French officer (Raft) is ordered to escort the daughter of a Moroc-can sultan (Windsor) back to her home. On the way, they fall in love, but the sultan, who vehemently hates the French, refuses the relationship. When he begins a revolution, nothing—not even his daughter's life—will come in the way of Morocco's independence. This forgettable comic adventure looks great on this DVD. Transferred from a combination of an original negative and a fine-grain master, the image varies in quality from good to excellent, but is far better than any previous release. The mono sound is good, with only occasional hissing in the background. —*DRL*
Movie: 🦴 ½ **DVD:** 🦴🦴🦴
Image Ent. (cat #9451, UPC 0143819451-26). Full frame. Mono. $19.99. Snapper. *LANG:* English. *FEATURES:* 9 chapters.
1949 92m/B George Raft, Marie Windsor, Akim Tamiroff, John Litel, Eduard Franz; **D:** Robert Florey; **W:** Charles Grayson, Paul de Sainte-Colombe; **C:** Lucien N. Andriot; **M:** Michel Michelet.

Outta Time

David (Lopez) is a college student whose bum knee causes him to lose his soccer scholarship. To continue his studies, he transports packages across the Mexico border for the mysterious Professor Darabont (Saxon). But the sealed packages aren't what Darabont claims. Reminiscent of a decent low-budget blaxploitation film of the mid-'70s, but prepare yourself for Z-movie straight-to-video production values. Good DVD transfer and sound. —*MO* **AKA:** The Courier.
Movie: 🦴🦴 ½ **DVD:** 🦴🦴🦴
Artisan Ent. (cat #12754, UPC 01223612-7543). Widescreen anamorphic. Dolby Digital 5.1; Dolby Surround. $24.98. Keepcase. *LANG:* English. *SUB:* English; Spanish. *CAP:* English. *FEATURES:* 20 chapters • Commentary: Lorena David, Mark Roberts, Mario Lopez, Ali Landry • Behind-the-scenes featurette • Interviews with director, producer, actors • Bios & filmographies of cast and filmmakers • Theatrical trailer • Photo gallery.
2001 (R) 90m/C Mario Lopez, John Saxon, Ali Landry, Nancy O'Dell, Tava Smiley, Tim Sitarz; **D:** Lorena David; **W:** Scott Duncan, Ned Kerwin; **C:** Lisa Wiegard; **M:** Scott Gilman.

Over the Hill Gang

A quirky cast is the only real reason to watch this made-for-TV western about a retired Texas Ranger and his pals who clean up a corrupt town. DVD image is exceptionally dark, faded, and poor. Sound is distorted. Title is available as part of *The Wild West* boxed set (cat.# 44213-9). —*MM*
Movie: 🦴🦴 **DVD:** 🦴 ½
Brentwood (cat #44086-9, UPC 78736440-8696). Full frame. $9.98. Keepcase. *LANG:* English. *FEATURES:* "Spooky Hooky" cartoon • 6 chapters • DVD dictionary • DVD-ROM features • Trivia game.
1969 75m/C Walter Brennan, Edgar Buchanan, Andy Devine, Jack Elam, Gypsy Rose Lee, Kristin Harmon, Ricky Nelson, Chill Wills, Edward Andrews; **D:** Jean Yarbrough; **W:** Jameson Brewer.

The Owl and the Pussycat

Tired of the noise and complaints, Felix (Segal) rats on his neighbor, Doris (Streisand), when he spots her making an illicit transaction. In return, she gets him thrown out as well, and the opposites find themselves on the streets together. The script is clever for the most part, although the opening barrage of gay jokes hasn't aged well. Streisand and Segal work very well together in this amiable comedy. The picture is a slight improvement over video, but the soundtrack doesn't handle high volumes very well, which is unfortunate in a movie that features this much yelling. —*BG*
Movie: 🦴🦴 ½ **DVD:** 🦴🦴 ½
Columbia Tristar (cat #04751, UPC 043-396047518). Widescreen (2.35:1) anamorphic; full frame. Dolby Mono. $19.95. Keepcase. *LANG:* English; French. *SUB:* English; French; Spanish; Portuguese; Chinese; Korean; Thai. *CAP:* English. *FEATURES:* 28 chapters • Trailers • Filmographies.
1970 (PG) 96m/C Barbra Streisand, George Segal, Robert Klein, Allen (Goorwitz) Garfield; **D:** Herbert Ross; **W:** Buck Henry; **C:** Harry Stradling Sr., Andrew Laszlo; **M:** Dick Halligan.

The Owl vs. Bombo

Any Sammo Hung picture is worth watching, but this one warrants extra attention as the film debut of Michelle Yeoh (*Supercop*). Master criminals Bombo (Hung) and the Owl (George Lam) pull their last heists and retire contentedly. That is, until frustrated police Inspector Fung (Stanley Fung) blackmails both criminals into working for him to bring down gangster Au Gun (James Tien). But first the odd couple is given a test assignment—volunteering as social workers. Yeoh plays a teacher at the youth center they're assigned to, trying to deal with tough inner-city kids. Later, their assignment includes harassment of Au Gun, which lands them into the expected hot water. Mix of light situation comedy, heavy social commentary, and kung fu fighting is unusual but entertaining. Sound is O.K., but the image highlights run a little hot. —*BT* **AKA:** Maau Tau Ying Yue Siu Fei Cheung; Mao Tou Ying Yu Xiao Fei Xiang; The Owl vs. Bumbo; The Owl and Dumbo.
Movie: 🦴🦴 ½ **DVD:** 🦴🦴
Tai Seng (cat #5167, UPC 48950249026-92). Widescreen letterboxed. $19.95. Keepcase. *LANG:* Cantonese; Mandarin. *SUB:* Chinese; English; Bahasa. *CAP:* English. *FEATURES:* 8 chapters • Trailers.
1984 101m/C *HK* Sammo Hung, Michelle Yeoh, George Lam, Stanley Fung, James Tien, Philip Ko; **D:** Sammo Hung; **C:** Arthur Wong.

Oxygen

A skinny psychopath with braces charms a rich woman on the street, only to smack her silly and haul her off to the woods. Harry (Brody) and his buddy bury her alive and send her rich husband a creepy ransom video. That's when NYPD detective Madeline Foster (Tierney) gets involved. She's supposed to catch the bad guy and save the woman who is about to suffocate in the coffin. The flick moves pretty well, until some long, drawn-out intense interrogation scenes. A fairly entertaining woman-buried-alive movie. The image is clear throughout with nice audio as well. An unexpected surprise is the quality of the commentary with director/writer Richard Shepard and stars Maura Tierney and Adrien Brody. It's both entertaining and informative—even better than the film itself. —GNG/DG

Movie: 🎵🎵 **DVD:** 🎵🎵 ½

A-PIX Entertainment Inc. (UPC 783722701-935). Widescreen (1.85:1) anamorphic. Dolby Digital 5.1 Surround. $19.98. Snapper. *LANG:* English. *SUB:* Spanish. *FEATURES:* Storyboards of the car chase • Commentary: director Shepard, actors Brody and Tierney • 28 chapters • Trailers.
1999 (R) 92m/C Adrien Brody, Maura Tierney, Terry Kinney, James Naughton, Laila Robins, Dylan Baker; *D:* Richard Shepard; *W:* Richard Shepard; *C:* Sarah Cawley; *M:* Rolfe Kent.

Oz: The Complete First Season

This three-disc set contains the first eight episodes of HBO's hard-hitting miniseries, set in the "Emerald City" unit of Oswald Maximum Security Prison. This complex and multiracial world explores questions of justice, punishment, revenge, honor, and forgiveness, but most of all the possibility of redemption. The directing is inconsistent and the series sometimes relies too much on stereotypes, but overall it is powerful and thought provoking, though not for the fainthearted. As is often the case, large areas of darkness reveal heavy grain, but for the most part the picture is bright and clean with sharp colors. The 5.1 soundtrack packs quite a punch and also serves the dialogue equally well. —BG

Movie: 🎵🎵🎵 **DVD:** 🎵🎵🎵 ½

HBO (cat #99204, UPC 026359920424). Full frame. Dolby 5.1; Dolby Surround; Stereo. $64.98. Custom cardboard. *LANG:* English; Spanish. *CAP:* English. *FEATURES:* 48 chapters • Commentary: series creator/writer Tom Fontana • Commentary: actor Lee Tergensen • Deleted scenes with optional commentary • Featurette • Music video • Cast & crew bios.
1997 451m/C Ernie Hudson, Terry Kinney, Harold Perrineau Jr., Eamonn Walker, Lee Tergesen; *D:* Darnell Martin, Nick Gomez, Jean De Segonzac, Leslie Libman, Larry Williams, Alan Taylor; *W:* Tom Fontana.

The Pact

A teenager witnesses the brutal murder of his parents and is enrolled in the Witness Protection Program. He is sent to private school in Montreal where his one and only friend turns out to be a young hitman hired to kill him. Ho-hum straight-to-video "thriller." Reasonable DVD transfer and sound. —MO **AKA:** The Secret Pact.

Movie: 🎵🎵 **DVD:** 🎵🎵🎵

Avalanche Ent. (cat #1562D, UPC 806-469). Full frame. Dolby Digital 2.0 Stereo. $19.99. Keepcase. *LANG:* English. *SUB:* French; Spanish. *CAP:* English; French; Spanish. *FEATURES:* 24 chapters • Theatrical trailer.
1999 (R) 94m/C CA Rider Strong, Adam Frost, John Heard, Nick Mancuso, Jack Langedijk, Lisa Zane; *D:* Rodney Gibbons; *W:* William Lee, Brian Cameron Fuld; *C:* Bert Tougas; *M:* Antonio Battista.

Paint Your Wagon

Lee Marvin plays wily and rambunctious Ben Rumson, who teams up with reserved Michigan farmer Pardner (Clint Eastwood) to mine gold and share a wife (Jean Seberg)—at *her* suggestion. Filmed against the breathtaking backdrop of the unspoiled Sierra Nevada, the film is full of grubby prospectors unabashedly belting out catchy musical numbers, especially Marvin and Eastwood. Sure, they're not the best vocalists around, but their gallant attempts are key to the charm and characterization of the production. The source print is clean, making for a transfer that is crisp and vibrant without any noticeable defects. The color is rich and true, delivering deep blue skies, lush terrain, and natural flesh tones. With deep blacks, balanced contrast, and remarkable detail, it's obvious the team at Paramount gave this transfer the attention and care it so richly deserves. Beginning with the title song, the orchestrations are so energetic and dimensional that you'd swear you've been seated smack dab in the middle of the orchestra pit. The remixed 5.1 also delivers plenty of ambient noise and directional effects that further envelop you in the on-screen hi-jinks, yet the dialogue is never upstaged or obscured. —DP

Movie: 🎵🎵🎵 **DVD:** 🎵🎵🎵 ½

Paramount (cat #06933, UPC 097360693-348). Widescreen (2.35:1) anamorphic. Dolby Digital 5.1 Surround Stereo; Dolby Digital Mono. $24.98. Keepcase. *LANG:* English; French. *SUB:* English. *FEATURES:* 18 chapters • Trailer.
1969 (PG) 164m/C Lee Marvin, Clint Eastwood, Jean Seberg, Harve Presnell; *D:* Joshua Logan; *W:* Paddy Chayefsky; *M:* Frederick Loewe, Andre Previn, Alan Jay Lerner. *AWARDS:* NOM: Oscars '69: Scoring/Musical.

The Pallisers, Vol. 2

Plantagenet Palliser (Latham) and Lady Glencora (Hampshire), the central characters in Anthony Trollope's political novels, continue with these middle episodes of the popular BBC series. Like the first release (reviewed in *Book 2*), DVD image quality is about equal to VHS tape. —MM

Movie: 🎵🎵🎵 **DVD:** 🎵🎵

Acorn Media (UPC 054961433995). Full frame. Dolby Digital Mono. $79.95. Keepcase boxed set. *LANG:* English. *FEATURES:* 24 chapters • Susan Hampshire interview • Cast filmographies.
1974 467m/C GB Susan Hampshire, Philip Latham, Roland Culver, Anna Massey, Donal McCann, Barbara Murray.

The Pallisers, Vol. 3

The political and social intrigues of Plantagenet Palliser (Latham) and Lady Glencora (Hampshire) and their family come to a conclusion in these final episodes of the popular BBC series. Like the first release (reviewed in *Book 2*), DVD image quality is no better than broadcast quality of 1974. Writing and acting are first-rate. —MM

Movie: 🎵🎵🎵 **DVD:** 🎵🎵

Acorn Media (UPC 054961465798). Full frame. Dolby Digital Mono. $79.95. Keepcase boxed set. *LANG:* English. *FEATURES:* 40 chapters • Susan Hampshire interview • Cast filmographies.
1974 468m/C GB Susan Hampshire, Philip Latham, Anthony Andrews, Jeremy Irons.

Panic

Hangdog Macy is perfect as middle-aged Alex, who is not having your average midlife crisis since he's a hitman. He learned the trade from his ruthless dad Michael (Sutherland), who's still calling the shots. But Alex has been keeping the truth from his wife Martha (Ullman) and his beloved son Sammy (Dorfman), and he needs to talk. So he goes to shrink Josh Parks (Ritter) and, in the waiting room, Alex meets neurotic Sarah (Campbell), with whom he contemplates an affair. But changes aren't easy for a professional killer. The image is clean and without blemishes, virtually free of grain or noise and without scratches or dust marks. Blacks are deep and shadows very well delineated, giving the image good dimensionality. The compression is also very well done, without introducing distracting artifacts in the presentation. Both English and Spanish language tracks are well produced with a natural quality. —MM/GH

Movie: 🎵🎵🎵 **DVD:** 🎵🎵🎵

Artisan Ent. (UPC 012236117285). Widescreen (2.35:1) anamorphic. Dolby Digital Surround Stereo. $24.98. Keepcase. *LANG:* English; Spanish. *SUB:* English. *FEATURES:* Commentary: director Henry Bromell • 5 deleted scenes • Trailers • Talent files.
2000 (R) 93m/C William H. Macy, John Ritter, Neve Campbell, Donald Sutherland, Tracey Ullman, Barbara Bain, David Dorfman; *D:* Henry Bromell; *W:* Henry Bromell; *C:* Jeffrey Jur; *M:* Brian Tyler.

Para Para Sakura

Color-blind aerobics instructor Aaron Kwok can only see colors in kooky heiress Cecilia Cheung. Romance, music, and comedy ensue. Surprisingly little is made of the color-blind angle, which you would think cinematographer/director Jingle Ma would turn into something spectacular. Perfect for Kwok's preteen fan club, but all others beware. Image and sound are both excellent. —*BT*

Movie: 🎬🎬 **DVD:** 🎬🎬
Tai Seng (UPC 4895043504785). Widescreen letterboxed. Dolby Digital 5.1 Surround. $24.95. Keepcase. *LANG:* Cantonese; Mandarin. *SUB:* Chinese; English. *FEATURES:* Character bios • Trailers • Documentary featurette.
2001 101m/C *HK* Aaron Kwok, Cecilia Cheung; **D:** Jingle Ma; **W:** Susan Chan; **C:** Jingle Ma.

Paradise Canyon
Please see review for *John Wayne: Western Classics.*
Movie: 🎬 ½
1935 59m/B John Wayne, Yakima Canutt, Marion Burns; **D:** Carl Pierson; **W:** Lindsley Parsons, Robert Emmett Tansey; **C:** Archie Stout.

Paradise Lost 2: Revelations
In 1993, three Arkansas teenagers were convicted of the murder of three little boys. The three teens, convicted with little actual evidence and a preponderance of irrational explanations, have become one of the most famous modern miscarriages of justice. This incredibly disturbing and frustrating follow-up documentary charts one of the teenagers' attempts to gain another trial and the defending attorney's efforts to introduce shocking, convincing evidence into the case. One of the parents of a murdered child (who seemed disturbingly violent and appeared to be the most likely suspect in the first film) is even more unsettling this time around. In the interim, his wife died (or was murdered) under mysterious causes and his stories constantly conflict one another. Not-for-the-squeamish film is just as maddening as the original, and just as riveting. The imagery is grainy, occasionally smeary, and prone to digital edging but is sharp. The sound is well recorded, clean, and crisp. —*DG*

Movie: 🎬🎬🎬 **DVD:** 🎬🎬 ½
New Video Group (cat #NVG-9483, UPC 767685948330). Full frame. Dolby Stereo. $24.95. Keepcase. *LANG:* English. *FEATURES:* 12 chapters • Filmmaker bios • Photo gallery • Trailers for other documentaries.
1999 133m/C D: Joe Berlinger, Bruce Sinofsky; **M:** Metallica.

A Paradise under the Stars
Impossible-to-synopsize Cuban comedy revolves around Sissy (Valdes) and Sergio (Cruz), would-be lovers who might be brother and sister. Sorting it out goes back a generation or so. Throw in professional jealousies and racial elements and

you've got a movie that's as complicated as Shakespeare with a strong streak of Felliniesque surrealism. DVD boasts a very good image that tends to be a bit pale in some scenes. Sound is O.K. Burned-in subtitles are easy to read. —*MM* **AKA:** Un Paraiso Bajo las Estrellas.
Movie: 🎬🎬 ½ **DVD:** 🎬🎬 ½
Vanguard Intl. Cinema (cat #VF9124, UPC 658769912432). Widescreen (1.66:1) letterboxed. $29.95. Keepcase. *LANG:* Spanish. *SUB:* English. *FEATURES:* 12 chapters • Trailer.
1999 90m/C *CU SP* Vladimir Cruz, Thais Valdes, Enrique Molina, Amparo Munoz, Daisy Granados, Litico Rodriguez, Satiago Alfonso, Jacqueline Arenal; **D:** Gerardo Chijona; **W:** Gerardo Chijona, Senel Paz; **C:** Raul Perez Ureta; **M:** Carlos Faruolo.

Paranoia
Jana Mercer's (Bako) family was murdered by a psycho killer when she was a child; 20 years later, said psycho Calvin Hawks (Drake) is about to be paroled and he's stalking her via the Internet. The woman-in-jeopardy clichés pile up faster than snow in Vermont, where much of this mid-budget horror was filmed. DVD appears to be an accurate reproduction of an often dark and underlit image. There was a curious digital "burp" that caused a brief pause in chapter 6 on this rental disc. —*MM*
Movie: 🎬🎬 ½ **DVD:** 🎬🎬 ½
Studio Home Ent. (cat #7155). Full frame. Stereo. $24.95. Keepcase. *LANG:* English. *SUB:* Spanish. *FEATURES:* Cast & crew thumbnail bios • Trailer • 24 chapters.
1998 (R) 86m/C Larry Drake, Sally Kirkland, Scott Valentine, Brigitte Bako; **D:** Larry Brand; **W:** Larry Brand; **M:** Martin Trum.

Parasite Eve
Hiroshi Mikami stars as Dr. Nagashima, a scientist who has discovered that mitochondria, the organisms which provide energy for cells, appear to have their own DNA and life-cycle. Nagashima has put this theory to work in his research, as he attempts to cure diseases in lab animals, using the mitochondrial energy. When Nagashima's young wife Kiyomi (Riona Hakuzi) is killed in an auto accident, Nagashima takes her liver in order to try and clone her, once again, using the energy of the mitochondria. He doesn't realize that her death may be the first step in an evolutionary leap, in which the mitochondria will rise up and dominate the world. The ending of *Parasite Eve* is somewhat confusing and convoluted, but the scenes leading up to the finale are very disturbing and contain some great imagery. This is not the best example of a Japanese horror film, but those of you who've grown bored with homegrown fare may want to "experiment" with it. The image here is simply beautiful. Aside from an occasional white spot, there are no defects from the source print. The picture is sharp and clear, rarely showing any grain. The most outstanding aspect of this transfer is the color. The

reds, blues, and greens simply leap off of the screen, and the fleshtones all appear natural. This great image gives the picture a great deal of depth, thus adding to Ochiai's visuals. Surround is used mainly for ambience, but in certain scenes, such as the storm, it does make its presence known. There are some problems with the recording level, as the volume would suddenly shift from loud to soft, but this is infrequent. The English subtitles are white and easy to read, but they do appear on the image itself. —*ML*
Movie: 🎬🎬🎬 **DVD:** 🎬🎬🎬
A.D.V. Films (UPC 702727012921). Widescreen (1.85:1) anamorphic. Dolby Digital Surround. $24.98. Keepcase. *LANG:* Japanese. *SUB:* English. *FEATURES:* Trailer (48 sec.).
1997 120m/C *JP* Hiroshi Mikami, Riona Hakuzi, Tomoko Nakajima; **D:** Masayuki Ochiai.

The Parent Trap
Classic Disney tale of twins who were separated in a divorce settlement who meet each other at summer camp. They hate each other on sight and engage in a series of pretty funny practical jokes designed by one to humiliate other. In the end, though, they realize they are sisters and decide to visit the parent they never knew by switching places. Hayley Mills (fresh from her special Academy Award for *Pollyanna*) plays both parts marvelously with Brian Keith and Maureen O'Hara as their parents. Also boasts a great supporting cast which includes Leo G. Carroll. The dual commentary by the now-adult Mills and director Swift (who also directed *Pollyanna*) is quite interesting, and is prefaced by a "commentary disclaimer" which notes that the opinions of Swift and Mills do not reflect the views of Disney. Digitally remastered print looks really good and the sound allows the ear-splitting theme song by Annette Funicello and Tommy Sands to cut right to your spine. —*CA*
Movie: 🎬🎬🎬 **DVD:** 🎬🎬🎬 ½
Buena Vista Home Ent. (cat #21551, UPC 786936143812). Widescreen (1.78:1) anamorphic. Dolby Digital 5.1 Surround; THX Optimizer. $29.99. Keepcase. *LANG:* English. *SUB:* Spanish. *CAP:* English. *FEATURES:* 24 chapters • Commentary: David Swift, Hayley Mills • Animated short, "Donald's Double Trouble" • "Making of."
1961 127m/C Hayley Mills, Maureen O'Hara, Brian Keith, Charlie Ruggles, Una Merkel, Leo G. Carroll, Joanna Barnes, Cathleen Nesbitt, Ruth McDevitt; **D:** David Swift; **W:** David Swift; **C:** Lucien Ballard; **M:** Paul J. Smith. *AWARDS: NOM:* Oscars '61: Film Editing, Sound.

Parental Guidance
Don't expect much in terms of image quality or production values in this comic drama about a black family's Christmas dinner. Sean (Lee) is already having problems with his girlfriend Lisa (Campbell),

but when he doesn't invite her over to his parents house, he's really in trouble. The relatives display an assortment of sexual, racial, and familial stereotypes. Similar material is handled with more polish in *Kingdom Come*, but if this film lacks style, its heart is in the right place. DVD presents an image that's incredibly grainy. The film appears to have been shot in suburban homes with minimal lighting. Writing and most of the acting are of higher quality. —*MM*

Movie: 🦴🦴 ½ **DVD:** 🦴🦴 ½
York Ent. (cat #YPD-1186, UPC 75072311-8628). Full frame. $14.99. Keepcase. *LANG:* English. *SUB:* Spanish. *FEATURES:* 30 chapters • Trailers.
2002 C Maia Campbell, Stacii Jae Johnson, Casey Lee; **D:** A.M. Cali; **W:** A.M. Cali; **C:** Scott Edelstein; **M:** Horace Washington.

Paris When It Sizzles

Screenwriter Richard Benson (Holden) and secretary Gabrielle Simpson (Hepburn) fall in love while cranking out a script in Paris and confusing themselves with the characters. Some of the humor is dated but the star-studded cast is still exceptionally studded, from Astaire to Sinatra to Noel Coward. Do not expect another *Charade*, however, despite the cast, setting, and time. Considering that age, image is acceptable but the heavy grain does make the bright, heavily saturated colors look a bit harsh. The Nelson Riddle score is terrific. —*MM*

Movie: 🦴🦴 **DVD:** 🦴🦴 ½
Paramount (cat #06314, UPC 0973606-3149). Widescreen (1.85:1) anamorphic. Dolby Digital Mono. $19.98. Keepcase. *LANG:* English; French. *SUB:* English. *CAP:* English. *FEATURES:* 17 chapters • Trailer.
1964 110m/C William Holden, Audrey Hepburn, Gregoire Aslan, Raymond Bussieres, Tony Curtis, Fred Astaire, Frank Sinatra, Noel Coward, Marlene Dietrich, Mel Ferrer; **D:** Richard Quine; **W:** George Axelrod; **C:** Charles B(ryant) Lang Jr.; **M:** Nelson Riddle.

Parisian Love / Down to the Sea in Ships

Clara Bow stars in two features before she had "It." In *Parisian Love*, the stronger of the two films, she plays a street hustler whose gang fleeces tourists. When her lover is shot during a heist, she plots seduction and revenge against the culprit, wealthy scientist Pierre Marcel (Tellegen). In the second feature, produced by the Whaling Film Corp., the plot and actors come second to the true star: the authentic, and impressive, whaling footage. The surrounding story is about a young businessman who will do anything, including signing onto a whaling ship, to win the heart of his love. Bow, in her first substantial role, plays a stowaway on the ship. Both prints show decay, but the transfers are very good. Each film has a new, though fairly weak, piano score. —*DL*
Movie: 🦴🦴🦴 **DVD:** 🦴🦴 ½

Kino on Video (cat #243, UPC 73832902-4321). Full frame. Mono. $29.99. Keepcase. *LANG:* Silent. *SUB:* English intertitles. *FEATURES:* 21 chapters.
1925 62m/B Clara Bow, Donald Keith, Lou Tellegen, Lillian (Lillianne, Lyllian) Leighton; **D:** Louis Gasnier; **W:** Lois Hutchinson; **C:** Allen Siegler.

Partners

All of the usual suspects are rounded up for this video premiere action comedy. Mild-mannered Bob (Paymer) steals a super-secret computer program from his company. Then it's stolen from him by hunky thief Axel (Van Dien). A series of double-crosses and chases—involving the obligatory Caddy convertible—ensue. Toss in the sexy girlfriend (Angel) and a cheap L.A. motel with a heart-shaped bed. DVD image is crisp and clear, making the so-so action look about as good as it could on home video. —*MM*

Movie: 🦴🦴 **DVD:** 🦴🦴 ½
Image Ent. (cat #OVED0816DVD, UPC 014-381081626). Widescreen (1.78:1) anamorphic. Dolby Digital 5.1 Surround Stereo; Dolby Digital Surround. $24.99. Keepcase. *LANG:* English. *FEATURES:* 12 chapters.
1999 (R) 90m/C Casper Van Dien, Vanessa Angel, David Paymer, Jenifer Lewis, Yuji Okumoto, Donna Pescow; **D:** Joey Travolta; **W:** Jeff Ferrell; **C:** Kristian Bernier; **M:** Jeff Lass.

The Party

Curious comedy is more enjoyable as a snapshot of entertainment folk in the mid-1960s than as a Seller vehicle, even though he does good work. He's Hrundi V. Bakshi, an actor who is mistakenly invited to a high-powered Hollywood dinner party. The supporting cast is filled with familiar faces. Some print wear is apparent and the opening exteriors are on the grainy side, but most of the film looks fine. Mono sound is completely acceptable, delivering understandable dialogue. —*MM*

Movie: 🦴🦴🦴 **DVD:** 🦴🦴 ½
MGM Home Ent. (cat #1002736, UPC 027-616869340). Widescreen (2.35:1) anamorphic. Dolby Digital Mono. $19.98. Keepcase. *LANG:* English; French; Spanish. *SUB:* English; French; Spanish. *CAP:* English. *FEATURES:* 16 chapters • Trailer.
1968 99m/C Peter Sellers, Claudine Longet, Marge Champion, Sharron Kimberly, Denny Miller, Gavin MacLeod, Carol Wayne; **D:** Blake Edwards; **W:** Blake Edwards; **C:** Lucien Ballard; **M:** Henry Mancini.

The Passion Network

Jana (Beaton) and Matt are happy hedonists who find themselves drawn into a group of wealthy folk who like to record their escapades and broadcast it on a private network. At least, that's what Jana explains to a couple of comic-relief cops after Matt has been shot. Sound is faint; the widescreen image is a bit better than VHS

tape, and the whole film is fairly ambitious for a made-for-cable production. —*MM*
Movie: 🦴🦴 ½ **DVD:** 🦴🦴 ½
Image Ent. (cat #ID1743PODVD, UPC 014-381174328). Widescreen (1.85:1) letterboxed. Dolby Digital Stereo. $24.98. Keepcase. *LANG:* English. *FEATURES:* 11 chapters.
2001 85m/C Stephanie Beaton, Tracie Turner, Nichole McAuley, Robert Knowlton, Carl Irwin; **D:** Paul S. Parco; **W:** Paul S. Parco; **C:** Philip Hurn; **M:** Cal Bennett.

Passport to Paris

Vive les Olsen Twins! Mel (Mary-Kate Olsen) and Ally (Ashley Olsen) are two junior high students who long to be part of the "cool" crowd. Things begin to look up for them when they are sent to Paris to visit their grandfather (Peter White). Aside from these facts, this vehicle doesn't have much of a plot. The girls travel around Paris taking in the famous sites and they meet two French boys and "fall in love." Considering the fact that the Twins are all of 13 years old, one can't help but question the appropriateness of the "falling in love" subplot. Aside from the travelogue views of some of France's most popular landmarks, there isn't much to recommend here for anyone over the age of 12. Aside from displaying realistic colors, this DVD doesn't offer much to differentiate the image quality from that of a VHS copy or the original TV broadcast. The picture isn't very sharp, and is actually quite hazy at times. Evidence of artifacting doesn't help this situation. Audio does provide clear dialogue with no perceivable distortion, but there is very little in the way of Surround sound effects. —*ML*

Movie: 🦴 ½ **DVD:** 🦴 ½
Warner (cat #36878, UPC 0853936878-23). Full frame. Dolby Surround Stereo. $19.98. Snapper. *LANG:* English; Spanish. *SUB:* English; Spanish; French. *CAP:* English. *FEATURES:* Fashion close-up • Trailers • Talent files • 28 chapters.
1999 (G) 87m/C Mary-Kate Olsen, Ashley (Fuller) Olsen; **D:** Alan Metter; **W:** Elizabeth Kruger, Craig Shapiro.

The Patriot [2 SB]

This "Superbit" edition improves somewhat on the image of the original release (reviewed in *Book 2*). There's not much to be done with the intentionally soft look of the period piece. It's flawless here. DTS Surround seems more dynamic and dramatic than the Dolby 5.1, but they're really quite similar. Perhaps the main improvement here is in the simple element of the menus. They've been redesigned, removing the nearly invisible arrows that lead to a second page of listings on the older disc. Here, the extras are on a second disc. Both are easy to navigate. —*MM*

Movie: 🦴🦴🦴 **DVD:** 🦴🦴🦴🦴
Columbia Tristar (cat #07910, UPC 043-396079106). Widescreen (2.35:1) anamorphic. DTS 5.1 Surround; Dolby 5.1 Surround. $29.98. Special packaging. *LANG:*

English. *SUB:* English; French; Spanish; Portuguese; Chinese; Korean; Thai. *FEATURES:* 28 chapters (film) ☞ Visual effects featurette ☞ Battlefield featurette ☞ "The True Patriots" featurette ☞ Conceptual art-to-film comparisons ☞ Deleted scenes ☞ Photo galleries ☞ Trailers ☞ Filmographies.
2000 (R) 164m/C Mel Gibson, Heath Ledger, Jason Isaacs, Chris Cooper, Tcheky Karyo, Joely Richardson, Tom Wilkinson, Donal Logue, Rene Auberjonois, Adam Baldwin; *D:* Roland Emmerich; *W:* Robert Rodat; *C:* Caleb Deschanel; *M:* John Williams. *AWARDS: NOM:* Oscars '00: Cinematog., Sound, Orig. Score.

Patton [2]

This is a non-special edition of the first disc of the two-disc *Patton* set (reviewed in *Book 1*) and the feature has an identical high quality transfer. The image is just as true and sharp as the Dimension-150 theatrical prints, as can be seen by the perfect lines of the giant American flag in the first scene. At this low price it's an amazing bargain. —*GE AKA:* Patton—Lust for Glory; Patton: A Salute to a Rebel.
Movie: 🎵🎵🎵 ½ *DVD:* 🎵🎵🎵 ½
20th Century Fox (UPC 024543026341). Widescreen (2.35:1) anamorphic. $19.98. Keepcase. *LANG:* English. *FEATURES:* Trailer ☞ Audio essay on the historical Patton.
1970 (PG) 171m/C George C. Scott, Karl Malden, Stephen Young, Michael Strong, Frank Latimore, James Edwards, Lawrence (Larry) Dobkin, Michael Bates, Tim Considine, Edward Binns, John Doucette, Morgan Paull, Siegfried Rauch, Paul Stevens, Richard Muench; *D:* Franklin J. Schaffner; *W:* Francis Ford Coppola, Edmund H. North; *C:* Fred W. Koenekamp; *M:* Jerry Goldsmith. *AWARDS:* Oscars '70: Actor (Scott), Art Dir./Set Dec., Director (Schaffner), Film Editing, Picture, Sound, Story & Screenplay; AFI '98: Top 100; Directors Guild '70: Director (Schaffner); Golden Globes '71: Actor—Drama (Scott); Natl. Bd. of Review '70: Actor (Scott); N.Y. Film Critics '70: Actor (Scott); Natl. Soc. Film Critics '70: Actor (Scott); Writers Guild '70: Orig. Screenplay; *NOM:* Oscars '70: Cinematog., Orig. Score.

Paul Simon: Graceland

Documentary produced by the VH-1 channel is something more than the usual collection of music videos. Paul Simon's 1986 album *Graceland* is a popular music landmark because it introduced American audiences to South African music. The film is an admittedly uncritical look at the project's genesis. Visually, the DVD is no better than broadcast quality, but the material is fascinating with well-chosen, extremely articulate interviews. The uncompressed PCM stereo sounds fine. —*MM*
Movie: 🎵🎵🎵 ½ *DVD:* 🎵🎵 ½
Rhino (cat #ID5845RHDVD, UPC 0143815-84523). Full frame. Uncompressed PCM Stereo. $19.98. Snapper. *LANG:* English. *FEATURES:* 17 chapters ☞ Discographies.

1997 78m/C Paul Simon, Philip Glass, Linda Ronstadt, Joseph Shabalala, Ray Phiri, Bakitki Kumalo; *D:* Jeremy Marre.

Pay It Forward

At Trevor's (Osment) first day of school his class is taught by Mr. Simonet (Spacey), a man whose face is scarred by burns, and whose intensity draws Trevor's interest. The teacher gives the children an assignment for the semester—think of an idea that will change the world. Trevor's idea is forward-thinking, if not terribly realistic: do something nice for three people, and have those three people do something nice for three additional people. Trevor helps a homeless person named Jerry, then tries to assist his alcoholic mother Arlene (Hunt) and Mr. Simonet in their lives by hitching them together. The acting is good, but Leder is not a subtle director and her audience manipulations are obvious. Many scenes seem designed as self-important "Oscar-worthy moments." The film starts off rather promisingly before heading into soap opera country and makes a terribly wrong decision with the ending. The two hours plus running time feels padded. The disc is a very good presentation, but slightly lacking. Sharpness detail and colors are usually good, although a few scenes are a tad soft, the preprint material used has a few marks and speckles, and some edge-enhancement is visible. This is a dialogue-driven feature, and as such, there really is hardly any activity to the sound presentation. Thomas Newman's score drifts through the room, sounding clear and crisp; it's really the only element that is taken beyond the front speakers. HBO First Look is a promotional featurette with the usual clips and interviews, but at least they're moderately interesting and do discuss more than the basics of the story. —*AB/DG*
Movie: 🎵🎵 *DVD:* 🎵🎵 ½
Warner Home Video (UPC 85391887720). Widescreen (1.85:1) anamorphic. Dolby Digital 5.1 Surround. $24.98. Snapper. *LANG:* English. *CAP:* English. *FEATURES:* Commentary: Leder ☞ Behind-the-scenes featurette ☞ Cast/production info.
2000 (PG-13) 122m/C Haley Joel Osment, Kevin Spacey, Helen Hunt, Jay Mohr, James Caviezel, Jon Bon Jovi, Angie Dickinson, David Ramsey, Gary Werntz; *D:* Mimi Leder; *W:* Leslie Dixon; *C:* Oliver Stapleton; *M:* Thomas Newman.

Pearl Harbor

Bottom line: a superb DVD (in a two-disc set) of an offensively dreadful movie. Captains Rafe McCawley (Affleck) and Danny Walker (Hartnett) grew up together, and became Army Air Corps pilots together. Rafe falls in love with nurse Evelyn Stewart (Beckinsale) just before rushing off to fight as a volunteer pilot in the Battle of Britain, where he's shot down and presumed dead. Danny and Evelyn ship out to Hawaii. All are reunited on December 6, 1941. Problems start with a script that lacks any suspense or genuine emotion,

arriving finally at a truly Strangelovian moment when Jon Voight's FDR stands up from his wheelchair! The direction of Michael Bay is not even direction, just a cluster of hyped scenes without feeling, or pace, or sensitivity of any kind. Even a lesser Spielberg work has an understanding of how older films worked, but Bay expresses nothing. Every image is like a shot in a television commercial—exact, functional, dead. The camera always moves, every shot is a perfect keeper, and absolutely meaningless. That said, the special effects are breathtaking, very pretty, and fun to watch in and of themselves. The planes look great, and the interaction of moving objects and water and smoke—tough media to animate digitally—is splendid. Too bad the attack sequence is so badly planned and directed. The awesome digital mastershots are all there is. Shots don't build into anything. Planes appear, torpedoes and bombs fall, ships blow up while thousands of ant-like men scramble for their lives. All the flaws of digital magic come through, too. Action is ridiculously optimized—we see everything, every detail, always from the perfect angle. We get a great sense of "being there," but no story is being told and we understand little of what we're seeing except boom, boom, splash, boom. With no action story to tell, video-game visuals take over. We zip between ships like the trench divers in *Star Wars*. The message is that *Pearl Harbor* is about really cool combat—we get torpedo points of view, bomb points of view: exploding planes carom into our faces. Almost no Japanese pilots are shown, but we are continually given their impossible points-of-view. Forget tragedy, iniquity, or understanding any of what we're seeing—all we learn is that the Japanese Naval Air Force clearly had the Right Nintendo Stuff, and those lucky enough to be at Pearl had one really cool day, man. Bay's direction skips over anything "fact" to concentrate on what know-nothing pubescent males want to see—grandiose video-game mayhem, and kick-ass payback. An innovative audio option is also available. The "Dolby headphone soundtrack" does a credible job of re-creating 5.1 Surround through conventional headphones. It's most noticeable in the flying scene in chapter 3, and the other larger action scenes. For a much better look at the events glossed over in the film, see *Tora! Tora! Tora!*, *30 Seconds Over Tokyo*, and, of course, *From Here to Eternity*. An even longer "director's cut" has been threatened. —*GE/MM*
Movie: 🎵 *DVD:* 🎵🎵🎵🎵
Buena Vista Home Ent. (cat #23889, UPC 786936164282). Widescreen (2.35:1) anamorphic. Dolby Digital 5.1 Surround; DTS 5.1 Surround; Dolby Headphone. $29.99. Special packaging. *LANG:* English; French. *SUB:* Spanish. *CAP:* English. *FEATURES:* 44 chapters ☞ "Making of" documentary ☞ History Channel documentary ☞ Music video.
2001 (PG-13) 183m/C Ben Affleck, Josh Hartnett, Kate Beckinsale, Alec Baldwin, Cuba Gooding Jr., Dan Aykroyd, Mako, Tom

Sizemore, Jon Voight, William Lee Scott, Colm Feore, Michael Shannon, Peter Firth, Jennifer Garner, Catherine Kellner, James King, Scott Wilson, William Fichtner, Ewen Bremner, Leland Orser, Graham Beckel, Tomas Arana, Guy Torry, Brian Haley, Tony Curran, Kim Coates, Glenn Morshower, John Fujioka, Tim Choate, John Diehl, Ted McGinley, Raphael Sbarge; **D:** Michael Bay; **W:** Randall Wallace; **C:** John Schwartzman; **M:** Hans Zimmer. *AWARDS: NOM:* Golden Globes '02: Song ("There You'll Be"), Score; Broadcast Film Critics '01: Song ("There You'll Be").

Pearl Harbor Before and After

This jingoistic collection is saved from its own excesses by the inclusion of one of the great forgotten WWII films, *Three Came Home*. It's the story of Agnes Keith (Colbert), who's imprisoned by the Japanese when they invade Borneo at the beginning of the war. She and her young son (Keuning) are separated from her husband (Knowles). The commander of her camp is Col. Suga (Hayakawa). Their curious relationship is at the center of the film. Though it will strike some contemporary viewers as too emotional and overstated, it does deal with issues that have not often been explored. DVD image displays irritating artifacts in almost every pan. The other films on the two-disc set are much worse in visual terms. "Dec. 7" (the long version) looks like it was created from a second-generation VHS tape. Contents: "Three Came Home" (106 min.), "Attack in the Pacific" (52 min.), "WWII G.I. Films," "6th Marine Division on Okinawa" (30 min.), "Dec. 7" (82 min.), "Return to Guam" (19 min.), "Payoff in the Pacific" (52 min.), "Pearl Harbor Clips" (22 min.). Also includes the "Star-Spangled Banner" and radio broadcast excerpts. —*MM*
Movie: 🎬🎬🎬 **DVD:** 🎬 ½
Triton Multimedia (cat #TDVD9259, UPC 017078925920). Full frame. Dolby Digital Mono. $19.98. Keepcase. *LANG:* English. *FEATURES:* 24 chapters in "Three Came Home."
2001 400m/C

Pearl Harbor: The View from Japan

This documentary will probably be an eye-opener for most American viewers. Despite the fact that it's a Japanese production, the film does not attempt to whitewash the attack. It does provide some historical background, and it views the architect of the plan, Admiral Isoroku Yamamoto, as something of a genius. He did, after all, change the very nature of 20th-century warfare. Until he showed how it could be done, naval combat was built around battleships and big guns. He demonstrated, in the most convincing fashion, that airplanes could be just as effective and much more versatile. He's the focus of the film. It appears to have been made for Japanese television and so

the DVD image is nothing spectacular. Most of the archival footage is so severely damaged that I suspect some of the imperfections have been emphasized or are intentional. Sound is fine. The "time line" extra includes interviews with history professors Theodore F. Cook and Haruko Taya Cook. —*MM*
Movie: 🎬🎬🎬 ½ **DVD:** 🎬🎬 ½
Central Park/U.S. Manga (cat #2148, UPC 719987214828). Full frame. Dolby Digital Stereo. $19.98. Keepcase. *LANG:* English; Japanese. *SUB:* English. *FEATURES:* 10 chapters ▪ Time line ▪ Yamamoto thumbnail bio ▪ DVD-ROM features ▪ Trailer.
1994 69m/C *JP* **D:** Kunio Kurita.

Pearl of the South Pacific

A trio of adventurers destroy a quiet and peaceful island when they ransack it for pearl treasures. An incredibly diffused picture is punctuated by unimpressive colors and poorly defined blacks. While the soundtrack fares a bit better, clear dialogue alone cannot save the disc from being below average. —*MJT* **AKA:** South Sea Woman.
Movie: 🎬🎬 **DVD:** 🎬🎬
VCI (cat #8290, UPC 089859829024). Full frame. Dolby Digital Mono. $19.99. Keepcase. *LANG:* English. *FEATURES:* 18 chapters ▪ Trailer gallery.
1955 85m/C Dennis Morgan, Virginia Mayo, David Farrar; **D:** Allan Dwan; **W:** Edwin Blum; **C:** John Alton; **M:** Louis Forbes.

Pecker (John Waters Collection Vol. 1)

When his photographs lead him to the top of the art world, Pecker (Furlong) finds out that fame isn't all it was cracked up to be, and that it also has an effect on everyone around him. In the meantime, viewers will get to learn all about teabagging and the evils of pubic hair. Waters takes plenty of shots at New York society and the art world in general, but it's all in good fun. The colors are lively without bleeding, and the overall transfer is very good. Surround sound only kicks in during the few party scenes. This version is double-billed with Waters's *Hairspray*. —*BG*
Movie: 🎬🎬 ½ **DVD:** 🎬🎬🎬
New Line (cat #N5230, UPC 7940435230-21). Widescreen (1.85:1) anamorphic. Dolby 5.1; Dolby Surround. $30.98. Custom cardboard. *LANG:* English. *CAP:* English. *FEATURES:* 20 chapters ▪ Trailer ▪ Commentary ▪ Interview with photographer Chuck Shacochis.
1998 (R) 87m/C Edward Furlong, Lili Taylor, Christina Ricci, Martha Plimpton, Mary Kay Place, Brendan Sexton III, Mark Joy, Mink Stole, Bess Armstrong, Patty (Patricia Campbell) Hearst, Mary Vivian Pearce, Lauren Hulsey, Jean Schertler; **D:** John Waters; **W:** John Waters; **C:** Robert Stevens; **M:** Stewart Copeland; **V:** John Waters. *AWARDS:* Natl. Bd. of Review '98: Support. Actress (Ricci).

The Penalty

A rash young doctor amputates the legs of an injured child. The child grows up to become vicious crimelord, Blizzard, who has macabre revenge planned for the doctor, his daughter, and her fiancé. Gripping, enjoyable penny dreadful is told in full melodramatic style. Chaney is excellent as Blizzard and performs most of the picture with his knees strapped painfully behind him. The ending is quite a surprise, but it's been prepared for beautifully. The image is predominantly sharp with moderate, acceptable contrasts but is prone to digital shimmer. The film is accurately and effectively tinted. The extras are informative and terrific, offering up a great degree of information on this old film. Michael Blake's passionately researched material and video tour give the supplements a tremendous sense of authenticity and are much appreciated. —*DG*
Movie: 🎬🎬🎬 **DVD:** 🎬🎬🎬
Kino on Video (cat #K216DVD, UPC 738-329021627). Full frame. Mono. $29.95. Keepcase. *LANG:* English. *FEATURES:* 12 chapters ▪ Video tour of Chaney's make-up case ▪ Essay on Chaney by Michael F. Blake ▪ Footage from Chaney's *The Miracle Man* ▪ "By the Sun's Rays," Chaney short ▪ Trailers for other Chaney films ▪ Photo and artwork gallery ▪ Budget sheet ▪ Essay on *The Penalty* ▪ Scene comparisons between novel, screenplay, film.
1920 93m/B Lon Chaney Sr., Claire Adams, Kenneth Harlan, Charles Clary; **D:** Wallace Worsley II; **W:** Charles Kenyon, Philip Lonergan; **C:** Don Short.

Pendulum

Sports Illustrated swimsuit babe Rachel Hunter makes a credible impression as Dallas police detective Amanda Reeve. She's distinctly de-glamorized and not a bad actress, though this script is so lame that it's difficult to judge. Reeve is working on a serial killer case when she's ordered to take over the investigation of the death of a college professor. The two cases become intertwined, and there's also a politically ambitious D.A. (Russo) to be dealt with. Full-frame image is about equal to tape, but enough distortion crops up in panning shots to make it a bit worse than VHS.
Movie: 🎬🎬 **DVD:** 🎬 ½
Artisan Ent. (cat #12486). Full frame. Dolby Digital Stereo. $24.98. Keepcase. *LANG:* English. *SUB:* Spanish. *FEATURES:* 27 chapters ▪ Trailer.
2001 (R) 94m/C Rachel Hunter, James Russo, Matt Battaglia; **D:** James D. Deck; **W:** Jason Kabolati; **C:** Bill Schwarz; **M:** William Richter.

The People That Time Forgot

Sequel to Edgar Rice Burroughs's *The Land That Time Forgot* finds a rescue team led by Wayne heading off to find lost explorer McClure. They discover a warm spot in the Arctic (actually the Canary

Islands) where dinosaurs and cave people live. The main attractions are star Gillespie's dramatic cleavage and some very funny model monsters. DVD displays a very sharp image. This one's far superior to the similar and contemporaneous *At the Earth's Core*. —*MM*
Movie: 🦴🦴 ½ **DVD:** 🦴🦴🦴
MGM Home Ent. (cat #1002646, UPC 027-616868466). Widescreen (1.85:1) anamorphic. Dolby Digital Mono. $14.95. Keepcase. *LANG:* English; French. *SUB:* French; Spanish. *CAP:* English. *FEATURES:* 16 chapters ▪ Trailer.
1977 (PG) 90m/C *GB* Doug McClure, Patrick Wayne, Sarah Douglas, Dana Gillespie, Thorley Walters, Shane Rimmer; *D:* Kevin Connor; *W:* Patrick Tilley; *C:* Alan Hume; *M:* John Scott.

Pep Squad
Director Steve Balderson does a John Waters riff with the story of evil Cherry (Brooke Balderson) who reacts inappropriately when she's not chosen for the high school pep squad. The Kansas production is driven by broad, nasty slapstick humor. Given a non-lavish budget, the DVD looks and sounds pretty good. One flashing green dress pattern is hard on the eyes. Otherwise, this is another nice package from York. —*MM*
Movie: 🦴🦴 ½ **DVD:** 🦴🦴 ½
York Ent. (cat #YPD-1139, UPC 75072311-3920). Widescreen letterboxed. $14.99. Keepcase. *LANG:* English. *FEATURES:* Trailer ▪ Filmmakers' commentary track.
1998 (R) 97m/C Brooke Balderson, Jennifer Dreiling, Adrian Pujoi, Summer Makovkin; *D:* Steve Balderson; *W:* Steve Balderson; *C:* Rhet W. Bear; *M:* Johnette Napolitano.

Percy
After an accident, young man-about-town Edwin (Bennett) receives the first penis transplant. Many British sexual jokes follow. (The film was made decades before the Lorena Bobbitt unpleasantness.) It's very light and silly and lots of fun in a nostalgic vein. DVD image is a bit on the (ahem) soft side, and that seems to come from well-preserved or restored original elements. Sound is thin. —*MM*
Movie: 🦴🦴 ½ **DVD:** 🦴🦴 ½
Anchor Bay (cat #DV11462, UPC 013131-146295). Widescreen (1.66:1) anamorphic. Dolby Digital Mono. $19.98. Keepcase. *LANG:* English. *FEATURES:* 25 chapters ▪ Trailer.
1971 (R) 101m/C *GB* Hywel Bennett, Denholm Elliott, Elke Sommer, Britt Ekland, Cyd Hayman, Julia Foster, Adrienne Posta; *D:* Ralph Thomas; *W:* Hugh Leonard; *C:* Ernest Steward; *M:* Ray Davies.

Perfect Love
Tumultuous relationship between 37-year-old twice-divorced Frederique (Renauld) and surly 28-year-old Christophe (Renaud). They meet at a wedding, think they're in love, and talk about it ad nauseum. The situation soon turns ugly, then graphically violent. The image and sound qualities as well as the production values are a major step up for the usually cheesy Breillat. The DVD looks and sounds pretty good. This unrated film contains explicit sex and some really disturbing violence. —*LA AKA: Parfait Amour.*
Movie: 🦴🦴 ½ **DVD:** 🦴🦴 ½
Winstar Home Ent. (cat #FLV5311, UPC 720917531120). Widescreen letterboxed. $24.98. Keepcase. *LANG:* French. *SUB:* English. *FEATURES:* Interactive menus ▪ Filmographies ▪ 16 chapters ▪ DVD-ROM features.
1996 110m/C *FR* Isabelle Renauld, Francis Renaud, Laura Saglio; *D:* Catherine Breillat; *W:* Catherine Breillat; *C:* Laurent Dailland.

The Perfect Wife
Liza (Sturges) is another of those vengeful blondes who, in the wake of *Hand That Rocks the Cradle*, thrive on video premieres. She goes after everyone she blames for her beloved brother's death, including the doctor (King) who did not save his life after an auto accident. How does she get close to the good doctor? She marries him, of course, and sets about to ruin everyone he cares for. The pace moves along briskly while production values are strictly of the made-for-TV level. Image is no real improvement over VHS tape. —*MM*
Movie: 🦴🦴 **DVD:** 🦴🦴 ½
York Ent. (cat #YPD-1122, UPC 75072311-2220). Full frame. Dolby Digital 5.1 Surround Stereo. $14.99. Keepcase. *LANG:* English. *SUB:* Spanish. *FEATURES:* 24 chapters ▪ Trailers.
2000 92m/C Shannon Sturges, Perry King, Lesley-Anne Down, William R. Moses; *D:* Don E. Fauntleroy; *W:* Frank Rehwaldt, George Saunders.

Perfume
Using improvised dialogue and an "all-star" cast, this confusing character drama revolves around Rita and Camille (Wilson, Mann), partners in an independent design firm. Three days before an important show, Camille receives, and accepts, an offer from the leading fashion conglomerate and the sparks fly. A number of loosely interweaving threads tell of the backstabbing that takes place in high-stakes fashion. The focus is placed on cameos rather than substance or story continuity. The image transfer looks good but the Surround sound is almost nonexistent. —*DRL*
Movie: 🦴 ½ **DVD:** 🦴🦴 ½
Studio Home Ent. (cat #7969, UPC 6581-49796928). Widescreen (1.85:1) anamorphic. Dolby 5.1 Surround. $24.99. Keepcase. *LANG:* English. *SUB:* Spanish. *CAP:* English. *FEATURES:* Trailer ▪ 24 chapters.
2001 (R) 106m/C Rita Wilson, Leslie Mann, Jared Harris, Michelle Forbes, Paul Sorvino, Peter Gallagher, Sonia Braga, Omar Epps, Jeff Goldblum, Harris Yulin, Michelle Williams, Joannne Baron, Mariel Hemingway, Carmen Electra, Coolio, Harry Hamlin, Mariska Hargitay, Gaby Hoffman, Robert Joy, Chris Sarandon, Angela Bettis, Kyle MacLachlan; *D:* Michael Rymer; *W:* Michael Rymer, L.M. Kit Carson; *C:* Rex Nicholson; *M:* Adam Plack.

Perpetrators of the Crime
Cute time passer about a kidnapping gone terribly wrong. Extra-lightweight *Fargo*, if you will. No guns, no wood chipper, just some college kids with a plan but very little else. They mean to kidnap the daughter of a wealthy industrialist (*The X-Files*'s Davis) but instead end up with her ditzy friend Lucy (Spelling) who needs the medication they left in her purse at the mall, or she becomes an annoying comedy routine ("Why won't you rape me; don't you find me attractive?"). Of course they don't know they have the wrong girl because they never meet up with their co-conspirator because they misread the directions to the hide out and are trapped in a cabin in the snow with no food instead of at the apartment the master planner set up for them. Strong and Burgess are very amusing as the argumentative kidnappers; they have a natural sense of comedic timing and sincerity in their delivery. With chapter titles like "Tampons" and "Smell," this could become a cult rental. Good-looking picture and good sound. —*CA*
Movie: 🦴 ½ **DVD:** 🦴🦴🦴
Avalanche Ent. (cat #VM1553D, UPC 806469155325). Full frame. Dolby Stereo. $19.99. Keepcase. *LANG:* English. *SUB:* English; French; Spanish. *CAP:* English. *FEATURES:* 24 chapters.
1998 (R) 85m/C *CA* Danny Strong, Tori Spelling, Mark Burgess, Sean Devine, William B. Davis; *D:* John Hamilton; *W:* Max Sartor.

A Personal Journey with Martin Scorsese through American Movies
A multi-part program originally produced for British TV, this overview of film history from the '20s through the '60s focuses particularly on films and filmmakers whose work had a strong influence on Scorsese or whose style of filmmaking was particularly important to the development of classic film genres. Westerns, films noir, and musicals are the primary focus, but melodramas and other genres are covered as well. The clips are very well-chosen, and illustrate most of Scorsese's points perfectly and he makes a genial, though nervous, host. Refreshingly, the program stays away from the usual tired examples and some much-needed exposure is given to several obscure films. In fact, some of the rare films sampled are so fascinating, most viewers will add them to their "must-see" list. A very likable compilation, but this is one that leaves you wishing for several

additional episodes. The disc overall is sharp, colorful, and pleasing, but some of the clips suffer from aliasing and pixelation. The sound is mono for the most part, due to the original audio of the clips, but it's clear and acceptable. The chapters are scant for a program of this size, making hunting down particular clips a bit of a chore. —DG

Movie: 🎬🎬🎬 **DVD:** 💿💿💿
Miramax Pictures (cat #20672, UPC 7179-5101047). Full frame. Dolby Digital Stereo. $32.99. Keepcase. *LANG:* English. *SUB:* English. *CAP:* English. *FEATURES:* 13 chapters ▪ Insert card with chapter index.
1997 226m/C D: Martin Scorsese, Michael Henry Wilson; **W:** Martin Scorsese, Michael Henry Wilson; **C:** Frances Reid, Jean-Yves Escoffier, Nancy Schreiber; **M:** Elmer Bernstein; **Nar:** Martin Scorsese.

The Personals

Fed up with her boring love life, Dr. Du Jia-zhen (Rene Liu) takes out a personal ad and gets 100 responses. The body of the film is made up of the interviews she conducts with these men—well, most of them are men. Other filmmakers have made more of the same premise, but director Kuo-fu Chen keeps his camera squarely on his characters. The Taiwan setting is a bit exotic. Rene Liu's performance is a model of restraint. Overall, DVD image is very good, though this import does not aspire to standards of Hollywood polish. English subtitles are easy to read and burned in. —MM

Movie: 💿💿 ½ **DVD:** 💿💿 ½
First Run Features (UPC 720229909778). Widescreen (1.66:1) letterboxed. $29.98. Keepcase. *LANG:* Chinese. *SUB:* English. *FEATURES:* 12 chapters ▪ Director bio.
1998 104m/C *TW* Rene Liu, Wu Bai; **D:** Kuo-fu Chen; **W:** Kuo-fu Chen, Shih-chich Chen; **C:** Nan-hong Ho.

Pet Sematary 2

Execrable sequel takes glee in its own sadism. King wasn't involved with this film, and the story isn't very coherent. Shock value and gross special effects are all it has to offer. Once again, DVD creates an excellent re-creation of a truly rotten movie. Image and sound are first-rate. —MM

Movie: woof **DVD:** 💿💿 ½
Paramount (cat #32747, UPC 097363274-742). Widescreen anamorphic. Dolby Digital 5.1 Surround; Dolby Digital Surround; Stereo. $24.98. Keepcase. *LANG:* English; French. *SUB:* English. *CAP:* English. *FEATURES:* Trailer ▪ 13 chapters.
1992 (R) 102m/C Anthony Edwards, Edward Furlong, Clancy Brown, Jared Rushton, Darlanne Fluegel, Lisa Waltz, Jason McGuire, Sarah Trigger; **D:** Mary Lambert; **W:** Richard Outten; **C:** Russell Carpenter.

Peter Gunn: Set One

The consummate cooler-than-cool detective was on television from 1958–61, first on NBC, and then on ABC. These two DVD sets represent the show's inaugural season. Los Angeles private investigator Peter Gunn (Stevens) is the epitome of hip; always calm under pressure, no matter how hairy the situation. And Gunn definitely gets in over his head at times, as he investigates murders and the mob. But with the help of his girlfriend Edie (Lola Albright) and his police contact Lieutenant Jacoby (Herschel Bernardi), Gunn always manages to come through. While the series was clearly influenced by the works of authors such as Mickey Spillane and Raymond Chandler, it was a first for television with a combination of action, producer Blake Edwards's trademark wit, and the famous cool-jazz score by Henry Mancini. The constant smoking and the treatment of the female characters are dated but the show is still entertaining. On disc, the shows look pretty good, but there are some problems. There are nearly constant flaws from the source print—scratches, lines, and white & black spots. Also, there is some flickering and darkening of the image. Otherwise, the image is sharp and clear, showing only occasional softening. The Dolby Digital Mono audio track provides clear dialogue, with only a minor amount of distortion. Most importantly, the music sounds fine here. A second two-disc set (UPC 733961703962) is also available. —GH/MM

Movie: 💿💿💿 **DVD:** 💿💿 ½
A&E (cat #AAE70393, UPC 7339617039-31). Full frame. Dolby Digital Mono. $35.98. 2-disc keepcase. *LANG:* English. *FEATURES:* Trivia game.
1958 400m/B Craig Stevens, Herschel Bernardi, Lola Albright.

Peter Pan [2 SE]

Disney classic about a boy who never wants to grow up, based on J.M. Barrie's book and play. Still stands head and shoulders above any recent competition in providing fun family entertainment. Terrific animation and lovely hummable music. This "Special Edition" (the first release is reviewed in *Book 1*) really does justice to the classic film. Lighter colors are sharp and bright, while blacks are extremely well defined and show no loss of clarity. The remixed soundtrack is similarly impressive. The musical score really stands out and dialogue is crisp and exhibits no distortion. The abundance and quality of the extras on the disc are too numerous to review in depth. Of particular note are the two "making of" featurettes. —MJT

Movie: 💿💿💿 **DVD:** 💿💿💿 ½
Buena Vista Home Ent. (cat #21620, UPC 786936144444). Full frame. Dolby Digital 5.1 Surround; Dolby Digital Stereo. $29.99. Keepcase. *LANG:* English; French; Spanish. *FEATURES:* 31 chapters ▪ "You Can Fly! The Making of *Peter Pan*" featurette ▪ "The *Peter Pan* Story" featurette ▪ Commentary: Roy Disney, Walt Disney, animators, Leonard Maltin ▪ Peter Pan still frame gallery ▪ "Following the Leader" sing-along song ▪ "Peter's Playful Prank" DVD storybook ▪ Pirate Treasure Hunt game ▪ *Return to Never Land* theatrical trailer ▪ DVD-ROM Weblinks.
1953 (G) 76m/C D: Hamilton Luske; **W:** Milt Banta, William Cottrell, Winston Hibler, Bill Peet, Erdman Penner, Joe Rinaldi, Ted Sears, Ralph Wright; **M:** Edward Plumb, Oliver Wallace; **V:** Bobby Driscoll, Kathryn Beaumont, Hans Conried, Heather Angel, Candy Candido, Bill Thompson; **Nar:** Tom Conway.

Petits Freres

This understated and poignant drama takes a close look at the lives of inner-city youth in France, following the story of young Talia and her dog, Kim. Talia flees from an abusive stepfather and falls in with a group of four boys. When Kim goes missing, Talia suspects her newfound friends, but must rely on them for help all the same. This slice of life film offers real characters and humanity, never feeling forced or exploitative. The picture quality is suitably grainy for the film's documentary feel, and the urban soundtrack comes through nicely. Chapters are accessible from the main menu only. —BG

Movie: 💿💿💿 ½ **DVD:** 💿💿💿
First Run Features (cat #FRF 909877D, UPC 720229909877). Widescreen (1.85:1) letterboxed. $29.95. Keepcase. *LANG:* French. *SUB:* English. *FEATURES:* 12 chapters ▪ Trailers ▪ Director bio ▪ Critic Kent Jones's views on *Petits Freres* ▪ Director's intro.
2000 92m/C *FR* Stephanie Touly, Ilies Sefraoui, Mustapha Goumane, Nassim Izem, Rachid Mansouri, Gerald Dantsoff, Dembo Goumane, Sabrina Mansar; **D:** Jacques Doillon; **W:** Jacques Doillon; **C:** Manuel Teran; **M:** Oxmo Puccino.

Petticoat Planet

Erotic sci-fi from prolific video auteur Dave DeCoteau has astronaut Steve Rogers (Vincent) land on an Old West planet (actually a few cheap sets) where he's the only male. The allegedly erotic action is tame. There's nothing that DVD can do with the underlit interiors, too-bright exteriors, and general soft-focus image. —MM

Movie: 💿 ½ **DVD:** 💿💿
Full Moon Pictures (cat #8020). Full frame. Dolby Digital Stereo. $24.95. Keepcase. *LANG:* English. *FEATURES:* Trailer ▪ 24 chapters ▪ Talent files ▪ Promotional material.
1995 (R) 78m/C Elizabeth Kaitan, Betsey Lynn George, Troy Vincent, Lesli Kay Sterling; **D:** David DeCoteau; **W:** Matthew Jason Walsh; **C:** Viorel Sergovici Jr.; **M:** Reg Powell.

Petula Clark: A Sign of the Times

Concert film of Petula Clark's performance at the Virginia Arts Festival was taped for PBS. Clark's actual performance is fine, as are her duets with Lou Rawls and Richard Carpenter (he plays the piano). However, the "video" footage that has been intercut with the concert scenes to make the performance look more MTVish is often just plain silly and makes the whole thing seem less than worthwhile. In terms of the video transfer, the concert footage looks great. Colors are bright and vibrant, and blacks are solid and well defined. Additional footage, however, looks blurry and quite awful in comparison to the concert portions. The soundtrack is excellent though it could have sounded fuller had it been spread out over a few more channels. Also included on the disc is a decent documentary that looks at Clark's career using interviews and archival footage. —*MJT*

Movie: 🎵🎵 **DVD:** 🎵🎵🎵
MPI (cat #DVD7499, UPC 0303067499-21). Widescreen (1.85:1) letterboxed; full frame. Dolby Digital Stereo. $14.98. Keepcase. *LANG:* English. *SUB:* English. *FEATURES:* 20 chapters • TV promos • Photograph gallery • Discography • Radio jingle • Duet with Dean Martin • "This Is My Song," documentary featurette.
2001 125m/C Petula Clark; *D:* Dennis Glore.

The Phantom from 10,000 Leagues

Dr. Taylor arrives at a beach to investigate death by sea monster. This monster is guarding an underwater deposit of uranium ore and is a mutation—a cross between a number of different ocean creatures—created by Dr. Whalen, who eventually regrets his experiment. Almost amusing. The "Phantom" monster is among the cheapest-looking of its kind, but at least has the dignity to show up immediately. Another transfer that looks exactly like VHS, with an annoying rippling in the last two chapters, as if shot through a heat wave. Hard to tell where the bad print ends and the bad DVD begins. Sound is better than average, including a very clean rendition of the hilariously melodramatic theme over the well-executed menu. "Vintage Intermission Spots and Trailers" alone are almost worth the price of the DVD. In "Drive-In Antics" and kindred bloopers, our host Fred presents himself as an aging biker alcoholic with Miss Kim as his buxom Goth girlfriend. Comedy is not their strength. —*MO*

Movie: 🎵 **DVD:** 🎵
Retromedia Entertainment Inc. (cat #RMED 007, UPC 802993011199). Full frame. $14.95. Snapper. *LANG:* English. *FEATURES:* 8 chapters • "Drive-In Antics" (and bloopers) with Fred & Miss Kim • Vintage drive-in intermission spots • Exclusive still gallery • Theatrical trailer (with 8 other Z-movie trailers). Trailers include *Beast of the Yellow Night, Hollywood Chainsaw Hookers, Evil Spawn*, to name a few.
1956 80m/B Kent Taylor, Cathy Downs, Michael Whalen, Helene Stanton, Phillip Pine; *D:* Dan Milner; *W:* Lou Rusoff; *C:* Brydon Baker; *M:* Ronald Stein.

The Phantom Lover

Director Ronny Yu handles his version of *Phantom of the Opera* (with a bit of *Romeo and Juliet*) as an adult fairy tale, not a horror story. In 1936, a theatrical troupe hopes to restore the burned-out opera house for their performances. Legendary singer Dan-Ping (Cheung) is thought to have died in the fire. Instead, horribly disfigured, he hides out in the ruins and dreams of his lost love (Chein-Lien). Letterboxed image transfer has a very good level of detail and the print is mostly clean and free of distracting blemishes, although the occasional dust mark is evident. The film's monochrome scenes look a bit flat, as the contrast of the footage does not allow for deep blacks, and the compression in these scenes creates a slightly noisy image. However, as soon as the film switches to its glorious color, the transfer becomes a bold representation of the original movie. The 5.1 tracks are very well done and feature a wide sound stage with good integration of the Surround channels, enhancing the haunting mood of the theatre, as well as the musical presentations performed. The English dub is expectedly disappointing with poor synchronization and poor voice acting. The DVD also contains two commentary tracks. The first one features director Ronny Yu, who delivers an engaging and interesting look at the film's origins, characters, and many other aspects of the production. Cinematographer Peter Pau—who received a well-deserved Academy Award for his work on *Crouching Tiger, Hidden Dragon*—discusses technical issues in a way that is easy to follow and always interesting. The second disc contains a lengthy behind-the-scenes documentary, two featurettes, and a selection of trailers. —*MM/GH* **AKA:** Ye Bang Ge Sheng.

Movie: 🎵🎵🎵 **DVD:** 🎵🎵🎵
Tai Seng (UPC 601643783246). Widescreen. Dolby Digital 5.1 Surround; Dolby Mono. $34.98. 2-disc keepcase. *LANG:* Cantonese; Mandarin; English. *FEATURES:* 2 commentary tracks • Documentary • Featurettes • Trailers.
1995 102m/C HK Leslie Cheung, Chien-Lien Wu, Philip Kwok, Roy Szeto; *D:* Ronny Yu; *W:* Roy Szeto, Raymond Wong; *C:* Peter Pau; *M:* Chris Babida.

Phantom of the Paradise

Rock producer and guru Swan (Williams) steals Winslow Leach's (Finley) Faust cantata and frames him, sending him to jail. After escaping, Winslow is disfigured in one of Swan's record pressing machines and presumably dies. As Swan prepares to open a new rock club named "The Paradise," Winslow makes his presence known and causes a behind-the-scenes accident. Swan strikes a deal with Winslow, promising to let Phoenix (Harper) sing the lead in his Faust cantata as long as Winslow signs a bargain and agrees to finish the composition. But Swan is more than just a slimy record producer, and Winslow discovers that his and Phoenix's immortal souls are at stake. This instant cult film has a kind of *Rocky Horror* sensibility to it, a little bit of truth and captures this strange era in rock fairly well. Unfortunately the film doesn't quite gel. The movie switches gears constantly, jumping from comedy to slapstick to camp to musical to backstage success drama to *Phantom of the Opera* knockoff to *Psycho* knockoff to *Faust* knockoff to *Picture of Dorian Gray* knockoff to Kiss concert to Grand Guignol to *Rocky Horror* take-off. Flashy and entertaining but the movie's tendency to abandon its story threads and its ever-shifting tones makes it ultimately unsatisfying. Graham (as an over-the-top rocker named "Beef") is an absolute hoot and steals the movie. It feels like the kind of film a hyperactive kid or impatient coke-addict might make. The framing of the opening logo is too tight but the rest of the film rarely shows signs of cropping. The stylized image is softer in scenes with fog, smoke, and surreal lighting, while close-ups reveal a razor-sharp image. The sound is fine but feels more like well-recorded mono than true stereo. —*DG*

Movie: 🎵🎵 ½ **DVD:** 🎵🎵🎵
20th Century Fox (cat #2002377, UPC 02454323777). Widescreen (1.85:1) anamorphic. Stereo. $19.98. Keepcase. *LANG:* English; French. *SUB:* English; Spanish. *CAP:* English. *FEATURES:* 32 chapters • Trailer • Additional Fox trailers.
1974 (PG) 92m/C Paul Williams, William Finley, Jessica Harper, Gerrit Graham, George Memmoli, Archie Hahn; *D:* Brian DePalma; *W:* Brian DePalma; *C:* Larry Pizer; *M:* George Aliceson Tipton, Paul Williams. *AWARDS: NOM:* Oscars '74: Orig. Song Score and/or Adapt.

Phat Beach

Harmless buddies-at-the-beach comedy has a hip-hop beat. Fast-talking Durrell (Hooks) manipulates sensitive, overweight pal Benny (Hopkins) into emptying his savings, borrowing his dad's Mercedes convertible, and heading off for some Southern California fun. Scores of scantily clad beach bunnies and just about every other cliché of the genre show up before it's over, but the likable Hopkins/Hooks comedy team is a hit with precise, low-brow humor. Given the strict limitations of the original budget, disc is no more than a minor improvement over VHS tape. —*MM*

Movie: 🎵🎵 **DVD:** 🎵🎵
Artisan Ent. (cat #12041, UPC 0122361-20414). Full frame. Dolby Digital Stereo. $14.98. Keepcase. *LANG:* English. *CAP:* English. *FEATURES:* 18 chapters • Production notes • Talent files.
1996 (R) 99m/C Jermaine "Huggy" Hopkins, Brian Hooks, Jennifer Lucienne, Claudia Kaleem, Gregg D. Vance, Tommy (Tiny) Lister, Erick Fleeks, Alma Collins, Candice Merideth, Sabrina De Pina, Coolio; *D:* Doug Ellin; *W:* Doug Ellin, Brian E. O'Neal, Ben Morris; *C:* Jurgen Baum; *M:* Paul Stewart.

Phenomenon— The Lost Archives: American Midnight / H.A.A.R.P.

The syndicated TV series that panders to the conspiratorial-minded continues with hyperbolic "examinations" of a drug deal that might have been part of the Iran/Contra mess and the High-Frequency Active Aural Research Project. As is the case with the other discs (reviewed in *Book 2*), overall image quality is no better than broadcast, particularly in the archival footage. Some of the original studio footage is exceptionally crisp. —*MM*
Movie: 🎬 **DVD:** 🎬🎬
Image Ent. (cat #ID0575LB DVD, UPC 014-381057522). Full frame. Dolby Digital Stereo. $24.98. Keepcase. *LANG:* English. *FEATURES:* 12 chapters.
1999 93m/C Nar: Dean Stockwell, Martin Sheen.

Phenomenon— The Lost Archives: Monopoly Men / An Unknown Encounter

The Federal Reserve Bank, long a favorite bugaboo of right-wing wackos, finds itself in the cross-hairs of the excitable syndicated TV series. The second program concerns a haunting and contains "interviews with one of the nation's leading parapsychologists." Sound and image are equal to others in the series. —*MM*
Movie: 🎬 **DVD:** 🎬🎬
Image Ent. (cat #ID0574LB DVD, UPC 014-381057423). Full frame. Dolby Digital Stereo. $29.98. Keepcase. *LANG:* English. *FEATURES:* 12 chapters.
1999 93m/C Nar: Dean Stockwell.

Picasso Trigger

Sequel to *Hard Ticket to Hawaii* finds our heroines Donna (Speir) and Taryn (Carlton) joined by no less than five more former *Playboy* Playmates in their efforts to defeat a group of villainous drug-dealing international assassins. Cool toys, gadgets, hot tubs, and bad guys who report to their superiors in rhymed couplets make this one of Andy Sidaris's more ambitious efforts. DVD contains the usual assortment of extras. Image and sound range between good and very good. The extras are virtually identical to the other entries in this series. —*MM*
Movie: 🎬🎬🎬 **DVD:** 🎬🎬🎬
Ventura Distribution (cat #1132-7, UPC 634991113229). Full frame. $19.98. Keepcase. *LANG:* English. *FEATURES:* 12 chapters • Behind-the-scenes featurette • Trailers • Andy Sidaris thumbnail bio • Liner notes • Commentary: Andy and Arlene Sidaris • Still gallery.
1989 (R) 99m/C Steve Bond, Dona Speir, John Aprea, Hope Marie Carlton, Guich Koock, Roberta Vasquez, Bruce Penhall, Harold Diamond, Rodrigo Obregon; **D:**

Andy Sidaris; **W:** Andy Sidaris; **C:** Howard Wexler; **M:** Gary Stockdale.

Picture of a Nymph

One of the best romantic fantasies produced in response to the hit *A Chinese Ghost Story*. Yuen Biao stars as the ghost-busting son of Taoist priest Wu Ma. Together, they face off against the demon King Ghost (Elizabeth Lee), who preys on brides in the area. A scholar spies on one of the ghost brides and paints her portrait. She hides from the King Ghost inside the picture. The third act comes through with dazzling supernatural spectacle, including flying palanquins, lightning bolts, explosions, and more. Director Wu Ma had done nothing before that matches the visual splendor on display here—every frame is breathtaking. —*BT* **AKA:** Ung Chung Sin; Hua Zhong Xian; Painting of a Nymph; Portrait of a Nymph.
Movie: 🎬🎬🎬 **DVD:** 🎬🎬🎬
Tai Seng (cat #5131, UPC 48950249038-73). Widescreen letterboxed. $19.95. Keepcase. *LANG:* Cantonese; Mandarin. *SUB:* Chinese; English; Bahasa. *CAP:* English. *FEATURES:* 8 chapters • Star profiles • Trailers.
1988 94m/C *HK* Yuen Biao, Joey Wong, Wu Ma, Elizabeth Lee, Lawrence Ng; **D:** Wu Ma; **W:** Wu Ma; **M:** James Wong.

Pie in the Sky: The Brigid Berlin Story

Born into wealth, Brigid Berlin rebelled against her tony upbringing when she met Andy Warhol and his artist friends. Though she's notorious as the oft-nude and least glamorous of the "Chelsea Girls," Berlin's obsessive nature, and her endless battles with an ever-shockable patrician mother, actually pushed her to become a groundbreaking artist herself. Still motor-mouthed and weight-obsessed at 60, Berlin may not be the easiest person to spend time with, but directors Vincent Freemont and Shelly Dunn Freemont have used her keen eye to paint a vivid picture of a raucous time. Image quality is about what you'd expect of a modestly budgeted documentary. —*JE*
Movie: 🎬🎬 **DVD:** 🎬🎬½
New Video Group (cat #NVG-9492, UPC 0767042514). Full frame. Dolby Digital Stereo. $24.95. Keepcase. *LANG:* English. *FEATURES:* Outtakes • Director bios.
2001 75m/C D: Vincent Freemont, Shelly Dunn Freemont.

Pigkeeper's Daughter / Sassy Sue

Like so many of the Something Weird Video soft-core releases, these look better on DVD than they probably did when they first played at the drive-in. Colors are bright; surface damage is at a minimum; mono sound is fine if unexceptional. As for the films, they're silly comedies of the *Beverly Hillbillies/Hee Haw* vein with lots of sex scenes. In *Sassy Sue*, family patriarch

Patrick Wright dreams of making a fortune in wooden outhouse seats. *The Pigkeeper's Daughter* is a sensitive coming-of-age about a teenaged girl. In that one, pigs, both large and small, figure prominently in many scenes. Don't miss Vince Bonavoglia's liner notes and interview with producer Harry Novak. He hits precisely the right tone. —*MM*
Movie: 🎬🎬½ **DVD:** 🎬🎬🎬
Something Weird Video (cat #ID0807SW-DVD, UPC 014381080728). Full frame. Dolby Digital Mono. $24.98. Keepcase. *LANG:* English. *FEATURES:* 16 chapters • "The Old Man's Bride" featurette • Trailers • Gallery of exploitation art and photos.
1975 92m/C Terry Gibson, Patty Smith, Gina Paluzzi, John Keith; **D:** Bethel Buckalew; **W:** Bethel Buckalew; **C:** Robert Wilson.

Pin...

Disturbed young Leon (played successively by Jacob Tierney, Steven Bednarski, and David Hewlett) is an apple who hasn't fallen far from the tree. His father, Dr. Linden (Terry O'Quinn), is a strange disciplinarian while his mother (Bronwen Mantel) keeps clear plastic slipcovers on all the furniture and thinks that Leon's friends are germ-ridden disease carriers. His younger sister Ursula (Michelle Anderson, Katie Shingler, and Cyndy Preston) has survived relatively unscathed. Pin is the transparent dummy in dad's office with which Leon develops an obsessive attachment. Few mainstream films deal with the changes in childhood and adolescence as well as this one. Writer/director Sandor Stern also delivers the goods with surprising scares that are developed through the characters. The picture is very sharp and stable, showing only the slightest hint of grain. There are no overt defects evident from the source print. The colors are bright and true, and the transfer displays even flesh-tones. The only discernable problem occurs during chapter 26, when Ursula is wearing a sweater with horizontal lines, causing aliasing artifacts, but that's simply a result of the NTSC television format and its inherent low resolution. The letterbox framing appears to be accurate and there are no noticeable problems resulting from compression issues. Surround mix delivers clear dialogue with no background hiss. Interview commentary track with director Stern and journalist Ted Newsom works well. Newsom is very familiar with the film and asks insightful questions. Stern has detailed memories of the production. —*MM/GH*
Movie: 🎬🎬🎬½ **DVD:** 🎬🎬🎬½
Anchor Bay (UPC 013131132298). Widescreen (1.85:1) anamorphic. Dolby Digital Surround. $24.98. Keepcase. *LANG:* English. *FEATURES:* Commentary • Trailer.
1988 (R) 103m/C Cyndy Preston, David Hewlett, Terry O'Quinn, Bronwen Mantel, Helene Udy, Patricia Collins, Steven Bednarski, Katie Shingler, Jacob Tierney, Michelle Anderson; **D:** Sandor Stern; **W:** Sandor Stern; **C:** Guy Defaux.

Pin Down Girls

Please see review of *Wrestling Women USA!* **AKA:** Racket Girls; Pin Down Girl.
Movie: 🎬
1951 81m/B Clara Mortensen, Rita Martinez.

Ping!

Have you ever wondered what *Home Alone* would have been like had the film starred a Chihuahua instead of Macauly Culkin? Well, it's your lucky day, because *Ping!* is here. Ethel (Shirley Jones) visits the local animal shelter to adopt a cat, but due to her thick glasses, gets the little Chihuahua Ping! instead and takes it home. When Ethel leaves Ping! "home alone," two bumbling crooks, Louie (Judge Reinhold) and Stu (Clint Howard), arrive to rob the house and it's up to Ping! to save the day. As most dogs would do in this situation, Ping! sets booby-traps and equips himself with a miniature hang-glider to fight off the bad guys. Sure, the dog is very cute, but otherwise this movie is pretty ridiculous. Jones, Reinhold, and Howard must have needed the money pretty badly. This should appeal only to Chihuahua lovers and those who wonder why they don't make more *Home Alone* movies. The full-frame image is sharp and clear, with very little grain. The colors are good and there is no distortion to the image. The Dolby Surround audio track provides clear dialogue and some nice Surround sound effects. It's as if Ping! is all around you! —*ML*
Movie: 🎬 ½ **DVD:** 🎬🎬 ½
20th Century Fox (cat #2002156, UPC 024543021568). Full frame. Dolby Surround. $19.98. Keepcase. *LANG:* English. *SUB:* English. *CAP:* English. *FEATURES:* Trailer • Cast & crew bios • Still gallery • 16 chapters.
1999 (PG) 93m/C Judge Reinhold, Clint Howard, Shirley Jones, Lou Ferrigno; **D:** Chris Baugh; **W:** Albert Ruis.

Pink Flamingos

In John Waters's original celebration of all things tasteless, Divine, the dainty 300-pound transvestite, has gone undercover as Babs Johnson, after a newspaper article proclaiming him/her to be the "filthiest person alive" has brought too much publicity. But an upscale couple believe themselves to be filthier, and set out to prove it. By the end of the film, there should be no doubt as to the contest's winner. Tasteless, crude, and hysterical film; this one earned Waters his title as "Prince of Puke." If there are any doubts about this honor—or Divine's rep—watch through to the end to catch Divine chewing real dog excrement, all the time wearing a you-know-what-eating grin. Wow! *Pink Flamingos* with a Dolby Surround soundtrack! Actually, there's not much difference between the mono and Dolby Surround mixes, but who cares. The DVD transfer of the restored version (BJ included) was obviously done from a fairly pristine, cleaned-up film print, and Waters's master-

piece can be seen in all its gritty near-home-movie glory. The Waters commentary is even more of a pleasure than the others in New Line's John Waters Collection discs, as Waters's nostalgic excitement is obvious throughout. The deleted scenes are presented as more of a featurette introduced by Waters and are the same as included in the 25th Anniversary Edition tape released several years ago. Available only as part of a double feature with *Female Trouble* (see separate entry). —*JO/BG*
Movie: 🎬🎬 **DVD:** 🎬🎬🎬
New Line (cat #N5232, UPC 7940435-23229). Widescreen (1.85:1) letterboxed. Dolby Surround; Dolby Digital Mono. $29.95. Custom. *LANG:* English. *SUB:* English. *CAP:* English. *FEATURES:* 26 chapters • Theatrical trailer • Commentary: John Waters • Deleted scenes with intro by John Waters.
1972 (NC-17) 95m/C Divine, David Lochary, Mary Vivian Pearce, Danny Mills, Mink Stole, Edith Massey, Cookie Mueller, Channing Wilroy, Paul Swift, Susan Walsh, Linda Olgierson, Elizabeth Coffey, Steve Yeager, Pat Moran, George Figgs; **D:** John Waters; **W:** John Waters; **C:** John Waters; **Nar:** John Waters.

Pink Lady and Jeff

This bizarre three-disc collection brings together all six episodes of the show that is considered by many to be the worst ever produced by network television executives. That's an impressive claim, but the idea of bringing together a Japanese pop duo—two girls who speak no English and have no fans beyond their home country—with an unfunny American comedian certainly covers a lot of potential badness and the show made full use of it. If nothing else, this was one of the final nails in the coffin in the variety show. These shows bring together such disparate guests as Blondie, Bert Parks, Hugh Hefner, Jim Varney, and Alice Cooper. DVD can do nothing to improve the mediocre image quality, and why should it? —*MM*
Movie: 🎬 **DVD:** 🎬🎬
Rhino (cat #R2 976019, UPC 603497601-929). Full frame. $39.98. Keepcase. *LANG:* English. *FEATURES:* 72 chapters.
1980 300m/C Jeff Altman, Keiko Masuda, Mitsuyo Nemoto.

Pirates! Long John Silver / Captain Kidd

The disc is transferred from a fairly clean print with good contrasts. It's a tad on the soft side and speckles appear at reel change points. The sound is a bit sharp, but the dialogue is intelligible. Digital noise is minimal. *Captain Kidd* is reviewed in *Book 2. Long John Silver* is a sequel to *Treasure Island*. After rescuing a kidnapped Governor's daughter, Silver (Newton) teams up with pal Jim Hawkins to find more gold. *Treasure* director Byron Haskin returns with this better than average follow-up. Newton is in fine, amusing form as

he reprises his legendary role. Not much in the way of originality, but it's consistently entertaining. The blind, white-eyed pirate must have been the source of many childhood nightmares. Aaarh! The disc features a transfer from a cropped 16mm TV print and suffers from few digital artifacts. It's overly splicy and scratched, but features subdued color. This CinemaScope release suffers much without its intended widescreen framing. The sound is adequate. —*DG*
Movie: 🎬🎬 ½ **DVD:** 🎬🎬
Marengo Films (cat #MRG-0010, UPC 807-013001020). Full frame. Mono. $14.98. Keepcase. *LANG:* English. *FEATURES:* 12 chapters.
2001 193m/C

Pitch

This documentary follows two filmmakers as they try to sell their comedy script, first at film festivals and then in Hollywood. It's a frustrating look at the industry until it becomes obvious how simple their problem is—they want to work within the Hollywood studio system, but don't want to deal with agents. The film demonstrates that you can't have it both ways. Both picture and sound reveal the film's low budget, and the transfer to DVD didn't help much. The "Director's Introduction" and "Cast Bios," advertised as special features, are just printed on the sleeve. —*BG*
Movie: 🎬🎬 **DVD:** 🎬🎬
Vanguard Intl. Cinema (cat #VFO265, UPC 658769026535). Full frame. $29.95. Keepcase. *LANG:* English. *FEATURES:* 10 chapters • Trailer.
2001 81m/C Spencer Rice, Kenny Hotz; **D:** Spencer Rice, Kenny Hotz; **W:** Spencer Rice, Kenny Hotz; **C:** Christopher J. Romeike.

A Place in the Sun

Melodramatic adaptation of Theodore Dreiser's fact-based novel *An American Tragedy* revolves around George Eastman (Clift), an ambitious young man whose aspirations to the high life with a gorgeous debutante (Taylor) are threatened by his lower-class lover's (Winters) pregnancy. All three stars are fine and the story holds up well. DVD does a fine job with well-detailed, Oscar-winning black-and-white photography. On their commentary track, the director's son, Stevens Jr., and Ivan Moffat, co-producer and friend, take an understandably reverential approach. Recommended. —*MM*
Movie: 🎬🎬🎬 **DVD:** 🎬🎬🎬
Paramount (cat #05815, UPC 097360581-546). Full frame. Dolby Digital 5.1 Surround Stereo. $29.99. Keepcase. *LANG:* English. *SUB:* English. *FEATURES:* 13 chapters • Commentary: George Stevens Jr., Ivan Moffat • Interviews with Elizabeth Taylor, Shelley Winters, Stevens Jr., Moffat • 2 George Stevens featurettes.
1951 120m/B Montgomery Clift, Elizabeth Taylor, Shelley Winters, Raymond Burr, Anne Revere; **D:** George Stevens; **W:** Harry

Brown, Michael Wilson; **C:** William Mellor; **M:** Franz Waxman. *AWARDS:* Oscars '51: B&W Cinematog., Costume Des. (B&W), Director (Stevens), Film Editing, Screenplay, Orig. Dramatic Score; AFI '98: Top 100; Directors Guild '51: Director (Stevens); Golden Globes '52: Film—Drama, Natl. Film Reg. '91; *NOM:* Oscars '51: Actor (Clift), Actress (Winters), Picture.

Places in the Heart

This is a great picture that didn't get anywhere near the attention it deserved back in 1984. Sally Field had already reached kitsch heaven with her Oscar acceptance gush for *Norma Rae,* a spectacle that didn't add to her star-power. She's even better in this film, which impresses because it's a real writer/director's picture in a decade when Hollywood forgot how to tell stories or make us care about characters. When her Sheriff Husband Royce (Baker) is suddenly killed, widow Edna Spalding (Field) determines not to lose her farm, despite the Depression and hostility to her sex from her banker. She takes in a blind boarder with a negative attitude (Malkovich), and with help from her sister Margaret Lomax (Crouse), and homeless sharecropper Moze (Glover), Edna faces up to everything Southern society and nature can throw at her. The conclusion is powerful. Benton gives us not a lame feel-good ending, but an almost mystical one, that wraps the film up in the warmth of its character's faith and hopes. Emotions that are inexpressible find expression, the unfaithful can be forgiven, the homeless can find a home, and the exiled can return. Even the murderer and victim can sit side by side and share bread and wine, with sins and tragedies forgiven. This is yet another of Columbia TriStar's exemplary discs, which can almost be taken for granted. The muted colors of Nestor Almendros's radiant photography are well-represented. There are some production notes but the only real extra is a trailer, and all those international subtitle choices. A flat version is encoded on the flip side for those who need it, but the 16:9 widescreen version is preferable by far. —GE
Movie: 🎞🎞🎞🎞 **DVD:** 🎞🎞🎞 ½
Columbia Tristar (cat #06976, UPC 04339-6069763). Widescreen (1.85:1) anamorphic; full frame. Dolby Digital Mono. $24.95. Keepcase. *LANG:* English; French. *SUB:* English; French; Spanish; Portuguese; Chinese; Korean; Thai. *CAP:* English. *FEATURES:* Trailers ● Production notes.
1984 (PG) 113m/C Sally Field, John Malkovich, Danny Glover, Ed Harris, Lindsay Crouse, Amy Madigan, Terry O'Quinn, Ned Dowd, Ray Baker; **D:** Robert Benton; **W:** Robert Benton; **C:** Nestor Almendros; **M:** Howard Shore. *AWARDS:* Oscars '84: Actress (Field), Orig. Screenplay; Golden Globes '85: Actress—Drama (Field); Natl. Bd. of Review '84: Support. Actor (Malkovich); N.Y. Film Critics '84: Screenplay; Natl. Soc. Film Critics '84: Support. Actor (Malkovich); *NOM:* Oscars '84: Costume Des., Director (Benton), Picture, Sup-

port. Actor (Malkovich), Support. Actress (Crouse).

Planet of the Apes

This obscure, short-lived series will be a welcome discovery for many *Apes* fanatics, as Galen the kindly chimp and his astro-pals challenge social conventions while also entertaining through their misadventures as fugitives. Stitched together as "TV movies" for syndication, this set presents them in their original episode form. Astronauts Alan Virdon and Pete Burke hit an interstellar pothole that hurtles their ship from 1980 to a smoldering crash on an alien planet in the year 3085. They're pulled from the wreckage by Farrow (Royal Dano), a slow-witted human who warns them that the apes who rule this land will surely kill them—himself having just been treed by a young primate and his dog. While nursing them back to health, Farrow shows off his forbidden "picture book" that features a stunning revelation for our heroes—a futuristic photo of New York City in the year—ta-da-dum—2503! They can't go home. They're there already. It's not long before Dr. Zaius (Booth Colman) catches wind of their arrival. They're captured, of course, and escape, thanks to Zaius's assistant Galen (Roddy McDowall). The rest of the series delineates their adventures until the open-ended finale. Each episode is presented with minor white dust spots or scratches throughout. Otherwise the picture quality is surprisingly crisp and colorful for this nearly 30-year-old series. Utilitarian mono track maintains consistent levels throughout. Excellent printed booklet features thumbnail synopses for each show along with original air date and credits. Another missed opportunity is the lack of commentaries or other extras directly related to the TV series. Let's hope the cartoon series isn't far behind! Recommended. —GNG/DG
Movie: 🎞🎞 **DVD:** 🎞🎞🎞
Fox/Lorber Home Video (UPC 024543025-214). Full frame. Mono. $49.98. Keepcase boxed set. *LANG:* English; French. *SUB:* English; Spanish. *CAP:* English. *FEATURES:* Booklet with notes ● Chapter links ● 14 episodes.
1974 644m/C Roddy McDowall, Ron Harper, James Naughton, Royal Dano, Booth Colman.

Planet of the Apes

Tim Burton calls his version of Pierre Boule's novel a "re-imagining" of the famous 1968 film, and that's accurate enough. Many of the funniest lines are riffs on dialogue that's familiar to many viewers. Does the whole thing work? Yes, kind of, sort of, to a degree. (Do I appear to equivocate?) The plot, involving Mark Wahlberg as the American astronaut trapped on a planet ruled by various monkeys and apes, moves along at a nice clip. He's a solid hero but the film belongs to Tim Roth as a maniacal chimp general. His furious energy is believable and he man-

ages to project a strong performance through Rick Baker's spectacular makeup. Paul Giamatti is equally believable as an orangutan. Helena Bonham Carter and David Warner look more like throwbacks to the '60s film. The less said the better about the let's-make-a-sequel! ending. Two-disc package delivers everything that a viewer could want from a special edition. Image is excellent; DTS Surround is much more impressive than it was in the theatre. Elfman's score is superb. In the end, if the film is not first-caliber Burton, it is entertaining and highly polished, until it reaches that ridiculous non-conclusion. —MM
Movie: 🎞🎞 ½ **DVD:** 🎞🎞🎞 ½
20th Century Fox (cat #2002897, UPC 024543028970). Widescreen (2.35:1) anamorphic. DTS 5.1 Surround; Dolby Digital 5.1; Dolby Digital Surround. $24.98. Keepcase. *LANG:* English; Spanish. *SUB:* English. *CAP:* English. *FEATURES:* 36 chapters ● Commentary: Tim Burton ● Commentary: Danny Elfman ● 6 documentaries ● HBO special ● 5 extended scenes ● Art gallery ● DVD-ROM features ● Music video ● Trailers and TV spots.
2001 (PG-13) 125m/C Mark Wahlberg, Tim Roth, Helena Bonham Carter, Michael Clarke Duncan, Paul Giamatti, Estella Warren, Cary-Hiroyuki Tagawa, David Warner, Kris Kristofferson, Erik Avari, Luke Eberl, Charlton Heston; **D:** Tim Burton; **W:** William Broyles Jr., Larry Konner, Mark Rosenthal; **C:** Philippe Rousselot; **M:** Danny Elfman. *AWARDS:* Golden Raspberries '01: Worst Remake/Sequel, Worst Support. Actor (Heston), Worst Support. Actress (Warren); *NOM:* British Acad. '01: Costume Des.

Planet of the Dinosaurs

A space ship gets lost and is forced to make an emergency landing on an unknown planet of dinosaurs. The crew hopes to be found and rescued, but they have to struggle to survive until then. Likewise, I braved a particularly dangerous part of town to catch this as a second feature when it came out. Jim Danforth, special effects wiz for *When Dinosaurs Ruled the Earth* and *The Seven Faces of Dr. Lao,* is credited as matte artist. I suspect his assistants may have decided to make this film, which has great stop-motion animation. It looks to be shot in 16mm and the signs of a professional production are otherwise lacking. Shot on the ever-so-familiar planet of Vasquez Rocks outside of L.A., landscape of *Star Trek* and many a western. Average DVD transfer and sound from a cheap print. —MO
Movie: 🎞🎞 ½ **DVD:** 🎞🎞 ½
Goodtimes Ent. (cat #05-81223, UPC 018713812230). Full frame. $7.49. Keepcase. *LANG:* English. *FEATURES:* 12 chapters.
1980 (PG) 85m/C James Whitworth, Michael Thayer, Louie Lawless, Pamela Bottaro, Charlotte Speer; **D:** James K. Shea; **W:** Ralph Lucas.

Planet of the Vampires

Astronauts search for missing comrades on a planet dominated by mind-bending forces. It's acceptable atmospheric filmmaking from Bava, but it's certainly not his most compelling work. The funky leather spacesuits with their industrial strength chin supports are difficult to overlook. Some grain is evident in the many dark scenes but overall, the image is exceptionally sharp and clear. (See *Video Watchdog* magazine no. 76 for Glenn Erickson's article about the difficulties in restoring the film.) —*MM* **AKA:** The Demon Planet; The Haunted Planet; The Outlawed Planet; Planet of Blood; Planet of Terror; Planet of the Damned; Space Mutants; Terror in Space; Terrore nello Spazio; Terreur dans l'Espace. **Movie:** ♫♫ ½ **DVD:** ♫♫ ½
MGM Home Ent. (cat #1002353, UPC 027-616865649). Widescreen (1.85:1) letterboxed. Dolby Digital Mono. $14.95. Keepcase. *LANG:* English. *SUB:* French; Spanish. *CAP:* English. *FEATURES:* 16 chapters ● Trailer.
1965 86m/C *IT SP* Barry Sullivan, Norma Bengell, Angel Aranda, Evi Marandi, Stelio Candelli, Ivan Rassimov, Fernando Villena; **D:** Mario Bava; **W:** Mario Bava, Alberto Bevilacqua, Callisto Cosulich, Louis M. Heyward, Ib Melchior, Antonio Roman, Rafael J. Salvia; **C:** Antonio Rinaldi; **M:** Gino Marinuzzi Jr.

The Plastic Age

Please see review of *The Show Off*. **Movie:** ♫♫ ½
1925 73m/B Clara Bow, Donald Keith, Gilbert Roland, Henry B. Walthall, Mary Alden; **D:** Wesley Ruggles; **W:** Eve Unsell, Frederica Sagor; **C:** Gilbert Warrenton, Allen Siegler.

Play for Me

After the death of his father, Carlos (Gaido) sets out on a quest to find out his mother, who died giving birth to him and whose name he never knew. His search takes him to a rural ghost town, where he is taken in by a prostitute and a curmudgeonly mechanic. The film manages to maintain a somber tone through its interesting diversions into magic realism, until it falls into sentimentalism in the last half-hour. Picture quality is grainy and not terribly sharp, while the sound is serviceable for such a dialogue-driven film. —*BG* **AKA:** Toca Para Mi. **Movie:** ♫♫ ½ **DVD:** ♫♫
Vanguard Intl. Cinema (cat #VFO238, UPC 658769023831). Full frame. $29.95. Keepcase. *LANG:* Spanish. *SUB:* English. *FEATURES:* 12 chapters.
2001 101m/C *AR* Hermes Gaido, Maria Laura Frigerio, Alejandro Fiore, Emilio Urdapilleta; **D:** Rodrigo Furth; **W:** Rodrigo Furth, Eduardo Ruderman; **C:** Paula Grandio; **M:** Fernando Manuel Dieguez.

Play It Again, Sam

Bogart-buff Allen is dumped by his current wife. During his frequently uproarious encounters with the opposite sex, he turns to a fantasized Bogie (a perfect Jerry Lacy) who offers clichéd tough-guy relationship advice. After repeated attempts by his married friends, Dick and Linda (Roberts, Keaton), to find someone for him, Allen and Linda find themselves falling in love and must decide what to do about it. Frequently hilarious and ultimately sad, the film rarely betrays its stage origins and keeps the pace bouncy and fast. Oddly enough, it's not directed by Allen, but rarely shows it. Perched about midway between Allen's slapstick and dialogue-driven comedies, this features effective smatterings of both. Keaton and Allen's on-screen chemistry (in their first collaboration) is amazing. The disc features a gorgeous picture transfer with rich fleshtones (Allen has rarely looked so freckly on-camera) and revelatory colors. Gone are the hideous brownish-yellow hues of the older VHS transfers. The sound is surprisingly crisp and strong for a mono track. —*DG* **Movie:** ♫♫♫ **DVD:** ♫♫♫ ½
Paramount (cat #08112, UPC 097360811-247). Widescreen (1.85:1) anamorphic. Mono. $29.99. Keepcase. *LANG:* English; French. *SUB:* English. *FEATURES:* 13 chapters ● Insert card.
1972 (PG) 86m/C Woody Allen, Diane Keaton, Tony Roberts, Susan Anspach, Jerry Lacy, Jennifer Salt, Joy Bang, Viva, Herbert Ross; **D:** Herbert Ross; **W:** Woody Allen; **C:** Owen Roizman; **M:** Billy Goldenberg.

Play-Mate of the Apes

A planet where man is ruled by apes? Yep—sexy, sexy apes. Col. Gaylor and her team of lesbian astronettes crashland on such a world, and struggle to avoid the natives' domination by dancing to disco music. Some of the makeup and visual effects in this silly romp are surprisingly competent. Others, not so much—most of the ape masks are from toy stores, and the ape décor favors fake paneling and shag carpet. The DVD extras offer even more nonsense. —*BT* **Movie:** ♫ ½ **DVD:** ♫♫♫
El Independent Cinema (cat #Sc1022, UPC 612385102295). Full frame. $19.98. Keepcase. *LANG:* English. *FEATURES:* Trailers ● Interviews ● Documentary featurettes.
2002 89m/C Misty Mundae, Debbie Rochon, Darian Caine, Anouchka, Zachary Winston Snygg, Shelby Taylor, Sharon Engert; **D:** John Bacchus; **W:** Debbie Rochon, John Bacchus, Joe Ned, Clancy Fitzsimmons; **C:** Giorgyorgy Benaskovich; **M:** John P. Fedele, Kevin Neblung.

Play Misty for Me

DJ Dave Garver (Eastwood) makes a big mistake when he lets Evelyn Draper (Walter) into his life. She's a lovely psychotic subject to uncontrollable rages. Similar themes are handled far less deftly in *Fatal Attraction* and a score of other more manipulative films. This one, Eastwood's directorial debut, stands up remarkably well. The script recognizes the dark side of what was then called "the sexual revolution." Eastwood handles the material without needless flourishes, and his character is a believably flawed protagonist. Evelyn is even a somewhat sympathetic figure—not so much a monster as an equally flawed woman. The "making of" featurette is filled with fascinating details. The film was shot entirely on location in Carmel, California, for a modest $725,000. No sets, no makeup, no studio meddling. DVD looks good, but it's less than perfect with some print damage visible through the original grain, which is heavy at times. Mono sound is fine for the story. —*MM* **Movie:** ♫♫♫ **DVD:** ♫♫♫
Universal Studios (cat #21428, UPC 025192142826). Widescreen (1.85:1) anamorphic. Dolby Digital Mono. $24.95. Keepcase. *LANG:* English; French; Spanish. *CAP:* English. *FEATURES:* "Making of" featurette ● Photo montage ● Evolution of a poster featurette ● Trailer ● Production notes ● Talent files ● DVD-ROM features.
1971 (R) 102m/C Jessica Walter, Donna Mills, John Larch, Irene Hervey, Jack Ging, Clint Eastwood, Donald Siegel; **D:** Clint Eastwood; **W:** Jo Heims, Dean Riesner; **C:** Bruce Surtees; **M:** Dee Barton.

Playgirl Killer

Bill's an artist. You can tell by his beatnik mustache and goatee. It also helps that he's quick to haul out a sketch pad when his lady friend is sunning on a big ol' rock by the lake. He frantically outlines her figure onto his paper until she changes positions. "DON'T MOVE!" he howls. She giggles and ignores him. In a rage, he snaps up his trusty speargun and fires. Bill's also a homicidal maniac who must now hoof it away from witnesses and the police. It's almost an hour into the flick before the next body falls. When it does, things get much more interesting, thanks to the creative use of a walk-in freezer and an archery set. A cheap knockoff of Corman's *A Bucket of Blood* and H.G. Lewis's *Color Me Blood Red*. Both approached the story with more panache, but Kerwin is a committed performer. The full-frame print is in remarkable shape given its age. Nothing troubling about its utilitarian mono track either. The modern teaser trailer has little to do with the flick. Nor does the buxom, knife-wielding woman on the cover. —*GNG/DG* **AKA:** Decoy for Terror. **Movie:** ♫ **DVD:** ♫ ½
Platinum Disc (UPC 096009022297). Full frame. Mono. $12.99. Keepcase. *LANG:* English. *FEATURES:* Trivia game ● Cast bios ● Teaser.
1966 86m/C *CA* William Kerwin, Jean Christopher, Andree Champagne, Neil Sedaka; **D:** Erick Santamaria.

Please Don't Eat My Mother

Unabashed soft-core remake of *Little Shop of Horrors* finds mama's boy Henry Fudd (Kartalian) attempting to raise a pair of carnivorous plants in his bedroom. He's also a voyeur who finds plant food in lover's lane. The bright image appears to have been made from a pristine original, reproducing a sometimes bilious color scheme with unfortunate accuracy. The film actually looks better on disc than some major studio releases of the early '70s. Only a few of the crazy clothing patterns flash. Producer Novak provides his usual off-the-cuff commentary. Extras are plentiful. —*MM* **AKA:** Hungry Pets; Glump.
Movie: 🎵🎵 *DVD:* 🎵🎵🎵
Image Ent. (cat #ID9747SWDVD, UPC 014-381974720). Full frame. Dolby Digital Mono. $24.99. Snapper. *LANG:* English. *FEATURES:* 16 chapters • Liner notes by Nathaniel Thompson • Commentary: producer Harry Novak • 6 theatrical trailers • 3 archival short films • Gallery of exploitation art and radio spots.
1972 95m/C Buck Kartalian, Lynn Lundgren, Art Hedberg, Alice Fredlund, Adam Blair, Flora Wiesel, Ric Lutze, Renee Bond, Dash Fremont; **D:** Carl Monson; **W:** Eric Norden; **C:** Jack Beckett; **M:** Dan Foly.

Please Not Now!

Sophie (Bardot) is young and innocent and desperately in love with Philippe (Riberolles), the owner of a small photo studio who regularly uses her as a model for advertising campaigns. Although the two had been an item for some time, Sophie would prefer a more solid relationship. When she learns that Philippe is seeing another woman, he breaks up with her. Devastated and desperate, she turns to Claude (Claude Brasseur), who tells her not to let herself be dragged down in humiliation, and suggests a plan to make Philippe jealous. From the first shot of Bardot driving her Citroen 2CV recklessly through the streets of Paris, this one's an enchanting blend of slapstick and witty humor. The setting of Paris in the early '60s is beautiful and romantic, skillfully captured by great black-and-white photography. The source print used for the transfer is virtually devoid of any defects, scratches, dust, or other blemishes. The black-and-white presentation looks incredibly sharp with great and naturally looking contrast. Blacks are deep and solid, but never lose any of their detail, while highlights are bright and clear. The grays in between are finely delineated without ever creating a harsh look. Monaural sound is very clean and without blips or distortions. The noise floor of the track is also very low, which indicates that quite some clean-up has been done. The original trailer from the American release (presented in full frame) actually contains footage that is even more revealing than the nude dance scenes in the movie. —*GH* **AKA:** Only for Love; La Bride sur le Cou.

Movie: 🎵🎵🎵 *DVD:* 🎵🎵🎵
Anchor Bay (UPC 013131106794). Widescreen (2.35:1) anamorphic. Dolby Digital Mono. $29.98. Keepcase. *LANG:* French. *SUB:* English. *FEATURES:* Trailer • Bardot bio.
1961 74m/B *FR IT* Brigitte Bardot, Josephine James, Michel Subor, Jacques Riberolles, Mireille Darc, Serge Marquand, Claude Brasseur, Jean Tissier, Bernard Fresson, Claude Berri; **D:** Roger Vadim, J(ack) D(unn) Trop; **W:** Roger Vadim, Claude Brule, J(ack) D(unn) Trop; **C:** Robert Lefebvre; **M:** James Campbell.

The Pledge

Retired Reno homicide detective Jerry Black (Nicholson) is obsessed with the unsolved murder of a little girl which bears a resemblance to past unsolved killings. He has promised the family that he will solve the matter. Nicholson and director Penn worked with similar compulsive material in the underrated *Crossing Guard*. Image and sound, of course, are excellent. The 5.1 does very nice things for Hans Zimmer's superb score, but the key is Nicholson's lived-in, worn-through performance. —*MM*
Movie: 🎵🎵🎵 *DVD:* 🎵🎵
Warner (cat #19053, UPC 0853919053-25). Widescreen anamorphic. Dolby Digital 5.1 Surround. $24.98. Snapper. *LANG:* English; French. *SUB:* English. *CAP:* English. *FEATURES:* 34 chapters • Trailer • Talent files.
2000 (R) 124m/C Jack Nicholson, Robin Wright Penn, Aaron Eckhart, Vanessa Redgrave, Patricia Clarkson, Benicio Del Toro, Costas Mandylor, Helen Mirren, Tom Noonan, Michael O'Keefe, Mickey Rourke, Sam Shepard, Lois Smith, Harry Dean Stanton, Dale Dickey, Pauline Roberts; **D:** Sean Penn; **W:** Jerzy Kromolowski, Mary Olson-Kromolowski; **C:** Chris Menges; **M:** Hans Zimmer.

Plenty [Anchor Bay]

Susan Traherne (Streep) found meaning and love in her life as an English spy helping with the French resistance during World War II. While in occupied France she fell in love with fellow spy, Lazar (Neill). But as interesting as all that could be, the story that writer David Hare focuses on is Susan's 20 years of struggle to find meaning in her life after the war. She gave up her love for Lazar to marry a diplomat, struggles with depression, and suffers from an insatiable appetite for satisfaction of any kind. The world she inhabits has plenty of everything, hence the title, but none of it is enough for Susan. Streep is, of course, terrific, but the story and struggle is an internal one and once the war is over, never very visually interesting. The action is emotional and such a task requires an actress of Streep's caliber (yes, there are others), but ultimately, the story should have remained a stage play. There are great performances by everyone involved: Tracy Ullman, John Gielgud, Ian

McKellan, Sting, and Charles Dance as Susan's suffering husband. Director Fred Schepisi's other big hit was the Steve Martin starrer *Roxanne*, a far cry from this brooding meditation on the burden of a well-lived life. The picture quality is slightly better than video, but it's hard to tell if a fresh print of the film was made for the DVD release. The Surround sound is almost a waste on this drawing room drama. —*JAS*
Movie: 🎵🎵 *DVD:* 🎵🎵🎵
Anchor Bay (cat #DV11463, UPC 0131311-46394). Widescreen (2.35:1) anamorphic. Dolby Surround. $9.98. Keepcase. *LANG:* English; French. *FEATURES:* 26 chapters • Talent bios • Days of Plenty: A Conversation with Fred Schepisi.
1985 (R) 119m/C Meryl Streep, Tracey Ullman, Sting, John Gielgud, Charles Dance, Ian McKellen, Sam Neill, Burt Kwouk; **D:** Fred Schepisi; **W:** David Hare; **C:** Ian Baker; **M:** Bruce Smeaton. *AWARDS:* L.A. Film Critics '85: Support. Actor (Gielgud); Natl. Soc. Film Critics '85: Support. Actor (Gielgud).

Plucking the Daisy

The anonymous author of a scandalous paperback, virgin Agnes Dumont (Brigitte Bardot) sneaks away to her disinherited brother in Paris rather than relocate to a convent as her father (Jacques Dumesnil) insists. She moves into her brother's mansion after hours, not knowing he's merely a curator at Balzac's home/museum, and not the owner. Before realizing what's up, she's sold a Balzac original edition for expense money. Getting enough cash to buy it back entangles Agnes with a ladykiller reporter, Daniel (Daniel Gélin) and a striptease contest, where she uses a disguise to again stay anonymous from family and boyfriend alike. Bardot's winning personality is what makes it all work; certainly not as va-va-voom as other European sex stars like Anita Ekberg, Bardot is sufficiently pert and perky enough to believe she might really be virgin convent school stock. The attitude of sex presented here is also entirely refreshing. Yup, it is a girly show, with lots of nudity probably snipped out of the original import versions, but all the skin is fleeting, directly presented, and not slobbered over as it would be in an American film. At this time Hollywood was still bogged down in lame teasing over possible nudity, in bathing scenes, etc., as if the idea that women could actually get naked was some kind of unconfirmed but heavenly rumor. Even with a striptease show the centerpiece of the film, you get the feeling that this was made by sophisticated dirty old men instead of the garden variety dirty old men, if such a distinction can be made. Naughty, yes, exploitative...well, only a little. Chris Gore's smarmy liner notes are an unwelcome touch that just come off as sleazy. Much nicer is the generous fanfold of cute French postcards, featuring BB, tucked discreetly into the case. —*GE* **AKA:** Please! Mr. Balzac; While Plucking the

Daisy; En Effeuillant la Marguerite; Mademoiselle Striptease.

Movie: 🎹🎹🎹 ½ **DVD:** 🎹🎹🎹 ½
Home Vision Cinema (cat #PLU010, UPC 037429160923). Full frame. $29.95. Keepcase. *LANG:* French. *SUB:* English. *FEATURES:* Liner notes by Chris Gore • Bardot filmography • Trailers • 18 chapters.
1956 100m/B FR Brigitte Bardot, Robert Hirsch, Daniel Gelin, Jacques Dumesnil; **D:** Marc Allegret; **W:** Marc Allegret, Roger Vadim; **C:** Louis Page; **M:** Paul Misraki.

Plughead Rewired: Circuitry Man 2

Acceptable sequel delivers about half the enjoyment of the first. Again, a tough cookie (Shelton) and a romantic robot (Metzler) are set against the nasty Plughead (Wells) in a post-Apocalyptic future. Image and sound are both slightly improved over the first film, *Circuitry Man* (please see review), which is included on the flip side of the disc. That means the image is virtually flawless. The commentary track is more relaxed than the first, too. It's nice to see these cult favorites getting some special treatment on disc. —*MM* **AKA:** Circuitry Man 2.

Movie: 🎹🎹 **DVD:** 🎹🎹🎹 ½
Columbia Tristar (cat #04865, UPC 043-396048652). Widescreen (1.85:1) anamorphic. Dolby Digital Surround; Dolby Stereo. $24.98. Keepcase. *LANG:* English. *SUB:* English; Spanish. *CAP:* English. *FEATURES:* 28 chapters • Trailers • Commentary: Steven & Robert Lovy, Vernon Wells, Tim Kelly.
1994 (R) 97m/C Vernon Wells, Deborah Shelton, Jim Metzler, Dennis Christopher, Nicholas Worth, Traci Lords; **D:** Steven Lovy, Robert Lovy; **W:** Steven Lovy, Robert Lovy; **C:** Stephen Timberlake; **M:** Tim Kelly.

Plunkett & Macleane

Macleane (Miller) and Plunkett (Carlyle) join together to rob from the rich. The two decide that with Macleane's connections to society and Plunkett's smarts, they can gain quite a haul. Macleane falls for Lady Rebecca (Tyler), who just happens to be the niece of the chief justice. So the two go on a spree, eventually become famous, and are chased by a number of farcical characters. There's little dialogue, and not much detail to the characters, so things happen without much explanation. The film is all style and no substance, an odd period thriller with the occasional techno song wandering into the soundtrack. The film's running time seems endless due to its lack of structure. The transfer quality is simply stunning. Many scenes take place in dimly lit scenes or in darkness, and the image is perfectly sharp and consistently detailed throughout. Colors are natural and gorgeous, with no flaws at all. The Surround channels come alive during some of the action scenes. Rich and dynamic, the score thumps away in the background and has terrific multi-channel

presence. Dialogue is clear, but occasionally a little thin sounding. —*AB/DG*

Movie: 🎹 ½ **DVD:** 🎹🎹🎹 ½
USA Home Ent. (UPC 44005868524). Widescreen (2.35:1) anamorphic; full frame. Dolby Digital 5.1 Surround; Dolby Digital Surround. $19.95. Keepcase. *LANG:* English. *SUB:* Spanish; French. *CAP:* English. *FEATURES:* Trailers • Featurette.
1998 (R) 102m/C GB Robert Carlyle, Jonny Lee Miller, Liv Tyler, Michael Gambon, Alan Cumming, Ken Stott, Terence Rigby, Claire Rushbrook, Iain Robertson, Dave Atkins; **D:** Jake Scott; **W:** Robert Wade, Neal Purvis, Charles McKeown; **C:** John Mathieson; **M:** Craig Armstrong.

Pocketful of Miracles

Capra's final film, a remake of his 1933 *Lady for a Day*, is just as corny and sentimental but doesn't work quite as well. Davis is delightful as Apple Annie, a street vendor who will go to any extreme to hide her circumstances from her daughter (Ann-Margret) who's bringing her fiancé for a visit and thinks that mom is a member of the upper crust. Ford is very good as bootlegger Dave the Dude, who hatches a scheme to fool the kid. Based on a Damon Runyon story. DVD could use some work. The image is pale and aliasing is a problem, but neither is as bad as the thin, wavering sound. —*MM*

Movie: 🎹🎹🎹 **DVD:** 🎹🎹 ½
MGM Home Ent. (cat #1002383, UPC 027616865946). Widescreen (2.35:1) letterboxed. Dolby Digital Mono. $14.98. Keepcase. *LANG:* English; Spanish. *SUB:* French; Spanish. *CAP:* English. *FEATURES:* 16 chapters • Trailer.
1961 136m/C Bette Davis, Glenn Ford, Peter Falk, Hope Lange, Arthur O'Connell, Ann-Margret, Thomas Mitchell, Jack Elam, Edward Everett Horton, David Brian, Mickey Shaughnessy; **D:** Frank Capra; **W:** Hal Kanter, Harry Tugend; **C:** Robert J. Bronner; **M:** Walter Scharf. *AWARDS:* Golden Globes '62: Actor—Mus./Comedy (Ford); *NOM:* Oscars '61: Costume Des. (C), Song ("Pocketful of Miracles"), Support. Actor (Falk).

Point Break

Kathryn Bigelow pumps up this off-kilter action flick with so much energy that it's pointless to criticize the complete lack of believability. Johnny Utah (Reeves) is a hot shot "blue flame" rookie who's come to the Los Angeles FBI office straight from training at Quantico. His first assignment is to catch the "ex-Presidents" gang who rob banks while wearing masks of Reagan, Carter, and Nixon. They're actually surfers led by Bodhi (Swayze). When Utah infiltrates the band, he finds himself attracted to their wild freedom. Don't ask any questions and don't dwell too long on the relationship between the two most study leads. Instead, appreciate the relentless pace that Bigelow maintains. DVD does justice to her big set pieces with a widescreen image that's flawless, as far as I could tell, and really strong

boomy sound. Even through headphones it helps to pump up the adrenaline. Lots of silly fun. A commentary track might have been equally enjoyable. —*MM*

Movie: 🎹🎹🎹 **DVD:** 🎹🎹🎹
20th Century Fox (UPC 024543014324). Widescreen (2.35:1) anamorphic. DTS 5.1; Dolby 5.1; Dolby 4.1; Dolby Surround. $24.98. Keepcase. *LANG:* English; French. *SUB:* English; Spanish. *FEATURES:* Trailers • Featurette • 20 chapters.
1991 (R) 117m/C Patrick Swayze, Keanu Reeves, Gary Busey, Lori Petty, John C. McGinley, Chris Pederson, Bojesse Christopher, Julian Reyes, Daniel Beer, Sydney Walsh, Vincent Klyn, James LeGros, John Philbin; **D:** Kathryn Bigelow; **W:** W. Peter Iliff; **C:** Don Peterman; **M:** Mark Isham. *AWARDS:* MTV Movie Awards '92: Most Desirable Male (Reeves).

The Point Men

A team of hired assassins knocks off one of Palestine's top terrorists, but Tony Eckhardt (Lambert) is convinced they were set up to kill the wrong man. No one believes him until the members of his team start meeting with unfortunate accidents, leaving it to Eckhardt to finish the job. A by-the-numbers thriller, where political intrigue is an excuse to blow things up. The picture quality is clear and bright and your rear speakers will be put to work often. As always, this reviewer prefers the widescreen version to the pan-and-scan one. —*BG*

Movie: 🎹 **DVD:** 🎹🎹🎹
Columbia Tristar (cat #06784, UPC 0433-96067844). Widescreen (1.85:1) anamorphic; full frame. Dolby 5.1; Dolby Surround. $24.95. Keepcase. *LANG:* English. *SUB:* English; French; Spanish; Chinese; Korean; Thai. *CAP:* English. *FEATURES:* 28 chapters • Trailers • Filmographies.
2001 (R) 90m/C Christopher Lambert, Kerry Fox, Vincent Regan, Donald (Don) Sumpter, Maryam D'Abo; **D:** John Glen; **W:** Ripley Highsmith; **C:** Alec Mills.

Point of View

This is an interactive thriller, meaning that the viewer chooses, at various points, where the story will go next, or even how it will end; essentially a "Choose your own adventure" on DVD. The story revolves around Jane, a mysterious artist who keeps to herself, with the exception of a few close friends. Soon she develops an attraction for neighbor Frank. Unfortunately for Jane, this turns more dangerous than she'd expected. Or, does it? As the viewer, you decide what will happen between these two. It's a potentially fascinating idea, but not one that's particularly well crafted. The low-budget production often looks like it was filmed in the apartments of the cast and crew on weekends. Fortunately, the cast isn't half bad. The interactive nature of the program is interesting and full of lots of surprise twists. I'd really love to see this kind of presentation done with a bigger film and a better

screenplay. *POV* was shot on digital video and although it doesn't look as smooth as film, it's fairly good. There are times during the low-light scenes that look rather soft in comparison to the outdoor sequences, but they're still moderately crisp and well defined. Some minor bits of shimmering and other artifacts pop up throughout, but these aren't too distracting. The audio (dialogue, ambient sounds) is also rather low-budget in quality, but the music (as cheesy as its rock/techno soundtrack sometimes is) is decent, with fair bass and good overall clarity. The "Making of" featurette is enjoyable, intimate, informative, and includes some behind-the-scenes footage. —*AB/DG*
Movie: 🎵🎵 ½ **DVD:** 🎵🎵 ½
A-PIX Entertainment Inc. (UPC 646610507-2720). Widescreen (1.85:1) letterboxed. Dolby Digital Surround. $29.98. Keepcase. *LANG:* English. *FEATURES:* Trailer • Production notes • "Making of" featurette.
2000 C Stefanie von Pfetten, Chris Bradford, Christopher Shyer, Sarah Rodgers; *D:* David Wheeler; *W:* David Wheeler; *C:* Calvin Kennedy; *M:* Payton Rule.

Poison

Kari Wuhrer plays a woman who decides to exact *Hand That Rocks the Cradle* revenge against a family. The machinations of her scheme are just as nutty as they can be with lots of nudity and hanky-panky. On the commentary track director Wynorski (here listed as Jay Andrews), director of photography Andrea Rossotto, and actor Jeff Trachta take an extremely lighthearted approach. Considering the limitations of budget and genre, the DVD image is not bad at all. Even the rain scenes look good. Sound is fine. —*MM*
AKA: Thy Neighbor's Wife.
Movie: 🎵🎵 **DVD:** 🎵🎵 ½
Artisan Ent. (cat #12217, UPC 01223612-2173). Widescreen (1.85:1) anamorphic. Dolby Digital 5.1 Surround Stereo; Dolby Digital Stereo. $24.98. Keepcase. *LANG:* English. *SUB:* English; Spanish. *CAP:* English. *FEATURES:* 16 chapters • Commentary: Wynorski, Andrea Rossotto, Jeff Trachta • Photo gallery • Trailer • Talent files.
2001 (R) 92m/C Kari Wuhrer, Jeff Trachta, Barbara Crampton, Michael Cavanaugh, Larry Poindexter; *D:* Jim Wynorski; *W:* Sean O'Bannon; *C:* Andrea V. Rossotto.

Pokemon: Mewtwo Returns

This feature-length Pokemon adventure is actually a sequel to *Pokemon: The First Movie* (1999), which told the origin of Mewtwo and his group of Pokemon clones. As opposed to the naturally occurring (?!) Pokemon creatures, Mewtwo and his super-clone ilk were created by the evil Dr. Giovanni. Stating that no one could control him, Mewtwo escaped from Giovanni, fought the other Pokemon, and then escaped to an island in the Johto region, using his powers to erase the minds of all of those who had encountered him. But

now after years of searching, Dr. Giovanni has discovered Mewtwo's hiding place and is determined to show the mutant creature who's boss. Ash, Pikachu, and the other familiar characters must come to Mewtwo's aid, as Giovanni puts all of the super-clones in danger. Unlike many of the *Pokemon* stories, this one presents an intriguing science-fiction plot, and Mewtwo is an interesting character. Unfortunately, any class that the film contains is destroyed by the typical silliness which permeates the TV show and the sub-standard animation. Fans will certainly love this continuation, but most others, especially devotees of serious anime, will find it weak and immature. The full-frame image is very sharp and clear, showing little grain and no flaws from the source material. Also, the colors here are outstanding, as the reds and blues jump off of the screen, with no oversaturation. (One can't help but notice how this image looks much better than the TV version.) The Dolby Surround stereo offers clear dialogue, nice bass response with the music, but only low-volume Surround effects. —*ML*
Movie: 🎵🎵 **DVD:** 🎵🎵 ½
Warner (cat #22142, UPC 0853922142-28). Full frame. Dolby Surround Stereo. $19.98. Snapper. *LANG:* English; French; Spanish. *SUB:* English; French; Spanish. *CAP:* English. *FEATURES:* Bonus short • Bonus trailers • 14 chapters.
2000 63m/C *JP*

Pokemon: The First Movie

The story goes like this: Pokemons (a shortening of the Japanese title "Pocket Monsters") are little creatures who are captured and trained by their new owners to fight in elaborate battles against other Pokemons. A new and evil Pokemon named Mewtwo is created and must be stopped. It's up to a character named Ash to lead the Pokemons into battle. It's all a bit hard to follow, strangely trippy, and plays like a 90-minute ad for the endless legions of Pokeproducts. I will give the franchise this: its popularity has gone on for much longer than I'd expected. This film was a smash hit theatrically in the U.S. and (at the time of release) was the second highest grossing Japanese animated film. Do I recommend the movie or not? Does it really matter? Kids will likely want it anyways. The animation isn't very impressive, but the DVD does present it very well. It's in full frame, cropped from the original theatrical ratio of 1.85:1. Images are pleasingly sharp, and colors are consistently vibrant looking. There's a scratch or two on the print used, but other than that, this is a pretty good image. The audio itself is quite impressive for a kid's movie, and most of the film offers up some very intense audio. Surrounds are used often and effectively, and there's some very solid bass as well. The Poke-dialogue is clear, as well. I'm fairly sure if you could play the movie backwards, you'd hear "buy more Pokemon...buy more Poke-

mon...." Unfortunately, the original Japanese dialogue track is *not* included. Kids probably aren't going to be too interested in listening to the commentary, but it's pretty interesting and it did explain some of the facts behind the story. —*AB/DG*
Movie: 🎵🎵 **DVD:** 🎵🎵🎵
Warner (cat #18020, UPC 0853918020-20). Full frame. Dolby Digital 5.1 Surround. $19.98. Snapper. *LANG:* English. *SUB:* English; French. *CAP:* English. *FEATURES:* Theatrical trailer • Short film, "Pikachu's Vacation" • Sneak preview of the second movie • Commentary: English adaptation director Haigney, producer Grossfeld • Music video, "Don't Say You Love Me" • 23 chapters.
1999 (G) 75m/C *D:* Kunihiko Yuyama, Michael Haigney; *W:* Michael Haigney, Takeshi Shudo; *C:* Hisao Shirai.

Pollock [SE]

First-time producer/director Harris (who also stars) makes an impressive debut with his biography of abstract expressionist artist Jackson Pollock (whom he resembles quite astonishingly). Pollock is a troubled soul, beset by alcoholism and insecurity, who leads himself down a path of self-destruction. The film covers the years 1941–56 as Pollock struggles to find an artistic-commercial breakthrough and marries fellow artist Lee Krasner (Harden, who won a well-deserved Supporting Actress Oscar). She's a tough New Yorker who takes his career in hand, but success only exacerbates Pollock's problems. Production is solid in all areas. Acting is flawless; despite a modest budget, the production design authentically reproduces mid–20th century New York, and the film is dramatically satisfying. This "Special Edition" contains the extras you'd expect to find with a serious film. The most important is Harris's commentary track; staying true to his subject, he's technically oriented, profane, and very funny in unexpected places. DVD is an accurate re-creation of the theatrical release with deeply saturated colors and heavy areas of darkness that reflect Harris's understanding of his subject. —*MM*
Movie: 🎵🎵🎵 ½ **DVD:** 🎵🎵🎵 ½
Columbia Tristar (cat #06454, UPC 0433-96064546). Widescreen (1.85:1) anamorphic. Dolby Digital 5.0 Surround; Dolby Surround. $24.98. Keepcase. *LANG:* English. *SUB:* English; French; Spanish. *CAP:* English. *FEATURES:* 28 chapters • Commentary: Ed Harris • Trailers • Filmographies • "Making of" featurette • Charlie Rose interview with Ed Harris • 4 deleted scenes • Production notes.
2000 (R) 122m/C Ed Harris, Marcia Gay Harden, Amy Madigan, Jennifer Connelly, Jeffrey Tambor, Bud Cort, John Heard, Val Kilmer; *D:* Ed Harris; *W:* Barbara Turner, Susan J. Emshwiller; *C:* Lisa Rinzler; *M:* Jeff Beal. *AWARDS:* Oscars '00: Support. Actress (Harden); N.Y. Film Critics '00: Support. Actress (Harden); *NOM:* Oscars '00: Actor (Harris); Ind. Spirit '01: Support. Actress (Harden).

Pollyanna

Based on the Eleanor Porter story about an enchanting young girl whose contagious enthusiasm and zest for life touches the hearts of all she meets. Mills is perfect in the title role and was awarded a special Oscar for outstanding juvenile performance. A distinguished supporting cast is the icing on the cake in this delightful Disney confection. Another amazing 2-DVD presentation in the Vault Disney series. By including the cartoon (in this case, Mickey Mouse in "Nifty Nineties") that was shown during the original theatrical run, Disney jump-starts the viewer's enjoyment with a nostalgic energy that helps re-create the theatre experience. The *Pollyanna* transfer is a good one with very little in the way of preprint scratches or speckling. Colors are saturated and the picture is amazingly sharp for a film of this vintage. The 5.1 remix (that seems to be standard in this series) offers added dimension for the score and slightly flatter mono dialogue. Still, the film is extremely enjoyable. Disc two offers the usual plethora of extras that would be overkill if not for the exceptional quality. The featurettes are all worth a look, but the most interesting may be the 1963 TV introduction to the film featuring Walt himself. Very few "Special Edition" DVDs can rival the amount of supplements included on these discs, and even less appear to be a real labor of love. —*JO*
Movie: ♫♫♫ ½ **DVD:** ♫♫♫ ½
Buena Vista Home Ent. (cat #21565, UPC 786936143928). Widescreen (1.75:1) anamorphic. Dolby Digital 5.1. $29.99. Keepcase. *LANG:* English. *SUB:* Spanish. *CAP:* English. *FEATURES:* 24 chapters • Theatrical trailer • Commentary: David Swift, Hayley Mills • Original theatrical animated short, "Nifty Nineties" • Featurette: "Pollyanna: Making of a Masterpiece" • Featurette: "Re-Creating Pollyanna's America" • Featurette: "1912!" • Lost Treasures—"Walt Disney TV Introduction" • Production archives • 1960 Disney studio album.
1960 134m/C Hayley Mills, Jane Wyman, Richard Egan, Karl Malden, Nancy Olson, Adolphe Menjou, Donald Crisp, Agnes Moorehead, Kevin Corcoran; **D:** David Swift; **W:** David Swift; **C:** Russell Harlan; **M:** Paul J. Smith.

Polyester (John Waters Collection Vol. 2)

Amusing satire on middle-class life, described by producer, director, and writer Waters as "*Father Knows Best* gone berserk." Forlorn housewife Francine Fishpaw (Divine) dreams of having a normal suburban family, even though she's an alcoholic, her husband is a local porn king, her teenage daughter wants to run off and work as a go-go dancer, and her son is a glue addict with a criminal foot fetish. Filmed in "Odorama," a hilarious gimmick in which theatre goers were provided with scratch 'n' sniff cards, containing specific scents corresponding to key scenes. The first of Waters's more mainstream films. Features songs by Murray and Harry. Don't worry, the DVD comes with a replica of the original Odorama card, so that *Polyester* can be enjoyed in all its smellerific glory. Since it was shot in 35mm, the image on the DVD looks considerably better than that of *Desperate Living,* which accompanies it. There's even a stereo soundtrack. Still, when compared to mainstream releases, *Polyester* comes across as rough as hell and trash fans will not be disappointed by the improvement. Look for (and listen to) the expected funny-as-hell Waters commentary which hops between production notes, childhood reminisces, and affectionate memories of his cast and crew. Available only as part of a double feature with *Desperate Living* (see separate entry). —*JO/BG*
Movie: ♫♫♫ **DVD:** ♫♫♫
New Line (cat #N5231, UPC 7940435231-20). Widescreen (1.85:1) letterboxed. Dolby Digital Stereo. $30.99. Custom. *LANG:* English. *SUB:* English. *FEATURES:* 21 chapters • Theatrical trailer • Commentary: John Waters • Reproduction of the "Odorama" scratch 'n' sniff card.
1981 (R) 86m/C Divine, Tab Hunter, Edith Massey, Mink Stole, Stiv Bators, David Samson, Mary Garlington, Kenneth King, Joni-Ruth White, Jean Hill, Hans Kramm, Mary Vivian Pearce, Cookie Mueller, Susan Lowe, George Stover, George Figgs, Steve Yeager; **D:** John Waters; **W:** John Waters; **C:** David Insley; **M:** Deborah Harry, Michael Kamen.

Poor Man's Orange

Miniseries is the sequel to *The Harp in the South,* both based on novels by Ruth Parks. And while the titles may lead one to believe that these films deal with the American South, they actually take place in Australia. This one continues the story of the Darcy family, who live in a poor section of Sydney in the 1950s. This Irish-Australian family has its share of troubles and must fight daily to survive. However, despite their socio-economic problems, the Darcys always stick together. Two families live under one roof. Mumma (Anne Phelan), Hughie (Martyn Sanderson), and daughter Dolour (Kaarin Fairfax) live downstairs, while older daughter Roie (Anna Hruby) lives upstairs with her husband Charlie (Shane Connor) and their daughter Moira (Emily Nicol). This three-hour plus miniseries introduces several plotlines, and each challenges the stability of the clan. The acting here is top-notch, but the film is simply far too depressing at times. It should be noted that the film was shot simultaneously with *Harp in the South.* The print used for this DVD transfer looks as if it may have come from the poor side of Sydney. The image is extremely blurry and hazy, and the colors often appear washed-out. There is a noticeable amount of grain on this full-frame transfer, and artifacting is evident throughout the film. It looks as if this transfer was mastered from a VHS copy. The Dolby Digital mono audio provides clear dialogue for the most part, but there are some scenes where the audio is muffled and there is an overt hissing on the track. —*ML*
Movie: ♫♫ **DVD:** ♫ ½
BFS Video (cat #30264-D, UPC 06680530-2640). Full frame. Dolby Digital Mono. $19.98. Keepcase. *LANG:* English. *FEATURES:* 12 chapters.
1987 192m/C *AU* Anne Phelan, Martyn Sanderson, Kaarin Fairfax, Anna Hruby, Shane Connor, Emily Nicol; **D:** George Whaley; **W:** George Whaley.

Poor White Trash

Raunchy independent comedy is a lot funnier than most of the big-budget "dumb and dumber" fare from Hollywood. Linda Bronco (Young) will do anything to make sure that her son (London) gets into college. A little robbery, a bit of mayhem...whatever works. The general level of humor is established early with an inflatable woman. Image is a cut above VHS tape, but the film is a low-budget production that's never going to sparkle on any medium. Sound is fine. —*MM*
Movie: ♫♫♫ **DVD:** ♫♫♫
Xenon Ent. (UPC 000799409329). Widescreen letterboxed. $14.98. Keepcase. *LANG:* English. *FEATURES:* 12 chapters • Trailers • Commentary • Talent files.
2000 (R) 85m/C Jacob Tierney, Sean Young, Jason London, Tony Denman, William Devane, Jaime Pressly, M. Emmet Walsh, Tim Kazurinsky; **D:** Michael Addis; **W:** Michael Addis; **C:** Peter Kowalski; **M:** Tree Adams.

Pootie Tang

Curious parody of blaxploitation films (and several other subjects) comes from comedian Chris Rock. The title character (Crouther) is a super-hero (sort of) with a magic belt. A millionaire (Vaughn) whose business is being harmed by Pootie Tang's public service announcements tries to do him in. Like almost all contemporary studio releases, this one arrives on DVD without any serious flaws, and, like almost all theatrical flops, it contains few extras. To date, it remains the only release from a major Hollywood studio to contain the word "pootie" in the title. —*MM*
Movie: ♫ **DVD:** ♫♫
Paramount Home Video (UPC 097363392-248). Widescreen. Dolby Digital 5.1 Surround; Dolby Digital Surround. $29.98. Keepcase. *LANG:* English. *SUB:* English. *CAP:* English. *FEATURES:* 8 chapters • Trailer • Music video.
2001 (PG-13) 81m/C Lance Crouther, Jennifer Coolidge, Robert Vaughn, Chris Rock, Reg E. Cathey, Wanda Sykes, Dave Attell, Mario Joyner, JB Smoove, Cathy Trien, Bob Costas; **D:** Louis CK; **W:** Louis CK; **C:** Willy Kurant.

Popcorn

Film students decide to hold an all-night horror movie festival at the closed-down

"Dreamland" Theater. During the screening, members of the class begin to be picked off by a murderer who uses goofy theatrical gimmicks (giant mosquito prop, electrified chairs, etc.) to kill them. Is the madman a legendary filmmaking lunatic who murdered members of his family onstage or someone else with different motives entirely? This clumsy, awkwardly scripted film (made entirely in Jamaica!) has dark, inadequate photography, but gets a few points for its interesting setting. Walston, Roberts, and Stone are wasted. Alan Ormsby co-wrote and co-directed the film but is uncredited. The disc (which appears to be reformatted from an old transfer) seems too tight on top and features muddy, dark blacks and muted flat colors. The sound pops around reel changes, leading one to believe it was mastered from a theatrical projection print. The promotional footage is just another trailer. —DG

Movie: ♫ ½ **DVD:** ♫
Elite Entertainment, Inc. (cat #EE7672, UPC 790594767228). Widescreen (1.85:1) anamorphic. Dolby Surround Stereo. $24.95. Keepcase. *LANG:* English. *FEATURES:* Insert card ◆ 12 chapters ◆ Trailers and TV spots ◆ Promotional footage.
1989 (R) 93m/C Jill Schoelen, Tom Villard, Dee Wallace Stone, Derek Rydell, Elliott Hurst, Kelly Jo Minter, Malcolm Danare, Ray Walston, Tony Roberts, Karen Witter; *D:* Mark Herrier, Alan Ormsby; *W:* Alan Ormsby; *C:* Ronnie Taylor.

The Pornographer
In his introduction, director Doug Atchison says that the inspiration for this story of a lonely guy (Degood) who becomes a porno filmmaker almost by accident came from his own situation. While trying to raise money for his own legitimate movies, Atchison briefly considered trying to make skin flicks to raise money. Instead, he came up with an intriguing little video premiere. DVD image ranges between good and very good. One striped shirt flashes nastily. Otherwise, it looks and sounds fine with a good selection of extras for an independent production. —MM

Movie: ♫♫ ½ **DVD:** ♫♫ ½
Vanguard Intl. Cinema (cat #VF9166, UPC 658769916638). Full frame. $29.95. Keepcase. *LANG:* English. *FEATURES:* 12 chapters ◆ Trailer ◆ Director's mission statement and commentary track ◆ Evolution of a scene featurette ◆ Deleted scenes.
2000 (R) 88m/C Michael Degood, Craig Wasson, Monique Parent, Katheryn Cain; *D:* Doug Atchison; *W:* Doug Atchison; *C:* Christopher Mosio; *M:* Warner David Jansen.

Possessed
Follow this, if you can: This film is based on a novel that documents an actual exorcism which took place in the United States in the 1949. This exorcism was also the inspiration for William Peter Blatty's novel *The Exorcist*, which was, of course, later made into the famous film. So, *Possessed* is extremely similar to *The Exorcist*, yet entirely different at the same time. Following the death of his grandmother, young Robbie (Jonathan Malen) begins to hear strange noises in his room and then his behavior becomes very erratic. Robbie's parents turn to the school counselor and then a psychiatrist for help, but to no avail. After Robbie attacks a ministry, the local Catholic church is consulted. Father Bowdern (Timothy Dalton), a World War II veteran whose faith has been shaken, is called in to examine the boy, along with Father McBride (Henry Czerny). They soon discover that Robbie is more than a pesky 12-year-old, and that they may not have much time left to save his soul. Knowing that he couldn't compete with *The Exorcist*, director Stephen E. de Souza (who wrote the script for *Die Hard*) avoids any lavish special effects shows or transformation makeup and tries to tell the story in a very concrete and linear fashion. This serves the film well, although it does fall apart in the final act. Dalton is excellent as the troubled Bowdern, as is Czerny as the ambitious yet ethical McBride. Those who find *The Exorcist* far too frightening may have an easier time with this possession tale. Despite the fact that *Possessed* was made for TV, the film is presented on this DVD in a letterboxed format. The image is sharp and clear, although there are some occasional white spots on the image. The colors are good, and the blacks are very deep and true. The Dolby Digital 5.1 audio track is quite good. The volume of the dialogue fluctuates at times, but the Surround sound effects are excellent, adding to the tension in the film. This DVD includes an interview with Father Halloran, who observed the real-life exorcism of the young boy. —ML

Movie: ♫♫ ½ **DVD:** ♫♫♫
Showtime Networks, Inc. (cat #SHO1045, UPC 7548445104523). Widescreen (1.85:1) letterboxed. Dolby Digital 5.1. $24.98. Keepcase. *LANG:* English; Spanish. *CAP:* English. *FEATURES:* Interview ◆ Filmographies ◆ 12 chapters.
2000 111m/C Timothy Dalton, Christopher Plummer, Henry Czerny, Jonathan Malen, Shannon Lawson, Piper Laurie, Michael Rhoades; *D:* Steven E. de Souza; *W:* Steven E. de Souza, Michael Lazarou; *C:* Edward Pei; *M:* John (Gianni) Frizzell.

Prancer
Jessica, poor apple farmer's daughter, still believes in Santa Claus, and when she comes across a reindeer with an injured leg, she assumes it's the same fake statue Prancer who has fallen from a Christmas display in town. She hides the reindeer in her barn until she can return it to Santa, but her father (Elliott) finds the reindeer and decides to sell it as an advertising display. Director John D. Hancock (*Bang the Drum Slowly*) has apparently fallen on some rough times, but manages to take a maudlin script and shoot it with surprising dignity and cleverness. O.K., so I was hugging my cats and crying at the end, it still doesn't make this *Babe*. Clean DVD transfer and sound. —MO

Movie: ♫♫ **DVD:** ♫♫♫ ½
MGM Home Ent. (cat #1002377, UPC 02761686588). Widescreen (1.85:1) anamorphic. Dolby Digital Surround; Dolby Digital Mono. $14.95. Keepcase. *LANG:* English; French. *SUB:* Spanish; French. *CAP:* English; Spanish; French. *FEATURES:* 16 chapters ◆ Theatrical trailer.
1989 (G) 102m/C Sam Elliott, Rebecca Harrell, Cloris Leachman, Rutanya Alda, John Joseph Duda, Abe Vigoda, Michael Constantine, Ariana Richards, Mark Rolston; *D:* John Hancock; *W:* Greg Taylor; *C:* Misha (Mikhail) Suslov; *M:* Maurice Jarre.

Prancer Returns
"If it ain't broke, don't fix it," the old saying goes and this appears to have been the mantra for the makers of this sequel, as it is basically a carbon-copy of the original 1989 film. After hearing the story of how a little girl found a lost deer and thought that it was Santa's Prancer, young Charlie (Gavin Fink) discovers a baby deer in the woods. Assuming that this must be Prancer as well (as he lives in the same town where the original tale took place), Charlie takes the deer home. Once there, he does everything in his power to return the deer to Santa Claus and in turn brings some much-needed magic to his family and the town. What can you say about a film which is almost exactly like its predecessor? Young Gavin Fink is great as Charlie and he receives support from a good cast which features John Corbett and Jack Palance. The film probably won't be considered a holiday classic, but it is appropriate family viewing and the deer is very cute. It's presented in an anamorphic widescreen transfer (not the full-frame ratio listed on the box). The image shows some grain, but is otherwise sharp, offering good colors and no video distortion. The Dolby Digital 5.1 audio track delivers clear dialogue, subtle yet effective Surround effects, and a nice LFE response. —ML

Movie: ♫♫ **DVD:** ♫♫ ½
USA Home Ent. (cat #96306 0287-2, UPC 696306028727). Widescreen (1.85:1) anamorphic. Dolby Digital 5.1; Dolby Stereo. $19.95. Keepcase. *LANG:* English. *CAP:* English. *FEATURES:* Music video ◆ 12 chapters.
2001 (G) 90m/C Jack Palance, John Corbett, Stacy Edwards, Gavin Fink, Michael O'Keefe; *D:* Joshua Butler; *W:* Greg Taylor.

Pre-Code Hollywood: Vol. 3, "Behind Office Doors"
Mary Linden (Astor) is the good woman behind Jim's (Ames) rise to the presidency of his paper company. But will Mary's dedication be rewarded, or will Jim continue to ignore her for a society girl? While this title may have been scandalous for 1931, it's now merely dull, probably of interest only to those with a particular interest in films of

this period or for those who need a refresher course in workplace sexual harassment. The picture and audio quality are adequate, considering the film's age. —BG
Movie: 🎬🎬 **DVD:** 🎬🎬
Roan Group (cat #AED-2053, UPC 785604-205326). Full frame. Dolby Mono. $19.95. Keepcase. *LANG:* English. *FEATURES:* 10 chapters • Film background.
1931 82m/C

Pre-Code Hollywood: Vol. 4, "Lonely Wives"
Wealthy Richard Smith (Horton), tired of being cooped up with his mother-in-law while his wife's away, hires an impersonator to take his place for the evening. The farce ensues when Mrs. Smith arrives home early. This film is primarily of historical interest; the double entendres seem pretty tame by today's standards. For a film of such age, the DVD looks and sounds quite good. —BG
Movie: 🎬🎬 **DVD:** 🎬🎬 ½
Roan Group (cat #AED-2058, UPC 785604-205821). Full frame. Dolby Mono. $19.95. Keepcase. *LANG:* English. *FEATURES:* 9 chapters • Cast bios.
1931 86m/B Edward Everett Horton, Patsy Ruth Miller, Laura La Plante, Esther Ralston; **D:** Russell Mack; **W:** Walter DeLeon; **C:** Edward Snyder.

The Pride and the Passion
Serious miscasting is the biggest problem with Stanley Kramer's period war romance. British Captain Trumbell (Grant) comes to Spain to recover a gigantic cannon for use against Napoleon's armies. He finds it, but also finds himself helping Miguel (Sinatra), leader of a war-weary Spanish faction, to liberate a city and falling in love with Miguel's girlfriend (Loren). The spectacle scenes are well done, with a cast of thousands, and the Technicolor photography is beautiful, but the script is often ridiculous and the production's problems come through in the final product. The transfer is rich in color, but lacks definition in the darker scenes. The mono sound is unspectacular. —DRL
Movie: 🎬🎬 ½ **DVD:** 🎬🎬 ½
MGM Home Ent. (cat #1003432, UPC 027-616875815). Widescreen (1.66:1) letterboxed. Dolby Digital Mono. $14.95. Keepcase. *LANG:* English; Spanish. *SUB:* English; French; Spanish. *CAP:* English. *FEATURES:* Trailer • 16 chapters.
1957 132m/C Cary Grant, Frank Sinatra, Sophia Loren, Theodore Bikel, John Wengraf, Jay Novello, Philip Van Zandt; **D:** Stanley Kramer; **W:** Edward Anhalt; **C:** Franz Planer; **M:** George Antheil.

The Prime Gig
Pendelton "Penny" Wise (Vaughn) is a telemarketer with a knack for closing the deal. After his latest fly-by-night employer goes belly up, Penny is approached by the beautiful Caitlin Carlson (Julia Ormond), who offers him a once-in-a-lifetime chance to go to work for the mysterious king of the con, Kelly Grant (Ed Harris). Grant has assembled a veritable A-Team of salespeople to push his latest venture, an untapped gold mine, from his very stylish boiler room phone center. While the other folks are swayed by Grant's promises of quick riches, Penny remains aloof and unconvinced. But a quick couple of thousand, as well as a heated affair with Caitlin, soon change his mind. Meanwhile, his down-and-out childhood pal, Joel (Rory Cochrane), is living on the street and spouting beatific odes to a life without entanglements. But a few nights of the hard life find Joel back on Penny's couch living off the good will of others. Story takes far too much time to get the ball rolling and even when it does kick into gear, remains predictable. The overall image quality for both transfers is quite good. The picture is very sharp (perhaps a little too sharp as diagonal lines get a bit jaggy at times) with little edge-enhancement noticeable. Colors are natural and solid and black levels are more than adequate. Neither of the Surround mixes is very active. The dialogue is planted front and center with a bit of the musical score spreading to the rest of the speakers. There is no deep bass to speak of but neither are there scenes that really warrant its presence. —MP
Movie: 🎬🎬 ½ **DVD:** 🎬🎬🎬
New Line Home Video (UPC 7940435475-22). Widescreen (2.35:1) anamorphic; full frame. Dolby Digital 5.1 Surround; Dolby Surround. $24.98. Snapper. *LANG:* English. *SUB:* English. *CAP:* English. *FEATURES:* 20 chapters.
2000 96m/C Vince Vaughn, Julia Ormond, Ed Harris, Rory Cochrane, Wallace Shawn, George Wendt, Stephen Tobolowsky; **D:** Gregory Mosher; **W:** William Wheeler; **C:** John A. Alonzo; **M:** David Robbins.

Primitive Love
Please see review of *Mondo Drive-In Double Feature.*
1964 77m/C *IT* Jayne Mansfield, Franco Franchi, Ciccio Ingrassia, Mickey Hargitay, Carlo Kechler; **D:** Luigi Scattini; **W:** Amedeo Sollazzo; **C:** Claudio Racca.

The Prince and the Showgirl
Elsie Marina, an American actress working in turn-of-the-century London (Monroe) has an accident with a dress strap while being introduced to the Regent of Carpathia (Olivier) backstage, and is invited to a reception at the embassy. The stuffy Regent is alternately pleased and annoyed with her, but attempts to send her away keep getting delayed, by Northbrook (Wattis), the British liaison, King Nicolas (Spenser), the Regent's young son who is planning a coup, and the Queen dowager (Thorndike), the Regent's mother, who insists on spouting fluffy French that Elsie cannot understand. The resourceful showgirl (she stays several days in the same dress, it seems) does understand German, however, which gives her an essential, if inadvertent role to play in the avoidance of a World War, the reconciliation of a royal family, and the softening of the Regent's chilly heart. The film reinforces the old adage that whenever Marilyn appears on screen, other actors cease to exist. She simply glows, and holds our interest no matter what she's doing. True, as she's the center of the action we follow her almost all the time, but for all his methods and acting finesse, Olivier just can't compete. Cinematographer Jack Cardiff gives Marilyn Monroe some of the handsomest shots of her career—lit better than most glamour photography, and dramatically sound, to boot. Some interiors in a large London Hall are distractingly undercranked to get enough light, but elsewhere Cardiff effortlessly mixes matte paintings and impressive sets. Notice how in the embassy set, there's always an awareness of the time of day. DVD is a minor disappointment. This should be a widescreen transfer, at least 1.66:1; and it looks as though an older element was used for the transfer, as opposed to going the admittedly expensive route of reworking the film back from original elements. Most scenes look fine, but quite a few have too much grain or are indistinct (especially the optical of the opening titles), and the color is nowhere as consistent as it should be. It never looks bad, exactly, but after seeing the excellent no-compromise job done on the first batch of Fox Monroe movies, this is nothing to write home about. Films released in Technicolor are always going to have this problem, and remastering them properly can be a costly process. Up until now, the bean counters in the studios have only approved a few titles, like *The Wizard of Oz,* for such treatment. Other dazzling shows, like John Huston's *Moulin Rouge,* sit in disrepair awaiting restoration funds. —GE
Movie: 🎬🎬🎬 **DVD:** 🎬🎬 ½
Warner Home Video (UPC 85391115427). Full frame. $19.98. Snapper. *LANG:* English. *FEATURES:* Newsreel • Trailer.
1957 127m/C Laurence Olivier, Marilyn Monroe, Sybil Thorndike, Jeremy Spenser, Richard Wattis; **D:** Laurence Olivier; **W:** Terence Rattigan; **C:** Jack Cardiff.

The Prince of Tides
Barbra Streisand and Nick Nolte star in this adaptation of Pat Conroy's beloved novel. Following a suicide attempt by his sister (Dillon), football coach Tom Wingo (Nolte) travels from his home in Charleston, South Carolina, to be with her in New York City. There, he meets psychiatrist Susan Lowenstein (Streisand), who needs information about the Wingo family's past to treat his sister. Tom is reluctant at first, but he soon opens up to Lowenstein, revealing a disturbing childhood and an unfulfilling life. This emotional outpouring leads Tom to make a romantic connection with Lowenstein. Director Streisand brings a very touching and engaging story to the screen, and presents a realistic portrayal of the mindset

of some Southerners. However, this emotional tale is at times hampered by the overacting of Nolte and the emotionless performance by Streisand. DVD looks fantastic. The newly mastered digital transfer gives us a sharp and clear picture, which shows virtually no grain and very few defects. The colors are excellent, showing natural-looking fleshtones. Ditto for the surprisingly rich Dolby 2.0 Surround soundtrack. This track provides clear dialogue, sweeping Surround sound effects, and impressive bass. —ML

Movie: 🎜🎜🎜 **DVD:** 🎜🎜🎜
Columbia Tristar (cat #23329, UPC 04336-9233294). Widescreen (1.85:1) anamorphic. Dolby 2.0 Surround. $24.98. Keepcase. *LANG:* English; French; Spanish; Portuguese. *SUB:* English; French; Spanish; Portuguese; Chinese; Korean; Thai. *CAP:* English. *FEATURES:* Theatrical teaser • Theatrical trailer • Talent files • Production notes • 28 chapters.
1991 (R) 132m/C Nick Nolte, Barbra Streisand, Blythe Danner, Kate Nelligan, Jeroen Krabbe, Melinda Dillon, George Carlin, Jason Gould, Brad Sullivan; *D:* Barbra Streisand; *W:* Pat Conroy, Becky Johnston; *C:* Stephen Goldblatt; *M:* James Newton Howard. *AWARDS:* Golden Globes '92: Actor—Drama (Nolte); L.A. Film Critics '91: Actor (Nolte); *NOM:* Oscars '91: Actor (Nolte), Adapt. Screenplay, Art Dir./Set Dec., Cinematog., Picture, Support. Actress (Nelligan), Orig. Score.

The Princess and the Pirate

Hope is at his craziest as Sylvester, a vaudevillian who falls for a beautiful princess (Mayo) who's traveling incognito. They're on the run from buccaneers on the Spanish Main. The gaudy colors are unfaded. There are very mild registration problems at the beginning along with some dust flecks. All of the grain appears to come from the original. For these ears, mono sound seems slightly superior to the remix. —MM

Movie: 🎜🎜🎜 **DVD:** 🎜🎜 ½
HBO (cat #90666). Full frame. Dolby Digital Stereo; Dolby Digital Mono. $24.95. Snapper. *LANG:* English; Spanish; French; Italian. *SUB:* English; French; Spanish. *FEATURES:* 22 chapters • Trailer • Talent files.
1944 94m/C Bob Hope, Walter Slezak, Walter Brennan, Virginia Mayo, Victor McLaglen, Bing Crosby; *D:* David Butler; *W:* Everett Freeman, Don Hartman, Melville Shavelson; *C:* Victor Milner; *M:* David Rose. *AWARDS:* NOM: Oscars '44: Orig. Dramatic Score.

The Princess and the Warrior

Tom Tykwer's follow-up to *Run, Lola, Run* lacks the dazzling kinetic energy that made that film so memorable but this one is concerned with some of the same ideas about chance and fate. Here Tykwer displays flashes of the same technical brilliance but in the end, this is a much less

meditative story that holds back key information until the last act. Sissi (Potente) is a nurse on a psychiatric ward. Bodo (Furmann) is a troubled veteran who's involved in some sort of complex heist. They meet during an auto accident and from that point, the story moves in one strange direction after another. Franka Potente continues to be one of the most interesting young actors around. Some of Tykwer's camerawork—particularly one shot on a bridge—will make you reverse the disc to appreciate what he's doing. Image and sound are very good, of course, with only some flashing within brickwork patterns worth noting. Both of the commentary tracks are excellent. —MM **AKA:** Der Krieger und die Kaiserin.

Movie: 🎜🎜🎜 **DVD:** 🎜🎜🎜
Columbia Tristar (cat #06390, UPC 0433-96063907). Widescreen (2.35:1) anamorphic. Dolby Digital 5.1 Surround; Dolby Digital Surround. $24.98. Keepcase. *LANG:* German. *SUB:* English; French; Spanish; Portuguese. *FEATURES:* 28 chapters • Commentary: director • Commentary: director & cast • "Making of" featurette • Deleted scenes • Music video • Filmographies • Trailers.
2000 (R) 130m/C GE Franka Potente, Benno Furmann, Joachim Krol, Marita Breuer, Lars Rudolph, Jurgen Tarrach, Melchior Beslon, Ludger Pistor; *D:* Tom Tykwer; *W:* Tom Tykwer; *C:* Frank Griebe; *M:* Tom Tykwer, Johnny Klimek, Reinhold Heil.

The Princess Bride [2 SE]

A kindly grandfather reads his grandson a bedtime story, a classic (and comic) tale of love and adventure as the beautiful Buttercup (Wright Penn) is kidnapped and held against her will to marry the evil Prince Humperdinck, and Westley (her childhood love, now returned as the Dread Pirate Roberts) attempts to save her. On the way Westley meets a swordsman and a giant, both of whom join up in the noble effort. His quest is hampered by various villains. This comedy directed by Rob Reiner and written by William Goldman has far too many fans (including my wife) to listen to my curmudgeon opinion of being singularly unmoved by the cleverness, sentiment, or cuteness. This DVD re-release has a lot of extras—along with great image and sound. (The first release was reviewed in *Book 2*.) —MO

Movie: 🎜🎜🎜 **DVD:** 🎜🎜🎜🎜
MGM Home Ent. (cat #1002362, UPC 027-61686573). Widescreen (1.85:1) anamorphic. Dolby Digital 5.1; Mono. $29.98. Keepcase. *LANG:* English; Spanish. *SUB:* English; Spanish; French. *CAP:* English; Spanish; French. *FEATURES:* 28 chapters • Commentary: Rob Reiner • Commentary: William Goldman • Brand-new "As You Wish" documentary with cast interviews • Elwes's own exclusive footage shot during the making of *Bride* • 2 original featurettes.
1987 (PG) 98m/C Cary Elwes, Mandy Patinkin, Robin Wright Penn, Wallace

Shawn, Peter Falk, Andre the Giant, Chris Sarandon, Christopher Guest, Billy Crystal, Carol Kane, Fred Savage, Peter Cook, Mel Smith; *D:* Rob Reiner; *W:* William Goldman; *C:* Adrian Biddle; *M:* Mark Knopfler. *AWARDS: NOM:* Oscars '87: Song ("Storybook Love").

The Princess Diaries

Director Garry Marshall retells *Pretty Woman* with a teenaged heroine who discovers that she's a princess and must learn to act the part. Mia Thermopolis (Hathaway) is a smart, insecure San Francisco girl who has no idea that her father was royalty until her grandmother (Andrews) arrives from Genovia. She and her trusty head of security (Elizondo) then set about to transform the gawky girl into a swan-like princess. The story slips a bit in the second half, but for the most part the film is thoroughly enjoyable fluff. Theatrical release was a surprise hit (a sequel must be in the works) and it gets commensurate treatment on DVD. Image, of course, is excellent. There may have been flaws but I, for one, was too charmed to notice. The extras contain all the expected bells and whistles. A separate full-frame edition is also available. —MM

Movie: 🎜🎜🎜 **DVD:** 🎜🎜🎜
Buena Vista Home Ent. (cat #23616, UPC 786936162134). Widescreen (1.85:1) anamorphic. Dolby Digital 5.1 Surround. $29.98. Keepcase. *LANG:* English; French. *SUB:* Spanish. *CAP:* English. *FEATURES:* 27 chapters • "Behind-the-scenes" featurette • 8 deleted scenes • Commentary: Julie Andrews, Anne Hathaway • Commentary: Garry Marshall • 2 music videos.
2001 (G) 114m/C Anne Hathaway, Julie Andrews, Hector Elizondo, Heather Matarazzo, Erik von Detten, Mandy Moore, Robert Schwartzman, Caroline Goodall, Larry Miller, Sandra Oh, Sean O'Bryan; *D:* Garry Marshall; *W:* Gina Wendkos; *C:* Karl Walter Lindenlaub; *M:* John Debney.

Princess of Thieves

While we are all familiar with the tale of Robin Hood and his great adventures, this film seeks to tell the next chapter of Robin's life-story. Here, we meet Gwyn (Keira Knightley), the daughter of Robin Hood and Maid Marion. Marion has passed away, and Robin Hood is always off on adventures, so Gwyn has grown up under the care of Friar Tuck (Roger Ashton-Griffiths) and her dear friend Froderick (Del Synnott). She desperately wants to travel with her father, but he forbids it. Things change when it is announced that King Richard is dying. Richard has decreed that his son Prince Philip take the throne. But the evil Prince John (Jonathan Hyde) and his loyal servant, the Sheriff of Nottingham (Malcolm McDowell), plot to kill Philip, so that Prince John will become king. Knowing that her father can't handle this fight alone, Gwyn springs into action seeking adventure and a possible romance with Prince Philip. Much of the story here is very familiar, but *Princess of Thieves* does offer a strong female lead and some exciting swashbuckling action. This one is good for the whole family, although younger viewers may be confused by the historically accurate references in the story (i.e. The Crusades), which add a certain seriousness to the proceedings. The image on the DVD is presented full frame (as this was originally made for TV) and looks very good. The picture is very sharp and clear, showing fine colors and virtually no grain. The Surround sound offers mostly musical cues from the rear speakers, but the dialogue is clear and the sound effects aren't overwhelming. In a sign that they aren't afraid to take that extra step, Disney has included an audio commentary from director Peter Hewitt here, which is informative and never boring. —ML

Movie: 🎬🎬🎬 **DVD:** 🎬🎬🎬

Buena Vista Home Ent. (cat #23615, UPC 786936162127). Full frame. Dolby 2.0 Surround. $29.99. Keepcase. *LANG:* English. *SUB:* French; Spanish. *CAP:* English. *FEATURES:* Commentary • Featurette • 24 chapters.
2001 88m/C Malcolm McDowell, Keira Knightley, Roger Ashton-Griffiths, Jonathan Hyde, Del Synnott; **D:** Peter Hewitt.

Prison on Fire 2

Many fans of Hong Kong action films believe that director Ringo Lam came into his own with this sequel, a prison drama that hinges on some complex moral choices. Star Chow Yun-Fat is excellent, as usual. Image is good, but not great; a bit above average for a Hong Kong import. Hex errors in the subtitles abound. Consider this incomprehensible rhetorical example: "What kind of world it is. Shoe the goose." —MM **AKA:** Tao Fan; Jian Yu Feng Yun Xu Ji.

Movie: 🎬🎬 ½ **DVD:** 🎬🎬 ½

Tai Seng (cat #26704). Widescreen letterboxed. Dolby Digital 5.1 Surround Stereo. $29.95. Keepcase. *LANG:* Chinese. *SUB:* Trad. & simpl. Chinese; Japanese; Bahasa (Ind. & Malay.); Thai; Korean; Vietnamese; English. *FEATURES:* 8 chapters • Talent files • Trailers.
1991 107m/C *HK* Chow Yun-Fat, Elvis Tsui, Kam-Kong Tsui, Yu Li; **D:** Ringo Lam; **M:** Lowell Lo.

The Prisoner

"Where am I?" "The Village." "Whose side are you on?" "That would be telling." "Who are you?" "I am the new Number 2." "Who is Number 1?" "You are Number 6." "I am not a number, I am a man!" Thus began each episode of one of the shortest-lived, most popular cult TV series ever made. The series was shot at a real location, the beach front Hotel Portmeirion in North Wales, and told the tale of a secret agent who was kidnapped just after resigning from his very classified job with an unknown agency. His kidnappers claim to want only the reason he resigned, but

are they from his agency or a counter agency? Everyone in the Village has a number, and an agenda, and despite Number 6's (McGoohan) constant denial that he is a man and not a number, we never know his name. Some fans believe that Number 6 was a continuation of *Danger Man* (*Secret Agent* in the U.S.) but McGoohan, one of the creators of the series, denied it. Of course the other creator of the series said it was absolutely true. Each episode deals with Number 6 attempting to escape the Village, and/or obtain the identity of Number 1. An amazingly creative series both in plot and visual presentation, it seems to be the basis for the images of many of today's most cutting-edge filmmakers. In one episode, Number 6 is physically taken from infancy to adulthood in an attempt to wrest information from his brain. In another he finds himself the Sheriff of an old west town, and in yet another the Village scientists invade his dreams to make him reveal the identity of his co-spys, only to have him turn the tables and feed them information he wants them to have. The Village has a very Disneyland-gone-wrong feel and look to it with lots of bright uniforms and many smiling faces that feel forced. McGoohan said that this series will always be ahead of its time and after re-watching the complete series there can be little argument. Only 17 episodes were made and each of them presented here is digitally re-mastered in a fan-approved order. The picture looks fabulous as far as color and clarity are concerned, but there are a few scratches on microscopic inspection. The sound is good, but a bit foggy at times when combined with the thick British accents. The extras are fun, especially the *Prisoner* trivia games on each set. Also included is an alternate version of "The Chimes of Big Ben," which is actually a version that was used to shop the series before the episode was completely finished. For *Prisoner* fans this is a fabulous find and for anyone who hasn't checked out this original series, it should go on their must-see list. (The series is contained on five sets, each $39.95.) —CA

Movie: 🎬🎬🎬 **DVD:** 🎬🎬🎬

A&E Home Video Full frame. Dolby Digital Mono. Keepcase (2 to a box). *LANG:* English. *FEATURES:* Sets 1,3,5: 3 chapters each; Sets 2, 4: 4 chapters each • Original broadcast trailers • Rarely seen foreign and textless footage • Prisoner trivia game • Footage of Hotel Portmeirion • Interview with production manager Bernie Williams • Interactive Map of the Village.
1968 52m/C *GB* Patrick McGoohan, Virginia Maskell, Guy Doleman, Paul Eddington, George Baker, Angelo Muscat, Barbara Yu Ling, Stephanie Randall; **D:** Don Chaffey.

Progeny

Familiar horror boasts some scary creatures. Craig (Vosloo) and Sherry (McWhirter) are zapped by a bright light while in bed and don't remember what happened until a shrink (Crouse) and UFO investigator Clavell

(Dourif) hypnotize them. Then Sherry remembers that she was abducted and impregnated by some slimy tentacled aliens and it's all just kind of predictably gross from there on out. For a relatively modestly budgeted SF film, this one gets exceptional treatment on DVD. Image, sound, and extras are well above average. The commentary track by director Yuzna and producers Jack Murphy and Henry Seggerman is mostly aimed at matters of production. Writers Aubrey Solomon and Stuart Gordon are more concerned with story. Both tracks are recommended to fans of the genre. —MM

Movie: 🎬🎬 **DVD:** 🎬🎬🎬

Studio Home Ent. (cat #7185). Widescreen (2.35:1) anamorphic. $29.95. Keepcase. *LANG:* English. *SUB:* Spanish. *FEATURES:* Storyboards • 2 commentary tracks by filmmakers • Storyboards • Talent files • Trivia game • Interviews • Slide show • "Making of Creatures" featurette.
1998 100m/C Arnold Vosloo, Jillian McWhirter, Brad Dourif, Lindsay Crouse, Wilford Brimley; **D:** Brian Yuzna; **W:** Aubrey Solomon; **C:** James Hawkinson; **M:** Steven Morrell.

The Projectionist

Fascinating, compulsively watchable exploration of the addictive fantasy world of movies. Structured around a 24-hour period in the life of a solitary film projectionist (McCann), it contrasts his dreary life with his amusing Saturday matinee–style black-and-white fantasies. In the real world, the projectionist is at odds with the boorish theatre owner (Dangerfield, in a subdued performance) who also appears as the mad villain in his serial fantasies! There's no story and a lack of forward momentum at times, but it features some highly thought-provoking sections and some astonishing impersonations by McCann. The transfer is sharp and accurately conveys the limited colors of the film's low-budget Eastmancolor photography. While restored and preserved by the Museum of Modern Art, the film occasionally features some marks and scratches, especially during reel changes. The sound is fine, but there's a very faint hiss. It's fairly unnoticeable, though. It's a shame there's no trailer or commentary tracks, as the film screams out for some discussion of its context, making, release, and intent. —DG

Movie: 🎬🎬🎬 **DVD:** 🎬🎬🎬

Image Ent. (cat #ID1424JHDVD, UPC 014381142426). Widescreen (1.78:1) anamorphic. Mono. $24.99. Keepcase. *LANG:* English. *FEATURES:* 10 chapters.
1971 (PG) 84m/C Rodney Dangerfield, Chuck McCann, Ina Balin, Jara Kohout, Harry Hurwitz, Stephen Phillips, Clara Rosenthal, Jacquelyn Glenn, Robert Staats; **D:** Harry Hurwitz; **W:** Harry Hurwitz; **C:** Victor Petrashevich; **M:** Igo Kantor, Erma E. Levin.

Proof of Life

When Alicia's (Ryan) engineer husband (Morse) is kidnapped by anti-government

guerrillas in South America, she hires professional negotiator Terry Thorne (Crowe) to get him back. Complications arise when Terry falls for the wife. Complications also arose when Ryan fell for Crowe and her marriage to Dennis Quaid fell apart. Crowe and Ryan subsequently broke up just in time for the marketing push, leaving director Hackford without his two biggest stars to promote the film. Despite the offscreen heat, the movie's a lot better when dealing with the husband's predicament and the rescue operations than when exploring Ryan's angst and the budding romance. The picture and sound quality on this DVD are close to as good as it gets. Even when watching for flaws, none are visible. The 5.1 sound is as dynamic as they come and on the action sequences it almost overcooks, throwing more than usual to both the subwoofer and the Surround tracks. Director Hackford's commentary is extremely dry and mostly uninteresting as he pretty much just tells the viewer what's happening on the screen. Only when he strays away from the obvious do his comments warrant attention. The "making of" documentary is nonstop with its 15-minute running time and throws in everything but the kitchen sink, including cast and director interviews, behind-the-scene glimpses, anecdotes, and even compares the film to the real-life kidnapping biz. —JO
Movie: 𝄢𝄢 ½ **DVD:** 𝄢𝄢𝄢𝄢
Warner (cat #19052, UPC 0853919052-26). Widescreen (2.35:1) anamorphic. Dolby Digital 5.1. $19.98. Snapper. *LANG:* English; French. *SUB:* English; French. *CAP:* English. *FEATURES:* 37 chapters ▪ Theatrical trailer ▪ Documentary, "The Making of *Proof of Life*" ▪ Commentary: director Taylor Hackford ▪ Talent files.
2000 (R) 135m/C Russell Crowe, Meg Ryan, David Morse, David Caruso, Pamela Reed, Anthony Heald, Stanley Anderson, Gottfried John, Alun Armstrong, Michael Kitchen, Margo Martindale, Mario Ernesto Sanchez, Pietro Sibille, Vicky Hernandez, Norma Martinez, Diego Trujillo; **D:** Taylor Hackford; **W:** Tony Gilroy; **C:** Slawomir Idziak; **M:** Danny Elfman.

Prophecy

And the prediction is...disappointment. The writer of *The Omen* and the director of *The Manchurian Candidate* team up for this failed attempt at a socially responsible horror film. Mutant creatures are appearing in the Maine woods. Dr. Verne (Foxworth), a public-health expert, and his cellist wife, Maggie (Shire), head to the forest to investigate the problem. There, they meet Isley (Dysart), a representative from the lumber company that may be responsible for toxic dumping, and John Hawks (Assante), a local Native American who is trying to stop the company from encroaching on his land. The majority of this film is made up of boring rhetoric, as Verne tries to piece together the source of such scary mutations as big salmon and a giant tadpole. Finally, at the 75-minute mark, a mutant bear shows up and begins

to menace the cast. Billing itself as "The Monster Movie," *Prophecy* features too much talking and not enough monster. To its credit, the last 22 minutes of the movie are fun, as the weary characters attempt to flee the hulking beast. But that's not enough to overcome the coma inducing first 2/3 of the film. The ecological message is still relevant today, but the bear special effects look a bit dated. Surprisingly, the print on this DVD doesn't look that bit dated. The anamorphic widescreen transfer is sharp and clear, showing only the occasional defect from the source print. The audio, which is listed as only being Dolby Stereo, actually offers a nice, discrete Surround mix, which is very effective during the finale. —ML
Movie: 𝄢𝄢 **DVD:** 𝄢𝄢 ½
Paramount (cat #01182, UPC 097360118-247). Widescreen (2.35:1) anamorphic. Dolby Digital Stereo. $24.99. Keepcase. *LANG:* English. *SUB:* English. *CAP:* English.
1979 (PG) 102m/C Talia Shire, Robert Foxworth, Armand Assante, Victoria Racimo, Richard Dysart, George Clutesi; **D:** John Frankenheimer; **W:** David Seltzer; **C:** Harry Stradling Jr.

Proud Rebel

Character study focuses on a stubborn widower (Ladd) who searches for a doctor to aid him in dealing with the problems of his mute son and the woman (de Havilland) who helps to tame the boy. Ladd's real-life son makes his acting debut. Moderate surface damage, mostly dust flecks, is visible throughout and the amount of grain is to be expected of a '50s western. A few shots are unusually pale, but that seems to come from the original. There's not much difference between the Surround remix and the original mono. —MM
Movie: 𝄢𝄢𝄢 **DVD:** 𝄢𝄢 ½
HBO (cat #91174). Full frame. Dolby Digital Surround Stereo; Mono. $24.98. Snapper. *LANG:* English; French; German; Italian; Spanish. *SUB:* French; Spanish. *CAP:* English. *FEATURES:* Cast & crew thumbnail bios ▪ 19 chapters.
1958 99m/C Alan Ladd, Olivia de Havilland, Dean Jagger, Harry Dean Stanton; **D:** Michael Curtiz; **W:** Lillie Hayward, Joseph Petracca; **C:** Ted D. McCord; **M:** Jerome Moross.

Psychic Killer

A wrongfully committed insane asylum inmate (Hutton) acquires psychic powers and uses them in deadly revenge against everyone who's ever done him wrong. The hollow-sounding audio is much as I remember it from the drive-in all those many years ago. DVD image is much sharper. —MM
Movie: 𝄢𝄢 **DVD:** 𝄢𝄢 ½
Elite Entertainment, Inc. (cat #7792). Widescreen letterboxed. Mono. $24.95. Keepcase. *LANG:* English. *FEATURES:* Trailer ▪ 15 chapters.
1975 (PG) 89m/C Jim Hutton, Paul Burke, Julie Adams, Neville Brand, Aldo

Ray, Rod Cameron, Della Reese; **D:** Ray Danton; **W:** Ray Danton, Mikel Angel, Greydon Clark; **C:** Herb Pearl; **M:** William Craft.

Psycho 2

Sequel finds Norman Bates (Perkins) returning home after 22 years in an asylum and still haunted by "mother" and caught up in a series of murders. Compared to most horror sequels, this one's actually very good and entertaining, with both Perkins and Miles reprising their roles from the original. The clear image and 5.1 audio are only a little better than VHS tape. —MM
Movie: 𝄢𝄢 ½ **DVD:** 𝄢𝄢 ½
Goodtimes Ent. (cat #81034). Full frame. Dolby Digital 5.1 Surround Stereo. $19.98. Snapper. *LANG:* English; French; Spanish. *SUB:* French; Spanish. *CAP:* English. *FEATURES:* 18 chapters ▪ Production notes.
1983 (R) 113m/C Claudia Bryar, Osgood Perkins II, Anthony Perkins, Vera Miles, Meg Tilly, Robert Loggia, Dennis Franz; **D:** Richard Franklin; **W:** Tom Holland; **C:** Dean Cundey; **M:** Jerry Goldsmith.

Pulp Cinema

A compendium of interesting previews from classic thrillers and films noir from the late '40s and early '50s. The trailers themselves are rare and interesting, and most feature exclusive footage shot specifically for them, but the audio and visual presentation are awful. The sound is filled with hiss and crackle and the audio level varies constantly. The trailers are dirty, scratched, and display inordinate amounts of print scratches and digital noise. If given a proper DVD presentation, the contents would have been a valuable addition to a collection, but as it stands, a VHS would be an improvement. —DG
Movie: 𝄢𝄢 **DVD:** woof
Image Ent. (cat #ADE0903DVD, UPC 0143-81090321). Full frame. Dolby Digital Mono. $24.99. Keepcase. *LANG:* English. *FEATURES:* 45 chapters.
2001 99m/B

The Puppetmaster

Not to be confused with the long-running horror series, this Taiwanese film uses historical re-creations and voice-over narration to tell the story of Li Tien-lu, the island's renowned puppeteer. It's essentially the story of Taiwan in the 20th century, covering the years 1909 to 1945. Director Hou Hsiao-Hsien's curious narrative technique allows important events to take place offscreen and then describes them. To audiences without a strong background in Taiwanese history, it's initially offputting. DVD image is not a significant improvement over VHS tape, but seems to be an accurate re-creation of the original. Subtitles are optional. The extras are text. —MM
Movie: 𝄢𝄢𝄢 **DVD:** 𝄢𝄢
Winstar Home Ent. (cat #FLV5286, UPC 720917528625). Full frame. Stereo. $24.98. Keepcase. *LANG:* Mandarin. *SUB:*

English. *FEATURES:* 16 chapters • Filmographies and awards • Li family tree • Traditional puppet roles • Director and the Puppetmaster • Trailer.

1993 142m/C *TW* Li Tien-lu, Lin Chung, Yang Li-Yin, I Toshiro, Tsai Chen-Nan; **D:** Hsiao-Hsien Hou; **W:** We Nien-Jen, Tien-Wen Chu; **C:** Mark Lee Pin-Bing; **M:** Chen Ming-Chang.

Purple Noon

French director René Clément made this version of Patricia Highsmith's novel *The Talented Mr. Ripley* several decades before the Anthony Minghella version. Lovers of noirish fare will probably prefer this foreign original—the plotting is coffin-tight, and the actors include some excellent, unfamiliar faces. It was also the star-making role for Gallic heartthrob Alain Delon. Rich American Phillip Greenleaf (Ronet) refuses to come home from Italy, despite his father's dispatching young Tom Ripley (Delon) to fetch him for a $5,000 fee. Phillip is perfectly happy spending the family money on a yacht and romancing his fiancée, Marge Duval (Laforet). Tom and Phillip spend their time getting drunk and carousing with other friends and acquaintances on the Italian coast, much to the consternation of the faithful and forgiving Marge. Tom, a pauper living on Phillip's nickel, is an adept conman, having already convinced Phillip's father that he was an old friend. Phillip admits that his promises to return are empty. But even though they joke about how easy it would be for Tom to kill his "best pal" and take his place, Phillip has no idea of the schemes that are running through Tom's head. Henri Decaë's color photography is splendid. The Italian seasides are beautiful, yet the film never becomes a travelog. Such is the extent of René Clément's expert control, that we are almost immediately pulled into the tale, and the picture's superior production values become a seamless part of the fabric. DVD is a satisfactory disc which could have been better if the company had seen fit to give it a 16:9 transfer. As it is, the show is very colorful and clean, but not all that well-digitized. There are more compression flaws than there should be. This doesn't hurt the impact of the story, but the picture never pops to life, as does *The Young Girls of Rochefort* from the same company. An English track is included but is not particularly recommended unless one wishes to hear what the film sounded like when imported to the States. The original French title, *Plein Soleil*, appears to mean "full sun" and may have something to do with the bad sunburn Tom receives early in the film. Nowhere does the disc explain the significance of the English title. —*GE* **AKA:** Plein Soleil; Lust for Evil.

Movie: ♫♫♫ ½ **DVD:** ♫♫♫
Buena Vista Home Ent. (UPC 786936-166705). Widescreen (1.66:1) letterboxed. $24.98. Keepcase. *LANG:* French; Italian; English. *SUB:* English.

1960 (PG-13) 118m/C *FR* Alain Delon, Maurice Ronet, Marie Laforet, Erno Crisa,

Billy Kearns; **D:** Rene Clement; **W:** Rene Clement, Paul Gegauff; **C:** Henri Decae; **M:** Nino Rota.

The Purple Rose of Cairo

During the Depression, waitress and abused wife Cecilia (Farrow) feeds her desires for beauty by attending glossy Hollywood movies. After a particularly horrible day, she goes to see *The Purple Rose of Cairo* again and sits in the audience for three consecutive showings. The lead character, Tom Baxter (Daniels), takes notice of her, and magically steps off the screen and into the "real" world. As the movie characters, the theatre managers, and the movie studio try to figure out what to do, Cecilia teaches the wildly naïve Tom about her world. Allen's film (another where he doesn't appear) is a bittersweet comedy that explores the relationship between reality and fantasy. It manages to be exhilarating, uproarious, thought provoking, and tragic. The film-within-a-film is an absolutely perfect reproduction of the films of the era and Daniels plays both his roles with charm and aplomb. Danny Aiello's character is so loathsome he makes you want to leap onto the screen and lump him for Cecilia! The cast is a knockout but the ending is incredibly downbeat. A must-see for movie buffs. The disc conveys the warm, brownish hues and flesh-tones with vividness and accuracy but is slightly grainy. The mono sound is excellent. —*DG*

Movie: ♫♫♫ ½ **DVD:** ♫♫♫
MGM Home Ent. (cat #1001747, UPC 027-616860477). Widescreen (1.85:1) anamorphic. Mono. $19.98. Keepcase. *LANG:* English; French; Spanish. *SUB:* English; French; Spanish. *CAP:* English. *FEATURES:* Booklet with notes • Theatrical trailer • 16 chapters.

1985 (PG) 82m/C Mia Farrow, Jeff Daniels, Danny Aiello, Dianne Wiest, Van Johnson, Zoe Caldwell, John Wood, Michael Tucker, Edward Herrmann, Milo O'Shea, Glenne Headly, Karen Akers, Deborah Rush; **D:** Woody Allen; **W:** Woody Allen; **C:** Gordon Willis; **M:** Dick Hyman. *AWARDS:* British Acad. '85: Film, Orig. Screenplay; Cesar '86: Foreign Film; Golden Globes '86: Screenplay; N.Y. Film Critics '85: Screenplay; *NOM:* Oscars '85: Orig. Screenplay.

Putney Swope

Infamous in the '60s for its outrageousness, this fundamentally silly and overrated comedy is nothing more than an anachronism. Putney Swope (Johnson), the token black executive in a Madison Avenue ad agency, winds up in charge and promptly turns the place on its ear. The spoofy commercials are the alleged highpoint of the film. The criticisms of '60s politics and society are as ham-fisted and blatant as the times they parody. The low-budget film has never had much to offer in visual terms and there's little DVD can (or should) do to

improve things. The full frame image still has a tightly framed, cramped feeling to it. Director Downey is the father of actor Robert Downey Jr. —*MM*

Movie: ♫♫ **DVD:** ♫♫
Rhino (cat #R2 976029, UPC 603497602-926). Full frame. $24.98. Keepcase. *LANG:* English. *FEATURES:* Interview with Robert Downey Sr • Robert Downey Sr. filmography • 13 chapters.

1969 (R) 84m/B Arnold Johnson, Laura Greene, Stanley Gottlieb, Mel Brooks; **D:** Robert Downey; **W:** Robert Downey; **C:** Gerald Cotts; **M:** Charles Cura.

Putting It Together: Stephen Sondheim—A Musical Review

Expertly filmed performance of the Cameron Mackintosh stage production that celebrates the music of Stephen Sondheim. Features the return of Carol Burnett to the Broadway musical stage. Also included in the cast are: George Hearn, John Barrowman, Ruthie Henshall, and Bronson Pinchot. The video transfer on this disc is exceptional. Colors are vivid and bright while blacks are crisp and suffer no loss of definition. The full, rich soundtrack is also quite impressive. A few entertaining extras (particularly the onstage blooper) round the disc out. —*MJT*

Movie: ♫♫ ½ **DVD:** ♫♫♫
Goodtimes Ent. (cat #0581268, UPC 018-713812681). Widescreen (1.85:1) anamorphic. Dolby Digital 5.1 Surround; Dolby Digital Stereo. $24.95. Keepcase. *LANG:* English. *FEATURES:* 34 chapters • Cast bios • Interview with Carol Burnett • Onstage "blooper."

2001 96m/C Carol Burnett, George Hearn, Bronson Pinchot, Ruthie Henshall, John Barrowman; **D:** Don Roy King; **M:** Stephen Sondheim.

QB VII

Knighted physician Dr. Adam Kelno (Hopkins) brings a libel suit against American Jewish novelist Abraham Cady (Gazarra) for implicating him in war crimes. The two stars are superb and the supporting cast is vast. The ending is a stunner but it takes a long hike to reach it. The epic TV miniseries is spread over two discs. Production values are exceptional and the image quality is virtually pristine. This one looks much better than similar works of the early '70s. Sound, however, is absolutely ordinary. —*MM*

Movie: ♫♫♫ ½ **DVD:** ♫♫ ½
Columbia Tristar (cat #05850, UPC 04339-6058507). Full frame. Dolby Digital Mono. $29.98. Keepcase. *LANG:* English; French. *SUB:* English; French; Spanish. *CAP:* English. *FEATURES:* 56 chapters • Production notes • Filmographies • Trailers.

1974 313m/C Anthony Hopkins, Ben Gazzara, Lee Remick, Leslie Caron, Juliet Mills, John Gielgud, Anthony Quayle; **D:** Tom Gries; **W:** Edward Anhalt; **M:** Jerry Goldsmith.

Quadrophenia

Townshend's excellent rock opera about an alienated youth looking for life's meaning in Britain's rock scene circa 1963. Music by The Who is powerful and apt. Fine performance by Sting in his acting debut. While the restoration job performed on this film is admirable and the film does look better than it has since its initial release, there are few sections that are far too dark and there is noticeable grain in some scenes. But that is most likely due to the age of the print and is entirely forgivable. The soundtrack is excellent. There is no distortion present and the music (essential to this film) is reproduced quite nicely. While the disc's extras are too numerous for this review to do justice to, the commentary track, recorded 23 years after the fact, should be singled out as an entertaining and informative highlight. —*MJT*
Movie: 🎬🎬🎬 **DVD:** 🎬🎬🎬
Rhino (cat #R2976624, UPC 603497-662425). Widescreen (1.85:1) letterboxed. Dolby Digital 5.1 Surround; Dolby Digital 2.0 Stereo. $24.95. Keepcase. *LANG:* English. *FEATURES:* 28 chapters • Theatrical trailer • Interview with Sting • Commentary: director Franc Roddam • Photo gallery: publicity photos, memorabilia, continuity from scripts • Rhino's film restoration • Subtitled trivia tracks • Animated location map • Quiz: Are You a Mod or a Rocker? • The Who discography • Cast & crew filmographies • Mod film list from Modculture.com • Easter Eggs: "Portrait of a Mod," film reviews, riot button, more.
1979 (R) 115m/C *GB* Phil Daniels, Mark Wingett, Philip Davis, Leslie Ash, Sting, Garry Cooper, Gary Shail, Toyah Willcox, Trevor Laird, Ray Winstone; *D:* Franc Roddam; *W:* Franc Roddam, Martin Stellman, Dave Humphries, Pete Townshend; *C:* Brian Tufano; *M:* John Entwhistle, Pete Townshend.

Que Viva Mexico

Eisenstein's grand unfinished folly on the history of Mexico was reconstructed and released in 1979 by his protégé Grigori Alexandrov. Divided into four sections: "Sandunga" covers Tehuantepec jungles and its inhabitants; "Manguei" is about a peasant and his bride; "Fiesta" devotes itself to bullfighting and romance; and "Soldadera" depicts the 1910 Mexican revolution through frescoes. Considering the project's checkered history, it's in fairly good shape with only moderate snow and flecks. Static on the soundtrack is really more distracting. DVD also includes two short films, "Romance Sentimentale" (1930; 20 min.) and "Misery and Fortune of Woman" (1929; 20 min.). —*MM* **AKA:** Da Zdravstvuyet Meksika.
Movie: 🎬🎬🎬 **DVD:** 🎬🎬 ½
Kino on Video (cat #K202, UPC 7383290-20224). Full frame. $29.95. Keepcase. *LANG:* Russian. *SUB:* English. *FEATURES:* 8 chapters • Press and PR clippings.

1932 85m/B *RU D:* Sergei Eisenstein; *W:* Sergei Eisenstein, Grigori Alexandrov; *C:* Eduard Tisse.

Queen Bee

Joan Crawford stars as the magnetic and monstrous Eva, the titular "Queen Bee" (a strained metaphor, at best). When her sister-in-law (Palmer) announces an engagement to Judson (Ireland), who is Eva's secret lover, Eva vows to halt the wedding at all costs. Her manipulations build to tragic consequences. The lukewarm screenplay calls for Crawford to carry the movie on her own, and she gives an admirable effort. The mono soundtrack is excellent for a film of this age. Likewise, the black-and-white video has been restored nicely, although the entire set seems to be comprised of shimmering shutters. —*BG*
Movie: 🎬🎬 **DVD:** 🎬🎬🎬
Columbia Tristar (cat #70889, UPC 0433-96708891). Widescreen (1.85:1) anamorphic. Dolby Mono. $24.95. Keepcase. *LANG:* English. *SUB:* English; Spanish; Portuguese; Thai; Chinese; Korean. *CAP:* English. *FEATURES:* 28 chapters • Production notes • Talent files • Trailers • Vintage advertising stills.
1955 94m/B Joan Crawford, Barry Sullivan, John Ireland, Lucy Marlow, Betsy Palmer, Fay Wray; *D:* Ranald MacDougall; *W:* Ranald MacDougall; *C:* Charles B(ryant) Lang Jr.; *M:* George Duning. *AWARDS: NOM:* Oscars '55: B&W Cinematog., Costume Des. (B&W).

Queens Logic

Sleeper ensemble comedy is in the tradition of *The Big Chill* with the trials and episodic adventures of the "old neighborhood gang" who gather for a wedding. Most of the film centers on Olin and girlfriend Webb. Will he bolt before the ceremony? The full-frame image is not significantly better than on VHS tape. —*MM*
Movie: 🎬🎬🎬 **DVD:** 🎬🎬
Pioneer Ent. (cat #DVD68923). Full frame. Dolby Digital Stereo. $24.98. Keepcase. *LANG:* English. *FEATURES:* Trailer • 16 chapters.
1991 (R) 116m/C John Malkovich, Kevin Bacon, Jamie Lee Curtis, Linda Fiorentino, Joe Mantegna, Ken Olin, Tom Waits, Chloe Webb, Ed Marinaro, Kelly Bishop, Tony Spiridakis; *D:* Steve Rash; *W:* Tony Spiridakis; *C:* Amir M. Mokri; *M:* Joe Jackson.

Queer As Folk: The Complete First Season

Predatory, gay 29-year-old Brian (Harold) takes 17-year-old innocent, Justin (Harrison) home for a one-night stand and finds the closeted lad becoming firmly enmeshed in his life. As Justin tries to establish a relationship with Brian, the series illuminates Brian's circle of friends, including Michael (Sparks), a longtime friend who also has a crush on Brian;

Michael's mom (Gless), a single woman who is proud of her gay son and Emmett, a camp but strong clothing store clerk. This landmark series is based on two British miniseries created by Russell T. Davies. While the initial episodes are almost carbon copy remakes, latter episodes wisely focus on new characters and tell different stories with the pre-existing ones. Once up and running, the U.S. series distinguishes itself, creating a brand new vibe and mood of its own. The performances are all strong (Gless's is absolute perfection), but Sparks's body language seems overly done and always seems enacted. The show features extremely graphic ("NC-17" style) scenes of gay and lesbian sex. It's refreshing to see a series so brashly "gay," but the sex scenes occasionally seem excessive and feel as if they were designed solely to shock Midwest Republican grandmothers. Also, the show deserves a much better title sequence than the cheap, awful, "punk" music–backed crap one used in this season. While the series should be applauded for avoiding stereotyped characters, it creates brand new (somewhat sexually irresponsible) ones. The discs feature sharp and colorful image transfers, but they seem excessively grainy and somewhat smeary. The sound is loud and terrific, making most Surround channel use from the club music that predominates the soundtrack. The set is jammed to the gills with extras but the audio commentaries are awkwardly designed. Assembled from snippets of videotaped cast and crew comments, they provide intermittent bits of interest. When commentators appear on the commentary, they share a split-screen with the episode. There are so many moments filled with dead air that waiting for comments becomes a chore. It would have played much better assembled into a "making of" featurette. What's particularly appalling is the lack of regard for the original British series. There's much talk by the executive producers about how important the staging of the early sex scenes were and how groundbreaking it is, but they don't bother to mention that these "fresh, original" scenes are simply remakes with identical staging and shot selection. The deleted scenes are interesting and are introduced in very funny Hal Sparks wraparound segments. The outtakes are hilarious. —*DG*
Movie: 🎬🎬🎬 **DVD:** 🎬🎬🎬
Showtime Networks, Inc. (cat #SHO2007, UPC 758445200720). Widescreen (1.78:1) anamorphic. Dolby Digital Surround. $119.98. Keepcase. *LANG:* English; Spanish. *SUB:* English. *CAP:* English. *FEATURES:* Episodes 1–22 • "Next on" episode teasers • Episode summaries • Commentary for episodes 1, 11, 18 • Deleted scenes • Outtakes • Bios and interviews with cast & crew • Season 2 trailer • Photo gallery • DVD-ROM website link with exclusive content.
2001 1205m/C Gale Harold, Scott Lowell, Randy Harrison, Hal Sparks, Peter Paige, Sharon Gless, Chris Potter; *D:* Russell Mulcahy.

Queer As F***k: Bizarre Short Films

A better-than-average collection of six odd, gay-themed short films. The best is the sick and hilarious "Jeffrey's Hollywood Screen Trick," which tells of one man's disastrous bar outing. Also of note is "The Trey Billings Show," a dead-on parody of a gay public access cable show. It hits several hilarious points and features an uproarious quadruple role lead performance but is a bit overlong at a half hour. Oddly enough, "Pyongyang Robogirl" has no story and zero gay interest, but it does document the strange, robotic gestures of a Pyongyang traffic cop. "Soda Pop" is pretty undistinguished and "Dirty Baby Does Fire Island" is more irritating than entertaining. "Shame No More" is an amusing, black-and-white parody of '50s classroom health films. The shorts are well presented, especially considering the variable quality of the source material. Most are somewhat grainy (especially "Shame No More") with occasional print marks. The sound is somewhat raw as well, but it's predominantly clean. The volume levels vary throughout. —DG
Movie: 🦴🦴½ **DVD:** 🦴🦴🦴
First Run Features (cat #FRF910187D, UPC 720229910187). Full frame. Mono. $29.95. Keepcase. *LANG:* English. *FEATURES:* Director bios • 1 chapter per short • Trailers.
2001 73m/C D: David Briggs, Todd Downing, Patrick McGuinn, John Krokidas.

Querelle

Sexually ambivalent sailor Querelle (Davis) arrives in the port of Brest where he smuggles drugs and involves himself in the area's sexually free inhabitants. A self-consciously artificial and pretentious adaptation of Jean Genet's *Querelle of Brest* from Germany's famous self-loathing homosexual filmmaker. While fascinating for its studio-bound set design and perpetual "sunset" lighting, it's dull and tortuous. There's no story on display and none ever develops. Jeanne Moreau looks like hell, but her song "Each Man Kills the Thing He Loves" will stick in your head, for better or worse. While *Querelle* is a gay-bar perennial (usually playing in the background with the sound off), its depiction of homosexual relations and sex is neither attractive nor self-affirming. The disc preserves the extremely wide framing that is essential to this film. The transfer itself is richly colored, but is soft and grainy. Images also have a tendency to smear during horizontal camera moves and there's some distracting jitter caused by poorly monitored DVNR (Digital Video Noise Reduction). Sound is fine. —DG
Movie: 🦴½ **DVD:** 🦴🦴
Columbia Tristar (cat #06745, UPC 043-396067455). Widescreen (2.35:1) anamorphic. Mono. $24.95. Keepcase. *LANG:* English; French. *SUB:* English; French; Spanish. *CAP:* English. *FEATURES:* Trailers • 28 chapters.

1983 (R) 106m/C *GE* Brad Davis, Jeanne Moreau, Franco Nero, Laurent Malet; **D:** Rainer Werner Fassbinder; **W:** Rainer Werner Fassbinder, Burkhard Driest; **C:** Xaver Schwarzenberger, Josef Vavra; **M:** Peer Raben.

Quigley Down Under

Western sharpshooter Matthew Quigley (Selleck) goes to Australia in search of employment, but is horrified to discover that he's been hired not to hunt wild dogs, "dingos," but the aborigines. It's essentially a '50s western moved to another continent, and that's exactly what it looks and sounds like on DVD. The image is not the sharpest, but excessive grain and artifacts are absent in the many panoramic landscapes. The three leads are first-rate, and so is Basil Poledouris's stirring score. —MM
Movie: 🦴🦴🦴 **DVD:** 🦴🦴🦴
MGM Home Ent. (cat #1002370, UPC 027-616865816). Widescreen (2.35:1) anamorphic. Dolby Digital Surround Stereo; Mono. $14.95. Keepcase. *LANG:* English; French; Spanish. *SUB:* French; Spanish. *CAP:* English. *FEATURES:* 16 chapters • "Rebirth of the Western" featurette • Trailer.
1990 (PG-13) 121m/C *AU* Tom Selleck, Laura San Giacomo, Alan Rickman, Chris Haywood, Ron Haddrick, Tony Bonner, Roger Ward, Ben Mendelsohn, Jerome Ehlers, Conor McDermottroe; **D:** Simon Wincer; **W:** John Hill; **C:** David Eggby; **M:** Basil Poledouris.

Rabid Grannies

Fans of alternative film have always loved this one for the title, if for nothing else. It's the story of two aging sisters (Aymerie and Brackman) who invite the relatives over for a birthday party. They receive a surprise from their devil-worshiping nephew that turns them into cannibalistic monsters. The bloody gore effects are on the amateurish side, but that's O.K. for this Belgian satire that's a bit too talky. DVD does no favors to the grainy, impoverished image. Dark clothes and shadows are featureless masses. The main benefit here—if it can be called that—is a director's commentary. The Troma folk treat all of their releases seriously and this one has all the expected extras. —MM
Movie: 🦴🦴½ **DVD:** 🦴🦴
Troma Team Video (UPC 790357997039). Full frame. $24.98. Keepcase. *LANG:* English. *FEATURES:* 9 chapters • Troma tour and game • Interviews • Photo album • Commentary: director.
1989 (R) 89m/C *BE* Catherine Aymerie, Caroline Brackman, Danielle Daven, Raymond Lescot, Anne Marie Fox, Richard Cotica, Patricia Davie; **D:** Emmanuel Kervyn; **W:** Emmanuel Kervyn; **C:** Hugh Labye; **M:** Jean-Bruno Castelain, Pierre-Damien Castelain.

Race the Sun

A decent cast and a mediocre story are strung up by a lousy script, dialogue cut

and pasted from every film about misfits who bicker amongst themselves and then triumph against a contrived bad guy. Halle Berry plays a new high school teacher saddled with a group of misfit teens and the losing prospect of racing their self-designed solar-powered car in an Australian road race. James Belushi plays the shop teacher dragged along for the adventure of a weekend. Reliable Steve Zahn, capable of spicing up any film with his Snoopy the beagle aura, plays the bad guy who has won the race in the past. Casey Affleck plays the "cute" team leader and J. Moki Cho is the stereotypical Hawaiian "fat kid." Contrary to the hyperbole on the box, Berry and Belushi do not end up together at the end, and in fact, there is no romance in the film for her. If you're wondering, as I did, why this tripe gets a DVD release, try to imagine it being called "Hey, Halle's Got an Oscar Now." There are no special features beyond the abundance of subtitle options that the studio almost always includes; the same sound and picture quality you would expect from any average DVD, and hey, it's great fodder for emotionally challenged 10-year-olds. —JAS
Movie: 🦴 **DVD:** 🦴🦴🦴
Columbia Tristar (cat #07755, UPC 0433-96077553). Full frame. Dolby Digital 5.1 Surround. $19.95. Keepcase. *LANG:* English. *SUB:* English; French; Spanish; Portuguese; Chinese; Korean; Thai. *FEATURES:* 28 chapters.
1996 (PG) 100m/C Halle Berry, James Belushi, Casey Affleck, Eliza Dushku, Kevin Tighe, Anthony Michael Ruivivar, J. Moki Cho, Dion Basco, Sara Tanaka, Nadja Pionilla, Steve Zahn, Bill Hunter; **D:** Charles Kanganis; **W:** Barry Morrow; **C:** David Burr; **M:** Graeme Revell.

Radical Jack

Country singer Billy Ray Cyrus and his funky mullet hairdo star as CIA agent Jack Reynolds who's brought out of retirement to catch a bunch of rural arms dealers. The action sequences are simply pitiful—slow and clumsily staged. DVD image and sound are equal to VHS tape. No-frills disc does not contain a menu. —MM
Movie: 🦴🦴 **DVD:** 🦴🦴
Studio Home Ent. (cat #VM7845D, UPC 031398784524). Full frame. Stereo. $14.99. Keepcase. *LANG:* English.
2000 (R) 95m/C Billy Ray Cyrus, Dedee Pfeiffer, Cassie Branham, Noah Blake, George "Buck" Flower; **D:** James Allen Bradley; **W:** James Allen Bradley; **C:** Carl Bartels.

Radio Days

Warmly told period drama about the golden days of radio centers on the exploits of a young Woody Allen–type child (Green) and his hilarious lower-class family. As their lives revolve around the omnipresent radio programming of the period, we are witness to a series of anecdotal remembrances of various episodic events in the lives of the family and unconnected fictional radio performers. It's not really satisfying (or developed) as a full-fledged drama (and not intended as one), but it's quite a funny, good-natured, and heartfelt film. Fans of classic radio will certainly appreciate the atmosphere of the film and its replication of this wonderful bygone era. The disc is strongly colored—primarily in brown and golden yellows—but a tad soft and excessively smeary with digital grain. Scenes with a foggy, overcast look suffer the most and tend to appear as if the film is being projected on a scratched and worn-out theatre screen. A bit of a step down from other Woody Allen releases. The mono sound is fine. —DG

Movie: 🎬🎬🎬 **DVD:** 🎬🎬
MGM Home Ent. (cat #1001748, UPC 027-616860484). Widescreen (1.85:1) anamorphic. Mono. $19.98. Keepcase. LANG: English; French; Spanish. SUB: English; French; Spanish. CAP: English. FEATURES: Booklet with notes • Theatrical trailer • 16 chapters.
1987 (PG) 89m/C Mia Farrow, Dianne Wiest, Julie Kavner, Michael Tucker, Wallace Shawn, Josh Mostel, Tony Roberts, Jeff Daniels, Kenneth Mars, Seth Green, William Magerman, Diane Keaton, Renee Lippin, Danny Aiello, Gina DeAngelis, Kitty Carlisle Hart, Mercedes Ruehl, Tito Puente; **D:** Woody Allen; **W:** Woody Allen; **C:** Carlo Di Palma; **Nar:** Woody Allen. AWARDS: NOM: Oscars '87: Art Dir./Set Dec., Orig. Screenplay.

Rage at Dawn

An outlaw gang is tracked by a special agent who must bend the rules a little to get the bad guys. Not surprisingly, he gets his girl as well. A solid standard of the genre with some clever plot twists. DVD displays a few registration problems and some print damage. Both clear up quickly and most of the film looks pretty good. Mild static is audible throughout. Barebones disc contains no links. —MM **AKA:** Seven Bad Men.

Movie: 🎬🎬 ½ **DVD:** 🎬🎬 ½
Troma Team Video (cat #2015). Widescreen letterboxed. Dolby Digital Mono. $19.95. Keepcase. LANG: English. FEATURES: Trailer.
1955 87m/C Randolph Scott, Forrest Tucker, Mala Powers, J. Carrol Naish, Edgar Buchanan; **D:** Tim Whelan; **W:** Horace McCoy; **C:** Ray Rennahan; **M:** Paul Sawtell.

Raiders of Leyte Gulf

Long-unavailable Philippine film from the early 1960s is a throwback to the propaganda that Hollywood produced during WWII. This one features sadistic buck-toothed Japanese soldiers. The protagonists are American POWs and Philippine guerrillas who are setting the stage for MacArthur's return. Director Romero would go on to a busy career in horror and other genres. This black-and-white effort exhibits surface damage of varying degrees throughout. Considering the film's age, it

still looks pretty good, though not that much better than VHS tape. Sound makes the discordant theme even worse. —MM

Movie: 🎬🎬 **DVD:** 🎬🎬
Winstar Home Ent. (cat #FLV5297, UPC 72-0917529721). Full frame. $14.98. Keepcase. LANG: English. FEATURES: 16 chapters • Filmographies • Trailers.
1963 80m/B PH Leopold Salcedo, Michael Parsons, Jennings Sturgeon, Liza Moreno; **D:** Eddie Romero; **W:** Carl Kuntze, E.F. Romero; **C:** F. Sacdalan; **M:** Tito Arevalo.

Railroaded

When a cop is murdered during a holdup, a young man is framed for the crime. His sister (Ryan) teams up with a cop (Beaumont) to prove his innocence. This tense, low-key film noir is surprisingly well-produced for a PRC cheapie and features memorable turns by Ireland as an ice-cold killer (who uses perfumed bullets!) and his moll Randolph. Some great hard-boiled dialogue adds spice to the mix. The print material used for the transfer shows its age with consistent, though light marks and scratches. Contrasts favor darker tones. The transfer shows a bit too much alias defects and digital noise. The mono sound is fine. —DG

Movie: 🎬🎬 ½ **DVD:** 🎬🎬
Kino on Video (cat #K145DVD, UPC 7383-29014520). Full frame. Mono. $29.95. Keepcase. LANG: English. FEATURES: 9 chapters • Insert card with contemporary review excerpts.
1947 72m/B John Ireland, Sheila Ryan, Hugh Beaumont, Ed Kelly, Jane Randolph; **D:** Anthony Mann; **W:** John C. Higgins; **C:** Guy Roe; **M:** Alvin Levin.

Rainbow Bridge

Unscripted experimental film is a trippy-dippy mess. Hippies search for their consciousness in Hawaii. Concert footage from Jimi Hendrix's final performance is the high point. The filmmakers must have had access to plentiful consciousness-altering substances. Note the introductory narration over the blank screen. Both image and sound are exceptionally rough, reflecting the original elements, the minuscule budget, and the talent behind the entire enterprise. —MM

Movie: 🎬 **DVD:** 🎬🎬
Rhino (cat #4461). Full frame. Mono. $24.98. Snapper. LANG: English. FEATURES: 3 trailers • 19 chapters • Jump to song • Jump to interview.
1971 (R) 74m/C Chuck Wein, Herbie Fletcher, Pat Hartley; **D:** Chuck Wein; **C:** Vilis Lapenieks.

Random Acts of Violence

Gangster Isaiah Knight (McCoy) is trying to go straight, but is forced back on the streets to avenge his mother and sister, murdered by Knight's fellow gang members. He won't stop until he has taken out his former friend and greatest foe, Lynch

(Mack-10). This low-budget urban drama moves along at a fast pace, although the performances are pretty poor. The picture is average, with some noticeable grain and scratching from the source material in the more brightly lit scenes. The Surround mix isn't used much except for some gunshots, but the bass is clear and heavy for the hip-hop soundtrack. —DRL

Movie: 🎬 ½ **DVD:** 🎬🎬
York Ent. (cat #1170, UPC 7507231170-27). Full frame. Dolby 5.1 Surround. $14.99. Keepcase. LANG: English. SUB: Spanish. FEATURES: 25 chapters • Behind-the-scenes featurette • Mack-10 discography and filmography • Trailers.
2002 (R) 85m/C Chyna McCoy, Mack-10, Jaih Baxter, Jason Morck, Nina James; **D:** Kantz; **W:** Kantz; **C:** Andy Steinman.

Random Encounter

Executive Berkley becomes involved in extortion and murder cover-up after she takes a shine to a mystery man and their rendezvous goes awry. Both image and sound are acceptable for a video premiere; no better than VHS tape. —MM

Movie: 🎬🎬 **DVD:** 🎬🎬
York Ent. (cat #1006). Full frame. $24.98. Keepcase. LANG: English. SUB: Spanish. FEATURES: Trailer • 25 chapters • Behind-the-scenes featurette.
1998 100m/C CA Elizabeth Berkley, Joel Wyner, Frank Schorpion, Barry Flatman, Mark Walker, Ellen David, Susan Glover, Frank Fontaine; **D:** Douglas Jackson; **W:** Matt Dorff; **C:** Georges Archambault; **M:** Daniel Scott.

Random Hearts

Dutch Van Den Broeck is an internal affairs cop played by Harrison Ford; Kristen Scott Thomas plays a congresswoman. Both believe their individual marriages are going well. When a plane carrying both of their significant others crashes, they learn that the two were having an affair. The rest of the movie is a look at how the two survivors cope with their loss and as a result, become closer together. There are enjoyable little moments and a good supporting performance by director Syndey Pollack, but getting to these points is a laborious journey. There is such a cold, bland feel to the movie that it's hard to become involved with any of the characters. It doesn't feel right to have these two characters get together after their losses and the two stars don't really have much chemistry together, either. Images are bright and consistently sharp and detailed. Colors are also vivid throughout, showcasing some beautiful scenery. There's a little bit of grain here and there, and in a couple of scenes there's a slight amount of shimmering. The sound captures the dialogue and music score with clarity and presence. The commentary is worthwhile and focuses more on the production than the actors. There are a few gaps but when Pollack really gets going on a particular subject, he does offer quite a bit of in-depth information. The deleted scenes aren't of too much interest but are a nice inclusion. Unfortunately, Pollack's commentary during these scenes is *not* optional. The featurette is the standard HBO promotional fluff piece. —AB/DG

Movie: 🎬🎬 **DVD:** 🎬🎬🎬

Columbia Tristar Home Video (UPC 4339-6040007). Widescreen (1.85:1) anamorphic. Dolby Digital 5.1 Surround; Dolby Digital Surround. $19.95. Keepcase. *LANG:* English. *SUB:* English. *CAP:* English. *FEATURES:* Theatrical trailer • Deleted scenes • Commentary: Pollack • Chapter links • "Making of" featurette • Isolated music score.

1999 (R) 133m/C Harrison Ford, Kristin Scott Thomas, Sydney Pollack, Charles S. Dutton, Bonnie Hunt, Dennis Haysbert, Richard Jenkins, Paul Guilfoyle, Susanna Thompson, Peter Coyote, Dylan Baker, Lynne Thigpen, Bill Cobbs, Susan Floyd, Edie Falco, Kate Mara; *D:* Sydney Pollack; *W:* Kurt Luedtke; *C:* Philippe Rousselot; *M:* Dave Grusin.

Ranma 1/2: Random Rhapsody—Wacky Winter Wonderland

Martial artists Ranma Saotome and his father are on a spiritual journey in China when they fall into enchanted pools. Now cursed, the two undergo transformations whenever they get wet: Ranma turns into a red-haired female and his father turns into a giant panda. Living with their friends, the Tendo family, wacky romantic hijinks ensue between Ranma and the lovely Akane. This hit Japanese animated series is based on the comics by Rumiko Takahashi and is charming, sweet, and hilarious. Included on this disc are three episodes: "A Xmas without Ranma" (title says all), "A Cold Day in Furinkan," featuring a strange little girl and a snowbeast, and (the strongest) "Akane Goes to the Hospital," where she recovers from a broken leg. Unfortunately, these late season episodes are fairly run-of-the-mill: amusing fare but never hilarious and forgettable. The disc transfers are appropriately colorful and predominantly free of digital noise. The dubbing job is strong and a worthy replication of the Japanese language track. Sound is limited but clear and strong. —DG

Movie: 🎬🎬 **DVD:** 🎬🎬🎬

Viz Video (cat #DRRR05, UPC 782009079-095). Full frame. Dolby Stereo Surround. $29.95. Keepcase. *LANG:* Japanese; English. *SUB:* English. *FEATURES:* 3 episodes • 5 chapters per episode • Insert card with chapter listings.

2001 72m/C JP

The Rape of the Vampire

This two-part movie was originally created as a half-hour short co-feature. The last hour was filmed to bring it to feature length. This, the premiere feature of

French avant-garde cinema-stylist Jean Rollin, is a pretty crude effort, but it conveys the director's flair for poetic visuals, gaudy pulp storytelling, and female nudity. Attempting to cure three sisters (who have been lead to believe they are vampires by their superstitious community) in a dilapidated old house brings a young man to disaster. The sisters are killed and he is (surprisingly) bitten, which turns him into a vampire. This puts them into conflict with the Queen of the Vampires. The plot is not very compelling and the film is slowly paced, but it is visual and unique. It's a horror camp mood piece than a horror film, and those expecting scares or traditional storytelling will be sorely disappointed. The disc features a sharp image, perfect contrasts, and rich blacks. The print element used has oft-visible marks, slight scratches, and the edges of objects have a tendency to shimmer. The sound is acceptable and mostly clean but occasionally distorts during loud sounds but this is more intrinsic to the low-budget nature of the motion picture, then to technical transfer flaws. —DG *AKA:* Le Viol du Vampire.

Movie: 🎬🎬 ½ **DVD:** 🎬🎬🎬

Image Ent. (cat #ID5638SADVD, UPC 014-381563825). Widescreen (1.66:1) letterboxed. Mono. $24.99. Keepcase. *LANG:* French. *SUB:* English. *FEATURES:* Trailer • Stills and poster gallery • 16 chapters • Insert booklet with notes.

1968 91m/B *FR* Solange Pradel, Bernard Letrou, Ursule Pauly, Catherine Deville; *D:* Jean Rollin; *W:* Jean Rollin; *C:* Guy Leblond, Antoine Harispe; *M:* Yvon Geraud, François Tusques.

Rappin'-N-Rhyming

Much of the action (too much) of this curious low-budget effort takes place in a high school classroom where the teens recite their efforts at verse. A little of it goes a very long way. Both acting and writing are on a semi-professional level. The exceptional amount of grain in the image makes it even harder to take. DVD image is worse than most tapes. —MM

Movie: 🎬 ½ **DVD:** 🎬 ½

York Ent. (cat #YPD-1165, UPC 75072311-6525). Full frame. $14.99. Keepcase. *LANG:* English. *FEATURES:* Trailers.

2000 90m/C Tami-Adrian George, Rahim Muhammad, Nicole Pulliam; *D:* Todd Ryan; *W:* Todd Ryan.

Raptor

The Corman organization recycles the basic ideas and effects from the *Carnosaur* series with dramatically less-effective results. It's more dinosaurs loose in the desert with Eric Roberts as the local sheriff and Corbin Bernsen as the semi-mad scientist. The critters are about as frightening as any sock puppet could be. On their commentary track between beers, director Jim Wynorski (as Jay Andrews) and star Melissa Brasselle admit as much. That's the only improve-

ment, dubious as it is, that DVD can make over VHS tape. —MM

Movie: 🎬🎬 **DVD:** 🎬🎬 ½

New Concorde (cat #NH20773 D, UPC 736991477491). Full frame. $19.98. Keepcase. *LANG:* English. *SUB:* Spanish. *FEATURES:* 24 chapters • Talent files • Trailers.

2001 (R) 81m/C Eric Roberts, Corbin Bernsen, Melissa Brasselle, Tim Abell, Harrison Paige, Lorissa McComas, Frank Novack; *D:* Jim Wynorski; *W:* Jim Wynorski, Michael B. Druxman, Frances Doel; *C:* Andrea V. Rossotto; *M:* James Horner.

Rashomon

Kurosawa's brilliant visual poem on the nature of truth is a certifiable classic by anyone's definition. When a woodcutter, a Samurai, the Samurai's wife, and a half-crazy bandit (Mifune) go before a judge, they can only agree on one thing: a man has been murdered. Their stories tell more about each of them than about the crime. Criterion has done their usual impeccable job of restoring and packaging this wonderful film that belongs in any serious collection. The Richie commentary is strictly optional, but the Altman introduction contains excellent observations and some great anecdotes. The booklet is beautifully produced. Newly translated subtitles are easy to read. The "Akira Kurosawa on Rashomon" extra is a reprinted excerpt from his book *Something Like an Autobiography*. Also included are excerpts from "The World of Kazuo Miyagawa," a documentary about the cinematographer, and reprints of the *Rashomon* source stories, Ryunosuke Akutagawa's "In a Grove" and "Rashomon." —LA *AKA:* In the Woods.

Movie: 🎬🎬🎬🎬 **DVD:** 🎬🎬🎬🎬

Criterion (cat #138, UPC 37429161821). Full frame. $39.98. Keepcase. *LANG:* Japanese; English. *SUB:* English. *FEATURES:* Commentary: Japanese film historian Donald Richie • Video intro by director Robert Altman • Excerpts from "The World of Kazuo Miyagawa" • Source stories, Akutagawa's "In a Grove" and "Rashomon" • 13 chapters • Trailer.

1951 83m/B *JP* Machiko Kyo, Toshiro Mifune, Masayuki Mori, Takashi Shimura, Minoru Chiaki, Kichijiro Ueda, Daisuke Kato; *D:* Akira Kurosawa; *W:* Akira Kurosawa, Shinobu Hashimoto; *C:* Kazuo Miyagawa; *M:* Fumio Hayasaka. *AWARDS:* Oscars '51: Foreign Film; Natl. Bd. of Review '51: Director (Kurosawa); Venice Film Fest. '51: Film; *NOM:* Oscars '52: Art Dir./Set Dec., B&W.

Rat

Imagine the Franz Kafka version of *Stuart Little* with an Irish setting. That's essentially what's going on in this story of Hubert Flynn (Postlethwaite), an ordinary man who turns into a rat one night. His wife Conchita (Staunton) is not amused, but when a reporter offers to turn poor Hubert's story into a book (and possibly a film), she considers the bright side. Perhaps it's the use of a real rat in most scenes—instead of a cuter animatronic or CGI critter—that gives this light material a dark sense. The image, however, is extraordinarily bright, detailed, and sharp. It's simply superb, making this Irish production the equal of similar Hollywood fare. Sound is fine. —*MM*

Movie: 🦴🦴½ **DVD:** 🦴🦴🦴
Universal Studios (cat #21390, UPC 0251-92139024). Widescreen (1.85:1) anamorphic. Dolby Digital 5.1 Surround Stereo. $26.98. Keepcase. *LANG:* English. *SUB:* French. *CAP:* English. *FEATURES:* 18 chapters • "Behind the Rat" featurette • Commentary: Steve Barron, Imelda Staunton • Trailer • Production notes.
2000 (PG) 91m/C Pete Postlethwaite, Imelda Staunton, Frank Kelly, David Wilmot; *D:* Steven Barron; *W:* Wesley Burrowes; *C:* Brendan Galvin; *M:* Pete Briquette, Bob Geldof.

Rat Race

Semi-remake of *It's a Mad, Mad, Mad, Mad World* follows a group of contestants (Goldberg, Chapman, Lovitz, Najimy, Gooding, Meyer, Smart, Atkinson, Knight, Green, and Vieluf) who are dashing from Las Vegas to Silver City, New Mexico, to win $2 million stashed in a train station locker by a casino owner (Cleese). The whole thing is meant to amuse his high-rollers. The slapstick and sight gags are well paced and, for my money, really funny. It ends on a note of coerced philanthropy that's perfect for our times. The film is put together with an inventive sense of style and a nice use of effects. Note the transition from the animated opening credits to live action. Unfortunately, the music doesn't hold up all the way through. Some of the better comic moments are weakened by familiar classical pieces. DVD image isn't as bright and sharp as some contemporary studio releases but it appears to be an accurate re-creation of the original. Surround effects really come into play during the big scenes involving the flying cow, rocket car, etc. —*MM*

Movie: 🦴🦴🦴 **DVD:** 🦴🦴🦴
Paramount (cat #33684, UPC 097363368-441). Widescreen anamorphic. Dolby Digital 5.1 Surround Stereo; Dolby Surround. $29.98. Keepcase. *LANG:* English; French. *SUB:* English. *CAP:* English. *FEATURES:* 15 chapters • "Making of" featurette • Deleted scenes • Bloopers • Interview with Zucker and Breckman • "Jerry and Andy Call the Actors."
2001 (PG-13) 92m/C John Cleese, Whoopi Goldberg, Cuba Gooding Jr., Jon Lovitz, Breckin Meyer, Amy Smart, Seth Green, Kathy Najimy, Rowan Atkinson, Wayne Knight, Kathy Bates, Dean Cain, Vince Vieluf, Lanei Chapman, Paul Rodriguez; *D:* Jerry Zucker; *W:* Andy Breckman; *C:* Thomas Ackerman; *M:* John Powell.

Rats

Two hundred and twenty five years after a nuclear holocaust, a gang of post-apoca-

lyptic punks finds a building with a secret stockpile of food and a mini-greenhouse with fresh vegetables. Unfortunately, the area is plagued by man-eating rats that lay siege to the building and pick off (or more accurately, gnaw off) the gang members. A hilariously inept film that displays barely adequate photography, a terrible script, and worse acting. The post-apocalyptic gang members all look laughably '80s and the black gang member is ridiculously (if not offensively) named "Chocolate." Worst of all, the ever placid "rats" (which appear to be white labs rats dyed gray) don't evoke any fear whatsoever. The only way these "rats" appear to attack is when an unseen production assistant dumps them on the actors from offscreen. One feels more sorry for the rats than the actors. Not aggravating or depressing, just dull and bereft of any tension or thrills. The finale is absolutely stupid. The disc is satisfying, if a tad soft. The softness may be an aspect of the photography as the opening and end titles are razor sharp and free of any distortion. The colors seem accurate. Framing seems a bit tight on top. Sound is flat with occasional distortion when dialogue is shouted. The featurette focuses solely on this film and *Hell of the Living Dead*, which are both released by the same distributor. Mattei seems amiable enough—it's just a shame none of these films shows any skill or aptitude for the genre. Mattei claims the "rats" were guinea pigs, but we're not convinced. The original poster (which is printed on the insert card and partially on the front cover) is terrific. (By the way, this one is not to be confused with the biopic *Minnesota Fats: The Knight of Terror.*) —*DG*
AKA: Rats: Night of Terror.
Movie: 🦴 **DVD:** 🦴🦴
Anchor Bay (cat #DV11752, UPC 0131311-75295). Widescreen (1.85:1) anamorphic. Mono. $19.98. Keepcase. *LANG:* English. *FEATURES:* "Hell Rats of the Living Dead: Interview with Director Bruno Mattei" • Theatrical trailer • Director bio • 25 chapters • Insert card.
1983 97m/C Richard Raymond, Richard Cross, Alex McBride; *D:* Bruno Mattei; *W:* Claudio Fragasso.

Ratz

Fun, but uneven "Cinderella" tale aimed directly at teenage girls. Marci (Vanessa Lengies) and Summer (Caroline Elliot) are unpopular girls who need dates to the big dance. When local curio shop owner Doris (Kathy Baker) finds a magic ring, things begin to get a little strange. Wanting to help the girls, Doris wishes for them to have dates, turning a pair of rats into teenage boys. The only problem is that they continue to act like rats. If the movie had stuck to this plot, it would have been much better, but instead there are several different subplots and *Ratz* never really seems to find its focus. Still, the target audience for *Ratz* should find it enjoyable and there is no objectionable material in the film. The DVD offers a full-frame trans-

fer of the film (as it was originally made for cable TV) and the image is broadcast quality. There is little grain and no overt distortion. The audio is adequate, giving clean dialogue and some moderate Surround effects. —*ML*
Movie: 🦴🦴½ **DVD:** 🦴🦴🦴
Showtime Networks, Inc. (cat #SHO3027, UPC 758445302721). Full frame. Dolby Surround. $19.98. Keepcase. *LANG:* English. *FEATURES:* Trailer • 18 chapters.
1999 95m/C Caroline Elliott, Vanessa Lengies, Jake Seeley, Levi James, Kathy Baker, Ron Silver, Barbara Tyson; *D:* Thom Eberhardt; *W:* Thom Eberhardt; *C:* Ric Waite.

The Ravagers

American and Philippine guerrillas take on the Japanese during World War II. They also deal with an American babe who's hiding out with nuns and a fortune in gold. It's difficult to say much about the DVD image because the original is such grainy, harshly lit black and white. Menu is a bit difficult to navigate in places. —*MM*
Movie: 🦴🦴 **DVD:** 🦴½
Winstar Home Ent. (cat #FLV5299, UPC 720917529929). Full frame. $14.98. Keepcase. *LANG:* English. *FEATURES:* 16 chapters • Filmographies • Trailers • DVD production credits.
1965 80m/B John Saxon, Fernando Poe Jr., Bronwyn Fitzsimons, Robert Arevalo, Mike Parsons; *D:* Eddie Romero; *W:* Eddie Romero, Cesar Amigo; *M:* Tito Arevalo.

Raven's Ridge

Imagine an exceptionally low-budget combination of Stanley Kubrick's heist movie *The Killing* and *Deliverance*. That's essentially what this story boils down to. A group of friends knock over an armored car at a racetrack then stash the loot out in the woods. When they go to retrieve it, they're attacked by a grizzled local. In his introduction, director Mike Upton admits that this is a "very independent" production, and the DVD is one of the grainiest you'll ever watch. —*MM*
Movie: 🦴🦴½ **DVD:** 🦴🦴
York Ent. (cat #YPD-1140, UPC 75072311-4026). Full frame. $14.99. Keepcase. *LANG:* English. *FEATURES:* Trailers • Director's intro.
1997 (R) 77m/C William Kendall, Dawn Howard, John Rizzi; *D:* Mike Upton.

Raw Deal

Joe (O'Keefe) escapes prison vowing to get even with the men who framed him. A top-notch and relatively unsung noir (like director Mann himself), this may be among my top 10 of its kind. A nearly pristine DVD transfer is marred by a slight ghost. Good sound. —*MO*
Movie: 🦴🦴🦴½ **DVD:** 🦴🦴½
VCI (cat #8310, UPC 089859831027). Full frame. Dolby Digital Mono. $14.99. Keepcase. *LANG:* English. *FEATURES:* 12 chapters • Classic original film noir trailers •

"Dark Reflections, Park 2," video "liner notes" by Max Allan Collins. **1948 79m/B** Dennis O'Keefe, Claire Trevor, Raymond Burr, Marsha Hunt, John Ireland, Curt Conway, Whit Bissell; **D:** Anthony Mann; **W:** John C. Higgins, Leopold Atlas; **C:** John Alton; **M:** Paul Sawtell.

Rawhead Rex

An ancient demon (a guy in a bad rubber suit) is released from his underground prison in Ireland by a plowing farmer and begins to decapitate and maim at will. (That's the demon, not the farmer.) Adapted by Clive Barker from his own short story but, be warned, the author later disowned the film. Bare-bones disc is equal to tape in every way. —MM
Movie: 🎵 ½ **DVD:** 🎵🎵
Pioneer Ent. (cat #DVD5217). Full frame. Dolby Digital Stereo. $24.98. Keepcase. LANG: English. FEATURES: 16 chapters.
1987 (R) 89m/C David Dukes, Kelly Piper, Niall Toibin, Niall O'Brien, Donal McCann, Gladys Sheehan, Cora Lunny, Heinrich von Schellendorf; **D:** George Pavlou; **W:** Clive Barker; **C:** John Metcalfe; **M:** Colin Towns.

Re–Animator 2 ME

This two-disc set upgrades the previously released Elite edition (reviewed in Book 1) with an improved anamorphic 16x9 film transfer, multiple Surround sound options, and some additional extras which raise this a few notches above the previous laser and DVD releases. The video interviews (about 90 minutes of them) offer interesting anecdotes (which occasionally overlap the commentaries) and information but they are completely static and could have benefited from some cutaways to clips or stills. The new Surround soundtracks are involving but are limited in their use of Surround channels and sound more like stereo...certainly a better option than re-recording the sound effects to create a new track, as some newly created Surround mixes have been known to do. —DG
Movie: 🎵🎵🎵 ½ **DVD:** 🎵🎵🎵🎵
Elite Entertainment, Inc. (cat #EE4325, UPC 790594432522). Widescreen (1.85:1) anamorphic. DTS; Dolby Digital 5.1 Surround; Mono. $29.95. Keepcase. LANG: English. FEATURES: 24 chapters • Insert card • Commentary: Stuart Gordon • Commentary: Yuzna, Combs, Sampson, Crampton, Abbott • THX Optimizer • Interviews: Gordon, Yuzna, Paoli, Band, Fangoria editor Timpone • 16 extended scenes • Deleted scene • Theatrical trailer and 5 TV spots • Music discussion with Richard Band • Behind-the-scenes photo gallery • 3 multi-angle storyboard/scene comparisons • Bios/filmographies.
1984 86m/C Jeffrey Combs, Bruce Abbott, Barbara Crampton, David Gale, Robert Sampson, Gerry Black, Carolyn Purdy-Gordon; **D:** Stuart Gordon; **W:** Stuart Gordon, Dennis Paoli, William J. Norris; **C:** Mac Ahlberg; **M:** Richard Band.

A Real American Hero

Brian Dennehy plays famous Tennessee sheriff Buford Pusser in this made-for-TV movie. Here he's up against moonshiners. Title is available on the Great Cop Movies triple feature. DVD is identical to tape. —MM **AKA:** Hard Stick.
Movie: 🎵 ½ **DVD:** 🎵🎵
BFS Video (cat #30174-D, UPC 06680530-1742). Full frame. $9.98. Keepcase. LANG: English. FEATURES: 4 chapters.
1978 94m/C Brian Dennehy, Brian Kerwin, Forrest Tucker; **D:** Lou Antonio.

Real Genius

A group of college geniuses find they are working on a secret weapon. They put their heads together and things get crazy. Fun movie with a good cast. Val Kilmer in his early days showing glimmers of future greatness, with Gabe Jarrett and Jonathan Gries. Cotton candy entertainment. DVD is as good as what you saw in the movie house and the sound zips around the room. —DE
Movie: 🎵🎵 ½ **DVD:** 🎵🎵 ½
Columbia Tristar (cat #07734, UPC 043-396077348). Widescreen; full frame. Dolby Surround. $24.98. Keepcase. LANG: English. SUB: English; French; Spanish. CAP: English. FEATURES: 28 chapters • Trailers.
1985 (PG) 108m/C Val Kilmer, Gabe Jarret, Jonathan (Jon Francis) Gries, Michelle Meyrink, William Atherton, Patti D'Arbanville, Severn Darden, Robert Prescott; **D:** Martha Coolidge; **W:** Peter Torokvei, Neal Israel, Pat Proft; **M:** Thomas Newman.

Real Time: Siege at Lucas Street Market

Real Time represents the rare work which was made specifically with DVD in mind. The film itself is quite short and not incredibly engaging, but the DVD features offer a wide range of selections. The movie deals with an armed robbery at a convenience store, which escalates into a hostage situation. What makes Real Time unique is that the story is played out through in-store security video, police-car cameras, and TV news footage. While this approach is interesting, it also depersonalizes the action, deflating the drama. At times, Real Time feels like an extended episode of Cops. Due to the nature of the production, the filmmakers were able to take advantage of the DVD player's seldom-used multi-angle function. Every scene can be viewed from a second angle, giving the movie the extra kick that it needs. Unfortunately, the inventiveness behind the camera never matches the on-screen action. The video transfer here is very sharp and clear, as all of the elements used look perfect (except where "real world" defects exist, such as the fuzziness of the patrol car footage). As noted above, the DVD is full of extras, including three audio commentaries, deleted scenes, and alternate takes. —ML
Movie: 🎵🎵 **DVD:** 🎵🎵🎵 ½

Troma Team Video (cat #9032, UPC 7903-57903238). Full frame. Digital Stereo. $19.98. Keepcase. LANG: English. FEATURES: Multi-angle • Commentaries • Deleted scenes • Audition excerpts • Trailers • Interviews • Interactive comic book • Audio book • Cast & crew.
2000 72m/C D: Max Allan Collins.

A Real Young Girl

Alice (Charlotte Alexandra) comes home from boarding school for the summer holidays with her hormones stuck in high gear. Her parents make no attempt to control her bored ramblings around their small village until they finally begin to suspect that she might get into some trouble with one of the local boys. Her father sets a shotgun in a boar trap in their cornfield leading to unintended consequences for Alice's would-be lover. This film has all the flat performances, bad photography, and aimless plot of a porn film with slightly less sex than the real McCoy. (It contains explicit sexual situations.) Only General Jack D. Ripper would share Alice's unhealthy obsession with her own bodily fluids. The original film was so inexpertly made that the DVD looks and sounds as rough as could be expected. —LA
Movie: 🎵 **DVD:** 🎵
Winstar Home Ent. (cat #FLV5310, UPC 720917531021). Widescreen letterboxed. $24.98. Keepcase. LANG: French. SUB: English. FEATURES: 16 chapters • Filmographies • Weblinks • DVD production credits.
1975 93m/C FR Charlotta Alexandra, Hiram Keller, Rita Meiden, Bruno Balp; **D:** Catherine Breillat; **W:** Catherine Breillat; **C:** Pierre Fattori; **M:** Mort Shuman.

Rebecca [Criterion]

Suspenseful and surprising, Hitchcock's uneasy collaboration with producer David O. Selznick is a gripping psychological drama. Based on Daphne Du Maurier's best-selling novel about a young woman (Fontaine) who marries a brooding, aristocratic widower (Olivier) who seems haunted by his dead first wife Rebecca. Fontaine's character is ill at ease about taking Rebecca's place, and the audience feels the same tension as the truth about Rebecca's fate gradually is revealed. Fontaine and Olivier turn in fine performances as the unlikely couple. But Anderson practically steals the show as Mrs. Danvers. "Danny" is the sinister servant who is more loyal to dead Rebecca than her living employers. Her final scene is a truly haunting affair that will stay with you long after the film's final reel is unspooled. Although Hitchcock had established himself as a masterful British director years before making Rebecca, this film marked his first assignment for Hollywood. His feuds with Selznick became legendary. Those behind-the-scenes stories and more are explored in depth within the ample supplement of bonus materials, including an informative commentary track by film

scholar Leonard J. Leff, author of *Hitchcock and Selznick,* and much more. The stuffed-with-extras, two-disc effort easily bests Criterion's previous laserdisc edition, which itself was loaded with extras. *Rebecca* has never looked or sounded better on home video, with the only quibble being the rather severe windowboxing used for the opening credits. —MB
Movie: ♫♫♫♫ **DVD:** ♫♫♫♫
Criterion (cat #CC1576D, UPC 71551501-2522). Full frame. Dolby Digital Mono. $39.95. Keepcase. *LANG:* English. *SUB:* English. *FEATURES:* 27 chapters ▪ Commentary: film scholar Leonard J. Leff ▪ Isolated music and effects track ▪ Rare screen, hair, makeup and costume tests ▪ Excerpts from Hitchcock's conversations with François Truffaut ▪ Phone interviews with Joan Fontaine and Judith Anderson, 1986 ▪ Behind-the-scenes photos ▪ Production correspondence and casting notes ▪ Deleted scene script excerpts ▪ 1939 test screening questionnaire ▪ Essay by author Daphne du Maurier ▪ Footage from the 1940 Academy Awards Ceremony ▪ Re-issue trailer ▪ 1938 Orson Welles and the Mercury Theatre adaptation ▪ 1941 Lux Radio Theatre adaptation ▪ 1950 Lux Radio Theatre adaptation ▪ 22-Page booklet with liner notes by Robin Wood.
1940 130m/B Joan Fontaine, Laurence Olivier, Judith Anderson, George Sanders, Nigel Bruce, Florence Bates, Gladys Cooper, Reginald Denny, Leo G. Carroll, Sir C. Aubrey Smith, Melville Cooper; **D:** Alfred Hitchcock; **W:** Joan Harrison, Robert Sherwood; **C:** George Barnes; **M:** Franz Waxman. *AWARDS:* Oscars '40: B&W Cinematog., Picture; *NOM:* Oscars '40: Actor (Olivier), Actress (Fontaine), Director (Hitchcock), Film Editing, Screenplay, Support. Actress (Anderson), Orig. Score.

Rebel Music: The Bob Marley Story

One of the most influential musicians of his time, Bob Marley has left his mark on countless people. The reggae superstar touched upon the social problems of his home country as well as issues of global politics. He never did so with a raised finger, though, like many other ambitious reggae stars, but always with songs that are full of poetic qualities and beauty. His fight for social equality and peace was a message that was heard across the world, catapulting the man from Trenchtown to international stardom. Sadly, Bob fell victim to cancer in 1981 and died at the early age of 36. But the legend lives on. Filled with interviews with friends and family members, this documentary sheds more light on Marley the man, the musician, and the victim. The quality of the footage varies naturally, but it has nonetheless been very well transferred to DVD. Even the Super-8 home footage looks considerably clear, giving us a good look at where Bob Marley and his ambitions came from. Of course, the newly done interview segments and additional footage are of much higher quality. Con-

cert footage is complemented by good audio mixes that help us understand the power of Bob's music. There is no distortion or other problems in the audio and the natural frequency response makes it enjoyable to watch and to listen to. —ML
Movie: ♫♫♫ **DVD:** ♫♫ ½
Palm Pictures (UPC 660200303723). Full frame. Dolby Digital Stereo. $24.95. Keepcase. *LANG:* English. *FEATURES:* Discography ▪ Previews.
2000 89m/C D: Jeremy Marre.

Rebel Rousers

A motorcycle gang wreaks havoc in a small town where a drag race is being held. The pregnant girlfriend of Dern's high-school buddy Mitchell is the prize. A young Nicholson in horizontally striped pants steals the show. DVD may be a slight improvement over a good tape, but there's not much to be done with the low-budget image and sound that was recorded on location. A terrific cast of character actors have become familiar since. —MM
Movie: ♫♫ **DVD:** ♫♫
Rhino (cat #2210). Full frame. $24.98. Keepcase. *LANG:* English. *FEATURES:* 18 chapters.
1969 81m/C Jack Nicholson, Cameron Mitchell, Diane Ladd, Bruce Dern, Harry Dean Stanton; **D:** Martin B. Cohen; **W:** Martin B. Cohen, Abe Polsky, Michael Kars; **C:** Laszlo Kovacs, Glen R. Smith; **M:** William Loose.

Rebirth of Mothra 1 & 2

Mothra is the creation of Ishiro Honda, who confronted the world with his creature for the first time in 1961. When the memorable encounter of *Godzilla vs. Mothra* hit theatres in 1964, Mothra quickly became a favorite among fans. After years of inactivity, Toho Studios decided in 1996 that it was time to bring the moth-shaped giant monster back to the big screen and has since created a trilogy of movies around this creature. The first one was *Mothra,* which is presented here as *Rebirth of Mothra.* The film is beautifully photographed and brings out the best of what people liked in Mothra, including the chanting fairy twins Moll and Lora. When humans come to their forests they accidentally stumble across the tomb of Desghidora, a fierce, three-headed monster. Soon Desghidora lays waste to Earth's green landscape and the only way to rid the world of this terrible creature is to call Mothra for help. One year later, Toho released *Rebirth of Mothra 2* to continue the environmental message that was carried by the colorful creature. This time, children uncover a hidden city and with it, Dagahra, a garbage-eating creature that soon threatens the Earth's oceans. Although not a bad movie, *2* oftentimes plays almost like a super-sized *Sesame Street* episode with its educational overtones. Once again, it is a fun-filled movie with plenty of explosive monster battles.

Taken from rather clean film prints, the material shows little to no damage and a high level of detail. Colors are strong but not oversaturated, making both the *Mothra* and *Godzilla* double features (please see review) spectacularly flashy movies. Shadow delineation is also perfect, with deep shadows that always maintain a high level of definition. The discs contain dubbed audio tracks in English language only; sadly, the original Japanese language tracks are not part of the release. The stereo audio tracks are well produced, however, and although the dubs are oftentimes out of sync and a little weary, the overall experience of the movies are great —GH **AKA:** *Mosura; Mothra.*
Movie: ♫♫ ½ **DVD:** ♫♫♫♫
Columbia Tristar Home Video (UPC 0433-96046917). Widescreen (1.85:1) anamorphic. Dolby Stereo. $27.98. Keepcase. *LANG:* English. *SUB:* English; French; Spanish. *CAP:* English. *FEATURES:* 28 chapters each.
1996 106m/C JP Megumi Kobayashi, Sayaka Yamaguchi, Hano Aki; **D:** Okihiro Yoneda.

Rebirth of Mothra 2

Please see review for *Rebirth of Mothra 1 & 2.* **AKA:** *Mosura 2; Mothra 2.*
Columbia Tristar Home Video
1997 103m/C JP Megumi Kobayashi, Sayaka Yamaguchi, Hano Aki; **D:** Kunio Miyoshi; **W:** Masumi Suetani.

Reborn from Hell: Jubei's Revenge

Samurai Jubei sets out to rescue a girl who is going to be used in a demonic ceremony. As Armageddon approaches, he continues to whittle down the sorcerer's army of dead warriors, one of which is his own father. This, the second-part of the *Reborn from Hell* series, seems just as cheap and sloppy as the first film, but is a notch above, thanks to a tighter, more streamlined story and improved action sequences. Frustratingly, the much threatened Armageddon doesn't happen. Though the story is essentially concluded in this film, the door is left wide open for a sequel. (Heck, at this rate, they might actually have a good film by part 4!) The disc is a *slight* step up from the previous disc. The image is centered for both versions and the image is a bit sharper. The transfer still seems too grainy and soft for a DVD, though. Sound is adequate, but there's little evidence of any stereo channel separation. —DG **AKA:** *Darkside Reborn: Path to Hell; Makai Tensho: Mado-Hen.*
Movie: ♫♫ **DVD:** ♫♫
Media Blasters (cat #TSDVD-0115, UPC 631595011586). Widescreen (1.85:1) letterboxed. Stereo. $29.95. Keepcase. *LANG:* Japanese; English. *SUB:* English. *FEATURES:* 8 chapters ▪ Trailers ▪ Character bios.
1996 83m/C JP Hiroyuki Watanabe, Yuko Moriyama, Hitomi Shimizu; **D:** Masakazu Shirai; **W:** Akinori Kikuchi; **C:** Yoshihiro Ito; **M:** Takashi Nakagawa, Sachi Sakamoto.

Reborn from Hell: Samurai Armageddon

This remake of 1981's *Samurai Reincarnation* is based on the same period fantasy novel. An evil sorcerer brings legendary dead warriors back to life to build an army for the coming Armageddon. It's up to one-eyed warrior Jubei to stop them. While the central idea is the stuff of great action/fantasy fodder, this pitiable version just doesn't work. The direction and photography are exceedingly poor; at times it seems almost like a home video shot by fans. Despite a plethora of (poorly choreographed) action sequences, demons, and gore, it neither thrills nor frightens. Everything seems terribly cheap and cheesy, evincing almost no technical polish or skill. Intended as the first of a two-part story, this part ends unresolved and should be seen in conjunction with its sequel. The disc is no earth-shaker. The image is colorful, but soft and grainy, as if mastered from a low-resolution source. The original Japanese titles are obscured by giant colored English text blocks and the subtitled version is presented at the top of the frame with the subtitles presented in the lower matting. The dubbed version is on a different disc layer and is centered within the screen. The audio is adequate but the sound mix has virtually no channel separation and is uninvolving. Oddly enough, the dubbed version seems a better choice. It matches the lip movements fairly well and the acting is just as hammy as the original track. Chapter stops are haphazardly located. —*DG* **AKA:** Darkside Reborn; Makai Tensho.

Movie: 🎵🎵 ½ **DVD:** 🎵🎵
Globalstage (cat #TSDVD-0090, UPC 631-595009026). Widescreen (1.85:1) letterboxed. Stereo. $29.95. Keepcase. *LANG:* Japanese; English. *SUB:* English. *FEATURES:* 8 chapters ⚫ Character bios ⚫ Trailers.
1996 83m/C *JP* Hiroyuki Watanabe, Yuko Moriyama, Hitomi Shimizu; **D:** Masakazu Shirai; **W:** Akinori Kikuchi; **C:** Yoshihiro Ito; **M:** Takashi Nakagawa, Sachi Sakamoto.

Recess Christmas: Miracle on Third Street

Based on the popular Saturday morning television program, *Recess Christmas: Miracle on Third Street* is a collection of four different stories disguised as one full-length movie. The wrap-around story involves three faculty members from the Third Street School: Principal Prickly (Dabney Coleman), Miss Finster (April Winchell), and Miss Grotke (Allyce Beasley) who are trapped in a car on the first day of Christmas vacation. They take this time to debate whether or not their students are good kids or troublemakers by reminiscing about four separate incidents, which involve things such as T.J. (Andrew Lawrence) being principal for a day and a canned-food drive. The seg-

ments are very similar to episodes of the show, with only the canned-food drive short standing out due to its positive Yuletide message. Good for fans of the show, but not as good as *Recess: School's Out.* The image on this DVD rivals digital broadcast quality, as it features a clear image and great colors. Strangely, this DVD offers both Dolby Digital 5.1 and DTS 5.1 audio, both giving clear dialogue, but not much in the way of Surround sound effects. —*ML*

Movie: 🎵🎵 ½ **DVD:** 🎵🎵🎵
Buena Vista Home Ent. (cat #22951, UPC 786936157017). Full frame. Dolby Digital 5.1; DTS 5.1. $29.99. Keepcase. *LANG:* English. *SUB:* English. *CAP:* English. *FEATURES:* Christmas slide shows ⚫ 8 chapters.
2001 65m/C D: Chuck Sheetz; **V:** Dabney Coleman, Allyce Beasley, April Winchell, Rickey D'Shon Collins, Andy Lawrence, Jason Davis, Ashley Johnson, Courtland Mead, Pamela Segall.

Recess: School's Out

The Third Street Elementary School is the site for a nefarious plot by ex-principal Benedict to eliminate summer vacation by creating an endless winter. It's the feature film debut of the Disney animated TV series. The quality of the art isn't close to the best that the studio can produce. It's much more in line with *Rugrats.* Even so, the DVD image is bright and shiny, though it's probably only a marginal improvement over VHS tape. Extras are extensive, including an indescribable music video of Robert Goulet singing that '60s ode to panhandling "Green Tambourine." The mind boggles. —*MM*

Movie: 🎵🎵 ½ **DVD:** 🎵🎵 ½
Buena Vista Home Ent. (cat #21945, UPC 786936147902). Widescreen (1.66:1) anamorphic. Dolby Digital 5.1 Surround Stereo. $29.99. Keepcase. *LANG:* English; Spanish. *FEATURES:* 21 chapters ⚫ 10 secrets of *Recess* TV show ⚫ "Recess" game ⚫ "Recess" animation camp ⚫ Digital comic book ⚫ "Green Tambourine" music video by Robert Goulet (full frame) ⚫ "Dancing in the Streets" music video by Myra (full frame) ⚫ Theatrical trailer ⚫ Previews ⚫ DVD-ROM features.
2001 (G) 82m/C D: Chuck Sheetz; **W:** Paul Germain, Joe Ansolabehere, Jonathan Greenberg; **M:** Denis M. Hannigan; **V:** Rickey D'Shon Collins, Jason Davis, Ashley Johnson, Courtland Mead, Pamela Segall, Dabney Coleman, Robert Goulet, Melissa Joan Hart, Peter MacNicol, James Woods, Diedrich Bader, Allyce Beasley.

Reckless and Wild

Party girls Francis (Paget Brewster, who is like Parker Posey without the skilled comedic timing) and Lily (the usually likable Christine Taylor) search for Lily's boyfriend (John Corbett), requiring them to run into a lot of boring, unfunny people, including a wannabe rock star named Gigi (a bored-looking Claudia Schiffer). The per-

formances add nothing to the movie. Brewster is shrill and unlikable. Taylor fares slightly better, but she's still stuck in a weak role. There's nothing particularly entertaining about watching two shallow people get into arguments with people who are surprisingly even more shallow and unlikable than they are. (I'm not surprised this film has been sitting on the shelf for three years.) Sharpness and detail are varied throughout the bland full-frame transfer. Some of the darker scenes appear murky and slightly undefined, while exteriors appear crisp, bright, and somewhat more defined. The 5.1 soundtrack fares better than the image quality. While certainly not very active, the music has decent presence (see the opening concert scene or, better yet, don't) and there are a fair amount of ambient sounds. Dialogue remained clear and crisp throughout. —*AB*

Movie: 🎵 **DVD:** 🎵🎵
20th Century Fox (UPC 024543036593). Full frame. Dolby Digital 5.1. $14.98. Keepcase. *LANG:* English. *CAP:* English. *FEATURES:* Trailer ⚫ Thumbnail bios.
2002 (R) 97m/C Christine Taylor, Paget Brewster, Claudia Schiffer, John Corbett, Joey Lawrence, Max Perlich, Henry Rollins; **D:** Bill Fishman; **W:** Nicole Coady, Halle Eaton, Abbe Wool.

Record of Lodoss War: Chronicles of the Heroic Knight

On the island of Lodoss, a world of fantasy exists. A group of disparate warriors, berserkers, elves, and sorcerers band together to fight an evil wizard and the forces of darkness. Based on the role-playing game, books, movie, and animated series, this latter attempt to revive the franchise is filled with exciting, colorful action, but is muddled and frequently incoherent. The reliance on magic powers and other fantastic elements to solve plot conflicts leaves the characters virtually empty ciphers. The plot and backstory will probably make sense to those familiar with the earlier series and movie, but it'll leave most viewers lost. The image transfer is colorful with digital video noise during fast motion. This four-disc collection is a step above a VHS release but is a bit lacking in sharpness and definition. The sound is strong. The bonuses are pretty slight; the relevant ones are on the DVD-ROM. The insert booklet does give some degree of insight into the complex world of Lodoss. —*DG*

Movie: 🎵🎵 **DVD:** 🎵🎵 ½
Central Park/U.S. Manga (cat #USMD-2008, UPC 719987200821). Full frame. Dolby Digital Surround. $129.99. Keepcase. *LANG:* Japanese. *SUB:* English. *FEATURES:* 1 chapter per episode ⚫ Cast page ⚫ Information guide ⚫ Comics ⚫ Character sketches ⚫ Sneak peaks ⚫ DVD-ROM: art gallery, character profiles & sketches, Japanese packaging, information guide, scripts, graphic novel pages, reviews.
1998 600m/C *JP*

The Red and the White

Epic war drama about the civil war between the Red Army and the non-communist Whites in Russia, 1919, is told from the perspective of the Hungarians who fought alongside the Reds. Unfortunately, the vast vistas are undercut by a very poor image transfer. Dust scratches and static are to be expected. The massively flashing artifacts in the backgrounds of bright landscapes are unacceptable. —*MM* *AKA:* Csillagosok, Katonak.

Movie: 🐾🐾🐾 **DVD:** 🐾
Winstar Home Ent. (cat #K223, UPC 7383-29022327). Widescreen (2.35:1) anamorphic. $24.98. Keepcase. *LANG:* Hungarian. *SUB:* English. *FEATURES:* 10 chapters.
1968 92m/B *HU* Tibor Molnar, Andras Kozak, Josef Madaras; **D:** Miklos Jancso; **W:** Miklos Jancso, Gyula Hernadi, Giorgi Mdivani; **C:** Tamas Somlo.

Red Cherry

Story of the aftermath of the Chinese revolution in 1940 is based on truth. The orphaned Chuchu (Ke-Yu) and Luo (Xiaoli) are sent to a Russian school outside Moscow and settle into their new lives. But their precarious happiness is shattered when German troops invade during WWII. Image lacks polish, but generally looks fine for an import. —*MM* *AKA:* Hong Ying Tao.

Movie: 🐾🐾 **DVD:** 🐾🐾🐾
Winstar Home Ent. (cat #5110). Widescreen letterboxed. Stereo. $29.98. Keepcase. *LANG:* Mandarin. *SUB:* English. *FEATURES:* 6 chapters • Production credits • Reviews and awards.
1995 (PG-13) 120m/C *CH* Guo Ke-Yu, Xu Xiaoli; **D:** Ye Ying.

Red Dirt

Griffith (Montgomery) longs to leave his hometown, but is unable to abandon his mentally unstable aunt (Black) and his cousin Emily (Palladino), who has been his lover since childhood. When his family rents their cottage to a young man (Goggins), longings begin to stir in Griffith and family secrets simmer to the surface. This melodrama is full of the clichés of both coming-out stories and small-town coming-of-age tales. The 5.1 mix is passable, but a high level of background hiss is present. Colors look faded, which may or may not have been the director's original intent. Some bleeding is also present. —*BG*
Movie: 🐾🐾 **DVD:** 🐾🐾½
Winstar Home Ent. (cat #FLV5296, UPC 720917529622). Widescreen letterboxed. Dolby 5.1; Dolby Stereo. $24.95. Keepcase. *LANG:* English. *FEATURES:* 16 chapters • "Peas N Corn"—short film by Tag Purvis • Trailer • Filmographies.
1999 111m/C Dan Montgomery Jr., Walton Goggins, Aleksa Palladino, Karen Black, Glenn Shadix, John Mese, Peg O'Keef; **D:** Tag Purvis; **W:** Tag Purvis; **C:** Ted Cohen; **M:** Nathan Barr.

Red Rock West

Top-notch neo-noir is consistently surprising. Down-on-his-luck nice guy and straight shooter Mike (Cage) is broke and jobless in the middle of Wyoming (well, all right, Arizona, as we learn on the commentary track), when he runs across a suspicious husband (Walsh), his seemingly faithless wife (Boyle), and a hitman (Hopper) with a poor sense of timing. The story is filled with unpredictable twists, fine characters, and a terrific sense of place. DVD presents an accurate version of an image that is not meant to be completely polished and sharp. I could spot no obvious artifacts in the bright dusty exteriors and intentionally dark interiors are handled equally well. Sound is all that the production requires. A real treat for any mystery fan. —*MM*
Movie: 🐾🐾🐾½ **DVD:** 🐾🐾½
Columbia Tristar Home Video (UPC 043-396269798). Widescreen anamorphic; full frame. Dolby Surround. $24.98. Keepcase. *LANG:* English; Spanish. *SUB:* English; French; Spanish. *FEATURES:* 28 chapters • Commentary: John Dahl, Richard Dahl, editor Scott Chesnut.
1993 (R) 98m/C Nicolas Cage, Dennis Hopper, Lara Flynn Boyle, J.T. Walsh, Timothy Carhart, Dan Shor, Dwight Yoakam, Bobby Joe McFadden, Craig Reay, Vance Johnson, Robert Apel, Dale Gibson, Ted Parks, Babs Bram, Robert Guajardo, Sarah Sullivan; **D:** John Dahl; **W:** John Dahl, Rick Dahl; **C:** Marc Reshovsky; **M:** William Olvis. *AWARDS: NOM:* Ind. Spirit '95: Director (Dahl), Screenplay.

Red Shoe Diaries: The Game

This disc includes three episodes of the late-night sexy adult drama series, a popular program from producer Zalman King. The quality of the DVD in terms of audio and video is what you would expect from a television program—the image has generally good color, but feels a little soft at times. Some scenes seem a little too dark, and occasionally, there is some slight pixelation. The audio actually isn't that bad, with a strong, clear score and very clear dialogue. The extras are very impressive. At the beginning of the movie, the opening screen says to watch out for the "red shoe" symbols to pop up. When you click on them, you're taken to the rehearsal footage of that particular scene. It's an extremely cool feature. Also on the disc is a commentary from producer Zalman King, who doesn't have too much to say. When he does talk he provides some interesting details about the production, but that's when he does talk—there are long periods without comments. A trivia game is included and if you guess the correct answer, you're shown the scene from the program where the answer comes from. In addition, there is part of an early draft of the screenplay, and viewers can skip from the draft to the final scene. Viewers can also play an animated "Red Shoe Diaries" game, read a text "diary," or look at some small bios for the actors. *Red Shoe Diaries* definitely isn't for everyone, but if you're a fan of the show, you'll definitely be pleased with the effort they've made with this disc. —*AB/DG*
Movie: 🐾🐾½ **DVD:** 🐾🐾🐾
Showtime Networks, Inc. (UPC 7584455-00325). Full frame. Dolby Digital Surround. $24.98. Keepcase. *LANG:* English; Spanish. *CAP:* English. *FEATURES:* Trivia game • Commentary: King • Re-creation of the game for home use • Link to extended, alternate scenes, unedited footage • Trailer • Original written diaries • Original script that links to the final scene • 27 chapters • Photo gallery.
2000 97m/C

Red Surf

Action abounds in this surfer flick. A couple of hard-nosed wave-riders (pre-*ER* Clooney and Savant) become involved with big money drug gangs. Beyond the deservedly minimal extras, there's little to differentiate this disc from VHS tape. —*MM*
Movie: 🐾🐾 **DVD:** 🐾🐾
Simitar Ent. (cat #4035). Full frame. $19.95. Keepcase. *LANG:* English. *FEATURES:* Trailer • Talent files • 18 chapters.
1990 (R) 104m/C George Clooney, Doug Savant, Dedee Pfeiffer, Gene Simmons, Rick Najera, Philip McKeon; **D:** H. Gordon Boos; **W:** Vincent Robert; **C:** John Schwartzman; **M:** Sasha Matson.

Red Zone Cuba

Please see review for *Mystery Science Theater 3000: "Red Zone Cuba."* *AKA:* Night Train to Mundo Fine.
1966 92m/C John Carradine, Coleman Francis, Tony Cordoza, Harold Saunders; **D:** Coleman Francis; **W:** Coleman Francis; **C:** Herb Roberts; **M:** John Bath.

Reflex Action

Lame action film has our hero coming home from Desert Storm to take on drug lords who want his family's land. There's not a cliché missed in this movie. DVD is about the same as VHS and the sound is passable. —*DE*
Movie: 🐾½ **DVD:** 🐾🐾
MTI (cat #50049, UPC 619935404939). Full frame. Dolby 5.1 Surround. $24.98. Keepcase. *LANG:* English. *SUB:* Spanish. *FEATURES:* 20 chapters • "Making of" • Deleted scenes • Photo montage • Bios • Trailer.
2002 (R) 95m/C Michael Baldoz, Richard Lynch, Michael Guerin, Monique Scott; **D:** Kevin Rapp; **W:** Kevin Rapp.

Regeneration / Young Romance

The early silent film *Regeneration* follows young Owen (Rockcliffe Fellowes) from an abusive foster home to the street gang he finds himself in charge of as an adult and his eventual triumphs over adversity. The first film by Raoul Walsh, who assisted D. W. Griffith on the landmark *Birth of a Nation,* doesn't quite rise to that film's level of technical achievement but is still an important step in cinema's development. The only surviving original print was badly scarred, and is almost unwatchable in some passages, but this is probably the best this film will ever look. Also included is the rediscovered comedy *Young Romance,* which is still an enjoyable romantic farce. The print of this film is from Cecil B. DeMille's library, and is in much better shape than *Regeneration.* —BG

Movie: 🎬🎬🎬 **DVD:** 🎬🎬🎬

Image Ent. (cat #ID0510DSDVD, UPC 014-381051025). Full frame. Dolby Stereo. $24.95. Keepcase. *LANG:* Silent. *SUB:* English intertitles. *FEATURES:* 12 chapters for *Redemption* • 11 chapters for *Young Romance.*
1915 72m/B Rockliffe Fellowes, Anna Q. Nilsson; *D:* Raoul Walsh; *W:* Raoul Walsh, Carl Harbaugh; *C:* Georges Benoit. *AWARDS:* Natl. Film Reg. '00.

A Regular Frankie Fan

Filmmaker Scott Mabbutt took his cameras to several midnight screenings of *The Rocky Horror Picture Show* in different cities, and then interviewed many of the regular fan/performers. He also goes "behind the scenes," as it were, to judge just how important the film is to them and to examine the elaborate plans they make. Production values are on the general level of home video and so the film gains little visually on DVD. Extras are extensive, but there's really nothing here to recommend the film beyond its core audience. —MM

Movie: 🎬🎬 **DVD:** 🎬🎬 ½

Liberty International Entertainment, Inc. (cat #LIP0800, UPC 801805080095). Widescreen letterboxed. $24.99. Keepcase. *LANG:* English. *FEATURES:* Commentary: director • Convention footage • Music video • Photo gallery • Trailers • Weblinks.
2001 75m/C *D:* Scott Mabbutt; *W:* Scott Mabbutt; *C:* Tom Clancey, Cary Caraway; *Nar:* Paul Williams.

Reindeer Games [Miramax DC]

This director's cut restores about 19 minutes worth of scenes into the movie (first reviewed in *Book 2*), while still keeping the film within an "R" rating. In the commentary, Frankenheimer explains that the testing process did not go as well as he expected and cuts were requested. Scenes are usually slightly extended, such as Affleck originally finding out about Theron's character in the prison, their original meeting, the sex scene, and some other bits when Affleck meets the bad guys and several other small alterations. The commentary seems to have been pulled from the track on the non–director's cut version with new comments pertaining

to this expanded version added. The new information added here is quite entertaining and informative, especially Frankenheimer's discussion on the testing process that reveals the pressure and nerves involved in the process. —AB/DG

Movie: 🎬🎬🎬 **DVD:** 🎬🎬🎬

Miramax Pictures Home Video (UPC 7869-36151565). Widescreen (2.35:1) anamorphic. Dolby Digital 5.1 Surround. $29.99. Keepcase. *LANG:* English. *FEATURES:* Commentary: Frankenheimer • Trailer • Featurette.
2000 (R) 124m/C Ben Affleck, Charlize Theron, Gary Sinise, Clarence Williams III, Dennis Farina, Donal Logue, James Frain, Isaac Hayes, Danny Trejo; *D:* John Frankenheimer; *W:* Ehren Kruger; *C:* Alan Caso; *M:* Alan Silvestri.

The Remains of the Day

British stiff upper lips work overtime in this Merchant-Ivory adaptation of Kazuo Ishiguro's novel. In 1930s England, steadfast butler Stevens (Anthony Hopkins) devotes his life to impeccably serving Lord Darlington (James Fox), measuring the exact placement of silverware on the dinner table and keeping the staff well disciplined for their duties at Darlington Hall. When the new housekeeper Miss Kenton (Emma Thompson) expresses a more-than-professional interest in Stevens, his entire world comes into question, especially with his employer courting sympathy among his peers for the emerging Nazi cause. Hopkins's impressive performance walks a tightrope between admiration for his duties and frustration that he doesn't just tell Darlington to stuff it and run off with Miss Kenton. Three separate times when watching the movie, I wished I could slap Stevens during yet another repressed emotion moment and yell in *Moonstruck*-fashion, "Snap out of it." Yet one cannot be too mad when watching two of the best actors of the day spar and parry with their unspoken feelings for each other. Transfer exhibits superb image definition and color rendition. Deep blacks, immaculate source print, and no digital artifacts means nothing gets between the viewer and the picture. The 5.1 digital tracks and standard Surround stereo emphasize dialogue clarity over multi-channel pyrotechnics, but the music fills all speakers nicely when necessary. —EP

Movie: 🎬🎬🎬 **DVD:** 🎬🎬🎬

Columbia Tristar (cat #71097, UPC 0433-96710979). Widescreen (2.35:1) anamorphic. Dolby Digital 5.1; Dolby Digital Surround. $24.95. Keepcase. *LANG:* French; Spanish; Portuguese. *SUB:* English; French; Spanish; Portuguese; Chinese; Korean; Thai. *FEATURES:* 28 chapters • Commentary: Emma Thompson • Behind-the-scenes documentary with new interviews • Deleted scenes • HBO "making of" featurette.
1993 (PG) 135m/C *GB* Anthony Hopkins, Emma Thompson, James Fox, Christopher

Reeve, Peter Vaughan, Hugh Grant, Michael (Michel) Lonsdale, Tim Pigott-Smith; *D:* James Ivory; *W:* Ruth Prawer Jhabvala; *C:* Tony Pierce-Roberts; *M:* Richard Robbins. *AWARDS:* British Acad. '93: Actor (Hopkins); L.A. Film Critics '93: Actor (Hopkins); Natl. Bd. of Review '93: Actor (Hopkins); *NOM:* Oscars '93: Actor (Hopkins), Actress (Thompson), Adapt. Screenplay, Art Dir./Set Dec., Costume Des., Director (Ivory), Picture, Orig. Score; British Acad. '94: Actress (Thompson), Adapt. Screenplay, Director (Ivory), Film; Directors Guild '93: Director (Ivory); Golden Globes '94: Actor—Drama (Hopkins), Actress—Drama (Thompson), Director (Ivory), Film—Drama, Screenplay; Writers Guild '93: Adapt. Screenplay.

Remember Pearl Harbor: America Taken by Surprise

This two-disc set is a fine introduction to the attack on Pearl Harbor. It is perhaps most valuable for the quick historical background it provides, focusing on the racial attitudes and nationalistic stereotypes that characterize so much of the 1930s and 1940s and seem, in some ways, so remote today. The original documentary is made up of the familiar newsreel footage. The newer material is generally of broadcast video quality. Some of the older scenes—both the real and the "re-created"—have been processed to look bad so it's pointless to be too hard on the disc in that regard. The extra "featurettes" are on the first disc. The second contains three of director John Ford's wartime documentaries, the short Oscar-winning version of "Dec. 7, 1941," "The Battle of Midway," and "The Fighting Lady," about the carrier USS *Yorktown.* —MM

Movie: 🎬🎬🎬 **DVD:** 🎬🎬 ½

Questar Video (cat #QD3240, UPC 03393-7032400). Full frame. $24.99. Keepcase. *LANG:* English. *FEATURES:* 10 chapters • "Stories from Battleship Row" featurette • "Hollywood's Pearl Harbor" featurette • "Attack of the Midget Subs" featurette • "Salvaging the Pacific Fleet" featurette • "Dec. 7, 1941" short film • "The Battle of Midway" short film • "The Fighting Lady" short film.
2001 240m/C *D:* Rolf Forsberg; *W:* Rolf Forsberg; *Nar:* Ed Ragazzino.

The Replacement Killers [2 SE]

The main difference between this "Special Edition" and the one reviewed in *Book 1* is director Antoine Fuqua's commentary track, and it's not the most expert you've ever heard. He actually seems a bit uncomfortable with long silent stretches and repetitions. The deleted and extended scenes are all in very rough shape, and were wisely removed. That said, this version, like the first, looks and sounds terrific. DVD does an excellent job with an often dark image. Even in this insubstan-

tial story, star Chow Yun-Fat's screen presence is undeniable. —*MM*
Movie: 🐾🐾 ½ **DVD:** 🐾🐾🐾 ½
Columbia Tristar (cat #07753, UPC 0433-96077539). Widescreen (2.35:1) anamorphic. Dolby Digital 5.1. $29.95. Keepcase. *LANG:* English; Spanish; French; Portuguese. *SUB:* English; Spanish; French; Portuguese; Chinese; Korean; Thai. *CAP:* English. *FEATURES:* 28 chapters ✱ Commentary: director ✱ Filmographies ✱ Trailers ✱ 2 featurettes.
1998 (R) 86m/C Chow Yun-Fat, Mira Sorvino, Michael Rooker, Kenneth Tsang, Juergen Prochnow, Danny Trejo, Til Schweiger, Clifton (Gonzalez) Collins Jr., Carlos Gomez, Frank Medrano; *D:* Antoine Fuqua; *W:* Ken Sanzel; *C:* Peter Collister; *M:* Harry Gregson-Williams.

Replicant

Yet again, Van Damme appears in a double-role, as himself and...himself. Once as a serial killer, and once as his clone. Not a very innovative story line, but neither is the rest of this formulaic and clichéd thriller. The transfer shows slight signs of grain in certain shots but is for the most part very stable. Colors are nicely reproduced, bringing out the best of the atmospheric shots, from the cool blues of the nighttime scenes, to the warm color schemes of the indoor settings. Black level is well balanced and creates deep blacks and well-defined shadows. No serious edge-enhancement has been applied and as a result, the transfer is mostly free of ringing artifacts. Pixelation is evident in a number of scenes where large portions of the frame are moving. While static shots are nicely compressed, those moments of movement lose some definition and wash out slightly. Audio is dynamic and aggressive, making good use of the Surround channels for an engrossing presentation. The disc also features an audio commentary by Jean-Claude Van Damme, which will make fans of the star happy, but offers very little of interest for other viewers. —*GH*
Movie: 🐾🐾 **DVD:** 🐾🐾 ½
Artisan Ent. (cat #11994, UPC 0122361-19944). Widescreen (1.85:1) anamorphic. Dolby Digital 5.1 Surround; Dolby Digital Surround. $24.98. Keepcase. *LANG:* English. *SUB:* Spanish. *CAP:* English. *FEATURES:* 19 chapters ✱ Commentary: Jean-Claude Van Damme ✱ Storyboards ✱ Trailer ✱ Talent files.
2001 (R) 100m/C Jean-Claude Van Damme, Michael Rooker, Ian Robinson, Catherine Dent; *D:* Ringo Lam; *W:* Lawrence Riggins, Les Weldon; *C:* Mike Southon; *M:* Guy Zerafa.

Reptilian

A remake of a favorite Korean monster movie from the 1960s, the retitled *Reptilian* is a fine example of id-release giant monster destruction that should satisfy the monster-movie lover in anyone. Ruthless Dr. Campbell is unearthing the largest dinosaur skeleton ever found, and he does-

n't mind losing a lot of workmen to mysterious "accidents" along the way. Alien puppets from beyond the galaxy park their huge, grungy mothership in Earth orbit and start zapping random satellites and space shuttles, planning to destroy the puny Earthlings by bringing the 200 million–year-old corpse of Yonggary back to life and sending it on a rampage. The DVD presents a trouble-free transfer, and comes with a few minor extras, the most valuable of which is the "production notes" section, which is upfront about the film's origins without putting it in a bad light. —*BT*
Movie: 🐾🐾🐾 **DVD:** 🐾🐾 ½
Columbia Tristar (cat #07226, UPC 0433-96-72268). Widescreen anamorphic. Dolby Digital 5.1 Surround; Dolby Surround. $24.95. Keepcase. *LANG:* English. *SUB:* English; Spanish; Portuguese. *CAP:* English. *FEATURES:* 24 chapters ✱ Trailer ✱ Image gallery.
2000 (PG-13) 99m/C *KN* Harrison Young, Donna Philipson, Richard B. Livingston; *D:* Hyung Rae Shim; *W:* Marty Poole; *C:* Hong Kim An; *M:* Chris Desmong, Seung Woo Cho.

Reptilicus

Oil drillers in Lapland bring up a sample of prehistoric flesh from a frozen bog deep below the earth, which is transported to a Copenhagen Akvarium/research establishment. It proves to be alive and growing; eventually a lightning storm frees it from its holding tank. Soon thereafter the army has a real problem on its hands when it reappears as a completely regenerated monster, crawling (and in the original Danish version, flying) across the landscape, crushing buildings and eating farmers. The authorities have no luck ridding themselves of the scaly, snake-like dragon, until they corner it in the main square in downtown Copenhagen. This alternative epic comes in dead last in the list of movies where giant monsters attack cities. The several hundred extras who run politely through the streets in "panic" look bored or amused, compared to the terror-stricken mobs in the same year's *Gorgo*, a far superior picture in every way. Most of Reptilicus's scenes are artlessly shot in broad daylight, making its general artificiality even more obvious. DVD transfer is flat, full-frame, and somewhat disappointing at first. It takes a while to realize that it is indeed newer than the old Orion element, and improves a few of the visual flaws where possible (nothing short of repainting every frame could have removed all the optical dirt in the effects scenes). It might not be full-frame all the time, as it is difficult to tell with the haphazard framing of so many shots. —*GE*
Movie: 🐾🐾 **DVD:** 🐾🐾
MGM Home Ent. (cat #1002354, UPC 027-616056656). Full frame. Dolby Digital Mono. $14.95. Keepcase. *LANG:* English; French. *SUB:* French; Spanish. *CAP:* English. *FEATURES:* Trailer.
1962 90m/C *DK* Carl Ottosen, Ann Smyrner, Mimi Heinrich, Asbjorn Andersen,

Bodil Miller, Bent Mejding, Dirch Passer, Ole Wisborg; *D:* Sidney Pink; *W:* Sidney Pink, Ib Melchior; *C:* Aage Wiltrup; *M:* Sven Gyldmark.

Requiem for a Heavyweight

At 37, after 17 years in the ring, Mountain Rivera (Anthony Quinn) is one punch away from being blind. His corrupt manager Rennick (Jackie Gleason) needs him to fight a few more fights, so he can clear up his gambling debts. Mountain is a mental and physical wreck with just barely enough smarts to be likable, when he meets up with Miss Miller (Julie Harris), a kindly social worker. She makes him realize he has no skills to survive outside the ring and when she does find him a job opportunity, Rennick conspires to screw it up. Rennick has plans to turn Mountain Rivera into a wrestling champ. Army (Mickey Rooney) is the devoted coach and friend who lacks the strength to steer things right. The script was written by Rod Serling for the live television series *Playhouse 90* in 1957. In 1962 he retooled it a bit for this film version. Anthony Quinn gives a great performance, showing Mountain Rivera to be a pile of a man's mental remains. This is one of the best performances of Jackie Gleason's career, right up there with *The Hustler*. Spivy LeVoe is creepy as lead mobster, Ma Greeny, this being one of her five film appearances. The DVD is a spotless transfer from film to digital format with much better sound quality than expected. No doubt it provided inspiration for *Rocky* and *Raging Bull*. Boxing fans will enjoy the cameo appearances of Jack Dempsey and Muhammad Ali when he was still known as Cassius Clay. It was released in the United Kingdom under the title *Blood Money*. —*JAS*
AKA: Blood Money.
Movie: 🐾🐾🐾 ½ **DVD:** 🐾🐾🐾 ½
Columbia Tristar (cat #08338, UPC 0433-96083387). Widescreen anamorphic; full frame. Mono. $24.95. Keepcase. *LANG:* English. *SUB:* English; French; Spanish; Portuguese. *FEATURES:* 28 chapters.
1962 100m/B Anthony Quinn, Jackie Gleason, Mickey Rooney, Julie Harris, Stanley Adams, Spivy Levoe, Muhammad Ali, Jack Dempsey; *D:* Ralph Nelson; *W:* Rod Serling; *C:* Arthur Ornitz; *M:* Laurence Rosenthal.

Requiem for Murder

Molly Ringwald stars in this substandard entry into the serial-killer genre as a classical music show host with an increasing number of unsettling suitors. One of them seems to be a killer, as her enemies are being knocked off while she's on the air. It's even duller than it sounds, and the ending comes from somewhere beyond left field. The picture is grainy but adequate, while the audio leaves something to be desired—patches of dialogue drop out almost all together in several places. —*BG*
Movie: 🐾 ½ **DVD:** 🐾🐾

Avalanche Ent. (cat #AV1546D, UPC 8064-69154625). Full frame. Ultra-Stereo. $19.95. Keepcase. *LANG:* English. *SUB:* English; French; Spanish. *CAP:* English. *FEATURES:* 24 chapters • Trailers.
1999 (PG-13) 95m/C Molly Ringwald, Chris Heyerdahl, Lynne Adams, Chris Mulkey, Jayne Heitmeyer; *D:* Douglas Jackson; *W:* Matt Dorff; *C:* Barry Gravelle; *M:* Milan Kymlicka.

Rescue from Gilligan's Island

Fifteen years after the cancellation of *Gilligan's Island* came this TV movie that reunited the principal cast (minus Tina Louise's original Ginger) and finally depicted the rescue of the castaways. When a tsunami sweeps the group's huts into the sea, they are discovered by the Coast Guard and return to their lives. Somewhat changed by their experiences on the island, the castaways face difficulties returning to modern life, while at the same time Gilligan is pursued by Russian spies sent to retrieve an information drive that landed on the island. This awkward return to the lame jokes and Keaton-inspired slapstick of the TV series seemed out of date even during the original broadcast, but the cast's chemistry is still evident. The early sections on the studio-bound island sets match the look and feel of the series, but the rest of the film (which is shot on location) just seems old. Series fans will enjoy many of the goings-on here and should kick this rating up an extra bone. The disc features a poor transfer of a faded 16mm print. Gilligan's red shirt looks predominantly orange in this edition and there are several sections that display picture noise, brief missing shots, and pixelation during rapid cutting. If you have a taped-off TV copy, there's little reason to bother with this disc. "Spooky Hooky" is a classic but looks just awful here: a digitized mess. —*DG*
Movie: 🎵½ *DVD:* 🎵
Brentwood (cat #44088-9, UPC 78736440-8894). Full frame. Mono. $4.99. Keepcase. *LANG:* English. *FEATURES:* "Little Rascals: Spooky Hooky" short • Trivia game • DVD dictionary • 6 chapters.
1978 92m/C Bob Denver, Alan Hale Jr., Russell Johnson, Jim Backus, Natalie Schafer, Dawn Wells, Judith Baldwin; *D:* Leslie Martinson; *W:* David Harmon, Sherwood Schwartz, Elroy Schwartz, Al Schwartz; *C:* Robert Primes; *M:* Gerald Fried.

Restless Spirits

This Canadian-lensed film is a ghost story that will be appropriate for the younger viewers, although they may not understand all of it. Following the death of their father, Katie (Juliana Wimbles) and Andy (Ben Cook) go to spend the summer with their grandmother (Marsha Mason). Once there, Katie discovers an odd occurrence at a nearby pond. There she meets two French aviators, who discuss their attempts to cross the Atlantic. These two

men are ghosts who are doomed to repeat their failed effort over and over again unless Katie can help them become "unstuck" in time. This mixture of a ghost story and *Groundhog Day* is an interesting idea, but the film is very sluggishly paced and the first 30 minutes drag by. The ghosts aren't of the scary variety, so the film is safe for family viewing. All of the performers in the film are fine, and the finale is exciting, but the movie seems to have borrowed a bit too much from other films to be highly recommended. Also known as *Dead Aviators,* which isn't all that surprising, considering that the director wrote the abysmal *Zombie Nightmare.* The full-frame made-for-TV image is sharp, but displays some obvious grain in the daytime scenes. The colors are nice, but the nighttime scenes are a bit too dark. The digital stereo audio track provides the viewer with clear dialogue and some minor Surround sound effects. There are no extra features on this DVD. —*ML* **AKA:** Dead Aviators.
Movie: 🎵🎵 *DVD:* 🎵🎵½
Showtime Networks, Inc. (cat #SHO3028, UPC 758445302820). Full frame. Digital Stereo. $19.98. Keepcase. *LANG:* English; Spanish. *CAP:* English. *FEATURES:* 12 chapters.
1999 95m/C *CA* Juliana Wimbles, Lothaire Bluteau, Michel Monty, Marsha Mason, Leslie Hope, Ben Cook, Eugene Lipinski, Nickolas Swan; *D:* David Wellington; *W:* Semi Chellas; *C:* Andre Pienaar; *M:* Ron Sures.

Retrievers

A young man and a former CIA agent team up to expose the unsavory practices of the organization in an ultra-low budget action flick that has nothing to do with dogs. Bare-bones disc (no menu; no links) is no better than tape. —*MM*
Movie: 🎵 *DVD:* 🎵½
Digital Versatile Disc (cat #111). Full frame. $19.95. Keepcase. *LANG:* English.
1982 90m/C Max Thayer, Roselyn Royce, Richard Anderson, Shawn Hoskins, Mary McCormick, Lenard Miller; *D:* Elliot Hong; *W:* Elliot Hong; *C:* Stephen Kim; *M:* Ted Ashford.

Retroactive

Scientist Brian (Whaley) has been experimenting with time reversal and finally manages to make his project work. Meanwhile, police psychologist Karen (Travis) has had car trouble and been given a ride by Frank (Belushi) and his wife Rayanne (Whirry). Karen soon realizes that Frank is a psycho and escapes to Brian's lab. But Brian's just reversed time and Karen winds up back in Frank's car. It's déjà vu all over again! Aliasing is noticeable in high-contrast scenes along bright lines. Surround is limited but effective. —*MM*
Movie: 🎵🎵 *DVD:* 🎵🎵½
MGM Home Ent. (cat #907788). Widescreen. Dolby Digital 5.1 Surround Stereo. $24.98. Keepcase. *LANG:* English; French.

SUB: English; French. *CAP:* English. *FEATURES:* Trailer • 32 chapters.
1997 (R) 91m/C James Belushi, Kylie Travis, Shannon Whirry, Frank Whaley, Jesse Borrego, M. Emmet Walsh, Guy Boyd; *D:* Louis Morneau; *W:* Robert Strauss, Phillip Badger; *C:* George Mooradian; *M:* Tim Truman.

Return of Captain Invincible

Captain Invincible (Arkin) was an American superhero who helped the allies during World War II. Accused of communism during the McCarthy era, the Captain left the states for the Australian outback where he became a drunken bum. When the Captain's arch nemesis Mr. Midnight (Lee) returns to cause more incoherent mayhem, an Australian policewoman tracks down the Captain and joins forces with him to stop the madman. It's a truly bizarre camp film with odd (dreadful) musical numbers and a strange feeling of patriotism. The script tends to settle for silly scenarios (Captain Invincible fighting living vacuum cleaners) rather than jokes, and the film is only enjoyable thanks to Arkin's considerable charms. His wry characterization, presumed improvisations, and knowing smirk give the film an air of self-parody which makes this uneven concoction entertaining. He and Lee even "sing!" Some songs are co-written by Richard O'Brien *(The Rocky Horror Picture Show)* but all of them are bad. A guilty pleasure, to be sure, but it does boast a spirited finale and enough fun moments to make it worth rewatching. The central idea may have inspired the has-been, overcoated horror host character in the *Commander USA's Groovie Movies* TV series which premiered three years later. The disc appears to be transferred from a theatrical print as it features muddy blacks and muted colors. The image is a bit prone to edge shimmer, but the preservation of the film's widescreen ratio gives this film an edge on other video versions. The newly remixed soundtrack is passable but usually feels like glorified mono. A film as odd as this one begs for a commentary, though. —*DG* **AKA:** Legend in Leotards.
Movie: 🎵🎵½ *DVD:* 🎵🎵🎵
Elite Entertainment, Inc. (cat #EE 7624, UPC 790594762421). Widescreen (2.35:1) anamorphic. Dolby Surround 5.1. $19.95. Keepcase. *LANG:* English. *FEATURES:* Trailer • 12 chapters • Insert card with chapter listing.
1983 (PG) 102m/C *AU* Alan Arkin, Christopher Lee, Kate Fitzpatrick, Bill Hunter, Graham Kennedy, Michael Pate, Hayes Gordon, Max Phipps, Noel Ferrier; *D:* Philippe Mora; *W:* Steven E. de Souza, Andrew Gaty; *C:* Louis Irving, Mike Molloy; *M:* William Motzig, Richard O'Brien.

Return of the Deadly Blade

A grand old epic of swordplay, magic, and hidden identities. Eighteen years ago,

Master Lee Wai killed his rival Kam the Invincible Golden Rings using his Deadly Blade, and disappeared. Kam's son uses Master Lee's name to publicly challenge all other fighters, hoping to draw out his father's killer. Meanwhile, a swordsman called The Lonely Winner battles assassins sent after him by a nobleman. The two warriors get in a battle various opponents before meeting at the Tomb of Heroes, where they learn some big secrets—and are taken to the Land of the Moon Goddess for an epic battle. The great variety of characters and weapons helps keep things interesting, but also makes the story difficult to follow. It seems more like one damn thing after another than a story, and it doesn't help that odd flashbacks keep popping up. As such, it's wacky fun, even if it makes your head hurt trying to follow it. The sound is of the usual poor quality of a dubbed 1970s kung fu flick. The image is squeezed and cropped, from a scratchy old print. Volume 8 of the *Wu Tang Clan Hidden Chambers Collection,* a series which makes up for the often poor quality of the prints presented with quite extensive extras. These include short bios of cast and crew members, contemporary interviews, clips from cast members' other films, image galleries, trailers, nice 3-D animated menus, interview footage of the Shaolin Temple Abbots, and more. —*BT AKA:* Shaolin Fighters vs. Ninja.
Movie: 🎬🎬 ***DVD:*** 🎬🎬
Xenon Ent. (cat #8, UPC 694795302427). Full frame. $14.95. Keepcase. *LANG:* English. *FEATURES:* Cast bios • Previews • Bonus footage • Wu Tang Clan music video • Wu Tang Clan interview.
1981 83m/C *HK* David Chiang, Jang-Lee Hwang, Bruce Liang, Norman Chu, Lo Lieh; *D:* Taylor Wong; *W:* Yu Chin; *C:* Hung Chuen Lau; *M:* Joseph Koo.

Return of the Killer Tomatoes!

Mad scientist Gangreen (Astin) has perfected his formula for turning ordinary tomatoes into Rambo-like warriors, and is ready to take over the world. Only a couple of pizza delivery boys and an escaped tomato-woman can stop him. But their most evil enemy has yet to strike—rampant product placement. This time out, everybody involved was trying way too hard to make a cult classic, a certain recipe for failure. The colors aren't terribly sharp, but both picture and audio are a step up from video. —*BG*
Movie: 🎬 ½ ***DVD:*** 🎬🎬 ½
Anchor Bay (cat #DV11465, UPC 0131311-46592). Full frame. Dolby Mono. $14.98. Keepcase. *LANG:* English. *CAP:* English. *FEATURES:* 24 chapters • Trailer.
1988 (PG) 98m/C Anthony Starke, George Clooney, Karen Mistal, Steve Lundquist, John Astin, Charlie Jones, Rock Peace, Frank Davis, C.J. Dillon, Teri Weigel; *D:* John DeBello; *W:* John DeBello, Constantine Dillon, Steve Peace; *C:* Stephen Kent Welch; *M:* Neal Fox, Rick Patterson.

The Return of the King

Inoffensive adaptation of the final volume of Tolkien's trilogy wraps up all of the conflicts with big battle scenes and grand derring-do. With static backgrounds and simply drawn characters, the film really doesn't do the books justice. DVD image and sound are fine but not a marked improvement over VHS tape, not that anything more is really needed. —*MM*
Movie: 🎬🎬 ***DVD:*** 🎬🎬 ½
Warner (cat #576, UPC 012569157623). Widescreen letterboxed. Dolby Digital Mono. $19.98. Snapper. *LANG:* English. *SUB:* English; French; Spanish. *CAP:* English. *FEATURES:* 30 chapters • Talent files • Trivia.
1980 120m/C *D:* Arthur Rankin Jr., Jules Bass; *M:* Maury Laws; *V:* Orson Bean, Roddy McDowall, John Huston, Theodore Bikel, William Conrad, Glen Yarborough, Paul Frees, Casey Kasem, Sonny Melendrez.

Return of the Living Dead 3

Disappointing entry into the *Living Dead* series is directed by Brian Yuzna (*Society*). Lacking the social commentary of *Night of the Living Dead* or *Dawn of the Dead,* or the intelligent slapstick humor of the first *Return of the Living Dead, Return 3* mires itself in an overly long first act, which finds the military experimenting with the flesh-eating zombie producing bio-toxin hoping to produce super soldiers. This initial plot point had good possibilities and great special effects but it takes a muddled turn when the son (Edmond) of the officer in charge (McCord) steals his father's key card to enter the facility where the experiments take place to impress his girlfriend (Clarke), because, of course, all you need to get into a super secret military facility is a key card. They watch as a reanimated corpse goes crazy and eats the brains of two lab techs too stupid to leave the room when it gets loose. Naturally, when his girlfriend ends up dead a few scenes later, he gets the brilliant idea to haul her dead body back to the lab and reanimate her with the bio-toxin, because for some reason the connection between the reanimation of the corpse and its propensity for eating humans just doesn't strike him as important. On top of that, it appears that it's really easy to get into the secret lab carrying your dead girlfriend over your shoulder. Cannibalistic hilarity ensues as his girlfriend rises from the dead. The odd couple is chased through town by a pissed-off street gang and the evil military while trying to find something that will satisfy her strange new hunger. There is nothing special to recommend this film beyond good gore and bad acting, with the exception of Kent McCord, who obviously decided to pretend he was in a different, better film. This is a pretty good DVD with a much sharper image than the pre-existing VHS version. The colors are also much

improved. No remix has been done of the low-budget feature's stereo soundtrack, which sounds good but not spectacular. The commentary by director Yuzna is a bit of a bore and is only recommended to fans who could "Beat the Geeks." However, the second commentary (who would have expected two commentaries for this film?), by Mindy Clarke and Tom Rainone, more than makes up for it with humorous anecdotes and an obvious chemistry between the two. —*CA/JO*
Movie: 🎬🎬🎬 ***DVD:*** 🎬🎬🎬
Lion's Gate Home Ent. (cat #VM7723D, UPC 031398772323). Widescreen (1.85:1) letterboxed. Dolby Digital Stereo. $19.99. Keepcase. *LANG:* English. *SUB:* English; French; Spanish. *CAP:* English. *FEATURES:* 24 chapters • Commentary: director • Production commentary • Theatrical trailer.
1993 (R) 97m/C Melinda (Mindy) Clarke, J. Trevor Edmond, Kent McCord, Basil Wallace, Fabio Urena; *D:* Brian Yuzna; *W:* John Penney; *C:* Gerry Lively; *M:* Barry Goldberg.

Return of the Street Fighter

Sonny Chiba is back for more eye-gouging fun, as the lethal mercenary Terry Tsurugi in this bone-snapping sequel. A crooked entrepreneur pressures martial arts schools, raising money to build a huge martial arts center. He hires Terry to kill the men out to expose the scheme. He refuses. Now targeted himself, Terry heads out to bring down the mafia villains. Amazingly, Terry's opposition includes a rematch with Junjo, who survived having his throat torn out in the original. Though not as outrageously violent as the original (except for one eye-popping incident), *Return* still delivers plenty of hard-hitting action. The Street Fighter's nasty disposition is also slightly mellowed. Its one great flaw is its simple-minded plot—one wonders just how much cash Otaguro could really raise through his scheme. However, it's really just an excuse to send waves of thugs against the hero. Image and sound quality are both very good, though the letterbox matte is a bit too soft. The disc contains a bargain triple feature of *Great Street Fighter Movies,* lacking only *Sister Street Fighter* from the collection. —*BT AKA:* Satsujin-ken 2.
Movie: 🎬🎬🎬 ***DVD:*** 🎬🎬 ½
BFS Video (cat #30234D, UPC 06680530-2343). Widescreen letterboxed. $14.99. Keepcase. *LANG:* English. *FEATURES:* 4 chapters • Bio • Selected filmography • Trivia quiz.
1974 88m/C *JP* Sonny Chiba, Claude Gannyon; *D:* Shigehiro (Sakae) Ozawa; *W:* Steve Autrey, Koji Takada; *C:* Teiji Yoshida.

Return to Cabin by the Lake

Please see review of *Cabin by the Lake / Return to Cabin by the Lake.*
Movie: 🎬 ½
2001 89m/C Judd Nelson, Brian Krause, Dahlia Salem, Michael P. Northey, Emman-

uelle Vaugier; **D:** Po Chich Leong; **W:** Jeffrey Reddick; **C:** Stephen M. Katz; **M:** Frankie Blue.

Return to Horror High

A group of low-budget filmmakers try to make a movie about a series of unsolved murders and shoot in the actual school where the crimes took place. Most of the cast and crew are killed in the process. As the police tally up the bodies (and body parts), the film flashes back to the gruesome events. Low-budget tongue-in-cheek parody of slasher films starts off fairly well, with some cute ironic gags and a memorable performance by Rocco as the producer. Around the halfway mark, though, the film completely self-destructs, becoming even more cheap and stupid than the one the characters are making! The (multiple) endings make little sense, the gore-effects are poor, and the movie is bereft of suspense. George Clooney appears but doesn't last long, ironically, as his character is walking off the set to star in a TV show. *Brady Bunch* fans might enjoy Maureen McCormick's quirky turn as a strange cop in the wraparound segments. The disc has been transferred from a pristine source and is appreciably sharp and colorful. There's a thin veil of grain throughout the duration but looks to be an aspect of the photography. The mono sound is clean, but undistinguished. The trailer features exclusively shot footage and is essentially a take off of the old U.S. *Suspiria* trailer. —DG
Movie: 🎬 **DVD:** 🎬🎬🎬
All Day Ent. (cat #DV11738, UPC 013131-173895). Widescreen (1.85:1) anamorphic. Mono. $14.98. Keepcase. *LANG:* English. *FEATURES:* Trailer • 24 chapters.
1987 (R) 95m/C Alex Rocco, Vince Edwards, Philip McKeon, Brendan Hughes, Lori Lethin, Scott Jacoby, George Clooney, Maureen McCormick; **D:** Bill Froelich; **W:** Bill Froelich, Mark Lisson, Dana Escalante, Greg H. Sims, Nancy Forner; **C:** Roy Wagner; **M:** Stacy Widelitz.

Revenge

Sequel to *Blood Cult* finds dog-worshipping murderers trying to get their hands on McGowan's land, or something to that effect. The violence is ample but not particularly believable. DVD presents an exceptionally grainy image that is no better than tape. As is the case with the first film, extras are relatively extensive. —MM
Movie: woof **DVD:** 🎬🎬 ½
VCI (cat #8246, UPC 089859824623). Full frame. Dolby Digital Stereo. $24.99. Keepcase. *LANG:* English. *FEATURES:* 20 chapters • Photo gallery • "Making of" featurette • Talent files • Trailer • Commentary: Christopher Lewis, Rod Slane, David Powell.
1986 (R) 104m/C Patrick Wayne, John Carradine, Bennie Lee McGowan, Josef Hanet, Stephanie Kropke; **D:** Christopher

Lewis; **W:** Christopher Lewis; **C:** Steve McWilliams; **M:** Rod Slane.

Revenge in the House of Usher

Once again, the prolific Jess Franco recycles ideas and characters from his earlier work. This time, he uses footage from *The Awful Dr. Orlof* as flashbacks for Howard Vernon's Usher character. The rest is a delirious hash of Poe and *Dracula* about vampires and women chained up in the dungeon of a castle. Overall, DVD image is very good considering age and budget. Light to moderate damage is visible throughout and sound is thin. —MM **AKA:** Neurosis; Zombie 5.
Movie: 🎬 **DVD:** 🎬🎬
Image Ent. (cat #ID9109BIDVD, UPC 014-381910926). Widescreen (1.78:1) anamorphic. Dolby Digital Mono. $24.99. Keepcase. *LANG:* English; French. *SUB:* English. *FEATURES:* 12 chapters • Trailer.
1982 90m/C *FR* Howard Vernon, Anthony (Jose, J. Antonio, J.A.) Mayans, Dan Villers, Lina Romay; **D:** Jess (Jesus) Franco; **C:** Alain Hardy; **M:** Daniel White.

Revenge of the Nerds / Revenge of the Nerds 2: Nerds in Paradise

In the first film, Lewis and Gilbert (Robert Carradine and Anthony Edwards) are college freshmen who are terrorized by the Alpha Betas, a rival athletic fraternity who want nothing more than to bash some nerds. Gilbert and Lewis find allies in some of their downtrodden college classmates as they attempt to outsmart the jocks. It's not a classic by any means but some of it is fairly funny and it gets across some successful and raunchy jokes. In the sequel, the nerds are transported to Florida for a meeting of fraternities or some such nonsense—it doesn't add up to as many laughs, although putting the characters in a new environment against their old enemies makes for some funny bits. The widescreen editions of these films give these fairly modest productions a bit of gloss. The image is fairly sharp and colorful, though a few scenes are a bit soft. The preprints on both occasionally display some nicks and scratches. The first film is presented with the original mono soundtrack and a new Surround presentation. Neither track is terribly impressive. The dialogue sounds somewhat flat, but is still clear and intelligible. The soundtrack for the second film sounds slightly fuller than in the first film, but it's a very limited presentation. —AB/DG
Movie: 🎬🎬 ½ **DVD:** 🎬🎬🎬
20th Century Fox (UPC 024543011712). Widescreen (1.85:1) anamorphic. Dolby Digital Surround; Mono. $24.98. Keepcase. *LANG:* English; French. *SUB:* English. *CAP:* English. *FEATURES:* Trailer • 32 chapters.
1984 (R) 89m/C Robert Carradine, Anthony Edwards, Timothy Busfield,

Andrew Cassese, Curtis Armstrong, Larry B. Scott, Brian Tochi, Julia Montgomery, Michelle Meyrink, Ted McGinley, John Goodman, Bernie Casey; **D:** Jeff Kanew; **W:** Tim Metcalfe, Jeff Buhai; **C:** King Baggot; **M:** Thomas Newman.

Revenge of the Nerds 2: Nerds in Paradise

Please see review for *Revenge of the Nerds / Revenge of the Nerds 2: Nerds in Paradise*.
Movie: 🎬
1987 (PG-13) 89m/C Robert Carradine, Curtis Armstrong, Timothy Busfield, Andrew Cassese, Ed Lauter, Larry B. Scott, Courtney Thorne-Smith, Anthony Edwards, James Hong; **D:** Joe Roth; **W:** Dan Guntzelman, Steve Marshall; **C:** Charles Correll; **M:** Mark Mothersbaugh.

Revenge of the Patriots

With the defeat of the Mings in the 1500s, the infamous Ching Dynasty began. The Ching emperor kills General Tsu, while Master Wu escapes with the princess to the house of Bruce Li. Wu seeks to hire Li as a guard while transporting the princess, some jewels, and the emperor's last will to the Ming patriots' camp. Li decides to get his sister Judy Lee to help them. Basically, it's the same plot the world would know in *Star Wars*, but with much better fight scenes, courtesy of the Lau Brothers' choreography. Distributors retitled this in some theatres to make it look like another Bruce Lee movie. The print for this once-lost feature was assembled from various sources, so the sound levels and image quality varies greatly. The layer change brings a brief pause, after which the time counter starts over. Volume 9 of the *Wu Tang Clan Hidden Chambers Collection,* a series which makes up for the often poor quality of the prints presented with quite extensive extras. These include short bios of cast and crew members, contemporary interviews, clips from cast members' other films, image galleries, trailers, nice 3-D animated menus, interview footage of the Shaolin Temple Abbots, and more. —BT **AKA:** The Ming Patriots; Bruce Lee's Big Secret; Dragon Reincarnate.
Movie: 🎬🎬🎬 **DVD:** 🎬 ½
Xenon Ent. (cat #9, UPC 694795302229). Widescreen letterboxed. $14.95. Keepcase. *LANG:* English. *FEATURES:* Cast bios • Theatrical trailers • Interviews • Bonus footage • Image gallery • Screensaver • Wu Tang Clan music video • Wu Tang Clan interview.
1976 (R) 87m/C *HK* Bruce Li, Chang Yi, Judy Lee; **D:** Ulysses Au; **W:** Yeung Kung, Shan Yi Cheung; **C:** Wing Him Ching; **M:** Fok Leung Chou.

Revenge Quest

In 2031, a serial killer escapes from a maximum security prison on Mars and seeks vengeance against the people who

put him there. Shot-on-video flick is completely sub-standard in every way, particularly lighting and sound, and so it's unwatchable on DVD or any other medium. Title is available as part of the *Action Arsenal* collection. —*MM*
Movie: woof *DVD:* woof
BCI-Eclipse (cat #44076-9, UPC 7873644-07699). Full frame. $19.98. Keepcase. *LANG:* English. *FEATURES:* 7 chapters.
1996 90m/C Brian Gluhak, Christopher Michael Egger, Jennifer Aguilar; *D:* Alan De Herrera; *W:* Alan De Herrera; *C:* Alan De Herrera; *M:* Joseph Andalino.

Revengeful Swordswoman

This is pure group fare. To watch it alone would be self-abuse of the most unpleasant sort. Forget the bad acting, story, wigs, and dubbing (any two of which could be forgiven for a martial arts film), but the print looks like it was washed with mud and scraped clean with a rock. Additionally, the pan-and-scan operator, or maybe the cinematographer (aghhh!), did the scan without the pan and there's more than a few shots of half of a face here and there on the screen. The dub track also has a load of annoying maniacal laughter from the bad guys. —*CA*
Movie: ♫ *DVD:* woof
Tai Seng (cat #77734, UPC 6016437773-44). Full frame. $9.95. Keepcase. *LANG:* English (dubbed). *FEATURES:* 9 chapters.
1980 88m/C *HK* Chia Ling.

Reversal of Fortune

This drama revolves around Claus Von Bulow (Irons), a member of high society who was convicted of attempting to murder his wife, Sunny (Close), with injections of insulin. After an opening that tells us what could have happened, the film takes us into trying to find out what really happened as Claus hires Alan Dershowitz (Silver) to defend him in an appeal. Much of the film switches between present day and flashbacks: a character drama and a legal one. Transitions between these varying worlds are nicely handled, and information is given out at just the right rate to keep us curious and engaged. Iron's performance is marvelously chilling, a calm man who rarely shows all of his cards—keeping his feelings and thoughts secret. Close plays Sunny well also, a depressed soul who was greatly unhappy with her marriage to Claus; her cold narration from her coma hangs over the film, leading the audience through to try to learn the truth. Although the disc's sharpness and detail are quite good, there are a couple of scenes throughout the movie that are a tad soft. The minor grain often present also keeps the image from looking as crisp as one might hope. Although pixelation is kept to a few very brief traces, there is some annoying image shimmer, although it appears in isolated incidents rather than consistently throughout the movie. Print flaws are sometimes noticeable. The film

is almost completely a dialogue-driven experience but the score does add some Surround presence now and then throughout the movie. Dialogue seemed a tiny bit soft now and then, but generally was easily heard and clear. The commentary is interesting and informative about the real events behind the film, but is marred by stretches of silence. —*AB/DG*
Movie: ♫♫♫ *DVD:* ♫♫ ½
Warner Home Video (UPC 85391193425). Widescreen (1.85:1) anamorphic. Dolby Digital Surround. $19.98. Snapper. *LANG:* English. *CAP:* English. *FEATURES:* Commentary: Schroder, Kazan • Trailer • Chapter links • Award index • Cast & crew notes.
1990 (R) 112m/C Jeremy Irons, Glenn Close, Ron Silver, Annabella Sciorra, Uta Hagen, Fisher Stevens, Julie Hagerty, Jack Gilpin, Christine Baranski, John David (J.D.) Cullum; *D:* Barbet Schroeder; *W:* Nicholas Kazan; *C:* Luciano Tovoli; *M:* Mark Isham. *AWARDS:* Oscars '90: Actor (Irons); Golden Globes '91: Actor—Drama (Irons); L.A. Film Critics '90: Actor (Irons), Screenplay; Natl. Soc. Film Critics '90: Actor (Irons); *NOM:* Oscars '90: Adapt. Screenplay, Director (Schroeder).

Rich and Famous / Tragic Hero

Featuring an incredible cast that shows off some of the best action stars of Hong Kong cinema, these films create a dark image of the Chinese Mob that is intensified by the look of Hong Kong's stark, urban streets. Not unlike Coppola's *Godfather* films, *Rich and Famous* and *Tragic Hero* manage to blend violent acts, action, romance, and humanity together for a lethal mixture—although with a very different tone. Stuck with gambling debts, the brothers Yung (Alex Man) and Kwok (Andy Lau) are in a precarious situation. Collectors are ready to cut off their fingers unless they don't pay up. Desperately they seek help from Lee Ah-Chai (Chow Yun-Fat), the local triad leader. Chai hires the brothers for his own enterprises. Energetic and reliable, Kwok soon becomes Chai's right-hand man, much to the dismay of Yung, who feels left out and overlooked. Frustration builds and as a confrontation with an opposing triad leader looms, Yung shows his real face. In a bloody showdown he changes sides and opposes the man who saved his life. In the sequel, *Tragic Hero*, Chai is driven by revenge. Yung has not only destroyed much of his work, but also put Chai's personal life in shambles. Without the help of Kwok, who has left Hong Kong for solitude, he tries to track down Yung, but the aspiring young mobster always seems to be one step ahead. Sadly, the source print that was used for these DVDs was in very bad shape, and the transfer is riddled with grain, scratches, and other blemishes. The transfer also has a very soft look and lacks detail definition. A number of scenes show slight signs of discoloration, although the majority of the film is presented with vivid colors. The Cantonese 5.1 audio track is

exceptionally well-produced with good dynamics and a frequency response that reproduces the events on the screen quite naturally. Explosions are voluminous despite the fact that the audio track does not have any notable bass extension. The mix is mostly front-loaded with the main focus on the center channel. Surrounds are hardly used and the LFE channel is practically never engaged. (The titles are also available separately.) —*GH*
Movie: ♫♫♫ *DVD:* ♫♫ ½
Tai Seng (UPC 601643801247). Widescreen letterboxed. Dolby Digital 5.1 Surround. $29.98. 2-disc keepcase. *LANG:* Cantonese; Mandarin; Spanish. *SUB:* English. *FEATURES:* 21 chapters • Trailers • Filmographies.
1987 104m/C *HK* Chow Yun-Fat, Andrew Lau, Alex Man, Carina Lau, Alan Tam; *D:* Taylor Wong.

Richard Pryor: Here and Now

This is a good DVD that would be better if it had been edited to perhaps 60 minutes. At 94 minutes it's too long. Yet Pryor is funny; he's at his best when he's giving it back to hecklers. DVD looks very good, and the sound is crisp and wonderful. —*DE*
Movie: ♫♫♫ *DVD:* ♫♫♫
Columbia Tristar (cat #06674, UPC 0433-96066748). Widescreen anamorphic; full frame. Dolby 5.1 Surround. $19.98. Keepcase. *LANG:* English. *SUB:* English; French; Spanish; Portuguese; Chinese; Korean; Thai. *CAP:* English. *FEATURES:* 20 chapters.
1983 (R) 94m/C Richard Pryor; *D:* Richard Pryor.

Richard Pryor: Live and Smokin'

Richard Pryor displays his comedic talents in this 1971 performance where he does his classic "The Wino and the Junkie" routine. A very bland, unimpressive video transfer has probably more to do with the quality of the source material than the transfer process. But the result is the same...a very lackluster disc. The soundtrack features clear dialogue, but that's about it for this already bare-bones disc. —*MJT*
Movie: ♫♫ ½ *DVD:* ♫♫
MPI (cat #DVD7233, UPC 0303067233-27). Full frame. Dolby Digital Stereo. $19.98. Keepcase. *LANG:* English. *SUB:* English. *FEATURES:* 18 chapters.
1981 47m/C Richard Pryor; *D:* Michael Blum.

Richard Rodgers: The Sweetest Sound

Excellent and entertaining documentary that chronicles the life and work of Richard Rodgers. His prolific career, including his partnerships with Lorenz Hart and Oscar Hammerstein II, is told through the use of archival footage, film clips, and interviews with a variety of contemporaries and admirers. Narrated by

Tony Roberts. Featuring interviews with Julie Andrews, Andrew Lloyd Webber, Trevor Nunn, and Celeste Holm, as well as classic performances by Judy Garland, Frank Sinatra, Diahann Carroll, Mary Martin, John Coltrane, and Barbra Streisand. This exceptional video transfer features well-represented colors and blacks. Even the archival footage is crisp and shows no loss of definition. The transfer is very impressive. Similarly, the soundtrack boasts clear, understandable dialogue, which is devoid of distortion. —*MJT*
Movie: 🎬🎬🎬 **DVD:** 🎬🎬🎬
Wellspring Media, Inc. (cat #73153, UPC 720917315324). Full frame. Dolby Digital Stereo. $24.98. Keepcase. *LANG:* English. *FEATURES:* 16 chapters • Musical chronology • Filmography • Weblinks.
2001 90m/C **D:** Roger Sherman; **W:** Laurence Maslon; **C:** Terry Hopkins, Buddy Squires; **Nar:** Tony Roberts.

Richard III

According to the American Film Institute, this is the oldest surviving American feature film and, in 1912, the most ambitious adaptation of Shakespeare ever attempted. Despite changes in conventions, it's still a lively work that's brightened considerably by a new Ennio Morricone score. For the most part, DVD image is nice and sharp but there's a serious registration wobble on the intertitle cards. —*MM* **AKA:** The Life and Death of King Richard III.
Movie: 🎬🎬 **DVD:** 🎬🎬 ½
Kino on Video (cat #K180, UPC 738-329018023). Full frame. $29.95. Keepcase. *LANG:* Silent. *SUB:* English intertitles. *FEATURES:* 16 chapters • "Rediscovery" documentary • Essay by scholar Douglas Brode • Frederick Warde on *Richard III*.
1912 58m/B Frederick Warde, Robert Gomp, Albert Gardner, Violet Stuart; **D:** James Keane.

Ricochet River

Rural coming-of-age story revolves around Lorna (Hudson) and her two buddies Wade (Richter) and Jesse Howl (Spain). The main attraction here is an early appearance by the blandly pretty young Hudson. Soft DVD image is no better than VHS tape. —*MM*
Movie: 🎬🎬 **DVD:** 🎬
Studio Home Ent. (cat #ST7876D, UPC 658149787629). Full frame. Stereo. $24.99. Keepcase. *LANG:* English. *SUB:* English; French; Spanish. *CAP:* English. *FEATURES:* 24 chapters • Trailer.
1998 (R) 111m/C Kate Hudson, Douglas Spain, Jason James Richter, Matthew Glave, Dan Lauria, John Cullum; **D:** Deborah Del Prete.

Riders of Destiny [Columbia]

Please see review for *John Wayne: Western Classics*.
Movie: 🎬🎬 ½
1933 59m/B John Wayne, George "Gabby" Hayes, Cecilia Parker, Forrest Taylor, Al

"Fuzzy" St. John; **D:** Robert North Bradbury; **W:** Robert North Bradbury; **C:** Archie Stout.

Riding in Cars with Boys

Director Penny Marshall tells the story of Beverly (Barrymore), a bright girl who has college on her mind but lust in her heart. She meets up with a sweet loser (Zahn), falls in love, gets pregnant and married (at her police sergeant father's insistence) by 16 and feels doomed by 20. Somewhere along the line she grows a backbone, kicks out her drug-addicted husband (who goes willingly realizing he is going to drag his family down), and eventually writes a book about her life. The story opens with an adult Beverly on her way to have her ex-husband sign a release that will allow her book to be published. This is a realistic coming-of-age story for girls and Marshall manages to balance a sense of humor with a sense of humanity. There are some truly inspired performances, especially by Zahn as the loser with a heart of gold and the always spectacular Brittany Murphy as Beverly's best friend. The disc has a beautiful transfer with vibrant color and very good sound. —*CA*
Movie: 🎬🎬🎬 **DVD:** 🎬🎬🎬
Columbia Tristar (cat #06456, UPC 04339-6064560). Widescreen anamorphic. Dolby Digital 5.1. $27.96. Keepcase. *LANG:* English; French. *SUB:* English; French; Chinese; Korean; Thai. *CAP:* English. *FEATURES:* 28 chapters • Commentary: Drew Barrymore • HBO "making of" special • 4 behind-the-scenes featurettes • Theatrical trailers.
2001 (PG-13) 132m/C Drew Barrymore, Steve Zahn, Brittany Murphy, Adam Garcia, Lorraine Bracco, James Woods, Sara Gilbert, Desmond Harrington, David Moscow, Maggie Gyllenhaal, Peter Facinelli, Marisa Ryan, Mika Boorem, Skye McCole Bartusiak, Logan Lerman; **D:** Penny Marshall; **W:** Morgan Ward; **C:** Miroslav Ondricek; **M:** Hans Zimmer.

The Riff

Old-fashioned music film tells a familiar story with a superb jazz score. Shoop (Fargas) is a Miles Davis–influenced trumpeter who's had a long and not completely happy relationship with producer/agent Adam Goodnight (Smith), who wants him to record another album. But there's a new kid on the scene in New Orleans. The plot is not particularly original, but it is handled with conviction and the score is wonderful. DVD image is fine but unexceptional. The trailer is presented widescreen but the film itself is full frame. Sound is better. —*MM*
Movie: 🎬🎬 **DVD:** 🎬🎬🎬
York Ent. (cat #YPD-1155, UPC 7507231-09928). Full frame. Dolby Digital 5.1 Surround. $14.99. Keepcase. *LANG:* English. *FEATURES:* 24 chapters • Trailers • Behind-the-scenes featurette.
2000 90m/C Antonio Fargas, Nia Peeples, Cameron Smith, Joe McBride; **D:** Mark W.

Allen; **W:** Mark W. Allen; **C:** Garett Griffin; **M:** Bob Belden.

Righting Wrongs

Much like a pulp hero of the 1930s, prosecutor Yuen Biao dishes out vigilante justice when he feels the courts have failed. Corrupt police Sergeant Melvin Wong assigns Inspector Cynthia Rothrock to his crimes, assisted by sloppy cop (and director) Corey Yuen. But Wong will go to any length to cover up his sins, including killing his own cops. A first-rate action picture—Yuen's matches with Rothrock and Wong are kung fu cinema classics. Side A contains the original 92-minute "tragic" version in Cantonese; side B has the 94-minute "happy" version in Mandarin. The image and sound quality on both sides seem identical—a trifle softer and brighter than the laserdisc. —*BT* **AKA:** Chap Faat Sin Fung; Zhi Fa Xian Feng; Above the Law.
Movie: 🎬🎬🎬 ½ **DVD:** 🎬🎬🎬
Tai Seng (cat #5121, UPC 48950249008-96). Widescreen letterboxed. Dolby Digital 5.1 Surround. $19.95. Keepcase. *LANG:* Cantonese; Mandarin. *SUB:* Chinese; English; Japanese; Bahasa; Thai; Korean; Vietnamese. *CAP:* English. *FEATURES:* 8 chapters • Star profiles • Trailers.
1986 93m/C **HK** Yuen Biao, Cynthia Rothrock, Melvin Wong, Wu Ma, James Tien, Corey Yuen; **D:** Corey Yuen; **W:** Barry Wong, Szeto Cheuk Hon; **C:** Tom Lau; **M:** Romeo Diaz.

Riki-Oh: The Story of Ricky

Based on a popular Japanese comic-book series, this is the most over-the-top violent and outrageous kung fu or prison movie (take your pick) ever made. The setting is the not-too-distant future year 2001, when the prison system has been handed over to private contractors. Ricky is sent to prison for 10 years for manslaughter and assault, which he earned by taking revenge on the creeps that killed his girlfriend. A legion of tough guys go into battle against our hero, who also must endure a series of incredible tortures, like being buried alive for days and getting ground glass blown in his eyes. Building on his inborn super-strength is a secret martial arts technique that feeds on its own power—so the more Ricky fights, the stronger he becomes. The martial arts choreography isn't that impressive, but the blood-drenched mayhem more than makes up for it. That may not be good, but at least it's incredibly tasteless. After years of only being able to see this film via smeary import tapes, viewing this crisp digital transfer is a pure joy. A theatrical trailer, dubbed in English, shows panels from the manga compared to matching characters from the film. The disc also has letterboxed Chinese theatrical trailers for several other Asian features. —*BT*
Movie: 🎬🎬🎬 **DVD:** 🎬🎬 ½
Media Blasters (cat #TSDVD0086, UPC 63-15950080623). Widescreen letterboxed.

$29.95. Keepcase. *LANG:* Cantonese; Mandarin; English. *SUB:* Chinese; English. *FEATURES:* 9 chapters • Trailers • Bilingual bios • Filmographies.
1989 90m/C *HK JP* Siu-wong Fan, William Ho; *D:* Ngai Kai Lam; *W:* Ngai Kai Lam; *M:* Philip Chan.

Rio Bravo

Border-town sheriff John T. Chance (John Wayne) locks up local bully Joe Burdette (Claude Akins) for murder, and then faces a blockade of gunmen. On his side are the town drunk, Dude (Martin); Stumpy (Brennan), an old coot; and quick-draw kid Colorado (Nelson). Hawks's answer to *High Noon* is simply one of the most entertaining westerns of its day. Widescreen transfer is mostly clean and clear, without distracting blemishes or other deficiencies. There seem to be a few color-timing problems with the print, however, and in a number of instances, frames appear incorrectly exposed just before splices occur. The level of detail is generally good, although edges appear a bit soft at times. Although a bit inconsistent, colors are typically faithfully rendered and skin tones look natural. The Monaural soundtrack is nicely presented, although the limited frequency response gives away the film's age. *—MM/GH*
Movie: 🎬🎬🎬 ½ *DVD:* 🎬🎬🎬
Warner Home Video (UPC 0853911050-22). Widescreen (1.85:1) anamorphic. Dolby Digital Mono. $19.98. Snapper. *LANG:* English. *SUB:* English; French; Spanish; Portuguese. *FEATURES:* Trailer • Thumbnail bios.
1959 140m/C John Wayne, Dean Martin, Angie Dickinson, Ricky Nelson, Walter Brennan, Ward Bond, Claude Akins, Bob Steele, John Russell, Harry Carey Jr., Pedro Gonzalez-Gonzalez; *D:* Howard Hawks; *W:* Leigh Brackett, Jules Furthman; *C:* Russell Harlan; *M:* Dimitri Tiomkin.

Ripper: Letter from Hell

Unwatchable dreck plays like a combination of the *Scream* and *Urban Legend* films, with a dose of the Jack the Ripper mythos thrown in as an attempt to give it some class. The film can't be accused of being boring, as it opens with a harrowing chase scene and then jumps immediately into a classroom discussion on serial killers. Unfortunately, *Ripper* also doesn't stop to tell the audience what in the world is going on. In the tradition of Pete Walker's fright films from the early '70s, the plot doesn't show up until some 45 minutes into the movie, and by that time, it's more than worn out its welcome. What little story there is deals with a group of students who are taking a class on serial killers. When someone begins to kill the students in a style reminiscent of Jack the Ripper, the kids decide to solve the murders themselves. The film tosses so many red herrings at the audiences, it begins to feel like a *Scary Movie*–type spoof, as one character after another mutters, "No, no,

it wasn't me..." To director John Eyres's credit, the film does have a nice look, but unfortunately, the writers felt that they needed to tack on one too many surprise endings. Interestingly, the on-screen title of the film is simply *Ripper*. One can't help but assume that the "Letter from Hell" subtitle was added after the Johnny Depp Jack the Ripper film *From Hell* opened at theatres. DVD has been letterboxed at 1.85:1 and delivers a print that is free from defects or distortion. The image is sharp and clear, and displays very nice colors. The packaging lists the audio as Dolby Digital 5.1, but in reality it is a Dolby 2.0 Surround mix. This delivers some decent Surround sound effects, but the dialogue is often mixed too low, making the music and sudden sound effects appear to be overly loud. *—ML*
Movie: 🎬 *DVD:* 🎬🎬 ½
Studio Home Ent. (cat #ST 7916D, UPC 658149791626). Widescreen (1.85:1) letterboxed. Dolby 2.0 Surround. $24.99. Keepcase. *LANG:* English. *SUB:* English; Spanish. *CAP:* English. *FEATURES:* Trailer • Commentary • Interviews • 24 chapters.
2001 (R) 113m/C A.J. Cook, Bruce Payne, Ryan Northcott, Juergen Prochnow, Claire Keim, Derek Hamilton, Emmanuelle Vaugier; *D:* John Eyres; *W:* Patrick Bermel; *C:* Thomas M. Harting; *M:* Peter Allen.

Risk

Australian made-for-cable thriller is an overachiever. Ben Morgan (Long) is new to his job as an insurance adjuster. Veteran John Kriesky (Brown) shows him the ropes and, with the assistance of his lawyer/girlfriend Louise (Karvan), lures Ben into a complex scam. The plot twists in all the right directions but the story works through believable characters. Though the cast may not be well known here, the acting is excellent throughout. DVD does all it can with a mid-budget image and an intentionally dark color scheme emphasizing blues and blacks. Detail tends to be lost in shadows and dark clothes. That comes from the original, not the transfer. Surround effects are used sparingly but effectively. A sleeper. Though a trailer is listed as an extra, I could not find it. Also, clicking the subtitle option on the menu led to the disc's cutting itself off. Subtitles could be accessed through the subtitle switch on the remote. *—MM*
Movie: 🎬🎬🎬 *DVD:* 🎬🎬 ½
Lion's Gate Home Ent. (cat #VM7969D, UPC 031398796923). Widescreen (1.85:1) letterboxed. Dolby Digital 5.1 Surround. $24.98. Keepcase. *LANG:* English. *SUB:* English; Spanish. *FEATURES:* 24 chapters • Cast interviews.
2000 (R) 89m/C *AU* Bryan Brown, Tom Long, Claudia Karvan, Jason Clarke; *D:* Alan White; *W:* John Armstrong; *C:* Simon Duggan; *M:* Don Miller-Robinson.

River of No Return

Gold rush times in the Northwest. No-good gambler Harry Weston (Calhoun) steals

the only rifle and only horse of farmer Matt Calder (Mitchum) and his son Mark (Rettig), leaving them defenseless. But Weston's songbird girlfriend Kay (Monroe) stays behind to make amends. Facing an Indian uprising, the trio must escape down a raging river by raft. Is Kay the gal for Matt, as Mark believes? Or is she the no-good tramp Matt thinks she is? As a western production, it's exciting enough, with enough baddies to go around, and peculiar Indians who show up on cue to provide a generic threat, and then go to great lengths to be slaughtered by the score. Although process work abounds, Preminger did indeed get some nice footage of his stars on real locations, and his direction is solid. Like some of the other films in the *Marilyn Monroe: The Diamond Collection, Vol. 2,* the main attraction here remains Monroe herself, who indeed is more romantically photogenic than all the scenery put together. Rigged though the situation may be, when she spreads herself across the 'Scope screen to sing, there's no denying that's what we've come to see. The show now looks like a BIG-screen western, and DVD is very satisfying pictorially. Made in the first year of CinemaScope, it is cropped to 2.35:1 from its original 2.55:1 aspect ratio, a fact which can be noticed in the target shooting scene—even though the view is widescreen, both the shooter and the target tree branch are crowding the frame on each side! *—GE*
Movie: 🎬🎬 ½ *DVD:* 🎬🎬🎬
20th Century Fox (UPC 024543035206). Widescreen (2.35:1) anamorphic. Dolby Digital 4.0 Surround; Stereo. $19.98. Keepcase. *LANG:* English; French. *SUB:* English; Spanish. *CAP:* English. *FEATURES:* Restoration comparison • Trailer • Still gallery.
1954 91m/C Robert Mitchum, Marilyn Monroe, Tommy Rettig, Rory Calhoun, Murvyn Vye, Douglas Spencer; *D:* Otto Preminger; *W:* Frank Fenton; *C:* Joseph LaShelle; *M:* Cyril Mockridge.

The Road

Manuel (Rodriguez) heads off across Patagonia, Argentina, on his motorcycle to find the father he has never known. On the way, he meets Carolina (Costa), a photographer/musician, and a cop with a bad attitude. The fairly conventional road story is sweet and sexy. DVD image is about equal to tape. Moderate grain seems to come from the original, which is generally of broadcast quality. Large yellow English subtitles are burned in. Sound is adequate. *—MM* *AKA: El Camino.*
Movie: 🎬🎬 ½ *DVD:* 🎬🎬
Vanguard Intl. Cinema (cat #VF9153, UPC 658769915334). Full frame. $29.95. Keepcase. *LANG:* Spanish. *SUB:* English. *FEATURES:* 12 chapters.
2000 107m/C *AR* Ezequiel Rodriquez, Antonella Costa, Daniel Valenzuela, Hector Anglada, Alejandro Awada, Ruben Patagonia; *D:* Javier Olivera; *W:* Hector Olivera, Javier Olivera; *C:* Cristian Cottet; *M:* Axel Krygier.

Road Dogz

In East L.A, three Latino youths struggle to escape both the ghetto and the clichés of *Boyz N the Hood*. They're more successful at the former. Picture quality is fairly good, but the dialogue sounds as if it was recorded through a microphone that had been wrapped up in a towel. —BG

Movie: ♪ ½ **DVD:** ♪♪ ½
Artisan Ent. (cat #12200, UPC 01223612-2005). Widescreen (1.85:1) anamorphic. Dolby 5.1; Dolby Stereo. $24.98. Keepcase. *LANG:* English. *SUB:* English; Spanish. *CAP:* English. *FEATURES:* 20 chapters ● Commentary: Alfredo Ramos, Jacob Vargas ● Filmographies ● Trailer ● Interviews ● Production notes.
2000 (R) 95m/C Jacob Vargas, Clifton (Gonzalez) Collins Jr., Greg Serano; **D:** Alfredo Ramos; **W:** Alfredo Ramos; **C:** Matt Faw.

The Road Home

Beautiful and delicate, Zhang Yimou's film deftly crosscuts two stories, one of familial duty and one of epic love. Upon receiving news of the death of his father, Luo Yusheng (Honglei Sun) returns to the tiny village of his youth to console his grieving mother and make peace with bad memories. His mother implores Yusheng to return his father's body (he died while traveling) by foot for a traditional burial. As Yusheng comes to grips with his mother's wishes, the story of Yusheng's father and mother unfolds in flashback. Yimou poignantly counterpoints the dual narratives by shooting the contemporary scenes in black and white and lush color for the lovers' back-story. Zhang Ziyi (*Crouching Tiger, Hidden Dragon*) is pitch-perfect as the steadfast Zhao Di, whose true love for Luo Changyu (Hao Zheng) must conquer social conventions, political peril, and even the elements. The disc offers 2.35:1 anamorphic and full-frame transfers, but widescreen is the only way to go here. The image is always sharp, brilliant, colorful, and, even during the black-and-white scenes, detailed to a fault. The Dolby Digital 5.1 perfectly compliments the film, with subtle Surround envelopment. Don't be fooled by the "G" rating; along with *Gone with the Wind* and *Doctor Zhivago*, this is a celluloid love story for the ages. —EP *AKA:* Wo De Fu Qin Mu Qin.

Movie: ♪♪♪ ½ **DVD:** ♪♪♪
Columbia Tristar (cat #06171, UPC 0433-96061712). Widescreen (2.35:1) anamorphic; full frame. Dolby 5.1 Surround. $29.98. Keepcase. *LANG:* Mandarin; French. *SUB:* English; French. *FEATURES:* 28 chapters ● Theatrical trailers ● Filmographies.
2001 (G) 89m/C *CH* Zhang Ziyi, Sun Honglei, Zheng Hao, Zhao Yuelin, Li Bin; **D:** Zhang Yimou; **W:** Bao Shi; **C:** Hou Yong; **M:** San Bao.

The Road to Morocco [Universal]

The third in the Hope/Crosby *Road* series is one of the best and funniest. This disc contains some extra features not found in the Image release (reviewed in *Book 1*). Picture quality is about the same, ranging between fair and very good, depending on the original photography. Few signs of wear are visible. Extras are nicely chosen. "Bob Hope and the Road to Success" is a 13-minute featurette that's included on several of the Bob Hope Collection discs. —MM

Movie: ♪♪♪ ½ **DVD:** ♪♪♪
Universal Studios (cat #21229, UPC 0251-92122927). Full frame. Dolby Digital Mono. $19.98. Keepcase. *LANG:* English. *SUB:* French; Spanish. *CAP:* English. *FEATURES:* 18 chapters ● "Bob Hope and the Road to Success" ● "Command Performance," 1945 short film ● Photo gallery ● Trailer ● Production notes ● Talent files ● DVD-ROM features.
1942 83m/C Bing Crosby, Bob Hope, Dorothy Lamour, Anthony Quinn, Dona Drake, Vladimir Sokoloff, Yvonne De Carlo; **D:** David Butler; **W:** Frank Butler, Don Hartman; **C:** William Mellor. *AWARDS:* Natl. Film Reg. '96; *NOM:* Oscars '42: Orig. Screenplay, Sound.

The Road to Ruin

Please see review of *Sex and Buttered Popcorn, Vol. 3*.
Movie: ♪♪
1928 45m/B Helen Foster, Grant Withers, Virginia Roye; **D:** Norton S. Parker; **W:** Erik Anjou; **C:** James Diamond.

The Road to Singapore

This is the beginning of the Hope/Crosby *Road*. The guys decide to swear off women and escape to Singapore to enjoy the free life. They meet Lamour, a showgirl who is abused by Quinn. The boys rescue her, both fall in love with her, and thereby set the formula for the rest of the series. Not surprisingly, this is not the sharpest black and white ever filmed, but, like the rest of the films in the Bob Hope Collection, the image transfer is fine, and the extras are well chosen. —MM

Movie: ♪♪ ½ **DVD:** ♪♪♪
Universal Studios (cat #21231, UPC 0251-92123122). Full frame. Dolby Digital Mono. $19.98. Keepcase. *LANG:* English. *SUB:* French; Spanish. *CAP:* English. *FEATURES:* 18 chapters ● "Bob Hope and the Road to Success" ● "Entertaining the Troops" short film ● Photo gallery ● Trailer ● Production notes ● Talent files ● DVD-ROM features.
1940 84m/C Bing Crosby, Bob Hope, Dorothy Lamour, Charles Coburn, Judith Barrett, Anthony Quinn, Jerry Colonna, Johnny Arthur, Pierre Watkin; **D:** Victor Schertzinger; **W:** Frank Butler, Don Hartman; **C:** William Mellor.

The Road to Utopia [Universal]

The fourth of the *Road* films finds the boys in Alaska. Image is a bit on the dark side and probably is not a huge improvement over the Image release (reviewed in *Book 1*). It does manage to reproduce a couple of garish checked suits with barely any flashing. Mono sound is fine for the snappy dialogue and songs. —MM

Movie: ♪♪♪ **DVD:** ♪♪♪
Universal Studios (cat #21230, UPC 0251-92123023). Full frame. Dolby Digital Mono. $19.98. Keepcase. *LANG:* English. *SUB:* French; Spanish. *CAP:* English. *FEATURES:* 18 chapters ● "Bob Hope and the Road to Success" ● "Hollywood Victory Caravan" short film ● Photo gallery ● Trailer ● Production notes ● Talent files ● DVD-ROM features.
1946 90m/B Bing Crosby, Bob Hope, Dorothy Lamour, Jack LaRue, Robert Benchley, Douglass Dumbrille, Hillary Brooke, Robert Barrat, Nestor Paiva; **D:** Hal Walker; **W:** Norman Panama, Melvin Frank; **C:** Lionel Lindon; **M:** Johnny Burke, Leigh Harline, James Van Heusen. *AWARDS:* *NOM:* Oscars '46: Orig. Screenplay.

The Road to Zanzibar

Hope and Crosby join Lamour and Merkel on safari in Africa. This is certainly not the finest entry in the series, but it's got all the trademark songs, jokes, and light romance. It's also one of the grainier of the *Road* films. That comes from the original. This is a clean transfer with no serious signs of wear. As always, mono sound gets the job done. —MM

Movie: ♪♪♪ **DVD:** ♪♪♪
Universal Studios (cat #21232, UPC 0251-92123221). Full frame. Dolby Digital Mono. $19.98. Keepcase. *LANG:* English. *SUB:* French; Spanish. *CAP:* English. *FEATURES:* 18 chapters ● "Bob Hope and the Road to Success" ● "Command Performance," 1944 short film ● Photo gallery ● Trailer ● Production notes ● Talent files ● DVD-ROM features.
1941 92m/C Bing Crosby, Bob Hope, Dorothy Lamour, Una Merkel, Eric Blore, Iris Adrian, Lionel Royce; **D:** Victor Schertzinger; **W:** Frank Butler, Don Hartman; **C:** Ted Tetzlaff.

The Robe

Tribune Marcellus Gallio (Burton) offends Caligula (Robinson) by purchasing the slave Demetrius (Mature) out from under him during an auction. To the dismay of his Senator father (Thatcher) and sweetheart Diana (Simmons), Marcellus is posted in the least desirable land under Roman rule, Palestine. There he ends up officiating at the crucifixion of Christ. He wins Jesus's robe in a dice game, but thinks it bewitched when he's stricken with anxiety attacks after cloaking himself in it for just a moment. Marcellus returns to Rome a mental case. An advisor to Emperor Tiberius (Thesiger of *The Bride of Frankenstein*) suggests that to break the spell he must return to Palestine and destroy the Robe. DVD is a good effort with what must have been less-than-optimal elements. The color is a bit drab and there's far too much grain, especially in

opticals. The quality is degraded just badly enough to make some of the lesser-quality matte paintings look perfectly awful. But it's still a far more powerful experience wide than it is pan and scan, and if you already like the film, this disc will probably not disappoint. The show certainly has flair—it starts with a fanfare befitting the introduction of a new Experience in Movies, and the credits play out over a scarlet curtain that finally pulls back to reveal a wide, wide arena full of gladiators. With the 4.0 Surround, I heard some of the directional-dialogue stereo effects common to films of this vintage. —GE
Movie: ♫♫ *DVD:* ♫♫ ½
20th Century Fox (cat #2002082, UPC 024543020820). Widescreen (2.55:1) anamorphic. Dolby Digital 4.0 Surround Stereo; Stereo; Mono. $19.98. Keepcase. *LANG:* English; French. *SUB:* English; Spanish. *CAP:* English. *FEATURES:* Trailer.
1953 133m/C Richard Burton, Jean Simmons, Victor Mature, Michael Rennie, Richard Boone, Dean Jagger, Jay Robinson, Dawn Addams, Ernest Thesiger, Torin Thatcher; *D:* Henry Koster; *W:* Albert (John B. Sherry) Maltz, Philip Dunne; *C:* Leon Shamroy. *AWARDS:* Oscars '53: Art Dir./Set Dec., Color, Costume Des. (C); Golden Globes '54: Film—Drama; Natl. Bd. of Review '53: Actress (Simmons); *NOM:* Oscars '53: Actor (Burton), Color Cinematog., Picture.

Robert Louis Stevenson's St. Ives

Harry Hook's period comedy recalls *Tom Jones* in its best moments. During the Napoleonic War, French Capt. Jacques St. Ives (Barr) is taken prisoner and sent to Scotland. There he escapes and falls for Flora (Friel). Meanwhile Flora's aunt (Richardson) takes up with British Maj. Chevening (Grant). Lots of chases (including one in a balloon), duels, and battles take place before it's over. The cast handles the light material with tongues firmly in cheeks. The British red coats tend to glow a bit. There's some softness in the candlelit interiors, too, but those are to be expected. Overall, the image is superb. —MM *AKA:* St. Ives; All for Love.
Movie: ♫♫♫ *DVD:* ♫♫♫
Miramax Pictures (cat #23547, UPC 7869-36161649). Widescreen (1.85:1) anamorphic. Dolby Digital Surround. $34.98. Keepcase. *LANG:* English. *CAP:* English. *FEATURES:* 16 chapters • Trailers.
1998 (R) 90m/C *GB* Jean-Marc Barr, Anna Friel, Richard E. Grant, Miranda Richardson, Michael Gough, Jason Isaacs, Tim Dutton, Cecile Pallas; *D:* Harry Hook; *W:* Allan Cubitt; *C:* Robert Alazraki.

Robin and the 7 Hoods

Typical Rat Pack fare with the brothers smoothly mimicking the story of Robin Hood and his merry men. Sinatra is Robo, Martin is John, and the list goes on. Some really great production numbers and the dialogue has some clever language plays and outright gags. When Falk is eulogizing a fellow fallen hood, he praises the dead guy by saying that "he didn't have any enemies, just a lot of friends who didn't like him." Times have changed a little since the golden days of Frank, though, as can be seen in a Sammy Davis production number where he sings, "I like the fun of reaching for a gun." Mostly good fun you can sing along to...unarmed. The print is good with little speckling and the sound is very good. —CA
Movie: ♫♫ ½ *DVD:* ♫♫ ½
Warner (cat #21493, UPC 0853921493-22). Widescreen (2.35:1) anamorphic. Dolby Digital Mono. $19.90. Snapper. *LANG:* English; French. *SUB:* English; French; Spanish. *CAP:* English. *FEATURES:* 38 chapters • Commentary: Frank Sinatra Jr. • Behind-the-scenes documentary.
1964 124m/C Frank Sinatra, Bing Crosby, Dean Martin, Sammy Davis Jr., Peter Falk, Barbara Rush, Victor Buono, Hank Henry, Robert Foulk, Allen Jenkins, Jack LaRue, Edward G. Robinson, Hans Conried, Tony Randall; *D:* Gordon Douglas; *W:* John Fenton Murray; *C:* William H. Daniels; *M:* Nelson Riddle, James Van Heusen. *AWARDS: NOM:* Oscars '64: Adapt. Score, Song ("My Kind of Town").

Robinson Crusoe

Barely released theatrically in 2001, this 1996 production takes considerable liberties with Defoe's novel. It is picture-postcard scenic and Pierce Brosnan looks funky in a long wig. Image is soft at first during the scenes in Scotland and England. It becomes much brighter and sharper once we reach the island (Papua, New Guinea). The whole castaway business and Crusoe's relationship with Man Friday (Takuku) is handled as an adventure tale. Production values are excellent; too good, really, for the story to have any semblance of realism. Grain becomes noticeable in the process shots, but that's not the fault of the disc. —MM *AKA:* Daniel Defoe's Robinson Crusoe.
Movie: ♫♫ ½ *DVD:* ♫♫♫
Miramax Pictures (cat #18543, UPC 7179-51005571). Widescreen (1.85:1) anamorphic. Dolby Digital Stereo. $34.98. Keepcase. *LANG:* English. *CAP:* English. *FEATURES:* Trailers • 16 chapters.
1996 (PG-13) 105m/C Pierce Brosnan, William Takuku; *D:* George Miller; *W:* Tracy Keenan Wynn, Christopher Canaan; *C:* David Connell.

Robotech: The Macross Saga— Extra Disc 1: Elements of Robotechnology

This bonus disc, only available in the *Robotech: Legacy Collection Vol. 1*, features the promotional TV special *CODE-NAME: ROBOTECH*, a compilation of scenes and sequences from the first dozen or so episodes of the show, intended to clue-in latecomers into the characters and story lines. Loosely held together by exclusive narration by the character of Captain Gloval, the program is a curio for fans, but features no new animation and is not essential. The audio commentary is interesting and very worthwhile, giving fans a nice insight into the work and dedication that went into constructing the series. The picture quality is sharp with fair colors but is prone to frequent frame jitter. The audio is fine for a mono track. The character designs are interesting, but one wishes the foreign language demonstration could have utilized a clip featuring more characters. Future extra discs will purportedly fill that need. —DG
Movie: ♫♫ ½ *DVD:* ♫♫ ½
A.D.V. Films (cat #DRT/BX1, UPC 702727-007521). Full frame. Dolby Digital Mono. $44.98. Keepcase. *LANG:* English. *FEATURES:* Commentary: Carl Macek • Character design drawings • Clip featuring English, French, Italian, Spanish, Portugese languages.
1985 74m/C *JP D:* Noboru Ishiguro.

Robotech: The Macross Saga, Vol. 2: Transformation

On this disc (episodes 7–12) the crew of the spaceship *SDF-1* continue their journey to Earth, constantly under siege from the alien Zentraedi. Amongst the highlights: Rick is promoted, Lisa confronts the fate of her fiancée on Mars, Minmei wins the Miss Macross competition, and Rick, Max, Ben, and Lisa are captured by the enemy. This addictive space opera continues to entertain, especially during the capture and escape episodes (10–12). The series episodes are nicely balanced between highly kinetic action sequences and melodramatic ones, with the whole thing tied together by the exciting music. The original commercial bumpers (which include voice-overs by the actors in character) are thoughtfully included. Episodes are a bit grainy, as the entire show was originally mastered on 16mm and the digital clarity shows every hair, dirty cell, and weakness in the original animation. Unfortunately, episodes 7, 8, 11, and 12 are cropped on all four sides, most apparent in the end credit sequences and a few parts where the headroom gets a bit tight. Episodes 9 and 10 look terrific. The sound is strong, but a bit thin. —DG
Movie: ♫♫♫ *DVD:* ♫♫ ½
A.D.V. Films (cat #DRT002, UPC 7027270-22029). Full frame. Dolby Digital Mono. $14.98. Keepcase. *LANG:* English. *FEATURES:* 5 chapters per episode • Previews for other ADV titles.
1985 140m/C *JP D:* Noboru Ishiguro.

Rocco and His Brothers

Modern masterpiece from top director Visconti is about four brothers (Delon, Focas,

Salvatori, Cartier) who move with their mother (Paxinou) from the Italian countryside to Milan. It's a long, sometimes ponderous but engrossing and complex drama. Image's DVD is a very handsome transfer that does a good job of showing off Giuseppe Rotunno's *(On the Beach)* wonderful B&W photography. Apparently heavily cut here in the states for its original release, the packaging takes pains to emphasize the fact that this is a full-length restoration at 168 minutes. Yet the IMDB says 182 in Italy and 175 for the U.S., which may, of course, be an error. There's certainly no feeling of anything being missing. There's no specific copyright holder listed on the DVD case, which is odd because Image usually acts as a semi-distributor for separate content providers. Nino Rota's music score is very impressive and deceptively unobtrusive; it's far more accomplished than his dour melodies for the Godfather films. —*MM/GE* **AKA:** Rocco et Ses Freres; Rocco E I Suoi Fratelli.

Movie: 🎵🎵🎵 ½ **DVD:** 🎵🎵🎵
Image Ent. (UPC 14381842425). Widescreen (1.66:1) letterboxed. Dolby Digital Mono. $29.99. Keepcase. *LANG:* Italian. *SUB:* English.

1960 168m/B *IT* Alain Delon, Renato Salvatori, Annie Girardot, Katina Paxinou, Claudia Cardinale, Roger Hanin, Alessandra Panaro, Spiros Focas, Max Cartier; **D:** Luchino Visconti; **W:** Luchino Visconti, Suso Cecchi D'Amico, Pasquale Festa Campanile, Enrico Medioli, Massimo Franciosa; **C:** Giuseppe Rotunno; **M:** Nino Rota.

Rock 'n' Roll High School [New Concorde SE]

This edition corrects some of the flaws of the earlier release (reviewed in *Book 1*), but it's still rough looking with some print damage. It contains more extras and the sound is stronger. It's the best on DVD to date, and cleaning it up too much would defeat the purpose. —*MM*

Movie: 🎵🎵🎵 **DVD:** 🎵🎵🎵
New Concorde (cat #NH20194, UPC 736-991219496). Widescreen (1.85:1) letterboxed. $19.98. Keepcase. *LANG:* English. *FEATURES:* Joey Ramone interview booklet • Intro & commentary by Allan Arkush • Commentary: Arkush, producer Michael Finnell, writer Richard Whitley • Audio outtakes of the Ramones • Trailers • Talent files.

1979 (PG) 94m/C P.J. Soles, Vincent Van Patten, Clint Howard, Dey Young, Mary Woronov, Alix Elias, Dick Miller, Paul Bartel, Don Steele, Dee Dee Ramone, Joey Ramone, Johnny Ramone, Marky Ramone; **D:** Allan Arkush; **W:** Joe Dante, Russ Dvonch, Joseph McBride, Richard Whitley; **C:** Dean Cundey; **M:** The Ramones.

Rock Star

In Pittsburgh in the mid-1980s, Chris Cole (Wahlberg) is a copy machine repairman by day, rocker by night. He's the lead singer in a hair "tribute" band to the stars Steel Dragon. When the lead singer for Steel Dragon gets the boot from the group, Chris is invited to join and, overnight, finds that all of his fantasies have been realized. His supportive girlfriend Emily (Aniston) is not as certain, and they both learn a lot about life in the music fast lane. The story is loosely based on the band Judas Priest, and all of the details look and sound right. Like the similarly themed *Almost Famous,* the film got uniformly positive reviews in theatrical release but couldn't find an audience. The truth is that there's not much to recommend this one to anyone who's not a fan of the music or the milieu. It's well told and well acted but of limited appeal. DVD is everything you'd expect of a new studio release. The image is bright and sharp with no flaws that I could see. Surround does more for the formulaic music than it really needs or deserves. —*MM*

Movie: 🎵🎵🎵 **DVD:** 🎵🎵🎵
Warner (cat #21327, UPC 0853921327-20). Widescreen anamorphic. Dolby Digital 5.1 Surround. $19.98. Snapper. *LANG:* English; French. *SUB:* English; French; Spanish. *FEATURES:* Commentary: Stephen Herek • Talent files • Music video • Trailer • 28 chapters.

2001 (R) 106m/C Mark Wahlberg, Jennifer Aniston, Timothy Olyphant, Timothy Spall, Jason Flemyng, Dominic West, Matthew Glave, Beth Grant, Stephan Jenkins, Jason Bonham, Heidi Mark, Michael Shamus Wiles, Dagmara Dominczyk, Rachel Hunter; **D:** Stephen Herek; **W:** John Stockwell; **C:** Ueli Steiger; **M:** Trevor Rabin.

Rockin' with a Bullet

Please see review of *Dealin' Dirty.* **AKA:** Sugar Hill, Part 2.

19?? 70m/C Divina Harris; **D:** J. Vincent Parris; **W:** J. Vincent Parris.

Rod Steele 0014: You Only Live Until You Die

According to director Rolfe Kanefsky, this soft-core parody was actually filmed at the beginning of 1996, before *Austin Powers* became a hit. It attempts the same kind of comedy on a shoestring budget—an exceptionally thin and frayed shoestring. Actually, it combines a James Bond spoof with Milo Manara's *Click* comic books. The two halves of the story really don't fit together very well, not that the target adolescent audience will care. The film was produced by the company that makes the *Emmanuelle* cable series and has virtually identical production values. Secret agent Rod Steele (Donavan, with a suitably silly Scottish accent) must save the world, etc., between love scenes. DVD image is not much better than VHS tape, but given the limitations, it looks O.K. The commentary was poorly recorded. Sound levels on the film are left so high that it's hard to understand the speakers. Film is also available in an "R"-rated version (UPC 736991465398). —*MM*

Movie: 🎵 ½ **DVD:** 🎵🎵 ½
New Concorde (UPC 736991665392). Full frame. $19.98. Keepcase. *LANG:* English. *FEATURES:* 24 chapters • Trailers • "Behind the behind" rehearsals and bloopers • Commentary: Kanefsky, Donavan, Hall, editor Cynthia Ludwig.

2002 93m/C Robert Donovan, Sita Thompson, D'Ann Power, John La Zar, Jacqueline Lovell, Michelle (McClellan) Bauer; **D:** Rolfe Kanefsky; **C:** Nils Erickson; **M:** Chris Farrell.

Rodgers & Hammerstein: The Sound of Movies [2 CE]

Introduction to two of the most influential men in American popular entertainment is fine but flawed (slightly). While this documentary, produced by the A&E cable channel, is short on personal details, it hits all the high spots of their film work, *Carousel, Oklahoma!, The King and I, South Pacific, Flower Drum Song,* and *The Sound of Music.* The clips are well chosen and so is the lesser-known background information. (Frank Sinatra almost played the lead in *Carousel.*) Shirley Jones is an attractive and informed host. She's saddled with some ungrammatical writing in the narration, and we're treated to two mercifully brief verses from "You'll Never Walk Alone" and "My Favorite Things," songs I cannot stand. You'll want to keep a notepad handy, though, because the rest of the program will send you to the video store to find copies of those great musicals. DVD delivers an image that's not really much better than its roots, but the sound is far superior to VHS tape, and the disc includes a wealth of extras, including some fascinating screen tests. Think of what *State Fair* might have been like with Andy Williams and Barbara Eden in the leads. That could've worked. And an unsuspecting world was spared Mia Farrow as Maria in *The Sound of Music.* —*MM*

Movie: 🎵🎵🎵 ½ **DVD:** 🎵🎵🎵
Image Ent. (cat #ID0971FSDVD, UPC 014-381097122). Widescreen letterboxed and full frame. Dolby Digital 5.1 Surround, DTS 5.1; Dolby Digital Surround. $24.98. Keepcase. *LANG:* English. *FEATURES:* 12 chapters • 7 screen tests • 3 Movietone News segments on premieres • 8 trailers.

1995 97m/C D: Kevin Burns.

Rodgers & Hammerstein's South Pacific

Authentic lush scenery and an earnest respect for its source mark this made-for-TV adaptation of Rodgers and Hammerstein's classic musical about heroism and racism. Stepping into the role previously essayed by Mary Martin on Broadway and Mitzi Gaynor in the 1958 film, Close (who also executive produces) stars as Nellie

Forbush, the "corny as Kansas" American Navy nurse stationed at a tropical island base during World War II. Nellie falls for the dashing Frenchman Emile de Becque (Rade Sherbedzija, taking a breather from playing Euro-trash villains) whose past threatens their fragile budding love. Actually, *South Pacific* charts two love stories. One thread follows Nellie and Emile, paralleled with the tribulations of Lt. Jim Cable (Harry Connick Jr.) coming to grips with his ingrained prejudice over his love for a Tonganese girl (Natalie Mendoza). Fifty years may have passed since *South Pacific* premiered, but R & H's tunes still pack a punch, even if some have dated badly. Sherbedzija does a splendid job with "Some Enchanted Evening," even if he doesn't hit the same baritone registers as Ezio Pinza. Pastorelli also earns points for his turn as Luther Billis, but comes up short against Ray Walston's definitive portrayal of the sailor/eternal con man. As for Close, her strengths come through when expressing Nellie's dilemma with her face, not her voice. Close is too realistic in demeanor and presence for me to believe she could spontaneously burst into "A Cockeyed Optimist." The full-frame transfer wows with excellent detail delineation, supported by vibrant and natural colors, leaving behind the original film's hokey theatrical lighting. Offering both Dolby Digital and DTS flavors, the 5.1 soundtrack houses few Surround effects, but does a good job of keeping the music flowing at the appropriate moments. —*EP* **AKA:** South Pacific.
Movie: 🎬🎬 ½ **DVD:** 🎬🎬🎬
Buena Vista Home Ent. (cat #23248, UPC 786936159479). Full frame. Dolby Digital 5.1; DTS 5.1. $29.99. Keepcase. *LANG:* English. *CAP:* English. *FEATURES:* 32 chapters ▪ Deleted scene ▪ "On Location with Glenn Close": A Behind-the-Scenes Look.
2001 135m/C Glenn Close, Rade Sherbedzija, Harry Connick Jr., Robert Pastorelli, Jack Thompson, Ilene Graff, Lori Tan Chinn, Natalie Mendoza, Simon Burke, Steve Le Marquand, Steve Bastoni, Damon Herriman; *D:* Richard Pearce; *W:* Lawrence D. Cohen; *C:* Stephen Windon; *M:* Richard Rodgers.

Rollerball

Abysmal remake of director Norman Jewison's 1975 film is given a slicker presentation, but all logic and sense have been thrown out the window. Chris Klein stars as Jonathan Cross, who's introduced while he's doing street-luge down the hills of San Francisco while narrowly dodging cars and even a truck or two. Why? Well, he's a risk-taker. He's saved by his friend Marcus (L.L. Cool J.), who tells him that rollerball teams play in what I think is Eastern Europe or somewhere in Asia. The film never really explains this very well. It doesn't explain the game, either. The rollerball sequences are a lot of images cut together in a way that makes positively no sense. If all of this weren't bad enough—and trust me, it is—McTiernan films an entire 15-minute

action scene in what looks to be green night-vision. The film was released theatrically (after delays) with a "PG-13" rating. DVD restores the film to an "R" rating and a 100-minute running time. From what I can tell, this is approximately three minutes or so of additional material—in other words, not a whole lot of differences. DVD sharpness and detail are very good, if only occasionally terrific. The game scenes look especially sharp and well-defined, with nice depth to the image. Other scenes can vary, but overall, the film never looks soft or hazy. The soundtrack is remarkably intense at times, often boasting some very strong bass. Dialogue remains crisp and clear throughout, as do effects. The box advertises a commentary by "The Horseman," which isn't a very good way to sell a feature that's actually a commentary from stars Rebecca Romijn-Stamos, Chris Klein, and L.L. Cool J. Klein and Romijn-Stamos. They are actually quite funny together and bounce some fairly informative comments back and forth. L.L. Cool J. (who was recorded separately), on the other hand, often simply chats about what's currently going on in the movie or adds goofy comments rather than talking about what went on behind-the-scenes. —*AB*
Movie: 🎬 **DVD:** 🎬🎬🎬
MGM Home Ent. (UPC 027616869982). Widescreen (2.35:1) anamorphic; full frame. Dolby Digital 5.1 Surround; Dolby Surround. $26.98. Keepcase. *LANG:* English; French; Spanish. *SUB:* English; Spanish; French. *CAP:* English. *FEATURES:* "Stunts of Rollerball" featurette ▪ Commentary ▪ Trailers ▪ Music video ▪ DVD production credits ▪ Rollerball Yearbook (talent files).
2002 (R) 100m/C Chris Klein, L.L. Cool J., Rebecca Romijn-Stamos, Jean Reno, Naveen Andrews, Oleg Taktarov, David Hemblen; *D:* John McTiernan; *W:* Larry Ferguson, John Pogue; *C:* Steve Mason; *M:* Eric Serra.

Romantic Comedy

Average romantic comedy about egocentric writer Jason (Moore), who takes on new writing partner Pheobe (Steenburgen) the day he gets married. Phoebe falls in love with Jason and lives a chaste life as his partner and he comes to count on her as his platonic best friend while jealously keeping other men away from her. Tension mounts and one thing leads to another, though the script gets points for not falling back on a Cinderella ending. There are a few fabulous scenes and overall the movie is good for romantic comedy fans. The strongest selling point is the back-and-forth banter between Moore and Steenburgen. The disc looks very good with some dust; the sound is the best mono it can be. — *CA*
Movie: 🎬🎬 **DVD:** 🎬🎬🎬
MGM Home Ent. (cat #1002757, UPC 027616869955). Widescreen (1.85:1) anamorphic. Dolby Digital Mono. $14.95. Keepcase. *LANG:* English. *SUB:* English;

French; Spanish. *CAP:* English. *FEATURES:* 16 chapters ▪ Trailer.
1983 (PG) 102m/C Dudley Moore, Mary Steenburgen, Frances Sternhagen, Ron Leibman; *D:* Arthur Hiller; *W:* Bernard Slade; *C:* David M. Walsh; *M:* Marvin Hamlisch.

Romeo Is Bleeding

This might have been the film noir love child of novelist Jim Thompson and feminist Camille Paglia. It's a wild mixture of sex and bizarre violence that tries to make virtues of its excesses. For those who can tune into the film's mordant humor, it's a fine guilty pleasure. The two central figures are Jack Grimaldi (Oldman), a corrupt cop, and Mona Demarkov (Olin), a professional hitwoman who really loves her work. Jack has squirreled away a tidy little retirement fund by fingering people in the witness protection program to the local mob. Neither his wife Natalie (Sciorra) nor his mistress Sheri (Lewis, as irritating as always) knows about his stash. Oldman is an old hand with this material, but the film belongs to Lena Olin. The role demands a full-tilt, no-prisoners approach, and she delivers. In spades. The picture on this no-frills disc is equal to what I remember from the theatrical release—acceptable, but nothing special. Sound is better. —*MM*
Movie: 🎬🎬🎬 **DVD:** 🎬🎬
MGM Home Ent. (cat #1003246, UPC 027-616873965). Widescreen (1.85:1) anamorphic. Dolby Digital Surround. $19.98. Keepcase. *LANG:* English. *SUB:* English; French; Spanish. *CAP:* English. *FEATURES:* 16 chapters ▪ Trailer.
1993 (R) 110m/C Gary Oldman, Lena Olin, Annabella Sciorra, Juliette Lewis, Roy Scheider, Michael Wincott, David Proval, Paul Butler, Will Patton, Larry Joshua, James Cromwell, Ron Perlman; *D:* Peter Medak; *W:* Hilary Henkin; *C:* Darius Wolski; *M:* Mark Isham. *AWARDS: NOM:* MTV Movie Awards '94: Action Seq.

Rookie of the Year

An inept 12-year-old Little Leaguer, Henry Rowengartner (Nicholas), breaks his arm in a bizarre accident during a game. When his cast comes off, he discovers that he can throw a strike from the centerfield bleachers at Chicago's Wrigley Field. The Cubs turn the city upside-down to find him and quickly coerce him into signing a contract. His hero, the fading star "Rocket" Steadman (Busey), helps him through the end of the season and falls in love with Rowengartner's mom in the bargain. With their new closer, the hapless Cubs actually find themselves winning the World Series. All aspects of this DVD look and sound great. Ironically, I wouldn't recommend this movie to real baseball fans because the filmmakers don't exhibit much respect for the sport. The only connection shows Barry Bonds, Bobby Bonilla, and Pedro Guerrero fanning some of Rowengartner's fictional high heat. —*LA*
Movie: 🎬🎬 ½ **DVD:** 🎬🎬🎬 ½

20th Century Fox (UPC 24543029205). Widescreen (1.85:1) anamorphic; full frame. Dolby Digital 5.1 Surround; Dolby Surround. $19.98. Keepcase. *LANG:* English; French. *SUB:* Spanish. *CAP:* English. *FEATURES:* 20 chapters • 3 theatrical trailers • Featurette • 8 TV spots.
1993 (PG) 103m/C Thomas Ian Nicholas, Daniel Stern, Gary Busey, Dan Hedaya; *D:* Daniel Stern; *W:* Sam Harper; *C:* Jack N. Green; *M:* Bill Conti. *AWARDS:* Blockbuster '95: Family Movie, V.

Roots

Dramatizing the shared heritage of millions of African Americans in an ennobling fashion, this milestone miniseries brought together dozens of black actors to create an accurate, if simplified, picture of several generations in one black family, as documented in Alex Haley's book. The story begins with Kunta Kinte (LeVar Burton) going through his manhood trials in his Gambian village in Africa, only to be captured by slavers and shipped away to America. *Roots* is about building dignity out of outrage and bitterness, and for 1977 television, it was pretty darn progressive. Every manner of negative expletive for blacks is used, but in a historical context that expresses the abject debasement that slavery was. This counters the old *Gone with the Wind* attitude taken that Individuals were responsible, instead of a corrupt society. The much-debated idea is presented that America began, grew, developed, and flourished as a racist nation, which thrived in no small part because of the suffering of exploited slaves. American movies about the issue had never quite settled on that viewpoint before and preferred to make excuses or change the subject, or concentrate on special situations about "good" whites. The message is that America is tainted, and that no amount of rationalizing can change it. By length alone, a miniseries can convince audiences of its importance just by wearing them down, but *Roots* stays interesting and coherent throughout. Even at 10 hours, the pace is fast. The necessity of getting across essential exposition results in some scenes playing like history lessons or simplified primers (as when the bitterness toward English taxation is hurriedly covered in part two). But the multigenerational, follow-the-family formula keeps a continuity of interest. DVD set is a giant undertaking well delivered. Three discs each have an episode per side; unlike other miniseries I've seen on DVD, the compression rate is excellent, and the shows look great. Most television shows from this period look pretty miserable, but *Roots* has rich colors and a terrific visual presence. The packaging is rather nicely designed, once you get by the usual drawback of a cardboard case that won't hold up to anything but delicate handling. Inside a slipcover is a threefold stack of double-sided discs that spreads nicely out, with the dozens of chapter stops clearly listed. There's a running commentary through most of the show, which I could only sample. With so many participants, only the James Bond documentaries are mounted on a larger scale. —*GE*
Movie: ♪♪♪♪ *DVD:* ♪♪♪♪
Warner Home Video (UPC 85393745622). Full frame. $59.98. Special packaging. *LANG:* English. *CAP:* English. *FEATURES:* Commentary • Behind-the-scenes documentary • DVD-ROM features.
1977 573m/C John Amos, Maya Angelou, Ed Asner, Lloyd Bridges, LeVar Burton, Chuck Connors, Cicely Tyson, Ben Vereen, Sandy Duncan, Tanya Boyd, Lynda Day George, Lorne Greene, Burl Ives, O.J. Simpson, Todd Bridges, Georg Stanford Brown, MacDonald Carey, Olivia Cole, Leslie Uggams, Ossie Davis; *D:* David Greene, Marvin J. Chomsky, John Erman, Gilbert Moses; *W:* William Blinn, Ernest Kinoy, M. Charles Cohen, James Lee; *C:* Stevan Larner, Joseph M. Wilcots; *M:* Quincy Jones, Gerald Fried.

Rough Air

As an overseas flight heads into a storm, a mechanical defect causes the cargo door to blow off. The pilot is knocked unconscious, fuel is running low, the controls aren't responding, and the only hope is a pilot (Roberts) on suspension for crashing his last flight. Every airborne cliché in the book is here, including an accused murderer being transferred and belligerent first-class passengers, but Roberts is likeable and manages to make the film enjoyable. Colors are nice, although the level of detail is low. The audio delivers on high-volume sound effects, but handles dialogue less well. The extra features include the world's worst filmography, which credits Eric Roberts with six of the dozens of features he has appeared in. —*BG*
Movie: ♪♪ *DVD:* ♪♪ ½
York Ent. (cat #YPD1168, UPC 750723-116822). Full frame. Dolby 5.1 Surround. $14.99. Keepcase. *LANG:* English. *SUB:* Spanish. *FEATURES:* 28 chapters • Trailers • Filmographies.
2002 90m/C Eric Roberts, Alexandra Paul; *D:* Jon Cassar; *W:* James Makichuk; *C:* Derick Underschultz.

Rough Night in Jericho

Martin plays unredeemable scum in this clichéd western. He's an ex-lawman trying to take over the town of Jericho when all that's left to own is the stagecoach line run by Simmons and McIntire. Coming to the rescue is Peppard as a former deputy marshal turned gambler. Overall, the disc is a good transfer of original elements that have been slightly damaged with light surface flecks in a few scenes. —*MM*
Movie: ♪ ½ *DVD:* ♪♪ ½
Goodtimes Ent. (cat #81042). Widescreen (2.35:1) letterboxed. $14.99. Keepcase. *LANG:* English. *SUB:* English; French; Spanish. *FEATURES:* 18 chapters • Production notes.

1967 104m/C Dean Martin, Jean Simmons, George Peppard, John McIntire, Slim Pickens, Don Galloway; *D:* Arnold Laven; *W:* Sydney Boehm, Marvin H. Albert; *C:* Russell Metty; *M:* Don Costa.

Roughnecks: Starship Troopers Chronicles— The Homefront Campaign

Following the events of *The Klendathu Campaign,* the Starship Troopers return to Earth, grateful that the war with the Bugs is over. However, psychic Carl Jenkins (voiced by Strong) feels that there is a Bug presence on Earth. High-ranking officials don't believe his claims, but Rico (Romano) convinces Lieutenant Razak (Hanes) to investigate Jenkin's intuitions. When the Troopers visit a small town in North Dakota, they uncover a Bug plot to destroy landmarks around the globe. The episodes presented here (representing shows 31–35) offer the same computer animation on which the show's foundation was built. (For a thorough assessment see *The Klendathu Campaign* review.) The story line is one of the best the series has to offer, as the familiar setting (the battles take place in several major cities) add drama to the proceedings. Each show displays a pristine transfer, showing no signs of artifacting, defects, or distortion. The image is as clear and stable as a digital broadcast. With the Dolby Digital 5.1 audio track, the viewer is treated to an impressive bass response and realistic Surround sound, which accompanies the crystal clear dialogue. —*ML*
Movie: ♪♪ ½ *DVD:* ♪♪♪ ½
Columbia Tristar (cat #08689, UPC 0433-96086890). Full frame. Dolby Digital 5.1; Dolby Surround. $24.99. Keepcase. *LANG:* English; French; Spanish. *SUB:* English; French; Spanish. *CAP:* English. *FEATURES:* Commentaries • Filmographies • Trailer • 28 chapters.
1999 96m/C *D:* Sam Liu, Alan Caldwell, Andre Clavel, Sean Song; *V:* Rider Strong, Rino Romano, Jamie Hanes.

Roughnecks: Starship Troopers Chronicles—The Klendathu Campaign

This collection features episodes 26–30 of the popular syndicated TV show based on the film *Starship Troopers* and the novel of the same name. Unlike most animated programs, *Roughnecks* offers intricate story arcs, which are played out over several episodes. As this story line opens, the Troopers, as well as the rest of the crew on the starship *Valley Forge* get a nasty surprise as pilot Zander (voiced by Guest) emerges from hyper-sleep as a hideous bug-monster. Rico (Romano), Ibanez (Hicks), and the others are helpless as the Zander-monster takes over control of the ship and pilots it towards a strange planet. As Zander suddenly jetti-

sons to the surface, the Troopers realize that the planet is Klendathu, home of the Bugs. Thus begins the Klendathu war, as the Troopers engage the Bugs on their home turf in an effort to finally end the war. Along the way, new alliances are formed and a deadly, mutant form of bug emerges. *Roughnecks* is a computer-animated show, and the quality of the animation varies widely. At times, the motion-captured images are photo-realistic, while some images aren't very detailed at all. The character faces look especially odd at times, as Rico bears a strong resemblance to something out of Archie Comics. (Ironically, the Ibanez character doesn't look anywhere near as fake as Denise Richards, the actress who portrayed Ibanez in the feature film.) The story line here is engrossing and well-paced, although episode 29 gets a little slow. Fans of the series should love this. The image is very sharp and clear, displaying no grain, defects, or distortion. The colors are perfect and the balance with dark areas is fine. In short, the transfer is digital broadcast quality. The bold Dolby Digital 5.1 audio track provides clear dialogue, along with a very deep bass response. The Surround sound effects are well placed, displaying a nice sound field and superior stereo separation. (For a good example, check out the gunfire in chapter 14.) The audio commentaries are fun and playful, giving detailed information about the production of the show. —ML
Movie: 🎵🎵 ½ **DVD:** 🎵🎵🎵 ½
Columbia Tristar (cat #08685, UPC 0433-96086852). Full frame. Dolby Digital 5.1; Dolby Surround. $24.95. Keepcase. *LANG:* English; French; Spanish. *SUB:* English; French; Spanish. *CAP:* English. *FEATURES:* Commentaries • Filmographies • Trailer • 28 chapters.
2002 95m/C **D:** David Hartman; **V:** Nicholas Guest, Rino Romano, Tish Hicks.

Roujin Z [Central Park]

The option of the original Japanese soundtrack is the main difference between this disc and the earlier Image release (reviewed in *Book 1*). Both provide very nice widescreen transfers. English subtitles are easy to read. The story of futuristic health care remains one of the best in anime. —MM
Movie: 🎵🎵🎵 **DVD:** 🎵🎵🎵
Central Park/U.S. Manga (cat #2168, UPC 719987216822). Widescreen (1.66:1) letterboxed. Dolby Digital Stereo. $24.98. Keepcase. *LANG:* English; Japanese. *SUB:* English. *FEATURES:* Katsuhiro Otomo thumbnail bio • 14 chapters • Trailers • Still gallery • Big Apple Anime Festival promotional short.
1995 (PG-13) 80m/C **D:** Katsuhiro Otomo.

Round Midnight

In 1959, Dale Turner (Gordon), an aging alcoholic black American sax player, goes to Paris seeking an escape from his self-

destructive ways. François (Cluzet), a devoted young French fan, spurs him to one last burst of creative brilliance. The film is a moody homage to such musicians as Bud Powell and Lester Young. DVD presents a very nice but subdued image that's altogether appropriate to the slow tempo. The score is so wonderful that the lack of an isolated soundtrack is a glaring omission. —MM
Movie: 🎵🎵🎵 **DVD:** 🎵🎵🎵
Warner (cat #11603). Widescreen. $24.98. Snapper. *LANG:* English and French. *SUB:* English; French; Spanish; Portuguese. *FEATURES:* 41 chapters • Talent files • Awards • Trailer.
1986 (R) 132m/C *FR* Dexter Gordon, Lonette McKee, François Cluzet, Martin Scorsese, Herbie Hancock, Sandra Reaves-Phillips; **D:** Bertrand Tavernier; **W:** Bertrand Tavernier, David Rayfiel; **C:** Bruno de Keyzer. *AWARDS:* Oscars '86: Orig. Score; *NOM:* Oscars '86: Actor (Gordon).

Route 666

Some very slick stylistic touches are brought to this action/horror that aspires to be another *From Dusk Til Dawn*. Marshals Jack (Phillips) and Stephanie (Petty) are escorting a witness to a grand jury in Los Angeles when they become lost on a remote highway. Years ago, a chain gang was murdered there, and they return as inmates of the living dead for revenge. The ultra-violence is silly but some of the visual tricks are pretty cool. DVD delivers an exceptionally sharp image that has no problems with the dramatic landscapes. Surround effects kick in for the big scenes. —MM
Movie: 🎵🎵 ½ **DVD:** 🎵🎵 ½
Studio Home Ent. (cat #ST7881D, UPC 658149788121). Widescreen letterboxed. Dolby Digital 5.1 Surround. $24.99. Keepcase. *LANG:* English. *SUB:* English; Spanish. *CAP:* English. *FEATURES:* Trailer • 30 chapters.
2001 (R) 90m/C Lou Diamond Phillips, Lori Petty, Steven Williams, Dale Midkiff, Alex McArthur, Mercedes Colon, L.Q. (Justus E. McQueen) Jones; **D:** William Wesley; **W:** William Wesley, Thomas N. Weber, Scott Fivelson; **C:** Philip Lee; **M:** Terry Plumeri.

Rowing Through

Tiff Wood (Ferguson), a top sculler at Harvard, sacrifices everything in his obsession to win gold at the 1980 Moscow Olympics. When the U.S decides to boycott the games, Tiff continues to work toward the '84 Olympics—even though that means proving himself against a younger group of competitors. The image has a curious orange tint that seems to come from the original. Barebones disc is no significant improvement over VHS tape. —MM
Movie: 🎵🎵 **DVD:** 🎵🎵
Vanguard Intl. Cinema (cat #VF0142). Full frame. $29.98. Keepcase. *LANG:* English. *FEATURES:* 12 chapters.
1996 115m/C *CA JP* Colin Ferguson, Leslie Hope, Peter Murnik, Kenneth Welsh, Michiko Hada, Helen Shaver, James Hynd-

man, Christopher Jacobs; **D:** Masato Harada; **W:** Masato Harada, Will Aitken; **C:** Sylvain Brault; **M:** Masahiro Kawasaki.

Roxanna

Please see review of *Roxanna* (2002).
1970 C Uschi Digart; **D:** Nick (Steve Millard) Phillips.

Roxanna

Credit the guys at El Independent with creativity in their choices of exploitation. This curious little film is a remake of an exceptionally low-budget 1970 original, which is included on the disc. Both tell very simply plotted stories of a sexually adventurous young woman (Mundae in the 2002 version). What separates them from the thousands of identical soft-core productions is the curious level of intensity they achieve. As for image, there's little DVD can (or should) do with a production that was shot in two days on digital video. It's clear enough and the older film is in remarkably good shape. Since it is silent with music and voice-over narration, sound is not really an issue either. —MM
Movie: 🎵🎵 ½ **DVD:** 🎵🎵 ½
El Independent Cinema (cat #sc-2214-dvd, UPC 612385221491). Full frame. $19.98. Keepcase. *LANG:* English. *FEATURES:* Commentary: Ted Crestview, Misty Mundae, Darian Caine • Trailers • "On Roxanna" featurette with exploitation historian 42nd Street Pete • "Despair" short film.
2002 120m/C Misty Mundae, Darian Caine, Katie Jordan; **D:** Ted Crestview.

The Royal Family

This parody of acting families is a flamboyantly told production of the 1927 Kaufman/Ferber Broadway hit. When stage legend and matriarch Fanny Cavendish (LeGallienne) learns that both her daughter and granddaughter are leaving their stage careers for marriage (to businessmen, no less), and that her son got in trouble in Hollywood, sparks fly. All the performances are very good and, though plays don't often transfer well to home viewing, it is a lot of fun. The image is as good or better than its original PBS airing, though there is an occasional, but slight, breakup of the picture. All the dialogue is perfectly clear with the mono sound, but it's nothing special. —DL
Movie: 🎵🎵🎵 ½ **DVD:** 🎵🎵 ½
Image Ent. (cat #879, UPC 0143810879-25). Full frame. Mono. $24.99. Keepcase. *LANG:* English. *FEATURES:* Filmographies • Trailers • 18 chapters.
1977 112m/C Rosemary Harris, Eva LeGallienne, Samm Levine, Ellis Rabb; **D:** Kirk Browning, Ellis Rabb; **W:** George S. Kaufman, Edna Ferber; **C:** Gordon S. Lewis.

R2PC: Road to Park City

Documentary-spoof follows aspiring filmmaker John Viener, who hopes to make a movie and take it to the Sundance Film Festival. Despite the fact that he's been a production assistant, John knows absolutely nothing about making movies; so, we follow him around New York as he tries to learn how. As John struggles to comprehend filmmaking (he seems to be obsessed with hair being in the film gate), the audience is treated to a crash-course in low-budget filmmaking, as we learn about the craft and why it is so hard to get a film made. The image is sharp, but there is a noticeable amount of grain. It's hard to discern if this was an artistic decision on the part of the director, or if it's the result of the transfer. Presumably, the film was shot on 16mm, so some grain is to be expected. The colors, while slightly washed-out at times, are realistic. Digital mono provides clear and audible dialogue. Despite the fact that the DVD box promises "DVD Video Extras," there are no special features. Also, it should be noted that the running time of 83 minutes listed on the packaging is incorrect. —*ML*

Movie: ♪♪♪ **DVD:** ♪♪ ½
Vanguard Intl. Cinema (cat #VF0154). Full frame. Dolby Digital Mono. $29.95. Keepcase. *LANG:* English.
1999 72m/C John Viener; *D:* Bret Stern; *W:* Bret Stern; *C:* Bret Stern; *M:* Daniel Gold.

Ruby

Ruby (Laurie) wants to send her deaf-mute teenaged daughter away, but the girl unleashes her telekinetic powers and causes havoc at the next-door drive-in. Comparisons to *Carrie* are not out of place. But this low-budget independent production is meant for the die-hard horror fan only. On their commentary track, director Harrington and Laurie have a nice trip down memory lane. Not surprisingly, they do not mention some of the unpersuasive effects. They do note the ending, which was filmed by the producer. (Apparently, Harrington's original version does not exist.) DVD image is generally clear but the darker scenes lose detail. That comes from the original. —*MM*

Movie: ♪♪ **DVD:** ♪♪♪
VCI (cat #8270, UPC 089859827020). Widescreen (1.85:1) letterboxed. Dolby Digital Mono. $24.99. Keepcase. *LANG:* English. *FEATURES:* 20 chapters • Talent files • Commentary: Curtis Harrington, Piper Laurie • Photo gallery • Trailer.
1977 (R) 85m/C Roger Davis, Janit Baldwin, Piper Laurie, Stuart Whitman; *D:* Curtis Harrington; *W:* Barry Schneider; *C:* William Mendenhall; *M:* Don Ellis.

Rudolph the Red-Nosed Reindeer: The Movie

Animated version of the famous song is strictly for the Saturday-morning cartoon set. Bright colors; no detail to speak of; cheery, forgettable musical numbers. DVD is a very good transfer of a run-of-the-mill production. —*MM*

Movie: ♪♪ **DVD:** ♪♪ ½
Goodtimes Ent. (cat #81059). Widescreen (1.78:1) letterboxed. Dolby Digital Surround Stereo. $14.99. Snapper. *LANG:* English; French; Spanish. *SUB:* French; Spanish. *CAP:* English. *FEATURES:* Trailer • 18 chapters.
1998 (G) 90m/C *D:* William R. Kowalchuk; *W:* Michael Aschner; *M:* Al Kasha, Michael Lloyd; *V:* John Goodman, Eric Idle, Bob Newhart, Debbie Reynolds, Richard Simmons, Whoopi Goldberg.

Rudy Blue

Minor tale of love found, love lost. The title character, Rudy Blue (Brian Patrick Sullivan), is a 35-year-old repressed history teacher who cares for his brain-damaged brother (Peter Stebbings) and nutty mother (Lauren Klein). Into his bleak little life comes his soul mate (played by Tari Signor, *A Midwife's Tale, The Doghouse*) and everything seems on the verge of change. A first-class example of moviemaking on a very, very small budget, with writer/director and co-producer John Werner (his debut film) connecting all the dots in fine style. Excellent DVD presentation, complete with commentary for both the film itself as well as the deleted scenes—perhaps best suited for film buffs and film school students. —*RJT*

Movie: ♪♪♪ **DVD:** ♪♪♪
York Ent. (cat #YPD-1118, UPC 75072311-1827). Full frame. Dolby Digital Surround. $14.99. Keepcase. *LANG:* English. *FEATURES:* 13 chapters • Commentary: director & lead actor • Deleted scenes with director's commentary • Trailer • 3 cross-promotional trailers.
2000 C Brian Patrick Sullivan, Peter Stebbings, Lauren Klein; *D:* John Werner; *W:* John Werner.

The Ruling Class

A combination of sophomoric sub–Monty Python jokes and bizarre Lewis Carroll–like speeches, this is basically a drawing-room comedy on acid. The 13th Earl of Gurney accidentally hangs himself while dressed in a military tunic and a ballet tutu, an embarrassment which throws the palatial Gurney Manor into a tizzy. Jack (O'Toole), the successor and heir to everything Gurney, is a total nutcase who thinks he's Jesus Christ and even relaxes on a 10-foot cross he erects in the middle of Gurney Hall. The various layabout relatives, mainly Sir Charles (Mervyn), connive to steer the title away from the completely unpredictable Jack, using music-hall "entertainer" Grace Shelley (Seymour) to seduce Jack into a marriage by pretending to be his lost love, The Lady of the Camelias. With the eccentric Lady Claire (Browne) trying to seduce him, the family doctor (Bryant) trying to shock him with a visit from the supernatural Electric Messiah (a wonderful Nigel Green), and the silly-ass Dinsdale (Villiers) worrying about what folks will think of the sometimes obscene proceedings at Gurney Manor, Jack is hav-

ing a tough time keeping about him those wits still in his possession. The film is handsomely photographed and, like most pictures from the era, this DVD easily looks far better than the miserable release prints we saw. The 16:9 transfer restores the show to its full length. (A lot was cut in the U.S., although I can't remember what.) There's a generous helping of Medak's home movies from the set, a stills section, and a commentary track with director Medak, O'Toole, and writer Barnes. They chat in a low-key manner about the history of the play (Barnes wanted Jack to be a midget at first!) and O'Toole has nice monologues about the actors he worked with, and offers his take on the "kitchen sink" genre of English films. The talk isn't going to pull viewers in from other rooms, but fans will love it. —*GE*

Movie: ♪♪♪ **DVD:** ♪♪♪ ½
Criterion (cat #132, UPC 715515012423). Widescreen (1.78:1) anamorphic. Dolby Digital 5.1 Surround. $39.98. Keepcase. *LANG:* English. *FEATURES:* Medak's home movies • Stills gallery • Commentary.
1972 (PG) 154m/C *GB* Peter O'Toole, Alastair Sim, Arthur Lowe, Harry Andrews, Coral Browne, Nigel Green, Michael Bryant, William Mervyn, Carolyn Seymour, James Villiers; *D:* Peter Medak; *W:* Peter Barnes; *C:* Ken Hodges; *M:* John Cameron. *AWARDS:* Natl. Bd. of Review '72: Actor (O'Toole); *NOM:* Oscars '72: Actor (O'Toole).

Run Silent, Run Deep

After his submarine is sunk by a Japanese destroyer in the Bungo Straits, Commander Richardson (Gable) is assigned to a desk back at Pearl Harbor. A year later, he's given another sub, but he takes command over Lt. Bledsoe (Lancaster), the executive officer who has every reason to expect a promotion to captain. Bledsoe is also popular with the crew, making Richardson's job harder. When Richardson announces that they're going into the Straits in defiance of orders to avoid the area, the two men come into direct conflict. Even if this isn't the best film ever made about submarine warfare—it's a far cry from *Das Boot*—it's a terrific showcase for two of Hollywood's best stars, one on the ascent, the other nearing the end of his career. Because the film was produced by Lancaster's company, it makes each of the leads roughly equal in the audience's estimation, and in that regard it can be seen as a precursor to the "buddy" pictures of the '80s and '90s. Even on VHS tape, the shortcomings of the special effects were obvious. On DVD, the wires pulling the model subs and torpedoes are easy to spot. As for the matte shots, the less said the better. Otherwise, the black-and-white photography is crisp and sharp in both aspect ratios. Mono sound is excellent. —*MM*

Movie: ♪♪♪ ½ **DVD:** ♪♪♪
Columbia Tristar Home Video (UPC 0276-16750020). Widescreen (2.35:1) anamorphic; full frame. Dolby Mono. $14.98. Keep-

case. *LANG:* English. *SUB:* English; French. *CAP:* English. *FEATURES:* 32 chapters.
1958 93m/B Burt Lancaster, Clark Gable, Jack Warden, Don Rickles, Brad Dexter, Nick Cravat, Joe Maross, Mary Laroche, Eddie Foy III, Rudy Bond, H.M. Wynant, Joel Fluellen, Ken Lynch, John Bryant; *D:* Robert Wise; *W:* John Gay; *C:* Russell Harlan; *M:* Franz Waxman; *Technical Advisor:* Rear Adm. Rob Roy McGregor.

The Runaway

In 1940s rural Georgia, Luke Winter (Newton) and Joshua Monroe (McLaughlin) are best friends, despite the fact that one is black and one white. While on an adventure, they make a discovery which leads new sheriff Frank Richards (Cain) to reopen an investigation into the unsolved murders of three local black men. The town wants to hush up the whole incident, but the sheriff wants justice to prevail. The situation divides the town along racial lines, and young Luke and Joshua find themselves caught in the middle, not knowing how to act towards one another. This moving drama offers good performances and some wonderful cinematography. The story is able to bring up important and sensitive issues without becoming overbearing. This DVD provides a nice transfer of this made-for-TV movie. The image is presented full frame and looks quite good, rivaling digital broadcast quality. The colors are quite good and there is only a minimal amount of grain in some shots. With the Dolby 2.0 Surround audio track, we get clear dialogue, wonderful music reproduction, and effective Surround effects. —ML
Movie: ♪♪ ½ *DVD:* ♪♪♪
Artisan Ent. (cat #011474, UPC 707729-114741). Full frame. Dolby Surround. $19.98. Keepcase. *LANG:* English. *CAP:* English. *FEATURES:* Production notes ▪ Cast information ▪ 15 chapters.
2000 98m/C Dean Cain, Maya Angelou, Debbi (Deborah) Morgan, Pat Hingle, Kathryn Erbe, Cliff DeYoung, Cody Newton, Duane McLaughlin, Roxanne Hart, Sonny Shroyer; *D:* Arthur Allan Seidelman; *W:* Ron Raley; *C:* Ron Garcia; *M:* Ernest Troost.

Runaway Bride

Roberts plays Maggie Carpenter, a woman famous in her small town of Hale, Maryland, for leaving three men at the altar at the last moment. Gere plays Ike Graham, who writes a rather anti-female column for *USA Today.* He's about to feature Maggie in his next article. Furious, Maggie writes a letter to the editor that results in Ike being fired. Offered a chance to write the tale for *GQ* magazine, Ike sets out to push himself into Maggie's life and save his career. He makes friends in the small town quickly, gaining allies to the horror of Maggie, who would like nothing else but to see him depart. Naturally the two are meant for each other and during Ike's stay, the two begin to warm to each other. Clearly

attempting to re-create the financial success of *Pretty Woman,* this picture reteams director Marshall with Gere and Roberts. She is winning and charming as expected, but Gere is surprising, delivering a fresh sarcastic energy to the role of Ike. Both definitely have great moments of dialogue and perform quite well. It's not perfect, but it certainly serves its purpose. As light entertainment it works. Detail is excellent throughout and flesh tones are natural as well. There is a wonderfully "film-like" feel throughout, with a clean picture that only has a few very minor flaws. There is a slight bit of shimmer, but it's only intermittent. The Surround track is fine, but fairly limited to dialogue and music. The disc includes an incredibly funny and charming commentary by director Gary Marshall. —AB/DG
Movie: ♪♪♪ *DVD:* ♪♪♪
Paramount Home Video (UPC 973632384-47). Widescreen (2.35:1) anamorphic. Dolby Digital 5.1 Surround; Dolby Digital Surround. $29.99. Keepcase. *LANG:* English; French. *SUB:* English. *CAP:* English. *FEATURES:* Trailer ▪ Music video: "Ready to Run" ▪ Commentary: Garry Marshall ▪ Production notes.
1999 (PG) 116m/C Julia Roberts, Richard Gere, Joan Cusack, Hector Elizondo, Christopher Meloni, Rita Wilson, Paul Dooley, Laurie Metcalf, Jean Schertler, Donal Logue, Reg Rogers, Yul Vazquez, Lisa Roberts Gillan, Sela Ward, Tom Mason; *D:* Garry Marshall; *W:* Josann McGibbon, Sara Parriott; *C:* Stuart Dryburgh; *M:* James Newton Howard. *AWARDS: NOM:* MTV Movie Awards '00: Female Perf. (Roberts).

Running Mates

On the eve of his nomination as Democratic Presidential candidate, Michigan governor James Pryce (Selleck) faces several choices for his VP. His savvy campaign manager Lauren Hartman (Linney) has one voice among many, including his wife (Travis) and others (Dunaway, Hatcher). The film is not as sharp (or as tense) as Gore Vidal's *The Best Man,* but writer Claudia Salter has cut it from the same cloth. Made-for-cable image gains little on DVD. The film looks and sounds fine; a filmmakers' commentary might have been called for. —MM
Movie: ♪♪♪ *DVD:* ♪♪ ½
Warner (cat #8349). Widescreen. $19.98. Snapper. *LANG:* English. *SUB:* English; French. *FEATURES:* 28 chapters ▪ Talent files ▪ Trailer.
2000 90m/C Tom Selleck, Laura Linney, Nancy Travis, Teri Hatcher, Bruce McGill, Bob Gunton, Faye Dunaway, Robert Culp, Caroline Aaron, Matt Malloy; *D:* Ron Lagomarsino; *W:* Claudia Salter; *C:* Alan Caso; *M:* John Debney.

Running Scared

Danny & Ray (Crystal & Hines) are two street-wise cops in Chicago. When they are almost killed on a case, they are

forced by their captain to take a vacation. Now Julio (Smits), the drug dealer who nearly killed them, has made bail and is trying to complete a giant deal, inspiring the cops to complete unfinished business. Basically a high-budget super TV cop show, but cast chemistry and Peter Hyams's notch-above-pedestrian direction make this a good movie to watch when home sick. Excellent DVD transfer and sound. —MO
Movie: ♪♪♪ *DVD:* ♪♪♪ ½
MGM Home Ent. (cat #1002577, UPC 027616867780). Widescreen (2.35:1) anamorphic. Dolby Digital Stereo; Dolby Digital Mono. $14.95. Keepcase. *LANG:* English; French; Spanish. *SUB:* French; Spanish. *CAP:* English; French; Spanish. *FEATURES:* 16 chapters ▪ Outtakes ▪ Theatrical trailer.
1986 (R) 107m/C Gregory Hines, Billy Crystal, Dan Hedaya, Jimmy Smits, Darlanne Fluegel, Joe Pantoliano, Steven Bauer; *D:* Peter Hyams; *W:* Gary De Vore; *C:* Peter Hyams.

Running Wild

Horror-industry vet Harry Alan Towers executive produced this made-for-TV family film, which was directed by the writer of the slasher classic *Happy Birthday to Me!* Gregory Harrison stars as Major Matt Robinson, a retired Air Force pilot who has taken a position with the United Nations to track elephant migrations in Africa. As a way to re-connect with his family, he has decided to take his children Angela (Brooke Nevin) and Nicholas (Cody Jones) with him. Once they arrive in Africa, Matt meets a pretty veterinarian, Rachel (Lori Hallier) and a guide, Isaac (Munyaradzi Kanaventi). The Robinson family is enjoying a great adventure on the veldt, until Matt realizes that there are many poachers in the area, who have been hunting the elephants for their valuable ivory. When the poachers threaten Angela and Nicholas, Matt and Rachel spring into action to rescue the children. This is a fun film for the entire family, although it does get a bit too preachy at times concerning the plight of endangered animals. It contains fine performances, as well as a wealth of breathtaking nature photography. The DVD presents the film in its original full-frame format (which does diminish the scope somewhat). The image is very sharp and clear, showing only the slightest amount of grain. The colors are very good, as the browns of the savannah mix with the more opulent colors of the trees and costumes. The digital stereo audio track offers clear dialogue, but it has been mixed at a very low volume, so it can be hard to hear at times. The track offers minimal Surround sound effects. There are no extras on the DVD. —ML
Movie: ♪♪ ½ *DVD:* ♪♪
Showtime Networks, Inc. (cat #SHO 3029, UPC 75844530292-9). Full frame. Digital Stereo. $19.98. Keepcase. *LANG:* English; Spanish. *CAP:* English. *FEATURES:* 12 chapters.

1999 92m/C Gregory Harrison, Lori Hallier, Cody Jones, Brooke Nevin, Munyaradzi Kanaventi; **D:** Timothy Bond.

Rush Hour 2

Detectives Carter (Tucker) and Lee (Chan) begin their second outing in Hong Kong, but the action doesn't really kick into high gear until they reach Las Vegas at the midpoint. The long set piece in a casino there is the film's finest sequence. John Lone, as usual, is a silky villain. Like virtually all sequels, this one lacks freshness, but the comic chemistry between the stars is still enjoyable. New Line has come up with a fully packed disc that's up to its high standards. Image and sound are fine, even in such challenging environments as the gaudy Hong Kong locations and the red-on-red interiors of the casino. The various "Infini-Film" features can either be accessed separately or as interruptions to the film. —*MM*
Movie: 🎵🎵 ½ **DVD:** 🎵🎵🎵 ½
New Line (cat #N5404-T, UPC 794043540-424). Widescreen anamorphic. Dolby Digital EX 5.1 Surround Stereo; DTS 6.1 Surround; DD Surround. $26.98. Keepcase. *LANG:* English. *FEATURES:* 16 chapters • 10 deleted scenes • Jackie Chan's Hong Kong intro • Commentary: Ratner, Nathanson • Ratner featurette • Ratner student film • "Evolution of a Scene" featurette • "Fashion" featurette • Visual effects deconstruction • Trailers and teasers • Talent files • DVD-ROM features.
2001 (PG-13) 91m/C Chris Tucker, Jackie Chan, Harris Yulin, Zhang Ziyi, John Lone, Alan King, Roselyn Sanchez, Kenneth Tsang, Ernie Reyes Jr., Jeremy Piven, Saul Rubinek, Don Cheadle; **D:** Brett Ratner; **W:** Jeff Nathanson; **C:** Matthew F. Leonetti; **M:** Lalo Schifrin, Kathy Nelson.

The Russia House

Ambitious film never quite hits its mark despite a more than competent script by Tom Stoppard. A disgruntled Russian scientist hopes to push Glasnost along by publishing Russian secrets in the U.K. He uses his ex-lover (Pfeiffer) to pass a manuscript along to a sympathetic publisher (Connery), but it's intercepted by British intelligence. They team up with American intelligence and recruit Connery to turn in the Russian scientist. Along the way Pfeiffer and Connery fall in love. It's all very spy vs. spy, but never really draws the viewer into any feeling for the characters. The disc looks and sounds fairly good with some bleeding and fading. —*CA*
Movie: 🎵🎵 ½ **DVD:** 🎵🎵 ½
MGM Home Ent. (cat #1002963, UPC 027-616871503). Widescreen (2.35:1) anamorphic. $14.95. Keepcase. *LANG:* English. *SUB:* English; French; Spanish. *FEATURES:* Theatrical trailer.
1990 (R) 122m/C Sean Connery, Michelle Pfeiffer, Roy Scheider, James Fox, John Mahoney, Klaus Maria Brandauer, Ken Russell, J.T. Walsh, Michael Kitchen,

David Threlfall, Ian McNeice, Christopher Lawford; **D:** Fred Schepisi; **W:** Tom Stoppard; **C:** Ian Baker; **M:** Jerry Goldsmith.

Ruthless People

DeVito and his mistress spend a romantic evening plotting his obnoxious wife's (Midler) untimely demise. Before he can put his plan into action, he's delighted to discover she's been kidnapped by some very desperate people—who don't stand a chance with Bette. High farcical entertainment is a variation on O. Henry's "The Ransom of Red Chief." Overall, the disc rates slightly above a VHS copy, but that's about all you can say for it. The video is often diffused. While bright colors appear crisp, darker hues lack definition and clarity. The soundtrack is merely decent. —*MJT*
Movie: 🎵🎵🎵 **DVD:** 🎵🎵
Buena Vista Home Ent. (cat #18324, UPC 717951005106). Widescreen (1.85:1) letterboxed. Dolby Digital Surround. $19.99. Keepcase. *LANG:* English. *SUB:* English. *FEATURES:* 12 chapters.
1986 (R) 93m/C Bette Midler, Danny DeVito, Judge Reinhold, Helen Slater, Anita Morris, Bill Pullman; **D:** David Zucker, Jim Abrahams, Jerry Zucker; **W:** Dale Launer; **C:** Jan De Bont; **M:** Michel Colombier.

Sabrina

The cast is fine in this story of an "ugly duckling" chauffeur's daughter (Ormond) who reinvents herself in Paris and comes home to be courted by both of the Larrabee brothers, straitlaced Linus (Ford) and ne'er-do-well David (Kinnear). Too often director Pollack lets the action meander when it ought to sparkle. Curiously, the DVD does a more than adequate job of adding a little liveliness to the pokey proceedings. Both image and sound are excellent, actually superior to the theatre where I first saw the film. —*MM*
Movie: 🎵🎵🎵 **DVD:** 🎵🎵🎵
Paramount (cat #33043, UPC 097363304-340). Widescreen anamorphic. Dolby Digital 5.1 Surround; Dolby Digital Surround; Stereo. $24.98. Keepcase. *LANG:* English; French. *SUB:* English. *CAP:* English. *FEATURES:* 17 chapters • Trailer.
1995 (PG) 127m/C Harrison Ford, Julia Ormond, Greg Kinnear, Nancy Marchand, John Wood, Richard Crenna, Angie Dickinson, Lauren Holly, Fanny Ardant, Dana Ivey, Patrick Bruel, Miriam Colon, Elizabeth Franz; **D:** Sydney Pollack; **W:** David Rayfiel, Barbara Benedek; **C:** Giuseppe Rotunno; **M:** John Williams. *AWARDS: NOM:* Oscars '95: Song ("Moonlight"), Orig. Score; Golden Globes '96: Actor—Mus./Comedy (Ford), Film—Mus./Comedy, Song ("Moonlight").

Sabrina, the Animated Series: Sabrina's World

Four episodes from the animated series following the exploits of our favorite teenage witch, as she saves her cat

Salem from an outer space trip and from a seductive feline witch, as well as navigating her own romantic binds. Young kids should enjoy these cartoons, but they don't have much to offer older children. Colors are sharp and vibrant and the menus are easy to navigate, making this a good introductory DVD. —*BG*
Movie: 🎵 ½ **DVD:** 🎵🎵 ½
Lion's Gate Home Ent. (cat #VM 7716D, UPC 031398771623). Full frame. $19.99. Keepcase. *LANG:* English; Spanish. *SUB:* English; Spanish. *CAP:* English. *FEATURES:* 4 chapters • Interactive trivia game • Trailer.
1999 90m/C D: Scott Heming; **V:** Melissa Joan Hart, Emily Anne Hart, Nicky Bakay.

The Sacrifice / Directed by Andrei Tarkovsky

Tarkovsky's enigmatic final film, released after his death, deals with a retired intellectual's spiritually worshipful efforts at self-sacrifice to save his family on the eve of a nuclear holocaust. Stunning cinematography by Nykvist, but the image has a slightly pale cast compared to similar American fare. The second film, which is presented both widescreen and full frame, was directed by Michal Leszcylowski, the editor of *The Sacrifice.* It's a loving portrait of Tarkovsky. Both films are more important for their intelligence and vision than for the brilliance of the DVD image. —*MM*
Movie: 🎵🎵🎵 **DVD:** 🎵🎵🎵
Kino on Video (cat #K149, UPC 73832901-4926). Full frame. $29.95. Keepcase. *LANG:* Swedish and Russian; English. *SUB:* English. *FEATURES:* 12 chapters, feature • 11 chapters, documentary.
1986 (PG) 145m/C *FR SW* Erland Josephson, Susan Fleetwood, Valerie Mairesse, Allan Edwall, Gudrun Gisladottir, Sven Wollter, Filippa Franzen; **D:** Andrei Tarkovsky; **W:** Andrei Tarkovsky; **C:** Sven Nykvist. *AWARDS:* British Acad. '87: Foreign Film.

Sadie Thompson

Swanson plays the hooker with a heart of gold—bawdy and good-natured—in the South Seas. A zealous missionary (Barrymore) arrives and falls in love with her. The last eight minutes of footage have been re-created, using stills and the original intertitle cards to replace the final reel, which had decomposed. Somerset Maugham's famous story "Rain" has been adapted many times; this is still one of the best. As an extra, the disc contains comparisons of fiction, play, and film. Image quality ranges widely throughout from very good to barely watchable. —*MM*
Movie: 🎵🎵🎵 **DVD:** 🎵🎵🎵
Kino on Video (cat #K194, UPC 7383290-19426). Full frame. $19.95. Keepcase. *LANG:* Silent. *SUB:* English intertitles. *FEATURES:* "Many Faces of Sadie Thompson" illustrated essay • Scene comparisons • Photo gallery • 12 chapters.

1928 97m/B Gloria Swanson, Lionel Barrymore, Raoul Walsh, Blanche Frederici, Charles Lane, James A. Marcus; **D:** Raoul Walsh; **W:** Raoul Walsh; **C:** George Barnes, Robert B. Kurrle, Oliver Marsh. *AWARDS: NOM:* Oscars '28: Actress (Swanson), Cinematog.

The Sadistic Baron Von Klaus

In a remote country village, the mysterious murders of young women cause local residents to remember Baron Von Klaus, who placed a curse on the town before his death in the 17th century. Does evil still run in his bloodlines? Although several scenes are quite sadistic for 1962, most of it is just boring. Fans of Italian giallos will be interested in the ways this film prefigures Argento, Bava, and other horror directors. The restoration is nice, although the sound in particular shows the film's age and low budget. —*BG* **AKA:** La Mano de un Hombre Muerto.
Movie: 🎬½ *DVD:* 🎬🎬🎬
Image Ent. (cat #ID9106BIDVD, UPC 0143-81910629). Widescreen (2.35:1) anamorphic. Dolby Mono. $24.95. Keepcase. *LANG:* French. *SUB:* English. *FEATURES:* 18 chapters ▪ Trailer ▪ Alternate footage.
1962 95m/B *SP* Howard Vernon, Hugo Blanco, Georges Rollin, Maria Frances; **D:** Jess (Jesus) Franco.

Sadistic City

Salary-man Taguchi Tomoro meets up with his old friend Hakuryu after 20 years. Afterward, he's drawn into their games of seduction and becomes more twisted and aggressive himself. The English subtitle translations are laughably bad, making it difficult to understand what's going on sometimes. But it's an artfully shot film, with cool music on the soundtrack from John Zorn. The sex scenes are relatively tame—it's the psychodrama that's twisted. Comes in a twin disc double feature with *Taboo.* —*BT* **AKA:** Maohgai.
Movie: 🎬🎬 *DVD:* 🎬🎬
Tai Seng (cat #68934, UPC 6016436893-40). Full frame. $24.95. Keepcase. *LANG:* Japanese; Cantonese; Mandarin. *SUB:* English; Chinese. *FEATURES:* 8 chapters.
1993 88m/C *JP* Akino Sakurako, Tomoroh Taguchi, Hakuryu, Hirota Reona, Rie Kondo; **D:** Ryuichi Hiroki; **W:** Ryuichi Hiroki; **C:** Yasushi Sakakibara; **M:** John Zorn.

Safe

Suburban California housewife Carol (Moore) literally becomes allergic to her environment and winds up seeking relief in a holistic center in Albuquerque, where director Haynes takes a shot at the New Age and finds a link to the AIDS crisis. Serious, stylistically detached look at a near future riddled with environmental toxins is led by Moore's performance as the sunny suburbanite undone by the unseen. Overall, Columbia's DVD transfer looks pretty good. Though director Hayne's sub-

dued colors may not make this a showpiece DVD, the colors are accurate and mostly free of bleed. The image is sharp, except during the lower-lit interior scenes where some noticeable grain appears. The "Dolby Surround" track is crisp, clear, and at least adequately full bodied. The problem is that it's hard to hear any separation at all, even a hint of left/right up front. Any sound sent to the rear Surround must have been zapped up by aliens between the A/V receiver and the speakers, because I didn't hear a thing—which is not necessarily a problem, but why not just call it mono, or at the very best, stereo? Listening to the commentary is more of a chore than it's worth, with far too many silent spaces and only actress Moore contributing some items of interest. —*JO*
Movie: 🎬🎬🎬 *DVD:* 🎬🎬½
Columbia Tristar (cat #06018, UPC 0433-96060180). Widescreen (1.85:1) anamorphic. Dolby Surround. $29.95. Keepcase. *LANG:* English. *SUB:* English; French. *CAP:* English. *FEATURES:* 28 chapters ▪ Theatrical trailer ▪ Talent files ▪ Director's production notes ▪ Commentary: Todd Haynes, Julianne Moore, Christine Vachon.
1995 (R) 119m/C Julianne Moore, Peter Friedman, Xander Berkeley, Susan Norman, James LeGros, Mary Carver, Kate McGregor Stewart, Jessica Harper, Brandon Cruz; **D:** Todd Haynes; **W:** Todd Haynes; **C:** Alex Nepomniaschy; **M:** Ed Tomney. *AWARDS: NOM:* Ind. Spirit '96: Actress (Moore), Director (Haynes), Film, Screenplay.

Sahara

Cut off behind enemy lines, the lone M3 Lee Tank Lulubelle commanded by Sergeant Gunn (Bogart) picks up some British troops and an Italian deserter (Naish) on its journey across the open desert, before holing up at a tiny spot on the map said to be an oasis. There's water, a few drips at a time from an underground well found by Sergeant Tambul (Ingram), but Gunn's problems contending with a vicious Nazi pilot (Kreuger) he's taken prisoner are compounded when a large German detachment surrounds the oasis, under the delusion that there's enough water for all. Gunn has to make his ragged group look heavily supplied and water-rich, if he's to keep his little international force from being overrun by hundreds of thirsty enemy soldiers. DVD is from a good 1998 transfer made for VHS, and has crisp hiss-less audio and only the few speckles and blemishes you'd expect from such an old feature. The disc is basically plainwrap, with the trailers turning out to be for other films and the filmographies just "highlights." The artwork for the package and the inside leaflet are very attractive, even though they've inexplicably included one still of Bogart with Lee J. Cobb, from *Sirocco.* Lloyd Bridges's name is also splashed all over the cover, even though his part is a bit that goes by fairly

unnoticed, and he doesn't even appear on the official cast list. —*GE*
Movie: 🎬🎬🎬🎬 *DVD:* 🎬🎬🎬
Columbia Tristar Home Video (UPC 433-96009899). Full frame. Dolby Digital Mono. $19.95. Keepcase. *LANG:* English; French. *SUB:* English; French; Spanish; Portuguese; Korean; Thai; Chinese. *CAP:* English. *FEATURES:* Trailers ▪ Vintage advertising ▪ Filmographies ▪ 28 chapters.
1943 97m/B Humphrey Bogart, Dan Duryea, Bruce (Herman Brix) Bennett, Lloyd Bridges, Rex Ingram, J. Carrol Naish, Richard Nugent, Pat O'Moore, Kurt Kreuger, John Wengraf, Carl Harbord, Louis Mercier, Guy Kingsford, Peter Lawford; **D:** Zoltan Korda; **W:** Zoltan Korda, John Howard Lawson, James O'Hanlon; **C:** Rudolph Mate; **M:** Miklos Rozsa. *AWARDS: NOM:* Oscars '43: B&W Cinematog., Sound, Support. Actor (Naish).

The Saint

The Saint television series, based on the pulp novels and stories by author Leslie Charteris, ran from 1962–1969. The program starred a pre-007 Roger Moore as dashing adventurer Simon Templar, a man who has dedicated his life to fighting injustice. Unlike other '60s shows in this vein, The Saint isn't a secret agent or private eye. Templar is a secretive man with a vague past, who works alone. He simply seeks out adventure and mystery and does whatever he can to help out those dealing with injustice. Because of these unique themes, the TV show holds up well to this day. Yes, some elements of the program are very dated, but the stories and the action are well done. Moore is very good as the dashing and heroic Templar, showing much of the satisfaction he would bring to the role of James Bond. A&E Home Video has brought *The Saint* to DVD in a series of box sets. These sets represent the 1966 and 1967 seasons of the program. Each set contains six or seven episodes and a host of special features. The presentation here is quite nice, and a great deal of care has clearly gone into restoring these shows. The episodes are presented full frame, and look very good, considering their age. The image here is sharp and quite clear, showing only a minute amount of grain, and surprisingly few defects from the source print. The colors are good, and only occasionally appear washed-out. The Dolby Digital Mono audio tracks deliver clear dialogue and adequate sound effects, but one can't help but wish for a new Dolby Digital 5.1 mix, as A&E did for their *Thunderbirds* DVD sets. Each set of *The Saint* features similar extras, consisting of the original commercial spots for each episode and in-depth information on Roger Moore and the program itself. —*ML*
Movie: 🎬🎬🎬 *DVD:* 🎬🎬🎬
A&E Home Video (UPC 733961702286). Full frame. Dolby Digital Mono. $39.95. Keepcase box set. *LANG:* English. *FEATURES:* Actor bio ▪ Original broadcast trailers ▪ Still gallery ▪ Production notes.

1966 364m/C *GB* Roger Moore, Ivor Dean.

St. Patrick's Day

The annual reunion of a dysfunctional family runs into a roadblock when the host (Laurie) swears off alcohol, and informs the guests that their celebration will be dry. Marriage announcements, a divorce, arguments, and plenty of limericks follow. It's not funny enough to be a comedy, and most of the characters are too one-dimensional for an engaging drama. The picture is grainy, with washed-out colors and a good deal of bleeding. The sound is fine, though for some of the musical numbers you'll wish it wasn't. —*BG*
Movie: 🎵🎵 **DVD:** 🎵🎵 ½
Image Ent. (cat #ID1323SIDVD, UPC 0143-81132328). Full frame. Dolby Stereo. $24.99. Keepcase. *LANG:* English. *FEATURES:* 12 chapters.
2001 (PG-13) 106m/C Piper Laurie, Joanne Baron, Jim Metzler, Julie Strain; **D:** Hope Perello; **W:** Hope Perello; **C:** Denise Brassard.

Salesman

The door-to-door salesman was once a very common, highly visible profession. Completely replaced over the last few decades by the television advertising, home shopping TV channels, and the Internet, these modern-day carpetbaggers would travel from city to city, using any tactic necessary to sell their current stock in trade. *Salesman* is a fascinating record of a group of four men who work in this precarious and lonely profession. As they make the rounds in Massachusetts and Florida, we are witness to the aggressive and sometimes morally questionable tactics they employ to sell an expensive, enormous, and gaudy edition of the Bible. The group members (given nicknames based on their sales tactics—"The Rabbit," "The Bull," etc.) are all featured but the primary focus is Paul Brennan, a once-able salesman whose defeatist attitude has started him down a slippery slope to failure and despair. The directors (highly acclaimed as masters of the documentary form) allow the events to unfold naturally without ever relying on interviews or voice-over narration. Their work is tightly edited and well-photographed. A true-life *Glengarry Glenn Ross, Salesman* manages to be both humorous and tragic. The film features a razor-sharp transfer of the black-and-white image. Though the DVD is extremely grainy, it is due to the original filmstock and the contrasts are rich and varied. The sound is clear (enough to detect a re-looped line or two) but occasionally suffers from the raw nature of the original recording. The commentary is excellent, offering interesting background into the making of the film. Hearing Maysles discuss his tactics for shooting and gaining the confidence of his subjects echoes the working methods employed by the salesmen featured in the film. This almost makes the commentary into a doc-

umentary as fascinating as the film itself! The interviews and photographs all make this disc an absolute must for documentary buffs. —*DG*
Movie: 🎵🎵🎵 **DVD:** 🎵🎵🎵
Criterion (cat #SAL120, UPC 037429158-92). Full frame. Dolby Digital Mono. $39.95. Keepcase. *LANG:* English. *SUB:* English. *FEATURES:* Still gallery • Insert booklet with essay and chapter listings • Commentary: Albert Maysles, Charlotte Zwerin • 22 chapters • Radio interview with "The Rabbit" • Trailer • Filmographies • 1968 TV interview with Albert and David Maysles by Jack Kroll.
1968 91m/B D: David Maysles, Albert Maysles, Charlotte Zwerin; **C:** Albert Maysles.

Same Guys, New Dresses: The Kids in the Hall

Documentary examines the 2000 North American Tour by the Canadian comedy troupe, The Kids in the Hall. But if the purpose of a documentary is to educate the viewer on a particular topic, then this one fails miserably. The film combines scenes from the group's live show with backstage footage. The seven scenes from the show are quite funny, and bring back many of the popular characters from the troupe's television show. The behind-the-scenes stuff is very hit or miss, as some of it goes on for far too long. There is a controversy over group member Dave Foley having laser eye surgery, which gets a bit tense, and a bizarre segment in which Scott Thompson becomes obsessed with a robot dog. The film was shot on video and apparently the mics in the video cameras were used to capture sound. Thus, for some of the back-stage scenes, the audio is muffled and it's difficult to make out what is being said. (This being The Kids in the Hall, one can't help but feel that some really funny lines are going unheard.) While this film should satisfy most die-hard fans of the group, its lack of cohesiveness will turn off many viewers. There's never an explanation of why or how the tour started in the first place, given the fact that the group hadn't worked together in five years. Also, their messy break-up is mentioned, but no details are given. The film was shot by a camera-crew and member Dave Foley got the task of overseeing the editing of many hours of footage. He may be a funny performer, but his editing instincts are questionable. The highlight of this DVD is the audio commentary, which features the Kids and special guests Jason Priestley, Mike Myers, Andy Richter, and Matt Stone and Trey Parker. It's very lively and entertaining. The speakers get way off topic at times, but it's still fun. For the most part, the image is clear, but as it was shot on video, there is some severe video distortion and streaking at times. Despite this, the colors are good. Aside from the audio problems mentioned above, the digital stereo track provides clear dialogue and

sounds great during the live performance scenes. Five deleted scenes are included, and one in particular, where the group does a series of phone interviews and provide a great deal of background information, would have helped the film tremendously. (DVD case promises the "Complete 2000 Tour Program," but that is nowhere to be found.) —*ML*
Movie: 🎵🎵 **DVD:** 🎵🎵 ½
Music Video Distributors (cat #VSC 1341, UPC 77884134195). Widescreen (1.78:1) letterboxed. Digital Stereo. $19.95. Keepcase. *LANG:* English. *FEATURES:* Commentary • Deleted scenes • Cast bios • Still gallery • 24 chapters.
2002 86m/C *CA* Dave Foley, Bruce McCulloch, Kevin MacDonald, Mark McKinney, Scott Thompson.

Samurai Jack

The shadow of the evil Aku has fallen across the land and enslaved its inhabitants in an effort to help their dark captor take over the world. Their only hope lies in Samurai Jack, a man who has spent many years abroad honing his skills as a warrior and waiting for the day he could return to his homeland and remove his country's greatest threat. But before Jack can defeat Aku, he will be pushed by his dark nemesis to the brink of his mental and combative skills. *Samurai Jack* is a more adult-themed cartoon developed by Genndy Tartakovsky, and does a good job of breaching an anime style while still retaining some of its innocent cartoonish nature. This DVD release features a good transfer with nice color quality and a crisp picture. There are no artifacts on the transfer, and no noticeable aliasing during the faster action scenes. The sound is good despite the inclusion of only a Dolby mono track, however due to the high-speed action nature of this film it would have greatly benefitted from a Surround track. —*EL*
Movie: 🎵🎵🎵 **DVD:** 🎵🎵🎵
Warner (cat #1902, UPC 014764190228). Full frame. Dolby Digital Stereo. $19.98. Keepcase. *LANG:* English; Spanish. *FEATURES:* Bonus episode • "Behind the Sword," documentary with Genndy Tartakovsky • "Inside the Making of Samurai Jack from Drawing Board to TV" • Powerpuff Girls theatrical movie sneak peek • 14 chapters. DVD-ROM features: screensaver; Samurai Jack game; weblinks.
2001 90m/C D: Genndy Tartakovsky; **M:** James L. Venable.

Sanctimony

Curiously unhinged thriller works in the same vein as *Seven* and *American Psycho*. Seattle police detectives Renart (Pare) and Smith (Rubin) are on the trail of the "Monkey Maker" serial killer. Wealthy Tom Gerrick (Van Dien) is a suspect. What begins in fairly standard fashion takes some surprising twists on the way to a crazed conclusion. DVD delivers an accurate reproduction of a glossy production. Bright daylight scenes have a blue cast. Darker moments are properly detailed. —MM

Movie: 🎞🎞 ½ **DVD:** 🎞🎞 ½
Pioneer Ent. (cat #PEAD 11531D, UPC 013023153196). Full frame. Dolby Stereo. $24.98. Keepcase. *LANG:* English. *FEATURES:* 20 chapters ● Trailer.
2001 87m/C Casper Van Dien, Eric Roberts, Michael Pare, Jennifer Rubin, Catherine Oxenberg; *D:* Uwe Boll; *W:* Uwe Boll; *C:* Mathias Neumann.

Sand

Below-average thriller features a great cast, but is strictly direct-to-video fare. After the death of his beloved mother, Ty (Michael Vartan) decides to visit her hometown, a small California beach community. There, he quickly befriends surfer Jack (Norman Reedus) and falls in love with Jack's sister Sandy (Kari Wuhrer). He's having a great time with his newfound friends and is determined to put his past behind him. Things go sour when Ty's estranged father Gus (Marshall Bell) arrives with his "business associate" Teddy (Denis Leary), along with Ty's two half-brothers. It seems that this quartet is on the run from the law and they want Ty to harbor them. When he refuses, a small war begins between Ty's friends and the nasty criminals. *Sand* plays like a very low-rent version of *Straw Dogs* at times, but it's very hard to identify or sympathize with any of the characters. The film is needlessly violent, and the editing can be unintentionally unnerving as the film shifts from one scene to the next. Even stranger is the bizarre accent coming from Jon Lovitz (in a cameo role), which sounds dubbed most of the time. *Sand* had a great deal of potential, but it was all swept out to sea. Equally unimpressive is the DVD presentation. The movie is presented full frame, but it's quite clear that it was shot in a widescreen format, as the pan-and-scan action is very noticeable. The image is sharp, but there is a questionable amount of grain in some shots. The colors are good, but there are some white "specks" on the print. The Dolby 2.0 Surround audio track is flat and lifeless for the most part, although the bass reproduction is quite good. —ML

Movie: 🎞 ½ **DVD:** 🎞🎞 ½
Studio Home Ent. (cat #VM7886D, UPC 031398788621). Full frame. Dolby Surround. $24.95. Keepcase. *LANG:* English. *SUB:* Spanish. *CAP:* English. *FEATURES:* Trailer ● 24 chapters.
2000 90m/C Michael Vartan, Denis Leary, Randy Quaid, Kari Wuhrer, Marshall Bell, Julie Delpy, Rodney Eastman, Bodhi (Pine) Elfman, Emilio Estevez, John Hawkes, Jon Lovitz, Norman Reedus, Peter Simmons, Harry Dean Stanton; *D:* Matt Palmieri; *W:* Matt Palmieri; *C:* John Skotchdopole.

The Sandlot

During a summer in 1962, one boy becomes part of a sandlot baseball team, nine boys bond as friends, and their leader becomes the local legend by confronting the spooky mystery that lies beyond the left field fence. Yearning to be a veritable tanning bed of heartwarmth and nostalgia, this one falls short of *A Christmas Story* and *My Dog Skip* with an average 20th Century Fox DVD transfer and decent sound. —MO

Movie: 🎞🎞 ½ **DVD:** 🎞🎞 ½
20th Century Fox (cat #2002924, UPC 024543029243). Widescreen anamorphic. 5.1 Dolby Surround; Dolby Surround. $19.98. Keepcase. *LANG:* English; French. *SUB:* English; Spanish. *CAP:* English; French; Spanish. *FEATURES:* 28 chapters ● Featurette ● Theatrical trailer & TV spots.
1993 (PG) 101m/C Tom Guiry, Mike Vitar, Patrick Renna, Chauncey Leopardi, Marty York, Brandon Adams, Denis Leary, Karen Allen, James Earl Jones, Maury Wills, Art LaFleur, Marley Shelton, Brooke Adams; *D:* David Mickey Evans; *W:* David Mickey Evans, Robert Gunter; *C:* Anthony B. Richmond; *M:* David Newman; *V:* Arliss Howard.

Sandra Bernhard: I'm Still Here...Damn It

This program is a document of Bernhard's most recent stand-up comedy tour, captured for an hour-long HBO special. It's an incredible performance, combining sharp observational humor with songs. The show at times seems almost improvised; Bernhard delivers a free-flowing performance full of energy, letting loose jokes and random creative observations left and right. When it's not hilarious, it's highly watchable. Bernhard's intensity and energetic performance style leave you constantly wondering just what she's going to say next. Her targets and commentary include discussions about Courtney Love, Melanie Griffith, Rosie O'Donnell, and the pairing of Celine Dion and Barbra Streisand. Although possibly more outrageous is the rather revealing outfit she comes out on stage in.... This performance was filmed by renowned award-winning cinematographer Haskell Wexler. His camerawork looks great in this presentation, coming through consistently crystal clear. The only problem is a very slight trace of pixelation in a couple of scenes, but definitely nothing distracting. The sound is 2.0, and it's fine for this kind of presentation. Everything comes through clearly, and the cheering of the crowd never overshadows anything Bernhard has to say. The bonus concert footage is included separately from the main presentation, but you can choose to watch each deleted scene one after another. It's too bad that a lot of this had to be cut out of the final show that ran on cable, because a lot of it is extremely funny. —AB/DG

Movie: 🎞🎞🎞 **DVD:** 🎞🎞🎞 ½
Palm Pictures (UPC 660200301422). Full frame. Dolby Digital Surround. $24.95. Keepcase. *LANG:* English. *FEATURES:* 30 mins. of bonus concert footage ● Production notes ● Previews ● 26 chapters.
1999 60m/C Sandra Bernhard; *W:* Sandra Bernhard; *C:* Haskell Wexler.

Santa Who?

One day during his Christmas preparations, Old Saint (Nielsen) Nick bumps his head quite badly and develops a serious case of amnesia. He's unable to remember who he is or what he is supposed to do, and so it is now up to a few heroes to bring back Santa's memory and save Christmas. No specks mar the print and although very slightly grainy at times, the picture is beautiful to behold. With very good contrast, the image ranges from the deepest blacks to the brightest, glaring whites without bleeding. Colors are very faithfully rendered, creating an image that is very natural looking. At the same time, the DVD does a great job reproducing the beautiful atmospheric, romanticized images of Christmas—as if taken right out of a Norman Rockwell painting. The movie has been transferred and compressed without flaws for this DVD and no compression artifacts are evident. Audio is well produced and has a good frequency response. Although not as bombastic as many newer productions, the sound here is fully sufficient for the subject matter. —GH

Movie: 🎞🎞 ½ **DVD:** 🎞🎞🎞
Buena Vista Home Ent. (cat #23226, UPC 786936159288). Full frame. Dolby Digital Surround. $29.99. Keepcase. *LANG:* English. *SUB:* French; Spanish. *CAP:* English. *FEATURES:* "The Art of Skiing" cartoon.
2000 88m/C Leslie Nielsen, Stephen Eckholdt, Robin (Robyn) Lively; *D:* William Dear.

The Saragossa Manuscript

Adapted from an early 19th-century book, the show is part Luis Borges, part *Canterbury Tales*, and part *Playboy*'s "Girls of Warsaw." A pair of soldiers begin reading a book found in a house in the embattled town of Saragossa, which one of them thinks is about his grandfather: In the story, Captain Alfons van Worden (Zbigniew Cybulski) is trying to get to Madrid but is delayed in the Sierra Morena by what seem to be the ghost demons of two hanged men. In cyclical waking dreams, he's seduced by a pair of Arabian princesses in a palace hidden under the decrepit Quemada (trans: burned) Inn. Yet every morning, he wakes up back out in the pass, under the gallows and its two corpses. Fleeing this dilemma, he's captured by the inquisition but rescued by some noblemen who invite him to a castle, where for a while it looks as if his ordeal was all a planned conspiracy. A passing gypsy tells a tale of the son of a Jewish merchant, which becomes a Chinese box of overlapping stories inside stories. Every nubile maiden in Poland would seem to have been recruited to play the various unholy vixens and mortal

temptresses met along the way, and their coquettish games remind us of the narrative tricks the author is pulling on Alfons—and us. Most of the relationships have aspects of a con in action; to watch the show is to constantly try to figure out what the heck is going on—whether the weird happenings will be revealed as a conspiracy, or perhaps the trick of the mind, or if Alfons is a soul already in hell. No sooner does one story begin, then a character in it begins telling another story. The tangents overlap and confusion is inevitable; not only is it difficult to figure out how storyteller #2 would learn the particulars of the tale told by storyteller #4, but it's impossible to keep them straight anyway. The good news is that the stories don't lead into conceptual cul-de-sacs, but pay off in the kind of ribald good humor that one would expect from a classic farce. The film is very good-looking, filmed in anamorphic black and white. Director Has's camera moves constantly and well; he's a very good director. DVD is presented with the flourish of its 1998 microrelease, that uses a Fillmore West–like poster to make the film seem as if Jerry Garcia (whose ardor for the film extended to paying for part of its restoration) directed it himself. The extras include some nice stills, an isolated music track, and very informative liner notes by Darren Gross. These were especially helpful when I became hopelessly confused at around the 30-minute mark. —GE **AKA:** Rekopis Znaleziony W Saragossie.
Movie: 🎵🎵🎵🎵 *DVD:* 🎵🎵🎵 ½
Image Ent. (cat #ID0563CVDVD, UPC 014-381056327). Widescreen (2:1) anamorphic. Dolby Digital Mono. $24.98. Keepcase. *LANG:* Polish. *SUB:* English. *FEATURES:* 44 chapters • Liner notes by Darren Gross • Notes by Alan Trist • Gallery of promotional art and photographs • Isolated music track.
1965 174m/B *PL* Zbigniew Cybulski, Iga Cembrzynska, Joanna Jedryka, Slawomir Linder; **D:** Wojciech Has; **W:** Tadeusz Kwiatkowski; **C:** Mieczyslaw Jahoda; **M:** Krzysztof Penderecki.

Sassy Sue
Please see review of *The Pigkeeper's Daughter.*
1972 84m/C Sharon Kelly, John Tull, Patrick Wright, Talie Cochrane; **D:** Bethel Buckalew; **W:** Bethel Buckalew; **M:** Hal Southern, Harold Hensley.

Satan in High Heels
Sideshow stripper Stacey (Myles) grabs $900 off her deadbeat husband (who's just been released from jail) and runs to the city to escape him. Making friends with nightclub owner Pepe (Hall), Stacey starts rehearsals for a saucy song-and-dance number and courts disaster by romancing the owner of the club and his son! Entertaining, hard-boiled grind house picture is interesting but lacks action and punch. Myles's wild song number "More

deadly than the male," complete with leather boots and whip, has become a camp classic. Hall (looking like she weighs about 45 pounds) gives a fun performance as a lovable lesbian. The ending is too low-key for its own good. The low-budget photography looks terrific in this disc transfer. The print is near-pristine and the image is sharp with strong contrasts. The sound is a clean and intelligible presentation of the somewhat raw and limited original materials. *The Wild and the Naked* is taken from an older video master (with a burned in SWV logo) from a pretty choppy print. The sound is squawky and frequently very tinny and rough on the ears. —DG
Movie: 🎵🎵 ½ *DVD:* 🎵🎵🎵
Image Ent. (cat #ID1177SWDVD, UPC 014-381117721). Full frame. Mono. $24.99. Keepcase. *LANG:* English. *FEATURES:* 12 chapters, *Satan in High Heels* • 13 chapters, *The Wild and the Naked* • "Satan and the Virgin!" short subject • "Latex She-Devils" short subject • *The Wild and the Naked,* full-length feature • Trailer gallery • Sexploitation art with audio rarities.
1961 90m/B Meg Myles, Grayson Hall, Del Tenney, Mike Keene, Robert Yuro, Sabrina, Earl Hammond, Paul Scott; **D:** Jerald Intrator; **W:** John T. Chapman; **C:** Bernard Herschensen; **M:** Mundell Lowe.

Satan's Bed
Please see review of *Scare Their Pants Off.*
1965 72m/B Yoko Ono, Val Avery, Gene Wesson, Glen Nielson; **D:** Tamijian Smith, Marshall Smith; **C:** Michael Findlay, Roberta Findlay; **M:** Thomas Valentino.

Satan's Cheerleaders
If only this one lived up to its inspired title, but, alas, it's fairly standard exploitation that's nearly done in by its own poverty-row production values. It's one of the grainiest, muddiest, murkiest discs you'll ever watch. As for a plot, we've got the devil's janitor (Kruschen) who works at a high school and kidnaps the ditzy Ms. Johnson (Cole) and four cheerleaders and delivers them to head satanist (Ireland) who's also sheriff. Sound is as weak as the image. —MM
Movie: woof *DVD:* 🎵
VCI (cat #8276, UPC 089859827624). Full frame. $9.99. Keepcase. *LANG:* English. *FEATURES:* Trailer • 12 chapters.
1977 (R) 92m/C John Carradine, John Ireland, Yvonne De Carlo, Kerry Sherman, Jacqulin Cole, Hilary Horan, Alisa Powell, Sherry Marks, Jack Kruschen, Sydney Chaplin; **D:** Greydon Clark; **W:** Greydon Clark, Alvin L. Fast; **C:** Dean Cundey; **M:** Gerald Lee.

Saturday Night and Sunday Morning
"Angry young man at the kitchen sink" drama finds the 23-year-old Finney at his youthful best as working-class Arthur Seaton, who's devoted to good times, spending his weekends with boozing, brawl-

ing, and willing women. He's having an affair with older married Brenda (Roberts) and pursuing the strictly moral Doreen (Field) who refuses to sleep with him without a commitment. Arthur thinks he's falling in love but not without complications and not before warning Doreen that he's unlikely to completely change his carefree ways. Reisz's first feature; Sillitoe adapted his novel. Finney was voted the most promising newcomer at the British Academy (BAFTA) awards. The superb black-and-white photography looks fine on DVD. The only noticeable problem is some flashing in Arthur's chalk stripe suit. The optional yellow subtitles are a help with some of the accents. Recommended. —MM
Movie: 🎵🎵🎵 ½ *DVD:* 🎵🎵🎵
MGM Home Ent. (cat #1003138, UPC 027-616873026). Widescreen (1.66:1) letterboxed. Dolby Digital Mono. $14.98. Keepcase. *LANG:* English. *SUB:* English; French; Spanish. *CAP:* English. *FEATURES:* 16 chapters • Trailer.
1960 98m/B *GB* Albert Finney, Rachel Roberts, Shirley Anne Field, Bryan Pringle, Norman Rossington, Hylda Baker, Robert Cowdra, Elsie Wagstaff, Frank Pettitt; **D:** Karel Reisz; **W:** Alan Sillitoe; **C:** Freddie Francis; **M:** John Dankworth. *AWARDS:* British Acad. '60: Actress (Roberts), Film; Natl. Bd. of Review '61: Actor (Finney).

Savage Pampas
Near the end of his career, Robert Taylor starred as an army officer in this South American spaghetti western. It's violent for its time. DVD is difficult to watch. Authoring appears to be fine, but disc was made from a very dinged up original. Title is also available as part of *The Wild West* boxed set. —MM
Movie: 🎵🎵 *DVD:* 🎵🎵
Brentwood (cat #44089-9, UPC 78736440-8993). Full frame. $9.98. Keepcase. *LANG:* English. *FEATURES:* 6 chapters • "A-Haunting We Will Go" cartoon • DVD dictionary • DVD-ROM features • Trivia game.
1966 100m/C *AR* Robert Taylor, Ty Hardin, Ron Randell; **D:** Hugo Fregonese; **W:** Hugo Fregonese, John Melson; **C:** Manuel Berenguer; **M:** Waldo de los Rios.

Saving Silverman
Darren Silverman (Biggs) hangs out with his boyhood friends Wayne (Zahn) and J.D. (Black), with whom he has formed a Neil Diamond tribute-band called "Diamonds in the Rough." Things are great until Darren meets Judith (Peet), a beautiful, sexy, manipulative control freak. After a disastrous meeting with Darren's friends, Judith forbids Darren from seeing Wayne and J.D., so they decide that they must take matters into their own hands and save him. Genuine laughs are few but this transfer looks fantastic, as there is practically no grain nor distortion or noise present on the image. The color scheme on this transfer is particularly pleasing, as the fleshtones are natural and the reds, blues, and greens look very realistic. The

framing appears to be accurate, and there are no overt problems from artifacting or compression. The 5.1 soundtrack is equally impressive. (Theatrical release is rated "PG-13"; DVD is rated "R".) —ML

Movie: 🎵🎵 **DVD:** 🎵🎵🎵
Columbia Tristar (cat #07066). Widescreen (1.85:1) anamorphic. Dolby Digital 5.1 Surround Stereo; Dolby Digital Surround Stereo. $24.98. Keepcase. *LANG:* English. *SUB:* English; French. *CAP:* English. *FEATURES:* Commentary: Dennis Dugan • Outtake and blooper reel • Trailer • Talent files.
2001 (R) 90m/C Jason Biggs, Steve Zahn, Jack Black, Amanda Peet, R. Lee Ermey, Amanda Detmer, Neil Diamond; **D:** Dennis Dugan; **W:** Hank Nelken, Greg DePaul; **C:** Arthur Albert; **M:** Mike Simpson.

Say Anything [SE]

Hands-down the best teen romance ever made gets the full treatment with a special edition. It's a little ditty about Lloyd (Cusack) and Diane (Skye). She's the straight-A valedictorian who's just won a prestigious scholarship to college in England; he's trying to figure out how to make a living from kick-boxing, and he's completely helplessly, senselessly in love with her. (The scene where he screws up his courage to call and ask her out is one of those rare moments of real truth. Every guy has gone through that fear.) She does agree to go out with him, and she even responds to his feelings, but then there's her proud father (Mahoney). Director Cameron Crowe resolutely avoids clichés as he shows us their relationship. The many deleted, extended, and alternate scenes are a tutorial on the filmmaking process. All of the material is interesting and the film is infinitely better without it. The commentary track is unusually serious; it begins with a 20-minute introduction (over still photographs) where Cameron talks about the extended genesis of the film before the picture actually begins. By contemporary standards, the image is rough, grainy, and dark, but that's what the late '80s production is supposed to look like. Within the muted color scheme, blacks tend to be solid masses. Surround effects are limited and really add little. This is a movie about really strong, likeable characters. At the price, this disc's a bargain that belongs in every collection. —MM

Movie: 🎵🎵🎵½ **DVD:** 🎵🎵🎵½
20th Century Fox (cat #2002452, UPC 024543024521). Widescreen (1.85:1) anamorphic. Dolby Digital 5.1 Surround; Dolby Surround; Dolby Stereo. $19.98. Keepcase. *LANG:* English; French. *SUB:* English; Spanish. *CAP:* English. *FEATURES:* 20 chapters • Commentary: Crowe, John Cusack, Ione Skye • 10 deleted scenes • 13 extended scenes • 5 alternate scenes • "Making of" featurette • Trailers • TV spots.
1989 (PG-13) 100m/C John Cusack, Ione Skye, John Mahoney, Joan Cusack, Lili Taylor, Richard Portnow, Pamela Segall, Jason Gould, Loren Dean, Bebe Neuwirth, Aimee Brooks, Eric Stoltz, Chynna Phillips, Joanna Frank, Jeremy Piven, Don "The Dragon" Wilson; **D:** Cameron Crowe; **W:** Cameron Crowe; **C:** Laszlo Kovacs; **M:** Anne Dudley, Richard Gibbs, Nancy Wilson.

Say It Isn't So

The Farrelly brothers produced this tale of boy-meets-girl, boy-gets-girl, boy-finds-out-girl-is-his-sister. They should've kept their money and done it themselves—it might've been a better movie. Klein stars as good-guy orphan Gilly, who meets cute Jo (Graham), an inept hairdresser with the most screwed-up family this side of the Mansons. Her mom (Field) decides Gilly isn't upwardly mobile enough so she makes everyone think the couple are kin. Gilly sets out to set things right amid Farrelly-approved gross-out gags and humiliations galore. First-time helmer Rogers lacks the Farrelly sense of timing and sentiment, which results in most of the jokes falling flat or not developing at all. The Fox DVD features a great transfer, a boring commentary, and has most likely captured the record for the shortest "making of" featurette ever produced. Of course, that's a good thing since this film doesn't really deserve any sort of special treatment. One would think that anything the Farrelly brothers were involved in would have at least inspired some goofiness on the commentary, but this one should be given out as penance by the local priest. Also included are six deleted scenes (one of which is just an extended scene), which are not funnier than the rest of the film and we can be grateful they were indeed cut. Back to the transfer: Sharp image, strong vibrant colors, deep inky blacks, and no artifacts, and a 5.1 mix that, although not offering the Surround tracks much more than musical enhancement, nonetheless does its job in fairly robust fashion. Despite the ample collection of extras, the DVD seems like a waste when all the votes are counted. —JO/MJT

Movie: 🎵½ **DVD:** 🎵🎵🎵
20th Century Fox (cat #2002058). Widescreen (1.85:1) anamorphic. Dolby Digital 5.1; Dolby Surround. $29.98. Keepcase. *LANG:* English; French. *SUB:* English; Spanish. *CAP:* English. *FEATURES:* Commentary: director James B. Rogers, Chris Klein • 6 deleted scenes with optional commentary • Trailer • 5 TV spots • "Making of" featurette • 20 chapters.
2001 (R) 95m/C Chris Klein, Heather Graham, Orlando Jones, Sally Field, Richard Jenkins, John Rothman, Jack Plotnick, Eddie Cibrian, Mark Pellegrino, Richard Riehle, Brent Briscoe, Suzanne Somers, Brent Hinkley, Henry Cho; **D:** James B. Rogers; **W:** Peter Gaulke, Gerry Swallow; **C:** Mark Irwin; **M:** Mason Daring.

Sayonara

Air Ace Major Lloyd Gruver (Brando) is yanked from fighter duty over Korea by General Webster (Smith), to come to Tokyo as part of his wife's (Scott) plan to accelerate his engagement to their daughter Eileen (Owens), into a quick marriage. But Lloyd is rather irked by the situation, and interested in the fact that one of his airmen, Joe Kelly (Buttons), is being persecuted by the U.S. Forces for his romance and eventual marriage to a Japanese woman, Katsumi (Umeki). Just sympathizing with Kelly earns Lloyd the ire of the brass, and thanks to the pushy attitude of Eileen's mother, the engagement falls apart. But Lloyd finds himself pulled into a relationship with a celebrity performer named Hana-ogi (Taka). When it comes to official prejudice, even the clout of a star fighter pilot can't protect Gruver and his Japanese sweetheart. Originally a Warner's release, *Sayonara* has found its way to DVD via MGM Home Entertainment through the Goldwyn collection, and the fact that MGM does not completely control the title may account for the less-than-stellar transfer on view here. The color and framing are basically good, but the film has not been 16:9 enhanced, and suffers when compared to other widescreen discs on a large monitor. The 2.35:1 aspect ratio is appropriate for Technirama. The stereo sound separation is mild, but the Franz Waxman score is as beautiful as ever. —GE

Movie: 🎵🎵½ **DVD:** 🎵🎵½
MGM Home Ent. (cat #1002384). Widescreen (2.35:1). Dolby Digital Mono. $19.98. Keepcase. *LANG:* English; French; Spanish. *SUB:* French; Spanish. *CAP:* English. *FEATURES:* Trailer.
1957 147m/C Marlon Brando, James Garner, Ricardo Montalban, Patricia Owens, Red Buttons, Miyoshi Umeki, Martha Scott, Kent Smith, Miiko Taka; **D:** Joshua Logan; **W:** Paul Osborn; **C:** Ellsworth Fredericks; **M:** Franz Waxman. *AWARDS:* Oscars '57: Art Dir./Set Dec., Sound, Support. Actor (Buttons), Support. Actress (Umeki); Golden Globes '58: Support. Actor (Buttons); *NOM:* Oscars '57: Actor (Brando), Adapt. Screenplay, Cinematog., Director (Logan), Film Editing, Picture.

Scandal

A congenial letch plucks an 18-year-old tart from his showgirl line, moves her into his flat, and proceeds to school her in the ways of rubbing elbows and OTHER body parts with posh London society folk. It's not long before Dr. Stephen Ward (Hurt) is taking Christine Keeler (Whalley) to swank dinner parties where he holds forth on the joys of "petting," only to be interrupted by the hostess bursting into the dining room wearing only a grass skirt. Of course, naughtiness ensues. When Christine breaks into an impromptu, poolside fan dance—nekkid as a jaybird—she literally bumps into Scandalsville. It's this chance meeting of Cabinet Minister John Profumo (McKellen) and a simultaneous affair with a commie spy (Krabbe) that later erupted into screaming headlines that caused the shameful downfall of Britain's Conservative party. Amidst the luridness of the story, and the unblinking way it's told, there's a profound sensitivity in the script, especially within the performances. John Hurt and Joanne Whalley enthuse seemingly base, torn-from-the-headlines characters with rich emotion. This transfer of the uncut version utilizes a clean print source. —GNG/DG

Movie: 🦴🦴 **DVD:** 🦴🦴

Anchor Bay (cat #DV11242, UPC 0131311-24293). Widescreen (1.85:1) anamorphic. Dolby Digital 5.1 Surround. $29.98. Keepcase. *LANG:* English. *FEATURES:* Theatrical trailer ➤ 32 chapters ➤ Insert card.

1989 (R) 105m/C *GB* John Hurt, Joanne Whalley, Ian McKellen, Bridget Fonda, Jeroen Krabbe, Britt Ekland, Roland Gift, Daniel Massey, Leslie Phillips, Richard Morant; ***D:*** Michael Caton-Jones; ***W:*** Michael Thomas; ***C:*** Mike Molloy; ***M:*** Carl Davis.

Scanners

Exploding head effects (chapter 3) burst onto the screen with David Cronenberg's story of dueling telepaths and government agents. Cronenberg presents telepathy as an uncontrollable babble of interior voices, and is then careful to point out that such a state is also called madness. At the film's worst, the special effects take over, and even though they have been surpassed by digital creations, they're still pretty good. Michael Ironside steals the show. Cronenberg would continue to work with these ideas in other films. DVD image is fine, though a little pale by today's standards. Same goes for the relatively thin sound. —MM

Movie: 🦴🦴🦴 **DVD:** 🦴🦴 ½

MGM Home Ent. (cat #1002330, UPC 027-616865496). Widescreen (1.85:1) anamorphic. Dolby Digital Mono. $14.95. Keepcase. *LANG:* English; French. *SUB:* French; Spanish. *CAP:* English. *FEATURES:* 16 chapters ➤ Trailer.

1981 (R) 102m/C *CA* Stephen Lack, Jennifer O'Neill, Patrick McGoohan, Lawrence Dane, Michael Ironside, Robert A. Silverman; ***D:*** David Cronenberg; ***W:*** David Cronenberg; ***C:*** Mark Irwin; ***M:*** Howard Shore.

Scare Their Pants Off / Satan's Bed

This goofy double feature is one of the Something Weird label's weirdest. *Scare Their Pants Off* is a sort of comedy exploitation about a couple of guys who pretend to kidnap women and torture them. One meets a masked figure; another is sacrificed (sort of) to a guy who wears a lot of makeup and professes to be the god Apu; the third is questioned by a fake Nazi. *Satan's Bed* boasts the screen debut of a young Yoko Ono playing a mail-order bride who's kidnapped by nutty crook. Both black-and-white features were made on shoe-string budgets but look very good for their age. And why not? They're simply too bizarre to be satisfying exploitation and so preserving the original elements probably wasn't too difficult. Of course, the usual

full helping of extras has been ladled onto the disc, including a third film, *Hot Skin and Cold Cash,* which doesn't come close to living up to its title. It's a slow-moving filmed-on-location account of one night in the life of a Times Square hooker. This one's still recommended for the most dedicated fans of cult oddities. —MM

Movie: 🦴 ½ **DVD:** 🦴🦴 ½

Something Weird Video (cat #ID0810SW-DVD, UPC 014381081022). Full frame. Dolby Digital Mono. $24.98. Keepcase. *LANG:* English. *FEATURES:* 10 trailers ➤ 4 short "grind house" films ➤ Gallery of exploitation art ➤ Radio spots.

1968 61m/B Sean Laney, Jon Woods, Mary St. Feint, Claire Adams; ***D:*** John Maddox; ***W:*** John Maddox; ***C:*** Arthur Marks.

Scarlett

Anyone who can get past star Joanne Whalley's hapless fingernails-on-the-blackboard attempts at a Southern accent might be able to enjoy this interminable sequel to *Gone with the Wind.* Our heroine tries to get back Tara and Rhett (Dalton), explores her Irish family ties, and even moves back to the Emerald Isle. The miniseries arrives on a double-disc set with the rich image intact. In fact, the colors of the lavish sets and costumes are so saturated that they appear a bit harsh in brighter shots. Stereo sound is very good. —MM

Movie: 🦴 **DVD:** 🦴🦴

Artisan Ent. (cat #11762). Full frame. Dolby Stereo. $19.98. Keepcase. *LANG:* English. *CAP:* English. *FEATURES:* Hallmark Channel trailer ➤ "Making of" documentary ➤ 46 chapters.

1994 (PG-13) 360m/C Joanne Whalley, Timothy Dalton, Ann-Margret, Barbara Barrie, Sean Bean, Brian Bedford, Stephen Collins, John Gielgud, Annabeth Gish, George Grizzard, Julie Harris, Tina Kellegher, Melissa Leo, Colm Meaney, Esther Rolle, Jean Smart, Elizabeth Wilson, Paul Winfield, Betsy Blair, Peter Eyre, Pippa Guard, Ronald Pickup, Gary Raymond, Dorothy Tutin; ***D:*** John Erman; ***W:*** William Hanley; ***M:*** John Morris.

The Scars of Dracula

A young couple tangles with Dracula (Lee) in their search for the man's missing brother. Gory, creepy, sexy tale is one of Hammer's last attempts to work with the famous character, and it's far from the studio's best work. The transfer has been cleaned up and is free of defects or speckles. The level of detail is incredibly high, making it a joy to watch. Rich in color and detail, with deep blacks that paint beautifully ominous pictures, and well-defined shadows. However, the transfer seems to have a bit of a problem with the strong blood-red hues found in a number of scenes, and some slight compression artifacts are evident there. Other than that, the presentation is meticulous. There is no sibilance and no distortion and the daring chord clusters of the score come

across powerful and menacing, as desired. Dialogue is always understandable and clear. Anchor Bay has included a second disc with the first 10,000 copies of the DVD. On that second disc you will find the 1995 full-length documentary *The Many Faces of Christopher Lee,* an exploration of Lee's career that no real fan can afford to miss. Hosted by Lee himself, this extensive documentary covers his entire career, and Lee is quite candid about the productions, offering valuable insight into the immense body of work he has done throughout his lengthy career and the people with whom he has worked. —GH

Movie: 🦴🦴 **DVD:** 🦴🦴 ½

Anchor Bay (UPC 13131146691). Widescreen (1.85:1) anamorphic. Dolby Digital Mono. $24.98. Keepcase. *LANG:* English. *FEATURES:* Commentary: Christopher Lee, Marcus Hearn, Roy Ward Baker ➤ Trailers ➤ TV spots ➤ Photo gallery.

1970 (R) 96m/C *GB* Christopher Lee, Jenny Hanley, Dennis Waterman, Wendy Hamilton, Patrick Troughton, Michael Gwynn, Anouska (Anoushka) Hempel, Michael Ripper, Christopher Matthews, Delta Lindsay; ***D:*** Roy Ward Baker; ***W:*** John (Anthony Hinds) Elder; ***M:*** James Bernard.

Scary Movie 2

A group of college students must spend a weekend in a haunted castle in exchange for receiving an A from their lascivious professor (Curry). Highlights include Tori Spelling as a hot and bothered psycho chick and James Woods as the old priest in an *Exorcist*-like prologue (attempting to replace the already-cast Marlon Brando who came down with pneumonia, a major loss for cult film history). As with *Scary Movie,* Keenen Ivory Wayans spoofs every horror film (and seemingly every film) of recent memory. This sequel, however, looks very hurried and the pacing is erratic both in plot and individual "skits." The DVD offers a huge amount of alternate takes and deleted scenes that suggest a trial-and-error approach that should have been less slap-dash. Competent image transfer and sound. —MO

Movie: 🦴🦴 ½ **DVD:** 🦴🦴🦴 ½

Buena Vista Home Ent. (cat #24014, UPC 786935166557). Widescreen. Dolby 5.1 Surround Sound. $29.99. Keepcase. *LANG:* English; French. *SUB:* Spanish. *CAP:* English; French; Spanish. *FEATURES:* 19 chapters ➤ Behind-the-scenes featurette ➤ Deleted and alternate scenes ➤ Special effects tour ➤ Behind the makeup ➤ Word from "The Perch" ➤ Still gallery.

2001 (R) 82m/C Anna Faris, Tim Curry, Shawn Wayans, Marlon Wayans, Chris Elliott, Tori Spelling, Christopher K. Masterson, Kathleen Robertson, Regina Hall, James Woods, David Cross, Andy Richter, Natasha Lyonne, Veronica Cartwright, Richard Moll; ***D:*** Keenen Ivory Wayans; ***W:*** Shawn Wayans, Marlon Wayans, Alyson Fouse, Greg Grabianski, Dave Polsky, Michael Anthony Snowden, Craig Wayans; ***C:*** Steven Bernstein.

The Scent of Green Papaya

Beautifully directed stream of consciousness for the eyes. Mui is sent to be the servant of a well-to-do family in Saigon in the 1950s. She is an observer of the people and things around her, and we too observe with her through the eye of the filmmaker. Ten years later when the family falls on hard times, she is sent to work at the home of a family friend, a bachelor musician who is eventually seduced by her simplicity and breaks the rules of his upper-class station to be with her. The art direction on this film is amazing, combining lush plant life with splashes of brilliant color. Written and directed by Tran Anh Hung, this is a visual feast that will leave you feeling sated. The disc is as smooth as velvet with beautiful color and clarity and the sound is very good. —CA **AKA:** Mui du du Xanh.

Movie: 🎹🎹🎹 **DVD:** 🎹🎹🎹🎹
Columbia Tristar (cat #07723, UPC 04339-6077232). Full frame. Dolby Digital Mono. $24.95. Keepcase. *LANG:* Vietnamese. *SUB:* English. *CAP:* English. *FEATURES:* 28 chapters ▪ Theatrical trailer.
1993 104m/C *VT* Tran Nu Yen-Khe, Lu Man San, Truong Thi Loc, Vuong Hoa Hoi; **D:** Tran Anh Hung; **W:** Tran Anh Hung, Patricia Petit; **C:** Benoit Delhomme; **M:** Ton That Tiet. *AWARDS:* NOM: Oscars '93: Foreign Film.

Schizo

This British shocker is a poor excuse for a murder mystery from the director of the far-superior *Frightmare*. In *Schizo*, young figure skater Samantha (played by Lynne Frederick, who was once married to Peter Sellers and later married David Frost) is convinced that someone is stalking her and attempting to ruin her impending wedding. In typical "whoddunit?" fashion, the bodies pile up and Samantha begins to snap under the strain. The ending offers an interesting twist, but it is too late to save this by-the-numbers thriller. *Schizo* resembles many other films from the period and there is little to distinguish it from its peers. Even director Pete Walker's trademark violence is downplayed here, making *Schizo* an impotent entry into the slasher genre. The DVD presentation of *Schizo* is a disappointment as well. The digital transfer shows many defects from the source print and the artifacting effects are hard to ignore. However, the garish '70s colors come across fine. The mono soundtrack makes the dialogue audible, but there is some hissing. —ML **AKA:** Amok; Blood of the Undead.

Movie: 🎹🎹 **DVD:** 🎹🎹
Image Ent. (cat #ID9347EUDVD, UPC 014-381934704). Widescreen (1.85:1) anamorphic. Dolby Digital Mono. $24.99. Keepcase. *LANG:* English. *FEATURES:* 14 chapters.
1977 (R) 109m/C *GB* Lynne Frederick, John Leyton, Stephanie Beacham, John Fraser, Jack Watson, John McEnery; **D:**

Pete Walker; **W:** John M. Watson Sr.; **C:** Peter Jessop.

Schlock

Neanderthal missing link Schlockthropus (director Landis, in an elaborate ape suit by Rick Baker) emerges from a hole in the ground in Agoura, California, to commit mass murder. Scientist Shirley Slivowitz (Emil Hamaty), newsman Joe Putzman (Eric Allison), and Detective Sergeant Wino (Saul Kahan) are immediately on his trail. But Schlock spends the day ambling from adventure to adventure with terrified locals, including the blind Mindy (Eliza Garrett), with whom he falls in love, even though she thinks he's a stray doggie. After various silent movie–style escapes, Schlock gravitates to the big school dance to see Mindy again, as the National Guard closes in. DVD looks far better than normal release prints or earlier videos. The disc is a definite treat for fans, featuring a sharp transfer with excellent colors. There are a few soft shots, but those are due to the low lighting/low-budget shooting conditions. The sound is mono but it's clear enough to distinguish post-synched dialogue from audio recorded on set. There are some nice production notes for the stars of the show, Landis and Baker. By far the best feature is the audio commentary, where they both tell the whole funny story in great, hilarious detail, beginning with Landis's first visit to Baker's house in West Covina, to see a "skinny hippie kid with long hair and a bedroom full of great models and makeup photos." —GE **AKA:** The Banana Monster.

Movie: 🎹🎹 **DVD:** 🎹🎹🎹
Anchor Bay (cat #DV11547, UPC 01313-1154795). Widescreen (1.85:1) anamorphic. Mono. $19.98. Keepcase. *LANG:* English. *FEATURES:* Commentary: John Landis, Rick Baker ▪ Radio spots ▪ Trailer ▪ Still gallery ▪ Talent bios ▪ 27 chapters.
1973 (PG) 78m/C John Landis, Saul Kahan, Joseph Piantadosi, Eliza (Simons) Garrett, Emil Hamaty, Eric Allison, Forrest J Ackerman; **D:** John Landis; **W:** John Landis; **C:** Robert E. Collins; **M:** David Gibson.

Schramm

This film delves into the everyday madness that ultimately drives Schramm (Florian Koerner von Gustorf) to do the heinous things he does. Chiefly, he's in love with the willowy prostitute next door (Monika M.) who thinks of him as a dopey brother—with a car. He's wholly inept at expressing himself, so he laces her nightcap with pills and takes Polaroids of her in her undies. He also suffers from superduper body dysmorphia, but instead of obsessing about his waistline, Schramm has gruesome hallucinations of waking to find his leg hacked away, or believing he can inspect his brain by merely parting his forehead with his fingertips. This haphazard assemblage of randomly ordered scenes chart the cluttered mind of the "Lipstick Killer" and curiously elicit a cer-

tain amount of pity for the guy. That is, when one's not retching. It's an aimless bore with not a single subplot to liven up the tedium. The clean full-frame transfer is taken from the original 16mm negative. Offers a German stereo remix or original mono tracks. Two English audio commentaries are included: one by the director and partner Franz Rodenkirchen and another track by actors Florian Koerner von Gustorf and Monika M. Includes a 35-minute "making of" with extensive behind-the-scenes footage, including how they were able to achieve some of the camerawork; and early Super-8 short films by Buttgereit: "Mein Papi," "Captain Berlin," and a music video he did for Mutter's "Die Neue Zeit" (about 30 minutes in all). Also included is a massive production photo gallery of more than 100 images. —GNG/DG

Movie: 🎹 **DVD:** 🎹🎹 ½
Image Ent. (UPC 690816600299). Full frame. Dolby Digital Surround; Mono. $34.98. Keepcase. *LANG:* German. *SUB:* English. *FEATURES:* Commentary: Buttgereit, Rodenkirchen ▪ Chapter links ▪ Commentary: Gustorf, Monika M. ▪ Short films ▪ "Making of" featurette ▪ Music videos.
1993 62m/C *GE* Florian Koerner von Gustorf, Micha Brendel, Carolina Harnisch, Volker Hauptvogel, Gerd Horvath, Monika M.; **D:** Jorg Buttgereit; **W:** Jorg Buttgereit; **C:** Manfred O. Jelinski; **M:** Max Muller, Gundula Schmitz.

Science and the Swastika

These four programs from Britain's Channel Four are not nearly as lurid or as exploitative as the box art suggests. They look at various aspects of social and "hard" sciences that became part of Nazi Germany. The first, "Hitler's Biological Soldiers," is about the racial ideas and eugenics that were part of the party philosophy. "The Deadly Experiment" and "The Wrong Stuff" show how those ideas led to the Holocaust and other horrors. "The Good German" looks at German efforts to create an atomic bomb. These are complex subjects and they get about as much depth of detail as one could expect of commercial television. Most of the experts who appear are authors of popular history books. DVD image improves on broadcast quality, but be warned. Not all of the chapter links lead to the beginnings of their programs. Use the main menu for that. —MM

Movie: 🎹🎹 ½ **DVD:** 🎹🎹 ½
BFS Video (cat #30255-D, UPC 066805-302558). Full frame. $24.99. Keepcase boxed set. *LANG:* English. *FEATURES:* 16 chapters ▪ "Campaign to Remember" with Ted Koppell ▪ Newsreel footage of liberation of death camps.
2001 196m/C *GB*

Scooby-Doo and the Reluctant Werewolf

Mediocre kids fare with uninspired animation. Tells the tale of cartoon regulars

Scooby, Shaggy (and his insipid girlfriend Goo), and Scrappy Doo (Scooby's nephew) and their forced entry into the Monster Road Rally. It seems Dracula needs a werewolf to complete his road team and since his werewolf quit, he casts a spell on the next greatest racer, Shaggy, and turns him into a werewolf to fill out the team. Absent are the rest of the Scooby crew: Daphne, Fred, and Velma. Guess they were too busy making the movie. Sound is really good but the picture is so-so with fuzzy lines and color accenting the poor animation. —CA

Movie: 🎵🎵 **DVD:** 🎵🎵
Warner (cat #H1878, UPC 0147641878-22). Full frame. Dolby Digital Mono. $19.90. Snapper. *LANG:* English; French; Spanish. *CAP:* English. *FEATURES:* 27 chapters • How to Draw Scooby Doo • Music video • DVD-ROM for PC game demos.
1989 95m/C

Scooby-Doo Goes Hollywood

There has been a resurgence of interest in Scooby-Doo over the last few years (not to mention the summer 2002 feature film), leading to the creation of several new movies containing the mystery-solving dog and his friends. And these movies have proven to be quite popular with both old and new fans. While the title *Scooby-Doo Goes Hollywood* may not be familiar, don't be fooled. This release is not one of those new movies; it is a Scooby special from 1979—the era when the heyday of *Scooby Doo, Where Are You!* and before the disastrous introduction of Scrappy-Doo—which means that it's mind-numbingly mediocre. This story takes place outside of the normal "Scooby-Doo" universe. Here, we go behind-the-scenes, where Scooby and Shaggy are tired of being chased by monsters and decide that they want to be in a new TV show. So, they go to the studio head and try to convince him that Scooby is suitable for any genre. This leads to spoofs of then popular shows, such as *Happy Days, Charlie's Angels,* and *Laverne & Shirley.* The film dispenses with all of the usual trappings and plays strictly as a comedy. But by removing the familiar (and popular) spook-chasing characteristics, all you're left with is a very unfunny series of set-pieces. Also, most of today's young fans won't recognize the shows that are being satirized. Even the most ardent should avoid this one. Full-frame image is clear, and the colors are very good, but the digital transfer highlights every speck of dirt and flaw on the original drawings. The mono soundtrack does an adequate job of reproducing the dialogue and music. As the main feature is only 49 minutes long, the DVD has many extras, the best of which is the "Mystery Inc. Yearbook," which gives a detailed overview of Scooby's history. —ML

Movie: 🎵 **DVD:** 🎵🎵
Warner (cat #H1378, UPC 0147641378-27). Full frame. Dolby Digital Mono. $19.98. Snapper. *LANG:* English; French;

Spanish. *CAP:* English. *FEATURES:* Set-top game • Featurette • Drawing featurette • Music videos • Bonus trailers • 10 chapters.
1979 49m/C

Scooby-Doo's Spookiest Tales

Scooby-Doo mania persists, with the release of this compilation of episodes from the 1970s TV shows. As with Warner's previous collection, there are five episodes on this DVD (four "main" episodes, and one "bonus" show). But unlike that earlier DVD, all of these episodes were not culled from *Scooby-Doo, Where Are You?* (which originally aired on CBS). Two of the five shows here are taken from the next Scooby incarnation, *The Scooby-Doo Show,* which was broadcast on ABC. While the shows are similar in tone and plot, the animation is slightly different (and less detailed) on *Show.* With these five episodes, Scooby-Doo and his crime-solving friends Shaggy, Fred, Daphne, and Velma face many spooky adversaries. In "Vampires, Bats and Scaredy Cat," the gang goes to a mysterious island to help an old friend and are chased by a vampire. (This episode is of interest because Scooby-Doo's cousin Scooby-Dum is featured.) The monsters in "A Gaggle of Galloping Ghosts" are actually an homage to the original Universal monsters, as the group finds themselves facing Dracula, the Wolfman, and Frankenstein's Monster in an old castle. Scooby and his friends have their ski trip interrupted by an electrified monster in "That's Snow Ghost," which is one of the best shows in the series. Another classic comes in the form of "Which Witch Is Witch?," in which (!) a witch and her zombie henchmen attempt to keep the kids from exploring an old riverboat. And finally, the title of "The Headless Horseman of Halloween" says it all, as the group attempts to outwit a headless rider seemingly inspired by the classic tale by Washington Irving. Each of these episodes helps to exemplify the thing that made *Scooby-Doo* great: the show's ability to combine genuinely creepy situations with comedic action. Oh yeah, and a talking dog. Fans of the old shows will love this, and a new generation of Scooby fans can explore the origins of the characters. This DVD presents the episodes in their original full-frame format. The images here are sharp and clear for the most part, and the colors are good. However, the digital transfer has revealed some flaws in the source material, consisting mainly of dirt and black spots. The Dolby Digital mono audio track offers clear dialogue, with no discernible hissing. The DVD contains an interesting extra which reveals detailed trivia about each of the five main characters. —ML

Movie: 🎵🎵🎵 **DVD:** 🎵🎵 ½
Warner (cat #H1759, UPC 0147641759-28). Full frame. Dolby Digital Mono. $19.98. Snapper. *LANG:* English; French; Spanish.

CAP: English. *FEATURES:* Bonus episode • Trivia game • Character bios • 4 chapters.
2001 110m/C

Score

Score is Japan's answer to the Hong Kong action films of John Woo, Tsui Hark, and Ronny Yu. If you've seen *Hard Boiled, City on Fire,* or Quentin Tarantino's *Reservoir Dogs,* then you can skip this one. Chance (Hitoshi Ozawa) is released from prison and forced to return to work for his old crime boss. Chance recruits three other thieves to rip-off a jewelry store. Following the robbery, distrust sets in amongst the crooks and a pair of hitchhikers interfere with their getaway plans. *Score* borrows liberally from the films mentioned above (all of which proceeded it) and is never exciting or engaging. Instead, it's morally ambiguous and boring. Also, this film features some of the thinnest and reddest blood ever seen in a movie. DVD offers a widescreen transfer that's clear for the most part, but generally dark. Flickering is evident at times, as is some artifacting. The colors appear slightly washed-out as well. The 2.0 Surround track does offer nice audio though, with rumbling explosions and a nice use of the rear speakers. Oddly, there is no menu on this DVD. —ML

Movie: woof **DVD:** 🎵🎵
Media Blasters (cat #TSDVD-0120, UPC 631595012088). Widescreen (1.85:1) letterboxed. Dolby 2.0 Surround. $29.95. Keepcase. *LANG:* Japanese. *SUB:* English. *FEATURES:* 24 chapters.
1995 94m/C *JP* Hitoshi Ozawa, Osamu Ebara, Ryuuji Minakami, Kazuyoshi Ozawa, Miyuki Takano, Masahiro Yamashita; **D:** Atsushi Muroga.

The Score

The thief who tries to pull off one last job was a popular theme in 2001. This variation is a relaxed take on the familiar material. Nick Wells (De Niro) is the master thief who wants to retire with enough cash to run his Montreal jazz club. Jack Teller (Norton) is the brash kid who's the inside man at the Customs House where a fabulous scepter is being stored. Max (Brando) is the fence who will pay for the dingus. Director Oz keeps the elements in proper balance and he got fine performances from his leads, despite the widely reported problems he had with Brando. The script's final twist is relatively tame but that's a quibble. The film delivers what caper fans want to see. DVD looks and sounds as sharp as you'd expect of a new big-budget studio release. The extras round up all of the usual suspects. —MM

Movie: 🎵🎵🎵 **DVD:** 🎵🎵🎵
Paramount (cat #33921, UPC 097363392-149). Widescreen anamorphic. Dolby Digital 5.1 Surround; Dolby Digital Surround. $29.95. Keepcase. *LANG:* English; French. *SUB:* English. *CAP:* English. *FEATURES:* 15 chapters • Trailer • "Making of" fea-

turette • Deleted scenes • Commentary: Frank Oz.
2001 (R) 124m/C Robert De Niro, Edward Norton, Marlon Brando, Angela Bassett, Gary Farmer, Paul Soles, Jamie Harold; **D:** Frank Oz; **W:** Kario Salem, Scott Marshall Smith, Lem Dobbs; **C:** Rob Hahn; **M:** Howard Shore.

The Scout

Al Percolo (Brooks) is an about-to-be-canned scout for the New York Yankees who discovers phenom Steve Nebraska (Fraser) on a trip to the backwaters of Mexico. The kid has a 100 mph fastball and he can hit like the Bambino. The question is: what's wrong with the kid? Is he immature? Nuts? Does it matter? The film tries at various times to be a sports comedy and a melodrama and doesn't really work as either. (The first half is much stronger than the second.) DVD image is somewhat paler than I remember from the theatre, but it handles the dusty rural Mexican scenes without a problem. Sound is fine. —MM
Movie: 🐾🐾 **DVD:** 🐾🐾 ½
MGM Home Ent. (cat #2001948, UPC 024-543019480). Widescreen (1.85:1) anamorphic. Dolby Digital 4.0 Surround. $19.98. Keepcase. *LANG:* English. *SUB:* English; Spanish. *CAP:* English. *FEATURES:* 28 chapters • TV spots • Featurette • Baseball strike news capsule.
1994 (PG-13) 101m/C Albert Brooks, Brendan Fraser, Dianne Wiest, Lane Smith, Michael Rapaport, Steve Garvey, Bob Costas, Roy Firestone, Anne Twomey, Tony Bennett; **D:** Michael Ritchie; **W:** Albert Brooks, Andrew Bergman, Monica Johnson; **C:** Laszlo Kovacs; **M:** Bill Conti.

A Scream in the Streets

This alternative classic is vintage exploitation. Technically, it's a serial killer movie about a couple of plainclothes cops (Kirkpatrick and Bannon) who catch several criminals, but not until the bad guys have engaged in their various sexual peccadilloes—spanking, voyeurism, cross-dressing—and, of course, the cops have their bedroom romps, too. The sexual material stays just this side of hard-core. The really astonishing thing here, though, is the clarity of the disc. It looks like it was made from a negative that just came out of the lab. It's nothing like the older double feature (with *Axe*) VHS tapes that are still floating around. All of the Something Weird extras are in place, too, including a short film with a very young Chuck Norris. —MM
Movie: 🐾 ½ **DVD:** 🐾🐾🐾
Something Weird Video (cat #ID0812SWD-VD, UPC 014381081220). Full frame. Dolby Digital Mono. $24.98. Keepcase. *LANG:* English. *FEATURES:* 12 chapters • 5 short films • 11 trailers • 2 galleries of exploitation art.
1973 (R) 90m/C John Kirkpatrick, Sharon Kelly, Frank Bannon, Linda York, Angela

Carnon; **D:** Carl Monson; **W:** Eric Norden; **C:** Jack Beckett.

Scream of the Wolf

Author and ex-hunter John (Graves) is called on to help the police in their investigation of a series of murders that seem to have been caused by a wolf that can walk on two legs. He turns to Byron (Walker), an old friend and obsessive hunter (think Zaroff in *The Most Dangerous Game*) for help, but Byron refuses, arguing that the murders are making the people in the community feel more alive than ever. Byron involves John in a battle of brawn and hunting skill that will ultimately reveal the truth behind the killings. Passable TV movie by director Curtis feels like another attempt to create a *Kolchak: The Night Stalker*–type TV series, complete with Graves's flashy red Corvette, and a jazzy '70s "wokka-chikka" soundtrack. The most astonishing thing about the film is the almost tangible sexual underpinnings of the story. It is strongly implied that Byron's primary motivation is his anger with John for not responding to his lusty, manly advances. That element alone makes it worth checking out. The ending (which may disappoint some) is still quite a surprise. The disc is transferred from a battered and occasionally scratched 16mm print with a strong yellow look. Reel changes (with their obvious soundtrack pops and clicks) are all too apparent. Pixelation tends to plague the image as well. The sound is clear but barely adequate. The disc copy makes several mistakes, including crediting this production not to Curtis but to a "Robert D. Webb." "Cobweb Hotel" is a fairly macabre but entertaining color cartoon. The print is faded and the quality is equal to that of the feature. —DG
Movie: 🐾🐾 **DVD:** 🐾
Brentwood (cat #44090-9, UPC 78736440-9099). Full frame. Mono. $4.99. Keepcase. *LANG:* English. *FEATURES:* "Cobweb Hotel" short • Trivia game • DVD dictionary • 6 chapters.
1974 74m/C Peter Graves, Clint Walker, JoAnn Pflug, Phil Carey, James Storm; **D:** Dan Curtis; **W:** Richard Matheson, David Case; **C:** Paul Lohmann; **M:** Robert Cobert.

Scrooge

Please see review for *A Classic Christmas*.
Movie: 🐾🐾🐾
1935 61m/B *GB* Sir Seymour Hicks, Maurice Evans, Robert Cochran, Donald Calthrop, Mary Glynne, Oscar Asche; **D:** Henry Edwards; **W:** Sir Seymour Hicks; **C:** Sydney Blythe, William Luff.

Sea People

Teen swimmer Amanda (Tegan Moss) rescues elderly John McRae (Hume Cronyn) after he leaps from a bridge into the water. But Amanda soon discovers that John wasn't trying to commit suicide and that he

and his wife Bridget (Joan Gregson) have a very unique relationship with the sea. As Amanda learns more about this strange couple and their peculiar habits, she can't help but wonder if they may be mermaids. *Sea People* is a fun and heart-warming film for the entire family. It shares an admirable lesson about judging others and offers a positive portrayal of a relationship between a pre-teen and a geriatric couple. As this film was made-for-TV, the DVD offers a full-frame representation. The image is near broadcast quality, as it is clear and sharp, showing some grain in the daytime shots. The audio track offers some ambient Surround sound effects (mostly musical cues) and clear dialogue. —ML
Movie: 🐾🐾 **DVD:** 🐾🐾
Showtime Networks, Inc. (cat #SHO3030, UPC 758445303025). Full frame. Dolby Surround. $19.98. Keepcase. *LANG:* English; Spanish. *CAP:* English. *FEATURES:* 12 chapters.
2000 92m/C Hume Cronyn, Tegan Moss, Joan Gregson, Ron Lea, Don McKellar, Cedric Smith; **D:** Vic Sarin.

The Seagull

Blythe Danner's sensitive performance as Nina, an aspiring actress with fragile emotions, highlights this filmed production of Chekhov's *The Seagull*, originally staged by the Williamstown Theatre Festival. Considering that this is a filmed play, image quality is not a prime consideration. Disc is really of historical interest. —JE
Movie: 🐾🐾 ½ **DVD:** 🐾🐾 ½
Image Ent. (cat #ID0880B DDVD, UPC 014-381188021). Full frame. Dolby Digital Mono. $24.99. Keepcase. *LANG:* English. *FEATURES:* Filmography of Frank Langella • Filmography of Blythe Danner • Filmography of Lee Grant.
1975 117m/C Blythe Danner, Olympia Dukakis, Lee Grant, Frank Langella; **D:** John J. Desmond, Nikos Psacharopoulos.

Searching for Bobby Fischer

Young Josh (Pomeranc) and his parents discover that he is a chess prodigy many consider equivalent to famed chess talent Bobby Fischer. Although his parents are surprised at first, they look out for Josh's best interest—his father (Mantenga) is a loving parent who encourages his child's gift and his mother (Allen) supports him as well. On the outside are a local park champion player (Fishburne) and a cold teacher (Kingsley). All of them become involved as Josh starts to enter competitions. Although chess games may not sound too interesting, visually, director Zaillian infuses them with enough energy to carry them through. James Horner's score may be a bit too emotional at times, but its pace helps along the film as well. The performances are excellent across the board (pun intended) and the film is a solid piece of entertainment. Sharpness varies, but is generally very pleasing with the majority of images clear and well defined. Colors are strong and flesh tones remain natural. Although primarily a quiet, dialogue-driven film, Surround sound effects are used for subtle background/environment sounds as well as the dramatic and emotional score from Horner. The disc's lack of extras (not even a trailer!) is disappointing. —AB/DG

Movie: 🎬🎬🎬 **DVD:** 🎬🎬 ½

Paramount Home Video (UPC 097363267-348). Widescreen (1.85:1) anamorphic. Dolby Digital 5.1 Surround; Dolby Digital Surround. $29.99. Keepcase. *LANG:* English; French. *SUB:* English. *CAP:* English.

1993 (PG) 111m/C Joe Mantegna, Max Pomeranc, Joan Allen, Ben Kingsley, Laurence "Larry" Fishburne, Robert Stephens, David Paymer, William H. Macy, Hal Scardino; **D:** Steven Zaillian; **W:** Steven Zaillian; **C:** Conrad L. Hall; **M:** James Horner. *AWARDS:* MTV Movie Awards '94: New Filmmaker (Zaillian); *NOM:* Oscars '93: Cinematog.

Second Skin

This small noir thriller would be at home with all of the similar features that are generally available on late-night cable TV, but parts of it are better than one might expect from a straight-to-video offering. Henstridge stars as Crystal Ball, a young woman who enters a bookstore in a small town and is injured in a hit-and-run when she leaves. The store's owner, Sam Kane (Macfadyen), cares for and falls in love with Crystal, who has amnesia. Henstridge isn't the finest actress in the business, but she looks great and has a presence. She can capably go from cheery and sweet to dark quite well. She also has good chemistry with Macfadyen. The dialogue and situations aren't terribly original and sometimes come across as rather generic noir. Interest flags by the time anything of consequence happens and the ending is awkwardly handled. The transfer is a bit soft at times. Colors are natural and occasionally beautiful. Most of the film is fairly mono-oriented, focusing on the film's dialogue. Surrounds are hardly used. —AB/DG

Movie: 🎬🎬 **DVD:** 🎬🎬

Artisan Ent. (UPC 12236117049). Widescreen (1.77:1) anamorphic. Dolby Digital 5.1 Surround. $24.98. Keepcase. *LANG:* English. *CAP:* English. *FEATURES:* 32 chapters ➧ Trailer.

2000 (R) 91m/C Angus Macfadyen, Natasha Henstridge, Peter Fonda, Liam Waite; **D:** Darrell Roodt.

Second to Die

Far-fetched, lethargic thriller is brightened by a few offbeat touches and an over-qualified cast. Sara Morgan (Eleniak) has taken a lover and decides to get rid of her boorish hubby (Shipp). She pulls it off swimmingly but there's still her sister (Rowe) to worry about. Colleen Camp camps it up shamelessly in a comic supporting role. The main problems are a plodding pace and made-for-TV production

values. The low-budget image has a dim, flat look that DVD cannot improve. Sound is acceptable. —MM

Movie: 🎬🎬 **DVD:** 🎬🎬

New Concorde (cat #NH20789 D, UPC 736991478992). Full frame. $19.98. Keepcase. *LANG:* English. *SUB:* Spanish. *FEATURES:* 18 chapters ➧ Filmographies ➧ Trailers.

2002 (R) 89m/C Erika Eleniak, Jerry Kroll, Colleen Camp, John Wesley Shipp, Kimberly Rowe, Brooke Davis; **D:** Sean Marlowe; **W:** George Morgan, Anita Doohan, Adrienne Armstrong; **C:** Moshe Levin; **M:** Andrew Dorfman.

Seconds

Lost in a dull world of disappointment and disillusion, middle-aged banker Arthur Hamilton (Randolph) is shocked to hear the voice of a dead friend contact him by phone and invite him to reinvent his own life through the services of a secret company with futuristic resources. Arthur takes the bait and transfers the bulk of his fortune into the company's hands; his own death is faked and futuristic medicine, plastic surgery, therapy, and coaching transform him into a much younger-looking man who goes by the name Tony Wilson (Hudson). Leaving his widow (Reid) behind, "Tony" is set up as a trendy Malibu artist, with a background and a clientele. All goes well, including a meeting with a sexy beach denizen named Norma Marcus (Jens), but Tony finds himself slowly reverting to Arthur's previous, apprehensive state of mind. He's intimidated instead of liberated by Norma's hedonistic friends, and worst of all, he's tempted to make contact with the life he's left behind. The second half ties up the story with a brutal irony, but even though most of the scenes are beautifully realized, something is lost along the way. As a moral tale, it's not clear whether Hudson's fate is sealed by his flawed desires, or whether he's the total pawn of this evil corporation (which must experience this kind of "failure" all the time). The movie excels at creating a first-person paranoid experience. In 1996, Paramount lengthened *Seconds* by replacing the original, racier cut of the scene at the Santa Barbara wine fair. It's been restored here without explanation, giving the film an "R" rating, and may confuse those who saw the original domestic release, which could never have contained this content. The nude scenes were found intact on an international negative for export, a French cut to be exact. Writer Bill Desowitz (now of *Animation Magazine*) realized the source for the restoration was a French print by watching the earlier laser release, which also cut a scene where Rock Hudson is given fake credentials for his new persona as a high-toned artist. Paramount's DVD is their dependable quality release, with the mind-bending visuals looking a lot better in widescreen than they did on flat television. I was a bit disappointed with some scenes that had more white negative speckling than they

should; this is the kind of stuff for which digital cleanup was invented. John Frankenheimer contributes one of his informative and self-critical commentaries, revealing that Rock Hudson had the idea of the main character being played by two actors, and that Rock was truly drunk during his breakdown scenes. The director's comments about the wild shooting for the wine vat scene are welcome, as is his candor about the movie's total inability to find an audience when new. This is a fine disc all around, with very minor reservations about the picture quality. —GE

Movie: 🎬🎬🎬 ½ **DVD:** 🎬🎬🎬

Paramount (cat #15691, UPC 097361569-147). Widescreen (1.78:1) anamorphic. Dolby Digital Mono. $24.98. Keepcase. *LANG:* English; French. *SUB:* English. *CAP:* English. *FEATURES:* Commentary ➧ Trailer ➧ 12 chapters.

1966 (R) 107m/B Rock Hudson, John Randolph, Salome Jens, Will Geer, Jeff Corey, Richard Anderson, Murray Hamilton, Karl Swenson, Khigh (Kaie Deei) Deigh, Frances Reid, Wesley Addy; **D:** John Frankenheimer; **W:** Lewis John Carlino; **C:** James Wong Howe; **M:** Jerry Goldsmith. *AWARDS:* *NOM:* Oscars '66: B&W Cinematog.

Secret Agent

Before Patrick McGoohan was *The Prisoner*, he was *Danger Man* (*Secret Agent* in the U.S. and in the A&E boxed set). Some *Prisoner* fans swear that John Drake was the Prisoner and if the hip theme song (yes, "Secret Agent Man") was any clue, they were right ("They've given you a number, and taken away your name.") Of course, even if that was true, this is the young Prisoner...I mean Drake, full of spunk and shown in black and white. Drake was Bond before the Fleming character had a chance to take hold; in fact, McGoohan was reportedly offered the role of Bond first, but turned it down because he felt it was demeaning to women. His chivalry didn't pay as well over the years as the Bond franchise did, but in 1965 when the series came to America, McGoohan was the highest paid actor on British TV. *Danger Man* shows the cold war spy at his best, clever with a slight sense of humor, but sober and honest as the day is long. This is your parent's version of *The Avengers*, no psychedelic costumes or sets, just plain black-and-white drama where the good guys always win. While a lot of the stories were written for the times, they still hold up today. Especially amusing is "A Date with Doris," which parodies Castro just after he had betrayed Che Guevera and taken over Cuba. Posing as a journalist visiting Cuba to interview the new leader, Drake is sent to recover an operative accused of murder. The operative has escaped jail and is running around injured. With the help of a disgruntled Cuban party member, Drake successfully gets the operative to his "date" with Doris, the submarine that is. Of course Cuba and Castro are never mentioned

directly—that just wasn't done back then—but the hilarious interview between Drake and "the leader" is worth the price of admission. *Danger Man* was created at a time when TV shows were used as political propaganda to stir public sentiment, not just to sell shampoo and diet aids, making *Secret Agent* an entertaining artifact from the past that plays well today. This set is not as full of extras as the *Prisoner* set simply because *Danger Man* never had quite the following of the more '60s oriented series, but it is still well worth looking at. The disc looks amazingly good for a TV series shot on film in the '60s, but there are a few dust motes dancing by and the sound is mono with all that implies. —*CA*
Movie: 🐾🐾 ½ **DVD:** 🐾🐾🐾
A&E Home Video Full frame. Dolby Digital Mono. $39.95. Keepcase boxed set. *LANG:* English. *FEATURES:* 2 discs per set, 8 chapters per disc ▪ Original U.S. opening ▪ Full-length version of "Secret Agent Man" theme song.
1965 B Patrick McGoohan, Lelia Goldoni.

Secret Defense
Superb Euro-thriller (French/Italian/Swiss) is leisurely paced but all the more fascinating for it. Scientist Sylvie (Bonnaire) is dubious when her brother Paul (Colin) tells her that he has discovered evidence suggesting that their father's death five years earlier was not an accident as they had believed. That sets in motion an imaginative, surprising plot that really shouldn't be revealed. It's spun out in long, carefully paced shots and scenes. Performances are understated and believable. Only those who are most adamantly opposed to subtitles should pass this one up. It's terrific. DVD image is remarkably sharp and subtle for an import. Recommended. Optional whitesubs are very clear. —*MM*
Movie: 🐾🐾🐾 ½ **DVD:** 🐾🐾🐾
Image Ent. (cat #ID0724SIDVDDVD, UPC 014381072426). Widescreen (1.85:1) letterboxed. Dolby Digital Surround. $24.98. Keepcase. *LANG:* French. *SUB:* English. *FEATURES:* 16 chapters.
1998 166m/C *FR SW IT* Sandrine Bonnaire, Jerzy Radziwilowicz, Laure Marsac, Gregoire Colin; **D:** Jacques Rivette; **W:** Jacques Rivette, Pascal Bonitzer; **C:** William Lubtchansky; **M:** Jordi Savall.

The Secret of NIMH
The story revolves around a mother mouse named Mrs. Brisby who has a number of things to worry about—her young son is sick and she needs medicine, and her family needs to move out of the way before the farmer's plow takes out their home. The only problem is, the young child's sickness could become worse if he's moved. She enlists the help of a group of intelligent rats to help her family, and finds a friend in a crow (DeLuise, providing comic relief.) Some of *NIMH* is rather dark and could be frightening for the youngest viewers, but older children

and adults will likely find its world of fantasy wonderfully engaging. What really makes the film is the combination of excellent voice talent and Bluth's superb animation. Although more advanced technology has made for animated pictures that look sharper and sleeker, Bluth's rich and beautiful traditional animation for this film still remains stunning. The film is unfortunately presented in a full-frame version, while its original aspect ratio was 1.85:1. Sharpness and detail are passable and the film occasionally has a "soft" look to it. Print flaws such as scratches, marks, and minor speckles become a mild distraction at times. The film's vibrant color palette remains bold and lively here, though. The Dolby 2.0 presentation sounds a bit dated in terms of sound quality, but all of the finer elements of the soundtrack still remain enjoyable. —*AB/DG*
Movie: 🐾🐾🐾 **DVD:** 🐾🐾
Buena Vista Home Ent. (UPC 276167037-29). Full frame. Dolby Digital Surround. $14.95. Keepcase. *LANG:* English. *SUB:* English; French. *CAP:* English. *FEATURES:* 32 chapters ▪ Trailer ▪ Booklet with background info.
1982 (G) 84m/C D: Don Bluth; **W:** Don Bluth; **M:** Jerry Goldsmith; **V:** John Carradine, Derek Jacobi, Dom DeLuise, Elizabeth Hartman, Peter Strauss, Aldo Ray, Edie McClurg, Wil Wheaton.

The Secret of Roan Inish
Fiona Coneely has been sent to live with her grandparents, but their abandoned and haunted ancestral home is the small island Roan Inish. Grandad tells of the day that the family left Roan Inish, and her infant brother Jamie was swept away to sea in his wooden cradle. Fiona, still heartbroken by the loss of her little brother, feels that the seals hanging out on the rocks about the island know more than they're telling, and she determines to visit Roan Inish herself and discover what really happened to her little brother. Columbia Tristar's transfer expertly captures Haskell Wexler's delicate cinematography, and delivers a solid Surround experience to those with the equipment. The widescreen matte feels somewhat tight in a lot of shots, pressing in on the actors' heads. However, while the full-frame transfer on the other side of the disc gives the characters more room to stand up in, once you've seen the widescreen, it can feel a bit cramped on the sides. The special features are accessible on both sides of the disc. —*BT*
Movie: 🐾🐾🐾 ½ **DVD:** 🐾🐾🐾
Columbia Tristar (cat #50929, UPC 0433-96509290). Widescreen letterboxed; full frame. Dolby Digital 2.0 Surround. $24.95. Keepcase. *LANG:* English. *SUB:* English; French; Spanish. *CAP:* English. *FEATURES:* 28 chapters ▪ Trailers ▪ Commentary ▪ Bio.
1994 (PG) 102m/C Jeni Courtney, Michael Lally, Eileen Colgan, John Lynch,

Richard Sheridan, Susan Lynch, Cillian Byrne; **D:** John Sayles; **W:** John Sayles; **C:** Haskell Wexler; **M:** Mason Daring. *AWARDS: NOM:* Ind. Spirit '96: Director (Sayles), Film, Screenplay.

Secret of the Andes
Archeologist Brooks Willings (Keith) has bet his career and his family's future on finding a relic that has supernatural powers. His wife Brenda (Allen) and his daughter (Belle) come to visit him from New York. Problems are happening with the dig and things look bleak but the daughter strikes up a friendship with a magician and saves the day. A delightful family film that will keep kids ages 5–12 engaged. The DVD is nicely presented but lacks any special features. —*DE*
Movie: 🐾🐾 ½ **DVD:** 🐾🐾 ½
MTI (cat #1073, UPC 3941451073). Full frame. Stereo. $24.95. Keepcase. *LANG:* English; Spanish. *SUB:* Spanish. *FEATURES:* 20 chapters ▪ Trailers ▪ Cast bios.
2001 (PG-13) 100m/C David Keith, Nancy Allen, Camilla Belle, John Rhys-Davies; **D:** Alejandro Azzano; **W:** Alejandro Azzano, Bernardo Nante.

The Secrets of the Warrior's Power
Further study for those that enjoyed *Shaolin: Wheel of Life*. This documentary, perfect for the Discovery Channel, explores the history of kung fu and how it survives in the modern era, starting with Bodhi Dharma and the Shaolin Temple. The rest of the program examines what kung fu masters are doing today. The extras include expanded versions of the interviews edited for the feature, along with more information. But the meaty section has more Hung Gar masters doing different hair-raising feats of chi focus, including one guy who can squeeze his fingers against his palm and make them *smoke*. Sure, it could be fake, but is it? —*BT*
Movie: 🐾🐾🐾 **DVD:** 🐾🐾 ½
Winstar Home Ent. (cat #WHE73147, UPC 7290917314723). Full frame. $24.99. Keepcase. *LANG:* English. *FEATURES:* 8 chapters ▪ Interviews ▪ Bios.
1997 52m/C *CA HK* Jim Grapek; **W:** Jim Grapek, Leo Johnson; **C:** Philip Earnshaw, Sheila Smith, Charles Kendall; **M:** Kenneth-Michael Veltz; **Nar:** Michael Weiner, Alice Chen.

Seducing Maarya
Maarya (Sen) comes from India to Canada for an arranged marriage to the son of a prosperous and recently widowed restaurateur. Problems begin when she discovers that her intended is gay. Then dad falls for her; then her brother arrives with secrets of his own. Characters and story are important here, not image. It's so grainy that the DVD is riddled with pixels and artifacts, some coming from the original elements, some popping up inexplicably on their own. Sound is fine but since rock

music is so important, with a separate soundtrack option, some sort of Surround remix might have been called for. —MM

Movie: ♫♫♫ **DVD:** ♫♫
Vanguard Intl. Cinema (cat #VF0190, UPC 658769019032). Widescreen (1.66:1) letterboxed. $29.95. Keepcase. *LANG:* English. *FEATURES:* 12 chapters ☛ Trailer ☛ Music clip ☛ Soundtrack.
1999 107m/C *CA* Nandana Sen, Mohan Agashe, Vijay Mehta, Ryan Holliman, Cas Anvar; *D:* Hunt Hoe; *W:* Hunt Hoe; *C:* Michael Wees; *M:* Dino Giancola, Janet Lumb.

Seduction of Mimi

Comic farce of politics and seduction follows a Sicilian laborer's escapades with the Communists and the local Mafia. Giannini is wonderful as the stubborn immigrant in the big city who finds himself in trouble. Contains one of the funniest love scenes ever filmed. Occasional specks of lint are visible. Overall, the image is only a small improvement over tape, save the optional subtitles. —MM
AKA: Mimi Metallurgico Ferito Nell'Onore.

Movie: ♫♫♫ **DVD:** ♫♫
Winstar Home Ent. (cat #5020). Widescreen (1.66:1) letterboxed. $29.98. Keepcase. *LANG:* Italian. *SUB:* English. *FEATURES:* Cast & crew thumbnail bios ☛ 8 chapters ☛ Awards ☛ Production notes.
1972 (R) 92m/C *IT* Giancarlo Giannini, Mariangela Melato, Turi Ferro, Agostina Belli, Elena Fiore; *D:* Lina Wertmuller; *W:* Lina Wertmuller; *C:* Dario Di Palma; *M:* Piero Piccioni.

See No Evil, Hear No Evil

This 1989 outing offers another teaming of Pryor and Wilder, hoping to recapture the success they shared with *Stir Crazy* and *Silver Streak*. Unfortunately, the third time isn't the charm. Wally (Pryor) is an out-of-work blind man. Dave (Wilder) runs a newsstand, and tries to downplay the fact that he is deaf. When a murder is committed in their presence, Wally and Dave become the prime suspects. It is now up to them to clear their names and find the real killers. The film is never very funny, despite the presence of two comedic geniuses, and today's audiences may find many of the gags to be politically incorrect. The film is notable for an early appearance by Oscar-winner Kevin Spacey. The transfer here is good, but not spectacular. The image is clear and sharp, showing no grain and offering nice colors. The audio track brings intelligible dialogue with no distortion, but Surround sound effects are seldom heard. Overall, a solid DVD offering. —ML

Movie: ♫♫ **DVD:** ♫♫♫
Columbia Tristar (cat #06600, UPC 04339-6066007). Widescreen (1.85:1) anamorphic; full frame. Dolby 2.0 Surround. $19.95. Keepcase. *LANG:* English; French. *SUB:* English; French; Spanish; Portuguese;

Chinese; Korean; Thai. *CAP:* English. *FEATURES:* Theatrical trailer ☛ 28 chapters.
1989 (R) 103m/C Gene Wilder, Richard Pryor, Joan Severance, Anthony Zerbe, Kevin Spacey; *D:* Arthur Hiller; *W:* Andrew Kurtzman, Eliot Wald, Earl Barret, Arne Sultan, Gene Wilder; *C:* Victor Kemper; *M:* Stewart Copeland.

See Spot Run

Just when you thought that every conceivable dog-infused comedy had been made and served to the public, along comes another one sadly elongating an already tired concept. After Agent 7 foils a mob racketeering outfit, the decorated canine must go into the witness protection program to protect him from Sonny Talia (Sorvino), the vengeful mob boss who lost not only his business but one of his family jewels to the canine cop. After a failed assassination attempt by inept mobsters, Agent 7 finds himself in the custody of Gordon (Arquette), a postman who has trouble with women, children, dogs, and life. In an effort to impress his neighbor (Bibb) and her son, James (Jones), Gordon tries to prove he is responsible for caring for both the young boy and the dog. The sound and picture on this DVD release are decent, but the weak plot, weaker acting, and tired concept earn this film a woof, woof, woof. —EL

Movie: woof **DVD:** ♫♫
Warner (cat #21250, UPC 0853921250-29). Widescreen anamorphic. Dolby 5.1 Surround Sound. $24.98. Snapper. *LANG:* English; French. *SUB:* English; French; Spanish. *CAP:* English. *FEATURES:* Commentary: director John Whitesell ☛ Spot's Silly Dog Tricks Contest winners ☛ "As Long As You're Loving Me" music video by Vitamin C ☛ Cast career highlights ☛ Theatrical trailer ☛ 30 chapters.
2001 (G) 97m/C David Arquette, Michael Clarke Duncan, Leslie Bibb, Angus T. Jones, Joe (Johnny) Viterelli, Paul Sorvino, Anthony Anderson; *D:* John Whitesell; *W:* George Gallo, Dan Baron, Chris Faber; *C:* John Bartley; *M:* John Debney.

Seems Like Old Times

This Neil Simon farce centers on Nick (Chase), a bumbling writer who is kidnapped and forced to rob a bank by two shy crooks. The law is after him and the only one he can turn to is overly sympathetic lawyer Glenda (Hawn), his ex-wife. She believes in Nick's innocence and agrees to help, but she needs to keep him out of the sight of Ira (Grodin), her new husband and the newly appointed Attorney General. The script is above average, with a lot of laughs, but the film lacks the energy of Simon's better work. The video quality is poor, with dirty source material and a lot of artifacts. The mono isn't outstanding, but it's clear enough. —DRL

Movie: ♫♫ ½ **DVD:** ♫ ½
Columbia Tristar (cat #8202, UPC 0433-96082021). Widescreen (1.85:1) anamorphic; full frame. Dolby Mono. $24.95.

Keepcase. *LANG:* English. *SUB:* English; French. *CAP:* English. *FEATURES:* Trailers ☛ 28 chapters.
1980 (PG) 102m/C Goldie Hawn, Chevy Chase, Charles Grodin, Robert Guillaume, Harold Gould, George Grizzard, T.K. Carter; *D:* Jay Sandrich; *W:* Neil Simon; *C:* David M. Walsh; *M:* Marvin Hamlisch.

Sell Out

A former spy living in Jerusalem is called out of retirement. His protégé (Reed), who defected to the Soviets, now wants out. DVD image is poor to fair, essentially equal to an old, tattered VHS tape. Title is available as part of *Great Spy Movies*. —MM

Movie: ♫♫ ½ **DVD:** ♫♫
BFS Video (cat #30176-D, UPC 06680530-1766). Full frame. $9.98. Keepcase. *LANG:* English. *FEATURES:* 4 chapters.
1976 (PG) 102m/C Richard Widmark, Oliver Reed, Gayle Hunnicutt, Sam Wanamaker; *D:* Peter Collinson; *W:* Judson Kinberg, Murray Smith; *C:* Arthur Ibbetson; *M:* Colin Frichter.

Separate Tables

A variety of guests, all lonely and dissatisfied with their lives, board at a British hotel. The film was quite daring for its time, discussing sexuality more frankly than was considered polite, but retains some embarrassingly outdated ways of thinking. Lancaster and Hayworth star as a divorced couple with thoughts of reconciling, while Oscars were awarded to Niven for his turn as a military gentleman hiding a secret, and Kerr for her portrayal of an unmarried woman held under the thumb of her overbearing mother. The transfer is very good for the most part, although it is occasionally bombarded with a flurry of specks and other crackles, and is not anamorphic. The mono soundtrack is adequate for such a dialogue-heavy film. Delbert Mann's commentary is a treat. —BG

Movie: ♫♫♫ **DVD:** ♫♫♫
MGM Home Ent. (cat #1002742, UPC 027-616869401). Widescreen (1.66:1) letterboxed. Mono. $19.98. Keepcase. *LANG:* English; French; Spanish. *SUB:* French; Spanish. *CAP:* English. *FEATURES:* 16 chapters ☛ Commentary: director Delbert Mann ☛ Trailer.
1958 98m/B Burt Lancaster, David Niven, Rita Hayworth, Deborah Kerr, Wendy Hiller, Rod Taylor, Gladys Cooper, Felix Aylmer, Cathleen Nesbitt, Audrey Dalton, May Hallatt, Priscilla Morgan, Hilda Plowright; *D:* Delbert Mann; *W:* John Gay; *C:* Charles B(ryant) Lang Jr.; *M:* David Raksin.
AWARDS: Oscars '58: Actor (Niven), Support. Actress (Hiller); Golden Globes '59: Actor—Drama (Niven); N.Y. Film Critics '58: Actor (Niven); *NOM:* Oscars '58: Actress (Kerr), Adapt. Screenplay, B&W Cinematog., Picture, Orig. Dramatic Score.

Serendipity

Featherweight romantic hokum about fate. Jonathan (Cusack) meets Sara (Beckinsale) in the accessories department at Bloomingdale's, they fall in love, then rely on fate to find each other again two years later. Their happy reunion prevents Jonathan from marrying his second-rate girlfriend and Sara from marrying a Yanni/John Tesh hybrid named Lars (Corbett). Eugene Levy does a nice bit as a sales clerk at Bloomie's. DVD quality is excellent; director's commentary and other bonus features pretty undistinguished. Chelsom's production diary is almost too fuzzy to be readable. —*LA*

Movie: 🐾🐾 ½ **DVD:** 🐾🐾🐾
Miramax Pictures (cat #24170, UPC 7869-36166583). Widescreen (1.85:1) anamorphic. Dolby Digital 5.1 Surround. $29.98. Keepcase. *LANG:* English; French. *SUB:* Spanish. *CAP:* English. *FEATURES:* Commentary: director Peter Chelsom • Behind-the-scenes Starz Encore "On the Set" • Chelsom's production diary • Deleted scenes with commentary by Chelsom • Still gallery • Storyboard comparisons • Theatrical trailer • 16 chapters.
2001 (PG-13) 87m/C John Cusack, Kate Beckinsale, Molly Shannon, John Corbett, Jeremy Piven, Bridget Moynahan, Eugene Levy; **D:** Peter Chelsom; **W:** Marc Klein; **C:** John de Borman; **M:** Alan Silvestri.

Serial Experiments: Lain

Shy 13-year-old student Lain receives an e-mail from a classmate who committed suicide days earlier. As Lain is drawn further into the world of the Internet (called "The Wired" here), she becomes isolated from her friends and discovers that her life and the world around her aren't as simple as they seem. Low-key, extremely challenging Japanese animated series reveals many intriguing ideas but is immensely cryptic and curiously unsatisfying. From an animation standpoint, though, it's an amazing piece of work. The characters are cleanly and simply drawn with pale, muted colors but the backgrounds and computer environments are enhanced by incredibly vibrant splashes of intense, eye-popping colors. In some scenes, more variant hues are used than in almost any other animated work. Repeated viewings reveal many layers to both the story and imagery. Aside from some visible pixels and digital "edging," the disc is incredibly sharp and pristine. The intensely colorful palette never causes any distortion or bleeding and the image is completely free of grain. The audio has been designed and recorded with such incredible artistry and care that it comes as quite a surprise that the disc mix is only stereo. It sounds incredible and is more crisp, enveloping, clean, and impressive than most feature film 5.1 Surround tracks! The English dubbing is passable, but the low-key tones of the original Japanese performances are hard to replicate. —*DG*

Movie: 🐾🐾🐾 **DVD:** 🐾🐾🐾 ½
Pioneer Ent. (cat #11608, UPC 013023-160197). Full frame. Dolby Digital Surround. $119.98. Keepcase boxed set. *LANG:* Japanese; English. *SUB:* English.

FEATURES: Textless opening and ending • Conceptual drawings • 8 chapters per episode. This boxed set contains all 13 episodes of this Japanese animated series; discs are also available individually for $29.98 each.
1998 325m/C *JP* **D:** Ryutaro Nakamura; **M:** Reiichi "Chabo" Nakaido.

Series 7: The Contenders

Sadly overlooked film is surely destined for cult status. With little fanfare director Minahan drops the viewer into an America where everyone is part of a lottery to play in *The Contenders,* a reality show where a group of average citizens are given guns and pitted against each other in a fight to the death. We join the series at the tail end of "Series 6" and meet Dawn (Smith)—who, by the way, is 8 1/2 months pregnant—as she storms into a convenience store and blows away her last competitor. This victory propels her into "Series 7," which, if she wins, will relieve her from ever having to play again. There is a snag when it's announced that the next game will be played in her hometown, where her estranged family live, and that one of her competitors will be Jeffrey, her ex-boyfriend and one true love—who, by the way, is dying of cancer. A film crew follows each contender as they are given notice that their family and friends are players via a surreal Publisher's Clearinghouse–style knock on the door, and as they plan and execute the deaths of the other contenders, or die miserably themselves. The cameras also capture the family squabble between Dawn and her family when they won't let Dawn borrow the new SUV to stalk and kill her competitors. During breaks in the action, we are treated to hilarious yet bleak promos for the show and what's coming up in the next episode. When Dawn and Jeffrey fall in love again and decide to buck the system, a showdown is inevitable and handled in the only way a television show could—with a "very special episode" of *The Contenders.* The way Minahan mixes reality TV and soap opera to create a brilliant satire on the voracious public love affair with violence that borders on primal, and the strange and volatile marriage between TV stars and their public, is something approaching brilliance. He never makes the mistake of trying to explain why such a show exists or suggests that something in America went terribly wrong and this is the result, he simply allows the characters and their actions to show you everything you need to know. Should appeal to those who hate reality shows, as well as to those who can't live without them. Shot to mimic the point of view of the camera, television broadcast and live footage, the picture is hard to rate; suffice to say each shot looks like broadcast TV, as it should, and the sound is good, but again edited to mimic different broadcast types. Of the extras, the most entertaining is the "Sundance Director's Lab," which contains clips from the first incarnation of

this film and commentary by director Minahan in which he describes his experiences with attempting to sell the show to the networks. Be sure to check out the deleted scenes section, which offers an alternate ending to the film. —*CA/ML*

Movie: 🐾🐾🐾 ½ **DVD:** 🐾🐾
USA Home Ent. (cat #9630602432, UPC 696306024323). Widescreen (1.85:1) anamorphic. Dolby Digital 5.1. $24.95. Keepcase. *LANG:* English. *SUB:* English. *CAP:* English. *FEATURES:* Commentary: director • Deleted scenes • 15 chapters • Theatrical trailers • The Sundance Filmmaker's Lab Scenes.
2001 (R) 86m/C Brooke Smith, Glenn Fitzgerald, Merritt Wever, Michael Kaycheck, Richard Venture, Donna Hanover, Marylouise Burke; **D:** Daniel Minahan; **W:** Daniel Minahan; **C:** Randy Drummond.

The Servant

Made at the peak of the art film craze, Joseph Losey's work is a dark tale of psychological domination in a class system. Described by its maker as a version of Faust, this sexy story has a sickly feeling of degradation that begs for interpretation. Resist it. Stick to the intricate relationships between the characters, and you can't go wrong. Back in London from Africa, the well-to-do Tony (Fox) takes a townhouse and hires impressively proper valet-butler Hugo Barrett (Bogarde) to "do everything" for him. Barrett takes charge and soon the house is a showplace of taste and organization. But something's amiss, although the dense Tony doesn't seem to be aware of it. Barrett has his life in such order that Tony's fiancée Susan (Craig) feels threatened. And Barrett's possessiveness may include a streak of malice, as he's passing off a tart acquaintance, Vera (Miles), as his sister. As Barrett's control and influence over Tony increase, things seem headed in an unpleasant direction.... DVD is as impeccably presented as Hugo Barrett himself, with a fine transfer of Douglas Slocombe's delicately photographed images, and very clear audio. There are no subtitles or closed captions. A trailer is included. The film is available as a single disc, or in "The Dirk Bogarde Collection" three-disc set, along with *The Mind Benders* and *Accident.* —*GE*

Movie: 🐾🐾🐾 ½ **DVD:** 🐾🐾🐾
Anchor Bay (cat #DV11580, UPC 0131311-58090). Full frame. Dolby Digital Mono. $19.98. Keepcase. *LANG:* English. *FEATURES:* Talent files • 24 chapters • Trailer.
1963 112m/B *GB* Dirk Bogarde, James Fox, Sarah Miles, Wendy Craig, Catherine Lacey, Richard Vernon; **D:** Joseph Losey; **W:** Harold Pinter; **C:** Douglas Slocombe; **M:** John Dankworth. *AWARDS:* British Acad. '63: Actor (Bogarde); N.Y. Film Critics '64: Screenplay.

Servants of Twilight

Religious zealots target a young boy (Lennon) for assassination because their cult leader (Zabriskie) says that he's the anti-Christ. Adaptation of the Dean R.

Koontz best-seller is packed with action but the shock ending undercuts all that has come before. DVD image and sound are about equal to VHS tape or broadcast. —MM

Movie: 🎵🎵/C **DVD:** 🎵🎵
Studio Home Ent. (cat #VM7802D, UPC 031398780229). Full frame. Dolby Digital Stereo. $19.99. Keepcase. LANG: English. SUB: English; French; Spanish. CAP: English. FEATURES: 24 chapters • Trailers.
1991 (R) 95m/C Bruce Greenwood, Belinda Bauer, Grace Zabriskie, Richard Bradford, Jarrett Lennon, Carel Struycken, Jack Kehoe, Kelli Maroney, Dale Dye; **D:** Jeffrey Obrow; **W:** Stephen Carpenter.

Sesame Street Presents: Follow That Bird

The Large Yellow-Feathered One decides that he needs to explore his roots and leaves Sesame Street to find his "real" bird family. After realizing the error of his ways, he heads back across country and runs into a series of adventures, including an encounter with a crop duster, straight from *North by Northwest*. DVD really can't do much with the full-frame image. Colors are bright and clear but undistinguished, which will mean absolutely nothing to a young audience. This one's a hit on any medium and will be enjoyed by Muppet fans of all ages. Any movie that allows Waylon Jennings to sing a duet with Big Bird earns an unqualified recommendation. Sound is fine for the jaunty songs. —MM **AKA:** Follow That Bird.
Movie: 🎵🎵🎵 **DVD:** 🎵🎵🎵
Warner (cat #13279, UPC 0853913279-29). Full frame. Dolby Stereo. $19.98. Snapper. LANG: English; French; Spanish. SUB: English; French; Spanish; Portuguese. CAP: English. FEATURES: Trailer • 27 chapters • Jump to song.
1985 (G) 92m/C Sandra Bernhard, John Candy, Chevy Chase, Joe Flaherty, Dave Thomas, Waylon Jennings; **D:** Ken Kwapis; **W:** Judy Freudberg, Tony Geiss; **C:** Curtis Clark; **M:** Lennie Niehaus; **V:** Carroll Spinney, Jim Henson, Frank Oz.

Session 9

Under the heavy financial pressures of a new family, Gordon Fleming (Mullan) says that his asbestos-removal company can clean out the abandoned Danvers Lunatic Asylum in one week. That puts his crew (Caruso, Gevedon, Guilfoyle, Lucas) under the gun. Each man has his own weakness and the ghosts that haunt the place still have power. The place itself has power, too. Danvers is real and Anderson filmed it using High-Definition video and natural light. The DVD image doesn't have quite the richness of film but it lacks the transparency that we tend to associate with shot-on-video productions. This one looks very good, with a muted color scheme and excellent sharpness throughout. More importantly, both acting and writing are first rate. This is a substantial horror film that

ought to find an appreciative audience on disc. One criticism, with the commentary track and some softly spoken dialogue, subtitles would have been useful. —MM
Movie: 🎵🎵🎵 **DVD:** 🎵🎵🎵
USA Home Ent. (cat #96306 0315-2, UPC 696306031529). Widescreen. Dolby Digital Surround. $26.98. Keepcase. LANG: English. FEATURES: 12 chapters • Commentary: Anderson, Gevedon • Story-to-screen scene comparisons • Trailer • "Haunted Palace" making-of featurette.
2001 (R) 100m/C Peter Mullan, David Caruso, Joshua Lucas, Brendan Sexton III, Paul Guilfoyle, Stephen Gevedon; **D:** Brad Anderson; **W:** Brad Anderson, Stephen Gevedon; **C:** Uta Briesewitz; **M:** Climax Gold Twins.

Seven Days to Live

Surprisingly engaging old country house/something's in the basement film from young German director Sebastian Niemann. Ellen (Plummer, in a normal human being role) and Martin (a creepy Pertwee) have bought a secluded Victorian house in the middle of a, possibly, English bog (the film was actually made in the Czech Republic) after the death of their young son. Ellen begins to get messages in various forms—the radio, road signs, written in blood on her forehead—that she only has seven days to live. Things get weirder as the history of the land is revealed and Martin begins to seem less than himself. A definite homage to films like *The Shining* (there's a copy of the book in a store window) and *Poltergeist*, this is a well-made suspense film for the drive-in crowd. The great lighting and cinematography look very good on the disc but the sound is a little muffled, which makes a few of the more accented actors hard to understand at times. —CA
Movie: 🎵🎵 **DVD:** 🎵🎵🎵
Studio Home Ent. (cat #ST7821D, UPC 658149782129). Widescreen letterboxed. Dolby Digital 5.1. $24.99. Keepcase. LANG: English. SUB: English; French; Spanish. CAP: English. FEATURES: 24 chapters • Cast & crew interviews • Trailer.
2001 (R) 96m/C Amanda Plummer, Sean Pertwee, Nick Brimble, Gina Bellman; **D:** Sebastian Niemann.

7 Lucky Ninja Kids

There is a belief among videophiles that DVD can make even the worst movie look good. That isn't always so. This film from the Far East has been retitled *7 Lucky Ninja Kids* and slapped onto DVD with no attention given to the presentation. The film was clearly filmed in a widescreen format, which hasn't been preserved for this transfer. To add insult to injury, the typical "pan & scan" technique hasn't been employed, so what we have is the center of the original image, meaning that action and characters are frequently falling off of the edge of the frame. As if that weren't bad enough, the image is grainy, hazy, and washed-out. Simply put, the image here is sub-VHS quality. (You know that something

has gone horribly wrong when the "Little Rascals" bonus feature looks better than the movie.) The digital mono sound isn't aided by the fact that the dialogue appears to have been dubbed by a kindergarten class who were asked to shout phrases at random. As for the story, it deals with a group of seven youngsters and their involvement with a stolen diamond. I'm sure that the original version of this film is fun and charming, but the incarnation presented here is an insult to the DVD medium. —ML **AKA:** 7 Ninja Kids.
Movie: woof **DVD:** woof
Brentwood (cat #44091-9, UPC 78736440-9198). Full frame. Digital Mono. $4.99. Keepcase. LANG: English. FEATURES: "Little Rascals" short • Trivia game • DVD Dictionary.
1989 (PG) 90m/C

Sex and Buttered Popcorn

Stylish and entertaining documentary examines the Hollywood exploitation moguls and their films, from the 1920s through the 1950s. These films shamelessly catered to audiences' prurient interests but typically delivered sugarcoated morality messages and stock footage of routine baby births or the horrible effects of sexually transmitted diseases. The main characters are David Friedman and Dan Sonney—two of the most important producers—and Mildred Babb, widow of Kroger Babb. The whole thing is just fascinating and host Ned Beatty approaches it with exactly the right amount of humor. Naturally enough, on DVD the new interview material looks fine; the older stuff varies widely in quality. Extras are extensive and properly sordid, stretching the total running time to 155 minutes. —MM
Movie: 🎵🎵🎵 **DVD:** 🎵🎵 ½
VCI (cat #KPF-508, UPC 089859050824). Full frame. $24.98. Keepcase. LANG: English. FEATURES: 3 striptease shorts with Lili St. Cyr and Tempest Storm • 10 trailers • "Queen of the B's" featurette • Exploitation poster gallery • Commentary: veteran roadshowmen.
1991 (R) 70m/C David Friedman; **D:** Sam Harrison.

Sex and Buttered Popcorn Collection

Boxed set collects all four volumes of the *Sex and Buttered Popcorn* discs. —MM
Movie: 🎵🎵 ½ **DVD:** 🎵🎵
VCI (cat #KPF-516, UPC 089859051623). Full frame. Dolby Digital Mono. $69.99. Keepcase boxed set. LANG: English.
2001 660m/C

Sex and Buttered Popcorn, Vol. 1: Tease, Sleaze, and Social Disease

Double feature begins with *Tomorrow's Children* (1934), an alarmist melodrama

warning against the threat of government-induced female sterilization. It asks the question: If a woman's family is weird, should her tubes be tied? The second, *The Story of DE 733* (1942), is a cautionary tale about venereal disease, contracted by a Navy ship's crew on shore leave. Curiously, on DVD, the older film looks much better. The image is sharp and sound is fine. *DE 733* is much grainier, but relatively free of pixels. —*MM*
Movie: 🦴🦴 *DVD:* 🦴🦴
VCI (cat #KPF-513, UPC 089859051326). Full frame. Dolby Digital Mono. $24.98. Keepcase. *LANG:* English. *FEATURES:* 14 chapters • Trailers • Poster gallery • 3 short films.
2000 143m/C

Sex and Buttered Popcorn, Vol. 2: Sex, Sin, and Salvation

Double feature begins with *She Shoulda Said No!* (AKA *Wild Weed,* 1949) in which funny-smelling cigarettes ruin the lives of all who inhale. Star Leeds's actual drug bust with Robert Mitchum got her the role. In the second, *Mad Youth* (1934), a teen dances the jitterbug and falls in love with the man her slutty, alcoholic mother had been chasing. Both look very good for their age on DVD, with the expected grainy black-and-white images but no excessive pixels. Extras are inventive, particularly the featurette on dancer Pearl Tolson. —*MM*
Movie: 🦴🦴 *DVD:* 🦴🦴
VCI (cat #KPF-514, UPC 089859051425). Full frame. Dolby Digital Mono. $24.98. Keepcase. *LANG:* English. *FEATURES:* 24 chapters • 2 nudie shorts • Exploitation poster gallery • Featurette on bit player Pearl Tolson.
2000 154m/C

Sex and Buttered Popcorn, Vol. 3: Granddad's Forbidden Follies

The first half of this double feature, *Elysia,* is an early nudist camp movie featuring lots of men walking away from the camera, when they're not playing leapfrog. DVD delivers a rough-looking image with registration jitters, heavy grain, and a scratchy soundtrack. The flaws come from a low-budget, well-worn original. The second film, *Road to Ruin,* shows that cigarettes lead to alcohol which leads to marijuana which leads to prostitution. Static fills the soundtrack and missing frames are obvious in several scenes. Extras are fine. —*MM*
Movie: 🦴🦴 *DVD:* 🦴½
VCI (cat #KPF-515, UPC 089859051524). Full frame. Dolby Digital Mono. $24.98. Keepcase. *LANG:* English. *FEATURES:* 10 chapters • "Expose of the Nudist Racket" short film • Bit player bio on Jimmy Tolson • Exploitation poster gallery • 1930s commercials.
2000 133m/C

Sex and the City: Season 1

Parker plays Carrie, a writer who discusses people's sex lives in her column; outside of work, she chats and gossips with her friends—Charlotte (Kirstin Davis), Miranda (Cynthia Nixon), and Samantha (Kim Catrall). Parker gets to showcase her playfulness and sense of style as Carrie. It's mainly a show aimed at women, but the performances are generally very good and the writing is funny. Some have dismissed the show as being too sexually active, but it isn't anything more than light, entertaining comedy that shouldn't be taken seriously enough to inspire anger. It's a very funny show and worth catching up with for those who haven't seen it. Colors are strong and occasionally vibrant and the image is fairly sharp. The episodes (especially the first one) tend to be very grainy and the occasional preprint scratch is visible. The sound quality is fine but fairly limited as far as Surround use is concerned. The music and dialogue is balanced perfectly—the musical score is clean and vibrant, and the dialogue is always clear. —*AB/DG*
Movie: 🦴🦴🦴 *DVD:* 🦴🦴🦴
HBO Home Video (UPC 26359930027). Full frame. Dolby Digital Surround. $39.94. Fold-out sleevecase. *LANG:* English. *CAP:* English. *FEATURES:* Chapter links • "Making of" featurette • DVD-ROM features • "Research" TV promo • List of awards and nominations.
2000 540m/C Sarah Jessica Parker, Kim Cattrall, Kristen Davis, Cynthia Nixon, Christopher Noth; *W:* Darren Star; *C:* Stuart Dryburgh; *M:* Douglas J. Cuomo.

Sex and the City: The Complete Third Season

Those bawdy Manhattanites are back in the third season of HBO's hit series. This three-disc set features all 18 episodes in their original, uncut form. Here, we get the continuing story of our four main characters, Carrie (Sarah Jessica Parker), sex columnist; Samantha (Kim Cattrall), PR guru; Charlotte (Kristin Davis), art gallery director; and Miranda (Cynthia Nixon), attorney. As in the first two seasons, the show focuses primarily on Carrie, but offers each character her own story line. Carrie is attempting to move on from her torrid relationship with Mr. Big (Chris Noth) and finds solace with the good-natured Aidan (John Corbett). But Mr. Big refuses to let Carrie go. Meanwhile, Charlotte meets the man of her dreams, Dr. Trey MacDougal (Kyle MacLachlan) and is able to have her dream wedding. But she learns dreams can turn into nightmares. During the latter half of the season, the four women head for Los Angeles, where Carrie hopes to turn her column into a movie. There, they discover that you don't have to be in New York to have fun. The episodes exemplify the quality of writing and care that goes into this show. Rarely

is a television program so funny, and yet so true and challenging. Part of the appeal is indeed the racy, "go for broke" attitude, where the women discuss things that most TV shows would never even imply, and this set is a great way to experience it. DVD image is sharp and clear, but there is a noticeable haze of grain in many of the shots. Still, the colors are very good, and the grain isn't all that distracting. Surround delivers clear and intelligible dialogue (which is very important with this show) and modest effects. Writer/producer/director Michael Patrick King provides a very informative audio commentary to four episodes on disc two, which should delight fans of the show. —*ML*
Movie: 🦴🦴🦴🦴 *DVD:* 🦴🦴🦴
HBO (cat #99232, UPC 026359923227). Full frame. Dolby 2.0 Surround; Mono. $49.99. Special packaging. *LANG:* English; French; Spanish. *CAP:* English. *FEATURES:* Commentary • Production notes • Cast & crew bios • Award & nominations • Promo spots.
2002 540m/C Sarah Jessica Parker, Kim Cattrall, Kristen Davis, Cynthia Nixon, John Corbett, Christopher Noth, Kyle MacLachlan; *D:* Michael Patrick King; *W:* Michael Patrick King.

Sex and the Emperor

Leering, grotesque freak show about the life of Emperor Tongzhi of China, whose life was cut short by syphilis. The tale of the teen monarch, told by his faithful eunuch, is used as an excuse to show dismemberment, urine drinking, grotesque syphilitic lesions, and other repellent sights. Image is a bit soft, and the non-removable subtitles are sometimes difficult to read. —*BT* *AKA:* Man Qing Jin Gong Qi An.
Movie: 🦴½ *DVD:* 🦴🦴
Mei Ah Laser Disc Co. (cat #DVD422, UPC 4890391104229). Widescreen letterboxed. $19.95. Keepcase. *LANG:* Cantonese; Mandarin. *SUB:* Chinese; English. *FEATURES:* 9 chapters.
1994 92m/C *HK* Jimmy Wong, Yvonne Yung Hung, Stuart Ong, Julie Lee; *D:* Sherman Wong; *W:* Cheuk Bing; *C:* Tony Miu; *M:* Marco Wan.

Sex Madness

Please see review of *The Madness Trilogy.*
AKA: They Must Be Told.
Movie: 🐶
1937 50m/B Duncey Taylor.

Sexual Chemistry

Silly soft-core sex comedy finds scientist Robert (Xander) developing a formula for a Viagra-like drug that works for women, too. He takes an experimental dose and, presto, he is transformed into Heidi (LaFleur). The film is made on far too small a budget for any transformation scenes. DVD image is fine in most interiors but any panning or tracking motion generates heavy artifacts. Skin tones (and there are a lot of those) tend to be far too red. —MM

Movie: 🐾 ½ **DVD:** 🐾 ½
Monarch (cat #BUZ005014D). Full frame. $19.98. Keepcase. LANG: English. FEATURES: 16 chapters.
1999 97m/C Steve Xander, Stephanie LaFleur; **D:** Mike Sedan; **W:** Helen Haxton; **C:** Mike Sedan; **M:** Todd Schroeder.

Sexual Predator

Parole officer Beth Spinella (Everhart) is almost sure that photographer J.C. Gale (Grieco) raped and murdered her friend. But the court said her death was accidental. Following the standard plotline for an erotic thriller, Beth decides she must get close, very close to her subject to learn the truth. Both production values and full-frame image are slightly above average for the genre, a bit better than VHS tape. Actually, the film's entire color scheme seems designed to highlight and flatter Ms. Everhart's long red hair, and said hair rises to the occasion and turns in a fine performance. On the minus side, one patterned shirt strobes in medium shots. Sound is acceptable on this few-frills disc. —MM

Movie: 🐾🐾 ½ **DVD:** 🐾🐾 ½
Columbia Tristar (cat #07068, UPC 043-396070684). Full frame. Dolby Digital Surround. $29.98. Keepcase. LANG: English; French. SUB: English; French; Spanish; Portuguese; Chinese; Korean; Thai. CAP: English. FEATURES: 28 chapters.
2001 (R) 85m/C Angie Everhart, Richard Grieco.

Sexy Beast

Gal Dove (Ray Winstone) is a retired London criminal, living an idyllic life on a secluded villa in Southern Spain, with his wife Deedee (Amanda Redman), and another couple, Aitch (Cavan Kendall) and Jackie (Julianne White). Then Don Logan (Ben Kingsley) shows up to bring Gal in on another heist, and he won't take no for an answer. Back in London, top crook Teddy Bass (Ian McShane) is preparing to break into the impregnable vault of Harry's (James Fox) bank—by digging an underwater tunnel. Already a swaggering, crass, abrasive thug, Don turns the heat up on Gal and his intimidated group—pressuring Gal, badgering Gal, lashing out with vicious invectives and uncontrollable violence that promises more. Gal's determined to stay retired, but Don's pushing far, far too hard to be satisfied with any kind of polite refusal. Jonathan Glazer's direction is direct; most of the story relies on the characters and their spatial relationships to one another—mostly to Ben Kingsley's Don Logan character. Like a boulder crashing down a mountainside, there's no stopping this wound-up mass of rage and venom: his first introduction, striding through an airport, eyes forward and every muscle taut, is reminiscent of Lee Marvin's corridor walk in Point Blank. The drama is a case of irresistible force come up against

immovable object. Director Glazer and his cameraman Ivan Bird stylize the images just enough to give the picture an edge, without toppling into fetish territory. Seen from above, Gal roasts happily on his pool deck, wa-ay over to the left of the Panavision screen. Two shots are never used when one will do—major sequences are sometimes covered from only one angle. The camera also doesn't move a great deal in the confrontation scenes—there's no eye candy to detract from the focus on the characters, who sit and stand in awkward groupings, too cowed by the horrid Don Logan to move. Their reactions and eyes tell it all. DVD has a nice menu with a perhaps overdone bullet-hole motif, framing lazy shots of Gal speaking to us from his suntanning pose. There's a full-length commentary from producer Jeremy Thomas and Ben Kingsley, that politely reacts to all the sights on-screen. Kingsley doesn't get into what made his role tick except to compliment the screenplay, and has uniform positive things to say about the other actors that don't become very interesting. One viewing suggestion: unless the English slang spoken in this film happens to be your own, you're going to want to use the English subtitle track. The first time I saw the show, I understood only half of the arcane lingo, and was unsure of the other half! —GE

Movie: 🐾🐾🐾 ½ **DVD:** 🐾🐾🐾 ½
20th Century Fox (cat #2002674, UPC 02-4543026747). Widescreen (2.35:1) anamorphic. Dolby Digital 5.1 Surround. $29.98. Keepcase. LANG: English. SUB: English. CAP: English. FEATURES: Commentary • Featurette • Trailers • TV spot • 20 chapters.
2000 (R) 88m/C GB Ray Winstone, Ben Kingsley, Ian McShane, Amanda Redman, James Fox, Robert Atiko, Julianne White, Cavan Kendall, Alvaro Monje; **D:** Jonathan Glazer; **W:** Louis Mellis, David Scinto; **C:** Ivan Bird; **M:** Roque Banos. AWARDS: Broadcast Film Critics '02: Support. Actor (Kingsley); NOM: Oscars '01: Support. Actor (Kingsley); Golden Globes '02: Support. Actor (Kingsley); Ind. Spirit '02: Foreign Film; Screen Actors Guild '01: Support. Actor (Kingsley).

The Sexy Sixth Sense

Filmed as I See Dead Strippers, this is yet another Seduction Cinema spoof. Harking back to the days of the Nudie Cuties, Frances is a lonely nerd who is the only one who can see the frolicking lesbian ghosts all around. An amusing behind-the-scenes clip shows the starlets waiting around in huge platform shoes while the crew sets up the lights. Image and sound are of professional camcorder quality. —BT

Movie: 🐾 **DVD:** 🐾🐾
EI Independent Cinema (cat #sc1019dvd, UPC 12385101991). Full frame. $19.98. Keepcase. LANG: English. FEATURES: 10 chapters • Behind-the-scenes • Interviews • Trailers.
2001 70m/C Terry West, Josh Robinson, Barbara Joyce, Darian Caine, Jade DuBoir,

Esmerelda Dellarocco, Natalia Ashe; **D:** Terry West, Josh Robinson; **W:** Terry West; **C:** Ted Crestview.

Shackleton

Exceptionally well-made version of Sir Ernest Shackleton's 1914 Antarctic expedition. To recruit men for this expedition, Shackleton (Branagh) posts this advertisement: "Men wanted for hazardous journey. Small wages, bitter cold. Long months of complete darkness. Constant danger. Safe return doubtful." Twenty-seven men boarded the Endurance in London and even after the ice took their ship, Shackleton inspired them to persevere. In spite of the overwhelming odds against their survival, they all returned to England safely. Sturridge has brought about as much passion to this project as Shackleton brought to his expedition. Everything about this production is top-notch. Even if you've read all the books about his expedition, this marvelous production won't disappoint you one bit. The bonus features illuminate Shackleton, the natural history, and the filmmaking very well. All-around great package with top sound and image quality. —LA

Movie: 🐾🐾🐾🐾 **DVD:** 🐾🐾🐾🐾
A&E (cat #AE-70430, UPC 7339617043-10). Widescreen (1.85:1) anamorphic. Dolby Digital Stereo. $49.95. Special packaging (slipcased keepcase). LANG: English. CAP: English. FEATURES: Part One: 12 chapters • Part Two: 12 chapters • "Making of" • A&E's bio of Shackleton • The History Channel's "Antarctica: A Frozen History" • Bio/filmography of Branagh. Discs are individually labeled: AAE-70431, AAE-70432, AAE-70433.
2002 200m/C Kenneth Branagh, Kevin McNally, Chris Larkin, Mark McGann, Lorcan Cranitch, Nicholas (Nick) Rowe, Pip Torrens, Shaun Dooley, Matt(hew) Day; **D:** Charles Sturridge; **W:** Charles Sturridge; **C:** Henry Braham; **M:** Adrian Johnston.

Shades of Darkness

Stephen King sort of story has to do with a woman (Trebilcock) who returns to her small hometown and finds that supernatural forces are at work. On his commentary track, director Johnson talks about the "pseudo-effects" that his meager budget forced him to employ. They are limited, but the film earns at least a qualified recommendation to horror fans for its energy. There's little that DVD can do for the grainy image, but the disc comes with the usual generous extras that York provides. —MM

Movie: 🐾🐾 ½ **DVD:** 🐾🐾 ½
York Ent. (cat #YPD-1159, UPC 75072311-5924). Widescreen letterboxed. $14.99. Keepcase. LANG: English. FEATURES: Trailers • "Making of" featurette • Deleted scenes • Director's Q&A and commentary track.
2000 (R) 90m/C John Maczko, Annie Trebilcock; **D:** Christopher Johnson.

Shadow Magic

Based on the true story of Westerner Raymond Wallace (Harris), who, in 1902, brought motion pictures to China. In the film, he hooks up with a local photographer Liu (Yu), who is enamored of modern mechanical things. They change each other's lives in dramatic ways by bridging their two cultures with the magic of movies. Yu's performance is simply captivating. Director's commentary has a lot of interesting historical information. The music is wonderfully evocative. Picture and sound quality are tops. —LA

Movie: 🎬🎬🎬 ½ **DVD:** 🎬🎬🎬 ½
Columbia Tristar (cat #06154, UPC 043-396061545). Widescreen (1.85:1) anamorphic. Dolby Surround. $29.98. Keepcase. *LANG:* Mandarin. *SUB:* English; French. *CAP:* English. *FEATURES:* Commentary: director • Theatrical trailers • 28 chapters • Filmographies • Link to official web site.
2000 (PG) 115m/C *GE* Jared Harris, Xia Yu, Liu Peiqi, Lu Liping, Xing Yufei, Wang Jingming, Li Yusheng; **D:** Ann Hu; **W:** Ann Hu, Huang Dan, Tang Louyi, Kate Raisz, Bob McAndrew; **C:** Nancy Schreiber; **M:** Zhang Lida.

A Shadow You Soon Will Be

After several years in Europe, a nameless computer programmer (Sola) returns to his native Argentina, where he finds a twisted and barren landscape. In his travels, he meets a host of bizarre characters, including a former carnival owner and a mysterious gambler. The soundtrack is heavy on background noise, and the picture is grainy with a noticeable red tint. —BG **AKA:** Una Sombra Ya Pronto Seras.

Movie: 🎬🎬 **DVD:** 🎬🎬
Vanguard Intl. Cinema (cat #VFO263, UPC 658769026337). Full frame. Dolby Stereo. $29.95. Keepcase. *LANG:* Spanish. *SUB:* English. *FEATURES:* 12 chapters.
1994 105m/C *AR* Miguel Angel Sola, Eusebio Poncela, Pepe Soriano, Alicia Bruzzo, Luis Brandoni, Diego Torres, Gloria Carra; **D:** Hector Olivera; **W:** Hector Olivera, Osvaldo Soriano; **C:** Felix Monti; **M:** Osvaldo Montes.

Shake, Rattle & Rock!

When rebellious teenager Susan (Renee Zellweger) and her friends open a teens' rock and roll nightclub, all the conservative parents band together to silence the storm. The musically besieged township eventually stages a telethon-style trial to decide if rock and roll is here to stay. Slight, mildly engaging remake of 1957 AIP teen flick keeps the 1950s setting, but has little else going for it other than Zellweger's game performance. Even the iconic supporting cast seems tired; i.e. Mary Woronov as the uptight community matron, Dick Miller as a caring cop, William Schallert as the mock judge. The only fleeting highlight is Paul Anka's

cameo as a cranky German cook waving a chicken carcass. Full-frame transfer is clean, colorful, and sharp. The Dolby Digital Surround sound ably pumps up such rock standards as "The Girl Can't Help It" and "Ain't That a Shame." —EP

Movie: 🎬🎬 **DVD:** 🎬🎬 ½
Buena Vista Home Ent. (cat #23293, UPC 786936159943). Full frame. Dolby Digital Surround Stereo. $29.99. Keepcase. *LANG:* English. *FEATURES:* 15 chapters.
1994 (PG-13) 83m/C Renee Zellweger, John Doe, Nora Dunn, Howie Mandel, Patricia Childress, Mary Woronov, Max Perlich, Dick Miller, William Schallert, Paul Anka; **D:** Allan Arkush; **W:** Trish Soodik; **C:** Jean De Segonzac; **M:** Joseph (Joey) Altruda.

Shakedown

Low-budget action flick from Roger Corman's organization tosses in just about everything. First there's the stolen Poplin virus. which can do terrible things to humanity. Then there's cult leader St. Joy (Perlman, channeling Marlon Brando's Col. Kurtz) who's predicting the apocalypse, and then there's the bank robbery where agent McKay (Larson) and Julie Hays (Eleniak) are trapped at the very moment that the big earthquake hits L.A.! Then the President (Dryer) considers nuking the city. With all that going on, the action trots along nicely. DVD image is fair in conventional scenes. It drops down to poor in the shaky-camera earthquake stuff, and when the dust rises it becomes exceptionally grainy with resultant artifacts. Throughout, it's clear to any viewer that cheap computer effects are as phony as cheap conventional effects. —MM

Movie: 🎬🎬 ½ **DVD:** 🎬🎬
New Concorde (cat #NH20702D, UPC 736-991470293). Widescreen letterboxed. $19.98. Keepcase. *LANG:* English. *SUB:* Spanish. *CAP:* English. *FEATURES:* Trailer • Talent files.
2002 92m/C Ron Perlman, Erika Eleniak, Fred (John F.) Dryer, Wolf Larson.

Shanghai Triad

The story revolves around a Chinese crime boss and his mistress, Jingbao (Li), as seen through the eyes of Shuisheng. Shuisheng is brought to China by his uncle, an older criminal who sets him to work as the assistant to Jingbao. Before long, though, he becomes more and more involved in the activities of the local mobs. The film's cinematography and sets are nothing short of beautiful, capturing the 1930's look perfectly. The images are washed in warm colors that make the film even more striking. Unfortunately, the characters and story aren't engaging and the slow, deliberate pace seems to work against the film. The movie is filmed intentionally soft—in addition to that, there are many scenes in nightclubs or other areas that are smoky and have a hazy look. Colors are beautiful, though. The movie is washed in deep, rich reds and golds, looking saturated and often gorgeous. Pixela-

tion and shimmering are occasionally noticeable. The audio is limited but strong. —AB/DG **AKA:** Yao a Yao Yao Dao Waipo Qiao.

Movie: 🎬🎬 **DVD:** 🎬🎬🎬
Columbia Tristar Home Video (UPC 433-96118577). Widescreen (1.85:1) letterboxed. Dolby Digital 5.1 Surround. $29.95. Keepcase. *LANG:* Chinese; Mandarin. *SUB:* English; Spanish. *CAP:* English. *FEATURES:* Cast bios • Production notes • Trailer • Chapter links.
1995 (R) 108m/C *FR CH* Gong Li, Li Bao-Tian, Li Xuejian, Shun Chun Shusheng, Wang Xiaoxiao Cuihua, Jiang Baoying; **D:** Zhang Yimou; **W:** Bi Feiyu; **C:** Lu Yue; **M:** Zhang Guangtain. *AWARDS:* NOM: Oscars '95: Cinematog.; Golden Globes '96: Foreign Film.

Shaolin Disciple

The Shaolin monks get involved in a slew of adventures, running into the vengeful spirit of a suicide and the infamous bandit Tiger, who has recently escaped from prison. There's a good deal of kung-foolery to boot—a fight breaks out when the patron of a brothel decides he's less interested in the girls than in one of the establishment's male managers. The picture and audio are what you'd expect for a bargain-basement DVD. —BG

Movie: 🎬 ½ **DVD:** 🎬 ½
Tai Seng (cat #77784, UPC 6016437778-49). Full frame. $9.98. Keepcase. *LANG:* English (dubbed). *FEATURES:* 9 chapters • Trailers for other Martial Art Theater titles.
1986 87m/C Kwok Fung, Kong Keung, Liu Gia Yung; **D:** Cheng Wing Keung.

Shaolin: Wheel of Life

In 2000, Chinese and British producers teamed up to present this unique touring stage show starring ordained Buddhist monks from the Shaolin Temple performing choreographed demonstrations, exercises, and rituals to tell the story of the temple's history and the development of kung fu. The show is wonderfully filmed using a multitude of camera angles, and techniques like close-ups and slow motion more fully capture the details of the presentation. The music and set designs are breathtaking. The DVD includes a 46-minute documentary about the show's creation. A text piece more fully explains the history of Shaolin Temple. —BT

Movie: 🎬🎬🎬 **DVD:** 🎬🎬🎬 ½
Universal Studios (cat #21419, UPC 02-519241928). Widescreen anamorphic. Dolby Digital 5.0 Surround. $24.98. Keepcase. *SUB:* English; French. *FEATURES:* 32 chapters • Documentary feature • Image gallery.
2000 83m/C *GB CH* **D:** Micha Bergese.

Shatter Dead

This is one of the best zombie flicks since *Night of the Living Dead*. It takes that premise one step further. The dead do rise up and walk but they're more of a nuisance, like panhandlers and petty thieves. Think of them as "inanimate Americans." Society has pretty much disintegrated, but that doesn't stop the resourceful Susan (Raven) from getting really ticked off when a charismatic preacher (Wells) steals her car. DVD does all it can with an image that appears to have been shot on 16mm. film. The picture is clear enough to make the homemade makeup effects and amateur acting all the more obvious. Sound is legible but nothing more. In an attempt to make up for the technical limitations, DVD comes with three commentary tracks, one with the director, a second with director and director of photography Matthew M. Howe, and a third with the director and the cast. All that's fine. The main problem with the disc is the lengthy introduction that precedes each menu. They're irritating and interminable. —MM

Movie: 🎬🎬🎬 **DVD:** 🎬🎬 ½
Sub Rosa Studios (UPC 674945102633). Full frame. Stereo. $29.99. Keepcase. *LANG:* English. *FEATURES:* 13 chapters • 3 commentary tracks • Trailers • Behind-the-scenes featurette • Tour of the "Shatter Dead" house.
2001 84m/C Stark Raven, Flora Fauna, Larry "Smalls" Johnson, Marina Del Rey, Robert Wells, Candy Coster; *D:* Scooter McCrae; *W:* Scooter McCrae; *C:* Matt Howe; *M:* Stephen Rajkumar.

She Creature

As part of the Creature Feature line of remakes of early AIP exploitation hits, *She Creature* sports a dandy (and sexy) Stan Winston mermaid, with a couple of extra monsters thrown in for good measure. The acting is fine, and the photography rich and evocative, but neither the script nor the direction of this monster potboiler are exciting enough to avoid boredom. An Irish carnival promoter named Angus (Sewell) and his girlfriend/fake mermaid Lillian (Gugino) visit a sea captain (Morris) who keeps a real mermaid, a dangerous murderess (Kihlstedt), in a fishtank. Angus steals the exhibit and heads out for fame and fortune on an America-bound sailing ship. But as the murders stack up, Lillian begins to believe she's experiencing an unwelcome telepathy with the mysterious creature, whose personal plans don't include captivity in a circus. DVD is a fine transfer that registers Tom Callaway's handsome photography well. The sound is also O.K., although the score is unmemorable and there's not much of a wooden sailing ship feel to the soundscape. The volume of the feature track is very low, especially when compared to the bubbly menu audio. A cable-TV featurette is included to remind us that Stan Winston is both producer and head of the monster makers. The director appears here and seems very, very young. Stan Winston keeps the commentary track for himself and his effects supervisor Shane Mahan. Three-quarters of the crew list are various

mermaid effects people. They did a fine job on a monster fit for a much more exciting vehicle than this. —GE **AKA:** Mermaid Chronicles Part 1: She Creature.
Movie: 🎬🎬 **DVD:** 🎬🎬🎬 ½
Columbia Tristar Home Video (UPC 043-396073647). Widescreen (1.78:1) anamorphic. $24.98. Keepcase. *LANG:* English. *FEATURES:* Commentary • Featurette.
2001 (R) 91m/C Rufus Sewell, Carla Gugino, Rya Kihlstedt, Aubrey Morris, Jim Piddock, Gil Bellows, Reno Wilson; *D:* Sebastian Gutierrez; *W:* Sebastian Gutierrez; *C:* Thomas Callaway; *M:* David Reynolds.

She-Devil

In this comic book version of the acidic Fay Weldon novel, *The Life and Loves of a She-Devil,* fat, dowdy Ruth (Roseanne) becomes a vengeful beast when smarmy romance novelist Mary (Streep) steals her husband (Begley Jr.). The wonderful comic touch that director Seidelman showed in *Desperately Seeking Susan* is noticeably absent, but then, these are caricatures, not characters. Even so, DVD delivers a faithful reproduction of a glossy Hollywood image. Sound is acceptable. —MM
Movie: 🎬🎬 **DVD:** 🎬🎬 ½
MGM Home Ent. (cat #1002578, UPC 027-616867797). Widescreen (1.85:1) anamorphic. Dolby Digital Surround; Mono. $24.99. Keepcase. *LANG:* English; French; Spanish. *SUB:* French; Spanish. *CAP:* English. *FEATURES:* Trailer • 16 chapters.
1989 (PG-13) 100m/C Meryl Streep, Roseanne, Ed Begley Jr., Linda Hunt, Elizabeth Peters, Bryan Larkin, A. Martinez, Sylvia Miles; *D:* Susan Seidelman; *W:* Mark Burns, Barry Strugatz; *C:* Oliver Stapleton; *M:* Howard Shore.

She Lives by Night

On his commentary track, Bret Hull makes no bones about the size of the budget he had to work with—"14 maxed-out credit cards"—to tell this contemporary vampire story about the amnesiac Angela (Cabal). Because of that, this extremely dark image makes for one of the grainiest DVDs you'll ever see. The bit rate is low and the amount of pixels and artifacts is enormous. Sound is hollow, too. —MM
Movie: 🎬🎬 ½ **DVD:** 🎬🎬 ½
York Ent. (cat #YPD-1141, UPC 75072311-4125). Widescreen letterboxed. $14.99. Keepcase. *LANG:* English. *FEATURES:* Trailer • Director's intro and commentary • Deleted scenes.
2001 (R) 90m/C Lilliana Cabal, John Woodhouse; *D:* Brett Hull.

She Shoulda Said No

Please see review of *Sex and Buttered Popcorn, Vol. 2.* **AKA:** The Devil's Weed; Wild Weed; Marijuana the Devil's Weed.
Movie: 🎬
1949 70m/B Lila Leeds, Alan Baxter, Lyle Talbot, Jack Elam, David Gorcey; *D:* Sam Newfield.

She Wolf of London

A series of brutal murders in a London park, thought to be from a dog or a wolf, throw soon-to-be-wed Phyllis Allenby (Lockhart) into a dither. She's all too aware of the legendary curse on her family name, and she's becoming certain that she's the monstrous She-Wolf who's been stalking the parks at midnight. Neither her "aunt" Martha Winthrop (Haden), Martha's daughter Carol (Wiley), or her fiancé Barry Lanfield (Porter) can shake her of this notion, especially after she starts waking up with blood on her hands and mud on her slippers. Title is available as half a double feature with *Werewolf of London.* (Please see review.) Both appear to be newer remasters than the VHS versions, and are stunning. —GE
Movie: 🎬 ½ **DVD:** 🎬🎬🎬
Universal Studios (cat #21410, UPC 025-192141027). Full frame. Dolby Digital Mono. $24.99. Keepcase. *LANG:* English; French; Spanish. *SUB:* French; Spanish. *CAP:* English. *FEATURES:* Trailer • Production notes.
1946 62m/B June Lockhart, Don Porter, Sara Haden, Jan Wiley, Lloyd Corrigan, Dennis Hoey, Martin Kosleck, Eily Malyon, Frederick Worlock; *D:* Jean Yarbrough; *W:* George Bricker, William Lava; *C:* Maury Gertsman.

Shelter

ATF agent Martin Roberts (Nelson) is set up by his commanding officer and has a bounty on his head. He takes refuge with a crime lord (Onorati), who's also on the feds' bad-guy hit list. They get even. Good to very good DVD image is only a marginal improvement over VHS tape, which is to be expected with this slightly above-average video premiere. —MM
Movie: 🎬🎬 **DVD:** 🎬🎬
Studio Home Ent. (cat #7015). Full frame. $24.95. Keepcase. *LANG:* English; Spanish. *FEATURES:* Cast & crew thumbnail bios • Notes • Trailer • 18 chapters.
1998 (R) 92m/C John Allen Nelson, Peter Onorati, Brenda Bakke, Costas Mandylor, Charles Durning, Linden Ashby, Kurtwood Smith; *D:* Scott Paulin; *W:* Max Strom; *C:* Eric Goldstein; *M:* David Williams.

Shiloh

Schmaltzy but redeeming story about Marty (Blake Heron), an 11-year-old boy living in a small town in West Virginia. After coming across a beagle named Shiloh, Marty seeks to rescue and care for the mistreated dog, who belongs to a mean hermit named Judd (Scott Wilson, who looks just like horror director Wes Craven!). This film goes beyond the usual "boy and his dog" theme, as it presents many moral and ethical issues that Marty faces when he takes the dog from its owner. Frannie (who plays Shiloh) is a very cute and expressive beagle, and newcomer Heron is great as Marty. The film was adapted from the Newberry Award–winning novel by Phyllis Reynolds Naylor. Both full-frame and widescreen images are sharp and clear, but there is some slight grain at times. The colors are good, and the fleshtones are realistic. This transfer does a fine job of showing off the beautiful scenery in the film. The Dolby Surround Stereo audio track offers clear dialogue and good musical reproduction, but the Surround effects are weak. With all of the scenes that take place in the forest, better Surround sound would have boosted the film's impact. The DVD includes a brief speech by noted film critic Roger Ebert, as he introduces the film at a festival. As one of the extras, this speech can be chosen from the "special features" menu. But it also appears at the beginning of the film, and cannot be skipped. —ML

Movie: 🎵🎵 ½ **DVD:** 🎵🎵🎵 Warner (cat #36200, UPC 0853936200-28). Widescreen (1.85:1) anamorphic; full frame. Dolby Surround Stereo. $19.98. Snapper. *LANG:* English; French. *SUB:* English; French; Spanish; Chinese; Thai; Korean. *CAP:* English. *FEATURES:* Cast & crew interviews ☞ Intro by Roger Ebert ☞ Theatrical trailer ☞ 26 chapters.
1997 (PG) 93m/C Blake Heron, Michael Moriarty, Scott Wilson, Rod Steiger, Ann Dowd, Bonnie Bartlett; **D:** Dale Rosenbloom; **W:** Dale Rosenbloom; **C:** Frank Byers; **M:** Joel Goldsmith.

Shiloh 2: Shiloh Season

Saccharine sequel finds 12-year-old Marty Preston (Browne) doing the boy-and-his-dog thing, while neighbor Judd (Wilson) has relapsed into nastiness. Before the story is over, many important lessons will be learned. Perhaps that assessment is a bit too skeptical but the jejune voice-over narration is made for those with stronger stomachs than mine. As the title character, Frannie remains a fine, lively young beagle. DVD image is what you'd expect for a film with a "2" at the end. It's nothing special but the disc earns extra marks for having both full-frame and widescreen options. —MM

Movie: 🎵🎵 **DVD:** 🎵🎵 ½ Warner Home Video (UPC 0853937315-26). Widescreen letterboxed; full frame. Dolby Surround Stereo. $17.98. Snapper. *LANG:* English; French. *SUB:* English; French; Spanish. *FEATURES:* 27 chapters ☞ Interviews ☞ Trailer ☞ Talent files.
1999 96m/C Zachary Browne, Scott Wilson, Michael Moriarty, Ann Dowd, Rod Steiger, Bonnie Bartlett, Joe Pichler; **D:** Sandy Tung; **W:** Dale Rosenbloom; **C:** Troy Smith; **M:** Joel Goldsmith.

The Shining [2 SE]

Those who were disappointed with Warner's initial DVD release of *The Shining* (reviewed in *Book 1*) will surely feel vindicated by the updated version. While the vast majority of this new release is identical to the previous version, it does sport newly remastered audio and video. Although some will still feel cheated that

The Shining is presented full frame, as per Kubrick's wishes, the improvements in the new transfer are definitely worth seeing. For a quick demonstration, simply jump to chapter 13, where Wendy (Duvall) and Danny (Lloyd) are running through the snow. On the old DVD, the grain on the image seemingly added another layer of snow to the scene and Wendy's coat appeared to be devoid of color. Here, there is virtually no grain, and the colors are quite striking. The fleshtones are realistic and true, and the snow surrounding the hotel now appears white, as opposed to gray. This sharp and clear presentation shows few, if any, signs of artifacting and no problems with compression. The newly remastered Dolby Digital 5.1 soundtrack adds much more presence to the film. As several of the scenes are played with little-to-no dialogue, the music of Wendy Carlos and Rachel Elkind, combined with the eerie sound effects used, helped to enhance the already creepy atmosphere of the film. This is a vast improvement over the old mono soundtrack. The dialogue here is clear and audible and there is no hiss on the track. While the Surround action is sparse, and the sound field isn't very wide, there is an impressive amount of bass response, once again, adding impact to the shock sound effects. The "making of" documentary, which is on the original DVD, appears here as well. However, it is now accompanied by an audio commentary by its director, Vivian Kubrick (Stanley's daughter). Here, she explains why she did the documentary, how she gained access to the stars, and what the shooting conditions were like. Her talk is upbeat and lively and it adds even greater insight to what is already an interesting documentary. —ML

Movie: 🎵🎵🎵 **DVD:** 🎵🎵🎵 ½ Warner Home Video (UPC 0853921156-24). Full frame. Dolby Digital 5.1 Surround Stereo. $24.98. Snapper. *LANG:* English; French. *SUB:* English; French; Spanish. *FEATURES:* "Making of" documentary ☞ Trailer.
1980 (R) 143m/C Jack Nicholson, Shelley Duvall, Danny Lloyd, Scatman Crothers, Joe Turkel, Barry Nelson, Philip Stone, Lia Beldam, Billie Gibson, Barry Dennan, David Baxt, Lisa Burns, Alison Coleridge, Kate Phelps, Anne Jackson, Tony Burton; **D:** Stanley Kubrick; **W:** Stanley Kubrick, Diane Johnson; **C:** John Alcott; **M:** Walter (Wendy) Carlos, Rachel Elkind.

Shock

Dora (Nicolodi) is the mother of a precocious little kid named Marco. His daddy died seven years ago and they haven't lived in the family home since. Mom remarries and decides to return to the old homestead. As soon as they're settled back in the house, Marco starts to act strangely. It soon becomes clear he's channeling his dead pop from the great beyond, and it turns out the guy's got a grudge. That pretty much sets the stage for the rest of the flick, which earns its title with numerous shocking and unsettling moments. This,

sadly, was director Bava's last film, though most of it evokes the work of his son Lamberto who reportedly helped finish the film. Though retitled *Beyond the Door 2* for U.S. release, it has nothing to do with the previous entry in that series. The disc features a fairly clean transfer from the original negative. Some grain and pixelation occur during the darker scenes. The mono sound is fine, though the bad English dubbing is flatly recorded and thin. The lack of subtitles is a regrettable judgment error as the Italian dialogue recording is much better. —GNG/DG **AKA:** Beyond the Door 2; Shock (Transfer Suspense Hypnos); Suspense; Al 33 di Via Orologio fa Sempre Freddo.

Movie: 🎵🎵 ½ **DVD:** 🎵 ½ Anchor Bay (cat #DV11072, UPC 0131311-07296). Widescreen (1.85:1) anamorphic. Mono. $29.98. Keepcase. *LANG:* English; Italian; French. *FEATURES:* Interview with assistant director Lamberto Bava ☞ International trailer ☞ U.S. TV spots ☞ Talent bios ☞ 15 chapters ☞ Insert card.
1979 (R) 90m/C *IT* John Steiner, Daria Nicolodi, David Colin Jr., Ivan Rassimov, Nicola Salerno; **D:** Mario Bava; **W:** Lamberto Bava, Franco Barbieri, Dardano Sacchetti, Paolo Brigenti; **C:** Alberto Spagnoli.

Shogun's Ninja

Henry Sanada reunites with his buddies in Japan, and plots the re-establishment of the Mimuchi clan destroyed by Shogun (Sonny Chiba). He holds one of two swords inscribed with a map to the Mimuchi gold mines, and Shogun will do anything to get it. Reunited with his girlfriend Sue Shiomi, whom he left in China, Sanada plots his revenge on Shogun. There's plenty of action, but it seems less with all the worthless meanderings of the plot. Available as part of a triple feature on one disc entitled *Classic Sonny Chiba Movies*. The image is vibrant (if a bit soft), cropped a bit on the sides and matted too tightly on the top. —BT

Movie: 🎵🎵 **DVD:** 🎵🎵 BFS Video (cat #30235D, UPC 06680530-2350). Widescreen letterboxed. $9.98. Keepcase. *LANG:* English. *FEATURES:* 4 chapters ☞ Bio ☞ Filmography ☞ Trivia.
1983 112m/C *JP* Henry Sanada, Sue Shiomi, Sonny Chiba; **D:** Noribumi Suzuki.

The Shootist

Aging gunfighter John Bernard Brooks (Wayne) gravitates to Carson City, Nevada, where Doctor E.W. Hostetler (Stewart) gives him the official word on his failing health—cancer, with six weeks to live. At first unwelcome at the boarding house of the widow Rogers (Bacall), he quickly strikes up a friendship with her and her son Gillom (Howard), even after the secret of his notoriety and his imminent demise leak out. In between fending off opportunists seeking to profit from his situation, and even a few would-be assassins, Brooks takes his doctor's advice and arranges to avoid a painful death in bed, by literally inviting three local toughs to a shootout at the local saloon. DVD looks great. The 16:9 enhancement can't make the redressed Burbank Studios streets look like Carson City, Nevada, but the colors and clarity are very pleasing to the eye. The sound is functional and Elmer Bernstein's uncharacteristically restrained score handsome. —GE

Movie: 🎵🎵🎵 ½ ***DVD:*** 🎵🎵🎵 ½
Paramount (cat #08904, UPC 0973608-90440). Widescreen (1.78:1) anamorphic. Dolby Digital Mono. $29.99. Keepcase. *LANG:* English; French. *SUB:* English. *FEATURES:* "Making of" documentary • Trailer.
1976 (PG) 100m/C John Wayne, Lauren Bacall, Ron Howard, James Stewart, Richard Boone, Hugh O'Brian, Bill McKinney, Harry (Henry) Morgan, John Carradine, Sheree North, Scatman Crothers; ***D:*** Donald Siegel; ***W:*** Scott Hale, Miles Hood Swarthout; ***C:*** Bruce Surtees; ***M:*** Elmer Bernstein. *AWARDS: NOM:* Oscars '76: Art Dir./Set Dec.

The Shop on Main Street

Engrossing story of a man's personal struggle with good and evil in fascist Slavakia. Antonin is a carpenter who has avoided toeing the fascist line much to his wife's displeasure, since this limits their financial options. However, a visit from his brother-in-law, a high-ranking fascist officer, forces him to do the dance of contrition and ask the hard moral question: Does he reject fascism on moral grounds or is he just unable to commit to anything? His brother-in-law informs him, over a raucous drunken dinner, that since Jews are no longer allowed to own businesses, each shop will be placed under the care of a Christian guardian. Antonin has been given a button and textile shop owned by a near-deaf Jewish widow. From here, it's one strange turn after another: Antonin and the widow fall into a strange platonic love. She is deaf and not really aware of the danger around her, which leads to some black comedy belly laughs amid, or perhaps because of, the impending doom everywhere. Antonin spends a lot of time trying to protect the widow yet still seem adequately fascist. There are some wistful fantasy sequences, and the cinematography is so beautifully plotted that it's almost a character. The film drags you kicking and screaming towards its last half-hour where the showdown between self-preservation and the good deed is played out. It is easy to understand why the film won the Academy Award for Best Foreign Language Film in 1968. Even so many years removed from the subject matter, its theme is timeless. This is a film that reminds you how it feels to feel strongly about something and how few absolutes you can afford when faced with a reality as stark as fascism. A part of the Criterion collection, the disc looks very good, and the sound is mono but clear. —CA ***AKA:*** The Shop on High Street; Obch Od Na Korze.
Movie: 🎵🎵🎵 ½ ***DVD:*** 🎵🎵🎵
Criterion (cat #130, UPC 037429156124). Full frame. Dolby Digital Mono. $29.95.

Keepcase. *LANG:* Czechoslovakian. *SUB:* English. *FEATURES:* 36 chapters • Theatrical trailer.
1965 111m/B *CZ* Ida Kaminska, Josef Kroner, Hana Slivkoua, Frantisek Holly, Martin Gregor; ***D:*** Jan Kadar, Elmar Klos; ***W:*** Jan Kadar, Elmar Klos; ***M:*** Zdenek Liska. *AWARDS:* Oscars '65: Foreign Film; N.Y. Film Critics '66: Foreign Film; *NOM:* Oscars '66: Actress (Kaminska).

Shopping

A crumbling industrial city (actually London's docklands) is the bleak setting for gangs of aimless youth who steal cars, crash into the windows of various shops, grab what they can, and lead the police on high-speed chases. Adrenaline junkie Billy (Law) is accompanied by thrill-seeking girlfriend Jo (Frost) on one such escapade while fending off rival Tommy (Pertwee). The *Rebel without a Cause* angst is nothing more than a posture, though the young cast has glamour to burn. That glamour is not served particularly well by an image that's dark and harsh. DVD can do little to improve on VHS tape. —MM
Movie: 🎵🎵 ½ ***DVD:*** 🎵🎵 ½
New Concorde (cat #NH20614 D, UPC 736991461499). Full frame. Dolby Digital Stereo. $14.98. Keepcase. *LANG:* English. *FEATURES:* 24 chapters • Trailers.
1993 (R) 86m/C *GB* Jude Law, Sadie Frost, Sean Pertwee, Fraser James, Sean Bean, Marianne Faithfull, Jonathan Pryce, Danny Newman; ***D:*** Paul Anderson; ***W:*** Paul Anderson; ***C:*** Tony Imi; ***M:*** Barrington Pheloung.

Short 6: Insanity

This volume in the series is weirdly funny, with a number of odd, hilarious short films. First off is "The Bad Plant," a well-animated short about a plant that wants to get away from its current confines in a small house. Offered with this great little film is director's commentary and storyboards, along with production notes. (Every feature on this DVD comes with those.) The most entertaining short feature is "Frankie Goes to Hollywood," a 12-minute "dogumentary" about the dog that appeared in one of the early scenes of *Armageddon*. Interviews are included with director Michael Bay and a number of stars from the film who talk about working with Frankie. Most hilarious are comments from Billy Bob Thornton, who gives the dog acting tips! It's a short with a great sense of humor. Another oddly interesting highlight is "Blue City," a story about a depressed man living in the inner city and the way his tale connects with that of two thieves. It also includes director's commentary. Other titles: "Midnight Dance," "Black Coffee," "Bovine Vendetta," "El Banquette" and "60 Channels—Beyond the Rhythm." As usual from both the "Short" and "Circuit" series, there are commentaries included for some of the features. Image quality of these short films varies due to the size and budget for

each, with some looking rather soft and some looking impressively sharp. Sound quality is very basic as well, but dialogue is always easily understood. —AB/DG
Movie: 🎵🎵🎵 ***DVD:*** 🎵🎵🎵
Warner Home Video (UPC 85393679927). Full frame. Dolby Digital 5.1 Surround; Dolby Digital Surround. $14.95. Snapper. *LANG:* English. *SUB:* English. *FEATURES:* Alternate audio & video tracks • Filmmaker commentaries • DVD-ROM features.
1999 120m/C

Short 7: Utopia

Shorts have become more and more popular in Hollywood and I can now see why—the work that is being done is absolutely remarkable. Mark Osborne's "More" is a six-minute feature that combines different forms of animation to tell the tale of an inventor that seeks to invent bliss for the inhabitants of his city. Not only does the director do a fantastic job with the animation but he tells the story perfectly without dialogue. The DVD provides an interview with the director at Sundance and also allows you to look at the film's storyboards. The next feature is "Zoltar from Zoron," an interesting if not too memorable 15-minute feature about a boy who claims to be from another planet. The disc offers a commentary from the director and a "roughcut alternate ending." "The Bar Channel" stars Richard Belzer as a guy trying to pick up a girl in a bar through his interactive television set. Good idea, but it's too short at three minutes to stick. Also included is a bonus short from the same director called "The Remote." "The Lion and The Lamb" is an award-winning short film that has little dialogue, only images of the chaos of life on the city streets, becoming more and more intense. The film has an intense visual style and is fascinating to watch. The alternate track offers a commentary from the filmmaker. "Images of Korea" is a claymation short. In the "Documentary" section, a number of subjects (including Devo's Mark Mothersbaugh) share their views on the future of man, and what will happen to society. An alternate segment shows Robot artist Christian Ristow at work. The video quality and audio quality for all of these short films was quite good. Although some of these are very small productions, the disc offers all of the shorts in 5.1 sound. As for the films themselves, I was really surprised at how good they were. If you're a fan of short features, you'll probably love this DVD. —AB/DG
Movie: 🎵🎵🎵 ½ ***DVD:*** 🎵🎵🎵
Warner Home Video (UPC 85393694326). Full frame. Dolby Digital 5.1 Surround; Dolby Digital Surround. $14.98. Snapper. *LANG:* English. *SUB:* English. *FEATURES:* Audio commentaries • DVD-ROM features • Production notes.
2000 100m/C

Short 10: Chaos

The latest edition of the *Short* series has scored with the inclusion of "Electronic

Labyrinth," a film that George Lucas did while at USC in 1967. It's the focus of the disc, although it's not the highlight. The film seems to be about an individual running through a maze, although since it has no dialogue and some rather experimental imagery, its point isn't exactly clear. More interesting is an interview with the professor that taught Lucas at USC, who chats about Lucas's early days as a filmmaker and the skills that he showed early on. Also included in this section is an interview with Francis Ford Coppola and Lucas about THX and the importance of film sound and sound presentation at your local theatre. Also included: "Five Feet High and Rising," the award-winning tale of kids in the city; the tale of a man who gets more to drink than he bargained for in "The Bottomless Cup"; and animation in "deliriouspink." The *Short* series has always been a great presentation, allowing young filmmakers to be able to not only have a forum for their work, but to add extra features such as commentaries and more. The video quality varies throughout the movie, with some of the low-budget shorts looking rather grainy and soft, but some of the newer ones are sharp and well defined. For the most part, though, the picture quality is pleasing with no instances of pixelation or shimmer. As for the sound, I can understand that the makers of this disc wanted to present these shorts in a bit more entertaining way by offering them in Dolby Digital 5.1, but for these films, which are mainly low-budget and dialogue-driven, they might almost work better in Dolby 2.0, as sometimes it seems here in 5.1 as if the same sound is coming from all sides at times. —AB/DG
Movie: ♫♫ ½ **DVD:** ♫♫ ½
Warner Home Video (UPC 85393724726). Full frame. Dolby Digital 5.1 Surround. $14.95. Snapper. *LANG:* English.
2000 140m/C

Short Circuit

Number Five, a newly developed robot for the military, is hit by lightning and begins to think for itself, to crave "input." Sheedy and Guttenberg help it hide from the mean people at the weapons lab who want to take it home. The letterbox framing on the transfer has been handled well, and there is no noticeable deficit of information at the top or bottom of the screen. This is a beautiful transfer, although it lacks some definition here and there as a result of the non-anamorphic presentation. There are some negligible defects from the source print. Color balancing has been handled rather well, with the cold metal look of Number Five standing out from the green and lush backgrounds of the Pacific Northwest. The audio has been re-mixed into a Dolby Digital 5.1 channel format that creates an elaborate sound field. My only complaint has to be that too much emphasis has been put on the Surround channels. The mix is by no means subtle, with musical cues, sound effects, or dialogue constantly streaming from the rear speak-

ers. While I'm a huge fan of Surround audio, too much of it creates an "artificial" and less natural atmosphere. In their laid-back commentary director John Badham and screenwriters S.S. Wilson and Brent Maddock show genuine affection for the film. —MM/GH
Movie: ♫♫ ½ **DVD:** ♫♫♫
Image Ent. (UPC 14381917321). Widescreen (2.35:1) letterboxed. Dolby Digital 5.1 Surround. $14.98. Keepcase. *LANG:* English. *FEATURES:* Commentary ● Isolated music and effects track ● Featurette ● Still galleries ● Theatrical trailer ● Talent files.
1986 (PG) 98m/C Steve Guttenberg, Ally Sheedy, Austin Pendleton, Fisher Stevens, Brian McNamara; **D:** John Badham; **W:** S.S. Wilson, Brent Maddock; **C:** Nick McLean; **M:** David Shire.

Short Circuit 2

In this sequel, lovable robot Johnny Five takes to the big city. Trying to blend in with society, Johnny Five quickly turns everything and everyone around himself upside down and goes on a hilarious rampage that ultimately helps make the city a little bit safer or unsafer, depending on your point of view. The image is clean and immediately reveals a good level of detail. Some slight grain is evident in occasional shots, but for the most part, the image is very stable and free of any blemishes or other distractions. Colors are strong and well delineated, creating a very pleasing and natural-looking image throughout. The transfer exhibits noticeable edge-enhancement, resulting in ringing artifacts and an unnatural crispness of the image, which can be distracting at times. The compression is generally good, but with slight pixelation artifacts that can become quite noticeable at times. The language tracks are well produced and create a lively sound field with adequate Surround usage. —GH
Movie: ♫♫ ½ **DVD:** ♫♫ ½
Columbia Tristar (cat #05995, UPC 0433-96059955). Widescreen (1.85:1) anamorphic; full frame. Dolby Digital Surround. $24.98. Keepcase. *LANG:* English; French; Spanish; Portuguese. *SUB:* English; French; Spanish; Portuguese; Chinese; Korean; Thai. *CAP:* English. *FEATURES:* "Making of" featurette ● Trailer.
1988 (PG) 95m/C Fisher Stevens, Cynthia Gibb, Michael McKean, Jack Weston, David Hemblen; **D:** Kenneth Johnson; **W:** Brent Maddock, S.S. Wilson; **C:** John McPherson; **M:** Charles Fox.

Shot in the Heart

Based on the story of Gary Gilmore (Koteas), the first person executed in the U.S. after a 10-year moratorium on the death penalty. Gary has rejected all appeals and requested a death by firing squad, so his younger brother Mikal (Ribisi) visits him in prison in hopes of convincing him to fight his sentence. While it does have a movie-of-the-week

quality, the film manages to avoid many clichés of death penalty stories, and is often understated and moving. The disc looks and sounds very good, and the extras also offer good information on the historical facts of the case. —BG
Movie: ♫♫ ½ **DVD:** ♫♫♫ ½
HBO (cat #91894, UPC 026359189425). Widescreen (1.85:1) anamorphic. Dolby Surround. $24.98. Snapper. *LANG:* English; Spanish. *SUB:* English; French; Spanish. *CAP:* English. *FEATURES:* 14 chapters ● Cast/director bios ● The Gary Gilmore Story ● Family photos ● Gary Gilmore's artwork ● The Music of *Shot in the Heart* ● Excerpt from the book *Shot in the Heart*.
2001 (R) 98m/C Giovanni Ribisi, Elias Koteas, Lee Tergesen, Sam Shepard, Amy Madigan, Eric Bogosian; **D:** Agnieszka Holland; **W:** Frank Pugliese; **C:** Jacek Petrycki.

Show Boat

Third film version of the 1927 musical about the lives and loves of a Mississippi riverboat troupe boasts terrific musical numbers with dance routines from Champion who went on to great fame as a choreographer. Grayson is somewhat vapid but lovely to look at and hear. Gardner didn't want to do the part of Julie, although she eventually received fabulous reviews—her singing was dubbed by Annette Warren. The 171-foot "Cotton Blossom" boat was built on the Tarzan lake set at the MGM backlot (at an astounding cost of $126,468). Warfield's film debut—his 'Ol' Man River'—was recorded in one take. There's some loss of definition in these bright Technicolor exteriors, but the supersaturated pink, orange, and lime satins are dazzling. Subtitles are a help with the often unintelligible lyrics. This appears to be a very good transfer with all of the flaws coming from age and the original elements. —MM
Movie: ♫♫ ½ **DVD:** ♫♫ ½
Warner (cat #906614). Full frame. Dolby Digital Mono. $24.98. Snapper. *LANG:* English. *SUB:* French; Spanish. *CAP:* English. *FEATURES:* Trailer ● 28 chapters.
1951 115m/C Kathryn Grayson, Howard Keel, Ava Gardner, William Warfield, Joe E. Brown, Agnes Moorehead, Gower Champion; **D:** George Sidney; **W:** George Wells, Jack McGowan; **C:** Charles Rosher; **M:** Jerome Kern, Oscar Hammerstein. *AWARDS: NOM:* Oscars '51: Color Cinematog., Scoring/Musical.

The Show Off / The Plastic Age

In the first feature on this double bill, Louise Brooks has a supporting role as the best friend of a young woman who marries the wrong man. The silent era sex symbol easily steals the film. In the second, Clara Bow is a co-ed who parties hearty at Prescott College. David Shepard's liner notes describe the differences between the source materials available for the films. It's immediately apparent to the viewer. *Show Off* was created from a virtu-

ally pristine 35mm. print, DVD delivers a breathtakingly sharp image with only a bit of surface damage in a few places. *Plastic Age*, on the other hand, was made from a 16mm. print. It's very dark and fuzzily focused. Both are recommended to students of early film. —*MM*
Movie: 🎞️🎞️ ½ **DVD:** 🎞️🎞️ ½
Image Ent. (cat #ID0511DSDVD, UPC 014-381051124). Full frame. Dolby Digital Stereo. $24.99. Keepcase. *LANG:* Silent. *SUB:* English intertitles. *FEATURES:* 16 chapters each.
1926 82m/B Ford Sterling, Lois Wilson, Louise Brooks, Claire McDowell, C.W. Goodrich, Gregory Kelly; *D:* Malcolm St. Clair; *W:* Pierre Collins; *C:* Lee Garmes; *M:* Timothy Brock.

Showdown

New Yorker Vinnie (Acovone) has left the family crime business and moved to California for a quieter life. When his fast-living nephew Anthony (LeBlanc) moves in, Vinnie finds himself drawn reluctantly back to violence. For a video premiere, the disc delivers an acceptable full-frame image, but it's only slightly superior to tape. The extras are the main difference. (The menu indicates 16 chapters, but the disc is divided into 12.) —*MM* **AKA:** Lookin' Italian.
Movie: 🎞️🎞️ **DVD:** 🎞️🎞️
MTI (cat #222). Full frame. $24.95. Keepcase. *LANG:* English. *FEATURES:* Cast & crew thumbnail bios • Commentary: Magar • Trailer • 12 chapters.
1994 (R) 90m/C Jay Acovone, Matt LeBlanc, Lou Rawls, John Lamotta, Stephanie Richards, Real Andrews; *D:* Guy Magar; *W:* Guy Magar; *C:* Gerry Lively; *M:* Jeff Beal.

Showgirl Stories

Anjelica Huston narrates this sometimes labored, sometimes erotic, sometimes touching look at the history of show dancing. We meet a bunch of elderly women who used to be considered hot back in the days when fellas went nuts over an exposed KNEE. They hold forth on the gentleman's entertainers of today—and they ain't pleased. They say the stage was an unspoken barrier between a performer and her audience. With table dances, and the "interactive" nature of today's strippers, that wall has fallen, and the veterans feel it's lowered their art form into the realm of prostitution. There's something oddly moving about listening to these women tell their stories—the obvious joy in their voices when they talk about their glory days. Days that are in stark contrast to those of the twilight of their years. Recommended. As one might expect, many of the scenes take place in dark nightclubs, and digital grain is present. The audio isn't anything spectacular. —*GNG/DG*
Movie: 🎞️🎞️ ½ **DVD:** 🎞️
A-PIX Entertainment Inc. (UPC 711027203-120). Full frame. DTS. $9.98. Keepcase. *LANG:* English.

1998 103m/C *D:* Agnieszka Piotrowska; *Nar:* Anjelica Huston.

Showgirls

This is the tender tale of a young woman's struggle toward a dream—to pick herself up by her g-string and put her lap-dancing days behind her. Between gigs at a strip club named Cheetahs, Nomi (Berkley) sees a hot new showgirl act at the Stardust hotel, called "Goddess." Now, Nomi knows *exactly* what she wants to be when she grows up. Nomi and Cristal (Gershon) trade barbs while Cristal inexplicably works to further the young dancer's career. Berkley is ultimately believable as Nomi, but where she fails is in her frequent fits of rage—she stomps around, chin out, teeth clasped in a sneer—which strike the funny bone, rather than fear. A legendary flop when released, the film is actually one of the best "B"-movies masquerading as a mainstream flick ever made. It has all the qualities one looks for: cheesy dialogue, paper-thin characters, barely recognizable plot, and tons of gratuitous nudity. It's deliciously awful. A true guilty pleasure. The audio is presented in a surprisingly robust, detailed 5.1 soundtrack. Equally sensational video quality. —*GNG/DG*
Movie: 🎞️🎞️ ½ **DVD:** 🎞️🎞️🎞️ ½
MGM Home Ent. (cat #908099, UPC 027-616804926). Widescreen (2.35:1) letterboxed. Dolby Digital 5.1 Surround; Dolby Digital Surround. $14.95. Keepcase. *LANG:* English; French; Spanish. *SUB:* French; Spanish. *FEATURES:* Featurette • Trailer.
1995 (NC-17) 131m/C Elizabeth Berkley, Gina Gershon, Kyle MacLachlan, Glenn Plummer, Alan Rachins, Robert Davi, Gina Ravera; *D:* Paul Verhoeven; *W:* Joe Eszterhas; *C:* Jost Vacano; *M:* David A. Stewart. *AWARDS:* Golden Raspberries '95: Worst Picture, Worst Actress (Berkley), Worst Director (Verhoeven), Worst Screenplay, Worst Song ("Walk into the Wind"), Worst New Star (Berkley); *NOM:* Golden Raspberries '95: Worst Actor (MacLachlan), Worst Support. Actor (Davi), Worst Support. Actress (Gershon).

Shrek [SE]

One of the best computer-animated films to date has humor that appeals to adults as well as kids and genuine emotion. Shrek (voice of Myers) is a big green ogre whose swamp becomes a holding pen for fairy tale characters when Lord Farquaad (Lithgow) orders them there. Then Shrek and his sidekick Donkey (Murphy) must rescue the Princess Fiona (Diaz) from the fire-breathing dragon and bring her to marry Lord F. The simple story is a delight. DVD, of course, presents a bright flawless image. The surprise here is the amount of extra material—more than 11 hours of games and such, according to the studio, and I, for one, will take their word for it. The menus are on the slow side, but cool. The "extended ending" is a karaoke col-

lection of bits from other pop songs. (It's an Easter egg on the widescreen disc, accessed by clicking on the music note.) This one belongs in every library. —*MM*
Movie: 🎞️🎞️🎞️ ½ **DVD:** 🎞️🎞️🎞️🎞️
DreamWorks Home Ent. (cat #89012, UPC 667068901221). Widescreen (1.78:1) anamorphic; full frame. Dolby Digital 5.1 Surround Stereo; DTS 5.1; Dolby Digital Surround. $26.99. Keepcase. *LANG:* English; French; Spanish. *SUB:* French; Spanish. *CAP:* English. *FEATURES:* 20 chapters • DKW Kids: games • Character interviews • Behind-the-scenes featurette • Karaoke dance party • Filmmakers' commentary track • Storyboard pitch of deleted scenes • Production featurette • Hints for Xbox video game • 3 music videos • International dubbing featurette • Outtakes • Trailer for *Spirit Stallion of the Cimarron* • Trailer • Production notes • Talent files.
2001 (PG) 89m/C *D:* Andrew Adamson, Victoria Jenson; *W:* Ted Elliott, Terry Rossio, Roger S.H. Schulman, Joe Stillman; *M:* Harry Gregson-Williams, John Powell; *V:* Mike Myers, Cameron Diaz, Eddie Murphy, John Lithgow, Vincent Cassel, Kathleen Freeman, Conrad Vernon. *AWARDS:* L.A. Film Critics '01: Animated Film; Broadcast Film Critics '01: Animated Film; *NOM:* Golden Globes '02: Film—Mus./Comedy; Broadcast Film Critics '01: Film.

Siberian Lady Macbeth

Katarina (Markovic), bored with life at her father-in-law's farm, will let nothing stand in the way of her affair with the new pigherder, Sergei (Tadic). As people find out, she dispatches them with cold-blooded cruelty. Director Wadja's brutal study of primal desire (based loosely on Nikolai Leskov's 1865 novel and Shostakovich's 1934 opera) is beautifully photographed and emotionally engaging. Katarina's savagery is unparalleled. Although the unenhanced image does no justice to the photography, the problems lie in the source material. The mono sound (backed by music from Shostakovich) is satisfactory. Subtitles are burned on the image. —*DRL* **AKA:** Fury Is a Woman; Sibirska Ledi Magbet.
Movie: 🎞️🎞️🎞️🎞️ **DVD:** 🎞️🎞️
Kino on Video (cat #250, UPC 738329025-021). Widescreen (2.35:1) letterboxed. Mono. $29.95. Keepcase. *LANG:* Serbo-Croatian. *SUB:* English. *FEATURES:* 15 chapters.
1961 93m/B *RU* Olivera Markovic, Ljuba Tadic, Kapitalina Eric; *D:* Andrzej Wajda; *W:* Sveta Lukic; *C:* Aleksandar Sekulovic.

The Sicilian

Adaptation of Mario Puzo's fact-based novel chronicles the exploits of Salvatore Giuliano (Lambert), a Robin Hood–like character who attempted to overthrow both the government and the church in 1940s Sicily and establish an American-style democracy. Disc is the full-length version of the heavily edited "R"-rated version that was distributed theatrically. Like so much of director Cimino's work, it's fun in a loopy sort of way with Lambert as an engaging hero. Virtually the entire film has a dusty, faded look. It appears to be intentional but it's also exceptionally grainy. Black clothes tend to lose definition in both darkened interiors and bright sunny exteriors. Pan-and-scan cropping of widescreen original image severely limits the landscapes which are so important to the story. Surround is exceptionally good. —*MM*

Movie: 🎬🎬 **DVD:** 🎬 ½
Artisan Ent. (cat #12051). Full frame. Dolby Digital Surround. $14.98. Keepcase. *LANG:* English. *FEATURES:* 21 chapters.
1987 146m/C Christopher Lambert, John Turturro, Terence Stamp, Joss Ackland, Barbara Sukowa; **D:** Michael Cimino; **W:** Steve Shagan; **C:** Alex Thomson; **M:** David Mansfield.

The Sid Caesar Collection: The Fan Favorites

Pulled from the long-running series *Your Show of Shows* and *Caesar's Hour*, this three-disc set represents the best comedy from TV's golden era. With an amazing display of screenwriting talent, including Woody Allen, Mel Brooks, and Neil Simon, many of these sketches are still hilarious today. Between the sketches are interviews with the writers and actors. The picture quality is marginal for DVD, and dialogue is sometimes difficult to understand. Includes three volumes: "Love and Laughter," "The Dream Team of Comedy," and "The Professor and Other Clowns." —*BG*

Movie: 🎬🎬 ½ **DVD:** 🎬🎬
Creative Light Video (cat #SV100305, UPC 692187103058). Full frame. $69.95. Keepcase. *LANG:* English. *CAP:* English. *FEATURES:* 20 chapters ➤ Bonus sketches ➤ Bonus interviews ➤ Original script ➤ Commentary: Sid Caesar on selected sketches ➤ Bios.
2001 231m/C Sid Caesar, Nanette Fabray, Carl Reiner, Imogene Coca; **W:** Sid Caesar, Woody Allen, Mel Brooks, Larry Gelbart, Neil Simon.

Sidewalks of New York

Six New Yorkers discuss life, love, and sex in front of documentary-style cameras in this romantic comedy/character study. Dramatizations of the events discussed reveal the truth behind what the characters say on camera. Burns is the beginning and end of this circle of six intertwining stories. Of these, the most interesting are Tucci's adulterous dentist and Rosario's guilt-ridden divorcee. Farina (in a tiny role) is hilarious as Burns's sleazy father. The improvised performances come off well, but the story gets very

tired. Shot to look like a documentary, the imperfect image is expected. The Surround channels are used for near-constant street noise. —*DRL*

Movie: 🎬🎬 ½ **DVD:** 🎬🎬 ½
Paramount (cat #33945, UPC 09736339-4549). Widescreen (1.85:1) anamorphic. Dolby 5.1 Surround. $29.99. Keepcase. *LANG:* English. *SUB:* English. *CAP:* English. *FEATURES:* Commentary: Edward Burns ➤ "Anatomy of a Scene" featurette ➤ 19 chapters.
2001 (R) 107m/C Edward Burns, Heather Graham, Rosario Dawson, Dennis Farina, David Krumholtz, Brittany Murphy, Stanley Tucci, Callie (Calliope) Thorne, Aida Turturro, Nadia Dajani, Michael Leydon Campbell; **D:** Edward Burns; **W:** Edward Burns; **C:** Frank Prinzi.

The Silence of the Lambs [MGM SE]

This "Special Edition" does not contain the commentary track of the Criterion laserdisc and DVD (reviewed in *Book 1*). It does have more deleted scenes—22, compared to Criterion's 8—though some of them are no more than snippets, and only one, a long monologue by Hopkins, might have been reincorporated. Image is not a major improvement over the earlier edition, either. Both are good but not great in visual terms. The performances, characters, and solid story construction are still the keys. A full-frame disc is also available. —*MM*

Movie: 🎬🎬🎬 ½ **DVD:** 🎬🎬🎬
MGM Home Ent. (cat #1002331, UPC 027-616865502). Widescreen (1.85:1) anamorphic. Dolby Digital 5.1 Surround Stereo; Dolby Digital Surround; Mono. $24.98. Keepcase. *LANG:* English; French; Spanish. *SUB:* English; French; Spanish. *CAP:* English. *FEATURES:* 22 deleted scenes ➤ "Inside the Labyrinth" documentary ➤ 1991 "making of" featurette ➤ Outtakes ➤ Photo gallery ➤ Booklet ➤ Trailers and TV spots ➤ Anthony Hopkins's phone message.
1991 (R) 118m/C Jodie Foster, Anthony Hopkins, Scott Glenn, Ted Levine, Brooke Smith, Charles Napier, Roger Corman, Anthony Heald, Diane Baker, Chris Isaak; **D:** Jonathan Demme; **W:** Ted Tally; **C:** Tak Fujimoto; **M:** Howard Shore. *AWARDS:* Oscars '91: Actor (Hopkins), Actress (Foster), Adapt. Screenplay, Director (Demme), Picture; AFI '98: Top 100; British Acad. '91: Actor (Hopkins), Actress (Foster); Directors Guild '91: Director (Demme); Golden Globes '92: Actress—Drama (Foster); Natl. Bd. of Review '91: Director (Demme), Film, Support. Actor (Hopkins); N.Y. Film Critics '91: Actor (Hopkins), Actress (Foster), Director (Demme), Film; Writers Guild '91: Adapt. Screenplay; *NOM:* Oscars '91: Film Editing, Sound.

Silent Fall

A young mute boy named Tim witnesses the murder of his parents. Tim is cared for by his sister Sylvie (Tyler, who has definite-

ly improved since this, her first performance). The psychologist who helps them is Jake Rainer (Dreyfuss); his competition is a less-than-kind doctor played by John Lithgow, who proposes more harsh treatment. The film has a number of good performers, but begins to seriously test the patience of the audience with a buildup that doesn't really develop to much of anything. Characters are underwritten and unsympathetic; dialogue isn't engaging and scenes don't serve to move along the plot. If that's not enough, the movie becomes completely silly towards the end and then totally falls apart as it becomes an oddball thriller with some weird twists. The disc is passable; colors are strong but dark scenes tend to look murky and there are some print flaws. The Surround track is used occasionally, but this is primarily a dialogue-driven film. —*AB/DG*

Movie: 🎬 **DVD:** 🎬🎬
Warner Home Video (UPC 85391356929). Widescreen (1.85:1) letterboxed. Dolby Digital Surround 5.1; Dolby Digital Surround. $14.98. Snapper. *LANG:* English; French. *SUB:* English; French. *FEATURES:* Trailers ➤ Production notes.
1994 (R) 101m/C Richard Dreyfuss, Ben Faulkner, John Lithgow, Liv Tyler, Linda Hamilton, J.T. Walsh; **D:** Bruce Beresford; **W:** Akiva Goldsman; **C:** Peter James; **M:** Stewart Copeland.

Silent Rage

It's a sci-fi variation on *Frankenstein* and it's a Chuck Norris kick-butt martial arts movie. Scientists of the semi-mad variety create a psychotic killer with superhuman strength. It's up to sheriff Stevens (Norris) and his bumbling comic deputy (Furst) to stop the monster, but first they've got to deal with a not-particularly-vicious motorcycle gang and Stevens's old flame Alison (Kalem). Ron Silver's serious approach to his role is completely out of place, though the film is not without a certain unpredictable charm. DVD image ranges between good and excellent. Both the widescreen and full-frame images are fine in bright sunny exteriors and exceptionally dim bars. Some grain is evident, of course, but it comes from the original. —*MM*

Movie: 🎬🎬 ½ **DVD:** 🎬🎬🎬
Columbia Tristar (cat #05277, UPC 0433-96052772). Widescreen (1.85:1) anamorphic; full frame. Dolby Digital Stereo. $19.98. Keepcase. *LANG:* English; French. *SUB:* English; French; Spanish; Portuguese; Chinese; Korean; Thai. *CAP:* English. *FEATURES:* 28 chapters ➤ Trailers.
1982 (R) 100m/C Chuck Norris, Ron Silver, Steven Keats, Toni Kalem, Brian Libby, Stephen Furst; **D:** Michael Miller; **W:** Joseph Fraley; **C:** Robert C. Jessup, Neil Roach; **M:** Peter Bernstein.

Silent Running [Universal]

When he learns that his space station must be destroyed, Lowell (Dern), the botanist who takes care of the vegetation,

kills his co-workers and commandeers the station to Saturn. Soon his "forest" begins to die. It seems odd that a botanist would be unaware that lack of sunlight would kill his "forest." The beginning of the film suggests a concern for environmental issues, but by the second act the nuttiness of Lowell takes over. The whole enterprise lacks wit and depth and has not dated well. Extras strictly for completists and film geeks. (An earlier Image release is reviewed in *Book 1*.) Monochromatic color scheme may have looked pretty good in a theatre, but it doesn't translate well on DVD. Sound is pretty good given the mostly silent nature of the story. —*LA*
Movie: 🎵🎵 *DVD:* 🎵🎵 ½
Universal Studios (cat #21243, UPC 0251-92124327). Widescreen (1.85:1) anamorphic. Dolby Digital Mono. $19.98. Keepcase. *LANG:* English; French; Spanish. *CAP:* English. *FEATURES:* "The Making of *Silent Running*" ● Commentary: director Douglas Trumbull, actor Bruce Dern ● "Silent Running" by Douglas Trumbull ● "Conversation with Bruce Dern" ● "Douglas Trumbull: Then and Now" ● Production notes ● Cast & filmmaker bios ● 20 chapters.
1971 (G) 90m/C Bruce Dern, Cliff (Potter) Potts, Ron Rifkin; *D:* Douglas Trumbull; *W:* Michael Cimino, Deric Washburn, Steven Bochco; *C:* Charles F. Wheeler; *M:* Prof. Peter Schickele.

The Silk Road

Excellent documentary of the silk road which runs through the length of China. Shot over 10 years, the film starts at the Great Wall, showing what was, in 1980, the first Quang Hang Di's clay army of life-sized soldiers and horses. For a mere 12 hours, it's amazing the scope of history, art, peoples, and architecture that the documentary covers. This is a good investment of time and a fine way to sharpen your ability to impress your friends with obscure historical details. The film stock, lenses, and cameras changed so much over 10 years that the film is also a historical document of the technical growth of the film industry. The first discs are grainy and jiggly but by the last disc, the color and clarity are amazing. The sound also evolves from average to good. The soundtrack is worth mentioning as it was scored by Kitaro, who may have single-handedly brought new age music to America, but don't blame him—his stuff is actually great and you can almost understand the attraction after listening to it. —*CA*
Movie: 🎵🎵🎵 ½ *DVD:* 🎵 ½
Central Park/U.S. Manga (cat #CPMD20-09, UPC 71998720090). Full frame. Dolby Digital Mono. $129.99. Keepcase 3-disc boxed set. *LANG:* English. *FEATURES:* 12 episodes, 4 per disc ● DVD ROM with press quotes and photo gallery.
1988 630m/C M: Kitaro.

Silver Bullet

In the mid-'80s, it seemed that everything Stephen King wrote suddenly became a

movie and this film came in the middle of the era. It's based on King's novella *Cycle of the Werewolf,* and King himself did the screenplay. The small town of Tarker's Mills is a quiet and peaceful place until a series of very savage murders begins. The local sheriff is stumped and the townspeople call for vigilante justice, as the bodies continue to pile-up. Things change when a young Marty (Haim) is confronted by a werewolf creature, and is able to defend himself, despite the fact that he is confined to a wheelchair. Convinced that this monster is responsible for the killings, Marty enlists the help of his sister Jane (Follows) and their alcoholic Uncle Red (Busey) to find and kill the werewolf. King's story was told in 12 chapters, as the werewolf would only kill once a month, under the full moon. In the film version, all of the murders seem to take place inside of a week, turning this into little more than a serial-killer film. To add insult to injury, the werewolf costume resembles a skinny bear instead of a wolf. Corey Haim is fine as Marty, but there are some instances where his believability as a wheelchair-bound person is questionable. There are moments when Busey acts as if he is in a different film. The final confrontation with the werewolf is exciting and well-shot, but the rest of the film is devoid of any suspense. Add this to the pile of Stephen King movie clunkers. DVD image is very sharp and clear, showing virtually no grain and only some minor black dots from the source print. There are some artifacting issues during fast camera motions, but otherwise, this is a fine-looking transfer. With the Dolby Digital mono audio track, we get clear dialogue with no distortion, but little else. —*ML* **AKA:** Stephen King's Silver Bullet.
Movie: 🎵 ½ *DVD:* 🎵🎵 ½
Paramount (cat #01827, UPC 09736018-2743). Widescreen (2.35:1) anamorphic. Dolby Digital Mono. $24.99. Keepcase. *LANG:* English; French. *SUB:* English. *CAP:* English. *FEATURES:* 18 chapters.
1985 (R) 94m/C Corey Haim, Gary Busey, Megan Follows, Everett McGill, Robin Groves, Leon Russom, Terry O'Quinn, Bill Smitrovich, Kent Broadhurst, Lawrence Tierney; *D:* Daniel Attias; *W:* Stephen King; *C:* Armando Nannuzzi.

Silver Wolf

A ranger (Biehn) and his 16-year-old nephew (Meier) struggle to save a wolf from a rancher (Scheider), who is out to kill it. Standard Disney-wannabe fare with strong Jack London influence. Biehn and Scheider are competent, as is director Peter Svatek, but straight to video this went, pleasing only little wolflings with a painfully conventional story of triumph in the face of obstacles. Very good DVD transfer and sound, though. —*MO*
Movie: 🎵🎵 ½ *DVD:* 🎵🎵🎵
York Ent. (cat #YPD-1069, UPC 750723-106922). Full frame. 5.1 Surround Sound. $14.99. Keepcase. *LANG:* English. *SUB:* Spanish. *FEATURES:* 30 chapters ● Theatrical trailers ● Filmographies.

1998 97m/C Michael Biehn, Roy Scheider, Shane Meier, Kimberly Warnat; *D:* Peter Svatek; *W:* Michael Amo; *C:* Curtis Petersen; *M:* Robert Carli.

The Simpsons: The Complete First Season

The hilarious adventures of the titular middle-class suburban American family originally began as a series of short vignettes on the *Tracy Ullman Show.* This wildly successful television series is a consistently witty and winning combination of sight gags and one-liners. Although conveyed with lightness and amiability, the program is frequently a savage mirror of contemporary society and values. Topical, literary, and filmic references abound and the gags come fast and furious. The oddball Simpsons are actually quite normal, truth be told, and one of the strengths of the occasional sentimental moment is that it reveals the sincere emotions that function within the dysfunction. Unlike a show like *Married with Children* (where the characters loathe each other so openly, it's a contrivance that they stay together) it's clear that the family has true love for one another. While the early episodes are less polished than those of later seasons, they are still successful and warrant repeated viewings. The Emmy-winning episode "Life in the Fast Lane" features Albert Brooks as a French bowling lothario who sweeps Marge off her feet. Brooks is an absolute scream and amidst the laughs are moments of touching drama. It's the highlight of a wonderful collection. Outtakes from the episode are included and they're also side-splitting. The image quality is disappointingly subpar. The episodes are sharp and colorful but excessively shimmery and prone to digital noise during movement. The Surround sound is clean and involving, but limited. The audio commentaries are informative and funny but much time is spent with the participants reacting to a particular scene or line of dialogue. The multi-language clips are particularly amusing and the outtakes and featurette are particularly worthwhile. —*DG*
Movie: 🎵🎵🎵 *DVD:* 🎵🎵
20th Century Fox (cat #2000900, UPC 02-4543009009). Full frame. Dolby Surround 5.1; Dolby Stereo. $39.98. 3-disc slip-sleeve box. *LANG:* English; French. *SUB:* English; Spanish. *CAP:* English. *FEATURES:* Commentaries on all episodes with Matt Groening, writers ● Outtakes from "Life in the Fast Lane" & "Some Enchanted Evening" ● Original scripts for 4 episodes ● Tracey Ullman short "Goodnight Simpsons" ● Early sketches by Matt Groening ● Featurette ● Insert booklet with episode notes ● 6 chapters per episode ● Clip in French, Spanish, Japanese, Portugese, Italian ● Animatics for "Bart the General" episode.
1989 298m/C M: Alf Clausen, Danny Elfman; *V:* Dan Castellaneta, Julie Kavner, Harry Shearer, Maggie Roswell, Nancy Cartwright, Yeardley Smith.

The Sinister Saga

The main problem with this inventive "making of" feature is that director Richard Rush essentially tells his version of the production and distribution of his innovative *The Stunt Man*. It's obviously a story that has multiple points of view, but we get only the creators'—Rush and members of his cast. That's not to say that this isn't interesting; it is. Objective, it's not. Much of the footage was shot on video and so the full-frame image really isn't much better than tape. The big deleted scene from the film is more than a little hysterical and the finished product is probably better without it. This documentary is also available as part of *The Stunt Man: Limited Edition.* —MM

Movie: ♫♫ ½ **DVD:** ♫♫ ½
Anchor Bay (cat #DV11940, UPC 0131311-94098). Full frame. Dolby Mono. $24.98. Keepcase. *LANG:* English. *CAP:* English. *FEATURES:* 28 chapters.
2000 114m/C Richard Rush, Peter O'Toole, Steve Railsback, Barbara Hershey, Charles "Chuck" Bail, Sharon Farrell; *D:* Richard Rush; *W:* Richard Rush; *C:* Bruce Schermer.

Sister Act

Surprising boxoffice hit casts Goldberg as a Reno lounge singer and inadvertent witness to a mob murder, who hides out in a convent—where she's as comfortable in a habit as a fish out of water. Much to the dismay of poker-faced Mother Superior Smith, she takes over the rag-tag choir and molds them into a swinging, religious version of a '60s girls group. Stock characters and situations are deflected by some genuinely funny moments and good performances, especially by Najimy and Makkena. Despite one's reaction to the film, there's no doubting the fact that the songs are very catchy. And those songs sound fine on this DVD, as the Dolby Digital 5.1 audio track provides a nice reproduction of the music and clear dialogue. However, there is little Surround sound, and basically no subwoofer response. The image here is sharp and clear, but is also slightly dark at times. —ML

Movie: ♫♫ ½ **DVD:** ♫♫♫
Buena Vista Home Ent. (cat #23231, UPC 786936159295). Widescreen (1.85:1) letterboxed. Dolby Digital 5.1. $29.99. Keepcase. *LANG:* English; French. *SUB:* English. *CAP:* English. *FEATURES:* Theatrical trailer ▪ Music videos ▪ "Making of" featurette ▪ 27 chapters.
1992 (PG) 100m/C Whoopi Goldberg, Maggie Smith, Harvey Keitel, Bill Nunn, Kathy Najimy, Wendy Makkena, Mary Wickes, Robert Miranda, Richard Portnow, Joseph Maher; *D:* Emile Ardolino; *W:* Joseph Howard; *C:* Adam Greenberg; *M:* Marc Shaiman.

Sister Street Fighter

When her brother is kidnapped, Sue Shiomi infiltrates the drug distribution gang that did it. Though usually included as part of the "Street Fighter" series, this is actually the first of a series of Lady Karate (or "Lethal Fist Woman") features Shiomi, the first woman to join Chiba's Japan Action Club. Sonny Chiba doesn't even play his Terry Tsurugi character. In some ways, this fluffier movie is more fun than the gritty "Street Fighter" movies, with cute Sue facing off against a variety of exotic fighters employed by the bad guys, including karate master Hammerhead, a speargun-toting priest, and seven Thai amazons wearing costumes straight out of *The Flintstones*. Available as part of a triple feature on one disc entitled *Classic Sonny Chiba Movies*. The image is vibrant (if a bit soft), cropped a bit on the sides and matted too tightly on the top. —BT

Movie: ♫♫♫ **DVD:** ♫♫
BFS Video (cat #30235D, UPC 0668053-02350). Widescreen letterboxed. $9.98. Keepcase. *LANG:* English. *FEATURES:* 4 chapters ▪ Bio ▪ Filmography ▪ Trivia.
1976 81m/C Sue Shiomi, Sonny Chiba; *D:* Kazuhiko Yamaguchi.

The 6th Day [2 SE]

This is one of the least special "special editions" ever released. Most of the extra features are already available on the first edition (reviewed in *Book 2*). It contains more subtitle options and seven more featurettes. Most of the extras are on a second disc. —MM

Movie: ♫♫♫ ½ **DVD:** ♫♫♫ ½
Columbia Tristar (cat #07740, UPC 0433-96077409). Widescreen (2.35:1) anamorphic. Dolby Digital 5.1 Surround; Dolby Digital Surround. $24.98. Keepcase. *LANG:* English; French; Spanish; Portuguese. *SUB:* English; French; Spanish; Portuguese; Chinese; Korean; Thai. *CAP:* English. *FEATURES:* 28 chapters ▪ 9 "making of" featurettes ▪ Isolated music score with commentary: composer Trevor Rabin ▪ Storyboard comparison ▪ Theatrical trailers ▪ Digitally mastered audio and anamorphic video ▪ RePet infomercial and TV spot ▪ Production notes ▪ Talent files ▪ DVD-ROM link to website ▪ Showtime special.
2000 (PG-13) 124m/C Arnold Schwarzenegger, Tony Goldwyn, Sarah Wynter, Michael Rooker, Robert Duvall, Michael Rapaport, Wendy Crewson, Rodney Rowland, Ken Pogue, Wanda Cannon, Christopher Lawford, Terry Crews, Colin Cunningham, Taylor Anne Reid, Jennifer Gareis, Don McManus, Steve Bacic; *D:* Roger Spottiswoode; *W:* Cormac Wibberly, Marianne S. Wibberly; *C:* Pierre Mignot; *M:* Trevor Rabin. AWARDS: NOM: Golden Raspberries '00: Worst Actor (Schwarzenegger).

The Sixth Sense [Buena Vista]

(For film and partial extras review, please see *Book 1*.) The film transfer looks identical to the one on the previous disc release. The main difference between this set and the previous edition is the inclusion of three substantial featurettes, which total more than 90 minutes. The shortest is one on the storyboard process and it reveals the tremendous amount of preparation, thought, and care Shyamalan puts into the pre-production process. "Between Two Worlds" is an intelligent analysis of the importance and function of ghost stories and the specific importance of films such as *The Sixth Sense* and *Ghost*. The interviews with William Peter Blatty, Bruce Joel Rubin, and Shyamalan (amongst others) are moving and thought provoking. "Reflections from the Set" is composed of behind-the-scenes footage and contemporary interviews with the primary cast on the development and creation of their performances. The elaborate endlessly folding sleevecase is a bit overdone and the discs are somewhat difficult to remove. The featurettes are terrific, though. —DG

Movie: ♫♫♫ ½ **DVD:** ♫♫♫ ½
Buena Vista Home Ent. (cat #22819, UPC 786936155853). Widescreen (1.85:1) anamorphic. Dolby Digital 5.1 Surround; DTS. $29.99. Special packaging. *LANG:* English; French. *SUB:* Spanish. *CAP:* English. *FEATURES:* "Reflections from the Set" featurette ▪ "Between Two Worlds" featurette on the paranormal ▪ "Moving Pictures: The Storyboard Process" featurette ▪ 19 chapters ▪ 4 deleted scenes ▪ "Music and Sound Design" featurette ▪ "Reaching the Audience" featurette ▪ Rules and clues ▪ Publicity ▪ Production bios ▪ Insert booklet ▪ Insert storyboard card.
1999 (PG-13) 107m/C Bruce Willis, Haley Joel Osment, Toni Collette, Olivia Williams, Donnie Wahlberg, Glenn Fitzgerald, Trevor Morgan, Mischa Barton, Bruce Norris; *D:* M. Night Shyamalan; *W:* M. Night Shyamalan; *C:* Tak Fujimoto; *M:* James Newton Howard. AWARDS: MTV Movie Awards '00: Breakthrough Perf. (Osment); Broadcast Film Critics '99: Breakthrough Perf. (Osment); NOM: Oscars '99: Director (Shyamalan), Film, Film Editing, Orig. Screenplay, Support. Actor (Osment), Support. Actress (Collette); British Acad. '99: Director (Shyamalan), Film, Film Editing, Orig. Screenplay; Directors Guild '99: Director (Shyamalan); Golden Globes '00: Screenplay, Support. Actor (Osment); MTV Movie Awards '00: Film, Male Perf. (Willis), On-Screen Duo (Bruce Willis/Haley Joel Osment); Screen Actors Guild '99: Support. Actor (Osment); Writers Guild '99: Orig. Screenplay.

61*

Crystal's nostalgic and meticulous telling of the 1961 home run race between Mickey Mantle (Jane) and Roger Maris (Pepper) clears the fence. Pepper and Jane are superb as the "M&M boys," and the rest of the cast is up to the task, as well. Fine script mixes baseball action with behind-the-scenes details well. Crystal and writer Steinberg take great pains to show the tremendous pressure and outside distractions with which both players had to contend. With the exception of a few sports writers (the obligatory villains), the characters are fleshed out nicely. For the most part, the baseball scenes and historical facts are on the mark. (Everybody smokes.) Crystal's daughter plays Mrs. Maris. DVD image is exceptionally sharp. The film looks and sounds much better than its made-for-cable roots or the period setting would suggest. The clarity of the image reveals the "painted" look of the computer-generated special effects. On the commentary track, Crystal's love of the material comes through without question. For an HBO disc, the list of features is impressive —*MM*

Movie: ♪♪♪ ½ **DVD:** ♪♪♪
HBO (cat #91782, UPC 026359178221). Widescreen anamorphic. Dolby Digital 5.1 Surround Stereo; Dolby Digital Surround; Stereo. $19.98. Snapper. *LANG:* English; Spanish. *SUB:* English; French; Spanish. *CAP:* English. *FEATURES:* 31 chapters • Commentary: Billy Crystal • "Making of" featurette • Theatrical trailer • Mantle bio and statistics • Maris bio and statistics • 1961 Roger Maris home run list • DVD-ROM weblinks.
2001 128m/C Thomas Jane, Barry Pepper, Chris Bauer, Christopher McDonald, Anthony Michael Hall, Bob Gunton, Bruce McGill, Richard Masur, Bobby Hosea, Donald Moffat, Renee Taylor, Joe Grifasi, Michael Nouri, Paul Borghese, Jennifer Crystal Foley, Seymour Cassel, Peter Jacobson, Robert Joy, Pat Crowley, Robert Costanzo; **D:** Billy Crystal; **W:** Hank Steinberg; **C:** Haskell Wexler; **M:** Marc Shaiman.

'68

Absolutely the only reason to watch this one is to hear the soundtrack from Hendrix, Joplin, et al. The story attempts to re-create one of the most tumultuous and pivotal years in American history and fails in almost every respect. The setting is San Francisco, where a Hungarian immigrant family tries to deal with the changes. Zoltan Szabo (Tecsi) runs a restaurant. His son Peter (Larson) tries on different identities—student, mechanic, writer—and winds up working for the Robert Kennedy campaign. His younger brother Sandy (Locke) discovers he's gay when he's drafted. Some of the sloganeering dialogue is embarrassingly accurate, but the film just doesn't look or feel right. The generational conflicts of those times were too deep for any film to cover. DVD presents an accurate re-creation of a relatively low-budget image. Like the monaural sound, it gets the job done and nothing more. —*MM*

Movie: ♪ ½ **DVD:** ♪♪
All Day Ent. (cat #DV11925, UPC 013131-192599). Widescreen (1.85:1) anamorphic. Dolby Digital Mono. $19.98. Keepcase. *LANG:* English. *CAP:* English. *FEATURES:* 23 chapters • Trailer.
1987 (R) 99m/C Eric Larson, Terra Vandergaw, Neil Young, Sandor Tecsi; **D:** Steven Kovacks; **C:** Daniel Lacambre; **M:** Shony Alex Braun, John Cipollinam.

Skipped Parts

Fourteen-year-old Sam Callahan (Hall) and his bad-girl mom, Lydia (Leigh), have been exiled to Wyoming in 1963 by Lydia's Southern big daddy, Caspar (Ermey). Lydia promptly takes up with the wrong guy (Greyeyes) and encourages Sam in sexual experimentation with schoolmate Maurey (Barton), with unfortunate results. Based on Sandlin's coming-of-age trilogy, the film is flat and predictable. This is a letterboxed rather than anamorphic transfer and it shows. Sharpness is generally good but often too soft and there is usually at least some noticeable grain on the screen. Fleshtones appear natural but the color is pretty lame needing both a brightness and contrast boost. The sound claims to be 5.1 and on one or two occasions, the Surrounds kick in and some dimension is added to the mix. In addition, very little is sent to the subwoofer, making the low end not much better than a Dolby Surround mix. Oh well, at least the dialogue is crisp and out front. Director Davis's commentary exhibits more energy than the soundtrack as she enthusiastically tells anecdotes about making the film and demonstrates her unabashed passion for her work and filmmaking in general. —*JO*

Movie: ♪ ½ **DVD:** ♪♪
Lion's Gate Home Ent. (cat #VM7670D, UPC 031398767022). Widescreen (1.85:1) letterboxed. Dolby Digital 5.1. $24.99. Keepcase. *LANG:* English. *SUB:* English; Spanish; French. *CAP:* English. *FEATURES:* 30 chapters • Theatrical trailer • Commentary: director Tamra Davis.
2000 (R) 93m/C Jennifer Jason Leigh, Bug Hall, Michael Greyeyes, Mischa Barton, Peggy Lipton, Brad Renfro, R. Lee Ermey, Angela Featherstone, Alison Pill, Drew Barrymore, Gerald Lenton-Young; **D:** Tamra Davis; **W:** Tim Sandlin; **C:** Claudio Rocha; **M:** Stewart Copeland.

The Skulls 2

What this sequel lacks in originality (and that's a lot) it makes up for with a very slick presentation. Story is essentially the same as the first film. Poor but smart and honest college student Ryan Sommers (Dunne) is invited to join the Skulls, a powerful secret society, and soon discovers that bad things go on at their meeting place. Veteran director Joe Chappelle directs the familiar material with real visual flair. Camera movement is inventive and active but not intrusive. Production values are solid throughout and he uses many different colored lights to tint key scenes. Surround sound is excellent, even through headphones. The young cast is attractive—particularly Ashley Lyn Cafagna as Ryan's girlfriend—but generally on the bland side. This Canadian video premiere is something of an overachiever. —*MM*

Movie: ♪♪ **DVD:** ♪♪♪
Universal Studios (cat #21490, UPC 025192149023). Widescreen (1.85:1) anamorphic. Dolby Digital 5.1 Surround; DTS 5.1. $26.98. Keepcase. *LANG:* Eng-

lish. *SUB:* French; Spanish. *CAP:* English. *FEATURES:* 18 chapters • "Making of" featurette • Talent files • Trailer.
2002 (R) 100m/C CA Robin Dunne, Aaron Ashmore, Ashley Lyn Cafagna, Christopher Ralph, Nathan West, James Callanders, Lindy Booth; **D:** Joe Chappelle; **W:** Hans Rodionoff, Michele Colucci-Zieger; **C:** Steve Danyluk; **M:** Christophe Beck.

Skyscraper

Playmate/celebrity Anna Nicole Smith is a curious choice to take the lead in a low-budget *Die Hard* rip-off. Quick, decisive physical action is not her forté. At least, not standing up. Here she's called upon to play helicopter pilot Carrie Wink, who must take on criminals holed up in a skyscraper. As an alternative classic—along the lines of *Mommie Dearest*—the film is a laugh riot. The double-sided DVD also contains *To the Limit* on the flip. Both are identical to VHS tape. —*MM*

Movie: ♪ **DVD:** ♪♪
Sunland Studios (cat #PM 800, UPC 757-449880013). Full frame. $19.98. Keepcase. *LANG:* English. *CAP:* English. *FEATURES:* 8 chapters.
1995 (R) 96m/C Anna Nicole Smith, Richard Steinmetz; **D:** Raymond Martino; **W:** William Applegate Jr.; **C:** Frank Harris; **M:** Jim Halfpenny.

Slackers

Once in a while a film comes along that can lower your IQ. This is one of those. And it will do with it fine digital sound and clear DVD images of bland visual direction. College guys Dave (Devon Sawa), Jeff (Micheal C. Maronna), and Sam (Jason Segal) are burdened by tests for classes they never attended. They are cheating and slacking off on their way to graduation when Ethan (Jason Schwartzman) catches them cheating. He blackmails them into getting him a date with Angela (James King). Golly, it's almost as if the filmmakers tried to cheat by hiring good talent, but they still failed. The plea for laughs ranges from farts to sponge bathing the elderly. In the end Dave and Ethan square off for Angela's affection. Dave and his pals decide to 'fess up to all their cheating to dodge Ethan's blackmail, and then they frame him for cheating and expose his freaky nature to Angela. (Ethan has a doll made of Angela's hair and has been taking pictures of her while stalking her around campus.) Part of the flick's failure lies in Ethan's actually being a more likable guy than Dave, but in the end, Dave wins. There, now you don't have to suffer through it. —*JAS*

Movie: woof **DVD:** ♪♪♪
Columbia Tristar (cat #08084, UPC 04339-6080843). Full frame; widescreen (1.85:1) letterboxed. Dolby Digital. $27.96. Keepcase. *LANG:* English. *CAP:* English. *FEATURES:* 28 chapters.
2002 (R) 86m/C Devon Sawa, Jason Schwartzman, James King, Jason Segel,

Michael Maronna, Laura Prepon, Mamie Van Doren, Joe Flaherty, Leigh Taylor-Young, Sam Anderson, Cameron Diaz; **D:** Dewey Nicks; **W:** David H. Steinberg; **C:** James R. Bagdonas; **M:** Joseph (Joey) Altruda.

Slap Shot [2]

Great satire of the world of professional sports. Reggie Dunlop (Paul Newman) puts together the ultimate hockey team. Watch this if for nothing else than to see the Hanson Brothers; they steal the show. Add in an on-the-ice strip tease by Braden (Michael Ontkean) and you have a howling great movie. Better than a seventh game in the Stanley Cup. DVD image is of excellent quality with good sound. This is one for your collection. (This second Universal release offers a commentary track and other extras not found on the first release.) —DE
Movie: 🎵🎵🎵 ½ **DVD:** 🎵🎵🎵
Universal Studios (cat #21793, UPC 251-9217932). Widescreen (1.85:1) anamorphic. Dolby 5.1 Surround. $26.98. Keepcase. *LANG:* English; French; Spanish. *CAP:* English. *FEATURES:* 18 chapters • Commentary: the Hanson Brothers • Hanson Brothers classic scenes • Puck talk with the Hansons • Theatrical trailer • Production notes • Cast and filmmakers.
1977 (R) 123m/C Allan Nicholls, Paul D'Amato, Brad Sullivan, Stephen Mendillo, Kathryn Walker, Paul Dooley, Yvon Barrette, Jeff Carlson, Steve Carlson, Dave Hanson, Ned Dowd, Paul Newman, Michael Ontkean, Jennifer Warren, Lindsay Crouse, Jerry Houser, Melinda Dillon, Strother Martin, Andrew Duncan, M. Emmet Walsh, Nancy Dowd, Swoosie Kurtz; **D:** George Roy Hill; **W:** Nancy Dowd; **C:** Victor Kemper; **M:** Elmer Bernstein.

Slap Shot 2: Breaking the Ice

Weak sequel to *Slap Shot,* but what do you expect when Stephen Baldwin is the star? He's coach of the Charleston Chiefs, who have been bought out by Gary Busey, a multi-millionaire who runs a Paxton-like family business. He turns the Chiefs into the patsies for a prep boy hockey squad. The whole thing is like the Ice Capades. A great idea that just doesn't translate, that's probably why this movie never saw a big screen. DVD is as good as VHS. Sound is O.K. —DE
Movie: 🎵🎵 **DVD:** 🎵🎵 ½
Universal Studios (cat #21456, UPC 2519-214562). Widescreen (1.85:1) anamorphic. Dolby 5.1 Surround. $26.98. Keepcase. *LANG:* English; Spanish; French. *SUB:* Spanish. *CAP:* English. *FEATURES:* 18 chapters • "Making of" featurette • Hanson Brothers interviews • Trailer • Production notes • Cast and filmmakers.
2002 (R) 104m/C Stephen Baldwin, Jeff Carlson, Steve Carlson, Dave Hanson, Gary Busey, Callum Keith Rennie, Jessica Steen; **D:** Steve Boyum; **W:** Broderick Miller; **C:** Joel Ransom.

Slapstick Encyclopedia (1909—27)

This five-disc set is a superb collection of early comedy. It covers the field from the obscure to the immortal. The films range in artistic quality from incredibly sophisticated to primitive. The special effects in "Barney Oldfield's Race for a Life" are still pretty impressive. In many of the other works, it's obvious that the filmmakers were still learning the vocabulary of their medium. In "One Too Many" for example, the spatial relationship between characters is confusing. That comes with the territory. Preservationists David Shepard and Joe Adamson have done excellent work with these. Image quality varies with the condition of the original elements. All of the damage that age and neglect can inflict is on display at different points here—burns, breaks, registration bounce, etc.—but the overall level ranges between very good and good. And, with any collection of this size, DVD provides superior accessibility. The new music makes the films more palatable to a younger audience while retaining a period feel. Contents: "One Too Many," "The Wrong Mr. Fox," "Mr. Flip," "Alkali Ike's Auto," "Fox Trot Finesse," "A Cure for Pokeritis," "Be My Wife," "A Natural Born Gambler," "Mabel's Dramatic Career," "Barney Oldfield's Race for a Life," "The Rounders," "A Muddy Romance," "A Movie Star," "Teddy at the Throttle," "Saturday Afternoon," "Super-Hooper-Dyne Lizzies," "Wandering Willies," "Circus Today," "His Marriage Wow," "All Night Long," "The Detectress," "One Wet Night," "Know Thy Wife," "Rowdy Ann," "Hearts and Flowers," "Fatty and Mabel Adrift," "Oh Doctor!," "The Garage," "The Boat," "The Iron Mule," "Oranges and Lemons," "Get Out and Get Under," "Mighty Like a Moose," "Big Moments from Little Pictures," "Haunted Spooks," "Laurel and Hardy Lafftoons," "Dogs of War," "Fluttering Hearts," "It's a Gift," "A Night at the Show," "Rare Chaplin Snippet," "The Rink," "Live Wires and Love Sparks," "He's in Again," "Pie-Eyed," "Only Me," "Water Wagons," "Outbound," "Chasing Choo-Choos," "Danger Ahead," "Yukon Jake," "Three of a Kind," "Dry and Thirsty," "Family Life," "Now You Tell One," and "The Grocery Clerk." —MM
Movie: 🎵🎵🎵 ½ **DVD:** 🎵🎵🎵
Image Ent. (cat #ID0699DSDVD, UPC 014-381069921). Full frame. Dolby Digital Stereo. $69.99. Keepcase boxed set. *LANG:* Silent. *SUB:* English intertitles. *FEATURES:* 57 chapters.
1998 1089m/B Harry Langdon, Harold Lloyd, Stan Laurel, Oliver Hardy, Charlie Chaplin, Ben Turpin.

Slaughter

After his parents are killed, a former Green Beret (Brown) goes after the murderers. It's vintage "blaxploitation" with all the requisite sex and violence. Bright image is very nice with only minimal grain in the night scenes and some shimmering in the overly bright daylight exteriors. —MM
Movie: 🎵🎵 **DVD:** 🎵🎵🎵
MGM Home Ent. (cat #1001469, UPC 027-616857897). Widescreen (2.35:1) anamorphic. Dolby Digital Mono. $14.98. Keepcase. *LANG:* English; French. *SUB:* French; Spanish. *CAP:* English. *FEATURES:* Trailer • 16 chapters.
1972 (R) 92m/C Jim Brown, Stella Stevens, Rip Torn, Cameron Mitchell, Don Gordon, Marlene Clark; **D:** Jack Starrett; **W:** Mark Hanna, Don Williams; **C:** R. Solano; **M:** Luchi De Jesus.

The Slayers

Petite, doe-eyed sorceress Lina Inverse joins with handsome lunk Gourry on farcical adventures in this cute fantasy series. Filled with the expected amount of enchanted swords, dragons, and evil sorcerers, *The Slayers* succeeds because of its knowing acknowledgment of fantasy genre clichés via Lina's frequent asides. All of the familiar scenarios are given a thorough ribbing and the series is a charming, successful light entertainment. The animation is colorful but somewhat average and occasionally limited. This set contains all 26 episodes. Follow-up series appeared (and are available) under the titles *The Slayers: Next* and *The Slayers: Try.* The dubbing job rewrites some of the jokes and can't quite match the spirit of the original voice artists. The original language is preferable. The image transfer occasionally displays shimmer and digital noise during fast-paced sections, but is acceptable overall. The audio is fine, but sounds more like mono than stereo. The majority of extras are contained on the DVD-ROM features; the rest are extremely insubstantial. The chapter links are quite underwhelming. —DG
Movie: 🎵🎵🎵 **DVD:** 🎵🎵 ½
Central Park/U.S. Manga (cat #SSDVD-6136, UPC 795243613628). Full frame. Dolby Digital Surround. $129.99. Keepcase. *LANG:* Japanese; English. *SUB:* English. *FEATURES:* 1 chapter per episode • "Meet the Cast" • Actor's bios • Graphic novel excerpt • Sneak peaks • DVD-ROM: art gallery, character gallery, cast, scripts, text interviews, graphic novel pages, reviews, character sketches.
1995 600m/C JP

Sleeping Murder / 4:50 from Paddington

Please see review of *Agatha Christie's Miss Marple Set 1.*
Movie: 🎵🎵 ½ **DVD:** 🎵🎵 ½
A&E (cat #AAE-70259, UPC 7339617025-90). Full frame. Dolby Digital Stereo. Keepcase. *LANG:* English.
1986 100m/C Joan Hickson, Geraldine Alexander, John Moulder-Brown, Frederick Treves, Jack Watson, Esmond Knight, Jean Anderson, Jean Heywood; **D:** John (Howard) Davies; **W:** Kenneth Taylor; **C:** Peter Hall.

Sleepless

A prostitute fleeing a client's apartment discovers a cache of elaborate knives and accidentally takes a scrapbook of all the murders he's committed. As the killer starts a series of murders based on a gruesome children's rhyme, retired police chief Moretti (von Sydow) teams up with the son of one of the victims (Dionisi) to solve the case. This ugly, nasty thriller steals ideas and scenes from Argento's other, better films resulting in an uneven, unsatisfying hodgepodge. The killer's identity is a surprise but it's so farfetched, and the actors are so poorly directed, it's doubtful you'll care. Particularly upsetting is the film's quite repellent misogyny; it feels at times as if the sole reason behind the movie is to enact scenes of brutal, hateful violence against screaming women. It's the kind of movie that reflects badly on the director's past works. The disc features a cropped transfer of a 1.85 film. As Argento's stylish visuals are usually the raison d'etre for the entire film, cropping them weakens an already poor film. The disc is also prone to shimmering, grain, and aliasing. The colors are there, but this is an ugly disc. The audio is involving as far as music and sound effects are concerned, but one frequently has to strain to hear (the terribly dubbed) dialogue. The cover art is particularly awful. —*AB/DG*

Movie: ♪ ½ **DVD:** ♪ ½
Artisan Ent. (cat #12404, UPC 01223612-4047). Full frame. Dolby Digital 5.1 Surround, Dolby Digital Surround. $24.98. Keepcase. *LANG:* English. *SUB:* English; Spanish. *FEATURES:* Director and cast filmographies • Trailers • 20 chapters.
2001 117m/C *IT* Max von Sydow, Stefano Dionisi, Chiara Caselli; *D:* Dario Argento; *W:* Dario Argento, Franco Ferrini; *C:* Ronnie Taylor; *M:* The Goblins.

Sleuth [2]

Anchor Bay has corrected the flaws in the first release of this tricky thriller (reviewed in *Book 1*). Absolutely clean and free of defects, the film has never looked better. The image reveals an incredible amount of detail and if it weren't for the muted color scheme of the movie itself, you would never guess its true age. Colors are nicely reproduced and always stable. Contrast is very good, giving the atmospheric cinematography an additional edge, as the image is full of little details, deep shadows, and good highlights. While sounding a bit dated with its limited frequency response, the mono soundtrack is absolutely sufficient for the mostly dialogue-driven presentation and never becomes a point of distraction. —*GH/MM*

Movie: ♪♪♪ ½ **DVD:** ♪♪♪ ½
Anchor Bay (cat #DV11740, UPC 01313-1174090). Widescreen (1.85:1) anamorphic. Dolby Digital Mono. $14.98. Keepcase. *LANG:* English; French. *CAP:* English. *FEATURES:* Featurette • Trailer and TV spot • Talent files • 25 chapters.

1972 (PG) 138m/C Laurence Olivier, Michael Caine, John Matthews, Alec Cawthorne, Teddy Martin; *D:* Joseph L. Mankiewicz; *W:* Anthony Shaffer; *C:* Oswald Morris; *M:* John Addison. *AWARDS:* N.Y. Film Critics '72: Actor (Olivier); *NOM:* Oscars '72: Actor (Caine), Actor (Olivier), Director (Mankiewicz), Orig. Dramatic Score.

Slightly Scarlet

Small-time hood Payne carries out an assignment from boss DeCorsia to smear a law-and-order politico running for mayor. He falls in love with the candidate's secretary, tries to go straight, and ends up running the mob when DeCorsia flees town. A spiffy, low-budget noir crime drama based on the James M. Cain novel *Love's Lovely Counterfeit*. While it's true that film noir utilizes shadows and varying degrees of light to its advantage, this disc is dark and diffused by even those standards. Consequently, the picture suffers from an overall lack of definition that proves very distracting. Dialogue is reproduced well enough to make the soundtrack passable. —*MJT*

Movie: ♪♪ ½ **DVD:** ♪♪ ½
VCI (cat #8292, UPC 089859829222). Widescreen (1.85:1) anamorphic. Dolby Digital Mono. $19.99. Keepcase. *LANG:* English. *FEATURES:* 18 chapters • Commentary by Max Allan Collins • Original theatrical trailer • Photo gallery • James Cain information • James Cain book gallery • Trailer gallery.
1956 99m/C Rhonda Fleming, Arlene Dahl, John Payne, Kent Taylor, Ted de Corsia; *D:* Allan Dwan; *W:* Robert Blees; *C:* John Alton; *M:* Louis Forbes.

The Slime People

Grade-Z schlock contains enough intentional tongue-in-cheek humor to save itself from a virtually non-existent budget. Huge prehistoric monsters—all right, a couple of guys in bad rubber suits—are awakened from hibernation by underground atomic testing in Los Angeles. They take over the city and create the fog that they need to live and to keep their slime wet, or something. Thank goodness for Professor Gelman (Burton) and his two lovely daughters who fight the good fight. DVD might ooze ahead of tape image-wise, but only by a drop. Light surface damage is evident throughout, but the disc comes with a cool glow-light. —*MM*

Movie: ♪♪ **DVD:** ♪♪
Rhino (cat #R2 971483, UPC 603497148-325). Full frame. $19.98. Snapper. *LANG:* English. *FEATURES:* 12 chapters • Glow light.
1963 76m/B Robert Hutton, Robert Burton, Susan Hart, William Boyce, Les Tremayne, John Close, Judee Morton; *D:* Robert Hutton; *W:* Vance Skarstedt; *C:* William G. Troiano.

Slipstream

Please see review of *Great Sci-Fi Thrillers*.

Movie: ♪♪
1989 (PG-13) 92m/C *GB* Mark Hamill, Bill Paxton, Bob Peck, Eleanor David, Kitty Aldridge, Robbie Coltrane, Ben Kingsley, F. Murray Abraham; *D:* Steven Lisberger; *W:* Tony Kayden; *C:* Frank Tidy; *M:* Elmer Bernstein.

Slow Burn

Driver stars as Trina, a woman obsessed with finding diamonds that she knows are out in the desert. As her quest begins to look grim, she considers moving towards a life outside of the burning hot sands. Two con artists (badly played by Spader and Brolin) enter her life and it becomes a matter of who's going to outsmart (which, in this case, is not saying a lot) whom. Flashbacks and other details are awkwardly revealed and the limp performances do nothing to speed up what often seems like three people wandering around the desert for an hour and a half. With some decent actors, it could have made for an interesting picture, but the final result is definitely less than a thrill. Skip it. A full-frame presentation is the only one present on this disc but the image never seems overtly cropped. Sharpness and detail are passable, and the limited color palette seems accurately conveyed. Other than a few scenes where a gust of wind blows, the presentation is geared almost completely towards the front of the room, with the music the primary focus. Dialogue occasionally sounds muffled and hard to understand. —*AB/DG*

Movie: ♪ ½ **DVD:** ♪♪
Artisan Ent. (UPC 12236106364). Full frame. Dolby Digital 5.1 Surround. $14.98. Keepcase. *LANG:* English. *CAP:* English. *FEATURES:* Production notes • Cast bios • Trailer.
2000 (R) 97m/C Minnie Driver, James Spader, Josh Brolin, Stuart Wilson; *D:* Christian Ford; *W:* Christian Ford, Roger Soffer; *C:* Mark Vicente; *M:* Anthony Marinelli.

Smash Cuts! Super Sci-Fi Shorts

This collection of seven short SF films runs the gamut from quirky to funny with an emphasis on the offbeat and shocking. Think ambitious student films with image and sound quality that range from fair to good. Contents: "In Transit," "Evil Hill," "Megahurtz," "Amplifier," "Big Day Off," "Sand Trooper," "Bubblepac." —*MM*

Movie: ♪♪ ½ **DVD:** ♪♪ ½
York Ent. (cat #YPD-1142, UPC 75072311-4224). Widescreen letterboxed and full frame. $14.99. Keepcase. *LANG:* English.
2000 (R) 92m/C *D:* Mike Daly, Ryan Schifrin, Darrin Plant, Glenn Forbes, David Janssen, Dalvatore Belleci, Rick Dublin.

Smash Cuts: Totally Twisted Shorts Fest

Totally twisted, gross, classless. Those words are not enough to describe these short movies that otherwise would have been smeared on a restroom wall somewhere. Each film contains a single funny premise that is stretched to the breaking point, except for the documentary about the crime-scene cleaning service, but even the guys in that film find themselves pretty funny and revel in their own coolness to the point of being loathsome. These are films by civilians desperate to be funny, and with few exceptions, they're just stupid or gross to the point of being more upsetting than amusing. More desperate for attention and laughs than are the films he's put together is Scott Forrest. He introduces the collection while playing Twister with two women: a midget and a virtually topless top-heavy elderly fat woman. In the animated short "The Hangnail," a skinny character rips his arm apart trying to bite off a hangnail and eventually his entire epidermis. In "The Dehumanized," two men with spare parts in their heads search for weird aliens, spiraling down into crap-soaked content. "Judgment Day" features Terry Gilliam–style animation with humor from third grade Catholic schoolboys making jokes about God swearing and crushing people for fun. "Shock Asylum" is the story of a man who goes to a mental hospital for a psychiatric evaluation and ends up being committed against his will because the people who run the asylum are crazy. This whole exercise is an argument to make the camera a registered weapon. This DVD's sound quality is at the mercy of the filmmakers and the menu design is clearly the cheapest and least helpful available. The shorts that are digitally shot look terrific, though the animated pieces look like some of the film was stepped on, and given the content, it wouldn't be surprising if a few prints were damaged by stomping fits. "Creature Nites of Ohio" is the simplest of the collection and actually very funny. The narrator takes you through a sort of field guild to creatures of Ohio, which have clearly been compiled from various parts of discarded stuffed animals and dolls. "Sunday's Game" features some nice film work and a morbidly funny story line of elderly ladies absurdly desperate for entertainment. If you're looking for family entertainment, run screaming from this DVD. If you like the idea of choking on your own vomit, give it a spin. —JAS

Movie: 𝄞𝄞 **DVD:** 𝄞𝄞
York Ent. (cat #YPD-1132, UPC 75072311-3227). Full frame. $14.99. Keepcase. *LANG:* English. *FEATURES:* Interviews with filmmakers.
2000 71m/C

Smile Now Cry Later

The two brothers Marcus and Smiley (Sir Dyno and A.L.G.) try to make it in the rap music business while surviving on the violent streets of the Barrio. A promising beginning suggests a Latino counterpart to the best of the black variations of this sub-genre. However, the acting is too amateurish and the camera too uninspired to

allow this to rise above its limitations. Decent DVD picture and sound. —MO
Movie: 𝄞𝄞 **DVD:** 𝄞𝄞𝄞
MTI (cat #7017, UPC 039414570175). Full frame. $24.95. Keepcase. *LANG:* English. *SUB:* Spanish. *FEATURES:* 20 chapters • Theatrical trailer • Darkroom Famila music videos • Cast bios.
2001 80m/C Sir Dyno, James Logan, Dub, A.L.G.; *D:* Jose Quiroz, Eduardo Quiroz; *W:* Jose Quiroz, Eduardo Quiroz; *C:* Rocky Robinson.

Smiling Fish & Goat on Fire

This "slice of life" film tells the story of two brothers Chris and Tony (real-life brothers Derick and Steven Martini), who have completely opposite personalities, but face similar problems in life. Chris is a happy-go-lucky actor who doesn't have a care in the world and likes to see several women at once. Tony is an uptight accountant who has trouble relaxing and insists on making his relationship with Alison (Amy Hathaway) work, despite the fact that she always cries during sex. Director Jordan follows the pair as they attempt to find happiness in committed relationships. The film has some very funny lines and the performances are good, but it never strives to tell us anything new. This film isn't all that different from dozens of other independents which explore life and love. DVD looks quite good for a low-budget production. The image is sharp and clear, showing occasional softening of the image and some defects from the source print. There is a minimal amount of grain. The Dolby Stereo soundtrack is adequate, as it offers clear dialogue with no distortion. For some insight into what life is like for those diagnosed with schizophrenia, check out the audio commentary featuring director Kevin Jordan and stars Derick & Steven Martini. On this commentary, the audio from the actual film has not been muted, so the listener is constantly being bombarded by the voices of the speakers on the commentary track and the actors from the movie, making for a most disorienting experience. —ML
Movie: 𝄞𝄞 ½ **DVD:** 𝄞𝄞 ½
Studio Home Ent. (cat #VM7853D, UPC 658149785328). Widescreen (1.85:1) letterboxed. Dolby Stereo. $24.99. Keepcase. *LANG:* English. *SUB:* English; Spanish; French. *CAP:* English. *FEATURES:* Commentary • Trailer • Deleted scenes • 24 chapters.
1999 (R) 90m/C Steven Martini, Derick Martini, Bill Henderson, Christa Miller, Amy Hathaway, Rosemarie Addeo, Heather Jae Marie, Nicole Rae, Wesley Thompson; *D:* Kevin Jordan; *W:* Kevin Jordan, Steven Martini, Derick Martini; *C:* Fred Iannone; *M:* Chris Horvath.

The Smokers

Three vacuous high schoolers are tired of feeling used by boys. When one of them steals a gun, they think they may have

found a way to reclaim power. If you're tired of movies trying to shock you with teenagers having sex, doing drugs, and talking about tampons, you'll want to stay far away from this. The DVD is fine, although the soundtrack reveals the film's low-budget origins with a high level of background hiss during dialogue. Both widescreen and full-frame versions are offered. —BG
Movie: 𝄞 **DVD:** 𝄞𝄞 ½
MGM Home Ent. (cat #1002277, UPC 027-61686486). Widescreen (1.85:1) anamorphic; full frame. Dolby Surround. $26.98. Keepcase. *LANG:* English. *SUB:* English; French; Spanish. *CAP:* English. *FEATURES:* 16 chapters.
2000 (R) 97m/C Dominique Swain, Keri Lynn Pratt, Busy Philipps, Oliver Hudson, Ryan Browning, Joel West, Thora Birch, Nicholas M. Loeb; *D:* Christina Peters; *W:* Christina Peters, Kenny Golde; *C:* J.B. Letchinger; *M:* Lawrence Gingold.

Snake and Crane Arts of Shaolin

A book describing "The Eight Steps of the Snake and Crane" somehow falls into the hands of a cocky young Jackie Chan, and all the clans are after it. He defends himself from all of them using his Snake and Crane. There's not much to the plot, but that leaves a lot of room for fighting, most of it quite good. New digital transfer is miles beyond any previous release of this title in quality. —BT
Movie: 𝄞𝄞 ½ **DVD:** 𝄞𝄞𝄞
Columbia Tristar (cat #08199, UPC 043-396081994). Widescreen anamorphic. $19.95. Keepcase. *LANG:* Mandarin; English. *SUB:* English; Spanish; Portuguese; French. *CAP:* English. *FEATURES:* 28 chapters • Trailer.
1978 95m/C *HK* Jackie Chan, Nora Miao, Kam Kong, Chin-lin Kim, Tin Miu; *D:* Chi-Hwa Chen; *W:* San Yee Cheung; *C:* Chung Yun Chan.

Snake in the Eagle's Shadow

Hwang Jang Lee has killed 3,000 followers of the Snake Fist style of kung fu to prove that his Eagle's Claw style is superior. Now the only fighters left to carry on the Snake Fist are old Simon Yuen and his young student Jackie Chan. After a string of failures, this was the first film really to let Chan do action scenes the way he wanted. The results made him a star. This edition is the first U.S. video release to contain the full 97-minute cut, in a vivid and sharp widescreen transfer. The mono sound is a bit fuzzy, especially on the Cantonese track. —BT
Movie: 𝄞𝄞 ½ **DVD:** 𝄞𝄞𝄞
Columbia Tristar (cat #08428, UPC 043-396084285). Widescreen anamorphic. $24.95. Keepcase. *LANG:* Cantonese; English. *SUB:* English; French; Spanish; Portuguese; Korean. *CAP:* English. *FEATURES:* 28 chapters • Trailers.

1978 (PG) 97m/C *HK* Jackie Chan, Simon Yuen, Hwang Jang Lee, Hark-On Fung, Dean Shek, Hsu Hsia; ***D:*** Woo-ping Yuen; ***W:*** Jackie Chan, See Yuen Ng, Siu Lung, Clifford Choi; ***C:*** Hai Chang; ***M:*** Fu-liang Chou.

Snapdragon

Police detective Peckham (Field) investigates a series of killings while her psychologist boyfriend (Bauer) romances a beautiful blonde tattooed amnesiac (Anderson) who's having nightmares that match the killings. Erotic thriller goes through the standard paces at a relatively slow pace en route to a "surprise" ending. DVD is virtually identical to VHS tape. —*MM*
Movie: 🦴🦴 ***DVD:*** 🦴🦴
Studio Home Ent. (cat #15248E, UPC 057-373152485). Full frame. $9.95. Keepcase. *LANG:* English. *FEATURES:* 12 chapters • Anderson and Bauer thumbnail bios.
1993 (R) 96m/C Steven Bauer, Pamela Anderson, Chelsea Field; ***D:*** Worth Keeter; ***W:*** Gene Church; ***C:*** James Mathers; ***M:*** Michael Linn.

Snatch [SE]

Turkish (Statham) and his partner in crime Tommy (Graham) are doing all right by their illegal gambling business but are anxious to make a big score in the world of underground boxing to fund their purchase of a nice new trailer. To this end they throw in with crime boss, and renowned sadist, Brick Top (Ford) to have their prize fighter, Gorgeous George (Fogerty), take a fall in an upcoming bout. But when George gets his butt whupped by the vagabond trailer-trading One Punch Mickey (Pitt), the boys instead recruit the marble-mouthed Mickey to fight. Unbeknownst to them, old Mickey doesn't quite know how to take a fall. Meanwhile, Frankie Four Fingers (Del Toro) is passing through London with a giant diamond he lifted in a Hasidic heist in Amsterdam. While waiting for his flight to New York, Frankie is informed about the bout by Doug the Head (Reid), a diamond broker who only thinks he's Jewish. Doug later mentions this tidbit in passing to Cousin Avi (Farina) back in New York and Avi, knowing that Frankie is a compulsive gambler, fears for his diamond and hops the Concord to Britain. When Avi arrives in London to find Frankie missing, he hires the unstoppable Bullet Tooth Tony (Jones) to find his gem, and that's just the beginning. The style of the film is grittily realistic with a very subdued color palette and natural lighting used throughout. While the transfer may look grainy at times, this is clearly the intent. Black levels aren't as deep as one might expect from a newer release due to the frequent low lighting but again, this is the way it's supposed to look. While the colors are intentionally washed-out, they are always solid and well-balanced. The image is quite sharp as well with very little edge-enhancement evident. The film elements do suffer from the occasional nick and blemish but these are never terribly distracting and add to the rough and tumble look of the movie. All in all, the video transfer is true to the director's intent and, while it isn't a glossy, impeccable show-off piece, the image mirrors the mood of the film perfectly. The soundtrack is quite immersive with the Surrounds and LFE channel coming to life for the action sequences and the often booming music. Dialogue is firmly centered and is quite clear although the heavy accents might necessitate the use of the subtitle track here and there (more on this later). Music, sound effects, and the spoken word are all given equal emphasis and this is one of the rare sound mixes that doesn't require frequent adjustments of the volume knob to achieve a comfortable listening level. As for the subtitles, there's a choice of English, French, or Pikey. The Pikey option is quite unusual in that it only offers subtitles when the character of One Punch Mickey is speaking in his nearly indecipherable brogue. Heck, even the subtitles can't always catch what the crazy Pikey is saying! The commentary track with director Guy Ritchie and producer Matthew Vaughn is an entertaining, casual discussion as the two happily munch away at their lunch and trade barbs while watching the film. Eventually, they are encouraged by unnamed men in suits to get a bit more focused but try as they might, they are unable to stay serious for long. Ritchie comes across as a very enthusiastic director who isn't afraid to be self-critical or to offer up compliments and criticism of his cast and crew and the style of the commentary matches perfectly the haphazard style of the film. Also included on the first disc is a special feature called "Stealing Stone." With this option enabled, a small diamond appears on screen during certain parts of the movie. Pressing the "Enter" key on the remote takes the viewer to the deleted scene that would have come next then returns them to the main feature when finished. The fact that the deleted scenes are in full frame, with mono sound, and with time-codes stamped across the bottom is really jarring and pulls the viewer out of the picture. All of these scenes are also included individually on the second disc and it's much more pleasing to view them in that fashion. —*MP*
Movie: 🦴🦴🦴 ***DVD:*** 🦴🦴🦴 ½
Columbia Tristar Home Video (UPC 043396062535). Widescreen (1.85:1) anamorphic; full frame. Dolby Digital 5.1 Surround; Dolby Surround. $27.98. Keepcase. *LANG:* English; French. *SUB:* English; French; Pikey. *CAP:* English. *FEATURES:* "Making of" documentary • 6 deleted scenes with optional commentary • 3 storyboard featurettes • Photo gallery • Trailers, TV spots, teasers • Filmographies.
2000 (R) 104m/C *GB* Benicio Del Toro, Dennis Farina, Brad Pitt, Vinnie Jones, Rade Serbedzija, Jason Statham, Lennie James, Ewen Bremner, Alan Ford, Mike Reid, Robbie Gee, Jason Flemyng, Sorcha Cusack, Stephen Graham; ***D:*** Guy Ritchie; ***W:*** Guy Ritchie; ***C:*** Tim Maurice-Jones; ***M:*** John Murphy.

Snow Dogs

Ted Brooks (Gooding Jr.) treks to Alaska to claim an inheritance that turns out to be a team of champion sled dogs. Problem is, old curmudgeon Thunder Jack (Coburn) wants the canines for an Arctic Circle dogsledding tournament. With a little effort, this one could have been fun for viewers over the age of eight, but it reeks of Disney Channel and poor Cuba is reduced to grinning idiotically or shrieking hysterically. With the added nostalgia of Nichelle Nichols and the out-of-left-field casting of rapper Sisqo. Extremely clean DVD transfer and sound are completely wasted. —*MO*
Movie: 🦴🦴 ***DVD:*** 🦴🦴🦴 ½
Buena Vista Home Ent. (cat #26508, UPC 786936184914). Full frame. Dolby Digital 5.1; DTS 5.1. $29.99. Keepcase. *LANG:* English; French. *CAP:* English. *FEATURES:* 24 chapters • Deleted & extended scenes • "Ted's Arctic Challenge" set-top game • Featurette: "Going to the Dogs" • Featurette: "Chillin' with the Actors" • Featurette: "Tolketna on Ice" • Commentary: director Brian Levant, producer Jordan Kerner.
2002 (PG) 99m/C Cuba Gooding Jr., James Coburn, Sisqo, Nichelle Nichols, M. Emmet Walsh, Graham Greene, Brian Doyle-Murray, Joanna Bascalso, Michael Bolton; ***D:*** Brian Levant; ***W:*** Jim Kouf, Tommy Swerdlow, Michael Goldberg, Mark Gibson, Philip Halprin; ***C:*** Thomas Ackerman; ***M:*** John Debney.

Snow White and the Seven Dwarfs [PE]

A young girl flees her murderous stepmother and moves in with seven miners. Disney's adaptation of the Grimm Brothers fairy tale is the first feature-length work of animation and it remains the standard against which all others are judged. In the years since 1937, it has been restored several times and this version is the sharpest and brightest that I've seen. The menus make good use of 5.1 effects and the Surround remix doesn't seem out of place, given the subject matter. (Traditionalists have the option of the original mono.) The studio has put its considerable resources into producing the best DVD possible and they have succeeded. Interestingly, the creative people elected not to "sanitize" the recorded comments by Walt Disney that are used as part of the commentary track (along with film historian John Canemaker's intelligent remarks). Traffic and other ambient sounds are clearly audible and that's somehow more appropriate than audio perfection. Most of the extras (almost three hours worth) are on the second disc. Probably the most interesting of them are the five deleted scenes, one fully animated. (All were wisely cut from this superbly concise film.) Details about story development, character, and animation are well chosen. Other extras are more promotional material for the studio. Some may question why a new version of "Someday My Prince Will Come" by Barbra Streisand was included, but she does a fine job with it. This set belongs in every collection. —MM

Movie: 🎞️🎞️🎞️🎞️ **DVD:** 🎞️🎞️🎞️🎞️
Buena Vista Home Ent. (cat #22254, UPC 786936150605). Full frame. Dolby Digital 5.1 Surround; Dolby Digital Surround; Mono. $29.99. Keepcase. *LANG:* English; French. *CAP:* English. *FEATURES:* 27 chapters ▪ 5 deleted scenes ▪ "Someday My Prince Will Come" by Barbra Streisand ▪ Video game ▪ Sing-along ▪ Storyboard to film comparisons ▪ Several sets of trailers and radio spots ▪ Abandoned concepts ▪ Restoration featurette ▪ Commentary: Walt Disney, John Canemaker.
1937 (G) 83m/C D: David Hand; **W:** Ted Sears, Otto Englander, Earl Hurd, Dorothy Blank, Richard Creedon, Dick Richard, Merrill De Maris, Webb Smith; **M:** Frank Churchill, Paul J. Smith, Larry Morey, Leigh Harline; **V:** Adriana Caselotti, Harry Stockwell, Lucille LaVerne, Moroni Olsen, Billy Gilbert, Pinto Colvig, Otis Harlan, Scotty Matraw, Roy Atwell, Stuart Buchanan, Marion Darlington, Jim Macdonald. *AWARDS:* AFI '98: Top 100, Natl. Film Reg. '89; *NOM:* Oscars '37: Score.

Snow White: The Fairest of Them All

The classic fairy tale receives a face-lift from Caroline Thompson, the co-creator of *Edward Scissorhands* and *The Nightmare before Christmas*. In this version, Snow White is a miracle-birth for her parents Josephine (Farmiga) and John (Irwin). But when her mother dies in childbirth, Snow White is left with her father, who is distraught and unsure of how to care for the infant. They are rescued by a creature known as the Green-Eyed One (Brown), who, using his magical powers, makes John a king and Snow White a princess. The Green-Eyed One then transforms his witch-like sister into the beautiful Elspeth (Richardson) for John to marry. As the years pass, Snow White (Kreuk) grows into a beautiful young woman, and Elspeth, envious of the princess's beauty, attempts to kill the young girl. Snow White flees from the castle, and finds solace in the forest with a group of seven dwarves, who are each named after a day of the week and identified by a trademark color. With the aid of the dwarves and Prince Alfred (Leitso), Snow White must make her way back to the castle and confront Elspeth. This new incarnation is quite entertaining and contains many good performances, most notably from newcomer Kreuk (TV's *Smallville*) and Brown. As with any good fairy tale, there are some dark moments here and the Green Eyed One is quite scary, so this may not be appropriate for the little ones. The story gets a bit convoluted at times (as if it's trying too hard to break away from the traditional tale), but

it's imaginative nonetheless. As this film was originally broadcast on television, it is presented in a full-frame format on this DVD. This transfer looks great and rivals digital broadcast quality. The picture is very sharp and clear, showing no grain and spectacularly vivid colors. The Dolby Digital 5.1 audio track provides clear dialogue, and some very well-placed Surround effects. But the track was recorded at a very low level, so you may have to adjust your volume higher than normal. The DVD contains a behind-the-scenes featurette, which offers interviews with the cast and crew. —ML

Movie: 🎞️🎞️ ½ **DVD:** 🎞️🎞️🎞️
Artisan Ent. (cat #11479, UPC 70772911-4796). Full frame. Dolby Digital 5.1; Dolby Surround. $19.98. Keepcase. *LANG:* English. *CAP:* English. *FEATURES:* Behind-the-scenes ▪ Cast & crew bios ▪ 10 chapters.
2002 90m/C Kristen Kreuk, Miranda Richardson, Tom Irwin, Vera Farmiga, Vincent Schiavelli, Warwick Davis, Michael J. Anderson, Clancy Brown, Tyron Leitso; **D:** Caroline Thompson; **W:** Caroline Thompson, Julie Hickson; **C:** Jon Joffin; **M:** Michael Covertino.

Soapdish

Backstage lives of the daytime soap opera *The Sun Also Sets* and its cast. When ratings fall, a character is written out of the script via decapitation and then is brought back to give things a lift. While the writer struggles to make the reincarnation believable, the cast juggles old and new romances, and professional jealousies abound. Several grandly funny moments blossom forth as film actors spoof the medium that gave many of them a start. Not surprisingly for a film of this age, DVD image is a little soft, but it's still very good. This one's just terrific. —MM

Movie: 🎞️🎞️🎞️ ½ **DVD:** 🎞️🎞️🎞️
Paramount (cat #32445, UPC 097363244-547). Widescreen anamorphic. Dolby Digital 5.1 Surround; Dolby Digital Surround; Stereo. $29.98. Keepcase. *LANG:* English; French. *SUB:* English. *CAP:* English. *FEATURES:* Trailer ▪ "Making of" featurette ▪ 15 chapters.
1991 (PG-13) 97m/C Sally Field, Kevin Kline, Robert Downey Jr., Cathy Moriarty, Whoopi Goldberg, Elisabeth Shue, Carrie Fisher, Garry Marshall, Teri Hatcher, Paul Johansson, Costas Mandylor, Stephen Nichols, Leeza Gibbons, John Tesh, Kathy Najimy, Sheila Kelley, Finola Hughes; **D:** Michael Hoffman; **W:** Andrew Bergman, Robert Harling; **C:** Ueli Steiger; **M:** Alan Silvestri.

Social Intercourse

Waste of celluloid concerning the social reclamation of cyber geek Todd (Steve Taylor, who also edited, produced, directed, and co-scripted) at a friend's blow-out bash. If horny hijinks, tough-talking chicks, and a water-balloon sniper constituted good plot elements, then *Social Intercourse* would be

the *Citizen Kane* of party films. Alas, despite the critical kudos of the Hermosa Beach Film Festival (nabbing the "Best Comedy" honors) and the Sydney Online Tribe (?), watching this film is as much fun as cleaning up the bathroom after a tequila chugging contest. Taylor even takes the time to tape an introduction. Naked with a strategically placed laptop computer, Taylor remarks that the film cost $15,000. The money would have been better spent buying clothes and acting lessons. The full-frame transfer offers desaturated colors and a constantly grainy image; during the night scenes, the picture looks like poor TV reception. The stereo sound is crisp and clear, all the better to hear such crafted gems as "Are my breasts in the shot?" Extras include a director's commentary track, trailers, and an interactive feature that allows the viewer to go behind the scenes whenever the "director's hat" electronically pops up in the frame. Short of a doorstop, I cannot think of a single reason to own this disc. —EP

Movie: woof **DVD:** 🎞️ ½
York Ent. (cat #YPD-1095, UPC 7-50723-10952-7). Full frame. Dolby Digital Stereo. $14.95. Keepcase. *LANG:* English. *FEATURES:* 14 chapters ▪ Theatrical trailers ▪ Intro by the director ▪ Commentary: director ▪ Extra party footage.
2001 88m/C Steve Taylor, Lee Abbott, Kim Little, Ashley Davis, Steve Grabowsky; **D:** Steve Taylor; **W:** Steve Taylor, Roger Kristian Jones; **C:** Armand Gazarian.

Some Folks Call It a Sling Blade

A young reporter (Ringwald) visits a mental institution to interview Karl Childers (Thornton) on the day of his release. Hickenlooper uses behind-the-scenes footage to whine about how he was wronged by Thornton and to make a case for how brilliant he is as a director. Thornton famously won that argument when the Academy of Motion Picture Arts and Sciences awarded him an Oscar for the feature screenplay version. Picture and sound are murky. —LA

Movie: 🎞️🎞️ ½ **DVD:** 🎞️🎞️ ½
Vanguard Intl. Cinema (cat #VF0232, UPC 658769023237). Widescreen letterboxed. $19.95. Keepcase. *LANG:* English. *FEATURES:* "The Making of 'Some Folks Call It a Sling Blade'" ▪ Additional behind-the-scenes with director's commentary ▪ Trailers of other works by George Hickenlooper ▪ 4 chapters.
1994 29m/B Billy Bob Thornton, Molly Ringwald, J.T. Walsh, Jefferson Mays, Suzanne Cryer; **D:** George Hickenlooper; **W:** Billy Bob Thornton; **C:** Kent Wakeford; **M:** Bill Boll.

Someone Like You

Here we have yet another film in which the perfect woman can't seem to find the perfect man. In this case, the film focuses on Jane Goodale (which is pronounced exactly like the famed gorilla expert), who is

portrayed by Ashley Judd. Jane has just left a bad relationship and moves in (on a platonic basis) with co-worker Eddie (Hugh Jackman), who is a habitual womanizer. Jane soon finds herself falling for another co-worker Ray (Greg Kinnear), who seems to be the perfect gentleman. Based on her observations of Ray and Eddie, Jane forms a hypothesis that men behave like animals in the way that they pursue women. This theory leads to unexpected national fame, as Jane tries to decide which man she should spend her life with. The "animal husbandry" angle gives an original edge to *Someone Like You*, but unfortunately, the rest of the film is a tired retread. From the outset, we know exactly who Jane is going to fall for, and most of the film is very predictable. Judd, Jackman, and Kinnear are all very good in their roles, but they can't save this script. *Someone Like You* does offer some funny moments and should spark discussion about gender differences, but the film is instantly forgettable. The DVD however, is very impressive, as the transfer is essentially flawless, showing no grain and revealing a true depth to the image. The Dolby Digital 5.1 audio track presents some fluctuations in volume, but the ambient Surround effects are impressive. The audio commentary by director Tony Goldwyn is of particular interest, as he discusses the work which went into making the film. —ML
Movie: 🎵🎵 ½ **DVD:** 🎵🎵🎵
20th Century Fox (cat #2002312, UPC 024543023128). Widescreen (1.85:1) anamorphic. Dolby Digital 5.1. $29.98. Keepcase. *LANG:* English; French. *SUB:* English; Spanish. *CAP:* English. *FEATURES:* Commentary • Extended scenes • Alternate ending • Featurette.
2001 (PG-13) 97m/C Ashley Judd, Hugh Jackman, Greg Kinnear, Marisa Tomei, Ellen Barkin, Peter Friedman, Catherine Dent, Laura Regan; *D:* Tony Goldwyn; *W:* Elizabeth Chandler; *C:* Anthony B. Richmond; *M:* Rolfe Kent.

Something within Me
Filmmakers Jerret Engle and Emma Joan Morris spent a year at St. Augustine's school in the South Bronx. When the Catholic school was about to close due to poor attendance, the faculty and staff turned it into an arts school with an emphasis on music. Enrollment has tripled and the film shows how the kids have prospered. It's an understated story that's much more inspiring than the seemingly endless parade of Hollywood stories wherein Meryl or Michelle save the poor children from life on the streets. DVD image is no better than VHS tape. Bits of fluff and dust pop up from time to time, but they are inconsequential. Technical sophistication is definitely not the point. —MM
Movie: 🎵🎵🎵 **DVD:** 🎵🎵
Vanguard Intl. Cinema (cat #VF0168). Full frame. $29.99. Keepcase. *LANG:* English. *FEATURES:* 8 chapters.

1993 61m/C *D:* Emma Joan Morris; *C:* Juan Cristobal Cobo. *AWARDS:* Sundance '93: Special Jury Prize, Aud. Award, Filmmakers Trophy.

Sometimes They Come Back
Jim Norman (Matheson) and his wife Sally (Adams) move back to the small town his parents left 27 years before. Jim finds that the horrors of his past haven't diminished and the ghosts are still there. Writers Lawrence Konner and Mark Rosenthal and director Tom McLoughlin effectively flesh out Stephen King's short story while retaining his weathered small-town atmosphere and his understanding of the enduring power of childhood bullies. Matheson's very good in a straight dramatic role. On video, the made-for-TV feature contains extra footage of violence and grotesque special effects. Inexplicably, this slender vehicle has become the basis for a moderately successful series. DVD image and sound is no improvement over tape. Title is also available on a two-sided disc with *Sometimes They Come Back...Again*. —MM
Movie: 🎵🎵🎵 **DVD:** 🎵🎵
Lion's Gate Home Ent. (cat #7145). Full frame. $14.99. Keepcase. *LANG:* English. *SUB:* French; Spanish. *FEATURES:* 16 chapters • Trailers.
1991 (R) 97m/C Tim Matheson, Brooke Adams, Robert Rusler, William Sanderson; *D:* Tom McLoughlin; *W:* Mark Rosenthal, Larry Konner; *C:* Bryan England; *M:* Terry Plumeri.

Sometimes They Come Back...Again
The plot to this sequel-remake is nothing special. It cannibalizes several other Stephen King works and tosses in a ton of witchcraft hokum. That said, the story of resurrected satanic teen bullies who terrorize John Porter (Gross) and his daughter Michelle (Swank) is not without style and polish. A few of the effects are really striking. Alexis Arquette is very good as the lead bad guy, and so are Gross and Swank. Image is slightly sharper than the first film, but it's still no real improvement over tape. On DVD, the title is available as a double feature with *Sometimes They Come Back*. —MM
Movie: 🎵🎵 ½ **DVD:** 🎵🎵
Lion's Gate Home Ent. (cat #6786). Full frame. Dolby Digital Stereo. $34.98. Keepcase. *LANG:* English. *SUB:* French; Spanish. *FEATURES:* Cast & crew thumbnail bios • Trailer • 16 chapters.
1996 (R) 98m/C Michael Gross, Hilary Swank, Alexis Arquette, Jennifer Elise Cox; *D:* Adam Grossman; *W:* Adam Grossman; *C:* Christopher Baffa; *M:* Peter Manning Robinson.

Son of Dracula
In this late-coming sequel to the Universal classic, a stranger named Alucard is invited to America by a Southern belle

obsessed with eternal life. It is actually Dracula himself, not his son, who wreaks havoc in this spine-tingling chiller. As with its companion film on the disc *(Dracula's Daughter)*, the viewer is treated to a good transfer from fairly poor source material that has numerous occurrences of white flicks, scratches, and film jitters. And, as with *Dracula's Daughter* it doesn't really detract from the film. The transfer itself is once again sharp and detailed with great blacks and graytones giving the beautiful black-and-white cinematography plenty of depth. There is a little more trouble with the sound on this one, which is mostly clear, but suffers from intermittent noise. Available only as part of a double feature with *Dracula's Daughter* (see separate entry). —JO **AKA:** *Young Dracula*.
Movie: 🎵🎵🎵 **DVD:** 🎵🎵🎵
Universal Studios Home Video Full frame. Dolby Digital Mono. Keepcase. *LANG:* English; Spanish. *SUB:* Spanish; French. *CAP:* English. *FEATURES:* Theatrical trailer • Talent files • Production notes.
1943 80m/B Lon Chaney Jr., Evelyn Ankers, Frank Craven, Robert Paige, Louise Allbritton, J. Edward Bromberg, Samuel S. Hinds; *D:* Robert Siodmak; *W:* Eric Taylor; *C:* George Robinson.

Son of Frankenstein
Wolf Frankenstein (Rathbone), son of Victor, returns to Vasaria with his wife Elsa (Hutchinson) and tiny son Peter (Dunagan) to claim his rightful estate. He meets hostility from the villagers, but installs his family successfully into the castle. Then Ygor (Lugosi) appears, a hanged murderer who survived the gallows and now haunts the Frankenstein ruins. He gloatingly reveals the inert but intact body of the Monster (Karloff), and goads Wolf into reviving it. Frankenstein fils becomes excited by the prospect, not knowing that Ygor wants to use the monster to settle the score with the jury that convicted him. This first non–James Whale Frankenstein film has a lot going for it, besides its powerhouse cast. The art direction is very impressive, taking advantage of the better lenses and film stocks available since *The Bride* premiered four years earlier. The combination sulphur pit—laboratory is splendidly atmospheric, with its steam and dark lighting. The cracked-egg appearance of the lab exterior (a nice matte painting) is also unique. DVD looks fine, but is perhaps a bit murkier than other, less popular entries in the series. The logical reason for this is that successful movies from the '30s were printed and reprinted countless times for reissues over the years, wearing out the original negative and probably most of the original printing dupes made from it. The audio is excellent, and accentuates the moody music, a custom score instead of the edited cues we're used to hearing later on in the series. The Realart trailer is included, along with some production notes that offer some interesting facts, such as an official mention of the notorious color test

footage for *Son* that fans have long been itching to see. Double feature disc also contains *Ghost of Frankenstein* (please see review). —*GE*
Movie: 🦴🦴 ½ **DVD:** 🦴🦴 ½
Universal Studios (cat #21404, UPC 0251-92140426). Full frame. Dolby Digital Mono. $24.98. Keepcase. *LANG:* English; French; Spanish. *SUB:* French; Spanish. *CAP:* English. *FEATURES:* Trailer ▪ Production notes.
1939 99m/C Basil Rathbone, Bela Lugosi, Boris Karloff, Lionel Atwill, Josephine Hutchinson, Donnie Dunagan, Emma Dunn, Edgar Norton, Lawrence Grant, Lionel Belmore; *D:* Rowland V. Lee; *W:* Willis Cooper; *C:* George Robinson.

The Son of Monte Cristo
Please see review of *Dueling DVD.*
Movie: 🦴🦴 ½ **DVD:** 🦴🦴
Marengo Films *FEATURES:* 12 chapters.
1940 102m/B Louis Hayward, Joan Bennett, George Sanders, Florence Bates, Montagu Love, Ralph Byrd, Clayton Moore; *D:* Rowland V. Lee; *W:* George Bruce; *C:* George Robinson; *M:* Edward Ward.

Son of the Sheik
The sequel to Valentino's star-making *The Sheik* (1921) also turned out to be his last film. Ahmed (Valentino) falls in love with dancing girl Yasmin (Banky). He's kidnapped by Ghabah (Love), the leader of a group of thieves, who tells the sheik's son that Yasmin has betrayed him. After his escape, Ahmed takes revenge by kidnapping Yasmin. DVD exhibits the normal wear—almost constant scratches and nicks. The fulsome romanticism on screen could use something more exotic than the droning organ score for accompaniment. —*MM*
Movie: 🦴🦴🦴 **DVD:** 🦴🦴 ½
Kino on Video (cat #K152, UPC 73832901-5220). Full frame. $29.95. Keepcase. *LANG:* Silent. *SUB:* English intertitles. *FEATURES:* 12 chapters.
1926 62m/B Rudolph Valentino, Vilma Banky, Montagu Love, George Fawcett, Karl (Daen) Dane, Agnes Ayres; *D:* George Fitzmaurice; *W:* Frances Marion; *C:* George Barnes.

Song for Cassavetes
Documentary takes a look at the state of modern underground music in America. Through interviews and musical performances, director Justin Mitchell examines a side of music that most people in mainstream culture don't get a chance to see. These aren't simply weirdos or freaks, these are simply music lovers, who love what they do. The life portrayed here isn't glamorous, as the bands play in small clubs, tour in cramped vans, and generally make little money. However, through the interviews, we learn that most of the artists featured here grew up listening to music, fell in love with it, and chose this lifestyle. Mitchell profiles 10 bands,

showcasing their live shows and conducting intimate interviews with each. He spent four years making the film and was inspired by a quote from rogue filmmaker John Cassavetes. As a nice touch, *Songs for Cassavetes* is subtitled "An All-Ages Film," referring to nightclub shows in which those under 21 can attend. This film will certainly appeal to fans of alternative rock, but anyone with a passion for music will appreciate the stance taken by the bands. The film was shot in 16mm black and white and the limits of that medium make themselves noticeable on DVD. The image is grainy and somewhat dark throughout, and there are some blurry shots. As the film was shot on location, Mitchell presumably couldn't control the lighting, and some shots are washed-out. The digital stereo audio does a fine job of reproducing the interviews, but there is some distortion during the live performances. Also, an audible hiss permeates from this track throughout the film. —*ML*
Movie: 🦴🦴🦴 **DVD:** 🦴 ½
Music Video Distributors (cat #DR-4327, UPC 022891432791). Full frame. Digital Stereo. $19.95. Keepcase. *LANG:* English. *FEATURES:* Video montage ▪ 18 chapters.
2000 90m/C *D:* Justin Mitchell.

Song of Freedom / Big Fella
In the first film, John Zinga (Robeson) is a British-born black dockworker whose vocal gifts are discovered by an opera impresario. After realizing a career as a concert performer, Zinga ventures to Africa to investigate his ancestry. He finds that he has royal roots, and that his people have fallen under the grip of corrupt spiritualists. In *Big Fella,* he's a dockworker again, this time in Marseilles. He's asked by the cops to find a young boy (Grant) who's missing from an ocean liner. It's a loose adaptation of the 1929 novel *Banjo* by Claude McKay. Though the original elements of *Big Fella* appear to have been knocked around, DVD image quality is above average for both films. Unfortunately, the same cannot be said for the sound. 1930s recording technology simply could not do justice to Robeson's incredible voice. I doubt that any remix or tweaking could improve these soundtracks. —*MM*
Movie: 🦴🦴 ½ **DVD:** 🦴🦴 ½
Kino on Video (cat #K151, UPC 73832901-5121). Full frame. $29.95. Keepcase. *LANG:* English. *FEATURES:* 16 chapters "Song of Freedom" ▪ 12 chapters *Big Fella.*
1936 80m/B *GB* Paul Robeson, Elisabeth Welch, George Mozart; *D:* J. Elder Wills; *W:* Ingram D'Abbes, Fenn Sherie; *C:* Eric Cross, Harry Rose.

Songmakers Collection
The early days of rock 'n' roll get a once-over-lightly introduction in this two-disc set. It contains five programs that were broadcast on the A&E cable channel. The

first, "The Hitmakers," is the best. It's a look at the songs that came out of the Brill Building in New York in the 1950s and '60s and the people who wrote them. Great clips, great stories. On the second disc, "Words and Music by Leiber & Stoller" is almost as good. Also included are specials about Dionne Warwick, Burt Bacharach, and Bobby Darin. DVD image doesn't offer much of an improvement over broadcast quality. Sound is fine and very important here. —*MM*
Movie: 🦴🦴 ½ **DVD:** 🦴🦴
New Video Group (cat #AAE-70320, UPC 733961703207). Full frame. Dolby Digital Stereo. $39.98. Keepcase boxed set. *LANG:* English. *FEATURES:* 36 chapters ▪ Thumbnail bios and discographies.
2001 300m/C

The Sopranos: The Complete Second Season
Though some considered the second season of the popular HBO series to be a disappointment after the first, a bit of distance has given the drama more depth and complexity. The central story revolves around Big Pussy's (Pastore) involvement with the FBI, and Tony's (Gandolfini) continuing struggles with his mother (Marchand) and Uncle Junior (Chianese), not to mention his prodigal sister Janice (Turturro). Like the first season (reviewed in *Book 2*), this one gains a new dimension on DVD. First, there's the option of watching the episodes at your own pace, then there are commentary tracks by four directors. Both DVD image and sound quality are measurable improvements over cablecast. The featurettes, "The Real Deal" and "Sit-down with the Sopranos," are something more than the usual mutual admiration and self-promotion. The "Season Review" extra is an episode by episode synopsis. And it all comes in a really neat box. —*MM*
Movie: 🦴🦴🦴🦴 **DVD:** 🦴🦴🦴🦴
HBO (cat #99247, UPC 026359924729). Widescreen (1.85:1) anamorphic. Dolby Digital 5.1 Surround Stereo; Dolby Digital Surround; Stereo. $99.98. Special packaging. *LANG:* English; French; Spanish. *CAP:* English. *FEATURES:* Talent files ▪ Awards ▪ DVD-ROM features ▪ 2 featurettes ▪ 4 directors' commentary.
2001 696m/C James Gandolfini, Lorraine Bracco, Edie Falco, Michael Imperioli, Dominic Chianese, Vincent Pastore, Stevie Van Zandt, G. Anthony "Tony" Sirico, Robert Iler, Aida Turturro, Nancy Marchand; *D:* Allen Coulter, Lee Tamahori, Timothy Van Patten, John Patterson, Martin Bruestle, Henry J. Bronchtein; *W:* Frank Renzulli, David Chase, Robin Green, Mitchell Burgess, Michael Imperioli, Jason Cahill, Terence Winter, Todd A. Kessler.

Sore Losers
Goof-ball movie is a combination of drive-in exploitation with quasi-experimental music video–inspired visuals. The plot is disposable stuff about a CGI flying saucer

that morphs into a red Chevy and an inter-galactic assassin who has returned to Earth. Pay no attention to it. Image and sound are no better than tape with exceptionally heavy grain in several scenes. No menu either. —MM
Movie: 🎵🎵 **DVD:** 🎵🎵
ETD (cat #9964). Full frame. $24.99. *LANG:* English.
1997 89m/C Jack Oblivian, Kerine Elkins, Mike Maker, D'lana Tunnell, Hugh Brooks, Ghetty Chasun; *D:* John Michael McCarthy; *W:* John Michael McCarthy; *C:* Darin Ipema.

Sorority Babes in the Slimeball Bowl-A-Rama

Dave DeCoteau's early creation helped cement the careers of three legendary B-sirens: Michelle Bauer, Brinke Stevens, and Linnea Quigley. Three chronically date-less losers get an eyeful outside the Tri Delta sorority house as they witness a buxom blonde smacking the behinds of squealing pledges with a canoe paddle. Being slightly drunk, the fellas naturally decide to sneak upstairs for a closer look, but are discovered doing that Three Stooges bit with their heads stacked atop each other in a partially open doorway. The grand paddler, Babs (Robin Stille), decides to make a two-for-one deal with the pledges and the horndogs: They're to steal a bowling trophy from the Plaza Camino mall. If they do, the girls are Tri Delts and the dweebs don't land in the pokey. Everything goes all right until they find the trophy and it starts rattling and smoking until out pops a jive-talkin' Imp. He promises them all wishes, but things go predictably haywire and the bugger turns a couple of the gals into blood-thirsty demons. This isn't a restoration print, that's for sure, but the quality is actually pretty good considering most saw this flick on early VCRs in the first place. The transfer is full frame and despite much of the film taking place at night, there's no noticeable digital grain. Utilitarian but sturdy Dolby Digital mono. —GNG/MM **AKA:** The Imp.
Movie: 🎵🎵🎵 **DVD:** 🎵🎵 ½
Koch Releasing (cat #8021, UPC 763843-802162). Full frame. Dolby Stereo. $9.98. Keepcase. *LANG:* English. *FEATURES:* 23 chapters • Trailers • Talent files.
1987 (R) 80m/C Linnea Quigley, Brinke Stevens, Andras Jones, John Wildman, Robin Rochelle, Michelle (McClellan) Bauer, George "Buck" Flower; *D:* David DeCoteau; *W:* Sergei Hasenecz; *C:* Scott Ressler, Stephen Blake; *M:* Guy Moon; *V:* Michael Sonye.

Sorry, Wrong Number

A wealthy, bedridden wife (Stanwyck) overhears two men plotting murder on a crossed telephone line. She suspects that one of the voices may be her husband's (Lancaster). The bracing, noir-tinged tale of

paranoia and suspense is based on the popular Lucille Fletcher radio play and its fictional adaptation. That means the story is solidly constructed, and it's well acted. Excellent black-and-white photography may reveal the barest hint of surface damage, but it means nothing. This is a fine transfer. Mono sound delivers crisp dialogue. The hyperventilating trailer is fun, too. —MM
Movie: 🎵🎵🎵 ½ **DVD:** 🎵🎵🎵
Paramount (cat #04801, UPC 097360480-146). Full frame. Dolby Digital Mono. $24.99. Keepcase. *LANG:* English; French. *SUB:* English. *CAP:* English. *FEATURES:* Trailer • 11 chapters.
1948 89m/B Barbara Stanwyck, Burt Lancaster, Ann Richards, Wendell Corey, Harold Vermilyea, Ed Begley Sr.; *D:* Anatole Litvak; *W:* Lucille Fletcher; *C:* Sol Polito; *M:* Franz Waxman. *AWARDS: NOM:* Oscars '48: Actress (Stanwyck).

S.O.S. Titanic

Not a bad stab at the Titanic story, and the first version in color, this expensive-looking two-part television movie has some strong performances and nice art direction on what must have been a modest budget. This DVD presentation, while otherwise better than adequate, has a crippling problem—a third of the show has been cut away, which plays havoc with the large cast of characters in the second half. Millionaire John Jacob Astor (Janssen) is enjoying his young bride Madeline (Beverly Ross) but enduring the cold-shoulder treatment from the other swells who resent his recent divorce. Cloris Leachman is a spirited, spunky Molly Brown, and has the most animated part. David Warner and Susan St. James play a *Goodbye, Mr. Chips*–inflected pair of schoolteachers who flirt with an affair before the Big Dunk—it is indeed refreshing to see Warner in a role where he's not a psycho or a villain. Ian Holm has little to do but act conflicted as the owner who abandons his ship along with the women and children. A grand Harry Andrews plays the captain with fine restraint. Unfortunately, this DVD appears to be a European theatrical cutdown of the longer television version, drastically reduced from 150 minutes to 103. The truncation can't help but massacre the show, which appears to play practically untouched until the disaster. The iceberg shows up at about the 70-minute mark. Before that time a regular soap-opera is developed, but the second half of the show, which used to be about these people, is now mostly limited to the mechanics of the sinking of the unsinkable ship. The struggle of the various parties to realize the scope of the disaster, and sort themselves out amid the panic are dropped, along with all sense of tension. DVD is a simple bare-bones presentation; its own jacket copy seems intimidated by the shadow of the 1997 best-picture winner. The widescreen image is the giveaway that this is a European theatrical version. The transfer is good and the elements used clean, but overall

the show looks a bit soft and a bit light, as if a lot of diffusion was used during filming, and the telecine couldn't compensate. Several notes of the "icebergs ahead" variety are rather hard to read. The sound is mono; there are no extras save for an isolated music and sound effects track. It's pretty much recommended for Titanic completists and fans of the individual stars. —GE
Movie: 🎵🎵 ½ **DVD:** 🎵🎵 ½
Image Ent. (UPC 014381067729). Widescreen (1.78:1) anamorphic. Dolby Digital Mono. $24.98. Keepcase. *LANG:* English. *FEATURES:* Music and sound effects track.
1979 103m/C *GB* Beverly Ross, David Janssen, Cloris Leachman, Susan St. James, David Warner, Ian Holm, Helen Mirren, Harry Andrews, David Battley, Ed Bishop, Peter Bourke, Shevaun Briars, Nick Brimble, Jacob Brooke, Catherine Byrne, Tony Caunter, Warren Clarke, Nicholas Davies, Deborah Fallender; *D:* Billy Hale; *W:* James Costigan; *C:* Christopher Challis; *M:* Howard Blake.

Soul Man

Strange story of reverse discrimination where an intelligent white boy (Howell) is forced to pass as black to get the only scholarship available at Harvard. He uses tanning pills rather than black face but the effect is still the same, rather awkward. As he becomes one with the black community at Harvard he shares their trials and tribulations with racism and fending off horny white girls. When he falls for a beautiful classmate played by Rae Dawn Chong he realizes that he needs to come clean and hope that she can see past his lack of color and love who he really is. Not as offensive as it could be, nor as funny as it promises, the film never quite hits the social commentary heights it's aiming toward. This is another excellent Anchor Bay transfer with good, um, color and sound. —CA
Movie: 🎵🎵 **DVD:** 🎵🎵🎵
Anchor Bay (cat #FLV5285, UPC 7209-17528526). Widescreen (1.85:1) anamorphic. Dolby Digital Surround. $14.90. Keepcase. *LANG:* English. *CAP:* English. *FEATURES:* 24 chapters • Commentary: director, Howell • Theatrical trailer.
1986 (PG-13) 112m/C C. Thomas Howell, Rae Dawn Chong, James Earl Jones, Leslie Nielsen, Arye Gross; *D:* Steve Miner; *W:* Carol Black; *C:* Jeffrey Jur; *M:* Tom Scott.

Soul Survivors

Perhaps the worst slash-and-burn editing job in the history of film was used to chop this muddled horror flick from an "R" to a "PG-13" rating. Cassie (Sagemiller) and her boyfriend Sean (Affleck) go to one last party with their friends Annabel (Dushku) and Matt (Bentley). The party is a nasty Goth rave held in a cathedral, seemingly run by juvenile delinquent vampires. Sean gets upset when he misinterprets an innocent kiss between Cassie and Matt, who

is also her ex. On the way home, a distracted Cassie crashes the car while trying to iron things out with Sean, killing him. Or not, as the case may be, because Cassie keeps seeing her dead boyfriend wherever she goes. Also, she keeps being chased by creepy Goth skanks. So is Cassie crazy? Is Sean alive? Frankly, you won't care even if you make it to the end of this contorted mess. Not too much to say about the DVD presentation other than it looks and sounds great. No grain in dark or light sequences, crisp saturated colors, deep inky blacks—the specs are all good. The 5.1 tracks will give your speakers a real workout especially on the near non-stop "alternative" soundtrack. Plenty of bass and Surround in the action scenes and even more at the club where the ambience is anything but discreet and the music is cranked up to "11." The commentary track offers little of interest and is limited to just a few scenes. The rest of the supplementals are not much better, including one of those short "making of" featurettes that plays more like a commercial than a documentary, and three deleted scenes that deserved to be cut. —JO
Movie: ♫ **DVD:** ♫♫♫ ½
Artisan Ent. (cat #12351, UPC 0122-36123514). Widescreen (1.77:1) anamorphic. Dolby Digital 5.1; Dolby Surround. $24.98. Keepcase. *LANG:* English. *SUB:* Spanish. *CAP:* English. *FEATURES:* 28 chapters • Theatrical trailer • Deleted scenes • Commentary: Melissa Sagemiller • Featurette: "Behind the Deathmask—The Making of Soul Survivors" • Featurette: "Living Dangerously—The Art of Harvey Danger" • Animated storyboards.
2001 (R) 85m/C Melissa Sagemiller, Wes Bentley, Casey Affleck, Eliza Dushku, Luke Wilson; **D:** Stephen Carpenter; **W:** Stephen Carpenter; **C:** Fred Murphy; **M:** Daniel Licht.

Soultaker: The Monster Within

Japanese series is filled with elements of Gothic horror, science fiction, mutants, and modern anime themes. It is a good mix as the series' main character Kyosuke tries to find out more about his real past as he discovers his mutant ability to transform into a creature much more powerful than himself. DVD contains three episodes, "The Crest of the Devil," "The World Is an Illusion," and "The Skull and the Maiden." The transfer is very clean and entirely free of defects or blemishes and also shows little grain. As a result the presentation is also very stable with bold colors that are nicely delineated. No signs of edge-enhancement are evident, giving the picture a natural look throughout. Blacks are deep, giving the high-contrast image good visual depth while highlights are also never overexposed. Color is strong and faithful, nicely reproducing the atmospheric, almost neo-Gothic quality of the series. The only distractions are a few compression artifacts in larger areas of low contrast where shadows break up, creating some pixelation. Other than that, the

presentation is very good. The audio is well produced and fairly natural sounding—if you can say so in regards to an English dub of any anime. Frequency response is good and the dynamic range of the track creates an engaging, though unspectacular, experience. —GH/MM
Movie: ♫♫♫ **DVD:** ♫♫♫ ½
Pioneer Ent. (cat #11698, UPC 01302316-9890). Widescreen (1.78:1) anamorphic. Dolby Digital Surround. $29.98. Keepcase. *LANG:* English; Japanese. *SUB:* English. *FEATURES:* Art gallery • Non-credit opening and ending • Booklet • 15 chapters.
2002 75m/C JP **D:** Akio Watanabe; **C:** Masahiko Matsuyama; **M:** Kou Otani.

Sound and Fury

The Cochlear implant has become a hotbed of controversy between the deaf and hearing communities. Once a person is implanted with the Cochlear device, sound is picked up, interpreted, and transmitted directly to the implanted person's audio receptors, enabling them to hear sound for possibly the first time in their lives. While the thought of being able to hear might seem appealing to someone who has never had this sense, the deaf community remains concerned about recipients losing touch with their deaf culture. *Sound and Fury* explores the range of emotions that surround a family deeply embroiled in this dispute, as a hearing brother chooses to implant his son, while his deaf brother decides not to use the implant for his daughter. Emotions and anger flare in this powerful and poignant documentary making it an engaging and enlightening 80 minutes of viewing. The sound on this DVD is good and contains no noticeable defects or loss of sound quality. While the film only contains a digital stereo track, it seems to be completely adequate for this type of feature. The picture quality is equally nice. It presents a very clear and crisp transfer with no apparent defects or artifacts. —EL
Movie: ♫♫♫ ½ **DVD:** ♫♫♫
New Video Group (cat #9484, UPC 76768-594843). Full frame. Dolby Digital Stereo. $24.95. Keeper. *LANG:* English. *CAP:* English. *FEATURES:* Deleted scenes and interviews • 12 chapters.
2000 80m/C D: Josh Aronson; **C:** Brian Danitz; **M:** Mark Suozzo.

South Bronx Heroes

An undercover cop (Van Peebles) helps two children when they run away from their foster home, the headquarters for a pornography ring. The soft image is no better than VHS tape. —MM *AKA:* The Runaways; Revenge of the Innocents.
Movie: ♫ ½ **DVD:** ♫ ½
BCI-Eclipse (cat #44116-9, UPC 7873644-11696). Full frame. $9.98. Keepcase. *LANG:* English. *FEATURES:* 6 chapters • "A-Haunting We Will Go" cartoon • Trivia game • DVD dictionary • DVD-ROM features.
1985 (R) 105m/C Brendan Ward, Mario Van Peebles, Megan Van Peebles, Melissa

Esposito, Martin Zurla, Jordan Abeles; **D:** William Szarka; **W:** William Szarka, Don Shiffrin; **C:** Eric Schmitz; **M:** Al Zima.

South of Heaven, West of Hell

Valentine Casey (Yoakam) is Marshal in the little town of Los Tragos in the Arizona Territory. He's up against the Henry gang, led by Taylor (Vaughn), and he has just fallen for actress Adalyne (Fonda). That brief synopsis hardly does justice to Yoakam's ambitious, dreamily paced western. It's not likely to satisfy purists, but it is a remarkable directorial debut. Yoakam displays an eye for strong images. That also leads to a certain self-indulgence and a two-hour plus running time. On DVD, the film simply looks great. The muted, dusty color scheme is reproduced with no excess grain. Surround is well employed. Recommended to adventurous audiences. —MM
Movie: ♫♫♫ **DVD:** ♫♫♫
Studio Home Ent. (cat #7657D, UPC 031-398765721). Widescreen letterboxed. Dolby Digital 5.1 Surround. $24.98. Keepcase. *LANG:* English. *SUB:* English; French; Spanish. *CAP:* English. *FEATURES:* 30 chapters • Isolated music score • Commentary • Trailer • Behind-the-scenes footage • Deleted scenes.
2001 (R) 133m/C Dwight Yoakam, Bridget Fonda, Vince Vaughn, Billy Bob Thornton, Peter Fonda, Bud Cort, Michael Jeter, Paul (Pee-wee Herman) Reubens; **D:** Dwight Yoakam; **W:** Dwight Yoakam; **C:** James Glennon; **M:** Dwight Yoakam.

South Park: Bigger, Longer and Uncut

The most unlikely critical darling of the summer of 1999 caught everybody's attention with its MPAA-baiting language and sexual subject matter, and made audiences laugh a lot along the way. Stan, Kenny, Cartman, and Kyle sneak into an "R"-rated movie and shock their families with what they learn (and what they say!). Concerned South Park parents form a censorship board to take on Canada, which results in a war with incredible amounts of bloody animated violence. The plot is tighter than you'd expect and the music is better. The animation is made up mostly of primary colors, and they shine on this version, without chroma noise and without oversaturation. The picture is very clear and there is no graininess or pixelation. The Surround mix is very good and the musical numbers sound fantastic. The battle scenes make good use of the split Surround sounds with good directional integration. The audio itself is well-balanced and the dialogue is always clear. —MM/GH
Movie: ♫♫♫ **DVD:** ♫♫♫
Paramount Home Video (UPC 097363368-243). Widescreen (1.85:1) anamorphic. Dolby Digital. $19.98. Keepcase. *LANG:* English; French. *SUB:* English. *FEATURES:* 3 theatrical trailers.

1999 (R) 80m/C D: Trey Parker; **W:** Trey Parker, Matt Stone, Pam Brady; **M:** Marc Shaiman, Trey Parker; **V:** Trey Parker, Matt Stone, Isaac Hayes, George Clooney, Minnie Driver, Mike Judge, Eric Idle, Mary Kay Bergman, Brent Spiner, Nick Rhodes, Stewart Copeland. *AWARDS:* NOM: Oscars '99: Song ("Blame Canada").

South Park: Insults to Injury

Four more episodes from those naughty animated boys, featuring the show's usual mix of biting social commentary and bathroom humor. These episodes push the envelope even further, and are sure to contain something to offend everyone. Includes "It Hits the Fan," "Cripple Fight," "Scott Tenorman Must Die," and the unspeakably crass "Proper Condom Use." Picture is about equal to the original broadcast; the sound is a two-channel Dolby mix that works fine. *—BG*
Movie: ♫♫ ½ **DVD:** ♫♫♫
Warner (cat #37535). Full frame. $19.98. Snapper. *LANG:* English. *SUB:* English; French. *FEATURES:* 4 chapters ☛ Trailers.
2002 88m/C D: Trey Parker, Matt Stone; **W:** Trey Parker, Matt Stone; **V:** Trey Parker, Matt Stone.

Southern Man

Turgid, undernourished drama revolves around an actor (Withers) who goes back to Nashville from Los Angeles to work out childhood problems involving sexual abuse. On DVD, color is faded and grain is heavy. The film appears to have been shot on video and the image somehow looks worse than most VHS tapes. *—MM*
Movie: ♫♫ **DVD:** ♫ ½
Vanguard Intl. Cinema (cat #VF0188). Full frame. $29.98. Keepcase. *LANG:* English. *FEATURES:* 14 chapters.
1999 104m/C Mark Withers, Ellia Vierling, Jesse Head, Leigh Rose, Jack Betts; **D:** Rick Rosenberg; **W:** Rick Rosenberg, Robert Northup; **C:** Ken Glassing; **M:** Matthew Ferrado.

The Southerner

A man (Scott) used to working for others is given some land by an uncle and decides to pack up his family and try farming for himself. They find hardships as they struggle to support themselves in this superb naturalistic celebration of a family fight to survive amid the elements. Novelist William Faulkner had an uncredited hand in the adaptation of George Sessions Perry's story "Hold Autumn in Your Hand." Faulkner thought Renoir the best contemporary director and later said this film gave him more pleasure than any of his Hollywood work, though given Faulkner's overall opinion of the movie business, that's faint praise. The black-and-white image is acceptable, though not markedly better than a decent tape. Sound is thin and staticky throughout. *—MM*
Movie: ♫♫♫♫ **DVD:** ♫♫

VCI (cat #8211). Full frame. $19.99. Keepcase. *LANG:* English. *FEATURES:* Cast & crew thumbnail bios ☛ Edgar Kennedy's comic short "Baby Daze" ☛ 20 chapters.
1945 91m/B Zachary Scott, Betty Field, Beulah Bondi, Norman Lloyd, Bunny Sunshine, Jay Gilpin, Estelle Taylor, Blanche Yurka, Percy Kilbride, J. Carrol Naish; **D:** Jean Renoir; **W:** Jean Renoir, Hugo Butler, William Faulkner; **C:** Lucien N. Andriot; **M:** Werner Janssen. *AWARDS:* Natl. Bd. of Review '45: Director (Renoir); Venice Film Fest. '46: Film; NOM: Oscars '45: Director (Renoir), Sound, Orig. Dramatic Score.

Southpaw

Documentary about Irish boxer Francis Barrett wears its rough visuals with pride. Barrett is a "Traveller," or gypsy. Travellers gather in "caravans" (mobile homes) and live in what appears to be extreme poverty. According to the film, they're also discriminated against by the rest of society and so Barrett's training and rise through the ranks is a story that has innate appeal. He's an attractive, knockabout protagonist, too. His accent and several others are so thick that the filmmakers provide yellow subtitles. The film may be a bit of a hard sell to audiences looking for typical Hollywood fare, but it's a solid sports film, recommended to fans of *On the Ropes.* DVD image is not really much better than tape, but again, that's intentional. Sound and subtitles are fine. *—MM*
Movie: ♫♫♫ **DVD:** ♫♫ ½
Image Ent. (cat #ID0599SLDVD, UPC 014-381059922). Full frame. Dolby Digital Stereo. $24.98. Keepcase. *LANG:* English. *SUB:* English. *FEATURES:* 10 chapters.
2000 76m/C D: Liam McGrath; **C:** Cian de Buitlear; **M:** Dario Marianelli.

Space Jam [2 EE]

(For film review, please see *Book 1.*) Unfortunately, this disc does not contain a widescreen transfer—so much for "enhancement." But for a pan-and-scan edition, this is a nicely above-average looking presentation. Sharpness is usually very good; there are a few scenes that look slightly on the soft side, but the majority of the movie is pleasing. What really impresses are the colors of the film—bold, bright, and vibrant. There are noticeable flaws—some parts look a bit grainy, but this isn't terribly distracting and only occasionally apparent. The score of rock, rap, and R&B (as well as the usual cartoon theme music) comes through with impressive impact and authority. Surround use is aggressive and usually very creative, making for a very entertaining experience. Dialogue is always clear, as well. The commentary is done mainly from the "Daffy Duck" and "Bugs Bunny" characters, with occasional insights by director Joe Pytka. Although there are some pauses during the commentary, when the two cartoons are chattering away, it becomes one of the funnier tracks I've heard in quite a while. Bugs and Daffy's discussion

over the opening credits alone is insanely funny. The human element (the director and some of the voice actors) serves to inform some of the more technical aspects of the film, but they don't really go into that much detail. *—AB/DG*
Movie: ♫♫ ½ **DVD:** ♫♫♫
Warner Home Video (UPC 0853918317-23). Full frame. Dolby Digital 5.1 Surround. $19.98. Snapper. *LANG:* English; French. *SUB:* English; French; Spanish. *FEATURES:* 3 music videos ☛ Talent bios ☛ Production notes ☛ Special effects notes ☛ Commentary: director Joe Pytka, Bugs Bunny, Daffy Duck ☛ Isolated music score.
1996 (PG) 87m/C Michael Jordan, Bill Murray, Wayne Knight, Theresa Randle; **D:** Joe Pytka; **C:** Michael Chapman; **M:** James Newton Howard; **V:** Danny DeVito. *AWARDS:* NOM: MTV Movie Awards '96: Song ("I Believe I Can Fly").

Space: 1999 Set 1

A nuclear waste dump on the moon is subject to a series of powerful, chain-reaction explosions that propel it out of Earth's orbit. As the moon passes out of the solar system, a colony of technicians lead by Koenig (Landau) encounter challenging forms of life and possibilities for escape. This welcome attempt at serious science fiction features a surplus of intelligent (if scientifically dubious) scripts but is too ponderous and somber for its own good. The leads are likable and the performances are strong, but there's not an ounce of comic relief and episodes tend to feel longer than they are. While the hairstyles, costumes, and set designs are dated (the computers are particularly impractical), they're not silly enough to turn the show into camp. The special effects are mostly successful and the design of the show is clearly influenced by *2001: A Space Odyssey.* While stars Bain and Landau were a married couple during this series' production, their characters are wisely allowed a relationship that builds gradually and realistically. Particular standout episodes are the pilot, "Breakaway," which sets the premise up with a nice buildup of suspense; "Black Sun," wherein the crew prepare for their deaths upon discovery that the moon is being drawn into the titular object; and "Earthbound," which features Christopher Lee in a story that has a particularly nasty, poetic sting in its tail. The discs feature stunningly vivid transfers with exceedingly sharp, film-like images and razor-sharp facial detail. There's an occasional instance of ghosting and some shimmer around the edges of diagonal objects, but it's doubtful the episodes have ever looked this good. "Another Time, Another Place" is particularly impressive. The mono sound is fine, but reveals its limits during excessively loud passages. The photo galleries feature seven images per episode. (Also available: Set 2: cat. #AAE-70151, UPC 733961701517; Set 3: cat. #AAE-70239, UPC 733961702392; Set 4: cat. #AAE-70242, UPC 733961702422; Set 5: cat.

#AAE-70403, UPC 733961704037; Set 6: cat. #AAE-70406, UPC 733961704068.) —DG

Movie: 🎬🎬 ½ **DVD:** 🎬🎬🎬
A&E (cat #AAE-70148, UPC 7339617014-87). Full frame. Mono. $39.95. Keepcases in slipsleeve. *LANG:* English. *FEATURES:* Still gallery ▪ Episodes 1–6.
1975 312m/C *GB* Martin Landau, Barbara Bain, Barry Morse, Nick (Nicholas) Tate, Jeremy Kemp, Barry Stokes, Alex Scott, Lawrence Trimble; *D:* Bob Kellett.

Spaceballs

Almost a classic of screwball comedy, Brooks's film is a remarkably hilarious *Star Wars* parody with a number of wonderful scenes. The story revolves around the evil Dark Helmet trying to steal the air from the little planet of Druidia. Pullman plays Lone Star, a jockey pilot who is, of course, meant to be similar to Han Solo. Candy is very funny as Barf, a "mog" (half man/half dog) and Moranis has his best role as Dark Helmet, the bungling master villain (sort of an early Dr. Evil from *Austin Powers*). Although it's more than a little silly and a bit sloppy, the jokes come fast and furious. The non-anamorphic disc is identical to the old laserdisc edition. The picture is a little soft at times, but sharpness is generally adequate. Colors are fine, but aren't terribly strong or vibrant. The sound quality is surprisingly good. Surrounds are used often and fairly aggressively on occasion. There's also some solid bass at times. The Brooks commentary is one of the worst I've ever heard, and it achieves an almost unintentionally hilarious level. He goes from subject to subject, rambling on without ever getting to a point. He follows a thought for about five seconds before moving on without warning to something new. A chore to listen to. —AB/DG

Movie: 🎬🎬🎬 **DVD:** 🎬🎬 ½
MGM Home Ent. (UPC 27616810021). Widescreen (1.85:1) letterboxed; full frame. Dolby Digital Surround. $14.95. Keepcase. *LANG:* English; French; Spanish. *SUB:* Spanish. *CAP:* English. *FEATURES:* Featurette ▪ Commentary: Mel Brooks.
1987 (PG) 96m/C Mel Brooks, Rick Moranis, John Candy, Bill Pullman, Daphne Zuniga, Dick Van Patten, John Hurt, George Wyner, Joan Rivers, Lorene Yarnell, Sal Viscuso, Stephen Tobolowsky, Dom DeLuise, Michael Winslow; *D:* Mel Brooks; *W:* Mel Brooks, Ronny Graham, Thomas Meehan; *M:* John Morris.

Spacehunter: Adventures in the Forbidden Zone

For the first 10 minutes, this one looks like it's going to be an outer space adventure. Any hopes of this happening are quickly crushed, as it becomes obvious that the film is little less than a rip-off of *The Road Warrior,* and other post-apocalyptic wasteland films. The story opens with an explosion aboard a luxury-liner spacecraft. Three

women use an escape pod to flee the ship and land on a desolate planet, where they are captured by odd-looking natives. Galactic adventurer Wolff (Strauss) intercepts an announcement that a reward is being offered for safe return of the women, and heads for the planet. Once there, he finds himself in the middle of a hostile environment, in which a violent war is taking place. Learning that the women were taken by a mutant named Overdog (Ironside), Wolff begins his search, and is soon joined by a headstrong orphan named Niki (Ringwald). Together, they battle many odd creatures on their way to Overdog's lair. When *Spacehunter* debuted in theatres in 1983, the only thing that set it apart from the other *Mad Max* clones was the fact that it was in 3-D. Shorn of that feature on home video, the film is a boring and pointless waste of time. The talented Strauss is completely wasted here, and it's doubly surprising to see *Ghostbusters* helmer Ivan Reitman listed as executive producer. DVD is anamorphic 1.85:1 (despite the fact that the DVD box claims it's 2.35:1). The image is sharp, but very grainy during the special effects sequences, otherwise, the grain is very subtle. Surprisingly, the film doesn't have the hazy look that most 3-D films have when they are shown "flat." The Dolby Digital 4.0 audio track provides clear dialogue, nice music reproduction, and occasional Surround sound effects. The stereo separation is noticeably good here. —ML

Movie: 🎬 ½ **DVD:** 🎬🎬 ½
Columbia Tristar (cat #06539, UPC 0433-9606539). Widescreen (1.85:1) anamorphic; full frame. Dolby 4.0 Surround. $19.95. Keepcase. *LANG:* English; French. *SUB:* English; French; Spanish; Portuguese; Chinese; Korean; Thai. *CAP:* English. *FEATURES:* Bonus trailers ▪ 28 chapters.
1983 (PG) 90m/C *CA* Peter Strauss, Molly Ringwald, Michael Ironside, Ernie Hudson, Andrea Marcovicci; *D:* Lamont Johnson; *W:* Len Blum; *C:* Frank Tidy; *M:* Elmer Bernstein.

Spanish Judges

It's con vs. con in this highly enjoyable independent film. Jack (Lillard) shows up at the apartment of Max (D'Onofrio) and Jamie (Golino) with an offer they can't refuse. He needs an armed escort when he delivers the coveted Spanish Judges, a pair of dueling pistols, to a buyer. They get a hundred thousand a piece from the take. What he doesn't tell them holds the key to their choosing wisely, which they don't, and the games begin. Slowly he tears their sense of duty and loyalty to each other to bits and then punishes them for their infidelity. Of course, they're no angels and have a few tricks up their sleeves. Lillard is great as Jack; it's nice to see him in an adult role. Dressed in a suit and speaking like a normal person, he's downright charismatic. D'Onofrio is always great to watch and Golino takes a humorous turn as Max's slightly ditzy girlfriend, who collects Barbies and deadly poisons. DVD looks very good but the disc

that was sent for review had a problem with the looping and in several sections of the film there is a lag between the movement of the actors' lips and the sound coming out of them. —CA

Movie: 🎬🎬 ½ **DVD:** 🎬🎬🎬
Studio Home Ent. (cat #7826D, UPC 658149782624). Widescreen letterboxed. $24.99. Keepcase. *LANG:* English. *SUB:* English; French; Spanish. *CAP:* English. *FEATURES:* 24 chapters ▪ Trailer.
1999 (R) 98m/C Vincent D'Onofrio, Matthew Lillard, Valeria Golino, Sam Hiona; *D:* Oz Scott; *W:* William Rehor; *C:* Stephen McNutt.

Speaking Parts

Writer/director Atom Egoyan continues his exploration of sex, lies, and videotape in his third feature. Lance (McManus) is a Los Angeles bellhop trying to break into the movie business but with nothing more than a handful of extra roles to his credit. When a screenwriter checks into the hotel, Lance tries to worm his way into a speaking role. The triangle's third corner is Lance's former lover Lisa (Khanjian), who also works at the hotel and spends her time renting films in which Lance appears as an extra. Although well constructed, this film lacks the humanity that separates Egoyan's best work. The transfer is a step up from video, but heavy grain is present in large areas of darkness. The soundtrack works fine for such a dialogue-heavy film. —BG

Movie: 🎬🎬 ½ **DVD:** 🎬🎬🎬
Zeitgeist Films (cat #Z1001, UPC 797-575100135). Full frame. Dolby Stereo. $29.99. Keepcase. *LANG:* English. *SUB:* English; French. *FEATURES:* 21 chapters ▪ Commentary: Atom Egoyan ▪ Egoyan interview ▪ Production stills ▪ Deleted scenes ▪ Bio/filmography.
1989 92m/C *CA* Michael McManus, Arsinee Khanjian, David Hemblen, Gabrielle Rose, Tony Nardi, Patricia Collins, Gerard Parkes; *D:* Atom Egoyan; *W:* Atom Egoyan; *C:* Paul Sarossy; *M:* Mychael Danna.

The Specialist

Lawyer Jerry Bounds (West) thinks he has seduced the stunning Landa (Capri), but she has been hired by the evil Pike Smith (Anderson) to lure Bounds into a compromising situation. Why? Because Bounds is a lawyer, of course. It's really silly exploitation that gathers a host of familiar faces from TV. West was Batman, of course; Bailiff Moore was Mr. Kimbell on *Green Acres,* and Anderson appeared on hundreds of series and soap operas. Given the age and budget of the production, the DVD is nothing short of astonishing. It looks very good, even those wild '70s polyesters and double-knits, and displays none of the flaws you usually find in this kind of low-budget material. —MM

Movie: 🎬🎬 **DVD:** 🎬🎬 ½
Rhino (cat #R2 976009, UPC 603497600-922). Widescreen letterboxed. $9.95. Snapper. *LANG:* English. *FEATURES:* 14 chapters.

1975 (R) 93m/C Adam West, John Anderson, Ahna Capri, Alvy Moore; **D:** Howard (Hikmet) Avedis; **W:** Howard (Hikmet) Avedis, Marlene Schmidt, Ralph B. Potts; **C:** Massoud Joseph; **M:** Shorty Rogers.

Speechless

Politically clueless romantic comedy has attractive leads but little else. Kevin (Keaton) is a TV comedy writer who's working for a conservative Republican senatorial candidate; Julia (Davis) is working for the liberal opposition. They fall in love before they realize who their respective employers are. (The film was written before the Mary Matalin–James Carville union.) Director Underwood does fine work as long as he keeps the camera focused on his two stars. They handle this sort of lightweight material with practiced ease. If their characters were involved in a reasonably believable and interesting larger conflict, the film might have been another *Adam's Rib* or *Desk Set*. But the political subplot is presented ineptly, with improbable details popping up at the last moment. (The embarrassing ending has virtually no connection to the rest of the story.) Viewers who demand nothing more than cute characters and slick scenery may get their money's worth, but for everyone else, this is thin, frivolous escapism. DVD image is nothing special, but then, neither was the theatrical release. It is presented in both widescreen and full-frame versions, though. —*MM*
Movie: 🎵🎵 **DVD:** 🎵🎵🎵
MGM Home Ent. (cat #1002747, UPC 027-616869456). Widescreen (1.85:1) anamorphic; full frame. Dolby Digital 5.1 Surround; Dolby Digital Surround; Mono. $14.98. Keepcase. LANG: English; French; Spanish. SUB: English; French; Spanish. CAP: English. FEATURES: 16 chapters • 3 trailers.
1994 (PG-13) 99m/C Michael Keaton, Geena Davis, Christopher Reeve, Bonnie Bedelia, Ernie Hudson, Charles Martin Smith, Gailard Sartain, Ray Baker, Mitchell Ryan; **D:** Ron Underwood; **W:** Robert King; **C:** Don Peterman; **M:** Marc Shaiman. AWARDS: NOM: Golden Globes '95: Actress—Mus./Comedy (Davis).

Spider–Man: The Ultimate Villain Showdown

While there are certainly some villains present in this Spider-Man DVD, it can hardly be called the "Ultimate Showdown." When Disney purchased the Fox Family Channel, they acquired the rights to the Fox *Spider-Man* animated series from the early '90s. This DVD offers four episodes from that show, which was notable for continuing its story lines over several episodes, mimicking the soap-opera style which is inherent to comic books. The four episodes on this disc come from a story line entitled "Sins of the Fathers," but strangely only chapters 2–5 here, meaning that we pick up the story already in progress. In the first two segments, Spider-Man battles his old foe Doctor Octopus, who uses four metallic arms to do his bidding. After a battle with Doc Oc causes serious damage to a medical lab, Spider-Man considers giving up the super-hero business. But his mind is changed by a little girl who admires him greatly. He tells her the story of how he gained his powers, and takes her for a swing across the city. This is interrupted by Octopus, who uses a mind-control machine to force Spider-Man to commit crimes. But with the help of the girl, our hero is able to come to his senses. In the third segment, we learn the origin of the Green Goblin, as industrialist Norman Osborn becomes the green menace and kidnaps all of those who feels have caused his demise, leaving it up to Spider-Man to rescue them. In the final segment, a small-time hood upgrades his skateboard to become the Rocket Racer and Spider-Man must show him the error of his ways. So, there you have it. Appearances by Doctor Octopus and Green Goblin, with a cameo by the Kingpin hardly constitute an "Ultimate Villain Showdown," nor does this DVD display the best episodes of this series. Still, the first two segments are entertaining, and one can never tire of hearing about how Spider-Man acquired his powers. The full-frame image is very sharp, showing no distortion or defects from the source material. The colors are fantastic and this transfer rivals digital broadcast quality. The Dolby 2.0 Surround audio track is lively, offering clear dialogue and nicely placed Surround effects. Marvel Comics fans will enjoy the comments from Spider-Man co-creator Stan Lee which appear before each episode. Also, an episode of the 1960s *Spider-Man* series is included, complete with bold psychedelic colors and twitchy animation. But that theme song is still one of the best ever. "Spider-Man, Spider-Man, Does whatever a spider can...." —*ML*
Movie: 🎵🎵🎵 **DVD:** 🎵🎵🎵
Buena Vista Home Ent. (cat #25898, UPC 786936179385). Full frame. Dolby Surround. $19.99. Keepcase. LANG: English; Spanish. CAP: English. FEATURES: Bonus Episode • Stan Lee interview • Enemy bios • Bonus trailers • 16 chapters.
2002 79m/C

Spike and Mike's Classic Festival of Animation

Spike and Mike have made a name for themselves touring their classic and sick and twisted animation festivals around the nation for over a decade. Now available for the first time on DVD is a cream-of-the-crop collection of 14 cartoons from independent animators that have appeared in the festival over the years. This cavalcade of animated madness is culled from the dark recesses of the animation void and features some of the best claymation, puppeteering, CGI, and traditional work to have graced the big screen since the inception of the Looney Tunes empire. The picture quality is extremely crisp and clear, and while there is no souped up audio track offered, the existing sound is still very clear and sounds good on a decent sound system. Extras vary from cartoon to cartoon. —*EL*
Movie: 🎵🎵🎵 ½ **DVD:** 🎵🎵🎵
SlingShot Ent. (cat #9148, UPC 0170789-14825). Full frame. $19.99. Keepcase. LANG: English. FEATURES: Selected film commentaries • Selected behind-the-scenes footage • Selected storyboards • Selected trailers • Selected production notes.
2001 110m/C

Spin the Bottle

Jonah (Holter Graham) invites four childhood friends, whom he hasn't seen in 10 years, for a weekend reunion at his Vermont lakefront summer house. This get-together leads to sexual hi-jinks and sweet revenge, as the group discovers that time can change people and that some old wounds never heal. The film is full of surprises, and the writing is witty, but the characters are difficult to like at times. This debut feature film from director Jamie Yerkes won several awards, as did his short film "Cowboy Jesus," which is also included on the DVD. The image on this DVD is surprisingly good given the low-budget nature of the film. It's clear, and the colors are very good. There are some noticeable defects from the source print, and a small amount of grain is visible at times. The digital stereo audio track provides clear dialogue, but a faint hiss is audible on the track. The disc includes an audio commentary with the director and screenwriter, which is very funny and involving. —*ML*
Movie: 🎵🎵 **DVD:** 🎵🎵 ½
First Run Features (cat #TLAD002, UPC 807839000023). Widescreen (1.85:1) anamorphic. Dolby Stereo. $29.99. Keepcase. LANG: English. FEATURES: Commentary • Theatrical trailer • Short film, "Cowboy Jesus" • Production notes • Cast & crew • 20 chapters.
1997 83m/C Holter Graham, Jessica Faller, Mitchell Riggs, Kim Winter, Heather Goldenhersch; **D:** Jamie Yerkes; **W:** Amy Sohn; **C:** Harlan Bosmajian.

Spirits of the Dead [Criterion]

This new edition is only a marginal improvement visually over the first Image disc (reviewed in *Book 1*). The audio track is a thorny issue. The buzz is that although the picture appears to be an uncut English-language export version entitled *Tales of Mystery and Imagination*, the track is straight French, with subtitles. Jane Fonda very clearly dubs her own voice for her few French language lines, but Terence Stamp is dubbed for both his French dialogue, and his English MacBeth soliloquy as well. The track is still well-mixed and detailed, but it is true that without Toby Dammit talking in his Cockney argot among all the continental voices, the dimension of displacement is missing. Not only that, but Stamp's audio performance in English was a full half of his achievement. Here, he's very good, but in English he was world-class great. What's wanted is an international version with Stamp dubbed Cockney, and all of Fellini's Italian characters speaking Italian, neither of which we get here. There are no extras except for an O.K. essay by Nathan Rabin that makes points about the essential conservatism of horror films, but tries to relate the film's debauched protagonists to the "libertine" (Huh?) '60s generation. He also spells Edgar Allan Poe's name wrong, always a bad sign. —*MM/GE* **AKA:** Histoires Extraordinaires; Tre Passi nel Delirio; Tales of Mystery; Tales of Mystery and Imagination; Trois Histoires Extraordinaires d'Edgar Poe.

Movie: 🎵🎵🎵 **DVD:** 🎵🎵🎵 ½
Criterion (cat #SPI120, UPC 0374291612-27). Widescreen (1.75:1) anamorphic. Mono. $29.95. Keepcase. *LANG:* French; Italian. *SUB:* English. *FEATURES:* 23 chapters • Essay by Nathan Rabin.
1968 (R) 117m/C *IT FR* Jane Fonda, Peter Fonda, Carla Marlier, Françoise Prevost, James Robertson Justice, Brigitte Bardot, Alain Delon, Katia Christine, Terence Stamp, Salvo Randone; **D:** Roger Vadim, Louis Malle, Federico Fellini; **W:** Roger Vadim, Louis Malle, Federico Fellini, Daniel Boulanger, Barnardino Zapponi; **C:** Tonino Delli Colli, Claude Renoir, Giuseppe Rotunno; **M:** Nino Rota, Diego Masson; **Nar:** Vincent Price, Clement Biddle Wood.

Split Second

In the futuristic world of 2008, London is a half-drowned city and maverick cop "Harley" Stone (Hauer) is hot on the trail of a serial killer who rips the hearts out of his victims. The genre-jumping film is thoroughly derivative with bits borrowed from *Alien, Blade Runner,* and many other better films. Curiously, the producers elected to use the Moody Blues' "Knights in White Satin" at the most inappropriate times. I vaguely remember the theatrical release being widescreen. The image here is full-frame, clear enough for the job at hand but not really an improvement over VHS tape. Same for the sound. —*MM*
Movie: 🎵 ½ **DVD:** 🎵🎵
HBO (cat #90804, UPC 026359080425). Full frame. Dolby Digital Surround. $19.98. Snapper. *LANG:* English. *SUB:* English; French; Spanish. *CAP:* English. *FEATURES:* 10 chapters • Talent files.
1992 (R) 91m/C *GB* Rutger Hauer, Kim Cattrall, Neil Duncan, Michael J. Pollard, Alun Armstrong, Pete Postlethwaite, Ian Dury, Roberta Eaton; **D:** Tony Maylam; **W:** Gary Scott Thompson; **C:** Clive Tickner; **M:** Francis Haines, Stephen Parsons.

Spongebob Squarepants: Nautical Nonsense and Sponge Buddies

This is the first collection of episodes from Nickelodeon's wildly popular animated series. The title character, Spongebob

Squarepants, is literally a sponge, adorned with shorts and a necktie. He lives under the sea in a community known as Bikini Bottom. (For the record, he lives in a pineapple!) Spongebob works in a fast-food restaurant called the Krusty Krab and when he's not working, he enjoys spending time with his friends—Patrick, a starfish; Sandy, a squirrel (who wears a spacesuit so that she may live underwater); and Squidward, Bob's dullard neighbor. Spongebob is always getting into trouble as he tries to impress Sandy and is constantly annoying Squidward. The animation is reminiscent of *Ren and Stimpy,* another Nickelodeon hit, but the overall tone of the show is nowhere near as crude. The jokes range from truly sophomoric (Spongebob rips his pants over and over) to more subtle (the episode in which Spongebob is afraid to go to the dumpster behind the Krusty Krab after dark is particularly sly). This broad scope in humor explains why the show has become popular with children and college students. Fans of the show will relish this DVD, which includes 10 episodes, encapsulating two recent VHS releases. The problem here is that this may not be a good intro to Spongebob Squarepants for the uninitiated. These are simply 10 random episodes and there is no show explaining who everyone is and what is going on. Despite this drawback, this DVD is quite impressive. The episodes are presented in their original full frame aspect ratio. The shows look perfect, as the colors are magnificent and there are no flaws to be seen. (This presentation certainly rivals digital broadcast quality.) The Dolby 2.0 Surround audio track provides clear dialogue and a nice, if subtle, use of Surround effects (mostly comprised of musical cues and aquatic sound effects). There are several different behind-the-scenes featurettes included here, which gives the viewer a nice tutorial on how Spongebob was created and what goes into making the show come to life. —*ML*
Movie: 🎵🎵 ½ **DVD:** 🎵🎵🎵
Paramount (cat #87679, UPC 097368767-942). Full frame. Dolby 2.0 Surround. $19.99. Keepcase. *LANG:* English. *CAP:* English. *FEATURES:* Behind-the-scenes featurettes • Music video.
2002 123m/C

Spreading Ground

Canadian serial killer flick is built on the murder of five children in one day. The mayor (Shepherd) orders top homicide cop Delongpre (Hopper) to catch the murderer fast and also makes a deal with the local crime boss to find the guy. Muddying the waters further, the mayor's aide (Hope) is Delongpre's estranged daughter. Though the film is handsomely photographed, I object to the use of violence against children as a subject for "entertainment." M it's not. The script is poorly written and the mayor's voice may have been over-dubbed by another actress because her mouth is so out of synch with her words.

Some grain is evident early on but that clears up and the image is exceptionally sharp. —*MM*
Movie: 🎵 **DVD:** 🎵🎵 ½
MTI (cat #9703, UPC 039414597035). Full frame. $24.98. Keepcase. *LANG:* English. *FEATURES:* 20 chapters • Talent files.
2001 98m/C *CA* Dennis Hopper, Leslie Hope, Frederic Forrest, Elizabeth Shepherd; **D:** Derek Vanlint; **C:** Derek Vanlint; **M:** Mark Katsumi Nakamura; **C:** Derek Vanlint; **M:** Mark Katsumi Nakamura, Mark Shannon.

Spy Game

In the film's 1991 present, CIA spy master Nathan Muir (Redford) is about to retire. Meanwhile, his protégé Tom Bishop (Pitt) has been caught during a mission at a Chinese prison. Top brass at the Agency is happy to write Bishop off. Extensive flashbacks (two-thirds of the film) reveal the complexity of the relationship between the two men. It begins in Vietnam and continues in Berlin and Beirut. In the hands of director Scott, the multi-faceted story is easy to follow, and suspenseful, despite the familiar nature of some of the material. That's O.K.; it's old-fashioned in the best sense. DVD does a very good job with visually demanding image. Scott uses a dark blue-black color scheme. It is slightly sharper and brighter on disc than it was in the theatre. The 5.1 sound is markedly superior to the theatrical presentation. On their commentary tracks, producers Douglas Wick and Marc Abraham tend to focus on the day-to-day work of filming. Scott is more interested in the story though there is some overlap. The alternate ending included as an extra is only slightly different from the original and doesn't change anything. —*MM*
Movie: 🎵🎵🎵 **DVD:** 🎵🎵🎵 ½
Universal Studios (cat #21552, UPC 0251-92155222). Widescreen (2.35:1) anamorphic. Dolby Digital 5.1 Surround; DTS 5.1. $26.98. Keepcase. *LANG:* English; French. *SUB:* Spanish. *CAP:* English. *FEATURES:* 22 chapters • Extended and deleted scenes • "Clandestine OPS" behind-the-scenes viewing option • Script-to-storyboard featurette • Commentary: Tony Scott • Commentary: Douglas Wick, Marc Abraham • Job description for CIA employment • DVD-ROM features.
2001 (R) 127m/C Robert Redford, Brad Pitt, Catherine McCormack, Stephen (Dillon) Dillane, Larry Bryggman, Michael Paul Chan, Marianne Jean-Baptiste, David Hemmings, Matthew Marsh, Todd Boyce, Charlotte Rampling; **D:** Tony Scott; **W:** Michael Frost Beckner, David Arata; **C:** Dan Mindel; **M:** Harry Gregson-Williams.

Spy Kids

Surprising treat can be enjoyed by adults and older children. Former spies Gregorio (Antonio Banderas) and Ingrid (Carla Gugino) Cortez have left the business to raise their two children, Carmen (Alexa Vega) and Juni (Daryl Sabara). When the

Cortezes decide to take on a mission to help an old friend, they are kidnapped by the bizarre Floop (Alan Cumming). Now, Carmen and Juni, who up until this point did not know about their parent's exciting past, must become spies themselves and rescue their parents, before Floop can initiate his play to take over the world. *Spy Kids* was designed as a "James Bond film for kids," and it works quite well on that level. Pre-adolescents will love the fact that it's the children who must rescue the parents and adults will enjoy the nonstop action and some cleverly placed humor. Also, writer/director Robert Rodriguez has recruited some of his old friends to appear in some fun cameos. This film may be too intense for children under eight, but all others should revel in it. The image and sound are flawless, but one must assume that a special edition DVD is inevitable in the future. Here, the anamorphic widescreen image is very sharp and clear, showing no defects and offering great colors. (Actually, this transfer is so good that it shows some of the flaws in the special effects.) Likewise, the Dolby Digital 5.1 mix is impressive, boasting nice Surround effects and a very deep bass. —*ML*

Movie: 🎜🎜🎜 **DVD:** 🎜🎜 ½
Buena Vista Home Ent. (cat #23539, UPC 786936161557). Widescreen (1.85:1) anamorphic. Dolby Digital 5.1. $24.99. Keepcase. *LANG:* English; Spanish; French. *SUB:* English. *CAP:* English. *FEATURES:* Theatrical trailers ☛ 23 chapters.
2001 (PG) 88m/C Alexa Vega, Daryl Sabara, Antonio Banderas, Carla Gugino, Alan Cumming, Tony Shalhoub, Teri Hatcher, Richard "Cheech" Marin, Robert Patrick, Danny Trejo, George Clooney; **D:** Robert Rodriguez; **W:** Robert Rodriguez; **C:** Guillermo Navarro; **M:** Robert Rodriguez, Danny Elfman, John Debney.

The Squeeze

Aging safecracker Ray Sloan (Van Cleef) is lured back into the business for one last job by the son (Albert) of an old friend. No cliché is left unturned as a double-cross is in the works. DVD presentation is thoroughly substandard. Transfer comes with heavy surface damage and equally damaged sound. Title is available on the *Classic Heist Movies* disc. —*MM* **AKA:** Diamond Thieves; The Heist; Rip-Off.

Movie: woof **DVD:** 🎜
BFS Video (cat #30295-D, UPC 066805-302954). Full frame. $9.98. Keepcase. *LANG:* English. *FEATURES:* 6 chapters ☛ Talent files.
1978 (R) 93m/C Lee Van Cleef, Karen Black, Edward Albert, Lionel Stander, Robert Alda; **D:** Anthony (Antonio Margheriti) Dawson; **W:** Paul Costello; **C:** Sergio d'Offizi; **M:** Paolo Vasile.

Squeeze

Self-conscious but not unappealing first effort was made on a shoestring budget, with a director who teaches acting at a Boston youth center and wrote his script based on the lives of his three teenaged lead actors. Tyson (Burton), Hector (Cutanda), and Boa (Duong) lead aimless lives on Boston's meaner streets where trouble finds them, despite their efforts to stay (more or less) clear. Faced on a daily basis with drugs, guns, and crime, the three boys do what it takes to get through the day alive. The young, inexperienced actors deliver great, realistic performances and writer/director Robert Patton-Spruill shows a true knack for storytelling. Not a very upbeat film, but an important one nonetheless. Despite its low-budget roots, the film looks pretty good on this DVD. The image is sharp and clear, showing only minimal grain and scant defects from the source print. There is some slight distortion at times, but this is rare. With the Dolby Digital Surround audio track, the viewer is treated to clear dialogue and some nice Surround effects. This DVD contains no extras, and it would have been nice to have some more behind-the-scenes information on how the filmmakers turned reality into fiction. —*ML*

Movie: 🎜🎜 **DVD:** 🎜🎜 ½
Miramax Pictures (cat #25014, UPC 7869-36172065). Widescreen (1.85:1) anamorphic. Dolby Digital Surround Sound. $29.99. Keepcase. *LANG:* English. *SUB:* English. *CAP:* English. *FEATURES:* 19 chapters.
1997 (R) 96m/C Tyrone Burton, Eddie Cutanda, Phuong Duong, Geoffrey Rhue, Russell Jones, Leigh Williams; **D:** Robert Patton-Spruill; **W:** Robert Patton-Spruill; **C:** Richard Moos; **M:** Bruce Flowers. *AWARDS: NOM:* Ind. Spirit '98: Debut Perf. (Burton), Debut Perf. (Cutanda, Duong).

Squeeze Play [DC]

The debut effort of the Troma studio contains what may well be the first wet T-shirt contest ever to appear in a feature film. Even so, on his commentary track, director Lloyd Kaufman swears that it's about liberated women. The story? Young women form a softball team to take on their boyfriends and teach the guys a lesson. On DVD, the image is remarkably sharp and free of wear. It looks and sounds every bit as good as many studio releases of its age. The real treat on the disc (and on the three other early Tromas released with it: *Waitress, Stuck on You!* and *First Turn-On!*) is Kaufman's commentary. Unlike establishment filmmakers who seldom have anything negative to say, Kaufman rants at length against the actress who, two days before filming was to begin, decided that she'd changed her mind and would not do any nudity. He then goes on to admit that he was wrong not to fire her then. Throughout the commentaries, he is profane, rude, and funny. He also provides what amounts to a tutorial on budget-stretching for the independent filmmaker. To access that commentary, switch to the second audio track after the introduction. (There is not a soundtrack option on the menu.) —*MM*

Movie: 🎜🎜 ½ **DVD:** 🎜🎜🎜

Troma Team Video (cat #9012, UPC 7903-57901234). Full frame. $19.98. Keepcase. *LANG:* English. *FEATURES:* 9 chapters ☛ Troma materials ☛ Featurette ☛ Commentary: director.
1979 92m/C Al Corley, Jennifer Hetrick, Jim Metzler, Jim Harris, Rick Gitlin, Helen Campitelli, Rick Kahn, Diana Valentien; **D:** Lloyd Kaufman; **W:** Charles Kaufman, Haim Pekelis; **C:** Lloyd Kaufman.

Stage Door Canteen

A young soldier (William Terry) on a pass in New York City visits the famed Stage Door Canteen, where stars of the theatre and screen appear for servicemen during World War II. The soldier also meets with romantic consequences. Not the most interesting work from director Frank Borzage *(Three Comrades, Moonrise)* by any means, but Image has found a print that seems complete, as this film is often shown running as much as 45 minutes short. Borzage manages to find a genuine warmth, wistfulness, and economy of exposition in what is basically a variety show, albeit an amazing time capsule of the top talent of the day, including Katherine Hepburn, Count Basie, and Benny Goodman. Reasonable DVD transfer and good sound. —*MO*

Movie: 🎜🎜🎜 **DVD:** 🎜🎜🎜
Image Ent. (cat #HRS 9548, UPC 0143-81945829). Full frame. Dolby Digital Mono. $19.99. Snapper. *LANG:* English. *FEATURES:* 8 chapters.
1943 135m/B Cheryl Walker, William Terry, Marjorie (Reardon) Riordan, Lon (Bud) McCallister, Sunset Carson, Tallulah Bankhead, Merle Oberon, Katharine Hepburn, Paul Muni, Ethel Waters, Judith Anderson, Ray Bolger, Helen Hayes, Harpo Marx, Gertrude Lawrence, Ethel Merman, Edgar Bergen, George Raft, Benny Goodman, Peggy Lee, Count Basie, Kay Kyser, Guy Lombardo, Xavier Cugat, Johnny Weissmuller; **D:** Frank Borzage; **W:** Delmer Daves; **C:** Harry Wild; **M:** Al Dubin, Freddie Rich. *AWARDS: NOM:* Oscars '43: Song ("We Mustn't Say Goodbye"), Scoring/Musical.

Stagefright

Before director Michele Soavi would team-up with Italian horror-master Dario Argento for *The Church* and *The Sect,* and then go on to international acclaim for *Dellamorte Dellamore,* he made his feature film directorial debut working with two of the most notorious names in Italian cinema, Luigi Montefiore and Aristide Massaccesi. This dubious pair had made films such as *The Grim Reaper* and *Erotic Nights of the Living Dead,* but Soavi's film would not carry any of the social stigmas which plagued Massaccesi's work. The plot of *Stagefright* is incredibly simple. A group of thespians rehearsing a play find themselves locked inside the theatre with a notorious serial killer, who slays them one by one. Soavi is able to expand Montefiore's weak script by filling the movie with energetic camerawork, unusual angles, and fast-paced edit-

ing. The normally tedious game of cat-and-mouse becomes quite interesting, as we watch the number of characters dwindle to just one. The last 30 minutes of *Stagefright* are very suspenseful and show what a skilled director can do with even the vaguest material. While some will find *Stagefright* a bit too shallow and silly, it is an excellent choice if you are looking for a horror film that doesn't ask you to think. While I'm sure the best possible materials were used for this transfer, there are some noticeable defects here, such as a vertical line that appears throughout the film. The image is also a bit dark in spots. Otherwise, the picture is sharp and clear, and the colors are fine. The Dolby Digital Surround EX audio track provides clear dialogue, and some nice Surround sound effects. This track is well-balanced, with the sound effects and music never overpowering the actors' voices. —*ML*
Movie: 𝅘𝅥𝅮𝅘𝅥𝅮𝅘𝅥𝅮 ½ ***DVD:*** 𝅘𝅥𝅮𝅘𝅥𝅮𝅘𝅥𝅮
Anchor Bay (cat #DV11754, UPC 013131-175493). Widescreen (1.85:1) anamorphic. Dolby Digital Surround EX. $19.98. Keepcase. *LANG:* English. *FEATURES:* Theatrical trailer • Director bio • 24 chapters. **1987 95m/C** David Brandon, Barbara Cupisti, Robert Gligorov; **D:** Michele (Michael) Soavi; **W:** Luigi Montefiore.

Stalker

Mack Maddox (Howell) serves on the jury of a murder trial. He had a fling with the victim but doesn't tell anyone. He then becomes the target of the insane hubby. It's a fairly standard video-premiere thriller that's handled with professional competence by all concerned. Production values are acceptable but modest. DVD provides an excellent image that's only slightly superior to VHS tape. —*MM* **AKA:** *Fatal Affair*.
Movie: 𝅘𝅥𝅮𝅘𝅥𝅮 ½ ***DVD:*** 𝅘𝅥𝅮𝅘𝅥𝅮 ½
Studio Home Ent. (cat #1556D, UPC 806-469155622). Full frame. Stereo. $19.98. Keepcase. *LANG:* English. *SUB:* English; French; Spanish. *CAP:* English. *FEATURES:* 24 chapters • 3 trailers. **1998 (R) 93m/C** *CA* C. Thomas Howell, Jay Underwood, Mark Camacho, Maxim Roy, Bryn McAuley; **D:** Marc S. Grenier; **W:** Michael Rauch; **C:** Georges Archambault; **M:** Normand Corbeil.

Stallone: Rambo Trilogy [SE]

Special-edition boxed sets are aimed at fans and this one delivers just about everything a Rambo fan could want. First, all three features are presented in widescreen and full-frame versions. Many of the features are also included with the previous DVD releases (reviewed in *Book 1*). Image and sound transfers are excellent. DTS and Dolby remixes for the first film are far superior to the theatrical release. Other supplemental materials—seven featurettes and three documentaries—are on a fourth disc. For my money, the screen size options are the most important additions for those who

already own the films, because the earlier discs look fine. The individual films are also available separately (cat. #12652, #12654, #12655) for $19.98. —*MM*
Movie: 𝅘𝅥𝅮𝅘𝅥𝅮𝅘𝅥𝅮 ***DVD:*** 𝅘𝅥𝅮𝅘𝅥𝅮𝅘𝅥𝅮𝅘𝅥𝅮
Artisan Ent. (cat #12537, UPC 0122-36125372). Widescreen (2.35:1) anamorphic; full frame. DTS 5.1 Surround; Dolby 5.1 Surround; Dolby Surround. $59.98. Special packaging. *LANG:* English. *SUB:* Spanish. *CAP:* English. *FEATURES:* 3 commentary tracks • 5 documentaries • 7 featurettes • Production notes • Trailers and teasers • Liner notes by author David Morrell • Talent files.
2002 293m/C

Star Blazers: The Comet Empire: Part 1

One year after the end of the last series, the Earth has been returned to its former glory. During a patrol in space, the Argo encounters a small group of powerful fighters that succeed in burning out the ship's circuitry before disappearing. An interstellar message is received during the battle and it is discovered to be both a warning and a call for help. Fearing an impending attack, the Argo's crew reassembles with the intention of responding to the distress call and intercepting the perceived threat to Earth. Forced to steal the ship, Wildstar and the crew must confront their own military forces who violently oppose the Argo's journey. This second series is interesting and more political but it's missing some of the inherent dramatic tension of the first season's story. Though the first few episodes start off a bit slow, the story begins to really take off (literally and figuratively) in episode 4, where layers of built-up tension begin to be felt and conflicts become gripping. Sadly, the disc is a big step down from the previous series releases. While colorful, the transfer's print source is soft and excessively bright, especially in ever-important facial details. Digital noise and aliasing are also somewhat abundant and the audio sounds thin, noisy, and somewhat muffled. The bonus illustrations and profiles are worthwhile, but the menus are clumsily programmed. The preferred option is to view the entire disc from beginning to end. Attempts to view complete episodes separately are extremely awkward. I hope these problems will be fixed in further volumes. —*DG*
Movie: 𝅘𝅥𝅮𝅘𝅥𝅮 ½ ***DVD:*** 𝅘𝅥𝅮 ½
Voyager Entertainment (UPC 7690710021-90). Full frame. Mono. $29.95. Keepcase. *LANG:* English. *FEATURES:* Episodes 1-5 • 4 chapters per episode • Insert card with episode titles • Character profiles • Earth 2201 AD designs • Clip from upcoming episodes.
1980 112m/C *JP* **D:** Leiji Matsumoto, Yoshinobu Nishizaki; **M:** Hiroshi Miyagawa.

Star Blazers: The Quest for Iscandar: Series 1

It is the year 2199. The Earth has been under attack by a race of blue-skinned

aliens called Gamilons. Driven underground by deadly radioactive planet bombs, humanity is given one last chance to escape extinction. Resurrecting the battleship *Yamato* (sunk in WWII), engineers turn it into a powerful space cruiser and launch it on a journey some 148,000 light years from Earth. There, on the planet Iscandar, is a machine that can rid the Earth of the deadly radioactivity that threatens to eradicate all life in just one year. The gruff but fatherly Captain Avatar, wounded in Earth's last battle, must face constant onslaught from the Gamilons and his own failing health to save the world. Possibly the most influential Japanese animated TV series, *Star Blazers* (original title: *Space Cruiser Yamato*) walks a tightrope between teenage science fiction and adult drama, and manages to both enrich and transcend the youth genre. Many of the story lines and concepts have been stolen for use in later science-fiction TV series. Originally produced in 1974, the series was unreleased in the U.S. until 1979 as part of the post–*Star Wars* science-fiction boom. The DVD set features the entire first season, which tells the complete 26-episode story of the Iscandar mission. The first and last disc feature some of the most intense and exciting battles. Additional standout episodes include disc 3's episode 10 (where the crew must say goodbye to their families for the last time) and episode 13 (young Derek Wildstar—whose family were victims of the war—confronts his own inner demons when he comes face to face with a Gamilon soldier for the first time). Disc 5's episode 19 is a standout dramatic episode as Conroy, faced with the knowledge that his father is dying back on Earth, has an agonizing emotional breakdown. All the transfers are extremely colorful and sharp. The added detail exposes every scuff and scratch in the somewhat primitive animation. There is an overabundance of digital artifacts on disc 1, but that situation was apparently remedied for the rest of the releases. All are recorded at an extremely high bit rate, but oddly enough only disc 2 has running time encoded on the disc. The sound is a clear, vibrant rendition of the old mono soundtrack. The dubbing is occasionally flat but the music is richly recorded and memorable. The brevity of the episodes is adequately served by the chapter links, though a few are misprogrammed and when keyed in, either start too late or bring you to an earlier chapter link. The bonus features are a delightful and satisfying treasure trove of interactive information and artwork. The "deleted scene" is actually taken from the feature film adaptation of this story and details the sinking of the original *Yamato*. The terrific color booklet is only available with the box set and is full of rich background details and an episode guide. Followed by two more seasons of TV episodes (planned for future DVD release) and several feature films. A compulsively addictive series and it comes highly recommended. —*DG*

Movie: 🎵🎵🎵 **DVD:** 🎵🎵🎵
Voyager Entertainment (UPC 7690710099-91). Full frame. Mono. $149.95. Keepcase. *LANG:* English. *FEATURES:* Deleted scene ☞ 4 chapters per episode ☞ Virtual tour of the Argo ☞ History of the Gamilon empire ☞ Character profiles ☞ 24-page illustrated booklet on the history of the show ☞ Map of the characters' journey ☞ Enemies and allies profiles ☞ Previews of future volumes.
1979 559m/C *JP*

Star Slammer

Lovely Taura (Brooke) is unjustly sentenced to a brutal intergalactic prison ship. She leads her fellow inmates to escape amid allegedly zany situations. It's spoofy but not particularly funny. Image on the no-frills disc is very good—surprisingly so, actually. Sound is good. —*MM*
Movie: 🎵 ½ **DVD:** 🎵🎵 ½
Image Ent. (cat #ID6620WEDVD, UPC 014-381662023). Widescreen (1.78:1) anamorphic. Dolby Digital Surround. $24.98. Keepcase. *LANG:* English. *FEATURES:* 12 chapters.
1987 (R) 85m/C Ross Hagen, John Carradine, Sandy Brooke, Aldo Ray; *D:* Fred Olen Ray; *W:* Michael Sonye; *C:* Paul Elliot; *M:* Anthony Harris.

Star Spangled Rhythm

Paramount studio guard (Moore) has told his son (Bracken) that he's actually the head of the place in this WWII musical/comedy. When he learns that his son and some of his Navy pals are coming for a visit, he enlists the aid of a friendly studio switchboard operator (Hutton) to pull off the impersonation. Plot, naturally, doesn't matter since it's just an excuse for a lot of Paramount stars to show up and perform. Image is slightly less sharp than some of the other titles in the Bob Hope Collection, but that's due to the original image, not the transfer. Wear is minimal; mono sound is clear. RSDL disc also includes *My Favorite Blonde.*
Movie: 🎵🎵🎵 **DVD:** 🎵🎵🎵
Universal Studios (cat #21363, UPC 025-192136320). Full frame. Dolby Digital Mono. $24.98. Keepcase. *LANG:* English. *SUB:* French; Spanish. *CAP:* English. *FEATURES:* 18 chapters ☞ Trailer ☞ Production notes ☞ Talent files.
1942 99m/B Betty Hutton, Eddie Bracken, Victor Moore, Bing Crosby, Ray Milland, Bob Hope, Veronica Lake, Dorothy Lamour, Susan Hayward, Dick Powell, Mary Martin, Alan Ladd, Paulette Goddard, Cecil B. DeMille, Arthur Treacher, Preston Sturges, Eddie Anderson, William Bendix; *D:* George Marshall; *W:* Melvin Frank, George S. Kaufman, Norman Panama, Arthur Ross, Harry Tugend; *C:* Theodor Sparkuhl, Leo Tover. *AWARDS: NOM:* Oscars '43: Song ("That Old Black Magic"), Scoring/Musical.

Star Trek: The Motion Picture [DE]

Created as a result of the post–*Star Wars* science-fiction boom, *Star Trek: The Motion Picture* reunites the cast of the original '60s series in a gripping, thought-provoking story. A gigantic ship, masked by a moving cloud, absorbs every ship it comes into contact with. A driven, ambitious Captain Kirk is given command of the newly renovated *Enterprise* and attempts to decipher the mystery of the cloud and stop it before it reaches Earth. Although the film lacks the camp humor and matinee adventure from the series, it succeeds because of its strong dramatic core and ambitious, intelligent premise. Its sense of wonder and tangibly realistic special effects sequences give it a feeling more akin to *2001: A Space Odyssey* than later sequels. Unfortunately, the production was extremely rushed and prone to endless script revisions. Several special effects sequences (which were incomplete in the original release) have been newly finished and restored to this film. In addition, Wise (whose final cut wasn't given the polish he desired) has editorially tweaked the film, adding some scenes and trimming others. The new digital effects have been seamlessly integrated into the film. Unlike the awkward, showy modern effects added to the *Star Wars* trilogy's "special edition" releases, all of the effects for this revision have been designed to appear as if they would have been achievable in 1979. It works perfectly. This version of the film is superior to every other edition. The image transfer is sharp and accurately colored, but prone to grain and occasional video noise. The Surround track gives incredible sweep and presence to the score and the sound effects. The supplements are incredibly thorough and informative. The retrospective documentaries cover all the salient points through well-conducted interviews. Wise is a fine commentator and his memories are strong, vivid, and consistently interesting. The rest of the commentary is more technical in nature, but it ends with a strongly impassioned monologue that every film buff should hear. The text commentary offers interesting trivia and technical information but it's an awkward feature that's too demanding for the casual viewer. Several cut scenes (and new scenes filmed full frame) were added to network television broadcasts and some previous video releases. The scenes that haven't been integrated into the director's cut have been included in the supplements. Most have wisely been left out of the film. Test special effects footage shots have also been included and the TV spots and trailers are particularly comprehensive. Highly recommended. —*DG*
Movie: 🎵🎵🎵 ½ **DVD:** 🎵🎵🎵
Paramount (cat #08858, UPC 097360885-842). Widescreen (2.40:1) anamorphic. Dolby Surround 5.1; Dolby Surround. $29.99. Keepcase. *LANG:* English. *SUB:* English. *CAP:* English. *FEATURES:* Commentary: Wise, Trumbull, Dykstra, Goldsmith,

Collins ☞ Text commentary by Michael Okuda ☞ 3 new retrospective documentary featurettes ☞ Original trailers ☞ Director's edition trailer ☞ 8 TV commercials ☞ 5 additional scenes ☞ 11 deleted scenes ☞ Storyboard archive ☞ *Enterprise* TV series promo spot ☞ Insert booklet with notes and Robert Wise intro.
1980 (G) 143m/C William Shatner, Leonard Nimoy, DeForest Kelley, James Doohan, Stephen Collins, Persis Khambatta, Nichelle Nichols, Walter Koenig, George Takei, Majel Barrett, Mark Lenard; *D:* Robert Wise; *W:* Harold Livingston; *C:* Richard H. Kline; *M:* Jerry Goldsmith. *AWARDS: NOM:* Oscars '79: Art Dir./Set Dec., Orig. Score.

Star Trek 3: The Search for Spock

This film starts where number two left off, and a great sadness remains as Spock's death still haunts the crew. As McCoy suffers from some sort of strange illness, Kirk soon figures out that he's carrying Spock's soul within him. The crew takes back the *Enterprise,* heading to the planet Genesis to bring back Spock. During all of this, the Klingons are making plans to use the Genesis project for their own good. It takes a little while to get started, but once the action begins, the film takes off at a fine pace. The acting is up to the usual standards for the first *Trek* crew, and the script and story remain solid. It's not the best of the series, but it's still fine entertainment. DVD provides a bright, clean and clear-looking image that is consistently strong and impressive. If not razor sharp, the picture consistently looks pleasingly crisp, with only a few flaws that remain rather minor. The audio is equally impressive. The wonderful score sounds pleasing and rich, enveloping the viewer well. Surrounds are used not terribly often, but they are used well when employed. —*AB/DG*
Movie: 🎵🎵🎵 **DVD:** 🎵🎵🎵
Paramount Home Video (UPC 097360162-141). Widescreen (2.35:1) anamorphic. Dolby Digital 5.1 Surround; Dolby Digital Surround. $29.99. Keepcase. *LANG:* English; French. *SUB:* English. *CAP:* English. *FEATURES:* Trailer ☞ 11 chapters.
1984 (PG) 105m/C William Shatner, Leonard Nimoy, DeForest Kelley, James Doohan, George Takei, Walter Koenig, Mark Lenard, Robin Curtis, Merritt Butrick, Christopher Lloyd, Judith Anderson, John Larroquette, James B. Sikking, Nichelle Nichols, Cathie Shirriff, Miguel Ferrer, Grace Lee Whitney; *D:* Leonard Nimoy; *W:* Harve Bennett; *C:* Charles Correll; *M:* James Horner.

Star Trek: The Next Generation—The Complete 1st Season

This, the best of the *Star Trek* spinoff series, started off somewhat awkwardly, but with a terrific cast and a fresh

approach to the look and feel of the franchise. This collection of the entire 25-episode first season is somewhat uneven and overly jokey (most episodes end with a quirky aside) but as the actors and writers begin to design and hone the characters and series, the episodes become stronger and the chemistry of the core cast becomes more apparent. Each episode tends to be designed as an "adventure of the week," but the death of a primary character near the end of the season is an important turning point. From that point the series begins to (brilliantly) build stories and characterizations by utilizing past events, instead of disregarding them as some episodic drama tends to do. Stewart makes a compelling (and wonderfully untraditional lead) and one of the series' strengths is that it doesn't attempt to copy the characters and relationships of the original series. This is a welcome collection on DVD but the quality is uneven. The discs appear to have been transferred from old sub-sub-masters and are excessively grainy and prone to visual noise. Exteriors of the ship's engine tend to blur and edges tend to suffer from excessive stair-stepping. The remixed Surround sound is terrific, though. It's used minimally in dialogue-heavy episodes, but the music and ship sound effects are given very strong presence. The opening titles have quite a bit of punch. The disc includes about 75 minutes of featurettes and interviews, including footage contemporary to the series' production, featuring the late Gene Roddenberry and the (then-fresh) cast and production team. They're much more interesting and worthwhile than the standard promotional clips. The featurettes are just as grainy as the episodes. The number of chapter links is particularly generous. —DG
Movie: 🎵🎵 ½ **DVD:** 🎵🎵
Paramount (cat #15692, UPC 097361569-246). Full frame. Dolby Digital 5.1 Surround; Dolby Digital Surround. $139.99. Keepcase. *LANG:* English. *SUB:* English. *CAP:* English. *FEATURES:* 8 chapters per episode ☛ "The Beginning" featurette ☛ "Crew Analysis" featurette ☛ "Making of a Legend" featurette ☛ "Memorable Missions" featurette.
1987 1183m/C Patrick Stewart, Michael Dorn, Jonathon Frakes, Gates (Cheryl) McFadden, Marina Sirtis, Denise Crosby, Brent Spiner, Wil Wheaton, LeVar Burton, DeForest Kelley; **W:** Gene Roddenberry.

Star Trek: The Next Generation—The Complete 2nd Season

The second season (featuring 22 episodes) finds the cast in solid form, enacting a batch of improved, meatier scripts. The strong-willed Dr. Pulaski (Diana Muldaur) replaces Dr. Crusher (McFadden), bringing some fire to her relations with Captain Picard (Stewart). Highlights of the season are the thought-provoking "The Measure of a Man," in which the android Data (Spiner) has to prove that

he has rights as a sentient being and "Q Who," the first episode featuring the popular cybernetic villains known as "The Borg." A strong, fairly well-balanced season with better stories, and strong episodes for the entire cast. The image and sound quality are equal to that in the "Season One" collection. The featurettes are terrific, feature little overlap and are all worthwhile. The "Inside Starfleet Archives" short is a tour of the enormous prop warehouse housing props from all of the TV series and films. All of the featurettes are overtly grainy and prone to digital noise whenever text appears on-screen. —DG
Movie: 🎵🎵🎵 **DVD:** 🎵🎵
Paramount (cat #15690, UPC 097361569-048). Full frame. Dolby Digital 5.1 Surround; Dolby Digital Surround. $139.99. Foldout keepcase. *LANG:* English. *SUB:* English. *CAP:* English. *FEATURES:* "Mission Overview: Year Two" featurette ☛ "Departmental Briefing: Production" featurette ☛ "Departmental Briefing: Memorable Missions" featurette ☛ "Selected Crew Analysis: Year Two" featurette ☛ "Inside Starfleet Archives" featurette ☛ Booklet.
1989 999m/C Diana Muldaur, Patrick Stewart, Jonathon Frakes, LeVar Burton, Michael Dorn, Marina Sirtis, Brent Spiner, Gates (Cheryl) McFadden, John de Lancie.

Star Warp'd

The *Star Wars* spoof is alive, and although we would like to believe it is doing well, it seems that *Star Warp'd* is out to prove the opposite. Taking characters from the popular *Star Wars* and *Star Trek* sagas (plus a host of other sci-fi favorites), dubbing them with less than imaginative names such as Darth Vapor, Mini Mall, and Mr. Spuck, and pitting them against one another in an effort to conquer the universe is the general modus operandi of this 32-minute feature. Unfortunately, the cheap claymation and sagging dialogue are a little too close to *Celebrity Deathmatch* and not close enough to being an original thought. The picture quality of this film is good with no noticeable artifacts. The colors are good and the picture is crisp and clear. The audio quality is equally decent making full use of both speakers on the Dolby stereo track with no noticeable defects throughout the course of the picture. —EL
Movie: 𝚆𝚘𝚘𝚏 **DVD:** 🎵🎵🎵
Synapse (cat #SFD0019, UPC 05439030-1999). Full frame. Dolby Digital Stereo. $12.95. Keepcase. *LANG:* English. *FEATURES:* 8 chapters ☛ Commentary ☛ Behind-the-scenes footage ☛ Upcoming sequel sneak peak.
2001 32m/C D: Pete Schuermann; **W:** Pete Schuermann, John Schuermann, Miko Davis.

Star Wars: Episode 1— The Phantom Menace

Lucas's first *Star Wars* film in 16 years is also the beginning of his "prequel" trilogy. Jedi Master Qui-Gon Jinn (Neeson) and rebellious apprentice Obi-Wan Kenobi

(McGregor) are sent to the peaceful planet of Naboo to aid young Queen Amidala (Portman) who is being forced to sign a Trade Federation treaty. When the Jedi escape to Tatooine with Amidala, they encounter a slave boy, Anakin (Lloyd), whom Qui-Gon Jinn realizes is empowered by the Force, and are pursued by the Federation and the evil Dark Lord, Darth Maul (Park). The story and characters are aimed at a younger audience than the original films, and the action sequences—particularly the famous Podrace—have more of a video game quality. DVD delivers an image much brighter and sharper than my multiplex can deliver, and that makes the film's shortcomings even more glaringly obvious. Despite the repeated claims of the filmmakers on the commentary track, the computer-generated effects, characters, and backgrounds are not "photorealistic." They're as easy to spot as a tutu on a buzzard. Not one moment of these million-dollar effects can match Darth Vader's entrance in *Star Wars*. Surround effects are equally important, again surpassing the theatrical experience. Most of the extensive extras are on the second disc of the set. With the film on the first disc is an exemplary commentary track with Lucas and six of his creative collaborators. They tend to stick to the technical details that fans are interested in, and their voices are identified with superscripts and presented on separate Surround speakers. Both of those are very helpful innovations that should become standard practice on future top-drawer discs. In the end, the extras are much more impressive than the feature itself. —MM
Movie: 🎵🎵 **DVD:** 🎵🎵🎵🎵
20th Century Fox (cat #2002391, UPC 024543023913). Widescreen (2.35:1) anamorphic. Dolby Digital 5.1 Surround EX; Dolby Digital Surround. $24.99. Keepcase. *LANG:* English; Spanish. *SUB:* English. *CAP:* English. *FEATURES:* 50 chapters ☛ Commentary ☛ 7 deleted scenes ☛ Trailers and TV spots ☛ Documentaries ☛ Featurettes ☛ Music video ☛ Storyboard-to-animatic-to-film comparisons of Podrace and Submarine ☛ Animatics and still galleries ☛ Advertising materials ☛ DVD-ROM features.
1999 (PG) 130m/C Liam Neeson, Ewan McGregor, Natalie Portman, Jake Lloyd, Ian McDiarmid, Samuel L. Jackson, Ray Park, Pernilla August, Terence Stamp, Brian Blessed, Oliver Ford Davies, Hugh Quarshie, Ralph Brown, Sofia Coppola; **D:** George Lucas; **W:** George Lucas; **C:** David Tattersall; **M:** John Williams; **V:** Ahmed Best, Frank Oz. AWARDS: MTV Movie Awards '00: Action Seq; NOM: Oscars '99: Sound, Visual FX; MTV Movie Awards '00: Villain (Park), Fight (Liam Neeson/Ewan McGregor/Ray Park); Golden Raspberries '99: Worst Picture, Worst Support. Actor (Lloyd), Worst Support. Actress (Coppola), Worst Director (Lucas), Worst Screenplay.

Stardom

Here is an interesting film from Canada which examines and lampoons the lives of the rich and famous. Shot as a pseudo-documentary, *Stardom* follows the life of Tina Menzhal (Jessica Pare), a young hockey player who is discovered by a modeling agency and becomes an overnight sensation. Various cameras follow Tina as she goes from the runway to talk shows to international scandals. What makes this film intriguing (besides the inventive camera-work) is that Tina is never allowed to express herself. Everything that we know about her is based on her appearance and what the media dredges up on her. Thus, *Stardom* is a diatribe against our media-age, which can create personalities without an individual's direct input. On DVD, *Stardom* offers a crisp clear transfer, showing only minimal grain. The Dolby 2.0 Surround track is very impressive, outdoing some 5.1 tracks. Sadly, this disc is shorn of extras, as a behind-the-scenes look at the making of the film would have been greatly appreciated. —ML

Movie: ♫♫♫ **DVD:** ♫♫♫
Universal Studios (cat #21260, UPC 025-192126024). Widescreen (1.85:1) anamorphic. Dolby Surround. $24.98. Keepcase. *LANG:* English; French. *SUB:* English. *CAP:* English. *FEATURES:* Theatrical trailer • 18 chapters.
2000 (R) 102m/C *FR CA* Jessica Pare, Dan Aykroyd, Thomas Gibson, Charles Berling, Frank Langella, Robert Lepage; **D:** Denys Arcand; **W:** Denys Arcand, Jacob Potashnik; **C:** Guy Dufaux; **M:** François Dompierre.

Startup.com

Timely, tragic documentary chronicles the creation of a new Internet company started by 20-something friends, who succeed in raising millions of dollars in capital and find themselves with a hundred employees, serious competition, and a crumbling marketplace. Serendipity brought director Noujaim in on the crucial, early stages of this project and it turned out to be a fascinating portrait of the possibilities and pitfalls of the American dream. One truly feels the sense of loss as business decisions effectively destroy Tom and Kaleil's long-term friendship and also as the multi-million dollar business collapses in ruin just a year and a half after launching. Recorded on digital video, the film itself is attractive but has occasional video noise. The audio is surprisingly clear. The featurettes are passable and the trailers are overdone camp, but the audio commentary is excellent. A must-see for anyone who's thinking of going into business. —DG

Movie: ♫♫♫ **DVD:** ♫♫♫
Artisan Ent. (cat #11986, UPC 012236-119869). Full frame. Dolby Surround 5.1. $24.98. Keepcase. *LANG:* English. *CAP:* English. *FEATURES:* Trailers • Featurette: "Documentarians on Documentary" • Cast and crew bios • Production notes • Commentary: Noujaim, Hegedus • 24 chapters.
2001 103m/C D: Chris Hegedus, Jehane Noujaim; **C:** Jehane Noujaim.

State and Main

Hollywood filmmakers descend on tiny Waterford, Vermont, where the locals are promptly dazzled by showbiz glitter and/or overcome by greed. Much of the action revolves around Hoffman playing a naïve writer who is forced to rewrite his script entitled *The Old Mill* when the director (Macy) discovers that the town's mill burned down years ago. Meanwhile, the star (Baldwin) has become involved with a local teenager (Stiles) who knows what she wants, and the leading lady (Parker) has decided that she won't do her nude scene after all. It's an entertaining, loosely woven take on material that writer/director Mamet has treated more seriously elsewhere. Ignore the loose ends and enjoy a talented ensemble cast that's having fun. DVD contains widescreen and full-frame versions of the film. Both look fine. I could see no visual flaws worth mentioning. Sound is acceptable. —MM

Movie: ♫♫♫ **DVD:** ♫♫♫ ½
New Line (cat #N5253, UPC 79404352-5322). Widescreen (2.35:1) anamorphic; full frame. Dolby Digital 5.1 Surround Stereo; Dolby Digital Surround. $24.98. Snapper. *LANG:* English. *SUB:* English. *CAP:* English. *FEATURES:* 17 chapters • Commentary: Parker, Macy, Gregg, Paymer, LuPone • DVD-ROM features • Trailer • Filmographies.
2000 (R) 90m/C Alec Baldwin, Philip Seymour Hoffman, William H. Macy, Julia Stiles, David Paymer, Rebecca Pidgeon, Sarah Jessica Parker, Charles Durning, Patti LuPone; **D:** David Mamet; **W:** David Mamet; **C:** Oliver Stapleton; **M:** Theodore Shapiro.

States of Control

Penetrating, disturbing character study follows Lisa (Van Dyck) as she transforms herself from secure Manhattan wife into something much different and difficult to define. Image is pale, grainy, and washed-out, with harshly shadowed areas of darkness. That's absolutely the right way for the film to look on any medium. DVD exhibits some aliasing, too, but that's not really worth consideration. This is one of those strange films that's going to repel as many viewers as it attracts. The director interview extra is text that is far too small to read on a conventionally sized monitor. —MM

Movie: ♫♫ ½ **DVD:** ♫♫
Vanguard Intl. Cinema (cat #VF0198). Widescreen letterboxed. $29.95. Keepcase. *LANG:* English. *FEATURES:* Trailer • 10 chapters.
1998 84m/C Jennifer Van Dyck, Stephen Bogardus, John Cunningham, Ellen Greene, Jennie Moreau, Nancy Giles; **D:** Zack Winestine; **W:** Zack Winestine; **C:** Susan Starr; **M:** Richard Termini.

Stavisky

Straight political-historical drama mostly breaks away from its director's penchant for splintered cinematic time experiments.

This lavish, beautifully executed film does what few French films have attempted—to make a compelling tale out of the corruption in France in the 1930s. The film classics most of us know deal with Stavisky-like schemers in abstract terms, such as Fritz Lang's *Dr. Mabuse* films. This show focuses on an historically real high-stakes swindler and his outlandish schemes, which led to a scandal that helped cripple the French Government, and in so doing aggravated conditions that led to WWII. Somewhat hard to follow at first, this is a story for grownups, as topical as the financial scandals which still make our headlines. In France of 1933, Serge Alexandre (Jean-Paul Belmondo) is a grand impresario and financier who runs a glamorous theatre and lives at the Claridge, and is promoting a grandiose multinational bank. He loses fortunes at casinos and can boast a beautiful wife, Arlette (Anny Duperey) and a loyal friend, The Baron Jean Raoul (Charles Boyer). But Alexandre's flamboyant lifestyle barely masks a mountain of duplicity that reaches into every corner of French life between the wars. By a constant infusion of bribes to policemen and officials in the liberal government, Serge manages to suppress the fact that he is indeed the notorious Stavisky, a con-man and gangster who's served time in prison. His grandiose finances are held afloat by false loan vouchers, and even his closest associates seem to stay in his hire only to see how long he can keep up the deception. Image Entertainment is to be commended for making such a rarified title available. Their DVD is handsomely transferred, and the soundtrack presents Stephen Sondheim's lyrical score in the best possible light. I fear that only the minority already indoctrinated into the interesting films of Alain Resnais will even be aware of the DVD, as the packaging isn't very attractive and there are no extras at all. Much attention can't have been expended in the marketing of a disc that misspells a famous director's name on its front cover. *Stavisky* is recommended for movie fans who can appreciate its complicated historical basis and dense political ideas. —GE

Movie: ♫♫♫ ½ **DVD:** ♫♫♫ ½
Image Ent. (cat #ID0668SRDVD, UPC 014-381066821). Widescreen (1.66:1) anamorphic. Dolby Digital Mono. $24.98. Keepcase. *LANG:* French. *SUB:* English. *FEATURES:* 16 chapters.
1974 117m/C Jean-Paul Belmondo, Anny (Annie Legras) Duperey, Charles Boyer, François Perier, Gerard Depardieu; **D:** Alain Resnais; **W:** Jorge Semprun; **C:** Sacha Vierny; **M:** Stephen Sondheim. *AWARDS:* N.Y. Film Critics '74: Support. Actor (Boyer).

Stay Tuned

This comedy takes a look at the nightmare that the Knables (Ritter and Dawber) are dropped into when they receive their new satellite dish. Soon enough, the couple finds that they become part of the evil shows they've watched. When sucked into the dish, they find themselves in a series of weird, dark TV show parodies. It's not quite as good as it could be, and the film mainly seems comfortable taking quick, light jabs as a soft satire of recent television shows. Performances from both Ritter and Dawber are strong, which helps give the material an unexpected energy. DVD transfer is a little soft at times, but is adequately sharp and crisp throughout much of the movie. Colors are bold, bright, and saturated. Flesh tones are natural. The audio is surprisingly active: most of the film is dialogue driven, but there are quite a few more intense sequences that make good use of the Surrounds. The sound seems a tiny bit bright at times, but overall this is a very entertaining film in terms of the audio presentation. —AB/DG

Movie: ♫♫ ½ **DVD:** ♫♫♫
Warner Home Video (UPC 85391688624). Widescreen (2.35:1) letterboxed. Dolby Digital 5.1 Surround; Dolby Digital Surround. $14.98. Snapper. *LANG:* English; French. *SUB:* English; French. *FEATURES:* Trailers • Featurette • Cast bios • Production notes.
1992 (PG-13) 90m/C John Ritter, Pam Dawber, Jeffrey Jones, Eugene Levy, David Tom, Heather McComb; **D:** Peter Hyams; **W:** Tom S. Parker; **C:** Peter Hyams; **M:** Bruce Broughton.

Stealing Beauty

Lucy Harmon (Tyler), an innocent abroad, spends the summer in Tuscany with family friends after her mother's suicide. Ostensibly artist Ian Grayson (McCann) is painting her portrait, but Lucy's more interested in finding neighbor lad Niccolo (Zibetti), who gave her her first kiss on a previous visit. Lucy's sunny nature and sexuality don't go unnoticed by the villa's other inhabitants, including dying playwright Alex (Irons). DVD image appears to be an accurate and offputting re-creation of the theatrical release. Colors are deeply saturated and slightly off, giving the entire picture a bilious quality. Oranges, reds, and greens are particularly noticeable. The 5.1 Surround effects are somewhat obtrusive, too. —MM

Movie: ♫♫ ½ **DVD:** ♫♫
20th Century Fox (UPC 024543028338). Widescreen anamorphic. Dolby Digital Surround. $19.98. Keepcase. *LANG:* English. *SUB:* English; Spanish. *FEATURES:* 32 chapters • "Making of" featurette • Trailer • TV spots.
1996 (R) 118m/C IT GB FR Liv Tyler, Jeremy Irons, Donal McCann, Sinead Cusack, Jean Marais, D.W. Moffett, Stefania Sandrelli, Carlo Cecchi, Roberto Zibetti, Joseph Fiennes, Jason Flemyng, Leonardo Treviglio; **D:** Bernardo Bertolucci; **W:** Susan Minot, Bernardo Bertolucci; **C:** Darius Khondji; **M:** Richard Hartley.

Stealing Home

A washed-up baseball player (Harmon) learns that his former babysitter (Foster), who was also his first love and inspiration,

has committed suicide. Their bittersweet relationship is told through flashbacks. Given the story's curious construction, the two stars never appear in the same scene. Beyond the appearance of heavy artifacts in a few exteriors, the full-frame image is no different from VHS tape. —MM

Movie: ♫♫ **DVD:** ♫♫
Warner (cat #11818). Full frame. Dolby Digital Stereo. $19.98. Snapper. *LANG:* English; French. *SUB:* French; Spanish. *CAP:* English. *FEATURES:* 32 chapters.
1988 (PG-13) 98m/C Mark Harmon, Jodie Foster, William McNamara, Blair Brown, Harold Ramis, Jonathan Silverman, John Shea, Helen Hunt, Richard Jenkins, Ted Ross, Thatcher Goodwin, Yvette Croskey; **D:** Steven Kampmann, Will Aldis; **W:** Steven Kampmann, Will Aldis; **C:** Bobby Byrne; **M:** David Foster.

Stealth Fighter

Turner (Ice-T) and Ryan (Costas Mandylor) are hot-shot pilots. Turner fakes his own death and gets involved with a Latin American arms dealer with a beef against the U.S. They steal a stealth fighter and also raise some hell with an attack satellite—including sinking an American nuclear submarine. Elsewhere, Ryan decides to give up his high-flying days, but he gets called away for one last mission. Will he succeed? This low-budget global intrigue picture was shot entirely in Los Angeles using a prop plane and lots of airplane stock footage. An average quickie, but it delivers occasionally. The disc features a clean, sharp image throughout but it also shows grain in the night scenes. The stereo Surround track strongly presents the various battles and explosions. —GNG/DG

Movie: ♫ **DVD:** ♫♫♫
Artisan Ent. (UPC 12236100942). Widescreen anamorphic. Dolby Digital Surround. $14.98. Keepcase. *LANG:* English. *FEATURES:* Production notes • Chapter link • "Legend of the Stealth Fighter" information • Video trailer.
1999 (R) 87m/C Ice-T, Costas Mandylor, Ernie Hudson, Erika Eleniak, Andrew Divoff, John Enos, Steve Eastin; **D:** Jim Wynorski; **W:** Lenny Juliano; **C:** J.E. Bash; **M:** Alex Wilkinson.

Stella Dallas

Uneducated Stella (Stanwyck) lets go of the daughter she loves when she realizes that her ex-husband can give the girl more advantages. What could be sentimental turns out believable and worthwhile under Vidor's steady hand. Stanwyck never makes a wrong step. It's adapted from a novel by Olive Higgins Prouty and was remade in 1989 as *Stella* with Bette Midler. The image is exceptionally grainy throughout, reflecting the state of black-and-white photography in 1937. Only the language options differentiate disc from tape. —MM

Movie: ♫♫♫ **DVD:** ♫♫
HBO (cat #90760). Full frame. Dolby Digital Mono; Stereo. $24.98. Snapper. *LANG:*

English; French; German; Italian, Spanish. *SUB:* French; Spanish. *FEATURES:* Cast & crew thumbnail bios • 18 chapters.
1937 106m/B Barbara O'Neil, Tim Holt, Barbara Stanwyck, Anne Shirley, John Boles, Alan Hale, Marjorie Main; **D:** King Vidor; **W:** Sarah Y. Mason, Victor Heerman; **C:** Rudolph Mate; **M:** Alfred Newman. *AWARDS: NOM:* Oscars '37: Actress (Stanwyck), Support. Actress (Shirley).

The Stepford Wives [2 SE]

This "Silver Anniversary Edition" of the 1975 cult classic replaces the earlier Anchor Bay DVD, which was released in late 1997 and reviewed in *Book 1*. This re-release features a newly made anamorphic widescreen transfer. For the most part, the image is sharp and clear, but some shots appear a bit soft and hazy, and at times, the colors, which would presumably be bold, are washed-out. Some defects from the source print are noticeable on the picture. However, the majority of this transfer looks pretty good, and it certainly beats the previous DVD release. The audio on this DVD is a Dolby Digital mono soundtrack. While we do get clear and audible dialogue, the sound level varies wildly throughout the film. The sound effects are loud and abrasive, while the dialogue has been recorded at a much lower level, resulting in constant volume control adjustments. The "making of" featurette is refreshingly contentious as director Forbes goes after writer William Goldman (who takes his own shots at the film in his book *Adventures in the Screen Trade*). —ML/MM

Movie: ♫♫♫ **DVD:** ♫♫♫
Anchor Bay (cat #DV11682, UPC 0131311-68297). Widescreen (1.85:1) anamorphic. Dolby Digital Mono. $24.99. Keepcase. *LANG:* English; French. *CAP:* English. *FEATURES:* "Making of" featurette • Trailer.
1975 115m/C Katharine Ross, Paula Prentiss, Peter Masterson, Nanette Newman, Patrick O'Neal, Tina Louise, Dee Wallace Stone, William Prince, Mary Stuart Masterson, Carol Rossen; **D:** Bryan Forbes; **W:** William Goldman; **C:** Owen Roizman; **M:** Michael Small.

Stephen King's Golden Years

A good solid science-fiction miniseries created by Stephen King. Harlan Williams (Szarabajka) is a janitor at a super secret government laboratory. He's about to lose his job because of a failed eye exam, but then an accident occurs and he suddenly begins to age backward. This solves the eye exam problem, but creates a few less manageable ones. The agency that funded the experiment, and the crazy professor responsible, want Williams for their new lab rat, but a renegade security chief (Huffman) from the agency lets his conscience get the best of her and spirits Williams and his wife Gina (Sternhagen) out of town. It's interesting to note that Huff-

man's character is pre–*X-Files* and yet is strangely familiar in shape and attitude to a certain red-headed FBI agent we would see a few years later. Aside from the specifics of the reason why he's running, the story of an everyman chased by forces beyond his control is not new. Fortunately, the people are interesting and the series takes its time developing the characters' relationships with one another. Especially touching are the conversations between Gina and Harlan. As he grows younger each day while she stays an old woman, they struggle with the knowledge that their love for each other may not be able to overcome this particular modern problem. Usually the resolution to shows like this have always been disappointing because you can't really sell the idea that the government can be stopped, but King found a resolution that is at once satisfying and hopeful. The final showdown and the resulting "escape" of Williams hops the fence from clever into the realm of brilliant. This is a must-see for King fans and highly recommended for fans of science fiction. The show was made for TV and the color and sound reflect this with pale colors and less-than-crisp sound. —CA *AKA:* Golden Years.
Movie: 🎵🎵🎵 ***DVD:*** 🎵🎵 ½
Artisan Ent. (cat #11958, UPC 01715311-9589). Full frame. Dolby Digital 2.0. $19.90. Keepcase. *LANG:* English. *CAP:* English. *FEATURES:* 51 chapters.
1991 232m/C Keith Szarabajka, Frances Sternhagen, Ed Lauter, R.D. Call, Stephen King, Felicity Huffman; *D:* Kenneth Fink, Stephen Tolkin, Allen Coulter, Michael G. Gerrick; *W:* Stephen King, Josef Anderson.

Stephen King's Rose Red

While Stephen King's stories have suffered when transferred into theatrical films, he has had a successful run of TV miniseries. That is, until *Rose Red* came along. The film borrows liberally from Shirley Jackson's classic, but the results are a lackluster and unoriginal haunted house tale. Rose Red is an immense mansion located in downtown Seattle. For years, stories have abounded concerning the mysterious events and disappearances which have occurred there. Psychology professor Dr. Joyce Reardon (Nancy Travis) assembles a group of psychics to explore the house and, she hopes, to find concrete evidence of paranormal activity. The group includes Annie (Kimberly J. Brown), an autistic girl who may be the key to unlocking Rose Red's secrets. Once the group reaches the mansion, strange things happen and they realize that they are in danger. King's intention was to create the "ultimate haunted house film," but the movie is boring and derivative. The first half spends far too much time explaining the history of Rose Red, and then the finale comes far too quickly leaving many story lines unexplained. Also, the film can't seem to make up its mind about how powerful the ghosts are. In one scene they can touch charac-

ters, but can't in others. Director Craig Baxley helmed King's *Storm of the Century* miniseries and did a much better job there of presenting a concise and original story. The film does contain some creepy moments, and the production design of the house is impressive, but one can't help but get the feeling that this sub-standard fare got the green-light simply because King's name was on it. The DVD presentation does its best to make the most of a bad situation. The film is presented full frame and looks great. There is no overt grain and the image is very sharp and clear, rivaling digital broadcast quality. The Dolby Digital 5.1 audio track is superb, as it offers a great bass response and impressive Surround effects. (This is one area where watching the DVD is preferable over catching the original TV broadcast.) A commentary is included on the disc, however Stephen King doesn't participate and it gets a bit too technical at times. A faux diary was released in conjunction with the series and the ABC special claiming to offer excerpts from the diary is included. This *Unsolved Mysteries* parody is actually better than the miniseries, as it is only 30 minutes and tells the entire story. —ML *AKA:* Rose Red.
Movie: 🎵 ½ ***DVD:*** 🎵🎵🎵
Lion's Gate Home Ent. (cat #8015D, UPC 031398801528). Full frame. Dolby Digital 5.1. $24.99. Keepcase. *LANG:* English; Spanish; French. *SUB:* English; Spanish. *CAP:* English. *FEATURES:* Commentary ▪ Still gallery ▪ Storyboards ▪ Featurettes ▪ 36 chapters.
2002 (PG-13) 254m/C Nancy Travis, Kimberly J. Brown, Matt Keeslar, David Dukes, Julian Sands, Judith Ivey, Melanie Lynskey, Matt Ross, Kevin Tighe, Julia Campbell, Jimmi Simpson; *D:* Craig R. Baxley; *W:* Stephen King; *C:* David Connell; *M:* Gary Chang.

Stephen King's The Langoliers

Miniseries adaptation of King's novella plays like a bloated *Twilight Zone* episode as a group of people on the L.A.-to-Bangor red eye awaken in flight to learn that most of the passengers have vanished and something strange is going on down on the ground. DVD makes the impoverished production values all the more evident, particularly in the heavily pixelated airline CGI effects. The critters are just as ridiculous but at least are unintentionally funny. —MM *AKA:* The Langoliers.
Movie: 🎵 ½ ***DVD:*** 🎵🎵
Artisan Ent. (cat #10021). Full frame. Dolby Digital 5.1 Surround Stereo. $19.98. Keepcase. *LANG:* English. *FEATURES:* 44 chapters.
1995 (PG-13) 180m/C David Morse, Bronson Pinchot, Patricia Wettig, Dean Stockwell, Kate Maberly, Christopher Collet, Kimber Riddle, Mark Lindsay Chapman, Frankie Faison, Baxter Harris, Stephen King, Tom Holland; *D:* Tom Holland; *W:* Tom Holland; *C:* Paul Maibaum; *M:* Vladimir Horunzhy.

Stiff Upper Lips

This period spoof on Merchant-Ivory movies revolves around Emily (Cates), who has reached the age of 22—the perfect age for getting married. Her Aunt Agnes tries to get sparks to fly with Cedric, who is hilariously more interested in books and speaking in Latin. When Agnes sees that nothing is working, she takes them all for a trip abroad while the whole time she has taken an interest in George, who had previously been the gardener. It's not a laugh riot, but a gentle and consistently amusing comedy. Sometimes the presentation looks overly sharp and often, slight marks and scratches are visible. Flesh tones are accurate and black level is good. Unfortunately, the transfer has a shimmery, digitized look. Good, but undistinguished sound on a dialogue-driven film. —AB/DG
Movie: 🎵🎵 ½ ***DVD:*** 🎵🎵
Miramax Pictures (cat #717951005618). Widescreen (1.85:1) anamorphic. Dolby Surround. $29.99. Keepcase. *LANG:* English. *SUB:* English. *CAP:* English. *FEATURES:* 29 chapters.
1996 85m/C *GB* Samuel West, Robert Portal, Georgina Cates, Sean Pertwee, Prunella Scales, Peter Ustinov, Brian Glover, Frank Finlay; *D:* Gary Sinyor; *W:* Gary Sinyor, Paul Simpkin; *C:* Simon Archer; *M:* David A. Hughes, John Murphy.

The Stillwell Road

This talky, dull World War II documentary short details the campaign to build an important supply road in the Burmese jungle. Narrated by Ronald Reagan, it's factual but deadly dull, filled with endless shots of maps and descriptions of geographical strategy. Never before has the real human drama of war been so stripped of the human element. The familiar background music track is taken from Franz Waxman's score for *Objective Burma!* The second film included in this set is "Battle of Saipan" and it too is dull and makes use of some overtly grisly and suggestive documentary attack footage in the latter half. The transfers are thoroughly miserable. Both films are prone to distracting digital noise and are transferred from bleary, ugly, and occasionally choppy prints. The sound is muffled, scratchy, and overtly hissy. —DG
Movie: 🎵 ***DVD:*** 🎵
Goodtimes Ent. (cat #05-81235, UPC 018-713812353). Full frame. Mono. $7.49. Keepcase. *LANG:* English. *FEATURES:* The Stilwell Road, 50 mins. ▪ "Battle of Saipan" (1944), 23 mins.
1947 50m/B *Nar:* Ronald Reagan.

Sting of Death

Please see review for *Death Curse of Tartu / Sting of Death*.
1965 76m/C Joe Morrison, John Vella, Doug Hobart, Neil Sedaka, Valerie Hawkins, Jack Nagle; *D:* William Grefe; *W:* Al Dempsey; *C:* Julio Chavez, Julio Roldan; *M:* Al Jacobs, Lon Norman.

Stonewall

Fictional account of the 1969 police raid on the Stonewall Inn, a Greenwich Village gay bar, which is considered to have launched the modern gay rights movement. White-bread Midwestern activist Matty Dean (Weller) arrives in New York and gets thrown in jail for defending streetwise drag queen LaMiranda (Diaz) from harassing cops. They become lovers but Matty is also involved with conservative prepster Ethan (Corbalis), who thinks flamboyant queens give the gay movement a bad name. Meanwhile, the drag queens at the mob-backed Stonewall are getting fed up with police raids and brutal treatment. The film is adapted from Martin Duberman's social history. Director Finch died during the final editing stages. Full-frame image is identical to VHS tape. The modest extras are the only improvement. —MM

Movie: 🎵🎵🎵 **DVD:** 🎵🎵 ½
Winstar Home Ent. (cat #5136). Full frame. Dolby Digital Stereo. $29.98. Keepcase. *LANG:* English. *FEATURES:* Cast & crew thumbnail bios • Production notes • Trailer • 6 chapters.
1995 (R) 93m/C Frederick Weller, Guillermo Diaz, Brendan Corbalis, Bruce MacVittie, Duane Boutte, Peter Ratray, Luis Guzman; *D:* Nigel Finch; *W:* Rikki Beadle Blair; *C:* Chris Seager; *M:* Michael Kamen.

Stop Making Sense

Reflecting the group's music, this concert film is stripped down to the essentials. It begins with David Byrne stepping onto an empty stage and then steadily fills both that stage (and the screen) with other musicians, props, instruments, effects, and songs. Director Demme doesn't go in for conventional interviews—a "self interview" with Byrne is an extra—montages, or backstage material. The commentary track is nice, but it does get in the way of the music. Byrne's "staggering dance" is based on Fred Astaire in *Royal Wedding*. Though the image lacks sparkle compared to a conventional feature, it's superb for a concert film. Sound is equally good, even through headphones. —MM

Movie: 🎵🎵🎵 ½ **DVD:** 🎵🎵🎵
Palm Pictures (UPC 660200301323). Widescreen anamorphic. Dolby Stereo. $29.98. Keepcase. *LANG:* English. *FEATURES:* Commentary • Storyboard comparison • David Byrne self interview • "Big Suit" (text) • Trailer • Montage • Discographies • Thumbnail bios • DVD-ROM features.
1984 99m/C *D:* Jonathan Demme; *C:* Jordan Cronenweth; *Performed by:* David Byrne, Tina Weymouth, Chris Franz, Jerry Harrison.

Storm in Summer

Peter Falk stars as Abel Shaddick, a New York City deli owner who finds out that his nephew (Andrew McCarthy) has agreed to sponsor a young African-American child from Harlem. He disagrees at first, telling the program sponsors that his nephew has skipped out on the project, but once the kid, Herman D. Washington (Aaron Meeks), arrives, his friendship with the young man grows stronger. Performances are really excellent. Falk's character has some delightfully funny lines early in the picture. Where these kinds of characters are usually grumpy and angered at those around them, Falk gives the character depth and humanity, while also providing the snippy lines with perfect timing. Eighties star McCarthy thankfully is not around too much as the nephew; he's a convincing jerk, but his performance is the least interesting in the picture. Aaron Meeks also makes a strong debut as Herman, a cynical, street-smart kid who gradually learns to befriend the older man. Director Wise has made enough films to have a terrific sense of tone, which is still in evidence here, as the film never becomes too sappy. Made-for-cable film arrives on disc with a very good, although not quite great, transfer. Sharpness and detail are very good; only a few scenes seem slightly soft in comparison. Oddly, the audio seemed unusually quiet, requiring turning up the volume to consistently hear dialogue. —AB

Movie: 🎵🎵🎵 **DVD:** 🎵🎵 ½
Showtime Networks, Inc. (UPC 7584453-04220). Full frame. Dolby Surround. $19.98. Keepcase. *LANG:* English. *FEATURES:* Filmographies • Trailers • Photo gallery.
2000 94m/C Peter Falk, Aaron Meeks, Nastassia Kinski, Andrew McCarthy, Ruby Dee; *D:* Robert Wise; *W:* Rod Serling; *C:* Bert Dunk; *M:* Cynthia Millar.

The Storm Riders

Conquer (Sonny Chiba) is the head of a large clan in medieval China who desires to expand his empire. The seer Mud Buddha (Lai Yu-hung) predicts that Conquer will have to earn the help of Wind and Cloud to achieve this goal. The emperor sends his troops to find Wind and Cloud, kills their parents, and adopts them as his children, raising them with Charity, his blood daughter. As the prophecy foretold, Conquer's empire flourishes for the next 10 years. As the boys grow up, helping their master to expand his reach, they both fall in love with Charity (Kristy Yeung). She returns the love of both and is torn between the two but one day Conquer makes the decision for them, not aware of the love triangle. He wants Wind (Ekin Cheng) to marry Charity, much to the dismay of Cloud (Aaron Kwok), who interrupts the wedding ceremony and attempts to spirit Charity away from his brother. Flawless transfer brings out the best of the painstakingly designed photography, unconventional framing, and lighting of the elaborate settings. The production design is extremely lush and much attention was paid to make sure every little detail of the image feels organic, well placed, and authentic. There are no signs of pixelation and the colors are vibrant and strong. This disc easily measures up with some of the best U.S. releases. Lively 5.1 soundtrack is not overly aggressive but nicely captures the ambiance of the scene on screen, giving it more dimensionality and bustling activity than a stereo soundtrack could offer. —GH

Movie: 🎵🎵🎵 **DVD:** 🎵🎵🎵 ½
Tai Seng (UPC 601643776248). Widescreen (2.35:1) letterboxed. Dolby Digital 5.1 Surround. $29.98. Keepcase. *LANG:* Cantonese; Mandarin. *SUB:* English; Chinese. *FEATURES:* Documentaries • Talent files • Trailers.
1998 (PG-13) 128m/C *HK* Sonny Chiba, Kristy Yeung, Ekin Cheng, Aaron Kwok, Yiu-Cheung Lai; *D:* Andrew Lau; *W:* Manfred Wong.

The Story of DE-733

Please see review for *Sex and Buttered Popcorn, Vol. 1*.
1942 47m/B Keefe Brasselle.

Strait-Jacket

A camp hoot starring Joan Crawford as Lucy Harbin, who axe-murders her philandering husband and is committed to an asylum. Released 20 years later, she tries to rebuild her life but when more murders begin, she doubts her sanity. Featuring better camerawork than most William Castle films, this one is effectively suspenseful and hilarious at the same time. Crawford (who seems to think she's in a big studio "A" production) devours the scenery with delicious aplomb. The scene where she hits on her daughter's boyfriend has to be seen to be believed. The disc transfer is excellent with perfect contrasts and a razor-sharp, pristine (if slightly grainy) image. The audio is fine. The test footage is a riot and the featurette is informative and interesting. It's a shame the extended promo featuring Castle, Crawford, and Robert Bloch (which is excerpted in the featurette) is not included in its entirety. A TV spot is included, but no theatrical trailer. —DG

Movie: 🎵🎵🎵 **DVD:** 🎵🎵🎵
Columbia Tristar (cat #06929, UPC 0433-96069299). Widescreen (1.85:1) letterboxed. Mono. $24.95. Keepcase. *LANG:* English. *SUB:* English; French; Spanish; Portuguese. *CAP:* English. *FEATURES:* 28 chapters • "Battle-Ax: The Making of Strait-Jacket" featurette • Joan Crawford costume and makeup tests • Joan Crawford axe-swinging screen test • Trailers.
1964 89m/B Joan Crawford, Leif Erickson, Diane Baker, George Kennedy, Howard St. John, Rochelle Hudson, Edith Atwater, Lee Majors, John Anthony Hayes, Mitchell Cox, Lee Yeary, Patricia Krest; *D:* William Castle; *W:* Robert Bloch; *C:* Arthur E. Arling; *M:* Van Alexander.

Strange Dawn— Strange World

Reluctant teenagers Emi and Yuko find themselves tossed into a mysterious land inhabited by a tiny race of people. To add to their dissatisfaction, the small inhabitants of the village "tingle think" that the teenage girls have been sent by the gods to be their great protectors against the other warring factions. Slowly the girls begin to change in the face of opposition and become what everyone hopes they are. Overall, there is not a lot that sets this series apart from many of the other anime releases on the market. The film transfer is clean with no noticeable defects. Although the sound has been re-mastered in 5.1, there is a noticeable sound vibration when watched on a regular television. Unfortunately, the only other sound option is a Japanese 2.0 soundtrack. This disc contains four episodes. —*EL*

Movie: 🎵🎵 **DVD:** 🎵🎵
Urban Vision Ent. (cat #1076, UPC 63865-2107602). Full frame. Dolby 5.1 Surround; Dolby Surround. $24.95. Keepcase. *LANG:* English; Japanese. *SUB:* English. *CAP:* English. *FEATURES:* Trailers • Art gallery • Link to Strange Dawn online.
2002 100m/C *JP*

Strange Dawn, Vol. 2—Strange Journey

Here are episodes 5–7 of the anime series about two girls from our world who are transported to a magic land of little people in the midst of civil war, where they are looked upon as the "Great Protectors." The girls are reluctant to help, but before they can return home, they must lend a hand. The animation is simple but good, and the story is very engaging. The English subtitles seem to be a literal translation from the Japanese, and make little sense, but the English dub is colloquial and easy to understand. The transfer is clear and the sound is distributed throughout the speakers in the Surround mix, making for fine family entertainment. —*DRL*

Movie: 🎵🎵🎵 **DVD:** 🎵🎵 ½
Urban Vision Ent. (cat #1077, UPC 6386-52107701). Full frame. Dolby 5.1 Surround. $22.95. Keepcase. *LANG:* Japanese; English. *SUB:* English. *FEATURES:* Trailers • 16 chapters.
2001 69m/C *JP* **D:** Junichi Sato; **W:** Michiko Yokote.

Strange Illusion

College student Paul Cartwright (Lydon) worries about a recurring dream in which a shadowy man has beguiled both his widowed mother Virginia (Eilers) and his easily impressed sister Dorothy (Hazard). His late father reportedly died in an accident, but details in Paul's dream, such as a distinctive bracelet and a piece of music, mysteriously have counterparts in real life. Paul begins to suspect that his mother's new beau Brett Curtis (William) is in fact a scoundrel, and that his father was murdered by him. Encouraged by family friend Dr. Vincent (Toomey) to clear up the mystery, Paul allows himself to become a "guest" at the psychiatric clinic of Professor Muhlbach (Arnt), not knowing that Muhlbach and Curtis are associates in

crime. The psychoanalytical plot is at its basis more sophisticated than other Hollywood attempts to dumb down Herr Freud (like Hitchcock's ridiculous *Spellbound* of the same year) and almost overcomes some clunky writing. DVD is a smart packaging of one of Ulmer's weirdest. Advertised as from 35mm elements, the image quality is not bad, but looks more like good 16mm. The dream sequences have lots of superimposed smoke that fluctuates in a way to suggest that the original film opticals were to blame for the variable quality there. There is some slight film damage along the way. The audio has been given a good cleaning and is very clear. The extras package includes a miniature reproduction of the movie's entire 1945 pressbook, that you'll need a magnifying glass to enjoy. —*GE* **AKA:** *Out of the Night.*

Movie: 🎵🎵🎵 **DVD:** 🎵🎵🎵
Troma Team Video (UPC 785604205920). Full frame. $19.98. Keepcase. *LANG:* English. *FEATURES:* Trailers • Edgar G. Ulmer documentary • Pressbook miniature.
1945 87m/B Jimmy Lydon, Warren William, Sally Eilers, Regis Toomey, Charles Arnt, George Reed, Jayne Hazard; **D:** Edgar G. Ulmer; **W:** Adele Comandini; **C:** Philip Tannura; **M:** Leo Erdody.

Strange Impersonation

Dreamy noir has chemist Nora Goodrich (Marshall) injecting herself to test a new anesthetic she's developing. (Never a good idea.) Then her life goes nuts when she can't separate reality from her dreams. DVD appears to have been made from exceptionally well-preserved original elements. Print damage is mostly fleeting. The black-and-white photography and evocative lighting are sharp. —*MM*

Movie: 🎵🎵 ½ **DVD:** 🎵🎵 ½
Kino on Video (cat #K153, UPC 7383290-15329). Full frame. $29.95. Keepcase. *LANG:* English. *FEATURES:* 12 chapters.
1946 68m/B Brenda Marshall, William Gargan, Hillary Brooke, George Chandler, Ruth Ford, H.B. Warner, Lyle Talbot, Mary Treen; **D:** Anthony Mann; **W:** Mindret Lord; **C:** Robert Pittack.

Strange Invaders

Body-snatchers-from-space SF with an attitude makes for a fun spoof of '50s alien flicks. Space folks have taken over a Midwestern town. When Professor Bigelow (LeMat) goes there, he has no idea what he's becoming involved with. On their commentary track, filmmakers William Condon and Michael Laughlin remember the early project fondly. DVD presents an accurate re-creation of a soft, fairly grainy image with no flaws that don't come from the original. Recommended. —*MM*

Movie: 🎵🎵🎵 **DVD:** 🎵🎵🎵
MGM Home Ent. (cat #1002647, UPC 027616868473). Widescreen (2.35:1) anamorphic. Dolby Digital Mono. $14.95. Keepcase. *LANG:* English. *SUB:* French;

Spanish. *CAP:* English. *FEATURES:* 16 chapters • Trailer • Commentary: Michael Laughlin, Bill Condon.
1983 (PG) 94m/C Paul LeMat, Nancy Allen, Diana Scarwid, Michael Lerner, Louise Fletcher, Wallace Shawn, Fiona Lewis, Kenneth Tobey, June Lockhart, Charles Lane, Dey Young, Mark Goddard; **D:** Michael Laughlin; **W:** Bill Condon; **C:** Louis Horvath; **M:** John Addison.

The Stranger [Delta/Laserlight]

Tight suspense made on a tight budget saved Welles's directorial career. He plays a Nazi hiding under a false identity in a small Connecticut town. Robinson is the Nazi hunter who's after him. The image on this disc is about the same as the Parade release (reviewed in *Book 1*), save the Delta "bug" in the lower right-hand corner in the first chapter. Extras are O.K. The "Orson Welles on Film" 30-minute featurette is mostly stills and trailers. It's an acceptable introduction to a complex individual and career. (See also the review for *Citizen Welles* for another release of this film.) —*MM*

Movie: 🎵🎵 ½ **DVD:** 🎵🎵🎵
Delta/Laserlight (cat #82053, UPC 0181-11205399). Full frame. $5.99. Keepcase. *LANG:* English. *FEATURES:* 22 chapters, film • 9 chapters, featurette • Intro by Tony Curtis • Trailer for *Touch of Evil.*
1946 95m/B Edward G. Robinson, Loretta Young, Martha Wentworth, Konstantin Shayne, Richard Long, Orson Welles; **D:** Orson Welles; **W:** Victor Trivas; **C:** Russell Metty; **M:** Bronislau Kaper. *AWARDS: NOM:* Oscars '46: Story.

Stranger than Paradise

Director Jim Jarmusch started his career with this low-budget effort. Lurie stars as unemployed Willie. He receives a call that his 16-year-old cousin Eva is coming to stay with him for a little under two weeks; he hates the idea and, at least for a little while, he doesn't make her feel welcome. After the period's up, she leaves for Cleveland; he finds himself missing her and decides to visit. The two of them and his friend then end up taking a journey to Florida. The film is incredibly low-budget ("no-budget," is more like it) and there are pauses where the two main characters are silent—and the silence goes on too long. Although Lurie is right for the role, we aren't given enough details about his life to care about him at all, which makes the slow points even slower. The film has a few moments as it goes onwards, but the opening half is definitely slow-going. After watching half of it, I felt as if I had already watched one whole movie. As the film was made on an extremely low budget, the black-and-white image is frequently very grainy. Sharpness actually is pretty decent in a few scenes, but most of the film looks soft and detail is fair at best. There are print flaws in the way of some marks and

scratches, but this is probably the best that this film has ever looked. The audio is thin and flat. Dialogue is occasionally a little muddy, but the majority of it is easily understood. There is some minor music in the background, but it certainly doesn't make much of an impression and sounds about the same as the rest of the audio in terms of quality. There is a weird and fairly lengthy featurette of the production behind-the-scenes in "Cleveland." The only problem is that this documentary was recorded without sound, so you just get to watch the footage, which is in color, but fairly worn looking. —AB/DG
Movie: 🎵🎵 **DVD:** 🎵🎵
MGM Home Ent. (cat #1000981, UPC 027-606852878). Widescreen (1.85:1) anamorphic. Mono. $19.98. Keepcase. *LANG:* English. *SUB:* French; Spanish. *CAP:* English. *FEATURES:* Featurette.
1984 (R) 90m/B *GE* John Lurie, Eszter Balint, Richard Edson, Sara Driver, Cecillia Stark, Danny Rosen; *D:* Jim Jarmusch; *W:* Jim Jarmusch; *C:* Tom DiCillo; *M:* John Lurie. *AWARDS:* Natl. Soc. Film Critics '84: Film.

The Street Fighter [BCI]

Fast-paced martial arts action finds freelance fighter Terry Tsuguri (Chiba) hired to spring a convicted killer from prison. But after he succeeds, his employers renege on their payment. Big mistake. The dubbing from the original Japanese is part of the film's trashy charm. Though BCI Eclipse is known for bargain-basement presentation of public domain titles, this is a good-looking disc. Image is bright, sharp, and well-focused, belying a modest budget. —MM *AKA:* Satsujim-ken.
Movie: 🎵🎵 ½ **DVD:** 🎵🎵 ½
BCI-Eclipse (cat #44120-9, UPC 7873644-12099). Widescreen (2.35:1) letterboxed. $9.98. Keepcase. *LANG:* English. *FEATURES:* 6 chapters ▪ "Have You Got Any Castles?" Cartoon ▪ DVD dictionary ▪ Trivia game ▪ DVD-ROM features.
1974 91m/C *JP* Sonny Chiba, Gerald (Waichi) Yamada, Tony Cetera, Doris (Yutaka) Nakajima; *D:* Shigehiro (Sakae) Ozawa; *W:* Steve Autrey, Koji Takada; *C:* Ken Tsukakoshi; *M:* Toshiaki Tsushima.

The Street Fighter [BFS]

Image and sound quality are both very good, though the letterbox matte is a bit too aggressive, cutting off the tops of heads in some scenes. The disc contains a bargain triple feature of *Great Street Fighter Movies*, lacking only *Sister Street Fighter* from the collection. —BT *AKA:* Satsujim-ken.
Movie: 🎵🎵🎵 ½ **DVD:** 🎵🎵 ½
BFS Video (cat #30234D, UPC 066805-302343). Widescreen letterboxed. $14.99. Keepcase. *LANG:* English. *FEATURES:* 4 chapters ▪ Bio ▪ Selected filmography ▪ Trivia quiz.

1974 91m/C *JP* Sonny Chiba, Gerald (Waichi) Yamada, Tony Cetera, Doris (Yutaka) Nakajima; *D:* Shigehiro (Sakae) Ozawa; *W:* Steve Autrey, Koji Takada; *C:* Ken Tsukakoshi; *M:* Toshiaki Tsushima.

The Street Fighter's Last Revenge

A yakuza drug lord is using a chemical plant as a front for his heroin business. He hires mercenary Sonny Chiba to retrieve a formula for synthetic heroin. Foolishly, he tries to double-cross the Street Fighter. With all the parties trying to manipulate each other for the formula—police, yakuza, the D.A., and various traitors within each organization, with Chiba in the middle—it's almost as if this were *The Maltese Falcon* with some martial arts written into the script. Director Teruo Ishii gives the final duel some style and spirit, but the film lacks the essential attitude that sets the Street Fighter apart from other movie heroes. Image and sound quality are both very good, though the letterbox matte is a bit too aggressive, cutting off the tops of heads in some scenes. The disc contains a bargain triple feature of *Great Street Fighter Movies*, lacking only *Sister Street Fighter* from the collection. —BT *AKA:* Revenge! The Killing Fist; Street Fighter Counterattacks.
Movie: 🎵🎵 ½ **DVD:** 🎵🎵 ½
BFS Video (cat #30234D, UPC 06680530-2343). Widescreen letterboxed. $14.99. Keepcase. *LANG:* English. *FEATURES:* 4 chapters ▪ Bio ▪ Selected filmography ▪ Trivia quiz.
1974 79m/C *JP* Sonny Chiba, Sue Shiomi; *D:* Teru Ishii.

Street Vengeance

Drug lord seeks vengeance against cop for death of brother. No-budget shot-on-video flick is atrocious in every way. DVD equals VHS tape. Title is available as part of the *Action Arsenal* collection. —MM
Movie: 🎵 **DVD:** 🎵
BCI-Eclipse (cat #44076-9, UPC 787364-407699). Full frame. $19.98. Keepcase. *LANG:* English. *FEATURES:* 10 chapters.
1995 85m/C Mari Blackwell, Michael Eugene; *D:* Rene Migliaccio; *W:* Michael Farakash.

Strictly Ballroom

Scott (Mercurio) is one of Australia's very best ballroom dancers. All signs point to his winning the local championships, but he strays from the traditional routines, and his career on the dance floor falls apart. When his partner Liz (Carides) leaves him, he's approached by a plain Jane amateur named Fran (Morice). Scott's initially against her plan, but as they practice, he thinks that the two of them might actually have potential as a team. The story provides fairly stereotypical plot devices and an obvious resolution, but Luhrmann makes the journey fun and vibrant. The result is something that could

easily be labeled as "light comedy," but pushes forward into something more substantial and enjoyable than that. The disc shows off Luhrmann's high-energy visuals quite wonderfully. Sharpness and detail are both quite good; a few slight instances of softness appear, but the picture otherwise appears film-like and well defined. Colors are wonderfully saturated: vivid, bright, and bold, without any instances of smearing or other flaws. The soundtrack is occasionally aggressive and provides high energy during crucial scenes. The commentary is particularly good, mixing some funny general chatter about the production along with in-depth detail about how some of the sequences were produced. "From Samba to Slow Fox" is an older 30-minute documentary about Australian dancing competitions. It's a rather odd piece that moves slowly and is only occasionally engaging. The extensive 3-D gallery features some animated stills and also features narration by Luhrmann. Definitely recommended. —AB
Movie: 🎵🎵🎵 **DVD:** 🎵🎵🎵🎵
Miramax Pictures (cat #24183, UPC 7869-36166712). Widescreen (1.85:1) anamorphic. Dolby Digital 5.1 Surround. $29.99. Keepcase. *LANG:* English. *SUB:* French; Spanish. *CAP:* English. *FEATURES:* 14 chapters ▪ "Samba to Slow Fox" featurette ▪ 3-D gallery ▪ Commentary: Luhrmann, Catherine Martin, John O'Connell.
1992 (PG) 94m/C *AU* Paul Mercurio, Tara Morice, Bill Hunter, Pat Thomsen, Barry Otto, Gia Carides, Peter Whitford, John Hannan, Sonia Kruger-Tayler, Kris McQuade, Pip Mushin, Leonie Page, Antonio Vargas, Armonia Benedito; *D:* Baz Luhrmann; *W:* Baz Luhrmann, Craig Pearce; *C:* Steve Mason; *M:* David Hirshfelder. *AWARDS:* Australian Film Inst. '92: Costume Des., Director (Luhrmann), Film, Film Editing, Screenplay, Support. Actor (Otto), Support. Actress (Thomsen); *NOM:* Golden Globes '94: Film—Mus./Comedy.

Stripes

Feeling like losers and trying to straighten out their lives, two friends (Murray and Ramis) enlist in the Army under the mistaken impression that boot camp is something like summer camp for adults. The shaggy comedy became a boxoffice hit due to Murray's charm, his sparring with Oates (who's memorable as the gruff sergeant), and fine support from the likes of Candy and other "Second City" players. It's really pointless to criticize the DVD image—this film has never been much to look at—so the choice of image size is the main improvement of disc over tape. —MM
Movie: 🎵🎵🎵 **DVD:** 🎵🎵 ½
Columbia Tristar (cat #79169). Widescreen letterboxed; full frame. $29.95. Keepcase. *LANG:* English; French. *SUB:* French; English. *FEATURES:* 28 chapters ▪ Trailer.
1981 (R) 105m/C Lance LeGault, Bill Murray, Harold Ramis, P.J. Soles, Warren Oates, John Candy, John Larroquette, Judge Reinhold, Sean Young, Dave Thomas, Joe Flaherty; *D:* Ivan Reitman; *W:*

Len Blum, Harold Ramis; **C:** Bill Butler; **M:** Elmer Bernstein.

Stroszek

Bruno Stroszek (S), having a difficult time making the transition from prison to society, convinces a prostitute (Mattes) and a neighbor (Scheitz) to come with him to America, which promises to offer them all a new start. Of course, things don't go as planned, and the true nature of the American dream is revealed. The story relies much on the events of Bruno S's life. He collaborated with Herzog on the screenplay, and his performance is unique and touching. The ending is legendary, and rightly so—a perfect blend of humor, social commentary, and sympathy without condescension. The transfer has a slight shimmering quality at the beginning, which gradually cleans itself up, but looks remarkable for a film of this age. The soundtrack is a very good mono remastering, and the extra features are useful and engaging. —BG
Movie: ♫♫♫♫ **DVD:** ♫♫♫ ½
Anchor Bay (cat #DV11565, UPC 0131-31156591). Widescreen (1.66:1) anamorphic. Dolby Mono. $29.98. Keepcase. *LANG:* German and English. *SUB:* English. *FEATURES:* 25 chapters • Commentary: Herzog, Norman Hill • Production notes • Trailer • Herzog bio.
1977 108m/C *GE* Eva Mattes, Bruno S, Clemens Scheitz; **D:** Werner Herzog; **W:** Werner Herzog; **C:** Thomas Mauch; **M:** Chet Atkins, Tom Paxton.

Stuart Bliss

Curious little comedy mixes elements of *The X-Files* and *The Truman Show.* Stuart Bliss (Zelnicker) is an ordinary guy who slowly succumbs to paranoia and apocalyptic religious visions. Of course, the question is: Is he crazy or well-informed? On DVD the film is much sharper and detailed than anyone should expect of a $30,000 production. (That's about what *Blair Witch Project* cost and this one looks much more professional.) Heavy grain and artifacts are visible in bright exteriors and some interiors. The filmmakers' commentary track is worth listening to. —MM
Movie: ♫♫ ½ **DVD:** ♫♫ ½
Vanguard Intl. Cinema (cat #VF9168, UPC 658769916836). Full frame. $29.95. Keepcase. *LANG:* English. *FEATURES:* Trailer • 10 chapters • Commentary: Neil Grieve, Michael Zelnicker.
1998 88m/C Michael Zelniker, Dea Lawrence, Derek McGrath, Ania Suli, Mark Fite; **D:** Neil Grieve; **W:** Michael Zelniker, Neil Grieve; **C:** Jens Sturup.

Stuart Little [2 DE]

This "deluxe edition" is actually a step back from the first release (reviewed in *Book 1*). Aimed at kids, it's a full-frame release and really serves more as a promo for the sequel. It contains all of the extras of the first film, plus a widescreen teaser for the second. —MM

Movie: ♫♫ ½ **DVD:** ♫♫♫
Columbia Tristar (cat #08974, UPC 0433-96089747). Full frame. Dolby Digital 5.1 Surround; Dolby Surround. $19.95. Keepcase. *LANG:* English. *SUB:* English. *CAP:* English. *FEATURES:* Games • Visual effects interactive featurette • Music videos • 28 chapters • Artists' screen tests • Deleted scenes • Visual effects gag reel • Production gag reel • Boat race early concept reel • Screen tests • HBO special • Cast & crew thumbnail bios • Trailers • Commentary: director and animation supervisor • Commentary: visual effects supervisor • Promotional material for *Stuart Little 2.*
1999 (PG) 92m/C Geena Davis, Hugh Laurie, Jonathan Lipnicki, Brian Doyle-Murray, Estelle Getty, Julia Sweeney, Dabney Coleman; **D:** Rob Minkoff; **W:** M. Night Shyamalan; **C:** Guillermo Navarro; **M:** Alan Silvestri; **V:** Michael J. Fox, Nathan Lane, Chazz Palminteri, Steve Zahn, Bruno Kirby, Jennifer Tilly, David Alan Grier, Jim Doughan. *AWARDS: NOM:* Oscars '99: Visual FX.

Stuck on You! [DC]

At the height of the "palimony" craze of the 1980s, Bill (Mukulski) and Carol (Penta) go before angelic Judge Gabriel (Corey) to arrange their separation. Via flashbacks, they patch things up. The comedy is vintage Troma. For comments on image quality and extras, please see review of *Squeeze Play.* —MM
Movie: ♫♫ ½ **DVD:** ♫♫♫
Troma Team Video (cat #9010, UPC 790357901036). Full frame. $19.98. Keepcase. *LANG:* English. *FEATURES:* 9 chapters • Troma materials • Featurette • Commentary: director.
1984 (R) 90m/C Prof. Irwin Corey, Virginia Penta, Mark Mikulski; **D:** Lloyd Kaufman, Michael Herz; **W:** Lloyd Kaufman, Michael Herz; **C:** Lloyd Kaufman.

The Stunt Man

Marvelous exercise in cinematic manipulation revolves around maniacal director Eli Cross (O'Toole). He cagily persuades Cameron (Railsback), who's on the lam from the law, to replace a stunt man who may have been killed in the line of duty. But the lines dividing truth, illusion, and lies are indistinct at best. The ambitious film manages to be a satisfying adventure, a psychological puzzle, and something more serious. DVD image is very grainy but that comes from the film's age. It looks better than a lot of productions from that era and it sounds much better. Anchor Bay has done its usual exemplary work. Extras—beginning with a commentary track by Rush, O'Toole, Railsback, Hershey, Rocco, Farrell, and Bail—are extensive. The screenplay and director's notes are DVD-ROM features. The film is also available in a "Limited Edition" set (cat. #DV11716) that includes the "making of" feature *Sinister Saga.* (Please see review.) —MM

Movie: ♫♫♫ ½ **DVD:** ♫♫♫♫ ½
Anchor Bay (cat #DV11655, UPC 01313-1165593). Widescreen (1.85:1) anamorphic. DTS Surround; Dolby Digital 5.1 Surround. $19.98. Keepcase. *LANG:* English. *CAP:* English. *FEATURES:* 28 chapters • Commentary • Trailers • Deleted scenes • Production and advertising art • DVD-ROM features.
1980 (R) 129m/C Peter O'Toole, Steve Railsback, Barbara Hershey, Charles "Chuck" Bail, Alex Rocco, Allen (Goorwitz) Garfield, Adam Roarke, Sharon Farrell, Philip Bruns; **D:** Richard Rush; **W:** Richard Rush, Lawrence B. Marcus; **C:** Mario Tosi; **M:** Dominic Frontiere. *AWARDS:* Golden Globes '81: Score; Montreal World Film Fest. '80: Film; Natl. Soc. Film Critics '80: Actor (O'Toole); *NOM:* Oscars '80: Actor (O'Toole), Adapt. Screenplay, Director (Rush).

Styx

When his brother Michael (MacFadyen) gets in deep with a bookie, safecracker Nelson (Weller) is brought back into the business with Art (Brown) for one last job. This is another of those movies where British thugs bully and torture each other; only this time, the Brits are South Africans. Barebones DVD (no menu) is identical to VHS tape in every way. Dark scenes are moderately grainy; most others are fine. —MM
Movie: ♫♫ **DVD:** ♫♫
Studio Home Ent. (cat #AV1600D, UPC 806469160022). Full frame. Stereo. $14.95. Keepcase. *LANG:* English. *CAP:* English.
2000 (R) 94m/C Peter Weller, Bryan Brown, Angus Macfadyen, Adrienne Pierce, Anthony Bishop, Nan Hamilton, Shane Howarth, Gerard Rudolf; **D:** Alexander Wright; **W:** George Ferris; **C:** Russell Lyster; **M:** Roy Hay.

Sublime: Stories, Tales, Lies and Exaggerations

This is a documentary about Sublime, the 1990s ska/rock group that broke up tragically early when lead singer Brad Nowell died. It takes a look at the band circa 1995 when they played on the "Warped" tour. There's a mixture of clips of concert footage as well as interviews with the band and their friends (including the band No Doubt) who discuss the origins and ideas behind the music. Unfortunately, songs really aren't allowed to play out fully and usually fade out as they go to the next interview. The program seems to be shot on home video, which makes the image quality hazy and the sound quality subpar. Fans of the band will probably be able to overlook the rough edges. There's not much DVD can do with the original video recordings. Much of it has a soft, hazy, and murky quality, and occasionally shows some pixelation. The stereo audio is definitely lacking; for such enjoyable music, it deserves at least a more polished sound for the concert footage, which is decent at times, but often rather muddy and slightly distorted. The band's CDs have better sound quality than this presentation often does. Comments in the interviews are occasionally difficult to discern. —AB/DG

Movie: 🎬🎬 **DVD:** 🎬 ½
Music Video Distributors (UPC 88377110-423). Full frame. Dolby Surround Stereo. $24.95. Keepcase. *LANG:* English. *FEATURES:* 22 chapters.
1999 130m/C

Submarine Attack

Unconventional war story posits an Italian submarine captain (Baldini) who decides to rescue the survivors of a Danish freighter that he has sunk. DVD comes from badly damaged original elements. The image is filled with blips, distortions, surface dirt, registration woes, and bad splices. Beyond those.... —MM *AKA:* Torpedo Zone; The Great Hope; La Grande Speranza.

Movie: 🎬🎬 **DVD:** 🎬
Winstar Home Ent. (cat #FLV5301, UPC 720917530123). Full frame. $14.98. Keepcase. *LANG:* English. *FEATURES:* 16 chapters • Filmographies • Trailers.
1954 92m/B *IT* Renato Baldini, Lois Maxwell, Folco Lulli, Carlo Bellini, Earl Cameron; *D:* Duilio Coletti; *C:* Leonida Barboni; *M:* Nino Rota.

The Suburbans

"The Suburbans" is the poorly named band that's the subject of the movie—an '80s one-hit wonder whose members find themselves wanting to get back together when an exec (Hewitt) think it's a good idea (for silly reasons I won't reveal) for them to reunite. While it starts off like a music biz satire, a lot of flat relationship material is thrown into the mix, most notably between Ward and Brenneman's characters. Brenneman is a fine actress, and deserving of better roles. Ben Stiller and dad Jerry Stiller pop up as record execs, and their few minutes of screen time is the highlight of the picture. Overall it's a pretty uneventful flick, and the brief running time feels much longer. Not only is the film not funny, it's almost painful to watch. Images are pleasantly sharp, and colors are bright, natural, and nicely saturated. The preprint material used is in impeccable shape. While the music in the film is clear and sounds excellent, the majority of the film is simply typical dialogue-driven comedy. Surrounds are used nicely on occasion and the dialogue is clear. —AB/DG

Movie: 🎬 **DVD:** 🎬🎬🎬
Columbia Tristar Home Video (UPC 433-96043879). Widescreen (1.85:1) anamorphic. Dolby Digital 5.1 Surround. $24.95. Keepcase. *LANG:* English. *SUB:* English. *CAP:* English. *FEATURES:* Trailers • Commentary: Donal Larder Ward • Production notes • Cast bios/filmographies.
1999 (R) 81m/C Jennifer Love Hewitt, Will Ferrell, Donal Lardner Ward, Craig Bierko, Amy Brenneman, Bridgette Wilson,

Tony Guma, Robert Loggia, Antonio Fargas, Ben Stiller, Jerry Stiller; *D:* Donal Lardner Ward; *W:* Donal Lardner Ward, Tony Guma; *C:* Michael Barrett; *M:* Robbie Kondor.

Sudden Manhattan

Delightfully quirky film about a woman who's having the strangest week of her life. Reminiscent of *After Hours,* it follows Donna (Shelly) as her English professor professes his love for her, her best friend gets over her ex by dating two men who seem a little fluffy, and the new man in her life (Tim Guinee) substitutes Dostoyevky for sex. There's also the little problem of her visions of murders on her favorite tree-lined street that are so disturbing they send her to a psychic (Lasser). Full of fun and funny slice-of-life insanity, this is a good little independent production. The transfer is average with a monochromatic look to the color and the sound is decent. —CA

Movie: 🎬🎬 ½ **DVD:** 🎬🎬
Vanguard Intl. Cinema (cat #VF0216, UPC 658769021639). Full frame. $29.95. Keepcase. *LANG:* English. *FEATURES:* 10 chapters • Commentary: director • Theatrical trailer.
1996 80m/C Adrienne Shelly, Tim Guinee, Roger Rees, Louise Lasser, Hynden Walch; *D:* Adrienne Shelly; *W:* Adrienne Shelly; *C:* Jim Denault; *M:* Pat Irwin.

Sugar & Spice

If there is such a thing as a smart cheerleader teen pic, this is it. It's a satire of offbeat pep squadders who cheer by day and rob banks by night. They include Suvari's rebellious Kansas, Shelton's permanently upbeat Diane, and the jealous Lisa (Sokoloff) who always wears green. Diane meets Jack (Marsden) and two American kids do the best they can when they learn that Diane is pregnant. This transfer is gorgeous, offering great colors and a very sharp image. For an example of the color scheme, simply go to the 0:13:00 mark, where the shot offers both natural and pastel colors, with both looking very realistic and sharp. The 5.1 audio mix is impressive as well. The dialogue is clear and the constant guitar rock heard in the film sounds great. There is consistently impressive use of the rear speakers and a nice utilization of the subwoofer as well. —MM/GH

Movie: 🎬🎬🎬 **DVD:** 🎬🎬🎬 ½
New Line (cat #N5298, UPC 79404-3529825). Widescreen (2.35:1) anamorphic. Dolby Digital 5.1 Surround Stereo. $24.98. Snapper. *LANG:* English. *SUB:* English. *CAP:* English. *FEATURES:* 4 deleted and extended scenes • Trailer • Talent files.
2001 (PG-13) 81m/C Marley Shelton, James Marsden, Mena Suvari, Marla Sokoloff, Rachel Blanchard, Melissa George, Alexandra Holden, Sara Marsh, Sean Young; *D:* Francine McDougall; *W:* Mandy Nelson; *C:* Robert Brinkmann; *M:* Mark Mothersbaugh.

Sullivan's Travels

Sturges's masterpiece is a sardonic, whip-quick romp about a Hollywood director tired of making comedies who decides to make a serious, socially responsible film and hits the road masquerading as a hobo in order to know hardship and poverty. Beautifully sustained, inspired satire mercilessly mocks the ambitions of Depression-era social cinema. Gets a little over-dark near the end before the happy ending: Sturges insisted on 20-year-old Lake as The Girl; her pregnancy forced him to rewrite scenes and design new costumes for her. As ever, she is stunning. Like most Criterion releases, this disc boasts an absolutely fabulous video transfer, featuring crisp blacks and extremely well-defined colors. The soundtrack is similarly impressive and includes clear dialogue and a flawlessly reproduced musical track. Of the potpourri of extras included on the disc, the documentary is probably the best of the lot. The interview with Sturges's widow is also quite enjoyable. The commentary track takes awhile to get endeared to as it begins as nothing more than fan club musings. But once the participants find their stride, the track becomes rather enjoyable. —MJT

Movie: 🎬🎬🎬🎬 **DVD:** 🎬🎬🎬🎬
Criterion (cat #118, UPC 715515012126). Full frame. Dolby Digital Mono. $39.95. Keepcase. *LANG:* English. *SUB:* English. *FEATURES:* 23 chapters • Commentary: Baumbach, Bowser, Christopher Guest, Michael McKean • 76-minute *American Masters* documentary by Kenneth Bowser • Interview with Preston Sturges's widow Sandy Sturges • Hedda Hopper interview with Preston Sturges • Audio of Sturges singing "My Love" and reciting "If I Were King" • Storyboards and blueprints • Production stills archive • Scrapbook of original publicity materials • Original theatrical trailer.
1941 90m/B Joel McCrea, Veronica Lake, William Demarest, Robert Warwick, Franklin Pangborn, Porter Hall, Eric Blore, Byron Foulger, Robert Greig, Torben Meyer, Jimmy Conlin, Margaret Hayes, Chester Conklin, Alan Bridge; *D:* Preston Sturges; *W:* Preston Sturges; *C:* John Seitz; *M:* Leo Shuken. *AWARDS:* Natl. Film Reg. '90.

Summer Catch

Predictable but enjoyable, in an empty calorie sort of way, "Bull Durham Jr." film. Ryan (Prinze) lives in a town where the elite Cape Cod summer leagues train and play for scouts that can recommend the guys to the big-time teams. He just has to get over his wrong-side-of-the-tracks job as a landscaper, a bitter unsupportive father, and his own ability to keep himself from succeeding to make it to the big leagues. Along the way he falls for a very shapely girl with a big lawn (Biel) and makes friends with some wacky summer stock players, including the always amusing Matthew Lillard and Buffy the Vampire Slayer's least popular boyfriend, Marc Blucas. But while things may seem bleak, this is a romantic comedy and in the end everyone gets what they want after learning a few valuable lessons. The print is clean and crisp with lots of bright green lawns, blue skies, and yards of young flesh. The sound is good—also crisp and clear. —CA

Movie: 🎵🎵 ½ **DVD:** 🎵🎵🎵
Warner (cat #21100, UPC 0853921100-25). Widescreen (1.85:1) anamorphic. Dolby Digital 5.1 Surround. $19.90. Snapper. *LANG:* English; French. *SUB:* English; French; Spanish. *CAP:* English. *FEATURES:* 30 chapters ▪ Commentary: director, writer ▪ Additional scenes.
2001 (PG-13) 108m/C Freddie Prinze Jr., Jessica Biel, Matthew Lillard, Brian Dennehy, Fred Ward, Jason Gedrick, Brittany Murphy, Marc Blucas, Bruce Davison, Wilmer Valderrama, Christian Kane, Gabriel Mann, Cedric Pendleton, Zena Grey, Corey Pearson; *D:* Mike Tollin; *W:* Kevin Falls, John Gatins; *C:* Tim Suhrstedt; *M:* George Fenton.

Summer of '42

Broad cinematography, muted color saturation, and haunting music all conspire to frame this coming-of-age story into a perfect picture of a time and a place that can only exist in films. Hermie (Grimes) passes the war torn summer of '42 playing with his fellow 15-year-old friends at a New England beach colony and being infatuated with an "older" woman, 22-year-old Dorothy (an ethereal O'Neill), who lives in a beach house with her soldier husband. When her husband is called back to service, Hermie begins helping her with small chores around the house. Intricate work by the actors under Robert Mulligan's almost invisible direction raise the innocence of Hermie and Dorothy's relationship to a more than believable level, and when tragedy strikes one of them, the comfort they take from one another is the stuff of fairy tales. But the film is not all stardust and gossamer wings, there is a classic condom-buying scene that never fails to elicit shrieks of laughter from first-time viewers. The disc looks great and the sound is good for mono. —CA

Movie: 🎵🎵🎵 **DVD:** 🎵🎵🎵
Warner (cat #1033, UPC 012569103320). Widescreen (1.85:1) anamorphic. Dolby Digital Mono. $19.90. Snapper. *LANG:* English; French. *SUB:* English; French; Spanish; Portuguese; Japanese; Thai; Korean. *CAP:* English. *FEATURES:* 29 chapters ▪ Theatrical trailer.
1971 (R) 102m/C Jennifer O'Neill, Gary Grimes, Jerry Houser, Oliver Conant; *D:* Robert Mulligan; *W:* Herman Raucher; *C:* Robert L. Surtees; *M:* Michel Legrand; *Nar:* Robert Mulligan. *AWARDS:* Oscars '71: Orig. Dramatic Score; *NOM:* Oscars '71: Cinematog., Film Editing, Story & Screenplay.

Summertime

Spinster Hepburn vacations in Venice and falls in love with Brazzi. She is hurt when she learns that he's married, but her life has been so bleak that she is not about to end her one great romance. Moving, funny, and richly photographed in a beautiful Old World city. Adapted from Arthur Laurents's play *The Time of the Cuckoo*. This disc contains fewer extras than most Criterion productions, but the film is dated. Image, as usual, is excellent with rich super-saturated colors. Sound is fine. —MM *AKA:* Summer Madness.

Movie: 🎵🎵🎵 ½ **DVD:** 🎵🎵🎵
Home Vision Cinema (cat #1307). Full frame. Dolby Digital Mono. $29.95. *LANG:* English. *CAP:* English. *FEATURES:* Trailer ▪ 18 chapters.
1955 98m/C Katharine Hepburn, Rossano Brazzi, Isa Miranda, Darren McGavin, Mari Aldon, MacDonald Parke, Jeremy Spenser; *D:* David Lean; *W:* David Lean, H.E. Bates; *C:* Jack Hildyard; *M:* Alessandro Cicognini. *AWARDS:* N.Y. Film Critics '55: Director (Lean); *NOM:* Oscars '55: Actress (Hepburn), Director (Lean).

Sumo Vixens

Cult actress Kei Mizutani stars in this sexy comedy about a former sumo wrestler excon who tries to start up a women's sumo dojo. Shot on video, the image is free of faults, and you can choose the original Japanese soundtrack or cartoony English dub. The DVD version includes an informative guide to the basics of sumo. This helps a bit, as there are plenty of gags and references that pass by Westerners and non-fans of the sport. Good dirty fun. —BT

Movie: 🎵🎵 **DVD:** 🎵🎵
Central Park/U.S. Manga (cat #APCD2091-DVD, UPC 719987209121). Widescreen letterboxed. $19.99. Keepcase. *LANG:* English; Japanese. *SUB:* English. *FEATURES:* 12 chapters ▪ Trailers ▪ Sumo FAQ.
1996 74m/C JP Kei Mizutani, Shouko Kudou, Kyoko Nakamura, Keisuke; *D:* Takao Nakano; *W:* Takao Nakano; *C:* Hideki Hasegawa; *M:* Hiroaki Yabunaka.

Super Kung Fu Kid

Because he always gets in fights, teenaged kid Cheung Lik and his mom have to move to live with his brother Kong Yeh. But Kong is working for the triad of Bolo Yeung. Cheung refuses to work for Yeung, pitting brother against brother. The martial arts footage is almost nonstop—but is also incredibly lame, except when better foes like Yeung (in an early role) are involved. For the most part, it looks like the combatants are just rehearsing their routines. The titles haven't been replaced for the U.S. release on the print—they've just been removed. The image looks cloudy, but it's likely just the age of the print. —BT *AKA:* Hong Kong Cat Named Karado; Superior Youngster.

Movie: 🎵 **DVD:** 🎵 ½
Tai Seng (cat #86644, UPC 6016438664-44). Full frame. $14.95. Keepcase. *LANG:* English. *FEATURES:* 8 chapters.
1986 86m/C HK Cheung Lik, Kong Yeh, Bolo Yeung, James Nam.

Superchick

Tara B. True (Jillson) is a mild-mannered stewardess by day but a free-swinging, karate-kicking blonde glamourpuss by night. There's not a single second of seriousness in this delightful dollop of early '70s exploitation, precisely the same cinematic stuff that the *Austin Powers* films have so much fun with. The sexual and violent aspects are downplayed, too, but nudie icon Uschi Digart shows up for an extended cameo. Psychedelic colors are reproduced with almost painful clarity. In fact, the gaudy low-budget image is virtually flawless. By the way, these days, Joyce Jillson is a syndicated newspaper astrologer. —MM

Movie: 🎵🎵 ½ **DVD:** 🎵🎵 ½
Rhino (cat #R2 976068, UPC 6034976-06825). Full frame. $9.99. Snapper. *LANG:* English. *FEATURES:* 12 chapters.
1971 (R) 94m/C Joyce Jillson, Louis Quinn, Thomas Reardon, Uschi Digart; *D:* Ed Forsyth; *W:* Gary Crutcher; *C:* Paul Hipp; *M:* Allan Alper.

Support Your Local Sheriff

Amiable, irreverent western spoof with more than its fair share of laughs. When a stranger stumbles into a gold rush town, he winds up becoming sheriff. Garner is perfect as the deadpan sheriff, particularly in the scene where he convinces Dern to remain in jail, in spite of the lack of bars. Neatly subverts every western cliché it encounters, yet keeps respect for formula western. Followed by *Support Your Local Gunfighter*. With the hit-and-miss (although mostly hit) quality of some of the catalog DVD releases by MGM, the great quality of this transfer is a pleasant surprise. The image has never looked this sharp, although it does vary on occasion. Since the film is more than 30 years old, this could be a film print issue or even due to something in a restoration process. It really doesn't matter since the DVD is such an improvement over the tape. Colors are excellent; good saturation and no bleed. There's not much to talk about with the mono soundtrack, but it's fine and most importantly, the dialogue is easy to understand, and only occasionally does the music clip a little. Well worth slappin' down a twenty at your local video store. —JO

Movie: 🎵🎵🎵 ½ **DVD:** 🎵🎵🎵
MGM Home Ent. (cat #1001596, UPC 027-616859068). Widescreen (1.85:1) anamorphic. Dolby Digital Mono. $19.98. Keepcase. *LANG:* English; French. *SUB:* Spanish; French. *CAP:* English. *FEATURES:* 16 chapters ▪ Theatrical trailer.
1969 (G) 92m/C James Garner, Joan Hackett, Walter Brennan, Bruce Dern, Jack Elam, Harry (Henry) Morgan; *D:* Burt Kennedy; *W:* William Bowers; *C:* Harry Stradling Jr.

Sure Death: Revenge

A class production of mystery and intrigue during the Edo period of Japan, highlighted

by strong performances and a captivating story, based on the long running *Hissatsu!* TV series about a secret group of contract killers who disguise their activities by posing as normal lower-class merchants. A new magistrate's arrival coincides with a number of mysterious deaths. Officer Mondo and a gruff stranger (Sonny Chiba) take the assignment to avenge the murders, leading to more deaths and a web of deceit. This is actually the eighth film in the *Hissatsu!* series, but the first to be released in the U.S., and generally considered the best. Mokoto Fujita makes for a fine, if unlikely, hard-boiled gum-clog detective. Chiba exudes his usual mix of valor and menace—though his use of tops as deadly weapons is in keeping with the series' humor. Image quality is fine throughout. Though the dubbing is very professional, there are also options to listen to the original Japanese voices with subtitles. —*BT* **AKA:** Sure-Fire Death 4: We Will Avenge You.
Movie: 🎵🎵🎵 ½ **DVD:** 🎵🎵🎵
Media Blasters (cat #TSDVD0116, UPC 631595011685). Full frame. $24.95. Keepcase. *LANG:* Japanese, English. *SUB:* English. *FEATURES:* 14 chapters ▪ Video trailers.
1987 130m/C *JP* Fujita Mokoto, Sonny Chiba, Henry Sanada; **D:** Kinji Fukasaku; **W:** Kinji Fukasaku, Tatsuo Nogami, Akira Nakahara; **C:** Ishihara Shigeru; **M:** Hirao Masaaki.

Survivors

The teaming of Robin Williams and Walter Matthau should have lead to the creation of a new "Odd Couple" and comic gold, but sometimes things just don't add up correctly. Donald (Williams) and Sonny (Matthau) are both down on their luck and out of work. This unlikely duo meet in a diner, which is robbed by a masked Jack (Jerry Reed). As Jack is attempting to get away, Sonny sees his face. Knowing that Sonny can identify him, Jack becomes determined to silence him. Meanwhile, Donald has become energized and enraged by the robbery attempt and the subsequent lack of help from the police, so he buys several guns and heads for a survival training retreat. Fearing for his life, Sonny joins Donald at his isolated cabin, unaware that Jack is hot on their trail. The film offers some nice one-liners and slapstick, but the result simply isn't funny or even interesting. Director Michael Ritchie has never shied away from tough topics in his films and this one tackles gun control and criminal justice with aplomb. Unfortunately, those subjects don't lend themselves to uproarious comedy. Williams rants, Matthau scowls, and the audience sleeps. DVD image is sharp and clear, showing little grain and only minor defects from the source print. However, the transfer is quite drab and the colors are lifeless. Audio provides clear dialogue and some minor Surround effects. The only extra here is the film's theatrical trailer (note that the majority of footage in

the trailer comes from the film's third act, highlighting just how boring most of the movie truly is). —*ML*
Movie: 🎵 ½ **DVD:** 🎵🎵 ½
Columbia Tristar (cat #03298, UPC 043396032989). Widescreen (1.85:1) letterboxed. Dolby Surround. $19.95. Keepcase. *LANG:* English; French. *SUB:* English; French; Spanish; Portuguese; Chinese; Korean; Thai. *CAP:* English. *FEATURES:* Trailer ▪ Bonus trailers ▪ 28 chapters.
1983 (R) 102m/C Robin Williams, Walter Matthau, Jerry Reed, John Goodman, James Wainwright, Kristen Vigard; **D:** Michael Ritchie; **W:** Michael Leeson; **C:** Billy Williams; **M:** Paul Chihara.

Suspect

Washington, D.C., public defender Kathleen Riley (Cher) is forced to represent a homeless Vietnam veteran (Neeson) in a grisly murder-case that appears fairly clear-cut. But soon into it, she realizes that this case is far from simple and that it has implications throughout the government. Her client is not the nutcase everyone thinks he is, but turns out to be a threat to very powerful people. With the help of lobbyist and jury member Eddie Sanger (Quaid), she connects the dots. Unrealistic plot is helped along by good performances and tight direction. The transfer is very clean and without notable blemishes. The film uses a very natural color palette and the DVD is able to reproduce it nicely with all its nuances and warm tones. Blacks are deep and shadows always maintain a good level of detail. Occasional edge-enhancement is evident in the transfer but it never gets too distracting, making for a pleasant presentation. The compression is also without flaws, maintaining a very good level of detail throughout the films. A good sound frequency response gives the film a natural quality that perfectly matches the style and feel of the film itself. Dialogue is well integrated and always remains highly intelligible. The disc also contains an informative commentary track by director Peter Yates that is full of valuable information and behind-the-scenes memories. —*GH*
Movie: 🎵🎵 ½ **DVD:** 🎵🎵🎵
Columbia Tristar Home Video (UPC 4339-6058576). Widescreen (1.85:1) anamorphic; full frame. Dolby Digital Surround Stereo. $24.95. Keepcase. *LANG:* English; French; Spanish; Portuguese. *SUB:* English; French; Spanish; Portuguese; Korean; Chinese; Thai. *CAP:* English. *FEATURES:* Commentary: Peter Yates ▪ Trailer ▪ Talent files.
1987 (R) 101m/C Dennis Quaid, Cher, Liam Neeson, E. Katherine Kerr, Joe Mantegna, John Mahoney, Philip Bosco; **D:** Peter Yates; **W:** Eric Roth; **C:** Billy Williams; **M:** Michael Kamen.

Suspiria

American dancer Suzy (Harper) arrives at a German ballet academy where she becomes aware of a strong malefic and

supernatural presence that fills the school with shuddering terror and violent death. Could the temperamental heads of school (Bennett, Valli) have something to do with it? Hmm.... Simple tale is structured as a combination of *The Wizard of Oz* and violent German fairy tales. Truly unique and utterly effective, the film attacks the audience with terrifying music, violent set pieces, and otherwordly atmosphere. One of the last films shot in three-strip Technicolor, *Suspiria* is an opulent, color-drenched nightmare, rich in primary colors and stylish visuals. Italian director Argento's control of the medium has never been stronger than it is here where the simplicity of the plot is justified. It's part one of a proposed trilogy and was followed by *Inferno*. One of the most successful Italian horror films ever. The DVD is stunning, with a beautiful, sharp, and vivid transfer of the film. Given the strong use of reds and other saturated colors, the lack of hue distortion is impressive, as is the speaker-rattling Surround soundtrack. Unfortunately, though the Italian and French dialogue tracks are included, there is no subtitle option. One must instead use the closed captioning, which obscures part of the image. The booklet and extras exclusive to the limited edition will be a pure delight for fans. The documentary is interesting, if a little heavy-handed. The CD is appreciated, but a track listing would have been nice. Highly recommended. —*DG*
Movie: 🎵🎵🎵 ½ **DVD:** 🎵🎵🎵 ½
Anchor Bay (cat #DV11610, UPC 013131-161090). Widescreen (2.35:1) anamorphic. Dolby 6.1; DTS-ES. $44.98. Keepcase. *LANG:* English; Italian; French. *CAP:* English. *FEATURES:* Theatrical trailers ▪ TV spots ▪ Radio spots ▪ Daemonia Music video ▪ Poster and still gallery ▪ Talent bios ▪ "Suspiria 25th Anniversary," 52-min. "making of" documentary ▪ Original soundtrack CD ▪ 32-page booklet with notes ▪ Lobby card reproductions ▪ 26 chapters ▪ Insert card with chapter listings.
1977 (R) 99m/C *IT* Jessica Harper, Joan Bennett, Alida Valli, Udo Kier, Stefania Casini, Flavio Bucci, Barbara Magnolfi, Rudolf Schuendler; **D:** Dario Argento; **W:** Dario Argento, Daria Nicolodi; **C:** Luciano Tovoli; **M:** Dario Argento, The Goblins.

Svengali

With a performance that could easily fill several breakfasts, John Barrymore hams it up as the hypnotic, domineering manipulator in Archie Mayo's brisk adaptation of George Du Maurier's novel *Trilby*. With long locks, Rasputin-esque face, and glowing eyes, Barrymore cuts an imposing figure as the opportunistic but strangely magnetic music teacher who guides some women to ruin and even death, yet finds in Trilby (17-year-old Marian Marsh) someone to potentially love as well as control. Many of the film's elements, like Barney McGill's atmospheric cinematography and Anton Grot's Expressionist sets, suggest this early Warner Bros./Vitaphone production attempted to cash in on the success of the early Universal horror classics. The scene where the camera pulls back from the trance-inducing Svengali to a miniature Parisian rooftop landscape still impresses. (For its influence, look no further than the opening shot of 1996's *Star Trek: First Contact*.) However, like the Universal monsters, the best special effect is the monster itself. Barrymore broods, leers, and sneers with relish, but all too recognizable in those moments when his human frailty breaks through his ruthless ambitions. For a 70-year-old film, the full-frame transfer impresses in sharpness and detail. Solid black and good gray tones help to overcome some of the source print deficiencies, namely the occasional emulsion wear and image softness. Constant hiss and pops plague the soundtrack, costing it half-a-bone in the Hound's technical rating. Well-written production notes constitute the only extra on the disc. Recommended for fans of Barrymore or early sound cinema. —EP

Movie: ♫♫♫ **DVD:** ♫♫
Roan Group (cat #AED-2052, UPC 785604-205227). Full frame. Dolby Digital Mono. $19.98. Keepcase. *LANG:* English. *FEATURES:* 9 chapters • Production notes.
1931 76m/B John Barrymore, Marian Marsh, Donald Crisp; **D:** Archie Mayo; **W:** J. Grubb Alexander; **C:** Barney McGill. *AWARDS: NOM:* Oscars '31: Cinematog.

Swamp Country

Please see review of *Swamp Girl / Swamp Country*.
1966 94m/C Rex Allen, Sue Casey, David DaLie, Lyle Waggoner, Carole Gilbert, Baker Knight; **D:** Robert Patrick; **W:** David DaLie; **C:** Mario Tosi; **M:** Baker Knight.

Swamp Girl / Swamp Country

The good ol' boys at Something Weird have come up with another of their exploitation double features. *Swamp Girl* is, I suppose, a vehicle for country singer Ferlin Husky. Most of the actors appear to be locals and anyone looking for the cheap thrills promised by the title will be disappointed. (It comes with an MPAA "GP" rating.) *Swamp Country* stars another country singer, Baker Knight, who's kidnapped by bad guys. Both look pretty rough on DVD. *Country* shows every sort of surface damage imaginable. Colors are still bright but it's hard to watch or to listen to with constant low-level static. *Girl* is much darker and grainier but not nearly as dinged up. —MM

Movie: ♫♫ **DVD:** ♫♫
Image Ent. (cat #ID1196SWDVD, UPC 014381119626). Full frame; widescreen (2.35:1) letterboxed. Dolby Digital Mono. $24.99. Keepcase. *LANG:* English. *FEATURES:* 28 chapters • "Swamp Virgin" featurette • Gallery of exploitation art • 6 Swamp trailers • "Swamp Buggy Race" short film.
1971 78m/C Ferlin Husky, Claude King, Harrison Page, Steve Drexel, Simone Grif-

fith; **D:** Donald A. Davis; **W:** Jay Kulp; **C:** Jay Kulp; **M:** Gene Kauer, Doug Lackey.

S.W.A.T.

Imagine, if you can, a classier version of TVs *Cops* and you'll have an idea of what this documentary is all about. The DVD is actually a series of three shows which originally aired on The Discovery Channel. Each segment examines the S.W.A.T. (Special Weapons and Tactics) teams in three different cities—Los Angeles, Las Vegas, and Detroit. The episodes are comprised of interviews with the team members and training footage. But the most interesting aspects are the scenes in which the S.W.A.T. teams must go into action. There are several exciting and suspenseful moments here, and the photography gets as close as possible. *S.W.A.T.* does a very good job of illustrating the pressures and dangers that these individuals experience on a daily basis. The interviews are candid and emotional and the training segments show how hard the team members work. This documentary isn't flashy or sensationalistic; it's simply a solidly made production which shows a valuable part of the police force at work. The full-frame image is sharp and clear, showing no distortion, artifacting, or overt grain. The picture here rivals digital broadcast quality. Audio provides clear dialogue and sound effects, with no hiss or distortion. —ML

Movie: ♫♫♫ **DVD:** ♫♫
BFS Video (cat #30269-D, UPC 06680-5302695). Full frame. Dolby Digital Stereo. $19.98. Keepcase. *LANG:* English. *FEATURES:* Still gallery.
2000 150m/C

Sweet Hearts Dance

In a small Vermont town, over the course of a fall and winter, two couples merge and separate. The Boons break up when Wiley (Johnson) becomes disenchanted. He moves out after an altercation at the family Thanksgiving dinner. His wife Sandra (Sarandon) responds to Wiley's inarticulate hostility with resentments of her own, and the winter is spent in cruel sniping, infidelity, and family unhappiness, especially with teenage son Kyle (Henry). Best friend Sam Manners (Daniels) tries to intervene, without much luck. A bachelor and high school principal, he falls in love with teacher Adie Nims (Perkins), a proud woman who becomes impatient with Sam's reticence and lack of decisiveness. The film is lazy, unfocused, and artificial. We have two couples in love in a Hallmark Cards version of a small town. Besides some worry about getting a gymnasium completed, there's no connection with economic reality. The actors try to make the characters seem complicated, but nothing like identifiable reality seeps through. DVD is greatly compromised by a pretty transfer that has been presented only flat—and pan 'n' scanned to boot. People are crowded onto the frame, and

wide compositions leave big empty spaces in the middle. To add insult to injury, the packaging proudly says this is a Hi-Def transfer. —GE

Movie: ♫ **DVD:** ♫ ½
Columbia Tristar (cat #06685, UPC 0433-96066854). Full frame. Dolby Digital Surround. $24.98. Keepcase. *LANG:* English. *SUB:* English; French. *CAP:* English. *FEATURES:* Trailers • 28 chapters.
1988 (R) 95m/C Don Johnson, Jeff Daniels, Susan Sarandon, Elizabeth Perkins, Justin Henry, Holly Marie Combs; **D:** Robert Greenwald; **W:** Ernest Thompson; **C:** Tak Fujimoto; **M:** Richard Gibbs.

Sweet Jane

Teenaged Tony (Gordon-Levitt) has AIDS and no family. He becomes infatuated with HIV-positive junkie Jane (Mathis) and follows her into a dangerous street life. Although she treats him badly, he sticks around to "protect" her and they slowly develop a genuine relationship. No-frills DVD image is about equal to tape and that's fine for a story about emotional and physical squalor. —MM

Movie: ♫♫ **DVD:** ♫♫
Vanguard Intl. Cinema (cat #VF0138, UPC 658769013832). Full frame. $29.95. Keepcase. *LANG:* English. *FEATURES:* 8 chapters.
1998 83m/C Samantha Mathis, Joseph Gordon-Levitt, Bud Cort, William McNamara, Mary Woronov; **D:** Joe Gayton; **W:** Joe Gayton; **C:** Greg Littlewood; **M:** Walter Werzowa.

Sweet November

An unfortunate remake of the 1968 film that starred Sandy Dennis and Anthony Newman. Sara Deever (Theron) is a terminally ill woman who has made it her life's goal to reform uptight, unloving, successful businessmen. During the course of a one-month love affair, she attempts to teach them the meaning of life and happiness. Nelson Moss (Reeves), an advertising guru, is Sara Deever's Mr. November. However, all of her plans change as the two become close and things get complicated. This film suffers from its less-than-firm grip on reality, and the fact that Mr. Reeves is utterly unbelievable in this role. The film falls very close to a woof rating, but is saved by a decent portrayal by Ms. Theron. The 5.1 Surround track makes ample use of the front three speakers, but did not seem to employ the full sound capacity. The transfer is nice and clear with no noticeable artifacts. It decently represents the colorful San Francisco backgrounds with lots of bright bay blues and foggy grays. —EL

Movie: ♫ ½ **DVD:** ♫♫
Warner (cat #18997, UPC 0853918997-23). Widescreen (1.85:1) anamorphic. Dolby 5.1 Surround. $24.98. Snapper. *LANG:* English; French. *SUB:* English; French. *CAP:* English. *FEATURES:* Documentary: "Sweet November: From the Heart" • Cast & crew bios • Theatrical trailer.

2001 (PG-13) 114m/C Keanu Reeves, Charlize Theron, Jason Isaacs, Greg Germann, Liam Aiken, Lauren Graham, Michael Rosenbaum, Robert Joy, Jason Kravits, Frank Langella; **D:** Pat O'Connor; **W:** Kurt Voelker; **C:** Edward Lachman; **M:** Christopher Young.

Sweet Talker

Following his release from prison, a charming con man (Brown) shows up in a coastal village, thinking that the townsfolk are ripe for the picking. What he doesn't know is that they can do some sweet talking of their own, and he soon finds himself caring for a pretty widow (Allen) and her son. Sleeper comedy works well thanks to the likeable leads. Full-frame DVD image is virtually identical to tape. Ditto sound. —*MM*
Movie: 🎵🎵🎵 **DVD:** 🎵🎵
Pioneer Ent. (cat #DVD68918). Full frame. Dolby Digital Stereo. $24.98. Keepcase. *LANG:* English. *CAP:* English. *FEATURES:* 17 chapters.
1991 (PG) 91m/C *AU* Bryan Brown, Karen Allen, Chris Haywood, Bill Kerr, Bruce Spence, Bruce Myles, Paul Chubb, Peter Hehir, Justin Rosniak; **D:** Michael Jenkins; **W:** Tony Morphett; **C:** Russell Boyd; **M:** Richard Thompson, Peter Filleul.

Sweet Thing

A well-constructed tale concerning a troubled young artist, Sean Fields (Fox), who begins a potentially meteoric rise with a series of controversial paintings. His abusive stepfather, Ray Fields (Lunning), a district judge, has announced his intention to run for U.S. Congress and his campaign success is mirrored by the growing popularity of Sean's work, although the graphic nature of the paintings sparks a warped media frenzy. The excellent video transfer is highlighted by crisp colors and well-defined blacks. Some scenes do seem to lose some clarity in their images, but that may have been the filmmakers' intentions. A decent soundtrack compliments the video with sharply reproduced dialogue and music. An ample collection of extras (of which the behind-the-scenes featurette is the best) augments the disc nicely. —*MJT*
Movie: 🎵🎵🎵 **DVD:** 🎵🎵🎵
York Ent. (cat #YPD1119, UPC 7507231-11926). Widescreen (1.85:1) letterboxed. Dolby Digital Stereo. $14.99. Keepcase. *LANG:* English. *FEATURES:* 12 chapters ▪ Director's intro ▪ Behind-the-scenes footage ▪ Theatrical trailer ▪ "First Rites" trailer gallery.
2000 (R) 115m/C Jeremy Fox, Amalia Stifter, Ev Lunning Jr.; **D:** Mark David; **W:** Mark David, Mark Spacek; **C:** Mark David, Levy Castleberry, Marc Wiskemann.

The Sweetest Sound

Documentary from filmmaker Alan Berliner starts out promising and then falls flat. Berliner decides to explore the significance of people's names: their origins, the popularity of particular names, and what

specific names mean to people. This interesting search loses steam when Berliner begins to explore his own name. He interviews his parents to find out why they picked "Alan Berliner"; he then discovers that he isn't the only "Alan Berliner" in the world and invites 12 other "Alan Berliner"s to a dinner party, to explore their similarities and differences. What began as a film to which anyone could relate winds up being far too self-indulgent. The high point is Berliner's discussion of "ego searching," which is the practice of entering one's name into an Internet search-engine. DVD gives the viewer an adequate presentation of the image and sound. The film is presented full-frame and the Digital Stereo mix offers clear dialogue. —*ML*
Movie: 🎵 **DVD:** 🎵🎵 ½
New Video Group (cat #NVG-9488, UPC 767685948835). Full frame. Dolby Digital Stereo. $24.95. Keepcase. *LANG:* English. *FEATURES:* Filmmaker bio.
2001 60m/C D: Alan Berliner; **W:** Alan Berliner.

The Swiss Family Robinson

A family, seeking to escape Napoleon's war in Europe, sets sail for New Guinea, but shipwrecks near a deserted tropical island. There they build an idyllic life, only to be confronted by a band of pirates. Lots of adventure for family viewing. Filmed on location on the island of Tobago. This new THX-approved DVD transfer looks great. The colors are vibrant and nearly dead-on in the fleshtone department. Combined with the improved contrast and brightness levels, the film looks much newer than it is. Disney also used a very fine print with very little damage. The soundtrack gets some juice with a new 5.1 mix that gives considerable boost via the subwoofer to cannon fire and storms. Vault Disney extras include the opening Donald Duck cartoon "Sea Salts," and another excellent commentary. Disc two follows with several very interesting featurettes, including "Adventure in the Making," as good a "making of" documentary as one could ever hope for. The four-minute "Lost Treasure," "Swiss Family Treehouse" documents the opening of the Swiss Family Treehouse at Disneyland. Don't miss the film clips from 1940 version of *Swiss Family Robinson*, narrated by Orson Welles. And there's plenty more. Like the other titles in the series, this one's worth adding to any collection. —*JO*
Movie: 🎵🎵🎵 **DVD:** 🎵🎵🎵 ½
Buena Vista Home Ent. (cat #21553, UPC 786936143836). Widescreen (2.35:1) anamorphic. Dolby Digital 5.1; Dolby Digital Mono. $29.99. Keepcase. *LANG:* English (DD5.1); Spanish (DD Mono). *CAP:* English. *FEATURES:* 18 chapters ▪ Theatrical trailer ▪ Commentary: Annakin, Kirk, James MacArthur, Kevin Corcoran ▪ Original theatrical animated short "Sea Salts" ▪ Featurette "Adventure in the Making" ▪ Featurette "Pirates!" ▪ Featurette Lost Treasures—"Swiss Family Treehouse" ▪

Production Archives ▪ Excerpts from the 1940 *Swiss Family Robinson* ▪ 1960 Disney studio album.
1960 126m/C John Mills, Dorothy McGuire, James MacArthur, Tommy Kirk, Janet Munro, Sessue Hayakawa; **D:** Ken Annakin; **W:** Lowell S. Hawley; **C:** Harry Waxman; **M:** William Alwyn.

Sword & the Sorcerer

Prince Talon (Horsley) must regain control of his kingdom now ruled by an evil sorcerer (Lynch) and rescue a princess (Beller), etc., etc. For an unashamed genre piece, this is a well-made film, carefully lit and photographed. The image may be slightly better than a widescreen tape. —*MM*
Movie: 🎵🎵 **DVD:** 🎵🎵 ½
Anchor Bay (cat #DV11332, UPC 0131-31133295). Widescreen (1.85:1) anamorphic. Dolby Digital 5.1 Surround Stereo; Dolby Digital Surround. $24.99. Keepcase. *LANG:* English. *FEATURES:* 27 chapters ▪ Trailers and TV spots.
1982 (R) 100m/C Lee Horsley, Kathleen Beller, George Maharis, Simon MacCorkindale, Richard Lynch, Richard Moll, Robert Tessier, Nina Van Pallandt, Anna Bjorn, Jeff Corey; **D:** Albert Pyun; **W:** Albert Pyun; **C:** Joseph Mangine; **M:** David Whitaker.

Swordfish

Hacker extraordinaire Stanley Jobson (Jackman) has just been released from prison, paroled under the condition that he stay away from computers. But he is offered one more job that he may not be able to turn down—the cyber-theft of a top secret government fund, known only as "Swordfish." The film doesn't have much to add to the genre, but it gets quite a few style points. The opening sequence is particularly impressive. The picture is near-reference quality, and the sound only a notch below that—with plenty of extra features, you've got the perfect disc for those nights when you just need to see lots of stuff blow up. —*BG*
Movie: 🎵🎵 **DVD:** 🎵🎵🎵 ½
Columbia Tristar (cat #21322, UPC 0853-92132225). Widescreen (2.35:1) anamorphic. Dolby 5.1. $24.98. Snapper. *LANG:* English; French. *SUB:* English; French; Spanish. *FEATURES:* 29 chapters ▪ Commentary: director ▪ 2 behind-the-scenes documentaries ▪ Trailers ▪ 2 alternate endings ▪ DVD-ROM features.
2001 (R) 99m/C John Travolta, Hugh Jackman, Halle Berry, Don Cheadle, Vinnie Jones, Sam Shepard, Zach Grenier, Camryn Grimes, Rudolf Martin, Drea De Matteo; **D:** Dominic Sena; **W:** Skip Woods; **C:** Paul Cameron; **M:** Christopher Young.

Swordsman 2

This furious Wire-Fu starts with some action-loaded martial arts moments, then slows down and introduces the viewer to the main characters and the general set-up. Upon his return from long travels, the young swordsman Ling (Jet Li) finds that some serious changes have occurred to the Sun Moon Sect during his absence. On their way to some remote mountains for retirement, he and his martial arts students find nothing but empty houses and signs of destruction. They search the woods and eventually find the remaining members of the sect who had been insidiously attacked. The chief of the Sun Moon Sect, Master Wu, has been overthrown and captured by Fong (Brigitte Lin Ching-Hsia), Chief of the Highlander clan, and a man who is hungry for the power over the entire region. With the help of the Sacred Scroll that he has stolen from the Sun Moon Sect, he is now studying the highest levels of Martial Arts. But there is an interesting side to achieving the ultimate Martial Arts powers; with the practicing of these powers found in the Scroll, he is slowly turning into a woman, as self-castration and a metastasis into a female is part of the exercise. Yikes! Although some dust and scratch marks are occasionally noticeable, the film print from which this non-anamorphic transfer has been struck is generally clean. The image is crisp and contains a good level of detail, bringing out the best of the highly atmospheric cinematography. DVD nicely restores the opulent colors without oversaturation, chroma noise or bleeding. Both language tracks are very well produced and boast a good number of directional Surround effects. Especially during the high-flying fight sequences, the split Surrounds are used to great effect. —GH

Movie: 🎵🎵🎵 **DVD:** 🎵🎵🎵

Tai Seng (UPC 601643273549). Widescreen (1.85:1) letterboxed. Dolby Digital 5.1 Surround. $29.98. Keepcase. *LANG:* Cantonese; Mandarin. *SUB:* English; Chinese; Korean; Vietnamese; Japanese; Malaysian. *FEATURES:* Trailers.

1991 109m/C *HK* Jet Li, Rosamund Kwan, Waise Lee, Brigitte (Lin Chinag-hsia) Lin, Michelle Reis; *D:* Siu-Tung Ching, Stanley Tong; *W:* Pik-yin Tang, Hanson Chan, Tsui Hark; *M:* Richard Yuen.

Sworn to Justice

Martial arts flick lives up to its generic title. Rothrock is a psychic psychologist who must avenge the killing of her sister and nephew. Lots of explosions and chopsocky ensue. DVD image is absolutely no improvement over VHS tape. —MM

Movie: 🎵🎵 **DVD:** 🎵🎵

MTI (cat #1074, UPC 039414510744). Full frame. $24.95. Keepcase. *LANG:* English. *SUB:* Spanish. *FEATURES:* 20 chapters • Talent files • Trailers • Behind-the-scenes featurette.

1997 (R) 90m/C Cynthia Rothrock, Kurt McKinney, Tony LoBianco, Brad Dourif, Mako, Kenn Scott; *D:* Paul Maslak; *W:* Robert Easter; *C:* Richard Benda; *M:* John Coda.

T-Men

United States Treasury agents O'Brien and Genaro infiltrate a counterfeiting ring. Supposedly based on actual Treasury cases. It's less interesting than his *Raw Deal* due to the sanitized Dragnet-style agents, but director Anthony Mann still manages to elude the script's routine moralizing. DVD transfer is very basic with a paint-by-numbers look—the print used may already have been duped. Sound is best they can manage. —MO

Movie: 🎵🎵🎵 **DVD:** 🎵🎵

VCI (cat #8308, UPC 089859830822). Full frame. Dolby Digital Mono. $14.99. Keepcase. *LANG:* English. *FEATURES:* 12 chapters • Classic original film noir trailers • "Dark Reflections, Part 1," video "liner notes" by Max Allan Collins.

1947 96m/B Alfred Ryder, Dennis O'Keefe, June Lockhart, Mary Meade, Wallace Ford, Charles McGraw; *D:* Anthony Mann; *W:* John C. Higgins; *C:* John Alton; *M:* Paul Sawtell. *AWARDS: NOM:* Oscars '47: Sound.

Taboo

When Yoji Maysuzaki dies, an odd request is found in his will: his last wish is that his widow and his best friend make love—in front of his coffin, on the day of his funeral! Flashbacks reveal how he'd been playing mind games with everyone for years. Years after the funeral, he's still screwing with people's heads. Another entry in Japan's cycle of sexual psychodramas from the 1990s, this one benefits from a strong lead performance by Maysuzaki, while Shindo's wide-eyed mugging fares not so well. Comes in a twin disc double feature with *Sadistic City*. —BT

Movie: 🎵🎵 **DVD:** 🎵🎵

Tai Seng (cat #68934, UPC 6016436893-40). Full frame. $24.95. Keepcase. *LANG:* Japanese; Cantonese; Mandarin. *SUB:* English; Chinese. *FEATURES:* 8 chapters.

1997 92m/C *JP* Noriko Hamada, Eisaku Shindo, Yoji Maysuzaki; *D:* Yutaka Kohira.

Taboo

Using spare intertitles and scenes of unusual beauty, director Oshima tells the story of a garrison of samurai militia during the decline of the shogunate power, when recruits were hard to come by. The militia needs recruits, and Captain Hijikata (Beat Takeshi) accepts two young applicants, the brash and lowbred Tashiro (Tadanobu Asano) and the very delicate and provocative Kano (Ryuhei). Kano's presence brings the not-uncommon homosexuality in the samurai militia to the surface of everyday affairs. He's rumored to be Tashiro's lover, and his looks attract the attention of other officers and men. Hijikata tries to let him find his own way for a while, and then assigns a sergeant to introduce Kano to women at the local geisha house. This fails miserably. When soldiers said to be involved with Kano turn up dead, the militia becomes a home for unspoken suspicions and rivalries. Because all the action and emotions remain rather remote and subdued, viewers who aren't reading between the lines may see the film as a samurai story where little happens and nothing is explained. Visually, the film is a treat. The settings are interesting and the camera is not used so formally as to become static. One entrance by a fully adorned geisha is a beautiful showstopper. Most of the fights happen at night and are not choreographed as action pieces, but the final confrontation takes place in a spooky stylized set. Although the "gay activity" on-screen is minimized, it will probably come as a very unwelcome surprise to viewers not expecting it. The film is not rated, indicating it did not get an American release, but the Canadian rating is 14A, which tells you that there's no nudity or graphic content. DVD is a flawless transfer of a beautifully photographed set of images. The only extras are some text biographies of the cast, director, and composer Riyuchi Sakamoto. —GE *AKA:* Gohatto.

Movie: 🎵🎵🎵 ½ **DVD:** 🎵🎵🎵 ½

Columbia Tristar (cat #08386, UPC 0433-96083868). Widescreen (1.78:1) anamorphic. $24.95. Keepcase. *LANG:* Japanese. *SUB:* English. *FEATURES:* Talent files.

1999 100m/C *JP* Takeshi "Beat" Kitano, Ryuhei Matsuda, Shinji Takeda, Tadanobu Asano; *D:* Nagisa Oshima; *W:* Nagisa Oshima; *C:* Toyomichi Kurita; *M:* Ryuichi Sakamoto.

The Tailor of Panama

Loose cannon British intelligence operative Andy Osnard (Pierce Brosnan) is exiled to Panama to ferret out possible threats to the canal. He blackmails tailor Harry Pendel (Geoffrey Rush) into using his client list to get news about revolutionaries. The cautionings of the stuffy local British mean nothing because Osnard's superiors are eager for any news they can give to the Americans as a pretext for seizing back the canal; Pendel's inventions and Osnard's recklessness soon cause enormous repercussions. DVD is one of Columbia TriStar's beautiful releases, visually and aurally pristine like almost all DVDs of big new pictures. There is a director's commentary by the usually outspoken John Boorman, who pretty much sticks to the production aspect of the movie, and a way-overlong and obnoxiously cut set of interviews with Rush and Brosnan. These become tiresome very quickly. There's also an alternate ending that I'm glad wasn't used, as it would have negated the film's truthfulness. The trailers try to make the show look like an action thriller, which must have helped it commit boxoffice suicide. Selling action, and delivering intellectual social criticism may have contributed to the negative word of mouth around this rather good movie. —GE

Movie: 🎵🎵🎵 **DVD:** 🎵🎵🎵 ½

Columbia Tristar (cat #06395, UPC 0433-96063952). Widescreen (2.35:1) anamorphic. Dolby Digital 5.1 Surround Stereo; Dolby Digital Surround. $24.95. Keepcase. *LANG:* English; French. *SUB:* English; French. *CAP:* English. *FEATURES:* Commentary: John Boorman • Extended interview with Rush

and Brosnan • Alternate ending • Trailer • Filmographies • 28 chapters.
2000 (R) 109m/C Pierce Brosnan, Geoffrey Rush, Jamie Lee Curtis, Brendan Gleeson, Catherine McCormack, Leonor Varela, Harold Pinter, Daniel Radcliffe, David Hayman, Mark Margolis, Martin Ferrero, John Fortune; **D:** John Boorman; **W:** John Boorman, Andrew Davies, John Le Carre; **C:** Philippe Rousselot; **M:** Shaun Davey.

Take It to the Limit
Troubled teen Rick (Fitzpatrick) is sent to stay with his uncle (Marlo) in hopes that it'll straighten him out. But that happens when Jill (Roenfeldt), a cute girl, introduces him to rock climbing. This is a pretty good movie for kids. It's a bit obvious, but it treats the characters seriously. Sound is much stronger than you normally find in a Corman production; image is so-so. Both are about the same as VHS. —MM
Movie: ♫♫ ½ **DVD:** ♫♫
New Concorde (cat #NH20697 D, UPC 736991369795). Full frame. Stereo. $14.98. Keepcase. *LANG:* English. *SUB:* Spanish. *FEATURES:* 24 chapters • Talent files • Trailers.
2000 87m/C Leo Fitzpatrick, John Marlo, Gretel Roenfeldt, Jason Bortz, Christin Couto; **D:** Sam Kieth; **W:** Arthur Jeon; **C:** Michael Anderson; **M:** Louis Gabriel Cowan.

Taking Care of Business
When he wins tickets to the World Series, car thief Jimmy Dworski (Belushi) breaks out of a minimum security prison and heads for the game. On the way, he finds workaholic ad man Spencer Barnes's (Grodin) organizer/planner which is crammed with credit cards, keys to the Malibu mansion, etc. Jimmy attempts to return the notebook for a reward but when everyone mistakes him for Spencer, who is supposed to be closing a big deal with a Japanese account, Jimmy takes the path of least resistance. The real Spencer, meanwhile, is stranded without ID or money. The result is a mildly diverting comedy. DVD is strictly a barebones affair. Full-frame image does nothing to improve on VHS tape. Sound might be a bit better but not much. —MM **AKA:** Filofax.
Movie: ♫♫ **DVD:** ♫♫
Hollywood Pictures (cat #24442, UPC 786-936119817). Full frame. Dolby Digital 5.1 Surround. $19.98. Keepcase. *LANG:* English. *CAP:* English. *FEATURES:* 12 chapters.
1990 (R) 108m/C James Belushi, Charles Grodin, Anne DeSalvo, Loryn Locklin, Veronica Hamel, Hector Elizondo, Mako, Gates (Cheryl) McFadden, Stephen Elliott; **D:** Arthur Hiller; **W:** Jeffrey Abrams; **C:** David M. Walsh; **M:** Stewart Copeland.

A Tale of Springtime
Jeanne (Teyssedre), a high school philosophy teacher, feels stifled by her present relationship. By chance, she meets Natascha (Darel), an emotional young piano student who invites her to stay at her flat while her widowed father (Quester) is away on a trip. It appears that Natascha wants to contrive a meeting between her father and Jeanne to drive away his young lover. Rohmer's films are always filled with sly musings on the differences between perception and reality and this film is no exception. It's the first in the series entitled "Tales of the Four Seasons." The color on this DVD is particularly vivid and the sound is great. —LA
Movie: ♫♫ ½ **DVD:** ♫♫♫
MGM Home Ent. (cat #1003249, UPC 27616873996). Widescreen (1.66:1) letterboxed. Mono. $19.98. Keepcase. *LANG:* French. *SUB:* English; Spanish. *CAP:* French. *FEATURES:* Original theatrical trailer • 16 chapters.
1989 (PG) 107m/C FR Anne Teyssedre, Hugues Quester, Florence Darel, Eloise Bennett, Sophie Robin; **D:** Eric Rohmer; **W:** Eric Rohmer; **C:** Luc Pages; **M:** Robert Schumann.

A Tale of Two Cities
Masterpiece Theatre production of the famous Dickens novel boasts excellent production values. Image is very good compared to other Granada television efforts. There's some increase in graininess in exteriors, but interiors are nice and sharp. Sound is adequate. —MM
Movie: ♫♫♫ **DVD:** ♫♫ ½
BFS Video (cat #30211-D, UPC 06680530-2114). Full frame. $29.98. Keepcase boxed set. *LANG:* English. *FEATURES:* 24 chapters.
1991 240m/C James Wilby, Serena Gordon, John Mills, Jean-Pierre Aumont, Anna Massey.

The Tale of Zatoichi
Blind, streetwise, ex-masseur Ichi avails himself of the hospitality of a local gang leader. A conflict with a rival gang is about to erupt into violence and Ichi's host wants his guest (and his incredible skills as a swordsman) on his side. While vacillating, the lowly Ichi (who is much wiser than he appears) befriends a local woman in crisis and a noble warrior who is dying of consumption. This endearing, first film in the popular series approaches the familiar story material with an air of humanity and tragedy. Ichi's relationship with his dying comrade is handled with an affecting poignancy, which is helped along by the sparse, but effective score. Much of this story material was revisited for the final Ichi film, 1989's *Zatoichi*. The disc features an appropriately sharp image, but the lack of 16x9 enhancement is quite a drawback for those with widescreen monitors. The contrasts are a little weak, with blacks that look a bit milky. The framing is a bit cramped on the top during the final "bridge" scene. Sound is unimpressive but fine. The liner notes do a nice job of putting the film in context and the stills (limited to 10) are an appreciated bonus.

—DG **AKA:** Blind Swordsman: The Tale of Zatoichi; Zatoichi Monogatari.
Movie: ♫♫♫ **DVD:** ♫♫ ½
Home Vision Cinema (cat #BLI020, UPC 037429168226). Widescreen (2.35:1) letterboxed. Mono. $19.95. Keepcase. *LANG:* Japanese. *SUB:* English. *FEATURES:* 19 chapters • 4 collector cards • Still gallery.
1962 96m/C JP Shintaro Katsu, Shigeru Amachi, Masayo Mari, Chitose Maki; **D:** Kenji Misumi; **W:** Minoru Inuzuka.

The Tale of Zatoichi Continues
Travelling blind masseur (and deadly swordsman), Ichi (AKA Zatoichi or "Blind Ichi") (Shintaro Katsu) is marked for death after he learns that the local clan leader is a giggling loony. The clan's hitmen and a group of infuriated gangsters make an aggressive attempt to kill him when he returns to pay respects at the grave of a dead friend (as seen in the first film). First sequel to the hit, *The Tale of Zatoichi* finds Katsu settling on a definitive set of mannerisms for Ichi and upping the action quotient. The melancholy, elegiac tone of the first film is also present, personified in the story of Zatoichi's estranged brother— a one-armed swordsman wanted by the police. Ichi's brother is played by Katsu's real-life sibling, Kenzaburo Jo (AKA Tomisaburo Wakayama, whose later *Lone Wolf and Cub* film series was produced by Katsu) which adds interesting resonance to the story line. The image is smeary and overbright with poor contrasts. There are instances of digital edging as well. It's a slight improvement over VHS. —DG **AKA:** Zoku Zatoichi Monogatari.
Movie: ♫♫ ½ **DVD:** ♫♫ ½
Home Vision Cinema (cat #BLI040, UPC 037429168424). Widescreen (2.35:1) letterboxed. Mono. $19.95. Keepcase. *LANG:* Japanese. *SUB:* English. *FEATURES:* 14 chapters • 4 collector cards • Still gallery.
1962 73m/B JP Shintaro Katsu, Tomisaburo Wakayama, Masayo Banri, Yoshie Mizutani; **D:** Kazuo Mori; **W:** Minoru Inuzuka; **C:** Shozo Honda; **M:** Ichiro Saito.

Tales from Europe: The Singing, Ringing Tree
This live-action film is based upon a story by the Brothers Grimm. A young prince (Eckart Dux) has pledged his love to a beautiful princess (Christel Bodenstein). But she requests that he procure the famous singing, ringing tree for her. The prince does indeed find the tree, but it is guarded by a wicked dwarf (Richard Kruger). The dwarf puts a curse on the prince, turning him into a bear. To return to normal, the prince must convince the princess to fall in love with him. This tale is a strange twist on the familiar story of "Beauty and the Beast" and is made all the weirder by the lavish production design

in this 1957 film from East Germany. Apparently, no expense was spared to create the enchanted kingdom. And although the special effects may look somewhat laughable today, they were most likely the cutting edge half a century ago. This engaging production is somewhat stunted by the economic route taken with the audio on this DVD. For those who speak German, the original dialogue is available on this disc. However, instead of dubbing the actors voices into English, French, and Spanish, simple narration has replaced the dialogue. This allows one to follow the story, but removes any dramatic involvement which the piece may have once had. That strange problem aside, the transfer here looks great, giving us a picture which is clear and displays very rich colors. There are some defects from the source print and the picture does flicker at times. The menus on this DVD are especially difficult to navigate. —*ML*

Movie: 🎵 ½ **DVD:** 🎵🎵🎵
ICESTORM International, Inc. (cat #69024, UPC 679126902422). Full frame. Dolby Digital Mono. $24.95. Keepcase. *LANG:* German; English; French; Spanish. *FEATURES:* Theatrical trailer • Bonus short film.
1957 70m/C *GE* Eckart Dux, Christel Bodenstein, Richard Kruger.

Tales from Europe: The Story of Little Mook

Icestorm International brings us another entry into their *Tales from Europe* series, with this 1953 East German production. Based on a fairy tale by Wilhelm Hauff, the film begins by describing the plight of Mook (Johannes Maus), a hunchbacked old man, who is constantly tormented by children whenever he travels through the streets. One day, Mook decides to confront the children and begins to tell them the story of his life. In these flashbacks, Little Mook (Thomas Schmidt) is seen being abused by his father, in quite the same manner as the children were admonished by the elder Mook. Leaving home, Little Mook sets out across the desert and becomes involved in one adventure after another. The film uses many creative (though dated looking) special effects to convey the tale of Little Mook's adventures. While the film isn't quite as colorful as some of the others in this series, it is still entertaining, although the youth of today may not know what to make of it. The full-frame image is sharp, but not entirely clear, as the picture becomes quite soft at times. This transfer has revealed many defects from the source print, comprised mainly of scratches and white spots. The colors here are true, but not very bright. The Dolby Digital Mono audio track offers dubbed English dialogue, which is always clear and audible. A very slight hiss is noticeable on this track. The DVD also includes an animated short from Germany. —*ML*

Movie: 🎵 ½ **DVD:** 🎵🎵
ICESTORM International, Inc. (cat #69025, UPC 679126902521). Full frame. Dolby

Digital Mono. $24.95. Keepcase. *LANG:* German; English; French; Spanish. *FEATURES:* Bonus short film • 6 chapters.
1953 96m/C *GE* Johannes Maus, Thomas Schmidt; *D:* Jesse White; *W:* Peter Podehl.

Tales from the Crypt: Robert Zemeckis Collection

These three tales from HBO's popular horror series were directed by Robert Zemeckis. In "All Through the House," an adulterous human kills her husband after years of frustration to collect his insurance policy. She splits his head with a fire-iron and then dumps the body into a well behind the house on a cold, snowy Christmas Eve. That same night an escapee from a local insane asylum prowls the neighborhood. He's dressed as Santa Claus and wields a sharp axe. "Yellow" features Kirk Douglas, Dan Aykroyd, and Lance Henriksen in a World War I story that's reminiscent of Stanley Kubrick's "Paths of Glory," which Douglas produced and starred in. "You, Murderer" is an exceptional entry. Not nearly as "horrific" as many other episodes, it's more of a crime-thriller. Using archival footage of the late Humphrey Bogart, it tells the story of an ex-crook who is murdered by his wife and his plastic surgeon after a set-up. The full-frame transfer is very good and contains plenty of detail. Colors are natural with deep shadows and good highlights. Dolby Stereo nicely brings the stories to life. —*GH*

Movie: 🎵🎵🎵 **DVD:** 🎵🎵🎵
HBO Home Video (UPC 026359128028). Full frame. Dolby Stereo. $14.98. Keepcase. *LANG:* English.
1995 90m/C Kirk Douglas, Dan Aykroyd, Lance Henriksen, John Lithgow, Isabella Rossellini; *D:* Robert Zemeckis.

Tales from the Darkside: The Movie

This collection of three horror stories is framed by a "wrap-around" involving a cannibalistic Deborah Harry who's preparing to cook a boy who tells her tales to delay the process. One involves a mummy; a second concerns a cat, a millionaire and a hitman; the third is a deal with the devil. They're all reasonably effective, but nothing really new for fans. DVD delivers an excellent image; grain in the darker scenes comes from the original. —*MM*

Movie: 🎵🎵 **DVD:** 🎵🎵🎵
Paramount (cat #32360, UPC 097363236-047). Widescreen anamorphic. Dolby Digital 5.1 Surround; Dolby Digital Surround; Mono. $24.98. Keepcase. *LANG:* English; French. *SUB:* English. *FEATURES:* 13 chapters • Commentary: director John Harrison, writer George Romero • Trailer.
1990 (R) 93m/C Deborah Harry, Christian Slater, David Johansen, William Hickey, James Remar, Rae Dawn Chong, Julianne Moore, Robert Klein, Steve Buscemi,

Matthew Lawrence; *D:* John Harrison; *W:* George A. Romero, Michael McDowell; *C:* Rob Draper.

Tales from the Gimli Hospital

Fans of movies where things actually happen will be sorely disappointed by this art-house favorite. In a hospital room where a woman is dying, a grandmother tells her grandchildren a story which took place in a hospital in the town of Gimli. This story concerns two men (Kyle McCulloch and Michael Gottli) who have adjacent hospital beds and recount stories from their lives. These "stories" amount to little more than odd and disturbing visuals which generally lack any sense of narrative. The film was clearly shot MOS, so there is scant dialogue—instead, there is an odd soundtrack of early 20th-century music. Fans of the surreal and the sublime will adore this film, but general audiences will find it lacking. For the DVD, *Tales from the Gimli Hospital* is presented full-frame. The black-and-white image is quite grainy and there are obvious defects from the source print. The audio is full of hissing and crackling, but it is difficult to discern if this was intentional on the filmmaker's part. The disc contains a commentary by director Guy Maddin (which does little to shed much logic on the film), as well as two of his early shorts. —*ML*

Movie: 🎵🎵 **DVD:** 🎵🎵
Kino on Video (cat #K183 DVD, UPC 738-329018320). Full frame. Digital Mono. $29.95. Keepcase. *LANG:* English. *FEATURES:* Commentary • Short films • 12 chapters.
1988 68m/B *CA* Kyle McCulloch, Michael Gottli, Angela Heck, Margaret Anne McLeod; *D:* Guy Maddin; *W:* Guy Maddin; *C:* Guy Maddin.

Tales of Frankenstein

This rather unfocused trailer collection showcases various film versions of *Frankenstein*, with the centerpiece being the presentation of the unsold pilot for the titular, proposed Columbia Pictures/Hammer studios anthology TV series. A bland, lifeless retelling of the story features Diffring as a doctor who exploits a woman's dead husband for use in his latest experiment. Sold into a package of other Columbia/Screen Gems short subjects, this pilot used to show up occasionally on television. The disc is made from one of these 16mm syndication prints and as such it is dark, scratchy, and features contrasts that are too strong. The optional audio commentary during the episode is informative but a bit too opinionated for a "historian's commentary" and seems to be miked solely on Newsom while the rest of the participants are forced to shout their opinions from the background. The additional video interviews are brief, but interesting. The Boris Karloff audio interview is a plus as is the longish fan interview with Glenn Strange. If the entire contents of the *Tales of Tomorrow* episode had been included, that might make this a must-have, simply for the novelty of owning these two unique TV works on legitimate digital video. But alas, the amount of digital noise and artifacting throughout all of the programs is distracting in the extreme and the result of an obviously poor authoring job. Menu navigation is a nightmare. A big disappointment from the usual exemplary All Day. At least we know the proceeds from this will go towards other, more worthy releases. —DG

Movie: 🐾 **DVD:** woof
Image Ent. (cat #ADED0905DVD, UPC 014-381090529). Full frame. Dolby Digital Mono. $24.99. Keepcase. *LANG:* English. *FEATURES:* 21 trailers from *Frankenstein* films ▪ Excerpts from *Tales of Tomorrow*, "Frankenstein" episode ▪ Boris Karloff, Peter Cushing, Michael Carreras interviews ▪ Boris Karloff, Glenn Strange audio interviews ▪ DVD-ROM text file of Mary Shelley's *Frankenstein* ▪ Commentary: Ted Newsom, Stuart Galbraith, Gary Smith ▪ Outtakes from *Abbott and Costello Meet Frankenstein*. There's no music credit, but at least one of the pieces is a library cue that was also used in *Night of the Living Dead* (1968).
1958 28m/B Anton Diffring, Helen Westcott, Don Megowan, Ludwig Stossel; *D:* Curt Siodmak; *W:* Curt Siodmak, Catherine Kuttner, Henry Kuttner; *C:* Gert Andersen.

The Tall Guy
Dexter King (Goldblum) plays straight man to an obnoxious British comedian (Atkinson) in a long-running stage show. The pay stinks but the work is steady and Dexter is only vaguely dissatisfied with his lot until he meets nurse Kate Lebon (Thompson), and falls hopelessly in love. Their wild Three-Stoogian love scene is one of the funniest ever put on film. The second half shifts gears slightly, becoming a wicked satire of contemporary British drama when Dexter takes part in a musical version of *The Elephant Man*. DVD does valiant work with a riotous, challenging color scheme that's heavy on oranges, greens, and reds, along with various tinted lights. All of that gives the image a flat, soft quality. The look comes from the original elements, I think, not the transfer. The 5.1 is not overly utilized and does not need to be. —MM
Movie: 🐾🐾🐾 ½ **DVD:** 🐾🐾 ½
Miramax Pictures (cat #21632, UPC 786936144550). Widescreen (1.85:1) anamorphic. Dolby Digital Surround. $19.98. Keepcase. *LANG:* English. *CAP:* English. *FEATURES:* 17 chapters.
1989 (R) 92m/C Jeff Goldblum, Emma Thompson, Rowan Atkinson, Geraldine James, Kim Thomson, Anna Massey; *D:* Mel Smith; *W:* Richard Curtis; *C:* Adrian Biddle; *M:* Peter Brewis.

Tank
Retired Army officer Garner's son is thrown into jail on a trumped-up charge by a small-town sheriff. Dad comes to the rescue in his restored Sherman tank. The trite and unrealistic portrayal of good vs. evil is made palatable by Garner's performance. The subtitle options are the only difference between disc and tape. —MM
Movie: 🐾 ½ **DVD:** 🐾🐾
Goodtimes Ent. (cat #81019). Full frame. Dolby Digital Mono. $19.98. Snapper. *LANG:* English. *SUB:* English; French; Spanish. *FEATURES:* 18 chapters.
1983 (PG) 113m/C James Garner, Shirley Jones, C. Thomas Howell, Mark Herrier, Sandy Ward, Jenilee Harrison, Dorian Harewood, G.D. Spradlin; *D:* Marvin J. Chomsky; *W:* Dan Gordon; *C:* Donald Birnkrant; *M:* Lalo Schifrin.

Taps
Fresh off his Oscar win for *Ordinary People*, Timothy Hutton stars as the leader of a serious teen rebellion at Bunker Hill Military Academy. The academy is deemed more valuable as real estate than as a school, so when the closing is announced, the kids take a stand. An accidental shooting of a local boy who was making trouble at the gates gets the Academy in deep trouble, costing them the year they had left to fight. Hutton leads the students in a stand off with local police and parents. The pleas of the parents come off as comic relief against the seriousness of the boy soldiers. Tom Cruise plays the gung-ho military fighter and Sean Penn is sedate as Hutton's roommate. George C. Scott is terrific as always playing General Bache. Scott draws a strong picture of Bache that provides motivation for the boys long after his removal from the Academy. His character casts a palpable shadow in the first half of the film that reaches all the way to the end as situations logically go from bad to worse. Hutton's acting falls just short of hitting the mark in this role, while Penn and Cruise stand out. Overall, not a bad film from the '80s genre of teen angst films. The DVD quality is up to snuff; the sound quality is good. —JAS
Movie: 🐾🐾🐾 **DVD:** 🐾🐾🐾
20th Century Fox (cat #20008, UPC 024-543009122). Widescreen (1.85:1) letterboxed. Dolby Surround. $19.98. Keepcase. *LANG:* English; French. *SUB:* English; Spanish. *FEATURES:* 32 chapters.
1981 (PG) 126m/C Timothy Hutton, George C. Scott, Ronny Cox, Sean Penn, Tom Cruise; *D:* Harold Becker; *W:* Robert Mark Kamen, Darryl Ponicsan; *C:* Owen Roizman; *M:* Maurice Jarre.

Tart
For 90 essentially plotless minutes, loner Cat (Swain) and her fellow teen friends wander from party to party and drink, smoke, and do whatever else they may find of interest at that particular moment. Cat gets involved with a popular kid (Renfro) who does various illegal things. At the end, she realizes that it's better (or at least healthier and less dangerous) to be yourself. *Cruel Intentions* covered the prep school ground in a much more entertaining fashion. In the end, it's difficult to care about a bunch of drug-addict prep school kids wandering around New York with little going on. The picture remains pleasantly crisp and clear throughout, with good detail, especially in the outdoor sequences. Light grain is occasionally visible, while the print displays infrequent marks and specks, along with slight edge-enhancement and a couple of traces of pixelation. Soundtrack is almost completely dialogue-driven. —AB
Movie: 🐾🐾 **DVD:** 🐾🐾 ½
Lion's Gate Home Ent. (UPC 031398798-828). Widescreen (1.85:1) anamorphic. Dolby Digital Surround. $24.98. Keepcase. *LANG:* English. *SUB:* English; Spanish. *FEATURES:* Trailer.
2001 (R) 94m/C Dominique Swain, Brad Renfro, Bijou Phillips, Mischa Barton, Lacey Chabert, Alberta Watson, Myles Jeffrey, Scott Thompson, Melanie Griffith; *D:* Christina Wayne; *W:* Christina Wayne; *C:* Stephen Kazmierski; *M:* Jeehun Hwang.

Tarzan and the Trappers
In the late 1950s, producer Sol Lesser filmed a trio of pilots for a proposed Tarzan TV series. The series—perhaps due to a lack of cowboys in those oater-crazed days of video—failed to sell, and the pilots were edited into this 69-minute feature for television sale in 1966. In the first part, Tarzan—aided by Boy and Jane—foils some poachers who've captured Cheetah. In the second, the brother of one of the poachers seeks revenge by trying to hunt down the ape man. The third concerns Tarzan driving off invaders searching for a lost city. The film features lots of nice stock footage from jungle documentaries, as well as footage shot when star Gordon Scott went to Africa to make some of the Tarzan features on location. Well photographed, with plenty of action, this might've made a fine series, but as a feature film, it's kind of a disjointed mess. The transfer doesn't look very good. For some reason, Laserlight's transfer is in letterbox format, the image obviously squeezed vertically and matted off at the top and bottom. This makes for unnecessary blur, and Scott's he-man shoulders look about six feet wide. Making things worse, the audio is also blurry and muffled. The disc also contains a companion feature *Tarzan the Fearless* —BT
Movie: 🐾🐾 **DVD:** 🐾 ½
Delta/Laserlight (cat #82051, UPC 01811-1205191). Widescreen letterboxed. $9.98. Keepcase. *LANG:* English. *FEATURES:* 25 chapters.
1958 70m/B Gordon Scott, Eve Brent, Ricky Sorenson, Maurice Marsac; *D:* Charles Haas, H. Bruce Humberstone, Sandy Howard.

Tarzan the Fearless
A 12-chapter serial has been condensed into this disjointed feature version. Mary

Brooks is searching for her scientist father, aided by her boyfriend Bob Hall. After rescuing her from a lost herd of Florida alligators, Tarzan becomes unofficial guardian of the expedition, slaying any lions and panthers that they happen across. It becomes apparent that the scientist has been captured by a lost tribe of Egyptians living in emerald-filled caves. There's a lot of action, with Buster Crabbe engaged in many fights with real lions, but the droning, monotonous library music that plays over everything is slumber inducing. Laserlight has released this feature frill-free in an attractively designed package. The print is scratchy, but given an acceptable transfer, the disc also contains a companion feature *Tarzan and the Trappers.* —BT

Movie: 🎬🎬 ½ **DVD:** 🎬 ½
Delta/Laserlight (cat #82051, UPC 01811-1205191). Widescreen letterboxed. $9.98. Keepcase. *LANG:* English. *FEATURES:* 21 chapters.
1933 84m/B Buster Crabbe, Julie (Jacqueline Wells) Bishop, E. Alyn Warren, Edward (Eddie) Woods, Philo (Philip, P.H., P.M.) McCullough, Matthew Betz; **D:** Robert F. "Bob" Hill; **W:** Walter Anthony; **C:** Joseph Brotherton, Harry Neumann.

The Taste of Others

This classy import is a hard sell to American audiences. For openers, it's in French with bright, optional English subtitles and captions. Second, it begins as if the first reel is missing; the low-key action opens with two banal conversations at separate restaurant tables. Director Jaoui takes time in sorting out relationships. Eventually it becomes clear that our main characters are gruff industrialist Jean-Jacques Castella (co-writer Bacri), his bodyguards, his wife and her dog named, umm, Flucky, and Mlle. Devaux (Alvaro), an English teacher. For me—and for fellow fans of Rohmer—it works. The characters are engagingly different and interesting. DVD image ranges between very good and excellent. The film looks as sharp and polished as a comparable Hollywood ensemble comedy. Sound is fine, but…Flucky? —MM **AKA:** Le Gout des Autres.
Movie: 🎬🎬🎬 **DVD:** 🎬🎬🎬
Buena Vista Home Ent. (cat #25405, UPC 786936175738). Widescreen (2.35:1) anamorphic. Dolby Digital 5.1 Surround. $24.98. Keepcase. *LANG:* French. *SUB:* English. *CAP:* English. *FEATURES:* 20 chapters.
2000 112m/C FR Jean-Pierre Bacri, Christiane Millet, Agnes Jaoui, Anne Alvaro, Gerard Lanvin, Wladimir Yordanoff, Brigitte Catillon, Xavier De Guillebon, Alain Chabet, Raphael Defour; **D:** Agnes Jaoui; **W:** Jean-Pierre Bacri, Agnes Jaoui; **C:** Laurent Dailland; **M:** Jean-Charles Jarrell.

The Tattered Web

Police detective Ed Stagg (Bridges) kills the woman his son-in-law is having an affair with. Then he's assigned to solve the case. When he tries to frame a wino, things get messy. Made-for-TV time-waster boasts O.K. performances and a tricky plot. DVD was made from a damaged print. It's full of scratches and nicks, essentially the same as VHS tape. Sound is acceptable. Title is available on the *Great Detective Movies* disc. —MM
Movie: 🎬🎬 **DVD:** 🎬 ½
BFS Video (cat #30292-D, UPC 06680530-2923). Full frame. $9.98. Keepcase. *LANG:* English. *FEATURES:* 6 chapters ● Talent files.
1971 74m/C Lloyd Bridges, Frank Converse, Broderick Crawford, Murray Hamilton, Sallie Shockley; **D:** Paul Wendkos; **M:** Robert Jackson Drasnin.

The Tavern

Film School 101 meets Business 101 in this bittersweet slice-of-life independent film (note: more bitter than sweet). Everything you could possibly ever want to know about the downside of running a bar is presented by writer, director, and the film's producer, Walter Foote. His lead character, played by Cameron Dye, is a middle-age bartender, who gets the bug about owning his own place. He quickly learns that it's all about raising money, the all-important non-compete clause (oops, forgot that one), raising more money, and ultimately seeing your dreams go up in smoke. No-frills DVD presentation of a truly independently produced film—commentary from the film's writer, director, and producer would have been nice. —RJT
Movie: 🎬🎬 ½ **DVD:** 🎬🎬
Wellspring Media, Inc. (cat #FLV5284, UPC 720917528427). Widescreen letterboxed. Dolby Digital Surround; Dolby Digital 5.1 Surround. $24.98. Keepcase. *LANG:* English. *FEATURES:* 16 chapters ● Trailer ● Filmographies.
2000 88m/C Cameron Dye, Kevin Geer, Margaret Cho, Greg Zittel, Nancy Ticotin, Steven Marcus, Carlo Alban, Kym Austin, Gary Perez; **D:** Walter Foote; **W:** Walter Foote; **C:** Kurt Lennig; **M:** Bill Lacey, Loren Toolajian.

Tchaikovsky

The glorious music is all that saves this pedestrian biography of the 19th-century Russian composer. It ignores his homosexuality and glosses over the dissolution of his marriage. Lead performance by Smoktunovsky does manage to rise above the script lapses. Kino has gone the extra mile on this one. First there are the multiple subtitles. Disc appears to have been made from very good original elements with bright colors and strong 5.1 sound. The film has been spread across two RSDL discs. —MM
Movie: 🎬🎬 ½ **DVD:** 🎬🎬🎬 ½
Kino on Video (cat #K190, UPC 738-329019020). Widescreen (2.35:1) letterboxed. Dolby Digital 5.1 Surround Stereo. $29.95. Keepcase. *LANG:* Russian; English; French. *SUB:* Russian; French; Spanish; Dutch; Japanese; Swedish; Arabic; English; Italian; Portuguese; Hebrew; Chinese. *FEATURES:* 32 chapters ● Interview with actress/dancer Maya Plisetskaya ● Interview with actor Innokenti Smoktunovsky ● Filmographies ● Featurette about cinematographer Margarita Pilikhina ● 2 photo galleries.
1971 153m/C RU Innokenti Smoktunovsky, Antonina Shuranova, Yevgeny Leonov, Maya Plisetskaya, Vladislav Strzeltchik, Alla Demidova, Kirill Lavrov; **D:** Igor Talankin; **W:** Igor Talankin, Yuri Nagibin, Budimir Metalnikov; **C:** Margarita Pilikhina. *AWARDS:* NOM: Oscars '71: Foreign Film, Orig. Song Score and/or Adapt.

Teenage Zombies

Teens pay a visit to a remote island and are captured by a sinister but fashionable mad scientist. The kids become subjects for her experiments in nerve gas research for commie spies. The print is battered, spliced, and bouncy, with plenty of speckles, a few awful sound drop-outs, and a puncture hole in the upper frame of the entire film. There are no extras or subtitles, and the disc also features BWF's usual ugly package design. —BT
Movie: 🎬 ½ **DVD:** 🎬
Beverly Wilshire Filmworks (cat #BWFD-82169, UPC 026617821692). Full frame. $14.99. Keepcase. *LANG:* English. *FEATURES:* 6 chapters.
1958 71m/B Don Sullivan, Katherine Victor, Chuck Niles; **D:** Jerry Warren; **W:** Jerry Warren; **C:** Allen Chandler.

Tekkaman Blade 2: Complete Collection

This DVD offers the complete six-episode cycle of the Japanese anime program *Tekkaman Blade 2.* As with many anime series, *Tekkaman* tells of humans who use robotic suits to enhance their strength. The story focuses on young Yuki François, a technician who has been chosen to join the elite Tekkaman fighting group. The Tekkaman has been given the task of protecting the galaxy from the evil Radham. Appearance-wise, *Tekkaman Blade* doesn't break any new ground in the anime genre, and there are times when the action borders on being too "cute." But when the Tekkaman begin battling the Radham, things do get interesting. The DVD offers a very nice transfer, with no grain and an impressive color scheme. There is some on-screen distortion at times, but it won't detract from the viewing experience. —ML
Movie: 🎬🎬 ½ **DVD:** 🎬🎬🎬
Urban Vision Ent. (cat #UV1071, UPC 638652107107). Full frame. Dolby Digital 5.1; Dolby 2.0 Surround. $29.95. Keepcase. *LANG:* English; Japanese. *SUB:* English. *FEATURES:* Fan art gallery ● Bonus trailers.
1994 (PG-13) 180m/C JP **D:** Hideki Tonokatsu.

Tell Me Something

This hit Korean thriller follows a detective assigned to the case when a serial killer starts leaving bags full of mismatched body parts all over Seoul. The leading clue: all the victims dated the same woman. The detective becomes a target as he's drawn toward the woman himself. The English dub is reasonably good, but the Korean preserves the performances better. The Korean soundtrack sometimes has an echo, and there is a significant pause at the layer change. —*BT*

Movie: 🎬🎬🎬 ½ **DVD:** 🎬🎬🎬
Kino on Video (cat #K237, UPC 738329-023720). Widescreen (1.85:1) letterbox. Dolby Digital 5.1 Surround. $29.95. Keepcase. *LANG:* Korean; English. *SUB:* English. *FEATURES:* 16 chapters ▪ Trailer ▪ Photo gallery.
1999 (R) 118m/C *KN* Suk-kyu Han, Eun-ha Shim, Hang-sun Chang, Jun-sang Yu, Jung-ah Yum; **D:** Yoon-Hyan Chang; **W:** Yoon-Hyan Chang, Su-chang Kong, Eun-ah In; **C:** Sung-bok Kim; **M:** Young-ook Cho.

The Temp

Neo-*femme fatale* thriller is fairly well made, with a refreshing sense of humor, but it falls apart completely in the last five minutes. Peter Derns (Hutton) is a young executive who's been in therapy for the paranoid jealousy that broke up his marriage. His doctor thinks that he's "cured" but pressures at work are building. His boss Charleen Townes (Dunaway) is about to introduce a new line of cookies and his secretary Lance is taking time off for a new son. Lance's temporary replacement, Kris Bolin (Boyle), turns out to be smarter, more ambitious and resourceful than anyone else who works for this cookie company. And she's devoted to Peter. Is it any coincidence that people who oppose him are removed from the picture? The guessing games are brightened by a sly bitchy sense of humor, and the kind of full-bore overacting that Faye Dunaway is so good at. When she and Hutton really cut loose, they're a joy to watch. Lara Flynn Boyle is effective, too. The fact that she and Hutton look like they were separated at birth is something of a distraction, but nothing is made of it. The cop-out ending is a much larger problem. It leaves dozens of unanswered questions. In fact, it's so abrupt and arbitrary that you might suspect the producers had no respect for the material or the form or the audience's expectations. The slightly grainy image is an accurate re-creation of the theatrical release, as I remember it. Details are quickly lost in dark interiors. The Dolby Digital 5.1 audio track is impressive. The stereo separation really stands out here (when the noise comes from the left, the character looks left!) and the Surround sound effects add to the ambience of the film (especially in chapter 13). Otherwise, this is a no-frills (not even a trailer) disc. —*MM/ML*

Movie: 🎬🎬 ½ **DVD:** 🎬🎬 ½
Paramount (cat #32793, UPC 097363279-341). Widescreen anamorphic. Dolby Digital 5.1; Dolby Surround; Stereo. $24.98. Keepcase. *LANG:* English; French. *SUB:* English. *CAP:* English. *FEATURES:* 13 chapters.

1993 (R) 99m/C Timothy Hutton, Lara Flynn Boyle, Faye Dunaway, Dwight Schultz, Oliver Platt, Steven Weber, Scott Coffey, Colleen Flynn, Dakin Matthews, Maura Tierney; **D:** Tom Holland; **W:** Kevin Falls; **C:** Steve Yaconelli; **M:** Frederic Talgorn. *AWARDS:* Golden Raspberries '93: Worst Support. Actress (Dunaway).

The Tempest

Derek Jarman's adaptation of Shakespeare is a wild and wooly affair, but it's also dark and gloomy for long stretches. On balance it is as much an imaginative independent production as a splashy, polished musical (though Elisabeth Welch's rendition of "Stormy Weather" is not to be missed). DVD appears to be a faithful reproduction of the original. Neither image nor sound is particularly notable. Jarman remains most well known for being one of the first openly gay filmmakers. —*MM*

Movie: 🎬🎬 ½ **DVD:** 🎬🎬 ½
Kino on Video (cat #K147, UPC 73832901-4728). Full frame. $29.95. Keepcase. *LANG:* English. *FEATURES:* 12 chapters ▪ "A Journey to Avebury" short film ▪ "Garden of Luxor" short film ▪ "Art of Mirrors" short film ▪ Original press kit.
1979 95m/C Heathcote Williams, Karl Johnson, Toyah Willcox, Elisabeth Welch; **D:** Derek Jarman; **W:** Derek Jarman; **C:** Peter Middleton.

The Temptations

Miniseries bio follows the Motown group from its high school beginnings in 1958 (under various names) through a meeting with Motown founder Berry Gordy (Babatunde) and major successes in the '60s. It's told from the viewpoint of the last original Temp, Otis Williams (Whitfield), as he and buddies Melvin Franklin (Woodside) and Paul Williams (Payton) hook up with first lead singer Eddie Kendricks (Brooks). When Kendricks goes solo, it's the turn of David Ruffin (Leon) but the group suffers various ego traumas and tragedies. Naturally, the music's the real highlight. Image is not a major improvement over VHS tape. Disc also offers a "jump to song" option. —*MM*

Movie: 🎬🎬 ½ **DVD:** 🎬🎬 ½
Hallmark Home Ent. (cat #99032). Full frame. Stereo. $19.98. Keepcase. *LANG:* English. *CAP:* English. *FEATURES:* 36 chapters ▪ Temptations discography ▪ Talent files ▪ Production notes ▪ Jump to song.
1998 150m/C Charles Malik Whitfield, DB Woodside, Terron Brooks, Christian Payton, Leon, Alan Rosenberg, Obba Babatunde, Charles Ley, Tina Lifford, Gina Ravera, Vanessa Bell Calloway, Chaz Lamar Shepherd; **D:** Allan Arkush; **W:** Kevin Arkadie, Robert P. Johnson; **C:** Jamie Anderson.

Ten Benny

Frustrated New Jersey shoe salesman Ray (Brody) borrows $10,000 from a local wiseguy to stake himself at the track and

set himself up in business. Bad idea. As his luck continues its downward spiral, he abuses his wife (Temchen) into the arms of his buddy (Gallagher) and becomes more desperate to climb out of the hole he has dug for himself. First-time director Bross has obviously studied at the Scorsese school of filmmaking, but he must have skipped the classes on originality and characterization. There's not much going here that hasn't been done (better) somewhere else, but Brody turns in a fine performance. Image is essentially identical to VHS tape, but that's not really a criticism of a character-driven story with modest production values. —*MM* **AKA:** Nothing to Lose.

Movie: 🎬🎬 ½ **DVD:** 🎬🎬
Winstar Home Ent. (cat #5137). Widescreen (1.66:1) letterboxed. Stereo. $29.98. Keepcase. *LANG:* English. *FEATURES:* Cast & crew thumbnail bios ▪ Trailer ▪ Production notes ▪ 6 chapters ▪ Photo gallery.
1998 (R) 98m/C Adrien Brody, Sybil Temchen, Michael Gallagher, Tony Gillan, James Moriarty, Frank Vincent; **D:** Eric Bross; **W:** Eric Bross, Tom Cudworth; **C:** Horacio Marquinez; **M:** Chris Hajian.

10 Magnificent Killers

Crime boss Bolo Yeung assembles a gang of 10 killers to dominate his province. While a new young constable trains to fight these criminals, a bounty hunter and his partner fight the killers one after another. It would've been better to concentrate more on the fights with the eccentric killers, and downplay the not-too-original twist ending. Fong Yeh's directorial style is straightforward, with almost every shot taking place outdoors—including some of those telephone poles they had in Old China. The sound is of the usual poor quality of a dubbed 1970s kung fu flick, though relatively free of noise. The letterboxed image is cropped a bit tight on both sides, cutting off the ends of credits. Volume 6 of the *Wu Tang Clan Hidden Chambers Collection*, a series that makes up for the often-poor quality of the prints presented with quite extensive extras. These include short bios of cast and crew members, contemporary interviews, clips from cast members' other films, image galleries, trailers, nice 3-D animated menus, interview footage of the Shaolin Temple Abbots, and more. —*BT*

Movie: 🎬🎬 **DVD:** 🎬🎬 ½
Xenon Ent. (cat #6, UPC 694795302021). Widescreen letterboxed. $14.95. Keepcase. *LANG:* English. *FEATURES:* Cast bios ▪ Previews ▪ Interviews ▪ Screensaver ▪ Wu Tang Clan music video ▪ Wu Tang Clan interview.
1977 (R) 86m/C *HK* Cheung Lik, Bolo Yeung, Yeh Fong, Kwai San; **D:** Yeh Fong; **W:** Yeh Fong; **C:** Hsin Yu Tsui; **M:** Ta Chiang Wu.

10 Violent Women

After failing to make a go of it with their gold mine (really!), 10 women decide to rob a jewel shop, and thereby put themselves in the way of a nasty Arab sheik, and then wind up in jail. Director Ted V. Mikels, who provides a commentary track, is a legendary exploitation auteur who makes Ed Wood Jr. look like Orson Welles. Extras are all that differentiate disc from VHS tape. Image is exceptionally grainy. —MM

Movie: woof **DVD:** ♪♪
Image Ent. (cat #ID1327TGDVD, UPC 014381132724). Full frame. Dolby Digital Mono. $24.98. Keepcase. *LANG:* English. *FEATURES:* 16 chapters ▪ Commentary ▪ Ted V. Mikels filmography and trailers ▪ Trailer.
1979 (R) 97m/C Sherri Vernon, Dixie Lauren, Sally Gamble; **D:** Ted V. Mikels; **W:** Ted V. Mikels; **C:** Yuval Shousterman; **M:** Nicholas Carras.

Tender Is the Heart

Young Dr. Freeman (Miller) can't get over memories of his dead wife—her ghost visits him in the shower—even though two live women (Noel and Gayle) have got the hots for him. Production values are generally better than average for a made-for-cable film. Sound is acceptable; image is better than VHS tape. —MM

Movie: ♪♪ ½ **DVD:** ♪♪ ½
Image Ent. (cat #ID1741PODVD, UPC 014-381174120). Widescreen (1.85:1) letterboxed. Dolby Digital Stereo. $24.98. Keepcase. *LANG:* English. *FEATURES:* 11 chapters.
2001 84m/C Staci Noel, Jennifer Gayle, Toby Miller, Todd Holliday, Robert Eastwood; **D:** Paul S. Parco; **W:** Paul S. Parco; **C:** Philip Hurn.

Tender Mercies [Anchor Bay]

Former country and western singer Mac Sledge (Duvall) gets another chance at a decent life when a buddy abandons him at a motel out in the middle of nowhere Texas. Fate comes in the form of Widow Rosa Lee (Harper) and her young son (Hubbard). Brilliant slice-of-life script by Horton Foote. Perfect cast lead by the Oscar-winner Duvall in one of his greatest roles. He can sing, too. Made-for-DVD documentary "Miracles and Mercies" contains new interviews with Robert Duvall, Tess Harper, Allen Hubbard, Bruce Beresford, and Horton Foote, and is worth a look. DVD looks and sounds great. —LA

Movie: ♪♪♪ ½ **DVD:** ♪♪♪
Anchor Bay (cat #DV11469, UPC 01313-1146998). Widescreen (1.77:1) anamorphic. $19.98. Keepcase. *LANG:* English; French. *CAP:* English. *FEATURES:* "Miracles and Mercies" documentary ▪ Theatrical trailer ▪ Talent bios ▪ 22 chapters.
1983 (PG) 88m/C Robert Duvall, Tess Harper, Betty Buckley, Ellen Barkin, Wilford Brimley, Lenny Von Dohlen, Allan Hubbard; **D:** Bruce Beresford; **W:** Horton Foote; **C:** Russell Boyd; **M:** George Dreyfus. *AWARDS:* Oscars '83: Actor (Duvall), Orig. Screenplay; Golden Globes '83: Actor—Drama (Duvall); L.A. Film Critics '83: Actor

(Duvall); N.Y. Film Critics '83: Actor (Duvall); Writers Guild '83: Orig. Screenplay; *NOM:* Oscars '83: Director (Beresford), Picture, Song ("Over You").

Tennessee's Partner

Enjoyable, unexceptional buddy western is adapted from a story by Bret Harte. Reagan intervenes in an argument and becomes Payne's pal. The video transfer lacks definition and is often quite dark. The soundtrack frequently sounds muddy and sports occasional distortion. —MJT

Movie: ♪♪ **DVD:** ♪♪
VCI (cat #8293, UPC 089859829321). Full frame. Dolby Digital Mono. $19.99. Keepcase. *LANG:* English. *FEATURES:* 12 chapters ▪ Original theatrical trailer ▪ Trailer gallery.
1955 87m/C Ronald Reagan, Rhonda Fleming, John Payne; **D:** Allan Dwan.

Tequila Body Shots

This movie plays like a sanitized high school theatre version of a horror film about reincarnation, true love, and demon vengeance. The sets are all just that—sets. Mexico looks like a Disney ride and even the dirt on the side of the road is clean. The dialogue is spoken so slowly and clearly that even an ESL student could follow the story. The script feels like it was taken from the back of a Cracker Jack box with lines like, "Have you ever met someone for the first time but you feel like you've known them for a very long time." Yawn. A group of three young guy friends meet a group of three young girl friends and it's kismet. There is, indeed, someone for everyone, and Johnny (Lawrence) is struck instantly by Tamlyn (Mouser) and the chase is on. By coincidence, they have all been invited to a party in Mexico for Halloween. Along the way the boys meet a warlock-like healer who gives our hero Johnny two bottles of magical tequila that he must drink. It's very important that he drink both, so of course he drinks one and loses track of the other. The one bottle is enough to give him the ability to hear what women are thinking (we never really know what the second bottle was supposed to do). This allows him to court Tamlyn and give his friends tips on women to hit on. With his new-found talent he also discovers that something sinister and otherworldly has brought them to Mexico. Yes, these middle-class, white kids are reincarnated souls from Mexico who have unfinished business.... There are a few obligatory flashes of flesh and some sophomoric fart and prison rape jokes to keep the action going, and to keep it out of complete family film territory, but in the end there's really no reason to care about any of these people, even in that bad-movie sort of way. The extras interviews are fluffy and go nicely with the film. The disc looks great, with bright even-toned colors and solid blacks, and the sound is good. —CA

Movie: ♪ ½ **DVD:** ♪♪ ½

Lion's Gate Home Ent. (cat #VM7761D, UPC 031398776123). Widescreen letterboxed. Dolby Digital 5.1 Surround. $24.99. Keepcase. *LANG:* English. *SUB:* English; French; Spanish. *CAP:* English. *FEATURES:* 24 chapters ▪ Theatrical trailer ▪ Interviews.
1999 (R) 94m/C Joey Lawrence, Dru Mouser, Rene L. Moreno, Nathan Anderson, Josh Marchette, Jennifer Lyons, Henry Darrow; **D:** Tony Shyu; **W:** Tony Shyu; **C:** Lawrence Schweich; **M:** Shayne Fair, Larry Herbstritt.

The Terminator [2 SE]

This "Special Edition" is only a marginal improvement visually over the earlier Image release (reviewed in *Book 1*). The image has always had a fair amount of grain. The 5.1 remix adds a new dimension of sound to the seminal action picture. More important are the numerous extras on the double-sided disc. The deleted scenes are mostly a curiosity; only one really adds much. Two new "making of" documentaries are essentially collections of interviews filmed at various times over the years. Many of the points made there are also included in the liner notes. —MM

Movie: ♪♪♪ ½ **DVD:** ♪♪♪ ½
MGM Home Ent. (cat #1001182, UPC 027616854735). Widescreen (1.85:1) anamorphic. Dolby Digital 5.1 EX Surround; Dolby Surround; Mono. $26.98. Keepcase. *LANG:* English; French; Spanish. *SUB:* English; French; Spanish. *FEATURES:* 32 chapters ▪ 2 "making of" documentaries ▪ Deleted scenes with commentary by James Cameron ▪ DVD-ROM features ▪ Original treatment ▪ Liner notes ▪ Trailers ▪ TV spots ▪ Stills gallery.
1984 (R) 108m/C Arnold Schwarzenegger, Michael Biehn, Linda Hamilton, Paul Winfield, Lance Henriksen, Bill Paxton, Rick Rossovich, Dick Miller, Earl Boen; **D:** James Cameron; **W:** James Cameron; **M:** Brad Fiedel.

Terminatrix

In the 21st century, an overpopulation crisis causes the world government to regulate all sex acts. One woman leads a rebellion against the tyranny. The leaders decide to send killer robot T-69 (Shouko Kudou) back in time to prevent the rebel from ever being born. Kei Mizutani time travels to the past as well, to warn horny bartender Naofumi Matsuda that he's to be the father of humanity's last hope, and that this Terminatrix is out to destroy his sexual potency. It's not as wild as *Weather Woman*, but it may please Mizutani's growing fanbase all the same. Image and sound quality are average. —BT

Movie: ♪♪ **DVD:** ♪♪
Central Park/U.S. Manga (cat #APCD2092, UPC 719987209220). Full frame. $29.99. Keepcase. *LANG:* Japanese; English. *SUB:* English. *FEATURES:* 10 chapters ▪ Trailers ▪ DVD-ROM features.
1995 75m/C *JP* Kei Mizutani, Naofumi Matsuda, Shouko Kudou, Saeko Ichijou,

Yuuki Fujisawa; **D:** Mikio Hirota; **W:** Mikio Hirota; **C:** Naoki Hashimoto; **M:** Tatsuo Nakanishi.

Territorial Men

Frontier family drama was created from the TV series *Sara*. It's sweet-natured but difficult to watch on DVD since the disc was made from a severely damaged print. It's dark and fuzzily focused. Title is available as part of *The Wild West* boxed set. —MM

Movie: 🎵🎵 **DVD:** 🎵🎵

Brentwood (cat #44213-9, UPC 78736442-1398). Full frame. $19.95. Keepcase. *LANG:* English. *FEATURES:* "Spooky Hooky" cartoon • 6 chapters • DVD dictionary • DVD-ROM features • Trivia game.

1976 100m/C Brenda Vaccaro, Mariclare Costello, Louise Latham, Sam Groom; **D:** Lawrence (Larry) Dobkin, William Claxton; **W:** James Dixon, Margaret Hatch.

Terror in the Haunted House

Newly married Sheila has a recurring nightmare about an ominous old house she can't recall having seen in waking life. Journeying with husband Philip to Florida, they go to live at a country house—gasp!...the house in her dream. Spooky events heap up—who's crazy?—with the answer rooted in the trauma of her past. Distinguished only by being filmed in "Psycho-Rama," where literal subliminal flashes show us single-frame cartoon skulls, bats, and demons that at first appear to be flaws in the print and then can be seen much as we catch Brad Pitt in *Fight Club*. In *Terror,* these blips in the center of the screen actually have a certain invasive visceral impact and probably would have flipped me out as a kid. Now, however, the film is stupid and dull. DVD image looks like VHS. Sound on the same par. —MO

AKA: My World Dies Screaming.

Movie: 🎵 **DVD:** 🎵🎵

Rhino (cat #R2971501, UPC 603497150-120). Full frame. $9.95. Snapper. *LANG:* English. *FEATURES:* 12 chapters.

1958 90m/C Gerald Mohr, Cathy O'Donnell, William Ching, John Qualen, Barry Bernard; **D:** Harold Daniels; **W:** Robert C. Dennis; **C:** Frederick E. West; **M:** Darrell Calker.

Terror in the Midnight Sun

Bizarre '50s Swedish sci-fi tale is difficult to describe. It's a first contact story with a big guy in a ratty fur suit who's one of the least frightening "monsters" ever to grace the screen. The snowy scenery is captured in black-and-white photography that ranges between fair and good. DVD is made from a print that's intermittently scratchy. There's some light static on the soundtrack and a nice commentary track by the film's producer. Disc also contains an American re-edit of the film under the title *Invasion of the Animal People.* (Please see review.) —MM **AKA:** Invasion of the Animal People; Space Invasion of Lapland; Space Invasion from Lapland; Horror in the Midnight Sun.

Movie: 🎵 ½ **DVD:** 🎵🎵 ½

Image Ent. (cat #ID9751SWDVD, UPC 014-381975123). Full frame. Dolby Digital Mono. $24.99. Snapper. *LANG:* English. *FEATURES:* 13 chapters • Commentary: Bertil Jernberg • Swedish exploitation trailers • 2 Swedish short subjects • "Girl in the Glacier" episode of Swedish TV show *13 Demon St.* • Gallery of exploitation art • Liner notes by Frank Henenlotter.

1958 70m/C Robert Burton, Barbara Wilson, Ake Gronberg; **D:** Virgil W. Vogel; **W:** Arthur C. Pierce; **C:** Hilding Bladh.

The Terror Within

In a post-apocalyptic world, mutants seek human women for breeding purposes. There's little that DVD can (or should) do to improve this low-budget, high-grain connect-the-dots genre piece. —MM

Movie: 🎵 **DVD:** 🎵

New Concorde (cat #NH20327 D, UPC 736991432796). Full frame. $9.99. Keepcase. *LANG:* English. *FEATURES:* 24 chapters • Trailers • Talent files.

1988 (R) 90m/C George Kennedy, Andrew Stevens, Starr Andreeff, Terri Treas; **D:** Thierry Notz; **W:** Thomas McKelvey Cleaver; **C:** Ronn Schmidt; **M:** Rick Conrad.

Testamento

Story told in flashback begins with the death of the wealthy Mr. Araujo (Xavier) and then examines the creation of his fortune (and his lively love life). Compared to American productions, the acting style here is a bit overstated in the big emotional scenes but that's not meant as a criticism. The film, made by Portuguese television, works well in every aspect—lighting, production design, pace, plotting. If the DVD image lacks high polish, it looks just fine. The photography is exceptional. Optional English subtitles are easy to read. —MM

Movie: 🎵🎵🎵 **DVD:** 🎵🎵 ½

Winstar Home Ent. (cat #FLV5281, UPC 720917528120). Full frame. $24.98. Keepcase. *LANG:* Portuguese. *SUB:* English. *FEATURES:* 16 chapters • Filmographies and awards • DVD credits.

1998 112m/C *PT* Nelson Xavier, Maria Ceica, Chico Diaz, Karla Leal; **D:** Francisco Manso; **W:** Mario Prata; **C:** Edgar Moura; **M:** Tito Paris.

Texas

Miniseries adaptation of massive James Michener best-seller epitomizes "made-for-TV." Stephen Austin (Duffy) sets up a colony in 1821 Texas where Mexican law requires all settlers to become Mexican citizens. Calls for statehood begin and Austin's initial resistance is overturned by rebellion and prodding from Sam Houston (Keach) and Jim Bowie (Keith). Lots of action amidst the history but it's a fairly pedestri-an extravaganza. The picture is simply atrocious on disc. The image is riddled with artifacts and pixels in bright panning shots. A definite step down from VHS tape. —MM **AKA:** James A. Michener's Texas.

Movie: 🎵 **DVD:** 🎵

Artisan Ent. (cat #12044). Full frame. Dolby Digital Stereo. $14.98. Keepcase. *LANG:* English. *FEATURES:* 27 chapters.

1994 180m/C Patrick Duffy, Stacy Keach, David Keith, Maria Conchita Alonso, Anthony Michael Hall, Rick Schroder, Benjamin Bratt, Chelsea Field, John Schneider, Grant Show, Randy Travis, Woody Watson; **D:** Richard Lang; **W:** Sean Meredith; **M:** Lee Holdridge.

Texas, Adios

Curious spaghetti western stars Franco Nero as a sheriff who goes to Texas with his kid brother Jim (Dell'Acqua) to get the man who murdered their father. The action has all of the affectations of this rarified branch of the genre, and that makes it lots of fun for fans and virtually unwatchable for everyone else. DVD presents an unusually good image. Those bright dusty landscapes can be brutal if they're not handled properly, but excess grain and artifacts are at a minimum. Go with the original Italian dialogue and English subtitles. They're far superior to the English dubbing. —MM **AKA:** The Avenger.

Movie: 🎵🎵 ½ **DVD:** 🎵🎵🎵

Anchor Bay (cat #DV11583, UPC 01313-1158397). Widescreen (2.35:1) anamorphic. Dolby Digital Mono. $24.99. Keepcase. *LANG:* English; Italian. *SUB:* English. *FEATURES:* 28 chapters • Trailer • Interview with Franco Nero.

1966 92m/C *IT* Franco Nero, Alberto Dell'Acqua, Cole Kitosch, Elisa Montes, Jose Suarez; **D:** Ferdinando Baldi; **W:** Ferdinando Baldi; **C:** Enzo Barboni.

Texas Rangers

I have to admit I really like a good western. This one is entertaining and action-filled, with a couple of good-looking females. A good cast (Van Der Beek, McDermott, Patrick, Travis, Cook, and Kutcher) gives a rousing performance about the formation and early days of the Texas Rangers. The Rangers in many cases weren't much different in their actions from the criminals they hunted. Over time, they helped clean up the state and brought real justice to the Wild West. A good ole "shoot 'em up." DVD image is clean and very crisp; Surround sound is outstanding, with bullets whizzing all around your viewing area. —DE

Movie: 🎵🎵 ½ **DVD:** 🎵🎵🎵

Buena Vista Home Ent. (cat #2167303, UPC 786936144987). Widescreen (2.35:1) anamorphic. Dolby Digital 5.1 Surround Sound. $29.98. Keepcase. *LANG:* English. *CAP:* English. *FEATURES:* 14 chapters • "Behind the Badge" featurette • Storyboard sequence • Still gallery • Theatrical trailer.

2001 (PG-13) 90m/C James Van Der Beek, Dylan McDermott, Ashton Kutcher, Usher Raymond, Robert Patrick, Rachael Leigh Cook, Leonor Varela, Randy Travis, Jon Abrahams, Matt Keeslar, Vincent Spano, Marco Leonardi, Oded Fehr, Joe Spano, Tom Skerritt, Alfred Molina; **D:** Steve Miner; **W:** Scott Busby, Martin Copeland; **C:** Daryn Okada; **M:** Trevor Rabin.

That Obscure Object of Desire

Luis Buñuel's final, perplexing film is well-served by this disc, which lives up to Criterion standards and then some. The strange tale of frustrated sex and cruel coquetry wraps up Buñuel's career with a cocktail of perversity and surrealism. The wealthy Mathieu (Rey) becomes infatuated with his new maid, Conchita (alternately, Carole Bouquet and Angela Molina), and pursues her across Paris and even to Spain in an unfulfilled "affair" that goes on for months with the woman unpredictably encouraging, and then repelling, his attentions. These escalate in intensity, as Mathieu keeps trying to buy Conchita in one way or another. He accepts her promises of intimacy only to be frustrated when she seemingly changes her mind at the last minute. DVD is another fine transfer from prime elements, with more pop and verve than their slightly dullish laserdisc from a decade ago. A racy original trailer is included that sells the film as *Last Tango in Seville;* it only serves to remind us what a conflicted, non-erotic response we have to all the sexual situations in the movie proper. In an interview extra, screenwriter and Buñuel collaborator Jean-Claude Carriere talks on-camera to a number of topics, including the dual-actress idea. The excellent liner notes by William Rothman are accompanied by a fascinating text interview with Buñuel that discusses the film's quirky mysteries satisfyingly, even though the Spanish trickster reveals next to nothing. Finally, the disc includes some sequences from a French silent movie version of the same story, *La Femme et la Pantin,* that includes a very erotic staging of Conchita's nude dance for the "tourists"—from 1929. —*GE* **AKA:** Cet Obscur Objet du Desir.
Movie: 🎜🎜🎜🎜 **DVD:** 🎜🎜🎜🎜
Criterion (cat #143, UPC 037429162026). Widescreen (1.78:1) anamorphic. Dolby Digital Mono. $39.95. Keepcase. *LANG:* French. *SUB:* English. *FEATURES:* Interview with Jean-Claude Carriere ▪ Text interview with Buñuel ▪ Sequences from French silent movie *La Femme et la Pantin* ▪ Liner notes by William Rothman.
1977 (R) 100m/C *SP* Fernando Rey, Carole Bouquet, Angela Molina, Julien Bertheau; **D:** Luis Buñuel; **W:** Luis Buñuel, Jean-Claude Carriere; **C:** Edmond Richard. *AWARDS:* L.A. Film Critics '77: Foreign Film; Natl. Bd. of Review '77: Director (Buñuel); Natl. Soc. Film Critics '77: Director (Buñuel); *NOM:* Oscars '77: Adapt. Screenplay, Foreign Film.

That Thing You Do!

The Wonders, a small-town foursome, hit the big time in 1964 after a substitute drummer adds some kick to the band's new song and sets the local kids a-dancin'. Developed by freshman director/screenwriter Hanks (who also appears as the band's record exec), it's nostalgic, mostly true to the times, and uncomplicated to a fault, but engaging nonetheless. Can't-get-it-out-of-your-head title track (played 11 times in the film!) was selected from more than 300 submissions after Hanks put out a call to music publishers. The transfer is clean and without defects and the image shows a good level of detail. However, at times the image appears a bit soft, which is a bit surprising given the film's relatively young age. Colors are strong and faithfully reproduced, creating natural-looking flesh tones and vibrant settings. Blacks are deep and never lose detail, producing an image that is nicely contrasted and offers plenty of visual depth. The compression is free of artifacts, creating a very pleasing presentation. Audio makes good use of Surround tracks, creating an enveloping sound stage, but as a whole the soundtrack is not nearly as aggressive as you may expect. —*MM/GH*
Movie: 🎜🎜🎜 **DVD:** 🎜🎜🎜
20th Century Fox (cat #2001641). Widescreen (1.85:1) anamorphic. Dolby Digital 5.0 Surround Stereo; Dolby Digital Surround. $19.98. Keepcase. *LANG:* English; French; Spanish. *SUB:* English; Spanish. *FEATURES:* Trailers and teasers ▪ 2 music videos ▪ Promotional featurette.
1996 (PG) 110m/C Giovanni Ribisi, Bryan Cranston, Holmes Osborne, Dawn Maxey, Sean M. Whalen, Clint Howard, Kathleen Kinmont, Barry Sobel, Gedde Watanabe, Jonathan Demme, Marc McClure, Colin Hanks, Tom Everett Scott, Johnathon Schaech, Liv Tyler, Steve Zahn, Ethan (Randall) Embry, Tom Hanks, Charlize Theron, Obba Babatunde, Peter Scolari, Alex Rocco, Bill Cobbs, Rita Wilson, Chris Isaak, Kevin Pollak; **D:** Tom Hanks; **W:** Tom Hanks; **C:** Tak Fujimoto; **M:** Howard Shore. *AWARDS: NOM:* Oscars '96: Song ("That Thing You Do!"); Golden Globes '97: Song ("That Thing You Do!").

Theatre of Blood

Companion piece to *The Abominable Dr. Phibes,* finds Price playing Edward Lionheart, a hammy Shakespearian actor who takes vengeance on any critic who has written an unfavorable review of his work. With the help of a mob of crazies and his daughter Edwina (Rigg, who spends far too much time in disguise), he concocts baroque schemes to get rid of them, each murder quoting a bloody moment from the Bard. Like so many films of its time, it's also about the establishment under siege by the rabble. The wit is sharp and the whole film plays to Price's strengths as an actor. (It ends with him literally attacking the scenery.) Douglas Hickox's energetic, swiftly paced direction keeps the theatrical aspects from ruining the film. A faint hiss is audible on the soundtrack and a few light flecks appear from time to time. The grain has always been there, so DVD is an acceptable presentation for a film of this age. —*MM* **AKA:** Much Ado about Murder.
Movie: 🎜🎜🎜 **DVD:** 🎜🎜 ½
MGM Home Ent. (cat #1002355, UPC 027-616865663). Widescreen (1.66:1) letterboxed. Dolby Digital Mono. $14.95. Keepcase. *LANG:* English; French; Spanish. *SUB:* French; Spanish. *CAP:* English. *FEATURES:* Trailer ▪ 16 chapters.
1973 (R) 104m/C *GB* Vincent Price, Diana Rigg, Ian Hendry, Robert Morley, Dennis Price, Diana Dors, Milo O'Shea, Harry Andrews, Coral Browne, Robert Coote, Jack Hawkins, Michael Hordern, Arthur Lowe; **D:** Douglas Hickox; **W:** Anthony Greville-Bell; **C:** Wolfgang Suschitzky; **M:** Michael Lewis.

Theatre of Death

Christopher Lee plays Phillipe Darvas, a manipulative theatre director who uses hypnosis on his lead actress to achieve believable terror in her performances. When a series of murders occur, Lee disappears, leaving the police to hunt him down. This somewhat unsatisfying thriller is noteworthy for its novel use of Grand Guignol theatre in a modern setting and a particularly vibrant use of its selective color palette. Lee plays a particularly unsympathetic lead and Glover is a moderately effective (though blandly written) foil. After Lee's disappearance, the film tends to flounder, sorely missing the immediate dramatic conflict of his confrontational character. It does deliver a few surprises and some atmospheric moments before the finale, though. The disc is fairly stunning with rich, dense, saturated colors and a clear, sharp picture. There's a bit of digital noise during a dressing room scene, but it's a minor quibble. The mono sound is fine. The Christopher Lee interview is candid and terrific, and one only wishes it were longer. —*DG* **AKA:** Blood Fiend; Female Fiend.
Movie: 🎜🎜 **DVD:** 🎜🎜🎜 ½
Anchor Bay (cat #DV11574, UPC 01313-1157499). Widescreen (2.35:1) anamorphic. Mono. $24.98. Keepcase. *LANG:* English. *FEATURES:* 25 chapters ▪ Insert card ▪ Interview with Christopher Lee ▪ Trailer ▪ TV spots ▪ Radio spots ▪ Poster and still gallery ▪ Christopher Lee bio.
1967 90m/C Christopher Lee, Lelia Goldoni, Julian Glover, Evelyn Laye, Jenny Till, Ivor Dean; **D:** Samuel Gallu; **W:** Ellis Kadison, Roger Marshall; **C:** Gilbert Taylor.

Thelonious Monk: Straight, No Chaser

This is a look at jazz pianist Thelonious Monk, both on and off stage. We learn about Monk's history, and see pictures and footage of his early performances. It also incorporates Christian and Michael Blackwell's 1968 footage of Monk, which is in excellent shape. The interviews that are included here are contemporary for this 1989 picture, and the associates and friends of Monk who are interviewed give insight into just who he was, and why he was important. An enjoyable film, which clearly will mean more to fans of the performer's work. The older, black-and-white footage looks fairly soft, but is still strong for its age. There is a mild amount of grain, but not enough to cause distraction. The more recent, color footage also is a little bit grainy at times, but often looks clear and clean. The audio for the older footage sounds rather flat and thin, with a tiny bit of background hiss. Most importantly, the music still manages to come through with acceptable clarity. The newer footage does sound smoother, if still limited by the mono audio. Both interviews and the narration sound clear and easily understood. —AB/DG

Movie: ♫♫♫ **DVD:** ♫♫ ½
Warner Home Video Full frame. Dolby Digital Surround. $19.98. Snapper. *LANG:* English. *SUB:* English; French; Spanish; Portugese. *FEATURES:* Cast & crew bios ➠ Trailer.
1989 (PG-13) 90m/C Thelonious Monk, Harry Colomby, Bob Jones, Baroness Nica De Koenigswarter; **D:** Charlotte Zwerin; **Nar:** Samuel E. Wright.

There's Nothing out There
Years before *Scream* or *Scary Movie,* this independent gem sent up the horror genre with real wit and originality. It gets the right treatment on DVD. Plot: Seven teens spend Spring Break at a secluded mountain cabin. One of the guys, who has seen every horror movie in the video store, recognizes the signs of impending doom. Despite the widescreen transfer, the image was shot on Super16mm film and so it's as grainy as it has always been. That comes with the territory, though, and is part of the game. So is the commentary track with selected cast and crew. They're lots of fun and the rest of the extras are the sort of things that fans love. Recommended. —MM

Movie: ♫♫♫ ½ **DVD:** ♫♫♫ ½
Image Ent. (cat #THEDO788DVD, UPC 014-381078824). Widescreen (1.78:1) anamorphic. Dolby Digital Stereo. $24.98. Keepcase. *LANG:* English. *FEATURES:* 14 chapters ➠ Commentary: Kanefsky, cast, crew ➠ Pre-production footage and video storyboards ➠ Rehearsals and bloopers ➠ Animation test footage and deleted shots ➠ Trailer ➠ Filmographies.
1990 91m/C Craig Peck, Wendy Bednarz, Mark Collver, Bonnie Bowers, John Carhart III, Claudia Flores, Jeff Dachis, Lisa Grant; **D:** Rolfe Kanefsky; **W:** Rolfe Kanefsky; **C:** Ed Hershberger; **M:** Christopher Thomas.

Therese Raquin
Kate Nelligan turns in an excellent performance as Zola's first famous adulterous heroine. Unfortunately, she is poorly served by a substandard image. DVD appears to have been created from a tape

that was played on a machine with dirty heads. The production is dark and somber to begin with. It's then marred by heavy grain and excessive pixelation and intermittent streaks and flecks. —MM

Movie: ♫♫♫ **DVD:** ♫ ½
BFS Video (cat #30125-D, UPC 06680530-1254). Full frame. $39.98. Keepcase boxed set. *LANG:* English. *FEATURES:* 18 chapters.
1980 173m/C *GB* Kate Nelligan, Brian Cox, Mona Washbourne, Kenneth Cranham, Alan Rickman, Richard Pearson; **D:** Simon Langton; **W:** Philip Mackie.

They Call It Murder
D.A. Doug Selby (Hutton) investigates the matter of a corpse found floating in a swimming pool. The characters are based on Erle Stanley Gardner. Production values are strictly made-for-TV. DVD does nothing to improve them. Image transfer was made from damaged original elements. Light static is constant. Artifacts blossom from the heavy grain. Title is available on the *Great Detective Movies* disc. —MM

Movie: ♫♫ **DVD:** ♫
BFS Video (cat #30292-D, UPC 06680530-2923). Full frame. $9.98. Keepcase. *LANG:* English.
1971 120m/C Jim Hutton, Lloyd Bochner, Jessica Walter, Leslie Nielsen, JoAnn Pflug, Nita Talbot, William Elliott, Vic Tayback; **D:** Walter Grauman; **W:** Sam Rolfe; **M:** Robert Jackson Drasnin.

They Do It with Mirrors
Please see review of *Agatha Christie's Miss Marple Set 2.*
Movie: ♫♫ ½ **DVD:** ♫♫ ½
A&E (cat #AAE-70383, UPC 7339617038-32). *FEATURES:* 12 chapters.
1991 100m/C *GB* Faith Brook, Gillian Barge, Joan Hickson, Joss Ackland, Jean Simmons; **D:** Norman Stone; **W:** T.R. Bowen; **C:** John Walker.

They Got Me Covered
Two WWII-era journalists become involved with a comic web of murder, kidnapping, and romance. Hope is very funny and carries the rest of the cast. Look for Doris Day in a bit part and listen for Bing Crosby singing whenever Hope opens his cigarette case. DVD delivers a very good black-and-white image. Grain intensifies in the special effects shots; that comes from the original. —MM

Movie: ♫♫ ½ **DVD:** ♫♫ ½
HBO (cat #91255). Full frame. Stereo; Mono. $24.98. Snapper. *LANG:* English; French; Italian; Spanish. *SUB:* English; French; Spanish. *FEATURES:* 21 chapters ➠ Talent files ➠ Trailer.
1943 95m/B Doris Day, Bob Hope, Dorothy Lamour, Otto Preminger, Eduardo Ciannelli, Donald Meek, Walter Catlett; **D:** David Butler; **W:** Harry Kurnitz; **C:** Rudolph Mate; **M:** Leigh Harline; **V:** Bing Crosby.

The Thief
Successful anti-Red thriller is also one of the best, mainly because it avoids obnoxious, argumentative political dialogue. In fact, it has no dialogue at all, a concept which United Artists was able to exploit for a marketing gimmick. Ray Milland does a one-man noir act as a tortured traitor, and the interesting direction contrasts expressive visuals with semi-documentary location work. It gets a bit slow, and the gimmick eventually turns out to be just that, but creatively it's still very interesting. Nuclear researcher Allan Fields (Milland) is photographing top nuclear secrets at his laboratory in Washington, D.C., and handing the film off to foreign agents who smuggle them to New York City, and from there out of the country. When an accident blows Allan's cover, he's given an escape route on an outbound freighter. He waits for a telephone code, stranded in a miserable Manhattan room across the hall from an exotic and interested woman (Rita Gam) he dares not approach. He shakes the G-Man sent to tail him, to meet his final contact atop the Empire State building, only to find that the F.B.I. agent has followed her. For all the hoopla, this is really just a silent movie with sound effects. The source materials are 35mm and in excellent shape, and the sound is very clear. We can really appreciate cameraman Sam Leavitt's blend of documentary techniques and low-key noir lighting. Only a steady sprinkling of negative dirt gets in the way of a perfect presentation. Perhaps when the technology becomes cheap enough, the relatively simple process of erasing this visual dandruff will be affordable to all...right now even studios use it only on their top titles, and then sometimes overuse it, erasing other picture details. —GE

Movie: ♫♫♫ ½ **DVD:** ♫♫♫ ½
Image Ent. (UPC 014381870626). Full frame. $24.98. Keepcase. *LANG:* English. *FEATURES:* Liner notes by Wade Williams.
1952 84m/B Ray Milland, Rita Gam, Martin Gabel, Harry Bronson, John McKutcheon; **D:** Russell Rouse; **W:** Russell Rouse, Clarence Greene; **C:** Sam Leavitt; **M:** Herschel Burke Gilbert. *AWARDS: NOM:* Oscars '52: Orig. Dramatic Score.

Thief in the Night
This film (the first in a series) follows the perils of Patty (Patty Dunning), a seemingly upright girl whose hubby got called up to heaven, with the rest of the good folks, and left her behind to deal with an Anti-Christ who enjoys seeing heads roll—literally. When we first meet Patty, she's just attended a service at Teen Town where a young preacher talks about Earth's final days when Christians believe Jesus Christ will return "like a thief in the night" and call his followers home. While strolling through the Iowa State Fair, Patty and friends contemplate the meaning of this sermon. Pig-tailed Jenny (Colleen Niday) feels compelled to go back to hear more, but Patty and her free-lovin' gal pal Diane

(Maryann Rachford) decide to go on a helicopter joyride with some cute boys as they can "always get converted later." Bad move, ladies. Full-frame transfer preserves all the spots and scratches of the original, but unfortunately, often suffers from the contemporary ill of frequent digital distortion. Tiny Dolby Digital mono track wavers in quality from shot to shot, but so does the source material. —NG

Movie: 🎜🎜 ½ **DVD:** 🎜🎜
Russ Doughten Films, Inc. (UPC 9781888-568646). Full frame. Mono. $29.95. Keepcase. *LANG:* English; Spanish; Portuguese. *FEATURES:* Commentary: Donald Thompson, Russ Doughten.
1972 69m/C Patty Dunning, Thom Rachford, Colleen Niday, Maryann Rachford; *D:* Donald W. Thompson; *W:* Jim Grant.

Thief of Hearts

In some ways, this flawed thriller can be seen as the progenitor of all the "erotic thrillers" that have become a staple of home video. The film enjoyed modest success in theatrical release, but then it was one of the first studio features to be re-edited with more sexual footage for VHS tape. This DVD, however, is the original version. Not that it matters, because the sexiest scene—the shooting lesson in chapter 8—remains intact (and still could be shown virtually uncut on network TV). The story concerns burglar Scott Muller (Bauer) who breaks into Ray (Getz) and Mickey's (Williams) house and steals, among other things, her diaries describing her sexual fantasies about a perfect man. The sexually frustrated second-story man decides to transform himself into her ideal. DVD is about what you'd expect of a film this old. The image is dark and grainy, just as it was in theatres. Sound is acceptable on another no-frills (not even a trailer) disc from Paramount. —MM

Movie: 🎜🎜 ½ **DVD:** 🎜🎜 ½
Paramount (cat #01660, UPC 0973601-66040). Widescreen anamorphic. Dolby Digital 5.1 Surround; Dolby Surround; Mono. $24.98. Keepcase. *LANG:* English; French. *SUB:* English. *CAP:* English. *FEATURES:* 14 chapters.
1984 (R) 101m/C Steven Bauer, Barbara Williams, John Getz, Christine Ebersole, George Wendt; *D:* Douglas Day Stewart; *W:* Douglas Day Stewart; *C:* Andrew Laszlo; *M:* Harold Faltermeyer.

Things I Left in Havanna

Three Cuban sisters arrive in Madrid searching for a better life. There they find an aunt who emigrated to Spain a long time ago and has become a devoted capitalist. They also encounter a Cuban man who tries to seduce them and attempts to exploit their inexperience in "comedic" ways. The box quotes *Variety* ("Energetic & accomplished") and *Village Voice* ("Lively & intelligent"). VideoHound says "Immediately uninteresting." Extremely crude DVD

transfer suggests some sort of video origin. Average sound. —MO

Movie: 🎜🎜 **DVD:** 🎜
Vanguard Intl. Cinema (cat #VF9186, UPC 658769918632). Widescreen. $29.95. Keepcase. *LANG:* Spanish. *SUB:* English. *FEATURES:* 11 chapters. Theatrical trailer.
1997 110m/C *SP* Jorge Perugorria, Violeta Rodrigues, Kiti Manver, Broselianda Hernandez; *D:* Manuel Gutierrez Aragon; *W:* Manuel Gutierrez Aragon, Senel Paz; *C:* Teodoro Escamilla; *M:* Jose Maria Vitier.

Things You Can Tell Just by Looking at Her

An anthology of slices in the lives of five main characters. All are women at a turning point, and all the actresses look fabulous as they are caressed by the camerawork of Emmanuel Lubezki *(Hearts in Atlantis, Sleepy Hollow)*. Close is a doctor caring for her indigent mother and looking for love in all the wrong men. Flockhart is a tarot card reader who comes over to her house to give her a reading, which turns out to be painfully accurate. The camera never wavers from Close's face as she tries to control her feelings and we are reminded joyfully what it is to watch a fabulous actress portraying big emotions with small movements. Holly Hunter is a single woman having a long-term affair with a doctor (Hines) who discovers she's pregnant. Hunter embodies the face of an angel as she endures the harsh words of a homeless woman because she feels she deserves it. Kathy Baker is a single mother who may be in love with the new neighbor across the street, a dwarf. This is perhaps one of the most endearing sections of the film. The awkward motions each of the characters go through make you believe in love at first sight. We go back to Flockhart, home-caring for her lover (Golino) who appears to be dying of cancer. All of the women in the film are complex and fascinating to watch. None of the stories are resolved, exactly, as the film is careful to show you what they are doing and how they feel rather than tell you how you should feel about what they are doing. Writer/director Garcia (who shot the amazing *Mi Vida Loca*) has managed to draw out performances from each of the actresses that reverberate with not only frailty and strength, but also sadness and hope. In each sequence we see a flash of a woman who we know from the beginning has committed suicide, but we never learn her story. Brenneman plays the detective who gets the case and realizes she went to high school with the woman, but even she is unable to find out what happened. The film leaves you melancholy, but somehow uplifted, and it will be a pleasure for people who like to see a movie unfold for them rather than chase them around with a hammer. Lubezki used a filter in every single shot in the film giving the disc a uniform, almost sepia quality, and the sound is very good. —CA

Movie: 🎜🎜🎜 ½ **DVD:** 🎜🎜🎜

MGM Home Ent. (cat #1001609, UPC 027-616859198). Widescreen (1.85:1) anamorphic; full frame. 5.1 Surround; Stereo Surround. $26.98. Keepcase. *LANG:* English; French; Spanish. *SUB:* French; Spanish. *CAP:* English. *FEATURES:* 32 chapters. Theatrical trailer.
2000 (PG-13) 106m/C Cameron Diaz, Glenn Close, Calista Flockhart, Holly Hunter, Amy Brenneman, Kathy Baker, Valeria Golino, Matt Craven, Gregory Hines, Noah Fleiss, Miguel (Michael) Sandoval, Danny Woodburn, Roma Maffia; *D:* Rodrigo Garcia; *W:* Rodrigo Garcia; *C:* Emmanuel Lubezki; *M:* Ed Shearmur.

Thirteen Days

The Cuban Missile Crisis is seen through the eyes of Presidential aide Kenny O'Donnell (Costner), JFK (Greenwood), and Attorney General Robert Kennedy (Culp). The film stays reasonably close to historical truth and manages to generate some tension, despite the fact that almost all of the action can be reduced to scenes of middle-aged guys walking into rooms, spouting self-important dialogue, looking grim, and then walking out. None of that provides any real challenge to DVD, which delivers the usual highly polished image. The 5.1 Surround does no favors to Costner's irritating Massachusetts accent. The disc's real value lies in the extensive "Infinifilm" extras which go into admirable historical detail. Because of them, DVD is far superior to any other form of home video and to the theatrical release. —MM

Movie: 🎜🎜🎜 **DVD:** 🎜🎜🎜 ½
New Line (cat #N5202, UPC 794043-520228). Widescreen anamorphic. Dolby Digital 5.1 Surround. $26.98. Keepcase. *LANG:* English. *CAP:* English. *FEATURES:* 32 chapters. Historical figures commentary. "Roots of the Cuban Missile Crisis" documentary. Historical figures biographical gallery. Historical information subtitles. Filmmakers' commentary track. "Bringing History to the Silver Screen" documentary. Visual effects scene deconstructions. Filmographies. DVD-ROM features.
2000 (PG-13) 145m/C Kevin Costner, Bruce Greenwood, Steven Culp, Dylan Baker, Michael Fairman, Kevin Conway, Tim Kelleher, Len Cariou, Bill Smitrovich, Dakin Matthews, Madison Mason, Christopher Lawford, Ed Lauter, Elya Baskin, Boris Krutonog, Peter White, James Karen, Tim Jerome, Olek Krupa, Lucinda Jenney, Henry Strozier, Frank Wood, Stephanie Romanov; *D:* Roger Donaldson; *W:* David Self; *C:* Andrzej Bartkowiak; *M:* Trevor Jones.

13 Gantry Row

After buying a house, wife Julie's (Gibney) life is endangered by creepy events that occurred there a century ago. Well-directed but completely warmed-over Ripper-type murdering ghost story line. Very clean DVD transfer of a source that looks like a video-to-film source. Good sound. —MO

Movie: 🎬🎬 **DVD:** 🎬🎬🎬
MTI Home Video (UPC 619935404236). Full frame. $24.95. Keepcase. *LANG:* English. *SUB:* Spanish. *FEATURES:* 20 chapters ▪ Theatrical trailers ▪ Cast bios.
1998 90m/C Rebecca Gibney, Mark Gerber, John Adam; **D:** Catherine Millar; **W:** Tony Morphett; **C:** Mark Wareham; **M:** Chris Neal.

13 Ghosts

The Zorba family inherits a furnished mansion from a reclusive uncle, which seems a stroke of luck as their finances are so poor they're selling their furniture. Moving in goes well until they're informed that their benefactor was an eccentric who believed he was collecting ghosts, 13 to be exact. Thanks to this DVD, producer William Castle's Illusion-O gimmick is back in all its glory. One side of the disc is the straight movie with no gimmick, so if you start playing the film and the title sequence is not in color, stop and flip. The single viewer supplied looks something like 3-D glasses, but with the red & blue filters placed over and under instead of side-by-side. Every Illusion-O sequence is printed in color, with the ghosts a colored overlay. View through the red gel, and the ghosts are visible. Watch through the blue, and they disappear (well, almost). Columbia TriStar's DVD is finally restored to its full Illusion-O majesty, for the curiosity of all. The picture quality changes during the special sequences, which were filmed on different Eastmancolor stock but were apparently not too difficult to restore. Overall, the 16:9-enhanced picture is excellent. —*GE*
Movie: 🎬🎬 ½ **DVD:** 🎬🎬🎬
Columbia Tristar Home Video (UPC 4339-6065505). Widescreen (1.78:1) anamorphic. Dolby Digital 5.1 Surround Stereo. $19.95. Keepcase. *LANG:* English; Spanish. *FEATURES:* "Making of Illusion-O" ▪ Notes ▪ Trailers ▪ Original William Castle introduction.
1960 88m/C Charles Herbert, Jo Morrow, Martin Milner, Rosemary DeCamp, Donald Woods, Margaret Hamilton, John van Dreelen; **D:** William Castle; **W:** Robb White; **C:** Joseph Biroc; **M:** Von Dexter.

13 Ghosts

Visually impressive remake is absolutely ridiculous and an empty mess otherwise. Eccentric millionaire Cyrus (Abraham) and his psychic assistant (Lillard) attempt to trap spirits to use for their own gain. Things don't go as planned; cut to present day. Cyrus's long-lost nephew Arthur (Shalhoub) finds out that a giant house has been left to him by his uncle. He packs up his children (Elizabeth and Roberts) and his nanny (rapper Rah Digga, stuck with unfunny lines) and sets out to the place. The house is a giant evil machine (powered by a group of very irritated ghosts) that is going to open the "eye of hell"—or some such business. The rest of the picture—no more, no less—is one very long chase sequence through glass hallways. By the end, the story becomes confusing—loud sounds attempting to make it appear as if things are actually happening. Even the film's sound mix is volume and fury, although not particularly inspired, using similar shock sounds over and over until they get annoying. Picture looks remarkably good throughout, as the vibrant cinematography and impressive production design are offered in top-notch fashion. Sharpness and detail are exceptional throughout; even dimly lit hallways provide a strong amount of visual information. Flaws are minimal and hardly bothersome. Very light grain is occasionally visible as is slight edge-enhancement. —*AB*
Movie: 🎬🎬 **DVD:** 🎬🎬🎬 ½
Warner (cat #22083, UPC 0853922083-26). Widescreen (1.85:1) anamorphic. Dolby Digital 5.1 Surround. $24.98. Snapper. *LANG:* English; French. *SUB:* English; French; Spanish. *CAP:* English. *FEATURES:* Commentary ▪ 18-min. "making of" featurette ▪ Talent files ▪ Trailer ▪ Music videos ▪ William Castle thumbnail bio ▪ 24 chapters ▪ "Ghost Files" featurette.
2001 (R) 91m/C Tony Shalhoub, Embeth Davidtz, Matthew Lillard, Shannon Elizabeth, Alec Roberts, Rah Digga, JR Bourne, F. Murray Abraham; **D:** Steve Beck; **W:** Richard D'Ovidio, Neal Marshall Stevens; **C:** Gale Tattersall; **M:** John (Gianni) Frizzell.

36 Crazy Fists

Early Jackie Chan martial arts flick is rendered virtually unwatchable by an abysmal image transfer. It looks worse than a worn VHS tape played on a machine with dirty heads. Chan directed the ho-hum fight scenes. English dubbing is goofy. —*MM*
Movie: 🎬 **DVD:** 🎬
BCI-Eclipse (cat #44189-9, UPC 7873644-18992). Full frame. $19.98. Keepcase. *LANG:* English. *FEATURES:* "Casper the Friendly Ghost" cartoon ▪ 6 chapters ▪ Trivia game ▪ DVD-ROM features ▪ DVD dictionary.
1977 90m/C *HK* Jackie Chan, Tony Leung Siu Hung, Wong Tai-Kwong; **D:** Jackie Chan, Chi-Hwa Chen.

This Is Not a Test

Please see review of *Atomic War Bride*.
Movie: 🎬🎬
1962 72m/B Seamon Glass, Mary Morlass, Thayer Roberts, Aubrey Martin; **D:** Frederic Gadette; **W:** Frederic Gadette, Peter Abenheim, Betty Laskey; **C:** Brick Marquard; **M:** Greig McRitchie.

Thomas Jefferson

Documentarian Ken Burns took his cameras to Thomas Jefferson's home, Monticello, and rounded up the usual suspects, including bloviator George Will, to comment on the man's life and work. It's the standard PBS glossy treatment with lots of mournful fiddles in the background. There's nothing wrong with the film. It's a good introduction to the man, but anyone who does not already have an interest in the subject probably isn't going to make it through three hours. Some pixels appear in the opening shots of the house and grounds in the fog. Otherwise, the image is fine with very sharp, artfully lit interiors. A solid step up from conventional broadcast quality. Stereo sound is all the material requires. Dialogue is crisp and clear. —*MM*
Movie: 🎬🎬 ½ **DVD:** 🎬🎬 ½
Warner (cat #B5594D, UPC 7940545594-22). Full frame. Stereo. $29.98. Keepcase. *LANG:* English. *FEATURES:* 10 chapters ▪ Conversation with Ken Burns ▪ "Ken Burns: Making History" featurette ▪ Weblink to Thomas Jefferson site.
2001 180m/C D: Ken Burns; **W:** Ken Burns, Geoffrey C. Ward; **C:** Allen Moore, Buddy Squires, Peter Hutton; **M:** Jennifer Dunnington; **V:** Ossie Davis, Sam Waterston, Philip Bosco, Blythe Danner, Amy Madigan, Michael W. Potts, Julie Harris, Derek Jacobi.

Those Who Love Me Can Take the Train

Bisexual artist Jean-Baptiste Emmerich (Trintignant) has died in Paris, but wished to be buried in his hometown of Limoges—a four-hour train trip for his motley group of mourners, which includes friends, relatives, and former lovers of both sexes. Things don't calm down at the cemetery, where yet more relatives await, including the artist's estranged twin brother. Rather than bonding in grief, the trip and funeral succeed in bringing out the old hurts and rivalries amongst the mourners, causing the shake-up of more than one relationship. The Dolby Digital 5.1 soundtrack is the highlight of this DVD, as it offers clear dialogue and a great sound field, most noticeable during the train trip. The film has been letterboxed at 2.35:1 and the image is clear, but has some problems. There is notable artifacting and a great deal of distortion with horizontal lines. —*ML AKA:* Ceux Qui M'Aiment Predront le Train.
Movie: 🎬🎬 **DVD:** 🎬🎬 ½
Kino on Video (cat #K160 DVD, UPC 738-329016029). Widescreen (2.35:1) letterboxed. Dolby Digital 5.1 Surround. $29.95. Keepcase. *LANG:* French. *SUB:* English. *FEATURES:* Theatrical trailer ▪ 12 chapters.
1998 122m/C *FR* Jean-Louis Trintignant, Pascal Greggory, Charles Berling, Bruno Todeschini, Valeria Bruni-Tedeschi, Vincent Perez, Dominique Blanc, Sylvain Jacques, Marie Daems; **D:** Patrice Chereau; **W:** Patrice Chereau, Daniele Thompson, Pierre Trividic; **C:** Eric Gautier. *AWARDS:* Cesar '99: Cinematog., Director (Chereau), Support. Actress (Blanc).

Three Amigos

Three unemployed silent screen stars (Martin, Short, Chase) are asked to defend a Mexican town from bandits. They think it's a public appearance. Spoof of the Three Stooges and Mexican bandito

movies somehow gets funnier with repeated viewings. Some of the routines are nothing short of brilliant. DVD displays some aliasing in the brighter scenes, but no more than you'd expect to find in a western. Also, the leads' ornate outfits suffer in some medium shots. —*MM*
Movie: 🎬🎬🎬 **DVD:** 🎬🎬 ½
HBO (cat #90007). Widescreen letterboxed. $24.98. Snapper. *LANG:* English. *SUB:* French; Spanish; English. *CAP:* English. *FEATURES:* Cast & crew thumbnail bios ▪ 20 chapters.
1986 (PG) 105m/C Chevy Chase, Steve Martin, Martin Short, Joe Mantegna, Patrice Martinez, Jon Lovitz, Phil Hartman, Randy Newman, Alfonso Arau; *D:* John Landis; *W:* Lorne Michaels, Steve Martin, Randy Newman; *C:* Ronald W. Browne; *M:* Elmer Bernstein.

Three Came Home
Please see review for *Pearl Harbor Before and After.*
Movie: 🎬🎬🎬
1950 106m/B Claudette Colbert, Patric Knowles, Sessue Hayakawa, Florence Desmond, Sylvia Andrew, Mark Keuning, Phyllis Morris, Howard Chuman; *D:* Jean Negulesco; *W:* Nunnally Johnson; *C:* William H. Daniels, Milton Krasner; *M:* Hugo Friedhofer.

Three Fugitives
Martin Short is an incredibly talented comedian and performer who has made some woefully mediocre films, and this is the perfect example. Nick Nolte stars as Lucas, who has just been released from prison and is determined to go straight. Unfortunately, he is in a bank when Perry (Short) decides to attempt his first robbery. Of course, the robbery is a complete failure, so Perry takes Lucas hostage, and suddenly Lucas is on the run from the law. The experienced criminal finds himself reluctantly watching out for Perry and Perry's young daughter Meg (Doroff). The film tries to combine action, comedy, and emotional drama, but only hits the mark half the time. Short is funny and Nolte is a good straight man, but the film never gels. Director Francis Veber here remakes his own film *Les Fugitives.* The image is clear, but there are noticeable white and black specks from the source print. The grain on the image is negligible and the colors are quite good. The Surround audio track offers surprisingly good stereo separation and Surround effects, rivaling some Dolby 5.1 tracks. —*ML*
Movie: 🎬🎬 **DVD:** 🎬🎬🎬
Buena Vista Home Ent. (cat #17592, UPC 717951003294). Widescreen (1.85:1) anamorphic. Dolby Digital Surround Sound. $19.99. Keepcase. *LANG:* English. *SUB:* English. *CAP:* English. *FEATURES:* 12 chapters.
1989 (PG-13) 96m/C Nick Nolte, Martin Short, James Earl Jones, Kenneth McMillan, Sarah Rowland Doroff, Alan Ruck; *D:* Francis Veber; *W:* Francis Veber; *C:* Haskell Wexler; *M:* David McHugh.

Three Men and a Baby
It may be hard to for many of today's younger viewers to believe that a film starring Tom Selleck, Steve Guttenberg, and Ted Danson was such a huge hit. Now, this amiable film has been overshadowed by the rumors that a "ghost" appears in the movie. Peter (Selleck), an architect, Michael (Guttenberg), a cartoonist, and Jack (Ted Danson), an actor, are successful bachelor roommates. That all changes when they find a baby girl on their doorstep. They have no choice but to take the infant in, and they quickly learn the difficulties of child-rearing. The film is very light, but also fun and sweet all the way and director Leonard Nimoy never lets things get dull or too sappy. A subplot involving some criminals and a mistaken identity does hurt the film, but this is only a small part of the movie. The three male leads are all very good, and a young Nancy Travis is also fine as the forlorn mother. At the 1:01:46 point in the film, a shadow appears in the window on the left side of the screen. For years, rumors claiming this to be a ghost have circulated, while the official word is that it's a prop that fell against the window. (Either way, it's creepy.) This widescreen image is not enhanced for 16x9 TVs (leading one to believe that this may be an older transfer taken from a previously released laserdisc). The image is sharp, but slightly grainy and hazy at times. The colors are good and there is only a hint of artifacting. The Dolby Digital 5.1 audio track is quite good, offering clear dialogue and some very exciting Surround sound effects. There are no extras on this DVD. —*ML*
Movie: 🎬🎬🎬 **DVD:** 🎬🎬 ½
Buena Vista Home Ent. (cat #24439, UPC 786936117738). Widescreen (1.85:1) letterboxed. Dolby Digital 5.1 Surround. $19.99. Keepcase. *LANG:* English. *SUB:* English; French; Spanish. *CAP:* English. *FEATURES:* 10 chapters.
1987 (PG) 102m/C Tom Selleck, Steve Guttenberg, Ted Danson, Margaret Colin, Nancy Travis, Philip Bosco, Celeste Holm, Derek De Lint, Cynthia Harris, Lisa Blair, Michelle Blair, Paul Guilfoyle; *D:* Leonard Nimoy; *W:* James Orr, Jim Cruickshank; *C:* Adam Greenberg; *M:* Marvin Hamlisch.

Three Men and a Little Lady
Following the success of *Three Men and a Baby,* the three happy bachelors Peter (Selleck), Michael (Guttenberg), and Jack (Danson), return in this sequel. Baby Mary (Weisman) is now five years old and the guys all love having her around. Sylvia (Travis), Mary's mother, attempts to woo Peter, but he doesn't get the message. So she decides to move back to England and take Mary with her. The resourceful men decide that they can't live without their two favorite ladies, so they head to Britain to try and get them back. This film actually has a more plausible plot than its prede-

cessor, but the jokes and sentimentality fall flat here. Director Emile Ardolino keeps the story moving along, but he doesn't have the deft touch that Leonard Nimoy brought to the first movie. If you are truly interested in what happened after the first film, then this sequel is worth seeing, otherwise stick with the original. Plus, there's no ghost in this one! Just as the sequel isn't as good as the first movie, this DVD isn't as impressive as the other disc, either. The film is presented full frame. Due to this blow-up, there is a noticeable amount of grain to the image, as well as some edge-enhancement flaws. The Dolby Digital Surround audio track offers clear dialogue, but it sounds very flat at times, and there is little response from the rear speakers. —*ML*
Movie: 🎬🎬 ½ **DVD:** 🎬🎬
Buena Vista Home Ent. (cat #24441, UPC 786936118605). Full frame. Dolby Digital Surround Sound. $19.99. Keepcase. *LANG:* English; French. *SUB:* English. *CAP:* English. *FEATURES:* 12 chapters.
1990 (PG) 100m/C Tom Selleck, Steve Guttenberg, Ted Danson, Nancy Travis, Robin Weisman, Christopher Cazenove, Fiona Shaw, Sheila Hancock, John Boswall, Jonathan Lynn, Sydney Walsh; *D:* Emile Ardolino; *W:* Charlie Peters, Sara Parriott, Josann McGibbon; *C:* Adam Greenberg; *M:* James Newton Howard.

3 Ninjas Kick Back
Sequel to the popular *3 Ninjas.* Three brothers help their grandfather (the late Victor Wong) protect a ceremonial knife won in a ninja tournament in Japan 50 years earlier. Gramps's ancient adversary in that tournament, now an evil tycoon, wants the sword back and he's willing to enlist the aid of his three American grandchildren, members of garage band Teenage Vomit, to get it. The showdown eventually heads to Japan, where *Kick Back,* unlike predecessors, dispenses with Japan-bashing. High-spirited action fare that kids will enjoy. Adults and kids will be able to choose from both letterboxed and full-frame versions on this DVD. The image here is clear, but slightly hazy at times. The audio is clean and provides surprisingly good ambient Surround sound effects. —*ML*
Movie: 🎬🎬 ½ **DVD:** 🎬🎬🎬
Columbia Tristar (cat #05983, UPC 0433-96059832). Widescreen (1.85:1) anamorphic; full frame. Dolby 2.0 Surround. $19.95. Keepcase. *LANG:* English; French; Spanish; Portuguese. *SUB:* English; French; Spanish; Portuguese; Chinese; Thai. *CAP:* English. *FEATURES:* Bonus trailers ▪ 28 chapters.
1994 (PG) 95m/C Victor Wong, Max Elliott Slade, Sean Fox, Evan Bonifant, Sab Shimono, Dustin Nguyen, Jason Schombing, Caroline Junko King, Angelo Tiffe; *D:* Charles Kanganis; *W:* Mark Saltzman; *C:* Christopher Faloona; *M:* Rick Marvin.

Three on the Trail
This fifth entry in the *Hopalong Cassidy* series is one of the more ambitious. The

fast-moving plot concerns Hoppy's (Boyd) efforts to help young schoolmarm Mary Stevens (Evans) from the clutches of an evil saloon keeper. Quality of image and sound are equal to the high standards of the other entries in the series. For technical comments, please see review of *Hopalong Cassidy*. Title is available as part of a double feature with *Hopalong Cassidy Returns* on volume 2 of *Hopalong Cassidy: The Early Years.* —MM
Movie: ♫♫♫ DVD: ♫♫ ½
Image Ent. (cat #ID9152UTDVD, UPC 014-38191528). Full frame. Dolby Digital 5.1 Surround Stereo; Dolby Digital Mono. $24.99. Keepcase. *LANG:* English. *FEATURES:* 12 chapters • Liner notes by Fred Romary.
1936 65m/B William Boyd, James Ellison, George "Gabby" Hayes, Onslow Stevens, Mary Evans, Claude King, William Duncan; *D:* Howard Bretherton; *W:* Doris Schroeder, Harrison Jacobs; *C:* Archie Stout.

Three Stooges: All Time Favorites

The title is misleading—this is actually a hodgepodge of little-seen Stooge films, including two never-aired television pilots ("Jerks of All Trades" and "Kook's Tour") and a documentary on the comedy troupe's history ("Family Album"). A short program of highlights from the 1998 Three Stooges convention is also included. As might be expected, there's a reason these programs haven't been shown too often, and all but the most die-hard fans should stay away. Picture and sound quality are both pretty abysmal, due to poor source material. Only two of the programs have chapter links. —BG
Movie: ♫ ½ DVD: ♫ ½
Anchor Bay (cat #DV12111, UPC 013131-211191). Full frame. Dolby Mono. $14.98. Keepcase. *LANG:* English. *FEATURES:* 18 chapters.
1998 120m/C Moe Howard, Larry Fine, Joe DeRita, Curly Howard, Shemp Howard; *D:* George McCahan, Norman Maurer; *W:* Henry Taylor, Norman Maurer, Steve Marmalstein.

Three Stooges Cartoon Classics, Volume 1

Three Stooges fans should be very excited about this release, which features four episodes of the obscure animated program from the 1960s. Each of the four episodes contains four short cartoons, with the Stooges involved in all sorts of madcap adventures. The real treasure here is that each cartoon short is introduced by the Stooges themselves, Moe, Larry, and Curly Joe. Yes, they all look incredibly old, but here they are in living color. The casual viewer may find the introductions and the cartoons themselves somewhat pedestrian, but Stooges fans should relish these rare gems. The transfer here was struck from the original 16mm negatives of the show. The images are clear and sharp, for the most part, although the title sequence to the show is quite blurry. The live-action sections look good, showing only a slight darkening of the image. The colors in the cartoons are rich and pleasing. Rhino Home Video continues to set a precedent with their animation releases, but it would have been nice if they could have included liner notes on the history of the show. —ML
Movie: ♫♫ ½ DVD: ♫♫♫
Rhino (cat #R2 976040). Full frame. Digital Mono. $14.95. Keepcase. *LANG:* English; Spanish. *FEATURES:* Producer interview • 16 chapters.
1965 113m/C

Three Stooges: Dizzy Doctors

Even the oldest of these short comedies has been exceptionally well preserved. That's always been the case with the studio's Stooge collections (reviewed in *Book 2*) on DVD. The black-and-white images are sharp with little bothersome surface damage. The best episodes here are the first two with Curly. (The other four have Shemp.) In "Dizzy Doctors," the guys try to sell a patent medicine called "Brighto" that works best as a paint remover. "Termites of 1938" contains what I consider to be the Stooges' single finest moment when they have dinner with socialites and teach them how to eat peas. First you take a scoop of mashed potatoes on the end of your knife; then you dip it into your peas and gracefully lift the sticky combination to your lips. When, at age eight, I demonstrated this technique to my mother, she was not at all amused. I still think it's hilarious. —MM
Movie: ♫♫♫ DVD: ♫♫♫
Columbia Tristar (cat #05893, UPC 04339-6058934). Full frame. Dolby Digital Mono. $19.99. Keepcase. *LANG:* English; Spanish; Portuguese. *SUB:* English; French; Spanish; Portuguese. *CAP:* English. *FEATURES:* 6 chapters.
1996 120m/B Larry Fine, Moe Howard, Curly Howard, Shemp Howard.

Three Stooges: Healthy, Wealthy, and Dumb

This is a particularly strong collection, all featuring Curly Howard. "Rockin' Thru the Rockies" is probably the best structured of the set while the rest of the stories are basically springboards for fun sight gags, wordplay, and slapstick. The quality of image and sound is directly proportional to the age of the work. Contents: "Gents without Cents" (1944), "Healthy, Wealthy, and Dumb" (1938), "If a Body Meets a Body" (1945), "Rockin' Thru the Rockies" (1939), "Phony Express" (1943), and "Whoops, I'm an Indian" (1936). —DG
Movie: ♫♫♫ DVD: ♫♫♫
Columbia Tristar (cat #05922, UPC 04339-6059221). Full frame. Mono. $24.95. Keep-case. *LANG:* English; Spanish; Portuguese. *SUB:* English; French; Spanish; Portuguese. *CAP:* English. *FEATURES:* 6 chapters.
2001 m/C Moe Howard, Larry Fine, Curly Howard.

Three Stooges: Three Smart Saps

This collection features a couple of fairly strong Shemp Howard episodes ("Three Arabian Nuts" features a perfectly executed special-effects shot) and the Curly Howard ones are not his best. "Three Loan Wolves" features a very sickly looking Howard in a very limited performance. As with other Stooge collections, image and sound quality depend on the age of the work. Contents: "Three Little Beers" (1935), "Three Smart Saps" (1942), "Three Loan Wolves" (1946), "Three Arabian Nuts" (1951), and "Three Dark Horses" (1952). —DG
Movie: ♫♫♫ DVD: ♫♫♫
Columbia Tristar (cat #07655, UPC 04339-6076556). Full frame. Mono. $24.95. Keepcase. *LANG:* English; Spanish; Portuguese. *SUB:* English; French; Spanish; Portuguese. *CAP:* English. *FEATURES:* 6 chapters.
1952 82m/B Moe Howard, Larry Fine, Curly Howard, Shemp Howard.

3:10 to Yuma

Fascinating variation on *High Noon* has rancher Dan Evans (Heflin) desperate for $200 to save his drought-stricken place and his family. He agrees to guard outlaw Ben Wade (Ford) for a few hours until the 3:10 train to Yuma arrives. Performances are rock solid and so is the perceptive script, based on an Elmore Leonard story. DVD does near-perfect work with excellent Charles Lawton Jr.'s sharp black-and-white cinematography. If you look really hard into the large dusty areas of the brightest exteriors, you'll spot some pixelation, but that's a meaningless quibble. It's a terrific western that simply looks great on disc. Worth owning. —MM
Movie: ♫♫♫ ½ DVD: ♫♫♫
Columbia Tristar (cat #07760, UPC 04339-6077607). Widescreen (1.85:1) anamorphic; full frame. Dolby Digital Mono. $19.98. Keepcase. *LANG:* English. *SUB:* English; French; Spanish; Portuguese. *CAP:* English. *FEATURES:* 28 chapters • Trailers.
1957 92m/B Glenn Ford, Van Heflin, Felicia Farr, Richard Jaeckel; *D:* Delmer Daves; *W:* Halsted Welles; *C:* Charles Lawton Jr.; *M:* George Duning.

3000 Miles to Graceland

Shockingly original pic sets Elvis impersonators in Vegas, only these Presleys wanna rob, not rock. Ex-cellmates Russell and Costner are the lead Kings, Michael and Murphy, who team up with Arquette, Slater, and Woodbine, and head to the quaint desert burg to relieve its wagering establishments of some extra cash. After a strong opening segment, only moments of comic relief are scattered throughout

the comedy, highlighted by the Elvii strutting through town in a *Reservoir Dogs* homage. Cox-Arquette is adept at playing the lovelorn, single mom Cybil, pining for Michael. Gratuitous violence and clichéd action don't help movie's one-note appeal but the look is slick and the boys drive cool cars. Wow, this DVD looks so good it almost makes up for the movie's shortcomings...almost. The colors are simply stunning and the blacks are inky black and true. On close-ups the picture is so sharp you can count the nose hairs and when the camera pulls back, even the longshots remain crystal clear. The 5.1 sound keeps up with the pic with plenty of Surround and sub-woofer drive on the plentiful action sequences. P.S. The movie still mostly sucks. —*JO*
Movie: 🎬 ½ ***DVD:*** 🎬🎬🎬 ½
Warner (cat #21188, UPC 0853921188-23). Widescreen (2.35:1) anamorphic. Dolby Digital 5.1 Surround Stereo. $19.98. Snapper. *LANG:* English; French. *SUB:* English; French. *CAP:* English. *FEATURES:* 35 chapters ▪ Theatrical trailer.
2001 (R) 125m/C Kevin Costner, Kurt Russell, Christian Slater, Bokeem Woodbine, David Arquette, Courteney Cox Arquette, Kevin Pollak, Jon Lovitz, Howie Long, Thomas Haden Church, Ice-T, David Kaye; **D:** Demian Lichtenstein; **W:** Demian Lichtenstein, Richard Recco; **C:** David Franco; **M:** George S. Clinton.

Three Wishes

Mysterious—and perhaps magical—stranger Jack (Swayze) moves into the lives of a 1950s suburban widow (Mastrantonio) and her kids (Mazzello and Mumy) after she hits him with her car. Jack proceeds to use Zen philosophy, stories of a genie disguised as a dog, and nude sunbathing to help the kids' Little League team, make a boy fly, and scandalize the neighborhood. Adults will recognize the beatnik, Kerouac-influenced philosophy of non-conformity. They'll also recognize the sell-out of that ideal with a sappy ending. Mumy is the son of former *Lost in Space* child star Billy Mumy. DVD image is acceptably sharp for a film that has never been particularly flashy in visual terms. The deleted scenes and the to-the-point commentary track by director Coolidge are the main improvement of disc over tape. —*MM*
Movie: 🎬🎬 ***DVD:*** 🎬🎬 ½
HBO (cat #91291). Widescreen. Dolby Digital 5.1 Surround Stereo; Dolby Digital Surround; Stereo. $19.95. Snapper. *LANG:* English; French; Spanish. *SUB:* English; French; Spanish. *FEATURES:* 23 chapters ▪ Talent files ▪ Deleted scenes ▪ Commentary: Martha Coolidge ▪ "Making of" featurette.
1995 (PG) 115m/C Patrick Swayze, Mary Elizabeth Mastrantonio, Joseph Mazzello, David Marshall Grant, Michael O'Keefe, John Diehl, Jay O. Sanders, Diane Venora, Seth Mumy; **D:** Martha Coolidge; **W:** Elizabeth Anderson; **C:** Johnny E. Jensen; **M:** Cynthia Millar.

The Three Worlds of Gulliver

Jonathan Swift's legendary combination of fantasy and social satire is approached as an amiable family film in this enjoyable adventure. Doctor Gulliver (Mathews), in search of fame and fortune, jumps aboard a ship and sails off, much to the chagrin of his fiancée (Morrow). Thrown overboard in a storm, Gulliver encounters the inhabitants of Lilliput, who are tiny, and their opposite, the Brobdingnagians, who are gigantic. The further adventures of Gulliver present in the book have been omitted. It's fun and Matthews is given more screen time than in other Harryhausen films, but the movie is occasionally dull and dated. The effects are colorful but unconvincing and the sound effects of the giant Gulliver are a bit grating. The film is presented open matte full frame instead of in its original widescreen ratio. The top and bottom occasionally reveal a bit too much, but it's better than a pan 'n' scan version would be. There's frequent digital edge noise, but the transfer is beautiful with rich, bright, perfect colors and a sharp image. There's visible dirt during special effects shots, but that's printed into the negative and would be present on the best of theatrical prints. The sound is fine. ("This Is Dynamation" featurette and "The Ray Harryhausen Chronicles" documentary are covered in the review for *Sinbad and the Eye of the Tiger* in Book 2.) —*DG* **AKA:** The Worlds of Gulliver.
Movie: 🎬🎬 ½ ***DVD:*** 🎬🎬🎬
Columbia Tristar (cat #05920, UPC 04339-6059207). Full frame. Dolby Digital Surround. $19.95. Keepcase. *LANG:* English; Spanish. *SUB:* English; French. *CAP:* English. *FEATURES:* "This Is Dynamation" featurette ▪ "The Ray Harryhausen Chronicles" documentary ▪ "Making of" ▪ Trailers ▪ Filmographies ▪ Production notes ▪ Insert booklet with notes ▪ 28 chapters.
1959 100m/C Kerwin Mathews, Jo Morrow, Basil Sydney, Mary Ellis; **D:** Jack Sher; **W:** Arthur Ross, Jack Sher; **M:** Bernard Herrmann.

Throw Momma from the Train

This extremely dark-edged comedy was generally met with a negative reaction from critics and audiences alike, but has become somewhat of a cult item in the years since. DeVito stars as Owen, a small, quiet man who still lives under the oppression of his mother (Ramsey), a tyrant whose scream induces a cringe. Crystal plays Larry, a novelist who has had to live with his anger over his ex-wife stealing his book and having it become a bestseller. Both are about to boil over, and both seek a favor from one another. Owen has fantasies of getting rid of his mother, and Larry's rage against his wife leads Owen to believe that he would like to have her gotten rid of as well. It's a knowing send up of *Strangers on a Train* but doesn't have enough laughs and some-

times comes across as rather flat. The picture appears a bit soft and undefined across the board. Not to the point of distraction, but it simply doesn't appear very crisp. Slight wear is visible as are a tiny bit of pixelation and edge-enhancement. Colors are fairly bland. The majority of the film has clean but fairly limited audio with the exception of the score. —*AB/DG*
Movie: 🎬🎬 ***DVD:*** 🎬🎬
MGM Home Ent. (UPC 27616861023). Widescreen (1.85:1) anamorphic. Dolby Surround Stereo. $19.98. Keepcase. *LANG:* English. *FEATURES:* Trailer ▪ 4 deleted scenes.
1987 (PG-13) 88m/C Danny DeVito, Billy Crystal, Anne Ramsey, Kate Mulgrew, Kim Greist, Branford Marsalis, Rob Reiner, Bruce Kirby; **D:** Danny DeVito; **W:** Stu Silver; **C:** Barry Sonnenfeld; **M:** David Newman. *AWARDS: NOM:* Oscars '87: Support. Actress (Ramsey).

Thumb Wars

Neither fall-down funny nor the ultimate parody of Lucas or his empire, this short film has little or no sense of irony or satire, just jokes, folks, so you don't get any sense of anything building while you watch, no sophomoric rush of coolness like that which accompanies the better episodes of *MST3K*. The novelty revolves around a single bizarre and creative visual—digitally transplanted human facial features that turn ordinary thumbs into talking, smirking, grimacing "finger puppets." An oversized mouth is topped by a pair of eyes cleverly pushed too close together. Using the limitless possibilities of the human face, this gag succeeds in sustaining interest no matter what happens on-screen. The disc looks just fine, with bright colors and nicely mixed sound-alike approximations of the Williams themes. Other attractions include storyboards, and an interview with the "Gabba the Butt" Thumb actor. —*GE*
Movie: 🎬🎬 ½ ***DVD:*** 🎬🎬🎬
Image Ent. (cat #ID036080DVD, UPC 014381036022). Full frame. Dolby Digital 5.1 Surround Stereo; Dolby Digital Surround. $9.99. Keepcase. *LANG:* English. *FEATURES:* Commentary: Steve Odekirk, Paul Marshall ▪ Storyboards ▪ Gag trailers.
1999 29m/C D: Steve Oedekerk, Paul Marshal; **W:** Steve Oedekerk, Paul Marshal.

Thumbelina [20th Century Fox]

Little girl Mia gets magically pulled into her *Thumbelina* storybook and finds all sorts of adventures. Featuring the voices of Charo and Carol Channing. One wonders if this was also secretly aimed at aging Ethel Merman fans who all have the first name "Mary." Arguably a better babysitter than Benadryl, it's below par even for Don *(Land That Time Forgot)* Bluth, with a very average DVD transfer cheapening things further and good sound for an excruciating Barry Manilow sound-

track that confirms the operating aesthetic (or this case, operation minus anesthetic). Let your kids watch *Iron Giant* again instead. —*MO* **AKA:** Hans Christian Andersen's Thumbelina.
Movie: 🎵 *DVD:* 🎵🎵
20th Century Fox (cat #2002928, UPC 023543029281). Widescreen anamorphic. Dolby Digital 2.0 Surround. $19.98. Keepcase. *LANG:* English. *SUB:* English; Spanish. *CAP:* English; Spanish. *FEATURES:* 20 chapters ▪ Featurette ▪ TV spots.
1994 (G) 86m/C D: Don Bluth, Gary Goldman; **W:** Don Bluth; **M:** William Ross, Barry Manilow, Barry Manilow, Jack Feldman, Bruce Sussman; **V:** Jodi Benson, Gary Imhoff, Charo, Gilbert Gottfried, Carol Channing, John Hurt, Will Ryan, June Foray, Kenneth Mars. *AWARDS:* Golden Raspberries '94: Worst Song ("Marry the Mole").

Thumbtanic

Re-creation of turgid blockbuster *Titanic* by a cast of costumed thumbs with animated human eyes and mouths. Mercifully shorter than the original, this version only hits the high spots, then quickly moves on. The humor of this "filmette" seems aimed at young adults, but the simple execution would most likely be funnier for small children. Audio commentary is about what you'd expect from the makers of this type of juvenile project. They think it's all very funny, but that's surely in the eye of the beholder. Bright colors and simple soundtrack transfer well to DVD. —*LA*
Movie: 🎵🎵 *DVD:* 🎵🎵 ½
Image Ent. (cat #ID1709BODVD0, UPC 14381170924). Full frame. Dolby Digital 5.1 Surround; Dolby 2.0 Stereo. $9.99. Keepcase. *LANG:* English. *FEATURES:* Trailers for *The Blair Thumb, Frankenthumb, Bat Thumb* ▪ Storyboards ▪ Commentary: Steve Oedekerk ▪ 15 chapters.
1999 27m/C D: Steve Oedekerk; **W:** Steve Oedekerk; **C:** Mike Deprez; **V:** Steve Oedekerk, Paul Greenberg, Mary Jo Keenan.

Thunder Kick

It's the old story about the young kung fu fighter who has promised not to fight with anyone because his father died in a fight, but then he has to fight when the bad guys kill his best friend. The kung fu is pretty standard in this Taiwanese production, with loud, silly sound effects. Bolo Yeung is top billed, but only has a small role. Picture and sound are vivid for the age of the print. —*BT*
Movie: 🎵 ½ *DVD:* 🎵🎵
Tai Seng (cat #89404, UPC 6016438940-41). Full frame. $14.95. Keepcase. *LANG:* English. *FEATURES:* 8 chapters.
1973 85m/C HK TW Bolo Yeung, Chin-kun Li, Kwok-Choi Han; **D:** Yung-tsu Yen.

Thunderbirds: Set 1

The hi-tech Tracy family runs a secret organization called "International Rescue"
from their remote tropical island. Monitoring the airwaves, the various members race to the rescue whenever there's a disaster. They are opposed by the evil "Hood," a bald villain and master of disguise. British, all-marionette TV series (in "Super-Marionation"!) is quite oddball and artificial on an intellectual level, but somehow manages to be gripping, silly fun. The focus of most episodes is on the tense procedural mechanics of the rescue operations and an inordinate amount of screen-time is given to launches and landings. The characters have the usual stock personalities but Lady Penelope (complete with pink limousine) is wonderfully camp fun. The series inspired two features, *Thunderbirds Are Go!* and *Thunderbird 6*. The discs utilize stunning transfers with rich filmic textures and vivid colors. The episodes are razor sharp and the only detriment is a tendency for edges to look overly digitized. The newly remixed 5.1 Surround track gives incredible punch to explosions and sound effects. All channels are used infrequently, but when they are utilized, the effect is incredibly effective. Good clean fun. (Also available are Set 2: cat. #AAE-70162, UPC 7339-61701623; Set 3: cat. #AAE-70329, UPC 733961703290; Set 4: cat. #AAE-70332, UPC 733961703-320; Set 5: cat. #AAE-70434, UPC 7339-61704341; and Set 6: cat. #AAE-70437, UPC 733961704372) —*DG*
Movie: 🎵🎵🎵 *DVD:* 🎵🎵🎵
A&E (cat #AAE-70159, UPC 7339617015-93). Full frame. Dolby Digital 5.1 Surround. $39.95. Keepcase (2-disc set). *LANG:* English. *FEATURES:* "Making of *Thunderbirds*" featurette ▪ Still gallery ▪ Episodes 1–6.
1965 312m/C GB

Tick Tock

In Bakersfield, California, trophy wife Rachel (Ward) and her pal Carla (Minter) plot to get rid of wealthy hubby (Dukes). That's only the beginning of a plot that stacks trick upon trick, double-cross upon double-cross. Think *Blood Simple* lite. It's a delightful guilty pleasure made all the more enjoyable by polished production values. DVD delivers an excellent image throughout. Sound is fine, too. All that's missing is a commentary track and the film is good enough to warrant one. —*MM*
Movie: 🎵🎵 ½ *DVD:* 🎵🎵🎵
Studio Home Ent. (cat #AV 1577D, UPC 806469157725). Widescreen (1.85:1) letterboxed. Dolby Digital Stereo. $19.98. Keepcase. *LANG:* English. *SUB:* English; French; Spanish. *CAP:* English. *FEATURES:* 24 chapters ▪ Trailer.
2000 (R) 93m/C Megan Ward, Kristin Minter, Linden Ashby, John Ratzenberger, David Dukes; **D:** Kevin S. Tenney; **W:** Kevin S. Tenney; **C:** Jack Conroy; **M:** Dennis Michael Tenney.

Ticker

Steven Seagal plays the bomb expert who's up against villain Dennis Hopper,
reprising the role he played in *Speed*. It's pretty much generic bang-bang boom-boom stuff, with the addition of a little snip-snip when the pony-tailed one cuts the wires. DVD delivers an exceptionally sharp image. The film also boasts handsome production values for a video premiere action flick. But in late 2001, any movie about terrorist bombs must have something substantial to offer and this one doesn't. —*MM*
Movie: 🎵🎵 *DVD:* 🎵🎵 ½
Artisan Ent. (UPC 012236122579). Widescreen anamorphic. Dolby Digital 5.1 Surround Stereo. $24.99. Keepcase. *LANG:* English. *SUB:* Spanish. *CAP:* English. *FEATURES:* Commentary ▪ Talent files ▪ Production notes ▪ 14 chapters.
2001 (R) 92m/C Tom Sizemore, Steven Seagal, Nas, Jaime Pressly, Dennis Hopper, Chilli; **D:** Albert Pyun; **W:** Paul B. Margolis.

Tie-Died: Rock 'n' Roll's Most Deadicated Fans

This film takes a look behind-the-music scene at a community of "Grateful Dead" followers who travel along with the band: a group of people who are simply there to enjoy the music and each other's company. It's an interesting subject, making for an entertaining documentary, but not one that's informative about just why the people who are involved do what they do. The film occasionally stumbles onto a commentator who shares some interesting thoughts about the society "out there" and the society "in here." That kind of discussion is the film at its best. On the other hand, there's a portion of the interviews that are fairly inane. It gets a little long after a while and begins to run out of things to say, but put all of the pieces together and you get a moderately interesting portrait of a community all its own. Not a great film, but it takes a very real, very relaxed look at these people. The picture is a tad on the soft side and colors are fairly good. Problems mainly involve print flaws; there are a handful of minor scratches and marks on the print used. The audio capably presents the atmosphere of the concert crowds, and does an especially nice job with the music, which sounds wonderfully clear. —*AB/DG*
Movie: 🎵🎵 ½ *DVD:* 🎵🎵 ½
Winstar Home Ent. (UPC 720917513027). Full frame. Dolby Digital Surround. $24.98. Keepcase. *LANG:* English. *FEATURES:* Theatrical trailer ▪ "A Conversation with Ken Kesey" short.
1995 (R) 88m/C D: Andrew Behar.

Tieta of Agreste

As a teenager Tieta (Braga) was tossed out of her little Brazilian village for her sexual adventurousness. Years later, she returns as the widow of a wealthy industrialist and upsets everything. The film is based on a novel by Jorge Amado (who appears at the beginning as a sort of nar-

rator), and it retains his finely tuned sense of the bawdy. Sonia Braga proves that mature women can generate a sexual heat that younger starlets can only dream about. DVD image is excellent. The soft red and brown color scheme looks fine. There's no noticeable grain in the bright beach exteriors. I'm not sure what the screen ratio is. On a conventional-sized monitor, letterboxing is so narrow as to be almost invisible. Recommended. —*MM*
Movie: 🐾🐾🐾 ***DVD:*** 🐾🐾🐾
Winstar Home Ent. (cat #FLV5038, UPC 720917503820). Widescreen letterboxed. $24.98. Keepcase. *LANG:* Portuguese. *SUB:* English. *FEATURES:* 9 chapters • "Making of"featurette • Filmographies.
1996 140m/C *BR* Sonia Braga, Marilia Pera, Zeze Motta, Jorge Amado; ***D:*** Carlos Diegues; ***W:*** Carlos Diegues; ***C:*** Edgar Moura; ***M:*** Caetano Veloso.

Tiger Claws

Brain-dead martial arts pic pits cops Masterson (Rothrock) and Richards (Merhi) against supernatural ancient evil. Threadbare special effects add nothing to pedestrian fight scenes. DVD can do little to improve an exceptionally cheap, dark, and grainy image. —*MM*
Movie: 🐾 ½ ***DVD:*** 🐾🐾
New Concorde (cat #NH20778 D, UPC 736991477896). Full frame. Stereo. $14.98. Keepcase. *LANG:* English. *SUB:* Spanish. *FEATURES:* 24 chapters • Trailers.
1991 (R) 93m/C Cynthia Rothrock, Bolo Yeung, Jalal Merhi; ***D:*** Kelly Markin; ***W:*** J. Stephen Maunder; ***C:*** Curtis Petersen, Mark Willis.

Tiger of Eschnapur

Architect Harald Berger (Hubschmid) travels to far off Eschnapur, there to build schools and hospitals for Chandra (Reyer), the district's all-powerful Maharaja. Along the way he falls in love with a temple dancer, Seetha (Paget), not knowing that Chandra has asked her to Eschnapur with the intention of making her his new Maharani. But Seetha and Berger become pawns in a plan by Chandra's brother Prince Ramigani (Deltgen) to seize the throne. The tone is somewhere between *The Thief of Bagdad* and *The Wind and the Lion,* minus massive battle scenes. There's nothing outright fantastical about the movie, but every scene has the feel of its exotic, alien locations. Where this show really kicks in, is of course the contribution of director Fritz Lang. There are huge sets of fascinating complexity, beautifully lit. They're purposefully rather empty-looking, and remind us of Lang's later American career. DVDs of this film and its sequel, *The Indian Tomb* (please see review), are a very handsome treat indeed. The transfer is very clean and blemish-free, with striking colors. Grain is apparent in some scenes, mostly during (and one curious shot in Seetha's temple dance in *Tiger*) and is easily overlooked. 16:9 enhancement would have made the

transfers perfect, but who's complaining. —*GE* ***AKA:*** Der Tiger von Eschnapur.
Movie: 🐾🐾🐾 ***DVD:*** 🐾🐾 ½
Fantoma Films (UPC 014381123821). Full frame. $29.98. Snapper. *LANG:* German and English. *SUB:* English. *FEATURES:* Stills collection.
1959 101m/C *GE* Debra Paget, Paul (Christian) Hubschmid, Walter Reyer, Claus Holm, Luciana Paluzzi; ***D:*** Fritz Lang; ***W:*** Werner Jorg Luddecke; ***C:*** Richard Angst; ***M:*** Michel Michelet.

Tiger over Wall

An Englishman's lost dog puts pressure on Corrupt Police Inspector Hwang Jang-Lee, who reacts by bullying the populace, until an old umbrella maker makes a deal with the cops to take the blame. But when it's learned that the scapegoat is being tortured for no reason, medical student Phillip Ko decides to kick some official ass. But what really happened to the little boxer Rover? Though it's a chore getting there, Ko's exhilarating duel with Hwang at the end is worth the wait. Oddly, actors' credits are still appearing on screen 41 minutes into the film, coinciding with the introduction of new players. The widescreen transfer, from a fairly worn print, is a bit cloudy throughout, and especially beat up at reel changes. The framing looks adequate, but is still tight enough to chop off credits on both sides. Released as a *Brooklyn Zoo Double Feature* with *Goose Boxer.* The packaging prominently features the World Trade Center towers and the package notes that "A portion of proceeds to benefit NYC relief charities." —*BT* ***AKA:*** Tiger over the Wall; Around the Jail Cell.
Movie: 🐾🐾 ***DVD:*** 🐾🐾
Xenon Ent. (UPC 694795305527). Widescreen letterboxed. Dolby Digital 2.0. $9.99. Keepcase. *LANG:* English. *FEATURES:* 6 chapters • Trailers.
1980 87m/C *HK* Jang-Lee Hwang, Philip Ko, Candy Wen; ***D:*** Tony Liu; ***C:*** Lu Ying Ho, Kuan Wah Ma; ***M:*** Tai Kong Ng.

Til Death Us Do Part

One of the BBC's longest-running programs, *Til Death Us Do Part* ran from 1966 to 1976 and has been on the air in some form or another since. The program also inspired a feature film version and was the credited basis for the U.S. TV series *All in the Family.* The show revolves around lower-class Alf Garnett (Mitchell), his wife (Nichols), and his live-in daughter (Stubbs) and son-in-law (Booth). Alf is a loud-mouthed bigot, a blowhard (of very little class) frequently at very vocal odds with his family and the people around him. For most audiences, the prime curiosity in the show will be the comparative similarities and differences between it and *All in the Family.* Certain compositional groupings are familiar and the deja vu feeling elicited by a few heated discussions would also seem to indicate some cross-pollination from the U.S. series as well. There are

plenty of differences between the two, notably the inclusion in this series of a scene-stealing drunken grandmother (Sims), a stronger wife character, and the absence of the sentiment and heart of the U.S. series. This is first and foremost a comedy, and at that it succeeds terrifically. While dated British topical, political, and football references will go over the heads of most viewers, the verbal gags and drunken set-pieces are frequently uproarious. This two-disc set presents seven episodes from the 1972 season. Highlights from the set are "Dock Pilfering," featuring Alf's sticky-fingered fellow workers; "Holiday in Bournemouth," where the family takes a stress-filled vacation; and "Alf's Broken Leg." It's a shame the disc series couldn't have begun with the pilot episode and the first season, but this is a welcome release and hopefully indicates further volumes to come. Though transferred from submasters of 30-year-old two-inch videotapes, the episodes are sharp and clean, accurately conveying the pale, bright colors. There are a few instances of slight tape damage and the filmed segments look as terrible as most present in British TV during this time. There's also a touch of grain, but overall these are terrific looking, especially considering the age of the materials. The bios/filmographies are limited to series creator Johnny Speight and star Warren Mitchell. The discs are also available separately. —*DG*
Movie: 🐾🐾🐾 ***DVD:*** 🐾🐾🐾
BFS Video (cat #30274-D, UPC 6680530-2749). Full frame. Mono. $39.98. Keepcase. *LANG:* English. *FEATURES:* 3 chapters per episode • Bios/filmographies.
1972 232m/C *GB* Warren Mitchell, Dandy Nichols, Anthony Booth, Una Stubbs, Joan Sims; ***D:*** Douglas Argent, Colin Strong; ***W:*** Johnny Speight.

Til There Was You

A love-it or hate-it romantic comedy. On the good side, the intended couple spends the entire movie crossing paths as circumstances build toward their eventual happily-ever-after thus fulfilling a generation-old promise. There's no drippy dialogue between people falling in love or long moonlit walks on the beach. You get to know the couple and see them working through their lives towards each other. On the bad side, the intended couple spends the entire movie crossing paths and you never get to see them coupled with all the wrong people. On both sides there's a great performance by Sarah Jessica Parker as a has-been child actress who's been in rehab more times than a rock star. Mushy and sometimes predictable, this is a film that will be enjoyed most by hardcore fans of romantic comedy. The color and texture of the image is very good, as is the sound. —*CA*
Movie: 🐾🐾🐾 ***DVD:*** 🐾🐾🐾
Paramount (cat #33248, UPC 097363324-83). Widescreen anamorphic. Dolby Digital 5.1 Surround; Dolby Surround; Stereo.

$29.99. Keepcase. *LANG:* English; French. *SUB:* English.

1996 (PG-13) 113m/C Dylan McDermott, Sarah Jessica Parker, Jeanne Tripplehorn, Jennifer Aniston, Ken Olin, Craig Bierko, Nina Foch, Alice Drummond, Christine Ebersole, Michael Tucker, Patrick Malahide, Kasi Lemmons, Karen Allen; *D:* Scott Winant; *W:* Winnie Holzman; *C:* Bobby Bukowski; *M:* Miles Goodman, Terence Blanchard.

Time and Tide

Tyler (Nicholas Tse) is a bartender who impregnates a lesbian policewoman, Ah Jo (Cathy Chui), during an alcohol-fueled one-night stand. Trying to do what is right, he's stopped at every turn by the woman who now wants nothing to do with him. Determined to provide for his unborn child, the restless Tyler hooks up with Uncle Ji's (Anthony Wong) bodyguard service to score some quick cash. During one assignment, Tyler stumbles upon Jack (Wu Bai), a disillusioned former mercenary married to the daughter of his old team's intended assassination target. Jack's wife, Ah Hui (Candy Lo), is also pregnant and, when the old gang comes to Hong Kong to take out their former partner, Tyler steps in to protect the lady and her unborn child while Jack sets out to destroy his one-time comrades in arms. Got all that straight? No? Well, good. This is an action film in the truest sense of the word and the plot is there only to provide a backdrop for Tsui Hark's imaginative and technically superb action sequences. The end result is a film that manages to bring some fresh ideas and a new look to what was fast becoming a very stale genre. The use of color is of primary importance and the diverse palette is used to great effect to set the mood—much in the same way that a musical score is used in a typical movie to give the audience emotional cues. As a result, colors are manipulated at will and can change radically from very subdued hues to an over-saturated, garish appearance—often within the same scene. The source elements are free of physical defects and the overall image is nice and sharp. Audio comes in both the original Cantonese as well as dubbed English Dolby Digital 2.0 and 5.1 mixes. The dialogue itself is a blend of English, Cantonese, and even Spanish, so just stick with the original soundtrack as the English dub just gets confusing. The 5.1 track is, in a word, incredible. Dynamic range is great with deep bass as well as even the subtlest atmospheric effects coming across strong. The LFE output is frequent and powerful and the subwoofer remains quite active from beginning to end. Tsui Hark's English is very understandable as he delves into all the minute details of the many action sequences and he talks almost nonstop from beginning to end on his commentary. —*MP* **AKA:** Seun-lau Ngaklau.
Movie: 🎬🎬🎬 **DVD:** 🎬🎬🎬 ½
Columbia Tristar Home Video (UPC 433-96066434). Widescreen (2.35:1) anamor-

phic. Dolby Digital Surround; Dolby Digital 5.1 Surround. $24.98. Keepcase. *LANG:* English; Cantonese, Spanish; English. *SUB:* English; French. *FEATURES:* Commentary • Trailers • Filmographies.
2000 (R) 113m/C HK Nicholas Tse, Wu Bai, Anthony Wong, Candy Lo, Cathy Chui, Joventino Couto Remotigue; *D:* Tsui Hark; *W:* Tsui Hark, Koan Hui; *C:* Herman Yau, Ko Chiu-lam; *M:* Tommy Wai.

Time Lapse

Spy thriller offers a unique plot device, which never pays off. Clayton Pierce (William McNamara) is a top-level secret agent who is working undercover on a heroin bust. When he realizes that the dealer is selling nuclear weapons and not drugs, Pierce blows his covers and thwarts the deal. Following this incident, things being to get strange. Pierce, who is known for his photographic memory, suddenly can't remember where he lives, or what kind of car he drives. It seems that he has been given a drug called Oblivion, which causes permanent memory loss. As he now has only a matter of hours before his memory is completely gone, Pierce turns to his ex-wife Kate (Dina Meyer) for help. The film plays as a cross between *D.O.A.* and *Memento,* but lacks any true originality. The action scenes are stale and even veteran actor Roy Scheider, as Pierce's boss, can't add much substance. The DVD is equally disappointing, as it offers the film in a full-frame format. The picture is sharp, but there is noticeable grain at times. The digital stereo is adequate, but lacks any real power when it comes to the shootouts and explosions. —*ML*
Movie: 🎬🎬 **DVD:** 🎬🎬 ½
Lion's Gate Home Ent. (cat #VM7839D, UPC 031398783923). Full frame. Dolby Digital Stereo. $24.99. Keepcase. *LANG:* English. *SUB:* English; Spanish. *CAP:* English. *FEATURES:* Trailer • 24 chapters.
2001 (PG-13) 88m/C Roy Scheider, William McNamara, Dina Meyer, Henry Rollins; *D:* David Worth.

Time of Your Life

Adaptation of William Saroyan's play is part of the Broadway Theatre Archives. It comes from the PBS "Great Performances" series. The story is set in a San Francisco bar, and, as is so often the case with these filmed plays, the lighting is dim and the sound is weak. The bare-bones productions are meant as a showcase for the actors and these are fine. DVD image is no better than VHS tape. —*MM*
Movie: 🎬🎬 ½ **DVD:** 🎬🎬 ½
Image Ent. (cat #ID0881B DDVD, UPC 014-381088120). Full frame. Dolby Digital Mono. $24.98. Keepcase. *LANG:* English. *FEATURES:* 18 chapters • Patti LuPone and Kevin Kline filmographies • Liner notes • Trailers.
1976 118m/C Patti LuPone, Kevin Kline, Gerald Gutierrez; *D:* Kirk Browning, Jack O'Brien; *W:* William Saroyan.

Timecop

Terminator rip-off is fodder for Van Damme followers with lots of action and special effects. 2004 policeman Max Walker (Van Damme) must travel back in time to prevent corrupt politician McComb (Silver) from altering history for personal gain. It's also Walker's chance to alter his personal history since his wife (Sara) was killed in an explosion he can now prevent. Based on a Dark Horse comic. The full-frame image is bright and sharp with no significant flaws. Overall, it's a slight improvement over tape. —*MM*
Movie: 🎬🎬 ½ **DVD:** 🎬🎬 ½
Universal Studios (cat #20147). Full frame. Dolby Digital 5.1 Surround Stereo. $24.98. Keepcase. *LANG:* English; French. *SUB:* English; Spanish. *FEATURES:* Cast & crew thumbnail bios • Production notes • Trailer • 16 chapters.
1994 (R) 98m/C Jean-Claude Van Damme, Ron Silver, Mia Sara, Bruce McGill, Scott Lawrence, Kenneth Welsh, Gabrielle Rose, Duncan Fraser, Ian Tracey, Gloria Reuben, Scott Bellis, Jason Schombing, Kevin McNulty, Sean O'Byrne, Malcolm Stewart, Alfonso Quijada, Glen Roald, Theodore Thomas; *D:* Peter Hyams; *W:* Mark Verheiden, Gary De Vore; *C:* Peter Hyams; *M:* Mark Isham.

Timerider

Fun, quick-witted story of a champion off-road motorcycle racer named Lyle Swann (a very young and handsome Fred Ward) who gets taken back 100 years in time when he crosses through a government-run experiment during a desert race. Armed with a map from an Exxon station and a deadpan sense of humor, he maneuvers through cowboys, cut-throats and, of course, a beautiful woman outlaw, who turns out to be his grandmother. Suspension of disbelief is a must for this time-travel tale brought to you by Michael Nesmith *(Repo Man),* but it proves its cult status with plenty of memorable lines and high-impact action. The picture looks above average with a little wash out, and the sound is fairly good. —*CA* **AKA:** The Adventure of Lyle Swan.
Movie: 🎬🎬🎬 **DVD:** 🎬🎬 ½
Anchor Bay (cat #DV11400, UPC 013131-40095). Widescreen (1.85:1) anamorphic. Dolby Digital Surround 5.1. $19.90. Keepcase. *LANG:* English. *CAP:* English. *FEATURES:* 25 chapters • Director commentary • Theatrical trailer • Director audio commentary.
1983 (PG) 93m/C Fred Ward, Belinda Bauer, Peter Coyote, Richard Masur, Ed Lauter, L.Q. (Justus E. McQueen) Jones, Tracey Walter; *D:* William Dear; *W:* Michael Nesmith, William Dear; *C:* Larry Pizer; *M:* Michael Nesmith.

Tin Men

In Baltimore, 1963, rival aluminum siding salesmen Bill (Dreyfuss) and Ernest (DeVito) first meet when their Cadillacs collide. Being typical men, neither will accept responsibility for the accident, and when they learn that they share the same profession, a personal war begins. Each tries to outdo the other, both professionally and by pulling childish pranks. But Bill decides to go for the coup de grace, when he discovers that Ernest has a lonely wife (Hershey) at home. The film does a good job of balancing the drama, comedy, and nostalgia for what most assume was a simpler time in America. Levinson lovingly photographs his native Baltimore and the cast is very good. It isn't the classic that one would hope for with two of today's best actors and the writer/director of *Diner*, but it certainly has its moments. The image is sharp and clear, but there is some noticeable grain at times and some slight artifacting. Still, the colors are good and there's no overt distortion to the image. The Dolby Surround audio track gives us clear dialogue, with no audible hiss on the track. The Surround sound effects are limited (musical cues, etc), but effective. This DVD features a great audio commentary with Levinson, producer Mark Johnson, costume designer Gloria Gresham, and actors Dreyfuss, Hershey, Bruno Kirby, Seymour Cassel, and John Mahoney. —*ML*

Movie: 🎬🎬 ½ **DVD:** 🎬🎬🎬
Buena Vista Home Ent. (cat #24443, UPC 786936119916). Widescreen (1.85:1) anamorphic. Dolby Digital Surround. $19.99. Keepcase. *LANG:* English. *SUB:* English; French; Spanish. *CAP:* English. *FEATURES:* Commentary • Theatrical trailer • Deleted scene • 14 chapters.
1987 (R) 112m/C Richard Dreyfuss, Danny DeVito, Barbara Hershey, John Mahoney, Jackie Gayle, Stan Brock, Seymour Cassel, Bruno Kirby, J.T. Walsh, Michael Tucker; *D:* Barry Levinson; *W:* Barry Levinson; *C:* Peter Sova; *M:* David Steele.

Titanic: The Complete Story

This two-disc set is a must have for any *Titanic* fan. I'll admit that I'm a history buff so I really enjoyed this set. The discs take you from the building of the ship, to how the passengers were loaded, all the way to why the *Titanic* had such a huge effect on our culture in this country and the world. DVD image is crystal clear and the sound is wonderful. —*DE*
Movie: 🎬🎬🎬 ½ **DVD:** 🎬🎬🎬 ½
A&E (cat #AAE-70411, UPC 3396170411). Full frame. Dolby Digital 5.1. $29.99. Keepcase. *LANG:* English. *FEATURES:* 36 chapters, 12 in each story • Time line of critical events • Bios of notable passengers • Text essay on the history of the tragedy as seen in popular culture.
2001 (G) 300m/C

T.N.T.

Gruner's managed to extricate himself from a covert fighting force but they're threatening his family unless he does what he's told. Video premiere gains noth-

ing but chapters and Spanish subtitles on DVD. Image is identical to VHS. —*MM*
Movie: 🎬🎬 **DVD:** 🎬🎬
Monarch (cat #7529). Full frame. Dolby Digital Surround Stereo. $19.95. Keepcase. *LANG:* English. *SUB:* Spanish. *FEATURES:* 16 chapters.
1998 (R) 87m/C Olivier Gruner, Eric Roberts, Randy Travis, Sam Jones, Rebecca Staab; *D:* Robert Radler; *C:* Bryan Duggan; *M:* Steve Edwards.

To Gillian on Her 37th Birthday

On her 35th birthday Gillian (Pfieffer) died in a horrible boating accident. Two years later, her husband David (Gallagher) is still meeting up with her spirit on the shore outside their Nantucket beach house. His sister in-law Esther (Baker) and her husband (Altman) come to visit for the weekend on the second anniversary of Gillian's death. They bring along a lady friend with hopes of she and David being a match. David's daughter Rachel (Danes) is getting the short end of the stick where her father's parenting is concerned, and she struggles to be 16 in spite of her father's grief. Enter every 16-year-old's dream, an eligible hunk played by Freddie Prinze Jr. Esther is overly protective of her niece and reveals during the weekend that she plans to take David to court for custody of Rachel. There are a few other bits used to fill the 92 minutes, but none noteworthy. The screenplay is by television titan David E. Kelly from the play by Michael Brady. The story is a bit sappy and the characters mope about, imagining their lives to be worse than they are. It's a boilerplate tear-jerker with good actors, pretty scenery, and a patchwork script that relies on one character's inability to separate from a ghost. Great image quality and O.K. sound; tissues not included. —*JAS*
Movie: 🎬🎬🎬 **DVD:** 🎬🎬🎬
Columbia Tristar (cat #06677, UPC 043-396066779). Full frame. Dolby Digital. $24.95. Keepcase. *LANG:* English. *SUB:* English; French. *FEATURES:* 28 chapters.
1996 (PG-13) 92m/C Peter Gallagher, Claire Danes, Kathy Baker, Wendy Crewson, Bruce Altman, Michelle Pfeiffer, Freddie Prinze Jr.; *D:* Michael Pressman; *W:* David E. Kelley; *C:* Tim Suhrstedt; *M:* James Horner.

To Kill with Intrigue

Jackie Chan plays a youth who escapes the massacre of his family, but finds himself indebted to the woman (Hsu Feng) responsible. A surprisingly beautifully shot picture, with wonderful Korean locations, especially the temple or garden where Chan's great climactic battle was shot. There's plenty of kung fu, both open hand and with strange weapons. Besides which, the openly insane story has a lot of entertaining facets. The widescreen image is a tremendous improvement on previous

video editions. —*BT* **AKA:** Jian Hua Yan Yu Jiang Nan.
Movie: 🎬🎬🎬 **DVD:** 🎬🎬🎬
Columbia Tristar (cat #08200, UPC 043-396082007). Widescreen anamorphic. $19.95. Keepcase. *LANG:* Cantonese; English. *SUB:* English; Spanish; Portuguese; French. *CAP:* English. *FEATURES:* 28 chapters • Trailers.
1977 107m/C HK Jackie Chan, Hsu Feng, George Wang Kuo, Ling-lung Yu; *D:* Lo Wei; *W:* Lung Ku; *C:* Chong-yuan Chen; *M:* Fang Chi Chen.

To Sir, with Love

Out-of-work engineer Mark Thackeray (Poitier) decides to take on a job as a teacher in London's rough East End. The students, children of dockworkers, are immediately hostile. He struggles with the class work and finally tosses out the books to focus on more basic life lessons. Fine acting from the star and his supporting ensemble keeps the material from falling victim to its inherent sentimentality. The full-frame presentation is an open matte transfer that adds additional image information at the top and bottom of the screen. Both transfers are richly detailed, although the slightest signs of film grain are evident at times—a technical limitation of the film material at the time the movie was produced. The disc faithfully reproduces the muted color scheme of the production, rendering fleshtones naturally throughout. Sound has obviously been carefully remastered, resulting in a much more natural presentation than you would expect from a film of this age. The frequency response is quite good without overly emphasized high ends and a rather natural bass roll-off. —*GH*
Movie: 🎬🎬🎬 **DVD:** 🎬🎬🎬
Columbia Tristar Home Video (UPC 43396-032965). Widescreen (1.85:1) anamorphic; full frame. Dolby Digital Mono. $24.98. Keepcase. *LANG:* English. *SUB:* English; Spanish; Portuguese; Korean; Chinese; Thai. *CAP:* English. *FEATURES:* Filmographies for James Clavell and Sidney Poitier • Trailers • 28 chapters.
1967 105m/C GB Sidney Poitier, Lulu, Judy Geeson, Christian Roberts, Suzy Kendall, Faith Brook; *D:* James Clavell; *W:* James Clavell; *C:* Paul Beeson; *M:* Ron Grainer.

To the Limit

Nutty thriller is relentlessly senseless. Pulchritudinous Colette (Smith) reveals to mobster Frank (Travolta) that she's a CIA agent (yeah, right) and that they are the targets of a rogue agent (Richmond). It really is worse than you can imagine, with Ms. Smith's shower scene arriving too late. The double-sided DVD also contains *Skyscraper* on the flip. Both are identical to VHS tape. —*MM*
Movie: 🎬 **DVD:** 🎬🎬
Sunland Studios (cat #PM 800, UPC 7574-49880013). Full frame. $19.98. Keepcase. *LANG:* English. *FEATURES:* 8 chapters.

1995 (R) 96m/C Anna Nicole Smith, Joey Travolta, Michael Nouri, Branscombe Richmond, John Aprea, Kathy Shower, Rebecca Ferratti, David Proval; **D:** Raymond Martino; **W:** Raymond Martino, Joey Travolta; **C:** Henryk Cymerman; **M:** Jim Halfpenny.

Todd McFarlane: The Devil You Know

Todd McFarlane writes, draws, and publishes one of the most popular comic books of all time, *Spawn*. Filmmaker Kenton Vaughan put together this 77-minute documentary about McFarlane's success story, and frankly, McFarlane is talented, but the story of how he became a multimillionaire is not very interesting. In short, he took skill and guts and turned it into cash. The friends and family that are interviewed about McFarlane are all securing their places in his will with their adoration and awe. The rare glimpse into "one of the world's most brilliant, intriguing, and creative minds" turns out to be a dull sycophantic jaunt through the life of one privileged man. How privileged? He paid $3 million for Mark McGuire's 70th home run baseball at auction. McFarlane justifies his Machiavellian approach to business by declaring himself to be a "man of contradictions." That makes it O.K. that he has become the very thing he rebelled against and hated about the corporate sector of the comic book world. Vaughan's filmmaking skill leaves a bit to be desired. He's up against a dull plot, and uses the same shots several times and fails to tell any semblance of an intriguing tale. The picture quality is crisp but don't expect great visual composition, it appears to be made for TV. It's a long stretch to the end of 77 minutes. —JAS
Movie: 🎵🎵 **DVD:** 🎵🎵🎵
New Video Group (cat #NVG-9497, UPC 767685949733). Full frame. Dolby Digital. $24.95. Keepcase. *LANG:* English. *FEATURES:* 12 chapters • *Spawn* promotional short • Todd McFarlane art gallery of unpublished images • McFarlane toys catalogue weblink.
2002 77m/C *CA* Todd McFarlane; **D:** Kenton Vaughan.

Tokyo Decameron: Three Tales of Madness & Sensuality

An anthology of three short stories telling us how screwed up modern society is in Tokyo. *Two Women Named Mariko* stars cult queen Kei Mizutani *(Weather Woman)* as the evil Mariko, the domineering leader of a gang of male hooligans. Marie Jino is her shy cousin Mariko. In *Lesbian Dream*, four lesbian friends on holiday in a mountain cabin find a dead body, and many accusing fingers are pointed. *The Man in the Pillory* finds fired construction worker Eisaku Shindo going on a bender and waking up bound to a chair. His tormentor accuses him of his sister's murder, and has him caught in a death trap, hoping to

torture the names of his three accomplices out of him. Average image quality. English dub track is pathetically bad. —BT
Movie: 🎵 ½ **DVD:** 🎵🎵
Central Park/U.S. Manga (cat #APCD1998, UPC 719987199828). Full frame. $19.99. Keepcase. *LANG:* English; Japanese. *SUB:* English. *FEATURES:* 10 chapters • Trailers • DVD-ROM features.
1996 90m/C *JP* Kei Mizutani, Hitomi Shiraishi, Hitoe Otake, Eisaku Shindo, Yu Kawai, Marie Jino; **D:** Koichi Kobayashi; **W:** Hono Misumi, Yuichiro Tatsumi; **C:** Norimasa Nakamoto; **M:** Seneca Park; **Nar:** Dave Mallow, Minori Terada.

Tokyo Mafia: Battle for Shinjuku

After three years of hiding out, Riki (Takeuchi) returns to Tokyo to rob the Teitokai yakuza's laundered money fund, and assembles a small group of crime veterans and green punks for the job. Superior in every way to the other Tokyo Mafia movies, *Battle for Shinjuku* benefits from an interesting story, good characters, and strong direction. In fact, this may not be a sequel at all, but a similar feature with the same leads, dubbed and subtitled to look like part of the series. The action is nicely choreographed, especially the unique guns vs. katana climax, which actually portrays the gunmen at a disadvantage in the match-up. Image and sound are better, too. —BT **AKA:** Gangster.
Movie: 🎵🎵 **DVD:** 🎵🎵
Central Park/U.S. Manga (cat #APCD2166, UPC 719987216624). Widescreen letterboxed. Dolby Digital Stereo. $29.95. Keepcase. *LANG:* Japanese; English. *SUB:* English. *FEATURES:* 10 chapters • Trailers • Character gallery • DVD-ROM features.
1996 84m/C *JP* Riki Takeuchi, Masayuki Imai, Bang-ho Cho, Asami Sawaki, Tomoroh Taguchi; **D:** Takeshi Miyasaka; **W:** Kosuke Hashimoto; **M:** Daisuke Suzuki.

Tokyo Mafia: Wrath of the Yakuza

Part 2 of the saga of the renegade crime gang begins as the Tokyo Mafia starts open warfare with the Teitokai yakuza. With plenty of money, but outnumbered 3,000 to 120, Tokyo Mafia head Riki Takeuchi decides to concentrate their efforts on the top men of the Teitokai. He clears the air with his old Yamaryu pal Sho Saimon (Masayuki Imai), and they team up to battle Yamaryu and the Blue Dragons together. It's a relief to see the leads finally get down to some action toward the end of this sequel, even though it's not very well performed. Both features have more of an atmosphere of condensed feature versions of a television series, with a hazy, shot-on-video look. —BT **AKA:** Tokyo Mafia 2.
Movie: 🎵🎵 **DVD:** 🎵🎵
Central Park/U.S. Manga (cat #APCD2152, UPC 719987215221). Widescreen letterboxed. Dolby Digital Stereo. $29.99. Keepcase. *LANG:* Japanese; English. *SUB:* Eng-

lish. *FEATURES:* 10 chapters • Trailers • Character gallery • DVD-ROM features.
1995 90m/C *JP* Riki Takeuchi, Masayuki Imai, Reiko Yasuhara, Hiroshi Miyauchi, Kojiro Hongo; **D:** Seiichi Shirai; **W:** Akinori Kikuchi; **M:** Takashi Nakagawa, Yuki Sakamoto.

Tokyo Mafia: Yakuza Wars

This is the first entry in the popular crime series starring Riki Takeuchi. It tells the story of a new organized crime gang in Japan, which is run more like a corporation than the old feudal system of the yakuza. The yakuza gets wind of the new gang, and is out for the Tokyo Mafia's blood. The only way out is for Tokyo Mafia to make war on the entire Teitokai yakuza. Scenes dealing with the adventures of the gang are interesting, but too often the story gets lost in the big picture. What action there is mostly consists of anonymous gangsters running around the streets chopping phony-looking pieces off of each other. The image has a hazy video look. Followed by *Wrath of the Yakuza*. —BT
Movie: 🎵🎵 **DVD:** 🎵🎵
Central Park/U.S. Manga (cat #APCD2082, UPC 719987208223). Widescreen letterboxed. Dolby Digital Stereo. $29.99. Keepcase. *LANG:* Japanese; English. *SUB:* English. *FEATURES:* 10 chapters • Trailers • Character gallery • DVD-ROM features.
1995 83m/C *JP* Riki Takeuchi, Masayuki Imai, Reiko Yasuhara, Kojiro Hongo, Shohei Yamamoto; **D:** Seiichi Shirai; **W:** Akinori Kikuchi; **M:** Takashi Nakagawa, Yuki Sakamoto.

Tom and Jerry: The Magic Ring

The classic cat and mouse team Tom and Jerry is back in a brand-new film. Unfortunately, they are doing the same old act. For reasons which are never fully explained, Tom and Jerry live in a creepy old house with a sorcerer. When he leaves for Calcutta (!), the sorcerer puts Tom in charge of a magic ring, which immediately gets stuck on Jerry's head. Seeing that Tom is furious over this, Jerry scampers from the house and heads for town. Knowing that he will be in hot water if he loses the precious ring, Tom gives chase. From here on out, the film is simply a series of chase scenes, with Three Stooges–like cartoon violence. There are cameos by other characters, like Droopy Dog, as well. There is never any further attempt at a plot, as Tom simply chases Jerry for an hour. Fans of the duo will love this, but many members of today's younger audience, who have been geared towards shorter attention spans, may find this redundant and boring. The animation is clean and colorful, but never rises above Saturday-morning cartoon quality. Full frame picture is razor-sharp, showing no overt flaws or defects. The colors are very good, and there is no video distortion, artifacting, or flaws from the source material.

The Dolby Digital 5.0 audio track provides clear dialogue and very nice musical reproduction. There are infrequent Surround effects, and despite the absence of a true LFE track, there is some noticeable bass response. The DVD features many text-only extra features, most focusing on the history of the Tom and Jerry universe. The two bonus shorts included on this DVD show some minor defects, but still look good given their age. —ML
Movie: ♫ ½ **DVD:** ♫♫♫
Warner (cat #65550, UPC 0125695550-20). Full frame. Dolby Digital 5.0; Dolby Surround Stereo. $19.98. Snapper. *LANG:* English; French; Spanish. *SUB:* English; French; Spanish. *CAP:* English. *FEATURES:* Bonus shorts • Featurette • Text files • Bonus trailers • 10 chapters.
2002 62m/C

Tom Clancy's Netforce

In 2005, technology has become so advanced that a special Netforce unit of the FBI has been established to police the Internet. Alex Michaels (Bakula, solid as always) heads the unit after the murder of predecessor Steve Day (Kristofferson), leading Michaels to believe that criminals are trying to cause a global computer crash. His two prime suspects are computer mogul Will Stiles (Reinhold) and crime boss Leong Cheng (Tagawa). DVD delivers an image that's a slight but definite improvement over broadcast quality. It can do nothing about the clichéd writing and acting. Two-sided disc must be turned over midway. —MM **AKA:** Netforce.
Movie: ♫♫ **DVD:** ♫♫ ½
Lion's Gate Home Ent. (cat #7087). Full frame. Dolby Digital Stereo. $29.99. Keepcase. *LANG:* English. *SUB:* English; French; Spanish. *FEATURES:* 30 chapters • Previews.
1998 (R) 90m/C Scott Bakula, Joanna Going, Brian Dennehy, Kris Kristofferson, Judge Reinhold, Cary-Hiroyuki Tagawa, CCH Pounder, Paul Hewitt, Chelsea Field, Frank Vincent; **D:** Robert Lieberman; **W:** Lionel Chetwynd; **C:** David Hennings; **M:** Jeff Rona.

Tombstone [2]

Wyatt Earp (Russell), his brothers (Elliott and Paxton), and Doc Holliday (Kilmer) decide to clean up Tombstone, Arizona, after the Clantons and their gang, the "cowboys" (who accessorize with dashing red sashes), go too far. Though many have criticized this interpretation of the events that led up to the O.K. Corral and what transpired afterward, it remains a lively and thoroughly enjoyable western that's somehow even more fun the second time around. (And given the liberties that so many filmmakers have taken with the material, this is an unusually accurate version.) The main reason is Kilmer, who is able to translate his normal obnoxiousness into an engaging performance. His Doc is a Byronic character, part Billy the Kid, part Poe. He and Russell make the

unlikely friendship between the two men seem completely real. Given the special treatment the film receives as part of the "Vista" series, it's no surprise that the image is excellent. This "director's cut" is four minutes longer than the theatrical release. I did not notice any serious differences between the two in terms of plot or content. DTS Surround is far superior to theatrical sound, as I remember it. Even conventional headphones provide a strong aural presentation. The extras, most on the second disc of the set, are not vast, though I do like the re-creation of the front page of the Tombstone Epitaph containing the first press account of the O.K. Corral unpleasantness. Cosmatos's affection for the film comes through strongly on his commentary. Highly recommended. —MM
Movie: ♫♫♫ ½ **DVD:** ♫♫♫ ½
Hollywood Pictures (cat #23118, UPC 786936158380). Widescreen (2.35:1) anamorphic. Dolby Digital 5.1 Surround; DTS 5.1. $29.98. Special packaging. *LANG:* English. *SUB:* French; Spanish. *CAP:* English. *FEATURES:* 27 chapters • "Making of" featurette • DVD-ROM features • O.K. Corral Time line • Facsimile map of Tombstone • Storyboards • Still gallery (Easter Egg) • Tombstone Epitaph newspaper account.
1993 (R) 130m/C Kurt Russell, Val Kilmer, Michael Biehn, Sam Elliott, Dana Delany, Bill Paxton, Powers Boothe, Stephen Lang, Jason Priestley, Dana Wheeler-Nicholson, Billy Zane, Thomas Haden Church, Joanna Pacula, Michael Rooker, Harry Carey Jr., Billy Bob Thornton, Charlton Heston, Robert John Burke, John Corbett, Buck Taylor, Terry O'Quinn, Pedro Armendariz Jr., Chris Mitchum, Jon Tenney; **D:** George P. Cosmatos; **W:** Kevin Jarre; **C:** William A. Fraker; **M:** Bruce Broughton; **Nar:** Robert Mitchum. *AWARDS: NOM:* MTV Movie Awards '94: Male Perf. (Kilmer), Most Desirable Male (Kilmer).

Tommy Boy

Not-too-bright rich kid Tommy (Farley) teams up with snide officious accountant Richard (Spade) to save the family auto parts business after dad (Dennehy) shuffles off this mortal coil. They must deal with a conniving stepmom (Derek) and stepbrother (Lowe), a ruthless rival (Aykroyd), and a road trip from hell to drum up new business. Not as bad as it sounds but inconsistent direction and too-familiar characters offset the chemistry between the two leads. DVD delivers a sharper image than tape. It actually looks better than the theatrical release, as I remember it. Strong good, too. —MM
Movie: ♫♫ **DVD:** ♫♫ ½
Paramount (cat #331317). Widescreen (1.85:1) anamorphic. Dolby Digital 5.1 Surround Stereo; Dolby Digital Surround. $29.99. Keepcase. *LANG:* English; French. *SUB:* English. *CAP:* English. *FEATURES:* Trailer • 24 chapters.
1995 (PG-13) 98m/C Chris Farley, David Spade, Brian Dennehy, Bo Derek, Dan Aykroyd, Julie Warner, Rob Lowe; **D:** Peter

Segal; **W:** Bonnie Turner, Terry Turner; **C:** Victor Kemper; **M:** David Newman. *AWARDS:* MTV Movie Awards '96: On-Screen Duo (Chris Farley/David Spade); *NOM:* MTV Movie Awards '96: Comedic Perf. (Farley).

The Tomorrow Man

Surprisingly engaging B-sci fi about the dangers of time travel and bad parenting. Corbin Bernsen plays Larry Mackey, a blue-collar father who rules his family with an iron fist. When his son Byron is kidnapped, he is pulled into the world of the future where he learns that the adult version of his son is a wanted criminal, and that it is this older son who kidnapped his younger son. Aided by a wicked-cool lady cop from the future (Kennedy), Mackey chases his "sons" across time and learns the hard way that his own actions may have ultimately created the situation he finds himself stuck in. Byron has kidnapped himself in an odd attempt to rescue his younger self from his abusive father, but when he shows Mackey a glimpse of what he is really like as a father, it seems there may be hope for everyone. A nice turn on the time travel genre with good acting and some fun "B"-movie action and snappy bad dialogue, this is a good rental and may appeal to some people for the long haul. The disc picture and sound are video quality. —CA
Movie: ♫♫ **DVD:** ♫♫ ½
MTI (cat #50046, UPC 619935404632). Full frame. $24.95. Keepcase. *LANG:* English. *SUB:* Spanish. *FEATURES:* 20 chapters • Additional trailers.
2001 (R) 95m/C Corbin Bernsen, Zach Galligan, Beth Kennedy, Morgan Rusler, Adam Sutton; **D:** Doug Campbell.

Tomorrow's Children

Please see review for *Sex and Buttered Popcorn, Vol. 1*.
Movie: ♫
1934 55m/B Sterling Holloway, Diana Sinclair, Sarah Padden, Don Douglas; **D:** Crane Wilbur.

Too Late the Hero

This above-average war movie finds American Lt. Sam Lawson (Robertson) assigned to a British battalion on a Japanese-occupied island in the Pacific. He must lead a mission into the jungle to take out a radio tower before the American Air Force arrives, but some unexpected complications leave him and Pct. Hearne (Caine) stranded deep within enemy territory. Well-directed and suspenseful, the film bends over backwards to humanize the Japanese officers. Anchor Bay's transfer is good, although some color inconsistencies in the original film detract from the overall look. Sound is adequate, though with a good deal of residual background hiss. —BG **AKA:** Suicide Run.
Movie: ♫♫♫ **DVD:** ♫♫♫

Anchor Bay (cat #DV11411, UPC 0131311-41191). Widescreen (1.85:1) anamorphic, full frame. Dolby 2.0. $24.98. Keepcase. *LANG:* English. *FEATURES:* 34 chapters • Trailer.

1970 (PG) 133m/C Michael Caine, Cliff Robertson, Henry Fonda, Ian Bannen, Harry Andrews, Denholm Elliott, William Beckley, Ronald Fraser, Percy Herbert, Patrick Jordan, Harvey Jason, Sam Kydd, Ken Takakura; *D:* Robert Aldrich; *W:* Robert Aldrich, Lois Heller; *C:* Joseph Biroc; *M:* Gerald Fried; **Technical Advisor:** Capt. Robert C. Lafever, Takashi Ohashi.

Too Many Ways to Be No. 1

The gangster genre stays alive in this black comedy, one of the twistiest. Lau Ching-wan is the frustrated leader of the hopelessly inept Hung Lok Gang. Each turn in the plot gets sharper and sharper. John Woo protégé Wai makes sure we don't somehow mistake this for a straight triad flick by keeping his camera doing tricks—turning upside down, zooming in and out, and so on. He crafts more than one send-up of a John Woo standoff—each with an increasing number of guns pointing at each other. Lau has the same sort of appeal Humphrey Bogart had. An offbeat joy, this would fit comfortably on a bill between *Run Lola Run* and *Pulp Fiction*. The image looks slightly soft, but that may just be part of the photography. There are a few splotchy artifacts in the transfer. —BT

Movie: 🎬🎬🎬 ½ **DVD:** 🎬🎬
Tai Seng (cat #NDVD129, UPC 60164381-4742). Widescreen letterboxed. $24.95. Keepcase. *LANG:* Cantonese; Mandarin. *SUB:* Chinese; English.
1997 91m/C *HK* Ching-Wan Lau, Carmen Lee, Frances Ng, Elvis Tsui, Ruby Wong, Matt Chow; *D:* Kai-Fai Wai; *W:* Kai-Fai Wai, Kam-yeun Szeto, Matt Chow; *C:* Horace Wong; *M:* Cacine Wong.

Top Dog

Another cop-and-dog-team-up-to-get-the-bad-guys flick. This one, however, is meant to appeal to kids who liked *Sidekicks*. Jake Wilder (Norris), a beer swillin' karate-choppin' loner cop, teams up with canine Reno whose ex-partner was killed by neo-Nazi terrorists. Weak script and erratic story line can't find a comfortable balance between the too-cute pooch scenes and the toned-down violence. Reno steals his scenes. DVD delivers an excellent reproduction of a good to very good image. —MM
Movie: 🎬 ½ **DVD:** 🎬🎬 ½
Artisan Ent. (cat #11278). Widescreen (1.85:1) letterboxed. $19.98. Keepcase. *LANG:* English. *FEATURES:* Trailer • 32 chapters.
1995 (PG-13) 93m/C Chuck Norris, Clyde Kusatsu, Michele Lamar Richards, Carmine Caridi, Peter Savard Moore, Erik von Detten, Herta Ware, Kai Wulff, Francesco Quinn, Timothy Bottoms; *D:* Aaron Norris; *W:* Ron Swanson; *C:* Joao Fernandes.

Topkapi

Like an Earth Mother for thieves, international adventuress Elizabeth Lipp (Mercouri) hires Swiss mastermind Walter Harper (Schell) to collect a number of professionals to help her crack Istanbul's fabulous Topkapi museum, there to steal a legendary jewel-encrusted dagger of inestimable value. Stuffy Englishman Cedric Page (Morley) is an expert on alarm systems; Hans (Hahn) and Giulio (Segal) are an acrobatic team, and ne'er-do-well Arthur Simon Simpson (Ustinov) is tapped as a patsy to get some guns across the Greek border. Their plan is hardly foolproof, as they have to outwit a sensitive alarm system, and find a way of escaping through a fierce security corps. Worse, their every move is being carefully observed by the local police, because Simpson has been caught at the border and forced to turn against them! DVD is O.K., but kind of a disappointment. This may be a new transfer, but I think it's identical to the 10-year-old laser version, and only looks better due to the higher resolution. The color doesn't quite gleam as it should. I'd say that the film is worn, due to the nicks and scratches in the colorful twinkly titles, but I've never seen a better copy, so the flaws might be built into the title negative. European opticals back then were never particularly great. The wonderful soundtrack sounds a tad distorted and thin, which also might be how the original played. But it's possible that some new work with the original picture and sound elements might have come up with major improvements. —GE
Movie: 🎬🎬🎬 **DVD:** 🎬🎬 ½
MGM Home Ent. (cat #1002743, UPC 027-616869418). Widescreen (1.66:1) anamorphic. Dolby Digital Mono. $19.98. Keepcase. *LANG:* English; French. *SUB:* French; Spanish. *CAP:* English. *FEATURES:* Trailer.
1964 122m/C Melina Mercouri, Maximilian Schell, Peter Ustinov, Robert Morley, Akim Tamiroff, Jess Hahn, Gilles Segal; *D:* Jules Dassin; *W:* Monja Danischewsky; *C:* Henri Alekan; *M:* Manos Hadjidakis. *AWARDS:* Oscars '64: Support. Actor (Ustinov).

Tormented

Please see review of *Monsters Crash the Pajama Party Spook Show Spectacular.*
Movie: 🎬 ½
1960 75m/B Richard Carlson, Susan Gordon, Juli Reding; *D:* Bert I. Gordon; *W:* Bert I. Gordon, George Worthing Yates; *C:* Ernest Laszlo; *M:* Albert Glasser, Calvin Jackson.

The Tormentors

They're the world's most clean-cut looking biker gang with their Junior League haircuts and khaki uniforms. Looks are deceiving, though, as they roar into town, hold up a bank in broad daylight, and motor away with a screaming blonde as a hostage. These fellas aren't just bad dudes—they're NAZIS!!! They haul the poor girl into the woods, rip off her top, and hold her to the ground while the head goose-stepper B. Rockwell Kemp rapes then strangles her with his blood-red swastika armband. For this they must pay! Anthony Eisley is her fiancé, who vows to exact vigilante justice by infiltrating the "Fourth Reich" when the cops are hesitant to do anything. He gains their confidence by craftily redecorating his one-room apartment in Hitler paraphernalia and acting real smarmy on Nazi orgy night. Sound and full-frame image are both slightly superior to VHS tape. —GNG/MM
Movie: 🎬🎬 ½ **DVD:** 🎬🎬
Platinum Disc (UPC 096009022693). Full frame. Mono. $12.99. Jewelcase. *LANG:* English; French. *FEATURES:* Trivia game • Talent files • Trailer.
1971 (R) 78m/C James Craig, Anthony Eisley, Chris Nole, William Dooley, Bruce Kemp, Inga Wede, James Gordon White; *D:* Boris Eagle; *W:* James Gordon White.

Tortilla Soup

Maria Ripoll's remake of Ang Lee's *Eat Drink Man Woman* sets the story in the Mexican-American neighborhoods of Los Angeles. That's where widowed master chef Martin Naranjo (Elizondo) cooks Sunday dinner every week for his three grown daughters (Pena, Obradors, and Mello) and their neighbor (Marie), a single mom. The family deals with a host of problems, not the least of which is the patriarch's fading sense of taste. Then there's the recently arrived widow (Welch) who's out to catch him. It's a fine story but for those who (like me) love the first version, this one lacks a certain freshness. That said, Ripoll manages to capture the loving spirit quite well, and Hector Elizondo has the same quiet commanding star power that Shiung Lung has. You can almost smell the kitchen in the opening credit sequence. DVD image is of medium clarity and sharpness, seemingly an accurate translation of the theatrical image. Beyond the choice of image size, disc is a bare-bones affair. —MM
Movie: 🎬🎬🎬 **DVD:** 🎬🎬 ½
Columbia Tristar (cat #08120, UPC 0433-96081208). Widescreen (1.85:1) anamorphic; full frame. Dolby Digital 5.1 Surround. $27.98. Keepcase. *LANG:* English; Spanish. *SUB:* English; Spanish. *CAP:* English. *FEATURES:* 28 chapters.
2001 (PG-13) 102m/C Hector Elizondo, Jacqueline Obradors, Elizabeth Pena, Tamara Mello, Nikolai Kinski, Raquel Welch, Paul Rodriguez, Joel Joan, Constance Marie; *D:* Maria Ripoli; *W:* Tom Musca, Ramon Menendez, Vera Blasi; *C:* Xavier Perez Grobet; *M:* Bill Conti.

Total Recall [2 SLE]

In revisiting Paul Verhoeven's 1990 futuristic epic (first reviewed in *Book 1*), Artisan pulled out all the stops in their new, truly packed special edition DVD. An excellent transfer, remastered sound, and a plethora of supplements including a commentary track by Verhoeven and Arnold

Schwarzenegger should more than please fans of this opulent but ultra-violent space opera. The 1.85:1 anamorphic transfer is stunning. Colors are accurate, constant, and vibrant. Deep blacks and superb detail delineation make for an exceptionally crisp image. Even in scenes with complex special effects, the picture is completely smooth, stable, and free of grain. The source print shows no blemishes nor digital or compression artifacts. The remixed Dolby Digital 5.1 soundtrack is very aggressive, with a wide front soundstage, active Surrounds, and window-cracking LFE at the necessary action moments. Even Jerry Goldsmith's pulsing score gets some low-end punch. Dialogue sounds well integrated. The 5.1 audio sounds like a genuine remix, rather than simply sprinkling in some discrete sound effects and cranking up the bass. A two-channel Dolby Surround audio option is also included, but if you have 5.1 capability, stick with the discrete soundtrack. Commentary by director Verhoeven and star Schwarzenegger too often lapses into the "let's-rehash-what-we're-watching" mode. While I am not a huge fan of the film, there is no mistaking that Artisan has mounted a lavish DVD edition. As a gimmick, the disc is housed in a red circular tin, brandishing Martian craters and even a "face." Keeping it from rolling out of its library slot has proved the most challenging facet of the DVD. —EP

Movie: ♫♫ ½ **DVD:** ♫♫♫
Artisan Ent. (cat #11957, UPC 0122361-19579). Widescreen (1.85:1) anamorphic. Dolby Digital 5.1 Surround Stereo; Dolby Digital Surround. $24.98. Special packaging. LANG: English. SUB: English; French; Spanish. CAP: English. FEATURES: Commentary ▪ Featurettes ▪ Storyboard comparisons ▪ Trailers & TV spots ▪ Production notes.
1990 (R) 113m/C Arnold Schwarzenegger, Rachel Ticotin, Sharon Stone, Michael Ironside, Ronny Cox, Roy Brocksmith, Marshall Bell, Mel Johnson Jr.; **D:** Paul Verhoeven; **W:** Gary Goldman, Dan O'Bannon; **C:** Jan De Bont; **M:** Jerry Goldsmith. AWARDS: Oscars '90: Visual FX; NOM: Oscars '90: Sound.

A Touch of Class
Steve Blackburn (Segal), an American insurance adjuster living in London, plans a quick and uncommitted affair with Vicki Elesio (Jackson in an Oscar-winning turn), but finds that things become emotionally complicated. The fairly realistic plotting is lightened with some slapstick and mild physical humor. DVD is made from an excellent transfer of an early '70s image. Surface damage is nearly non-existent. Sound is O.K., and doesn't need to be much more since Jackson's cool performance is the point of it all. —MM
Movie: ♫♫♫ **DVD:** ♫♫ ½
Warner (cat #T8361, UPC 0539398361-27). Widescreen (2.35:1) anamorphic. Dolby Mono. $19.98. Snapper. LANG: English; French. SUB: English; French. CAP:

English. FEATURES: Talent files ▪ Trailer ▪ Awards ▪ 30 chapters.
1973 (PG) 105m/C George Segal, Glenda Jackson, Paul Sorvino, Hildegard(e) Neil, K. Callan, Mary Barclay, Cec Linder; **D:** Melvin Frank; **W:** Jack Rose; **C:** Austin Dempster; **M:** John Cameron. AWARDS: Oscars '73: Actress (Jackson); Golden Globes '74: Actor—Mus./Comedy (Segal), Actress—Mus./Comedy (Jackson); Writers Guild '73: Orig. Screenplay; NOM: Oscars '73: Picture, Song ("All That Love Went to Waste"), Story & Screenplay, Orig. Dramatic Score.

Town and Country
Typically when a film has been ravaged by critics, there is at least some component of the movie which general audiences would find compelling. Such is not the case here. In this pointless film, we watch two rich couples (Warren Beatty & Diane Keaton and Garry Shandling & Goldie Hawn) deal with infidelity and divorce. Ultimately, the message of the film is: Don't Cheat! There is nothing original and the film is strangely edited, as many scenes simply end without having gone anywhere. Shandling does have a couple of funny lines, but they were most likely improvised. If you find people who can't speak English and topless fat men funny, then this is the movie for you! Otherwise, most need not apply. Despite the fact that Town & Country is the epitome of a stinker, the DVD is nearly flawless. The letterboxed image is beautiful, showing a superior sharpness and no defects. The colors are nice and there is no overt artifacting. The 5.1 audio is splendid as well, offering clean dialogue and excellent Surround sound effects. What a waste of digital quality! —ML
Movie: woof **DVD:** ♫♫♫
New Line (cat #N5354, UPC 79404-3535420). Widescreen (1.85:1) anamorphic; full frame. Dolby Digital 5.1; Dolby 2.0 Surround. $24.98. Snapper. LANG: English. SUB: English. CAP: English. FEATURES: Theatrical trailer ▪ Cast & crew ▪ 20 chapters.
2001 (R) 104m/C Warren Beatty, Diane Keaton, Goldie Hawn, Andie MacDowell, Jenna Elfman, Garry Shandling, Charlton Heston, Marian Seldes, Tricia Vessey, Josh Hartnett, Nastassia Kinski, Katharine Towne, Buck Henry, Holland Taylor, William Hootkins, Del Zamora, Ian McNeice, Azura Skye; **D:** Peter Chelsom; **W:** Buck Henry, Michael Laughlin; **C:** William A. Fraker; **M:** Rolfe Kent.

Town without Pity
Though the subject of this courtroom drama remains far too timely, its treatment is dated in some key scenes. In 1960, four American G.I.s (Blake, Jaeckel, Sutton, Sondock) stationed in Germany are accused of raping a local girl, Karin (Kaufmann). Lawyer Steve Garrett (Douglas) is brought in to defend them and elects to put the young woman on trial. DVD appears to have been

made from less than perfect original elements. It suffers minor registration jitters in a few places. Black-and-white photography ranges between good and very good; sound isn't as strong. It's often clipped and sharp. —MM AKA: Stadt ohne Mitleid.
Movie: ♫♫ ½ **DVD:** ♫♫ ½
MGM Home Ent. (cat #1003140, UPC 027616873040). Full frame. Dolby Digital Mono. $14.98. Keepcase. LANG: English; French. SUB: English; French; Spanish. CAP: English. FEATURES: 16 chapters ▪ Trailer.
1961 103m/B GE Kirk Douglas, E.G. Marshall, Robert (Bobby) Blake, Richard Jaeckel, Frank Sutton, Alan Gifford, Barbara Rutting, Christine Kaufmann, Mal Sondock; **D:** Gottfried Reinhardt; **W:** Silvia Reinhardt, Georg Hurdalek; **C:** Kurt Hasse; **M:** Dimitri Tiomkin. AWARDS: Golden Globes '62: Song (Tiomkin); NOM: Oscars '62: Song (Tiomkin).

The Toxic Avenger, Part 3: The Last Temptation of Toxie [DC]
Early in his typically candid and cutting commentary, Troma honcho Lloyd Kaufman admits that this movie was created because he shot too much film making Toxic Avenger 2 and wanted to make use of his extra footage. Who'd have thought that this auteur would stoop to crass commercialism to tell the next chapter in the story of Tromaville's favorite superhero and his blind girlfriend (Legere)? As is so often the case with Troma releases, DVD image is a faithful reproduction of an ultra–low budget original. The extensive extras, many of them promotional materials, are the selling point. One glitch: the menu option for Kaufman's commentary track did not activate it. I switched to it using the audio option after the feature had begun. (This is the unrated "director's cut.") —MM
Movie: ♫♫ ½ **DVD:** ♫♫♫
Troma Team Video (cat #9036, UPC 7903-57903634). Full frame. $19.98. Keepcase. LANG: English. SUB: English. FEATURES: 13 chapters ▪ Commentary: Kaufman, editors Ronnie Thomas, Sean McGrath ▪ Commentary: actor Jo Fleishaker ▪ Interviews ▪ Promotional materials ▪ Trailers ▪ "Where in the World Is Toxie?" film clips.
1989 (R) 102m/C Ron Fazio, Phoebe Legere, John Altamura, Rick Collins, Lisa Gaye, Jessica Dublin; **D:** Michael Herz, Lloyd Kaufman; **W:** Gay Partington Terry, Lloyd Kaufman; **C:** James London; **M:** Christopher De Marco.

The Toy
This pitiful comedy stars Pryor as a penniless reporter who finds himself the new "toy" of the spoiled son of a multimillionaire oilman, played by Gleason. The bulk of the film deals with Pryor being tortured by his new "owner," while the final reel gets far too sappy. There is no chemistry

whatsoever between Pryor and Gleason, and the young boy (Schwartz) is simply annoying. The film is never funny and often borders on being extremely racist. This slow and terrible remake of *Le Jouet* offers heavy-handed lecturing about earning friends. Director Donner, who is better known for his action films, should have known better. Faring somewhat better is the DVD release, which offers a sharp picture, but there is some artifacting of the image at times. The colors are fine, and no distortion clouds the screen. The audio track provides clear dialogue, with practically no Surround sound or bass. Also, the music is muffled at times. —ML
Movie: ♪ ½ **DVD:** ♪♪ ½
Columbia Tristar (cat #06542, UPC 0433-96065420). Widescreen (1.85:1) anamorphic; full frame. Dolby Surround. $19.95. Keepcase. *LANG:* English; French. *SUB:* English; French; Spanish; Portuguese; Chinese; Korean; Thai. *CAP:* English. *FEATURES:* Bonus trailers ● 28 chapters.
1982 (PG) Richard Pryor, Jackie Gleason, Ned Beatty, Wilfrid Hyde-White, Scott Schwartz; *D:* Richard Donner; *W:* Carol Sobieski; *C:* Laszlo Kovacs; *M:* Patrick Williams.

Toys

Disappointingly earnest comedy about Leslie (Williams), the whimsical son of a toy manufacturer who must fight to keep the playful spirit of the factory alive after it passes into the hands of his deranged uncle (Gambon). The uncle is a general who attempts to transform the factory into an armaments plant. Leslie receives assistance in this battle from his sister Alsatia (Cusack) and his cousin Patrick (L.L. Cool J.). Film offers flat characters and generally falls short by trying too hard to send a message to viewers about the folly of war. The one positive aspect of *Toys* is the colorful production design of Ferdinando Scarfiotti, who gives the film a wonderful primary color look, similar to that of *Dick Tracy*. This film is certainly one of the weakest efforts for both Williams and director Barry Levinson. This DVD is somewhat of a disappointment as well. The image here is on the dark side, which mutes the wonderful color palette of the film. Otherwise, the image is sharp and shows little grain. The audio track fares much better, as the Dolby Digital 5.1 sound offers clear dialogue, good Surround effects, and a resonating bass. The DVD includes the memorable theatrical trailers for the film in which Robin Williams stands in a field of tall grass. This may be the best thing about this disc. —ML
Movie: ♪ ½ **DVD:** ♪♪ ½
20th Century Fox (cat #2002053, UPC 024543020530). Widescreen (1.85:1) anamorphic. Dolby Digital 5.1; Dolby Surround. $19.98. Keepcase. *LANG:* English; French. *SUB:* English; Spanish. *CAP:* English. *FEATURES:* Featurette ● Trailers ● TV spots ● 20 chapters.
1992 (PG-13) 121m/C Robin Williams, Joan Cusack, Michael Gambon, L.L. Cool

J., Robin Wright Penn, Donald O'Connor; *D:* Barry Levinson; *W:* Valerie Curtin, Barry Levinson; *C:* Adam Greenberg. *AWARDS:* NOM: Oscars '92: Art Dir./Set Dec., Costume Des.

Traffic [Criterion]

The movie is of course excellent, a remake of the equally good *Traffik* U.K. miniseries. This DVD is essentially the same as the earlier USA disc (reviewed in *Book 2*), with a remastered transfer; if all you want to do is see the movie, the USA release will suffice. The extras on this two-disc set are extensive. On his commentary track, director Soderbergh is open, honest, and gracious in his praise without turning the track into a group hug. He and his writer Stephen Gaghan analyze each and every scene. Soderbergh's not above saying that he simply had a rotten day without inspiration, to describe the scene where Catherine Zeta-Jones's kid is almost kidnapped on the beach. No excuses. We also find out that he started serving as his own director of photography on this film (under a pseudonym) for creative reasons, not because he wanted to hog credit. His explanations are very interesting and artistically sound. Disc 2's deleted scenes are fairly fascinating. I listened to them first with the commentary, and then by themselves. It's interesting to hear a director express ambivalence about whether a scene belongs in or out, as all of these play well, and in most cases would have enriched the movie. Soderbergh stresses that USA Films allowed him to shoot his entire overlong script with the idea that it would have to be shaped in the editing room, which he did with a vengeance. The color-stylization demonstration is elaborate and thorough but not very compelling. The lab process to make the Mexico scenes look as if they were shot on an inferior, yellowed film stock seems almost arbitrary. It's the kind of thing you have to admire Soderbergh for—going to the trouble to get an organic photochemical look instead of just processing the scenes digitally. But since we don't get a full rationale for why he went for this style, it doesn't make that big of an impression. Other extras give nice insights to Soderbergh's sophisticated shooting style, while picture and dialogue editing demonstrations show the talent required to keep up with him. The editing demonstration given by cutter Stephen Mirrione shows the Avid interface and might not mean much to civilians, but is interesting to see from an editor's point of view. The dialogue editing demo by sound cutter Larry Blake is even more exacting, as he shows us the intricacies of his craft. Location tracks with recording problems are addressed, as well as the creation of a flawlessly replaced ADR line. After all that, the trailers and TV spots seem almost superfluous. —GE/MM
Movie: ♪♪♪♪ **DVD:** ♪♪♪♪
Criterion (UPC 696306038924). Widescreen (1.78:1) anamorphic. Dolby Digital

5.1 Surround. $39.98. 2-disc keepcase. *LANG:* English. *SUB:* English. *CAP:* English. *FEATURES:* Commentary: Soderbergh, writer Stephen Gaghan ● Commentary: producers, consultants ● Commentary: composer Cliff Martinez (with cues not heard in film) ● 25 deleted scenes with commentary ● Film processing demonstration ● Editing demonstration ● Dialogue editing demonstration ● 30 minutes of multi-angle coverage of 2 scenes ● Trailers ● TV spots ● U.S. Customs trading cards of drug-sniffing dogs.
2000 (R) 147m/C Michael Douglas, Catherine Zeta-Jones, Benicio Del Toro, Dennis Quaid, Benjamin Bratt, Albert Finney, Amy Irving, Don Cheadle, Luis Guzman, Steven Bauer, James Brolin, Erika Christensen, Clifton (Gonzalez) Collins Jr., Miguel Ferrer, Tomas Milian, D.W. Moffett, Marisol Padilla Sanchez, Peter Riegert, Jacob Vargas, Rena Sofer, Stacy Travis, Salma Hayek, Topher Grace, Beau Holden, Enrique Murciano; *D:* Steven Soderbergh; *W:* Stephen Gaghan; *C:* Steven Soderbergh; *M:* Cliff Martinez. *AWARDS:* Oscars '00: Adapt. Screenplay, Director (Soderbergh), Film Editing, Support. Actor (Del Toro); British Acad. '00: Adapt. Screenplay, Support. Actor (Del Toro); Golden Globes '01: Screenplay, Support. Actor (Del Toro); L.A. Film Critics '00: Director (Soderbergh); Natl. Bd. of Review '00: Director (Soderbergh); N.Y. Film Critics '00: Director (Soderbergh), Film, Support. Actor (Del Toro); Natl. Soc. Film Critics '00: Director (Soderbergh), Support. Actor (Del Toro); Screen Actors Guild '00: Actor (Del Toro), Cast; Writers Guild '00: Adapt. Screenplay; Broadcast Film Critics '00: Adapt. Screenplay, Director (Soderbergh); *NOM:* Oscars '00: Film; Directors Guild '00: Director (Soderbergh).

Traffik

Hamburg detectives capture middleman drug trafficker Ledesert (Lakenmacher) and force him to name names, which brings about the arrest of businessman Kurt (Hinz), a seemingly benign millionaire who does great public works in Pakistan. His trophy wife Helen (Duncan) is forced to take over her husband's racket, fending off the advances of their lawyer Domenguez (Benestante) and outsmarting the cops on her own. In Pakistan, venal drug czar Tariq Butt (Hussain) takes on a new assistant, Fazal (Jamal Shah), a farmer driven from growing poppy crops by government troops. Fazal is soon learning the drug trade, but at a high price, because Butt wants him to commit ever-greater crimes, while holding his family as virtual hostages. Minister Jack Lithgow (Paterson) is in Pakistan getting completely snowed by corrupt local officials, who want the financial aid package he's come to investigate. At a reception, the activist sister of his consulate contact, Roomana (Feryal Gauhar Shah) tells him that the government anti-heroin activities are a sham, and points out Tariq Butt as a guest at the reception. Jack has problems back in London, too: his daughter Caroline (Ormond) is becoming an uncontrollable heroin addict herself. Acorn Media's DVD set of the British TV series (upon which Steven Soderbergh's film is based) is an efficient but plainwrap package, with no real extras. Three episodes are on each disc, which do not have closed captions (Americans have trouble with U.K. dialogue at times). About half of the German and Pakistani dialogue is dubbed, and half subtitled, without any pattern that I could discern. The camerawork, probably 16mm, is good and the image is clean but still has the slightly (very slightly) soft look of PAL to NTSC conversion. —GE

Movie: 🎬🎬🎬 ½ **DVD:** 🎬🎬 ½
Acorn Media (UPC 054961480098). Full frame. $39.99. Keepcase boxed set. *LANG:* English.
1990 360m/C *GB* Lindsay Duncan, Bill Paterson, Jamal Shah, Talat Hussain, Fritz Muller-Scherz, Julia Ormond, Knut Hinz, Feryal Gauhar Shah, Peter Lakenmacher, Vincenzo Benestante; **D:** Alastair Reid; **W:** Simon Moore; **C:** Clive Tickner; **M:** Tim Souster.

Tragic Hero

Please see review of *Rich and Famous / Tragic Hero*.
1987 96m/C *HK* Chow Yun-Fat, Andrew Lau, Carina Lau, Alex Man, Pauline Wong; **D:** Taylor Wong.

Trail Beyond [Columbia]

Please see review for *John Wayne: Western Classics*.
Movie: 🎬 ½
1934 57m/B John Wayne, Noah Beery Sr., Verna Hillie, Noah Beery Jr.; **D:** Robert North Bradbury; **W:** Lindsley Parsons; **C:** Archie Stout.

Trailer, the Movie

Goofy experimental comedy combines elements of *Last Action Hero* and *Purple Rose of Cairo*. In a black-and-white introduction, two lonely guys (McCrudden and Pope) sneak into a theatre one night and fall in love with two actresses (Hicks and Crigler) they see in a trailer. After the guys are tossed out, they wish their way into a color world where the rules of movies apply. Unfortunately, this well-meaning independent production lacks the wit to make full use of the engaging premise. And the thrift-shop budget is so meager that the (shot on video?) image is second rate. On DVD, focus is soft; colors and sound are weak. —MM

Movie: 🎬🎬 **DVD:** 🎬🎬
Vanguard Intl. Cinema (cat #VF9180, UPC 658769918038). Full frame. $29.98. Keepcase. *LANG:* English. *FEATURES:* 11 chapters.
1999 101m/C Ian McCrudden, Will Pope, Miranda Hicks, Marjorie Crigler; **D:** Ian McCrudden; **C:** Matthew Uhry.

Training Day

Jake Hoyt (Hawke) has been on the police force for 19 months and wants to move up in rank to provide his wife and child with a nicer home. He has one "training" day (ta-daa!) to prove himself to older officer, Alonzo (Washington). Alonzo wastes no time testing the rookie: taunting him and eventually forcing him to try narcotics before they head out on the streets. Is Alonzo, who has arrested dozens of criminals, trying to give Jake a crash course in undercover investigation or does he have a hidden agenda? With Alonzo, Washington takes his usual intensity to the limit. He goes over the top, but there are enough subtle moments sprinkled throughout the performance to make Alonzo unpredictable. It's a genuinely stunning performance and Washington is not alone; Hawke's effort is good enough that he actually stands up fairly well to Washington's powerhouse effort. The film has little pieces here and there that aren't as effective as the whole and it isn't flawless, but this is a very impressive leap forward from director Fuqua's previous pictures. DVD sharpness and detail are impressive, and the image is crisp and well defined. It often shows nice depth. There's a slight trace or two of edge-enhancement, which is hardly noticeable. This is an excellent disc that is, if not reference quality, is about as close as it gets. The Surround channels are used frequently throughout the movie, providing strong ambience and support for the music. On the commentary, Fuqua provides a very interesting discussion of the obstacles that occurred during filming. There are a few silent stretches but he talks throughout most of the film and provides several great stories as well as an analysis of the story and the production experience. The featurette is probably one of the best HBO "making of"s that I've seen in recent times. While there is a lot of discussion of what happens in the story, there's also insight into the characters and some good behind-the-scenes footage. The 12 minutes of deleted scenes are actually quite good. It's too bad that no commentary is available for these scenes, because it would have been interesting to learn why they were deleted. Recommended. —AB

Movie: 🎬🎬🎬 ½ **DVD:** 🎬🎬🎬 ½
Warner (cat #21962, UPC 0853921962-27). Widescreen (2.35:1) anamorphic. Dolby Digital 5.1 Surround. $26.98. Snapper. *LANG:* English; French. *SUB:* English; French; Spanish. *CAP:* English. *FEATURES:* Alternate ending ⬤ 28 chapters ⬤ 2 music videos ⬤ Theatrical trailer ⬤ Deleted scenes ⬤ Commentary: director Fuqua ⬤ Behind-the-scenes documentary ⬤ HBO "making of" featurette ⬤ Cast & crew bios.
2001 (R) 120m/C Denzel Washington, Ethan Hawke, Scott Glenn, Clifford Curtis, Dr. Dre, Snoop Dogg, Tom Berenger, Harris Yulin, Raymond J. Barry, Charlotte Ayanna, Macy Gray, Eva Mendez, Nicholas Chinlund, Jaime Gomez, Raymond Cruz; **D:** Antoine Fuqua; **W:** David Ayer; **C:** Mauro Fiore; **M:** Mark Mancina. *AWARDS:* Oscars '01: Actor (Washington); L.A. Film Critics '01: Actor (Washington); *NOM:* Oscars '01: Support. Actor (Hawke); Golden Globes '02: Actor—Drama (Washington); Screen Actors Guild '01: Actor (Washington), Support. Actor (Hawke).

Trans

Shot documentary-style in what seems like digital video (DV), film tells the story of Ryan, a 15-year-old living in a juvenile detention center. He escapes with several of the other boys one day when some of the other inmates on the road crew he is working on start a fight. The rest of the film covers his ill-conceived attempt to get from Florida to Colorado to reconcile with his mother. Ryan Daugherty is pitch-perfect as Ryan, emotionally frail but with a defective moral compass, which makes him fodder for the wrong crowd. He seems doomed from the start of his story and probably before that, but it is his journey the film is concerned with and not his fate. This might make the story seem slow for anyone more interested in mainstream pacing, but the art-house crowd will be thrilled with the slowly evolving character study. The picture has the fuzzy look of digital and the night scenes are especially rough. The sound is muffled at times, though the dialogue still comes through. —CA

Movie: 🎬🎬 ½ **DVD:** 🎬🎬
Fox/Lorber (cat #FLV5292, UPC 7209175-29226). Full frame. 5.1 Stereo. $24.90. Keepcase. *LANG:* English. *FEATURES:* 16 chapters.
1999 80m/C Ryan Daugherty, Jon Daugherty, Justin Lakes; **D:** Julian Goldberger; **W:** Julian Goldberger; **C:** Jesse Rosen.

Transformers: Season 1

Some franchises refuse to die off; these shape-changing robots re-emerge every few years with a new animated series or line of toys. This DVD box set from Rhino encompasses the first season of the original animated show from 1986, containing all 16 episodes. The shows are spread out over three DVDs, with a fourth disc of bonus features. The shows begin with the origin of "The Transformers," who originated from the planet Cybertron, millions of years ago. Cybertron is facing an energy crisis, and two separate factions, the benevolent Autobots and the malevolent Decepticons, fight for control of resources and the planet. Realizing that Cybertron is a dying world, Optimus Prime, the leader of the Autobots, decides to take his group into outer space in hopes of finding energy. The Decepticons follow, a battle ensues, and all crashland on Earth. The robots lie dormant for millions of years, but are suddenly revived by an earthquake. Decepticon leader Megatron quickly surmises that Earth is rich with energy and commands his 'bots to begin pillaging the planet. The Autobots, along with their human companion Spike, vow to stop the evil Decepticons. Once this basic premise

is established, the remaining episodes focus on the war between the two sides and the introduction of new Transformers, such as the Dinobots and the Insecticons. In an unusual move for an animated show, this one offers continuing story lines and a season-ending cliff-hanger. The animation looks woefully dated and sluggish, but Transformers fans should love this. The images are sharp and clear, but there are numerous noticeable flaws and defects. (One of the extras in this set describes the restoration process and how these problems were unavoidable.) The colors are good and the picture is relatively free from distortion or artifacting. The newly created Dolby Digital 5.1 audio track is impressive, as it features clear dialogue, well-timed Surround effects, and a deep bass response. The bulk of the extra features should appeal only to hard-core fans, as they focus on the differences between this show and its Japanese cousin, and many outtake and animation flaws. Also, there is a brief look at a convention for fans of the Transformers. —*ML*
Movie: ♪♪♪ ***DVD:*** ♪♪♪
Rhino (cat #R2 976039, UPC 603497603-923). Full frame. Dolby Digital 5.1; Dolby Surround. $59.95. Box set. *LANG:* English. *FEATURES:* Restoration process • Outtakes & alternate sequences • Original script • Convention featurette • 96 chapters • 2 post-card sized animation cels.
1986 490m/C

Transylvania 6–5000

This comedy covers all the bases as it spoofs the classic horror monsters. The problem is that it's just not that funny. Tabloid reporters Jack Harrison (Goldblum) and Gil Turner (Begley Jr.) are sent to Transylvania to seek out Frankenstein's Monster. What they find are a slew of monsters, including the wolfman, a mummy, and a female vampire (played by Goldblum's future ex-wife Geena Davis, whose outfit is more entertaining than this film), but few funny jokes. The film features many familiar faces—Carol Kane, John Byner, Joseph Bologna, and a pre-*Seinfeld* Michael Richards, but it simply tries too hard. Yes, some of the jokes are funny and there are some nice sight gags, but overall, the film is a loser. And while the scenery isn't all that impressive either, the film was actually shot in Yugoslavia. (For a better take on the old Universal monsters, track down Fred Dekkers's *Monster Squad*.) Despite the lackluster reputation of the film, Anchor Bay has given the film good treatment on DVD. The image is sharp and clear, but there is some slight grain at times. The colors are good and there is very little artifacting. The Dolby Digital mono audio track offers clear dialogue, but a very slight hiss can be heard. This DVD contains an audio commentary with writer/director Rudy DeLuca and visual consultant Steve Haberman. While there are some silent patches, this is a fun commentary, as DeLuca has many good anecdotes about the film's production. —*ML*

Movie: ♪ ***DVD:*** ♪♪♪
Anchor Bay (cat #DV11485, UPC 0131-31148596). Widescreen (1.85:1) anamorphic. Dolby Digital Mono. $14.98. Keepcase. *LANG:* English. *FEATURES:* Commentary • Theatrical trailers • TV spots • Storyboards • Still gallery • 25 chapters.
1985 (PG) 93m/C Jeff Goldblum, Joseph Bologna, Ed Begley Jr., Carol Kane, John Byner, Geena Davis, Jeffrey Jones, Norman Fell, Michael Richards; **D:** Rudy DeLuca; **W:** Rudy DeLuca; **C:** Tomislav Pinter; **M:** Lee Holdridge.

Treasure Island

Near the end of WWII, two officers of the fictional intelligence compound called "Treasure Island" are given a dead body and a covert assignment: construct a fake "backstory," including made-up letters to girlfriends, family members, etc., and fill the body's pockets with information. When dumped in the ocean, it is hoped that the false information will send the Japanese in the wrong direction. The two officers find themselves consumed by visions of the body, which seems to show up everywhere, including invading their (quite unusual) sex lives. Challenging and ambitious puzzle of a film which is filled from sprocket hole to sprocket hole with coded messages, encrypted dialogue, and implied meanings. Certainly not for all audiences, but a funny and fascinating exercise in style and cinematic invention. The basics of the story are simple and easy to follow, but the female characters (and their relationship to our protagonists) are a bit muddled. In a '40s period style, the film begins with a brief serial and newsreel that are absolutely perfect. All Day Entertainment has pulled out all the stops for this stupendous set. The disc is cleverly concealed in the pages of a small book that also includes essays about the production. The transfer itself is sharp and artifact-free, accurately conveying the contrast, soft focus, and grain of the original photography. Sound is crisp and well recorded, and the isolated music score is an appreciated bonus. The three deleted scenes are interesting, and the two featurettes are amusing and worthwhile. The real assets in the set are two audio commentaries by King, one focused on the making and meaning of the film, and the other on the photography. King is an entertaining host and makes both commentaries essential by filling them with candid explanations and examinations of the finished film and the work that went into it. Both give one a stronger appreciation and greater understanding of the film itself. —*DG*

Movie: ♪♪ ½ ***DVD:*** ♪♪♪♪
All Day Ent. (cat #ADED0266, UPC 01438-1026634). Full frame. Dolby Digital Mono. $29.99. Keepcase. *LANG:* English. *FEATURES:* Two audio commentaries with King • Isolated music score • Behind-the-scenes featurette • 3 deleted scenes • Sundance featurette • Theatrical trailer • Storyboards • Insert book with notes

• DVD-ROM with screenplay and promotional materials.
1999 83m/B Lance Baker, Nick Offerman, Jonah Blechman; **D:** Scott King; **W:** Scott King; **C:** Scott King, Phillip Glau; **M:** Chris Anderson.

The Treat

Overqualified ensemble cast meanders through a slight comedy (based on a play) involving three hookers, Francesca (Delpy), Mimi (Cates), and Dolly (Gidley). The low-budget indie image really gains nothing on DVD. The whole thing feels like an acting class exercise. —*MM*
Movie: ♪ ½ ***DVD:*** ♪ ½
MTI (cat #1076, UPC 039414510768). Full frame. $24.95. Keepcase. *LANG:* English. *SUB:* Spanish. *FEATURES:* 20 chapters • Talent files • Trailers.
1998 (R) 87m/C Julie Delpy, Georgina Cates, Pamela Gidley, Daniel Baldwin, Patrick Dempsey, Seymour Cassel, Vincent Perez, Alfred Molina, Michael York, Yancy Butler, Mark Boone Jr., Richmond Arquette; **D:** Jonathan Gems; **W:** Jonathan Gems; **C:** Joey Forsyte; **M:** Stephen Croes.

Tremors 3: Back to Perfection

It's been 11 years since the Graboids showed up in the little desert town of Perfection, but survivalist Burt Gummer (Gross) knows they'll be back and he's ready. The series continues with the same offbeat humor and more inventive computer-generated effects. DVD was made with a high bit-rate that makes for an excellent image. This video premiere looks as good as most theatrical releases. Surround tracks are well used for the critters. —*MM*
Movie: ♪♪ ½ ***DVD:*** ♪♪♪
Universal Studios (cat #21264, UPC 025-192126420). Widescreen (1.85:1) anamorphic. Dolby Digital 5.1 Surround Stereo. $24.95. Keepcase. *LANG:* English; French. *SUB:* French. *CAP:* English. *FEATURES:* 18 chapters • "Spotlight on Location" featurette • Trailers • Production notes • Talent files.
2001 (PG-13) 104m/C Michael Gross, Charlotte Stewart, Shawn Christian, Ariana Richards, Susan Chung; **D:** Brent Maddock; **W:** John Whelpley; **C:** Virgil Harper; **M:** Kevin Kiner.

The Trial

Please see review for *Citizen Welles.* **AKA:** Le Proces; Der Prozess; Il Processo.
Movie: ♪♪♪
1963 118m/B *FR* Anthony Perkins, Jeanne Moreau, Orson Welles, Romy Schneider, Akim Tamiroff, Elsa Martinelli; **D:** Orson Welles; **W:** Orson Welles; **C:** Edmond Richard; **M:** Jean Ledrut.

Trial by Jury

There's a fine thriller somewhere inside this one, struggling to get out. The story concerns juror and single mom Valerie

Alston (Whalley-Kilmer) being threatened by gangster Rusty Pirone (Assante), who's on trial. If everyone else had been as smooth and convincing as William Hurt is in a supporting role, the film might have been terrific. They're not and it isn't. Barebones DVD presents a serviceable transfer of an acceptable image. —MM

Movie: 🐾🐾 **DVD:** 🐾🐾

Warner (cat #13515). Widescreen. $19.95. Snapper. *LANG:* English; French. *SUB:* English; French; Spanish. *FEATURES:* Trailer • Talent files • 31 chapters.

1994 (R) 107m/C Joanne Whalley, William Hurt, Gabriel Byrne, Armand Assante, Kathleen Quinlan, Stuart Whitman, Margaret Whitton, Ed Lauter, Joe Santos, Richard Portnow; **D:** Heywood Gould; **W:** Heywood Gould; **C:** Frederick Elmes; **M:** Terence Blanchard.

The Triangle

Pals Stu (Perry) and Tommy (Cortese) head off into the Bermuda Triangle on a charter boat and are shocked to discover a computer-generated ocean liner. That unspecial effect is one of the most laughable ever committed to celluloid. It looks like a cardboard cutout, and the action that takes place upon it is no more persuasive. It has to do with past lives, etc., etc. The made-for-TV production is a paint-by-numbers effort from all concerned. Beyond the negligible extras, DVD is identical to VHS tape. —MM

Movie: 🐾🐾 **DVD:** 🐾🐾

York Ent. (cat #YPD-1171, UPC 75072311-7126). Full frame. Dolby Digital 5.1 Surround Stereo. $14.99. Keepcase. *LANG:* English. *SUB:* Spanish. *FEATURES:* Trailers • Filmographies.

2001 92m/C Luke Perry, Dan Cortese, Olivia D'Abo, Dorian Harewood, Polly Shannon, David Hewlett; **D:** Lewis Teague; **W:** Ted Humphrey; **C:** Ric Waite; **M:** Lawrence Shragge.

The Trio

An older gay man, his daughter, and his partner are a trio of lower-echelon pickpockets. When one of them is hurt, they bring a young man of questionable sexuality into the group. As they travel around Germany, both father and daughter become attracted to him. Although billed as a comedy, it isn't very funny and the story material is used almost primarily for dramatic effect. Unfortunately, the characters are sleazy, not very likable or interesting and the film never goes anywhere. George makes a fairly unpleasant gay romantic lead. The story seems to change gears and tones several times but it never reaches a satisfactory conclusion. The image is sharp with accurate, muted colors. Digital grain appears occasionally. The sound is very good. The director interview is fairly insubstantial. The cover artwork is a bit of a bait and switch. —DG

Movie: 🐾🐾 **DVD:** 🐾🐾🐾

TLA Video (cat #TLAD003, UPC 807839-000030). Widescreen (1.85:1) letterboxed.

Dolby Digital Surround. $29.99. Keepcase. *LANG:* German. *SUB:* English. *FEATURES:* Trailer • Director text interview • 20 chapters • Cast and crew bios • Picture gallery.

1997 97m/C *GE* Goetz George, Jeanette Hain, Felix Eitner, Christian Redl; **D:** Hermine Huntgeburth; **W:** Hermine Huntgeburth, Horst Sczerba, Volker Einrauch; **C:** Martin Kukula; **M:** Niki Reiser.

Triumph of the Spirit

Of the 11 million people killed by the Nazis during the Holocaust, 6 million were Jewish, but 5 million other people of other origins were also killed. This is a brutal no-frills presentation of the Holocaust from the Gypsy perspective. Dafoe plays Salamo Arouch, a Gypsy who was an Olympic class boxer before he and his family were shipped to Auschwitz. Once there he is recognized by a Nazi officer and offered the option of a slow brutal death or the possibility of life if he boxes other inmates in a regular life and death match. He chooses life all the while knowing that each victory he has is the life of another camp prisoner. He also knows that each victory brings extra bread for his aging father (Loggia). Edward James Olmos plays the ringmaster of the entertainment in the ring and the mediator of Salamo's conscience. Not a happy film, but a powerful one about the need to survive. DVD boasts rich colors, good night scenes, and great train smoke. The sound is good and clear. —CA

Movie: 🐾🐾🐾 **DVD:** 🐾🐾🐾

MGM Home Ent. (cat #1003338, UPC 027616874870). Widescreen (1.85:1) anamorphic; full frame. Dolby Digital Surround. $19.90. Keepcase. *LANG:* English; Spanish. *SUB:* English; French; Spanish. *CAP:* English. *FEATURES:* 16 chapters.

1989 (R) 115m/C Willem Dafoe, Robert Loggia, Edward James Olmos, Wendy Gazelle, Kelly Wolf, Costas Mandylor, Kario Salem; **D:** Robert M. Young; **W:** Robert M. Young, Shimon Arama, Andrzej Krakowski, Laurence Heath, Arthur Coburn, Millard Lampell; **M:** Cliff Eidelman.

Trixie

Watson is miscast as Trixie Zurbo, a casino security guard (?!). Trixie's main trait is confusing her sayings (she nabs criminals "by hook or by ladder"). She meets another set of colorful characters in the casino, including a lounge singer (Lane), sleazy local (Mulroney), and even Nolte as a corrupt senator. The plot revolves around some scandal nonsense with the Nolte character but the characters are so unengaging that we really don't care a great deal about what's going on. Trixie's ability to spout malapropisms is funny once but gets tedious about five minutes into the film. The rest of the cast overplays already dull material; Mulroney and Murphy find themselves lost in poorly defined characters. It's supposed to be a "noir-screwball comedy," but the material isn't at all funny, though

some of it could have been saved if it was played better. Sharpness and detail are fair; much of the movie seems to be intentionally given a slightly soft look. Some of the interior scenes, such as at the casino, end up looking a little too dark, murky, and undefined. The cinematography gives the film a rather drab look that doesn't really make it any easier to watch. The Surround track really only comes alive during the casino scenes, where there are strong ambient sounds from the rear channels. Otherwise, the sound here folds up completely to being dialogue-driven. On the commentary, Rudolph often sounds as excited while talking about his movie as I was while watching it (read: not very). An unintentionally funny remark comes at the very beginning of the track when he says, "I tried to do this film with no visual style." (Success!) The rest of the commentary proves to be a mildly involving listen, as the director talks about some of the details of the production and some of his feelings about the story. It won't make you think the movie is any better, though. —AB/DG

Movie: 🐾 **DVD:** 🐾🐾 ½

Columbia Tristar Home Video (UPC 4339-6052819). Full frame; widescreen (1.85:1) anamorphic. Dolby Digital 5.1 Surround; Dolby Digital Surround. $29.95. Keepcase. *LANG:* English. *SUB:* English; Spanish; French. *CAP:* English. *FEATURES:* Trailers • Talent files • 28 chapters • Commentary: Rudolph.

2000 (R) 117m/C Emily Watson, Nick Nolte, Dermot Mulroney, Nathan Lane, Brittany Murphy, Lesley Ann Warren, Will Patton, Stephen Lang; **D:** Alan Rudolph; **W:** Alan Rudolph; **C:** Jan Kiesser; **M:** Mark Isham, Roger Neill.

Trois

Jermaine (Dourdan) and Jasmine (Moore) have lost their boom-boom in the bedroom. Jermaine thinks adding another chick will do the trick. Jasmine whines to her friend about how lame her once studly hubby has become in the sack. The situation seems dire for the young couple until the buxom bride awakes from a horrible nightmare and suddenly agrees to indulge her husband. After the sheets are flung from one corner of the boudoir to the other, all heck breaks loose and the plot plays Wheel-of-Deception like any number of previous erotic thrillers—but, without the customary skin appeal. For a flick centered on a threesome, it's pretty darn chaste. But the escalation of revenge pranks and the multi-twist ending pay nearly adequate penance. The disc utilizes a relatively clean print. The low-budget production values are of the direct-to-video realm, but there's only a tiny bit of digital grain, limited mostly to one bar scene. The audio delivers a purely utilitarian stereo track. This is the "unrated version" with "additional footage," but there's really not much to shout about. It features a chummy audio commentary with director Rob Hardy and producer William Packer who are old friends that love saying "menage-a-trois" almost as much as "it's all good." The video interviews feature the same fellas, speaking about the film's financing, distribution, screenplay—the usual stuff. The alternate ending tosses in another, but clichéd, twist. —GNG/DG

Movie: 🐾 ½ **DVD:** 🐾 ½

Columbia Tristar Home Video (UPC 4339-6059122). Widescreen (1.85:1) anamorphic. Dolby Digital Surround. $29.95. Keepcase. *LANG:* English. *SUB:* English; Spanish; French. *CAP:* English. *FEATURES:* Theatrical trailer • 28 chapters • Commentary: director Rob Hardy • Filmmakers' interview.

2000 (R) 93m/C Gary Dourdan, Gretchen Palmer, Kenya Moore, Chrystale Wilson, Bryce Wilson; **D:** Rob Hardy; **W:** Rob Hardy; **C:** Charles Mills; **M:** Steve Gutheinz.

A Troll in Central Park

Because of his uncharacteristic kindness, a young troll, Stanley (voice of DeLouise), is ousted from his clan by the evil queen Gnorga (Leachman) and sent to live in a remote place where it is believed that nothing green can grow. Unbeknown to the deceptive matriarch is that the place she has chosen to exile the goodhearted troll is the beautiful backdrop of Central Park in New York City. Stanley soon befriends two young children, whom he quickly invites to share in his magical adventures, and everything seems fine until Gnorga realizes her error and decides to unleash her magic on the unsuspecting Big Apple. Featuring the trademarked "Don Bluth" look, this musical comedy falls short in its plot and does not seem to keep the viewer interested when stacked up with other Bluth films such as *An American Tail* and *Titan A.E.* The DVD features a clean transfer with no noticeable artifacts, and the cell colors seem bright and vibrant for a film that has been out for almost a decade. The Surround track does a good job of utilizing the front three speakers, but failed to impress on the rear monitors. There was also some noticeable top-end distortion during some of the musical numbers. —EL

Movie: 🐾🐾🐾 **DVD:** 🐾🐾🐾

20th Century Fox (cat #2932, UPC 0245-42029328). Widescreen (1.78:1) anamorphic; full frame. Dolby Digital Surround. $19.98. Keepcase. *LANG:* English. *SUB:* English; Spanish. *CAP:* English. *FEATURES:* Theatrical trailer • Featurette.

1994 (G) 76m/C D: Don Bluth, Gary Goldman; **W:** Stu Krieger; **M:** Robert Folk; **V:** Dom DeLuise, Cloris Leachman, Jonathan Pryce, Hayley Mills, Charles Nelson Reilly, Phillip Glasser, Robert Morley, Sy Goraleb, Tawney Sunshine Glover, Jordan Metzner.

Troma's Edge TV: Vol. 1

Troma's signature style and "wit" corrupts the small screen in five episodes from the variety show that originally aired on Britain's Channel 4. Skit comedy and film clips hosted by Troma film regulars Shepis and Haaga are put together in a show barely worthy of public access. As in many Troma productions, after wading through two hours of muck, there is little more than a minute of good material. The image and sound look as good as broadcast television. The disc, however, is loaded with extras and Easter eggs that will delight Troma fanatics. —DRL

Movie: woof **DVD:** 🐾🐾🐾

Troma Team Video (cat #9040, UPC 7903-57904037). Full frame. Stereo. $14.98. Keepcase. *LANG:* English. *FEATURES:* "Radiation March" short • "Too Hot" segments • Photo gallery • Trailers • 10 chapters.

2000 112m/C Tiffany Shepis, Trent Haaga, Debbie Rochon, Lloyd Kaufman.

Tron [2 CE]

(For film review see *Book 1*.) The remastered 70mm film transfer features strong, vivid colors with very little bleed-through. The animated sequences are better than live-action sequences which look as ugly as they always have. Except for some instances of digital noise during action sequences this is an impressive transfer. The sound is satisfactory but (obviously) doesn't have as strong channel separations as tracks designed later. The extras cover all the bases with an impressive collection of featurettes and supplementary material. The feature-length documentary is terrific and includes test footage, behind-the-scenes stills, and interviews with all of the key participants. The only aspect left out is Wendy Carlos's synthesizer music score. While two alternate music tracks are included on the disc, her pioneering synthesizer work and important contribution are barely acknowledged. The commentary isn't very scene-specific but it's an interesting counterpart to the documentary. There's very little repetition and having the participants interact makes for a more dynamic track. While the exhaustive supplements won't convince the non-enthusiasts, it does compel a greater appreciation of the ground-breaking (and exhaustive) computer animation work that's on display. The fully produced deleted scenes don't belong in the film but are very fun to see. —DG

Movie: 🐾🐾 **DVD:** 🐾🐾🐾 ½

Buena Vista Home Ent. (cat #23569, UPC 786936161878). Widescreen (2.20:1) anamorphic. Dolby Digital 5.1 Surround. $29.99. Keepcase. *LANG:* English. *SUB:* Spanish; French. *CAP:* English. *FEATURES:* "The Making of *Tron*" documentary • Deleted scenes introduced by Bruce Boxleitner • Photo gallery • Storyboards showcasing the Light Cycles • Storyboard to film comparisons • Commentary: Lisberger, Donald Kushner • Commentary: Harrison Ellenshaw, Richard Taylor • Insert card • 19 chapters.

1982 (PG) 96m/C Jeff Bridges, Bruce Boxleitner, David Warner, Cindy Morgan, Barnard Hughes, Dan Shor, Peter Jurasik, Tony Stephano; **D:** Steven Lisberger; **W:** Steven Lisberger; **C:** Bruce Logan; **M:** Walter (Wendy) Carlos. *AWARDS: NOM:* Oscars '82: Costume Des., Sound.

Troubles

Troubled World War I veteran Maj. Brendan Archer (Charleson) goes to Ireland to be with his fiancée at the Hotel Majestic owned by her eccentric family. Like so many British television productions, this one is brilliantly acted and written with real wit and intelligence. The DVD image is a cut above the norm for imports, too. It's bright and on the pale side with comparatively little grain. Sound is fair to good. —MM

Movie: 🐾🐾🐾 **DVD:** 🐾🐾 ½

BFS Video (cat #30212-D, UPC 06680530-2121). Full frame. $39.98. Keepcase boxed set. *LANG:* English. *FEATURES:* 24 chapters.

1988 208m/C *GB* Ian Charleson, Ian Richardson, Sean Bean, Emer Gillespie, Susannah Harker; **D:** Christopher Morahan; **W:** Charles Sturridge.

True Blue

Clichéd cop action/suspense film boasts some good performances and a polished look. NYPD (well, Toronto) detective Rem Macy (Berenger) drinks too much, smokes too much, and is getting fat. Naturally beautiful young blonde Nikki (Heuring, whose resemblance to Sarah Jessica Parker is played up for all it's worth on the box art and in the film) hops into the sack with him because he's such a stud muffin. Or could she have something to do with the mystery of the severed hand that Macy's investigating? The image is built around undersaturated colors with lots of pale blues and grays and heavy shadows. DVD handles all of them with no flaws. Sound is fine for a nice score (by Tim Jones) that recalls Miles Davis's "Kind of Blue." In both execution and presentation, the familiar material is handled well. —MM

Movie: 🐾🐾 ½ **DVD:** 🐾🐾🐾

Columbia Tristar (cat #07795, UPC 0433-96077959). Widescreen (1.85:1) anamorphic; full frame. Dolby Digital 5.1 Surround; Dolby Surround. $24.98. Keepcase. *LANG:* English; French. *SUB:* English; French; Spanish; Portuguese; Thai; Chinese; Korean. *CAP:* English. *FEATURES:* 28 chapters • Trailers.

2001 (R) 101m/C Tom Berenger, Lori Heuring, Barry Newman, Pamela Gridley, Soon-Teck Oh, Richard Chevolleau, Leo Lee; **D:** J.S. Cardone; **W:** J.S. Cardone; **C:** Darko Suvak; **M:** Timothy S. Jones.

True Crime

Director/actor Eastwood does a good job developing his seriously flawed character Steve Everett, a boozing, philandering reporter whose ways have gotten him fired. He's working for the Oakland *Tribune* when, at the last minute, he's given an assignment to interview death row inmate Frank Beachum (Washington). Everett becomes convinced that Beachum is innocent and the plot erodes into a trite race against time to save the innocent man. DVD image is so bright, clear, and sharply focused that it reveals how unflattering Eastwood was on himself. He wears every year of his age on his face. Sound is fine. —MM

Movie: 🎬🎬 ½ **DVD:** 🎬🎬🎬
Warner (cat #16323, UPC 0853916323-20). Widescreen anamorphic. Dolby Digital 5.1 Surround. $19.98. Snapper. LANG: English. CAP: English. FEATURES: 39 chapters ▪ Talent files ▪ Music video ▪ 2 behind-the-scenes documentaries ▪ Trailer.
1999 (R) 127m/C Clint Eastwood, James Woods, Isaiah Washington IV, Denis Leary, Frances Fisher, Diane Venora, Mary McCormack, Lisa Gay Hamilton, Bernard Hill, Michael McKean, Michael Jeter, Hattie Winston, Laila Robins, Christine Ebersole, Anthony Zerbe, John Finn, Marissa Ribisi, Erik King, Graham Beckel, Sydney Tamiia Poitier, Penny Rae Bridges; **D:** Clint Eastwood; **W:** Larry Gross, Paul Brickman, Stephen Schiff; **C:** Jack N. Green; **M:** Lennie Niehaus.

Truly, Madly, Deeply

The recent death of her lover Jamie (Rickman) drives Nina (Stevenson) into despair and anger until he turns up at her apartment one day. Tender, well-written tale of love and the supernatural works through believable, thoroughly likeable characters and an inventive plotline. On his commentary track, director Minghella is justifiably proud and affectionate toward his debut effort. His remarks tend to be scene-specific and he's interesting. DVD does nothing to improve the graininess of the image. It's always been that way. —MM

Movie: 🎬🎬🎬 **DVD:** 🎬🎬🎬
MGM Home Ent. (cat #1002758, UPC 027616869562). Full frame. Dolby Digital Surround Stereo; Mono. $19.98. Keepcase. LANG: English; French; Spanish. SUB: English; French; Spanish. CAP: English. FEATURES: Commentary ▪ 16 chapters ▪ Trailers ▪ Interview with Anthony Minghella.
1991 (PG) 107m/C GB Juliet Stevenson, Alan Rickman, Bill Paterson, Michael Maloney, Christopher Rozycki, Keith Bartlett, David Ryall, Stella Maris; **D:** Anthony Minghella; **W:** Anthony Minghella; **C:** Remi Adefarasin; **M:** Barrington Pheloung. AWARDS: Australian Film Inst. '92: Foreign Film; British Acad. '91: Orig. Screenplay.

The Trumpet of the Swan

Translating a novel to the screen is always a daunting task, and even if one gets the story right, it can be hard to capture the spirit of a great book. Such is the case with the animated adaptation of this E.B. White classic. The movie does a fine job of condensing the great story, but loses all of the book's charm. It tells the story of Louie, a swan who is born mute. His parents (voiced by Jason Alexander and Mary Steenburgen) are supportive, but they'd

hoped that he would be a great trumpeter swan like his dad. Louie tries to play and fit in with the other swans, but his lack of voice makes him an outsider. He meets a human boy named Sam Beaver (voiced by Sam Gifaldi) and they form a friendship. Louie follows Sam to school, where he learns to read and write, hoping that this will allow him to communicate with the other swans, especially Serena (voiced by Reese Witherspoon), an attractive female swan. When this ploy fails, Louie nearly gives up, until he discovers how to play the trumpet, thus finding his voice. The main problem with this version is that it tries way too hard to be contemporary and hip, while losing sight of the classic nature of the story. The film contains some lame songs and stale references, which simply come across as pathetic. The animation here is very nicely done (although some of the humans look a bit weird), so if the filmmakers had let the story work on its own, this could have been a much better movie. Children may be content to sit through this film once, but it won't be one of those videos that gets played over and over. This DVD offers a very nice transfer. Both full-frame and widescreen images are pristine, showing no defects or distortion. The colors are very good, as they contrast well with no oversaturation. The Dolby Digital 5.1 audio track offers clear dialogue, nice Surround sound effects, and (unfortunately) nice reproduction of the music. —ML

Movie: 🎬 ½ **DVD:** 🎬🎬🎬
Columbia Tristar (cat #05847, UPC 0433-96058477). Widescreen (1.78:1) anamorphic; full frame. Dolby Digital 5.1; Dolby Surround. $24.95. Keepcase. LANG: English; French; Spanish. SUB: English; Spanish; French. CAP: English. FEATURES: Theatrical trailer ▪ Bonus trailers ▪ Set-top game ▪ 28 chapters.
2001 (G) 75m/C D: Richard Rich, Terry L. Noss; **W:** Judy Rothman Rofe; **M:** Marcus Miller; **V:** Dee Baker, Jason Alexander, Mary Steenburgen, Reese Witherspoon, Seth Green, Carol Burnett, Joe Mantegna, Sam Gifaldi.

Trust Me U Die

This odd drama from director Billy Chung (Killer) uses a sci-fi premise to explore problems in the Hong Kong medical community. Scientist Simon Yam discovers a super-soldier serum, which can boost strength, speed, mental agility, and endurance. He and his assistant/girlfriend Chan Ying Lai go to old friend Dr. Mark Cheng, who agrees to help them. When Yam discovers Cheng and Chan having an affair, he decides to get his revenge by using Mike as a test subject, along with other victims, including skinny constable Sam Lee, with disastrous results. It may be meant as a cautionary tale or social commentary, but for the most part, Trust Me U Die is just plain uncomfortable to watch. Some scenes flirt with comedy or horror, while others are agonizing. Sound and image quality are both bland, though that may have been intentional. —BT **AKA:**

San Giu Cheung Yee Sang; Xin Gao Yang Yi Sheng.

Movie: 🎬 ½ **DVD:** 🎬🎬
Tai Seng (cat #5235, UPC 60164662749). Widescreen letterboxed. $19.95. Keepcase. LANG: Cantonese; Mandarin. SUB: Chinese; English; Bahasa. CAP: English. FEATURES: 8 chapters ▪ Star profiles ▪ Trailers.
1999 94m/C HK Simon Yam, Ying Lai Chan, Sam Lee, Mark Cheng, Joey Tan; **D:** Billy Chung; **W:** Kam Fai Law; **C:** Daniel Chan; **M:** Kam Cheung Chow.

Tupac Shakur: Thug Angel

This frustrating documentary traces the meteoric career of rapper Tupac Shakur by combining interview footage from various stages of Shakur's life with reminisces from friends and collaborators. The most striking feature is Shakur's thoughtful articulation as a high school student, compared with the nonsense he speaks in the interviews following his first record deal. This transition is left unexplored, making for an extremely puzzling exploration of a complex character. Since much of the film is taken from home videos, both the audio and picture quality are inconsistent. The DVD offers a number of complete interviews that were excerpted for the film. —BG **AKA:** Thug Angel: The Life of an Outlaw.

Movie: 🎬🎬 **DVD:** 🎬🎬🎬
Image Ent. (cat #ID1585QDDVD, UPC 014-381158526). Full frame. Dolby 5.1. $19.99. Keepcase. LANG: English. FEATURES: 28 chapters ▪ Unedited interviews ▪ Tupac Audio Recordings ▪ Photo gallery.
2002 92m/C Tupac Shakur, Treach (Anthony Criss), Shock G; **D:** Peter Spirer.

Turbulence 2: Fear of Flying

A group of fearful fliers try to overcome their phobia aboard a flight from Seattle to Los Angeles. What do they run into? A storm, nerve gas in the cockpit, terrorists, and Pearl Harbor on the in-flight movie. All of the familiar aerial clichés are trotted out at a brisk pace. It's completely derivative stuff but it's handled with such spirit that this is definitely an overachieving sequel, much better than it has any right (or need) to be. DVD is similarly exceptional. Widescreen image and Surround sound range between very good and good. All of the grain seems to come from the original. —MM

Movie: 🎬🎬 ½ **DVD:** 🎬🎬 ½
Lion's Gate Home Ent. (cat #7450D, UPC 031398745020). Widescreen letterboxed. Dolby Digital 5.1 Surround. $24.98. Keepcase. LANG: English. SUB: English; French; Spanish. CAP: English. FEATURES: 24 chapters ▪ 4 interviews on parts of the film ▪ Trailer.
1999 100m/C Tom Berenger, Craig Sheffer, Jennifer Beals, Jeffrey Nordling; **D:** David Mackay; **W:** Kevin Bernhardt, Brendan Broderick, Rob Kerchner.

Turbulence 3: Heavy Metal

Those who can suspend enough disbelief to buy into a nutball premise may be able to enjoy the excesses of this installment in an otherwise inexplicable series. Metal superstar Slade Craven decides to celebrate his imminent retirement with a concert on board a 747 to be broadcast over the Internet. Crazed fans, hijackers, explosions, shootouts, you know the drill. A familiar cast has no trouble with the formulaic material. (What in the world is Joe Mantegna doing here?) DVD image is completely acceptable, actually better than it needs to be. Sound is excellent. —*MM*
Movie: ♫ ½ **DVD:** ♫♫ ½
Studio Home Ent. (cat #7677D, UPC 0313-98767725). Widescreen letterboxed. Dolby Digital 5.1 Surround. $24.98. Keepcase. *LANG:* English. *SUB:* English; French; Spanish. *CAP:* English. *FEATURES:* 24 chapters ● Commentary: producer Ogden Gavanski, Wade Ferley, John Mann ● Trailer.
2000 (R) 96m/C Craig Sheffer, Gabrielle Anwar, Monika Schnarre, Rutger Hauer, Joe Mantegna; **D:** Jorge Montesi; **W:** Wade Ferley; **C:** Philip Linzey; **M:** John McCarthy.

Turner and Hooch

Turner (Hanks) and Hooch (a De Bordeaux dog) are an Odd Couple for the late '80s. The human is a compulsively neat cop and the incurably sloppy dog slobbers all over the place. We're not just talking about a little spit here; this pooch is a veritable Niagara of saliva. The two are brought together when Hooch's owner is killed. Turner considers the dog a witness and takes him home for protective custody. The mystery elements of the plot are sacrificed to lots of long scenes of the dog destroying things and puddling spit all over them. In the end, though, Hanks's comic performance and the dog's adorable ugliness make this one better than you might expect. Bare-bones DVD, however, is no great shakes. The film is a mid-budget production with heavier-than-normal grain. It's not the brightest, sharpest image ever put on disc. If memory serves, it is accurate. Sound is all that the material requires. —*MM*
Movie: ♫♫♫ **DVD:** ♫♫ ½
Buena Vista Home Ent. (cat #17370, UPC 717951002747). Widescreen (1.85:1) letterboxed. Dolby Digital Surround. $19.98. Keepcase. *LANG:* English; French. *CAP:* English. *FEATURES:* 12 chapters.
1989 (PG) 99m/C Tom Hanks, Mare Winningham, Craig T. Nelson, Scott Paulin, J.C. Quinn; **D:** Roger Spottiswoode; **W:** Michael Blodgett, Jim Cash, Jack Epps Jr.; **C:** Adam Greenberg; **M:** Charles Gross.

The Turning

Cliff Harnish (Dolan) returns home after a four-year absence to shock his family with strident neo-Nazi beliefs. The film's main claim to fame is the presence of a pre-*X-Files* Anderson in a dark kitchen sex scene with brief nudity. Based on a play by Ceraso. So-so image and sound are no real improvement over tape. This is such a dreary-looking and -feeling film that it's never going to sparkle. —*MM* **AKA:** Home Fires Burning.
Movie: ♫ ½ **DVD:** ♫♫
MTI (cat #216). Full frame. Dolby Digital Stereo. $24.95. Keepcase. *LANG:* English. *FEATURES:* Cast & crew thumbnail bios ● Trailer ● Production notes ● 32 chapters.
1992 92m/C Michael Dolan, Raymond J. Barry, Karen Allen, Tess Harper, Gillian Anderson; **D:** L.A. Puopolo; **W:** L.A. Puopolo, Chris Ceraso; **C:** J. Michael McClary.

Twelve o'Clock High

Gregory Peck was nominated for a Best Actor Academy Award for his portrayal of Gen. Frank Savage in one of Hollywood's best serious war films. The subject is the precision daylight bombing raids on Germany by American B-17s. The 918th Bomber Group is known as a "hard luck" division that's suffering catastrophic losses with every mission. When Savage takes over, he kicks ass and takes names. The physical details of flying and life in Quonset huts all seem accurate, but the psychological details concerning the pressures of command and combat are just as accurate and infinitely more important. Despite the odd dust fleck here and there, DVD does justice to cinematographer Leon Shamroy's crisp black-and-white photography. The interiors are deliberately dark and heavily shadowed. The mono sound won an Oscar, too, and the disc also comes with a stereo remix. It may be slightly better than the original but both are acceptable for a work of this age. On any medium, this is a terrific film that belongs in the library of every fan of war films. Given its importance, a commentary track by a military or aviation historian would not have been out of place. —*MM*
Movie: ♫♫♫ ½ **DVD:** ♫♫♫
20th Century Fox (UPC 024543013143). Full frame. Dolby Digital Stereo; Mono. $19.98. Keepcase. *LANG:* English; French. *SUB:* English; Spanish. *CAP:* English. *FEATURES:* 16 chapters.
1949 132m/B Gregory Peck, Hugh Marlowe, Gary Merrill, Millard Mitchell, Dean Jagger, Paul Stewart, Robert Arthur, John Kellogg, Sam Edwards, Russ Conway, Lawrence (Larry) Dobkin; **D:** Henry King; **W:** Sy Bartlett, Beirne Lay Jr.; **C:** Leon Shamroy; **M:** Alfred Newman; **Technical Advisor:** John H. DeRussy. *AWARDS:* Oscars '49: Sound, Support. Actor (Jagger), Natl. Film Reg. '98; *NOM:* Oscars '49: Actor (Peck), Picture; N.Y. Film Critics '50: Actor (Peck).

2103: Deadly Wake

Curious Canadian/British SF attempts to use CGI effects to create a futuristic seagoing epic. Burnt-out case Sean Murdock (McDowell) is hired to captain the *Lilith*, a corporate prison ship for the criminally insane, that also carries another secret cargo. The pulpy plot rattles right along, a capable cast handles it seriously, too, and the costumes and sets have a tongue-in-cheek quality. (Co-star Michael Pare walks around with big "E" on his chest.) DVD delivers a very sharp image with no serious flaws and active Surround sound. —*MM*
Movie: ♫♫ ½ **DVD:** ♫♫ ½
York Ent. (cat #YPD-1096, UPC 75072310-9626). Full frame. Dolby Digital 5.1 Surround Stereo. $14.99. Keepcase. *LANG:* English. *SUB:* Spanish. *FEATURES:* 30 chapters ● Trailers ● Talent files.
1997 100m/C CA GB Malcolm McDowell, Michael Pare, Heidi von Palleske, Gwynyth Walsh, Hal Eisen; **D:** G. Philip Jackson; **W:** Timothy Lee, Andrew Dowler, Doug Bagot.

Twice-Told Tales

Three horror stories based on the writings of Nathaniel Hawthorne. "Dr. Heidegger's Experiment" attempts to restore the youth of four elderly friends. "Rappaccini's Daughter" is inoculated with poison by her demented father so she may never leave her garden of poisonous plants. In "The House of the Seven Gables," one brother frames the other for murder while fighting over an inheritance. No tie-in between the three stories other than a book's turning pages. Vincent Price is in all three—one of the drearier Corman/Poe style rip-offs. MGM does its usual top-notch DVD image and sound transfers, but the film doesn't rate it. —*MO* **AKA:** Nathaniel Hawthorne's "Twice Told Tales."
Movie: ♫ **DVD:** ♫♫♫ ½
MGM Home Ent. (cat #1002356, UPC 027616865670). Widescreen (1.66:1) letterboxed. Dolby Digital 2.0 Mono. $14.95. Keepcase. *LANG:* English. *SUB:* Spanish; French. *CAP:* English; Spanish; French. *FEATURES:* 16 chapters ● Theatrical trailer.
1963 120m/C Beverly Garland, Richard Denning, Vincent Price, Sebastian Cabot, Brett Halsey; **D:** Sidney Salkow; **W:** Robert E. Kent; **C:** Ellis W. Carter; **M:** Richard LaSalle.

Twin Peaks: Fire Walk with Me

Following the demise of the *Twin Peaks* TV series in 1991, fans of the program cried out for more. Series director and co-creator answered that call with a feature film which only left the faithful confused and angry. The TV show had focused on the events following the murder of Laura Palmer (Sheryl Lee), as the town of Twin Peaks reacted to the death of this popular teenager and her assailant was sought. *Fire Walk with Me* focuses on the events that take place prior to Laura's death, specifically her activities during the final week of her life. Here, we learn that Laura is a troubled and haunted girl, involved in drugs and prostitution. Also, she feels that a mystery man known only as "Bob" is trying to kill her. As the week progresses, we watch Laura spin out of control as her risky behaviors and paranoia lead to her doom. It certainly isn't an overstatement to say

that this is one of the oddest films ever made. (But that is to be expected, coming from Lynch.) The first 35 minutes are dreadfully boring, as Lynch explores a murder which pre-dates Laura's demise. Then, when the action finally shifts to *Twin Peaks,* the tone is so different from that of the show that many viewers will be left numb by it. Still, the film has its positive aspects. Whereas *Twin Peaks* the TV show was an over-the-top spoof of soap operas, this feature plays like an existentialist horror movie, with Lynch creating an incredibly tense and scary atmosphere at times. While there is still a great deal of debate over this film among fans, those who find the show to be too tame or who love alternative cinema should get a kick out of it. The new transfer looks very good. The image is sharp, but a bit dark and soft at times. The colors look very good, most notably the green trees. The DTS 5.1 and Dolby Digital 5.1 audio tracks are very similar in the sense that the dialogue is mixed quite low, while the music and sound effects are much louder. (Apparently, this is the way that Lynch wanted it.) That creates a very uneven audio experience, where the volume must constantly be adjusted. The documentary contains some interesting sound-bites from the cast and crew (sans Lynch), but it was edited so as to resemble the film, so it is disconcerting and hard to watch. —*ML*
Movie: ♪♪♪ **DVD:** ♪♪ ½
New Line (cat #5081, UPC 7940435081-27). Widescreen (1.85:1) anamorphic. Dolby Digital 5.1; DTS 5.1; Stereo Surround. $19.98. Keepcase. *LANG:* English; French. *SUB:* English; French. *CAP:* English. *FEATURES:* Theatrical trailer • Documentary • 40 chapters. Although the DVD has chapter stops, there is no chapter selection menu.
1992 (R) 135m/C FR Kyle MacLachlan, Sheryl Lee, Moira Kelly, David Bowie, Chris Isaak, Harry Dean Stanton, Ray Wise, Kiefer Sutherland, Peggy Lipton, Dana Ashbrook, James Marshall, David Lynch, Catherine Coulson, Julee Cruise, Eric (DaRe) Da Re, Miguel Ferrer, Heather Graham, Madchen Amick, Juergen Prochnow, Grace Zabriskie; *D:* David Lynch; *W:* David Lynch; *C:* Ron Garcia; *M:* Angelo Badalamenti.

Twin Peaks: The First Season
"She's dead. Wrapped in plastic." With the discovery of the corpse of prom queen Laura Palmer (Lee), television's most bizarre mystery is off and running. Unfortunately, *Twin Peaks: The First Season,* as presented in this boxed DVD set, doesn't start with that discovery—or the first episode at all. Because of complicated rights issues, the double-length pilot film that began the series when it debuted on ABC television on April 8, 1990, isn't included here. Regrettably, neither the video nor the sound quality on that disc match the high level achieved in this domestic set, which boasts the next seven installments that comprise the first

season. Set in a weirdville of the Pacific Northwest, *Twin Peaks* is populated by oddballs ranging from the Log Lady (Coulson) to the dwarf who inhabits FBI Special Agent Dale Cooper's (MacLachlan) dreams. Cooper, who via his tape recorder sends notes to his never-seen assistant Diane, has come to town to help Sheriff Harry Truman (Ontkean) solve the Palmer murder. He also helps himself to some damn fine cherry pie. The prequel theatrical film *Twin Peaks: Fire Walk with Me* (also on DVD) is optional viewing, but by all means track down the elusive pilot episode before looking at anything on these four marvelous platters. Once that's done and you've watched Season 1, tackle the extras as you ponder a forthcoming DVD release of the second—and final—season. *Twin Peaks* debuted to huge ratings, but its Nielsen numbers dwindled with each episode as the general audience realized the story as told by creators David Lynch (*Blue Velvet*) and Mark Frost (*Hill Street Blues*) was going nowhere. But the core fans realized then and now that the fun is in the journey itself. *Twin Peaks* delivers a quirky ride. The audio and video quality here easily bests all previous laserdisc and VHS releases, especially the VHS box set that was recorded in low-quality LP mode. An alternate "European" version of the pilot episode, with a different ending from the American broadcast, has been available on LD. But again, seek out the DVD import of the pilot episode in its preferred original form. —*MB*
Movie: ♪♪♪ ½ **DVD:** ♪♪♪ ½
Artisan Ent. (cat #10089, UPC 01715-3100891). Full frame. DTS Surround; Dolby Digital 5.1; Dolby Surround. $59.98. Custom. *LANG:* English. *CAP:* English. *FEATURES:* 70 chapters • Select episode analysis by the directors • New interviews with cast and crew • Optional Log Lady intros to each episode • Script notes: optional guide to the "Unseen Twin Peaks" • Rare archival material from *Wrapped in Plastic,* the official *Twin Peaks* magazine.
1990 336m/C Michael Ontkean, Kyle MacLachlan, Joan Chen, Piper Laurie, Sherilyn Fenn, Peggy Lipton, Madchen Amick, Lara Flynn Boyle, Michael Horse, Russ Tamblyn, Richard Beymer, Dana Ashbrook, Warren Frost, Everett McGill, Jack Nance, Ray Wise, Eric (DaRe) Da Re, Catherine Coulson, Harry Goaz, Sheryl Lee; *D:* David Lynch; *W:* Mark Frost; *M:* Angelo Badalamenti.

Twisted Justice
Heavener is a cop in 2020 who must stop a ruthless killer. Matters become complicated when his gun is taken away and he must rely on his wits. D'oh! DVD adds considerable pixels and artifacts to a low-budget video-premiere image that was pretty poor to begin with. Title is available as part of the *Action Arsenal* collection. —*MM*
Movie: ♪ **DVD:** ♪
BCI-Eclipse (cat #44076-9, UPC 7873644-07699). Full frame. $19.98. Keepcase. *LANG:* English. *FEATURES:* 6 chapters.

1989 90m/C David Heavener, Erik Estrada, Jim Brown, Shannon Tweed, James Van Patten, Don Stroud, Karen Black, Lori Warren; *D:* David Heavener; *W:* David Heavener; *C:* David Hue.

Two Can Play That Game
When high-powered executive Shanté's (Fox) man steps out of line, she sets in motion a 10-day plan designed to make Keith (Chestnut) come crawling back. Some amusing moments (especially Bobby Brown's cameo as a "scary-curl" brother), but none of it would be happening if anyone would act remotely like a grown-up. The transfer looks very good, with only some moments of shimmering to mar the picture, while the two available sound options are virtually identical. Complete with three featurettes, where we learn how much everyone on the cast and crew loves each other. —*BG*
Movie: ♪♪ **DVD:** ♪♪♪
Columbia Tristar (cat #07107, UPC 043-396071070). Widescreen (1.85:1) anamorphic; full frame. Dolby 5.1; Dolby Surround. $27.96. Keepcase. *LANG:* English. *SUB:* English; French; Spanish; Portugese; Chinese; Korean; Thai. *CAP:* English. *FEATURES:* 28 chapters • Commentary: director • 3 featurettes • Music video • Trailers • Filmographies.
2001 (R) 90m/C Vivica A. Fox, Morris Chestnut, Anthony Anderson, Gabrielle Union, Wendy Raquel Robinson, Tamala Jones, Mo'Nique, Ray Wise, Bobby Brown, Dondre T. Whitfield; *D:* Mark Brown; *W:* Mark Brown; *C:* Alexander Grusynski; *M:* Marcus Miller.

Two Coyotes
Ambitious video premiere attempts to cover some of the same territory as *Traffic.* If the results are not as accomplished, the film is an impressive debut. Rafael (Cordova) and Carlos (Guilak) are ambitious young drug pushers who break the rules when they try to outfox the big boss Acosta (video vet Estevez). The film was made on a very low budget and so the DVD image is very grainy throughout and never any better than VHS tape. Sound is fine. The ensemble commentary track is engaging and focuses on the shortcuts necessary to get this kind of project finished. —*MM*
Movie: ♪♪ ½ **DVD:** ♪♪ ½
Xenon Ent. (cat #XE XX 4098DVD, UPC 000799409824). Full frame. $24.98. Keepcase. *LANG:* English; Spanish. *FEATURES:* 14 chapters • Commentary: Bencomo, Cordova, Guilak, Duran • Trailer.
2001 (R) 85m/C Joe Estevez, Jorge Cordova, Nico Guilak, Ricardo Molina, Jorge Soriano; *D:* Jose Reyes Bencomo; *W:* Jose Reyes Bencomo, Jose Quintanilla; *C:* Armand Gazarian.

Two Family House
A great romantic comedy about learning to love yourself and reaching out for what

you want. Buddy Visalo (Rispoli) is trying to be a good Italian husband in 1950s New York, but he wants to be his own boss and runs through a lot of failed businesses in the attempt. It doesn't help that his traditional Italian wife is happy to live with her parents while Buddy works at a factory job, and she is willing to go to extreme lengths—sabotaging his finances for example—to make sure he fails so she can have the simple life she wants. Things take a strange turn when Buddy's latest attempt at self employment leads him to buy a two-family house, where he plans to live on the top story and turn the lower half into a bar. There is a problem, though: the tenants on the second story, an old Irish wino and his very young, very pregnant wife (Macdonald), won't leave. The stalemate doesn't last long; when the wife has a baby that is obviously not a product of the union of his white parents, the husband abandons both child and wife. Buddy's reaction to the situation and his genuinely good heart lead him to a crossroads where he must choose between tradition and a happy life. The story is narrated by the now-grown child, which of course gives some foreshadowing as to the outcome, but also provides a homey feel. The story line may not be totally fresh for all viewers, but the film itself is so full of good acting and strong writing that you can't help but be taken in by it. This is a lush, warm, romantic film with strong themes of tolerance and hope. Also of note, for those who care about such things, it was the winner of the 2000 Sundance Audience Award. The disc looks and sounds great. —CA

Movie: 🎬🎬🎬 ½ **DVD:** 🎬🎬🎬
Universal Studios (cat #21261, UPC 025192126123). Widescreen anamorphic. Dolby Digital Surround. $24.90. Keepcase. *LANG:* English. *SUB:* English. *CAP:* English. *FEATURES:* 18 chapters.
1999 (R) 109m/C Michael Rispoli, Kelly Macdonald, Kathrine Narducci, Matt Servitto, Kevin Conway, Michele Santopietro; **D:** Raymond De Felitta; **W:** Raymond De Felitta; **C:** Mike Mayers; **M:** Stephen Endelman. *AWARDS:* Sundance '00: Aud. Award; *NOM:* Ind. Spirit '01: Actress (Macdonald), Screenplay.

Two-Fisted Law
Please see review for *John Wayne: Western Classics.*
Movie: 🎬 ½
1932 58m/B Tim McCoy, Tully Marshall, Wheeler Oakman, Alice Day, Wallace Macdonald, John Wayne, Walter Brennan; **D:** David Ross Lederman; **W:** Kurt Kempler; **C:** Benjamin (Ben H.) Kline.

Two Friends
Two childhood friends, grown apart after one enrolls in a private school, try to reconnect with each other. The film works backwards over the last year of their friendship to explore their divergent paths. The two leads are likeable but the script doesn't give them much to work with, so

the film will probably interest only fans of Campion's later work. The picture quality is only a small step up from video, and the dialogue is often buried beneath background noises. —BG
Movie: 🎬🎬 **DVD:** 🎬🎬 ½
Image Ent. (cat #ID1296MLSDVD, UPC 014381129625). Full frame; widescreen (1.66:1) anamorphic. Dolby Mono. $29.99. Keepcase. *LANG:* English. *FEATURES:* 12 chapters • Press kit • Stills gallery • Short feature: Campion's "Mishaps of Seduction and Conquest."
1986 76m/C AU Kris Bidenko, Emma Coles, Peter Hehir, Kris McQuade; **D:** Jane Campion; **W:** Helen Garner; **C:** Julian Penney; **M:** Martin Armiger.

Two Ninas
Nice-guy Marty Sachs (Livingston) is fed up with his lack of success with women and has decided to move from New York back to his hometown. Then he meets Nina Cohen (Buono) and then he meets Nina Harris (Peet) and falls hard for both of them. He's trying to decide what to do when he learns that they know each other. So-so romantic comedy never generates any real chemistry despite attractive leads. DVD image ranges between good and very good; sound is acceptable. —MM
Movie: 🎬🎬 ½ **DVD:** 🎬🎬 ½
Studio Home Ent. (cat #AV1565D, UPC 806469156520). Widescreen letterboxed. Dolby Digital Stereo. $19.98. Keepcase. *LANG:* English. *SUB:* English; French; Spanish. *CAP:* English. *FEATURES:* 24 chapters • Bloopers and outtakes • Trailer.
2000 (R) 90m/C Ron Livingston, Cara Buono, Amanda Peet, Bray Poor, Jill(ian) Hennessey; **D:** Neil Turitz; **W:** Neil Turitz; **C:** Joaquin Baca-Asay; **M:** Joseph Saba.

2000 Year Old Man
In 1961, Mel Brooks and Carl Reiner came up with this piece of classic American comedy. Brooks is the title character; Reiner is the straight man who's interviewing him about all of the changes he has seen and how things were "back then." Many sources report that it was improvised. Then in the 1970s, Leo Salkin took the original routine and used it as the soundtrack for a short (26 minutes) animated film. I'm not sure that the animation really adds much to Brooks's inspired fantasy, but it remains a wonderful piece of work on any medium. And there's not much that DVD can do for the simple drawing style. Image and sound are not much of an improvement over VHS tape, but so what? The words and the timing are what's important, and even though this one falls far short of feature-length, the VideoHound is always willing to make an exception for Mel. —MM
Movie: 🎬🎬 **DVD:** 🎬🎬
Rhino (cat #R2 2168, UPC 6034972168-26). Full frame. $14.98. Keepcase. *LANG:* English. *FEATURES:* 5 chapters.
1982 (G) 25m/C D: Leo Salkin; **V:** Carl Reiner, Mel Brooks.

2001: A Space Travesty
Marshal Dix (Nielsen) journeys to the moon to stop a plot to replace top political figures with clones. Another terrible, unfunny *Naked Gun* rip-off starring Nielsen in ever-bumbling mode. (Haven't they made enough of these yet?) This particular cash-in steals the structure, plot elements, and in some cases, full sequences from its inspiration, but delivers a zero on the laugh meter. The jokes are often painfully unfunny and labored. The slickness of this Canadian/German co-production reveals both a significant budget...and the investors' stupidity. (Please read the script next time, before signing the checks, guys, O.K.?) Stick through the unfunny credits if fart noises are your cup of tea. The disc showcases the bright, colorful images with a vivid, razor-sharp image and seemingly perfect framing. The image aliases occasionally, but overall it looks terrific. Sound is clean and the Surrounds are fairly well used. —DG
Movie: 🎬 **DVD:** 🎬🎬🎬
Columbia Tristar (cat #07372, UPC 04339-6073722). Full frame. Dolby Digital 5.1 Surround. $24.95. Keepcase. *LANG:* English. *SUB:* English. *CAP:* English. *FEATURES:* 28 chapters • Trailers.
2000 (R) 99m/C Leslie Nielsen, Ezio Greggio, Peter Egan, Ophelie Winter; **D:** Allan Goldstein; **W:** Alan Shearman; **C:** Sylvain Brault; **M:** Claude Foisy.

2069: A Sex Odyssey
Beautiful sensuous astronauts are sent from Venus to Earth to obtain male sperm. They land in the German alps and are mistaken for the French ski team. Tongue-in-cheek soft-core SF spoof. DVD displays lots of print damage to an original that was never very sharp. It's equal to tape. —MM
Movie: 🎬 ½ **DVD:** 🎬🎬
El Independiente Cinema (cat #sc-2203-dvd, UPC 612385220395). Full frame. $19.98. Keepcase. *LANG:* English. *FEATURES:* Trailers • "Seduction of Cyber Jane" featurette.
1978 (R) 73m/C Alena Penz, Nina Fredric, Gerti Sneider, Raul Retzer, Catherine Conti, Heidi Hammer, Michael Mein, Herb Heesel; **D:** George Keil; **W:** Willi Frisch; **C:** Michael Marszalek, Georg Mondi; **M:** Hans Hammerschmid.

UHF
Daydreamer George Newman (Yankovic) stumbles into a job managing a struggling UHF station, channel 62, and inadvertently turns it into a ratings smash. His programs include *Wheel of Fish*, where contestants can win their weight in red snapper; a topical talk show featuring "Lesbian Nazi Hookers Abducted by UFOs and Forced into Weight-Loss Programs," and the kid's show *Stanley Spadowski's Clubhouse*, which is so weird it makes *Pee Wee's Playhouse* look like *Masterpiece Theatre*. Of course, he's a success. "Weird"

Al's parodies are the funniest parts of the film. Overall, DVD delivers an excellent image of a modestly budgeted picture that was shot primarily at an abandoned shopping center in Tulsa, Oklahoma. The commentary track is of a piece with the content. It's more than a little surprising and heartening to see so many extras on an older catalog title like this one. —*MM*

Movie: 🎟🎟 ½ **DVD:** 🎟🎟 ½
MGM Home Ent. (cat #1003515, UPC 027-616876652). Widescreen (1.85:1) anamorphic; full frame. Dolby Digital Surround; Mono. $14.98. Keepcase. *LANG:* English; French; Spanish. *SUB:* English; French; Spanish. *CAP:* English. *FEATURES:* Commentary • Deleted scenes • Behind-the-scenes footage • Production stills • Promotional material • Music video.
1989 (PG-13) 97m/C Weird Al Yankovic, Kevin McCarthy, Victoria Jackson, Michael Richards, David Bowe, Anthony Geary, Stan Brock, Trinidad Silva, Gedde Watanabe, Dr. Demento, Fran Drescher, John Paragon, Emo Phillips, Billy Barty; **D:** Jay Levey; **W:** Jay Levey, Weird Al Yankovic; **C:** David Lewis; **M:** John Du Prez.

Ulee's Gold

Ulee Jackson (Fonda) is a widowed Vietnam vet who cares less for his family than for his bees, and not without reason. His troubled son Jimmy (Wood) and daughter-in-law Helen (Dunford) have left him in charge of their daughters Casey (Biel) and Penny (Zima). Now Jimmy's in jail and Helen shows up with two thugs who demand that Ulee come up with $100,000. Though it sounds like the stuff of a thriller, Victor Nunez is more interested in character development and the importance of place (the Florida panhandle) to the film. On those counts, it succeeds nicely. DVD delivers an image that's excellent for an independent production filmed on location. Compared to more lavish studio productions, it's not great. Disc's main asset is the availability of both screen ratios. A commentary track by star and director might have been worthwhile. —*MM*

Movie: 🎟🎟🎟 **DVD:** 🎟🎟 ½
MGM Home Ent. (UPC 027616778727). Widescreen (1.85:1) letterboxed; full frame. $14.98. Keepcase. *LANG:* English; French. *SUB:* English; French. *FEATURES:* 44 chapters • Trailer.
1997 (R) 111m/C Peter Fonda, Tom Wood, Vanessa Zima, Jessica Biel, Christine Dunford, Patricia Richardson, Steve Flynn, Dewey Weber, J. Kenneth Campbell; **D:** Victor Nunez; **W:** Victor Nunez; **C:** Virgil Marcus Mirano; **M:** Charles Engstrom. *AWARDS:* Golden Globes '98: Actor—Drama (Fonda); N.Y. Film Critics '97: Actor (Fonda); *NOM:* Oscars '97: Actor (Fonda); Ind. Spirit '98: Actor (Fonda), Director (Nunez), Film, Screenplay, Support. Actress (Richardson); Screen Actors Guild '97: Actor (Fonda).

Ultimate Fights

A collection of 16 different film fights from the likes of *Rumble in the Bronx, Scarface,*

Crouching Tiger, Hidden Dragon, Gladiator, and *Snatch.* You probably have seen virtually every one of these, which still runs only a total of 54 minutes. None of the clips are letterboxed, although at least the transfer of *Scarface* is better than the shamelessly crude and overpriced "Collector's Edition" DVD of that film. The clips in general are average in transfer quality. An avid action fan myself, I'm amazed to see how much more listless these fights prove to be when taken out of context. A "techno party" alternate soundtrack is offered, much more robustly mixed than the sound on many of the clips themselves, but proves to be the warmed-over rave equivalent of a Reno lounge band. One can imagine the drunken frat house festivities ending with head-butting contests after this is slapped on. —*MO*

Movie: 🎟🎟 **DVD:** 🎟🎟🎟
Universal Studios (cat #21374, UPC 0251-9213742). Full frame. Dolby Digital 5.1. $19.98. Keepcase. *LANG:* English. *SUB:* Spanish; French. *CAP:* English; Spanish; French. *FEATURES:* 18 chapters • "Behind the Punches," staging-your-own-movie fight featurette • "How Did They Do That?" commentary • Commentary: producer/director Tsui Hark • The Ultimate Rumble party mix score • Name That Frame Game • Fighter profiles • Flix facts • Fight cards • My Top 5—programmable scene selection • Theatrical trailers.
2002 54m/C D: Tsui Hark.

Ultimate G's

IMAX feature loses a lot on a conventional monitor (and on most home theatre systems, for that matter), but the Surround sound is really impressive. This one has a plot, of sorts, about Zac (McNichol) and his friend Laura (Campbell) and their desire to fly. It's really a light framework for some very nice aerial sequences which appear to have been filmed without computer effects. There is some curious distortion in some scenes—windows on an airplane hanger seem to move—and aliasing, but most of the flying stuff looks fine and that's the point. Still, the sound is more impressive. Disc also has a 3-D option that requires special wireless glasses and other equipment. —*MM*

Movie: 🎟🎟 **DVD:** 🎟🎟🎟
SlingShot Ent. (cat #SEDVD9174, UPC 017078917420). Full frame. Dolby Digital 5.1 Surround. DTS Surround. $24.98. Keepcase. *LANG:* English; French; German; Japanese. *SUB:* English. *FEATURES:* 10 chapters • 3 featurettes • Commentary: producer/director • Trailer.
2001 104m/C Joel McNichol, Emma Campbell, Frayne McCarthy; **D:** Keith Melton; **W:** Jean Bergeron; **C:** Peter Anderson; **M:** Benoit Jutras.

Ultimatum

Hong Kong police chief inspector Michael Wong fails to protect witnesses from a mysterious assassin in black (Yoyo Mung), an ex-cop crime reporter who is on a

vendetta against the entire gang responsible for her father's death. Mainland forensic psychologist Dr. James Fong is sent to help out on the case. After he sees her in action saving a witness from an assassination attempt, Fong puts the pieces together and guesses the truth. The police scenes are handled conventionally, but whenever the film heads into assassin territory, it's almost like a superhero show. It's a slightly uneven mix, thrown off even further by the soap opera elements. However, the action scenes are quite satisfying. Picture looks clean and sharp, but the sound mix is slightly flat. —*BT*

Movie: 🎟🎟 ½ **DVD:** 🎟🎟🎟
Tai Seng (cat #5774, UPC 48950249252-33). Widescreen letterboxed. Dolby Digital 5.1 Surround. $24.95. Keepcase. *LANG:* Mandarin. *SUB:* Chinese; English. *CAP:* Chinese. *FEATURES:* 8 chapters • Star profiles • Trailers.
2001 90m/C *HK* Michael Wong, Yoyo Mung, Yuen Wah, Joe Lee, Kant Leung, William Tuen; **D:** Kant Leung; **W:** Kant Leung, Jessica Chan; **C:** Wai Ying Yip.

Ultraviolet

The best, freshest vampire tale since Bigelow's *Near Dark,* only with that famous English restraint, and no cool Cramps tunes. The story goes that vampires (referred to here as Code Vs) and humans have co-existed for years, but with the current human trend towards self-destruction on a global level, the vampires have organized to protect their food supply. In six one-hour episodes we meet the CIB team through the experiences of their latest reluctant recruit, Michael (Davenport). Michael is a cop in the homicide division and when his partner Jack goes missing the day of his wedding, Michael gets drawn into the battle between humans and vampires. The leader of the CIB is Pearse Harman (Quast), a Catholic priest who only found his faith when faced with the reality of the evil he sees in the Code Vs. One of the best episodes pits Harman and one of the vampire elite in a philosophical debate about the existence of God. Their residing scientist is Dr. Angela Marsh (Harker). When the vampires tried to recruit her and her husband, a noted blood specialist, she lost both her husband and one of her twin daughters when she refused to go. As Vaughan (Elba) tells Michael later, "They say they only take those who what to go, but they don't tell you what they do to make you want to go." Her husband was turned but now resides as dust in deep storage below the CIB offices. The brawn of the team is Vaughan Rice, a military specialist who lost his whole team to the vampires and now hates them with a cold vengeance that only elite military members seem capable of feeling. He carries a torch for Marsh, but keeps his distance from her pedestal. In a particular touching scene, Vaughan believes he is going to die and he uses his cell phone to call Marsh, but doesn't speak, only listens to the sound of her

voice and hangs up. The story follows Michael as he learns about the vampires through their attempts to control their food supply, namely us. The CIB uncovers hospices used as cover to test fake blood and a possible plot to throw the world into a nuclear winter if the fake blood can be perfected. All through the story we meet the enemy and they claim to be misunderstood and persecuted minorities. Through clever scripting, there is always a small hint that this might be true, and you can't help but wonder if the Code Vs appear evil simply because they threaten humans. This is an intelligent series that uses fantasy to discuss such real issues as global warming, abortion, and pedophilia, with a deft hand. Amazing story lines, and first-rate acting and production make this a must-see series for anyone who loves a good political thriller with a little bloodletting. Even the score is notable. This is a two-disc set with three episodes on each disc. There is rumor of an American version in the making, but there is little doubt, given past American remakes of English series, that this will remain the best version. Extras include some good interactive character "personal files." The picture quality is very good with a lot of night shots that are easy to see and the sound is also good. —*CA*
Movie: 🎬🎬🎬🎬 **DVD:** 🎬🎬🎬
Palm Pictures (cat #PALM3034 2, UPC 660200303426). Full frame. Dolby Digital Stereo. $24.99. Keepcase. *LANG:* English. *FEATURES:* 4 chapters per episode, 6 episodes ▪ Character bio files ▪ Joe Ahearne interview.
1998 360m/C *GB* Jack Davenport, Susannah Harker, Philip Quast, Idris Elba, Corin Redgrave, Stephen Moyer, Thomas Lockyer, Collette Brown, Fiona Dolman; *D:* Joe Ahearne; *W:* Joe Ahearne; *C:* Peter Greenhalgh; *M:* Sue Hewitt.

Ulysses' Gaze

Moving and pessimistic depiction of the Balkan conflict is seen through a filmmaker's eyes. Nameless Greek-American filmmaker (Keitel) journeys across the Balkans from Athens to Sarajevo while making a documentary on pioneer filmmakers, the Manakia brothers, who ignored national and ethnic strife to record the lives of ordinary people. Keitel has heard that some undeveloped film shot by the brothers has turned up in Sarajevo and he's determined to see it despite the turmoil in Bosnia. The picture is fine with crisp colors and solid blacks, although some darker scenes seem to give up some detail. The sound is acceptable while never really overpoweringly good. — *MJT* **AKA:** The Look of Ulysses; To Vlemma Tou Odyssea; The Gaze of Ulysses.
Movie: 🎬🎬 **DVD:** 🎬🎬🎬
Winstar Home Ent. (cat #FLV5067, UPC 720917506722). Widescreen (1.66:1) letterboxed. Dolby Digital Stereo. $34.90. Keepcase. *LANG:* English; Greek. *SUB:* English. *FEATURES:* 8 chapters ▪ Theatrical

trailer ▪ Filmographies ▪ Production notes.
1995 173m/C *GR FR IT* Harvey Keitel, Maia Morgenstern, Erland Josephson, Thanassis Vengos, Yorgos Michalokopoulos, Dora Volonaki; *D:* Theo Angelopoulos; *W:* Theo Angelopoulos, Tonino Guerra, Petros Markaris; *C:* Yorgos Arvanitis; *M:* Eleni Karaindrou. *AWARDS:* Cannes '95: Grand Jury Prize.

Un Flic

Edouard Coleman (Delon) is a burned-out Paris detective, always waiting for the next glimpse into the darkness just below the "city of lights." Simon (Crenna) is a nightclub owner who augments his income with daytime bank robberies and drug heists. Edouard is having an affair with Simon's girlfriend, Cathy (Deneuve, with golden locks that would seduce a blind man). Simon overconfidently believes that he has every contingency planned for when it comes to fleshing out his criminal schemes. Edouard and Simon slowly chart a collision course that not only tests their "friendship," but also finds Edouard confronting his unflinching pessimism about the citizens he is sworn to protect. Transfer looks flawless. The source print shows nary a wrinkle, blemish, or speckle. Melville paints the frame with a slight bluish-gray wash, but the colors read accurate and strong. Whites are pure white, blacks run deep, and detail delineation is superb, accenting the muted vertical stripes on Delon's suit and bringing out the purples and blues in the plumes of the showgirl costumes. Fleshtones are completely natural and smooth. There is some hiss on the soundtrack, but I had to place my ear directly on the center channel speaker to catch it. A few sound effects like cars driving on gravel and unlocking doors are a bit "in your face," but otherwise the Dolby Digital mono sounds crisp and vital. The film is presented in the original French with optional English subtitles. —*GH* **AKA:** Dirty Money.
Movie: 🎬🎬🎬 ½ **DVD:** 🎬🎬🎬
Anchor Bay (cat #DV11412, UPC 0131311-41290). Widescreen (1.85:1) anamorphic. Dolby Digital Mono. $24.98. Keepcase. *LANG:* French. *SUB:* English. *FEATURES:* 23 chapters ▪ Trailer ▪ Thumbnail bios.
1972 100m/C *FR* Alain Delon, Richard Crenna, Catherine Deneuve, Riccardo Cucciolla, Michael Conrad, Paul Crauchet; *D:* Jean-Pierre Melville; *W:* Jean-Pierre Melville; *C:* Walter Wottitz; *M:* Michel Colombier.

The Unborn

On the box copy, producer Roger Corman admits the many other (and better) films that inspired this one. It's still a distasteful but occasionally effective horror about a woman (Adams) who undergoes fertility treatments at a mysterious clinic with nasty results. DVD presents an image that's not as rough as some of New Con-

corde's other low-budget efforts, but it's still not a significant improvement over VHS tape. —*MM*
Movie: 🎬🎬 **DVD:** 🎬🎬
New Concorde (cat #NH20401 D, UPC 736991440197). Full frame. $9.98. Keepcase. *LANG:* English. *FEATURES:* 20 chapters ▪ Talent files ▪ Trailers.
1991 (R) 85m/C Brooke Adams, Jeff Hayenga, James Karen, K. Callan, Jane Cameron; *D:* Rodman Flender; *W:* Henry Dominic; *C:* Wally Pfister; *M:* Gary Numan, Michael R. Smith.

Unbreakable

When the train he's on crashes, security guard David Dunn (Willis) finds he's the only survivor and emerges completely unscathed. Shocked and confused by this apparent miracle, Dunn finds an unlikely answer from crippled comic book expert Elijah (Jackson), who has a novel idea. Skeptical at first, Dunn begins to realize that there may be something to Elijah's theory after all. Low-key and dramatic, the tale is told with sincerity and warmth by Shyamalan, producing some truly wonderful, believable moments and genuine thrills. Though very similar to *The Sixth Sense* in structure, it has a completely different theme and resolution. The ending is a shocker, but it enriches further viewings of the film. A must for comic-book fans. The disc is absolutely superb, featuring a stunning transfer (with only occasional minimal grain) of a frequently dark, pale, and rain-drenched film. The sound is also superb, with rich bass, and a very involving Surround mix. The additional features are all valuable, but one wishes the theatrical trailer (which featured dialogue not in the finished film) and audio commentary were included. The deleted scenes are a must, especially one where Dunn breaks down in the shower—a powerful sequence, hauntingly performed by Willis. Though billed as a multi-angle feature, "train station" sequence feature actually offers a comparison between the storyboard and the scene. No alternate angles are featured. —*DG*
Movie: 🎬🎬🎬 **DVD:** 🎬🎬🎬 ½
Buena Vista Home Ent. (cat #21656, UPC 786936144772). Widescreen (2.35:1) anamorphic. DTS 5.1 Surround. $29.99. 2-disc slipsleeve case. *LANG:* English; French; Spanish. *SUB:* English. *CAP:* English. *FEATURES:* 2 Alex Ross illustration cards ▪ Excerpt from early film by Shyamalan ▪ Deleted scenes introduced by Shyamalan ▪ Behind-the-scenes featurette ▪ Comic books and superheroes featurettes ▪ Storyboard/film train station sequence comparison ▪ 28 chapters ▪ Insert booklet with notes.
2000 (PG-13) 107m/C Bruce Willis, Samuel L. Jackson, Robin Wright Penn, Spencer (Treat) Clark, Charlaine Woodard, James Handy, Elizabeth Lawrence, Leslie Stefanson, Eamonn Walker; *D:* M. Night Shyamalan; *W:* M. Night Shyamalan; *C:* Eduardo Serra; *M:* James Newton Howard.

Uncorked

Minnie Driver and Rufus Sewell star in this whimsical comedy which features a little too much whimsy and not enough comedy. Sewell is Ross, a dreamer, who has tried many schemes in the past to get rich. He thinks that he's finally struck the mother-lode in his efforts to purchase a manganese mine. If he is successful, he will then finally be able to marry his girlfriend Kendal (Driver). But Ross's eccentric Uncle Cullen (Nigel Hawthorne) is determined for Ross to better himself through more spiritual means and constantly sabotages all of Ross's plans. The film has some funny moments, but the eccentricities of the characters dominate the film, squeezing out what little plot there is. *Uncorked* does have a positive message, and features some fine performances, but many will find it very dull. The film pops onto DVD in a full-frame format. The image is sharp and clear, but there is some shimmering of the image at times, and the fleshtones appear a tad too shiny. The dialogue is clear and audible, but there is very little in the way of Surround sound effects. The only extra on the DVD is a trailer for the film. —*ML* *AKA*: At Sachem Farm; Higher Love.
Movie: ♫♫ **DVD:** ♫♫ ½
Studio Home Ent. (cat #VM 7827D, UPC 031398782728). Full frame. Dolby Surround. $24.99. Keepcase. *LANG*: English. *SUB*: English; Spanish. *CAP*: English. *FEATURES*: Trailer ▪ 24 chapters.
1998 (PG) 95m/C Rufus Sewell, Nigel Hawthorne, Minnie Driver, Michael E. Rodgers, Gregory Sporleder, Amelia Heinle, Keone Young; **D:** John Huddles; **W:** John Huddles; **C:** Mark Vicente; **M:** Jeff Danna.

Under Fire

Three journalists—Russell (Nolte), Claire (Cassidy), and Alex (Hackman)—old friends from the past, find themselves working in Managua, witnessing the 1979 Nicaraguan revolution. Their jobs demand objectivity, but the situation forces them to take sides. Those messy, realistic conflicts don't gel quite as solidly as they need to for good, compelling drama. Even so, performances are excellent, particularly Harris as a mercenary. DVD presents an accurate reproduction of a fairly soft and necessarily grainy image. Sound is acceptable. —*MM*
Movie: ♫♫ ½ **DVD:** ♫♫ ½
MGM Home Ent. (cat #1002364, UPC 027616865755). Widescreen (1.85:1) anamorphic. Dolby Digital Surround Stereo. $14.95. Keepcase. *LANG*: English; French. *SUB*: French; Spanish. *CAP*: English. *FEATURES*: Trailer ▪ 16 chapters.
1983 (R) 128m/C Gene Hackman, Nick Nolte, Joanna Cassidy, Ed Harris, Richard Masur, Hamilton Camp, Jean-Louis Trintignant; **D:** Roger Spottiswoode; **W:** Clayton Frohman, Ron Shelton; **C:** John Alcott; **M:** Jerry Goldsmith. *AWARDS: NOM:* Oscars '83: Orig. Score.

Under the Sand

François Ozon's psychological puzzle will remind some viewers of George Sluizer's *The Vanishing* and Anthony Minghella's *Truly, Madly, Deeply*, but it's an original that provides star Charlotte Rampling one of her most memorable roles. She's Marie. On vacation at the beach, Jean (Cremer), her husband of 25 years, inexplicably disappears. The rest of the film is about the ways in which she deals with that. DVD image ranges between good and very good. The 5.1 Surround is incorporated as a narrative tool most effectively. Small optional yellow subtitles are clear. —*MM*
AKA: Sous le Sable.
Movie: ♫♫♫ ½ **DVD:** ♫♫♫ ½
Winstar Home Ent. (cat #FLV5306, UPC 720917530628). Widescreen anamorphic. $24.98. Keepcase. *LANG*: French and English. *SUB*: English; Spanish. *FEATURES*: Trailer ▪ 14 chapters ▪ Commentary: François Ozon ▪ Filmographies ▪ Charlotte Rampling interview.
2000 95m/C *FR* Charlotte Rampling, Bruno Cremer, Jacques Nolot, Alexandra Stewart, Pierre Vernier, Andree Tainsey; **D:** François Ozon; **W:** François Ozon, Marina de Van, Emmanuele Bernheim, Marcia Romano; **C:** Jeanne Lapoirie, Antoine Heberle; **M:** Philippe Rombi.

Undercurrent

Ex-cop Mike Aguayo (Lamas) arrives in Puerto Rico and is persuaded by a gangster to romance the man's wife, Renee (Strong), supposedly to give him ammunition for a divorce. Of course, it's more complicated. This is one of those completely clichéd video premieres with many scenes in a strip club. Neither sound nor image is really superior to VHS tape. Minimal extras are the only differences. —*MM*
Movie: ♫♫ **DVD:** ♫♫
Avalanche Ent. (cat #13921). Full frame. $24.95. Keepcase. *LANG*: English. *SUB*: Spanish. *FEATURES*: Cast and crew thumbnail bios ▪ Trailer ▪ Synopsis ▪ 12 chapters.
1999 (R) 99m/C Lorenzo Lamas, Frank Vincent, Brenda Strong; **D:** Frank Kerr; **C:** Carlos Gaviria; **M:** Christopher Lennertz.

Underdog [CE]

This DVD presents three uncut Underdog adventures, complete and digitally remastered. "The Vacuum Gun" features mad scientist Simon Barsinister, who invents the title weapon, and uses it to consolidate the city's top criminals together into a crook army, with plans to steal "all the money in the country." In "From Hopeless to Helpless," canine gangster Riff Raff replaces the hero with look-alike Tap Tap the chiseler, who smears Underdog's reputation. In "Underdog vs. Overcat," an alien dictator from the planet Felina steals all the cows on Earth after their milk wells run dry. Four shorter episodes are included. One is the little-seen pilot cartoon for the series. Most prints are in very good shape. The DVD is fun to navigate through

with its amusing animated menus. Other extras are split between the interests of kids and grown-ups. There's also an inter-view with Underdog's co-creator Joe Harris in his studio. —*BT*
Movie: ♫♫♫ **DVD:** ♫♫♫ ½
Sony Wonder (cat #LVD55406, UPC 0746-45540696). Full frame. $19.98. Keepcase. *LANG*: English. *CAP*: English. *FEATURES*: 12 chapters ▪ Interview ▪ Trivia game ▪ Screensaver ▪ Sound files.
2000 75m/C D: Joseph Harris; **W:** Joseph Harris, W. Watt Biggers; **M:** W. Watt Biggers, Winston Sharples; **V:** Wally Cox.

Undersea Kingdom

This Republic serial essentially re-creates *Flash Gordon* (produced the same year) with the sunken continent of Atlantis substituting for the planet Mongo and Ray "Crash" Corrigan in place of Buster Crabbe. The model submarines, aircraft, and castles are virtual duplicates, too. And so is the sense of fun. This one's a real kick in the pants with fast-moving plots, funny dialogue, and great props. My favorites are the robots that look like walking trash cans. The double-sided DVD contains 12 episode A few registration problems are the only flaw. Thin sound is of the period. —*MM*
Movie: ♫♫♫ **DVD:** ♫♫
Troma Team Video (cat #AED-2060, UPC 785604206026). Keepcase. Dolby Digital Mono. $19.98. Keepcase. *LANG*: English. *FEATURES*: 12 chapters.
1936 226m/B Ray Corrigan, Lon Chaney Jr., Lois Wilde, Monte Blue, William Farnum, Smiley Burnette; **D:** B. Reeves Eason.

Unforgettable

David Krane (Liotta) is a city medical examiner who has just been acquitted of his wife's murder. Martha Briggs (Fiorentino) is a researcher developing a process by which memories and experiences can be moved in chemical form from one person to another, but they have to be extreme experiences, unforgettable moments. Krane steals a sample of Briggs's drug so that he can share his wife's memories and thereby determine the identity of the real killer. It's an interesting premise that goes a bit awry toward the end of the film when Krane is suffering through the memories of the different people on his trail to justice. The drug he takes to share the memories of others causes him heart trouble, so every injection is another major risk. The DVD transfer provides a clear picture but the sound is annoying. The sound effects that play during the moments of memory flashbacks are considerably louder than any dialogue in the film and that gets really annoying. Otherwise, not a bad "B" flick. —*JAS*
Movie: ♫♫ ½ **DVD:** ♫♫♫
MGM Home Ent. (cat #1003516, UPC 027616876669). Full frame; widescreen anamorphic. Dolby Digital. $14.95. Keepcase. *LANG*: English; French. *SUB*: English; Spanish; French. *FEATURES*: 16 chapters ▪ Original theatrical trailer.
1996 (R) 116m/C Ray Liotta, Linda Fiorentino, Peter Coyote, Christopher

McDonald, Kim Cattrall, David Paymer, Kim Coates, Duncan Fraser, Garwin Sanford; **D:** John Dahl; **W:** Bill Geddie; **C:** Jeffrey Jur; **M:** Christopher Young.

Unlawful Entry

After a terrifying break-in, Karen and Michael Carr call the police. Unassuming Officer Pete (Liotta) is quickly on the scene and, after making them feel safe, befriends them. Slowly, however, Michael begins to realize that Pete is a psychopath who is obsessed with Karen. The predictable series of events in this "cop-from-Hell" thriller leads to the boring, but inevitable, final battle between the two suitors (Kaplan, in his commentary, claims it is this derivative predictability that viewers want). The enhanced widescreen image and Surround sound are as good as the theatrical release. —*DRL*
Movie: 🦴 ½ **DVD:** 🦴🦴🦴
20th Century Fox (cat #2001441, UPC 02454014416). Widescreen (1.85:1) anamorphic. DTS; Dolby 4.0 Surround; Dolby Stereo Surround. $22.98. Keepcase. *LANG:* English; French. *SUB:* English; Spanish. *CAP:* English. *FEATURES:* Commentary: director • Featurette • Trailer & TV spots • 28 chapters.
1992 (R) 107m/C Kurt Russell, Ray Liotta, Madeleine Stowe, Roger E. Mosley, Ken Lerner, Deborah Offner, Carmen Argenziano, Andy Romano, Barry W. Blaustein, Dick Miller; **D:** Jonathan Kaplan; **W:** Lewis Colick; **C:** Jamie Anderson; **M:** James Horner.

The Untold Story 2

Sequel takes a more comic approach to the distasteful subject matter (murder and unintentional cannibalism) of the original. Hong Kong restaurateur Cheung (Cheung Kam Ching) is the henpecked husband of a beautiful wife. His cousin Fung (Paulyn Sun) comes to work at his place. Turns out she's a psychotic killer with a hair-trigger temper. Anthony Wong plays a comic cop. The pale, slightly translucent image is about average for an import. The many shades of red tend to bleed. English subtitles are riddled with humorous and inexplicable "hex" errors. A newspaper article describes a massacre as "an obtrude-and-destroy tragedy by a mysterious woman." —*MM*
Movie: 🦴🦴 **DVD:** 🦴🦴 ½
Tai Seng (cat #184, UPC 890391101846). Widescreen letterboxed. Dolby Digital Stereo. $24.98. Keepcase. *LANG:* Cantonese; Mandarin. *SUB:* Simpl. & Trad. Chinese; English; Korean; Malaysian; Japanese; Vietnamese; Spanish; Thai. *FEATURES:* 9 chapters • Trailers • 2 interviews • Talent files.
1998 90m/C *HK* Anthony Wong, Kam Ching Cheung, Paulyn Sun; **D:** Yiu-Kuen Ng.

Up against Amanda

Amanda (Priestly) is a teen psycho-babe who's released from a nuthouse, kills her abusive doctor, and sets her sights on her new next-door neighbor (DeWitt). He presents an easy target because his wife

(Grosso) is an aspiring singer who's on the road. The film is such a low-budget effort that DVD actually works against it. The clarity of the medium makes the flat lighting all the more apparent. It gives the action a lifeless look while, at the same time emphasizing the star's heavy makeup. Dialogue has a hollow sound, too. —*MM*
Movie: 🦴🦴 ½ **DVD:** 🦴🦴
New Concorde (cat #NH20781 D, UPC 73-6991478190). Full frame. $14.98. Keepcase. *LANG:* English. *SUB:* Spanish. *FEATURES:* Talent files • Trailers • 24 chapters.
2001 (R) 102m/C Justine Priestley, David DeWitt, Karen Grosso, Chuck Williams; **D:** Michael Rissi; **W:** Michael Rissi; **M:** Mladen Milicevic, Karen Lawrence.

Uprising

TV miniseries tells the fact-based story of Jewish resistance in the Warsaw ghetto to the Holocaust. The story begins in 1939. The main protagonists in the large cast are teacher Yitzhak Zuckerman (Schwimmer) and Mordechai Anielewicz (Azaria). Director Avnet combines new footage with digitally reworked archival film. Disc does a very nice job. Production values are comparable to a Hollywood feature, and the widescreen image is noticeably sharper and more detailed than conventional broadcast. Sound is very good, too; extras are extensive. On his commentary track, Avnet takes a fairly serious, technically oriented approach. A second actors' commentary is also included. Other extras are on a second disc. —*MM*
Movie: 🦴🦴🦴 **DVD:** 🦴🦴🦴
Warner (cat #21891, UPC 085392189120). Widescreen (1.85:01) anamorphic. Dolby Digital Surround. $24.98. Special packaging. *LANG:* English. *SUB:* English; French; Spanish. *CAP:* English. *FEATURES:* 39 chapters • Commentary: Jon Avnet • Commentary: Azaria, Schwimmer, Sobieski, Voigt • Talent files • Trailer • "Making of" documentary • Resistance documentary.
2001 177m/C Leelee Sobieski, Hank Azaria, David Schwimmer, Jon Voight, Donald Sutherland, Cary Elwes, Stephen Moyer, Sadie Frost, Radha Mitchell, Mili Avital, Alexandra Holden, John Ales, Eric Lively, Jesper Christensen; **D:** Jon Avnet; **W:** Jon Avnet, Paul Brickman; **C:** Denis Lenoir; **M:** Maurice Jarre.

Upstairs, Downstairs: The Complete First Season

The "classy" miniseries was introduced to American audiences by this British import that examines various levels of pre-World War I society as seen within the Bellamy household where Mr. Hudson (Jackson), Mrs. Bridges (Baddeley), and Rose (co-creator Marsh) run things. Not surprisingly, the image is very rough and grainy. Black clothes merge seamlessly with any dark background and production values are thin by today's standards. But all those flaws come from the original elements. DVD

does as much with the material as any medium could. Recommended. —*MM*
Movie: 🦴🦴🦴🦴 **DVD:** 🦴🦴🦴🦴
A&E (cat #AAE-70260, UPC 7339617026-06). Full frame. Dolby Digital Stereo. $79.95. Keepcase boxed set. *LANG:* English. *FEATURES:* 78 chapters • Series Retrospective: 25th Anniversary Special.
1971 663m/C *GB* Angela Baddeley, Pauline Collins, Gordon Jackson, Nicola Pagett, David Langton, Jean Marsh, Simon Williams, Rachel Gurney; **D:** Raymond Menmuir, Brian Parker, Herbert Wise, Derek Bennett, Joan Kemp-Welch; **W:** Charlotte Bingham, John Harrison, Jeremy Paul, Julian Bond, John Hawkesworth, Alfred Shaughnessy, Rosemary Anne Sisson, Fay Weldon, Maureen Duffy, Terence Brady.

Upstairs, Downstairs: The Second Season

The second season of the seminal Masterpiece Theatre series looks a bit better than the first. It's still not going to compete with contemporary video productions, but the image appears a bit sharper. Yes, it's grainy at times and exteriors are pale, but I doubt that these shows are ever going to look any better. —*MM*
Movie: 🦴🦴🦴 ½ **DVD:** 🦴🦴 ½
A&E (cat #AAE-70372, UPC 7339617037-26). Full frame. Dolby Digital Stereo. $79.95. Boxed set keepcase. *LANG:* English.
1972 663m/C *GB*

Urbania

Urban legends and painful confusing flashbacks are plentiful in this disturbing feature that finds Charlie (Futterman) restlessly wandering the night streets of New York in search of the handsome homophobic stranger (Ball) who turns out to be more than he seems. It's stylishly made and hip to a fault; definitely not to all tastes. The image is intentionally distressed and distorted in some scenes and so it's difficult and not very useful to comment on quality. The film doesn't look good but it looks like it's supposed to look. Sound is fine. One of the featurettes may be a put-on. —*MM*
Movie: 🦴🦴 **DVD:** 🦴🦴 ½
Lion's Gate Home Ent. (cat #7610D, UPC 031398761020). Widescreen (1.85:1) letterboxed. Dolby Digital 5.1 Surround. $24.98. Keepcase. *LANG:* English. *SUB:* English; French; Spanish. *CAP:* English. *FEATURES:* 24 chapters • Deleted scenes • Commentary • 2 featurettes.
2000 (R) 104m/C Dan Futterman, Matt Keeslar, Josh Hamilton, Samuel Ball, William Sage, Megan Dodds, Alan Cumming, Lothaire Bluteau, Barbara Sukowa, Paige Turco, Gabriel Olds; **D:** Jon Shear; **W:** Daniel Reitz; **C:** Shane Kelly; **M:** Marc Anthony Thompson.

Urusei Yatsura: TV Series 1

Teenager Ataru is cursed with extremely bad karma. Dragged home by shady government agents, Ataru discovers that he is a randomly chosen champion picked to decide the fate of Earth. If Ataru can successfully tag buxom alien Lum's horns, Earth will be spared. After successfully (and lewdly) winning the challenge, Ataru ends up accidentally married to Lum and finds his home life constantly besieged by annoying aliens! Farcical, side-splittingly silly comedy series was one of the pioneering Japanese animation releases to gain a U.S. cult audience, thanks to years of science-fiction convention exposure. Although the animation is simple and dated by today's standards, the show is still gag-packed and uproarious. Each half-hour episode contains two stories and the series (a smash hit in Japan) ran to 192 installments. Animeigo's disc release features excellent subtitles and superlative liner notes that go way beyond trivial history to explain Japanese topical and language references. Given the age of the series and master tapes, this is a fine, acceptable release. Colors are bright, if a bit flat and there are occasional marks on the print material. Digital edging is kept to a minimum, but is occasionally noticeable. Sound is adequate. —DG

Movie: 🎜🎜🎜 **DVD:** 🎜🎜🎜
AnimEigo Inc. (cat #AV000-101, UPC 7371-87003301). Full frame. Mono. $24.95. Keepcase. LANG: Japanese. SUB: English. FEATURES: 20 chapters ● Insert notes.
1981 120m/C JP

U.S. Seals 2

Sequel-in-title-only is a generic video-premiere shoot-'em-up. It has to do with the conflict between by-the-book Sheppard (Worth) and loose-cannon Ratliff (Chapa), friends who become enemies when one goes to work for a terrorist. Martial arts scenes are the point and these do not even come close to the best. The pedestrian story looks very good on disc. DVD image is bright and crisp; even night scenes are carefully lit to reveal a high level of detail. Sound is fine. —MM
Movie: 🎜 ½ **DVD:** 🎜🎜 ½
Artisan Ent. (cat #123154). Full frame. Dolby Digital Stereo. $14.98. Keepcase. LANG: English. FEATURES: 19 chapters ● Trailer.
2001 (R) 95m/C Damian Chapa, Mike Worth, Marshall Teague, Sophia Crawford; **D:** Isaac Florentine; **W:** Michael D. Weiss; **C:** Peter Belcher; **M:** Steve Edwards.

Used Cars

Outrageous, raunchy comedy is based in part on apocryphal and legendary used-car tales. Conniving dealer Roy L. Fuchs (Warden) knows there's a freeway overpass coming that will blow away his thriving business, so he schemes to seize the competing lot across the street—which happens to be owned by his twin brother Luke (also Warden). Luke's crooked establishment uses every sleazy trick in the book to pawn off some of the worst cars ever offered for sale. His top salesmen Jeff (Graham) and

Rudy Russo (Russell) hijack Roy's customers, and steal commercial airtime by tapping into local broadcasts. Then Luke's long-lost daughter Barbara (Deborah Harmon) shows up for a reunion with daddy. DVD is a perfectly dandy transfer of the film that looks and sounds fine. A commentary track from Zemeckis, Gale, and star Russell is almost as much fun as the movie—they come off as a trio of genial nuts. Every scene has several funny stories behind it, and the trio have no trouble at all being brutally honest with their mistakes, etc. "Outtakes" is a reel of funny odds and ends spliced together, including an alternate scene with Gerritt Graham wearing pornographic glasses. The gallery of ads is nice, but they're small in the frame and hard to read. Also with radio spots, and a low-tech Mesa Arizona TV local dealership spot where Kurt Russell actually went on the air hawking a car for the owner. There are three trailers, but none for this film. —GE
Movie: 🎜🎜🎜 **DVD:** 🎜🎜🎜 ½
Columbia Tristar Home Video (UPC 04339-6058514). Widescreen (1.78:1) anamorphic. $19.98. Keepcase. LANG: English. FEATURES: Commentary ● Advertising material ● Trailers ● Outtakes.
1980 (R) 113m/C Kurt Russell, Jack Warden, Deborah Harmon, Gerrit Graham, Joe Flaherty, Michael McKean, David Lander, Al Lewis, Wendie Jo Sperber, Dick Miller, Rita Taggart; **D:** Robert Zemeckis; **W:** Robert Zemeckis, Bob Gale; **C:** Donald M. Morgan; **M:** Patrick Williams.

The Usual Suspects [MGM SE]

Finally, the commentaries we've all been waiting for. Director Bryan Singer and writer Christopher McQuarrie provide one; composer/editor John Ottman does a second. As for the film itself, this version looks every bit as good as the first DVD release (reviewed in Book 1), and that means that it's superior to the theatrical experience, particularly when viewed on a widescreen monitor. I could see no flaws, even in the night scenes on the burning ship. With that clarity, it's even more surprising when Singer admits that one shot in the scene was actually filmed in his backyard! Not many films are really worth going back through a second (or third) time with a commentary track. This one is. Even though the deleted scenes are exceptionally rough, it's obvious that they were properly deleted. They really add nothing and slow the pace. This disc belongs in every library. —MM
Movie: 🎜🎜🎜 ½ **DVD:** 🎜🎜🎜🎜
MGM Home Ent. (cat #1003332, UPC 027-616874818). Widescreen (2.35:1) anamorphic. Dolby Digital 5.1 Surround; Stereo. $24.98. Special packaging keepcase. LANG: English; French. SUB: English; French; Spanish. CAP: English. FEATURES: 32 chapters ● Commentary: Bryan Singer, Christopher McQuarrie ● Commentary: John Ottman ● 4 featurettes ● 5 deleted scenes ● TV spots and trailers.

1995 (R) 105m/C Kevin Spacey, Gabriel Byrne, Chazz Palminteri, Kevin Pollak, Stephen Baldwin, Benicio Del Toro, Giancarlo Esposito, Pete Postlethwaite, Dan Hedaya, Suzy Amis, Paul Bartel, Peter Greene; **D:** Bryan Singer; **W:** Christopher McQuarrie; **C:** Newton Thomas (Tom) Sigel; **M:** John Ottman. AWARDS: Oscars '95: Orig. Screenplay, Support. Actor (Spacey); British Acad. '95: Orig. Screenplay; Ind. Spirit '96: Screenplay, Support. Actor (Del Toro); Natl. Bd. of Review '95: Support. Actor (Spacey); N.Y. Film Critics '95: Support. Actor (Spacey); Broadcast Film Critics '95: Support. Actor (Spacey); NOM: British Acad. '95: Film; Golden Globes '96: Support. Actor (Spacey); Ind. Spirit '96: Cinematog.; Screen Actors Guild '95: Support. Actor (Spacey).

Utu

Utu is set in colonial New Zealand in the year 1870. British sympathizer Ta Wheke (Anzac Wallace) is devastated when he learns that his village has been destroyed by colonial troops and he seeks vengeance against the English settlers. Violent and uncompromising, Utu has a lot to say about the treatment which New Zealand natives received at the hands of the British. Director Geoff Murphy (Freejack, Young Guns 2) keeps things well-paced and the movie is alternately an action film (very similar to a western) and a morality play. This DVD version reinstates 14 minutes of footage which have never been seen in the U.S. Unfortunately, the image on this DVD is grainy and there are numerous defects from the source print. The colors are somewhat washed-out as well. The audio is adequate, with clear dialogue and realistic sound effects. —ML
Movie: 🎜🎜 ½ **DVD:** 🎜🎜
Kino on Video (cat #K189 DVD, UPC 7383-29018924). Widescreen (1.78:1) letterboxed. Digital Stereo. $29.95. Keepcase. LANG: English.
1983 (R) 122m/C NZ Anzac Wallace, Kelly Johnson, Tim Elliot, Bruno Lawrence; **D:** Geoff Murphy; **W:** Geoff Murphy, Keith Aberdein; **C:** Graeme Cowley; **M:** John Charles.

V

Down from the clouds lumber a horde of flying saucers that creep eerily across the skies before parking over the population centers of the world. Earthlings cower below, their puny fighter jets utterly unable to approach even one of the craft, when finally, a message emanates from the invaders. It turns out they're visitors from somewhere near Sirius, who just stopped by for a few billion cups of some mineral we've got that'd save their dying planet. In exchange, they'll give us technology. Things are great until a nosey reporter by the name of Mike Donovan (Marc Singer) stows aboard the ship hovering over Los Angeles and comes face to scales with the truth—the visitors are giant lizards masquerading as Earth people. It's actually an allegory for the unspeakable tyranny of the Nazi regime and the corrupting influence of power. Well, as much as it could be in a May Sweeps miniseries on NBC. Despite some deliciously cringe-worthy FX, this alien invasion epic is every bit as powerful today as when it first aired—and it's certainly never looked or sounded better. Highly recommended. For the first time, the series can be seen in the original widescreen (1.85:1) aspect ratio in which it was filmed. The print is amazingly clean and without obvious blemishes. Some softness or tint to scenes are intentional and were achieved with camera lenses at the time of filming. Devoted fans have murmured ever so slightly that some of the sound effects were "enhanced" for the brand new Dolby Digital Surround 2.0 track but it should be noted that writer/director Kenneth Johnson oversaw the creation of the robust new audio master. Johnson somehow manages to avoid repeating himself, or losing his voice, during nearly three and a half hours of commentary. Even after almost two decades, Johnson has amazing recall of every aspect of the project. The informative and personable track is no small effort on his part, and will truly be appreciated by even those with only a casual interest in the flick. Also included is a 25-minute documentary featuring on-set footage and interviews with stars Marc Singer and Faye Grant. —GNG/DG

Movie: 🎦🎦🎦 **DVD:** 🎦🎦 ½
Warner (cat #WB D011489D, UPC 8539-1148920). Widescreen (1.85:1) letterboxed. Dolby Digital Surround. $19.98. Snapper. *LANG:* English. *SUB:* English; Spanish; French. *CAP:* English. *FEATURES:* Trailer ▪ "Making of" featurette ▪ Commentary: Kenneth Johnson.
1983 190m/C Marc Singer, Jane Badler, Faye Grant, Robert Englund, Michael Durrell, Peter Nelson, Neva Patterson, Andrew Prine, Richard Herd, Rafael Campos; *D:* Kenneth Johnson; *W:* Kenneth Johnson.

Va Savoir

Camille (Balibar) and her Italian lover Ugo (Castellitto) are in Paris to perform Pirandello's *As You Desire Me*, a play about the questionable identity of a woman who is most likely an imposter. Romantic misadventures ensue when Camille reunites with an old lover who is now married. Ugo spends his off-hours searching for a long lost play by Goldoni. He falls for a young girl whose family has a library containing some very rare items. It's a complicated, but very charming look at love Rivette-style. The muted colors and dark locations tend to look a little murky on the DVD, but not to a distracting degree. It sounds great. —LA *AKA:* Who Knows?.
Movie: 🎦🎦🎦 ½ **DVD:** 🎦🎦🎦
Sony Music Video (cat #07900, UPC 4339-6079007). Widescreen (1.85:1) anamorphic. French Dolby Surround. $29.98. Keepcase. *LANG:* French; Italian. *SUB:* English. *FEATURES:* 28 chapters ▪ Theatrical trailer.

2001 (PG-13) 154m/C *FR IT GE* Jeanne Balibar, Sergio Castellitto, Jacques Bonnaffe, Marianne Basler, Helene de Fougerolles, Bruno Todeschini, Catherine Rouvel, Claude Berri; *D:* Jacques Rivette; *W:* Jacques Rivette, Christine Laurent, Pascal Bonitzer; *C:* William Lubtchansky.

Vacas

Visually stunning film that follows three generations of two Northern Spain families who can't seem to get along. It takes three generations and two wars for the male and female of the neighbors to finally get life right. There is an easygoing nature to the production that makes what could be a boring film utterly engaging, and its story seems to be more revealed than told. The imagery and cinematography are breathtaking. Offers an above-average picture, and crisp clear sound that showcases the sound effects editing. —CA *AKA:* Cows.
Movie: 🎦🎦🎦 **DVD:** 🎦🎦 ½
Vanguard Intl. Cinema (cat #VF0211, UPC 658769021134). Full frame. Dolby Digital Stereo. $29.95. Keepcase. *LANG:* Spanish. *SUB:* English. *FEATURES:* 12 chapters.
1991 96m/C *SP* Carmelo Gomez, Ana Torrent, Emma Suarez, Pilar Bardem, Kandito Uranga; *D:* Julio Medem; *W:* Julio Medem, Michel Gaztambide; *C:* Carles Gusi; *M:* Alberto Iglesias.

Valdez Is Coming

The influence of spaghetti westerns is obvious from the first frame, but this film is based on an Elmore Leonard novel with a solid plot. Lancaster is a semi-retired Mexican-American sheriff who confronts the local land baron (Cypher). Characters and acting are well above average. If this isn't one of Lancaster's great films, it is one of his more serious works. It appears that the DVD producers have punched up the bit rate to handle the bright western (all right, Spanish) exteriors where grain is particularly heavy. The dimness of a few scenes comes from the original. Some print damage is also evident, but the film rates a solid recommendation to any of the star's fans who may well have missed it. —MM
Movie: 🎦🎦🎦 **DVD:** 🎦🎦 ½
MGM Home Ent. (cat #1002372, UPC 027-616865830). Widescreen (1.66:1) letterboxed. Dolby Digital Mono. $14.95. Keepcase. *LANG:* English; French; Spanish. *SUB:* French; Spanish. *CAP:* English. *FEATURES:* 16 chapters ▪ Trailer.
1971 (PG-13) 90m/C Burt Lancaster, Susan Clark, Jon Cypher, Barton Heyman, Richard Jordan, Frank Silvera, Hector Elizondo; *D:* Edwin Sherin; *W:* David Rayfiel; *M:* Charles Gross.

Valentine

Standard-issue slasher plot deals with five girls who teased a boy in junior high school. Now grown, these five women are being stalked by a killer wearing a cherub mask. Boring. The only time that anything happens is when the killer is on-screen

and that is very rare, except for the finale. And to make matters worse, the ending doesn't really make any sense. The picture here is pristine, without grain or distortion. The colors are lavish, as the film is filled with rich reds, and natural flesh-tones. There are no artifacting problems, and the framing is accurate. It's a shame that this sharp image is showing such a bad film. Even better is the audio; the most impressive aspect is the accuracy of the on-screen to speaker sound placement. This is the kind of movie where people are always hearing a "bump" offscreen and you get the feeling that you're there. Also, the film features a rocking soundtrack, which comes across nicely on the audio track. —ML
Movie: 🎦 **DVD:** 🎦🎦🎦
Warner (cat #21187). Widescreen (2.35:1) anamorphic. Dolby Digital 5.1 Surround Stereo. $24.98. Snapper. *LANG:* English; French. *SUB:* English; French; Spanish. *FEATURES:* Commentary: director Jamie Blanks ▪ Behind-the-scenes featurette ▪ Deleted scene ▪ Trailer ▪ Talent files ▪ Music video.
2001 (R) 96m/C David Boreanaz, Denise Richards, Marley Shelton, Jessica Capshaw, Katherine Heigl, Johnny Whitworth, Hedy Burress, Jessica Cauffiel, Fulvio Cecere, Daniel Cosgrove; *D:* Jamie Blanks; *W:* Donna Powers, Wayne Powers, Gretchen J. Berg, Aaron Harberts; *C:* Rick Bota; *M:* Don Davis.

Vamp

Three college boys (Makepeace, Rusler, and Watanabe) go to the city to find an ecdysiast for a frat party and wind up in the strip joint of the undead. Grace Jones is the lead dancer. Her "chair" routine in white face and adhesive tape is too bizarre for words, and, in one incarnation, her makeup is based on the original *Nosferatu*. The story takes place over one long night, and the joke wears thin early. As usual, Anchor Bay gives this marginal little horror flick the best treatment possible. The dark interiors often have wildly colored lighting don't lend themselves to a particularly sharp image. This is an accurate re-creation of the original with no serious flaws or damage. On the giggly commentary track, director Wenk admits that he was given the job on the basis of his short film "Dracula Bites the Big Apple" (included) and poster art that had been created before the script. —MM
Movie: 🎦🎦 **DVD:** 🎦🎦🎦
Anchor Bay (cat #DV11418, UPC 1301311-41894). Widescreen (1.85:1) anamorphic. Dolby Digital Mono. $24.98. Keepcase. *LANG:* English. *CAP:* English. *FEATURES:* Commentary: Wenk, Makepeace, Pfeiffer, Watanabe ▪ Trailers and TV spots ▪ Rehearsal footage ▪ Blooper reel ▪ "Dracula Bites the Big Apple" short film ▪ Poster and still gallery.
1986 (R) 93m/C Grace Jones, Chris Makepeace, Robert Rusler, Gedde Watanabe, Sandy Baron, Dedee Pfeiffer, Billy Drago,

Lisa Lyons; **D:** Richard Wenk; **W:** Richard Wenk; **C:** Elliot Davis; **M:** Jonathan Elias.

Vampire Hunter D: Bloodlust

Anime fans who thought that there would never be another film as powerful as *Akira* will be enraptured by this one. But more importantly, the film will appeal to those who usually don't enjoy Japanese animation. It's set in a very distant future, where most of the Earth is a desolate wasteland, and vampires rule the night. The vampire threat is so great that every house and building is adorned with a cross. The film opens with the kidnapping of the beautiful Charlotte Elbourne (voiced by Wendee Lee) by a powerful vampire named Meier (voiced by John Rafter Lee). Charlotte's father and brother turn to the most vicious vampire hunter in the world, D (voiced by Andrew Philpot) to rescue her. D is half-human, half-vampire, and is a very determined and skillful hunter. From this point on, the film becomes a "road movie" of sorts, as D tracks Meier, while trying to avoid the other bounty hunters who are trying to rescue Charlotte. *Bloodlust* is an amazing horror/sci-fi hybrid. It embraces all of the familiar vampire legends, while introducing the viewer to a world which is strange and terrifying. Unlike most anime, this film never gets mired down with cutesy creatures or a confusing plot. The animation is top-notch and at times, breathtaking. The animators have given a great deal of detail to the characters and the multi-plane images in the action scenes are amazing. This film should appeal to anyone who likes horror, sci-fi, or any film that tells an imaginative and moving story. The DVD is equally impressive. The image is very sharp and clear, showing no distortion or defects from the source print. A small amount of grain can be seen in some shots, but this is the only real flaw. The colors look good, although most of the film is populated with very drab hues. The Dolby Digital 5.1 audio track offers fantastic Surround sound, at the expense of the center channel, which has been mixed too low, making some of the dialogue inaudible. Still, the rear speaker effects are awesome, especially when the bats take flight. The featurette offered here is a disappointment, but the international trailers and TV spots are interesting. —*ML*
Movie: 🎬🎬🎬🎬 **DVD:** 🎬🎬🎬 ½
Urban Vision Ent. (cat #UV1093, UPC 638-652109309). Widescreen (1.85:1) anamorphic. Dolby Digital 5.1. $29.95. Keepcase. *LANG:* English. *CAP:* English. *FEATURES:* Featurette • Storyboards • Theatrical trailers • TV spots • 20 chapters.
2001 105m/C *JP* **D:** Yoshiaki Kawajiri; **W:** Yoshiaki Kawajiri; **V:** Wendee Lee, John Rafter Lee, Andrew Philpot.

Vampire in Brooklyn

Maximillian (Murphy), a Caribbean vampire from a dying clan, travels to Brooklyn to locate a woman (Bassett) who is unaware that she is part vampire. Various fish-out-of-water antics ensue as Maximillian tries to capture her heart. Wes Craven attempts the same balance between horror and comedy that he would later achieve with *Scream,* but meets with far less success. The most humorous moments are offered by supporting players Hardison and Witherspoon. The picture quality is top-notch; even the many exterior night scenes appear sharp and relatively free of grain. The rear speakers are seldom used, even for shock effects. —*BG*
Movie: 🎬🎬 **DVD:** 🎬🎬🎬
Paramount (cat #32982, UPC 097363298-243). Widescreen anamorphic. Dolby 5.1; Dolby Surround. $24.98. Keepcase. *LANG:* English; French. *SUB:* English. *FEATURES:* 17 chapters • Trailer.
1995 (R) 103m/C Eddie Murphy, Angela Bassett, Kadeem Hardison, Allen Payne, Zakes Mokae, John Witherspoon; **D:** Wes Craven; **W:** Charles Murphy, Christopher Parker, Michael Lucker; **C:** Mark Irwin; **M:** J. Peter Robinson.

Vampire Obsession

One afternoon, hooker Wendy (Anouchka) is propositioned by Alexis (Caine) in a cemetery. She goes back to Alexis's apartment and learns that her newest John (or should that be Joan?) is a vampire. Judged by El Independent's standards, the mix of erotic action and blood is pretty extreme. Production values are on a par with the studio's other releases. The shot-on-video image is soft and grainy and there's little DVD can do to improve it. —*MM*
Movie: 🎬 **DVD:** 🎬🎬
El Independent Cinema (cat #sc-1032, UPC 612385103292). Full frame. $19.98. Keepcase. *LANG:* English. *FEATURES:* 17 chapters (no menu) • Trailers.
2002 160m/C Anouchka, Darian Caine, Jade DuBoir; **D:** John Bacchus; **W:** John Bacchus; **M:** Don Mike.

Vampires in Havana

Very funny romp with animated vampires in 1930s Havana. Vampire scientist Professor Von Dracula invents the formula "Vampisol" which allows vampires to spend time out in the sun. His trumpet-playing nephew Pepito doesn't know he's a vampire because he's been drinking it since he was five years old. When the Vampire Mafia of Chicago and a group of German Vampires from Dusseldorf converge on Havana to take control of the formula, a wild chase ensues. Great trumpet solos by Sandoval. Unfortunately, the muted colors don't transfer well. The sound is a bit muddy. —*LA* **AKA:** Vampiros en la Habana.
Movie: 🎬🎬🎬 **DVD:** 🎬🎬 ½
Vanguard Intl. Cinema (cat #VF0254, UPC 658769025439). Full frame. $29.95. Keepcase. *LANG:* Spanish. *SUB:* English. *FEATURES:* 12 chapters.
1987 80m/C *CU* **D:** Juan Padron; **W:** Juan Padron; **C:** Adalberto Hernandez; **M:** Rembert Egues; **V:** Frank Gonzalez, Manuel Marin, Irela Bravo, Carlos Gonzalez, Juan Padron.

The Van

A recent high school graduate passes on college so he can spend more time picking up girls in his van. Typical early '70s drive-in teen sex comedy arrives on disc with no significant improvements to image or sound. Picture is harsh; it always has been. This is one of the cheapest of the low-budget sex comedies, very poorly lit, and so it's never going to look any better. —*MM* **AKA:** Chevy Van.
Movie: 🎬🎬 ½ **DVD:** 🎬🎬
Rhino (cat #5736). Full frame. $14.95. Snapper. *LANG:* English. *FEATURES:* 6 chapters • Talent files • Stills.
1977 (R) 92m/C Stuart Getz, Deborah White, Danny DeVito, Harry Moses, Maurice Barkin; **D:** Sam Grossman; **W:** Robert J. Rosenthal, Celia Susan Cotelo; **C:** Irv Goodnoff; **M:** Steve Eaton.

Vanilla Sky

Which parts of this film are a dream and which parts are real? That's the problem faced by David Aames (Cruise) as he makes his way from scene to scene getting into trouble through his confusion. He flits between two women, Julie (Diaz) and Sofia (Cruz). One is his true love. The other is for casual sex. Both are causing him stress. Director Cameron Crowe fills the movie with mood-infusing music rather than achieving his own moods through dialogue or film style. The terrific sound quality of the DVD is on his side when it comes to the songs. The visual quality of the film seems to be enhanced by the DVD transfer. You couldn't ask for a cleaner print. The director's commentary reveals how heavily the studio and Cameron rely on audience testing for their final product. He also waxes on about "hints" contained in the movie, and behind-the-scenes minutia that will fascinate the Cameron Crowe fans he so desperately hopes are out there. If you don't get the clues that this film is a dream, you may be mildly retarded. Instead of being a conspiracy theorist, Crowe tries to create in an insider mentality for what turns out to be a vacuous film. As a victim of self-aggrandizement, Crowe confuses what is "cool" with what is actually true or interesting, both in the film and in his commentary. We know Cameron is cool, because he can just dial Cruise on whim during his taping of the commentary. Following the great tradition of America being an international bully, Crowe saw a Spanish film he wished he had made, bought the rights to it and made his own version. Unfortunately, Crowe dumbed the thing down by transforming it into Hollywood's idea of originality, infusing the picture with meanings which he's more than happy to explain and then expecting audiences to relate to a gorgeous multi-millionaire media mogul whose life is changed when his face is disfigured. Sympathize with the privileged? Weep for their losses? Cheer for the shallowness of the unjustifiably entitled? Not this viewer. If you're a fan of everything Tom Cruise does, you will find the picture an intellectual challenge. If you are a fan of a good story or even decent films, you'll be better off watching the Spanish original *Abre Los Ojos (Open Your Eyes).* The very last thing the Hollywood machine—of which Cameron and Cruise are cogs—wants to suggest to the American entertainment culture that fills its coffers is "Open Your Eyes." —JAS

Movie: 🐾 **DVD:** 🐾🐾🐾🐾
Paramount (cat #33936, UPC 097363393-641). Widescreen anamorphic. Dolby Digital 5.1 Surround; Dolby Surround. $29.99. Keepcase. *LANG:* English; French. *SUB:* English. *CAP:* English. *FEATURES:* 28 chapters • Featurettes: "Prelude to a Dream," "Hitting It Hard" • Commentary: director Crowe, composer Nancy Wilson • Music video "Afrika Shox" by Lettfiel/Afrika Bambaataa • Photo gallery with audio intro by photographer Neal Preston • Interview with Paul McCartney • Unreleased trailer • Theatrical trailer.
2001 (R) 135m/C Tom Cruise, Penelope Cruz, Cameron Diaz, Jason Lee, Kurt Russell, Noah Taylor, Timothy Spall, Tilda Swinton, Alicia Witt, Johnny Galecki, Michael Shannon; *D:* Cameron Crowe; *W:* Cameron Crowe; *C:* John Toll; *M:* Nancy Wilson. *AWARDS: NOM:* Oscars '01: Song ("Vanilla Sky"); Golden Globes '02: Song ("Vanilla Sky"), Support. Actress (Diaz); Screen Actors Guild '01: Support. Actress (Diaz); Broadcast Film Critics '01: Song ("Vanilla Sky"), Support. Actress (Diaz).

The Vanishing [Criterion]

This widescreen edition of George Sluizer's masterpiece of horror gets a nod over the previously released Image disc (reviewed in *Book 1*). The story of the disappearance of a young woman (Ter Steege) and its chilling resolution is one of the most frightening ever made. Criterion's presentation is flawless, of course. In this case, any commentary track would, I think, have been a distraction. The only extra is Kim Newman's succinct liner notes. —MM **AKA:** Spoorloos.
Movie: 🐾🐾🐾 ½ **DVD:** 🐾🐾🐾 ½
Criterion (cat #133, UPC 037429161623). Widescreen anamorphic. Dolby Digital Mono. $29.98. Keepcase. *LANG:* French and Dutch. *SUB:* English. *FEATURES:* 24 chapters • Liner notes by Kim Newman.
1988 107m/C *NL FR* Barnard Pierre Donnadieu, Johanna Ter Steege, Gene Bervoets, Gwen Eckhaus, Bernadette Le Sache, Tania Latarjet, Lucille Glenn, Roger Souza; *D:* George Sluizer; *W:* George Sluizer, Tim Krabbe; *C:* Toni Kuhn; *M:* Henry Vrienten.

Vengeance of the Dead

This homegrown horror flick never manages to live up to the big ideas which it introduces. Eric (Micheal Galvin) journeys to the town of Harvest, to visit his Grandpa (Mark Vollmers). (Although we're never told where he's been or given an idea of how long he's going to stay.) Once he's settled in, Eric has strange nightmares concerning a little girl, an act of violence, and a burning house. These dreams lead him to sleepwalk through the town and commit strange acts of vengeance. The dreams and Eric's behaviors are linked to a crime from many years ago, and a ghostly presence is seeking revenge on those responsible. *Vengeance of the Dead* has an interesting premise, but the film is slow, boring, and hard to follow at times. Kudos to filmmakers Don Adams and Harry James Picardi for squeezing as much as possible out of their limited budget, but this movie can't overcome its amateur roots. DVD offers the film in a full-frame transfer. The image is clear, but slightly hazy at times. There is a noticeable amount of grain to the picture and the colors are sometimes slightly oversaturated. The 2.0 Surround audio track brings clear dialogue and atmospheric touches of Surround sound. The DVD contains a second film from Adams and Picardi entitled *Schrek,* another horror quickie which should not be confused with the hit animated film. —ML
Movie: 🐾 ½ **DVD:** 🐾🐾 ½
Tempe Ent. (cat #CUV-DV 8077, UPC 763-843807761). Full frame. Digital 2.0 Surround. $14.99. Keepcase. *LANG:* English. *FEATURES:* Commentary • Bonus feature film • Featurettes • Music video • Trailers • 20 chapters.
2001 85m/C Michael Galvin, Mark Vollmers; *D:* Don Adams, Harry James Picardi.

Vengeance Valley

Lancaster and Walker are foster brothers with Walker being an envious weasel who always expects Lancaster to get him out of scrapes. Lancaster is even accused of a crime committed by Walker and must clear himself. Good cast is let down by uneven direction. Film was made in the famous three-strip Technicolor process and so it remains fairly bright, with vivid colors and a softish focus. Almost no surface damage is visible on the print. Overall, the disc looks much better than you'd expect for a film of this age. DVD contains no chapter links or features. —MM
Movie: 🐾🐾 ½ **DVD:** 🐾🐾 ½
Troma Team Video (cat #2016). Full frame. $19.95. Keepcase. *LANG:* English.
1951 83m/C Burt Lancaster, Joanne Dru, Robert Walker, Sally Forrest, John Ireland, Hugh O'Brian; *D:* Richard Thorpe; *W:* Irving Ravetch; *C:* George J. Folsey; *M:* Rudolph Kopp.

Venomous

Government conspiracies and rattlers with Ebola-laced venom? Sounds like a job for Treat Williams. He plays a doctor who discovers a bizarre link between a spreading epidemic and snakebite victims. He enlists the help of his wife (Keller), a viral biologist for the government, and together they uncover the true horror of this disease. Sharp direction by Ray (under the pseudonym "Ed Raymond") makes the reptile horror, while sometimes cheesy, fairly effective. The transfer is excellent. It may be too good, actually, as it reveals some of the shortcomings of the film. The Surround sound is good and Ray's commentary—a discussion of making the movie on the cheap—is interesting. —DRL
Movie: 🐾🐾 **DVD:** 🐾🐾🐾
20th Century Fox (cat #2003323, UPC 024543033233). Widescreen (1.85:1) anamorphic. Dolby 5.1 Surround; Dolby 2.0 Surround; French Dolby Stereo. $34.99. Keepcase. *LANG:* English. *SUB:* English; Spanish. *CAP:* English. *FEATURES:* Commentary: director • Photo gallery • Filmographies • Trailer • 20 chapters.
2001 (PG-13) 97m/C Treat Williams, Mary Page Keller, Brian Poth, J.B. Gaynor, Hannes Jaenicke, Geoffrey Pierson, Catherine Dent; *D:* Fred Olen Ray; *W:* Dan Golden, Sean McGinley; *C:* Andrea V. Rossotto; *M:* Neal Acree.

Vertical Limit [2 SB]

The "Superbit" edition boasts of a higher sampling bit-rate for clearer picture and sound quality. The picture and audio are impressive, but unless you have a high-end system you'll be hard pressed to detect an improvement over the regular release (reviewed in *Book 2*). In addition, this disc dispenses with the extra features found on the earlier disc. —BG
Movie: 🐾🐾 **DVD:** 🐾🐾🐾
Columbia Tristar (cat #08834, UPC 043396088344). Widescreen anamorphic. Dolby 5.1; DTS 5.1. $27.96. Keepcase in cardboard slipcase. *LANG:* English. *SUB:* English; French; Spanish; Portuguese; Chinese; Korean; Thai. *CAP:* English. *FEATURES:* 28 chapters.
2000 (PG-13) 126m/C Chris O'Donnell, Robin Tunney, Bill Paxton, Scott Glenn, Izabela Scorupco, Temuera Morrison, Stuart Wilson, Nicholas Lea, Alexander Siddig, Robert Taylor, Roshan Seth, David Hayman, Ben Mendelsohn, Steve Le Marquand; *D:* Martin Campbell; *W:* Robert King, Terry Hayes; *C:* David Tattersall; *M:* James Newton Howard.

The Vertical Ray of the Sun

Another beautiful film from writer/director Tran Anh Hung (*The Scent of Green Papaya*) about family life in Vietnam. Not all is as it seems as three sisters move about their daily routines with their clan members. Two of the sisters are married, one has a child, and the third sister shares a space in the clan's large house and gardens with her brother. The complicated relationships full of love and betrayal are slowly revealed, and the story takes on a surreal feeling as scenes earlier told as family history or anecdotal tales are

acted out in current events. The filmmaker loves his subjects and takes time to show the strength of their ties through actions rather than exposition. Especially enchanting is a brief respite the girls take to wash their hair in the garden. The comfort that the girls take in the casual intimacy of family is striking and the cinematography makes them into a rich oil painting alive on your TV. The disc looks incredibly good with the bright colors and rich black tones radiating from the screen and the sound is very good. —CA
Movie: 🎬🎬🎬 ½ **DVD:** 🎬🎬🎬🎬
Columbia Tristar (cat #06391, UPC 0 433-96). Widescreen. Dolby Digital Stereo; Dolby Digital Surround. $29.95. Keepcase. *LANG:* Vietnamese. *SUB:* English. *CAP:* English. *FEATURES:* 28 chapters • Theatrical trailer.
2000 (PG-13) 112m/C *VT FR* Tran Nu Yen-Khe, Nguyen Nhu Quynh, Le Khanh, Tran Manh Cuong, Chu Ngoc Hung, Ngo Quang Hai; *D:* Tran Anh Hung; *W:* Tran Anh Hung; *C:* Mark Lee Ping-Bin; *M:* Ton That Tiet.

Very Private Lessons
Anime is typical male wish-fulfillment about teacher Oraku who is lusted after by his beautiful student Aya, daughter of a powerful gangster. The sexual content is relatively mild by Japanese animation standards, but the mixture of titillation and slapstick is still unusual by western standards. DVD image is nice and sharp but animation and storytelling are strictly by the numbers. —MM
Movie: 🎬🎬 **DVD:** 🎬🎬
Media Blasters (cat #0107, UPC 6315950-10770). Full frame. $19.95. Keepcase. *LANG:* English; Japanese. *SUB:* English; Japanese. *FEATURES:* 18 chapters • Director's notes • Trailers.
2001 80m/C *JP* **D:** Masakazu Yamada, Etsuro Tokuda, Rubin Arvizu; *W:* Kazuto Okada, Rubin Arvizu.

Vibration
Writer Mauritz (Taube) travels to an island off the Swedish coast to enjoy some fun in the sun and immediately becomes involved with blonde cutie-pie Barbro (Sjodin). But she can't compete with Eliza (Persson), who claims that she wants to be alone but still finds time for a romp in the greenhouse. This once-racy number is now of curiosity value only. Lots of crackle and static riddle the soundtrack. The pale black-and-white image has been fairly well preserved with only moderate surface damage. —MM *AKA:* Lejonsommar.
Movie: 🎬🎬 ½ **DVD:** 🎬🎬
First Run Features (UPC 72022299097-09). Widescreen (1.85:1) letterboxed. $24.98. Keepcase. *LANG:* Swedish. *SUB:* English. *FEATURES:* 12 chapters • Vintage trailers • Essy Persson photo gallery.
1968 84m/B *SW* Sven-Bertil Taube, Essy Persson, Margareta Sjodin; *D:* Torbjorn Axelman; *W:* Torbjorn Axelman; *C:* Hans Dittmer; *M:* Ulf Bjorlin.

Victim of Love
A therapist (Williams) doesn't know what to believe when she learns that she and one of her more neurotic patients (Madsen) are sharing the same boyfriend (Brosnan). Only the patient claims the man murdered his wife-to-be with his lover. Who will be the next victim? Made-for-television production values make the DVD no real improvement over VHS tape. Extras are limited. —MM
Movie: 🎬🎬 **DVD:** 🎬🎬
Studio Home Ent. (cat #4015). Full frame. $24.95. Keepcase. *LANG:* English. *FEATURES:* Cast and crew thumbnail bios • Trailer • 18 chapters.
1991 (PG-13) 92m/C Pierce Brosnan, JoBeth Williams, Virginia Madsen, Georgia Brown; *D:* Jerry London, James Desmarais; *C:* Billy Dickson; *M:* Richard Stone.

Victoria & Albert
Another lavish BBC production that makes you long to be British. Fabulous sets and costumes frame the story of Victoria, the girl who would be Queen, and Albert, the husband she weds by arrangement. This is a romantic tale of two people who are put together through politics but come to depend on and love each other through trust and mutual respect. The story is historically accurate, but little things pertaining to the personal relationship and family life are painted a little too rosy. It's well known that Victoria didn't like children but she's shown as quite the doting mother in a few scenes. Literary license aside, this is a great, romantic, period drama that makes historical figures from a distant land accessible and friendly while teaching you a little about potentially dry English history. Filmed for TV, DVD picture quality and sound are first rate with rich colors and textures mostly unmarred by bleeding or overexposure, and the sound is very good. —CA
Movie: 🎬🎬 ½ **DVD:** 🎬🎬🎬
A&E (cat #AAE 70344, UPC 7339617034-43). Full frame. Dolby Digital Stereo. $39.95. Keepcase (2-disc boxed set). *LANG:* English. *FEATURES:* 14 chapters • Filmographies.
2001 200m/C Victoria Hamilton, Jonathan Firth, David Suchet, Diana Rigg, Patrick Malahide, Penelope Wilton, Peter Ustinov, Nigel Hawthorne.

Video Girl Ai
After renting a video from a curiously new video store, the lonely Yota Moteuchi is taken by surprise as the beautiful Video Ai girl from his VHS rental literally leaps from her one-dimensional world on the small screen into the three-dimensional reality of his bedroom. After the shock and surprise wears off, Yota learns that Ai has been loaned to him for a one-month period in which her sole job is to make him happy. The two strike a deal to help Yota claim his true love and achieve his much-desired happiness. However, after spending all of their time together working to help him claim his secret love, Yota and Ai begin to develop feelings for each other, but there is a time limit to their love. Masakazu Katsura developed Video Girl Ai from his wildly popular manga series of the same name into a six-episode mini feature. Although this anime series does not break any borders in the realm of new material, the story line is fun and cohesive, and the characters are engaging. Video and audio quality are both good on this feature, though it does lack a 5.1 soundtrack. —EL
Movie: 🎬🎬🎬 **DVD:** 🎬🎬🎬
Viz Video (cat #11643, UPC 7820090845-32). Full frame. Dolby Digital Stereo. $29.98. Keepcase. *LANG:* English; Japanese. *SUB:* English. *FEATURES:* Director's interview • Character info.
1992 180m/C *JP*

The Vigil
Laid-back road picture is short on production values, long on solid characterizations. After rocker Kurt Cobain shuffles off this mortal coil, five friends (Johnson, Lucas, Franz, White, Awan) make a pilgrimage from their small town in Alberta, Canada, to Seattle. Along the way, they pick up a musician (Spence) and a grad student (Beiser). As expected, there's much more talk than action, but it's good smart talk. DVD is an accurate reproduction of an unpolished, damaged image. Large white flecks and snow are visible throughout. —MM
Movie: 🎬🎬 ½ **DVD:** 🎬🎬 ½
Vanguard Intl. Cinema (cat #VF9198, UPC 658769919837). Widescreen (1.66:1) letterboxed. $29.98. Keepcase. *LANG:* English. *FEATURES:* Trailer • Director's intro • 11 chapters.
1998 86m/C *CA* Damon Johnson, Donny Lucas, Allan Franz, Trevor White, Tahina Awan, Jane Spence, Brendan Beiser; *D:* Justin MacGregor; *W:* Justin MacGregor; *C:* James Wallace; *M:* Helen Siwak.

Vigilante [2 DC]
This version of William Lustig's violent exploitation melodrama (reviewed in *Book 1*) presents a much sharper image. Colors are still flat, as they're supposed to be, but the excessive grain has been cleaned up admirably. Sound is excellent. —MM
AKA: Street Gang.
Movie: 🎬🎬 **DVD:** 🎬🎬🎬
Anchor Bay (cat #DV11647, UPC 01313-1164794). Widescreen (2.35:1) anamorphic. Dolby Digital 5.1; DTS 6.1; Dolby Digital Surround. $24.98. Keepcase. *LANG:* English; French; Italian; German. *SUB:* Spanish. *CAP:* English. *FEATURES:* 28 chapters • Commentary • Trailers, TV and radio spots • Promo reel • Still gallery.
1983 (R) 91m/C Robert Forster, Fred Williamson, Carol Lynley, Rutanya Alda, Richard Bright, Woody Strode, Donald Blakely, Joseph Carberry, Joe Spinell, Frank Pesce; *D:* William Lustig; *W:* Richard Vetere; *C:* James (Momel) Lemmo; *M:* Jay Chattaway.

The Vikings

The main attractions of this glorious period piece have always been the impressive locations, the big battle scenes, the authentic-looking Viking ships, and the stars in wonderfully overwrought roles. All of those qualities arrive intact on a handsome disc. First, the widescreen transfer does justice to Jack Cardiff's cinematography. The Norwegian locations are just great. Colors are bright. There may have been some visual flaws, but I'm such a fan of this one, I didn't notice or care. A Surround remix would have gilded the lily for the memorable score by Mario Nascimbene and Gérard Schumann. According to director Richard Fleischer in his featurette, the ships were built from plans based on ones that had been recovered from wrecks. As for the cast, Curtis and Leigh are fine as the romantic leads, but the film belongs to Douglas (who also produced), and Borgnine as Ragnar whose death remains one of his finest professional moments. In short, this one belongs in everyone's permanent collection, and, at the price, it's a steal. —MM
Movie: 🎬🎬🎬 ½ **DVD:** 🎬🎬🎬 ½
MGM Home Ent. (cat #1003433, UPC 027616878522). Widescreen (2.35:1) anamorphic. Dolby Digital Mono. $14.98. Keepcase. *LANG:* English; French; Spanish. *SUB:* English; French; Spanish. *CAP:* English. *FEATURES:* Featurette with Richard Fleischer ▪ Trailer ▪ 16 chapters.
1958 116m/C Kirk Douglas, Ernest Borgnine, Janet Leigh, Tony Curtis, James Donald, Alexander Knox; **D:** Richard Fleischer; **W:** Calder Willingham; **C:** Jack Cardiff; **M:** Mario Nascimbene, Gerard Schumann; **Nar:** Orson Welles.

The Villain

An unfunny spoof of "B" westerns that is almost like a live-action "Roadrunner" cartoon. Douglas plays Cactus Jack, a highwayman who keeps trying to kidnap fair damsel Ann-Margret. Hero Schwarzenegger keeps rescuing her. Lynde is amusing as the uptight Indian chief Nervous Elk. The DVD claims re-mastered in high definition. Who knows what they mean by that. Maybe it's just a misprint. This disc looks pretty horrible right from the start. To start with the film is presented pan and scan. It looks dirty and the transfer is grainy. Film damage also results in far more jumps and jitters than should be acceptable on a DVD release from a major studio. It's not like we're talking about some lost classic from the '20s. To be fair, there are quite a few sequences that are watchable, but the bad parts ruin the viewing experience. Oh, the sound is at least passable, but though the specs say stereo, it sure sounds mono, and a very flat mono at that. —JO
AKA: Cactus Jack.
Movie: 🎬 ½ **DVD:** 🎬
Columbia Tristar (cat #07875, UPC 04339-6078758). Full frame. Dolby Digital Stereo. $24.95. Keepcase. *LANG:* English. *SUB:* English; Spanish; French; Portuguese; Chinese; Korean; Thai. *CAP:* English. *FEATURES:* 28 chapters.
1979 (PG) 93m/C Kirk Douglas, Ann-Margret, Arnold Schwarzenegger, Paul Lynde, Foster Brooks, Ruth Buzzi, Jack Elam, Strother Martin, Robert Tessier, Mel Tillis; **D:** Hal Needham; **W:** Robert G. Kane; **C:** Bobby Byrne; **M:** Bill Justis.

Violent City

A predictably violent reworking of the classic film noir *Out of the Past*, Sergio Sollima's gangster melodrama is essentially a vehicle for the Charles Bronson/Jill Ireland acting duo. Some good photography and story surprises are the high points; bad acting and an overriding sense of gratuitousness eventually do the picture in, like one of hitman Bronson's hapless victims. Top-notch killer-for-hire Jeff (Bronson) is vacationing in the Caribbean with beautiful model Vanessa (Ireland) when he's involved in a car chase and shootout. A number of assailants are left dead—but not racecar driver Coogan (Constantin), who escapes with Vanessa. Back in the states after serving a prison sentence, Jeff tracks down and kills Coogan in the middle of a road race, only to find out that evidence of the act is in the hands of crime boss Weber (Savalas), who wishes to force Jeff to join his New Orleans–based crime syndicate, The Family. Worse, Vanessa still claims fidelity to Jeff, even though she's now married to Weber. Sergio Sollima's direction is fairly standard, his camera zoom-happy, and his transitions cheapened with dull focus-pull tricks to avoid opticals. The picture is fairly lavish for locations, but cheap on actors. Third-lead Savalas is only seen in three interiors, probably never left Cinecittá, and could have phoned-in his colorless turn as the crime kingpin. Ennio Morricone's growling, prowling main theme expresses an intensity the movie itself never approaches, and is mainly used for transitions, not action scenes. Anchor Bay gives the film a flattering DVD sendoff. The main extra eight minutes of scenes cut from the American release, which will immediately make it a must-have for Bronson fans. These are integrated into the show perfectly, except that they have no English dialogue, so it's easy to tell when they occur—Bronson suddenly speaks al Italiana with subtitles. One long restored scene in a Virgin Islands prison has the best fake spider, or the strangest real spider, I've ever seen. Most if not all of the film appears to be shot in English, so the fact that there are no English subs to go with the full Italian and French tracks is not a drawback. —GE **AKA:** Citta Violenta; The Family.
Movie: 🎬🎬 ½ **DVD:** 🎬🎬🎬
Anchor Bay (UPC 13131189193). Widescreen (2.35:1) anamorphic. $19.98. Keepcase. *LANG:* English; French; Italian. *FEATURES:* Interview/documentary, "Shooting Violent City" ▪ Artwork and stills ▪ Talent files ▪ Trailer.
1970 108m/C Charles Bronson, Jill Ireland, Michel Constantin, Telly Savalas, Umberto Orsini; **D:** Sergio Sollima; **W:** Massimo De Rita, Arduino (Dino) Maiuri, Sauro Scavolini, Sergio Sollima, Lina Wertmuller; **C:** Aldo Tonti; **M:** Ennio Morricone.

Violent Zone

After a preface set during the last days of World War II, we shift to 1988 where mercenaries go on a supposed rescue mission in the wilderness to fetch a millionaire's son held by the North Vietnamese. Cheap action flicks don't come much cheaper than this one. It's such a poorly lit production that even bright daylight scenes have a dim aura of twilight. The generic score sounds distorted but that seems to come from the original. Disc comes without extras, save a trailer at the beginning which might be considered a fair warning not to proceed any farther. —MM
Movie: 🎬 **DVD:** 🎬
Digital Versatile Disc (cat #112). Full frame. $19.95. Keepcase. *LANG:* English. *FEATURES:* Trailer.
1989 92m/C John Douglas, Chad Hayward, Christopher Weeks; **D:** John Garwood; **W:** David Pritchard, John Bushelman.

Virtual Sexuality

An odd little British teen film mainly targeted towards girls who will likely enjoy the lively and energetic performance from lead actress Fraser, who fires out dialogue at a hyperactive pace. She plays a girl named Justine who's spent a little too much time in her own mind looking for Mr. Right. When a visit to a virtual reality machine goes wrong, she turns into the guy she was dreaming about. Sort of. There isn't much to the movie, or to the characters for that matter, but the level of energy that this import has to offer is impressive. London is photographed with flair and the film's (almost cartoonish) bright color palette and production design is nicely done. The techno/pop soundtrack becomes a little too much after awhile, but it's a fairly entertaining light comedy. The transfer features sharp, crisp images and bold colors but is prone to small amounts of pixelation and image shimmer. The audio is impressive. The pop/techno music comes through with solid impact and envelops the viewer. There's quite a bit of Surround use at times, even if the way they're used is a bit goofy on occasion. A series of cast video diaries is included. The cast members were given camcorders to capture each other at work, and this is the edited result. It's actually pretty funny but the clip is a little more than a minute long and ends suddenly. —AB/DG
Movie: 🎬🎬 ½ **DVD:** 🎬🎬🎬
Columbia Tristar Home Video (UPC 04339-6047563). Widescreen (1.85:1) anamorphic. Dolby Digital 5.1 Surround; Dolby Digital Surround. $24.95. Keepcase. *LANG:* English. *SUB:* English; Spanish. *CAP:* Eng-

lish. *FEATURES:* Cast video diaries • Trailers • Featurette • Production notes.
1999 (R) 92m/C *GB* Laura Fraser, Rupert Penry-Jones, Kieran O'Brien, Luke De Lacey, Natasha Bell, Steve John Sheperd, Laura Macaulay, Marcelle Duprey; **D:** Nick Hurran; **W:** Nick Fisher; **C:** Brian Tufano; **M:** Rupert Gregson-Williams.

The Visit

Hill Harper leads an excellent cast in this story of Alex, a man imprisoned for a rape he may not have committed, who seeks only the acceptance and love of his family. Through visits with his estranged, successful brother (Obba Babatunde), his loving mother (Marla Gibbs, of *The Jeffersons*), and his disapproving father (Billy Dee Williams), as well as a prison psychiatrist (Phylicia Rashad) and a childhood friend (Rae Dawn Chong), Alex finds the peace he seeks. Yes, it sounds hokey, but the excellent performances and steady subtle direction make it all work. Based on a stage play. This DVD offers a very good transfer of the film. The image is very sharp and clear, showing no overt defects. There is some slight grain during daylight shots, but that's the only real flaw here. The audio offers clear dialogue (very important here) and some low-volume Surround sound effects. —*ML*
Movie: 🎦🎦🎦 *DVD:* 🎦🎦🎦
HBO (cat #91872, UPC 026359187223). Widescreen anamorphic. Dolby Surround. $19.98. Snapper. *LANG:* English; Spanish. *SUB:* English; French; Spanish. *CAP:* English. *FEATURES:* Theatrical trailer • Cast & crew • 16 chapters.
2000 (R) 107m/C Hill Harper, Obba Babatunde, Billy Dee Williams, Marla Gibbs, Rae Dawn Chong, Phylicia Rashad, Talia Shire, David Clennon, Glynn Turman, Efrain Figueroa, Amy Stiller; **D:** Jordan Walker-Pearlman; **W:** Jordan Walker-Pearlman; **C:** John Ndiaga Demps; **M:** Michael Bearden.

Viy

A Russian seminary student, Thomas is plagued by an old witch while on a school break. Hopping on his back, she rides him around the countryside like a broom. After making a narrow escape, Thomas is asked to sit watch over a young girl's body. The girl proves to be the old witch and as he prays over her body for three nights in a church, he is besieged by the forces of evil who try to break through his protective circle. One of the few Russian films that could be considered a horror film, *Viy* is a groundbreaking and stylish work, mixing fantasy elements and comedy into the supernatural fable. The first two thirds of the film function almost solely as a light folk tale, but the movie comes alive in the last section. This beautifully realized and wonderfully creepy set piece boasts terrific special effects and some truly bizarre imagery. A film that gets even better with repeated viewings. The picture is razor sharp and satisfying, but the print source

is a tad on the pale side. All the scenes inside the church are as richly hued and luscious as one could wish, so the muted tones of the rest of the film may be intentional. The sound is excellent, but is fairly limited on Surround effects. Unfortunately, a couple of the film's traditional Russian songs are not translated. The clips from earlier silent-era Russian horror films are incredibly valuable to genre film historians as they offer rare glimpses of some of the only known Soviet essays into the macabre before this film. The clips are not presented with any score but instead with odd "projector noise" accompaniment. —*DG* **AKA:** *Spirit of Evil.*
Movie: 🎦🎦🎦 *DVD:* 🎦🎦🎦
Image Ent. (cat #RUSD0257DVD, UPC 014-381025729). Full frame. Dolby Digital 5.1 Surround. $29.99. Keepcase. *LANG:* Russian; English; French. *SUB:* Russian; English; French; German; Hebrew; Spanish; and others. *FEATURES:* Theatrical trailer • 3 additional trailers from other releases • Filmography • Photos • Documentary on the works of Nikolai Gogol • Episodes from 3 silent Russian horror movies • Bios • 20 chapters • Insert card with menu guide.
1967 72m/C *RU* Leonid Kuravlyov, Natalia Varley, Alexei Glazyrin; **D:** Konstantin Yershov, Georgy Kropachov; **W:** Alexander Ptushko, Konstantin Yershov, Georgy Kropachov; **C:** Fyodor Provorov, Victor Pishchalnikov; **M:** Karen Khachaturyan.

A Voice from Heaven

Documentary examines the life and career of Sufi singer Nusrat Fateh Ali Khan. He was a Pakistani who died in 1997. He performed traditional Muslim songs with such passion that many in his audiences were transported into ecstatic trances. His music also crossed over into the popular realm when it was remixed into dance numbers. The man's undeniable charisma comes through even to viewers who do not have a background in the Sufi mystical tradition and earns the film a recommendation to a wide audience. New interviews look very sharp. Older footage varies in visual quality. If the monaural sound is not as dazzling as a Surround track might have provided, it is appropriate to the material. —*MM*
Movie: 🎦🎦🎦 *DVD:* 🎦🎦 ½
Winstar Home Ent. (cat #WHE73145, UPC 720917314525). Full frame. $24.98. Keepcase. *LANG:* English. *FEATURES:* 12 chapters • Production credits.
2001 75m/C D: Giuseppe Asaro; **W:** Giuseppe Asaro.

Voices from Beyond

Here's another oddity from legendary Italian horror director Lucio Fulci. After wealthy Giorgio Mainardi hemorrhages to death, his daughter Rosy (Karina Huff) returns home from college to attend the funeral. She soon begins to have strange dreams in which her father claims that he was murdered, and begs Rosy to discover the identity of the killer. In flashbacks, we

learn that Giorgio did something to enrage everyone in the household before he died, so there are many suspects. While the revelation of the murderer is actually surprising, the rest of *Voices from Beyond* is a boring mess. While Fulci is well-known for his liberal use of gore and his occasionally creepy visuals, this film has neither. The acting isn't very good, and the atrocious dubbing only makes matters worse. The transfer presented on this DVD is surprisingly clear, but the picture is very soft at times. Also, there is some artifacting present. Still, there is only a small amount of grain to speak of, and the colors are fine. The Dolby Digital Mono audio track provides clear dialogue, but there is hissing present here and the voice-overs by the Giorgio character create some distortion. —*ML* **AKA:** *Voci dal Profondo.*
Movie: 🎦 ½ *DVD:* 🎦🎦
Image Ent. (cat #ID07401XDVD, UPC 014-381074024). Widescreen (1.78:1) anamorphic. Dolby Digital Mono. $24.99. Keepcase. *LANG:* English. *FEATURES:* 15 chapters.
1990 91m/C *IT* Dulio Del Prete, Karina Huff, Pascal Persiano, Lorenzo Flaherty, Bettina Giovannini, Damiano Azzos; **D:** Lucio Fulci; **W:** Piero Regnoli; **M:** Stelvio Cipriano.

Volunteers

Ivy League playboy Laurence Bourne III (Hanks) joins the newly formed Peace Corps to escape gambling debts. He joins genuine idealists Tom Tuttle (Candy) and Beth Wexler (Wilson) in building a bridge in Thailand. The film has a certain uninhibited quality that is hard to pinpoint, but makes for a very refreshing comedy with plenty of absurd situations. Widescreen transfer reveals a great level of detail. Some grain is evident in a few select scenes but for the most part the source print is in good condition without distracting defects or scratches. Colors do appear slightly washed-out, an indication of the movie's age and period. Shadows are well defined and with good detail while blacks are deep and solid. Audio is well integrated and natural sounding. Although the bass extension on the track appears slightly limited, the overall frequency response is quite pleasing without creating the harshness found in many other movies of the time. —*GH/MM*
Movie: 🎦🎦 ½ *DVD:* 🎦🎦 ½
HBO Home Video (UPC 026359298325). Widescreen (1.85:1) anamorphic. Dolby Digital Stereo. $14.98. Snapper. *LANG:* English. *SUB:* English; French; Spanish. *FEATURES:* Trailer • Talent files.
1985 (R) 107m/C Tom Hanks, John Candy, Rita Wilson, Tim Thomerson, Gedde Watanabe, George Plimpton, Ernest Harada; **D:** Nicholas Meyer; **W:** David Isaacs, Ken Levine; **C:** Ric Waite; **M:** James Horner.

Von Ryan's Express

Diverting star vehicle is fine for Sinatra fans. Those expecting another *Guns of*

Navarone or *Great Escape* will be disappointed. Ol' Blue Eyes plays American Air Force Col. Ryan, whose P-38 is shot down over Italy near the end of the war. He's taken to a prison camp where he locks horns with Maj. Finchan (Howard), who's in charge of the British POWs. Conflicts in the first half are fairly realistic, but then the prisoners decide to take over a train and escape, and the film becomes standard shoot-'em-up stuff. DVD image is a bit on the dark side in a few scenes, but that seems to come from the original. Throughout, colors are sharp and there's virtually no surface damage. To my ears, the original mono soundtrack was superior to the stereo remix. —*MM*

Movie: 🐾🐾 ½ **DVD:** 🐾🐾 ½
20th Century Fox (UPC 024543013112). Widescreen (2.35:1) anamorphic. Dolby Digital Stereo; Mono. $19.98. Keepcase. *LANG:* English; French. *SUB:* English; Spanish. *FEATURES:* Trailer • 30 chapters.
1965 117m/C Frank Sinatra, Trevor Howard, Brad Dexter, Raffaella Carra, Sergio Fantoni, John Leyton, Vito Scotti, Edward Mulhare, Adolfo Celi, James Brolin, James B. Sikking, Wolfgang Preiss, John van Dreelen, Richard Bakalyan, Michael Goodliffe, Michael St. Clair, Ivan Triesault; *D:* Mark Robson; *W:* Wendell Mayes, Joseph Landon; *C:* William H. Daniels; *M:* Jerry Goldsmith.

Voodoo Nightmare

A young woman leads a group of friends on a trek into the Malaysian jungle in search of her mother. They end up lost and haunted by the resident Pontianak, the spirit of a woman who has died a violent death at the hands of a man and returns to make things unpleasant for others. If you think you've heard this before, I'm sure you're right. The Hound tries to cut low-budget indie films some slack, but this disc looks and sounds pretty awful. —*BG*

Movie: woof **DVD:** 🐾
Vanguard Intl. Cinema (cat #VFO 242, UPC 658769024232). Full frame. $29.95. Keepcase. *LANG:* English. *FEATURES:* 6 chapters.
2000 84m/C Thi Le Hiep, Fadzlind, Jaffar Aris, Steven Banks, Victor Khong, Eleanor Lee Fadali; *D:* Djinn; *W:* Djinn; *C:* Minh Nguyen.

Voyeur.com

Even though a psycho killer is stalking Los Angeles glamour photographers, three guys decide to set up a house filled with tiny digital cameras where seven girls will live and, presumably, take frequent showers. They're a varied lot. Innocent Mary (Romano) signs on because she is so desperate for work that she's been living in her beat-up car. Low-budget exploitation was shot on video and so DVD can do little to improve a clear but impoverished image. —*MM*

Movie: 🐾🐾 **DVD:** 🐾🐾
MTI Home Video (UPC 039414510751). Full frame. $24.98. Keepcase. *LANG:* English. *SUB:* Spanish. *FEATURES:* Trailers • 20 chapters.

2000 95m/C Jena Romano, Adam Weiner, Tawnya Richardson, Travis Shakespeare; *D:* Miles Feldman; *W:* Miles Feldman; *C:* John Turk; *M:* Evan Evans.

W. Eugene Smith: Photography Made Difficult

Docudrama on the life and work of photographer W. Eugene Smith—an unusually lean and compelling entry in a traditionally tepid and poorly acted sub-genre. The actor who plays Smith (Riegert) is the best I've seen in this kind of format, a first-rate performer who is not a star. You will recognize photographer Smith's work even though you may not know his name—the photos were widely circulated in *Life* magazine circa the 1940s and have been frequently reprinted. My only objections: Smith himself is a difficult man to like, as the title seems to anticipate, and both the original video and DVD transfer are very average (per Image Entertainment's track record)—particularly evident when it comes to showing Smith's work, which should be a crisp and clear black and white but winds up lacking sharpness with evident video lines. Good sound, though. —*MO*

Movie: 🐾🐾🐾 **DVD:** 🐾🐾
Image Ent. (cat #ID9338RADVD, UPC 014381933826). Full frame. Dolby Digital Mono. $24.99. Keepcase. *LANG:* English. *FEATURES:* 14 chapters.
1989 88m/B Peter Riegert; *D:* Gene Lasko; *W:* Jan Hartman; *C:* William Megalos.

Waiting

Dumb and dumber semi-gross out comedy made in Philadelphia. Young Sean McNutt (Keenan) has just broken up with his girlfriend—passed out at dinner with her folks, and he's been given 30 days to find an apartment before his parents kick him out of his house. Working as a waiter at Broccoletti's Italian restaurant, he has to wear a hideous greenish/yellow shirt and undergoes all sorts of ill treatment. The episodic action is stylishly put together by Patrick Hasson. He uses colored filters to jazz up the unpolished indie-prod look. DVD image captures them accurately, but the real benefit of the disc lies in the extensive extras. The menu boasts about several hidden Easter eggs which, doubtless, are there but I was not moved to search. The film is funny enough on its own. —*MM*

Movie: 🐾🐾🐾 **DVD:** 🐾🐾🐾
First Run Features (cat #TLAD005, UPC 807839000122). Widescreen (1.66:1) anamorphic. Dolby Digital Mono. $24.98. Keepcase. *LANG:* English. *FEATURES:* 20 chapters • Behind-the-scenes featurette • Previews • Easter eggs • Commentary: Patrick Hasson, Will Keenan. • Deleted scenes and outtakes.
2001 80m/C Will Keenan, Hannah Dalton, Kerri Kenney, Harry Philabosian, Lloyd Kaufman, Ron Jeremy; *D:* Patrick Hasson; *W:* Patrick Hasson; *C:* Michael Pearlman.

Waiting for Guffman

The eccentric citizens of Blaine, Missouri, plan an original musical ("Red, White, and Blaine") to celebrate the town's 150th anniversary. Leading the pack is former New Yorker and semi-hysteric Corky St. Claire (Christopher Guest) as the director. Everyone's very game—and almost completely talentless. The Guffman of the title is the Broadway producer Corky knows and whom he's invited to see their disaster-in-the-making. This movie has some classic moments, but it's a little too quirky for its own good. The film plays much better if you know going in that the majority of the dialogue and jokes were improvised. Most of the individuals involved in this film would reassemble for Guest's *Best in Show*. DVD offers a very nice package. The image presented here is quite sharp, although it does show some grain and is slightly dark at times. The audio track provides clear and audible dialogue, but little in the way of Surround sound. This disc contains 14 deleted scenes, which offers over 30 minutes of new material, some of which is quite funny. Also amusing is the audio commentary with Guest and star Eugene Levy. —*ML*

Movie: 🐾🐾 **DVD:** 🐾🐾
Warner (cat #C2526, UPC 0539392526-20). Widescreen anamorphic. Dolby 2.0 Surround. $19.98. Snapper. *LANG:* English. *SUB:* English; French; Spanish; Portuguese. *CAP:* English. *FEATURES:* Commentary • Deleted scenes • Theatrical trailer • Cast & crew • 28 chapters.
1996 (R) 84m/C Bob Odenkirk, Christopher Guest, Eugene Levy, Catherine O'Hara, Parker Posey, Fred Willard, Lewis Arquette, Matt Keeslar, Paul Dooley, Paul Benedict, Bob Balaban, Larry Miller, Brian Doyle-Murray; *D:* Christopher Guest; *W:* Christopher Guest, Eugene Levy; *C:* Roberto Schaefer; *M:* Michael McKean, Harry Shearer, Christopher Guest. *AWARDS:* NOM: Ind. Spirit '98: Actor (Guest), Film, Screenplay.

Waitress [DC]

Troma's second comedy follows three waitresses—an aspiring actress, a magazine reporter, and a preppy—who work in a New York beanery where the chef is a drunk, the kitchen explodes, the customers riot, and most of the women seem to find a reason to take their clothes off. Troma fans know what to expect. For comments on image quality and extras, please see review of *Squeeze Play*. —*MM* *AKA:* Soup to Nuts.

Movie: 🐾🐾 ½ **DVD:** 🐾🐾🐾
Troma Team Video (cat #9011, UPC 790357901135). Full frame. $19.98. Keepcase. *LANG:* English. *FEATURES:* 9 chapters • Troma materials • Featurette • Commentary: director.
1981 (R) 85m/C Jim Harris, Carol Drake, Carol Bever; *D:* Lloyd Kaufman; *W:* Charles Kaufman, Michael Stone; *C:* Lloyd Kaufman.

Waking Life

Gen X-er Wiley Wiggins wanders through a surreal dreamscape, meeting a variety of characters who offer their views on existence, God, and the meaning of life. The animation is brilliant, using constantly shifting shapes and colors to create an evocative and unsettling mood. Unfortunately, the script sounds like a pretentious introductory philosophy course, and the repetitive structure and lack of plot quickly grow tiresome. The transfer brings out the broad color-spectrum of the film, and the soundtrack is equally excellent. The extra features are plentiful, but largely uninteresting. —BG
Movie: ♪♪ **DVD:** ♪♪♪ ½
20th Century Fox (cat #2004068). Widescreen (1.85:1) anamorphic. Dolby 5.1. $29.98. Keepcase. *LANG:* English; Spanish. *SUB:* English; French. *CAP:* English. *FEATURES:* 20 chapters ☞ Commentary: Richard Linklater ☞ Commentary: film's animation staff ☞ Text commentary ☞ Deleted animation scenes ☞ Takes from live-action version ☞ Shorts by art director Bob Sabiston ☞ Featurette ☞ Animation software tutorial ☞ Trailers.
2001 (R) 99m/C Richard Linklater, Glover Gill, Julie Delpy, Wiley Wiggins, Ethan Hawke, Adam Goldberg, Nicky Katt, Steven Soderbergh; *D:* Richard Linklater; *W:* Richard Linklater; *C:* Richard Linklater, Tommy Pallotta; *M:* Glover Gill. *AWARDS:* N.Y. Film Critics '01: Animated Film; *NOM:* Ind. Spirit '02: Director (Linklater), Film, Screenplay.

Walking and Talking

Long-time friends Laura (Heche) and Amelia (Keener) are facing the big 3-0. Laura is getting married to Frank (Field), but Amelia has settled for a video store clerk (Kevin Corrigan) who takes her out to a monster movie convention for their first date. Commitment crises abound in this low-budget, lighthearted indie-prod estrogen romp. The characters are well-written and realized, with dialogue that's natural and often entertaining. Rather than force this fine material, the actors underplay nicely and really pull the audience into the situations. The New York City locations are also wonderfully captured by cinematographer Michael Spiller. The streets and stores really become a character and the film feels more realistic as a result. Sharpness and detail aren't exceptional, but the picture remained consistently crisp and pleasantly defined. Flaws are really few and far between. The print for this 1996 picture looks unexpectedly clean, with only a couple of little specks during the whole feature. Very slight grain was occasionally present, but this was hardly an issue. Disc is also free of pixelation and edge-enhancement. Dialogue remains crisp, clear, and easily heard without turning the volume way up. —AB/MM
Movie: ♪♪♪ **DVD:** ♪♪♪
Miramax Pictures Home Video (UPC 7869-36184945). Widescreen (1.85:1) anamorphic. Dolby Surround. $19.98. Keepcase. *LANG:* English. *FEATURES:* Trailers.

1996 (R) 86m/C Anne Heche, Catherine Keener, Liev Schreiber, Todd Field, Kevin Corrigan, Randall Batinkoff, Joseph Siravo, Vincent Pastore, Lynn Cohen, Andrew Holofcener; *D:* Nicole Holofcener; *W:* Nicole Holofcener; *C:* Michael Spiller; *M:* Billy Bragg. *AWARDS: NOM:* Ind. Spirit '97: Actress (Keener), Support. Actor (Corrigan).

Walking with Dinosaurs

This fantastic 180-minute series is both educational and extremely entertaining. The documentary brings the entire story of the dinosaurs back to life using a combination of CGI, animatronic, and other effects, and the result is amazing. Rather than feeling cold and withdrawn, such as some nature documentaries do, this one brings the camera right into the action, making viewers feel as if they're right in the middle of all of the confrontations. The documentary is split into six episodes and each introduces a new environment and a new cast of characters. It's unbelievable how well the effects have been integrated into the surrounding area. Dinosaurs convincingly interact with each other, and walk through the world around them, and the effect is flawless. The disc transfer has a couple of minor instances of shimmering, but the picture quality is otherwise so breathtaking that any flaws pretty much are thrown out the window. The sharpness and detail are magnificent, almost three-dimensional looking. Colors are almost impossibly beautiful and this image shows off every little detail. This is a nice, although somewhat basic soundtrack with minimal Surround effects. The "picture-in-picture" feature is a wonderfully creative extra; a little window opens featuring a narrator who talks in greater detail about the making of that particular sequence. The excellent 55-minute "making of" documentary is also presented in anamorphic widescreen. It's impressive and in depth, examining everything from the history and environment of these dinosaurs to the bones being found today to the special effects that bring these creatures to life. Historians and experts take us through each of the dinosaurs, pointing out all of the characteristics of each creature and their behavior. Recommended. —AB/DG
Movie: ♪♪♪ ½ **DVD:** ♪♪♪ ½
Warner Home Video (UPC 7940511504-24). Widescreen anamorphic. Dolby Digital Surround. $29.98. Keepcase. *LANG:* English. *SUB:* English; Spanish. *FEATURES:* "Picture within a Picture" feature ☞ "Making of" documentary ☞ 44 chapters.
1999 180m/C *D:* Jasper James; *Nar:* Kenneth Branagh.

Walls of Hell

Philippine war movie is a virtual companion piece to *Raiders of Leyte Gulf.* It's another story of American G.I.s and native guerrillas fighting the Japs toward the end of the occupation. Dialogue is turgid and anachronistic details of clothing and hairstyles abound. Black-and-white photography is fairly sharp and original elements have been pretty well maintained. Faint static hiss is audible throughout; light vertical scratches are intermittent. —MM
Movie: ♪♪ **DVD:** ♪♪
Winstar Home Ent. (cat #FLV5298, UPC 720917529820). Full frame. $14.98. Keepcase. *LANG:* English. *FEATURES:* 16 chapters ☞ Filmographies ☞ Production notes.
1964 88m/B PH Jock Mahoney, Fernando Poe Jr., Mike Parsons; *D:* Gerardo (Gerry) De Leon, Eddie Romero; *W:* Eddie Romero, Cesar Amigo, Ferde Grofe Jr.; *C:* F. Sacdalan; *M:* Tito Arevalo.

Walt Disney Treasures: Davy Crockett

This two-disc set comes in a tin box and contains all five of the Davy Crockett shows produced for television. As Leonard Maltin notes in his introduction, the "Crockett craze" was not something that the studio manufactured. It came from the then-young baby boomers' heart. We thought Davy Crockett and his coonskin cap were cool and we liked the song. The shows are presented here with the introductions from the original broadcasts. They've been well preserved (and/or restored). They look terrific on DVD, and the extras are nicely done. Mono sound is just fine; a Surround remix wouldn't have been right. Contents: "Davy Crockett Indian Fighter," "Davy Crockett Goes to Congress," "Davy Crockett at the Alamo," "Davy Crockett's Keelboat Race," and "Davy Crockett and the River Pirates." —MM
Movie: ♪♪♪ **DVD:** ♪♪♪♪
Buena Vista Home Ent. (cat #23092, UPC 786936158229). Full frame. Dolby Digital Mono. $32.99. Special packaging. *LANG:* English. *CAP:* English. *FEATURES:* Leonard Maltin intros ☞ "Davy Crockett Craze" featurette ☞ Conversation with Fess Parker.
2001 (PG) 268m/C Fess Parker, Buddy Ebsen, Hans Conried, Ray Whiteside, Pat Hogan, William "Billy" Bakewell, Basil Ruysdael, Kenneth Tobey; *D:* Norman Foster; *M:* George Bruns.

Walt Disney Treasures: Disneyland USA

This two-disc set contains four early episodes of the popular Disney TV series. Today, their value is mostly historic, particularly "Dateline Disneyland," a show that was broadcast live on July 17, 1955, when the famous theme park was dedicated. Of course, the black-and-white and color footage varies in quality but it's all been perfectly preserved. The discs look and sound fine. Contents: "The Disneyland Story," "Dateline Disneyland," "Disneyland After Dark," and "Disneyland Tenth Anniversary Show." —MM
Movie: ♪♪ ½ **DVD:** ♪♪♪♪
Buena Vista Home Ent. (cat #23093, UPC 786936158236). Full frame. Dolby Digital Mono. $32.99. Special packaging. *LANG:* English. *CAP:* English. *FEATURES:* Leonard Maltin intros ☞ Still gallery ☞ "The Magic Kingdom and the Magic of Television" featurette.
2001 228m/C

Walt Disney Treasures: Silly Symphonies

Disney's Silly Symphonies short films were hugely successful with audiences and they provided invaluable experience for the studio's animators. They won many awards and the ground-breaking "Old Mill" was a testing ground for some of the techniques used in *Snow White*. The picky will be able to find some minor visual quibbles in the 32 cartoons included on these discs, but the colors are bright and sharp, and the overall look is terrific. Also, the menus contain several Easter eggs. Click on the saxophone's hat to find "Farmyard Symphony." Contents: The Grasshopper and the Ants; The Tortoise and the Hare; The Flying Mouse; The Country Cousin; Wynken, Blynken and Nod; Three Little Pigs; Mother Goose Melodies; Babes In the Woods; Lullaby Land; The Golden Touch; The Robber Kitten; Elmer Elephant; The Wise Little Hen; Three Little Wolves; The Big Bad Wolf; Toby Tortoise Returns; The Skeleton Dance; Flowers and Trees; Music Land; The Ugly Duckling (1931 and 1939); The China Plate; Egyptian Melodies; The Cookie Carnival; Woodland Café; Birds of a Feather; The Busy Beavers; Just Dogs; Father Noah's Ark; Funny Little Bunnies; Peculiar Penguins; Mother Pluto; The Old Mill; Farmyard Symphonies. —*MM*
Movie: ♪♪♪ **DVD:** ♪♪♪♪
Buena Vista Home Ent. (cat #23091, UPC 786936158212). Full frame. Dolby Digital Mono. $32.99. Special packaging. *LANG:* English. *CAP:* English. *FEATURES:* "Song of the Silly Symphonies" featurette • "Silly Symphonies Souvenirs" featurette • Still gallery • Leonard Maltin intros.
2001 305m/C

Wanted: Dead or Alive

Nick Randall (Hauer), the great-grandson of the character played by Steve McQueen in his '50s TV series, is a modern-day bounty hunter who heads out to catch a terrorist (Simmons) who's setting off bombs in L.A. Gunplay and pyrotechnics are the point and they're presented with adequate sharpness on DVD. Image is excellent; the grainy night scenes have always looked that way. —*MM*
Movie: ♪♪ **DVD:** ♪♪♪
Anchor Bay (cat #DV11409, UPC 0131311-40996). Widescreen (1.85:1) anamorphic. Dolby Digital Stereo. $24.98. Keepcase. *LANG:* English. *CAP:* English. *FEATURES:* 26 chapters • Trailers.
1986 (R) 104m/C Rutger Hauer, Gene Simmons, Robert Guillaume, William Russ, Jerry Hardin, Mel Harris; *D:* Gary Sherman; *W:* Brian Taggert; *C:* Alex Nepomniaschy; *M:* Joe Renzetti.

War Gods of the Deep

Loopy comedy/adventure is a companion piece to *At the Earth's Core* and *People That Time Forgot*. Vincent Price plays the Capt. Nemo-esque ruler of an undersea kingdom. He sends his gill-men to kidnap beautiful Jill (Hart). Then it's up to her stalwart beau (Hunter) and his sidekick (Tomlinson) and his sidekick's chicken to get her back! Though the lighting tends to be heavily shadowed, image is sharp and virtually grain-free. DVD appears to have been made from well-preserved original elements. —*MM* **AKA:** City under the Sea.
Movie: ♪♪♪ **DVD:** ♪♪♪
MGM Home Ent. (cat #1002650, UPC 027616868497). Widescreen (2.35:1) anamorphic. Dolby Digital Mono. $14.98. Keepcase. *LANG:* English. *SUB:* French; Spanish. *CAP:* English. *FEATURES:* 16 chapters • Trailer.
1965 85m/C Tab Hunter, Vincent Price, Susan Hart, David Tomlinson; *D:* Jacques Tourneur; *W:* Charles Bennett, Louis M. Heyward; *C:* Stephen Dale; *M:* Stanley Black.

The War of the Roses [SE]

Acidic black comedy about a well-to-do suburban couple who can't agree on a property settlement during their divorce so they wage unreserved and ever-escalating combat on each other, using their palatial home as a battleground. Expertly and lovingly directed by DeVito, who plays the lawyer. Turner and Douglas are splendid. Adapted from the novel by Warren Adler. The video transfer represents colors extremely well. The film's visuals tend to a darker hue in some scenes, which leads to a loss of clarity in a few scenes, but the transfer is solid regardless. The soundtrack is also well done, featuring reasonably crisp and clear dialogue, though it could have benefited from a remastered 5.1 mix. While the sheer volume of extras on the disc is impressive, with assorted production materials, deleted scenes, promotional clip, etc., director DeVito's commentary track occasionally disappoints with long pauses (though it is informative when he does finally speak). —*MJT*
Movie: ♪♪♪ **DVD:** ♪♪♪
20th Century Fox (cat #2002339, UPC 024543023395). Widescreen (1.85:1) anamorphic. Dolby Digital Surround. $19.98. Keepcase. *LANG:* English; French. *SUB:* English; Spanish. *FEATURES:* 18 chapters • Commentary: director Danny DeVito • Deleted scenes • Computer sketches • Storyboards • Still galleries • Theatrical trailers and TV spots.
1989 (R) 116m/C Michael Douglas, Kathleen Turner, Danny DeVito, Marianne Saegebrecht, Sean Astin, G.D. Spradlin, Peter Donat, Heather Fairfield, Dan Castellaneta, Danitra Vance, Tony Crane; *D:* Danny DeVito; *W:* Michael Leeson; *C:* Stephen Burum; *M:* David Newman.

Warm Blooded Killers

When baseball card–collecting hitman John Portenza (Murray) whacks the nephew of a local crime boss for taking advantage of his sister (Zimmer), his profession and his reputation quickly unravel. He is immediately dispatched on assignment to snuff out the man believed responsible for the death of his boss's nephew. Portenza desperately tries to stay ahead of his suspecting boss to avoid becoming the mark for the crime he has committed. The film attempts vainly to step into the ring with other intelli-crime hits such as *Reservoir Dogs* and *Pulp Fiction*, but falls sadly short of its intended target. Most of the dialogue comes off as cliché or a cheap rip-off of an original, and the acting lacks depth of talent to support its intended style of delivery. The DVD sports a clear transfer with no noticeable artifacts. The colors are bright and the film sports a crisp image with no noticeable aliasing. The sound is fairly well done, but comes across a little muffled in certain scenes, possibly a side effect of its low-budget nature. —*EL*
Movie: ♪ **DVD:** ♪♪
Key East Ent. (cat #2004, UPC 69159720-0425). Widescreen letterboxed. Stereo. $14.95. Keepcase. *LANG:* English. *FEATURES:* 24 chapters.
2001 (R) 84m/C Mick Murray, Constance Zimmer, F. William Parker, Carmen Argenziano; *D:* Nicholas Siapkaris, Stephen Langford; *W:* Stephen Langford; *C:* Charles L. Barbee; *M:* Matthew Olivo.

The Wash

With the rent due and his car repossessed, Sean (Dr. Dre) struggles with his best friend and roommate Dee Loc (Snoop Dog) to come up with some fast cash. The solution: get jobs at the local car wash. Then Sean is made Dee Loc's supervisor and forced-comedy ensues. Sex, drugs, music, gangstas, etc., all make their way into the clichéd plot somehow and then it really gets funny. The disc has a solid video transfer, but nothing spectacular. Colors and darker hues are well represented. But while colors are bright and crisp, definition is lost in some darker-lit scenes. The musical score is the highlight of the soundtrack. It is full and really takes advantage of the format. Unfortunately, some dialogue tends to be muffled and a bit hard to discern. Yet it's a decent transfer overall. —*MJT*
Movie: ♪♪ ½ **DVD:** ♪♪ ½
Lion's Gate Home Ent. (cat #VM7964D, UPC 031398796428). Widescreen (1.85:1) anamorphic. Dolby Digital 5.1 Surround. $24.99. Keepcase. *LANG:* English. *SUB:* English; Spanish. *FEATURES:* 24 chapters • Premiere coverage • "Bad Intentions" music video • Cast and crew interviews • Theatrical trailer • Complete CD soundtrack.
2001 (R) 96m/C Snoop Dogg, Dr. Dre, DJ Pooh, George Wallace, Tommy (Tiny) Lister, Alex Thomas, Arif S. Kinchen, Demetrius Navarro, Thomas Chong, Pauly Shore, Lamont Bentley, Bruce Bruce, Shari Watson, Shawn Fonteno, Angell Conwell; *D:* DJ Pooh; *W:* DJ Pooh; *C:* Keith L. Smith.

The Wasp Woman [Elite]

Please see review for *Drive-in Discs, Vol. 2*.
Movie: 🎬 ½
1959 84m/B Susan Cabot, Anthony Eisley, Barboura Morris, Michael Marks, William Roerick, Frank Gerstle, Bruno VeSota, Frank Wolff, Lynn Cartwright, Roy Gordon; ***D:*** Roger Corman; ***W:*** Leo Gordon; ***C:*** Harry Neumann; ***M:*** Fred Katz.

The Watcher in the Woods

A misconceived Disney horror film made at a time when the studio was at its lowest ebb, this one is mostly a stack of problems—casting, story conception, special effects. It has the ring of studio interference, cowardice, and indecisiveness. The original tale is no winner, and the smart casting of Bette Davis and some good photography can't do enough to make things right. After a well-publicized disastrous preview, the ending was reworked at the last minute, and the scenes that were jettisoned have since become legendary. Now, thanks to Anchor Bay, we can finally see not just two but all three endings that were cobbled together in an effort to save the picture. The Curtis family rents a secluded country house from elderly Mrs. Aylwood (Bette Davis), who only agrees after perceiving the "sensitivity" of older daughter Jan (Lynn-Holly Johnson). Both she and her sister Ellie (Kyle Richards) are immediately bombarded with supernatural phenomena—reflections of a blindfolded girl in a mirror, glass that breaks in a triangular pattern, blue light that forms into circles—that Jan investigates, much to the consternation of her mother Helen (Carroll Baker). The mystery is directly connected to the disappearance 30 years before of Mrs. Aylwood's daughter Karen, under suspicious circumstances witnessed by neighbors Mary Fleming (Frances Cuka), Tom Colley (Richard Pasco), and John Keller (Ian Bannen): something is in the woods, something fearsome, and it's not Karen's ghost. Anchor Bay's DVD is laudable for its thoroughness. The film's confused birth was a cinematic mystery, and all the puzzle pieces are presented here for us to pick over. Director John Hough provides a commentary that repeatedly claims that the film works fine, right up to the ending, which he had nothing to do with—the IMDb suggests that the Disney journeyman Vincent McEveety directed the reshoots. I saw several moments in the woods, particularly one with mottled light filtering down through the trees, that did indeed conjure up a nice mood. But that, and the isolated pleasure of watching Bette Davis do her stuff, is about it. Seeing the two alternate endings (making three in all) is worth the price of the disc. They're an education in Film Doctoring 101. I've seen lots of films that have been completely worked over in post through reshoots (*The Whip Hand, The Night They Raided Minsky's*), or have had their endings blunted by tampering (Fritz Lang's *Fury* and *Cloak and Dagger*), but this one takes the cake. —GE
Movie: 🎬🎬 ***DVD:*** 🎬🎬🎬 ½
Anchor Bay (cat #DV10832, UPC 01313-1083293). Full frame. Dolby Digital 5.1 Surround; DTS Surround. $24.98. Keepcase. *LANG:* English. *CAP:* English. *FEATURES:* 23 chapters • Booklet • Commentary • Trailers • TV spot • John Hough thumbnail bio • Alternate endings.
1981 (PG) 83m/C Bette Davis, Carroll Baker, David McCallum, Ian Bannen, Lynn-Holly Johnson, Kyle Richards, Frances Cuka, Richard Pasco; ***D:*** John Hough; ***W:*** Brian Clemens; ***C:*** Alan Hume; ***M:*** Stanley Myers.

Water Damage

Curiously constructed mystery begins with the death of a child then attempts to become a convoluted thriller. Paul Pretty (Baldwin) goes to his high school reunion and discovers that only two other classmates have been invited. A few days later, a cop (Stockwell) tells him that they have been brutally murdered. The whole thing is more distasteful than it needs to be. Barebones (no menu) DVD image is no improvement over VHS tape. —MM
Movie: 🎬🎬 ***DVD:*** 🎬🎬
Studio Home Ent. (cat #VM#7848D, UPC 031398784821). Full frame. Stereo. $14.99. Keepcase. *LANG:* English.
2001 85m/C Daniel Baldwin, Leslie Hope, John Neville, Roberta Maxwell, Dean Stockwell; ***D:*** Murray Battle; ***W:*** Tony Johnston; ***C:*** Rene Ohashi.

Water Drops on Burning Rocks

Surprisingly charming sex comedy is adapted from an unproduced play by ultra-prolific German filmmaker R.W. Fassbinder. Sexual predator Leopold (Giraudeau) seduces Franz (Zidi) who abandons his fiancée Anna (Sagnier) for an unpredictable life with his demanding new lover. Anna pops in during Leopold's absence and seduces Franz back, but not for long. Leopold returns home just in time to initiate a ménage-a-trois with the transsexual Vera (Thomson), his ex, who can't live without him. Image and sound quality are excellent. Sing-a-long feature is cheesy, but effective. —LA ***AKA:*** Gouttes d'Eau sur Pierres Brulantes.
Movie: 🎬🎬 ½ ***DVD:*** 🎬🎬🎬
Zeitgeist Films (cat #Z1006, UPC 79597-5100632). Widescreen (1.66:1) letterboxed. Dolby 2.0 Sound. $29.98. Keepcase. *LANG:* French. *SUB:* English. *FEATURES:* Theatrical trailers • Sing-a-long lyrics • François Ozon bio • R.W. Fassbinder bio • Filmographies • 12 chapters.
1999 82m/C FR Bernard Giraudeau, Anna Thomson, Malik Zidi, Ludivine Sagnier; ***D:*** François Ozon; ***W:*** François Ozon; ***C:*** Jeanne Lapoirie.

Waterproof

Burt Reynolds is oddly cast but very effective as Eli, a Jewish shopkeeper who is shot by a young would-be robber, Thaniel (Cordereau Dye). To protect him from prosecution, Thaniel's mother, Tyree (April Grace), whisks her son and Eli to her childhood home in Waterproof, Louisiana. She's been away for 15 years and finds a great deal of tension with her family, but they are willing to take Tyree and Thaniel in to assist them. The film examines the struggles that exist between family members and individuals from differing ethnic backgrounds. Without becoming overwrought, the film delivers a positive message while being entertaining. Special kudos to Orlando Jones, who overcomes his comic reputation by portraying a man with severe brain damage. DVD offers the film in both a full-frame and widescreen format. The image is clear and sharp, showing little grain and no distortion. The colors are nice, with no oversaturation. The 2.0 Surround soundtrack gives clear dialogue, with no obvious hiss on the track. The extra features are standard fare, but they do give some insight into the making of the film. —ML
Movie: 🎬🎬🎬 ***DVD:*** 🎬🎬🎬
Cloud Ten Pictures (cat #503, UPC 74563-8005033). Widescreen (1.85:1) letterboxed; full frame. Dolby 2.0 Surround. $29.95. Keepcase. *LANG:* English. *FEATURES:* "Making of" featurette • Theatrical trailer • Deleted scenes • Filmmaker bios • Weblinks • 12 chapters.
1999 (PG-13) 94m/C Burt Reynolds, April Grace, Cordereau Dye, Whitman Mayo, Anthony Lee, Orlando Jones, Ja'net DuBois; ***D:*** Barry Berman.

Watership Down

Beautifully designed and animated feature makes no concessions whatsoever to the kiddie cartoon market. Its story of survival and bravery among rabbit warrens in the English countryside is less like Peter Rabbit and more like Mad Max. It's the harrowing tale of a few daring rabbits journeying in hope of finding a home of their own. Crowded and unhappy in their regimented warren, Hazel (voice of Hurt) leads a group of similarly disenchanted rabbits in search of a new home. Fiver (Briers) foresees dangers and finds them a perfect hilltop; but they are threatened by a nearby warren more dictatorial than the one they left. Needing mates, which only their enemies can provide, they prevail only through their wits and courage. Beginning with an interesting origin story for the whole rabbit race, the film builds a fascinating world of rabbits, who live in terror of predators, while oppressed by the patriarchal dictatorships of their underground warren communities. The rabbits here are by no means cute bunny characters—they're hard-bitten veterans and hopeful souls struggling against the legendary curse against their species. Prey for half the animals of creation, speed and cunning are their only defenses. The story seems to be about humanity's struggle for basic security, but what we see is too intricate on its own terms to become a simple allegory. There's a tendency to figure out an *Animal Farm*–like analog for the show, until the predicament of the hero rabbits sinks in and you realize that it's about nature and survival and life and death, as simple as that. An English production, the voices have the appropriate accents, but are always clear—you won't need the subtitles. DVD is a fine entertainment. The anamorphic-enhanced image captures all the beauty of the watercolor backgrounds and the fine points of the animation. The audio is forceful and sharp, with the music especially delicately rendered. The contents list some interesting extras, all of which turn out to be one or two-page text items. An inviting listing called "Watership Down Today," instead of being a documentary, is three lines of text telling us that the real location for the story is now the property of Andrew Lloyd Webber. Gee, thanks. —*GE*

Movie: 🎬🎬🎬 ½ **DVD:** 🎬🎬🎬 ½
Warner Home Video (UPC 0853937501-21). Full frame. $19.98. Snapper. *LANG:* English; French. *SUB:* English; French; Spanish; Portuguese. *CAP:* English. *FEATURES:* Text extras ▪ Trailer ▪ Liner notes.
1978 (PG) 92m/C *GB D:* Martin Rosen; *W:* Martin Rosen; *V:* Richard Briers, Ralph Richardson, Zero Mostel, John Hurt, Denholm Elliott, Harry Andrews, Michael Hordern, Joss Ackland.

Wayne's World

Aurora, Illinois, wannabe misfits Wayne Campbell (Myers) and Garth Algar (Carvey) run a ragtag cable access show from the Campbell family basement. Fueled solely with their own demented suburban-loser wit, the show is a local success until promoter Benjamin Oliver (Lowe) snags it as a marketing vehicle for a proprietor of arcade halls, Noah Vanderhoff (Doyle-Murray). Ben also tries to co-opt Mike's hot new girlfriend Cassandra (Carrere), a rock 'n' roller from Hong Kong. DVDs of this film and the sequel (please see review) are technically top-notch, with bright pictures and punchy audio. The audio commentaries are O.K., but not standouts. (Both films are available as a boxed set, cat. #15667, UPC 097361566740, for $50.) —*GE*

Movie: 🎬🎬🎬 ½ **DVD:** 🎬🎬🎬 ½
Paramount (cat #32706, UPC 0973632-70645). Widescreen (1.78:1) anamorphic. Dolby Digital 5.1 Surround Stereo; Dolby Digital Surround. $29.98. Keepcase. *LANG:* English; French. *SUB:* English. *CAP:* English. *FEATURES:* 23 chapters ▪ Commentary: Penelope Spheeris ▪ Cast and crew interviews.
1992 (PG-13) 93m/C Mike Myers, Dana Carvey, Rob Lowe, Tia Carrere, Brian Doyle-Murray, Lara Flynn Boyle, Kurt Fuller, Colleen Camp, Donna Dixon, Ed O'Neill, Alice Cooper, Meat Loaf Aday; *D:* Penelope Spheeris; *W:* Mike Myers, Bonnie Turner, Terry Turner; *C:* Theo van de Sande; *M:* J.

Peter Robinson. *AWARDS:* MTV Movie Awards '92: On-Screen Duo (Mike Myers/Dana Carvey).

Wayne's World 2

A year later in their saga, Wayne and Garth (Myers and Carvey) are now living in loft space instead of at home with their parents, but their cable show is still a local anomaly, and Wayne's girlfriend Cassandra (Carrere) is now being courted by an even shadier promoter, Bobby (Walken). Wayne is contacted in his dreams by Jim Morrison (Nickles), who tells him to promote a big rock festival in Aurora, with huge name acts like Aerosmith. Following Morrison's cryptic instructions, Wayne and Garth take a trip to England to collect legendary roadie Del Preston (Brown), who also has been receiving telepathic messages from the late lead singer of the Doors. They hold a fund raiser at a Communist-themed nightclub, but all looks grim as Wayne alienates both Cassandra and Garth—who's seduced by hot-chick Honey Horneé (Basinger) to kill her husband—and is afraid nobody will buy a ticket to their self-styled "WayneStock." Visually, the DVD is equal to the first. I sampled Stephen Surjik's commentary track in half a dozen places, and everything he had to say was pretty predictable, like "Mike really wanted the Kung-Fu parody," or "Chuck Heston was a nice guy." The best gag on the disc is the clever menu setup, which mimics a cable channel guide. —*GE*

Movie: 🎬🎬🎬 **DVD:** 🎬🎬🎬
Paramount (cat #32845, UPC 097363-284543). Widescreen (1.78:1) anamorphic. Dolby Digital 5.1 Surround Stereo; Dolby Digital Surround. $29.98. Keepcase. *LANG:* English; French. *SUB:* English. *CAP:* English. *FEATURES:* 21 chapters ▪ Commentary: Stephen Surjik ▪ Cast and crew interviews.
1993 (PG-13) 94m/C Mike Myers, Dana Carvey, Tia Carrere, Christopher Walken, Ralph Brown, Kim Basinger, James Hong, Chris Farley, Ed O'Neill, Olivia D'Abo, Kevin Pollak, Drew Barrymore, Charlton Heston, Rip Taylor, Bob Odenkirk, Michael A. (M.A.) Nickles; *D:* Stephen Surjik; *W:* Bonnie Turner, Terry Turner, Mike Myers; *C:* Francis Kenny; *M:* Carter Burwell. *AWARDS: NOM:* MTV Movie Awards '94: On-Screen Duo (Mike Myers/Dana Carvey), Kiss (Dana Carvey/Kim Basinger).

We Dive at Dawn

Interesting, tense British submarine drama follows the *Sea Tiger* as it attempts to sink the German battleship *Brandenburg* off Denmark. A solid cast is led by Mills, who prepared for the role by riding in a submarine and turning "a pale shade of pea-green" when it crash-dived. Title is available on the *Great WWII Movies* disc. Image quality in BFS's *Great* and *Classic* series tends to be poor. This one's an exception. It's not great, but the film looks pretty good and lacks the surface flaws

that plague so many older releases. Sound is O.K., too. —*MM*

Movie: 🎬🎬🎬 **DVD:** 🎬🎬
BFS Video (cat #30294-D, UPC 06680-5302947). Full frame. $9.98. Keepcase. *LANG:* English. *FEATURES:* 6 chapters ▪ Talent files.
1943 98m/B *GB* Eric Portman, John Mills; *D:* Anthony Asquith; *W:* Val Valentine; *C:* Jack Cox.

We Take New Guinea

Dull compilation of four World War II newsreels/short documentaries focused on the battles for islands in the Pacific. "We Take New Guinea" is the longest, running 39 minutes and encompasses the battle for the Admiralty Islands. It is narrated in detached but typically racist propaganda tones of the period by Ronald Reagan. "The Pacific War" runs 15 minutes and briefly covers the Pacific battles leading up to and after the attack on Pearl Harbor. It is the only color film in the batch and is mostly composed of still photos and narration. "Battles of Tarawa & Makin" (11 minutes) and "Fury in the Pacific" (20 minutes) offer their takes on further island battles. While an important document historically, these mini-documents are deadly dull and drained of drama. Endless maps and diagrams are presented and vague history is reported. Although there's some impressive combat footage on display, the dreary tone robs the images of most of their tragic, heroic, and disturbing power. "The Pacific War" is fairly clean and acceptable but the rest of the films look absolutely atrocious. They're all grainy, muddy, soft prints transferred with a never-ending stream of digital noise. The opening and end titles are missing or incomplete on all of the films, necessitating video burned in titles. The audio is poor, particularly on "Fury in the Pacific," which sounds as if the audio was transferred from a drive-in speaker. —*DG*

Movie: 🎬 ½ **DVD:** 🎬
Goodtimes Ent. (cat #05-811233, UPC 018713812339). Full frame. Mono. $7.49. Keepcase. *LANG:* English.
19?? 86m/C Nar: Ronald Reagan.

Weather Report Girl

Animated version of the popular Japanese character begins with her debut on TV. Keiko is an ambitious young woman who fills in for the normal weather forecaster and causes a sensation by raising her skirt. From there, her attempts to gain attention become more explicit. Compared to the excesses of some "adult" anime, this one's fairly tame. There's nothing really innovative about the juvenile writing or the animation. It's bright, overexposed with lots of aliasing and flashing within patterns. DVD image and sound are no improvement over VHS. —*MM*

Movie: 🎬🎬 **DVD:** 🎬 ½
Central Park/U.S. Manga (UPC 74261769-5322). Full frame. $24.98. Keepcase.

LANG: Japanese; English. SUB: English. FEATURES: 8 chapters. **2001 90m/C** *JP D:* Kunihiko Yuyama.

The Wedding Planner

Mary Fiore (Lopez) is a workaholic wedding planner in San Francisco who has no love life of her own. The driven Mary meets cute aw-shucks doctor Steve Edison (McConaughey) who, naturally, turns out to be the fiancé of her client, heiress Fran (Wilson). The transfer has a high level of detail but edge-enhancement is quite noticeable in a number of scenes. Colors are very faithful and create a natural-looking picture throughout that exhibits strong colors and natural look skin tones. Blacks are deep and solid and shadows always maintain good level of detail without breaking up. The compression has been done without flaws, maintaining the high definition of the transfer. The audio is well produced and has a very wide and natural sounding frequency response. The dynamic range is good, although the film itself doesn't lend itself to overly aggressive dynamic use of the Surround tracks. — *MM/GH*
Movie: ♫♫ ½ **DVD:** ♫♫ ½
Columbia Tristar (cat #06157, UPC 04339-6061576). Widescreen (2.35:1) anamorphic. Dolby Digital 5.1 Surround Stereo; Dolby Digital Surround. $24.99. Keepcase. LANG: English. SUB: English; French; Spanish. FEATURES: Commentary: director Adam Shankman ▪ Deleted scenes ▪ "Making of" featurette ▪ Trailers. **2001 (PG-13) 105m/C** Jennifer Lopez, Matthew McConaughey, Bridgette Wilson, Justin Chambers, Alex Rocco, Judy Greer, Kevin Pollak, Joanna Gleason, Charles Kimbrough, Fred Willard, Kathy Najimy; *D:* Adam Shankman; *W:* Michael Ellis, Pamela Falk; *C:* Julio Macat; *M:* Mervyn Warren.

Welcome to Death Row

Unlike most documentaries about rap music, this one aspires to an audience that is not already familiar with the material. Miraculously, it succeeds. The focus is "Shug" Knight's Death Row Records and the violence that is such an important part of the business. Most of the major stars are interviewed, and the film tells its story without narration. DVD is also remarkably polished compared to many others. Some concert footage is little better than home-video quality but the interviews look and sound very good. In short, the filmmakers tell a good interesting story about American ambition. On their commentary track director Savidge and producers Scheftel and Housden's enthusiasm for their work comes through clearly. Recommended to anyone with even a passing interest in rap. —*MM*
Movie: ♫♫♫ **DVD:** ♫♫♫
Xenon Ent. (cat #XE XX 4094DVD, UPC 000799409428). Widescreen (1.85:1) anamorphic. $24.98. Keepcase. LANG:

English. FEATURES: Trailers ▪ Extra interviews and outtakes ▪ 18 chapters ▪ Commentary. **2000 104m/C** *D:* Leigh Savidge; *M:* Tommy Coster.

The Well

Promising but ultimately disappointing tale of spinster Hester (Rabe) who develops an obsession with the young girl, Katherine (Otto), she has brought home from a shelter to do housework at her isolated farm where she lives with her father. Katherine's resentment at her situation is kept tightly under wraps but when the father dies, Hester sells the farm in an ever-increasing attempt to keep Katherine's attention by giving her everything she wants, and to allow herself some much missed fun in life. As time goes by you begin to wonder who is using whom; then a moment of crisis on a dark highway forces the hand of both women and the ending, while not surprising, is a good theatre. The film takes its time developing and only picks up speed in the last 20 minutes. Beautifully shot and filtered with cold blue lenses, the disc looks great with beautiful open shots of vast landscapes. The sound is good but not great. The accents can be hard to decipher, but not so distracting it hurts the enjoyment of the film. —*CA*
Movie: ♫ ½ **DVD:** ♫♫♫
Fox/Lorber (cat #FLV5293, UPC 7209175-29325). Full frame. Stereo. $24.90. Keepcase. LANG: English. FEATURES: 16 chapters ▪ Filmographies ▪ Trailer. **1997 101m/C** *AU* Pamela Rabe, Miranda Otto, Paul Chubb; *D:* Samantha Lang; *W:* Laura Jones; *C:* Mandy Walker; *M:* Stephen Rae. AWARDS: Australian Film Inst. '97: Actress (Rabe), Adapt. Screenplay, Art Dir./Set Dec; NOM: Australian Film Inst. '97: Actress (Otto), Cinematog., Costume Des., Director (Lang), Film, Film Editing, Sound, Score.

Werewolf of London

English botanist Wilfred Glendon (Hull) finds the rare flowering plant he seeks in Tibet, but not before he is bitten by a feral monster-man. Back at his greenhouse lab outside London, he wows his guests with exotic (and utterly fantastic) plant specimens, but is having trouble getting new blooms to form from his imported Tibetan buds, which legend has it only open under the rays of the full moon. Already neglected, his wife Lisa (Hobson) becomes further estranged when Wilfred acts oddly, even more reclusive than normal. A doctor Yogami (Oland) has appeared to tell him that the flowers are the only antidote for "WereWolfry," and that he'll be "transvected" every night of the full moon to seek a murder victim. The title is available on a double feature with *She-Wolf of London* (please see review). Both appear to be newer remasters than the VHS versions, and are stunning. —*GE*
Movie: ♫♫♫ ½ **DVD:** ♫♫♫ ½

Universal Studios (cat #21410, UPC 025192141027). Full frame. Dolby Digital Mono. $24.98. Keepcase. LANG: English; French; Spanish. SUB: Spanish; French. CAP: English. FEATURES: Trailer ▪ Production notes.
1935 75m/B Henry Hull, Warner Oland, Valerie Hobson, Lester Matthews, Spring Byington, Lawrence Grant, Zeffie Tilbury; *D:* Stuart Walker; *W:* Robert Harris, John Colton; *C:* Charles Stumar.

West of the Divide

Please see review for *John Wayne: Western Classics.*
Movie: ♫♫ ½
1933 53m/B John Wayne, George "Gabby" Hayes, Lloyd Whitlock, Yakima Canutt; *D:* Robert North Bradbury; *W:* Robert North Bradbury; *C:* Archie Stout.

Wet Hot American Summer

Part of the reason for this comedy's lack of theatrical success can be traced to a title that sounds like it belongs on a cheap skin flick. Instead, it's a summer camp comedy with Janeane Garofalo largely wasted as a counselor. It's the last day at Camp Firewood in 1981. Romances must be wrapped up and there's the talent show that night if a piece of Skylab doesn't land on the camp first. Most of the jokes were done with more spirit and humor in *Meatballs*, but the cast gives it their best shot. Everyone involved on the commentary track admits that this was a very low-budget production and so there's little to recommend the DVD image. It's good enough but nothing special. Among the plentiful extras is a soundtrack with extra farts, and that pretty much tells you all you need to know about the disc and the movie. —*MM*
Movie: ♫♫ **DVD:** ♫♫ ½
USA Home Ent. (cat #96306 0314-2). Widescreen (1.85:1) letterboxed. Dolby Digital Stereo. $26.98. Keepcase. LANG: English. FEATURES: 12 chapters ▪ Commentary ▪ Trailer ▪ Behind-the-scenes featurette ▪ Deleted scenes with optional commentary ▪ Talent files ▪ Soundtrack with extra farts ▪ Production stills. **2001 (R) 97m/C** Janeane Garofalo, David Hyde Pierce, Michael Showalter, Marguerite Moreau, Paul Rudd, Zak Orth, Christopher Meloni, A.D. Miles, Molly Shannon, Ken Marino, Michael Ian Black, Marisa Ryan, Bradley Cooper; *D:* David Wain; *W:* Michael Showalter, David Wain; *C:* Ben Weinstein; *M:* Theodore Shapiro, Craig (Shudder to Think) Wedren.

What Your Eyes Don't See

A high-powered magazine editor is murdered, and a temp writer's new boyfriend, the magazine's attorney, is charged. Of course, we wouldn't have a movie if she didn't set out to prove his innocence. Picture quality is full of grain and often lacks

detail. The soundtrack is full of excess background hiss. The disc features two trailers, which are in Spanish without subtitles. —BG **AKA:** Ojos Que No Ven.
Movie: 🎵½ **DVD:** 🎵🎵
Vanguard Intl. Cinema (cat #VF0240, UPC 658769024036). Full frame. $29.95. Keepcase. *LANG:* Spanish. *SUB:* English. *FEATURES:* 12 chapters • Trailers.
1999 90m/C *AR* Mauricio Dayub, Luis Luque, Malena Solda, Gaston Pauls, Alejandra Flechner; **D:** Beda Docampo Feijoo; **W:** Beda Docampo Feijoo, Enrique Cortes; **C:** Ricardo Rodriguez; **M:** Ivan Wyszogrod.

What's Eating Gilbert Grape

Depp stars as Gilbert Grape, the titular head of a very dysfunctional family living in a big house in a small Iowa town. His Momma (Cates) weighs more than 500 pounds and hasn't left the house in seven years; he has two squabbling teenage sisters, and 17-year-old brother Arnie (DiCaprio) is mentally retarded and requires constant supervision. What's a goodhearted grocery clerk to do? Well, when free-spirited Becky (Lewis) is momentarily marooned in town, Gilbert may have found a true soulmate. Performances, especially DiCaprio's, save this from the oddball/cute factor although the flick would have benefited from streamlining, particularly the scenes involving Depp and bad-haircut Lewis. Based on the novel by Hedges. The disc boasts an excellent video transfer; colors are crisp and vibrant while blacks are sharp and solid throughout. A similarly impressive soundtrack features clear dialogue and a well-reproduced musical score. —MJT **AKA:** Gilbert Grape.
Movie: 🎵🎵🎵 **DVD:** 🎵🎵½
Paramount (cat #32955, UPC 097363295-549). Widescreen (1.85:1) anamorphic. Dolby Digital 5.1 Surround; Dolby Digital Surround. $24.99. Keepcase. *LANG:* English. *SUB:* English. *FEATURES:* 17 chapters • Theatrical trailer.
1993 (PG-13) 118m/C Johnny Depp, Leonardo DiCaprio, Juliette Lewis, Mary Steenburgen, Darlene Cates, Laura Harrington, Mary Kate Schellhardt, Kevin Tighe, John C. Reilly, Crispin Glover, Penelope Branning; **D:** Lasse Hallstrom; **W:** Peter Hedges; **C:** Sven Nykvist; **M:** Alan Parker, Bjorn Isfalt. *AWARDS:* Natl. Bd. of Review '93: Support. Actor (DiCaprio); *NOM:* Oscars '93: Support. Actor (DiCaprio); Golden Globes '94: Support. Actor (DiCaprio).

What's the Worst That Could Happen? [SE]

Max (DeVito), a billionaire trying to stave off bankruptcy, crosses paths with the wrong thief when Kevin (Lawrence) is caught breaking into his mansion. Max turns the tables on Kevin, which sets off a maelstrom of revenge and other antics. Lawrence and DeVito have their moments,

but the quirky supporting cast is what keeps the comedy rolling. Fichtner, as a gender-ambiguous detective, and Miller, as Max's head of security, really steal the show. Picture is fine, though it runs into a horde of shimmering skyscrapers and venetian blinds. The audio track is merely serviceable, without much use made of the rear speakers. Plenty of extras are thrown on, with both wide- and full-frame versions, two commentary tracks, trailers, outtakes, featurettes, etc. —BG
Movie: 🎵🎵½ **DVD:** 🎵🎵🎵
MGM Home Ent. (cat #1002563, UPC 027-6168676443). Widescreen (1.85:1) anamorphic; full frame. Dolby 5.1. $26.98. Keepcase. *LANG:* English; French; Spanish. *SUB:* English; French; Spanish. *FEATURES:* 32 chapters • Deleted/alternate scenes • Outtakes • Behind-the-scenes featurette • Commentary: director, producer • Commentary: cast members • Music video: "Music," by Erick Sermon • Trailers.
2001 (PG-13) 95m/C Martin Lawrence, Danny DeVito, Nora Dunn, William Fichtner, Glenne Headly, John Leguizamo, Bernie Mac, Carmen Ejogo, Larry Miller, Richard Schiff, Ana Gasteyer, Sascha Knopf, Siobhan Fallon, Lenny Clarke, Michael Mulheren, Cam Neely, Dana Wheeler-Nicholson; **D:** Sam Weisman; **W:** Matthew Chapman; **C:** Anastas Michos; **M:** Tyler Bates.

Wheels on Meals

A private eye (Hung) and a street food merchant (Chan) try to find an heiress (Forner) who has been kidnapped. The two main stars are at their youthful best here. DVD delivers an acceptable widescreen image which, like so many Asian imports, is on the soft side. Sound is acceptable. —MM **AKA:** Meals on Wheels; Million Dollar Heiress.
Movie: 🎵🎵½ **DVD:** 🎵🎵½
Tai Seng (cat #56344). Widescreen letterboxed. Dolby Digital Surround. $29.95. Keepcase. *LANG:* Mandarin; Cantonese. *SUB:* Traditional Chinese; simplified Chinese; English; Japanese; Bahasa (Indonesia); Bahasa (Malaysian); Thai; Korean; Vietnamese. *FEATURES:* 8 chapters • Talent files • Trailer.
1984 100m/C *HK* Jackie Chan, Yuen Biao, Lola Forner, Sammo Hung, Herb Edelman, Richard Ng; **D:** Sammo Hung; **W:** Edward Tong.

When a Stranger Calls

Archetypal babysitter/horror begins with Carol Kane being threatened by the caller who's in the house and then takes some very interesting plot turns and a solid sense of place. On DVD, the age of the movie is immediately evident, as the film stock is very grainy and muted, and blemishes in the print are abundant. Overall, the image has a very dark look with dark, muted colors and soft edges, all of which is part of the movie's original art direction. Colors are mostly stable, but occasional color shifts are visible. Some slight edge-

enhancement is visible in the transfer and occasionally pixelation artifacts are present despite the fact that a fairly good bitrate was used for the video stream. Sibilance is audible on rare occasions, but for the most part, the audio presentation is sufficient. —MM/GH
Movie: 🎵🎵🎵 **DVD:** 🎵🎵🎵
Columbia Tristar (cat #06551, UPC 043-396065512). Widescreen (1.85:1) anamorphic; full frame. Dolby Digital Mono. $19.95. Keepcase. *LANG:* English; French. *SUB:* English; French; Spanish. *FEATURES:* Trailers.
1979 (R) 97m/C Carol Kane, Charles Durning, Colleen Dewhurst, Rachel Roberts, Rutanya Alda, Carmen Argenziano, Kirsten Larkin, Ron O'Neal, Tony Beckley; **D:** Fred Walton; **W:** Fred Walton, Steve Feke; **C:** Don Peterman.

When Good Ghouls Go Bad

This made-for-TV Halloween special is surprisingly good, that is until the second half, when things begin to fall apart (literally). Twelve-year-old Danny Walker (Joe Pichler) moves from Chicago to his father's hometown of Walker Falls, Minnesota. There, they live with his grandfather, who is known to everyone as Uncle Fred (Christopher Lloyd). The Walker's once ran a successful chocolate factory, until a mysterious curse caused the town of Walker Falls to stop celebrating Halloween, thus closing the candy factory. But Danny's dad has a plan to bring back Halloween and re-open the factory. Things go awry when Uncle Fred is killed; however, death isn't going to stop this spry fellow, as he returns from the grave to help Danny battle the supernatural forces which have invaded Walker Falls. *When Good Ghouls Go Bad* is based on a story by *Goosebumps* creator R.L. Stine and should appeal to his legions of fans. The first half of the film is very good and surprisingly dark-natured, as we learn about the superstitions surrounding Halloween in Walker Falls and observe the reactions of the townspeople to the attempt to resurrect the holiday. However, the final act becomes very convoluted and silly, thus hurting the film overall. Appropriate for adolescents familiar with the *Goosebumps* books, but is definitely too scary for the little ones. Fox has given this film the same DVD treatment which it lavishes upon its big-budget titles. The image here is pristine. The picture is razor sharp and has amazing clarity, showing no grain, even in the brightest shots. The colors are fantastic, as the rich greens and reds mix with the traditional Halloween hues. The Dolby Digital 5.1 Surround sound is equally impressive, as there are continuous rear speaker effects throughout the movie, and a nice bass response as well. —ML
Movie: 🎵🎵🎵 **DVD:** 🎵🎵🎵
Fox/Lorber (cat #2002165, UPC 024543-021650). Widescreen (1.78:1) anamorphic. Dolby Digital 5.1; Dolby 2.0 Surround. $19.98. Keepcase. *LANG:* English. *SUB:*

English; Spanish. *CAP:* English. *FEATURES:* Featurette • 12 chapters.
2001 93m/C Christopher Lloyd, Tom Amandes, Joe Pichler; *D:* Patrick Read Johnson; *W:* Patrick Read Johnson; *C:* Brian J. Breheny; *M:* Christopher Gordon.

When Justice Fails
Fairly standard video-premiere cop flick has a few interesting twists. First, police detective Chaney (Fahey) discovers that his new partner Lambeau (Malotte) is gay. Then Chaney becomes involved with a lawyer (Matlin), who may be a suspect in a series of killings. DVD image is no improvement over VHS tape. Surround is used mostly for music. The menu on this rental disc malfunctioned. Some unreadable text was crowded off the bottom of the screen. —*MM*
Movie: 🎵🎵 ½ *DVD:* 🎵 ½
Sunland Studios (cat #3362). Full frame. Dolby Digital Surround Stereo. $24.95. Keepcase. *LANG:* English. *FEATURES:* 6 chapters.
1998 (R) 90m/C Jeff Fahey, Marlee Matlin, Monique Mercure, Carl Marotte; *D:* Allan Goldstein; *W:* Tony Kayden; *C:* Barry Gravelle.

When the Sky Falls
Loose biography of martyred Irish journalist Veronica Gerin laments the state of Ireland's justice system and the hardships a journalist must suffer to tell the truth. Sinead Hamilton (Allen) expertly reports on gangs and drugs in Dublin's streets. As she digs deeper, she receives increasingly dire threats that only make her more determined. This diligence, however, causes her undoing. Unfortunately, while gritty and well acted, it's not very compelling. The rough image is purposeful. Surround sound is crisp and clear in all channels. The featurette helps give some historical significance to the story. —*DRL*
Movie: 🎵🎵 ½ *DVD:* 🎵🎵🎵
Lion's Gate Home Ent. (cat #7688, UPC 031398768821). Widescreen (1.78:1) anamorphic. Dolby 5.1 Surround. $24.99. Keepcase. *LANG:* English. *SUB:* English; French; Spanish. *CAP:* English. *FEATURES:* Commentary: director • Featurette • Trailer • 24 chapters.
1999 107m/C *IR* Joan Allen, Patrick Bergin, Liam Cunningham, Gerard Flynn, Kevin McNally, Jimmy Smallhorne, Jason Barry, Pete Postlethwaite, Des McAleer, Ruaidhri Conroy; *D:* John MacKenzie; *W:* Michael J. Sheridan, Ronan Gallagher, Colum McCann; *C:* Seamus Deasy; *M:* Pol Brennan.

When Trumpets Fade
John Irvin's fine war film is essentially a remake of Don Siegel's *Hell Is for Heroes*. They tell virtually identical stories set in the autumn of 1944 on the Siegfried Line. More importantly, both are made with the same tough, pared down, laconic style. In many ways, Irvin's film is the more success-

ful because it begins on a strong note and never really lessens the tension. A bizarre opening scene introduces Manning (Eldard), the only survivor of his platoon to make it back from a patrol. The situation is tense, with the Allied forces stretched thin against Germans who are now defending their own country. Capt. Pritchett (Donovan) immediately gives Manning a battlefield promotion to sergeant. He doesn't want it and tries to explain, "in the woods...I've done things." But Pritchett doesn't have time. He gives Manning command of a group of untried replacements and sends them out to the snowy front. The rest is as brutal and moving as the strongest moments of *Saving Private Ryan* but without the large-scale action sequences. This one works on a more personal level. Production values are first-rate. Irvin uses a muted palette, creating a color scheme that recalls the black and white of the best 1950s war films. The widescreen image is a solid step up from broadcast quality (the film was made for HBO) with a fine combination of clarity and graininess. Highest recommendations. —*MM*
Movie: 🎵🎵🎵🎵 *DVD:* 🎵🎵🎵🎵
HBO Home Video (UPC 026359148026). Widescreen (1.85:1) letterboxed. $14.98. Snapper. *LANG:* English; Spanish. *SUB:* English; French; Spanish. *CAP:* English. *FEATURES:* 14 chapters • Talent files.
1998 (R) 93m/C Ron Eldard, Zak Orth, Frank Whaley, Dylan Bruno, Martin Donovan, Timothy Olyphant, Dan Futterman, Dwight Yoakam, Devon Gummersall, Jeffrey Donovan; *D:* John Irvin; *W:* W.W. Vought; *C:* Thomas Burstyn; *M:* Geoffrey Burgon.

When Worlds Collide
Early SF tale exhibits the clunky plotting and bad dialogue familiar to fans of the genre, but it's also an instructive snapshot of the '40s/'50s apocalyptic mindset. The Oscar-winning special effects—particularly the flooding—are really not that much different from today's CGI. The matte paintings do look dated. DVD was made from well preserved original elements. The bright colors still are sharply defined. The heavy grain in some shots has always been there. Mono sound isn't bad either. —*MM*
Movie: 🎵🎵 ½ *DVD:* 🎵🎵🎵
Paramount (cat #05106, UPC 097360-510645). Full frame. Dolby Digital Mono. $26.99. Keepcase. *LANG:* English; French. *SUB:* English. *CAP:* English. *FEATURES:* 11 chapters • Trailer.
1951 (G) 81m/C Richard Derr, Barbara Rush, Larry Keating, Peter Hanson; *D:* Rudolph Mate; *W:* Sydney Boehm; *C:* William Howard Greene; *M:* Leith Stevens. *AWARDS: NOM:* Oscars '51: Color Cinematog.

Where a Good Man Goes
Johnny To (*Heroic Trio*) delivers a change of pace with a fine romantic melodrama.

Gangster Lau Ching-Wan has just got out of prison, and is touched by the patience and kindness of widowed innkeeper Ruby Wong and her son. Though his efforts are a bit raw for her, the lonely widow finds herself warming to Michael as well. But crooked cop Lam Suet seems obsessed with putting him back in jail. The film shows both the soft and hard parts of gangster life, but painted in To's earth-tones and foggy blue colors. The excellent soundtrack by Cacine Wong creates a pleasant mood, and dominates many scenes. —*BT* **AKA:** Joi Gin A Long; Zai Jian A Lang.
Movie: 🎵🎵🎵 *DVD:* 🎵🎵 ½
Tai Seng (cat #DVD-243, UPC 489039110-2430). Widescreen letterboxed. $19.95. Pretty blue keepcase. *LANG:* Cantonese; Mandarin. *SUB:* Chinese; English. *FEATURES:* 9 chapters • Trailer for *Gigolo of Chinese Hollywood*.
1999 98m/C *HK* Ching-Wan Lau, Ruby Wong, Wayne Lai, Suet Lam, Raymond Wong; *D:* Johnny To; *W:* Nai-Hoi Yau; *C:* Siu Keung Cheng; *M:* Cacine Wong.

Where Angels Dance
Ultra–low budget drama can boast some of the slowest and most poorly staged scenes of physical action ever put on film. Auteur Coppola is Alex Blake, an ex-boxer who hangs out in the seediest parts of the seedy side of town and finally finds redemption. Not surprisingly, the image gains nothing on this bare-bones disc. It's identical to VHS tape. —*MM*
Movie: 🎵 ½ *DVD:* 🎵 ½
Brentwood (cat #44190-9, UPC 78736441-9098). Full frame. Dolby Digital Stereo. $14.98. Keepcase. *LANG:* English. *FEATURES:* 7 chapters.
2001 135m/C Patrick Coppola, Lauren Martin, John Fiore, Ayo Haynes, Andrew Scudiero; *D:* Patrick Coppola; *W:* Patrick Coppola; *C:* John Rosnell; *M:* Woody Giessmann.

Where the Red Fern Grows
A young boy in Dust Bowl–era Oklahoma learns maturity from his love and responsibility for two Redbone hounds. Family fare is well produced but a little hokey. Followed by a sequel nearly 20 years later. DVD is no improvement over tape. Soundtrack is very scratchy. Image is marred by heavy grain, light surface damage, and registration instability. —*MM*
Movie: 🎵🎵 ½ *DVD:* 🎵 ½
United American Video (cat #40083). Full frame. Dolby Digital Surround Stereo. $14.99. Snapper. *LANG:* English. *FEATURES:* 9 chapters • Trailers.
1974 (G) 97m/C James Whitmore, Beverly Garland, Jack Ging, Lonny (Loni) Chapman, Stewart Peterson; *D:* Norman Tokar; *W:* Douglas Day Stewart, Eleanor Lamb; *C:* Dean Cundey; *M:* Lex de Azevedo.

Where the Red Fern Grows: Part 2

Sequel to the popular family movie stars Brimley as Grandpa Coleman. It's a coming-of-age story set deep in the Louisiana woods. DVD appears to have been copied from a VHS tape. It's noticeably less detailed than conventional broadcast television. —*MM*

Movie: 🎵🎵 ½ **DVD:** 🎵
United American Video (cat #40093). Full frame. Dolby Digital Surround Stereo. $14.99. Keepcase. *LANG:* English. *FEATURES:* 9 chapters • Trailers • Title is also available from Universal (cat. # 40093) for $19.99.
1992 (G) 105m/C Wilford Brimley, Doug McKeon, Lisa Whelchel, Chad McQueen; *D:* Jim McCullough; *W:* Samuel Bradford; *C:* Joseph M. Wilcots; *M:* Robert Sprayberry.

Whispers: An Elephant's Tale

Odd anthropomorphic film made up entirely of nature footage is similar in some respects to *The Adventures of Milo & Otis*. As with that film, here we have animals photographed in the wilds of Africa, with various actors supplying voices for the animals. The film opens with the birth of Whispers (voiced by Debi Derryberry), an elephant. While his herd is roaming, he gets lost and can't find his mother Gentle Heart (voiced by Anne Archer). Wandering through the bush, he meets another elephant named Groove (voiced by Angela Bassett). Groove isn't very fond of Whispers at first, but she ultimately decides to help him find his mom. Along the way, they meet a variety of interesting animals and encounter some evil poachers. *Whispers* is an entertaining film, but it also feels very artificial. Clearly, the filmmakers waded through tons of footage to piece this story together and then added the human voices. The end result is a film with some amazing photography, but a story which comes across as hollow. And, that amazing photography looks very nice on this DVD. The image is clear and fairly sharp, showing only a dense grain. This last point is especially impressive, given the fact that the film takes place in the bright, African sun. The colors are true, and there is no distortion to the image. The audio track brings clear dialogue and a nice reproduction of the score, but not much in the way of Surround sound. Oddly, the DVD box claims that "This film has been modified from its original version. It has been formatted to fit your screen." Yet the film is definitely letterboxed. —*ML*

Movie: 🎵🎵 ½ **DVD:** 🎵🎵 ½
Buena Vista Home Ent. (cat #23406, UPC 786936160789). Widescreen (1.85:1) letterboxed. Dolby Surround. $29.99. Keepcase. *LANG:* English. *SUB:* English. *CAP:* English. *FEATURES:* Animated shorts • 14 chapters.
2000 (G) 72m/C D: Derek Joubert; *W:* Derek Joubert, Jordan Moffet, Holly Goldberg Sloan; *C:* Derek Joubert; *M:* Trevor

Rabin; *V:* Debi Derryberry, Anne Archer, Angela Bassett, Joanna Lumley, Kevin M. Richardson, Alice Ghostley, Betty White, Kathryn Cressida, Joan Rivers.

White Badge

In 1979, reporter Han (Sung Ki Ahn) is ordered to write about his service in Vietnam. (The Korean Army sent troops there to serve with the Americans.) The assignment along with a telephone call from one of his men, brings on a series of flashbacks where Sgt. Han remembers what happened during the war. DVD colors tend to be on the dark, harsh side and some night scenes are almost impossible to make out. That appears to come from the original elements, which have been well preserved, and the rough look is certainly appropriate to the story. Sound is muffled and some of the dialogue is difficult to hear, though that will be important only to speakers of Korean. Clear subtitles are burned in. —*MM*

Movie: 🎵🎵🎵 **DVD:** 🎵🎵 ½
Vanguard Intl. Cinema (cat #VF152). Widescreen letterboxed. $29.98. Keepcase. *LANG:* Korean. *SUB:* English. *FEATURES:* 15 chapters.
1997 122m/C *KN* Sung-Ki Ahn, Kyung-Young Lee, Hae-Jin Shim, Junho Huh, Sejun Kim, Yongjae Tokko; *D:* Ji-Yong Chung; *W:* Ji-Yong Chung.

White Fang to the Rescue

Live-action adventure film contains a few too many rough elements (dog fights) to recommend it to very young audiences. The atrocious DVD image quality precludes any recommendation to older viewers. Canadian locations may be excellent. Who knows? The poor sound distorts the score painfully. —*MM*

Movie: 🎵 ½ **DVD:** 🎵
BCI-Eclipse (cat #44097-9, UPC 787364-409792). Full frame. Dolby Digital Stereo. $14.99. Keepcase. *LANG:* English. *FEATURES:* "Came the Brawn" Little Rascals short film • Trivia game • DVD Dictionary • DVD-ROM features • 6 chapters.
1974 100m/C *IP* Henry Silva, Maurizio Merli, Gisela Hahn, Renzo Palmer, Matteo Zoffoli; *D:* Tonino Ricci; *W:* Alessandro Continenza, Giovanni Bergamini; *M:* Carlo Rustichelli.

The White Pony

A young girl who's always wanted a pony goes to stay in Ireland with her uncle (Gruner). She meets a leprechaun (Davis, taking a break from the *Leprechaun* horror series) and a magic pony. The film doesn't even come close to the brilliant *Into the West*, but it is a satisfying effort for kids. Though production values are very good for a low-budget film, DVD is but scant improvement over VHS tape. —*MM*

Movie: 🎵🎵 ½ **DVD:** 🎵🎵
New Concorde (cat #NH20732 D, UPC 736991173293). Full frame. Stereo.

$19.98. Keepcase. *LANG:* English. *FEATURES:* 24 chapters • Talent files • Trailers.
1999 (G) 86m/C *IR* Olivier Gruner, Warwick Davis, Carly Anderson, Natalie Anderson; *D:* Brian Kelly; *W:* Laura Ambler; *C:* Ed Talavera; *M:* Derek Gleason.

White River

A fine cast does what it can with less-than-stellar comic material. Two Deep South con men, Brother Edward (Hoskins) and Pittman (Banderas), make the mistake of trying to help another felon, The White River Kid (Bentley). But the Kid takes them and his fiancée Apple Lisa (Dickens) hostage. Toss in the blind hooker Eva Nell (Barkin) and the Weeds (Bridges and Kurtz) and this is surely one of the more expensive video premieres. Beyond the pricey ensemble, the production has the highly polished look of a major studio release. DVD reproduces it without flaw and even contains a respectable list of extras. —*MM* **AKA:** The White River Kid.

Movie: 🎵🎵 ½ **DVD:** 🎵🎵🎵
Columbia Tristar (cat #06765, UPC 043396067653). Widescreen (1.85:1) letterboxed; full frame. Dolby Digital Surround; 5.1 Surround. $24.95. Keepcase. *LANG:* English. *SUB:* English; French. *CAP:* English. *FEATURES:* 28 chapters • Commentary: director • Filmographies • Trailers.
1999 (R) 99m/C Bob Hoskins, Antonio Banderas, Wes Bentley, Kim Dickens, Ellen Barkin, Randy Travis, Beau Bridges, Swoosie Kurtz; *D:* Arne Glimcher; *W:* David Leland; *C:* Michael Chapman; *M:* John (Gianni) Frizzell.

White Sands

Convoluted mystery begins well with rural New Mexico sheriff Ray Dozzell (Dafoe) finding a corpse and a briefcase full of cash. When he assumes the dead man's identity to find out what he was up to, credibility is stretched to the breaking point. However, the cast is capable, and DVD makes the most of some well-chosen Southwestern landscapes. Image on the few-frills disc ranges between good and very good. Same for sound. —*MM*

Movie: 🎵🎵 **DVD:** 🎵🎵
Warner (cat #12532). Widescreen (2.35:1) anamorphic. Dolby Digital 5.1 Surround Stereo. $19.98. Snapper. *LANG:* English; French. *SUB:* English; French; Spanish. *FEATURES:* 33 chapters • Talent files • Trailer.
1992 (R) 101m/C Willem Dafoe, Mary Elizabeth Mastrantonio, Mickey Rourke, Mimi Rogers, Samuel L. Jackson, M. Emmet Walsh, James Rebhorn, Maura Tierney, Beth Grant, Miguel (Michael) Sandoval, John Lafayette, Fred Dalton Thompson, John P. Ryan; *D:* Roger Donaldson; *W:* Daniel Pyne; *C:* Peter Menzies Jr.; *M:* Patrick O'Hearn.

The White Warrior

In this standard Italian adventure flick, musclehead Steve Reeves leads a band of merry mountain men against the tyrannical Czar, winning the hearts of several ladies in the process. Cameraman Mario Bava went on to become a cult favorite as a horror director, and rumor has it that he was actually in charge of this film, with credited director Freda serving as a producer. Picture and audio are slightly above average for a bargain-basement disc, although colors still look washed-out. It claims to be enhanced for widescreen monitors, but somebody's lying. —BG
Movie: 🐾 ½ **DVD:** 🐾🐾
VCI (cat #8277, UPC 089859827723). Widescreen (1.85:1) letterboxed. Dolby Mono. $9.98. Keepcase. LANG: English. FEATURES: 12 chapters • Trailers.
1961 81m/C IT Steve Reeves, Georgia Moll; **D:** Riccardo (Robert Hampton) Freda; **W:** Gino DeSanctis, Alcos Tolnay; **C:** Mario Bava.

Who the Hell Is Juliette?

Documentary is both sad and intriguing (and a bit confusing at times). While shooting a music video with model Fabiola Quiroz, director Carlos Marcovich casts a 16-year-old Cuban girl named Yuliet Ortega to be in the shoot. Marcovich is so intrigued by Yuliet's story that he decides to make a film about her, tracing her life in Cuba. Yuliet has not had an easy life, as her father escaped to America and her mother committed suicide. Living with her grandmother, Yuliet is now a streetwise girl, seemingly old beyond her years. Marcovich juxtaposes Yuliet's story with that of Fabiola's, a beautiful model living in New York City. Yuliet's story is certainly touching and poignant, but the editing of the film makes the facts difficult to follow at times. This is certainly one of the most accurate accounts of life in Cuba that one is likely to see. DVD offers a crisp transfer which exhibits some defects from the source material. However, given the low-budget nature of the film, and the occasional black-and-white photography, the low level of grain is quite acceptable. The audio brings clear dialogue and the subtitles are easy to read. The DVD contains in-depth liner notes from the director describing the making of the film. —ML
Movie: 🐾🐾 **DVD:** 🐾🐾 ½
Kino on Video (cat #K162 DVD, UPC 738-329016227). Widescreen (1.85:1) letterboxed. Dolby Digital Surround. $29.95. Keepcase. LANG: Spanish. SUB: English. FEATURES: Theatrical trailer • 15 chapters.
1997 91m/C D: Carlos Marcovich; **W:** Carlos Marcovich.

Who'll Stop the Rain?

Temperamental Vietnam vet Ray Hicks (Nolte) is enlisted in a scheme to smuggle a large amount of heroin into California.

He manages to bring the war with him, too. The blend of comedy, action, suspense, and drama—based on Robert Stone's novel *Dog Soldiers*—has aged well. Some might say that the period soundtrack could use a 5.1 remix, but not me. It sounds the way I remember it from the theatre. Minor grain is evident in darker scenes and some light print damage shows through, too, but overall, this one has the rough look that's found in most '70s films. —MM **AKA:** Dog Soldiers.
Movie: 🐾🐾🐾 **DVD:** 🐾🐾 ½
MGM Home Ent. (cat #1002208, UPC 027616864390). Widescreen (1.85:1) letterboxed. Dolby Digital Mono. $19.95. Keepcase. LANG: English; Spanish. SUB: French; Spanish. CAP: English. FEATURES: 16 chapters • Trailer.
1978 (R) 126m/C Nick Nolte, Tuesday Weld, Michael Moriarty, Anthony Zerbe, Richard Masur, Ray Sharkey, David Opatoshu, Charles Haid, Gail Strickland; **D:** Karel Reisz; **W:** Judith Rascoe; **C:** Richard H. Kline; **M:** Laurence Rosenthal.

Why Do They Call It Love When They Mean Sex?

Gloria (Forqué) works in a live-sex act but is forced to change partners and take on inexperienced Manu (Sanz) who needs some quick cash to pay off gambling debts. Everything goes well until Manu's respectable parents meet Gloria and think the duo are just a nice conventional couple. DVD image is violently colorful, but extremely soft. That appears to come from the original. Transfer is fine. Subtitles are burned in. —MM **AKA:** Por Que Lo Llaman Amor Cuando Quieren Decir Sexo?.
Movie: 🐾🐾 ½ **DVD:** 🐾🐾
Vanguard Intl. Cinema (cat #VF017). Widescreen letterboxed. $29.98. Keepcase. LANG: Spanish. SUB: English. FEATURES: 14 chapters • Trailer.
1992 115m/C SP Jorge Sanz, Veronica Forque, Fernando Colomo, Fernando Guillen, Rosa Maria Sarda, Alejandra Grepi, Elisa Matilla, Isabel Ordaz; **D:** Manuel Gomez Pereira; **W:** Manuel Gomez Pereira; **C:** Hans Burman; **M:** Manuel Tena.

The Wicker Man [SE]

Strictly devout and slighty priggish, Police Sergeant Howie (Woodward) uses a small seaplane to visit the many scattered islands in the North of Scotland. He goes to balmy Summerisle to check a report of a missing child, Rowan Morrison, and lands in the middle of a situation that outrages him and warps his judgment. The cheerfully boorish Lord Summerisle (Lee) counters Howie's every protest with a calm defense of his religion, backed up by his casual lover, schoolmarm Miss Rose (Cilento). And the local strumpet Willow (Eklund) further confuses Howie with an attempted seduction that may be aided by drugs, or magic. Anchor Bay has issued two separate disc packages. A flawless but short (88-minute) theatrical cut is on

their standard disc (UPC 013131142297, $19.98), accompanied by an informative documentary, and an Easter egg television interview with Christopher Lee. A 99-minute special edition boxed (or wickered) set adds a version where the cut scenes have been fuzzily reintegrated into the show from a fairly pathetic one-inch source. Now restored to their springtime brilliance, the visuals of *The Wicker Man* have greatly improved (on the theatrical cut) the overall look of the show. The efficient and professional documentary is to the point and uses prime sources (Corman, Shaffer, etc.) to tell the movie's woeful production tale, but see the film first, as it gives away everything, spoiler-wise. The extra interview, from an ancient video source, is also a welcome find for *Wicker* addicts. —GE
Movie: 🐾🐾🐾 **DVD:** 🐾🐾🐾
Anchor Bay (cat #DV11652, UPC 01313-1165296). Widescreen (1.78:1) anamorphic. Dolby Digital 5.1 Surround Stereo. $39.98. Special packaging. LANG: English. CAP: English. FEATURES: Trailers and TV spots • Documentary • TV interview with Christopher Lee.
1975 103m/C GB Edward Woodward, Christopher Lee, Britt Ekland, Diane Cilento, Ingrid Pitt, Lindsay Kemp, Irene Sunters, Walter Carr, Geraldine Cowper, Lesley Mackie; **D:** Robin Hardy; **W:** Anthony Shaffer; **C:** Harry Waxman; **M:** Paul Giovanni.

The Widow of Saint-Pierre

This beautiful French film opens with two men committing a bizarre murder on the island of Saint-Pierre. When one of them, Auguste (Emir Kusturica), is sentenced to death, a guillotine must be requested from the French mainland. While waiting for his death, Auguste is housed in the local jail, to be watched over by Jean (Daniel Auteuil), the local police chief. Jean's wife Pauline (Juliette Binoche) becomes interested in Auguste and asks him to assist her in the garden. From this, a friendship blooms in which Pauline and Jean begin to see Auguste as a human being, and not just a prisoner. With this new enlightenment, Jean and Pauline attempt to halt the execution and save their new friend. Wonderfully shot by director Patrice Leconte, this is a haunting, lyrical film which should move even the coldest heart. The fantastic performances and beautiful scenery only help to enhance it. These great images are perfectly captured on the DVD. The image does show some minor grain and scratches at times, but the picture is very sharp and the colors (dominated by reds and blues) look fantastic. The Dolby Digital 5.1 audio track is also impressive, balancing the film's quiet moments with rich Surround effects during the crowd scenes. —ML **AKA:** La Veuve de Saint-Pierre.
Movie: 🐾🐾🐾 **DVD:** 🐾🐾🐾 ½
Lion's Gate Home Ent. (cat #7744D, UPC 031398774426). Widescreen letterboxed. Dolby Digital 5.1 Surround. $24.99. Keep-

case. *LANG:* French. *SUB:* English; French; Spanish. *CAP:* English. *FEATURES:* "Making of" featurette ▪ Trailer ▪ Cast & crew interviews ▪ 24 chapters.
2000 (R) 112m/C *FR* Juliette Binoche, Daniel Auteuil, Emir Kusturica, Michael Duchaussoy, Sylvie Moreau, Sarah McKenna, Reynald Bouchard, Philippe Magnan; *D:* Patrice Leconte; *W:* Claude Faraldo; *C:* Eduardo Serra; *M:* Pascal Esteve. *AWARDS: NOM:* Cesar '01: Actress (Binoche), Support. Actor (Kusturica); Golden Globes '01: Foreign Film.

The Wild Child

Truffaut directs himself as a 19th-century physician who attempts to educate a young boy (Cargol) found living in the wilderness. Based on a true account, as chronicled in the real doctor's journal, about the attempts to acquaint the boy with civilization after his years in the wild. When he is introduced to society in Paris, an unscrupulous opportunist makes a sideshow of him, charging admission to see the boy. It is the good doctor who saves him from a fate that might have included years in an insane asylum. Brilliant coming-of-age tale is conveyed in a documentary-like fashion, with measured pace and no music track. Sensitive performances by Truffaut and, especially, Cargol prevent the film from becoming inappropriately farcical. Monaural soundtrack gets the job done, with little necessary for it to convey through the French dialogue and the boy's grunts. Image is slightly letterboxed to preserve the 1.66:1 framing. The DVD is devoid of extras, save for a trailer and optional English, French, or Spanish subtitles to accompany the original French soundtrack. Subtitles are legible, although their yellow color is inappropriate for the black-and-white cinematography. The picture source, while only very occasionally marked by small blemishes, suffers from low contrast and a lack of deep, rich blacks. —*MB* **AKA:** L'Enfant Sauvage.
Movie: 🎞🎞 ½ *DVD:* 🎞🎞 ½
MGM Home Ent. (cat #1002218, UPC 027616864499). Widescreen (1.66:1) letterboxed. Dolby Digital Mono. $19.98. Keepcase. *LANG:* English. *SUB:* English; Spanish; French. *CAP:* English. *FEATURES:* 16 chapters ▪ Original theatrical trailer.
1970 (G) 85m/B *FR* Jean-Pierre Cargol, François Truffaut, Jean Daste, Françoise Seigner, Paul Ville; *D:* François Truffaut; *W:* Jean Gruault, François Truffaut; *C:* Nestor Almendros; *M:* Antoine Duhamel. *AWARDS:* Natl. Bd. of Review '70: Director (Truffaut); Natl. Soc. Film Critics '70: Cinematog.

Wild Guitar / The Choppers

A double bill starring Arch Hall Jr. and produced by his father. *Wild Guitar* has Hall Jr. arrive in Hollywood looking like a male hustler and becoming an instant teen idol. *The Choppers* features Hall Jr. at his Michael Pollard look-a-like best operating

a car theft ring. Ray Dennis Steckler *(The Thrill Killers)* directs *Guitar* with his usual better-than-average thrift store delirium. In contrast, Leigh Jason's *Choppers* is a monstrous bore of crude direction, though I was shocked to hear the trailer narrated by my own father, character actor Nelson Olmsted. *Guitar* sports a first-class print and DVD transfer, with a runner-up *Choppers* looking almost as good. Both have the best sound you could hope for, given the source. —*MO*
Movie: 🎞🎞 ½ *DVD:* 🎞🎞🎞
Image Ent. (cat #ID11995WDVD, UPC 014-381119923). Full frame. Dolby Digital 2.0 Mono. $24.99. Keepcase. *LANG:* English. *FEATURES: Wild:* 12 chapters, *Choppers:* 10 chapters ▪ Theatrical trailers ▪ Twist-o-Mania Short Subject #1: Dance Craze ▪ Twist-o-Mania Short Subject #2: Twist Craze ▪ Anti-Choppers Police Science Short Subject #3: Hot Car ▪ Gallery of Trash-o-Rama exploitation art with radio-spot rarities.
1962 92m/B Arch Hall Jr., Cash (Ray Dennis Steckler) Flagg, Ray Dennis Steckler, Carolyn Brandt, Bob Crumb, Nancy Czar, Marie Denn, Arch (Archie) Hall Sr.; *D:* Ray Dennis Steckler; *W:* Joe Thomas, Bob Wehling, Arch (Archie) Hall Sr.; *C:* Joseph Mascelli; *M:* Alan O'Day.

Wild Orchid

After a carefully constructed "controversy" in 1990, wherein the original cut of the film was given an "X" rating by the MPAA, *Wild Orchid* went on to become a minor sensation on home video and was at least partially responsible for the many "erotic thrillers" that have followed it. (Star Mickey Rourke stated that he and his costar/girlfriend Carré Otis actually "did it" in one scene—chapter 15, for inquiring minds.) Director King has certainly had a lucrative career creating more glossy, elegant soft-core eroticism for cable television with his *Red Shoes Diaries* series. This one's cut from the same cloth. Otis is beautiful but innocent international lawyer Emily Reed who goes to Rio to do a real estate deal with enigmatic millionaire Wheeler (Rourke, who appears to have slapped several bottles of tanning goop on his face and chest). Jacqueline Bissett, as Emily's boss, is apparently the only member of the cast who realized that this is a comedy. The others are dead serious. A surprising amount of grain is present in most scenes, but that might be a reaction to Rourke's goop and the other gaudy colors. It leads to fairly heavy pixels. Double-sided DVD contains both the "international" unrated version (at 112 minutes) and the "R." Rourke and King scholars can study both to discern the subtle differences. —*MM*
Movie: 🎞 *DVD:* 🎞🎞 ½
MGM Home Ent. (cat #1003253, UPC 027616874030). Widescreen (1.85:1) anamorphic. Dolby Digital Surround. $14.98. Keepcase. *LANG:* English. *SUB:* English; French; Spanish; Portuguese. *CAP:* English. *FEATURES:* 16 chapters ▪ Trailer.

1990 (R) 107m/C Mickey Rourke, Jacqueline Bisset, Carre Otis, Assumpta Serna, Bruce Greenwood; *D:* Zalman King; *W:* Zalman King; *C:* Gale Tattersall; *M:* Simon Goldenberg, Geoff MacCormack.

Wild Strawberries

Bergman's landmark film of fantasy, dreams, and nightmares. An aging professor, on the road to accept an award, must come to terms with his anxieties and guilt. Brilliant performance by Sjostrom, Sweden's first film director and star. Excellent use of flashbacks and film editing. An intellectual and emotional masterpiece. Although the age of the print is evident from time to time, Criterion has done another excellent restoration job with this disc. The image is sharp and blacks are extremely well defined. My only complaint about the presentation is that the captions appeared a bit low on the screen, which could be a problem for viewers with varying monitor settings. The soundtrack is also a triumph and boasts crisp, understandable dialogue as well as a lush musical score. The superb documentary by Jorn Donner included on the disc is worthy of a disc unto itself. —*MJT* **AKA:** Smultron-Stallet.
Movie: 🎞🎞🎞🎞 *DVD:* 🎞🎞🎞
Criterion (cat #139, UPC 037429162422). Full frame. Dolby Digital Mono. $39.95. Keepcase. *LANG:* Swedish. *SUB:* English. *FEATURES:* 24 chapters ▪ Commentary: film scholar Peter Cowie ▪ "Ingmar Bergman on Life and Work," documentary by Jorn Donner ▪ Stills gallery.
1957 90m/B *SW* Victor Sjostrom, Bibi Andersson, Max von Sydow, Ingrid Thulin, Gunnar Bjornstrand, Folke Sundquist, Bjorn Bjelvenstam; *D:* Ingmar Bergman; *W:* Ingmar Bergman; *C:* Gunnar Fischer; *M:* Erik Nordgren. *AWARDS:* Golden Globes '60: Foreign Film; *NOM:* Oscars '59: Story & Screenplay.

The Wild West

Image quality on these 10 imports and American made-for-TV movies is no better than tape, but for die-hard fans of westerns, they're a real bargain at $2 apiece. Please see individual reviews for *Cry Blood, Apache, Crazy Horse & Custer, Fistful of Lead, The Gunfighters, The New Daughters of Joshua Cabe, The Over the Hill Gang, Territorial Men, Daniel Boone: Trailblazer, The Jackals,* and *Savage Pampas.* —*MM*
Movie: 🎞🎞 *DVD:* 🎞🎞
BCI-Eclipse (cat #44213-9, UPC 7873644-21398). Full frame. $19.98. 5-disc keepcase. *LANG:* English.
2001 907m/C

Wilde

Low-key, fairly standard biopic of genius playwright and famous wit, Oscar Wilde. It details the loving relationship Wilde (Fry) had with his wife as well as his disastrous liaisons with the impetuous, selfish Alfred

Douglas (Law). Fry is excellent as Wilde but the film doesn't quite come off, failing to successfully penetrate the self-destructive Wilde's skin. The gay love scenes are rather passionless and feel a bit timid. Still, it's a worthwhile re-creation of the period and has some beautiful moments. The transfer is excessively grainy and smeary and is prone to shimmer and digital noise. Movement occasionally appears sped up and lens distortion is occasionally noticeable at the edges of the frames. Sound is clean but undistinguished. The documentaries add up to over an hour of interesting historical information about Wilde and interesting background on the genesis of the film. —DG
Movie: 🎬🎬 ½ **DVD:** 🎬🎬 ½
Columbia Tristar (cat #02297, UPC 043-396022973). Widescreen (2.35:1) anamorphic. Dolby Digital Surround. $29.95. Keepcase. *LANG:* English. *SUB:* English. *CAP:* English. *FEATURES:* 28 chapters ● "Simply Wilde" featurette ● Commentary: filmmakers ● "Still Wild about Wilde" featurette ● Trailers ● DVD-ROM: complete official Wilde website content ● Photo montage ● Filmographies ● Production notes.
1997 (R) 115m/C *GB* Stephen Fry, Jude Law, Vanessa Redgrave, Jennifer Ehle, Michael Sheen, Zoe Wanamaker, Tom Wilkinson, Gemma Jones, Judy Parfitt; **D:** Brian Gilbert; **W:** Julian Mitchell; **C:** Martin Fuhrer; **M:** Debbie Wiseman. *AWARDS: NOM:* British Acad. '97: Support. Actress (Ehle), Support. Actress (Wanamaker); Golden Globes '99: Actor—Drama (Fry).

Will Penny

Charlton Heston turns in one of the best performances of his career as aging illiterate cowboy Will Penny. He plays against heroic stereotypes to inhabit the role from the inside out. He gets considerable help from a solid script and a sense of cold realism that's rarely seen in the genre. The story concerns a winter where Will meets Catherine (Hackett) and her son (Gries, son of the director), and, for the first time in his life considers a loving family relationship. At the same time, he has to deal with a psychotic preacher (Pleasence) and his sadistic son (Dern). You may be able to spot some inconsequential surface damage but, on DVD, the film looks better than I've ever seen it. Colors are bright. The grain comes from the original. The featurettes are short and though they contain no startling revelations, they're worth watching. One of the best sleepers around. —MM
Movie: 🎬🎬🎬 ½ **DVD:** 🎬🎬🎬 ½
Paramount (cat #06723, UPC 09736-0672343). Widescreen (1.85:1) anamorphic. Dolby Digital Mono. $24.99. Keepcase. *LANG:* English; French. *SUB:* English. *CAP:* English. *FEATURES:* "Remembering Will Penny" featurette (13 min.) ● "The Cowboys of Well Penny" featurette (3 min.) ● 12 chapters.
1967 109m/C Charlton Heston, Joan Hackett, Donald Pleasence, Lee Majors, Bruce Dern, Anthony Zerbe, Ben Johnson, Clifton James, Jonathan (Jon Francis) Gries; **D:** Tom Gries; **W:** Tom Gries; **C:** Lucien Ballard; **M:** Elmer Bernstein.

Willow

The elfin Willow Ufgood (Davis) leaves his town and young family to try to deliver a giant (normal) infant to safety in the next kingdom, knowing that evil knights dispatched by the even more evil Queen Bavmorda (Marsh) are out for its blood. Willow collects helpers along the way, a pair of diminutive brownies, a sorceress (Hayes) who's been transformed into a lemur-like animal, and Madmartigan (Kilmer), a condemned thief who nevertheless offers stalwart assistance. Complicating matters is the fact that Queen Bavmorda's warrior daughter Sorsha (Whalley) is leading the search for the baby, even though she and Madmartigan are soon attracted to each other. By adult standards, this one's too long and has an unimaginative story, and a lazy screenplay with too many clunker dialogue lines. But that doesn't keep it from being an entertaining kid's film in the sub–*Lord of the Rings* genre. *Willow* can be enjoyed as perhaps the last major effects film not dominated by digital enhancements. Time-consuming traveling mattes and optical superimpositions account for most of the fantastic scenes, with the matting of the brownies into countless shots done particularly well. Phil Tippet provides a socko scene of real, honest, old-fashioned stop-motion animation with a very impressive and interesting-looking two-headed dragon. It's just one facet of the film's most complicated setpiece, that includes fire, water, fighting knights, flying arrows, and a pair of scary ape-like trolls who scramble over the castle walls like cockroaches. DVD will please everyone, with its pristine picture and strong audio tracks. James Horner's slightly too emphatic score comes across well. Besides an original featurette, added-value producer Jeffrey Schwarz has created a snappy short documentary that concentrates on just one facet of the effects, the morphing illusions done with the "primitive" computer graphics of 1988. This is better than trying to tell the full production story in boring detail. A good commentary is voiced by the very likeable Warwick Davis, who makes for a perfectly informative and entertaining host, with nicely judged observations on the entire filming process. —GE
Movie: 🎬🎬🎬 **DVD:** 🎬🎬🎬 ½
20th Century Fox (UPC 24543026174). Widescreen (2.35:1) anamorphic. Dolby Digital 5.1 Surround. $26.98. Keepcase. *LANG:* English; Spanish. *CAP:* English. *FEATURES:* Commentary: Warwick Davis ● Mini-documentary on morphing ● "Making of" featurette ● Still gallery ● Trailers and TV spots.
1988 (PG) 118m/C Warwick Davis, Val Kilmer, Jean Marsh, Joanne Whalley, Billy Barty, Pat Roach, Ruth Greenfield, Patricia Hayes, Gavan O'Herlihy, Kevin Pollak; **D:** Ron Howard; **W:** Bob Dolman; **C:** Adrian Biddle; **M:** James Horner.

Wind River

In 1855 Utah, young Nicholas Wilson (Heron) leaves his widowed mom (Allen) and joins the Shoeshone tribe. They accept him because his presence fulfills a prophecy. The impressive Wes Studi appears too briefly as the leader of another tribe. The film is an acceptable but clichéd western adventure for kids. Locations are terrific. DVD image is only a small improvement over VHS tape. —MM
Movie: 🎬🎬 **DVD:** 🎬🎬 ½
Studio Home Ent. (cat #AV1597D, UPC 806469159729). Full frame. Stereo. $19.98. Keepcase. *LANG:* English. *SUB:* English; Spanish. *CAP:* English. *FEATURES:* 24 chapters ● 3 trailers.
1998 (PG-13) 97m/C Blake Heron, A. Martinez, Russell Means, Wes Studi, Karen Allen, Patricia Van Ingen, Joe Wandell; **D:** Tom Shell; **W:** Tom Shell, Elizabeth Hansen; **C:** Lawrence Schweich; **M:** Jeff Marsh.

A Wing and a Prayer

Aircraft Carrier "X" (its name changed to protect military "secrets") is ordered to race across the Pacific and back, to avoid fights and be seen anywhere but near Midway. After convincing the enemy that our ships are scattered and our morale too low to engage in battle, the carrier reports to Midway to help out in a whopping big battle. Running the ship are Captain Waddell (Bickford) and stern flight commander Bingo Harper (Ameche). Among the frustrated fliers are Hallam Scott (Eythe), an Oscar-winning actor who's sometimes unreliable about following orders; Malcolm Brainard (Morgan), a scratched pilot who wants back up in a plane; Cookie Cunningham (O'Shea), an Ace who thinks he's lost his touch; and Ed Moulton (Andrews), the flight leader who tries to hold them all together. But when they finally cross planes with the Japanese at Midway, all rise to the occasion as fierce warriors. DVD looks in top shape, but the transfer is a mite compromised by white highlights around dark objects on screen. These ring many images and outline the headlines in newspapers in white light. Overall it's not too distracting, but I'm told this is a result of digital processing done indiscriminately to improve overall contrast and picture punch. I think I'd rather let the 1944 picture look as it should instead. You might not even notice it on your monitor. —GE
Movie: 🎬🎬 **DVD:** 🎬🎬 ½
20th Century Fox (cat #2002536, UPC 024543024368). Full frame. Stereo; Mono. $19.98. Keepcase. *LANG:* English; French. *SUB:* English; Spanish. *CAP:* English. *FEATURES:* Trailer.
1944 97m/B Don Ameche, Dana Andrews, William Eythe, Charles Bickford, Cedric Hardwicke, Kevin O'Shea, Richard Jaeckel, Harry (Henry) Morgan; **D:** Henry Hathaway; **W:** Jerome Cady; **C:** Glen MacWilliams; **M:**

Hugo Friedhofer. *AWARDS: NOM:* Oscars '44: Orig. Screenplay.

Winning London

Mary-Kate and Ashley Olsen are back in another made-for-TV, jet-set globetrotting adventure, but unlike their other films, this one at least offers some positive messages. The twins play Chloe and Riley Lawrence, two high-school students who are chosen to travel to London for a Model United Nations competition. Once there, they take in the sights, chat about cute guys, and become involved in a hostage situation. But most importantly, they wear all of the latest fashions. The majority of the action is the same lightweight fluff which can be found in all of the other Olsen Twins films, but this one stands out. Despite all the distractions London offers, the girls realize that it's the educational portion of their trip that got them to the U.K. in the first place, and is the most important part of their journey. Fans of the Olsen Twins will certainly love this one, although most adults will find it boring and banal. The picture offers good colors and is adequately sharp, but there is a noticeable amount of grain, which can be distracting at times. Audio provides clear dialogue and some decent Surround sound effects. —ML

Movie: ♪ ½ **DVD:** ♪♪
Warner (cat #37332, UPC 0853937332-23). Full frame. Dolby Surround Stereo. $19.98. Snapper. *LANG:* English; Spanish. *SUB:* English; Spanish; French. *CAP:* English. *FEATURES:* Talent files ● Behind-the-scenes ● Fashion Close-up ● 30 chapters.
2001 (G) 93m/C Mary-Kate Olsen, Ashley (Fuller) Olsen; **D:** Craig Shapiro; **W:** Karol Ann Hoeffner.

The Winslow Boy

This film revolves around a young boy named Ronnie Winslow who is accused of stealing a postal order. The son pleads his innocence to his family and especially his father, who decides to start an intense battle to prove that his child is innocent. Sir Robert Morton (Northam) is called in to defend the boy. Soon the family and the lawyer find that the intensity of their fight is draining their finances and beginning to ruin them. Although there are times when the story feels dragged out a little, some wonderful things are done with the plot. When it seems that the story will be a courtroom drama about the fight for justice for the boy, it turns out to be something completely different, a film mainly about character, and Mamet is able to build tension from the simplest of sequences. The sharp delivery adds to the riveting conversations. The performances are excellent, especially Hawthorne and Northam. This is a gorgeous transfer and aside from a few small scratches here and there, it's beautiful and very close to perfect. The image is perfectly sharp and clear, but the rich, deep colors are impressive. It's a very basic, dialogue-driven

sound mix. There really isn't anything to the audio besides conversations between characters. Dialogue sounds clear, but a little on the soft side at times. A great deal of the commentary is devoted to the group's thoughts on acting style, as well as comments on the way that members of the cast played their parts. There really isn't much discussion into the technical aspects of the movie but it is informative and occasionally funny. The featurette is above average and provides interviews with all of the cast members as well as Mamet, and gives the viewer a good look behind the production and history of the play. —AB/DG

Movie: ♪♪♪ **DVD:** ♪♪♪
Columbia Tristar (cat #04057, UPC 433-96040571). Widescreen. Dolby Surround. $27.98. Keepcase. *LANG:* English. *CAP:* English. *FEATURES:* Commentary: Mamet, Northam, Pidgeon, Hawthorne ● Featurette ● Trailers ● Talent files.
1998 (G) 104m/C Nigel Hawthorne, Jeremy Northam, Rebecca Pidgeon, Gemma Jones, Guy Edwards, Matthew Pidgeon, Colin Stinton, Aden (John) Gillett, Perry Fenwick, Sarah Flind, Sara Stewart, Alan Polanski, Neil North; **D:** David Mamet; **W:** David Mamet; **C:** Benoit Delhomme; **M:** Alaric Jans.

Winter Lily

This Canadian Gothic builds a nice atmosphere, but cannot deliver in the end. Danny Gilmore (who looks like a cross between Julian Lennon, Keanu Reeves, and Hilary Swank in *Boys Don't Cry*) stars as Clive, a young photographer who is traveling the isolated roads of snowy New Hampshire (although these are most likely Canadian locations) looking for photogenic spots. He comes across the Memory Lane Inn Bed & Breakfast and inquires about a room. It seems that the only people about are the hostess Agatha (Berryman) and a surly handyman. Clive is made to feel welcome, but becomes slightly uncomfortable when Agatha begins to speak of her daughter Lily, who is apparently bedridden. Despite the fact that he can hear Agatha speaking with someone, Clive doubts Lily's existence. Writer/director Roshel Bissett does a fine job of cranking up the tension during the first half, but cannot maintain the suspense through the final reel. The film is slow at times, and while the finale does bring some much-needed action, it leaves too many questions unanswered. Kudos to the filmmakers for not pulling any punches and dealing with disturbing themes that harken back to the rural psycho films of the mid-1980s. (Content note: There is some nudity and, more importantly, sex with a corpse.) DVD delivers a disappointing transfer. The full-frame image is very grainy (and the snow-covered landscapes make this grain very apparent). The picture is sharp, for the most part, and the colors are fine, but the fleshtones are very waxy. The audio mix is a mixed bag. There are some subtle Surround effects, but the dialogue is muffled at times, and the sound

effects drown out the speech at times. There are no extras. —ML/LA

Movie: ♪♪ **DVD:** ♪♪
Vanguard Intl. Cinema (cat #VF0230, UPC 658769023039). Full frame. Digital Stereo Surround. $29.95. Keepcase. *LANG:* English. *FEATURES:* 10 chapters.
1998 90m/C *CA* Dorothee Berryman, Danny Gilmore, Jean-Pierre Bergeron, Kimberley Laferriere; **D:** Roshel Bissett; **W:** Roshel Bissett.

Wirey Spindell

The title character (played by writer/director Shaeffer) is scheduled to be married in a few days, but has a problem: he can't seem to make love to women that he actually cares about. As the date approaches, he takes a trip down memory lane to revisit his sexual history, starting at seven years old with the next-door neighbor. It's amusing at times but extremely shallow, and the resolution it arrives at is pathetic. Both sound options have a high level of background hiss and colors are not always consistent, but both of these problems are most likely due to the quality of the source material rather than the transfer. —BG

Movie: ♪ ½ **DVD:** ♪♪ ½
Winstar Home Ent. (cat #FLV5241, UPC 720917523122). Widescreen (1.85:1) letterboxed. Dolby 5.1; Dolby Surround. $19.98. Keepcase. *LANG:* English. *FEATURES:* 16 chapters ● Filmographies ● Commentary ● Trailer.
1999 101m/C Eric Schaeffer, Callie (Calliope) Thorne, Eric Mabius, Samantha Buck; **D:** Eric Schaeffer; **W:** Eric Schaeffer; **C:** Kramer Morgenthau; **M:** Amanda Kravat.

Wishmaster 3: Beyond the Gates of Hell

The most frightening moment in this film occurs early in the commentary track when director Chris Angel admits that *Wishmaster 4* has already been made. That means this low-budget horror series about an evil genie could go on as long as *Friday the 13th*. Now, that's scary. Generic story has the critter (Novak) coming to a college campus where he goes after a group of students. The Canadian locations look nice. The special effects are fine and the whole production has a nicely polished look that's pretty amazing when you consider the modest budget that the film must have had. Add in a full slate of extras and you've got an overachieving entry in a so-so series. (Title is also available with the first two films, UPC 012236126218.) —MM

Movie: ♪♪ **DVD:** ♪♪ ½
Artisan Ent. (cat #12206, UPC 0122-36122067). Widescreen (1.85:1) anamorphic. Dolby Digital Surround. $19.98. Keepcase. *LANG:* English. *SUB:* Spanish. *FEATURES:* 16 chapters ● Filmmakers' commentary track ● Trailer ● Production notes ● Talent files ● Storyboard gallery.
2001 (R) 92m/C A.J. Cook, Jason Connery, Tobias Mehler, Aaron Smolinksi,

Louisette Geiss, John Novak; **D:** Chris Angel; **W:** Alexander Wright.

W.I.S.O.R. The Robo Welder

This documentary about the attempts to build a robot welder to unleash in the steam lines of New York City is interesting, but not as interesting as the history of the NYC steam lines that is told as a side bar to all the technology-intensive footage of W.I.S.O.R.'s creators. NYC uses steam to heat a great many buildings, the Chrysler Building and Empire State buildings for example, as well as steam for laundry businesses and for heating water. The original lines were built in the 1880s and most of the pipes have never been replaced or upgraded. This results in the occasional steam explosion that destroys streets, tangles traffic, and sometimes, kills people. The goal of the team is to create a robot that will stop at each pipe connection, block off the steam and then make a new weld in the pipe. Watching the team of experts go through the paces of testing ideas for the robot is like watching a mystery being solved. Additionally, the team has to learn to weld in order to teach the robot to weld. At the close of the documentary, the robot is not yet finished and the team is way over budget, but the project clearly should go on to its completion. One of the film's stranger conceits is a weird voice-over in the "voice" of W.I.S.O.R. recounting the history of NYC's steam lines and becoming ever more egomaniacal about his place in solving the problems the steam lines are having. This should be fun, educational, and generally interesting to anyone who watches the Discovery or History channel and engineers everywhere. The filmmaker chose to use different film stock for different parts of the film so there is an uneven nature to the color of the disc, but overall it looks good and the sound quality is above average. —*CA*
Movie: 🎬🎬 ½ **DVD:** 🎬🎬 ½
New Video Group (cat #NVG9489, UPC 767685948934). Full frame. Dolby Digital Stereo. $24.95. Keepcase. *LANG:* English. *FEATURES:* 12 chapters • Interview with Marvin Minsky • Jupiter's Wife trailer • Photos of W.I.S.O.R.
2001 75m/C D: Michel Negroponte; **W:** Gabriel Morgan; **C:** Michel Negroponte.

Witch Hunter

Deceptive advertising is the order of the day, as this Canadian film offers no witch, nor any hunting. What we do have is an interesting film which focuses on the plight of Canadian Indians and how white men have encroached on their land. Three childhood friends return to their hometown for a reunion and decide to hike into the woods, which legend says contains the lost gold of the Ar'Lei tribe. The trio soon becomes lost and must seek the help of an Ar'Lei elder to get out of the woods alive. Added to the mix is an archaeologist

who is on a quest to find the lost gold. All of these characters are soon confronted by the spirits for fallen Ar'Lei who died at the hands of White men. *Witch Hunter* is a lyrical film which escapes classification. The movie makes a strong point about the treatment of Indians, and it is very well shot, but it is never very entertaining. The DVD presents the film full frame, and the image is noticeably grainy, leading one to believe that the movie was shot on 16mm film. The audio is questionable, as most of the dialogue is muffled, but the music sounds fine. Also, note that the end credits are for another film entirely! The DVD box claims that *Witch Hunter* is based on a true story. It would have been nice to get more details on that. —*ML*
Movie: 🎬🎬 **DVD:** 🎬 ½
Leo Films (cat #1026, UPC 6778801026-90). Full frame. Digital 2.0 Surround. $19.95. Keepcase. *LANG:* English.
2001 90m/C *CA* Jean François Beaupre, Ray Galleth; **D:** Denis Paquet.

Witchouse 3: Demon Fire

J.R. Bookwalter's *Witchouse 2* was one of the most extra features–laden direct-to-video DVDs ever, and he's aimed to top that feat with *Witchouse 3: Demon Fire. 3* is totally unrelated to the first two films in the series and brings us a new cast of characters. Stevie (Debbie Rochon) and Rose (Tina Krause) are filming a documentary on witchcraft, when their old friend Annie (Tanya Dempsey) comes to visit. Annie is seeking refuge from her abusive boyfriend and her buddies are glad to oblige. As part of the documentary, the three women conduct a mock séance, and inadvertently raise the spirit of the evil witch Lilith (Brinke Stevens). Soon, strange things happen and the corpses start piling up. Is Lilith real, or has one of the girls gone insane? As with the other films in this series, Bookwalter is able to put every nickel up on-screen and create an interesting movie. This one isn't great art, nor does it want to be. It's simply a horror film that offers cheap thrills, attractive ladies, and a brief escape from reality. Surprisingly, considering that the movie was shot on video, it is presented in an anamorphic widescreen and has been letterboxed at 1.85:1. The image is sharp and clear, although this is some video lens flare at times. The Dolby Digital 5.1 audio track (which Bookwalter paid for himself!) is particularly effective, as the speakers fill with odd sound effects during the terror scenes. This DVD is overflowing with extra features, but the best is "Home Movies," which give a humorous and entertaining look at the set of a very low-budget movie. —*ML*
Movie: 🎬🎬 **DVD:** 🎬🎬🎬
Full Moon Pictures (cat #TD-1103, UPC 802993110397). Widescreen (1.85:1) anamorphic. Dolby Digital 5.1. $19.99. Keepcase. *LANG:* English. *FEATURES:* Commentaries • Cast interviews • Outtakes

• Behind-the-scenes • Still gallery • Bonus film • Trailers • Cast & crew.
2001 (R) 77m/C Debbie Rochon, Tanya Dempsey, Tina Krause, Brinke Stevens; **D:** J.R. Bookwalter.

With a Friend Like Harry

Twisted, surprisingly funny black comedy is about a character who is either a sociopath or extremely helpful. Michel (Lucas), his wife Claire (Seigner), and their three young daughters are on the vacation from hell when they happen to meet Harry (Lopez), a high school acquaintance who remembers Michel very well. Michel's not quite as clear on Harry, but before they know it, Michel and Claire are sharing their farmhouse with Harry and his sexy, full-figured girlfriend Plum (Guillemin). As Harry learns about the various problematic aspects of Michel's life, he decides to lend assistance as best he can. English dialogue is available, but the original French track is strongly recommended. It captures the subtle nuances of voice that are so important to the story. Image is excellent, but then, I'm such a fan of this one, that any flaws are easy to ignore. Recommended particularly to Hitchcock fans. —*MM* **AKA:** Harry, He's Here to Help; Harry, un Ami Qui Vous Veut du Bien; Harry, A Friend Who Wishes You Well.
Movie: 🎬🎬🎬 ½ **DVD:** 🎬🎬🎬
Miramax Pictures (cat #23564, UPC 7869-36161816). Widescreen (2.35:1) anamorphic. Dolby Digital 5.1 Surround. $34.98. Keepcase. *LANG:* French; English. *SUB:* English. *FEATURES:* 30 chapters.
2000 (R) 117m/C *FR* Sergei Lopez, Laurent Lucas, Mathilde Seigner, Sophie Guillemin; **D:** Dominik Moll; **W:** Dominik Moll, Gilles Marchand; **C:** Mathieu Poirot-Delpech; **M:** David Whitaker. *AWARDS:* Cesar '01: Actor (Lopez), Director (Moll), Film Editing, Sound; *NOM:* Cesar '01: Film, Screenplay, Support. Actress (Seigner).

With Friends Like These

Low-budget ensemble comedy is virtually unwatchable on DVD. The image is indescribably grainy. (It might have been made from a second-generation VHS dupe.) The writing is clichéd and tedious and there's nothing about the characters to attract any interest. The whole project appears to be the work of enthusiastic amateurs. Given the number of people who worked behind the scenes, it's no wonder that the result is such a shapeless mess. Menuless disc contains no features. —*MM*
Movie: 🎬 **DVD:** 🎬
Digital Versatile Disc (cat #145). Full frame. $19.95. Keepcase. *LANG:* English.
1990 85m/C Deidre Fitzsimons, Mark Ruel, Beth Lechance, Michael Burns, Norman Fell; **D:** Chris Malazdrewicz, Alain Zaloum, Tom Parkinson; **W:** Chris Malazdrewicz, Alain Zaloum, Tom Parkinson, Jim C. Dioro, Antoinette Martella; **C:** Stephen

Reizes, Bruno Philip, Micheal Lamothe; **M:** Richard Cresko.

Withnail and I

One of the defining cult films of the 1980s charts the comic misadventures of two unemployed actors, Withnail (Richard E. Grant) and Marwood (Paul McGann), in late 1960s England. In a moment of altered reality, they decide the country life is for them and bound off for Withnail's Uncle Monty's (Richard Griffiths) country residence. Short of the Ten Plagues of Egypt, our besotted duo must contend with randy relatives, scarce supplies, and a less-than-idyllic English pastoral setting. Robinson's first directorial turn drips with black comic wit, whether Withnail violently reacting to a pyramid of dirty dishes in his squalid flat or Marwood vainly convincing himself that "things aren't all that bad." Grant and McGann don't play their roles as much as inhabit them, their chemistry perfectly mixed by Robinson's sour-milk remembrance of his salad days (the film is adapted from his semi-autobiographical novel). The 1.85 non-anamorphic transfer looks terrific under the circumstances. The source print radiates with nary a blemish, but the intentional low lighting (which vexed co-executive producer Denis O'Brien, according to Grant in the retrospective documentary) contributes to consistent film grain in the image. Colors are solid but stark and gritty, perfectly in tune with the hostile environment. The mono soundtrack exhibits a surprising degree of fidelity. The dialogue sounds nice and clear, all the better to appreciate every syllable of the acidic script. The look-back documentary features 1999 video interviews with Robinson, Grant, and McGann, among others. Chapter-encoded with titles like "W is for wasted youth" and "T is for trainspotters," the retrospective examines the film's genesis and creation with the same dark humor as the film itself. The disc is another Criterion winner, an absolute must for appreciators of black comedies, cult films, 1980s cinema, or just plain good writing. —EP
Movie: ♫♫♫ ½ **DVD:** ♫♫♫
Criterion (cat #CC1573D, UPC 71551501-2225). Widescreen (1.85:1) letterboxed. Dolby Digital Mono. $29.95. Keepcase. *LANG:* English. *SUB:* English. *FEATURES:* 22 chapters • Retrospective documentary • Rare pre-production photos • Reproduction of original film poster • Theatrical trailer.
1987 (R) 108m/C *GB* Richard E. Grant, Paul McGann, Richard Griffiths, Ralph Brown, Michael Elphick; **D:** Bruce Robinson; **W:** Bruce Robinson; **C:** Peter Hannan; **M:** David Dundas.

Witness for the Prosecution

Unemployed Leonard Vole (Power) is accused of murdering a wealthy widow whom he befriended. Ailing defense attorney (Laughton) can't resist an intriguing case, and a straightforward matter becomes increasingly complicated in this energetic adaptation of an Agatha Christie story and stage play. Outstanding performances by Laughton, Lancaster (his real wife was a patient nurse), Power, and femme fatale Dietrich. DVD image is nothing short of superb. The terrific black-and-white cinematography (from director Wilder and D.P. Russell Harlan) has never looked better. Mono sound is more than adequate for a dialogue-heavy courtroom drama. Highest recommendations for this perennial favorite. —MM
Movie: ♫♫♫♫ **DVD:** ♫♫♫
MGM Home Ent. (cat #1002744, UPC 027616869425). Widescreen (1.66:1) letterboxed. Dolby Digital Mono. $19.98. Keepcase. *LANG:* English; French. *SUB:* French; Spanish. *CAP:* English. *FEATURES:* 16 chapters • Trailer.
1957 116m/B Charles Laughton, Tyrone Power, Marlene Dietrich, Elsa Lanchester, John Williams, Henry Daniell, Una O'Connor; **D:** Billy Wilder; **W:** Billy Wilder, Harry Kurnitz; **C:** Russell Harlan; **M:** Matty Malneck. *AWARDS:* Golden Globes '58: Support. Actress (Lanchester); *NOM:* Oscars '57: Actor (Laughton), Director (Wilder), Film Editing, Picture, Sound, Support. Actress (Lanchester).

The Wizard of Oz

A toymaker reads L. Frank Baum's tale to an impatient little girl who enters his shop. The tale (which is a mishmash of new ideas as well as plot elements from several classic Oz books except *The Wizard of Oz*) tells of a conspiracy to prevent Dorothy from discovering that she is the lost heir to the throne of Oz. It's essentially a vehicle for (virtually forgotten) silent film director and star Larry Semon, as the focus tends to be on his slapstick and run-around routines. There are some interesting special effects (flying barns, people falling off of great heights, hand-drawn lightning, etc.) but the film and Oz are completely lacking in any of Baum's atmosphere of wonder, magic, and imagination. While Semon and Hardy (sans Laurel) disguise themselves as "The Scarecrow" and "The Tin Man," the much-beloved characters do not appear in the film at all. A wasted opportunity co-written by L. Frank Baum Jr.—Frank Joslyn Baum. This video version is a hideous travesty of the original film. Mastered from a print that's so extensively damaged, it appears to have been dragged behind an automobile. It's a muddy, flickery, contrasty mess with an image cropped on all four sides. The music is a repetitive, inappropriate modern synthesizer score that never seems to fit the on-screen action. This version also features intertitles which are read aloud, storybook style. To be charitable, it's an unnecessary and stupid addition. Some sequences of the film also seem to be projected at an incorrect, slower speed, making those parts move at a glacial, twitchy pace. Given the exceedingly poor rendition of this edition, I've given the film a higher rating than it would seem to deserve; there may be qualities to the movie itself that would be apparent in a correct, pristine edition. As far as I'm concerned, the jury's still out. The "Little Rascals" short is a cute, entertaining entry in that series and features a wrestling match between Alfalfa and a local bully. The print is passable but the transfer is digitally noisy and the sound is sharp and tinny. —DG
Movie: ♫ ½ **DVD:** woof
Brentwood (cat #44098-9, UPC 78736440-9891). Full frame. Mono. $4.99. Keepcase. *LANG:* English. *FEATURES:* "Little Rascals: Came the Brawn" short • Trivia game • DVD dictionary.
1925 96m/B Larry Semon, Dorothy Dwan, Bryant Washburn, Charles Murray, Oliver Hardy, Josef Swickard, Virginia Pearson; **D:** Larry Semon; **W:** L. Frank Baum Jr., Larry Semon; **C:** Leonard Smith, Frank Good, Hans Koenekamp.

The Wolfman

Colin Glasgow is summoned back to his family manor to attend the funeral of his father. Unbeknownst to Colin, his father was actually murdered by his children who are in thrall to a satanist priest. The family stalls Colin, hoping their father's "curse" will be passed on to him at the next full moon. It does, and Colin turns into a werewolf and begins a small rural rampage. A virtually un-remarked upon staple on home video, *Wolfman* is an extremely amateurish Gothic horror attempt in the Universal/*Dark Shadows* vein. The sets and models look flimsy and the acting is like that of a bad stage-play. While it takes place in the 19th century, ugly modern wallpaper and the occasional visible powerline betray the production's modern origins. Owensby (who also stars as cinema's flabbiest werewolf) also produced, giving this the flavor of an Andy Milligan film done North Carolina style. Although the actors are supposed to be in the same family, Owensby's N.C. accent sticks out like a sore thumb. The first werewolf transformation doesn't happen until an hour in, and not much of interest happens after that. Owensby does attempt to create some atmosphere, though. Transferred from a fairly clean print source, the disc has accurate colors and is fairly sharp. Wider shots have a tendency to display digitized edges and some shots exhibit an overly processed look. The sound is adequate. All in all, a notch above a VHS. —DG
Movie: ♫ **DVD:** ♫♫
Brentwood (cat #44099-9, UPC 78736-4409990). Full frame. Mono. $4.99. Keepcase. *LANG:* English. *FEATURES:* "Little Rascals: Spooky Hooky" short • Trivia game • DVD dictionary.
1982 102m/C Earl Owensby, Kristina Reynolds, Sid Rancer, Julian Morton; **D:** Worth Keeter; **W:** Worth Keeter; **C:** Darrell Cathcart; **M:** David Floyd, Arthur Smith.

The Wolves of Kromer

A gay parable told as a fairy tale reversal of "Little Red Riding Hood." On the outskirts of the English village of Kromer live a group of "wolves"—essentially runaway gay men with fur coats, pointy ears, and tails. Young Seth (Williams) joins the wolves and falls in love with Gabriel (Layton) and the two have a playful, on-again, off-again relationship. When two despicable old women murder their mistress and lay the blame on the wolves, the town (led by the priest, Moore) takes arms against them. Based on a play, this film is certainly original and interesting, but lacks proper story development to make a full-length feature. More of the spare running time is spent on the old woman plot and the family than on the wolves, which makes the main story line with Seth and Gabriel somewhat unsatisfying. The epilogue is terrific, though, and Williams is quite an attractive lead. The lush photography gives the film an air of legitimacy that makes the central idea seem less silly than if it had been used in a threadbare production. The brief opening narration is by Boy George. The disc features a clear, crisp image with very slight grain. Colors are vivid and strong, though a few scenes have a bit of a purple cast to them. Except for one shot where the tops of heads are lopped off, the compositions seem appropriately framed. The soundtrack and audio recording are excellent. The commentary is worthwhile and the featurette is mostly comprised of valuable and interesting behind-the-scenes footage. —DG

Movie: 🎵🎵 ½ ***DVD:*** 🎵🎵🎵
First Run Features (cat #FRF909679D, UPC 720229909679). Widescreen (1.78:1) anamorphic. Dolby Digital Surround. $29.95. Keepcase. *LANG:* English. *FEATURES:* Behind-the-scenes featurette ● Commentary: Will Gould, Charles Lambert, Kevin Moore ● 11 chapters.
1998 77m/C *GB* Lee Williams, James Layton, Rita Davies, Margaret Towner, Rosemary Dunham, Angharad Rees, Kevin Moore, Leila Lloyd-Evelyn, Matthew Dean, David Prescott; ***D:*** Will Gould; ***W:*** Charles Lambert, Matthew Read; ***C:*** Laura Remacha; ***M:*** Basil Moore-Asfouri; ***Nar:*** Boy George.

Woman in Black

Chilling ghost story set in 1925 is adapted from Susan Hill's novel, which is also the basis of a long-running London stage play. Solicitor Arthur Kidd (Rawlings) is sent to a remote seaside house to settle the estate of a client. He's haunted by the mysterious figure of a woman in black, who, according to the locals, has put a curse on the village. He learns first hand exactly what they're talking about. This is a beautifully told tale that was made for British television. As such, there's little DVD can do with a so-so image that's no better than broadcast. Adding to the problems, the viewer must fast-forward through an ad for the company's *Sharpe* series. —MM

Movie: 🎵🎵🎵 ***DVD:*** 🎵🎵
BFS Video (cat #98553-D, UPC 06680591-5536). Full frame. Dolby Digital Mono.

$29.98. Keepcase. *LANG:* English. *FEATURES:* 12 chapters.
1989 100m/C *GB* Adrian Rawlins, Bernard Hepton, David Daker, Pauline Moran; ***D:*** Herbert Wise; ***W:*** Nigel Kneale.

Women in Cages

As the title suggests, this is one of the early and archetypal babes-behind-bars exploitation flicks. Pam Grier seems to be having a dandy time as Alabama, the vicious matron. Jennifer Gan is the innocent American girl who is cruelly tricked by her sleazeball boyfriend into taking the rap for his criminal activities. The rest has to do with de-lousing, showers, and some of the most outrageous torture scenes to be found in the genre. DVD image is very grainy but the disc was made from well-preserved original elements that display only minor surface damage. The funky sound comes from the original dubbing. It's alternately clipped and so harsh as to be unintelligible. —MM **AKA:** Women's Penitentiary 3.

Movie: 🎵🎵 ½ ***DVD:*** 🎵🎵
New Concorde (cat #NH20111 D, UPC 736991411197). Full frame. $14.98. Keepcase. *LANG:* English. *FEATURES:* 24 chapters ● Trailers ● Filmographies.
1971 (R) 78m/C Jennifer Gan, Judy Brown, Roberta Collins, Pam Grier; ***D:*** Gerardo (Gerry) De Leon; ***W:*** James H. Watkins, David R. Osterhout; ***C:*** F. Sacdalan; ***M:*** Tito Arevalo.

The Wood

Although not always perfect, this is an occasionally effective and entertaining story about a group of men remembering the times they spent growing up together in Inglewood, California (AKA: "The wood"). In present day, we're introduced to Mike (Epps), whose friend Roland (Diggs), who is about to be married, has gone missing. He's more than a little scared and more than a little drunk, so as the group prepares him to get hitched, we're introduced to more flashbacks about their high school years. The majority of their teen years seems like it's spent in pursuit of girls. The film is an entertaining look at these characters growing up. It skips back and forth smoothly between past and present and is frequently funny. Although the film goes on a little bit longer than it should have, it still manages to glide along on charming performances from both leads in the past and present scenes. Images are sharp and clear, and reveal very good detail throughout. Colors are strong, natural, and have no instances of bleeding. There are a couple of instances of shimmering and a few small marks on the print used. Dialogue is pretty much the focus of the audio department, although the few songs on the soundtrack occasionally kick in a little bit of bass. Everything sounds clear and without problems and dialogue is clean and free of flaws. —AB/DG

Movie: 🎵🎵🎵 ***DVD:*** 🎵🎵🎵

Paramount Home Video (UPC 973633699-43). Widescreen (1.85:1) anamorphic. Dolby Digital 5.1 Surround; Dolby Digital Surround. $29.98. Keepcase. *LANG:* English. *SUB:* English. *CAP:* English. *FEATURES:* Trailer ● 13 chapters.
1999 (R) 107m/C Omar Epps, Sean Nelson, Richard T. Jones, Taye Diggs, Trent Cameron, Malinda Williams, Duane Finley, Sanaa Lathan, De'Aundre Bonds, (Lisa Ray MacCoy) LisaRaye, Cynthia Martells, Tamala Jones, Elayne J. Taylor; ***D:*** Rick Famuyiwa; ***W:*** Rick Famuyiwa; ***C:*** Steven Bernstein; ***M:*** Robert Hurst.

Woodstock 99

Aah! The fires, the riots, the rapes, the broken toilets! 1999's warm, non-commercial follow-up to 1969's legendary "three days of peace and music" event at Woodstock, New York, became the antithesis of its inspiring event. This program captures one song from each of the many bands that played at the festival, and in between shows what went on during the event with plenty of interviews with the concert goers, some of whom are a little goofy, but still interesting to listen to. The artists on this disc include: Kid Rock, Everclear, Insane Clown Posse, Dave Matthews Band, and Alanis Morissette, among others. When the video steps into the crowds, it keeps to the lighter side of things, whitewashing the event by refusing to show the near-apocalyptic newsworthy events. Image quality, aside from a few little traces of pixelation, is excellent throughout, with strong colors and sharp images. The audio is simply fantastic. During some of the more metal numbers like Rage Against The Machine's "Bulls on Parade" or the techno of the Chemical Brothers "Block Rockin' Beats," the audio is incredibly powerful, with strong bass. Your neighbors will hate this one! The sound re-creates the feeling of a live concert. The "behind-the-scenes" footage runs 17 minutes and features extra footage of the crowds and a few interviews. —AB/DG

Movie: 🎵🎵🎵 ***DVD:*** 🎵🎵🎵 ½
Sony Music Video (UPC 74645020792). Full frame. Dolby Surround 5.1. $19.98. Keepcase. *LANG:* English. *FEATURES:* Photo gallery ● Behind-the-scenes footage.
1999 155m/C

The Woody Allen Collection

Please see individual reviews of *Broadway Danny Rose, Hannah and Her Sisters, Midsummer Night's Sex Comedy, Purple Rose of Cairo, Radio Days,* and *Zelig.* —MM

Movie: 🎵🎵🎵 ½ ***DVD:*** 🎵🎵🎵 ½
MGM Home Ent. (cat #1001750, UPC 027616860507). Widescreen (1.85:1) anamorphic. Dolby Digital Mono. $99.96. Boxed set. *LANG:* English; French; Spanish. *SUB:* English; French; Spanish. *CAP:* English. *FEATURES:* 16 chapters per film ● Booklet.
2001 528m/C

Working

This is a television version of the stage musical of Studs Terkel's book of interviews about work. Fans of the cast are the target audience since this is hardly a milestone of the genre. It's part of the Broadway Theatre Archives and the PBS American Playhouse series and so there's little DVD can do to improve the image. It's no better than broadcast or VHS quality. Sound is nothing special. —*MM*
Movie: ♫♫ *DVD:* ♫♫
Image Ent. (cat #ID0882B DDVD, UPC 014381088229). Full frame. Dolby Digital Stereo. $24.98. Keepcase. *LANG:* English. *FEATURES:* 25 chapters • Trailers • Liner notes.
1982 88m/C Barry Bostwick, Rita Moreno, James Taylor, Eileen Brennan, Charles Durning, Barbara Hershey, Patti LaBelle, Scatman Crothers; **D:** Stephen Schwartz, Kirk Browning; **M:** James Taylor, Stephen Schwartz, Craig Carnelia, Mickey Grant, Mary Rodgers, Susan Birkenhead.

The World according to Garp

Screenwriter Steve Tesich is relatively faithful to John Irving's popular novel which chronicles the life of T.S. Garp (Williams), who struggles to maintain his optimism while pummeled by various forces of modern society. At the core of the film is a subplot involving a group of extreme feminists inspired in part by Garp's mother (Close). She and Lithgow (as a giant transsexual) are spectacular while Williams takes a low-key approach to the beleaguered Garp. (Irving has a cameo as a wrestling referee.) DVD delivers a fine image for a film of this age. It ranges between good and very good. Subtitles are helpful with the sometimes muffled dialogue. Even though the film is no cinematic milestone, some kind of commentary track would seem to be called for. —*MM*
Movie: ♫♫♫ *DVD:* ♫♫ ½
Warner (cat #11261). Widescreen. $19.98. Snapper. *LANG:* English; French. *SUB:* English; French; Portuguese; Spanish. *FEATURES:* 44 chapters • Trailer • Talent files • Awards.
1982 (R) 136m/C Robin Williams, Mary Beth Hurt, John Lithgow, Glenn Close, Hume Cronyn, Jessica Tandy, Swoosie Kurtz, Amanda Plummer, Warren Berlinger, Brandon Maggart, George Roy Hill; **D:** George Roy Hill; **W:** Steve Tesich; **C:** Miroslav Ondricek; **M:** David Shire. *AWARDS:* L.A. Film Critics '82: Support. Actor (Lithgow), Support. Actress (Close); Natl. Bd. of Review '82: Support. Actress (Close); N.Y. Film Critics '82: Support. Actor (Lithgow); *NOM:* Oscars '82: Support. Actor (Lithgow), Support. Actress (Close).

The World at War

Jeremy Isaacs's ambitious miniseries documentary about World War II remains the standard against which all others are judged. As he notes in his introduction, since it was brought to America in the early 1970s, it has never been off the air. That's completely understandable. The one-hour episodes deliver a superb mix of history and fascinating entertainment that combines archival film with new footage and interviews. Holding it all together is Laurence Olivier's pitch-perfect narration. The focus is on the English experience. DVD image is not a huge improvement over VHS tape or broadcast. The material filmed in the 1970s is pretty grainy and that leads to blossoming artifacts in almost all panning and tracking shots. There's also a moderate amount of surface damage, but technical polish has never been the point here. With a work of this size, accessibility is much more important and the five double-sided discs are broken into more than 700 chapters. Extras are well chosen. The programs are also available as individual discs. —*MM*
Movie: ♫♫♫ ½ *DVD:* ♫♫♫
HBO Home Video (UPC 026359924620). Full frame. $119.98. Keepcase (5-disc boxed set). *LANG:* English. *FEATURES:* 732 chapters • "Making of" documentary • Time line • Thumbnail bios • Photo galleries • Weblinks • Brief history-text • Episode summaries.
1973 1920m/C D: Ted Childs, Michael Darlow, David Elstein, John Pett, Hugh Raggett, Martin Smith; **Nar:** Laurence Olivier.

World History of Organized Crime

History Channel documentary is the usual straightforward, well-paced introduction to its subject. The two-disc set contains five programs that examine the roots and contemporary activities of organized criminals in Sicily, Russia, Colombia, China, and India, with a combination of travelogue footage, interviews, and dramatic re-creations. Some of the material is rough, of course, but the new footage looks very good. Sound is fine, too. The "time lines" extra is text. —*MM*
Movie: ♫♫ ½ *DVD:* ♫♫ ½
New Video Group (cat #AAE-70400, UPC 733961704006). Full frame. $39.98. Keepcase boxed set. *LANG:* English. *FEATURES:* 30 chapters • Time lines.
2001 250m/C W: Scott M. Alexander.

The World of Sid & Marty Krofft

This indispensable 3-disc box-set collects episodes from the Saturday morning shows created by Sid & Marty Krofft. These shows combined live-action actors and sets with imaginative puppetry and costumed characters. While these shows come off as incredibly dated and silly today, the memories will come flooding in for anyone who grew up with these peculiar TV oddities. The set contains one episode from each of the following programs: *H.R. Pufnstuf, Bugaloos, Lidsville, Sigmund & the Sea Monsters, Land of the Lost, Far Out Space Nuts, The Lost Saucer, ElectraWoman and Dynagirl, Dr. Shrinker,* *Wonderbug, Magic Mongo, Bigfoot and Wildboy,* and *Pryor's Place.* While none of the shows are as good today as they seemed to be 20–30 years ago, some of them, such as *Sigmund & the Sea Monsters* and *Land of the Lost,* still have a certain playful charm. Besides the incredible trip back in time that this set offers, it's also interesting to examine the "name" actors who appeared in these shows. While none of them are superstars, most everyone would recognize Jim Nabors, Ruth Buzzi, Bob Denver, Deidre Hall, Charles Nelson Reilly, and Martha Raye. And then *Pryor's Place* is a cultural archive unto itself. Richard Pryor had a children's show? Who knew?! It's clear that Rhino put a great deal of work into this set. Most of the shows here were produced on videotape, so the quality of the transfers are quite good, offering clear pictures and good colors. However, *H.R. Pufnstuf* and *Bigfoot and Wildboy* were shot on film, and these two episodes display a number of defects from the source material. (*Pufnstuf* looks especially bad.) The audio track here is a digital stereo, which provides a clarity and volume, making each of the incredibly convoluted theme-songs easy to understand. There are no extra features here, which is a glaring error, as this set should have contained some sort of history or biography for the Kroffts. —*ML*
Movie: ♫♫ *DVD:* ♫♫♫
Rhino (cat #R2 2625, UPC 6034972625-26). Full frame. Digital Stereo. $49.95. Trifold Case. *LANG:* English.
2002 390m/C

World Trade Center— A Modern Marvel: 1973–2001

Completed just months prior to the destruction of the World Trade Center, this archival documentary is destined to become something of a landmark in its own right. This stunning film is filled with interviews of the people who planned, fought for, and built the famed twin towers that would come to symbolize America's industrial and financial might. The picture quality is good with very few noticeable artifacts throughout the course of the 50-minute feature. A decent 5.1 Surround track makes adequate use of all six speakers. The special features are light, providing only a time line of the towers. —*EL*
Movie: ♫♫♫ *DVD:* ♫♫♫
New Video Group (cat #70487, UPC 7339-61704897). Full frame. Dolby 5.1 Surround Sound. $19.95. Keepcase. *LANG:* English. *FEATURES:* World Trade Center time line • 9 chapters.
2001 50m/C D: Bruce Nash; **W:** Nancy Dey, Bob Petrella.

World War I Films of the Silent Era

These four films have more historical value than entertainment value. Two of them, "Fighting the War" (1916) and "The Log of the U-35" (1919/20), are essentially plotless "reality footage." American Donald C. Thompson (who, according to the liner notes, lived a life that cries out to be turned into a film) actually went into the trenches and onto fields that were being shelled to capture the action on motion picture film. Image quality is very rough by contemporary standards and some stretches have been badly damaged but this is still an invaluable record of what happened. Lothar Von Arnauld de la Perrière was the captain of a German U-boat and an amateur filmmaker. He shot home movies of his boat's finest moments—the sinking of ships and the handling of survivors—along with more routine activities. This version of the film was created from the German release "Der Magische Gürtel." "The Secret Game" is an early fictional look at espionage during the war directed by William B. DeMille (older brother of Cecil). It stars Sessue Hayakawa as a Japanese man who helps the American army capture German spies. (At that time, the Japanese were allies.) Parts of the film have been well preserved; others display severe chemical burns and lesser signs of wear. Finally, "The Moving Picture Boys in the Great War" (1975) is a documentary that incorporates some footage from the first two films. It's narrated by Lowell Thomas. For anyone who's interested in this crucially important but almost forgotten part of our history, the disc is required viewing. —MM

Movie: 𝄞𝄞𝄞 ½ **DVD:** 𝄞𝄞𝄞
Image Ent. (cat #ID0512DSDVD, UPC 014381051223). Full frame. Dolby Digital Stereo; Mono. $24.98. Keepcase. *LANG:* Silent. *SUB:* English intertitles. *FEATURES:* 53 chapters • Liner notes by David Shepard • Music by Eric Beheim.
2002 167m/C Sessue Hayakawa, Jack Holt, Florence Vidor, Raymond Hatton, Charles Ogle; *D:* William C. deMille, Larry Ward, Donald C. Thompson; *W:* Marion Fairfax; *C:* Charles Rosher; *Nar:* Lowell Thomas.

The Worm Eaters

Mean developers want to take over a reclusive worm farmer's land. He unleashes his livestock on them. The bad guys turn into—eeck!—"worm people." A truck runs over our hero nearly 75 minutes too late to save the viewer. Those who thought that director Mikels had hit bottom with *10 Violent Women* have been proved wrong. This one's much worse. For humor, imagine a lost episode of *Hee Haw* but production values on *Hee Haw* were a bit better than these. It's rough, grainy, and cheap throughout and there's nothing that DVD can do about it. —MM

Movie: woof **DVD:** 𝄞𝄞
Image Ent. (cat #ID0836TGDVD, UPC 014-381083620). Widescreen (1.78:1) anamorphic. Dolby Digital Mono. $24.98. Keepcase. *LANG:* English. *FEATURES:* Trailer • Commentary: Ted V. Mikels • 13 chapters.
1977 (PG) 75m/C Herb Robins, Barry Hostetler, Lindsay Armstrong Black,

Joseph Sacket, Robert Garrison, Mike Garrison; *D:* Herb Robins; *W:* Herb Robins; *C:* Willis Hawkins; *M:* Theodore Stern.

The Worst Witch

Not to be confused with the 1986 TV film starring Fairuza Balk and Tim Curry, this is instead a late '90s British/Canadian television series based on *The Worst Witch* novels by author Jill Murphy. The story is set at Miss Cackle's Academy for Witches, a school where young witches go to be trained to perform spells and fly on brooms. The Academy is turned upsidedown when young Mildred Hubble (Georgina Sherrington) enters the school. Mildred desperately wants to be a witch, but the problem is that she's not very good at it. She can't fly very well, and often botches her spells, but she never stops trying, despite the discouragement of evil teacher Miss Hardbroom (Kate Duchene) and the taunting of fellow student Ethel Hallow (Felicity Jones). With the assistance of her friend Maud (Emma Brown) and the gentle guidance of Miss Cackle (Clare Coulter), Mildred is usually able to find her way out of even the stickiest messes. The series follows Mildred through her first year at the Academy, as she makes new friends, attempts to perfect her abilities, and learns a great deal about herself. The show is good-spirited fun which never takes itself too seriously. In an interesting twist, the character of Mildred is a bit unlikable at first, and must grow on the viewer, as she does on her classmates. The DVDs included in these newly released boxed sets (each DVD is also available separately) feature the program in its original full-frame format. The image is sharp and relatively clear, but this digital transfer has revealed some of the budgetary constraints of the show. A great deal of "green screen" FX are used here and they look simply awful on this DVD presentation. Also, there is some video noise visible in shots where the camera is moving quickly. The Dolby Digital Stereo audio track is satisfactory, as it offers clear dialogue, with no distortion or hissing. It's interesting to note that the original British dialogue track is offered here, but there is also a dubbed English track where the actors have no accents! —ML

Movie: 𝄞𝄞 ½ **DVD:** 𝄞𝄞
BFS Video (UPC 066805301568). Full frame. Dolby Digital Stereo. $29.99. Keepcase box set. *LANG:* English; Spanish; French; German; U.K. English. *FEATURES:* Photo gallery • 24 chapters • Set 2 runs 175 minutes, UPC 066805301599.
1998 150m/C *GB CA* Georgina Sherrington, Kate Duchene, Felicity Jones, Emma Brown, Clare Coulter, Una Stubbs; *D:* Andrew Morgan; *W:* Martin Riley.

The Wrecking Crew

Ice-T plays a bloodthirsty bounty hunter hired by the government to "handle" warring gangs. There are three gangs. Two

form an alliance to wipe out the third, but Ice and his boys monkey up their plans. Of the 80-minute running time, about 15 minutes are frittered away in title sequences. The remaining time is skillfully used to see how many bombs can be dropped, and corpses stacked, in an hour. There's a somewhat moralistic, hollow ending. Not enough gang violence in your neighborhood? This is for you. Without a doubt one of the worst 5.1 audio tracks ever mastered. The dialogue sounds as though it was recorded in an echo chamber. However, the music and fireworks rumble nicely. Switch to the 2.0 track instead. There's also an isolated music track. The video quality is generally awful also, but at least it's presented in its original widescreen ratio. Director Albert Pyun's commentary deals mostly with the production process. He talks in detail about the decision to split the movie up (during shooting this became three films) and how the film was shot so quickly. Actors David Askew and Ernie Hudson Jr. see the film together for the first time during their commentary track. The soft-spoken pair (who played rival gang leaders) don't seem entirely comfortable with the film's violence, or language. Roughly three minutes of behind-the-scenes footage is included. —GNG/DG

Movie: 𝄞 ½ **DVD:** 𝄞 ½
Studio Home Ent. (UPC 658149741522). Widescreen (1.85:1) letterboxed. Dolby Digital 5.1 Surround; Dolby Digital Surround. $29.95. Keepcase. *LANG:* English. *SUB:* Spanish. *FEATURES:* Commentary: Pyun, Hudson, Askew • DVD-ROM—script feature • Behind-the-scenes footage • Trailers • Chapter links • Isolated music track • Still gallery.
1999 (R) 81m/C Ice-T, Snoop Dogg, David Askew, Ernie Hudson Jr.; *D:* Albert Pyun; *W:* Hannah Blue.

Wrestling Women USA!

The good folks at Something Weird Video certainly live up to their name with this collection of short films and one short feature, all apparently from the 1950s and early '60s, about women wrestling. Most of the bouts take place in a conventional ring. Some are outdoors and one, "Glamazon Living Room Rumble," really does take place in what appears to be somebody's living room, complete with shag carpet and ugly furniture. The four women involved are giggling and the ferocity is strictly on the level of a pillow fight. The feature, "Pin Down Girl," is all about the dirty side of the business with gangsters who fix fights and engage in other slimeball activities. "Girls of the Mat" contains six matches. The quality of the films varies considerably. The feature is considerably nicked up. Many of the short works are essentially home movies and look it. The commentary by Johnny Legend is appropriately lighthearted. —MM

Movie: 𝄞𝄞 **DVD:** 𝄞𝄞𝄞
Something Weird Video (cat #ID0808SWD-VD, UPC 014381080827). Full frame.

Dolby Digital Mono. $24.98. Keepcase. *LANG:* English. *FEATURES:* 14 chapters ▪ 5 short films ▪ Commentary: Johnny Legend ▪ Stills gallery.
2001 212m/C Timothy Farrell, Clara Mortensen, Rita Martinez, Peaches Page.

Written on the Wind

Sirk's frenzied glossy melodrama created the template that would be copied by *Dallas* and a host of other (and lesser) TV soaps. Based on Robert Wilder's novel (itself loosely based on the famous Libby Holman/Smith Reynolds scandal), the film tells the story of the Hadley family—weak-willed but libidinous son Kyle (Stack) who marries Lucy (Bacall) who really loves Kyle's best friend Mitch (Hudson), who is also lusted after by Kyle's sister Marylee (Malone). The fevered story, told in flashback, is as entertaining today as it has ever been. DVD can boast a near-perfect image that captures the sumptuous production design and the stylized acting. Sound is a bit clipped, however, and lacks clarity in a few moments. That comes from the technology of the times, though and is not really a weakness. Great fun with well-chosen extras, including an annotated and illustrated Sirk filmography. —*MM*
Movie: ♪♪♪ ½ **DVD:** ♪♪♪ ½
Criterion (cat #96, UPC 715515011525). Widescreen (1.77:1) anamorphic. Dolby Digital Mono. $29.98. Keepcase. *LANG:* English. *SUB:* English. *FEATURES:* Liner notes by film theorist Laura Mulvey ▪ 23 chapters ▪ 2 trailers ▪ Sirk filmography.
1956 99m/C Lauren Bacall, Rock Hudson, Dorothy Malone, Robert Stack, Robert Keith, Grant Williams, Edward Platt, Harry Shannon; *D:* Douglas Sirk; *W:* George Zuckerman; *C:* Russell Metty. *AWARDS:* Oscars '56: Support. Actress (Malone); *NOM:* Oscars '56: Song ("Written on the Wind"), Support. Actor (Stack).

Wuthering Heights

Fuest's version of Emily Bronte's romance (the third film adaptation) features excellent photography, fine performances by Dalton and Calder-Marshall as Heathcliff and Cathy, and good Yorkshire locations. All right, it's not the equal of the William Wyler film, but younger audiences will find it more accessible. Both the widescreen and full-frame images are excellent, even in the darker interiors. The DVD was created from exceptionally well-preserved original elements. —*MM*
Movie: ♪♪♪ **DVD:** ♪♪♪
MGM Home Ent. (cat #1002748, UPC 027-616869463). Widescreen (1.85:1) anamorphic; full frame. Dolby Digital Mono. $14.98. Keepcase. *LANG:* English; French. *SUB:* English; French; Spanish. *CAP:* English. *FEATURES:* Trailers ▪ 16 chapters.
1970 (G) 105m/C *GB* Anna Calder-Marshall, Timothy Dalton, Harry Andrews, Pamela Brown, Judy Cornwell, James Cossins, Rosalie Crutchley, Hilary Dwyer, Hugh Griffith, Ian Ogilvy; *D:* Robert Fuest;

W: Patrick Tilley; *C:* John Coquillon; *M:* Michel Legrand.

X

In the near future, two groups of citizens (with amazing telekinetic powers) battle each other with the existence of humanity at stake. Young student and warrior Kamui returns to Tokyo to protect his friends, Fuma and Kotoro, but eventually discovers that Fuma is also a psychic warrior and has chosen to try to bring about the apocalypse. As all of the warriors engage in combat, Tokyo falls in ruin and Kamui and Fuma find themselves forced to fight each other to the death. Based on the comic by the woman's collective "CLAMP" the film does a nice job of condensing the material and providing the story with an ending, but suffers from some confusing character relationships and a lack of character development. The animation is beautiful and impressive (several shots are breathtaking), and the pace never drags. Unfortunately, the disc does not sport an anamorphic transfer, but the imagery is sharp, colorful, and detailed. The transfer is prone to digital noise and aliasing at times. Still, it's better than a VHS and the audio track is involving and excellent. The English dub is better than most, but the subtitled version is still preferable. —*AB/DG* **AKA:** X:1999.
Movie: ♪♪♪ **DVD:** ♪♪♪
Manga Ent. (cat #MANGA40462 WR01, UPC 660200404628). Widescreen (1.85:1) letterboxed. Dolby Surround 5.1; Dolby Surround. $29.95. Keepcase. *LANG:* Japanese; English. *SUB:* English. *FEATURES:* Booklet with chapter listings ▪ 15 chapters ▪ Theatrical trailer ▪ Character bios ▪ Text interview with the director ▪ Photo gallery ▪ Manga DVD previews.
1996 (R) 98m/C *JP D:* Taro Rin; *W:* Mami Watanabe, Nanase Ohkawa; *M:* Yasuaki Shimizu.

The X-Files: Season 4

While the DVD package is perfect, the content is more of a mixed bag. Season 4 saw FBI agent Fox Mulder (David Duchovny) drawn deeper into the conspiracy involving an alien takeover of Earth. And while his partner, Agent Dana Scully (Gillian Anderson) had always been a skeptic who attempted to keep Mulder grounded in reality, she too got dragged into the cover-up, as her character developed an alien-abduction related cancer. The true highlights of this set are those "stand alone" episodes which don't fit in with the conspiracy story arc. Episodes such as the eerie "Home" or "El Mundo Gira" (which deals with the mythical Chupacabra!) show that while *The X-Files* may have lost some of its luster, it hadn't lost its ability to frighten and entertain. The episodes here are all presented full frame and they look very nice—equal to or better than broadcast quality. The image is clear and sharp, and the colors are realistic. The 2.0 Surround audio track provides a

nice layer of ambience which adds to the effectiveness of the show. Fans of the show will surely be pleased by the sheer volume of extras in this package. While audio commentaries and a season-overview documentary provide a look behind-the-scenes, the inclusion of over 60 TV promos for the show should satiate even the most obsessive fan. —*ML*
Movie: ♪♪♪ ½ **DVD:** ♪♪♪♪
20th Century Fox (cat #2002005, UPC 024543020059). Full frame. Dolby 2.0 Surround. $149.97. Special Box Set. *LANG:* English; French. *SUB:* English; Spanish. *CAP:* English. *FEATURES:* Deleted scenes ▪ Documentary ▪ Interviews ▪ TV spots ▪ Special effects feature ▪ Commentary ▪ International clips.
2000 148m/C David Duchovny, Gillian Anderson.

Xena: Warrior Princess— Series Finale

When the campy hit television series finished after six seasons, the producers decided to end the show with a bang, resulting in this feature-length special. And for some reason, USA Films decided to make the last episode of the show mark Xena's Region 1 DVD debut. Xena (Lawless) and Gabrielle (O'Connor) head east to Japan and are forced to battle Yodoshi (Brown), the eater of souls, because of a favor Xena had granted her friend Hakimi (Ang) many years earlier. The episode was directed by series producer (and Lawless's husband) Robert Tapert, who paces the show quite well, with secrets being revealed every few minutes. (Although Tapert went too far by emulating old pal Sam Raimi in one shot which comes straight out of *Evil Dead*.) DVD includes a "Director's Cut" of the show, which incorporates 16 minutes of footage that wasn't seen on broadcast television. The full-frame image is very sharp and clear, rivaling digital broadcast quality. There are no defects and the image is basically free of grain. Audio is quite lively, as it provides clear dialogue, nice sound effects, and active Surround action. Commentary features Tapert, Lawless, and O'Connor. Unfortunately, Lawless doesn't seem to take the proceedings very seriously and O'Connor is obviously busy with her infant child. So, Tapert does most of the talking and does make some good comments about the production of the episode and the Xena legacy. The 30-minute "making of" featurette contains some nice behind-the-scenes footage and interviews. —*ML/LA*
Movie: ♪♪♪ **DVD:** ♪♪♪
USA Home Ent. (cat #963060352-2, UPC 696306305220). Full frame. Dolby 2.0 Surround. $24.95. Keepcase. *LANG:* English. *CAP:* English. *FEATURES:* Featurette ▪ Commentary ▪ Still gallery.
2001 100m/C Lucy Lawless, Renee O'Connor, Michelle Ang, Adrian Brown; *D:* Robert Tapert; *W:* R.J. Stewart.

The Yellow Fountain

This Spanish thriller doesn't match the quality of other recent films from Spain. Following the mysterious suicide of her boyfriend, Lola (Silvia Abascal) heads for Madrid to research the Chinese side of her family, and to get clues surrounding her beau's strange behavior. There, she meets Sergio (Eduardo Noriega), a nerdy government employee whose hobby is collecting data on Chinese immigrants. Together, they uncover an illegal immigrant smuggling ring, and Lola decides to take on the ruthless Triads. Director Miguel Santesmases allows the film to unfold at a deliberate pace, as another piece of the puzzle is revealed every few minutes. The problem is that most of the story seems very hackneyed. We've all seen the movie where the fearless girl influences the bookish guy, and the image of Chinese only being gangsters is getting very old. The bright spot in the film is Noriega, who sheds his playboy image from *Tesis* and *Abre Los Ojos* and is quite good as the quiet Sergio. The film is presented in a widescreen format and offers an average transfer. The image is dark and there are some defects from the source print. A Dolby 2.0 Surround audio track gives clear dialogue and occasional rear-speaker action. The subtitles are clear and easy to read. —*ML* **AKA:** La Fuente Amarilla.

Movie: 🎬🎬 **DVD:** 🎬🎬
Vanguard Intl. Cinema (cat #TF1012, UPC 681116101227). Widescreen (1.85:1) letterboxed. Dolby Digital Surround. $29.95. Keepcase. *LANG:* Spanish. *SUB:* English. *FEATURES:* 12 chapters.
1999 94m/C SP Silvia Abascal, Eduardo Noriega, Carlos Wu, Chuen Lam; **D:** Miguel Santesmases; **W:** Miguel Santesmases; **C:** Javier Aguirresarobe.

You Are Here *

Pretentious, undistributed digital video feature about four jobless losers in New York City. Moe (Peters), Jason (Jaynes), Sanjay (Naidu), and Sallie (Hall) aimlessly wander around and talk but never really say anything. Peters has a vague charisma. Director's commentary fails to illuminate the point of this movie. Transfer looks O.K. considering the low production values and bad lighting. Letterbox masking isn't always black. Sound is badly mixed with constant intrusive background music. —*LA*

Movie: 🎬 **DVD:** 🎬
Vanguard Intl. Cinema (cat #VF0228, UPC 658769022834). Widescreen letterboxed. $29.95. Keepcase. *LANG:* English. *FEATURES:* Director's intro and commentary • Deleted scenes • Trailer • 12 chapters.
2000 (R) 86m/C Todd Peters, Randall Jaynes, Ajay Naidu, Caroline Hall, Larry Fessenden, Heather Burns; **D:** Jeff Winner; **W:** Jeff Winner; **C:** Bryan Pryzpek; **M:** Byron Estep.

You Light Up My Life

Unendurable, sappy excuse to showcase songs by writer/director Brooks. Laurie Robinson (Conn), aspiring actress and songwriter, tries to please her obnoxious father Si (Silver) by attempting to make a go of it as a comedienne. One note performance by squeaky-voiced Conn is unbearable. Image and sound quality are very good, but it was hardly worth the effort. The overlit, garish color scheme gave me a headache. —*LA*

Movie: woof **DVD:** 🎬🎬🎬 ½
Columbia Tristar (cat #07964, UPC 0433-96079649). Widescreen anamorphic; full frame. Digitally Mastered Mono. $24.98. Keepcase. *LANG:* English; French. *SUB:* French; Spanish; Portuguese; Chinese; Korean; Thai. *CAP:* English. *FEATURES:* 28 chapters.
1977 (PG) 91m/C Didi Conn, Michael Zaslow, Melanie Mayron, Joe Silver, Stephen Nathan; **D:** Joseph Brooks; **W:** Joseph Brooks; **C:** Eric Saarinen; **M:** Joseph Brooks. *AWARDS:* Oscars '77: Song ("You Light Up My Life"); Golden Globes '78: Song ("You Light Up My Life").

The Young Bruce Lee

A young boy named Bruce Lee and his friend both learn the martial arts in order to defend themselves from bullies. As they grow up Lee sets his sights on becoming a movie star while his friend performs in acrobatic stage shows. Though Lee achieves stardom, he finds himself hounded by martial artists that want to challenge him. This unauthorized biopic follows the major events in Bruce Lee's life but most of it is clichéd fabrication. The film is cheap and poorly crafted, but Lung (AKA Bruce Li) does a fairly successful job of mimicking Lee and he's helped by an accurate hairdo and wardrobe. As far as Bruce Lee wannabe films, you could do a lot worse. Despite the packaging, there is no Lee footage in the film—only a newsphoto of his body. The disc features a pale, soft, faded transfer of an occasionally tattered theatrical print. The cropped image is a poor representation of its much wider Techniscope compositions. The dubbing and sound effects are flatly recorded. —*DG*

Movie: 🎬🎬 **DVD:** 🎬 ½
Goodtimes Ent. (cat #05-81189, UPC 018-713811899). Full frame. Mono. $7.49. Keepcase. *LANG:* English. *FEATURES:* 12 chapters • Insert card with chapter listings.
1980 80m/C Bruce Li.

The Young Girls of Rochefort

Jacques Demy's impressively mounted production almost captures the effortless charm of the American dancing musicals it emulates. The sentiment is in the right place, but whether or not the magic comes will depend on the particular viewer. Easy to like but too lengthy to sustain its energy, this colorful and bright show is perfect for diehard musical fans and lovers of director Jacques Demy and composer Michel Legrand. In this collaboration they employ jazz rhythms in a musical that's concerned more with Demy's theories of romance than Hollywood conventions. A boat and recreation show comes to the port town of Rochefort, but dancers Etienne (George Chakiris) and Bill (Grover Dale) have to look for replacements for their female counterparts when entertainers Esther (Leslie North) and Judith (Pamela Hart) decide to run off with sailors. Enter the Garnier twins, ballet teacher Delphine (Catherine Deneuve) and piano teacher Solange (Françoise Dorléac), and the unwinding of a complex web of romantic entanglements. Delphine is breaking up with art gallery owner Guillaume Lancien (Jacques Riberolles). He displays a painting by young soldier Maxence (Jacques Perrin) that looks just like Delphine, although Maxence has never met her. Maxence has met Delphine's mother Yvonne (Danielle Darrieux), and tells her that he's searching the world for the feminine ideal of his painting. Meanwhile, Yvonne pines for the lover she spurned 10 years before for frivolous reasons. He's Simon Dame (Michel Piccoli), who's just returned to Rochefort thinking Yvonne's long gone to Mexico. He's soft on Solange, who wants to go to Paris to meet successful composer Andy Miller (Gene Kelly), not realizing she's already met him here in town. Add to that several other characters whose random destinies hinge on chance encounters on Rochefort's charming streets, and it's hard to tell who will end up with whom. DVD can't be faulted. Some reviews criticized the early Fox-Lorber release of Demy's *The Umbrellas of Cherbourg* as poorly framed and even time-compressed, but this disc looks accurate and uncompromised. The softer French color palate is well-represented. The slight warping at the edges of the image in some shots appears to be part of the original photography. The Dolby Digital audio is mono. There are no real extras; the trailers on board are recent promos prepped for video release. On my player, no English subtitles came up until I hit the appropriate remote button, so if you want a clean start, set them beforehand. —*GE* **AKA:** Les Demoiselles de Rochefort.

Movie: 🎬🎬🎬 ½ **DVD:** 🎬🎬🎬 ½
Buena Vista Home Ent. (UPC 7179510-05007). Widescreen (2.35:1) anamorphic. Dolby Digital Mono. $34.98. Keepcase. *LANG:* French. *SUB:* English. *CAP:* English.
1968 125m/C FR Catherine Deneuve, Françoise Dorleac, George Chakiris, Grover Dale, Gene Kelly, Jacques Perrin, Danielle Darrieux, Michel Piccoli, Pamela Hart, Jacques Riberolles, Leslie North; **D:** Jacques Demy; **W:** Jacques Demy; **C:** Ghislan Cloquet; **M:** Michel Legrand.

The Young Land

Idealistic sheriff Patrick Wayne decides to inject some law and order into his frontier town by calling in a federal judge to try a Mexican-hating gunslinger (Hopper) for murder. Also on trial is the American judicial system, as groups of white settlers and Mexicans prepare to stir up trouble if they aren't happy with the verdict. An extremely young Dennis Hopper brings his usual bundle of nervous energy to his role as the defendant. This is a standard bargain-basement disc with lots of grain, inconsistent colors, and a picture that seems to have been cropped from widescreen. The sound is indistinguishable from tape. —BG

Movie: 🦴 ½ **DVD:** 🦴 ½
VCI (cat #8324, UPC 089859832420). Full frame. Dolby Mono. $9.99. Keepcase. *LANG:* English. *FEATURES:* 12 chapters ▪ Trailers.
1959 88m/C Dennis Hopper, Patrick Wayne, Dan O'Herlihy, Yvonne Craig, Ken Curtis, Pedro Gonzalez-Gonzalez; **D:** Ted Tetzlaff; **W:** Norman S. Hall; **C:** Winton C. Hoch, Henry Sharp; **M:** Dimitri Tiomkin. *AWARDS: NOM:* Oscars '59: Song ("Strange Are the Ways of Love").

The Young Lions

Sensitive German Army Lieutenant Christian Diestl (Brando) doesn't understand the harsh attitudes of his peers and superiors, and undergoes a slow demoralization as the war proceeds in North Africa. Meanwhile, singer Michael Whiteacre (Martin) is drafted, and makes friends with Jewish-American Noah Ackerman (Clift), who falls in love with whitebread New England girl Hope Plowman (Lange) before shipping off to Europe. The soldiers on opposite sides suffer through their predicaments until their fates eventually cross paths at a concentration camp in Western Germany, near the very end of the conflict. The main complaint with the show is that it looks so cheap and flat, the same quality Dmytryk was somehow able to impart to the very expensive *Raintree County*. All of the money must have gone into the actors, because it's not in the production. Half of a scene in North Africa is stolen from (I think) *The Immortal Sergeant*, an older Fox film. Stock shots don't mix with the new CinemaScope lensing very well, especially those that have just been cut in flat and allowed to squash out horizontally. DVD looks clean and neat, and spreads out nice 'n' wide in black and white. This points up all of those production deficiencies but gives you a front row seat at all the good acting in view. —GE

Movie: 🦴🦴 **DVD:** 🦴🦴🦴
20th Century Fox (cat #2002540, UPC 024543025405). Widescreen (2.35:1) anamorphic. Stereo. $19.98. Keepcase. *LANG:* English; French. *SUB:* English; Spanish. *CAP:* English. *FEATURES:* Trailers ▪ 40 chapters.
1958 167m/B Marlon Brando, Montgomery Clift, Dean Martin, Hope Lange, Barbara Rush, Lee Van Cleef, Maximilian Schell, May Britt, Dora Doll, Liliane Montevecchi, Parley Baer, Arthur Franz, Hal Baylor, Richard Gardner, Herbert Rudley, L.Q. (Justus E. McQueen) Jones; **D:** Edward Dmytryk; **W:** Edward Anhalt; **C:** Joe MacDonald; **M:** Hugo Friedhofer; **Technical Advisor:** Allison A. Conrad. *AWARDS: NOM:*

Oscars '58: B&W Cinematog., Sound, Orig. Dramatic Score.

Your Place or Mine!

Another romantic romp starring Tony Leung Chiu-wei, who narrates. An advertising creative director who has trouble holding onto women finds himself involved with two at once: his sophisticated new boss, and a naïve young model. Meanwhile, his womanizing best friend goes into shock when he meets the right girl and doesn't want to cheat on her. Plenty of modern soap opera, but comedy? Not so much. Transfer and features are acceptable. —BT

Movie: 🦴 **DVD:** 🦴🦴
Tai Seng (cat #5224, UPC 48950249014-66). Widescreen letterboxed. $19.95. Keepcase. *LANG:* Cantonese; Mandarin. *SUB:* Chinese; English. *FEATURES:* 8 chapters ▪ Star profiles ▪ Outtakes ▪ Trailers.
1998 101m/C *HK* Tony Leung Chiu-Wai, Vivian Hsu, Ada Choi, Alex Fong, Suki Kwan, Eileen Tung, Spencer Lam; **D:** James Yuen; **W:** James Yuen; **C:** Man Po Cheung; **M:** Lincoln Lo.

Zebra Lounge

Where *Hand That Rocked the Cradle* posited a nanny who threatened a family, this Canadian thriller has spouse-swappers. Young parents Alan (Daddo) and Wendy (Ledford) are looking to spice things up romantically. They place an ad and eventually wind up meeting Louise (Swanson) and Jack (Baldwin), who turn out to be more than they had expected. Director Skogland handles the material with more attention to characters than the "erotic thriller" synopsis might lead you to expect. She also gives the production the polish of a major studio release and DVD captures it with a flawless image. Sound is fine, too. —MM

Movie: 🦴🦴 ½ **DVD:** 🦴🦴 ½
Columbia Tristar (cat #07604, UPC 0433-96076044). Widescreen (1.85:1) letterboxed. Dolby Digital 5.1 Surround Stereo; Dolby Digital Surround. $24.95. Keepcase. *LANG:* English; Spanish. *SUB:* English; Spanish. *FEATURES:* 23 chapters ▪ Still gallery ▪ Trailer.
2001 93m/C *CA* Stephen Baldwin, Kristy Swanson, Cameron Daddo, Brandy Ledford; **D:** Keri Skogland; **W:** Claire Montgomery, Monte Montgomery; **C:** Barry Parrell.

Zebrahead

Zach (Rappaport) and Nikki (Wright) are two teens in love—which would be fine but he's white and she's black. Writer/director Drazan's impressive debut features exceptional work from the two leads and one of the last performances by Sharkey as Zach's dad. Music's very good, too, and it gets a nice presentation on the Surround audio. A minute amount of surface lint is visible, but only if you look hard for it. Overall, the image here is much richer than the one I remember from VHS tape. Recommended. —MM

Movie: 🦴🦴🦴 **DVD:** 🦴🦴🦴
Columbia Tristar (cat #08337, UPC 04339-6083370). Widescreen (1.85:1) anamorphic. Dolby Digital Surround. $24.98. Keepcase. *LANG:* English. *SUB:* English; French. *FEATURES:* 28 chapters ▪ Trailers.
1992 (R) 102m/C Michael Rapaport, N'Bushe Wright, Ray Sharkey, DeShonn Castle, Ron Johnson, Marsha Florence, Paul Butler, Abdul Hassan Sharif, Dan Ziskie, Candy Ann Brown, Helen Shaver, Luke Reilly, Martin Priest, Kevin Corrigan; **D:** Tony Drazan; **W:** Tony Drazan; **C:** Maryse Alberti; **M:** Taj Mahal. *AWARDS:* Sundance '92: Filmmakers Trophy.

Zelig

Note-perfect faux-documentary about bogus legendary Jazz Age personality Leonard Zelig (Allen). Zelig's obsession with trying to fit in has given him the ability to physically change himself into another person, at times becoming a doctor, a rabbi, an American Indian, or a black musician! Newly shot (and appropriately battered-looking) footage is perfectly integrated into real newsreel footage, period photographs, newspaper articles, etc., making this seem incredibly genuine. Amazing, but tends to lose its novelty around the one-hour mark. More impressive as a technical feat than as a comedy, it still delivers moments of hilarity and drama. One wonders if it fooled foreign audiences who may not have gotten the dialogue-driven jokes! The disc features a sharp transfer and the film looks appropriately scratchy, grainy, and worn. The sound is clear with the various artificial "source recordings" and period songs sounding as thin and squawky as they should. The notes in the booklet are up to the high standard of the other MGM Woody Allen releases. The optional foreign subtitles occasionally appear (awkwardly positioned) over people's faces so as not to interfere with the actual on-screen burned-in captions. —DG

Movie: 🦴🦴🦴🦴 **DVD:** 🦴🦴🦴
MGM Home Ent. (cat #1001749, UPC 027-616860491). Widescreen (1.85:1) anamorphic. Mono. $19.98. Keepcase. *LANG:* English. *SUB:* English; French; Spanish. *CAP:* English. *FEATURES:* Booklet with notes ▪ Theatrical trailer ▪ 16 chapters.
1983 (PG) 79m/B Woody Allen, Mia Farrow, Susan Sontag, Saul Bellow, Irving Howe; **D:** Woody Allen; **W:** Woody Allen; **C:** Gordon Willis. *AWARDS:* N.Y. Film Critics '83: Cinematog; *NOM:* Oscars '83: Cinematog., Costume Des.

Zeram 2

Imagine an episode of *Mighty Morphin' Power Rangers* hopped up on steroids crossed with the nightmarish imagery of H.R. Giger, and you'll have an idea of what *Zeram 2* is like. Yuko Moriyama returns to play Investigator Iria, an intergalactic bounty hunter, who is assisted by her computer, Bob. Iria has been given a new android as a trainee, but it malfunctions during a battle and turns on her. The android is infected with a Zeram, an evil alien force. To

make matters worse, Iria's partner Fujikuro has betrayed her and is trying to steal an ancient artifact which Iria possesses. Trapped and in need of assistance, Iria calls on her old friends Teppei and Kamiya, two bumbling electricians to help her. *Zeram 2* is nonstop fun, as it mixes amazing action scenes, gross monsters, and slapstick comedy seamlessly to create an entertaining sci-fi treat. The only problem with the film is that it makes no attempt to recap the events from *Zeram*, so if you haven't seen that film, you may be lost. This DVD offers a widescreen transfer of the film and has a nice amount of space at the bottom of the screen for the English subtitles. The transfer is sharp, but there are moments where the image goes soft. Also, the screen is a bit dark at times and the colors are somewhat muted. However, for the most part, the transfer is acceptable. The 2.0 Surround soundtrack is very good, giving us clear dialogue, but more importantly realistic sound effects with a good bass response. *—ML* **AKA:** Zeiram 2; Zeiramu.
Movie: 🐾🐾🐾 **DVD:** 🐾🐾 ½
Media Blasters (cat #TSDVD-0107, UPC 631595010787). Widescreen (1.85:1) letterboxed. Dolby Surround. $29.95. Keepcase. *LANG:* English; Japanese. *SUB:* English; Japanese. *FEATURES:* 18 chapters.
1994 100m/C *JP* Yukihiro Hotaru, Kunihiko Iida, Yuko Moriyama; **D:** Keito Amamiya.

Zero Degrees Kelvin

A tale of trappers in 1920s Greenland. Henrik Larsen (Eidsvold), a poet living in Oslo, decides to join the band of trappers after his girlfriend Gertrude (Martens) spurns his marriage proposal. On his arrival in the stark and frozen landscape, he is forced to share a cabin with the stoic, silent Holm (Sundquist) and the lewd, violent Randbaek (Skarsgard). Randbaek holds the newcomer and his city-boy ways in disdain, creating an air of tension and menace that inevitably results in a clash between the two. Instead of dwelling on the action aspect, director Moland uses the minimalist landscape to echo the psychological battles the men must face with the frigid terrain and between themselves. This DVD offers little more than a workable transfer. The image is clear for the most part, but there is grain evident during the extremely snowy scenes. The audio is very clear, and those with subwoofers will notice a nice bass response. However, the white subtitles can be difficult to make out at times. *—ML* **AKA:** Zero Kelvin; Kjaerlighetens Kjotere.
Movie: 🐾🐾 ½ **DVD:** 🐾🐾 ½
Kino on Video (cat #K210 DVD, UPC 7383-29021023). Widescreen (1.66:1) letterboxed. Digital Stereo. $29.95. Keepcase. *LANG:* Norwegian. *SUB:* English. *FEATURES:* 18 chapters.
1995 113m/C *NO* Gard B. Eidsvold, Stellan Skarsgard, Bjorn Sundquist, Camilla Martens; **D:** Hans Petter Moland; **W:** Hans Petter Moland, Lars Bill Lundheim; **C:** Philip Ogaard; **M:** Terje Rypdal.

Zeta One

First, ignore both of the bone ratings. This movie is impossible to judge. It's a silly SF spy spoof (sort of) with really harsh color and often atrocious lighting. It's almost an experimental exploitation film that might be the fevered brainchild of a gonzo teenage boy in the mid-'60s who had seen all of the original *Avengers* TV shows. Then throw in elements of *Invasion of the B-Girls* and *Benny Hill*. It all has to do with secret agent James Word (Hawdon), who's after Maj. Bourdon (Justice) who, in turn, is after alien women who practice their martial arts in panties and pasties. DVD was made from very clean original elements, but given the pitiful production values, the film does not (and could not) look as sharp as similar Something Weird Video, Image Entertainment, or Anchor Bay releases from the same period. *—MM* **AKA:** Alien Women; The Love Factor.
Movie: 🐾🐾 ½ **DVD:** 🐾🐾 ½
Image Ent. (cat #ID0928SGDVD, UPC 014-381092820). Full frame. Dolby Digital Mono. $14.99. Keepcase. *LANG:* English. *FEATURES:* 15 chapters • Stills and ad materials • Trailer.
1969 86m/C *GB* James Robertson Justice, Charles Hawtrey, Robin Hawdon, Anna Gael, Brigitte Skay, Dawn Addams, Valerie Leon, Yutte Stensgaard, Wendy Lingham, Rita Webb, Caroline Hawkins; **D:** Michael Cort; **W:** Michael Cort, Christopher Neame, Alistain McKenzie; **C:** Jack Atcheler; **M:** John Hawksworth.

Zoolander

Popular comic-actor Ben Stiller travels into risky territory here, centering a feature-length film on a character which he created for the *VH-1 Fashion Awards.* Derek Zoolander (Stiller) is the world's most popular male fashion model, and one of the most vapid and self-absorbed people that you've ever seen. But his success is being threatened by up-and-coming model Hansel (Owen Wilson). Seeing that his time in the spotlight may be over, Derek decides to retire. But he's lured back into the game by fashion designer Mugatu (Will Ferrell), who wants Derek to model his new line of clothes. What Derek doesn't know (besides, well, *everything*), is that Mugatu is going to use Derek to assassinate the Prime Minister of Malaysia, as a way of protesting that country's ban on child labor. Derek's only hope is to seek help from Hansel and beautiful reporter Matilda (Christine Taylor). Can Derek stop Mugatu while still remaining ridiculously good-looking? This is an incredibly silly film that spoofs the fashion industry in general and models in particular. And while it is silly, the humor here is very subtle at times, playing on a *Spinal Tap* or *Monty Python* level. It's slow at first, as it introduces the viewer to its bizarre concepts, but picks up towards the end. Stiller is great as Zoolander, and he does a wonderful job of playing "stupid." However, it's Wilson who steals the show, and we learn in the audio commentary that many of his lines were ad-

libbed. Look for cameos by dozens of famous faces. Derek Zoolander's whole life is built around looking good, and he certainly looks fine on this DVD. This transfer gives us a very sharp and clear picture, which shows only the slightest amount of grain during the daytime scenes. The only flaw is an occasional sign of edge-enhancement. The colors are fantastic, as the movie displays many garishly colored costumes. The Dolby Digital 5.1 audio track is good as well, as it offers clear dialogue and some nice Surround effects. However, the subwoofer response was somewhat lacking. (Also, note that this audio track is recorded somewhat lower than the average DVD, so you may need to adjust your volume higher than usual.) Paramount has given *Zoolander* the deluxe treatment by filling the disc with extras. There are some funny moments to be had in the deleted scenes and outtakes—the last deleted scene is priceless!—and the original *VH-1 Fashion Award* skits. Director/co-writer/co-producer/star Ben Stiller and his two co-writers provide an entertaining audio commentary. All together, a very solid package. *—ML*
Movie: 🐾🐾 ½ **DVD:** 🐾🐾🐾 ½
Paramount (cat #33737, UPC 097363-373742). Widescreen (2.35:1) anamorphic. Dolby Digital 5.1; Dolby Surround. $29.99. Keepcase. *LANG:* English; French. *SUB:* English. *CAP:* English. *FEATURES:* Commentary • Deleted scenes • Extended scenes • Outtakes • Original character skits • Promotional spots • Music video • Still galleries • Alternate end title sequence • 30 chapters.
2001 (PG-13) 89m/C Ben Stiller, Owen C. Wilson, Christine Taylor, Will Ferrell, Milla Jovovich, Jerry Stiller, Jon Voight, David Duchovny; **D:** Ben Stiller; **W:** Ben Stiller, John Hamburg, Drake Sather; **C:** Barry Peterson; **M:** David Arnold.

Zorro, the Gay Blade

Hamilton plays both the swashbuckling crusader Don Diego and his long-lost cousin Bunny Wigglesworth who steps in when DD is felled by a sprained ankle. Some changes have to be made since Bunny thinks that he looks much better in plum than in the traditional black. Everyone involved seems to have been in the spirit of things. A few flecks and snow are particularly noticeable in the night scenes and the colors have never been particularly bright. Still, this is an acceptable no-frills disc of a frivolous little mid-budget comedy. *—MM*
Movie: 🐾🐾 ½ **DVD:** 🐾🐾 ½
Image Ent. (cat #ID9176CUDVD, UPC 014-381917628). Widescreen (1.78:1) anamorphic. Dolby Digital Mono. $19.98. Keepcase. *LANG:* English. *FEATURES:* 16 chapters.
1981 (PG) 96m/C George Hamilton, Lauren Hutton, Brenda Vaccaro, Ron Leibman, Donovan Scott, James Booth, Helen Burns, Clive Revill; **D:** Peter Medak; **W:** Greg Alt; **C:** John A. Alonzo; **M:** Ian Fraser.

"DVD Connections" offers lists of DVD-related magazines and newsletters, books, websites (including retail and rental sources), and newsgroups to help you keep abreast of this fast-paced new technology.

Magazines/Newsletters

DVD—Laser Disc Newsletter
Laser Disc Newsletter
PO Box 420
East Rockaway, NY 11518
800-551-4914
(516)594-9307 (fax)
www.dvdlaser.com

Monthly. $47.5/year; $75/2 years in North America ($70/year; $130/2 years outside North America).

Inside DVD
Versatile Media One, Inc.
2400 N. Lincoln Ave.
Altadena, CA 91001
(626)296-6361 (fax)

Bimonthly. $29.95/year in U.S. (Published in DVD format.)

Laser Disc Gazette DVD & CD Report
Rad Bennett
Rd. 2, Box 654
Harpers Ferry, WV 25425
(304)725-0525
(304)725-0525 (fax)

Bimonthly. $19.95/year in U.S.; $19.95 elsewhere.

Widescreen Review
27645 Commerce Center Dr., Ste. 105
Temecula, CA 92590
(909)676-4914
888-977-7827
(909)693-2960 (fax)
www.widescreenreview.com

Monthly. $34/year in U.S. ($40/year in Canada and Mexico; $75/year elsewhere).

Websites

Ace VCD DVD
www.acevcddvd.com

Sells Asian and Japanese movies, music, adult, and animation.

Active Buyer's Guide: DVDs
www.dvdplayers.activebuyersguide.com

Consumer guide to purchasing DVD players.

Active DVD
www.activewin.com/dvd

DVD news, tips, reviews, and other related articles.

All DVD Links
www.alldvdlinks.com

DVD reviews, articles, and links.

All Star DVD
www.alldvdmovies.com

Mail-order distributor of video movies, CD-ROMS, laserdiscs, and books.

Animania
www.animania-ent.com

Mail-order anime and manga.

Anime Castle
www.animecastle.com

DVD retail.

Anime on DVD
www.animeondvd.com

Anime articles and reviews.

Apollo Movie Guide
www.apolloguide.com/dvd.htm

Includes reviews of DVDs.

Asian DVD Guide
www.asiandvdguide.com

Guide to DVD movies from Hong Kong, Japan, and Korea.

AsianXpress
www.asianxpress.net

Hong Kong DVD retailer.

Askew Reviews
www.askewreviews.com

Movie, DVD, and music reviews.

Bargain Central
www.bargain-central.com

Provides links to DVD-specific purchases.

BargainFlix
www.bargainflix.com

Source for DVD bargains and coupons on the Internet.

Big Picture DVD Review Page
www.thebigpicturedvd.com/bigpicmain.shtml

DVD reviews and discussion, with emphasis on high-resolution display.

BinaryFlix
www.binaryflix.com

DVD discussion and menu details.

Blackstar
www.blackstar.co.uk

DVD retail for U.K. and international customers.

Blowout Video
www.blowoutvideo.com

Retail DVD and VHS.

BlueDVD.com
www.bluedvd.com

Adult DVD rental by mail.

C & L Internet Club
www.cnl.com

Canadian DVD retailer.

Cafe DVD
www.cafedvd.com

DVD rental.

CD/DVD Playwright
www.cdplayright.com

Sells products to protect CDs and DVDs.

Cinema Classics
www.cinemaclassics.com

DVD retail.

Cinema Laser
www.thecinemalaser.com

Laserdisc and DVD reviews and links.

DC DVD
www.dc-dvd.net

Retails Region 1 DVD in the U.K.

DealCatcher.com
www.dealcatcher.com

DesiFilms.com
www.desifilms.com

Indian DVD rental.

DesiPadam.com
www.desipadam.com

Indian DVD rental.

Digital Bits, The
www.thedigitalbits.com

DVD reviews and other articles.

Digital Entertainment, Inc.
www.indianfilmsdvd.com

Indian DVD retail.

Digital Eyes
www.digitaleyes.net

DVD retail.

Digital Video Depot
www.dv-depot.com

DVD retail.

DiscountFlix
www.discountflix.com

DVD comparison shopping service.

DiVerse DVD
www.attrill.com
Price comparison for DVDs.

DVD Angle
www.dvdangle.com
DVD reviews.

DVD AniMania
www.ij.net/wildcoast/anime/
News and reviews on anime DVD.

The DVD Answer Man
www.dvdanswerman.com
DVD info and reviews.

DVD Arena
www.dvdarena.com
Buys and sells used DVDs.

DVD Authority
www.dvdauthority.com
DVD reviews.

DVD Bargain Update
www.dvdbargainupdate.com
Newsletter for DVD bargain hunters.

DVD Box Office
www.dvdboxoffice.com
DVD retail.

DVD Buying Guide
www.dvdbuyingguide.com
Offers info on DVD players and related issues.

DVD Channel News
www.dvdchannelnews.com
DVD reviews and news.

DVD Corner Net
www.dvdcorner.net
Weekly e-zine offering DVD news and reviews.

DVD Coupon Post
www.dvdcouponpost.com
Information on DVD bargains.

DVD Cyber Center
www.dvdcc.com
DVD reviews and articles.

DVD Demystified
www.dvddemystified.com
DVD information, including an exhaustive DVD FAQ.

DVD Digital Domain
www.dvddigital.com
DVD retail.

DVD Easter Eggs
www.dvdeastereggs.com
Provides info on DVD hidden features.

DVD Empire
www.dvdempire.com
DVD retailer.

DVD ESP
www.dvdesp.com
DVD shopping service.

DVD Essentials
www.dvdessentials.co.uk
Reviews and information on Region 2 DVDs.

DVD Express
www.dvdexpress.com
DVD retailer.

DVD File
www.dvdfile.com
DVD information.

DVD Journal
www.dvdjournal.com
DVD news, reviews, and commentary.

DVD King
www.dvdking.com
DVD retail.

DVD Mon
www.dvdmon.com
DVD news, reviews, and resources.

DVD Movie Guide
www.dvdmg.com
DVD releases, reviews, and links.

DVD Now
www.geocities.com/Hollywood/Academy/6586
Consumer-based site for DVD technology information.

DVD Overnight
www.dvdovernight.com
DVD rental.

DVD Palace
www.dvdpalace.com
Adult DVD retail.

DVD pizza.com
www.dvdpizza.com
DVD retail.

DVD Planet
www.dvdplanet.com
DVD retail.

DVD Price Compare
www.dvdpricecompare.com
DVD bargain search service.

DVD Price Search
www.dvdpricesearch.com
Offers DVD price comparisons.

DVD Review
www.dvdreview.com
DVD reviews, news, interviews, links, and chat.

DVD Reviewer
www.dvd.reviewer.co.uk
DVD news, articles, and forums.

DVD Store
www.dvd1.com
DVD retail.

DVD Street
www.dvdstreet.co.uk/
DVD retail.

DVD Talk
www.dvdtalk.com
DVD news, chats, and reviews.

DVD Times
www.dvdtimes.co.uk
DVD news, reviews, and forums.

DVD Tracker
www.dvdtracker.com
DVD purchase cataloging service.

DVD Verdict
www.dvdverdict.com
DVD movie and hardware reviews, forums, and news.

DVD Web
www.dvdweb.co.uk
DVD news, reviews, links, and competitions.

dvdfuture.com
www.dvdfuture.com
DVD reviews, features, and forums.

DVDinsider
www.dvdinsider.com
DVD news and reviews for the professional.

DVDirect.net
www.dvdirect.net
DVD retail.

DVDLaser.com
www.DVDLaser.com
DVD reviews, info, commentary, links, and news.

DVDLink
www.dvdlink.co.uk
Directory of DVD-related sites.

DVDs 1 2 3
www.dvds123.com
Sells used DVDs.

DVDspotlight
www.dvdspotlight.com
DVD news and reviews for the consumer.

DVDTOWN.COM
www.dvdtown.com
DVD news and reviews.

Entertainme.com
www.entertainme.com
DVD and CD retail.

Entertainment Warehouse
www.dvd-plus.com
Canadian DVD retail.

Fight DIVX Association
www.fightdivx.com
DVD news and links.

Guide to Current DVD
www.currentfilm.com
DVD reviews and other info.

HorrorDVDs.com
www.horrordvds.com
Horror DVD news, forums, reviews, contests, and links.

Incredible DVD
www.incredibledvd.com
DVD coupons, bargains, and freebies.

IndiaWeekly
www.digibuster.com
Indian DVD rental and sales.

Jeff's Used LD/DVD Finder
www.rtr.com/~jeff/
Searches for used laserdisc and DVDs.

Laser's Edge
www.lasersedge.com
DVD retail.

Laserific
www.laserific.com
DVD rental/retail in Orlando, FL.

Lasertown Video Discs, Inc.
www.lasertown.com
DVD and laserdisc retail.

Movie Store, The
www.themovie-store.com
DVD retail.

Movietrak.com
www.movietrak.com
DVD rental in the U.K.

MyDVDsource.com
www.mydvdsource.com
New and used DVD retail.

Netflix
www.netflix.com
DVD rental.

OpenDVD Group
www.opendvd.org
Comprehensive resource for developers looking to implement DVD technology, and for users to take full advantage of all the technology has to offer.

Play247
www.play.com
DVD retail.

Right Stuff International
www.rightstuf.com
Anime DVD retail.

Second Chance DVDs
www.scdvd.com

Buys and sells used DVDs.

Splatterhouse
www.splatterhouse.net

Reviews and other info on horror DVDs.

Starship Industries' Laser & DVD Home Page
www.starlaser.com

DVD and laserdisc retail.

Thomas Video
www.thomasvideo.com

DVD, VHS, and laserdisc retail.

Ultimate Guide to Anamorphic Widescreen DVD (for Dummies!)
www.thedigitalbits.com/articles/anamorphic

In simple language, explains anamorphic format and its benefits.

Undercover DVD
www.hewittco.com/bstreet/verification.tpl

Sells adult DVDs.

Video Tropic
www.videotropic.com

Guide to coupons, discounts, and promotions for DVDs.

Video Zone
www.video-zone.com

DVD retail.

Widescreen Review Magazine
www.widescreenreview.com

DVD reviews.

Yanman's DVD Reviews
www.yanman.com

DVD reviews and discussion.

Books

The Dictionary of New Media: The New Digital World of Video, Audio, and Print
James Monaco. 1999. Harbor Electronic Publishing. $39.95; $19.95 (paperback).

Digital Video for Dummies
Martin Doucette. 1999. IDG Books. $24.99 (paperback w/CD-ROM).

Doug Pratt's DVD-Video Guide
Douglas Pratt. 1999. Harbor Electronic Publishing. $49.95; $19.95 (paperback).

DVD Authoring and Production
Ralph Labarge. 2001. CMP Books. $54.95 (paperback w/DVD).

DVD Demystified
Jim Taylor. 2nd ed., 2000. McGraw Hill. $49.95 (paperback w/DVD).

DVD Player Fundamentals
John Ross. 2000. Howard W. Sams & Co. $34.95 (paperback).

DVD Production
Phil De Lancie and Mark Ely. 2001. Focal Press. $39.95 (paperback w/CD).

How to Use Digital Video
Dave Johnson. 2000. Howard W. Sams & Co. $29.99 (paperback w/CD-ROM).

The Ultimate Widescreen DVD Movie Guide
2001. *Widescreen Review* magazine. $9.95 (paperback).

Newsgroups

alt.media.dvd.cracked
alt.video.digital-tv
alt.video.divx
alt.video.dvd
alt.video.dvd.complain
alt.video.dvd.friends-of-joe
alt.video.dvd.non-anamorphic
alt.video.dvd.software
alt.video.dvd.tech
alt.video.laserdisc
aus.dvd
rec.video.dvd
rec.video.dvd.advocacy
rec.video.dvd.marketplace
rec.video.dvd.misc
rec.video.dvd.players
rec.video.dvd.tech
rec.video.dvd.titles
uk.media.dvd

Looking for *Spinal Tap*? You can find this entry in the Ts, because the correct title is *This Is Spinal Tap*. How would you know this? By using this handy-dandy "Alternative Titles Index." Variant and translated titles for the DVDs reviewed in this book are provided below in alphabetical order followed by a cross-reference to the appropriate entry in the main review section. Please remember that English-language initial articles ("a," "an," and "the") are ignored in the sort, but non-English initial articles (such as "la" or "el" or "das") are NOT ignored. Enjoy.

A Bout de Souffle
See Breathless (1959)
Above the Law
See Righting Wrongs (1986)
Abraxas
See Abraxas: Guardian of the Universe (1990)
Abre Los Ojos
See Open Your Eyes (1997)
Adorenarin Doraibu
See Adrenaline Drive (1999)
The Adventure of Lyle Swan
See Timerider (1983)
AFO
See Air Force One (1997)
Against All Hope
See One for the Road (1982)
Al 33 di Via Orologio fa Sempre Freddo
See Shock (1979)
The Alien Files
See Alien Exotica: The Secret Files (1998)
Alien Women
See Zeta One (1969)
All for Love
See Robert Louis Stevenson's St. Ives (1998)
All Forgotten
See Lover's Prayer (1999)
All Mixed Up
See Manji (1964)
Amazon: Savage Adventure
See Cut and Run (1985)
American Warrior
See American Ninja (1985)
Amok
See Schizo (1977)
Amor Perjudica Seriamente la Salud
See Love Can Seriously Damage Your Health (1996)
And Woman...Was Created
See And God Created Woman (1957)
Any Special Way
See Business Is Business (1971)
Ape Girl
See Lady Iron Monkey (1983)
Apocalipsis Canibal
See Hell of the Living Dead (1983)
Apocalypse 4: Judgment
See Judgment (2001)
Armored Attack
See The North Star (1943)
Around the Jail Cell
See Tiger over Wall (1980)
At Sachem Farm
See Uncorked (1998)
Atlantic City U.S.A.
See Atlantic City (1981)
Attack of the Giant Horny Gorilla
See A*P*E* (1976)
Auggie Rose
See Beyond Suspicion (2000)

Avalanche
See Escape from Alaska (2002)
The Avenger
See Texas, Adios (1966)
Ballada o Soldate
See Ballad of a Soldier (1960)
The Banana Monster
See Schlock (1973)
The Battle for Anzio
See Anzio (1968)
The Beating of the Butterfly's Wings
See Happenstance (2000)
Below Utopia
See Body Count (1997)
Berry Gordy's The Last Dragon
See The Last Dragon (1985)
Beyond Control
See The Amy Fisher Story (1993)
Beyond the Door 2
See Shock (1979)
Biker Zombies from Detroit
See Biker Zombies (2001)
Birds of a Feather
See La Cage aux Folles (1978)
Black Evil
See Ganja and Hess (1973)
Black Out: The Moment of Terror
See Ganja and Hess (1973)
Black Vampire
See Ganja and Hess (1973)
Blackout
See Contraband (1940)
Blind Swordsman: The Tale of Zatoichi
See The Tale of Zatoichi (1962)
A Blonde in Love
See Loves of a Blonde (1965)
Blood Couple
See Ganja and Hess (1973)
Blood Fiend
See Theatre of Death (1967)
Blood Money
See Requiem for a Heavyweight (1962)
Blood of the Undead
See Schizo (1977)
Bob the Gambler
See Bob le Flambeur (1955)
Body Parts
See Harold Robbins' Body Parts (2001)
Boli Zhi Cheng
See City of Glass (1998)
Born to the West
See Helltown (1938)
The Boys from Brooklyn
See Bela Lugosi Meets a Brooklyn Gorilla (1952)
Bride of Fengriffen
See And Now the Screaming Starts (1973)
Bruce Lee's Big Secret
See Revenge of the Patriots (1976)

Bruce Li the Invincible
See Bruce Lee the Invincible (1977)
Bruno
See The Dress Code (1999)
Buckaroo Banzai
See The Adventures of Buckaroo Banzai Across the Eighth Dimension (1984)
The Burning Man
See Dangerous Summer (1982)
Caccia alla Volpe
See After the Fox (1966)
Cactus Jack
See The Villain (1979)
Caged Females
See Caged Heat (1974)
California Axe Massacre
See Axe (1974)
Cannibals in the City
See Cannibal Apocalypse (1980)
Cannibals in the Streets
See Cannibal Apocalypse (1980)
Captain Conan
See Capitaine Conan (1996)
Captured
See Agent Red (2000)
Caravan
See Himalaya (1999)
Cathy Tippel
See Katie Tippel (1975)
Cavegirl
See Cave Girl (1985)
Celos
See Jealousy (1999)
Cet Obscur Objet du Desir
See That Obscure Object of Desire (1977)
Ceux Qui M'Aiment Predront le Train
See Those Who Love Me Can Take the Train (1998)
Challenge
See Drunken Master (1978)
Chamber of Fear
See The Fear Chamber (1968)
Champ vs. Champ
See Champ against Champ (1983)
Chap Faat Sin Fung
See Righting Wrongs (1986)
The Charcoal People of Brazil
See The Charcoal People (2001)
Chevy Van
See The Van (1977)
Chrome Hearts
See C.C. & Company (1970)
Chui Kuen
See Drunken Master (1978)
Circuitry Man 2
See Plughead Rewired: Circuitry Man 2 (1994)
Citta Violenta
See Violent City (1970)

City Hunter: Secret Police
See City Hunter: Secret Service (1996)
City under the Sea
See War Gods of the Deep (1965)
Cleo de 5 a 7
See Cleo from 5 to 7 (1961)
Cobra Nero
See The Black Cobra (1987)
Confessions of a Lap Dancer
See Illicit Confessions (1977)
Cop Killers
See Bad Cop Chronicles 2: Corrupt (1984)
The Courier
See Outta Time (2001)
Cows
See Vacas (1991)
Crocodile
See Blood Surf (2000)
The Cry
See Il Grido (1957)
Crystal Fist
See Jade Claw (1979)
Csillagosok, Katonak
See The Red and the White (1968)
Cutter and Bone
See Cutter's Way (1981)
Da Zdravstvuyet Meksika
See Que Viva Mexico (1932)
Daikyoju Gappa
See Gappa the Trifibian Monster (1967)
The Dangerous Chase
See Blood of the Dragon (1971)
Daniel Defoe's Robinson Crusoe
See Robinson Crusoe (1996)
Dao Shou
See Killer (2000)
Dark Prince: Intimate Tales of Marquis de Sade
See Marquis de Sade (1996)
Dark Prince: The True Story of Dracula
See Dracula: The Dark Prince (2001)
Darkside Reborn
See Reborn from Hell: Samurai Armageddon (1996)
Darkside Reborn: Path to Hell
See Reborn from Hell: Jubei's Revenge (1996)
Das Indische Grabmal
See The Indian Tomb (1959)
Das tagebuch einer verlorenen
See Diary of a Lost Girl (1929)
The Daughter of Frankenstein
See Lady Frankenstein (1972)
Dayereh
See The Circle (2000)
Dead Aviators
See Restless Spirits (1999)
Deadly Harvest
See Children of the Corn 4: The Gathering (1996)
The Deadly Rays from Mars
See Flash Gordon: The Deadly Ray from Mars (1939)
Death for Five Voices
See Gesualdo: Death for Five Voices (1995)
Death Rides a Carousel
See Carnival of Blood / Curse of the Headless Horseman (1971)
Decoy for Terror
See Playgirl Killer (1966)
The Demon Planet
See Planet of the Vampires (1965)
Demons of the Swamp
See Attack of the Giant Leeches (1959)
Der Blaue Engel
See The Blue Angel (1930)
Der Golem, wie er in die Welt kam
See The Golem (1920)
Der Krieger und die Kaiserin
See The Princess and the Warrior (2000)
Der Letzte Mann
See The Last Laugh (1924)
Der Prozess
See The Trial (1963)
Der Tiger von Eschnapur
See Tiger of Eschnapur (1959)
Der Unhold
See The Ogre (1996)
The Desperate Chase
See Blood of the Dragon (1971)
Destruction, Inc.
See Just for the Hell of It (1968)

Detention: The Siege at Johnson High
See Hostage High (1997)
The Devil's Commandment
See I Vampiri (1956)
The Devil's Weed
See She Shoulda Said No (1949)
Diamond Thieves
See The Squeeze (1978)
Diary of a Hooker
See Business Is Business (1971)
Dick Tracy Meets Karloff
See Dick Tracy Meets Gruesome (1947)
Dick Tracy's Amazing Adventure
See Dick Tracy Meets Gruesome (1947)
Die Stille Nach Dem Schuss
See The Legend of Rita (1999)
Die Zwolfte Stunde
See Nosferatu (1922)
Dirty Money
See Un Flic (1972)
Diy Sau
See Killer (2000)
Dr. Mabuse, Parts 1 & 2
See Dr. Mabuse, The Gambler (1922)
Dr. Orloff's Invisible Monster
See Orloff and the Invisible Man (1970)
Doctors Wear Scarlet
See The Bloodsuckers (1970)
Dog Soldiers
See Who'll Stop the Rain? (1978)
Doktor Mabuse der Spieler
See Dr. Mabuse, The Gambler (1922)
Don Juan 73
See Don Juan (Or If Don Juan Were a Woman) (1973)
Dona Herlinda y Su Hijo
See Dona Herlinda & Her Son (1986)
Double Possession
See Ganja and Hess (1973)
Dracula
See Bram Stoker's Dracula (1992)
The Dragon and the Cobra
See Fist of Fear, Touch of Death (1980)
Dragon Claw
See Dragon's Claws (1979)
Dragon Reincarnate
See Revenge of the Patriots (1976)
Dragon's Claw
See Dragon's Claws (1979)
Drunk Monkey
See Drunken Master (1978)
Drunken Monkey in a Tiger's Eye
See Drunken Master (1978)
Dynamite Women
See The Great Texas Dynamite Chase (1976)
Eagle Claw Snake Fist Cat's Paw Part 2
See Drunken Master (1978)
Eagle's Claw
See Eagle Fist (1977)
East Great Falls High
See American Pie (1999)
Ekstase
See Ecstasy (1933)
El Beso Que Me Diste
See The Kiss You Gave Me (2000)
El Camino
See The Road (2000)
El Cazador de la Muerte
See Deathstalker (1983)
El Jardin del Eden
See Garden of Eden (1994)
El Mariachi 2
See Desperado (1995)
Elektra
See Electra (1962)
En Effeuillant la Marguerite
See Plucking the Daisy (1956)
En el Pais de No Pasa Nada
See In the Country Where Nothing Happens (1999)
Enter the Lone Ranger
See The Legend of the Lone Ranger (1959)
Epsilon
See Alien Visitor (1995)
Erotic Boundaries
See Boundaries (1997)
Et Dieu Crea la Femme
See And God Created Woman (1957)
Eu Tu Eles
See Me You Them (2000)

European Vacation
See National Lampoon's European Vacation (1985)
Eva the Devil's Woman
See Eva (1962)
Extase
See Ecstasy (1933)
The Family
See Violent City (1970)
Fatal Affair
See Stalker (1998)
Father Goose
See Fly Away Home (1996)
Faust-Eine deutsche Volkssage
See Faust (1926)
Fearless Dragons
See Fearless Dragon (1979)
Federico Fellini's 8 1/2
See 8 1/2 (1963)
Female Fiend
See Theatre of Death (1967)
Fengriffen
See And Now the Screaming Starts (1973)
Fiendish Ghouls
See The Flesh and the Fiends (1960)
Fight Zone
See The Avenging Fist (2001)
Fighting Justice
See Lady Iron Monkey (1983)
A Film about Love
See Love Film (1970)
Filofax
See Taking Care of Business (1990)
First Gundam
See Mobile Suit Gundam: The Battle Begins! Vol. 1 (1979)
Fist of Fear
See Fist of Fear, Touch of Death (1980)
A Fist Too Fast
See The Legendary Strike (1978)
Fixing the Shadow
See Beyond the Law (1992)
Flash Gordon's Trip to Mars
See Flash Gordon: The Deadly Ray from Mars (1939)
Flying Wild
See Fly Away Home (1996)
Fo Zhang Huang Di
See Buddha Assassinator (1979)
Follow That Bird
See Sesame Street Presents: Follow That Bird (1985)
Fong Sai-yuk 2
See The Legend 2 (1993)
Four Horsemen of the Apocalypse
See Four of the Apocalypse (1975)
Frank Herbert's Dune
See Dune (2000)
The Freedom Seekers
See The Bloodsuckers (1970)
Funny Little Dirty War
See Funny, Dirty Little War (1983)
Fury Is a Woman
See Siberian Lady Macbeth (1961)
Game of the Dragon
See Bruce Lee the Invincible (1977)
Gangster
See Tokyo Mafia: Battle for Shinjuku (1996)
Gangster at Bay
See Gunman in the Streets (1950)
The Gaze of Ulysses
See Ulysses' Gaze (1995)
Gedo
See Fatal Blade (2000)
The George McKenna Story
See Hard Lessons (1986)
Ghosts from the Past
See Ghosts of Mississippi (1996)
Ghosts of Mars
See John Carpenter's Ghosts of Mars (2001)
The Giant Leeches
See Attack of the Giant Leeches (1959)
Gilbert Grape
See What's Eating Gilbert Grape (1993)
Ginga Tetsudo No Yoru
See Night on the Galactic Railroad (1985)
The Girl
See Catherine Cookson's The Girl (1996)
The Girls
See Les Bonnes Femmes (1960)

Giulietta Degli Spiriti
See Juliet of the Spirits (1965)

Glump
See Please Don't Eat My Mother (1972)

Go and See
See Come and See (1985)

God of Fist Style
See The Avenging Fist (2001)

Godzilla vs. Destroia
See Godzilla vs. Destroyah (1995)

Godzilla vs. Destroyer
See Godzilla vs. Destroyah (1995)

Godzilla vs. Desutoroia
See Godzilla vs. Destroyah (1995)

Gohatto
See Taboo (1999)

Gojira
See Godzilla, King of the Monsters (1956)

Gojitmal
See Lies (1999)

Golden Years
See Stephen King's Golden Years (1991)

The Good Girls
See Les Bonnes Femmes (1960)

Gouttes d'Eau sur Pierres Brulantes
See Water Drops on Burning Rocks (1999)

Grand Larceny
See Larceny (1991)

The Great Hope
See Submarine Attack (1954)

The Grinch
See Dr. Seuss' How the Grinch Stole Christmas (2000)

Guards of Shaolin
See Ninja vs. Shaolin Guards (1984)

Guns, Sin and Bathtub Gin
See Lady in Red (1979)

Haishang Hua
See Flowers of Shanghai (1998)

Hallelujah, I'm a Tramp
See Hallelujah, I'm a Bum (1933)

Hang Zhou Wang Ye
See The Lord of Hangzhou (1998)

Hans Christian Andersen's Thumbelina
See Thumbelina (1994)

Hao xia
See Last Hurrah for Chivalry (1978)

Haonan haonu
See Good Men, Good Women (1995)

Happy Go Lucky
See Hallelujah, I'm a Bum (1933)

Hard Stick
See A Real American Hero (1978)

Hard Way Out
See Bloodfist 8: Hard Way Out (1996)

Harry, A Friend Who Wishes You Well
See With a Friend Like Harry (2000)

Harry, He's Here to Help
See With a Friend Like Harry (2000)

Harry Potter and the Philosopher's Stone
See Harry Potter and the Sorcerer's Stone (2001)

Harry, un Ami Qui Vous Veut du Bien
See With a Friend Like Harry (2000)

The Haunted and the Hunted
See Dementia 13 (1963)

The Haunted Planet
See Planet of the Vampires (1965)

Haxan
See Haxan: Witchcraft through the Ages (1922)

The Head that Wouldn't Die
See The Brain that Wouldn't Die (1963)

The Heart of New York
See Hallelujah, I'm a Bum (1933)

Heftig og begeistret
See Cool and Crazy (2001)

Heisser Sommer
See Hot Summer (1968)

The Heist
See The Squeeze (1978)

Hellraiser 2
See Hellbound: Hellraiser 2 (1988)

Hero Defeating Japs
See Ninja in the Deadly Trap (1983)

Heroes Defeat Japs
See Ninja in the Deadly Trap (1983)

Herz aus Glas
See Heart of Glass (1974)

Higher Love
See Uncorked (1998)

Hijack
See The Last Siege (1999)

Himalaya - L'Enfance d'un Chef
See Himalaya (1999)

Himalaya - The Youth of a Chief
See Himalaya (1999)

Histoires Extraordinaires
See Spirits of the Dead (1968)

The Hoary Legends of the Caucasus
See Ashik Kerib (1988)

The Hole
See Le Trou (1959)

Home Fires Burning
See The Turning (1992)

Hong Chow Wong Yow
See The Lord of Hangzhou (1998)

Hong Kong Cat Named Karado
See Super Kung Fu Kid (1986)

Hong Qiang dao Ying
See Millennium Dragon (1993)

Hong Ying Tao
See Red Cherry (1995)

Hopalong Cassidy Enters
See Hopalong Cassidy (1935)

Hori, ma panenko
See The Firemen's Ball (1968)

L'Horloger de Saint-Paul
See The Clockmaker (1973)

Horror Hotel
See The City of the Dead (1960)

Horror in the Midnight Sun
See Invasion of the Animal People (1962)

Horror in the Midnight Sun
See Terror in the Midnight Sun (1958)

Hot Car Girl
See Hot Rod Girl (1956)

Hot Sweat
See Katie Tippel (1975)

How the Grinch Stole Christmas
See Dr. Seuss' How the Grinch Stole Christmas (2000)

Hua Zhong Xian
See Picture of a Nymph (1988)

Hung Cheung do Ying
See Millennium Dragon (1993)

Hungry Pets
See Please Don't Eat My Mother (1972)

Hustler Squad
See The Doll Squad (1973)

I Coltelli Del Vendicatore
See Knives of the Avenger (1965)

I Have No Mouth But I Must Scream
See And Now the Screaming Starts (1973)

I Quattro dell'Apocalisse
See Four of the Apocalypse (1975)

Idi i Smotri
See Come and See (1985)

Iedereen Beroemd!
See Everybody's Famous! (2000)

Il Buco
See Le Trou (1959)

Il Giardino Del Finzi-Contini
See The Garden of the Finzi-Continis (1971)

Il Montagna di Dio Cannibale
See Mountain of the Cannibal God (1979)

Il Processo
See The Trial (1963)

The Imp
See Sorority Babes in the Slimeball Bowl-A-Rama (1987)

In the Woods
See Rashomon (1951)

Incense for the Damned
See The Bloodsuckers (1970)

Independence
See Best Men (1998)

Inferno in Diretta
See Cut and Run (1985)

Invasion of Mars
See The Angry Red Planet (1959)

Invasion of the Animal People
See Terror in the Midnight Sun (1958)

Invasion of the Flesh Hunters
See Cannibal Apocalypse (1980)

The Invincible
See Bruce Lee the Invincible (1977)

The Invisible Dead
See Orloff and the Invisible Man (1970)

Iron Maiden
See The Legendary Strike (1978)

Iron Monkey: The Young Wong Fei-hung
See Iron Monkey (1993)

It Stalked the Ocean Floor
See Monster from the Ocean Floor (1954)

It! The Vampire from Beyond Space
See It! The Terror from Beyond Space (1958)

Jack Frost
See Father Frost (1966)

Jakob der Lugner
See Jacob the Liar (1974)

James A. Michener's Texas
See Texas (1994)

Ji Zhao
See Jade Claw (1979)

Jian Hua Yan Yu Jiang Nan
See To Kill with Intrigue (1977)

Jian Yu Feng Yun Xu Ji
See Prison on Fire 2 (1991)

Jim Henson's Jack and the Beanstalk
See Jack and the Beanstalk: The Real Story (2001)

Joe! Cercati un Posto Per Morire
See Find a Place to Die (1968)

Joi Gin A Long
See Where a Good Man Goes (1999)

Journey to Planet Four
See The Angry Red Planet (1959)

Juen Sun
See The Avenging Fist (2001)

Kakushi Toride No San Akunin
See The Hidden Fortress (1958)

Karakkaze yaro
See Afraid to Die (1960)

Kat and Allison
See Lip Service (2000)

Katie's Passion
See Katie Tippel (1975)

Keetje Tippel
See Katie Tippel (1975)

Kei Chiu
See Jade Claw (1979)

Kido Senshi Gundam
See Mobile Suit Gundam: The Battle Begins! Vol. 1 (1979)

Kill and Go Hide
See The Child (1976)

Killer Bats
See The Devil Bat (1941)

Killing Cars
See Blitz (1985)

Kjaerlighetens Kjotere
See Zero Degrees Kelvin (1995)

Krampack
See Nico and Dani (2000)

Kuen San
See The Avenging Fist (2001)

Kung Fu Kids
See Dreaming Fists with Slender Hands (1980)

Kung Fu Rascals
See Adventures of the Kung Fu Rascals (1992)

Kyojin to Gangu
See Giants and Toys (1958)

La Bete
See The Beast (1975)

La Bride sur le Cou
See Please Not Now! (1961)

La Camara del Terror
See The Fear Chamber (1968)

La Chiesa
See The Church (1998)

La Figlia di Frankenstein
See Lady Frankenstein (1972)

La Fuente Amarilla
See The Yellow Fountain (1999)

La Gran Vida
See Living It Up (2000)

La Grande Speranza
See Submarine Attack (1954)

La Leggenda del Pianista Sull'Oceano
See The Legend of 1900 (1998)

La Mano de un Hombre Muerto
See The Sadistic Baron Von Klaus (1962)

La Matriarca
See The Libertine (1969)

La Patinoire
See The Ice Rink (1999)

La Traque
See Gunman in the Streets (1950)

La Vendetta di Ercole
See Goliath and the Dragon (1961)

La Veuve de Saint-Pierre
See The Widow of Saint-Pierre (2000)
La Vida Es Silbar
See Life Is to Whistle (1998)
La Virgen de los Sicarios
See Our Lady of the Assassins (2001)
L'Amant
See The Lover (1992)
Lanford Wilson's Fifth of July
See Fifth of July (1982)
Lang Zi Yi Zhao
See The Legendary Strike (1978)
The Langoliers
See Stephen King's The Langoliers (1995)
Lap Dancer
See Friction (1995)
Lasky Jedne Plavovlasky
See Loves of a Blonde (1965)
The Last Adventurers
See Down to the Sea in Ships (1922)
The Last Battle
See Le Dernier Combat (1984)
The Last Days of Man on Earth
See The Final Programme (1973)
Lazy Bones
See Hallelujah, I'm a Bum (1933)
Le Battement d'Ailes du Papillon
See Happenstance (2000)
Le Cri du Hibou
See The Cry of the Owl (1987)
Le Gout des Autres
See The Taste of Others (2000)
Le Placard
See The Closet (2000)
Le Proces
See The Trial (1963)
Le Viol du Vampire
See The Rape of the Vampire (1968)
Legend in Leotards
See Return of Captain Invincible (1983)
Legend of Tekken
See The Avenging Fist (2001)
Legend of the Fist Master
See The Avenging Fist (2001)
The Legend of the Pianist on the Ocean
See The Legend of 1900 (1998)
The Legend of Wisely
See Bury Me High (1990)
Legenda Suramskoi Kreposti
See The Legend of Suram Fortress / Ashik Kerib (1985)
Lejonsommar
See Vibration (1968)
L'Enfant Sauvage
See The Wild Child (1970)
Les Bijoutiers du Clair de Lune
See The Night Heaven Fell (1957)
Les Demoiselles de Rochefort
See The Young Girls of Rochefort (1968)
Les Enfants du Paradis
See Children of Paradise (1944)
Les Feluettes
See Lilies (1996)
Les Raisins de la Mort
See The Grapes of Death (1978)
Les Rivieres Pourpres
See The Crimson Rivers (2001)
Les Valseuses
See Going Places (1974)
Letyat Zhuravit
See The Cranes Are Flying (1957)
Liar
See Deceiver (1997)
The Life and Death of King Richard III
See Richard III (1912)
Lisa, Lisa
See Axe (1974)
Lo Sbarco di Anzio
See Anzio (1968)
The Lone Ranger
See The Legend of the Lone Ranger (1959)
Long Ji Yat Chiu
See The Legendary Strike (1978)
Long John Silver Returns to Treasure Island
See Long John Silver (1954)
The Look of Ulysses
See Ulysses' Gaze (1995)
Lookin' Italian
See Showdown (1994)

Love and Larceny
See Larceny (1991)
The Love Factor
See Zeta One (1969)
The Lovelorn Minstrel
See Ashik Kerib (1988)
Love's a Bitch
See Amores Perros (2000)
The Loves of Count Yorga, Vampire
See Count Yorga, Vampire (1970)
L'Ultimo Uomo Della Terra
See The Last Man on Earth (1964)
Lust for Evil
See Purple Noon (1960)
Lust of the Vampires
See I Vampiri (1956)
Maau Tau Ying Yue Siu Fei Cheung
See The Owl vs. Bombo (1984)
Madame Frankenstein
See Lady Frankenstein (1972)
Mademoiselle Strip-tease
See The Nude Set (1961)
Mademoiselle Striptease
See Plucking the Daisy (1956)
The Magnificent One
See Le Magnifique (1976)
Makai Tensho
See Reborn from Hell: Samurai Armageddon (1996)
Makai Tensho: Mado-Hen
See Reborn from Hell: Jubei's Revenge (1996)
Making It
See Going Places (1974)
The Making of Mermaid Avenue
See Billy Bragg & Wilco: Man in the Sand (2001)
Man Qing Jin Gong Qi An
See Sex and the Emperor (1994)
Manchester Prep
See Cruel Intentions 2 (1999)
Manhattan Project: The Deadly Game
See The Manhattan Project (1986)
Mania
See The Flesh and the Fiends (1960)
Mao Tou Ying Yu Xiao Fei Xiang
See The Owl vs. Bombo (1984)
Maohgai
See Sadistic City (1993)
Marijuana the Devil's Weed
See She Shoulda Said No (1949)
Mark of the Claw
See Dick Tracy's Dilemma (1947)
Mark Twain
See Ken Burns' Mark Twain (2001)
The Marsupials: Howling 3
See Howling 3: The Marsupials (1987)
Mas Que Amor Frenesi
See Not Love Just Frenzy (1996)
Meals on Wheels
See Wheels on Meals (1984)
Mermaid Chronicles Part 1: She Creature
See She Creature (2001)
Midnight Movie Massacre
See Attack from Mars (1988)
Million Dollar Heiress
See Wheels on Meals (1984)
Mimi Metallurgico Ferito Nell'Onore
See Seduction of Mimi (1972)
The Ming Patriots
See Revenge of the Patriots (1976)
A Miracle Can Happen
See On Our Merry Way (1948)
Moju
See The Blind Beast (1969)
Monster from a Prehistoric Planet
See Gappa the Trifibian Monster (1967)
Monster Maker
See Monster from the Ocean Floor (1954)
The Monster Meets the Gorilla
See Bela Lugosi Meets a Brooklyn Gorilla (1952)
Morgan!
See Morgan: A Suitable Case for Treatment (1966)
Morozko
See Father Frost (1966)
Mosura
See Rebirth of Mothra 1 & 2 (1996)
Mosura 2
See Rebirth of Mothra 2 (1997)

Mothra
See Rebirth of Mothra 1 & 2 (1996)
Mothra 2
See Rebirth of Mothra 2 (1997)
Ms. Don Juan
See Don Juan (Or If Don Juan Were a Woman) (1973)
Much Ado about Murder
See Theatre of Blood (1973)
Mui du du Xanh
See The Scent of Green Papaya (1993)
Musime si Pomahat
See Divided We Fall (2000)
My Private War
See Mein Krieg (1990)
My World Dies Screaming
See Terror in the Haunted House (1958)
Nan Yang Tang Ren Jie
See Bruce Lee the Invincible (1977)
Nanguo Zaijian, Nanguo
See Goodbye South, Goodbye (1996)
Nathaniel Hawthorne's "Twice Told Tales"
See Twice-Told Tales (1963)
Neil Simon's Lost in Yonkers
See Lost in Yonkers (1993)
Nelly and Mr. Arnaud
See Nelly et Monsieur Arnaud (1995)
Netforce
See Tom Clancy's Netforce (1998)
Neurosis
See Revenge in the House of Usher (1982)
Night Legs
See Fright (1971)
Night of the Anubis
See Night of the Living Dead (1968)
Night of the Flesh Eaters
See Night of the Living Dead (1968)
Night of the Zombies
See Hell of the Living Dead (1983)
Night on the Milky Way Railroad
See Night on the Galactic Railroad (1985)
Night Train to Mundo Fine
See Red Zone Cuba (1966)
The Night Watch
See Le Trou (1959)
Ninja Kung Fu
See Ninja in the Deadly Trap (1983)
Ninjutsu
See Ninja in the Deadly Trap (1983)
No Hambra mas Penas ni Olvido
See Funny, Dirty Little War (1983)
Nosferatu, A Symphony of Horror
See Nosferatu (1922)
Nosferatu, A Symphony of Terror
See Nosferatu (1922)
Nosferatu, Eine Symphonie des Grauens
See Nosferatu (1922)
Nosferatu, the Vampire
See Nosferatu (1922)
Nothing to Lose
See Ten Benny (1998)
Notre Dame de Paris
See The Hunchback of Notre Dame (1957)
Obch Od Na Korze
See The Shop on Main Street (1965)
Ojos Que No Ven
See What Your Eyes Don't See (1999)
Only for Love
See Please Not Now! (1961)
The Oracle
See The Horse's Mouth (1958)
Order of Death
See Bad Cop Chronicles 2: Corrupt (1984)
Orloff against the Invisible Man
See Orloff and the Invisible Man (1970)
Os Carvoeiros
See The Charcoal People (2001)
Ostre Siedovane Vlaky
See Closely Watched Trains (1966)
Otto E Mezzo
See 8 1/2 (1963)
L'Ours
See The Bear (1989)
Out of Rosenheim
See Bagdad Cafe (1988)
Out of the Night
See Strange Illusion (1945)
The Outcry
See Il Grido (1957)

The Outlawed Planet
See Planet of the Vampires (1965)
The Owl and Dumbo
See The Owl vs. Bombo (1984)
The Owl vs. Bumbo
See The Owl vs. Bombo (1984)
The Pace That Kills
See Cocaine Fiends (1936)
Painting of a Nymph
See Picture of a Nymph (1988)
Pane e Cioccolata
See Bread and Chocolate (1973)
Pane e Tulipani
See Bread and Tulips (2001)
Parfait Amour
See Perfect Love (1996)
Patton: A Salute to a Rebel
See Patton (1970)
Patton—Lust for Glory
See Patton (1970)
Pin Down Girl
See Pin Down Girls (1951)
Planet of Blood
See Planet of the Vampires (1965)
Planet of Terror
See Planet of the Vampires (1965)
Planet of the Damned
See Planet of the Vampires (1965)
Plankton
See Creatures from the Abyss (1994)
Please! Mr. Balzac
See Plucking the Daisy (1956)
Plein Soleil
See Purple Noon (1960)
Poirot: The ABC Murders
See Agatha Christie's Poirot: The ABC Murders (1992)
Por Que Lo Llaman Amor Cuando Quieren Decir Sexo?
See Why Do They Call It Love When They Mean Sex? (1992)
Portrait of a Nymph
See Picture of a Nymph (1988)
Preparez Vous Mouchoirs
See Get Out Your Handkerchiefs (1978)
Preppies
See Making the Grade (1984)
Preston Tylk
See Bad Seed (2000)
The Professional
See Le Professionnel (1981)
Promenons Nous dans les Bois
See Deep in the Woods (2000)
The Promise
See La Promesse (1996)
Psycho Killers
See The Flesh and the Fiends (1960)
Quan Shen
See The Avenging Fist (2001)
Quien Sabe?
See A Bullet for the General (1968)
Racket Girls
See Pin Down Girls (1951)
The Radical
See Katherine (1975)
Rape Me
See Baise Moi (2000)
Rat
See Atomic War Bride / This Is Not a Test (1960)
Rats: Night of Terror
See Rats (1983)
Red Dragon
See Manhunter (1986)
Red Square Thieves
See Millennium Dragon (1993)
Rekopis Znaleziony W Saragossie
See The Saragossa Manuscript (1965)
Renegade Girls
See Caged Heat (1974)
Revenge of the Dead
See Night of the Ghouls (1959)
Revenge of the Innocents
See South Bronx Heroes (1985)
Revenge! The Killing Fist
See The Street Fighter's Last Revenge (1974)
Rip-Off
See The Squeeze (1978)
Robert Ludlum's the Apocalypse Watch
See The Apocalypse Watch (1997)

Rocco E I Suoi Fratelli
See Rocco and His Brothers (1960)
Rocco et Ses Freres
See Rocco and His Brothers (1960)
Rose Red
See Stephen King's Rose Red (2002)
Rudyard Kipling's Jungle Book
See The Jungle Book (1942)
Rukajarven Tie
See Ambush (1999)
Run for the Money
See Hard Cash (2001)
The Runaways
See South Bronx Heroes (1985)
Ruthless Tactics
See Ninja in the Deadly Trap (1983)
St. Ives
See Robert Louis Stevenson's St. Ives (1998)
San Giu Cheung Yee Sang
See Trust Me U Die (1999)
Sang sei Kuen Chuk
See The Fist Power (1999)
Sardonicus
See Mr. Sardonicus (1961)
Satsujim-ken
See The Street Fighter (1974)
Satsujin-ken 2
See Return of the Street Fighter (1974)
Savage Apocalypse
See Cannibal Apocalypse (1980)
Sayat Nova
See The Color of Pomegranates (1969)
Scarlet Countess
See The Erotic Rites of Countess Dracula (2001)
The Secret of Blue Water
See Nadia: Secret of Blue Water, Vol. 1: The Adventure Begins (1989)
The Secret Pact
See The Pact (1999)
Sedmikrasky
See Daisies (1996)
The Sentinel
See La Sentinelle (1992)
Seunlau Ngaklau
See Time and Tide (2000)
Seven Bad Men
See Rage at Dawn (1955)
7 Ninja Kids
See 7 Lucky Ninja Kids (1989)
Sha Sha Ren
See Ballistic Kiss (1998)
Shao Nian Huang Fei Hong Zhi Tie Ma Liu
See Iron Monkey (1993)
Shaolin Fighters vs. Ninja
See Return of the Deadly Blade (1981)
She Demons of the Swamp
See Attack of the Giant Leeches (1959)
Sheng Si Quan Su
See The Fist Power (1999)
Shisenjiyou No Aria
See The Bedroom (1992)
Shock (Transfer Suspense Hypnos)
See Shock (1979)
Shogun Massacre
See Buddha Assassinator (1979)
The Shop on High Street
See The Shop on Main Street (1965)
Si Don Juan Etait une Femme
See Don Juan (Or If Don Juan Were a Woman) (1973)
Sibirska Ledi Magbet
See Siberian Lady Macbeth (1961)
The Silence After the Shot
See The Legend of Rita (1999)
Siunin Wong Fei-hung Tsi Titmalau
See Iron Monkey (1993)
The Slaughterers
See Cannibal Apocalypse (1980)
Slave Coast
See Cobra Verde (1988)
Slave of the Cannibal God
See Mountain of the Cannibal God (1979)
Smultron-Stallet
See Wild Strawberries (1957)
The Soldiers
See Les Carabiniers (1963)
Soul
See Earth (1930)

Soup to Nuts
See Waitress (1981)
Sous le Sable
See Under the Sand (2000)
South Pacific
See Rodgers & Hammerstein's South Pacific (2001)
South Sea Woman
See Pearl of the South Pacific (1955)
Space Invasion from Lapland
See Invasion of the Animal People (1962)
Space Invasion from Lapland
See Terror in the Midnight Sun (1958)
Space Invasion of Lapland
See Invasion of the Animal People (1962)
Space Invasion of Lapland
See Terror in the Midnight Sun (1958)
Space Mutants
See Planet of the Vampires (1965)
Spiklenci Slasti
See Conspirators of Pleasure (1993)
Spirit of Evil
See Viy (1967)
Spoorloos
See The Vanishing (1988)
Stadt ohne Mitleid
See Town without Pity (1961)
Stephen King's Graveyard Shift
See Graveyard Shift (1990)
Stephen King's Silver Bullet
See Silver Bullet (1985)
The Story of Drunken Master
See Drunken Master (1978)
Straight to Hell
See Cut and Run (1985)
Street Fighter Counterattacks
See The Street Fighter's Last Revenge (1974)
Street Gang
See Vigilante (1983)
Sudden Terror
See Eye Witness (1970)
Sugar Hill, Part 2
See Rockin' with a Bullet (19??)
Suicide Run
See Too Late the Hero (1970)
A Suitable Case for Treatment
See Morgan: A Suitable Case for Treatment (1966)
Summer Madness
See Summertime (1955)
Superior Youngster
See Super Kung Fu Kid (1986)
Sure-Fire Death 4: We Will Avenge You
See Sure Death: Revenge (1987)
Suspense
See Shock (1979)
Swing, Teacher, Swing
See College Swing (1938)
Symphony of Love
See Ecstasy (1933)
Szerelmesfilm
See Love Film (1970)
Tales of Mystery
See Spirits of the Dead (1968)
Tales of Mystery and Imagination
See Spirits of the Dead (1968)
Tao Fan
See Prison on Fire 2 (1991)
Terreur dans l'Espace
See Planet of the Vampires (1965)
Terror at the Opera
See Opera (1988)
Terror in Space
See Planet of the Vampires (1965)
Terror in the Midnight Sun
See Invasion of the Animal People (1962)
Terror in Toyland
See Christmas Evil (1980)
Terror of Dracula
See Nosferatu (1922)
Terrore nello Spazio
See Planet of the Vampires (1965)
They Must Be Told
See Sex Madness (1937)
Three Bad Men in the Hidden Fortress
See The Hidden Fortress (1958)
Three Rascals in the Hidden Fortress
See The Hidden Fortress (1958)
Thug Angel: The Life of an Outlaw
See Tupac Shakur: Thug Angel (2002)

Thy Neighbor's Wife
  See Poison (2001)
Ti Tian Xing Dao Zhi Sha Xiong
  See Brother of Darkness (1994)
Tiao Tiao Miu
  See Ballistic Kiss (1998)
Tiger over the Wall
  See Tiger over Wall (1980)
Time Running Out
  See Gunman in the Streets (1950)
To Love a Vampire
  See Lust for a Vampire (1971)
To Vlemma Tou Odyssea
  See Ulysses' Gaze (1995)
Toca Para Mi
  See Play for Me (2001)
Tokyo Mafia 2
  See Tokyo Mafia: Wrath of the Yakuza (1995)
Tomb Raider
  See Lara Croft: Tomb Raider (2001)
Torpedo Zone
  See Submarine Attack (1954)
Torture Chamber
  See The Fear Chamber (1968)
Torture Zone
  See The Fear Chamber (1968)
Tre Passi nel Delirio
  See Spirits of the Dead (1968)
Trmavomodry Svet
  See Dark Blue World (2001)
Trois Histoires Extraordinaires d'Edgar Poe
  See Spirits of the Dead (1968)
The Trollenberg Terror
  See The Crawling Eye (1958)
The Truth about Fidel Castro Revolution
  See Cuban Story (1959)
Tsvet Granata
  See The Color of Pomegranates (1969)
The Umbrella Woman
  See The Good Wife (1986)
Un Paraiso Bajo las Estrellas
  See A Paradise under the Stars (1999)
Una Sombra Ya Pronto Seras
  See A Shadow You Soon Will Be (1994)
Unagi
  See The Eel (1996)
Ung Chung Sin
  See Picture of a Nymph (1988)
Vampiros en la Habana
  See Vampires in Havana (1987)

Vercingetorix
  See Druids (2001)
Viking Massacre
  See Knives of the Avenger (1965)
Viktor Vogel: Commercial Artist
  See Advertising Rules! (2001)
Virus
  See Cannibal Apocalypse (1980)
Viskingar Och Rop
  See Cries and Whispers (1972)
Viva Las Nowhere
  See Dead Simple (2001)
Voci dal Profondo
  See Voices from Beyond (1990)
Vredens Dag
  See Day of Wrath (1943)
Watchtower
  See Cruel and Unusual (2001)
Wei Si Li Zhi ba Wang Xie Ji
  See Bury Me High (1990)
Wes Craven Presents: Dracula 2000
  See Dracula 2000 (2000)
When the Heart Speaks
  See Cuando Habla El Corazon (1942)
While Plucking the Daisy
  See Plucking the Daisy (1956)
The White River Kid
  See White River (1999)
A White White Boy
  See The Mirror (1975)
Who Killed Atlanta's Children?
  See Echo of Murder (2000)
Who Knows?
  See Va Savoir (2001)
Wilbur Falls
  See Dead Silence (1998)
Wild Weed
  See She Shoulda Said No (1949)
Witchcraft through the Ages
  See Haxan: Witchcraft through the Ages (1922)
Wo De Fu Qin Mu Qin
  See The Road Home (2001)
Women's Penitentiary 2
  See The Big Bird Cage (1972)
Women's Penitentiary 3
  See Women in Cages (1971)
The Word
  See Ordet (1955)
The Worlds of Gulliver
  See The Three Worlds of Gulliver (1959)
Wrestling Women vs. the Aztec Ape
  See Doctor of Doom (1962)

Wu Tang Champ vs. Champ
  See Champ against Champ (1983)
  See Champ vs. Champ (1983)
X:1999
  See X (1996)
Xin Gao Yang Yi Sheng
  See Trust Me U Die (1999)
XX Beautiful Beast
  See Beautiful Beast (1995)
XX Beautiful Hunter
  See Beautiful Hunter (1994)
XX: Utukushiki Gakuen
  See Beautiful Beast (1995)
Yao a Yao Yao Dao Waipo Qiao
  See Shanghai Triad (1995)
Ye Bang Ge Sheng
  See The Phantom Lover (1995)
You Better Watch Out
  See Christmas Evil (1980)
Young Dracula
  See Son of Dracula (1943)
Zai Jian A Lang
  See Where a Good Man Goes (1999)
Zatoichi Monogatari
  See The Tale of Zatoichi (1962)
Zeiram 2
  See Zeram 2 (1994)
Zeiramu
  See Zeram 2 (1994)
Zemlya
  See Earth (1930)
Zerkalo
  See The Mirror (1975)
Zero Kelvin
  See Zero Degrees Kelvin (1995)
Zhi Fa Xian Feng
  See Righting Wrongs (1986)
Zigs
  See Double Down (2001)
Zoku Zatoichi Monogatari
  See The Tale of Zatoichi Continues (1962)
Zombie 5
  See Revenge in the House of Usher (1982)
Zombie Creeping Flesh
  See Hell of the Living Dead (1983)
Zorro
  See The Mask of Zorro (1998)
Zui Quan
  See Drunken Master (1978)

The Cast Index provides a listing of cast members and the DVDs in which they appeared that are covered in this book. The listings for the actor names follow an alphabetical sort by last name (although the names appear in a first name, last name format). The videographies are listed chronologically, with the most recent appearance first. A (V) beside a movie title indicates voice-over work; an (N) indicates narration.

Angela Aames
Bachelor Party '84

Willie Aames
Cut and Run '85

Caroline Aaron
Joe Dirt '01
Running Mates '00
House Arrest '96

Silvia Abascal
The Yellow Fountain '99

Tony Abatemarco
All over the Guy '01

Sean Abbananto
Bikini Med School / Bikini
House Calls '98

Bruce Abbott
Re-Animator [2 ME] '84

Bud Abbott
Abbott and Costello Meet the
Mummy '55

Diahnne Abbott
Jo Jo Dancer, Your Life Is Calling '86

Lee Abbott
Social Intercourse '01

Kareem Abdul-Jabbar
Bruce Lee: A Warrior's Journey '01

Umar Abdurrahman
Daughters of the Dust '91

Hiroshi Abe
Moon over Tao '97

Yael Abecassis
Kadosh '99

Alfred Abel
Dr. Mabuse, The Gambler '22

Jordan Abeles
South Bronx Heroes '85

Tim Abell
Dead Simple '01
Raptor '01
Attack of the 60-Foot Center-
fold '95

Sebastian Abineri
Flambards '78

F. Murray Abraham
13 Ghosts '01
Dillinger and Capone '95
Slipstream '89

Jon Abrahams
Texas Rangers '01

Michele Abrams
Buffy the Vampire Slayer '92

Yussef Abu-Warda
Kadosh '99

Forrest J Ackerman
Attack of the 60-Foot Center-
fold '95
The Howling '81
Schlock '73

Joss Ackland
Bill & Ted's Bogus Journey
'91
They Do It with Mirrors '91
The Sicilian '87
Watership Down '78 (V)

Mario Acosta
Drive By '01

Jay Acovone
Showdown '94

Acquanetta
The Lost Continent '51

Eddie Acuff
Guadalcanal Diary '43
Jungle Girl '41

John Adam
13 Gantry Row '98

Ashot Adamian
Calendar '93

Amy Adams
Cruel Intentions 2 '99

Brandon Adams
The Sandlot '93

Brooke Adams
The Sandlot '93
Sometimes They Come Back
'91
The Unborn '91
Cuba '79

Claire Adams
Scare Their Pants Off /
Satan's Bed '68
The Penalty '20

Edie Adams
It's a Mad, Mad, Mad, Mad
World '63

Jane Adams
The Anniversary Party '01

Joey Lauren Adams
Dr. Dolittle 2 '01 (V)
Jay and Silent Bob Strike
Back '01
The Dress Code '99
Bio-Dome '96

Julie Adams
Psychic Killer '75
Creature from the Black
Lagoon '54

Lynne Adams
Requiem for Murder '99

Maud Adams
The Man with the Golden Gun
'74

Polly Adams
Murder at the Vicarage '86

Stanley Adams
Requiem for a Heavyweight '62

Meat Loaf Aday
Blacktop '01
Focus '01
Wayne's World '92
Motorama '91

Jill Adcock
Carnivore '01

Anthony Addabbo
The Gunfighters '87

Dawn Addams
Zeta One '69
The Robe '53

Rosemarie Addeo
Smiling Fish & Goat on Fire
'99

Mark Addy
Down to Earth '01
A Knight's Tale '01

Wesley Addy
Seconds '66

Luther Adler
The Brotherhood '68

Iris Adrian
The Fast and the Furious '54
The Road to Zanzibar '41

Ben Affleck
Jay and Silent Bob Strike
Back '01
Pearl Harbor '01
Reindeer Games [Miramax
DC] '00
Dogma [2 SE] '99

Casey Affleck
American Pie 2 '01
Ocean's Eleven '01
Soul Survivors '01
Committed '99
Race the Sun '96

John Agar
The Daughter of Dr. Jekyll '57

Mohan Agashe
Seducing Maarya '99

Tetchie Agbayani
Mission Manila '87

Tim Agee
Boundaries '97

Jennifer Agular
Revenge Quest '96

Jenny Agutter
An American Werewolf in London [CE Universal] '81

Abolfazi Ahankhah
Close-Up '90

Mehrdad Ahankhah
Close-Up '90

Sung-Ki Ahn
White Badge '97

Danny Aiello
Dead Silence '98
Harlem Nights '89
The January Man '89
Radio Days '87
The Purple Rose of Cairo '85

Shou Aikawa
The Eel '96

Liam Aiken
Sweet November '01

Anouk Aimee
8 1/2 '63

Mary Ainslee
Mad Youth '40

Franklin Ajaye
Fraternity Vacation '85

Karen Akers
The Purple Rose of Cairo '85

Hano Aki
Rebirth of Mothra 2 '97
Rebirth of Mothra 1 & 2 '96

**Adewale Akinnuoye-
Agbaje**
The Mummy Returns '01
Lip Service '00

Claude Akins
The Devil's Brigade '68
Inherit the Wind '60
Rio Bravo '59

Denis Akiyama
Johnny Mnemonic [2 SB] '95

Carlo Alban
The Tavern '00

George Nicholas Albergo
Ninja in the U.S.A. '88

Hans Albers
The Blue Angel '30

Edward Albert
Extreme Honor '01
Mimic 2 '01
The Squeeze '78
Butterflies Are Free '72

Julius Albert
Daisies '96

Giorgio Albertazzi
Eva '62

Luis Alberto Garcia
Life Is to Whistle '98

Regine Albrecht
Hot Summer '68

Ariauna Albright
Mom's Outta Sight '01

Lola Albright
Peter Gunn: Set One '58

Alan Alda
The Object of My Affection
'98
California Suite '78
Free to Be...You and Me '74

Robert Alda
The Squeeze '78

Rutanya Alda
Prancer '89
Vigilante [2 DC] '83
Mommie Dearest '81
Christmas Evil '80
When a Stranger Calls '79
The Fury '78

Mary Alden
The Plastic Age '25

Norman Alden
The Devil's Brigade '68

Mari Aldon
Summertime '55

Tom Aldredge
Into the Woods '90
King Lear '74

Kitty Aldridge
Slipstream '89

Norma Aleandro
Cousins '89

M. Aleksanian
The Color of Pomegranates
'69

John Ales
Uprising '01

Toni Alessandra
Bachelor Party '84

Geraldine Alexander
Forgotten '99
Sleeping Murder / 4:50 from
Paddington '86

Jace Alexander
Crocodile Dundee 2 '88

Jane Alexander
Kramer vs. Kramer '79

Jason Alexander
The Hunchback of Notre
Dame 2 '01 (V)
The Trumpet of the Swan '01
(V)
The Hunchback of Notre
Dame '96 (V)
Blankman '94

Sasha Alexander
All over the Guy '01

Sherrie Alexander
The Last Warrior '99

Charlotta Alexandra
A Real Young Girl '75

Satiago Alfonso
A Paradise under the Stars
'99

A.L.G.
Smile Now Cry Later '01

Muhammad Ali
The Greatest '77
Requiem for a Heavyweight
'62

Carlo Alighiero
The Cat o' Nine Tails '71

William Alland
Citizen Kane '41

Louise Allbritton
Son of Dracula '43

Debbie Allen
Jo Jo Dancer, Your Life Is Calling '86

Ginger Lynn Allen
Mind, Body & Soul '92

Gracie Allen
College Swing '38

Joan Allen
Mists of Avalon '01
When the Sky Falls '99
The Ice Storm '97
Searching for Bobby Fischer
'93
Manhunter [LE] '86

Jonelle Allen
Next Time '99

Judith Allen
Bright Eyes '34

Karen Allen
The Basket [SE] '99
Wind River '98
Til There Was You '96
The Sandlot '93
The Turning '92
Sweet Talker '91

Nancy Allen
Secret of the Andes '01
Strange Invaders '83
Blow Out '81
Dressed to Kill [SE] '80
Carrie '76

Rex Allen
Me, Myself, and Irene '00 (V)
Swamp Country '66

Sage Allen
Mr. Saturday Night [MGM] '92

Steve Allen
Great Balls of Fire '89

Woody Allen
Company Man '01
The Curse of the Jade Scorpi-
on '01
Husbands and Wives '92
Radio Days '87 (N)
Hannah and Her Sisters '86
Broadway Danny Rose '84
Zelig '83
A Midsummer Night's Sex
Comedy '82
Play It Again, Sam '72

Kirstie Alley
Look Who's Talking Now '93

Eric Allison
Schlock '73

Mariam Palvin Almani
The Circle '00

Almayvonne
Mo' Money '92

Maria Conchita Alonso
High Noon '00
Blackheart '98
Texas '94
The House of the Spirits '93
Colors '88
Moscow on the Hudson '84

John Altamura
The Toxic Avenger, Part 3: The
Last Temptation of Toxie
[DC] '89

Bruce Altman
L.I.E. '01
To Gillian on Her 37th Birth-
day '96

Jeff Altman
Holiday in the Sun '01
Pink Lady and Jeff '80

John L. Altom
Freez'er '00

Angela Alvarado
Boss of Bosses '99

Anne Alvaro
The Taste of Others '00

Shigeru Amachi
The Tale of Zatoichi '62

Chisco Amado
Nico and Dani '00

Jorge Amado
Tieta of Agreste '96

Nadjiwarra Amagula
The Last Wave '77

Walter Amagula
The Last Wave '77

Tom Amandes
When Good Ghouls Go Bad
'01

Tangie Ambrose
Jackie's Back '99

Don Ameche
Hidden Hollywood: Treasures
from the 20th Century Fox
Vaults '99
A Wing and a Prayer '44

Tony Amendola
The Mask of Zorro [2 SE] '98

Ramsay Ames
The Mummy's Ghost '44

Robert Ames
Behind Office Doors '31

Warren Ames
House on Bare Mountain '62

Madchen Amick
Twin Peaks: Fire Walk with
Me '92
Twin Peaks: The First Season
'90

Suzy Amis
The Usual Suspects [MGM
SE] '95

Luigi Amodeo
Art House '98

John Amos
American Flyers '85
Beastmaster '82
Roots '77

Sean Amsing
Bones '01

Julie Andelman
Blood Cult '85

Donna Anders
Count Yorga, Vampire '70

Luana Anders
Goin' South '78
Dementia 13 [Roan] '63

Asbjorn Andersen
Reptilicus '62

John Andersen
Haxan: Witchcraft through the
Ages '22

Adisa Anderson
Daughters of the Dust '91

Anthony Anderson
Exit Wounds '01
Kingdom Come '01
See Spot Run '01
Two Can Play That Game '01
Me, Myself, and Irene '00

Carly Anderson
The White Pony '99

Dan Anderson
Extreme Honor '01

Donna Anderson
Inherit the Wind '60
On the Beach '59

Eddie Anderson
It's a Mad, Mad, Mad, Mad
World '63
Star Spangled Rhythm '42

Flex Anderson
Out Cold '01

Gillian Anderson
The X-Files: Season 4 '00
The Turning '92

Herbert Anderson
I Bury the Living '58

Jean Anderson
Sleeping Murder / 4:50 from
Paddington '86

Jeff Anderson
Dogma [2 SE] '99

John Anderson
The Specialist '75
Five Card Stud '68

Judith Anderson
Star Trek 3: The Search for
Spock '84
And Then There Were None
[Image] '45

Stage Door Canteen '43
Rebecca [Criterion] '40

Kevin Anderson
Liebestraum '91

Michael J. Anderson
Snow White: The Fairest of
Them All '02
Mulholland Drive '01

Michelle Anderson
Pin... '88

Natalie Anderson
The White Pony '99

Nathan Anderson
Tequila Body Shots '99

Pamela Anderson
Snapdragon '93

Raffaela Anderson
Baise Moi '00

Richard Anderson
The Glass Shield '95
Retrievers '82
Seconds '66

Sam Anderson
Slackers '02

Stanley Anderson
Proof of Life '00
He Said, She Said '91

Warner Anderson
Go for Broke! [VCI] '51

Bibi Andersson
I Never Promised You a Rose
Garden '77
Wild Strawberries '57

Harriet Andersson
Cries and Whispers '72

Mansanobu Ando
Adrenaline Drive '99

Peter Andorai
Mephisto '81

Annette Andre
A Funny Thing Happened on
the Way to the Forum '66

Gaby Andre
Goliath and the Dragon '61

Andre the Giant
The Princess Bride [2 SE] '87

Vitalba Andrea
Bread and Tulips '01

Felice Andreasi
Bread and Tulips '01

Starr Andreeff
The Terror Within '88

Frederic Andrei
Diva [Anchor Bay] '82

Ursula Andress
Mountain of the Cannibal
God '79
Four for Texas '63

Sylvia Andrew
Three Came Home '50

Anthony Andrews
Haunted '95
The Pallisers, Vol. 3 '74

Brian Andrews
Halloween [Extended Edition]
'78

Dana Andrews
The Devil's Brigade '68
A Wing and a Prayer '44
The North Star '43

David Andrews
Graveyard Shift '90

Edward Andrews
Over the Hill Gang '69

Harry Andrews
S.O.S. Titanic '79
Watership Down '78 (V)
The Final Programme '73
Theatre of Blood '73
The Ruling Class '72
Too Late the Hero '70
Wuthering Heights '70
The Charge of the Light
Brigade '68

Julie Andrews
The Princess Diaries '01
Hollywood Screen Tests: Take
1 '00
The Man Who Loved Women
'83

Naveen Andrews
Rollerball '02

Real Andrews
Showdown '94

Tod Andrews
Destination Nightmare '54

Michelle Ang
Xena: Warrior Princess—
Series Finale '01

Heather Angel
Peter Pan [2 SE] '53 (V)

Jack Angel
A.I.: Artificial Intelligence '01
(V)

Melanie Angel
Crash & Byrnes '99

Vanessa Angel
Firetrap '01
Partners '99

Maya Angelou
The Runaway '00
Roots '77

Hector Anglada
The Road '00

Jean-Hugues Anglade
Nelly et Monsieur Arnaud '95

Jennifer Aniston
Rock Star '01
The Object of My Affection
'98
Til There Was You '96
Friends: The Complete First
Season '95

Paul Anka
Shake, Rattle & Rock! '94

Evelyn Ankers
Son of Dracula '43
The Ghost of Frankenstein
'42

Morris Ankrum
Jack the Ripper: 4 Tales of
the Supernatural '58
Borderline '50
Hopalong Cassidy Returns
'36

Ann-Margret
Hollywood Screen Tests: Take
1 '00
Scarlett '94
Newsies '92
The Villain '79
The Cheap Detective '78
C.C. & Company '70
Pocketful of Miracles '61

Eve Annenberg
Dogs: The Rise and Fall of an
All-Girl Bookie Joint '96

Imogen Annesley
Howling 3: The Marsupials
'87

Val Avery
Firehouse '72
Satan's Bed '65

John G. Avildsen
The Karate Kid: Part 3 '89

Maricarmen Aviles
The Kiss You Gave Me '00

Mili Avital
Uprising '01
Bad Seed '00

Alejandro Awada
The Road '00

Tahina Awan
The Vigil '98

Charlotte Ayanna
Training Day '01
Dancing at the Blue Iguana
'00

Dan Aykroyd
The Curse of the Jade Scorpi-
on '01
Earth vs. the Spider '01
Evolution '01
Pearl Harbor '01
Stardom '00
Tales from the Crypt: Robert
Zemeckis Collection '95
Tommy Boy '95
The Best of the Blues Broth-
ers '93

Felix Aylmer
The Mummy '59
Separate Tables '58

John Aylward
Just Visiting '01

Catherine Aymerie
Rabid Grannies '89

Agnes Ayres
Son of the Sheik '26

Fraser Ayres
Intimacy '00

Hank Azaria
America's Sweethearts '01
Uprising '01

Annette Azcuy
Bill & Ted's Bogus Journey '91

Damiano Azzos
Voices from Beyond '90

Obba Babatunde
How High '01
The Visit '00
Introducing Dorothy Dan-
dridge '99
The Temptations '98
That Thing You Do! '96

Barbara Babcock
The Heart of Dixie '89

Lauren Bacall
The Shootist '76
Designing Woman '57
Written on the Wind '56
Key Largo '48

Donna Baccala
The Dunwich Horror '70

Barbara Bach
Caveman '81
Force 10 from Navarone '78

Karen Bach
Baise Moi '00

Steve Bacic
The 6th Day [2 SE] '00

Jim Backus
Rescue from Gilligan's Island
'78
It's a Mad, Mad, Mad, Mad
World '63
Don't Bother to Knock '52

Kevin Bacon
Novocaine '01
The Hollow Man [2 SB] '00
He Said, She Said '91
Queens Logic '91
Diner '82

Jean-Pierre Bacri
The Taste of Others '00

Angelo Badalamenti
Mulholland Drive '01

Michael Badalucco
The Man Who Wasn't There
'01

Angela Baddeley
Upstairs, Downstairs: The
Complete First Season '71

Sarah Badel
Just Visiting '01
Not without My Daughter '90

Diedrich Bader
Jay and Silent Bob Strike
Back '01
Recess: School's Out '01 (V)

Nuria Badia
Barcelona '94

Mina (Badiyi) Badie
The Anniversary Party '01

Annette Badland
Angels and Insects '95
Jabberwocky '77

Jane Badler
V '83

Parley Baer
The Young Lions '58

Kyoko Baertsoen
Haunted Castle '01 (V)

Paloma Baeza
The Odyssey '97

William Bagdad
The Doll Squad '73

Vladas Bagdonas
Come and See '85

Wu Bai
Time and Tide '00
The Personals '98

Charles "Chuck" Bail
The Sinister Saga '00
The Stunt Man '80

Bill Bailey
Just Visiting '01

Eion Bailey
Almost Famous: Untitled—
The Bootleg Cut '00

G.W. Bailey
Mannequin '87

Lauren Bailey
Flooding '97

Pearl Bailey
Carmen Jones '54

Barbara Bain
Panic '00
Space: 1999 Set 1 '75
Murder Once Removed '71

Jimmy Baio
The Bad News Bears in
Breaking Training '77

Harry Baird
Four of the Apocalypse '75

Scott Bairstow
Dead in the Water '01

Mitsuko Baisho
The Eel '96

Jon Robin Baitz
One Fine Day '96

Sidiki Bakaba
Le Professionnel '81

Richard Bakalyan
Von Ryan's Express '65

Nicky Bakay
Sabrina, the Animated
Series: Sabrina's World '99
(V)

Betsy Baker
Evil Dead [LE] '83

Blanche Baker
The Handmaid's Tale '90

Carroll Baker
The Watcher in the Woods
'81

David Aaron Baker
Kate & Leopold '01

Dee Baker
The Trumpet of the Swan '01
(V)

Diane Baker
The Net [2 SE] '95
The Silence of the Lambs
[MGM SE] '91
Marnie '64
Strait-Jacket '64

Dylan Baker
Along Came a Spider '00
Thirteen Days '00
Oxygen '99
Random Hearts '99
Love Potion 9 '92

George Baker
At Bertram's Hotel '86
The Prisoner '68

Hylda Baker
Saturday Night and Sunday
Morning '60

Jill Baker
Catherine Cookson's The Girl
'96

Joe Don Baker
Joe Dirt '01
Citizen Cohn '92
Cape Fear '91
Mitchell '75

Kathy Baker
The Glass House '01
Things You Can Tell Just by
Looking at Her '00
Ratz '99
To Gillian on Her 37th Birth-
day '96

Kenny Baker
The Elephant Man '80

Kenny L. Baker
The Harvey Girls '46

Lance Baker
Treasure Island '99

Ray Baker
Speechless '94
Places in the Heart '84

Robyn Baker
The Black Cat / The Fat
Black Pussycat '65

Stanley Baker
Accident '67
Eva '62

William "Billy" Bakewell
Walt Disney Treasures: Davy
Crockett '01
The Iron Mask '29

Brenda Bakke
Shelter '98

Tami Bakke
Mind, Body & Soul '92

Elwon Bakly
The Basket [SE] '99

Brigitte Bako
Paranoia '98

Scott Bakula
A Girl Thing '01
Life As a House '01
Luminarias '99
Major League 3: Back to the
Minors '98
Tom Clancy's Netforce '98

Bob Balaban
Ghost World '01
The Mexican '01
Waiting for Guffman '96

Pablo Canche Balam
Chac: The Rain God '74

Belinda Balaski
The Howling '81

Brooke Balderson
Pep Squad '98

Renato Baldini
Submarine Attack '54

Michael Baldoz
Reflex Action '02

Adam Baldwin
Double Bang '01
Jackpot '01
Dr. Jekyll & Mr. Hyde '00
The Patriot [2 SB] '00
800 Leagues down the Ama-
zon '93
Full Metal Jacket [2 SE] '87
My Bodyguard '80
Ordinary People '80

Alec Baldwin
Final Fantasy: The Spirits
Within '01 (V)
Pearl Harbor '01
State and Main '00
Ghosts of Mississippi '96
Great Balls of Fire '89

Daniel Baldwin
Bare Witness '02
Water Damage '01
The Treat '98

Janit Baldwin
Ruby '77

Judith Baldwin
Rescue from Gilligan's Island
'78

Stephen Baldwin
Slap Shot 2: Breaking the Ice
'02
Zebra Lounge '01
Bio-Dome '96
The Usual Suspects [MGM
SE] '95

William Baldwin
Double Bang '01

Christian Bale
Captain Corelli's Mandolin
'01
Newsies '92
Empire of the Sun '87

Michael Balfour
The Flesh and the Fiends '60

Jeanne Balibar
Va Savoir '01

Ina Balin
The Projectionist '71

Andras Balint
Colonel Redl '84
Love Film '70

Eszter Balint
Stranger than Paradise '84

Fairuza Balk
Almost Famous: Untitled—
The Bootleg Cut '00

Lucille Ball
Lured '47

Samuel Ball
The Last Castle '01
Urbania '00

Ruth Ballan
The Child '76

Carl Ballantine
Mr. Saturday Night [MGM] '92

J.G. Ballard
Empire of the Sun '87

Kaye Ballard
Alice in Wonderland '83

Pamela Ballard
Carnival of Souls [DC] '62
Carnival of Souls / Dementia
13 '62

Edoardo Ballerini
Looking for an Echo '99

Anderson Ballesteros
Our Lady of the Assassins
'01

Bruno Balp
A Real Young Girl '75

Martin Balsam
Cape Fear '91
Mitchell '75
Bad Cop Chronicles: Confes-
sions of a Police Captain
'72
After the Fox '66
Cape Fear '61

Allison Balson
Best Seller '87

Jamie Bamber
Horatio Hornblower: The
Adventure Continues '01

Judy Bamber
A Bucket of Blood / Attack of
the Giant Leeches [Maren-
go] '59

Eric Bana
Black Hawk Down '01
Chopper '01

Anne Bancroft
Heartbreakers '01
Home for the Holidays '95
Love Potion 9 '92
84 Charing Cross Road '86
Agnes of God '85
The Elephant Man '80
Don't Bother to Knock '52

Bradford Bancroft
Bachelor Party '84

George Bancroft
Mr. Deeds Goes to Town '36

Antonio Banderas
The Body '01
Original Sin '01
Spy Kids '01
White River '99
The Mask of Zorro [2 SE]
'98
Desperado [2 SB] '95
The House of the Spirits '93

Yasosuke Bando
Mishima: A Life in Four Chapters '85

Doru Bandol
Because Why? '93

Lisa Banes
The Hotel New Hampshire
'84

Sean Bean
Don't Say a Word '01
Bravo Two Zero '99
Scarlett '94
Shopping '93
The Field [Artisan] '90
Troubles '88

Brett Beardslee
The Dead Hate the Living '99

Amanda Bearse
Fraternity Vacation '85

Emmanuelle Beart
Nelly et Monsieur Arnaud '95
Date with an Angel '87

Allyce Beasley
Recess Christmas: Miracle
on Third Street '01 (V)
Recess: School's Out '01 (V)
Motorama '91

John Beasley
The Gift '00

Stephanie Beaton
The Passion Network '01

Ned Beatty
The Toy '82

Warren Beatty
Town and Country '01
Dick Tracy '90

Hugh Beaumont
The Lost Continent '51
Railroaded '47

Kathryn Beaumont
Peter Pan [2 SE] '53 (V)

Michel Beaune
Le Professionnel '81

Jean Francois Beaupre
Witch Hunter '01

Paul Beauvais
Le Petit Soldat '60

Fernando Becerril
In the Time of the Butterflies
'01

John Beck
King of the Pecos '36

John Beck
Extreme Limits '01
Audrey Rose '77
Lawman '71

Stanley Beck
Lenny '74

Graham Beckel
Hardball '01
Pearl Harbor '01
True Crime '99

Gerry Becker
Mickey Blue Eyes '99

Tony Becker
Agent Red '00

Kate Beckinsale
Pearl Harbor '01
Serendipity '01
The Golden Bowl '00
Haunted '95

Tony Beckley
When a Stranger Calls '79

William Beckley
Too Late the Hero '70

Claire Beckman
Fallout '01

Henry Beckman
Marnie '64

Don Beddoe
Jack the Giant Killer '62

Bonnie Bedelia
Speechless '94
Die Hard [FS 2] '88

Rodney Bedell
Just for the Hell of It '68

Brian Bedford
Scarlett '94

Steven Bednarski
Pin... '88

Wendy Bednarz
There's Nothing out There '90

Daniel Beer
Point Break '91

Noah Beery, Sr.
Trail Beyond [Columbia] '34
Mark of Zorro [2] / Don Q,
Son of Zorro '20

Noah Beery, Jr.
Inherit the Wind '60
Trail Beyond [Columbia] '34
Mark of Zorro [2] / Don Q,
Son of Zorro '20

Max Beesley
Glitter '01
Kill Me Later '01

Chris Beetem
Black Hawk Down '01

Bibiana Beglau
The Legend of Rita '99

Ed Begley, Sr.
The Dunwich Horror '70
Sorry, Wrong Number '48

Ed Begley, Jr.
Diary of a Sex Addict '01
Get over It! '01
She-Devil '89
Transylvania 6-5000 '85
Goin' South '78

Jennifer Behr
Adventures of Justine '00

Yerye Beirut
The Fear Chamber '68

Brendan Beiser
The Vigil '98

Barbara Bel Geddes
The Long Night '47

Harry Belafonte
Free to Be...You and Me '74
Carmen Jones '54

Patricia Belcher
Jeepers Creepers '01

Lia Beldam
The Shining [2 SE] '80

Ana Belen
Love Can Seriously Damage
Your Health '96

E.E. Bell
800 Leagues down the Ama-
zon '93

Marshall Bell
Sand '00
Total Recall [2 SLE] '90

Natasha Bell
Virtual Sexuality '99

Rini Bell
Bring It On '00

Diana Bellamy
The Nest '88

Ralph Bellamy
The Boy in the Plastic Bubble
[2] '76
The Ghost of Frankenstein '42

Clara Bellar
A.I.: Artificial Intelligence '01

Camilla Belle
Back to the Secret Garden
'01
Secret of the Andes '01

Kathleen Beller
Sword & the Sorcerer '82

Agostina Belli
Seduction of Mimi '72

Carlo Bellini
Submarine Attack '54

Scott Bellis
Timecop '94

Sonja Belliveau
Abraxas: Guardian of the Universe [BFS] '90

Gina Bellman
Seven Days to Live '01

Saul Bellow
Zelig '83

Gil Bellows
She Creature '01
Chasing Sleep '00

Jean-Paul Belmondo
Le Professionnel '81
Le Magnifique '76
Stavisky '74
Breathless '59

Lionel Belmore
Son of Frankenstein '39

Robert Beltran
Luminarias '99

Mark Beltzman
Mo' Money '92

James Belushi
Echo of Murder '00
Retroactive '97
Gang Related '96
Race the Sun '96
Abraxas: Guardian of the Uni-
verse [BFS] '90
Taking Care of Business '90
The Fury '78

John Belushi
The Best of the Blues Broth-
ers '93
Goin' South '78

Robert Benchley
The Road to Utopia [Univer-
sal] '46

Russ Bender
I Bury the Living '58

William Bendix
Guadalcanal Diary '43
Star Spangled Rhythm '42

Jitka Bendova
Closely Watched Trains '66

Pierre Benedetti
The Beast '75

Paul Benedict
Waiting for Guffman '96

Armonia Benedito
Strictly Ballroom '92

Vincenzo Benestante
Traffik '90

Eric Benet
Glitter '01

John Benfield
Hidden Agenda '90

Norma Bengell
Planet of the Vampires '65

Paul Benjamin
The Five Heartbeats '91
Across 110th Street '72

Benji
Benji [Ventura] '74

David Bennent
Legend [UE] '86

**Bruce (Herman Brix)
Bennett**
Daniel Boone: Trail Blazer '56
Sahara '43

Dorothy Bennett
Hitch Hike to Hell / Kid-
napped Coed '97

Eloise Bennett
A Tale of Springtime '89

Hywel Bennett
Percy '71

Jill Bennett
The Charge of the Light
Brigade '68

Joan Bennett
Suspiria '77
Dark Shadows: DVD Collec-
tion 1 '67
The Son of Monte Cristo '40
Little Women '33

Tony Bennett
The Scout '94

Jack Benny
It's a Mad, Mad, Mad, Mad
World '63

Victor Benoit
A Fool There Was '14

Jodi Benson
Balto 2: Wolf Quest '02 (V)
Thumbelina [20th Century
Fox] '94 (V)

Wendy Benson
Luck of the Draw '00

James Bentley
The Others [CE] '01

Lamont Bentley
The Wash '01

Wes Bentley
Soul Survivors '01
White River '99

Barbi Benton
Deathstalker '83

Dean Benton
Cocaine Fiends '36

Mark Benton
Catherine Cookson's The Girl
'96

Michael Bentt
Ali '01

Daniel Benzali
Boss of Bosses '99

John Beradino
Moon of the Wolf '72

Iris Berben
Companeros '70

Luca Bercovici
Hard Luck '01
American Flyers '85

Tom Berenger
Cruel and Unusual '01
Training Day '01
True Blue '01
Turbulence 2: Fear of Flying '99
The Last of the Dogmen '95
Major League 2 '94
The Field [Artisan] '90
Eddie and the Cruisers '83
The Dogs of War '81

Peter Berg
Corky Romano '01
A Midnight Clear '92

Candice Bergen
Gandhi '82
Bite the Bullet '75

Edgar Bergen
The Muppet Movie '79
Stage Door Canteen '43

Polly Bergen
Cape Fear '61

Tushka Bergen
Barcelona '94

Helmut Berger
The Garden of the Finzi-Continis '71

Senta Berger
Blitz '85
De Sade '69
Cast a Giant Shadow '66

Sidney Berger
Carnival of Souls [DC] '62
Carnival of Souls / Dementia
13 '62

William Berger
Keoma '76

Jean-Pierre Bergeron
Winter Lily '98

Phillipe Bergerone
The Mangler 2 '01

Patrick Bergin
Amazons and Gladiators '01
The Devil's Prey '01
When the Sky Falls '99
The Apocalypse Watch '97

Emily Bergl
Happy Campers '01
Chasing Sleep '00

Ingrid Bergman
Cactus Flower '69
Indiscreet '58

Mary Kay Bergman
South Park: Bigger, Longer
and Uncut '99 (V)
Batman & Mr. Freeze: Subzero '97 (V)

Sandahl Bergman
Hell Comes to Frogtown '88

Ulla Bergryd
The Bible '66

Christine Bergstrom
Medium Cool [SE] '69

Xander Berkeley
Air Force One [2 SB] '97
Safe '95

Elizabeth Berkley
The Curse of the Jade Scorpi-
on '01
Random Encounter '98
Showgirls '95

Steven Berkoff
Beverly Hills Cop [CE] '84

James Berland
Luminous Motion '00

James Berlau
Olive Juice '01

Milton Berle
Broadway Danny Rose '84
The Muppet Movie '79
It's a Mad, Mad, Mad, Mad
World '63
Let's Make Love '60
Mark of Zorro [2] / Don Q,
Son of Zorro '20

Francois Berleand
Capitaine Conan '96

Charles Berling
Stardom '00
Those Who Love Me Can
Take the Train '98
Nelly et Monsieur Arnaud '95

Brian Bloom
Dance 'til Dawn '88

Claire Bloom
The Mirror Cracked from Side to Side '92
Look Back in Anger '58

John Bloom
Bachelor Party '84

Orlando Bloom
Black Hawk Down '01

Verna Bloom
The Journey of Natty Gann '85
Medium Cool [SE] '69

Eric Blore
The Lady Eve '41
The Road to Zanzibar '41
Sullivan's Travels '41

Lisa Blount
Great Balls of Fire '89
Cut and Run '85

Marc Blucas
Summer Catch '01

Ben Blue
The Big Broadcast of 1938 '38
College Swing '38

Callum Blue
In Love and War '01

Monte Blue
Helltown '38
Undersea Kingdom '36

Mark Blum
Blind Date '87
Crocodile Dundee '86

Graeme Blundell
Idiot Box '97

Erin Blunt
The Bad News Bears Go to Japan '78
The Bad News Bears in Breaking Training '77
The Bad News Bears '76

Lothaire Bluteau
Urbania '00
Restless Spirits '99
Black Robe [MGM] '91

John Bluthal
The Fifth Element [2 SB] '97

Benedick Blythe
The Apocalypse Watch '97

Catherine Blythe
Finding Buck McHenry '00

Erik Blythe
Invasion U.S.A. '52

Peter Blythe
The Luzhin Defence '00
Carrington '95

Victor Bo
Deathstalker '83

Bruce Boa
Full Metal Jacket [2 SE] '87

Freddie Boath
The Mummy Returns '01

Michael Boatman
The Glass Shield '95

Anne Bobby
Nightbreed '90

Barbara Bobulova
In Love and War '01

Hart Bochner
Die Hard [FS 2] '88

Lloyd Bochner
They Call It Murder '71
The Dunwich Horror '70

Francisco Bodalo
Companeros '70

Christel Bodenstein
Tales from Europe: The Singing, Ringing Tree '57

Henri Boeck
Nekromantik '87

Earl Boen
The Terminator [2 SE] '84

Dirk Bogarde
Accident '67
The Mind Benders '63
The Servant '63

Stephen Bogardus
States of Control '98

Humphrey Bogart
Key Largo '48
Sahara '43

Eric Bogosian
Shot in the Heart '01

Robert Bogue
Matthew Blackheart: Monster Smasher '99

Richard Bohringer
Diva [Anchor Bay] '82

John Boles
Stella Dallas '37

Ray Bolger
The Harvey Girls '46
Stage Door Canteen '43

Joseph Bologna
Citizen Cohn '92
Transylvania 6-5000 '85

Michael Bolton
Snow Dogs '02

Jon Bon Jovi
Pay It Forward '00
Little City '97

Ivan Bonar
MacArthur '77

Renee Bond
Please Don't Eat My Mother '72

Rudy Bond
Run Silent, Run Deep '58

Steve Bond
Picasso Trigger '89

Ward Bond
Rio Bravo '59
The Long Gray Line '55

Beulah Bondi
The Southerner '45

De'Aundre Bonds
The Wood '99

Peter Bonerz
Medium Cool [SE] '69

Jason Bonham
Rock Star '01

Helena Bonham Carter
Novocaine '01
Planet of the Apes '01

Evan Bonifant
3 Ninjas Kick Back '94

Jacques Bonnaffe
Va Savoir '01

Sandrine Bonnaire
Secret Defense '98

Beverly Bonner
Basket Case [2 SE] '82

Tony Bonner
Quigley Down Under '90
Eye Witness '70

Hugh Bonneville
Blow Dry '00

Sonny Bono
Hairspray (John Waters Collection Vol. 1) '88

Daneen Boone
Adventures of Justine '00

Mark Boone, Jr.
Memento [1]'00
Memento [2 SE] '00
The Treat '98

Richard Boone
The Hobbit '78 (V)
The Shootist '76
I Bury the Living '58
The Robe '53
The Halls of Montezuma '50

Mika Boorem
Hearts in Atlantis '01
Riding in Cars with Boys '01

Imogen Boorman
Hellbound: Hellraiser 2 [2 THX] '88

Anthony Booth
Til Death Us Do Part '72

James Booth
Zorro, the Gay Blade '81
Brannigan '75

Lindy Booth
The Skulls 2 '02

Robert Booth
Great Fighting Machines of WWII: Allied & Axis Bombers '01 (N)
Great Fighting Machines of WWII: Allied & Axis Fighters '01 (N)
Great Fighting Machines of WWII: Allied & Axis Tanks '01 (N)

Powers Boothe
Tombstone [2] '93

Mac Bootsie
Get Down on It '01

Steve Boozer
Carnival of Souls [DC] '62
Carnival of Souls / Dementia 13 '62

Caterina Boratto
Juliet of the Spirits [Criterion] '65
8 1/2 '63

David Boreanaz
Valentine '01

Veda Ann Borg
Fog Island '45

Paul Borghese
61* '01

Ernest Borgnine
Gattaca [2 SB] '97
High Risk '81
All Quiet on the Western Front '79
The Greatest '77
Barabbas '62
The Vikings '58

Matt Borlenghi
Blood Surf '00

Katherine Borowitz
The Man Who Wasn't There '01

Jesse Borrego
Retroactive '97

Anthony Borrows
Liam '00

Jason Bortz
Take It to the Limit '00

John Yong Bosch
Extreme Heist '99

Philip Bosco
Kate & Leopold '01
Thomas Jefferson '01 (V)
Borough of Kings '98
My Best Friend's Wedding [2 SE] '97
Suspect '87
Three Men and a Baby '87

Barry Bostwick
800 Leagues down the Amazon '93
Working '82

John Boswall
Three Men and a Little Lady '90

Pamela Bottaro
Planet of the Dinosaurs '80

Maria Botto
Jealousy '99

Sam Bottoms
Apocalypse Now [Redux] '79
The Outlaw Josey Wales [2] '76

Timothy Bottoms
Top Dog '95
Invaders from Mars [MGM] '86

Reynald Bouchard
The Widow of Saint-Pierre '00

Jean Bouise
Le Dernier Combat '84

Daniel Boulanger
Breathless '59

Lily Boulogne
Happenstance '00

Carole Bouquet
That Obscure Object of Desire '77

Frederique Bouraly
Happenstance '00

John Bourgeois
Ginger Snaps '00

Peter Bourke
S.O.S. Titanic '79

JR Bourne
13 Ghosts '01

Antoine Bourseiller
Cleo from 5 to 7 '61

Duane Boutte
Stonewall '95

Jean-Luc Boutte
La Sentinelle '92

Jean-Pierre Bouyxou
The Grapes of Death '78

Clara Bow
It '27
Parisian Love / Down to the Sea in Ships '25
The Plastic Age '25
Down to the Sea in Ships '22

David Bowe
UHF '89

Michael Bowen
Echo Park '86

Roger Bowen
M*A*S*H [FS] '70

Malick Bowens
Ali '01
Out of Africa '85

Antoinette Bower
The Evil That Men Do '84

Megan Bower
Finding Buck McHenry '00

Michael Ray Bower
Evolution '01

Tom Bower
Hearts in Atlantis '01

Bonnie Bowers
There's Nothing out There '90

David Bowie
The Hunger: Smoke, Mirrors, and Paranoia '00
Mr. Rice's Secret '00
Twin Peaks: Fire Walk with Me '92

Peter Bowles
In Love and War '01
The Legend of Hell House '73
The Charge of the Light Brigade '68

Jessica Bowman
Joy Ride '01

Michael Bowman
Me, Myself, and Irene '00

Bruce Boxleitner
Tron [2 CE] '82

Boy George
The Wolves of Kromer '98 (N)

Todd Boyce
Spy Game '01

William Boyce
The Slime People '63

Brittany Boyd
Lassie '94

Darren Boyd
High Heels and Low Lifes '01

Guy Boyd
Retroactive '97

Karin Boyd
Mephisto '81

Stephen Boyd
The Bible '66
The Night Heaven Fell '57

Tanya Boyd
Roots '77

William Boyd
Hopalong Cassidy Returns '36
Three on the Trail '36
Bar 20 Rides Again '35
Hopalong Cassidy '35

Charles Boyer
Stavisky '74

Sully Boyer
The Manhattan Project '86

Lara Flynn Boyle
Baby's Day Out '94
Red Rock West '93
The Temp '93
Wayne's World '92
Twin Peaks: The First Season '90

Peter Boyle
Joe '70
Medium Cool [SE] '69

Marcel Bozzuffi
La Cage aux Folles 2 '81
The French Connection [SE] '71

Teda Bracci
The Big Bird Cage '72
C.C. & Company '70

Lorraine Bracco
Riding in Cars with Boys '01
The Sopranos: The Complete Second Season '01

Eddie Bracken
Star Spangled Rhythm '42

Louise Brooks
Diary of a Lost Girl '29
The Show Off / The Plastic
Age '26

Lowry Brooks, Jr.
Dead or Alive '02

Martin Brooks
Drawing Flies '02

Mel Brooks
Spaceballs '87
2000 Year Old Man '82 (V)
The Muppet Movie '79
Free to Be...You and Me '74
Putney Swope '69

Randi Brooks
Colors '88

Terron Brooks
The Temptations '98

Van Brooks
Blood Simple '85

Edward Brophy
Dumbo '41 (V)

Pierce Brosnan
The Tailor of Panama '00
Robinson Crusoe '96
Victim of Love '91
Nomads '86

Ben Browder
Farscape, Vol. 1 '00

Adrian Brown
Xena: Warrior Princess—
Series Finale '01

Art Edler Brown
Best Men '98

Barry Brown
Bad Company '72

Bille Brown
The Dish '00

Blair Brown
Follow the Stars Home '01
In His Life: The John Lennon
Story '00
Stealing Home '88
Kennedy '83

Bobby Brown
Two Can Play That Game '01

Bruce Brown
Eddie and the Cruisers '83

Bryan Brown
Risk '00
Styx '00
Sweet Talker '91
The Good Wife '86
The Irishman '78

Candy Ann Brown
Zebrahead '92

Clancy Brown
Snow White: The Fairest of
Them All '02
Boss of Bosses '99
The Batman Superman Movie
'97 (V)
Pet Sematary 2 '92
Highlander [Anchor Bay] '86
The Bride '85
The Adventures of Buckaroo
Banzai Across the Eighth
Dimension [SE] '84
Bad Boys [Anchor Bay] '83

Collette Brown
Ultraviolet '98

Divine Brown
Black Spring Break 2 '01

Emma Brown
The Worst Witch '98

Georg Stanford Brown
Roots '77

Georgia Brown
Victim of Love '91

Jim Brown
Twisted Justice '89
Slaughter '72

Joe E. Brown
It's a Mad, Mad, Mad, Mad
World '63
Show Boat '51

Johnny Mack Brown
Helltown '38
Fire Alarm '32

Juanita Brown
Caged Heat '74

Judy Brown
Women in Cages '71

June Brown
Gormenghast '00

Kimberly J. Brown
Stephen King's Rose Red '02

Lou Brown
The Irishman '78

L.P. Brown, III
Choke '01

Pamela Brown
Wuthering Heights '70

Paul Brown
Morons from Outer Space '85

Ralph Brown
Star Wars: Episode 1—The
Phantom Menace '99
Ivanhoe '97
Wayne's World 2 '93
Impromptu '90
Withnail and I '87

Ruth Brown
Hairspray (John Waters Collection Vol. 1) '88

Timothy Brown
M*A*S*H [FS] '70

Tom Brown
The Choppers '61

W. Earl Brown
Dancing at the Blue Iguana
'00

Woody Brown
The Accused '88

Coral Browne
Theatre of Blood '73
The Ruling Class '72

Diana Browne
Basket Case [2 SE] '82

Roscoe Lee Browne
Oliver & Company '88 (V)
Black Like Me '64

Zachary Browne
Shiloh 2: Shiloh Season '99

Ricou Browning
Creature from the Black
Lagoon '54

Ryan Browning
The Smokers '00

Mongo Brownlee
Me, Myself, and Irene '00

Bruce Bruce
The Wash '01

Cheryl Lynn Bruce
Daughters of the Dust '91

Clifford Bruce
A Fool There Was '14

Joan Bruce
Dot & the Kangaroo '77 (V)

Nigel Bruce
Rebecca [Criterion] '40

Patrick Bruel
Sabrina '95

Eddie Brugman
Katie Tippel '75

Valeria Bruni-Tedeschi
Those Who Love Me Can
Take the Train '98

Dylan Bruno
When Trumpets Fade '98

Philip Bruns
The Stunt Man '80

Eric Bruskotter
Major League 3: Back to the
Minors '98
Major League 2 '94

Robert Bruzio
Mr. Vincent '97

Alicia Bruzzo
A Shadow You Soon Will Be
'94

Darrell Bryan
Hard Luck '01

John Bryant
Run Silent, Run Deep '58

Michael Bryant
The Ruling Class '72
The Mind Benders '63

Pablo Bryant
Big Empty '98

Claudia Bryar
Psycho 2 '83

Larry Bryggman
Spy Game '01

Yul Brynner
Light at the Edge of the World
'71
Cast a Giant Shadow '66

Dan Bucatinsky
All over the Guy '01

Flavio Bucci
Suspiria '77

Edgar Buchanan
Over the Hill Gang '69
Rage at Dawn '55

Stuart Buchanan
Snow White and the Seven
Dwarfs [PE] '37 (V)

Horst Buchholz
The Enemy '01

Detlev Buck
Aimee & Jaguar '98

Samantha Buck
Wirey Spindell '99

Betty Buckley
Tender Mercies [Anchor Bay]
'83
Carrie '76

William F. Buckley
New York in the Fifties '01

Jillian Buckshaw
Biker Zombies '01

Gerard Buhr
Bob le Flambeur '55

Genevieve Bujold
Choose Me '84
Obsession '76

Richard Bull
Lawman '71

Maurice Bullard
The Last Castle '01

Donna Bullock
Air Force One [2 SB] '97

Sandra Bullock
The Net [2 SE] '95
Love Potion 9 '92

Alan Bunce
Homicidal '61

Cara Buono
Two Ninas '00
In a Class of His Own '99

Victor Buono
Robin and the 7 Hoods '64
Four for Texas '63

Sonny Bupp
Citizen Kane '41

Maud Buquet
Deep in the Woods '00

Steve Burce
Black and Blue '01

Hugh Burden
Blood from the Mummy's
Tomb '71
Funeral in Berlin '66

Mark Burgess
Perpetrators of the Crime '98

Michael Burgess
Black Knight '01

Gary Burghoff
M*A*S*H [FS] '70

Billy Burke
Along Came a Spider '00

David Burke
The Adventures of Sherlock
Holmes, Vol. 3 '83

Joe Michael Burke
The Last Warrior '99

Marylouise Burke
Series 7: The Contenders '01

Michelle Burke
Major League 2 '94

Paul Burke
Psychic Killer '75

Robert John Burke
Tombstone [2] '93

Robert Karl Burke
The Basket [SE] '99

Simon Burke
Rodgers & Hammerstein's
South Pacific '01
The Irishman '78

Walter Burke
Jack the Giant Killer '62

Dennis Burkley
Bummer '73

Tam Dean Burn
The Acid House '98

Carol Burnett
Putting It Together: Stephen
Sondheim—A Musical
Review '01
The Trumpet of the Swan '01
(V)

Smiley Burnette
Dick Tracy [Marengo] '37
Dick Tracy [VCI] '37
Undersea Kingdom '36

Edward Burns
15 Minutes '01
Sidewalks of New York '01

George Burns
18 Again! '88
College Swing '38

Heather Burns
You Are Here * '00

Helen Burns
Zorro, the Gay Blade '81

Jere Burns
Crocodile Dundee in Los
Angeles '01

Lisa Burns
The Shining [2 SE] '80

Marion Burns
Paradise Canyon '35

Mark Burns
The Charge of the Light
Brigade '68

Megan Burns
Liam '00

Michael Burns
With Friends Like These '90

Tim Burns
Mad Max [MGM SE] '80

Raymond Burr
Godzilla, King of the Mon-
sters [Goodtimes] '56
A Place in the Sun '51
Borderline '50
Raw Deal '48

Ty Burrell
Black Hawk Down '01
Evolution '01

Hedy Burress
Valentine '01
Cabin by the Lake / Return to
Cabin by the Lake '00

Jackie Burroughs
Lost and Delirious '01
Careful '92

William S. Burroughs
Haxan: Witchcraft through the
Ages '22 (N)

Ellen Burstyn
Mermaid '00
Deceiver '97
The Exorcist [2]: The Version
You've Never Seen '73

Clarissa Burt
NeverEnding Story 2: The
Next Chapter '91

Corey Burton
Cinderella 2: Dreams Come
True '02 (V)
Atlantis: The Lost Empire
[CE] '01 (V)

Jeff Burton
Night Divides the Day '01

Julian Burton
A Bucket of Blood / Attack of
the Giant Leeches [Maren-
go] '59

Kate Burton
The Ice Storm '97
Alice in Wonderland '83

LeVar Burton
Ali '01
Dancing in September '00
Star Trek: The Next Genera-
tion—The Complete 2nd
Season '89
Star Trek: The Next Genera-
tion—The Complete 1st
Season '87
The Hunter '80
Roots '77

Norman Burton
Crimes of Passion [2] '84

Richard Burton
Alice in Wonderland '83
Hamlet '64
Look Back in Anger '58
The Robe '53

Robert Burton
The Slime People '63
Invasion of the Animal People
'62
Terror in the Midnight Sun '58

Steve (Stephen) Burton
The Last Castle '01

Tony Burton
The Shining [2 SE] '80

Tyrone Burton
Squeeze '97

Warren Burton
Bloodfist 8: Hard Way Out '96

Steve Buscemi
Domestic Disturbance '01
Final Fantasy: The Spirits
Within '01 (V)
Ghost World '01
Desperado [2 SB] '95
Airheads '94
Tales from the Darkside: The
Movie '90

Gary Busey
Slap Shot 2: Breaking the Ice
'02
Rookie of the Year '93
Point Break '91
Silver Bullet '85
Angels Hard As They Come '71

Jake Busey
Fast Sofa '01

Timothy Busfield
Revenge of the Nerds 2:
Nerds in Paradise '87
Revenge of the Nerds /
Revenge of the Nerds 2:
Nerds in Paradise '84

Billy Green Bush
The Hitcher '86

Grand Bush
Boa '02
Extreme Honor '01
Colors '88

Akosua Busia
Hard Lessons '86

Manuel Busquets
Our Lady of the Assassins
'01

Raymond Bussieres
Paris When It Sizzles '64

Humberto Busto
Amores Perros '00

Brett Butler
The Dress Code '99

Gerard Butler
Dracula 2000 '00

Kerry Butler
Borough of Kings '98

Paul Butler
Romeo Is Bleeding '93
Zebrahead '92

Tom Butler
Josie and the Pussycats '01

Yancy Butler
The Treat '98

Merritt Butrick
Star Trek 3: The Search for
Spock '84

Jorg Buttgereit
Nekromantik '87

Red Buttons
18 Again! '88
Hatari! '62
Sayonara '57

Ruth Buzzi
The Villain '79

Dave Buzzotta
Children of the Corn 5: Fields
of Terror '98

Lee Byers
Curse of the Headless Horseman '72

Spring Byington
Werewolf of London '35
Little Women '33

John Byner
Transylvania 6-5000 '85

Ralph Byrd
Dick Tracy Meets Gruesome
'47
Dick Tracy's Dilemma '47
Guadalcanal Diary '43
The Jungle Book '42
The Son of Monte Cristo '40
Dick Tracy [Marengo] '37
Dick Tracy [VCI] '37

Barbara Byrne
Into the Woods '90

Catherine Byrne
S.O.S. Titanic '79

Cillian Byrne
The Secret of Roan Inish '94

Eddie Byrne
The Mummy '59

Gabriel Byrne
The Usual Suspects [MGM
SE] '95
Trial by Jury '94

Jenna Byrne
Lip Service '00

Michael Byrne
Mists of Avalon '01
The Musketeer '01

Delma Byron
Dimples '36

James Caan
Dead Simple '01
A Glimpse of Hell '01
Luckytown '00
Mickey Blue Eyes '99
Flesh and Bone '93
Dick Tracy '90
Comes a Horseman '78
Funny Lady '75
The Gambler '74

Scott Caan
American Outlaws '01
Novocaine '01
Ocean's Eleven '01
Bongwater '98

Lilliana Cabal
She Lives by Night '01

Bruce Cabot
Hatari! '62
Goliath and the Dragon '61

Sebastian Cabot
Twice-Told Tales '63

Susan Cabot
The Wasp Woman [2] '59

Nicolas Cabre
Brain Drain '98

Jason Cadieux
Lilies '96

Adolph Caesar
Fist of Fear, Touch of Death
'80

Sid Caesar
The Sid Caesar Collection:
The Fan Favorites '01
The Cheap Detective '78
It's a Mad, Mad, Mad, Mad
World '63

Ashley Lyn Cafagna
The Skulls 2 '02

Jose Maria Caffarell
Doctor Zhivago '65

Nicolas Cage
Captain Corelli's Mandolin
'01
Family Man '00
Red Rock West '93
The Cotton Club '84

James Cagney
Blood on the Sun [Image] '45

Jeanne Cagney
Don't Bother to Knock '52

Dean Cain
Boa '02
Firetrap '01
Rat Race '01
The Runaway '00
Best Men '98

Katheryn Cain
The Pornographer '00

Darian Caine
Play-Mate of the Apes '02
Roxanna '02
Vampire Obsession '02
The Erotic Mirror '01
Mummy Raider '01
The Sexy Sixth Sense '01

Michael Caine
Dirty Rotten Scoundrels
[MGM] '88
Hannah and Her Sisters '86
Dressed to Kill [SE] '80
California Suite '78
Sleuth [2] '72
Too Late the Hero '70
Funeral in Berlin '66

John Cairney
The Flesh and the Fiends '60

Jonathan Cake
Catherine Cookson's The Girl
'96

Anna Calder-Marshall
Wuthering Heights '70

Paul Calderon
The Last Castle '01

Linda Lee Caldwell
Bruce Lee: A Warrior's Journey '01

Sandra Caldwell
Love Songs '99

Zoe Caldwell
The Purple Rose of Cairo '85

Monica Calhoun
Bagdad Cafe '88

Rory Calhoun
Hell Comes to Frogtown '88
River of No Return '54

R.D. Call
Stephen King's Golden Years
'91
Colors '88

K. Callan
Frankie and Johnny '91
The Unborn '91
A Touch of Class '73

James Callanders
The Skulls 2 '02

Joseph Calleia
Lured '47
The Jungle Book '42

James Callis
Bridget Jones's Diary '01

Simon Callow
No Man's Land '01

Vanessa Bell Calloway
The Temptations '98

Donald Calthrop
Scrooge '35

Philippe Calvario
Intimacy '00

Phyllis Calvert
Indiscreet '58

Felipe Camacho
Drive By '01

Mark Camacho
Nowhere in Sight '01
Stalker '98
The Kid '97

Christian Camargo
Lip Service '00

Earl Cameron
Submarine Attack '54

Jane Cameron
The Unborn '91

Kirk Cameron
The Miracle of the Cards '00

Rod Cameron
Psychic Killer '75
Evel Knievel '72

Trent Cameron
The Wood '99

Tony Camilieri
Bill & Ted's Excellent Adventure '89

Terry Camillieri
Bill & Ted's Excellent Adventure '89

Colleen Camp
Second to Die '02
Wayne's World '92
Apocalypse Now [Redux] '79

Hamilton Camp
Under Fire '83

Joseph Campanella
Murder Once Removed '71

Billy Campbell
Bram Stoker's Dracula [SB]
'92

Bruce Campbell
The Ice Rink '99
Evil Dead [LE] '83

Cheryl Campbell
Murder at the Vicarage '86

Christian Campbell
Next Time '99

Elizabeth Campbell
Doctor of Doom '62

Emma Campbell
Ultimate G's '01

Gerardo Campbell
Amores Perros '00

J. Kenneth Campbell
Ulee's Gold '97

Joseph Campbell
Joseph Campbell Mythos '97
Joseph Campbell: The Power
of Myth '88

Julia Campbell
Stephen King's Rose Red '02

Maia Campbell
Parental Guidance '02

Michael Leydon
Campbell
Sidewalks of New York '01

Neve Campbell
Panic '00

Rob Campbell
Hedwig and the Angry Inch '00

Ruby Campbell
Love Goggles '99

William Campbell
Dementia 13 [Roan] '63

Helen Campitelli
Squeeze Play [DC] '79

Wally Campo
The Beast from Haunted
Cave '60

Bruno Campos
Mimic 2 '01

Rafael Campos
V '83
The Doll Squad '73

Ron Canada
Dean Koontz's Black River
'01

Gianna Maria Canale
I Vampiri '56
Go for Broke! [VCI] '51

David Canary
Johnny Firecloud / Bummer
'75
Incident on a Dark Street '72

Stelio Candelli
Planet of the Vampires '65

Candy Candido
Peter Pan [2 SE] '53 (V)

John Candy
Spaceballs '87
Brewster's Millions [Univer-
sal] '85
Sesame Street Presents: Fol-
low That Bird '85
Volunteers '85
Stripes '81

Roberto Canedo
Doctor of Doom '62

Hugh Cannon
House on Bare Mountain '62

J.D. Cannon
Lawman '71

Wanda Cannon
The 6th Day [2 SE] '00

Jack Canon
Kidnapped Coed '77
Axe '74

Joanna Canton
The Convent '01

Yakima Canutt
King of the Pecos '36
Paradise Canyon '35
West of the Divide '33

Virginia Capers
Jo Jo Dancer, Your Life Is Calling '86
Five on the Black Hand Side
'73

Lino Capolicchio
The Garden of the Finzi-Continis '71

Truman Capote
Murder by Death '76

Ahna Capri
The Specialist '75

Vittorio Caprioli
Le Magnifique '76

Jessica Capshaw
Valentine '01
The Locusts '97

Kate Capshaw
A Girl Thing '01
The Locusts '97

Paul Carafotes
All the Right Moves '83

Joseph Carberry
Vigilante [2 DC] '83

Antony Carbone
A Bucket of Blood / Attack of the Giant Leeches [Marengo] '59

Richard Cardella
The Crater Lake Monster '77

Linda Cardellini
Legally Blonde '01

Bill "Chilly Billy" Cardille
Night of the Living Dead [Elite ME] '68

Tantoo Cardinal
The Education of Little Tree '97
Black Robe [MGM] '91

Claudia Cardinale
8 1/2 '63
Rocco and His Brothers '60

Anthony Cardoza
Night of the Ghouls '59

Harry Carey, Sr.
Beyond Tomorrow '40

Harry Carey, Jr.
Tombstone [2] '93
Breaking In '89
The Devil's Brigade '68
Rio Bravo '59

Helen Carey
Black Knight '01

MacDonald Carey
Roots '77

Mariah Carey
Glitter '01

Phil Carey
Scream of the Wolf '74
The Long Gray Line '55

Timothy Carey
Echo Park '86
Head '68

Shantel Cargle
Better Dayz '02

Jean-Pierre Cargol
The Wild Child '70

John Carhart, III
There's Nothing out There '90

Timothy Carhart
Beverly Hills Cop 3 '94
Candyman 2: Farewell to the Flesh '94
Red Rock West '93

Gia Carides
Maze '01
The Extreme Adventures of Super Dave '98
Letters from a Killer '98
Strictly Ballroom '92

Carmine Caridi
Top Dog '95

Len Cariou
Thirteen Days '00

George Carlin
Jay and Silent Bob Strike Back '01
Dogma [2 SE] '99
Bill & Ted's Bogus Journey '91
The Prince of Tides '91
Bill & Ted's Excellent Adventure '89

Bruce Carlisle
The Fast and the Furious '54

Kitty Carlisle Hart
Radio Days '87

Christine Carlo
All or Nothing '01

Jeff Carlson
Slap Shot 2: Breaking the Ice '02
Slap Shot [2] '77

Karen Carlson
Man Next Door '97
Fleshburn '84

Richard Carlson
Tormented '60
Creature from the Black Lagoon '54
It Came from Outer Space '53
Behind Locked Doors '48
The Little Foxes [MGM] '41
Beyond Tomorrow '40
The Ghost Breakers '40

Steve Carlson
Slap Shot 2: Breaking the Ice '02
Slap Shot [2] '77

Hope Marie Carlton
Picasso Trigger '89
Hard Ticket to Hawaii '87

Robert Carlyle
Plunkett & Macleane '98

Katy Carmichael
Mood Swingers '00

Art Carney
The Muppets Take Manhattan '84
Katherine '75

Angela Carnon
A Scream in the Streets '73

Morris Carnovsky
Cyrano de Bergerac '50

Sheila Carol
The Beast from Haunted Cave '60

Adam Carolla
Art House '98

Leslie Caron
QB VII '74

Charisma Carpenter
Buffy the Vampire Slayer: Season 1 '97

John Carpenter
Night of the Ghouls '59

Linda Carpenter
Apocalypse Now [Redux] '79

Hayley Carr
Mood Swingers '00

Walter Carr
The Wicker Man [SE] '75

Gloria Carra
A Shadow You Soon Will Be '94

Raffaella Carra
Von Ryan's Express '65

David Carradine
Balto 2: Wolf Quest '02 (V)
Cybercity '99
Children of the Corn 5: Fields of Terror '98
Lone Wolf McQuade '83
Boxcar Bertha '72

Ever Carradine
Life without Dick '01

John Carradine
Star Slammer '87
Revenge '86
The Secret of NIMH '82 (V)

The Howling '81
Satan's Cheerleaders '77
The Shootist '76
Boxcar Bertha '72
Red Zone Cuba '66
Invasion of the Animal People '62
Captain Kidd [Marengo] '45
Bluebeard '44
House of Frankenstein '44
The Mummy's Ghost '44
Dimples '36

Keith Carradine
The Diamond of Jeru '01
Andre '94
Choose Me '84
Maria's Lovers '84

Robert Carradine
Revenge of the Nerds 2: Nerds in Paradise '87
Revenge of the Nerds / Revenge of the Nerds 2: Nerds in Paradise '84
Coming Home '78

Don Carrara
Curse of the Headless Horseman '72

Barbara Carrera
Lone Wolf McQuade '83
Never Say Never Again '83
The Island of Dr. Moreau '77

Tia Carrere
Wayne's World 2 '93
Wayne's World '92

Jim Carrey
Dr. Seuss' How the Grinch Stole Christmas '00
Me, Myself, and Irene '00
The Dead Pool '88

Corey Carrier
After Dark, My Sweet [2] '90

Matthieu Carriere
Don Juan (Or If Don Juan Were a Woman) '73

Elpidia Carrillo
Bread and Roses '00

Beeson Carroll
Coming Home '78

Diahann Carroll
The Five Heartbeats '91
Carmen Jones '54

Leo G. Carroll
The Parent Trap '61
The Bad and the Beautiful '52
Rebecca [Criterion] '40

Madeleine Carroll
My Favorite Blonde '42

Peter Carroll
The Last Wave '77

Julius J. Carry, III
The Last Dragon '85

Hunter Carson
Invaders from Mars [MGM] '86

John David Carson
Empire of the Ants '77

Sunset Carson
Stage Door Canteen '43

Terrence "T.C." Carson
Gang Related '96

Alex Carter
Hitched '01

Jim Carter
Haunted Honeymoon '86

John N. Carter
The Doll Squad '73

T.K. Carter
Seems Like Old Times '80

Max Cartier
Rocco and His Brothers '60

Katrin Cartlidge
From Hell [DLE] '01
No Man's Land '01

Lynn Cartwright
The Wasp Woman [2] '59

Nancy Cartwright
The Simpsons: The Complete First Season '89 (V)

Veronica Cartwright
Scary Movie 2 '01
Money Talks '97
Candyman 2: Farewell to the Flesh '94
Goin' South '78

David Caruso
Session 9 '01
Proof of Life '00

Brigitte Carva
Orloff and the Invisible Man '70

Brent Carver
Deeply '99
Lilies '96
Larceny '91

Mary Carver
Safe '95

Dana Carvey
Wayne's World 2 '93
Wayne's World '92

Maria Casares
Children of Paradise '44

Regina Case
Me You Them '00

Max Casella
Newsies '92

Chiara Caselli
Sleepless '01

Adriana Caselotti
Snow White and the Seven Dwarfs [PE] '37 (V)

Bernie Casey
Bill & Ted's Excellent Adventure '89
Revenge of the Nerds / Revenge of the Nerds 2: Nerds in Paradise '84
Never Say Never Again '83
Cornbread, Earl & Me '75
Boxcar Bertha '72

Sue Casey
Swamp Country '66

Johnny Cash
Murder in Coweta County '83

June Carter Cash
Murder in Coweta County '83

Rosalind Cash
The Adventures of Buckaroo Banzai Across the Eighth Dimension [SE] '84
Cornbread, Earl & Me '75
Amazing Grace '74
King Lear '74

Stefania Casini
Suspiria '77

Philip Casnoff
Kiss Tomorrow Goodbye '00

John Cassavetes
The Fury '78

Jean-Pierre Cassel
The Crimson Rivers '01
The Ice Rink '99

Seymour Cassel
61* '01
Just One Night '00
The Treat '98
Indecent Proposal '93
Dick Tracy '90
Colors '88
Best Seller '87
Tin Men '87
The Mountain Men '80

Vincent Cassel
The Crimson Rivers '01
Shrek [SE] '01 (V)

Andrew Cassese
Revenge of the Nerds 2: Nerds in Paradise '87
Revenge of the Nerds / Revenge of the Nerds 2: Nerds in Paradise '84

Gabriel Casseus
Black Hawk Down '01

Elaine Cassidy
The Others [CE] '01

Joanna Cassidy
John Carpenter's Ghosts of Mars '01
Barbarians at the Gate '93
1969 '89
Under Fire '83

Ted Cassidy
MacKenna's Gold '69

Claudio Cassinelli
The New Gladiators '83
Mountain of the Cannibal God '79

Carla Cassola
Demonia '90

Jean-Pierre Castaldi
The Musketeer '01

Carlos Castanon
Cabeza de Vaca '90

Lou Castel
A Bullet for the General '68

Dan Castellaneta
The Simpsons: The Complete First Season '89 (V)
The War of the Roses [SE] '89
Nothing in Common '86

Richard S. Castellano
Incident on a Dark Street '72

Vincent Castellanos
Mulholland Drive '01

Sergio Castellitto
Va Savoir '01
For Sale '98

Willy Castello
Mad Youth '40
Cocaine Fiends '36

DeShonn Castle
Zebrahead '92

John Castle
The Mirror Cracked from Side to Side '92

Nick Castle
Halloween [Extended Edition] '78

Peggy Castle
Invasion U.S.A. '52

Antonio Catania
Bread and Tulips '01

Darlene Cates
What's Eating Gilbert Grape '93

Georgina Cates
The Treat '98
Stiff Upper Lips '96

Joe Cates
Eddie and the Cruisers '83

Phoebe Cates
The Anniversary Party '01
The Heart of Dixie '89
Date with an Angel '87

Reg E. Cathey
Boycott '02
Pootie Tang '01

Brigitte Catillon
The Taste of Others '00

Walter Catlett
They Got Me Covered '43
Mr. Deeds Goes to Town '36

Michael Caton
The Animal '01

Kim Cattrall
Sex and the City: The Complete Third Season '02
15 Minutes '01
Sex and the City: Season 1 '00
Unforgettable '96
Split Second '92
Mannequin '87

Daniel Cauchy
Bob le Flambeur '55

Jessica Cauffiel
Legally Blonde '01
Valentine '01

Maxwell Caulfield
Facing the Enemy '00

Tony Caunter
S.O.S. Titanic '79

Gary Cavagnaro
The Bad News Bears '76

Megan Cavanagh
The Blair Thumb '01 (V)

Michael Cavanaugh
Poison '01
Dancing in September '00

Lumi Cavazos
In the Time of the Butterflies '01

James Caviezel
Angel Eyes '01
Pay It Forward '00

Kary Cawley
Flooding '97

Alec Cawthorne
Sleuth [2] '72

Christopher Cazenove
A Knight's Tale '01
Three Men and a Little Lady '90

Carlo Cecchi
Stealing Beauty '96

Fulvio Cecere
Valentine '01

Cedric the Entertainer
Kingdom Come '01

Maria Ceica
Testamento '98

Adolfo Celi
Von Ryan's Express '65

Iga Cembrzynska
The Saragossa Manuscript '65

Jitka Cerhova
Daisies '96

Mike Cerrone
Me, Myself, and Irene '00

Tony Cetera
The Street Fighter [BCI] '74
The Street Fighter [BFS] '74

Michael Ceveris
The Mexican '01

Lacey Chabert
Balto 2: Wolf Quest '02 (V)
Not Another Teen Movie '01
Tart '01

Alain Chabat
The Taste of Others '00

George Chakiris
The Young Girls of Rochefort '68

Feodor Chaliapin, Jr.
The Church '98

William Challee
The Lone Ranger: Volume 1 '56

Charla Challoner
Circus of Horrors '60

Richard Chamberlain
The Last Wave '77

Justin Chambers
The Musketeer '01
The Wedding Planner '01

Andree Champagne
Playgirl Killer '66

Gower Champion
Show Boat '51

Marge Champion
The Party '68

Jackie Chan
Rush Hour 2 '01
Wheels on Meals '84
Drunken Master '78
Snake and Crane Arts of Shaolin '78
Snake in the Eagle's Shadow '78
36 Crazy Fists '77
To Kill with Intrigue '77

Jordan Chan
The Cheaters '00
Killer '00
Biozombie '98

Kwok-Bong Chan
The Lord of Hangzhou '98

Mario Chan
Eagle vs. Silver Fox '83

Michael Paul Chan
Spy Game '01
Molly '99

Ringo Chan
Lady Iron Monkey '83

Sing Chan
The Legendary Strike '78

Wai Lau Chan
Fists of Bruce Lee '78

Weiman Chan
The Invincible Killer '81

Ying Lai Chan
Trust Me U Die '99

Chick Chandler
The Lost Continent '51

George Chandler
Strange Impersonation '46

Tanis Chandler
Lured '47

Lon Chaney, Sr.
The Penalty '20

Lon Chaney, Jr.
The Defiant Ones '58
Daniel Boone: Trail Blazer '56
House of Frankenstein '44
The Mummy's Curse '44
The Mummy's Ghost '44
Son of Dracula '43

Frankenstein Meets the Wolf-man '42
The Ghost of Frankenstein '42
The Mummy's Tomb '42
Undersea Kingdom '36

Hang-sun Chang
Tell Me Something '99

Simon Chang
Flowers of Shanghai '98

Sylvia Chang
Eat Drink Man Woman '94

Carol Channing
Thumbelina [20th Century Fox] '94 (V)

Stockard Channing
A Girl Thing '01
The Cheap Detective '78

Winston Chao
Eat Drink Man Woman '94

Damian Chapa
U.S. Seals 2 '01
Cypress Edge '99

Tom Chapin
Lord of the Flies '63

Charlie Chaplin
Slapstick Encyclopedia (1909–27) '98

Deborah Chaplin
Bruce Lee Fights Back from the Grave '76

Dolores Chaplin
The Ice Rink '99

Geraldine Chaplin
The Odyssey '97
Home for the Holidays '95
The Age of Innocence '93
Doctor Zhivago '65

Sydney Chaplin
Satan's Cheerleaders '77

Alexander Chapman
Lilies '96

Ben Chapman
Creature from the Black Lagoon '54

Lanei Chapman
Rat Race '01

Lonny (Loni) Chapman
Where the Red Fern Grows '74

Marguerite Chapman
Flight to Mars '52

Mark Lindsay Chapman
Stephen King's The Langoliers '95

Sean Chapman
Hellbound: Hellraiser 2 [2 THX] '88

Cyd Charisse
The Harvey Girls '46

Josh Charles
Little City '97

Ian Charleson
Opera '88
Troubles '88
Gandhi '82

Charlita
Bela Lugosi Meets a Brooklyn Gorilla '52

Charo
Thumbelina [20th Century Fox] '94 (V)

Chevy Chase
Cops and Robbersons '94
Three Amigos '86

National Lampoon's European Vacation '85
Sesame Street Presents: Follow That Bird '85
Seems Like Old Times '80

Stephan Chase
Macbeth '71

Don Chastain
Black Godfather '74

Ghetty Chasun
Sore Losers '97

Glenndon Chatman
Love and Basketball '00

Ruth Chatterton
Dodsworth [MGM] '36

Jonathon Chaus
Loser '97

Alonso Chavez
Bread and Roses '00

Oscar Chavez
Break of Dawn '88

Sandra Chavez
The Fear Chamber '68

Jeff Chayette
Cave Girl '85

Maury Chaykin
The Mask of Zorro [2 SE] '98
Breaking In '89

Don Cheadle
Ocean's Eleven '01
Rush Hour 2 '01
Swordfish '01
Family Man '00
Traffic [Criterion] '00
Colors '88

Molly Cheek
American Pie 2 '01

Alice Chen
The Secrets of the Warrior's Power '97 (N)

Chang Chen
Crouching Tiger, Hidden Dragon [2 SB] '00

Joan Chen
In a Class of His Own '99
Twin Peaks: The First Season '90

Lai Chen
In the Mood for Love [SE] '00

Lester Chen
Eat Drink Man Woman '94

Terry Chen
Almost Famous: Untitled—The Bootleg Cut '00
Crash & Byrnes '99

Tsai Chen-Nan
The Puppetmaster '93

Adam Cheng
The Legend 2 '93

Ekin Cheng
Goodbye, Mr. Cool '01
The Duel '00
The Storm Riders '98

Kent Cheng
Dr. Lamb '92

Mark Cheng
Killer '00
Trust Me U Die '99

Pei Pei Cheng
The Fist Power '99

Philip Cheng
Eat My Dust '93

Sammi Cheng
Love on a Diet '01

Cher
Suspect '87

Christopher Scott Cherot
Hav Plenty '97

Morris Chestnut
Two Can Play That Game '01

Cecilia Cheung
Para Para Sakura '01

Chi Lan Cheung
Comic King '00

Emotion Cheung
The Demon's Baby '98

Julian Cheung
Comic King '00

Kam Ching Cheung
The Untold Story 2 '98

Leslie Cheung
The Phantom Lover '95

Maggie Cheung
In the Mood for Love [SE] '00
Dragon Inn '92

Nick Cheung
The Duel '00

Nicola Cheung
City of Glass '98

Philip Cheung
Fury in the Shaolin Temple '82

Roy Cheung
The Avenging Fist '01
Jiang Hu—"The Triad Zone" '00
City on Fire [Dimension] '87

Richard Chevolleau
True Blue '01

Kwan Chun Chi
Eagle Fist '77
Master of Death '75

Minoru Chiaki
The Hidden Fortress '58
Rashomon '51

Dominic Chianese
The Sopranos: The Complete Second Season '01

David Chiang
Return of the Deadly Blade '81

Sheng Chiang
Ninja in the Deadly Trap '83

Chiao Chiao
Blood of the Dragon '71

Sofiko Chiaureli
Ashik Kerib '88
The Color of Pomegranates '69

Sonny Chiba
The Storm Riders '98
Sure Death: Revenge '87
Shogun's Ninja '83
The Bodyguard [BFS] '76
Sister Street Fighter '76
Return of the Street Fighter '74
The Street Fighter [BCI] '74
The Street Fighter [BFS] '74
The Street Fighter's Last Revenge '74

Michael Chick
Money Buys Happiness '99

Hazel Childers
The Cheat [Kino] '15

Patricia Childress
Shake, Rattle & Rock! '94

Jeremy Childs
The Last Castle '01

Chilli
Ticker '01

Costas Dino Chimona
Full Metal Jacket [2 SE] '87

Ka-Lok Chin
The Avenging Fist '01
Bury Me High '90

William Ching
Terror in the Haunted House '58

Nicholas Chinlund
Training Day '01

Lori Tan Chinn
Rodgers & Hammerstein's South Pacific '01

Charles Chiodo
Killer Klowns from Outer Space '88

Jimmy Chisholm
Ivanhoe '97

Erik Chitty
Doctor Zhivago '65
First Men in the Moon '64

Bang-ho Cho
Tokyo Mafia: Battle for Shinjuku '96

Charlie Cho
Millennium Dragon '93

Henry Cho
Say It Isn't So '01

J. Moki Cho
Race the Sun '96

John Cho
Earth vs. the Spider '01

Margaret Cho
Margaret Cho: I'm the One That I Want '00
The Tavern '00

Seung Woo Cho
Chunhyang '00

Tim Choate
Pearl Harbor '01

Ada Choi
Your Place or Mine! '98

Mink-sik Choi
Happy End '99

Billy Chong
Jade Claw '79

Elton Chong
Invincible Obsessed Fighter '82

Jason Chong
Dr. Jekyll & Mr. Hyde '00

Mona Chong
On Her Majesty's Secret Service '69

Rae Dawn Chong
The Visit '00
Tales from the Darkside: The Movie '90
Soul Man '86
American Flyers '85
Cheech and Chong's The Corsican Brothers '84
Choose Me '84

Richard Chong
Dr. Jekyll & Mr. Hyde '00

Thomas Chong
The Wash '01
Ferngully '92 (V)

Cheech and Chong's The Corsican Brothers '84
Cheech and Chong's Nice Dreams '81

Sarita Choudhury
The House of the Spirits '93

China Chow
Head over Heels '01
The Big Hit [2 SB] '98

Lily Chow
Ballistic Kiss '98

Matt Chow
Too Many Ways to Be No. 1 '97

Emmanuelle Chriqui
A.I.: Artificial Intelligence '01
On the Line '01
100 Girls '00

Erika Christensen
Traffic [Criterion] '00

Hayden Christensen
Life As a House '01

Jesper Christensen
Uprising '01

Claudia Christian
Atlantis: The Lost Empire [CE] '01 (V)

Shawn Christian
Tremors 3: Back to Perfection '01

Benjamin Christiansen
Haxan: Witchcraft through the Ages '22

Emil Hass Christiansen
Ordet '55

Helen Christie
Lust for a Vampire '71

Julie Christie
Memoirs of a Survivor '81
Doctor Zhivago '65
Billy Liar '63

Katia Christine
Spirits of the Dead [Criterion] '68

Mayra Christine
The Death Curse of Tartu / Sting of Death '66

Virginia Christine
The Mummy's Curse '44

Bojesse Christopher
Point Break '91

Dennis Christopher
Plughead Rewired: Circuitry Man 2 '94
Circuitry Man '90
Breaking Away '79

Jean Christopher
Playgirl Killer '66

Kay Christopher
Dick Tracy's Dilemma '47

Johnny Chu
Eat My Dust '93

Norman Chu
Return of the Deadly Blade '81

Paul Chu
Bury Me High '90

Paul Chubb
The Well '97
Sweet Talker '91

Alan Chui
Ninja vs. Shaolin Guards '84

Cathy Chui
Time and Tide '00

Howard Chuman
Three Came Home '50

Do-yeon Chun
Happy End '99

Christy Chung
Cold War '00

Chuen Yung Chung
Ninja in the Deadly Trap '83

Lily Chung
Brother of Darkness '94
Daughter of Darkness '93
Millennium Dragon '93

Lin Chung
The Puppetmaster '93

Susan Chung
Tremors 3: Back to Perfection '01

Thomas Haden Church
3000 Miles to Graceland '01
Tombstone [2] '93

Berton Churchill
Dimples '36

Marguerite Churchill
Dracula's Daughter '36

Inna Churikova
Father Frost '66

Eduardo Ciannelli
MacKenna's Gold '69
They Got Me Covered '43
The Mummy's Hand '40

Eddie Cibrian
Say It Isn't So '01

Diane Cilento
The Wicker Man [SE] '75

Charles Cioffi
Newsies '92
All the Right Moves '83
Klute '71

Patty Cipoletti
Harvesters '02

George Cisar
Attack of the Giant Leeches [Marengo] '59

Joe Clair
Axe 'Em '02

Cyrielle Claire
Le Professionnel '81

Jennifer Claire
The Good Wife '86

Anna Clark
Introduction to Antiques '95

Blake Clark
Joe Dirt '01

Candy Clark
Buffy the Vampire Slayer '92
Blue Thunder '83

Dan Clark
The Item '01

Dane Clark
Gunman in the Streets '50

Kenneth (Ken) Clark
Attack of the Giant Leeches [Marengo] '59

Marlene Clark
Ganja and Hess '73
Slaughter '72

Matt Clark
Barbarians at the Gate '93
The Adventures of Buckaroo Banzai Across the Eighth Dimension [SE] '84
An Eye for an Eye '81
The Outlaw Josey Wales [2] '76

Petula Clark
Petula Clark: A Sign of the Times '01

Robin Clark
A Girl, 3 Guys and a Gun '01

Spencer (Treat) Clark
Unbreakable '00

Susan Clark
Valdez Is Coming '71

Caitlin Clarke
The Kid Brother '87

David Clarke
The Great St. Louis Bank Robbery '59

Jason Clarke
Risk '00

Joe Clarke
Basket Case [2 SE] '82

Lenny Clarke
What's the Worst That Could Happen? [SE] '01
Me, Myself, and Irene '00

Melinda (Mindy) Clarke
Return of the Living Dead 3 '93

Robert Clarke
Attack from Mars '88

Warren Clarke
Blow Dry '00
Greenfingers '00
S.O.S. Titanic '79

Lana Clarkson
Barbarian Queen 2: The Empress Strikes Back '89
Barbarian Queen '85
Deathstalker '83

Patricia Clarkson
The Pledge '00
The Dead Pool '88

Charles Clary
The Penalty '20

Kira Clavel
Dr. Jekyll & Mr. Hyde '00

Christian Clavier
Just Visiting '01

Eric Clawson
The Dead Hate the Living '99

Nicholas Clay
The Odyssey '97

June Clayworth
Dick Tracy Meets Gruesome '47

John Cleese
Harry Potter and the Sorcerer's Stone '01
Rat Race '01
Clockwise '86
The Great Muppet Caper '81

Paul Clemens
The Beast Within '82

Pierre Clementi
Belle de Jour '67

John Clements
The Mind Benders '63

David Clennon
The Visit '00
Falling in Love '84

Karen Cliche
Dr. Jekyll & Mr. Hyde '00

Jack Clifford
King of the Pecos '36

Richard Clifford
Carrington '95

Montgomery Clift
The Young Lions '58
A Place in the Sun '51

Debra Clinger
Midnight Madness '80

E.E. Clive
The Little Princess [Marengo] '39

Al Cliver
Demonia '90

George Clooney
Ocean's Eleven '01
Spy Kids '01
South Park: Bigger, Longer and Uncut '99 (V)
One Fine Day '96
Red Surf '90
Return of the Killer Tomatoes! '88
Return to Horror High '87

Eric Close
Follow the Stars Home '01

Glenn Close
Rodgers & Hammerstein's South Pacific '01
Things You Can Tell Just by Looking at Her '00
Air Force One [2 SB] '97
The House of the Spirits '93
Hook '91
Reversal of Fortune '90
Fatal Attraction [SCE] '87
The World according to Garp '82

John Close
The Slime People '63

Martin Clunes
Lorna Doone '01
The Acid House '98

George Clutesi
Prophecy '79

Francois Cluzet
Round Midnight '86

Jeremy Clyde
The Musketeer '01

Kim Coates
Black Hawk Down '01
Pearl Harbor '01
Beyond Suspicion '00
Unforgettable '96

Phyllis Coates
Invasion U.S.A. '52

Kacey Cobb
The Crater Lake Monster '77

Lee J. Cobb
The Exorcist [2]: The Version You've Never Seen '73
Lawman '71
MacKenna's Gold '69
On the Waterfront '54

Bill Cobbs
Random Hearts '99
Ghosts of Mississippi '96
That Thing You Do! '96
Dominick & Eugene '88

Roberto Cobo
Cabeza de Vaca '90

Charles Coburn
Monkey Business '52
Lured '47
The Lady Eve '41
The Road to Singapore '40

James Coburn
Snow Dogs '02
Hollywood Screen Tests: Take 2 '00
Deep Water '99
High Risk '81
The Muppet Movie '79
Midway [Universal CE] '76
Bite the Bullet '75

Rachael Leigh Cook
Josie and the Pussycats '01
Texas Rangers '01
Blow Dry '00

Ron Cook
The Odyssey '97

Jennifer Cooke
Friday the 13th, Part 6: Jason
Lives '86

Jennifer Coolidge
American Pie 2 '01
Down to Earth '01
Legally Blonde '01
Pootie Tang '01
American Pie [2 UE] '99

Philip Coolidge
Inherit the Wind '60

Coolio
The Convent '01
Get over It! '01
Perfume '01
Phat Beach '96

Kevin Cooney
Full Moon in Blue Water '88

Alice Cooper
The Alice Cooper Story '01
Wayne's World '92

Bradley Cooper
Wet Hot American Summer
'01

Chris Cooper
Me, Myself, and Irene '00
The Patriot [2 SB] '00
Breast Men '97

Garry Cooper
Quadrophenia '79

Gary Cooper
Along Came Jones '45
Mr. Deeds Goes to Town '36
It '27

Gladys Cooper
Separate Tables '58
Now, Voyager '42
Rebecca [Criterion] '40

Maggie Cooper
An Eye for an Eye '81

Maria Cooper
Axe 'Em '02

Melville Cooper
The Lady Eve '41
Rebecca [Criterion] '40

Stephen Cooper
The Amy Fisher Story '93

Trevor Cooper
Ivanhoe '97

Robert Coote
Theatre of Blood '73
The Horse's Mouth '58
Lured '47

Stewart Copeland
South Park: Bigger, Longer
and Uncut '99 (V)

**Zane R. (Lil' Zane)
Copeland, Jr.**
Dr. Dolittle 2 '01

Michael Copeman
Focus '01

Alicia Coppola
Double Down '01

Francis Ford Coppola
Apocalypse Now [Redux] '79

Patrick Coppola
Where Angels Dance '01

Sofia Coppola
Star Wars: Episode 1—The
Phantom Menace '99

Jean-Paul Coquelin
Le Trou '59

Brendan Corbalis
Stonewall '95

Glenn Corbett
Homicidal '61

Harry H. Corbett
Jabberwocky '77

John Corbett
Reckless and Wild '02
Sex and the City: The Com-
plete Third Season '02
Prancer Returns '01
Serendipity '01
Tombstone [2] '93

Barry Corbin
Crossfire Trail '01
Nothing in Common '86
Any Which Way You Can '80

Donna Corcoran
Don't Bother to Knock '52

Kevin Corcoran
Pollyanna '60
Old Yeller '57

Alex Cord
Air Rage '01
The Brotherhood '68

Rita (Paula) Corday
Dick Tracy vs. Cueball '46

Jorge Cordova
Two Coyotes '01

Tony Cordoza
Red Zone Cuba '66

Nick(y) Corello
Blankman '94
Colors '88

David Corey
Liam '00

Prof. Irwin Corey
The Curse of the Jade Scorpi-
on '01
Stuck on You! [DC] '84

Isabel Corey
Bob le Flambeur '55

Jeff Corey
Sword & the Sorcerer '82
Seconds '66

Wendell Corey
Sorry, Wrong Number '48

Al Corley
Squeeze Play [DC] '79

Annie Corley
Along for the Ride '00

Pat Corley
Coming Home '78

Maddie Corman
Mickey Blue Eyes '99

Roger Corman
The Silence of the Lambs
[MGM SE] '91
The Howling '81

Ellie Cornell
Halloween 4: The Return of
Michael Myers [MGM LE]
'88

Judy Cornwell
The Mirror Cracked from Side
to Side '92
Wuthering Heights '70

Georges Corraface
Impromptu '90
Not without My Daughter '90

Adrienne Corri
Doctor Zhivago '65
Devil Girl from Mars '54

Kevin Corrigan
Walking and Talking '96
Zebrahead '92

Lloyd Corrigan
She Wolf of London '46

Ray Corrigan
It! The Terror from Beyond
Space '58
Undersea Kingdom '36

Odile Corso
Extreme Honor '01

Bud Cort
South of Heaven, West of
Hell '01
Pollock [SE] '00
Dogma [2 SE] '99
Sweet Jane '98
Invaders from Mars [MGM]
'86
Maria's Lovers '84
M*A*S*H [FS] '70

Dan Cortese
The Triangle '01

Valentina Cortese
Juliet of the Spirits [Criterion]
'65

Ricardo Cortez
Behind Office Doors '31

Jerry Cortwright
The Giant Gila Monster '59

Bill Cosby
California Suite '78

Howard Cosell
Broadway Danny Rose '84

Daniel Cosgrove
Valentine '01
The Object of My Affection
'98

James Cosmo
Ivanhoe '97

James Cossins
At Bertram's Hotel '86
Wuthering Heights '70

Antonella Costa
The Road '00

James Costa
L.I.E. '01

Paulo Costanzo
Josie and the Pussycats '01

Robert Costanzo
61* '01

Bob Costas
Pootie Tang '01
The Scout '94

Lou Costello
Abbott and Costello Meet the
Mummy '55

Mariclare Costello
Territorial Men '76

Ward (Edward) Costello
MacArthur '77

Candy Coster
Shatter Dead '01

Nicolas Coster
MacArthur '77

Nikolaj Coster-Waldau
Black Hawk Down '01

Kevin Costner
3000 Miles to Graceland '01
Thirteen Days '00
Bull Durham [MGM SE] '88
American Flyers '85

Laurence Cote
Gang of Four '88

Richard Cotica
Rabid Grannies '89

Kevin Cotteleer
Dead Pet '01

Joseph Cotten
The Hearse '80
Lady Frankenstein '72
Niagara '52
Citizen Kane '41

Ralph Cotterill
Howling 3: The Marsupials
'87

Curtis Cotton, III
George Washington '00

James Cotton
After Dark, My Sweet [2] '90

Pierre Couderc
His Majesty, the Scarecrow of
Oz '14

Marisa Coughlan
Freddy Got Fingered '01

George Coulouris
Blood from the Mummy's
Tomb '71
Citizen Kane '41

Bernie Coulson
Cabin by the Lake / Return to
Cabin by the Lake '00
The Accused '88

Catherine Coulson
Twin Peaks: Fire Walk with
Me '92
Twin Peaks: The First Season
'90

Clare Coulter
The Worst Witch '98

Richard Council
The Manhattan Project '86

Clotilde Courau
Deep in the Woods '00

Hazel Court
Devil Girl from Mars '54

Margaret Courtenay
The Mirror Cracked from Side
to Side '92

Tom Courtenay
Doctor Zhivago '65
Billy Liar '63

Bob Courtney
The Jackals '67

Jeni Courtney
The Secret of Roan Inish '94

Marguerite Courtot
Down to the Sea in Ships '22

Christopher Cousins
Earth vs. the Spider '01

Christin Couto
Take It to the Limit '00

Casey Cowan
The Basket [SE] '99

Jerome Cowan
Fog Island '45

Richard Cowan
Madame Butterfly '95

Noel Coward
Paris When It Sizzles '64

Robert Cowdra
Saturday Night and Sunday
Morning '60

Victor Cowie
Careful '92

John Cowley
The Field [Artisan] '90

Geraldine Cowper
The Wicker Man [SE] '75

Alan Cox
The Odyssey '97

Brian Cox
L.I.E. '01
Hidden Agenda '90
Directed by Andrei Tarkovsky
'88 (N)
Manhunter [LE] '86
Therese Raquin '80

Deborah Cox
Love Come Down '00

Jennifer Elise Cox
Sometimes They Come
Back...Again '96

Jim Cox
Ferngully '92 (V)

Julie Cox
Dune [2 SE] '00

Mitchell Cox
Strait-Jacket '64

Paul Cox
Careful '92

Richard Cox
American Tragedy '00

Ronny Cox
American Outlaws '01
Total Recall [2 SLE] '90
Beverly Hills Cop 2 '87
Beverly Hills Cop [CE] '84
The Beast Within '82
Taps '81

Tony Cox
Me, Myself, and Irene '00

Wally Cox
Underdog [CE] '00 (V)

Courteney Cox Arquette
3000 Miles to Graceland '01
Friends: The Complete First
Season '95
Masters of the Universe '87

Jonathan Coy
Conspiracy '01

Brendan Coyle
Conspiracy '01

Richard Coyle
Lorna Doone '01

Peter Coyote
The Basket [SE] '99
Random Hearts '99
Unforgettable '96
Cross Creek '83
Timerider '83

Buster Crabbe
Flash Gordon: The Peril from
Planet Mongo '40
Flash Gordon: The Purple
Death from Outer Space
'40
Flash Gordon: The Deadly
Ray from Mars '39
Flash Gordon: Spaceship to
the Unknown '36
Tarzan the Fearless '33

Andrew Craig
Hard As Nails '01

Daniel Craig
Lara Croft: Tomb Raider '01

James Craig
The Tormentors '71
The Devil's Brigade '68

Michael Craig
The Irishman '78

Wendy Craig
The Mind Benders '63
The Servant '63

The Hound of the
Baskervilles '59
The Mummy '59

Eddie Cutanda
Squeeze '97

Zbigniew Cybulski
The Saragossa Manuscript
'65

Jon Cypher
Valdez Is Coming '71

Charles Cyphers
Big Bad Mama 2 '87
Halloween 2: The Nightmare
Isn't Over! [Universal] '81
Coming Home '78
Halloween [Extended Edition]
'78

Myriam Cyr
Kill by Inches '99

Billy Ray Cyrus
Mulholland Drive '01
Radical Jack '00

Nancy Czar
Wild Guitar / The Choppers
'62

Henry Czerny
Possessed '00
Cement '99
The Ice Storm '97

Zsuzsi Czinkoczi
An American Rhapsody '01

Da Brat
Glitter '01

Eric (DaRe) Da Re
Twin Peaks: Fire Walk with
Me '92
Twin Peaks: The First Season
'90

Howard da Silva
Mommie Dearest '81

Maryam D'Abo
The Point Men '01

Olivia D'Abo
The Enemy '01
The Triangle '01
Wayne's World 2 '93

Mark Dacascos
Dragstrip Girl '94

Jeff Dachis
There's Nothing out There '90

Amedo D'Adamo
Dogs: The Rise and Fall of an
All-Girl Bookie Joint '96

Cameron Daddo
Zebra Lounge '01

Marie Daems
Those Who Love Me Can
Take the Train '98

Willem Dafoe
White Sands '92
Triumph of the Spirit '89

Jensen Daggett
Major League 3: Back to the
Minors '98

Liza D'Agostino
Bar Girls '95

Lil Dagover
Dr. Mabuse, The Gambler '22

Arlene Dahl
Slightly Scarlet '56

Nadia Dajani
Sidewalks of New York '01

David Daker
Woman in Black '89

Badgett Dale
Lord of the Flies '90

Grover Dale
The Young Girls of Rochefort
'68

Jennifer Dale
Love Come Down '00
Larceny '91

David DaLie
Swamp Country '66

Beatrice Dalle
The Blackout '97

Joe Dallesandro
The Cotton Club '84

Audrey Dalton
Mr. Sardonicus '61
Separate Tables '58
The Monster That Challenged
the World '57

Hannah Dalton
Waiting '01

Timothy Dalton
American Outlaws '01
Possessed '00
Scarlett '94
Wuthering Heights '70

Roger Daltrey
Dracula: The Dark Prince '01

Carson Daly
Josie and the Pussycats '01

Timothy Daly
The Object of My Affection
'98
The Batman Superman Movie
'97 (V)
Diner '82

Tom Daly
The Angry Red Planet '59

Tyne Daly
The Aviator '85
The Enforcer '76

Paul D'Amato
Slap Shot [2] '77

Marcus D'Amico
Full Metal Jacket [2 SE] '87

Janet Damon
The Fat Black Pussycat '63

Mark Damon
Anzio '68

Matt Damon
Jay and Silent Bob Strike
Back '01
Ocean's Eleven '01
Dogma [2 SE] '99
Courage Under Fire '96

Stuart Damon
Cinderella '64

Mike Damus
Lost in Yonkers '93

Bill Dana
Lena's Holiday '90

Leora Dana
Kings Go Forth '58

Malcolm Danare
Popcorn '89

Charles Dance
Dark Blue World '01
China Moon '91
Plenty [Anchor Bay] '85

Hugh Dancy
Black Hawk Down '01

Dorothy Dandridge
Carmen Jones '54

Eric Dane
The Basket [SE] '99

Karl (Daen) Dane
Son of the Sheik '26

Lawrence Dane
Scanners '81

Claire Danes
To Gillian on Her 37th Birth-
day '96
Home for the Holidays '95

Jean Danet
The Hunchback of Notre
Dame '57

Beverly D'Angelo
An Eye for an Eye '95
High Spirits '88
National Lampoon's Euro-
pean Vacation '85
Honky Tonk Freeway '81
Every Which Way But Loose
'78

Carlo D'Angelo
I Vampiri '56

Rodney Dangerfield
The Projectionist '71

Leslie Daniel
The Brain That Wouldn't Die
'63

Emma Danieli
The Last Man on Earth '64

Henry Daniell
Witness for the Prosecution
'57

Ben Daniels
Conspiracy '01

Gary Daniels
Fatal Blade '00

Jeff Daniels
Chasing Sleep '00
Fly Away Home [2 SE] '96
The Butcher's Wife '91
Sweet Hearts Dance '88
Radio Days '87
The Purple Rose of Cairo '85
Fifth of July '82

Jody Daniels
Girl in Gold Boots '69

Phil Daniels
The Bride '85
Quadrophenia '79

William Daniels
Blind Date '87

Richard Danielson
Body Count '97

Ignat Daniltsev
The Mirror '75

Blythe Danner
Thomas Jefferson '01 (V)
Husbands and Wives '92
The Prince of Tides '91
The Seagull '75

Paul Franklin Dano
L.I.E. '01

Royal Dano
Killer Klowns from Outer
Space '88
House 2: The Second Story
'87
The Outlaw Josey Wales [2]
'76
Planet of the Apes '74
Moon of the Wolf '72

Ted Danson
Three Men and a Little Lady
'90
Cousins '89
Three Men and a Baby '87

Michael Dante
Crazy Horse and Custer: "The
Untold Story" '90

Gerald Dantsoff
Petits Freres '00

Tony Danza
Angels in the Outfield '94

Maia Danzinger
The Ice Storm '97

Ho Chung Dao
Bruce Lee the Invincible '77

Patti D'Arbanville
Real Genius '85

Mireille Darc
Please Not Now! '61

Jake D'Arcy
Gregory's Girl '80

Severn Darden
Real Genius '85

Florence Darel
A Tale of Springtime '89

Marion Darlington
Snow White and the Seven
Dwarfs [PE] '37 (V)

Linda Darlow
The Amy Fisher Story '93

Gerard Darmon
Diva [Anchor Bay] '82

Danielle Darrieux
The Young Girls of Rochefort
'68

Henry Darrow
Tequila Body Shots '99

Tony Darrow
Mickey Blue Eyes '99

Jane Darwell
Bright Eyes '34

Stacey Dash
Mo' Money '92

Jean Daste
The Wild Child '70

Jon Daugherty
Trans '99

Ryan Daugherty
Trans '99

Kiami Davael
The Dress Code '99

Danielle Daven
Rabid Grannies '89

Jack Davenport
Ultraviolet '98

Nigel Davenport
The Island of Dr. Moreau '77

Garry Davey
The Amy Fisher Story '93

Robert Davi
Showgirls '95
Cops and Robbersons '94
Die Hard [FS 2] '88
The Goonies '85

Eleanor David
Slipstream '89
84 Charing Cross Road '86

Ellen David
Random Encounter '98

Joanna David
4:50 from Paddington '87

Keith David
Final Fantasy: The Spirits
Within '01 (V)
Ken Burns' Mark Twain '01
(N)
Novocaine '01
An Eye for an Eye '95
Men at Work '90

Trevor David
Love Goggles '99

**Lolita (David)
Davidovich**
Intersection '93

Embeth Davidtz
Bridget Jones's Diary '01
13 Ghosts '01

Patricia Davie
Rabid Grannies '89

Jeremy Davies
The Locusts '97

Nicholas Davies
S.O.S. Titanic '79

Oliver Ford Davies
Star Wars: Episode 1—The
Phantom Menace '99

Rita Davies
The Wolves of Kromer '98

Stephen Davies
Bloodfist 7: Manhunt '95
Dillinger and Capone '95
The Nest '88

Alex Davion
The Bloodsuckers '70

Ashley Davis
Social Intercourse '01

Bette Davis
The Watcher in the Woods
'81
Pocketful of Miracles '61
Now, Voyager '42
The Little Foxes [MGM] '41

Brad Davis
Querelle '83

Brooke Davis
Second to Die '02

**Carole (Raphaelle)
Davis**
Mannequin '87

Chuck Davis
How High '01

Clifton Davis
Kingdom Come '01

Frank Davis
Return of the Killer Tomatoes! '88

Geena Davis
Stuart Little [2 DE] '99
Speechless '94
Transylvania 6-5000 '85

Hope Davis
Final '01
Hearts in Atlantis '01

Jason Davis
Recess Christmas: Miracle
on Third Street '01 (V)
Recess: School's Out '01 (V)

Jim Davis
Comes a Horseman '78
Bad Company '72

Judy Davis
Life with Judy Garland—Me
and My Shadows '01
Husbands and Wives '92
Impromptu '90

Kristen Davis
Sex and the City: The Com-
plete Third Season '02
Blacktop '01
Sex and the City: Season 1
'00

Mac Davis
Jackpot '01

Matthew Davis
Legally Blonde '01

John Derek
All the King's Men '49

Lisa Dergan
The Arena '01

Joe DeRita
Three Stooges: All Time Favorites '98
Four for Texas '63
It's a Mad, Mad, Mad, Mad World '63

Bruce Dern
The Glass House '01
After Dark, My Sweet [2] '90
1969 '89
Coming Home '78
Silent Running [Universal] '71
Rebel Rousers '69
Support Your Local Sheriff '69
Will Penny '67
Marnie '64

Laura Dern
Focus '01
I Am Sam '01
Jurassic Park 3 [CE] '01
Novocaine '01

Richard Derr
When Worlds Collide '51

Cleavant Derricks
Moscow on the Hudson '84

Debi Derryberry
Whispers: An Elephant's Tale '00 (V)

Michael Des Barres
Diary of a Sex Addict '01
Mulholland Drive '01

Jean Desailly
Le Professionnel '81

Anne DeSalvo
Taking Care of Business '90

Stanley DeSantis
Head over Heels '01
I Am Sam '01

Zooey Deschanel
Almost Famous: Untitled—The Bootleg Cut '00

Donna Desmond
Naughty Stewardesses '74

Florence Desmond
Three Came Home '50

Louis D'Esposito
Eddie and the Cruisers '83

Amanda Detmer
Saving Silverman '01

Bruce Detrick
Invasion of the Blood Farmers '72

Ernst Deutsch
The Golem '20

William Devane
The Hollow Man [2 SB] '00
Poor White Trash '00
Honky Tonk Freeway '81
The Bad News Bears in Breaking Training '77

Cherie Devanney
A Glimpse of Hell '01

Devin Devasquez
House 2: The Second Story '87

Nathaniel DeVeaux
In a Class of His Own '99

Marie Devereux
The Mark '61

Syndy Devil
Erotic Survivor 2 '01

Catherine Deville
The Rape of the Vampire '68

Sebastian DeVincente
Dead in the Water '01

Andy Devine
Over the Hill Gang '69

George Devine
Look Back in Anger '58

Loretta Devine
I Am Sam '01
Kingdom Come '01
Introducing Dorothy Dandridge '99

Margaret Devine
1999 '98

Sean Devine
Perpetrators of the Crime '98

Stuart Devine
Meet the Feebles '89 (V)

Danny DeVito
Heist '01
What's the Worst That Could Happen? [SE] '01
Space Jam [2 EE] '96 (V)
Look Who's Talking Now '93 (V)
The War of the Roses [SE] '89
Throw Momma from the Train '87
Tin Men '87
Ruthless People '86
Goin' South '78
The Van '77

Patrick Dewaere
Get Out Your Handkerchiefs '78
Going Places '74

Colleen Dewhurst
Alice in Wonderland '83
The Blue and the Gray '82
When a Stranger Calls '79
A Moon for the Misbegotten '75

David DeWitt
Up against Amanda '01

Jackie DeWitt
Kiss Me Quick! '64

Brad Dexter
Von Ryan's Express '65
Run Silent, Run Deep '58

Susan Dey
Echo Park '86

Cliff DeYoung
The Runaway '00
Dance 'til Dawn '88

Margarita d'Francisco
Fidel '02

Caroline Dhavernas
Out Cold '01

Barry Diamond
Bachelor Party '84

Don Diamond
Borderline '50

Harold Diamond
Picasso Trigger '89
Hard Ticket to Hawaii '87

Neil Diamond
Saving Silverman '01

Reed Edward Diamond
High Noon '00

Cameron Diaz
Slackers '02
Shrek [SE] '01 (V)
Vanilla Sky '01
Things You Can Tell Just by Looking at Her '00
My Best Friend's Wedding [2 SE] '97

Chico Diaz
Testamento '98

Guillermo Diaz
Fidel '02
Stonewall '95

Vic Diaz
The Big Bird Cage '72
Blood Thirst '65

Kem Dibbs
Daniel Boone: Trail Blazer '56

Leonardo DiCaprio
What's Eating Gilbert Grape '93

George DiCenzo
Exorcist 3: Legion '90
18 Again! '88

Andy Dick
Dr. Dolittle 2 '01 (V)
Best Men '98
Bongwater '98

Kim Dickens
The Gift '01
The Hollow Man [2 SB] '00
White River '99

Bonnie Dickenson
Little Shots of Happiness '97

Beach Dickerson
The Dunwich Horror '70

George Dickerson
After Dark, My Sweet [2] '90
Cutter's Way '81

Dale Dickey
The Pledge '00

Angie Dickinson
Ocean's Eleven '01
Pay It Forward '00
Sabrina '95
Big Bad Mama 2 '87
Dressed to Kill [SE] '80
Cast a Giant Shadow '66
Ocean's 11 '60
Rio Bravo '59

Joan Didion
New York in the Fifties '01

Gabino Diego
Love Can Seriously Damage Your Health '96

Juan Diego
Cabeza de Vaca '90

John Diehl
Jurassic Park 3 [CE] '01
Pearl Harbor '01
Three Wishes '95
Mo' Money '92
Motorama '91

John Dierkes
The Daughter of Dr. Jekyll '57

Charles Dierkop
Angels Hard As They Come '71

Vin Diesel
The Fast and the Furious '01

Marlene Dietrich
Paris When It Sizzles '64
Witness for the Prosecution '57
The Blue Angel '30

Anton Diffring
Circus of Horrors '60
Tales of Frankenstein '58

Ted DiFilippo
Major League 3: Back to the Minors '98

Tim DiFilippo
Major League 3: Back to the Minors '98

Tom DiFilippo
Major League 3: Back to the Minors '98

Uschi Digart
Superchick '71
Roxanna '70

Taye Diggs
The Wood '99

Mark Dignam
The Charge of the Light Brigade '68

Stephen (Dillon) Dillane
Spy Game '01

Victoria Dillard
Ali '01
Out of Sync '95

Bradford Dillman
The Enforcer '76
The Disappearance of Flight 412 '74
Moon of the Wolf '72

C.J. Dillon
Return of the Killer Tomatoes! '88

Jyl Dillon
Lady in Blue '96

Kevin Dillon
A Midnight Clear '92

Matt Dillon
One Night at McCool's '01
Kansas '88
My Bodyguard '80

Melinda Dillon
The Prince of Tides '91
Slap Shot [2] '77

Charles Dingle
The Little Foxes [MGM] '41

Ernie Dingo
Crocodile Dundee 2 '88

Stefano Dionisi
Sleepless '01

Timothy DiPri
Adventures of Justine '00

John DiResta
15 Minutes '01

Divine
Hairspray (John Waters Collection Vol. 1) '88
Polyester (John Waters Collection Vol. 2) '81
Female Trouble '74
Pink Flamingos '72

Andrew Divoff
Faust: Love of the Damned '00
Stealth Fighter '99

Donna Dixon
Wayne's World '92

Russell Dixon
Liam '00

Branko Djuric
No Man's Land '01

DMX
Exit Wounds '01

Peter J. D'Noto
Monsters Crash the Pajama Party Spook Show Spectacular '65

Khoa Do
The Diamond of Jeru '01

Alan Dobie
The Charge of the Light Brigade '68

Lawrence (Larry) Dobkin
Patton [2] '70
Twelve o'Clock High '49

Gosia Dobrowolska
Careful '92

Kevin Dobson
Midway [Universal CE] '76

Peter Dobson
Double Down '01

Vernon Dobtcheff
The Body '01

Gina Doctor
Dead Pet '01

Megan Dodds
Urbania '00

John Doe
Shake, Rattle & Rock! '94
Great Balls of Fire '89

Chris Doerk
Hot Summer '68

Shannen Doherty
Jay and Silent Bob Strike Back '01
Jailbreakers '94
Heathers [2 THX] '89

Michael Dolan
The Turning '92

Guy Doleman
The Prisoner '68
Funeral in Berlin '66

Mickey Dolenz
Head '68

Dora Doll
The Nude Set '61
The Young Lions '58

Fiona Dolman
Ultraviolet '98

John Doman
The Opponent '01

Andrea Domburg
Katie Tippel '75

Myrtle Domerel
A Bucket of Blood / Attack of the Giant Leeches [Marengo] '59

Dagmara Dominczyk
Rock Star '01

Jamie Donahue
The Dead Hate the Living '99

James Donald
Cast a Giant Shadow '66
The Vikings '58

Norma Donaldson
The Five Heartbeats '91

Peter Donat
The Deep End '01
The War of the Roses [SE] '89

Yolande Donlan
Expresso Bongo '59
The Devil Bat '41

Brian Donlevy
Cowboy '58

Barnard Pierre Donnadieu
Druids '01
The Vanishing [Criterion] '88

Ruth Donnelly
Mr. Deeds Goes to Town '36

Tony Donnelly
L.I.E. '01

Vincent D'Onofrio
Spanish Judges '99
Fires Within '91
Full Metal Jacket [2 SE] '87
First Turn On [DC] '83

Charles Durning
L.A.P.D.: To Protect and Serve
'01
State and Main '00
Shelter '98
One Fine Day '96
Home for the Holidays '95
Dick Tracy '90
Working '82
The Muppet Movie '79
When a Stranger Calls '79
The Fury '78

Michael Durrell
V '83

Ian Dury
Split Second '92

Dan Duryea
Along Came Jones '45
Sahara '43
The Little Foxes [MGM] '41

Jaroslav Dusek
Divided We Fall '00

Ann Dusenberry
Cutter's Way '81

Eliza Dushku
Jay and Silent Bob Strike
Back '01
Soul Survivors '01
Bring It On '00
Race the Sun '96

Sanjay Dutt
Mission Kashmir '00

Charles S. Dutton
Random Hearts '99
Crocodile Dundee 2 '88

Tim Dutton
Robert Louis Stevenson's St.
Ives '98

James Duval
Donnie Darko '01

Clea DuVall
John Carpenter's Ghosts of
Mars '01

Robert Duvall
The 6th Day [2 SE] '00
Newsies '92
The Handmaid's Tale '90
Colors '88
Tender Mercies [Anchor Bay]
'83
Apocalypse Now [Redux] '79
The Greatest '77
Breakout '75
Lawman '71
M*A*S*H [FS] '70

Shelley Duvall
The Shining [2 SE] '80

Eckart Dux
Tales from Europe: The
Singing, Ringing Tree '57

Ann Dvorak
The Long Night '47

Dorothy Dwan
The Wizard of Oz '25

Bill Dwyer
Little Shots of Happiness '97

Hilary Dwyer
Wuthering Heights '70

Valentine Dyall
The City of the Dead '60

Cameron Dye
The Tavern '00
Fraternity Vacation '85

Cordereau Dye
Waterproof '99

Dale Dye
Servants of Twilight '91
Casualties of War '89
Invaders from Mars [MGM] '86

Danny Dyer
High Heels and Low Lifes '01
Greenfingers '00

Richard Dysart
Prophecy '79
The Autobiography of Miss
Jane Pittman '74

George Dzundza
Batman & Mr. Freeze: Subze-
ro '97 (V)
Basic Instinct [2 SE] '92
The Butcher's Wife '91

Kristian Ealey
In His Life: The John Lennon
Story '00

Chan Eason
Comic King '00

Carlos East
The Fear Chamber '68

Ben Easter
Holiday in the Sun '01

Henry Easterday
The Kid Brother '87

Jesse Easterday, Jr.
The Kid Brother '87

Steve Eastin
Agent Red '00
Stealth Fighter '99

Marilyn Eastman
Night of the Living Dead [Elite
ME] '68

Rodney Eastman
The Caveman's Valentine '01
Sand '00

Joyce Easton
The Fury '78

Robert Easton
Just One Night '00

Sheena Easton
Indecent Proposal '93

Clint Eastwood
True Crime '99
The Dead Pool '88
Any Which Way You Can '80
Every Which Way But Loose
'78
The Enforcer '76
The Outlaw Josey Wales [2]
'76
Magnum Force '73
Dirty Harry [2] '71
Play Misty for Me '71
Paint Your Wagon '69

Kyle Eastwood
The Outlaw Josey Wales [2]
'76

Robert Eastwood
Tender Is the Heart '01

Roberta Eaton
Split Second '92

Osamu Ebara
Score '95

Luke Eberl
Planet of the Apes '01

Jake Eberle
The Breed '01

Christine Ebersole
True Crime '99
Til There Was You '96
Thief of Hearts '84

Buddy Ebsen
Walt Disney Treasures: Davy
Crockett '01

Christopher Eccleston
The Others [CE] '01

Emilio Echeverria
Amores Perros '00

Randy Echols
Hitch Hike to Hell / Kid-
napped Coed '97

Aaron Eckhart
The Pledge '00
Molly '99

Gwen Eckhaus
The Vanishing [Criterion] '88

Stephen Eckholdt
Santa Who? '00

Billy Eckstine
Jo Jo Dancer, Your Life Is Calling '86

Paul Eddington
Murder at the Vicarage '86
The Prisoner '68

Herb Edelman
Wheels on Meals '84

Lisa Edelstein
Dean Koontz's Black River
'01

Laura Eden
House on Bare Mountain '62

Mark Eden
Doctor Zhivago '65

Earle Edgerton
Carnival of Blood / Curse of
the Headless Horseman
[SE] '71

J. Trevor Edmond
Return of the Living Dead 3
'93

**Kenneth "Babyface"
Edmonds**
Hav Plenty '97

Louis Edmonds
Dark Shadows: DVD Collec-
tion 1 '67

Peter Edmund
Full Metal Jacket [2 SE] '87

Beatie Edney
Highlander [Anchor Bay] '86

Richard Edson
Let It Ride '89
Stranger than Paradise '84

Allan Edwall
The Sacrifice / Directed by
Andrei Tarkovsky '86

Anthony Edwards
Jackpot '01
Pet Sematary 2 '92
Revenge of the Nerds 2:
Nerds in Paradise '87
Revenge of the Nerds /
Revenge of the Nerds 2:
Nerds in Paradise '84

Cliff Edwards
Dumbo '41 (V)

Guy Edwards
The Winslow Boy '98

Hugh Edwards
Lord of the Flies '63

James Edwards
Patton [2] '70

Jennifer Edwards
The Man Who Loved Women
'83
Heidi '67

Luke Edwards
Newsies '92

Mark Edwards
Blood from the Mummy's
Tomb '71

Rory Edwards
Ivanhoe '97

Sam Edwards
Twelve o'Clock High '49

Shanee Edwards
Dead Silence '98

Stacy Edwards
Driven '01
Mexico City '01
Prancer Returns '01
Four Dogs Playing Poker '00

Vince Edwards
Jailbreakers '94
Motorama '91
Return to Horror High '87
Firehouse '72
The Devil's Brigade '68

Charles Egan
Monsters Crash the Pajama
Party Spook Show Spectac-
ular '65

Eddie Egan
The French Connection [SE]
'71

Peter Egan
2001: A Space Travesty '00

Richard Egan
Pollyanna '60

Julie Ege
On Her Majesty's Secret Service '69

Samantha Eggar
Light at the Edge of the World
'71

**Christopher Michael
Egger**
Revenge Quest '96

Atom Egoyan
Calendar '93

Julieta Egurrola
In the Country Where Nothing
Happens '99

Jennifer Ehle
Wilde '97

Jerome Ehlers
Quigley Down Under '90

Lisa Eichhorn
Cutter's Way '81

Gard B. Eidsvold
Zero Degrees Kelvin '95

Christopher Eigeman
Barcelona '94

David Eigenberg
The Mothman Prophecies '02

Jill Eikenberry
The Manhattan Project '86

Lisa Eilbacher
Beverly Hills Cop [CE] '84

Sally Eilers
Strange Illusion '45

Bob Einstein
The Extreme Adventures of
Super Dave '98

Hal Eisen
2103: Deadly Wake '97

Robin Eisenman
Mission Manila '87

Anthony Eisley
The Doll Squad '73
The Tormentors '71
The Wasp Woman [2] '59

Felix Eitner
The Trio '97

Carmen Ejogo
Boycott '02
What's the Worst That Could
Happen? [SE] '01

Anita Ekberg
Four for Texas '63

Britt Ekland
Scandal '89
Fraternity Vacation '85
The Wicker Man [SE] '75
The Man with the Golden Gun
'74
Percy '71
After the Fox '66

Gosta Ekman
Faust '26

Linda Ekoian
Little Shots of Happiness '97

Jack Elam
The Villain '79
The New Daughters of
Joshua Cabe '76
Over the Hill Gang '69
Support Your Local Sheriff
'69
Four for Texas '63
Pocketful of Miracles '61
She Shoulda Said No '49

Idris Elba
Ultraviolet '98

Ron Eldard
Black Hawk Down '01
When Trumpets Fade '98

Kevin Eldon
High Heels and Low Lifes '01

Florence Eldridge
Inherit the Wind '60

Carmen Electra
Perfume '01

Erika Eleniak
Second to Die '02
Shakedown '02
First Degree '01
The Opponent '01
Stealth Fighter '99

Sandor Eles
And Soon the Darkness '70

Bodhi (Pine) Elfman
Sand '00
The Others '97

Jenna Elfman
Mr. Bill Goes to Hollywood /
Mr. Bill Does Vegas '01
Town and Country '01

Alix Elias
Rock 'n' Roll High School
[New Concorde SE] '79

Hector Elias
Katherine '75

Shannon Elizabeth
American Pie 2 '01
Jay and Silent Bob Strike
Back '01
13 Ghosts '01
American Pie [2 UE] '99

Hector Elizondo
How High '01
The Princess Diaries '01
Tortilla Soup '01
Runaway Bride '99
Beverly Hills Cop 3 '94
Frankie and Johnny '91
Taking Care of Business '90
Nothing in Common '86
Cuba '79
Valdez Is Coming '71
The Fat Black Pussycat '63

Karen Elkin
Matthew Blackheart: Monster
Smasher '99

Timothy Farrell
Wrestling Women USA! '01

Mia Farrow
A Girl Thing '01
Husbands and Wives '92
Radio Days '87
Hannah and Her Sisters '86
The Purple Rose of Cairo '85
Broadway Danny Rose '84
Zelig '83
A Midsummer Night's Sex
Comedy '82
Avalanche '78

Bart Fasbender
Daria, The Movie: Is It Fall
Yet? '01 (V)

Joey Fatone
On the Line '01

Faudel
Happenstance '00

Ben Faulkner
Silent Fall '94

Lisa Faulkner
The Lover '92

Flora Fauna
Shatter Dead '01

Jon Favreau
Made [SE] '01

Farrah Fawcett
Extremities '86

George Fawcett
Son of the Sheik '26

Alice Faye
Hidden Hollywood: Treasures
from the 20th Century Fox
Vaults '99
Hidden Hollywood 2: More
Treasures from the 20th
Century Fox Vaults '99

Denise Faye
American Pie 2 '01

Ron Fazio
The Toxic Avenger, Part 3: The
Last Temptation of Toxie
[DC] '89

Michael Feast
A Caribbean Mystery / The
Mirror Cracked from Side
to Side '89

Angela Featherstone
Skipped Parts '00

Birgitte Federspiel
Ordet '55

John Fedevich
Almost Famous: Untitled—
The Bootleg Cut '00

Caroleen Feeney
Escape from Alaska '02

Roy Fegan
The Five Heartbeats '91

Brendan Fehr
The Forsaken '01
Kill Me Later '01
Christina's House '99

Oded Fehr
The Mummy Returns '01
Texas Rangers '01

Lung Fei
Dreaming Fists with Slender
Hands '80
Buddha Assassinator '79
Blood of the Dragon '71

Frances Feist
Carnival of Souls [DC] '62
Carnival of Souls / Dementia
13 '62

Corey Feldman
Friday the 13th, Part 5: A
New Beginning '85
The Goonies '85

Eric Feldman
Happenstance '00

Tovah Feldshuh
Brewster's Millions [Univer-
sal] '85

Norman Fell
With Friends Like These '90
Transylvania 6-5000 '85
It's a Mad, Mad, Mad, Mad
World '63
Inherit the Wind '60
Ocean's 11 '60

Rockliffe Fellowes
Regeneration / Young
Romance '15

Tom Felton
Harry Potter and the Sorcerer's Stone '01

Verna Felton
Dumbo '41 (V)

Hsu Feng
To Kill with Intrigue '77

Zhang Fengyi
The Assassin '93

Sherilyn Fenn
Cement '99
Of Mice and Men '92
Twin Peaks: The First Season
'90

Tod Fennell
The Kid '97

George Fenneman
How to Succeed in Business
without Really Trying '67

Lance Fenton
Heathers [2 THX] '89

Andy Fenwick
Christmas Evil '80

Perry Fenwick
The Winslow Boy '98

Colm Feore
The Caveman's Valentine '01
Pearl Harbor '01

Chloe Ferguson
Alien Visitor '95

Colin Ferguson
Daydream Believers: The
Monkees Story '00
Rowing Through '96

Craig Ferguson
Life without Dick '01
Born Romantic '00

Matthew Ferguson
Lilies '96

Phoebe Ferguson
Alien Visitor '95

Danielle Ferland
Into the Woods '90

Jodelle Ferland
Mermaid '00

Colin Fernandes
An American Werewolf in London [CE Universal] '81

Evelina Fernandez
Luminarias '99

Juan Fernandez
Crocodile Dundee 2 '88

Olympia Fernandez
Hell Asylum '01

**Wilhelmenia Wiggins
Fernandez**
Diva [Anchor Bay] '82

Rebecca Ferratti
To the Limit '95

Will Ferrell
Jay and Silent Bob Strike
Back '01
Zoolander '01
The Suburbans '99

Annette Ferrer
Animated Christmas DVD
Double Feature '79 (V)

Jose Ferrer
The Evil That Men Do '84
A Midsummer Night's Sex
Comedy '82
Cyrano de Bergerac '50

Leilani Sarelle Ferrer
Barbarians at the Gate '93
Basic Instinct [2 SE] '92

Mel Ferrer
Catherine the Great '95
Brannigan '75
Paris When It Sizzles '64

Miguel Ferrer
Traffic [Criterion] '00
Twin Peaks: Fire Walk with
Me '92
Star Trek 3: The Search for
Spock '84

Martin Ferrero
The Tailor of Panama '00
High Spirits '88

Eve Ferret
Haunted Honeymoon '86

Noel Ferrier
Return of Captain Invincible
'83

Lou Ferrigno
Ping! '01

Pam Ferris
The Darling Buds of May '91

Dan Ferro
Blow '01

Turi Ferro
Seduction of Mimi '72

Yarmis Fertis
Electra '62

Gabriele Ferzetti
On Her Majesty's Secret Service '69

Larry Fessenden
You Are Here * '00

Stepin Fetchit
Amazing Grace '74

William Fichtner
Black Hawk Down '01
Pearl Harbor '01
What's the Worst That Could
Happen? [SE] '01

Shelby Fiddis
Cheech and Chong's The Corsican Brothers '84

Betty Field
The Southerner '45

Chelsea Field
Tom Clancy's Netforce '98
Andre '94
Texas '94
Snapdragon '93

David Field
Chopper '01

Sally Field
Say It Isn't So '01
An Eye for an Eye '95

Forrest Gump [SCE] '94
Soapdish '91
Not without My Daughter '90
Places in the Heart '84

Shirley Anne Field
Saturday Night and Sunday
Morning '60

Todd Field
New Port South '00
Walking and Talking '96

Alexis Fields
House Party 4: Down to the
Last Minute '00

W.C. Fields
Hidden Hollywood 2: More
Treasures from the 20th
Century Fox Vaults '99
The Big Broadcast of 1938
'38

Joseph Fiennes
Enemy at the Gates '00
Stealing Beauty '96

George Figgs
Polyester (John Waters Col-
lection Vol. 2) '81
Female Trouble '74
Pink Flamingos '72

Efrain Figueroa
The Visit '00

Jon Finch
The Final Programme '73
Macbeth '71

Peter Finch
First Men in the Moon '64
Girl with Green Eyes '64
Fighting Rats of Tobruk '44

Yolande Finch
Girl with Green Eyes '64

Larry Fine
Three Stooges: Healthy,
Wealthy, and Dumb '01
Three Stooges: All Time
Favorites '98
Three Stooges: Dizzy Doctors
'96
Four for Texas '63
It's a Mad, Mad, Mad, Mad
World '63
Three Stooges: Three Smart
Saps '52

Gavin Fink
Prancer Returns '01

Frank Finlay
Stiff Upper Lips '96

**Stewart Finlay-
McLennan**
Christy—A Change of Sea-
sons '01
Christy—A New Beginning '01
Christy—Return to Cutter
Gap '01

Jon Finlayson
Lonely Hearts '82

Duane Finley
The Wood '99

William Finley
The Fury '78
Phantom of the Paradise '74

John Finn
True Crime '99

Albert Finney
Traffic [Criterion] '00
Saturday Night and Sunday
Morning '60

Shirley Jo Finney
Echo Park '86

Eugenia Tettoni Fior
The Last Days of Pompeii '13

Alejandro Fiore
Play for Me '01

Elena Fiore
Seduction of Mimi '72

John Fiore
Where Angels Dance '01

Linda Fiorentino
Dogma [2 SE] '99
Unforgettable '96
Beyond the Law '92
Queens Logic '91

Roy Firestone
The Scout '94

Scott Firestone
The Bad News Bears '76

Colin Firth
Bridget Jones's Diary '01
Conspiracy '01

Jonathan Firth
Victoria & Albert '01

Peter Firth
Pearl Harbor '01
Chill Factor '99

Kate Fischer
Blood Surf '00

Nancy Fish
Exorcist 3: Legion '90

**Laurence "Larry"
Fishburne**
Osmosis Jones '01 (V)
Higher Learning '94
Searching for Bobby Fischer
'93
Apocalypse Now [Redux] '79
Cornbread, Earl & Me '75

B.G. Fisher
Curse of the Headless Horseman '72

Carrie Fisher
Jay and Silent Bob Strike
Back '01
Soapdish '91
Hannah and Her Sisters '86

Frances Fisher
True Crime '99

L.B. Fisher
Daydream Believers: The
Monkees Story '00

Shug Fisher
The Giant Gila Monster '59

Mark Fite
Stuart Bliss '98

Barry Fitzgerald
And Then There Were None
[Image] '45

Geraldine Fitzgerald
Kennedy '83

Glenn Fitzgerald
Series 7: The Contenders '01
The Sixth Sense [Buena
Vista] '99

Tac Fitzgerald
Black Hawk Down '01

Tara Fitzgerald
Dark Blue World '01

**Colleen (Ann) (Vitamin
C) Fitzpatrick**
Dracula 2000 '00
Hairspray (John Waters Col-
lection Vol. 1) '88

Kate Fitzpatrick
Return of Captain Invincible
'83

Leo Fitzpatrick
Bully '01
Take It to the Limit '00

Jim Frangione
Heist '01

Astrid Frank
Au Pair Girls '72

Joanna Frank
Say Anything [SE] '89

Elena Franklin
Osmosis Jones '01

Pamela Franklin
The Legend of Hell House '73
And Soon the Darkness '70

Philip Franks
The Darling Buds of May '91

Adrienne Frantz
Jimmy Zip '00

Allan Franz
The Vigil '98

Arthur Franz
The Young Lions '58
Flight to Mars '52

Dennis Franz
Psycho 2 '83
Blow Out '81
Dressed to Kill [SE] '80
The Fury '78

Eduard Franz
Outpost in Morocco '49

Elizabeth Franz
Sabrina '95

Filippa Franzen
The Sacrifice / Directed by
Andrei Tarkovsky '86

Peter Franzen
Ambush '99

Daniel Franzese
Bully '01

Brendan Fraser
Monkeybone '01
The Mummy Returns '01
Mrs. Winterbourne '96
Airheads '94
The Scout '94

Duncan Fraser
Unforgettable '96
Timecop '94

Hugh Fraser
Agatha Christie's Poirot:
Dumb Witness '01
Agatha Christie's Poirot: Her-
cule Poirot's Christmas '01
Agatha Christie's Poirot: The
ABC Murders '92
Agatha Christie's Poirot: Peril
at End House '90

John Fraser
Schizo '77

Laura Fraser
A Knight's Tale '01
Forgive and Forget '99
Virtual Sexuality '99
Left Luggage '98

Ronald Fraser
Too Late the Hero '70

Tomiko Fraser
Head over Heels '01

Barbara Frawley
Dot & the Kangaroo '77 (V)

Rupert Frazer
Empire of the Sun '87

Sheila Frazier
Firehouse '72

Stan Freberg
It's a Mad, Mad, Mad, Mad
World '63

Blanche Frederici
Sadie Thompson '28

Lynne Frederick
Schizo '77
Four of the Apocalypse '75

Alice Fredlund
Please Don't Eat My Mother
'72

Nina Fredric
2069: A Sex Odyssey '78

Bert Freed
Evel Knievel '72
The Halls of Montezuma '50

Bill Freeman
Basket Case [2 SE] '82

Cheryl Freeman
Fresh '94

Howard Freeman
The Long Night '47

Kathleen Freeman
Shrek [SE] '01 (V)

Morgan Freeman
Along Came a Spider '00
Clint Eastwood: Out of the
Shadows '00 (N)

Paul Freeman
The Dogs of War '81

Paul Frees
The Return of the King '80 (V)

Wolf Frees
Doctor Zhivago '65

Matthias Freihof
Coming Out '89

Dash Fremont
Please Don't Eat My Mother
'72

Bruce French
Coming Home '78

Dawn French
Maybe Baby '99

Sadie French
The Black Cat / The Fat
Black Pussycat '65

Susan French
House '86

Victor French
Chato's Land '71

Mabel Frenyear
A Fool There Was '14

Bernard Fresson
French Connection 2 '75
Please Not Now! '61

Matt Frewer
Breast Men '97

Glenn Frey
Jerry Maguire [2 SE] '96

Leonard Frey
Fiddler on the Roof [2 SE] '71

Sami Frey
Cleo from 5 to 7 '61

Brenda Fricker
Angels in the Outfield '94
The Field [Artisan] '90

Jonathan Frid
Dark Shadows: DVD Collec-
tion 1 '67

Tom Fridley
Friday the 13th, Part 6: Jason
Lives '86

Frederick Friedel
Axe '74

Will Friedle
Batman Beyond: Return of
the Joker [2 Uncut] '00 (V)

David Friedman
Mau Mau Sex Sex '00
Sex and Buttered Popcorn
'91

Peter Friedman
Someone Like You '01
Safe '95
Christmas Evil '80

John Friedrich
The Boy in the Plastic Bubble
[2] '76

Anna Friel
An Everlasting Piece '00
Robert Louis Stevenson's St.
Ives '98

Colin Friels
Child Star: The Shirley Temple Story '01

Maria Laura Frigerio
Play for Me '01

David Frishberg
Breaking In '89

Nikki Fritz
Attack of the 60-Foot Centerfold '95

Milton Frome
Batman: The Movie '66

Troy Fronin
Adventures of the Kung Fu
Rascals '92

Renata Fronzi
Dead in the Water '01

Adam Frost
The Pact '99

Jake Frost
Hammers over the Anvil '91

Mark Frost
Faust: Love of the Damned
'00

Robert Frost
The Black Cat / The Fat
Black Pussycat '65

Sadie Frost
Uprising '01
Shopping '93
Bram Stoker's Dracula [SB]
'92

Warren Frost
Twin Peaks: The First Season
'90

Stephen Fry
Wilde '97
Jeeves & Wooster: The Com-
plete Second Season '96

Dwight Frye
Frankenstein Meets the Wolfman '42
The Ghost of Frankenstein
'42

Virgil Frye
Colors '88

Amalia Fuentes
Curse of the Vampires '70

Warner Fuetterer
Faust '26

Athol Fugard
Gandhi '82

Patrick Fugit
Almost Famous: Untitled—
The Bootleg Cut '00

Tatsuya Fuji
Gappa the Trifibian Monster
'67

John Fujioka
Pearl Harbor '01

Yuuki Fujisawa
Terminatrix '95

Susumu Fujita
The Hidden Fortress '58

**Kamatari (Keita)
Fujiwara**
The Hidden Fortress '58

Kei Fujiwara
Organ '96

Lucio Fulci
Demonia '90

Christopher Fulford
Immortal Beloved '94

Kurt Fuller
Wayne's World '92

Gene Fullmer
The Devil's Brigade '68

Eiji Funakoshi
The Blind Beast '69
Manji '64
Afraid to Die '60

Hark-On Fung
Snake in the Eagle's Shadow
'78

Kwok Fung
Shaolin Disciple '86

Paul Fung
Guadalcanal Diary '43

Stanley Fung
The Owl vs. Bombo '84

Stephen Fung
The Avenging Fist '01

Annette Funicello
Head '68

Edward Furlong
Pecker (John Waters Collec-
tion Vol. 1) '98
Pet Sematary 2 '92

John Furlong
Man Next Door '97

Benno Furmann
The Princess and the Warrior
'00

Yvonne Furneaux
The Mummy '59

Chris Furrh
Lord of the Flies '90

Stephen Furst
Silent Rage '82
Midnight Madness '80

Toshio Furukawa
Metropolis '01 (V)

Dan Futterman
Urbania '00
1999 '98
When Trumpets Fade '98

Herbert (Fuchs) Fux
Lady Frankenstein '72

Marianne Gaba
The Choppers '61

Martin Gabel
Marnie '64
The Thief '52

Clark Gable
Run Silent, Run Deep '58

Monique Gabrielle
Deathstalker 2: Duel of the
Titans '87
Bachelor Party '84

Jacqueline Gadsdon
It '27

Anna Gael
Zeta One '69

Jim Gaffigan
Final '01

Kevin Gage
Blow '01

Marie Gahva
Cry Blood, Apache '70

Hermes Gaido
Play for Me '01

Max Gail
Facing the Enemy '00

M.C. Gainey
Breakdown '96

Courtney Gains
Colors '88

Michel Galabru
La Cage aux Folles 2 '81
La Cage aux Folles '78

Alastair Galbraith
Intimacy '00

David Gale
Re-Animator [2 ME] '84

Eddra Gale
8 1/2 '63

Peter Gale
Empire of the Sun '87

Genevieva Galea
Les Carabiniers '63

Johnny Galecki
Vanilla Sky '01

Tony Galento
On the Waterfront '54

Zach Galifianakis
Out Cold '01

Stacy Galina
Children of the Corn 5: Fields
of Terror '98

Nacho Galindo
Borderline '50

Balazs Galko
An American Rhapsody '01

Frank Gallagher
Orphans '97

Matt Gallagher
Green '01

Michael Gallagher
Ten Benny '98

Nicholas Gallagher
In Love and War '01

Peter Gallagher
Perfume '01
To Gillian on Her 37th Birth-
day '96
High Spirits '88

Carlos Gallardo
Bravo '98
Desperado [2 SB] '95

Ray Galleth
Witch Hunter '01

Zach Galligan
The Tomorrow Man '01

Michaela Gallo
Beethoven's 4th '01

Vincent Gallo
The House of the Spirits '93

Don Galloway
Rough Night in Jericho '67

V. Galstian
The Color of Pomegranates
'69

Tyrese Gibson
Baby Boy '01

Tyrone Gibson
All or Nothing '01

Pamela Gidley
The Treat '98
Liebestraum '91

John Gielgud
Haunted '95
Scarlett '94
Plenty [Anchor Bay] '85
Gandhi '82
The Elephant Man '80
QB VII '74
The Charge of the Light
  Brigade '68
Hamlet '64

Stefan Gierasch
Carrie '76

Sam Gifaldi
The Trumpet of the Swan '01
  (V)

Alan Gifford
Town without Pity '61

Frances Gifford
Jungle Girl '41

Roland Gift
Scandal '89

Vincent (Vince Gill) Gil
Mad Max [MGM SE] '80

Andrew S. Gilbert
Idiot Box '97

Billy Gilbert
Snow White and the Seven
  Dwarfs [PE] '37 (V)

Carole Gilbert
Swamp Country '66

Lewis Gilbert
Across 110th Street '72

Ron Gilbert
Hard Luck '01

Sara Gilbert
Riding in Cars with Boys '01

Alexandra Gilbreath
Mood Swingers '00

Connie Gilchrist
Long John Silver '54

Nancy Giles
States of Control '98

Jack Gilford
Caveman '81
A Funny Thing Happened on
  the Way to the Forum '66

Glover Gill
Waking Life '01

Tony Gillan
Ten Benny '98

Aidan Gillen
Lorna Doone '01

Max Gilles
The Coca-Cola Kid '84

Dana Gillespie
The People That Time Forgot
  '77

Emer Gillespie
Troubles '88

Aden (John) Gillett
The Winslow Boy '98
Ivanhoe '97

Seth Gilliam
Courage Under Fire '96

Danny Gilmore
Winter Lily '98
Lilies '96

Ian Gilmour
Dangerous Summer '82

Jack Gilpin
Barcelona '94
Reversal of Fortune '90

Jay Gilpin
The Southerner '45

Peri Gilpin
Final Fantasy: The Spirits
  Within '01 (V) Cacho

Daniel Gimenez Cacho
Jealousy '99
Cabeza de Vaca '90

Jack Ging
Where the Red Fern Grows
  '74
Play Misty for Me '71

Robert Ginty
Coming Home '78

Lim Giong
Goodbye South, Goodbye '96
Good Men, Good Women '95

Rocky Giordani
After Dark, My Sweet [2] '90

Daniela Giordano
Find a Place to Die '68

Maria Angela Giordano
Killer Barbys '96

Arnaud Giovanietti
The Lover '92

Bettina Giovannini
Voices from Beyond '90

Carmine D. Giovinazzo
Black Hawk Down '01
The Learning Curve '01

Annie Girardot
Rocco and His Brothers '60

Bernard Giraudeau
Water Drops on Burning
  Rocks '99

Annabeth Gish
Scarlett '94
Hiding Out '87

Lillian Gish
Broken Blossoms [Kino] '19

Sheila Gish
Highlander [Anchor Bay] '86

Gudrun Gisladottir
The Sacrifice / Directed by
  Andrei Tarkovsky '86

Robert Gist
Jack the Giant Killer '62

Rod Gist
Lady in Red '79

Rick Gitlin
Squeeze Play [DC] '79

Robin Givens
Blankman '94

Michael Glaser
Butterflies Are Free '72

Paul Michael Glaser
Fiddler on the Roof [2 SE] '71

Philip Glass
Paul Simon: Graceland '97

Seamon Glass
This Is Not a Test '62

Phillip Glasser
A Troll in Central Park '94 (V)

Matthew Glave
Corky Romano '01
Rock Star '01
Ricochet River '98
Baby's Day Out '94

Eugene Glazer
The Five Heartbeats '91
Harlem Nights '89
Hollywood Shuffle '87

Alexei Glazyrin
Viy '67

Jackie Gleason
Nothing in Common '86
The Toy '82
Requiem for a Heavyweight
  '62

Joanna Gleason
The Wedding Planner '01
Into the Woods '90

Paul Gleason
Not Another Teen Movie '01
Money Talks '97
Die Hard [FS 2] '88

Nicholas Gledhill
Careful, He Might Hear You
  '84

Brendan Gleeson
A.I.: Artificial Intelligence '01
The Tailor of Panama '00

Paul Gleeson
Idiot Box '97

Iain Glen
Lara Croft: Tomb Raider '01
Beautiful Creatures '00
Mararia '98

Philip Glenister
Horatio Hornblower: The
  Adventure Continues '01

Robert Glenister
Just Visiting '01

Jacquelyn Glenn
The Projectionist '71

Lucille Glenn
The Vanishing [Criterion] '88

Roy Glenn
Carmen Jones '54

Scott Glenn
Training Day '01
Vertical Limit [2 SB] '00
Courage Under Fire '96
The Silence of the Lambs
  [MGM SE] '91
Apocalypse Now [Redux] '79
Angels Hard As They Come
  '71

Sharon Gless
Queer As Folk: The Complete
  First Season '01

Robert Gligorov
Stagefright '87

Brian Glover
Stiff Upper Lips '96
An American Werewolf in Lon-
  don [CE Universal] '81

Bruce Glover
Big Bad Mama 2 '87
C.C. & Company '70

Crispin Glover
Fast Sofa '01
What's Eating Gilbert Grape
  '93

Danny Glover
Boesman & Lena '00
Angels in the Outfield '94
Places in the Heart '84

Jamie Glover
In His Life: The John Lennon
  Story '00

John Glover
The Evil That Men Do '84
The Mountain Men '80

Julian Glover
Theatre of Death '67
Girl with Green Eyes '64

Susan Glover
Random Encounter '98

Tawney Sunshine Glover
A Troll in Central Park '94 (V)

William Glover
Oliver & Company '88 (V)

Vadim Glowna
Advertising Rules! '01

Brian Gluhak
Revenge Quest '96

Mary Glynne
Scrooge '35

Harry Goaz
Twin Peaks: The First Season
  '90

Karen Goberman
Brooklyn Babylon '00

Jean-Luc Godard
Cleo from 5 to 7 '61
Le Petit Soldat '60

Mark Goddard
Strange Invaders '83

Paulette Goddard
On Our Merry Way '48
Star Spangled Rhythm '42
The Ghost Breakers '40

Arthur Godfrey
Four for Texas '63

Adam Godley
Cor, Blimey! '00

Alexander Godunov
Die Hard [FS 2] '88

Dave Goelz
The Muppet Movie '79 (V)

Bernhard Goetzke
Dr. Mabuse, The Gambler '22

Gary Goetzman
Caged Heat '74

Walton Goggins
Red Dirt '99
Major League 3: Back to the
  Minors '98

Joanna Going
Tom Clancy's Netforce '98
Little City '97

Eleanor Gold
The New Gladiators '83

Tracey Gold
Dance 'til Dawn '88

Adam Goldberg
All over the Guy '01
Fast Sofa '01
Waking Life '01

Whoopi Goldberg
Call Me Claus '01
Kingdom Come '01
Monkeybone '01
Rat Race '01
Jackie's Back '99
Mary Pickford: A Life on Film
  '99 (N)
Rudolph the Red-Nosed Rein-
  deer: The Movie '98 (V)
Ghosts of Mississippi '96
Sister Act 2 '92
Soapdish '91

Harold Goldblatt
The Mind Benders '63

Jeff Goldblum
Perfume '01
Beyond Suspicion '00
The Tall Guy '89
Transylvania 6-5000 '85

**The Adventures of Buckaroo
  Banzai Across the Eighth
  Dimension [SE] '84**

Heather Goldenhersh
Spin the Bottle '97

Lelia Goldoni
Theatre of Death '67
Secret Agent '65

Bob(cat) Goldthwait
Blow '01

Ellen Goldwasser
Big Empty '98

Tony Goldwyn
An American Rhapsody '01
The 6th Day [2 SE] '00
The Last Tattoo '94

Valeria Golino
Things You Can Tell Just by
  Looking at Her '00
Spanish Judges '99
Immortal Beloved '94

Isabel Gomes
Glitter '01

Carlos Gomez
The Replacement Killers [2
  SE] '98
Desperado [2 SB] '95

Carmelo Gomez
Living It Up '00
Mararia '98
Vacas '91

Cesar Gomez
Dirty Kopz '01

Jaime Gomez
Training Day '01

Michelle Gomez
The Acid House '98

Sandra Gomez
Doomsdayer '99

Thomas Gomez
Key Largo '48

Robert Gomp
Richard III '12

George Gonzales
The Bad News Bears Go to
  Japan '78
The Bad News Bears in
  Breaking Training '77
The Bad News Bears '76

Humberto Gonzales
The Kiss You Gave Me '00

Carlos Gonzalez
Vampires in Havana '87 (V)

Frank Gonzalez
Vampires in Havana '87 (V)

Pedro Gonzalez-Gonzalez
Rio Bravo '59
The Young Land '59

Michael Gooch
Bad Taste [LE] '88

Caroline Goodall
Mists of Avalon '01
The Princess Diaries '01
Hook '91
After the War '89

Conrad Goode
Don't Say a Word '01

Cuba Gooding, Jr.
Snow Dogs '02
Pearl Harbor '01
Rat Race '01
Chill Factor '99
Jerry Maguire [2 SE] '96

Cuba Gooding, Sr.
Fatal Blade '00

Omar Gooding
Baby Boy '01

Michael Goodliffe
Von Ryan's Express '65

Benny Goodman
Stage Door Canteen '43

Brian Goodman
The Last Castle '01

John Goodman
My First Mister '01
One Night at McCool's '01
Rudolph the Red-Nosed Rein-
deer: The Movie '98 (V)
Maria's Lovers '84
Revenge of the Nerds /
Revenge of the Nerds 2:
Nerds in Paradise '84
Survivors '83

C.W. Goodrich
The Show Off / The Plastic
Age '26

Michael Goodwin
The Dead Pool '88
Date with an Angel '87

Thatcher Goodwin
Stealing Home '88

Sy Goraleb
A Troll in Central Park '94 (V)

David Gorcey
She Shoulda Said No '49

Leo Gorcey
It's a Mad, Mad, Mad, Mad
World '63

Carl Gordon
Love Songs '99

Dexter Gordon
Round Midnight '86

Don Gordon
The Beast Within '82
Slaughter '72

Gavin Gordon
The Bat [Goodtimes] '59

Gerald Gordon
Hell up in Harlem '73

Hannah Taylor Gordon
Anne Frank '01

Hayes Gordon
Return of Captain Invincible
'83

Julia Swayne Gordon
It '27

Keith Gordon
Dressed to Kill [SE] '80
Jaws 2 '78

Roy Gordon
The Wasp Woman [2] '59

Ruth Gordon
Any Which Way You Can '80
My Bodyguard '80
Every Which Way But Loose
'78

Serena Gordon
A Tale of Two Cities '91
After the War '89

Susan Gordon
Tormented '60

Joseph Gordon-Levitt
Along for the Ride '00
Sweet Jane '98
Angels in the Outfield '94

Eydie Gorme
Ocean's Eleven '01

Frank Gorshin
Luck of the Draw '00
Batman: The Movie '66

Louis Gossett, Jr.
Deceived '01
Love Songs '99
Enemy Mine '85
J.D.'s Revenge '76

Robert Gossett
Jimmy Zip '00

Gilbert Gottfried
Thumbelina [20th Century
Fox] '94 (V)
Beverly Hills Cop 2 '87

Michael Gottli
Tales from the Gimli Hospital
'88

Franz Gottlieb
M*A*S*H [FS] '70

Stanley Gottlieb
Putney Swope '69

John Gottowt
Nosferatu '22

Michael Gough
Robert Louis Stevenson's St.
Ives '98
The Age of Innocence '93
Out of Africa '85
The Legend of Hell House '73
The Horse's Mouth '58

Elliott Gould
Ocean's Eleven '01
Hollywood Screen Tests: Take
2 '00
The Big Hit [2 SB] '98
The Glass Shield '95
The Muppet Movie '79
M*A*S*H [FS] '70

Harold Gould
Seems Like Old Times '80

Jason Gould
The Prince of Tides '91
Say Anything [SE] '89

Robert Goulet
Recess: School's Out '01 (V)

Dembo Goumane
Petits Freres '00

Mustapha Goumane
Petits Freres '00

Olivier Gourmet
La Promesse '96

Harry Goz
Mommie Dearest '81

Bernie Gozier
Creature from the Black
Lagoon '54

GQ
On the Line '01

Betty Grable
Hidden Hollywood: Treasures
from the 20th Century Fox
Vaults '99
Hidden Hollywood 2: More
Treasures from the 20th
Century Fox Vaults '99
College Swing '38

Steve Grabowsky
Social Intercourse '01

Anna Grace
Fiona '98

April Grace
Waterproof '99

Frank Grace
Confessions of a Psycho Cat
/ Hot Blooded Woman '68

Topher Grace
Ocean's Eleven '01
Traffic [Criterion] '00

Ana Gracia
Nico and Dani '00

Ilene Graff
Rodgers & Hammerstein's
South Pacific '01

Todd Graff
Dominick & Eugene '88

C.J. Graham
Friday the 13th, Part 6: Jason
Lives '86

Gerrit Graham
Used Cars '80
Phantom of the Paradise '74

Heather Graham
From Hell [DLE] '01
Say It Isn't So '01
Sidewalks of New York '01
Committed '99
Twin Peaks: Fire Walk with
Me '92

Holter Graham
Spin the Bottle '97

Jeff Dylan Graham
Dead and Rotting '02

John Michael Graham
Halloween [Extended Edition]
'78

Kenny Graham
Chopper '01

Lauren Graham
Sweet November '01

Marcus Graham
Mulholland Drive '01

Stephen Graham
Snatch [SE] '00

Gloria Grahame
The Big Heat '53
The Bad and the Beautiful
'52

Kelsey Grammer
15 Minutes '01
Dance 'til Dawn '88

Alexander Granach
Nosferatu '22

Daisy Granados
A Paradise under the Stars
'99

Tracy Grandstaff
Daria, The Movie: Is It Fall
Yet? '01 (V)

Farley Granger
The North Star '43

Philip Granger
The Amy Fisher Story '93

Beth Grant
Rock Star '01
White Sands '92

Cary Grant
The Grass Is Greener '61
Operation Petticoat '59
Indiscreet '58
The Pride and the Passion
'57
Monkey Business '52

Cy Grant
At the Earth's Core '76

David Marshall Grant
Three Wishes '95
American Flyers '85

Eldon Grant
Big Fella '37

Faye Grant
V '83

Hugh Grant
Bridget Jones's Diary '01

Mickey Blue Eyes '99
The Remains of the Day '93
Impromptu '90
The Lady and the Highway-
man '89

Lawrence Grant
Son of Frankenstein '39
Werewolf of London '35

Lee Grant
Mulholland Drive '01
Citizen Cohn '92
The Seagull '75

Lisa Grant
There's Nothing out There '90

Richard E. Grant
Robert Louis Stevenson's St.
Ives '98
Jack and Sarah '95
The Age of Innocence '93
Bram Stoker's Dracula [SB]
'92
How to Get Ahead in Advertis-
ing '89
Withnail and I '87

Bonita Granville
Lone Ranger '56
Now, Voyager '42

Christiane Graskoff
Mephisto '81

Peter Graves
Scream of the Wolf '74

Fernand Gravet
Gunman in the Streets '50

David Barry Gray
Cops and Robbersons '94

Dolores Gray
Designing Woman '57

Dorian Gray
Il Grido '57

Jane Gray
The House of the Spirits '93

Macy Gray
Training Day '01

Pam Gray
Dogs: The Rise and Fall of an
All-Girl Bookie Joint '96

Sam Gray
Burnzy's Last Call '95
Christmas Evil '80

Spalding Gray
How High '01
Kate & Leopold '01

Vivean Gray
The Last Wave '77

Kathryn Grayson
Show Boat '51

Al Green
On the Line '01
Beverly Hills Cop 3 '94

Rev. Ervin Green
Daughters of the Dust '91

Kerri Green
The Goonies '85

Nigel Green
The Ruling Class '72
Khartoum '66

Seth Green
America's Sweethearts '01
Josie and the Pussycats '01
Rat Race '01
The Trumpet of the Swan '01
(V)
Radio Days '87
The Hotel New Hampshire
'84

Tom Green
Freddy Got Fingered '01

Paul Greenberg
The Blair Thumb '01 (V)
Thumbtanic '99 (V)

Daniel Greene
Me, Myself, and Irene '00

Ellen Greene
States of Control '98
One Fine Day '96

Graham Greene
Snow Dogs '02
Lost and Delirious '01
The Education of Little Tree
'97

Laura Greene
Putney Swope '69

Lorne Greene
Animated Christmas DVD
Double Feature '79 (V)
Roots '77

Peter Greene
The Usual Suspects [MGM
SE] '95

Richard Greene
The Little Princess [Marengo]
'39

Tim Greene
Creepin' '01

Ruth Greenfield
Willow '88

Brad Greenquist
Gang Related '96

Bruce Greenwood
The Magnificent Ambersons
'02
A Girl Thing '01
Thirteen Days '00
Servants of Twilight '91
Wild Orchid '90

Dabbs Greer
It! The Terror from Beyond
Space '58

Jane Greer
Dick Tracy, Detective '45

Judy Greer
The Wedding Planner '01

Virginia Gregg
Operation Petticoat '59
Love Is a Many Splendored
Thing '55

Ezio Greggio
2001: A Space Travesty '00

Pascal Greggory
Those Who Love Me Can
Take the Train '98

Martin Gregor
The Shop on Main Street '65

Rose Gregorio
Maze '01

Andre Gregory
Alice in Wonderland '83

Brendan Gregory
Dead Creatures '01

James Gregory
Clambake '67

Mary Gregory
Coming Home '78

Natalie Gregory
Oliver & Company '88 (V)

Joan Gregson
Sea People '00

John Gregson
Fright '71

Robert Greig
Sullivan's Travels '41

Kim Greist
Throw Momma from the Train '87
Manhunter [LE] '86

Adrian Grenier
A.I.: Artificial Intelligence '01

Zach Grenier
Swordfish '01
Chasing Sleep '00
The Kid Brother '87

Alejandra Grepi
Why Do They Call It Love When They Mean Sex? '92

Googy Gress
First Turn On [DC] '83

Jennifer Grey
American Flyers '85
The Cotton Club '84

Nan Grey
Dracula's Daughter '36

Virginia Grey
All That Heaven Allows '55

Zena Grey
Summer Catch '01

Michael Greyeyes
Skipped Parts '00

Robert Gribbin
Hitch Hike to Hell / Kidnapped Coed '97

Pamela Gridley
True Blue '01

Richard Grieco
Harold Robbins' Body Parts '01
Sexual Predator '01
Blackheart '98

Helmut Griem
McKenzie Break '70

David Alan Grier
15 Minutes '01
Stuart Little [2 DE] '99 (V)
Blankman '94

Pam Grier
Bones '01
John Carpenter's Ghosts of Mars '01
Bill & Ted's Bogus Journey '91
Bucktown '75
The Big Bird Cage '72
Women in Cages '71

Roosevelt "Rosie" Grier
Free to Be...You and Me '74

Jonathan (Jon Francis) Gries
Jackpot '01
Real Genius '85
Will Penny '67

Joe Grifasi
61* '01
Looking for an Echo '99
One Fine Day '96

Rachel Griffin
A Midnight Clear '92

Robert E. (Bob) Griffin
Jack the Ripper: 4 Tales of the Supernatural '58

Andy Griffith
Murder in Coweta County '83

Hugh Griffith
The Final Programme '73
Wuthering Heights '70

Julian Griffith
Hardball '01

Kenneth Griffith
Circus of Horrors '60

Melanie Griffith
Tart '01
Along for the Ride '00
Harrad Experiment '73

Simone Griffith
Swamp Girl / Swamp Country '71

Thomas Ian Griffith
Escape from Alaska '02
The Karate Kid: Part 3 '89

Tracy Griffith
The First Power '89

Rachel Griffiths
Blow '01
Blow Dry '00
My Best Friend's Wedding [2 SE] '97

Richard Griffiths
Harry Potter and the Sorcerer's Stone '01
Gormenghast '00
Withnail and I '87

Camila Griggs
Bar Girls '95

Eva Grimaldi
The Black Cobra '87

Camryn Grimes
Swordfish '01

Gary Grimes
Summer of '42 '71

Jim Grimshaw
Chill Factor '99

Rupert Grint
Harry Potter and the Sorcerer's Stone '01

David Grisman
Grateful Dawg '01

Stephen Grives
Flambards '78

George Grizzard
Scarlett '94
Bachelor Party '84
Seems Like Old Times '80
Comes a Horseman '78

Charles Grodin
Taking Care of Business '90
The Great Muppet Caper '81
Seems Like Old Times '80

Clare Grogan
Gregory's Girl '80

Ake Gronberg
Terror in the Midnight Sun '58

Sam Groom
Territorial Men '76

Arye Gross
A Midnight Clear '92
House 2: The Second Story '87
Soul Man '86

Frances B. Gross
Faces of Death 2 '81 (N)
Faces of Death 3: Scenes from the Underground '81

Michael Gross
Tremors 3: Back to Perfection '01
Sometimes They Come Back...Again '96

Karen Grosso
Up against Amanda '01

Sonny Grosso
The French Connection [SE] '71

Robin Groves
Silver Bullet '85

Ioan Gruffudd
Black Hawk Down '01
Horatio Hornblower: The Adventure Continues '01
Horatio Hornblower '99

Greg Grunberg
The Hollow Man [2 SB] '00

Olivier Gruner
Extreme Honor '01
The White Pony '99
T.N.T. '98

Ah-Leh Gua
Eat Drink Man Woman '94

Robert Guajardo
Red Rock West '93

Christopher Guard
Memoirs of a Survivor '81
The Lord of the Rings '78 (V)

Pippa Guard
Scarlett '94

Harry Guardino
Any Which Way You Can '80
The Enforcer '76
Dirty Harry [2] '71

Michael Guerin
Reflex Action '02

Alvaro Guerrero
Amores Perros '00
In the Country Where Nothing Happens '99

Evelyn Guerrero
Cheech and Chong's Nice Dreams '81

Christopher Guest
Waiting for Guffman '96
The Princess Bride [2 SE] '87

Lance Guest
Halloween 2: The Nightmare Isn't Over! [Universal] '81

Nicholas Guest
Roughnecks: Starship Troopers Chronicles—The Klendathu Campaign '02 (V)

Carla Gugino
The Center of the World '01
She Creature '01
Spy Kids '01

Wandisa Guida
I Vampiri '56

Nico Guilak
Two Coyotes '01

Paul Guilfoyle
Company Man '01
Session 9 '01
Random Hearts '99
Air Force One [2 SB] '97
Cadillac Man '90
Beverly Hills Cop 2 '87
Three Men and a Baby '87

Robert Guillaume
Wanted: Dead or Alive '86
Seems Like Old Times '80

Sophie Guillemin
With a Friend Like Harry '00

Fernando Guillen
Why Do They Call It Love When They Mean Sex? '92

Cayetana Guillen Cuervo
Not Love Just Frenzy '96

Tim Guinee
Courage Under Fire '96
Sudden Manhattan '96

Alec Guinness
Murder by Death '76

Doctor Zhivago '65
The Horse's Mouth '58

Tom Guiry
Black Hawk Down '01
Lassie '94
The Sandlot '93

Clu Gulager
Hit Lady '74

Amo Gulinello
The Object of My Affection '98

David Gulpilil
Crocodile Dundee '86
The Last Wave '77

Tony Guma
The Suburbans '99

Devon Gummersall
Earth vs. the Spider '01
When Trumpets Fade '98

Larry Gund
Lady in Blue '96

Bill Gunn
Ganja and Hess '73

Janet Gunn
Marquis de Sade '96

Moses Gunn
The NeverEnding Story '84
Cornbread, Earl & Me '75
Amazing Grace '74

Robert Gunner
The Jackals '67

Bob Gunton
61* '01
Running Mates '00

Rachel Gurney
Upstairs, Downstairs: The Complete First Season '71

Eric Gurry
Bad Boys [Anchor Bay] '83

Gerald Gutierrez
Time of Your Life '76

Zaide Silvia Gutierrez
In the Country Where Nothing Happens '99

Steve Guttenberg
Home for the Holidays '95
Three Men and a Little Lady '90
High Spirits '88
Three Men and a Baby '87
Short Circuit '86
Diner '82
Can't Stop the Music '80

Melanie Gutteridge
Amazons and Gladiators '01

Stefan Guttler
Heart of Glass '74

Jasmine Guy
Harlem Nights '89

Murphy Guyer
Lewis and Clark: Journey of the Corps of Discovery '97 (V)

Luis Guzman
Luckytown '00
Traffic [Criterion] '00
Stonewall '95

Michael Gwynn
The Scars of Dracula '70

Anne Gwynne
Dick Tracy Meets Gruesome '47
House of Frankenstein '44

Fred Gwynne
Fatal Attraction [SCE] '87
The Cotton Club '84

Agi Gyenes
Just for the Hell of It '68

Jake Gyllenhaal
Bubble Boy '01
Donnie Darko '01
Highway '01

Maggie Gyllenhaal
Donnie Darko '01
Riding in Cars with Boys '01

Emily Haack
I Spit on Your Corpse, I Piss on Your Grave '02

Trent Haaga
Dead and Rotting '02
Troma's Edge TV: Vol. 1 '00

Eva Habermann
Lexx Series 2, Vol. 1 '98

Matthias Habich
Enemy at the Gates '00

Buddy Hackett
It's a Mad, Mad, Mad, Mad World '63
God's Little Acre '58

Claire Hackett
Liam '00

Joan Hackett
Support Your Local Sheriff '69
Will Penny '67

Gene Hackman
Behind Enemy Lines '01
Heartbreakers '01
Heist '01
Heroes of Iwo Jima '01 (N)
The Mexican '01
Full Moon in Blue Water '88
Under Fire '83
Bite the Bullet '75
French Connection 2 '75
The French Connection [SE] '71

Michiko Hada
Flowers of Shanghai '98
Rowing Through '96

Ron Haddrick
Quigley Down Under '90

Krystof Hadek
Dark Blue World '01

Sara Haden
She Wolf of London '46

Reed Hadley
Guadalcanal Diary '43

Mark Hadlow
Meet the Feebles '89 (V)

Hendrick Haese
The Enemy '01

Dudley Hafner
Mission to Death '66

Ross Hagen
Star Slammer '87

Uta Hagen
Reversal of Fortune '90

Ron Hagerthy
The Lone Ranger: Volume 1 '56

Julie Hagerty
Freddy Got Fingered '01
Jackie's Back '99
Reversal of Fortune '90
A Midsummer Night's Sex Comedy '82

Dan Haggerty
Escape to Grizzly Mountain '99

Archie Hahn
Phantom of the Paradise '74

Robert Harper
Molly '99

Ron Harper
Body Count '97
Planet of the Apes '74

Tess Harper
The Turning '92
Tender Mercies [Anchor Bay]
'83

Georgia Harrell
First Turn On [DC] '83

Rebecca Harrell
Prancer '89

Woody Harrelson
Grass '00 (N)
Indecent Proposal '93

Laura Harring
Mulholland Drive '01

Desmond Harrington
My First Mister '01
Riding in Cars with Boys '01

Kevin Harrington
The Dish '00

Laura Harrington
What's Eating Gilbert Grape
'93

Barbara Harris
Dirty Rotten Scoundrels
[MGM] '88

Baxter Harris
Stephen King's The Lan-
goliers '95

Cynthia Harris
Three Men and a Baby '87

Danielle Harris
Halloween 4: The Return of
Michael Myers [MGM LE]
'88

Divina Harris
Rockin' with a Bullet

Ed Harris
Enemy at the Gates '00
Pollock [SE] '00
The Prime Gig '00
Jackson Pollock: Love and
Death on Long Island '99
An Eye for an Eye '95
China Moon '91
Places in the Heart '84
Under Fire '83

Estelle Harris
Good Advice '01

George Harris
Black Hawk Down '01

Harriet Harris
Memento [1] '00
Memento [2 SE] '00

Hope Harris
Ice Grill '02

Jamie Harris
The Lost Battalion '01

Jared Harris
How to Kill Your Neighbor's
Dog '01
Lush '01
Perfume '01
Shadow Magic '00

Jim Harris
Waitress [DC] '81
Squeeze Play [DC] '79

John Harris
Carnival of Blood / Curse of
the Headless Horseman
[SE] '71

Julie Harris
Thomas Jefferson '01 (V)

Scarlett '94
Requiem for a Heavyweight
'62

Julius W. Harris
Hell up in Harlem '73

Kirk Harris
Hard Luck '01
Loser '97

Mel Harris
Firetrap '01
Out of Time '00
Wanted: Dead or Alive '86

Richard Harris
Harry Potter and the Sorcer-
er's Stone '01
The Field [Artisan] '90
The Bible '66

Ricky Harris
Bones '01

Rosalind Harris
Fiddler on the Roof [2 SE] '71

Rosemary Harris
Blow Dry '00
The Gift '00
The Royal Family '77

Abigail Harrison
Elizabeth '02

Gabriel Harrison
The Legend of a Professional
'00

Gregory Harrison
Running Wild '99

Jenilee Harrison
Tank '83

Randy Harrison
Queer As Folk: The Complete
First Season '01

Jamie Harrold
A Glimpse of Hell '01

Kathryn Harrold
The Hunter '80

Deborah Harry
Tales from the Darkside: The
Movie '90
Hairspray (John Waters Col-
lection Vol. 1) '88

Christina Hart
Johnny Firecloud / Bummer
'75

David Hart
Liam '00

Emily Anne Hart
Child Star: The Shirley Tem-
ple Story '01
Sabrina, the Animated
Series: Sabrina's World '99
(V)

Ian Hart
Harry Potter and the Sorcer-
er's Stone '01
Aberdeen '00
Born Romantic '00
Liam '00

Melissa Joan Hart
Recess: School's Out '01 (V)
Batman Beyond: Return of
the Joker [2 Uncut] '00 (V)
Sabrina, the Animated
Series: Sabrina's World '99
(V)

Pamela Hart
The Young Girls of Rochefort
'68

Roxanne Hart
Follow the Stars Home '01
The Runaway '00
Highlander [Anchor Bay] '86

Susan Hart
War Gods of the Deep '65
The Slime People '63

Mariette Hartley
1969 '89
Marnie '64

Pat Hartley
Rainbow Bridge '71

Elizabeth Hartman
The Secret of NIMH '82 (V)

Phil Hartman
Blind Date '87
Three Amigos '86

Josh Hartnett
Black Hawk Down '01
O '01
Pearl Harbor '01
Town and Country '01
Blow Dry '00

Michael Hartson
Olive Juice '01

Don Harvey
Casualties of War '89

Harold (Herk) Harvey
Carnival of Souls [DC] '62
Carnival of Souls / Dementia
13 '62

Laurence Harvey
Expresso Bongo '59

Megan Taylor Harvey
Joe Dirt '01

Terence Harvey
From Hell [DLE] '01

Jun Hashizume
Godzilla vs. Space Godzilla /
Godzilla vs. Destroyah '94

Colleen Haskell
The Animal '01

Susan Haskell
Mrs. Winterbourne '96

Imogen Hassall
The Bloodsuckers '70

David Hasselhoff
Jekyll & Hyde: The Musical
'01

Teri Hatcher
Spy Kids '01
Running Mates '00
Fever '99
Soapdish '91

Amy Hathaway
Smiling Fish & Goat on Fire
'99

Anne Hathaway
The Princess Diaries '01

Noah Hathaway
The NeverEnding Story '84

Yoram Hattab
Kadosh '99

Rohini Hattangady
Gandhi '82

Raymond Hatton
World War I Films of the
Silent Era '02

Chiu Sing Hau
Jade Claw '79

Rutger Hauer
Turbulence 3: Heavy Metal
'00
Arctic Blue '93
Buffy the Vampire Slayer '92
Split Second '92
The Hitcher '86
Wanted: Dead or Alive '86
Katie Tippel '75

Ullrich Haupt
The Iron Mask '29

Volker Hauptvogel
Schramm '93

Cole Hauser
Higher Learning '94

Fay Hauser
Candyman 2: Farewell to the
Flesh '94
Jo Jo Dancer, Your Life Is Call-
ing '86

Wings Hauser
Mind, Body & Soul '92
Jo Jo Dancer, Your Life Is Call-
ing '86

Nigel Havers
Empire of the Sun '87

Alex Haw
Following '99

Robin Hawdon
Zeta One '69

Ethan Hawke
Training Day '01
Waking Life '01
Gattaca [2 SB] '97
A Midnight Clear '92

John Hawkes
Hardball '01
Sand '00

Caroline Hawkins
Zeta One '69

Jack Hawkins
Theatre of Blood '73

Valerie Hawkins
Sting of Death '65

Goldie Hawn
Town and Country '01
Seems Like Old Times '80
Butterflies Are Free '72
Cactus Flower '69

Nigel Hawthorne
Call Me Claus '01
Victoria & Albert '01
The Object of My Affection
'98
Uncorked '98
The Winslow Boy '98
Memoirs of a Survivor '81

Charles Hawtrey
Zeta One '69

Sessue Hayakawa
World War I Films of the
Silent Era '02
The Swiss Family Robinson
'60
Three Came Home '50
The Cheat [Kino] '15

Nora Hayden
The Angry Red Planet '59

Sterling Hayden
The Blue and the Gray '82
The Final Programme '73

Salma Hayek
In the Time of the Butterflies
'01
Living It Up '00
Traffic [Criterion] '00
Dogma [2 SE] '99
Desperado [2 SB] '95

Jeff Hayenga
The Unborn '91

Allison Hayes
The Crawling Hand '63

George "Gabby" Hayes
Hopalong Cassidy Returns
'36
Three on the Trail '36
Bar 20 Rides Again '35

Hopalong Cassidy '35
Riders of Destiny [Columbia]
'33
West of the Divide '33

Helen Hayes
Stage Door Canteen '43

Isaac Hayes
Dr. Dolittle 2 '01 (V)
Reindeer Games [Miramax
DC] '00
South Park: Bigger, Longer
and Uncut '99 (V)

John Anthony Hayes
Strait-Jacket '64

Margaret Hayes
Sullivan's Travels '41

Patricia Hayes
Willow '88
The NeverEnding Story '84

Sherman Hayes
The Death Curse of Tartu /
Sting of Death '66

Cyd Hayman
Percy '71

David Hayman
The Tailor of Panama '00
Vertical Limit [2 SB] '00

Ayo Haynes
Where Angels Dance '01

Dennis Haysbert
Love and Basketball '00
Random Hearts '99
Major League 3: Back to the
Minors '98
Major League 2 '94

Chad Hayward
Violent Zone '89

Louis Hayward
And Then There Were None
[Image] '45
The Son of Monte Cristo '40

Rachel Hayward
Cruel and Unusual '01

Susan Hayward
I Want to Live! '58
Star Spangled Rhythm '42

Chris Haywood
Sweet Talker '91
Quigley Down Under '90
The Coca-Cola Kid '84

Rita Hayworth
Separate Tables '58

Jayne Hazard
Strange Illusion '45

Jonathan Haze
Monster from the Ocean
Floor '54

Anthony Head
Buffy the Vampire Slayer:
Season 1 '97

Jesse Head
Southern Man '99

Lena Headey
Aberdeen '00

Glenne Headly
A Girl Thing '01
What's the Worst That Could
Happen? [SE] '01
Dick Tracy '90
Dirty Rotten Scoundrels
[MGM] '88
The Purple Rose of Cairo '85

Anthony Heald
Proof of Life '00
The Silence of the Lambs
[MGM SE] '91

Candace Hilligoss
Carnival of Souls [DC] '62
Carnival of Souls / Dementia 13 '62

Richard Hillman
Bring It On '00

George Hilton
Fistful of Lead '70

Nichole Hiltz
Amazons and Gladiators '01

Madeline Hinde
The Bloodsuckers '70

Art Hindle
The Gunfighters '87

Earl Hindman
Murder in Coweta County '83

Ciaran Hinds
Ivanhoe '97

Samuel S. Hinds
Son of Dracula '43

Gregory Hines
Echo of Murder '00
Things You Can Tell Just by Looking at Her '00
Running Scared '86
The Cotton Club '84
The Muppets Take Manhattan '84

Pat Hingle
The Runaway '00
Citizen Cohn '92
Brewster's Millions [Universal] '85

Brent Hinkley
Say It Isn't So '01

Skip Hinnant
Nine Lives of Fritz the Cat '74 (V)
Fritz the Cat '72 (V)

James D. Hinton
Galaxina '80

Knut Hinz
Traffik '90

Bill (William Heinzman) Hinzman
Night of the Living Dead [Elite ME] '68

Sam Hiona
Spanish Judges '99

Akihiko Hirata
Godzilla, King of the Monsters [Goodtimes] '56

Judd Hirsch
Ordinary People '80

Karl T. Hirsch
Green '01

Robert Hirsch
The Hunchback of Notre Dame '57
Plucking the Daisy '56

Jeff Hirschfield
Lexx Series 2, Vol. 1 '98

Alice Hirson
Blind Date '87

Josie Ho
The Legend of a Professional '00

Ka Chun Ho
The Legend of a Professional '00

William Ho
Brother of Darkness '94
Daughter of Darkness '93
Riki-Oh: The Story of Ricky '89

Florence Hoath
Back to the Secret Garden '01

Doug Hobart
The Death Curse of Tartu / Sting of Death '66
Sting of Death '65

Mara Hobel
Mommie Dearest '81

Valerie Hobson
Contraband '40
Werewolf of London '35

Danny Hoch
Black Hawk Down '01

Mike Hodge
Boycott '02
Fiona '98

Eddie Hodges
A Hole in the Head '59

Runa Hodges
A Fool There Was '14

John Hodiak
The Harvey Girls '46

Dennis Hoey
She Wolf of London '46

Connie Hoffman
Naughty Stewardesses '74

Dustin Hoffman
Goldwyn: The Man and His Movies '01 (N)
Hollywood Screen Tests: Take 1 '00
Hook '91
Dick Tracy '90
Kramer vs. Kramer '79
Lenny '74

Gaby Hoffman
Perfume '01

Philip Seymour Hoffman
Almost Famous: Untitled— The Bootleg Cut '00
State and Main '00

Charlie Hofheimer
Black Hawk Down '01

Suzi Hofrichter
How to Kill Your Neighbor's Dog '01

Marco Hofschneider
Immortal Beloved '94

Chris Hogan
Dancing at the Blue Iguana '00

Jonathan Hogan
Fifth of July '82

Pat Hogan
Walt Disney Treasures: Davy Crockett '01

Paul Hogan
Crocodile Dundee in Los Angeles '01
Crocodile Dundee 2 '88
Crocodile Dundee '86

Robert Hogan
Maze '01
Lady in Red '79

Ian Hogg
Forgotten '99

San Lee Hoi
Last Hurrah for Chivalry '78

Vuong Hoa Hoi
The Scent of Green Papaya '93

Hal Holbrook
Lewis and Clark: Journey of the Corps of Discovery '97 (V)

Midway [Universal CE] '76
Magnum Force '73

Alexandra Holden
Sugar & Spice '01
Uprising '01

Beau Holden
Traffic [Criterion] '00

Donald Holden
George Washington '00

Gloria Holden
Dracula's Daughter '36

William Holden
The Devil's Brigade '68
Paris When It Sizzles '64
Love Is a Many Splendored Thing '55

Bobby Holiday
Creepin' '01

Josh Holland
A Girl, 3 Guys and a Gun '01

Tom Holland
Stephen King's The Langoliers '95

Adam Hollander
Halloween [Extended Edition] '78

Tom Hollander
Maybe Baby '99

Todd Holliday
Tender Is the Heart '01

Earl Holliman
Anzio '68

Ryan Holliman
Seducing Maarya '99

Laurel Holloman
Lush '01

Sterling Holloway
Dumbo '41 (V)
Tomorrow's Children '34

Ellen Holly
King Lear '74

Frantisek Holly
The Shop on Main Street '65

Lauren Holly
Sabrina '95

Astrid Holm
Haxan: Witchcraft through the Ages '22

Celeste Holm
Three Men and a Baby '87
Cinderella '64

Claus Holm
Tiger of Eschnapur '59

Ian Holm
From Hell [DLE] '01
The Fifth Element [2 SB] '97
S.O.S. Titanic '79

Rex Holman
The Choppers '61

Katie Holmes
The Gift '00
The Ice Storm '97

Andrew Holofcener
Walking and Talking '96

Jack Holt
World War I Films of the Silent Era '02

Sandrine Holt
1999 '98
Black Robe [MGM] '91

Tim Holt
The Monster That Challenged the World '57
Stella Dallas '37

Gary Holtz
The Death Curse of Tartu / Sting of Death '66

Skip Homeier
The Halls of Montezuma '50

Oscar Homolka
Funeral in Berlin '66
Mr. Sardonicus '61

James Hong
Wayne's World 2 '93
Revenge of the Nerds 2: Nerds in Paradise '87

Leanne Hong
Full Metal Jacket [2 SE] '87

Sun Honglei
The Road Home '01

Kojiro Hongo
Tokyo Mafia: Wrath of the Yakuza '95
Tokyo Mafia: Yakuza Wars '95

Darla Hood
The Bat [Goodtimes] '59

Brian Hooks
Phat Beach '96

Wendy Hoopes
Daria, The Movie: Is It Fall Yet? '01 (V)

William Hootkins
The Magnificent Ambersons '02
Town and Country '01

Tom Hoover
Dead and Rotting '02

Bob Hope
The Muppet Movie '79
The Road to Utopia [Universal] '46
The Princess and the Pirate '44
They Got Me Covered '43
My Favorite Blonde '42
The Road to Morocco [Universal] '42
Star Spangled Rhythm '42
The Road to Zanzibar '41
The Ghost Breakers '40
The Road to Singapore '40
The Big Broadcast of 1938 '38
College Swing '38

Leslie Hope
Spreading Ground '01
Water Damage '01
Bruiser '00
Restless Spirits '99
Rowing Through '96
Men at Work '90
Kansas '88

Tamara Hope
The Deep End '01

William Hope
Hellbound: Hellraiser 2 [2 THX] '88

Anthony Hopkins
Hearts in Atlantis '01
Dr. Seuss' How the Grinch Stole Christmas '00 (N)
The Mask of Zorro [2 SE] '98
The Remains of the Day '93
Bram Stoker's Dracula [SB] '92
The Silence of the Lambs [MGM SE] '91
Desperate Hours '90
84 Charing Cross Road '86
The Elephant Man '80
Audrey Rose '77
QB VII '74

Jermaine "Huggy" Hopkins
Phat Beach '96

Rolf Hoppe
Mephisto '81

Dennis Hopper
Firestarter 2: Rekindled '02
Choke '01
L.A.P.D.: To Protect and Serve '01
Spreading Ground '01
Ticker '01
Luck of the Draw '00
The Blackout '97
Red Rock West '93
Apocalypse Now [Redux] '79
Head '68
The Young Land '59

Hedda Hopper
Dracula's Daughter '36

Hilary Horan
Satan's Cheerleaders '77

Michael Hordern
Watership Down '78 (V)
Theatre of Blood '73
A Funny Thing Happened on the Way to the Forum '66
Khartoum '66

Katsuosuke Hori
Hermes—Winds of Love '97 (V)

Sami Hori
Kadosh '99

Tad Horino
Galaxina '80

Camilla Horn
Faust '26

Paul Hornung
The Devil's Brigade '68

David Horovitch
Ivanhoe '97
The Mirror Cracked from Side to Side '92
4:50 from Paddington '87

Jane Horrocks
Absolutely Fabulous: Series 4 '01
Born Romantic '00

Michael Horse
Twin Peaks: The First Season '90

Brian Horsey
Dead or Alive '02

Alyah Horsford
Deep Trouble '01

Anna Maria Horsford
How High '01
Along Came a Spider '00
Dancing in September '00
One Fine Day '96

Lee Horsley
Sword & the Sorcerer '82

Edward Everett Horton
It's a Mad, Mad, Mad, Mad World '63
Pocketful of Miracles '61
College Swing '38
Pre-Code Hollywood: Vol. 4, "Lonely Wives" '31

Peter Horton
Into Thin Air: Death on Everest '97

Gerd Horvath
Schramm '93

Bobby Hosea
61* '01

Bob Hoskins
Enemy at the Gates '00

Breakout '75
De Sade '69
The Bible '66 (N)

Virginia Huston
Flight to Mars '52

Walter Huston
And Then There Were None
[Image] '45
The North Star '43
Dodsworth [MGM] '36

Geoffrey Hutchings
Cor, Blimey! '00

Will Hutchins
Clambake '67

Josephine Hutchinson
Son of Frankenstein '39

Doug Hutchison
I Am Sam '01

Betty Hutton
Star Spangled Rhythm '42

Jim Hutton
Psychic Killer '75
They Call It Murder '71

Lauren Hutton
Zorro, the Gay Blade '81
The Gambler '74

Robert Hutton
The Slime People '63

Timothy Hutton
Just One Night '00
The Temp '93
Taps '81
Ordinary People '80

Jang-Lee Hwang
Fist of Fury '95
Return of the Deadly Blade
'81
Tiger over Wall '80
Dragon's Claws '79
Drunken Master '78

Jonathan Hyde
Princess of Thieves '01

Alex Hyde-White
Deep Water '99

Wilfrid Hyde-White
The Toy '82

Martha Hyer
First Men in the Moon '64

Diana Hyland
The Boy in the Plastic Bubble
[2] '76

Jane Hylton
Circus of Horrors '60

Richard Hylton
The Halls of Montezuma '50

Bob Hyman
The Crater Lake Monster '77

Crystal Hyman
Ice Grill '02

James Hyndman
Rowing Through '96

Steve Hytner
Air Rage '01

Mirta Ibarra
Mararia '98

Masato Ibu
Empire of the Sun '87

Ice Cube
John Carpenter's Ghosts of
Mars '01
The Glass Shield '95
Higher Learning '94

Ice-T
Air Rage '01
3000 Miles to Graceland '01

The Guardian '00
Luck of the Draw '00
Stealth Fighter '99
The Wrecking Crew '99
Body Count '97
Johnny Mnemonic [2 SB] '95

Etsuko Ichihara
The Eel '96

Saeko Ichijou
Terminatrix '95

Eric Idle
South Park: Bigger, Longer
and Uncut '99 (V)
Rudolph the Red-Nosed Rein-
deer: The Movie '98 (V)
Jabberwocky '77

James Iglehart
Angels Hard As They Come
'71

Kunihiko Iida
Zeram 2 '94

Robert Iler
The Sopranos: The Complete
Second Season '01

Masayuki Imai
Tokyo Mafia: Battle for Shin-
juku '96
Tokyo Mafia: Wrath of the
Yakuza '95
Tokyo Mafia: Yakuza Wars '95

Iman
Out of Africa '85

Gary Imhoff
Thumbelina [20th Century
Fox] '94 (V)

Yuka Imoto
Metropolis '01 (V)

Michael Imperioli
The Sopranos: The Complete
Second Season '01

Pedro Infante
Cuando Habla El Corazon '42

Sonia Infante
Doctor of Doom '62

Rex Ingram
Sahara '43

Ciccio Ingrassia
Primitive Love '64

Neil Innes
Jabberwocky '77

Annie Shizuka Inoh
Flowers of Shanghai '98
Goodbye South, Goodbye '96

Dan Inosanto
Bruce Lee: A Warrior's Journey '01

Michael Irby
The Last Castle '01

Jill Ireland
Breakout '75
Violent City '70

John Ireland
Satan's Cheerleaders '77
Queen Bee '55
The Fast and the Furious '54
Vengeance Valley '51
All the King's Men '49
Raw Deal '48
Railroaded '47

Jeremy Irons
Stealing Beauty '96
The House of the Spirits '93
Reversal of Fortune '90
The French Lieutenant's
Woman '81
The Pallisers, Vol. 3 '74

Michael Ironside
Children of the Corn: Revela-
tion '01
Extreme Honor '01
The Glass Shield '95
Total Recall [2 SLE] '90
Spacehunter: Adventures in
the Forbidden Zone '83
Scanners '81

Amy Irving
Traffic [Criterion] '00
The Fury '78
Carrie '76

Richard Irving
Borderline '50

Bill Irwin
Dr. Seuss' How the Grinch
Stole Christmas '00

Carl Irwin
The Passion Network '01

Tom Irwin
Snow White: The Fairest of
Them All '02

Jason Isaacs
Black Hawk Down '01
Sweet November '01
The Patriot [2 SB] '00
Robert Louis Stevenson's St.
Ives '98

Chris Isaak
That Thing You Do! '96
Twin Peaks: Fire Walk with
Me '92
The Silence of the Lambs
[MGM SE] '91

Katharine Isabelle
Bones '01
Ginger Snaps '00

**Maria (Isasi-Isasmendi)
Isasi**
In the Country Where Nothing
Happens '99

Takaaki Ishibashi
Major League 3: Back to the
Minors '98
Major League 2 '94

Hikari Ishida
Adrenaline Drive '99

Noboru Ishiguro
Macross: Box Set '85

Guts Ishimatsu
Empire of the Sun '87

Gerard Ismael
Money Talks '97

Irene Ismailoff
Happenstance '00

Kiyomi Ito
The Bedroom '92

Miki Ito
Hermes—Winds of Love '97
(V)

Robert Ito
The Adventures of Buckaroo
Banzai Across the Eighth
Dimension [SE] '84

Yunosuke Ito
Giants and Toys '58

Gregory Itzin
Evolution '01
Original Sin '01

Zeljko Ivanek
Black Hawk Down '01
Courage Under Fire '96

Stefan Ivanov
Druids '01

Diana Ivarson
The Jackals '67

Vladimir Ivashov
Ballad of a Soldier '60

Burl Ives
Roots '77

Dana Ivey
Sabrina '95
Hamlet '90
Dirty Rotten Scoundrels
[MGM] '88

Judith Ivey
Stephen King's Rose Red '02

Nassim Izem
Petits Freres '00

Eduard Izotov
Father Frost '66

Ja Rule
The Fast and the Furious '01

Hugh Jackman
Kate & Leopold '01
Someone Like You '01
Swordfish '01

Jim Jackman
The Blair Thumb '01 (V)

Anne Jackson
The Shining [2 SE] '80

Donald G. Jackson
Hell Comes to Frogtown '88

Glenda Jackson
A Touch of Class '73

Gordon Jackson
Upstairs, Downstairs: The
Complete First Season '71

John M. Jackson
The Hitcher '86

Jonathan Jackson
On the Edge '00

Joshua Jackson
Ocean's Eleven '01
Andre '94

Leonard Jackson
Five on the Black Hand Side
'73
Ganja and Hess '73

Michael Jackson
Free to Be...You and Me '74

Peter Jackson
Bad Taste [LE] '88

Philip Jackson
Agatha Christie's Poirot: The
ABC Murders '92

Samuel L. Jackson
The Caveman's Valentine '01
Unbreakable '00
Star Wars: Episode 1—The
Phantom Menace '99
Fresh '94
White Sands '92

Selmer Jackson
Guadalcanal Diary '43

Sherry Jackson
Daughters of the Dust '91

Victoria Jackson
UHF '89

John C. Jacob
Carnivore '01

Derek Jacobi
The Body '01
Thomas Jefferson '01 (V)
Cadfael—The Raven in the
Foregate '94
The Secret of NIMH '82 (V)

Christopher Jacobs
Rowing Through '96

Jon Jacobs
Hard Luck '01

Peter Jacobson
61* '01

Billy Jacoby
Beastmaster '82

Scott Jacoby
Return to Horror High '87

Steven Peacock Jacoby
Love Goggles '99

Sylvain Jacques
Those Who Love Me Can
Take the Train '98

Richard Jaeckel
Firehouse '72
The Devil's Brigade '68
Town without Pity '61
Cowboy '58
3:10 to Yuma '57
A Wing and a Prayer '44
Guadalcanal Diary '43

Elizabeth Jaegen
Barbarian Queen 2: The
Empress Strikes Back '89

Hannes Jaenicke
Extreme Limits '01
Mom's Outta Sight '01
Venomous '01
Catherine the Great '95

Sam Jaffe
The Dunwich Horror '70

Saeed Jaffrey
Gandhi '82

Dean Jagger
Proud Rebel '58
The Robe '53
Twelve o'Clock High '49
The North Star '43

Brion James
The Fifth Element [2 SB] '97
Enemy Mine '85

Clifton James
The Bad News Bears in
Breaking Training '77
The Man with the Golden Gun
'74
Will Penny '67
Black Like Me '64

Fraser James
Shopping '93

Geraldine James
The Luzhin Defence '00
Lover's Prayer '99
The Tall Guy '89

Godfrey James
At the Earth's Core '76

Hawthorne James
The Five Heartbeats '91

Jesse James
Blow '01

Jessica James
Diner '82

Jim James
Jade Claw '79

Josephine James
Please Not Now! '61

Lennie James
Snatch [SE] '00

Levi James
Ratz '99

Nina James
Random Acts of Violence '02

Reginald James
Hav Plenty '97

Steve James
Bloodfist 5: Human Target '93
Hero and the Terror '88
American Ninja '85

Jeffrey Jones
Dr. Dolittle 2 '01
Heartbreakers '01
How High '01
Stay Tuned '92
Transylvania 6-5000 '85

Jennifer Jones
Love Is a Many Splendored
   Thing '55
Dick Tracy [Marengo] '37
Dick Tracy [VCI] '37

Jerome Jones
House Party 4: Down to the
   Last Minute '00

Jocelyn Jones
The Great Texas Dynamite
   Chase '76

Keisha Jones
Get Down on It '01

**L.Q. (Justus E.
McQueen) Jones**
Route 666 '01
The Mask of Zorro [2 SE] '98
Lone Wolf McQuade '83
Timerider '83
The Beast Within '82
The Young Lions '58

Marcia Mae Jones
The Little Princess [Marengo]
   '39
Heidi '37

Mark Lewis Jones
Mists of Avalon '01

Nicholas Jones
Horatio Hornblower: The
   Adventure Continues '01

Orlando Jones
Evolution '01
Say It Isn't So '01
Waterproof '99

Renee Jones
Friday the 13th, Part 6: Jason
   Lives '86

Richard T. Jones
Beyond Suspicion '00
The Wood '99

Russell Jones
Squeeze '97

Sam Jones
Dead Sexy '01
T.N.T. '98

Shirley Jones
Ping! '99
Tank '83

Tamala Jones
On the Line '01
Two Can Play That Game '01
The Wood '99

Tammi Katherine Jones
Hav Plenty '97

Terry Jones
Jabberwocky '77

Toby Jones
In Love and War '01

Vinnie Jones
Swordfish '01
Snatch [SE] '00

Walter Emmanuel Jones
Backyard Dogs '00

Palina Jonsdottir
In His Life: The John Lennon
   Story '00

Jin-mo Joo
Happy End '99

Tim Joosten
One for the Road '82

Katie Jordan
Roxanna '02
Erotic Survivor 2 '01

Marsha Jordan
Count Yorga, Vampire '70

Michael Jordan
Space Jam [2 EE] '96

Michael Jordan
Hardball '01

Patrick Jordan
Too Late the Hero '70

Richard Jordan
Chato's Land '71
Lawman '71
Valdez Is Coming '71

Sydney Jordan
Naughty Stewardesses '74

Victor Jory
The Mountain Men '80

Edward Jose
A Fool There Was '14

Paterson Joseph
Greenfingers '00
The Long Run '00

Erland Josephson
Light Keeps Me Company '00
   (N)
Ulysses' Gaze '95
Directed by Andrei Tarkovsky
   '88 (N)
The Sacrifice / Directed by
   Andrei Tarkovsky '86
Cries and Whispers '72

Larry Joshua
Romeo Is Bleeding '93
A Midnight Clear '92

Ljubisa Jovanovic
Atomic War Bride / This Is
   Not a Test '60

Milla Jovovich
Zoolander '01
The Fifth Element [2 SB] '97

Leatrice Joy
Manslaughter / The Cheat
   '22

Mark Joy
Pecker (John Waters Collection Vol. 1) '98

Robert Joy
Perfume '01
61* '01
Sweet November '01
Larceny '91
Atlantic City '81

Barbara Joyce
The Sexy Sixth Sense '01

Mario Joyner
Down to Earth '01
Pootie Tang '01

Ashley Judd
Someone Like You '01
The Locusts '97

Edward Judd
Flambards '78
First Men in the Moon '64

Arline Judge
The Crawling Hand '63
Mysterious Mr. Wong '35

Mike Judge
South Park: Bigger, Longer
   and Uncut '99 (V)

Raul Julia
King Lear '74

Julissa
The Fear Chamber '68

Gordon Jump
Making the Grade '84

Eric Jungmann
Not Another Teen Movie '01

Katy Jurado
Barabbas '62

Peter Jurasik
Tron [2 CE] '82

Curt Jurgens
And God Created Woman '57

Albert Juross
Les Carabiniers '63

**James Robertson
Justice**
Zeta One '69
Spirits of the Dead [Criterion]
   '68

Katherine Justice
Five Card Stud '68

Richard Jutras
Nowhere in Sight '01

Suzanne Kaaren
The Devil Bat '41

Jane Kaczmarek
Falling in Love '84

David Kagen
Friday the 13th, Part 6: Jason
   Lives '86

Saul Kahan
Schlock '73

Madeline Kahn
The Muppet Movie '79
The Cheap Detective '78

Rick Kahn
Squeeze Play [DC] '79

Khalil Kain
Bones '01

Oldrich Kaiser
Dark Blue World '01

Elizabeth Kaitan
Petticoat Planet '95

Claudia Kaleem
Phat Beach '96

Toni Kalem
Silent Rage '82

Jean-Pierre Kalfon
The Cry of the Owl '87

Fung Kam
Lady Iron Monkey '83

Danny Kamekona
The Karate Kid: Part 2 '86

Ida Kaminska
The Shop on Main Street '65

Melina Kanakaredes
15 Minutes '01

Steve Kanaly
Fleshburn '84

Sean Kanan
The Karate Kid: Part 3 '89

Munyaradzi Kanaventi
Running Wild '99

Carol Kane
My First Mister '01
The Princess Bride [2 SE] '87
Transylvania 6-5000 '85
The Muppet Movie '79
When a Stranger Calls '79

Christian Kane
Crossfire Trail '01
Summer Catch '01

Michael Kane
The Gunfighters '87

Tayler Kane
The Dish '00

Jack Kao
Flowers of Shanghai '98
Goodbye South, Goodbye '96
Good Men, Good Women '95

Chris Kapanke
Beverly Hills Bordello '01

John Kapelos
Nothing in Common '86

Herb Kaplowitz
Galaxina '80

Selan Karay
Hell of the Living Dead '83

Ivana Karbanova
Daisies '96

James Karen
Mulholland Drive '01
Thirteen Days '00
The Unborn '91

Robin Karfo
Eddie and the Cruisers '83

Rita Karin
He Said, She Said '91

Anna Karina
Bread and Chocolate '73
Les Carabiniers '63
Cleo from 5 to 7 '61
Le Petit Soldat '60

Richard Karlan
Abbott and Costello Meet the
   Mummy '55

John Karlen
Dark Shadows: DVD Collec-
   tion 1 '67

Boris Karloff
The Fear Chamber '68
Mondo Balordo '64 (N)
Jack the Ripper: 4 Tales of
   the Supernatural '58
Destination Nightmare '54
Dick Tracy Meets Gruesome
   '47
Lured '47
House of Frankenstein '44
The Fatal Hour '40
Son of Frankenstein '39
Mr. Wong, Detective '38

Buck Kartalian
Please Don't Eat My Mother
   '72

Vincent Kartheiser
Bad Seed '00
Luckytown '00

Claudia Karvan
Risk '00

Tcheky Karyo
Kiss of the Dragon '01
The Patriot [2 SB] '00
The Bear '89

Renate Kasche
Lady Frankenstein '72

Casey Kasem
The Return of the King '80 (V)

Anna Kashfi
Cowboy '58

Csongor Kassai
Divided We Fall '00

Mathieu Kassovitz
The Fifth Element [2 SB] '97

Kurt Katch
Abbott and Costello Meet the
   Mummy '55
The Mummy's Curse '44

Christian Kane
Crossfire Trail '01
Summer Catch '01

Kimberley Kates
First Degree '01
Highway '01

Daisuke Kato
Rashomon '51

Masaya Kato
Brother '01

Rosanne Katon
Bachelor Party '84

Masako Katori
Afraid to Die '60

Aleka Katselli
Electra '62

Shintaro Katsu
The Tale of Zatoichi '62
The Tale of Zatoichi Contin-
   ues '62

Nicky Katt
Waking Life '01

William Katt
House '86
Carrie '76

Chris Kattan
Corky Romano '01
Monkeybone '01

Barbara Katz-Norrod
Dead and Rotting '02

Lloyd Kaufman
Waiting '01
Troma's Edge TV: Vol. 1 '00

Christine Kaufmann
Bagdad Cafe '88
Town without Pity '61

Maurice Kaufmann
Fright '71

Christine Kavanagh
In His Life: The John Lennon
   Story '00

Julie Kavner
The Simpsons: The Complete
   First Season '89 (V)
Radio Days '87
Hannah and Her Sisters '86
Katherine '75

Hiroshi Kawaguchi
Giants and Toys '58

Yu Kawai
Tokyo Decameron: Three
   Tales of Madness & Sensu-
   ality '96

Tamio Kawaji
Gappa the Trifibian Monster
   '67

Sabu Kawara
The Eel '96

Keizo Kawasaki
Afraid to Die '60

Yusuke Kawazu
Manji '64

Barnaby Kay
Conspiracy '01

Bernard Kay
Doctor Zhivago '65

Billy Kay
L.I.E. '01

Stephen Kay
Angel Eyes '01

Michael Kaycheck
Series 7: The Contenders '01

David Kaye
3000 Miles to Graceland '01
Mermaid '00

Jesse Kaye
Mind, Body & Soul '92

Lila Kaye
An American Werewolf in London [CE Universal] '81

Sung Nyu Kim
Chunhyang '00

Tae Yeon Kim
Lies '99

Anne Kimball
Monster from the Ocean
Floor '54

Sharron Kimberly
The Party '68

Charles Kimbrough
The Wedding Planner '01
The Hunchback of Notre
Dame '96 (V)

Taky Kimura
Bruce Lee: A Warrior's Journey '01

Arif S. Kinchen
The Wash '01
Beverly Hood '99

Alan King
Rush Hour 2 '01

Caroline Junko King
3 Ninjas Kick Back '94

Claude King
Swamp Girl / Swamp Country
'71
Three on the Trail '36

Damu King
Black Godfather '74

Erik King
True Crime '99
Casualties of War '89

Ginger King
Olive Juice '01

James King
Slackers '02
Blow '01
Happy Campers '01
Pearl Harbor '01

Jieh-Wen King
Good Men, Good Women '95

Kenneth King
Polyester (John Waters Collection Vol. 2) '81

Larry King
America's Sweethearts '01

Mabel King
Ganja and Hess '73

Perry King
The Perfect Wife '00

Regina King
Down to Earth '01
Jerry Maguire [2 SE] '96
Higher Learning '94

Stephen King
Stephen King's The Lan-
goliers '95
Stephen King's Golden Years
'91

Steven King
Harvesters '02

Tony King
Cannibal Apocalypse '80

Yolanda King
Ghosts of Mississippi '96

Guy Kingsford
Sahara '43

Walter Kingsford
My Favorite Blonde '42

Ben Kingsley
A.I.: Artificial Intelligence '01
(N)
Anne Frank '01
Sexy Beast '00

Searching for Bobby Fischer
'93
Slipstream '89
Gandhi '82

Alex Kingston
Carrington '95

Graeme Kingston
Mummies Alive! '97 (V)

Kinko
Cold War '00

Laurence Kinlan
An Everlasting Piece '00

Kathleen Kinmont
That Thing You Do! '96
Halloween 4: The Return of
Michael Myers [MGM LE]
'88
Fraternity Vacation '85

Melanie Kinnaman
Friday the 13th, Part 5: A
New Beginning '85

Melinda Kinnaman
Light Keeps Me Company '00
(N)

Greg Kinnear
Dinner with Friends '01
Someone Like You '01
The Gift '00
Sabrina '95

Terry Kinney
Luminous Motion '00
Oxygen '99
Oz: The Complete First Sea-
son '97
Fly Away Home [2 SE] '96

Klaus Kinski
Cobra Verde '88
A Bullet for the General '68
Doctor Zhivago '65

Nastassia Kinski
An American Rhapsody '01
Diary of a Sex Addict '01
Town and Country '01
Storm in Summer '00
The Hotel New Hampshire
'84
Maria's Lovers '84

Nikolai Kinski
Tortilla Soup '01

Stephen Kinyanjui
Out of Africa '85

Zourab Kipchidze
The Legend of Suram
Fortress / Ashik Kerib '85

Bruce Kirby
Throw Momma from the Train
'87

Bruno Kirby
American Tragedy '00
Stuart Little [2 DE] '99 (V)
Tin Men '87
Harrad Experiment '73

Luke Kirby
Lost and Delirious '01

Tommy Kirk
Attack of the 60-Foot Center-
fold '95
Mars Needs Women '66
The Swiss Family Robinson
'60
Old Yeller '57

Sally Kirkland
Dead Silence '98
Paranoia '98
Bite the Bullet '75
Coming Apart '69

John Kirkpatrick
A Scream in the Streets '73

Bryan Kirkwood
The Devil's Prey '01

Mia Kirshner
Not Another Teen Movie '01

Kyoko Kishida
Manji '64

Ildiko Kishonti
Mephisto '81

Tawny Kitaen
Bachelor Party '84

Takeshi "Beat" Kitano
Brother '01
Taboo '99
Gonin '95
Johnny Mnemonic [2 SB] '95

Michael Kitchen
Lorna Doone '01
Proof of Life '00
The Russia House '90
Out of Africa '85

Cole Kitosch
Texas, Adios '66

Johnny Kitt
Ice Grill '02

Barry Kivel
One Fine Day '96

Uri Klauzner
Kadosh '99

Chris Klein
Rollerball '02
American Pie 2 '01
Say It Isn't So '01
American Pie [2 UE] '99

Dan Klein
Fishing with Gandhi '98

Lauren Klein
Rudy Blue '00

Robert Klein
One Fine Day '96
Tales from the Darkside: The
Movie '90
The Owl and the Pussycat '70

Rudolf Klein-Rogge
Dr. Mabuse, The Gambler '22

Kevin Kline
The Anniversary Party '01
The Hunchback of Notre
Dame 2 '01 (V)
Life As a House '01
The Ice Storm '97
The Hunchback of Notre
Dame '96 (V)
Soapdish '91
Hamlet '90
The January Man '89
Time of Your Life '76

Brian Klinknett
Helter Skelter Murders '71

Miljen Kreka Kljakovic
Dune [2 SE] '00

Heidi Klum
Blow Dry '00

Vincent Klyn
Point Break '91

Skelton Knaggs
Dick Tracy Meets Gruesome
'47
Dick Tracy vs. Cueball '46

Baker Knight
Swamp Country '66

Cindi Knight
Murder in Coweta County '83

Esmond Knight
Sleeping Murder / 4:50 from
Paddington '86
Contraband '40

Michael E. Knight
Date with an Angel '87

Ronald J. Knight
Galaxina '80

Shirley Knight
Angel Eyes '01

Wayne Knight
Rat Race '01
Space Jam [2 EE] '96
Basic Instinct [2 SE] '92

Keira Knightley
Princess of Thieves '01

Sascha Knopf
What's the Worst That Could
Happen? [SE] '01

Don Knotts
It's a Mad, Mad, Mad, Mad
World '63

Patric Knowles
The Devil's Brigade '68
Three Came Home '50
Frankenstein Meets the Wolf-
man '42

Robert Knowlton
The Passion Network '01

Alexander Knox
Accident '67
Khartoum '66
The Vikings '58

Elyse Knox
The Mummy's Tomb '42

Johnny Knoxville
Life without Dick '01

Eddy Ko
Fist of Fury '95

Philip Ko
The Owl vs. Bombo '84
Fury in the Shaolin Temple
'82
Tiger over Wall '80
Fearless Dragon '79
Goose Boxer '78
Eagle Fist '77

Kei Kobayashi
Metropolis '01 (V)

Ken Kobayashi
The Eel '96

Megumi Kobayashi
Rebirth of Mothra 2 '97
Rebirth of Mothra 1 & 2 '96

Jeff Kober
American Tragedy '00
The First Power '89

Momoko Kochi
Godzilla vs. Destroyah '95
Godzilla, King of the Mon-
sters [Goodtimes] '56

Jiri Kodet
Divided We Fall '00

Barbara Kodetova
Dune [2 SE] '00

Walter Koenig
Star Trek 3: The Search for
Spock '84
Star Trek: The Motion Picture
[DE] '80

Lacey Kohl
Dead Simple '01

Fred Kohler, Jr.
Daniel Boone: Trail Blazer '56

Juliane Kohler
Aimee & Jaguar '98

Jara Kohout
The Projectionist '71

Yoshi Koizumi
Afraid to Die '60

Vincent Kok
Ballistic Kiss '98

Blanche Kommerell
Jacob the Liar '74

Rie Kondo
Sadistic City '93

Kam Kong
The Legendary Strike '78
Snake and Crane Arts of
Shaolin '78

Queen Kong
Deathstalker 2: Duel of the
Titans '87

Richard Kong
Eagle vs. Silver Fox '83

Guich Koock
Picasso Trigger '89
American Ninja '85

K. Korieniev
The Amphibian Man '61

Josh Kornbluth
Haiku Tunnel '00

Mary Kornman
Desert Trail '35

Lidya Korolyova
Barbara the Fair with the
Silken Hair '69

Alix Koromzay
Mimic 2 '01

Charlie Korsmo
Hook '91
Dick Tracy '90

Sylva Koscina
Juliet of the Spirits [Criterion]
'65

Martin Kosleck
She Wolf of London '46
The Mummy's Curse '44

Mitchell Kosterman
Cruel and Unusual '01

Elias Koteas
Novocaine '01
Shot in the Heart '01
Dancing at the Blue Iguana
'00
Gattaca [2 SB] '97
Desperate Hours '90
Full Moon in Blue Water '88

Yaphet Kotto
Out of Sync '95
Across 110th Street '72
Five Card Stud '68

Anna Kournikova
Me, Myself, and Irene '00

Martin Kove
Extreme Honor '01
The Karate Kid: Part 3 '89
The Karate Kid: Part 2 '86

Taketo Koyasu
Hermes—Winds of Love '97
(V)

Andras Kozak
The Red and the White '68

Harley Jane Kozak
The Amy Fisher Story '93
The Favor '92

Mikhail Kozakov
The Amphibian Man '61

Mark Kozelek
Almost Famous: Untitled—
The Bootleg Cut '00

Sonny Landham
Fleshburn '84

John Landis
The Muppets Take Manhattan '84
Schlock '73

Hal Landon, Jr.
Bill & Ted's Bogus Journey '91

Michael Landon
God's Little Acre '58

Ali Landry
Outta Time '01

Tamara Landry
Bikini Med School / Bikini House Calls '98

Ruth Landshoff
Nosferatu '22

Charles Lane
Sadie Thompson '28
Dr. Jekyll and Mr. Hyde [Kino] '20

Charles Lane
Date with an Angel '87
Strange Invaders '83
Borderline '50

Diane Lane
The Glass House '01
Hardball '01
The Cotton Club '84

Lenita Lane
The Bat [Goodtimes] '59

Nathan Lane
Trixie '00
Stuart Little [2 DE] '99 (V)
Frankie and Johnny '91
He Said, She Said '91
Alice in Wonderland '83

Sirpa Lane
The Beast '75

Sean Laney
Scare Their Pants Off / Satan's Bed '68

Judith Lang
Count Yorga, Vampire '70

Robert Lang
Murder at the Vicarage '86

Stephen Lang
Trixie '00
Tombstone [2] '93
Manhunter [LE] '86

Harry Langdon
Slapstick Encyclopedia (1909–27) '98

Allison Lange
Christina's House '99

Hope Lange
Pocketful of Miracles '61
The Young Lions '58

Jessica Lange
Cape Fear '91
Frances [Anchor Bay] '82

Jack Langedijk
The Pact '99

Frank Langella
Sweet November '01
Stardom '00
Masters of the Universe '87
The Seagull '75

Wallace (Wally) Langham
Daydream Believers: The Monkees Story '00

Lisa Langlois
The Nest '88

David Langton
Upstairs, Downstairs: The Complete First Season '71

Paul Langton
It! The Terror from Beyond Space '58

Holly Laningham
Fashionably L.A. '99

Jenya Lano
Fashionably L.A. '99

Victor Lanoux
National Lampoon's European Vacation '85

Angela Lansbury
The Harvey Girls '46

Joi Lansing
A Hole in the Head '59

Robert Lansing
The Nest '88
Empire of the Ants '77

Luis Lantigua
Fresh '94

Gerard Lanvin
The Taste of Others '00

Anthony LaPaglia
Company Man '01
Lantana '01
He Said, She Said '91

Daniel Lapaine
1999 '98

Joe Lara
Doomsdayer '99

John Larch
Dirty Harry [2] '71
Play Misty for Me '71

Vincent Laresca
Hard Cash '01

Leon Larive
Children of Paradise '44

Bryan Larkin
She-Devil '89

Chris Larkin
Shackleton '02
Angels and Insects '95

Kirsten Larkin
When a Stranger Calls '79

Mary Laroche
Run Silent, Run Deep '58

Michele Laroque
The Closet '00
Nelly et Monsieur Arnaud '95

Catalina Larranaga
Bare Witness '02

John Larroquette
Blind Date '87
Choose Me '84
Star Trek 3: The Search for Spock '84
Stripes '81

Eric Larson
'68 '87

Wolf Larson
Shakedown '02
Avalanche Alley '01
Crash & Byrnes '99

Ali Larter
American Outlaws '01
Jay and Silent Bob Strike Back '01
Legally Blonde '01

Gerard Lartigau
Indochine '92

Jack LaRue
Robin and the 7 Hoods '64
The Road to Utopia [Universal] '46

Robert LaSardo
Gang Related '96

Jerry Lasater
Mission to Death '66

Louise Lasser
Sudden Manhattan '96

Sarah Lassez
The Blackout '97

Sydney Lassick
Carrie '76

Tania Latarjet
The Vanishing [Criterion] '88

Lyle Latell
Dick Tracy Meets Gruesome '47
Dick Tracy's Dilemma '47
Dick Tracy vs. Cueball '46
Dick Tracy, Detective '45

Louise Latham
Territorial Men '76
Marnie '64

Philip Latham
The Pallisers, Vol. 2 '74
The Pallisers, Vol. 3 '74

Sanaa Lathan
Love and Basketball '00
The Wood '99

Frank Latimore
Patton [2] '70

Andrew Lau
Love on a Diet '01
The Duel '00
Rich and Famous / Tragic Hero '87
Tragic Hero '87

Carina Lau
Rich and Famous / Tragic Hero '87
Tragic Hero '87

Chi Wing Lau
Fist of Fury '95

Ching-Wan Lau
Where a Good Man Goes '99
Too Many Ways to Be No. 1 '97

Damian Lau
Legend of the Red Dragon '94
Last Hurrah for Chivalry '78

Kar Wing Lau
The Fist Power '99
Dragon's Claws '79

Lap Cho Lau
Dreaming Fists with Slender Hands '80

Siu-ming Lau
Dr. Lamb '92

Wesley Lau
I Want to Live! '58

Lubomiras Lauciavicus
Come and See '85

Jack Laufer
The Learning Curve '01
Lost in Yonkers '93

John Laughlin
Motorama '91
Crimes of Passion [2] '84

Charles Laughton
Witness for the Prosecution '57
Captain Kidd [Marengo] '45

Matthew Laurance
Eddie and the Cruisers '83

Carole Laure
Get Out Your Handkerchiefs '78

Stan Laurel
Slapstick Encyclopedia (1909–27) '98

Dixie Lauren
10 Violent Women '79

Rod Lauren
The Crawling Hand '63

Ashley Laurence
Cypress Edge '99
Hellbound: Hellraiser 2 [2 THX] '88

Agnes Laurent
The Nude Set '61

Remy Laurent
La Cage aux Folles '78

Dan Lauria
Ricochet River '98

Hugh Laurie
Life with Judy Garland—Me and My Shadows '01
Maybe Baby '99
Stuart Little [2 DE] '99
Jeeves & Wooster: The Complete Second Season '96

John Laurie
Devil Girl from Mars '54

Piper Laurie
St. Patrick's Day '01
Possessed '00
Twin Peaks: The First Season '90
Ruby '77
Carrie '76

Ed Lauter
Not Another Teen Movie '01
Thirteen Days '00
Trial by Jury '94
Stephen King's Golden Years '91
Revenge of the Nerds 2: Nerds in Paradise '87
Timerider '83

June Laverick
The Flesh and the Fiends '60

Lucille LaVerne
Snow White and the Seven Dwarfs [PE] '37 (V)

Linda Lavin
The Muppets Take Manhattan '84

Gladys Lavitan
Kidnapped Coed '77

Kirill Lavrov
Tchaikovsky '71

Helena Law
The Legend of a Professional '00

Jude Law
A.I.: Artificial Intelligence '01
Enemy at the Gates '00
Gattaca [2 SB] '97
Wilde '97
Shopping '93

Kon Lan Law
The Legend of a Professional '00

Christopher Lawford
The 6th Day [2 SE] '00
Thirteen Days '00
The Russia House '90

Peter Lawford
Ocean's 11 '60
Sahara '43

Louie Lawless
Planet of the Dinosaurs '80

Lucy Lawless
Xena: Warrior Princess— Series Finale '01

Andy Lawrence
Recess Christmas: Miracle on Third Street '01 (V)

Bruno Lawrence
Utu '83

Dea Lawrence
Stuart Bliss '98

Elizabeth Lawrence
Unbreakable '00

Gail Lawrence
Maniac [LE] '80

Gertrude Lawrence
Stage Door Canteen '43

Joey Lawrence
Reckless and Wild '02
Tequila Body Shots '99
Oliver & Company '88 (V)

Marc Lawrence
The Man with the Golden Gun '74

Martin Lawrence
Black Knight '01
What's the Worst That Could Happen? [SE] '01

Matthew Lawrence
Tales from the Darkside: The Movie '90

Scott Lawrence
Timecop '94

Steve Lawrence
Ocean's Eleven '01

Dean Lawrie
Bad Taste [LE] '88

Bianca Lawson
Bones '01

Christina Lawson
Bloodfight '89

Denis Lawson
Horatio Hornblower '99

Leigh Lawson
Back to the Secret Garden '01

Priscilla Lawson
Flash Gordon: Spaceship to the Unknown '36

Richard Lawson
Coming Home '78

Shannon Lawson
Possessed '00

Me Me Lay
Au Pair Girls '72

Evelyn Laye
Theatre of Death '67

James Layton
The Wolves of Kromer '98

John Lazar
Attack of the 60-Foot Centerfold '95
Deathstalker 2: Duel of the Titans '87

Paul Lazar
Mickey Blue Eyes '99

George Lazenby
Four Dogs Playing Poker '00
On Her Majesty's Secret Service '69

Bruce Le
Bruce Lee Fights Back from the Grave '76

Ngoc Le
Full Metal Jacket [2 SE] '87

Thuy Thu Le
Casualties of War '89

Samm Levine
Not Another Teen Movie '01
The Royal Family '77

Ted Levine
Ali '01
Evolution '01
The Fast and the Furious '01
Joy Ride '01 (V)
Harlan County War '00
The Silence of the Lambs [MGM SE] '91

Stan Levitt
Carnival of Souls [DC] '62
Carnival of Souls / Dementia 13 '62

Spivy Levoe
Requiem for a Heavyweight '62

Eugene Levy
American Pie 2 '01
Down to Earth '01
Serendipity '01
American Pie [2 UE] '99
Waiting for Guffman '96
Stay Tuned '92

Mickey Levy
Human Prey '95

Jose Lewgoy
Cobra Verde '88

Al Lewis
Used Cars '80

Buddy Lewis
Beverly Hood '99

Fiona Lewis
Strange Invaders '83

Gary Lewis
Orphans '97

Geoffrey Lewis
Any Which Way You Can '80
Every Which Way But Loose '78
The New Daughters of Joshua Cabe '76
Moon of the Wolf '72
The Fat Black Pussycat '63

Greg Lewis
Frankie and Johnny '91

Jenifer Lewis
Dancing in September '00
Jackie's Back '99
Partners '99

Jerry Lewis
Mr. Saturday Night [MGM] '92
It's a Mad, Mad, Mad, Mad World '63

Juliette Lewis
Romeo Is Bleeding '93
What's Eating Gilbert Grape '93
Husbands and Wives '92
Cape Fear '91

Keisha Lewis
Black Spring Break 2 '01

Leigh Lewis
Judgment '01

Matthew Lewis
Harry Potter and the Sorcerer's Stone '01

Ronald Lewis
Mr. Sardonicus '61

Steve Lewis
Inbred Rednecks '97

Lance Lewman
Breeders '86

Charles Ley
The Temptations '98

John Leyton
Schizo '77
Von Ryan's Express '65

Thierry Lhermitte
The Closet '00

Thinlen Lhondup
Himalaya '99

Bruce Li
The Young Bruce Lee '80
Fists of Bruce Lee '78
Bruce Li the Invincible '77
Revenge of the Patriots '76

Chin-kun Li
Thunder Kick '73

Fei Li
The Fist Power '99

Gong Li
Shanghai Triad '95

Jet Li
Kiss of the Dragon '01
Legend of the Red Dragon '94
The Legend 2 '93
Swordsman 2 '91

Yu Li
Prison on Fire 2 '91

Yang Li-Yin
The Puppetmaster '93

Bruce Liang
Return of the Deadly Blade '81

Liu Chang Liang
Fighting Ace '79

Ning Liang
Madame Butterfly '95

Brian Libby
Silent Rage '82

Nicole Liberty
The Erotic Rites of Countess Dracula '01

Andrea Libman
Dragon Tales '99 (V)

Peter Licassi
Killer Klowns from Outer Space '88

Lo Lieh
Lady Iron Monkey '83
Return of the Deadly Blade '81
Fists of Bruce Lee '78
Master of Death '75

Madeleine Lierck
Hot Summer '68

Tina Lifford
Letters from a Killer '98
The Temptations '98
Colors '88

Marilyn Lightstone
Abraxas: Guardian of the Universe [BFS] '90

Cheung Lik
Super Kung Fu Kid '86
10 Magnificent Killers '77

Marie Liljedahl
Inga '67

Matthew Lillard
Summer Catch '01
13 Ghosts '01
Spanish Judges '99

Andrew C. Lim
Luminarias '99

Kwan Hi Lim
Hard Ticket to Hawaii '87

Brigitte (Lin Chinaghsia) Lin
Dragon Inn '92
Swordsman 2 '91

Ruby Lin
Comic King '00

Peter Linari
The Curse of the Jade Scorpion '01

Lar Park Lincoln
House 2: The Second Story '87

Gillian Lind
And Now the Screaming Starts [SE] '73

Traci Lind
The Handmaid's Tale '90

Chad Lindberg
The Fast and the Furious '01

Hal Linden
The Others '97

Cec Linder
A Touch of Class '73

Slawomir Linder
The Saragossa Manuscript '65

Viveca Lindfors
Exorcist 3: Legion '90
Coming Apart '69

Carl Michael Lindner
The Extreme Adventures of Super Dave '98

Delroy Lindo
Heist '01
The Last Castle '01
First Time Felon '97

Sandra Lindquist
Crash & Byrnes '99

Delta Lindsay
The Scars of Dracula '70

Lois Lindsay
Cocaine Fiends '36

Robert Lindsay
Horatio Hornblower: The Adventure Continues '01
Horatio Hornblower '99

Amy Lindsey
Illicit Confessions '77

Rosaleen Linehan
About Adam '00

Bai Ling
The Breed '01

Chia Ling
Revengeful Swordswoman '80

Wendy Lingham
Zeta One '69

Richard Linklater
Waking Life '01

Rex Linn
Crossfire Trail '01
Breakdown '96

Laura Linney
The Mothman Prophecies '02
Lush '01
Maze '01
Running Mates '00

Kent Linville
Black Hawk Down '01

Alex D. Linz
The Dress Code '99
One Fine Day '96

Ray Liotta
Blow '01
Heartbreakers '01

Unforgettable '96
Unlawful Entry '92
Dominick & Eugene '88

Lu Liping
Shadow Magic '00

Eugene Lipinski
Restless Spirits '99

Jonathan Lipnicki
Stuart Little [2 DE] '99
Jerry Maguire [2 SE] '96

Enrique Liporace
Brain Drain '98

Renee Lippin
Radio Days '87

Peggy Lipton
Jackpot '01
Skipped Parts '00
Twin Peaks: Fire Walk with Me '92
Twin Peaks: The First Season '90

(Lisa Ray MacCoy) LisaRaye
The Wood '99

Theodore Liscinski
Hedwig and the Angry Inch '00

Virna Lisi
Eva '62

Tommy (Tiny) Lister
The Wash '01
Never 2 Big '98
Body Count '97
The Fifth Element [2 SB] '97
Phat Beach '96
Beverly Hills Cop 2 '87

Litefoot
The Indian in the Cupboard '95

John Litel
Outpost in Morocco '49

John Lithgow
Shrek [SE] '01 (V)
Tales from the Crypt: Robert Zemeckis Collection '95
Silent Fall '94
The Manhattan Project '86
The Adventures of Buckaroo Banzai Across the Eighth Dimension [SE] '84
The World according to Garp '82
Blow Out '81
Obsession '76

Brandy Little
American Nightmare '00

Cleavon Little
High Risk '81

Kim Little
Social Intercourse '01

Natasha Little
Greenfingers '00

Sacheen Little Feather
Johnny Firecloud / Bummer '75

Iris Little-Thomas
Boycott '02

Gary Littlejohn
Angels Hard As They Come '71

Leighanne Littrell
Olive Juice '01

Gordon Liu
Fury in the Shaolin Temple '82

Harrison Liu
Black Robe [MGM] '91

Jimmy Liu
Dragon's Claws '79

Lucy Alexis Liu
Molly '99

Rene Liu
The Personals '98

Denny Live
Creepin' '01

Eric Lively
Uprising '01

Jason Lively
National Lampoon's European Vacation '85

Robin (Robyn) Lively
Santa Who? '00
The Karate Kid: Part 3 '89

John Livingston
The Others '97

Richard Livingston
Bravo '98

Richard B. Livingston
Reptilian '00

Ron Livingston
Two Ninas '00

Stanley Livingston
Attack of the 60-Foot Centerfold '95

Robert Livingstone
Naughty Stewardesses '74

L.L. Cool J.
Rollerball '02
Kingdom Come '01
Out of Sync '95
Toys '92

Desmond Llewelyn
The Man with the Golden Gun '74
On Her Majesty's Secret Service '69

Christopher Lloyd
When Good Ghouls Go Bad '01
Angels in the Outfield '94
The Adventures of Buckaroo Banzai Across the Eighth Dimension [SE] '84
Star Trek 3: The Search for Spock '84
Lady in Red '79
Goin' South '78

Danny Lloyd
The Shining [2 SE] '80

Eric Lloyd
Luminous Motion '00

Harold Lloyd
Slapstick Encyclopedia (1909–27) '98

Jake Lloyd
Star Wars: Episode 1—The Phantom Menace '99

Norman Lloyd
Audrey Rose '77
The Southerner '45

William Lloyd
Eegah! '62

Leila Lloyd-Evelyn
The Wolves of Kromer '98

Candy Lo
Time and Tide '00

Robyn Loau
Idiot Box '97

Tony LoBianco
Sworn to Justice '97
The French Connection [SE] '71

Kelly Lynch
Desperate Hours '90

Ken Lynch
Run Silent, Run Deep '58

Richard Lynch
Reflex Action '02

Richard Lynch
Cut and Run '85
Invasion U.S.A. '85
Sword & the Sorcerer '82

Susan Lynch
From Hell [DLE] '01
Beautiful Creatures '00
Ivanhoe '97
The Secret of Roan Inish '94

Paul Lynde
The Villain '79

Simon Lyndon
Chopper '01

Carol Lynley
Vigilante [2 DC] '83

Jonathan Lynn
Three Men and a Little Lady '90

Meredith Scott Lynn
Legally Blonde '01

Melanie Lynskey
Stephen King's Rose Red '02

Sue Lyon
Evel Knievel '72

Natasha Lyonne
American Pie 2 '01
Fast Sofa '01
Kate & Leopold '01
Scary Movie 2 '01
American Pie [2 UE] '99

Jennifer Lyons
Tequila Body Shots '99

Lisa Lyons
Vamp '86

Monika M.
Schramm '93
Nekromantik '87

Wu Ma
Picture of a Nymph '88
Righting Wrongs '86

Adrian Maben
Helmut Newton: Frames from the Edge '88 (N)

Kate Maberly
Stephen King's The Langoliers '95

Eric Mabius
On the Borderline '01
Wirey Spindell '99

Moms (Jackie) Mabley
Amazing Grace '74

Bernie Mac
Ocean's Eleven '01
What's the Worst That Could Happen? [SE] '01

Anne MacAdams
The Black Cat / The Fat Black Pussycat '65

James MacArthur
The Swiss Family Robinson '60

Laura Macaulay
Virtual Sexuality '99

Ralph Macchio
The Karate Kid: Part 3 '89
The Karate Kid: Part 2 '86

Simon MacCorkindale
Sword & the Sorcerer '82

Jim Macdonald
Snow White and the Seven Dwarfs [PE] '37 (V)

Kelly Macdonald
Two Family House '99

Kevin MacDonald
Same Guys, New Dresses: The Kids in the Hall '02

Norm MacDonald
Dr. Dolittle 2 '01 (V)

Wallace MacDonald
Two-Fisted Law '32

Andie MacDowell
Dinner with Friends '01
Town and Country '01
Groundhog Day [2 SE] '93

Angus Macfadyen
Second Skin '00
Styx '00

Niall MacGinnis
Jack the Ripper: 4 Tales of the Supernatural '58

Jack MacGowran
The Exorcist [2]: The Version You've Never Seen '73
Doctor Zhivago '65

Gabriel Macht
American Outlaws '01
Behind Enemy Lines '01

Stephen Macht
Graveyard Shift '90
Galaxina '80

Mack-10
Random Acts of Violence '02

J.C. MacKenzie
Final '01

Peter M. MacKenzie
Major League 3: Back to the Minors '98

Allison Mackie
Original Sin '01

Lesley Mackie
The Wicker Man [SE] '75

Albert Macklin
Date with an Angel '87

Kyle MacLachlan
Sex and the City: The Complete Third Season '02
Perfume '01
Showgirls '95
Twin Peaks: Fire Walk with Me '92
Twin Peaks: The First Season '90

Caterpillar MacLaggan
Late Night Sessions '99

Shirley MacLaine
The Dress Code '99
Mrs. Winterbourne '96
Irma La Douce '63
Ocean's 11 '60

Barton MacLane
The Mummy's Ghost '44

Gavin MacLeod
The Party '68

Violet MacMillan
His Majesty, the Scarecrow of Oz '14

Fred MacMurray
Borderline '50
On Our Merry Way '48

Patrick Macnee
The Howling '81
The Bloodsuckers '70
The Avengers '68 '68

Peter MacNeill
Angel Eyes '01

Tress MacNeille
Cinderella 2: Dreams Come True '02 (V)

Peter MacNicol
Recess: School's Out '01 (V)

Elle Macpherson
A Girl Thing '01

Michael Macready
Count Yorga, Vampire '70

John Macurdy
Don Giovanni '79

Bruce MacVittie
Stonewall '95

William H. Macy
Focus '01
Jurassic Park 3 [CE] '01
Panic '00
State and Main '00
Air Force One [2 SB] '97
Ghosts of Mississippi '96
Searching for Bobby Fischer '93

John Maczko
Shades of Darkness '00

Josef Madaras
The Red and the White '68

Ciaran Madden
Ivanhoe '97

Peter Madden
Doctor Zhivago '65

Amy Madigan
Shot in the Heart '01
Thomas Jefferson '01 (V)
Pollock [SE] '00
Places in the Heart '84

Noel Madison
Cocaine Fiends '36

Madonna
Dick Tracy '90

Gerda Madsen
Haxan: Witchcraft through the Ages '22

Michael Madsen
Choke '01
Extreme Honor '01
L.A.P.D.: To Protect and Serve '01
High Noon '00
Luck of the Draw '00
Beyond the Law '92
One for the Road '82

Virginia Madsen
Crossfire Trail '01
The Apocalypse Watch '97
Ghosts of Mississippi '96
Victim of Love '91
The Heart of Dixie '89

Mia Maestro
In the Time of the Butterflies '01

Roma Maffia
Things You Can Tell Just by Looking at Her '00

Patrick Magee
And Now the Screaming Starts [SE] '73
The Final Programme '73
Anzio '68
Dementia 13 [Roan] '63

William Magerman
Radio Days '87

Brandon Maggart
The World according to Garp '82
Christmas Evil '80
Dressed to Kill [SE] '80

Licia Maglietta
Bread and Tulips '01

Philippe Magnan
The Widow of Saint-Pierre '00

Barbara Magnolfi
Suspiria '77

Ann Magnuson
The Caveman's Valentine '01
Glitter '01

Felicia Maguire
Fiona '98

Tobey Maguire
The Ice Storm '97

George Maharis
Sword & the Sorcerer '82

Alan Maher
About Adam '00

Bill Maher
House 2: The Second Story '87

Joseph Maher
Sister Act '92
The Evil That Men Do '84

Jock Mahoney
Walls of Hell '64

John Mahoney
Atlantis: The Lost Empire [CE] '01 (V)
The Russia House '90
Say Anything [SE] '89
Suspect '87
Tin Men '87
The Manhattan Project '86

Diane Mahree
Manos, the Hands of Fate '66

Sharon Maiden
Clockwise '86

Marjorie Main
The Harvey Girls '46
Stella Dallas '37

Valerie Mairesse
The Sacrifice / Directed by Andrei Tarkovsky '86

Tina Majorino
Andre '94

Lee Majors
Out Cold '01
Will Penny '67
Strait-Jacket '64

Shirley Mak
Invincible Obsessed Fighter '82

Heike Makatsch
Aimee & Jaguar '98

Chris Makepeace
Vamp '86
My Bodyguard '80

Mike Maker
Sore Losers '97

Mohsen Makhmalbaf
Close-Up '01

Chitose Maki
The Tale of Zatoichi '62

Kuroudo Maki
Brother '01

Wendy Makkena
Sister Act '92

Mako
Pearl Harbor '01
Sworn to Justice '97
Taking Care of Business '90
An Eye for an Eye '81

Summer Makovkin
Pep Squad '98

Patrick Malahide
Captain Corelli's Mandolin '01
Victoria & Albert '01
Til There Was You '96
After the War '89

Christophe MaLavoy
The Cry of the Owl '87

Henrik Malberg
Ordet '55

Karl Malden
The Cat o' Nine Tails '71
Patton [2] '70
Pollyanna '60
On the Waterfront '54
The Halls of Montezuma '50

Jonathan Malen
Possessed '00

Arthur Malet
Hook '91
Halloween [Extended Edition] '78

Laurent Malet
Querelle '83

Keram Malicki-Sanchez
Happy Campers '01

Art Malik
After the War '89

John Malkovich
The Ogre '96
Of Mice and Men '92
Queens Logic '91
Empire of the Sun '87
Places in the Heart '84

Dave Mallow
Tokyo Decameron: Three Tales of Madness & Sensuality '96 (N)

Matt Malloy
The Great Gatsby '01
Running Mates '00

Bonz Malone
Brooklyn Babylon '00

Dorothy Malone
Basic Instinct [2 SE] '92
Written on the Wind '56
The Fast and the Furious '54

Jena Malone
Donnie Darko '01
Life As a House '01

Patrick Malone
Hostage High '97

Michael Maloney
Truly, Madly, Deeply '91

Eily Malyon
She Wolf of London '46

Anatoly Mambetrov
The Arena '01

Nargess Mamizadeh
The Circle '00

Alex Man
Rich and Famous / Tragic Hero '87
Tragic Hero '87

Al Mancini
Mission Manila '87

Nick Mancuso
Avalanche Alley '01
Judgment '01
The Pact '99
Matter of Trust '98
Marquis de Sade '96
Lena's Holiday '90

Howie Mandel
Shake, Rattle & Rock! '94

Miles Mander
Guadalcanal Diary '43
The Little Princess [Marengo] '39

Costas Mandylor
The Pledge '00
Deep Water '99
Stealth Fighter '99
Shelter '98
Soapdish '91
Triumph of the Spirit '89

Louis Mandylor
Double Deception '01

Tyler Mane
Joe Dirt '01

Luisa Maneri
La Cage aux Folles '78

Nino Manfredi
Bread and Chocolate '73

Xiem Mang
The Lover '92

Silvana Mangano
Barabbas '62

Camryn Manheim
A Girl Thing '01

Blu Mankuma
Mermaid '00

Alakina Mann
The Others [CE] '01

Gabriel Mann
Josie and the Pussycats '01
Summer Catch '01
New Port South '00

Leonard Mann
Cut and Run '85
Bad Cop Chronicles 2: Corrupt '84

Leslie Mann
Perfume '01

Paul Mann
Fiddler on the Roof [2 SE] '71

Ron Mann
Grass '00

Ettore Manni
Mademoiselle '66

Marilyn Manning
Eegah! '62

Taryn Manning
crazy/beautiful '01

Tom Mannion
Beautiful Creatures '00

Sheila (Manors) Mannors
Cocaine Fiends '36

Dinah Manoff
Ordinary People '80

Sabrina Mansar
Petits Freres '00

Jayne Mansfield
Primitive Love '64

Martha Mansfield
Dr. Jekyll and Mr. Hyde [Kino] '20

Rachid Mansouri
Petits Freres '00

Joe Mantegna
The Trumpet of the Swan '01 (V)
Turbulence 3: Heavy Metal '00
An Eye for an Eye '95
Airheads '94
Baby's Day Out '94
Searching for Bobby Fischer '93

Queens Logic '91
Suspect '87
Three Amigos '86

Bronwen Mantel
Pin... '88

Randolph Mantooth
Agent Red '00

Kiti Manver
Things I Left in Havanna '97

Dagmar Manzel
Coming Out '89

Angela (Mao Ying) Mao
The Legendary Strike '78

Kate Mara
Random Hearts '99

Mary Mara
K-PAX '01
Love Potion 9 '92
Mr. Saturday Night [MGM] '92

Jean Marais
Stealing Beauty '96

Evi Marandi
Planet of the Vampires '65

Fredric March
Inherit the Wind '60

Jane March
Dracula: The Dark Prince '01
The Lover '92

Georges Marchal
Belle de Jour '67

Corinne Marchand
Cleo from 5 to 7 '61

Nancy Marchand
The Sopranos: The Complete Second Season '01
Sabrina '95

Josh Marchette
Tequila Body Shots '99

Ron Marchini
Murder in the Orient '73

Paul Marco
Night of the Ghouls '59

Bill Marcos
The Death Curse of Tartu / Sting of Death '66

Andrea Marcovicci
Spacehunter: Adventures in the Forbidden Zone '83

James A. Marcus
Sadie Thompson '28

Richard Marcus
Enemy Mine '85

Steven Marcus
The Tavern '00

Vladimir Marek
Divided We Fall '00

Mark Margolis
Hardball '01
The Tailor of Panama '00

Miriam Margolyes
Immortal Beloved '94
The Age of Innocence '93
The Butcher's Wife '91

David Margulies
Looking for an Echo '99
Dressed to Kill [SE] '80

Julianna Margulies
Mists of Avalon '01

Masayo Mari
The Tale of Zatoichi '62

Constance Marie
Tortilla Soup '01

Heather Jae Marie
Smiling Fish & Goat on Fire '99

Lisa Marie
Breast Men '97

Eli Marienthal
American Pie 2 '01

Manuel Marin
Vampires in Havana '87 (V)

Richard "Cheech" Marin
Spy Kids '01
Luminarias '99
Desperado [2 SB] '95
Ferngully '92 (V)
Oliver & Company '88 (V)
Echo Park '86
Cheech and Chong's The Corsican Brothers '84
Cheech and Chong's Nice Dreams '81

Rikki Marin
Cheech and Chong's The Corsican Brothers '84

Ed Marinaro
Avalanche Alley '01
Queens Logic '91

Sonny Marinelli
Boss of Bosses '99

Ken Marino
Wet Hot American Summer '01

P.J. Marino
Little Shots of Happiness '97

Richard Marion
Godmonster of Indian Flats '73

Howard Marion-Crawford
The Charge of the Light Brigade '68

Stella Maris
Truly, Madly, Deeply '91

Heidi Mark
Rock Star '01

Jane (Jeanne) Marken
Children of Paradise '44

Monte Markham
Hot Pursuit '87

Brian Markinson
The Curse of the Jade Scorpion '01

Olivera Markovic
Siberian Lady Macbeth '61

Leo Marks
Dogs: The Rise and Fall of an All-Girl Bookie Joint '96

Michael Marks
The Wasp Woman [2] '59

Sherry Marks
Satan's Cheerleaders '77

John Marley
The Greatest '77

Carla Marlier
Spirits of the Dead [Criterion] '68

John Marlo
Take It to the Limit '00

Lucy Marlow
Queen Bee '55

Hugh Marlowe
Monkey Business '52
Twelve o'Clock High '49

Kelli Maroney
Servants of Twilight '91

Michael Maronna
Slackers '02

Joe Maross
Run Silent, Run Deep '58

Carl Marotte
When Justice Fails '98

Christian Marquand
And God Created Woman '57

Serge Marquand
The Grapes of Death '78
Please Not Now! '61

Alan Marriott
Devil Man '87 (V)

John Marriott
Black Like Me '64

Hyla Marrow
Maniac [LE] '80

Kenneth Mars
Thumbelina [20th Century Fox] '94 (V)
Radio Days '87

Laure Marsac
Secret Defense '98

Maurice Marsac
Tarzan and the Trappers '58

Branford Marsalis
Throw Momma from the Train '87

James Marsden
Sugar & Spice '01

Matthew Marsden
Black Hawk Down '01

Jean Marsh
Willow '88
Upstairs, Downstairs: The Complete First Season '71

Marian Marsh
Svengali '31

Matthew Marsh
Spy Game '01

Michele Marsh
Fiddler on the Roof [2 SE] '71

Sara Marsh
Sugar & Spice '01

William Marsh
Mood Swingers '00

Brenda Marshall
Strange Impersonation '46

E.G. Marshall
Kennedy '83
Town without Pity '61

Garry Marshall
Soapdish '91

Herbert Marshall
The Little Foxes [MGM] '41

James Marshall
Luck of the Draw '00
Twin Peaks: Fire Walk with Me '92

Tully Marshall
Two-Fisted Law '32

Gabriel Marshall-Thomson
Enemy at the Gates '00

Christina Marsillach
Opera '88

Henri Marteau
Indochine '92

Cynthia Martells
The Wood '99

Felix Marten
The Grapes of Death '78

Camilla Martens
Zero Degrees Kelvin '95

Andrea Martin
All over the Guy '01
Hedwig and the Angry Inch '00

Aubrey Martin
This Is Not a Test '62

Dean Martin
Five Card Stud '68
Rough Night in Jericho '67
Robin and the 7 Hoods '64
Four for Texas '63
Ocean's 11 '60
Rio Bravo '59
The Young Lions '58

D'Urville Martin
Five on the Black Hand Side '73

George Martin
One Fine Day '96
Falling in Love '84

Helen Martin
Hollywood Shuffle '87

Jared Martin
Aenigma '87
The New Gladiators '83

Lauren Martin
Where Angels Dance '01

Lori Martin
Cape Fear '61

Mary Martin
Star Spangled Rhythm '42

Pamela Sue Martin
Lady in Red '79

Rudolf Martin
Dracula: The Dark Prince '01
Swordfish '01

Steve Martin
Novocaine '01
Dirty Rotten Scoundrels [MGM] '88
Three Amigos '86
The Muppet Movie '79

Strother Martin
The Villain '79
Slap Shot [2] '77

Teddy Martin
Sleuth [2] '72

Victor Huggo Martin
Fidel '02

Vince Martin
Nightmaster '87

Margo Martindale
Proof of Life '00

Elsa Martinelli
The Trial '63
Hatari! '62

A. Martinez
Wind River '98
She-Devil '89

Fele Martinez
Open Your Eyes '97

Norma Martinez
Proof of Life '00

Patrice Martinez
Three Amigos '86

Rita Martinez
Wrestling Women USA! '01
Pin Down Girls '51

Derick Martini
Smiling Fish & Goat on Fire '99

Steven Martini
Smiling Fish & Goat on Fire '99

Lee Marvin
Paint Your Wagon '69
The Big Heat '53

Brett Marx
The Bad News Bears Go to Japan '78
The Bad News Bears in Breaking Training '77
The Bad News Bears '76

Harpo Marx
Stage Door Canteen '43

Masasa
Kingdom Come '01

Joseph Mascolo
Jaws 2 '78

Marino (Martin) Mase
Les Carabiniers '63

Vladimir Mashkov
Behind Enemy Lines '01
Dancing at the Blue Iguana '00

Giulietta Masina
Juliet of the Spirits [Criterion] '65

Virginia Maskell
The Prisoner '68

James Mason
Hopalong Cassidy '35

James Mason
Dangerous Summer '82

Laurence Mason
Ali '01

Madison Mason
Thirteen Days '00

Marsha Mason
Restless Spirits '99
The Cheap Detective '78
Audrey Rose '77

Tom Mason
Looking for an Echo '99
Runaway Bride '99
The Amy Fisher Story '93
Apocalypse Now [Redux] '79
Night of the Ghouls '59

Walter Mason
Black Like Me '64

Michael Massee
One Fine Day '96

Anna Massey
Dark Blue World '01
Angels and Insects '95
Haunted '95
A Tale of Two Cities '91
Impromptu '90
The Tall Guy '89
The Pallisers, Vol. 2 '74
De Sade '69

Athena Massey
Harold Robbins' Body Parts '01

Daniel Massey
Scandal '89

Edith Massey
Polyester (John Waters Collection Vol. 2) '81
Desperate Living (John Waters Collection Vol. 2) '77
Female Trouble '74
Pink Flamingos '72

Ilona Massey
Frankenstein Meets the Wolfman '42

Raymond Massey
MacKenna's Gold '69

Marina Massironi
Bread and Tulips '01

Christopher K. Masterson
Scary Movie 2 '01

Danny Masterson
Dracula 2000 '00

Fay Masterson
Cops and Robbersons '94

Mary Stuart Masterson
The Stepford Wives [2 SE] '75

Peter Masterson
The Stepford Wives [2 SE] '75
The Exorcist [2]: The Version You've Never Seen '73

Walter Masterson
L.I.E. '01

Mary Elizabeth Mastrantonio
Three Wishes '95
White Sands '92
The January Man '89

Marcello Mastroianni
8 1/2 '63

Keiko Masuda
Pink Lady and Jeff '80

Richard Masur
61* '01
Hard Lessons '86
Timerider '83
Under Fire '83
Who'll Stop the Rain? '78

Adam Matalon
Devil Man '87 (V)

Heather Matarazzo
The Princess Diaries '01
Blue Moon '00

Hans Matheson
Mists of Avalon '01

Tim Matheson
Sometimes They Come Back '91
Magnum Force '73

Kerwin Mathews
Jack the Giant Killer '62
The Three Worlds of Gulliver '59

Thom Mathews
Friday the 13th, Part 6: Jason Lives '86

Heather Mathieson
Because Why? '93

Samantha Mathis
Mists of Avalon '01
Attraction '00
Mermaid '00
Sweet Jane '98
Jack and Sarah '95
Ferngully '92 (V)

Elisa Matilla
Why Do They Call It Love When They Mean Sex? '92

Marlee Matlin
When Justice Fails '98

Scotty Matraw
Snow White and the Seven Dwarfs [PE] '37 (V)

Naofumi Matsuda
Terminatrix '95

Ryuhei Matsuda
Taboo '99

Seiko Matsuda
Fatal Blade '00

Eva Mattes
Enemy at the Gates '00
Stroszek '77

Walter Matthau
Survivors '83
California Suite '78
The Bad News Bears '76
Cactus Flower '69

Christopher Matthews
The Scars of Dracula '70

Dakin Matthews
Thirteen Days '00
The Temp '93

John Matthews
Sleuth [2] '72

Lester Matthews
Werewolf of London '35

Liesl Matthews
Air Force One [2 SB] '97

Victor Mature
Head '68
After the Fox '66
The Robe '53

Yataka Matushige
Adrenaline Drive '99

John Matuszak
The Goonies '85
Caveman '81

Wayne Maunder
Crazy Horse and Custer: "The Untold Story" '90

Peggy Maurer
I Bury the Living '58

Paula Maurice
The Brain That Wouldn't Die '63

Claire Maurier
La Cage aux Folles '78

Johannes Maus
Tales from Europe: The Story of Little Mook '53

Dawn Maxey
That Thing You Do! '96

Antonina Maximova
Ballad of a Soldier '60

Yelena Maximova
Earth '30

Chenoa Maxwell
Hav Plenty '97

Lois Maxwell
The Man with the Golden Gun '74
On Her Majesty's Secret Service '69
Submarine Attack '54

Roberta Maxwell
Water Damage '01

Elaine May
California Suite '78

Mathilda May
The Cry of the Owl '87

Rik Mayall
An American Werewolf in London [CE Universal] '81

Anthony (Jose, J. Antonio, J.A.) Mayans
Revenge in the House of Usher '82

Debra Mayer
Hell Asylum '01

Ferdinand "Ferdy" Mayne
Au Pair Girls '72

Virginia Mayo
Man Next Door '97
Pearl of the South Pacific '55
The Princess and the Pirate '44

Whitman Mayo
Boycott '02
Waterproof '99

Melanie Mayron
You Light Up My Life '77

Jefferson Mays
Some Folks Call It a Sling Blade '94

Yoji Maysuzaki
Taboo '97

Debi Mazar
Little Man Tate '91

Monet Mazur
Angel Eyes '01
The Learning Curve '01

Mike Mazurki
Dick Tracy, Detective '45

Joseph Mazzello
Three Wishes '95

Des McAleer
When the Sky Falls '99
Hidden Agenda '90

Alex McArthur
Route 666 '01

Bryn McAuley
Stalker '98

Nichole McAuley
The Passion Network '01

Alex McBride
Rats '83

Chi McBride
Dancing in September '00

Joe McBride
The Riff '00

Ruth McCabe
An Everlasting Piece '00

James McCaffrey
Burnzy's Last Call '95

Toussaint McCall
Hairspray (John Waters Collection Vol. 1) '88

Holt McCallany
Kiss Tomorrow Goodbye '00

Lon (Bud) McCallister
Stage Door Canteen '43

David McCallum
The Watcher in the Woods '81

Michael McCallum
Night Divides the Day '01

Macon McCalman
Fleshburn '84

Mercedes McCambridge
The Exorcist [2]: The Version You've Never Seen '73 (V)
All the King's Men '49

Chuck McCann
The Projectionist '71

Donal McCann
Stealing Beauty '96
Rawhead Rex '87
Out of Africa '85
The Pallisers, Vol. 2 '74

Andrew McCarthy
Nowhere in Sight '01
Storm in Summer '00
Kansas '88
Less Than Zero '87
Mannequin '87

Frayne McCarthy
Ultimate G's '01

Kevin McCarthy
UHF '89
The Howling '81

Maureen McCarthy
One for the Road '82

Molly McCarthy
The Great St. Louis Bank Robbery '59

Nobu McCarthy
The Karate Kid: Part 2 '86

Sheila McCarthy
House Arrest '96
Larceny '91

Nancy McCauley
Galaxina '80

Leigh McCloskey
Fraternity Vacation '85

Doug McClure
The People That Time Forgot '77
At the Earth's Core '76

Marc McClure
That Thing You Do! '96

Edie McClurg
Dance 'til Dawn '88
Cheech and Chong's The Corsican Brothers '84
The Secret of NIMH '82 (V)
Carrie '76

Stephen McCole
The Acid House '98
Orphans '97

Lorissa McComas
Hard As Nails '01
Raptor '01

Heather McComb
Stay Tuned '92

Matthew McConaughey
The Wedding Planner '01

Kent McCord
Return of the Living Dead 3 '93

Catherine McCormack
Spy Game '01
Born Romantic '00
The Tailor of Panama '00

Gary McCormack
The Acid House '98

Mary McCormack
High Heels and Low Lifes '01
K-PAX '01
True Crime '99

Patty McCormack
Acceptable Risk '01

Will McCormack
American Outlaws '01

Carolyn McCormick
Enemy Mine '85

Mary McCormick
Retrievers '82

Maureen McCormick
Return to Horror High '87

Myron McCormick
The Iceman Cometh '60

Alec McCowen
The Age of Innocence '93
Hanover Street '79

Chyna McCoy
Random Acts of Violence '02

Jamie McCoy
Children of the Living Dead '00

Matt McCoy
Fraternity Vacation '85

Sid McCoy
Medium Cool [SE] '69

Two Friends '86
The Coca-Cola Kid '84

Butterfly McQueen
Amazing Grace '74

Chad McQueen
Where the Red Fern Grows:
Part 2 '92

Steve McQueen
The Hunter '80
The Great St. Louis Bank
Robbery '59

Phillip McQuillan
In His Life: The John Lennon
Story '00

Carmen McRae
Jo Jo Dancer, Your Life Is Calling '86

Leslie McRae
Girl in Gold Boots '69

Gerald McRaney
Danger beneath the Sea '02
The NeverEnding Story '84

Peter McRobbie
Kill by Inches '99

Ian McShane
Sexy Beast '00

Janet McTeer
Carrington '95

Tyler McVey
Attack of the Giant Leeches
[Marengo] '59

Margaret McWade
Mr. Deeds Goes to Town '36

Jillian McWhirter
Progeny '98
Bloodfist 7: Manhunt '95

Courtland Mead
Recess Christmas: Miracle
on Third Street '01 (V)
Recess: School's Out '01 (V)

Mary Meade
T-Men '47

Arlene Meadows
Focus '01

Colm Meaney
Scarlett '94

Russell Means
Wind River '98

Julio Mechoso
Heartbreakers '01
Jurassic Park 3 [CE] '01

Kay Medford
Funny Girl '68

Frank Medrano
The Replacement Killers [2
SE] '98

Donald Meek
They Got Me Covered '43

Ralph Meeker
Brannigan '75
Johnny Firecloud / Bummer
'75

Aaron Meeks
Storm in Summer '00

Don Megowan
The Devil's Brigade '68
Tales of Frankenstein '58

Tobias Mehler
Avalanche Alley '01
Wishmaster 3: Beyond the
Gates of Hell '01

Vijay Mehta
Seducing Maarya '99

Rita Meiden
A Real Young Girl '75

Shane Meier
Silver Wolf '98
Andre '94

Thomas Meighan
Manslaughter / The Cheat
'22

John Meillon
Crocodile Dundee 2 '88
Crocodile Dundee '86

Michael Mein
2069: A Sex Odyssey '78

Frederique Meininger
The Lover '92

Lysaine Meis
Happenstance '00

Petr Meissel
Conspirators of Pleasure '93

Bent Mejding
Reptilicus '62

Gerardo Mejia
Colors '88

Mariangela Melato
Seduction of Mimi '72

John Melendez
Airheads '94

Migdalia Melendez
Go Fish '94

Sonny Melendrez
The Return of the King '80 (V)

Harry Melling
Harry Potter and the Sorcerer's Stone '01

Leonie Mellinger
Memoirs of a Survivor '81

Tamara Mello
Tortilla Soup '01

Christopher Meloni
Wet Hot American Summer
'01
Runaway Bride '99

Sid Melton
The Lost Continent '51

Jean-Pierre Melville
Breathless '59

George Memmoli
Phantom of the Paradise '74

Ben Mendelsohn
Vertical Limit [2 SB] '00
Idiot Box '97
Quigley Down Under '90

Eva Mendez
Exit Wounds '01
Training Day '01
Children of the Corn 5: Fields
of Terror '98

Alonzo Mendez Ton
Chac: The Rain God '74

Stephen Mendillo
Slap Shot [2] '77

Natalie Mendoza
Moulin Rouge [SE] '01
Rodgers & Hammerstein's
South Pacific '01

Victor Manuel Mendoza
Cowboy '58
Cuando Habla El Corazon '42

Joey Meng
Fist of Fury '95

Adolphe Menjou
Pollyanna '60

Laszlo Mensaros
Colonel Redl '84

Julino Mer
The Last Warrior '99

Hector Mercado
Nomads '86

Vivien Merchant
Accident '67

Louis Mercier
Sahara '43

Melina Mercouri
Topkapi '64

Monique Mercure
When Justice Fails '98

Micole Mercurio
Bandits '01
Colors '88

Paul Mercurio
Strictly Ballroom '92

Burgess Meredith
Full Moon in Blue Water '88
MacKenna's Gold '69
Batman: The Movie '66
On Our Merry Way '48

Judi Meredith
Jack the Giant Killer '62

Jalal Merhi
Tiger Claws '91

Candice Merideth
Phat Beach '96

Lee Meriwether
Batman: The Movie '66

Una Merkel
The Parent Trap '61
The Road to Zanzibar '41

Vasily Merkuryev
The Cranes Are Flying '57

Maurizio Merli
White Fang to the Rescue '74

Ethel Merman
It's a Mad, Mad, Mad, Mad
World '63
Stage Door Canteen '43

Dina Merrill
The Greatest '77
Operation Petticoat '59

Gary Merrill
Clambake '67
Twelve o'Clock High '49

George Merritt
Jekyll & Hyde: The Musical
'01

Susan Merson
Lost in Yonkers '93

William Mervyn
The Ruling Class '72

John Mese
Red Dirt '99

Daniel Mesguich
The Musketeer '01

Debra Messing
The Mothman Prophecies '02

Laurie Metcalf
Runaway Bride '99

Saul Meth
Night to Dismember '83

Method Man
How High '01

Veronkia Metonidze
Ashik Kerib '88

Jim Metzler
St. Patrick's Day '01

**Plughead Rewired: Circuitry
Man 2** '94
Circuitry Man '90
Squeeze Play [DC] '79

Jordan Metzner
A Troll in Central Park '94 (V)

Christian Meunier
The Grapes of Death '78

Raymond Meunier
Le Trou '59

Jason Mewes
Drawing Flies '02
Jay and Silent Bob Strike
Back '01
Dogma [2 SE] '99

Breckin Meyer
Josie and the Pussycats '01
Kate & Leopold '01
Rat Race '01

Daniel Meyer
The Locusts '97

Dina Meyer
Time Lapse '01
Johnny Mnemonic [2 SB] '95

Hans Meyer
Le Magnifique '76

Torben Meyer
Sullivan's Travels '41

Jeannie Meyers
Killer Instinct '00

Michelle Meyrink
Real Genius '85
Revenge of the Nerds /
Revenge of the Nerds 2:
Nerds in Paradise '84

Arturo Meza
Dona Herlinda & Her Son '86

Yiur Mgoyan
Ashik Kerib '88

Robert Miano
Luckytown '00
Matter of Trust '98

Nora Miao
Snake and Crane Arts of
Shaolin '78

**Jordan Christopher
Michael**
Motorama '91

Dario Michaelis
I Vampiri '56

Yorgos Michalokopoulos
Ulysses' Gaze '95

Jason Michas
Dragon Tales '99 (V)

Marc Michel
Le Trou '59

Michael Michele
Ali '01

Helena Michell
At Bertram's Hotel '86

Frank Middlemass
A Caribbean Mystery / The
Mirror Cracked from Side
to Side '89

Charles Middleton
Flash Gordon: The Peril from
Planet Mongo '40
Flash Gordon: The Purple
Death from Outer Space
'40
Flash Gordon: The Deadly
Ray from Mars '39
Flash Gordon: Spaceship to
the Unknown '36
Hopalong Cassidy '35

Robert Middleton
Harrad Experiment '73

Dale Midkiff
Route 666 '01
Love Potion 9 '92

Bette Midler
Oliver & Company '88 (V)
Ruthless People '86

Mako Midori
The Blind Beast '69

Toshiro Mifune
Midway [Universal CE] '76
The Hidden Fortress '58
Rashomon '51

Hiroshi Mikami
Parasite Eve '97

George Miki
Go for Broke! [VCI] '51

Izabella Miko
The Forsaken '01

Mark Mikulski
Stuck on You! [DC] '84

Alyssa Milano
Body Count '97
Dance 'til Dawn '88

Christina Milano
Fishing with Gandhi '98

A.D. Miles
Wet Hot American Summer
'01

Joanna Miles
Crossfire Trail '01

Sarah Miles
The Servant '63

Sylvia Miles
She-Devil '89

Vera Miles
Psycho 2 '83

Penelope Milford
Heathers [2 THX] '89
Coming Home '78

Tomas Milian
Traffic [Criterion] '00
Four of the Apocalypse '75
Companeros '70

Ivana Milicevic
Head over Heels '01

Frank Military
The Last Castle '01

Hugh Millais
The Dogs of War '81

Ray Milland
The Thief '52
Star Spangled Rhythm '42

Andrew Miller
The Last of the Dogmen '95

Ann Miller
Mulholland Drive '01

Bodil Miller
Reptilicus '62

Christa Miller
Smiling Fish & Goat on Fire
'01

Dax Miller
Blood Surf '00

Dennis Miller
Joe Dirt '01
The Net [2 SE] '95

Denny Miller
The Party '68

Dick Miller
Shake, Rattle & Rock! '94
Unlawful Entry '92

Motorama '91
The Terminator [2 SE] '84
All the Right Moves '83
The Howling '81
Used Cars '80
Lady in Red '79
Rock 'n' Roll High School
[New Concorde SE] '79
A Bucket of Blood / Attack of
the Giant Leeches [Maren-
go] '59

Jason Miller
Exorcist 3: Legion '90
The Exorcist [2]: The Version
You've Never Seen '73

Jonny Lee Miller
Dracula 2000 '00
Plunkett & Macleane '98

Kathleen Miller
Coming Home '78

Larry Miller
The Princess Diaries '01
What's the Worst That Could
Happen? [SE] '01
Waiting for Guffman '96
The Favor '92

Lenard Miller
Retrievers '82

Patsy Ruth Miller
Pre-Code Hollywood: Vol. 4,
"Lonely Wives" '31

Penelope Ann Miller
Along Came a Spider '00
Along for the Ride '00
Little City '97

Toby Miller
Tender Is the Heart '01

Christiane Millet
The Taste of Others '00

Dana Millican
Green '01

Danny Mills
Pink Flamingos '72

Donna Mills
Play Misty for Me '71

Frank Mills
Flambards '78

Gary Landon Mills
Full Metal Jacket [2 SE] '87

Hayley Mills
A Troll in Central Park '94 (V)
The Parent Trap '61
Pollyanna '60

John Mills
Cats [UE Universal] '98

John Mills
A Tale of Two Cities '91
The Lady and the Highway-
man '89
Gandhi '82
The Swiss Family Robinson
'60
We Dive at Dawn '43

Judson Mills
Chill Factor '99
Major League 3: Back to the
Minors '98

Juliet Mills
QB VII '74

Kaly Mills
Carnival of Blood / Curse of
the Headless Horseman
[SE] '71

Georgy Millyar
Barbara the Fair with the
Silken Hair '69
Father Frost '66

Martin Milner
13 Ghosts '60
The Halls of Montezuma '50

Sandra Milo
Juliet of the Spirits [Criterion]
'65
8 1/2 '63

Sofia Milos
The Order '01

Josh Milrad
Beastmaster '82

Yvette Mimieux
Hit Lady '74

Ryuuji Minakami
Score '95

Jan Miner
Lenny '74

Rachel Miner
Bully '01

Mike Minett
Bad Taste [LE] '88

Tsui Siu Ming
Bury Me High '90

Ming Na
Final Fantasy: The Spirits
Within '01 (V)

Claudette Mink
Children of the Corn: Revelation '01

Liza Minnelli
Jackie's Back '99
The Muppets Take Manhattan
'84

Kylie Minogue
Moulin Rouge [SE] '01
Bio-Dome '96

Kelly Jo Minter
Popcorn '89

Kristin Minter
Tick Tock '00

Miou-Miou
Going Places '74

Carmen Miranda
Hidden Hollywood 2: More
Treasures from the 20th
Century Fox Vaults '99

Isa Miranda
Summertime '55

Robert Miranda
Lost in Yonkers '93
Sister Act '92

Olga Mironova
Come and See '85

Helen Mirren
Greenfingers '00
The Pledge '01
S.O.S. Titanic '79

Yukio Mishima
Afraid to Die '60

Karen Mistal
Return of the Killer Tomatoes! '88

Mr. T
Judgment '01
Not Another Teen Movie '01

Jimi Mistry
Born Romantic '00

Cameron Mitchell
Slaughter '72
Rebel Rousers '69
Knives of the Avenger '65
Flight to Mars '52

Darryl (Chill) Mitchell
Black Knight '01

Duke Mitchell
Bela Lugosi Meets a Brooklyn
Gorilla '52

E. Roger Mitchell
Boycott '02

Elizabeth Mitchell
Double Bang '01
Molly '99

John Cameron Mitchell
Hedwig and the Angry Inch
'00

Mary Mitchell
Dementia 13 [Roan] '63

Millard Mitchell
Twelve o'Clock High '49

Radha Mitchell
Uprising '01

Sasha Mitchell
Luck of the Draw '00

Scoey Mitchell
Jo Jo Dancer, Your Life Is Calling '86

Sharon Mitchell
Maniac [LE] '80

Thomas Mitchell
Pocketful of Miracles '61

Warren Mitchell
Jabberwocky '77
Til Death Us Do Part '72
The Crawling Eye '58

Chris Mitchum
Tombstone [2] '93

John Mitchum
The Enforcer '76
The Outlaw Josey Wales [2]
'76

Robert Mitchum
Tombstone [2] '93 (N)
Cape Fear '91
Maria's Lovers '84
Midway [Universal CE] '76
Anzio '68
Five Card Stud '68
Cape Fear '61
The Grass Is Greener '61
River of No Return '54

Koji Mitsui
The Hidden Fortress '58

Tin Miu
Snake and Crane Arts of
Shaolin '78
Blood of the Dragon '71

Tse Miu
Legend of the Red Dragon
'94

Jerod Mixon
Me, Myself, and Irene '00

Hiroshi Miyauchi
Tokyo Mafia: Wrath of the
Yakuza '95

Yukio Mishima

Eiko Miyoshi
The Hidden Fortress '58

Kei Mizutani
Sumo Vixens '96
Tokyo Decameron: Three
Tales of Madness & Sensu-
ality '96
Terminatrix '95

Yoshie Mizutani
The Tale of Zatoichi Continues '62

Mary Ann Mobley
Crazy Horse and Custer: "The
Untold Story" '90

Roger Mobley
Jack the Giant Killer '62

Matthew Modine
Jack and the Beanstalk: The
Real Story '01
The Blackout '97
Full Metal Jacket [2 SE] '87
The Hotel New Hampshire
'84

Gaston Modot
Children of Paradise '44

Donald Moffat
61* '01

Katherine Moffat
The Beast Within '82

D.W. Moffett
Kill Me Later '01
Traffic [Criterion] '00
Molly '99
Stealing Beauty '96

Aribert Mog
Ecstasy '33

Victor Mohica
Johnny Firecloud / Bummer
'75

Gerald Mohr
The Angry Red Planet '59
Terror in the Haunted House
'58
Invasion U.S.A. '52
Jungle Girl '41

Jay Mohr
Dean Koontz's Black River
'01
Pay It Forward '00
Jerry Maguire [2 SE] '96

Karen Mok
Goodbye, Mr. Cool '01

Max Mok
The Assassin '93

Zakes Mokae
Vampire in Brooklyn '95

Fujita Mokoto
Sure Death: Revenge '87

Albert Mol
Business Is Business '71

Gretchen Mol
Attraction '00

Henk Molenberg
Business Is Business '71

Alfred Molina
Texas Rangers '01
The Treat '98
Not without My Daughter '90

Angela Molina
That Obscure Object of
Desire '77

Enrique Molina
A Paradise under the Stars
'99

Ricardo Molina
Two Coyotes '01

Rolando Molina
crazy/beautiful '01

Georgia Moll
The White Warrior '61

Richard Moll
Evolution '01
Scary Movie 2 '01
House '86
Sword & the Sorcerer '82

Jordi Molla
Blow '01

Tibor Molnar
The Red and the White '68

Taylor Momsen
Dr. Seuss' How the Grinch
Stole Christmas '00

Jeff Monahan
Bruiser '00

Rene Monclova
The Kiss You Gave Me '00

Merwin Mondesir
Bones '01

Mo'Nique
Two Can Play That Game '01

Alvaro Monje
Sexy Beast '00

Isabell Monk
Black Knight '01

Thelonious Monk
Thelonious Monk: Straight,
No Chaser '89

Yvonne Monlaur
Circus of Horrors '60

Marilyn Monroe
Let's Make Love '60
The Prince and the Showgirl
'57
River of No Return '54
Don't Bother to Knock '52
Monkey Business '52
Niagara '52

Renzo Montagnani
The Libertine '69

Ricardo Montalban
Sayonara '57

Yves Montand
Let's Make Love '60

Ted Monte
Attack of the 60-Foot Centerfold '95

Elisa Montes
Texas, Adios '66

Liliane Montevecchi
The Young Lions '58

Dan Montgomery, Jr.
On the Line '01
Red Dirt '99

Douglass Montgomery
Little Women '33

Julia Montgomery
Revenge of the Nerds /
Revenge of the Nerds 2:
Nerds in Paradise '84

Lafayette Montgomery
Mulholland Drive '01

Anna Maria Monticelli
Nomads '86

Rita Montone
Maniac [LE] '80

Michel Monty
Restless Spirits '99

Jim Moody
Bad Boys [Anchor Bay] '83

Lynne Moody
Las Vegas Lady '76

Ralph Moody
Lone Ranger and the Lost
City of Gold '58

Dennis Mooney
Hollywood Chainsaw Hookers
'88

Saba Moor
Cave Girl '85

Alvy Moore
The Specialist '75
Designing Woman '57

Cedric Moore
Black and Blue '01

Clayton Moore
The Legend of the Lone Ranger '59
Lone Ranger and the Lost City of Gold '58
Lone Ranger '56
The Lone Ranger: Volume 1 '56
The Son of Monte Cristo '40

Demi Moore
The Hunchback of Notre Dame 2 '01 (V)
The Hunchback of Notre Dame '96 (V)
Indecent Proposal '93
The Butcher's Wife '91

Dennis Moore
The Mummy's Curse '44

Dudley Moore
Romantic Comedy '83

Duke Moore
Night of the Ghouls '59

Frank Moore
His Majesty, the Scarecrow of Oz '14

Joanna Moore
The Dunwich Horror '70

Julianne Moore
Evolution '01
Safe '95
Tales from the Darkside: The Movie '90

Kaycee Moore
Daughters of the Dust '91

Kenya Moore
Trois '00

Kevin Moore
The Wolves of Kromer '98

Mandy Moore
The Princess Diaries '01

Mary Tyler Moore
Ordinary People '80

Matt Moore
I Bury the Living '58

Michael Moore
The Awful Truth: The Complete Second Season '01

Peter Savard Moore
Top Dog '95

Roger Moore
The Enemy '01
In the Footsteps of the Holy Family '01 (N)
The Man with the Golden Gun '74
The Man Who Haunted Himself '70
The Saint '66

Shemar Moore
Mama Flora's Family '98
Never 2 Big '98

Stephen Moore
Clockwise '86

Victor Moore
On Our Merry Way '48
Star Spangled Rhythm '42

Agnes Moorehead
Pollyanna '60
The Bat [Goodtimes] '59
All That Heaven Allows '55
Show Boat '51
Citizen Kane '41

Esai Morales
Bad Boys [Anchor Bay] '83

Nick Moran
The Musketeer '01

Pat Moran
Desperate Living (John Waters Collection Vol. 2) '77
Female Trouble '74
Pink Flamingos '72

Pauline Moran
Agatha Christie's Poirot: Peril at End House '90
Woman in Black '89

Peggy Moran
The Mummy's Hand '40

Rob Moran
Me, Myself, and Irene '00

Rick Moranis
Spaceballs '87
Brewster's Millions [Universal] '85

Richard Morant
Scandal '89

Jason Morck
Random Acts of Violence '02

Jeanne Moreau
Catherine the Great '95
The Lover '92 (N)
Querelle '83
Going Places '74
Mademoiselle '66
The Trial '63
Eva '62

Jennie Moreau
States of Control '98

Marguerite Moreau
Firestarter 2: Rekindled '02
Wet Hot American Summer '01

Sylvie Moreau
The Widow of Saint-Pierre '00

Andre Morell
The Hound of the Baskervilles '59

Antonio Moreno
Creature from the Black Lagoon '54
It '27

Liza Moreno
Raiders of Leyte Gulf '63

Rene L. Moreno
Tequila Body Shots '99

Rita Moreno
Blue Moon '00
Working '82

Cindy Morgan
Tron [2 CE] '82

Debbi (Deborah) Morgan
Love and Basketball '00
The Runaway '00

Dennis Morgan
Pearl of the South Pacific '55

Frank Morgan
Dimples '36
Hallelujah, I'm a Bum '33

Harry (Henry) Morgan
The Shootist '76
Support Your Local Sheriff '69
Inherit the Wind '60
A Wing and a Prayer '44

Nancy Morgan
The Nest '88

Priscilla Morgan
Separate Tables '58

Red Morgan
The Adventures of Buckaroo Banzai Across the Eighth Dimension [SE] '84

Trevor Morgan
The Glass House '01
Jurassic Park 3 [CE] '01
The Sixth Sense [Buena Vista] '99

Maia Morgenstern
Ulysses' Gaze '95

John Morghen
Cannibal Apocalypse '80

Masayuki Mori
Rashomon '51

Cathy Moriarty
The Hunger: Smoke, Mirrors, and Paranoia '00
Soapdish '91

James Moriarty
Ten Benny '98

Michael Moriarty
Along Came a Spider '00
Shiloh 2: Shiloh Season '99
Shiloh '97
Courage Under Fire '96
Who'll Stop the Rain? '78

P. H. Moriarty
Dune [2 SE] '00

Tara Morice
Strictly Ballroom '92

Alanis Morissette
Jay and Silent Bob Strike Back '01
Dogma [2 SE] '99

Noriyuki "Pat" Morita
Beyond Barbed Wire '97 (N)
Lena's Holiday '90
The Karate Kid: Part 3 '89
The Karate Kid: Part 2 '86

Henning Moritzen
Cries and Whispers '72

Yuko Moriyama
Reborn from Hell: Jubei's Revenge '96
Reborn from Hell: Samurai Armageddon '96
Zeram 2 '94

Mary Morlass
This Is Not a Test '62

Robert Morley
A Troll in Central Park '94 (V)
The Lady and the Highwayman '89
The Great Muppet Caper '81
Theatre of Blood '73
Topkapi '64

Anita Morris
18 Again! '88
Ruthless People '86
The Hotel New Hampshire '84
Maria's Lovers '84
The Magic Show '81

Aubrey Morris
She Creature '01

Barboura Morris
The Dunwich Horror '70
A Bucket of Blood / Attack of the Giant Leeches [Marengo] '57
The Wasp Woman [2] '59

Garrett Morris
Jackpot '01
Motorama '91

Iona Morris
Next Time '99

Jane Morris
Frankie and Johnny '91
Nothing in Common '86

Kirk Morris
The Conqueror of Atlantis '65

Phil Morris
Atlantis: The Lost Empire [CE] '01 (V)

Phyllis Morris
Three Came Home '50

Jenny Morrison
Intersection '93

Joe Morrison
Sting of Death '65

Kenny Morrison
NeverEnding Story 2: The Next Chapter '91

Temuera Morrison
Vertical Limit [2 SB] '00

David Morrissey
Captain Corelli's Mandolin '01
Born Romantic '00

Jeff Morrow
The Robe '53

Jo Morrow
13 Ghosts '60
The Three Worlds of Gulliver '59

Kirby Morrow
Barbie in the Nutcracker '01 (V)

Rob Morrow
Maze '01

Vic Morrow
The Bad News Bears '76
God's Little Acre '58

Barry Morse
Space: 1999 Set 1 '75

David Morse
Hearts in Atlantis '01
Proof of Life '00
Stephen King's The Langoliers '95
Desperate Hours '90

Robert Morse
How to Succeed in Business without Really Trying '67

Terry Morse
Fog Island '45

Glenn Morshower
Black Hawk Down '01
Pearl Harbor '01

Clara Mortensen
Wrestling Women USA! '01
Pin Down Girls '51

Joe Morton
Ali '01
Of Mice and Men '92

Judee Morton
The Slime People '63

Julian Morton
The Wolfman '82

David Moscow
Riding in Cars with Boys '01
Newsies '92

Bill Moseley
The Convent '01

Edda Moser
Don Giovanni '79

Harry Moses
The Van '77

Rick Moses
Avalanche '78

William R. Moses
The Perfect Wife '00
Alone with a Stranger '99

Nthati Moshesh
The Long Run '00

Roger E. Mosley
Letters from a Killer '98
Unlawful Entry '92
The Greatest '77

Carrie-Anne Moss
Memento [1] '00
Memento [2 SE] '00

Jesse Moss
Ginger Snaps '00

Paige Moss
Killer Instinct '00

Ron Moss
Hard Ticket to Hawaii '87

Tegan Moss
Sea People '00

Josh Mostel
Little Man Tate '91
Radio Days '87

Zero Mostel
Watership Down '78 (V)
A Funny Thing Happened on the Way to the Forum '66

Masahiro Motoki
Gonin '95

Zeze Motta
Tieta of Agreste '96

John Moulder-Brown
Sleeping Murder / 4:50 from Paddington '86

Dru Mouser
Tequila Body Shots '99

Lisbeth Movin
Day of Wrath '43

Alan Mowbray
Lured '47
My Man Godfrey [Criterion] '36

Patrick Mower
The Bloodsuckers '70

Angela Moya
Luminarias '99

Stephen Moyer
Uprising '01
Ultraviolet '98

Bill Moyers
Joseph Campbell: The Power of Myth '88

Bridget Moynahan
Serendipity '01

George Mozart
Song of Freedom / Big Fella '36

Umberto Mozzato
Cabiria '14

Cookie Mueller
Polyester (John Waters Collection Vol. 2) '81
Desperate Living (John Waters Collection Vol. 2) '77
Female Trouble '74
Pink Flamingos '72

Armin Mueller-Stahl
The Long Run '00
The Ogre '96
The House of the Spirits '93
Colonel Redl '84
Jacob the Liar '74

Richard Muench
Patton [2] '70

Amanda Muggleton
Idiot Box '97

Rahim Muhammad
Rappin'-N-Rhyming '00

Separate Tables '58

Michael Nesmith
Head '68

Loni Nest
The Golem '20

John Nettleton
And Soon the Darkness '70

Jack Neubeck
Invasion of the Blood Farmers '72

Ruth Neuman
Basket Case [2 SE] '82

Bebe Neuwirth
Say Anything [SE] '89

John Neville
Water Damage '01
The Fifth Element [2 SB] '97
Baby's Day Out '94

Sarah Neville
Careful '92

Brooke Nevin
Running Wild '99

Robyn Nevin
Careful, He Might Hear You '84
The Irishman '78

Patrick Newall
Borough of Kings '98

Milton Newberger
Bela Lugosi Meets a Brooklyn Gorilla '52

Bob Newhart
Rudolph the Red-Nosed Reindeer: The Movie '98 (V)

Alec Newman
Dune [2 SE] '00

Barry Newman
Good Advice '01
True Blue '01
The Mirror Cracked from Side to Side '92

Danny Newman
Shopping '93

Laraine Newman
Invaders from Mars [MGM] '86

Nanette Newman
The Stepford Wives [2 SE] '75

Paul Newman
Slap Shot [2] '77

Randy Newman
Three Amigos '86

Julie Newmar
MacKenna's Gold '69

Pauline Newstone
Mummies Alive! '97 (V)

Cody Newton
The Runaway '00

Margit Evelyn Newton
Hell of the Living Dead '83

Robert Newton
Long John Silver '54

Wayne Newton
Mr. Bill Goes to Hollywood / Mr. Bill Does Vegas '01
Ocean's Eleven '01

Ben Ng
Millennium Dragon '93

Carrie Ng
City on Fire [Dimension] '87

Daniel Ng
City of Glass '98

Frances Ng
Too Many Ways to Be No. 1 '97

Frankie Ng
Cops on a Mission '01

Hugo Ng
Brother of Darkness '94
Daughter of Darkness '93

Lawrence Ng
Picture of a Nymph '88

Mark Ng
Eat My Dust '93

Richard Ng
Wheels on Meals '84

Sandra Ng
Jiang Hu—"The Triad Zone" '00

Dustin Nguyen
3 Ninjas Kick Back '94

Philippe Nicaud
The Nude Set '61

Harold Nicholas
The Five Heartbeats '91

Thomas Ian Nicholas
American Pie 2 '01
American Pie [2 UE] '99
Rookie of the Year '93

Allan Nicholls
Slap Shot [2] '77

Dandy Nichols
Til Death Us Do Part '72

Nichelle Nichols
Snow Dogs '02
Star Trek 3: The Search for Spock '84
Star Trek: The Motion Picture [DE] '80

Stephen Nichols
Soapdish '91

Taylor Nichols
Jurassic Park 3 [CE] '01
Barcelona '94

Jack Nicholson
The Pledge '00
The Shining [2 SE] '80
Goin' South '78
Rebel Rousers '69

Grant Nickalls
Glitter '01

Michael A. (M.A.) Nickles
Wayne's World 2 '93

Alex Nicol
A*P*E* '76

Emily Nicol
Poor Man's Orange '87

Daria Nicolodi
Opera '88
Shock '79

Steve Nicolson
Bravo Two Zero '99

Colleen Niday
Thief in the Night '72

Brigitte Nielsen
Doomsdayer '99
Beverly Hills Cop 2 '87

Leslie Nielsen
Hollywood Screen Tests: Take 2 '00
Santa Who? '00
2001: A Space Travesty '00
Soul Man '86
They Call It Murder '71

Glen Nielson
Satan's Bed '65

Yvonne Nielson
Blood Thirst '65

Karl Niemiec
Narcotic Justice

Pepe Nieto
The Night Heaven Fell '57

Bill Nighy
Blow Dry '00

Jan Niklas
The House of the Spirits '93
Colonel Redl '84

Chuck Niles
Teenage Zombies '58

Anna Q. Nilsson
Regeneration / Young Romance '15

Leonard Nimoy
Atlantis: The Lost Empire [CE] '01 (V)
Mind Meld: Secrets behind the Voyage of a Lifetime '01
Star Trek 3: The Search for Spock '84
Star Trek: The Motion Picture [DE] '80

Najwa Nimri
Open Your Eyes '97

Yana Nirvana
Echo Park '86

Aud Egede Nissen
Dr. Mabuse, The Gambler '22

Barbara Niven
Alone with a Stranger '99

David Niven
Murder by Death '76
Separate Tables '58
Dodsworth [MGM] '36

Kip Niven
Magnum Force '73

Alessandro Nivola
Jurassic Park 3 [CE] '01

Cynthia Nixon
Sex and the City: The Complete Third Season '02
Sex and the City: Season 1 '00
Let It Ride '89
The Manhattan Project '86
Fifth of July '82

Chiharu Niyama
The Dimension Travelers '98

Christian Noble
Human Desires '97
Illegal Affairs '96

Nancy Lee Noble
Just for the Hell of It '68

Staci Noel
Tender Is the Heart '01

Philippe Noiret
The Clockmaker '73

John Nolan
Following '99

Lloyd Nolan
Hannah and Her Sisters '86
Guadalcanal Diary '43

Michelle Nolden
Deceived '91

Chris Nole
The Tormentors '71

Jacques Nolot
Under the Sand '00

Nick Nolte
The Golden Bowl '00
Trixie '00

Cape Fear '91
The Prince of Tides '91
Three Fugitives '89
Under Fire '83
Who'll Stop the Rain? '78

Kerry Noonan
Friday the 13th, Part 6: Jason Lives '86

Tom Noonan
The Pledge '00
Manhunter [LE] '86

Jeffrey Nordling
Turbulence 2: Fear of Flying '99

Eduardo Noriega
The Yellow Fountain '99
Open Your Eyes '97

Susan Norman
Safe '95

Zack Norman
Cadillac Man '90

Bruce Norris
The Sixth Sense [Buena Vista] '99

Chuck Norris
Top Dog '95
Hero and the Terror '88
Invasion U.S.A. '85
Lone Wolf McQuade '83
Silent Rage '82
An Eye for an Eye '81
Good Guys Wear Black '78

Hermione Norris
Born Romantic '00

Alan North
Highlander [Anchor Bay] '86

J.J. North
Attack of the 60-Foot Centerfold '95

Leslie North
The Young Girls of Rochefort '68

Neil North
The Winslow Boy '98

Sheree North
The Shootist '76
Breakout '75
Lawman '71

Jeremy Northam
The Golden Bowl '00
The Winslow Boy '98
Carrington '95
The Net [2 SE] '95

Ryan Northcott
Ripper: Letter from Hell '01

Michael P. Northey
Return to Cabin by the Lake '01

Alex Norton
Beautiful Creatures '00
Orphans '97
Gregory's Girl '80

Edgar Norton
Son of Frankenstein '39

Edward Norton
The Score '01

Jim Norton
Hidden Agenda '90

Richard Norton
Amazons and Gladiators '01

Brandy Norwood
Osmosis Jones '01 (V)

Jack Noseworthy
Breakdown '96

Christopher Noth
Sex and the City: The Complete Third Season '02
The Glass House '01
Sex and the City: Season 1 '00
Burnzy's Last Call '95

Michael Nouri
61* '01
To the Limit '95

Frank Novack
Raptor '01

John Novak
Wishmaster 3: Beyond the Gates of Hell '01

Kim Novak
Liebestraum '91

Don Novello
Atlantis: The Lost Empire [CE] '01 (V)
Mr. Bill Goes to Hollywood / Mr. Bill Does Vegas '01
Just One Night '00

Jay Novello
The Pride and the Passion '57

Tom Novembre
The Ice Rink '99

Nancho Novo
Not Love Just Frenzy '96

Pavel Novy
Conspirators of Pleasure '93

Hitomi Nozoe
Giants and Toys '58

Esther Nubiola
Nico and Dani '00

Danny Nucci
Firestarter 2: Rekindled '02

Richard Nugent
Sahara '43

Bill Nunn
The Legend of 1900 '98
Candyman 2: Farewell to the Flesh '94
Sister Act '92

Rudolf Nureyev
Nureyev '91

Michael Nyuis
Late Night Sessions '99

Barbara O
Daughters of the Dust '91

Simon Oakland
Chato's Land '71
I Want to Live! '58

Wheeler Oakman
Two-Fisted Law '32

Simon Oates
Doomwatch '72

Warren Oates
Blue Thunder '83
The Blue and the Gray '82
Stripes '81
Dixie Dynamite '76

Merle Oberon
Stage Door Canteen '43

Jack Oblivian
Sore Losers '97

Jacqueline Obradors
Atlantis: The Lost Empire [CE] '01 (V)
Tortilla Soup '01

Rodrigo Obregon
Picasso Trigger '89
Hard Ticket to Hawaii '87

Hugh O'Brian
The Shootist '76

Maureen O'Sullivan
Hannah and Her Sisters '86

Michael O'Sullivan
Careful '92

Richard O'Sullivan
Au Pair Girls '72

Hitoe Otake
Tokyo Decameron: Three Tales of Madness & Sensuality '96

Carre Otis
Wild Orchid '90

Peter O'Toole
The Sinister Saga '00
High Spirits '88
The Stunt Man '80
The Ruling Class '72
The Bible '66

Barry Otto
Strictly Ballroom '92
Howling 3: The Marsupials '87

Miranda Otto
The Well '97

Carl Ottosen
Reptilicus '62

Assita Ouedraogo
La Promesse '96

Rasmane Ouedraogo
La Promesse '96

Sverre Anker Ousdal
The Last Place on Earth '94

Maria Ouspenskaya
Frankenstein Meets the Wolfman '42
Beyond Tomorrow '40
Dodsworth [MGM] '36

Levan Outchanechvili
The Legend of Suram Fortress / Ashik Kerib '85

Alexander Outhred
Hammers over the Anvil '91

Stacy Oversier
The Guardian '00

Rick Overton
Beverly Hills Cop [CE] '84

Baard Owe
Gertrud '64

Chris Owen
American Pie 2 '01
American Pie [2 UE] '99

Clive Owen
Greenfingers '00

Reginald Owen
Captain Kidd [Marengo] '45

Patricia Owens
Sayonara '57

Earl Owensby
The Wolfman '82

Catherine Oxenberg
Sanctimony '01
The Miracle of the Cards '00

Frank Oz
Star Wars: Episode 1—The Phantom Menace '99 (V)
Sesame Street Presents: Follow That Bird '85 (V)
The Muppets Take Manhattan '84 (V)
An American Werewolf in London [CE Universal] '81
The Great Muppet Caper '81 (V)
The Muppet Movie '79 (V)
Emmet Otter's Jug-Band Christmas '77 (V)

Hitoshi Ozawa
Score '95

Kazuyoshi Ozawa
Score '95

Lloyd Pace
Basket Case [2 SE] '82

Tom Pace
Girl in Gold Boots '69

Al Pacino
Frankie and Johnny '91
Dick Tracy '90

Roger Lloyd Pack
Fright '71

Joanna Pacula
Crash & Byrnes '99
Tombstone [2] '93
Death Before Dishonor '87

Sarah Padden
Tomorrow's Children '34

Pilar Padilla
In the Time of the Butterflies '01
Bread and Roses '00

Juan Padron
Vampires in Havana '87 (V)

Bartolomeo Pagano
Cabiria '14

Elaine Page
Cats [UE Universal] '98

Genevieve Page
Belle de Jour '67

Geraldine Page
The Bride '85
Honky Tonk Freeway '81

Harrison Page
Swamp Girl / Swamp Country '71

Ken Page
Cats [UE Universal] '98

Leonie Page
Strictly Ballroom '92

Peaches Page
Wrestling Women USA! '01

Debra Paget
The Indian Tomb '59
Tiger of Eschnapur '59

Robert Paget
The Choppers '61

Nicola Pagett
Upstairs, Downstairs: The Complete First Season '71

Harrison Paige
Raptor '01

Peter Paige
Queer As Folk: The Complete First Season '01

Robert Paige
Son of Dracula '43

Nestor Paiva
Creature from the Black Lagoon '54
The Road to Utopia [Universal] '46

Luca Palanca
Double Down '01

Jack Palance
Prancer Returns '01
Cops and Robbersons '94
Bagdad Cafe '88
Chato's Land '71
Companeros '70
Barabbas '62
The Halls of Montezuma '50

Michael Palin
Jabberwocky '77

Aleksa Palladino
Red Dirt '99

Erik Palladino
Life without Dick '01

Cecile Pallas
Robert Louis Stevenson's St. Ives '98

Aubert Pallascio
Lilies '96

Eugene Pallette
The Lady Eve '41
My Man Godfrey [Criterion] '36

Gabriella Pallotta
Il Grido '57

Betsy Palmer
The Long Gray Line '55
Queen Bee '55

Cynthia Palmer
Escape to Grizzly Mountain '99

Gretchen Palmer
Trois '00

Lilli Palmer
De Sade '69

Rebecca Palmer
Intimacy '00

Renzo Palmer
White Fang to the Rescue '74

Chazz Palminteri
Down to Earth '01
Boss of Bosses '99
Stuart Little [2 DE] '99 (V)
Hurlyburly '98
The Usual Suspects [MGM SE] '95

Gwyneth Paltrow
The Anniversary Party '01
Flesh and Bone '93
Hook '91

Gina Paluzzi
Pigkeeper's Daughter / Sassy Sue '75

Luciana Paluzzi
Tiger of Eschnapur '59

Rebecca Pan
In the Mood for Love [SE] '00

Alessandra Panaro
Rocco and His Brothers '60

Michael Panes
The Anniversary Party '01

Franklin Pangborn
Sullivan's Travels '41
My Man Godfrey [Criterion] '36

Stuart Pankin
Fatal Attraction [SCE] '87

John Pankow
The Object of My Affection '98

Joe Pantoliano
Memento [1] '00
Memento [2 SE] '00
Baby's Day Out '94
Empire of the Sun '87
Running Scared '86
The Goonies '85
Eddie and the Cruisers '83

Irene Papas
Captain Corelli's Mandolin '01
The Odyssey '97
The Brotherhood '68
Electra '62

Anna Paquin
Almost Famous: Untitled—The Bootleg Cut '00
Hurlyburly '98
Fly Away Home [2 SE] '96

John Paragon
UHF '89

Kip Pardue
Driven '01

Jessica Pare
Lost and Delirious '01
Stardom '00

Michael Pare
Sanctimony '01
2103: Deadly Wake '97
Eddie and the Cruisers '83

Monique Parent
Beverly Hills Bordello '01
The Pornographer '00
Illegal Affairs '96

Judy Parfitt
Wilde '97

Woodrow Parfrey
The Outlaw Josey Wales [2] '76

Dale Paris
Night Orchid '97

Simone Paris
The Nude Set '61

Ray Park
Star Wars: Episode 1—The Phantom Menace '99

MacDonald Parke
Summertime '55

Cecilia Parker
Riders of Destiny [Columbia] '33

Edwin Parker
Abbott and Costello Meet the Mummy '55

Eleanor Parker
A Hole in the Head '59

F. William Parker
Warm Blooded Killers '01

Fess Parker
Walt Disney Treasures: Davy Crockett '01
Old Yeller '57

Jean Parker
Bluebeard '44
Beyond Tomorrow '40
Lady for a Day '33
Little Women '33

Kevin Parker
Dirty Kopz '01

Molly Parker
The Center of the World '01

Nathaniel Parker
Lover's Prayer '99
Into Thin Air: Death on Everest '97

Nicole Ari Parker
Dancing in September '00

Sarah Jessica Parker
Sex and the City: The Complete Third Season '02
Life without Dick '01
Sex and the City: Season 1 '00
State and Main '00
Til There Was You '96

Trey Parker
South Park: Insults to Injury '02 (V)
South Park: Bigger, Longer and Uncut '99 (V)
Cannibal! The Musical '96

Gerard Parkes
Speaking Parts '89

Shaun Parkes
The Mummy Returns '01

Michael Parks
The Bible '66

Tammy Parks
Attack of the 60-Foot Centerfold '95

Ted Parks
Red Rock West '93

Alan Parnaby
Flambards '78

Jay Parris
Ice Grill '02

Frederick Parslow
The Last Wave '77

Estelle Parsons
Dick Tracy '90

Michael Parsons
Raiders of Leyte Gulf '63

Mike Parsons
The Ravagers '65
Walls of Hell '64

Dolly Parton
Jackie's Back '99

Christine Pascal
The Clockmaker '73

Marie-Georges Pascal
The Grapes of Death '78

Richard Pasco
The Watcher in the Woods '81

Dirch Passer
Reptilicus '62

George Pastell
The Mummy '59

Clara Pastor
Anguish '88

Vincent Pastore
Made [SE] '01
The Sopranos: The Complete Second Season '01
Blue Moon '00
Mickey Blue Eyes '99
Walking and Talking '96

Robert Pastorelli
Rodgers & Hammerstein's South Pacific '01
Beverly Hills Cop 2 '87

Ruben Patagonia
The Road '00

Michael Pataki
Halloween 4: The Return of Michael Myers [MGM LE] '88

Tom Patchett
The Muppets Take Manhattan '84 (V)

Michael Pate
Howling 3: The Marsupials '87
Return of Captain Invincible '83

Bill Paterson
Truly, Madly, Deeply '91
Traffik '90

Mandy Patinkin
Dick Tracy '90
Impromptu '90
The Princess Bride [2 SE] '87

Angela Paton
Groundhog Day [2 SE] '93

Laurie Paton
The Amy Fisher Story '93

Linh Dan Pham
Indochine '92

Anne Phelan
Poor Man's Orange '87
The Harp in the South '86

Kate Phelps
The Shining [2 SE] '80

Peter Phelps
Lantana '01

Mekhi Phifer
O '01

Harry Philabosian
Waiting '01

John Philbin
Point Break '91

Regis Philbin
The Bad News Bears Go to
Japan '78

Busy Philipps
The Smokers '00

Donna Philipson
Reptilian '00

Ryan Phillippe
Company Man '01

Bijou Phillips
Bully '01
Fast Sofa '01
Tart '01
Almost Famous: Untitled—
The Bootleg Cut '00

Chynna Phillips
Say Anything [SE] '89

Emo Phillips
UHF '89

Gina Phillips
Jeepers Creepers '01

Leslie Phillips
Lara Croft: Tomb Raider '01
Scandal '89
Empire of the Sun '87

Lou Diamond Phillips
Route 666 '01
In a Class of His Own '99
The Big Hit [2 SB] '98
Courage Under Fire '96
The First Power '89

Michelle Phillips
Let It Ride '89

Sally Phillips
Bridget Jones's Diary '01

Sian Phillips
Ivanhoe '97

Stephen Phillips
The Projectionist '71

Andrew Philpot
Vampire Hunter D: Bloodlust
'01 (V)

Max Phipps
Return of Captain Invincible
'83

Ray Phiri
Paul Simon: Graceland '97

Rain Phoenix
O '01

Joseph Piantadosi
Schlock '73

Maureen Picard
Little Shots of Happiness '97

Robert Picardo
Motorama '91
The Howling '81

Michel Piccoli
Atlantic City '81

The Young Girls of Rochefort
'68
Belle de Jour '67

Irving Pichel
Dick Tracy [Marengo] '37
Dick Tracy [VCI] '37
Dracula's Daughter '36

Elissa Pichelli
Knives of the Avenger '65

Joe Pichler
Beethoven's 4th '01
When Good Ghouls Go Bad
'01
Shiloh 2: Shiloh Season '99

James Pickens, Jr.
Ghosts of Mississippi '96

Slim Pickens
Crazy Horse and Custer: "The
Untold Story" '90
The Howling '81
Rough Night in Jericho '67
The Lone Ranger: Volume 1
'56

Blake Pickett
Illicit Confessions '77

Ronald Pickup
Horatio Hornblower '99
Ivanhoe '97
Scarlett '94

Molly Picon
Fiddler on the Roof [2 SE] '71

Kane Picoy
Double Down '01

Jim Piddock
She Creature '01

Matthew Pidgeon
The Winslow Boy '98

Rebecca Pidgeon
Heist '01
State and Main '00
The Winslow Boy '98

Walter Pidgeon
Funny Girl '68
Cinderella '64
The Bad and the Beautiful
'52

Adrienne Pierce
Styx '00

David Hyde Pierce
Osmosis Jones '01 (V)
Wet Hot American Summer
'01
Jackie's Back '99
Little Man Tate '91

Richard Pierce
Basket Case [2 SE] '82

Geoffrey Pierson
Venomous '01

Tim Pigott-Smith
The Remains of the Day '93

Alison Pill
Skipped Parts '00

Daniel Pilon
Brannigan '75

Bronson Pinchot
Putting It Together: Stephen
Sondheim—A Musical
Review '01
Courage Under Fire '96
Stephen King's The Lan-
goliers '95
Beverly Hills Cop 3 '94
Beverly Hills Cop [CE] '84

Phillip Pine
The Phantom from 10,000
Leagues '56

Robert Pine
Body Count '97
Empire of the Ants '77
Incident on a Dark Street '72

Fred Pinero
The Death Curse of Tartu /
Sting of Death '66

Siu Ping-Lam
In the Mood for Love [SE] '00

Jada Pinkett Smith
Ali '01
Kingdom Come '01

Dick Pinner
Monster from the Ocean
Floor '54

Steven Pinner
Link '86

Dominique Pinon
Diva [Anchor Bay] '82

Harold Pinter
The Tailor of Panama '00
Accident '67

Elith Pio
Haxan: Witchcraft through the
Ages '22

Nadja Pionilla
Race the Sun '96

Emma Piper
Empire of the Sun '87

Kelly Piper
Rawhead Rex '87
Maniac [LE] '80

Roddy Piper
Cybercity '99
Hell Comes to Frogtown '88

Danuel Pipoly
Lord of the Flies '90

Marie-France Pisier
The Ice Rink '99

Luigi Pistilli
The Libertine '69

Ludger Pistor
The Princess and the Warrior
'00

Mario Pisu
Juliet of the Spirits [Criterion]
'65

Anne Pitoniak
Best Seller '87
Agnes of God '85

Brad Pitt
The Mexican '01
Ocean's Eleven '01
Spy Game '01
Snatch [SE] '00
The Favor '92

Ingrid Pitt
The Wicker Man [SE] '75

Michael Pitt
Bully '01
Hedwig and the Angry Inch '00

Veronica Pitts
Dead or Alive '02

ZaSu Pitts
It's a Mad, Mad, Mad, Mad
World '63

Jeremy Piven
Black Hawk Down '01
Highway '01
Rush Hour 2 '01
Serendipity '01
Say Anything [SE] '89

Mary Kay Place
My First Mister '01
Pecker (John Waters Collec-
tion Vol. 1) '98

Tony Plana
Fidel '02
Break of Dawn '88

Edward Platt
Designing Woman '57
Written on the Wind '56

Oliver Platt
Don't Say a Word '01
Indecent Proposal '93
The Temp '93

Alice Playten
Legend [UE] '86

Donald Pleasence
A Caribbean Mystery / The
Mirror Cracked from Side
to Side '89
Halloween 4: The Return of
Michael Myers [MGM LE]
'88
Halloween 2: The Nightmare
Isn't Over! [Universal] '81
All Quiet on the Western
Front '79
Halloween [Extended Edition]
'78
Will Penny '67
Circus of Horrors '60
The Flesh and the Fiends '60
Look Back in Anger '58

Wanda Plimmer
Cremains '01

George Plimpton
Just Visiting '01
Little Man Tate '91
Volunteers '85

Martha Plimpton
Pecker (John Waters Collec-
tion Vol. 1) '98
The Goonies '85

Maya Plisetskaya
Tchaikovsky '71

Jack Plotnick
Say It Isn't So '01

Hilda Plowright
Separate Tables '58

Joan Plowright
Back to the Secret Garden
'01
Britannia Hospital '82

Amanda Plummer
Seven Days to Live '01
Joe versus the Volcano '90
The Hotel New Hampshire
'84
The World according to Garp
'82

Christopher Plummer
American Tragedy '00
Dracula 2000 '00
Hollywood Screen Tests: Take
1 '00
Possessed '00
Blackheart '98
Hanover Street '79

Glenn Plummer
Love Beat the Hell outta Me
'00
Showgirls '95
Colors '88

Fernando Poe, Jr.
The Ravagers '65
Walls of Hell '64

Ken Pogue
Crossfire Trail '01
Out of Time '00
The 6th Day [2 SE] '00
The Amy Fisher Story '93

Larry Poindexter
Poison '01

Deep Water '99

Sidney Poitier
To Sir, with Love '67
The Defiant Ones '58

Sydney Tamiia Poitier
True Crime '99

Alan Polanski
The Winslow Boy '98

Beverly Polcyn
Not Another Teen Movie '01

Jon Polito
The Man Who Wasn't There
'01
Mimic 2 '01
Blankman '94
Highlander [Anchor Bay] '86

Boleslav Polivka
Divided We Fall '00

Cheryl Pollack
Art House '98

Sydney Pollack
Random Hearts '99
Husbands and Wives '92

Kevin Pollak
Dr. Dolittle 2 '01
3000 Miles to Graceland '01
The Wedding Planner '01
House Arrest '96
That Thing You Do! '96
The Usual Suspects [MGM
SE] '95
Wayne's World 2 '93
Willow '88

Michael J. Pollard
Along for the Ride '00
The Odyssey '97
Split Second '92
Motorama '91
Dick Tracy '90
Four of the Apocalypse '75

Luciano Pollentin
Knives of the Avenger '65

Sarah Polley
Love Come Down '00

David Pollock
The Bad News Bears Go to
Japan '78
The Bad News Bears in
Breaking Training '77
The Bad News Bears '76

Teri Polo
Domestic Disturbance '01
The House of the Spirits '93

John Polson
Idiot Box '97

Max Pomeranc
Searching for Bobby Fischer
'93

Ada Pometti
Lady Frankenstein '72

Eusebio Poncela
A Shadow You Soon Will Be
'94

Brent Ponder
Inbred Rednecks '97

Clara Pontoppidan
Haxan: Witchcraft through the
Ages '22

DJ Pooh
The Wash '01

Bray Poor
Two Ninas '00
Anima '98

Will Pope
Trailer, the Movie '99

The Road to Morocco [Universal] '42
The Ghost Breakers '40
The Road to Singapore '40

Colin Quinn
Crocodile Dundee 2 '88

Francesco Quinn
Top Dog '95

J.C. Quinn
Turner and Hooch '89

Ken Quinn
Abraxas: Guardian of the Universe [BFS] '90

Louis Quinn
Superchick '71

Martha Quinn
Motorama '91

Luis Quiroz
Brain Drain '98

Nguyen Nhu Quynh
The Vertical Ray of the Sun '00

Francesco Rabal
Belle de Jour '67

Ellis Rabb
The Royal Family '77

Pamela Rabe
The Well '97

Kazimir Rabetsky
Come and See '85

Maryann Rachford
Thief in the Night '72

Thom Rachford
Thief in the Night '72

Alan Rachins
Showgirls '95

Victoria Racimo
Prophecy '79

Daniel Radcliffe
Harry Potter and the Sorcerer's Stone '01
The Tailor of Panama '00

Ronald Radd
The Iceman Cometh '60

Natalie Radford
Agent Red '00

Gilda Radner
Haunted Honeymoon '86

Jerzy Radziwilowicz
Secret Defense '98

John Rae
Morgan: A Suitable Case for Treatment '66

Nicole Rae
Smiling Fish & Goat on Fire '99

Stephen Rae
Idiot Box '97

Bob Rafelson
Head '68

Chips Rafferty
Fighting Rats of Tobruk '44

George Raft
Ocean's 11 '60
Outpost in Morocco '49
Stage Door Canteen '43

Ed Ragazzino
Remember Pearl Harbor: America Taken by Surprise '01 (N)

Rah Digga
13 Ghosts '01

Rahzel
Brooklyn Babylon '00

Steve Railsback
The Sinister Saga '00
The Stunt Man '80

Sam Raimi
Evil Dead [LE] '83

Theodore (Ted) Raimi
Evil Dead [LE] '83

Ruggero Raimondi
Don Giovanni '79

Douglas Rain
Larceny '91

Jackson Raine
The Diamond of Jeru '01

Frances Raines
Breeders '86

Pam Raines
Bar Girls '95

Claude Rains
Now, Voyager '42

Christopher Ralph
The Skulls 2 '02

Sheryl Lee Ralph
Oliver & Company '88 (V)

Esther Ralston
Pre-Code Hollywood: Vol. 4, "Lonely Wives" '31

Fernando Ramallo
Nico and Dani '00

Dack Rambo
Hit Lady '74

Harold Ramis
Stealing Home '88
Stripes '81

Dee Dee Ramone
Rock 'n' Roll High School [New Concorde SE] '79

Joey Ramone
Rock 'n' Roll High School [New Concorde SE] '79

Johnny Ramone
Rock 'n' Roll High School [New Concorde SE] '79

Marky Ramone
Rock 'n' Roll High School [New Concorde SE] '79

Rudy Ramos
Colors '88

Charlotte Rampling
Spy Game '01
Aberdeen '00
Under the Sand '00
Hammers over the Anvil '91

Anne Ramsey
Throw Momma from the Train '87
The Goonies '85
Goin' South '78
The Boy in the Plastic Bubble [2] '76

David Ramsey
Pay It Forward '00

Logan Ramsey
The Beast Within '82
Head '68

Sid Rancer
The Wolfman '82

Brick Randall
The Erotic Rites of Countess Dracula '01

Stephanie Randall
The Prisoner '68

Tony Randall
Robin and the 7 Hoods '64
Let's Make Love '60

Ron Randell
Savage Pampas '66

Mary Jo Randle
The Hollow Man [2 SB] '00

Theresa Randle
Space Jam [2 EE] '96
Beverly Hills Cop 3 '94

Jane Randolph
Railroaded '47

John Randolph
Frances [Anchor Bay] '82
Seconds '66

Salvo Randone
Spirits of the Dead [Criterion] '68

Tim Ransom
Courage Under Fire '96

Caleb Ranson
Forgotten '99

Michael Rapaport
Dr. Dolittle 2 '01 (V)
The 6th Day [2 SE] '00
Higher Learning '94
The Scout '94
Zebrahead '92

David Rappaport
The Bride '85

Phylicia Rashad
The Visit '00

Eddy Rasimi
Le Trou '59

Fritz Rasp
Diary of a Lost Girl '29
The Love of Jeanne Ney '27

Ivan Rassimov
Shock '79
Planet of the Vampires '65

Thalmus Rasulala
Bucktown '75

Jeremy Ratchford
Angel Eyes '01
Fly Away Home [2 SE] '96

Basil Rathbone
Son of Frankenstein '39

Peter Ratray
Stonewall '95

John Ratzenberger
Tick Tock '00
House 2: The Second Story '87

Siegfried Rauch
Patton [2] '70

Mike Raven
Lust for a Vampire '71

Stark Raven
Shatter Dead '01

Raven-Symone
Dr. Dolittle 2 '01

Gina Ravera
The Temptations '98
Showgirls '95

Adrian Rawlins
Forgotten '99
Woman in Black '89

Lou Rawls
Showdown '94

Aldo Ray
Star Slammer '87
The Secret of NIMH '82 (V)
Psychic Killer '75
God's Little Acre '58

Martha Raye
The Big Broadcast of 1938 '38
College Swing '38

Gary Raymond
Scarlett '94
Look Back in Anger '58

Richard Raymond
Rats '83

Usher Raymond
Texas Rangers '01

Stephen Rea
The Musketeer '01
On the Edge '00

Ronald Reagan
We Take New Guinea '?0s (N)
Tennessee's Partner '55
The Stillwell Road '47 (N)

Thomas Reardon
Superchick '71

James Reason
Monsters Crash the Pajama Party Spook Show Spectacular '65

Sandra Reaves-Phillips
Round Midnight '86

Craig Reay
Red Rock West '93

James Rebhorn
White Sands '92

Lance Reddick
Don't Say a Word '01

Robert Redford
The Last Castle '01
New York in the Fifties '01
Spy Game '01
Indecent Proposal '93
Out of Africa '85
The Iceman Cometh '60

Corin Redgrave
Ultraviolet '98
The Charge of the Light Brigade '68

Jemma Redgrave
The Acid House '98

Lynn Redgrave
How to Kill Your Neighbor's Dog '01
Deeply '99
Girl with Green Eyes '64

Michael Redgrave
Heidi '67

Vanessa Redgrave
Jack and the Beanstalk: The Real Story '01
The Pledge '00
Wilde '97
The House of the Spirits '93
The Charge of the Light Brigade '68
Morgan: A Suitable Case for Treatment '66

Juli Reding
Tormented '60

Nick Reding
In Love and War '01

Christian Redl
The Trio '97

Redman
How High '01

Amanda Redman
Sexy Beast '00

George Reed
Strange Illusion '45

Jerry Reed
Survivors '83

Kira Reed
Alien Exotica: The Secret Files '98
Lady in Blue '96

Oliver Reed
The Lady and the Highwayman '89
Sell Out '76

Pamela Reed
Proof of Life '00
Cadillac Man '90

Robert Reed
The Boy in the Plastic Bubble [2] '76

Norman Reedus
Bad Seed '00
Sand '00

Angharad Rees
The Wolves of Kromer '98

Roger Rees
Sudden Manhattan '96

Della Reese
Mama Flora's Family '98
Harlem Nights '89
Psychic Killer '75

Christopher Reeve
Speechless '94
The Remains of the Day '93
The Aviator '85

Keanu Reeves
Hardball '01
Sweet November '01
The Gift '00
Johnny Mnemonic [2 SB] '95
Bram Stoker's Dracula [SB] '92
Bill & Ted's Bogus Journey '91
Point Break '91
Bill & Ted's Excellent Adventure '89

Saskia Reeves
Dune [2 SE] '00

Steve Reeves
The White Warrior '61

Steve Reevis
The Last of the Dogmen '95

Laura Regan
Someone Like You '01

Vincent Regan
Black Knight '01
The Point Men '01

Duncan Regehr
Blood Surf '00

Benoit Regent
Gang of Four '88

Meg Register
Demonia '90

James Reichmuth
Fishing with Gandhi '98

John Reichmuth
Fishing with Gandhi '98

Alex Reid
Arachnid '01

Anne Reid
Liam '00

Carl Benton Reid
The Little Foxes [MGM] '41

Ella Reid
Caged Heat '74

Elliott Reid
Inherit the Wind '60

Frances Reid
Seconds '66

Terence Rigby
Plunkett & Macleane '98

Diana Rigg
Victoria & Albert '01
The Great Muppet Caper '81
Theatre of Blood '73
On Her Majesty's Secret Service '69

Mitchell Riggs
Spin the Bottle '97

Michael Riley
Because Why? '93

Shane Rimmer
Out of Africa '85
The People That Time Forgot '77

Vince Rimmer
Careful '92

Noelle Rimmington
Macbeth '71

Ita Rina
Atomic War Bride / This Is Not a Test '60

Meredith Rinehart
The Erotic Rites of Countess Dracula '01

Molly Ringwald
Not Another Teen Movie '01
Requiem for Murder '99
Some Folks Call It a Sling Blade '94
Spacehunter: Adventures in the Forbidden Zone '83

David Rintoul
Horatio Hornblower: The Adventure Continues '01

Marjorie (Reardon) Riordan
Stage Door Canteen '43

Michael Ripper
The Scars of Dracula '70
The Mummy '59

Leon Rippy
The Patriot [2 SB] '00
Beyond the Law '92

Michael Rispoli
Two Family House '99

Bob (Kid Rock) Ritchie
Joe Dirt '01

John Ritter
Panic '01
Stay Tuned '92

Thelma Ritter
A Hole in the Head '59

Geoffrey Rivas
Luminarias '99

Joan Rivers
Whispers: An Elephant's Tale '00 (V)
Spaceballs '87
The Muppets Take Manhattan '84

Leslie Ann Rivers
Kidnapped Coed '77

Victor Rivers
Fatal Blade '00

Andrea Rivette
Jekyll & Hyde: The Musical '01

John Rizzi
Raven's Ridge '97

Adrian R'Mante
All or Nothing '01

Pat Roach
Willow '88

Glen Roald
Timecop '94

Adam Roarke
The Stunt Man '80

Jason Robards, Sr.
The Fatal Hour '40

Jason Robards, Jr.
Comes a Horseman '78
A Moon for the Misbegotten '75
The Iceman Cometh '60

Sam Robards
A.I.: Artificial Intelligence '01
Life As a House '01
Casualties of War '89

Glenn Robbins
Lantana '01

Herb Robbins
The Doll Squad '73

Tim Robbins
Cadillac Man '90
Bull Durham [MGM SE] '88
Fraternity Vacation '85

David Roberson
House Party 4: Down to the Last Minute '00

Alec Roberts
13 Ghosts '01

Christian Roberts
To Sir, with Love '67

Doris Roberts
All over the Guy '01

Emma Roberts
Blow '01

Eric Roberts
Rough Air '02
Fast Sofa '01
The King's Guard '01
Raptor '01
Sanctimony '01
Luck of the Draw '00
T.N.T. '01
The Odyssey '97
The Coca-Cola Kid '84

Francesca Roberts
The Heart of Dixie '89

Glenn Roberts
The Crater Lake Monster '77

Ian Roberts
Bring It On '00

Julia Roberts
America's Sweethearts '01
The Mexican '01
Ocean's Eleven '01
Runaway Bride '99
My Best Friend's Wedding [2 SE] '97
Hook '91

Pauline Roberts
The Pledge '00

Rachel Roberts
When a Stranger Calls '79
Saturday Night and Sunday Morning '60

Roy Roberts
Borderline '50
He Walked by Night [BFS] '48
Guadalcanal Diary '43

Scott Roberts
Chicks, Man '99

Tanya Roberts
Beastmaster '82

Thayer Roberts
This Is Not a Test '62

Tony Roberts
Richard Rodgers: The Sweetest Sound '01 (N)
Popcorn '89
18 Again! '88
Radio Days '87
Hannah and Her Sisters '86
A Midsummer Night's Sex Comedy '82
Play It Again, Sam '72

Lisa Roberts Gillan
Runaway Bride '99

Cliff Robertson
Midway [Universal CE] '76
Obsession '76
Too Late the Hero '70
The Devil's Brigade '68

Iain Robertson
Plunkett & Macleane '98

Jenny Robertson
Bull Durham [MGM SE] '88

Kathleen Robertson
Scary Movie 2 '01

Paul Robeson
Big Fella '37
King Solomon's Mines '37
Song of Freedom / Big Fella '36

Kim Robillard
Ali '01
Breakdown '96

Liliane Robin
Breathless '59

Sophie Robin
A Tale of Springtime '89

Herb Robins
The Worm Eaters '77

Laila Robins
Oxygen '99
True Crime '99

Andrew (Andy) Robinson
Dirty Harry [2] '71

Ann (Robin) Robinson
Attack from Mars '88

Eartha D. Robinson
Daughters of the Dust '91

Edward G. Robinson
MacKenna's Gold '69
Robin and the 7 Hoods '64
A Hole in the Head '59
Key Largo '48
The Stranger [Delta/Laserlight] '46

Ian Robinson
Replicant '01

Jay Robinson
The Robe '53

Josh Robinson
The Sexy Sixth Sense '01

Roger Robinson
Burnzy's Last Call '95

Wendy Raquel Robinson
Two Can Play That Game '01

Jorge Robles
Mexico City '01

May Robson
Lady for a Day '33

Wayne Robson
Harlan County War '00

Alex Rocco
The Wedding Planner '01
That Thing You Do! '96
Return to Horror High '87
The Stunt Man '80

Mario Roccuzzo
Earth vs. the Spider '01

Jean Rochefort
The Closet '00
The Clockmaker '73

Robin Rochelle
Sorority Babes in the Slimeball Bowl-A-Rama '87

Debbie Rochon
Dead and Rotting '02
Play-Mate of the Apes '02
Witchouse 3: Demon Fire '01
American Nightmare '00
Troma's Edge TV: Vol. 1 '00

Lela Rochon
The Big Hit [2 SB] '98
Gang Related '96

Martine Rochon
Because Why? '93

Chris Rock
A.I.: Artificial Intelligence '01 (V)
Down to Earth '01
Jay and Silent Bob Strike Back '01
Osmosis Jones '01 (V)
Pootie Tang '01
Dogma '01
Beverly Hills Cop 2 '87

Charles Rocket
Fraternity Vacation '85

Jeffrey Rockland
Doctor Zhivago '65

Sam Rockwell
Heist '01

Jay Rodan
The Caveman's Valentine '01
The Lost Battalion '01

Ebbe Rode
Gertrud '64

Nina Pens Rode
Gertrud '64

Karel Roden
15 Minutes '01

Anton Rodgers
Impromptu '90
Dirty Rotten Scoundrels [MGM] '88

Michael E. Rodgers
Uncorked '98

Sarah Rodgers
Point of View '00

Violeta Rodrigues
Things I Left in Havanna '97

Litico Rodriguez
A Paradise under the Stars '99

Michelle Rodriguez
The Fast and the Furious '01

Paul Rodriguez
Ali '01
Crocodile Dundee in Los Angeles '01
Rat Race '01
Tortilla Soup '01

Ezequiel Rodriquez
The Road '00

Norman Rodway
The Mirror Cracked from Side to Side '92

Daniel Roebuck
A Glimpse of Hell '01
Money Talks '97
Cave Girl '85

Gabriela Roel
Garden of Eden '94

Gretel Roenfeldt
Take It to the Limit '00

William Roerick
The Wasp Woman [2] '59

Maurice Roeves
Beautiful Creatures '00
Forgive and Forget '99
The Acid House '98
Hidden Agenda '90

Alva Rogers
Daughters of the Dust '91

Ginger Rogers
Hidden Hollywood 2: More Treasures from the 20th Century Fox Vaults '99
Cinderella '64
Monkey Business '52

Jean Rogers
Flash Gordon: The Deadly Ray from Mars '39
Flash Gordon: Spaceship to the Unknown '36

Mimi Rogers
Ginger Snaps '00
Cruel Intentions 2 '99
White Sands '92
Desperate Hours '90

Paul Rogers
The Mark '61

Reg Rogers
Runaway Bride '99

Wayne Rogers
Ghosts of Mississippi '96

Jaromir Rogoz
Ecstasy '33

Claudia Rojas
Life Is to Whistle '98

Maria Rojo
Break of Dawn '88

Gilbert Roland
Incident on a Dark Street '72
The Bad and the Beautiful '52
Captain Kidd [Marengo] '45
The Plastic Age '25

Guy Rolfe
And Now the Screaming Starts [SE] '73
Mr. Sardonicus '61

Esther Rolle
Scarlett '94

Georges Rollin
The Sadistic Baron Von Klaus '62

Henry Rollins
Reckless and Wild '02
Time Lapse '01
Johnny Mnemonic [2 SB] '95

Mark Rolston
Letters from a Killer '98
Prancer '89

Candice Roman
The Big Bird Cage '72

Andy Romano
Unlawful Entry '92

Christy Romano
Looking for an Echo '99

Jena Romano
Voyeur.com '00

Rino Romano
Roughnecks: Starship Troopers Chronicles—The Klendathu Campaign '02 (V)
Roughnecks: Starship Troopers Chronicles—The Homefront Campaign '99 (V)

Stephanie Romanov
Thirteen Days '00

Richard Romanus
Cops and Robbersons '94

Lina Romay
Revenge in the House of
Usher '82

Piet Romer
Business Is Business '71

Cesar Romero
Batman: The Movie '66
Ocean's 11 '60
The Lost Continent '51
The Little Princess [Marengo]
'39

George A. Romero
Night of the Living Dead [Elite
ME] '68

Rebecca Romijn-Stamos
Rollerball '02

Eric Romley
Little Shots of Happiness '97

Hugh Romney
The Fat Black Pussycat '63

Maurice Ronet
Don Juan (Or If Don Juan
Were a Woman) '73
Purple Noon '60

Linda Ronstadt
Paul Simon: Graceland '97

Michael Roof
Black Hawk Down '01

Michael Rooker
Replicant '01
The 6th Day [2 SE] '00
The Replacement Killers [2
SE] '98
Deceiver '97
Tombstone [2] '93

Mickey Rooney
It's a Mad, Mad, Mad, Mad
World '63
Requiem for a Heavyweight
'62

Thorkild Roose
Day of Wrath '43

Stephen (Steve) Root
Crocodile Dundee 2 '88

Pamela Rosas
The Fear Chamber '68

Gabrielle Rose
Timecop '94
Speaking Parts '89
Family Viewing / Next of Kin
'87

George Rose
The Flesh and the Fiends '60

Jamie Rose
Holiday in the Sun '01

Leigh Rose
Southern Man '99

Roseanne
She-Devil '89

Danny Rosen
Stranger than Paradise '84

Michael Rosenbaum
Sweet November '01

Alan Rosenberg
The Temptations '98

Joseph Rosenberg
I Am Sam '01

Clara Rosenthal
The Projectionist '71

Sheila Rosenthal
Not without My Daughter '90

Hrithik Roshan
Mission Kashmir '00

Justin Rosniak
Sweet Talker '91

Beverly Ross
S.O.S. Titanic '79

Chelcie Ross
The Gift '00
Basic Instinct [2 SE] '92
Bill & Ted's Bogus Journey
'91

Diana Ross
Free to Be...You and Me '74

Gene Ross
Halloween 4: The Return of
Michael Myers [MGM LE]
'88

Herbert Ross
Play It Again, Sam '72

Howard (Red) Ross
The New Gladiators '83

Katharine Ross
Donnie Darko '01
The Stepford Wives [2 SE]
'75

Matt Ross
Stephen King's Rose Red '02
Just Visiting '01

Shavar Ross
Friday the 13th, Part 5: A
New Beginning '85

Shirley Ross
The Big Broadcast of 1938
'38

Ted Ross
Stealing Home '88

Isabella Rossellini
Left Luggage '98
The Odyssey '97
Tales from the Crypt: Robert
Zemeckis Collection '95
Immortal Beloved '94
Cousins '89

Carol Rossen
The Fury '78
The Stepford Wives [2 SE]
'75

Leo Rossi
One Night at McCool's '01
The Accused '88

**Giacomo "Jack" Rossi-
Stuart**
Knives of the Avenger '65
The Last Man on Earth '64

Norman Rossington
The Charge of the Light
Brigade '68
Saturday Night and Sunday
Morning '60

Leonard Rossiter
Britannia Hospital '82

Angelo Rossitto
The Corpse Vanishes '42

Rick Rossovich
The Terminator [2 SE] '84

Emmy Rossum
An American Rhapsody '01

Maggie Roswell
The Simpsons: The Complete
First Season '89 (V)
Midnight Madness '80

Gene Roth
Attack of the Giant Leeches
[Marengo] '59

Tim Roth
The Musketeer '01
Planet of the Apes '01
The Legend of 1900 '98
Deceiver '97

Bendt Rothe
Gertrud '64

Teryl Rothery
Mr. Rice's Secret '00

Will Rothhaar
Hearts in Atlantis '01

John Rothman
Say It Isn't So '01

Cynthia Rothrock
Sworn to Justice '97
Tiger Claws '91
Righting Wrongs '86

Richard Roundtree
Corky Romano '01
An Eye for an Eye '81
Firehouse '72

Mickey Rourke
The Pledge '00
White Sands '92
Desperate Hours '90
Wild Orchid '90
Diner '82

Catherine Rouvel
Va Savoir '01

Jean Rouveral
Bar 20 Rides Again '35

Josef Rovensky
Diary of a Lost Girl '29

Kelly Rowan
Candyman 2: Farewell to the
Flesh '94

Brad Rowe
Christina's House '99

Kimberly Rowe
Second to Die '02
Adventures of Justine '00

Nicholas (Nick) Rowe
Shackleton '02

Rodney Rowland
Dancing at the Blue Iguana
'00
The 6th Day [2 SE] '00

Richard Roxburgh
Moulin Rouge [SE] '01

Maxim Roy
Stalker '98

Cornell (Kofi) Royal
Daughters of the Dust '91

Lionel Royce
My Favorite Blonde '42
The Road to Zanzibar '41

Roselyn Royce
Retrievers '82

Virginia Roye
The Road to Ruin '28

Selena Royle
The Harvey Girls '46

Christopher Rozycki
Truly, Madly, Deeply '91

Jennifer Rubin
Amazons and Gladiators '01
Sanctimony '01

Saul Rubinek
Rush Hour 2 '01

Zelda Rubinstein
Anguish '88

Ingrid Rubio
Not Love Just Frenzy '96

Jack Rubio
Loser '97

Jose Rubio
Dr. Orloff's Monster '64

Richard Ruccolo
All over the Guy '01
Luck of the Draw '00

Alan Ruck
Three Fugitives '89

Paul Rudd
The Great Gatsby '01
Wet Hot American Summer
'01
The Object of My Affection
'98
The Locusts '97

Herbert Rudley
The Young Lions '58

Gerard Rudolf
Styx '00

Lars Rudolph
The Princess and the Warrior
'00

Mercedes Ruehl
Lost in Yonkers '93
Radio Days '87
84 Charing Cross Road '86

Mark Ruel
With Friends Like These '90

Mark Ruffalo
The Last Castle '01

Leonora Ruffo
Goliath and the Dragon '61

Charlie Ruggles
The Parent Trap '61

Vyto Ruginis
The Fast and the Furious '01
The Glass House '01

**Anthony Michael
Ruivivar**
Race the Sun '96

Janice Rule
American Flyers '85

Sig Rumann
House of Frankenstein '44

Jenny Runacre
The Final Programme '73

Tygh Runyan
Cruel and Unusual '01

Jennifer Runyon
18 Again! '88

Al Ruscio
Boss of Bosses '99

Elizabeth Ruscio
Letters from a Killer '98

Barbara Rush
Moon of the Wolf '72
Robin and the 7 Hoods '64
The Young Lions '58
It Came from Outer Space
'53
When Worlds Collide '51

Deborah Rush
The Purple Rose of Cairo '85

Geoffrey Rush
Lantana '01
The Tailor of Panama '00

Richard Rush
The Sinister Saga '00

Claire Rushbrook
Plunkett & Macleane '98

Jared Rushton
Pet Sematary 2 '92

Sheila Ruskin
A Caribbean Mystery / The
Mirror Cracked from Side
to Side '89

Morgan Rusler
The Tomorrow Man '01

Robert Rusler
Sometimes They Come Back
'91
Vamp '86

William Russ
Wanted: Dead or Alive '86

Clive Russell
Mists of Avalon '01

Elizabeth Russell
The Corpse Vanishes '42

John Russell
The Outlaw Josey Wales [2]
'76
Rio Bravo '59

Ken Russell
The Russia House '90

Kurt Russell
3000 Miles to Graceland '01
Vanilla Sky '01
Breakdown '96
Tombstone [2] '93
Unlawful Entry '92
Used Cars '80

Lucy Russell
Following '99

Raymond Russell
His Majesty, the Scarecrow of
Oz '14

Robert Russell
Dune [2 SE] '00

Theresa Russell
Earth vs. the Spider '01
Luckytown '00

James Russo
Double Deception '01
Pendulum '01
Jimmy Zip '00
Extremities '86
Beverly Hills Cop [CE] '84

John A. Russo
Night of the Living Dead [Elite
ME] '68

Leon Russom
Silver Bullet '85

Kelly Rutherford
Acceptable Risk '01

Barbara Rutting
Town without Pity '61

Basil Ruysdael
Walt Disney Treasures: Davy
Crockett '01

David Ryall
Truly, Madly, Deeply '91

Christopher Ryan
American Nightmare '00

Ger Ryan
Forgive and Forget '99

Jeri Ryan
Dracula 2000 '00

John P. Ryan
White Sands '92

Marisa Ryan
Riding in Cars with Boys '01
Wet Hot American Summer
'01

Meg Ryan
Kate & Leopold '01
Proof of Life '00
Hurlyburly '98
Courage Under Fire '96
Flesh and Bone '93
Joe versus the Volcano '90

Mitchell Ryan
Speechless '94
Magnum Force '73

Dark Shadows: DVD Collection 1 '67

Paddy Ryan
An American Werewolf in London [CE Universal] '81

Robert Ryan
Lawman '71
Anzio '68
God's Little Acre '58

Sheila Ryan
Railroaded '47

Will Ryan
Thumbelina [20th Century Fox] '94 (V)

Linda Rybova
Dark Blue World '01

Christopher Rydell
Flesh and Bone '93

Derek Rydell
Popcorn '89

Alfred Ryder
T-Men '47

Winona Ryder
The Age of Innocence '93
The House of the Spirits '93
Bram Stoker's Dracula [SB] '92
Great Balls of Fire '89
Heathers [2 THX] '89
1969 '89

Mark Rylance
Intimacy '00
Angels and Insects '95
Institue Benjamenta or This Dream People Call Human Life '95

Okubo Ryu
Organ '96

Bruno S
Stroszek '77

Raelyn Saalman
Attack of the 60-Foot Centerfold '95

Daryl Sabara
Spy Kids '01

William Sabatier
The Clockmaker '73

Antonio Sabato, Jr.
Fatal Error '99
The Big Hit [2 SB] '98
Jailbreakers '94

Elham Saboktakin
The Circle '00

Marcel Sabourin
Lilies '96

Sabrina
Satan in High Heels '61

Sabu
The Jungle Book '42

Hossain Sabzian
Close-Up '90

Joseph Sacket
The Worm Eaters '77

William Sadler
Bill & Ted's Bogus Journey '91

Marianne Saegebrecht
Left Luggage '98
The War of the Roses [SE] '89
Bagdad Cafe '88

Issei Sagawa
The Bedroom '92

William Sage
Urbania '00

Melissa Sagemiller
Get over It! '01
Soul Survivors '01

Ray Sager
Just for the Hell of It '68
Blast-Off Girls / Just for the Hell of It '67

Laura Saglio
Perfect Love '96

Ludivine Sagnier
Water Drops on Burning Rocks '99

Rosario Sagrav
Garden of Eden '94

Elena Sahagun
Firetrap '01

Yam Sai-kun
Iron Monkey [Miramax] '93

Eric Saiet
Body Count '97

Eva Marie Saint
Nothing in Common '86
On the Waterfront '54

Julie St. Clair
Extreme Limits '01

Michael St. Clair
Von Ryan's Express '65

Mary St. Feint
Scare Their Pants Off / Satan's Bed '68

Michael St. Gerard
Great Balls of Fire '89
Hairspray (John Waters Collection Vol. 1) '88

Soledad St. Hilaire
crazy/beautiful '01

Raymond St. Jacques
The Evil That Men Do '84

Susan St. James
S.O.S. Titanic '79

Al "Fuzzy" St. John
Riders of Destiny [Columbia] '33

Betta St. John
The City of the Dead '60

Howard St. John
Strait-Jacket '64

John St. John
Lady in Blue '96

Trevor St. John
The King's Guard '01

Irma St. Paul
Fever '99

Lucile Saint-Simon
Les Bonnes Femmes '60

Sachio Sakai
Godzilla, King of the Monsters [Goodtimes] '56

Amy Sakasitz
House Arrest '96

Akino Sakurako
Sadistic City '93

Leopold Salcedo
Raiders of Leyte Gulf '63

Theresa Saldana
The Evil That Men Do '84

Zoe Saldana
Get over It! '01

Dunia Saldivar
Amores Perros '00

Robert Sale
Ali '01

Norman Salect
Loser '97

Dahlia Salem
Return to Cabin by the Lake '01

Kario Salem
Triumph of the Spirit '89

Pamela Salem
Never Say Never Again '83

Meredith Salenger
The Journey of Natty Gann '85

Nicola Salerno
Shock '79

Chucho Salinas
Doctor of Doom '62

Jorge Salinas
Amores Perros '00

Raul Salinas
Drive By '01

Diane Salinger
The Butcher's Wife '91

Emmanuel Salinger
Kill by Inches '99
La Sentinelle '92

Albert Salmi
Breaking In '89
Empire of the Ants '77
Lawman '71

Lyda Salmonava
The Golem '20

Louis Salou
Children of Paradise '44

Jennifer Salt
Play It Again, Sam '72

Renato Salvatori
Rocco and His Brothers '60

Aldo Sambrel
Killer Barbys '96

Emma Samms
The Lady and the Highwayman '89

Tatyana Samoilova
The Cranes Are Flying '57

Robert Sampson
Re-Animator [2 ME] '84

Will Sampson
The Outlaw Josey Wales [2] '76

David Samson
Polyester (John Waters Collection Vol. 2) '81

Joanne Samuel
Nightmaster '87
Mad Max [MGM SE] '80

Kwai San
10 Magnificent Killers '77

Lu Man San
The Scent of Green Papaya '93

Laura San Giacomo
Quigley Down Under '90

Henry Sanada
Sure Death: Revenge '87
Shogun's Ninja '83

Mario Ernesto Sanchez
Proof of Life '00

Marisol Padilla Sanchez
Traffic [Criterion] '00
Fever '99

Roselyn Sanchez
Rush Hour 2 '01

Aitana Sanchez-Gijon
Jealousy '99

Fernando (Fernand) Sancho
Orloff and the Invisible Man '70

Jose Sancho
Arachnid '01

Barry Sand
Eddie and the Cruisers '83

Michele Sand
Don Juan (Or If Don Juan Were a Woman) '73

Paul Sand
Can't Stop the Music '80

Dominique Sanda
The Crimson Rivers '01
The Garden of the Finzi-Continis '71

George Sanders
Doomwatch '72
Lured '47
Rebecca [Criterion] '40
The Son of Monte Cristo '40

Harland "Colonel" Sanders
Blast-Off Girls / Just for the Hell of It '67

Jay O. Sanders
Along Came a Spider '00
Boss of Bosses '99
Three Wishes '95
Angels in the Outfield '94

Martyn Sanderson
Poor Man's Orange '87
The Harp in the South '86

William Sanderson
Crossfire Trail '01
Sometimes They Come Back '91

Adam Sandler
Airheads '94

Miguel (Michael) Sandoval
Blow '01
Things You Can Tell Just by Looking at Her '00
Mrs. Winterbourne '96
White Sands '92

Stefania Sandrelli
Stealing Beauty '96

Billy (Billie) Sands
Harrad Experiment '73

Julian Sands
Stephen King's Rose Red '02
Impromptu '90

Ellen Sandweiss
Evil Dead [LE] '83

Erskine Sanford
Citizen Kane '41

Garwin Sanford
Mr. Rice's Secret '00
Unforgettable '96

Thomas Sangster
The Miracle of the Cards '00

Carles Sans
Love Can Seriously Damage Your Health '96

Santanon
The Fear Chamber '68

Beatriz Santiago
Not Love Just Frenzy '96

Zak Santiago Alam
Late Night Sessions '99

Ruben Santiago-Hudson
Domestic Disturbance '01
American Tragedy '00

Sebastian Santis
Chac: The Rain God '74

Reni Santoni
Bad Boys [Anchor Bay] '83
Dirty Harry [2] '71
Anzio '68

Michele Santopietro
Two Family House '99

Isabel Santos
Life Is to Whistle '98

Joe Santos
Beyond Suspicion '00
Trial by Jury '94
Mo' Money '92

Michael Sanville
First Turn On [DC] '83

Jorge Sanz
Why Do They Call It Love When They Mean Sex? '92

Eric Sapp
Little Shots of Happiness '97

Mia Sara
Jack and the Beanstalk: The Real Story '01
Timecop '94
Legend [UE] '86

Richard Sarafian
Dr. Dolittle 2 '01 (V)

Chris Sarandon
Perfume '01
The Princess Bride [2 SE] '87
Cuba '79

Susan Sarandon
Joseph Campbell Mythos '97
The January Man '89
Bull Durham [MGM SE] '88
Sweet Hearts Dance '88
Atlantic City '81
Joe '70

Rosa Maria Sarda
Why Do They Call It Love When They Mean Sex? '92

Michael Sarrazin
Lena's Holiday '90

Peter Sarsgaard
The Center of the World '01

Gailard Sartain
Ali '01
Speechless '94

Fabio Sartor
The Luzhin Defence '00

Jacqueline Sassard
Accident '67

Cat Sasson
Bloodfist 6: Ground Zero '94

Ines Sastre
Druids '01

Tura Satana
The Doll Squad '73

Koichi Sato
Gonin '95

Yasue Sato
The Dimension Travelers '98

Kenpachiro Satsuma
Godzilla vs. Destroyah '95

Barry Sattels
Fatal Blade '00

Jeff Saumier
The Kid '97

Harold Saunders
Red Zone Cuba '66

Jennifer Saunders
Absolutely Fabulous: Series 4 '01
Absolutely Fabulous: Series 1 '94

Jean Seberg
Paint Your Wagon '69
Breathless '59

Septula Sebogodi
The Long Run '00

Kyle Secor
The Heart of Dixie '89

Jon Seda
Double Bang '01

Neil Sedaka
Playgirl Killer '66
Sting of Death '65

Margaret Seddon
Mr. Deeds Goes to Town '36

Kyra Sedgwick
Kansas '88

Natalya Sedykh
Father Frost '66

Xenia Seeberg
Lexx Series 2, Vol. 1 '98

Jake Seeley
Ratz '99

Ilies Sefraoui
Petits Freres '00

George Segal
Look Who's Talking Now '93
A Touch of Class '73
The Owl and the Pussycat '70

Gilles Segal
Topkapi '64

Pamela Segall
Recess Christmas: Miracle
   on Third Street '01 (V)
Recess: School's Out '01 (V)
Say Anything [SE] '89

Jason Segel
Slackers '02

Santiago Segura
Killer Barbys '96

Francoise Seigner
The Wild Child '70

Mathilde Seigner
With a Friend Like Harry '00

Johnny Sekka
The Bloodsuckers '70
Khartoum '66

David Selby
Intersection '93

Nicholas Selby
Macbeth '71

Marian Seldes
Town and Country '01

Tom Selleck
Crossfire Trail '01
Running Mates '00
Quigley Down Under '90
Three Men and a Little Lady
   '90
Three Men and a Baby '87
Midway [Universal CE] '76

Peter Sellers
Murder by Death '76
The Party '68
After the Fox '66

Charles Sellon
Bright Eyes '34
Behind Office Doors '31

Larry Semon
The Wizard of Oz '25

Nandana Sen
Seducing Maarya '99

Noriko Sengoku
The Blind Beast '69

Greg Serano
Road Dogz '00

Rade Serbedzija
Rodgers & Hammerstein's
   South Pacific '01
Snatch [SE] '00

Zoltan Seress
An American Rhapsody '01

Brian Sergent
Meet the Feebles '89 (V)

Assumpta Serna
Wild Orchid '90

Pepe Serna
The Adventures of Buckaroo
   Banzai Across the Eighth
   Dimension [SE] '84

Michel Serrault
Nelly et Monsieur Arnaud '95
La Cage aux Folles 2 '81
La Cage aux Folles '78

Matt Servitto
Two Family House '99

Roshan Seth
Vertical Limit [2 SB] '00
Not without My Daughter '90
Gandhi '82

Peter Settelen
Flambards '78

Matthew Settle
Attraction '00

Joan Severance
Matter of Trust '98
See No Evil, Hear No Evil '89

Rufus Sewell
A Knight's Tale '01
She Creature '01
Uncorked '98
Carrington '95

Brendan Sexton, III
Black Hawk Down '01
Session 9 '01
Pecker (John Waters Collec-
   tion Vol. 1) '98

Coleen Sexton
Jekyll & Hyde: The Musical '01

Anne Seymour
All the King's Men '49

Carolyn Seymour
The Ruling Class '72

Dan Seymour
Abbott and Costello Meet the
   Mummy '55
Key Largo '48

Ralph Seymour
Empire of the Sun '87

Delphine Seyrig
Accident '67

Joseph Shabalala
Paul Simon: Graceland '97

Glenn Shadix
Red Dirt '99
Heathers [2 THX] '89

Feryal Gauhar Shah
Traffik '90

Jamal Shah
Traffik '90

Gary Shail
Quadrophenia '79

Travis Shakespeare
Voyeur.com '00

Tupac Shakur
Tupac Shakur: Thug Angel '02
Gang Related '96

Victoria Shalet
Haunted '95

Tony Shalhoub
The Man Who Wasn't There
   '01
Spy Kids '01
13 Ghosts '01
Gattaca [2 SB] '97

Brendan Shanahan
Me, Myself, and Irene '00

Garry Shandling
Town and Country '01
Hurlyburly '98
The Larry Sanders Show: The
   Complete First Season '92

John Herman Shaner
A Bucket of Blood / Attack of
   the Giant Leeches [Maren-
   go] '59

Frank Shannon
Flash Gordon: The Peril from
   Planet Mongo '40
Flash Gordon: The Purple
   Death from Outer Space
   '40
Flash Gordon: Spaceship to
   the Unknown '36

Harry Shannon
Written on the Wind '56
Citizen Kane '41

Michael Shannon
Pearl Harbor '01
Vanilla Sky '01

Molly Shannon
Osmosis Jones '01
Serendipity '01
Wet Hot American Summer
   '01
Dr. Seuss' How the Grinch
   Stole Christmas '00

Polly Shannon
The Triangle '01

Vicellous Reon Shannon
Dancing in September '00

Abdul Hassan Sharif
Zebrahead '92

Omar Sharif
Catherine the Great '95
Funny Lady '75
MacKenna's Gold '69
Funny Girl '68
Doctor Zhivago '65

Ray Sharkey
Zebrahead '92
Who'll Stop the Rain? '78

Anastasia Sharp
Go Fish '94

Leslie Sharp
From Hell [DLE] '01

William Shatner
Mind Meld: Secrets behind
   the Voyage of a Lifetime
   '01
Osmosis Jones '01 (V)
Bill & Ted's Bogus Journey
   '91
Star Trek 3: The Search for
   Spock '84
Star Trek: The Motion Picture
   [DE] '80
Incident on a Dark Street '72

Mickey Shaughnessy
Pocketful of Miracles '61
Designing Woman '57

Michael Shaun
Creepin' '01

Helen Shaver
Rowing Through '96
Zebrahead '92

Fiona Shaw
Harry Potter and the Sorcerer's Stone '01
Three Men and a Little Lady
   '90

Glen Byam Shaw
Look Back in Anger '58

Martin Shaw
The Last Place on Earth '94
Macbeth '71

Natalie Shaw
Just One Night '00

Robert Shaw
Force 10 from Navarone '78

Stan Shaw
Bingo Long Traveling All-Stars
   & Motor Kings '76

Vinessa Shaw
Corky Romano '01

Dick Shawn
It's a Mad, Mad, Mad, Mad
   World '63

Wallace Shawn
The Curse of the Jade Scorpi-
   on '01
The Prime Gig '00
House Arrest '96
The Princess Bride [2 SE] '87
Radio Days '87
The Hotel New Hampshire
   '84
Strange Invaders '83

Konstantin Shayne
The Stranger
   [Delta/Laserlight] '46

Zhai Nai She
Empire of the Sun '87

John Shea
The Apocalypse Watch '97
Stealing Home '88
Kennedy '83

Katt Shea
Barbarian Queen '85

Harry Shearer
Haunted Castle '01 (V)
The Simpsons: The Complete
   First Season '89 (V)

Ally Sheedy
The Heart of Dixie '89
Short Circuit '86
Bad Boys [Anchor Bay] '83

Gladys Sheehan
Rawhead Rex '87

Charlie Sheen
Good Advice '01
Money Talks '97
Major League 2 '94
Beyond the Law '92
Men at Work '90

Martin Sheen
O '01
Phenomenon—The Lost
   Archives: American Mid-
   night / H.A.A.R.P. '99 (N)
Dillinger and Capone '95
Kennedy '83
Gandhi '82
Apocalypse Now [Redux] '79

Michael Sheen
Wilde '97

Craig Sheffer
Maze '01
Turbulence 3: Heavy Metal
   '00
Turbulence 2: Fear of Flying
   '99
Nightbreed '90

Dean Shek
Snake in the Eagle's Shadow
   '78

Rachel Shelley
Lagaan: Once upon a Time in
   India '01

Adrienne Shelly
Sudden Manhattan '96

Deborah Shelton
Plughead Rewired: Circuitry
   Man 2 '94

Marley Shelton
Bubble Boy '01
On the Borderline '01
Sugar & Spice '01
Valentine '01
The Sandlot '93

Paul Shenar
Best Seller '87

Chien Yueh Sheng
Buddha Assassinator '79

Ben Shenkman
Chasing Sleep '00

Jan Shepard
Attack of the Giant Leeches
   [Marengo] '59

Sam Shepard
Black Hawk Down '01
Shot in the Heart '01
Swordfish '01
The Pledge '00
Frances [Anchor Bay] '82

Steve John Sheperd
Virtual Sexuality '99

Chaz Lamar Shepherd
The Temptations '98

Elizabeth Shepherd
Spreading Ground '01

Jack Shepherd
Lorna Doone '01

John Shepherd
Friday the 13th, Part 5: A
   New Beginning '85

Steve John Shepherd
Forgive and Forget '99

Tiffany Shepis
Troma's Edge TV: Vol. 1 '00

Mark Sheppard
Boa '02

Anthony Sher
Horatio Hornblower '99

Dave Sheridan
Bubble Boy '01
Corky Romano '01
Ghost World '01

Jamey Sheridan
Life As a House '01
Luminous Motion '00
The Ice Storm '97

Kelly Sheridan
Barbie in the Nutcracker '01
   (V)

Richard Sheridan
The Secret of Roan Inish '94

Donna Sherman
Harvesters '02

Kerry Sherman
Satan's Cheerleaders '77

Babette Sherrill
The Death Curse of Tartu /
   Sting of Death '66

Georgina Sherrington
The Worst Witch '98

Arthur Shields
The Daughter of Dr. Jekyll '57

Jeremy Slate
The Devil's Brigade '68

Christian Slater
Hard Cash '01
3000 Miles to Graceland '01
Ferngully '92 (V)
Tales from the Darkside: The Movie '90
Heathers [2 THX] '89

Helen Slater
Nowhere in Sight '01
Lassie '94
Ruthless People '86

Justine Slater
Bar Girls '95

Imogen Slaughter
Elizabeth '02

Bobby Slayton
Bandits '01

Walter Slezak
The Princess and the Pirate '44

Grace Slick
Jackie's Back '99

Hana Slivkoua
The Shop on Main Street '65

Everett Sloane
Citizen Kane '41

Lindsay Sloane
Bring It On '00

Joey Slotnick
The Hollow Man [2 SB] '00

Neva Small
Fiddler on the Roof [2 SE] '71

Jimmy Smallhorne
When the Sky Falls '99

Amy Smart
Rat Race '01

Jean Smart
Scarlett '94

Richard Smedley
Naughty Stewardesses '74

Tava Smiley
A Girl, 3 Guys and a Gun '01
Outta Time '01

Yakov Smirnoff
The Adventures of Buckaroo Banzai Across the Eighth Dimension [SE] '84

Alexis Smith
The Age of Innocence '93

Anna Nicole Smith
Skyscraper '95
To the Limit '95

Brandon Smith
Jeepers Creepers '01

Brooke Smith
Series 7: The Contenders '01
The Silence of the Lambs [MGM SE] '91

Sir C. Aubrey Smith
And Then There Were None [Image] '45
Beyond Tomorrow '40
Rebecca [Criterion] '40

Cameron Smith
The Riff '00

Carolyn Smith
Boundaries '97

Cedric Smith
Sea People '00

Charles Martin Smith
Speechless '94

Cheryl "Rainbeaux" Smith
Caged Heat '74

Craig Smith
Bad Taste [LE] '88

Cynthia Smith
Benji [Ventura] '74

Ebbe Roe Smith
Big Bad Mama 2 '87

Gregory Smith
American Outlaws '01

Hal Smith
Animated Christmas DVD Double Feature '79 (V)

Hillary Bailey Smith
Love Potion 9 '92

Howard Smith
I Bury the Living '58

Jamie Renee Smith
Children of the Corn 4: The Gathering '96

Jason Smith
Hairdo U '02

John W. Smith
Hot Rod Girl '56

Keith Randolph Smith
Fallout '01

Kent Smith
Sayonara '57

Kerr Smith
The Forsaken '01

Kevin Smith
Drawing Flies '02
Jay and Silent Bob Strike Back '01
Dogma [2 SE] '99

Kurtwood Smith
Shelter '98
The Last of the Dogmen '95
The Heart of Dixie '89

Lane Smith
The Scout '94
Frances [Anchor Bay] '82

Lauren Lee Smith
Christy—Return to Cutter Gap '01

Lewis Smith
The Adventures of Buckaroo Banzai Across the Eighth Dimension [SE] '84

Lionel Smith
Galaxina '80

Lois Smith
The Pledge '00

Maggie Smith
Harry Potter and the Sorcer- er's Stone '01
Sister Act '92
Hook '91
California Suite '78
Murder by Death '76

Mel Smith
The Princess Bride [2 SE] '87
Morons from Outer Space '85

Oliver Smith
Hellbound: Hellraiser 2 [2 THX] '88

Patty Smith
Pigkeeper's Daughter / Sassy Sue '75

Paul Smith
Haunted Honeymoon '86

Quinn Smith
The Bad News Bears in Breaking Training '77
The Bad News Bears '76

Riley Smith
Not Another Teen Movie '01

R.W. Smith
Cremains '00

Shawn Smith
It! The Terror from Beyond Space '58

Shawnee Smith
Desperate Hours '90

Terri Susan Smith
Basket Case [2 SE] '82

Will Smith
Ali '01

William Smith
Any Which Way You Can '80
C.C. & Company '70

Yeardley Smith
The Simpsons: The Complete First Season '89 (V)

Bill Smitrovich
Thirteen Days '00
Air Force One [2 SB] '97
Silver Bullet '85

Jimmy Smits
Fires Within '91
Running Scared '86

Innokenti Smoktunovsky
Tchaikovsky '71

Aaron Smolinksi
Wishmaster 3: Beyond the Gates of Hell '01

JB Smoove
Pootie Tang '01

Dick Smothers
Mr. Bill Goes to Hollywood / Mr. Bill Does Vegas '01

Tom Smothers
Mr. Bill Goes to Hollywood / Mr. Bill Does Vegas '01

Victoria Smurfit
Ivanhoe '97

Ann Smyrner
Reptilicus '62

Johnny Sneed
American Nightmare '00

Gerti Sneider
2069: A Sex Odyssey '78

Carl Snell
The Dish '00

Carrie Snodgress
The Forsaken '01
The Fury '78

Snoop Dogg
Baby Boy '01
Bones '01
Training Day '01
The Wash '01
The Wrecking Crew '99

Shaun Snow
I Spit on Your Corpse, I Piss on Your Grave '02

Suzanne Snyder
Killer Klowns from Outer Space '88

Zachary Winston Snygg
Play-Mate of the Apes '02

Barry Sobel
That Thing You Do! '96

Leelee Sobieski
The Glass House '01
Joy Ride '01
My First Mister '01
Uprising '01

Ron Soble
The Beast Within '82

Maria Socas
Deathstalker 2: Duel of the Titans '87

Steven Soderbergh
Waking Life '01

Rena Sofer
Traffic [Criterion] '00

Marilyn Sokol
Emmet Otter's Jug-Band Christmas '77 (V)

Marla Sokoloff
Sugar & Spice '01
Dude, Where's My Car? '00

Vladimir Sokoloff
Mr. Sardonicus '61
The Road to Morocco [Univer- sal] '42

Miguel Angel Sola
A Shadow You Soon Will Be '94
Funny, Dirty Little War '83

Malena Solda
What Your Eyes Don't See '99

Paul Soles
The Score '01

P.J. Soles
Stripes '81
Rock 'n' Roll High School [New Concorde SE] '79
Halloween [Extended Edition] '78
The Boy in the Plastic Bubble [2] '76
Carrie '76

Yulia Solntseva
Earth '30

Ian Somerhalder
Life As a House '01

Suzanne Somers
Say It Isn't So '01

Geraldine Somerville
Haunted '95

Elke Sommer
Percy '71

Josef Somr
Closely Watched Trains '66

Gale Sondergaard
My Favorite Blonde '42

Tiffany Sonders
Erotic Survivor 2 '01

Mal Sondock
Town without Pity '61

Dan Sonney
Mau Mau Sex Sex '00

Susan Sontag
Zelig '83

Michael Sonye
Sorority Babes in the Slime- ball Bowl-A-Rama '87 (V)

Agnes Soral
Blitz '85

Jean Sorel
Belle de Jour '67

Ricky Sorenson
Tarzan and the Trappers '58

Paula Sorge
Bar Girls '95

Jorge Soriano
Two Coyotes '01

Pepe Soriano
A Shadow You Soon Will Be '94

Mira Sorvino
The Great Gatsby '01
The Replacement Killers [2 SE] '98
Barcelona '94

Paul Sorvino
Perfume '01
See Spot Run '01
Money Talks '97
Dick Tracy '90
The Gambler '74
King Lear '74
A Touch of Class '73

Roberto Sosa
Cabeza de Vaca '90

Shannyn Sossamon
A Knight's Tale '01

Brian Sostek
Dead Pet '01

David Soul
The Disappearance of Flight 412 '74
Magnum Force '73

Charles Southwood
Fistful of Lead '70

Roger Souza
The Vanishing [Criterion] '88

Filip Sovagovic
No Man's Land '01

Agnes Spaak
Dr. Orloff's Monster '64

Catherine Spaak
The Cat o' Nine Tails '71
The Libertine '69
Le Trou '59

Sissy Spacek
Carrie '76
Katherine '75

Kevin Spacey
K-PAX '01
Pay It Forward '00
Hurlyburly '98
The Usual Suspects [MGM SE] '95
See No Evil, Hear No Evil '89

David Spade
Joe Dirt '01
Tommy Boy '95

James Spader
Slow Burn '00
Less Than Zero '87
Mannequin '87

Douglas Spain
Ricochet River '98

Fay Spain
God's Little Acre '58

Kim Spalding
It! The Terror from Beyond Space '58

Timothy Spall
Rock Star '01
Vanilla Sky '01
Intimacy '00

Joe Spano
Texas Rangers '01

Vincent Spano
Texas Rangers '01
Maria's Lovers '84

Hal Sparks
Queer As Folk: The Complete First Season '01

Ned Sparks
Lady for a Day '33

Wendy Speake
The Dead Hate the Living '99

Empire of the Sun '87
Hot Pursuit '87

Jerry Stiller
On the Line '01
Zoolander '01
The Suburbans '99
Hairspray (John Waters Collection Vol. 1) '88
Hot Pursuit '87

Sting
The Bride '85
Plenty [Anchor Bay] '85
Quadrophenia '79

Colin Stinton
The Winslow Boy '98

Rachael Stirling
Maybe Baby '99

Amy Stock-Poynton
Bill & Ted's Bogus Journey '91
Bill & Ted's Excellent Adventure '89

Vaclav Stockel
The Firemen's Ball '68

Dean Stockwell
Water Damage '01
Phenomenon—The Lost Archives: American Midnight / H.A.A.R.P. '99 (N)
Phenomenon—The Lost Archives: Monopoly Men / An Unknown Encounter '99 (N)
Air Force One [2 SB] '97
Stephen King's The Langoliers '95
Beverly Hills Cop 2 '87
The Dunwich Horror '70

Guy Stockwell
The Disappearance of Flight 412 '74

Harry Stockwell
Snow White and the Seven Dwarfs [PE] '37 (V)

John Stockwell
Breast Men '97
Eddie and the Cruisers '83

Malcolm Stoddard
Catherine Cookson's The Girl '96

Barry Stokes
Space: 1999 Set 1 '75

Mink Stole
Pecker (John Waters Collection Vol. 1) '98
Hairspray (John Waters Collection Vol. 1) '88
Polyester (John Waters Collection Vol. 2) '81
Desperate Living (John Waters Collection Vol. 2) '77
Female Trouble '74
Pink Flamingos '72

Brad Stoll
Lost in Yonkers '93

Georgina Stoll
The Arena '01

Robert Stolper
Mission to Death '66

Eric Stoltz
Jerry Maguire [2 SE] '96
Say Anything [SE] '89

Christopher Stone
The Howling '81

Danton Stone
He Said, She Said '91

Harold J. Stone
Mitchell '75

Matt Stone
South Park: Insults to Injury '02 (V)
South Park: Bigger, Longer and Uncut '99 (V)
Cannibal! The Musical '96

Paula Stone
Hopalong Cassidy '35

Philip Stone
The Shining [2 SE] '80

Sharon Stone
Intersection '93
Basic Instinct [2 SE] '92
He Said, She Said '91
Total Recall [2 SLE] '90

Stuart Stone
Donnie Darko '01
Joy Ride '01

Gale Storm
My Little Margie: Collection 2 (1952–55) '02

James Storm
Firetrap '01
Scream of the Wolf '74

Peter Stormare
Happy Campers '01
Bruiser '00

Ludwig Stossel
Tales of Frankenstein '58

Ken Stott
Plunkett & Macleane '98

Count Stovall
Deep Trouble '01

George Stover
Harvesters '02
Attack of the 60-Foot Centerfold '95
Hairspray (John Waters Collection Vol. 1) '88
Polyester (John Waters Collection Vol. 2) '81
Desperate Living (John Waters Collection Vol. 2) '77
Female Trouble '74

Madeleine Stowe
The Magnificent Ambersons '02
Unlawful Entry '92
China Moon '91

Julie Strain
St. Patrick's Day '01

Chantal Strand
Dragon Tales '99 (V)

Glenn Strange
The Legend of the Lone Ranger '59
House of Frankenstein '44
The Black Raven '43

Susan Strasberg
The Brotherhood '68

Marcia Strassman
The Aviator '85

David Strathairn
Home for the Holidays '95
Lost in Yonkers '93
Dominick & Eugene '88

Dorothy Stratten
Galaxina '80

Peter Strauss
Spacehunter: Adventures in the Forbidden Zone '83
The Secret of NIMH '82 (V)

Meryl Streep
A.I.: Artificial Intelligence '01 (V)
The House of the Spirits '93
She-Devil '89

Out of Africa '85
Plenty [Anchor Bay] '85
Falling in Love '84
The French Lieutenant's Woman '81
Kramer vs. Kramer '79

Elliot Street
Harrad Experiment '73

Russell Streiner
Night of the Living Dead [Elite ME] '68

Barbra Streisand
Hollywood Screen Tests: Take 2 '00
The Prince of Tides '91
Funny Lady '75
The Owl and the Pussycat '70
Funny Girl '68

Alexia Stresi
Deep in the Woods '00

Oscar Stribolt
Haxan: Witchcraft through the Ages '22

Connie Strickland
Bummer '73

Gail Strickland
Who'll Stop the Rain? '78

John Stride
Macbeth '71

Sherry Stringfield
Dead Simple '01
Burnzy's Last Call '95

Edward Strode
First Love and Other Pains / One of Them '99

Woody Strode
Vigilante [2 DC] '83
Keoma '76

Tara Strohmeier
The Great Texas Dynamite Chase '76

Monica Strommerstedt
Inga '67

Tami Stronach
The NeverEnding Story '84

Brenda Strong
Undercurrent '99

Danny Strong
Perpetrators of the Crime '98

Gwyneth Strong
Forgotten '99

Johnny Strong
Black Hawk Down '01
The Fast and the Furious '01

Michael Strong
Patton [2] '70

Rider Strong
The Pact '99
Roughnecks: Starship Troopers Chronicles—The Homefront Campaign '99 (V)

Dorothy Strongin
Basket Case [2 SE] '82

Don Stroud
Dillinger and Capone '95
Twisted Justice '89

Duke Stroud
Human Desires '97

David Strowell
Night Divides the Day '01

Henry Strozier
Thirteen Days '00

Shepperd Strudwick
All the King's Men '49

Sally Struthers
All in the Family: The Complete First Season '71

Carel Struycken
Servants of Twilight '91

Vladislav Strzeltchik
Tchaikovsky '71

John Stuart
The Mummy '59

Violet Stuart
Richard III '12

Imogen Stubbs
Jack and Sarah '95

Una Stubbs
The Worst Witch '98
Til Death Us Do Part '72

Wes Studi
Wind River '98

John Stump
Night Divides the Day '01

Jennings Sturgeon
Raiders of Leyte Gulf '63

Preston Sturges
Star Spangled Rhythm '42

Shannon Sturges
The Perfect Wife '00

Hans Sturm
The Golem '20

Emma Suarez
Vacas '91

Jose Suarez
Texas, Adios '66

Michel Subor
Please Not Now! '61
Le Petit Soldat '60

David Suchet
Agatha Christie's Poirot: Dumb Witness '01
Agatha Christie's Poirot: Hercule Poirot's Christmas '01
Victoria & Albert '01
Agatha Christie's Poirot: The ABC Murders '92
Agatha Christie's Poirot: Peril at End House '90

Christopher Suciu
Dead and Rotting '02

Holger Suhr
Nekromantik '87

Kwan Suki
Cops on a Mission '01

Barbara Sukowa
Urbania '00
Johnny Mnemonic [2 SB] '95
The Sicilian '87

Ania Suli
Stuart Bliss '98

Barry Sullivan
Planet of the Vampires '65
Queen Bee '55
The Bad and the Beautiful '52

Brad Sullivan
The Prince of Tides '91
Slap Shot [2] '77

Brian Patrick Sullivan
Rudy Blue '00

Don Sullivan
The Giant Gila Monster '59
Teenage Zombies '58

Erik Per Sullivan
Joe Dirt '01

Jenny Sullivan
Katherine '75

Sarah Sullivan
Red Rock West '93

Susan Sullivan
My Best Friend's Wedding [2 SE] '97

Cree Summer
Atlantis: The Lost Empire [CE] '01 (V)

Diane Summerfield
Black Godfather '74

Debra Summers
Beverly Hills Bordello '01

Donald (Don) Sumpter
The Point Men '01

Paulyn Sun
The Untold Story 2 '98

Bjorn Sundquist
Zero Degrees Kelvin '95

Folke Sundquist
Wild Strawberries '57

Bunny Sunshine
The Southerner '45

Irene Sunters
The Wicker Man [SE] '75

Silcia Superstar
Killer Barbys '96

Ethan Suplee
Blow '01
Evolution '01

Nicolas Surovy
All over the Guy '01

Vincent Survinski
Night of the Living Dead [Elite ME] '68

Todd Susman
Beverly Hills Cop 2 '87

Donald Sutherland
Final Fantasy: The Spirits Within '01 (V)
Uprising '01
Panic '00
Buffy the Vampire Slayer '92
Ordinary People '80
Klute '71
M*A*S*H [FS] '70

Kiefer Sutherland
An Eye for an Eye '95
Twin Peaks: Fire Walk with Me '92
1969 '89

Kristine Sutherland
Buffy the Vampire Slayer: Season 1 '97

Adam Sutton
The Tomorrow Man '01

Frank Sutton
Town without Pity '61

John Sutton
The Bat [Goodtimes] '59

Michael Sutton
Dracula: The Dark Prince '01

Mena Suvari
American Pie 2 '01
The Musketeer '01
Sugar & Spice '01
American Pie [2 UE] '99

Semyon Svashenko
Earth '30

Josef Svet
The Firemen's Ball '68

Anna Svierker
Day of Wrath '43

Chelse Swain
The Mangler 2 '01

John Terry
Of Mice and Men '92
Full Metal Jacket [2 SE] '87

William Terry
Stage Door Canteen '43

Terry-Thomas
It's a Mad, Mad, Mad, Mad World '63

Lorenzo Terzon
Lady Frankenstein '72

Richard Tesarik
Divided We Fall '00

John Tesh
Soapdish '91

Robert Tessier
Sword & the Sorcerer '82
The Villain '79
Cry Blood, Apache '70

Fabio Testi
Four of the Apocalypse '75
The Garden of the Finzi-Continis '71

Tia Texada
Glitter '01

Gilda Texter
Angels Hard As They Come '71

Anne Teyssedre
A Tale of Springtime '89

G. Thang
Black Spring Break 2 '01

Torin Thatcher
Jack the Giant Killer '62
Love Is a Many Splendored Thing '55
The Robe '53

Brynn Thayer
Hero and the Terror '88

Max Thayer
Retrievers '82

Michael Thayer
Planet of the Dinosaurs '80

Jeremy Theobald
Following '99

Charlize Theron
The Curse of the Jade Scorpion '01
15 Minutes '01
Sweet November '01
Reindeer Games [Miramax DC] '00
That Thing You Do! '96

Justin Theroux
Mulholland Drive '01
Body Count '97

Ernest Thesiger
The Robe '53

Virginie Thevenet
The Cry of the Owl '87

Joseph Thiaka
Out of Africa '85

Jack Thibeau
Apocalypse Now [Redux] '79

Alan Thicke
Dance 'til Dawn '88

Melanie Thierry
The Legend of 1900 '98

Lynne Thigpen
Novocaine '01
Random Hearts '99

Alex Thomas
The Wash '01

Dave Thomas
Sesame Street Presents: Follow That Bird '85
Stripes '81

Eddie Kaye Thomas
American Pie 2 '01
Freddy Got Fingered '01
American Pie [2 UE] '99

Eugene Thomas
Ninja in the U.S.A. '88

Henry Thomas
Dead in the Water '01
Fever '99

Jake Thomas
A.I.: Artificial Intelligence '01

Lowell Thomas
World War I Films of the Silent Era '02 (N)

Marlo Thomas
Free to Be...You and Me '74

Richard Thomas
The Miracle of the Cards '00
Fifth of July '82
All Quiet on the Western Front '79

Sean Patrick Thomas
Dracula 2000 '00

Theodore Thomas
Timecop '94

Tressa Thomas
The Five Heartbeats '91

Marsha Thomason
Black Knight '01

Tim Thomerson
The Devil's Prey '01
Volunteers '85

Bill Thompson
Peter Pan [2 SE] '53 (V)

Brian Thompson
The Order '01

Christopher Thompson
The Luzhin Defence '00

Cindy Ann Thompson
Cave Girl '85

Emma Thompson
Maybe Baby '99
Carrington '95
The Remains of the Day '93
Impromptu '90
The Tall Guy '89

Fred Dalton Thompson
Baby's Day Out '94
Barbarians at the Gate '93
White Sands '92
Cape Fear '91

Jack Thompson
Original Sin '01
Rodgers & Hammerstein's South Pacific '01

John Thompson
Born Romantic '00

Lea Thompson
All the Right Moves '83

Marshall Thompson
It! The Terror from Beyond Space '58

Sarah Thompson
Cruel Intentions 2 '99

Scott Thompson
Same Guys, New Dresses: The Kids in the Hall '02
Tart '01
Mickey Blue Eyes '99

Shawn Thompson
Hairspray (John Waters Collection Vol. 1) '88

Sita Thompson
Rod Steele 0014: You Only Live Until You Die '02

Susanna Thompson
High Noon '00
Random Hearts '99
Ghosts of Mississippi '96

Victoria Thompson
Harrad Experiment '73

Wesley Thompson
Smiling Fish & Goat on Fire '99

Pat Thomsen
Strictly Ballroom '92

Anna Thomson
Water Drops on Burning Rocks '99
Fiona '98

Kenneth Thomson
Hopalong Cassidy '35

Kim Thomson
The Tall Guy '89

Sybil Thorndike
The Prince and the Showgirl '57

Callie (Calliope) Thorne
Sidewalks of New York '01
Wirey Spindell '99

Courtney Thorne-Smith
Revenge of the Nerds 2: Nerds in Paradise '87

Billy Bob Thornton
Bandits '01
The Man Who Wasn't There '01
South of Heaven, West of Hell '01
Some Folks Call It a Sling Blade '94
Indecent Proposal '93
Tombstone [2] '93

Sven-Ole Thorsen
Abraxas: Guardian of the Universe [BFS] '90

Linda Thorson
The Avengers '68 '68

David Threlfall
Conspiracy '01
The Russia House '90

Frank Thring, Jr.
Howling 3: The Marsupials '87

Ingrid Thulin
Cries and Whispers '72
Wild Strawberries '57

Beverly Thurman
The Giant Gila Monster '59

Julia Anna Thurman
The Erotic Rites of Countess Dracula '01

Uma Thurman
The Golden Bowl '00
Gattaca [2 SB] '97

Gerard Tichy
Doctor Zhivago '65

Nancy Ticotin
The Tavern '00

Rachel Ticotin
First Time Felon '97
Total Recall [2 SLE] '90

James Tien
Bruce Lee: A Warrior's Journey '01
Righting Wrongs '86
The Owl vs. Bombo '84

Li Tien-lu
The Puppetmaster '93

Andrew Tiernan
Horatio Hornblower '99

Tommy Tiernan
About Adam '00

Adian Tierney
Family Viewing / Next of Kin '87

Jacob Tierney
Poor White Trash '00
Pin... '88

Lawrence Tierney
Silver Bullet '85

Malcolm Tierney
The Apocalypse Watch '97

Maura Tierney
Oxygen '99
The Temp '93
White Sands '92

Patrick Tierney
Next of Kin '84

Angelo Tiffe
3 Ninjas Kick Back '94

Kevin Tighe
Stephen King's Rose Red '02
Race the Sun '96
What's Eating Gilbert Grape '93
Newsies '92

Zeffie Tilbury
Werewolf of London '35

Yevgeni Tilicheyev
Come and See '85

Jenny Till
Theatre of Death '67

Mel Tillis
The Villain '79

Jennifer Tilly
The Magnificent Ambersons '02
Fast Sofa '01
Dancing at the Blue Iguana '00
The Dress Code '99
Stuart Little [2 DE] '99 (V)
House Arrest '96
Let It Ride '89
High Spirits '88

Meg Tilly
Agnes of God '85
Psycho 2 '83

Corbin Timbrook
Forbidden Sins '99

Yau Tin
Blood of the Dragon '71

Jean Tissier
Please Not Now! '61
The Hunchback of Notre Dame '57

Kenneth Tobey
Walt Disney Treasures: Davy Crockett '01
Strange Invaders '83
The Howling '81

Stephen Tobolowsky
Dean Koontz's Black River '01
Memento [1] '00
Memento [2 SE] '00
The Prime Gig '00
Groundhog Day [2 SE] '93
Basic Instinct [2 SE] '92
Breaking In '89
Great Balls of Fire '89
Spaceballs '87

Brian Tochi
Revenge of the Nerds / Revenge of the Nerds 2: Nerds in Paradise '84

Lisa Todd
The Doll Squad '73

Tony Todd
Never 2 Big '98
Burnzy's Last Call '95
Candyman 2: Farewell to the Flesh '94
Colors '88

Bruno Todeschini
Va Savoir '01
Those Who Love Me Can Take the Train '98
La Sentinelle '92

Ugo Tognazzi
La Cage aux Folles 2 '81
La Cage aux Folles '78

Niall Toibin
Rawhead Rex '87

Yongjae Tokko
White Badge '97

Michael Toland
Eddie and the Cruisers '83

Goya Toledo
Amores Perros '00
Mararia '98

John Toles-Bey
K-PAX '01

James Tolkan
Dick Tracy '90

Marilu Tolo
Bad Cop Chronicles: Confessions of a Police Captain '72

David Tom
Stay Tuned '92

Dara Tomanovich
Bio-Dome '96

Marisa Tomei
Someone Like You '01

Frances Tomelty
The Field [Artisan] '90

Joseph Tomelty
Devil Girl from Mars '54

Tamlyn Tomita
The Karate Kid: Part 2 '86

Lily Tomlin
The Celluloid Closet '95 (N)

David Tomlinson
War Gods of the Deep '65

Tone Loc
Ferngully '92 (V)

James N. Toney
Ali '01

Jacqueline Tong
How to Get Ahead in Advertising '89

Karen Tong
Ballistic Kiss '98

Renato Tontini
I Vampiri '56

Regis Toomey
Strange Illusion '45

Chaim Topol
Left Luggage '98
Fiddler on the Roof [2 SE] '71
Cast a Giant Shadow '66

Kendra Torgan
Just Visiting '01

Peter Tork
Head '68

Angelica Torn
Domestic Disturbance '01

Rip Torn
Freddy Got Fingered '01
Beyond the Law '92
Cross Creek '83

Liv Ullmann
Cries and Whispers '72

Skeet Ulrich
Chill Factor '99

Martin Umbach
NeverEnding Story 2: The
Next Chapter '91

Miyoshi Umeki
Sayonara '57

Blair Underwood
Mama Flora's Family '98

Jay Underwood
Dancing in September '00
Stalker '98

Deborah Kara Unger
Luminous Motion '00

Gabrielle Union
Two Can Play That Game '01
Bring It On '00

Kandito Uranga
Vacas '91

Emilio Urdapilleta
Play for Me '01

Mary Ure
The Mind Benders '63
Look Back in Anger '58

Fabio Urena
Return of the Living Dead 3
'93

Justin Urich
Horror 101 '00

Robert Urich
Magnum Force '73

Peter Ustinov
Victoria & Albert '01
Stiff Upper Lips '96
The Great Muppet Caper '81
Topkapi '64

Kari Vaananen
Ambush '99

Brenda Vaccaro
Zorro, the Gay Blade '81
Territorial Men '76

David Vadim
Exit Wounds '01
Brooklyn Babylon '00
Air Force One [2 SB] '97

Pierre Val
Capitaine Conan '96

Serge-Henri Valcke
No Man's Land '01

Wilmer Valderrama
Summer Catch '01

Thais Valdes
A Paradise under the Stars
'99

Vladimir Valenta
Closely Watched Trains '66

Diana Valentien
Squeeze Play [DC] '79

Scott Valentine
Paranoia '98

Rudolph Valentino
Son of the Sheik '26
Blood and Sand '22

Daniel Valenzuela
The Road '00

Rosa Valetti
The Blue Angel '30

Paco Valladares
Orloff and the Invisible Man
'70

Rudy Vallee
How to Succeed in Business
without Really Trying '67

Amber Valletta
Family Man '00

Alida Valli
Suspiria '77
Il Grido '57
The Night Heaven Fell '57

Romolo Valli
The Garden of the Finzi-Continis '71

Vera Valmont
The Nude Set '61

Tito Valverde
Living It Up '00

Vampira
Night of the Ghouls '59

Lee Van Cleef
The Squeeze '78
The Young Lions '58

Ron Van Cliff
Fist of Fear, Touch of Death
'80

Jean-Claude Van Damme
The Order '01
Replicant '01
Timecop '94

Monique Van De Ven
Katie Tippel '75

James Van Der Beek
Jay and Silent Bob Strike
Back '01
Texas Rangers '01

Eva Van der Gucht
Everybody's Famous! '00

Jean Van Derpyl
Animated Christmas DVD
Double Feature '79 (V)

Trish Van Devere
The Hearse '80

Casper Van Dien
Danger beneath the Sea '02
Sanctimony '01
Partners '99

Mamie Van Doren
Slackers '02

John van Dreelen
Von Ryan's Express '65
13 Ghosts '60

Jennifer Van Dyck
States of Control '98

Dick Van Dyke
Dick Tracy '90

Kevin Van Hentenryck
Basket Case [2 SE] '82

Brian Van Holt
Black Hawk Down '01

Patricia Van Ingen
Wind River '98

Peter Van Norden
The Accused '88

Ed Van Nuys
Murder in Coweta County '83

Nina Van Pallandt
Sword & the Sorcerer '82
Cutter's Way '81

Dick Van Patten
Spaceballs '87

James Van Patten
Twisted Justice '89

Joyce Van Patten
The Bad News Bears '76

Vincent Van Patten
Backyard Dogs '00
Rock 'n' Roll High School
[New Concorde SE] '79
Peebles

Mario Van Peebles
Ali '01
The Guardian '00
Mama Flora's Family '98
Full Eclipse '93
South Bronx Heroes '85

Megan Van Peebles
South Bronx Heroes '85

Gus Van Sant
Jay and Silent Bob Strike
Back '01

Edward Van Sloan
Dracula's Daughter '36

**Deborah Van
Valkenburgh**
Firestarter 2: Rekindled '02

Steve Van Wormer
The Extreme Adventures of
Super Dave '00

Philip Van Zandt
The Pride and the Passion
'57
Citizen Kane '41

Stevie Van Zandt
The Sopranos: The Complete
Second Season '01

Courtney B. Vance
Beyond the Law '92

Danitra Vance
Little Man Tate '91
The War of the Roses [SE]
'89

Gregg D. Vance
Phat Beach '96

Jim Vance
Blood Cult '85

Terra Vandergaw
'68 '87

Alexandra Vandernoot
The Closet '00

Vanity
The Last Dragon '85

Victor Varconi
My Favorite Blonde '42

Leonor Varela
Texas Rangers '01
The Tailor of Panama '00

Antonio Vargas
Strictly Ballroom '92

Jacob Vargas
Dr. Dolittle 2 '01 (V)
Road Dogz '00
Traffic [Criterion] '00

Natalia Varley
Viy '67

Jim Varney
Atlantis: The Lost Empire
[CE] '01 (V)

Diane Varsi
I Never Promised You a Rose
Garden '77

Michael Vartan
Mists of Avalon '01
Sand '00

Luiz Carlos Vasconcelos
Me You Them '00

Roberta Vasquez
Picasso Trigger '89

Romeo Vasquez
Curse of the Vampires '70

Frankie Vaughan
Let's Make Love '60

Greg Vaughan
Children of the Corn 5: Fields
of Terror '98

Paris Vaughan
Buffy the Vampire Slayer '92

Peter Vaughan
Lorna Doone '01
The Remains of the Day '93
Haunted Honeymoon '86

Betty Vaughn
Hav Plenty '97

Ned Vaughn
Courage Under Fire '96

Robert Vaughn
Pootie Tang '01

Vince Vaughn
Domestic Disturbance '01
Made [SE] '01
South of Heaven, West of
Hell '01
The Prime Gig '00
The Locusts '97

Emmanuelle Vaugier
Return to Cabin by the Lake
'01
Ripper: Letter from Hell '01

Yul Vazquez
Runaway Bride '99
Fresh '94

Alex Veadov
Adventures of Justine '00

Alexa Vega
Follow the Stars Home '01
Spy Kids '01

Isela Vega
The Fear Chamber '68

Conrad Veidt
Contraband '40

Reginald Vel Johnson
Die Hard [FS 2] '88

Dawn Marie Velasquez
The Item '01

Patricia Velasquez
Fidel '02
The Mummy Returns '01
Committed '99

John Vella
Sting of Death '65

Coralia Veloz
Life Is to Whistle '98

Thanassis Vengos
Ulysses' Gaze '95

Chick Vennera
Deep Water '99
High Risk '81

Diane Venora
Megiddo: The Omega Code 2
'01
Looking for an Echo '99
True Crime '99
Three Wishes '95
Hamlet '90
The Cotton Club '84

John Ventimiglia
Mickey Blue Eyes '99

Vincent Ventresca
The Learning Curve '01

Jesse Ventura
Abraxas: Guardian of the Universe [BFS] '90

Richard Venture
Series 7: The Contenders '01

Gwen Verdon
The Dress Code '99
The Cotton Club '84

Elena Verdugo
Cyrano de Bergerac '50
House of Frankenstein '44

Peter Vere-Jones
Meet the Feebles '89 (V)
Bad Taste [LE] '88

Ben Vereen
Fosse '01
Roots '77
Funny Lady '75

Simon Verhoeven
Bride of the Wind '01

Tom Verica
800 Leagues down the Ama-
zon '93

Harold Vermilyea
Sorry, Wrong Number '48

Pierre Vernier
Under the Sand '00

Conrad Vernon
Shrek [SE] '01 (V)

Glenn Vernon
I Bury the Living '58

Howard Vernon
Revenge in the House of
Usher '82
Orloff and the Invisible Man
'70
The Sadistic Baron Von Klaus
'62
Bob le Flambeur '55

John Vernon
Mob Story [BFS] '90
Killer Klowns from Outer
Space '88
Fraternity Vacation '85
The Outlaw Josey Wales [2]
'76
Brannigan '75
Dirty Harry [2] '71

Kate Vernon
Mob Story [BFS] '90

Richard Vernon
The Servant '63

Sherri Vernon
10 Violent Women '79

Todd Verow
Little Shots of Happiness '97

Cec Verrell
Hell Comes to Frogtown '88

Veruschka
The Bride '85

Victor Verzhbitsky
The Arena '01

Bruno VeSota
The Choppers '61
Attack of the Giant Leeches
[Marengo] '59
A Bucket of Blood / Attack of
the Giant Leeches [Maren-
go] '59
The Wasp Woman [2] '59

Tricia Vessey
Town and Country '01
On the Edge '01

Ondrej Vetchy
Dark Blue World '01

Yvette Vickers
Attack of the Giant Leeches
[Marengo] '59

Charles Victor
Contraband '40

Steve Wang
Adventures of the Kung Fu Rascals '92

Yu-Wen Wang
Eat Drink Man Woman '94

George Wang Kuo
To Kill with Intrigue '77

Karma Wangiel
Himalaya '99

Patrick Warburton
The Dish '00

Brendan Ward
South Bronx Heroes '85

Burt Ward
Hollywood Screen Tests: Take 1 '00
Batman: The Movie '66

Donal Lardner Ward
The Suburbans '99

Fannie Ward
The Cheat [Kino] '15

Fred Ward
Corky Romano '01
Joe Dirt '01
Summer Catch '01
Best Men '98
Timerider '83

Harlen Ward
The Monster That Challenged the World '57

Jonathan Ward
Ferngully '92 (V)

Megan Ward
Tick Tock '00

Rachel Ward
After Dark, My Sweet [2] '90
How to Get Ahead in Advertising '89
The Good Wife '86

Richard Ward
Across 110th Street '72

Roger Ward
Quigley Down Under '90
Mad Max [MGM SE] '80

Sandy Ward
Tank '83

Sela Ward
Runaway Bride '99
Nothing in Common '86

Zack (Zach) Ward
Almost Famous: Untitled— The Bootleg Cut '00

Frederick Warde
Richard III '12

Jack Warden
The Aviator '85
The Great Muppet Caper '81
Used Cars '80
Run Silent, Run Deep '58

Rick Warden
Bravo Two Zero '99

Herta Ware
Top Dog '95

William Warfield
Show Boat '51

John Warnaby
In Love and War '01

Kimberly Warnat
Silver Wolf '98

Amelia Warner
Lorna Doone '01

David Warner
Back to the Secret Garden '01

Horatio Hornblower: The Adventure Continues '01
Planet of the Apes '01
Money Talks '97
Tron [2 CE] '82
S.O.S. Titanic '79
Morgan: A Suitable Case for Treatment '66

H.B. Warner
Strange Impersonation '46
Mr. Deeds Goes to Town '36

Julie Warner
Tommy Boy '95
Mr. Saturday Night [MGM] '92

DeWayne Warren
Hardball '01

E. Alyn Warren
Tarzan the Fearless '33

Estella Warren
Driven '01
Planet of the Apes '01

Fred Warren
Mysterious Mr. Wong '35

Hal P. Warren
Manos, the Hands of Fate '66

Jennifer Warren
Slap Shot [2] '77

Jennifer Leigh Warren
Matter of Trust '98

Joshua P. Warren
Inbred Rednecks '97

Lesley Ann Warren
Trixie '00
Choose Me '84
Cinderella '64

Lori Warren
Twisted Justice '89

Harold Warrender
Contraband '40

Ruth Warrick
Citizen Kane '41

Robert Warwick
Sullivan's Travels '41
Hopalong Cassidy '35

Mona Washbourne
Therese Raquin '80

Beverly Washburn
Old Yeller '57

Bryant Washburn
The Wizard of Oz '25

Denzel Washington
Training Day '01
Courage Under Fire '96
Hard Lessons '86

Isaiah Washington, IV
Exit Wounds '01
Dancing in September '00
True Crime '99

Vernon Washington
Friday the 13th, Part 5: A New Beginning '85

Craig Wasson
Boa '02
The Pornographer '00

David Wasson
Fallout '01

Gedde Watanabe
That Thing You Do! '96
UHF '89
Vamp '86
Volunteers '85

Hiroyuki Watanabe
Reborn from Hell: Jubei's Revenge '96
Reborn from Hell: Samurai Armageddon '96

Dennis Waterman
Fright '71
The Scars of Dracula '70

Felicity Waterman
Lena's Holiday '90

Ethel Waters
Stage Door Canteen '43

John Waters
Pecker (John Waters Collection Vol. 1) '98 (V)
Hairspray (John Waters Collection Vol. 1) '88
Pink Flamingos '72 (N)

William Waters
Eegah! '62

James Waterson
Christy—A Change of Seasons '01
Christy—A New Beginning '01
Christy—Return to Cutter Gap '01

Sam Waterston
Thomas Jefferson '01 (V)
Lewis and Clark: Journey of the Corps of Discovery '97 (V)
Hannah and Her Sisters '86

Pierre Watkin
The Road to Singapore '40

James L. Watkins
J.D.'s Revenge '76

Miles Watkins
The Great Texas Dynamite Chase '76

Alberta Watson
Tart '01
Hedwig and the Angry Inch '00
Deeply '99

Douglas Watson
King Lear '74

Emily Watson
The Luzhin Defence '00
Trixie '00

Emma Watson
Harry Potter and the Sorcerer's Stone '01

Jack Watson
Sleeping Murder / 4:50 from Paddington '86
Schizo '77
McKenzie Break '70
The Devil's Brigade '68

Minor Watson
Guadalcanal Diary '43

Shari Watson
Ali '01
The Wash '01

Woody Watson
Texas '94

Vernee Watson-Johnson
The Boy in the Plastic Bubble [2] '76

Cameron J. Watt
First Love and Other Pains / One of Them '99

Richard Wattis
The Prince and the Showgirl '57

Naomi Watts
Mulholland Drive '01
Children of the Corn 4: The Gathering '96

Al Waxman
Mob Story [BFS] '90
Atlantic City '81

Damon Wayans
Blankman '94
Mo' Money '92
Colors '88
Hollywood Shuffle '87
Beverly Hills Cop [CE] '84

Keenen Ivory Wayans
Hollywood Shuffle '87

Marlon Wayans
Scary Movie 2 '01
Mo' Money '92

Shawn Wayans
Scary Movie 2 '01

Sam Waymon
Ganja and Hess '73

Carol Wayne
The Party '68

John Wayne
The Shootist '76
Brannigan '75
Cast a Giant Shadow '66
Hatari! '62
Rio Bravo '59
Helltown '38
King of the Pecos '36
Desert Trail '35
Paradise Canyon '35
Trail Beyond [Columbia] '34
Riders of Destiny [Columbia] '33
West of the Divide '33
Two-Fisted Law '32

Keith Wayne
Night of the Living Dead [Elite ME] '68

Patrick Wayne
Revenge '86
The People That Time Forgot '77
The Young Land '59

Vickey We
Good Men, Good Women '95

Robert Weatherby
In Love and War '01

Jeff Weatherford
Money Buys Happiness '99

Michael Weatherly
Cabin by the Lake / Return to Cabin by the Lake '00

Carl Weathers
Force 10 from Navarone '78

Dennis Weaver
High Noon '00

Fritz Weaver
Alice in Wonderland '83

Sigourney Weaver
Company Man '01
Heartbreakers '01
The Ice Storm '97

Chloe Webb
Queens Logic '91

Jack Webb
The Halls of Montezuma '50
He Walked by Night [BFS] '48

Rita Webb
Zeta One '69

Amy Weber
Art House '98

Dewey Weber
Ulee's Gold '97

Steven Weber
The Temp '93

Angela Webster
House on Bare Mountain '62

Nick Wechsler
Chicks, Man '99

Inga Wede
The Tormentors '71

Frank Weed
The Death Curse of Tartu / Sting of Death '66

Jeannette Weegar
Black Knight '01

Christopher Weeks
Violent Zone '89

Paul Wegener
The Golem '20

Hsiao-hui Wei
Flowers of Shanghai '98

Paul Wei
Fists of Bruce Lee '78

Teri Weigel
Return of the Killer Tomatoes! '88

Chuck Wein
Rainbow Bridge '71

Mike Weinberg
Life As a House '01

Adam Weiner
Voyeur.com '00

Michael Weiner
The Secrets of the Warrior's Power '97 (N)

Carl Weintraub
Oliver & Company '88 (V)

Gabe Weisert
Fishing with Gandhi '98

Robin Weisman
Three Men and a Little Lady '90

Michael T. Weiss
Bones '01

Johnny Weissmuller
Stage Door Canteen '43

Rachel Weisz
The Mummy Returns '01
Beautiful Creatures '00
Enemy at the Gates '00

Bruce Weitz
Facing the Enemy '00

Elisabeth Welch
The Tempest '79
Big Fella '37
Song of Freedom / Big Fella '36

Raquel Welch
Legally Blonde '01
Tortilla Soup '01
Hollywood Screen Tests: Take 1 '00

Gertrude Welcker
Dr. Mabuse, The Gambler '22

Tuesday Weld
Hollywood Screen Tests: Take 2 '00
Who'll Stop the Rain? '78

Frederick Weller
Stonewall '95

Peter Weller
The Contaminated Man '01
Dracula: The Dark Prince '01
Styx '00
The Adventures of Buckaroo Banzai Across the Eighth Dimension [SE] '84

Mel Welles
Abbott and Costello Meet the Mummy '55

Orson Welles
The Muppet Movie '79
The Trial '63

The Vikings '58 (N)
The Stranger
  [Delta/Laserlight] '46
Citizen Kane '41

Carole Wells
Funny Lady '75

Dawn Wells
Rescue from Gilligan's Island
  '78

Robert Wells
Shatter Dead '01

Tico Wells
The Five Heartbeats '91

Vernon Wells
Plughead Rewired: Circuitry
  Man 2 '94
Circuitry Man '90

Kenneth Welsh
Focus '01
Love Come Down '00
Rowing Through '96
Timecop '94
Larceny '91
Crocodile Dundee 2 '88

Candy Wen
Tiger over Wall '80

Alan J. Wendl
Hairspray (John Waters Collection Vol. 1) '88

George Wendt
The Prime Gig '00
House '86
Thief of Hearts '84
My Bodyguard '80

John Wengraf
The Pride and the Passion
  '57
Sahara '43

David Wenham
Moulin Rouge [SE] '01

Jann Wenner
Almost Famous: Untitled—
  The Bootleg Cut '00

Martha Wentworth
The Stranger
  [Delta/Laserlight] '46

Fritz Wepper
Le Dernier Combat '84

Gary Werntz
Pay It Forward '00

Dick Wessel
Dick Tracy vs. Cueball '46

Dick Wesson
Calamity Jane '53

Gene Wesson
Satan's Bed '65

Adam West
Hollywood Screen Tests: Take
  1 '00
The Specialist '75
Batman: The Movie '66

Dominic West
Rock Star '01

Joel West
Blood Surf '00
The Smokers '00

Kevin West
Bio-Dome '96

Nathan West
The Skulls 2 '02

Samuel West
Horatio Hornblower '99
Stiff Upper Lips '96
Carrington '95

Shane West
Get over It! '01

Terry West
The Sexy Sixth Sense '01

Wendi Westbrook
Narcotic Justice

Helen Westcott
Tales of Frankenstein '58

Robert Westenberg
Into the Woods '90

Jim Westerbrook
Mission to Death '66

James Westerfield
Homicidal '61

Helen Westley
Heidi '37
Dimples '36

Lucy Westmore
Doctor Zhivago '65

Matt Westmore
Hard As Nails '01

Celia Weston
Hearts in Atlantis '01
K-PAX '01
Little Man Tate '91

Jack Weston
Short Circuit 2 '88
Cuba '79
Cactus Flower '69

Anna Wetlinska
Conspirators of Pleasure '93

Patricia Wettig
Bongwater '98
Stephen King's The Lan-
  goliers '95

Merritt Wever
Series 7: The Contenders '01

Cynthia Whalen
Money Buys Happiness '99

Michael Whalen
The Phantom from 10,000
  Leagues '56

Sean M. Whalen
That Thing You Do! '96

Frank Whaley
When Trumpets Fade '98
Retroactive '97
A Midnight Clear '92

Joanne Whalley
Scarlett '94
Trial by Jury '94
Scandal '89
Willow '88

Wil Wheaton
Star Trek: The Next Genera-
  tion—The Complete 1st
  Season '87
The Secret of NIMH '82 (V)

Jane Wheeler
The Kid '97

Dana Wheeler-Nicholson
What's the Worst That Could
  Happen? [SE] '01
Tombstone [2] '93
Circuitry Man '90

Lisa Whelchel
Where the Red Fern Grows:
  Part 2 '92

Shannon Whirry
Me, Myself, and Irene '00
Retroactive '97

Forest Whitaker
Four Dogs Playing Poker '00

Betty White
Whispers: An Elephant's Tale
  '00 (V)

Dan(iel) White
Attack of the Giant Leeches
  [Marengo] '59

Deborah White
The Van '77

De'voreaux White
Die Hard [FS 2] '88

James Gordon White
The Tormentors '71

Jesse White
Designing Woman '57

John Patrick White
Bloodfist 8: Hard Way Out '96

Joni-Ruth White
Polyester (John Waters Collection Vol. 2) '81

Julianne White
Sexy Beast '00

Kenneth White
Dead Sexy '01

Michael Jai White
Exit Wounds '01

Peter White
Thirteen Days '00

Slappy (Melvin) White
Mr. Saturday Night [MGM] '92
Amazing Grace '74

Steve White
Just for the Hell of It '68

Trevor White
The Vigil '98

Paxton Whitehead
Kate & Leopold '01

Billie Whitelaw
The Flesh and the Fiends '60

Paul Whiteman
Lady Frankenstein '72

Hugh Whitemore
84 Charing Cross Road '86

Ray Whiteside
Walt Disney Treasures: Davy
  Crockett '01

Charles Malik Whitfield
Behind Enemy Lines '01
The Temptations '98

Dondre T. Whitfield
Two Can Play That Game '01

Lynn Whitfield
A Girl Thing '01
Love Songs '99
Hard Lessons '86

Mitchell Whitfield
Best Men '98

Bradley Whitford
Kate & Leopold '01

Peter Whitford
Strictly Ballroom '92

Kym E. Whitley
Beverly Hood '99

Lloyd Whitlock
West of the Divide '33

Kipp Whitman
Bummer '73

Mae Whitman
An American Rhapsody '01
One Fine Day '96

Stuart Whitman
Trial by Jury '94
Ruby '77
Las Vegas Lady '76
The Mark '61

James Whitmore
Where the Red Fern Grows
  '74
Harrad Experiment '73
Chato's Land '71
Black Like Me '64

Grace Lee Whitney
Star Trek 3: The Search for
  Spock '84

Leanne Whitney
Little Shots of Happiness '97

Margaret Whitton
Major League 2 '94
Trial by Jury '94

James Whitworth
Planet of the Dinosaurs '80

Johnny Whitworth
Valentine '01

David Whorf
On Our Merry Way '48

Mary Wickes
The Hunchback of Notre
  Dame '96 (V)
Sister Act '92

Saskia Wickham
Angels and Insects '95

Kathleen Widdoes
Courage Under Fire '96

Richard Widmark
Sell Out '76
Don't Bother to Knock '52
The Halls of Montezuma '50

Flora Wiesel
Please Don't Eat My Mother
  '72

Dianne Wiest
I Am Sam '01
Cops and Robbersons '94
The Scout '94
Little Man Tate '91
Radio Days '87
Hannah and Her Sisters '86
The Purple Rose of Cairo '85
Falling in Love '84

Peter Wigfield
The Miracle of the Cards '00

Wiley Wiggins
Waking Life '01

George P. Wilbur
Halloween 4: The Return of
  Michael Myers [MGM LE]
  '88

James Wilby
A Tale of Two Cities '91

Larry Wilcox
Mission Manila '87

Collin Wilcox-Paxton
Jaws 2 '78

Colette Wilde
Circus of Horrors '60

Lois Wilde
Undersea Kingdom '36

Gene Wilder
See No Evil, Hear No Evil '89
Haunted Honeymoon '86

James Wilder
First Degree '01

John Wildman
Sorority Babes in the Slimeball Bowl-A-Rama '87

Dawn Wildsmith
Hollywood Chainsaw Hookers
  '88

Jason Wiles
Higher Learning '94

Michael Shamus Wiles
Rock Star '01

Jan Wiley
She Wolf of London '46

Gabriela Wilhelmova
Conspirators of Pleasure '93

Kathleen Wilhoite
Breast Men '97

Keith Wilkes
Cornbread, Earl & Me '75

Tom Wilkinson
Black Knight '01
The Patriot [2 SB] '00
Wilde '97

Fred Willard
How High '01
The Wedding Planner '01
Waiting for Guffman '96

Toyah Willcox
Quadrophenia '79
The Tempest '79

Warren William
Strange Illusion '45
Lady for a Day '33

Barbara Williams
Love Come Down '00
Jo Jo Dancer, Your Life Is Call-
  ing '86
Thief of Hearts '84

Billy Dee Williams
The Visit '00
Bingo Long Traveling All-Stars
  & Motor Kings '76

Cara Williams
The Defiant Ones '58

Chris(topher) Williams
Cremains '00

Chuck Williams
Up against Amanda '01

Clarence Williams, III
Reindeer Games [Miramax
  DC] '00
The Legend of 1900 '98

Cynda Williams
Introducing Dorothy Dan-
  dridge '99

Darnell Williams
Firestarter 2: Rekindled '02

Erik Williams
Better Dayz '02

Gareth Williams
Hard Luck '01

Grant Williams
Written on the Wind '56

Harland Williams
Freddy Got Fingered '01

Heathcote Williams
The Odyssey '97
The Tempest '79

Hugh Williams
Khartoum '66

JoBeth Williams
Jackie's Back '99
Little City '97
Victim of Love '91
The Dogs of War '81
Kramer vs. Kramer '79

John Williams
Witness for the Prosecution
  '57

Kimberly Williams
Follow the Stars Home '01

Lee Williams
In His Life: The John Lennon
  Story '00
The Wolves of Kromer '98

Leigh Williams
Squeeze '97

Malinda Williams
Dancing in September '00
The Wood '99

Mark Williams
High Heels and Low Lifes '01

Michelle Williams
Perfume '01
Lassie '94

Olivia Williams
The Body '01
Born Romantic '00
Four Dogs Playing Poker '00
The Sixth Sense [Buena
Vista] '99

Paul Williams
A Regular Frankie Fan '01 (N)
The Muppet Movie '79
The Cheap Detective '78
Phantom of the Paradise '74

Peter Williams
Love Come Down '00

Robin Williams
A.I.: Artificial Intelligence '01
(V)
Ferngully '92 (V)
Toys '92
Hook '91
Cadillac Man '90
Moscow on the Hudson '84
Survivors '83
The World according to Garp
'82

Samm-Art Williams
Blood Simple '85

Saul Williams
K-PAX '01

Scot Williams
In His Life: The John Lennon
Story '00

Simon Williams
Upstairs, Downstairs: The
Complete First Season '71

Steven Williams
Firetrap '01
Route 666 '01
Crash & Byrnes '99
Bloodfist 7: Manhunt '95

Treat Williams
Extreme Limits '01
Venomous '01
The Heart of Dixie '89

**Vanessa L(ynne)
Williams**
The Odyssey '97

Fred Williamson
Children of the Corn 5: Fields
of Terror '98
The Black Cobra '87
The New Gladiators '83
Vigilante [2 DC] '83
Fist of Fear, Touch of Death
'80
Bucktown '75
Hell up in Harlem '73
M*A*S*H [FS] '70

Melissa Williamson
Mom's Outta Sight '01

Mykelti Williamson
Ali '01
Forrest Gump [SCE] '94
The First Power '89

Nicol Williamson
Exorcist 3: Legion '90
The Cheap Detective '78

Bruce Willis
Bandits '01
Unbreakable '00

**The Sixth Sense [Buena
Vista] '99**
The Fifth Element [2 SB] '97
Die Hard [FS 2] '88
Blind Date '87

Noel Willman
Doctor Zhivago '65

Chill Wills
Over the Hill Gang '69
The Harvey Girls '46

Damien "Bolo" Wills
Ali '01

Maury Wills
The Sandlot '93

David Wilmot
Rat '00

Channing Wilroy
Desperate Living (John
Waters Collection Vol. 2)
'77
Female Trouble '74
Pink Flamingos '72

Alec Wilson
Crocodile Dundee in Los
Angeles '01

Barbara Wilson
Invasion of the Animal People
'62
Terror in the Midnight Sun '58

Beverly Wilson
Dead Creatures '01

Bridgette Wilson
Just Visiting '01
The Wedding Planner '01
The Suburbans '99

Bryce Wilson
Trois '01

Chrystale Wilson
Trois '00

David Wilson
Eddie and the Cruisers '83

Don Wilson
Niagara '52

**Don "The Dragon"
Wilson**
Bloodfist 8: Hard Way Out '96
Bloodfist 7: Manhunt '95
Bloodfist 6: Ground Zero '94
Bloodfist 5: Human Target
'93
Say Anything [SE] '89

Elizabeth Wilson
Scarlett '94

Kristen Wilson
Dr. Dolittle 2 '01

Lois Wilson
Bright Eyes '34
The Show Off / The Plastic
Age '26
Manslaughter / The Cheat
'22

Luke Wilson
Legally Blonde '01
Soul Survivors '01
Bad Seed '00
Committed '99
Best Men '98
Bongwater '98

Melanie Wilson
Facing the Enemy '00

Owen C. Wilson
Behind Enemy Lines '01
Zoolander '01

Peta Wilson
Loser '97

Reno Wilson
She Creature '01

Richard Wilson
How to Get Ahead in Advertising '89

Rita Wilson
The Glass House '01
Perfume '01
Runaway Bride '99
That Thing You Do! '96
Volunteers '85

Scott Wilson
Pearl Harbor '01
Shiloh 2: Shiloh Season '99
Shiloh '97
Flesh and Bone '93
Exorcist 3: Legion '90
The Aviator '85

Sheree J. Wilson
Fraternity Vacation '85

Stuart Wilson
The Luzhin Defence '00
Slow Burn '00
Vertical Limit [2 SB] '00
Narcotic Justice
The Mask of Zorro [2 SE] '98
The Age of Innocence '93

Trey Wilson
Great Balls of Fire '89
Bull Durham [MGM SE] '88

Penelope Wilton
Victoria & Albert '01
Carrington '95
Clockwise '86

Juliana Wimbles
Restless Spirits '99

Wendi Winburn
Amazons and Gladiators '01

April Winchell
Recess Christmas: Miracle
on Third Street '01 (V)

Michael Wincott
Along Came a Spider '00
Romeo Is Bleeding '93

William Windom
Children of the Corn 4: The
Gathering '96

Barbara Windsor
Cor, Blimey! '00

Marie Windsor
Abbott and Costello Meet the
Mummy '55
Outpost in Morocco '49

Paul Winfield
Scarlett '94
Death Before Dishonor '87
The Terminator [2 SE] '84
The Greatest '77

Pui-Shan Wing
Eagle vs. Silver Fox '83

Mark Wingett
Quadrophenia '79

Henry Winkler
Hostage High '97
Katherine '75

Kitty Winn
The Exorcist [2]: The Version
You've Never Seen '73

Charles Winninger
Beyond Tomorrow '40

Mare Winningham
Turner and Hooch '89

George Winslow
Monkey Business '52

Michael Winslow
Spaceballs '87

Hattie Winston
True Crime '99

Robert Winston
Blood Thirst '65

Ray Winstone
Sexy Beast '00
Quadrophenia '79

Maurice Dean Wint
Hedwig and the Angry Inch
'00

Alex Winter
Bill & Ted's Bogus Journey
'91
Bill & Ted's Excellent Adventure '89

Kim Winter
Spin the Bottle '97

Ophelie Winter
2001: A Space Travesty '00

Jonathan Winters
It's a Mad, Mad, Mad, Mad
World '63

Shelley Winters
A Place in the Sun '51

Karen Winther
Haxan: Witchcraft through the
Ages '22

Estelle Winwood
Murder by Death '76

Ole Wisborg
Reptilicus '62

Ray Wise
Two Can Play That Game '01
Twin Peaks: Fire Walk with
Me '92
Twin Peaks: The First Season
'90
The Journey of Natty Gann
'85

Joseph Wiseman
Lawman '71

Grant Withers
The Fatal Hour '40
Mr. Wong, Detective '38
The Road to Ruin '28

Jane Withers
The Hunchback of Notre
Dame 2 '01 (V)
Bright Eyes '34

Mark Withers
Southern Man '99

Jimmy Witherspoon
Black Godfather '74

John Witherspoon
Vampire in Brooklyn '95

Reese Witherspoon
Legally Blonde '01
The Trumpet of the Swan '01
(V)

Glenn Withrow
Lady in Red '79

Alicia Witt
Vanilla Sky '01
Bongwater '98

Karen Witter
Popcorn '89

Johanna Wokalek
Aimee & Jaguar '98

Fred Wolf
Joe Dirt '01

Jennifer Wolf
Friction '95

Kelly Wolf
Graveyard Shift '90
Triumph of the Spirit '89

Lynn Wolfbrandt
Night Divides the Day '01

Nancy Allison Wolfe
Bar Girls '95

Frank Wolff
The Beast from Haunted
Cave '60
The Wasp Woman [2] '59

Rikard Wolff
Light Keeps Me Company '00
(N)

Donald Wolfit
The Charge of the Light
Brigade '68
The Mark '61

Louis Wolheim
Dr. Jekyll and Mr. Hyde [Kino]
'20

Sven Wollter
The Sacrifice / Directed by
Andrei Tarkovsky '86

Tommy Wonder
Mad Youth '40

Alex Wong
First Love and Other Pains /
One of Them '99

Anthony Wong
Jiang Hu—"The Triad Zone"
'00
The Legend of a Professional
'00
Time and Tide '00
The Fist Power '99
The Demon's Baby '98
The Untold Story 2 '98
Brother of Darkness '94
Daughter of Darkness '93

Carter Wong
The Legendary Strike '78

Casanova Wong
The Legendary Strike '78

Don Wong
Eagle Fist '77

Jimmy Wong
Ballistic Kiss '98
Sex and the Emperor '94

Jing Wong
Legend of the Red Dragon
'94

Joey Wong
Picture of a Nymph '88

Karel Wong
The Legend of a Professional
'00

Ken Wong
The Cheaters '00
Killer '00

Lung Wong
Ninja vs. Shaolin Guards '84

Mark Wong
Champ Against Champ [BFS]
'83
Champ vs. Champ [Xenon]
'83

Melvin Wong
Righting Wrongs '86

Michael Wong
Ultimatum '01
Invincible Obsessed Fighter
'82

Parkman Wong
Dr. Lamb '92

Pauline Wong
Tragic Hero '87

Quincy Wong
Mo' Money '92

Raymond Wong
Where a Good Man Goes '99

Michael York
Megiddo: The Omega Code 2 '01
The Treat '98
The Lady and the Highway-man '89
The Island of Dr. Moreau '77
Accident '67

Rachel York
One Fine Day '96

Sarah York
Evil Dead [LE] '83

Susannah York
After the War '89

Troy Yorke
Children of the Corn: Revelation '01

Aden Young
Black Robe [MGM] '91

Alan Young
Beverly Hills Cop 3 '94

Bill Young
Chopper '01

Blumen Young
Narcotic Justice

Bruce A. Young
Jurassic Park 3 [CE] '01
Basic Instinct [2 SE] '92

Burt Young
Blue Moon '00
Mickey Blue Eyes '99
The Gambler '74
Carnival of Blood / Curse of the Headless Horseman [SE] '71

Chris Young
Dance 'til Dawn '88

Dey Young
Frankie and Johnny '91
Strange Invaders '83
Rock 'n' Roll High School [New Concorde SE] '79

Faron Young
Daniel Boone: Trail Blazer '56

Harrison Young
Reptilian '00

Karen Young
Maria's Lovers '84

Keone Young
Uncorked '98

Loretta Young
The Stranger [Delta/Laserlight] '46
Along Came Jones '45

Neil Young
'68 '87

Polly Ann Young
The Invisible Ghost '41

Richard Young
Friday the 13th, Part 5: A New Beginning '85

Roland Young
And Then There Were None [Image] '45
King Solomon's Mines '37

Sean Young
Sugar & Spice '01
Poor White Trash '00
Cousins '89
Stripes '81

Stephen Young
Patton [2] '70

Jun-sang Yu
Tell Me Something '99

Ling-lung Yu
To Kill with Intrigue '77

Rongguang Yu
Iron Monkey [Miramax] '93

Wang Yu
Blood of the Dragon '71

Xia Yu
Shadow Magic '00

Barbara Yu Ling
The Prisoner '68

Sun Yueh
City on Fire [Dimension] '87

Zhao Yuelin
The Road Home '01

Brandy Yuen
Jade Claw '79

Corey Yuen
The Legend 2 '93
Righting Wrongs '86

David Yuen
Champ Against Champ [BFS] '83
Champ vs. Champ [Xenon] '83

Simon Yuen
Jade Claw '79
Drunken Master '78
Snake in the Eagle's Shadow '78

Simpson Yuen
Eagle vs. Silver Fox '83

Stan Yuen
Champ Against Champ [BFS] '83
Champ vs. Champ [Xenon] '83

Xing Yufei
Shadow Magic '00

Harris Yulin
American Outlaws '01
Perfume '01
Rush Hour 2 '01
Training Day '01

Jung-ah Yum
Tell Me Something '99

Chow Yun-Fat
Crouching Tiger, Hidden Dragon [2 SB] '00
The Replacement Killers [2 SE] '98
Prison on Fire 2 '91
City on Fire [Dimension] '87
Rich and Famous / Tragic Hero '87
Tragic Hero '87

Rick Yune
The Fast and the Furious '01

Liu Gia Yung
Shaolin Disciple '86

Yvonne Yung Hung
Sex and the Emperor '94

Blanche Yurka
The Southerner '45

Robert Yuro
Satan in High Heels '61

Li Yusheng
Shadow Magic '00

Rod Z.
Black Spring Break 2 '01

William Zabka
The Karate Kid: Part 2 '86
National Lampoon's European Vacation '85

Grace Zabriskie
Ferngully '92 (V)
Twin Peaks: Fire Walk with Me '92
Servants of Twilight '91

Ramy Zada
Out of Sync '95

Pia Zadora
Hairspray (John Waters Collection Vol. 1) '88

Frank Zagarino
Barbarian Queen '85

Caveh Zahedi
Money Buys Happiness '99

Steve Zahn
Dr. Dolittle 2 '01 (V)
Joy Ride '01
Riding in Cars with Boys '01

Saving Silverman '01
Stuart Little [2 DE] '99 (V)
The Object of My Affection '98
Race the Sun '96
That Thing You Do! '96

Tracy Zahoryin
A Girl, 3 Guys and a Gun '01

Del Zamora
Town and Country '01

Johnny Zander
Mexico City '01

Billy Zane
The Diamond of Jeru '01
Tombstone [2] '93

Lisa Zane
Monkeybone '01
The Pact '99

Bob Zany
Joe Dirt '01

Frank Zappa
Head '68

Dominique Zardi
Le Trou '59

Michael Zaslow
You Light Up My Life '77

Maria Luisa Zea
Cuando Habla El Corazon '42

Renee Zellweger
Bridget Jones's Diary '01
Me, Myself, and Irene '00
Deceiver '97
Jerry Maguire [2 SE] '96
Shake, Rattle & Rock! '94

Michael Zelniker
Stuart Bliss '98

Bo Zena
Adventures of Justine '00

Anthony Zerbe
True Crime '99
See No Evil, Hear No Evil '89
Who'll Stop the Rain? '78
Will Penny '67

Catherine Zeta-Jones
America's Sweethearts '01
Traffic [Criterion] '00
The Mask of Zorro [2 SE] '98
Catherine the Great '95
The Darling Buds of May '91

Mai Zetterling
Hidden Agenda '90

Vincent Zhou
The Fist Power '99

Roberto Zibetti
Stealing Beauty '96

Malik Zidi
Water Drops on Burning Rocks '99

Joseph Ziegler
Focus '01

Sonja Ziemann
De Sade '69

Chip Zien
Into the Woods '90

Vanessa Zima
Ulee's Gold '97

Constance Zimmer
Warm Blooded Killers '01

Preity Zinta
Mission Kashmir '00

Daniel Zirilli
Black Spring Break 2 '01

Dan Ziskie
Zebrahead '92

Greg Zittel
The Tavern '00

Zhang Ziyi
The Road Home '01
Rush Hour 2 '01
Crouching Tiger, Hidden Dragon [2 SB] '00

Adrian Zmed
Bachelor Party '84

Moses Znaimer
Abraxas: Guardian of the Universe [BFS] '90

Matteo Zoffoli
White Fang to the Rescue '74

George Zucco
Lured '47
Fog Island '45
House of Frankenstein '44
The Mummy's Ghost '44
The Black Raven '43
The Mummy's Tomb '42
My Favorite Blonde '42
The Mummy's Hand '40

Daphne Zuniga
800 Leagues down the Amazon '93
Spaceballs '87

Vincente Zuniga C
Drive By '01

Martin Zurla
South Bronx Heroes '85

The Director Index provides a listing for all directors of movies reviewed in this book. The listings for the director names follow an alphabetical sort by last name (although the names appear in a first name, last name format). The videographies are listed chronologically, from most recent film to the oldest. If a director helmed more than one film in the same year, these movies are listed alphabetically within the year.

Dodo Abashidze
Ashik Kerib '88

Jim Abrahams
Ruthless People '86

Mark Achbar
Manufacturing Consent:
Noam Chomsky and the
Media '93

Robert Ackerman
Life with Judy Garland—Me
and My Shadows '01

Don Adams
Vengeance of the Dead '01

Al Adamson
Naughty Stewardesses '74

Andrew Adamson
Shrek [SE] '01

Michael Addis
Poor White Trash '00

Percy Adlon
Bagdad Cafe '88

Ed Adlum
Invasion of the Blood Farmers '72

Joe Ahearne
Ultraviolet '98

Alfonso Albacete
Not Love Just Frenzy '96

Kevin Alber
Adventures of Justine '00

Will Aldis
Stealing Home '88

Robert Aldrich
Too Late the Hero '70
Four for Texas '63

Marc Allegret
Plucking the Daisy '56

Corey Allen
Avalanche '78

Debbie Allen
Out of Sync '95

Mark W. Allen
The Riff '00

Woody Allen
The Curse of the Jade Scorpion '01
Husbands and Wives '92
Radio Days '87

Hannah and Her Sisters '86
The Purple Rose of Cairo '85
Broadway Danny Rose '84
Zelig '83
A Midsummer Night's Sex
Comedy '82

Robert Altman
M*A*S*H [FS] '70

Keito Amamiya
Moon over Tao '97
Zeram 2 '94

Alejandro Amenabar
The Others [CE] '01
Open Your Eyes '97

Julian Amyes
Murder at the Vicarage '86

Ed Anders
L.A.P.D.: To Protect and Serve '01

Brad Anderson
Session 9 '01

Lindsay Anderson
Britannia Hospital '82

Paul Anderson
Shopping '93

Chris Angel
Wishmaster 3: Beyond the
Gates of Hell '01

Robert Angelo
Dead Sexy '01
Forbidden Sins '99

Theo Angelopoulos
Ulysses' Gaze '95

Ken Annakin
The Swiss Family Robinson '60

Jean-Jacques Annaud
Enemy at the Gates '00
The Lover '92
The Bear '89

Eve Annenberg
Dogs: The Rise and Fall of an
All-Girl Bookie Joint '96

Hideaki Anno
Nadia: Secret of Blue Water,
Vol. 1: The Adventure
Begins '89

Reverge Anselmo
Lover's Prayer '99

Pedrag (Peter) Antonijevic
Hard Cash '01

Lou Antonio
A Real American Hero '78

Michelangelo Antonioni
Il Grido '57

Tetsuro Aoki
Devil Hunter Yohko: The Complete Collection, Vol. 1 '93

Michael Apted
42 Up '00
Me & Isaac Newton '99

Manuel Gutierrez Aragon
Things I Left in Havanna '97

Vicente Aranda
Jealousy '99

Alfonso Arau
The Magnificent Ambersons '02

Fatty Arbuckle
Arbuckle & Keaton, Vol. 1
(1917–19) '00
Arbuckle & Keaton, Vol. 2
(1918–20) '00

Denys Arcand
Stardom '00

Emile Ardolino
Sister Act '92
Three Men and a Little Lady '90

Douglas Argent
Til Death Us Do Part '72

Dario Argento
Sleepless '01
Opera '88
Suspiria '77
The Cat o' Nine Tails '71

Allan Arkush
The Temptations '98
Shake, Rattle & Rock! '94
Rock 'n' Roll High School
[New Concorde SE] '79

Gillian Armstrong
Fires Within '91

Jack Arnold
Creature from the Black
Lagoon '54
It Came from Outer Space '53

Newton Arnold
Blood Thirst '65

Josh Aronson
Sound and Fury '00

Isaac Artenstein
Break of Dawn '88

Rubin Arvizu
Very Private Lessons '01
Fortune Quest: Journey to
Terrason '97

Giuseppe Asaro
A Voice from Heaven '01

Anthony (Giuliano Carnimeo) Ascot
Find a Place to Die '68

Hal Ashby
Coming Home '78

Peter Askin
Company Man '01

Anthony Asquith
We Dive at Dawn '43

Doug Atchison
The Pornographer '00

David Atkins
Novocaine '01

Mark Atkins
Night Orchid '97

Vic Atkinson
Animated Christmas DVD
Double Feature '79

Richard Attenborough
Gandhi '82

Daniel Attias
Silver Bullet '85

David Attwood
Fidel '02

Ulysses Au
Revenge of the Patriots '76

Bille August
The House of the Spirits '93

Howard (Hikmet) Avedis
The Specialist '75

Brian Avenet-Bradley
Freez'er '00

John G. Avildsen
The Karate Kid: Part 3 '89
The Karate Kid: Part 2 '86
Joe '70

Jon Avnet
Uprising '01

Torbjorn Axelman
Vibration '68

Alejandro Azzano
Secret of the Andes '01

John Bacchus
Play-Mate of the Apes '02
Vampire Obsession '02
Erotic Survivor 2 '01

Clarence Badger
It '27

John Badham
Short Circuit '86
American Flyers '85
Blue Thunder '83
Bingo Long Traveling All-Stars
& Motor Kings '76

John Bailey
China Moon '91

Roy Ward Baker
And Now the Screaming
Starts [SE] '73
Dr. Jekyll and Sister Hyde '71
The Scars of Dracula '70
Don't Bother to Knock '52

Ralph Bakshi
The Lord of the Rings '78
Fritz the Cat '72

Steve Balderson
Pep Squad '98

Ferdinando Baldo
Texas, Adios '66

Carroll Ballard
Fly Away Home [2 SE] '96

Albert Band
I Bury the Living '58

Ken Barbet
Killer Instinct '00

Miguel Bardem
Not Love Just Frenzy '96

Clive Barker
Nightbreed '90

Mike Barker
Lorna Doone '01

Steven Barron
Rat '00

Mariano Barroso
In the Time of the Butterflies '01

Ian Barry
The Diamond of Jeru '01

Andrzej Bartkowiak
Exit Wounds '01

Charles T. Barton
Helltown '38

David P. Barton
Dead and Rotting '02

Jules Bass
The Return of the King '80
The Hobbit '78

Murray Battle
Water Damage '01

Chris Baugh
Ping! '99

L. Frank Baum
His Majesty, the Scarecrow of Oz '14

Mario Bava
Shock '79
Knives of the Avenger '65
Planet of the Vampires '65
I Vampiri '56

Craig R. Baxley
Stephen King's Rose Red '02

Michael Bay
Pearl Harbor '01

Edgar Beatty
The Hippie Revolt '67

Warren Beatty
Dick Tracy '90

William Beaudine
Bela Lugosi Meets a Brooklyn Gorilla '52

Steve Beck
13 Ghosts '01

Harold Becker
Domestic Disturbance '01
Taps '81

Jacques Becker
Le Trou '59

Ford Beebe
Flash Gordon: The Peril from Planet Mongo '40
Flash Gordon: The Purple Death from Outer Space '40
Flash Gordon: The Deadly Ray from Mars '39

Andrew Behar
Tie-Died: Rock 'n' Roll's Most Deadicated Fans '95

Jean-Jacques Beineix
Diva [Anchor Bay] '82

Timour Bekmambetov
The Arena '01

Earl Bellamy
The Lone Ranger: Volume 1 '56

Dalvatore Belleci
Smash Cuts! Super Sci-Fi Shorts '00

Roberto Benabib
Little City '97

Jose Reyes Bencomo
Two Coyotes '01

Tony Benedict
Animated Christmas DVD Double Feature '79

Richard Benjamin
Mrs. Winterbourne '96

Derek Bennett
Upstairs, Downstairs: The Complete First Season '71

Edward Bennett
Agatha Christie's Poirot: Dumb Witness '01
Agatha Christie's Poirot: Hercule Poirot's Christmas '01

Rodney Bennett
The Darling Buds of May '91

Robert Benton
Places in the Heart '84
Kramer vs. Kramer '79
Bad Company '72

Luca Bercovici
Luck of the Draw '00

Bruce Beresford
Bride of the Wind '01
Silent Fall '94
Black Robe [MGM] '91
Tender Mercies [Anchor Bay] '83

Micha Bergese
Shaolin: Wheel of Life '00

Ingmar Bergman
Cries and Whispers '72
Wild Strawberries '57

Gabriel Beristain
Bloody Proof '99

William Berke
Dick Tracy, Detective '45

Alan Berliner
The Sweetest Sound '01

Joe Berlinger
Paradise Lost 2: Revelations '99

Barry Berman
Waterproof '99

Dale Berry
Hot Blooded Woman '65

John Berry
Boesman & Lena '00
The Bad News Bears Go to Japan '78

Peter Berry
Kiss Me Quick! '64

Bernardo Bertolucci
Stealing Beauty '96

Irvin Berwick
Hitch Hike to Hell / Kidnapped Coed '97

Luc Besson
The Fifth Element [2 SB] '97
Le Dernier Combat '84

Antonio J. Betancor
Mararia '98

Frank Beyer
Jacob the Liar '74

Kathryn Bigelow
Point Break '91

Tony Bill
Harlan County War '00
My Bodyguard '80

Kevin Billington
Light at the Edge of the World '71

Bruce Bilson
The New Daughters of Joshua Cabe '76

Mike Binder
Blankman '94

Steve Binder
Elvis: '68 Comeback Special '68

Roshel Bissett
Winter Lily '98

Betsy Blankenbaker
New York in the Fifties '01

Jamie Blanks
Valentine '01

William Peter Blatty
Exorcist 3: Legion '90

Jeff Bleckner
Dean Koontz's Black River '01

Bertrand Blier
Get Out Your Handkerchiefs '78
Going Places '74

Jason Bloom
Dead Simple '01
Bio-Dome '96

Michael Blum
Richard Pryor: Live and Smokin' '81

Don Bluth
Thumbelina [20th Century Fox] '94
A Troll in Central Park '94
The Secret of NIMH '82

Carl Boese
The Golem '20

Budd Boetticher
Behind Locked Doors '48

Jon Bokenkamp
Bad Seed '00

Uwe Boll
Sanctimony '01

Ben Bolt
Forgotten '99

Timothy Bond
Running Wild '99

Peter Bonerz
Friends: The Complete First Season '95

Ted Bonnitt
Mau Mau Sex Sex '00

J.R. Bookwalter
Witchouse 3: Demon Fire '01

John Boorman
The Tailor of Panama '00

H. Gordon Boos
Red Surf '90

Robert Boris
Backyard Dogs '00

Walerian Borowczyk
The Beast '75

Clay Borris
The Gunfighters '87

Frank Borzage
Stage Door Canteen '43

Roy Boulting
The Moving Finger '85

George Bowers
The Hearse '80

Chuck Bowman
Christy—Return to Cutter Gap '01

Steve Boyum
Slap Shot 2: Breaking the Ice '02

Robert North Bradbury
Desert Trail '35
Trail Beyond [Columbia] '34
Riders of Destiny [Columbia] '33
West of the Divide '33

James Allen Bradley
Radical Jack '00

Larry Brand
Paranoia '98

Andre Braugher
Love Songs '99

Paddy Breathnach
Blow Dry '00

Catherine Breillat
Perfect Love '96
A Real Young Girl '75

Alfonso Brescia
The Conqueror of Atlantis '65

Martin Brest
Beverly Hills Cop [CE] '84

Howard Bretherton
Three on the Trail '36
Bar 20 Rides Again '35
Hopalong Cassidy '35

Salome Breziner
Fast Sofa '01

Marshall Brickman
The Manhattan Project '86

David Briggs
Queer As F**k: Bizarre Short Films '01

Henry Bromell
Panic '00

Henry J. Bronchtein
The Sopranos: The Complete Second Season '01

Peter Brook
Lord of the Flies '63

Joseph Brooks
You Light Up My Life '77

Lowry Brooks, Jr.
Dead or Alive '02

Mel Brooks
Spaceballs '87

Richard Brooks
Bite the Bullet '75

Eric Bross
On the Line '01
Ten Benny '98

Karl Brown
Fire Alarm '32

Mark Brown
Two Can Play That Game '01

Melville Brown
Behind Office Doors '31

Kirk Browning
Hamlet '91
Alice in Wonderland '83
Working '82
The Royal Family '77
Time of Your Life '76

Martin Bruestle
The Sopranos: The Complete Second Season '01

Todd Brunswick
Biker Zombies '01

Franco Brusati
Bread and Chocolate '73

Joseph Brutsman
Diary of a Sex Addict '01

Larry Buchanan
Mars Needs Women '66

Dimitri Buchowetzki
Othello '22

Bethel Buckalew
Pigkeeper's Daughter / Sassy Sue '75
Sassy Sue '72

Colin Budds
Dr. Jekyll & Mr. Hyde '00

Veljko Bulajic
Atomic War Bride / This Is Not a Test '60

Peter Gathings Bunche
Never 2 Big '98

Luis Bunuel
That Obscure Object of Desire '77
Belle de Jour '67

Charles Burnett
Finding Buck McHenry '00
The Glass Shield '95

Edward Burns
Sidewalks of New York '01

Ken Burns
Ken Burns' Mark Twain '01
Thomas Jefferson '01
Ken Burns: Jazz '00
Frank Lloyd Wright—A Film by Ken Burns and Lynn Novick '98
Lewis and Clark: Journey of the Corps of Discovery '97

Kevin Burns
Rodgers & Hammerstein: The Sound of Movies [2 CE] '95

Jon Burroughs
Beverly Hills Bordello '01

James Burrows
Friends: The Complete First Season '95

Jeff Burton
Night Divides the Day '01

Tim Burton
Planet of the Apes '01

David Butler
Calamity Jane '53
The Princess and the Pirate '44
They Got Me Covered '43
The Road to Morocco [Universal] '42
Bright Eyes '34

Joshua Butler
Prancer Returns '01

Jorg Buttgereit
Schramm '93
Nekromantik '87

Reggie Rock Bythewood
Dancing in September '00

Christy Cabanne
The Mummy's Hand '40

Michael Cacoyannis
Electra '62

David Caesar
Idiot Box '97

Edward L. Cahn
It! The Terror from Beyond Space '58

Alan Caldwell
Roughnecks: Starship Troopers Chronicles—The Homefront Campaign '99

A.M. Cali
Parental Guidance '02

Mars Callahan
Double Down '01

James Cameron
The Terminator [2 SE] '84

Ken Cameron
The Good Wife '86

Joe Camp
Benji [Ventura] '74

Pasquale Festa Campanile
The Libertine '69

Doug Campbell
The Tomorrow Man '01

Martin Campbell
Vertical Limit [2 SB] '00
The Mask of Zorro [2 SE] '98

Norman Campbell
The Magic Show '81

Jane Campion
Two Friends '86

Erik Canuel
Matthew Blackheart: Monster Smasher '99

Frank Capra
Pocketful of Miracles '61
A Hole in the Head '59
Mr. Deeds Goes to Town '36
Lady for a Day '33

Rene Cardona, Sr.
Doctor of Doom '62

J.S. Cardone
The Forsaken '01
True Blue '01

Marcel Carne
Children of Paradise '44

Charles Robert Carner
Echo of Murder '00

John Carney
On the Edge '00

Giuliano Carnimeo
Fistful of Lead '70

Heiner Carow
Coming Out '89

John Carpenter
John Carpenter's Ghosts of Mars '01
Halloween [Extended Edition] '78

Steve Carpenter
Soul Survivors '01

Steve Carr
Dr. Dolittle 2 '01

David Carson
In His Life: The John Lennon Story '00
Letters from a Killer '98

Steve Carver
Lone Wolf McQuade '83
An Eye for an Eye '81

Mario Caserini
The Last Days of Pompeii '13

Jon Cassar
Danger beneath the Sea '02
Rough Air '02

Enzo G. Castellari
Keoma '76

William Castle
Strait-Jacket '64
Homicidal '61
Mr. Sardonicus '61
13 Ghosts '60

William Allen Castleman
Johnny Firecloud / Bummer '75
Bummer '73

Joe Castro
Legend of the Chupacabra '97

Mark Catalena
Goldwyn: The Man and His Movies '01

Michael Caton-Jones
Scandal '89

Antonio Caudri
Living It Up '00

Kelley Cauthen
Bare Witness '02

Robert Celestino
Mr. Vincent '97

Claude Chabrol
The Cry of the Owl '87
Les Bonnes Femmes '60

Don Chaffey
The Prisoner '68

Benny Chan
Fist of Fury '95

Billy Chan
The Legend of a Professional '00

Jackie Chan
36 Crazy Fists '77

Aman Chang
The Fist Power '99

Yoon-Hyan Chang
Tell Me Something '99

Michael Chapman
All the Right Moves '83

Joe Chappelle
The Skulls 2 '02
Dracula: The Dark Prince '01

Charles Chauvel
Fighting Rats of Tobruk '44

Peter Chelsom
Serendipity '01
Town and Country '01

Chi-Hwa Chen
Lady Iron Monkey '83
Snake and Crane Arts of Shaolin '78
36 Crazy Fists '77

Kuo-fu Chen
The Personals '98

Wai-man Cheng
Fist of Fury '95

Patrice Chereau
Intimacy '00
Those Who Love Me Can Take the Train '98

Christopher Scott Cherot
Hav Plenty '97

Mabel Cheung
City of Glass '98

Pierre Chevalier
Orloff and the Invisible Man '70

Gerardo Chijona
A Paradise under the Stars '99

Ted Childs
The World at War '73

Andy (Wing Keung Chien) Chin
The Lord of Hangzhou '98

Siu-Tung Ching
Swordsman 2 '91

Stephen Chiodo
Killer Klowns from Outer Space '88

Lee Chiu
Fearless Dragon '79

Marvin J. Chomsky
Catherine the Great '95
Tank '83
Roots '77
Evel Knievel '72

Thomas Chong
Cheech and Chong's The Corsican Brothers '84
Cheech and Chong's Nice Dreams '81

Vidhu Vinod Chopra
Mission Kashmir '00

Benjamin Christiansen
Haxan: Witchcraft through the Ages '22

Grigori Chukhraj
Ballad of a Soldier '60

Billy Chung
The Cheaters '00
Killer '00
Trust Me U Die '99
The Assassin '93

Ji-woo Chung
Happy End '99

Ji-Yong Chung
White Badge '97

Simon Chung
First Love and Other Pains / One of Them '99

William Chung Kei
Ninja vs. Shaolin Guards '84

Vera Chytilova
Daisies '96

Michael Cimino
Desperate Hours '90
The Sicilian '87

Louis CK
Pootie Tang '01

Rene Clair
And Then There Were None [Image] '45

Dan Clark
The Item '01

Greydon Clark
Satan's Cheerleaders '77

Larry Clark
Bully '01

Lawrence Gordon Clark
Flambards '78

Andre Clavell
Roughnecks: Starship Troopers Chronicles—The Homefront Campaign '99

James Clavell
To Sir, with Love '67

William Claxton
Territorial Men '76

Tom Clegg
Bravo Two Zero '99

Rene Clement
Purple Noon '60

Graeme Clifford
Frances [Anchor Bay] '82

Elmer Clifton
Down to the Sea in Ships '22

Joel Coen
The Man Who Wasn't There '01
Blood Simple '85

Larry Cohen
Hell up in Harlem '73

Martin B. Cohen
Rebel Rousers '69

Rob Cohen
The Fast and the Furious '01

Lionel Coleman
Margaret Cho: I'm the One That I Want '00

Duilio Coletti
Submarine Attack '54

Bill Colleran
Hamlet '64

Max Allan Collins
Real Time: Siege at Lucas Street Market '00

Peter Collinson
Sell Out '76
Fright '71

Chris Columbus
Harry Potter and the Sorcerer's Stone '01

Ryan Combs
Dirty Kopz '01

Bill Condon
Candyman 2: Farewell to the Flesh '94

Frank Conniff
4:50 from Paddington '87

Kevin Connor
The Apocalypse Watch '97
The People That Time Forgot '77
At the Earth's Core '76

Martha Coolidge
Introducing Dorothy Dandridge '99
Three Wishes '95
Lost in Yonkers '93
Real Genius '85

Kyle Cooper
New Port South '00

Francis Ford Coppola
Bram Stoker's Dracula [SB] '92
The Cotton Club '84
Apocalypse Now [Redux] '79
Dementia 13 [Roan] '63

Patrick Coppola
Where Angels Dance '01

Sergio Corbucci
Companeros '70

Craig Corman
Harold Robbins' Body Parts '01

Roger Corman
A Bucket of Blood / Attack of the Giant Leeches [Marengo] '59
The Wasp Woman [2] '59

John Cornell
Crocodile Dundee 2 '88

Michael Cort
Zeta One '69

Don A. Coscarelli
Beastmaster '82

George P. Cosmatos
Tombstone [2] '93

Vittorio Cottafavi
Goliath and the Dragon '61

Kevin Cotteleer
Dead Pet '01

Allen Coulter
The Sopranos: The Complete Second Season '01
Stephen King's Golden Years '91

David Cove
Adventures of Justine '00

Rich Cowan
The Basket [SE] '99

James Cox
Highway '01

Paul Cox
Lonely Hearts '82

Wes Craven
Vampire in Brooklyn '95

Ted Crestview
Roxanna '02

Donald Crisp
Don Q, Son of Zorro '25

Michael Cristofer
Original Sin '01

Donald Crombie
The Irishman '78

David Cronenberg
Scanners '81

David Cross
Mr. Show: The Complete First & Second Seasons '02

Cameron Crowe
Vanilla Sky '01
Almost Famous: Untitled—The Bootleg Cut '00
Jerry Maguire [2 SE] '96
Say Anything [SE] '89

Billy Crystal
61* '01
Mr. Saturday Night [MGM] '92

Michael Cuesta
L.I.E. '01

George Cukor
Let's Make Love '60
Little Women '33

Alan Cumming
The Anniversary Party '01

Paul Currie
Lionheart '00

Dan Curtis
Scream of the Wolf '74

Vondie Curtis-Hall
Glitter '01

Michael Curtiz
Proud Rebel '58

John Dahl
Joy Ride '01
Unforgettable '96
Red Rock West '93

Anthony Dalesandro
Escape to Grizzly Mountain '99

Mike Daly
Smash Cuts! Super Sci-Fi Shorts '00

Damiano Damiani
Bad Cop Chronicles: Confessions of a Police Captain '72
A Bullet for the General '68

Harold Daniels
Terror in the Haunted House '58

Joe Dante
The Howling '81

Ray Danton
Psychic Killer '75

Jean-Pierre Dardenne
La Promesse '96

Luc Dardenne
La Promesse '96

Michael Darlow
The World at War '73

Julie Dash
Daughters of the Dust '91

Jules Dassin
Topkapi '64

Nina Davenport
Always a Bridesmaid '00

Delmer Daves
Cowboy '58
Kings Go Forth '58
3:10 to Yuma '57

Lorena David
Outta Time '01
Bravo '98

Mark David
Sweet Thing '00

Martin Davidson
Looking for an Echo '99
The Heart of Dixie '89
Eddie and the Cruisers '83

John (Howard) Davies
Sleeping Murder / 4:50 from
Paddington '86

Desmond Davis
Girl with Green Eyes '64

Donald A. Davis
Swamp Girl / Swamp Country
'71

Julie Davis
All over the Guy '01

Michael Davis
100 Girls '00

Nick Davis
1999 '98

Tamra Davis
Skipped Parts '00
Best Men '98

**Anthony (Antonio
Margheriti) Dawson**
Cannibal Apocalypse '80
The Squeeze '78

Michael de Avila
Burnzy's Last Call '95

Philippe de Broca
Le Magnifique '76

Raymond De Felitta
Two Family House '99

Rolf de Heer
Alien Visitor '95

Alan De Herrera
Revenge Quest '96

Maricarmen de Lara
In the Country Where Nothing
Happens '99

Gerardo (Gerry) De Leon
Women in Cages '71
Curse of the Vampires '70
Walls of Hell '64

Jean De Segonzac
Mimic 2 '01
Oz: The Complete First Sea-
son '97

Vittorio De Sica
The Garden of the Finzi-Conti-
nis '71
After the Fox '66

Steven E. de Souza
Possessed '00

Oscar de Waard
Castles of War '00

William Dear
Santa Who? '00
Angels in the Outfield '94
Timerider '83

Basil Dearden
The Man Who Haunted Him-
self '70
Khartoum '66
The Mind Benders '63

John DeBello
Return of the Killer Tomatoes! '88

James D. Deck
Pendulum '01

David DeCoteau
Petticoat Planet '95
Sorority Babes in the Slime-
ball Bowl-A-Rama '87

Russell DeGrazier
Attraction '00

Deborah Del Prete
Ricochet River '98

Jean Delannoy
The Hunchback of Notre
Dame '57

Lionel Delplanque
Deep in the Woods '00

Rudy DeLuca
Transylvania 6-5000 '85

Cecil B. DeMille
Manslaughter / The Cheat
'22
The Cheat [Kino] '15

William C. deMille
World War I Films of the
Silent Era '02

Jonathan Demme
The Silence of the Lambs
[MGM SE] '91
Stop Making Sense '84
Caged Heat '74

Ted (Edward) Demme
Blow '01

Jacques Demy
The Young Girls of Rochefort
'68

Ruggero Deodato
Cut and Run '85

Brian DePalma
Casualties of War '89
Blow Out '81
Dressed to Kill [SE] '80
The Fury '78
Carrie '76
Obsession '76
Phantom of the Paradise '74

Dominique Deruddere
Everybody's Famous! '00

James Desmarais
Victim of Love '91

John J. Desmond
The Seagull '75

Virginie Despentes
Baise Moi '00

Arnaud Desplechin
La Sentinelle '92

Danny DeVito
The War of the Roses [SE]
'89
Throw Momma from the Train
'87

Matthew Diamond
Fosse '01

Ernest R. Dickerson
Bones '01

Mary Dickinson
Confessions of Robert Crumb
'87

Carlos Diegues
Tieta of Agreste '96

Karen Disher
Daria, The Movie: Is It Fall
Yet? '01

Djinn
Voodoo Nightmare '00

Edward Dmytryk
Anzio '68
The Young Lions '58

Lawrence (Larry) Dobkin
Territorial Men '76

Jacques Doillon
Petits Freres '00

Andrew Dominik
Chopper '01

Roger Donaldson
Thirteen Days '00
White Sands '92
Cadillac Man '90

Harris Done
Firetrap '01

Stanley Donen
The Grass Is Greener '61
Indiscreet '58

Diane Doniol-Valcroze
Kill by Inches '99

Richard Donner
The Goonies '85
The Toy '82

Nick Doob
Down from the Mountain '00

Jacques Dorfman
Druids '01

Richard Dornhelm
Anne Frank '01

Robert Dornhelm
Echo Park '86

Gordon Douglas
Robin and the 7 Hoods '64
Dick Tracy vs. Cueball '46

Alexander Dovzhenko
Earth '30

Robert Downey
Putney Swope '69

Todd Downing
Queer As F**k: Bizarre Short
Films '01

Danny Draven
Hell Asylum '01

Tony Drazan
Hurlyburly '98
Zebrahead '92

Carl Theodor Dreyer
Gertrud '64
Ordet '55
Day of Wrath '43

Charles S. Dubin
Murder Once Removed '71
Cinderella '64

Rick Dublin
Smash Cuts! Super Sci-Fi
Shorts '00

James Glenn Dudelson
Horror 101 '00

Peter Duffell
Flambards '78

Dennis Dugan
Saving Silverman '01

John Duigan
Molly '99

Charles S. Dutton
First Time Felon '97

Allan Dwan
Slightly Scarlet '56
Pearl of the South Pacific '55
Tennessee's Partner '55
Heidi '37
The Iron Mask '29

Jesse Dylan
How High '01

Boris Eagle
The Tormentors '71

Bill Eagles
Beautiful Creatures '00

Ellen Earnshaw
Human Desires '97

B. Reeves Eason
Undersea Kingdom '36

Clint Eastwood
True Crime '99
The Outlaw Josey Wales [2]
'76
Play Misty for Me '71

Thom Eberhardt
Ratz '99

Nicolas Echevarria
Cabeza de Vaca '90

Stephen Eckelberry
First Degree '01

Uli Edel
Mists of Avalon '01

Harriet Eder
Mein Krieg '90

Blake Edwards
Blind Date '87
The Man Who Loved Women
'83
The Party '68
Operation Petticoat '59

Henry Edwards
Scrooge '35

Arthur Egeli
Friction '95

Atom Egoyan
Calendar '93
Speaking Parts '89
Family Viewing / Next of Kin
'87
Next of Kin '84

Sergei Eisenstein
Que Viva Mexico '32

Harry Elfont
Josie and the Pussycats '01

Doug Ellin
Phat Beach '96

David Elstein
The World at War '73

Ben Elton
Maybe Baby '99

Sheri Elwood
Deeply '99

Roland Emmerich
The Patriot [2 SB] '00

Cy Endfield
De Sade '69

John English
Jungle Girl '41
Dick Tracy [Marengo] '37
Dick Tracy [VCI] '37

Robert Epstein
The Celluloid Closet '95

Gordon Eriksen
Lena's Dreams '97

John Erman
Scarlett '94
Roots '77

Emilio Estevez
Men at Work '90

David Mickey Evans
Beethoven's 4th '01
The Sandlot '93

John Evans
Black Godfather '74

John Eyres
Ripper: Letter from Hell '01

Roberto Faenza
Bad Cop Chronicles 2: Corrupt '84

Peter Faiman
Crocodile Dundee '86

Ferdinand Fairfax
The Last Place on Earth '94

Rick Famuyiwa
The Wood '99

Max Farberbock
Aimee & Jaguar '98

James Fargo
Every Which Way But Loose
'78
The Enforcer '76

Michele Farinola
Hollywood at Your Feet: The
Story of the Chinese The-
ater Footprints '00

Bobby Farrelly
Osmosis Jones '01
Me, Myself, and Irene '00

Peter Farrelly
Osmosis Jones '01
Me, Myself, and Irene '00

**Rainer Werner
Fassbinder**
Querelle '83

Don E. Fauntleroy
The Perfect Wife '00

Jon Favreau
Made [SE] '01

John Fawcett
Ginger Snaps '00

Neill Fearnley
Daydream Believers: The
Monkees Story '00

Beda Docampo Feijoo
What Your Eyes Don't See
'99

Miles Feldman
Voyeur.com '00

Federico Fellini
Spirits of the Dead [Criterion]
'68
Juliet of the Spirits [Criterion]
'65
8 1/2 '63

Leslie Fenton
On Our Merry Way '48

Larry Ferguson
Beyond the Law '92

Abel Ferrara
The Blackout '97

Mark Fielder
Elizabeth '02

Mike Figgis
Liebestraum '91

Nigel Finch
Stonewall '95

Travis Fine
The Others '97

Kenneth Fink
Stephen King's Golden Years
'91

Joe Finley
Barbarian Queen 2: The
Empress Strikes Back '89

Laurent Firode
Happenstance '00

Ken Grieve
Cadfael—The Raven in the Foregate '94

Neil Grieve
Stuart Bliss '98

D.W. Griffith
Broken Blossoms [Kino] '19

Mark Griffiths
The Miracle of the Cards '00

Teresa Griffiths
Jackson Pollock: Love and Death on Long Island '99

Gillian Grisman
Grateful Dawg '01

Ulu Grosbard
Falling in Love '84

Yoram Gross
Dot & the Kangaroo '77

Adam Grossman
Sometimes They Come Back...Again '96

Sam Grossman
The Van '77

Christopher Guest
Waiting for Guffman '96

Val Guest
Au Pair Girls '72
Expresso Bongo '59

Charles Guggenheim
The Great St. Louis Bank Robbery '59

Bill Gunn
Ganja and Hess '73

Sebastian Gutierrez
She Creature '01

Charles Haas
Tarzan and the Trappers '58

Philip Haas
Angels and Insects '95

Taylor Hackford
Proof of Life '00

Michael Haigney
Pokemon: The First Movie '99

Billy Hale
S.O.S. Titanic '79

Arch (Archie) Hall, Sr.
Eegah! '62

Daniel Haller
The Dunwich Horror '70

Lasse Hallstrom
What's Eating Gilbert Grape '93

Guy Hamilton
Force 10 from Navarone '78
The Man with the Golden Gun '74
Funeral in Berlin '66

John Hamilton
Perpetrators of the Crime '98
The Kid '97

Michael Hamilton-Wright
The Mangler 2 '01

Joshua B. Hamlin
Late Night Sessions '99

Christopher Hampton
Carrington '95

John Hancock
Prancer '89

David Hand
Snow White and the Seven Dwarfs [PE] '37

Tom Hanks
That Thing You Do! '96

Masato Harada
Rowing Through '96

Rob Hardy
Trois '00

Robin Hardy
The Wicker Man [SE] '75

Rod Hardy
High Noon '00

Tsui Hark
Ultimate Fights '02
Time and Tide '00

Renny Harlin
Driven '01

Robert Harmon
The Hitcher '86

Curtis Harrington
Ruby '77

Ed Harris
Pollock [SE] '00

Joseph Harris
Underdog [CE] '00

Kirk Harris
Loser '97

Mark Jonathan Harris
Into the Arms of Strangers: Stories from the Kindertransport '00

John Harrison
Dune [2 SE] '00
Tales from the Darkside: The Movie '90

John Kent Harrison
In Love and War '01

Sam Harrison
Sex and Buttered Popcorn '91

Robert Hartford-Davis
The Bloodsuckers '70

Richard Hartley
Kennedy '83

David Hartman
Roughnecks: Starship Troopers Chronicles—The Klendathu Campaign '02

Harold (Herk) Harvey
Carnival of Souls [DC] '62
Carnival of Souls / Dementia 13 '62

Wojciech Has
The Saragossa Manuscript '65

Byron Haskin
Long John Silver '54

Joachim Hasler
Hot Summer '68

Patrick Hasson
Waiting '01

Ken Hastings
Olive Juice '01

Henry Hathaway
Five Card Stud '68
Niagara '52
A Wing and a Prayer '44

Howard Hawks
Hatari! '62
Rio Bravo '59
Monkey Business '52

Sidney Hayers
Circus of Horrors '60

Blair Hayes
Bubble Boy '01

Peter Hayman
Cybercity '99

Todd Haynes
Safe '95

David Heavener
Twisted Justice '89

Amy Heckerling
National Lampoon's European Vacation '85

Chris Hegedus
Startup.com '01
Down from the Mountain '00

Stuart Heisler
Lone Ranger '56
Along Came Jones '45

Brian Helgeland
A Knight's Tale '01

Monte Hellman
The Beast from Haunted Cave '60

Scott Heming
Sabrina, the Animated Series: Sabrina's World '99

Frank Henenlotter
Basket Case [2 SE] '82

Brian Henson
Jack and the Beanstalk: The Real Story '01

Jim Henson
The Great Muppet Caper '81
Emmet Otter's Jug-Band Christmas '77

Stephen Herek
Rock Star '01
Bill & Ted's Excellent Adventure '89

Jaime Humberto Hermosillo
Dona Herlinda & Her Son '86

Mark Herrier
Popcorn '89

Joel Hershman
Greenfingers '00

Michael Herz
The Toxic Avenger, Part 3: The Last Temptation of Toxie [DC] '89
Stuck on You! [DC] '84
First Turn On! [DC] '83

John Herzfeld
15 Minutes '01

Werner Herzog
Little Dieter Needs to Fly '97
Gesualdo: Death for Five Voices '95
Fata Morgana '92
Lessons of Darkness '92
Cobra Verde '88
Stroszek '77
Heart of Glass '74

Jon Hess
Crash & Byrnes '99

David L. Hewitt
Monsters Crash the Pajama Party Spook Show Spectacular '65

Peter Hewitt
Princess of Thieves '01
Bill & Ted's Bogus Journey '91

George Hickenlooper
Some Folks Call It a Sling Blade '94

Anthony Hickox
The Contaminated Man '01
Jill the Ripper '00
Full Eclipse '93

Douglas Hickox
Brannigan '75
Theatre of Blood '73

James D.R. Hickox
Blood Surf '00

Katherine Hicks
Knight Chills '01

Scott Hicks
Hearts in Atlantis '01

George Roy Hill
The World according to Garp '82
Slap Shot [2] '77

Jack Hill
The Big Bird Cage '72
The Fear Chamber '68

Robert F. "Bob" Hill
Flash Gordon: The Deadly Ray from Mars '39
Tarzan the Fearless '33

Walter Hill
Brewster's Millions [Universal] '85

Arthur Hiller
Taking Care of Business '90
See No Evil, Hear No Evil '89
Romantic Comedy '83

Lambert Hillyer
Dracula's Daughter '36

Ryuichi Hiroki
Sadistic City '93

Rin Hiroo
Kizuna '94

Mikio Hirota
Terminatrix '95

Karl T. Hirsch
Green '01

Alfred Hitchcock
Marnie '64
Rebecca [Criterion] '40

Godfrey Ho
Champ Against Champ [BFS] '83
Champ vs. Champ [Xenon] '83
Eagle vs. Silver Fox '83
Fury in the Shaolin Temple '82

Fredric Hobbs
Godmonster of Indian Flats '73

Mike Hodges
Morons from Outer Space '85

Hunt Hoe
Seducing Maarya '99

Harold Hoffman
The Black Cat / The Fat Black Pussycat '65

Michael Hoffman
One Fine Day '96
Soapdish '91

P.J. Hogan
My Best Friend's Wedding [2 SE] '97

Agnieszka Holland
Shot in the Heart '01

Tom Holland
Stephen King's The Langoliers '95
The Temp '93

William A. Hollins
Black and Blue '01

Nicole Holofcener
Walking and Talking '96

Seth Holt
Blood from the Mummy's Tomb '71

Inoshiro Honda
Godzilla, King of the Monsters [Goodtimes] '56

Elliot Hong
Retrievers '82

Harry Hook
Robert Louis Stevenson's St. Ives '98
Lord of the Flies '90

Tobe Hooper
Invaders from Mars [MGM] '86

Dennis Hopper
Colors '88

Kenny Hotz
Pitch '01

Hsiao-Hsien Hou
Flowers of Shanghai '98
Goodbye South, Goodbye '96
Good Men, Good Women '95
The Puppetmaster '93

John Hough
The Lady and the Highwayman '89
The Watcher in the Woods '81
The Legend of Hell House '73
Eye Witness '70

Ellen Hovde
Grey Gardens '75

Frank Howard
Helter Skelter Murders '71

Ron Howard
Dr. Seuss' How the Grinch Stole Christmas '00
Willow '88

Sandy Howard
Tarzan and the Trappers '58

Jan Hrebejk
Divided We Fall '00

Talun Hsu
Fatal Blade '00

Ann Hu
Shadow Magic '00

John Huddles
Uncorked '98

Albert Hughes
From Hell [DLE] '01
American Pimp '99

Allen Hughes
From Hell [DLE] '01

Terry Hughes
The Butcher's Wife '91

Brett Hull
She Lives by Night '01

H. Bruce Humberstone
Tarzan and the Trappers '58

Hwa Yi Hung
Jade Claw '79

Sammo Hung
The Owl vs. Bombo '84
Wheels on Meals '84

Sui Hung
The Assassin '93

Tran Anh Hung
The Vertical Ray of the Sun '00
The Scent of Green Papaya '93

Peter Hunt
On Her Majesty's Secret Service '69

Koichi Kobayashi
Tokyo Decameron: Three Tales of Madness & Sensuality '96

Kenji Kodama
City Hunter: Secret Service '96

Yutaka Kohira
Taboo '97

Amos Kollek
Fiona '98

Kazuya Konaku
The Dimension Travelers '98

Andrei Konchalovsky
The Odyssey '97
Maria's Lovers '84

Masaura Konuma
Beautiful Hunter '94

Zoltan Korda
Sahara '43
The Jungle Book '42

Jacob Kornbluth
Haiku Tunnel '00

Josh Kornbluth
Haiku Tunnel '00

John Korty
The Autobiography of Miss Jane Pittman '74

Henry Koster
The Robe '53

Jim Kouf
Gang Related '96

Steven Kovacks
'68 '87

William R. Kowalchuk
Rudolph the Red-Nosed Reindeer: The Movie '98

Bernard L. Kowalski
Attack of the Giant Leeches [Marengo] '59

Jeroen Krabbe
Left Luggage '98

Stanley Kramer
It's a Mad, Mad, Mad, Mad World '63
Inherit the Wind '60
On the Beach '59
The Defiant Ones '58
The Pride and the Passion '57

Lars Kraume
Advertising Rules! '01

John Kretchmer
Buffy the Vampire Slayer: Season 1 '97

John Krokidas
Queer As F**k: Bizarre Short Films '01

Piet Kroon
Osmosis Jones '01

Georgy Kropachov
Viy '67

Steve Kroschel
Escape from Alaska '02

Bill Kroyer
Ferngully '92

Lisa Krueger
Committed '99

Stanley Kubrick
Full Metal Jacket [2 SE] '87
The Shining [2 SE] '80

Thomas Kufus
Mein Krieg '90

Buzz Kulik
The Hunter '80
Incident on a Dark Street '72

Roger Kumble
Cruel Intentions 2 '99

Joseph Kuo
Dragon's Claws '79

Kunio Kurita
Pearl Harbor: The View from Japan '94

Akira Kurosawa
The Hidden Fortress '58
Rashomon '51

F. Joseph Kurtz
Carnivore '01

Fran Rubel Kuzui
Buffy the Vampire Slayer '92

Ken Kwapis
He Said, She Said '91
Sesame Street Presents: Follow That Bird '85

Philip Kwok
Ninja in the Deadly Trap '83

Gregory La Cava
My Man Godfrey [Criterion] '36

Gregg Lachow
Money Buys Happiness '99

Ron Lagomarsino
Running Mates '00

Christine Lahti
My First Mister '01

Ivan Lai
Daughter of Darkness '93

Dante Lam
Jiang Hu—"The Triad Zone" '00

Ngai Kai Lam
Riki-Oh: The Story of Ricky '89

Ringo Lam
Replicant '01
Prison on Fire 2 '91
City on Fire [Dimension] '87

Mary Lambert
Dragstrip Girl '94
Pet Sematary 2 '92

Charles Lamont
Abbott and Costello Meet the Mummy '55

John Landis
Beverly Hills Cop 3 '94
Three Amigos '86
An American Werewolf in London [CE Universal] '81
Schlock '73

Paul Landres
Destination Nightmare '54

Eric Laneuville
Hard Lessons '86

Sidney Lanfield
My Favorite Blonde '42

Fritz Lang
The Indian Tomb '59
Tiger of Eschnapur '59
The Big Heat '53
Dr. Mabuse, The Gambler '22

Richard Lang
Texas '94
The Mountain Men '80

Samantha Lang
The Well '97

Walter Lang
The Little Princess [Marengo] '39

Stephen Langford
Warm Blooded Killers '01

Simon Langton
Jeeves & Wooster: The Complete Second Season '96
Therese Raquin '80

James Lapine
Impromptu '90
Into the Woods '90

Gene Lasko
W. Eugene Smith: Photography Made Difficult '89

Stan Lathan
Amazing Grace '74

Andrew Lau
The Avenging Fist '01
The Duel '00
The Storm Riders '98

Michael Laughlin
Strange Invaders '83

Dale Launer
Love Potion 9 '92

Georges Lautner
Le Professionnel '81

Arnold Laven
Rough Night in Jericho '67
The Monster That Challenged the World '57

Quentin Lawrence
The Crawling Eye '58

Ray Lawrence
Lantana '01

Harold Lea
The Fat Black Pussycat '63

David Lean
Doctor Zhivago '65
Summertime '55

Timothy Leary
Cheech and Chong's Nice Dreams '81

Reginald LeBorg
The Mummy's Ghost '44

Conan LeClaire
Faces of Death 2 '81
Faces of Death 3: Scenes from the Underground '81

Patrice Leconte
The Widow of Saint-Pierre '00

Mimi Leder
Pay It Forward '00

Paul Leder
A*P*E* '76

David Ross Lederman
Two-Fisted Law '32

Ang Lee
Crouching Tiger, Hidden Dragon [2 SB] '00
The Ice Storm '97
Eat Drink Man Woman '94

Bruce Lee
Bruce Lee: A Warrior's Journey '01

Damian Lee
Agent Red '00
Abraxas: Guardian of the Universe [BFS] '90

Danny Lee
Dr. Lamb '92

Raymond Lee
Dragon Inn '92

Rowland V. Lee
Captain Kidd [Marengo] '45
The Son of Monte Cristo '40
Son of Frankenstein '39

Tso Nam Lee
Eagle Fist '77

Michael Lehmann
Airheads '94
Heathers [2 THX] '89

Jennifer Jason Leigh
The Anniversary Party '01

Danny Leiner
Dude, Where's My Car? '00

Mitchell Leisen
The Big Broadcast of 1938 '38

Kasi Lemmons
The Caveman's Valentine '01

Umberto Lenzi
Bruce Lee Fights Back from the Grave '76

Terry J. Leonard
Death Before Dishonor '87

Po Chich Leong
Return to Cabin by the Lake '01
Cabin by the Lake / Return to Cabin by the Lake '00

Carl Lerner
Black Like Me '64

Richard Lester
Cuba '79
A Funny Thing Happened on the Way to the Forum '66

Michael Leszczylowski
Directed by Andrei Tarkovsky '88

Sheldon Lettich
The Order '01
The Last Warrior '99

Kant Leung
Ultimatum '01
The Demon's Baby '98

Kar-yan Leung
Cold War '00

Yun-chuen Leung
Fist of Fury '95

Brian Levant
Snow Dogs '02

Jay Levey
UHF '89

Marc Levin
Brooklyn Babylon '00

Barry Levinson
Bandits '01
An Everlasting Piece '00
Toys '92
Tin Men '87
Diner '82

Elyse Lewin
Borough of Kings '98

Christopher Lewis
Revenge '86
Blood Cult '85

Herschell Gordon Lewis
Just for the Hell of It '68
Blast-Off Girls / Just for the Hell of It '67

Joseph H. Lewis
The Invisible Ghost '41

Louis Lewis
Brief Affair '96

Mark Lewis
Cane Toads: An Unnatural History '87

Bruce Li
Fists of Bruce Lee '78

Karl Liao
Dreaming Fists with Slender Hands '80

Peter Paul Liapis
Alone with a Stranger '99

Leslie Libman
Oz: The Complete First Season '97

Demian Lichtenstein
3000 Miles to Graceland '01

Robert Lieberman
Tom Clancy's Netforce '98

Richard Linklater
Waking Life '01

Norman C. Linton
Better Dayz '02

Gustavo Lipzstein
Dead in the Water '01

Steven Lisberger
Slipstream '89
Hot Pursuit '87
Tron [2 CE] '82

Dwight Little
Boss of Bosses '99
Halloween 4: The Return of Michael Myers [MGM LE] '88

John Little
Bruce Lee: A Warrior's Journey '01

Anatole Litvak
Sorry, Wrong Number '48
The Long Night '47

Sam Liu
Roughnecks: Starship Troopers Chronicles—The Homefront Campaign '99

Tony Liu
Tiger over Wall '80

Luis Llosa
800 Leagues down the Amazon '93

Frank Lloyd
Blood on the Sun [Image] '45

Ken Loach
Bread and Roses '00
Hidden Agenda '90

Jayne Loader
The Atomic Cafe [SE] '82

Joshua Logan
Paint Your Wagon '69
Sayonara '57

Jerry London
Victim of Love '91

Robert Longo
Johnny Mnemonic [2 SB] '95

Joseph Losey
Don Giovanni '79
Accident '67
The Servant '63
Eva '62

Robert Lovy
Plughead Rewired: Circuitry Man 2 '94

Steven Lovy
Plughead Rewired: Circuitry Man 2 '94
Circuitry Man '90

Dick Lowry
The Diamond of Jeru '01
Follow the Stars Home '01

George Lucas
Star Wars: Episode 1—The Phantom Menace '99

NeverEnding Story 2: The Next Chapter '91
The Aviator '85

George Miller
Robinson Crusoe '96
Mad Max [MGM SE] '80

Michael Miller
Silent Rage '82

Dan Milner
The Phantom from 10,000 Leagues '56

Daniel Minahan
Series 7: The Contenders '01

Steve Miner
Texas Rangers '01
House '86
Soul Man '86

Anthony Minghella
Truly, Madly, Deeply '91

Rob Minkoff
Stuart Little [2 DE] '99

Vincente Minnelli
Designing Woman '57
The Bad and the Beautiful '52

David Mirkin
Heartbreakers '01

Randy Misho
Narcotic Justice

Kenji Misumi
The Tale of Zatoichi '62

John Cameron Mitchell
Hedwig and the Angry Inch '00

Justin Mitchell
Song for Cassavetes '00

Frederic Mitterrand
Madame Butterfly '95

Takeshi Miyasaka
Tokyo Mafia: Battle for Shinjuku '96

Hayao Miyazaki
The Castle of Cagliostro '80

Kunio Miyoshi
Rebirth of Mothra 2 '97

Hans Petter Moland
Aberdeen '00
Zero Degrees Kelvin '95

Edouard Molinaro
La Cage aux Folles 2 '81
La Cage aux Folles '78

Dominik Moll
With a Friend Like Harry '00

Carl Monson
A Scream in the Streets '73
Please Don't Eat My Mother '72

Robert Montero
Mondo Balordo '64

Jorge Montesi
Turbulence 3: Heavy Metal '00

Guy Moore
Daria, The Movie: Is It Fall Yet? '01

John Moore
Behind Enemy Lines '01

Jonathan Moore
Great Fighting Machines of WWII: Allied & Axis Bombers '01
Great Fighting Machines of WWII: Allied & Axis Fighters '01

Great Fighting Machines of WWII: Allied & Axis Tanks '01

Michael Moore
The Awful Truth: The Complete Second Season '01

Robert Moore
The Cheap Detective '78
Murder by Death '76

Philippe Mora
Howling 3: The Marsupials '87
Return of Captain Invincible '83
The Beast Within '82

Christopher Morahan
Troubles '88
Clockwise '86

Andrew Morgan
The Worst Witch '98

Kazuo Mori
The Tale of Zatoichi Continues '62

Louis Morneau
Retroactive '97

Emma Joan Morris
Something within Me '93

Rob Morrow
Maze '01

Terry Morse
Godzilla, King of the Monsters [Goodtimes] '56
Fog Island '45

Gilbert Moses
Roots '77

Gregory Mosher
The Prime Gig '00

Jonathan Mostow
Breakdown '96

John Llewellyn Moxey
The City of the Dead '60

Russell Mulcahy
The Lost Battalion '01
Queer as Folk: The Complete First Season '01
Highlander [Anchor Bay] '86

Peter Mullan
Orphans '97

Robert Mulligan
Summer of '42 '71

Robert Munic
In a Class of His Own '99

F.W. Murnau
Faust '26
The Last Laugh '24
Nosferatu '22

Atsushi Muroga
Score '95

Eddie Murphy
Harlem Nights '89

Geoff Murphy
Utu '83

Tab Murphy
The Last of the Dogmen '95

Fernando Musa
Brain Drain '98

Arthur Nadel
Clambake '67

Chris Nahon
Kiss of the Dragon '01

Ryutaro Nakamura
Serial Experiments: Lain '98

Takao Nakano
Sumo Vixens '96

Bruce Nash
World Trade Center—A Modern Marvel: 1973–2001 '01

Ronald Neame
The Horse's Mouth '58

Hal Needham
The Villain '79

Michel Negroponte
W.I.S.O.R. The Robo Welder '01

Jean Negulesco
Three Came Home '50

Roy William Neill
Frankenstein Meets the Wolfman '42

Gary Nelson
Murder in Coweta County '83

Jessie Nelson
I Am Sam '01

Ralph Nelson
Requiem for a Heavyweight '62

Tim Blake Nelson
O '01

Sam Newfield
The Lost Continent '51
She Shoulda Said No '49
The Black Raven '43

Yiu-Kuen Ng
The Untold Story 2 '98

Fred Niblo
Blood and Sand '22
Mark of Zorro [2] / Don Q, Son of Zorro '20

Andrew Niccol
Gattaca [2 SB] '97

Paul Nicholas
Luckytown '00

Jack Nicholson
Goin' South '78

Dewey Nicks
Slackers '02

Sebastian Niemann
Seven Days to Live '01

William Nigh
The Fatal Hour '40
Mr. Wong, Detective '38
Mysterious Mr. Wong '35

Leonard Nimoy
Three Men and a Baby '87
Star Trek 3: The Search for Spock '84

Akihiko Nishiyama
The Gatchaman Collection '94

Yoshinobu Nishizaki
Star Blazers: The Comet Empire: Part 1 '80

Nigel Noble
The Charcoal People '01

Haruyasu Noguchi
Gappa the Trifibian Monster '67

Christopher Nolan
Memento [1] '00
Memento [2 SE] '00
Following '99

Aaron Norris
Top Dog '95

Terry L. Noss
The Trumpet of the Swan '01

Noel Nosseck
Las Vegas Lady '76

Thierry Notz
The Terror Within '88

Jehane Noujaim
Startup.com '01

Maria Novaro
Garden of Eden '94

Lynn Novick
Frank Lloyd Wright—A Film by Ken Burns and Lynn Novick '98

Victor Nunez
Ulee's Gold '97

Trevor Nunn
Cats [UE Universal] '98

Carl-Gustaf Nykvist
Light Keeps Me Company '00

Sing Pui O
Comic King '00

Michael Oblowitz
The Breed '01
On the Borderline '01

Jack O'Brien
Time of Your Life '76

Jeffrey Obrow
Servants of Twilight '91

Masayuki Ochiai
Parasite Eve '97

Pat O'Connor
Sweet November '01
The January Man '89

William A. O'Connor
Cocaine Fiends '36

Bob Odenkirk
Mr. Show: The Complete First & Second Seasons '02

Steve Oedekerk
The Blair Thumb '01
Thumb Wars '99
Thumbtanic '99

Tommy O'Haver
Get over It! '01

Shundo Ohkawa
Double Deception '01

Takao Okawara
Godzilla vs. Destroyah '95

David Oliver
Cave Girl '85

Hector Olivera
A Shadow You Soon Will Be '94
Barbarian Queen '85
Funny, Dirty Little War '83

Javier Olivera
The Road '00

Laurence Olivier
The Prince and the Showgirl '57

Tamara Olson
Fashionably L.A. '99

Lawrence O'Neil
Breast Men '97

Wyott Ordung
Monster from the Ocean Floor '54

Josh Oreck
The Matrix Revisited '01

Stuart Orme
Ivanhoe '97

Kenny Ortega
Newsies '92

Nagisa Oshima
Taboo '99

Katsuhiro Otomo
Roujin Z [Central Park] '95

Frank Oz
The Score '01
The Indian in the Cupboard '95
Dirty Rotten Scoundrels [MGM] '88
The Muppets Take Manhattan '84

Shigehiro (Sakae) Ozawa
Return of the Street Fighter '74
The Street Fighter [BCI] '74
The Street Fighter [BFS] '74

Francois Ozon
Under the Sand '00
Water Drops on Burning Rocks '99

G.W. Pabst
Diary of a Lost Girl '29
The Love of Jeanne Ney '27

Juan Padron
Vampires in Havana '87

Anthony Page
I Never Promised You a Rose Garden '77

Victor Pahlen
Cuban Story '59

Alan J. Pakula
Comes a Horseman '78
Klute '71

Matt Palmieri
Sand '00

Robert Palumbo
Fallout '01

Jafar Panahi
The Circle '00

Denis Paquet
Witch Hunter '01

Sergei Paradjanov
Ashik Kerib '88
The Legend of Suram Fortress / Ashik Kerib '85
The Color of Pomegranates '69

Arto Paragamian
Because Why? '93

Paul S. Parco
The Passion Network '01
Tender Is the Heart '01

Nick Park
Creature Comforts '90

Brian Parker
Upstairs, Downstairs: The Complete First Season '71

Dave Parker
The Dead Hate the Living '99

Norton S. Parker
The Road to Ruin '28

Trey Parker
South Park: Insults to Injury '02
South Park: Bigger, Longer and Uncut '99
Cannibal! The Musical '96

Andrew Parkinson
Dead Creatures '01

Tom Parkinson
With Friends Like These '90

J. Vincent Parris
Dealin' Dirty Rockin' with a Bullet

Lee Rose
A Girl Thing '01

Martin Rosen
Watership Down '78

Steve Rosen
Beyond Barbed Wire '97

Rick Rosenberg
Southern Man '99

Dale Rosenbloom
Shiloh '97

Rick Rosenthal
Bad Boys [Anchor Bay] '83
Halloween 2: The Nightmare
Isn't Over! [Universal] '81

Herbert Ross
California Suite '78
Funny Lady '75
Play It Again, Sam '72
The Owl and the Pussycat '70

Robert Rossen
All the King's Men '49

Joe Roth
America's Sweethearts '01
Revenge of the Nerds 2:
Nerds in Paradise '87

Phillip J. Roth
Boa '02

Russell Rouse
The Thief '52

Alexander Row
Barbara the Fair with the
Silken Hair '69
Father Frost '66

Jack Rubio
Hard Luck '01

Alan Rudolph
Trixie '00
Choose Me '84

Oscar Rudolph
The Lone Ranger: Volume 1
'56

Wesley Ruggles
The Plastic Age '25

Richard Rush
The Sinister Saga '00
The Stunt Man '80

Steven Rush
Extreme Honor '01

Ken Russell
Crimes of Passion [2] '84

Todd Ryan
Rappin'-N-Rhyming '00

Mark Rydell
Intersection '93

Renny Rye
Agatha Christie's Poirot: Peril
at End House '90

Michael Rymer
Perfume '01

Olli Saarela
Ambush '99

William Sachs
Galaxina '80

Daniel Sackheim
The Glass House '01

Malcolm St. Clair
The Show Off / The Plastic
Age '26

Hironobu Sakaguchi
Final Fantasy: The Spirits
Within '01

Koichi Sakamoto
Extreme Heist '99

Gene Saks
Cactus Flower '69

Leo Salkin
2000 Year Old Man '82

Sidney Salkow
The Last Man on Earth '64
Twice-Told Tales '63

Mikael Salomon
A Glimpse of Hell '01

Victor Salva
Jeepers Creepers '01

Edwards Sampson
The Fast and the Furious '54

Barry Samson
Bloodfist 8: Hard Way Out '96

Jay Sandrich
Seems Like Old Times '80

Jimmy Sangster
Lust for a Vampire '71

Erick Santamaria
Playgirl Killer '66

Miguel Santesmases
The Yellow Fountain '99

Joseph Sargent
MacArthur '77

Vic Sarin
Sea People '00

Maurice Sarli
The Bodyguard [BFS] '76

Michael J. Sarna
Doomsdayer '99

Joe Sarno
Inga '67

Peter Sasdy
Doomwatch '72

Eiichi Sato
Fortune Quest: Journey to
Terrason '97

Hisayasu Sato
The Bedroom '92

Junichi Sato
Strange Dawn, Vol. 2—
Strange Journey '01

Tatsuo Sato
Martian Successor Nadesico:
Endgame '96

Claude Sautet
Nelly et Monsieur Arnaud '95

Leigh Savidge
Welcome to Death Row '00

Seiko Sayama
Angel Sanctuary '00

John Sayles
The Secret of Roan Inish '94

Luigi Scattini
Primitive Love '64

Eric Schaeffer
Wirey Spindell '99

Franklin J. Schaffner
Patton [2] '70

Fred Schepisi
The Russia House '90
Plenty [Anchor Bay] '85

Shawn Schepps
Lip Service '00

Victor Schertzinger
The Road to Zanzibar '41
The Road to Singapore '40

Ryan Schifrin
Smash Cuts! Super Sci-Fi
Shorts '00

Lawrence Schiller
American Tragedy '00

John Schlesinger
An Eye for an Eye '95
Honky Tonk Freeway '81
Billy Liar '63

Volker Schlondorff
The Legend of Rita '99
The Ogre '96
The Handmaid's Tale '90

Paul Schneider
Dance 'til Dawn '88

Paul Schrader
Mishima: A Life in Four Chapters '85

Barbet Schroeder
Our Lady of the Assassins
'01
Reversal of Fortune '90
General Idi Amin Dada: A Self
Portrait '74

Pete Schuermann
Star Warp'd '01

Carl Schultz
Careful, He Might Hear You
'84

Michael A. Schultz
The Last Dragon '85

Joel Schumacher
Cousins '89

Eric Schwab
The Learning Curve '01

Stephen Schwartz
Working '82

Martin Scorsese
A Personal Journey with Mar-
tin Scorsese through Amer-
ican Movies '97
The Age of Innocence '93
Cape Fear '91
The Last Waltz [SE] '78
Boxcar Bertha '72

Campbell Scott
Final '01

Jake Scott
Plunkett & Macleane '98

Oz Scott
Spanish Judges '99

Ridley Scott
Black Hawk Down '01
Legend [UE] '86

T.J. Scott
Blacktop '01

Tony Scott
Spy Game '01
Beverly Hills Cop 2 '87

George Scribner
Oliver & Company '88

Richard Sears
Bongwater '98

Mike Sedan
Sexual Chemistry '99
Boundaries '97
Illicit Confessions '77

John Sedwick
Dark Shadows: DVD Collec-
tion 1 '67

Peter Segal
Tommy Boy '95

Jose Segura
Cuando Habla El Corazon '42

Arthur Allan Seidelman
The Runaway '00

Susan Seidelman
She-Devil '89

Lewis Seiler
Guadalcanal Diary '43

William A. Seiter
Borderline '50
Dimples '36

George B. Seitz
The Legend of the Lone
Ranger '59
The Lone Ranger: Volume 1
'56

Lesley Selander
Lone Ranger and the Lost
City of Gold '58
Flight to Mars '52

Henry Selick
Monkeybone '01

Larry Semon
The Wizard of Oz '25

Dominic Sena
Swordfish '01

Steve Sessions
Cremains '00

Adam Shankman
The Wedding Planner '01

John Patrick Shanley
Joe versus the Volcano '90

L.L. Shapira
Adventures of Justine '00

Arnold Shapiro
Heroes of Iwo Jima '01

Craig Shapiro
Winning London '01

Ben Sharpsteen
Dumbo '41

Melville Shavelson
Cast a Giant Shadow '66

James K. Shea
Planet of the Dinosaurs '80

Barry Shear
Across 110th Street '72

Jon Shear
Urbania '00

Chuck Sheetz
Recess Christmas: Miracle
on Third Street '01
Recess: School's Out '01

Tom Shell
Wind River '98

Adrienne Shelly
Sudden Manhattan '96

Ron Shelton
Bull Durham [MGM SE] '88

Richard Shepard
Mexico City '01
Oxygen '99

Jack Sher
The Three Worlds of Gulliver
'59

Jim Sheridan
The Field [Artisan] '90

Edwin Sherin
King Lear '74
Valdez Is Coming '71

Gary Sherman
Wanted: Dead or Alive '86

Roger Sherman
Richard Rodgers: The Sweetest Sound '01

Dominic Shiach
Blackheart '98

Barry Shils
Motorama '91

Hyung Rae Shim
Reptilian '00

Masakazu Shirai
Reborn from Hell: Jubei's
Revenge '96
Reborn from Hell: Samurai
Armageddon '96

Seiichi Shirai
Tokyo Mafia: Wrath of the
Yakuza '95
Tokyo Mafia: Yakuza Wars '95

Jack Sholder
Arachnid '01

Haruhiko Shono
Gadget Trips—Mindscapes
'95

M. Night Shyamalan
Unbreakable '00
The Sixth Sense [Buena
Vista] '99

Melville Shyer
Mad Youth '40

Tony Shyu
Tequila Body Shots '99

Nicholas Siapkaris
Warm Blooded Killers '01

Andy Sidaris
Picasso Trigger '89
Hard Ticket to Hawaii '87

George Sidney
Show Boat '51
The Harvey Girls '46

David Siegel
The Deep End '01

Donald Siegel
The Shootist '76
Dirty Harry [2] '71

Marisa Silver
He Said, She Said '91

Bryan Singer
The Usual Suspects [MGM
SE] '95

John Singleton
Baby Boy '01
Higher Learning '94

Ralph S. Singleton
Graveyard Shift '90

Gary Sinise
Of Mice and Men '92

Bruce Sinofsky
Paradise Lost 2: Revelations
'99

Gary Sinyor
Stiff Upper Lips '96

Curt Siodmak
Tales of Frankenstein '58

Robert Siodmak
Son of Dracula '43

Douglas Sirk
Written on the Wind '56
All That Heaven Allows '55
Lured '47

Rob Sitch
The Dish '00

Tom Sito
Osmosis Jones '01

John Sjogren
Choke '01

Bix Skahill
Life without Dick '01

Keri Skogland
Zebra Lounge '01

Neil Slavin
Focus '01

Please Not Now! '61
And God Created Woman '57
The Night Heaven Fell '57

Jose Luis Valenzuela
Luminarias '99

Eric Valli
Himalaya '99

Andre Van Heerden
Deceived '01
Judgment '01

Buddy Van Horn
The Dead Pool '88
Any Which Way You Can '80

Timothy Van Patten
The Sopranos: The Complete Second Season '01

Derek Vanlint
Spreading Ground '01

Agnes Varda
Cleo from 5 to 7 '61

Kenton Vaughan
Todd McFarlane: The Devil You Know '02

Francis Veber
The Closet '00
Three Fugitives '89

Gore Verbinski
The Mexican '01

Michael Verhoeven
Blitz '85

Paul Verhoeven
The Hollow Man [2 SB] '00
Showgirls '95
Basic Instinct [2 SE] '92
Total Recall [2 SLE] '90
Katie Tippel '75
Business Is Business '71

Mark Verkerk
Castles of War '00

Todd Verow
Little Shots of Happiness '97

King Vidor
On Our Merry Way '48
Stella Dallas '37

Joe Viola
Angels Hard As They Come '71

Clement Virgo
Love Come Down '00

Luchino Visconti
Rocco and His Brothers '60

Virgil W. Vogel
Invasion of the Animal People '62
Terror in the Midnight Sun '58

Josef von Sternberg
The Blue Angel '30
It '27

Robert Voskanian
The Child '76

Kurt Voss
Body Count '97

Andrucha Waddington
Me You Them '00

Jeremy Wagener
Chicks, Man '99

Kai-Fai Wai
Love on a Diet '01
Too Many Ways to Be No. 1 '97

David Wain
Wet Hot American Summer '01

Andrzej Wajda
Siberian Lady Macbeth '61

Grant Austin Waldman
Gator King '70

Dorian Walker
Making the Grade '84

Hal Walker
The Road to Utopia [Universal] '46

Michael Walker
Chasing Sleep '00

Nancy Walker
Can't Stop the Music '80

Pete Walker
Schizo '77

Stuart Walker
Werewolf of London '35

Jordan Walker-Pearlman
The Visit '00

Aisling Walsh
Forgive and Forget '99

Raoul Walsh
College Swing '38
Sadie Thompson '28
Regeneration / Young Romance '15

Fred Walton
When a Stranger Calls '79

Steve Wang
Adventures of the Kung Fu Rascals '92

Wayne Wang
The Center of the World '01

David S. Ward
Major League 2 '94

Donal Lardner Ward
The Suburbans '99

Larry Ward
World War I Films of the Silent Era '02

Regis Wargnier
Indochine '92

Hal P. Warren
Manos, the Hands of Fate '66

Jerry Warren
Invasion of the Animal People '62
Teenage Zombies '58

John Warren
Major League 3: Back to the Minors '98

Joshua P. Warren
Inbred Rednecks '97

Akio Watanabe
Soultaker: The Monster Within '02

Daniel Waters
Happy Campers '01

John Waters
Pecker (John Waters Collection Vol. 1) '98
Hairspray (John Waters Collection Vol. 1) '88
Polyester (John Waters Collection Vol. 2) '81
Desperate Living (John Waters Collection Vol. 2) '77
Female Trouble '74
Pink Flamingos '72

Mark Waters
Head over Heels '01

Michael W. Watkins
Hostage High '97

Charlie Watson
The Enemy '01

John Watson
Deathstalker '83

Nate Watt
Hopalong Cassidy Returns '36

Keenen Ivory Wayans
Scary Movie 2 '01

Christina Wayne
Tart '01

Robert D. Webb
The Jackals '67

David Wechter
Midnight Madness '80

Paul Wegener
The Golem '20

Lo Wei
To Kill with Intrigue '77

Chuck Wein
Rainbow Bridge '71

Phil Weinstein
Balto 2: Wolf Quest '02

Zachary Weintraub
Amazons and Gladiators '01

Peter Weir
The Last Wave '77

Gabe Weisert
Fishing with Gandhi '98

Sam Weisman
What's the Worst That Could Happen? [SE] '01

Chris Weitz
Down to Earth '01
American Pie [2 UE] '99

Paul Weitz
Down to Earth '01
American Pie [2 UE] '99

Mel Welles
Lady Frankenstein '72

Orson Welles
The Trial '63
The Stranger [Delta/Laserlight] '46
Citizen Kane '41

David Wellington
Restless Spirits '99

Paul Wendkos
The Tattered Web '71

Richard Wenk
Vamp '86

Alfred Werker
He Walked by Night [BFS] '48

John Werner
Rudy Blue '00

Peter Werner
Call Me Claus '01
Mama Flora's Family '98

Lina Wertmuller
Seduction of Mimi '72

William Wesley
Route 666 '01

Simon West
Lara Croft: Tomb Raider '01

Terry West
The Sexy Sixth Sense '01

Haskell Wexler
Medium Cool [SE] '69

George Whaley
Poor Man's Orange '87
The Harp in the South '86

David Wheatley
Catherine Cookson's The Girl '96

David Wheeler
Point of View '00

Tim Whelan
Rage at Dawn '55

Alan White
Risk '00

Jesse White
Tales from Europe: The Story of Little Mook '53

John Whitesell
See Spot Run '01

James Wignall
The Knights Templar '00

Crane Wilbur
The Bat [Goodtimes] '59
Tomorrow's Children '34

Billy Wilder
Irma La Douce '63
Witness for the Prosecution '57

Gene Wilder
Haunted Honeymoon '86

Gavin Wilding
Christina's House '99

Ethan Wiley
Children of the Corn 5: Fields of Terror '98
House 2: The Second Story '87

Larry Williams
Oz: The Complete First Season '97

Oscar Williams
Five on the Black Hand Side '73

Walter Williams
Mr. Bill Goes to Hollywood / Mr. Bill Does Vegas '01

J. Elder Wills
Big Fella '37
Song of Freedom / Big Fella '36

Andy Wilson
Gormenghast '00

Michael Henry Wilson
A Personal Journey with Martin Scorsese through American Movies '97

Scott Winant
Til There Was You '96

Simon Wincer
Crocodile Dundee in Los Angeles '01
Crossfire Trail '01
Quigley Down Under '90

Harry Winer
House Arrest '96

Zack Winestine
States of Control '98

Jonathan Winfrey
Bloodfist 7: Manhunt '95

Irwin Winkler
Life As a House '01
The Net [2 SE] '95

Terence H. Winkless
The Nest '88

Jeff Winner
You Are Here * '00

Michael Winner
Chato's Land '71
Lawman '71

Alex Winter
Fever '99

Peter Wintonick
Manufacturing Consent: Noam Chomsky and the Media '93

Herbert Wise
Woman in Black '89
Upstairs, Downstairs: The Complete First Season '71

Kirk Wise
Atlantis: The Lost Empire [CE] '01
The Hunchback of Notre Dame '96

Robert Wise
Storm in Summer '00
Star Trek: The Motion Picture [DE] '80
Audrey Rose '77
I Want to Live! '58
Run Silent, Run Deep '58

Doris Wishman
Night to Dismember '83

Fung Wong
The Legendary Strike '78

Gum-miu Wong
Fist of Fury '95

Jing Wong
Legend of the Red Dragon '94

Kirk Wong
The Big Hit [2 SB] '98

Sherman Wong
Sex and the Emperor '94

Taylor Wong
Rich and Famous / Tragic Hero '87
Tragic Hero '87
Return of the Deadly Blade '81

John Woo
Last Hurrah for Chivalry '78

Edward D. Wood, Jr.
Night of the Ghouls '59

Rowan Woods
Farscape, Vol. 1 '00

Wallace Worsley, II
The Penalty '20

David Worth
Time Lapse '01

Alexander Wright
Styx '00

Dennis Wu
Ninja in the U.S.A. '88

Ming-hoi Wu
Fist of Fury '95

William Wyler
Funny Girl '68
The Little Foxes [MGM] '41
Dodsworth [MGM] '36

Tracy Keenan Wynn
Hit Lady '74

Jim Wynorski
Extreme Limits '01
Poison '01
Raptor '01
Stealth Fighter '99
Big Bad Mama 2 '87
Deathstalker 2: Duel of the Titans '87

Shinobu Yaguchi
Adrenaline Drive '99

Boaz Yakin
Fresh '94

Katsuhisa Yamada
Devil Hunter Yohko: The Complete Collection, Vol. 1 '93

Masakazu Yamada
Very Private Lessons '01

Kazuhiko Yamaguchi
Sister Street Fighter '76

Kensho Yamashita
Godzilla vs. Space Godzilla /
    Godzilla vs. Destroyah '94

Jean Yarbrough
Over the Hill Gang '69
She Wolf of London '46
The Devil Bat '41

Peter Yates
Suspect '87
Breaking Away '79

Donnie Yen
Ballistic Kiss '98

Yung-tsu Yen
Thunder Kick '73

Jamie Yerkes
Spin the Bottle '97

Konstantin Yershov
Viy '67

Zhang Yimou
The Road Home '01
Shanghai Triad '95

Ye Ying
Red Cherry '95

Wilson (Wai-Shun) Yip
Biozombie '98

Dwight Yoakam
South of Heaven, West of
    Hell '01

Makoto Yokoyama
Extreme Heist '99

Okihiro Yoneda
Rebirth of Mothra 1 & 2 '96

Jeff Yonis
Bloodfist 5: Human Target
    '93

Harold Young
The Mummy's Tomb '42

Robert M. Young
Triumph of the Spirit '89
Dominick & Eugene '88
Extremities '86

Ronny Yu
The Phantom Lover '95

Corey Yuen
The Avenging Fist '01
Legend of the Red Dragon
    '94
The Legend 2 '93
Bury Me High '90
Righting Wrongs '86

James Yuen
Your Place or Mine! '98

Woo-ping Yuen
Iron Monkey [Miramax] '93
Magnificent Butcher '87
Drunken Master '78
Snake in the Eagle's Shadow
    '78

Kunihiko Yuyama
Weather Report Girl '01

Pokemon: The First Movie '99

Brian Yuzna
Faust: Love of the Damned
    '00
Progeny '98
Return of the Living Dead 3
    '93

Steven Zaillian
Searching for Bobby Fischer
    '93

Alain Zaloum
With Friends Like These '90

Robert Zemeckis
Tales from the Crypt: Robert
    Zemeckis Collection '95
Forrest Gump [SCE] '94
Used Cars '80

Scott Ziehl
Earth vs. the Spider '01

Paul Ziller
Avalanche Alley '01

Fred Zinnemann
From Here to Eternity '53

Daniel Zirilli
Black Spring Break 2 '01

Joseph Zito
Invasion U.S.A. '85

David Zucker
Ruthless People '86

Jerry Zucker
Rat Race '01
Ruthless People '86

Harald Zwart
One Night at McCool's '01

Charlotte Zwerin
Thelonious Monk: Straight,
    No Chaser '89
Salesman '68

Edward Zwick
Courage Under Fire '96

Terry Zwigoff
Ghost World '01

The Screenwriter Index lists all writers with at least one credit in the DVDs reviewed in this book. The listings for the writer names follow an alphabetical sort by last name (although the names appear in a first name, last name format). The videographies are listed chronologically, from most recent film to their first. If a writer wrote (or script doctored) more than one film in the same year, these movies are listed alphabetically within the year.

D. Avelo
Friction '95

Brian Avenet-Bradley
Freez'er '00

Jon Avnet
Uprising '01

Robert J. Avrech
Into Thin Air: Death on Everest '97

Torbjorn Axelman
Vibration '68

George Axelrod
Paris When It Sizzles '64

David Ayer
The Fast and the Furious '01
Training Day '01

Dan Aykroyd
The Best of the Blues Brothers '93

Alejandro Azzano
Secret of the Andes '01

John Bacchus
Play-Mate of the Apes '02
Vampire Obsession '02
Erotic Survivor 2 '01

Danilo Bach
Beverly Hills Cop [CE] '84

Jean-Pierre Bacri
The Taste of Others '00

Phillip Badger
Retroactive '97

Giya Badridze
Ashik Kerib '88

Doug Bagot
2103: Deadly Wake '97

Elliott Baker
Breakout '75

Ralph Bakshi
Fritz the Cat '72

Nigel Balchin
Barabbas '62

Steve Balderson
Pep Squad '98

Ferdinando Baldo
Texas, Adios '66

Coven Balfour
Demon Lust '01

Melissa Balin
Beverly Hood '99

Milt Banta
Peter Pan [2 SE] '53

Jack Baran
Great Balls of Fire '89

Dana Baratta
Andre '94

Franco Barbieri
Shock '79

Miguel Bardem
Not Love Just Frenzy '96

Clive Barker
Nightbreed '90
Rawhead Rex '87

Peter Barnes
The Ruling Class '72

Dan Baron
See Spot Run '01

Jackson Barr
800 Leagues down the Amazon '93

Earl Barret
See No Evil, Hear No Evil '89

Julian Barry
Lenny '74

Odile Barski
The Cry of the Owl '87

Sy Bartlett
Twelve o'Clock High '49

Hal Barwood
MacArthur '77
Bingo Long Traveling All-Stars & Motor Kings '76

Ronald Bass
My Best Friend's Wedding [2 SE] '97

H.E. Bates
Summertime '55

L. Frank Baum
His Majesty, the Scarecrow of Oz '14

L. Frank Baum, Jr.
The Wizard of Oz '25

Thomas Baum
Dracula: The Dark Prince '01
The Manhattan Project '86

Lamberto Bava
Shock '79

Mario Bava
Knives of the Avenger '65
Planet of the Vampires '65

George L. Baxt
Circus of Horrors '60
The City of the Dead '60

Peter S. Beagle
The Lord of the Rings '78

Simon Beaufoy
Blow Dry '00

Phil Beauman
Not Another Teen Movie '01

Jacques Becker
Le Trou '59

Jurek Becker
Jacob the Liar '74

Michael Frost Beckner
Spy Game '01

S.N. Behrman
Hallelujah, I'm a Bum '33

Jean-Jacques Beineix
Diva [Anchor Bay] '82

John Bellucci
Haiku Tunnel '00

Peter Bellwood
Highlander [Anchor Bay] '86

Roberto Benabib
Little City '97

Jose Reyes Bencomo
Two Coyotes '01

Michael G. Bender
Not Another Teen Movie '01

Jessica Bendinger
Bring It On '00

Barbara Benedek
Sabrina '95

Tony Benedict
Animated Christmas DVD Double Feature '79

Charles Bennett
War Gods of the Deep '65

Harve Bennett
Star Trek 3: The Search for Spock '84

Robert Benton
Places in the Heart '84
Kramer vs. Kramer '79
Bad Company '72

Clara Beranger
Dr. Jekyll and Mr. Hyde [Kino] '20

Gretchen J. Berg
Valentine '01

Scott Berg
Goldwyn: The Man and His Movies '01

Giovanni Bergamini
White Fang to the Rescue '74

Stephen Berger
Children of the Corn 4: The Gathering '96

Jean Bergeron
Ultimate G's '01

Andrew Bergman
The Scout '94
Soapdish '91

Ingmar Bergman
Cries and Whispers '72
Wild Strawberries '57

Erik Bergquist
The Fast and the Furious '01

Eric Bergren
Frances [Anchor Bay] '82
The Elephant Man '80

Stan Berkowitz
The Batman Superman Movie '97

Alan Berliner
The Sweetest Sound '01

Patrick Bermel
Ripper: Letter from Hell '01

Sam Bernard
Blood Surf '00

Sandra Bernhard
Sandra Bernhard: I'm Still Here...Damn It '99

Kevin Bernhardt
Jill the Ripper '00
Turbulence 2: Fear of Flying '99

Emmanuele Bernheim
Under the Sand '00

John Berry
Boesman & Lena '00

Matthew Berry
Crocodile Dundee in Los Angeles '01

Peter Berry
The Luzhin Defence '00

Bernardo Bertolucci
Stealing Beauty '96

Brendon Beseth
Luckytown '00

Luc Besson
Kiss of the Dragon '01
The Fifth Element [2 SB] '97
Le Dernier Combat '84

Antonio J. Betancor
Mararia '98

Minoru Betsuyaku
Night on the Galactic Railroad '85

Alberto Bevilacqua
Planet of the Vampires '65

W. Watt Biggers
Underdog [CE] '00

Cheuk Bing
Sex and the Emperor '94

Charlotte Bingham
Upstairs, Downstairs: The Complete First Season '71

William Birdthistle
Fishing with Gandhi '98

Wes Bishop
Dixie Dynamite '76

Roshel Bissett
Winter Lily '98

Jerome Bixby
It! The Terror from Beyond Space '58

Alan Black
Faces of Death 2 '81
Faces of Death 3: Scenes from the Underground '81

Carol Black
Soul Man '86

Darby Black
Deep Water '99

Karen Black
First Degree '01

Rikki Beadle Blair
Stonewall '95

Dorothy Blank
Snow White and the Seven Dwarfs [PE] '37

Michael Blankfort
The Halls of Montezuma '50

Vera Blasi
Tortilla Soup '01

William Peter Blatty
Exorcist 3: Legion '90
The Exorcist [2]: The Version You've Never Seen '73

Corey Blechman
Dominick & Eugene '88

Robert Blees
Slightly Scarlet '56

William Bleich
The Hearse '80

Seymour Blicker
The Kid '97

Bertrand Blier
Get Out Your Handkerchiefs '78
Going Places '74

Stephan Blinn
Megiddo: The Omega Code 2 '01

William Blinn
Roots '77

Robert Bloch
Strait-Jacket '64

Michael Blodgett
Turner and Hooch '89
Hero and the Terror '88

Rick Bloggs
Luck of the Draw '00

Tom Blomquist
Christy—Return to Cutter Gap '01

Hannah Blue
The Wrecking Crew '99

Edwin Blum
Pearl of the South Pacific '55

Len Blum
Spacehunter: Adventures in the Forbidden Zone '83
Stripes '81

Don Bluth
Thumbelina [20th Century Fox] '94
The Secret of NIMH '82

Steven Bochco
Silent Running [Universal] '71

Sydney Boehm
Rough Night in Jericho '67
The Big Heat '53
When Worlds Collide '51

Jon Bokenkamp
Bad Seed '00

Uwe Boll
Sanctimony '01

Robert Bolt
Doctor Zhivago '65

Julian Bond
Upstairs, Downstairs: The Complete First Season '71

Vittorio Bonicelli
The Bible '66

Pascal Bonitzer
Va Savoir '01
Secret Defense '98
Gang of Four '88

Ted Bonnitt
Mau Mau Sex Sex '00

Greg Booker
Stuart Little [2 DE] '99

John Boorman
The Tailor of Panama '00

Robert Boris
Backyard Dogs '00

Walerian Borowczyk
The Beast '75

Pierre Bost
The Clockmaker '73

David Bottrell
Kingdom Come '01

Michel Marc Bouchard
Lilies '96

Daniel Boulanger
Spirits of the Dead [Criterion] '68

Andrew Bovell
Lantana '01

T.R. Bowen
The Mirror Cracked from Side to Side '92
They Do It with Mirrors '91
A Caribbean Mystery / The Mirror Cracked from Side to Side '89
4:50 from Paddington '87
Murder at the Vicarage '86
Nemesis '86

William Bowers
Support Your Local Sheriff '69

Douglas Bowie
Larceny '91

Bill Boyd
Confessions of a Psycho Cat / Hot Blooded Woman '68

Bill Bozzone
Full Moon in Blue Water '88

Gerard Brach
The Lover '92
The Bear '89
Maria's Lovers '84

Stephen J. Brackely
The Last Warrior '99

Charles Brackett
Niagara '52

Leigh Brackett
Hatari! '62
Rio Bravo '59

Ray Bradbury
It Came from Outer Space '53

Christopher Scott Cherot
Hav Plenty '97

Lionel Chetwynd
Tom Clancy's Netforce '98

Hoi Ching Cheung
Goose Boxer '78

San Yee Cheung
Snake and Crane Arts of
Shaolin '78
Eagle Fist '77

Shan Yi Cheung
Revenge of the Patriots '76

Li Ngai Chi
Millennium Dragon '93

Ping Han Chiang
Dragon's Claws '79

Gerardo Chijona
A Paradise under the Stars
'99

Amy Chin
Jiang Hu—"The Triad Zone"
'00

Yu Chin
Return of the Deadly Blade
'81

Charles Chiodo
Killer Klowns from Outer
Space '88

Stephen Chiodo
Killer Klowns from Outer
Space '88

Margaret Cho
Margaret Cho: I'm the One
That I Want '00

Clifford Choi
Snake in the Eagle's Shadow
'78

Thomas Chong
Cheech and Chong's The Cor-
sican Brothers '84
Cheech and Chong's Nice
Dreams '81

Vidhu Vinod Chopra
Mission Kashmir '00

Matt Chow
Too Many Ways to Be No. 1 '97

Benjamin Christiansen
Haxan: Witchcraft through the
Ages '22

Dick Christie
Molly '99

Tien-wen Chu
Flowers of Shanghai '98
Goodbye South, Goodbye '96
Good Men, Good Women '95
The Puppetmaster '93

Grigori Chukhraj
Ballad of a Soldier '60

Billy Chung
Killer '00

Ji-woo Chung
Happy End '99

Ji-Yong Chung
White Badge '97

Paul Chung
The Cheaters '00

Simon Chung
First Love and Other Pains /
One of Them '99

Yao Chung
Dreaming Fists with Slender
Hands '80

Mikhail Chuprin
Barbara the Fair with the
Silken Hair '69

Gene Church
Snapdragon '93

Vera Chytilova
Daisies '96

Cynthia Cidre
Fires Within '91

Santo Cilauro
The Dish '00

David Ciminello
The Dress Code '99

Michael Cimino
Magnum Force '73
Silent Running [Universal] '71

Louis CK
Down to Earth '01
Pootie Tang '01

Rene Clair
And Then There Were None
[Image] '45

Anna Clark
Introduction to Antiques '95

Dan Clark
The Item '01

Dennis Lynton Clark
Comes a Horseman '78

Greydon Clark
Satan's Cheerleaders '77
Psychic Killer '75

John Clarke
Lonely Hearts '82

James Clavell
To Sir, with Love '67

Christian Clavier
Just Visiting '01

**Thomas McKelvey
Cleaver**
The Terror Within '88

Brian Clemens
The Watcher in the Woods
'81
Dr. Jekyll and Sister Hyde '71
And Soon the Darkness '70

Rene Clement
Purple Noon '60

John Clifford
Carnival of Souls [DC] '62
Carnival of Souls / Dementia
13 '62

Edward Clinton
Honky Tonk Freeway '81

Daniel Clowes
Ghost World '01

Nicole Coady
Reckless and Wild '02

Arthur Coburn
Triumph of the Spirit '89

Jay Cocks
The Age of Innocence '93

Ethan Coen
The Man Who Wasn't There
'01
Blood Simple '85

Joel Coen
The Man Who Wasn't There
'01
Blood Simple '85

Catherine Cohen
Indochine '92

David M. Cohen
Friday the 13th, Part 5: A
New Beginning '85

Howard R. Cohen
Barbarian Queen 2: The
Empress Strikes Back '89
Barbarian Queen '85
Deathstalker '83

Joel Cohen
Money Talks '97

Larry Cohen
Best Seller '87
Hell up in Harlem '73

Lawrence D. Cohen
Rodgers & Hammerstein's
South Pacific '01
Carrie '76

M. Charles Cohen
Roots '77

Martin B. Cohen
Rebel Rousers '69

Alice Colaris
The Nude Set '61

Lester Cole
Blood on the Sun [Image] '45

Lewis Colick
Domestic Disturbance '01
Ghosts of Mississippi '96
Unlawful Entry '92

Boon Collins
Escape to Grizzly Mountain
'99

Pierre Collins
The Show Off / The Plastic
Age '26

John Colton
Werewolf of London '35

Michele Colucci-Zieger
The Skulls 2 '02

Chris Columbus
The Goonies '85

Adele Comandini
Strange Illusion '45
Beyond Tomorrow '40

Ryan Combs
Dirty Kopz '01

Jacques Companeez
Gunman in the Streets '50

Bill Condon
Strange Invaders '83

J.C. (Chris) Conkling
The Lord of the Rings '78

Pat Conroy
The Prince of Tides '91

William Conselman
Bright Eyes '34

Alessandro Continenza
White Fang to the Rescue '74

Deborah Cook
Ivanhoe '97

T.S. Cook
High Noon '00

Willis Cooper
Son of Frankenstein '39

Martin Copeland
Texas Rangers '01

Francis Ford Coppola
The Cotton Club '84
Apocalypse Now [Redux] '79
Patton [2] '70
Dementia 13 [Roan] '63

Patrick Coppola
Where Angels Dance '01

Sergio Corbucci
Companeros '70

Craig Corman
Harold Robbins' Body Parts
'01

John Cornell
Crocodile Dundee '86

John W. Corrington
The Arena '01
Boxcar Bertha '72

Joyce H. Corrington
Boxcar Bertha '72

Michael Cort
Zeta One '69

Enrique Cortes
What Your Eyes Don't See
'99

Don A. Coscarelli
Beastmaster '82

Jean Cosmos
Capitaine Conan '96

Paul Costello
The Squeeze '78

James Costigan
S.O.S. Titanic '79

Callisto Cosulich
Planet of the Vampires '65

Celia Susan Cotelo
The Van '77

Kevin Cotteleer
Dead Pet '01

Joe Cottonmouth
Night Divides the Day '01

William Cottrell
Peter Pan [2 SE] '53

Rich Cowan
The Basket [SE] '99

Jim Cox
Ferngully '92
Oliver & Company '88

Paul Cox
Lonely Hearts '82

Kerry Crabbe
Memoirs of a Survivor '81

H.A.L. Craig
Anzio '68

David Crane
Friends: The Complete First
Season '95

Bruce Craven
Fast Sofa '01

Richard Creedon
Snow White and the Seven
Dwarfs [PE] '37

Michael Cristofer
Original Sin '01
Falling in Love '84

Donald Crombie
The Irishman '78

David Cronenberg
Scanners '81

David Cross
Mr. Show: The Complete First
& Second Seasons '02

Lance Crouther
Down to Earth '01

Cameron Crowe
Vanilla Sky '01
Almost Famous: Untitled—
The Bootleg Cut '00
Jerry Maguire [2 SE] '96
Say Anything [SE] '89

John Crowther
The Evil That Men Do '84

Jim Cruickshank
Three Men and a Baby '87

Robert Crumb
Confessions of Robert Crumb
'87

Gary Crutcher
Superchick '71

Billy Crystal
America's Sweethearts '01
Mr. Saturday Night [MGM] '92

Allan Cubitt
Robert Louis Stevenson's St.
Ives '98

Tom Cudworth
Ten Benny '98

Gerald Cuesta
L.I.E. '01

Michael Cuesta
L.I.E. '01

Mike Cullen
Horatio Hornblower '99

Alan Cumming
The Anniversary Party '01

J.M. Cunilles
Hell of the Living Dead '83

Jack Cunningham
Don Q, Son of Zorro '25

Jere P. Cunningham
Boss of Bosses '99

Valerie Curtin
Toys '92

Nathaniel Curtis
Blood on the Sun [Image] '45

Richard Curtis
Bridget Jones's Diary '01
The Tall Guy '89

Ingram D'Abbes
Big Fella '37
Song of Freedom / Big Fella
'36

John Dahl
Red Rock West '93

Rick Dahl
Red Rock West '93

David DaLie
Swamp Country '66

Walter Dallenbach
Las Vegas Lady '76

Damiano Damiani
Bad Cop Chronicles: Confessions of a Police Captain
'72

Suso Cecchi D'Amico
Rocco and His Brothers '60

Huang Dan
Shadow Magic '00

William Danch
Monster from the Ocean
Floor '54

Monja Danischewsky
Topkapi '64

Gabriele D'Annunzio
Cabiria '14

Marcello Danon
La Cage aux Folles '78

Joe Dante
Rock 'n' Roll High School
[New Concorde SE] '79

Ray Danton
Psychic Killer '75

Jean-Pierre Dardenne
La Promesse '96

David Mickey Evans
The Sandlot '93

John Evans
Black Godfather '74

Clive Exton
Agatha Christie's Poirot: Hercule Poirot's Christmas '01
Agatha Christie's Poirot: Peril at End House '90
Doomwatch '72

Diego Fabbri
Barabbas '62

Chris Faber
See Spot Run '01

Roberto Faenza
Bad Cop Chronicles 2: Corrupt '84

Douglas Fairbanks, Sr.
The Iron Mask '29
Mark of Zorro [2] / Don Q, Son of Zorro '20

Marion Fairfax
World War I Films of the Silent Era '02

Pamela Falk
The Wedding Planner '01

Kevin Falls
Summer Catch '01
The Temp '93

Rick Famuyiwa
The Wood '99

Michael Farakash
Street Vengeance '95

Claude Faraldo
The Widow of Saint-Pierre '00

Max Farberbock
Aimee & Jaguar '98

Herman Daniel Farrell, III
Boycott '02

Bobby Farrelly
Me, Myself, and Irene '00

Peter Farrelly
Me, Myself, and Irene '00

John Farris
The Fury '78

John Fasano
Megiddo: The Omega Code 2 '01

Rainer Werner Fassbinder
Querelle '83

Alvin L. Fast
Satan's Cheerleaders '77
Bummer '73

William Faulkner
The Southerner '45

Jon Favreau
Made [SE] '01

Terence Feely
The Lady and the Highwayman '89

Beda Docampo Feijoo
What Your Eyes Don't See '99

Bi Feiyu
Shanghai Triad '95

Steve Feke
When a Stranger Calls '79

Miles Feldman
Voyeur.com '00

Federico Fellini
Spirits of the Dead [Criterion] '68

Juliet of the Spirits [Criterion] '65
8 1/2 '63

Ben Fello
Curse of the Vampires '70

Frank Fenton
River of No Return '54

Peggy Fenwick
All That Heaven Allows '55

Edna Ferber
The Royal Family '77

Larry Ferguson
Rollerball '02
Beyond the Law '92
Beverly Hills Cop 2 '87
Highlander [Anchor Bay] '86

Wade Ferley
Turbulence 3: Heavy Metal '00

Evelina Fernandez
Luminarias '99

Abel Ferrara
The Blackout '97

Jeff Ferrell
Partners '99

Franco Ferrini
Sleepless '01
The Church '98
Opera '88

George Ferris
Styx '00

Michael Ferris
The Net [2 SE] '95

Walter Ferris
The Little Princess [Marengo] '39
Heidi '37

Iaia Fiastri
Bread and Chocolate '73

Pat Fielder
The Monster That Challenged the World '57

Helen Fielding
Bridget Jones's Diary '01

Jacques Fieschi
Nelly et Monsieur Arnaud '95

Mike Figgis
Liebestraum '91

Diane Fine
Firetrap '01

Travis Fine
The Others '97

Harry Julian Fink
Dirty Harry [2] '71

Rita M. Fink
Dirty Harry [2] '71

Laurent Firode
Happenstance '00

Nick Fisher
Virtual Sexuality '99

Jeffrey Alladin Fiskin
Cutter's Way '81

Clancy Fitzsimmons
Play-Mate of the Apes '02
The Erotic Mirror '01

Scott Fivelson
Route 666 '01

Ennio Flaiano
Juliet of the Spirits [Criterion] '65
8 1/2 '63

Arthur Flam
Kill by Inches '99

Hugh Fleetwood
Bad Cop Chronicles 2: Corrupt '84

R. Lee Fleming, Jr.
Get over It! '01

Lucille Fletcher
Sorry, Wrong Number '48

Ruth Fletcher
The Breed '01

Brent Florence
A Girl, 3 Guys and a Gun '01

Rich Fogel
The Batman Superman Movie '97

James Foley
After Dark, My Sweet [2] '90

Yeh Fong
10 Magnificent Killers '77

Tom Fontana
Oz: The Complete First Season '97

Lloyd Fonvielle
The Bride '85

Horton Foote
Of Mice and Men '92
Tender Mercies [Anchor Bay] '83

Walter Foote
The Tavern '00

Bryan Forbes
Eye Witness '70
The Man Who Haunted Himself '70

Christian Ford
Slow Burn '00

Carl Foreman
High Noon '52
MacKenna's Gold '69
Cyrano de Bergerac '50

Milos Forman
The Fireman's Ball '68
Loves of a Blonde '65

Nancy Forner
Return to Horror High '87

Rolf Forsberg
Remember Pearl Harbor: America Taken by Surprise '01

Bill Forsyth
Gregory's Girl '80

Garrett Fort
Dracula's Daughter '36

Alyson Fouse
Scary Movie 2 '01

Claudio Fragasso
Hell of the Living Dead '83
Rats '83

Tracy Fraim
Best Men '98

Randall Frakes
Hell Comes to Frogtown '88

Joseph Fraley
Silent Rage '82

M. Francesconi
Bloody Proof '99

Massimo Franciosa
Rocco and His Brothers '60

Coleman Francis
Red Zone Cuba '66

Jess (Jesus) Franco
Killer Barbys '96

Melvin Frank
A Funny Thing Happened on the Way to the Forum '66
The Road to Utopia [Universal] '46
Star Spangled Rhythm '42

Scott Frank
Little Man Tate '91

Jill Franklyn
My First Mister '01

David Franzoni
Citizen Cohn '92

L. Alan Fraser
Next Time '99

Juan J. Frausto
Drive By '01

Michael Frayn
Clockwise '86

Kevin R. Frech
On the Borderline '01

David Freed
A Glimpse of Hell '01

Everett Freeman
The Princess and the Pirate '44

Hugo Fregonese
Savage Pampas '66

Eric Freiwald
Lone Ranger and the Lost City of Gold '58

Judy Freudberg
Sesame Street Presents: Follow That Bird '85

Kurt Frey
Haunted Castle '01

Frederick Friedel
Kidnapped Coed '77
Axe '74

Richard Friedenberg
The Education of Little Tree '97

Ken Friedman
Cadillac Man '90

Willi Frisch
2069: A Sex Odyssey '78

Sonia Fritz
The Kiss You Gave Me '00

Bill Froelich
Return to Horror High '87

Clayton Frohman
Under Fire '83

Lee Frost
Dixie Dynamite '76

Mark Frost
Twin Peaks: The First Season '90

Cesare Frugoni
Cut and Run '85

Christopher Fry
The Bible '66
Barabbas '62

Robert Fuest
The Final Programme '73

Kei Fujiwara
Organ '96

Kinji Fukasaku
Sure Death: Revenge '87

Lucio Fulci
Demonia '90
Aenigma '87

Brian Cameron Fuld
The Pact '99

Charles Fuller
Love Songs '99

Kim Fuller
High Heels and Low Lifes '01

Rodrigo Furth
Play for Me '01

Jules Furthman
Rio Bravo '59

Frederic Gadette
This Is Not a Test '62

Beth Gage
Fleshburn '84

Christos N. Gage
The Breed '01

George Gage
Fleshburn '84

Stephen Gaghan
Traffic [Criterion] '00

Claude Gagnon
The Kid Brother '87

Bob Gale
Used Cars '80

Henrik Galeen
Nosferatu '22
The Golem '20

John A. Gallagher
Blue Moon '00

Ronan Gallagher
When the Sky Falls '99

Mark Gallini
Fallout '01

George Gallo
See Spot Run '01

Lowell Ganz
Mr. Saturday Night [MGM] '92

Rodrigo Garcia
Things You Can Tell Just by Looking at Her '00

Louis Gardel
Indochine '92

Eva Gardos
An American Rhapsody '01

Brian Garfield
Fleshburn '84

Louis Garfinkle
I Bury the Living '58

Helen Garner
Two Friends '86

David Garrett
Corky Romano '01

Jerome Gary
Dragstrip Girl '94

Tudor Gates
Fright '71
Lust for a Vampire '71

John Gatins
Hardball '01
Summer Catch '01

John Gatliff
Death Before Dishonor '87

Andrew Gaty
Return of Captain Invincible '83

Peter Gaulke
Black Knight '01
Say It Isn't So '01

Cesc Gay
Nico and Dani '00

John Gay
Run Silent, Run Deep '58
Separate Tables '58

Timothy Harris
Brewster's Millions [Universal] '85

Joan Harrison
Rebecca [Criterion] '40

John Harrison
Dune [2 SE] '00
Upstairs, Downstairs: The Complete First Season '71

Lindsay Harrison
Fraternity Vacation '85

Noel Harrison
Adventures of Justine '00

Jim V. Hart
Jack and the Beanstalk: The Real Story '01
Bram Stoker's Dracula [SB] '92

Don Hartman
The Princess and the Pirate '44
My Favorite Blonde '42
The Road to Morocco [Universal] '42
The Road to Zanzibar '41
The Road to Singapore '40

Jan Hartman
W. Eugene Smith: Photography Made Difficult '89

Ron Harvey
Fist of Fear, Touch of Death '80

Derek Harvie
Freddy Got Fingered '01

Naoko Hasegawa
Oh My Goddess! Vol. 1 '93

Sergei Hasenecz
Sorority Babes in the Slimeball Bowl-A-Rama '87

Gustav Hasford
Full Metal Jacket [2 SE] '87

Kosuke Hashimoto
Tokyo Mafia: Battle for Shinjuku '96

Shinobu Hashimoto
The Hidden Fortress '58
Rashomon '51

Patrick Hasson
Waiting '01

Ken Hastings
Olive Juice '01

Margaret Hatch
Territorial Men '76

Richard Hatem
The Mothman Prophecies '02

Juen Hau
Lady Iron Monkey '83

John Hawkesworth
Upstairs, Downstairs: The Complete First Season '71

Lowell S. Hawley
The Swiss Family Robinson '60

Helen Haxton
Sexual Chemistry '99
Boundaries '97
Illicit Confessions '77

Phil Hay
crazy/beautiful '01

Joseph Hayes
Desperate Hours '90

Terry Hayes
From Hell [DLE] '01
Vertical Limit [2 SB] '00

Todd Haynes
Safe '95

Lillie Hayward
Proud Rebel '58

Laurence Heath
Triumph of the Spirit '89

David Heavener
Twisted Justice '89

Ben Hecht
Monkey Business '52
Hallelujah, I'm a Bum '33

Peter Hedges
What's Eating Gilbert Grape '93

Victor Heerman
Stella Dallas '37
Little Women '33

Richard T. Heffron
The Great St. Louis Bank Robbery '59

Jo Heims
Play Misty for Me '71

Robert Held
Looking for an Echo '99

Brian Helgeland
A Knight's Tale '01

Lois Heller
Too Late the Hero '70

Lillian Hellman
The North Star '43
The Little Foxes [MGM] '41

Alex Hencken
Night Divides the Day '01

Frank Henenlotter
Basket Case [2 SE] '82

Hilary Henkin
Romeo Is Bleeding '93

Paul Henning
Dirty Rotten Scoundrels [MGM] '88

Buck Henry
Town and Country '01
The Owl and the Pussycat '70

Brian Henson
Jack and the Beanstalk: The Real Story '01

Peter Hepworth
Hammers over the Anvil '91

Jaime Humberto Hermosillo
Dona Herlinda & Her Son '86

Gyula Hernadi
The Red and the White '68

Michael Herr
Full Metal Jacket [2 SE] '87
Apocalypse Now [Redux] '79

Joel Hershman
Greenfingers '00

Adam Herz
American Pie 2 '01
American Pie [2 UE] '99

Michael Herz
Stuck on You! [DC] '84
First Turn On! [DC] '83

John Herzfeld
15 Minutes '01

Werner Herzog
Little Dieter Needs to Fly '97
Fata Morgana '92
Lessons of Darkness '92
Cobra Verde '88
Stroszek '77
Heart of Glass '74

Fraser Heston
The Mountain Men '80

David L. Hewitt
Monsters Crash the Pajama Party Spook Show Spectacular '65

Louis M. Heyward
Planet of the Vampires '65
War Gods of the Deep '65

Winston Hibler
Peter Pan [2 SE] '53

Sir Seymour Hicks
Scrooge '35

Nicholas Hicks-Beach
Letters from a Killer '98

Julie Hickson
Snow White: The Fairest of Them All '02

John C. Higgins
He Walked by Night [BFS] '48
Raw Deal '48
Railroaded '47
T-Men '47

Ripley Highsmith
The Point Men '01

Tony Hiles
Bad Taste [LE] '88

Benny Hill
Benny Hill Golden Greats '89

Debra Hill
Jailbreakers '94
Halloween 2: The Nightmare Isn't Over! [Universal] '81
Halloween [Extended Edition] '78

Ethel Hill
The Little Princess [Marengo] '39

Jack Hill
The Big Bird Cage '72
The Fear Chamber '68

John Hill
Quigley Down Under '90

Al Hine
Find a Place to Die '68

Hilary Hinkle
Barbie in the Nutcracker '01

Ryuichi Hiroki
Sadistic City '93

Mikio Hirota
Terminatrix '95

Karl T. Hirsch
Green '01

Michael Hitchcock
House Arrest '96

Doane R. Hoag
The Lone Ranger: Volume 1 '56

Fredric Hobbs
Godmonster of Indian Flats '73

Adrian Hodges
Lorna Doone '01

Hunt Hoe
Seducing Maarya '99

Karol Ann Hoeffner
Winning London '01

Harold Hoffman
The Black Cat / The Fat Black Pussycat '65

Lauran Hoffman
Bar Girls '95

Michael Hogan
King Solomon's Mines '37

Paul Hogan
Crocodile Dundee 2 '88
Crocodile Dundee '86

Brian Hohlfield
He Said, She Said '91

Carlton Holder
Extreme Heist '99

Tom Holland
Stephen King's The Langoliers '95
Psycho 2 '83
The Beast Within '82

William A. Hollins
Black and Blue '01

Nicole Holofcener
Walking and Talking '96

Winnie Holzman
Til There Was You '96

Szeto Cheuk Hon
Righting Wrongs '86

Inoshiro Honda
Godzilla, King of the Monsters [Goodtimes] '56

Elliot Hong
Retrievers '82

Edward Hope
The Long Gray Line '55

Andrew Horn
East Side Story '97

Robert Horn
Good Advice '01

Ed Horowitz
Exit Wounds '01

Kenny Hotz
Pitch '01

David Houston
Attack from Mars '88

Joseph Howard
Sister Act '92

Karin Howard
NeverEnding Story 2: The Next Chapter '91

Sidney Howard
Dodsworth [MGM] '36

Nina Howatt
Mysterious Mr. Wong '35

Jean Howell
The Fast and the Furious '54

Duke Howze
Helter Skelter Murders '71

Tim Hoy
Bloody Proof '99

Talun Hsu
Fatal Blade '00

Ann Hu
Shadow Magic '00

Tom Hubbard
Daniel Boone: Trail Blazer '56

John Huddles
Uncorked '98

Rob Hudnut
Barbie in the Nutcracker '01

Dick Huemer
Dumbo '41

Allen Hughes
American Pimp '99

James Hughes
New Port South '00

John Hughes
Just Visiting '01
Baby's Day Out '94
National Lampoon's European Vacation '85

Koan Hui
Time and Tide '00

Ted Humphrey
The Triangle '01

Dave Humphries
Quadrophenia '79

Tran Anh Hung
The Vertical Ray of the Sun '00
The Scent of Green Papaya '93

Hermine Huntgeburth
The Trio '97

Earl Hurd
Snow White and the Seven Dwarfs [PE] '37

Georg Hurdalek
Town without Pity '61

Harry Hurwitz
The Projectionist '71

John Huston
Key Largo '48

Siri Hustvedt
The Center of the World '01

Lois Hutchinson
Parisian Love / Down to the Sea in Ships '25

Peter Hyams
The Hunter '80
Hanover Street '79

Jill Hyem
At Bertram's Hotel '86

Marc Hyman
Osmosis Jones '01

Eric Idle
National Lampoon's European Vacation '85

Tsutomu Iida
Devil Man '87

W. Peter Iliff
Point Break '91

Shohei Imamura
The Eel '96

Michael Imperioli
The Sopranos: The Complete Second Season '01

Eun-ah In
Tell Me Something '99

Malcolm Ingram
Drawing Flies '02

Minoru Inuzuka
The Tale of Zatoichi '62
The Tale of Zatoichi Continues '62

Paxti Irigoyen
Killer Barbys '96

David Isaacs
Volunteers '85

Takashi Ishii
Gonin '95

Neal Israel
Real Genius '85

Lewis Jackson
Christmas Evil '80

Peter Jackson
Meet the Feebles '89
Bad Taste [LE] '88

Alan Jacobs
Just One Night '00

Harrison Jacobs
Three on the Trail '36

Matthew Jacobs
Lassie '94

Andrew Jacobson
Not Another Teen Movie '01

Jacob Kornbluth
Haiku Tunnel '00

Josh Kornbluth
Haiku Tunnel '00

Jim Kouf
Snow Dogs '02
Gang Related '96

Tim Krabbe
The Vanishing [Criterion] '88

Andrzej Krakowski
Triumph of the Spirit '89

Norman Krasna
Let's Make Love '60
Indiscreet '58

Lars Kraume
Advertising Rules! '01

Steven Kreinberg
Dance 'til Dawn '88

Howard B. Kreitsek
Breakout '75

Stu Krieger
A Troll in Central Park '94

Jerzy Kromolowski
The Pledge '00

Jeremy Joe Kronsberg
Every Which Way But Loose
'78

Georgy Kropachov
Viy '67

Steve Kroschel
Escape from Alaska '02

Lisa Krueger
Committed '99

Ehren Kruger
Reindeer Games [Miramax
DC] '00

Elizabeth Kruger
Passport to Paris '99

Mark Kruger
Candyman 2: Farewell to the
Flesh '94

Ester Krumbachova
Daisies '96

Lung Ku
The Legendary Strike '78
To Kill with Intrigue '77

Yi Kuang
Buddha Assassinator '79

Stanley Kubrick
Full Metal Jacket [2 SE] '87
The Shining [2 SE] '80

Robert Kuhn
Mickey Blue Eyes '99

Jay Kulp
Swamp Girl / Swamp Country
'71

Roger Kumble
Cruel Intentions 2 '99

Yeung Kung
Revenge of the Patriots '76

Carl Kuntze
Raiders of Leyte Gulf '63

Harry Kurnitz
Witness for the Prosecution
'57
They Got Me Covered '43

Akira Kurosawa
The Hidden Fortress '58
Rashomon '51

F. Joseph Kurtz
Carnivore '01

Andrew Kurtzman
See No Evil, Hear No Evil '89

Catherine Kuttner
Tales of Frankenstein '58

Henry Kuttner
Tales of Frankenstein '58

Tadeusz Kwiatkowski
The Saragossa Manuscript
'65

Hans Kyser
Faust '26

Gregory La Cava
My Man Godfrey [Criterion]
'36

Dee La Duke
Jackie's Back '99

Gregg Lachow
Money Buys Happiness '99

Ivan Lai
Daughter of Darkness '93

Don Lake
The Extreme Adventures of
Super Dave '98

Paul LaLonde
Deceived '01

Ngai Kai Lam
Riki-Oh: The Story of Ricky
'89

Ross LaManna
Arctic Blue '93

Eleanor Lamb
Where the Red Fern Grows
'74

Charles Lambert
The Wolves of Kromer '98

Gavin Lambert
I Never Promised You a Rose
Garden '77

Leonard Lamensdorf
Cornbread, Earl & Me '75

Beau L'Amour
The Diamond of Jeru '01

Millard Lampell
Triumph of the Spirit '89

Bill Lancaster
The Bad News Bears Go to
Japan '78
The Bad News Bears '76

Richard H. Landau
The Lost Continent '51

John Landis
An American Werewolf in Lon-
don [CE Universal] '81
Schlock '73

Joseph Landon
Von Ryan's Express '65

Fritz Lang
Dr. Mabuse, The Gambler '22

Stephen Langford
Warm Blooded Killers '01

Kate Lanier
Glitter '01

T.L. Lankford
Hollywood Chainsaw Hookers
'88

Dale Lanner
Ruthless People '86

James Lapine
Into the Woods '90

Edward Laraby
Adventures of Justine '00

Bob Larbey
The Darling Buds of May '91

Ring Lardner, Jr.
The Greatest '77
M*A*S*H [FS] '70

Wolf Larson
Crash & Byrnes '99

Kendrew Lascelles
Focus '01

Betty Laskey
This Is Not a Test '62

Steve Latshaw
The Last Siege '99

Tai-Muk Lau
Iron Monkey [Miramax] '93

Michael Laughlin
Town and Country '01

Dale Launer
Love Potion 9 '92
Dirty Rotten Scoundrels
[MGM] '88
Blind Date '87

Salvatore Laurani
Bad Cop Chronicles: Confessions of a Police Captain
'72
A Bullet for the General '68

Christian Laurent
Gang of Four '88

Christine Laurent
Va Savoir '01

Georges Lautner
Le Professionnel '81

William Lava
She Wolf of London '46

Paul Laverty
Bread and Roses '00

Alex Law
City of Glass '98

Kam Fai Law
Trust Me U Die '99
Dr. Lamb '92

John Howard Lawson
Sahara '43

J.F. Lawton
Blankman '94

Beirne Lay, Jr.
Twelve o'Clock High '49

Michael Lazarou
Possessed '00

Auguste Le Breton
Bob le Flambeur '55

John Le Carre
The Tailor of Panama '00

Harold Lea
The Fat Black Pussycat '63

David Lean
Summertime '55

Charles Leavitt
K-PAX '01

Paul Leder
A*P*E* '76

Reuben Leder
A*P*E* '76

Charles Lederer
Ocean's 11 '60
Monkey Business '52

Ang Lee
Eat Drink Man Woman '94

Bruce Lee
Bruce Lee: A Warrior's Journey '01

Chris Chan Lee
Double Deception '01

Damian Lee
Agent Red '00
Abraxas: Guardian of the Uni-
verse [BFS] '90

James Lee
Roots '77

Timothy Lee
2103: Deadly Wake '97

William Lee
The Pact '99

Michael Leeson
The War of the Roses [SE]
'89
Survivors '83

William P. Leicester
The Last Man on Earth '64

Jennifer Jason Leigh
The Anniversary Party '01

David Leland
White River '99

James (Momel) Lemmo
Nowhere in Sight '01

Peter M. Lenkov
Dr. Jekyll & Mr. Hyde '00

Isobel Lennart
Funny Girl '68

**Fernando Leon de
Aranda**
Living It Up '00

Hugh Leonard
Percy '71

Doriana Leondeff
Bread and Tulips '01

Rudolf Leonhard
Diary of a Lost Girl '29

Carl Lerner
Black Like Me '64

Gerda Lerner
Black Like Me '64

Ali LeRoi
Down to Earth '01

Michael Leszcylowski
Directed by Andrei Tarkovsky
'88

Kant Leung
Ultimatum '01
The Demon's Baby '98

Kar-yan Leung
Cold War '00

Jay Levey
UHF '89

Larry Levin
Dr. Dolittle 2 '01

Marc Levin
Brooklyn Babylon '00

Ken Levine
Volunteers '85

Barry Levinson
Toys '92
Tin Men '87
Diner '82

Eugene Levy
Waiting for Guffman '96

Marilyn Levy
Bride of the Wind '01

Raoul Levy
And God Created Woman '57

Robert L. Levy
Blood Surf '00

Andy Lewis
Klute '71

Christopher Lewis
Revenge '86

Dave Lewis
Klute '71

Herschell Gordon Lewis
Blast-Off Girls / Just for the
Hell of It '67

Keisha Lewis
Black Spring Break 2 '01

Mark Lewis
Cane Toads: An Unnatural
History '87

Russell Lewis
Horatio Hornblower '99

Lauren Lexton
Heroes of Iwo Jima '01

Chan Wai Li
Jade Claw '79

Tu Liang-Ti
Buddha Assassinator '79

Peter Paul Liapis
Alone with a Stranger '99

Alberto Liberati
Knives of the Avenger '65

Demian Lichtenstein
3000 Miles to Graceland '01

Robert Liebmann
The Blue Angel '30

Louis D. Lighton
It '27

Eugene Ling
Behind Locked Doors '48

Wang Hui Ling
Crouching Tiger, Hidden Dragon [2 SB] '00

Richard Linklater
Waking Life '01

David Linter
Dancing at the Blue Iguana
'00

Norman C. Linton
Better Dayz '02

Steven Lisberger
Tron [2 CE] '82

Mark Lisson
Return to Horror High '87

Jay Lister
Monsters Crash the Pajama
Party Spook Show Spectac-
ular '65

John Little
Bruce Lee: A Warrior's Journey '01

Ezra Litwack
The Butcher's Wife '91

Harold Livingston
Star Trek: The Motion Picture
[DE] '80

Bey Logan
Ballistic Kiss '98

Philip Lonergan
The Penalty '20

Pamela K. Long
The Last Warrior '99

Zachary Long
Bully '01

Mindret Lord
Strange Impersonation '46

Hope Loring
It '27

Chris Lou
Comic King '00

Irene Mecchi
The Hunchback of Notre
  Dame '96

Julio Medem
Vacas '91

Enrico Medioli
Rocco and His Brothers '60

Mark Medoff
Good Guys Wear Black '78

Thomas Meehan
Spaceballs '87

Ib Melchior
Planet of the Vampires '65
Reptilicus '62
The Angry Red Planet '59

Frank Melford
Blood on the Sun [Image] '45

Louis Mellis
Sexy Beast '00

John Melson
Savage Pampas '66

Jean-Pierre Melville
Un Flic '72
Bob le Flambeur '55

Ramon Menendez
Tortilla Soup '01

David Menkes
Not Love Just Frenzy '96

Joe Menosky
Hiding Out '87

Furio M. Menotti
The Last Man on Earth '64

Jiri Menzel
Closely Watched Trains '66

David Mercer
Morgan: A Suitable Case for
  Treatment '66

Sean Meredith
Texas '94

Budimir Metalnikov
Tchaikovsky '71

Stephen Metcalfe
Cousins '89

Tim Metcalfe
Revenge of the Nerds /
  Revenge of the Nerds 2:
  Nerds in Paradise '84

Menno Meyjes
Empire of the Sun '87

Michael Mfume
Axe 'Em '02

Lorne Michaels
Three Amigos '86

Ted V. Mikels
10 Violent Women '79
The Doll Squad '73

John Milius
Apocalypse Now [Redux] '79
Magnum Force '73
Evel Knievel '72

Broderick Miller
Slap Shot 2: Breaking the Ice
  '02

George Miller
Mad Max [MGM SE] '80

Merle Miller
Kings Go Forth '58

Yvette Mimieux
Hit Lady '74

Daniel Minahan
Series 7: The Contenders '01

Anthony Minghella
Truly, Madly, Deeply '91

Joe Minion
Motorama '91

Susan Minot
Stealing Beauty '96

Hono Misumi
Tokyo Decameron: Three
  Tales of Madness & Sensu-
  ality '96

John Cameron Mitchell
Hedwig and the Angry Inch
  '00

Julian Mitchell
Wilde '97

Frederic Mitterrand
Madame Butterfly '95

Jordan Moffet
Whispers: An Elephant's Tale
  '00

Hans Petter Moland
Aberdeen '00
Zero Degrees Kelvin '95

Edouard Molinaro
La Cage aux Folles '78

Dominik Moll
With a Friend Like Harry '00

John Mollica
Mr. Vincent '97

Paul Monash
All Quiet on the Western
  Front '79

Justin Monjo
Cement '99

Eric Monte
Nine Lives of Fritz the Cat '74

Luigi Montefiore
Stagefright '87

Claire Montgomery
Zebra Lounge '01

Monte Montgomery
Zebra Lounge '01

Brian Moore
Black Robe [MGM] '91

Simon Moore
Traffik '90

Frank Moorhouse
The Coca-Cola Kid '84

Philippe Mora
Howling 3: The Marsupials
  '87

Julian More
The Bloodsuckers '70

Gabriel Morgan
W.I.S.O.R. The Robo Welder
  '01

George Morgan
Second to Die '02

Miyoo Morita
Kizuna '94

J. Everitt Morley
Deep Water '99

Tony Morphett
13 Gantry Row '98
Sweet Talker '91
The Last Wave '77

Ben Morris
Phat Beach '96

Barry Morrow
Race the Sun '96

Rob Morrow
Maze '01

John Mortimer
In Love and War '01

Michael H. Moss
Along Came a Spider '00

Jonathan Mostow
Breakdown '96

Danny Mulheron
Meet the Feebles '89

Peter Mullan
Orphans '97

Eddie Muller
Mau Mau Sex Sex '00

Robert Munic
In a Class of His Own '99

Kaj Munk
Ordet '55

Rona Munro
Aimee & Jaguar '98

Takeo Murata
Godzilla, King of the Monsters [Goodtimes] '56

Charles Murphy
Vampire in Brooklyn '95

Eddie Murphy
Harlem Nights '89

Geoff Murphy
Utu '83

Tab Murphy
Atlantis: The Lost Empire
  [CE] '01
The Hunchback of Notre
  Dame '96
The Last of the Dogmen '95

John Fenton Murray
Robin and the 7 Hoods '64

Michael J. Murray
Acceptable Risk '01

Fernando Musa
Brain Drain '98

Tom Musca
Tortilla Soup '01

Mike Myers
Wayne's World 2 '93
Wayne's World '92

Fred Myton
The Black Raven '43

Yuri Nagibin
Tchaikovsky '71

Hoi Nai
Love on a Diet '01

Akira Nakahara
Sure Death: Revenge '87

**Mark Katsumi
Nakamura**
Spreading Ground '01

Ryuzo Nakanishi
Gappa the Trifibian Monster
  '67

Takao Nakano
Sumo Vixens '96

Art Names
Girl in Gold Boots '69

Bernardo Nante
Secret of the Andes '01

Jeff Nathanson
Rush Hour 2 '01

Terry Nation
And Soon the Darkness '70

Christopher Neame
Zeta One '69

Joe Ned
Play-Mate of the Apes '02

Rob Neighbors
L.A.P.D.: To Protect and Serve
  '01

Terry Neish
Boa '02

Hank Nelken
Saving Silverman '01

Jessie Nelson
I Am Sam '01

Mandy Nelson
Sugar & Spice '01

Dennis Nemec
Murder in Coweta County '83

Michael Nesmith
Timerider '83

E. Jack Neuman
Incident on a Dark Street '72

John Thomas Neville
The Devil Bat '41

Craig J. Nevius
Marquis de Sade '96

Patrick Newall
Borough of Kings '98

David Newman
Bad Company '72

Randy Newman
Three Amigos '86

See Yuen Ng
Drunken Master '78
Snake in the Eagle's Shadow
  '78

Hong Ngai
Blood of the Dragon '71

Andrew Niccol
Gattaca [2 SB] '97

Dudley Nichols
And Then There Were None
  [Image] '45

Jack Nicholson
Head '68

Peggy Nicoll
Daria, The Movie: Is It Fall
  Yet? '01

Daria Nicolodi
Suspiria '77

Karl Niemiec
Narcotic Justice

We Nien-Jen
The Puppetmaster '93

Tatsuo Nogami
Sure Death: Revenge '87

Christopher Nolan
Memento [1] '00
Memento [2 SE] '00
Following '99

Ken Nolan
Black Hawk Down '01

Eric Norden
A Scream in the Streets '73
Please Don't Eat My Mother
  '72

Marc Norman
The Aviator '85
Breakout '75

William J. Norris
Re-Animator [2 ME] '84

Edmund H. North
Patton [2] '70
Cowboy '58

Robert Northup
Southern Man '99

William W. Norton, Sr.
Brannigan '75
McKenzie Break '70

Betriz Novaro
Garden of Eden '94

Maria Novaro
Garden of Eden '94

Victor Nunez
Ulee's Gold '97

Dan O'Bannon
Total Recall [2 SLE] '90
Invaders from Mars [MGM]
  '86
Blue Thunder '83

Rockne S. O'Bannon
Fatal Error '99

Sean O'Bannon
Air Rage '01
Mom's Outta Sight '01
Poison '01

Edna O'Brien
Girl with Green Eyes '64

Pat O'Connor
The January Man '89

David Odell
Masters of the Universe '87

Bob Odenkirk
Mr. Show: The Complete First
  & Second Seasons '02

Jerome Odlum
The Fast and the Furious '54

Dan O'Donahue
Art House '98

Steve Oedekerk
The Blair Thumb '01
Thumb Wars '99
Thumbtanic '99

Hideo Oguni
The Hidden Fortress '58

James O'Hanlon
Calamity Jane '53
Sahara '43

Michael O'Hara
In His Life: The John Lennon
  Story '00

Nanase Ohkawa
X '96

Shundo Ohkawa
Double Deception '01

Kazuto Okada
Very Private Lessons '01

David Oliver
Cave Girl '85

Hector Olivera
The Road '00
A Shadow You Soon Will Be
  '94
Funny, Dirty Little War '83

Javier Olivera
The Road '00

Tamara Olson
Fashionably L.A. '99

**Mary Olson-
Kromolowski**
The Pledge '00

Kazuki Omori
Godzilla vs. Destroyah '95

Brian E. O'Neal
Phat Beach '96

Eugene O'Neill
A Moon for the Misbegotten
  '75

Alan Ormsby
Popcorn '89
My Bodyguard '80

James Orr
Three Men and a Baby '87

Erik Orsenna
Indochine '92

Paul Osborn
Sayonara '57

John Osborne
Look Back in Anger '58

Nagisa Oshima
Taboo '99

David R. Osterhout
Women in Cages '71

Katsuhiro Otomo
Metropolis '01

Richard Outten
Pet Sematary 2 '92

Frank Oz
The Muppets Take Manhattan '84

Francois Ozon
Under the Sand '00
Water Drops on Burning Rocks '99

Jose Padilha
The Charcoal People '01

Juan Padron
Vampires in Havana '87

Victor Pahlen
Gunman in the Streets '50

Rospo Pallenberg
Druids '01

Matt Palmieri
Sand '00

Robert Palumbo
Fallout '01

Norman Panama
The Road to Utopia [Universal] '46
Star Spangled Rhythm '42

Edmund Pang
The Cheaters '00
Killer '00

Dennis Paoli
Re-Animator [2 ME] '84

Jaroslav Papousek
The Firemen's Ball '68
Loves of a Blonde '65

Sergei Paradjanov
The Color of Pomegranates '69

Arto Paragamian
Because Why? '93

Paul S. Parco
The Passion Network '01
Tender Is the Heart '01

Ruth Park
The Harp in the South '86

Christopher Parker
Vampire in Brooklyn '95

Dave Parker
The Dead Hate the Living '99

Tom S. Parker
Stay Tuned '92

Trey Parker
South Park: Insults to Injury '02
South Park: Bigger, Longer and Uncut '99
Cannibal! The Musical '96

Andrew Parkinson
Dead Creatures '01

Tom Parkinson
With Friends Like These '90

Sara Parriott
Runaway Bride '99

The Favor '92
Three Men and a Little Lady '90

J. Vincent Parris
Dealin' Dirty
Rockin' with a Bullet

Lindsley Parsons
Desert Trail '35
Paradise Canyon '35
Trail Beyond [Columbia] '34

Kambozia Partovi
The Circle '00

Ivan Passer
The Firemen's Ball '68
Loves of a Blonde '65

Allan Passes
Institue Benjamenta or This Dream People Call Human Life '95

Giovanni Pastrone
Cabiria '14

Jonas Pate
Deceiver '97

Josh Pate
Deceiver '97

John Patrick
Daniel Boone: Trail Blazer '56
Love Is a Many Splendored Thing '55

Robert Patton-Spruill
Squeeze '97

John Patus
Deceived '01

Cinco Paul
Bubble Boy '01

Jeremy Paul
Upstairs, Downstairs: The Complete First Season '71

John Paxton
On the Beach '59

Alexander Payne
Jurassic Park 3 [CE] '01

Senel Paz
A Paradise under the Stars '99
Things I Left in Havanna '97

Steve Peace
Return of the Killer Tomatoes! '88

Craig Pearce
Moulin Rouge [SE] '01
Strictly Ballroom '92

Tony Peck
Diary of a Sex Addict '01

Anthony Peckham
Don't Say a Word '01

Bill Peet
Peter Pan [2 SE] '53

Haim Pekelis
Squeeze Play [DC] '79

John L.E. Pell
Down to the Sea in Ships '22

Zak Penn
Behind Enemy Lines '01

Erdman Penner
Peter Pan [2 SE] '53

John Penney
The Contaminated Man '01
The Enemy '01
Matter of Trust '98
Return of the Living Dead 3 '93

Paul Pepperman
Beastmaster '82

Hope Perello
St. Patrick's Day '01

Fernando Perez
Life Is to Whistle '98

Ivo Perilli
Barabbas '62

Annabelle Perrichon
Deep in the Woods '00

Nat Perrin
Dimples '36

Frank Perry
Mommie Dearest '81

Michael Pertwee
A Funny Thing Happened on the Way to the Forum '66

Roland Pertwee
King Solomon's Mines '37

Charlie Peters
Three Men and a Little Lady '90

Christina Peters
The Smokers '00

Wolfgang Petersen
The NeverEnding Story '84

Patricia Petit
The Scent of Green Papaya '93

Joseph Petracca
Proud Rebel '58

Bob Petrella
World Trade Center—A Modern Marvel: 1973-2001 '01

Dan Petrie, Jr.
Beverly Hills Cop [CE] '84

Harley Peyton
Bandits '01
Less Than Zero '87

Marco Piccolo
Goliath and the Dragon '61

Jack Pichesin
The Doll Squad '73

John Pielmeier
Agnes of God '85

Arthur C. Pierce
Invasion of the Animal People '62
Terror in the Midnight Sun '58

Tseng Pik-Yin
Iron Monkey [Miramax] '93

Tullio Pinelli
Juliet of the Spirits [Criterion] '65
8 1/2 '63

Sidney Pink
Reptilicus '61
The Angry Red Planet '59

Harold Pinter
The Handmaid's Tale '90
The French Lieutenant's Woman '81
Accident '67
The Servant '63

Robert Pirosh
Go for Broke! [VCI] '51

George Plympton
Flash Gordon: The Peril from Planet Mongo '40

Peter Podehl
Tales from Europe: The Story of Little Mook '53

Rick Podell
Nothing in Common '86

John Pogue
Rollerball '02

Jean-Marie Poire
Just Visiting '01

Jean Poiret
La Cage aux Folles '78

Roman Polanski
Macbeth '71

Mark Polish
Jackpot '01

Michael Polish
Jackpot '01

Jack Pollexfen
The Daughter of Dr. Jekyll '57

Abe Polsky
Rebel Rousers '69

Dave Polsky
Scary Movie 2 '01

Darryl Ponicsan
Taps '81

DJ Pooh
The Wash '01

Marty Poole
Reptilian '00

Petru Popescu
The Last Wave '77

Todd Portugal
Flooding '97

Jacob Potashnik
Stardom '00

Johann Potgieter
The Long Run '00

Sally Potter
The Man Who Cried '00

Ralph B. Potts
The Specialist '75

Michael Powell
Contraband '40

Donna Powers
Valentine '01

Wayne Powers
Valentine '01

Tim Prager
Haunted '95

Mario Prata
Testamento '98

Richard Preston, Jr.
Firetrap '01

Jacques Prevert
The Hunchback of Notre Dame '57
Children of Paradise '44

Jeffrey Price
Dr. Seuss' How the Grinch Stole Christmas '00

Jonathan Prince
18 Again! '88

Gina Prince-Bythewood
Love and Basketball '00

David Pritchard
Violent Zone '89

Steve Procko
Golf Balls! '99

Pat Proft
Real Genius '85
Bachelor Party '84

Richard Pryor
Jo Jo Dancer, Your Life Is Calling '86

Alexander Ptushko
Viy '67

Frank Pugliese
Shot in the Heart '01

Roger Pullis
Bully '01

L.A. Puopolo
The Turning '92

Neal Purvis
Plunkett & Macleane '98

Tag Purvis
Red Dirt '99

Mario Puzo
The Cotton Club '84

Daniel Pyne
White Sands '92

Albert Pyun
Sword & the Sorcerer '82

Darryl Quarles
Black Knight '01

Bruce Quarrie
Great Fighting Machines of WWII: Allied & Axis Tanks '01

Stephen Quay
Institue Benjamenta or This Dream People Call Human Life '95

Timothy Quay
Institue Benjamenta or This Dream People Call Human Life '95

David Quinn
Faust: Love of the Damned '00

Jose Quintanilla
Two Coyotes '01

Gene Quintano
The Musketeer '01
Making the Grade '84

Eduardo Quiroz
Smile Now Cry Later '01

Jose Quiroz
Smile Now Cry Later '01

William Quist
Four Dogs Playing Poker '00

David Rabe
Hurlyburly '98
Casualties of War '89

Martin Rackin
Long John Silver '54

Michael Radford
Dancing at the Blue Iguana '00

Bob Rafelson
Head '68

Stewart Raffill
High Risk '81

Sam Raimi
Evil Dead [LE] '83

Norman Reilly Raine
Captain Kidd [Marengo] '45

Kate Raisz
Shadow Magic '00

Ron Raley
The Runaway '00

Harold Ramis
Groundhog Day [2 SE] '93
Stripes '81

Alfredo Ramos
Road Dogz '00

Al Ramrus
The Island of Dr. Moreau '77

Ben Ramsey
The Big Hit [2 SB] '98

Dana Ranga
East Side Story '97

Simuel Rankins
Get Down on It '01

Frederic Raphael
After the War '89

Kevin Rapp
Reflex Action '02

Judith Rascoe
Who'll Stop the Rain? '78

Terence Rattigan
The Prince and the Showgirl '57

Michael Rauch
Stalker '98

Herman Raucher
Summer of '42 '71

Irving Ravetch
Vengeance Valley '51

Rand Ravich
Candyman 2: Farewell to the Flesh '94

Fred Olen Ray
Hollywood Chainsaw Hookers '88

David Rayfiel
Sabrina '95
Intersection '93
Round Midnight '86
Valdez Is Coming '71

Jan Read
First Men in the Moon '64

Matthew Read
The Wolves of Kromer '98

Richard Recco
3000 Miles to Graceland '01

Eric Red
The Hitcher '86

Jeffrey Reddick
Return to Cabin by the Lake '01

Robert Redlin
After Dark, My Sweet [2] '90

Piero Regnoli
Demonia '90
Voices from Beyond '90

William Rehor
Spanish Judges '99

Frank Rehwaldt
The Perfect Wife '00

James Reichmuth
Fishing with Gandhi '98

John Reichmuth
Fishing with Gandhi '98

Al Reinert
Final Fantasy: The Spirits Within '01

Silvia Reinhardt
Town without Pity '61

Walter Reisch
Niagara '52

Daniel Reitz
Urbania '00

Jacques Remy
The Night Heaven Fell '57

Jean Renoir
The Southerner '45

Frank Renzulli
The Sopranos: The Complete Second Season '01

Robert Resnikoff
The First Power '89

Shonda Rhimes
Introducing Dorothy Dandridge '99

Griff Rhys Jones
Morons from Outer Space '85

Spencer Rice
Pitch '01

Dick Richard
Snow White and the Seven Dwarfs [PE] '37

Craig Richardson
Anima '98

Tony Richardson
The Hotel New Hampshire '84

Maurice Richlin
Operation Petticoat '59

W.D. Richter
Home for the Holidays '95

Richmond Riedel
First Degree '01

Dean Riesner
Dirty Harry [2] '71
Play Misty for Me '71

Lawrence Riggins
Replicant '01

Martin Riley
The Worst Witch '98

Joe Rinaldi
Peter Pan [2 SE] '53

David W. Rintels
Not without My Daughter '90

Robert Riskin
Mr. Deeds Goes to Town '36
Lady for a Day '33

Michael Rissi
Up against Amanda '01

Guy Ritchie
Snatch [SE] '00

Stephen J. Rivele
Ali '01

Jacques Rivette
Va Savoir '01
Secret Defense '98
Gang of Four '88

Matthew Robbins
MacArthur '77
Bingo Long Traveling All-Stars & Motor Kings '76

Thomas Roberdeau
Adventures of Justine '00

Vincent Robert
Red Surf '90

Jonathan Roberts
The Hunchback of Notre Dame '96

Marguerite Roberts
Five Card Stud '68

William Roberts
The Devil's Brigade '68

R.J. Robertson
Big Bad Mama 2 '87

Herb Robins
The Worm Eaters '77

Bruce Robinson
How to Get Ahead in Advertising '89
Withnail and I '87

Casey Robinson
Now, Voyager '42

Matt Robinson
Amazing Grace '74

Sally Robinson
Follow the Stars Home '01

Todd Robinson
Mermaid '00

Debbie Rochon
Play-Mate of the Apes '02

Chris Rock
Down to Earth '01

Lisa-Marie Rodano
Mrs. Winterbourne '96

Robert Rodat
The Patriot [2 SB] '00
Fly Away Home [2 SE] '96

Franc Roddam
Quadrophenia '79

Gene Roddenberry
Star Trek: The Next Generation—The Complete 1st Season '87

Franz Rodenkirchen
Nekromantik '87

Hans Rodionoff
The Skulls 2 '02

Serge Rodnunsky
Cypress Edge '99

Robert Rodriguez
Spy Kids '01
Desperado [2 SB] '95

Judy Rothman Rofe
The Trumpet of the Swan '01

Randy Rogel
Batman & Mr. Freeze: Subzero '97

John Rogers
American Outlaws '01

Steven Rogers
Kate & Leopold '01

Eric Rohmer
A Tale of Springtime '89

Sam Rolfe
They Call It Murder '71

Mino Roli
Keoma '76

Jean Rollin
The Grapes of Death '78
The Rape of the Vampire '68

Antonio Roman
Planet of the Vampires '65

Marcia Romano
Under the Sand '00

Eddie Romero
The Ravagers '65
Walls of Hell '64

E.F. Romero
Raiders of Leyte Gulf '63

George A. Romero
Bruiser '00
Tales from the Darkside: The Movie '90
Night of the Living Dead [Elite ME] '68

Brunello Rondi
Juliet of the Spirits [Criterion] '65
8 1/2 '63

Wells Root
The Lone Ranger: Volume 1 '56

Tom Ropelewski
Look Who's Talking Now '93

Bernard Rose
Immortal Beloved '94

Jack Rose
The Great Muppet Caper '81
A Touch of Class '73

Tania Rose
It's a Mad, Mad, Mad, Mad World '63

William Rose
It's a Mad, Mad, Mad, Mad World '63

Martin Rosen
Watership Down '78

Steve Rosen
Beyond Barbed Wire '97

Henry Rosenbaum
The Dunwich Horror '70

C.A. Rosenberg
Maniac [LE] '80

Jeanne Rosenberg
The Journey of Natty Gann '85

Rick Rosenberg
Southern Man '99

Scott Rosenberg
Highway '01

Dale Rosenbloom
Shiloh 2: Shiloh Season '99
Shiloh '97

Mark Rosenthal
Planet of the Apes '01
Sometimes They Come Back '91
Desperate Hours '90

Robert J. Rosenthal
The Van '77

Arthur Ross
The Three Worlds of Gulliver '59
Creature from the Black Lagoon '54
Star Spangled Rhythm '42

Gary Ross
Lassie '94

Jerry Ross
The Magic Show '81

Robert Rossen
All the King's Men '49

Terry Rossio
Shrek [SE] '01
The Mask of Zorro [2 SE] '98

Leo Rosten
Lured '47

Eric Roth
Ali '01
Forrest Gump [SCE] '94
Suspect '87

Phillip J. Roth
Boa '02

Robert Roth
Luminous Motion '00

Jeff Rothberg
Hiding Out '87

Russell Rouse
The Thief '52

Alexander Row
Barbara the Fair with the Silken Hair '69
Father Frost '66

Tom Rowe
Light at the Edge of the World '71

Viktor Rozov
The Cranes Are Flying '57

Daniel F. Rubin
Groundhog Day [2 SE] '93

Eduardo Ruderman
Play for Me '01

Alan Rudolph
Trixie '00
Choose Me '84

Ed Rugoff
Mannequin '87

Albert Ruis
Ping! '99

Richard Rush
The Sinister Saga '00
The Stunt Man '80

Steven Rush
Extreme Honor '01

Lou Rusoff
The Phantom from 10,000 Leagues '56

Charlie Russell
Five on the Black Hand Side '73

Ray Russell
Mr. Sardonicus '61

John A. Russo
Night of the Living Dead [Elite ME] '68

Tim Ryan
Bela Lugosi Meets a Brooklyn Gorilla '52

Todd Ryan
Rappin'-N-Rhyming '00

Stephen M. Ryder
L.I.E. '01

Michael Rymer
Perfume '01

Morrie Ryskind
My Man Godfrey [Criterion] '36

Olli Saarela
Ambush '99

Dardano Sacchetti
The New Gladiators '83
Cannibal Apocalypse '80
Shock '79

William Sachs
Galaxina '80

Howard Sackler
Jaws 2 '78

Frederica Sagor
The Plastic Age '25

Mary St. Feint
Butterflies Are Free '72

Nao Sakai
Fatal Blade '00

Pierre L. Salas
Curse of the Vampires '70

Alfredo Salazar
Doctor of Doom '62

Kario Salem
The Score '01

Claudia Salter
Running Mates '00

Mark Saltzman
3 Ninjas Kick Back '94

Victor Salva
Jeepers Creepers '01

Rafael J. Salvia
Planet of the Vampires '65

Richard Sam
Champ Against Champ [BFS] '83
Champ vs. Champ [Xenon] '83

Holly Goldberg Sloan
Whispers: An Elephant's Tale '00
Angels in the Outfield '94

Rick Sloane
Mind, Body & Soul '92

Alfred Slote
Finding Buck McHenry '00

Shawn Slovo
Captain Corelli's Mandolin '01

George Sluizer
The Vanishing [Criterion] '88

Bob Small
Golf Balls! '99

Harold Jacob Smith
Inherit the Wind '60
The Defiant Ones '58

Juney Smith
Deep Trouble '01

Kevin Smith
Jay and Silent Bob Strike Back '01
Dogma [2 SE] '99

Kirsten Smith
Legally Blonde '01

Mel Smith
Morons from Outer Space '85

Murray Smith
Sell Out '76

Richard Dana Smith
Alone with a Stranger '99

Robert Smith
Invasion U.S.A. '52

Roger Smith
C.C. & Company '70

Scott Marshall Smith
The Score '01

Todd Smith
Human Desires '97

Webb Smith
Snow White and the Seven Dwarfs [PE] '37

Michael Anthony Snowden
Scary Movie 2 '01

Stephen So
Fury in the Shaolin Temple '82

Elena Soarez
Me You Them '00

Michele (Michael) Soavi
The Church '98

Carol Sobieski
The Toy '82

Gerard Soeteman
Katie Tippel '75
Business Is Business '71

Roger Soffer
Slow Burn '00

Amy Sohn
Spin the Bottle '97

Joel Soisson
Mimic 2 '01
Dracula 2000 '00

Alec Sokolow
Money Talks '97

Silvio Soldini
Bread and Tulips '01

Chris Solimine
The Odyssey '97

Franco Solinas
A Bullet for the General '68

Amedeo Sollazzo
Primitive Love '64

Sergio Sollima
Violent City '70

Aubrey Solomon
Progeny '98

Cary Solomon
Earth vs. the Spider '01

Edward Solomon
Bill & Ted's Bogus Journey '91
Bill & Ted's Excellent Adventure '89

Bernie Somers
Cops and Robbersons '94

Stephen Sommers
The Mummy Returns '01

Manuel G. Songo
Murder in the Orient '73

Michael Sonye
Star Slammer '87

Trish Soodik
Shake, Rattle & Rock! '94

Osvaldo Soriano
A Shadow You Soon Will Be '94

Laura Sosa
In the Country Where Nothing Happens '99

Mark Spacek
Sweet Thing '00

David Spade
Joe Dirt '01

Johnny Speight
Til Death Us Do Part '72

Greg Spence
Children of the Corn 4: The Gathering '96

Steven Spielberg
A.I.: Artificial Intelligence '01
The Goonies '85

Evan Spiliotopoulos
Bare Witness '02

Joe Spinell
Maniac [LE] '80

Norman Spinrad
Druids '01

Tony Spiridakis
Queens Logic '91

Ron Sproat
Dark Shadows: DVD Collection 1 '67

Laurence Stallings
On Our Merry Way '48
The Jungle Book '42

Sylvester Stallone
Driven '01

Paul Stanton
On the Line '01

Eric Stanze
I Spit on Your Corpse, I Piss on Your Grave '02

Darren Star
Sex and the City: Season 1 '00

Philip Stark
Dude, Where's My Car? '00

Jaison Starkes
J.D.'s Revenge '76

David Starkey
Elizabeth '02

Ben Stassen
Haunted Castle '01
Alien Adventure '99

Joseph Stein
Fiddler on the Roof [2 SE] '71

David H. Steinberg
Slackers '02

Hank Steinberg
61* '01

Danny Steinmann
Friday the 13th, Part 5: A New Beginning '85

Martin Stellman
Quadrophenia '79

Gerard Stembridge
About Adam '00

Lucki Stepetic
Gesualdo: Death for Five Voices '95

C. David Stephens
Cabin by the Lake / Return to Cabin by the Lake '00

Mark Stephens
Legend of the Chupacabra '97

Bret Stern
R2PC: Road to Park City '99

Jonathan Stern
Mexico City '01

Sandor Stern
Pin... '88

David Stevens
Mama Flora's Family '98

Neal Marshall Stevens
13 Ghosts '01

Douglas Day Stewart
Thief of Hearts '84
The Boy in the Plastic Bubble [2] '76
Where the Red Fern Grows '74

R.J. Stewart
Xena: Warrior Princess—Series Finale '01
Major League 2 '94

Robert Banks Stewart
The Darling Buds of May '91

Ben Stiller
Zoolander '01

Joe Stillman
Shrek [SE] '01

Whit Stillman
Barcelona '94

Mark Stock
Attack from Mars '88

John Stockwell
Rock Star '01
Breast Men '97

Christopher Stone
Killer Instinct '00

Matt Stone
South Park: Insults to Injury '02
South Park: Bigger, Longer and Uncut '99

Michael Stone
Waitress [DC] '81

Tom Stoppard
The Russia House '90
Empire of the Sun '87

Robert Strauss
Retroactive '97

Arthur Strawn
Flight to Mars '52

Wesley Strick
The Glass House '01
Hitched '01
Cape Fear '91

Herbert L. Strock
The Crawling Hand '63

Max Strom
Shelter '98

Raymond Stross
The Mark '61

Troy Stroud
Beverly Hood '99

Barry Strugatz
She-Devil '89

Stuart Strutin
First Turn On [DC] '83

John Stu
Ice Grill '02

Jeb Stuart
Die Hard [FS 2] '88

Preston Sturges
The Lady Eve '41
Sullivan's Travels '41

Charles Sturridge
Shackleton '02
Troubles '88

Hel Styverson
Forbidden Sins '99

Milton Subotsky
At the Earth's Core '76

Henry Sucher
The Mummy's Ghost '44
The Mummy's Tomb '42

Ging On Suen
Daughter of Darkness '93

Masumi Suetani
Rebirth of Mothra 2 '97

Larry Sulkis
John Carpenter's Ghosts of Mars '01

Tim Sullivan
Jack and Sarah '95

Arne Sultan
See No Evil, Hear No Evil '89

Sai-shing Sum
Ninja in the Deadly Trap '83

Phoef Sutton
Mrs. Winterbourne '96

Jan Svankmajer
Conspirators of Pleasure '93

Zdenek Sverak
Dark Blue World '01

Gerry Swallow
Black Knight '01
Say It Isn't So '01

Ron Swanson
Top Dog '95

Miles Hood Swarthout
The Shootist '76

Tommy Swerdlow
Snow Dogs '02

David Swift
How to Succeed in Business without Really Trying '67
The Parent Trap '61
Pollyanna '60

Frank Swoboda
The Basket [SE] '99

Tessa Swoboda
The Basket [SE] '99

Istvan Szabo
Mephisto '81
Love Film '70

Laszlo Szabo
Colonel Redl '84

William Szarka
South Bronx Heroes '85

Kam-yeun Szeto
Too Many Ways to Be No. 1 '97

Roy Szeto
The Phantom Lover '95

Matthew Tabak
Beyond Suspicion '00

Brian Taggert
Wanted: Dead or Alive '86

Hisaya Takabayashi
Devil Hunter Yohko: The Complete Collection, Vol. 1 '93

Koji Takada
Return of the Street Fighter '74
The Street Fighter [BCI] '74
The Street Fighter [BFS] '74

Hiroshi Takehashi
Beautiful Beast '95

Tamiya Takehashi
Beautiful Beast '95

Igor Talankin
Tchaikovsky '71

Ted Tally
The Silence of the Lambs [MGM SE] '91

Cheung Tan
Iron Monkey [Miramax] '93

Billy Tang
Brother of Darkness '94

Pik-yin Tang
Iron Monkey [Miramax] '93
Swordsman 2 '91

Danis Tanovic
No Man's Land '01

Robert Emmett Tansey
Paradise Canyon '35

Daniel Taplitz
Dean Koontz's Black River '01

Daniel Taradash
Don't Bother to Knock '52

Andrei Tarkovsky
The Sacrifice / Directed by Andrei Tarkovsky '86
The Mirror '75

Clay Tarver
Joy Ride '01

Yuichiro Tatsumi
Tokyo Decameron: Three Tales of Madness & Sensuality '96

Bertrand Tavernier
Capitaine Conan '96
Round Midnight '86
The Clockmaker '73

Eric Taylor
Dick Tracy Meets Gruesome '47
Dick Tracy, Detective '45
Son of Dracula '43

Greg Taylor
Prancer Returns '01
Prancer '89

Henry Taylor
Three Stooges: All Time Favorites '98

Jim Taylor
Jurassic Park 3 [CE] '01

Kenneth Taylor
Sleeping Murder / 4:50 from Paddington '86

Herschel Weingrod
Brewster's Millions [Universal] '85

Zachary Weintraub
Amazons and Gladiators '01

Peter Weir
The Last Wave '77

Brenda Weisberg
The Mummy's Ghost '44

Gabe Weisert
Fishing with Gandhi '98

Eric Weiss
Bongwater '98

Michael D. Weiss
U.S. Seals 2 '01

David Weissman
Evolution '01
Family Man '00

Fay Weldon
Upstairs, Downstairs: The Complete First Season '71

Les Weldon
The Order '01
Replicant '01

Halsted Welles
3:10 to Yuma '57

Orson Welles
The Trial '63
Citizen Kane '41

George Wells
Designing Woman '57
Show Boat '51

Peter Wells
First Love and Other Pains / One of Them '99

Irvine Welsh
The Acid House '98

Gina Wendkos
The Princess Diaries '01

Richard Wenk
Vamp '86

John Werner
Rudy Blue '00

Michael Werner
Harrad Experiment '73

Lina Wertmuller
Seduction of Mimi '72
Violent City '70

William Wesley
Route 666 '01

Terry West
The Sexy Sixth Sense '01

Haskell Wexler
Medium Cool [SE] '69

Norman Wexler
Joe '70

John Wexley
The Long Night '47

George Whaley
Poor Man's Orange '87
The Harp in the South '86

Joss Whedon
Buffy the Vampire Slayer: Season 1 '97

Buffy the Vampire Slayer '92

David Wheeler
Point of View '00

Paul Wheeler
The Darling Buds of May '91

William Wheeler
The Prime Gig '00

John Whelpley
Tremors 3: Back to Perfection '01

Bradley White
Maze '01

James Gordon White
The Tormentors '71

Noni White
The Hunchback of Notre Dame '96

Robb White
Homicidal '61
13 Ghosts '60

Robertson White
Dick Tracy Meets Gruesome '47

Hugh Whitemore
84 Charing Cross Road '86

Richard Whitley
Rock 'n' Roll High School [New Concorde SE] '79

Cormac Wibberly
The 6th Day [2 SE] '00

Marianne S. Wibberly
The 6th Day [2 SE] '00

Christopher Wicking
Blood from the Mummy's Tomb '71

Gregory Widen
Highlander [Anchor Bay] '86

Joe Wiesenfeld
Back to the Secret Garden '01
Child Star: The Shirley Temple Story '01

James Wignall
The Knights Templar '00

Crane Wilbur
The Bat [Goodtimes] '59

Billy Wilder
Irma La Douce '63
Witness for the Prosecution '57

Gene Wilder
See No Evil, Hear No Evil '89
Haunted Honeymoon '86

Ethan Wiley
Children of the Corn 5: Fields of Terror '98
House 2: The Second Story '87
House '86

Rich Wilkes
Airheads '94

J.J. Wilkie
Helter Skelter Murders '71

Christopher Wilkinson
Ali '01

Don Williams
Slaughter '72

Hugh Williams
The Grass Is Greener '61

Calder Willingham
The Vikings '58

Carey Wilson
Behind Office Doors '31

Gerald Wilson
Chato's Land '71
Lawman '71

Lanford Wilson
Fifth of July '82

Lee Wilson
The Miracle of the Cards '00

Michael Wilson
A Place in the Sun '51

Michael Henry Wilson
A Personal Journey with Martin Scorsese through American Movies '97

S.S. Wilson
Short Circuit 2 '88
Short Circuit '86

Zack Winestine
States of Control '98

Terence H. Winkless
The Howling '81

Jeff Winner
You Are Here * '00

Alex Winter
Fever '99

Terence Winter
The Sopranos: The Complete Second Season '01

Doris Wishman
Night to Dismember '83

William Witney
Jungle Girl '41

Dan Witt
Cruel and Unusual '01

Wolfram Witt
Coming Out '89

P.G. Wodehouse
Jeeves & Wooster: The Complete Second Season '96

Fred Wolf
Joe Dirt '01

Karen Wolf
Children of the Living Dead '00

Barry Wong
Righting Wrongs '86

Jing Wong
Legend of the Red Dragon '94
Magnificent Butcher '87

Manfred Wong
The Storm Riders '98

Raymond Wong
The Phantom Lover '95

John Woo
Last Hurrah for Chivalry '78

Charles Wood
Cuba '79
The Charge of the Light Brigade '68

Edward D. Wood, Jr.
Night of the Ghouls '59

Bronte Woodard
Can't Stop the Music '80

Skip Woods
Swordfish '01

Abbe Wool
Reckless and Wild '02

Alexander Wright
Wishmaster 3: Beyond the Gates of Hell '01

Ralph Wright
Peter Pan [2 SE] '53

Alvin Wyckoff
The Cheat [Kino] '15

J.H. Wyman
The Mexican '01
Mr. Rice's Secret '00

Tracy Keenan Wynn
Robinson Crusoe '96
The Autobiography of Miss Jane Pittman '74

Jim Wynorski
Raptor '01
Big Bad Mama 2 '87
Deathstalker 2: Duel of the Titans '87

Frank Yablans
Mommie Dearest '81

Jeff Yagher
The Guardian '00

Shinobu Yaguchi
Adrenaline Drive '99

Boaz Yakin
Fresh '94

Hiroshi Yamaguchi
Blue Submarine No. 6—Episode 1: Blues '98
Blue Submarine No. 6—Episode 2: Pilots '98
Blue Submarine No. 6—Episode 3: Hearts '98
Blue Submarine No. 6—Episode 4: Minasoko '98

Weird Al Yankovic
UHF '89

George Worthing Yates
Tormented '60

Nai-Hoi Yau
Where a Good Man Goes '99

Konstantin Yershov
Viy '67

Valentin Yezhov
Ballad of a Soldier '60

Rafael Yglesias
From Hell [DLE] '01

Dwight Yoakam
South of Heaven, West of Hell '01

Michiko Yokote
Strange Dawn, Vol. 2—Strange Journey '01

Jeff Yonis
Bloodfist 5: Human Target '93

Phillip Yordan
God's Little Acre '58

Sawaguchi Yoshiaki
Bloodfight '89

Graham Yost
The Last Castle '01

Robert Yost
Helltown '38

Dalene Young
Cross Creek '83

Nedrick Young
Inherit the Wind '60
The Defiant Ones '58

Robert M. Young
Triumph of the Spirit '89

Corey Yuen
Bury Me High '90

James Yuen
Your Place or Mine! '98

Shiro Yumeno
The Bedroom '92

Jon Zack
Out Cold '01

Steven Zaillian
Searching for Bobby Fischer '93

Alain Zaloum
With Friends Like These '90

Barnardino Zapponi
Spirits of the Dead [Criterion] '68

Cesare Zavattini
The Garden of the Finzi-Continis '71
After the Fox '66
Atomic War Bride / This Is Not a Test '60

Michael Zelniker
Stuart Bliss '98

Robert Zemeckis
Used Cars '80

Bill Zide
Fatal Blade '00

Paul Ziller
Avalanche Alley '01

John Zinman
Lara Croft: Tomb Raider '01

Chris Zois
The Blackout '97

Archibald Zounds, Jr.
Goliath and the Dragon '61

George Zuckerman
Written on the Wind '56

Carl Zuckmayer
The Blue Angel '30

Vincente Zuniga C
Drive By '01

Terry Zwigoff
Ghost World '01

The Cinematographer Index lists all cinematographers, or Directors of Photography (D.P.), as they are also known, credited in at least one DVD reviewed in this book. The listings for the cinematographer names follow an alphabetical sort by last name (although the names appear in a first name, last name format). The videographies are listed chronologically, from most recent to oldest film. If a cinematographer lensed more than one film in the same year, these movies are listed alphabetically within the year.

Alfonso Beato
Ghost World '01
Great Balls of Fire '89

Andres Leon Becker
Bloody Proof '99

Jack Beckett
A Scream in the Streets '73
Please Don't Eat My Mother '72

Terry Bedford
Jabberwocky '77

Dion Beebe
Along for the Ride '00

Paul Beeson
To Sir, with Love '67

Peter Belcher
U.S. Seals 2 '01

Ted C. Bemiller
Fritz the Cat '72

Giorgyorgy Benaskovich
Play-Mate of the Apes '02
The Erotic Mirror '01
Erotic Survivor 2 '01

Richard Benda
Sworn to Justice '96

Henning Bendtsen
Gertrud '64
Ordet '55

Peter Benison
Cruel and Unusual '01

Mark Benjamin
Brooklyn Babylon '00

Georges Benoit
Regeneration / Young
Romance '15

Christopher Benson
Hairdo U '02

Manuel Berenguer
Savage Pampas '66

Gabriel Beristain
Molly '99

Monty Berman
The Flesh and the Fiends '60

Michael Bernard
On the Line '01

Kristian Bernier
Partners '99

Steven Bernstein
Corky Romano '01
The Forsaken '01
Scary Movie 2 '01
The Wood '99

Paul Berriff
Lessons of Darkness '92

Renato Berta
Kadosh '99

Thom Best
Ginger Snaps '00

Amit Bhattacharya
Adventures of Justine '00

Corwin Bibb
Dirty Kopz '01

Adrian Biddle
The Mummy Returns '01
The Tall Guy '89
Willow '88
The Princess Bride [2 SE] '87

Luca Bigazzi
Bread and Tulips '01

Adam Biggs
Mind Meld: Secrets behind
the Voyage of a Lifetime '01

Robert Birchall
Bucktown '75

Ivan Bird
Sexy Beast '00

Donald Birnkrant
Tank '83

Joseph Biroc
Too Late the Hero '70
13 Ghosts '60
The Bat [Goodtimes] '59
On Our Merry Way '48

Billy (G.W.) Bitzer
Broken Blossoms [Kino] '19

Hilding Bladh
Invasion of the Animal People '62
Terror in the Midnight Sun '58

Stephen Blake
Sorority Babes in the Slimeball Bowl-A-Rama '87

Ken Blakey
Extreme Honor '01
Agent Red '00

John Blick
The Last Tattoo '94

Sydney Blythe
Scrooge '35

Ralf Bode
Cousins '89
The Accused '88
Dressed to Kill [SE] '80

Uwe Bohrer
Nekromantik '87

Francisco Bojorquez
Barbarian Queen 2: The
Empress Strikes Back '89

Gene Borghi
Fritz the Cat '72

Harlan Bosmajian
Spin the Bottle '97

Rick Bota
Valentine '01

David Boyd
Firestarter 2: Rekindled '02

Russell Boyd
American Outlaws '01
Company Man '01
Sweet Talker '91
Crocodile Dundee 2 '88
Crocodile Dundee '86
Tender Mercies [Anchor Bay] '83
The Last Wave '77

Charles P. Boyle
Old Yeller '57

Kurt Brabbee
Dead Silence '98

Henry Braham
Shackleton '02

Denise Brassard
St. Patrick's Day '01

Sylvain Brault
2001: A Space Travesty '00
Rowing Through '96

Elwood "Woody" Bredell
The Mummy's Hand '40

Brian J. Breheny
When Good Ghouls Go Bad '01

Jules Brenner
1969 '89
Cornbread, Earl & Me '75

Uta Briesewitz
Session 9 '01

Robert Brinkmann
Sugar & Spice '01

Cyril Bristow
Big Fella '37

Robert J. Bronner
Pocketful of Miracles '61

Joseph Brotherton
Tarzan the Fearless '33

Blain Brown
Double Deception '01

Edward R. Brown
Amazing Grace '74

Ronald W. Browne
Three Amigos '86

Michael J. Bruggemeyer
Chicks, Man '99

Bobby Bukowski
Til There Was You '96

Don Burgess
Forrest Gump [SCE] '94
Mo' Money '92
Death Before Dishonor '87

Robert Burks
Marnie '64

Hans Burman
Open Your Eyes '97
Why Do They Call It Love
When They Mean Sex? '92

Ken Burns
Ken Burns' Mark Twain '01
Ken Burns: Jazz '00
Lewis and Clark: Journey of
the Corps of Discovery '97

David Burr
Crocodile Dundee in Los
Angeles '01
Race the Sun '96

Thomas Burstyn
When Trumpets Fade '98
Andre '94
Arctic Blue '93

Stephen Burum
He Said, She Said '91
Casualties of War '89
The War of the Roses [SE] '89
The Bride '85

Dick Bush
The Journey of Natty Gann '85
Crimes of Passion [2] '84

Bill Butler
Deceiver '97
Stripes '81
Can't Stop the Music '80
Bingo Long Traveling All-Stars
& Motor Kings '76

Michael C. Butler
Jaws 2 '78

Frank Byers
Shiloh '97

Bobby Byrne
Bull Durham [MGM SE] '88
Stealing Home '88
The Villain '79

John Cabrera
Hell of the Living Dead '83

Thomas Callaway
Earth vs. the Spider '01
She Creature '01

Tom Calloway
The Dead Hate the Living '99

Nesto Calvo
Living It Up '00
Not Love Just Frenzy '96

Grant Scott Cameron
Orphans '97

Paul Cameron
Swordfish '01

John Campbell
Just One Night '00

Marco Cappetta
Hard As Nails '01

Cary Caraway
A Regular Frankie Fan '01

Jack Cardiff
The Dogs of War '81
The Vikings '58
The Prince and the Showgirl '57

Russell Carpenter
Money Talks '97
The Indian in the Cupboard '95
Pet Sematary 2 '92

Beat Carroll
The Fat Black Pussycat '63

Ellis W. Carter
Twice-Told Tales '63

Owen Casey
Ninja in the U.S.A. '88

Alan Caso
Reindeer Games [Miramax DC] '00
Running Mates '00

Levy Castleberry
Sweet Thing '00

Darrell Cathcart
The Wolfman '82

Francois Catonne
Indochine '92

Sarah Cawley
Oxygen '99

Christopher Challis
S.O.S. Titanic '79
Force 10 from Navarone '78
The Grass Is Greener '61

Benoit Chamaillard
Baise Moi '00

Caroline Champetier
Lush '01
La Sentinelle '92
Gang of Four '88

Chung Yun Chan
The Demon's Baby '98
Lady Iron Monkey '83
Snake and Crane Arts of Shaolin '78

Daniel Chan
The Cheaters '00
Trust Me U Die '99

Allen Chandler
Teenage Zombies '58

Hai Chang
Drunken Master '78
Snake in the Eagle's Shadow '78

Yao Chu Chang
Last Hurrah for Chivalry '78

Gu Changwei
Hurlyburly '98
Life on a String '90

Michael Chapman
Evolution '01
White River '99
Space Jam [2 EE] '96
The Last Waltz [SE] '78

Colin Chase
Confessions of Robert Crumb '87

Julio Chavez
The Death Curse of Tartu /
Sting of Death '66
Sting of Death '65

Chong-yuan Chen
To Kill with Intrigue '77

How-chung Chen
Dreaming Fists with Slender
Hands '80

Hwai-en Chen
Goodbye South, Goodbye '96
Good Men, Good Women '95

Siu Keung Cheng
Love on a Diet '01
Where a Good Man Goes '99

Man Po Cheung
Jiang Hu—"The Triad Zone" '00
Your Place or Mine! '98

Wing Him Ching
Revenge of the Patriots '76

Steven Chivers
High Heels and Low Lifes '01

Alain Choquart
Boesman & Lena '00
Capitaine Conan '96

Fook Leung Chow
Goose Boxer '78

Luis Ciccarese
Demonia '90

Richard Ciupka
Atlantic City '81

Josep Civit
Anguish '88

Richard Clabaugh
Children of the Corn 4: The
Gathering '96

Tom Clancey
A Regular Frankie Fan '01

Curtis Clark
Dominick & Eugene '88
Extremities '86
Sesame Street Presents: Fol-
low That Bird '85

Tony Clark
Alien Visitor '95

Charles Clarke
Guadalcanal Diary '43

Ross Clarkson
Cold War '79

Robert C. Cline
The Black Raven '43

Wilfrid M. Cline
The Giant Gila Monster '59
Calamity Jane '53

Ghislan Cloquet
The Young Girls of Rochefort '68
Le Trou '59

William Clothier
The Devil's Brigade '68

Juan Cristobal Cobo
Something within Me '93

Daniel Cohen
Mood Swingers '00

Ted Cohen
Red Dirt '99

Robert E. Collins
Schlock '73

Peter Collister
The Animal '01
The Replacement Killers [2 SE] '98
Higher Learning '94
Halloween 4: The Return of
Michael Myers [MGM LE] '88

Roy Collodi
Just for the Hell of It '68

Giovanni Fiore Coltellacci
In Love and War '01

David Connell
Stephen King's Rose Red '02
Robinson Crusoe '96
NeverEnding Story 2: The Next Chapter '91
The Aviator '85

Jack Conroy
Tick Tock '00
The Field [Artisan] '90

Alfio Contini
The Libertine '69

James A. Contner
The Last Dragon '85

Denys Coop
And Now the Screaming Starts [SE] '73
Billy Liar '63
The Mind Benders '63

Wilkie Cooper
First Men in the Moon '64

John Coquillon
The Last Place on Earth '94
Clockwise '86
All Quiet on the Western Front '79
Wuthering Heights '70

Ericson Core
The Fast and the Furious '01
Dancing at the Blue Iguana '00

Charles Correll
Revenge of the Nerds 2: Nerds in Paradise '87
Star Trek 3: The Search for Spock '84
Cheech and Chong's Nice Dreams '81

Stanley Cortez
The Angry Red Planet '59

Andrew M. Costikyan
The Beast from Haunted Cave '60

Cristian Cottet
The Road '00

Gerald Cotts
Putney Swope '69

Michael Coulter
Breaking In '89
Gregory's Girl '80

Raoul Coutard
Les Carabiniers '63
Le Petit Soldat '60
Breathless '59

Graeme Cowley
Utu '83

Jack Cox
Devil Girl from Mars '54
We Dive at Dawn '43

James A. Crabe
The Karate Kid: Part 2 '86
The Autobiography of Miss Jane Pittman '74

Ted Crestview
The Sexy Sixth Sense '01

Jordan Cronenweth
Stop Making Sense '84
Cutter's Way '81

Edward Cronjager
On Our Merry Way '48

Floyd Crosby
The Fast and the Furious '54
Monster from the Ocean Floor '54

James A. Crosby
His Majesty, the Scarecrow of Oz '14

Eric Cross
Song of Freedom / Big Fella '36

Richard Crudo
Down to Earth '01
Out Cold '01
American Pie [2 UE] '99
Bongwater '98

Xavier Cruz
The Evil That Men Do '84

Augustin Cubano
The Kiss You Gave Me '00

Dean Cundey
Hook '91
Psycho 2 '83
Halloween 2: The Nightmare Isn't Over! [Universal] '81
Galaxina '80
Rock 'n' Roll High School [New Concorde SE] '79
Halloween [Extended Edition] '78
Satan's Cheerleaders '77
Where the Red Fern Grows '74

Neve Cunningham
Horatio Hornblower '99

Alec Curtis
Horatio Hornblower '99

Henryk Cymerman
To the Limit '95

Laurent Dailland
The Taste of Others '00
Perfect Love '96

Bernard Daillencourt
The Beast '75

Stephen Dale
War Gods of the Deep '65

John Daly
Greenfingers '00

Arch R. Dalzell
The Boy in the Plastic Bubble [2] '76

Reggie Danials
Axe 'Em '02

William H. Daniels
Von Ryan's Express '65
Robin and the 7 Hoods '64
Ocean's 11 '60
A Hole in the Head '59
Three Came Home '50
Lured '47

Brian Danitz
Sound and Fury '00

Steve Danyluk
The Skulls 2 '02

Alex D. Darvounis
Olive Juice '01

Andreas Daub
Advertising Rules! '01

Nina Davenport
Always a Bridesmaid '00

Allen Daviau
Empire of the Sun '87

Mark David
Sweet Thing '00

Elliot Davis
Happy Campers '01
I Am Sam '01
The Glass Shield '95
Vamp '86

Matt Davis
A Girl, 3 Guys and a Gun '01

Jan De Bont
Basic Instinct [2 SE] '92
Total Recall [2 SLE] '90
Die Hard [FS 2] '88
Ruthless People '86
All the Right Moves '83
Katie Tippel '75
Business Is Business '71

John de Borman
Serendipity '01

Cian de Buitlear
Blow Dry '00
Southpaw '00

Segundo de Chomon
Cabiria '14

William de Diego
Hitch Hike to Hell / Kidnapped Coed '97

Alan De Herrera
Revenge Quest '96

Bruno de Keyzer
About Adam '00
The Ogre '96
Impromptu '90
Round Midnight '86

Arturo de la Rosa
In the Country Where Nothing Happens '99

Jean De Segonzac
Shake, Rattle & Rock! '94

Roger Deakins
The Man Who Wasn't There '01
Courage Under Fire '96

Seamus Deasy
An Everlasting Piece '00
When the Sky Falls '99

Henri Decae
Le Professionnel '81
Don Juan (Or If Don Juan Were a Woman) '73
Light at the Edge of the World '71
Joe '70
Les Bonnes Femmes '60
Purple Noon '60
Bob le Flambeur '55

Guy Defaux
Pin... '88

Thomas Del Ruth
Barbarians at the Gate '93

Benoit Delhomme
The Winslow Boy '98
The Scent of Green Papaya '93

Franco Delli Colli
The Last Man on Earth '64

Tonino Delli Colli
Spirits of the Dead [Criterion] '68

Frank DeMarco
Hedwig and the Angry Inch '00

Peter Deming
From Hell [DLE] '01
Mulholland Drive '01
Hollywood Shuffle '87

John L. Demps, Jr.
Finding Buck McHenry '00
The Visit '00

Austin Dempster
A Touch of Class '73

Daniil Demutsky
Earth '30

Jim Denault
Chasing Sleep '00
Sudden Manhattan '96

Mike Deprez
Thumbtanic '99

Joe DeSalvo
Fever '99

Dominic Desantis
Dead or Alive '02

Caleb Deschanel
The Patriot [2 SB] '00
Fly Away Home [2 SE] '96

Kerwin Devonish
Hav Plenty '97

Joe Di Gennaro
The Opponent '01

Carlo Di Palma
Husbands and Wives '92
Radio Days '87
Hannah and Her Sisters '86

Dario Di Palma
Seduction of Mimi '72

Gianni Di Venanzo
Juliet of the Spirits [Criterion] '65
8 1/2 '63
Eva '62
Il Grido '57

James Diamond
The Road to Ruin '28

Craig DiBona
Blue Moon '00

Louis DiCesare
Lena's Holiday '90

Tom DiCillo
Stranger than Paradise '84

Desmond Dickinson
The Bloodsuckers '70
The City of the Dead '60

Billy Dickson
Victim of Love '91

Bill Dill
Dancing in September '00
The Five Heartbeats '91

George E. Diskant
Dick Tracy vs. Cueball '46

Hans Dittmer
Vibration '68

Conrad Dobler
Beverly Hills Bordello '01

Sergio d'Offizi
The Squeeze '78

Raul Dominguez
The Fear Chamber '68

Rudy Donovan
Barbarian Queen '85

Dermott Downs
Dracula: The Dark Prince '01

Christopher Doyle
Made [SE] '01
In the Mood for Love [SE] '00

Jack Draper
Daniel Boone: Trail Blazer '56

Rob Draper
Tales from the Darkside: The Movie '90

Randy Drummond
Series 7: The Contenders '01
Anima '98

Stuart Dryburgh
Bridget Jones's Diary '01
Kate & Leopold '01
Sex and the City: Season 1 '00
Runaway Bride '99

Guy Dufaux
The Great Gatsby '01
Stardom '00

Bryan Duggan
T.N.T. '98

Simon Duggan
Risk '00

Victor Duncan
The Great St. Louis Bank Robbery '59

Bert Dunk
Megiddo: The Omega Code 2 '01
Storm in Summer '00

Andrew Dunn
Monkeybone '01
Liam '00

Edwin DuPar
Lone Ranger '56

Jean-Rene Duveau
Happenstance '00

John Dyer
Matthew Blackheart: Monster Smasher '99

Philip Earnshaw
The Secrets of the Warrior's Power '97

Scott Edelstein
Parental Guidance '02

Eric Alan Edwards
On the Edge '01
Garden of Eden '94

David Eggby
Crossfire Trail '01
Quigley Down Under '90
Kansas '88
Mad Max [MGM SE] '80

Miguel Ehrenberg
Dona Herlinda & Her Son '86

Paul Elliot
Citizen Cohn '92
Star Slammer '87

Frederick Elmes
The Ice Storm '97
Trial by Jury '94

Robert Elswit
Heist '01
The Heart of Dixie '89

Susan Emerson
First Degree '01

Bryan England
Sometimes They Come Back '91

Nils Erickson
Rod Steele 0014: You Only Live Until You Die '02

Teodoro Escamilla
Things I Left in Havanna '97

Jean-Yves Escoffier
15 Minutes '01
A Personal Journey with Martin Scorsese through American Movies '97
Jack and Sarah '95

Christopher Faloona
3 Ninjas Kick Back '94

James Fan
Invincible Obsessed Fighter '82

Daniel F. Fapp
Five Card Stud '68
Let's Make Love '60
On the Beach '59
Kings Go Forth '58

Pierre Fattori
A Real Young Girl '75

Don E. Fauntleroy
Jeepers Creepers '01

Matt Faw
Road Dogz '00

Zhao Fei
The Curse of the Jade Scorpion '01

Jock Feindel
Bluebeard '44

Joao Fernandes
Top Dog '95
Invasion U.S.A. '85

David Ferrara
Kill Me Later '01

Michael Ferris
Bar Girls '95

A. Jafa Fielder
Daughters of the Dust '91

Vilko Filac
Novocaine '01

Michael Findlay
Satan's Bed '65

Roberta Findlay
Satan's Bed '65

Russell Fine
O '01

Mauro Fiore
The Center of the World '01
Driven '01
Highway '01
Training Day '01

Harry Fischbeck
The Big Broadcast of 1938 '38

Gunnar Fischer
Wild Strawberries '57

Cary Fisher
Jailbreakers '94

Dick Fisher
Mr. Vincent '97

Gerry Fisher
Cops and Robbersons '94
Exorcist 3: Legion '90
Highlander [Anchor Bay] '86
The Island of Dr. Moreau '77
Brannigan '75
Accident '67

Mike Flash
Britannia Hospital '82

Brenden Flint
Better Dayz '02

Pili Flores-Guerra
800 Leagues down the Amazon '93

George J. Folsey
Vengeance Valley '51
The Harvey Girls '46

Cinders Forshaw
The Long Run '00

Joey Forsyte
Bad Seed '00
The Treat '98

Steve Fraasa
Golf Balls! '99

Robert Fraisse
Enemy at the Gates '00
The Lover '92

William A. Fraker
Town and Country '01
Tombstone [2] '93

Freddie Francis
Cape Fear '91
The French Lieutenant's Woman '81
The Elephant Man '80
Saturday Night and Sunday Morning '60

David Franco
3000 Miles to Graceland '01

Ellsworth Fredericks
Sayonara '57

Jonathan Freeman
Hitched '01
The Lost Battalion '01

Karl Freund
Key Largo '48
The Last Laugh '24
The Golem '20

Martin Fuhrer
Wilde '97
Lord of the Flies '90

Tak Fujimoto
The Sixth Sense [Buena Vista] '99
That Thing You Do! '96
The Silence of the Lambs [MGM SE] '91
Sweet Hearts Dance '88
Caged Heat '74

Kei Fujiwara
Organ '96

Vicky Funari
Live Nude Girls Unite! '00

Steve Gainer
Bully '01

Ricardo Jacques Gale
The Nest '88

Michael Gallagher
Bloodfist 7: Manhunt '95
Bloodfist 6: Ground Zero '94

Brendan Galvin
Behind Enemy Lines '01
Rat '00

Ron Garcia
The Runaway '00
Twin Peaks: Fire Walk with Me '92

Mike Garfath
The Enemy '01

David Garfinkel
The Last Warrior '99

Lee Garmes
The Jungle Book '42
The Show Off / The Plastic Age '26

Frederick Gately
I Bury the Living '58

Eric Gautier
Intimacy '00
Those Who Love Me Can Take the Train '98

Carlos Gaviria
Undercurrent '99

Armand Gazarian
Social Intercourse '01
Two Coyotes '01

David Geddes
Fatal Error '99

Paul Gentry
The Crater Lake Monster '77

Laszlo George
Christy—A Change of Seasons '01
Christy—A New Beginning '01
Christy—Return to Cutter Gap '01

Henry W. Gerrard
Little Women '33

Maury Gertsman
She Wolf of London '46

Pierre Gill
Lost and Delirious '01

Dan Gillham
Final '01

Ken Glassing
Southern Man '99

Phillip Glau
Treasure Island '99

Pierre William Glenn
Avalanche '78

Bert Glennon
Dimples '36

James Glennon
Dead Simple '01
Life without Dick '01
South of Heaven, West of Hell '01
Best Men '98

Richard C. Glouner
Moon of the Wolf '72
The Dunwich Horror '70

Michael Gol
Echo of Murder '00
Fatal Blade '00
Forbidden Sins '99

Stephen Goldblatt
Conspiracy '01
The Prince of Tides '91
Joe versus the Volcano '90
The Cotton Club '84

Eric Goldstein
Shelter '98

Carlos Gonzalez
Arachnid '01

Frank Good
The Wizard of Oz '25

Irv Goodnoff
The Van '77

Paula Grandio
Play for Me '01

Arthur Grant
Blood from the Mummy's Tomb '71

Barry Gravelle
Requiem for Murder '99
When Justice Fails '98

Gary Graver
Attack of the 60-Foot Centerfold '95

Mark W. Gray
Firetrap '01

Kreso Grcevic
Atomic War Bride / This Is Not a Test '60

Richard Greatrex
A Knight's Tale '01

Jack N. Green
True Crime '99
The Net [2 SE] '95
Rookie of the Year '93

Adam Greenberg
Sister Act '92
Toys '92
Three Men and a Little Lady '90
Turner and Hooch '89
Three Men and a Baby '87

Robbie Greenberg
Introducing Dorothy Dandridge '99

Tim Greene
Creepin' '01

William Howard Greene
When Worlds Collide '51

Jack Greenhalgh
The Lost Continent '51

Peter Greenhalgh
Ultraviolet '98

David Gribble
Chill Factor '99
Fires Within '91
Cadillac Man '90

Frank Griebe
The Princess and the Warrior '00

Garett Griffin
The Riff '00

Marcel Grignon
The Beast '75

Xavier Perez Grobet
In the Time of the Butterflies '01
Tortilla Soup '01

Eyal Grodin
Acceptable Risk '01

Alexander Grusynski
Two Can Play That Game '01

Ennio Guarnieri
The Garden of the Finzi-Continis '71

Paul Guffee
Confessions of a Psycho Cat / Hot Blooded Woman '68

Burnett Guffey
How to Succeed in Business without Really Trying '67
Homicidal '61
Mr. Sardonicus '61
All the King's Men '49

Eric Guichard
Himalaya '99

Carles Gusi
Vacas '91

Eugeny Guslinsky
Marquis de Sade '96

Carl Guthrie
Long John Silver '54

Rob Hahn
The Score '01

Jacques Haitkin
Faust: Love of the Damned '00
Making the Grade '84

Stephen Hajinal
The Brain That Wouldn't Die '63

Conrad L. Hall
Searching for Bobby Fischer '93

Geoffrey Hall
Chopper '01

Peter Hall
Sleeping Murder / 4:50 from Paddington '86

Hans J. Haller
God's Little Acre '58

Takashi Hamada
Adrenaline Drive '99

Fenton Hamilton
Hell up in Harlem '73

Victor Hammer
Major League 2 '94

Peter Hannan
Not without My Daughter '90
How to Get Ahead in Advertising '89
Withnail and I '87
Dangerous Summer '82

Charles Hannawalt
Dementia 13 [Roan] '63

Alain Hardy
Revenge in the House of Usher '82

Antoine Harispe
The Rape of the Vampire '68

Russell Harlan
Hatari! '62
Pollyanna '60
Operation Petticoat '59
Rio Bravo '59
Run Silent, Run Deep '58
Witness for the Prosecution '57

Virgil Harper
Tremors 3: Back to Perfection '01

Frank Harris
Skyscraper '95

Harvey Harrison
Cheech and Chong's The Corsican Brothers '84

Thomas M. Harting
Ripper: Letter from Hell '01

Hideki Hasegawa
Sumo Vixens '96

Youichi Hasegawa
City Hunter: Secret Service '96

Naoki Hashimoto
Terminatrix '95

Kurt Hasse
Town without Pity '61

Yudeo Hato
The Kid Brother '87

Willis Hawkins
The Worm Eaters '77

James Hawkinson
Progeny '98

Robert Hayes
Mind, Body & Soul '92

James Hayman
Buffy the Vampire Slayer '92

John Hazard
Fist of Fear, Touch of Death '80

George Heath
Fighting Rats of Tobruk '44

Antoine Hebale
For Sale '98

Antoine Heberle
Under the Sand '00

Dan Heigh
The Basket [SE] '99
Matter of Trust '98

Bernd Heinl
The Extreme Adventures of Super Dave '98
Bagdad Cafe '88

Wolfgang Held
Fallout '01
Maze '01
Dogs: The Rise and Fall of an All-Girl Bookie Joint '96

Otto Heller
Funeral in Berlin '66

Thomas Hencz
Amazons and Gladiators '01

David Hennings
Boycott '02
Tom Clancy's Netforce '98

Adalberto Hernandez
Vampires in Havana '87

Bernard Herschensen
Satan in High Heels '61

Ed Hershberger
There's Nothing out There '90

David L. Hewitt
Monsters Crash the Pajama
Party Spook Show Spectacular '65

Jack Hildyard
Summertime '55

Ian Hilton
The Moving Finger '85

James E. Hinton
Ganja and Hess '73

Paul Hipp
Superchick '71

Lu Ying Ho
Tiger over Wall '80

Nan-hong Ho
The Personals '98

Winton C. Hoch
The Young Land '59
The Halls of Montezuma '50

Ken Hodges
The Ruling Class '72

Andreas Hofer
The Legend of Rita '99

Carl Hoffmann
Faust '26
Dr. Mabuse, The Gambler '22

Michael Hofstein
The Learning Curve '01

Adam Holender
Fresh '94

Tom Hollyman
Lord of the Flies '63

Aslaug Holm
Cool and Crazy '01

David Holmes
Eye Witness '70

Shozo Honda
The Tale of Zatoichi Continues '62

Jamie Hook
Money Buys Happiness '99

William Hooke
Next Time '99

Nathan Hope
Diary of a Sex Addict '01
Mimic 2 '01

Terry Hopkins
Richard Rodgers: The Sweetest Sound '01

John Hora
The Howling '81

David S. Horsley
Jack the Giant Killer '62

Louis Horvath
Strange Invaders '83

Frank Howard
Helter Skelter Murders '71

David Howe
Carnival of Blood / Curse of
the Headless Horseman
[SE] '71

James Wong Howe
Funny Lady '75
Seconds '66
The North Star '43

Matt Howe
Shatter Dead '01

Roger Hubert
Children of Paradise '44

David Hue
Twisted Justice '89

Albert Hughes
American Pimp '99

Michael Hugo
The Mountain Men '80
Head '68

Alan Hume
Caveman '81
The Watcher in the Woods
'81
The People That Time Forgot
'77
At the Earth's Core '76
The Legend of Hell House '73

Shane Hurlbut
crazy/beautiful '01

Philip Hurn
The Passion Network '01
Tender Is the Heart '01

Nick Hutak
Adventures of Justine '00

Peter Hutton
Thomas Jefferson '01

Peter Hyams
The Musketeer '01
Timecop '94
Stay Tuned '92
Running Scared '86

Fred Iannone
Smiling Fish & Goat on Fire
'99

Arthur Ibbetson
Sell Out '76
The Horse's Mouth '58

Jeremy Ides
A Galaxy Far Far Away '00

Slawomir Idziak
Black Hawk Down '01
Proof of Life '00
Gattaca [2 SB] '97

Tony Imi
Aimee & Jaguar '98
Shopping '93
Enemy Mine '85

David Insley
Hairspray (John Waters Collection Vol. 1) '88
Polyester (John Waters Collection Vol. 2) '81

Darin Ipema
Sore Losers '97

Louis Irving
Howling 3: The Marsupials
'87
Return of Captain Invincible
'83

Mark Irwin
American Pie 2 '01
Freddy Got Fingered '01
Osmosis Jones '01
Say It Isn't So '01
Me, Myself, and Irene '00
Vampire in Brooklyn '95
Scanners '81

Hiroshi Isakawa
Devil Hunter Yohko: The Complete Collection, Vol. 1 '93

Kinichi Ishikawa
Devil Hunter Yohko: The Complete Collection, Vol. 1 '93

Yoshihiro Ito
Reborn from Hell: Jubei's
Revenge '96
Reborn from Hell: Samurai
Armageddon '96

Donald G. Jackson
Hell Comes to Frogtown '88

Harry Jackson
The Halls of Montezuma '50

Peter Jackson
Bad Taste [LE] '88

Mieczyslaw Jahoda
The Saragossa Manuscript
'65

Peter James
Bride of the Wind '01
Silent Fall '94
Black Robe [MGM] '91
The Irishman '78

Manfred O. Jelinski
Schramm '93

Devereaux Jennings
Helltown '38

Johnny E. Jensen
Three Wishes '95

Peter Jessop
Schizo '77

Robert C. Jessup
Silent Rage '82
Mars Needs Women '66

Joseph Robert Jobe
Demon Lust '01

Daniel Jobin
Lilies '96

Jon Joffin
Snow White: The Fairest of
Them All '02
Mermaid '00

Bruce Douglas Johnson
The Contaminated Man '01

Shelly Johnson
Jurassic Park 3 [CE] '01
The Last Castle '01

Lawrence Jones
In His Life: The John Lennon
Story '00

Massoud Joseph
The Specialist '75

Dereck Joubert
Whispers: An Elephant's Tale
'00

Il Sung Jung
Chunhyang '00

Jeffrey Jur
Joy Ride '01
My First Mister '01
Panic '00
Unforgettable '96
Soul Man '86

Janusz Kaminski
A.I.: Artificial Intelligence '01
Jerry Maguire [2 SE] '96

William Kaplan, Jr.
Chac: The Rain God '74

Norayr Kasper
Calendar '93

Stephen M. Katz
Return to Cabin by the Lake
'01
18 Again! '88
Las Vegas Lady '76

Boris Kaufman
The Brotherhood '68
On the Waterfront '54

Lloyd Kaufman
Stuck on You! [DC] '84
First Turn On [DC] '83
Waitress [DC] '81
Squeeze Play [DC] '79

Mori Kawa
The Hearse '80

Stephen Kazmierski
Tart '01

Michel Kelber
The Hunchback of Notre
Dame '57

Shane Kelly
Urbania '00

Ken Kelsch
The Blackout '97

Victor Kemper
Tommy Boy '95
See No Evil, Hear No Evil '89
Audrey Rose '77
Slap Shot [2] '77
The Gambler '74

Nils Kenaston
Borough of Kings '98

Charles Kendall
The Secrets of the Warrior's
Power '97

Calvin Kennedy
Point of View '00

Francis Kenny
How High '01
Kingdom Come '01
Wayne's World 2 '93
Heathers [2 THX] '89

Olugbeck Khamraev
The Arena '01

Darius Khondji
Stealing Beauty '96

Gary B. Kibbe
John Carpenter's Ghosts of
Mars '01

Jan Kiesser
Trixie '00
The Dress Code '99
Choose Me '84

Stephen Kim
Retrievers '82

Sung-bok Kim
Tell Me Something '99

Woo-Hyoung Kim
Happy End '99
Lies '99

Jeffrey L. Kimball
Beverly Hills Cop 2 '87

Adam Kimmel
Beyond Suspicion '00

Scott King
Treasure Island '99

Alar Kivilo
The Glass House '01

Yuri Klimenko
The Legend of Suram
Fortress / Ashik Kerib '85

Benjamin (Ben H.) Kline
Two-Fisted Law '32

Richard H. Kline
Star Trek: The Motion Picture
[DE] '80
The Fury '78
Who'll Stop the Rain? '78
Harrad Experiment '73

Edward Klosinski
Kill Cruise '90

Nicholas D. Knowland
Cats [UE Universal] '98
Institue Benjamenta or This
Dream People Call Human
Life '95
Barbarians at the Gate '93

Cyril Knowles
King Solomon's Mines '37

Ko Chiu-lam
Time and Tide '00

Setsuo Kobayashi
The Blind Beast '69
Manji '64

Fred W. Koenekamp
The Adventures of Buckaroo
Banzai Across the Eighth
Dimension [SE] '84
The Hunter '80
The Bad News Bears in
Breaking Training '77
Patton [2] '70

Hans Koenekamp
The Wizard of Oz '25

Karl Kofler
Echo Park '86

Lajos Koltai
The Legend of 1900 '98
Home for the Holidays '95
Colonel Redl '84
Mephisto '81

Shigeru Komatsubara
The Eel '96

Sergei Koslov
The Odyssey '97

Simon Kosoff
Agatha Christie's Poirot:
Dumb Witness '01
Agatha Christie's Poirot: Hercule Poirot's Christmas '01

Laszlo Kovacs
My Best Friend's Wedding [2
SE] '97
The Scout '94
Say Anything [SE] '89
Frances [Anchor Bay] '82
The Toy '82
Rebel Rousers '69
The Hippie Revolt '67
Mondo Mod / The Hippie
Revolt '67
Kiss Me Quick! '64

Peter Kowalski
Poor White Trash '00

Gunther Krampf
Nosferatu '22

Jon Kranhouse
Friday the 13th, Part 6: Jason
Lives '86

Milton Krasner
Monkey Business '52
Three Came Home '50
Along Came Jones '45
The Ghost of Frankenstein
'42

Svein Krovel
Cool and Crazy '01

Tom Krueger
Committed '99

Howard Krupa
1999 '98

Jaroslav Kucera
Daisies '96

Toni Kuhn
The Vanishing [Criterion] '88

Martin Kukula
The Trio '97

Jay Kulp
Swamp Girl / Swamp Country
'71

Fang Chi Kuo
Blood of the Dragon '71

Woo Kuo-Hsiao
Buddha Assassinator '79

Willy Kurant
Pootie Tang '01
China Moon '91

Ellen Kuras
Blow '01

Toyomichi Kurita
Taboo '99

Robert B. Kurrle
Sadie Thompson '28

Chi Ken Kwan
Killer '00

Flavio Labiano
Bones '01
Harlan County War '00

Hugh Labye
Rabid Grannies '89

Daniel Lacambre
'68 '87
Lady in Red '79

Edward Lachman
Sweet November '01
Less Than Zero '87

Richard Lacy
Gator King '70

Kjell Lagerros
Ambush '99

Wan Hsiung Lai
Fists of Bruce Lee '78

Yiu-fai Lai
The Avenging Fist '01

Harry Lake
The Magic Show '81

Rodrigo Lalinde
Our Lady of the Assassins '01

Micheal Lamothe
With Friends Like These '90

Charles B(ryant) Lang, Jr.
Butterflies Are Free '72
Cactus Flower '69
Paris When It Sizzles '64
Separate Tables '58
Queen Bee '55
The Big Heat '53
The Ghost Breakers '40

Roger Lanser
Maybe Baby '99

Vilis Lapenieks
Rainbow Bridge '71
Eegah! '62

Jeanne Lapoirie
Under the Sand '00
Water Drops on Burning
Rocks '99

Stevan Larner
Dance 'til Dawn '88
Roots '77

Joseph LaShelle
River of No Return '54

Walter Lassally
Memoirs of a Survivor '81
Electra '62

Andrew Laszlo
Thief of Hearts '84
The Owl and the Pussycat '70

Ernest Laszlo
Four for Texas '63
It's a Mad, Mad, Mad, Mad
World '63
Inherit the Wind '60
Tormented '60
On Our Merry Way '48

Andrew Lau
City on Fire [Dimension] '87

Hung Chuen Lau
Return of the Deadly Blade '81

Tom Lau
Legend of the Red Dragon '94
Righting Wrongs '86

Wan Shing Law
Fearless Dragon '79

Charles Lawton, Jr.
Cowboy '58
3:10 to Yuma '57
The Long Gray Line '55

Marcel Le Picard
The Invisible Ghost '41

Sam Leavitt
Cape Fear '61
The Defiant Ones '58
Hot Rod Girl '56
Carmen Jones '54
The Thief '52

Guy Leblond
The Rape of the Vampire '68

Henry Lebo
The Miracle of the Cards '00

Hoo-gon Lee
Bruce Lee: A Warrior's Journey '01

Kwok Keung Lee
Daughter of Darkness '93

Philip Lee
Route 666 '01

Pin Bang Lee
The Legend 2 '93

Robert Lefebvre
Please Not Now! '61

James (Momel) Lemmo
Vigilante [2 DC] '83

Kurt Lennig
The Tavern '00

Denis Lenoir
Uprising '01
Carrington '95

Dean Lent
Fast Sofa '01

Don Lenzer
Into the Arms of Strangers:
Stories from the Kindertransport '00

John R. Leonetti
Joe Dirt '01

Matthew F. Leonetti
Rush Hour 2 '01
Along Came a Spider '00
Angels in the Outfield '94
Breaking Away '79

J.B. Letchinger
The Smokers '00

Moshe Levin
Second to Die '02

David Lewis
Holiday in the Sun '01
Children of the Corn 5: Fields
of Terror '98
UHF '89

Gordon S. Lewis
The Royal Family '77

Dennis C. Lewiston
The Apocalypse Watch '97

Matthew Libatique
Josie and the Pussycats '01

Stephen Lighthill
Break of Dawn '88

Jong Lin
Eat Drink Man Woman '94

Karl Walter Lindenlaub
One Night at McCool's '01
The Princess Diaries '01
The Last of the Dogmen '95

Lionel Lindon
I Want to Live! '58
The Road to Utopia [Universal] '46

Robert Lindsay
Maniac [LE] '80

Richard Linklater
Waking Life '01

Philip Linzey
Cabin by the Lake / Return to
Cabin by the Lake '00
Turbulence 3: Heavy Metal '00

Greg Littlewood
Sweet Jane '98

Gerry Lively
Showdown '94
Return of the Living Dead 3 '93

Bruce Logan
Kiss Tomorrow Goodbye '00
Tron [2 CE] '82
I Never Promised You a Rose
Garden '77

Paul Lohmann
Mommie Dearest '81
Scream of the Wolf '74

Thomas Loizeaux
Desperate Living (John Waters
Collection Vol. 2) '77

James London
The Toxic Avenger, Part 3: The
Last Temptation of Toxie
[DC] '89

Dave Long
Green '01

Jose Luis Lopez-Linares
Calle 54 '01

Josef Lorinc
Love Film '70

Randall Love
Little City '97

Dudley Lovell
The Mark '61

Emmanuel Lubezki
Ali '01
Things You Can Tell Just by
Looking at Her '00

William Lubtchansky
Va Savoir '01
Secret Defense '98

William Luff
Scrooge '35

Victor Lukens
Black Like Me '64

Igor Luther
The Handmaid's Tale '90

Bernard Lutic
The Luzhin Defence '00

Russell Lyster
Styx '00

Jingle Ma
Para Para Sakura '01
City of Glass '98

Kuan Wah Ma
Tiger over Wall '80
Dragon's Claws '79

Julio Macat
The Wedding Planner '01

Joe MacDonald
MacKenna's Gold '69
The Young Lions '58
Niagara '52

Robert MacDonald
Family Viewing / Next of Kin
'87

Kenneth Macmillan
Lassie '94
Of Mice and Men '92

Glen MacPherson
Exit Wounds '01
The Amy Fisher Story '93

Glen MacWilliams
A Wing and a Prayer '44
King Solomon's Mines '37

Guy Maddin
Careful '92
Tales from the Gimli Hospital
'88

Joey Mah
Champ Against Champ [BFS]
'83
Champ vs. Champ [Xenon]
'83

Kwok Wah Mah
Fury in the Shaolin Temple
'82

Paul Maibaum
Stephen King's The Langoliers '95

Stewart Main
First Love and Other Pains /
One of Them '99

David Makin
Daydream Believers: The
Monkees Story '00

Jan Malir
Divided We Fall '00

Denis Maloney
Luckytown '00
Bikini Med School / Bikini
House Calls '98
Body Count '97
Illegal Affairs '96
Lady in Blue '96

Joseph Mangine
Sword & the Sorcerer '82

Teodoro Maniaci
Luminous Motion '00

Isidore Mankofsky
Out of Sync '95
Hard Lessons '86
The Muppet Movie '79

Nikolas Mann
Black Spring Break 2 '01

Alain Marcoen
La Promesse '96

Gunter Marczinkowski
Jacob the Liar '74

Michael D. Margulies
My Bodyguard '80

William Margulies
Clambake '67

Arthur Marks
Breeders '86
Scare Their Pants Off /
Satan's Bed '68

Brick Marquard
This Is Not a Test '62

John Marquette
A Bucket of Blood / Attack of
the Giant Leeches [Marengo] '59

Horacio Marquinez
Ten Benny '98

Oliver Marsh
Sadie Thompson '28

Michael Marszalek
2069: A Sex Odyssey '78

Jack Marta
King of the Pecos '36

Jessie Martin
Lionheart '00

Kinley Martin
It '27

Arthur Martinelli
The Devil Bat '41

Joseph Mascelli
Wild Guitar / The Choppers
'62

Steve Mason
Rollerball '02
Strictly Ballroom '92

Stelvio Massi
Fistful of Lead '70

Rudolph Mate
Sahara '43
They Got Me Covered '43
Stella Dallas '37
Dodsworth [MGM] '36

Rene Mathelin
Le Magnifique '76

James Mathers
Deep Water '99
Snapdragon '93

John Mathieson
K-PAX '01
Plunkett & Macleane '98

Masahiko Matsuyama
Soultaker: The Monster Within '02

Thomas Mauch
Stroszek '77

Shawn Maurer
Bring It On '00
Big Empty '98

Tim Maurice-Jones
Snatch [SE] '00

Robert Maxwell
Girl in Gold Boots '69

Harry J. May
J.D.'s Revenge '76

Mike Mayers
Two Family House '99

Michael Mayhew
The Item '01

Albert Maysles
Grey Gardens '75
Salesman '68

David Maysles
Grey Gardens '75

Donald McAlpine
Moulin Rouge [SE] '01
Moscow on the Hudson '84

J. Michael McClary
The Turning '92

Ted D. McCord
Proud Rebel '58

William McGann
Mark of Zorro [2] / Don Q,
Son of Zorro '20

Barney McGill
Svengali '31

Austin McKay
Monsters Crash the Pajama
Party Spook Show Spectacular '65

Austin McKinney
Kidnapped Coed '77
Axe '74
The Fear Chamber '68

Robert McLachlan
High Noon '00

Nick McLean
Short Circuit '86
The Goonies '85

Dylan Mcleod
Love Come Down '00

Geary McLeod
Cement '99**

Mr. Saturday Night [MGM] '92
Point Break '91
When a Stranger Calls '79

Curtis Petersen
Silver Wolf '98
Tiger Claws '91
Abraxas: Guardian of the Universe [BFS] '90

Barry Peterson
Zoolander '01

Victor Petrashevich
The Projectionist '71

Jacek Petrycki
Shot in the Heart '01

Wally Pfister
Memento [1] '00
Memento [2 SE] '00
The Unborn '91

Bruno Philip
Nowhere in Sight '01
With Friends Like These '90

Alex Phillips, Jr.
Luminarias '99
High Risk '81
Chac: The Rain God '74

Frank Phillips
Midnight Madness '80

Tim Philo
Evil Dead [LE] '83

Joseph Pickering
Idiot Box '97

Andre Pienaar
Restless Spirits '99

Tony Pierce-Roberts
The Golden Bowl '00
Haunted '95
The Remains of the Day '93

Margarita Pilikhina
Tchaikovsky '71

Mark Lee Ping-Bin
In the Mood for Love [SE] '00
The Vertical Ray of the Sun '00
Flowers of Shanghai '98
Goodbye South, Goodbye '96
The Puppetmaster '93

Guiseppe Pinori
Bad Cop Chronicles 2: Corrupt '84
The New Gladiators '83

Tomislav Pinter
Transylvania 6-5000 '85

Victor Pishchalnikov
Viy '67

Robert Pittack
Strange Impersonation '46

Larry Pizer
Murder in Coweta County '83
Timerider '83
Phantom of the Paradise '74
Morgan: A Suitable Case for Treatment '66

Franz Planer
The Pride and the Passion '57
Cyrano de Bergerac '50

Mark Plummer
Head over Heels '01
After Dark, My Sweet [2] '90

Mathieu Poirot-Delpech
With a Friend Like Harry '00

Gene Polito
The Bad News Bears Go to Japan '78
Five on the Black Hand Side '73

Sol Polito
Sorry, Wrong Number '48

The Long Night '47
Now, Voyager '42

Christopher Poncin
Beverly Hood '99

Stephen Posey
Friday the 13th, Part 5: A New Beginning '85

Steven Poster
Donnie Darko '01

Vinod Pradhan
Mission Kashmir '00

Maurice Prather
Carnival of Souls [DC] '62
Carnival of Souls / Dementia 13 '62

Michael Price
Attraction '00

Jack Priestley
Across 110th Street '72

Rodrigo Prieto
Original Sin '01
Amores Perros '00

Robert Primes
Money Talks '97
Rescue from Gilligan's Island '78

Frank Prinzi
Sidewalks of New York '01

Francois Protat
Johnny Mnemonic [2 SB] '95

Fyodor Provorov
Viy '67

Bryan Pryzpek
You Are Here * '00

Tak Yip Pun
The Legend of a Professional '00

Jean Rabier
The Cry of the Owl '87
Cleo from 5 to 7 '61

Claudio Racca
Primitive Love '64

Elemer Ragalyi
An American Rhapsody '01
Anne Frank '01
Catherine the Great '95

Claudio Ragona
Bad Cop Chronicles: Confessions of a Police Captain '72

Clark Ramsey
The Choppers '61

Stephen Ramsey
Nomads '86

Joel Ransom
Slap Shot 2: Breaking the Ice '02

Ousama Rawi
Blackheart '98

Andreu Rebes
Nico and Dani '00

Don Reddy
Benji [Ventura] '74

Frank Redman
Dick Tracy Meets Gruesome '47
Dick Tracy's Dilemma '47
Dick Tracy, Detective '45

Michael Reed
McKenzie Break '70

Frances Reid
A Personal Journey with Martin Scorsese through American Movies '97

Stephen Reizes
With Friends Like These '90

Laura Remacha
The Wolves of Kromer '98

Christian Remde
Legend of the Chupacabra '97

Ray Rennahan
Rage at Dawn '55

Claude Renoir
French Connection 2 '75
Spirits of the Dead [Criterion] '68
Gunman in the Streets '50

Georgy Rerberg
The Mirror '75

Marc Reshovsky
Red Rock West '93

Scott Ressler
Hollywood Chainsaw Hookers '88
Sorority Babes in the Slimeball Bowl-A-Rama '87

Brian Reynolds
Boss of Bosses '99
Gang Related '96

Edmond Richard
That Obscure Object of Desire '77
The Trial '63

Jack L. Richards
The Beast Within '82

Anthony B. Richmond
Legally Blonde '01
Someone Like You '01
The Sandlot '93

Tom Richmond
Hardball '01
A Midnight Clear '92

Bruce Ricker
Clint Eastwood: Out of the Shadows '00

Antonio Rinaldi
Planet of the Vampires '65

Lisa Rinzler
Pollock [SE] '00

Joe Ripple
Harvesters '02

Gunther Rittau
The Blue Angel '30

Neil Roach
Mama Flora's Family '98
Silent Rage '82

Herb Roberts
Red Zone Cuba '66

Jean-Francois Robin
The Ice Rink '99
Nelly et Monsieur Arnaud '95

George Robinson
Abbott and Costello Meet the Mummy '55
House of Frankenstein '44
Son of Dracula '43
Frankenstein Meets the Wolfman '42
The Mummy's Tomb '42
The Son of Monte Cristo '40
Son of Frankenstein '39
Dracula's Daughter '36

Rocky Robinson
Smile Now Cry Later '01

Claudio Rocha
Four Dogs Playing Poker '00
Skipped Parts '00

Steven R. Rocha
The Erotic Rites of Countess Dracula '90

Alexei Rodionov
Come and See '85

Ricardo Rodriguez
What Your Eyes Don't See '99

Bill Roe
Hostage High '97

Guy Roe
Godzilla, King of the Monsters [Goodtimes] '56
Behind Locked Doors '48
Railroaded '47

Nicolas Roeg
A Funny Thing Happened on the Way to the Forum '66

Owen Roizman
Taps '81
The Stepford Wives [2 SE] '75
The Exorcist [2]: The Version You've Never Seen '73
Play It Again, Sam '72
The French Connection [SE] '71

Julio Roldan
Sting of Death '65

Christopher J. Romeike
Pitch '01

George A. Romero
Night of the Living Dead [Elite ME] '68

Harry Rose
Song of Freedom / Big Fella '36

Jesse Rosen
Trans '99

Steve Rosen
Beyond Barbed Wire '97

Charles Rosher
World War I Films of the Silent Era '02
Show Boat '51

John Rosnell
Where Angels Dance '01

Ann T. Rossetti
Go Fish '94

Andrea V. Rossotto
Extreme Limits '01
Poison '01
Raptor '01
Venomous '01

Giuseppe Rotunno
Sabrina '95
Anzio '68
Spirits of the Dead [Criterion] '68
The Bible '66
Rocco and His Brothers '60

Denis Rouden
Deep in the Woods '00

Sylvain Rougerie
The Clockmaker '73

Philippe Rousselot
Planet of the Apes '01
The Tailor of Panama '00
Random Hearts '99
The Bear '89
Diva [Anchor Bay] '82

Kevin Rowley
Forgive and Forget '99

Juan Ruiz-Anchia
Focus '01
New Port South '00
Mararia '98
Liebestraum '91
Maria's Lovers '84

Brad Rushing
Adventures of Justine '00

John L. "Jack" Russell
Invasion U.S.A. '52

Richard Rutkowski
Kill by Inches '99

Viktor Ruzicka
Cobra Verde '88

Paul Ryan
Fraternity Vacation '85

Eric Saarinen
You Light Up My Life '77

F. Sacdalan
The Big Bird Cage '72
Women in Cages '71
Walls of Hell '64
Raiders of Leyte Gulf '63

Pierre Saint-Blancat
Don Giovanni '79

Scott St. John
Burnzy's Last Call '95

Yasuhi Sakakibara
Sadistic City '93

Anthony Salinas
The Doll Squad '73

A. Samvelyan
The Color of Pomegranates '69

Hector Rosario Sanchez
Erotic Survivor 2 '01

Paul Sarossy
Speaking Parts '89

Yasushi Sasakibara
Gonin '95

Edward Scaife
Khartoum '66

Roberto Schaefer
Waiting for Guffman '96

Walter Schenk
The Black Cat / The Fat Black Pussycat '65

Bruce Schermer
The Sinister Saga '00

Martin Schlesinger
Coming Out '89

Tobias Schliessler
Candyman 2: Farewell to the Flesh '94

Ronn Schmidt
The Terror Within '88

Jorge Schmidt-Reitwein
Heart of Glass '74

Eric Schmitz
South Bronx Heroes '85

George Schneiderman
A Fool There Was '14

Nancy Schreiber
Shadow Magic '00
Never 2 Big '98
A Personal Journey with Martin Scorsese through American Movies '97
The Celluloid Closet '95

Eugene Schufftan
Gunman in the Streets '50

Fred Schuler
Haunted Honeymoon '86

Howard Schwartz
Batman: The Movie '66

John Schwartzman
Pearl Harbor '01
Airheads '94
Red Surf '90

Jiri Tirl
Deceived '01

Romeo Tirone
L.I.E. '01

Eduard Tisse
Que Viva Mexico '32

Gregg Toland
December 7th / The Fleet
    That Came to Stay '43
Citizen Kane '41
The Little Foxes [MGM] '41

John Toll
Captain Corelli's Mandolin '01
Vanilla Sky '01
Almost Famous: Untitled—
    The Bootleg Cut '00

Aldo Tonti
Violent City '70
Cast a Giant Shadow '66
Barabbas '62

Bruce Torbet
Basket Case [2 SE] '82

Carlos Torlaschi
Brain Drain '98

Mario Tosi
The Stunt Man '80
MacArthur '77
Carrie '76
Swamp Country '66

Bert Tougas
The Pact '99

Leo Tover
Star Spangled Rhythm '42

Luciano Tovoli
The Closet '00
Reversal of Fortune '90
Suspiria '77
Bread and Chocolate '73

William G. Troiano
The Slime People '63

Hal Trussel
Bachelor Party '84

Hsin Yu Tsui
10 Magnificent Killers '77

Ken Tsukakoshi
The Street Fighter [BCI] '74
The Street Fighter [BFS] '74

Brian Tufano
Virtual Sexuality '99
Quadrophenia '79

Christopher Tufty
Jimmy Zip '00

John Turk
Voyeur.com '00

Andre Turpin
Because Why? '93

Muneo Ueda
Gappa the Trifibian Monster '67

Matthew Uhry
Trailer, the Movie '99
Fishing with Gandhi '98

Alejandro Ulloa
Companeros '70

Derick Underschultz
Danger beneath the Sea '02
Rough Air '02

Sergei Urusevsky
The Cranes Are Flying '57

Jost Vacano
The Hollow Man [2 SB] '00
Showgirls '95
The NeverEnding Story '84

Theo van de Sande
Wayne's World '92
The First Power '89

Willard Van der Veer
The Crawling Hand '63

Charles Van Enger
Bela Lugosi Meets a Brooklyn
    Gorilla '52

Walther Vanden Ende
No Man's Land '01
Left Luggage '98

Derek Vanlint
Spreading Ground '01

Checco Varese
Fidel '02

Carlo Varini
Le Dernier Combat '84

Josef Vavra
Querelle '83

Todd Verow
Little Shots of Happiness '97

Mark Vicente
Slow Burn '00
Uncorked '98

Robin Vidgeon
Nightbreed '90
Hellbound: Hellraiser 2 [2
    THX] '88

Sacha Vierny
The Man Who Cried '00
Stavisky '74
Belle de Jour '67

Reynaldo Villalobos
Not Another Teen Movie '01
Love and Basketball '00

Amelia Vincent
The Caveman's Valentine '01

Paul Vogel
Go for Broke! [VCI] '51

William Wages
Love Potion 9 '92

Fritz Arno Wagner
Diary of a Lost Girl '29
Nosferatu '22

Roy Wagner
Return to Horror High '87

Ric Waite
The Triangle '01
Ratz '99
Brewster's Millions [Univer-
    sal] '85
Volunteers '85

Kent Wakeford
Loser '97
Some Folks Call It a Sling
    Blade '94

David Wald
Extreme Heist '99

Alasdair Walker
The Acid House '98

Brad Walker
American Nightmare '00

John Walker
The Mirror Cracked from Side
    to Side '92
They Do It with Mirrors '91
A Caribbean Mystery / The
    Mirror Cracked from Side
    to Side '89
4:50 from Paddington '87
At Bertram's Hotel '86
Murder at the Vicarage '86
Nemesis '86

Joseph Walker
Mr. Deeds Goes to Town '36
Lady for a Day '33

Mandy Walker
Lantana '01
The Well '97

Enrique Wallace
Doctor of Doom '62

James Wallace
The Vigil '98

David M. Walsh
Taking Care of Business '90
Romantic Comedy '83
Seems Like Old Times '80
California Suite '78
Murder by Death '76
Evel Knievel '72

Mark Wareham
Dr. Jekyll & Mr. Hyde '00
13 Gantry Row '98

John F. Warren
The Daughter of Dr. Jekyll '57

Gilbert Warrenton
The Plastic Age '25

Norman Warwick
The Final Programme '73
Dr. Jekyll and Sister Hyde '71

John Waters
Female Trouble '74
Pink Flamingos '72

David Watkin
Lover's Prayer '99
Out of Africa '85
The Hotel New Hampshire '84
Cuba '79
Hanover Street '79
The Charge of the Light
    Brigade '68
Mademoiselle '66

Harry Waxman
The Wicker Man [SE] '75
The Swiss Family Robinson
    '60

Michael Wees
Seducing Maarya '99

Curtis J. Wehr
Let It Ride '89

Ben Weinstein
Wet Hot American Summer
    '01

Charles S. Welbourne
Creature from the Black
    Lagoon '54

Stephen Kent Welch
Return of the Killer Toma-
    toes! '88

James Welland
Beautiful Creatures '00

Philippe Welt
Madame Butterfly '95

Brian West
84 Charing Cross Road '86

Frederick E. West
Terror in the Haunted House
    '58

Haskell Wexler
61* '01
Sandra Bernhard: I'm Still
    Here...Damn It '99
The Secret of Roan Inish '94
Three Fugitives '89
Colors '88
The Man Who Loved Women
    '83
Coming Home '78
Medium Cool [SE] '69

Howard Wexler
Attack of the 60-Foot Center-
    fold '95
Picasso Trigger '89
Hard Ticket to Hawaii '87

Charles F. Wheeler
Silent Running [Universal] '71
C.C. & Company '70

Paul Wheeler
Cor, Blimey! '00

Lester White
The Monster That Challenged
    the World '57
Beyond Tomorrow '40

Noni White
Newsies '92

William F. Whitley
The Lone Ranger: Volume 1
    '56

Lisa Wiegard
Outta Time '01

Joseph M. Wilcots
Where the Red Fern Grows:
    Part 2 '92
Roots '77

John Wilcox
Au Pair Girls '72
Expresso Bongo '59

Harry Wild
Stage Door Canteen '43

Billy Williams
Suspect '87
The Manhattan Project '86
Survivors '83
Gandhi '82
The Exorcist [2]: The Version
    You've Never Seen '73

Gordon Willis
The Purple Rose of Cairo '85
Broadway Danny Rose '84
Zelig '83
A Midsummer Night's Sex
    Comedy '82
Comes a Horseman '78
Bad Company '72
Klute '71

Mark Willis
Tiger Claws '91

Ian Wilson
Back to the Secret Garden '01
Fright '71
And Soon the Darkness '70

Robert Wilson
Pigkeeper's Daughter / Sassy
    Sue '75

Aage Wiltrup
Reptilicus '62

Stephen Windon
The Diamond of Jeru '01
Rodgers & Hammerstein's
    South Pacific '01

Marc Wiskemann
Sweet Thing '00

**Michael G.
Wojciechowski**
Bloodfist 5: Human Target
    '93

Darius Wolski
The Mexican '01
Romeo Is Bleeding '93

Arthur Wong
Iron Monkey [Miramax] '93
The Owl vs. Bombo '84

Horace Wong
Too Many Ways to Be No. 1
    '97

Kai Fei Wong
Ballistic Kiss '98

Man-Wan Wong
Jade Claw '79

Ping Hung Wong
First Love and Other Pains /
    One of Them '99

Graeme Wood
The Dish '00

Oliver Wood
Bill & Ted's Bogus Journey
    '91

David Worth
Any Which Way You Can '80

Walter Wottitz
The Last Train '74
Un Flic '72

Alvin Wyckoff
Blood and Sand '22
Manslaughter / The Cheat
    '22

Manny Wynn
Girl with Green Eyes '64

Joseph Yacoe
Motorama '91

Steve Yaconelli
The Temp '93
The Karate Kid: Part 3 '89

Jack Yager
Coming Apart '69

Kazuo Yamazaki
The Hidden Fortress '58

Katsumi Yanagishima
Brother '01

Herman Yau
Time and Tide '00

Robert Yeoman
Dogma [2 SE] '99

Wai Ying Yip
Ultimatum '01

Hou Yong
The Road Home '01

Teiji Yoshida
Return of the Street Fighter
    '74

**Frederick A. (Freddie)
Young**
Doctor Zhivago '65
Indiscreet '58
Contraband '40

Ching Yu
Last Hurrah for Chivalry '78

Jimmy Wang Yu
Eagle vs. Silver Fox '83

Kam-chun Yu
Ninja in the Deadly Trap '83

Lu Yue
Shanghai Triad '95

Miyaki Yukio
Ninja vs. Shaolin Guards '84

Ali Reza Zaiindast
Close-Up '90

Flavio Zangrandi
The Charcoal People '01

Peter Zeitlinger
Little Dieter Needs to Fly '97
Gesualdo: Death for Five
    Voices '95

Jerzy Zielinski
Bubble Boy '01
The January Man '89

Bernard Zitzermann
Angels and Insects '95

Vilmos Zsigmond
The Body '01
Life As a House '01
Mists of Avalon '01
Intersection '93
Blow Out '81
Obsession '76
The Hippie Revolt '67
Mondo Mod / The Hippie
    Revolt '67

The Composer Index provides a listing for all composers, arrangers, lyricists, and bands that have provided an original music score for any of the DVDs reviewed in this book. The listings for the composer names follow an alphabetical sort by last name (although the names appear in a first name, last name format). The videographies are listed chronologically, from most recent film to the first. If a composer provided music for more than one film in the same year, these movies are listed alphabetically within the year.

Stripes '81
Slap Shot [2] '77
The Shootist '76
Will Penny '67
Cast a Giant Shadow '66
God's Little Acre '58
Kings Go Forth '58

Leonard Bernstein
On the Waterfront '54

Peter Bernstein
Megiddo: The Omega Code 2 '01
Silent Rage '82

Peter Best
Crocodile Dundee 2 '88
Crocodile Dundee '86

Harry Betts
Cheech and Chong's Nice Dreams '81

W. Watt Biggers
Underdog [CE] '00

Jean-Marie Billy
La Promesse '96

Susan Birkenhead
Working '82

Georges Bizet
Carmen Jones '54

Ulf Bjorlin
Vibration '68

Stanley Black
War Gods of the Deep '65
The Flesh and the Fiends '60
The Crawling Eye '58

Damon Blackman
Exit Wounds '01

Howard Blake
S.O.S. Titanic '79

Terence Blanchard
The Caveman's Valentine '01
Glitter '01
Original Sin '01
Love and Basketball '00
Til There Was You '96
Trial by Jury '94

George Blondheim
Avalanche Alley '01

Alexander Blonksteiner
Cannibal Apocalypse '80

Michael Bloomfield
Medium Cool [SE] '69

Frankie Blue
Dracula: The Dark Prince '01
Return to Cabin by the Lake '01
Cabin by the Lake / Return to Cabin by the Lake '00

Chris Boardman
The Dress Code '99

Michael Boddicker
The Adventures of Buckaroo Banzai Across the Eighth Dimension [SE] '84

Ed Bogas
Fritz the Cat '72

Bill Boll
Some Folks Call It a Sling Blade '94

Claude Bolling
California Suite '78
Le Magnifique '76

Jay Bolton
Mom's Outta Sight '01

Wong Bong
Brother of Darkness '94
Daughter of Darkness '93

Zoran Boris
The Learning Curve '01

Simon Boswell
Born Romantic '00
Jack and Sarah '95

Perry Botkin
Goin' South '78

Pieter Bourke
Ali '01

Richard Bowers
Facing the Enemy '00

Euel Box
Benji [Ventura] '74

Jean Boyer
Bob le Flambeur '55

Don Braden
Lena's Dreams '97

Billy Bragg
Walking and Talking '96

Shony Alex Braun
'68 '87

Pol Brennan
When the Sky Falls '99

Peter Brewis
The Tall Guy '89
Morons from Outer Space '85

Ales Brezina
Divided We Fall '00

Pete Briquette
Rat '00

Timothy Brock
Diary of a Lost Girl '29
Faust '26
The Show Off / The Plastic Age '26

Bruce Brody
Diner '82

Garth Brooks
Call Me Claus '01

Joseph Brooks
You Light Up My Life '77

Bruce Broughton
House Arrest '96
Baby's Day Out '94
Tombstone [2] '93
Stay Tuned '92
The Blue and the Gray '82

Andre Brummer
Monster from the Ocean Floor '54

George Bruns
Walt Disney Treasures: Davy Crockett '01 Transeau)

BT (Brian Transeau)
Driven '01
The Fast and the Furious '01

Walter Bullock
The Little Princess [Marengo] '39

Geoffrey Burgon
When Trumpets Fade '98
The Dogs of War '81

Johnny Burke
The Road to Utopia [Universal] '46

Pip Burley
The Darling Buds of May '91

Ralph Burns
The Muppets Take Manhattan '84
Lenny '74

Jeff Burton
Night Divides the Day '01

Carter Burwell
A Knight's Tale '01
The Man Who Wasn't There '01
The Locusts '97
The Celluloid Closet '95
Airheads '94
Wayne's World 2 '93
Buffy the Vampire Slayer '92
Blood Simple '85

Artie Butler
Harrad Experiment '73

David Buttolph
Lone Ranger '56
Long John Silver '54
Guadalcanal Diary '43
My Favorite Blonde '42

Donald Byrd
Cornbread, Earl & Me '75

Emil Cadkin
Mission to Death '66

John Cafferty
Eddie and the Cruisers '83

Doug Caldwell
Cement '99

John Cale
Caged Heat '74

Darrell Calker
Terror in the Haunted House '58

John Cameron
A Touch of Class '73
The Ruling Class '72

David (Richard) Campbell
All the Right Moves '83

James Campbell
Please Not Now! '61

Xavier Capellas
Faust: Love of the Damned '00

Robert Carli
Silver Wolf '99

Walter (Wendy) Carlos
Tron [2 CE] '82
The Shining [2 SE] '80

Hoagy Carmichael
College Swing '38

Craig Carnelia
Working '82

Stefan Carow
Coming Out '89

John Carpenter
John Carpenter's Ghosts of Mars '01
Halloween 4: The Return of Michael Myers [MGM LE] '88
Halloween 2: The Nightmare Isn't Over! [Universal] '81
Halloween [Extended Edition] '78

Nicholas Carras
10 Violent Women '79
The Doll Squad '73
Girl in Gold Boots '69

Tristram Cary
Blood from the Mummy's Tomb '71

Jean-Bruno Castelain
Rabid Grannies '89

Pierre-Damien Castelain
Rabid Grannies '89

Teddy Castellucci
The Animal '01
Good Advice '01

Mario Castelnuovo-Tedesco
And Then There Were None [Image] '45

William Allen Castleman
The Big Bird Cage '72

Matthieu Chabrol
The Cry of the Owl '87

Yves Chamberland
Lost and Delirious '01

Frankie Chan
The Legendary Strike '78

Philip Chan
Riki-Oh: The Story of Ricky '89

Ricky Chan
Champ Against Champ [BFS] '83
Champ vs. Champ [Xenon] '83
Eagle vs. Silver Fox '83
Fury in the Shaolin Temple '82

Gary Chang
Stephen King's Rose Red '02

John Charles
The Last Tattoo '94
Utu '83

Pierre Charvet
Druids '01

Peter Chase
Happenstance '00

Jay Chattaway
Invasion U.S.A. '85
Vigilante [2 DC] '83
Maniac [LE] '80

Fang Chi Chen
To Kill with Intrigue '77

Chen Ming-Chang
The Puppetmaster '93

Shung Chi Chen
Jade Claw '79

Tsun Chi Chen
Dragon's Claws '79

Paul Chihara
Survivors '01
The Bad News Bears Go to Japan '78
I Never Promised You a Rose Garden '77

Seung Woo Cho
Reptilian '00

Young-ook Cho
Tell Me Something '99

Edmund Choi
The Dish '00

Fok Leung Chou
Revenge of the Patriots '76

Fu-liang Chow
Drunken Master '78
Snake in the Eagle's Shadow '78

Kam Cheung Chow
Trust Me U Die '99

Sherman Chow
Ninja in the U.S.A. '88

Frank Churchill
Dumbo '41
Snow White and the Seven Dwarfs [PE] '37

Alessandro Cicognini
Summertime '55

John Cipollinam
'68 '87

Stelvio Cipriano
Voices from Beyond '90

Chuck Cirino
Big Bad Mama 2 '87
Deathstalker 2: Duel of the Titans '87

Stanley Clarke
The Five Heartbeats '91

Alf Clausen
The Simpsons: The Complete First Season '89

Les Claypool
Adventures of the Kung Fu Rascals '92

Climax Gold Twins
Session 9 '01

George S. Clinton
3000 Miles to Graceland '01

Elia Cmiral
Bones '01

Robert Cobert
Scream of the Wolf '74
Dark Shadows: DVD Collection 1 '67

John Coda
Sworn to Justice '97

Leonard Cohen
Fata Morgana '92

Serge Colbert
The Body '01
Along for the Ride '00

Lisa Coleman
Hav Plenty '97

Michel Colombier
Major League 2 '94
Ruthless People '86
Un Flic '72

Alberto Colombo
Go for Broke! [VCI] '51

Eric Colvin
Crossfire Trail '01

Joseph Conlan
Hot Pursuit '87

Rick Conrad
The Nest '88
The Terror Within '88

Bill Conti
Tortilla Soup '01
American Tragedy '00
The Scout '94
Rookie of the Year '93
The Bear '89
The Karate Kid: Part 3 '89
Masters of the Universe '87
The Karate Kid: Part 2 '86
Nomads '86
Bad Boys [Anchor Bay] '83
The Garden of the Finzi-Continis '71

Michael Convertino
Bull Durham [MGM SE] '88

Ry Cooder
Brewster's Millions [Universal] '85

Ray Cook
Careful, He Might Hear You '84

Stewart Copeland
On the Line '01
Skipped Parts '00
Pecker (John Waters Collection Vol. 1) '98
Silent Fall '94
Hidden Agenda '90
Men at Work '90
Taking Care of Business '90
The First Power '89
See No Evil, Hear No Evil '89

Pierre Foldes
L.I.E. '01

Robert Folk
Major League 3: Back to the Minors '98
A Troll in Central Park '94
NeverEnding Story 2: The Next Chapter '91
Bachelor Party '84

Dan Foly
Please Don't Eat My Mother '72

Louis Forbes
The Bat [Goodtimes] '59
Slightly Scarlet '56
Pearl of the South Pacific '55

David Foster
Stealing Home '88

Charles Fox
Short Circuit 2 '88
National Lampoon's European Vacation '85

Neal Fox
Return of the Killer Tomatoes! '88

David Michael Frank
The Last Warrior '99
Hero and the Terror '88

Ian Fraser
Zorro, the Gay Blade '81

Terry Frewer
Out of Time '00

Colin Frichter
Sell Out '76

Gerald Fried
Rescue from Gilligan's Island '78
Roots '77
Too Late the Hero '70
I Bury the Living '58

Hugo Friedhofer
Homicidal '61
The Young Lions '58
Three Came Home '50
A Wing and a Prayer '44

Irving Friedman
Behind Locked Doors '48

John (Gianni) Frizzell
Josie and the Pussycats '01
13 Ghosts '01
Possessed '00
White River '99

Dominic Frontiere
The Aviator '85
The Stunt Man '80
Brannigan '75

Giovanni Fusco
Il Grido '57

Michael Galasso
In the Mood for Love [SE] '00

Eduardo Gamboa
Bloody Proof '99

Douglas Gamley
And Now the Screaming Starts [SE] '73

Peter Gannan
American Nightmare '00

Bob Geldof
Rat '00

Lynne Geller
1999 '98

Francesc Gener
Arachnid '01

Yvon Geraud
The Rape of the Vampire '68

Alexander Gerens
The Fast and the Furious '54

Lisa Gerrard
Ali '01

Joseph Gershenson
Abbott and Costello Meet the Mummy '55
All That Heaven Allows '55

Irving Gertz
It Came from Outer Space '53

Dino Giancola
Seducing Maarya '99

Michael Gibbs
Breaking In '89

Richard Gibbs
Barbarians at the Gate '93
Say Anything [SE] '89
Sweet Hearts Dance '88

David Gibson
Schlock '73

Woody Giessmann
Where Angels Dance '01

Gilberto Gil
Me You Them '00

Herschel Burke Gilbert
The Thief '52

Glover Gill
Waking Life '01

Scott Gilman
Outta Time '01

Lawrence Gingold
The Smokers '00

Marcello Giombini
Knives of the Avenger '65

Lim Giong
Goodbye South, Goodbye '96

Paul Giovanni
The Wicker Man [SE] '75

Michael Paul Girard
Lady in Blue '96

Philip Glass
Candyman 2: Farewell to the Flesh '94
Mishima: A Life in Four Chapters '85

Albert Glasser
Tormented '60
Invasion U.S.A. '52

Derek Gleason
The White Pony '99

The Goblins
Sleepless '01
Suspiria '77

Daniel Gold
R2PC: Road to Park City '99

Ernest Gold
It's a Mad, Mad, Mad, Mad World '63
Inherit the Wind '60
On the Beach '59

Murray Gold
Beautiful Creatures '00

Barry Goldberg
Return of the Living Dead 3 '93

Billy Goldenberg
18 Again! '88
Play It Again, Sam '72

Simon Goldenberg
Wild Orchid '90

Elliot Goldenthal
Final Fantasy: The Spirits Within '01

Jerry Goldsmith
The Last Castle '01
Along Came a Spider '00
The Hollow Man [2 SB] '00
Air Force One [2 SB] '97
Basic Instinct [2 SE] '92
Not without My Daughter '90
The Russia House '90
Total Recall [2 SLE] '90
Legend [UE] '86
Link '86
Psycho 2 '83
Under Fire '83
The Secret of NIMH '82
Star Trek: The Motion Picture [DE] '80
MacArthur '77
Breakout '75
QB VII '74
Patton [2] '70
Seconds '66
Von Ryan's Express '65

Joel Goldsmith
Shiloh 2: Shiloh Season '99
Shiloh '97

William Goldstein
An Eye for an Eye '81
Bingo Long Traveling All-Stars & Motor Kings '76

Osvaldo Golijov
The Man Who Cried '00

Miles Goodman
Til There Was You '96
The Indian in the Cupboard '95
Blankman '94
He Said, She Said '91
Dirty Rotten Scoundrels [MGM] '88

Ronald Goodwin
Force 10 from Navarone '78

Christopher Gordon
When Good Ghouls Go Bad '01

Alison Gordy
Fiona '98

Michael Gore
The Butcher's Wife '91

Louis F. Gottschalk
Broken Blossoms [Kino] '19

John Graham
Bloodfist 6: Ground Zero '94

Ron Grainer
To Sir, with Love '67

Mickey Grant
Working '82

Stephane Grappelli
Going Places '74

Al Greene
The Death Curse of Tartu / Sting of Death '66

Harry Gregson-Williams
Shrek [SE] '01
Spy Game '01
The Replacement Killers [2 SE] '98
Deceiver '97

Rupert Gregson-Williams
Virtual Sexuality '99

Jeremy C. Grody
Double Deception '01

Andrew Gross
Dead Simple '01
The Extreme Adventures of Super Dave '98
Bio-Dome '96

Charles Gross
Turner and Hooch '89
King Lear '74
Valdez Is Coming '71

Louis Gruenberg
All the King's Men '49

Dave Grusin
Random Hearts '99
The Goonies '85
Falling in Love '84
My Bodyguard '80
Murder by Death '76

Jay Gruska
Mo' Money '92

Zhang Guangtain
Shanghai Triad '95

Pedro Guerra
Mararia '98

Christopher Guest
Waiting for Guffman '96

Gib Guilbeau
Boxcar Bertha '72

Steve Gurevitch
Jill the Ripper '00

Steve Gutheinz
Trois '00

Sven Gyldmark
Reptilicus '62

Scott Hackwith
Four Dogs Playing Poker '00

Manos Hadjidakis
Topkapi '64

Chris Hagian
Mr. Vincent '97

Francis Haines
Split Second '92

Chris Hajian
Ten Benny '98

Joe Hajos
Gunman in the Streets '50

Jim Halfpenny
Dead Silence '98
Skyscraper '95
To the Limit '95

Arch Hall, Jr.
Eegah! '62

Dick Halligan
The Owl and the Pussycat '70

Marvin Hamlisch
Frankie and Johnny '91
The January Man '89
Three Men and a Baby '87
Romantic Comedy '83
Ordinary People '80
Seems Like Old Times '80

Hans Hammerschmid
2069: A Sex Odyssey '78

Wolfgang Hammerschmid
Mickey Blue Eyes '99

Oscar Hammerstein
Cinderella '64
Carmen Jones '54
Show Boat '51

Herbie Hancock
Harlem Nights '89
Colors '88
Hard Lessons '86
Jo Jo Dancer, Your Life Is Calling '86

Denis M. Hannigan
Recess: School's Out '01

Leigh Harline
Monkey Business '52
The Road to Utopia [Universal] '45
They Got Me Covered '43
Snow White and the Seven Dwarfs [PE] '37

Udi Harpaz
Hollywood Shuffle '87

Don Harper
Beyond Suspicion '00

Anthony Harris
Star Slammer '87

Ken Harrison
The Miracle of the Cards '00

Deborah Harry
Polyester (John Waters Collection Vol. 2) '81

Lorenz Hart
Hallelujah, I'm a Bum '33

Mickey Hart
Gang Related '96

Richard Hartley
Stealing Beauty '96

Mick Harvey
Chopper '01

Paul Haslinger
crazy/beautiful '01

Wayne Hawkins
Bruce Lee: A Warrior's Journey '01

John Hawksworth
Zeta One '69

Roy Hay
Styx '00

Fumio Hayasaka
Rashomon '51

Richard Hazard
Bela Lugosi Meets a Brooklyn Gorilla '52

Reinhold Heil
The Princess and the Warrior '00

Harold Hensley
Sassy Sue '72

Larry Herbstritt
Tequila Body Shots '99

Bernard Herrmann
Cape Fear '91
Obsession '76
Marnie '64
Cape Fear '61
The Three Worlds of Gulliver '59
Citizen Kane '41

Sue Hewitt
Ultraviolet '98

Werner R. Heymann
Faust '26

Richard Hieronymous
Angels Hard As They Come '71

David Hirshfelder
Strictly Ballroom '92

Joe Hisaishi
Brother '01

Brian Hodgson
The Legend of Hell House '73

Michael Hoenig
The Contaminated Man '01
The Amy Fisher Story '93

Gabriel Holden
Dead or Alive '02

Lee Holdridge
Mists of Avalon '01
Texas '94
Transylvania 6-5000 '85
Beastmaster '82

Deborah Holland
Circuitry Man '90

Company Man '01
Life without Dick '01
American Pie [2 UE] '99

Karen Lawrence
Up against Amanda '01

Maury Laws
The Return of the King '80
The Hobbit '78

Ronnie Laws
Love Songs '99

Jean Ledrut
The Trial '63

Gerald Lee
Satan's Cheerleaders '77

Michel Legrand
Never Say Never Again '83
Atlantic City '81
The Mountain Men '80
Summer of '42 '71
Wuthering Heights '70
The Young Girls of Rochefort '68
Eva '62
Cleo from 5 to 7 '61

Jed Leiber
Love Potion 9 '92

Melvyn Lenard
The Daughter of Dr. Jekyll '57

Christopher Lennertz
Undercurrent '99
Art House '98

Patrick Leonard
Nothing in Common '86

Raymond Leppard
Lord of the Flies '63

Cory Lerios
Beyond the Law '92

Alan Jay Lerner
Paint Your Wagon '69

Maurice Leroux
Le Petit Soldat '60

Sylvester Levay
Mannequin '87
Invaders from Mars [MGM] '86

Alvin Levin
Railroaded '47

Erma E. Levin
The Projectionist '71

Geoff Levin
Extreme Honor '01
Jimmy Zip '00

Michael Lewis
Theatre of Blood '73
The Man Who Haunted Himself '70

Jason Libs
Olive Juice '01

Daniel Licht
Soul Survivors '01
Cabin by the Lake / Return to Cabin by the Lake '00

Zhang Lida
Shadow Magic '00

Hal Lindes
Forgive and Forget '99

Michael Linn
Snapdragon '93
American Ninja '85

Michael Linnen
George Washington '00

Zdenek Liska
The Shop on Main Street '65

Michael Lloyd
Rudolph the Red-Nosed Reindeer: The Movie '98 Webber

Andrew Lloyd Webber
Cats [UE Universal] '98

Lincoln Lo
Cops on a Mission '01
The Demon's Baby '98
Your Place or Mine! '98

Lowell Lo
The Legend 2 '93
Prison on Fire 2 '91

Joseph LoDuca
Evil Dead [LE] '83

Frank Loesser
How to Succeed in Business without Really Trying '67
College Swing '38

Frederick Loewe
Paint Your Wagon '69

Doug Lofstrom
Carnivore '01

William Loose
Johnny Firecloud / Bummer '75
The Big Bird Cage '72
Rebel Rousers '69
Mission to Death '66

Los Lobos
Desperado [2 SB] '95

Mundell Lowe
Satan in High Heels '61

Guido Luciani
Grass '00

Janet Lumb
Seducing Maarya '99

John Lunn
Lorna Doone '01

John Lurie
Stranger than Paradise '84

Geoff MacCormack
Wild Orchid '90

Mader
Eat Drink Man Woman '94

Matty Malneck
Witness for the Prosecution '57

William V. Malpede
Fast Sofa '01

Josh Mancell
Bongwater '98

Mark Mancina
Domestic Disturbance '01
Training Day '01
Beyond Suspicion '00

Henry Mancini
Blind Date '87
The Man Who Loved Women '83
Mommie Dearest '81
The Party '68
Hatari! '62
Creature from the Black Lagoon '54
It Came from Outer Space '53

Johnny Mandel
M*A*S*H [FS] '70
I Want to Live! '58

Harry Manfredini
Friday the 13th, Part 6: Jason Lives '86
House '86

Barry Manilow
Thumbelina [20th Century Fox] '94

Hummie Mann
Jailbreakers '94

David Mansfield
Desperate Hours '90
The Sicilian '87

Keith Mansfield
Fist of Fear, Touch of Death '80

Chris Many
Hollywood Screen Tests: Take 1 '00
Hollywood Screen Tests: Take 2 '00

Jim Manzie
Blood Surf '00

Charles Marawood
The Irishman '78

Karel Mares
The Firemen's Ball '68

Dario Marianelli
Southpaw '00

Mariano Marin
Open Your Eyes '97

Anthony Marinelli
15 Minutes '01
Just One Night '00
Slow Burn '00

Gino Marinuzzi, Jr.
Planet of the Vampires '65

Jeff Marsh
Wind River '98

Jack Marshall
The Giant Gila Monster '59

Phil Marshall
Full Moon in Blue Water '88

Philip Martell
Dr. Jekyll and Sister Hyde '71

Barrett Martin
Lush '01

Cliff Martinez
Traffic [Criterion] '00

Rick Marvin
The Lost Battalion '01
3 Ninjas Kick Back '94

Bill Marx
Count Yorga, Vampire '70

Hirao Masaaki
Sure Death: Revenge '87

John Massari
Killer Klowns from Outer Space '88

Michael Masser
The Greatest '77

Diego Masson
Spirits of the Dead [Criterion] '68

Greg Mathieson
American Flyers '85

Muir Mathieson
Circus of Horrors '60

Sasha Matson
Red Surf '90

Yuji Matsuyama
Mobile Suit Gundam: The Battle Begins! Vol. 1 '79

Stuart Matthewman
Jackpot '01

Marie Maxwell
Heroes of Iwo Jima '01

Thad Maxwell
Boxcar Bertha '72

Brian May
Death Before Dishonor '87
Mad Max [MGM SE] '80

Toshiro Mayuzumi
The Bible '66

Jim McBride
Great Balls of Fire '89

Dennis McCarthy
In His Life: The John Lennon Story '00
Letters from a Killer '98
Breast Men '97

John McCarthy
Turbulence 3: Heavy Metal '00

John McCulloch
Careful '92

Garry McDonald
Dr. Jekyll & Mr. Hyde '00

Francis Anthony McGlynn
The Erotic Mirror '01

David McHugh
Three Fugitives '89
Moscow on the Hudson '84

Rich McHugh
Boa '02

Scotty McKay
The Black Cat / The Fat Black Pussycat '65

Michael McKean
Waiting for Guffman '96

Joel McNeely
Lover's Prayer '99

Greig McRitchie
This Is Not a Test '62

Abigail Mead
Full Metal Jacket [2 SE] '87

Peter Melnick
Mermaid '00
Arctic Blue '93

Wendy Melvoin
Hav Plenty '97

Alan Menken
The Hunchback of Notre Dame '96
Newsies '92

Johnny Mercer
The Harvey Girls '46

Metallica
Paradise Lost 2: Revelations '99

Micki Meuser
Deeply '99

Robert Jan Meyer
Advertising Rules! '01

Lenny Meyers
Bar Girls '95

Michel Michelet
The Indian Tomb '59
Tiger of Eschnapur '59
Outpost in Morocco '49
Lured '47

Jean-Michael Michenaud
Big Empty '98

Don Mike
Vampire Obsession '02

Mladen Milicevic
Up against Amanda '01

Cynthia Millar
Storm in Summer '00
Three Wishes '95

Marcus Miller
The Trumpet of the Swan '01
Two Can Play That Game '01

Randy Miller
Hitched '01

Don Miller-Robinson
Risk '00

Paul Misraki
Les Bonnes Femmes '60
And God Created Woman '57
Plucking the Daisy '56

Hiroshi Miyagawa
Star Blazers: The Comet Empire: Part 1 '80

Fonce Mizell
Hell up in Harlem '73

Yuichi Mizusawa
Hermes—Winds of Love '97

Cyril Mockridge
River of No Return '54

Charlie Mole
High Heels and Low Lifes '01

Fred Mollin
Daydream Believers: The Monkees Story '00

Osvaldo Montes
A Shadow You Soon Will Be '94

Guy Moon
Sorority Babes in the Slimeball Bowl-A-Rama '87

Gene Moore
Carnival of Souls [DC] '62
Carnival of Souls / Dementia 13 '62

Basil Moore-Asfouri
The Wolves of Kromer '98

Jacques Morali
Can't Stop the Music '80

Benny More
Life Is to Whistle '98

Larry Morey
Snow White and the Seven Dwarfs [PE] '37

Christopher Morford
Drive By '01

Giorgio Moroder
Let It Ride '89
The NeverEnding Story '84

Jerome Moross
Proud Rebel '58

Steven Morrell
Progeny '98

Ennio Morricone
The Legend of 1900 '98
Casualties of War '89
Bad Cop Chronicles 2: Corrupt '84
La Cage aux Folles 2 '81
Le Professionnel '81
La Cage aux Folles '78
The Cat o' Nine Tails '71
Companeros '70
Violent City '70

John Morris
Scarlett '94
Spaceballs '87
The Elephant Man '80

Boris Morros
The Big Broadcast of 1938 '38
College Swing '38

Mark Mothersbaugh
Sugar & Spice '01
Best Men '98
Bongwater '98

Peter Manning Robinson
Sometimes They Come Back...Again '96

Rockwilder
How High '01

Al Rodger
Mr. Rice's Secret '00

Mary Rodgers
Working '82

Nile Rodgers
Beverly Hills Cop 3 '94

Richard Rodgers
Rodgers & Hammerstein's South Pacific '01
Cinderella '64
Hallelujah, I'm a Bum '33

Robert Rodriguez
Spy Kids '01

Heinz Roemheld
The Monster That Challenged the World '57
On Our Merry Way '48

Shorty Rogers
The Specialist '75

Tim Rogers
Idiot Box '97

Philippe Rombi
Under the Sand '00

Jeff Rona
Exit Wounds '01
Tom Clancy's Netforce '98

David Rose
Operation Petticoat '59
The Princess and the Pirate '44

David Rosenblad
American Nightmare '00

Leonard Rosenman
Cross Creek '83

Laurence Rosenthal
Catherine the Great '95
Who'll Stop the Rain? '78
Requiem for a Heavyweight '62

William Ross
Cops and Robbersons '94
Thumbelina [20th Century Fox] '94
Look Who's Talking Now '93

Nino Rota
Spirits of the Dead [Criterion] '68
Juliet of the Spirits [Criterion] '65
8 1/2 '63
Purple Noon '60
Rocco and His Brothers '60
Submarine Attack '54

Bruce Rowland
Andre '94

Miklos Rozsa
The Atomic Cafe [SE] '82
Blood on the Sun [Image] '45
Sahara '43
The Jungle Book '42

Michel Rubini
Manhunter [LE] '86

Donald Rubinstein
Bruiser '00

Payton Rule
Point of View '00

Patrice Rushen
Hollywood Shuffle '87

Gus Russo
Basket Case [2 SE] '82

Carlo Rustichelli
White Fang to the Rescue '74

Terje Rypdal
Zero Degrees Kelvin '95

Joseph Saba
Two Ninas '00

Riqui Sabates
Nico and Dani '00

Craig Safan
Good Guys Wear Black '78
The Bad News Bears in Breaking Training '77
The Great Texas Dynamite Chase '76

Shiroh Sagisu
Nadia: Secret of Blue Water, Vol. 1: The Adventure Begins '89

Jon St. James
Cave Girl '85

Ichiro Saito
The Tale of Zatoichi Continues '62

Ryuichi Sakamoto
Taboo '99
The Handmaid's Tale '90

Sachi Sakamoto
Reborn from Hell: Jubei's Revenge '96
Reborn from Hell: Samurai Armageddon '96

Yuki Sakamoto
Tokyo Mafia: Wrath of the Yakuza '95
Tokyo Mafia: Yakuza Wars '95

Hans J. Salter
Abbott and Costello Meet the Mummy '55
Creature from the Black Lagoon '54
Borderline '50
The Mummy's Ghost '44
The Mummy's Hand '40

Bennett Salvay
Jeepers Creepers '01

Roman Sang
Invincible Obsessed Fighter '82

Gustavo Santaolalla
Amores Perros '00

Philippe Sarde
Nelly et Monsieur Arnaud '95
Lord of the Flies '90
The Last Train '74
The Clockmaker '73

Masaru Sato
The Hidden Fortress '58

Camile Sauvage
Orloff and the Invisible Man '70

Jordi Savall
Secret Defense '98

Paul Sawtell
The Last Man on Earth '64
Jack the Giant Killer '62
It! The Terror from Beyond Space '58
Rage at Dawn '55
Raw Deal '48
Dick Tracy Meets Gruesome '47
Dick Tracy's Dilemma '47
T-Men '47

Walter Scharf
Funny Girl '68
Pocketful of Miracles '61

Johnny Lee Schell
The Forsaken '01

Prof. Peter Schickele
Silent Running [Universal] '71

Poul Schierbeck
Day of Wrath '43

Lalo Schifrin
Rush Hour 2 '01
Money Talks '97
The Dead Pool '88
Tank '83
Caveman '81
Magnum Force '73
Dirty Harry [2] '71
The Brotherhood '68

Gundula Schmitz
Schramm '93

Todd Schroeder
Sexual Chemistry '99

Gerard Schumann
The Vikings '58

Robert Schumann
A Tale of Springtime '89

Stephen Schwartz
The Hunchback of Notre Dame '96
Working '82
The Magic Show '81

Louis Sclavis
Kadosh '99

Bobby Scott
Joe '70

Daniel Scott
Random Encounter '98

John Scott
The People That Time Forgot '77

Lee Scott
Me, Myself, and Irene '00

Tom Scott
Soul Man '86
Firehouse '72

Ben Scribner
Green '01

Michelle Scullion
Bad Taste [LE] '88

Misha Segal
The Last Dragon '85

Bernardo Segall
Moon of the Wolf '72
The Great St. Louis Bank Robbery '59

Eric Serra
Rollerball '02
The Fifth Element [2 SB] '97
Le Dernier Combat '84

Luis Maria Serra
Brain Drain '98

Patrick Seymour
Me & Isaac Newton '99

Marc Shaiman
One Night at McCool's '01
61* '01
Jackie's Back '99
South Park: Bigger, Longer and Uncut '99
Ghosts of Mississippi '96
Speechless '94
Mr. Saturday Night [MGM] '92
Sister Act '92

Ray Shanklin
Fritz the Cat '72

Mark Shannon
Spreading Ground '01

Theodore Shapiro
Heist '01
Not Another Teen Movie '01
Wet Hot American Summer '01
State and Main '00

Jamshield Sharifi
Down to Earth '01

Jennifer Sharpe
Go Fish '94

Winston Sharples
Underdog [CE] '00

George Newman Shaw
Kidnapped Coed '77

Harry Shearer
Waiting for Guffman '96

Ed Shearmur
K-PAX '01
Things You Can Tell Just by Looking at Her '00

Bert Shefter
The Last Man on Earth '64
Jack the Giant Killer '62
It! The Terror from Beyond Space '58

Michael Shields
Ginger Snaps '00

Umebayashi Shigeru
In the Mood for Love [SE] '00

Yasuaki Shimizu
X '96

David Shire
Short Circuit '86
The World according to Garp '82

Howard Shore
The Score '01
Dogma [2 SE] '99
That Thing You Do! '96
The Silence of the Lambs [MGM SE] '91
She-Devil '89
Places in the Heart '84
Scanners '81

Lawrence Shragge
The Triangle '01

Leo Shuken
Sullivan's Travels '41

Mort Shuman
A Real Young Girl '75

Siegfried
For Sale '98

Louis Silvers
Dimples '36

Alan Silvestri
The Mexican '01
The Mummy Returns '01
Serendipity '01
Reindeer Games [Miramax DC] '00
Stuart Little [2 DE] '99
Forrest Gump [SCE] '94
Ferngully '92
Soapdish '91
Las Vegas Lady '76

Claudio Simonetti
Opera '88
Cut and Run '85

Mike Simpson
Freddy Got Fingered '01
Saving Silverman '01

Helen Siwak
The Vigil '98

Marlin Skiles
Flight to Mars '52

Frank Skinner
All That Heaven Allows '55

Rod Slane
Revenge '86
Blood Cult '85

Helen Slater
Nowhere in Sight '01

Jiri Slitr
Daisies '96

Michael Small
1969 '89
Comes a Horseman '78
The Stepford Wives [2 SE] '75
Klute '71

Bruce Smeaton
Plenty [Anchor Bay] '85

Arthur Smith
The Wolfman '82

Doug Smith
Diary of a Sex Addict '01

Michael R. Smith
The Unborn '91

Paul J. Smith
The Parent Trap '61
Pollyanna '60
Snow White and the Seven Dwarfs [PE] '37

Mark Snow
High Risk '81
The Boy in the Plastic Bubble [2] '76

Martial Solal
Breathless '59

Marc Oliver Sommer
La Sentinelle '92

Stephen Sondheim
Putting It Together: Stephen Sondheim—A Musical Review '01
Dick Tracy '90
Into the Woods '90
Stavisky '74

Ondrej Soukup
Dark Blue World '01

Tim Souster
Traffik '90

Hal Southern
Sassy Sue '72

Mischa Spoliansky
King Solomon's Mines '37

Robert Sprayberry
Where the Red Fern Grows: Part 2 '92

Lenny Stack
C.C. & Company '70

Paul Stasi
Fishing with Gandhi '98

David Steele
Tin Men '87

Mulius Steffaro
Business Is Business '71

Herman Stein
It Came from Outer Space '53

Ronald Stein
Dementia 13 [Roan] '63
The Phantom from 10,000 Leagues '56

Max Steiner
Key Largo '48
Now, Voyager '42
Little Women '33

Theodore Stern
The Worm Eaters '77

Leith Stevens
When Worlds Collide '51

David A. Stewart
Showgirls '95

Paul Stewart
Phat Beach '96

Gary Stockdale
Picasso Trigger '89
Hard Ticket to Hawaii '87

Richard Stone
Victim of Love '91

David Storrs
Invaders from Mars [MGM] '86

David Stout
Chicks, Man '99

Jule Styne
Funny Girl '68

Jerry Styner
Mitchell '75

Andy Summers
Motorama '91

Mark Suozzo
Sound and Fury '00
Barcelona '94

Ron Sures
Restless Spirits '99

Bruce Sussman
Thumbelina [20th Century Fox] '94

Jiri Sust
Daisies '96
Closely Watched Trains '66

Daisuke Suzuki
Tokyo Mafia: Battle for Shinjuku '96

Jorge Tafur
800 Leagues down the Amazon '93

Taj Mahal
Zebrahead '92

Fujio Takano
Kizuna '94

Frederic Talgorn
The Temp '93

Zdenko Tamassy
Colonel Redl '84
Mephisto '81

Shin'ichi Tanaka
Gadget Trips—Mindscapes '95

Danis Tanovic
No Man's Land '01

Graham Tardiff
Alien Visitor '95

James Taylor
Working '82

Stephen James Taylor
Boycott '02
Finding Buck McHenry '00
The Glass Shield '95

Bob Telson
Bagdad Cafe '88

Manuel Tena
Why Do They Call It Love When They Mean Sex? '92

Dennis Michael Tenney
Tick Tock '00

Richard Termini
States of Control '98

Maurice Thiriet
Children of Paradise '44

Christopher Thomas
There's Nothing out There '90

John Thomas
Heroes of Iwo Jima '01

Marc Anthony Thompson
Urbania '00

Richard Thompson
Sweet Talker '91

Ken Thorne
The Apocalypse Watch '97
The Evil That Men Do '84
Head '68
A Funny Thing Happened on the Way to the Forum '66

Mike Thron
Memoirs of a Survivor '81

Ton That Tiet
The Vertical Ray of the Sun '00
The Scent of Green Papaya '93

Dimitri Tiomkin
Town without Pity '61
Rio Bravo '59
The Young Land '59
Cyrano de Bergerac '50
The Long Night '47

George Aliceson Tipton
Hit Lady '74
Phantom of the Paradise '74

Tomandandy
The Mothman Prophecies '02

Ed Tomney
Safe '95

Loren Toolajian
The Tavern '00

Colin Towns
Maybe Baby '99
Ivanhoe '97
Rawhead Rex '87

Pete Townshend
Quadrophenia '79

Stephen Trask
Hedwig and the Angry Inch '00

Ernest Troost
The Runaway '00

Armando Trovajoli
The Libertine '69

Martin Trum
Paranoia '98

Tim Truman
Retroactive '97

Michael Tscanz
Olive Juice '01

Tetsuo Tsukahara
Giants and Toys '58

Toshiaki Tsushima
The Street Fighter [BCI] '74
The Street Fighter [BFS] '74

Jonathan Tunick
Alice in Wonderland '83

Francois Tusques
The Rape of the Vampire '68

Tom Tykwer
The Princess and the Warrior '00

Brian Tyler
Four Dogs Playing Poker '00
Panic '00

Christopher Tyng
The Diamond of Jeru '01

Steve Tyrell
Out of Sync '95

Koji Ueno
Gadget Trips—Mindscapes '95

Moisej Vajnberg
The Cranes Are Flying '57

Thomas Valentino
Satan's Bed '65

Raymond van het Groenewoud
Everybody's Famous! '00

James Van Heusen
Robin and the 7 Hoods '64
The Road to Utopia [Universal] '46

Roger van Otterloo
Katie Tippel '75

Kenny Vance
The Heart of Dixie '89
Hairspray (John Waters Collection Vol. 1) '88

Nana Vasconcelos
Because Why? '93

Paolo Vasile
The Squeeze '78

Caetano Veloso
Tieta of Agreste '96

Kenneth-Michael Veltz
The Secrets of the Warrior's Power '97

James L. Venable
Jay and Silent Bob Strike Back '01
Samurai Jack '01
Iron Monkey [Miramax] '93

Giovanni Venosta
Bread and Tulips '01

James Verboort
Echo of Murder '00

Mike Verta
Extreme Heist '99

Michael Vickers
At the Earth's Core '76

Manuel Villalta
Living It Up '00

Michael Vista
Bare Witness '02

Jose Maria Vitier
Things I Left in Havanna '97

Henry Vrienten
Left Luggage '98
The Vanishing [Criterion] '88

Popul Vuh
Cobra Verde '88
Heart of Glass '74

Louis Vyncke
Alien Adventure '99

Waddy Wachtel
Joe Dirt '01

Kaoru Wada
Harlock Saga '99

Tommy Wai
Jiang Hu—"The Triad Zone" '00
Time and Tide '00
The Fist Power '99

Rick Wakeman
Crimes of Passion [2] '84

Oliver Wallace
Old Yeller '57
Peter Pan [2 SE] '53
Dumbo '41

Rob Wallace
The Child '76

Jeff Walton
Attack of the 60-Foot Centerfold '95

Gast Waltzing
The Enemy '01

Marco Wan
Sex and the Emperor '94

Michael Wandmacher
On the Borderline '01

Sat San Wang
Lady Iron Monkey '83

Stephen Warbeck
Captain Corelli's Mandolin '01

Edward Ward
The Son of Monte Cristo '40

Harry Warren
The Harvey Girls '46

Joshua P. Warren
Inbred Rednecks '97

Mervyn Warren
The Wedding Planner '01

Horace Washington
Parental Guidance '02

Hiroya Watanabe
Devil Hunter Yohko: The Complete Collection, Vol. 1 '93

Takeo Watanabe
Mobile Suit Gundam: The Battle Begins! Vol. 1 '79

Franz Waxman
Run Silent, Run Deep '58
Sayonara '57
A Place in the Sun '51
Sorry, Wrong Number '48
Rebecca [Criterion] '40

Sam Waymon
Ganja and Hess '73

Roger Webb
Au Pair Girls '72

Roy Webb
Dick Tracy, Detective '45

Paul Francis Webster
Calamity Jane '53

Julius Wechter
Midnight Madness '80

Craig (Shudder to Think) Wedren
Wet Hot American Summer '01

Larry Wellington
Just for the Hell of It '68

Oliver Wells
Black and Blue '01

Rick Wentworth
The Alchemists '99
How to Get Ahead in Advertising '89

Walter Werzowa
Sweet Jane '98

David Whitaker
With a Friend Like Harry '00
Sword & the Sorcerer '82
Dr. Jekyll and Sister Hyde '71

Daniel White
Revenge in the House of Usher '82

Maurice White
The Gatchaman Collection '94

Stacy Widelitz
Return to Horror High '87

Alex Wilkinson
Escape from Alaska '02
Stealth Fighter '99

John Willhelm
Kidnapped Coed '77

Andy Williams
Hollywood Screen Tests: Take 1 '00

David Williams
Shelter '98
Children of the Corn 4: The Gathering '96

John Williams
A.I.: Artificial Intelligence '01
Harry Potter and the Sorcerer's Stone '01
The Patriot [2 SB] '00
Star Wars: Episode 1—The Phantom Menace '99
Sabrina '95
Hook '91
Empire of the Sun '87
The Fury '78
Jaws 2 '78
Midway [Universal CE] '76
Fiddler on the Roof [2 SE] '71
Heidi '67

Joseph Williams
Never 2 Big '98
Body Count '97

Ken Williams
Crash & Byrnes '99

Patrick Williams
The Toy '82
Used Cars '80
Breaking Away '79
Cuba '79
Evel Knievel '72

Paul Williams
The Muppet Movie '79
Emmet Otter's Jug-Band Christmas '77
The Boy in the Plastic Bubble [2] '76
Phantom of the Paradise '74

Meredith Willson
The Little Foxes [MGM] '41

Nancy Wilson
Vanilla Sky '01
Almost Famous: Untitled—The Bootleg Cut '00
Jerry Maguire [2 SE] '96
Say Anything [SE] '89

David Wingo
George Washington '00

Debbie Wiseman
Wilde '97
Haunted '95

Bon Yin Wong
Fist of Fury '95

Cacine Wong
Love on a Diet '01
Where a Good Man Goes '99
Too Many Ways to Be No. 1 '97

James Wong
Picture of a Nymph '88

Jonathan Wong
Dr. Lamb '92

Christine Woodruff
Lionheart '00

Phil Woods
Choose Me '84

Lyle Workman
Made [SE] '01

Ta Chiang Wu
10 Magnificent Killers '77

David Wurst
Agent Red '00
Dillinger and Capone '95
Bloodfist 5: Human Target '93

Eric Wurst
Agent Red '00
Dillinger and Capone '95
Bloodfist 5: Human Target '93

Tim Wynn
Adventures of Justine '00

Ivan Wyszogrod
What Your Eyes Don't See '99

Hiroaki Yabunaka
Sumo Vixens '96

Seiichi Yamamoto
Adrenaline Drive '99

Tadashi Yamauchi
Manji '64

Oleg Yanchenko
Come and See '85

Yoshihiro Yanno
Flowers of Shanghai '98

Tatsumi Yano
City Hunter: Secret Service
   '96

Gabriel Yared
The Lover '92

Takeshi Yasuda
Oh My Goddess! Vol. 1 '93

Goro Yasukawa
Gonin '95

Dwight Yoakam
South of Heaven, West of
   Hell '01

Peter Yorn
Me, Myself, and Irene '00

Christopher Young
Bandits '01
The Glass House '01
Sweet November '01
Swordfish '01
The Gift '00
Unforgettable '96
Barbarian Queen 2: The
   Empress Strikes Back '89
Hellbound: Hellraiser 2 [2
   THX] '88
Invaders from Mars [MGM]
   '86
Barbarian Queen '85

Bob Yuen
Eat My Dust '93

Richard Yuen
Swordsman 2 '91

Oguchi Yuji
Bloodfight '89

Allan Zavod
Howling 3: The Marsupials
   '87

Guy Zerafa
Replicant '01

Al Zima
South Bronx Heroes '85

Hans Zimmer
Black Hawk Down '01
Pearl Harbor '01
Riding in Cars with Boys '01
An Everlasting Piece '00
The Pledge '00
Chill Factor '99
The House of the Spirits '93

Daniel Zirilli
Black Spring Break 2 '01

Mikhail Ziv
Ballad of a Soldier '60

John Zorn
Sadistic City '93

The Category Index includes subject terms ranging from straight genre descriptions (Action-Adventure, Slapstick Comedy, etc.) to more off-the-wall themes (Hurling, Mermaids). These terms can help you identify unifying themes (Baseball, Heists), characters (Dracula, Zorro), settings (Cold Spots, Period Pieces), events (The Great Depression, World War II), occupations (Cops, Going Postal), or ensembles (Monty Python, the Muppets). You will also find categories for films produced outside the U.S. (see individual nationalities). Category terms are listed alphabetically; corresponding movie lists are also alphabetical.

Action-Adventure
See also: Action-Comedy; Adventure Drama; Boom!; Comic Adventure; Disaster Flicks; Martial Arts; Romantic Adventures; Swashbucklers

Ballistic Kiss
The Breed
Brother
Bury Me High
Dead or Alive
Dirty Kopz
Doomsdayer
Eat My Dust
The Fist Power
Gator King
Goodbye, Mr. Cool
The Guardian
Hard As Nails
Human Prey
Ice Grill
The Lord of Hangzhou
Narcotic Justice
Radical Jack
Raven's Ridge
Reflex Action
Score
Shakedown
36 Crazy Fists
Ticker
Tiger of Eschnapur
Where a Good Man Goes

Action-Comedy
See also: Action-Adventure; Comedy

Adventures of the Kung Fu Rascals
Chill Factor
Comic King
Extreme Heist
Partners
Ranma 1/2: Random Rhapsody—Wacky Winter Wonderland

Adaptations
See: Cartoon Adaptations; Comics/Comic Book Adaptations; Fairy Tale Adaptations; Game Adaptations; Memoirs or Diary Adaptations; Opera Adaptations; Poetry Adaptations; Television Adaptations.

Adolescence
See: Coming of Age; Hell High School; Summer Camp; Teen Angst

Adoption & Orphans
Andre
Back to the Secret Garden
Dick Tracy
The Education of Little Tree
Love Come Down
Oliver & Company
Pollyanna
Red Cherry
Snow Dogs
Snow White and the Seven Dwarfs [PE]
Stuart Little [2 DE]

Adultery
Hitched
In the Mood for Love [SE]
Lantana
The Man Who Wasn't There
Sidewalks of New York
The Taste of Others
Therese Raquin

Adventure Drama
See also: Action-Adventure; Boom!; Drama

Air Force One [2 SB]
Apocalypse Now [Redux]
Arctic Blue
The Aviator
The Blue and the Gray
Blue Thunder
Breakdown
Casualties of War
Danger beneath the Sea
Dick Tracy
Die Hard [2 FS]
Down to the Sea in Ships
Escape to Grizzly Mountain
Evel Knievel
Fire Alarm
Full Eclipse
Guadalcanal Diary
The Halls of Montezuma
Hamlet
Himalaya
Horatio Hornblower
Horatio Hornblower: The Adventure Continues
The Indian Tomb
Into Thin Air: Death on Everest
The Iron Mask
Johnny Mnemonic [2 SB]
The Journey of Natty Gann
Jurassic Park 3 [CE]
The Karate Kid: Part 2
The Karate Kid: Part 3
Knives of the Avenger
The Last Place on Earth

The Mask of Zorro [2 SE]
Midway [Universal CE]
Mountain of the Cannibal God
The New Daughters of Joshua Cabe
The North Star
The Odyssey
The Replacement Killers [2 SE]
Sell Out
The Swiss Family Robinson
Tank
Taps
Twisted Justice
Von Ryan's Express
We Dive at Dawn
White Fang to the Rescue
A Wing and a Prayer

Advertising
Advertising Rules!
Giants and Toys
How to Get Ahead in Advertising
Kramer vs. Kramer
Nothing in Common
Putney Swope
Sweet November

African America
Ali
The Autobiography of Miss Jane Pittman
Baby Boy
Better Dayz
Bingo Long Traveling All-Stars & Motor Kings
Black Godfather
Black Knight
Black Like Me
Boesman & Lena
Boycott
Bucktown
Carmen Jones
Comedy in Da Hood
Dancing in September
Daughters of the Dust
The Defiant Ones
Finding Buck McHenry
The Five Heartbeats
Fresh
Ghosts of Mississippi
The Glass Shield
The Greatest
Hard Lessons
Harlem Nights
Hav Plenty
Higher Learning
Hollywood Shuffle

How High
Introducing Dorothy Dandridge
J.D.'s Revenge
Jo Jo Dancer, Your Life Is Calling
Kingdom Come
The Last Dragon
The Last of the Blue Devils
Love Beat the Hell outta Me
Love Songs
Mama Flora's Family
Mo' Money
Out of Sync
Phat Beach
Pootie Tang
Putney Swope
Richard Pryor: Here and Now
Roots
Snow Dogs
Song of Freedom / Big Fella
The Temptations
To Sir, with Love
Two Can Play That Game
The Wash
The Wood
Zebrahead

Airborne
Air Force One [2 SB]
Air Rage
The Aviator
Blue Thunder
Dark Blue World
Dumbo
Extreme Limits
Fly Away Home [2 SE]
Jurassic Park 3 [CE]
Look Who's Talking Now
The Man with the Golden Gun
Pearl Harbor
Restless Spirits
Rough Air
Stealth Fighter
Stephen King's The Langoliers
Turbulence 2: Fear of Flying
Turbulence 3: Heavy Metal
Twelve o'Clock High
Ultimate G's
A Wing and a Prayer

Alcoholism
See: On the Rocks

Alien Beings—Benign
See also: Alien Beings—Vicious; Space Operas

Enemy Mine
It Came from Outer Space

K-Pax
Morons from Outer Space
Star Trek 3: The Search for Spock
Star Wars: Episode 1—The Phantom Menace
Zeta One

Alien Beings—Vicious
See also: Alien Beings—Benign; Space Operas

The Adventures of Buckaroo Banzai Across the Eighth Dimension [SE]
The Angry Red Planet
Attack from Mars
Bad Taste [LE]
Devil Girl from Mars
Evolution
The Fear Chamber
The Fifth Element [2 SB]
Final Fantasy: The Spirits Within
Flight to Mars
Invaders from Mars [MGM]
Invasion of the Animal People
It Came from Outer Space
It! The Terror from Beyond Space
John Carpenter's Ghosts of Mars
Killer Klowns from Outer Space
Macross: Box Set
Mars Needs Women
Planet of the Vampires
Progeny
Reptilian
Space Jam [2 EE]
Split Second
Star Trek: The Motion Picture [DE]
Star Trek 3: The Search for Spock
Star Wars: Episode 1—The Phantom Menace
Stephen King's The Langoliers
Strange Invaders
Terror in the Midnight Sun
2001: A Space Travesty
V
Zeram 2

American Indians
See: Native America

American South
The Autobiography of Miss Jane Pittman

Black Like Me
Boxcar Bertha
Boycott
Bucktown
Cape Fear
Christy—A Change of Seasons
Christy—A New Beginning
Christy—Return to Cutter Gap
Cypress Edge
Forrest Gump [SCE]
Ghosts of Mississippi
The Gift
God's Little Acre
Great Balls of Fire
Harlan County War
The Heart of Dixie
Inbred Rednecks
Jackpot
The Mothman Prophecies
Murder in Coweta County
The Patriot [2 SB]
The Prince of Tides
Queen Bee
A Real American Hero
Red Dirt
Roots
The Runaway
Scarlett
The Southerner
Tank
Tender Mercies [Anchor Bay]

Amnesia
Mulholland Drive
Santa Who?
She Lives by Night
Shock
Time Lapse
Total Recall [2 SLE]
Virtual Sexuality

Amusement Parks
See also: Carnivals & Circuses

Alien Adventure
Beverly Hills Cop 3
Carnival of Blood / Curse of the Headless Horseman [SE]
Carnival of Souls / Dementia 13
Curse of the Headless Horseman
Fatal Attraction [SCE]
Walt Disney Treasures: Disneyland USA

Angels
Angel Sanctuary
Angels in the Outfield
Date with an Angel
Dogma [2 SE]
Down to Earth

Animals
See: Bears; Cats; Dogs; Killer Apes & Monkeys; Killer Dogs; Killer Rodents; Nice Mice; Rabbits; Talking Animals; Wild Kingdom

Animated Musicals
See also: Animation & Cartoons; Musicals

Barbie in the Nutcracker
Emmet Otter's Jug-Band Christmas
The Hunchback of Notre Dame
Madeline at the North Pole
Snow White and the Seven Dwarfs [PE]
South Park: Bigger, Longer and Uncut
Thumbelina [20th Century Fox]

Animated Sci Fi
See also: Anime

Alien Adventure

Beast Wars: Transformers, Vol. 1
Final Fantasy: The Spirits Within
Harlock Saga
Roughnecks: Starship Troopers Chronicles—The Homefront Campaign
Roughnecks: Starship Troopers Chronicles—The Klendathu Campaign
Samurai Jack
Star Warp'd

Animation & Cartoons
See also: Animated Musicals; Animated Sci Fi; Anime

Animated Christmas DVD Double Feature
Atlantis: The Lost Empire [CE]
Balto 2: Wolf Quest
Batman & Mr. Freeze: Subzero
Batman Beyond: Return of the Joker [2 Uncut]
The Batman Superman Movie
Batman: The Animated Series—The Legend Begins
The Brothers Quay Collection
The Castle of Cagliostro
Cinderella 2: Dreams Come True
Creature Comforts
Daria, The Movie: Is It Fall Yet?
Disney's American Legends
Dot & the Kangaroo
Dragon Tales
Dumbo
Ferngully
Fritz the Cat
Gadget Trips—Mindscapes
Gumby, Vol. 1
Haunted Castle
The Hobbit
The Hunchback of Notre Dame 2
Justice League
The Lord of the Rings
The Many Adventures of Winnie the Pooh
Max Fleischer's Superman
Mickey Mouse in Living Color
Mickey's Magical Christmas
Mummies Alive!
Muppet Family Christmas
Nine Lives of Fritz the Cat
Oliver & Company
Peter Pan [2 SE]
Recess Christmas: Miracle on Third Street
Recess: School's Out
The Return of the King
Rudolph the Red-Nosed Reindeer: The Movie
Sabrina, the Animated Series: Sabrina's World
Scooby-Doo and the Reluctant Werewolf
Scooby-Doo Goes Hollywood
Scooby-Doo's Spookiest Tales
The Secret of NIMH
Shrek [SE]
The Simpsons: The Complete First Season
South Park: Insults to Injury
Spider-Man: The Ultimate Villain Showdown
Spike and Mike's Classic Festival of Animation
Spongebob Squarepants: Nautical Nonsense and Sponge Buddies
Star Blazers: The Comet Empire: Part 1
Star Blazers: The Quest for Iscandar: Series 1
Three Stooges Cartoon Classics, Volume 1

Tom and Jerry: The Magic Ring
Transformers: Season 1
A Troll in Central Park
The Trumpet of the Swan
2000 Year Old Man
Underdog [CE]
Vampires in Havana
Waking Life
Walt Disney Treasures: Silly Symphonies
Watership Down

Anime
See also: Animation & Cartoons

Amon Saga
Angel Sanctuary
Battle of the Planets, Vol. 1
Battle of the Planets, Vol. 2
Battle of the Planets, Vol. 3
Blood: The Last Vampire
Blue Submarine No. 6—Episode 1: Blues
Blue Submarine No. 6—Episode 2: Pilots
Blue Submarine No. 6—Episode 3: Hearts
Blue Submarine No. 6—Episode 4: Minasoko
The Castle of Cagliostro
City Hunter: Secret Service
Devil Hunter Yohko: The Complete Collection, Vol. 1
Devil Man
Fortune Quest: Journey to Terrason
The Gatchaman Collection
Harlock Saga
Hermes—Winds of Love
Kizuna
Lady Blue
Macross: Box Set
Martian Successor Nadesico: Endgame
Masquerade: Eternal Life
Metropolis
Mobile Suit Gundam: The Battle Begins! Vol. 1
Mobile Suit Gundam Wing: Operation 1
Nadia: Secret of Blue Water, Vol. 1: The Adventure Begins
Night on the Galactic Railroad
Oh My Goddess! Vol. 1
Pokemon: Mewtwo Returns
Pokemon: The First Movie
Ranma 1/2: Random Rhapsody—Wacky Winter Wonderland
Record of Lodoss War: Chronicles of the Heroic Knight
Robotech: The Macross Saga—Extra Disc 1: Elements of Robotechnology
Robotech: The Macross Saga, Vol. 2: Transformation
Roujin Z [Central Park]
Serial Experiments: Lain
The Slayers
Soultaker: The Monster Within
Strange Dawn—Strange World
Strange Dawn, Vol. 2—Strange Journey
Tekkaman Blade 2: Complete Collection
Urusei Yatsura: TV Series 1
Vampire Hunter D: Bloodlust
Very Private Lessons
Video Girl Ai
Weather Report Girl
X

Anthologies
See also: Comedy Anthologies; Horror Anthologies; Serials

The Acid House
The Best of Resfest: Resfest Shorts 1
The Best of Tromadance Christmas Past
The Educational Archives Volume 1: Sex & Drugs
The Educational Archives Volume 2: Social Engineering 101
A Girl Thing
Listen to Britain and other Films by Humphrey Jennings
Love Songs
Queer As F**k: Bizarre Short Films
Red Shoe Diaries: The Game
Short 6: Insanity
Short 7: Utopia
Short 10: Chaos
Smash Cuts! Super Sci-Fi Shorts
Smash Cuts: Totally Twisted Shorts Fest
Tokyo Decameron: Three Tales of Madness & Sensuality
Twice-Told Tales
With Friends Like These
World War I Films of the Silent Era

Anti-Heroes
See also: Rebel with a Cause

The Dead Pool
Dirty Harry [2]
The Enforcer
Gang Related
Magnum Force
Ten Benny
True Crime

Anti-War War Movies
All Quiet on the Western Front
Apocalypse Now [Redux]
The Charge of the Light Brigade
Come and See
Coming Home
Les Carabiniers
M*A*S*H [FS]
A Midnight Clear
Mission to Death
No Man's Land
Too Late the Hero
The Young Lions

Apartheid
See also: Civil Rights

Boesman & Lena

Archaeology
See: Big Digs

Argentinean (Production)
Funny, Dirty Little War
Play for Me
The Road
Savage Pampas
A Shadow You Soon Will Be
What Your Eyes Don't See

Art & Artists
See also: Biopics: Artists; Struggling Musicians; Writers

Advertising Rules!
Baby Van Gogh
The Blind Beast
Bluebeard
Bride of the Wind
A Bucket of Blood / Attack of the Giant Leeches [Marengo]
Fly Away Home
The Horse's Mouth
Jimmy Zip
Morgan: A Suitable Case for Treatment
Something within Me

Stealing Beauty
Sweet Thing

Assassinations
See also: Camelot (New); Foreign Intrigue; Hit Men/Women; Homicide; Spies & Espionage

All the King's Men
The Assassin
Beautiful Beast
Beautiful Hunter
Blow Out
The Clockmaker
The Evil That Men Do
Ghosts of Mississippi
Hit Lady
The Man with the Golden Gun
The Point Men
The Terminator [2 SE]
Ultimatum
Zoolander

At the Movies
See also: Behind the Scenes

Anguish
Attack from Mars
Polyester (John Waters Collection Vol. 2)
Popcorn
The Projectionist
The Purple Rose of Cairo
The Replacement Killers [2 SE]
South Park: Bigger, Longer and Uncut
Trailer, the Movie

Australian (Production)
Alien Visitor
Black Robe [MGM]
Careful, He Might Hear You
Chopper
The Coca-Cola Kid
Crocodile Dundee
Dangerous Summer
The Dish
Dr. Jekyll & Mr. Hyde
Dot & the Kangaroo
Echo Park
Fighting Rats of Tobruk
The Good Wife
Hammers over the Anvil
The Harp in the South
Howling 3: The Marsupials
Idiot Box
The Irishman
Lantana
The Last Wave
Lonely Hearts
Long John Silver
Mad Max [MGM SE]
Moulin Rouge [SE]
Nightmaster
Poor Man's Orange
Quigley Down Under
Return of Captain Invincible
Risk
Strictly Ballroom
Sweet Talker
Two Friends
The Well

Automobiles
See: Checkered Flag; Motor Vehicle Dept.

Babysitting
Don't Bother to Knock
Fright
Halloween [EE]
See Spot Run
When a Stranger Calls

Bad Dads
See also: Monster Moms; Parenthood

Aberdeen
Flesh and Bone
Freddy Got Fingered
La Promesse
L.I.E.

Kiss Tomorrow Goodbye
The Locusts
Manhunter [LE]
Novocaine
Purple Noon
Red Rock West
Romeo Is Bleeding
The Silence of the Lambs [MGM SE]
The Usual Suspects [MGM SE]
Who'll Stop the Rain?
Wild Orchid

Cooking
See: Edibles

Cops
See also: Comic Cops; Detectives; Future Cop; Loner Cops; Police Detectives; Private Eyes; Small Town Sheriffs; Women Cops

Abraxas: Guardian of the Universe [BFS]
Across 110th Street
Angel Eyes
The Animal
Bad Cop Chronicles: Confessions of a Police Captain
Best Seller
Beverly Hills Cop [CE]
Beverly Hills Cop 2
Beverly Hills Cop 3
Beyond the Law
The Big Heat
Bloodfist 7: Manhunt
Blue Thunder
Brannigan
The Breed
Cement
China Moon
Colors
Cops and Robbersons
Cornbread, Earl & Me
The Crimson Rivers
Deceiver
Dirty Kopz
Diva [Anchor Bay]
Exorcist 3: Legion
An Eye for an Eye
The Fast and the Furious
Fever
15 Minutes
The French Connection [SE]
French Connection 2
Full Eclipse
The Glass Shield
He Walked by Night [BFS]
The January Man
John Carpenter's Ghosts of Mars
L.A.P.D.: To Protect and Serve
Mad Max [MGM SE]
Matter of Trust
Mimic 2
Mind, Body & Soul
Mitchell
One Night at McCool's
Random Hearts
A Real American Hero
The Replacement Killers [2 SE]
Replicant
The Road
The Runaway
Slipstream
Snapdragon
Stonewall
Timecop
Traffic [Criterion]
Twisted Justice
Ultraviolet
Unforgettable
The Usual Suspects [MGM SE]
Vampire in Brooklyn

Corporate Shenanigans
See also: Advertising; Salespeople

The Alchemists
Barbarians at the Gate
Behind Office Doors
The Closet
The Coca-Cola Kid
Dodsworth [MGM]
Firetrap
Giants and Toys
Haiku Tunnel
How to Get Ahead in Advertising
How to Succeed in Business without Really Trying
Jack and the Beanstalk: The Real Story
Johnny Mnemonic [2 SB]
Mo' Money
Never 2 Big
Out Cold
Perfume
Pootie Tang
The Prime Gig
Putney Swope
Race the Sun
Sabrina
The 6th Day [2 SE]
Startup.com
The Taste of Others
The Temp
Tommy Boy
The Toxic Avenger, Part 3: The Last Temptation of Toxie [DC]
Toys

Courtroom Drama
See: Order in the Court

Creepy Houses
Bones
Chasing Sleep
The Ghost Breakers
The Glass House
Haunted
House
House 2: The Second Story
The Legend of Hell House
Monsters Crash the Pajama Party Spook Show Spectacular
The Others [CE]
Psycho 2
Revenge in the House of Usher
Scary Movie 2
Seven Days to Live
The Shining [2 SE]
Shock
Stephen King's Rose Red
Terror in the Haunted House
13 Gantry Row
13 Ghosts

Crime & Criminals
See: Crime Drama; Crime Sprees; Crimes of Passion; Disorganized Crime; Frame-Ups; Fugitives; Gangs; Heists; Hit Men/Women; Organized Crime; Scams, Stings & Cons; Serial Killers; Smuggler's Blues; Triads; True Crime; Urban Drama; Vigilantes; Yakuza

Crime Drama
See also: Drama

Bad Boys [Anchor Bay]
Borough of Kings
Brother of Darkness
Cement
Cops on a Mission
Dillinger and Capone
The Fat Black Pussycat
15 Minutes
Gang Related
Gonin
Gunman in the Streets
Key Largo
Killer
Memento [1]

Memento [2 SE]
Millennium Dragon
The Night Heaven Fell
Parisian Love / Down to the Sea in Ships
Petits Freres
Purple Noon
Railroaded
Red Zone Cuba
Reindeer Games [Miramax DC]
Satan's Bed
The Score
Sexy Beast
Showdown
Spanish Judges
They Call It Murder
Tom Clancy's Netforce
Violent City
Warm Blooded Killers
When the Sky Falls

Crime Sprees
See also: Fugitives; Lovers on the Lam

Baise Moi
15 Minutes
Idiot Box
Shopping

Crimes of Passion
The Amy Fisher Story
China Moon
Fatal Attraction [SCE]
Niagara

Crop Dusters
Earth
The Field [Artisan]
God's Little Acre
A Moon for the Misbegotten
Places in the Heart
The Southerner
Vacas
The Well

Cuban (Production)
Life Is to Whistle
A Paradise under the Stars
Vampires in Havana

Cults
See also: Occult; Satanism

The Devil's Prey
Helter Skelter Murders
Mind, Body & Soul
Putney Swope
Revenge
Safe
Servants of Twilight
Withnail and I

Culture Clash
An American Rhapsody
Beverly Hood
Black Robe [MGM]
crazy/beautiful
Crocodile Dundee in Los Angeles
Just Visiting
Moscow on the Hudson
Quigley Down Under
Rescue from Gilligan's Island
Rodgers & Hammerstein's South Pacific
Shadow Magic
Snow Dogs

Cuttin' Heads
Blow Dry
An Everlasting Piece
Hairdo U
Hairspray (John Waters Collection Vol. 1)
The Man Who Wasn't There

Cyberpunk
The Fifth Element [2 SB]
Johnny Mnemonic [2 SB]
Mad Max [MGM SE]
The Terminator [2 SE]
Total Recall [2 SLE]
Tron [2 CE]

Czech (Production)
Closely Watched Trains
Conspirators of Pleasure
Daisies
Dark Blue World
Divided We Fall
Ecstasy
The Firemen's Ball
Loves of a Blonde
The Shop on Main Street

Dance Fever
See also: Ballet; Disco Musicals

Girl in Gold Boots
The Harvey Girls
Mad Youth
Showgirls
Strictly Ballroom

Danish (Production)
Day of Wrath
Gertrud
Light Keeps Me Company
Ordet
Reptilicus

Deafness
See also: Physical Problems

Immortal Beloved
See No Evil, Hear No Evil
Sound and Fury
Suspect

Death & the Afterlife
See also: Angels; Funerals; Ghosts, Ghouls & Goblins; Occult; Suicide; Zombies

Angel Eyes
Audrey Rose
Beyond Tomorrow
Bill & Ted's Bogus Journey
Bowery at Midnight
Carnival of Souls / Dementia 13
The Child
Courage Under Fire
The Death Curse of Tartu / Sting of Death
Down to Earth
Faces of Death 2
Faces of Death 3: Scenes from the Underground
High Spirits
I Bury the Living
The Legend of Hell House
Macbeth
Mannequin
Mermaid
Monkeybone
Night of the Living Dead [Elite ME]
Scrooge
Seven Days to Live
The Sixth Sense [Buena Vista]
Sometimes They Come Back
South Park: Bigger, Longer and Uncut
Star Trek 3: The Search for Spock
Tequila Body Shots
13 Ghosts
To Gillian on Her 37th Birthday
Truly, Madly, Deeply
Under the Sand

Death Row
See also: Men in Prison; Women in Prison

I Want to Live!
Letters from a Killer
A Place in the Sun
Shot in the Heart
True Crime
The Widow of Saint-Pierre

Dedicated Teachers
See also: Hell High School; School Daze

Coming Out
Institue Benjamenta or This Dream People Call Human Life
Race the Sun
The Road Home
To Sir, with Love

Deep Blue
See also: Killer Sea Critters; Shipwrecked; Submarines

Andre
The Big Broadcast of 1938
Danger beneath the Sea
Dead in the Water
Deep Water
Down to the Sea in Ships
Horatio Hornblower
Horatio Hornblower: The Adventure Continues
Jaws 2
Kill Cruise
The Legend of 1900
Light at the Edge of the World
Lionheart
Long John Silver
The Odyssey
Operation Petticoat
Run Silent, Run Deep
She Creature
Spongebob Squarepants: Nautical Nonsense and Sponge Buddies
Thumbtanic
To Gillian on Her 37th Birthday
The Triangle
2103: Deadly Wake

Demons & Wizards
See also: Occult

The Church
Deathstalker
The Demon's Baby
Evil Dead [LE]
The Hobbit
Picture of a Nymph
Possessed
Rawhead Rex
The Return of the King
Sword & the Sorcerer
Willow

Dental Mayhem
See also: Doctors & Nurses; Evil Doctors

Novocaine
Snow Dogs

Deserts
Dune [2 SE]
Evolution
Fatal Attraction [SCE]
Mad Max [MGM SE]
The Road to Morocco [Universal]
Sahara
Slow Burn
Son of the Sheik
White Sands

Detectives
See also: Comedy Mystery; Cops; Feds; Police Detectives; Private Eyes

The Adventures of Sherlock Holmes, Vol. 3
The Cheap Detective
City on Fire [Dimension]
The Hound of the Baskervilles
Sleepless

Dinosaurs
At the Earth's Core
Caveman
The Crater Lake Monster
Fantastic Dinosaurs of the Movies
Jurassic Park 3 [CE]
The Lost Continent
The People That Time Forgot

Fists of Bruce Lee
The Five Heartbeats
Frances [Anchor Bay]
The French Connection [SE]
French Connection 2
Fresh
Green
High Risk
Jo Jo Dancer, Your Life Is Call-
ing
Lenny
Less Than Zero
Loser
Love Come Down
Mission Manila
Mood Swingers
Ninja in the U.S.A.
Out of Sync
Red Surf
Riding in Cars with Boys
Running Scared
She Shoulda Said No
Sweet Jane
The Temptations
Tombstone [2]
Traffic [Criterion]
Traffik
Twin Peaks: Fire Walk with
Me
Ulee's Gold
The Usual Suspects [MGM
SE]
Who'll Stop the Rain?
Withnail and I

Drugs
*See: Drug Abuse; On the
Rocks; Reefer Madness; Smug-
gler's Blues*

Dutch (Production)
Business Is Business
Katie Tippel
The Vanishing [Criterion]

Eating
See: Cannibalism; Edibles

Eco-Vengeance!
See also: Killer Bugs & Slugs
Ferngully
Jaws 2
Prophecy

Edibles
See also: Cannibalism

The Age of Innocence
The Big Hit [2 SB]
Eat Drink Man Woman
Tortilla Soup

Egypt—Ancient
The Mummy
The Mummy Returns

Elephants
See also: Carnivals & Circuses
Dumbo
Freddy Got Fingered
Whispers: An Elephant's Tale

Elevators
Basic Instinct [2 SE]
Die Hard [2 FS]
Fatal Attraction [SCE]
The Silence of the Lambs
[MGM SE]

Erotic Thrillers
See also: Sex & Sexuality
Bare Witness
Basic Instinct [2 SE]
Boundaries
Dead Sexy
Diary of a Sex Addict
The Passion Network
Poison
Sexual Predator
Snapdragon
Trois

Escaped Cons
*See also: Great Escapes; Men
in Prison*
Bandits
The Defiant Ones
Prison on Fire 2
Slow Burn
The Stunt Man

Evil Doctors
*See also: Doctors & Nurses;
Mad Scientists*
Dr. Jekyll and Mr. Hyde [Kino]
Dr. Jekyll and Sister Hyde
Dr. Mabuse, The Gambler

Exploitation
See also: Sexploitation
Elysia
Faces of Death 2
Faces of Death 3: Scenes
from the Underground
Hot Blooded Woman
Mau Mau Sex Sex
Pin Down Girls
The Road to Ruin
Satan's Cheerleaders
Scare Their Pants Off /
Satan's Bed
Sex and Buttered Popcorn
Collection
Sex and Buttered Popcorn,
Vol. 1: Tease, Sleaze, and
Social Disease
Sex and Buttered Popcorn,
Vol. 2: Sex, Sin, and Salva-
tion
Sex and Buttered Popcorn,
Vol. 3: Granddad's Forbid-
den Follies
She Shoulda Said No
Slaughter
Tomorrow's Children

Explorers
Atlantis: The Lost Empire
[CE]
Cabeza de Vaca
The Last Place on Earth
Lewis and Clark: Journey of
the Corps of Discovery
Shackleton

Eyeballs!
See also: Hearts!
Anguish
The Crawling Eye
The Fury
Halloween 2: The Nightmare
Isn't Over! [Universal]
Scanners
Silver Bullet
The Terminator [2 SE]

Fairy Tale Adaptations
Barbie in the Nutcracker
Cinderella
Cinderella 2: Dreams Come
True
Father Frost
Into the Woods
Jack and the Beanstalk: The
Real Story
The NeverEnding Story
Peter Pan [2 SE]
Pin...
The Princess Bride [2 SE]
Snow White: The Fairest of
Them All
Tales from Europe: The
Singing, Ringing Tree
Tales from Europe: The Story
of Little Mook
Thumbelina [20th Century
Fox]

Family Ties
*See also: Bad Dads; Brothers & Sis-
ters; Incest; Monster Moms;
Parenthood; Stepparents;
Twins*

Fantasy
*See also: Animation & Car-
toons; Anime; Musical Fantasy*
The Amphibian Man
Ashik Kerib
Atlantis: The Lost Empire
[CE]
Barbarian Queen
Beastmaster
Beyond Tomorrow
Bill & Ted's Excellent Adven-
ture
Deathstalker
Deathstalker 2: Duel of the
Titans
The Demon's Baby
Desperate Living (John
Waters Collection Vol. 2)
Devil Man
Father Frost
The Final Programme
Fortune Quest: Journey to
Terrason
The Golem
Goliath and the Dragon
Gormenghast
Harry Potter and the Sorcer-
er's Stone
His Majesty, the Scarecrow of
Oz
The Hobbit
Hook
The Indian in the Cupboard
Jack the Giant Killer
The Jungle Book
Le Magnifique
Legend [UE]
The Legend of Suram
Fortress / Ashik Kerib
The Lord of the Rings
The Lost Continent
Masters of the Universe
Mr. Rice's Secret
Mists of Avalon
Monkeybone
Moon over Tao
The NeverEnding Story
NeverEnding Story 2: The
Next Chapter
Night on the Galactic Rail-
road
Nine Lives of Fritz the Cat
The Ogre
Peter Pan [2 SE]
Picture of a Nymph
Pokemon: Mewtwo Returns
Prancer
Ranma 1/2: Random Rhap-
sody—Wacky Winter Won-
derland
Rat
Reborn from Hell: Jubei's
Revenge
Reborn from Hell: Samurai
Armageddon
Restless Spirits
Return of the Deadly Blade
The Return of the King
Rookie of the Year
The Saragossa Manuscript
Sea People
The Secret of NIMH
The Secret of Roan Inish
Secret of the Andes
Serial Experiments: Lain
Shrek [SE]
The Slayers
Snow White: The Fairest of
Them All
Strange Dawn—Strange
World
Strange Dawn, Vol. 2—
Strange Journey
Sword & the Sorcerer
Tales from Europe: The
Singing, Ringing Tree
Three Wishes
The Three Worlds of Gulliver
A Troll in Central Park
Undersea Kingdom
Watership Down

The White Pony
Willow
The Wizard of Oz
The Wolves of Kromer
Xena: Warrior Princess—
Series Finale

Farming
See: Crop Dusters

Fashion
Fashionably L.A.
Perfume

Feds
*See also: Detectives; Spies &
Espionage*
Best Men
Bloodfist 5: Human Target
Bloodfist 8: Hard Way Out
Boss of Bosses
Corky Romano
Crash & Byrnes
Dillinger and Capone
Extreme Limits
Hard Cash
Kill Me Later
Manhunter [LE]
Paradise Canyon
Plughead Rewired: Circuitry
Man 2
Point Break
See Spot Run
The Silence of the Lambs
[MGM SE]
Swordfish
T-Men
Time Lapse
To the Limit
Traffic [Criterion]
White Sands
The X-Files: Season 4

Femme Fatale
See also: Wonder Women
The Amy Fisher Story
Basic Instinct [2 SE]
Beautiful Beast
Beautiful Hunter
The Blue Angel
Dr. Jekyll and Sister Hyde
A Fool There Was
Intersection
Jay and Silent Bob Strike
Back
Kill Cruise
Lady Frankenstein
Novocaine
On Her Majesty's Secret Ser-
vice
One Night at McCool's
Scandal
Second Skin
Snow White and the Seven
Dwarfs [PE]
The Specialist
The Temp
The Wasp Woman [2]

Fencing
See also: Swashbucklers
Terror in the Midnight Sun

Fifties
See: Period Piece: 1950s

Filipino (Production)
Blood Thirst
Curse of the Vampires
Murder in the Orient
Raiders of Leyte Gulf
Walls of Hell

Film History
The Celluloid Closet
Hidden Hollywood: Treasures
from the 20th Century Fox
Vaults
Hidden Hollywood 2: More
Treasures from the 20th
Century Fox Vaults

Hollywood at Your Feet: The
Story of the Chinese The-
ater Footprints
Hollywood Screen Tests: Take
1
Hollywood Screen Tests: Take
2
Mary Pickford: A Life on Film
The Movies Begin
(1894–1913)
A Personal Journey with Mar-
tin Scorsese through Amer-
ican Movies
Pulp Cinema
Sex and Buttered Popcorn
Shadow Magic

Film Noir
See also: Contemporary Noir
The Big Heat
Bob le Flambeur
Don't Bother to Knock
Gunman in the Streets
He Walked by Night [BFS]
Key Largo
The Long Night
Niagara
Railroaded
Raw Deal
Sorry, Wrong Number
Strange Illusion
Strange Impersonation
T-Men

Filmmaking
*See also: At the Movies;
Behind the Scenes*
Art House
Clint Eastwood: Out of the
Shadows
Close-Up
Dario Argento: An Eye for Hor-
ror
The Dead Hate the Living
Directed by Andrei Tarkovsky
The Directors: Roger Corman
Fantastic Dinosaurs of the
Movies
Goldwyn: The Man and His
Movies
The Haunted World of Edward
D. Wood, Jr.
The Horror of Hammer
Light Keeps Me Company
The Matrix Revisited
Mau Mau Sex Sex
Oliver Stone Collection
Pitch
The Pornographer
R2PC: Road to Park City
The Sinister Saga
The Stunt Man
Sullivan's Travels
Ulysses' Gaze

Finnish (Production)
Ambush

Fires & Firemen
*See also: Boom!; Disaster
Flicks*
Evolution
Fire Alarm
Firehouse
Firemen
The Fireman's Ball
Firestarter 2: Rekindled
Firetrap

Flashback
Amores Perros
Bandits
Boss of Bosses
Cement
Citizen Kane
Company Man
Courage Under Fire
Dark Blue World
Deeply
Don Juan (Or If Don Juan
Were a Woman)
Eagle vs. Silver Fox

Hardball
Indecent Proposal
Las Vegas Lady
Let It Ride
Luckytown
Ocean's Eleven
Rat Race
Showgirls
Support Your Local Sheriff
The Tailor of Panama
Ten Benny
Tennessee's Partner
3000 Miles to Graceland

Game Adaptations
Final Fantasy: The Spirits
   Within
Lara Croft: Tomb Raider

Gangs
See also: Crime & Criminals;
Organized Crime

Beyond the Law
Big Bad Mama 2
The Black Cobra
Borderline
Broadway Danny Rose
C.C. & Company
Colors
Designing Woman
Dick Tracy vs. Cueball
Diva [Anchor Bay]
Drive By
The Enforcer
Every Which Way But Loose
Full Eclipse
Hard As Nails
Hard Lessons
Key Largo
Lady in Red
Mob Story [BFS]
Random Acts of Violence
Robin and the 7 Hoods
Stavisky
The Wrecking Crew

Gays
See also: Bisexuality; Gender
Bending; Lesbians

All over the Guy
Carrington
The Celluloid Closet
The Closet
Colonel Redl
Coming Out
The Deep End
Fifth of July
First Love and Other Pains /
   One of Them
Forgive and Forget
Go Fish
Kizuna
La Cage aux Folles
La Cage aux Folles 2
L.I.E.
Lilies
Luminarias
The Mexican
My Best Friend's Wedding [2
   SE]
Nico and Dani
The Object of My Affection
Our Lady of the Assassins
Perfume
Queer As Folk: The Complete
   First Season
Queer As F**k: Bizarre Short
   Films
Querelle
Red Dirt
Seducing Maarya
Stonewall
Sweet November
Taboo
Those Who Love Me Can
   Take the Train
The Trio
Urbania
Water Drops on Burning
   Rocks
Wilde

Withnail and I
The Wolves of Kromer

Gender Bending
See also: Gays; Lesbians; Role
Reversal

Desperate Living (John
   Waters Collection Vol. 2)
Dressed to Kill [SE]
Hairspray (John Waters Col-
   lection Vol. 1)
Hedwig and the Angry Inch
La Cage aux Folles
La Cage aux Folles 2
Lilies
Pink Flamingos
Polyester (John Waters Col-
   lection Vol. 2)
The Silence of the Lambs
   [MGM SE]
Stonewall
Those Who Love Me Can
   Take the Train
Water Drops on Burning
   Rocks
The World according to Garp

Genetics
See also: Cloning Around; Mad
Scientists

Gattaca [2 SB]
Rats

Genre Spoofs
See also: Satire & Parody

Cannibal! The Musical
Corky Romano
Galaxina
Hell Comes to Frogtown
Murder by Death
Not Another Teen Movie
Phantom of the Paradise
Return of Captain Invincible
Rod Steele 0014: You Only
   Live Until You Die
Scary Movie 2
The Sexy Sixth Sense
Soapdish
Spaceballs
Star Warp'd
Strange Invaders
Support Your Local Sheriff
Three Amigos
Transylvania 6-5000
2069: A Sex Odyssey
UHF
The Villain
Wet Hot American Summer

German (Production)
Advertising Rules!
Aimee & Jaguar
Bagdad Cafe
The Blue Angel
The Cat o' Nine Tails
Catherine the Great
Cobra Verde
Colonel Redl
Coming Out
Companeros
Diary of a Lost Girl
Dr. Mabuse, The Gambler
East Side Story
Enemy at the Gates
Faust
Gesualdo: Death for Five
   Voices
The Golem
Heart of Glass
Hot Summer
The Indian Tomb
Jacob the Liar
The Last Laugh
The Legend of Rita
Lessons of Darkness
Lexx Series 2, Vol. 1
Liam
Little Dieter Needs to Fly
The Love of Jeanne Ney
Mein Krieg
Nekromantik

Nelly et Monsieur Arnaud
Nosferatu
The Ogre
Othello
The Princess and the Warrior
Querelle
Schramm
Shadow Magic
Stranger than Paradise
Stroszek
Tales from Europe: The
   Singing, Ringing Tree
Tales from Europe: The Story
   of Little Mook
Tiger of Eschnapur
Town without Pity
The Trio
Va Savoir

Ghosts, Ghouls &
Goblins
See also: Death & the Afterlife;
Demons & Wizards; Occult

Beyond Tomorrow
Destination Nightmare
The Ghost Breakers
Haunted
Haunted Honeymoon
High Spirits
The Mummy's Ghost
The Others [CE]
Restless Spirits
Scary Movie 2
The Sexy Sixth Sense
The Sixth Sense [Buena
   Vista]
Sometimes They Come
   Back...Again
13 Ghosts
To Gillian on Her 37th Birth-
   day
Under the Sand
The Watcher in the Woods
When Good Ghouls Go Bad
Woman in Black

Giants
Attack of the 60-Foot Center-
   fold
The Princess Bride [2 SE]

Gifted Children
Little Man Tate
Real Genius
Rookie of the Year
Searching for Bobby Fischer

Godzilla & Friends
Gappa the Trifibian Monster
Godzilla, King of the Mon-
   sters [GoodTimes]
Godzilla vs. Destroyah
Godzilla vs. Space Godzilla /
   Godzilla vs. Destroyah
Rebirth of Mothra 1 & 2
Rebirth of Mothra 2

Going Postal
84 Charing Cross Road
Letters from a Killer
See Spot Run

Golf
Golf Balls!
Space Jam [2 EE]

Grand Hotel
See also: No-Exit Motel

America's Sweethearts
Psycho 2
Separate Tables
The Shining [2 SE]

Grand Theft Auto
The Fast and the Furious
Rat Race

Great Depression
See also: Hard Knock Life;
Homeless

All the King's Men
Big Bad Mama 2
Boxcar Bertha

Dillinger and Capone
Hallelujah, I'm a Bum
The Journey of Natty Gann
The Life and Times of Hank
   Greenberg
Of Mice and Men
Places in the Heart
Sullivan's Travels

Great Escapes
See also: Escaped Cons; Men
in Prison; POW/MIA; War;
Women in Prison

Breakout
Die Hard [2 FS]
Le Trou
McKenzie Break
Not without My Daughter
Raw Deal
Robert Louis Stevenson's St.
   Ives
The Shining [2 SE]
Von Ryan's Express

Greek (Production)
Ulysses' Gaze

Growing Older
See also: Death & the Afterlife;
Late Bloomin' Love

Anima
Atlantic City
Blue Moon
Citizen Kane
The Field [Artisan]
The Firemen's Ball
42 Up
The Last Laugh
Mr. Saturday Night [MGM]
Our Lady of the Assassins
Queens Logic
Rabid Grannies
Sea People
The Shootist
Stephen King's Golden Years
The Wasp Woman [2]
Wild Strawberries

Gypsies
The Hunchback of Notre
   Dame
The Hunchback of Notre
   Dame
The Hunchback of Notre
   Dame 2
Love Potion 9
Snatch [SE]
Triumph of the Spirit

Hackers
See also: Computers

The Net [2 SE]
Swordfish

Halloween
American Nightmare
Halloween [EE]
Halloween 2: The Nightmare
   Isn't Over! [Universal]
Halloween 4: The Return of
   Michael Myers [MGM LE]
When Good Ghouls Go Bad

Hallucinations/Illusions
Final
Monkeybone
The Mothman Prophecies
Waking Life

Hammer Horror
Dr. Jekyll and Sister Hyde
Hammer House of Horror
The Hound of the
   Baskervilles
Lust for a Vampire
The Mummy
The Scars of Dracula
Theatre of Blood

Hard Knock Life
See also: Great Depression;
Homeless

Boesman & Lena

Broken Blossoms [Kino]
Liam
Mama Flora's Family
Me You Them
Pay It Forward
Pocketful of Miracles
The Road Home

Hearts!
See also: Eyeballs!

Split Second
The Terminator [2 SE]

Heists
See also: Scams, Stings &
Cons

Bandits
Best Men
Bob le Flambeur
Body Count
City on Fire [Dimension]
The Curse of the Jade Scorpi-
   on
Dillinger and Capone
Extreme Heist
Extreme Honor
Firetrap
Four Dogs Playing Poker
The Great St. Louis Bank
   Robbery
Hard Cash
Heist
High Risk
Ice Grill
Kill Me Later
Motorama
Ocean's 11
Ocean's Eleven
Point Break
Reindeer Games [Miramax
   DC]
The Score
Sexy Beast
Snatch [SE]
The Squeeze
Styx
3000 Miles to Graceland
Topkapi
Un Flic
The Usual Suspects [MGM
   SE]
Who'll Stop the Rain?

Hell
Bill & Ted's Bogus Journey
Faust: Love of the Damned
Hellbound: Hellraiser 2 [2
   THX]
South Park: Bigger, Longer
   and Uncut

Hell High School
See also: Campus Capers;
School Daze; Teen Angst

Bill & Ted's Excellent Adven-
   ture
Buffy the Vampire Slayer
Buffy the Vampire Slayer:
   Season 1
Carrie
Cruel Intentions 2
Dance 'til Dawn
Ginger Snaps
Hard Lessons
Heathers [2 THX]
Hiding Out
Hostage High
Lust for a Vampire
Making the Grade
My Bodyguard
New Port South
The Others
Pep Squad
Return to Horror High
Rock 'n' Roll High School
   [New Concorde SE]
Satan's Cheerleaders
To Sir, with Love

The Help: Female
Au Pair Girls
The Others [CE]

Jurassic Park 3 [CE]
Mararia
The Others [CE]
Pearl of the South Pacific
Rescue from Gilligan's Island
Robinson Crusoe
Undercurrent
Vibration
The Widow of Saint-Pierre

Israeli (Production)
Kadosh

Italian (Production)
After the Fox
Bad Cop Chronicles: Confessions of a Police Captain
Bad Cop Chronicles 2: Corrupt
Barbarian Queen
Barbarian Queen 2: The Empress Strikes Back
The Black Cobra
Bread and Chocolate
Bread and Tulips
A Bullet for the General
Cabiria
Cannibal Apocalypse
The Cat o' Nine Tails
The Church
Companeros
The Conqueror of Atlantis
Creatures from the Abyss
The Cry of the Owl
Cut and Run
Demonia
8 1/2
Eva
Find a Place to Die
Fistful of Lead
Four of the Apocalypse
The Garden of the Finzi-Continis
Goliath and the Dragon
Hell of the Living Dead
Il Grido
Juliet of the Spirits [Criterion]
Keoma
Knives of the Avenger
Lady Frankenstein
The Last Days of Pompeii
The Last Man on Earth
Les Carabiniers
The Libertine
Mountain of the Cannibal God
Nelly et Monsieur Arnaud
The New Gladiators
The Night Heaven Fell
No Man's Land
Opera
Orloff and the Invisible Man
Planet of the Vampires
Please Not Now!
Primitive Love
Rocco and His Brothers
Secret Defense
Seduction of Mimi
Shock
Sleepless
Spirits of the Dead [Criterion]
Stealing Beauty
Submarine Attack
Suspiria
Texas, Adios
Ulysses' Gaze
Va Savoir
Voices from Beyond
The White Warrior

It's a Conspiracy, Man!
See also: Capitol Capers; Mystery & Suspense

The Alchemists
Echo of Murder
The Last Tattoo
Rush Hour 2
Tom Clancy's Netforce
Venomous
The X-Files: Season 4

Jack the Ripper
From Hell [DLE]
Jack the Ripper: 4 Tales of the Supernatural
Ripper: Letter from Hell

Japanese (Production)
Adrenaline Drive
Afraid to Die
Amon Saga
Angel Sanctuary
Battle of the Planets, Vol. 1
Battle of the Planets, Vol. 2
Battle of the Planets, Vol. 3
Beautiful Beast
Beautiful Hunter
The Bedroom
The Blind Beast
Blood: The Last Vampire
Bloodfight
Blue Submarine No. 6—Episode 1: Blues
Blue Submarine No. 6—Episode 2: Pilots
Blue Submarine No. 6—Episode 3: Hearts
Blue Submarine No. 6—Episode 4: Minasoko
The Bodyguard [BFS]
Brother
The Castle of Cagliostro
City Hunter: Secret Service
Devil Hunter Yohko: The Complete Collection, Vol. 1
Devil Man
The Dimension Travelers
The Eel
Fatal Blade
Flowers of Shanghai
Gappa the Trifibian Monster
The Gatchaman Collection
Giants and Toys
Godzilla, King of the Monsters [GoodTimes]
Godzilla vs. Destroyah
Godzilla vs. Space Godzilla / Godzilla vs. Destroyah
Gonin
Good Men, Good Women
Goodbye South, Goodbye
Harlock Saga
Hermes—Winds of Love
Kizuna
Macross: Box Set
Manji
Martian Successor Nadesico: Endgame
Metropolis
Mobile Suit Gundam: The Battle Begins! Vol. 1
Mobile Suit Gundam Wing: Operation 1
Moon over Tao
Nadia: Secret of Blue Water, Vol. 1: The Adventure Begins
Night on the Galactic Railroad
Oh My Goddess! Vol. 1
Organ
Parasite Eve
Pearl Harbor: The View from Japan
Pokemon: Mewtwo Returns
Ranma 1/2: Random Rhapsody—Wacky Winter Wonderland
Rashomon
Rebirth of Mothra 1 & 2
Rebirth of Mothra 2
Reborn from Hell: Jubei's Revenge
Reborn from Hell: Samurai Armageddon
Record of Lodoss War: Chronicles of the Heroic Knight
Return of the Street Fighter
Riki-Oh: The Story of Ricky
Robotech: The Macross Saga—Extra Disc 1: Elements of Robotechnology

Robotech: The Macross Saga, Vol. 2: Transformation
Rowing Through
Sadistic City
Score
Serial Experiments: Lain
Shogun's Ninja
The Slayers
Soultaker: The Monster Within
Star Blazers: The Comet Empire: Part 1
Star Blazers: The Quest for Iscandar: Series 1
Strange Dawn—Strange World
Strange Dawn, Vol. 2—Strange Journey
The Street Fighter [BCI]
The Street Fighter [BFS]
The Street Fighter's Last Revenge
Sumo Vixens
Sure Death: Revenge
Taboo
Taboo
The Tale of Zatoichi
The Tale of Zatoichi Continues
Tekkaman Blade 2: Complete Collection
Terminatrix
Tokyo Decameron: Three Tales of Madness & Sensuality
Tokyo Mafia: Battle for Shinjuku
Tokyo Mafia: Wrath of the Yakuza
Tokyo Mafia: Yakuza Wars
Urusei Yatsura: TV Series 1
Vampire Hunter D: Bloodlust
Very Private Lessons
Video Girl Ai
Weather Report Girl
X
Zeram 2

Jealousy
Amores Perros
Fast Sofa

Journalism
See: Front Page

Judaism
See also: The Holocaust

Aimee & Jaguar
Divided We Fall
Fiddler on the Roof [2 SE]
Funny Girl
The Garden of the Finzi-Continis
The Golem
Jacob the Liar
Kadosh
Left Luggage
The Life and Times of Hank Greenberg
The Man Who Cried
Radio Days
The Shop on Main Street
Uprising

Jungle Stories
Bela Lugosi Meets a Brooklyn Gorilla
The Diamond of Jeru
The Jungle Book
Jungle Girl
The Lost Continent
The Road to Zanzibar
Tarzan and the Trappers
Tarzan the Fearless
Volunteers
Voodoo Nightmare

Justice Prevails...?
See also: Order in the Court

The Accused
An Eye for an Eye

Ghosts of Mississippi
I Am Sam
Lawman
Reversal of Fortune
The Runaway
Wilde
The Winslow Boy
The Young Land

Kiddie Viddy
See also: Animation & Cartoons

Animated Christmas DVD Double Feature
Baby Dolittle: Neighborhood Animals
Baby Dolittle: World Animals
Baby Mozart
Bear in the Big Blue House: Potty Time with Bear
Caillou: Family Collection, Vol. 1
Dragon Tales
Emmet Otter's Jug-Band Christmas
Madeline at the North Pole
Muppet Family Christmas
Three Stooges Cartoon Classics, Volume 1
Tom and Jerry: The Magic Ring
The World of Sid & Marty Krofft

Kidnapped!
See also: Hostage!; Missing Persons

Along Came a Spider
Baby's Day Out
Benji [Ventura]
The Big Hit [2 SB]
Bravo
Contraband
Don't Say a Word
Double Deception
Everybody's Famous!
I Spit on Your Corpse, I Piss on Your Grave
In the Country Where Nothing Happens
Kidnapped Coed
The Mummy Returns
The Order
Perpetrators of the Crime
Proof of Life
Ruthless People
Son of the Sheik
The Wash
Wheels on Meals

Killer Apes & Monkeys
A*P*E*
Doctor of Doom
Link
Planet of the Apes

Killer Brains
See also: Renegade Body Parts

The Brain that Wouldn't Die

Killer Bugs & Slugs
Arachnid
Attack of the Giant Leeches [Marengo]
Earth vs. the Spider
Empire of the Ants
Mimic 2
The Monster That Challenged the World
The Nest
Rebirth of Mothra 1 & 2
Rebirth of Mothra 2
Roughnecks: Starship Troopers Chronicles—The Homefront Campaign
Roughnecks: Starship Troopers Chronicles—The Klendathu Campaign
The Wasp Woman [2]
The Worm Eaters

Killer Cars
See also: Motor Vehicle Dept.

The Hearse
Mad Max [MGM SE]

Killer Dogs
See also: Dogs

The Hound of the Baskervilles
Pet Sematary 2
Revenge

Killer Dreams
Strange Impersonation
Waking Life

Killer Kiddies
See also: Childhood Visions

The Child
Children of the Corn 5: Fields of Terror
Children of the Corn: Revelation

Killer Plants
Please Don't Eat My Mother
Return of the Killer Tomatoes!

Killer Reptiles
See also: Godzilla & Friends

The Giant Gila Monster
Reptilian
Reptilicus

Killer Rodents
The Bat [GoodTimes]
The Devil Bat
Rats

Killer Sea Critters
See also: Deep Blue

Attack of the Giant Leeches [Marengo]
Blood Surf
Creature from the Black Lagoon
Creatures from the Abyss
Jaws 2
Monster from the Ocean Floor
The Monster That Challenged the World
Obsession
The Phantom from 10,000 Leagues
She Creature

Stephen King (Adaptations)
Carrie
Graveyard Shift
Hearts in Atlantis
The Shining [2 SE]
Silver Bullet
Sometimes They Come Back
Sometimes They Come Back...Again
Stephen King's Golden Years
Stephen King's Rose Red
Stephen King's The Langoliers
Tales from the Darkside: The Movie

Korean (Production)
A*P*E*
Bruce Lee: A Warrior's Journey
Chunhyang
Cold War
Eagle vs. Silver Fox
Fury in the Shaolin Temple
Happy End
Lies
Reptilian
Tell Me Something
White Badge

Korean War
The Korean War in Color
MacArthur
M*A*S*H [FS]

The Last Place on Earth
Shackleton
Stiff Upper Lips
Troubles
The Winslow Boy

Period Piece: 1920s
The Cotton Club
The Great Gatsby
Haunted
The Lover
The Luzhin Defence
Woman in Black

Period Piece: 1930s
Break of Dawn
Child Star: The Shirley Temple Story
The Education of Little Tree
The Field [Artisan]
Liam
The Man Who Cried
The Mummy Returns
The Phantom Lover
The Remains of the Day
Shanghai Triad

Period Piece: 1940s
Aimee & Jaguar
Back to the Secret Garden
The Curse of the Jade Scorpion
Focus
Lost in Yonkers
The Man Who Wasn't There
Mararia
The Others [CE]
Pollock [SE]
Possessed
The Runaway

Period Piece: 1950s
An American Rhapsody
Boycott
Dark Blue World
Diner
The Heart of Dixie
In His Life: The John Lennon Story
Introducing Dorothy Dandridge
Jailbreakers
New York in the Fifties
Pollock [SE]
The Road Home
Round Midnight
The Scent of Green Papaya
Shake, Rattle & Rock!
Strange Invaders
Three Wishes
Two Family House

Period Piece: 1960s
See also: Beatniks
Ali
Angels Hard As They Come
Blast-Off Girls / Just for the Hell of It
Company Man
The Dish
Fritz the Cat
Head
Hearts in Atlantis
The Hippie Revolt
In His Life: The John Lennon Story
In the Mood for Love [SE]
The Locusts
Mondo Mod / The Hippie Revolt
Rainbow Bridge
Riding in Cars with Boys
The Sandlot
61*
'68
Skipped Parts
That Thing You Do!
Thirteen Days
Who'll Stop the Rain?

Period Piece: 1970s
Ali

Almost Famous: Untitled—The Bootleg Cut
Blow
Hedwig and the Angry Inch
The Ice Storm
Jill the Ripper
Left Luggage
The Legend of Rita
Riding in Cars with Boys
Shot in the Heart
Spy Game
Water Drops on Burning Rocks

Period Piece: 1980s
Blow
Donnie Darko
An Everlasting Piece
Hurlyburly
The Legend of Rita
Riding in Cars with Boys
Rock Star
Spy Game
Wet Hot American Summer
The Wood

Persian Gulf War
See also: Desert War/Foreign Legion
Courage Under Fire
Reflex Action

Phone Terror
Sorry, Wrong Number
When a Stranger Calls

Photography
See: Shutterbugs

Physical Problems
See also: Blindness; Deafness; Mental Retardation; Savants
Coming Home
Don't Say a Word
The Elephant Man
Follow the Stars Home
Freddy Got Fingered
The Hunchback of Notre Dame
The Hunchback of Notre Dame
The Kid Brother
Orphans
The Penalty
Silver Bullet
What's Eating Gilbert Grape

Pirates
See also: Island Fare; Swashbucklers
Captain Kidd [Marengo]
Hook
Long John Silver
Peter Pan [2 SE]
The Princess and the Pirate
The Princess Bride [2 SE]
The Swiss Family Robinson

Poetry
The Color of Pomegranates

Poetry Adaptations
Cats [Universal UE]
The Charge of the Light Brigade
The Odyssey

Poisons
Doomwatch
Safe

Police Detectives
Along Came a Spider
Beautiful Creatures
Dead Sexy
Dick Tracy
Dick Tracy [Marengo]
Dick Tracy [VCI]
Dick Tracy, Detective
Dick Tracy Meets Gruesome
Dick Tracy vs. Cueball
Dick Tracy's Dilemma
The Enforcer

From Hell [DLE]
Hitched
Jill the Ripper
Lantana
Magnum Force
Revenge Quest
Tell Me Something
True Blue
Un Flic
What Your Eyes Don't See
When the Sky Falls

Polish (Production)
The Saragossa Manuscript

Politics
See also: Presidency
Citizen Cohn
crazy/beautiful
Fidel
Fires Within
General Idi Amin Dada: A Self Portrait
The House of the Spirits
Indochine
Medium Cool [SE]
The Pallisers, Vol. 2
The Pallisers, Vol. 3
Richard III
Running Mates
Speechless
Timecop

Pornography
See also: Sex & Sexuality; Sexploitation
The Pornographer
South Bronx Heroes

Portuguese (Production)
Me You Them
Testamento

Post Apocalypse
See also: Negative Utopia; Technology—Rampant
A.I.: Artificial Intelligence
Circuitry Man
The Handmaid's Tale
Hell Comes to Frogtown
The Last Man on Earth
Le Dernier Combat
Lord of the Flies
Mad Max [MGM SE]
Memoirs of a Survivor
On the Beach
Plughead Rewired: Circuitry Man 2
Rats
Silent Running [Universal]
The Slime People

Postwar
See also: Veterans
After the War
Courage Under Fire
House
Le Dernier Combat
Love Is a Many Splendored Thing
Maria's Lovers
Plenty [Anchor Bay]
QB VII
Who'll Stop the Rain?

POW/MIA
See also: Vietnam War; War; World War II
Empire of the Sun
In Love and War
McKenzie Break
Raiders of Leyte Gulf
Robert Louis Stevenson's St. Ives
Three Came Home
Three Wishes
Von Ryan's Express

Pregnant Men
Enemy Mine

Pregnant Pauses
See also: Bringing Up Baby
The Circle
Coming Out
Divided We Fall
Hell Comes to Frogtown
Maybe Baby
Maze
Me You Them
Mists of Avalon
The Object of My Affection
Progeny
Riding in Cars with Boys
Saturday Night and Sunday Morning
Seducing Maarya
Skipped Parts
Sugar & Spice
Time and Tide
Two Family House
The Unborn

Prep School
See also: Hell High School; Teen Angst
Harry Potter and the Sorcerer's Stone
The Smokers
Tart

Presidency
See also: Camelot (New); Politics
Air Force One [2 SB]
Forrest Gump [SCE]
Kennedy
Thirteen Days

Price of Fame
See also: Rags to Riches
The Bad and the Beautiful
Citizen Kane
The Cotton Club
Echo Park
Eddie and the Cruisers
The Five Heartbeats
Frances [Anchor Bay]
Jo Jo Dancer, Your Life Is Calling
Lenny
The Magnificent Ambersons
Mephisto
Mommie Dearest
Pecker (John Waters Collection Vol. 1)
Stardom
You Light Up My Life

Prison
See: Great Escapes; Men in Prison; POW/MIA; Women in Prison

Private Eyes
Bad Seed
Big Empty
The Curse of the Jade Scorpion
Human Desires
Mr. Wong, Detective
Murder by Death
Peter Gunn: Set One
Trixie

Propaganda
See also: Patriotism & Paranoia; Politics
The Atomic Cafe [SE]
Blood on the Sun [Image]
Cuban Story
Guadalcanal Diary
Invasion U.S.A.
Que Viva Mexico
Sex Madness
The Thief
Tomorrow's Children

Prostitutes
See: Oldest Profession

Protests
See also: Rebel with a Cause
Forrest Gump [SCE]
Hairspray (John Waters Collection Vol. 1)

Psychiatry
See: Shrinks

Psychic Abilities
See also: Mystery & Suspense; Supernatural Comedies
Firestarter 2: Rekindled
From Hell [DLE]
The Gift
Hearts in Atlantis
Life without Dick
The Mothman Prophecies
Roughnecks: Starship Troopers Chronicles—The Homefront Campaign
The Sixth Sense [Buena Vista]
Stephen King's Rose Red

Psycho-Thriller
See also: Mystery & Suspense
Cape Fear
Day of Wrath
Deceiver
Facing the Enemy
Fatal Attraction [SCE]
The Glass House
Haunted
I Never Promised You a Rose Garden
The Invisible Ghost
Jealousy
Joy Ride
Kill by Inches
Les Bonnes Femmes
Letters from a Killer
The Man Who Haunted Himself
The Mark
Marnie
The Mind Benders
The Net [2 SE]
Paranoia
Play Misty for Me
Playgirl Killer
Requiem for Murder
Seconds
The Silence of the Lambs [MGM SE]
The Sixth Sense [Buena Vista]
Snapdragon
Sorry, Wrong Number
Strange Illusion
Svengali
The Temp
Unforgettable
Unlawful Entry
The Vanishing [Criterion]
Vengeance of the Dead
Victim of Love

Psychotics/Sociopaths
See also: Roommates from Hell
Breakdown
Cape Fear
Carrie
Fatal Attraction [SCE]
Helter Skelter Murders
Mademoiselle
Mommie Dearest
Mondo Balordo
Playgirl Killer
Psycho 2
Retroactive
The Shining [2 SE]
The Temp
Twin Peaks: Fire Walk with Me
Unlawful Entry
With a Friend Like Harry
Zero Degrees Kelvin

He Said, She Said
Head over Heels
High Spirits
Impromptu
Indiscreet
Irma La Douce
It
Jerry Maguire [2 SE]
Joe versus the Volcano
Just One Night
Kate & Leopold
Kill Me Later
The Lady Eve
Le Magnifique
Lena's Holiday
Let's Make Love
Life without Dick
Little City
Lonely Hearts
Lost in Yonkers
Love Can Seriously Damage
    Your Health
Love Goggles
Love on a Diet
Love Potion 9
Luminarias
The Man Who Loved Women
Mannequin
Me, Myself, and Irene
Mickey Blue Eyes
Mrs. Winterbourne
Money Buys Happiness
Morgan: A Suitable Case for
    Treatment
My Best Friend's Wedding [2
    SE]
Olive Juice
On the Line
One Fine Day
The Owl and the Pussycat
Para Para Sakura
A Paradise under the Stars
The Personals
Play It Again, Sam
Please Not Now!
The Prince and the Showgirl
The Princess and the Pirate
The Purple Rose of Cairo
Queens Logic
Robert Louis Stevenson's St.
    Ives
Romantic Comedy
Runaway Bride
Sabrina
Seems Like Old Times
Serendipity
Short Circuit
Sidewalks of New York
Smiling Fish & Goat on Fire
Soapdish
Someone Like You
Speechless
Strictly Ballroom
Sweet Talker
The Tall Guy
They Got Me Covered
Tieta of Agreste
Til There Was You
A Touch of Class
Two Ninas
The Wedding Planner

Romantic Drama
The Age of Innocence
Aimee & Jaguar
All That Heaven Allows
Angel Eyes
Angels and Insects
The Beast
Blood and Sand
Breathless
Bride of the Wind
Brooklyn Babylon
Cabiria
Calendar
Carrington
Chunhyang
City of Glass
Cor, Blimey!
The Cranes Are Flying
crazy/beautiful
Cuando Habla El Corazon

Cyrano de Bergerac
Doctor Zhivago
Ecstasy
84 Charing Cross Road
Falling in Love
Fires Within
First Love and Other Pains /
    One of Them
The French Lieutenant's
    Woman
Girl with Green Eyes
Glitter
Good Men, Good Women
The Great Gatsby
Hammers over the Anvil
Hanover Street
Husbands and Wives
In Love and War
In the Mood for Love [SE]
Indecent Proposal
Indochine
Jailbreakers
Kings Go Forth
Lagaan: Once upon a Time in
    India
The Last Train
Le Petit Soldat
Lies
Lorna Doone
Love and Basketball
Love Is a Many Splendored
    Thing
The Love of Jeanne Ney
Love Songs
The Lover
The Luzhin Defence
The Man Who Cried
Nelly et Monsieur Arnaud
Next Time
Pay It Forward
Perfect Love
Proof of Life
Queen Bee
Queer As Folk: The Complete
    First Season
Random Hearts
Regeneration / Young
    Romance
The Road Home
Sadie Thompson
Sayonara
Scarlett
Summertime
Tender Mercies [Anchor Bay]
Therese Raquin
To Gillian on Her 37th Birth-
    day
Wuthering Heights
You Light Up My Life

Romantic Triangles
    See also: Otherwise Engaged

The Age of Innocence
Amores Perros
Bandits
Bride of the Wind
Bull Durham [MGM SE]
Cactus Flower
Calendar
Captain Corelli's Mandolin
Carrington
Coming Out
Dark Blue World
Dead in the Water
Driven
The Favor
The Golden Bowl
Happy End
Indecent Proposal
Intersection
Mararia
Matter of Trust
Maze
Mists of Avalon
My Best Friend's Wedding [2
    SE]
Olive Juice
Out of Africa
Pearl Harbor
Risk
Sabrina

Saturday Night and Sunday
    Morning
Stonewall
The Storm Riders
Summer Catch
Town and Country
The Trio
Two Ninas
Un Flic

Roommates from Hell
    See also:
    Psychotics/Sociopaths

Lip Service
Zero Degrees Kelvin

Royalty
    See also: Biopics: Royalty; His-
    torical Drama; Medieval
    Romps; Period Piece

Atlantis: The Lost Empire
    [CE]
Barbarian Queen 2: The
    Empress Strikes Back
Black Knight
Catherine the Great
Dracula: The Dark Prince
Dune [2 SE]
Elizabeth
Hamlet
The Iron Mask
Ivanhoe
King Lear
The King's Guard
Macbeth
Mists of Avalon
The Musketeer
The Prince and the Showgirl
The Princess Bride
The Princess Diaries
Richard III
The Saragossa Manuscript
Sex and the Emperor
Shrek [SE]
Snow White and the Seven
    Dwarfs [PE]
Snow White: The Fairest of
    Them All
Sword & the Sorcerer
Victoria & Albert
Willow

Running
Forrest Gump [SCE]
The Long Run

Russian (Production)
The Amphibian Man
The Arena
Ashik Kerib
Ballad of a Soldier
Barbara the Fair with the
    Silken Hair
The Color of Pomegranates
Come and See
The Cranes Are Flying
Earth
Father Frost
The Legend of Suram
    Fortress / Ashik Kerib
The Mirror
Que Viva Mexico
Siberian Lady Macbeth
Tchaikovsky
Viy

Salespeople
    See also: Corporate Shenani-
    gans

Cadillac Man
My First Mister
Risk
Salesman
Tin Men

Samurai
The Legendary Strike
Moon over Tao
Rashomon
Reborn from Hell: Jubei's
    Revenge

Reborn from Hell: Samurai
    Armageddon
Taboo

Sanity Check
    See also: Mental Hospitals;
    Shrinks

Along for the Ride
Anguish
Behind Locked Doors
The Caveman's Valentine
Chasing Sleep
Clockwise
Cobra Verde
Dementia 13 [Roan]
Desperate Living (John
    Waters Collection Vol. 2)
The Devil Bat
Dr. Jekyll and Mr. Hyde [Kino]
Dr. Mabuse, The Gambler
Donnie Darko
Don't Say a Word
Fever
Final
Frances [Anchor Bay]
Fright
The Gift
A Girl Thing
Hamlet
Hard Luck
How to Get Ahead in Advertis-
    ing
I Never Promised You a Rose
    Garden
The Invisible Ghost
K-PAX
The Locusts
Manhunter [LE]
Mr. Deeds Goes to Town
Morgan: A Suitable Case for
    Treatment
Open Your Eyes
The Others [CE]
Pecker (John Waters Collec-
    tion Vol. 1)
Play Misty for Me
Psychic Killer
Psycho 2
Return to Cabin by the Lake
Revenge in the House of
    Usher
The Ruling Class
Schramm
The Scout
Session 9
The Shining [2 SE]
The Silence of the Lambs
    [MGM SE]
Some Folks Call It a Sling
    Blade
Soul Survivors
Strait-Jacket
Strange Illusion
Stuart Bliss
Twin Peaks: Fire Walk with
    Me
Under the Sand
White Badge
Woman in Black

Satanism
    See also: Demons & Wizards;
    Devils; Occult

The Bloodsuckers
The Devil's Prey
The Exorcist [2]: The Version
    You've Never Seen
Mind, Body & Soul
Revenge
Satan's Cheerleaders
Servants of Twilight

Satire & Parody
    See also: Black Comedy; Com-
    edy; Genre Spoofs

The Awful Truth: The Com-
    plete Second Season
Bill & Ted's Bogus Journey
Bill & Ted's Excellent Adven-
    ture
The Blair Thumb

Bread and Chocolate
Bring It On
Britannia Hospital
Caveman
The Cheap Detective
Clockwise
The Coca-Cola Kid
Galaxina
Going Places
Hairspray (John Waters Col-
    lection Vol. 1)
Jabberwocky
Jay and Silent Bob Strike
    Back
Monty Python Live
Monty Python's Flying Circus
    Set 1
Murder by Death
Polyester (John Waters Col-
    lection Vol. 2)
The Princess Bride [2 SE]
Putney Swope
Return of Captain Invincible
Romeo Is Bleeding
The Ruling Class
Running Mates
Seduction of Mimi
Series 7: The Contenders
The Sexy Sixth Sense
The Sid Caesar Collection:
    The Fan Favorites
Stay Tuned
Stiff Upper Lips
Strange Invaders
Sullivan's Travels
Thumb Wars
Thumbtanic
Transylvania 6-5000
2001: A Space Travesty
UHF
Waiting for Guffman
The Worm Eaters
Zelig
Zeta One
Zoolander
Zorro, the Gay Blade

Savants
    See also: Mental Retardation

Forrest Gump [SCE]
King Lear

Scams, Stings & Cons
    See also: Heists

After the Fox
Blackheart
The Cheaters
Dangerous Summer
The Dead Pool
Dirty Rotten Scoundrels
    [MGM]
Gang Related
Heartbreakers
The Lady Eve
The Learning Curve
Mo' Money
Never Again Never Again
The Prime Gig
Risk
The Road to Zanzibar
Ruthless People
Slackers
Stavisky
Sweet Talker
White River

School Daze
    See also: Campus Capers; Hell
    High School

Accident
American Pie [2 UE]
Baby Shakespeare
crazy/beautiful
The Educational Archives Vol-
    ume 1: Sex & Drugs
The Educational Archives Vol-
    ume 2: Social Engineering
    101
Get Over It!
Hard Lessons
In a Class of His Own

Showbiz Comedies

America's Sweethearts
The Big Broadcast of 1938
Everybody's Famous!
Hollywood Shuffle
Jackie's Back
Jay and Silent Bob Strike Back
Josie and the Pussycats
Let's Make Love
Mr. Saturday Night [MGM]
The Muppet Movie
The Muppets Take Manhattan
The Party
The Prince and the Showgirl
The Royal Family
Soapdish
Star Spangled Rhythm
Waiting for Guffman

Showbiz Dramas

The Anniversary Party
Blast-Off Girls / Just for the Hell of It
Child Star: The Shirley Temple Story
Cor, Blimey!
Dancing in September
Frances [Anchor Bay]
Funny Girl
Funny Lady
Introducing Dorothy Dandridge
Lena's Dreams
Lenny
Mommie Dearest
State and Main

Showbiz Musicals

See also: Musical Fantasy; Musicals; Showbiz Comedies

Glitter
Hedwig and the Angry Inch
Moulin Rouge [SE]
The Suburbans
The Temptations
That Thing You Do!

Showbiz Thrillers

The Dead Pool
Kiss Tomorrow Goodbye
Return to Cabin by the Lake
Return to Horror High
Satan in High Heels
The Stunt Man

Shrinks

See also: Mental Hospitals; Sanity Check

Agnes of God
Coming Apart
Dark Asylum
Diary of a Sex Addict
Don't Say a Word
Final
A Girl Thing
Halloween [EE]
Human Prey
I Never Promised You a Rose Garden
K-PAX
Lantana
The Man Who Loved Women
Monkeybone
On the Edge
One Fine Day
Open Your Eyes
Panic
The Prince of Tides
Progeny
Silent Fall
The Sixth Sense [Buena Vista]
Sometimes They Come Back...Again
Victim of Love
The Visit

Shutterbugs

See also: Front Page

Calendar

Helmut Newton: Frames from the Edge
Memento [1]
Memento [2 SE]
Pecker (John Waters Collection Vol. 1)
Perfume
Shadow Magic
W. Eugene Smith: Photography Made Difficult

Silent Films

Blood and Sand
Broken Blossoms [Kino]
Cabiria
The Cheat [Kino]
Diary of a Lost Girl
Dr. Jekyll and Mr. Hyde [Kino]
Dr. Mabuse, The Gambler
Don Q, Son of Zorro
Down to the Sea in Ships
Earth
Faust
A Fool There Was
The Golem
Haxan: Witchcraft through the Ages
His Majesty, the Scarecrow of Oz
The Iron Mask
It
The Last Laugh
The Love of Jeanne Ney
Mark of Zorro [2] / Don Q, Son of Zorro
Nosferatu
Othello
The Penalty
The Plastic Age
Regeneration / Young Romance
The Road to Ruin
Sadie Thompson
Slapstick Encyclopedia (1909–27)
The Thief
The Wizard of Oz

Neil Simon (Adaptations)

California Suite
The Cheap Detective
Lost in Yonkers
Murder by Death
Seems Like Old Times

Single Parents

See also: Bringing Up Baby; Parenthood

Hearts in Atlantis
I Am Sam
Kramer vs. Kramer
One Fine Day
Pay It Forward
The Sixth Sense [Buena Vista]
Things You Can Tell Just by Looking at Her

Sixties

See: Period Piece: 1960s

Skating

See also: Hockey

The Ice Rink
Schizo

Skiing

Avalanche
On Her Majesty's Secret Service
Out Cold

Skydiving

Point Break

Slapstick Comedy

See also: Comedy; Screwball Comedy

Abbott and Costello Meet the Mummy

The Adventures of Buckaroo Banzai Across the Eighth Dimension [SE]
After the Fox
The Animal
Any Which Way You Can
Arbuckle & Keaton, Vol. 1 (1917–19)
Arbuckle & Keaton, Vol. 2 (1918–20)
Baby's Day Out
The Bad News Bears
The Bad News Bears Go to Japan
The Bad News Bears in Breaking Training
Benny Hill Golden Greats
Cheech and Chong's The Corsican Brothers
Corky Romano
Drunken Master
Fishing with Gandhi
Freddy Got Fingered
It's a Mad, Mad, Mad, Mad World
The New Daughters of Joshua Cabe
The Party
Rescue from Gilligan's Island
Say It Isn't So
Slapstick Encyclopedia (1909–27)
Stripes
Three Stooges: All Time Favorites
Three Stooges: Dizzy Doctors
Three Stooges: Healthy, Wealthy, and Dumb
Three Stooges: Three Smart Saps

Slavery

See also: Civil Rights

Candyman 2: Farewell to the Flesh
Cobra Verde
Planet of the Apes
The Road to Morocco [Universal]
The Robe
Roots

Small-Town Sheriffs

Hard Luck
The Mothman Prophecies
Red Rock West

Smuggler's Blues

See also: Crime & Criminals; Drug Abuse

Blow
Exit Wounds
Jimmy Zip
Memento [1]
Memento [2 SE]
Millennium Dragon
Our Lady of the Assassins
Outta Time
The Street Fighter's Last Revenge
Street Vengeance
The Taste of Others
Time and Tide
Training Day
Two Coyotes

Snakes

See also: Killer Reptiles

Boa
Venomous

South African (Production)

The Long Run

Southern Belles

See also: American South

Queen Bee
Scarlett

Space Operas

See also: Alien Beings— Benign; Alien Beings—Vicious

The Dish
First Men in the Moon
Flight to Mars
Gattaca [2 SB]
Mars: The Red Planet
Planet of the Apes
Planet of the Dinosaurs
Planet of the Vampires
Silent Running [Universal]
Spaceballs
Star Slammer
Star Trek: The Motion Picture [DE]
Star Trek 3: The Search for Spock
Star Trek: The Next Generation—The Complete 1st Season
2001: A Space Travesty

Spaghetti Western

See also: Western Comedy; Westerns

A Bullet for the General
Find a Place to Die
Four of the Apocalypse

Spanish (Production)

Anguish
Cabeza de Vaca
Companeros
Dr. Orloff's Monster
Hell of the Living Dead
Jealousy
Killer Barbys
Life Is to Whistle
Living It Up
Love Can Seriously Damage Your Health
Mararia
Nico and Dani
Not Love Just Frenzy
Open Your Eyes
A Paradise under the Stars
Planet of the Vampires
The Sadistic Baron Von Klaus
That Obscure Object of Desire
Things I Left in Havanna
Vacas
Why Do They Call It Love When They Mean Sex?
The Yellow Fountain

Spanish Civil War

Vacas

Spies & Espionage

See also: Feds; Foreign Intrigue; Terrorism

The Apocalypse Watch
The Avengers '68
Company Man
Contraband
The Doll Squad
Funeral in Berlin
Hard Ticket to Hawaii
Head over Heels
La Cage aux Folles 2
Le Magnifique
Le Professionnel
The Man with the Golden Gun
The Mind Benders
My Favorite Blonde
Never Say Never Again
On Her Majesty's Secret Service
Picasso Trigger
Rescue from Gilligan's Island
Retrievers
The Russia House
Secret Agent
Sell Out
Spy Game
Spy Kids
The Stranger [Delta/Laserlight]
Swordfish

The Tailor of Panama
They Got Me Covered
The Thief
Wanted: Dead or Alive
Zeta One

Sports

See: Baseball; Basketball; Bicycling; Biopics: Sports; Boxing; Football; Golf; Hockey; The Olympics; Running; Skating; Skiing; Skydiving; Sports Comedies; Sports Dramas; Surfing

Sports Comedies

Angels in the Outfield
The Bad News Bears
The Bad News Bears Go to Japan
The Bad News Bears in Breaking Training
Bingo Long Traveling All-Stars & Motor Kings
Bull Durham [MGM SE]
Jerry Maguire [2 SE]
Major League 2
Major League 3: Back to the Minors
Rookie of the Year
The Sandlot
The Scout
Slap Shot [2]
Slap Shot 2: Breaking the Ice
Space Jam [2 EE]
Squeeze Play [DC]

Sports Dramas

All the Right Moves
American Flyers
Backyard Dogs
Breaking Away
The Long Run
Love and Basketball
O
Red Surf
Requiem for a Heavyweight
Rollerball
Rowing Through
61*
Summer Catch
Where Angels Dance

Spousal Abuse

See also: Sexual Abuse

Angel Eyes
The Gift
Love Come Down
The Opponent

Stagestruck

See also: Showbiz Comedies; Showbiz Dramas; Showbiz Thrillers

Broadway Danny Rose
Carnegie Hall
Let's Make Love
The Phantom Lover
Stagefright
Va Savoir

Stalked!

See also: Obsessive Love

Christina's House
Fatal Attraction [SCE]
Klute
Stalker

Stepparents

See also: Family Ties; Parenthood

Domestic Disturbance
Lassie
Snow White: The Fairest of Them All

Stewardesses

See also: Airborne

Naughty Stewardesses

Strained Suburbia

Desperate Hours

Cowboy
Dracula: The Dark Prince
The Elephant Man
Evel Knievel
The Hunter
Lenny
The Life and Times of Hank Greenberg
Manufacturing Consent: Noam Chomsky and the Media
Nostradamus: His Life and Prophecies / Prophecy and Prediction
The Sicilian

3-D Flicks
Alien Adventure
Creature from the Black Lagoon
Haunted Castle
It Came from Outer Space
Spacehunter: Adventures in the Forbidden Zone

Thrillers
See: Erotic Thrillers; Mystery & Suspense; Psycho-Thrillers; Showbiz Thrillers

Thumbs Up
Blood Simple
The Forsaken
The Hitcher
Pink Flamingos

Time Travel
See also: Rescue Missions Involving Time Travel

Bill & Ted's Bogus Journey
Bill & Ted's Excellent Adventure
The Indian in the Cupboard
Just Visiting
The Terminator [2 SE]
Terminatrix
Timecop
Timerider
The Tomorrow Man

Time Warped
Black Knight
Groundhog Day [2 SE]
Kate & Leopold
Matthew Blackheart: Monster Smasher
Retroactive

Torn in Two (or More)
Dr. Jekyll and Mr. Hyde [Kino]
Dr. Jekyll and Sister Hyde
Exorcist 3: Legion
Jekyll & Hyde: The Musical
Me, Myself, and Irene

Torrid Love Scenes
See also: Sex & Sexuality; Sex on the Beach; Sexploitation

Atlantic City
Basic Instinct [2 SE]
Bram Stoker's Dracula [SB]
Bull Durham [MGM SE]
Crimes of Passion [2]
Fatal Attraction [SCE]
The Lover
Wild Orchid

Tragedy
See also: Drama; Tearjerkers

Electra
The French Lieutenant's Woman
Gandhi
Hamlet
The Hunchback of Notre Dame
Il Grido
King Lear
Love Is a Many Splendored Thing
Macbeth
Madame Butterfly

The Mummy
O
Othello
A Place in the Sun
Queen Bee
The World according to Garp
Wuthering Heights

Trains
See also: Subways

Boxcar Bertha
Closely Watched Trains
Courage Under Fire
The Harvey Girls
The Journey of Natty Gann
The Lady Eve
The Last Siege
Mrs. Winterbourne
Running Scared
Those Who Love Me Can Take the Train
3:10 to Yuma
Throw Momma from the Train
Unbreakable
Von Ryan's Express

Transvestites & Transsexuals
See: Gender Bending

Trapped with a Killer!
See also: Psychotics/Sociopaths

Air Force One [2 SB]
Extremities
Fatal Attraction [SCE]
Manhunter [LE]
The Shining [2 SE]
The Silence of the Lambs [MGM SE]
When a Stranger Calls

Treasure Hunt
Abbott and Costello Meet the Mummy
The Diamond of Jeru
The Goonies
Lara Croft: Tomb Raider
Legend of the Red Dragon
Rat Race
Slow Burn
The Triangle

Trees & Forests
See also: Wilderness

Axe 'Em
Dr. Dolittle 2
Evil Dead [LE]
Ferngully
The Many Adventures of Winnie the Pooh
Out of Time
The Watcher in the Woods

Triads
See also: Gangs

Cops on a Mission
Fists of Bruce Lee
Rich and Famous / Tragic Hero
Time and Tide
Too Many Ways to Be No. 1
Tragic Hero

Troma Films
The Best of Tromadance
Cannibal! The Musical
Christmas Evil
Rabid Grannies
Squeeze Play [DC]
Stuck on You! [DC]
The Toxic Avenger, Part 3: The Last Temptation of Toxie [DC]
Troma's Edge TV: Vol. 1

True Crime
See also: Crime & Criminals; This Is Your Life; True Stories

American Tragedy
Bully
Daughter of Darkness

Echo of Murder
From Hell [DLE]
The Great St. Louis Bank Robbery
Helter Skelter Murders
Murder in Coweta County
Paradise Lost 2: Revelations
When the Sky Falls

True Stories
See also: Biopics; This Is My Life; This Is Your Life; True Crime

The Accused
Aimee & Jaguar
The Amy Fisher Story
Andre
Black Hawk Down
Blow
Breast Men
Cabeza de Vaca
Casualties of War
Chopper
The Dish
84 Charing Cross Road
Empire of the Sun
Enemy at the Gates
First Time Felon
Ghosts of Mississippi
Greenfingers
Hard Lessons
Harlan County War
He Walked by Night [BFS]
Hostage High
In a Class of His Own
In Love and War
In the Time of the Butterflies
Inherit the Wind
Into Thin Air: Death on Everest
The Last Place on Earth
The Miracle of the Cards
The Mothman Prophecies
Not without My Daughter
Possessed
The Puppetmaster
A Real American Hero
Red Cherry
Reversal of Fortune
Riding in Cars with Boys
Scandal
Searching for Bobby Fischer
Shackleton
Shot in the Heart
Southpaw
Stonewall
Thirteen Days
Three Came Home
Triumph of the Spirit
The Wild Child

TV Series
All in the Family: The Complete First Season
The Avengers '68
The Awful Truth: The Complete Second Season
Dark Shadows: DVD Collection 1
The Darling Buds of May
Destination Nightmare
Elvis: '68 Comeback Special
Friends: The Complete First Season
Gumby, Vol. 1
Jack the Ripper: 4 Tales of the Supernatural
Jeeves & Wooster: The Complete Second Season
The Larry Sanders Show: The Complete First Season
The Legend of the Lone Ranger
Lone Ranger and the Lost City of Gold
Mr. Show: The Complete First & Second Seasons
Monty Python Live
Monty Python's Flying Circus Set 1
My Little Margie: Collection 2 (1952–55)

Oz: The Complete First Season
The Prisoner
Queer As Folk: The Complete First Season
The Saint
Secret Agent
Sex and the City: Season 1
Sex and the City: The Complete Third Season
The Sid Caesar Collection: The Fan Favorites
The Simpsons: The Complete First Season
The Sopranos: The Complete First Season
The Sopranos: The Complete Second Season
Space: 1999 Set 1
Star Trek: The Next Generation—The Complete 1st Season
Star Trek: The Next Generation—The Complete 2nd Season
Til Death Us Do Part
Upstairs, Downstairs: The Complete First Season
Upstairs, Downstairs: The Second Season
Walt Disney Treasures: Davy Crockett
Walt Disney Treasures: Disneyland USA
The World of Sid & Marty Krofft

Twins
See also: Family Ties

Basket Case [2 SE]
Holiday in the Sun
Major League 3: Back to the Minors
The Parent Trap
Passport to Paris
Rebirth of Mothra 1 & 2
Rebirth of Mothra 2
Winning London
The Young Girls of Rochefort

Unexplained Phenomena
Carrie
The Disappearance of Flight 412
The Fury
Mondo Balordo
Nomads
Phenomenon—The Lost Archives: American Midnight / H.A.A.R.P.
Phenomenon—The Lost Archives: Monopoly Men / An Unknown Encounter
Truly, Madly, Deeply
Twin Peaks: The First Season
Unbreakable
The X-Files: Season 4

Universal's Classic Horror
Creature from the Black Lagoon
Dracula's Daughter
Frankenstein Meets the Wolfman
The Ghost of Frankenstein
House of Frankenstein
The Mummy's Curse
The Mummy's Ghost
The Mummy's Hand
The Mummy's Tomb
Son of Dracula
Son of Frankenstein
Werewolf of London

Urban Drama
All or Nothing
Baby Boy
Better Dayz
Black and Blue
Colors
Dealin' Dirty

Deep Trouble
Drive By
Fresh
Gang Related
Hard Lessons
Loser
Out of Sync
Random Acts of Violence
Rappin'-N-Rhyming
Road Dogz
Rockin' with a Bullet
Squeeze
Ten Benny
Training Day
Zebrahead

Urban Gangstas
See also: Gangs; Urban Drama

Better Dayz

U.S. Marshals
See also: Loner Cops; Westerns

South of Heaven, West of Hell
Texas Rangers
Tombstone [2]

Vacations
American Pie 2
An American Werewolf in London [CE Universal]
Bread and Tulips
California Suite
Fraternity Vacation
Hot Pursuit
Hot Summer
Lena's Holiday
National Lampoon's European Vacation
Nico and Dani
Stealing Beauty
Vibration
With a Friend Like Harry

Vampire Babes
See also: Vampires

Blood: The Last Vampire
Dracula's Daughter
The Erotic Rites of Countess Dracula
The Forsaken
Lust for a Vampire
Vamp
Vampire Obsession

Vampires
See also: Dracula; Vampire Babes

Attack from Mars
Blood Thirst
The Bloodsuckers
Bram Stoker's Dracula [SB]
The Breed
Buffy the Vampire Slayer
Buffy the Vampire Slayer: Season 1
Count Yorga, Vampire
Curse of the Vampires
Dark Shadows: DVD Collection 1
The Devil Bat
Dracula 2000
The Forsaken
Ganja and Hess
House of Frankenstein
The Last Man on Earth
Nosferatu
Planet of the Vampires
The Rape of the Vampire
The Scars of Dracula
Scooby-Doo and the Reluctant Werewolf
She Lives by Night
Son of Dracula
Theatre of Death
Ultraviolet
Vampire Hunter D: Bloodlust
Vampire in Brooklyn
Vampires in Havana

Rabbits; Talking Animals; Wilderness

Andre
The Animal
Animals at Play: Cute and Cuddly
Baby Dolittle: Neighborhood Animals
Baby Dolittle: World Animals
The Bear
Beastmaster
Dr. Dolittle 2
Dumbo
Escape to Grizzly Mountain
Every Which Way But Loose
Fly Away Home [2 SE]
Hatari!
The Many Adventures of Winnie the Pooh
Pet Sematary 2
Running Wild
The Secret of NIMH
Watership Down
Whispers: An Elephant's Tale

Wilderness
See also: Trees & Forests

Arctic Blue
The Bear
Black Robe [MGM]
Cannibal! The Musical
Cross Creek
Silver Wolf
Violent Zone
Walt Disney Treasures: Davy Crockett
Zero Degrees Kelvin

Witchcraft
See also: Demons & Wizards; Occult

The City of the Dead
Day of Wrath
Dead and Rotting
Sabrina, the Animated Series: Sabrina's World
Snow White: The Fairest of Them All
Viy
Witchouse 3: Demon Fire
The Worst Witch

Witness Protection Program
See also: Organized Crime; U.S. Marshals

The Pact
Romeo Is Bleeding
Sister Act

The Wolfman
See also: Werewolves

Frankenstein Meets the Wolfman
House of Frankenstein
The Wolfman

Women
See: Femme Fatale; Monster Moms; Westrogens; Women Cops; Women in Prison; Wonder Women

Women Cops
See also: Cops

Corky Romano
The Enforcer
Lady in Blue
Pendulum
The Silence of the Lambs [MGM SE]

Women in Prison
See also: Exploitation; Men in Prison; Sexploitation

The Big Bird Cage
Caged Heat
The Circle
I Want to Live!
Star Slammer
10 Violent Women
Women in Cages

Women in War
See also: Korean War; Vietnam War; Wonder Women; World War I; World War II

Courage Under Fire
Rodgers & Hammerstein's South Pacific

Wonder Women
Amazons and Gladiators
Attack of the 60-Foot Centerfold
Barbarian Queen
Barbarian Queen 2: The Empress Strikes Back
Big Bad Mama 2
Buffy the Vampire Slayer
Crouching Tiger, Hidden Dragon [2 SB]
Doctor of Doom
The Great Texas Dynamite Chase
Lara Croft: Tomb Raider
Not without My Daughter
The Silence of the Lambs [MGM SE]
Skyscraper
Superchick
Terminatrix
Xena: Warrior Princess—Series Finale

World War I
All Quiet on the Western Front
Capitaine Conan
Dr. Mabuse, The Gambler
Flambards
The Lost Battalion
World War I Films of the Silent Era

World War II
See also: The Holocaust; Nazis & Other Paramilitary Slugs; Postwar; POW/MIA

Ambush
Anzio
Attack—The Battle for New Britain
The Basket [SE]
Beyond Barbed Wire
Blood on the Sun [Image]
Captain Corelli's Mandolin
Closely Watched Trains
Come and See
Conspiracy
Contraband
The Cranes Are Flying
Dark Blue World
December 7th / The Fleet That Came to Stay
The Devil's Brigade
Divided We Fall
Empire of the Sun
Enemy at the Gates
Fighting Rats of Tobruk
The Fleet that Came to Stay
Force 10 from Navarone
The Garden of the Finzi-Continis
Go for Broke! [VCI]
Great Fighting Machines of WWII: Allied & Axis Bombers
Great Fighting Machines of WWII: Allied & Axis Fighters
Great Fighting Machines of WWII: Allied & Axis Tanks
Guadalcanal Diary
The Halls of Montezuma
Hanover Street
Heroes of Iwo Jima
In Love and War
Into the Arms of Strangers: Stories from the Kindertransport
Jacob the Liar
Kings Go Forth
The Last Tattoo
The Last Train
Little Dieter Needs to Fly
MacArthur
Maria's Lovers
McKenzie Break
Mein Krieg
Mephisto
A Midnight Clear
Midway [Universal CE]
The Mirror
Mission to Death
The North Star
The Ogre
Patton [2]
Pearl Harbor
Pearl Harbor Before and After
Pearl Harbor: The View from Japan
Raiders of Leyte Gulf
The Ravagers
Red Cherry
Remember Pearl Harbor: America Taken by Surprise
Rodgers & Hammerstein's South Pacific
Run Silent, Run Deep
Sahara
The Shop on Main Street
Stage Door Canteen
Star Spangled Rhythm
The Stillwell Road
Submarine Attack
Three Came Home
Too Late the Hero
Treasure Island
Triumph of the Spirit
Twelve o'Clock High
Uprising
Von Ryan's Express
Walls of Hell
We Dive at Dawn
We Take New Guinea
When Trumpets Fade
A Wing and a Prayer
The World at War
The Young Lions

Wrestling
Backyard Dogs
Doctor of Doom
Pin Down Girls
Sumo Vixens
The World according to Garp
Wrestling Women USA!

Writers
See also: Biopics: Writers

Best Seller
Cabin by the Lake / Return to Cabin by the Lake
Eva
Hav Plenty
How to Kill Your Neighbor's Dog
Impromptu
Ken Burns' Mark Twain
Letters from a Killer
The Master of the Rings
Maybe Baby
Moulin Rouge [SE]
Our Lady of the Assassins
Out of Africa
Romantic Comedy
Two Ninas
White Badge
The World according to Garp

The Wrong Man
See also: Frame-Ups; Mistaken Identity

Bad Seed
Bloodfist 7: Manhunt
Kiss of the Dragon
The Winslow Boy

Wrong Side of the Tracks
See also: Rags to Riches

Bachelor Party
Breaking Away
Careful, He Might Hear You
crazy/beautiful
Dragstrip Girl
Eegah!
It
My Man Godfrey [Criterion]
Outpost in Morocco
A Place in the Sun
Rappin'-N-Rhyming
The Servant

Yakuza
See also: Crime & Criminals; Organized Crime

Adrenaline Drive
Afraid to Die
Beautiful Beast
The Bodyguard [BFS]
Brother
Fatal Blade
Gonin
Johnny Mnemonic [2 SB]
The Street Fighter's Last Revenge
Tokyo Mafia: Battle for Shinjuku
Tokyo Mafia: Wrath of the Yakuza
Tokyo Mafia: Yakuza Wars

You Lose, You Die
See also: Post Apocalypse

The Arena
Rollerball
Tron [2 CE]

Yugoslavian (Production)
Atomic War Bride / This Is Not a Test

Zombie Soldiers
See also: Zombies

House
Reborn from Hell: Jubei's Revenge
Reborn from Hell: Samurai Armageddon

Zombies
See also: Death & the Afterlife; Ghosts, Ghouls & Goblins; Zombie Soldiers

Biker Zombies
Biozombie
Bowery at Midnight
Carnival of Souls / Dementia 13
Children of the Living Dead
The Convent
Dead Creatures
The Dead Hate the Living
The Death Curse of Tartu / Sting of Death
The Grapes of Death
The Mummy
Night of the Ghouls
Night of the Living Dead [Elite ME]
Pet Sematary 2
Re-Animator [2 ME]
Return of the Living Dead 3
Shatter Dead
Svengali
Teenage Zombies

Zorro
Don Q, Son of Zorro
Mark of Zorro [2] / Don Q, Son of Zorro
The Mask of Zorro [2 SE]
Zorro, the Gay Blade

The "Distributor Index" provides contact information for the distributors indicated within the reviews, and the DVDs reviewed in this book which they offer. Beware: DVDs sometimes change hands frequentloy; we've tried to provide cross-references where applicable. Also, studio distributors do not usually sell to the public—they generally act as wholesalers, selling only to retail outlets. Many video stores provide an ordering service; check out the "DVD Connections" section on p. xx for some websites to help you track down a title.

A-PIX ENTERTAINMENT INC.
200 Madison Ave., 24th Fl.
New York, NY 10016
(206)284-4700
800-245-6472
Fax: (206)286-4433

Mars: The Red Planet '99
Oxygen '99
Point of View '00
Showgirl Stories '98

A&E HOME VIDEO
PO Box 2284
South Burlington, VT 05407
888-423-1212
Fax: (802)864-9846

Agatha Christie's Miss Marple Set 1 '87
Agatha Christie's Miss Marple Set 2 '02
At Bertram's Hotel '86
The Avengers '68 '68
A Caribbean Mystery / The Mirror Cracked from Side to Side '89
Catherine the Great '95
Christianity: The First Two Thousand Years '00
Elizabeth '02
The Great Gatsby '01
Hammer House of Horror '80
Heroes of Iwo Jima '01
Horatio Hornblower '99
Horatio Hornblower: The Adventure Continues '01
In the Footsteps of the Holy Family '01
Ivanhoe '97
Jeeves & Wooster: The Complete Second Season '96
Lorna Doone '01
The Lost Battalion '01
The Magnificent Ambersons '02
Monty Python Live '72
Monty Python's Flying Circus Set 1 '69
The Moving Finger '85
Murder at the Vicarage '86
Nemesis '86
Peter Gunn: Set One '58
The Prisoner '68
The Saint '66
Secret Agent '65
Shackleton '02
Sleeping Murder / 4:50 from Paddington '86

Space: 1999 Set 1 '75
They Do It with Mirrors '91
Thunderbirds: Set 1 '65
Titanic: The Complete Story '01
Upstairs, Downstairs: The Complete First Season '71
Upstairs, Downstairs: The Second Season '72
Victoria & Albert '01

ACORN MEDIA PUBLISHING
7910 Woodmont Ave., Ste. 350
Bethesda, MD 20814
(301)907-0030
800-999-0212
Fax: (301)907-9049

Agatha Christie's Poirot: Dumb Witness '01
Agatha Christie's Poirot: Hercule Poirot's Christmas '01
Agatha Christie's Poirot: Peril at End House '90
Agatha Christie's Poirot: The ABC Murders '92
Cadfael—The Raven in the Foregate '94
Lexx Series 2, Vol. 1 '98
The Pallisers, Vol. 2 '74
The Pallisers, Vol. 3 '74
Traffik '90

A.D.V. FILMS
5750 Bintliff, No. 216
Houston, TX 77036-2123
(713)341-7100
Fax: (713)341-7195

City Hunter: Secret Service '96
Devil Hunter Yohko: The Complete Collection, Vol. 1 '93
Farscape, Vol. 1 '00
Farscape, Vol. 6 '01
Martian Successor Nadesico: Endgame '96
Nadia: Secret of Blue Water, Vol. 1: The Adventure Begins '89
Parasite Eve '97
Robotech: The Macross Saga—Extra Disc 1: Elements of Robotechnology '85
Robotech: The Macross Saga, Vol. 2: Transformation '85

ALL DAY ENTERTAINMENT
3109 Batter Sea Ln.
Alexandria, VA 22309

Bluebeard '44
The Cry of the Owl '87
The Daughter of Dr. Jekyll '57
Ganja and Hess '73
Get Out Your Handkerchiefs '78
Gunman in the Streets '50
Heart of Glass '74
Highlander [Anchor Bay] '86
The Horror of Hammer '01
Memoirs of a Survivor '81
Return to Horror High '87
'68 '87
Treasure Island '99

ANCHOR BAY
1699 Stutz Dr.
Troy, MI 48084
(248)816-0909
800-786-8777
Fax: (248)816-3335

Accident '67
The Amy Fisher Story '93
And Soon the Darkness '70
Anguish '88
Bad Boys [Anchor Bay] '83
Bad Taste [LE] '88
Beastmaster '82
Blood from the Mummy's Tomb '71
Britannia Hospital '82
A Bullet for the General '68
Business Is Business '71
Can't Stop the Music '80
The Cat o' Nine Tails '71
The Church '98
Circus of Horrors '60
Clockwise '86
Cobra Verde '88
Colonel Redl '84
Companeros '70
Crimes of Passion [2] '84
Cross Creek '83
Cut and Run '85
Date with an Angel '87
Death Before Dishonor '87
Diva [Anchor Bay] '82
Dr. Jekyll and Sister Hyde '71
18 Again! '88
Evil Dead [LE] '83
Eye Witness '70
The Final Programme '73
Four of the Apocalypse '75
Frances [Anchor Bay] '82

Fraternity Vacation '85
Fright '71
Going Places '74
Halloween [EE] '78
Heathers [2 THX] '89
Hell Comes to Frogtown '88
Hell of the Living Dead '83
Hellbound: Hellraiser 2 [2 THX] '88
Hiding Out '87
Honky Tonk Freeway '81
House '86
House 2: The Second Story '87
Katie Tippel '75
Keoma '76
The Last Tattoo '94
Lessons of Darkness '92
Link '86
Little Dieter Needs to Fly '97
Lust for a Vampire '71
The Man Who Haunted Himself '70
Manhunter [LE] '86
Maniac [LE] '80
Mephisto '81
Midnight Madness '80
The Mind Benders '63
Morgan: A Suitable Case for Treatment '66
Mountain of the Cannibal God '79
Opera '88
Percy '71
Pin... '88
Please Not Now! '61
Plenty [Anchor Bay] '85
Rats '83
Return of the Killer Tomatoes! '88
Scandal '89
The Scars of Dracula '70
Schlock '73
The Servant '63
Shock '70
The Sinister Saga '00
Sleuth [2] '72
Soul Man '86
Stagefright '87
The Stepford Wives [2 SE] '75
Stroszek '77
The Stunt Man '80
Suspiria '77
Sword & the Sorcerer '82
Tender Mercies [Anchor Bay] '83
Texas, Adios '66
Theatre of Death '67

Three Stooges: All Time Favorites '98
Timerider '83
Too Late the Hero '70
Transylvania 6-5000 '85
Un Flic '72
Vamp '86
Vigilante [2 DC] '83
Violent City '70
Wanted: Dead or Alive '86
The Watcher in the Woods '81
The Wicker Man [SE] '75

ANIMEIGO INC.
PO Box 989
Wilmington, NC 28402-0989
(910)251-1850
800-242-6463
Fax: (910)763-2376

Macross: Box Set '85
Oh My Goddess! Vol. 1 '93
Urusei Yatsura: TV Series 1 '81

ARIZTICAL ENTERTAINMENT
405 E. Wetmore, Ste. 117-516
Tucson, AZ 85705
(520)622-2400
800-356-4386

Kizuna '94

ARTISAN ENTERTAINMENT
15400 Sherman Way
PO Box 10124
Van Nuys, CA 91410-0124
(818)988-5060
800-677-0789
Fax: (818)778-3259

Acceptable Risk '01
After Dark, My Sweet [2] '90
All Quiet on the Western Front '79
Along for the Ride '00
The Apocalypse Watch '97
Back to the Secret Garden '01
Backyard Dogs '00
Bad Seed '00
Barbie in the Nutcracker '01
Basic Instinct [2 SE] '92
Beyond the Law '92
Body Count '97
Brooklyn Babylon '00
The Center of the World '01

Children of the Living Dead
'00
Dead Simple '01
Deep in the Woods '00
Double Bang '01
Down from the Mountain '00
Dracula: The Dark Prince '01
Drive By '01
Dune [2 SE] '00
Fatal Error '99
Fidel '02
The Field [Artisan] '90
Follow the Stars Home '01
Ginger Snaps '00
Good Advice '01
The Grass Is Greener '61
Hard Cash '01
Hard Lessons '86
Haunted '95
High Noon '00
Hostage High '97
The House of the Spirits '93
How to Kill Your Neighbor's
Dog '01
In Love and War '01
Indiscreet '58
The Item '01
Jack and the Beanstalk: The
Real Story '01
King of the Pecos '36
The Last Siege '99
The Last Warrior '99
Luck of the Draw '00
Made [SE] '01
Mama Flora's Family '98
The Mangler 2 '01
Never 2 Big '98
Novocaine '01
The Odyssey '97
Open Your Eyes '97
Operation Petticoat '59
Out of Sync '95
Outta Time '01
Panic '00
Pendulum '01
Phat Beach '96
Poison '01
Replicant '01
Road Dogz '00
The Runaway '00
Scarlett '94
Second Skin '00
The Sicilian '87
Sleepless '01
Slow Burn '00
Snow White: The Fairest of
Them All '02
Soul Survivors '01
Stallone: Rambo Trilogy [SE]
'02
Startup.com '01
Stealth Fighter '99
Stephen King's Golden Years
'91
Stephen King's The Lan-
goliers '95
Texas '94
Ticker '01
Top Dog '95
Total Recall [2 SLE] '90
Twin Peaks: The First Season
'90
U.S. Seals [2] '01
Wishmaster 3: Beyond the
Gates of Hell '01

**AVALANCHE
ENTERTAINMENT**
595 Burrard St., Ste. 3123
Bentall Three
Vancouver, BC, Canada V7X
1J1
(416)944-0104

Double Down '01
The Enemy '01
The Pact '99
Perpetrators of the Crime '98
Requiem for Murder '99
Undercurrent '99

**BANDAI
ENTERTAINMENT**
5551 Katella Ave.
PO Box 6054
Cypress, CA 90630

Blue Submarine No. 6—
Episode 2: Pilots '98
Blue Submarine No. 6—
Episode 3: Hearts '98
Blue Submarine No. 6—
Episode 4: Minasoko '98
Mobile Suit Gundam: The
Battle Begins! Vol. 1 '79
Mobile Suit Gundam Wing:
Operation 1 '95

**BBC/WORLDWIDE
AMERICAS**
BBC Direct
PO Box 2284
South Burlington, VT 05407-
2284
800-216-IBBC
Fax: (802)864-9846

Absolutely Fabulous: Series 1
'94
Absolutely Fabulous: Series 4
'01

BCI-ECLIPSE, LLC
706 Executive Blvd., Ste. C
Valley Cottage, NY 10989-
2013
(845)267-2459
Fax: (845)267-2438

Action Arsenal '01
All Night Movies '00
Bad Cop Chronicles: Confes-
sions of a Police Captain
'72
Bad Cop Chronicles 2: Cor-
rupt '84
Bikini Med School / Bikini
House Calls '98
The Black Cobra '87
Black Godfather '74
Blitz '85
The Choppers '61
Cops '01
Crazy Horse and Custer: "The
Untold Story" '90
Cremains '00
Cry Blood, Apache '70
Dealin' Dirty
Great Adventures '00
The Hard Road '00
Human Prey '95
Illegal Affairs '96
The Jackals '67
Kill Cruise '90
The Lady and the Highway-
man '89
The Last Train '74
Mind, Body & Soul '92
Murder in the Orient '73
Narcotic Justice
One for the Road '82
Revenge Quest '96
South Bronx Heroes '85
The Street Fighter [BCI] '74
Street Vengeance '95
36 Crazy Fists '77
Twisted Justice '89
White Fang to the Rescue '74
The Wild West '01

**BEVERLY WILSHIRE
FILMWORKS**
PO Box 111, Prince Street Sta.
New York, NY 10012

Doctor of Doom '62
Teenage Zombies '58

BFS VIDEO
360 Newkirk Rd.
Richmond Hill, ON, Canada
L4C 3G7
(905)884-2323
Fax: (905)884-8292

After the War '89
Angels Hard As They Come
'71
Animals at Play: Cute and
Cuddly '01
Blood of the Dragon '71
Bloodfight '89
The Bodyguard [BFS] '76
Borderline '50
Brothers in Arms '01
Bruce Lee Fights Back from
the Grave '76
Castles of War '00
Catherine Cookson's The Girl
'96
Champ Against Champ [BFS]
'83
Classic Biker Movies '02
Classic Dick Tracy Movies '01
Classic Heist Movies '02
Classic Seventies Movies '02
Classic Sonny Chiba Movies
'01
Cor, Blimey! '00
Dangerous Summer '82
The Darling Buds of May '91
The Devil Bat '41
Evel Knievel '72
Fire Alarm '32
Firehouse '72
Fist of Fear, Touch of Death
'80
Fists of Bruce Lee '78
Flambards '78
Forgotten '99
Great Bloodsucking Movies
'01
Great Cop Movies '78
Great Detective Movies '02
Great Fire Movies '02
Great John Wayne Movies '00
Great Mafia Movies 2 '02
Great Martial Arts Movies '02
Great Racing Movies '00
The Great St. Louis Bank
Robbery '59
Great Scary Movies '01
Great Sci-Fi Thrillers '02
Great Spy Movies '00
Great WWII Movies '02
The Harp in the South '86
High Risk '81
Introduction to Antiques '95
The Irishman '78
Jane Austen: Her Life, Her
Works, Her Society '98
Katherine '75
The Knights Templar '00
Larceny '91
The Last Man on Earth '64
The Last Place on Earth '94
Legendary Sherlock Holmes
Movies '00
Murder Once Removed '71
The North Star '43
Nostradamus: His Life and
Prophecies / Prophecy and
Prediction '94
Poor Man's Orange '87
A Real American Hero '78
Return of the Street Fighter
'74
Science and the Swastika '01
Sell Out '76
Shogun's Ninja '83
Sister Street Fighter '76
The Squeeze '78
The Street Fighter [BFS] '74
The Street Fighter's Last
Revenge '74
S.W.A.T. '00
A Tale of Two Cities '91
The Tattered Web '71
Therese Raquin '80
They Call It Murder '71
Til Death Us Do Part '72
Troubles '88
We Dive at Dawn '43
Woman in Black '89
The Worst Witch '98

BMG
1540 Broadway
New York, NY 10036
(216)543-6466

The Alice Cooper Story '01

**BRENTWOOD HOME
VIDEO**
810 Lawrence Dr., Ste. 100
Newbury Park, CA 91320
(805)375-9998
Fax: (805)375-9908

Daniel Boone: Trail Blazer '56
Fistful of Lead '70
The Gunfighters '87
His Majesty, the Scarecrow of
Oz '14
Moon of the Wolf '72
The New Daughters of
Joshua Cabe '76
Over the Hill Gang '69
Rescue from Gilligan's Island
'78
Savage Pampas '66
Scream of the Wolf '74
7 Lucky Ninja Kids '89
Territorial Men '76
Where Angels Dance '01
The Wizard of Oz '25
The Wolfman '82

**BUENA VISTA HOME
ENTERTAINMENT**
500 S. Buena Vista St.
Burbank, CA 91521-1120
800-723-4763

Angels in the Outfield '94
Anne Frank '01
Atlantis: The Lost Empire
[CE] '01
Baby Bach '00
Baby Dolittle: Neighborhood
Animals '01
Baby Dolittle: World Animals
'01
Baby Einstein: Language
Nursery '01
Baby Mozart '00
Baby Shakespeare '99
Baby Van Gogh '00
Belle de Jour '67
Bravo Two Zero '99
Bubble Boy '01
Child Star: The Shirley Tem-
ple Story '01
Children of the Corn 4: The
Gathering '96
Children of the Corn 5: Fields
of Terror '98
Children of the Corn: Revela-
tion '01
Cinderella 2: Dreams Come
True '02
City on Fire [Dimension] '87
Committed '99
Corky Romano '01
crazy/beautiful '01
David Blaine: Fearless '02
Dick Tracy '90
Disney's American Legends
'02
Dracula 2000 '00
Dragstrip Girl '94
Dumbo '41
High Heels and Low Lifes '01
The Hunchback of Notre
Dame '96
The Hunchback of Notre
Dame 2 '01
Jailbreakers '94
Jay and Silent Bob Strike
Back '01
The Journey of Natty Gann
'85
Kate & Leopold '01
The Legend [2] '93
The Many Adventures of Win-
nie the Pooh '77
Mexico City '01

Mickey Mouse in Living Color
'01
Mickey's Magical Christmas
'01
Mimic [2] '01
New Port South '00
Newsies '92
Old Yeller '57
Oliver & Company '88
The Others [CE] '01
Out Cold '01
The Parent Trap '61
Pearl Harbor '01
Peter Pan [2 SE] '53
Pollyanna '60
The Princess Diaries '01
Princess of Thieves '01
Purple Noon '60
Recess Christmas: Miracle
on Third Street '01
Recess: School's Out '01
Rodgers & Hammerstein's
South Pacific '01
Ruthless People '86
Santa Who? '00
Scary Movie 2 '01
The Secret of NIMH '82
Shake, Rattle & Rock! '94
Sister Act '92
The Sixth Sense [Buena
Vista] '99
Snow Dogs '02
Snow White and the Seven
Dwarfs [PE] '37
Spider-Man: The Ultimate Vil-
lain Showdown '02
Spy Kids '01
The Swiss Family Robinson
'60
The Taste of Others '00
Texas Rangers '01
Three Fugitives '89
Three Men and a Baby '87
Three Men and a Little Lady
'90
Tin Men '87
Tron [2 CE] '82
Turner and Hooch '89
Unbreakable '00
Walt Disney Treasures: Davy
Crockett '01
Walt Disney Treasures: Dis-
neyland USA '01
Walt Disney Treasures: Silly
Symphonies '01
Whispers: An Elephant's Tale
'00
The Young Girls of Rochefort
'68

**CARLTON
INTERNATIONAL MEDIA
LTD.**
35-38 Portman Sq.
London W1H 6NU, England
(44)20-7224-3339
Fax: (44) 20-7486-1707

Kennedy '83

**CENTRAL PARK
MEDIA/U.S. MANGA
CORPS**
250 W. 57th St., Ste. 317
New York, NY 10107
(212)977-7456
800-833-7456
Fax: (212)977-8709

Angel Sanctuary '00
Beautiful Beast '95
Beautiful Hunter '95
The Dimension Travelers '98
Harlock Saga '99
Lady Blue '01
Masquerade: Eternal Life '00
Night on the Galactic Rail-
road '85
Pearl Harbor: The View from
Japan '94

Legally Blonde '01
The Mexican '01
Shrek [SE] '01

DVD DRIVE-IN
G & P Productions
Box 366
Setauket, NY 11733

Lady Frankenstein '72

EI INDEPENDENT CINEMA
PO Box 371
Glenwood, NJ 07418
(973)838-3030
Fax: (973)509-3530

Demon Lust '01
The Erotic Mirror '01
The Erotic Rites of Countess Dracula '01
Erotic Survivor 2 '01
Inga '67
Mummy Raider '01
Naughty Stewardesses '74
Night Divides the Day '01
Play-Mate of the Apes '02
Roxanna '02
The Sexy Sixth Sense '01
2069: A Sex Odyssey '78
Vampire Obsession '02

ELITE ENTERTAINMENT, INC.
PO Box 1177
Scarborough, ME 04070-1177
(207)883-0200
Fax: (207)883-2579

Drive-in Discs, Vol. 2 '01
Howling 3: The Marsupials '87
Night of the Living Dead [Elite ME] '68
Night to Dismember '83
Popcorn '89
Psychic Killer '75
Re-Animator [2 ME] '84
Return of Captain Invincible '83

ETD
13950 Senlac Dr., Ste. 300
Farmers Branch, TX 75234
(972)406-0866
800-541-1008

Sore Losers '97

FACETS MULTIMEDIA, INC.
1517 W. Fullerton Ave.
Chicago, IL 60614
(773)281-9075
800-331-6197
Fax: (773)929-5437

Close-Up '90
Daisies '96

FANTOMA FILMS
660A Bryant St.
San Francisco, CA 94107
(415)348-8840
415-348-8849

The Educational Archives Volume 1: Sex & Drugs '01
The Educational Archives Volume 2: Social Engineering 101 '01
The Indian Tomb '59
Tiger of Eschnapur '59

FIRST LOOK PICTURES
8800 Sunset Blvd.
Los Angeles, CA 90069
(310)855-1199
Fax: (310)855-0152

Escape from Alaska '02

FIRST RUN FEATURES
153 Waverly Pl.
New York, NY 10014
(212)243-0600
800-229-8575
Fax: (212)989-7649

Aberdeen '00
Cane Toads: An Unnatural History '87
Coming Out '89
Cool and Crazy '01
First Love and Other Pains / One of Them '99
42 Up '00
Hot Summer '68
The Libertine '69
Light Keeps Me Company '00
Live Nude Girls Unite! '00
New York in the Fifties '01
The Nude Set '61
The Personals '98
Petits Freres '00
Queer As F**k: Bizarre Short Films '01
Spin the Bottle '97
Vibration '68
Waiting '01
The Wolves of Kromer '98

FOCUSFILM
PO Box 1177
Scarborough, ME 04070

Citizen Welles '01

FOX/LORBER HOME VIDEO
419 Park Ave. S., 20th Fl.
New York, NY 10016
(212)686-6777
Fax: (212)685-2625

Hammers over the Anvil '91
Planet of the Apes '74
Trans '99
The Well '97
When Good Ghouls Go Bad '01

FULL MOON PICTURES
8721 Santa Monica Blvd., Ste. 526
West Hollywood, CA 90069
(323)468-0599
877-315-MOON
Fax: (323)468-0598

Dead and Rotting '02
The Dead Hate the Living '99
Hell Asylum '01
Petticoat Planet '95
Witchouse 3: Demon Fire '01

GLOBALSTAGE
465 California, Ste. 525
San Francisco, CA 94104
(415)217-5800
Fax: (415)217-5819

Reborn from Hell: Samurai Armageddon '96

GOLDHIL HOME MEDIA
137 E. Thousand Oaks Blvd., Ste. 207
Thousand Oaks, CA 91360
(805)495-0735
Fax: (805)373-1603

The Korean War in Color '02

GOODTIMES ENTERTAINMENT
16 E. 40th St., 8th Fl.
New York, NY 10016-0113
(212)951-3000
Fax: (212)213-9319

Attack—The Battle for New Britain '44
The Bat [Goodtimes] '59
Bruce Lee and Kung Fu Mania '92

Bruce Lee the Invincible '77
December 7th / The Fleet That Came to Stay '43
Fantastic Dinosaurs of the Movies '90
Godzilla, King of the Monsters [Goodtimes] '56
Jack the Giant Killer '62
Jekyll & Hyde: The Musical '01
The Jungle Book '42
Megiddo: The Omega Code 2 '01
Planet of the Dinosaurs '80
Psycho 2 '83
Putting It Together: Stephen Sondheim—A Musical Review '01
Rough Night in Jericho '67
Rudolph the Red-Nosed Reindeer: The Movie '98
The Stillwell Road '47
Tank '83
We Take New Guinea
The Young Bruce Lee '80

GORGON VIDEO
c/o MPI Home Video
16101 S. 108th Ave.
Orland Park, IL 60462
800-777-2223
Fax: (708)460-0175

Faces of Death 2 '81
Faces of Death 3: Scenes from the Underground '81

HALLMARK HOME ENTERTAINMENT
6100 Wilshire Blvd., Ste. 1400
Los Angeles, CA 90048
(213)634-3000
Fax: (213)549-3760

The Temptations '98

HBO HOME VIDEO
1100 6th Ave.
New York, NY 10036
(212)512-7400
Fax: (212)512-7498

Barbarians at the Gate '93
Benny Hill Golden Greats '89
Blacktop '00
Boycott '02
Breast Men '97
Citizen Cohn '92
Conspiracy '01
Dancing in September '00
Dinner with Friends '01
First Time Felon '97
Full Eclipse '93
Good Guys Wear Black '78
The Hitcher '86
House Arrest '96
Introducing Dorothy Dandridge '99
The Last of the Dogmen '95
Mr. Show: The Complete First & Second Seasons '02
Oz: The Complete First Season '97
The Princess and the Pirate '44
Proud Rebel '58
Sex and the City: Season 1 '00
Sex and the City: The Complete Third Season '02
Shot in the Heart '01
61* '01
The Sopranos: The Complete Second Season '01
Split Second '92
Stella Dallas '37
Tales from the Crypt: Robert Zemeckis Collection '95
They Got Me Covered '43
Three Amigos '86
Three Wishes '95
The Visit '00

Volunteers '85
When Trumpets Fade '98
The World at War '73

HEN'S TOOTH VIDEO
2805 E. State Blvd.
Fort Wayne, IN 46805
(219)471-4332
Fax: (219)471-4449

Bread and Chocolate '73
Dance 'til Dawn '88
Dot & the Kangaroo '77
Free to Be...You and Me '74
Jacob the Liar '74

HOLLYWOOD PICTURES HOME VIDEO
Fairmont Bldg. 526
500 S. Buena Vista St.
Burbank, CA 91505-9842
(818)562-3560

Just Visiting '01
Taking Care of Business '90
Tombstone [2] '93

HOME VISION CINEMA
5547 N. Ravenswood Ave.
Chicago, IL 60640-1199
(773)878-2600
800-826-3456
Fax: (773)878-8406

Confessions of Robert Crumb '87
Don Juan (Or If Don Juan Were a Woman) '73
Grass '00
Jackson Pollock: Love and Death on Long Island '99
Me & Isaac Newton '99
The Night Heaven Fell '57
Plucking the Daisy '56
Summertime '55
The Tale of Zatoichi '62
The Tale of Zatoichi Continues '62

ICESTORM INTERNATIONAL, INC.
78 Main St., Ste. 401
Northampton, MA 01060
(413)587-9334
Fax: (413)587-9305

Tales from Europe: The Singing, Ringing Tree '57
Tales from Europe: The Story of Little Mook '53

IMAGE ENTERTAINMENT
9333 Oso Ave.
Chatsworth, CA 91311
(818)407-9100
800-473-3475
Fax: (818)407-9111

Adrenaline Drive '99
Aenigma '87
Afraid to Die '60
Alice in Wonderland '83
Alien Exotica: The Secret Files '98
The Amphibian Man '61
And Now the Screaming Starts [SE] '73
And Then There Were None [Image] '45
A*P*E* '76
Atomic War Bride / This Is Not a Test '60
Attack from Mars '88
Au Pair Girls '72
Axe '74
Bar 20 Rides Again '35
Barbara the Fair with the Silken Hair '69
Basket Case [2 SE] '82
Bela Lugosi Meets a Brooklyn Gorilla '52
The Black Cat / The Fat Black Pussycat '65

Blackheart '98
The Blair Thumb '01
Blast-Off Girls / Just for the Hell of It '67
The Blind Beast '69
Blood on the Sun [Image] '45
Blood Thirst '65
The Bloodsuckers '70
Bongwater '98
Cannibal Apocalypse '80
Careful, He Might Hear You '84
Carnival of Blood / Curse of the Headless Horseman [SE] '71
Chac: The Rain God '74
The Child '76
Chopper '01
Christoph Von Dohnanyi: In Rehearsal—Philharmonia Orchestra '98
The Crawling Eye '58
Creature Comforts '90
Cuban Story '59
Dario Argento: An Eye for Horror '00
Devil Girl from Mars '54
Dr. Mabuse, The Gambler '22
Dr. Orloff's Monster '64
The Doll Squad '73
Doomwatch '72
Earth '30
Ecstasy '33
Father Frost '66
Fifth of July '82
Flash Gordon: Spaceship to the Unknown '36
Flash Gordon: The Deadly Ray from Mars '39
Flash Gordon: The Peril from Planet Mongo '40
Flash Gordon: The Purple Death from Outer Space '40
The Flesh and the Fiends '60
Flight to Mars '52
For Sale '98
Fosse '01
Gadget Trips—Mindscapes '95
Gang of Four '88
Gesualdo: Death for Five Voices '95
Giants and Toys '58
Girl in Gold Boots '69
Godmonster of Indian Flats '73
God's Little Acre '58
Goliath and the Dragon '61
Hamlet '64
Hamlet '90
The Haunted World of Edward D. Wood, Jr. '95
Helmut Newton: Frames from the Edge '88
Helter Skelter Murders '71
Hermes—Winds of Love '97
Hidden Hollywood: Treasures from the 20th Century Fox Vaults '99
Hidden Hollywood 2: More Treasures from the 20th Century Fox Vaults '99
Hitch Hike to Hell / Kidnapped Coed '97
Hollywood at Your Feet: The Story of the Chinese Theater Footprints '00
Hollywood Screen Tests: Take 1 '00
Hollywood Screen Tests: Take 2 '00
Hopalong Cassidy '35
Hopalong Cassidy Returns '36
House on Bare Mountain '62
I Vampiri '56
The Iceman Cometh '60
Into the Woods '90
Invasion of the Animal People '62

Cornbread, Earl & Me '75
The Cotton Club '84
Count Yorga, Vampire '70
Cuba '79
Cutter's Way '81
De Sade '69
Deceiver '97
The Defiant Ones '58
Desperate Hours '90
The Devil's Brigade '68
Dirty Rotten Scoundrels [MGM] '88
Dodsworth [MGM] '36
The Dogs of War '81
Dominick & Eugene '88
The Dress Code '99
Dressed to Kill [SE] '80
The Dunwich Horror '70
Eat Drink Man Woman '94
Echo Park '86
Eddie and the Cruisers '83
Electra '62
Empire of the Ants '77
Escape to Grizzly Mountain '99
The Extreme Adventures of Super Dave '98
Extremities '86
An Eye for an Eye '81
The Favor '92
Fiddler on the Roof [2 SE] '71
Fires Within '91
Firestarter 2: Rekindled '02
The First Power '89
Five on the Black Hand Side '73
Force 10 from Navarone '78
The French Lieutenant's Woman '81
Fritz the Cat '72
Full Moon in Blue Water '88
A Funny Thing Happened on the Way to the Forum '66
Gang Related '96
Ghost World '01
Girl with Green Eyes '64
Go Fish '94
The Good Wife '86
Great Balls of Fire '89
Gregory's Girl '80
Hallelujah, I'm a Bum '33
Halloween 4: The Return of Michael Myers [MGM LE] '88
The Handmaid's Tale '90
Hannah and Her Sisters '86
Haunted Honeymoon '86
The Heart of Dixie '89
Heartbreakers '01
Hell up in Harlem '73
Hero and the Terror '88
Hidden Agenda '90
High Spirits '88
A Hole in the Head '59
Hollywood Shuffle '87
Home for the Holidays '95
The Hotel New Hampshire '84
The Hound of the Baskervilles '59
How to Succeed in Business without Really Trying '67
The Howling '81
I Bury the Living '58
I Want to Live! '58
Impromptu '90
In the Time of the Butterflies '01
Inherit the Wind '60
Invaders from Mars [MGM] '86
Invasion U.S.A. '85
Irma La Douce '63
The Island of Dr. Moreau '77
It! The Terror from Beyond Space '58
It's a Mad, Mad, Mad, Mad World '63
Jack and Sarah '95
The January Man '89
J.D.'s Revenge '76

Jeepers Creepers '01
Joe '70
Kansas '88
Khartoum '66
Killer Klowns from Outer Space '88
King Solomon's Mines '37
Kings Go Forth '58
La Cage aux Folles '78
La Cage aux Folles 2 '81
The Last Waltz [SE] '78
Lawman '71
The Learning Curve '01
Lenny '74
Less Than Zero '87
Liebestraum '91
The Little Foxes [MGM] '41
Little Man Tate '91
The Locusts '97
Lone Wolf McQuade '83
Lonely Hearts '82
Look Back in Anger '58
Lord of the Flies '90
The Lover '92
Mad Max [MGM SE] '80
Mademoiselle '66
Making the Grade '84
The Man with the Golden Gun '74
The Manhattan Project '86
Mannequin '87
Maria's Lovers '84
Mars Needs Women '66
McKenzie Break '70
Men at Work '90
A Midsummer Night's Sex Comedy '82
Mr. Saturday Night [MGM] '92
Molly '99
The Monster That Challenged the World '57
Morons from Outer Space '85
Never Say Never Again '83
Nine Lives of Fritz the Cat '74
1969 '89
No Man's Land '01
Nomads '86
Not without My Daughter '90
Of Mice and Men '92
On Her Majesty's Secret Service '69
On the Beach '59
Original Sin '01
The Party '68
The People That Time Forgot '77
Planet of the Vampires '65
Pocketful of Miracles '61
Prancer '89
The Pride and the Passion '57
The Princess Bride [2 SE] '87
The Purple Rose of Cairo '85
Quigley Down Under '90
Radio Days '87
Reptilicus '62
Retroactive '97
Rollerball '02
Romantic Comedy '83
Romeo Is Bleeding '93
Running Scared '86
The Russia House '90
Saturday Night and Sunday Morning '60
Sayonara '57
Scanners '81
The Scout '94
Separate Tables '58
She-Devil '89
Showgirls '95
The Silence of the Lambs [MGM SE] '91
Slaughter '72
The Smokers '00
Spaceballs '87
Speechless '94
Strange Invaders '83
Stranger than Paradise '84
Support Your Local Sheriff '69
A Tale of Springtime '89

The Terminator [2 SE] '84
Theatre of Blood '73
Things You Can Tell Just by Looking at Her '00
Throw Momma from the Train '87
Topkapi '64
Town without Pity '61
Triumph of the Spirit '89
Truly, Madly, Deeply '91
Twice-Told Tales '63
UHF '89
Ulee's Gold '97
Under Fire '83
Unforgettable '96
The Usual Suspects [MGM SE] '95
Valdez Is Coming '71
The Vikings '58
War Gods of the Deep '65
What's the Worst That Could Happen? [SE] '01
Who'll Stop the Rain? '78
The Wild Child '70
Wild Orchid '90
Witness for the Prosecution '57
The Woody Allen Collection '01
Wuthering Heights '70
Zelig '83

MIRAMAX PICTURES HOME VIDEO
500 S. Buena Vista St.
Burbank, CA 91521
800-413-5566

About Adam '00
Alien Visitor '95
Blow Dry '00
Bridget Jones's Diary '01
Calle 54 '01
The Closet '00
Everybody's Famous! '00
Fresh '94
Get Over It! '01
The Glass Shield '95
Hav Plenty '97
The Hunchback of Notre Dame '57
Iron Monkey [Miramax] '93
The Kid '97
Life with Judy Garland—Me and My Shadows '01
Little City '97
On the Line '01
A Personal Journey with Martin Scorsese through American Movies '97
Reindeer Games [Miramax DC] '00
Robert Louis Stevenson's St. Ives '98
Robinson Crusoe '96
Serendipity '01
Squeeze '97
Stiff Upper Lips '96
Strictly Ballroom '92
The Tall Guy '89
Walking and Talking '96
With a Friend Like Harry '00

MONARCH HOME VIDEO
2 Ingram Blvd.
La Vergne, TN 37086-7006
(615)287-4632
Fax: (615)287-4992

American Nightmare '00
Sexual Chemistry '99
T.N.T. '98

MPI HOME VIDEO
16101 S. 108th Ave.
Orland Park, IL 60467
(708)460-0555
800-777-2223
Fax: (708)873-3177

The Adventures of Sherlock Holmes, Vol. 3 '83

Dark Shadows: DVD Collection 1 '67
Let Freedom Ring: Images of the American Spirit '01
Men Are from Mars, Women Are from Venus '97
Petula Clark: A Sign of the Times '01
Richard Pryor: Live and Smokin' '81

MTI HOME VIDEO
14216 SW 136th St.
Miami, FL 33186
(305)255-8684
Fax: (305)233-6943

The Alchemists '99
Carnivore '01
Choke '01
Cypress Edge '99
Dead Creatures '01
Dead Silence '98
Dean Koontz's Black River '01
Deep Trouble '01
Dr. Jekyll & Mr. Hyde '00
Doomsdayer '99
Double Deception '01
Extreme Heist '99
Extreme Honor '1
Fatal Blade '00
Kiss Tomorrow Goodbye '00
L.A.P.D.: To Protect and Serve '01
Lena's Dreams '97
Lip Service '00
Luminarias '99
Matthew Blackheart: Monster Smasher '99
Mr. Rice's Secret '00
Reflex Action '02
Secret of the Andes '01
Showdown '94
Smile Now Cry Later '01
Spreading Ground '01
Sworn to Justice '97
13 Gantry Row '98
The Tomorrow Man '01
The Treat '98
The Turning '92
Voyeur.com '00

MUSIC VIDEO DISTRIBUTORS
PO Box 280
Oaks, PA 19456
800-888-0486

Same Guys, New Dresses: The Kids in the Hall '02
Song for Cassavetes '00
Sublime: Stories, Tales, Lies and Exaggerations '99

NAVARRE CORP.
7400 49th Ave. N.
New Hope, MN 55428
(763)535-8333
800-728-4000
Fax: (763)533-2156

Hollywood Chainsaw Hookers '88

NEW CONCORDE
11600 San Vincente Blvd.
Los Angeles, CA 90049
(310)820-6733
Fax: (310)207-6816

Adventures of Justine '00
Alone with a Stranger '99
The Arena '01
Attack of the 60-Foot Centerfold '95
Avalanche '78
Avalanche Alley '01
Barbarian Queen '85
Barbarian Queen 2: The Empress Strikes Back '89
Big Bad Mama 2 '87
The Big Bird Cage '72

Bloodfist 5: Human Target '93
Bloodfist 6: Ground Zero '94
Bloodfist 7: Manhunt '95
Bloodfist 8: Hard Way Out '96
Cabeza de Vaca '90
Caged Heat '74
Cybercity '99
Daydream Believers: The Monkees Story '00
Deathstalker '83
Deathstalker 2: Duel of the Titans '87
Dillinger and Capone '95
800 Leagues down the Amazon '93
Facing the Enemy '00
A Girl, 3 Guys and a Gun '01
The Great Texas Dynamite Chase '76
Hard As Nails '01
Harold Robbins' Body Parts '01
I Never Promised You a Rose Garden '77
Lady in Red '79
Marquis de Sade '96
The Nest '88
Raptor '01
Rock 'n' Roll High School [New Concorde SE] '79
Rod Steele 0014: You Only Live Until You Die '02
Second to Die '02
Shakedown '02
Shopping '93
Take It to the Limit '00
The Terror Within '88
Tiger Claws '91
The Unborn '91
Up against Amanda '01
The White Pony '99
Women in Cages '71

NEW LINE HOME VIDEO
116 N. Robertson Blvd.
Los Angeles, CA 90048
(310)967-6670
Fax: (310)854-0602

The Anniversary Party '01
Blow '01
Bones '01
Desperate Living (John Waters Collection Vol. 2) '77
Female Trouble '74
15 Minutes '01
Hairspray (John Waters Collection Vol. 1) '88
Happy Campers '01
Hedwig and the Angry Inch '00
Highway '01
House Party 4: Down to the Last Minute '00
Hurlyburly '98
I Am Sam '01
Life As a House '01
Love and Basketball '00
Money Talks '97
Pecker (John Waters Collection Vol. 1) '98
Pink Flamingos '72
Polyester (John Waters Collection Vol. 2) '81
The Prime Gig '00
Rush Hour 2 '01
State and Main '00
Sugar & Spice '01
Thirteen Days '00
Town and Country '01
Twin Peaks: Fire Walk with Me '92

NEW VIDEO GROUP
126 5th Ave., 15th Fl.
New York, NY 10017
(212)206-8600
800-314-8822
Fax: (212)206-9001

Borough of Kings '98
Bread and Roses '00
Bruiser '00
Bully '01
Cement '99
Chasing Sleep '00
The Contaminated Man '01
The Convent '01
Dancing at the Blue Iguana '00
Dark Asylum '01
Deeply '99
The Devil's Prey '01
Fast Sofa '01
Fever '99
Firetrap '01
The Guardian '00
In His Life: The John Lennon Story '00
Kill Me Later '01
The King's Guard '01
Letters from a Killer '98
Lost and Delirious '01
Love Come Down '00
Luckytown '00
Lush '01
Madeline at the North Pole '00
Maze '01
Murder in Coweta County '83
Nowhere in Sight '01
O '01
Olive Juice '01
On the Borderline '01
100 Girls '00
Paranoia '98
Perfume '01
Progeny '98
Radical Jack '00
Ricochet River '98
Ripper: Letter from Hell '01
Route 666 '01
Sand '00
Servants of Twilight '91
Seven Days to Live '01
Shelter '98
Smiling Fish & Goat on Fire '99
Snapdragon '93
South of Heaven, West of Hell '01
Spanish Judges '99
Stalker '98
Styx '00
Tick Tock '00
Turbulence 3: Heavy Metal '00
Two Ninas '00
Uncorked '98
Victim of Love '91
Water Damage '01
Wind River '98
The Wrecking Crew '99

SUB ROSA STUDIOS
5858 E. Malloy Rd., Ste. 163A
Syracuse, NY 13211
(315)454-5608
Fax: (315)478-1410

I Spit on Your Corpse, I Piss on Your Grave '02
Inbred Rednecks '97
Shatter Dead '01

SUNLAND STUDIOS
9450 Chivers Ave.
Sun Valley, CA 91352
(818)504-6332
800-934-2111
Fax: (818)504-6380

Skyscraper '95
To the Limit '95
When Justice Fails '98

SYNAPSE
PO Box 1860
Bloomington, IL 61702
(309)661-9201
Fax: (309)661-9140

The Beast from Haunted Cave '60
The Grapes of Death '78
Invasion U.S.A. '52
Organ '96
Star Warp'd '01

TAI SENG VIDEO MARKETING
170 S. Spruce Ave., Ste. 200
South San Francisco, CA 94080
(415)871-8118
800-888-3836
Fax: (415)871-2392

The Assassin '93
The Avenging Fist '01
Ballistic Kiss '98
Brother of Darkness '94
Bury Me High '90
The Cheaters '00
City of Glass '98
Cold War '00
Comic King '00
Cops on a Mission '01
Daughter of Darkness '93
The Demon's Baby '98
Dragon Inn '92
Dragon's Claws '79
Dreaming Fists with Slender Hands '80
The Duel '71
Eat My Dust '93
Fist of Fury '95
The Fist Power '99
Gonin '95
Goodbye, Mr. Cool '01
Happy End '99
The Invincible Killer '81
Jiang Hu—"The Triad Zone" '00
Killer '00
Last Hurrah for Chivalry '78
The Legend of a Professional '00
The Legendary Strike '78
The Lord of Hangzhou '98
Magnificent Butcher '87
Master of Death '75
Millennium Dragon '93
Ninja in the Deadly Trap '83
Ninja in the U.S.A. '88
Ninja vs. Shaolin Guards '84
The Owl vs. Bombo '84
Para Para Sakura '01
The Phantom Lover '95
Picture of a Nymph '88
Prison on Fire 2 '91
Revengeful Swordswoman '80
Rich and Famous / Tragic Hero '87
Righting Wrongs '86
Sadistic City '93
Shaolin Disciple '86
The Storm Riders '98
Super Kung Fu Kid '86
Swordsman 2 '91
Taboo '97
Thunder Kick '73
Too Many Ways to Be No. 1 '97
Trust Me U Die '99
Ultimatum '01
The Untold Story 2 '98
Wheels on Meals '84
Where a Good Man Goes '99
Your Place or Mine! '98

TAURUS
465 McGill St.
Montreal, QC, Canada H2Y A46

Horror 101 '00

TEMPE ENTERTAINMENT
3727 W. Magnolia Blvd., No. 241
Burbank, CA 91510-7711
(818)762-5707

Vengeance of the Dead '01

TLA VIDEO
234 Market St.
Philadelphia, PA 19106
(215)733-0608
800-333-8521

Forgive and Forget '99
The Trio '97

TRITON MULTIMEDIA
15030 Ventura Blvd., No. 912
Sherman Oaks, CA 91403

The Black Raven '43
Crime Stoppers, Vol. 2 '01
Fog Island '45
German Silent Masterpieces '00
Pearl Harbor Before and After '01

TROMA TEAM VIDEO
733 9th Ave.
New York, NY 10019
(212)957-5678
800-83-TROMA
Fax: (212)957-4497

The Best of Tromadance '02
Bowery at Midnight '42
Cannibal! The Musical '96
Christmas Evil '80
Dementia 13 [Roan] '63
First Turn On [DC] '83
The Invisible Ghost '41
Legend of the Chupacabra '97
Mysterious Mr. Wong '35
The New Gladiators '83
Rabid Grannies '89
Rage at Dawn '55
Real Time: Siege at Lucas Street Market '00
Squeeze Play [DC] '79
Strange Illusion '45
Stuck on You! [DC] '84
The Toxic Avenger, Part 3: The Last Temptation of Toxie [DC] '89
Troma's Edge TV: Vol. 1 '00
Undersea Kingdom '36
Vengeance Valley '51
Waitress [DC] '81

TVA INTERNATIONAL
Address Unknown

Intimacy '00

20th CENTURY FOX HOME ENTERTAINMENT
PO Box 900
Beverly Hills, CA 90213
(310)369-3900
888-223-4FOX
Fax: (310)369-5811

All the Right Moves '83
Baby's Day Out '94
Bachelor Party '84
Batman: The Movie '66
Behind Enemy Lines '01
Beyond Suspicion '00
The Bible '66
Black Knight '01
Breaking Away '79
Bright Eyes '34
Buffy the Vampire Slayer '92
Buffy the Vampire Slayer: Season 1 '97
Carmen Jones '54
Courage Under Fire '96
The Deep End '01
Deep Water '99
Die Hard [FS 2] '88
Dimples '36
Dr. Dolittle 2 '01
Donnie Darko '01
Don't Bother to Knock '52
Don't Say a Word '01
Dude, Where's My Car? '00
Enemy Mine '85

Extreme Limits '01
Ferngully '92
The Five Heartbeats '91
Freddy Got Fingered '01
The French Connection [SE] '71
French Connection 2 '75
From Hell [DLE] '01
The Fury '78
A Glimpse of Hell '01
Guadalcanal Diary '43
The Halls of Montezuma '50
Heidi '37
The Ice Storm '97
Joy Ride '01
Kingdom Come '01
Kiss of the Dragon '01
The Legend of Hell House '73
Let's Make Love '60
The Life and Times of Hank Greenberg '99
Love Is a Many Splendored Thing '55
Love Potion 9 '92
Marilyn Monroe: The Diamond Collection, Vol. 2 '02
M*A*S*H [FS] '70
Me, Myself, and Irene '00
Mom's Outta Sight '01
Monkey Business '52
Monkeybone '01
Moulin Rouge [SE] '01
My Bodyguard '80
Niagara '52
The Object of My Affection '98
One Fine Day '96
Patton [2] '70
Phantom of the Paradise '74
Ping! '99
Planet of the Apes '01
Point Break '91
Reckless and Wild '02
Revenge of the Nerds / Revenge of the Nerds 2: Nerds in Paradise '84
River of No Return '54
The Robe '53
Rookie of the Year '93
The Sandlot '93
Say Anything [SE] '89
Say It Isn't So '01
Sexy Beast '00
The Simpsons: The Complete First Season '89
Someone Like You '01
Star Wars: Episode 1—The Phantom Menace '99
Stealing Beauty '96
Taps '81
That Thing You Do! '96
Thumbelina [20th Century Fox] '94
Toys '92
A Troll in Central Park '94
Twelve o'Clock High '49
Unlawful Entry '92
Venomous '01
Von Ryan's Express '65
Waking Life '01
The War of the Roses [SE] '89
Willow '88
A Wing and a Prayer '44
The X-Files: Season 4 '00
The Young Lions '58

UNITED AMERICAN VIDEO
PO Box 7647
Charlotte, NC 28241
(803)548-7300
Fax: (803)548-3335

Where the Red Fern Grows '74
Where the Red Fern Grows: Part 2 '92

UNIVERSAL STUDIOS HOME VIDEO
100 Universal City Plz.
Universal City, CA 91608-9955
(818)777-1000
Fax: (818)866-1483

Abbott and Costello Meet the Mummy '55
American Pie [2 UE] '99
American Pie 2 '01
An American Werewolf in London [CE Universal] '81
Balto 2: Wolf Quest '02
Beautiful Creatures '00
Beethoven's 4th '01
The Big Broadcast of 1938 '38
Bingo Long Traveling All-Stars & Motor Kings '76
Blood Simple '85
Boogeymen '01
Brewster's Millions [Universal] '85
Bring It On '00
Burn the Floor '00
Cape Fear '61
Cape Fear '91
Captain Corelli's Mandolin '01
Cats [UE Universal] '98
The Caveman's Valentine '01
College Swing '38
Creature from the Black Lagoon '54
Dr. Seuss' How the Grinch Stole Christmas '00
Dracula's Daughter '36
Family Man '00
The Fast and the Furious '01
Frankenstein Meets the Wolfman '42
The Ghost Breakers '40
The Ghost of Frankenstein '42
Halloween 2: The Nightmare Isn't Over! [Universal] '81
Head over Heels '01
House of Frankenstein '44
How High '01
It Came from Outer Space '53
Jaws 2 '78
Josie and the Pussycats '01
Jurassic Park 3 [CE] '01
K-PAX '01
Legend UE '86
The Long Run '00
MacArthur '77
The Man Who Cried '00
Marnie '64
Midway [Universal CE] '76
Muhammad Ali—Through the Eyes of the World '02
Mulholland Drive '01
The Mummy Returns '01
The Mummy's Curse '44
The Mummy's Ghost '44
The Mummy's Hand '40
The Mummy's Tomb '42
The Musketeer '01
My Favorite Blonde '42
On the Edge '00
Out of Africa '85
Play Misty for Me '71
Rat '00
The Road to Morocco [Universal] '42
The Road to Singapore '40
The Road to Utopia [Universal] '46
The Road to Zanzibar '41
Shaolin: Wheel of Life '00
She Wolf of London '46
Silent Running [Universal] '71
The Skulls 2 '02
Slap Shot [2] '77
Slap Shot 2: Breaking the Ice '02
Son of Dracula '43

Tieta of Agreste '96
Ulysses' Gaze '95
Under the Sand '00
A Voice from Heaven '01
Walls of Hell '64
Wirey Spindell '99

WOLFE VIDEO
PO Box 64
New Almaden, CA 95042
(408)268-6782
800-438-9653
Fax: (408)268-9449

Lilies '96

**XENON
ENTERTAINMENT**
1440 9th St.
Santa Monica, CA 90401
(310)451-5510
800-829-1913
Fax: (310)395-4058

Bravo '98
Buddha Assassinator '79
Champ vs. Champ [Xenon]
  '83

Eagle Fist '77
Eagle vs. Silver Fox '83
Fearless Dragon '79
Fighting Ace '79
Fury in the Shaolin Temple '82
Goose Boxer '78
Invincible Obsessed Fighter
  '82
Jackie's Back '99
Jade Claw '79
Lady Iron Monkey '83
Poor White Trash '00
Return of the Deadly Blade
  '81
Revenge of the Patriots '76
10 Magnificent Killers '77
Tiger over Wall '80
Two Coyotes '01
Welcome to Death Row '00

YORK ENTERTAINMENT
16133 Ventura Blvd., Ste.
1140
Encino, CA 91436
(818)788-4050
800-84-MOVIE
Fax: (818)788-4011

Adventures of the Kung Fu
  Rascals '92
Art House '98
Axe 'Em '02
Better Dayz '02
Beverly Hills Bordello '01
Beverly Hood '99
Black and Blue '01
Boundaries '97
Chicks, Man '99
Creepin' '01
Danger beneath the Sea '02
Dead or Alive '02
Dead Pet '01
Dirty Kopz '01
Fallout '01
Fashionably L.A. '99
First Degree '01
Fishing with Gandhi '98
Flooding '97
Friction '95
Get Down on It '01
Green '01
Hairdo U '02
The Hunger: Smoke, Mirrors,
  and Paranoia '00
Ice Grill '02

Illicit Confessions '77
Lady in Blue '96
Late Night Sessions '99
Loser '97
Man Next Door '97
Night Orchid '97
1999 '98
The Others '97
Parental Guidance '02
Pep Squad '98
The Perfect Wife '00
Random Acts of Violence '02
Random Encounter '98
Rappin'-N-Rhyming '00
Raven's Ridge '97
The Riff '00
Rough Air '02
Rudy Blue '00
Shades of Darkness '00
She Lives by Night '01
Silver Wolf '98
Smash Cuts! Super Sci-Fi
  Shorts '00
Smash Cuts: Totally Twisted
  Shorts Fest '00
Social Intercourse '01
Sweet Thing '00

The Triangle '01
2103: Deadly Wake '97

ZEITGEIST FILMS LTD.
247 Centre St., 2nd Fl.
New York, NY 10013
(212)274-1989
Fax: (212)274-1644

The Acid House '98
Aimee & Jaguar '98
Calendar '93
Family Viewing / Next of Kin
  '87
Manufacturing Consent:
  Noam Chomsky and the
  Media '93
Next of Kin '84
Speaking Parts '89
Water Drops on Burning
  Rocks '99

Listed below are all titles covered in "Book 1," "Book 2," and this volume, "Book 3." Each DVD is labelled **1, 2, or 3,** in bold, to indicate in which volume of the series a particular DVD title may be found. Note that there are duplicates of some DVDs; if the title was put out by more than one distributor, the distributor's name will be indicated. If a distributor re-released a title, then the notations [1] and [2] will appear. Finally, some titles are annotated with the following codes to indicate designations specificed by the distributors: [CE] (Collector's Edition), [CS] (Collector's Series), [DC] (Director's Cut), [DLE] (Director's Limited Edition), [EE] (Enhanced Edition), [FS] (Five Star Edition), [LE] (Limited Edition), [ME] (Millennium Edition), [PE] (Platinum Edition), [SE] (Special Edition), [SB] (Superbit), [UE] (Ultimate Edition).

Andre '94 **3**
Andrei Rublev '66 **1**
The Andromeda Strain '71 **1**
Andy Warhol '88 **2**
Andy Warhol's Dracula '74 **1**
Andy Warhol's Frankenstein '74 **1**
Angel and the Badman '47 **1**
Angel Blue '97 **3**
Angel Eyes '01 **3**
Angel Heart '87 **1**
Angel Heart '95 **1**
Angel in Training '99 **1**
Angel of the Night '98 **2**
Angel on My Shoulder '46 **2**
Angel Sanctuary '00 **3**
Angela's Ashes '99 **2**
Angels and Insects '95 **3**
Angel's Dance '99 **1**
Angels Hard As They Come '71 **3**
Angels in the Outfield '94 **3**
Angels' Wild Women '72 **2**
The Angry Red Planet '59 **3**
Anguish '88 **3**
Anima '98 **3**
The Animal '01 **3**
Animal Crackers '30 **1**
Animal Factory '00 **2**
Animal Instincts '92 **2**
Animal Instincts 3: The Seductress '95 **1**
Animal Room '95 **1**
Animaland '48 **1**
Animals at Play: Cute and Cuddly '01 **3**
Animated Christmas DVD Double Feature '79 **3**
Animation Greats '97 **2**
Animation Legend: Winsor McCay '93 **2**
Anna and the King '99 **3**
Anna Karenina '48 **2**
Anne Frank '01 **3**
Annie '82 **2**
Annie '99 **3**
Annie Get Your Gun '50 **2**
Annie Hall '77 **1**
The Anniversary Party '01 **3**
Another Day, Another Man '66 **2**
Another Day in Paradise '98 **1**
Another 48 Hrs. '90 **1**
Another Man's Poison '52 **1**
Another 9 1/2 Weeks '96 **1**
Another Woman '88 **2**
Antarctica '91 **1**
Antitrust '00 **2**
Antonia's Line '95 **1**
Antz '98 **1**
Any Given Sunday '99 **2**
Any Number Can Win '63 **1**
Any Which Way You Can '80 **3**
Anywhere But Here '99 **1**
Anzio '68 **3**
The Apartment '60 **2**
A*P*E* '76 **3**
The Apocalypse '96 **1**
Apocalypse Now '79 **3**
Apocalypse Now [Redux] '79 **3**
The Apocalypse Watch '97 **3**
Apollo 13 '95 **1**
The Apostate '98 **2**
The Apostle '97 **1**
Apt Pupil '97 **1**
Arabian Nights '74 **1**
Arachnid '01 **3**
Arachnophobia '90 **1**
Arbuckle & Keaton, Vol. 1 (1917–19) '00 **3**
Arbuckle & Keaton, Vol. 2 (1918–20) '00 **3**
The Architecture of Doom '91 **1**
Arctic Blue '93 **3**
The Arena '73 **2**
The Arena '01 **3**
Aria '88 **1**
The Aristocats '70 **2**

Arlington Road '99 **1**
Armageddon '97 **1**
Armageddon '98 **1**
Armistead Maupin's More Tales of the City '97 **1**
Armitage 3: Polymatrix '94 **1**
Armstrong '97 **2**
Army of Darkness '92 **1**
Around the Fire '98 **2**
Around the World in 80 Days '89 **1**
Around the World with Orson Welles '55 **2**
The Arrangement '99 **2**
The Arrival '96 **1**
Arsenic and Old Lace '44 **2**
Art and Jazz in Animation '85 **1**
Art House '98 **3**
Art of Fighting '93 **2**
The Art of War '00 **2**
Arthur '81 **1**
As Good As It Gets '97 **1**
As You Like It '36 **1**
Ashes of Time '94 **2**
Ashik Kerib '88 **3**
The Asphyx '72 **2**
Assassin '86 **1**
The Assassin '93 **3**
Assassin of Youth '35 **2**
Assassins '95 **1**
The Assault '97 **1**
Assault of the Killer Bimbos '88 **1**
Assault of the Party Nerds '89 **2**
Assault of the Party Nerds 2: Heavy Petting Detective '95 **2**
Assault on Precinct 13 '76 **1**
The Assignment '97 **1**
The Associate '96 **1**
Asteroid '97 **2**
The Astounding She-Monster '58 **2**
The Astro-Zombies '67 **2**
The Astronaut's Wife '99 **1**
Asylum '72 **2**
Asylum of Terror '98 **2**
At Bertram's Hotel '86 **3**
At Close Range '86 **2**
At First Sight '98 **1**
At the Earth's Core '76 **3**
At War with the Army '50 **2**
Atlantic City '81 **3**
Atlantis: The Lost Empire [CE] '01 **3**
The Atomic Cafe [SE] '83 **3**
Atomic Submarine '59 **1**
Atomic Train '99 **1**
Atomic War Bride / This Is Not a Test '60 **3**
Attack from Mars '88 **3**
Attack of the Giant Leeches [SlingShot] '59 **2**
Attack of the Giant Leeches [Marengo] '59 **3**
Attack of the Puppet People '58 **2**
Attack of the 60-Foot Center-fold '95 **3**
Attack—The Battle for New Britain '44 **3**
Attention Shoppers '99 **2**
Attila '01 **2**
Attila 74: The Rape of Cyprus '75 **2**
Attraction '00 **3**
Au Pair Girls '72 **3**
The Audrey Hepburn Story '00 **2**
Audrey Rose '77 **3**
Austin Powers: International Man of Mystery '97 **3**
Austin Powers 2: The Spy Who Shagged Me '99 **1**
The Autobiography of Miss Jane Pittman '74 **3**
Autopsy '78 **1**
Autumn in New York '00 **2**
Avalanche '78 **3**

Avalanche Alley '01 **3**
Avalon '90 **2**
The Avengers 1964–66 '67 **2**
The Avengers '67 '67 **1**
The Avengers '68 '68 **3**
The Avengers '98 **1**
The Avenging Fist '01 **3**
The Aviator '85 **3**
Awakening of Gabriella '99 **1**
Awakenings '90 **1**
Awakenings of the Beast '68 **2**
Away All Boats '56 **2**
The Awful Dr. Orlof '62 **2**
The Awful Truth: The Complete Second Season '01 **3**
Axe '74 **3**
Axe 'Em '02 **3**
Ayn Rand: A Sense of Life '98 **1**

B
B. Monkey '97 **2**
Babar: King of the Elephants '99 **2**
Babe '95 **1**
Babe: Pig in the City '98 **1**
Babette's Feast '87 **2**
The Baby '72 **1**
Baby Bach '00 **3**
Baby Boom '87 **2**
Baby Boy '01 **3**
Baby Dolittle: Neighborhood Animals '01 **3**
Baby Dolittle: World Animals '01 **3**
Baby Einstein: Language Nursery '01 **3**
Baby Geniuses '98 **1**
Baby Mozart '00 **3**
Baby Shakespeare '99 **3**
Baby Van Gogh '00 **3**
Baby's Day Out '94 **3**
The Babysitter's Seduction '96 **1**
The Bachelor '99 **1**
Bachelor Party '84 **3**
Back to Back '96 **2**
Back to God's Country / Something New '19 **2**
Back to School '86 **2**
Back to the Secret Garden '01 **3**
Backdraft '91 **1**
Backlash '99 **2**
Backstage '00 **2**
Backyard Dogs '00 **3**
The Bad and the Beautiful '52 **3**
Bad Boys [Republic] '83 **1**
Bad Boys [Anchor Bay] '83 **3**
Bad Boys '95 **3**
Bad Company '72 **3**
Bad Cop Chronicles: Confessions of a Police Captain '72 **3**
Bad Cop Chronicles 2: Corrupt '84 **3**
Bad Girls Go to Hell / Another Day, Another Man '65 **2**
Bad Lieutenant '92 **1**
Bad Love '95 **1**
Bad Manners '98 **2**
Bad Man's River '72 **2**
Bad Moon '96 **2**
The Bad News Bears '76 **3**
The Bad News Bears Go to Japan '78 **3**
The Bad News Bears in Breaking Training '77 **3**
Bad Seed '00 **3**
Bad Taste [LE] '88 **3**
Badlands '74 **1**
Bagdad Cafe '88 **3**
Baise Moi '00 **3**
Bait '00 **2**
Baker's Hawk '76 **1**
The Balcony '63 **2**
Ball of Fire '41 **1**
Ballad of a Soldier '60 **3**
The Ballad of Ramblin' Jack '00 **2**

Ballistic Kiss '98 **3**
Balto 2: Wolf Quest '02 **3**
Bamboozled '00 **2**
Bananas '71 **2**
Bandit Queen '94 **2**
Bandits '99 **2**
Bandits '01 **3**
The Bank Dick '40 **2**
Banzai Runner '86 **2**
Bar-B-Q '00 **2**
Bar Girls '95 **3**
Bar 20 Rides Again '35 **3**
Barabbas '62 **3**
Baraka '93 **1**
Barb Wire '96 **2**
Barbara the Fair with the Silken Hair '69 **3**
Barbarella '68 **1**
Barbarian Queen '85 **3**
Barbarian Queen 2: The Empress Strikes Back '89 **3**
Barbarians at the Gate '93 **3**
Barbie in the Nutcracker '01 **3**
Barcelona '94 **3**
Bare Witness '02 **3**
The Barefoot Contessa '54 **2**
Barefoot in the Park '67 **1**
Barney's Great Adventure '98 **2**
Barry Lyndon '75 **1**
Bartok the Magnificent '99 **1**
The Base '99 **2**
BASEketball '98 **1**
Basic Instinct [1] '92 **1**
Basic Instinct [2 SE] '92 **3**
The Basket [SE] '99 **3**
Basket Case [1] '82 **1**
Basket Case [2 SE] '82 **3**
The Basketball Diaries '94 **1**
Bastard out of Carolina '96 **1**
The Bat [Roan] '59 **1**
The Bat [Goodtimes] '59 **3**
The Bat Whispers '30 **1**
Bataan '43 **1**
Batman '89 **1**
Batman & Mr. Freeze: Subzero '97 **3**
Batman and Robin '97 **1**
Batman Beyond: Return of the Joker [1] '00 **2**
Batman Beyond: Return of the Joker [2 Uncut] '00 **3**
Batman Forever '95 **1**
Batman: Mask of the Phantasm '93 **2**
Batman Returns '92 **1**
The Batman Superman Movie '97 **3**
Batman: The Animated Series—The Legend Begins '92 **3**
Batman: The Movie '66 **3**
Bats '99 **2**
*batteries not included '87 **1**
Battle beyond the Stars '80 **2**
Battle for the Planet of the Apes '73 **2**
Battle of the Amazons '74 **2**
Battle of the Planets, Vol. 1 '78 **3**
Battle of the Planets, Vol. 2 '78 **3**
Battle of the Planets, Vol. 3 '78 **3**
Battle of the Sexes '28 **2**
Battle Queen 2020 '99 **2**
Battlecade: Extreme Fighting '95 **1**
Battlecade: Extreme Fighting 2 '96 **1**
Battlefield Earth '00 **2**
The Battleship Potemkin '25 **1**
Battlestar Galactica '78 **1**
Battling Butler '26 **1**
Bay of Blood '71 **2**
Baywatch: Nightmare Bay / River of No Return '94 **2**
The Beach '00 **2**

Beach Blanket Bingo '65 **2**
Beach Girls '82 **2**
Beach Party '63 **2**
Bean '97 **1**
The Bear '89 **3**
Bear in the Big Blue House: Party Time with Bear '00 **2**
Bear in the Big Blue House: Potty Time with Bear '99 **3**
Bear in the Big Blue House: Shapes, Sounds & Colors '00 **2**
The Bears & I '74 **1**
The Beast '75 **3**
The Beast '88 **2**
Beast Cops '98 **1**
The Beast from Haunted Cave '60 **3**
The Beast Must Die '75 **2**
The Beast of Yucca Flats '61 **2**
The Beast That Killed Women / The Monster of Camp Sunshine '65 **2**
Beast Wars: Transformers, Vol. 1 '96 **3**
The Beast Within '82 **3**
Beastmaster '82 **1**
Beat the Devil '53 **2**
The Beatles: A Celebration '96 **3**
The Beatles: The First U.S. Visit '91 **1**
The Beatles: The Ultimate DVD Collection '00 **2**
Beau Pere '81 **1**
Beautiful '00 **2**
Beautiful Beast '95 **3**
Beautiful Creatures '00 **3**
Beautiful Girls '96 **1**
Beautiful Hunter '94 **3**
Beautiful Joe '00 **2**
Beautiful People '99 **2**
Beauty and the Beast '46 **1**
Beauty and the Beast: The Enchanted Christmas '97 **2**
Beauty Investigator '93 **1**
Beavis and Butt-Head Do America '96 **1**
Because of You '95 **2**
Because Why? '93 **3**
Bed and Board '70 **2**
Bed of Roses '95 **1**
The Bed You Sleep In '93 **2**
Bedazzled [SE] '00 **2**
Bedknobs and Broomsticks '71 **2**
The Bedroom '92 **3**
The Bedroom Window '87 **2**
Bedrooms and Hallways '98 **2**
Beethoven '36 **2**
Beethoven '00 **2**
Beethoven's 2nd '93 **1**
Beethoven's 3rd '00 **2**
Beethoven's 4th '01 **3**
Beetle Bailey / Hagar the Horrible / Betty Boop '89 **2**
Beetlejuice '88 **1**
Before Night Falls '00 **2**
Before Sunrise '94 **1**
The Beguiled '70 **1**
Behind Enemy Lines '01 **3**
Behind Locked Doors '48 **3**
Behind Office Doors '31 **3**
Behind the Planet of the Apes '98 **2**
Being John Malkovich '99 **1**
Being There '79 **2**
Bela Lugosi Double Feature: The Corpse Vanishes / Invisible Ghost '01 **3**
Bela Lugosi Meets a Brooklyn Gorilla '52 **3**
Bell, Book and Candle '58 **1**
Belle de Jour '67 **3**
Belle of the Nineties '34 **1**
The Bells / The Crazy Ray '26 **1**
The Bells of St. Mary's '45 **1**
Belly '98 **1**

Breaker Morant '80 **1**
Breakfast at Tiffany's '61 **1**
The Breakfast Club '85 **1**
Breakfast of Champions '98 **2**
Breakheart Pass '76 **2**
Breaking Away '79 **3**
Breaking In '89 **3**
Breaking the Waves '95 **2**
Breakout '75 **3**
Breast Men '97 **3**
Breathless '59 **3**
The Breed '01 **3**
Breeders '86 **3**
Breeders '97 **1**
Brenda Starr '86 **1**
Brewster's Millions [Good-times] '85 **1**
Brewster's Millions [Universal] '85 **3**
Brian's Song '71 **2**
The Bride '85 **3**
Bride of Chucky '98 **1**
The Bride of Frankenstein '35 **1**
Bride of Re-Animator '89 **2**
Bride of the Monster '55 **1**
Bride of the Wind '01 **3**
The Bride with White Hair '93 **1**
The Bride with White Hair 2 '93 **1**
The Bride Wore Black '68 **2**
The Bridge '00 **2**
The Bridge at Remagen '69 **2**
Bridge of Dragons '99 **2**
The Bridge of San Luis Rey '44 **1**
The Bridge on the River Kwai [LE] '57 **2**
A Bridge Too Far '77 **1**
The Bridges at Toko-Ri '55 **2**
The Bridges of Madison County '95 **1**
Bridget Jones's Diary '01 **3**
Brief Affair '96 **3**
Brief Encounter '46 **2**
Brigadoon '54 **1**
Bright Eyes '34 **3**
A Bright Shining Lie '98 **1**
Brighton Beach Memoirs '86 **1**
Bring It On '00 **3**
Bringing Out the Dead '99 **2**
Britannia Hospital '82 **3**
The British Invasion Returns '00 **2**
Broadcast News '87 **1**
Broadway Danny Rose '84 **3**
Brokedown Palace '99 **1**
Broken Arrow '95 **1**
Broken Blossoms [Image] '19 **1**
Broken Blossoms [Kino] '19 **3**
Broken Harvest '94 **2**
The Broken Hearts Club '00 **2**
Broken Vessels '98 **2**
Bronco Billy '80 **2**
A Bronx Tale '93 **1**
Brooklyn Babylon '00 **3**
Brother '01 **3**
Brother Cadfael: The Devil's Novice '94 **2**
Brother, Can You Spare a Dime? '75 **1**
Brother of Darkness '94 **3**
The Brotherhood '68 **3**
Brothers in Arms '01 **3**
A Brother's Kiss '97 **1**
The Brothers McMullen '94 **2**
The Brothers Quay Collection '00 **3**
Bruce Lee: A Warrior's Journey '01 **3**
Bruce Lee and Kung Fu Mania '92 **3**
Bruce Lee Fights Back from the Grave '76 **3**

Bruce Lee the Invincible '77 **3**
Bruiser '00 **3**
The Brutal Truth '99 **2**
Brute Force '46 **1**
The Brute Man '46 **1**
The Brylcreem Boys '96 **2**
Bubble Boy '01 **3**
Bubblegum Crisis Tokyo 2040 '00 **2**
Buck Privates '41 **1**
Buck Privates Come Home '47 **1**
A Bucket of Blood [Slingshot] '59 **2**
A Bucket of Blood / Attack of the Giant Leeches [Marengo] '59 **3**
Bucktown '75 **3**
Buddha Assassinator '79 **3**
Buddhist Fist '80 **1**
Buddy '97 **2**
The Buddy Holly Story '78 **1**
Buena Vista Social Club '99 **1**
Buffalo Bill & the Indians '76 **2**
Buffalo 66 '97 **1**
Buffet Froid '79 **1**
Buffy the Vampire Slayer '92 **3**
Buffy the Vampire Slayer: Season 1 '97 **3**
Bug Buster '99 **1**
A Bug's Life [CE] '98 **1**
Bugsy '91 **1**
Bull Durham [Image] '88 **1**
Bull Durham [MGM SE] '88 **3**
Bulldog Drummond Escapes '37 **2**
Bulldog Drummond's Secret Police '39 **2**
A Bullet for the General '68 **3**
A Bullet in the Head '90 **1**
Bulletproof '96 **2**
Bullets over Broadway '94 **1**
Bullitt '68 **1**
Bully '01 **1**
Bulworth '98 **1**
Bummer '73 **3**
The 'Burbs '89 **1**
Burglar '87 **1**
Burlesque on Carmen '16 **2**
Burn the Floor '03 **3**
Burnzy's Last Call '95 **3**
Bury Me High '90 **3**
Bury Me in Niagara '93 **1**
Bus Stop '56 **2**
Business Is Business '71 **3**
Buster Keaton Rides Again / The Railrodder '65 **2**
Bustin' Loose '81 **2**
But I'm a Cheerleader '99 **2**
Butch Cassidy and the Sundance Kid '69 **1**
The Butcher's Wife '91 **3**
Butterfield 8 '60 **2**
Butterflies Are Free '72 **3**
Butterfly '00 **2**
Buzz Lightyear of Star Command: The Adventure Begins '00 **2**
Bye, Bye, Birdie '63 **1**
Bye Bye Monkey '77 **1**

C
Cabaret '72 **1**
Cabeza de Vaca '90 **3**
Cabin by the Lake / Return to Cabin by the Lake '00 **3**
The Cabinet of Dr. Caligari '19 **1**
Cabiria '14 **3**
The Cable Guy '96 **1**
Cabo Blanco / U.S. Marshal '81 **1**
Cactus Flower '69 **3**
Caddyshack '80 **1**
Caddyshack 2 '88 **1**
Cadfael—The Raven in the Foregate '94 **3**
Cadillac Man '90 **3**

Caged Heat '74 **3**
Caillou: Family Collection, Vol. 1 '01 **3**
The Caine Mutiny '54 **1**
Calamity Jane '53 **3**
Calendar '93 **3**
California Suite '78 **3**
Caligula '80 **1**
Call Me Claus '01 **3**
Call of the Wild '72 **2**
Calle 54 '01 **3**
Camelot '67 **1**
Camille Claudel '89 **2**
Camille 2000 '69 **1**
Canadian Bacon '94 **2**
The Candidate '72 **1**
Candleshoe '78 **1**
Candy '68 **2**
Candyman '92 **1**
Candyman 2: Farewell to the Flesh '94 **3**
Cane Toads: An Unnatural History '87 **3**
Cannibal Apocalypse '80 **3**
Cannibal Ferox '84 **2**
Cannibal! The Musical '96 **3**
Cannonball Run '81 **2**
Cannonball Run 2 '84 **1**
Can't Hardly Wait '98 **1**
Can't Stop the Music '80 **3**
The Canterbury Tales '71 **1**
The Canterville Ghost '98 **2**
Cape Fear '61 **3**
Cape Fear '91 **3**
Capitaine Conan '96 **3**
Capone '89 **1**
Capricorn One '78 **1**
Captain Corelli's Mandolin '01 **3**
Captain Kidd [Troma] '45 **2**
Captain Kidd [Marengo] '45 **3**
Captive '00 **2**
The Car '77 **1**
Car Wash '76 **2**
Caracara '00 **2**
Career Opportunities '91 **1**
Careful '92 **3**
Careful, He Might Hear You '84 **3**
Caress of the Vampire [CE] '96 **1**
Caress of the Vampire 2: Teenage Girl a Go-Go '96 **1**
A Caribbean Mystery / The Mirror Cracked from Side to Side '89 **3**
Carl Theodore Dreyer Box Set '00 **3**
Carlito's Way '93 **1**
Carmen / The Cheat '15 **2**
Carmen, Baby '66 **1**
Carmen Jones '54 **3**
Carmen Miranda: Bananas Is My Business '95 **2**
Carnal Crimes '91 **1**
Carnegie Hall '47 **3**
Carnival of Blood / Curse of the Headless Horseman [SE] '71 **3**
Carnival of Souls [DC] '62 **3**
Carnival of Souls / Dementia 13 '62 **3**
Carnival of Souls '98 **1**
Carnivore '01 **3**
Carnosaur '93 **2**
Carnosaur 2 '94 **2**
Carnosaur 3: Primal Species '96 **2**
Carolina Skeletons '92 **1**
Carousel '56 **1**
Carrie '76 **3**
Carrington '95 **3**
Cartel '90 **1**
Cartoon Crazys '97 **1**
Cartoon Crazys 2 '98 **1**
Cartoon Crazys: And the Envelope, Please '99 **1**
Cartoon Crazys: Banned & Censored '00 **2**
Cartoon Crazys Christmas '98 **1**

Cartoon Crazys Comic Book Heroes '00 **2**
Cartoon Crazys Goes to War '98 **1**
Cartoon Crazys: Kids All-Time Favorites '99 **1**
Cartoon Crazys Sci-Fi '99 **1**
Cartoon Crazys Spooky Toons '00 **2**
Cartoon Crazys: The Great Animation Studios: Famous Studios '00 **2**
Cartoon Noir '00 **2**
Casablanca '42 **1**
Casino '95 **1**
Casper's Haunted Christmas '00 **2**
The Cassandra Crossing '76 **2**
Cast a Giant Shadow '66 **3**
Castaway '00 **2**
The Castle '97 **1**
Castle Freak '95 **1**
The Castle of Cagliostro '80 **1**
Castles of War '00 **3**
Casual Sex? '88 **1**
Casualties of War '89 **3**
The Cat and the Canary '27 **1**
Cat Ballou [SE] '65 **2**
Cat City '87 **1**
The Cat from Outer Space '78 **1**
The Cat o' Nine Tails '71 **3**
Cat on a Hot Tin Roof '84 **1**
Cat People '82 **1**
Cat Women of the Moon '53 **2**
Catch-22 '70 **2**
Catherine Cookson's The Cinder Path '94 **2**
Catherine Cookson's The Girl '96 **3**
Catherine Cookson's The Secret '00 **3**
Catherine the Great '95 **3**
Cats [USA] '98 **1**
Cats [UE Universal] '98 **3**
Caught Up '98 **1**
Cause of Death '90 **1**
Cave Girl '85 **3**
Cave of the Living Dead '65 **2**
Caveman '81 **3**
The Caveman's Valentine '01 **3**
C.C. & Company '70 **3**
Cecil B. Demented '00 **2**
Celebrity '98 **1**
The Cell '00 **2**
The Celluloid Closet '95 **3**
Cement '00 **3**
The Cement Garden '93 **2**
The Center of the World '01 **3**
Center Stage '91 **1**
Center Stage '00 **2**
Central Station '98 **1**
C'est la Vie, Mon Cherie '93 **1**
Chac: The Rain God '74 **3**
Chained Heat 3: Hell Mountain '98 **2**
Chairman of the Board '97 **1**
The Challenge of Flight: Disc One '99 **1**
The Chamber '96 **1**
Champ Against Champ [BFS] '83 **3**
Champ vs. Champ [Xenon] '83 **3**
Champions '96 **1**
Chances Are '89 **2**
Chang: A Drama of the Wilderness '27 **2**
The Changeling '80 **2**
Changing Habits '96 **1**
Chaplin '92 **1**
The Chaplin Mutuals, Vol. 1 '97 **1**
The Chaplin Mutuals, Vol. 2 '97 **1**

The Chaplin Mutuals, Vol. 3 '97 **1**
Chaplin's Art of Comedy '66 **1**
Chaplin's Essanay Comedies, Vol. 1 '99 **1**
Chaplin's Essanay Comedies, Vol. 2 '99 **1**
Chaplin's Essanay Comedies, Vol. 3 '99 **1**
Chappaqua '66 **1**
Charade '63 **1**
The Charcoal People '01 **3**
The Charge of the Light Brigade '68 **3**
Chariots of Fire '81 **1**
Charles Chaplin—A First National Collection '?? **1**
Charlie, the Lonesome Cougar '67 **1**
Charlie's Angels '00 **2**
Charlie's Angels: Angels Undercover '76 **2**
Charlotte's Web '73 **2**
Charming Billy '99 **1**
Chasers '94 **2**
Chasing Amy '97 **2**
Chasing Sleep '00 **3**
Chato's Land '71 **3**
The Cheap Detective '78 **3**
Cheap Trick: Music for Hangovers '98 **3**
The Cheat [Image] '15 **2**
The Cheat [Kino] '15 **3**
The Cheaters '00 **3**
Cheaters '00 **2**
Cheech and Chong: Still Smokin' '83 **2**
Cheech and Chong's Nice Dreams '81 **3**
Cheech and Chong's The Corsican Brothers '84 **3**
Cheech and Chong's Up in Smoke '79 **2**
Cherry Falls / Terror Tract '00 **2**
Cherry 2000 '88 **2**
Chicken Run '00 **2**
Chicks, Man '99 **3**
The Child '76 **3**
Child Star: The Shirley Temple Story '01 **3**
Children of a Lesser God '86 **1**
Children of Paradise '44 **3**
Children of the Corn '84 **2**
Children of the Corn 4: The Gathering '96 **3**
Children of the Corn 5: Fields of Terror '98 **3**
Children of the Corn 666: Isaac's Return '99 **1**
Children of the Corn: Revelation '01 **3**
Children of the Living Dead '00 **3**
Children Shouldn't Play with Dead Things '72 **1**
Child's Play '88 **1**
Child's Play 2 '90 **1**
Chill Factor '99 **3**
China Moon '91 **1**
China O'Brien '88 **2**
The China Syndrome '79 **1**
Chinatown '74 **1**
Chinese Box '97 **1**
A Chinese Ghost Story '87 **1**
Chinese Ghost Story II '90 **2**
Chinese Ghost Story III '91 **2**
A Chinese Ghost Story: The Tsui Hark Animation '97 **2**
Chinese Odyssey, Part One: Pandora's Box '94 **3**
Chinese Odyssey, Part Two: Cinderella '94 **1**
Chino / Man with a Camera '75 **1**
Chitty Chitty Bang Bang '68 **1**
Chloe in the Afternoon '72 **1**
Choices '81 **2**

Dawn Rider / Trail Beyond '35 **2**
A Day in Black and White '01 **2**
Day of the Animals '77 **2**
Day of the Dead '85 **1**
The Day of the Jackal '73 **1**
Day of Wrath '43 **3**
The Day the Earth Caught Fire '61 **2**
Daydream Believers: The Monkees Story '00 **3**
Daylight '96 **1**
Days of Heaven '78 **1**
Days of Thunder '90 **1**
The Daytrippers '96 **2**
Dazed and Confused '93 **1**
De Sade '69 **3**
Deacon Brodie '98 **2**
Dead Again '91 **1**
Dead Alive '93 **1**
Dead and Buried '81 **2**
Dead and Rotting '02 **3**
Dead Are Alive '72 **2**
Dead Bang '89 **1**
Dead Calm '89 **1**
Dead Creatures '01 **3**
Dead End '98 **1**
The Dead Hate the Living '99 **3**
Dead in the Water '01 **3**
Dead Man '95 **2**
Dead Man on Campus '97 **1**
Dead Man Walking '95 **2**
Dead Men Don't Wear Plaid '82 **2**
The Dead Next Door '89 **2**
Dead of Night '99 **2**
Dead or Alive '02 **3**
Dead Pet '01 **3**
Dead Poets Society '89 **1**
The Dead Pool '88 **3**
Dead Presidents '95 **1**
Dead Ringers '88 **1**
Dead Sexy '01 **3**
Dead Silence '98 **3**
Dead Simple '01 **3**
Dead Waters '94 **2**
Dead Zone '83 **2**
Deadbeat at Dawn '88 **2**
Deadfall '93 **1**
Deadful Melody '92 **1**
Deadly Beauty: Snow's Secret Life '01 **2**
Deadly Weapons '70 **2**
Deal of a Lifetime '99 **2**
Dealin' Dirty '?? **3**
Dean Koontz's Black River '01 **3**
Dean Koontz's Mr. Murder '98 **1**
Dear Santa '98 **2**
Death and the Compass '96 **2**
Death Becomes Her '92 **1**
Death Before Dishonor '87 **3**
The Death Curse of Tartu / Sting of Death '66 **3**
Death Mask '98 **2**
Death on the Nile '78 **2**
Death Race 2000 '75 **1**
Death Sentence '74 **2**
Death Warrant '90 **2**
Death Wish '74 **2**
Death Wish 5: The Face of Death '94 **2**
Deathstalker '83 **3**
Deathstalker 2: Duel of the Titans '87 **3**
Deathtrap '82 **1**
The Decalogue '88 **1**
The Decameron '70 **1**
Deceived '01 **3**
Deceiver '97 **3**
December 7th / The Fleet That Came to Stay '43 **3**
December 7th: The Pearl Harbor Story '43 **2**
Deconstructing Harry '97 **1**
Dee Snider's Strangeland '98 **1**

The Deep '77 **1**
Deep Blue Sea '99 **1**
Deep Cover '92 **1**
The Deep End '01 **3**
The Deep End of the Ocean '98 **1**
Deep Impact '98 **1**
Deep in the Heart (of Texas) '98 **2**
Deep in the Woods '00 **3**
Deep Red: Hatchet Murders '75 **1**
Deep Rising '98 **1**
Deep Trouble '01 **3**
Deep Water '99 **3**
Deeply '99 **3**
Deepstar Six '89 **2**
The Deer Hunter '78 **1**
Def by Temptation '90 **1**
Def Jam's How to Be a Player '97 **1**
The Defender '94 **2**
Defending Your Life '91 **2**
The Defiant Ones '58 **3**
The Defilers '65 **2**
Deliverance '72 **1**
Delivered '98 **2**
The Delivery '99 **2**
Delta Force '86 **2**
Delta Force 2: Operation Stranglehold '90 **2**
Dementia '55 **2**
Dementia '98 **2**
Dementia 13 [Madacy] '63 **2**
Dementia 13 [Roan] '63 **3**
Dementia 13 [Marengo] '63 **3**
Demetrius and the Gladiators '54 **2**
Demolition Man '93 **1**
The Demolitionist '95 **1**
Demon City Shinjuku '93 **3**
Demon Lust '01 **3**
Demonia '90 **3**
The Demoniacs '74 **1**
Demons '86 **1**
Demons 2 '87 **1**
The Demon's Baby '98 **3**
The Dentist '96 **1**
The Dentist 2: Brace Yourself '98 **1**
Dersu Uzala '75 **2**
The Descendant of Wing Chun '78 **1**
Desecration '99 **1**
Desert Blue '98 **1**
Desert Hearts '86 **2**
Desert Heat '99 **1**
Desert Thunder '99 **2**
Desert Trail '35 **3**
Desert Winds '95 **2**
The Designated Mourner '97 **1**
Designing Woman '57 **3**
Desolation Angels '95 **1**
Desperado [1] '95 **1**
Desperado [2 SB] '95 **3**
Desperado / El Mariachi '95 **1**
Desperate Crimes '93 **1**
Desperate Hours '90 **1**
Desperate Living (John Waters Collection Vol. 2) '77 **3**
Desperate Measures '98 **1**
Desperately Seeking Susan '85 **2**
Destination Moon '50 **1**
Destination Nightmare '54 **3**
Destination Vegas '95 **2**
Destiny '21 **2**
Detention '98 **2**
Deterrence '00 **2**
Detour '46 **2**
Detroit 9000 '73 **2**
Detroit Rock City '99 **1**
Deuce Bigalow: Male Gigolo '99 **2**
The Devil & Max Devlin '81 **2**
The Devil Bat '41 **3**

The Devil Bat's Daughter '46 **1**
Devil Girl from Mars '54 **3**
Devil Hunter Yohko: The Complete Collection, Vol. 1 '93 **3**
Devil in a Blue Dress '95 **1**
Devil in the Flesh '98 **1**
Devil Man '87 **3**
The Devil Rides Out '68 **2**
The Devil's Advocate '97 **1**
The Devil's Brigade '68 **3**
Devil's Island '96 **2**
The Devil's Nightmare '71 **1**
The Devil's Own '96 **1**
The Devil's Prey '01 **3**
Devil's Rain '75 **1**
Devonsville Terror '83 **1**
Diabolique '55 **1**
Diabolique '96 **2**
The Diamond of Jeru '01 **3**
Diamond Run '00 **2**
Diamondbacks '99 **2**
Diamonds '99 **2**
Diamonds Are Forever [SE] '71 **2**
Diary of a Chambermaid '64 **2**
Diary of a Lost Girl '29 **3**
Diary of a Serial Killer '97 **2**
Diary of a Sex Addict '01 **3**
Dick '99 **2**
Dick Tracy '90 **3**
Dick Tracy, Detective '45 **3**
Dick Tracy DVD Double Feature '45 **3**
Dick Tracy [VCI] '37 **3**
Dick Tracy [Marengo] '37 **3**
Dick Tracy Meets Gruesome '47 **3**
Dick Tracy vs. Cueball '46 **3**
Dick Tracy's Dilemma '47 **3**
Die! Die! Die! '00 **2**
Die Hard [1] '88 **1**
Die Hard [FS 2] '88 **3**
Die Hard 2: Die Harder '90 **1**
Die Hard: With a Vengeance '95 **1**
Die, Monster, Die! '65 **2**
Die Screaming, Marianne '73 **2**
Die Watching '93 **1**
Digging to China '98 **2**
Digimon: The Movie '00 **2**
Dilemma '97 **2**
Dillinger '73 **2**
Dillinger and Capone '95 **3**
The Dimension Travelers '98 **3**
Dimples '36 **3**
Diner '82 **3**
The Dinner Game '98 **2**
Dinner with Friends '01 **3**
Dinosaur [CE] '00 **2**
Dinosaur Valley Girls '96 **2**
Dinosaurus! '60 **2**
Diplomatic Siege '99 **2**
Directed by Andrei Tarkovsky '88 **3**
The Directors: Roger Corman '01 **3**
Dirty Dancing [1] '87 **1**
Dirty Dancing [2 CE] '87 **1**
The Dirty Dozen '67 **1**
Dirty Duck '75 **2**
The Dirty Girls '64 **1**
Dirty Harry [1] '71 **1**
Dirty Harry [2] '71 **3**
Dirty Kopz '01 **3**
Dirty Pictures '00 **2**
Dirty Rotten Scoundrels [Image] '88 **1**
Dirty Rotten Scoundrels [MGM] '88 **3**
Dirty Work '97 **2**
The Disappearance of Flight 412 '74 **3**
Disclosure '94 **1**
The Discreet Charm of the Bourgeoisie '72 **2**
The Disenchanted '90 **1**

The Dish '00 **3**
Dish Dogs '98 **2**
Disney's American Legends '02 **3**
Disney's The Kid '00 **2**
The Distinguished Gentleman '92 **1**
Disturbing Behavior '98 **1**
Diva [Fox/Lorber] '82 **1**
Diva [Anchor Bay] '82 **3**
Divided We Fall '00 **3**
Divided We Stand '00 **2**
Divine Madness '80 **1**
Divine Trash '98 **2**
Dixie Dynamite '76 **3**
Django '68 **1**
Django Strikes Again '87 **1**
Do the Right Thing [1] '89 **1**
Do the Right Thing [2] '89 **2**
D.O.A. [Image] '49 **1**
D.O.A. [Roan] '49 **2**
D.O.A.: The End '99 **3**
Doc Hollywood '91 **1**
Doctor Dolittle '67 **2**
Dr. Dolittle '98 **1**
Dr. Dolittle 2 '01 **3**
Dr. Frankenstein's Castle of Freaks '74 **2**
Dr. Giggles '92 **2**
Dr. Goldfoot and the Bikini Machine '66 **2**
Dr. Jekyll and Mr. Hyde [Image] '20 **1**
Dr. Jekyll and Mr. Hyde [Kino] '20 **3**
Dr. Jekyll & Mr. Hyde '00 **3**
Dr. Jekyll and Sister Hyde '71 **3**
Dr. Lamb '92 **3**
Dr. Mabuse, The Gambler '22 **3**
Dr. No [SE] '62 **1**
Doctor of Doom '62 **3**
Dr. Orloff's Monster '64 **3**
Doctor Phibes Rises Again '72 **2**
Dr. Seuss' How the Grinch Stole Christmas '00 **3**
Dr. Strangelove, or: How I Learned to Stop Worrying and Love the Bomb [1] '64 **1**
Dr. Strangelove, or: How I Learned to Stop Worrying and Love the Bomb [2 SE] '64 **2**
Dr. T & the Women '00 **2**
Doctor Zhivago '65 **3**
Dodsworth [HBO] '36 **1**
Dodsworth [MGM] '36 **3**
Dog Day Afternoon '75 **1**
Dogma [1] '99 **2**
Dogma [2 SE] '99 **3**
The Dogs of War '81 **3**
Dogs: The Rise and Fall of an All-Girl Rookie Joint '96 **3**
Dolemite '75 **1**
The Doll Squad '73 **3**
Dolores Claiborne '94 **1**
Dolphins '00 **2**
Domestic Disturbance '01 **3**
Dominick & Eugene '88 **3**
Dominion Tank Police '89 **1**
Don Giovanni '79 **3**
Don Juan DeMarco '94 **1**
Don Juan (Or If Don Juan Were a Woman) '73 **3**
Don Q, Son of Zorro '25 **3**
Dona Herlinda & Her Son '86 **3**
Donnie Brasco [1] '96 **1**
Donnie Brasco [2] '96 **2**
Donnie Darko '01 **3**
Donovan's Brain '53 **2**
Donovan's Reef '63 **2**
Don's Party '76 **1**
Don't Answer the Phone '80 **2**
Don't Be a Menace to South Central While Drinking Your Juice in the Hood '95 **1**

Don't Bother to Knock '52 **3**
Don't Do It '93 **1**
Don't Go in the House '80 **2**
Don't Let Me Die on a Sunday '99 **2**
Don't Look in the Basement '73 **1**
Don't Mess with My Sister! '85 **2**
Don't Say a Word '01 **3**
Don't Tell Mom the Babysitter's Dead '91 **2**
Don't Torture a Duckling '72 **2**
Don't Touch the White Woman! '74 **1**
Doomsdayer '99 **3**
Doomwatch '72 **3**
The Doors [1] '91 **1**
The Doors [2 SE] '91 **2**
Dope Case Pending '00 **2**
Dot & the Kangaroo '77 **3**
Double Agent 73 '80 **2**
Double Bang '01 **3**
Double Deception '01 **3**
Double Down '01 **3**
Double Dragon '94 **2**
Double Impact '91 **2**
Double Indemnity '44 **1**
Double Jeopardy '99 **2**
Double Parked '00 **2**
Double Suicide '69 **2**
Double Team '97 **1**
Down from the Mountain '00 **3**
Down in the Delta '98 **1**
Down to Earth '01 **3**
Down to the Sea in Ships '22 **3**
Down to You '00 **2**
Downhill Willie '96 **2**
Dracula '73 **1**
Dracula / Strange Case of Dr. Jekyll & Mr. Hyde '73 **2**
Dracula '79 **1**
Dracula, Prince of Darkness '66 **1**
Dracula: The Dark Prince '01 **3**
Dracula 2000 '00 **3**
Dracula vs. Frankenstein '71 **2**
Dracula's Daughter '36 **3**
Dragnet '87 **1**
The Dragon Chronicles '94 **2**
The Dragon Fist '80 **1**
Dragon from Shaolin '96 **1**
Dragon Inn '92 **3**
Dragon Princess '81 **2**
Dragon Tales '99 **3**
Dragon: The Bruce Lee Story '93 **1**
Dragonheart [SE] '96 **1**
Dragonheart: A New Beginning '00 **2**
Dragon's Claws '79 **3**
Dragons Forever '88 **1**
Dragons of the Orient '88 **1**
Dragstrip Girl '94 **3**
Dralion '00 **2**
The Draughtsman's Contract '82 **1**
Drawing Flies '02 **3**
Dream Lovers '86 **1**
Dreaming Fists with Slender Hands '80 **3**
The Dreamlife of Angels '98 **1**
Dreams of Gold: The Mel Fisher Story '86 **1**
Dreamscape '84 **1**
The Dress Code '99 **3**
Dressed to Kill '46 **2**
Dressed to Kill [SE] '80 **3**
The Drifter '88 **1**
Driller Killer '74 **1**
Drive '96 **1**
Drive By '01 **3**
Drive-in Discs, Vol. 1 '00 **2**
Drive-in Discs, Vol. 2 '01 **3**
Drive Me Crazy '99 **2**

Driven '01 **3**
Driving Miss Daisy '89 **1**
Drop Dead Gorgeous '99 **1**
Drop Dead Rock '95 **2**
DROP Squad '94 **1**
Drop Zone '94 **2**
Drowning Mona '00 **2**
Drugstore Cowboy '89 **2**
Druids '01 **3**
Drunken Master '78 **3**
Drunks '96 **1**
Duck Soup '33 **1**
Dude, Where's My Car? '00 **3**
Dudley Do-Right '99 **1**
The Duel '00 **3**
Duel in the Sun '46 **1**
Dueling DVD: Cyrano de Berg-
  erac / The Son of Monte
  Cristo '01 **3**
Duets '00 **2**
Dumb & Dumber '94 **1**
Dumb Luck in Vegas '97 **1**
Dumbo '41 **3**
Dune '84 **1**
Dune [1] '00 **2**
Dune [2 SE] '00 **3**
Dungeons and Dragons '00 **2**
The Dunwich Horror '70 **3**

E
Eagle Fist '77 **3**
The Eagle Has Landed '77 **2**
Eagle vs. Silver Fox '83 **3**
Earth '30 **3**
Earth Girls Are Easy '89 **1**
Earth vs. the Spider '01 **3**
Earthly Possessions '99 **2**
Earthquake '74 **1**
East Is East '99 **2**
East Side Story '97 **3**
East-West '99 **3**
Eastern Condors '87 **2**
Tha Eastsidaz '00 **2**
Easy Rider '69 **1**
Eat Drink Man Woman '94 **3**
Eat My Dust '76 **1**
Eat My Dust '93 **3**
Eat Your Heart Out '96 **2**
Eaten Alive '76 **1**
Echo of Murder '00 **3**
Echo Park '86 **3**
Ecstasy '33 **3**
Ecstasy of the Angels '72 **2**
Ed McBain's 87 Precinct '96
  1
Eddie '96 **1**
Eddie and the Cruisers '83 **3**
Eden '98 **2**
Edgar Ulmer Collection, Vol. 1
  '00 **2**
The Edge '97 **1**
EDtv '99 **1**
The Education of Little Tree
  '97 **3**
The Educational Archives Vol-
  ume 1: Sex & Drugs '01 **3**
The Educational Archives Vol-
  ume 2: Social Engineering
  101 '01 **3**
Edvard Grieg: What Price
  Immortality? '00 **2**
Edward Scissorhands [SE]
  '90 **2**
Eegah! '62 **3**
The Eel '96 **3**
An Egyptian Story '82 **2**
The Eiger Sanction '75 **1**
8 1/2 '63 **3**
8 1/2 Women '99 **2**
800 Leagues down the Ama-
  zon '93 **3**
8 Man '92 **1**
8 Man After: The Perfect Collection '93 **2**
Eight Men Out '88 **2**
8 Seconds '94 **1**
18 Again! '88 **3**
8mm '98 **1**
84 Charing Cross Road '86 **3**
El Diablo '90 **2**
El Mariachi '93 **1**
Election '99 **1**

Electra '62 **3**
The Electric Horseman '79 **1**
The Element of Crime '84 **2**
Element of Doubt '96 **2**
An Elephant Called Slowly '69
  2
The Elephant Man '80 **3**
Elephant Parts '81 **2**
Elizabeth '98 **1**
Elizabeth '02 **3**
The Elm-Chanted Forest '97 **1**
Elvira Madigan '67 **1**
Elvis: '68 Comeback Special
  '68 **3**
Elysia '34 **3**
Embrace of the Vampire '95
  1
Embrace the Darkness '98 **1**
Embryo '76 **2**
The Emerald Forest '85 **2**
Emma '96 **1**
Emmanuelle '74 **1**
Emmanuelle: First Contact
  '99 **2**
Emmanuelle in Space: A
  World of Desire '99 **3**
Emmanuelle: Queen of the
  Desert '93 **3**
Emmanuelle, the Joys of a
  Woman '76 **1**
Emmet Otter's Jug-Band
  Christmas '77 **3**
The Emperor and the Assas-
  sin '99 **2**
The Emperor's New Groove
  [SE] '00 **2**
The Emperor's Shadow '96 **1**
Empire of the Ants '77 **3**
Empire of the Sun '87 **3**
Empire Records '95 **2**
Encino Man '92 **1**
The End '78 **2**
End of Days '99 **1**
End of the Affair '55 **2**
The End of the Affair '99 **2**
Endless Night '71 **2**
The Endless Summer '66 **1**
The Enemy '01 **3**
Enemy at the Gates '00 **3**
Enemy Mine '85 **3**
Enemy of the State '98 **1**
The Enforcer '76 **3**
The English Patient '96 **1**
The Englishman Who Went up
  a Hill But Came down a
  Mountain '95 **1**
Enter the Dragon [SE] '73 **1**
The Entertainer '60 **2**
Entrapment '99 **1**
Entre-Nous '83 **1**
Eraser '96 **1**
The Eric Rohmer Collection:
  The Moral Tales '62 **1**
Erin Brockovich '00 **2**
The Erotic Adventures of
  Zorro '72 **2**
The Erotic Ghost '00 **2**
Erotic Ghost Story '90 **1**
Erotic Ghost Story: Perfect
  Match '97 **1**
The Erotic Mirror '01 **3**
The Erotic Rites of Countess
  Dracula '01 **3**
Erotic Survivor '00 **2**
Erotic Survivor 2 '01 **3**
The Erotic Witch Project [CE]
  '99 **2**
Erotic Witch Project 2: Book
  of Seduction '00 **2**
Errol Flynn / Randolph Scott
  Double Feature '00 **2**
Escape from Alaska '02 **3**
Escape from Alcatraz '79 **1**
Escape from Hell '89 **2**
Escape from L.A. '96 **1**
Escape from New York '81 **2**
Escape from the Planet of
  the Apes '71 **2**
Escape to Grizzly Mountain
  '99 **3**
Escape under Pressure '00 **2**

Essex Boys '99 **2**
The Eternal '99 **1**
Eternal Evil '87 **1**
Eternal Love '29 **2**
Eva '62 **3**
Evangeline '29 **2**
Evel Knievel '72 **3**
Even Dwarfs Started Small
  '69 **1**
The Evening Star '96 **2**
An Evening with Sherlock
  Holmes '00 **2**
Event Horizon '97 **1**
Ever After: A Cinderella Story
  '98 **1**
An Everlasting Piece '00 **3**
Every Which Way But Loose
  '78 **3**
Everybody's Famous! '00 **3**
Everyone Says I Love You '96
  1
Everything You Always Want-
  ed to Know about Sex (But
  Were Afraid to Ask) '72 **2**
Eve's Bayou '97 **1**
Evil Dead '83 **1**
Evil Dead [LE] '83 **3**
Evil Dead 2: Dead by Dawn
  [1] '87 **1**
Evil Dead 2: Dead by Dawn [2
  THX] '87 **2**
Evil Dead Trap '88 **2**
Evil Ed '96 **1**
The Evil That Men Do '84 **3**
Evil under the Sun '82 **2**
Evita '96 **1**
Evolution '01 **3**
Evolver '94 **1**
Excalibur '81 **1**
Excellent Cadavers '99 **2**
Excess Baggage '96 **1**
Exclusive '82 **1**
The Executioners '93 **1**
Executive Decision '96 **1**
eXistenZ '99 **1**
Exit Wounds '01 **3**
The Exorcist [1 SE] '73 **1**
The Exorcist [2]: The Version
  You've Never Seen '73 **3**
Exorcist 3: Legion '90 **3**
Exotica '94 **1**
Expect the Unexpected '98 **1**
Expert Weapon '93 **1**
Expresso Bongo '59 **3**
Exterminator '80 **1**
Extramarital '98 **2**
The Extreme Adventures of
  Super Dave '98 **3**
Extreme Heist '99 **3**
Extreme Honor '01 **3**
Extreme Justice '93 **1**
Extreme Limits '01 **3**
An Extremely Goofy Movie '99
  1
Extremities '86 **3**
An Eye for an Eye '81 **3**
An Eye for an Eye '95 **3**
Eye of the Beholder '99 **2**
Eye of the Killer '99 **2**
Eye of the Serpent '92 **1**
Eye Witness '70 **3**
Eyes of Laura Mars '78 **2**
The Eyes of Tammy Faye '00
  2
Eyes Wide Shut '99 **1**

F
F/X '86 **2**
F/X 2: The Deadly Art of Illu-
  sion '91 **2**
The Fabulous Baker Boys '89
  1
Face/Off '97 **1**
Face the Evil '97 **1**
Faces of Death '78 **1**
Faces of Death 2 '81 **3**
Faces of Death 3: Scenes
  from the Underground '81
  3
Facing the Enemy '00 **3**
The Faculty '98 **1**
Fade to Black '80 **1**

Fahrenheit 451 '66 **1**
Fail-Safe '64 **2**
Fair Game '85 **2**
Fair Game '89 **2**
Fair Game '95 **1**
The Falcon and the Snowman
  '85 **1**
Fall of the House of Usher
  '28 **2**
The Fall of the House of
  Usher '60 **2**
Fall Time '94 **2**
Fallen '97 **1**
Fallen Angel '99 **2**
Fallen Angels '95 **1**
Falling Down '93 **1**
Falling for a Dancer '98 **2**
Falling in Love '84 **3**
Falling in Love Again '80 **1**
Fallout '01 **3**
Family Enforcer '76 **2**
Family Man '00 **3**
Family of Cops '95 **2**
Family of Cops 2: Breach of
  Faith '97 **2**
Family of Cops 3 '98 **2**
Family Plot '76 **2**
Family Reunion '79 **1**
A Family Thing '96 **2**
Family Viewing / Next of Kin
  '87 **3**
The Fan '96 **1**
Fanatic '82 **2**
Fando and Lis '68 **1**
The Fantasia Anthology '00 **2**
Fantasia/2000 '00 **2**
Fantastic Dinosaurs of the
  Movies '90 **3**
The Fantastic Night '42 **1**
Fantastic Planet '73 **1**
Fantastic Voyage '66 **2**
The Fantasy Film Worlds of
  George Pal '82 **2**
Fantasy Mission Force '84 **2**
The Fantasy Worlds of Irwin
  Allen '95 **2**
Far and Away '92 **1**
The Far Pavilions '84 **2**
Farewell My Concubine '93 **1**
Farewell, My Lovely '75 **1**
A Farewell to Arms '32 **2**
Fargo '96 **1**
Farinelli '94 **2**
The Farmer's Wife '28 **1**
Farscape, Vol. 1 '00 **3**
Farscape, Vol. 2 '00 **2**
Farscape, Vol. 3 '01 **2**
Farscape, Vol. 6 '01 **3**
Fascination '79 **1**
Fashionably L.A. '99 **3**
The Fast and the Furious '54
  3
The Fast and the Furious '01
  3
Fast Sofa '01 **3**
Fast Times at Ridgemont
  High '82 **2**
The Fat Black Pussycat '63 **3**
Fata Morgana '92 **3**
Fatal Attraction [SCE] '87 **3**
Fatal Beauty '87 **2**
Fatal Blade '00 **3**
Fatal Error '99 **3**
The Fatal Hour '40 **3**
The Fatal Image '90 **1**
Fatal Pursuit '98 **1**
Father Frost '66 **3**
Father of the Bride '91 **1**
Father of the Bride Part II '95
  2
Father's Day '96 **1**
Father's Little Dividend '51 **2**
Faust '26 **3**
Faust: Love of the Damned
  '00 **3**
The Favor '92 **3**
Fay Wray Collection '00 **2**
The Fear '94 **1**
Fear '96 **1**
Fear and Loathing in Las
  Vegas '98 **1**

The Fear Chamber '68 **3**
Fear City '85 **2**
The Fear: Halloween Night
  '99 **1**
Fear Runs Silent '99 **2**
Fearless '93 **1**
Fearless Dragon '79 **3**
Fearless Hyena '79 **1**
Fearless Hyena: Part 2 '83 **1**
Feeling Minnesota '96 **1**
Felicia's Journey '99 **1**
Fellini Satyricon '69 **2**
Female Convict Scorpion—
  Jailhouse 41 '72 **2**
Female Trouble '74 **3**
Female Vampire '73 **2**
Femalien '96 **2**
Femalien 2 '98 **2**
The Fence '94 **1**
Ferngully '92 **3**
Ferngully 2: The Magical Res-
  cue '97 **2**
Ferris Bueller's Day Off '86 **1**
Fetishes '96 **1**
Fever '99 **3**
Fever Pitch '96 **2**
A Few Good Men '92 **1**
Fiddler on the Roof [1] '71 **1**
Fiddler on the Roof [2 SE] '71
  3
Fidel '02 **3**
The Field [Artisan] '90 **3**
The Field [Pioneer] '90 **2**
Fiend without a Face '58 **2**
Fierce Creatures '96 **1**
15 Minutes '01 **3**
Fifth Day of Peace '72 **1**
The Fifth Element [1] '97 **1**
The Fifth Element [2 SB] '97
  3
Fifth of July '82 **3**
54 '98 **1**
Fight Club '99 **1**
Fight for the Title '57 **2**
The Fighter '52 **2**
Fighting Ace '79 **3**
Fighting Rats of Tobruk '44 **3**
The Fighting Sullivans '42 **1**
The Filth and the Fury '99 **2**
Final '01 **3**
Final Analysis '92 **1**
Final Destination '00 **2**
Final Fantasy: The Spirits
  Within '01 **3**
Final Justice '84 **1**
Final Payback '02 **2**
The Final Programme '73 **2**
Final Voyage '99 **2**
Find a Place to Die '68 **3**
Finding Buck McHenry '00 **3**
Finding Forrester '00 **2**
Finding Graceland '98 **1**
Finding North '97 **1**
Fiona '98 **2**
Fire '96 **2**
Fire Alarm '32 **3**
Fire Down Below '97 **1**
Fire on the Amazon '93 **1**
Fire over England '37 **2**
Firehouse '72 **3**
Firehouse '87 **1**
The Firemen's Ball '68 **3**
Fires Within '91 **3**
Firestarter '84 **1**
Firestarter 2: Rekindled '02 **3**
Firestorm '97 **1**
Firetrap '01 **3**
Fireworks '97 **2**
The Firing Line '91 **2**
The Firm '93 **1**
First Blood '82 **1**
The First Deadly Sin '80 **1**
First Degree '01 **3**
First Knight '95 **1**
First Love and Other Pains /
  One of Them '99 **3**
First Man into Space '59 **3**
First Men in the Moon '64 **3**
First Name: Carmen '83 **1**
The First 9 1/2 Weeks '98 **2**
First Option '96 **1**

The First Power '89 **3**
First Spaceship on Venus '60 **2**
First Time Felon '97 **3**
The First to Go '97 **3**
First Turn On [DC] '83 **3**
The First Wives Club '96 **1**
A Fish Called Wanda '88 **1**
The Fisher King '91 **2**
Fishing with Gandhi '98 **3**
Fist of Fear, Touch of Death '80 **3**
Fist of Fury '95 **3**
Fist of Legend '94 **1**
Fist of the North Star '86 **1**
Fist of the North Star '95 **2**
The Fist Power '99 **3**
A Fistful of Dollars '64 **1**
Fistful of Lead '70 **3**
Fists of Bruce Lee '78 **3**
Fists of Fury '73 **1**
Fitzcarraldo '82 **1**
Five Card Stud '68 **3**
Five Corners '88 **1**
Five Dolls for an August Moon '70 **2**
Five Easy Pieces '70 **2**
The Five Heartbeats '91 **3**
Five on the Black Hand Side '73 **3**
The Five Senses '99 **2**
The 5000 Fingers of Dr. T '53 **2**
Flambards '78 **3**
The Flamingo Kid '84 **1**
Flash Gordon '80 **1**
Flash Gordon: Space Soldiers '36 **2**
Flash Gordon: Spaceship to the Unknown '36 **3**
Flash Gordon: The Deadly Ray from Mars '39 **3**
Flash Gordon: The Peril from Planet Mongo '40 **3**
Flash Gordon: The Purple Death from Outer Space '40 **3**
Flashfire '94 **2**
Flatliners '90 **1**
Flawless '99 **2**
Fled '96 **2**
The Fleet That Came to Stay '46 **3**
Flesh '68 **1**
Flesh and Bone '93 **3**
The Flesh and the Fiends '60 **3**
Flesh Gordon '72 **1**
Flesh Gordon 2: Flesh Gordon Meets the Cosmic Cheerleaders '90 **2**
Fleshburn '84 **3**
Fletch '85 **1**
Flight to Mars '52 **3**
The Flintstones [CE] '94 **1**
The Flintstones in Viva Rock Vegas '00 **2**
Flirting with Disaster '95 **1**
Floating '97 **2**
Flooding '97 **3**
The Florentine '98 **2**
Floundering '94 **1**
Flowers in the Attic '87 **2**
Flowers of Shanghai '98 **3**
Flubber '97 **1**
Fluke '95 **2**
The Fly / Return of the Fly '58 **2**
The Fly / The Fly 2 '86 **2**
The Fly 2 '89 **2**
Fly Away Home [1] '96 **1**
Fly Away Home [2 SE] '96 **3**
The Flying Deuces / Utopia '39 **2**
The Flying Saucer '50 **2**
The Flying Serpent '55 **1**
Flynn '96 **2**
Flypaper '97 **2**
FM '78 **1**
Focus '01 **3**
Fog Island '45 **3**

Follow the Stars Home '01 **3**
Follow Your Heart '98 **1**
Following '99 **3**
Fong Sai Yuk '93 **1**
A Fool There Was '14 **3**
Foolish '99 **1**
Foolish Wives '22 **2**
Fools Rush In '97 **1**
Footsteps '98 **2**
For a Few Dollars More '65 **1**
For Hire '98 **2**
For Love of a Child '90 **1**
For Love of the Game '99 **2**
For Love or Country: The Arturo Sandoval Story '00 **3**
For Pete's Sake '74 **2**
For Richer or Poorer '97 **1**
For Sale '98 **3**
For the Boys '91 **2**
For the Love of Benji '77 **1**
For Whom the Bell Tolls '43 **1**
For Your Eyes Only [SE] '81 **1**
Forbidden Planet '56 **1**
Forbidden Sins '99 **3**
Force 10 from Navarone '78 **3**
Forces of Nature '99 **1**
Forever and a Day '43 **1**
Forever Mine '99 **2**
Forever Together '00 **2**
Forever Young '92 **1**
Forgive and Forget '99 **3**
Forgotten '99 **3**
Forgotten City '99 **1**
Forgotten Silver '96 **2**
Forrest Gump [SCE] '94 **3**
The Forsaken '01 **3**
Fort Apache, the Bronx '81 **2**
Fortune Quest: Journey to Terrason '97 **3**
42 Up '99 **3**
42nd Street '33 **2**
The 47 Ronin, Parts 1 & 2 '42 **1**
Fosse '01 **3**
Four Dogs Playing Poker '00 **3**
4:50 from Paddington '87 **3**
Four for Texas '63 **3**
The 400 Blows [Winstar] '59 **1**
The 400 Blows [Criterion] '59 **1**
Four Little Girls '97 **2**
The Four Musketeers '75 **2**
Four of the Apocalypse '75 **3**
Four Rooms '95 **1**
Four Sided Triangle '53 **2**
Four Times That Night '69 **2**
Four Weddings and a Funeral '94 **1**
The 4D Man '59 **1**
The 4th Floor '99 **2**
The 4th Man '79 **2**
The Fox and the Hound '81 **2**
Foxfire '96 **2**
Foxy Brown '74 **2**
Fractured Follies '88 **1**
Frances [Republic] '82 **2**
Frances [Anchor Bay] '82 **3**
Francesco '89 **1**
Frank and Jesse '94 **2**
Frank Lloyd Wright—A Film by Ken Burns and Lynn Novick '98 **3**
Frankenstein '31 **1**
Frankenstein Created Woman '66 **2**
Frankenstein Meets the Wolfman '42 **3**
Frankenstein's Daughter '58 **2**
Frankie and Johnny '65 **2**
Frankie and Johnny '91 **3**
Frantic '88 **1**
Fraternity Demon '92 **1**
Fraternity Vacation '85 **3**
Freddy Got Fingered '01 **3**
Freddy's Dead: The Final Nightmare '91 **1**

Free Enterprise '98 **1**
Free to Be...You and Me '74 **1**
Free Willy '93 **1**
Freedom Strike '98 **1**
Freejack '92 **2**
Freez'er '00 **3**
The French Connection [SE] '71 **3**
French Connection 2 '75 **3**
French Kiss '95 **1**
The French Lieutenant's Woman '81 **3**
Frenzy '72 **2**
Frequency '00 **2**
Fresh '94 **3**
The Freshman '90 **1**
Friction '95 **3**
Friday '95 **1**
Friday Foster '75 **2**
Friday the 13th '80 **1**
Friday the 13th, Part 2 '81 **1**
Friday the 13th, Part 3 '82 **2**
Friday the 13th, Part 4: The Final Chapter '84 **2**
Friday the 13th, Part 5: A New Beginning '85 **3**
Friday the 13th, Part 6: Jason Lives '86 **3**
Fried Green Tomatoes '91 **1**
Friend of the Family '95 **1**
Friend of the Family 2 '96 **1**
Friendly Persuasion '56 **2**
Friends: The Complete First Season '95 **3**
Fright '71 **3**
Fright Night '85 **2**
The Frightened Woman '71 **2**
The Frighteners '96 **1**
Frightmare '74 **2**
Fritz the Cat '72 **3**
From a Whisper to a Scream '00 **2**
From Dusk Till Dawn [1] '95 **1**
From Dusk Till Dawn [2 CS] '95 **2**
From Dusk Till Dawn 2: Texas Blood Money '98 **1**
From Dusk Till Dawn 3: The Hangman's Daughter '99 **1**
From Hell [DLE] '01 **3**
From Here to Eternity '53 **3**
From Mao to Mozart: Isaac Stern in China '80 **2**
From Russia with Love [1] '63 **1**
From Russia with Love [2 SE] '63 **2**
From the Earth to the Moon '98 **3**
From the Journals of Jean Seberg '95 **1**
The Front Page '74 **1**
Frostbiter: Wrath of the Wendigo '94 **2**
Frozen '98 **1**
The Fruit Is Swelling '97 **1**
Fruits of Passion: The Story of "O" Continued '82 **2**
The Fugitive '93 **1**
Fugitive Champion '99 **2**
Full Contact '92 **1**
Full Disclosure '00 **2**
Full Eclipse '93 **3**
Full Metal Jacket [1] '87 **1**
Full Metal Jacket [2 SE] '87 **3**
The Full Monty '96 **1**
Full Moon in Blue Water '88 **3**
Full Moon in Paris '84 **1**
Full Throttle '95 **2**
Fun & Fancy Free '47 **2**
The Funeral '84 **1**
Funeral in Berlin '66 **3**
The Funhouse '81 **1**
Funny Dirty Little War '83 **3**
Funny Farm '88 **1**
Funny Games '97 **1**
Funny Girl '68 **3**
Funny Lady '75 **3**
A Funny Thing Happened on the Way to the Forum '66 **3**

The Fury '78 **3**
Fury in the Shaolin Temple '82 **3**
Fusion One '00 **2**
Futuresport '98 **1**

G

Gadget Trips—Mindscapes '95 **3**
Galaxina '80 **3**
A Galaxy Far Far Away '00 **3**
Galaxy Quest '99 **2**
Gallipoli '81 **1**
The Gambler '74 **3**
The Game '97 **1**
Gandhi '82 **3**
Gang of Four '88 **3**
Gang Related '96 **3**
Ganja and Hess '73 **3**
Gappa the Trifibian Monster '67 **3**
The Garden of Allah '36 **2**
Garden of Eden '94 **3**
The Garden of the Finzi-Continis '71 **3**
Gargoyles '72 **1**
Gary Cooper Double Feature '00 **2**
Gasaraki 1: The Summoning '00 **2**
The Gatchaman Collection '94 **3**
Gator King '70 **3**
Gattaca [1] '97 **1**
Gattaca [2 SB] '97 **3**
The Gauntlet '77 **1**
The Gay Deceivers '69 **2**
The Gay Desperado '36 **2**
Gen-X Cops '99 **2**
The General '26 **1**
The General '98 **1**
General Idi Amin Dada: A Self Portrait '74 **3**
The General's Daughter '99 **1**
Generator 1: Gawl '00 **2**
Gentleman's Agreement '47 **1**
Gentlemen Prefer Blondes '53 **2**
George Balanchine's The Nutcracker '93 **1**
George of the Jungle '97 **1**
George Washington '00 **3**
Georgia '95 **1**
German Silent Masterpieces '00 **3**
Geronimo: An American Legend '93 **1**
Gertrud '64 **3**
Gesualdo: Death for Five Voices '95 **3**
Get Carter '71 **2**
Get Carter '00 **2**
Get Down on It '01 **3**
Get On the Bus '96 **2**
Get Out Your Handkerchiefs '78 **3**
Get over It! '01 **3**
Get Shorty '95 **1**
The Getaway '72 **1**
The Getaway '93 **1**
Getting Even with Dad '94 **2**
Getting Gertie's Garter '45 **2**
Gettysburg '93 **2**
Ghost '90 **2**
The Ghost and the Darkness '96 **1**
The Ghost Breakers '40 **3**
Ghost Chase '88 **2**
Ghost Dog: The Way of the Samurai '99 **2**
The Ghost Goes Gear '66 **1**
Ghost in the Shell '95 **1**
The Ghost of Frankenstein '42 **3**
Ghost Story '81 **1**
Ghost World '01 **3**
Ghostbusters '84 **1**
Ghostbusters 2 '89 **1**
Ghosts of Mississippi '96 **3**
Ghosts on the Loose '43 **2**
G.I. Jane '97 **1**

Gia '98 **2**
Giant from the Unknown '58 **2**
The Giant Gila Monster '59 **3**
Giants and Toys '58 **3**
The Gift '00 **3**
Gigi '58 **1**
Gilda '46 **2**
Gimme Shelter '70 **2**
Ginger Snaps '00 **3**
The Gingerbread Man '97 **1**
Girl '98 **2**
Girl Explores Girl: The Alien Encounter [CE] '00 **2**
Girl Gang '54 **2**
Girl Hunters '63 **1**
Girl in Black '56 **2**
Girl in Gold Boots '69 **3**
Girl, Interrupted '99 **2**
The Girl on a Motorcycle '68 **1**
A Girl Thing '01 **3**
A Girl, 3 Guys and a Gun '01 **3**
The Girl Who Knew Too Much '63 **2**
Girl with Green Eyes '64 **3**
Girlfight '99 **2**
Girls Just Want to Have Fun '85 **2**
Girls of the White Orchid '85 **1**
Girls School Screamers '86 **1**
Gladiator '92 **2**
Gladiator '00 **2**
Gladiator Eroticus '00 **2**
Gladiators: Bloodsport of the Colosseum '02 **3**
The Glass House '01 **3**
The Glass Shield '95 **3**
Glastonbury: The Movie '95 **2**
Glen or Glenda? '53 **1**
The Glimmer Man '96 **1**
A Glimpse of Hell '01 **3**
Glitch! '88 **1**
Glitter '01 **3**
Gloria '98 **1**
Glory [1] '89 **1**
Glory [2 SE] '89 **2**
Go '99 **1**
Go Fish '94 **3**
Go for Broke! [BFS] '51 **2**
Go for Broke! [VCI] '51 **3**
Go, Go Second Time Virgin '69 **2**
Go West '25 **1**
God.com '99 **1**
God of Cookery '96 **1**
God of Gamblers '89 **1**
God of Gambler's Return '94 **1**
The Godfather DVD Collection '72 **2**
The Godfather, Part 2 '74 **2**
The Godfather, Part 3 '90 **2**
Godmoney '99 **1**
Godmonster of Indian Flats '73 **3**
Gods and Monsters '98 **1**
God's Comedy '95 **2**
God's Little Acre '58 **3**
Godzilla '98 **1**
Godzilla, King of the Monsters [Simitar] '56 **1**
Godzilla, King of the Monsters [Goodtimes] '56 **3**
Godzilla 2000 '99 **2**
Godzilla vs. Destroyah '95 **3**
Godzilla vs. Monster Zero '68 **1**
Godzilla vs. Mothra '92 **1**
Godzilla vs. Space Godzilla / Godzilla vs. Destroyah '94 **3**
Godzilla's Revenge '69 **3**
Goin' South '78 **3**
Going My Way / Holiday Inn '44 **1**
Going Overboard '89 **1**
Going Places '74 **3**

The Hollywood Knights '80 **2**
Hollywood Rhythm, Vol. 1:
    Best of Jazz and Blues
    (1929–41) '00 **3**
Hollywood Rhythm, Vol. 2:
    Best of Big Bands Swing
    (1929–39) '00 **3**
Hollywood Screen Tests: Take
    1 '00 **3**
Hollywood Screen Tests: Take
    2 '00 **3**
Hollywood Shuffle '87 **3**
Hollywood Vice Sqaud '86 **2**
Holy Man '98 **1**
Holy Smoke '99 **2**
Home Alone '90 **1**
Home Alone 2: Lost in New
    York '92 **1**
Home Alone 3 '97 **1**
Home for Christmas '93 **2**
Home for the Holidays '95 **3**
Home Fries '98 **1**
A Home of Our Own '93 **2**
Homegrown '97 **2**
Homeward Bound: The
    Incredible Journey '93 **1**
Homicidal '61 **3**
Homicide: The Movie '00 **2**
Honey & Ashes '96 **2**
Honeymoon in Vegas '92 **1**
Hong Kong 1941 '84 **1**
Honky Tonk Freeway '81 **3**
Honor Among Thieves '68 **2**
Honor Thy Father '73 **2**
The Hoodlum '51 **1**
Hoodlum '96 **2**
Hook '91 **1**
Hooper '78 **1**
Hoosiers '86 **1**
Hopalong Cassidy '35 **3**
Hopalong Cassidy Returns
    '36 **3**
Hope and Glory '87 **2**
Hope Floats '98 **1**
Horatio Hornblower '99 **3**
Horatio Hornblower: The
    Adventure Continues '01 **3**
The Horrible Dr. Bones '00 **2**
Horror Express [Simitar] '72
    1
Horror Express [Image] '84 **1**
Horror Hospital '73 **1**
Horror Hotel '60 **2**
The Horror of Hammer '01 **3**
Horror 101 '00 **3**
Horrors of Spider Island '59
    2
Horse Feathers '32 **1**
The Horse Soldiers '59 **2**
The Horse Whisperer '97 **1**
The Horse's Mouth '58 **3**
Horton Foote's Alone '97 **1**
Hostage High '97 **3**
Hot Blooded '98 **1**
Hot Blooded Woman '65 **3**
Hot Boyz '99 **2**
Hot Pursuit '87 **3**
Hot Rod Girl '56 **3**
The Hot Spot '90 **1**
Hot Summer '68 **3**
Hot Vampire Nights '00 **2**
Hot War '98 **1**
The Hotel New Hampshire
    '84 **3**
H.O.T.S. '79 **2**
The Hound of the
    Baskervilles '59 **3**
The Hound of the
    Baskervilles '83 **1**
House '86 **3**
House 2: The Second Story
    '87 **3**
House Arrest '96 **3**
The House by the Cemetery
    [Anchor Bay] '83 **2**
The House by the Cemetery
    [Diamond] '83 **2**
House of Frankenstein '44 **3**
House of Games '87 **2**
House of Mirth '00 **2**

The House of Seven Corpses
    '73 **2**
The House of the Spirits '93
    3
House of Whipcord '75 **1**
The House of Yes '97 **1**
House on Bare Mountain '62
    3
House on Haunted Hill '58 **1**
House on Haunted Hill '99 **1**
The House on Sorority Row
    '83 **2**
House Party '90 **2**
House Party 2: The Pajama
    Jam '91 **2**
House Party 3 '94 **2**
House Party 4: Down to the
    Last Minute '00 **3**
How Green Was My Valley '41
    2
How High '01 **3**
How Stella Got Her Groove
    Back '98 **1**
How the West Was Won '63 **1**
How to Be a Woman and Not
    Die in the Attempt '91 **1**
How to Commit Marriage '69
    2
How to Get Ahead in Advertis-
    ing '89 **3**
How to Kill Your Neighbor's
    Dog '01 **3**
How to Make an American
    Quilt '95 **1**
How to Marry a Millionaire
    '53 **2**
How to Succeed in Business
    without Really Trying '67 **3**
Howard's End '92 **1**
The Howling '81 **3**
Howling 3: The Marsupials
    '87 **3**
The Hubley Collection: Every-
    body Rides the Carousel
    '99 **1**
The Hubley Collection, Vol. 1
    '99 **1**
The Hubley Collection, Vol. 2
    '99 **1**
Hudson Hawk '91 **1**
The Hudsucker Proxy '93 **1**
Hugo Pool '97 **1**
Hum Dil De Chuke Sanam
    '99 **1**
The Human Condition: No
    Greater Love '58 **1**
The Human Condition: Road
    to Eternity '59 **1**
Human Desires '97 **3**
Human Prey '95 **3**
Human Traffic '99 **2**
Humanity '99 **2**
Humanoids from the Deep
    '80 **1**
The Hunchback of Notre
    Dame '39 **1**
The Hunchback of Notre
    Dame '57 **3**
The Hunchback of Notre
    Dame '96 **3**
The Hunchback of Notre
    Dame 2 '01 **3**
The Hunger: Smoke, Mirrors,
    and Paranoia '00 **3**
The Hunt for Red October '90
    1
The Hunted '94 **1**
The Hunter '80 **3**
Hunter's Moon '97 **1**
Hurlyburly '98 **3**
The Hurricane '37 **1**
The Hurricane '99 **2**
Husbands and Wives '92 **3**
Hush '98 **1**
Hush Little Baby '93 **1**
Hyper Space '89 **1**
Hysterical '83 **2**

I

I, a Woman '66 **1**
I Am Cuba '64 **1**
I Am Sam '01 **3**

I Bury the Living '58 **3**
I, Claudius '91 **2**
I Dreamed of Africa '00 **2**
I Know What You Did Last
    Summer '97 **1**
I Know Where I'm Going '45
    2
I Like the Girls Who Do '73 **2**
I Like to Play Games '95 **3**
I Love Maria '88 **1**
I Love Trouble '94 **1**
I Love You, I Love You Not '97
    1
I Married a Strange Person
    '97 **2**
I Never Promised You a Rose
    Garden '77 **3**
I Saw What You Did '65 **1**
I Shot Andy Warhol '96 **2**
I Spit on Your Corpse '74 **2**
I Spit on Your Corpse, I Piss
    on Your Grave '02 **3**
I Spit on Your Grave '77 **1**
I Spy '65 **2**
I Still Know What You Did
    Last Summer '98 **1**
I Vampiri '56 **3**
I Want to Live! '58 **3**
I Was a Teenage Zombie '87
    1
I, Zombie '99 **2**
Ice Castles '79 **2**
Ice from the Sun '00 **2**
Ice Grill '02 **3**
The Ice Rink '99 **3**
The Ice Storm '97 **1**
The Iceman Cometh '60 **3**
An Ideal Husband '99 **1**
Idiot Box '97 **3**
Idle Hands '99 **2**
If Lucy Fell '96 **2**
If These Walls Could Talk 2
    '00 **2**
Igor & the Lunatics '85 **1**
Iguana '89 **2**
Il Bidone '55 **2**
Il Grido '57 **3**
I'll Be Home for Christmas
    '98 **2**
Ill-Gotten Gains '97 **2**
I'll Never Forget What's
    'Isname '67 **2**
I'll Remember April '99 **2**
Illegal Affairs '96 **3**
Illicit Confessions '77 **3**
Illuminata '98 **2**
Ilsa, Harem Keeper of the Oil
    Sheiks '76 **2**
Ilsa, She-Wolf of the SS '74 **2**
Ilsa, the Wicked Warden '78
    1
I'm Gonna Git You Sucka '88
    1
I'm Losing You '98 **2**
I'm No Angel '33 **1**
Image of an Assassination: A
    New Look at the Zapruder
    Film '98 **1**
Imaginary Crimes '94 **2**
Immoral Tales '74 **2**
Immortal Battalion '44 **2**
Immortal Beloved '94 **3**
Immortal Combat '94 **1**
Immortality '98 **2**
Impact '49 **1**
The Impossible Spy '87 **2**
The Imposters '98 **1**
Impromptu '90 **3**
Impulse '84 **1**
In a Class of His Own '99 **3**
In and Out '97 **1**
In Country '89 **2**
The In Crowd '00 **2**
In Dreams '98 **1**
In God's Hands '98 **2**
In Harm's Way '65 **2**
In His Life: The John Lennon
    Story '00 **3**
In Love and War '96 **1**
In Love and War '01 **3**
In Pursuit '00 **2**

In Pursuit of Honor '95 **2**
In Search of Dracula '76 **1**
In the Beginning... '00 **2**
In the Company of Men '96 **1**
In the Country Where Nothing
    Happens '99 **3**
In the Flesh / Blood Bullets
    Buffoons '00 **2**
In the Footsteps of the Holy
    Family '01 **3**
In the Heat of the Night '67 **2**
In the Line of Duty 3 '88 **1**
In the Line of Duty 4 '89 **1**
In the Line of Duty 5 '90 **1**
In the Line of Fire [1] '93 **1**
In the Line of Fire [2 SE] '93
    2
In the Mood for Love [SE] '00
    3
In the Mouth of Madness '95
    1
In the Name of the Father '93
    1
In the Navy '41 **1**
In the Realm of Passion '80
    1
In the Realm of the Senses
    '76 **1**
In the Shadows '98 **1**
In the Time of the Butterflies
    '01 **3**
In This House of Brede '75 **2**
In Too Deep '99 **1**
Inbred Rednecks '97 **3**
Incident on a Dark Street '72
    3
Incognito '97 **1**
Incubus '65 **2**
Indecent Proposal '93 **3**
Independence Day '96 **1**
The Indestructible Man / The
    Amazing Transparent Man
    '56 **2**
The Indian in the Cupboard
    '95 **3**
The Indian Tomb '21 **2**
The Indian Tomb '59 **3**
Indiscreet '58 **3**
Indochine '92 **3**
Indomitable Teddy Roosevelt
    '83 **1**
Inferno '80 **1**
Inferno '99 **2**
Infinity '96 **1**
Inga '67 **3**
Inherit the Wind '60 **3**
The Inheritance '76 **1**
Inhumanity '00 **2**
The Inland Sea '93 **2**
Inn of 1000 Sins '75 **2**
Innocent Blood '92 **1**
Inseminoid '80 **2**
The Inside Man '84 **2**
The Insider '99 **1**
Insomnia '97 **1**
Inspector Gadget '99 **1**
The Inspector General '49 **2**
Inspector Wears Skirts '88 **1**
Instinct '99 **1**
Institue Benjamenta or This
    Dream People Call Human
    Life '95 **3**
Interceptor '92 **1**
Interceptor Force '99 **2**
Interiors '78 **2**
Interlocked '98 **1**
Intermezzo '36 **1**
Intern '00 **2**
Internal Affairs '90 **2**
Intersection '93 **3**
The Interview '98 **2**
Interview with the Vampire
    '94 **1**
Intimacy '00 **3**
Into the Arms of Strangers:
    Stories from the Kinder-
    transport '00 **3**
Into the Woods '90 **3**
Into Thin Air: Death on Ever-
    est '97 **3**
Intolerance '16 **1**

Introducing Dorothy Dan-
    dridge '99 **3**
Introduction to Antiques '95
    3
The Intruder '61 **2**
Invaders from Mars '53 **1**
Invaders from Mars [Anchor
    Bay] '86 **1**
Invaders from Mars [MGM]
    '86 **3**
Invasion of the Animal People
    '62 **3**
Invasion of the Blood Farm-
    ers '72 **3**
Invasion of the Body Snatch-
    ers '56 **1**
Invasion of the Body Snatch-
    ers '78 **1**
Invasion U.S.A. '52 **3**
Invasion U.S.A. '85 **3**
Inventing the Abbotts '97 **2**
The Invincible Killer '81 **3**
Invincible Obsessed Fighter
    '82 **3**
The Invisible Ghost '41 **3**
The Invisible Man '33 **2**
Invisible Mom '96 **2**
The Invisible Strangler '76 **1**
The Ipcress File '65 **1**
Irene Dunne Romance Clas-
    sics '00 **2**
The Irishman '78 **3**
Irma La Douce '63 **3**
Irma Vep '96 **1**
Iron Eagle 4 '95 **1**
Iron Giant '99 **1**
The Iron Mask '29 **3**
Iron Maze '91 **1**
Iron Monkey [Tai Seng] '93 **1**
Iron Monkey [Miramax] '93 **3**
Isaac Asimov's Nightfall '00 **2**
The Island at the Top of the
    World '74 **3**
The Island of Dr. Moreau '77
    3
The Island of Dr. Moreau '96
    1
Island of Greed '97 **1**
Isn't She Great '00 **2**
It '27 **3**
It Came from Outer Space
    '53 **3**
It Could Happen to You '94 **2**
It Happened Here '65 **1**
It Happened One Night '34 **1**
It! The Terror from Beyond
    Space '58 **3**
Italian Movie '93 **2**
The Italians '00 **2**
The Item '01 **3**
It's a Mad, Mad, Mad, Mad
    World '63 **3**
It's a Wonderful Life '46 **1**
It's Good to Be Alive '74 **2**
It's Raining on Santiago '74 **2**
It's the Rage '99 **2**
Ivan the Terrible, Part 1 '44 **1**
Ivan the Terrible, Part 2 '46 **1**
Ivanhoe '97 **3**
I've Been Waiting for You '98
    1
Ivory Tower '97 **2**

J

Jabberwocky '77 **3**
Jack and Sarah '95 **3**
Jack & the Beanstalk '52 **2**
Jack and the Beanstalk: The
    Real Story '01 **3**
Jack Be Nimble '94 **1**
The Jack Bull '99 **2**
Jack Frost '97 **1**
Jack Frost '97 **1**
Jack Frost 2: Revenge of the
    Mutant Killer Snowman '00
    3
Jack-O '95 **1**
Jack the Giant Killer '62 **3**
Jack the Ripper: 4 Tales of
    the Supernatural '58 **3**
The Jackal [CE] '97 **1**
The Jackals '67 **3**

Lawrence of Arabia '62 **2**
Lawyer Lawyer '97 **1**
Le Beau Mariage '82 **1**
Le Dernier Combat '84 **3**
Le Magnifique '76 **3**
Le Petit Soldat '60 **3**
Le Professionnel '81 **3**
Le Trou '59 **3**
The Leading Man '96 **1**
A League of Their Own '92 **1**
Lean on Me '89 **1**
The Learning Curve '01 **3**
Leave It to Beaver '97 **1**
Leaving Las Vegas '95 **1**
Leaving Scars '97 **1**
Lee Rock '91 **1**
Left Behind: The Movie '00 **2**
Left Luggage '98 **3**
Legacy of Rage '86 **1**
Legal Eagles '86 **1**
Legally Blonde '01 **3**
Legend [UE] '86 **3**
The Legend '93 **2**
The Legend 2 '93 **3**
The Legend of a Professional '00 **3**
The Legend of Bagger Vance '00 **2**
The Legend of Drunken Master '94 **2**
The Legend of Hell House '73 **3**
The Legend of 1900 '98 **3**
The Legend of Rita '99 **3**
The Legend of Suram Fortress / Ashik Kerib '85 **3**
Legend of the Chupacabra '93 **3**
Legend of the Drunken Tiger '92 **1**
The Legend of the Lone Ranger '59 **3**
Legend of the Red Dragon '94 **3**
The Legend of the 7 Golden Vampires '73 **1**
Legendary Sherlock Holmes Movies '00 **3**
The Legendary Strike '78 **3**
Legendary WWII Movies '00 **2**
Legends of the Fall [1] '94 **1**
Legends of the Fall [2 SE] '94 **2**
Legionnaire '98 **1**
The Lemon Drop Kid '51 **1**
The Lemon Sisters '90 **2**
Lena's Dreams '97 **3**
Lena's Holiday '90 **3**
L'Enfer '93 **1**
L'Ennui '98 **2**
Lenny '74 **2**
Leon, the Professional '94 **2**
Leonard Bernstein: Reaching for the Note '98 **1**
Leprechaun '93 **1**
Leprechaun 2 '94 **2**
Leprechaun 3 '95 **2**
Leprechaun 4: In Space '96 **2**
Leprechaun 5: In the Hood '99 **2**
Les Bonnes Femmes '60 **3**
Les Carabiniers '63 **3**
Les Miserables '97 **2**
A Lesson Before Dying '99 **2**
Lessons of Darkness '92 **3**
Let Freedom Ring: Images of the American Spirit '01 **3**
Let It Ride '89 **3**
Let Sleeping Corpses Lie '74 **2**
Let the Devil Wear Black '99 **2**
Lethal Seduction '97 **2**
Lethal Weapon '87 **1**
Lethal Weapon 2 '89 **1**
Lethal Weapon 3 '92 **1**
Lethal Weapon 4 '98 **1**
Let's Make Love '60 **3**

Letters from a Killer '98 **3**
Leviathan '89 **1**
Lewis and Clark and George '97 **2**
Lewis and Clark: Journey of the Corps of Discovery '97 **3**
Lexx Series 2, Vol. 1 '98 **3**
Liam '00 **3**
Liar Liar '96 **1**
The Libertine '69 **3**
Liberty Heights '99 **2**
License to Kill '89 **1**
The Lickerish Quartet '70 **1**
Liebestraum '91 **3**
Lies '99 **3**
Life '99 **1**
Life According to Muriel '97 **2**
The Life and Times of Hank Greenberg '99 **2**
Life As a House '01 **3**
The Life Before This '99 **2**
Life Is Beautiful '98 **1**
Life Is to Whistle '98 **3**
A Life Less Ordinary '97 **1**
Life of a Gigolo '98 **1**
The Life of Jesus '96 **2**
Life on a String '90 **3**
Life with Father '47 **3**
Life with Judy Garland—Me and My Shadows '01 **1**
Life without Dick '01 **3**
Lifeforce '85 **1**
The Lifestyle '99 **2**
Light at the Edge of the World '71 **3**
Light It Up '99 **2**
Light Keeps Me Company '00 **3**
Light Sleeper '92 **1**
Lightning Jack '94 **2**
Like It Is '98 **3**
Like Water for Chocolate '93 **3**
Lilian's Story '95 **2**
Lilies '96 **3**
Lilies of the Field '63 **2**
Limbo '99 **1**
Limelight '52 **1**
The Limey '99 **1**
Lingerie '01 **2**
Link '86 **3**
The Lion in Winter '68 **2**
The Lion King: Simba's Pride '98 **1**
Lion of the Desert '81 **1**
Lionheart '00 **3**
Lionheart '90 **1**
Lip Service '00 **3**
Lips of Blood '75 **1**
Lipstick Camera '93 **1**
Lisa and the Devil / The House of Exorcism '75 **1**
The List '99 **3**
Listen to Britain and other Films by Humphrey Jennings '40 **3**
A Little Bit of Soul '97 **2**
Little Buddha '93 **1**
Little City '97 **3**
Little Dieter Needs to Fly '97 **3**
The Little Foxes [HBO] '41 **1**
The Little Foxes [MGM] '41 **3**
Little Fugitive '53 **2**
Little Lord Fauntleroy '36 **2**
Little Man Tate '91 **3**
The Little Mermaid '89 **1**
The Little Mermaid 2: Return to the Sea '00 **2**
Little Mother '71 **1**
Little Nicky '00 **2**
A Little Princess '95 **1**
The Little Princess [Slingshot] '39 **2**
The Little Princess [Marengo] '39 **3**
The Little Rascals '94 **1**
Little Shop of Horrors '86 **1**

Little Shots of Happiness '97 **3**
The Little Vampire '00 **2**
Little Voice '98 **1**
Little Witches '96 **1**
Little Women '33 **3**
Little Women [1] '94 **1**
Little Women [2 SE] '94 **2**
The Littlest Horse Thieves '76 **1**
Live and Let Die '73 **1**
Live Flesh '97 **2**
Live Nude Girls Unite! '00 **3**
The Living Daylights '87 **2**
The Living Dead Girl '82 **1**
Living It Up '00 **3**
Living Out Loud '98 **1**
Local Hero '83 **2**
Lock, Stock and 2 Smoking Barrels '98 **2**
Lock Up '89 **1**
Lockdown '90 **2**
The Locusts '97 **3**
The Lodger '26 **1**
Logan's Run '76 **1**
Lola Montes '55 **1**
Lolida 2000 '97 **2**
Lolita '62 **1**
Lolita '97 **2**
Lone Justice 2 '93 **2**
Lone Justice 3: Showdown at Plum Creek '90 **2**
Lone Ranger '56 **3**
Lone Ranger and the Lost City of Gold '58 **3**
The Lone Ranger: Volume 1 '56 **3**
Lone Wolf McQuade '83 **3**
The Lonely Guy '84 **1**
Lonely Hearts '82 **3**
Lonely Wives '31 **3**
Long Arm of the Law '84 **1**
Long Arm of the Law II '87 **1**
The Long Good Friday '80 **1**
The Long Gray Line '55 **3**
Long John Silver '54 **3**
The Long Kiss Goodnight '96 **1**
The Long Night '47 **3**
The Long Riders '80 **2**
The Long Run '00 **3**
The Long Shadow '92 **3**
The Long Way Home '97 **2**
The Longest Day '62 **1**
Longest Nite '92 **1**
The Longest Yard '74 **2**
Longtime Companion '90 **2**
Look Back in Anger '58 **3**
Look Who's Talking '89 **1**
Look Who's Talking Now '93 **3**
Look Who's Talking, Too '90 **2**
Looking for an Echo '99 **3**
Looking for Lola '98 **1**
Lord Edgeware Dies '99 **2**
The Lord of Hangzhou '98 **3**
Lord of Illusions '95 **1**
Lord of the Flies '63 **3**
Lord of the Flies '90 **3**
The Lord of the Rings '78 **3**
The Lords of Flatbush '74 **2**
Lorna Doone '01 **3**
Loser '93 **3**
Loser '00 **2**
Losin' It '82 **2**
The Loss of Sexual Innocence '98 **2**
Lost and Delirious '01 **3**
Lost and Found '99 **1**
The Lost Battalion '01 **3**
The Lost Boys '87 **1**
The Lost Continent '51 **3**
Lost Continent '68 **3**
The Lost Films of Laurel and Hardy, Vol. 1 '98 **1**
The Lost Films of Laurel and Hardy, Vol. 2 '98 **1**
The Lost Films of Laurel and Hardy, Vol. 3 '99 **1**
The Lost Films of Laurel and Hardy, Vol. 5 '99 **1**

The Lost Films of Laurel and Hardy, Vol. 6 '99 **1**
Lost Horizon '37 **1**
Lost in America '85 **2**
Lost in Space '98 **1**
Lost in Yonkers '93 **3**
Lost Souls '00 **2**
The Lost Weekend '45 **2**
The Lost World [SlingShot] '25 **1**
The Lost World [Image] '25 **2**
The Lost World: Jurassic Park 2 [CE] '97 **2**
Lotto Land '95 **1**
Louis Prima: The Wildest! '99 **2**
Loulou '80 **2**
Love Affair '39 **2**
Love After Love '94 **2**
Love and a .45 '94 **1**
Love and Anarchy '73 **1**
Love and Basketball '00 **3**
Love and Death '75 **2**
Love and Death on Long Island '97 **1**
Love Beat the Hell outta Me '00 **3**
Love by Appointment '76 **2**
Love Can Seriously Damage Your Health '96 **3**
Love Come Down '00 **3**
Love, etc. '96 **1**
Love Field '91 **2**
Love Film '70 **3**
The Love Goddesses '65 **1**
Love Goggles '99 **3**
Love, Honour & Obey '00 **2**
Love Is a Many Splendored Thing '55 **3**
Love Jones '96 **1**
Love Kills '98 **2**
The Love Letter '99 **1**
Love Letters '83 **2**
The Love Master '97 **2**
The Love of Jeanne Ney '27 **3**
Love on a Diet '01 **3**
Love Potion #9 '92 **3**
Love Songs '99 **3**
Love Stinks '99 **3**
Love Story '70 **2**
Love to Kill '97 **1**
Loveblind '98 **1**
The Lover '92 **3**
Lover of the Last Empress '95 **1**
Lovers and Liars '81 **2**
Lover's Prayer '99 **3**
Love's Labour's Lost '00 **2**
Loves of a Blonde '65 **3**
The Loves of Carmen '48 **2**
Lovesick '83 **1**
Loving Jezebel '99 **2**
Lower Level '91 **2**
Lucinda's Spell '00 **2**
Luck of the Draw '00 **3**
Lucky Luke '94 **1**
Lucky Numbers '00 **2**
Lucky Texan '34 **2**
Luckytown '00 **3**
Lulu on the Bridge '98 **1**
Lumiere and Company '96 **1**
The Lumiere Brothers' First Films '97 **1**
Luminaria '83 **1**
Luminous Motion '00 **3**
Lupin III: The Mystery of Mamo '78 **1**
Lured '47 **3**
Lush '01 **3**
Lust for a Vampire '71 **1**
Lust for Frankenstein '88 **2**
Lust in the Dust '85 **2**
The Luzhin Defence '00 **3**

M
M '31 **1**
Ma Saison Preferee '93 **1**
Ma Vie en Rose '97 **2**
Maborosi '95 **2**
Macabre '80 **2**
MacArthur '77 **3**
Macbeth '71 **3**

Mach 2 '00 **2**
MacKenna's Gold '69 **3**
Macross: Box Set '85 **3**
The Mad Butcher '72 **3**
Mad City '97 **1**
Mad Dog and Glory '93 **1**
Mad Love '95 **1**
Mad Max [Image] '80 **1**
Mad Max [MGM SE] '80 **3**
Mad Max: Beyond Thunderdome '85 **1**
Mad Youth '40 **3**
Madadayo '92 **2**
Madame Butterfly '95 **3**
Made for Each Other '39 **1**
Made in America '93 **1**
Made [SE] '01 **3**
Made Men '99 **1**
Madeline '98 **2**
Madeline at the North Pole '00 **3**
Mademoiselle '66 **3**
Madigan '68 **1**
Madman '82 **2**
The Madness of King George '94 **2**
The Madness Trilogy: Reefer Madness, Cocaine Fiends, Sex Madness '00 **3**
Madron '72 **2**
Mafia! '98 **2**
The Magic Show '81 **3**
The Magic Voyage '93 **1**
The Magical Legend of the Leprechauns '99 **2**
Magical Mystery Tour '67 **1**
The Magnificent Ambersons '02 **3**
Magnificent Butcher '87 **3**
The Magnificent Seven '60 **2**
Magnificent Warriors '87 **1**
Magnolia '99 **2**
Magnum Force '73 **3**
Mah Jong Dragon '97 **1**
Mahler '74 **1**
Mailer on Mailer '00 **2**
Major League 2 '94 **3**
Major League 3: Back to the Minors '98 **3**
Major Payne '95 **1**
Make Mine Music '46 **2**
Making the Grade '84 **3**
Male and Female '19 **2**
Malice [Polygram] '93 **1**
Malice [MGM] '93 **2**
Mallrats '95 **1**
The Maltese Falcon '41 **2**
Mama Flora's Family '98 **3**
Man Called Hero '99 **2**
A Man for All Seasons '66 **2**
The Man from Laramie '55 **2**
The Man from Planet X '51 **2**
Man from Utah / Sagebrush Trail '34 **2**
The Man in the Iron Mask '98 **1**
A Man in Uniform '93 **1**
Man Next Door '97 **3**
Man of a Thousand Faces '57 **1**
Man of the Year '95 **1**
Man on the Moon '99 **1**
Man Wanted '94 **1**
The Man Who Cried '00 **3**
The Man Who Fell to Earth '76 **1**
The Man Who Haunted Himself '70 **3**
The Man Who Knew Too Little '97 **1**
The Man Who Knew Too Much '34 **1**
The Man Who Knew Too Much '56 **2**
The Man Who Loved Women '77 **2**
The Man Who Loved Women '83 **3**
The Man Who Shot Liberty Valance '62 **2**

The Movies Begin
(1894–1913) '02 **3**
The Moving Finger '85 **3**
Moving Target '96 **1**
Moving Target '00 **2**
Ms. 45 '81 **1**
Much Ado about Nothing '93
1
Muhammad Ali—Through the
Eyes of the World '02 **3**
Mulan '98 **1**
Mulholland Drive '01 **3**
Multiplicity '96 **1**
Mumford '99 **1**
Mumia: A Case for Reason-
able Doubt? '96 **1**
Mummies Alive! '97 **3**
The Mummy '32 **1**
The Mummy '59 **1**
The Mummy [1] '99 **1**
The Mummy [2 SE] '99 **2**
Mummy Raider '01 **3**
The Mummy Returns '01 **3**
The Mummy's Curse '44 **3**
The Mummy's Ghost '44 **3**
The Mummy's Hand '40 **3**
The Mummy's Shroud '67 **2**
The Mummy's Tomb '42 **3**
Munster, Go Home! '66 **2**
The Munsters' Revenge '81 **2**
Muppet Family Christmas '95
3
The Muppet Movie '79 **3**
Muppets from Space '99 **1**
The Muppets Take Manhattan
'84 **3**
Murder '30 **1**
Murder at 1600 '97 **1**
Murder at the Vicarage '86 **3**
Murder by Death '76 **3**
Murder in Coweta County '83
3
Murder in the First '95 **2**
Murder in the Orient '73 **3**
A Murder of Crows '99 **1**
The Murder of Roger Ackroyd
'99 **2**
Murder Once Removed '71 **3**
The Muse '99 **1**
The Music Man '62 **1**
Music of the Heart [CS] '99 **2**
The Musketeer '01 **3**
Mutant '83 **2**
MVP: Most Valuable Primate
'00 **2**
My Best Fiend '99 **2**
My Best Friend's Wedding [1]
'97 **1**
My Best Friend's Wedding [2
SE] '97 **3**
My Best Girl '27 **1**
My Blue Heaven '90 **1**
My Bodyguard '80 **3**
My Cousin Vinny '92 **2**
My Dinner with Andre '81 **1**
My Dog Skip '99 **2**
My Fair Lady '64 **1**
My Favorite Blonde '42 **3**
My Favorite Brunette '47 **2**
My Favorite Martian '98 **1**
My Fellow Americans '96 **1**
My First Mister '01 **3**
My 5 Wives '00 **2**
My Giant '98 **1**
My Girl '91 **1**
My Left Foot '89 **1**
My Life '93 **2**
My Life As a Dog '85 **1**
My Life So Far '98 **1**
My Life to Live '62 **1**
My Little Margie: Collection 2
(1952–55) '02 **3**
My Lucky Stars '85 **1**
My Man Godfrey [Madacy] '36
1
My Man Godfrey [Criterion]
'36 **3**
My Mom's a Werewolf '89 **2**
My Night at Maud's '69 **1**
My Science Project '85 **1**

My Sex Life...Or How I Got
into an Argument '96 **2**
My Son the Fanatic '97 **1**
My Son, the Vampire '52 **2**
My Stepmother Is an Alien
'88 **1**
My Teacher's Wife '95 **2**
Mysterious Mr. Wong '35 **3**
Mystery, Alaska '99 **2**
Mystery Men '99 **1**
Mystery of the Necronomicon
'00 **2**
Mystery Science Theater
3000: "Eegah!" '93 **3**
Mystery Science Theater
3000: "Manos, the Hands
of Fate" '93 **3**
Mystery Science Theater
3000: "Mitchell" '93 **3**
Mystery Science Theater
3000: "Red Zone Cuba"
'94 **3**
Mystery Science Theater
3000: "The Brain that
Wouldn't Die" '93 **3**
Mystery Science Theater
3000: The Movie '96 **1**
Mystic Pizza '88 **2**
The Myth of Fingerprints '97
2

N

Nadia: Secret of Blue Water,
Vol. 1: The Adventure
Begins '89 **3**
The Naked City '48 **1**
Naked Gun 2 1/2: The Smell
of Fear '91 **2**
Naked Gun 33 1/3: The Final
Insult '94 **2**
The Naked Gun: From the
Files of Police Squad '88 **2**
Naked Killer '92 **2**
Naked Kiss '64 **1**
The Naked Truth '92 **1**
Napoleon '96 **2**
Napoleon and Samantha '72
1
Narcotic Justice '?? **3**
Nashville '75 **2**
National Lampoon's Animal
House '78 **1**
National Lampoon's Christ-
mas Vacation '89 **1**
National Lampoon's Class
Reunion '82 **1**
National Lampoon's Euro-
pean Vacation '85 **3**
National Lampoon's Golf
Punks '99 **2**
National Lampoon's Loaded
Weapon 1 '93 **1**
National Lampoon's Vacation
'83 **1**
National Velvet '44 **1**
The Natural '84 **2**
Natural Born Killers [DC] '94
2
Naughty Stewardesses '74 **3**
Nautilus '99 **2**
The Navigator '24 **1**
The Navigator '88 **2**
Navy SEALS [Image] '90 **1**
Navy SEALS [MGM] '90 **2**
Necessary Roughness '91 **2**
Necromancer: Satan's Ser-
vant '88 **2**
Needful Things '93 **1**
The Negotiator '98 **1**
Neil Simon's The Odd Couple
2 '98 **1**
Nekromantik '87 **3**
Nelly et Monsieur Arnaud '95
3
Nemesis '86 **3**
Nemesis '93 **1**
Neon Genesis Evangelion
Collection '99 **2**
The Nest '88 **3**
The Net [1] '95 **1**
The Net [2 SE] '95 **3**
Network '76 **1**

Neurotica: Middle-Age Spread
and Other Life Crises '97 **2**
Never Been Kissed '99 **1**
Never Cry Wolf '83 **2**
Never Say Never Again '83 **1**
Never Talk to Strangers '95 **1**
Never Too Late '98 **2**
Never 2 Big '98 **3**
The NeverEnding Story '84 **3**
NeverEnding Story 2: The
Next Chapter '91 **3**
The New Adventures of Pippi
Longstocking '88 **3**
The New Daughters of
Joshua Cabe '76 **3**
The New Eve '98 **2**
New Fist of Fury '76 **1**
The New Gladiators '83 **3**
New Jack City '91 **1**
New Jersey Drive '95 **1**
New Legend of Shaolin '96 **2**
New Orleans '47 **1**
New Port South '00 **3**
New Rose Hotel '98 **1**
New World Disorder '99 **1**
New York in the Fifties '01 **3**
New York Ripper '82 **1**
News from the West '99 **2**
Newsbreak '00 **2**
Newsies '92 **3**
The Newton Boys '97 **1**
The Next Best Thing '00 **2**
Next Friday [Platinum Series]
'00 **2**
Next of Kin '84 **3**
Next of Kin '89 **1**
The Next Step '95 **2**
Next Stop, Wonderland '98 **2**
Next Time '99 **3**
Niagara '52 **3**
Nice Guys Sleep Alone '99 **2**
Nicholas and Alexandra '71 **1**
Nick of Time '95 **2**
Nico and Dani '00 **3**
Nico Icon '95 **1**
A Night at the Roxbury '98 **1**
Night Caller from Outer
Space '66 **1**
Night Calls: The Movie '98 **1**
Night Calls: The Movie 2 '99
1
Night Divides the Day '01 **3**
Night Falls on Manhattan '96
1
Night Fire '94 **1**
The Night Heaven Fell '57 **3**
A Night in the Life of Jimmy
Reardon '88 **2**
Night of the Ghouls '59 **3**
Night of the Hunted '80 **3**
Night of the Living Dead
[Anchor Bay LE] '68 **2**
Night of the Living Dead
[Madacy] '68 **2**
Night of the Living Dead
[Elite] '68 **2**
Night of the Living Dead [Elite
ME] '68 **3**
Night of the Living Dead '90
2
Night of the Warrior '91 **1**
Night on the Galactic Rail-
road '85 **3**
Night Orchid '97 **3**
Night Screams '87 **1**
Night Shift '82 **1**
The Night Stalker '71 **1**
The Night Strangler '72 **1**
The Night That Never Hap-
pened '97 **1**
Night Tide '61 **3**
Night to Dismember '83 **3**
A Night to Remember '58 **1**
Night Train to Terror '84 **1**
Nightbreed '90 **3**
Nighthawks '81 **1**
Nightmare at Noon '87 **1**
The Nightmare before Christ-
mas [1] '93 **1**
The Nightmare before Christ-
mas [2 SE] '93 **2**

A Nightmare on Elm Street
'84 **1**
A Nightmare on Elm Street 2:
Freddy's Revenge '85 **1**
A Nightmare on Elm Street 3:
Dream Warriors '87 **1**
A Nightmare on Elm Street 4:
Dream Master '88 **1**
A Nightmare on Elm Street 5:
Dream Child '89 **1**
The "Nightmare on Elm
Street" Collection '99 **1**
Nightmares '83 **1**
Nightmaster '87 **3**
Nights of Cabiria '57 **1**
Nightwatch '94 **2**
Nightwatch '96 **2**
Nikki, the Wild Dog of the
North '61 **1**
9 1/2 Weeks '86 **1**
Nine Lives of Fritz the Cat '74
3
Nine Months '95 **2**
9 to 5 '80 **2**
1941 '79 **1**
1969 '89 **3**
1999 '98 **3**
90 Degrees South: With
Scott to the Antarctic '33 **1**
Ninja in the Deadly Trap '83 **3**
Ninja in the U.S.A. '88 **3**
Ninja Scroll '93 **1**
Ninja vs. Shaolin Guards '84
3
The Ninth Gate '99 **2**
Ninth Street '98 **2**
Nixon '95 **1**
No Code of Conduct '98 **2**
No Dessert Dad, 'Til You Mow
the Lawn '94 **2**
No Escape '94 **1**
No Looking Back '98 **2**
No Man's Land '01 **3**
No Mercy '86 **1**
No Safe Haven '87 **2**
No Strings Attached '98 **1**
No Way Out '87 **2**
Noah's Ark '99 **2**
Nomads '86 **3**
Norma Rae '79 **2**
The North Avenue Irregulars
'79 **1**
North by Northwest '59 **2**
North Dallas Forty '79 **2**
The North Star '43 **3**
Northanger Abbey '87 **2**
Nosferatu [Image 1] '22 **1**
Nosferatu [Image 2] '22 **2**
Nosferatu [Triton] '22 **3**
Nosferatu the Vampyre '79 **1**
Nostalghia '83 **1**
Nostradamus: His Life and
Prophecies / Prophecy and
Prediction '94 **3**
Not Another Teen Movie '01 **3**
Not Love Just Frenzy '96 **3**
Not of This Earth '88 **2**
Not without My Daughter '90
3
Nothin' 2 Lose '00 **2**
Nothing but Trouble '91 **1**
Nothing in Common '86 **3**
Nothing Sacred '37 **1**
Nothing to Lose '96 **1**
Notorious '46 **1**
The Notorious Daughter of
Fanny Hill / Head Mistress
'66 **2**
Notting Hill '99 **1**
Novel Desires '92 **1**
Novocaine '01 **3**
Now and Then '95 **1**
Now, Voyager '42 **3**
Nowhere in Sight '01 **3**
Nowhere to Run '93 **1**
Nude for Satan '74 **1**
Nude on the Moon '61 **2**
The Nude Set '61 **3**
No. 17 '32 **1**
Nunsense '93 **1**

Nunsense 2: The Sequel '94
1
Nuremberg '00 **2**
Nureyev '91 **3**
Nurse Betty '00 **2**
The Nutt House '92 **1**
The Nutty Professor '63 **2**
The Nutty Professor '96 **1**
Nutty Professor 2: The
Klumps [1 CE] '00 **2**
Nutty Professor 2: The
Klumps [2 Uncensored] '00
1
A Nymphoid Barbarian in
Dinosaur Hell [SE] '94 **2**

O

O '01 **3**
O Brother Where Art Thou?
'00 **2**
Oasis of the Zombies '82 **2**
The Object of Beauty '91 **2**
The Object of My Affection
'98 **3**
Object of Obsession '95 **1**
Obsession '76 **3**
An Occasional Hell '96 **1**
Ocean's 11 '60 **3**
Ocean's Eleven '01 **3**
October Sky '99 **1**
October 22 '98 **2**
Octopus '00 **2**
Octopussy '83 **2**
The Odd Couple '68 **2**
Odd Man Out '47 **1**
The Odessa File '74 **1**
The Odyssey '97 **3**
Of Human Bondage '34 **2**
Of Mice and Men '39 **1**
Of Mice and Men '92 **3**
Office Space '98 **1**
An Officer and a Gentleman
'82 **2**
The Ogre '96 **3**
Oh My Goddess! Vol. 1 '93 **3**
Oklahoma '55 **1**
The Old Dark House '32 **1**
The Old Man and the Sea '58
2
Old Yeller '57 **3**
Olive Juice '01 **3**
Oliver! '68 **1**
Oliver & Company '88 **3**
Oliver Stone Collection '00 **3**
Oliver Twist '48 **1**
The Omega Code '99 **2**
The Omen [SE] '76 **2**
Omen 3: The Final Conflict
'81 **2**
Omen 4: The Awakening '91
1
The Omen Collection '00 **2**
On Approval '44 **1**
On Deadly Ground '94 **1**
On Golden Pond '81 **1**
On Her Majesty's Secret Ser-
vice '69 **3**
On Our Merry Way '48 **3**
On the Beach '59 **3**
On the Border '98 **2**
On the Borderline '01 **3**
On the Edge '00 **3**
On the Line '01 **3**
On the Ropes '99 **1**
On the Waterfront '54 **3**
Once a Thief '96 **1**
Once Upon a Time in China
'91 **2**
Once Upon a Time in China II
'92 **1**
Once Upon a Time in China III
'93 **1**
Once Upon a Time...When We
Were Colored '95 **2**
One Day in September '99 **2**
187 '97 **2**
One-Eyed Jacks '61 **2**
One False Move '91 **2**
One Fine Day '96 **3**
One Flew Over the Cuckoo's
Nest '75 **1**
One for the Road '82 **3**

Pretty Woman '90 **1**
A Price above Rubies '97 **1**
The Price of Desire '96 **1**
Price of Glory '00 **2**
Pride and Prejudice '95 **1**
The Pride and the Passion '57 **3**
The Pride of the Yankees '42 **1**
Priest '94 **1**
Primal Fear '96 **1**
Primary Colors '98 **1**
The Prime Gig '00 **3**
Prime Suspect '82 **1**
Primitive Love '64 **3**
The Prince and the Pauper '78 **2**
The Prince and the Showgirl '57 **3**
Prince of Central Park '00 **2**
Prince of Darkness '87 **1**
Prince of Egypt '98 **1**
The Prince of Tides '91 **3**
The Princess and the Pirate '44 **3**
The Princess and the Pirate '95 **1**
The Princess and the Warrior '00 **3**
The Princess Bride [1] '87 **3**
The Princess Bride [2 SE] '87 **3**
Princess Caraboo '94 **2**
The Princess Diaries '01 **3**
Princess Mononoke '98 **2**
Princess of Thieves '01 **3**
Princess Warrior '90 **1**
Prison on Fire '87 **1**
Prison on Fire 2 '91 **3**
The Prisoner '68 **3**
The Prisoner '90 **2**
Prisoner Maria: The Movie '95 **2**
Private Benjamin '80 **1**
The Private Eyes [SE] '80 **2**
Private Navy of Sgt. O'Farrell '68 **2**
Private Obsession '94 **1**
Private Parts '96 **1**
Prizzi's Honor '85 **1**
The Prodigy '98 **2**
The Professional '94 **1**
The Professionals '66 **1**
Progeny '98 **3**
Project A '83 **2**
Project A-ko '86 **2**
Project: Eliminator '91 **1**
Project Moon Base '53 **1**
The Projectionist '71 **3**
Prom Night '80 **1**
Proof of Life '00 **3**
Prophecy '79 **3**
The Prophecy '95 **1**
The Prophecy 2: Ashtown '97 **1**
The Prophecy 3: The Ascent '99 **1**
The Prophet's Game '99 **2**
The Proposal '00 **2**
Protector '97 **1**
Protocol '84 **1**
Proud Rebel '58 **3**
Psychic Killer '75 **3**
Psycho [CE] '60 **1**
Psycho '98 **1**
Psycho 2 '83 **3**
Psycho 3 '86 **1**
Psycho Sisters '98 **2**
Psychomania '73 **2**
Public Access '93 **1**
Pulp Cinema '01 **3**
Pulp Fiction '94 **1**
Pump Up the Volume '90 **1**
Pumpkinhead '88 **2**
The Punisher '90 **1**
Puppet Films of Jiri Trnka '51 **1**
Puppet Master '89 **2**
Puppet Master 2 '90 **2**
Puppet Master 3: Toulon's Revenge '90 **2**

Puppet Master 4 '93 **2**
Puppet Master 5: The Latest Chapter '94 **2**
Puppet Master Collection '00 **2**
The Puppetmaster '93 **3**
The Puppetoon Movie '87 **2**
Pure Country '92 **1**
Purple Noon '60 **3**
Purple Rain '84 **1**
The Purple Rose of Cairo '85 **3**
Pusher '96 **2**
Pushing Hands '92 **1**
Pushing Tin '99 **1**
Putney Swope '69 **3**
Putting It Together: Stephen Sondheim—A Musical Review '93 **1**
Pyaar Kiya to Darna Kya '98 **1**
Pyar to Hona Hi Tah '98 **1**
Pygmalion '38 **2**
Python '00 **2**

Q
Q & A '90 **1**
Q: The Movie '99 **2**
Q (The Winged Serpent) '82 **1**
QB VII '74 **3**
Quackser Fortune Has a Cousin in the Bronx '70 **2**
Quadrophenia '79 **3**
Quantum Leap: The Pilot Episode '89 **1**
The Quarrel '93 **1**
The Quarry '98 **2**
Quatermass 2 '57 **2**
Quatermass and the Pit '67 **1**
Que Viva Mexico '32 **3**
Queen Bee '55 **3**
Queens Logic '91 **3**
Queens of Comedy '01 **2**
Queer As Folk: The Complete First Season '01 **3**
Queer As F**k: Bizarre Short Films '01 **3**
Querelle '83 **3**
The Quest '96 **1**
Quest for Camelot '98 **1**
The Quick and the Dead '94 **1**
Quicksand '50 **2**
Quidam '99 **2**
Quiet Days in Hollywood '97 **2**
The Quiet Man '52 **1**
Quigley Down Under '90 **3**
Quills '00 **1**
Quiz Show '94 **1**

R
Rabid '77 **2**
Rabid Dogs '74 **1**
Rabid Grannies '89 **3**
Race '99 **1**
Race Against Time '00 **2**
Race the Sun '96 **3**
Race to Freedom: The Story of the Underground Railroad '94 **2**
Rachel's Man '75 **2**
Radical Jack '00 **3**
Radio Days '87 **3**
Radioland Murders '94 **1**
Rage at Dawn '55 **3**
The Rage: Carrie 2 '99 **1**
Raging Bull '80 **2**
Raid on Rommel '71 **1**
Raiders of Leyte Gulf '63 **3**
Railroaded '47 **3**
Railrodder '65 **2**
Rain '32 **2**
Rain Man '88 **1**
Rainbow Bridge '71 **3**
A Raisin in the Sun '61 **2**
Raising Cain '92 **1**
Raising the Mammoth '00 **2**
Rambling Rose [1] '91 **1**
Rambling Rose [2 SE] '91 **2**
Rambo: First Blood, Part 2 '85 **1**
Rambo 3 '88 **1**

Ran '85 **1**
Rancho Deluxe '75 **2**
Random Acts of Violence '02 **3**
Random Encounter '98 **3**
Random Hearts '99 **3**
Randy Rides Alone '34 **2**
Rangers '00 **2**
Ranma 1/2: Random Rhapsody—Wacky Winter Wonderland '01 **3**
Ransom '96 **1**
The Rape of the Vampire '68 **3**
Rappin'-N-Rhyming '00 **3**
Raptor '01 **3**
Rashomon '51 **3**
Rasputin the Mad Monk '66 **1**
Rat '00 **3**
The Rat Pack '98 **1**
Rat Race '01 **3**
Ratas, Ratones, Rateros '99 **2**
Rated X '00 **2**
Rats '83 **3**
Ratz '99 **3**
The Ravagers '65 **3**
Raven '97 **1**
Raven's Ridge '97 **3**
Raw Deal '48 **3**
Raw Deal '86 **1**
Rawhead Rex '87 **3**
Razor Blade Smile '98 **1**
Re-Animator [1] '84 **1**
Re-Animator [2 ME] '84 **3**
Ready to Rumble '00 **2**
Ready to Wear '94 **1**
A Real American Hero '78 **3**
The Real Blonde '97 **2**
Real Genius '85 **3**
Real Life '79 **2**
The Real McCoy '93 **1**
Real Time: Siege at Lucas Street Market '00 **3**
A Real Young Girl '75 **3**
Reality Bites '94 **1**
Reap the Wild Wind '42 **1**
Rear Window '54 **2**
Rebecca [Anchor Bay] '40 **1**
Rebecca [Criterion] '40 **3**
Rebel Music: The Bob Marley Story '00 **3**
Rebel Rousers '69 **3**
Rebel without a Cause '55 **1**
Rebirth of Mothra 1 & 2 '96 **3**
Rebirth of Mothra 2 '97 **3**
Reboot: Season III '97 **2**
Reborn from Hell: Jubei's Revenge '96 **3**
Reborn from Hell: Samurai Armageddon '96 **3**
Recess Christmas: Miracle on Third Street '01 **3**
Recess: School's Out '01 **3**
Reckless and Wild '92 **3**
Record of Lodoss War '90 **1**
Record of Lodoss War: Chronicles of the Heroic Knight '98 **3**
The Red and the White '68 **3**
Red Cherry '95 **3**
Red Corner '97 **1**
Red Dawn '84 **1**
The Red Desert '64 **1**
Red Dirt '99 **3**
The Red Dwarf '99 **2**
Red Heat '88 **1**
The Red House '47 **1**
Red Letters '00 **2**
Red Line '96 **1**
Red Planet '00 **2**
Red River '48 **1**
Red Rock West '93 **3**
Red Scorpion '89 **2**
Red Shoe Diaries: Four on the Floor '96 **2**
Red Shoe Diaries: Luscious Lola '00 **2**

Red Shoe Diaries: Strip Poker '96 **2**
Red Shoe Diaries: Swimming Naked '00 **2**
Red Shoe Diaries: The Game '00 **3**
The Red Shoes '48 **1**
Red Surf '90 **3**
The Red Violin '98 **1**
Red Zone Cuba '66 **3**
Redline '97 **1**
Reefer Madness '38 **2**
Reflex Action '02 **3**
Reform School Girls '86 **2**
Regeneration / Young Romance '15 **3**
Regina '83 **1**
A Regular Frankie Fan '01 **3**
Rehearsal for Murder '82 **1**
The Reincarnation of Isabel '72 **1**
Reindeer Games [Buena Vista] '00 **1**
Reindeer Games [Miramax DC] '00 **3**
Relative Values '99 **2**
The Relic '96 **1**
The Remains of the Day '93 **3**
Rembrandt '36 **2**
Rembrandt Films' Greatest Hits '00 **2**
Remember Pearl Harbor: America Taken by Surprise '01 **3**
Remember the Titans '00 **2**
Remembering the Cosmos Flower '99 **2**
Rent-A-Cop '88 **1**
The Replacement Killers [1] '98 **1**
The Replacement Killers [2 SE] '98 **3**
The Replacements '00 **2**
Replicant '01 **3**
Repo Man '83 **2**
The Reptile '66 **1**
Reptilian '00 **3**
Reptilicus '62 **3**
Requiem for a Dream '00 **2**
Requiem for a Heavyweight '62 **3**
Requiem for a Vampire '71 **1**
Requiem for Murder '99 **3**
Rescue from Gilligan's Island '78 **3**
The Rescuers Down Under '90 **2**
Reservoir Dogs '92 **1**
Restaurant '98 **2**
Restless Spirits '99 **3**
Restoration '94 **1**
Restraining Order '99 **2**
Resurrection '99 **1**
Retrievers '82 **3**
Retro Puppet Master '99 **2**
Retroactive '97 **3**
Return of Captain Invincible '83 **3**
The Return of Martin Guerre '83 **1**
Return of the Blind Dead '75 **1**
Return of the Boogeyman '94 **1**
Return of the Deadly Blade '81 **3**
Return of the Dragon '73 **1**
Return of the Fly '59 **2**
Return of the Killer Tomatoes! '88 **3**
The Return of the King '80 **3**
Return of the Living Dead 3 '93 **3**
Return of the Magnificent Seven '66 **2**
Return of the Street Fighter '74 **3**
Return to Cabin by the Lake '01 **3**
Return to Horror High '87 **3**

Return to Me '00 **2**
Return to Oz '85 **1**
Return to Paradise '98 **1**
Revelation '00 **2**
Revenge '86 **3**
Revenge '90 **1**
Revenge in the House of Usher '82 **3**
Revenge of the Nerds / Revenge of the Nerds 2: Nerds in Paradise '84 **3**
Revenge of the Nerds 2: Nerds in Paradise '87 **3**
Revenge of the Patriots '76 **3**
Revenge of the Pink Panther '78 **1**
Revenge Quest '96 **3**
Revengeful Swordswoman '80 **3**
Reversal of Fortune '90 **3**
Revolt of the Zombies '36 **1**
Rich and Famous / Tragic Hero '87 **3**
Rich and Strange '32 **1**
The Rich Man's Wife '96 **2**
Richard Pryor: Here and Now '83 **3**
Richard Pryor: Live and Smokin' '81 **3**
Richard Pryor: Live in Concert '79 **1**
Richard Pryor: Live on the Sunset Strip '82 **1**
Richard Rodgers: The Sweetest Sound '01 **3**
Richard III '12 **3**
Ricochet '91 **1**
Ricochet River '98 **3**
Ride in the Whirlwind '66 **2**
Ride with the Devil '99 **2**
Riders of Destiny [Columbia] '33 **3**
Riders of Destiny / Star Packer '33 **2**
Riding in Cars with Boys '01 **3**
The Riff '00 **3**
Rififi '54 **2**
The Right Stuff '83 **1**
The Right Temptation '00 **2**
Righting Wrongs '86 **3**
Riki-Oh: The Story of Ricky '89 **3**
Rikyu '90 **2**
The Ring '27 **1**
Ring of Bright Water '69 **2**
The Ring Virus '99 **2**
Ringmaster '98 **1**
Rio Bravo '59 **3**
Rio Grande '50 **1**
Ripper: Letter from Hell '01 **3**
Rising Sun '93 **1**
Risk '00 **3**
Risky Business '83 **1**
Rites of Passage '99 **1**
The River '84 **2**
River of No Return '54 **3**
A River Runs Through It '92 **1**
The River Wild '94 **1**
River's Edge '87 **2**
The Road '00 **3**
Road Dogz '00 **3**
Road Movie '72 **2**
The Road to Bali '53 **2**
The Road to El Dorado '00 **2**
The Road to Morocco [Image] '42 **1**
The Road to Morocco [Universal] '42 **3**
The Road to Rio '47 **2**
The Road to Ruin '28 **3**
The Road to Singapore '40 **3**
The Road to Utopia [Image] '46 **1**
The Road to Utopia [Universal] '46 **3**
The Road to Zanzibar '41 **3**
Road Trip '00 **2**
The Road Warrior '82 **1**
Rob Roy '95 **1**

Shadows '22 **2**
Shadows and Fog '92 **2**
Shadrach '98 **1**
Shaft '71 **1**
Shaft '00 **2**
Shaft in Africa '73 **2**
Shaft's Big Score '72 **2**
Shag: The Movie '89 **2**
Shake, Rattle & Rock! '94 **3**
Shakedown '88 **1**
Shakedown '02 **3**
Shakes the Clown '92 **2**
Shakespeare in Love [CS] '98 **1**
Shalako '68 **1**
Shallow Grave '94 **1**
Shameless '94 **1**
Shane '53 **2**
The Shanghai Gesture '42 **1**
Shanghai Noon '00 **2**
Shanghai Triad '95 **3**
Shaolin Avengers '94 **1**
Shaolin Disciple '86 **3**
Shaolin: Wheel of Life '00 **3**
Shark Attack '99 **1**
Shark Attack 2 '00 **2**
Sharky's Machine '81 **1**
Sharpe's Battle '94 **2**
Sharpe's Company '94 **2**
Sharpe's Eagle '93 **2**
Sharpe's Enemy '94 **2**
Sharpe's Gold '94 **2**
Sharpe's Honour '94 **2**
Sharpe's Justice '97 **2**
Sharpe's Mission '96 **2**
Sharpe's Regiment '96 **2**
Sharpe's Revenge '97 **2**
Sharpe's Rifles '93 **2**
Sharpe's Siege '96 **2**
Sharpe's Sword '94 **2**
Sharpe's Waterloo '97 **2**
Shatter Dead '01 **3**
Shattered Image '98 **1**
The Shawshank Redemption '94 **1**
She '35 **1**
She Creature '01 **3**
She Demons '58 **2**
She-Devil '89 **3**
She Devils in Chains '76 **1**
She-Freak '67 **2**
She Killed in Ecstasy '70 **2**
She Lives by Night '01 **3**
She Shoulda Said No '49 **3**
She Wolf of London '46 **3**
Sheba, Baby '75 **2**
Shelter '98 **3**
Sherlock Holmes and the Secret Weapon '42 **1**
Sherlock Holmes Consulting Detective, Vol. 1 '91 **1**
She's All That '99 **1**
She's Having a Baby '88 **2**
She's So Lovely '97 **2**
She's the One '96 **2**
Shiloh '97 **3**
Shiloh 2: Shiloh Season '99 **3**
Shine '95 **1**
The Shining [1] '80 **1**
The Shining [2 SE] '80 **3**
The Shiver of the Vampires '70 **1**
Shock '79 **3**
Shock Corridor '63 **1**
Shocker '89 **1**
Shogun's Ninja '83 **3**
Shoot Out '71 **1**
Shoot the Piano Player '62 **1**
The Shooting '66 **2**
Shooting Fish '98 **1**
The Shootist '76 **3**
The Shop on Main Street '65 **3**
Shopping '93 **3**
Short 1: Invention '99 **1**
Short 2: Dreams '00 **1**
Short 6: Insanity '99 **3**
Short 7: Utopia '00 **3**
Short 10: Chaos '00 **3**
Short Circuit '86 **3**

Short Circuit 2 '88 **3**
A Shot in the Dark '64 **1**
Shot in the Heart '01 **3**
Show Boat '51 **3**
The Show Off / The Plastic Age '26 **3**
Showdown '94 **3**
Showdown in Little Tokyo '91 **1**
Showgirl Stories '98 **3**
Showgirls '95 **3**
Shrek [SE] '01 **3**
Shriek If You Know What I Did Last Friday the 13th '00 **2**
Siberian Lady Macbeth '61 **3**
The Sicilian '87 **3**
Sid & Nancy [Criterion] '86 **1**
Sid & Nancy [MGM] '86 **2**
The Sid Caesar Collection: The Fan Favorites '01 **3**
Sideshow '00 **3**
Sidewalks of New York '01 **3**
The Siege '98 **1**
The Sign of Four '83 **2**
Silence of the Lambs [Criterion] '91 **1**
Silence of the Lambs [MGM SE] '91 **3**
Silent Fall '94 **3**
Silent Rage '82 **3**
Silent Running [Image] '71 **1**
Silent Running [Universal] '71 **3**
Silent Shakespeare '00 **2**
Silk 'n' Sabotage '94 **1**
The Silk Road '88 **3**
Silkwood '83 **1**
Silver Bullet '85 **3**
Silver Wolf '98 **3**
Silverado [SE] '85 **2**
Simon Birch '98 **1**
Simon Sez '99 **1**
Simpatico '99 **2**
A Simple Plan '98 **1**
A Simple Wish '97 **1**
Simply Irresistible '99 **1**
The Simpsons: The Complete First Season '89 **3**
Sin: The Movie '98 **2**
Sinbad and the Eye of the Tiger '77 **2**
Sinbad: Beyond the Veil of Mists '00 **2**
The Sinful Nuns of Saint Valentine '74 **1**
Singin' in the Rain '52 **1**
A Single Girl '96 **2**
Single White Female '92 **1**
Singles '92 **1**
The Sinister Saga '00 **3**
Sink or Swim '97 **1**
Sirens '94 **1**
Sister Act '92 **3**
Sister Act 2: Back in the Habit '93 **1**
Sister My Sister '94 **1**
Sister, Sister '87 **2**
Sister Street Fighter '76 **3**
Sisters '73 **2**
Six Days, Seven Nights '98 **1**
Six Degrees of Separation '93 **2**
Six Ways to Sunday '99 **1**
Sixteen Candles '84 **1**
The 6th Day [1] '00 **2**
The 6th Day [2 SE] '00 **3**
The Sixth Sense [Hollywood Pictures] '99 **1**
The Sixth Sense [Buena Vista] '99 **3**
The '60s '99 **1**
61* '01 **3**
'68 '87 **3**
Sizzle Beach U.S.A. '74 **1**
Skin Game '31 **1**
Skinner '93 **1**
Skipped Parts '00 **1**
The Skulls '00 **2**
The Skulls 2 '02 **3**
Skylark '93 **1**
Skyscraper '95 **3**

Slackers '02 **3**
Slam '98 **1**
Slap Shot [1] '77 **1**
Slap Shot [2] '77 **3**
Slap Shot 2: Breaking the Ice '02 **3**
Slapstick Encyclopedia (1909–27) '98 **3**
Slaughter '72 **3**
Slaughterhouse '87 **2**
Slaughterhouse Five '72 **1**
Slaughter's Big Ripoff '73 **2**
Slave Girls from Beyond Infinity '87 **1**
Slaves to the Underground '96 **1**
The Slayers '95 **3**
SLC Punk! '99 **1**
Sleepaway Camp '83 **2**
Sleeper '73 **2**
Sleepers '96 **1**
Sleeping Murder / 4:50 from Paddington '86 **3**
Sleepless '01 **3**
Sleepless in Seattle '93 **1**
Sleepwalkers '92 **2**
Sleepy Hollow '99 **1**
Sleuth [1] '72 **1**
Sleuth [2] '72 **3**
Sliding Doors '97 **1**
Slightly Scarlet '56 **3**
The Slime People '63 **3**
Sling Blade '96 **1**
The Slipper and the Rose '76 **1**
Slippery When Wet '58 **2**
Slipstream '89 **3**
Slow Burn '97 **1**
Slugs '87 **2**
Slumber Party Massacre '82 **2**
Slumber Party Massacre 2 '87 **2**
Slumber Party Massacre 3 '90 **2**
Slums of Beverly Hills '98 **1**
Small Change '76 **2**
Small Soldiers '98 **1**
Small Time Crooks '00 **2**
Smart Money '97 **1**
Smash Cuts! Super Sci-Fi Shorts '00 **3**
Smash Cuts: Totally Twisted Shorts Fest '00 **3**
Smashing Time '67 **1**
Smile Now Cry Later '01 **3**
Smiling Fish & Goat on Fire '99 **3**
Smilla's Sense of Snow '96 **2**
Smoke Signals '98 **1**
The Smokers '00 **3**
Smokey and the Bandit '77 **1**
Snake and Crane Arts of Shaolin '78 **3**
Snake Eyes '98 **1**
Snake in the Eagle's Shadow '78 **3**
Snapdragon '93 **3**
Snatch [SE] '00 **3**
Sneakers '92 **1**
Sniper '92 **2**
Snow Day '00 **2**
Snow Dogs '02 **3**
Snow Falling on Cedars '99 **2**
Snow White: A Tale of Terror '97 **1**
Snow White and the Seven Dwarfs [PE] '37 **3**
Snow White: The Fairest of Them All '02 **3**
The Snows of Kilimanjaro '52 **2**
So I Married an Axe Murderer '93 **1**
Soapdish '91 **3**
Social Intercourse '01 **3**
Social Misfits '00 **2**
The Soft Skin '64 **1**
Sol Bianca: The Legacy '90 **2**
Solar Crisis '92 **1**
Soldier '98 **1**

Soldier of Orange '78 **2**
A Soldier's Story '84 **2**
A Soldier's Tale '91 **1**
Solo '96 **1**
Solomon and Gaenor '98 **2**
Some Folks Call It a Sling Blade '94 **3**
Some Like It Hot [SE] '59 **2**
Somebody Has to Shoot the Picture '90 **2**
Someone Like You '01 **3**
Someone to Watch Over Me '87 **1**
Something about Sex '98 **1**
Something More '99 **2**
Something New '20 **2**
Something Weird '68 **2**
Something Wicked This Way Comes '83 **1**
Something Wild '86 **2**
Something within Me '93 **3**
Sometimes They Come Back '91 **3**
Sometimes They Come Back...For More '99 **2**
Sometimes They Come Back...Again '96 **3**
Somewhere in Time '80 **1**
Sommersby '93 **1**
Son-in-Law '93 **1**
Son of Dracula '43 **3**
Son of Frankenstein '39 **3**
Son of Gascogne '95 **2**
The Son of Monte Cristo '40 **3**
Son of Paleface '52 **3**
Son of the Sheik '26 **3**
Song for Cassavetes '00 **3**
Song of Freedom / Big Fella '36 **3**
Songmakers Collection '01 **3**
Sons of Katie Elder '65 **2**
Sophie's Choice '82 **1**
The Sopranos: The Complete First Season '00 **2**
The Sopranos: The Complete Second Season '01 **3**
Sorcerer '77 **1**
Sorcerer Hunters: Magical Encounters '00 **2**
Sorceress '94 **1**
Sore Losers '97 **3**
Sorority Babes in the Slimeball Bowl-A-Rama '87 **3**
Sorority House Massacre '86 **2**
Sorority House Massacre 2: Nighty Nightmare '92 **3**
The Sorrow and the Pity '71 **2**
Sorry, Wrong Number '48 **3**
S.O.S. Titanic '79 **3**
Soul Food '97 **1**
Soul Man '86 **3**
Soul of the Game '96 **2**
Soul Survivors '01 **3**
The Souler Opposite '97 **2**
Soultaker '90 **1**
Soultaker: The Monster Within '02 **3**
Sound and Fury '00 **3**
The Sound of Music [FS] '65 **2**
Sour Grapes '98 **2**
The Source '96 **2**
South Bronx Heroes '85 **3**
South Central '92 **2**
South of Heaven, West of Hell '01 **3**
South Pacific '58 **1**
South Park: Bigger, Longer and Uncut '99 **3**
South Park: Insults to Injury '02 **3**
Southern Comfort '81 **2**
Southern Man '99 **3**
The Southerner '45 **3**
Southie '98 **1**
Southpaw '99 **3**
Space Cowboys '00 **2**
Space Jam [1] '96 **1**
Space Jam [2 EE] '96 **3**

Space: 1999 Set 1 '75 **3**
Space-Thing '67 **2**
Space Truckers '97 **1**
Spaceballs '87 **3**
Spacehunter: Adventures in the Forbidden Zone '83 **3**
Spaceways '53 **2**
Spanish Judges '99 **3**
The Spanish Prisoner '97 **1**
Sparrows '26 **1**
Spartacus [Universal] '60 **1**
Spartacus [Criterion] '60 **2**
Spawn [SE] '97 **1**
Speaking Parts '89 **3**
The Specialist '75 **3**
The Specialist '94 **1**
The Specials '00 **2**
Specimen '97 **1**
Speechless '94 **3**
Speed '94 **1**
Speed 2: Cruise Control '97 **1**
Speed Racer: The Movie '93 **2**
Spellbound '45 **1**
Sphere '97 **1**
Spice World: The Movie '97 **1**
Spider Baby '64 **1**
Spider-Man: The Ultimate Villain Showdown '02 **3**
Spiders '18 **3**
Spiders '00 **2**
Spies Like Us '85 **1**
Spike and Mike's Classic Festival of Animation '01 **3**
Spin the Bottle '97 **3**
The Spiral Staircase '46 **2**
Spirit of the Eagle '90 **1**
Spirits of the Dead [Image] '68 **1**
Spirits of the Dead [Criterion] '68 **3**
Spiritual Kung Fu '78 **1**
Splash '84 **2**
Splendor '99 **2**
Split Second '92 **3**
Spoiler '98 **3**
Spongebob Squarepants: Nautical Nonsense and Sponge Buddies '02 **3**
Spooky Encounters '80 **2**
Spreading Ground '01 **3**
Spring Symphony '86 **1**
Sprung '96 **1**
Spy Game '01 **3**
Spy Hard '96 **1**
Spy Kids '01 **3**
The Spy Who Loved Me [SE] '77 **1**
The Squeeze '78 **3**
Squeeze '97 **3**
Squeeze Play [DC] '79 **3**
Stage Door Canteen '43 **3**
Stagecoach '39 **1**
Stagefright '87 **3**
Stalingrad '94 **1**
Stalked '99 **2**
Stalker '98 **3**
Stallone: Rambo Trilogy [SE] '02 **3**
Stand and Deliver '88 **1**
Stand by Me [1] '86 **1**
Stand by Me [2 SE] '86 **2**
Stand-Ins '97 **3**
Star Blazers: The Comet Empire: Part 1 '80 **3**
Star Blazers: The Quest for Iscandar: Series 1 '79 **3**
Star 80 '83 **1**
A Star Is Born '37 **1**
A Star Is Born '54 **2**
The Star Packer '34 **2**
Star Slammer '87 **3**
Star Spangled Rhythm '42 **3**
Star Trek: The Motion Picture [DE] '80 **3**
Star Trek 2: The Wrath of Khan '82 **2**
Star Trek 3: The Search for Spock '84 **3**

There's No Business Like Show Business '54 **2**
There's Nothing out There '90 **3**
There's Something about Mary '98 **1**
Therese & Isabelle '67 **1**
Therese Raquin '80 **3**
Thesis '96 **1**
They Call It Murder '71 **3**
They Call Me Mr. Tibbs! '70 **2**
They Came from Within '75 **1**
They Do It with Mirrors '91 **3**
They Got Me Covered '43 **3**
They Live '88 **1**
They Made Me a Criminal '39 **2**
They Might Be Giants '71 **1**
They Shoot Horses, Don't They? '69 **1**
They Were Expendable '45 **1**
Thick As Thieves '99 **2**
The Thief '52 **3**
Thief '81 **1**
The Thief '97 **2**
Thief in the Night '72 **3**
Thief of Hearts '84 **3**
A Thin Line Between Love and Hate '96 **1**
The Thin Red Line '64 **1**
The Thin Red Line '98 **1**
The Thing '82 **1**
The Thing with Two Heads '72 **2**
Things I Left in Havanna '97 **3**
Things to Come '36 **2**
Things to Do in Denver When You're Dead '95 **1**
Things You Can Tell Just by Looking at Her '00 **3**
The Third Man '49 **1**
Third World Cop '99 **2**
Thirteen Days '00 **3**
13 Gantry Row '98 **3**
13 Ghosts '60 **3**
13 Ghosts '01 **3**
The Thirteenth Floor '99 **1**
The 13th Warrior '99 **1**
32 Short Films about Glenn Gould '93 **2**
36 Crazy Fists '77 **3**
36 Fillete '88 **1**
The 39 Steps [Criterion] '35 **1**
The 39 Steps [Delta/Laserlight] '35 **1**
This Is My Father '99 **1**
This Is Not a Test '62 **3**
This Is Spinal Tap [Criterion] '84 **1**
This Is Spinal Tap [MGM] '84 **2**
This Night I'll Possess Your Corpse '66 **2**
This Sporting Life '63 **1**
Thomas and the Magic Railroad '00 **2**
The Thomas Crown Affair '99 **1**
Thomas Jefferson '01 **3**
Those Bedroom Eyes '92 **1**
Those Who Love Me Can Take the Train '98 **3**
Thou Shalt Not Kill. . .Except '87 **2**
A Thousand Acres '97 **1**
The Thousand Eyes of Dr. Mabuse '60 **2**
Three Ages '23 **1**
Three Amigos '86 **3**
Three Businessmen '99 **2**
The Three Caballeros '45 **2**
Three Came Home '50 **3**
Three Days of the Condor '75 **1**
Three Fugitives '89 **3**
Three Kings '99 **1**
Three Men and a Baby '87 **3**
Three Men and a Little Lady '90 **3**

The Three Musketeers '21 **1**
Three Musketeers '74 **1**
Three Musketeers '88 **1**
The Three Musketeers '93 **1**
3 Ninjas Kick Back '94 **3**
Three on the Trail '36 **3**
Three Stooges: All the World's a Stooge '00 **2**
Three Stooges: All Time Favorites '98 **3**
Three Stooges Cartoon Classics, Volume 1 '65 **3**
Three Stooges: Dizzy Doctors '96 **3**
Three Stooges: Healthy, Wealthy, and Dumb '01 **3**
Three Stooges: Merry Mavericks '01 **2**
Three Stooges: Nutty but Nice '00 **3**
Three Stooges: Spook Louder '00 **2**
Three Stooges: Three Smart Saps '52 **3**
Three Strikes '00 **2**
3:10 to Yuma '57 **3**
3000 Miles to Graceland '01 **3**
Three Wishes '95 **3**
The Three Worlds of Gulliver '59 **3**
Threesome '94 **2**
Thrill Seekers '99 **3**
Throw Down '00 **2**
Throw Momma from the Train '87 **3**
Thug Immortal '97 **2**
Thug Life '00 **3**
Thumb Wars '99 **3**
Thumbelina [Warner] '94 **2**
Thumbelina [20th Century Fox] '94 **3**
Thumbtanic '99 **3**
Thunder Kick '73 **3**
Thunderball '65 **1**
Thunderbolt & Lightfoot '74 **2**
Thunderbirds: Set 1 '65 **3**
Thunderheart '92 **2**
The Tic Code '99 **2**
Tick Tock '00 **3**
Ticker '01 **3**
Ticket to Heaven '81 **1**
Tie-Died: Rock 'n' Roll's Most Deadicated Fans '95 **3**
Tie Me Up! Tie Me Down! '90 **2**
The Tie That Binds '95 **2**
Tierra '96 **3**
Tieta of Agreste '96 **3**
Tiger Bay '59 **1**
Tiger Claws '91 **3**
Tiger of Eschnapur '59 **3**
Tiger over Wall '80 **3**
Tigerland '00 **2**
The Tigger Movie '00 **2**
Til Death Us Do Part '72 **3**
Til There Was You '96 **3**
Till the Clouds Roll By '46 **2**
Tillie's Punctured Romance '14 **1**
Time and Tide '00 **3**
Time Bandits '81 **1**
Time Code '00 **2**
Time Lapse '01 **3**
The Time Machine '60 **2**
Time Masters '82 **1**
Time of Your Life '76 **3**
A Time to Kill '96 **1**
Timecop '94 **3**
Timeless '96 **2**
Timelock '99 **2**
Timerider '83 **3**
Times Square '80 **2**
Tin Cup '96 **1**
Tin Drum '79 **1**
Tin Men '87 **3**
The Tingler '59 **1**
Titan A.E. '00 **2**
Titanic '97 **1**
Titanic: The Complete Story '01 **3**

Titanic 2000 '00 **2**
Titanica '98 **1**
Tito and Me '92 **2**
Titus '98 **3**
T.N.T. '98 **3**
To Catch a Killer '92 **1**
To Cross the Rubicon '91 **1**
To Die For '95 **1**
To Gillian on Her 37th Birthday '96 **3**
To Kill a Mockingbird '62 **1**
To Kill with Intrigue '77 **3**
To Kill with Intrigue '85 **1**
To Play or to Die '91 **1**
To Sir, with Love '67 **3**
To the Limit '95 **3**
Todd McFarlane: The Devil You Know '02 **3**
Todd McFarlane's Spawn '97 **1**
Todd McFarlane's Spawn 2 '98 **1**
Tokyo Decadence '91 **1**
Tokyo Decameron: Three Tales of Madness & Sensuality '96 **3**
Tokyo Drifter '66 **1**
Tokyo Fist '96 **1**
Tokyo Mafia: Battle for Shinjuku '96 **3**
Tokyo Mafia: Wrath of the Yakuza '95 **3**
Tokyo Mafia: Yakuza Wars '95 **3**
Tokyo Raiders '00 **2**
Tol'able David '21 **1**
The Toll Gate ' **1**
Tom and Jerry: The Magic Ring '02 **3**
Tom & Jerry's Greatest Chases '45 **2**
Tom Clancy's Netforce '98 **3**
Tom Jones [HBO] '63 **1**
Tom Jones [MGM] '63 **2**
Tom Sawyer '99 **1**
Tom Thumb '58 **2**
Tombs of the Blind Dead '72 **1**
Tombstone [1] '93 **1**
Tombstone [2] '93 **3**
Tommy '75 **2**
Tommy and the Computoys '95 **1**
Tommy Boy '95 **3**
The Tomorrow Man '01 **3**
Tomorrow Never Dies [SE] '97 **1**
Tomorrow the World '44 **2**
Tomorrow's Children '34 **3**
Tonight or Never '31 **2**
Too Late the Hero '70 **3**
Too Many Ways to Be No. 1 '97 **3**
Tootsie '82 **2**
Top Dog '95 **3**
Top Gun '86 **1**
Top of the World '97 **1**
Topaz '69 **3**
Topkapi '64 **3**
Topper Returns '41 **2**
Topsy Turvy '99 **2**
Tora! Tora! Tora! [1] '70 **1**
Tora! Tora! Tora! [2 SE] '70 **2**
Tormented '60 **3**
The Tormentors '71 **3**
Torn Curtain '66 **2**
Tornado Run '95 **1**
Torso '73 **1**
Tortilla Soup '01 **3**
Torture Chamber of Baron Blood '72 **1**
Total Eclipse '95 **1**
Total Reality '97 **1**
Total Recall [1] '90 **1**
Total Recall [2 SLE] '90 **3**
Total Recall 2070: Machine Dreams '99 **1**
A Touch of Class '73 **3**
Touch of Evil [SE] '58 **2**
Tourist Trap '79 **2**
Tower of Evil '72 **1**

Tower of Song: The Canadian Music Hall of Fame '01 **2**
The Towering Inferno '74 **1**
Town and Country '01 **3**
A Town Has Turned to Dust '98 **2**
Town without Pity '61 **3**
The Toxic Avenger [DC] '86 **1**
The Toxic Avenger, Part 2 '89 **1**
The Toxic Avenger, Part 3: The Last Temptation of Toxie [DC] '89 **3**
The Toy '82 **3**
Toy Story '95 **2**
Toy Story 2 '99 **2**
Toy Story: The Ultimate Toybox '00 **2**
Toys '92 **2**
The Tracker '88 **2**
Trader Hornee '70 **1**
Traffic [Criterion] '00 **3**
Traffic [USA] '00 **2** –
Traffik '89 **1**
Tragic Hero '87 **3**
Trail Beyond [Madacy] '34 **2**
Trail Beyond [Columbia] '34 **3**
Trailer, the Movie '99 **3**
The Train '65 **1**
Train Ride to Hollywood '75 **1**
Training Day '01 **3**
Trainspotting '95 **1**
Traitor's Heart '98 **2**
Trans '98 **3**
Transformers: Season 1 '86 **3**
Transformers: The Movie '86 **2**
Transylvania 6-5000 '85 **3**
Trapper County War '89 **1**
Trash '70 **1**
Traveller '96 **2**
Treasure Island '97 **1**
Treasure Island '99 **3**
Treasures from the American Film Archives: 50 Preserved Films '00 **2**
The Treat '98 **3**
Treehouse Hostage '99 **1**
Trees Lounge '96 **1**
Tremors '89 **1**
Tremors 2: Aftershocks '96 **1**
Tremors 3: Back to Perfection '01 **3**
Trespass '92 **1**
The Trial [Image] '63 **1**
The Trial [FOCUSfilm] '63 **1**
The Trial '93 **1**
Trial & Error '62 **1**
Trial and Error '96 **1**
Trial by Jury '94 **3**
The Triangle '01 **3**
Tribulation '00 **2**
Trick '99 **1**
The Trigger Effect '96 **1**
Trilogy of Terror '75 **1**
Trinity and Beyond: The Atomic Bomb Movie '99 **1**
The Trio '97 **3**
Triumph of the Spirit '89 **3**
Triumph of the Will '34 **2**
Trixie '00 **3**
Trois '00 **3**
A Troll in Central Park '94 **3**
Troma's Edge TV: Vol. 1 '00 **3**
Troma's War [DC] '88 **1**
Tromeo & Juliet '95 **1**
Tron [1] '82 **1**
Tron [2 CE] '82 **3**
The Trouble with Harry '55 **2**
Troublemakers '94 **1**
Troubles '88 **3**
Truck Turner '74 **2**
Trucks '97 **1**
True Believer '89 **2**
True Blue '01 **3**
True Crime '96 **1**
True Crime '99 **3**
True Friends '98 **1**
True Lies '94 **1**
True Romance '93 **1**

True Stories '86 **1**
Truly, Madly, Deeply '91 **3**
The Truman Show '98 **1**
The Trumpet of the Swan '01 **3**
Trust Me U Die '99 **3**
The Truth about Cats and Dogs '96 **2**
Truth or Consequences, N.M. '97 **1**
Truth or Dare '91 **1**
Tucker: The Man and His Dream '88 **2**
Tuff Turf '85 **2**
Tumbleweeds '98 **2**
The Tune '92 **1**
Tupac Shakur: Thug Angel '02 **3**
Turbo: A Power Rangers Movie '96 **1**
Turbulence '96 **1**
Turbulence 2: Fear of Flying '99 **3**
Turbulence 3: Heavy Metal '00 **3**
Turkish Delight '73 **2**
Turn It Up '00 **2**
Turner and Hooch '89 **3**
The Turning '92 **3**
The Tuskegee Airmen '95 **2**
Twelve Angry Men '57 **2**
The Twelve Chairs '70 **1**
12 Monkeys '95 **1**
Twelve o'Clock High '49 **3**
20th Century Fox: The First 50 Years '96 **2**
20,000 Leagues under the Sea '16 **1**
2103: Deadly Wake '97 **3**
28 Days [SE] '00 **2**
Twice-Told Tales '63 **3**
Twice upon a Yesterday '98 **1**
Twilight '98 **1**
The Twilight of the Golds '97 **1**
Twin Dragons '92 **1**
Twin Falls Idaho '99 **2**
Twin Peaks: Fire Walk with Me '92 **3**
Twin Peaks: The First Season '90 **3**
Twin Warriors '93 **3**
Twins '88 **1**
Twisted '96 **1**
Twisted Justice '89 **3**
Twister '96 **1**
Twitch of the Death Nerve '71 **2**
Two Can Play That Game '01 **3**
Two Coyotes '01 **3**
Two English Girls '72 **1**
Two Family House '99 **3**
Two-Fisted Law '32 **3**
Two Friends '86 **3**
2 G's and a Key '00 **3**
200 Cigarettes '98 **1**
Two If by Sea '95 **2**
The Two Jakes '90 **1**
Two Lane Blacktop '71 **1**
Two Lost Worlds '50 **1**
Two Minute Warning '76 **1**
Two Moon Junction '88 **2**
Two Ninas '00 **3**
2000 Maniacs '64 **1**
2000 Year Old Man '82 **3**
2001: A Space Odyssey [Warner] '68 **1**
2001: A Space Odyssey [MGM] '68 **1**
2001: A Space Travesty '00 **3**
2010: The Year We Make Contact '84 **1**
2069: A Sex Odyssey '78 **3**
Two Undercover Angels '68 **1**
Two Women '61 **1**
Tycus '98 **2**

U
U-571 [CE] '00 **2**
U-Turn '97 **1**

UFOs Above and Beyond '97 **1**
The Ugly '96 **1**
UHF '89 **3**
Ulee's Gold '97 **3**
Ultimate Attraction '98 **2**
Ultimate Fights '02 **3**
Ultimate G's '01 **3**
Ultimatum '01 **3**
Ultraviolet '98 **3**
Ulysses '67 **2**
Ulysses' Gaze '95 **3**
Ulzana's Raid '72 **1**
Umbrellas of Cherbourg '64 **1**
Un Air de Famille '96 **1**
Un Flic '72 **3**
The Unbearable Lightness of
    Being '88 **1**
The Unbelievable Truth '90 **2**
The Unborn '91 **3**
Unbreakable '00 **3**
Uncensored Bosko, Vol. 1 '91
    2
Uncensored Bosko, Vol. 2 '91
    2
Uncle Buck '89 **1**
Uncle Sam '96 **1**
Uncle Tom's Cabin '27 **1**
Uncommon Valor '83 **2**
Uncorked '98 **3**
Under Fire '83 **3**
Under Oath '97 **2**
Under Siege '92 **1**
Under Siege 2 '95 **1**
Under Suspicion '00 **2**
Under the Gun '95 **1**
Under the Sand '00 **3**
Undercover '94 **1**
Undercurrent '99 **3**
Underdog [CE] '00 **3**
Underground '90 **1**
The Underneath '95 **1**
Undersea Kingdom '36 **3**
The Undertaker and His Pals
    '67 **2**
Underworld '96 **1**
Unforgettable '96 **3**
Unforgiven '92 **1**
Unidentified Flying Oddball
    '79 **1**
Uninvited Guest '99 **2**
Union City '81 **1**
U.S. Seals '98 **2**
Universal Soldier '92 **1**
Universal Soldier: The Return
    '99 **1**
Unknown Island '48 **1**
The Unknown Marx Brothers
    '93 **1**
Unlawful Entry '92 **3**
Unlikely Angel '97 **1**
Unmade Beds '00 **2**
The Unsinkable Molly Brown
    '64 **2**
Unspeakable '00 **2**
Untamed Heart '93 **2**
The Untold Story '93 **1**
The Untold Story 2 '98 **3**
The Untouchables '87 **2**
Up against Amanda '01 **3**
Up at the Villa '00 **2**
Up Close and Personal '96 **1**
Up in Mabel's Room '44 **2**
Uprising '01 **3**
Upstairs, Downstairs: The
    Complete First Season '71
    3
Upstairs, Downstairs: The
    Second Season '72 **3**
Urban Legend '98 **1**
Urban Legends 2: Final Cut
    '00 **2**
Urban Menace '99 **1**
Urbania '00 **3**
Urotsukidoji: Perfect Collec-
    tion '89 **1**
Urusei Yatsura Movie 2:
    Beautiful Dreamer '84 **1**
Urusei Yatsura: TV Series 1
    '81 **3**
U.S. Marshals '98 **1**

U.S. Seals 2 '01 **3**
Used Cars '80 **3**
The Usual Suspects [Poly-
    gram] '95 **1**
The Usual Suspects [MGM
    SE] '95 **3**
Utopia '51 **2**
Utu '83 **3**
U2: Rattle and Hum '88 **2**

V
V '83 **3**
Va Savoir '01 **3**
Vacas '91 **3**
Valdez Is Coming '71 **3**
Valentine '01 **3**
Vamp '86 **3**
The Vampire Bat '32 **2**
The Vampire Happening '71 **2**
Vampire Hunter D [SE] '85 **2**
Vampire Hunter D: Bloodlust
    '01 **3**
Vampire in Brooklyn '95 **3**
Vampire Journals '96 **1**
Vampire Obsession '02 **3**
Vampires in Havana '87 **3**
Vamps: Deadly Dreamgirls
    '95 **2**
Vampyr '31 **1**
Vampyres '74 **2**
Vampyros Lesbos '70 **2**
The Van '77 **3**
Vanilla Sky '01 **3**
The Vanishing [Image] '88 **1**
The Vanishing [Criterion] '88
    3
The Vanishing American '25 **2**
Varietease '54 **2**
Variety Lights '51 **2**
Varsity Blues '98 **1**
The Vault '00 **2**
Vegas Vacation '96 **1**
Velocity '99 **2**
Velocity Trap '99 **2**
Velvet Goldmine '98 **1**
Vengeance '68 **2**
The Vengeance of She '68 **1**
Vengeance of the Dead '01 **3**
Vengeance Valley '51 **3**
Venomous '01 **3**
Venus in Furs '94 **2**
The Venus Wars '89 **1**
Vera Cruz '53 **2**
Vertical Limit [1] '00 **2**
Vertical Limit [2 SB] '00 **3**
The Vertical Ray of the Sun
    '00 **3**
Vertigo [CE] '58 **1**
Very Bad Things '98 **1**
A Very Natural Thing '73 **1**
Very Private Lessons '01 **3**
The Very Thought of You '98
    1
Vibration '68 **3**
Vice Girls '96 **2**
Victim of Love '91 **3**
Victoria & Albert '01 **3**
Victory '81 **1**
Video Girl Ai '92 **3**
Videodrome '83 **1**
Vietnam: The Ten Thousand
    Day War '80 **2**
A View to a Kill [SE] '85 **2**
The Vigil '98 **3**
Vigilante [1] '83 **1**
Vigilante [2 DC] '83 **3**
The Viking Queen '67 **1**
The Vikings '58 **3**
Village of Dreams '97 **1**
Village of the Damned '95 **1**
Village of the Giants '65 **2**
The Villain '79 **3**
The Vineyard '89 **2**
Violent City '70 **3**
The Violent Years / Girl Gang
    '56 **2**
Violent Zone '89 **3**
Virasat '97 **1**
The Virgin Suicides '99 **2**
Virtual Combat '95 **1**
Virtual Desire '95 **1**
Virtual Sexuality '99 **3**

Virtuosity '95 **1**
Virus '98 **1**
Vision Quest '85 **1**
Visions of Light: The Art of
    Cinematography '93 **1**
The Visit '00 **3**
Vive l'Amour '94 **1**
Viy '67 **3**
A Voice from Heaven '01 **3**
Voices from Beyond '90 **3**
Volcano '97 **1**
Voltage Fighters! Gowcaizer:
    The Movie '98 **1**
Volunteers '85 **3**
Von Ryan's Express '65 **3**
Voodoo '95 **1**
Voodoo Academy [DC] '00 **2**
Voodoo Nightmare '00 **3**
Voyage to the Bottom of the
    Sea / Fantastic Voyage '61
    2
Voyeur.com '00 **3**

W
W. Eugene Smith: Photogra-
    phy Made Difficult '89 **3**
Wag the Dog '97 **1**
Wages of Fear '55 **1**
Waiting '01 **3**
Waiting for Guffman '96 **3**
The Waiting Game '99 **2**
Waitress [DC] '81 **3**
Waking Life '01 **3**
Waking Ned Devine '98 **1**
Waking the Dead '00 **2**
Waking Up Horton '99 **1**
A Walk in the Clouds '95 **2**
A Walk in the Sun '46 **2**
A Walk on the Moon '99 **1**
Walkabout '71 **1**
Walking and Talking '96 **3**
Walking Tall '73 **1**
Walking the Edge '83 **2**
Walking with Dinosaurs '99 **3**
Wall Street '87 **2**
Wallace & Gromit: The First
    Three Adventures '99 **1**
Walls of Hell '64 **3**
Walt Disney Treasures: Davy
    Crockett '01 **3**
Walt Disney Treasures: Dis-
    neyland USA '01 **3**
Walt Disney Treasures: Silly
    Symphonies '01 **3**
Waltz of the Toreadors '62 **1**
Wanted '98 **1**
Wanted: Dead or Alive '86 **3**
The War '94 **1**
War Gods of the Deep '65 **3**
The War of the Roses [SE]
    '89 **3**
The War of the Worlds '53 **1**
The War Room '93 **1**
The War Wagon '67 **1**
The War Zone '98 **2**
WarGames '83 **1**
Warlock: The Armageddon
    '93 **2**
Warlock 3: The End of Inno-
    cence '98 **1**
Warm Blooded Killers '01 **3**
The Warriors '79 **2**
Warriors of Virtue '97 **1**
The Wash '01 **3**
The Wasp Woman [Slingshot]
    '59 **2**
The Wasp Woman [Elite] '59
    2
Watch Me '96 **1**
The Watcher '00 **2**
The Watcher in the Woods
    '81 **3**
Water Damage '01 **3**
Water Drops on Burning
    Rocks '99 **3**
The Waterboy '98 **1**
The Watermelon Woman '97
    2
Waterproof '99 **3**
Watership Down '78 **3**
Waterworld '95 **1**
Wax Mask '97 **2**

Way Down East ' **1**
Way of the Gun '00 **2**
The Way We Were [SE] '73 **2**
Wayne's World '92 **3**
Wayne's World 2 '93 **3**
W.C. Fields 6 Short Films '33
    2
We Dive at Dawn '43 **3**
We Take New Guinea '???? **3**
Weather Report Girl '01 **3**
Weather Woman '99 **2**
Web of Seduction '99 **1**
The Wedding Planner '01 **3**
The Wedding Singer '97 **1**
Weekend at Bernie's '89 **1**
Weird Science '85 **1**
Welcome to Death Row '00 **3**
Welcome to the Dollhouse
    '95 **1**
Welcome II the Terrordome
    '95 **2**
The Well '97 **3**
We'll Meet Again '82 **2**
Went to Coney Island on a
    Mission from God...Be
    Back by Five '98 **2**
Werewolf '95 **1**
Werewolf of London '35 **3**
Werther '88 **1**
Wes Craven's New Nightmare
    '94 **1**
West of the Divide '33 **3**
West Side Story '61 **1**
The Westerner '40 **1**
Westworld '73 **1**
Wet Hot American Summer
    '01 **3**
Wham-Bam, Thank You
    Spaceman '75 **2**
What about Bob? '91 **2**
What Dreams May Come '98
    1
What Ever Happened to Baby
    Jane? '62 **1**
What Lies Beneath '00 **2**
What Planet Are You From?
    '00 **2**
What Women Want '00 **2**
What Your Eyes Don't See
    '99 **3**
Whatever Happened to Aunt
    Alice? '69 **2**
Whatever It Takes '97 **1**
Whatever It Takes '00 **2**
What's Cooking? '00 **2**
What's Eating Gilbert Grape
    '93 **3**
What's Love Got to Do with
    It? '93 **1**
What's the Worst That Could
    Happen? [SE] '01 **3**
Wheels on Meals '84 **3**
When a Man Loves a Woman
    '94 **1**
When a Stranger Calls '79 **3**
When a Stranger Calls Back
    '93 **1**
When Good Ghouls Go Bad
    '01 **3**
When Harry Met Sally... [SE]
    '89 **2**
When Justice Fails '98 **3**
When the Sky Falls '99 **3**
When Trumpets Fade '98 **3**
When Worlds Collide '51 **3**
Where a Good Man Goes '99
    3
Where Angels Dance '01 **3**
Where the Buffalo Roam '80
    1
Where the Heart Is '00 **2**
Where the Money Is '00 **2**
Where the Red Fern Grows
    '74 **3**
Where the Red Fern Grows:
    Part 2 '92 **3**
Where the Rivers Flow North
    '94 **1**
While You Were Sleeping '95
    1
The Whip and the Body '63 **2**

Whipped '00 **2**
Whisper Kill '88 **1**
Whispers: An Elephant's Tale
    '00 **3**
White Badge '97 **3**
White Christmas '54 **2**
White Fang to the Rescue '74
    3
White Lies '98 **2**
The White Lioness '96 **2**
White Man's Burden '95 **1**
White Men Can't Jump '92 **2**
White Palace '90 **1**
The White Pony '99 **3**
White River '99 **3**
White Sands '92 **3**
White Squall '96 **1**
The White Warrior '61 **3**
White Wolves 2: Legend of
    the Wild '94 **2**
White Wolves 3: Cry of the
    White Wolf '98 **3**
Whity '70 **2**
Who Framed Roger Rabbit
    '88 **1**
Who the Hell Is Juliette? '97
    3
The Whole Nine Yards '00 **2**
Who'll Stop the Rain? '78 **3**
Who's Afraid of Virginia
    Woolf? '66 **1**
Why Do Fools Fall in Love?
    '98 **1**
Why Do They Call It Love
    When They Mean Sex? '92
    3
Why Has Bodhi-Darma Left
    for the East '89 **1**
Wicked City '92 **1**
Wicked City [SE] '89 **2**
Wicked Ways '99 **1**
The Wicked, Wicked West '97
    1
The Wicker Man [SE] '75 **3**
Wide Awake '97 **2**
The Widow of Saint-Pierre '00
    3
The Wife '95 **1**
Wild America '97 **1**
The Wild Angels '66 **2**
Wild Bill '95 **2**
The Wild Bunch '69 **1**
The Wild Child '70 **3**
Wild Guitar / The Choppers
    '62 **3**
The Wild One '54 **1**
Wild Orchid '90 **3**
Wild Reeds '94 **1**
Wild Strawberries '57 **3**
Wild Things '98 **1**
The Wild West '01 **3**
Wild Wild West '99 **1**
Wilde '97 **3**
Wilderness '96 **2**
Will Penny '67 **3**
William Shakespeare's A Mid-
    summer Night's Dream '99
    1
William Shakespeare's
    Romeo and Juliet '96 **1**
Willow '88 **3**
Willy Wonka & the Chocolate
    Factory '71 **1**
The Wind '87 **3**
A Wind Named Amnesia '93
    1
Wind River '98 **3**
Winds of the Wasteland '36 **2**
A Wing and a Prayer '44 **3**
Wing Commander '99 **1**
The Wings of the Dove '97 **1**
Winner Takes All '99 **2**
Winning London '01 **3**
The Winslow Boy '98 **3**
Winstanley '75 **1**
Winter Lily '98 **3**
Winter People '89 **2**
Winter Sleepers '97 **2**
Wirey Spindell '99 **3**
Wishful Thinking '92 **2**
Wishmaster '97 **1**

Wishmaster 2: Evil Never Dies '98 **1**
Wishmaster 3: Beyond the Gates of Hell '01 **3**
W.I.S.O.R. The Robo Welder '01 **3**
Witch Hunter '01 **3**
Witchcraft '88 **1**
Witchcraft 2: The Temptress '90 **1**
Witchcraft 9: Bitter Flesh '96 **1**
The Witches '66 **2**
The Witches '90 **1**
The Witches of Eastwick '87 **1**
Witchouse '99 **1**
Witchouse 2: Blood Coven '00 **2**
Witchouse 3: Demon Fire '01 **3**
With a Friend Like Harry '00 **3**
With Byrd at the South Pole: The Story of Little America '30 **1**
With Friends Like These '90 **3**
With Honors '94 **1**
Within the Rock '96 **1**
Withnail and I '87 **3**
Without Air '95 **1**
Without Limits '97 **1**
Witness '85 **1**
Witness for the Prosecution '57 **3**
The Wiz '78 **1**
The Wizard of Gore '70 **1**
The Wizard of Oz '25 **3**
The Wizard of Oz '39 **1**
Wolf '94 **1**
The Wolf Man '41 **1**

The Wolfman '82 **3**
The Wolves of Kromer '98 **3**
A Woman Called Moses '78 **2**
A Woman Called Sada Abe '75 **2**
A Woman, Her Men and Her Futon '92 **2**
Woman in Black '89 **3**
The Woman in Green / Dressed to Kill '45 **2**
A Woman Is a Woman '60 **1**
Woman of the Year '42 **1**
Woman on Top '00 **2**
A Woman under the Influence '74 **2**
The Woman Who Came Back '45 **1**
The Womaneater '59 **2**
Women '97 **2**
Women in Cages '71 **3**
Women in Revolt '71 **1**
The Women of Brewster Place '89 **2**
Women of Valor '86 **1**
Women on the Verge of a Nervous Breakdown '88 **2**
Wonder Boys '00 **2**
Wonder Man '45 **2**
The Wonderful, Horrible Life of Leni Riefenstahl '93 **1**
Wonderland '99 **2**
Wonderwall: The Movie '69 **2**
The Wood '99 **3**
Woodstock [DC] '70 **1**
Woodstock 99 '99 **3**
The Woody Allen Collection '01 **3**
Word of Mouth '99 **1**
Working '82 **3**

Working Girl '88 **2**
Working Girls '87 **2**
The World according to Garp '82 **3**
The World at War '73 **3**
World History of Organized Crime '01 **3**
The World Is Not Enough [SE] '99 **2**
The World of Sid & Marty Krofft '02 **3**
World Trade Center—A Modern Marvel: 1973–2001 '01 **3**
World War I Films of the Silent Era '02 **3**
World War II '42 **2**
The World's Greatest Animation '93 **1**
The Worm Eaters '77 **3**
The Worst Witch '98 **3**
The Wounds '98 **2**
Woyzeck '78 **2**
The Wrecking Crew '99 **3**
Wrestling Women USA! '01 **3**
Written on the Wind '56 **3**
Wrongfully Accused '98 **1**
Wuthering Heights '39 **1**
Wuthering Heights '70 **3**

X
X '96 **3**
The X-Files '98 **1**
The X-Files: Season 1 [CE] '00 **2**
The X-Files: Season 2 '00 **2**
The X-Files: Season 4 '00 **3**
X-Men '00 **2**

X-Men: The Phoenix Saga '92 **2**
X: The Man with X-Ray Eyes '63 **2**
X The Unknown '56 **2**
Xanadu '80 **1**
Xchange '00 **2**
Xena: Warrior Princess—Series Finale '01 **3**
Xiu Xiu: The Sent Down Girl '97 **1**
Xtro 3: Watch the Skies '95 **1**

Y
The Yards '00 **2**
The Year of Living Dangerously '82 **1**
Year of the Horse '97 **3**
Yellow '98 **2**
The Yellow Fountain '99 **3**
Yellow Submarine '68 **1**
Yes Boss! '97 **1**
Yi Yi '00 **2**
You Are Here * '00 **3**
You Can't Do That: The Making of "A Hard Day's Night" '94 **2**
You Light Up My Life '77 **3**
You Only Live Twice [SE] '67 **2**
You So Crazy '94 **2**
Young and Innocent '37 **1**
The Young Bruce Lee '80 **3**
Young Frankenstein '74 **1**
The Young Girls of Rochefort '68 **3**
Young Guns '88 **1**
The Young Land '59 **3**
The Young Lions '58 **3**
Youngblood '86 **2**

Your Friends & Neighbors '98 **1**
Your Place or Mine! '98 **3**
Yours, Mine & Ours '68 **2**
You've Got Mail '98 **1**

Z
Zachariah '70 **1**
Zardoz '73 **2**
Zebra Lounge '01 **3**
Zebrahead '92 **3**
A Zed & Two Noughts '88 **1**
Zeder '83 **1**
Zelig '83 **3**
Zeram '91 **1**
Zeram 2 '94 **3**
Zero Degrees Kelvin '95 **3**
Zero Effect '97 **1**
Zeta One '69 **3**
Zeus and Roxanne '96 **1**
Ziggy Stardust and the Spiders from Mars '83 **3**
Zombie '80 **1**
Zombie Lake '80 **2**
Zoolander '01 **3**
Zorro, the Gay Blade '81 **1**
Zu: Warriors of the Magic Mountain '83 **2**